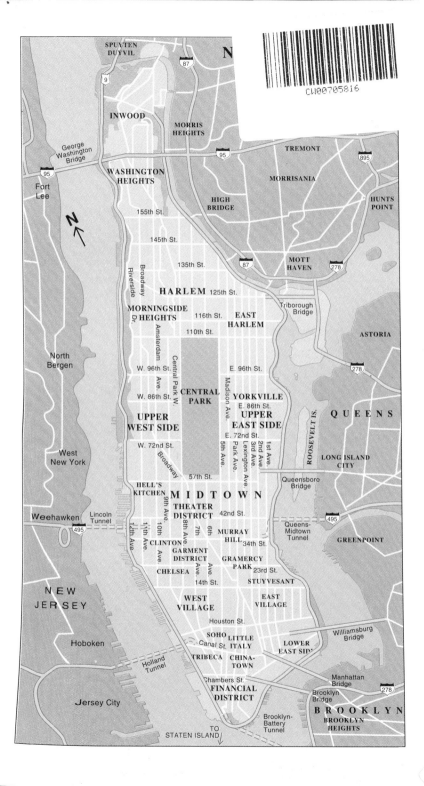

# New York City Subways

## Subways

Stops are not served by all trains at all times.
Refer to Transit Authority map for descriptions of express, local, and limited service.

**LEGEND**

K,B  Line
168 St  Terminal

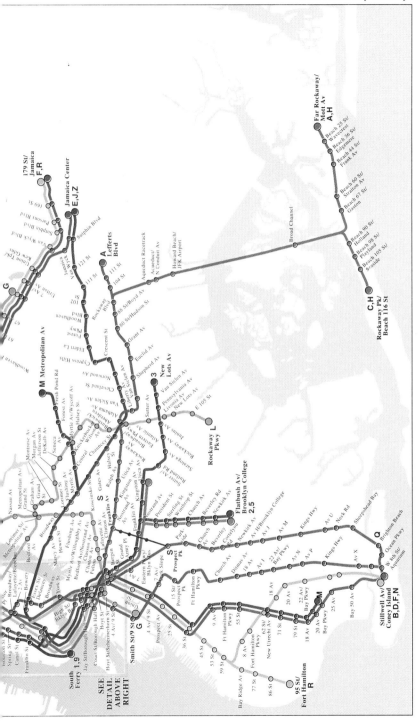

# Downtown Manhattan

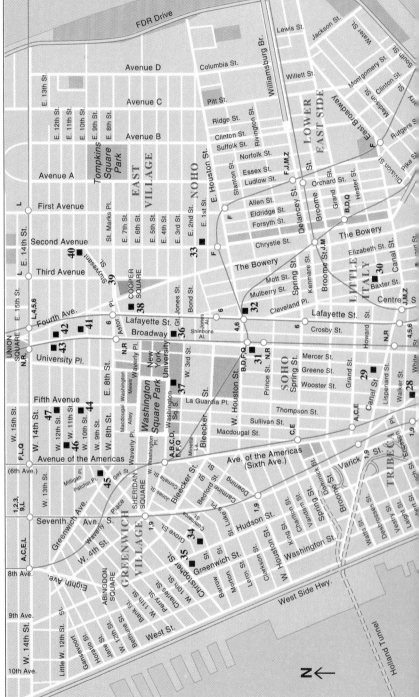

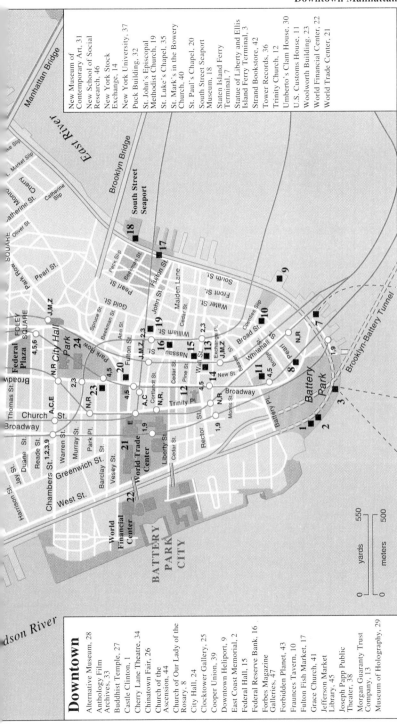

# Midtown Manhattan

East River

Queensboro Bridge

Queens-Midtown Tunnel

FDR Dr.

First Ave.

Second Ave.

Third Ave.

Lexington Ave.

Park Ave.

Madison Ave.

Fifth Ave.

TURTLE BAY

United Nations

MURRAY HILL

Empire State Building

Grand Central Terminal

New York Public Library

Bryant Park

Rockefeller Center

Museum of Modern Art

Carnegie Hall

Central Park South

Grand Army Plaza

COLUMBUS CIRCLE

New York Convention & Visitors Bureau

HERALD SQUARE

GARMENT DISTRICT

Port Authority Bus Terminal

General Post Office

TIMES SQUARE

Broadway

Seventh Ave.

Eighth Ave.

Ninth Ave.

Tenth Ave.

Eleventh Ave.

Twelfth Ave.

Dyer Ave.

Lincoln Tunnel

HELL'S KITCHEN

Citicorp Center

E. 56th St.
E. 55th St.
E. 54th St.
E. 53rd St.
E. 52nd St.
E. 51st St.
E. 50th St.
E. 49th St.
E. 48th St.
E. 47th St.
E. 46th St.
E. 45th St.
E. 44th St.
E. 43rd St.
E. 42nd St.
E. 41st St.
E. 40th St.
E. 39th St.
E. 38th St.
E. 37th St.
E. 36th St.
E. 35th St.
E. 34th St.
E. 33rd St.

E. 60th St.
E. 59th St.
E. 58th St.
E. 57th St.

W. 60th St.
W. 59th St.
W. 58th St.
W. 57th St.
W. 56th St.
W. 55th St.
W. 54th St.
W. 53rd St.
W. 52nd St.
W. 51st St.
W. 50th St.
W. 49th St.
W. 48th St.
W. 47th St.
W. 46th St.
W. 45th St.
W. 44th St.
W. 43rd St.
W. 42nd St.
W. 41st St.
W. 40th St.
W. 39th St.
W. 38th St.
W. 37th St.
W. 36th St.
W. 35th St.
W. 34th St.

A,B,C,D
1,2,3,9
N,R
N,R,9
1,2,3
4,5,6
B,C
N,F
B,Q
B,D,E
B,D,F,Q
C,E
A,C,E
E,F
7
6
1,2,3,9
P,B,Q

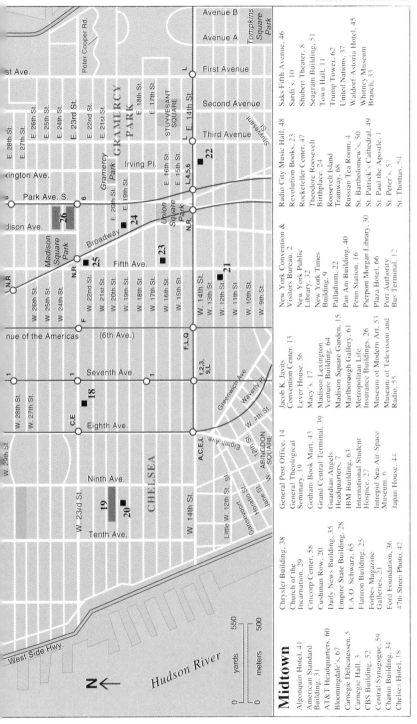

# Midtown Manhattan

## Midtown

Algonquin Hotel, 41
American Standard
Building, 31
AT&T Headquarters, 60
Bloomingdale's, 67
Carnegie Delicatessen, 5
Carnegie Hall, 3
CBS Building, 52
Central Synagogue, 59
Chanin Building, 34
Chelsea Hotel, 18

Chrysler Building, 38
Church of the
Incarnation, 29
Citicorp Center, 58
Cushman Row, 20
Daily News Building, 35
Empire State Building, 28
Flatiron Building, 25
Forbes Magazine
Galleries, 21
Ford Foundation, 36
47th Street Photo, 42

General Post Office, 14
General Theological
Seminary, 19
Gotham Book Mart, 43
Grand Central Terminal, 39
Guardian Angels
Headquarters, 7
IBM Building, 63
International Student
Hospice, 27
Intrepid Sea-Air-Space
Museum, 6
Japan House, 44

Jacob K. Javits
Convention Center, 13
Lever House, 56
Macy's, 17
Madison Lexington
Venture Building, 64
Madison Square Garden, 15
Marlborough Gallery, 61
Metropolitan Life
Insurance Buildings, 27
Museum of Modern Art, 53
Museum of Television and
Radio, 55

New York Convention &
Visitors Bureau, 2
New York Public
Library, 32
New York Times
Building, 9
Palladium, 22
Pan Am Building, 40
Penn Station, 16
Pierpont Morgan Library, 26
Plaza Hotel, 66
Port Authority
Bus Terminal, 12

Radio City Music Hall, 48
Revolution Books, 23
Rockefeller Center, 47
Theodore Roosevelt
Birthplace, 24
Roosevelt Island
Tramway, 68
Russian Tea Room, 4
St. Bartholomew's, 50
St. Patrick's Cathedral, 49
St. Paul the Apostle, 1
St. Peter's, 57
St. Thomas, 54

Saks Fifth Avenue, 46
Sardi's, 10
Shubert Theater, 8
Seagram Building, 51
Town Hall, 11
Trump Tower, 62
United Nations, 37
Waldorf-Astoria Hotel, 45
Whitney Museum
Branch, 33

# Uptown

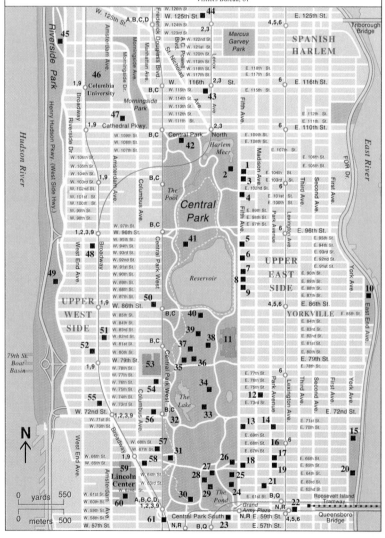

Downtown Washington, D.C.

# Central Washington, D.C.

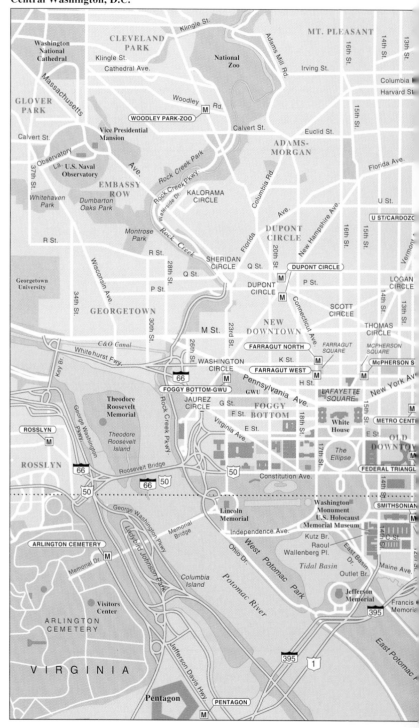

Central Washington, D.C.

# The Mall Area, Washington, D.C.

Lafayette Park
White House
The Ellipse
Treasury Pl.
Penn. Ave. S.
Constitution Ave.
Madison Dr.

H St. — McPHERSON SQUARE
New York Ave.
G St. — METRO CENTER
Penn. Ave. N.
Pennsylvania Ave.
FEDERAL TRIANGLE
ARCHIVES
GALLERY PL
THE MALL
SMITHSONIAN
Independence Av
L'ENFANT PL
Madison Pl. · 15th St. · 14th St. · 13th St. · 12th St. · 11th St. · 10th St. · 9th St. · 8th St. · 7th St.
G St. · F St. · E St. · D St. · C St.
Indiana

3 Department of the Treasury
4 White House
Warner Theatre
2 National Theatre
1
Ford's Theatre 11
9:30 club 13
14 Natl. Museum & of American Art Natl. Portrait Gallery
Federal Bureau of Investigation 12
District Building 6
Department of Commerce & National Aquarium 5
Interstate Commerce Commission 7
Old Post Office 9
10 Internal Revenue Service
15 Department of Justice
16 National Archives
National Museum of American History 8
National Museum of Natural History 21
Ice Rink
Washington Monument 22
Sylvan Theatre 23
Department of Agriculture 26
Smithsonian Castle 28
Freer Gallery 27
30 31 Sackler Gallery
National Museum of African Art
Arts & Industries Building 29
Hirshhorn Museum & Sculpture Garden 32
35 NASA
U.S. Holocaust Memorial Museum 24
Raoul Wallenberg Pl.
Bureau of Engraving & Printing 25
34 Department of Energy
East Basin Dr.
12th St. Expwy.
L'Enfant Plaza 36
37 Department of Housing & Urban Development
38 Department of Transportation
Outlet Br.
Maine Ave.
Virginia Av
395
N

## Mall Area

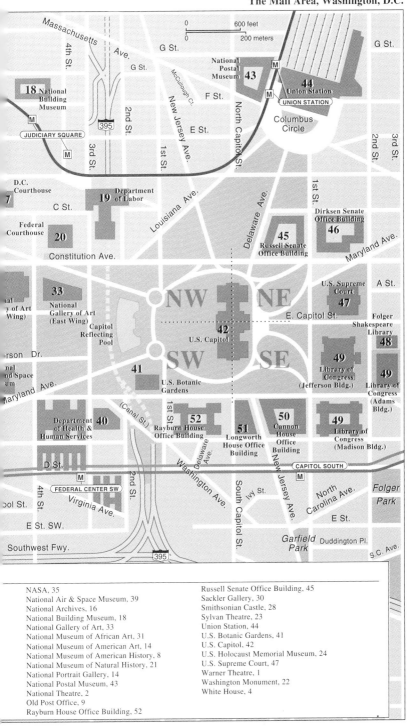

## White House Area, Foggy Bottom, and Nearby Arlington

N St.

Prospect St.

GEORGETOWN

Old Stone House

Olive St.

M St.

Rock Creek

33rd St.

31st St.

C&O Creek

South St.

Whitehurst Fwy.

L St.

26th St.

25th St.

24th St.

WASHINGTON CIRCLE

N

29

K St.
(under expressway)

FOGGY BOTTOM-GWU

M

Potomac River

Francis Scott Key Br.

66

G.W.
Ho

Ge
Was
Uni

Thompson Boat Center

Watergate Hotel

Watergate Hotel Complex

JUAREZ CIRCLE

24th St.

23rd St.

FOGG
BOTTO

Fort Myer Dr.

N. Lynn St.

N. Moore St.

19th St.

George Washington Pkwy.

Theodore Roosevelt Memorial

Theodore Roosevelt Island

Rock Creek Pkwy.

Kennedy Center for the Performing Arts

ROSSLYN

M

N. Kent St.

Wilson Blvd.

Arlington Ridge Rd.

Depar

Na
Ac
of S

ROSSLYN

Fairfax Dr.

66

Theodore Roosevelt Br.

66

50

5

N. Nash St.

50

NW

SW

12th St.

Mead Dr.

Marine Corps War Memorial (Iwo Jima Statue)

Netherlands Carillon

George Washington Memorial Pkwy.

Arlington Memorial Br.

Linc
Men

Ericsson Memorial

ARLINGTON

M

ARLINGTON CEMETERY

Memorial Dr.

Ladybird Johnson Park

Columbia Island

Grave of President John F. Kennedy

Arlington House

Robert E. Lee Memorial

Visitor Center

Jefferson Davis Hwy.

ARLINGTON NATIONAL CEMETERY

Tomb of the Unknown Soldier

Lyndon B. Johnson Memorial

V I R G I N I A

0 ———— 1500 feet

0 ———— 500 meters

Pentagon, National Airport

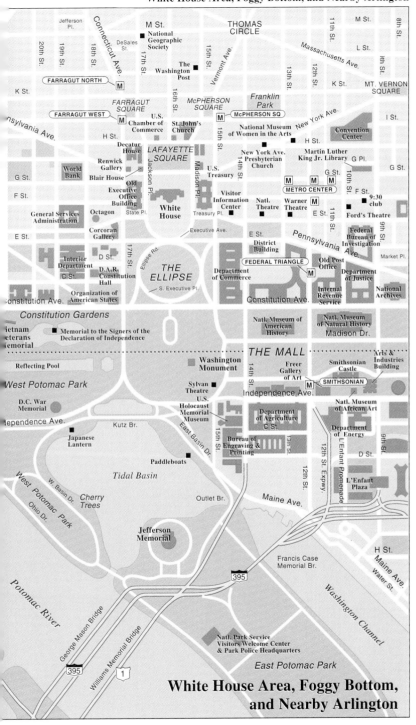

# White House Area, Foggy Bottom, and Nearby Arlington

# Metrorail System, Washington, D.C.

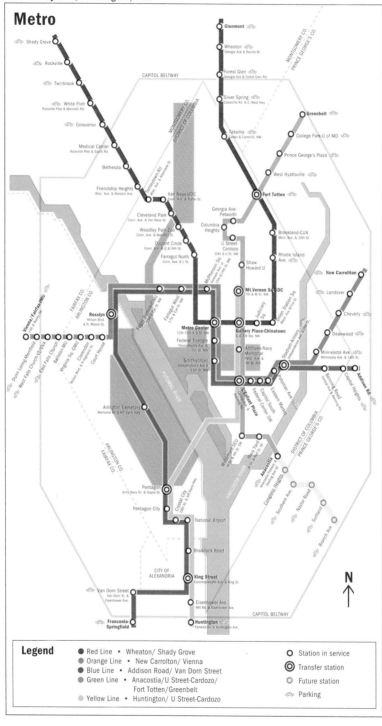

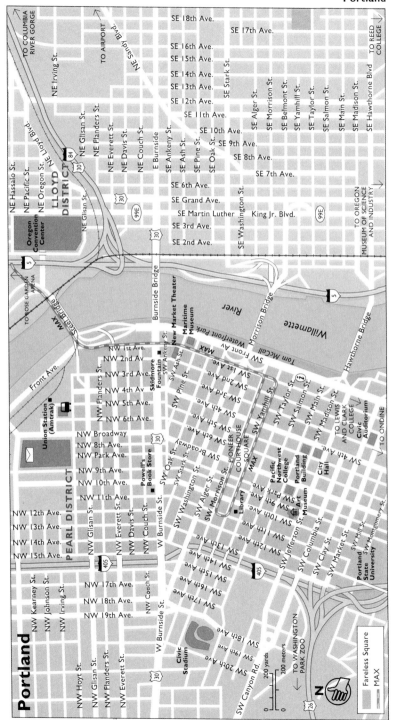

Portland

# Seattle

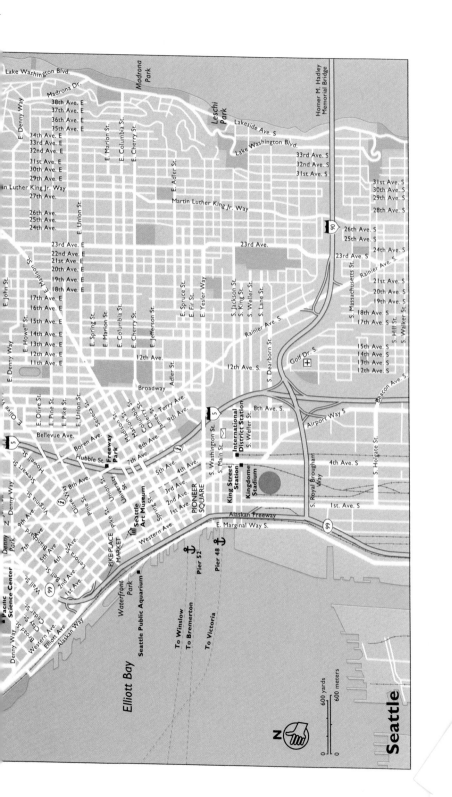

# Vancouver

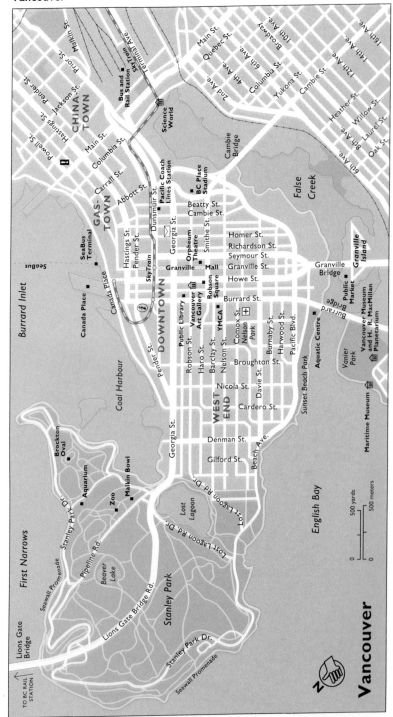

Los Angeles

# San Francisco

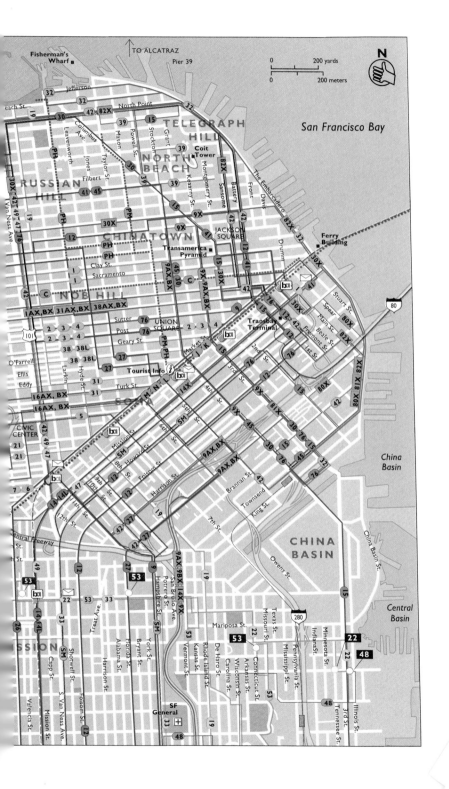

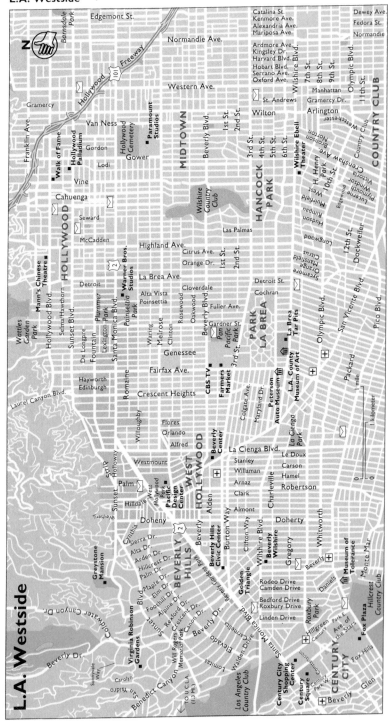

## ⬛ Let's Go writers travel on your budget.

"Guides that penetrate the veneer of the holiday brochures and mine the grit of real life."

—*The Economist*

"The writers seem to have experienced every rooster-packed bus and lunar-surfaced mattress about which they write."

—*The New York Times*

"All the dirt, dirt cheap."

—*People*

## ⬛ Great for independent travelers.

"The guides are aimed not only at young budget travelers but at the independent traveler; a sort of streetwise cookbook for traveling alone."

—*The New York Times*

"Flush with candor and irreverence, chock full of budget travel advice."

—*The Des Moines Register*

"An indispensible resource, *Let's Go*'s practical information can be used by every traveler."

—*The Chattanooga Free Press*

## ⬛ Let's Go is completely revised each year.

"Only *Let's Go* has the zeal to annually update every title on its list."

—*The Boston Globe*

"Unbeatable: good sightseeing advice; up-to-date info on restaurants, hotels, and inns; a commitment to money-saving travel; and a wry style that brightens nearly every page."

—*The Washington Post*

## ⬛ All the important information you need.

"*Let's Go* authors provide a comedic element while still providing concise information and thorough coverage of the country. Anything you need to know about budget traveling is detailed in this book."

—*The Chicago Sun-Times*

"Value-packed, unbeatable, accurate, and comprehensive."

—*Los Angeles Times*

# Let's Go Publications

Let's Go: Alaska & the Pacific Northwest 2000
Let's Go: Australia 2000
Let's Go: Austria & Switzerland 2000
Let's Go: Britain & Ireland 2000
Let's Go: California 2000
Let's Go: Central America 2000
Let's Go: China 2000 **New Title!**
Let's Go: Eastern Europe 2000
Let's Go: Europe 2000
Let's Go: France 2000
Let's Go: Germany 2000
Let's Go: Greece 2000
Let's Go: India & Nepal 2000
Let's Go: Ireland 2000
Let's Go: Israel 2000 **New Title!**
Let's Go: Italy 2000
Let's Go: Mexico 2000
Let's Go: Middle East 2000 **New Title!**
Let's Go: New York City 2000
Let's Go: New Zealand 2000
Let's Go: Paris 2000
Let's Go: Perú & Ecuador 2000 **New Title!**
Let's Go: Rome 2000
Let's Go: South Africa 2000
Let's Go: Southeast Asia 2000
Let's Go: Spain & Portugal 2000
Let's Go: Turkey 2000
Let's Go: USA 2000
Let's Go: Washington, D.C. 2000

## Let's Go *Map Guides*

| | |
|---|---|
| Amsterdam | New Orleans |
| Berlin | New York City |
| Boston | Paris |
| Chicago | Prague |
| Florence | Rome |
| London | San Francisco |
| Los Angeles | Seattle |
| Madrid | Washington, D.C. |

**Coming Soon:** Sydney and Hong Kong

# USA

## INCLUDING COVERAGE OF CANADA

**T.J. Kelleher**
Editor

**Ana Laguarda**
Associate Editor

**Georgia Young**
Associate Editor

Researcher-Writers:

**Randy Bell**

**Eli Poliakoff**

**Nathan Foley-Mendelssohn**

**Matthew Smith**

**Emily Griffin**

**Zach Towne-Smith**

**Bryce Pickering**

**Kevin Yip**

**Jennifer Westhagen**

with:

**David Mihalyfy**

St. Martin's Press ☙ New York

**HELPING LET'S GO** If you want to share your discoveries, suggestions, or corrections, please drop us a line. We read every piece of correspondence, whether a postcard, a 10-page email, or a coconut. Please note that mail received after May 2000 may be too late for the 2001 book, but will be kept for future editions. **Address mail to:**

> Let's Go: USA
> 67 Mount Auburn Street
> Cambridge, MA 02138
> USA

Visit Let's Go at **http://www.letsgo.com,** or send email to:

> feedback@letsgo.com
> Subject: "Let's Go: USA"

In addition to the invaluable travel advice our readers share with us, many are kind enough to offer their services as researchers or editors. Unfortunately, our charter enables us to employ only currently enrolled Harvard students.

# HOW TO USE THIS BOOK

The **United States of America,** and its great neighbor to the north, **Canada,** present untold millions of opportunities for travel and adventure. Over the past seven months, we at Let's Go have been working hard to bring these two countries to you, gentle reader, but be forewarned: we did not cover it all in our 976 pages, and we could not, not even with 2000. Don't be afraid to explore a town we did not list.

But this is still the most useful budget travel guide to the old colonies in the New World. The book is divided into four main parts. The first of these, **Discover the USA and Canada,** highlights the two countries' bounteous offerings, and provides some sample itineraries of can't-miss destinations and road trips—they're ready to go, or ready just to jog the mind and stir the imagination.

The next section, **Life and Times,** details the histories and cultures of these two countries—not to mention a few little known facts about Canada (see p. 152).

Following the gripping tale of the U.S.'s and Canada's foundings and development comes the section entitled **Essentials,** which gives a good grounding in hard facts and travel aids for both the first-time traveler and the long-time vet. The section itself is split in three parts. The first part contains all the information necessary to **plan a trip** to the U.S. and Canada, including documents, money, entrance requirements, exchange rates, certain laws and customs, health and safety advice, and travel advice for women, seniors, bisexuals, gays, and lesbians, and disabled travelers. The second part is called **Getting There,** and covers travel to North America from around the globe. Finally is **Once There,** a discussion of getting around, finding a bed, exploring the outdoors, and keeping in touch with home.

The real meat of the book comes next: 14 chapters, dividing the two countries into 14 regions. These are: **New England, Eastern Canada, the Mid-Atlantic, the South, Florida, the Great Lakes, the Great Plains, Texas, the Rockies, the Southwest, California, the Pacific Northwest, Western Canada,** and **Alaska.** Each chapter begins with a **Highlights of the Region** box, which provides a flavor of what each region is most famous for. Each state, province, or territory's coverage begins with the most accesible destination, and moves outward from there.

All this is capped by a mileage chart, and, in the inside backcover, a list of commonly needed phone numbers, including **Greyhound Bus Lines, Amtrak,** and major U.S. and Canadian air carriers. Also included is a map key.

For all major destinations in the USA and Canada, we include **⌐Accommodations, ⌐Food, ⌐Sights,** and **⌐Nightlife/Entertainment** headers. Within these groups, the listings have been ranked by researcher-writers and editors, and the very best are given thumbs-up ⌐. **⌐Practical Information** will help visitors navigate destinations. Finally, **"Near: X"** sections provide day trip suggestions. The book also makes heavy use of abbreviations in order to facilitate covering more cities and sites.

Don't forget about our regional guides if you are planning to stay for a long time in one locale. These include: *Alaska & the Pacific Northwest,* and *California,* as well as *New York City* and *Washington, D.C.* Our map guides provide excellent maps of all the following cities: Chicago, New Orleans, Boston, New York, Washington, D.C., San Francisco, Los Angeles, and Seattle. Now—**LET'S GO!**⌐⌐⌐⌐

# Hawaii
## Aloha Hostels

# CONTENTS

# MAPS

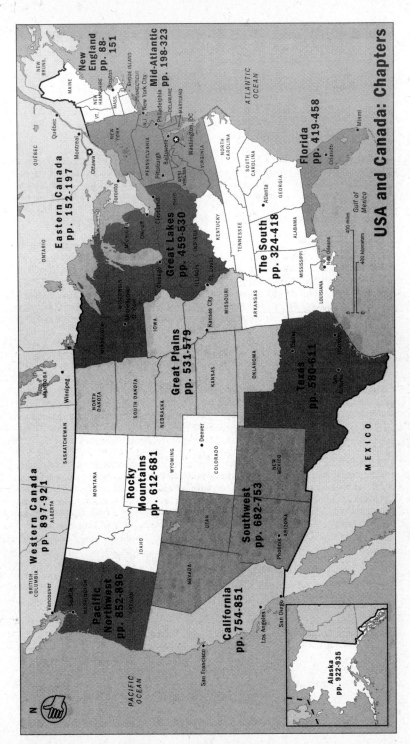

# USA and Canada: Chapters

New England pp. 88-151
Mid-Atlantic pp. 198-323
Eastern Canada pp. 152-197
Great Lakes pp. 459-530
The South pp. 324-418
Florida pp. 419-458
Great Plains pp. 531-579
Texas pp. 580-611
Western Canada pp. 897-921
Rocky Mountains pp. 612-681
Southwest pp. 682-753
Pacific Northwest pp. 852-896
California pp. 754-851
Alaska pp. 922-935

# RESEARCHER-WRITERS

**Randy Bell**                    *Montana, Wyoming, the Dakotas, Iowa, Nebraska*
Fresh from months in the editing room and his film on Bob Dylan, Randy hoped to find one thing on his trip: weird old America. Replete with full hookups and a Crazy Creek chair, Randy's stellar copy was launched directly from the wild, wild west via his tent site. He gaped at Crazy Horse, a nude statue of David, and all of Iowa's exciting tourist opportunities.

**Nathan Foley-Mendelssohn**            *Texas, Louisiana, Mississippi, Arkansas, Oklahoma*
Nathan never liked saying good-bye, and it saddened Team USA to bid him, his top-notch work, and Texas farewell. A hardy soul, he went unfazed by empty gas tanks and topless New Orleans tourists. An excellent researcher, he kept us in the office waiting for copy like a Louisiana belle awaits beads from a carnival Rex. We hope he'll always remember his days and days (and days) on the road fondly.

**Emily Griffin**          *Southern New England, New York, Toronto, Pennsylvania, Ohio, Indiana*
Emily was a modern woman traveling alone, and she wouldn't take any crap; nor did she give any to us—only spot-on work. Traversing the wilds of the Rust Belt isn't easy, but Emily kept chugging and didn't stop until she hit Indiana, turned around, and said, "It's time to go home." By the time she got there, we'd realized that she'd taken an ornery itinerary and whipped it right into shape, giving us copy that dispensed with the tired and so-called "alternative," replacing it with what we think are the ingredients for a smashing jaunt.

**Bryce Pickering**              *Northern New England, Québec, Ontario, the Maritimes*
Bryce loved Montréal, he loved Ottawa, he loved New Hampshire, and he had a certain fondness for Mexican food—but that's what happens when you send a French Canadian living in New England north. Like any well adjusted individual, he transferred his energy for an object into great research and well constructed copybatches. We hope this regional expert will be back for more food, folks, and fun, but we're certain that any traveler through his coverage areas will be standing on the shoulders of a giant.

**Eli Poliakoff**                    *The Carolinas, Georgia, Alabama, Florida*
We actually *paid* Eli to go to Florida—not a bad deal—and he repaid us in kind with fastidious research. But it was really our pleasure to read reports from a South Carolinan so enamored with his home region, holding out visions of grandeur in a time of so many tarnished memories. He will love *Let's Go* forever for giving him the chance to ride in a NASCAR car; his hearing will recover shortly, but the thrill will never die.

**Matthew Smith**      *Illinois, Missouri, Kansas, Arkansas, Mississippi, Tennessee, North Carolina*
Longtime friend to Team USA, Matt was like a good son. He called home very often, he sent us presents, and he stuck us with the phone bill. Though enthralled with the flatlands of Illinois, Kansas, and Missouri, Matt found his inner middle-aged man at the Jim Beam factory in Kentucky, and was lucky enough to enjoy the Great Smokey Mountains in the summertime. Our oldest has moved on to Hawaii, where he teaches math, is the faculty advisor for the snorkeling cabal, and gallivants about in a 4WD, but we hope he'll still call to say hello.

**Zach Towne-Smith**                    *Minnesota, Wisconsin, Illinois, Iowa*
A veteran traveler, and a man who knows the only thing necessary to stare down an anaconda is a telephoto lens, Zach picked up and went just when we needed him most. He breezed through his itinerary, as his hair grew ever-longer. Blazing a route from Minneapolis along the U.S.'s interior coast to Chi-town, Zach set a new

standard for pinch hitters and research in the Great Lakes. Now he's off to photograph the more exotic terrain of Guatemala, but we know he'll save a soft spot for those locals in Door County, WI.

**Kevin Yip**                                         *Arizona, Utah, Colorado, New Mexico, Texas*
A hostel-owner in Arizona sent us a postcard telling us how stellar "our researcher" was, and we agree. Kevin delivered an attention to Native American culture and history long missing from the Southwest, and we know, wherever he goes next, someone is going to be writing another one of those postcards.

**Jennifer Westhagen**                                         *Idaho, Wyoming, Colorado, Utah*
Jennifer always believed that fine copy is like fine wine—you have to wait for it. And, like an expectant vintner, we awaited every batch like a bunch of chardonnay grapes. Westhagen brought a thesis-writer's keen eye to a region she had studied exhaustively, and ultimately gave the coverage of the book a much needed overhauling. She loved the food in Salt Lake City, Utah, and the backcountry of the entire region, and we all hope that our readers find as many distractions in the awe-inspiring Rocky Mountains as she did.

with

**David Mihalyfy**                                         *Michigan*
The second week of deer camp can be rough, but David made sure we'll always recognize Michigan from outer space.

# REGIONAL RESEARCHER-WRITERS

| | |
|---|---|
| **Weston Eguchi** | *Western Washington, Portland* |
| **Matt Elliott** | *Vancouver Island, Southern BC, Calgary, and the Rockies* |
| **David Friedland** | *Southcentral, Interior, and Southwest Alaska* |
| **Maja Groff** | *Vancouver Island, Northern BC, and the Yukon* |
| **Ken Haig** | *Southeast and Interior Alaska* |
| **Ana Morrel-Samuels** | *Oregon, Eastern Washington* |
| **Teresa Crockett** | *Northern Interior, Sierra Nevada, Fresno, Reno* |
| **Melissa Debayle** | *The Desert, Las Vegas, Rt. 66, San Diego* |
| **Zachary Fultz** | *Central Coast, Stockton, North Coast, Ojai* |
| **Julio V. Gambuto** | *Los Angeles, South Bay, Catalina Island, Orange County, Santa Barbara* |
| **Jenny Weiss** | *San Francisco, Bay Area, Wine Country* |
| **Brandee Butler** | *Queens, Brooklyn, Atlantic City, Manhattan* |
| **Edward Borey** | *Bronx, Staten Island, Liberty/Ellis Island, Fire Island, Manhattan* |
| **Rachel Farbiarz** | *Brooklyn, Bronx, Long Island, Manhattan* |
| **Colleen Gargan** | *Daytrips throughout MD, DE, VA and WV* |
| **Michelle Robinson** | *Washington, D.C. and environs* |
| **Katarina Wong** | *Washington, D.C. and environs* |
| **Eli Ceryak** | *Sydney and Northern New South Wales* |

# REGIONAL EDITORS

| | |
|---|---|
| **Tom Davidson** | *Editor, Alaska & The Pacific Northwest (not neglecting Western Canada)* |
| **James Wilson** | *Associate Editor, Alaska & The Pacific Northwest (God Save the Queen!)* |
| **Elena DeCoste** | *Editor, California (there's goald in them thar hills!)* |
| **Sarah A. Knight** | *Associate Editor, California* |
| **Lucia Brawley** | *Editor, New York City* |
| **Erin Billings** | *Editor, Washington, D.C.* |
| **Nicholas Grossman** | *Editor, Nick Time* |
| **Kaya Stone** | *Editor, Puerto Rico* |
| **Christian Lorentzen** | *Typesetter and DJ* |

# LET'S GO PICKS

**NATURALLY SPLENDID: Denali National Park,** AK (p. 928). Landscape, wildlife, and the largest vertical relief in the world; can you top 18,000 ft.? The **White Mountains National Forest,** NH (p. 99). Crowded with greenhorns, the aged Whites seem pretty tame—but fierce wind and weather make for quite an alpine adventure. **Jasper National Park,** AB (p. 917). Big mountains, big glaciers, big valleys, and one very small town. And you gotta see the **Grand Canyon,** AZ (p. 710).

**ARTIFICIAL WONDERS: Carhenge,** NE (p. 557), where Druid meets Buick. **Cross in the Woods,** MI (p. 483). Truly God's country, the woods of Petoskey, MI, shelter the nation's tallest crucifix. **Coral Castle,** FL (p. 444). This coral rock fortress near the entrance to the Everglades was built by a recluse to honor his lost love. A work in progress, and someday to be the largest sculpture in the world, the 563 ft. **Crazy Horse Memorial** (p. 540) stands in protest to nearby **Mount Rushmore** (p. 540).

**HOSPITABLE HOSTELS: Lake Louise Hostel,** AB (p. 914), the best of Banff, hosteled. **Gram's Place B&B** in Tampa, FL (p. 450). Unique amenities devoted to Gram Parsons. **Shadowcliff Hostel,** Rocky Mountain NP, CO (p. 664). A lodge with a view.

**CAMP HERE: Jenny Lake, Grand Teton National Park,** WY (p. 640). This may be the most spectacular spot in the nation to pitch a tent. **Big Sur,** CA (p. 795). Surrounded by Cali's redwoods and adjacent to the Pacific Ocean. **Padre Island,** TX (p. 604). Silky sands and crashing waves make this a Texan paradise. **John Pennekamp State Park,** FL (p. 446), has a beautiful campground right next to a 25mi. coral reef lapped by the waters of the Florida Keys.

**TOWNS WE HATE TO LEAVE: Cambridge,** MA (p. 125). We haven't left yet. Make sure to rub John Harvard's foot for extra special good luck.

**SCENIC DRIVES: The Kancamangus Hwy.,** NH (p. 100). Premium autumn foliage. **Telluride to Durango,** CO (p. 676). This bucolic journey is what road-tripping is all about. **Rt. 20,** WA (p. 876). A verdant loop winding through the North Cascades. **Icefields Prkwy.,** AB (p. 916). Massive hunks of stone and ice line the road through Banff and Jasper National Parks. **Rt. 1** up the Cali coast (p. 791). Surf, sun, cliffs, fog, and really, really big trees.

**SUSTENANCE IN STYLE:** Food in **New York City** (p. 208)—everything, in every flavor, at every hour; to work off that bowling-ball stomach, drink a beer and play some glo-in-the-dark rounds to the DJ house beat at **Bowlmor** (p. 237). **Dushanbe Teahouse** in Boulder, CO (p. 663). The building, built by artists in Tajikstan, was moved piecemeal across two continents and an ocean. **Nita's Place** in Savannah, GA (p. 382), explains the necessity of soul food in your diet.

**FAB FESTIVALS: Ashland Shakespeare Festival,** OR (p. 893). Year-round bard on the east banks of the Pacific, not the Thames. **Cheyenne Frontier Days,** Cheyenne WY, the largest outdoor rodeo in the nation, makes even city slickers yippee.

**MUSEUMS THAT WON'T INDUCE DROWSINESS: Center for Southern Folklore** in Memphis, TN (p. 347). Music history as it should be: down-home and performed live. **Museum of Contemporary Art** in North Adams, MA (p. 140). A bucolic setting for the newest and largest modern art museum. **J. Paul Getty Museum and Getty Center** in Los Angeles, CA (p. 768). A fabulous building housing fabulous "old" art. The **Biodome** in Montreal, PQ (p. 171). Literally a living museum.

**BEST BAR:** The **Cantab Lounge,** Cambridge, MA (p. 127). Live music upstairs, Boston's best poetry slamming downstairs. Good beer and nice, how you say, locals, all around.

**BEST CHEESEBURGER: Charlie's Kitchen,** Cambridge, MA (p. 126).

# ACKNOWLEDGMENTS

**TEAM USA THANKS:** Alex, our tireless ME. Jon Stein, the map boy and former R-W. The Domestic Room. Our R-Ws. And The Boss.

**T.J. THANKS:** Ana and Georgia, who made every day a pleasure. The DR. My mom, who convinced me years ago that I should apply to Harvard. Grandad, your postcards and slide-shows convinced me a long time ago that the traveling life is best. My whole family. John L., a better friend than I ever deserved. Xian, Sonesh, and Kaya, without whom nothing would have been the same. Pierce, Mateo, and Eli: for the ups and downs and four good years. JP, Drake, and Aaron. Nick G. and Chutz. D.P.G. to James and Tom. To Elena for the beer. To Lucky Wilbury, of course. Anne C., the indomitable. Irene, for hiring me in the first place. DJ. And Sarah J., for realizing I'm a jerk.

**GEORGIA THANKS:** "TeeJaaaay!" for answering questions. Ana, the smartest & bestest girl in the world. Rach & Dave; roomates can be family. Sarah for herself. ME for 4 yrs. of listening. Matt O. for opening my eyes. Beccah for knee-injuries and runs. Laura for being here this summer. Yuki for a road-trip? Greg & Becky for the menage-a-trois that could have been. John Lotz and Australia. Rolán, my partner-in-crime. C. Killip. John Duda. Petey Peehose. Cory for reconnections. My green bike. Brook & Yumi. FOP leaders & all their smelly armpits. Allegra & Becky. DGM, wherever. My parents; I'll always be their little girl. Xan, my sis. Hayden for that last really great hug.

**ANA THANKS:** ♥T.J. for making me laugh, ♥Georgia for dancing on the couch. Mum and Pli for warm meals and hearts. Ita y su czar de Rusia. Nanano for unending help. Meb and Boo-Boo for listening. Emster for speaking my language, a smiley life, and driving. Sofia for MEHHH. McKenzie for being my B2. Erica for trusting me. Al-i-son. Diego, mi amigo "derecho." My bike, my feet, my doggies. Angie for ocean commutes. Kyle. Weej for a better summer. Kate for a job. Kurt. Bill and Jules. My boys, especially Flynny. Mosquito Head. F.P. Jeff and Ben for bath-like hugs. Lewis R. for reading my poems. Tia Lucia. Raz. The locals.

**Editor**
T.J. Kelleher
**Associate Editors**
Ana Laguarda and Georgia Young
**Managing Editor**
Alexandra Leichtman

**Publishing Director**
Benjamin Wilkinson
**Editor-in-Chief**
Bentsion Harder
**Production Manager**
Christian Lorentzen
**Cartography Manager**
Daniel J. Luskin
**Design Managers**
Matthew Daniels, Melissa Rudolph
**Editorial Managers**
Brendan Gibbon, Benjamin Paloff, Kaya Stone, Taya Weiss
**Financial Manager**
Kathy Lu
**Personnel Manager**
Adam Stein
**Publicity & Marketing Managers**
Sonesh Chainani, Alexandra Leichtman
**New Media Manager**
Maryanthe Malliaris
**Map Editors**
Kurt Mueller, Jon Stein
**Production Associates**
Steven Aponte, John Fiore
**Office Coordinators**
Elena Schneider, Vanessa Bertozzi, Monica Henderson

**Director of Advertising Sales**
Marta Szabo
**Associate Sales Executives**
Tamas Eisenberger, Li Ran

**President**
Noble M. Hansen III
**General Managers**
Blair Brown, Robert B. Rombauer
**Assistant General Manager**
Anne E. Chisholm

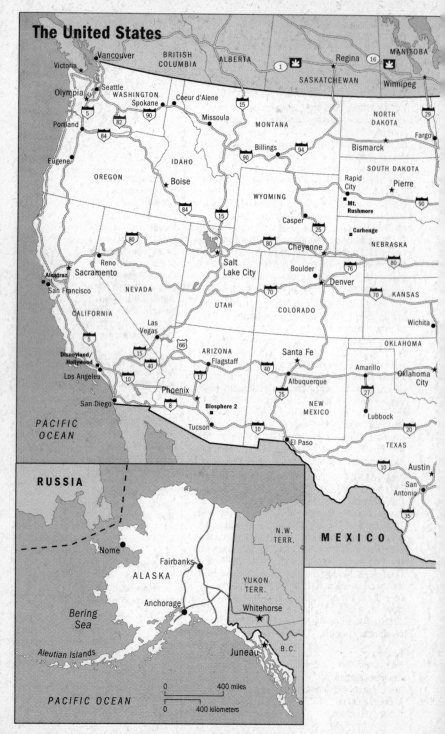

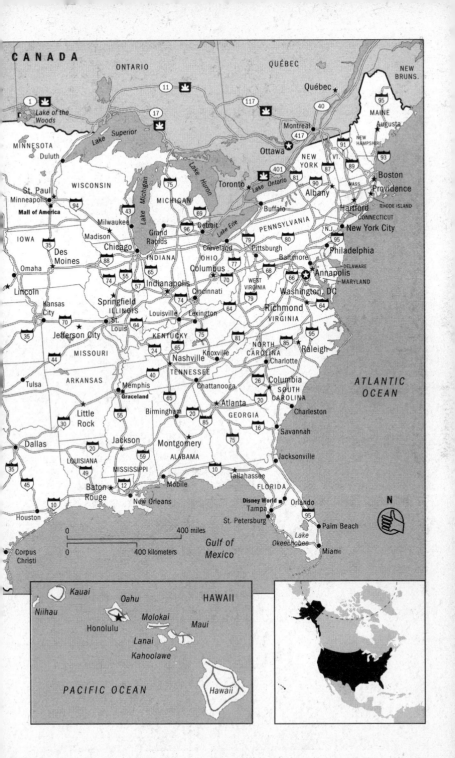

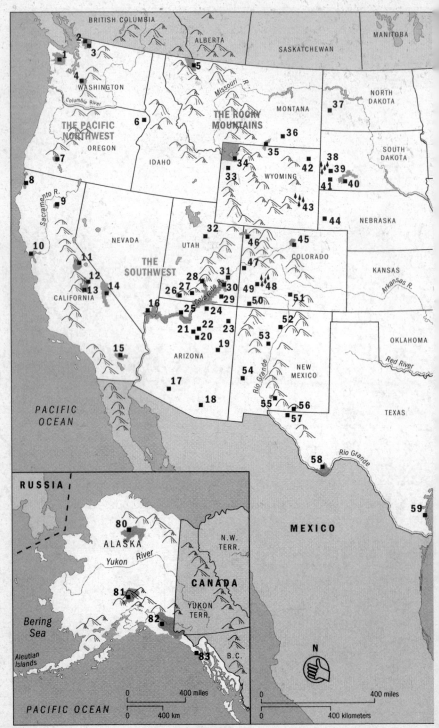

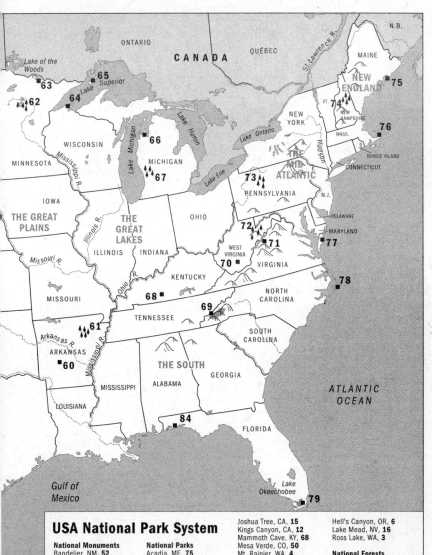

## USA National Park System

**National Monuments**
Bandelier, NM, **52**
Black Canyon, CO, **49**
Canyon de Chelly, AZ, **23**
Colorado, CO, **47**
Devils Tower, WY, **42**
Dinosaur, CO, **46**
Gila Cliff Dwellings, NM, **54**
Great Sand Dunes, CO, **51**
Lassen Volcanic, CA, **9**
Little Bighorn, MT, **36**
Mt. Rushmore, SD, **39**
Natural Bridges, UT, **29**
Navajo, AZ, **24**
Organ Pipe, AZ, **17**
Petroglyph, NM, **53**
Scotts Bluff, NE, **44**
Sunset Crater, AZ, **21**
Timpanogos Cave, UT, **32**
Walnut Canyon, AZ, **20**
White Sands, NM, **55**
Wupatki, AZ, **22**

**National Parks**
Acadia, ME, **75**
Arches, UT, **31**
Badlands, SD, **40**
Big Bend, TX, **58**
Bryce Canyon, UT, **27**
Canyonlands, UT, **30**
Capitol Reef, UT, **28**
Carlsbad Caverns, NM, **56**
Crater Lake, OR, **7**
Death Valley, CA, **14**
Denali, AK, **81**
Everglades, FL, **79**
Gates of the Arctic, AK, **80**
Glacier, MT, **5**
Glacier Bay, AK, **83**
Grand Canyon, AZ, **25**
Grand Teton, WY, **33**
Great Smoky Mts., TN, **69**
Guadalupe Mts., TX, **57**
Hot Springs, AR, **60**
Isle Royale, MI, **65**

Joshua Tree, CA, **15**
Kings Canyon, CA, **12**
Mammoth Cave, KY, **68**
Mesa Verde, CO, **50**
Mt. Rainier, WA, **4**
New River Gorge, WV, **70**
North Cascades, WA, **2**
Olympic, WA, **1**
Petrified Forest, AZ, **19**
Redwood, CA, **8**
Rocky Mt., CO, **45**
Saguaro, AZ, **18**
Sequoia, CA, **13**
Shenandoah, VA, **71**
Theodore Roosevelt, ND, **37**
Voyageurs, MN, **63**
Wind Cave, SD, **41**
Wrangell-St. Elias, AK, **82**
Yellowstone, WY, **34**
Yosemite, CA, **11**
Zion, UT, **26**

**National Recreation Areas**
Bighorn Canyon, MT, **35**
Golden Gate, CA, **10**

Hell's Canyon, OR, **6**
Lake Mead, NV, **16**
Ross Lake, WA, **3**

**National Forests**
Allegheny, PA, **73**
Black Hills, SD, **48**
Chippewa, MN, **62**
Grand Mesa, CO, **48**
Manistee, MI, **67**
Medicine Bow, WY, **43**
Monongahela, WV, **72**
Ozark, AR, **61**
White Mts., NH, **74**

**National Lakeshores**
Apostle Islands, WI, **64**
Sleeping Bear Dunes, MI, **66**

**National Seashores**
Assateague, MD, **77**
Cape Cod, MA, **76**
Cape Hatteras, NC, **78**
Padre Island, TX, **59**
Gulf Islands, FL, **84**

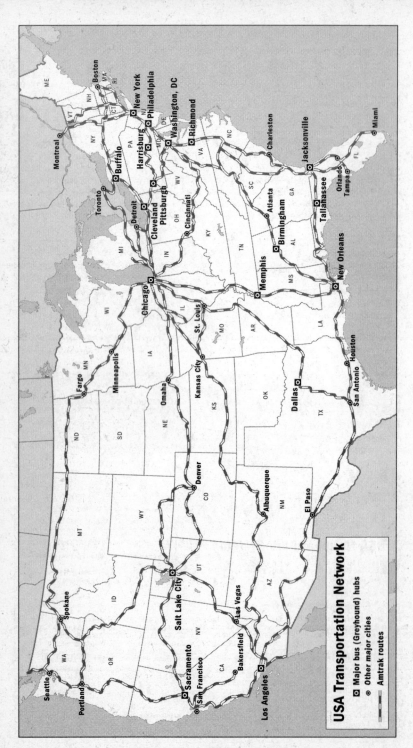

## USA Transportation Network

- ◎ Major bus (Greyhound) hubs
- ⊙ Other major cities
- Amtrak routes

# DISCOVER
# THE USA AND CANADA

## THE UNITED STATES

Stretching from below the Tropic of Cancer to above the Arctic Circle and spanning the North American continent, the United States is big. It is a country defined by open spaces and an amazing breadth of terrain. From sparse deserts to lush forests to snow-capped peaks to rolling fields of grain, the American landscape sprouts new views from state to state—even from neighborhood to neighborhood.

America's accumulation of wealth and prestige since WWII has heightened both its patriotism and its interior divisions. Americans have reason to be proud: in this fair country, world-class creature comforts exist minutes away from acres of country quiet—and most of it is accessible, at least in theory, to everyone. However, the contrast between the overall abundance of wealth and the homeless who line city streets is a constant confrontation. Though class lines aren't openly acknowledged, they drive people's daily lives, aspirations, and politics. Wealthy people may run the big show, but the middle-class masses define America's ideological orientation towards unpretentious family values. Through centuries of immigration, the U.S. has absorbed and integrated millions of immigrants to create the cultural amalgamation that now defines the population, contributing to the proud spirit of diversity which pervades the country, and also clashing in situations of discrimination and misunderstanding.

America does indeed live up to its reputation as the land of plenty, but plentiness leads often to too-muchness, as the proliferation of Blockbuster video stores and expanding acres of cookie-cutter suburbs attests to. As this child of many continents has risen from a colonial experiment to a position of supreme economic and political power, its largesse continues to both impress and overwhelm.

## CANADA

Canucks will beat you silly if they hear you say that Canada is "just like America." Canada is also a huge, prosperous, educated country; but up north the terrain is wilder, the distribution of wealth is more thorough, and a third of the population speaks French. The second largest country in the world, Canada covers almost 10 million square kilometers (3.85 million square miles), and only 29 million people inhabit its 10 provinces and two territories; well over half of the population crowds into Ontario and Québec. Though its cities are cosmopolitan, Canada's vast tracts of underpopulated forest and frozen tundra lend it a wild edge that no amount of cultural savvy can subdue.

Early French colonists were largely independent hunters, trappers, and traders who depended on Native Canadians, especially the powerful Huron-Iriquois tribe, as allies and hunting instructors. The country originated as a system of trading posts stretching through Quebec and Ontario, areas which to this day are largely French-speaking. The British colonists were relatively distant and culturally distinct, eventually settling along the two coasts. Since then, each population has fought to retain political dominance. Native Canadian concerns and a rapidly increasing allophone population—people whose first language is neither English nor French—have convoluted the cultural struggle. Divergent economic foundations have exacerbated inter-regional tensions; bankrupt fisheries have drained the Maritime provinces while the West Coast booms with trans-Pacific trade.

| USA FACTS | CANADA FIGURES |
|---|---|
| ■ **Population:** 270,311,756, of which 90% live next to their televisions. | ■ **Population:** 30,675,398, of which 90% live within 160km of the U.S. border. |
| ■ **Airports:** 5167 with paved runways; 9407 with unpaved runways. | ■ **Airports:** 515 with paved runways; 878 with unpaved runways. |
| ■ **Captial:** Washington, D.C. | ■ **Capital:** Ottawa |

# AMERICANA

The United States specializes in tackiness. Beyond the pink flamingos and year-round Christmas tree lights found in (too) many American front yards, commercial America enshrines the largest, smallest, and wackiest of everything and puts it on public display (most often for a fee). A few of the best...Drunken revelry or lots of road-side can-collecting helped John Mikovisch build the **beer can house,** in Houston, TX (p. 595). The **largest kaleidoscope** in the world spins in Mt. Tremper, NY (p. 240). Visitors can attempt to phone home at the **alien crash site** in Roswell, NM (p. 752). **The Mall of America,** the country's largest commercial playground, waits in Bloomington, MN (p. 524), outside of Minneapolis-St. Paul. Visitors watch what they eat at the **largest FDA food pyramid** in the world, in Wichita, KS (p. 559). **Graceland,** Elvis' old home in Memphis, Tenessee (p. 347), is the ultimate in tac-o-rama. The **Miracle of America Museum** cashes in, with a magnificient collection in Polson, MT (between Missoula and Glacier; p. 627). A **600 pound ball of stamps** can be found at Father Flanagan's Boys' Home in Omaha, NE (p. 553).

# HISTORICAL SIGHTS

Most historical sights are dusty meccas overrun with elementary school field trips and fathers armed with narrated car tapes, determined to educate their children. A trip down history lane can be quite a kick, however. Patriotic Americans have a die-hard love of Revolutionary and Civil War sites which, at least in the words of interpretive signs, reflect the values our forebearers fought to protect. Boston is over-run with Revolution-mania; the **Freedom Trail** (p. 118) traverses the modern city on its historical trek—the U.S.S. Constitution and the Old South Meeting house are two memorable sites—and city pleasures such as excellent oysters and tiramasu sweeten the deal along the way. The Civil War battlefields spattering Pennsylvania and Virginia are best summed up by the cannon-ball littered fields of **Gettysburg National Cemetery, PA** (p. 270), forcing reflection on what it must have been like to fight a brotherly enemy face to face.

Most of the numerous "recreated historical villages" which line the East Coast are tacky and expensive, but a few are informative. **Williamsburg, VA** (p. 307), tastefully restores the 18th-century capital of the colony. At **Plimoth Plantation, MA** (p. 129), costumed actors play their roles as toughened founders of the New World with straight faces. **Monticello** (p. 314), Thomas Jefferson's plantation in Virginia, has been restored with magnificent accuracy, including the slave quarters out back.

West of the Appalacians, colonial history is a more recent phenomenon. The bygone days of the Wild West coagulate in recreated cowboy towns such as **Cody,** Wyoming (p. 647). Numerous sites and museums memorialize the pioneers' covered wagon trek along the Oregon Trail. 150 year-old wagon ruts seem dinky in comparison with the ancient pueblo cities left by Native American tribes in the the Southwest; the **Gila Cliff Dwellings** in New Mexico (p. 750) are the most impressive.

# NATIONAL PARKS

Together, the U.S. and Canada cover most of the North American continent, containing a diverse series of ecosystems and geographic formations. Some of the most spectacular land is protected as national parkland, where development and logging are prohibited and use is strictly controlled. America's most popular parks—**Yellowstone,** WY (p. 632), the **Grand Canyon N.P.,** AZ (p. 710), **Yosemite N.P.,** CA (p. 844), and the **Great Smoky Mountains N.P.,** TN (p. 340), are over-run with tourists, though are still well worth visiting. Other parks are more quiet; at the desert **Joshua Tree N.P.,** CA (p. 789), imagination (and some other substances which *Let's Go* cannot recommend) turn the park's boulders into fantastic animals. South Dakota's **Wind Cave N.P.** (p. 541) remains 95% undiscovered, waiting, perhaps, for you. **North Cascades N.P.,** WA (p. 876), **Bryce Canyon N.P.,** UT (p. 704), and **Wrangell St. Elias N.P.,** AK (p. 927), are spots remarkable for backcountry hiking. From Maine's **Acadia N.P.** (p. 97), numerous remote islands are accessible.

Canada's national parks tend to be much less crowded, offering purists a more pristine experience. At **Fundy N.P.,** NB (p. 160), the tide rises at 1 ft. per min. and deer are still common. **Yoho N.P.** (p. 919) and **Kluane N.P.** (p. 911) are deliciously barren of folks. **Jasper N.P.,** AB (p. 917), is the largest of Canada's 4 mountain parks, which also include the popular **Banff N.P.,** AB (p. 914). **Prince Edward Island N.P.** (p. 162), a northern marine beauty, cradles 32 km of Canada's best beaches.

## BREWERIES

Beer is an American pastime; from paper napkin barbecues to yuppie bars, beer is the drink of choice. In the midwest, where Miller (Milwaukee, WI) and Anheuser-Busch (St. Louis, MO) are home institutions, the masses drink **Budweiser** and **Miller Light** from cans. In fact, the masses elsewhere drink the stuff, too. Bottled **Microbrew** is the newest thing in beer. Hand-made in local breweries—usually in towns where the primary activity is outdoor recreation—microbrews tend to have inventive names like "Hair of the Dog" and "Magic Hat #9." Microbrew was invented in the West, and the best beers still come from west of the Rockies, but now-a-days, micro breweries and their subsidiaries on tap, "brewpubs," are almost everywhere. Most breweries, large and small, offer tours and tastings.

# SUGGESTED ITINERARIES

**SUMMER ROADTRIP: THE EAST COAST (6 WEEKS)** U.S. 1 and I-95 parallel each other from the northern wilds of Maine down to the gorgeous coasts of the Florida Keys; a tour of the original 13 colonies provides a true cross-section of American culture north to south. Beware, however, I-95 is laced with toll booths, and a trip on that strip will cost considerably more money. The rogues and other assorted characters of the far-south of Florida await in Key West (p. 447), chumming with Hemingway's ghost. Don't miss the swampy mystery, danger, and beauty of the Everglades (p. 443), or the nearby glitz of Miami Beach (p. 438). Disney World beckons (p. 428), as does the oldest city in the United States, St. Augustine (p. 420). Georgia's coast offers feral and heavenly Cumberland Island (p. 384), and the more refined pleasures of Savannah (p. 381). Farther north, that port city finds a soul-

mate in Charleston, SC (p. 362), where Confederate Gen. Beauregard fired the first shots of the Civil War. The coasts of the Carolinas—SC's Grand Strand (p. 368), and NC's Outer Banks (p. 359)—offer pirate history, American kitsch, and all-around fun. The beaches of Virginia are nothing to smirk at, nor are historic spots like Jamestown and Yorktown (p. 309). The nation's capital (p. 286) deserves a couple of days, although the days of Mr. Smith are long gone. The coasts of Delaware (p. 277) and New Jersey (p. 285) offer more classic American beachfront fun, but they quickly give way to the myth builder of America, New York City (p. 198). Give it a least a weekend—some people take a lifetime—but *caveat emptor*: these people aren't the least bit ironic about how great they or their city is. Boston and Cambridge (p. 113) await in Massachusetts. The beauty of the White Mountains (p. 99) in New Hampshire

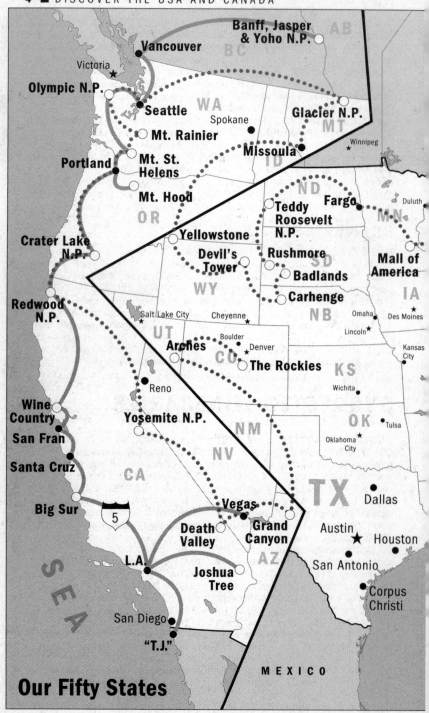

**Our Fifty States**

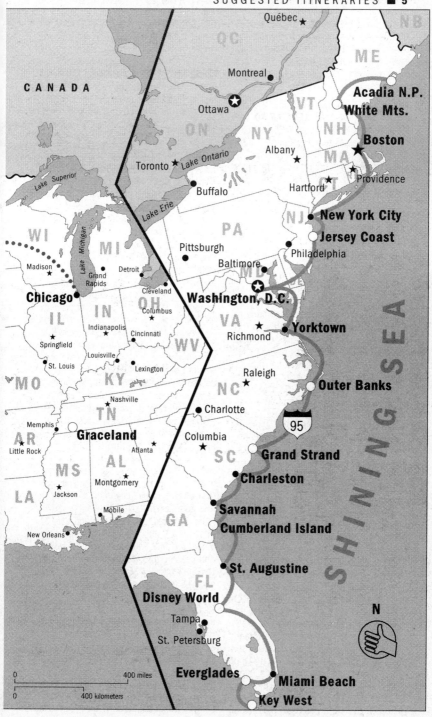

should not be ignored on the way to Maine's Mt. Desert Island (p. 94); this final drive is lined with quaint beach towns and natural beauty.

## AMERICA'S WESTERN WILDERNESS: FROM CHICAGO TO SEATTLE TO LAS VEGAS TO CHICAGO (6 WEEKS)

The first western explorers boasted of its natural wonder...the only problem is that spots preserved in their natural state tend to be few and far between. Disparate national parks protect some of the most spectacular areas. Chicago (p. 493) can trap you for days, but there truly is something better out there. Point the hood ornament toward Theodore Roosevelt N.P. in North Dakota (p. 534). The journey there leads through Minneapolis-St. Paul and the artificial jungle of the Mall of America (p. 524), as well as the Cohen brothers' favorite city, Fargo (p. 531). Mt. Rushmore (p. 540) and the Badlands (p. 537) wait to the south, along with Carhenge (p. 557), where the road then leads westward to Wyoming where Devil's Tower (p. 650) and Yellowstone (p. 632) spew from the earth. Past Missoula, MT (p. 625) the natural splendors of America's northern Rockies accompanies travelers to Glacier N.P. (p. 627). Crossing the Great Divide, blip through the bare neck of Idaho and eastern Washington to the funky metropolis of Seattle (p. 853), where the nature-weary can re-fuel with high-octane coffee and the freshest grub. The snowy tips of the Olympic Mtns. are visible across the bay but the remote beaches and lush rainforest are more hidden (p. 870). Two major mountains lie along the road towards Portland (p. 879); Mt. Ranier (p. 874) is a monolith, but Mt. St. Helens (p. 873) is more fascinating because of what's missing: it's entire top half, due to a 1980 eruption. Bookin' on to southern Oregon, Crater Lake (p. 892) is the deepest (and bluest) freshwater lake. The ancient Redwoods (p. 835) populate the N. California coast. Inland, the jagged spine of the Sierra Nevada Mtns. runs through Yosemite (p. 844), of Ansel Adams and rock-climbing fame. Past the aptly named Death Valley (p. 790) lie gluttonous rewards—Las Vegas (p. 682). Everyone has seen pictures of

the Grand Canyon (p. 710), but you don't know it 'til you see it. The (not golden) Arches (p. 700) provide more natural wonder of the architectural sort. The Rocky Mountains (p. 663) in Colorado boast acres of the highest peaks—one last wahoo before the road back to Chicago flattens into gridded Midwest farmland.

## THE WEST COAST: FROM LA TO VANCOUVER, B.C. (2-6 WEEKS).

Though it no longer takes months in a covered wagon to reach the West Coast, and much of the land has been gobbled up by urban sprawl, there still exists a raw, escapist quality to the West Coast. People are less stuck in their ways, life is cleaner, and it's still possible to penetrate forests so dense that they feel undiscovered. A tour of the West Coast offers the most cosmopolitan diversity, mountainscapes, and oceanfront property for your buck; from sunny, boisterous Los Angeles to lush, mellow Vancouver, B.C. there lies much natural (and artificial) diversion in-between. L.A. (p. 754), America's western outpost of high culture, provides access to Hollywood (p. 756), famous art, and quintessential beach culture. Las Vegas (p. 682), Tijuana (p. 786), and Joshua Tree (p. 789) are viable side trips. The 400 mi. stretch of shore-hugging Rt. 1 between LA and San Francisco—through Big Sur (p. 795), and Santa Cruz (p. 792)—is pure California: rolling surf, secluded beaches, dramatic cliffs, and quirky folks. San Francisco (p. 800), a groovin' city in itself, is only 3-4hr. from Yosemite National Park (p. 844). From San Fran, the slightly inland Rt. 101 hits Napa Valley wine country (p. 830) before reuniting with Rt. 1 (and the coast) and passing through primordial Redwood National Park (p. 835). Once past the trees, rejoin I-5 for a speedy trip through Oregon to Portland (p. 879). Side trips to Crater Lake (p. 892) and Mt. Hood (p. 885) are worth it for nature-junkies. Before resettling with a cappucino in Seattle, the moonscape of Mt. St. Helens (p. 873) and the rainforests of Olympic National Park (p. 870) lie in waiting. Vancouver, B.C. (p. 897)—just 3 hr. away but in a whole new country—offers access to the outdoor havens of Vancouver Is. (p. 904) and Yoho NP (p. 919).

# LIFE AND TIMES

## THE UNITED STATES

## HISTORY

### IN THE BEGINNING

Archaeologists estimate that the first Americans crossed the Bering Sea from Siberia, either by land bridge or boat, during the last **Ice Age,** about 15,000 years ago. Recent archaeological digs have uncovered evidence of earlier habitation, but the data leaves room for speculation. By 9000 BC hunter-gatherer populations lived in every corner of North America. These settlers adapted remarkably well to their new environment; on the plains Native Americans hunted buffalo, on the West Coast Aleuts and Eskimos caught whales and other sea mammals, and on the East Coast the forests provided vast foraging grounds. By the time Europeans arrived, around a hundred civilizations composed nine distinct cultural areas of North America.

### EUROPEAN EXPLORATION AND COLONIZATION

The date of the first European exploration of North America is also disputed. The earliest Europeans to stumble upon the "New World" were likely sea voyagers blown off-course by storms. *The Saga of the Greenlanders* and *The Saga of Erik the Red* describe the travels of Icelanders who sailed to Greenland, the Labrador coast, and possibly northern New England in 982. The traditional "discovery" of the Americas was in 1492, when **Christopher Columbus** found his voyage to the East blocked by Hispaniola in the Caribbean Sea. Believing he had reached the spice islands of the East Indies, he erroneously dubbed the inhabitants **"Indians."** In return for an efficient agricultural system, suitable for survival in the New World, the Europeans gave the Native Americans pestilence, persecution, and slavery.

Many Europeans came to the Americas (named after Italian explorer **Amerigo Vespucci**) in search of gold and silver; most were unsuccessful, but European colonization persisted. The Spanish originally boasted the most extensive American empire (today's New Mexico, Arizona, California, and Florida). **St. Augustine** (p. 420), founded in Florida in 1565, was the first permanent European settlement in the present-day United States. Meanwhile, the French and Dutch created more modest empires to the north. It was the English, however, who most successfully settled the vast New World. After a few unsuccessful attempts, like the "lost colony" at **Roanoke** in North Carolina (p. 360), the English finally managed to establish a colony at **Jamestown** in 1607 (p. 309). Their success hinged on a strain of native American weed called tobacco, which achieved wild popularity in England. **English Puritans** landed first in **Provincetown** (p. 134) in 1620 (*not* **Plymouth Rock,** p. 129) in what is now Massachusetts, but quickly left for better land and sailed into the history books. Native Americans helped teach them to survive in a harsh land. The Pilgrims, grateful for their hard-won survival, celebrated with a huge feast. **Thanksgiving,** one of the most treasured holidays in American culture, continues to stuff families with turkey, gravy, and cranberry sauce every fourth Thursday in November. Although Britain's American empire grew to encompass 13 diverse colonies up and down the eastern seaboard, the New England Puritans exerted a strong political and cultural influence over all regions until well after the Revolution.

# CONSOLIDATION AND REVOLUTION

Throughout the first half of the 18th century, the English colonies expanded as valleys were settled, fields plowed, and babies born. A quarter-million settlers had grown into 2.5 million by 1775. The expanding British colonies gradually imposed upon the French, who also sought to expand their neighboring empire. Several military clashes resulted; the most explosive of these encounters was the **French and Indian War,** a side-show to the world-wide Seven Years' War. From 1756 to 1763, the English fought the French and their Native American allies, who joined the battle in exchange for French aid in inter-tribal conflicts. The British emerged victorious, and the 1763 **Peace of Paris** ceded French Canada to Britain's King George III.

Determined to make the colonists help pay the debts incurred in assuring their safety, the British government levied a number of taxes in the 1760s and early 1770s. The colonists reacted with indignation, protesting **"no taxation without representation."** Agitation over the taxes came to a head with the **Boston Massacre** in 1770 and then the **Boston Tea Party** in December of 1774, in which a group of revolutionaries dressed as Native Americans dumped several ship loads of taxed English tea into Boston Harbor. The British response, dubbed the Intolerable Acts, was swift and harsh. Boston was effectively placed under siege, but the red-coated British soldiers who poured into town were met with armed rebellion, beginning in Lexington, MA in April of 1775. On July 4, 1776, the Continental Congress formally issued the **Declaration of Independence,** announcing the 13 colonies' desire to be free of British rule. Initially a guerilla band composed of homespun militia known as **Minutemen,** the Continental forces eventually grew into an effective army under the leadership of **George Washington.** Despite many setbacks, the revolutionaries prevailed in 1871 after vanquishing British General Lord Cornwallis at **Yorktown, Virginia** (p. 309), with the help of the French fleet.

## LIFE, LIBERTY, AND THE CONSTITUTION

The country experimented with a loose confederate government until 1787, when the several state legislatures sent a distinguished group of 55 men convened to draft what is now the world's oldest written **Constitution.** While the **Federalists** supported a strong central government uninfluenced by popular whim, their opposition, the **Jeffersonians** (Anti-Federalists), favored states' rights and feared the cutthroat individualism and domineering government that capitalism would bring.

The Constitution's **Bill of Rights,** which included the rights to free speech, freedom of the press, and freedom of religion, remains a controversial cornerstone of the American political system. In spite of the supposed inalienability of these rights, the original words of the document's authors are still interpreted differently according to the political climate of each era. In 1896, **Justice Henry Billings Brown** used the Constitution to support segregation in **Plessy v. Ferguson,** whereas **Chief Justice Earl Warren** cited the same document to destroy the practice in the 1950s. The Constitution, with its malleability and responsiveness to changing mores, reflects the country's longing for just governance.

## ONWARD AND OUTWARD: MANIFEST DESTINY

Looking toward the land beyond the Mississippi River, in 1803 **President Thomas Jefferson** purchased the **Louisiana Territory** (one-fourth of the present-day United States) from Napoleon for less than 3¢ an acre. The next year, Jefferson sent the **Lewis and Clark expedition** to explore the new territory and to find an aqueous trade route through to the Pacific Ocean. Lewis and Clark never found a trade route, but they did chart the vast extent of land which lay west of Louisiana. After the War of 1812 with Britain, the westward movement gained momentum. **Manifest Destiny,** a belief that the United States was destined by God to rule the continent, captured the ideological imagination of the era. The annexation of Texas in 1846 and war with Mexico in 1848 added most of the Southwest and California to the territorial fold. Britain was pressured into relinquishing its Pacific Coast claims south of the 49th parallel, and the Oregon territory was added to a burgeoning nation which now straddled two coasts. Droves of people migrated west in covered wagons along the grueling **Oregon Trail** in search of cheap, fertile land, elusive gold, and a new life.

**The Homestead Act** of 1862, which distributed government land to those who would farm and live on it, prompted the cultivation of the Great Plains. This large-scale settlement led to bloody battles with the Sioux, Hunkpapas, the Cheyenne tribes who had long inhabited the plains. From 1866-1891 the U.S. fought a continuous war against the remaining 300,000 "Indians." At **Custer's Last Stand** in 1876, a group of Native Americans led by **Crazy Horse** and **Sitting Bull** massacred General Custer's army, which prompted a furious reaction. The Native Americans were routed out, their land taken away, and their communities relegated to reservations. Much of the legend of the **Wild West** revolves around tales of brave white settlers and stoic cowboys fending off attacks by the Indians. These stories are largely distortions, created to justify the actions of a government which displaced Native Americans through random surges of violence and breaches of treaties. However, the West was a place furnished by adventurous fantasies, capturing the popular imagination of Americans fed up with the stodginess of more established Eastern society. For more, see **Navajo Reservation,** p. 719.

## AMERICA'S PECULIAR INSTITUTION

The first **Africans** came to America in 1619, prisoners aboard a Dutch slave ship headed for Jamestown, VA. Their arrival marked the decline of indentured servitude, a system by which poor Europeans would pay for crossing the Atlantic with labor, typically for seven years. From the late-16th century and into the 17th century, as the demand for cheap labor increased, white settlers systematically invaded and terrorized Native American communities in search of "slaves." As white indentured servitude tapered off and Native Americans suffered fatally from European diseases, white America relied heavily on the African slave trade to fill the gap. Thousands of Africans were plucked from their homes and forced across the Atlantic in the dark and moldy bellies of slave ships, a harrowing journey known as the **Middle Passage.** Once in the U.S., they were auctioned. This practice would last until the late 19th century, forming one of the most brutal chapters in the country's short history.

American victory in the Revolutionary War proved a mixed bag for African Americans. While northern blacks earned a large degree of freedom for themselves and their families as soldiers, nurses, and spies in the War, wealthy southern whites gained greater autonomy to exploit the enslaved population. Slavery was not an easy system for southerners to maintain. After contending with fierce uprisings, slaveowners dealt with more subtle means of black rebellion, as slaves created their own secret culture in resistance to their inescapable lot. Some slaves did escape, though most were caught before they'd gone far. Free African Americans and abolitionist whites formed the elusive **Underground Railroad,** an escape route into the free northern states. **Harriet Tubman,** a former slave, led at least a thousand African Americans on foot across the United States. Southerners who invaded the north to retrieve their "property" fueled existing tensions between North and South over slavery and states' rights. These two separate halves of a nation, split by economic and societal differences, coexisted uneasily during the first half of the 19th century—it would take a fierce and bloody call to arms to decide which identity would prevail.

## "A HOUSE DIVIDED"—THE CIVIL WAR

Tensions between the North and South came to a head when an anti-slavery President, **Abraham Lincoln,** was elected in 1860. South Carolina seceded from the Union, but Lincoln refused to officially recognize the secession. Twelve states (AL, AR, FL, GA, KY, LA, MS, MO, NC, TN, TX, and VA) followed in 1861, and 1862 witnessed the birth of a united southern Confederacy, under the lead of **Jefferson Davis.** When the South Carolina militia attacked the Union's **Fort Sumter** in Charleston, South Carolina, it was war. For four years the country endured a savage and bloody war, fought by the North to restore the Union and by the South to break it. Lincoln issued the **Emancipation Proclamation** in 1863 to free slaves in Southern-held territory (but not in the few Union slave states, or occupied southern land). Despite the Proclamation's modest aims, blacks throughout the U.S. were encouraged by its promise; widespread plantation walk-outs ensued. The battle at **Gettysburg** (p. 270), Pennsylvania in July 1863, where the northern advance of **General Robert E. Lee's** Confederate army was defeated by Union forces under **General Ulysses S. Grant,** turned the tide of the war. After four bloody years, the North overcame the South. On April 9, 1865, General Lee surrendered to General Grant at Appomatox Court House, Virginia.

Lincoln led the North to victory, but the price was high. The war claimed more American lives than any other in history, and many families were divided against each other as brothers took up different uniforms and loyalties. Lincoln was assassinated on April 14 by John Wilkes Booth, a Southern sympathizer. The **13th Amendment** ended slavery in 1865, and Abe Lincoln was forever memorialized in public memory as the President who saved the union and abolished slavery.

## RECONSTRUCTION AND INDUSTRIALIZATION

The period after the war brought Reconstruction to the South, and Industrial Revolution to the North. The North's rapid industrialization rendered it a formidable contender in the world economy, while the South's agricultural economy began a slow decline. The South, injured and embittered by the war and dependent on an outdated agricultural tradition, struggled to readjust to the new economic and social situations forced upon them. The newly-freed blacks faced a difficult transition from plantation to free life. **Jim Crow** laws continued to restrict blacks' freedom; white politicians espousing the "separate but equal" doctrine, prohibited blacks from frequenting the same establishments, schools, and even drinking fountains as whites. Though black colleges were established and prominent blacks were able to gain some degree of political power, many blacks were relegated to a life of share-cropping for white landowners and were manipulated by white politicians who needed their votes. A group of white southerners, bitter that their way of life had been abolished, established the **Ku Klux Klan** in 1867, a white supremacist, stealth organization dedicated to terrorizing blacks and prohibiting them from gaining power. They performed numerous lynchings, burnings, and beatings.

During the North's **"Gilded Age,"** so-called because it was beautiful on the surface but tarnished underneath, captains of industry such as George Vanderbilt, Andrew Carnegie, and John D. Rockefeller built commercial empires and enormous personal fortunes amidst an atmosphere of widespread political and economic corruption. The downside of the concentration of massive wealth in a few hands landed most heavily on the powerless masses—on hapless farmers toiling in a dying agricultural economy, and on workers, who faced low wages, violent strike break-ups, and unsafe working conditions. Yet the fruits of the industrial age, including railroads, telegraphs, and telephones, made transportation and communication across the vast nation easier. America became an increasingly mobile nation and remains one to this day; if Americans don't like where they are, they pick up and move far, far away.

## GLOBAL IMPERIALISM AND WWI

The racism expressed in Jim Crow laws and Native American genocide didn't end at domestic borders. The United States' victory in the **Spanish-American War** in 1898 validated the American sense of Anglo-Saxon superiority, and the cocky belief that their influence could be extended world-wide. The United States caught imperial fever, acquiring colonies in the Philippines, Puerto Rico, and Cuba. Meanwhile, large industrial monopolies came under attack from the Progressive Party. A new breed of journalists, nicknamed **"muckrakers,"** began exposing the corruption rampant in big business.

In 1901 at age 42, **Teddy Roosevelt** became the youngest president in history, and one never afraid to use the **"big stick."** In response to the corrupt, monopolistic practices of big business, Roosevelt promoted anti-trust reforms to regulate large companies. In foreign affairs Roosevelt established the U.S. as an "international police power," reflecting a reassessment of the traditional isolationist sentiment.

After vowing to keep the U.S. out of "Europe's War," President **Woodrow Wilson** reluctantly entered **World War I** in its closing stages. U.S. troops landed in Europe in 1917, and fought until Germany's defeat two years later. Though the metal-eating war jump-started America's industrial economy and established the United States as a major international power, the frightful toll of the Great War—ten million people dead, including 130,174 Americans—disillusioned and shocked Americans.

# ROARING 20S, GREAT DEPRESSION, AND WWII

Americans returned their attentions to their own continent, busting with money but ruffled by the winds of change. A conservative administration routed "foreign" influences, unleashing the **Red Scare;** politicians slanderously accused Socialists of being Russian sympathizers. The perceived "moral decline" of America was addressed by establishing the immensely unpopular **Prohibition** in 1919, which outlawed all alcohol. Among the younger populous, however, restrictive conventions were exuberantly tossed aside. In celebration of the free-wheelin', booze-smugglin', **"Jazz Age"** women shucked their undergarments aside and bared their shoulders to dance the Charleston. Women **suffragists** also mobilized for the right to vote, which the **19th Amendment** to the Constitution granted in 1920.

European immigrants struggled to assimilate into an American identity, often by unifying to push black Americans and Asian immigrants out of white, European immigrant neighborhoods. Yet a common thread ran through each of these postwar communities; all grabbed for a slice of the seemingly abundant capitalist pie. The "Roaring 20s," however, were largely supported by overextended credit. The facade crumbled on "Black Thursday," October 24, 1929, when the New York Stock Exchange crashed, launching the **Great Depression.** In an urbanized, mechanized age, millions of workers (25-50% of the work force) were left unemployed and they had no farms to fall back on for survival. The United States was unable to rebound from the Great Depression as it had from previous depressions. Many people suffered, struggling to provide food and housing for their families. The experience of the Depression imprinted a generation of Americans with a compulsion to hoard, an appreciation of money, and a skepticism of the economy.

Under the firm hand of President **Franklin D. Roosevelt,** the United States began a decade-long recovery. Roosevelt's **New Deal** implemented reform legislation and economic management by increasing social spending. Farm prices were subsidized, financial institutions put under federal jurisdiction, minimum wages set, and the Social Security Act brought the U.S. into the era of the welfare state.

As the German Nazi regime plowed through Europe, anxious Americans largely stood aside and watched, regretfully unaware of the Holocaust. The Japanese attack on **Pearl Harbor,** Hawaii, on December 7, 1941, brought America reluctantly into World War II. The U.S. played a key role in the invasion of the Normandy coast on June 6, 1944—**D-Day,** the battle that turned the tide of the war. The Germans formally surrendered on May 7, 1945, ending the war in Europe. The war in the Pacific continued until August, when the U.S. dropped two newly-developed nuclear bombs on Japan, at **Hiroshima** on August 6, 1945, and at Nagasaki three days later, killing 80,000 civilians. Despite major debate over the morality of detonating a hugely destructive bomb in civilian territory, this move established the United States as a nuclear power to be reckoned with.

# THE COLD WAR, VIETNAM, AND CIVIL RIGHTS

Spared the wartime devastation of Europe and East Asia, the U.S. economy boomed in the post-war era, solidifying the status of the United States as the world's foremost economic and military power. The **"fifties"** (which really began in 1945) are nostalgically recalled as a time of prosperity and social normality; T.V. sitcoms and suburban houses with glowing green lawns and dishwashers typified the American dream. This veneer of comfortability disguised deeper societal rifts. A generation of **"beats,"** self-proclaimed social outcasts led by writers such as Jack Kerouac and Allen Ginsberg (p. 18), questioned the increasing conformity of American life.

The ideological gulf between the two nuclear powers—the democratic, capitalist America and the totalitarian, communist Soviet Union—initiated a half-century of **Cold War** between the two nations. Tension with the Soviet Union heightened as President **Harry Truman** exaggerated the Soviet threat in order to gain support for his foreign policy of **Communist containment.** Fear of Russia and communism was exacerbated by the **Alger Hiss** case, in which a prominent Washington official was tried for espionage, and the **Rosenburg** trial, in which Julius and Ethel Rosenburg were executed after being convicted of handing over atomic secrets to the Russians. Amidst this cloud of anti-Communist hysteria, **McCarthyism** took root. A powerful congressional committee, the "House Un-American Activities Committee" led by Senator Joseph McCarthy, saw communists everywhere: thousands of civil servants, writers, actors, and academics were blacklisted. McCarthyism was meant to be a patriotic stand against Communism, but in retrospect the era is seen as a smear campaign of groundless accusations.

Fear of communism had grown in the U.S. since the Russian Revolution in 1917, but the feverish intensity it gained during the McCarthy era ultimately led to American military involvement in Asia, where communism was beginning to take hold. From 1950-3, the United States fought the **Korean War** on behalf of the South Koreans who were attacked by the Communist North Korean government. Though it cost more than 100,000 American lives, this war was largely a forgotten war. However, the premises established in Korea were carried over to the Vietnam conflict. The Soviet's launch of **Sputnik**, the first artificial satellite, in 1957, renewed fears that communism was getting ahead. The **Cuban Missile Crisis** in 1962, when President **John F. Kennedy** narrowly negotiated the removal of Soviet missiles from a Cuban base, reinforced the notion that the United States must protect the world from Soviet invasion and nuclear assault.

In 1963, President Kennedy was assassinated during a campaign parade in Dallas, Texas by a lone gunman, **Lee Harvey Oswald,** aiming out the window of the nearby Texas Book Depository (p. 583). Though numerous conspiracy theories have been suggested, it appears that Oswald acted alone. The assassination of the young, charismatic President evoked the loss of innocence America was confronting. Playing into a larger cultural revolution unfolding in America, the **"60s"** witnessed mounting social unrest linked to entrenched racism and the escalation of the Vietnam conflict.

High on their role as global policemen staying the tide of communism, the United States became entrenched in Vietnamese politics, culminating in the large-scale deployment of combat troops in 1967 to protect the south Vietnamese government from Ho Chi Minh's socialist government to the north. The **Vietnam War** became a symbol for America's credibility and power to protect struggling nations from communism; thus it was very difficult for the government to back out of the war, even when it became apparent that the situation in Vietnam was not clear-cut and that victory seemed unlikely. Though Americans had at first supported the war, opposition grew as it dragged on and its moral premises were questioned. The use of TV and photographic media to convey war coverage contributed to the harsh and hopeless vision of the situation in Vietnam. In 1968, a platoon of American GI's slaughtered 560 civilians, mostly women and children, in the village of **My Lai.** An army photographer captured the incident on a secret camera. To the American public, My Lai embodied the immorality of the American position. The mounting human costs of Vietnam—and growing suspicion of America's motives—catalyzed wrenching generational clashes reflected vividly in the stacks of burning draft cards and anti-war demonstrations on college campuses. Riots disrupted the **1968 Democratic Convention,** and in 1970 four student protesters were killed by National Guardsmen at **Kent State.** The mantra "Make Love, Not War," shouted among long-haired, scantily-clad bodies rolling in the mud at the 1969 **Woodstock** music festival, came to symbolize the **hippie** generation.

The Vietnam War was not the only cause that captured the hearts and lungs of idealistic young Americans. **Rosa Parks'** refusal to give up a bus seat in Montgomery, Alabama in 1955 sparked the **civil rights movement,** a time of intense protests by African Americans, who organized countless demonstrations, marches, and sit-ins in the heart of a defiant and often violent South. Activists were drenched with fire hoses, arrested, and even killed by local whites and policemen. The movement peaked with the **March on Washington** in 1963, where **Dr. Martin Luther King, Jr.** delivered his famous "I Have A Dream" speech calling for non-violent racial integration. The tone of the civil rights movement changed as blacks became fed up with peaceful moderation, and gathered around the more aggressive rhetoric of **Malcolm X,** a converted Black Muslim who espoused separatist "Black Power." The militant **Black Panthers** resorted to terrorist tactics to assert the rights of African Americans. One summer day in 1965, when a policeman in the **Watts** neighborhood of L.A. pulled over a young black man to check him for drunk driving, a mob gathered, screaming angry charges of racism, and hostile riots ensued. The Watts riots were only a prelude to a string of violent urban riots prompted by racial unrest nationwide. King, the foremost leader of the original civil rights movement, was gunned down in Memphis, Tennessee in 1968, just as he became increasingly vocal about stifling poverty and decrying the moral depravity of the Vietnam War.

The second wave of the **women's movement** accompanied the civil rights movement. Sparked by Betty Friedan's landmark book, *The Feminine Mystique*, American women sought far more than a vote; they sought to change the delineation between men's and women's roles in society, demanding access to male-dominated professions and equal pay. The sexual revolution, fueled by the birth control pill, heightened debate over a woman's right to choose abortion. The 1973 Supreme Court decision **Roe v. Wade** legalized abortion, but the battle between abortion opponents and pro-choice advocates still divides the nation today.

Despite a spate of civil rights legislation and anti-poverty measures passed under President **Lyndon B. Johnson's** Great Society agenda, the specter of the war overshadowed his presidency. By the end of these tumultuous years, the nation had dropped 7 million tons of bombs on Indochina—twice the amount used against America's World War II enemies—and victory was still unattainable. In 1972, as President **Richard Nixon** was attempting to "honorably" extricate the United States from Vietnam, five burglars were caught breaking into the Democratic National Convention Headquarters in the **Watergate** apartment complex. Their botched attempt to bug the Democratic offices was eventually tied to a broader scandal involving the President himself. Caught by his own audiotape, Nixon fought Congress and the people but ultimately led to his resignation.

## STAYIN' ALIVE IN THE 70S

By the mid-70s, America was firmly disillusioned with the idealistic counter culture of the previous decade. The happy-go-lucky **Jimmy Carter** was elected President in 1976. More frivolous forms of fun, such as dancing in platform shoes and powder blue suits under flashing colored lights, a phenomenon known as **"disco,"** became the mark of a generation that just wanted to have fun. Unfortunately, the international situation continued to be tenuous. The oil-rich Arab nations boycotted the U.S., causing an **energy crisis** which drove up gas prices, frustrated autophiliac Americans, and precipitated an economic recession. The oil crisis also forced the U.S. to develop more energy-efficient technology, lending economic credibility to the **environmentalist** movement.

# BIG 80S

In 1980 **Ronald Reagan,** a politically conservative actor and former California governor was elected to the White House. Reagan knew how to give the people what they wanted: money. He cut government spending on public programs and lowered taxes. Influxed with **the "Me" generation**, college campuses grew quieter and more conservative as graduates flocked to Wall Street to become investment bankers. Though the decade's conservatives did embrace certain right-wing social goals like school prayer and the campaign against abortion, the Reagan revolution was essentially economic. **Reaganomics** handed tax breaks to big business, spurred short-term consumption, deregulated savings and loans, and laid the groundwork for economic downturn in the early 1990s.

On the foreign policy front, Reagan aggressively swelled the military budget and sent weapons and aid to right-wing "freedom fighters" in Guatemala, Nicaragua, and Afghanistan, as well as selling arms to Iran and using the profits to help the Contras in Nicaragua The shady, covert action of the **Iran-Contra** affair sullied the Republican administration, but Reagan left office soon after anyway, leaving the brunt of the blame on **Oliver North.** Though Reagan has been endlessly ridiculed for his detached, placid presidency, he was a popular president, seeming to strike a chord with the "forgotten majority" of people with traditional values who were more interested in living their own lives than in raising a ruckus for social causes.

# 90S—WE ARE THE WORLD

The nineties dawned with Supreme Court Justice **Clarence Thomas** being accused of sexual harassment by **Anita Hill.** This high-profile case reflected a general movement towards **political correctness.** As women and minorities became more vigilant about asserting their rights, college campuses and workplaces turned "P.C." (politically correct); racist and slanderous words and actions became officially offensive. **Generation X,** the people who grew up in the materialistic, spoiled 80s and found themselves disillusioned but knowing only to play Nintendo when life hurt, became the cultural trendsetters.

The United States did not give up her love of sending troops to foreign countries and bombing innocent civilians, however. President **George Bush** instigated "Operation Desert Storm," an attempt to thwart **Saddam Hussein,** free Kuwait, and maintain oil prices. The war managed to free Kuwait and keep gas at $1.20, but Saddam is still going strong. **Dan Quayle,** Bush's right-hand man, managed to embarrass the nation more than once, as when he mispelled "potato[e]" at a spelling bee.

In 1992 Los Angeles was consumed in fire and riots after **Rodney King** was convicted and the four policemen who had brutally abused him were acquitted. The trial was charged with racial tension: jurors were shown tapes of the beating, so when the policemen were acquitted, angry mobs attributed the "not guilty" verdict to the color of King's skin. (King is black and the policemen are white.) The day after the trial ended 25 murders had taken place, 1000 fires had swept the city, and 2400 National Guardsmen had moved in. These numbers only increased by the second day. It was obvious from the nature of the pillaging and looting that occurred that the riots were not purely racial, but also the product of civil unrest. The similar nationwide racial tension and upset occurred when a more famous Southern Callifornian, a star, black football player—**O.J. Simpson**—was aquitted of the alleged murder of his wife and her lover in 1995 in a nationally televised trial.

At his election in 1992, a young, saxophone-tooting **Bill Clinton** promised a new era of governmental activism after years of laissez-faire rule. The promise of universal health care, the most ambitious of Clinton's policy goals, best captured the new attitude. The **Whitewater** real estate scam and Clinton's alleged extramarital affairs with **Gennifer Flowers** and **Paula Jones** called Clinton's legitimacy into question, but he bounced back from these tabloid setbacks and regained public face. His health care legislations died young, however, after vigorous lobbying from the health insurance industry, and pressure from the newly-Republican Congress. An eager Republican majority attempted radical economic reforms and environmental rollbacks, which led to two government shut-downs between 1995 and 1996 and nationwide protests against the harsh proposals. A more conservative Clinton beat the Republicans at their own game in 1996, signing a welfare bill that ended the federal guarantee to the poor in exchange for bloc grants to the state—the administration's own estimate predicted that 1.2 million children would be thrown into poverty. The move enabled the savvy Clinton to capture the political center and an easy win in his 1996 reelection bid. His sails caught too much wind when news of "improper" relations with a former intern, 24-year-old **Monica Lewinsky,** blew across the nation. Chief investigator **Kenneth Starr's** proceedings caused national debate and embarrassment as America's president turned into the number one soap opera story for the nation. Clinton was impeached, but not convicted, so he was able to finish his term with some dignity. Clinton seems uncannily resiliant to scandals that in other times would have cut his career short—assuming, of course, that the past's more formal press would have published the stories in the first place.

America faces voter apathy, persistent racism, a massive but shrinking deficit, an underfunded education system, and a sustained assault on social spending. Right-winged, bushy-eyebrowed adults complain about the loss of the "good old days," but many changes are for the better. The publicity devoted to AIDS, the death penalty, disabled access, and gay rights have awarded visibility and rights to a wider variety of people, and America's massive economy continues to expand.

# 1999'S NEWS

Pre-adolescents have begun to take up arms against their oppressors. Students have opened fire at schools in 10 states, spanning from Virginia to Alaska, leaving the nation searching for the cause of this latest plague. Answers range from video games to violent movies to the dissolution of the American family; the only thing for sure is that support for gun-control legislation has risen, challenging the fundamental American right to bear arms.

Seeking to carry on hubby President Clinton's good name, **Hillary Rodham Clinton** (who picked up her maiden name to appeal to feminists, and then dropped it so as not to offend the cookie-making crowd) declared her candicay for Senatorship of New York (a state in which she has never lived). Meanwhile, the **2000 Presidential race** fills up with equally juicy characters: **Senator Bill Bradley,** a Rhodes Scholar, former Princeton and NBA Knicks basketball star, and member of the Hall of Fame; Texas **Governor George W. Bush,** son of former-President George Bush; **Steve Forbes,** a rich publisher who seems to think the Presidency is sold to whoever spends the most on advertising; **Elizabeth Dole,** following in the footsteps of unsuccesful 1996 candidate and Viagra-toting husband **Senator Bob Dole;** and **Vice-President Al Gore,** who, despite scandal, is the leading Democrat, placidly swearing to protect the environment from toxins.

On July 17, **John F. Kennedy, Jr.,** who as a father-less toddler evoked the nation's sympathy, and as a young man became America's most wanted bachelor, crashed into the sea while flying his private plane. Dying with him were his wife, Caroline Bessette Kennedy, and his sister-in-law, Lauren Bessette. From a family of risk-takers, on his first solo flight JFK Jr. steered his state-of-the-art rig into the open ocean off Martha's Vineyard, where the couple was attending a family wedding.

The effects of *El Niño* continue to cause screwy **weather.** *El Niño* winters were unusualy mild over the Northern states; in the South, "the child" dumped buckets of rain. Droughts in the midwest have parched crops and hurricanes have ravaged the Gulf Coast. North Carolina was hardest hit in Aug. and Sept. by Hurricanes Dennis and Floyd, the first in eight predicted hurricanes for the East Coast season. In California, Montana, Utah, and Idaho, large and practically uncontrollable fires scorched more than 130,000 acres, leaving many without a home.

America seems to have gotten a job—**unemployment rates** for college graduates are at a 30yr. low, and the jobless rate has dropped for everyone else too. A study released by the International Labor Organization showed that **Americans work longer hours** than any other industrialized nation in the world. Unfortunately, she is still overweight. A recent study by LSU's Calpennington Biomedical Research Institute suggests that the "couch potato" syndrome which has for years been cited as the cause for overweight kids and adults might be just that. **Potato chips and French fries are the bulk of much of America's "vegetable" consumption,** and together they make up one fourth of childrens' and one third of teenagers' diets.

# A CIVICS PRIMER

The U.S. federal government has **three branches:** the executive, legislative, and judicial. The **executive branch,** which is headed by the **president** and **vice-president,** is elected every 4 years. The executive branch administers most federal agencies, which fall under the jurisdiction of 13 government departments. The heads of these departments make up the Cabinet, and they aid the president in policy decisions. The **House of Representatives** and the **Senate** comprise the **legislative branch,** where laws and budgets are debated. House representatives are allocated seats based on state population, but every state sends two senators to Washington. Senators and representatives (collectively known as Congress) are directly elected by the people of their state. The **judicial branch** consists of the **Supreme Court of the United States** and 90 district courts. The Supreme Court's nine justices, appointed for life by the President, hold the power to strike down laws that violate Constitutional principles.

Elected representatives in the U.S. are usually members of the **Republican** or **Democratic Parties,** which span a narrow (and right-leaning) political spectrum. The Republican Party is more conservative and is divided into two warring camps: Christian traditionalists grudgingly share a tent with their libertarian, pro-business colleagues. The Democrats are also plagued by internal conflict, as the centrist, "New Democrats" lock horns with the party's dwindling liberal contingent.

# THE ARTS

While the arts in the U.S. hearken back to age-old European tradition, American artists have infused literature, music, theatre, painting, architecture, and film with a fresh perspective. Especially in the last century, American art has established a fervent, and for the most part justified, presence in the global canon.

## LITERATURE

The **first best-seller** printed in America, the *Bay Psalm Book*, was published in Cambridge in 1640. Like much of the literature read and published in 17th- and 18th-century America, this chart buster was religious in nature. Most of these early works gather dust on academic bookshelves—America did not create any enduring classics until the early 1800s, when she became more established and began to cultivate a substantial literary tradition expressing the unique American experience. **Herman Melville's** *Moby Dick*, **James Fenimore Cooper's** *Last of the Mohicans*, and **Nathaniel Hawthorne's** *Scarlet Letter* all featured strong yet innocent individualists negotiating the raw American landscape. By the mid-nineteenth century, the New England Renaissance writers began writing sparse, less romantic works, in a firm attempt to portray a down-to-earth culture distinct from that of their European forbearers. The work of **Henry David Thoreau** (*Walden Pond*), **Ralph Waldo Emerson,** and **Walt Whitman** (*Leaves of Grass, Song of Myself*) revolved around the spartan retreat into nature and self-reflection.

In the latter half of the 19th century, women became a strong cultural force. In 1852, **Harriet Beecher Stowe** published *Uncle Tom's Cabin*, an expose of slavery life that became internationally popular and was a major factor in starting the Civil War. The poet **Emily Dickinson** secretly scribbled away in her native Amherst, Massachusetts, home; her untitled, unpunctuated, and uncapitalized verses weren't discovered until after her death in 1886. Three decades later, later, naturalist **Edith Wharton** (*The Age of Innocence*) astutely detailed the genteel yet vicious life of upper-class New York society from a women's point of view.

By the end of the nineteenth century, the older generation of academic New England writers had been displaced by more middle-class, journalistic "realists" who sought to portray life as it really was, focusing on the ordinary and the local rather than the magnificent and remote. **Mark Twain** captured the lazy riverboat days along the Mississippi from the point of view of a boy and a black slave in *The Adventures of Huckleberry Finn*, an American masterpiece. **Kate Chopin** and **Henry James** were other short story writers who provided regional tales full of local color from East, West, North, and South.

The reverberations of the Civil War, the upheaving ideas of Darwinism, and the rampant corruption and poverty which accompanied industrialization led to a backlash against the happy-go-lucky outlook conveyed by realism. By the early twentieth century, literary "naturalists" such as **Jack London** (*The Call of the Wild*), and **Stephen Crane** (*Red Badge of Courage*) were attempting to portray a harsher realism, exposing the lives of lower social and economic classes.

Though many of these earlier works have grown a bit musty, the mundane, optimistic elements of realism and the socially conscious, shock-value elements of naturalism continued to be distinct participles of American literature as it seesawed through the twentieth century. In the early part of the century, **Willa Cather** (*My Antonia*) captured the stark beauty of the Plains and the American desire to control, but care for, the land. **Robert Frost** reverted to plain speech and natural symbolism in his poetry, which probes the unapparent depths of simplicity. Written simultaneously, **Carl Sandburg's** poetry portrays the smoke, steam, and corruption of Chicago. **William Carlos Williams,** living a double life as a country doctor in New Jersey, broke from literary convention and wrote free-form poems detailing the decreptitude of common American scenes, while maintaining a sense of traditional, neighborly values.

The 1920s marked a time of increasing angst, and a reflective, self-centered movement fermented in American literature. **F. Scott Fitzgerald's** works (*The Great Gatsby, This Side of Paradise*) portray restless individuals, financially secure but unfulfilled by their conspicuous consumption. Many writers moved abroad in search of refuge during this tumultuous time. This **"lost generation"** included **Ernest Hemingway** (*The Sun Also Rises*), **T.S. Eliot** ("The Waste Land"), **Ezra Pound**, and **e.e. cummings,** poets and writers whose sophisticated works often took place in other countries, but intrinsically included existentialist critiques of America. On the home front, the **Harlem Renaissance,** a timely gathering of African-American artistic energy in New York City, fed off the excitement of the Jazz Age. **Langston Hughes, Nella Larsen,** and **Zora Neale Hurston** (*Their Eyes Were Watching God*) exposed the black American experience to a broad scope of readers.

As America struggled to recover from the Great Depression, the plight of decaying agricultural life in the Deep South and West began to infiltrate literature. **William Faulkner** (*The Sound and the Fury*, "A Rose for Emily") juxtaposed avantgarde stream-of-consciousness techniques with subjects rooted in the rural South. The plays of **Tennessee Williams** (*The Glass Menagerie, A Streetcar Named Desire*) portray the family dynamics within lower-class, uprooted Southern families. **John Steinbeck** (*The Grapes of Wrath, Of Mice and Men*) treated the social problems of his time, particularly the hardship confronting dispossessed farmers and migrant workers in California. In his remarkable autobiography, *Black Boy*, and the ground-breaking novel, *Native Son*, **Richard Wright** recounts the harsher side of the African-American experience in the South and Harlem.

In the conforming 50s, literature provided alternative commentary on America's underlying social problems. **Ralph Ellison's** *Invisible Man*, published in 1952, confronted a broad audience with the division between white and black identities in

America. **Gwendolyn Brooks,** the first black writer to win a Pulitzer Prize, published intense poetry which highlighted social problems such as abortion, gangs, and drop-outs. The Beatniks, spearheaded by cult heroes **Jack Kerouac** (*On the Road*) and **Allen Ginsberg** ("Howl"), lived wildly and proposed a more free-wheeling attitude. The playwright **Arthur Miller** stared into the American psyche with *The Crucible*, an allegory of McCarthyism (**p. 12**). Rural images and simple, everyday reality continued to be a strong vein in American literature. **Robert Lowell** and **Elizabeth Bishop** were two poets whose work vacillated between homey sentimentality and social commentary.

As the rules of established society began to crumble in the sixties, writers began to explore more outrageous material. **Anne Sexton** and **Sylvia Plath** led the movement towards "confessional poetry"; Sexton delves into the depths of her own mental breakdown, while Plath exposes her psychological deterioration and eventual suicide in *The Bell Jar*. **James Baldwin's** essays and stories warn white America of the explosions to come and caution black America against the self-destructive excesses of racial hatred. Amidst calm Southern society, **Flannery O'Connor's** ("A Good Man is Hard to Find") characters confront a world of eerie violence and evil underneath a surface of tranquility. **John Cheever** (*Bullet Park*) and **John Updike** (*Rabbit, Run*) explore the terrifying ennui of suburban America. **Joyce Carol Oates** depicts the torments and frightening derangements suffered by ordinary people in the modern world.

In more recent fiction, the search for identity and the attempt to reconcile artistic and social agendas has continued. **Toni Morrison** (*Beloved*) won the Nobel Prize, viscerally interpreting the tension between gender, ethnic, and cultural identities. **Tim O'Brien** (*Going After Caccatio*) writes about the issues faced by Vietnam veterans. **Wallace Stegner** (*Angle of Repose*) explores the myth of the West and how American ideals were partially recreated by Western expansion. **Raymond Carver,** in his numerous short stories, charts the hopelessly misdirected, yet strangely hopeful lives of people stuck amidst the fog of modern society. The fast pace and commercialism of modern society has been the subject of many a novel. In *Bright Lights Big City*, **Jay McIntire** exposes the fast-living Wall Street of the 1980's. **Bret Easton Ellis** (*Less Than Zero*) deals with similarly drug-ridden populations of rich kids passing life by in LA. **Don Delillo's** *White Noise* heats up to the tune of a chemical holocaust. Most of **Richard Ford's** books (*Independence Day*) are about guys in mid-life crises—which everyone seems to be going through these days.

Since before the days of Thoreau, American writing has forever been infused with an obsession with the **outdoors.** In the 1930's, **Aldo Leopold** explored the mountain ecosystems that seemed to provide an allegory on life, and proposed the concept of **environmental ethics**. Later **Edward Abbey** and **Barry Lopez** further expounded upon the importance of the environment in a rapidly industrializing world. Literature from the western states and the Pacific Northwest, especially, has focused on how environmental issues are tied up with human lives.

The most popular **children's books** are widely read under bedcovers nationwide and have an immeasurable effect on young minds. It is assumed by parents that reading encourages intelligence, so even toddlers have tons of **picture books.** Some perpetual favorites are *The Hungry, Hungry Caterpillar* and *Goodnight, Moon*. **Pop-up books** and anything by the recently deceased, kind-rhyme-is-fine **Dr. Seuss** are also popular. Teen fiction tends to focus on coming-of-age tales, ranging from **Laura Ingalls Wilder's** classic *Little House on the Prarie* series to the more modern **Beverly Cleary's** Ramona Quimby books and **Judy Blume's** young adult fodder.

# MUSIC

The United States has given birth to a plethora of musical genres and artists, whose styles and songs have intermingled to produce the many distinct styles that can be heard on the radio today. From the South came **Scott Joplin,** who meshed African- American harmony and rhythm with classical European style to develop the first American pianistic form, **ragtime.** The **blues,** another style that developed in the South, is thought to have come from the calls of slaves from Northwest Africa, as well as from Native American musical and verse forms. Blues were originally sung by men and accompanied by a banjo. Later, they became popular through **W.C. Handy** and female singers **Mamie Smith** and **Bessie Smith. Billie Holiday** took the blues up North in the thirties and more recently **Jimi Hendrix, Stevie Ray Vaughn, Eric Clapton,** and **B.B. King** are said to be "down and out." Military Brass Band music is best known because of the work of **John Phillip Sousa.** Sousa wrote hundreds of marches, conducted the White House band, and played a mean violin.

Ragtime, blues, and military brass combined in New Orleans to create America's classical music, **jazz.** Old-time jazz greats include the late **Jelly Roll Morton** and **Louis Armstrong.** Jazz expanded from the music of these artists to big band **(Duke Ellington)**, bebop **(Dizzy Gillespie)**, post bebop **(Thelonius Monk)**, cool jazz **(Bill Evans)**, fusion **(Miles Davis)**, and has also influenced the work of classical composers such as **Leonard Bernstein** and **George Gershwin.** Today, **Ellis Marsalis** and sons **Wynton** and **Branford** dominate the American jazz scene.

Another strong influence on jazz music was gospel music. Gospel music is similar to jazz and blues, but its content is purely religious. This genre was pioneered by **Thomas A. Dorsey's** lyrics and **Mahalia Jackson's** beautiful, sonorous voice. Other popular gospel singers include **Marion Williams** and the **Blackwood Brothers Quartet.** Rhythm & blues (R&B) emerged from the gospel tradition into the love-making, slow jam tradition. Artists like **Aretha Franklin, Professor Longhair, The Temptations,** and a modern generation including **Erykah Badhu** took it there.

Also from the South came zydecho, country, and bluegrass. Zydecho is an accordion based sound whose roots lie in Creole, blues, Caribbean, R&B, and rock & roll. Zydecho has evolved from a low down blues sung mostly in creole **(Clifton Chenier)** to a party music sung in English **(Nathan Williams)**. Country music and her fans owe everything to an alcoholic genius, **Hank Williams.** In sixteen years, Hank produced seven hundred songs and an honest style which few modern artists have been able to feign. **Johnny Cash,** part Cherokee and wholly an excellent singer, came very close. Recently, country music artists **Garth Brooks, George Straight,** and **Alan Jackson** have conquered both a southern, cowboy-hat-wearin' and a Northern wanna-be audience. Bluegrass, a twanky string style invented by **Bill Monroe** and expanded by **Earl Scruggs'** three-fingered banjo technique, originated in Kentucky and has since spread as far north as Virginia.

Mahalia Jackson said that **rock and roll** "was stolen out of the sanctified church." Rock has come a long way since its kidnapping. Parented not only by gospel but by blues and country as well, rock and roll has produced most of America's more famous music icons—first **Chuck Berry** and **Jerry Lee Lewis,** and eventually The King, **Elvis Presley.** Elvis and his contemporaries are thought of as "oldies," while artists such as **Billy Joel** and **Bruce Springsteen** are "classic" rock. Today, the rock music genre spans heavy metal **(Metallica)**, pop **(Madonna, Brandy, Michael Jackson)**, soft rock **(Kenny G)**, and angsty "alternative" **(Counting Crows, Dave Mathews).**

Apart from rock, American music in the past several decades has seen many more new genres and artists. **Woody Guthrie's** folk lyrics were like a Russian novel, honest and insightful. Thanks to **Bob Dylan,** folk music caught fire in the sixties and spoke to social protesters across the nation. **Arlo Guthrie's** 45-minute song, *Alice's Restaurant* criticizes the Vietnam draft. Also from the sixties came the long-living **Grateful Dead,** a band and mentality which survives even the recent death of the lead singer, Jerry Garcia. New folk artists include **The Indigo Girls** and **Ani Difranco.** In the seventies, punk bands **Sonic Youth** and **Yo La Tengo** contended with disco and sixties holdover groups like **The Doors.** Spawned by East Coast stars **Sugar Hill Gang, Public Enemy,** and the **Beastie Boys,** the eighties witnessed a rap revolution which is still going strong today through "the entertainer" **Puff Daddy's** efforts. In the early nineties, grunge music made a short appearance largely because of Seattle's **Nirvana** and **Pearl Jam.** Also in the nineties, hip-hop, which infiltrated styles around the world through the creative lyrics of **A Tribe Called Quest** and the late **Notorious B.I.G.,** gained popularity. The West Coast birthed the "gangsta rap" move-

> **✎ THE BOSS** Bruce Springsteen is just a reg'lar guy, but he has the heart of a poet and the stamina of a superhero. Born in 1949 to a working class family in Freehold, NJ, Bruce faced many of the same problems that any American faces. His dad wanted him to be a lawyer, but he wanted to be Elvis. Of course, Springsteen has become something entirely different, a troubadour for the working man, tugging at heartstrings that most Americans, whether from Los Angeles, New Jersey, or the suburbs of Dallas, TX can appreciate. The Boss, as his fans like to call him, has even attracted the attention of Harvard Professor Robert Coles, and he's occasionally rumored to be accepting a teaching job in one of Coles' classes. It hasn't happened yet, but Springsteen has spent long years teaching America a few things, not least of which is this sage wisdom: that everyone deserves cold beer at a reasonable price.
>
> *Let's Go: USA Including Coverage of Canada* recommends the following Bruce albums and songs...
>
> *Greetings from Asbury Park NJ:* "Does This Bus Stop At 82nd Street?" "Growin' Up."
> *The River:* "The River." "Wreck on the Highway." "Independence Day."
> *Born to Run:* "Thunder Road." "Born to Run."
> *Born in the USA:* "I'm on Fire." "Dancing in the Dark." "Bobby Jean."
> *Tunnel of Love:* among some silly songs are some sublime silkies—"Tougher than the Rest." "Walk Like a Man."

ment **(Snoop Doggy Dog, Dr. Dre),** which has sparked much debate because of the lyric's heavy espousal of violence and drugs.

Speaking of violence and drugs, perhaps the greatest American music tradition is the musical. Although musicals were not born (gasp) in the United States, they have, since their earliest roots in England and France, developed a distinctly "only-in-the-U.S." feel. Musicals in the United States began with variety shows of song and dance, mostly centered around two characters, **Jim Crow** and **Zip Coon,** whose antics played upon ignorant racism. Eventually, these bawdy and usually tasteless shows were cleaned up by good standing men like **Tony Pastor.** In the 1860s **Black Crook,** an obnoxiously elaborate musical, gained great success and marked the beginning of the end. Since then, musical popularity has grown exponentially. From **Gilbert & Sullivan** shows to the touring shows after railroad expansion, from the works of **Cole Porter** to those of Brit **Andrew Lloyd Webber,** musicals, whether on Broadway or on the big screen, have become a national obsession. Popular musicals include *The Sound of Music, Oklahoma, Fiddler on the Roof, West Side Story, Phantom of the Opera, Les Miserables, Hair,* and *Rent.*

## FILM

Since the invention of the motion picture, the democratic access and glorious fanfare of the movies has appealed to the fundamental American psyche. Movies are a mainstay of American popular culture, and people rich and poor, short and tall, stand in lines and shell out $8 a head (plus $4 for a bucket of popcorn) in cineplexes across the nation to view the latest releases.

American film has come a long way since viewers were first awed by Thomas Edison's 30-second film of a galloping horse. Since the 1910's, **Hollywood, CA**—where the perpetual sunshine made lighting easier and the West Coast isolation helped independent filmmakers evade the New York movie trust—has been the capital of the movie industry. It's taken a while to perfect fake rain and it's been difficult to convince the crew to get out of the swimming pool, but Hollywood has been so successful as a movie mecca that it now defines the mainstream.

American movies have always been ruled by the **"star system";** actors are hero-worshipped figures who can attract audiences regardless of what movie they're in. The first wave of movie stars were speechless; **Mary Pickford, Charlie Chaplin,** and **Buster Keaton** all starred in silent movies. In the 1920's, the silent screen began to talk, and the Golden Age of Hollywood ensued. *Gone With the Wind* was the first large-scale movie extravaganza, employing exorbitant budgets, flamboyant costumes, **Scarlett O'Hara,** and a cast of thousands. **Ginger Rogers** and **Fred Astaire** swept across the floor in numerous musicals. Hollywood's love of tiny-tots is evident in the huge career of the child star, **Shirley Temple** (*The Little Princess*). **Judy Garland** tapped her ruby slippers in *The Wizard of Oz.* The classic movie *It's a Wonderful Life* continues to warm the hearts of generations every holiday season. In *Casablanca,* the moody **Humphrey Bogart** slumped across the screen with the utmost class. Not all stars were flesh and blood—Walt Disney established his mark with the animated *Snow White.* And not all movies were resolutely happy-go-lucky; in 1941 **Orson Welles** unveiled his intricate masterpiece, *Citizen Kane,* a landmark work whose innovations expanded contemporary ideas about the potential of film.

Cloaked in glitz, glamour, and scandal, sexy stars **Marilyn Monroe, James Dean** (*Rebel Without a Cause*), and **Elizabeth Taylor** ruled the silver screen into the 50s. Though their gas burned up fast (Monroe and Dean both lived wildly and died young; Taylor went through 8 husbands) the unbridled adoration of these stars established the actor as a sex symbol. Some stars survived the hubbub more or less intact and went on to long careers; **Marlon Brando,** the hot, sweaty stud in *A Streetcar Named Desire,* gained some weight, perfected his slur and starred in the **Godfather** movies. **Audrey Hepburn,** the elegant, mini-waisted star of *Breakfast at Tiffany's* introduced the waif-like, gamine look to a previously curvacious Hollywood, and grew into her wrinkles with aplomb. Alfred Hitchcock perfected suspense and the careers of **James Stewart** (*Vertigo*) and **Cary Grant** (*North By Northwest*).

By the late 60's and 70s, the most memorable movies were more grim and experimental, moving away from happy-go-lucky Hollywood. In *The Graduate* Dustin Hoffman plays a disillusioned, aimless college graduate seduced by a family friend, Mrs. Robinson. Martin Scorsese's *Taxi Driver* stars Robert DeNiro as a NYC taxi driver gone mad. Francis Ford Coppola's *Apocalypse Now* adapted Joseph Conrad's *Heart of Darkness* to Vietnam. A stylin' John Travolta captured the disillusioned nightlife of the 70s disco era in *Saturday Night Fever. Chinatown,* with Jack Nicholson, moved back to L.A., but the dark complexity of its script belied the Hollywood bubblegum. The prolifically neurotic Woody Allen initiated his neverending exploration of New York angst with *Annie Hall.*

Driven by the global mass distribution of American cinema and the rise of high-tech special effects, the eighties witnessed the revitalization of the "Big Blockbuster." Some masterpieces of technology and massive budgets include *The Terminator* and *Terminator 2,* starring the bulging muscled Aaaaahnold Schwarzenegger. The *Star Wars* trilogy proved to be a cult classic, inspiring a generation of Jedi wanna-be's. Another action movie that spawned a bunch of sequels is *Indiana Jones,* the Harrison Ford archaeology adventure trilogy. Oliver Stone's *Platoon* showed what the Vietnam War was really like. *Top Gun* was the best of the cheesy, boy-meets-girl-and-woos-her-with-a-fast-motorcycle genre. Another Tom Cruise movie, *Rainman,* was a more thoughtful critique of 80s materialism and self-absorption. *Pretty Woman* had a winningly dumb prostitute-turned-princess storyline—and a grinning Julia Roberts to do the deed. *The Little Mermaid* marked the comeback of the Disney animated musical. *Who Framed Roger Rabbit* was a terrible movie, but the first one to merge animated images with live-action ones.

The 80s teen flick enjoyed a brief but glorious career, starring a group of California-native teen idols known as the "Brat Pack." In *Pump Up the Volume,* Christian Slater leads a mass rebellion against the monotony of suburbia. *Ferris Bueller's Day Off* inspired teens to skip school on sunny days. Molly Ringwald was the girl that everyone wanted to be in the John Hughes' movies *Sixteen Candles* and *The Breakfast Club. Bill and Ted's Excellent Adventure* was the last 80's teen flick, and unfortunately launched the career of Keanu Reeves.

In the last decade, the low-budget **indie film** scene arose in direct opposition to the excesses of Hollywood. The 21 year-old John Singleton directed *Boyz N the Hood,* a hard-hitting portrayal of life in poverty-stricken South Central L.A. The photographer Larry Clark switched mediums to make the quasi-documentary, *Kids,* so we could all see skinny kids shooting up on drugs. The fabulous documentary, **Hoop Dreams,** details the American dream of going "pro" (professional basketball, that is). The Coen brothers created the gruesome slapstick of **Fargo** and **The Big Lebowski.** A video store clerk, Quentin Tarantino, swarmed onto the scene with the ultra-cool **Reservoir Dogs,** and the next, more polished, installment of swank, **Pulp Fiction.** Single boys everywhere found a soulmate in **Swingers.** The more recent **Rushmore** justifies the mean-spirited humor that people laugh at despite better sensibilities.

Even Hollywood movies disguised themselves in the indie cloak; toning down their special effects and budgets. Cameron Crowe's **Singles** follows the hip, grunge, answering-machine dependent life of single people in the espresso mecca of Seattle. **The Player,** Robert Altman's mirror trick of a motion picture, cooly dissects the studio biz. Spike Lee's in-your-face **Do the Right Thing** brought racial misunderstandings into the pop cultural limelight. **Reality Bites** chews over the reality of twenty-something Generation Xers in Austin, Texas. Nicolas Cage renders a hopeless alcoholic in **Leaving Las Vegas. Out of Sight** is the most underrated film of late, after its unspectacular box office run it enjoyed video mania. The much-hailed retro-film noir **L.A. Confidential** brought back the police drama.

Despite the success of the indie scene, the blockbuster has far from disappeared. In fact, the development of computer technology has made movies bigger than ever. Disney's magic waved on with **Aladdin,** starring the voice of the comedian/actor Robin Williams. The usual plethora of action movies with massive car chases and firepower stunts continue to be released; the best of 90s high-tech fare includes **Speed, Independence Day, Face-Off,** and **The Matrix.** The Saturday Night Live TV show has spawned many spoof-babies, including Adam Sandler's **Billy Madison** and Mike Meyers' **Austin Powers. There's Something About Mary** and Jim Carrey's **Ace Ventura: Pet Detective** are other truly hilarious comedies. The teen flick has refused to die; **Clueless, Can't Hardly Wait,** and **Scream** mercilessly poke fun at the soap opera that is American high school. The tear-jerker is also still around, though modern tears are usually mixed with some good 'ole violent bloodshed. Stephen Spielberg's **Schindler's List** and **Saving Private Ryan** rehash the horror of WWII, while **Titanic** captured America's still-credulous heart.

After their initial run in the theatres, movies are released on **video.** Video rentals and sales have become a huge portion of gross sales, and allowed for the proliferation of movies into living rooms nationwide. More recently, high-quality **DVD** (digital visual display) has made its mark on the home movie front. Far from destroying the cinema as an institution, video has only increased American's love of movies—even today, nothing beats the crackle of the big screen.

## VISUAL ART

Like literature, American art didn't come into its own until the mid-19th century. Grandiose landscape paintings captured the mythic beauty of the American West, while **Andrew Wyeth** painted stormy seaside scenes and Civil-War-era farmscapes and **John Singer Sargent** painted smooth, impressionistic portraits.

In the early 20th century, **Alfred Stieglitz** championed photography as a legitimate art form, while his wife, **Georgia O'Keefe,** painted surreal, pastel visions of desert bones and sexually oriented flowers. In colorful, narrative paintings of American scenes, **Edward Hopper** and **Thomas Hart Benton** explored the innocence and mythic values of the country during its emergence as a superpower. Photography became the medium of choice for artists with a social conscience; **Lewis Hine** photographed the urban poor while **Dorthea Lange** and **Walker Evans** captured the plight of destitute farmers during the Great Depression. **Ansel Adams'** crisp photographs of pristine landscapes helped establish the National Park system.

By the 40s, the abstract expressionist movement in Europe caught on overseas. **Willem deKooning's** masterful work documents the movement from realistic to abstracted images. The obscure images of **Arshile Gorky** and **Robert Rauchenburg,** along with **Jackson Pollock's** energetic drip paintings, display both the swaggering confidence and frenetic insecurity rampant in Cold War America. **Mark Rothko's** color field paintings perfect the subtle aesthetics and emotional impact of abstract art. **Jasper Johns** incorporated iconic images, such as American flags and tools, into his art, ushering in the age of "pop" art. Practiced most memorably by **Roy Lichtenstein** and **Andy Warhol**, pop art created graphic, cartoonish images which satirize the icons of American life and pop culture, and blurred the line between art and advertisement.

In the seventies, photography finally came into its own, as the back-to-basics 35mm photographs of **Gary Winnogrand** and **Lee Friedlander** and the freakish **Diane Arbus** stretched notions of art photography. **William Eggleston's** exhibit at the MOMA in NYC was ill-received, but eventually established the legitimacy of color photography. The 80s art boom, stationed around private galleries in NYC on the East Coast and L.A. on the West Coast, ushered in a decade of slick art. **Julian Schnabel** and **David Hockney** garnered the adoring accolades of savvy art investors. As the gold plating wore off, ultra-realistic art depicting the harsh reality of everyday life was produced in response to the materialism of the 80s, and the bare-all photographs of **Nan Goldin** became all the rage. **Cindy Sherman** (a photographer who places herself in various scenes from movie stills to gruesome pornography) and **Kiki Smith** (who makes body part sculptures) are typical of recent artists who deconstruct the meaning of identity and the human body. Abstract art hasn't died on the gallery floor, however; **Brice Marden's** squiggly lines are also big sellers.

American architecture in the early days scrapped up the leftovers of previous European eras, but the 20th-century architect **Frank Lloyd Wright** gave America its own style of abode—angular and environmentally cohesive. Wright's opuses—the Falling Waters house in Pennsylvania and the Guggenheim Museum in NYC—testify to the angular aesthetic and environmentally cohesive technique that typifies modern American architecture. More recently, **Frank Gehry** has moved the notion of architecture into the 21st century with his fabulously impossible feats of optical engineering. **Public art** has an established role in American cities; many devote 1% of their funds to art. Officially, sculptures adorn city parks and installations decorate lobbies; unofficially, **graffitti art,** an outgrowth of the underground hip-hop culture, decorates the backs of buildings and freeway underpasses.

# THE MEDIA

America is wired. Images, sounds, and stories from the boob tube, radio, internet, and advertisements infiltrate every aspect of the American lifestyle. Because of the media's power, constant debate centers on censorship and freedom. Censored or not, new forms of media sprout and spread like (poison) ivy every second.

## TELEVISION

There are television sets in 98% of U.S. homes. Competition between the six national networks (ABC, CBS, NBC, Fox, and two newcomers: UPN and WB), cable television, and satellite TV has triggered exponential growth in TV culture over the last few years. The most popular shows airing during prime time (8-11pm EST) are the drama *ER*, the paranoid thriller *The X-Files*, and the witty, animated sitcom *The Simpsons*. Gen X-ers and wanna-be teenagers are glued to *Beverly Hills 90210*, *Melrose Place*, and *Dawson's Creek*. **Day-time programming** is dominated by trashy talk shows like *Oprah* and *Jerry Springer*, full of bare-all sex stories, and steamy soap operas, including *Days of Our Lives* and *The Young and the Restless*.

Over 100 **cable** channels offer around-the-clock news, sports, movies, weather, and home shopping. **MTV,** offering dazzling displays of random visceral images set to music. **HBO** brings Hollywood movies into the living room *sans* commercials. **Pay-per-view** channels charge about $7 for a movie or sporting event. **ESPN** satiates sports fans with round-the-clock sports coverage.

Recently, many TV shows from the 70s, like *The Brady Bunch*, have come back in style. This follows the obsession with "retro" camp that has infected America's youth since the early 90s. Old shows are revived through **reruns,** which play over and over again on cable channels. Reruns of recent shows that were taken off the air too soon, like *My So Called Life* and *Seinfeld*, are also shown again and again and again for nostalgic fans that never say die.

Television is the point of entry to world-wide news for most Americans. Twenty-four hour news coverage is available on **CNN,** a cable station. Each network presents local and national nightly news, usually at 5 or 10 p.m., while programs like *60 Minutes* and *Dateline* specialize in investigate reporting and exposés.

The **Public Broadcasting Station (PBS)** is commercial-free, funded by viewer contributions, the federal government, and corporate grants. Its repertoire includes educational children's shows like *Sesame Street* and *Mister Roger's Neighborhood,* nature programs, mystery shows, and odd British comedy shows.

## PRINT MEDIA

What's fit to print? In the early days of American printing, media meant government-supported articles, sermons, and almanacs. Print centers were huddled around large ports (like Boston), and most of the material that they put out was heavily censored. In 1690 **Benjamin Harris** published the first newspaper, **Publick Occurences.** His journal was supposed to run monthly, but only the first issue was printed; due to censorship, no further issues were permitted. **James Franklin,** another journalist, was put in jail after the publishing of his paper, **The New England Courrant.** Eventually, brash young hotheads like Franklin and Harris were not considered quite so brash anymore. New ideas about what could and should be done were brought over by European printers. By the early 18th century, such radical things as primers and advertisements were being published all over the Northeast. Eventually, printing centers spread throughout the New World.

Today, the most influential newspapers in the U.S. are the *New York Times*, the *Washington Post*, and the *Los Angeles Times*. They all roughly stand in the center politically, and they have wide distributions throughout the U.S. *The Christian Science Monitor* and the *Wall Street Journal* are also well-respected dailies. *USA Today* is not as well respected, but is nationally the most readily available and easy to read. The three major weekly newsmagazines, *Time, Newsweek,* and *U.S. News & World Report,* cover national news and cultural trends in short, glossy articles. Other widely read magazines in the U.S. include *People,* which chronicles American gossip; *Spin* and *Rolling Stone,* which focus on the music industry; *Sports Illustrated* which showcases athletes and bathing-suit clad models; and the *New Yorker,* which combines Big Apple happenings with short stories and essays on current events. Women aspiring to be underweight and over-dressed read *Cosmopolitan* and *Vogue,* and those wishing to be in shape read *Shape* and *Self.* Their younger counterparts read *Seventeen* and *YM.* Men who pluck their eyebrows read *Details* and *Maxim.* Americans on the left read *The Nation* or *In These Times,* while conservatives subscribe to the *National Review* or Rupert Murdoch's new *Weekly Standard.* The business world reads *Fortune, Forbes,* and *Business Week.*

## RADIO

Families used to gather around the radio to be entertained and informed. Today televisions and the internet have replaced this need. Nevertheless, the radio lives on in the hearts (and cars) of millions of Americans. Every city's radio waves carry at least one rock, country, jazz, classic rock, easy listening, Top 40, classical, all-talk, and all-news station; however, most of the nation is dominated by country-western, rock, and Christian evangelism. Radio is generally divided into AM and FM; talk-radio compromises most of the low-frequency AM slots, and the high-powered FM stations feature most of the music. Each broadcaster owns a four-letter call-name, with "W" as the first letter for those east of the Mississippi River (as in WJMN), and "K" to the west (as in KPFA).

The U.S. public network, **National Public Radio (NPR),** has a local station in every major market. Popular offerings include the hodge-podge feature *All Things Considered*, Ray Suarez's call-in *Talk of the Nation*, and the hilarious auto junkies Tom and Ray Magliozzi's *Car Talk*.

# SPORTS

Start your engines; although baseball is officially America's favorite past time, it is **NASCAR** auto racing that draws the most fans of any sport on Memorial Day weekend (late May) with the **Indianapolis 500**. Average family vehicles are transformed into 185+ m.p.h. powerhouses and are driven hundreds of times around a banked track, while open-mouthed and wide-eyed fans throw down countless beers and hot dogs. Cars are sponsored by different automobile manufacturers in conjunction with large brand-name companies such as Spam, Cheerios, and Caterpillar. Top drivers include **Jeff Gordon, Dale Earnhardt,** and **Rusty Wallace**. Other divisions of auto racing include **Formula One Racing,** (where team budgets are usually around $100 million), **CART,** and the **Indy Car League**.

For those who don't like fast-paced sports, pollution, or noisy fans, professional ("pro") atheletes participate in the internationally publicized **U.S. Open** (tennis) and **U.S. Open** (golf). The **Kentucky Derby** (horse racing) is a peculiarly American event replete with boozing and betting. Professional basketball teams in almost every major city make up the **National Basketball Association (NBA),** where the best players in the world duke it out. NBA players have come a long way since the first teams were playing with peach baskets and Converse All Stars. Today, players can jump so high and pass so fast that they had to move the three-point shooting line out to compensate for it, and American basketball has become a playground institution. Most large cities also host professional teams in **Major League Baseball (MLB)**. Baseball games are often cheap and easy to get tickets to, and they are worth the price. America's favorite past time, baseball captures the hearts of many dreaming boys and the spirits of grown men as well. The **National Football League (NFL)** is a third major sport network. Full of beefy men and even beefier shoulder pads, football is especially popular in the mid-west. Ice hockey's popularity is concentrated in the north-east; the **National Hockey League (NHL)** is heavily influenced by it's competitor's up north, in Canada. **Major League Soccer (MLS)** and **women's basketball (WNBA)** are both budding, but not yet maniacal, sports. In complaint against over-paid athletes, or maybe just to relive their college days, many Americans are known to live, bet large amounts of money, and die by their state college's football team in the **bowl games** or their college's basketball team in the **NCAA tournament,** fondly called **March Madness**.

Many young Americans play football, basketball, baseball, soccer, and, especially in Northern states, ice and field hockey. Tennis is popular in upper-middle class suburbia, and **street basketball** in Venice Beach, California, and New York City rivals that of many professional teams. In the past decade, enthusiasm for athletics and being in shape has risen. Work-out enthusiasts have gone from **Jane Fonda** classic aerobic workouts to step aerobics, **Cindy Crawford** (personal trainer) style exercise to spinning (group bike workouts set to pumping music) and kick boxing; there is always a new way to burn fat. The **X-Games** give athletic and slightly psychotic Gen-Xers a chance to gain national attention while engaging in life- threatening "sports." Along the beaches of California, you'll find skin-cancer poster children equipped with surf boards and in-line skates. In the Northeast, numerous suburban yuppies have been spotted powerwalking and cycling on expensive custom-made bikes. Of course, Americans like to do it all in as little time and as much style as possible; thus, the **eight minute work-out** and matching **spandex gear**. In the winter, **skiing, snowboarding,** and **ice skating** are popular recreational sports, while during the rest of the year, families and bored teenagers nationwide resort to **bowling** and **miniature golf** for good, and usually clean, fun.

# TAKE ME OUT TO THE BALL GAME To many visitors to the United States (and even to the occasional American), the game of **baseball** can be as hard to understand as why the American League ever adopted the "Designated Hitter" rule. Here's a brief run-down of the American Pastime's basic rules to make that first trip to Wrigley Field (or a Rookie League game in a small-town park) a little less confusing.

The structure of a baseball field is straight-forward. There are four **bases** 90 ft. apart, arranged in a diamond. The **infield** is grass, bounded by dirt base paths. The **outfield** is the grass beyond, bounded by the fences (usually 370-410 ft. away from homeplate). The chalk lines running down each side of the field are the **foul lines;** balls landing here are out of play.

The game is played by two teams, each with 9 active players at all times. There are **9 innings** in major and minor league games. Innings are divided into halves (the **top half** and the **bottom half**), representing each team's turn at bat. A half-inning ends when the team in the field (the defense) makes 3 outs.

**Outs** in the field are typically made when: a player is tagged out by a fielder with the ball, the ball is caught on the fly, or the ball gets to a base before an advancing runner. The field positions are chiefly divided between the **outfielders** (rightfielder, centerfielder, and leftfielder) and the **infielders** (first-baseman, second-baseman, shortstop, and third-baseman). There is also a **pitcher** on the mound, and the **catcher** behind the homeplate.

A team's **batting order** is determined by the **manager,** or skipper. It is based on power, speed, and overall batting prowess. The first batter, or **lead-off man,** is typically a good hitter with good speed; the fourth, or **clean-up man,** often has the best power. In the American League, many minor leagues, colleges, and high schools, there is a **designated hitter,** who bats in favor of the weakest hitting fielder (often the pitcher).

A batter can reach base in many ways. These are the most common: a **walk** (taking 4 bad pitches), a **hit** (safely reaching first base on a hit ball), and an **error** (when a fielder mistake allows the runner to reach first safely). **Runs** are scored when runners cross homeplate. A **homerun** occurs when the ball is hit over the fence, allowing all runners to score.

But the key to any baseball experience is to know what to say. Try these lines: "I can't believe that (Baseball Commisioner) Bud Selig! Give me Bart Giaomatti anyday." "Good change of pace on that last pitch." "Is that bat corked?" "Baseball shoud ban all growth hormones."

# FOOD

If it's individually wrapped, Americans will buy it. From six packs of soda and beer to serving size bags of Doritos, Americans gobble up millions of dollars in one serving containers every year. Besides causing major landfill issues, this lifestyle is usually conducive to **couch potato syndrome,** otherwise known as obesity. In many towns, McDonalds, Burger Kings, Roy Rogers, and Kentucky Fried Chickens dominate the stomachs of children, teenagers, and many adults. Despite attempts to add healthy options, like "fish" sandwiches and stale salads to their repetoire, fast food remains the number one cause of **Slim Fast** and **Weight Watchers' popularity.**

Apart from junk food, traditional American cuisine is divided regionally. From the Northeast, largely thanks to the Native Americans, comes the year-round Thangsgiving palate: **corn on the cob, chicken pot pie, apple pie, cornbread,** and **turkey.** For the best **seafood** and **lobster** on the East Coast, go to the rocky coast of Maine, where lobster pots crowd the bays. Vermont and New Hampshire's maple trees mean delicious **maple syrup.** New York loads on the meat in enormous "New York Style" submarine sandwiches. Also, Boston's **baked beans** and **clam chowda** will satisfy. Washington D.C. and Maryland are famous for their **soft-shell crabs.** In the South, food varies greatly according to state, but pork and fried chicken are common most places. Cajun and Creole rules in Louisiana; spice flavors yummy gumbo, catfish, and jambalaya to boot. Also, check out the seafood in Florida. In Texas, **beef barbecue** is always fresh from the slaughter and **Tex-Mex** (Americanized Mexican food) ranges from delicious to blatantly non-authentic. **Grits** in Mississippi and Georgia taste yummy, if you like the taste of cardboard. From middle America, we are lucky to have been blessed with **seven layer dip, recipes that use Kellogg's Cornflakes,** and **fried pork rinds.** Courtesy of the Midwest, we have the great American **steak.** The Rocky Mountain states have been all but depleted of buffalo, but locally-ranched **beef** stampedes the dinner table. **Rocky Mountain oysters** may sound out of place in such an inland realm, but these fried bull testicles are far from amphibious. In California, where people need to maintain their hot bods for the beach, the nutritive style is cool and light; super **salads** and multi-fruit **smoothies** with wheatgrass were invented here, and **sushi** has been greedily imported. Closer to the border, next-to-authentic **Mexican food** is all the rage. Farther north, in the wild woods of the Pacific Northwest, gourmet restaurants in Portland and Seattle serve wild delicacies such as **chantrelle mushrooms,** Pacific **salmon,** and **berries** picked along roadsides.

Recently, U.S. diners have made a strong movement towards **organic** food. Perhaps a product grade-school indoctrination with the **Food Pyramid,** a set of dietary reccomendations, or maybe just an offshoot of increasing health-awareness and extra money to spend, new organic food stores are popping up everywhere. At supermarkets and smaller specialty shops, one can find tomatos that were spoken to in the growing process, and turkeys that received a first-grade education. Yuppie Americans, Gen-Xers, and bored housewives buy up these products at any expense, which usually means a big one.

The other new food (or drink) trend is **coffee.** Although Americans always liked coffee, now they *love* it. With the arrival of flavored coffee and frozen coffee creations, America has found a way to satisfy her sweet tooth while feining to be sophisticated. On public transportation, on the streets, and even on the highways, businessmen and women gulp down moccha-frappe-latte creations with glee.

# CANADA

O Canada! The second largest country in the world, Canada covers almost 10 million square kilometers (3.85 million square miles). Still, only 29 million people inhabit Canada's 10 provinces and two territories; well over half the population crowds into either Ontario or Québec. Framed by the Atlantic coastline in the east and the Pacific Ocean in the west, Canada extends from fertile southern farmlands to frozen northern tundra.

The name Canada is thought to be derived from the Huron-Iroquois word **"kanata,"** meaning "village" or "community." This etymology reveals the dependence of early settlers on the Native Canadians as well as the country's origins in a system of important trading posts. The early colonists, the French and English, were relatively distant and culturally distinct. Each population has fought to retain political dominance, but it was only in the 1970s that ethnic and linguistic differences between the two communities flared briefly into quasi-terrorist acts of violence. Native Canadian concerns and a rapidly increasing **allophone** population—people whose first language is neither English nor French—have also become intertwined in the cultural struggle. Inter-regional tensions have been exacerbated by divergent economic foundations; bankrupt fisheries have drained the Maritime provinces while the West Coast booms with trans-Pacific trade. For crucial info on travel in Canada, see **Essentials,** in the front of this book (p. 31).

## NATIVES AND NEWCOMERS

Although archaeologists are uncertain about the exact timing, recent data indicates that the first Canadians arrived about 11,000 years ago, by either crossing **Beringia,** the Asian-Alaskan land bridge, or by migrating north from sea-faring populations that reached South America about 3,000 years before. Their descendants flooded the continent, fragmenting into disparate tribes. Arriving Europeans intensified inter-tribal warfare by trading guns for fur, and by exchanging aid in pre-existing conflicts for knowledge of the local terrain.

Such bargains proved a raw deal for the tribes. As the English and French became more familiar with the land, they squeezed the Native Canadians out by force and by less-than-just land agreements. Natives found themselves confined to large settlements such as **Moose Factory** in Ontario or **Oka** in Québec. Recently, the **Assembly of First Nations,** the umbrella aboriginal organization, has taken legal action to secure long overdue compensation.

The first Europeans known to explore the area were the Norse, who apparently settled in northern Newfoundland around the year 1000. England came next; **John Cabot** sighted Newfoundland in 1497. When **Jacques Cartier,** landing on the gulf of the St. Lawrence River, claimed the mainland for the French crown in 1534, he touched off a rivalry that persisted until Britain's 1759 capture of Québec in the Seven Years' War and France's total capitulation four years later.

The movement to unify the British North American colonies gathered speed after the American Civil War, when U.S. military might and economic isolationism threatened the independent and continued existence of the British colonies. On March 29, 1867, **Queen Victoria** signed the **British North America (BNA) Act,** uniting Nova Scotia, New Brunswick, Upper Canada, and Lower Canada (now Ontario and Québec). Though still a dominion of the British throne, Canada had its country—and its day: the BNA was proclaimed on July 1, now known as Canada Day.

## IN RECENT HISTORY

The past 130 years have witnessed Canadian territorial expansion and burgeoning power. The years following consolidation witnessed sustained economic growth and settlement in the west with the completion of the trans-continental railway; the country quickly grew to encompass most of the land it covers today. Participation in World War I earned the Dominion international respect and a charter membership in the **League of Nations.** It joined the **United Nations** in 1945 and was a founding member of the **North Atlantic Treaty Organization** in 1949. The Liberal government of the following decade created a national social security system and a national health insurance program. **Pierre Trudeau's** government repatriated Canada's constitution in 1981, freeing the nation from Britain in constitutional legality (though **Elizabeth II** remains nominal head of state). Free to forge its own alliances, the country signed the **North American Free Trade Agreement (NAFTA)** in 1992 under the leadership of Conservative **Brian Mulroney.**

Mulroney will go down in Canadian history as the leader who almost tore the nation apart in an effort to bring it back together. His numerous attempts to negotiate a constitution that all 10 provinces would ratify (Canada's present constitution lacks Québec's support) consistently failed, flaring century-old regional tensions and spelling the end of his government. Riding on a wave of backlash, the 1993 election saw Conservative support collapse to a mere two seats in the Commons and the election in Québec of a separatist government at both federal and provincial levels. The question of Québec still drives recent politics. An October 1996 referendum rejected separation by a mere 1.2% margin.

# LANGUAGE

Canada has two official languages, English and French, but there are numerous other native languages. **Inuktitut** is widely spoken in the Northwest Territories. Listen for French in most provinces. *Québécois* pronunciation of French can be perplexing, but natives are generally sympathetic toward attempts to speak their language. The Québécois are also less formal than European French-speakers.

# THE MEDIA

Most Canadian literature is post-1867. The opening of the Northwest and the Klondike Gold Rush (1898) provided fodder for the adventure tale—**Jack London** and **Robert Service** both penned stories of wolves and prospectors based on their mining experience. In the Maritimes, **L.M. Montgomery** authored one of the greatest coming of age/romance novels of all times, *Anne of Green Gables*. In the *Deptford Trilogy*, **Robertson Davies** chronicled the roving Canadian identity.

Canada also boasts three of the world's most authoritative cultural and literary critics: **Northrop Frye, Hugh Kenner,** and pop phenom **Marshall McLuhan.** Prominent contemporary authors include **Margaret Atwood,** best known for the futuristic bestseller *The Handmaid's Tale,* and Sri Lankan-born poet and novelist **Michael Ondaatje,** whose *The English Patient* received the prestigious Booker Prize.

Canada's contribution to the world of popular music includes a range of artists with varying levels of musical ability. **Neil Young, Joni Mitchell, Bruce Cockburn, Rush, Cowboy Junkies, Bare Naked Ladies, k.d. lang, Bryan Adams, Crash Test Dummies, Sarah McLachlan,** and the **Tragically Hip** are all Canucks. Recent chart-toppers include **Alanis Morisette,** country goddess **Shania Twain,** and **Céline Dion,** who's everything she is because we loved her. Catch them on **MuchMusic,** Canada's MTV. Canada is also home to *Québécois* folk music and to several world-class orchestras, including the Montréal, Toronto, and Vancouver Symphonies.

On the silver screen, **Canada's National Film Board (NFB),** which finances many documentaries, has gained worldwide acclaim. The first Oscar given to a documentary went to the NFB's 1941 *Churchill Island.* Since then, *Québécois* filmmakers have caught the world's eye with Oscar-nominated movies like *Le declin de l'empire americain,* directed by **Denys Arcand.** He also directed the striking *Jesus de Montréal.* Art flick *Léolo* was deemed a classic by critics. **François Girard** provoked gasps with *Thirty-two Short Films about Glenn Gould,* and actress **Sheila McCarthy** shone in *I Have Heard the Mermaids Singing.*

Many famous television actors and comedians are of Canadian origin, including **Dan Aykroyd, Mike Meyers** *(Saturday Night Live, Wayne's World, and Austin Powers),* **Michael J. Fox** *(Family Ties, Back to the Future),* newscaster **Peter Jennings,** *Jeopardy* host **Alex Trebek,** and Captain James T. Kirk (of *Star Trek*) himself, **William Shatner.** The Canadian comedy troupe **SCTV** spawned the careers of big-time laughmasters **Martin Short,** the late **John Candy,** and **Rick Moranis.**

The *Toronto Globe and Mail* is Canada's national newspaper, distributed six days a week across the entire country. Every Canadian city has at least one daily paper; the weekly news magazine is *Maclean's.* The publicly-owned **Canadian Broadcasting Corporation (CBC)** provides two national networks for both radio and TV, one in English and one in French. A host of private networks serve limited areas; CTV broadcasts nationally. Cable and satellite access U.S. TV networks.

# SPORTS

On the field, Canada is best known for sports appropriate to its northern latitudes. Winter sports include curling, ice skating, skiing, and, of course, the ultimate winter sport in Canada, **ice hockey.** Some of Canada's other popular sports are derived from those of the aboriginal peoples. **Lacrosse,** the national game, was played long before the colonists arrived. Finally, sports played in the U.S. have crossed the border. There is a Canadian Football League (CFL) and two teams in both Major League Baseball and the National Basketball Association.

# THIS YEAR'S NEWS

USA

Canada faces ever-increasing Americanization pressure. Not only do Canadian policy-makers have to worry about protecting themselves from the **"brain drain,"** a southward emigration of Canada's top intellectuals, American media has begun to strain Canadian pride. Radio stations are required to play 30% Canadian music to counteract America's boombox take-over, print media is being forced into dire straights because of cheaper advertisement prices for American magazines, and after the Colorado highschool shootings in the United States, a 14-year-old boy in **Taber, Alberta** killed one student and injured another in his former school. At the same time, Canada's economic growth is second highest among the top industrial economies and unemployment levels are steadily decreasing.

As usual, one of the biggest puzzles for most Canadians is whether or not **Québec** will secede. Some worry that the implications of a succession could mean economic woe for Québeckers, but Seperatists argue that the French-speaking people would not go anywhere, thus creating a solid economic base.

For the first time since 1971, a major political party in Canada won back-to-back majorities, when tax-cutting Progressive Conservative Mike Harris was reelected for **Ontario** government. Mr. Harris cut 30% of the provincial income tax, which, according to the Liberal and left-wind New Democratic parties, had led to dire consequences for both health care and eduction. Harris' popularity lies mostly in the prosperous suburbs and rural sections of the province.

**British Columbia** premier Glen Clark is suffering scant popular support after a string of allegations about his and his party's stewardship and reporting of the province's deficit and funds. A highly publicized search of his home—caught on television, no less—in relation to a friend's application for a casino nearly forced his resignation in March. The moderately socialist NDP still has a couple of years before they need to call an election.

Contrary to the desire of the frontier to divest itself of obligations to the feds, the rest of Canada would like to the leave the **Yukon Territory** to its own devices: Ottawa has recently made it clear that it intends the Yukon to take on powers normally devolved only to provinces—control over land and natural resources—as well as bearing more responsibility, along with all of Canada's provinces, for the administration of its well-subscribed social safety net.

# ESSENTIALS

## FACTS FOR THE TRAVELER

### WHEN TO GO

Climate and happenings vary greatly across these two enormous countries, so when to go depends on where you are going. In general, tourist season for the U.S. runs from Memorial Day to Labor Day, (May 28-Sept. 3, 2000). In Canada, the high season is from mid-July to early September. In the off season, hostels might be cheaper and slightly less crowded, but sights might also be closed. On national holidays, many sights will be closed. In general, call ahead to the tourist office in the region to which you are going. See below for more specific information.

### NATIONAL HOLIDAYS

| USA | | CANADA | |
|---|---|---|---|
| Date in 2000 | Holiday | Date in 2000 | Holiday |
| January 1 | New Year's Day | January 1 | New Year's Day |
| January 17 | Martin Luther King, Jr. Day | April 23 | Easter Sunday |
| February 21 | Presidents Day | April 24 | Easter Monday |
| May 29 | Memorial Day | May 22 | Victoria Day |
| July 4 | Independence Day | July 1 | Canada Day |
| September 4 | Labor Day | September 4 | Labour Day |
| October 9 | Columbus Day | October 9 | Thanksgiving |
| November 11 | Veterans Day | November 11 | Remembrance Day |
| November 23 | Thanksgiving | December 25 | Christmas Day |
| December 25 | Christmas Day | December 26 | Boxing Day |

### FESTIVALS

Some of the most popular festivals are listed below, along with the page numbers of their respective descriptions in the guide. This list is not exhaustive; refer to Sights and Entertainment sections of individual city listings for more festivals.

| Month | Festival and Location |
|---|---|
| **USA** | |
| January | Elvis Presley's Birthday Tribute, Memphis, TN (p. 343) |
| | National Western Stock Show, Rodeo, and Horse Show, Denver, CO (p. 655) |
| | Winterskol, Aspen, CO (p. 667) |
| | Winter Carnival, St. Paul, MN (p. 519) |
| February | Mardi Gras, New Orleans, LA (p. 398) |
| | Ashland Shakespeare Festival, Ashland, OR (p. 893) |
| | Gasparilla Pirate Festival, Tampa, FL (p. 450) |
| March | South by Southwest, Austin, TX (p. 586) |
| April | New Orleans Jazz and Heritage Festival, New Orleans, LA (p. 398) |
| | Fiesta San Antonio, San Antonio, TX (p. 597) |
| May | Memphis in May International Festival, Memphis, TN (p. 343) |
| | Spoleto Festival USA, Charleston, SC (p. 362) |
| June | Portland Rose Festival, Portland, OR (p. 879) |

| | |
|---|---|
| June | **Chisholm Trail Round-up,** Fort Worth, TX (**p. 586**) |
| | **Chicago Blues Festival,** Chicago, IL (**p. 493**) |
| | **Summerfest,** Milwaukee, WI (**p. 508**) |
| | **Aspen Music Festival,** Aspen, CO (**p. 667**) |
| July | **Tanglewood,** Lenox, MA (**p. 140**) |
| | **Frontier Days,** Cheyenne, WY (**p. 652**) |
| | **Aquatennial,** Minneapolis, MN (**p. 519**) |
| August | **Newport Folk Festival and JVC Jazz Festival,** Newport, RI (**p. 146**) |
| September | **Bumbershoot,** Seattle, WA (**p. 853**) |
| | **La Fiesta de Santa Fe,** Santa Fe, NM (**p. 737**) |
| November | **Hot Air Balloon Rally,** Albuquerque, NM (**p. 743**) |
| | **Macy's Thanksgiving Day Parade,** New York, NY (**p. 198**) |

### CANADA

| | |
|---|---|
| January | **Annual Polar Bear Swim,** Vancouver, B.C. (**p. 897**) |
| February | **Winterlude,** Ottawa, ON (**p. 191**) |
| | **Winter Carnival,** Québec City, QC (**p. 174**) |
| May | **Stratford Festival,** Stratford, ON (**p. 190**) |
| | **Canadian Tulip Festival,** Ottawa, ON (**p. 191**) |
| June | **International Jazz Festival,** Montréal, QC (**p. 164**) |
| July | **Nova Scotia International Tattoo Festival,** Halifax, NS (**p. 155**) |
| | **Juste Pour Rire,** Montréal, QC (**p. 164**) |

## CLIMATE

The following chart gives the average temperatures in degrees Farenheit and the average rainfall in inches during four months of the year. To convert from Farenheit to Celsius, subtract 32 and divide by 2.

| Temperature in °F | January | | April | | July | | October | |
|---|---|---|---|---|---|---|---|---|
| Rain in inches | Temp | Rain | Temp | Rain | Temp | Rain | Temp | Rain |
| Atlanta | 51° | 4.9" | 73° | 4.4" | 89° | 4.7" | 74° | 2.5" |
| Chicago | 29° | 1.6" | 59° | 3.7" | 83° | 3.6" | 64° | 2.3" |
| Dallas | 54° | 1.7" | 84° | 3.6" | 98° | 2.0" | 80° | 2.5" |
| Las Vegas | 56° | 0.5" | 77° | 0.2" | 105° | 0.5" | 82° | 0.3" |
| Los Angeles | 67° | 3.7" | 71° | 1.2" | 84° | 0.0" | 79° | 0.2" |
| New Orleans | 62° | 5.0" | 79° | 4.5" | 91° | 6.7" | 79° | 2.7" |
| New York | 68° | 3.2" | 61° | 3.8" | 85° | 3.8" | 66° | 3.4" |
| Seattle | 45° | 5.9" | 58° | 2.5" | 74° | 0.9" | 60° | 3.4" |

# DOCUMENTS AND FORMALITIES

## EMBASSIES AND CONSULATES

Contact your nearest embassy or consulate to obtain info regarding visas and passports to the United States and Canada. The U.S. **State Dept.** provides contact information for U.S. overseas stations which can be found on the Internet at www.state.gov/www/about_state/contacts/keyofficer_index.html. A similar listing for the Canadian Ministries of Foreign Affairs can be found at www.dfait-maeci.gc.ca/dfait/missions/menu-e.asp.

**U.S. EMBASSIES:** In **Australia,** Moonah Pl., Canberra, ACT 2600 (02 6214 5600; fax 6214 5970); in **Canada,** 100 Wellington St., Ottawa, ON K1P 5T1 (613-238-5335 or 238-4470; fax 238-5720); in **Ireland,** 42 Elgin Rd., Ballsbridge, Dublin 4 (01 668 8777; fax 668 9946); in **New Zealand,** 29 Fitzherbert Terr., Thorndon, Wellington (04 472 2068; fax 472 3537); in **South Africa,** 877 Pretorius St., Arcadia 0083, P.O. Box 9536 Pretoria 0001 (012 342 1048; fax 342 2299); in the **U.K.,** 24/31 Grosvenor Sq., London W1A 1AE (0171 499 9000; fax 495 5012).

**U.S. CONSULATES:** In **Australia,** MLC Centre, 19-29 Martin Pl., 59th fl., Sydney NSW 2000 (02 9373 9200; fax 9373 9125); 553 St. Kilda Rd., P.O. Box 6722, Melbourne, VIC 3004 (03 9625 1583; fax 9510 4646); 16 St. George's Terr., 13th fl., Perth, WA 6000 (08 9231 9400; fax 9231 9444); in **Canada,** 615 Macleod Trail, #1050, S.E., Calgary, AB T2G 4T8, (403-266-8962; fax 264-6630); Cogswell Tower, #910, Scotia Sq., Halifax, NS, B3J 3K1, (902-429-2480; fax 423-6861); P.O. Box 65, Postal Station Desjardins, Montreal, QC H5B 1G1 (514-398-9695; fax 398-0973); 2 Place Terrasse Dufferin, C.P. 939, Quebec, QC, G1R 4T9 (418-692-2095; fax 692-4640); 360 University Ave., Toronto, ON, M5G 1S4 (416-595-1700; fax 595-0051); 1095 West Pender St., Vancouver, BC V6E 2M6 (604-685-4311; fax 685-5285); in **New Zealand,** Yorkshire General Bldg., 4th fl., 29 Shortland St., Auckland (09 303 2724; fax 366 0870); Price Waterhouse Center, 109 Armagh St., 11th fl., Christchurch (03 379 0040; fax 379 5677); in **South Africa,** Broadway Industries Centre, P.O. Box 6773, Heerengracht, Foreshore, Cape Town (021 214 280; fax 211 130); Durban Bay House, 333 Smith St., 29th fl., Durban (031 304 4737; fax 301 8206); 1 River St. c/o Riviera, Killarney, Johannesburg (011 646 6900; fax 646 6913); in the **U.K.,** Queen's House, 14 Queen St., Belfast, N. Ireland BT1 6EQ, PSC 801, Box 40, APO AE 09498-4040 (0123 232 8239; fax 224 8482); 3 Regent Terr., Edinburgh, Scotland EH7 5BW, PSC 801 Box 40, FPO AE 90498-4040 (0131 556 8315; fax 557 6023).

**CANADIAN EMBASSIES:** In **Australia,** Commonwealth Ave., Canberra, ACT 2600 (02 6273 3844; fax 6273 3285); in **Ireland,** 65 St. Stephen's Green, Dublin 2 (01 478 1988; fax 478 1285); in **New Zealand,** 61 Molesworth St., 34th fl., Thorndon, Wellington (04 473 9577; fax 471 2082); in **South Africa,** 1103 Arcadia St. Hatfield, Pretoria 0028 (012 422 3000; fax 422 3052); in the **U.K.,** Macdonald House, 1 Grosvenor Sq., London W1X 0AB (0171 258 6600; fax 258 6333); in the **U.S.,** 501 Pennsylvania Ave. NW, Washington, D.C. 20001 (202-682-1740; fax 682-7726).

**CANADIAN CONSULATES:** In **Australia,** Quay West Bldg., 111 Harrington St., Level 5, Sydney NSW, 2000 (02 9364 3000; fax 9364 3098); 123 Camberwell Rd., Hawthorn East, Melbourne, VIC 3123 (03 9811 9999; fax 9811 9969); 267 St. George's Terr., 3rd fl., Perth WA (08 9322 7930; fax 9261 7700); in **New Zealand,** Level 9, Jetset Centre, 48 Emily Pl., Auckland (09 309 3680; fax 307 3111); in **South Africa,** Reserve Bank Bldg., 360 St. George's Mall St., 19th fl., Cape Town 8001 (021 423 5240; fax 423 4893); 25/27 Marriott Rd., Durban 4001 (031 309 8434; fax 309 8432); in the **U.K.,** 30 Lothian Rd., Edinburgh, Scotland EH2 2XZ (0131 220 4333; fax 246 6010); in the **U.S.,** 1251 6th Ave., New York, NY 10020-1175 (212-596-1683; fax 596-1790); 550 S. Hope St. 9th fl., Los Angeles, CA 90071 (213-346-2700; fax 620-8827); 2 Prudential Plaza, 180 N. Stetson, Ave., Ste. 2400, Chicago, IL 60601 (312-616-1860; fax 616-1877).

## EMBASSIES IN THE USA AND CANADA

### IN WASHINGTON, DC (USA):

**Australia,** 1601 Massachussetts Ave., 20036; (202-797-3000; fax 797-3040). **Canada,** 501 Pennsylvania Ave., 20001; (202-682-1740; fax 682-7726). **Ireland,** 2234 Mass. Ave., 20008, (202-462-3939; fax 232-5993). **New Zealand,** 37 Observatory Circle, 20008; (202-328-4800; fax 667-5227). **U.K.,** 3100 Mass. Ave., 20008, (202-588-6500; fax 588- 6500). **South Africa,** 3051 Mass. Ave., 20008; (202- 966- 1650; fax 244- 9417).

**IN OTTAWA, ONTARIO (CANADA):**

**Australia,** 50 O' Connor St. #710, K1P 6I2; (613-238-5707; fax 236-4376). **Ireland,** 130 Albert St. #700, K1P 5G4; (613-233-6281; fax 233-5835). **New Zealand,** 727 Bank St. #99, K1P 6G3; (613- 238- 5991; fax 238-5707). **U.K.,** 310 Summerset St., K2P 0J9; (613-230-2961; fax 230-2400). **U.S.,** 100 Wellington St., K1P 5T1; (613-238-3335). **South Africa,** 130 Albert St. #700, K1P 5G4; (613-744-0330; fax 741-1639).

## ENTRANCE REQUIREMENTS

**Passport** (p. 34). Required for all visitors to the U.S. and Canada.

**Visa** In genereal a visa is required for visitng the U.S. and Canada, but it can be waived. (See p. 37 for more specific information.)

**Work Permit** (p. 37). Required for all foreigners planning to work in Canada or the U.S.

**Driving Permit** (p. 78). Required for all those planning to drive.

## PASSPORTS

**REQUIREMENTS.** Citizens of Australia, Ireland, New Zealand, South Africa, and the U.K. need valid passports to enter the United States and Canada, and to re-enter their own country. Returning home with an expired passport is illegal, and may result in a fine.

**PHOTOCOPIES.** It is a good idea to photocopy the page of your passport that contains your photograph, passport number, and other identifying information, along with other important documents such as visas, travel insurance policies, airplane tickets, and traveler's check serial numbers, in case you lose anything. Carry one set of copies in a safe place apart from the originals and

leave another set at home. Consulates also recommend that you carry an expired passport or an official copy of your birth certificate in a part of your baggage separate from other documents.

**LOST PASSPORTS.** If you lose your passport, immediately notify the local police and the nearest embassy or consulate of your home government. To expedite its replacement, you will need to know all information previously recorded and show identification and proof of citizenship. A replacement may take weeks to process, and it may be valid only for a limited time. Any visas stamped in your old passport will be irretrievably lost. In an emergency, ask for immediate temporary traveling papers that will permit you to re-enter your home country. Your passport is a public document belonging to your nation's government. You may have to surrender it to a foreign government official, but if you don't get it back in a reasonable amount of time, inform the nearest mission of your home country.

**NEW PASSPORTS.** All applications for new passports or renewals should be filed several weeks or months before your planned departure date—you are relying on government agencies to complete these transactions. Most passport offices offer emergency passport services for an extra charge. Citizens residing abroad needing a passport or renewal should contact their nearest embassy or consulate.

**Australia** Citizens must apply for a passport in person at a post office, a passport office, or an Australian diplomatic mission overseas. Passport offices are located in Adelaide, Brisbane, Canberra, Darwin, Hobart, Melbourne, Newcastle, Perth, and Sydney. New adult passports cost A$126 (for a 32-page passport) or A$188 (64-page), and a child's is A$63 (32-page) or A$94 (64-page). Adult passports are valid for 10 years and child passports for 5 years. For more info, call toll-free (in Australia) 13 12 32, or visit www.dfat.gov.au/passports.

**Canada** Citizens may cross the U.S.-Canada border withany proof of citizenship.

**Ireland** Citizens can apply for a passport by mail to either the Department of Foreign Affairs, Passport Office, Setanta Centre, Molesworth St., Dublin 2 (tel. (01) 671 16 33; fax 671 1092; www.irlgov.ie/iveagh), or the Passport Office, Irish Life Building, 1A South Mall, Cork (tel. (021) 27 25 25). Obtain an application at a local Garda station or post office, or request one from a passport office. Passports cost IR£45 and are valid for 10 years. Citizens under 18 or over 65 can request a 3-year passport (IR£10).

**New Zealand** Application forms for passports are available in New Zealand from most travel agents. Applications may be forwarded to the Passport Office, P.O. Box 10526, Wellington, New Zealand (tel. 0800 22 50 50; www.govt.nz/agency_info/forms.shtml). Standard processing time in New Zealand is 10 working days for correct applications. The fees are adult NZ$80, and child NZ$40. Children's names can no longer be endorsed on a parent's passport—they must apply for their own, which are valid for up to 5 years. An adult's passport is valid for up to 10 years.

**South Africa** South African passports are issued only in Pretoria. However, all applications must still be submitted or forwarded to the applicable office of a South African consulate. Tourist passports, valid for 10 years, cost around SAR80. Children under 16 must be issued their own passports, valid for 5 years, which cost around SAR60. Time for the completion of an application is normally 3 months or more from the time of submission. For further information, contact the nearest Department of Home Affairs Office (www.southafrica-newyork.net/passport.htm).

**United Kingdom** Full passports are valid for 10 years (5 years if under 16). Application forms are available at passport offices, main post offices, and many travel agents. Apply by mail or in person to one of the passport offices, located in London, Liverpool, Newport, Peterborough, Glasgow, or Belfast. The fee is UK£31, UK£11 for children under 16. The process takes about four weeks, but the London office offers a five-day, walk-in rush service; arrive early. The U.K. Passport Agency can be reached by phone at (0870) 521 04 10. More info is available at www.open.gov.uk/ukpass/ukpass.htm.

**United States** Citizens may cross the U.S.-Canada border with any proof of citizenship.

# VISAS

A visa, stamped into a traveler's passport by the government of a host country, allows the bearer to stay in that country for a specified purpose and period of time. The **Center for International Business and Travel** (CIBT), 23201 New Mexico Ave. NW, #210, Washington, D.C. 20016 (202-244-9500 or 800-925-2428), secures travel visas to and from all possible countries for a variable service charge, usually around $45. To obtain a U.S. or Canadian visa, contact the nearest embassy or consulate. Residents of Canada do not need a visa to enter the U.S. if their stay is planned for 180 days or less; citizens of Australia and South Africa need a visa to enter. Citizens of France, Germany, Ireland, Italy, Japan, New Zealand, and the U.K can waive the U.S. visa through the **Visa Waiver Pilot Program** if staying 90 days or less; work and study is prohibited to those who waiver visas. Visitors qualify as long as they are staying for 90 days or less, have proof of intent to leave (e.g., a returning plane ticket), a completed I-94W form (arrival/departure certificate attached to your visa upon arrival), and are traveling on particular air or sea carriers. Contact a U.S. consulate for more info; countries are added frequently.

Most visitors obtain a **B-2,** or "pleasure tourist," visa at the nearest U.S. consulate or embassy, which normally costs $45 and is usually valid for 6 months. For general visa inquiries, consult the Bureau of Consular Affair's Webpage (travel.state.gov/visa_services.html). If you lose your I-94 form, you can replace it at the nearest **Immigration and Naturalization Service (INS)** office, though it's very unlikely that the form will be replaced within the time of your stay. **Extensions** for visas are sometimes attainable with a completed I-539 form; call the forms request line 800-870-3676. For more info, contact the INS at 800-755-0777 or 202-307-1501 (www.ins.usdoj.gov).

Citizens of Australia, France, Germany, Ireland, Italy, Japan, Mexico, New Zealand, the U.K., and the U.S. may enter Canada without visas for stays of 90 days or less if they carry proof of intent to leave; South Africans need a visa to enter Canada ($75 for a single person, $400 for a family). Citizens of other countries should contact their Canadian consulate for more info. Write to Citizenship and Immigration Canada for the useful booklet *Applying for a Visitor Visa* at Information Centre, Public Affairs Branch, Journal Tower South, 365 Laurier Ave. W., Ottawa, ON K1A 1L1 (888-242-2100 or 613-954-9019; fax 954-2221), or consult the electronic version at http://cicnet.ci.gc.ca. Extensions are sometimes granted; phone the nearest Canada Immigration Centre listed in the phone directory.

# IDENTIFICATION

When you travel, always carry two or more forms of identification on your person, including at least one photo ID. A passport combined with a driver's license or birth certificate usually serves as adequate proof of your identity and citizenship. Many establishments, especially banks, require several IDs before cashing traveler's checks. Never carry all your forms of ID together because you risk being left entirely without ID or funds in case of theft or loss. It is useful to carry extra passport-size photos to affix to the various IDs or railpasses you may acquire.

**STUDENT AND TEACHER IDENTIFICATION.** The **International Student Identity Card (ISIC)** is the most widely accepted form of student identification. Flashing this card can procure you discounts for sights, theaters, museums, accommodations, meals, train, ferry, bus, and airplane transportation, and other services. Cardholders have access to a toll-free 24hr. ISIC helpline whose multilingual staff can provide assistance in medical, legal, and financial emergencies overseas (800-626-2427 in the U.S. and Canada; elsewhere call collect (tel (181) 666 90 25).

Many student travel agencies around the world issue ISICs, including STA Travel in Australia and New Zealand; Travel CUTS in Canada; USIT in Ireland and Northern Ireland; SASTS in South Africa; Campus Travel and STA Travel in the U.K.; Council Travel, STA Travel, and via the web (www.counciltravel.com/

idcards/default.asp) in the U.S. (See p.32). When you apply for the card, request a copy of the *International Student Identity Card Handbook*, which lists some of the available discounts in the U.S. and Canada. You can also write to Council for a copy. The card is valid from September of one year to December of the following year and costs A$15, CDN$15, or $20. Applicants must be at least 12 years old and degree-seeking students of a secondary or post-secondary school. Because of the proliferation of phony ISICs, many airlines and some other services require additional proof of student identity, such as a signed letter from the registrar attesting to your student status that is stamped with the school seal or your school ID card. The **International Teacher Identity Card (ITIC)** offers similar but limited discounts The fee is A$13, UK£5, or $20. For more info on these cards, contact the **International Student Travel Confederation (ISTC)**, Herengracht 479, 1017 BS Amsterdam, Netherlands (from abroad call 31 20 421 28 00; fax 421 28 10; email istcinfo@istc.org; www.istc.org).

**YOUTH IDENTIFICATION.** The International Student Travel Confederation also issues a discount card to travelers who are 25 years old or younger, but not students. This one-year card, known as the International Youth Travel Card (IYTC) and formerly as the GO25, offers many of the same benefits as the ISIC, and most organizations that sell the ISIC also sell the IYTC. To apply, you will need either a passport, valid driver's license, or copy of a birth certificate, and a passport-sized photo with your name printed on the back. The fee is $20.

# CUSTOMS

Upon entering the United States or Canada, you must declare certain items from abroad and pay a duty on the value of those articles that exceed the allowance established by the U.S. or Canada's customs service. Keeping receipts for purchases made abroad will help establish values when you return. It is wise to make a list, including serial numbers, of any valuables that you carry with you from home; if you register this list with customs before your departure and have an official stamp it, you will avoid import duty charges and ensure an easy passage upon your return. Be especially careful to document items manufactured abroad, and don't try to bring perishable food over the border.

Upon returning home, you must declare all articles acquired abroad and pay a **duty** on the value of articles that exceed the allowance established by your country's customs service. Goods and gifts purchased at **duty-free** shops abroad are not exempt from duty or sales tax at your point of return; you must declare these items as well. "Duty-free" merely means that you need not pay a tax in the country of purchase. For more specific information on customs requirements, contact the following information centers:

**Australia** Australian Customs National Information Line 1 300 363; www.customs.gov.au.

**Canada** Canadian Customs, 2265 St. Laurent Blvd., Ottawa, ON K1G 4K3 (tel. 613-993-0534 or 24hr. automated service 800-461-9999; www.revcan.ca).

**Ireland** The Collector of Customs and Excise, The Custom House, Dublin 1 (tel. (01) 679 27 77; fax 671 20 21; email taxes@revenue.iol.ie; www.revenue.ie/customs.htm).

**New Zealand** New Zealand Customhouse, 17-21 Whitmore St., Box 2218, Wellington (tel. (04) 473 6099; fax 473 7370; www.customs.govt.nz).

**South Africa** Commissioner for Customs and Excise, Private Bag X47, Pretoria 0001 (tel. 120 314 99 11; fax 328 64 78).

**United Kingdom** Her Majesty's Customs and Excise, Custom House, Nettleton Road, Heathrow Airport, Hounslow, Middlesex TW6 2LA (tel. (0181) 910 36 02/35 66; fax 910 37 65; www.hmce.gov.uk).

**United States** U.S. Customs Service, Box 7407, Washington D.C. 20044 (tel. 202-927-6724; www.customs.ustreas.gov).

ESSENTIALS

# Money From Home In Minutes.

If you're stuck for cash on your travels, don't panic. Millions of people trust Western Union to transfer money in minutes to 165 countries and over 50,000 locations worldwide. Our record of safety and reliability is second to none. For more information, call Western Union: USA 1-800-325-6000, Canada 1-800-235-0000. Wherever you are, you're never far from home.

**www.westernunion.com**

**WESTERN UNION | MONEY TRANSFER®**

*The fastest way to send money worldwide:*

# MONEY

**Accommodations** start at about $12 per night in a hostel bed, while a basic sit-down meal costs about $10 depending on the region. If you stay in hostels and prepare your own food, you can spend anywhere from $25-60 per person per day. Transportation will increase these figures. No matter how low your budget, if you plan to travel for more than a couple of days, you will need to keep handy a larger amount of cash than usual. Carrying it around with you, even in a money belt, is risky, and personal checks from another country, or even another state, will probably not be accepted no matter how many forms of identification you have (some banks even shy away from accepting checks).

Many Canadian shops, as well as vending machines and parking meters, accept U.S. coins at face value. Stores often convert the price of your purchase for you, but they are not legally obligated to offer a fair exchange. During the past several years, the Canadian dollar has been worth roughly 30% less than the U.S. dollar.

> All prices in the Canada section of this book are listed in Canadian dollars unless otherwise noted.

## CURRENCY AND EXCHANGE

The main unit of currency in the U.S. and Canada is the **dollar**, which is divided into 100 **cents**. Paper money is green in the U.S.; bills come in denominations of $1, $5, $10, $20, $50, and $100. Coins are 1¢ (penny), 5¢ (nickel), 10¢ (dime), and 25¢ (quarter). Paper money in Canada comes in denominations of $5, $10, $20, $50, and $100, which are all the same size but color coded by denomination. Coins are 1¢, 5¢, 10¢, 25¢, $1, and $2. The $1 coin is known as the **Loonie**.

The currency chart below is based on published exchange rates from Sept. 1999.

**THE GREENBACK (THE U.S. DOLLAR)**

| | |
|---|---|
| CDN$1 = $0.67 | US$1 = CDN$1.49 |
| UK£1 = $1.60 | US$1 = UK£0.62 |
| IR£1 = $1.34 | US$1= IR£0.74 |
| A$1 = $0.65 | US$1= A$1.54 |
| NZ$1 = $0.52 | US$1 = NZ$1.92 |
| SAR1=$0.17 | US$1 = SAR6.03 |

**THE LOONIE (THE CANADIAN DOLLAR)**

| | |
|---|---|
| US$1 = $1.49 | CDN$1 = US$0.67 |
| UK£1 = $2.39 | CDN$1 = UK£0.42 |
| IR£1 = $2.00 | CDN$1= IR£0.50 |
| A$1 = $0.96 | CDN$1= A$1.04 |
| NZ$1 = $0.78 | CDN$1 = NZ$1.29 |
| SAR1=$0.25 | CDN$1 = SAR4.05 |

Watch out for commission rates and check newspapers for the standard rate of exchange. Banks generally have the best rates. A good rule of thumb is only to go to banks or money-exchanging centers/*bureaux de change* that have at most a 5% margin between their buy and sell prices. Since you lose money with each transaction, convert in large sums. Also, using an ATM card or a credit card (see p. 43) will often get you the best possible rates.

If you use traveler's checks or bills, carry some in small denominations ($50 or less), especially for times when you are forced to exchange money at disadvantageous rates. However, it is good to carry a range of denominations since charges may be levied per check cashed.

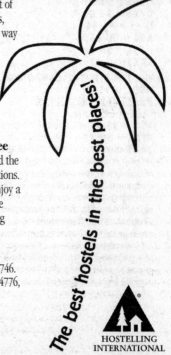

# TRAVELER'S CHECKS

Traveler's checks are one of the safest and least troublesome means of carrying funds, since they can be refunded if stolen. Also, in both the United States and Canada, traveler's checks are widely accepted in both rural and urban areas. Several agencies and banks sell them, usually for face value plus a small percentage commission. **American Express** and **Visa** are the most widely recognized. If you're ordering checks, do so well in advance, especially if you are requesting large sums.

Each agency provides refunds if your checks are lost or stolen, and many provide additional services, such as toll-free refund hotlines in the countries you're visiting, emergency message services, and stolen credit card assistance.

In order to collect a **refund for lost or stolen checks,** keep your check receipts separate from your checks and store them in a safe place or with a traveling companion. Record check numbers when you cash them, leave a list of check numbers with someone at home, and ask for a list of refund centers when you buy your checks. Never countersign your checks until you are ready to cash them, and always bring your passport with you when you plan to use the checks.

**American Express:** Call (800) 251-902 in Australia; in New Zealand (0800) 441 068; in the U.K. (0800) 52 13 13; in the U.S. and Canada 800-221-7282. Elsewhere, call U.S. collect 1-801-964-6665; www.aexp.com. American Express traveler's checks are available in U.S. (but not Canadian) dollars. Checks can be purchased for a small fee (1-4%) at American Express Travel Service Offices, banks, and American Automobile Association offices. AAA members (see p. 79) can buy the checks commission-free. American Express offices cash their checks commission-free (except where prohibited by national governments), but often at slightly worse rates than banks. *Cheques for Two* can be signed by either of two people traveling together.

**Citicorp:** Call 800-645-6556 in the U.S. and Canada; in Europe, the Middle East, or Africa, call the London office at 44 171 508 7007; from elsewhere, call U.S. collect 1-813-623-1709. Traveler's checks in 7 currencies. Commission 1-2%. Guaranteed hand-delivery of traveler's checks when a refund location is not convenient. Call 24hr.

**Thomas Cook MasterCard:** From the U.S., Canada, or Caribbean call 800-223-7373; from the U.K. call (0800) 622 101; from elsewhere, call (44) 1733 318 950 collect. Available in 13 currencies. Commission 2%. Offices cash checks commission-free.

**Visa:** Call 800-227-6811 in the U.S.; in the U.K. (0800) 895 078; from elsewhere, call 44 1733 318 949 and reverse the charges. Any of the above numbers can tell you the location of their nearest office.

# CREDIT CARDS

Credit cards are generally accepted in all but the smallest businesses in both the United States and Canada. Major credit cards—**MasterCard** and **Visa** are welcomed most often—can be used to extract cash advances in dollars, (both U.S. and Canadian) from associated banks and teller machines throughout both countries. Credit card companies get the wholesale exchange rate, which is generally 5% better than the retail rate used by banks and other currency exchange establishments. **American Express** cards also work in some ATMs, as well as at AmEx offices and major airports. All such machines require a **Personal Identification Number (PIN).** You must ask your credit card company for a PIN before you leave; without it, you will be unable to withdraw cash with your credit card outside your home country. If you already have a PIN, check with the company to make sure it will work in Canada and the U.S. Credit cards often offer an array of other services, from insurance to emergency assistance; check with your company.

**Visa** (U.S. 800-336-8472) and **MasterCard** (U.S. 800-307-7309) are issued in cooperation with individual banks and some other organizations. **American Express** (800-843-2273) has an annual fee of up to $55, depending on the card. Cardholder services include the option of cashing personal checks at AmEx offices, a 24-hour hotline with medical and legal assistance in emergencies (800-554-2639 in U.S. and

Canada; from abroad call U.S. collect 1-202-554-2639), and the American Express Travel Service. Benefits include assistance in changing airline, hotel, and car rental reservations, baggage loss and flight insurance, sending mailgrams and international cables, and holding your mail at one of the more than 1700 AmEx offices around the world. The **Discover Card** (U.S. 800-347-2683; outside U.S., call 1-801-902-3100) offers small cashback bonuses on most purchases, but it may not be readily accepted in Canada or the U.S. **Diner's Club** (U.S. 800-234-6377; outside U.S., call collect 1-303-799-1504) is another popular option.

## CASH CARDS

Cash cards—popularly called ATM (Automated Teller Machine) cards—are widespread in both rural and urban parts of the U.S. and Canada. Depending on the system that your home bank uses, you can probably access your own personal bank account whenever you need money. ATMs get the same wholesale exchange rate as credit cards. Despite these perks, do some research before relying too heavily on automation. There is often a limit on the amount of money you can withdraw per day (usually about $500, depending on the type of card and account), and computer networks sometimes fail. If your PIN is longer than four digits, ask your bank whether the first four digits will work, or whether you need a new number.

The two major international money networks are **Cirrus** (800-424-7787) and **PLUS** (800-843-7587 for the "Voice Response Unit Locator"). To locate ATMs in the U.S. and Canada, use www.visa.com/pd/atm or www.mastercard .com/atm. A typical ATM transaction fee is $1-3 in the U.S. and $5 outside of the U.S.

## GETTING MONEY FROM HOME

**American Express:** Cardholders can withdraw cash from their checking accounts at any of AmEx's major offices and many of its representatives' offices, up to $1000 every 21 days (no service charge, no interest). AmEx also offers Express Cash at any of their ATMs in the U.S. or Canada. Express Cash withdrawals are automatically debited from the Cardmember's checking account or line of credit. Green card holders may withdraw up to $1000 in a seven day period. There is a 2% transaction fee for each cash withdrawal, with a $2.50 minimum/$20 maximum. To enroll in Express Cash, cardmembers may call 800-CASH NOW (227-4669) in the U.S.; outside the U.S. call collect 1-336-668-5041. The AmEx national number in the United States and Canada is 800-221-7282.

**Western Union** Travelers from the U.S., Canada, and the U.K. can wire money abroad through Western Union's international money transfer services. In the U.S., call 800-325-6000; in Canada, call 800-235-0000. To cable money within the U.S. using a credit card (Visa, MasterCard, Discover), call 800-CALL-CASH (225-5227). The rates for sending cash are generally $10-11 cheaper than with a credit card, and the money is usually available at the place you're sending it to within an hour.

## TIPPING AND BARGAINING

In the U.S., it is customary to tip waitstaff and cab drivers 15-20%, at your discretion. Tips are usually not included in restaurant bills, unless you are in a party of 6 or more. At the airport and in hotels, porters expect at least a $1 per bag tip to carry your bags. Tipping is less compulsory in Canada; a good tip signifies remarkable service. Bargaining is generally frowned upon and fruitless in both countries.

## TAXES

The U.S. sales tax is the equivalent of the European Value-Added Tax and ranges from 4-10% depending on the item and the place; in many states, groceries are not taxed. *Let's Go* lists sales tax rates in the introduction to each state; usually these taxes are not included in the prices of items.

In Canada, you'll quickly notice the 7% goods and services tax (GST) and an additional sales tax in some provinces. See the provinces' introductions for info on local taxes. Visitors can claim a rebate of the GST they pay on accommodations of less than 1 month and on most goods they buy and take home, so be sure to save your receipts and pick up a GST rebate form while in Canada. The total claim must be at least CDN$7 of GST (equal to CDN$100 in purchases) and made within 1 year of the date of the purchase; further goods must be exported from Canada within 60 days of purchase. A brochure detailing restrictions is available from local tourist offices or through Revenue Canada, Visitor's Rebate Program, 275 Pope Rd., Summerside, PEI C1N 6C6 (800-668-4748 or 902-432-5608 outside of Canada.)

# TIME ZONES

North Americans tell **time** on a 12hr. clock cycle. Hours before noon are "am" *(ante meridiem)*; hours after noon are "pm" *(post meridiem)*. The four time zones in the continental U.S. are (east to west, each zone 1hr. earlier than the preceding): **Eastern, Central, Mountain,** and **Pacific. Alaska, Hawaii,** and the **Aleutian Islands** have their own time zones. Canada has six: **Newfoundland, Atlantic, Eastern, Central, Mountain,** and **Pacific.**

# MEASUREMENTS

Although the metric system has made considerable inroads into American business and science, the English system of weights and measures prevails here. Refer to the inside back cover of this guide for a metric/English conversion chart.

# SAFETY AND SECURITY

Crime is mostly concentrated in the cities, but being safe is a good idea no matter where you are. Wahington D.C.; Newark, N.J.; New Orleans, LA; Richmond, Virginia; Atlanta, GA; Los Angeles, CA; Detroit MI; and St. Louis, MO are the most dangerous cities in the United States, but that does not mean you should not visit them. Common sense and a little bit of thought will go a long way in helping you to avoid dangerous situations.

**BLENDING IN.** Tourists are particularly vulnerable to crime because they often carry large amounts of cash and are not as street savvy as locals. To avoid unwanted attention, try to blend in as much as possible: leave the fanny pack, pulled-up socks, and weird shoes at home. The gawking camera-toter is a more obvious target than the low-profile traveler. Familiarize yourself with your surroundings before setting out; if you must check a map on the street, duck into a cafe or shop. Also, carry yourself with confidence. If you are traveling alone, remember Little Red Riding Hood: be sure that someone at home knows your itinerary and *never admit that you're traveling alone.*

**EXPLORING.** Extra vigilance is always wise, but there is no need to panic when exploring a new city or region. Find out about unsafe areas from tourist offices, from the manager of your hotel or hostel, or from a local whom you trust. You may want to carry a **whistle** to attract attention, and you must memorize the emergency number of the city or area. Whenever possible, *Let's Go* warns of unsafe neighborhoods and areas, but there are some good general tips to follow.

When walking at night, stick to busy, well-lit streets and avoid dark alleyways. Do not attempt to cross through parks, parking lots or other large, deserted areas. Buildings in disrepair, vacant lots, and unpopulated areas are all bad signs. The distribution of people can reveal a great deal about the relative safety of the area; look for children playing, women walking in the open, and other signs of an active community. Keep in mind that a district can change character drastically between blocks. If you feel uncomfortable, leave as quickly and directly as you can, but don't allow fear to turn you into a hermit. Careful, persistent exploration will build confidence and make your stay in an area that much more rewarding.

**GETTING AROUND. Driving** in the U.S. and Canada is, in general, safe. It is a good idea to drive during the day, because you can get help faster if you run into trouble on the highways, and you can avoid trouble in the city streets at night. Learn local driving signals and wear a seatbelt. (Seatbelt laws vary by state, but seatbelts save lives.) Children under 40 lbs. should ride only in a specially-designed carseat, available for a small fee from most car rental agencies. Study route maps before you hit the road, and, if possible, figure out gas station availibility before you set out. (You should have no problem finding stations if you are driving on major roads.) If you plan on spending a lot of time on the road, you may want to bring spare parts. Also, if traveling in the winter, it is a good idea to have a blanket, a shovel, emergency flares, a needle and thread, and some chocolate, in case of getting stuck in a snowstorm. For long drives in desolate areas, invest in a cellular phone and a roadside assistance program (see p. 79). If your car breaks down, wait for the police to assist you. Be sure to park your vehicle in a garage or well-traveled area, and use a steering wheel locking device in larger cities. **Sleeping in your car** is one of the most dangerous (and often illegal) ways to get your rest.

**Public transportation** across states (buses and trains) is generally safe. Occasionally, the stations that the buses or trains leave you at are dangerous; *Let's Go* warns of these stations where applicable. If possible, avoid using public transportation late at night unless you are in a large group. **Taxis** are oftentimes driven by people who don't speak English, but they are safe.

*Let's Go* does not recommend **hitchhiking** under any circumstances, particularly for women—see **Getting Around,** p. 76 for more information.

**SELF-DEFENSE.** There is no sure-fire set of precautions that will protect you from all of the situations you might encounter when you travel. A good self-defense course will give you more concrete ways to react to different types of aggression. **Impact, Prepare, and Model Mugging** can refer you to local self-defense courses in the United States (800-345-5425) and Vancouver, Canada (604-878-3838). Workshops (2-3hrs.) start at $50 and full courses run $350-500. Both women and men are welcome.

# FINANCIAL SECURITY

**PROTECTING YOUR VALUABLES.** Theft in the U.S. is more rampant in big cities, and at night. To prevent easy theft, don't keep all your valuables (money, important documents) in one place. **Photocopies** of important documents allow you to recover them in case they are lost or filched. Carry one copy separate from the documents and leave another copy at home. Label every piece of luggage both inside and out. *Don't put a wallet with money in your back pocket.* Never count your money in public and carry as little as possible—keep some aside in case of an emergency. If you carry a purse, buy a sturdy one with a secure clasp, and carry it crosswise on the side, away from the street with the clasp against you. Secure packs with small combination padlocks which slip through the two zippers. A **money belt** is the best way to carry cash; you can buy one at most camping supply stores. A nylon, zippered pouch with a belt that sits inside the waist of your pants or skirt combines convenience and security. A **neck pouch** is equally safe, although far less accessible and discreet. Valuables in a fanny pack will be stolen.

**CON ARTISTS AND PICKPOCKETS.** Among the more colorful aspects of large cities are **con artists.** Con artists and hustlers often work in groups, and children are among the most effective. They possess an innumerable range of ruses. Be aware of certain classics: sob stories that require money, rolls of bills "found" on the street, mustard spilled (or saliva spit) onto your shoulder, directions asked—all distracting you for enough time to snatch your bag. Try to rent a car with a phone so you can call the police, be careful when driving, and if you get bumped, be wary. In general, if you are harrassed, do not respond or make eye contact, walk away quickly, and keep a solid grip on your belongings. Contact the police if a hustler is particularly insistent or aggressive.

In city crowds and especially on public transportation, **pickpockets** are amazingly deft at their craft. Rush hour is no excuse for strangers to press up against you on the metro. If someone stands uncomfortably close, move to another car and hold your bags tightly. Also, be alert in public telephone booths. If you must say your calling card number, do so very quietly; if you punch it in, make sure no one can look over your shoulder.

**ACCOMMODATIONS AND TRANSPORTATION.** Never leave your belongings unattended; crime occurs in even the most demure-looking hostel or hotel. If you feel unsafe, look for places with either a curfew or a night attendant. *Let's Go* lists locker availability in hostels and train stations, but you'll need your own **padlock**. Lockers are useful if you plan on sleeping outdoors or don't want to lug everything with you, but don't store valuables in them. Most hotels also provide lock boxes free or for a minimal fee.

Be particularly careful on **buses;** carry your backpack in front of you, avoid checking baggage on trains, and don't trust anyone to "watch your bag for a second." Thieves thrive on **trains;** professionals wait for tourists to fall asleep and then carry off everything they can. When traveling in pairs, sleep in alternating shifts; when alone, use good judgement in selecting a train compartment: never stay in an empty one, and use a lock to secure your pack to the luggage rack. Keep important documents and other valuables on your person.

If you travel by **car,** try not to leave valuable possessions—such as radios or luggage—in it while you are away. If your tape deck or radio is removable, hide it in the trunk or take it with you. If it isn't, at least conceal it under something else. Similarly, hide baggage in the trunk—although savvy thieves can tell if a car is heavily loaded by the way it sits on its tires.

# DRUGS AND ALCOHOL

In the U.S., the drinking age is 21; in Canada the drinking age is 19, except in Alberta, Manitoba, and Québec, where it is 18. Some areas of the United States are "dry", meaning they do not sell alcohol. If you carry prescription drugs while you travel, it is vital to have a copy of the prescriptions themselves and a note from a doctor, both readily accessible at country borders.

# HEALTH

Common sense is the simplest prescription for good health. Travelers complain most often about their feet and their gut, so take precautionary measures: drink lots of fluids to prevent dehydration and constipation, wear sturdy, broken-in shoes and clean socks, and use talcum powder to keep your feet dry. To minimize the effects of jet lag, "reset" your body's clock by adopting the time of your destination as soon as you board the plane.

# BEFORE YOU GO

Preparation can help minimize the likelihood of contracting a disease and maximize the chances of receiving effective health care in the event of an emergency.

For minor health problems, bring a compact **first-aid kit,** including bandages, aspirin or another pain killer, antibiotic cream, a thermometer, a Swiss army knife with tweezers, moleskin, decongestant for colds, motion sickness remedy, medicine for diarrhea or stomach problems (Pepto Bismol tablets or liquid and Immodium), sunscreen, insect repellent (you might want to get an extra-strength repellent if you plan on camping), burn ointment, and a syringe for emergency medical purposes (get a letter of explanation from your doctor). **Contact lens** wearers should bring an extra pair, a copy of the prescription, a pair of glasses, extra solution, and eyedrops. Those who use heat disinfection might consider switching to chemical cleansers for the duration of the trip.

**ESSENTIALS**

In your **passport,** write the names of any people you wish to be contacted in case of a medical emergency, and also list any **allergies** or medical conditions you would want doctors to be aware of. Allergy sufferers might want to obtain a full supply of any necessary medication before the trip. Matching a prescription to a foreign equivalent is not always easy, safe, or possible. Carry up-to-date, legible prescriptions or a statement from your doctor stating the medication's trade name, manufacturer, chemical name, and dosage. While traveling, be sure to keep all medication with you in your carry-on luggage.

**USEFUL ORGANIZATIONS.** The U.S. **Centers for Disease Control and Prevention (CDC)** (888-232-3299; www.cdc.gov) is an excellent source of information for travelers around the world and maintains an international fax information service for travelers. The CDC also publishes the booklet *Health Information for International Travelers* ($20), an annual global rundown of disease, immunization, and general health advice. This book may be purchased by sending a check or money order to the Superintendent of Documents, U.S. Government Printing Office, P.O. Box 371954, Pittsburgh, PA, 15250-7954. Orders can be made by phone (202-512-1800) with a major credit card (Visa, MasterCard, or Discover).

**MEDICAL ASSISTANCE ON THE ROAD.** Health care in the U.S. and Canada is good. One thing to do before you leave: make sure you have some sort of travel insurance. Medicare (for U.S. citizens in Canada) and most health insurance plans cover members' medical emergencies during trips abroad, but you should check with your insurance carrier to be sure, because you may have to purchase additional coverage. (For more information, see **Insurance,** p. 57).

**MEDICAL CONDITIONS.** Those with medical conditions (e.g., diabetes, allergies to antibiotics, epilepsy, heart conditions) may want to obtain a stainless steel **Medic Alert** identification tag ($35 the 1st year, and $15 annually thereafter), which identifies the condition and gives a 24-hour collect-call information number. Contact the Medic Alert Foundation, 2323 Colorado Ave., Turlock, CA 95382 (800-825-3785; www.medicalert.org). Diabetics can contact the **American Diabetes Association,** 1660 Duke St., Alexandria, VA 22314 (800-232-3472), to receive copies of the article "Travel and Diabetes" and a diabetic ID card, which carries messages in 18 languages explaining the carrier's diabetic status.

If you are **HIV positive**, contact the Bureau of Consular Affairs, #4811, Department of State, Washington, D.C. 20520 (202-647-1488; auto-fax 647-3000; http://travel.state.gov). According to U.S. law, HIV positive persons are not permitted to enter the U.S. However, HIV testing is conducted only for those who are planning to immigrate permanantly. Travelers from areas with particularly high concetrations of HIV positive persons or persons with AIDS may be required to provide more information when applying. Travelers to Canada who are suspected of being HIV- positive will be required to submit to HIV testing.

# ENVIRONMENTAL HAZARDS

**Heat exhaustion and dehydration:** Heat exhaustion, characterized by dehydration and salt deficiency, can lead to fatigue, headaches, and wooziness. Avoid heat exhaustion by drinking plenty of fluids (enough to keep your urine clear) and eating salty foods, like crackers. Alcoholic beverages are dehydrating, as are coffee, strong tea, and caffeinated sodas. Wear a hat, sunglasses, and a lightweight longsleeve shirt in hot sun, and take time to acclimate to a hot destination before seriously exerting yourself. Continuous heat stress can eventually lead to **heatstroke,** characterized by rising body temperature, severe headache, and cessation of sweating. Heatstroke is rare but serious, and victims must be cooled off with wet towels and taken to a doctor as soon as possible. You are more at risk for heat exhaustion and dehydration in the South and in the desert, because the heat is dry and sweat evaporates very quickly.

**Sunburn:** If you're prone to sunburn, bring sunscreen with you, or buy some (it can be bought at most drug stores, supermarkets, and some tourist centers), and apply it liberally and often to avoid burns and risk of skin cancer. If you are planning on spending time near water, in the desert, or in the snow, you are at risk of getting burned, even through clouds. Protect your eyes with good sunglasses, since ultraviolet rays can damage the retina of the eye after too much exposure. If you get sunburned, drink more fluids than usual and apply Calamine or an aloe-based lotion.

**Hypothermia and frostbite:** A rapid drop in body temperature is the clearest warning sign of overexposure to cold. Victims may shiver, feel exhausted, have poor coordination or slurred speech, hallucinate, or suffer amnesia. Seek medical help, and *do not let hypothermia victims fall asleep*—their body temperature will continue to drop and they may die. To avoid hypothermia, keep dry, wear layers, and stay out of the wind. In wet weather, wool and synthetics such as pile retain heat. Most other fabric, especially cotton, will make you colder. When the temperature is below freezing, watch for **frostbite.** If a region of skin turns white, waxy, and cold, do not rub the area. Drink warm beverages, get dry, and slowly warm the area with dry fabric or steady body contact, until a doctor can be found.

**High altitude:** Travelers to high altitudes (e.g. in the Rocky Mountains) must allow their bodies a couple of days to adjust to lower oxygen levels in the air before exerting themselves. Alcohol is more potent at high elevations. High altitudes mean that ultraviolet rays are stronger, as well, and the risk of sunburn is therefore greater.

## PREVENTING DISEASE

**INSECT-BORNE DISEASES.** Many diseases are transmitted by insects—mainly mosquitoes, fleas, ticks, and lice. Be aware of insects in wet or forested areas, while hiking, and especially while camping. Mosquitoes are most active from dusk to dawn. Use insect repellents, such as DEET. Wear long pants and long sleeves (fabric need not be thick or warm; tropic-weight cottons can keep you comfort-

able in the heat) and buy a mosquito net. Wear shoes and socks, and, if no one can see you, tuck long pants into socks. Wear a hat. Soak or spray your gear with permethrin, which is licensed in the U.S. for use on clothing. Natural repellents can be useful supplements: taking vitamin B-12 pills regularly can repel insects, as can garlic pills. Calamine lotion or topical cortisones (like Cortaid) may stop insect bites from itching, as can a bath with a half-cup of baking soda or oatmeal. Ticks—responsible for Lyme and other diseases—can be particularly dangerous in rural and forested regions. Pause periodically while walking to brush off ticks using a fine-toothed comb on your neck and scalp. Do not try to remove ticks by burning them or coating them with nail polish remover or petroleum jelly.

> **Lyme disease,** carried by ticks, is a bacterial infection. Symptoms include a circular bull's-eye rash of 2 in. or more around the bite, fever, headache, tiredness, and aches and pains. Antibiotics are effective if administered early. Untreated, Lyme can cause problems in joints, the heart, and the nervous system. If you find a tick attached to your skin, grasp the tick's head parts with tweezers as close to your skin as possible and apply slow, steady traction. Removing a tick within 24hrs. greatly reduces risk of infection.

## AIDS, HIV, STDS

**Acquired Immune Deficiency Syndrome (AIDS)** is a growing problem around the world. The World Health Organization estimates that there are 30 million people infected with HIV, and women now represent 40% of all new HIV infections.

The easiest mode of HIV transmission is through direct blood-to-blood contact with an HIV-positive person; *never* share intravenous drug, tattooing, or other needles. The most common mode of transmission is sexual intercourse. Health professionals recommend the use of latex condoms.

For more information on AIDS, call the **U.S. Centers for Disease Control's** 24-hour hotline at 800-342-2437. In Europe, contact the **World Health Organization,** Attn: Global Program on AIDS, Ave. Appia 20, 1211 Geneva 27, Switzerland (tel. 44 22 791 21 11, fax 791 31 11), for statistical material on AIDS internationally. Council's brochure, *Travel Safe: AIDS and International Travel,* is available at all Council Travel offices and at their website (www.ciee.org/study/safety/travelsafe.htm).

**Sexually transmitted diseases** (STDs) such as gonorrhea, chlamydia, genital warts, syphilis, and herpes are easier to catch than HIV, and some can be just as deadly. **Hepatitis B** and **C** are also serious sexually-transmitted diseases. Warning signs for STDs include: swelling, sores, bumps, or blisters on sex organs, rectum, or mouth; burning and pain during urination and bowel movements; itching around sex organs; swelling or redness in the throat, flu-like symptoms with fever, chills, and aches. If these symptoms develop, see a doctor immediately. When having sex, condoms may protect you from certain STDs, but oral or even tactile contact can lead to transmission.

## WOMEN'S HEALTH

Women traveling in unsanitary conditions are vulnerable to **urinary tract** and **bladder infections,** common and severely uncomfortable bacterial diseases that cause a burning sensation and painful and sometimes frequent urination. To try to avoid these infections, drink plenty of vitamin-C-rich juice and clean water, and urinate frequently, especially right after intercourse. Untreated, these infections can lead to kidney infections, sterility, and even death. If symptoms persist, see a doctor.

Women who need an **abortion** while traveling in the USA should contact the National Abortion Federation Hotline, 1755 Massachusetts Ave. NW, Washington, D.C. 20036 (800-772-9100; open M-F 9am-7pm).

### FURTHER READING

> *International Travel Health Guide,* Stuart Rose, MD (Travel Medicine, $20): Detailed information and tips on travel health, including an overview of diseases and a list of clinics in the USA. Information is also available at www.travmed.com.

**American Red Cross:** A trove of information, the ARC publishes *First-Aid and Safety Hand-book* ($5) available for purchase by calling or writing to the American Red Cross, 285 Columbus Ave., Boston, MA 02116-5114 (tel. 800-564-1234, M-F 8:30am-4:30pm). *Handbook for Women Travellers,* Maggie and Gemma Moss. Piatkus Books ($15).

# INSURANCE

Travel insurance generally covers four basic areas: medical/health problems, property loss, trip cancellation/interruption, and emergency evacuation. Although your regular insurance policies may well extend to travel-related accidents, you may consider purchasing travel insurance if the cost of potential trip cancellation/ interruption is greater than you can absorb.

**Medical insurance** (especially university policies) often covers costs incurred abroad; check with your provider. Medicare covers travel to Canada. Canadians are protected by their home province's health insurance plan for up to 90 days after leaving the country; check with the provincial Ministry of Health or Health Plan Headquarters for details. **Homeowners' insurance** (or your family's coverage) often covers theft during travel and loss of travel documents (passport, plane ticket, railpass, etc.) up to $500.

**ISIC** and **ITIC** provide basic insurance benefits, including $100 per day of in-hospital sickness for a maximum of 60 days, $3000 of accident-related medical reimbursement, and $25,000 for emergency medical transport (see **Identification,** p. 37). Cardholders have access to a toll-free 24-hour helpline whose multilingual staff can provide assistance in medical, legal, and financial emergencies overseas (800-626-2427 in the U.S. and Canada; elsewhere call the U.S. collect 713-267-2525. **American Express** (800-528-4800) grants most cardholders automatic car rental insurance (collision and theft, but not liability) and ground travel accident coverage of $100,000 on flight purchases made with the card.

Prices for travel insurance purchased separately generally run about $50 per week for full coverage, while trip cancellation/interruption may be purchased separately at a rate of about $5.50 per $100 of coverage.

**INSURANCE PROVIDERS. Council** and **STA** (see p. 73 for complete listings) offer a range of plans to supplement insurance coverage. Other private insurance providers in the **U.S.** and **Canada** include: **Access America** (800-284-8300; fax 804-673-1491); **Berkely Group/Carefree Travel Insurance** (800-323-3149 or 516-294-0220; fax 516-294-1095; email info@berkely.com; www.berkely.com); **Globalcare Travel Insurance** (800-821-2488; fax 781-592-7720; www.globalcare-cocco.com); and **Travel Assistance International** (800-821-2828 or 202-828-5894; fax 202-828-5896; email wassist@aol.com; www.worldwide-assistance.com). Providers in the **U.K.** include **Campus Travel** (01865 258 000; fax 792 378) and **Columbus Travel Insurance** (0171 375 0011; fax 375 0022). In **Australia** try **CIC Insurance** (02 9202 8000; fax 9202 8220).

# PACKING

Pack according to the extremes of climate you may experience and the type of travel you'll be doing. **Pack light:** a good rule is to lay out only what you absolutely need, then take half the clothes and twice the money. The less you have, the less you have to lose (or store, or carry on your back). Don't forget the obvious things: no matter where you're traveling, it's always a good idea to bring a rain jacket (Gore-Tex is a miracle fabric that's both waterproof and breathable), a warm jacket or wool sweater, and sturdy shoes and thick socks. You may also want to add one outfit beyond the jeans and t-shirt uniform, a collared shirt and a nicer pair of shoes if you have the room. Remember that wool will keep you warm even when soaked through, whereas wet cotton is colder than wearing nothing at all.

**Backpack** See p. 46 for information about different types of backpacks. Before you leave, pack your bag, strap it on, and imagine yourself walking uphill on hot asphalt for three hours; this should give you a sense of how important it is to pack lightly. Organizations that sell packs through mail-order are listed on p. 65.

**Suitcase or Trunk** They're fine if you plan to live in one or two cities and explore from there, but a very bad idea if you're going to be moving around a lot. Make sure suitcases have wheels and consider how much they weigh even when empty. Hard-sided luggage is more durable but more weighty and cumbersome. Soft-sided luggage should have a PVC frame, a strong lining to resist bad weather and rough handling, and its seams should be triple-stitched for durability.

**Daypack** In addition to your main vessel, a small backpack may be useful as a **daypack** for sight-seeing expeditions; it doubles as an airplane **carry-on.** An empty, lightweight **duffel bag** packed in your luggage may also be useful for dirty clothes or purchases.

**SLEEPSACKS.** Some youth hostels require that you have your own sleepsack or rent one of theirs. If you plan to stay in hostels you can avoid linen charges by making the requisite sleepsack yourself: fold a full size sheet in half the long way, then sew it closed along the open long side and one of the short sides. Sleepsacks can also be bought at any Hostelling International outlet store.

**WASHING CLOTHES.** Laundromats are common in North America, but it may be cheaper and easier to use a sink. Bring a small bar or tube of detergent soap, a small rubber ball to stop up the sink, and a travel clothes line.

**ELECTRIC CURRENT.** In the USA and Canada, electricity is 110V. 220V electrical appliances don't like 110V current. Visit a hardware store for an adapter (which changes the shape of the plug) and a converter (which changes the voltage). Don't make the mistake of using only an adapter (unless appliance instructions explicitly state otherwise).

**CONTACT LENSES.** Machines which heat-disinfect contact lenses will require a small converter (about $20) to 110V. Consider switching temporarily to a chemical disinfection system, but check with your lens dispenser to see if it's safe to switch; some lenses may be damaged by a chemical system. Contact lens supplies are generally easy to find..

**FILM.** If you're not a serious photographer, you might want to consider bringing a **disposable camera** or two rather than an expensive permanent one. Despite disclaimers, airport security X-rays *can* fog film, so either buy a lead-lined pouch, sold at camera stores, or ask the security to hand inspect it. Always pack it in your carry-on luggage, since higher-intensity X-rays are used on checked luggage.

**OTHER USEFUL ITEMS.** No matter how you're traveling, it's always a good idea to carry a first-aid kit including sunscreen, insect repellent, and vitamins (see **Health,** p. 51). Other useful items include: an umbrella; sealable plastic bags (for damp clothes, soap, food, shampoo, and other spillables); alarm clock; waterproof matches; sun hat; moleskin (for blisters); needle and thread; safety pins; sunglasses; pocketknife; plastic water bottle; compass; rope (makeshift clothesline and lashing material); towel; padlock; whistle; rubber bands; flashlight; cold-water soap; earplugs; electrical tape (for patching tears); tweezers; garbage bags; a small calculator for currency conversion; a pair of flip-flops for the shower; a money-belt for carrying valuables; deodorant; razors; tampons; and condoms (see **AIDS, HIV, and STDs,** p. 55).

**FURTHER READING: PACKING**

*The Packing Book,* Judith Gilford. Ten Speed Press ($9).

*Backpacking One Step at a Time,* Harvey Manning. Vintage ($15).

# ACCOMMODATIONS

## HOSTELS

Hostels are generally dorm-style accommodations, often in single-sex large rooms with bunk beds, although some hostels do offer private rooms for families and couples. They sometimes have kitchens and utensils for your use, bike or moped rentals, storage areas, and laundry facilities. There can be drawbacks: some hostels close during certain daytime "lock-out" hours, have a curfew, don't accept reservations, impose a maximum stay, or, less frequently, require that you do chores. In the USA and Canada, a bed in a hostel will average around $15.

For their various services and lower rates at member hostels, hostelling associations, especially **Hostelling International (HI),** can definitely be worth joining. HI hostels are scattered throughout both countries, and many accept reservations via the International Booking Network (tel. 2261 1111 from Australia, 800-663-5777 from Canada, 171 836 1036 from England, 1301 766 from Ireland, 9379 4224 from New Zealand, 800-909-4776 from U.S.; www.hiayh.org/ushostel/reserva/ibn3.htm) for a nominal fee. HI's umbrella organization's web page lists the web addresses and phone numbers of all national associations and can be a great place to begin researching hostelling in a specific region (www.iyhf.org). Other comprehensive hostelling websites include www.hostels.com. To join HI, contact one of the following organizations in your home country:

**Australian Youth Hostels Association (AYHA),** 422 Kent St., Sydney NSW 2000 (tel. (02) 9261 1111; fax 9261 1969; email yha@yhansw.org.au; www.yha.org.au). One-year membership A$44, under 18 A$13.50.

**Hostelling International-Canada (HI-C),** 400-205 Catherine St., Ottawa, ON K2P 1C3 (tel. 800-663-5777 or 613-237-7884; fax 237-7868; email info@hostellingintl.ca; www.hostellingintl.ca). One-year membership CDN$25, under 18 CDN$12; 2-yr. CDN$35.

ESSENTIALS

**An Óige (Irish Youth Hostel Association),** 61 Mountjoy St., Dublin 7 (tel. (1) 830 4555; fax 830 5808; email anoige@iol.ie; www.irelandyha.org). One-year membership IR£10, under 18 IR£4, families IR£20.

**Youth Hostels Association of New Zealand (YHANZ),** P.O. Box 436, 173 Cashel St., Christchurch 1 (tel. (643) 379 9970; fax 365 4476; email info@yha.org.nz; www.yha.org.nz). One-year membership NZ$24, ages 15-17 NZ$12, under 15 free.

**Hostelling International South Africa,** P.O. Box 4402, Cape Town 8000 (tel. (021) 24 2511; fax 24 4119; email info@hisa.org.za; www.hisa.org.za). One-year membership SAR50, under 18 SAR25, lifetime SAR250.

**Scottish Youth Hostels Association (SYHA),** 7 Glebe Crescent, Stirling FK8 2JA (tel. (01786) 891 400; fax 891 333; email info@syha.org.uk; www.syha.org.uk). Membership UK£6, under 18 UK£2.50.

**Youth Hostels Association of England and Wales (YHA),** 8 St. Stephen's Hill, St. Albans, Hertfordshire AL1 2DY, England (tel. (01727) 855 215 or 845 07; fax 844 126; email yhacustomerservices@compuserve.com; www.yha.org.uk). One-year membership UK£11, under 18 UK£5.50, families UK£22.

**Hostelling International Northern Ireland (HINI),** 22-32 Donegall Rd., Belfast BT12 5JN, Northern Ireland (tel. (01232) 324 733 or 315 435; fax 439 699; email info@hini.org.uk; www.hini.org.uk). One-year membership UK£7, under 18 UK£3, families UK£14.

**Hostelling International-American Youth Hostels (HI-AYH),** 733 15th St. NW, Suite 840, Washington, D.C. 20005 (tel. 202-783-6161 ext. 136; fax 783-6171; www.hiayh.org). One-year membership $25, over 54 $15, under 18 free.

## BED AND BREAKFASTS

For a cozy alternative to hotel rooms, B&Bs (private homes with rooms available to travelers) range from the acceptable to the sublime. Hosts will sometimes go out of their way to be accommodating of travelers with pets, giving personalized tours, or offering home-cooked meals. On the other hand, many B&Bs do not provide phones, TVs, or private bathrooms. Rooms in B&Bs generally cost $50-70 for a single and $70-90 for a double. For more info see **Nerd World's Bed and Breakfasts by Region** (www.nerdworld.com/users/dstein/nw854) or use a booking agency:

**Bed and Breakfast: The National Network (TNN) of Reservation Services,** Box 764703, Dallas, TX 75376 (tel. 888-866-4262; fax 972-298-7118; email bdtxstyle1@aol.com; www.go-lodging.com), can book reservations at 7000+ B&Bs in the U.S. and Canada.

## YMCA AND YWCAS

Not all **Young Men's Christian Association (YMCA)** locations offer lodging; those that do are often located in urban downtowns, which can be convenient but a little gritty. YMCA rates are usually lower than a hotel's but higher than a hostel's and may include TV, air conditioning, pools, gyms, access to public transportation, tourist information, safe deposit boxes, luggage storage, daily housekeeping, multilingual staff, and 24-hour security. Many YMCAs accept women and families (group rates often available), and some will not lodge people under 18 without parental permission. There are several ways to make a reservation, all of which must be made at least two weeks in advance and paid for in advance with a traveler's check, U.S. money order, certified check, Visa, or Mastercard in US dollars.

**YMCA of the USA,** 101 North Wackers Drive, Chicago, IL 60606 (800-872-9622; fax 312-977-9063; www.ymca.net). A listing of the nearly 1000 Y's across the U.S. and info on prices, phone numbers and addresses, but no reservation service.

**YMCA Canada,** 42 Charles St. 6th flr., Toronto ON M4Y 1T4 (416-967-9622; fax 967-9618; email sevices@ymca.ca; www.ymca.ca), offers info on Ys throughout Canada.

**YWCA of the USA,** Empire State Building, 350 Fifth Avenue #301, New York, NY 10118 (212-273-7800; fax 465-2281; www.ywca.org). Publishes a directory ($8) on YWCAs across the USA.

## DORMS

Many **colleges and universities** open their residence halls to travelers when school is not in session (May-Sept.)—some do so even during term-time. These dorms are often close to student areas—good sources for information on things to do—and are usually very clean. Getting a room may take a couple of phone calls and require advanced planning, but rates tend to be low, and many offer free local calls. *Let's Go* lists colleges which rent dorm rooms among the accommodations for appropriate cities.

### FURTHER READING: ACCOMMODATIONS

*Campus Lodging Guide (18th Ed.).* B&J Publications ($15).

*The Complete Guide to Bed and Breakfasts, Inns and Guesthouses in the U.S., Canada, and Worldwide,* Pamela Lanier. Ten Speed Press ($17).

## CAMPING AND THE OUTDOORS

### USEFUL PUBLICATIONS AND WEB RESOURCES

A variety of publishing companies offer hiking guidebooks to meet the educational needs of novice or expert. For information about camping, hiking, and biking, write or call the publishers listed below to receive a free catalogue.

**Sierra Club Books,** 85 Second St. 2nd fl., San Francisco, CA 94105-3441 (800- 935-1056 or 415-977-5500; www.sierraclub.org/books). Books on many national parks and several series on different regions of the U.S., all with an adventurous bent.

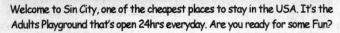

ESSENTIALS

**The Mountaineers Books,** 1001 SW Klickitat Way, #201, Seattle, WA 98134 (800- 553-4453 or 206-223-6303; email alans@mountaineers.org; www.mountaineers.org). Over 400 titles on hiking (the *100 Hikes* series), biking, mountaineering, natural history, and conservation.

**Wilderness Press,** 2440 Bancroft Way, Berkeley, CA 94704 (253-891-2500 or 800-443-7227; or 510-558-1666; email mail@wildernesspress.com; www.wildernesspress.com). Over 100 hiking guides and maps for the western U.S. including *Backpacking Basics* ($10), as well as guides to New England and Minnesota

**Woodall Publications Corporation,** 13975 W. Polo Trail Dr., Lake Forest, IL 60045-5000 (888-226-7328 or 847-362-6700; email emd@woodallpub.com; www.woodalls.com). Covering the U.S. and Canada, Woodall publishes the annually updated *Woodall's Campground Directory* ($22) and *Woodall's Plan-it, Pack-it, Go!: Great Places to Tent, Fun Things To Do* ($13).

For topographical maps of Canada, write the **Center for Topographic Information,** Canada Map Office, 130 Bentley Ave., Nepean, ON K1A 0E9 (800-465-6277 or 613-952-7000; http://maps.NRCan.gc.ca). In the USA, contact the **U.S. Geological Survey Information Services,** Box 25286, Denver CO 80225 (800-HELP-MAP/435-7627; http://mapping.usgs.gov/mac/findmaps.html).

# CAMPING AND HIKING EQUIPMENT

Good camping equipment is both sturdy and light. Camping equipment is generally more expensive in Australia, New Zealand, and the U.K. than in North America.

**Sleeping Bag:** Most good sleeping bags are rated by "season," or the lowest outdoor temperature at which they will keep you warm ("summer" means 30-40°F at night and "four-season" or "winter" often means below 0°F). Sleeping bags are made either of down (warmer and lighter, but more expensive, and miserable when wet) or of synthetic material (heavier, more durable, and warmer when wet). Prices range from $80-210 for a summer synthetic to $250-500 for a good down winter bag. **Sleeping bag pads,** including foam pads ($10-20) and air mattresses ($15-50) cushion your back and neck and insulate you from the ground. **Therm-A-Rest** self-inflating sleeping pads are part foam and part air-mattress and partially inflate when you unroll them, but cost $45-80. Bring a **"stuff sack"** lined with a plastic bag to store your sleeping bag.

**Tent:** The best tents are free-standing, with their own frames and suspension systems; they set up quickly and only require staking in high winds. Low-profile dome tents are the best all-around. When pitched their internal space is almost entirely usable, which means little unnecessary bulk. Tent sizes can be somewhat misleading: two people *can* fit in a two-person tent, but will find life more pleasant in a four-person. If you're traveling by car, go for the bigger tent, but if you're hiking, stick with a smaller tent that weighs no more than 5-6 lbs (2-3kg). Good two-person tents start at $120, four-person tents at $300. Seal the seams of your tent with waterproofer, and make sure it has a rain fly. Other tent accessories include a **battery-operated lantern,** a **plastic ground-cloth,** and a **nylon tarp.**

**Backpack:** If you intend to do a lot of hiking, you should have a frame backpack. **Internal-frame packs** mold better to your back, keep a lower center of gravity, and can flex adequately to allow you to hike difficult trails that require a lot of bending and maneuvering. If your trip involves significant numbers of flights, consider an "adventure travel" pack, which is designed to go weather baggage handling systems as well as wilderness. NorthFace and Lowe-Alpine make durable models. **External-frame packs** are more comfortable for long hikes over even terrain since they keep the weight higher and distribute it more evenly. Whichever you choose, make sure your pack has a strong, padded hip belt, which transfers the weight from the back to the legs. Any serious backpacking requires a pack of at least 4000 cubic inches (65litres). Allow an additional 500 cubic inches for your sleeping bag in internal-frame packs. Sturdy backpacks cost anywhere from $125-420. This is one area where it doesn't pay to economize—cheaper packs may be less comfortable, and the straps are more likely to fray or rip. Before you buy

any pack, try filling it with something heavy and walking around the store to get a sense of how it distributes weight. A **waterproof backpack cover** or plastic garbage bags will prove invaluable if it rains.

**Boots:** Be sure to wear hiking boots with good **ankle support** which are appropriate for the terrain you plan to hike. **Gore-tex** fabric or **part-leather** boots are appropriate for day-hikes or 2-3 day overnights over moderate terrain, but for longer trips or trips in mountainous terrain, stiff **leather** boots are highly preferable. Your boots should fit snugly and comfortably over one or two wool socks and a thin liner sock. Breaking in boots properly before setting out requires wearing them for several weeks; doing so will spare you from painful and debilitating blisters. Waterproof your boots with waterproofing treatment before going out in the woods.

**Other Necessities: Raingear** in two pieces, a top and pants, is far superior to a poncho. **Gore-Tex** is the best material if you are doing aerobic activity and need breathable raingear; **rubber** raingear will keep you completely dry but will get clammy if you sweat. For warm layers, **synthetics,** like polypropylene tops, socks, and long underwear, along with a pile jacket, are preferable to cotton or because they will keep you warm even when wet and dry quickly. **Wool** also stays warm when wet, but much heavier. When camping in autumn, winter, or spring, bring along a **"space blanket,"** which helps you to retain your body heat and doubles as a groundcloth ($5-15). Plastic **canteens** or water bottles keep water cooler than metal ones do, and are virtually shatter- and leakproof. Large, collapsible **water sacks** will significantly improve your lot in primitive campgrounds and weigh practically nothing when empty, though they are bulky and heavy when full. Bring **water-purification tablets** for when you can't boil water, unless you are willing to shell out money for a portable water-purification system. Though most campgrounds provide campfire sites, you may want to bring a small **metal grate** or **grill** of your own. For those places that forbid fires or the gathering of firewood, you'll need a **camp stove**. The classic propane-powered Coleman stove starts at about $40; the more expensive **Whisperlite** stoves ($60-100), which run on cleaner-burning white gas, are much lighter and more versatile. You will need to purchase a **fuel bottle** and fill it with fuel to operate stoves. A **first aid kit, swiss army knife, insect repellent, calamine lotion,** and **waterproof matches** or a **lighter** are other essential camping items.

The mail-order/online companies listed below offer lower prices than many retail stores, but a visit to a local camping or outdoors store will give you a good sense of items' look and weight. Many local outdoor stores also have message boards where used equipment can be found.

**Campmor,** P.O. Box 700, Upper Saddle River, NJ 07458-0700 (888-226-7667, outside U.S.call 201-825-8300; email customer-service@campmor.com; www.campmor.com).

**Discount Camping,** 880 Main North Rd., Pooraka, South Australia 5095, Australia (08) 8262 3399; fax 8260 6240; www.discountcamping.com.au.

**Eastern Mountain Sports (EMS),** 327 Jaffrey Rd., Peterborough, NH 03458 (888-463-6367 or 603-924-7231;email emsmail@emsonline.com; www.emsonline.com.) Call the above number for the branch nearest you.

**L.L. Bean,** Freeport, ME 04033-0001 (U.S./Canada 800-441-5713; U.K. (0800) 962 954; elsewhere, call U.S. 207-552-6878; www.llbean.com). They refund/replace products which don't meet your expectations. The main store and the 800 number are both open 24hr.

**Mountain Designs,** P.O. Box 1472, Fortitude Valley, Queensland 4006, Australia (07 3252 8894; fax 3252 4569; www.mountaindesign.com.au).

**Recreational Equipment, Inc. (REI),** Sumner, WA 98352 (800-426-4840 or 253-891-2500; www.rei.com).

**YHA Adventure Shop,** 14 Southampton St., London, WC2E 7HA, U.K. (tel. (01718) 36 85 41). The main branch of one of Britain's largest outdoor equipment suppliers.

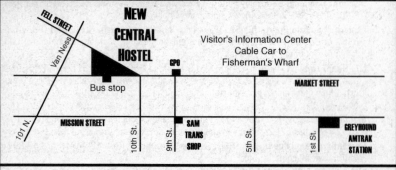

# WILDERNESS SAFETY

**Stay warm, stay dry, and stay hydrated.** The vast majority of life-threatening wilderness situations result from a breach of this simple dictum. On any hike, however brief, you should pack enough equipment to keep you alive should disaster befall. This includes **raingear, hat** and **mittens,** a **first-aid kit,** a **reflector,** a **whistle, high energy food,** and extra **water.** Dress in warm layers of **synthetic materials** designed for the outdoors, or **wool.** Pile fleece jackets and Gore-Tex raingear are excellent choices. Never rely on **cotton** for warmth. This "death cloth" will be absolutely useless should it get wet. Make sure to check all equipment for any defects before setting out, and see **Camping and Hiking Equipment,** above, for more information.

Check **weather forecasts** and pay attention to the skies when hiking. Weather can change suddenly. Whenever possible, let someone know when and where you are going hiking, either a friend, your hostel, a park ranger, or a local hiking organization. Do not attempt a hike beyond your ability—you may endanger your life. See **Health,** p. 51 for information about outdoor ailments such as heatstroke, hypothermia, giardia, rabies, and insects, as well as basic medical concerns and first-aid.

If you are hiking in an area which might be frequented by bears, ask local rangers for information on bear behavior before entering any park or wilderness area, and obey posted warnings. No matter how irresistibly cute a bear appears, don't be fooled—they're powerful and unpredictable animals who are not intimidated by humans. If you're close enough for a bear to be observing you, you're too close.

Don't leave food or other scented items (trash, toiletries, the clothes that you cooked in) near your tent. **Bear-bagging,** hanging edibles, trash, toiletries, sunscreen, used tampons, and other smelly objects from a tree out of reach of hungry paws, is the best way to keep your toothpaste from becoming a condiment. Bears are also attracted to any perfume, as are bugs, so cologne, scented soap, deodorant, and hairspray should stay at home.

If you see a bear at a distance, calmly walk (don't run) in the other direction. If it seems interested, back away slowly while speaking to the bear in firm, low tones and head in the opposite direction or toward a settled area. If you stumble upon a sweet-looking bear cub, leave immediately lest its over-protective mother stumble upon you. If you are attacked by a bear, get in a fetal position to protect yourself, put your arms over the back of your neck, and play dead. In all situations, remain calm, as loud noises and sudden movements can trigger an attack.

### FURTHER READING: WILDERNESS SAFETY

*How to Stay Alive in the Woods,* Bradford Angier. Macmillan ($8).

*Everyday Wisdom: 1001 Expert Tips for Hikers,* Karen Berger. Mountaineer ($17).

*Making Camp,* Steve Howe, et al. Mountaineer ($17).

## CAMPERS AND RVS

Much to the chagrin of more purist outdoorspeople, the U.S. and Canada are havens for the corpulent, home-and-stove on wheels known as **"recreational vehicles" (RVs).** Most national parks and small towns cater to RV travelers, providing campgrounds with large parking areas and electric outlets ("full hookup"). Especially for older travelers or families, RV's can be a convenient way to view the continent without sacrificing independence, mobility, and creature comforts.

Renting an RV will always be more expensive than tenting or hostelling, but the costs compare favorably with the price of staying in hotels and renting a car (see **Rental Cars,** p. 82), and the convenience of bringing along your own bedroom, bathroom, and kitchen makes it an attractive option.

# ORGANIZED ADVENTURE TRIPS

**Organized adventure** tours offer another way of exploring the wild. Activities include hiking, biking, skiing, canoeing, kayaking, rafting, climbing, photo safaris and archaeological digs. Consult tourism bureaus, which can suggest parks, trails, and outfitters. Other good sources for organized adventure options are the stores and organizations specializing in camping and outdoor equipment listed above. Sales reps at REI, EMS, or Sierra often know of a range of cheap, convenient trips. They also often offer training programs for people who want to have an independent trip. The **Specialty Travel Index**, 305 San Anselmo Ave., #313, San Anselmo, CA 94960 (888-624-4030 or 415-455-1643; fax 459-4974; email spectrav@ix.netcom.com; www.specialtytravel.com) is a directory listing hundreds of tour operators worldwide. The **Sierra Club** (email national.outings@sierraclub.org; www.sierraclub.org/outings) plans many adventure outings at all of its branches throughout Canada and the U.S. **TrekAmerica,** P.O. Box 189, Rockaway, NJ 07866 (800-221-0596; fax 973-983-8551; email info@trekamerica.com; www.trekamerica.com) operates small group active adventure tours throughout the U.S., including Alaska and Hawaii, and Canada. These tours are for 18- to 38-year olds, and run from 1 to 9 weeks. **Footloose** (www.footloose.com) is their open-age adult program. **Roadrunner Hostelling Treks,** 9741 Canoga Ave., Chatsworth, CA 91311 (818-721-6080 or 800-873-5872 or 44 1892 51 27 00 in Europe and the U.K; www.americanadventures.com) offers inexpensive guided trips (max. 13 travelers) in the U.S. and Canada.

# NATIONAL PARKS

**National Parks** protect some of the most spectacular scenery in North America. Though their primary purpose is preservation, the parks also host recreational activities such as ranger talks, guided hikes, marked trails, skiing, and snowshoe expeditions. For info, contact the **National Park Service**, Office of Public Inquiries, 1849 C St. NW, #1013, Washington, D.C. 20240 (202-208-4747). The slick and informative webpage (www.nps.gov) lists info on all the parks, detailed maps, and fee and reservation data. The **National Park Foundation**, 1101 17th St. NW, #1102, Washington, D.C. 20066 (202-785-4500) distributes *The Complete Guide to America's National Parks* by mail-order ($16, plus $3 shipping); a guide to national parks is available online at www.nationalparks.org.

Entrance fees vary. The larger and more popular parks charge a $4-20 entry fee for cars and sometimes a $2-7 fee for pedestrians and cyclists. The **Golden Eagle Passport** ($50), available at park entrances, allows the passport-holder's party entry into all national parks for 1 year. Golden Eagle Passports can also be bought by writing to Golden Eagle Passport, 1100 Ohio Dr. SW, #138, Washington, D.C. 20242. U.S. citizens or residents 62 and over qualify for the lifetime **Golden Age Passport** ($10 one-time fee), which entitles the holder's party to free park entry, a 50% discount on camping, and 50% reductions on various recreational fees for the passport holder. Persons eligible for federal benefits on account of disabilities can enjoy the same privileges with the **Golden Access Passport** (free). Golden Age and Golden Access Passports must be purchased at a park entrance with proof of age or federal eligibility, respectively. All passports are also valid at National Monuments, Forests, Wildlife Preserves, and other national recreation sites.

Most national parks have both backcountry and developed tent **camping**; some welcome RVs, and a few offer grand lodges. At the more popular parks in the U.S. and Canada, reservations are essential, available through MISTIX (800-365-CAMP/2267 or 619-452-8787 outside the U.S.) no more than 5 months in advance. Lodges and indoor accommodations should be reserved months in advance. Campgrounds often observe first come, first served policies. Many campgrounds fill up by late morning. Some limit your stay and/or the number of people in a group.

**Www.recreation.gov** provides coalated information on various kinds of public land available for recreational purposes, including National Parks, National Wildlife Refuges, National Forests, and Bureau of Land Management (BLM) sites.

## NATIONAL FORESTS

Often less accessible and less crowded, U.S. **National Forests** (www.fs.fed.us) are a purist's alternative to parks. While some have recreation facilities, most are equipped only for primitive camping—pit toilets and no water are the norm. Entrance fees, when charged, are $10-20, but camping is generally free, or $3-4. Some specially designated wilderness areas have regulations barring all vehicles. Necessary wilderness permits for backpackers can be obtained at the U.S. Forest Service field office in the area. If you are interested in exploring a National Forest, *The Guide to Your National Forests* is available at all Forest Service branches, or call or write the main office (USDA, Forest Service, Office of Communications, Sydney R. Yates Building, 201 14th St. SW, Washington, D.C. 20090; 202-205-0957; fax 205-0885). This booklet includes a list of all national forest addresses; request maps and other info directly from the forest(s) you plan to visit. Reservations, with a one-time $16.50 service fee, are available for most forests, but are usually unnecessary except during high season at the more popular sites. Write or call up to 1 year in advance to National Recreation Reservation Center, P.O. Box 900, Cumberland, MD 21501-0900 (800-280-2267; fax 301-722-9802).

## CANADA'S NATIONAL PARKS

Less trammeled than their southern counterparts, these parks boast at least as much natural splendor. Park entrance fees range from CDN$3-7 per person, with family and multi-day passes available. Reservations are offered for a limited number of campgrounds with a CDN$7 fee. For these reservations, or for info on the over 40 parks and countless historical sites in the network, call **Parks Canada**, 25 Edy St., Hull, QC, Canada K1A 0M5 (888-773-8888 for trip planning info), or consult the useful webpage (http://parkscanada.pch.gc.ca). A patchwork of regional passes are available at relevant parks; the best is the Western Canada Pass, which covers admission to all the parks in the Western provinces for a year (CDN$35 per adult, CDN$70 per group— up to 7 people).

# KEEPING IN TOUCH

## MAIL

### SENDING AND RECEIVING MAIL

**Airmail** letters under 1 oz. between North America and the world are $1. Envelopes should be marked "air mail" or "par avion" to avoid having letters sent by sea. There are several ways to arrange pick-up of letters sent to you by friends and relatives while you are abroad.

> **General Delivery:** Mail can be sent to the USA through **General Delivery** to almost any city or town with a post office. Address letters to:
> Elvis PRESLEY
> General Delivery
> Post Office Street Address
> Memphis, TN 38101 or VICTORIA, BC V8W 1L0
> USA or Canada.

The mail will go to a special desk in the central post office, unless you specify a post office by street address or postal code. As a rule, it is best to use the largest post office in the area, and mail may be sent there regardless of what is written on the envelope. It is usually safer and quicker to send mail express or registered. When picking up your mail, bring a form of photo ID, preferably a passport. There is generally no surcharge; if there is a charge, it generally does not exceed the cost of domestic postage. If the clerks insist that there is nothing for you, have them check under your first name as well. *Let's Go* lists post offices in the Practical Information section for each city and most towns.

**American Express:** AmEx's travel offices throughout the world will act as a mail service for cardholders if you contact them in advance. Under this free **Client Letter Service,** they will hold mail for up to 30 days and forward upon request. Address the letter in the same way shown above. Some offices will offer these services to non-cardholders (especially those who have purchased AmEx Travelers Cheques), but you must call ahead to make sure. A complete list is available free from AmEx (tel. 800-528-4800).

If regular airmail is too slow, **Federal Express** (U.S. tel. for international operator 800-247-4747) can get a letter from New York to Sydney in 2 days for a whopping $30. By **U.S. Express Mail,** a letter from Cambridge would arrive within 4 days and would cost $15.

**Surface mail** is by far the cheapest and slowest way to send mail. It takes 1-3 months to cross the Atlantic and 2-4 to cross the Pacific—appropriate for sending large quantities of items you won't need to see for a while. When ordering books and materials from abroad, always include one or two **International Reply Coupons (IRCs)**—a way of providing the postage to cover delivery. IRCs should be available from your local post office and those abroad ($1.05).

## SENDING MAIL HOME FROM THE USA AND CANADA

**Aerogrammes,** printed sheets that fold into envelopes and travel via airmail, are available at post offices. It helps to mark "airmail," though "par avion" is universally understood. Most post offices will charge exorbitant fees or simply refuse to send aerogrammes with enclosures. Airmail from the USA averages 4 to 7 days, although times are more unpredictable from smaller towns.

# TELEPHONES

## CALLING THE USA AND CANADA FROM HOME

To call direct from home, dial
1. The international access code of your home country. **International access codes** include: Australia 0011; Ireland 00; New Zealand 00; South Africa 09; U.K. 00; U.S. 011. Country codes and city codes are sometimes listed with a zero in front (e.g., 033), but after dialing the international access code, drop successive zeros (with an access code of 011, e.g., 011 33).
2. 1 (USA and Canada's country code).
3. The area code (see the city's **Practical Information** section) and local number.

## CALLING HOME FROM CANADA AND THE USA

A **calling card** is probably your best and cheapest bet. Calls are billed either collect or to your account. **MCI WorldPhone** also provides access to MCI's Traveler's Assist, which gives legal and medical advice, exchange rate information, and translation services. Other phone companies provide similar services to travelers. **To obtain a calling card** from your national telecommunications service before you leave home, contact the appropriate company below.

**USA: AT&T** (888-288-4685); **Sprint** (800-877-4646); or **MCI** (800-444-4141; from abroad dial the country's MCI access number).

**Canada:** Bell Canada **Canada Direct** (tel.(800) -565-4708).

**U.K.:** British Telecom **BT Direct** (tel. (0800) 34 51 44).

**Ireland:** Telecom Éireann **Ireland Direct** (tel. 800 250 250).

**Australia:** Telstra **Australia Direct** (tel. 13 22 00).

**New Zealand:** Telecom New Zealand (tel. 0800 000 000).

**South Africa: Telkom South Africa** (tel. 09 03).

ESSENTIALS

**ESSENTIALS**

**To call home with a calling card,** contact the North American operator for your service provider by dialing:

**BT Direct:** AT&T 800-445-5667, MCI 800-444-2162 , Sprint 800-800-0008.

**Australia Direct:** AT&T 800-682-2878, MCI 800-937-6822, Sprint 800-676-0061.

**Telkom South Africa Direct:** 800-949-7027.

Wherever possible, use a calling card for international phone calls; long-distance rates for national phone services are often exorbitant. You can usually make direct international calls from pay phones, but if you aren't using a calling card you may need to drop your coins as quickly as your words. Prepaid phone cards and occasionally credit cards can be used for direct international calls, but they are still less cost-efficient. In-room hotel calls invariably include an arbitrary surcharge.

If you do dial direct, you must first insert the appropriate amount of money or a prepaid card, then dial 011 (the international access code for USA and Canada), and then dial the country code and number of your home. **Country codes** include: Australia 61; Ireland 353; New Zealand 64; South Africa 27; U.K. 44.

The expensive alternative to dialing direct or using a calling card is using an international operator to place a **collect call.** An English-speaking operator from your home nation can be reached by dialing the appropriate service provider listed above, and they will typically place a collect call even if you don't possess one of their phone cards.

### CALLING WITHIN USA AND CANADA

The simplest way to call within the country is to use a coin-operated phone. You can also buy **prepaid phone cards**, which carry a certain amount of phone time depending on the card's denomination. The time is measured in minutes or talk units (e.g. one unit/one minute), and the card usually has a toll-free access telephone number and a personal identification number (PIN). To make a phone call, you dial the access number, enter your PIN, and at the voice prompt, enter the phone number of the party you're trying to reach. Phone rates tend to be highest in the morning, lower in the evening, and lowest on Sunday and late at night.

## EMAIL AND INTERNET

The internet can be accessed at internet cafes, copy centers (like Kinkos), libraries, and many college campuses. *Let's Go* lists suggestions in the Practical Information of city listings. **Cybercafe Guide** (www.cyberiacafe.net/cyberia/guide/ccafe.htm) can help you find cybercafes in USA and Canada.

Free, web-based email providers include Hotmail (www.hotmail.com) and Yahoo! Mail (www.yahoo.com). Almost every internet search engine has an affiliated free email service.

Travelers who have the luxury of a laptop with them can use a **modem** to call an internet service provider. Long-distance phone cards specifically intended for such calls can defray normally high phone charges. Check with your long-distance phone provider to see if they offer this option.

# GETTING THERE

## BY PLANE

When it comes to airfare, a little effort can save you a bundle. If your plans are flexible enough to deal with the restrictions, courier fares are the cheapest. Tickets bought from consolidators and standby seating are also good deals, but last-minute specials, airfare wars, and charter flights often beat these fares. The key is to hunt around, to be flexible, and to persistently ask about discounts. Students, seniors, and those under 26 should never pay full price for a ticket.

## DETAILS AND TIPS

**Timing:** Airfares to USA and Canada peak in the summer, and holidays are also expensive periods in which to travel. Midweek (M-Th morning) round-trip flights run $40-50 cheaper than weekend flights, but the latter are generally less crowded and more likely to permit frequent-flier upgrades. Return-date flexibility is usually not an option for the budget traveler; traveling with an "open return" ticket can be pricier than fixing a return date when buying the ticket and paying later to change it.

**Route:** Round-trip flights are by far the cheapest; "open-jaw" (arriving in and departing from different cities) and round-the-world, or RTW, flights are pricier but reasonable alternatives. Patching one-way flights together is the least economical way to travel. Flights between capital cities or regional hubs will offer the most competitive fares.

**Boarding:** Whenever flying internationally, pick up tickets for international flights well in advance of the departure date, and confirm by phone within 72 hours of departure. Most airlines require that passengers arrive at the airport at least two hours before departure. One carry-on item and two pieces of checked baggage is the norm for non-courier flights. Consult the airline for weight allowances.

**Fares:** Round-trip fares from Western Europe to the U.S. range from $100-400 (during the off-season) to $200-550 (during the summer).

# BUDGET AND STUDENT TRAVEL AGENCIES

A knowledgeable agent specializing in flights to the U.S. and Canada can make your life easy and help you save, too, but agents may not spend the time to find you the lowest possible fare—they get paid on commission. Those holding **ISIC and IYTC cards** (see **Identification,** p. 37), respectively, qualify for big discounts from student travel agencies. Most flights from budget agencies are on major airlines, but in peak season some may sell seats on less reliable chartered aircraft.

**Campus/Usit Youth and Student Travel** 52 Grosvenor Gardens, **London** SW1W 0AG (in London call (0870) 240 1010; www.usitcampus.co.uk). Other offices include: 19-21 Aston Quay, O'Connell Bridge, **Dublin** 2 (tel (01) 677 8117; fax 679 8833); New York Student Center, 895 Amsterdam Ave., **New York,** NY, 10025 (212-663-5435; email usitny@aol.com). Additional offices in Cork, Galway, Limerick, Waterford, Coleraine, Derry, Belfast, and Greece.

**Council Travel** (www.counciltravel.com). U.S. offices include: Emory Village, 1561 N. Decatur Rd., **Atlanta,** GA 30307 (404-377-9997); 273 Newbury St., **Boston,** MA 02116 (617-266-1926); 1160 N. State St., **Chicago,** IL 60610 (312-951-0585); 10904 Lindbrook Dr., **Los Angeles,** CA 90024 (310-208-3551); 205 E. 42nd St., **New York,** NY 10017 (212-822-2700); 530 Bush St., **San Francisco,** CA 94108 (415-421-3473); 1314 NE 43rd St., #210, **Seattle,** WA 98105 (206-632-2448); 3300 M St. NW, **Washington, D.C.** 20007 (tel. 202-337-6464). **For U.S. cities not listed,** call 800-2-COUNCIL (226-8624). Also 28A Poland St. (Oxford Circus), **London,** W1V 3DB (tel. (0171) 287 3337), **Paris** (01 44 41 89 89), and **Munich** (089 39 50 22).

**CTS Travel,** 44 Goodge St., W1 (tel. (0171) 636 00 31; fax 637 53 28; email ctsinfo@ctstravel.com.uk).

**STA Travel,** 6560 Scottsdale Rd. #F100, Scottsdale, AZ 85253 (tel. 800-777-0112 fax 602-922-0793; www.sta-travel.com). A student and youth travel organization with over 150 offices worldwide. Ticket booking, travel insurance, railpasses, and more. In the U.S.: 297 Newbury St., **Boston,** MA 02115 (617-266-6014); 429 S. Dearborn St., **Chicago,** IL 60605 (312-786-9050); 7202 Melrose Ave., **Los Angeles,** CA 90046 (323-934-8722); 10 Downing St., **New York,** NY 10014 (212-627-3111); 4341 University Way NE, **Seattle,** WA 98105 (206-633-5000); 2401 Pennsylvania Ave., Ste. G, **Washington, D.C.** 20037 (202-887-0912); 51 Grant Ave., **San Francisco,** CA 94108 (415-391-8407). In the U.K., 6 Wrights Ln., **London** W8 6TA (tel. (0171) 938 47 11 for North American travel). In New Zealand, 10 High St., **Auckland** (tel. (09) 309 04 58). In Australia, 222 Faraday St., **Melbourne** VIC 3053 (tel. (03) 9349 2411).

**Travel CUTS (Canadian Universities Travel Services Limited)**, 187 College St., Toronto, ON M5T 1P7 (tel. 416-979-2406; fax 979-8167; www.travelcuts.com). 40 offices in Canada. Also in the U.K., 295-A Regent St., **London** W1R 7YA (tel. (0171) 255 19 44).

Other organizations that specialize in finding cheap fares include:

**Cheap Tickets** (800-377-1000; www.cheaptickets.com) offers cheap flights around the U.S.

**Travel Avenue** (800-333-3335) rebates commercial fares to or from the U.S. and offers low fares for flights anywhere in the world. They also offer package deals, which include car rental and hotel reservations, to many destinations.

# COMMERCIAL AIRLINES

The commercial airlines' lowest regular offer is the **APEX** (Advance Purchase Excursion) fare, which provides confirmed reservations and allows "open-jaw" tickets. Generally, reservations must be made 7 to 21 days in advance, with 7- to 14-day minimum and up to 90-day maximum-stay limits, and hefty cancellation and change penalties (fees rise in summer). Book peak-season APEX fares early, since by May you will have a hard time getting the departure date you want.

Although APEX fares are probably not the cheapest possible fares, they provide a sense of the average commercial price, from which to measure other bargains. Many airlines offer "**e-fares**," special, last-minute fares available over the internet; check airline webpages for details. Www.sta-travel.com is a pretty reliable website offering deals for student travelers. Specials in newspapers may be cheaper but have more restrictions and fewer available seats. Popular carriers include:

**Air Tran** (800-AIRTRAN/247-8726; www.airtran.com). Consumer Relations, Dept. INT, 9955 AirTran Blvd., Orlando, FL 32827. A budget carrier which also offers the "X-Fares Standby Program" for 18 to 22 year-olds (888-4-X-Fares).

**Air Canada** (800-776-3000 from the US, 888-247-2262 from Canada; www.aircanada.ca). Ask about "Websaver" fares (800-776-3030 in US, 888-776-3030 in Canada, W-F).

**Alaska Airlines** (800-252-7522; www.alaska-air.com). P.O. Box 68900. Seattle, WA 98168. AA's subsidiary, **Horizon Air** (800-547-9308) services the Northwest.

**America West** (800-235-9292; www.americawest.com). 4000 Sky Harbor Blvd., Phoenix, AZ 85034. Services primarily the Western U.S.

**American** (800-433-7300; www.americanair.com). P.O. Box 619612, Dallas-Ft. Worth International Airport, TX 75261. Offers "College SAAvers" fares for full-time college students.

**Continental** (800-525-0280; www.flycontinental.com). Great deals for senior citizens in the "Freedom Club;" call 800-441-1135.

**Delta** (800-2414141; www.delta-air.com).

**Northwest** (800-225-2525; www.nwa.com). 5101 Northwest Dr., St. Paul, MN 55111-3034.

**Southwest** (800-435-9792; www.iflyswa.com). P.O.Box 36611, Dallas, TX 75235.-1611 A budget carrier with an ultra-friendly, laissez-faire attitude.

**TWA** (800-221-2000; www.twa.com). Customer Relations, 1415 Olive St., St. Louis, MO 63103. Offers last minute "TransWorld specials" via email.

**United** (800-241-6522; www.ual.com). P.O. Box 66100, Chicago, IL 60666. .

**USAir** (800-428-4322; www.usair.com). Office of Consumer Affairs, P.O. Box 1501, Winston-Salem, NC 27102-1501.

# OTHER CHEAP ALTERNATIVES

**CHARTER FLIGHTS.** Charters are flights a tour operator contracts with an airline to fly extra loads of passengers during peak season. Charters can sometimes be cheaper than flights on scheduled airlines, some operate nonstop, and restrictions on minimum advance-purchase and minimum stay are more lenient. However, charter flights fly less frequently than major airlines, make refunds particularly difficult, and are almost always fully booked. Schedules and itineraries may also change or be cancelled at the last moment (as late as 48 hours before the trip, and without a full refund), and check-in, boarding, and baggage claim are often much slower. As always, pay with a credit card if you can, and consider traveler's insurance against trip interruption.

**Discount clubs** and **fare brokers** offer members savings on last-minute charter and tour deals. Study their contracts closely; you don't want to end up with an unwanted overnight layover. **Travelers Advantage**, Stamford, CT (800-548-1116; www.travelersadvantage.com; $60 annual fee includes discounts, newsletters, and cheap flight directories) specializes in travel and tour packages.

**STANDBY FLIGHTS.** To travel standby, you will need considerable flexibility in the dates and cities of your arrival and departure. Companies that specialize in standby flights don't sell tickets but rather the promise that you will get to or near your destination within a certain window of time (anywhere from 1-5 days). You may only receive a refund if all available flights which depart within your date-range from the specified region are full, but future travel credit is always available.

Carefully read agreements with any company offering standby flights, as tricky fine print can leave you in the lurch. To check on a company's service record, call the Better Business Bureau of New York City (tel. 212-533-6200). It is difficult to receive refunds, and clients' vouchers will not be honored when an airline fails to receive payment in time.

**Airhitch**, 2641 Broadway, 3rd fl., New York, NY 10025 (tel. 800-326-2009 or 212-864-2000; fax 864-5489; www.airhitch.org) and Los Angeles, CA (tel. 310-726-5000). Primarily offers flights to and from Europe, but also has travel rates within the USA ranging from $79-$139.

**TICKET CONSOLIDATORS.** **Ticket consolidators,** or **"bucket shops,"** buy unsold tickets in bulk from commercial airlines and sell them at discounted rates. The best place to look is in the Sunday travel section of any major newspaper, where many bucket shops place tiny ads. Call quickly, as availability is typically extremely limited. Not all bucket shops are reliable establishments, so insist on a receipt that gives full details of restrictions, refunds, and tickets, and pay by credit card. For more information, check the website **Consolidators FAQ** (www.travel-library.com/air-travel/consolidators.html).

## FURTHER READING: BY PLANE

*Consolidators: Air Travel's Bargain Basement,* Kelly Monaghan (Intrepid Traveler, $8)

*The Worldwide Guide to Cheap Airfare,* Michael McColl. Insider Publications ($15).

*Discount Airfares: The Insider's Guide,* George Hobart. Priceless Publications ($14).

*The Official Airline Guide,* an expensive tome available at many libraries, has flight schedules, fares, and reservation numbers.

*Travelocity* (www.travelocity.com). A searchable online database of published airfares. Online reservations.

*Air Traveler's Handbook* (www.cs.cmu.edu/afs/cs.cmu.edu/user/mkant/Public/Travel/airfare.html).

*TravelHUB* (www.travelhub.com). A directory of travel agents that includes a searchable database of fares from over 500 consolidators.

# GETTING AROUND

## BY TRAIN

Locomotion is still one of the cheapest (and most pleasant) ways to tour the U.S. and Canada, but keep in mind that discounted air travel may be cheaper, and much faster, than train travel. As with airlines, you can save money by purchasing your tickets as far in advance as possible, so plan ahead and make reservations early. It is essential to travel light on trains; not all stations will check your baggage.

**Amtrak** (800-USA-RAIL/872-7245; www.amtrak.com) is the only provider of inter-city passenger train service in the U.S. Most cities have Amtrak offices which directly sell tickets, but tickets must be bought thorugh an agent in some small towns. The informative web page lists up-to-date schedules, fares, arrival and departure info, and makes reservations. **Discounts** on full rail fares are given to: senior citizens (15% off), students with a Student Advantage card (15% off; call 800-96-AMTRAK to purchase the $20 card), travelers with disabilities (15% off), children 2-15 accompanied by an adult (50% off), children under 2 (free), and current members of the U.S. armed forces, active-duty veterans, and their dependents (25% off). "Rail SALE" offers online discounts of up to 90%; visit the Amtrak web site for details and reservations. Amtrak also offers some **special packages**:

**All-aboard America**: This fare divides the Continental U.S. into 3 regions: Eastern, Central, and Western.

**Air-Rail Vacations**: Amtrak and United Airlines allow you to travel in 1 direction by train and return by plane, or to fly to a distant point and return home by train. The train portion of the journey can last up to 30 days and include up to 3 stopovers. A multitude of variations are available; call 800-437-3441.

**North America Rail Pass**: A 30-day pass offered in conjunction with Canada's VIA Rail which allows unlimited travel and unlimited stops throughout the U.S. and Canada for 30 consecutive days; $645 during peak season (June 1-Oct. 15) and $450 during off-season. A 15-day Northeastern North America Pass is available to international residents only; $400 during peak season, $300 off-season.

**VIA Rail**, P.O. Box 8116, Station A, Montreal, QC H3C 3N3 (800-842-7733; http://arail.ca), is Amtrak's Canadian analogue. **Discounts** on full fares are given to: students with ISIC card and youths under 24 (40% off full fare); seniors 60 and over (10% off); ages 2-15, accompanies by an adult (50% off); children under 2 (free on the lap of an adult). Reservations are required for first-class seats and sleep car accomodations. "Supersaver" fares offer discounts of up to 50%. Call for details. The **Canrail Pass** allows unlimited travel on 12 days within a 30-day period. Between early June and mid-October, a 12-day pass costs CDN$589 (seniors and youths under 24 CDN$529). Off-season passes cost CDN$379 (seniors and youths CDN$345). Add CDN$29-50 for each additional day of travel. Call for information on seaonal promotions such as discounts on Grayline Sightseeing Tours.

## BY BUS

Buses generally offer the most frequent and complete service between the cities and towns of the U.S. and Canada. Often a bus is the only way to reach smaller locales without a car. In rural areas and across open spaces, however, bus lines tend to be sparse. *Russell's Official National Motor Coach Guide* ($15.70 including postage) is an invaluable tool for constructing an itinerary. Updated each month, *Russell's Guide* has schedules of every bus route (including Greyhound) between any two towns in the United States and Canada. Russell's also publishes two semiannual *Supplements* which are free when ordered with the main issue; a Directory of Bus Lines and Bus Stations, and a series of Route Maps (both $8.40 if ordered separately). To order any of the above, write Russell's Guides, Inc., P.O. Box 278, Cedar Rapids, IA 52406 (319-364-6138; fax 364-4853).

## GREYHOUND

Greyhound (800-231-2222; www.greyhound.com) operates the largest number of routes in the U.S., though local bus companies may provide more extensive services within specific regions. Schedule information is available at any Greyhound terminal, on the web page, or by calling the 800 number. Reserve with a credit card over the phone at least 10 days in advance, and the ticket can be mailed anywhere in the U.S. Otherwise, reservations are available only up to 24hr. in advance. You can buy your ticket at the terminal, but arrive early.

If **boarding at a remote "flag stop,"** be sure you know exactly where the bus stops. You must call the nearest agency and let them know you'll be waiting and at what time. Catch the driver's attention by standing on the side of the road and flailing your arms wildly—better to be embarrassed than stranded. If a bus passes (usually because of overcrowding), a later, less-crowded bus should stop. Whatever you stow in compartments underneath the bus should be clearly marked; be sure to get a claim check for it and make sure your luggage is on the same bus as you.

**Advance purchase fares:** Reserving space far ahead of time ensures a lower fare, although expect a smaller discount during the busy summer months (June 5-Sept. 15). For tickets purchased more than 7 days in advance, the one-way fare anywhere in the U.S. will not exceed $79, while the round-trip price is capped at $158 (from June-Sept., the one-way cap is $89 and the round-trip $178). Fares are often reduced even more for 14-day or 21-day advance purchases on many popular routes; call the 800 number for up to the date pricing, or consult the user-friendly web page.

**Discounts on full fares:** Senior citizens (10% off); children ages 2 to 11 (50% off); travelers with disabilities and special needs and their companions ride together for the price of 1. Active and retired U.S. military personnel and National Guard Reserves (10% off with valid ID) and their spouses and dependents may take a round-trip between any 2 points in the U.S. for $169. With a ticket purchased 3 or more days in advance, a friend can travel along for free; during the summer months, if purchased 7 days in advance, the free-loadin' friend gets half off.

**Ameripass:** Call 888-GLI-PASS (454-7277). Allows adults unlimited travel for 7 days ($199), 15 days ($299), 30 days ($409), or 60 days ($549). Prices for students with a valid college ID and for senior citizens are slightly less: 7 days ($189), 15 days ($279), 30 days ($379), or 60 days ($509). Children's passes are half the price of adults. The pass takes effect the first day used. Before purchasing an Ameripass, total up the separate bus fares between towns to make sure that the pass is really more economical, or at least worth the unlimited flexibility it provides. **TNMO Coaches, Vermont Transit, Carolina Trailways,** and **Valley Transit** are Greyhound subsidiaries, and as such will honor Ameripasses; actually, most bus companies in the U.S. will do so, but check for specifics.

**International Ameripass:** For travelers from outside North America. A 7-day pass is $179, 15-day pass $269, 30-day pass $369, 60-day pass $499. Call 888-GLI-PASS (454-7277) for info. International Ameripasses are not available at the terminal; they can be purchased in foreign countries at Greyhound-affiliated agencies; telephone numbers vary by country and are listed on the web page. Passes can also be ordered at the web page, or purchased in Greyhound's International Office, in Port Authority Bus Station, 625 Eighth Ave., New York, NY 10018 (800-246-8572 or 212-971-0492; fax 402-330-0919; email intlameripass@ greyhound.com). **Australia:** 049 342 088. **New Zealand:** (64) 9 479 65555. **South Africa:** (27) 11 331 2911. **United Kingdom:** (44) 01342 317 317.

## GREYHOUND CANADA TRANSPORTATION

Unrelated to Greyhound Lines, Greyhound Canada Transportation, 877 Greyhound Way, Calgary, AB T3C 3V8 (800-661-TRIP/ (8747); www.greyhound.ca) is Canada's main intercity bus company. The web page has full schedule info.

**Discounts:** Seniors (10% off); students (10% off in Ontario, 25% off in West with purchase of CDN$15 discount card); a companion of a disabled person free; ages 3-7 50%; under 3 free. If reservations are made 7 days or more in advance, a friend travels ½-off. A child under 16 rides free with an adult if reserved 7 days in advance.

**Canada Pass:** Offers 7-, 15-, 30-, and 60-day unlimited travel on all routes for North American residents, including limited links to northern U.S. cities. 7 day advance purchase required. (7-day pass CDN$230; 15-day pass CDN$360; 30-day pass CDN$420; 60-day pass CDN$535).

**International Canada Pass:** For foreign visitors. Slightly lower prices (7-day pass CDN$199; 15-day pass CDN$270; 30-day pass CDN$365; 60-day pass CDN$465). The "Plus" pass adds travel to Québec and the Maritime provinces for a few dollars more; this pass can be purchased only overseas at select travel agencies, including those listed above for Greyhound Lines. Goods and services tax (GST) is added to fares.

## GREEN TORTOISE

**Green Tortoise,** 494 Broadway, San Francisco, CA 94133 (415-956-7500 or 800-867-8647; www.greentortoise.com, email tortoise@greentortoise.com), offers a more slow-paced, whimsical alternative to straighforward transportation. Green Tortoise's communal "hostels on wheels"--remodeled diesel buses done up for living and eating on the road--traverse the U.S. on aptly named Adventure Tours. Prices include transportation, sleeping space on the bus, and tours of the regions through which you pass, often including such treats as hot springs and farm stays. Meals are prepared communally, and incur an additional food charge. Cross-country trips run May-Oct. between Hartford, Boston, or New York City and San Francisco, Los Angeles, or Seattle (14 days; $389 plus $121 for food, 10 days; $349 plus $111 for food). Round-trip vacation loops start in San Francisco, winding through Yosemite National Park, Northern California, Baja California, or the Grand Canyon. The grand Alaska extravaganza takes 28 days to work up from S.F. to the huge, wide open ($1500 plus $250 for food; includes return airfare). Prepare for an earthy trip; buses have no toilets and little privacy. Reserve one to two months in advance, deposits ($100) are generally required. Many trips have space available at departure. Reservations can be made over the phone or through the web.

## EAST COAST EXPLORER

East Coast Explorer, 245 Eighth Ave., Suite 144, New York, NY 10011 (718-694-9667 or 800-610-2680 outside NYC, call between 8-11 pm for reservations; or email llustig@delphi.com; hostels. com/transport/trans.ece.html), is an inexpensive and interesting way to tour between New York City and Boston or Washington, D.C. For $3-7 more than Greyhound, you and 13 other passengers travel all day (10-11hr.) on back roads, stopping at natural and historic sites. Buses run a couple times a week; call or check out the website for routes and schedules. Trips run between New York City and Washington, D.C. ($32) and between New York City and Boston ($29). The air-conditioned bus will pick up and drop off at most hostels and budget hotels. (Reservations required. Two bags per person allowed.)

## ADVENTURE NETWORK FOR TRAVELLERS (ANT)

Adventure Network for Travellers, 870 Market St., #416, San Francisco, CA 94102 (415-399-0880 or 800-336-6049; fax 415-399-0949; www.theant.com; email anttrips@theant.com). The ANT is a flexible hop-on, hop-off backpacker transportation and adventure network operating between popular cities, towns, and national parks in California and the Southwest U.S. Transportation is in 15-seat mini-vans driven by knowledgable guides, providing fun company. Travel passes ($89-$279, depending on which destinations are included) are valid for up to 6 months.

# BY CAR

"I" (as in "I-90") refers to Interstate highways, "U.S." (as in "U.S. 1") to United States highways, and "Rte." (as in "Rte. 7") to state and local highways. For Canadian highways, "TCH" refers to the Trans-Canada Hwy., while "Hwy." or "autoroute" refers to standard automobile routes.

## AUTOMOBILE CLUBS

**American Automobile Association (AAA),** (for emergency road service call 800-AAA-HELP/800-222-4357; www.aaa.com). Offers free trip-planning services, roadmaps and guidebooks, 24-hour emergency road service anywhere in the U.S., free towing, and commission-free traveler's checks from American Express with over 1,000 offices scattered across the country. Discounts on Hertz car rental (5-20%), Amtrak tickets (10%), and various motel chains and theme parks. AAA has reciprocal agreements with the auto associations of many other countries, which often provide you with full benefits while in the U.S. AAA has 2 types of memberships, basic and plus, although the services do not differ greatly. Memberships vary depending on which AAA branch you join, but hover between $50-60 for the first year and less for renewals and additional family members; call 800-JOIN-AAA/800-564-6222 to sign up.

**Canadian Automobile Association (CAA),** 1145 Hunt Club Rd., #200, Ottawa, ON K1V 0Y3 (800-CAA-HELP/(800-222-4357); www.caa.ca). Affiliated with AAA (see above), the CAA provides nearly identical membership benefits, including 24hr. emergency roadside assistance, free maps and tourbooks, route planning, and various discounts. Basic membership is CDN$66 and CDN$24 for associates; call 800-JOIN-CAA (800-564-6222) to sign up.

**Mobil Auto Club,** 200 N. Martingale Rd., Schaumbourg, IL 60174 (800-621-5581 for information; 800-323-5880 for emergency service). Benefits include locksmith reimbursement, towing (free up to 10 mi.), roadside service, and car-rental discounts. $7/month covers you and another driver.

## ON THE ROAD

Tune up the car before you leave, make sure the tires are in good repair and have enough air, and get good maps. *Rand McNally's Road Atlas*, covering all of the U.S. and Canada, is one of the best (available at bookstores and gas stations, $10). A **compass** and a **car manual** can also be very useful. You should always carry a **spare tire** and **jack, jumper cables, extra oil, flares,** a **flashlight,** and **blankets** (in case you break down at night or in the winter). Those traveling long undeveloped stretches of road may want to consider renting a **car phone** in case of a breakdown. When traveling in the summer or in the desert bring five gallons of **water** for drinking and for the radiator. In extremely hot weather, use the air conditioner with restraint; if you see the car's temperature gauge climbing, turn it off. Turning the heater on full blast will help cool the engine. If radiator fluid is steaming, turn off the car for half an hour. *Never pour water over the engine to cool it.* Never lift a searing hot hood. In remote areas, remember to bring emergency food and water.

   **Sleeping in a car or van parked in the city is extremely dangerous**—even the most dedicated budget traveler should not consider it an option. While driving, be sure to buckle up—seat belts are **required by law in many regions of the U.S. and Canada. The speed limit** in the U.S. varies considerably from region to region. Most urban highways have a limit of 55 miles per hour (63km per hr.), while rural routes range from 65 mph (104kph) to 80 mph (128kph). Heed the limit; not only does it save gas, but most local police forces and state troopers make frequent use of radar to catch speed demons. The **speed limit in Canada** is 100kph (63 mph). **Gas** in the U.S. costs about $1.10 per gallon ($0.33 per L), but prices vary widely according to state gasoline taxes. In Canada, gas costs CDN60-65¢ per L (CDN$2-2.65 per gallon).

   Drivers should take necessary precautions against **carjacking,** which has become one of the most frequent crimes committed in this country. Carjackers, who are usually armed, approach their victims in their vehicles, and force them to turn over the automobile. Carjackers prey on cars parked on the side of the road and cars stopped at red lights. If you are going to pull over on the side of the road, keep your doors locked and windows up at all times and do not pull over to help a car in the breakdown lane; call the police instead.

## HOW TO NAVIGATE THE INTERSTATES

In the 1950s, President Eisenhower envisioned an **interstate system,** a federally funded network of highways designed primarily to subsidize American commerce. His dream has been realized, and there is actually an easily comprehensible, consistent system for numbering interstates. Even-numbered interstates run east-west and odd ones run north-south, decreasing in number toward the south and the west. North-south routes begin on the West Coast with I-5 and end with I-95 on the East Coast. The southernmost east-west route is I-4 in Florida. The northernmost east-west route is I-94, stretching from Montana to Wisconsin. Three-digit numbers signify branches of other interstates (e.g., I-285 is a branch of I-85), which are often bypasses skirting around large cities.

## RENTING

The cost of car rental is often prohibitive for one-way trips between two cities, but local trips may be reasonable. **Rental agencies** fall into two categories: national companies with hundreds of branches, and local agencies serving a city or region.

National chains usually allow cars to be picked up in one city and dropped off in another (for a hefty charge, sometimes in excess of $1000); occasional promotions linked to coastal inventory imbalances may cut the fee dramatically. By calling a toll-free number, you can reserve a reliable car anywhere in the country. Generally, airport branches carry the cheapest rates. However, like airfares, car rental prices change constantly and often require scouting around for the best rate. Drawbacks include steep prices (a compact rents for about $35-45 per day) and high minimum ages for rentals (usually 25). Most branches rent to ages 21-24 with an additional fee, but policies and prices vary from agency to agency. If you're 21 or older and have a major credit card in your name, you may be able to rent where the minimum age would otherwise rule you out. **Alamo** (800-327-9633; www.goalamo.com) rents to ages 21-24 with a major credit card for an additional $20 per day. Some branches of **Avis** (800-230-4898; www.avis.com), in New York state and Québec province, and **Budget** (800-527-0700) rent to drivers under 25 with a surcharge that varies by location. **Hertz** (800-654-3131; www.hertz.com) policy varies with city. **Enterprise** (800-Rent-A-Car/736-8222) rents to customers aged 21-24 with a variable surcharge. Most **Dollar** (800-8-00-4000; dollarcar.com) branches allow it, and various **Thrifty** (800-367-2277; www.thrifty.com) locations allow ages 21-24 to rent for an additional daily fee of about $20. **Rent-A-Wreck** (800-421-7253; email gene@raw.com; www.rent-a-wreck.com), specializes in supplying vehicles that are past their prime for lower-than-average prices; a bare-bones compact less than 8 years old rents for around $20 per day; cars 3-5 years old average under $25.

Most rental packages offer unlimited mileage, although some allow you a certain number of miles free before the usual charge of 25-40¢ per mile takes effect. Most quoted rates do not include gas or tax, so ask for the total cost before handing over the credit card; many large firms have added airport surcharges not covered by the designated fare. Return the car with a full tank unless you sign up for a fuel option plan that stipulates otherwise. When dealing with any car rental company, ask whether the price includes insurance against theft and collision. There may be an additional charge for a collision and damage waiver (CDW), which usually comes to about $12-15 per day. Some major credit cards (including MasterCard and American Express) will cover the CDW if you use their card to rent a car; call your credit card company or inquire at the rental agency for specifics.

A cheaper rental option for large groups is **The Green Machine** (P.O. Box 573, Acton, CA 93510; 805-269-0360, fax 269-2835; www.donbarnett.com/gmachine; e-mail gmachinetravel@hotmail.com) which rents renovated school buses, equipped with camping gear, to groups with a driver 18 years or older. Starting at $350 per week, rental includes insurance and unlimited mileage.

## BUYING

**Adventures on Wheels,** 42 Hwy. 36, Middletown, NJ 07748 (800-WHEELS-9/(943-3579) or 732-583-8714; fax 583-8932; email info@wheels9.com; www.wheels9.com), will sell domestic and international travelers a motorhome, a camper or station wagon, organize its registration and provide insurance, and guarantee that they will buy it back from you after you have finished your travels. Cars with a buy-back guarantee start at $2500. Buy a camper for $6000-9000, use it for 5-6 months, and sell it back for $3000-5000. The main office is in New York/ New Jersey; there are other offices in Los Angeles, San Francisco, and Miami. Vehicles can be picked up at one office and dropped off at another.

## AUTO TRANSPORT COMPANIES

These services match drivers with car owners who need cars moved from one city to another. Would-be travelers give the company their desired destination and the company finds a car which needs to go there. The only expenses are gas, tolls, and your own living expenses. Some companies insure their cars; with others, your security deposit covers any breakdowns or damage. You must be at least 21, have a valid license, and agree to drive about 400 mi. per day on a fairly direct route. Companies regularly inspect current and past job references, take your fingerprints, and require a cash bond. Cars are available between most points, although it's easiest to find cars for traveling from coast to coast; New York and Los Angeles are popular transfer points. If offered a car, look it over first. Think twice about accepting a gas guzzler, since you'll be paying for the gas. With the company's approval, you may be able to share the cost with several companions.

**Auto Driveaway Co.,** 310 S. Michigan Ave., Chicago, IL 60604 (800-346-2277 or 312-341-1900; fax 312-341-9100; email autodrv@aol.com; www.autodriveaway.com).

**Across America Driveaway,** 3626 Calumet Ave., Hammond, IN 46320 (800-619-7707 or 219-852-0134; fax 800-334-6931; www.schultz-international.com, e-mail Schultz!@gte.net). Other offices in L.A. (800-964-7874 or 310-798-3377) and Dallas (214-745-8892).

## BY BICYCLE

Before you pedal furiously onto the byways of America astride your banana-seat Huffy, remember that safe and secure cycling requires a quality helmet and lock. A good helmet costs about $40—much cheaper than critical head surgery. U-shaped **Kryptonite** or **Citadel** locks ($30-60) carry insurance against theft for 1 or 2 years if your bike is registered with the police. **Bike Nashbar,** 4111 Simon Rd., Youngstown, OH 44512 (800-627-4227; fax 456-1223), will beat any nationally advertised in-stock price by 5¢, and ships anywhere in the U.S. and Canada. They fields questions about repairs and maintenance (330-788-6464; open M-F 8am-6pm).

**Adventure Cycling Association,** P.O. Box 8308, Missoula, MT 59807 (800-755-2453 or 406-721-1776; fax 721-8754; email acabike@aol.com; www.adv-cycling.org). A national, non-profit organization that researches and maps long-distance routes and organizes bike tours long and short for members (75-day Great Divide Expedition, $2800, 9-day trip $650). Annual membership $30; includes access to maps and routes and a subscription to *Adventure Cyclist* magazine.

**The Canadian Cycling Association,** 1600 James Naismith Dr., #212A, Gloucester, ON K1B 5N4 (613-748-5629; fax 748-5692; email general@canadian-cycling.com; www.canadian-cycling.com). Provides information for cyclists of all abilities, from recreational to racing. Distributes *The Canadian Cycling Association's Complete Guide to Bicycle Touring in Canada* (CDN$24), plus guides to specific regions of Canada, Alaska, and the Pacific Coast.

**Backroads,** 801 Cedar St., Berkeley, CA 94710-1800 (800-462-2848; fax 510-527-1444; email goactive@backroads.com; www.backroads.com), offers cushy tours in 20 states, including Montana, Hawaii, California, Utah, and Maine. Travelers ride from accommodation to accommodation; prices include most meals, guide services, maps and directions, and van support (6-day trip with camping accomodation, $848).

**ESSENTIALS**

## BY MOTORCYCLE

It may be cheaper than car travel, but it takes a tenacious soul to endure a motorcycle tour. The wind-in-your-face thrill, burly leather, and revving crackle of a motorcycle engine unobscured by windows or upholstery has built up quite a cult following, but motorcycling is the most dangerous of roadtop activities. Of course, **safety** should be your primary concern. Motorcycles are incredibly vulnerable to crosswinds, drunk drivers, and the blind spots of cars and trucks. *Always ride defensively.* Dangers skyrocket at night. **Helmets** are required by law in many states; wear the best one you can find. Americans should ask their State's Dept. of Motor Vehicles for a motorcycle operator's manual; the AMA webpage (see below) lists relevant laws and regulations for all 50 states. If you must carry a load, keep it low and forward where it won't distort the cycle's center of gravity. Fasten it either to the seat or over the rear axle in saddle or tank bags.

Those considering a long journey should contact the **American Motorcyclist Association,** 13515 Yarmouth Dr. Pickering, OH 43147 (800-AMA-JOIN/262-5646 or 614-856-1900; fax 856-1920; email ama@ama-cycle.org; ama-cycle.org), the linchpin of U.S. biker culture. A full membership ($29 per year) includes a subscription to the extremely informative *American Motorcyclist* magazine, discounts on insurance, rentals, and hotels, and a kick-ass patch for your riding jacket. For an additional $25, members benefit from emergency roadside assistance, including pick-up and delivery to a service shop.

**Americade** (email info@tourexpo.com; www.tourexpo.com) is an enormous week-long annual touring rally. In 2000 it will be held June 5-10 in Lake George, NY. Call 518-798-7888; fax 798-0169 or write Americade, P.O. Box 2205, Glen Falls, NY 12801 to register.

## BY THUMB

*Let's Go* urges you to consider the great risks and disadvantages of **hitchhiking** before thumbing it. Hitching means entrusting your life to a randomly selected person who happens to stop beside you on the road. While this may be comparatively safe in some areas of Europe and Australia, it is generally *not* so in the U.S. We do not recommend it. We strongly urge you to find other means of transportation and to avoid situations where hitching is the only option.

# ADDITIONAL INFORMATION
## SPECIFIC CONCERNS
### WOMEN TRAVELERS

In the U.S., a woman should expect to be treated just as a man would be, no matter what they are wearing or how they act; though sexism still exists, it is considered unacceptable behavior. If you are treated unfairly because you are a woman, this is grounds for compaint.

Women exploring on their own inevitably face some additional safety concerns, but it's easy to be adventurous without taking undue risks. Generally, it is safe to travel in the U.S. as a woman, but common sense still applies; women are targeted for muggings and swindlings, as well as general harassment. Watch out for vendors who may try to take advantage of you. Avoid downtrodden neighborhoods, especially at night, and avoid solitary, late-night treks or subway rides. If you are camping in isolated areas or travelling in big cities you are unfamiliar with, try to travel with partners. In more rural areas, rowdy bars can also be sketchy. Wherever you go, walk purposefully and self-confidently; women who look like they know what they are doing and where they are going are less likely to be harassed. When traveling, always carry extra money for a phone call, bus, or taxi. **Hitching** is never safe for lone women, or even for two women traveling together. Consider approaching older women or couples if you're lost or feel uncomfortable.

Don't hesitate to seek out a police officer or a passerby if you are being harassed. *Let's Go: USA* lists emergency numbers (including rape crisis lines) in the Practical Information listings of most cities, and you can always dial **911.** An **IMPACT Model Mugging** self-defense course will not only prepare you for a potential attack, but will also raise your level of awareness of your surroundings as well as your confidence (see **Self Defense,** p. 49). Women also face some specific health concerns when traveling (see **Women's Health,** p. 55).

The **National Organization for Women (NOW)** (email now@now.org; now.org) can refer women travelers to rape crisis centers and counseling services. Main offices include 150 W. 28th St., # 304, New York, NY 10001 (212-627-9895) and 1000 16th St. NW, # 700, Washington, D.C. 20036 (202-331-0066).

# TRAVELING ALONE

There are many benefits to traveling alone, among them greater independence and challenge. As a lone traveler, you have greater opportunity to interact with the region you're visiting. Without distraction, you can write a great travel log in the grand tradition of Mark Twain, John Steinbeck, and Charles Kuralt.

On the other hand, any solo traveler is a more vulnerable target of harassment and street theft. Lone travelers need to be well-organized and look confident at all times. Try not to stand out as a tourist, and be especially careful in deserted or very crowded areas. If questioned, never admit that you are traveling alone. Maintain regular contact with someone at home who knows your itinerary.

A number of organizations supply information for solo travelers, and others find travel companions for those who don't want to go alone. A few are listed here.

**Connecting: Solo Traveler Network,** P.O. Box 29088, 1996 W. Broadway, Vancouver, BC V6J 5C2, Canada (604-737-7791; email info@cstn.org; www.cstn.org). Bi-monthly newsletter features going solo tips, single-friendly tips and travel companion ads. Annual directory lists holiday suppliers that avoid single supplement charges. Advice and lodging exchanges facilitated between members. Membership $25-35.

**Travel Companion Exchange,** P.O. Box 833, Amityville, NY 11701 (516-454-0880 or 800-392-1256; www.travelalone.com). Publishes the pamphlet *Foiling Pickpockets & Bag Snatchers* ($4) and *Travel Companions,* a bi-monthly newsletter for single travelers seeking a travel partner (subscription $48).

### FURTHER READING; TRAVELING ALONE

*Traveling Solo,* Eleanor Berman. Globe Pequot ($17).

*The Single Traveler Newsletter,* P.O. Box 682, Ross, CA 94957 (415-389-0227). 6 issues $29.

# OLDER TRAVELERS

Senior citizens are eligible for a wide range of discounts on transportation, museums, movies, theaters, concerts, restaurants, and accommodations. If you don't see a senior citizen price listed, ask, and you may be delightfully surprised.

Agencies for senior group travel are growing in enrollment and popularity. These are only a few:

**ElderTreks,** 597 Markham St., Toronto, ON, Canada, M6G 2L7 (tel. 800-741-7956 or 416-588-5000; fax 588-9839; email passages@inforamp.net; www.eldertreks.com).

**Elderhostel,** 75 Federal St., Boston, MA 02110-1941 (617-426-7788 or 877-426-8056; email registration@elderhostel.org; www.elderhostel.org). Programs at colleges, universities, and other learning centers in the U.S. on varied subjects lasting 1-4 weeks. Must be 55 or over (spouse can be of any age).

**The Mature Traveler,** P.O. Box 50400, Reno, NV 89513 (775-786-7419 or 800-460-6676). Soft-adventure tours for seniors. Subscription $30.

**FURTHER READING: OLDER TRAVELERS**

*No Problem! Worldwise Tips for Mature Adventurers,* Janice Kenyon. Orca Book Publishers ($16).

*A Senior's Guide to Healthy Travel,* Donald L. Sullivan. Career Press. ($15).

*Unbelievably Good Deals and Great Adventures That You Absolutely Can't Get Unless You're Over 50,* Joan Rattner Heilman. Contemporary Books ($13).

# BISEXUAL, GAY, AND LESBIAN TRAVELERS

American cities are generally accepting of all sexualities, and thriving gay and lesbian communities can be found in most cosmopolitan areas. Most college towns are gay-friendly as well. In rural areas, however, homophobia can be rampant. In light of the anti-gay legislative measures narrowly defeated in various states, and not-so-isolated gay-bashing incidents, homophobia is still all too common.

## BOOKSTORES AND INFORMATION SERVICES

**Gay's the Word,** 66 Marchmont St., London WC1N 1AB (tel. (0171) 278 7654; email gays.theword@virgin.net; www.gaystheword.co.uk). The largest gay and lesbian bookshop in the U.K. Mail-order service available. No catalogue of listings, but they will provide a list of titles on a given subject.

**Giovanni's Room,** 345 S. 12th St., Philadelphia, PA 19107 (215-923-2960; fax 923-0813; email giophilp@netaxs.com). An international feminist, lesbian, and gay bookstore with mail-order service which carries the publications listed below.

**International Gay and Lesbian Travel Association,** 4331 N. Federal Hwy., #304, Fort Lauderdale, FL 33308 (954-776-2626 or 800-448-8550; fax 954-776-3303; email IGLTA@aol.com; www.iglta.com). An organization of 1350+ companies serving gay and lesbian travelers worldwide. Call for lists of travel agents, accommodations, and events.

**International Lesbian and Gay Association (ILGA),** 81 rue Marché-au-Charbon, B-1000 Brussels, Belgium (tel./fax 32 2 502 24 71; email ilga@ilga.org; www.ilga.org). Not a travel service. Provides information such as homosexuality laws of individual countries.

## FURTHER READING: BISEXUAL, GAY, AND LESBIAN TRAVELERS

*Spartacus International Gay Guide.* Bruno Gmunder Verlag. ($33).

*Damron Men's Guide, Damron Road Atlas, Damron's Accommodations,* and *The Women's Traveller.* Damron Travel Guides ($14-19). For more information, call 415-255-0404 or 800-462-6654 or check their website (www.damron.com).

*Ferrari Guides' Gay Travel A to Z, Ferrari Guides' Men's Travel in Your Pocket, Ferrari Guides' Women's Travel in Your Pocket,* and *Ferrari Guides' Inn Places.* Ferrari Guides ($14-16). For more information, call 602-863-2408 or 800-962-2912 or check their web site (www.q-net.com).

*Gayellow Pages* ($16). (212-674-0120; gayellowpages.com; email gayellow@banet.net).

# TRAVELERS WITH DISABILITIES

Federal law dictates that all public buildings should be handicap accessible, and recent laws governing building codes have made disabled access more the norm than the exception. Businesses, transportation companies, national parks, and public services are complied to assist the disabled in using their facilities. However, traveling with a disability still requires planning and flexibility.

Those with disabilities should inform airlines, buses, trains, and hotels of their disabilities when making arrangements for travel; some time may be needed to prepare special accommodations. Call ahead to restaurants, hotels, parks, and other facilities to find out about the existence of ramps, the widths of doors, the dimensions of elevators, etc. Major airlines and **Amtrak** (800-872-7245; see p. 39) will accomodate disabled passengers if notified at least 72hr. in advance. Amtrak offers 15% discounts to disabled passengers, and hearing impaired travelers may contact Amtrak using teletype printers (800-872-7245). **Greyhound** (see p. 40) will provide free travel for a companion; if you are without a fellow traveler, call Greyhound (800-752-4841) at least 48hr., but no more than 1 week, before you leave and they'll arrange assistance where needed. Hertz, National, and Avis **car rental** agencies have hand-controlled vehicles at some locations (see **Renting**, p. 42). If planning to visit a national park or any other sight managed by the U.S. National Park Service, you can obtain a free **Golden Access Passport** (see **National Parks**, p. 69).

### FOR MORE INFORMATION

**Access-Able Travel Source**, LLC, P.O. Box 1796, Wheat Ridge, CO 80034 (303-232-2979, fax 239-8486; www.access-able.com, e-mail bill@access-able.com). A database on traveling the U.S. for disabled travelers, started by two avid disabled travellers. Provides info on access, transportation, accomodations, and various other resources.

**Mobility International USA (MIUSA),** P.O. Box 10767, Eugene, OR 97440 (541-343-1284 voice and TDD; fax 343-6812; email info@miusa.org; www.miusa.org). Sells *A World of Options: A Guide to International Educational Exchange, Community Service, and Travel for Persons with Disabilities* ($35).

**Moss Rehab Hospital Travel Information Service** (215-456-9600; www.mossresourcenet.org). A telephone and internet information resource center on travel accessibility and other travel-related concerns for those with disabilities.

**Society for the Advancement of Travel for the Handicapped (SATH),** 347 Fifth Ave., #610, New York, NY 10016 (212-447-1928; fax 725-8253; email sathtravel@aol.com; www.sath.org). Advocacy group which publishes quarterly color travel magazine *OPEN WORLD* (free for members or $13 for nonmembers). and a wide range of information sheets on disability travel facilitation and accessible destinations. Annual membership $45, students and seniors $30.

The following organizations arrange tours or trips for disabled travelers:

**Directions Unlimited,** 720 N. Bedford Rd., Bedford Hills, NY 10507 (tel. 800-533-5343; in NY 914-241-1700; fax 241-0243; email cruisesusa@aol.com). Specializes in arranging individual and group vacations, tours, and cruises for the physically disabled. Group tours for blind travelers.

**The Guided Tour Inc.,** 7900 Old York Rd.,#114B, Elkins Park, PA 19027-2339 (800-783-5841 or 215-782-1370; email gtour400@aol.com; www.guidedtour.com). Runs travel programs for persons with developmental and physical challenges around the U.S.

### FURTHER READING: DISABLED TRAVELERS
*Resource Directory for the Disabled*, Richard Neil Shrout. Facts on file ($45).

## MINORITY TRAVELERS

Racial and ethnic minorities sometimes face blatant and, more often, subtle discrimination and/or harassment, though regions in the U.S. and Canada differ drastically in their general attitudes towards race relations. Verbal harassment is now less common than unfair pricing, false information on accomodations, or inexcusably slow or unfriendly service at restaurants. The best way to deal with such encounters is to remain calm and report individuals to a supervisor and establishments to the Better Business Bureau for the region (the operator will provide local listings); contact the police in extreme situations. *Let's Go* always welcomes reader input regarding discriminating establishments.

In larger cities, African-Americans can uaually consult chapters of hte Urban League and the **National Association for the Advancement of Colored People** (**NAACP**) (www.naacp.org) for info on events of interest to African-Americans.

### FURTHER READING: MINORITY TRAVELERS
*Go Girl! The Black Woman's Book of Travel and Adventure*, Elaine Lee. Eighth Mountain Press ($18).

*The African-American Travel Guide*, Wayne Robinson. Hunter Publishing ($16).

*Traveling Jewish in America*, Jane Moskowitz. Wandering You Press ($14.50).

**ESSENTIALS**

# TRAVELERS WITH CHILDREN

Family vacations often require that you slow your pace, and always require that you plan ahead. When deciding where to stay, remember the special needs of young children; if you pick a B&B or a small hotel, call ahead and make sure it's child-friendly. If you rent a car, make sure the rental company provides a car seat for younger children. Be sure that your child carries some sort of ID in case of an emergency or he or she gets lost, and arrange a reunion spot in case of separation when sight-seeing.

Restaurants often have children's menus and discounts. Virtually all museums and tourist attractions also have a children's rate. Children under two generally fly for free or 10% of the adult airfare on domestic flights (this does not necessarily include a seat). Fares are usually discounted 25% for children from two to 11. Finding a private place for **breast feeding** can be a problem while traveling.

## FURTHER READING: TRAVELERS WITH CHILDREN

*Backpacking with Babies and Small Children,* Goldie Silverman. Wilderness Press ($10).

*Have Kid, Will Travel: 101 Survival Strategies for Vacationing With Babies and Young Children,* Claire and Lucille Tristram. Andrews and McMeel ($9).

*Kidding Around Boston, San Francisco, Washington D.C., Atlanta, Austin, Chicago, Miami, Nashville* OR *Portland.* John Muir ($8).

*Adventuring with Children: An Inspirational Guide to World Travel and the Outdoors,* Nan Jeffrey. Avalon House Publishing ($15).

# DIETARY CONCERNS

**Vegetarians** should have no problem finding suitable cuisine on either coast (the West Coast, especially, is extremely vegetarian friendly) and in most major cities, although small-town America may meet veggie requests with a long, blank stare and a pile of mashed potatos. *Let's Go* tries to indicate vegetarian options in it's restaurant listings; other places to look for vegetarian and vegan cuisine is at local health food stores and co-ops, as well as large natural food chains such as Wild Harvest, Wild Oats, Bread and Circus, Nature's, and Trader Joes. Vegan options are often more difficult to find outside of the Southern California health-freak zone; be prepared to make your own food, request tailored dishes, or seek out specialty cafes. For more information about vegetarian travel, contact:

**North American Vegetarian Society,** P.O. Box 72, Dolgeville, NY 13329 (518-568-7970; email navs@telenet.com; www.cyberveg.org/navs/). Publishes *Transformative Adventures,* a guide to vacations and retreats ($15), and the *Vegetarian Journal's Guide to Natural Food Restaurants in the U.S. and Canada* ($12).

Travelers who keep **kosher** should contact synagogues in larger cities for information on kosher restaurants; your own synagogue or college Hillel should have access to lists of Jewish institutions across the nation. If you are strict in your observance, you may have to prepare your own food on the road.

**The Jewish Travel Guide** lists synagogues, kosher restaurants, and Jewish institutions in the U.S. and Canada. Available from Vallentine-Mitchell Publishers, Newbury House 890-900, Eastern Ave., Newbury Park, Ilford, Essex, U.K. IG2 7HH (tel. (0181) 599 88 66; fax 599 09 84). It is available in the U.S. ($16) from ISBS, 5804 NE Hassalo St., Portland, OR 97213-3644 (800-944-6190).

## FURTHER READING: DIETARY CONCERNS

*The Vegetarian Traveler: Where to Stay if You're Vegetarian,* Jed Civic. Larson Pub. ($16).

# OTHER RESOURCES

## USEFUL PUBLICATIONS

### MISCELLANEOUS

**Specialty Travel Index,** 305 San Anselmo Ave., #313, San Anselmo, CA 94960 (415-455-1643 or 888-624-4030; fax 459-4974; email spectrav@ix.netcom.com; www.spectrav.com). Published twice yearly, this is an extensive listing of "off the beaten track" travel opportunities. One copy $6, one-year subscription (2 issues) $10.

### TRAVEL BOOK PUBLISHERS

**Hippocrene Books, Inc.,** 171 Madison Ave., New York, NY 10016 (212-685-4371; orders 718-454-2366; fax 454-1391; email contact@hippocrenebooks.com; www.netcom.com/~hippocre). Free catalogue. Publishes travel reference books and guides.

**Hunter Publishing,** 130 Campus Drive, Edison, NJ 08818-7816 (800-255-0343; fax 417-0482; email kimba@mediasoft.net; www.hunterpublishing.com). Has an extensive catalogue of travel books, guides, language learning tapes, and quality maps, and the *Charming Small Hotel Guide to New England* or *Florida* ($15).

**Rand McNally,** 150 S. Wacker Dr., Chicago, IL 60606 (tel. 800-234-0679 or 312-332-2009; fax 443-9540; email storekeeper@randmcnally.com; www.randmcnally.com). Publishes a number of comprehensive road atlases (each $8).

## THE WORLD WIDE WEB

The Internet can provide factual information without the hassle of calling, and can facillitate hotel, hostel, and car rental reservations. Listed below are sights that would be useful to a budget traveler.

**Microsoft Expedia** (expedia.msn.com) has everything you'd ever need to make travel plans on the web: compare flight fares, look at maps, make reservations. FareTracker, a free service, sends you monthly mailings about the cheapest fares to any destination.

**The CIA World Factbook** (www.odci.gov/cia/publications/factbook/index.html) has tons of vital statistics on the United States and Canada. Check it out for an overview of either country's economy, and an explanation of its system of government.

**Shoestring Travel** (www.stratpub.com), an alternative to Microsoft's monolithic site, is budget travel e-zine that features listings of home exchanges, links, and accommodations information.

**Tourism Offices Worldwide Directory** (http://mbnet.mb.ca/lucas/travel/tourism-offices.html), will give you tourism offices for all fifty states and Canada, as well as consulate and embassy addresses.

**City Net** (www.city.net) dispenses info on renting a car, restaurants, hotel rates, and weather for a wide array of cities and regions across the U.S. and Canada.

### FURTHER READING: THE WORLD WIDE WEB

*How to Plan Your Dream Vacation Using the Web.* Elizabeth Dempsey. Coriolis Group ($25).

*Nettravel: How Travelers Use the Internet,* Michael Shapiro. O'Reilly & Associates. ($25).

*Travel Planning Online for Dummies,* Noah Vadnai. IDG Books. ($25).

# NEW ENGLAND

New England has fancied itself an intellectual and political center since before the States were United. Students and scholars funnel into New England's colleges each fall, and town meetings still evoke the spirit of popular government which inspired American colonists to create a nation. Numerous historic landmarks recount every step of the young country's break from "Old" England.

The region's unpredictable climate can be particularly dismal during the harsh, wet winter from November to March, when rivers, campgrounds, and tourist attractions freeze up. Nevertheless, today's visitors find adventure in the rough edges that irked early settlers, flocking to New England's dramatic, salty coastline to sun on the sand; or heading to the slopes and valleys of the Green and White Mountains to ski, hike, bike, and canoe. In the fall, the nation's most brilliant foliage bleeds and burns, transforming the entire region into a giant kaleidoscope, one of New England's most memorable sights.

## HIGHLIGHTS OF NEW ENGLAND

■ **Seafood.** Head to Maine (see below) for the best lobster around, and don't forget to try New England clam chowda before you leave.

■ **Skiing.** Enthusiasts flock to the mountains of New Hampshire and Vermont; the most famous resorts include Stowe (p. 108) and Killington (p. 104).

■ **Beaches.** Cape Cod, MA (p. 130) and Nantucket, MA (p. 136) may have the region's best.

■ **Colonial landmarks.** They're everywhere, but a walk along the Freedom Trail in Boston, MA (p. 118) is a great place to start.

■ **Scenic New England.** Take a drive along Rt. 100 in the fall, when the foliage is at its most striking, or hike the Appalachian Trail (p. 93) for a view on foot.

# MAINE

Nearly a thousand years ago, Leif Ericson and his band of Viking explorers set foot on the coasts of Maine. Moose roamed the sprawling evergreen wilderness, the cry of the Maine coon cat echoed through towering mountains, and countless lobsters crawled in the ocean deep. A millennium has not changed much. Forests still cover nearly 90% of Maine's land, an area larger than the entire stack of New England states below, and the inner reaches of the state stretch on for mile after uninhabited mile. The more populated locales dot a harsh and jagged coastline; rather than trying to conquer the wilderness like the urbanites to the south, the deeply independent Maine "Downeaster" has adapted to this rough wilderness with rugged pragmatism. The beauty of the place has inspired writers like Stephen King, Henry Wadsworth Longfellow, and Edna St. Vincent Millay.

# ⊠ PRACTICAL INFORMATION

**Capital:** Augusta.

**Visitor Info: Maine Publicity Bureau,** 325B Water St., Hallowell (207-623-0363 or 888-624-6345; www.visitmaine.com). Send mail to P.O. Box 2300, Hallowell 04347. **Bureau of Parks and Lands,** State House Station #22 (AMHI, Harlow Bldg.), Augusta 04333 (207-287-3821). **Maine Forest Service,** Bureau of Forestry, State House Station #22, Harlow Bldg., 2nd fl., Augusta 04333 (207-287-2791).

**Postal Abbreviation:** ME. **Sales Tax:** 6%. **Area code:** 207.

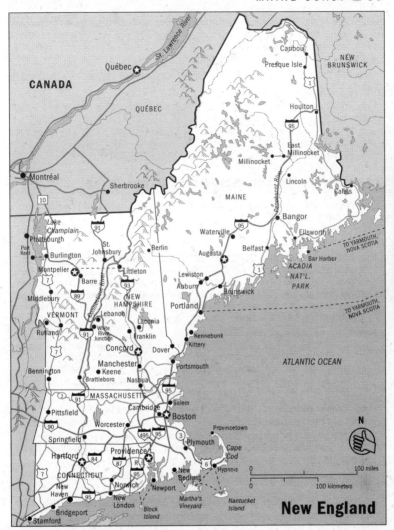

**New England**

# MAINE COAST

As the bird flies, the Maine coast from Kittery to Lubec measures 228mi., but if untangled, all of the inlets and rocky promontories would stretch out 3478mi. Fishing, the earliest business here, was later augmented by a vigorous shipbuilding industry; both traditions are still visible. Unfortunately, rampant overfishing and overcatching have depleted the North Atlantic cod and lobster populations and left Maine workers wondering about the future of their livelihood. Lobster, at least for now, is still ubiquitous in coastal Maine. It's worth stopping at one of the innumerable makeshift red wooden lobster signs that speckle the roadsides for a freshly boiled lobster. Lobsters are tastiest before July, when most start to molt.

**U.S. 1** hugs the coastline, stringing the port towns together. Lesser roads and small ferry lines connect the remote villages and offshore islands. **Visitor Info: Maine Information Center** (207-439-1319), in Kittery, 3mi. north of the Maine-New

Hampshire bridge (open daily 8am-6pm; mid-Oct. to June 9am-5pm). **Greyhound** serves points between Portland and Bangor along I-95, the coastal town of Brunswick, and on to Boston. Reaching most coastal points of interest is virtually impossible by bus; a car or bike is necessary.

# PORTLAND

During the July 4th fireworks of 1866, a young boy playing on a Portland wharf inadvertently started a fire which destroyed over ¾ of the city. The Victorian reconstruction that survives, in the Old Port Exchange, stands in stark contrast to Portland's spirited youth culture. Ferries run to the nearby Casco Bay Islands; Sebago Lake provides sunning and water skiing opportunities.

## 🛈 ORIENTATION AND PRACTICAL INFORMATION

Downtown sits near the bay, along **Congress St.** between State and Pearl St. A few blocks south lies the **Old Port** on Commercial and Fore St. These 2 districts contain most of the city's sights and attractions. **I-295** (off I-95) forms the western boundary of downtown.

**Buses: Concord Trailways,** 100 Sewall St. (828-1151). To Boston (2hr., 10 per day, $16.50) and Bangor (2hr., 3 per day, $20). Metro buses #5 and #3 run to and from the station (774-0351). Office open daily 5:30am-8:30pm. **Greyhound/Vermont Transit,** 950 Congress St. (772-6587), on the western outskirts of town. *Be cautious here at night.* Take bus #1 "Congress St." downtown. Open daily 6:30am-7:15pm. To Boston (2hr., 9 per day, $13) and Bangor (2½-3½hr., 6 per day, $17).

**Ferries: Prince of Fundy Cruises,** P.O. Box 4216, 468 Commercial St. (800-341-7540, 800-482-0955 or 775-5616 in ME). Ferries to Yarmouth, NS leave from the Portland International Ferry Terminal, on Commercial St. near the Million Dollar Bridge. Runs May to mid-June and mid-Sept. to late Oct. $60, ages 5-14 $30, car $80, bike $7; late June to mid-Sept. $80/$40/$98/$10. Reservations strongly recommended. Boats depart Portland at 9pm; the 11hr. trip takes the whole night. Cabins available.

**Public Transit: Metro Bus** (774-0351) offers service within and beyond downtown. Most routes run 6am-7pm. $1, students 75¢, seniors 50¢, under 5 free, transfers free.

**Visitor Info: Visitors Information Bureau,** 305 Commercial St. (772-5800), at Center St. Open M-F 8am-6pm, Sa-Su 10am-6pm; mid-Oct. to mid-May M-F 9am-5pm, Sa-Su 10am-5pm.

**Hotlines: Rape Crisis,** 774-3613. **Crisis Intervention Hotline,** 800-660-8500. Both 24hr.

**Hospitals: Maine Medical Center,** 22 Bramhall St. (871-0111). **Women's Community Health Services,** 773-7247 or 800-666-7247. Open daily 9am-5pm.

**Internet Access: JavaNet Café,** 37 Exchange St. (773-2469). Open M-Th 8am-11pm, F-Sa 8am-midnight, Su 8am-10pm. $6 per hr.

**Post Office:** 622 Congress St. (871-8449). Open M-F 8:30am-5pm, Sa 9am-noon. **ZIP code:** 04104. **Area code:** 207.

## ⬛ ACCOMMODATIONS

Portland has some inexpensive accommodations, but prices jump during the summer. At exit 8 off I-95, **Super 8** (854-1881) and budget rates (a few singles at $35; most start around $60) congregate.

🛏 **Portland Youth Hostel (HI-AYH),** 645 Congress St. (874-3281). Centrally located in a university dorm (Portland Hall), near the best restaurants, sights, and nightlife spots. 48 beds in clean triples with bath and shower. Energetic and helpful staff. Common room with TV, kitchen, bike storage. $16, nonmembers $19. $10 deposit required. Check-out 11am. Free parking. Reservations recommended. Open June-Aug.

**YMCA,** 70 Forest Ave. (874-1111), on the north side of Congress St., 1 block from post office. Men only. Access to kitchen, pool, and exercise facilities. 85 rooms. Singles $26 per night, $87 per week. Key deposit $10. Check-in 11am-8:30pm.

**The Inn at St. John,** 939 Congress St. (773-6481 or 800-636-9127), across from the bus station. An upscale environment makes for a pricier alternative to the hostel. Free local calls and parking. Continental breakfast included. Kitchen, laundry facilities, and bike storage available. Tidy, tasteful singles and doubles start at $50, $40 in winter. Rooms with private bath are available.

**Wassamki Springs,** 56 Saco St. (839-4276), in Scarborough. Closest campground (10min. drive) to Portland. Drive 6mi. west on Congress St. (becomes Rt. 22, then County Rd.), then turn right on Saco St. Full facilities plus a sandy beach. Flocks of migrant Winnebagos nest among cozy, fairly private sites bordering a lake. Sites $21 for 2 people, with hookup $23-25; $4 per additional person; add $2 for lakefront sites. Free showers. Reserve 2 weeks in advance, especially July-Aug. Open May to mid-Oct.

## ⚫ FOOD

Life is de bubbles for seafood lovers; Portland loves to chop *le poisson* and make it taste nice, as well as to boil lobsters and sauté clams in ze spice. Do-it-yourselfers can buy seafood, dead or alive—or just roam—at the port on **Commercial St.**

**Federal Spice,** 225 Federal St. (774-6404), just off Congress St. This Portland favorite whips up cheap, bold, healthy home-cooking in a hurry using spicy hot elements from Caribbean, South American, and Asian cuisine all under $6. Open M-Sa 11am-9pm.

**Gilbert's Chowder House,** 92 Commercial St. (871-5636). The local choice for seafood. A large bowl of chowder in a bread bowl is a meal in itself ($5). On summer nights Gilbert's patio on the water is one of the nicest spots in town. Open Su-Th 11am-9pm, F-Sa 11am-11pm; Oct.-May call for hrs.

**Seamen's Club,** 375 Fore St. (774-7777), at Exchange St. in the Old Port, with a harbor view. Top-notch seafood steeped in briny lore. Salads and sandwiches around $6, dinner around $13. Fresh lobster year-round. Near all the best nightspots on Fore St. Open M-F 10:30am-9:30pm, Sa-Su 10am-10:30pm.

## ⚫ SIGHTS

Many of Portland's spectacular sights lie outside the city proper, along the rugged coast or on the beautiful, secluded islands a short ferry ride offshore. **Two Lights State Park,** across the Million Dollar Bridge on State St. and south along Rt. 77 to Cape Elizabeth, is a wonderful place to picnic and relax, and is not usually crowded. *(799-5871.)* America's oldest ferry service, **Casco Bay Lines** on State Pier near the corner of Commercial and Franklin, runs year-round to the nearby islands. *(774-7871.)* Daily **ferries** depart approximately every hour for nearby **Peaks Island.** *(M-Sa 5:45am-10:30pm. Round-trip $5.25.)* On the island, you can rent a bike at **Brad's Recycled Bike Shop.** *(115 Island Ave. 766-5631; $4 per hr., $7.50 for up to 3hr., $10 per day.)* Waves crash on **Long Island's** quiet, unpopulated beach; Casco Bay Lines runs 10 ferries there daily. Starting at Long Island, you can island-hop by catching later ferries to other islands. *(Same price as Peaks ferry.)* Getting to more than 2 islands will take all day.

The sea calls, but Portland does have landlubber activities. The **Portland Museum of Art,** at the intersection of Congress, High, and Free St.; collects American art by John Singer Sargent, Wyeth, and Winslow Homer. *(7 Congress Sq. 775-6148 or 800-639-4067. Open May 31-Oct. 11 M-W and Sa-Su 10am-5pm, Th-F 10am-9pm. $6, students and seniors $5, ages 6-12 $1.)* The **Wadsworth-Longfellow House** was the home of 19th century poet Henry Wadsworth Longfellow, and is now a museum of social history and U.S. literature focusing on late 18th- and 19th-century antiques as well as on the life of the poet. *(489 Congress St. 879-0427. Purchase tickets at 489 Congress St. House open June-Oct. daily 10am-4pm. Gallery and museum store also open Nov.-May W-Sa noon-4pm. $5, seniors $4, under 12 $1. Price includes admission to a neighboring history museum with rotating exhibits. Tours every 30-40min.)*

NEW ENGLAND

## 🎵 ENTERTAINMENT AND NIGHTLIFE

During the summer months, Portland brims with performing arts. Signs advertising concerts and theatrical productions are posted in the city; the visitors center (see **Practical Information,** above) has schedules. The **Portland Symphony** presents concerts renowned throughout the northeast (842-0800; 50% student discount).

Traditionally on the first Sun. in June, the **Old Port Festival** fills several blocks from Federal to Commercial St. with as many as 50,000 people (772-6828). On summer afternoons during the **Noontime Performance Series,** a variety of bands perform in Portland's Monument Sq. and Congress Sq. (772-6828; mid-June to Aug.).

For a taste of the hometown spirit, the **Portland Sea Dogs,** an AA minor-league baseball team, take the field from Apr. to mid-Sept. at **Hadlock Field** on Park Ave. (tickets 879-9500; $4-6, under 17 $2-5).

After dark, the Old Port area, known as "the strip," especially **Fore St.** between Union and Exchange Sts., livens up with pleasant "shoppes" and a few good pubs. **Brian Boru,** 57 Center St., provides a mellow pub scene. The brew nachos ($5) are nice, as are $2 pints all day Su. (780-1506. Open daily 11:30am-1am.) **Gritty MacDuff's,** 396 Fore St., brews its own sweet beer for adoring locals; tasty pints are worth the $3. (772-2739. Open daily 11:30am-1am.) The English pub around the corner, **Three Dollar Dewey's,** 241 Commercial St., serves over 100 varieties of beer and ale (36 on tap at $3-3.50), along with great chili (cup $3.50) and free popcorn (772-3310; open Su-Th 11:30am-midnight, F-Sa 11:30am-1am). The **Dry Dock Restaurant & Tavern,** 84 Commercial St., is a great place to relax with a few drinks and friends. The bar is outside with a great waterfront view. (774-3550. Open daily 11am-1am). Info on Portland's jazz, blues, and club scene packs the *Casco Bay Weekly* and *FACE*, both of which are free in many restaurants and stores.

## SOUTH OF PORTLAND

**Old Orchard Beach,** a kingdom of tackiness and middle-aged Bud drinkers, reigns 10mi. south of Portland on U.S. 1. The plastic jewel in the beach's crown is the **Wonderland Arcade,** "the First Amusement Park in New England." Parking costs $3, and the cheapest hotels cost around $40 for a double.

More tasteful (and expensive) is **Kennebunk,** and, 8mi. east on Rt. 35, its coastal counterpart **Kennebunkport** of Presidential fame. If you want to bypass busy U.S. 1, take the Maine Turnpike (I-95) south of Portland to exit 3, then take Fletcher St. east into Kennebunk. Spending the night in Kennebunk ain't cheap; avoid penury by camping. **Salty Acres Campground,** 4½mi. northeast of Kennebunkport on winding Rt. 9, offers swimming, a grocery store, laundry, phones, showers, and a convenient location about 1mi. from beaches. Sites are small and closely packed. (967-8623. 185 sites for 2 $16, with electricity $18, full hookup $22; $8 per additional adult; $2 per additional child. Open May-Oct. No reservations.) A little farther out, the **Mousam River Campground,** on Alfred Rd. just west of exit 3 off I-95 in west Kennebunk, has free showers, a small pool, and tightly packed but tidy campsites. (985-2507. 115 RV sites for 2 $22, $21 with AAA; $4 per additional adult; $3 per additional person ages 13-17. Open mid-May to mid-Oct.)

Both of these towns are popular hideaways for wealthy authors and artists. Rare and used bookstores line U.S. 1 just south of Kennebunk, while art galleries fill the town itself. You could spend a day, and a fortune, exploring all the little shops in town. The blue-blooded (and gray-haired) meet at Kennebunkport, which reluctantly grew famous as the summer home of former President Bush. The **Kennebunk-Kennebunkport Chamber of Commerce,** 17 U.S. 100/Western Ave. (967-0857), in Kennebunkport, has a free guide (open daily 9am-6pm; off-season 9am-5pm).

South of Kennebunk on U.S. 1 lies **Ogunquit,** which means "beautiful place by the sea." The long, sandy shoreline is probably the best beach north of Cape Cod. Ogunquit also has one of New England's largest (although seasonal) gay communities. The **Ogunquit Information Bureau** (646-2939), on U.S. 1, has info. (Open M-Th noon-5pm, F and Su noon-6pm, Sa 10am-6pm; early Sept. to late May daily 9am-

## THE APPALACHIAN TRAIL

Stretching 2160mi. from Mt. Katahdin, ME, to Springer Mountain, GA, the Appalachian Trail, or "AT," follows the path of the Appalachian Mountains along the eastern United States. Use of the AT is free, although only foot travelers may access the trail. The trail cuts through 14 states, 8 national forests, and 6 national parks; 98% of the Trail is on public land. Generally, the trail is very accessible, crossed by roads along its entire length except for the northernmost 100mi. Although many sections of the trail makes excellent day hikes or overnights, about 2500 "through-hikers" attempt a continuous hike of the AT annually. 3-sided first come, first served shelters dot the trail, spaced about a day's journey apart. Hikers take advantage of the many streams and nearby towns to stock up on water and supplies. White blazes on rocks and trees mark the entire length of the main trail, while blue blazes mark side trails. Numerous publications are available to facilitate your journey; contact the **Center for AT Studies,** P.O. Box 525, Hot Springs, NC 28743 (704-622-7601, M-Sa 10am-10pm; fax 704-622-7601; email atcenter@trailplace.com; www.trailplace.com) for more information, including a list of publications.

5pm.) Weather-permitting, biking is the best way to travel Maine's rocky shores and spare yourself the thick summer traffic. **Wheels and Wares,** U.S. 1 on the Wells/Ogunquit border, rents mountain bikes (646-5774; $20 per day, $25 per 24hr.; open daily 10am-6pm). **Moody,** just south of Ogunquit, has budget motels.

The **Rachel Carson National Wildlife Refuge,** ½mi. off U.S. 1 on Rt. 9, provides a secluded escape from tourist throngs to the west. A trail winds through the salt marsh, home to over 200 species of shorebirds and waterfowl. (646-9226. Open M-F 8am-4:30pm, Sa-Su 10am-2pm; off-season M-F 8am-4:30pm. Trail open daily sunrise-sunset. Free.) In nearby Wells, the **National Estuarine Research Reserve,** at the junction of U.S. 1 and Rt. 9, sprawls over meadows and beaches and offers tours of the estuary, bird life, and wildflowers (open daily 8am-5pm).

Nearby **Perkins Cove,** which is accessible only by a very windy and narrow road, charms the argyle socks off the polo shirt crowd with boutiques hawking seashell sculptures. The 2 **Barnacle Billy's** restaurants (646-5575), 20 yd. apart on Oar Weed Rd., practice an interesting division of labor. The original (a lobster pound) broils, bakes, and sautes lobsters, while their newer full-service location has a bigger menu. (Both open daily noon-9:30pm with free parking for patrons.)

# NORTHERN MAINE COAST

Much like the coastal region south of Portland, the north offers the traveler unforgettable beaches, windswept ocean vistas, and verdant forests—for a price. Lodging in L.L. Bean country isn't cheap, but camping or just passing through can give all the flavor, without the guilt. Although traffic can be horrendous, public transportation is virtually non-existent. Driving along U.S. 1 does offer a charming and unadulterated (if slow-moving) view of coastal Maine.

**FREEPORT.** About 20mi. north of Portland on I-95, Freeport once garnered glory as the "birthplace of Maine." The 1820 signing of documents declaring the state's independence from Massachusetts took place at the historic **Jameson Tavern,** 115 Main St., right next to L. L. Bean. Freeport is now known as the factory outlet capital of the world, with over 100 downtown stores attracting urbanite travelers sick of the woods. The granddaddy of them all, **L.L. Bean,** began manufacturing Maine Hunting Shoes in Freeport in 1912. Bean sells everything in outdoor gear, and clothes that have come to epitomize preppy *haute couture;* many a college student and politician can be summed up as "L.L. Bean-y." The **factory outlet,** 11 Depot St., behind Bannister Shoes, is the place for bargains (865-4057 or 800-341-4341; open daily 9am-10pm; Jan. to late May 9am-9pm). The **retail store,** 95 Main St., is open 24hr., 365 days a year. Only 3 events have ever caused the store to close: a nearby fire in the late 1980s, the death of President Kennedy, and the death of L.L. Bean founder Leon Leonwood Bean. (865-4761.)

In a town where even fast food is fancy (McDonald's and Arby's are housed in stately Victorian mansions), unpretentious eateries are welcome sights. **DeRosier's,** 120 Main St., across from L.L. Bean, has good pizza sandwiches, and ice cream (865-6290; open M-Sa 9am-9pm, Su 11am-9pm; closed Su in winter). **Chowder Express and Sandwich Shop,** 2 Mechanic St., sells delicious sandwiches ($4-5), steaming bowls of chowder ($4-5), and some of the best bagels in town (about $2 with cream cheese; 865-3404). For the past 100yrs., the soil at the **Desert of Maine Campground,** 2mi. west of exit 19 off I-95, has eroded, exposing acres upon acres of beach-like sand. The campground has 48 sites, nature trails, amazing dunes, a museum, and shuttles into downtown Freeport (sites $19, with hookup $25).

**CAMDEN.** In the summer, khaki-clad crowds flock to Camden, 100mi. north of Portland, to dock their yachts alongside the tall-masted schooners in Penobscot Bay. Cruises are generally out of the budgeteer's price range, but the **Rockport-Camden-Lincolnville Chamber of Commerce** (236-4404, outside ME 800-223-5459), on the public landing in Camden behind Cappy's Chowder House, can tell you which are most affordable. They also have info on the sparse budget accommodations. (Open M-F 9am-5pm, Sa 10am-5pm, Su noon-2pm; mid-Oct. to mid-May closed Su.) The **Camden Hills State Park,** 1¼mi. north of town on U.S. 1, is almost always full in July and Aug. but you are fairly certain to get a site if you arrive before 2pm. This beautiful coastal retreat offers more than 25mi. of trails, including one which leads up to **Mt. Battie** and has a harbor view. (236-3109; reservations 800-332-1501 in ME, 287-3824 out of state. Sites $12, day use $2. Free showers. Open mid-May to mid-Oct.). The folks at **Maine Sports,** on U.S. 1, in Rockport just south of Camden, teach/lead/rent/sell a wide array of sea-worthy vehicles. **Kayaks** will only be rented to those with paddling experience, but anyone can join a tour. (236-8797. 24hr. singles rental $40, doubles $55; ask about overnights to nearby islands. Open daily 8am-9pm; Sept.-May Su-Th 9am-6pm, F 9am-8pm. 2hr. harbor tour $30.)

Parking in Camden is nearly impossible, and driving around to find a spot can take hours; allow extra time. Eating in Camden is never cheap, but the oceanside experience may be worth it. In the heart of downtown is **Cappy's Chowder House,** 1 Main St., a kindly, comfortable hangout where great seafood draws tourists and townspeople alike. The seasonal seafood pie ($9), made with scallops, shrimp, and clams, is exquisite. The line goes out the door and around the corner; be ready to wait. (236-2254. Open daily 11am-midnight; in winter 11am-10pm.) **Fitzpatrick's,** on Sharp's Wharf, has omelettes, sandwiches, and burgers, all for less than $7 (236-2041; open May-Oct. Su-Th 7am-8pm, F-Sa 7am-8:30pm; call for winter hrs.).

The **Maine State Ferry Service** (624-7777 or 800-491-4883), 5mi. north of Camden in Lincolnville, takes you across the Bay to Islesboro Island. (20min.; 7-9 per day; last return trip 4:30pm; round-trip $4.50, ages 5-11 $2, bike $4, car and driver $13. Parking $4.) The ferry also has an agency on U.S. 1 in **Rockland,** 517A Main St. (596-2202), that shuttles to North Haven, Vinalhaven, and Matinicus. Rates and schedules change with the weather.

# MT. DESERT ISLAND AND BAR HARBOR

Mt. Desert Island is anything but deserted. During the summer, the island swarms with tourists lured by the thick forests and mountainous landscape. Roughly half of the island is covered by Acadia National Park, which harbors some of the last protected marine, mountain, and forest environments on the New England coast. Bar Harbor, on the eastern side, is by far the most crowded and glitzy part of the island, sandwiched between the Blue Hill and Frenchmen Bays. Once a summer hamlet for the very wealthy, the town now welcomes a motley *mélange* of R&R-seekers; the monied have fled to the more secluded Northeast and Seal Harbor, but the town still maintains its overpriced traditions.

# ⁊ ORIENTATION AND PRACTICAL INFORMATION

Mt. Desert Island is shaped roughly like a really big lobster claw, 14mi. long and 12mi. wide. To the east on Rt. 3 lie Bar Harbor and Seal Harbor. South on Rt. 198 near the cleft is **Northeast Harbor.** Across Somes Sound on Rt. 102 is **Southwest Harbor,** where fishing and shipbuilding thrive without the taint of tacky tourism. **Rt. 3** runs through Bar Harbor, becoming **Mt. Desert St.;** it and **Cottage St.** are the major east-west arteries. **Rt. 102** circuits the western half of the island.

**Buses: Greyhound/Vermont Transit** (800-451-3292) leaves for Bangor ($9) and Boston ($39) daily May-June and Sept.-Oct. 6:45am; July-Aug. 8am; in front of **Fox Run Travel,** 4 Kennebec St. (288-3366). Tickets are sold at Fox Run (open M-F 7:30am-5pm). 15% discount for students, 10% for seniors. Fox Run's owner comes to meet the bus for last-minute ticket purchases 30min. before departure.

**Ferries: Beal & Bunker,** from Northeast Harbor on the town dock (244-3575). To: Great Cranberry Island (20min.; 6 per day; $10, under 12 $5). Open late June to Sept. 6 M-F 7:30am-6pm, Sa-Su 10am-6pm; call for winter hrs. **Bay Ferries** (888-249-7245), Bar Harbor. To Yarmouth, NS. (2½hr.; 2 per day; $46, ages 5-12 $23, seniors $41, car $108, bike $15. Reservations recommended, $5 fee.)

**Bike Rental: Bar Harbor Bicycle Shop,** 141 Cottage St. (288-3886). Mountain bikes $10 for 4hr., $15 per day. Helmet, lock, and map. 20% discount for rentals of 5 days or longer. Driver's license, cash deposit, or credit card required. Open daily 8am-8pm; Sept.-June 9am-6pm.

**National Park Canoe Rentals** (244-5854), north end of Long Pond off Rt. 102. Canoe rental $22 for 4hr., $32 per day; kayak rental $25 per ½-day, $50 per day. Open mid-May to mid-Oct. daily 8am-5pm. Reservations are strongly recommended.

**Visitor Info: Acadia National Park Visitors Center** (288-4932 or 288-5262), 3mi. north of Bar Harbor on Rt. 3. Open daily mid-June to mid-Sept. 8am-6pm; mid-Apr. to mid-June and mid-Sept. to Oct. 8am-4:30pm. **Park Headquarters** (288-3338), 3mi. west of Bar Harbor on Rt. 233. Open M-F 8am-4:30pm. **Bar Harbor Chamber of Commerce** (288-5103), in the Marine Atlantic Ferry Terminal, Rt. 3. Open M-F 8am-5pm, Sa 10am-5pm, Su noon-5pm; in winter M-F 8am-4pm. **Mt. Desert Island Regional Chamber of Commerce** (288-3411), on Rt. 3 at the entrance to Thompson Island. In the same building is an **Acadia National Park Information Center** (288-9702). Both open daily July-Aug. 9am-8pm; mid-May to July and Sept. 6 to mid-Oct. 10am-6pm.

**Hotlines: Downeast Sexual Assault Helpline,** 800-228-2470. **Mental Health Crisis Line,** 800-245-8889. Both 24hr.

**Emergency: Acadia National Park Law Enforcement,** 288-3369.

**Post Office:** 55 Cottage St. (288-3122). Open M-F 8am-4:45pm, Sa 9am-noon. **ZIP code:** 04609. **Area code:** 207.

# ▟ ACCOMMODATIONS

Grand hotels and prices linger from the island's exclusive resort days. Still, a few reasonable establishments do exist, particularly on **Rt. 3** north of Bar Harbor. Camping spots cover the island, especially **Rt. 198** and **102,** well west of town.

**Bar Harbor Youth Hostel (HI-AYH),** 27 Kennebec St. (288-5587), Bar Harbor; mailing address P.O. Box 32. In the parish house of St. Saviour's Episcopal Church, adjacent to the bus stop. 2 large dorm rooms which accommodate 20 in cheery red-and-white bunks. Common room, full kitchen, and a perfect location. Organized activities include movie nights. $12, nonmembers $15. Linen $2. Occasional pancake breakfast ($3). Lockout 9am-5pm. Curfew 11pm. Open mid-June to Sept.

**Mt. Desert Island YWCA,** 36 Mt. Desert St. (288-5008), Bar Harbor, near downtown. Women only. Common space, full kitchen, laundry. Singles with hallway bath $30 per night; doubles $25 per person; solarium with 7 beds $20 per bed; weekly rates $90/$75/$65. $25 deposit. Open daily 9am-9pm; off-season M-F 9am-4pm. Reserve early.

**White Birches Campground** (244-3797), Southwest Harbor, on Seal Cove Rd. 1mi. west of Rt. 102. 60 widely spaced, wooded sites offer an escape from the touristy areas. $18 for up to 4 people, with hookup $22; weekly $108/$132; $2 per additional person. Free hot showers, fireplace, bathrooms. Open mid-May to mid-Oct. daily 8am-9pm for check-in. Reservations recommended, especially in July-Aug.

**Acadia National Park Campgrounds: Blackwoods** (288-3274, reservations 800-365-2267), 5mi. south of Bar Harbor on Rt. 3. Over 300 sites. Mid-June to mid-Sept. $16; mid-May to mid-June and mid-Sept. to mid-Oct. $14; mid-Dec. to mid-Mar. free. Group sites also available. Reserve in summer. **Seawall** (244-3600), Rt. 102A on the western side of the island, 4mi. south of Southwest Harbor. 10min. walk from the ocean. Toilets but no hookups. Showers available ($1 per 6min.). First come, first served walk-in sites $10, drive-in $14, RV sites $14. Open late May to Sept. daily 7:15am-9pm.

## 🔆 🎵 FOOD, NIGHTLIFE, AND ENTERTAINMENT

🦞 **Beal's** (244-7178 or 800-245-7178), Southwest Harbor, at the end of Clark Point Rd. Superb prices for lobster. Pick a live crustacean from a tank ($10-13); Beal's does the rest. Kitchen closed off-season, but fresh seafood is sold. Open daily mid-May to early Sept. 9am-8pm; off-season 9am-5pm. Hrs. vary with weather.

**Jordan's,** 80 Cottage St. (288-3586), Bar Harbor. A favorite of locals and visitors, especially those who love muffins (6 for $4.25) and plate-sized blueberry pancakes ($3). Breakfast is served all day. Open daily 5am-2pm except for 3 weeks in Nov.

**The Colonel's Deli Bakery and Restaurant** (276-5147), on Main St. in Northeast Harbor. Sandwiches so big it's hard to get one into your mouth (around $4.50). Taking one with you makes a cheap dinner in the national park. The desserts are unusual and delicious ($1-2). Open mid-Apr. to Oct. daily 6:30am-9pm.

Most after-dinner pleasures on the island are simple. **Ben and Bill's Chocolate Emporium,** 66 Main St., near Cottage St., boasts 50 flavors of homemade ice cream, including (no kidding) lobster (cone $2.50-3.75), which is almost certainly an acquired taste, and enough luscious chocolates to challenge Willy Wonka (288-3281; open mid-Feb. to Jan. daily 9am-midnight). **Geddy's Pub,** 19 Main St., is a three-tiered entertainment complex with a bar, dancing, and live music until 10:30pm; a DJ takes over until closing. Geddy's serves up a decent dinner until 9:30pm and pizzas until 10pm. (288-5077. No cover. Open Apr.-Oct. daily 11:30-12:30am; winter hrs. vary.) Locals prefer the **Lompoc Café & Brew Pub,** 36 Rodick St., off Cottage St., which features Bar Harbor Real Ale and live jazz, blues, Celtic, rock, or folk. (288-9392. Shows F-Sa nights; cover $1-2. Open May-Oct. daily 11:30am-1am; winter hrs. vary.) The Art Deco **Criterion Theater,** on Cottage St., shows movies in the summer. (288-3441. 2 evening shows daily. $6.50, under 12 $4, balcony seats $7.50, seniors $5.50. Box office open 30min. before show.)

## 👁 SIGHTS

The staff at the **Mt. Desert Oceanarium,** at the end of Clark Pt. Rd. near Beals in Southwest Harbor, knows its sea stuff. The main museum, reminiscent of a grammar school science fair, fascinates children and some adults. (244-7330. Open mid-May to late Oct. M-Sa 9am-5pm. Ticket for all 3 facilities $12.20, ages 4-12 $9.15.) Cruises head out to sea from a number of points. **Whale Watcher, Inc.,** Harbor Pl., offers sailing trips (2hr., $26); lobstering and seal watching trips (1½hr., $16.75); and whale-watching trips. (1 West St. 288-3322. 3hr., $32; operates May-Oct.; reservations recommended; call for schedule.) The **Acadian Whale Watcher,** Golden Anchor Pier, West St., has occasional sunset cruises. (288-9794. Buy tickets at corner of Cottage and Main St. 4 trips per day, whale watch/puffin tour combo $34, $20 for kids ages 6-14. Operates May-Nov.)

**Wildwood Stables,** along Park Loop Rd. in Seal Harbor, takes tourists on explorations of the island via horse and carriage. (276-3622. 1hr. tour $13, seniors $12, ages 6-12 $7, ages 2-5 $4. 2hr. tour $16.50/$15.50/$8/$5. Reservations recommended.)

## ACADIA NATIONAL PARK

The 33,000 acres that comprise Acadia National Park offer strolls and hikes galore. Millionaire and expert horseman John D. Rockefeller, fearing the island would someday be overrun by cars, funded the park's 120mi. of trails. These **carriage roads** make for easy walking, fun mountain biking, and pleasant carriage rides.

**Precipice Trail,** one of the most popular hikes, is closed June to late Aug. to accommodate nesting peregrine falcons. The 5mi. **Eagle Lake Carriage Rd.** is graded for bicyclists. Touring the park by auto costs $10 for 7 days, $5 per pedestrian or cyclist. Seniors can purchase a lifetime pass for $10. The *Biking and Hiking Guide to the Carriage Roads* ($6), available at the visitors center and in bookstores, offers invaluable directions for the more labyrinthine trails.

About 4mi. south of Bar Harbor on Rt. 3, **Park Loop Rd.** runs along the shore of the island, where great waves crash against steep granite cliffs. The sea comes into **Thunder Hole** with a bang at half-tide. Swimming can be found in the relatively warm **Echo Lake** or at **Sand Beach,** both of which have lifeguards in the summer. To be the first person in the U.S. to see the sunrise, climb Cadillac Mountain just before dawn (4-4:30am in summer). Cadillac Mountain, at 1530 feet, is also the highest point on the Atlantic seaboard north of Brazil.

# NEW HAMPSHIRE

There are two sides to New Hampshire; the rugged landscape and natural beauty that covers 90% of the land, and the tax-free outlets, tourist traps, and state liquor stores that line most of the highways. The first colony to declare its independence from Great Britain, New Hampshire has kept its backwoods libertarian charm, still shouting "Live Free or Die!"

## ■ PRACTICAL INFORMATION

**Capital:** Concord.
**Visitor Info: Office of Travel and Tourism,** P.O. Box 856, Concord 03302 (603-271-2666, 800-386-4664; www.visitnh.gov). **Outdoor report:** 800-258-3608, 24hrs. **Fish and Game Dept.,** 2 Hazen Dr., Concord 03301 (603-271-3421), furnishes info on hunting and fishing regulations and license fees. **U.S. Forest Service,** 719 North Main St., Laconia 03246 (603-528-8721). Open M-F 8am-4:30pm.
**Postal Abbreviation:** NH. **Sales Tax:** 8% on meals and rooms. **Area Code:** 603.

## PORTSMOUTH

Although New Hampshire's seacoast is the smallest in the nation, with only 13mi. fronting the Atlantic Ocean, the state makes the most of it's toehold on the water. Portsmouth, once the colonial capital, is one of the nicest seaside towns north of Boston. Most buildings date to the 18th century, while a handful were built in the mid 1600s. Although not large by any standards, Portsmouth is exceptionally cultured—and expensive. History is the main attraction, seafood reigns supreme, and a pint of local ale is the mainstay after dinner.

■ **PRACTICAL INFORMATION.** Just 57mi. north of Boston, Portsmouth is situated at the junction of U.S. 1, 1A, and I-95. The town is most easily navigated by foot; leave your car in one of the inexpensive parking lots ($2-4) downtown. State St. runs north/south through downtown and is bisected by Pleasant and Fleet St. **Buses: Vermont Transit/Greyhound,** 1 Market Sq., heads to Portsmouth from Boston (7 per day, 1hr., $12). **Wade's Taxi:** 436-0044. **Visitor Info: Greater Portsmouth Chamber of Commerce** (436-1118), 500 Market St., outside downtown. In summer, open 8:30am-5pm M-W; 8:30am-7pm Th-F; 10am-5pm Sa-Su; rest of year, open 8:30am-5pm M-F. **Public Transit: Seacoast Trolley** (431-6975) runs hourly in summer from 10am-5pm, with 17 stops in and around Portsmouth. $2. **Hospital: Portsmouth General** (436-5110), a few mi.mi. from town at 333 Borthwick Ave. **Post Office:** 80 Daniel St. (431-1300). Open M-F 8am-5pm, Sa 9am-noon. **Zip code:** 03801. **Area code:** 603.

**ACCOMMODATIONS AND FOOD.** Portsmouth is not the best place to spend the night if you can't afford to part with your Ben Franklins. Accommodations in town are pricey; try U.S. 1A south of Portsmouth for typically drab motels. A nice alternative is **Camp Eaton** in York Harbor, ME. It's about 15mi. north of Portsmouth off Rt. 1. The bathrooms are immaculate and the showers are hot. (207-363-3424. Sites $29 for 2.) The best bet may be to splurge and stay right in Portsmouth to take advantage of the great nightlife without having to drive out of town late at night.

■ **Pier II,** 10 State St. on the waterfront under the Rt. 1 bridge to Kittery, offers some of the best food in town. Lunch is your best bet here, with hearty sandwiches ($6-8), steamed mussels or clams ($9), and other traditional New England seafood. (436-0669. Open daily May-Nov. 11:30am-1am. Closed Dec.-Apr.) Portsmouth offers plenty of other dining options, with many fine establishments dotting Market St. Unfortunately, prices are not the budget traveler's friend in Portsmouth. For inexpensive baked goods, try **Cafe Brioche,** 14 Market St. (430-9225. Open M-F 6:30am-11pm, Sa-Su 6:30am-9pm.)

**SIGHTS AND ENTERTAINMENT.** Modern Portsmouth sells itself with its colonial past. The most prestigious and well-known example is **Strawberry Banke,** on the corner of Marcy and Hancock streets. The community was first settled as Strawberry Banke in 1630 and did not assume the name of Portsmouth until 1653. The museum is a collection of several dozen original buildings from the pre-Portsmouth period. Costumed interpreters and craftsmen give visitors a feel for what life was like before the Revolution. (433-1100. Open daily 10am-5pm from Apr.-Oct. $12, under 18 $8; tickets are good for 2 days.) For something more modern, try the **U.S.S. Albacore,** a research submarine built locally at the Portsmouth Naval Shipyard. The sub was retired in 1972 and returned to Portsmouth in 1984, and has since served as a museum of both marine exploration and naval life. (436-3680. Open daily 9:30am-5:30pm, May-Oct. Hours vary in winter. $4, seniors $3, children under 18 $2.) Step back into the past with **Ghostly Tours of Portsmouth, NH.** Tours begin at either 7pm or 8pm and begin from the **Rusty Hammer Restaurant** at 49 Pleasant St. Hooded guides lead visitors on a candlelit tour through Old Portsmouth, recounting ghost stories and witch tales along the way (433-8888. Open June-Oct., tour times vary, call for reservations.) Once you've had the bejesus scared out of you, you'll be ready to relax with a cold brew at the **Portsmouth Gaslight Company,** 64 Market St. The Gaslight Co. offers a very mellow, fun atmosphere (430-9122. Open Su-Th 11:30am-10pm, F-Sa 11:30am-11pm. Music F-Sa on deck until 1am; $5 cover for deck.)

## NEW HAMPSHIRE SKI RESORTS

The various ranges within the White Mountains offer numerous opportunities for skiing. **Ski-93** is a service which provides information and reservations for 5 ski resorts in the White Mountains (745-8101 or 800-937-5493, PO Box 517, Lincoln 03251). Winters in New England are long, so skiing is generally available from Nov. through Apr., but can vary drastically with weather changes.

**CRANMORE.** Very close to North Conway, and especially convenient if you wish to combine skiing with shopping at the outlets in town. *(Lift tickets: $29, ages 6-12 $15; lift operates from 8:30am-4pm.)*

**ATTITASH.** Located along U.S. 302 near North Conway, Attitash is expensive, but offers lots of trails and 2 mountains. In the summer, Attitash runs a very popular alpine slide. *(Lift tickets for weekends, weekdays, and holidays: $48/$42/$50, children $30/ $27/$30. Alpine slide open 10am-6pm. Single ride $9, double $15, unlimited $21.)*

**WILDCAT MOUNTAIN.** Just outside Pinkham Notch on Rt. 16, Wildcat offers yet another choice in the dizzying array. *(Lift tickets for weekends and weekdays: $46/$39, teens $39/$39, children $29/$25.)*

**LOON MOUNTAIN.** 3mi. east of Lincoln on Rt. 112. Guarantees less-crowded ski conditions by limiting ticket sales, so come early. Loon offers summer activities, including biking and horseback riding. Around the third week of Sept., Loon hosts the annual **Highland Games,** attracting more than 20,000 spectators. *(745-8111. Lift tickets for weekends and weekdays: $44/$37, teens $40/$32, children $28/$25.)*

**WATERVILLE VALLEY.** Off exit 28, about 20min. south of Franconia Notch, with excellent alpine and nordic ski trails. *(Lift tickets for weekends and weekdays: $46/$40, students $41/$33.)*

**CANNON MOUNTAIN.** Conveniently located within Franconia Notch State Park and somewhat less expensive than other local resorts. *(823-5563. Lift tickets for weekends and weekdays: $39/$28, teens $32/$19, children and seniors $27/$19.)*

## WHITE MOUNTAINS

In the late 19th century, the White Mountains was an immensely popular summer retreat for wealthy New Englanders and New Yorkers. Grand hotels and stately homes were scattered across the terrain, and frequent train service whisked passengers to the region. One hundred years later, public transportation is virtually non-existent, and the region is less accessible. Although many spots retain the high prices of yesteryear, the White Mountains still make an excellent vacation destination for the spirited vacationer willing to bypass the strip malls and mini-golf parks and rough it a bit. Campsites and cabins can be found throughout the mountains, by lakes and rivers, and deep within the forest. Use caution, as the weather can change quickly, making a sunny afternoon wet in a matter of minutes.

**7 PRACTICAL INFORMATION.** Finding the White Mountains by bus is considerably easier than getting around once there. **Concord Trailways** (228-3300 or 800-639-3317) runs from Boston to Concord (18 per day, $12); Conway (1 per day, $26); and Franconia (1 per day, $26). **Vermont Transit** (800-451-3292) stops its Boston-to-Vermont buses in Concord (3 daily, $11) at the Trailways terminal, 30 Stickney Ave. The **Appalachian Mountain Club (AMC)** runs a **shuttle service** (466-2727) among locations along the Appalacian Trail in the White Mountains. Consult AMC's *The Guide* for a complete map of routes and times; reservations are recommended for all stops and required for some. (Service operates early June to early Oct. daily 8:45am-3:30pm. $7, nonmembers $8.) Local travel info can be obtained from the **White Mountain Attraction Center,** P.O. Box 10, N. Woodstock 03262 (745-8720), at exit 32 from Interstate 93 (open daily 8:30am-5:30pm). **U.S. Forest Service Ranger Stations** dot the main highways throughout the forest: **Androscoggin** (466-2713), on Rt. 16, 5mi. south of the U.S. 2 junction in Gorham; **Ammonoosuc** (869-2626), on Trudeau Rd. in Bethlehem, west of U.S. 3 on U.S. 302; and **Saco** (447-5448), on the Kancamangus Hwy. in Conway, 100 yd. off Rt. 16. Each station provides info on trail locations and conditions and a handy free guide to the local **backcountry facilities** (stations open daily 8am-4:30pm, however Ammonoosuc is only open M-F). **Pinkham Notch Visitors Center** (466-2721 or 466-2727 for reservations), 10mi. north of Jackson on Rt. 16 in Gorham, is the area's best source of info on weather and trail conditions. The center, run by the AMC, also handles reservations at any of the AMC lodgings and sells the complete line of AMC books, trail maps ($3-9), and camping and hiking accessories. (Open daily 6:30am-10pm.)

**ACCOMMODATIONS.** The AMC has its main base in the mountains at the Pinkham Notch Visitors Center, on Rt. 16 between Gorham and Jackson (see **Practical Information,** above). The area's primary source of info on camping, food, and lodging, the AMC also sells an assortment of camping and hiking accessories. The club runs 2 car-accessible lodgings in the White Mountains: **Joe Dodge Lodge** (see Pinkham Notch, p. 103) and the **Crawford Hostel,** adjoining the **Crawford Notch Depot** east of Bretton Woods on U.S. 302. The **depot** has trail guides, maps, food, camping necessities, film, and restrooms (open May to early Oct. daily 9am-5pm). The **hos-**

**tel** has 24 bunks that fill up quickly, so make reservations. (846-7773, reservations 466-2727. $18, members $16. Clean toilets, showers, functioning kitchen. Bring a sleeping bag and food. Curfew 9:30pm.) The AMC also operates a system of 8 **huts,** spaced about a day's hike apart along the **Appalachian Trail.** Guests must provide their own sleeping bags or sheets. Meals at the huts, while not as good as those back at the Dodge lodge, are ample and appetizing. (Bunk with 2 meals $56, children $35; nonmembers $62/$39.) All huts stay open for full service June to mid-Oct.; self-service rates with no meals provided are available at other times ($16, nonmembers $18; call the AMC for reservations.)

Camping is free in a number of backcountry areas throughout the **White Mountains National Forest (WMNF),** but a $20 recreation pass is needed for any car parked within the forest. Other campsites, mainly lean-tos and tent platforms with no showers or toilets, pepper the mountain trails. Most run $5 per night on a first come, first served basis, but many are free. The **U.S. Forest Service** (528-8721) or the AMC's free 2-page handout, *Backpacker Shelters, Tentsites, Campsites, and Cabins in the White Mountains* are both good sources of info. Neither camping nor fires are allowed above the tree line (approximately 4000 ft.), within 200 ft. of a trail, or within ¼mi. of roads, huts, shelters, tent platforms, lakes, or streams. Rules vary depending on forest conditions; backpackers should call the Forest Service before settling into a campsite. The Forest Service can also direct you to one of their 23 **designated campgrounds.** (800-280-2267 or 877-444-6777 for info. Sites $12-16. Bathrooms and firewood usually available. Reservation fee $10. Reserve 2 weeks in advance, especially July-Aug.)

⚠ **HIKING AND BIKING.** If you intend to spend a lot of time in the area, and are planning to do a significant amount of hiking, the *AMC White Mountain Guide* is invaluable ($22; available in most bookstores and huts). The guide includes full maps and descriptions of all the mountain trails. Hikers should bring 3 layers of clothing in all seasons: one for wind, one for rain, and at least one for warmth, as weather conditions change at a moment's notice. Black flies and swarms of mosquitoes can ruin a trip, particularly in June, so carry insect repellent.

Next to hiking, bicycling is one of the most popular ways to tour the White Mountains. Many areas are easily accessible by bike, and paths are specifically provided for bikers in some locations. The *New Hampshire Bicycle* guide and map, available at info centers, the U.S. Forest Service's bike trail guides, or *30 Bicycle Tours in New Hampshire* ($13), available at local bookstores and outdoor equipment stores, can help with planning.

## FRANCONIA NOTCH AREA

Formed by glacial movements that began during an ice age 400 million years ago, Franconia Notch boasts imposing granite cliffs, waterfalls, endless woodlands, and the famous rocky profile known as the "Old Man of the Mountain." The twin towns of Lincoln and North Woodstock make excellent bases for venturing into the notch, and are located off I-93 just south of Franconia Notch State Park. Lincoln also provides access to the **Pemigewasset Wilderness,** as it is located along Rt. 112, (or the Kancamangus Highway). This scenic route, nicknamed ⚡ **"The Kanc,"** twists its way 35mi. east through beautiful mountain landscapes to the resort town of North Conway. This wilderness area has been attracting guests for over a century. Today, backpackers and skiers will be at home; the mountains of the **Sandwich Range** provide breathtaking views and challenging outdoor opportunities.

The **Flume Visitors Center** (745-8391) off Parkway exit 1 on I-93 north of Lincoln, shows an excellent 15 min. film that acquaints visitors with the landscape and geological history of the area. (Open daily May-Oct., 9am-5pm. Open until 5:30pm in July and Aug.) The center sells tickets to **The Flume,** a 2mi. walk through a spectacular granite gorge. The walls of the gorge are 90 ft. high, and the walk takes visitors over covered bridges and past waterfalls ($7, ages 6-12 $4). A 9mi. recreational **bike path** begins at the Visitors Center and parallels I-93 north through the park.

The westernmost of the notches, Franconia is best known for the **Old Man of the Mountain,** a 40 ft. human profile formed by 5 ledges of stone atop a 1200 ft. cliff on Cannon Mountain. Nathaniel Hawthorne addressed this geological visage in his 1850 story "The Great Stone Face," and the landmark has since graced state licence plates as the symbol of the granite state. The Old Man has required a major face-lift in recent years; cables and turnbuckles now support his forehead and nose. **Profile Lake,** a 10min. walk from the base of the Cannon Mountain Aerial Tramway, (see below) has the best view of his profile, but several other viewing locations are set aside along the interstate.

The 80-passenger ▓ **Cannon Mountain Aerial Tramway** carries visitors to the summit of The Great Cannon Cliff, a 1000 ft. sheer drop into the cleft between Mt. Lafayette and Cannon Mountain. The tram offers unparalleled vistas of Franconia Notch along its ascent, and even better views can be had from the summit. (823-8800. Open daily 9am-4:30pm May-Oct., open until 5:30pm July-Aug. One-way $7; roundtrip $9; 6-12 $5). Skilled mountaineers might enjoy climbing instead, via the aptly named "Sticky Fingers" or "Meat Grinder" routes.

Myriad trails lead up into the mountains on both sides of Franconia Notch, providing excellent day hikes and spectacular views. Be prepared for severe weather, especially above 4000 ft. The **Lonesome Lake Trail,** a relatively easy hike, winds its way 1½mi. from Lafayette Place Campground to **Lonesome Lake,** where the AMC operates its westernmost summer hut (see **Practical Information, p. 99**). The **Greenleaf Trail** (2½mi.), which starts at the Aerial Tramway parking lot, and the **Old Bridle Path** (3mi.), from Lafayette Place, are much more ambitious. Both lead up to the AMC's Greenleaf Hut near the summit of Mt. Lafayette and overlooking Echo Lake. This is a favorite destination for sunset photographers. From Greenleaf, a 7½mi. trek east along **Garfield Ridge** leads to the AMC's most remote hut, the **Galehead;** this area can keep you occupied for days; adequate supplies and equipment are needed before starting out. A campsite on Garfield ridge costs $5.

Between parkway exits 1 and 2 on I-93, visitors can find a well-marked turnoff for **The Basin,** a whirlpool along the Pemigewasset River that has been carved out as a 15ft waterfall erodes a massive base of granite. It's fully wheelchair-accessible—the path is paved—and it makes a nice spot for a quick picnic by the water.

On steamy **summer** days, the lifeguard-protected beach at **Echo Lake** just off parkway exit 3 offers cool waters, but crowds are guaranteed. The lake is accessible even when the lifeguard is not on duty. (823-5563. Lifeguard on duty mid-June to Sept. daily 10am-5pm. Park admission $2.50, under 12 and over 65 free.) **Lost River,** located 6mi. west of North Woodstock on Rt. 112, is a gorge with a series of caves and rock formations that was created 25,000 years ago as the last glacier receded. The reservation, which was started by the Society for the Protection of New Hampshire Forests, also maintains an elaborate nature garden as well as a forestry museum. The walk through the gorge is less than a mile in length, but can take quite a while as each creatively named cavern (such as the Lemon Squeeze) is open for exploration. Friendly staff members are conveniently located at intervals along the walk and are well-versed in the natural history of the area. Lost River embodies the natural beauty that makes New Hampshire famous and should not be missed. (745-8031. $8; children 6-12 $5. Open daily May-Oct. 9am-5pm, last ticket sold 1 hour prior to close.)

The beauty of Fraconia Notch makes it an ideal place for **camping. Lafayette Place Campground,** with nearly 100 sites, is nestled smack in the middle of the Franconia Notch State Park. (388-4373. Open mid-May to mid-Oct., weather permitting. Lafayette's location makes it extremely popular; reservations are recommended at least 1wk. in advance. Coin-operated showers. Sites for 2 $15, $8 per additional person.) **Fransted Campground,** 3mi. north of the Notch on route 18, is one option if Lafayette is already full. (823- 5675. Showers and bathroom. Sites $18, with water and electricity $20. Open May to mid-Oct) **Woodstock Inn & Station** offers a nice alternative to camping, plus the menu at the restaurant isn't shabby either. Breakfast (daily 7am-11:30am) and brunch (runs until 2pm on Su) menus include omelettes ($6), waffles ($5), and excellent crepes ($5). (745-3951. Rooms start at $55.)

NEW ENGLAND

If you are feeling hungry **Polly's Pancake Parlor** on Rt. 117 in Sugar Hill, just 2mi. from exit 38 off I-93, offers tremendous portions of delicious food at extremely reasonable prices. The parlor offers a stack of 6 pancakes ($6), unlimited pancakes ($11) or waffles ($12), and a friendly staff. Polly's location is also remarkable, with the dining room overlooking both Franconia Notch and Mount Washington, so guests can enjoy the view while packing down a hearty meal. (823-5575. Open weekends Apr. and Nov. 7am-2pm, then daily May-Oct. 7am-3pm.)

## NORTH CONWAY

North Conway serves as one of New Hampshire's most popular vacation destinations because of its proximity to ski resorts in winter, foliage in the fall, and hiking and shopping year- round. Rt. 16, the traffic-infested main road, houses **outlet stores** from big buck labels like Banana Republic, J. Crew, Liz Claiborne, and Brooks Brothers. The town of Conway, just a few mi. south, is identical, except that it numbers its buildings on Main St. while North Conway does not.

A number of stores in the North Conway area rent outdoor equipment. For ski goods in winter or biking gear during other seasons, **Joe Jones,** in North Conway on Main St. at Mechanic, is good. A second branch lies a few mi. north of town on Rt. 302. (356-9411. Alpine skis, boots, and poles $12 for 1 day, $22 for 2 days. Cross-country equipment $10/$16. Open July-Aug. daily 9am-9pm; Sept.-Nov. and Apr.-June Su-Th 10am-6pm, F-Sa 9am-6pm.) **Eastern Mountain Sports (EMS),** on Main St. in the Eastern Slope Inn, distributes free mountaineering pamphlets and books on the area. EMS also sells (slightly pricey) camping equipment and rents tents and sleeping bags. The knowledgeable staff can provide first-hand info on climbing and hiking in North Conway. Visitors heading into the wilderness for a few days might want to stop by to pick up freeze-dried meals ($6) and other last minute necessities. (356-5433. Open June-Sept. M-Sa 9am-9pm, Su 9am-6pm; Oct.-May 9am-6pm.)

**White Mountains Hostel (HI-AYH),** 36 Washington St., occupies a great location in the heart of Conway. Washington St. is off Route 16 at the intersection of Route 153. The hostel has 43 bunks on several floors, and each bed comes with clean linen and a pillow. (447-1001 or 800-909-4776, ext. 51. $16, nonmembers $19, includes light breakfast; private rooms $45/$48. Kitchen and computer use. Reception 7-10am and 5-10pm. Check-out 10am. Reservations recommended during the summer and peak foliage season. Open Dec.-Oct.) The hostel at the beautiful **Mt. Cranmore Lodge,** 859 Kearsarge Rd., has 40 bunks. Although the lodge is a few mi. from downtown, it makes up for the distance with its wonderful setting and array of offerings. A recreation room, pool, jacuzzi, trails, cable, refrigerator, microwave, and duck pond are all at the disposal of guests. In addition, a full country breakfast is included with each overnight stay. (356-2044 or 800-356-3596. $17, linen and towel included. No curfew; no lockout. No smoking. Check-in 3pm. Check-out 11am.)

Breakfast and lunch spots line North Conway's Main St. **Café Noche,** 147 Main St. offers surprisingly authentic Mexican food with many vegetarian choices, and all menu items are made from fresh ingredients. While everything is tasty, local patrons recommend the $7 Montezuma Pie, a sort of Mexican lasagna, or the $4.25 garden burger. (447-5050. Open M-F 11:30am-9pm, Sa-Su 11:30am-9:30pm.) **Horsefeathers** serves hearty meals in the heart of North Conway. Burgers cost $7-7.50. (356-2687. Kitchen open daily 11:30am-11:45pm; bar open until 1am.) **Alpenglow Grill**, located at 78 Main St. in Conway, serves up some traditional grilled fare with a spicy twist. Try the barbecued pork sandwich for a filling meal. (447-5524. Open daily from late May to early Oct, 12pm-9:30; or 5pm-9:30pm during the rest of the year). Get a day in the mountains or on the slopes off to a great start by grabbing a cup of freshly roasted coffee at **Morning Dew,** next to Olympia Sports in North Conway village, (open daily 7am-9pm). While enjoying a stroll in North Conway, be sure to check out **Zeb's Country Store** right on Main St. Zeb's sells 100% New England products, ranging from gourmet foods to home decorations. This knick-knack shop makes a great browsing spot. (356-9294. Open 9am-10pm from mid-June to Dec., with hours varying during other months.)

## PINKHAM NOTCH

New Hampshire's easternmost Notch lies in the shadow of the tallest mountain in the Northeast, Mt. Washington. Due to its practical location near this ego-inflating mountain, Pinkham Notch is often crowded and less than peaceful. The **Pinkham Notch Visitors Center**, the AMC's main info center in the White Mountains and the starting point for most trips up Mt. Washington, lies between Gorham and Jackson on Rt. 16. To get to Pinkham Notch from I-93 S, take exit 35 from I-93 and travel north on U.S. Rt, 3 until it meets U.S. Rt. 302; travel east on 302 until its junction with Rt. 16, then travel north on 16.

From just behind the Pinkham Notch Visitors Center all the way up to the summit of Mt. Washington, **Tuckerman's Ravine Trail** takes 4-5hr. of steep hiking each way. Authorities urge caution when climbing—Mt. Washington claims at least one life every year. A gorgeous day here can suddenly turn into a chilling storm, with whipping winds and rumbling thunderclouds. It has never been warmer than 72°F atop Mt. Washington, and the average temperature on the peak is a bone-chilling 26.7°F. With an *average* wind speed of 35 mph and gusts that have been measured up to an astounding 231 mph, Mt. Washington is the windiest place in the world. As long as you take proper measures, the climb is stellar and the view well worth it. Motorists can take the **Mt. Washington Auto Rd.,** a paved and dirt road that winds 8mi. to the summit. When you opt to drive the mountain, you get a free flashy bumper sticker reading "This Car Climbed Mt. Washington"—it's certain to impress folks when you cruise back through town, although locals will probably snicker. The road begins at Glen House, 3mi. north of the visitors center on Rt. 16. (466-3988. Road open daily mid-June to mid-Sept. 7:30am-6pm; mid-May to mid-June and mid-Sept. to mid-Oct. 8:30am-5pm. $15 per car and driver, $6 per passenger, ages 5-12 $4.) **Guided van tours** to the summit include a 30min. presentation on the mountain's natural history ($20, ages 5-12 $10). On even the most beautiful summer days, the summit is likely to be covered with clouds, giving you a slim chance of getting a good view. So enjoy the **snack bar** (466-3347; open late May to mid-Oct. daily 8am-6pm), and a **museum** run by the **Mt. Washington Observatory** (466-3388; museum open late May to mid-Oct. daily 9am-7pm).

AMC's huts offer the best lodging near the mountain. At **Joe Dodge Lodge,** immediately behind the Pinkham Notch Visitors Center, a stay includes a comfy bunk with a delicious and sizeable breakfast and dinner. ($42, children $27; nonmembers $47/$31. Off-season $39, children $26; nonmembers $44/$29. Without meals $27, children $18; nonmembers $30/$20.) **Hermit Lake Shelter,** situated about 2hr. up the Tuckerman Ravine Trail, has bathrooms but no shower, and sleeps 72 people in 8 lean-tos and 3 tent platforms ($7 per night; buy nightly passes at the visitors center). **Carter Notch Hut** lies to the east of the visitors' center, a 4mi. hike up the 19mi. **Brook Trail.** Just 1½mi. from Mt. Washington's summit sits **Lakes of the Clouds,** the largest, highest, and most popular of the AMC's huts (room for 90); additional sleeping space for 6 backpackers in its basement refuge room can be reserved from any other hut ($16, nonmembers $18).

# VERMONT

Perhaps no other state is as aptly named as Vermont. The lineage of the name extends back to Samuel de Champlain, who in 1609 dubbed the area "green mountain" in his native French *(mont vert)*. The Green Mountain range shapes and defines Vermont, spanning the length of the state from north to south and covering most of its width as well. Over the past few decades, ex-urbanite yuppies have invaded, creating some tension between the original, pristine Vermont and the packaged Vermont of organic food stores and mountaineering shops. Happily, the former still seems to prevail; visitors can frolic in any of the 30 state forests, 80 state parks, or the mammoth 186,000-acre Green Mountain National Forest.

# ⚡ PRACTICAL INFORMATION

**Capital:** Montpelier.

**Visitor Info: Vermont Information Center,** 134 State St., Montpelier 05602 (802-828-3237; www.travel-vermont.com). Open M-F 8am-8pm. **Dept. of Forests, Parks and Recreation,** 103 S. Main St., Waterbury 05676 (802-241-3670). Open M-F 7:45am-4:30pm. **Vermont Snowline** (802-229-0531). Nov.-May 24hr. recording on snow conditions.

**Postal Abbreviation:** VT. **Sales Tax:** 5%; 9% on meals and lodgings. **Area code:** 802.

## VERMONT SKI RESORTS

Come winter, skiers pour into Vermont to hit some of the Northeast's finest resort areas, which become havens for bikers and hikers in the summer and fall. Numerous small towns feature budget accommodation options for travelers beyond the pricey inns and lodges at the resorts themselves; shared rooms with bunks cost significantly less than private rooms. For more information, contact **Ski Vermont,** 26 State St., P.O. Box 368, Montpelier 05601 (802-223-2439; fax 802-229-6917, open M-F 7:45am-4:45pm), or visit the comprehensive website at www.skivermont.com, which also provides links to the websites of major resorts. Helpful information can also be obtained from the Vermont Information Center (see **Practical Information** above). Cheaper tickets can be found off-season before mid-Dec. and after mid-Mar.

**MT. SNOW:** West of Brattleboro on Rt. 100 in the town of West Dover, (see p. 111), this popular resort boasts 134 trails and 26 lifts, as well as the first snowboard park in the Northeast. In the summer, bikers can take advantage of 45mi. of trails across the "Mountain Biking Capital of the East." *(800-245-7669. Open mid-Nov. to late Apr. M-F 9am-4pm, Sa-Su 8am-4pm. Adults: weekends $52 and weekdays $49, ages 13-19 $46/$44, seniors and 12 and under $33/$31.)*

**KILLINGTON:** At the junction of U.S. 4 and Rt. 100 N in Sherburne, Killington's 7 mountains make for the East's longest ski season (mid-Oct. to early June), as well as the most terrain for novice and advanced skiers in New England. Killington offers many other winter activities and provides a wide assortment of restaurants and clubs for evening entertainment. *(802-422-3333 or 800-621-6867. Adults $52, teens 13-18 $39, kids 6-12 $26.)*

**BURKE:** For some of the most reasonable lift ticket prices in Vermont, head to Burke, off I-91 in northern Vermont. In summer, visitors can partake in almost any recreational activity from rock climbing to fishing, as well as hike and bike across 200mi. of trails. *(802-626-3305. Sa-Su adults $42, ages 13-18 $37, 12 and under $28; M-F $25; off-season $20).*

**JAY PEAK:** In Jay on Rt. 242, Jay Peak sits just across the U.S. border with Canada in Vermont's Northeast Kingdom. Some of the East's most challenging Glades and ample opportunities for woods skiing make Jay Peak an appealing option for thrill-seekers; in summer, excellent fishing and mountain biking opportunities abound. *(800-451-4449 or 802-988-2611. Adults $49, under 15 $37, after 2:45pm $12.)*

**OTHER RESORTS: Stratton** (802-297-2200 or 800-787-2886; 90 trails, 12 lifts), on Rt. 30 N in Bondville; **Sugarbush** (802-583-2381 or 800-537-8427; 112 trails, 18 lifts, 4 mountains); and **Stowe** (p. 109). **Cross-country resorts** include the **Trapp Family Lodge, Stowe** (p. 109); **Mountain Meadows, Killington** (802-775-7077; 90mi. of trails); and **Woodstock** (802-457-6674; 40mi. of trails).

# BURLINGTON

Tucked between Lake Champlain and the Green Mountains, the largest city in Vermont successfully bridges the gap between the urban and the outdoors. Five colleges, including the University of Vermont (UVM), give the area a youthful, progressive flair; bead shops pop up next door to mainstream clothing stores without disrupting local harmony. Along Church St., downtown's bustling marketplace, numerous sidewalk cafes offer both a taste of the middle-class hippie atmosphere and a great venue for people-watching.

## 🛈 PRACTICAL INFORMATION

**Trains: Amtrak,** 29 Railroad Ave., Essex Jct. (879-7298), 5mi. east of Burlington on Rt. 15. To New York (9¾hr., 1 per day, $56-62) and White River Junction (2hr., 1 per day, $13). Station open daily 7:30am-noon and 8-9pm. CCTA bus to downtown runs every 30min. M-F 5:55am-6:05pm, Sa 6:45am-7:40pm.

**Buses: Vermont Transit,** 345 Pine St. (864-6811 or 800-451-3292), at Main St. can get you to and from Burlington pretty cheaply. To: Boston (4¾hr., 5 per day, $45); Montreal (2½hr., 5 per day, $18-19); White River Junction (2hr., 5 per day, $14.50); Middlebury (1hr., 3 per day, $7.50); and Albany (4¾hr., 3 per day, $34). 15% discount with student ID. Connections made with Greyhound; Ameripasses accepted. Open daily 6am-8:15pm.

**Public Transit: Chittenden County Transit Authority (CCTA)** (864-0211). Downtown Burlington is definitely walkable, but if visitors are planning to venture out of the city center, CCTA provides unbeatable access. Frequent, reliable service. Downtown hub at Cherry and Church St. Connections with Shelburne and other outlying areas. Buses operate every 30min. M-Sa roughly 6:15am-9:20pm, depending on routes. Fare $1; seniors, disabled, and under 18 50¢; under 5 free.

**Visitor Info: Lake Champlain Regional Chamber of Commerce,** 60 Main St., Rt. 100 (863-3489). Open M-F 8:30am-5pm, Sa-Su 11am-3pm; Oct.-May M-F 8:30am-5pm.

**Bike Rental: Ski Rack,** 85 Main St. (658-3313 or 800-882-4530). Mountain bikes $8 for 1hr., $14 for 4hr., and $22 for 24hr. Helmet and lock included. In-line skates $8 for 4hr., $12 per day. Credit card required for rental. Open M-Th 9am-8pm, F 9am-9pm, Sa 9am-6pm, Su 10am-5pm; mid-Aug. to mid-Apr. M-Th 10am-7pm, F 10am-8pm, Sa 9am-6pm, Su 11am-5pm.

**Hotlines: Women's Rape Crisis Center,** 863-1236. **Crises Services of Chittenden County,** 863-2400. Both 24hr.

**Internet Access: Kinko's,** 199 Main St. (658-2561). $12 per hr. Open 24hr.

**Post Office:** 11 Elmwood Ave. (863-6033), at Pearl St. Open M-F 8am-5pm, Sa 8am-1pm. **ZIP code:** 05401.

## ⌂ A PLACE TO LAY YOUR HEAD

The chamber of commerce has the complete rundown on area accommodations. B&Bs are generally found in the outlying suburbs. Reasonably priced hotels and guest houses line **Shelburne Rd.** south of downtown. **Mrs. Farrell's Home Hostel (HI-AYH),** 3mi. north of downtown via North Ave., is accessible by public transportation; get directions when you call for reservations. Six beds are split between a clean, comfortable basement and a lovely garden porch. Even if she has no available beds, she can refer you to an overflow location. (865-3730. $17, nonmembers $20. Free linen, coffee, and bagels. Wheelchair access in summer.) The **North Beach Campsites,** on Institute Rd. beside the high school 1½mi. north of town by North Ave., have a spectacular view and access to a pristine beach on Lake Champlain. Take Rt. 127 to North Ave., or the "North Ave." bus from the main terminal on Pine St. (862-0942. 137 sites. $18, with electricity $22, full hookup $25. Showers 25¢ per 5min. Beach is free but closes at 9pm, and parking costs $3. Snack bar. Open May to mid-Oct.) The **Shelburne Campground,** on Shelburne Rd., lies 1mi. north of Shelburne and 5mi. south of Burlington by Rt. 7; buses to Shelburne South stop right next to the campground. (985-2540. Sites for 2 $19, with water and electricity $21, full hookup $27; $2 per additional person. Pool, laundry facilities. Showers are 25 cents for 5 minutes. Open May-Oct.) See **Near Burlington,** p. 107, for more camping.

NEW ENGLAND

## ⃝ FOOD AND ICE CREAM

**Sweetwater's,** 120 Church St. (864-9800), with its incredibly high ceilings and vast wall paintings, dwarf those who come for delicious $3-3.50 soups and $6-7 sandwiches. Try the Duck Quesadillas for $9, served with cranberry mayo. In the summer, ask to be seated outdoors so you can observe the goings-on of Church St. Marketplace. Open M-Sa 11:30am-2am, Su 10:30am-midnight; food served M-Sa until 1am, Su until 11pm.

**Oasis Diner,** 189 Bank St. (864-5308), has fried up the ultimate American diner experience since 1954. Hamburger, fries, and a small soda go for $5. The ghost of Elvis might enjoy the $3 grilled bacon and peanut butter sandwich. Open M-F 5am-3pm, Sa 5am-2pm, Su 8am-2pm.

**Cheese Outlet and Fresh Market,** 400 Pine St. (863-3968), sells cheese, wine, and other gourmet items about a mile south of the city center. Visitors planning a picnic might want to stop here and get a few goodies before heading off to lake shore. Veggie enchilada $6. Open M-Sa 8am-7pm, Su 10am-5pm.

**Ben & Jerry's,** 36 Church St. (862-9620), is considered the company's birthplace (see p. 111) after its original shop, a converted gas station at 169 Cherry St., had burned down and been abandoned. Come here for yummy ice cream. Cones $2-3. Open Apr.-Nov. Su-Th 11am-11pm, F- Sa 11am-midnight; Dec.-Mar. Su-Th 11:30am-10pm, F- Sa 11:30am-11pm.

**Church Street Marketplace**, and its adjacent sidestreets, has approximately 85 restaurants, making Burlington a food-lover's paradise. Visitors could eat downtown for weeks without hitting the same place twice; not bad for a city of only 40,000.

## ⃝ ⃝ SIGHTS, NIGHTLIFE, AND ENTERTAINMENT

Despite its suburban appearance, Burlington offers lively cultural and artistic entertainment. The popular pedestrian mall at historic **Church St. Marketplace** provides a haven for tie-dye and ice cream lovers, and it sells works by local artists. Amateur historians delight in Victorian **South Willard St.,** where you'll find **Champlain College** and the **University of Vermont,** founded in 1797. **City Hall Park,** in the heart of downtown, and **Battery St. Park,** on Lake Champlain near the edge of downtown, are bucolic. For insomniac boaters, the **Burlington Community Boathouse,** at the base of College St. at Lake Champlain, is open late to rent light craft for a cruise on the lake. (865-3377. Open June 2-Aug. 24hr.; mid-May to June 1 and Sept. to mid-Oct. daily 6am-10pm. Sailboats $20-35 per hr.) The **Spirit of Ethan Allen** scenic cruise departs from the boathouse at the bottom of College St. The boat cruises along the Vermont coast, giving passengers a close-up view of the famous **Thrust Fault,** which is not visible from land. (862-9685. Cruises late May to mid-Oct. daily 10am, noon, 2, and 4pm. $8.67, ages 3-11 $4.15. Sunset cruise lasts 1 hour longer and sails at 6:30pm Sun-Th; adults $9.98, ages 3-11 $5.20.)

The **Shelburne Museum,** 7mi. south of Burlington in Shelburne, houses one of the best collections of Americana in the country. The 45-acre museum has 37 buildings transported from all over New England, a covered bridge, a lighthouse and Degas, Cassatt, Manet, Monet, Rembrandt, and Whistler paintings. (985-3346. Open daily 10am-5pm from mid-May to Oct. Tickets are valid for 2 days; $17.50, 14 and under $7. Hours vary from Oct.-May; several buildings only open in summer). Five mi. farther south on U.S. 7, the **Vermont Wildflower Farm** has a seed shop and 6½ acres of wildflower gardens. (425-3641. Open Apr.-Oct. daily 10am-5pm. $3; off-season admission only $1.50, but don't expect many blossoms.)

The **Ethan Allen Homestead** rests northeast of Burlington on Rt. 127. In the 1780s, Allen forced the surrender of Fort Ticonderoga and helped establish the state of Vermont. He built his cabin in what is now the Winooski Valley Park; it's worth a visit for history buffs. (865-4556. Open mid-May to mid-June daily 1-5pm; June to mid-Oct. M-Sa 10am-5pm, Su 1-5pm. Last tour 4:15pm. Admission $4, seniors $3.50, ages 5-17 $2, families $12. Reserved tours available late Oct. to mid-May.)

Immortalized by ex-regulars Phish on their album *A Picture of Nectar*, **Nectar's** 188 Main St., rocks with inexpensive food, (fries $2-5), and nightly tunes. (658-4771. No cover; open M-F 5:45am-2am, Sa 7:30am-1am, Su 7:30am-2am). The **Red Square,** 136 Church St., is one of Burlington's most popular night spots with live music nightly. Bands play in the alley if the crowd gets large. (859-8909. No cover.)

In the summer, the **Vermont Mozart Festival** (862-7352 or 800-639-9097) sends Bach, Beethoven, and Mozart to barns, farms, and meadows throughout the area and the **Discover Jazz Festival** (863-7992) features over 1000 international and Vermont musicians in both free and ticketed performances. The **Flynn Theater Box Office,** 153 Main St. (863-5966), handles sales for the Mozart and jazz performances (open M-F 10am-5pm, Sa 11am-4pm). The **Champlain Valley Folk Festival** (800-769-9176) entertains in early Aug.

## NEAR BURLINGTON: CHAMPLAIN VALLEY

**Lake Champlain,** a 100mi. long lake between Vermont's Green Mountains and New York's Adirondacks, is often referred to as "Vermont's West Coast." You can take a bridge or a ferry over the lake; the ferry offers fantastic views. The **Lake Champlain Ferry,** located on the dock at the bottom of King St., sails daily from Burlington to Port Kent, NY, and back. (864-9804. 1hr. Late June to Aug. 12-14 per day, 8am-7:30pm; mid-May to late June and Sept. to mid-Oct. 9 per day, 8am-6:35pm. $3.25, ages 6-12 $1.25, car $12.75). The same company also travels from Grand Isle to Plattsburg, NY and 14mi. south of Burlington from Charlotte, VT, to Essex, NY (either fare $2, ages 6-12 50¢, with car $6.75).

**Mt. Philo State Park,** 15mi. south of Burlington off Rt. 7, offers pleasant camping and gorgeous views of the Champlain Valley; take the Vermont Transit bus from Burlington south along U.S. 7 toward Vergennes. (425-2390. 8 tent sites without hookups $11, 2 lean-tos $15. Entrance fee $2, ages 4-14 $1.50. Open mid-May to mid-Oct. daily 10am-sunset.) The marsh of the **Missisquoi National Wildlife Refuge** sits at the northern end of the lake west of Swanton, VT along route 78. Also north of the lake, **Burton Island State Park** is accessible only by ferry from **Kill Kare State Park**, 35mi. north of Burlington and 3½mi. southwest off U.S. 7 near St. Albans Bay. (524-6353. Open late May to early Sept. daily 8:30am-6:30pm; $2. Call for schedule.) The campground has 19 tent sites ($13) and 26 lean-tos ($17; $4 per additional person). The state park on **Grand Isle,** just off U.S. 2 north of Keeler Bay, also offers camping. (372-4300. 123 sites for 4 $13, $3 per additional person; 34 lean-tos $17/$4; 1 cabin $34. Reservations are highly recommended, especially for weekends in the summer. Open mid-May to mid-Oct.)

# MIDDLEBURY

Unlike the many Vermont towns that seem to shy away from association with local colleges, Middlebury, "Vermont's Landmark College Town," welcomes the energy and culture stimulated by Middlebury College. The result is a traditional Vermont atmosphere tinged both with vitality and history.

**⊞ PRACTICAL INFORMATION.** Middlebury stretches along U.S. 7, 42mi. south of Burlington. **Vermont Transit** (388-4373) stops at the Exxon station, 16 Court St., west of Main St. (station open M-Sa 6am-9pm, Su 7am-9pm). Buses run to Burlington (1hr., 3 per day, $7.50); Rutland (1½hr., 3 per day, $7.50); Albany (3hr., 3 per day, $28); and Boston (6hr., 3 per day, $43). There is no public transportation in Middlebury, but the **Bike Center,** 74 Main St. (388-6666), rents bikes on the cheap (as low as $15 per day and $50 per week). The staff at the **Addison County Chamber of Commerce,** 2 Court St. (388-7951; www.midvermont.com), in the historic Gamaliel Painter House, has area info (open M-F 9am-5pm; limited weekend hrs. in summer; maps of Middlebury are outside if you arrive after hours). **Post Office:** 10 Main St. (388-2681; open M-F 8am-5pm, Sa 8am-12:30pm). **ZIP code:** 05753.

**▶ ACCOMMODATIONS.** Lodging with 4 walls and no mosquitoes does not come cheaply in Middlebury; prepare to trade an arm and a leg for an extended stay. The **Sugar House Motor Inn,** just north of Middlebury on Rt. 7, offers basic motel rooms with free local calls, refrigerators, and microwaves. (388-2770. Singles $59-69; doubles $69-79; extra rollaway beds $15; prices jump to $90/$95 during fall foliage season and Middlebury graduation). On the southern edge of Middlebury, the **Greystone Motel,** 2mi. south of the town center on Rt. 7, has 10 rooms (388-4935; singles $57-60; doubles $67-70). The best budget accommodations are in the great outdoors. Situated on a Lake Dumore, **Branbury State Park,** 7mi. south on U.S. 7, then 4mi. south on Rt. 53, is all abuzz with campers, picnickers, and water lovers. Visitors should take advantage of the beautiful beach to cool off when the temperatures soar in July and Aug. (247-5925. 40 sites $13; lean-tos $17. Canoe rentals $5 per hr., $30 per day; paddle boats $5 per 30min. Showers 25¢ per 5 min. Open late May to mid-Oct.) **River's Bend Campground,** 3mi. north of Middlebury off Rt. 7 on the Dog Team Rd. in New Haven, is clean and appropriately named, but can be difficult to find. (388-9092 or 888-505-5159. 65 sites for 2 with water and electricity $20, river sites $24; $6 per additional adult. Showers 25¢ per 5min. Fishing, swimming, picnicking facilities $3. Canoe rental $6 per hr.)

**▶◼ FOOD AND NIGHTLIFE.** Middlebury's many fine restaurants cater chiefly to plump wallets, but the year-round presence of students ensures the survival of cheaper places. **Noonie's Deli,** in the Marbleworks building just behind Main St., is a student favorite and makes terrific sandwiches ($4-5) on homemade bread, and fresh baked desserts. Try the Vermonter ($4.50) for a delightful maple and ham local specialty. (388-0014. Open daily 8am-8pm.) Students also flock to **Mister Up's**, a popular night-time hangout on Bakery Ln. just off Main St., for an impressively eclectic menu including sandwiches ($6-$9), hamburgers ($5-7) and an extensive salad bar (388-6724. Open M-Sa 11:30am-midnight, Su 11am-midnight.) If you are still itching for food or a good time after midnight, head up to **Angela's** on Park St. next to the Sheldon Museum; it's a local pub and it's open until 1am or 2am, depending on the day of the week. **Amigos,** 4 Merchants Row, befriends weary travelers with Mexican food ($5-12) and live local music 9:30pm-12:30am on summer F and Sa. Check with the waitress about other special events such as disco nights. (388-3624. Open M-Th 11:30am-9pm, F-Sa 11:30am-9:30pm, Su 4-9pm; bar open daily until midnight, depending on the crowd.)

**◙ SIGHTS.** The **Vermont State Craft Center** at Frog Hollow, exhibits and sells the artistic productions of Vermonters *(388-3177. Open M-Th 9:30am-5:30pm, F-Sa 9am-6pm, Su 11am-5pm.* **Middlebury College** hosts cultural events; the architecturally striking concert hall in the college **Arts Center,** just outside of town, resonates with a terrific concert series. The campus **box office** has details on events sponsored by the college. *(443-6433. Open Sept.-May Tu-Sa 11am-4pm.)* Tours from the **Admissions Office,** in Emma Willard Hall on S. Main St., showcase the campus. *(443-3000. Tours Sept. to late May daily 10-11am and 2-3pm. In July and Aug., an additional tour is run at 12pm. Self-guided tour brochures available.)* The beer runs freely at the **Otter Creek Brewery,** 793 Exchange St., ¾mi. north of town. *(800-473-0727. Tours daily at 1, 3, and 5pm.)* Fifteen mi. east of the Middlebury College campus, the **Middlebury College Snow Bowl** entertains skiers with 15 trails and lifts. *(802-388-4356.)*

# STOWE

Stowe winds gracefully up the side of Mt. Mansfield (Vermont's highest peak, at 4393 ft.). The village self-consciously fancies itself an American skiing hotspot on par with its ritzier European counterparts: Stowe has something of an obsession with all things Austrian, so visitors will notice the Austrian restaurants, lodges, and shops lining the streets.

**⛄ PRACTICAL INFORMATION.** Stowe is 12mi. north of I-89's exit 10, which is 27mi. southwest of Burlington. The ski slopes lie along **Rt. 108** (Mountain Road) northwest of Stowe. **Vermont Transit** (244-6943 or 800-451-3292; open daily 8am-8pm) comes only as close as the **Gateway Motel**, 73 S. Main St. (Rt. 100) in Waterbury, 10mi. from Stowe. **Peg's Pick-up DBA Stowe Taxi:** 253-9433. In winter, the **Stowe Trolley** (253-7585) runs irregularly between the important locations in the village. (In summer, 1¼hr. tours M, W, F 11am; $5. In winter, every 20min. 8-10am and 2-4:20pm; every hr. 11am-1pm and 5-10pm; $1, weekly pass $10.) **Visitors Info: Stowe Area Association** (253-7321 or 800-247-8693), on Main St. (Open M-F 9am-8pm, Sa 10am-6pm, Su 10am-5pm; late Apr. to early May closed Sa-Su.) **Post Office:** 105 Depot St. (253-7521), off Main St. (open M-F 7:15am-5pm, Sa 9am-noon). **ZIP code:** 05672. **Area code:** 802.

**⛄⛄ ACCOMMODATIONS AND FOOD.** At the base of Mt. Mansfield, **Mt. Mansfield Hostel** 6992 Mountain Rd., 7mi. from town (shuttles run to town during ski season), is Stowe's best lodging bargain by far. Also, meals are gigantic: excellent breakfast $5, dinner $7. (253-4010. 48 beds; $12 in the summer, $15 in the spring and fall; in ski season Su-Th $19, F-Sa $24. Reserve by phone far in advance for ski and foliage seasons.) **Foster's Place**, on Mountain Rd., offers dorm rooms with a lounge and a game room in a recently renovated school building. (253-9404. Singles with shared bath $39; private bath $49; quad $69.)

  **Gold Brook Campground**, 1½mi. south of the town center on Rt. 100, offers a camping experience without all that roughing-it business. This is the only camping area open year round in Stowe, so it's the place if you're visiting in cooler weather. (253-7683. Showers, laundry, horseshoes, skateboard ramp. Tent sites for 2 $18; with hookup $20-27; $5 per additional person.) **Smuggler's Notch State Park,** 7248 Mountain Rd./Rt. 108, 8mi. west of Stowe, just past the hostel, keeps it simple with hot showers (limited hot water available), tent sites, and lean-tos. (253-4014. Sites for 4 $12, $3 per additional person up to 8; lean-tos $16/$4. Reservations recommended. Open late May to mid-Oct.)

  Big deli sandwiches ($3), subs ($4), or an excellent seafood salad ($6 per lb.) and locals are at **Mac's Deli,** inside Mac's Stowe Grocery Store, S. Main St. by the intersection of 100 and 108. In winter, they also serve piping hot soups ($2.25 per pint). (253-4576. Open daily 7am-9pm.) The **Depot Street Malt Shoppe,** 57 Depot St., is another local favorite known for its delicious food and great prices. Visitors enjoy classic diner fare and salivate over hot fudge sundaes in an artfully recreated 50s soda shop. (253-4269. Meals $3-8. Open daily 11am-9pm.) The **Sunset Grille and Tap Room,** on 140 Cottage Club Rd. off Mountain Rd., sells generous meals ($5-15) and a vast selection of domestic beers in a friendly, down-home barbecue restaurant/bar. This is the only sports bar in town, and with 20 TVs, it draws a large crowd of locals and visitors late at night. (253-9281. Open daily for dining 11:30am-midnight; bar 11:30am-2am, closes at 1am on Sat.)

**⛄⛄ UNDER THE SUN.** Stowe's ski offerings consist of the **Stowe Mountain Resort** (253-3000 or 800-253-4754) and **Smuggler's Notch** (664-1118 or 800-451-8752). At both areas lift tickets cost about $52-$54 for adults, $32-$34 for children 6-12. Nearby, the hills are alive with the sound of the area's best cross-country skiing at the **Von Trapp Family Lodge,** Luce Hill Rd., 2mi. off Mountain Rd. Yes, it *is* the family from *The Sound of Music*, and it is divine. Don't stay here unless you have a rich uncle in Stowe—prices for lodging climb to $345 in the high season. There's no charge to visit, however. The lodge does offer fairly inexpensive rentals and lessons (253-8511. Trail fee $12, ski rentals $13, lessons $14-40 per hr.; discounts for kids). **A.J.'s Ski and Sports,** at the base of Mountain Rd., rents snow equipment. (253-4593. Skis, boots, and poles: downhill $24 per day, 2 days $46; cross-country $12/$22. Snowboard and boots $24 per day. Discount with advance reservations. Open in summer daily 9am-6pm; in winter Su-Th 8am-8pm, F-Sa 8am-9pm.)

NEW ENGLAND

In summer, Stowe's frenetic pace drops off—as do its prices. **Action Outfitters,** 2160 Mountain Rd., rents mountain bikes ($8 per hr., $20 per ½-day, $34 per day) and in-line skates ($6/$12/$18). Action also rents canoes ($30 per day), and will transport the canoe to the reservoir on Sa and Su (253-7975; open daily 9am-5:30.) **The Mountain Bike Shop,** on Mountain Rd. near Stowe Center, also rents bikes and in-line skates ($7 per hr., $16 for 4hr., $25 full day; children $5/$12/$18; helmet included), as well as cross-country skis and snowshoes ($12 per day. 253-7919 or 800-682-4534. Open in summer M-Sa 9am-6pm, Su 9am-5pm; in winter daily 9am-5pm.) Stowe's 5½mi. **asphalt recreation path,** perfect for cross-country skiing in the winter and biking, skating, or strolling in the summer, runs parallel to the Mountain Road's ascent and begins behind the church on Main St. in Stowe. Before you set out on the path check out **Shaw's General Store,** 207 Main St. across from the Church, for pretty much anything, including Vermont-made shoes (253-4040).

**Fly fisherfolk** should head to the **Fly Rod Shop,** 3mi. south of Stowe on Rt. 100, to pick up the necessary fishing licenses ($20 for Vermont residents, $38 for everyone else) and rent fly rods and reels for $11 per day or $25 per week. The owner can show you how to tie a fly, or you can stick around for free fly-fishing classes on the shop's own pond. (253-7346 or 800-535-9763. Open Apr.-Oct. M-F 9am-6pm, Sa 9am-5pm, Su 10am-4pm; after fishing season, M-F 9am-5pm, Sa 9am-4pm, Su 10am-4pm.) To canoe on the nearby Lamoille River, **Umiak,** Rt. 100, 1mi. south of Stowe Center, can help. The store (named after a unique type of kayak used by the Inuit) rents regular ol' kayaks and canoes in the summer and offers a full-day river trip for $25. (253-2317. Rental and transportation to the river included. Open Apr.-Oct. daily 9am-6pm; winter hrs. vary. Sport kayaks $8/hr., $15/ 4hr.; canoes $10/hr., $25/ 4hr.) Located in a rustic red barn, **Topnotch Stowe,** 4000 Mountain Rd. (253-6433), offers 1hr. horseback-riding tours from late May through Sept. (tours daily 11am, 1, and 3pm; $25; reservations required).

## NEAR STOWE: ROUTE 100 GLUTTONY

If you haven't already made yourself sick on **Ben & Jerry's** ice cream (see p. 111), Rt. 100 features a veritable food fiesta south of Stowe. Begin at Ben & Jerry's and drive north on Rt. 100 towards Stowe. The first stop is the **Green Mountain Chocolate Company** (244-1139) and **Cabot Annex Store** (244-6334), home to rich chocolate truffles and Vermont's best cheddar (open daily 9am-6pm). The samples are free. Leave room in your stomach for the **Cold Hollow Cider Mill.** In addition to the potent beverage, cider spin-offs on sale include jelly and donuts (35¢. 244-8771; call for a cider making schedule; open daily 8am-6pm.) Finally, maple is everywhere at the **Stowe Maple Products** maple museum and candy kitchen. Mar. and Apr. is syrup season, but they sell the goods all year (253-2508, open daily 8am-6pm).

# WHITE RIVER JUNCTION

Named for its location at the confluence of the White and Connecticut Rivers, White River Junction was once the focus of railroad transportation in the northeastern U.S. Today, near the intersection of I-89 and I-91, the Junction serves as the bus center for most of Vermont. **Vermont Transit** (295-3011 or 800-552-8737; office open daily 7am-9pm), on U.S. 5, behind the Mobil station 1mi. south of downtown White River Junction, makes connections to New York (8hr., 3-4 per day, $58); Burlington (2hr., 5 per day, $14.50); Montréal (5hr., 5 per day, $39-$45); and smaller centers on a less regular basis. **Amtrak** (295-7160; office open daily 9am-noon and 5-7pm), on Railroad Rd. off N. Main St., rockets once per day to New York (7½hrs., $57 M-Th and Sa; $63 on F and Su); Essex Jct (near Burlington, 2hrs., $15/$23); Montreal (4½hrs., $29/$29); and Philadelphia (9hrs., $67/$74).

There's not much in White River Junction to attract tourists, but if you must stay in town, virtually the only choice for lodging is the old-style **Hotel Coolidge (HI-AYH),** 17 S. Main St., across the road from the retired Boston and Maine steam engine. From the bus station, walk to the right on U.S. 5 and down the hill past 2 stop lights (1mi.) into town. The Coolidge boasts a 26-bed dorm-style hostel-ette and tidy pri-

> ## BEN & JERRY: TWO MEN, ONE DREAM, AND LOTS OF CHUNKS
> In 1978, Ben Cohen and Jerry Greenfield enrolled in a Penn State correspondence course in ice cream making, converted a gas station into their first shop, and launched themselves on the road to a double scoop success story. Today, **Ben and Jerry's Ice Cream Factory,** north of Waterbury on Rt. 100, is a cow-spotted mecca for ice cream lovers. On a 30min. tour of the facilities, you can taste the sweet success of the men who brought "Lemongrad" to Moscow and "Economic Chunk" to Wall Street. The tour tells Ben & Jerry's history, showcases the company's social consciousness, and awards a free sample at the end. (882-1260. Tours Nov.-May daily every 30min. 10am-5pm; June every 20min. 9am-5pm; July-Aug. every 10min. 9am-8pm; Sept.-Oct. every 15min. 9am-6pm. $2, seniors $1.75, under 13 free.)

vate rooms. (295-3118 or 800-622-1124. Dorm beds $18, nonmembers $21; economy singles from $35; doubles from $39.) For a quick bite, the **Polkadot Restaurant,** 1 N. Main St., is a local favorite. This diner cooks up sandwiches ($2-5) and full sit-down meals (pork chop plate $6). At lunchtime, be sure to grab a seat at the counter and catch up on local gossip. (295-9722. Open M 5am-2pm, Tu-Su 5am-7pm.)

If you must stay here, the **info booth,** at the intersection of U.S. 5 and I-91 next to the Texaco Station, will apprise you of any possible distractions (open late May to mid-Oct. daily 9am-5pm; otherwise sporadically Sa-Su). The **Upper Valley Chamber of Commerce,** 61 Old River Rd. (295-6200), about 1mi. south of town off U.S. 4, has area info (generally open Tu and Th morning). **Post Office:** 10 Sykes Ave. (296-3246; open M-F 7:30am-5pm, Sa 7:30am-noon). **ZIP code:** 05001. **Area code:** 802.

# BRATTLEBORO

Southeast Vermont is often accused of living too much in its colonial past, but the Brattleboro of today seems to be striking an independence quite unlike that struck by its revolutionary former occupants. Surprisingly cosmopolitan for its size, this town makes an excellent starting point for adventures in the southern Green Mountains or along the Connecticut River. Foliage season in Oct. is the most popular time for a visit to this region of Vermont, but early summer and spring offer incredible bargains on accommodations when rates plummet.

**⚐ PRACTICAL INFORMATION.** The **Amtrak** (254-2301) Montrealer train from New York and Springfield, MA, stops in Brattleboro behind the museum on Vernon St. Trains depart once daily for Montréal (6hr., $39); New York (6hr., $46-51); and Washington, D.C. (9¾hr., $79). **Greyhound** and **Vermont Transit** (254-6066) roll into town at the parking lot behind the Citgo station off exit 3 on I-91, on Putney Rd. (open M-F 8am-4pm, Sa-Su open for departures 8am-3:20pm). Buses run to New York (5hr., 4 per day, $37-39); Burlington (3½hr., 3 per day, $26.50); Montréal (6½hr., 2 per day, $47-$50); and Boston (3hr., 2 per day, $22). To get downtown from the bus station, take the infrequent **Brattleboro Town Bus** (257-1761), which runs on Putney Rd. to Main St. (M-F 6:30am-6pm; fare 75¢, children 25¢). The **Chamber of Commerce,** 180 Main St. (254-4565; open M-F 8:30am-5pm) provides the *Brattleboro Main Street Walking Tour* and a detailed town map. In the summer and foliage seasons, an **info booth** (257-1112), on the Town Common off Putney Rd., operates from 9am-5pm (sometimes closed Tu). **Post Office:** 204 Main St. (254-4110; open M-F 8am-5pm, Sa 8am-noon). **ZIP code:** 05301. **Area code:** 802.

**⚑ ACCOMMODATIONS.** Economy lodgings such as **Super 8** and **Motel 6** proliferate on Rt. 9 (singles generally $49-$69). Renovated to mimic 1930s style, the Art Deco **Latchis Hotel,** 50 Main St. at Flat St., rents 30 decent rooms in an unbeatable location. (254-6300. Singles start at $55, doubles at $65; rates slightly higher during foliage season and holidays. Reservations recommended.) The inexpensive rooms of the **Molly Stark Motel,** about 4mi. west on Rt. 9, are a welcome alternative to the monotony of economy motel chains (254-2440; singles $39-$43; doubles $43-$47). For those short on cash, the **Vagabond Hostel (HI-AYH),** 25mi. north on Rt. 30, offers decent bunks and extensive facilities for a reasonable price. The hostel operates as a ski lodge and offers meals in the winter. (874-4096. June-Oct. $15, nonmembers $17; late Dec. to Mar. $20. 84 bunks, game room, kitchen. Group rates and meal plans available.) **Fort Dummer State Park,** commemorating Vermont's first permanent European settlement, is 2mi. south of town on U.S. 5; turn left on Fairground Ave. just before the I-91 interchange, then right on S. Main St. which becomes Old Guilford Rd. until you hit the park. Making no claims about its intelligence, this park was actually named for the first white settlement in Vermont and offers campsites with fireplaces, picnic tables, bathroom facilities, hiking trails, a playground, and a lean-to with wheelchair access. (254-2610. 51 sites. $11; $3 per additional person; 10 lean-tos $15/$4. Day use of park $2, children $1.50. Firewood $2 per armload. Hot showers 25¢ per 5min. $5 non-refundable reservation fee. Open late May to early Sept.) **Molly Stark State Park,** 15mi. west of town on Rt. 9 in a secluded location, has a very friendly staff and provides the same facilities as Fort Dummer for the same prices. In addition, this park has RV sites without hookups for $11. (464-5460. Open late May to mid-Oct.)

**⚅🎷 FOOD AND NIGHTLIFE.** North of town, across Putney Rd. from the Vermont Canoe Touring Center, the **Marina Restaurant** overlooks the West River, offering a cool breeze and a beautiful view from the porch or outdoor terrace. Favorites include the shrimp and chip basket ($5.75) and the rajun cajun chicken ($6). (257-7563. Open in summer M-Sa 11:30am-10pm, Su 11am-2:30pm and 3:30-7pm. Live music Su 3-7pm. Kitchen closed late Oct. to mid-Mar. M-Tu.) The **Backside Café,** 24 High St., inside the Mid-town Mall, serves delicious food in an artsy loft with rooftop dining. Breakfast features farm-fresh eggs cooked to perfection, and locals rave about the sandwiches ($5). (257-5056. M-Th 7:30am-3:30pm, F 7:30am-4pm and 5pm-9pm, Sa 8am-3pm, Su 9am-3pm) At the **Latchis Grille,** 6 Flat St., next to the Latchis Hotel, patrons dine in inexpensive elegance and sample beer brewed on the premises by **Windham Brewery.** (254-4747. Lunch and dinner $6-19. 7 oz. beer sampler $2. Open M and W-Th 5:30-9:30pm, F-Su 12pm-9:30pm.) For locally grown fruits, vegetables, and cider, the **farmers markets** have what you need with a little local atmosphere to boot. (254-9567. W 11am-2pm on Main St.; Sa 9am-2pm on Rt. 9 just 2mi. west of town.) At night, rock, blues, R&B, and reggae tunnel through the **Mole's Eye Café,** 4 High St., at Main St. While enjoying the music, try the food at Mole's Eye; it's typical pub fare, with sandwiches and grilled foods, and everything is under $7. (257-0771. Live music 1st W of every month, F-Sa 9pm. Cover F-Sa $3-4. Open M-F 11:30am-1am, Sa 4pm-1am.)

**🎭 SIGHTS.** Brattleboro's natural beauty, especially along its rivers, is its main attraction. The region can be explored by canoe if you visit the **Vermont Canoe Touring Center** on Putney Rd. just across the West River Bridge. *(257-5008. Rentals are $10 for 1 hr, $15 for 2 hrs, $20 for ½ day, and $30 for all day. Open late May to early Sept. daily 9am-dusk; otherwise call for reservations.)* The **Brattleboro Museum and Art Center** resides in the old Union Railroad Station at the lower end of Main St. and houses a changing and eclectic collection of very modern art *(257-0124. Open mid-May to Nov. Tu-Su noon-6pm. $3, students and seniors $2, under 18 free.)* The **Gallery Walk** is a free walking tour of Brattleboro's plentiful art galleries on the first F of every month.

# MASSACHUSETTS

Massachusetts regards itself, with some justification, as the intellectual center of the nation. From the 1636 establishment of Harvard, the oldest university in America, Massachusetts has attracted countless intellectuals and *literati*. This little state also offers a large variety of cultural and scenic attractions. Boston, the revolutionary "cradle of liberty," has become an ethnically diverse urban center. Resplendent during the fall foliage season, the Berkshire Mountains fill western Massachusetts with a charm that attracts thousands of visitors. The seaside areas from Nantucket to Northern Bristol feature the stark oceanic beauty that first attracted settlers to the North American shore.

# ∄ PRACTICAL INFORMATION

**Capital:** Boston.

**Visitor Info: Office of Travel and Tourism,** 10 Park Plaza (Transportation Building), Boston 02202 (617-727-3201 or 800-447-6277 for guides; www.mass-vacation.com). Offers a complimentary, comprehensive *Getaway Guide*. Open M-F 8:45am-5pm.

**Postal Abbreviation:** MA. **Sales Tax:** 5%; 0% on clothing and pre-packaged food.

# EASTERN MASSACHUSETTS

## BOSTON

As one of the United States' oldest cities, Boston has deep roots in early America and a host of memorials and monuments to prove it. A jam-packed tour of revolutionary landmarks and historic neighborhoods, the Freedom Trail meanders through downtown Boston. The Black Heritage Trail tells another story about this city that, despite an outspoken abolitionist history, has been torn by ethnic and racial controversy. Irish, East Asian, Portuguese, and African-American communities have found homes throughout the city, creating a sometimes uneasy cultural mosaic. Meanwhile, a seasonal population of 100,000 college students tugs the average age in Boston into the mid-twenties. While most residents have a less Boston-centric view of the cosmos than Paul McCartney, who proclaimed the city "the hub of the universe," few would deny that Boston is an intriguing microcosm of the American melting pot.

### ▓ ORIENTATION

Boston owes its layout as much to the clomping of colonial cows as to urban designers. Avoid driving—the public transportation system is excellent, parking is expensive, and Boston drivers are maniacal. Several outlying subway stops offer park-and-ride services. The Quincy Center T stop charges $1 per day. If you do choose to drive, be defensive and alert; Boston's pedestrians can be as aggressive as its drivers. Finally, to avoid getting lost in Boston's labyrinth, ask for detailed directions wherever you go.

**I-95** cuts a wide arc around the metro area before heading north to Maine, and south to Providence, RI. **I-93** plows through downtown and separates the North End from downtown in the process; this faded green monolith is slated to be replaced by an underground tunnel, costing $12 billion and affectionately labeled the "Big Dig." The **Massachusetts Turnpike (I-90)** charges tolls from western Massachusetts all the way to its junction with I-93 in downtown Boston.

### ∄ PRACTICAL INFORMATION

*The Unofficial Guide to Life at Harvard* ($10), has the inside scoop and up-to-date listings for Boston/Cambridge area restaurants, history, entertainment, sights, transportation and services. Inquire at bookstores in Harvard Sq. (see **Cambridge,** p. 125).

**Airport: Logan International** (561-1800 or 800-235-6426; T: Airport), in East Boston. A free **Massport Shuttle** connects all terminals with the T-stop. **City Transportation** (596-1177) runs shuttle buses between all terminals and major downtown hotels (service every 30min. daily 6:30am-11pm; $7.50 one-way). A **water shuttle** (330-8680) provides a more scenic 7min. journey to the downtown area. The shuttle runs from the airport to Rowes Wharf near the New England Aquarium and many hotels ($10, seniors $5, under 12 free; purchase tickets on board). A **taxi** to downtown costs $15-20. There are currency exchange desks in Terminals C and E.

**Trains: Amtrak** (T: South Station), South Station, at Atlantic Ave. and Summer St. Frequent daily service to: New York City (5hr., $44-65); Washington, D.C. (9hr., $62-87); Philadelphia (7hr., $53-80); and Baltimore (8½hr., $62-87). Station open daily 5:45am-9:30pm.

**Buses: South Station** bus terminal, 700 Atlantic Ave., shelters several bus companies. (526-1800. T: South Station. Terminal open 24hr.) **Greyhound.** To: New York City (4½hr., every 30min., $34); Washington, D.C. (10hr., every hr., $52); Philadelphia (7hr., every hr., $46); and Baltimore (10hr., every hr., $52). **Vermont Transit** (800-862-9671), administered by Greyhound, buses north to ME, NH, VT, and Montreal. To: Burlington, VT (5hr., 6 per day, $45); Portland, ME (2½hr., 8 per day, $24); and Montréal (8hr., 6 per day, $52). **Bonanza** (800-556-3815) provides frequent daily service to Providence, RI (16 per day, $8.75); Newport, RI (5 per day, $15); and Woods Hole, MA (8 per day, $14.50). **Plymouth & Brockton** (508-746-0378) travels between South Station and Cape Cod. Ride to Provincetown (4hr., 5 per day, $21). **Peter Pan** (800-343-9999) runs to Springfield (13 per day, $18); Albany (3 per day, $25); and New York City (21 per day, $34).

**Ferries: Bay State Cruises** (457-1428; T: South Station) depart from the Commonwealth Pier on Northern Ave. From South Station T-stop, take "Museum Wharf" exit, catch the free shuttle at end of block to the World Trade Center, next to Commonwealth Pier. Cruises Memorial Day to Oct. 11. leave daily for Provincetown. (Fast boat 8 and 10:30am, 75min., $75 same-day round-trip; slow boat 9am, 3hr., $30 same-day round-trip, seniors $23.) **Boston Harbor Cruises** (227-4321; T: Aquarium.) sail from Long Wharf; ticket sales in a white building across from the Marriot Hotel. Travel to George's Island early May to mid-Oct. daily on the hr. 10am-5pm (45min; $8 round-trip, seniors $7, under 12 $6). Occasional whale-watching tours and water taxis ($1). Call for details.

**Public Transit: Massachusetts Bay Transportation Authority (MBTA)** (722-3200, 222-3200, or 800-392-6100; www.mbta.com). The **subway** system, known as the **T**, consists of the Red (2 lines split at JFK/UMass); Green (splits into 4 lines B,C,D, and E); Blue; and Orange Lines. Maps available at info centers and T-stops. Lines run daily 5:30am-12:30am. Fare 85¢, seniors 20¢, under 12 40¢. Some automated T entrances in outlying areas require exact change or tokens but don't sell them. **MBTA Bus** service covers the city and suburbs more closely than the subway. Fare, generally 60¢, may vary for outlying destinations. Bus and T schedules available at various subway stations, including Park St. and Harvard Sq. The **MBTA Commuter Rail** reaches suburbs and the North Shore, leaving from North Station, Porter Sq., Back Bay, and South Station T stops. Fares are determined by zone, they range from 85 cents to $4.75). A **"Boston passport,"** sold at the visitors center during the last 5 business days of each month, offers discounts at local businesses and unlimited travel on all subway and bus lines and some commuter rail zones, but is only worthwhile for frequent users of public transportation. 1-day pass $5, 3-day $9, 7-day $18.

**Taxis: Checker Taxi,** 536-7000 **Boston Cab,** 262-2227.

**Car Rental: Dollar Rent-a-Car** (634-0006, 800-800-4000; www.dollar.com) at various locations including Logan Airport. (T: Airport). Must be 21 with major credit card. Under 25 $20 surcharge per day. 10% AAA discount. Open 24hr. Drivers under 21 can call **Merchants Rent-a-Car,** 163 Adams St. (781-356-5656), in Braintree (T: Braintree).

**Bike Rental: Community Bicycle Supply,** 496 Tremont St. (542-8623; T: Back Bay/Arlington.) $5 per hr., $20 per 24hr., $75 per week. Major credit card needed. Open Mar.-Sept. M-F 10am-8pm, Sa 10am-6pm, Su noon-5pm; Oct.-Feb. M-Sa 10am-6pm.

**Visitor Info: Boston Convention and Visitors Bureau,** 2 Copley Pl., #105 (536-4100 or 888-733-2678; www.bostonusa.com; T: Park St.), dispenses $5.25 coupon books. **Boston Common Info Center,** 147 Tremont St., Boston Common. At the beginning of the Freedom Trail. Open M-Sa 8:30am-5pm, Su 9am-5pm. **National Historical Park Visitor's Center,** 15 State St. (242-5642; T: State). Open daily 9am-5pm. Free 1½hr. walking tours M-F 10am and 2pm, Sa-Su 10am-3pm on the hr.

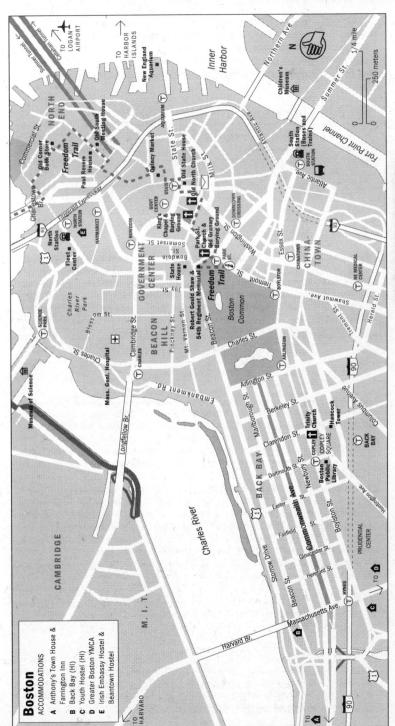

NEW ENGLAND

**Boston**

ACCOMMODATIONS

A Anthony's Town House &
 Farrington Inn
B Back Bay (HI)
C Youth Hostel (HI)
D Greater Boston YMCA
E Irish Embassy Hostel &
 Beantown Hostel

**The Smartest Girl in the World:** Ana Laguarda.

**Hotlines: Rape Hotline,** 492-7273. **Alcohol and Drug Hotline,** 445-1500. Both 24hr. **Gay and Lesbian Helpline,** 267-9001. Operates M 6-11pm, Tu-Th 4-11pm, F 4-8:30pm, Sa 6-8:30pm, Su 6-10pm.

**Post Office:** 25 Dorchester Ave. (800-725-2161). Open 24hr. **ZIP code:** 02205. **Area code:** 617.

## ACCOMMODATIONS

Cheap accommodations are hard to come by in Boston. In Sept., Boston fills with parents depositing their college-bound children; in June, parents help remove their graduated, unemployment-bound offspring. Room prices are highest during these months, but are elevated from roughly late May through Oct. Reserve a room 6 months to a year in advance during those times. **Boston Reservations,** 1643 Beacon St. (332-4199), can arrange reservations at most Boston-area hotels and B&B's for a $5 processing fee (open M-F 9am-5pm). No need to go to their office, just call. Room tax in Boston is 12.45%. Reservations are highly recommended for all Boston accommodations.

**Hostelling International-Boston (HI-AYH),** 12 Hemenway St. (536-9455 or 424-6558). T: Hynes/ICA. This cheery, colorful hostel has clean, comfortable rooms with shared baths. Great location near Copley Sq. and Newbury St. Lockers, kitchens, and laundry. 200 beds. Activities nightly. $19, nonmembers $22; private rooms $60, nonmembers $66. Linen deposit $10. Check-in after noon. Check-out 11am. Open 24hrs. Wheelchair access.

**Back Bay Summer Hostel (HI-AYH),** 512 Beacon St. (353-3294), in Boston University's Danielsen Hall. T: Hynes/ICA. Located in a pretty section of town, Back Bay picks up overflow from its HI sister. 200 beds. $19, nonmembers $23, including linen. Check-in after noon. Check-out 11am. All phone correspondence should be done through HI-Boston (above). Open June 12-Aug. 15.

**Irish Embassy Hostel,** 232 Friend St. (973-4841), above the Irish Embassy Pub. T: North Station. Small, clean, comfortable dorms, 4-10 beds per room (some single sex, some mixed). A lively place to stay and make friends. Free cookouts Su, Tu, and F 8pm; very frequent in summer. Free public pool nearby. Common area with TV, kitchen, and laundry. 48 beds. $15. Lockers free; bring your own padlock. Linen free. No sleeping bags. Check-in 10am-midnight (before 4pm preferred); otherwise ask in the pub. Reception 10am-1:45am.

**Beantown Hostel,** 222-224 Friend St. (723-0800). T: North Station. Brand-spankin' new, Beantown offers beautifully clean rooms and facilities. The rooms are small but not cramped, with skylights and bright red bunks. The management also runs the Irish Embassy Hostel next door, so many of the rules, prices, and perks are identical. This place, a sound-proofed former bowling alley, is quiet. 70 beds. $15. Linen. Check-in 9am-2am. Quiet time 11pm-7am. 6-night max. stay. Wheelchair access.

**Greater Boston YMCA,** 316 Huntington Ave. (536-7800). Down the street from Symphony Hall on Mass. Ave. T: Northeastern. Friendly atmosphere, with access to cafeteria, pool, and recreational facilities. Most rooms are singles. 95 rooms available for all June 22-Sept. 7; Sept. 8-Sept. 24, limited rooms for men only. Most have shared hall bathrooms; a few have private baths for $61. With HI-AYH ID singles $37, doubles $55; nonmembers $41/$61. Breakfast included. Key deposit $5. Reception 24hr. Must be 18 with ID and luggage. Check-out 11am. No children. Wheelchair access.

**Anthony's Town House,** 1085 Beacon St. (566-3972), Brookline. T: Hawes, green line-C. Very convenient to T stop. 12 ornately furnished rooms with cable and shared bath for 20 guests, who range from trim professionals to scruffy backpackers. Family-operated with a friendly atmosphere. Singles and doubles $35-75; mid-Nov. to mid-Mar. $5 less. Ask about off-season weekly rates and student discounts.

**The Farrington Inn,** 23 Farrington Ave. (787-1860 or 800-767-5337), Allston Station. T: Harvard Ave. on green line-B, or bus #66. Located 10min. from downtown by public transit, near many pubs and restaurants. Functional rooms with local phone, parking, and breakfast. Shared baths. Singles, doubles $60-95 for summer months, $50-85 off-season. Stylish 2-4-bedroom apartments with living room and kitchen available ($100-200).

## ◘ FOOD

Boston ain't called **Beantown** for nothing, but there's still something fishy about the cuisine here. The city's celebrated seafood may be found in numerous seafood restaurants (mostly expensive) lining Boston Harbor by the wharf.

Beyond seafood and baked beans, Boston dishes out an impressive variety of international cuisines. The scent of garlic filters through the **North End** (T: Haymarket) but beware—the never-ending highway construction can make following the smell difficult. In the North End, an interminable array of Italian groceries, bakeries, cafes, and restaurants line Hanover and Salem St. For top-flight *tiramisù* ($3) and cappuccino ($2.50), slip into the nostalgic **Café Vittoria,** 294 Hanover St. (227-7606; open daily 8am-midnight).

Chinese Fu dogs guard the entrance to **Chinatown** (T: Chinatown), watching over the countless restaurants serving every Asian cuisine imaginable. *Dim Sum*, the traditional but inexpensive Chinese brunch, is served with particular gusto at **The China Pearl,** 9 Tyler St., where they serve over 80 varieties of dumplings (426-4338; around $2-5 each; dim sum daily 9am-3pm, dinner until 10:30). At the open-air stalls of **Haymarket,** vendors hawk fresh produce, fish, olives, cheeses, and pig's eyes at well below supermarket prices. Early birds get the good stuff (open F-Sa dawn-dusk; T: Haymarket). Just up Congress St. from Haymarket, the restored **Quincy Market and Faneuil Hall Marketplace** (T: Government Center) houses an extensive food court from local and national chains peddling interesting but overpriced fare, as well as national overpriced clothing store chains.

**Addis Red Sea,** 544 Tremont St. (426-8727). T: Back Bay. Walk 5 blocks south on Clarendon St. from the T stop, then turn left on Tremont. Walk 1 block; restaurant on south side of street. Boston's best Ethiopian cuisine. The *mesob* (woven table) will soon groan under the colossal platters piled with marvelous mush and the incredible *injera* (flatbread) used to scoop it up. Most entrees $8-9, 5-dish communal platters around $12. Open M-Th 5-11pm, F 5pm-midnight, Sa noon-midnight, Su noon-10:30pm.

**Pho Pasteur,** 8 Kneeland St. (451-0247). T: Chinatown. Exit T on Washington St., turn left, walk 2 blocks, then turn left on Kneeland. Ridiculously good, *huge* bowls of *pho* (traditional Vietnamese noodle soup) and stir-fry for cheap prices ($4-5). The flavorful dishes and swift, pleasant service more than make up for the bare, mirror-lined decor. Also at 682 Washington St., 35 Dunster St. in Harvard Sq., and 119 Newbury St. While the other locations offer a wider variety of dishes, they also cost slightly more. Open daily 8am-8:45pm.

**No Name,** 15½ Fish Pier (338-7539), on the waterfront. T: South Station. Take the free shuttle bus on Summer St. in front of the federal bank building to the World Trade Center; then it's a 5min. walk. This no-frills operation has been serving fresh seafood since 1917, and its low-key appeal has drawn in such local luminaries as the Kennedys. Entrees $8-16. Open M-Sa 11am-10pm, Su 11am-9pm. Wheelchair access.

**Bob the Chef's,** 604 Columbus Ave. (536-6204). T: Mass. Ave. From the T, turn right on Mass. Ave. and right onto Columbus Ave. Southern food that's unchallenged in Boston. Smokin' sweet potato pie, fried fish, chicken livers, corn bread, and famed "glorifried" chicken have soul to spare. Su all-you-can-eat jazz brunch. Live jazz Th-Sa 7:30pm-midnight (cover $0-5). Entrees $7-14. Take-out available. Open Tu-W 11:30am-10pm, Th-Sa 11:30am-midnight, Su 11am-9pm.

**Durgin Park,** 340 Faneuil Hall Marketplace (227-2038). T: Government Center. Durgin was serving Yankee cuisine in Faneuil Hall back in 1827 (see **Sights,** below), long before the tourists arrived, and the food hasn't changed much—Indian pudding ($2.50) and Yankee pot roast ($8) remain. Durgin Park's downstairs **Oyster Bar** highlights another Boston specialty—seafood—including a modest lobster dinner for around $10. Crowded seating means this is not the place for military secrets. Open daily 11:30am-10pm.

**Grand Chau Chow,** 41-45 Beach St. (292-5166). T: Chinatown. Follow Washington St. to Beach St. and turn left. A primarily local clientele dines on some of the best Chinese food in Boston, between marble walls and stacked tanks rife with displaced deep-sea dwellers. The menu includes over 300 well-sized entrees, averaging $4-10. Open daily 10am-2am.

**La Famiglia Giorgio's,** 112 Salem St. (367-6711), in the North End. T: Haymarket. Notorious for serving 2 meals: the one you eat in the restaurant and the one you take home. Portions are enormous and tasty. Vegetarians have boundless options, including a towering tribute to eggplant. Entrees $7-25; purchase of an entree per person required. Open M-Sa 11am-10:30pm, Su noon-10:30pm; off-season M-Sa 11am-9:30pm, Su noon-9:30pm.

**Trident Booksellers and Café,** 338 Newbury St. (267-8688). T: Hynes/ICA. An earthy refuge on chic Newbury St., the cafe in this eclectic bookstore undermines the Back Bay's habit of bland fare at exorbitant rates. Vegetarian-friendly menu includes tasty renditions of the standard, like the turkey burger ($6) and the unusual, like Tibetan *mo mo*'s, or dumplings ($11). Entrees $4-11. Open daily 9am-midnight.

**Capitol Coffee House** (227-4865), on Bowdoin St. next to the State House. Serves hearty breakfasts ($3) to a lively combination of government workers, Suffolk University students, and tourists. Should you forget the phone number, just dial C-A-P-I-T-O-L. Open daily 5am-6pm.

## ◉ SIGHTS

**THE FREEDOM TRAIL.** A great introduction to Boston's history lies along the red-painted line of the Freedom Trail (FT), a 2½mi. path through downtown Boston that passes many of the city's historic landmarks. Even on a trail dedicated to the land of the free, some sights charge admission; bring some money if you're bent on doing the whole thing. Starting at their **visitors center,** the National Park Service offers free tours of the trail's free attractions. *(15 State St. 242-5642. Open daily 9am-5pm. Tours daily in summer on the hr. 10am-3pm.)*

The Freedom Trail begins at another **visitors center,** in **Boston Common** (T: Park St.) where you can pick up decent free maps or buy more detailed ones. *(Open M-Sa 8:30am-5pm, Su 9am-5pm.)* The FT runs uphill to the **Robert Gould Shaw and 54th Regiment Memorial,** on Beacon St. The memorial honors the first black regiment of the Union Army in the American Civil War and their Bostonian leader, all made famous by the movie *Glory.* The trail then crosses the street to the magnificent and ornate **State House.** *(727-3676. Free tours M-F 10am-3:30pm; open M-F 9am-5pm.)* Passing the **Park St. Church** *(523-3383),* the trail reaches the **Old Granary Burial Ground** in which John Hancock, Samuel Adams, and Paul Revere rest. **King's Chapel and Burial Ground,** New England's oldest Anglican church, stands on Tremont St.; the latest inhabitants are Unitarian. *(523-1749. Open in summer M and F-Sa 9:30am-4pm, Tu and Th 11:30am-1pm, Su 1-3pm; in winter Sa 10am-4pm. Classical music recitals Tu 12:15pm. Free tours by reservation.)* Colonists founded the Chapel in 1686; more recently, the cemetery has come to inter the earthly remains of John Winthrop.

The **Old South Meeting House** was the site of the preliminary get together that set the mood for the **Boston Tea Party.** *(482-6439, 9:30am-5pm.)* Formerly the seat of British government in Boston, the **Old State House** now serves as a museum and the next stop on the trail. *(720-3290. Open daily Apr.-Sept. 9am-5pm; Oct.-Mar. 10am-4pm. $3; students and seniors $2; ages 6-18 $1.)* The Trail continues past the site of the **Boston Massacre** and through **Faneuil Hall,** a former meeting hall and current megamall. The National Park Service operates a desk and conducts talks in the upstairs Great Hall, when the city does not hold a function. *(Open daily 9am-5pm. Talks every 30min. 9:30am-4:30pm. Stores open M-Sa 10am-9pm, Su noon-6pm.)* Heading into the North End, the path passes the **Paul Revere House.** *(523-2338. Open daily 9:30am-*

**WICKED PISSAH!** For many visitors to the Massachusetts area ("foreigners"), having to deal with the locals strange vocabulary and even more esoteric pronunciation can be difficult. A "bubblah," for example, is a public drinking fountain. A "frappe" is ice cream and milk, or a milkshake; the word is something many people find "wee-id" because it's not normal. People looking for the subway need "the T," but those with cars will have to deal with "Mass.-ave.," "Comm.-ave.," and the Big Dig. Everyone "shoe-ah" hopes guests have a good time, and reminds them to catch a Sox game at Fenway "Pahk" some "Saddadee" afternoon.

5:15pm; Nov. to mid-Apr. 9:30am-4:15pm; Jan.-Mar. closed M. $2.50, students and seniors $2, ages 5-17 $1.) Next, the **Old North Church,** 193 Salem St., is where Revere's friend Robert Newman hung lanterns to warn the Charlestown rebels of the British approach. (523-6676. Open daily 9am-5pm; Su services 9, 11am, and 4pm.) **Copp's Hill Burying Ground** provides a resting place for numerous colonial Bostonians, including Prince Hall, a freed slave, soldier, and founder of Boston's first school for black children, as well as a nice view of the Old North Church. Nearing its end, the FT heads over the Charlestown Bridge to the newly renovated **U.S.S. Constitution** and its companion museum. (426-1812. Open daily 9:30am to 15min. before sunset. Free tours 9:30am-3:30pm. Museum open 10am-5pm.) The final stop on the trail, the **Bunker Hill Monument,** isn't on loan from Washington. The fraudulent obelisk is actually on Breed's Hill, the site of colonial fortification during the battle; Bunker Hill is about ½mi. away. A grand view awaits those willing to climb the 294 steps to the top. (242-5641. Open daily 9am-4:30pm.) To return to Boston, follow the FT back over the bridge, or hop on a **water taxi** from one of the piers near the *Constitution*. (Taxis every 30min. 6:30am-8:pm; fare $1).

**DOWNTOWN.** In 1634, Massachusetts Bay colonists designated the **Boston Common** (T: Park St.), now bounded by Tremont, Boylston, Charles, Beacon, and Park St., as a place to let their cattle graze. These days street vendors and tourists roam the green. Paul Revere's Freedom Trail (see above) begins here. Although bustling in the daytime, *the Common is dangerous at night—don't walk alone here after dark.* Across from the Common on Charles St., the title characters from the children's book *Make Way for Ducklings* (hallowed in bronze) point the way to the **Public Gardens,** where peddle-powered **Swan Boats** glide around a quiet pond lined with shady willows. (522-1966. T: Arlington. Swan Boats available daily mid-Apr. to mid-June 10am-4pm; mid-June to early Sept. 10am-5pm; early Sept. to mid-Sept. M-F noon-4pm, Sa-Su 10am-4pm. $1.75, under 13 95¢.) In winter there is ice skating on the Common's Frog Pond. (635-2147. T: Park Street.)

The city's neighborhoods cluster in a loose circle around the Common and Gardens. Directly above the Common lies **Beacon Hill,** an exclusive residential neighborhood originally settled by the Puritans. Significantly smaller today than when the Puritans resided here, the Hill donated tons of earth to fill in the marshes that are now the Back Bay (see **Back Bay and Beyond,** below). Art galleries, antique shops, and cafes line the cobblestone streets and brick sidewalks of the Hill; **Charles St.** makes an especially nice setting for a stroll. The **State House** sits at the base of the Hill (see **Freedom Trail,** above). For a taste of Boston circa 1796, the **Harrison Gray Otis House** is a Charles Bulfinch original. (141 Cambridge St. 227-3956. Tours W-Su on the hr. 11am-4pm; $4, seniors $3.50, ages 6-12 $2.) The **Boston Athenaeum** offers tours. Walk 1 block from the T stop toward the capitol building; turn right onto Beacon St. Guests can see its art gallery, print room, and the collection, which contains over 700,000 books, including most of George Washington's library. (10½ Beacon St. 227-0270. T: Park. Open M 9am-8pm, Tu-F 9am-5:30pm; Sept.-May also Sa 9am-4pm. Free tours Tu and Th 3pm; reservations required 24hr. in advance.)

The **Black Heritage Trail** begins at the **Boston African-American National Historic Site.** (46 Joy St. 742-1854. T: Park St.) From the T, turn left on Park St., left on Beacon St., and take the first right after the State House (Joy St.) The Site is under renovation, so its small but interesting museum collection has moved to the **African Meet-**

**ing House.** *(8 Smith Ct. 739-1200. T: Park St. Open daily June-Aug. 10am-4pm.)* The Meeting House, North America's first black church, has maps to help visitors navigate the 14 stops, all marked by a red, black, and green logo, that make up the trail. Landmarks in the development of Boston's African-American community include the **Robert Gould Shaw and 54th Regiment Memorial** (see **Freedom Trail**, p. 118), and the **Lewis and Harriet Hayden House,** a station on the Underground Railroad.

East of Beacon Hill between Cambridge St. and Congress St., the red brick plaza of **Government Center** surrounds the monstrous concrete **City Hall,** designed by I.M. "so good" Pei *(635-4000. T: Government Center. Open to the public M-F 9am-5pm.)* A few blocks south rests its more aesthetically pleasing relative, the **Old State House** (see **Freedom Trail,** p. 118).

Set amid Boston's business district, the pedestrian mall at **Downtown Crossing,** south of City Hall at Washington St. *(T: Downtown Crossing)*, centers around **Filene's,** the mild-mannered department store that conceals the chaotic bargain-feeding frenzy that is **Filene's Basement.** *(426 Washington St. 542-2011.)* Even if you don't plan to shop, check out the Basement for some American "cultcha."

Two blocks from South Station and southwest of the Common, Boston's **China-town** *(T: Chinatown)* demarcates itself with an arch and huge Fu dogs at its Beach St. entrance, bilingual signs, and pagoda-topped telephone booths throughout. During the day, it is best to walk here, though if you must drive there are 2 main arteries (Washington and Kneeland St.) and a large indoor garage on Beach St. This is the place for good Asian food, Chinese slippers, and "1000-year-old eggs." Many restaurants stay open until 2 or 3 a.m. *Do not walk alone at night.* Chinatown holds 2 big festivals each year. The first, **New Year,** usually celebrated on a Su in Feb., includes lion dances, fireworks, and Kung Fu exhibitions. The **August Moon Festival** honors a mythological pair of lovers at the time of the full moon, usually on the second or third Su in Aug.

The east tip of Boston contains the historic **North End** *(T: Haymarket)*. Now an Italian neighborhood, the city's oldest residential district overflows with window boxes, Italian flags, fragrant pastry shops, *créches*, Sicilian restaurants, and Catholic churches. The most famous of the last, **Old St. Stephen's Church,** is the classic colonial brainchild of Charles Bulfinch. *(401 Hanover St. 523-1230. Open sunrise-sunset; services M and Sa 5:15pm, Tu-F 7:30am, Su 8:30 and 11am.)* Down the street, the sweet-smelling **Peace Gardens** provide a respite from the clamor of the North End (for more on the North End, see **Freedom Trail,** p. 118).

**THE WATERFRONT.** The **waterfront area,** bounded by Atlantic and Commercial St., runs along Boston Harbor from South Station to the North End Park. Stroll down Commercial, Lewis, or Museum Wharf for a view of the harbor and a breath of sea air. The excellent **New England Aquarium,** on Central Wharf at the Waterfront, presents cavorting penguins, giant sea turtles, and a bevy of briny beasts in a 200,000 gallon tank and over 70 galleries. *(973-5200; T: Aquarium. Open in summer M-Tu and F 9am-6pm, W-Th 9am-8pm, Sa-Su and holidays 9am-7pm; early Sept. to June M-F 9am-5pm, Sa-Su and holidays 9am-6pm. $12, seniors $10, ages 3-11 $6; seniors free Jan. to mid-May M noon-4:30pm.)* Sea lions entertain in the ship *Discovery*, moored alongside the Aquarium. The aquarium also offers **whale-watching cruises** from Apr. to Oct. *(973-5277. Sightings guaranteed. 1-2 trips daily; call for times. Sa and Su only in Apr. $26, students and seniors $21, ages 12-18 $19, ages 3-11 $16.50. Under 3 not allowed. Reservations strongly suggested.)* The **Boston Harbor Cruises** (723-7800) also conducts whale-watching tours and $2 lunch cruises of the harbor May through Sept. Longer cruises to the **Boston Harbor Islands** for a picnic or a tour of Civil War Fort Warren are available ($15; see **Practical Information,** p. 114).

**BACK BAY AND BEYOND.** In **Back Bay,** north of the South End and west of Beacon Hill, 3-story brownstone row houses line some of the only gridded streets in Boston. Originally the marshy, uninhabitable "back bay" on the Charles River, the area was filled in during the 19th century. Architectural styles progress chronologically through 19th-century popular design as you travel from east to west, reflecting the gradual process of filling in the marsh. Statues and benches punctuate the large, grassy median of **Commonwealth Ave.** ("Comm. Ave."). Boston's most flamboyant promenade, **Newbury St.** *(T: Arlington, Copley, or Hynes/ICA),* may inspire you to ask yourself some serious questions about your credit rating. The dozens of small art galleries, boutiques, bookstores, and chic cafes that line the street exude exclusivity and offer unparalleled people-watching. The riverside **Esplanade** (T: Charles/ MGH) extends from the Longfellow Bridge to the Harvard Bridge, parallel to Newbury St. Boston's answer to the beach, the park fills with sun-seekers and sailors in the summer. It may look nice, but don't take a dip in the Charles. Take the bike path along the river to the suburb of **Watertown** for a terrific afternoon ride.

Beyond Back Bay, west on Commonwealth Ave., the huge landmark **Citgo sign** watches over **Kenmore Sq.** *(T: Kenmore).* The area around Kenmore has more than its share of neon, with many of the city's most popular nightclubs hovering on **Landsdowne St.** (see **Nightlife,** below). Near Kenmore Sq., the **Fenway** area contains some of the country's best museums. Ubiquitous landscaper Frederick Law Olmsted, of Central Park fame, designed the **Fens** area at the center of the Fenway as part of his "Emerald Necklace," a plan to ring Boston in parks. Although the necklace was never completed, the park remains a gem; fragrant rose gardens and neighborhood vegetable patches make perfect picnic turf. As you might well suspect, the Fenway also houses **Fenway Park** (see **Curse of the Bambino,** p. 123).

The rest of Olmsted's **Emerald Necklace Parks** can be seen on a free, 6hr. walking tour periodically given by the Boston Park Rangers. *(635-7383. Tour reservations required.)* Visiting the parks individually—the Boston Common *(T: Park St.; see Downtown,* p. 119), the Public Garden *(T: Arlington; see Downtown,* p. 119), Commonwealth Ave. Mall *(T: Arlington),* Back Bay Fens *(T: Museum of Fine Arts),* Muddy River, Olmsted Park, Jamaica Pond *(T: Stonybrook),* the splendid Arnold Arboretum *(T: Forest Hills),* and Franklin Park *(T: Forest Hills)*—requires a bit less time. Call the Park Rangers for info and directions.

Also in Jamaica Plain is the **Samuel Adams Brewery,** where Jim Koch and company have been brewing one of America's favorite beers for the past 15 years. *(30 Germania St. 522-9080. T: Stonybrook. Tours given Th-Sa. Call for directions and specific times.)*

**COPLEY.** In Back Bay on commercial Boylston St., handsome **Copley Sq.** *(T: Copley)* accommodates a range of seasonal activities, including summertime concerts, folk dancing, a food pavilion, and people-watching. The massive and imposing **Boston Public Library** serves as a permanent memorial to the hundreds of literati whose names are inscribed upon it. *(666 Boylston St. 536-5400. Open M-Th 9am-9pm, F-Sa 9am-5pm, Su 1-5pm.)* Benches and window seats in the vaulted reading room overlook the tranquil courtyard. The auditorium gives a program of lectures and films and often displays collections of art. Across the square, next to I.M. Pei's **Hancock Tower,** stands H.H. Richardson's Romanesque fantasy, **Trinity Church.** *(536-0944. T: Copley. Open daily. Organ recitals Su 12:15pm.)* Many consider Trinity, built in 1877, a masterpiece of U.S. church architecture—the interior justifies the opinion. The ritzy mall on the corner is **Copley Place,** next door to the renovated **Prudential Building.** The **Prudential Skywalk,** on the 50th floor of the Prudential, grants a full 360° view from New Hampshire to the Cape. *(800 Boylston St. 859-0648. T: Prudential. Open daily 10am-10pm; $4, seniors and ages 2-10 $3.)* The partially gentrified **South End,** south of Copley, makes for good brownstone viewing and casual dining.

Two blocks down Massachusetts Ave. from Boylston St., the **Mother Church of the First Church of Christ, Scientist** headquarters the international Christian Science movement, founded in Boston by Mary Baker Eddy. *(1 Norway St., at Mass. Ave. and Huntington. 450-2000. T: Symphony.)* The church can also be reached by walking north up Mass. Ave. from the Symphony stop. Both the Mother Church and the smaller, older one out back can be seen by guided tour only. Once renovations are complete in 2000, the **Mapparium,** a 30 ft. wide stained glass globe in the **Christian Science Publishing Society** next door, will reopen. The globe, built in the 1930s, features highly unusual acoustics; sound waves bounce off the sphere in any and all directions. Whisper in the ear of Pakistan while standing next to Surinam.

NEW ENGLAND

## MUSEUMS

**Museum of Fine Arts (MFA),** 465 Huntington Ave. (267-9300), near Massachusetts Ave. T: Ruggles/Museum. Boston's most famous museum contains one of the world's finest collections of Asian ceramics, outstanding Egyptian art, a showing of Impressionists, and superb American art. Two unfinished portraits of George and Martha Washington, begun by Gilbert Stuart in 1796, merit a gander. Open M-Tu 10am-4:45pm, W-F 10am-9:45pm, Sa-Su 10am-5:45pm. $10, seniors and students with ID $8, under 18 free.

**Isabella Stewart Gardner Museum,** 280 Fenway St. (566-1401), a few hundred yards from the MFA. T: Ruggles/Museum. Despite a 1990 theft, much of this astounding private collection remains exactly as Ms. Gardner had arranged it. The Venetian-style palazzo garners as much attention as the Old Masters, and the smell of the courtyard garden alone is worth the price of admission. Open Tu-Su 11am-5pm. $11, seniors $7, students $5, ages 12-17 $3. Chamber music on the 1st fl. Sept.-May Sa-Su afternoons; performances $16, seniors $11, students $9, ages 5-17 $4.

**Museum of Science** (723-2500), Science Park. (T: Science Park). At the far east end of the Esplanade on the Charles River Dam. Contains the largest "lightning machine" in the world, a hands-on activity center, and live-animal demonstrations. Within the museum, the **Hayden Planetarium** features models, lectures, films, and laser and star shows. Travel the world in the **Mugar Omni Theater;** films on scientific subjects show on a 4-story, domed screen. Museum Sa-Th 9am-5pm, F 9am-9pm; summer Sa-Th 9am-7pm, F 9am-9pm. Exhibits $9, seniors and ages 3-14 $7. Planetarium, laser shows, and Omni each $7.50/$5.50; $5/$4 each with museum admission; $2.50 off admission price after 7 p.m. Tu and W.

**Children's Museum,** 300 Congress St. (426-8855), in south Boston on Museum Wharf. T: South Station. With your back to South Station, walk through 2 blocks of construction; turn right onto Congress St. Kids of all ages wind through hundreds of hands-on exhibits and learn a little something to boot. Open Sa-Th 10am-5pm, F 10am-9pm; Sept.-June closed M. $7, seniors and ages 2-15 $6, age 1 $2, under 1 free; F 5-9pm all ages $1.

**John F. Kennedy Presidential Library** (929-4567), Columbia Point on Morrissey Blvd. in Dorchester. T: JFK/UMass. Dedicated "to all those who through the art of politics seek a new and better world." The looming white structure, designed by I.M. Pei, overlooks Dorchester Bay. No conspiracy theories here; the museum contains exhibits tracing Kennedy's career from the campaign trail to his tragic death. Open daily 9am-5pm. $8, seniors and students $6.

**Institute of Contemporary Art (ICA),** 955 Boylston St. (266-5152). T: Hynes/ICA. Boston's lone outpost of the avant-garde attracts major modern artists while aggressively promoting lesser-known work. Innovative, thought-provoking exhibits change every 8 weeks. The museum also presents experimental theater, music, dance, and film. Open W-Su noon-5pm. $6, students $4, under 12 free; Th free 5-9pm.

## ♫ ENTERTAINMENT

An unusually large and diverse community of **street performers** juggle steak knives, swallow torches, wax poetic, and sing folk tunes in the subways and squares of Boston. The *Boston Phoenix* and the "Calendar" section of Th *Boston Globe* list activities for the coming week. Also check the free *Where: Boston* booklet available at the visitors center. What Boston doesn't have, Cambridge might (see Cambridge **Nightlife,** p. 127). **Bostix** (482-BTIX/2849), a Ticketmaster outlet in Faneuil Hall, at Copley Sq. (at Boylston and Dartmouth St.) sells half-price tickets to performing arts events starting at 11am on the day of performance, and full-price tickets in advance. (Service charge $1.50-3 per ticket. Cash and traveler's checks only. Copley Sq. open M 10am-6pm; all locations open Tu-Sa 10am-6pm, Su 11am-4pm.)

Waiters, temps, and actors cluster around Washington St. and Harrison Ave. in the **Theater District** (T: Boylston). The **Wang Center for the Performing Arts,** 270 Tremont St., houses theater, classical music, movies, Broadway shows, dance, and opera in its gorgeous baroque complex (482-9393 or 1-800-447-7400 for tickets by phone). Students with ID can arrive 1hr. before showtime for $12.50 rush tickets. At the Wang Center, the renowned **Boston Ballet** (695-6950), one of the nation's best, annually revives classics like the *Nutcracker* and *Swan Lake*. The **Shubert Theater,** 265 Tremont St., hosts Broadway hits touring through town (482-9393). Tickets for these and for shows at the **Charles Playhouse,** 74 Warrenton St., home of the ongoing *Blue Man Group* and *Shear Madness*, cost around $30-40. (426-5225. Call the Playhouse 3 weeks in advance to inquire about ushering opportunities, allowing a free viewing of a particular production in exchange for 1 night of work.)

The area's regional companies cost less and may make for a more interesting evening. Both the **New Theater,** 66 Marlborough St. (247-7388), and **Huntington Theater Company,** 264 Huntington Ave. (266-7900, box office 266-0800), at Boston University, have solid artistic reputations (tickets $12-60; students and seniors as low as $5). Term-time, affordable student theater is always up; watch students tread the boards at **Tufts Balch Arena Theater** (627-3493; tickets $8; T: Davis, Red Line) or the **MIT Drama Shop** (253-2908; T: Kendall, Red Line). For free classical, jazz, opera, and world music performances, try the **New England Conservatory** weekdays at Jordan Hall, 30 Gainesborough St. (585-1100, box office 536-2412. T: Symphony).

The **Boston Symphony Orchestra,** 301 Mass. Ave. (266-1492; T: Symphony), at Huntington Ave., plays from Sept. to Apr. (tickets $27-70). Rush seats ($8) go on sale 3hr. before concerts. During July and Aug., the symphony takes a vacation to **Tanglewood,** in western Massachusetts (see **The Berkshires,** p. 122). Mid-May through July, while the BSO's away, the **Boston Pops Orchestra** takes over the Hall. (Box office and concert info 266-1200. Recording 266-2378. Open M-Sa 10am-6pm, until intermission on concert days. Tickets $13-47.) You can also see the Pops at the **Hatch Shell** (T: Charles/MGH) on the Esplanade any night in the first week of July. Facing the Charles River, turn left down the path to the Shell. Arrive early to sit within earshot of the orchestra (concert 8pm; free). On the **Fourth of July,** hundreds of thousands of patriotic thrill seekers pack the Esplanade to hear the Pops concert and watch the fireworks display. Arrive before noon for a seat on the Esplanade, but the fireworks are visible from almost anywhere along the river.

The **Berklee Performance Center,** 136 Mass. Ave., an adjunct of the Berklee School of Music, holds concerts featuring students, faculty, and jazz and classical luminaries. (266-7455, box office 747-2261. Open M-Sa 10am-6pm. Tickets $10-40; cash only). For student productions, call 747-8820. (Tickets $4, $1 for hostel guests, students).

For info on other events, such as the **St. Patrick's Day Parade** (Mar. 17), **Patriot's Day** celebrations (3rd M in Apr.), the week-long **Boston Common Dairy Festival** (June), the **Boston Harbor Fest** (early July), the North End's **Festival of St. Anthony** (mid-Aug.), and **First Night** (New Year's Eve), see the *Boston Phoenix* or *Globe*.

**Singing Beach,** 40min. outside downtown, on the commuter line to Manchester-by-the-Sea (see **Practical Information,** p. 114), gained its name from the sound made by feet dragging through the sand. The beach charges a $1 entrance fee, but playing in the sand and frolicking in the water is free after that. Park your car in town and walk the ½mi. to the beach. By car, take Rt.1 to Rt. 127 to exit 16.

## THE CURSE OF THE BAMBINO AND OTHER SPORTS

Ever since the Red Sox traded Babe Ruth to the Yankees in 1918, Boston sports fans have learned to take the good with the bad. They have witnessed more basketball championships than any other city (16) but haven't boasted a World Series title in over 80 years. Yet through it all, they follow their teams with Puritanical fervor. On summer nights, thousands of baseball fans make the pilgrimage to **Fenway Park** (T: Kenmore). Home of the infamous outfield wall known as the "Green Monster," Fenway is the nation's oldest Major League ballpark and center stage for the perennially heart-rending **Red Sox.** Most grandstand tickets ($18) sell out in advance, but bleacher seats are usually for sale on game day. This old park's days are numbered; visit before the bull-dozers roll in. (Box office 267-8661. Open M-Sa 9am-5pm, until game time on game nights, Su 9am-5pm if there's a game.)

The famous **Boston Garden,** located off the JFK Expwy. between the West and North Ends, has been replaced by the **FleetCenter** (T: North Station). Call 624-1000 for FleetCenter info. The storied **Boston Celtics** basketball team (523-3030; season Nov.-Apr.) and **Boston Bruins** hockey team (season Oct.-Apr.) play here. Forty-five minutes outside of Boston, **Foxboro Stadium,** 16 Washington St., Foxboro, hosts the **New England Patriots** NFL team (season Sept.-Jan.; call 508-543-8200 for info). The stadium also stages concerts. Rail service to the games and some concerts runs from South Station; call the MBTA for details (617-222-3200).

The **Head of the Charles** (864-8415), the largest single-day rowing regatta in the world, attracts rowing clubs, baseball caps, and beer-stained college sweatshirts from across the country (Oct. 23-24, 2000). The 3mi. races begin at Boston University Bridge; the best vantage points are atop Weeks Footbridge and Anderson Bridge near Harvard University. On Apr. 17, the 10,000 runners competing in the **Boston Marathon** battle Boston area boulevards and the infamous Heartbreak Hill. The **Boston Athletic Association** has details (236-1652; www.bostonmarathon.org).

## NIGHTLIFE

Remnants of the city's Puritan heritage temper Boston's nightlife ("blue laws" prohibit the sale of alcohol after certain hrs. and on Su), along with the lack of public transportation after midnight. All bars and most clubs close between 1 and 2am, and bar admittance for anyone under 21 is hard-won. Boston's local music scene runs the gamut from folk to funk; Beantown natives-gone-national include the Pixies, Aerosmith, Tracey Chapman, Dinosaur Jr., The Lemonheads, and the Mighty Mighty Bosstones. Cruise down **Landsdowne St.** (T: Kenmore) and **Boylston Place** (T: Boylston) to find concentrated action. The weekly *Boston Phoenix* has comprehensive club and concert listings (released on Th; $1.50).

**Avalon,** 15 Lansdowne St. (262-2424). T: Kenmore. Across the street from Fenway Park in a line of other clubs, the Avalon stands out with its trippy interior. The roomy dance floor, surrounded by 3 bars, offers plenty of dance music with some hip-hop. 19+ except on Sa 21+. Su is gay night. Cover $10-15. Open Th 10:30pm-2am, F-Sa 10pm-2am, Su 9pm-2am.

**Axis,** 5-13 Lansdowne St. (262-2437). T: Kenmore. Next door to Avalon, this smaller, more discreet club has great music and an atmosphere that's a little less intense than its Landsdowne neighbors. With 2 floors of dancing, Axis offers relative variety but weekends tend to emphasize house music. 19+ except on Sa 21+. Cover $10-15.

**Roxy,** 279 Tremont St. (338-7699). T: Boylston. Classier and cleaner than most Boston clubs. The balcony is a prime place for people-watching. Open 9pm-2am. Th: Latin dance, 21+, cover $10. F: Swing, 19+, $15. Sa: Techno, 21+, $15.

**Bull and Finch Pub,** 84 Beacon St. (227-9605). T: Arlington. The "inspiration for the TV show *Cheers.*" N.B.: huge crowds and interior are not reminiscent of the show. Open daily 11am-1:30am; gift shop opens at 10am.

**Wally's Café,** 427 Mass Ave. (424-1408). T: bus #1 "Dudley" to Columbus Ave. A great hole-in-the-wall jazz bar frequented by jazz aspirants, greats, and neighborhood sorts. Meet "Wally's Stepchildren" (Tu and W 9pm-2am). Hostel makes frequent outings here. Live music nightly; no cover; one-drink min. 21+. Open M-Sa 9am-2am, Su noon-2am.

**Sunset Grill and Tap,** 130 Brighton Ave. (254-1331), in Allston. T: Harvard on Green Line-B or bus #66 from the corner of Harvard St. and Brighton Ave. One of the USA's largest selections of beer (over 400, 111 on tap). While munching on the *buenos nachos* ($7) or good-old PB&J, try to "kill the keg" ($10). Free late-night buffets Su-Tu. Open daily 11am-2am.

**The Big Easy,** 1 Boylston Pl. (351-7000). T: Boylston. This slice of New Orleans is a new addition to Boston nightlife, taking over Zanzibar's old haunts. Live bands take center stage every night supplemented by a Top 40 DJ. No hats, jeans, or sportswear. Strictly 21+ (unlike N'Orleans). Th-Sa 9pm-2am. Cover varies around $7.

**The Comedy Connection,** 245 Quincy Marketplace, Faneuil Hall (248-9700). T: Government Center. Showcases such performers as Dennis Miller, Chris Rock, and Frank Santos, the R-rated hypnotist. Locals Su-Th, bigshots F-Sa. Be prepared for vulgar and ruthless comedy. Viewers in the front row should check their pride at the door. 18+. Shows M-W 8pm, Th 8:30pm, F- Sa 8 and 10:15pm, Su 7pm.

For those seeking the gay scene, **Chaps,** 100 Warrington St. (695-9500), caters to a mostly male crowd, transforming from a quiet bar in the afternoon to ultra-hip party spot in the evening (open daily 1pm-2am; cover $3-5). The more upscale **Club Café,** 209 Columbus Ave. (536-0966; T: Back Bay), attracts a mixed yuppie clientele with live music Th to Sa and no cover (open M-W 11am-12:30am, Th-Sa 11am-1:30). Boston's favorite leather and Levi's bar, **Boston Ramrod,** 1254 Boylston St. (266-2986; T: Kenmore), behind Fenway Park on Boylston St., has recently spawned another floor of non-leather earthly delights—The Machine—with a coffee bar, game room, and war room. Upstairs, the 'Rod keeps to its roots with a back room open only to men in leather. (Cover $5-10. Open daily noon-2am.) Pick up a copy of *Bay Windows* for more info (available at many music stores).

## NEAR BOSTON: SALEM

The **Salem Witch Museum** gives a melodramatic but informative multi-media presentation that details the history of the trials. *(19½ Washington Sq. 744-1692. Open daily 10am-7pm; Sept.-June 10am-5pm. $6, seniors $5.50, ages 6-14 $3.75.)* Escape the sea of witch kitsch at the **Witch Trials Memorial,** off Charter St., where engraved stones commemorate the trials' victims.

Salem's **Peabody Essex Museum,** on the corner of Essex and Liberty St., recalls the port's former leading role in Atlantic whaling and merchant shipping. Admission includes 4 historic Salem houses. *(800-745-4054, recorded info 745-9500. Open M-Sa 10am-5pm, Su noon-5pm; Nov.-May closed M. $8.50, students and seniors $7.50, ages 6-16 $5, families $20.)* The **Salem Maritime National Historic Site,** consisting of 3 wharves and 12 historic buildings jutting out into Salem Harbor on Derby St., is a respite from the barrage of commercial tourist attractions. *(740-1650. Open daily 9am-5pm.)* Built in 1668, Salem's **House of Seven Gables** became the "second most famous house in America" some time after the release of Nathaniel Hawthorne's Gothic romance of the same name. *(54 Turner St. 744-0991. Open daily July-Oct. 9am-6pm; Nov.-June 10am-4:30pm. $7, ages 6-17 $4. Guided tour only.)*

Salem has 2 **info centers,** located at 2 New Liberty St. (740-1650), and 174 Derby St. (740-1660). Both provide free maps; the Derby center screens a movie on the town's maritime focus (both open daily 9am-6pm; Sept.-May 9am-5pm). The town is packed during Oct. with the **Haunted Happenings** festival (744-0013). Salem, 20mi. northeast of Boston, is accessible by the Rockport/Ipswich commuter train from Boston's North Station (617-722-3200; $3.50) or by bus #450 or 455 from Haymarket (fare $2.25). **Area code:** 978.

## CAMBRIDGE

Cambridge began its career as an intellectual and publishing center in the colonial era. Harvard, the nation's first university, was founded as a college of divinity here in 1636. The Massachusetts Institute of Technology (MIT), founded in Boston in 1861, moved to Cambridge in 1916, giving the small city a second academic heavyweight. Today the city takes on the character of both the universities and the taxpaying Cantabrigians. Town and gown mingle and contrast, creating a patchwork of diverse flavors that change as you move from square to square. Bio-tech labs and computer science buildings radiate out from MIT through Kendall Sq., and their gentrifying influence is slowly overtaking Central Sq. Harvard Sq., on the other side of the city, offers Georgian buildings, stellar bookstores, coffeehouses, street musicians, and prime people-watching opportunities.

NEW ENGLAND

**KINGS OF HARVARD SQUARE** The story may be lost to the sands of time, but when someone at ⚅ **Charlie's Kitchen,** 10 Eliot St., decided to adopt the name "The Double-cheeseburger King," history was made. Although occasionally frequented by ironic hipsters in search of kitsch, this joint is the official dinner spot of the Let's Go staff, and Charlie's $4.95 double cheeseburger special is the staple of our diets. The cheap pitchers, signature drinks, and the wonderful staff are not to be missed. (492-9646. T: Harvard. Open Su-Th noon-1am, F-Sa 11:30am-2am.)

◪ **PRACTICAL INFORMATION.** Cambridge is best reached by a 10min. T-ride outbound from downtown Boston. The city's main artery, **Massachusetts Ave.** ("Mass. Ave."), parallels the Red Line, which makes stops at a series of squares along the ave. The **Kendall Sq./MIT** stop is just across the Longfellow Bridge from Boston. The subway continues outbound through **Central Sq., Harvard Sq.,** and **Porter Sq.** The *Old Cambridge Walking Guide* provides an excellent self-guided tour ($2). **Post Office:** 125 Mt. Auburn St. (876-9280; open M-F 7:30am-6pm, Sa 7:30am-3pm; self-service available M-F 7am-6:30pm, Sa 7am-3:30pm). **ZIP code:** 02138. **Area code:** 617. For budget **accommodations,** head back to Boston (see p. 116).

◖ **FOOD.** Every night, hundreds of college students renounce cafeteria fare and head to the funky eateries of Harvard Sq. The weekly *Square Deal*, usually thrust in one's face by distributors near the T stop, has coupons on local eats. Known affectionately to Harvard students as "Nocch's," ⚅ **Pinocchio's,** 74 Winthrop St., offers the best pizza deal in town with 2 slices of sizzling Sicilian for $3.50, and a huge cheeseburger sub for $4.60 (876-4897; open M-Th 11am-1am, F-Sa 11am-2am, Su 11am-midnight). **Campo de' Fiori,** 1350 Massachusetts Ave., in the Holyoke Center Arcade, has staggeringly delicious tuna, bread, and tomatoes, among other great Italian fare (354-3805; sandwiches $4-5; M-Sa 8am-10pm, off-season M-Sa 8am-8pm). For some of the tastiest and cheapest (everything under $5) Mexican fare in town, try **Boca Grande,** 1728 Mass. Ave., in between Porter and Harvard Sq. (354-7400; open Su-F 11am-10pm, Sa 11am-10:30pm). A hangout for MIT math whizzes and all sorts of types, **Mary Chung Restaurant,** 464 Mass. Ave., in Central Sq., dishes out excellent Szechuan and Mandarin cuisine including a flavorful $6 Yu-Hsiang Eggplant. (864-1991. Open Su-M and W-Th 11:30am-10pm, F-Sa 11:30am-11pm. *Dim Sum* brunch Sa-Su 11:30am-2:30pm.) A 10-15min. walk from Harvard, the **S&S Restaurant and Deli,** 1334 Cambridge St., offers a deli-style lunch or breakfast served all day. Take the #69 bus to the intersection of Cambridge and Beacon/Hampshire St. Filling entrees like Penne Pasta Primavera average $8-14. Hot beef knishes ($4) and an abundance of beers and desserts are worth the trek. "Ess and ess" means "eat and eat" in Yiddish. (354-0777. Open M-Tu 7am-11pm, W-Sa 7am-midnight, Su 8am-11pm.)

◉ **SIGHTS.** The **Massachusetts Institute of Technology (MIT)** supports cutting-edge work in the sciences. Free campus tours highlight the Chapel, designed by Eero Saarinen, and an impressive collection of modern outdoor sculpture. Contact **MIT Information** for more details *(77 Mass. Ave. 253-1875. T: Kendall/MIT. Open M-F 9am-5pm; tours, M-F 10am and 2pm, meet in the lobby.)* The **MIT Museum** contains a slide rule collection and wonderful photography exhibits, including the famous stop-action photos of Harold Edgerton. *(265 Mass. Ave. 253-4444. Open Tu-F 10am-5pm, Sa-Su noon-5pm; $3, students and seniors $1, under 5 free.)*

In all its red-brick-and-ivy dignity, **Harvard University,** farther down Mass. Ave. from Boston, finds space for Nobel laureates, students from around the world, and the occasional party. The **Harvard Events and Information Center,** at the Holyoke Center in Harvard Sq., distributes free guides to the university, its museums, and all upcoming events, as well as offering 1hr. tours of Harvard Yard. Pick up a comprehensive map of Harvard for $1. *(1350 Mass. Ave. 495-1573. Tours in summer M-Sa 10, 11:15am, 2 and 3:15pm, Su 1:30 and 3pm; Sept.-May M-F 10am and 2pm, Sa 2pm.)* The university revolves around **Harvard Yard**, a grassy oasis amid the Cantabrigian bustle. The **Harry Elkins Widener Memorial Library** stands as the largest academic library in the world, containing 4.5 million of the university's 13.4 million books. Visitors are not allowed inside. The extravagantly ornate **Memorial Hall,** just outside the Yard's northern gate, is a secular cathedral dedicated to the Union dead.

The most notable of Harvard's museums, the **Fogg Art Museum** gathers a considerable collection of works ranging from ancient Chinese jade to contemporary photography, as well as the largest Ingres collection outside of France. Across the street, the modern exterior of the **Arthur M. Sackler Museum** holds a rich collection of ancient Asian and Islamic art. Another of Harvard's art museums, the **Busch-Reisinger Museum,** on the 2nd floor of the Fogg, displays Northern and Central European sculpture, painting, and decorative arts, especially German Expressionism. *(32 Quincy St. and 485 Broadway. 495-9400 for all 3. All open M-Sa 10am-5pm, Su 1-5pm. $5, students $3, seniors $4; free on W, Sa before noon, and for guests under 18. Wheelchair access on Prescott St.)* Peering down at the Fogg, Le Corbusier's piano-shaped **Carpenter Center** displays student and professional work with especially strong photo exhibits and a great, largely foreign, film series at the **Harvard Film Archives,** located inside the Center. Pick up schedules outside the door. *(24 Quincy St. 495-3251. Center open M-Sa 9am-11pm, Su noon-11pm; during term-time, always 9am-11pm. Most shows $6, students and seniors $5, under 8 free.)* The **Botanical Museum,** one of Harvard's several **Museums of Natural and Cultural History** draws huge crowds to view the Ware collection of glass flowers. *(24 Oxford St. 495-3045. Open M-Sa 9am-5pm, Su 1-5pm. $5, students and seniors $4, ages 3-13 $3. Admission includes all the museums.)*

The **Longfellow House,** now a National Historic Site, headquartered the Continental Army during the early stages of the Revolution. The poet Henry Wadsworth Longfellow, for whom the house is named, lived here later. *(105 Brattle St. 876-4491. Closed until fall 2000.)* The **Mt. Auburn Cemetery** lies about 1mi. up the road at the end of Brattle St. The nation's first botanical garden/cemetery has 174 acres of beautifully landscaped grounds fertilized by Louis Agassiz, Charles Bulfinch, Dorothea Dix, Mary Baker Eddy, and Longfellow. Locals say it's the best birdwatching site in Cambridge. The central tower offers a stellar view of Boston and Cambridge. *(580 Mt. Auburn St. 547-7105. 8am-7pm. Open Su-Sa 8am-7pm; tower closes 1hr. earlier. Greenhouse: M- Sa 8am-4pm. Free. Wheelchair access.)*

🎵 **ENTERTAINMENT AND NIGHTLIFE.** In warm weather, street performers ranging from Andean folk singers to magicians crowd every brick sidewalk of Harvard Sq. and nearby **Brattle Sq.** The **American Repertory Theater (ART),** 64 Brattle St., in the Loeb Drama Center, produces shows from late Nov. to early June. (547-8300. Box office open M 11am-5pm, Tu-Su 10am-5pm, or until showtime. Tickets $25-55. Student rush tickets available 30min. before shows, $12 cash only; seniors $5 off ticket price.)

🍸 **The Cellar**, 991 Mass. Ave., has a devoted Th night crowd of whiskey sour-drinking Hemingway types and Radcliffe lushes. (876-2580. 16oz. mixed drink $3.75. Downstairs open daily 4pm-1am; upstairs open M-Sa noon-1am.) Cambridge's club scene centers around a 1 block area in Central Sq., while countless bars can be found in both Harvard and Central Sq. The **Middle East,** 472 Mass. Ave., in Central Sq., a 3-stage nirvana for the musically adventurous, offers a mixture of local alternative and rock (354-8238; cover $5-12; open Su-W 11am-1am, Th-Sa 11am-2am). The **Green St. Grill,** 280 Green St., in Central Sq., hosts local art work, a top-notch jukebox, a critically-acclaimed kitchen and great live music—everything form Latin to bluegrass to reggae, although on Tu a magic show takes the stage (876-1655; cover $0-5; bar open daily 3pm-1am, restaurant 7pm-midnight). For over 15 years, Little Joe Cook and his blues band have been packing the 🍸 **Cantab Lounge,** 738 Mass. Ave., in Central Sq., with hard-rocking and hard-drinking Cantabrigians. (354-2685. Cover $3-6. Open M-W 8am-1am, Th-Sa 8am-2am, Su noon-1am. The Cantab also hosts poetry readings and slams downstairs on W nights.) A fantastic Irish bar, 🍸 **The Field,** 20 Prospect St., in Central Sq., surrounds visitors with signs pointing everywhere from Galway to Ballybunion, and the mood runs the gamut from mellow to meleé. Incidentally, this bar burns through

25 kegs of Guinness per week. (534-7345. Open M-Sa 11am-1am, Su noon-1am.) **ManRay,** 21 Brookline St., is your basic leather bar catering to the area's gay crowd Th (21+) and Sa (19+) nights with an all-out dance party. Wear black. (864-0400. Cover $3-5 W-F, $5-10 Sa. Open W until 1 am, Th-Sa until 2am.)

## LEXINGTON AND CONCORD

**LEXINGTON.** "Stand your ground. Don't fire unless fired upon, but if they mean to have a war, let it begin here," said Captain John Parker to the colonial Minutemen on April 19, 1775. Although no one is certain who fired the first shot, the American Revolution did indeed erupt in downtown Lexington. The site of the fracas lies in the center of town (Mass Ave.) at the **Battle Green,** where a **Minuteman Statue** still watches over Lexington. The fateful command itself was issued from across the street at the **Buckman Tavern,** 1 Bedford St., which housed the minutemen on the eve of their decisive battle. The nearby **Hancock-Clarke House,** 36 Hancock St., and the **Munroe Tavern,** 1332 Mass. Ave., also played significant roles in the birth of the Revolution. (Buckman: 862-5598. House: 861-0928. Munroe: 674-9238. All open mid-Apr. to Oct. M-Sa 10am-5pm, Su 1-5pm. $4 per site, ages 6-16 $2. Combination ticket for all 3 houses, $10.) All 3 can be seen on a 30min. tour that runs continuously. You can also survey exhibits on the Revolution at the **Museum of Our National Heritage,** 33 Marrett Rd./Rt. 2A, which emphasizes a historical approach to understanding popular American life (861-6559; open M-Sa 10am-5pm, Su noon-5pm; wheelchair access; free). An excellent model and description of the Battle of Lexington decorates the **visitors center,** 1875 Mass. Ave., behind the Buckman Tavern (862-1450; open mid-Apr. to Oct daily 9am-5pm, 10am-4pm off-season).

Picky eaters flock to the 33-acre **Wilson Farm,** 10 Pleasant St., for freshly picked fruits and veggies and over 30 varieties of freshly baked bread and pastry (862-3900. Open M and W-F 9am-8pm, Sa 9am-7pm, Su 9am-6:30pm; call for winter hrs.). The road from Boston to Lexington is easy. Drive straight up Mass. Ave. from Boston or Cambridge, or bike up the **Minuteman Commuter Bike Trail,** which runs into downtown Lexington (access off Mass. Ave. in Arlington, or Alewife in Cambridge). MBTA bus #62 from Alewife in Cambridge runs to Lexington (60¢). **Area code:** 781.

**CONCORD.** Concord, the site of the second conflict of the American Revolution, is famous for both its military history and its status as a 19th-century intellectual center. The **Concord Museum** on the Cambridge Turnpike, near its intersection with Lexington St. lies across the street from Ralph Waldo Emerson's 19th-century home. This impressive museum houses a reconstruction of Emerson's study alongside Paul Revere's lantern. (369-9763. Open M-Sa 9am-5pm, Su noon-5pm; Jan.-Mar. M-Sa 10am-4pm, Su 1-4pm. $6, students $4, seniors $5, under 18 $3, families $12.) Right down the road from the Concord Museum, you'll find the **Orchard House,** 399 Lexington Rd., where Louisa May Alcott wrote *Little Women.* (369-4118. Open M-Sa 10am-4:30pm, Su 1-4:30pm; Nov.-Mar. M-F 11am-3pm, Sa 10am-4:30pm, Su 1-4:30pm. $6, students and seniors $5, ages 6-17 $4, families $16. Guided tour only.) Still further down the road lies **Wayside,** 455 Lexington Rd., the former residence of the Alcotts and Hawthornes. (369-6975. Open May to Oct. M-Th 10am-5pm. $4, under 16 free. Guided tour only.) Today, Emerson, Hawthorne, Alcott, and Thoreau reside on "Author's Ridge" in the peaceful **Sleepy Hollow Cemetery** on Rt. 62, 3 blocks from the center of town.

Past The Minuteman statue and over the **Old North Bridge,** you'll find the spot from which "the shot heard 'round the world" was fired. From the parking lot, a 5min. walk brings you to the **North Bridge Visitors Center,** 174 Liberty St. (369-6993; open Apr.-Oct. daily 9am-5pm; 9am-4pm in winter). The **Minuteman National Historical Park,** best explored along the adjacent 5½mi. **Battle Rd. Trail,** includes a mediocre and out-of-the-way **visitors center,** off Rt. 2A between Concord and Lexington (781-862-7753; open Apr.-Nov. daily 9am-5pm; 9am-4pm in winter). Concord, 20mi. north of Boston, is served by commuter rail trains from **North Station** (722-3200; fare $2.50, seniors and ages 5-11 $1.25). **Area code:** 978.

**WALDEN POND.** In 1845, Thoreau retreated 1½mi. south of Concord "to live deliberately, to front only the essential facts of life" (though the harsh essence of *his* life was eased from time to time by his mother's home cooking; she lived within walking distance of his cabin). Here he wrote his famous book *Walden*. The **Walden Pond State Reservation,** on Rt. 126, draws picnickers, swimmers, and boaters and is mobbed in summer (though still mighty pleasant). No camping, pets, or novelty flotation devices are allowed. (978-369-3254. Open daily 7am-8pm. Parking $2.) When Walden Pond swarms with crowds, head east from Concord center on Rt. 62 to another of Thoreau's haunts, **Great Meadows National Wildlife Refuge,** on Monsen Rd. (978-443-4661; open daily dawn-dusk; free).

## PLYMOUTH

Despite what American high school textbooks say, the Pilgrims' first step onto the New World was *not* at Plymouth. They stopped first at Provincetown, but promptly left because the soil was so inadequate. **Plymouth Rock** itself is a rather diminutive stone that has dubiously been identified as the actual rock on which the Pilgrims disembarked although this distinction is highly doubtful. A stepping stone to the nation, it served as a symbol of liberty during the American Revolution, then was moved 3 times, and was chipped away by tourists before landing at its current home beneath an extravagant portico on Water St., at the foot of North St. After several vandalization episodes, it's under high security.

Three mi. south of town off Rt. 3A, the historical theme-park of **Plymouth Plantation** recreates the Pilgrims' early settlement. In the **Pilgrim Village,** costumed actors play the roles of actual villagers carrying out their daily tasks, based upon William Bradford's record of the year 1627, while the **Wampanoag Summer Encampment** represents a Native American village of the same period. To make sure they know their stuff, the plantation sends a historian to England each summer to gather more info about each villager. (746-1622. Open Apr.-Nov. daily 9am-5pm. $16, ages 6-12 $9. Pass good for 2 consecutive days.) The **Mayflower II,** built in the 1950s to recapture the atmosphere of the original ship, is docked off Water St. (Open Apr.-Nov. daily 9am-5pm. $6.50, ages 6-12 $4. Admission to both sights $19, students and seniors $16.50, ages 6-12 $11.) The nation's oldest museum in continuous existence, the **Pilgrim Hall Museum,** 75 Court St., houses Puritan crafts, furniture, books, paintings, and weapons. (746-1620. open Feb.-Dec. daily 9:30am-4:30pm; $5, seniors $4.50, ages 5-17 $3, families $13.) The **Plymouth National Wax Museum,** 16 Carver St. overlooking Plymouth Rock, is yet another pilgrim exhibit, retracing history through extremely life-like exhibits. (746-6468. Open Jul.-Aug. 9am-9pm; June and Sept.-Oct. 9am-7pm; Nov.-May 9am-5pm. $5.50, children $2.25.)

Bogged down in history? A trip down Federal Furnace Rd. or Rt. 44 in early fall leads you to the heart of **Cranberry Country. Cranberry World,** 225 Water St., celebrates one of the 3 indigenous American fruits (the others are the blueberry and the Concord grape). Exhibits, including a small cranberry bog in front of the museum, show how cranberries are grown, harvested, and sold. (747-2350. Free samples. Open May-Nov. daily 9:30am-5pm. Free.) **The Plymouth Bay Winery,** 114 Water St. has free wine tasting. Try peach, raspberry, blueberry, and the local favorite: cranberry! (746-2100. Open daily 10am-5pm. 21+.)

**Plymouth Visitor's Information Center:** 130 Water St. (800-872-1620 or 747-7525. Open daily Apr.-May 9am-5pm; June 9am-6pm; July-Aug. 9am-9pm; Sept.-Nov. 9am-5pm.) A few blocks from the center of town, the **Bunk and Bagel,** 51 Pleasant St., has a cheerful, homey atmosphere and the cheapest beds in Plymouth. Bunks come with a bagel. (830-0914. 5-8 hostel beds with common bath. $20-25. Linen provided. Reception daily 7am-9pm.) Majestic **Myles Standish Forest,** 7mi. south of Plymouth via exit 3 off Rt. 3, offers 450 wooded sites. (866-2526. Sites $6-7. Office open daily Apr.-June 8am-10pm; July-Aug. 24hr.; Sept.-Oct. 8am-midnight.) The natives bite at **Wood's Seafood Restaurant,** Town Pier. A fish sandwich with fries is $4; prices vary with fresh market prices. (746-0261. Open daily June-Aug. 11am-9pm; Sept.-May 11am-8:30pm.) Zip back to modern times at **Sean O'Toole's Public House,** 22 Main St., with live music and a traditional Irish pub atmosphere (746-3388; open daily 4:30pm-12:30am). **Area code:** 508.

NEW ENGLAND

# CAPE COD

Henry David Thoreau once said: "At present [this coast] is wholly unknown to the fashionable world, and probably it will never be agreeable to them." Think again, Hank. In 1602, when English navigator and Jamestown colonist Bartholomew Gosnold landed on this peninsula in southeastern Massachusetts, he named it in honor of all the codfish he caught in the surrounding waters. In recent decades, tourists have replaced the plentiful cod, and the area has as many taffy shops as fishermen. This small strip of land supports a diverse set of landscapes—long, unbroken stretches of beach, salt marshes, hardwood forests, deep freshwater ponds carved by glaciers, and desert-like dunes sculpted by the wind. Thankfully, the Cape's natural landscape has been protected from the tide of commercialism by the establishment of the **Cape Cod National Seashore.** Blessed with an excellent hostel system, Cape Cod can be an option for budget travellers, though in general it services more spendy tourists. The Cape also serves as the gateway to **Martha's Vineyard** and **Nantucket,** 2 islands with unsurpassed natural beauty. Ferries shuttle from Falmouth, Woods Hole, and Hyannis to Martha's Vineyard, and from Hyannis to Nantucket; see **Martha's Vineyard** (p. 136) and **Nantucket** (p. 138) for info.

Terminology for locations on the Cape can be confusing. **Upper Cape** refers to the more suburbanized and developed part of Cape Cod, closer to the mainland. Proceeding eastward away from the mainland, you travel "down Cape" until hitting the **Lower Cape;** the National Seashore encompasses much of this area. Cape Cod resembles a bent arm, with **Woods Hole** at its armpit, **Chatham** at the elbow, and **Provincetown** at its clenched fist. Travel times on the peninsula are often inconsistent; a drive from the Sagamore bridge to Provincetown can take anywhere from 2 to 4hrs. Leaving the Cape can be equally annoying; the area's weekend warriors can turn a Su departure into a hellacious 6hr. odyssey.

If you're up for some exercise, cycling is the best way to travel the Cape's gentle slopes. The park service can give you a free map of trails or sell you the detailed *Cape Cod Bike Book* ($3; available at most Cape bookstores). The 135mi. **Boston-Cape Cod Bikeway** connects Boston to Provincetown at land's end. If you want to bike this route, pick up a bicycle trail map of the area. These are available at some bookstores and most bike shops. The trails which line either side of the **Cape Cod Canal** in the National Seashore rank among the country's most scenic, as does the 25mi. **Cape Cod Rail Trail** from Dennis to Wellfleet. For discount coupons good for bargains at restaurants, sights, and entertainment venues throughout the Cape, pick up a free copy of *The Official 2000 Guide to Cape Cod* or the *Cape Cod Best Read Guide*, available at most Cape info centers. **Area code:** 508.

## UPPER CAPE

**HYANNIS.** Hyannis is not the Cape Cod idyll most people expect. JFK spent his summers on the beach in nearby Hyannisport, but the town itself sees more action as a transportation hub than as a tourist mecca. Island ferries and buses to destinations throughout the Cape leave from Hyannis; hop on one and get out of town—the Kennedys *aren't* going to meet you at the bus station.

About 3mi. up the road from the bus station, the **Hyannis Area Chamber of Commerce,** 1481 Rt. 132, distributes the free *Hyannis Guidebook* and has a campground guide for the whole Cape. (362-5230 or 800-449-6647. Open June-Sept. M-Sa 9am-5pm, Su 10am-2pm; Oct.-May M-Sa 9am-5pm.) You probably won't want to spend more than a few hours in Hyannis, but if you must, there are a bunch of your run-of-the-mill cheap motels.

Hyannis is tattooed midway across the Cape's upper arm, 3mi. south of Rt. 6 on Nantucket Sound. **Plymouth & Brockton** (771-6191) runs 5 Boston-to-Provincetown buses per day with 30min. layovers at the **Hyannis Bus Station,** 17 Elm St. Other stops besides Boston (1¾hr., $12) and Provincetown (1½hr., $9) include Plymouth, Barnstable, Yarmouth, Eastham, Wellfleet, and Truro. **Bonanza Bus Lines**

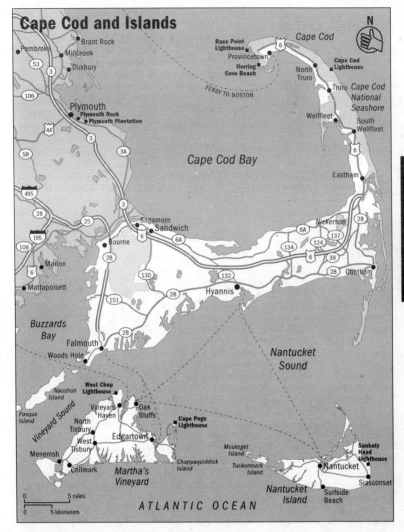

Cape Cod and Islands

(800-556-3815) operates a line through Providence to New York City (6hr., 7 per day, $29). See the listings for **Martha's Vineyard** (p. 136) and **Nantucket** (p. 138) for info on ferry service to the islands.

**SANDWICH.** The oldest town on the Cape, Sandwich cultivates an old-fashioned charm, more old New England-esque than touristy. The beauty and workmanship of Sandwich glass was made famous by the Boston & Sandwich Glass Company, founded in Sandwich in 1825. Master glassblowers shape works of art from blobs of molten sand at **Pairpoint Crystal**, on Rt. 6A just across the town border in Sagamore (888-2344; open M-F 9am-noon and 1-4:30pm; free). To enjoy the town's considerable collection of older pieces, tiptoe through the light-bending exhibits at **The Sandwich Glass Museum**, 129 Main St., in Sandwich center. (888-0251. Open Apr.-Oct. daily 9:30am-5pm; Nov.-Mar. W-Su 9:30am-4pm; closed in Jan. $3.50.) The gorgeously floral **Heritage Plantation of Sandwich,** Grove St., features a working 1912 carousel, antique automobiles, military and art museums, and 76 acres of landscaped gardens. (888-3300. Open mid-May to mid-Oct. daily 10am-5pm. $9, seniors $8, ages 6-18 $4.50. Wheelchair access.)

The best beach on the Upper Cape, the **Sandy Neck Beach,** on Sandy Neck Rd. 3mi. east of Sandwich off Rt. 6A, extends 6mi. along Cape Cod Bay with beautifully polished, egg-sized granite cobbles and verdant dunes. Hike only on marked trails; the plants are very fragile. The **Shawme-Crowell State Forest,** at Rt. 130 and Rt. 6, provides 285 wooded campsites with showers and campfires, but no hookups (888-0351; $6). Parking is at **Scusset Beach,** on the canal near the junction of Rt. 6 and Rt. 3. Scusset Beach also offers swimming and a fishing jetty (888-0859; $2 per car). The family-oriented **Peters Pond Park Campground,** on Cotuit Rd. in south Sandwich, combines waterside sites with swimming, fishing, rowboat rentals ($15 per day), showers, and a grocery store. No pets are allowed. (477-1775. Sites $24-28, with hookup $30-50. Open mid-Apr. to mid-Oct.)

Sandwich lies at the intersection of Rt. 6A and Rt. 130, about 13mi. from Hyannis. The **Plymouth & Brockton** bus makes its closest stop in Sagamore, 3mi. northwest along Rt. 130.

# LOWER CAPE

**CAPE COD NATIONAL SEASHORE.** As early as 1825, the Cape had suffered so much man-made damage that the town of Truro required local residents to plant beach grass and keep their cows off the dunes. Further efforts toward conservation culminated in 1961 with the creation of the **Cape Cod National Seashore,** which includes much of the Lower Cape from Provincetown south to Chatham. Over 30mi. of wide, soft, uninterrupted beaches lie under the tall clay cliffs and towering 19th-century lighthouses of this protected area. Thanks to conservationists, the shore has largely escaped the commercialism which afflicts most American seacoasts. Just a short walk away from the lifeguards, the sea of umbrellas and coolers fades into the distance. The National Seashore Beaches aren't geared towards suntanning and beach volleyball; they offer sights of natural beauty and untouched shores instead. Hike one of the seashore's beautiful nature trails and you're sure to be impressed by the variety of natural habitats and creatures that occupy them. Grassy dunes give way to inland forests, and salt marshes play host to migrating and native waterfowl, while warm freshwater ponds, such as **Gull Pond** in Wellfleet or **Pilgrim Lake** in Truro, are perfect for more secluded swimming.

Beachgoers at the Cape face a difficult question: ocean or bay? While the ocean beaches entice with whistling winds and surging waves, the water on the bay side rests calmer and gets a bit warmer. The National Seashore oversees 6 beaches: **Coast Guard** and **Nauset Light** in Eastham; **Marconi** in Wellfleet; **Head of the Meadow** in Truro, and **Race Point** and **Herring Cove** in Provincetown. Herring Cove has special facilities which allow disabled travelers access to the water. (Parking at all beaches $7 per day, $20 per season; mid-Sept. to late June free.)

To park at any other beach, a town permit is required. While each town has a different beach-parking policy, all require proof of lodging in their town. Permits generally cost $5-10 per day, $20-25 per week, or $50-100 per season, and can be bought at town halls. Call the appropriate town hall before trying to get around the parking permit; beaches are sometimes mi. from any other legal parking and police with tow trucks flock like vultures. Parking lots fill up by 11am or earlier; it is often easier to rent a bike and ride in. Most town beaches do not require bikers and walkers to pay an entrance fee. Wellfleet and Truro stand out among the ocean beaches as great examples of the Cape's famous endangered sand dunes. **Cahoon Hollow Beach,** with spectacular, cliff-like dunes, and **Duck Harbor Beach,** overlooking the bay in Wellfleet, provide 2 particularly beautiful vistas.

Among the best of the seashore's 11 self-guiding **nature trails,** the **Great Island Trail,** in Wellfleet, traces an 8mi. loop through pine forests and grassy marshes and along a ridge with a view of the bay and Provincetown. The **Atlantic White Cedar Swamp Trail,** a 1¼mi. walk, leads to dark, swampy waters under towering trees, beginning at Marconi Station site in south Wellfleet. The **Buttonbush Trail,** a ¼mi. walk with braille guides and a guide rope for the blind, leaves the Salt Pond Visitors Center (see below). There are also 3 park **bike trails:** Nauset Trail (1.6mi.), Head of the Meadow Trail (2mi.), and Province Lands Trail (5mi.). The accessible **National Seashore's Salt Pond Visitors Center,** at Salt Pond, off Rt. 6 in Eastham, offers a free 10min. film every 30min. and a free museum with exhibits on the Cape's natural and contemporary history. (255-3421. Open daily 9am-5pm; Sept.-June 9am-4:30pm.) **Camping** on the national seashore is illegal. Permits for fishing and campfires can be purchased at the visitors center.

**EASTHAM.** The **Eastham Windmill,** on Rt. 6 at Samoset Rd. in Eastham, has had its nose to the grindstone since 1680, but has only resided in it's current location for the past 191 years. Cape Cod's oldest windmill still works, demonstrating how the corn crops were put to use by industrious Cape Codders. (Open July-Aug. M-Sa 10am-5pm, Su 1-5pm. Free.) Off Rt. 6, **Fort Hill** grants a survey of Nauset Marsh and the surrounding forest and ocean, as well as the paths which access them. For a classic view of the dunes and sea, drive to **Nauset Light,** on Salt Pond Rd. Popular with Cape bikers, the **Mid-Cape Hostel (HI-AYH),** 75 Goody Hallet Dr., occupies a quiet, wooded spot in Eastham, convenient to the lower part of the Cape. On the Plymouth-Brockton bus to Provincetown, ask to be let off at the traffic circle in Orleans (not the Eastham stop). Walk out on the exit to Rock Harbor, turn right on Bridge Rd., and take a right onto Goody Hallet Rd. ½mi. from Rt. 6. The hostel has 8 cabins with a total of 78 beds, a kitchen, and a relaxed atmosphere that attracts groups. (255-2785. Members $14, nonmembers $17. 5-day max. stay. Reception daily 7:30-10am and 5-10pm. Reservations essential July-Aug. Open mid-May to mid-Sept.) **Town Hall:** 240-5900. Rt. 6, directly across from the Eastham Windmill. Open M-F 8am-4pm.

**WELLFLEET.** Hundreds of bird species inhabit the **Wellfleet Wildlife Sanctuary,** on Rt. 6, follow signs for Audobon Society. Seven walking trails wind through salt marshes, tidal flats, and fields. (349-2615. Open daily 8:30am-5pm; mid-Oct. to May Tu-Su 8:30am-5pm. $3, seniors $2, ages 6-12 $2.) **Gull Pond,** off Gull Pond Rd., which is off Rt. 6 past the town center in Wellfleet, provides for some of the Cape's best paddling; heading north on Rt. 6, take the first right after the police/fire department. **Maurice's Campground,** 80 Rt. 6 offers 200 sites as well as a playground, basketball court, and direct access to the Cape Cod Rail Trail. (349-2029. Office open mid-May to mid-Oct. daily 9am-9pm. Tent sites $22, with hookup $25.) **Paine's Campground,** 180 Old County Rd., is harder to find, but avoids noise conflicts with special sections for families and quiet couples. To get there on Rt. 6 E., turn right just before the Citgo station and follow the signs to Paine's. (349-3007 or 800-479-3017. Office open May to mid-Oct. 9am-9pm; tent sites for 2 $18-24.) Family-owned **Moby Dick's Restaurant,** on Rt. 6, offers Cape Cod favorites, including scrumptious clam chowder ($3.75) and lobster rolls ($11.95) No liquor is served, but patrons can bring their own beer or wine. (349-9795. Credit cards accepted, open mid-May to late Sept. daily 11:30am-10pm.) **Town Hall:** 349-9818.

**TRURO.** Head down Highland Rd., off Rt. 6, to visit one of Thoreau's favorite places and catch a panoramic view of the Lower Cape from the **Cape Cod Lighthouse.** Recently moved over 400 ft. inland, the lighthouse lies adjacent to the **Truro Historical Museum,** a former hotel that transports visitors back in history with shipwreck mementos, early whaling gear, and Victorian-style furnished rooms. (487-3397. Open June-Oct. daily 10am-4:30pm. $3, $5 for a lighthouse/museum combo ticket, under 12 free.) The picturesque ½mi. **Cranberry Bog Trail,** North Pamet Rd., provides a secluded, spectacular setting for a walk; get a map at the Salt Pond Visitors Center (see above). Directly across the road from the trail lies the noteworthy **Truro Hostel (HI-AYH),** N. Pamet Rd. Take the N. Pamet Rd. Exit off Rt. 6; follow it 1½mi. to the east. The hostel offers an escape from the crowds with plenty of space, 42 beds, a large kitchen, great ocean views, and access to Ballston Beach.

NEW ENGLAND

(349-3889 or 800-909-4776 ext. 15. $14, nonmembers $17. Reception daily 8-10am and 5-10pm. Reservations essential in July and Aug. Open late June to early Sept.) Several popular campgrounds nestle among the dwarf pines by the dunes of North Truro. Just 7mi. southeast of Provincetown on Rt. 6, **North Truro Camping Area,** on Highland Rd. ½mi. east of Rt. 6, has small sandy sites, heated restrooms, hot showers, and cable TV with hookup (487-1847; sites for 2 $16, full hookup $24;-$8 per additional person). **Horton's Camping Resort,** 71 South Highland Rd., offers 200 wooded and open sites with views of the ocean, as well as restrooms and hot showers. (487-1220. Sites for 2 $17-21, with hookup $24-26. $8 per additional person.) **North of Highland** offers yet more sites in Truro. Take the Head of the Meadow exit off Rt. 6, and follow the signs. (487-1191. 237 sites for family camping, restrooms, laundromat, and hot showers from $18. No wood fires, but grilles are allowed.) **Town Hall:** 349-3635.

## PROVINCETOWN

At Provincetown, Cape Cod ends and the wide Atlantic begins. The National Seashore protects two-thirds of "P-Town" as conservation land; the inhabited third touches the harbor on the south side of town. This former whaling village has diversified, and now includes a prominent gay and lesbian contingent. P-Town is far from inexpensive, but there are many options for the budget travelers. Commercial St., the town's main drag is home to countless art galleries, novelty shops, and trendy eateries, as well as hosting parades and drag shows.

**7 PRACTICAL INFORMATION.** Provincetown rests in the clenched fist at the end of the arm that is Cape Cod, 123mi. from Boston by car and 3hr. by ferry across Massachusetts Bay. Parking spots are hard-won, especially on cloudy days when the Cape's frustrated sun-worshippers flock to Provincetown. Follow the parking signs on **Bradford St.,** the auto-friendly thoroughfare, to dock your car for $4-8 per day, or try to find free public parking on Bradford St. or **Commercial St.** at the east end of town. Whale-watching boats, the Boston ferry, and buses depart from **MacMillan Wharf,** off Commercial St., at the center of town, just down the hill from the Pilgrim Monument.

**Plymouth and Brockton Bus** (746-0378) heads to Boston (4hr., in summer 5 per day, $20) at the stop on MacMillan Wharf. **Bay State Cruises** (617-748-1428), sends a ferry to Boston (3hr., $18) from MacMillan wharf. (Ferries mid-June to early Sept. daily; late May to mid-June F-M, and early Sept. to mid-Oct. Sa-Su.) To get around in Provincetown and Herring Cove Beach, take the **Provincetown Shuttle Bus** (240-0050). One route travels the length of Bradford St.; the other goes from MacMillan Wharf to Herring Cove Beach. (Operates late June to early Sept. daily on the hr. 8am-midnight, 10am-6pm for the beach. Tickets at the Chamber of Commerce, see below; $1.25, seniors 75¢.) Rented bikes from **Arnold's Where You Rent the Bicycles,** 329 Commercial St. (487-0844), are another popular mode of transport. ($2.50-3.50 per hr., 2hr. min. $10-15 per day. 24hr. rental $2 more. Deposit and ID required; credit cards accepted. Open daily 8:30am-5:30pm.) You'll find the exceptionally helpful **Provincetown Chamber of Commerce,** 307 Commercial St. (487-3424), on MacMillan Wharf (open daily June-Sept. 9am-5pm; Apr.-May 10am-4pm; Oct.-Dec. M-Sa 10am-4pm). Limited winter hrs., call for more information. **Visitor Info: Province Lands Visitors Center,** Race Point Rd. (487-1256; open mid-Apr. to late Nov. 9am-5pm). **Post Office:** 211 Commercial St. (487-0163; open M-F 8:30am-5pm, Sa 9:30am-3pm). **ZIP code:** 02657. **Area code:** 508.

**? ACCOMMODATIONS.** Provincetown teems with expensive places to lay your head. The most affordable options are the wonderful hostels 10mi. away in nearby Truro and a bit further away in Eastham. But if the roaring Provincetown nightlife makes a late-night drive home undesirable, a few decent quasi-budget accommodations exist in P-town. In the quiet east end of town, the excellent **Cape Codder,** 570 Commercial St., welcomes you in classic Cape Cod style, right down to the wicker furniture and private beach access. (487-0131. Singles and doubles $40-$65; mid-Sept. to mid-June $10 less. Parking and continental breakfast included in summer. Open May-Oct. Reservations recommended.) For the cheapest beds in town, try **The Outermost Hostel,** 28 Winslow St., 100 yd. from the Pilgrim Monument. Thirty beds in 5 cramped but cozy cottages go for $15 each, including kitchen access and free parking. (487-4378. Linen rental $3. Key deposit $10. Reception daily 8-9:30am and 5:30-9:30pm. Check-out 9:30am. Reservations recommended for weekends and in July and Aug. Open mid-May to mid-Oct.) Catering to a slightly older clientele, **Dunham's Guest House,** 3 Dyer St., has 5 rooms (named and colored according to squares on a Monopoly board) available in a Victorian house near the beach, a 5min. walk from the center of town. (487-3330. Singles $44; doubles $54; rates vary on holidays. 1 free night per week of stay.) When the great American Realist Edward Hopper wanted to paint a guest house, he chose what is now the **Sunset Inn,** 142 Bradford St.; it inspired his famous *Rooms For Tourists*. The house has changed little, and the warmth and light he depicted still welcome weary travelers. (487-9810. Free parking available. Rates July-Aug. $59-$125; mid-Apr. to June and Sept.-Nov. $45-$69; includes continental breakfast. Closed in winter.)

   **Camping** in Provincetown will cost you. **Dune's Edge Campground,** off Rt. 6 on the east end of town, has 100 shady, spacious sites. (487-9815. Sites $25, with partial hookup $31. Office open July-Aug. 8am-10pm, May-June and Sept. 9am-8pm.) The **Coastal Acres Camping Court,** a 1mi. walk from the center of town, west on Bradford or Commercial St. and right on W. Vine St., has over 110 crowded sites—try to snag one on the waterside. (487-1700. Office open July-Aug. 8am-9pm, Apr.-June and Sept. to late Oct. 8am-11am. Sites $23, full hookup $32; Apr.-June and mid-Sept. to late Oct. $22/$30. Open Apr.-Nov. 1.)

📷 **FOOD.** Sit-down meals in Provincetown cost a bundle. Grab a bite at **Mojo's,** 5 Ryder St. Ext. by MacMillan Wharf, a fast-food shack serving up excellent home-made french fries ($2-3) and a wide selection of Mexican, seafood, and vegetarian platters (487-3140; $4-9; open May to mid-Oct. M-Th 11am-midnight, F-Sa 10:30am-10:30pm). For a monstrous burrito ($4.25-5.25), head down to **Big Daddy's Burritos,** 205 Commercial St. (487-4432) in the Aquarium Mall (open July-Sept. daily 11am-10pm, May-June Su-Th 11am-8pm, F-Sa 11am-10pm). Since 1921, **Mayflower Family Dining,** 300 Commercial St. (487-0121), has given visitors walls lined with ancient caricatures and stomachs lined with solid food. Try the Portuguese beef tips ($9.95), the Italian spaghetti ($5.25), or the $7 crab cakes. (Open Apr.-Nov. daily 11:30am-10pm. Cash only.) **Spiritus,** 190 Commercial St., dishes out a spirit-lifting whole-wheat pizza. (487-2808. Slices $2. Open daily Apr.-early Nov. noon-2am. Continental breakfast on weekends, 8am-noon.) **Cafe Crudite,** 336 Commercial St., a casual restaurant advertising "International Vegetarian Fare," offers deliciously fresh vegetarian and vegan options, such as open-face veggie melts ($6.95), or cold spicy sesame noodles ($5.50), topped off with fresh-baked Toll House cookies (75¢) (487-6237; lunch served from 11:30am-4:30pm, dinner from 5:30-8pm).

🏛 **SIGHTS.** Provincetown's natural waterfront resources provide spectacular walks. Directly across from Snail Rd. on Rt. 6, an unlikely path will lead you to a world of towering, rolling **sand dunes;** look for the shacks where writers like Tennessee Williams, Norman Mailer, and John Dos Passos penned their days away. The 1.2mi. **Breakwater Jetty,** at the west end of Commercial St., whisks you away from the crowds and onto a secluded peninsula of endless beach bearing two working lighthouses and the remains of a Civil War fort.

   Provincetown is acknowledged as the original site of the Pilgrims' 1620 arrival in Massachusetts at the **Pilgrim Monument and Provincetown Museum** on High Pole Hill. The nation's tallest all-granite structure (253 ft.), the monument looms over Provincetown and commemorates that 17-day Pilgrim layover. It also offers a gorgeous panoramic view of the Cape and an intense workout if you choose to climb all the way to the top. *(800-247-1620 or 487-1310. Open Apr.-Nov. daily 9am-5pm. $5, ages*

**NEW ENGLAND**

*4-12 $3.)* At the **Provincetown Heritage Museum** you can see a half-scale model of a fishing schooner, paintings, and other exhibits. *(356 Commercial St. 487-7098. Open June to mid-Oct. daily 10am-6pm. $3, under 12 free with adult.)*

The **Provincetown Art Association and Museum,** lies near the artsy East End and was founded during Provincetown's heyday as a seasonal colony for painters and other artists. It is both a museum with changing exhibits and a center from which to explore the plethora of **galleries** in town—there are more than 20. *(400 Commercial St. 487-1750. Most galleries are free and lie east of MacMillan Wharf on Commercial St. In general, galleries stay open in the afternoon and evening until 11pm, but close during a 2hr. dinner break. The free Provincetown Gallery Guide has complete details.)*

■ **ENTERTAINMENT AND NIGHTLIFE.** Today, Provincetown seafarers carry telephoto lenses, not harpoons, when they go whale hunting. **Whale-watch cruises** are some of P-town's most popular attractions. Several companies take you out to the feeding waters in about 40 min., then cruise around them for 2hr. The companies claim that whales are sighted on 99% of the journeys, and most promise free trips to the unlucky 1%. Tickets cost about $18; discount coupons can be found in most local publications. **Dolphin Fleet** (349-1900 or 800-826-9300), **Portuguese Princess** (487-2651 or 800-442-3188), and **Ranger V** (487-3322 or 800-992-9333) operate ticket booths and leave from MacMillan Wharf.

Provincetown's nightlife is almost totally gay- and lesbian-oriented, but all are welcome. Most of the clubs and bars on Commercial St. charge around $5, and shut down at 1am. Live music drives **Antro,** 258 Commercial St., with nightly drag shows and techno dance music after 11pm (487-2505; cover varies; open May-Oct. daily 11am-1am). Proud to be the "oldest gay bar on the seacoast," **Atlantic House,** 6 Masonic Ave., off Commercial St., more commonly known as the "A House," offers dancing and 2 bars (487-3821; cover $10; open daily noon-1am). The lively and crowded **Governor Bradford,** 312 Commercial St., has karaoke, female impersonators, and other entertainment (487-2781; cover varies; open daily 11:30am-10pm). **Steve's Alibi,** 293 Commercial St., is a local hangout that attracts a diverse, mixed gay and straight crowd. The laid-back atmosphere and tiny tables crunched together promote both conversation and socializing. The bar features live pop music at night, along with the locally renowned comedy routine of Khris Francis. (487-2890. Open year-round M-Sa 10am-1am, Su noon-10pm. Cover $3, 2 beverage minimum per table per show.)

# MARTHA'S VINEYARD

Once home to several of the most successful whaling ports in New England, Martha's Vineyard now offers a haven for many vacationing luminaries. Visitors from the late Princess Di to President Clinton have frequented this island for its dunes, inland woods, pastel houses, and weathered cottages. Seven communities comprise Martha's Vineyard. The western side of the island is called "up island" because sailors have to tack up wind to get to it. The 3 largest towns; Oak Bluffs, Vineyard Haven, and Edgartown; are "down island" and have flatter terrain. Oak Bluffs and Edgartown are the only "wet" (alcohol-selling) towns on the island.

■ **PRACTICAL INFORMATION**

**Buses: Bonanza** (800-556-3815) stops at the Ferry Terminal in Woods Hole and departs, via Bourne, for Boston (1½hr.; 12 per day, Sept. to late June 10 per day; $14.50) and New York (6hr.; 6 per day, early Sept. to late June 5 per day; $45).

**Ferries:** The **Steamship Authority** (693-9130) sends 24 boats per day on the 45min. ride from Woods Hole to Vineyard Haven and Oak Bluffs. (Ticket office open M-Th and Sa 5am-9:45pm, F and Su 5am-10:45pm. $5, ages 5-12 $2.50, car $44, bike $3. Reserve cars months in advance in summer.) The company has 3 parking lots ($7.50 per day) as well as shuttles to the dock. **Hyline Cruises** serves the island from Hyannis

(778-2600; 1¾hr.; June-Sept. 4 per day, Oct.-May 3 per day; $12); **Ferry Schamoinchi** leaves from New Bedford (997-1688; 1½hr.; July-Aug. 7 per day; mid-May to June and Sept. to mid-Oct. M-F, 3 per day, Sa-Su 1 per day; $9). The shortest and cheapest ride leaves from Falmouth on the **Island Queen** (548-4800; 30min., late May to early Sept. 7 per day, $5). The **Chappy "On Time" Ferry** (627-9427) connects Edgartown Town Dock and Chappaquiddick Island. (Open daily 7am-midnight; mid-Oct. to May 7am-7:30pm, 9-10pm, and 11-11:15pm. Round-trip $1, car $5, motorcycle $4, bicycle $3.)

**Taxis: Oak Bluffs:** 800-396-0003. **Edgartown:** 627-4677. **Vineyard Haven:** 693-3705.

**Public Transit: Island Transport** (693-1589) runs shuttle buses between Vineyard Haven (Union St.), Oak Bluffs (Ocean Park), and Edgartown (Church St.) late June through Aug., daily 6am-12:45am, every 15min. May to late June and early Sept. to Oct. every 30min. Su-Th 10am-6pm, F-Sa 10am-11pm. Vineyard Haven to Oak Bluffs $1.50, to Edgartown $3.) Buses run up-island from Vineyard Haven (Union St.) and Oak Bluffs (Ocean Park) to Gay Head ($4.75), West Tisbury (Alley's General Store, $2.25), and Chilmark (Chilmark Store, $4.75; late June to Aug., 4 buses daily from Vineyard Haven, 6 from Oak Bluffs). **Martha's Vineyard Regional Transit Authority (VTA)** runs summer shuttles between and within the various towns on the island; call 627-7448 for recorded information or 693-4833 for paratransit and additional information. (In-town passes $25 for summer, students $15, disabled patrons $12.50. Island-wide $50, students $30, disabled patrons $25. Individual fares 50¢ to $1.50.)

**Bike Rental: Martha's Bike Rental** (693-6593), at the corner of Beach St. and Beach Rd. in Vineyard Haven. $12 per day for a 3-speed, $18 per day for a mountain or hybrid. Open daily Apr.1-mid-Oct. 8am-6pm; mid-Oct.-Apr.1 8am-6pm. Prices similar for rental companies from Oak Bluffs or Edgartown. Scenic **bike paths** run along the state beach between Oak Bluffs and Edgartown, and through the State Forest between West Tisbury and Edgartown.

**Visitor Info: Martha's Vineyard Chamber of Commerce** (693-0085), Beach Rd., Vineyard Haven. Open M-F 9am-5pm.

**Medical Services: Vineyard Walk-In Medical Center,** 108 State Rd. (693-6399). Open daily June-Oct. 9am-1pm; Nov.-May 9am-noon. Call for afternoon appts.

**Post Office:** Beach Rd., Vineyard Haven (693-2815). Open M-F 8:30am-5pm, Sa 930am-1pm. **ZIP code:** 02568. **Area code:** 508.

# ▌ ACCOMMODATIONS

Cheap places to stay in Martha's Vineyard are almost nonexistent. The chamber of commerce provides a list of inns and guest houses; all recommend reservations for July and Aug., especially weekends.

**Martha's Vineyard Hostel (HI-AYH),** Edgartown-West Tisbury Rd. (693-2665), West Tisbury. The fantastic hostel provides the 78 cheapest beds on the island. Located right next to the bike path, great kitchen and a volleyball court. $14, nonmembers $17. Linen $2. Open Apr. to early Nov. daily 7:30-10am and 5-10pm. Curfew 11pm. Light chores required. Reservations essential.

**Martha's Vineyard Family Campground** (693-3772), 1½mi. from Vineyard Haven on Edgartown Rd. 185 shaded sites in an oak forest. Groceries and metered showers nearby. Office open daily 8am-9pm; reduced hrs. off-season. Sites for 2 $30; ages 2-18 $2, $10 per additional person. No pets or motorcycles. Open mid-May to mid-Oct.

# ▐ FOOD

Cheap sandwich and lunch places speckle the Vineyard, especially in Vineyard Haven and Oak Bluffs. Fried-food shacks across the island sell clams, shrimp, and potatoes, which generally cost at least $15. Several **farm stands** sell inexpensive produce; the chamber of commerce map shows their locations.

NEW ENGLAND

**Main Street Diner** (627-9337), under the Edgartown Cinema on Main St. Hearty sandwiches ($5-8) and a meatloaf that would make a mother proud ($7-11). Open daily 7am-9pm; Oct-May 7am-8pm.

**Louis'**, 350 State Rd. (693-3255), Vineyard Haven. Take-out Italian food that won't break the bank. Try the fresh pasta with meat sauce ($5.25) or the vegetable calzone for $5.50. Open M-Sa 11:30am-9pm, Su 4-8:30pm.

**Black Dog Bakery** (693-4786), on Beach St., in Vineyard Haven A range of creative and delicious pastries and breads (40¢-$3.25) tempt patrons, but for the love of God, please don't buy another sweatshirt. Open in summer daily 5:30am-6pm.

**Mad Martha's** (693-9151), on Circuit Ave. in Oak Bluffs. This island institution scoops out homemade ice cream and frozen yogurt ($2.50-3.20). Open daily 11am-midnight; in season only. One of 5 locations throughout the island.

## ▣ SIGHTS

Exploring the Vineyard can involve much more than zipping around on a moped. Head out to the countryside, hit the beach, or trek down one of the great trails. **Felix Neck Wildlife Sanctuary,** on the Edgartown-Vineyard Haven Rd., offers 5 trails which meander through 350 acres. *(627-4850. Office open M-Sa 8:30am-4pm, Su 10am-3pm; $3, seniors and under 12 $2.)* **Memensha Hills Reservation,** off North Rd. in Menemsha, has 4mi. of trails along the rocky Vineyard Sound beach leading to the island's second-highest point. **Cedar Tree Neck** on the western shore harbors 250 acres of headland off Indian Hill Rd. with trails throughout, while the **Long Point** park in West Tisbury preserves 550 acres and a shore on the Tisbury Great Pond. The largest conservation area on the island, **Cape Pogue Wildlife Refuge and Wasque Reservation,** floats on Chappaquiddick Island. *(627-3599.)*

Two of the best beaches on the island, **South Beach,** at the end of Katama Rd., 3mi. south of Edgartown; and **State Beach,** on Beach Rd. between Edgartown and Oak Bluffs, are free and open to the public. South Beach boasts sizeable surf and an occasionally nasty undertow. State Beach's warmer waters once set the stage for parts of *Jaws*, the granddaddy of classic beach-horror films. For the best sunsets on the island, stake out a spot at **Gay Head** or the **Menemsha Town Beach.**

**Chicama Vineyards,** off State Rd. in West Tisbury, offers free tours and wine tasting. *(888-244-2262. Open June to Sept. M-Sa 11am-5pm, Su 1-5pm.)* **Oak Bluffs,** 3mi. west of Vineyard Haven on Beach Rd., is the most youth-oriented of the Vineyard villages. Highlights of a tour of **Trinity Park** near the harbor include the famous "Gingerbread Houses" (minutely detailed, elaborate pastel Victorian cottages) and the Oak Bluffs's **Flying Horses Carousel,** at the end of Circuit Ave. It's the oldest in the nation (built in 1876), and composed of 20 handcrafted horses with real horsehair. *(693-9481. Open mid-June to Aug. daily 10am-10pm; Aug. to mid-June hrs. vary. Fare $1.)* **Gay Head,** 22mi. southwest of Oak Bluffs on State Rd., offers just about the best view of the sea in all of New England. The native Wampanoag frequently saved sailors whose ships wrecked on the breathtaking **Gay Head Cliffs.** The 100,000-year-old precipice shines in brilliant colors and supports one of 5 lighthouses on the island. **Menemsha** and **Chilmark,** a little northeast of Gay Head, share a scenic coastline; Chilmark claims to be the only working fishing town on the island. Tourists can fish off the pier. **Vineyard Haven** has more artsy boutiques and fewer tacky t-shirt shops than other towns on the island.

## NANTUCKET

Nantucket is far enough away to ward off tourists, but not so secluded that it is not worth the 2hr. ferry ride to get there. Once the home of the biggest whaling port in the world—Herman Melville's *Moby Dick* is based on a Nantucket whaling incident—Nantucket has a lot of history to be proud of. Beyond its rich past, Nantucket offers dune-covered beaches, beautiful wild flowers, cobblestone streets, and spectacular bike paths. Although famed to be a mecca for privileged preppies, it is possible to enjoy a stay on the island without holding up a convenience store to do so. During the first or last weeks of the tourist season, prices tend to drop. There is only one town on the island, where the ferries unload their passengers. The hostel is a few mi. south.

**⟁ PRACTICAL INFORMATION. Hyline** (778-2600) operates a faster **ferry** service to Nantucket's Straight Wharf from Hyannis (late May to Sept., 3-6 per day; late Sept. to Oct., 1 per day; $12 one-way, $2 discount for HI-AYH members; no cars) and from Martha's Vineyard (early May to late Oct., 4 per day. $12). **Steamship Authority** (477-8600), docked at Steamboat Wharf on Nantucket, runs ferries from Hyannis only but carries automobiles (6 per day, $12 one-way). Both charge $5 for bikes. **Nantucket Regional Transit Authority** (228-7025) runs 5 shuttle bus routes throughout the island. (Bus to Madaket leaves from Peter Foulger Museum on Broad St. Bus to Sconset leaves from corner of Main St. and Washington St. Buses depart every 30min. 7am-11:30pm. 50¢-$1, seniors and under 6 free. Multi-day passes available at the visitors center.) **Visitor services and information center:** 25 Federal St. (228-0925; open daily 9am-5:30pm). Some say that hitchhiking is the best way to get around Nantucket, but *Let's Go* does not recommend it. Renting bikes is a great option: there are 3 beautiful **bike paths** which wind from town through wild flower paths and along dune-covered beaches (to Madaket Beach 5mi., Surfside Beach 2½mi., and Siasconset 6mi.). Rent from **Nantucket Bike Shop** (228-1999), Steamboat and Straight Wharfs. (Bikes $6 per hr. or $20 per day. Open Apr.-Oct. daily 8am-6pm; off-season 10am-6pm.) **Area code:** 508.

**⟁⟁ ACCOMMODATIONS AND FOOD.** Occupying an old life-saving station, the **Nantucket Hostel (HI-AYH),** 31 Western Ave., sits pretty at Surfside Beach, 3½mi. from town at the end of the Surfside Bike Path. Take the Miacomet Loop Shuttle to Surfside Rd. and walk 1mi. south on Surfside. (228-0433. 49 beds, full kitchen. $14, nonmembers $17. Linen $2. Reception 7:30-10am and 5-10pm. Lockout 10am-5pm. Curfew 11pm. Reservations essential. Open late Apr. to mid-Oct.) In the heart of Nantucket Town, **Nesbitt Inn,** 21 Broad St., offers 13 rooms, each with a sink and shared baths in the oldest Victorian guest house on the island. The friendly owners make sure guests are comfortable with a fireplace, deck, and free continental breakfast. (228-0156. Singles $65; doubles $75; triples or quads $105. Oct.-Apr. $10 less. Closed Jan. and Feb. Reception 7am-10pm. Reservations and deposit required.) Meals on Nantucket are pricey. The standard entree runs about $15-20, but the frugal gourmet can still dine well. **Black Eyed Susan's,** 10 India St., offers a rotating breakfast and dinner menu with interesting dishes such as buttermilk pancakes with Jarlsberg cheese. (325-0308. Full order $6.25. Breakfast daily 7am-1pm, dinner M-Sa 6-10pm.) **Henry's Sandwiches,** Steamboat Wharf, piles 'em high with cold cuts and tons of toppings (228-0123; open daily 10am-7pm). **Muse Pizza,** 44 Surfside Rd., offers the cheapest and best pizza on the island. Muses eat among pool players and live rock 'n' roll, ska, and acoustic music nightly. (228-1471 or 228-6873. Slices $2.50-3. Open daily 11am-1am.)

**⟁ SIGHTS.** The remarkable natural beauty of Nantucket is well protected; over 36% of the island's land can never be built upon. For a great bike trip, head east from Nantucket Town on Milestone Rd. and turn left onto any path that looks promising. For a day on the sand, **Dionis Beach,** on the northwest end of the island, has the smallest crowds and impressive dunes. **Cisco Beach** appeals to the younger set, while **Surfside** offers the largest waves. For another sort of aquatic adventure, **Sea Nantucket** will set you up in a rental **sea kayak.** The boats aren't difficult to maneuver, but paddling works up a sweat. If you take one out to a nearby salt marsh, or head across the harbor to an isolated beach on the Coatue peninsula, you'll be able to enjoy a picnic undisturbed by other beachgoers. *(228-7499, at the end of Washington St. at the waterfront. Single $30 for ½-day, double $50; full-day $40/$60. Open daily 8:30am-5:30pm.)* Those who prefer to stand on the strand between land and sea can rent **surf fishing** equipment from **Barry Thurston's.** Thurtston's provides up-to-date info on where the fish are biting. *(228-9595, at Harbor Sq. near the A&P. Necessary equipment $20 for 24hr. Open daily Apr.-Dec. 8am-6pm.)* The fascinating **Nantucket Whaling Museum** explains the glories and hardships of the old whaling community through exhibits and talks on whales and methods of whaling. The **Peter Foulger Museum** gives an overview of Nantucket's history. The most economical way to see both museums is to buy a visitor's pass, which allows access to both museums and 7 other historical sights run by the historical association. *(Whaling: 228-1736, Broad St. in Nantucket Town. Foulger: 228-1894, Broad St. 3 lectures per day. $4, children $3. Both museums open early June to mid-Oct. daily 10am-5pm; May to early June and mid-Oct. to early Dec. daily 11am-3pm. Visitors pass $10, children $5.)* The free publication *Yesterday's Island* runs listings of nature walks, concerts, lectures, and art exhibitions.

# WESTERN MASSACHUSETTS

Famous for cultural events in the summer, rich foliage in the fall, and skiing in the winter, the Berkshire Mountains have long been a vacation destination for Boston and New York urbanites seeking a relaxing country escape. Filling the western third of Massachusetts, the Berkshire Region is bordered to the north by Rt. 2 (the Mohawk Trail) and Vermont, to the west by Rt. 7 and New York, to the south by the Mass. Pike and Connecticut, and to the east by I-91.

## THE BERKSHIRES

■ **PRACTICAL INFORMATION.** Sprinkled with small New England towns, the Berkshires offer a plethora of churches, fudge shops, antique boutiques, and country stores. To see sights located far from the town centers, you'll have to drive. Winding and sometimes pocked with potholes, the region's roads are nevertheless scenic. **Visitor Info: Berkshire Visitors Bureau,** 2 Berkshire Common (443-9186 or 800-237-5747), Plaza Level, in Pittsfield (open M-F 8:30am-5pm) and an **information booth** (open M-F 9am-5pm) on the east side of Pittsfield's rotary circle. Berkshire County's 12 state parks and forests cover 100,000 acres and offer numerous camping and hiking options. For info, stop by the **Region 5 Headquarters,** 740 South St., in Pittsfield (442-8928; open M-F 8am-5pm). **Area code:** 413.

### THE MOHAWK TRAIL

Perhaps the most famous highway in the state, the **Mohawk Trail** (Rt. 2) provides a meandering drive that showcases the beauty of the Berkshires. During fall foliage weekends, the awe-inspiring reds and golds of the surrounding mountains draw crowds of leaf-peepers. The town of Millers Falls marks its eastern terminus.

**CHARLEMONT.** Five mi. west of Charlemont, off Rt. 2, the **Mohawk Trail State Forest** offers campsites along a river ($6) and rents cabins. (339-5504; partial hook-ups small $8, large $10; reservations required at least 2 wks. in advance.) Whitewater raft on the **Deerfield River** (Apr.-Oct.) with **Crabapple Whitewater,** in Charlemont (800-553-7238; differing skill levels available).

**NORTH ADAMS.** The recently opened ■ **Museum of Contemporary Art,** 87 Marshall St., the largest center for contemporary visual and performing arts in the country. Many sorts of media are represented in the museum's extensive collection, which is housed in several old factory buildings. (662-2111. Open June-Oct. Su-Th 10am-5pm, F-Sa 10am-7pm, Nov.-May Tu-Su 10am-4pm. $8, ages 6-16 $3, Nov.-May $6, seniors $4, ages 6-16 $2.) North Adams is home to the **Western Gateway,** on Furnace St. bypass off Rt. 8, a railroad museum, gallery, and one of Massachusetts's five Heritage State Parks. (663-6312. Open daily 10am-5pm. Free, donations encouraged. Live music in summer Th 7pm.) **The Freight Yard Pub,** within the Western Gateway park, offers inexpensive salads ($2-7) and, on weekdays, a huge $6 lunch buffet (663-6547; open Su-W 11:30am-1am, Th-Sa 11:30am-2am). On Rt. 8, ½mi. north of downtown North Adams, lies **Natural Bridge State Park,** a white marble bridge formed during the last Ice Age and the only natural, water-eroded bridge on the continent. (In summer 663-6392, in winter 663-6312. Open late May to mid-Oct. M-F 8am-4pm, Sa-Su 10am-6pm. $2 per vehicle.)

**MT. GREYLOCK.** The highest peak in Massachusetts (3491 ft.), it's south of the Mohawk Trail, and only accessible by Rt. 2 to the north and U.S. 7 to the west. By car, take Notch Rd. from Rt. 2 between North Adams and Williamstown, or take Rockwell Rd. from Lanesboro on U.S. 7. The roads up are rough but the views of the surrounding area are breathtaking in all seasons. Hiking trails begin from nearly all the towns around the mountain; grab free maps at the **Mt. Greylock Visitors Information Center,** Rockwell Rd. (499-4262; open daily 9am-5pm). Climb the **War Memorial** at the top for a breathtaking view. The nearby **Bascom Lodge** is built from the rock excavated for the monument (743-1591; $27; under 12 $13; private doubles $65). The lodge offers breakfast ($6), lunch ($6), and dinner ($12; open mid-May to mid-Oct. 6am-10pm; snack bar open daily 10am-5pm). Two mi. shy of the summit off Rockwell Rd., **primitive camping** is offered at 35 sites, 27 of them reservable at 1-877-422-6762 (443-0011; $4; water available at Bascom Lodge).

**WILLIAMSTOWN.** The Mohawk Trail ends in Williamstown at its junction with U.S. 7. Here, an **information booth** provides an abundance of free local maps and seasonal brochures, and can help find a place to stay in one of Williamstown's many reasonably priced B&Bs (458-4922; staffed July-Oct. daily 10am-6pm, May-June Sa-Su 10am-6pm). At **Williams College,** the second-oldest in Massachusetts (est. 1793), lecturers compete with the beautiful scenery of surrounding mountains for the students' attention. Campus maps are available from the **Admissions Office,** 988 Main St., in Mather House (597-2211; open M-F 8:30am-4:30pm; tours 10, 11:15am, 1:15, 3:30pm). **Chapin Library,** in Stetson Hall, displays a number of rare U.S. manuscripts, including early copies of the Declaration of Independence, Articles of Confederation, Constitution, and Bill of Rights (597-2462; open M-F 10am-noon and 1-5pm; free). The small but impressive **Williams College Museum of Art,** off Main St. (Rt. 2), between Spring and Water St., merits a visit. Rotating exhibits have included Soviet graphic art, postmodern architecture, and Impressionist works. (597-2429. Open Tu-Sa 10am-5pm, Su 1-5pm. Free.) Also of artistic note in Williamstown, the **Sterling and Francine Clark Art Institute,** 225 South St., houses an impressive assortment of Impressionist paintings and collections of silver and sculpture. (458-9545. Open July to late Oct. W-M 10am-5pm, Tu 10am-8pm, Nov.-June daily 10am-5pm. $5, students and under 18 free; free Tu.)

In the summer months, be sure to check out the **Williamstown Theater Festival** (597-3400). Past performers include Gwyneth Paltrow, along with her mother, Blythe Danner, and countless other acting luminaries. Call ahead for information on performances and tickets, as it's a popular attraction.

Williamstown has many affordable motels east of town on Rt. 2. The welcoming **Maple Terrace Motel,** 555 Main St./Rt. 2, has bright rooms with a heated outdoor pool and free continental breakfast (458-9677; singles $44-83; doubles $54-88; office open daily 8am-10:30pm). Williamstown's surrounding wooded hills beckon from the moment you arrive. The **Hopkins Memorial Forest** offers over 2250 acres that are free for hiking and cross-country skiing. Take U.S. 7 N, turn left on Bulkley St., follow Bulkley to the end, and turn right onto Northwest Hill Rd. (597-2346). Popular **Pappa Charlie's Deli,** 28 Spring St., offers sandwiches such as the "Dick Cavett" and the $4.25 "Dr. Johnny Fever." (458-5969. Open M-Sa 8am-11pm, Su 9am-9pm; Sept.-June M-Sa 8am-9pm, Su 9am-9pm.)

# ROUTE 7

Paralleling the Appalachian Trail as it meanders through western Massachusetts, Rt. 7 offers the road-bound some of the same natural beauty that the brave through-hikers are treated to on the way from Georgia to Maine.

**PITTSFIELD.** South of Williamstown, the first major town along Rt. 7 is Pittsfield, the county seat of Berkshire County and the town credited with the creation of the county fair. Recreational possibilities abound at the **Pittsfield State Forest,** 4mi. northwest of town, off Rt. 20. There's camping and scheduled outdoor activities (442-8992; $4-5). **Herman Melville's** home, **Arrowhead,** is 3½mi. south of Pittsfield, off Rt. 7. (780 Holmes Rd. 442-1793. Open late May to late Oct. 9:30am-5pm, Nov.-May by appointment only. $5, seniors $4.50, students with ID $3, ages 6-15 $1. 40 min. tours on the hr.) Inside, the **Berkshire County Historical Society** has exhibits on 19th-century country life and the role of women on the farm. The **Berkshire Museum** has Hudson River School paintings, natural history exhibits, and an aquarium. (39 South St. 443-7171. Open Aug. M-Sa 10am-5pm, Su 1-5pm; Sept.-July Tu-Sa 10am-5pm, Su 1-5pm. $6, seniors $5, 3-18 $4. Free W and Sa 10am-noon.)

**LENOX.** **Tanglewood** is the famed summer home of the **Boston Symphony Orchestra,** one of the Berkshires' greatest treasures. South on Rt. 7, a short distance west of Lenox Center on Rt. 183 (West St.), Tanglewood concerts include a variety of music styles, from Ray Charles to James Taylor, but its bread-and-butter is top-notch classical music. Lawn tickets and picnics make for a great evening or Su afternoon. There are chamber concerts on Th evenings, and the Boston Pops give 2 summer concerts. The summer ends with a jazz festival over Labor Day weekend. (637-5165. Orchestral concerts held July-Aug. F 8:30pm with 6:30pm prelude, Sa 8:30pm, Su 2:30pm. Tickets $16-82, lawn seats $13.50-17. Open rehearsals held Sa 10:30am. Call for schedule of special events and prices.) The **Edith Wharton Restoration at the Mount,** at the junction of Rt. 7 and 7A, showcases the home of the turn-of-the-century Pulitzer Prize-winner. (2 Plunkett St. 637-1899. Open late May to Oct. daily 9am-2pm. $6, seniors $5.50, ages 13-18 $4.50. Tours on the hr.)

**STOCKBRIDGE.** The must-see ⊠ **Norman Rockwell Museum,** on Rt. 183, ½mi. south from the junction of Rt. 7 and 102, contains over 1000 items, including many of Rockwell's *Saturday Evening Post* covers. (298-4100. Open May-Oct. daily 10am-5pm; Nov.-Apr. M-F 11am-4pm, Sa-Su 10am-5pm. $9, children $2.)

Rt. 7 south passes the **Wagon Wheel Motel,** at the junction with Rt. 20 (445-4532; off-season $35-55, varying in summer). Summer weekend rates are high throughout the Berkshires, starting at $100. A cheaper option is to continue north on U.S. 20 for about 3mi. to Walker Rd., which takes you to **October Mountain State Forest** with toilets and showers (243-1778; sites $6).

**NORTHAMPTON AND AMHERST.** The last 2 sides of the Berkshire square are major interstate routes. Although time-saving, these interstates prevent visitors from seeing as much natural scenery. However, there are alternate routes for beauty-seekers with time on their hands. Rt. 20 meanders above, below, and around the Mass Pike (Rt. 90), and in the north-south direction, Rt. 91 can be supplanted by Rt. 47 and 63, which snake along the Connecticut River.

On Rt. 91, about 15min. north of Springfield, lie educational hubs **Northampton** and **Amherst.** The **Five-College Consortium** consists of five area schools which form a larger academic community. The largest is the gargantuan **University of Massachusetts-Amherst** in Amherst (545-0222; tours daily 11am and 1:15pm; June-Aug. M-F 11am and 1:15pm). Prestigious **Amherst College** shares the town with the main UMass campus. (542-2328. Open M-F 8:30am-4:30pm. Tours depend on availability of student guides; call ahead.) The all-female **Smith** and **Mount Holyoke** colleges, and the small, alternative **Hampshire College** complete the community.

Northampton is a beautiful town that boasts a number of restaurants and shops, on Main and Pleasant St. The **Smith College Museum of Art,** on Elm St. at Bedford Terrace in Tyron Hall, has a collection of 19th- and 20th-century European and American paintings, and offers tours and gallery talks (585-2760; open Tu-W and F-

Sa 9:30am-4pm, Th and Su 2-8pm; free). **Look Memorial Park,** on the Berkshire Trail (Rt. 9) not far from Northampton, is bordered by the Mill River. Its 200 acres make for a pleasant picnic spot. (584-5457. Open daily dawn-dusk. Facilities open late May to early Sept. daily 11am-7pm. $2 per vehicle Sa-Su, $1 M-F.) Award-winning **La Veracruzana,** 31 Main St. in Northampton, is the hot spot for Mexican food. Try the excellent enchiladas ($6-7) with any one of the eight salsas at their salsa bar. (586-7181. Open Su-M 11am-10pm, Tu-Sa 11am-midnight.)

The ☒ **Black Sheep Deli and Bakery,** 79 Main St. in Amherst, is another popular eating option, offering huge, ultra-fresh gourmet sandwiches, along with pastas and salads. Vegetarian choices also available (253-3442). Dubbed "the mecca of the Northeast" by Amherst students, **Antonio's,** 31 N. Pleasant St. in Amherst, makes deliciously creative pizza with toppings like pesto chicken or beef taco (slices $1.25-2.75; 253-0808; open daily 10am-10pm).

For more info, visit or call the **Greater Northampton Chamber of Commerce,** 99 Pleasant St. (584-1900; open M-F 9am-5pm, July-early Oct. Sa-Su 10am-2pm). **Peter Pan Trailways,** 1 Roundhouse Plaza (586-1030; station open daily 7am-6pm), runs buses to Boston (14 per day, $21) and New York (12 per day, $29). **Area code:** 413.

**SPRINGFIELD.** As the largest city in the western half of Massachusetts, **Springfield** serves the region as an industrial and transportation center, and a counterbalance to its rival Shelbyville. Springfield fills the southeast quadrant of the intersection of I-90 and I-91, the main north-south artery in the region. It's a transportation hub, so get in and get out. **Visitor Info: Greater Springfield Convention and Visitors Bureau,** in the Tower Sq. building at 1500 Main St. (787-1548; open M-F 8:30am-5pm). Most budget motels are in West Springfield, at exits 13A and 13B off I-91.

It's not only Peter Pan bus lines that call Springfield home: in 1891, Dr. James Naismith invented the game of basketball here, and the city has been identified with it ever since. Today, visitors to the **Basketball Hall of Fame,** 1150 W. Columbus Ave., adjacent to I-91, can see Bob Lanier's size 22 sneakers and play a virtual one-on-one with Bill Walton. (781-6500. Open July to early Sept. M-Sa 9am-7pm, Su 9:30am-5:30pm, mid-Sept.-June daily 9:30am-5pm. $8, seniors and ages 7-15 $5.)

30min. east is **Old Sturbridge Village,** on Rt. 20 in Sturbridge at the intersection of I-90 and I-84. Home to costumed "villagers," this recreated 1830s town has over 40 exhibits such as a cider mill, blacksmith shop, and clock gallery, spread out over 200 acres of rural countryside. (Open late Mar. to Oct. 9am-5pm. 2-day admission $16, seniors $15, ages 6-15 $8.) **Peter Pan Bus Line** provides service to Springfield from Boston; call 617-426-7838 for info and tickets. **Area code:** 413.

# RHODE ISLAND

Despite its diminutive stature (it is the smallest state in the Union), Rhode Island has never felt pressure to conform. It was founded by Roger Williams, a religious outcast during colonial days, and it was the first state to pass laws against slavery. Though you can drive through the body of Rhode Island in 45 minutes, the state's 400mi. coastline deserves a longer look. Small, elegant hamlets speckle the shores winding to Connecticut, and the inland roads remain quiet, unpaved thoroughfares lined with family fruit stands.

# ⓘ PRACTICAL INFORMATION

**Capital:** Providence.

**Visitor Info: Dept. of Tourism,** 1 West Exchange St., Providence 02903 (401-222-2601 or 800-556-2484; www.visitrhodeisland.com). Open M-F 8:30am-5pm. **Division of Parks and Recreation,** 2321 Hartford Ave., Johnston 02919 (401-222-2632). Open M-F 8:30am-4pm.

**Postal Abbreviation:** RI. **Sales Tax:** 7%.

# PROVIDENCE

Seven colleges inhabit the seven hills of Providence, luring a community of students, artists, and academics to join the native working class and state representatives. Providence has cobbled sidewalks and colonial buildings, a college town atmosphere, and more than its share of bookstores and cafes. In the area around the colleges, students on tight budgets support a plethora of inexpensive restaurants and shops. Its local color stems in part from constant allegations of corrupt city government: the current mayor, Buddy Cianci, served a jail term and a term of office while on probation for attacking his estranged wife's suspected lover.

## ■ PRACTICAL INFORMATION

The state capitol and the downtown business district cluster just east of the intersection of **I-95** and **I-195**. **Brown University** and the **Rhode Island School of Design (RISD)** sit atop a steep hill, a 10min. walk east of downtown. **Amtrak,** 100 Gaspee St. (727-7379 or 800-872-7245; station open daily 5:30am-11pm), operates from a gleaming white structure behind the state capitol, a 10min. walk from Brown or downtown. Trains set out for Boston (50min., 6 per day, $12) and New York (4hr., 9 per day, $37-52). **Greyhound,** 102 Fountain St. in downtown Providence, (station open daily 6:30am-6:30pm) runs buses to Boston (1 hr., 12 per day, $8 one-way). **Bonanza,** 1 Bonanza Way (454-0790; station open daily 6am-8pm), exit 25 off I-95, also has frequent service to Boston (1hr., 17 per day, $8.50) and New York (4hr., 7 per day, $35). **Rhode Island Public Transit Authority (RIPTA),** 265 Melrose St. (781-9400; M-F 7am-6pm, Sa 8am-6pm), runs an **info booth** at Kennedy Plaza, which provides route and schedule assistance and free bus maps. RIPTA's service includes Newport ($3) and other points. (Buses run daily 6am-1:30am; hrs. vary by route. Fare 25¢-$3; within Providence, generally $1.) **Visitor Info: Greater Providence Convention and Visitors Bureau,** 38 Exchange Terrace (274-1636 or 800-233-1636), in downtown, (open M-F 10am-5pm, Sa-Su 10am-4pm). The **Providence Preservation Society,** 21 Meeting St. (831-7440), at the foot of College Hill, provides detailed info on historic Providence (open M-F 9am-5pm). **Post Office:** 2 Exchange Terrace (421-4361; open M-F 7:30am-5:30pm, Sa 8am-2pm). **ZIP code:** 02903. **Area code:** 401.

## ■ ACCOMMODATIONS

Downtown motel rates make Providence an expensive overnight stay. Rooms fill up far in advance for the graduation season in May and early June. Head 10mi. south on I-95 to Warwick/Cranston for cheap motels.

Catering largely to the international visitors of the universities, the stained-glass-windowed **International House of Rhode Island,** 8 Stimson Ave., off Hope St. near the Brown campus, has 3 comfortable, welcoming rooms, but they are often full. Amenities include kitchen, private bath, TV, and a fridge. (421-7181. Singles $50, students $35; doubles $60/$45; $5 per night off for stays of 5 nights or more. 2-night min. stay. Reception M-F 9:30am-5pm. Reservations required.) If you don't mind that cheap motel smell, the **Town 'n' Country Motel,** 3mi. outside of Providence on Rt. 6 in Seekonk, MA, rents out reasonable rooms (508-336-8300; singles $44; doubles $47). The nearest **campgrounds** lie a 30min. drive from downtown. One of the closest, in Coventry, R.I., **Colwell's Campground,** provides showers and hookups for 75 sites on the shore of the Flat River Reservoir. From Providence, take I-95 S to exit 10, then head west 9½mi. on Rt. 117 to Peckham Ln. (397-4614; sites $12-17, depending on proximity to the waterfront).

## ■ FOOD

A variety of impressive food is found in 3 areas in Providence: **Atwells Ave.** in the Italian district, on Federal Hill just west of downtown; **Thayer St.,** on College Hill to the east, home to off-beat student hangouts and ethnic restaurants; and **Broad St.,** in the southwest part of town, with many inexpensive international eateries. **Geoff's Superlative Sandwiches,** 163 Benefit St., attracts corporate, punky, and student types with 60 different sandwiches, named after local stars like Buddy Cianci (751-2248; sandwiches $4-6; open M-F 8am-9pm, Sa-Su 10am-9pm). They have swivel stools and good home-cookin' at the **Seaplane Diner,** 307 Allens Ave., in East Providence. Around "since Grandma was a girl," Seaplane has perfected cheap homestyle breakfast and lunches (941-9547; $3.50-5; open M-F 5am-3pm, Sa 5am-1pm, F-Sa midnight-4am). **Louis' Family Restaurant,** 286 Brook St., has made the entire community its family because of its friendly service. Students swear by the prices and donate artwork for the walls. Try the #1 special: 2 eggs, homefries, toast, and coffee for $2.65. (861-5225; Open daily 5am-3pm.)

# ◎ SIGHTS

The most notable historic sights in Providence cluster around the 350-year-old neighborhood surrounding **College Hill. Brown University,** established in 1764, includes several 18th-century buildings and provides a fitting starting point for a historic walking tour of Providence. The Office of Admissions, housed in the historic **Carliss-Brackett House,** gives free 1hr. walking tours of the campus *(45 Prospect St. 863-2378. Open M-F 8am-4pm. Tours M-F 10, 11am, 1, 3, and 4pm.)* In addition to founding Rhode Island, in 1775 Roger Williams founded the *first* **First Baptist Church of America.** *(75 N. Main St. 454-3418. Open M-F 10am-noon and 1pm-3pm, Sa 10am-1pm. Free.)* Down the hill, the **Rhode Island State Capitol** supports the 4th-largest free-standing marble dome in the world. *(222-2357. Open M-F 8:30am-4:30pm. Free tours M-F 10 and 11am; reservations appreciated. Free self-guide booklets available in room 220.)* John Quincy Adams called it "the most magnificent and elegant private mansion." On College Hill sits the **John Brown House Museum,** the 18th-century home of the Rhode Island entrepreneur and revolutionary. *(52 Power St. 331-8575. Open Tu-Sa 10am-5pm, Su noon-4pm. $6, students and seniors $4.50, ages 7-17 $3.)* The nearby **RISD Museum of Art** gathers a fine collection of Greek, Roman, Asian, and Impressionist art, as well as a gigantic 10th-century Japanese Buddha. *(224 Benefit St. 454-6500. Open W-Th and Sa-Su. 10am-5pm, F 10am-8pm. $5, students $2, seniors $4, ages 5-18 $1. Free every 3rd Th 5-9pm and last Sa of month.)* The New England textile industry was born in 1793 when Samuel Slater used plans smuggled out of Britain to build the first water-powered factory in America. In Pawtucket, the **Slater Mill Historic Site** preserves the fabric heritage with operating machinery. *(67 Roosevelt Ave. 725-8638. Open June-Oct. M-Sa 10am-5pm, Su 1-5pm; Mar.-June and Nov.-Dec. Sa-Su 1-5pm. Tours leave roughly every 2hr. $6.50, seniors $5.50, 6-12 $5.)*

# ♫ ENTERTAINMENT AND NIGHTLIFE

The nationally acclaimed **Trinity Repertory Company,** 201 Washington St., offers $10 student rush tickets 2hr. before performances when available, except on Sa (351-4242; tickets $26-38). For splashier productions, contact the **Providence Performing Arts Center,** 220 Weybosset St., which hosts a variety of concerts and Broadway musicals (421-2787). The **Cable Car Cinema and Café,** 204 S. Main St., shows artsy and foreign films in a kinder, gentler setting—on couches instead of chairs (272-3970; tickets $6.50).

If you're in the mood for a little hardball, the **Pawtucket Red Sox** (AAA) take the field Apr. through Aug. in Pawtucket's **McCoy Stadium,** 1 Columbus Ave. (724-7300; Box seats $6; general admission $4, seniors and under 12 $3).

Read the "Weekend" section of the *Friday Providence Journal* or the *Providence Phoenix* for film, theater, and nightlife listings. Brownies, townies, and RISDs rock the night away at several hot spots throughout town. Mingle with the local artist community at **AS220,** 115 Empire St. between Washington and Westminster St., a cafe/bar/gallery/performance space. (831-9327. Cover $2-5. Open M 10am-5pm, Tu-F 10am-1am, Sa 1pm-1am, Su 7pm-1am.) **The Living Room,** 23 Rathbone St., hosts both dancing and live alternative bands (521-5200; open daily 8pm-

1am). Both gay and straight patrons favor **Gerardo's,** 1 Franklin Sq. on Allens Ave., where karaoke blasts in addition to a DJ (274-5560; cover varies; open Su-Th 4pm-1am, F-Sa 4pm-2am).

# NEWPORT

Money has always found its way into Newport. Once supported by slave trade profits, the town later became the summer home of the elite and the site of some of the nation's most opulent mansions. The city's monied residents played the first game of polo in North America, hosted the America's Cup race for 35 years, and watched John F. Kennedy wed Jacqueline Bouvier. Today, the city attracts throngs of tourists with deep pockets and a passion for high-priced boats. For those on a tight budget, events such as the jazz and folk festivals are reason enough to visit.

◪ **PRACTICAL INFORMATION.** The place to start any visit to Newport is the **Newport County Convention and Visitors Bureau,** 23 America's Cup Ave. (845-9123 or 800-976-5122), in the Newport Gateway Center (open Su-Th 9am-5pm, F-Sa 9am-6pm). **Bonanza Buses** (846-1820) depart from the Center, as do the buses of **Rhode Island Public Transit Authority (RIPTA)** (781-9400 or 800-244-0444); station open daily 7:30am-9pm; fare $1.25). RIPTA routes run daily 5:30am-9:30pm. RIPTA also heads north to Providence (1hr., $1.25), to points on Rt. 114, and to the Kingston Amtrak station (1 hr., $1.25, June to mid-Oct.). There are no 10-speeds at **Ten Speed Spokes,** 18 Elm St. (847-5609). (Mountain bikes $5 per hr., $25 per day. Must have credit card and photo ID. Open M-Th 10am-6pm, F-Sa 9am-6pm, Su 11am-5pm.) **Post Office:** 320 Thames St. (847-2329; open M-F 8:30am-5pm, Sa 9am-1pm). **ZIP code:** 02840. **Area code:** 401.

◪◪ **ACCOMMODATIONS AND FOOD.** Guest houses account for the bulk of Newport's accommodations. Most offer a bed and continental breakfast with colonial intimacy. Those willing to share a bathroom or forego a sea view might find a double for $65; singles are almost nonexistent. Many hotels and guest houses book solid 2 months in advance for summer weekends. Fortunately for the budget traveler, Newport is blessed with a **Motel 6,** 249 J.T. Connel Hwy. Follow Broadway out of Newport into Middletown, turn left on W. Main St., and follow Connelton Hwy. for 1.5mi. (848-0600 or 800-466-8356. 1 person $55-65, 2 people $62-72, $3 per additional person). **Campsites** await at **Fort Getty Recreation Area,** on Fort Getty Rd. on Conanicut Island. The nearby Fox Hill Salt Marsh has great birdwatching. (423-7264, reservations 423-7311. 100 RV sites in summer $25; 20 year-round. 15 tent sites $20. Showers and beach access. Reservations recommended 1-2 months in advance. Tent sites available late May to Oct.)

Despite what you might expect, cheap food *does* exist in Newport. Most of Newport's restaurants line up on **Thames St.** where wrap joints and ice cream parlors abound. Mighty good food can be consumed at the **Franklin Spa,** 229 Spring St., like the $4 banana pancakes or $6 grilled chicken club (open daily 6am-3pm). Shack up with some choice mollusks alongside a severely incapacitated lobster boat at **Flo's Clam Shack,** Rt. 138A/Aquidneck Ave., across from Easton Beach (847-8141; fried clams $9. Open Su-Th 11am-9pm, F-Sa 11am-10pm). **Dry Dock Seafood,** 448 Thames St., fries 'em and serves 'em with a minimum of fuss (847-3974; entrees $6-13; open daily 11am-10pm, in summer closes at 9pm).

◪ **SIGHTS.** George Noble Jones built the first "summer cottage" here in 1839, thereby kicking off an extravagant string of palatial summer estates. Five of the mansions lie south of town on Bellevue Ave. A self-guided walking tour or a guided tour by the **Preservation Society of Newport** will allow you to ogle at the extravagance; purchase tickets at any mansion. *(424 Bellevue Ave. 847-1000. Open M-F 9am-5pm. $3.50-10, students $2-6, ages 6-11 $0-4. Combination tickets available.)* **The Marble House** is the must-see of the mansions. Built in 1892 as a weekend/summer home for William K. Vanderbilt, it contains over 500,000 cubic ft. of marble, silk walls, and rooms covered entirely in gold. *(847-1000. Open Apr.-Oct. 10am-5pm; Jan.-Mar. Sa-Su 10am-4pm. $8, students $5, ages 6-11 $3.50.)* Eight mi. north of Newport in Portsmouth, the **Green Animals Topiary Gardens,** Cory's Lane, holds 21 shrubs amazingly sculpted into the likes of giraffes and lions. *(847-1000. $8, students $5, ages 6-11 $3; open May-Oct. daily 10am-5pm.)* The father of William Mayes, a notorious Red Sea pirate, opened the **White Horse Tavern** Marlborough St. and Farewell St., as a tavern in 1687, making it the oldest continuously operated drinking establishment in the country and there's food too. *(849-3600, beer $3-4, open W-M noon-3 and dinner daily from 6pm.)* The oldest synagogue in the U.S., the beautifully restored Georgian **Touro Synagogue,** dates back to 1763. *(85 Touro St. 847-4794. Visits by free tour only. Tours every 30min. late May to early July M-F 1-2:30pm, Su 11am-2:30pm every 30min.; early July to early Sept. Su-F. 10am-4pm; call for off-season tour schedule.)* Die-hard tennis fans will feel right at home in Newport, where the newly renovated **Tennis Hall of Fame** hosts grass court tournaments and dedicates a museum to the game. *(194 Bellevue Ave. 849-3990. Open daily 9am-5pm. $8, students and seniors $6, under 17 $4, families $20.)*

Newport's gorgeous beaches are frequently as crowded as the streets. The most popular is **Easton's Beach,** or First Beach, on Memorial Blvd. *(848-6491. Open late May to early Sept. M-F 9am-9pm, Sa-Su 8am-9pm. Parking M-F $8, Sa-Su $10.)* **Fort Adams State Park,** south of town on Ocean Dr. 2½mi. from the Visitors Center, offers showers, picnic areas, and 2 fishing piers. *(847-2400. Entrance booth open M-F 7:30am-4pm, Sa-Su 7:30am-6pm; park open sunrise to sunset. Entrance fee $4 per car.)* Good beaches also line Little Compton, Narragansett, and the shore between Watch Hill and Point Judith; for more details the free *Ocean State Beach Guide*, available at the Visitors Center, ought not be missed.

🎭 **ENTERTAINMENT.** In July and Aug., Newport gives lovers of classical, folk, blues, and jazz each a festival to call their own. The oldest and best-known jazz festival in the world, the **Newport Jazz Festival** has seen the likes of Duke Ellington and Count Basie; bring your beach chairs and coolers to Fort Adams State Park to join the fun Aug. 11-13, 2000 (847-3700; tickets $40 per day, under 12 $15). Also at Fort Adams State Park, on Aug. 4-6, 2000, folk singers (former acts include the Indigo Girls and Susan Vega) entertain at the **Newport Folk Festival** (847-3709 in summer; tickets $40, under 12 $15). **Newport Music Festival,** July 7-23, 2000, attracts pianists, violinists, and other classical musicians from around the world for 2 weeks of concerts in the ballrooms and lawns of the mansions (846-1133, box office 849-0700; box office open daily 10am-5pm; tickets $30-35).

Newport's nightlife centers around the bars and clubs on the Newport Harborfront. **One Pelham East,** 274 Thames St., packs 'em in for alternative cover bands (847-9460; live music nightly; cover F-Sa $10; open daily 1pm-1am).

## NEAR NEWPORT: BLOCK ISLAND

A popular daytrip 10mi. southeast of Newport in the Atlantic, sand-blown **Block Island** possesses an untamed natural beauty. Block Island was originally called by its Mohegan name Manisses, or "Isle of Little God." One-quarter of the island is protected open space; local conservationists hope to increase that to 50%. From Old Harbor where the ferry lets you off, a 4mi. journey brings you to the **National Wildlife Refuge,** a great spot for a picnic. Two mi. south of Old Harbor, the **Mohegan Bluffs** invite the adventurous, cautious, and strong to wind their way down to the Atlantic 200 ft. below. High in the cliffs, the **Southeast Lighthouse** has warned fog-bound fisherfolk since 1875; its beacon shines the brightest of any on the Atlantic coast. Located at the top of a 150 ft. cliff, the lighthouse was on the verge of falling into the sea until 1993, when the whole structure was moved 20 ft. back.

**Block Island Chamber of Commerce:** (466-2982) at the ferry dock in Old Harbor Drawer D and in an office behind Finn's Fish Market (open daily in summer 9am-5pm; mid-Oct. to mid-May 10am-4pm). Cycling is the ideal way to explore the tiny (7mi. by 3mi.) island; the **Old Harbor Bike Shop,** directly to the left of the ferry exit, rents just about anything on wheels. (466-2029. Mountain bikes $5-8 per hr., $20-30 per day; mopeds $17/60. Cars $79 per day plus 20¢ per mi. Must be 21+ with credit card. Open mid-May to mid-Oct. daily 8:30am-7pm.) The **Interstate Navigation Co.** (783-4613) provides **ferry service** to Block Island from Galilee Pier in Point Judith, RI. (1¼hr. 7 per day, Sept. 7 to May 31 1-4 per day. $8.40, ages 5-11 $4.60. Cars by reservation $26.30 1-way, driver and passengers extra; bikes $2.30), and summer service from Newport, RI (2hr., late June to early Sept. 1 per day, $7.40) and New London, CT (2hr., mid-June to mid-Sept. 1 per day, $13.50).

The island does not permit camping; it's best to take a daytrip unless you're willing to shell out $60 or more for a room in a guest house. Most restaurants hover near the ferry dock in Old Harbor, where cheap, casual, and filling options abound; several cluster at New Harbor 1mi. inland.

# CONNECTICUT

Connecticut, the third-smallest state in the Union, resembles a patchwork quilt stitched from industrialized centers (like Hartford and New Haven), serene New England villages, and lush woodland beauty. Perhaps it is this diversity that attracted such famous residents as Mark Twain, Harriet Beecher Stowe, Noah Webster, and Eugene O'Neill, and inspired the birth of the American Impressionist movement and the American musical—both Connecticut originals. Home to Yale University and the nation's first law school, Connecticut has an equally rich intellectual history. This doesn't mean that the people of Connecticut don't know how to let their hair down—this is the state that brought us the lollipop, the 3-ring circus, and the largest casino in the United States.

## ◪ PRACTICAL INFORMATION

**Capital:** Hartford.

**Visitor Info: Connecticut Vacation Center**, 865 Brook St., Rocky Hill 06067 (800-282-6863; www.state.ct.us/tourism). Open M-F 9am-4:30pm.

**Postal Abbreviation:** CT. **Sales Tax:** 6%.

## HARTFORD

In 1687, the English governor demanded the surrender of the charter that Charles II had granted Hartford 25 years before. Hartfordians obstinately hid the charter in a tree trunk until the infuriated governor returned to England. Today, a plaque marks the spot at Charter Oak Place. Over the last 300 years, Hartford has grown from a colony of rebels into the world's insurance capital. The city's skyline is shaped by towering granite structures financed by some of the larger firms, including the monolithic oval of the Boat Building, America's first two-sided building.

The ◪ **Wadsworth Athenaeum**, 600 Main St., has absorbing collections of contemporary and Baroque art, including one of three Caravaggios in the U.S. (278-2670. Open Tu-Su 11am-5pm. $7, seniors and students $5, ages 6-17 $3. Free Th and Sa before noon. Call ahead for tour and lecture information.) Designed by Charles Bullfinch in 1796, the gold-domed **Old State House**, 800 Main St., housed the state government until 1878. Now, well-dressed historic actors welcome tourists to the chambers, a rotating art exhibit hall, and a museum of oddities including a mounted 2-headed calf. (522-6766. Open M-F 10am-4pm, Sa 11am-4pm.) The **Mark Twain House**, 351 Farmington Ave., and **Harriet Beecher Stowe House**, 71 Forest St., both just west of the city center on Farmington Ave are engaging and interesting. From the Old State House, take any "Farmington Ave." bus west. The rambling, richly colored Twain place housed the author for 17 years, during which he composed his masterpiece *Huckleberry Finn*. Stowe, whom Abraham Lincoln called "the little lady that started the big war," lived next door after the publication of *Uncle Tom's Cabin*. (Twain House: 493-6411. Open M-Sa 9:30am-4pm, Su 11am-4pm; Oct.-May closed Tu. $9, seniors $8, ages 6-12 $3.50. Stowe House: 525-9317. Open June to early Oct. daily 9:30am-4pm, off-season Tu-Sa 9:30am-4pm, Su noon-4pm; $6.50/$6/$2.75.)

NEW HAVEN ■ 149

The excellent **Mark Twain Hostel (HI-AYH),** 131 Tremont St., offers welcoming accommodations in a homey atmosphere, not far from the center of town (523-7255. $14, nonmembers $18; check-in 9am-10pm). Tremont St. is past the Mark Twain House on Farmington Ave. and is accessible by the "Farmington Ave." bus west. In the heart of downtown, the **YMCA,** 160 Jewell St., by Bushnell Park, offers dorm-like rooms at reasonable rates, and use of a gym, pool, and racquetball courts. (522-4183. Singles $19, with private bath $24. $5 key deposit. Must be 18+ with ID. Check-in 7:30am-10pm. Check-out noon. No reservations accepted.)

Many restaurants hover within a few blocks of the downtown area. Hartford's eldest eatery, the **Municipal Cafe,** 485 Main St., is a popular and friendly place to catch a good breakfast or lunch. The breakfast special means bacon, ham, or sausage with 2 eggs, toast, and coffee or tea for $4. Hot lunches go for $4-6. (278-4844. Open daily 7am-3:30pm.) **The Hartford Brewery,** 35 Pearl St., one of Connecticut's only brew-pubs, serves up sandwiches ($6-7), burgers ($7), and a changing menu of 6 freshly brewed beers (246-2337. Open M 11:30am-2pm, bar open until 8pm; both open Tu-F 11:30am-midnight, Sa noon-2am.)

Hartford marks the intersection of I-91 and I-84. Union Place, in the northeast part of the city, between Church and Asylum St., houses **Amtrak** (727-1776), which runs 9 trains daily both north and south (office open daily 5:30am-9pm), and **Greyhound** (station open daily 6am-9pm), at Union Place, run buses to New York (2½hr., 19 per day, $20) and Boston (2½hr., 19 per day, $20). **Visitor Info: Greater Hartford Convention and Visitors Bureau,** 1 Civic Center Plaza, 3rd fl. (728-6789 or 800-446-7811; open M-F 8:30am-4:30pm), and the **Old State House,** 800 Main St. (522-6766; open M-F 10am-4pm, Sa 11am-4pm). In front of the Old State House, **Connecticut Transit's Information Center** (525-9181), at State and Market St., doles out helpful downtown maps and public transportation info (basic bus fare $1; open M-F 7am-6pm). **Post Office:** 141 Weston St. (524-6074; open M-F 8am-5pm, Sa 7am-2pm). **ZIP code:** 06101. **Area code:** 860.

# NEW HAVEN

Simultaneously university town and depressed city, New Haven has gained a reputation as something of a battleground—academic types and a working-class population live uneasily side by side. Every facet of life in the city, from architecture to safety, reflects this difference. While most of New Haven continues to decay, Yale has begun to renovate its neo-Gothic buildings, convert its concrete sidewalks to brick, and created a thriving collegiate coffeehouse, bar, and bookstore scene.

**◪ PRACTICAL INFORMATION.** New Haven lies at the intersection of I-95 and I-91, 40mi. south of Hartford. New Haven is laid out in 9 squares. Between Yale University and City Hall, the central square, called the Green, provides a pleasant escape from the hassles of city life. *At night, don't wander too far from the immediate downtown and campus areas; surrounding sections are notably less safe.* On the Green, on Chapel St. between Church and Temple St., **CT Transit** runs an info booth with free bus maps and route and schedule assistance (open M-F 7:30am-5:30pm). Nineteen bus routes head to all points in Greater New Haven. Buses generally run daily 6am-midnight; hours vary by route. (Fare within New Haven $1 with a few exceptions.) **Amtrak** (ticket office open daily 6am-10:15 pm), Union Station on Union Ave. exit 1 off I-91, runs out of a newly renovated station. *Be careful; the area is unsafe at night.* Trains chug-a-lug to New York City (1½hr, every hr., $22); Boston (2½hr., every 2hr., $33); Washington, D.C. (6hr., every 3 hr., $61); and Mystic ($15). Also at Union Station, **Greyhound** (772-2470; ticket office open daily 6:15am-8pm) runs frequently to New York (1½hr., 11 per day, $14); Boston (4hr., 14 per day, $19); and Providence (2½hr., 7 per day, $19).

**Visitor Info: Greater New Haven Convention and Visitors Bureau,** at exit 46 off I-95. (Open May to early Sept. M-Th 11am-7pm, F-Su 10am-7pm and early Sept.-late Nov. F-Su 10am-7pm) and at 350 Long Wharf Dr. (777-8550). For a weekly **recorded events update,** call 498-5050, ext. 1310. **Yale Visitors Center:** 149 Elm St. (432-2300), facing the Green (open M-F 9am-4:45pm, Sa-Su 10am-4pm. Free tours M-F 10:30am and 2pm, Sa-Su 1:30pm. Tours last 1¼hr.). From Apr.-Oct., the Visitor Center offers a walking tour of the historic New Haven Green (Th noon). **Area code:** 203.

NEW ENGLAND

**▟▛ ACCOMMODATIONS AND FOOD.** Inexpensive lodgings are sparse in New Haven; the hunt quickens around Yale Parents Weekend (mid-Oct.) and commencement (early June). Head 10mi. south on I-95 to **Milford** for affordable motels. **Hotel Duncan,** 1151 Chapel St. is located in downtown New Haven, close to Yale, has old-fashioned charm, inexpensive rooms with cable TV, and the oldest manually operated elevator in the state (787-1273; singles $44; doubles $60; reservations recommended for F-Su). **Motel 6,** 270 Foxon Blvd., exit 8 off I-91, keeps 58 rooms at good prices. (469-0343 or 800-466-8356. Su-Th singles $52, doubles $58; F-Sa singles $58, doubles $64.) **Hammonasset Beach State Park,** 20min. east on I-95 N from New Haven, exit 62 in Madison, offers 558 sites in a beautiful setting for $12 (245-1817; office open mid-May to Oct. 8am-11pm).

For great authentic Italian cuisine, work your way along Wooster St. The finest brick oven pizza can be found at **Pepe's,** 157 Wooster St. Try a large, crispy, thin-crust pizza with their special sauce for $11. (865-5762. Open M, W-Th 4-10:30pm, F-Sa 11:30am-midnight, Su 2:30-10:30pm.) No condiments are allowed at **Louis' Lunch,** 263 Crown St. Cooked vertically in original cast iron grills, these $3 burgers are too fine for ketchup or mustard. (562-5507. Open Tu-W 11am-4pm, Th-Sa noon-2am.) The $6 all-you-can-eat lunch buffet at **India Palace,** 65 Howe St., is one of the best deals in town (776-9010; open until 10:30pm; lunch served M-F 11:30am-3pm).

**◙ SIGHTS.** The Yale University Campus provides the bulk of the city's sights and museums. Each campus building was designed in the English Gothic and Georgian Colonial styles, many of them with detailed, intricate moldings and a few with gargoyles. Wander into the charming Old Campus, bordered by Chapel, College, Elm, and High St., and view Connecticut Hall, the 299-year-old unviersity's oldest building. One block north, on the other side of Elm St., **Sterling Memorial Library,** 120 High St., is designed to resemble a monastery. Even the telephone booths are shaped like confessionals. Designer James Gambel Rodgers spared no expense in making Yale look "authentic," even decapitating the figurines on the library's exterior to imitate those at Oxford. Just outside the Sterling, is a fountain designed by Yale Design School alum Maya Lin, whose other credits include Montgomery's Civil Rights Memorial and the Vietnam Memorial.

Apparently the creator of the massive **Beinecke Rare Book and Manuscript Library** wasn't fond of windows: this massive modern white structure lacks them. It is paneled with Vermont marble cut thin enough to be translucent. The building, protecting one of only five Gutenberg Bibles in the U.S. and an extensive collection of William Carlos Williams's writings, could probably survive a nuclear war. *(121 Wall St. 432-2977. Open M-F 8:30am-5pm, Sa 10am-5pm. Closed Sa in Aug.)*

On New Haven's own **Wall St.,** between High and Yale St., the gargoyles perched on the Law School building portray cops and robbers. Open since 1832, the **Yale University Art Gallery,** on the corner of York, claims to be the oldest university art museum in the Western Hemisphere. The museum holds over 100,000 pieces from around the world, including works by Monet, Picasso, and 13th-century Italian artists. *(1111 Chapel St. 432-0600. Open Sep.-July Tu-Sa 10am-5pm, Su 1-6pm. Free.)* Just across the street, The **Yale Center for British Art** boasts the largest collection of, well, British art, outside of the United Kingdom. *(1080 Chapel St. 432-2800 or 432-2850. Open Tu-Sa 10am-5pm, Su noon-5pm. Free.)* The **Peabody Museum of Natural History,** off I-91 at exit 3, houses Rudolph F. Zallinger's Pulitzer Prize-winning mural, which portrays the North American continent as it appeared 350 to 70 million years ago. Other exhibits include a hall displaying the skeleton of an apatosaurus, and a cat mummy and tomb from ancient Egypt. *(170 Whitney Ave. 432-5050. Open M-Sa 10am-5pm, Su noon-5pm. $5, seniors and ages 3-15 $3.)*

**▟▛ ENTERTAINMENT AND NIGHTLIFE.** Pick up a free copy of *The Advocate* to find out what's up. **The Shubert Theater,** 247 College St., brings in top Broadway productions. (562-5666 or 800-228-6622. Box office open M-F 10am-5pm, Sa-Su 11am-3pm.) **The Yale Repertory Theater,** 1120 Chapel St., boasts such illustrious alums as Meryl Streep, Glenn Close, and James Earl Jones, and continues to produce excellent shows. (432-1234. Open Oct.-May M-Sa 11am-5pm, June-Sept. M-F

10am-5pm. Tickets $10-30. ½-price student rush tickets on the day of a show.) In summer, the city hosts **concerts** on the Green (787-8956), including **New Haven Symphony** concerts (865-0831, box office 776-1444; open M-F 10am-5pm).

**Toad's Place,** 300 York St., has hosted gigs by Bob Dylan and the Stones. (562-5694, recorded info 624-8623. Box office open daily 11am-6pm; buy tickets at the bar after 8pm. Bar open Su-Th 8pm-1am, F-Sa 8pm-2am.) Yalie jocks and fratboys get drunk on $2.75 beers at the **Union League Café,** 1032 Chapel St. (562-4299; open daily 5:30pm-2am). **Bar,** 254 Crown St., is anything but generic—the place for drinking is also the gay hotspot on Tu, and they make their own beer and brick-oven pizzas (495-8924; open M-Th 4pm-1am, F-Sa 4pm-2am, Su 1pm-1am).

## MYSTIC AND THE CONNECTICUT COAST

Connecticut's coastal towns were busy seaports in the days of Melville and Richard Henry Dana, but the dark, musty inns filled with tattooed sailors swapping sea journeys are history. Today, the coast is mainly a resort and sailing base. **Mystic Seaport,** 1mi. south on Rt. 27 from I-95 at exit 90, offers a look back at Melville's Connecticut, with 17 acres of recreated village, tall ships (including the Mar. 2000 installation of the *Amistad*), and a maritime museum. (572-5315. Open daily July-Sept 9am-6pm, Oct-June 9am-5pm. $16, seniors $15, ages 6-12 $8. Admission is free on the 2nd consecutive day of your visit. Audio tours $3.50.) Seaport admission entitles visitors to **Sabino Charters** 1½hr. tour on the **Mystic River,** for a few dollars more. (572-5351. 30min. trips mid-May to early Oct. daily on the hr. 11am-4pm. $3.50, ages 6-12 $2.50 after Seaport admission.) Evening excursions do not require museum admission. (late May to late Sept. daily 5pm; July to early Sept. daily at 5pm and F-Sa 5 and 7pm. $8.50, ages 6-12 $7.)

If walking through a fishing village puts you in the mood for aquatic life, seals, penguins, sharks, and dolphins await at one of the northeast's finest aquariums, the **Mystic Marinelife Aquarium,** at exit 90 off I-95. (55 Coogan Blvd. 572-5955. Open daily 9am-5pm; July to early Sept. 9am-6pm. $15, seniors $14, ages 3-12 $10.) The **Denison Pequotsepos Nature Center,** 109 Pequotsepos Rd., offers a refuge from the droves of tourists with great bird watching and 7½mi. of scenic trails through meadows, fields, streams, ponds, and woodland. (536-1216. Park center open M-Sa 9am-5pm, Su noon-5pm; park open dawn-dusk. $4, seniors $3 ages 6-12 $2.) One of Mystic's oft-missed treasures is the **Mystic Drawbridge,** which connects East and West Main St. Built in 1922, it is one of only a few working drawbridges east of the Mississippi, and the riverbank next to it offers a picturesque view of the Mystic area. (Raises May-Oct. every 15min. past the hr. 7:15am-7:15pm.)

It may be difficult to secure cheap lodgings in Mystic, and pricier offerings need to be reserved well in advance. Close to Mystic is **Seaport Campgrounds,** on Rt. 184, 3mi. north on Rt. 27 from Mystic. (536-4044. Sites $28, with water and electricity $32; $5 per additional person; seniors 10% discount. Open daily mid-Apr. to late Oct.) **Stonington** makes a more affordable base from which to explore the shore and also boasts a beautiful downtown area on the water. The **Sea Breeze Motel,** 812 Stonington Rd./Rt. 1, rents big, clean rooms with A/C and cable TV (535-2843; singles $50, F-Su $85; doubles $75-95; rates much lower in winter).

While Mystic's most renowned eatery carries the namesake of the 1988 film, **Mystic Pizza,** 56 W. Main St., it lacks flavorful fame. Don't expect Julia Roberts to sweep up after you, though she's featured in a wall photograph doing so. (536-3737 or 536-3700. Slices $2; small pizza $5; large $9.25. Open Sa-Su 10am-midnight, M-F 10am-11pm.) A better bet is **Christine's Cafe,** 4 Pearl St. off W. Main St. Try the enormous 3D sandwiches, such as the "Good Rockin' Daddy" or the "Mercy Mercy Me." (536-1244 or 536-2068. Sandwiches $3-6. Open M-W 8:30am-8pm, Th 8:30am-11pm, F-Sa 8:30am-midnight, Su 9am-8pm. Hours vary off-season. Live acoustic music Th-Sa nights.) **Trader Jack's,** 14 Holmes St., near downtown, pours $2 domestic beers. Happy hour (M-F 4:30-6:30pm) will have you smiling with half-price appetizers and 50¢ off all drinks except wine. Frequent live music will spice up your $5 burger. (572-8550. No cover. Food Su-Th 5-10pm, F-Sa 5pm-midnight; last call for drinks Su-Th 1am, F-Sa 2am.) The **Mystic Tourist and Information Center,** Bldg. 1d in Olde Mysticke Village, off Rt. 27, has oodles of info on sights and accommodations (536-1641; open M-Sa 9am-6pm, Su 10am-6pm). **Area code:** 860.

NEW ENGLAND

# EASTERN CANADA

 **A NOTE TO OUR READERS.** Canada is **not** a part of the United States.

## NOVA SCOTIA

### HIGHLIGHTS OF EASTERN CANADA

- ■ **Food.** Fresh seafood abounds, particularly on Prince Edward Island (p. 161). Delicious *québecois* cuisine fills the restaurants of Québec City, QC (p. 177).
- ■ **Coastal towns.** Say "cheese" in the photo-opportune, picturesque towns of Yarmouth, NS (p. 154) and Fundy, NB (p. 160).
- ■ **Nightlife.** Québec offers up terrific nightlife opportunities in Montréal (p. 173) and Hull (p. 196). (Drinking age 18).
- ■ **Toronto.** Ethnic neighborhoods and fabulous museums provide fodder for long days of exploration (p. 181).

Around 1605, French colonists joined the indigenous Micmac Indians in the Annapolis Valley and on the shores of Cape Breton Island. During the American Revolution, Nova Scotia declined the opportunity to become the 14th American state, establishing itself as a refuge for fleeing British loyalists. Subsequent immigration waves infused Pictou and Antigonish Counties with a Scottish flavor. As a result of these multinational immigrants, Nova Scotia's population is a cultural "mixed salad." This diversity is complemented by the province's 4 breathtaking geographies: the rugged Atlantic coast, the lush Annapolis Valley, the calm of the Northumberland Strait, and the magnificent highlands of Cape Breton Island.

## 📏 PRACTICAL INFORMATION

**Capital:** Halifax.

**Visitor Info: Tourism Nova Scotia,** P.O. Box 519, Halifax, NS B3J 2R7 (800-565-0000 in U.S. and Canada, 902-425-5781 elsewhere; www.explore.gov.ns.ca/virtualns).

**Drinking Age:** 19.

**Postal Abbreviation:** NS. **Provincial Sales Tax:** 11%, plus 7% GST.

 All prices in this chapter are listed in Canadian dollars unless otherwise noted.

### ATLANTIC COAST

On Nova Scotia's **Lighthouse Rt.,** south on Hwy. 3 from Halifax to a number of tiny coastal villages, boats and lobster traps are tools of a trade, not just props for tourists. **MacKenzie Bus Lines** (902-543-2491) runs between Halifax and Yarmouth, at the tip of the peninsula (call for details M-Sa 8:30am-5pm; 1 per day Su-F, $38).

A quintessential Nova Scotia lighthouse overlooks **Peggy's Cove,** off Hwy. 333, 43km southwest of Halifax, now perhaps equally famous as the sight of a Swissair plane crash in 1998. The fishing village earned a reputation for selflessness and bravery as the locals used their own boats to begin searching for survivors in the thick fog. Even on the rainiest of day, you have zero chance of being alone out on the smooth, slippery rocks that surround the lighthouse. No public transportation serves the town, but most bus companies offer packages including a stop there. The cove's declared population is 60, but tourists are aplenty. Early arrivals avoid the crowds, and early birds wake up with espresso ($1.50) and freshly baked goods from **Beales Bailiwick** (902-823-2099; open Apr.-Nov. daily 9am-8pm).

Eastern Canada

N

100 kilometers
100 miles
0

NEWFOUNDLAND

Channel-Port-aux-Basques

TO ARGENTIA, NEWFOUNDLAND

Cape Breton Island

Sydney

Cape Breton Highlands Nat'l Park

Iles de la Madeleine

Antigonish

Gulf of St. Lawrence

Ile d'Anticosti

NOVA SCOTIA

Charlottetown

Wood Islands

Dartmouth
Halifax

PRINCE EDWARD ISLAND

Cap-aux

Lunenburg

Borden

Amherst

Byfield

ATLANTIC OCEAN

Gaspé

Percé

Baie des Chaleurs

Moncton

Yarmouth

Digby

Sept-Iles

Fleuve St-Laurent

Parc de la Gaspésie

Matane

NEW BRUNSWICK

Bathurst

Dalhousie

Edmundston

Fredericton

Saint John

Bay of Fundy

Fundy N.P.

Calais

Bar Harbor

Réserve de Sept-Iles

Baie-Comeau

Forestville

Les Escoumins

Mont-Joli

Trois-Pistoles

Rivière-du-Loup

Presque Isle

MAINE

Bangor

Portland

TO LABRADOR CITY

Alma

Lac St-Jean

Jonquière

St-Siméon

Ste Anne de Beaupré

Québec

Trois Rivières

Sherbrooke

Granby

Augusta

Mistassini

Réserve des Laurentides

Grand-Mère

Montréal

Lake Champlain

Berlin

Montpelier

N.H.

Concord

Chibougamau

Parc du Mont-Tremblant

Laval

Burlington

N.Y.

V.T.

Adirondacks Park

Val-d'Or

Mont Tremblant

Mont-Laurier

Cornwall

NEW YORK

QUÉBEC

Réserve la Vérendrye

Ottawa

Kingston

Ottawa River

ONTARIO

Algonquin Provincial Park

Huntsville

Lake Ontario

Toronto

Take Hwy. 333 W to Hwy. 3 and head west for about 90km to find **Mahone Bay,** a slightly larger coastal town. The **tourist office** is at 165 Edgewater St. (624-6151; open daily July-Sept. 9am-7:30pm; May-June and Oct. 9am-6pm). The **Wooden Boat Festival,** a celebration of the region's ship-building heritage, includes a boat building contest and race (participants are supplied with wood and glue), and a parade of old-style schooners (early Aug.; 624-8443). Avast, ye scurvy dog! ✪ **Mug & Anchor Pub,** 634 Main St., tames a mate's appetite for seafood and draft beer beneath wooden beams laden with a collection of coasters. Specialties include meat pie ($9), fish and chips ($8), and seafood pasta ($8-9). The entire town floods here for lunch, so be prepared to wait a few minutes for a table. (624-6378. Open daily 11am-9:30pm; bar open Su-Th 11am-midnight, F-Sa 11am-1am.)

The undefeated racing schooner **Bluenose,** which graces the Canadian dime and the Nova Scotia license plate, saw its start in the shipbuilding center of **Lunenburg,** which claims to be Canada's oldest German settlement, 11km west of Mahone Bay on Hwy. 3. Explore the schooner and ocean-going history at the **Fisheries Museum of the Atlantic,** on Bluenose Dr. by the harbor front. (634-4794. Open mid-May to mid-Oct. daily 9:30am-5:30pm; call for winter hrs. $7, seniors $5.50, ages 6-17 $2.) Several bed and breakfasts dot the roadsides in this area, but don't aim for bargains. **Brook House B&B,** 3 Old Blue Rocks Rd., is as good as it gets. (634-3826. Singles $45; doubles $60. Includes continental breakfast. Reservations recommended.) The **tourist office** (634-8100 or 634-3656) provides info in the new blockhouse on Blockhouse Hill Rd. (open daily July-Sept. 9am-8pm; May-June and Oct. 8am-6pm).

From Lunenburg, follow the signs 16km to **Ovens Natural Park,** west on Hwy. 3, then south and east on Rt. 332. Steeped in lore that extends from Native Canadian legends to tales of the Nova Scotia Gold Rush, the park has an almost spiritual quality, marred only by efforts to package it for tourists. The park features a spectacular trail along a cliff to a set of natural sea caves (the "ovens" from which the area takes its name) and the region's best **campground.** Overlooking the ocean, amenities include access to the caves, free hot showers, a heated swimming pool, flush toilets, a restaurant, and a store. (902-766-4621. 65 sites $18, with water and electricity $20, full hookup $22-25. Private cottages from $45. Open May-Oct.)

Hwy. 332 continues along the shore and into the town of **East LaHave,** where a **cable ferry** runs across the LaHave River to **LaHave** (every 30min. 7am-11pm, by demand 11pm-7am; $1.75 per car or person). There is no actual ferry terminal, just a small turnoff from the road with a sign, so be on the lookout or you might just drive right by. The **LaHave Bakery,** about 100m from the ferry dock on the left, emits the mouth-watering scent of cheese-and-herb bread ($2.75). Upstairs, in a homey apartment with a wood-burning stove, the **LaHave Marine Hostel (HI-C)** is run by the bakery proprietor, specializing in small town hospitality; call ahead or arrive during bakery hours. (688-2908. Bakery open daily 9am-7pm; mid-Sept. to June 10am-5pm. Hostel beds $10, nonmembers $12. Hostel open June-Oct.) **Area code:** 902.

**YARMOUTH.** The port of **Yarmouth,** 339km from Halifax on the southwestern tip of Nova Scotia, has a major **ferry terminal,** 58 Water St., from which boats shuttle across the **Bay of Fundy** to Maine (open daily 8am-5pm). Life here seems to revolve around the ferries. **Bay Ferries** (742-6800 or 888-249-7245) provides service to Bar Harbor, ME. (2½hr.; 2 per day; U.S. $46, ages 5-12 U.S. $23, seniors U.S. $41, car U.S. $108, bike U.S. $15. Reservations recommended, $5 fee.) **Prince of Fundy Cruises** (800-341-7540) sails from Yarmouth to Portland, ME. (11hr.; early May to mid-Oct. daily 10am; early May to mid-June; U.S. $60, ages 5-14 U.S. $30, car U.S. $80, bike U.S. $7; mid-June to mid-Oct. U.S. $80/$40/$98/$10. Add U.S. $3 passenger tax.) **Avis** is at 42 Starr's Rd., and at a desk in the ferry terminal. (742-3323. Reserve ahead. $45-70 per day with 200 free km, 15¢ per additional km; must be 21+.) The **info center,** 228 Main St., uphill and visible from the ferry terminal, houses both **Nova Scotia Information** (742-5033) and **Yarmouth Town and County Information** (742-6639; both open mid-June to mid-Oct.; hrs. vary). The **Ice House Hostel** and adjacent **Churchill Mansion Inn** overlook Darling Lake, 15km from Yarmouth on Rt. 1; take Old Post Rd. on the left; the Inn and hostel are on your right. 7 hostel beds are split between the hostel and a cabin outside the inn. Guests have access to all inn facilities, and when the hostel is full, guests can stay at the inn for hostel rates. With enough guests, a delicious seafood buffet is served at night. (649-2818. Shared bath. Pick-up from ferry. $10 or U.S. $7. Open May-Nov. Reservations recommended.) **Area code:** 902.

# HALIFAX

The British erected the Halifax Citadel in 1749 to counter the French Fortress of Louisbourg on the northeastern shoulder of Cape Breton Island. As it was never attacked, the Citadel has ended up seeing more French tourists than French soldiers. Its location, with access to the Atlantic Ocean, made Halifax an important strategic port in both World Wars. Now the largest city in Atlantic Canada, Halifax claims its beautiful port for more peaceful visitors.

## ORIENTATION AND PRACTICAL INFORMATION

**Barrington St.,** the major north-south thoroughfare, runs straight through downtown. Approaching the Citadel and the Public Garden, **Sackville St.** cuts east-west parallel to **Spring Garden Rd.,** Halifax's shopping thoroughfare. Downtown is flanked by the less affluent **North End** and the mostly quiet and arboreal **South End,** on the ocean. Traffic is light, and parking is available by the waterfront for $3-7.

**Airport: Halifax International,** 40km from the city on Hwy. 102 into town. The **Airbus** (873-2091; 21 per day, 7:45am-11:15pm; $12, under 10 free with adult) and **Ace Y Share-A-Cab** (429-4444; 5am-9pm; phone 1 day ahead; $18, $30 for 2) will get you to and from the airport and town.

**Trains: VIA Rail,** 1161 Hollis St., at South St. in the South End near the harbor. To Montréal ($180). Open daily 9am-5:30pm.

**Buses: Acadian Lines** and **MacKenzie Bus Lines** share a terminal at 6040 Almon St. (454-9321), near Robie St.; take bus #7 or 80 on Robie St. MacKenzie travels down the coast to Yarmouth (6hr., M-F 1 per day, $38). Acadian covers most of the remainder of Nova Scotia and Canada: Annapolis Royal (3-5hr., 1 per day, $30); Charlottetown, PEI (8½hr., 1 per day, $57); and North Sydney (6-8hr., 2 per day, $53.25). Seniors 20% discount, ages 5-11 50% discount. Station open daily 6:30am-11:30pm.

**Public Transit: Metro Transit,** 490-6600. Efficient and thorough; maps and schedules at any info center. Fare $1.65 adults, $1.15 seniors and ages 5-15, under 5 free. Buses run daily roughly 6am-11pm. Station open M-F 8am-4pm.

**Ferries: Dartmouth-Halifax Ferry** (490-6600), on the harbor front. 15min. crossings depart from both terminals every 15-30min. June-Sept. M-F 7am-11:30pm, Sa 6:30am-11:30pm, Su noon-5:30pm; no Su service Oct.-May. Same fares as Metro Transit.

**Taxi: Ace Y Cab,** 429-4444.

**Car Rental: Rent-a-Wreck,** 2823 Robie St. (454-2121); vehicles at 130 Woodlawn Rd. $40 per day (varies) with 200 free km, 12¢ per additional km. Insurance $13 per day, ages 21-25 $15. Must be 21+ with credit card. Open M-F 8am-5:30pm, Sa 8am-noon.

**Visitor Info: Halifax International Visitors Center,** 1595 Barrington St. (490-5946). Open daily 8:30am-8pm; off-season closes between 5-7pm. Free **Internet access** (15 min.).

**Hotlines: Sexual Assault,** 425-0122. **Crisis Centre,** 421-1188. Both 24hr.

**Royal Canadian Mounted Police** (the Mounties), 426-1323.

**Post Office:** Main Station, 1680 Bedford Row (494-4000). Open M-F 8am-5:15pm. **Postal code:** B3K 5M9. **Area code:** 902.

## ACCOMMODATIONS

Affordable summer accommodations come easy, but popular ones, like the universities and the hostel, are usually booked. Expect trouble during major events, such as the Tattoo Festival (see **Entertainment,** below). **Halifax Heritage House Hostel (HI-**

C), 1253 Barrington St., a 3min. walk from the heart of downtown, 1½ blocks from the train station, has immaculate rooms with access to TV lounge, kitchen, and laundry. 1st fl. rooms enjoy a low people-to-bathroom ratio. (422-3863. $15, non-members $20. Linen $1.55. Free parking. Office closed noon-4pm. Check-in 4-11pm.) **St. Mary's University,** 923 Robie St., just a short distance from pubs and clubs has hundreds of rooms in the summer, some with private baths, some with shared. (420-5485 or 888-547-5555. Singles $23, doubles $33. Students and seniors lower rates. Call for reservations.) **Dalhousie University** ("Dal"), 6136 University Ave., recently merged with the Technical University, so it has a large selection of summer housing options in various locations. (494-8840, after 8pm 494-2108. Singles from $21; doubles from $42. Call ahead for reservations and directions. Open May-Aug.) **Laurie Provincial Park,** 25km north of Halifax on Hwy. 2 has rustic campsites on Grand Lake (861-1623; $10; no showers, pit toilets; open 24hr.).

## FOOD

Downtown venues provide many options for appeasing the demons of hunger. Pubs peddle cheap grub and inner peace, but their kitchens often close down around 10pm. For fresh local produce and baked goods, visit the **farmers' market** in the old brewery on Lower Water St. (492-4043, open Sa 7am-1pm). The Donair, a meat sandwich creation prepared in a funky Maritime manner, is available for less than $6 at many locations.

A microbrewery with some of the best pub food around, **Granite Brewery,** 1222 Barrington St, produces 3 beer labels; the "Peculiar" is strangely appealing ($5) and goes well with the hearty beef-and-beer stew ($5.25. 423-5660. Open M-Sa 11:30am-1am, Su noon-11:30pm.) At **Mediterraneo Restaurant,** 1571 Barrington St., students and civilians gather over Middle Eastern dishes. (423-4403. Tabouleh with 2 huge pita pockets $3-4, falafel sandwich $3-5, full breakfast served until 11am for $2.50-3. Open M-Sa 7am-10pm, Su 7am-8pm.) For killer food in a casual, fun atmosphere try **The Atrium,** 1740 Argyle St. (422-5453. Seafood dishes around $6-8, daily specials $6-7. Famous 15¢ wings daily 4-9pm. Also a popular nightspot. Open M-Tu 11am-2am, W-Su 11am-3:30am. Kitchen closes at 9pm.)

## SIGHTS

The star-shaped **Halifax Citadel National Historic Park,** in the heart of Halifax on Sackville St., and the old **Town Clock,** at the foot of **Citadel Hill,** anchor the city to its past. A walk along the fortress walls affords a fine view of the city and harbor. Small exhibits and a 1hr. film relays the relevant history. Come any day at noon to see the pageantry of preparation for the **noonday cannon firing.** *(426-5080. Open daily mid-June to early Sept. 9am-6pm; early Sept. to mid-Oct. and mid-May to mid-June 9am-5pm. In summer $5.75, seniors $4.25, ages 6-16 $3. Parking $2.50. No charge Nov.-Apr.)*

The **Halifax Public Gardens,** across from the Citadel near the intersection of South Park and Sackville St. are a relaxing break spot. The Roman statues, Victorian bandstand, gas lamps, exquisite horticulture, and overfed loons on the pond are all properly British. From July through Sept., watch for concerts on Su afternoons at 2pm. *(424-4248. Open daily 8am-sunset.)*

**Point Pleasant Park,** 186 car-free wooded acres at the southern tip of Halifax (take bus #9 from Barrington St. downtown), remains one of England's last imperial holdings, leased to the city of Halifax for 999 years at the bargain rate of one shilling per year. Inside the park, the **Prince of Wales Martello Tower,** an odd fort built by the British in 1797, stands as testimony to one of Prince Edward's 2 fascinations: round buildings and his mistress—both of which he kept in Halifax. *(Tower open daily 10am-6pm, Jul.-Sept.)* A little farther from downtown, **The Dingle** or **Sir Sandford Fleming Park** (Dingle Rd.), provides an ocean for escaping summer heat that can transform Halifax into Houston. But if you're really *HOT,* (wink wink) go to **Crystal Crescent Beach,** off Rt. 349, Halifax's clothing-optional locale.

**BOOM!!** What do you get when you cross 225 tons of TNT, a few barrels of butane, a hell of a lot of picric acid, and a lone spark? On Dec. 6, 1917 the citizens of Halifax discovered the answer—the biggest boom before the Atomic Age. Tragically, over 2000 people lost their lives when a French ship, the acid and TNT-heavy *Mont Blanc*, collided with the *Imo*, a Belgian relief ship. Both vessels began to burn, luring hapless spectators to the docks. Frantic soldiers evacuated the *Mont Blanc* by paddling lifeboats to the opposite shore, unable to warn the Halifax citizenry. An hour later, the explosion leveled 325 acres of the city, throwing a half-ton anchor 2 mi, and a cannon barrel 3½mi. in the opposite direction. Windows shattered 50mi. away, and shock waves were felt for 270mi. The **Maritime Museum of the Atlantic** has an exhibit and short film on the explosion. *(1675 Lower Water St. 424-7490. Open M-Sa 9:30am-5:30pm, Su 1pm-5:30pm. In winter, open Tu-Sa 8:30am-5pm, Su 1-5pm. June to mid.-Oct. $4.50, seniors $3.50, ages 6-17 $1; mid-Oct. to May 31 free.)*

## 🎵 ENTERTAINMENT AND NIGHTLIFE

The **Neptune Theater**, 1593 Argyle St., presents the area's most noteworthy professional stage productions (429-7070, tickets $18-33). **The Nova Scotia International Tattoo Festival** is Halifax's biggest summer event. The festival runs through the first week of July, featuring military groups and international performers; at noon, the Metro area overflows with free entertainment. Later, a 3hr. **show** takes place in the Metro Centre (420-1114, tickets 451-1221. Tickets $12-24, seniors and under 13 $10-22). The **Atlantic Jazz Festival** jams for a week in mid-July with ticketed and free concerts throughout the city (492-2225 or 800-567-5277). In Aug., street performers from around the world display random talents at **Buskerfest** (429-3910). At the end of Sept., the **Atlantic Film Festival** wraps up the season with Canadian and international films (422-3456). The **Halifax Event Line** says what's going on (451-1202).

Halifax boasts an intoxicating nighttime scene—the pub per capita ratio is "the highest in Canada," which makes bar-hopping common and easy. The free *Coast* lists special goings-on. **The Dome** (that's the **Liquordome** to locals), 1740 Argyle St., houses eating, drinking, and dancing establishments that draw young people. Inside, **The Atrium** has a DJ and live bands (422-5453; Th-Sa cover $2-4; open M-Tu 11am-2am, W-Su 11am-3:30am). The **Seahorse Tavern**, 1665 Argyle St., is the oldest tavern in Nova Scotia. Purple-haired students chat with paralegals in a dark basement room with carved woodwork. (423-7200. Open M-W noon-1am, Th-Sa noon-2am.) Amidst nautical decor, the **Lower Deck** in the Historic Properties region on Upper Water St., offers excellent Irish folk music (425-1501; cover $2-4; open daily 11am-12:30am). Huge and always packed, **Peddler's Pub**, in Barrington Place Mall on Granville St., is favored for good pub food like wings ($4.50), steamed mussels ($4.25), and $1.50 food specials M-F after 4pm (423-5033; open M-Sa 11am-10:30pm, Su 11am-8pm). **J.J. Rossy's**, 1883 Granville St., across the street from Peddler's, attracts nocturnal crowds with a dance floor and tremendous drink specials—during the "power hours" (W and F-Sa 9-10pm and midnight-1am, Th all night), a draft falls to $1-1.50 and shots to $1-2. (422-4411. Cover after 8pm $2.50. Open M-Sa 11am-2am; kitchen open M-Tu 11am-4pm, W-Sa 11am-8pm.) **Reflections Cabaret**, 5184 Sackville St., is one of the hottest gay spots in town (422-2957).

# NEW BRUNSWICK

Powerful South Indian Ocean currents sweep around the tip of Africa and ripple thousands of mi. through the Atlantic before coming to a spectacular finish at New Brunswick. The Bay of Fundy witnesses the world's highest tides, which can ebb and flow through a staggering 48 ft. cycle. Away from the ocean's violent influence, vast unpopulated stretches of forest swathe the land in timeless wilderness. In the 17th century, French pioneers established the farming and fishing nation of *l'Acadie* on the northern and eastern coasts. Later, British Loyalists, fleeing in the wake of the American Revolution, settled on the shores of the bay. After complaining about the distant government in Halifax, the colonists were granted self-government by the Crown, and New Brunswick was born. Over a third of the province's population is French-speaking, but English is more widely used.

# 🛈 PRACTICAL INFORMATION

**Capital:** Fredericton.

**Visitor Info: Dept. of Economic Development and Tourism,** P.O. Box 6000, Fredericton E3B 5C3. Call **Tourism New Brunswick** (800-561-0123) from anywhere in Canada.

**Postal Abbreviation:** NB. **Drinking Age:** 19. **Sales Tax:** 15%. **Area Code:** 506

# SAINT JOHN

The city of Saint John (never abbreviated in order to prevent confusion with St. John's, Newfoundland) was founded literally overnight on May 18, 1783, by the United Empire Loyalists, a band of about 10,000 American colonists holding allegiance to the British crown. Saint John's Loyalist tradition shows through in its architecture, festivals, and institutions; however, some areas have become very Americanized. Saint John's location on the Bay of Fundy means cool summers and mild winters, though it often makes the city foggy and wet. Locals joke that Saint John is where you get your car, and body, washed for free.

## 🛈 ORIENTATION AND PRACTICAL INFORMATION

Saint John's busy downtown is bounded by **Union St.** to the north, **Princess St.** to the south, **King Sq.** to the east, and **Market Sq.** and the harbor to the west. Find free 3hr. parking outside the city's malls. Fort Latour Harbor Bridge (toll 25¢) on Hwy. 1 connects Saint John to West Saint John, as does a free bridge on Hwy. 100.

**Trains: Via Rail** (857-9830) has a station in Moncton; take an SMT bus from Saint John. A train ticket or a Canrail pass will cover bus fare. Call for prices and schedules.

**Buses: SMT,** 300 Union St. (648-3555). To: Moncton (2hr., 2 or 4 per day, $22); Montréal (14hr., 2 per day, $94); and Halifax (6-6½hr., 2 or 3 per day, $62). Open daily 7:30am-9pm.

**Public Transit: Saint John Transit** (658-4700) runs until roughly 12:30am. Fare $1.45, under 14 $1.20. Late June to early Oct., 2hr. tour of historic Saint John leaves from Barbara General Store at Loyalist Plaza and Reversing Falls. $14, ages 6-14 $5.

**Ferries: Marine Atlantic** (636-4048 or 800-341-7981 from the U.S.), on Lancaster St. extension near the mouth of Saint John Harbor. Take "West Saint John" bus, then walk 10min. Crosses to Digby, NS (3hr.; 1-3 per day; $23, seniors $22, ages 5-12 $12, bikes $11.25, cars $55).

**Taxis: Royal Taxi,** 652-5050. **Diamond,** 648-8888.

**Visitor Info: Saint John Visitors and Convention Bureau,** 15 Market Sq. (658-2990), on the 11th fl. of City Hall, at the foot of King St. Open M-F 8:30am-4:30pm. The **City Center** info center (658-2855), at Market Sq., is open daily 9am-6pm. **Weather:** 636-4991.

**Hotlines: Crisis,** 658-3737. **Suicide Crisis Line,** 633-0001. Operates daily 5pm-midnight.

**Post Office:** Station B, 41 Church Ave. W. (672-6704), in west Saint John (open M-F 8am-5pm). **Postal code:** E2L 3W9.

## 🛏 ACCOMMODATIONS

A number of nearly identical motels on the 1100 to 1300 blocks of **Manawagonish Rd.** charge $35-45 for a single. Saint John Transit has bus directions (see **Practical Information,** above); by car, avoid the 25¢ bridge toll by taking Hwy. 100 into

West Saint John, turn right on Main St., and head west until it turns into Manawagonish Rd. The rooms at the **Saint John YMCA/YWCA (HI-C)**, 19-25 Hazen Ave. are clean and unremarkable. Access to recreational facilities, pool, workout room is included. From Market Sq., head 2 blocks up Union St. on the left. (634-7720. Singles $20, nonmembers $25; doubles $25/30. Open daily 5am-11pm; guests arriving on evening ferry can check in later. Summer reservations recommended.) 5min. north of downtown, the Sir James Dunn Residence Hall at the **University of New Brunswick at Saint John,** on Tucker Park Rd., offers neat and furnished rooms. (648-5768. Singles $29, students $18; doubles $42/$30. Reception M-F 8am-4pm. Check-out noon. Reservations recommended. Open May-Aug.) Partially wooded tent sites at the **Rockwood Park Campground** are just off Lake Drive S. in Rockwood Park. Take the "University" bus to the Mt. Pleasant stop, and follow the signs. (652-4050. Sites $15, with hookup $18; weekly $65/$95; showers included; open May-Sept.)

## ⍾ FOOD

The butcher, baker, fishmonger, produce dealer, and cheese merchant sell fresh goodies at **City Market,** 47 Charlotte St., between King and Brunswick Sq. The market may be the best place to look for **dulse,** sun-dried seaweed from the Bay of Fundy; it is best described as "ocean jerky." A $1 bag is more than a sample. (658-2820. Open M-Th 7:30am-6pm, F 7:30am-7pm, Sa 7:30am-5pm.) **Billy's Seafood Company,** 49-51 Charlotte St. is delicious. While the restaurant specializes in fresh oysters ($9 for 6) and lobster, almost anything on the menu is good. (672-3474. Seasonal prices. Open M-Th 11am-10pm, F-Sa 11am-11pm, Su 4-10pm.) **Reggie's Restaurant,** 26 Germain St., provides homestyle renditions of basic North American fare in a relaxed atmosphere. The sandwiches ($2-4), made with famous smoked meat from Ben's Deli in Montréal, may not fill you up, but the breakfast special will: 2 eggs, sausage, homefries, and toast go for $3.50, served daily 6-11am. (657-6270. Open M-Tu 6am-7pm, W-F 6am-8pm, Sa-Su 6am-6pm.)

## ⍾ SIGHTS

Saint John's main attraction is the **Reversing Falls,** a natural phenomenon caused by the powerful Bay of Fundy tides (for more on the tides see **Fundy,** below). Though the name may suggest 100 ft. walls of gravity-defying water, the "falls" are actually beneath the surface of the water. At high tide, patient spectators see the flow of water at the nexus of the Saint John River and Saint John Harbor slowly halt and change direction. More amazing than the event itself may be the number of people captivated by it. The **Reversing Falls Tourist Centre,** at the west end of the Hwy. 100 bridge (take the west-bound "East-West" bus), distributes tide schedules and shows a 12min. film on the phenomenon. (658-2937. Screenings every 15min.; $1.25. Center open June-Aug. daily 8am-8pm.) **Jet boat rides,** though overpriced, are the latest in Reversing Falls excitement. (634-8987. In summer 10am-dusk. 20min. $20.)

    **Moosehead Breweries,** in West Saint John, is the oldest independent brewery in Canada. (89 Main St. 635-7000. Free 1hr. tours with samples mid-June to Aug. 9:30am and 2pm. Call for times. Tours limited to 20 people; make reservations 2-3 days in advance.)

    Tourist info centers have maps for 3 nostalgic, self-guided **walking tours** (each about 2hr.). **The Victorian Stroll** roams past some old homes; **Prince William's Walk** details commerce in the port city; **The Loyalist Trail** traces the places where the Loyalist founders hung out. **Trinity Church,** on the Loyalist Trail tour, displays amazing stained-glass windows and the Royal Coat of Arms of George III's House of Hanover. (115 Charlotte St. 693-8558. Open Tu-Sa 9am-5:30pm, M 10am-4:30pm.) **Fort Howe Lookout,** originally erected to protect the harbor from dastardly Americans, affords an impressive view of the city and its harbor. (open 24hr. Free.)

# FUNDY

**Fundy National Park** occupies 260 sq. km of New Brunswick's coast (a 1hr. drive southeast of Moncton on Hwy. 114). Approximately every 12hr., the world's largest tides draw back over 1km into the Bay of Fundy. Don't get caught too far out without your running shoes; the water rises 1 ft. per min. when the tide comes in. When you're not fleeing the surf, or the wanna-be marine biologists who cover the beaches in search of starfish and periwinkles, Fundy's extensive hiking trails, forests, campgrounds, and recreational facilities should keep you occupied.

**◪ PRACTICAL INFORMATION. Park Headquarters,** P.O. Box 40 (887-6000), Alma, E0A 1B0, in the southeastern corner of the Park facing the Bay, across the Upper Salmon River from the town of Alma, includes the administration building and the **visitors reception center** (open daily Jun.-Sept. 8am-10pm; Oct.-May. daily 8am-4:30pm). The other visitors center, **Wolfe Lake Information** (432-6026), is at the northwest entrance off Hwy. 114 (open late June to early Sept. daily 10am-6pm). No public transportation serves Fundy, nearest bus depots are in Moncton and Sussex. (Mid-May to early Oct. entrance fee $3.50 per day; ages 6-16 $1.75; $7 max. per family.) The free and invaluable park newspaper *Salt and Fir*, available at the entrance stations and info centers, includes a map of hiking trails and campgrounds, as well as a schedule of activities. For **weather info,** call 887-6000.

**⌖⌂ ACCOMMODATIONS AND FOOD.** The park operates 4 **campgrounds** totaling over 600 sites. Getting a site is seldom a problem, but landing one at your campground of choice may be a little more difficult. The park accepts no reservations; all sites are first come, first served. **Headquarters Campground,** closest to facilities, is usually in highest demand. If a site is full, put your name on the waiting list; at noon, the names of those admitted for the night are read. (Sites $12, with hookup $19. Open mid-May to early Oct.) The only other campground with hookups, **Chignecto North Campground,** off Hwy. 114, 5km inland from the headquarters, provides greater privacy (sites $12, with hookup $17-19; open mid-May to mid-Oct.). **Point Wolfe Campground,** scenically located along the coast 7km west of headquarters, stays cooler and more insect-free than the inland campgrounds (sites $12; open late June to early Sept.). These 3 campgrounds have showers and washrooms. The **Wolfe Lake Campground,** near the northwest park entrance, a 1min. walk from the lake, does not (sites $10; open mid-May to mid-Oct.). Year-round wilderness camping is also available in some of the most scenic areas of the park, especially **Goose River** along the coast. The campsites, all with fireplaces, wood, and an outhouse, carry a $3 per person per night permit fee. The **Fundy National Park Hostel (HI-C),** near Devil's Half Acre about 1km south of the park headquarters, has a full kitchen, showers, and a common room with TV. Ask the staff for the lowdown on park nightlife. (887-2216. $10, nonmembers $13. Check-in 8-10am and 5-10pm. Open mid-May to mid-Oct. Wheelchair access.)

For a cheap, home-cooked meal, the **Harbor View Market and Coffee Shop,** on Main St. in Alma, will fit the bill. Dinner specials are $7, and the breakfast special of 2 eggs, toast, bacon, and coffee runs $4. (887-2450. Open daily Jul.-Aug. 7:30am-8:30pm; Sept.-June M-F 8am-6pm, Sa-Su 8am-7pm.)

**⚐ ACTIVITIES.** The park maintains about 104km of park trails year-round, about 35km of which are open to mountain bikes. Unless you're ready to hoof it, bring your own bike; no rental outfits serve the island. *Salt and Fir* contains detailed descriptions of all trails, including where to find waterfalls and ocean views. The easy but breathtaking 1½km **Dickson Falls** trail is especially recommended. Deer are declining in number, but still fairly common; thieving raccoons run thick; peregrine falcons are hard to spot; moose come out around dusk.

Most recreational facilities operate only during the summer season (mid-May to early Oct.), including free daily interpretive programs designed to help visitors get to know the park. The park staff leads beach walks, evening programs, and weekly campfire programs. Visits to the park in chillier Sept. and Oct. catch the fall foliage and avoid the crush of vacationers.

## NEAR FUNDY: KOUCHIBOUGUAC

Unlike Fundy's rugged forests and high tides, **Kouchibouguac** (meaning "river of the long tides" in Micmac) **National Park** shows off warm lagoon waters, salt marshes, peat bogs, and white sandy beaches. Bask in the sun along the 25km stretch of barrier islands and sand dunes, or swim through canoe waterways that were once highways for the Micmacs. Rent canoes ($6 per hr., $30 per day), kayaks ($4.60 per hr.), and bikes ($4.60 per hr., $26 per day) at **Ryans Rental Center** in the park between the South Kouchibouguac Campground and Kelly's Beach (876-3733; open June-Aug. daily 8:30am-9pm; May Sa-Su 8am-5pm). The park operates 2 campgrounds in the summer. **South Kouchibouguac** has 311 sites with showers. (Late June to early Sept. $16.25, with hookup $22; mid-May to late June and early Sept. to mid-Oct. $13/$18. Reservations recommended July-Aug.) **Côte-à-Fabien** has 32 sites ($14), but no showers. Off-season campers take advantage of primitive sites within the park and several commercial campgrounds just outside of the park (park entrance fee $3.50, ages 6-16 $1.75). The **park info center** is at the park entrance on Hwy. 117 just off Hwy. 11, 90km north of Moncton (open daily 8am-8pm; mid-Sept. to mid-June 9am-5pm). The park administration is open year-round (876-2443; M-F 8am-4:30pm).

# PRINCE EDWARD ISLAND

Prince Edward Island, now more commonly called "P.E.I." or "the Island," began as St. John's Island. In 1799, residents renamed the area for Prince Edward, son of King George III, in thanks for his interest in the territory's welfare. The smallest province in Canada attracts most of its visitors thanks to the beauty made famous by Lucy Maud Montgomery's novel *Anne of Green Gables*. The fictional work did not exaggerate the wonders of natural life on the island; the soil, made red by its high iron-oxide content, complements the green crops and shrubbery, turquoise waters, and purple roadside lupin. On the north and south shores, some of Canada's finest beaches extend for mi. Relentlessly quaint, Island towns seem to exist more for visitors than for residents, consisting mainly of restaurants and shops. From lawn bowling, a favorite of the older set, to nightly public parties (Celtic music is big here), P.E.I. comes alive during the summer.

The newly constructed Confederation Bridge, the longest continuous marine span bridge in the world, extends over the 9mi. from P.E.I. to the mainland. The Bridge authorities charge a toll of $35.50 to exit the island.

## ▨ PRACTICAL INFORMATION

**Queen St.** and **University Ave.** are Charlottetown's main thoroughfares, straddling **Confederation Centre** along the west and east, respectively. The most popular beaches—**Cavendish, Brackley,** and **Rustico Island**—lie on the north shore in the middle of the province, opposite Charlottetown. **Confederation Bridge** meets P.E.I. at Borden-Carleton, 56km west of Charlottetown on Hwy. 1.

**Capital:** Charlottetown.

**Postal Abbreviation:** P.E.I. **Drinking Age:** 19.

**Provincial Sales Tax:** 10%, plus 7% GST.

**Beach Shuttles:** 566-3243. Picks up at the **P.E.I. Visitor Information Centre** at 178 Water St. and the hostel (call for additional points) and drops off in Cavendish (45min.; 2 per day June and Sept., 4 per day July-Aug.; $9, same-day round-trip $15).

**Ferries: Northumberland Ferry** (566-3838 or 800-565-0201 from P.E.I. and Nova Scotia), in Wood Islands 61km east of Charlottetown on Trans-Canada Hwy. To Caribou, NS (1¼hr.; 6-10 per day; pedestrians $10.75, vehicles $47).

**Taxis: City Cab,** 892-6567. Open 24hr.

**Bike Rental: MacQueens,** 430 Queen St. (368-2453). Road and mountain bikes $25 per day, $100 per week; children ½-price. Must have credit card or $75 deposit. Open M-Sa 8:30am-5:30pm.

**Visitor Info: P.E.I. Visitor Information Centre,** P.O. Box 940, C1A 7M5 (368-4444 or 888-734-7529), by the waterfront in Charlottetown. Open daily June 8am-8pm; July-Aug. 8am-10pm; Sept. to mid-Oct. 9am-6pm; mid-Oct. to May 9am-4:30pm M-F only. The **Charlottetown Visitors Bureau,** 199 Queen St. (566-5548), hides inside City Hall. Open daily 8am-5pm; Sept.-June 8:30am-5pm.

**Crisis Line: Crisis Centre,** 566-8999. 24hr.

**Police: Charlottetown,** 368-2677. **Royal Canadian Mounted Police,** 566-7111.

**Post Office:** 135 Kent St. (628-4400). Open M-F 8am-5:15pm. **Postal code:** C1A 7N7. **Area code:** 902.

# ▚ ACCOMMODATIONS

**B&Bs** and **country inns** crowd every nook and cranny of the province; some are open year-round, but the most inexpensive are closed off-season. Rates hover around $28 for singles and $35 for doubles, but you won't land those prices unless you call in advance. Fifteen farms participate in a provincial **Farm Vacation** program, in which tourists spend time with a farming family. Call the **Farm Vacation Association** (651-2620), or pick up a brochure at the visitors center.

The **Charlottetown International Hostel (HI-C),** 153 Mt. Edward Rd., across the yard from the University of P.E.I. (UPEI), is in a large green barn. Take Belvedere 1 long block east of University Ave., then turn left onto Mt. Edward Rd. The green-and-white sign marking the turn-off leads to neat, spacious rooms, friendly staff, and a diverse clientele. (894-9696. $14, nonmembers $16.80. Kitchen facilities, showers, TV lounge. Linen $1. Bike rental $15. Check-in 7-10am and 4pm-midnight. Curfew midnight. Lockout 10am-4pm. Open June to early Sept.) The UPEI runs a mass B&B (with the second "B" included) in **Marion Hall** (July-Aug. singles $29.50; doubles $38; May-June $26/$32). **Bernadine Hall,** is another option in the summer (July-Aug. singles $38.50; doubles $44, breakfast included; May-June $36/$39). Check in for all locations at **Blanchard Hall** (Sept.-May 566-0362, June-Aug. 566-0442).

**Prince Edward Island National Park** operates 3 campgrounds during the summer and one off-season. (672-6350 or 963-2391. Summer: 462 primitive sites with showers, toilets, kitchen access, laundry facilities $13-19; 110 sites with hookup $20-21. Winter: primitive sites $8.) **Cavendish Campground** has a beach-side location—reservations are particularly handy. The many other provincial parks that offer camping, as well as the plentiful private campgrounds scattered throughout the Island, ensure that there will always be a campsite available. (Open seasons vary, but expect to find a campground open mid-June to mid-Sept.)

# ◖ FOOD

The quest for food often boils down to the search for **lobster.** The coveted crustaceans start around $9 per lb. Fresh seafood, including world-famous **Malpeque oysters,** is sold along the shores of the island, especially in North Rustico on the north shore. The back of the *P.E.I. Visitor's Guide* lists fresh seafood outlets. The **Charlottetown Farmers' Market** on Belvedere Ave. opposite UPEI, sells the freshest food around (368-4444; open July-Sept. 9am-2pm on W and Sa, 12pm-4pm on Su).

The cosmopolitan young clientele at **Beanz,** 52 University Ave., bask on a sunny outdoor terrace and wash down homemade sandwiches ($3-4) with great espresso. (892-8797. Open M-F 6:30am-8pm, Sa 8am-5pm, Su 9am-5pm.) **Shaddy's,** 44 University Ave., has non-aquatic Lebanese and Canadian fare, and lots of people enjoying it (sandwiches $4-7; 368-8886; open daily 7:30am-9:30pm).

**SIGHTS**

**THE ISLAND AT LARGE. Green Gables House,** off Rt. 6 in Cavendish just west of Rt. 13, is a shrine for adoring Lucy Maud Montgomery readers—a surprising number of them from Japan. Don't confuse the real thing with other "Green Gables" establishments. Green Gables House gets crowded between late July and Sept.; it's best to arrive in the early morning or the evening. *(963-3370. Open daily July-Aug. 9am-8pm; May-June and Sept.-Oct. 9am-5pm. $5, seniors $4, ages 6-16 $2.50, families $12. Off-season discounts.)*

**Prince Edward Island National Park,** consists of a 32km coastal strip embracing some of Canada's finest beaches. Wind-sculpted sand dunes and salt marshes undulate along the park's terrain. The park is home to many of the Island's 300-odd species of birds, including the endangered piping plover. *(963-7830 or 963-7831. Campgrounds, programs, and services from early Jul. to mid-Aug.)*

The stretches of beach on the **eastern coast** of P.E.I. are considerably less touristed than those in the west, perhaps due to a rougher surf. **Lakeside,** a beach 35km east of Charlottetown on Rt. 2, is unsupervised and often nearly deserted on July and Aug. weekdays. Trot along the surf atop a sturdy steed from **Gun Trail Ride,** located right beside the golf course. *(961-2076. $9 per hr., with trail guide $9, June to early Sept. daily 9am-9pm.)* **Basin Head Beach,** 95km east of Charlottetown, makes a relaxing daytrip, with over 7mi. of unsupervised white sand.

**CHARLOTTETOWN.** The province's capital prides itself on being the "Cradle of Confederation." Visitors won't be surprised; *all* of PEI's landmarks have the word "confederation" in their official names. Delegates from the British North American colonies met in 1864 inside the brownstone **Province House** on the corner of Great George and Richmond St., to discuss the union that would become the Dominion of Canada in 1867. *(566-7626. Open July-Aug. daily 9am-6pm; June and Sept. to mid-Oct. daily 9am-5pm; mid-Oct. to May M-F 9am-5pm. Free.)* Adjoining the Province House, the modern national arts complex at **Confederation Centre of the Arts,** on the corner of Queen and Grafton St., contains theaters, restaurants, gift shops, an art gallery, and gives tours June-Sept. *(628-1864. Box office open M-Sa 9am-9pm; Sept. to mid-June M-Sa noon-5:30pm.)* Every summer, a musical production of *Anne of Green Gables* is presented as part of the **Charlottetown Festival.** *(June to early Sept. M-W and Sa 8pm; tickets $20-38. Matinees M and W 1:30pm; tickets $20-32. Seniors and children 10% off. For ticket info, call 566-1267 or 800-565-0278.)*

# QUÉBEC

Home to 90% of Canada's French-speaking population, Québec continues to fight for political and legal recognition of its separate cultural identity. Originally populated by French fur trading settlements along the St. Lawrence River, Québec was ceded to the British in 1759. Ever since, anti-federalist elements within *québecois* society have rankled under control of the largely Anglicized national government. French is spoken by 95% of Québec's population; all signs are printed in French, as required by provincial law. The failure of the 1990 Meech Lake Accord to recognize Québec as a "distinct society" and the more recent election of the Parti Québecois, a separatist party, to run the provincial government, signal more uncertainty for the province. Visitors will likely never notice these underlying tensions—the majority of the struggle goes on behind closed doors in Ottawa—but the entire country wonders if this province will choose to stay a part of the whole. In recent years, voters in Québec have narrowly rejected separation from Canada, but the separatist government promises another referendum in the near future.

# ⓘ PRACTICAL INFORMATION

**Capital:** Québec City.

**Visitor Info: Tourisme Québec,** C.P. 979, Montréal, PQ H3C 2W3 (800-363-7777, 514-873-2015 in Montréal; www.tourisme.gouv.qc.ca). Open daily 9am-5pm. **Canadian Parks Service, Québec Region,** 3 Passage du D'or, C.P. Box 6060, Haute-Ville, PQ GIR 4V7 (800-463-6769, 418-648-4177 in Québec City).

**Postal Abbreviation:** PQ. **Drinking Age:** 18.

**Provincial Sales Tax:** 7.5%, plus 7% GST.

# ⓘ ACCOMMODATIONS INFORMATION

The following organizations offer assistance in locating accommodations throughout the province.

**Hospitalité Canada,** 1001 Square-Dorchester, Montréal H3B 4V4 (800-322-2932). Info and reservations throughout Québec, primarily in Montréal and Québec City.

**Camping: Association des terrains du camping du Québec (Camping Association of Québec),** 2001 de la Metropole St., #700, Longueil, Québec J4G 1S9 and **Fédération québecoise du camping et de caravaning (Québec Camping and RV Federation),** 4545 ave. Pierre-de-Coubertin, Stade Olympique, C.P. 1000, succursale "M," Montréal H1V 3R2 (Same number for both: 514-252-3003).

**Hostels: Regroupement Tourisme Jeunesse (HI-C)** (514-252-3117), at the Fédération address. For reservations in any Québec hostel and a few in neighboring Ontario, call 800-461-8585 at least 24hr. in advance, with a credit card.

# MONTRÉAL

This island city, named for the royal mountain in its midst, has been coveted territory for over 300 years. Wars and sieges have brought governments in and out like the tide, including a brief takeover by American revolutionaries in late 1775. Despite, or perhaps due to, these conflicts, Montréal has grown into a diverse city with a cosmopolitan air seen in few other cities on the continent. Although less than an hour from the U.S.-Canada border, Montréal's European legacy is immediately evident. Fashion that rivals Paris, a nightlife comparable to London, and cuisine from around the globe all attest to this international influence. Whether you credit the international flavor or the large student population of the city, it is hard not to be swept up by the vibrancy that courses through Montréal's *centre-ville*.

# ⓘ ORIENTATION AND PRACTICAL INFORMATION

Two major streets divide the city, making orientation convenient. The one-way **bd. St-Laurent** (also called **"The Main"**) runs north through the city, splitting Montréal and its streets east-west. The Main also serves as the unofficial French/English divider; English **McGill University** lies to the west, while slightly east is **St-Denis,** a parallel 2-way thoroughfare which defines the French student quarter (also called the *quartier latin* or the "student ghetto"). **Rue Sherbrooke,** which is paralleled by **de Maisonneuve** and **Ste-Catherine** downtown, runs east-west almost the entire length of Montréal. The **Underground City** runs north-south, stretching from **rue Sherbrooke** to **rue de la Gauchetière** and **rue St. Antoine.** For easy navigation, a free map from the tourist office will help. Parking is expensive (meters are 25¢ for 10min. and $30 tickets are common) and often difficult. Searching for a convenient spot can take hours, particularly during winter when snowbanks narrow the streets and slow traffic. The **Métro** avoids the hassle by whisking riders throughout the city. Montréal's population is 85% Francophone, but most are bilingual.

**Airports: Dorval** (info 394-7377), 20-30min. from downtown by car. From the Lionel Groulx Métro stop, take bus #211 to Dorval Train Station, then transfer to bus #204. Handles international and domestic flights. **Autocar Connaisseur-Grayline** (394-7369) runs a minivan to Dorval from 777 rue de la Gauchetière, at University St., stopping at any downtown hotel if you call in advance. Vans run 5:20am-11:00pm M-F every 20min., Sa-Su every 30min. $9.25, under 5 free. Taxi to downtown $30-35. **Mirabel International** (450-476-3010), 45min. from downtown by car, handles all flights from outside the U.S. or Canada. Taxi to downtown $60. **Information:** 800-465-1213.

**Trains: Central Station,** 895 rue de la Gauchetière Ouest, under Queen Elizabeth Hotel. Métro: Bonaventure. Served by **VIA Rail** (989-2626 or 800-561-9181, from U.S. 800-842-7245). To: Québec City (3hr., 3-4 per day, $37); Ottawa (2hr., 4 per day, $29); and Toronto (4-5½hr., 6 per day, $69). Discounts for students, seniors, and tickets bought 5 or more days in advance. Ticket counter open daily 6am-9pm. **Amtrak** (800-872-7245). To New York (10hr., 1 per day, U.S. $58) and Boston (13hr., 1 per day, U.S. $120). Ticket counter open daily 8am-5pm.

**Buses: Voyageur,** 505 bd. de Maisonneuve Est (842-2281). Métro: Berri-UQAM. To: Toronto (6¾hr.; 7 per day; $74, students $51); Ottawa (2½hr., 17-18 per day, $28/$28); and Québec City (3hr., 18 per day, $37/$27). **Greyhound** (287-1580). To New York City (7½-8¾hr., 7 per day, $89-98) and Boston (7hr., 7 per day, $52-55).

**Public Transit: STCUM Métro and Bus** (288-6287). Safe and extremely efficient. The 4 Métro lines and most buses operate daily 5:30am-12:30am; some have early morning schedules as well. Get maps at the tourist office, or any Métro station booth. Buses are well-integrated; transfer tickets from bus drivers are valid as subway tickets, and vice versa. Fare for train or bus $1.85, 6 tickets $8. 1-day unlimited tourist pass $5, 3-day $12; weekly $12.25. Passes sold at any downtown metro station.

**Taxis: Taxi Pontiac,** 761-5522. **Champlain Taxi Inc.,** 273-2435.

**Car Rental: Via Route,** 1255 rue MacKay (871-1166), at Ste-Catherine. Rates vary depending on mileage, insurance, and model, but start around $40 for the bare minimum. Must be 21 with credit card. Open M-F 7am-9pm, Sa 7:30am-5pm, Su 9am-9pm.

**Driver/Rider Service: Allo Stop,** 4317 rue St-Denis (985-3032). Matches passengers with member drivers; part of the rider fee goes to the driver. To: Québec City ($15), Ottawa ($10), Toronto ($26), Sherbrooke ($9), New York City ($50), and Boston ($42). Riders and drivers fix their own fees for rides over 1000mi. Annual membership fee required ($6, drivers $7). Open daily 9am-6pm.

**Bike Rental: Cycle Pop,** 1000 Rachel Est (526-2525). Métro: Mont-Royal. 21-speeds $20 per day, $40 per weekend. Open M-W 10am-6pm, Th-F 10am-9pm, Sa-Su 10am-5pm. Credit card or $250 deposit required.

**Visitor Info: Infotouriste,** 1001 rue de Square-Dorchester (873-2015 or 800-363-7777; www.tourisme.montreal.org), at Peel and Ste-Catherine between rue Peel and rue Metcalfe. Metro: Peel. Open daily 8am-7:50pm; Sept.-June 9am-6pm. In **Old Montréal,** 174 rue Notre-Dame Est at Place Jacques Cartier. Open daily 9am-7pm; Sept.-Oct. daily 9am-5pm; Nov. to early Mar. Th-Su 9am-5pm; late Mar. to early daily June 9am-5pm.

**Youth Travel Office: Tourisme Jeunesse,** 4008 rue St-Denis (252-3117 or 844-0287). Métro: Sherbrooke. A non-profit organization that inspects and ranks all officially recognized youth hostels in Québec. Open M-W 10am-6pm, Th-F 10am-9pm, Sa 10am-6pm, Su 10am-5pm. **Travel CUTS,** McGill Student Union, 3480 rue McTavish (398-0647). Métro: McGill. Specializes in budget travel for college students. Open M-F 9am-5pm.

**Currency Exchange: Currencies International,** 1250 rue Peel (392-9100). Métro: Peel. Open in summer M-W 8:30am-8pm, Th-F 8:30am-9pm, Sa 8:30am-7pm, Su 9am-6pm; call for winter hours. **Thomas Cook,** 777 rue de la Gauchetière Ouest (397-4029). Métro: Bonaventure. Open M-F 8:30am-7pm, Sa 9am-4pm, Su 10am-3pm. Most **ATMs** are on the PLUS system and charge only the normal transaction fee for withdrawals abroad; ask your bank about fees.

**American Express,** 1141 rue de Maisonneuve (284-3300), at Peel. Métro: Peel. Travel agency. Traveler's checks and currency exchange. Open M-F 9am-5pm.

**EASTERN CANADA**

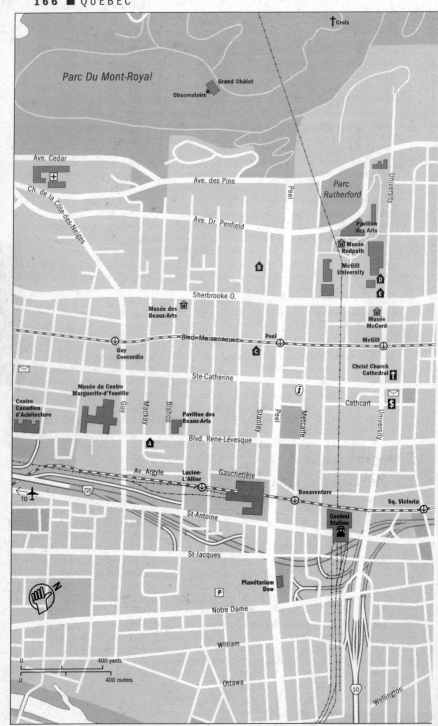

† Croix

Parc Du Mont-Royal

Grand Chálet
Observatoire

Ave. Cedar

Ch. de la Côte-des-Neiges

Ave. des Pins

Parc Rutherford

University

Peel

Ave. Dr. Penfield

Pavillon des Arts

Musée Redpath

B

McGill University

D

E

Sherbrooke O.

Musée des Beaux-Arts

Musée McCord

Blvd. Maisonneuve

Peel

McGill

Guy Concordia

C

Christ Church Cathedral

Ste-Catherine

*i*

Cathcart

Centre Canadien d'Achitecture

Musée du Centre Marguerite-d'Youville

Guy

Mackay

Bishop

Pavillon des Beaux-Arts

Stanley

Peel

Metcalfe

University

$

Blvd. Rene-Lévesque

A

Av. Argyle

Lucien-L'Allier

Gauchetière

720

TO ✈

Bonaventure

Sq. Victoria

St-Antoine

Central Station

St-Jacques

Planétarium Dow

P

Notre Dame

William

0        400 yards
0        400 meters

Ottawa

10

Wellington

**Montréal**
ACCOMMODATIONS

**A** Auberge de Jeunesse (HI)
**B** Manoir Ambrose
**C** YMCA
**D** McGill University
**E** Maison André
**F** Hôtel le Breton
**G** Hôtel de Paris

**Hotlines: Tel-aide,** 935-1101. **Sexual Assault,** 934-4504. **Suicide-Action,** 723-4000. All 3 operate 24hr. **Rape Crisis,** 278-9383. Operates M-F 9:30am-4:30pm.

**Post Office: Succursale (Postal Station) "B,"** 1250 rue Université (395-4539), at Cathcourt. Open M and W-Th 8am-5:45pm, Tu and F 8am-9pm, Sa 9:30am-5pm. **Postal code:** H3B 3B0. **Area code:** 514.

# ACCOMMODATIONS

The **Québec Tourist Office** is the best resource for info about hostels, hotels, and *chambres touristiques* (rooms in private homes or small guest houses). B&B singles cost $25-40, and doubles run $35-75. The most extensive B&B network is **Bed & Breakfast à Montréal,** P.O. Box 575, Snowdon Station, H3X 3T8 (738-9410; fax 735-7493). Reserve early by phone, fax, or mail. (Singles from $40; doubles from $60; $15 per night deposit upon confirmation. Leave a message if the owners are out.) The **Downtown Bed and Breakfast Network,** 3458 ave. Laval, H2X 3C8 (289-9749 or 800-267-5180), near Sherbrooke, lists 80 homes downtown (singles $25-55, doubles $35-65; open daily 9am-9pm). Most B&Bs have bilingual hosts.

Many of the least expensive *maisons touristiques* and hotels cluster around **rue St-Denis,** ranging from quaint to seedy. The area, which abuts Vieux Montréal, flaunts lively nightclubs and a number of funky cafes and bistros.

**Auberge de Jeunesse, Montréal Youth Hostel (HI-C),** 1030 rue MacKay (843-3317). Métro: Lucien-L'Allier. Airport shuttle drivers will stop here if asked. Relatively new, large, and complemented by great service. Downtown location near both a metro stop and the Molson Centre where the popular Montréal Canadiens play hockey. The friendly, upbeat staff knows the nightlife lowdown and gives free tours and outings. Biweekly pub crawl (F and Tu 8:30pm). Dorm rooms have 3-10 beds (246 total; with baths). $18, Canadian nonmembers $20, non-Canadian nonmembers $22.10, under 13 free with parent. Private doubles $26/$31/$31 per person. New cafe with kitchen facilities. Linen $2.10. Prices include tax. Laundry facilities, A/C, and extensive ride board. Some parking. 1-week max. stay; in winter 10 days. Reception 24hr.

**Hotel Le Breton,** 1609 rue St-Hubert (524-7273), around the corner from the bus station and 2 blocks east of St-Denis. Métro: Berri-UQAM. Although the neighborhood is neither particularly wholesome nor attractive, the 13 rooms are clean and comfortable with a TV, some with A/C. Rooms $40-$55. Reception 8am-midnight. Make reservations 2 weeks in advance. Non-smoking rooms available. Front door remains locked.

**McGill University, Bishop Mountain Hall,** 3935 rue de l'Université, H3A 2B4 (398-6367). Métro: McGill. Follow Université through campus. Ideally located singles $38, students and seniors $31; weekly $217/$186; prices include tax. Full breakfast $6, served M-Th 7:30-9:30am. Kitchenettes on each floor. 1000 beds. Common room with TV and laundry facilities. Reception daily 7am-10pm; a guard will check you in late. Open May 15-Aug. 15. Popular with anglophone travelers.

**Université de Montréal, Residences,** 2350 rue Edouard-Montpetit, H2X 2B9, (343-6531), off Côte-des-Neiges. Métro: Edouard-Montpetit. Located on the edge of a beautiful campus; try the East Tower for great views. Singles $26.46 plus tax; doubles $38. Student discounts. Laundry facilities. Free local calls, sink in each room. Parking will run you $7 per day, and the noon check-out is strictly enforced—trust us. Reception 24hr. Cafe with basic foods open M-F 7:30am-2:30pm. Open early May to mid-Aug.

**Hôtel de Paris,** 901 Sherbrook E. (522-6861). Métro: Sherbrook. In cahoots with the pricier Dansereau Mansion, the Hotel has been painting, hammering, sweeping, and setting up a kitchen, all to bring you a splendidly outfitted brand new hostel with 90 beds. Single-sex dorm rooms $17. Linen rental $2.

**Maison André Tourist Rooms,** 3511 rue Université (849-4092). Métro: McGill. Mme Zanko spins great yarns in her old, well located house. Guests have been returning to this bastion of European cleanliness and decor for over 30 years. Singles $26-35; doubles $38-45; $10 per additional person. Reservations recommended. No smoking.

EASTERN CANADA

**YMCA,** 1450 rue Stanley (849-8393), downtown. Métro: Peel (right across the street from the station). 350 rooms. Co-ed. Access to newly renovated facilities. Tiny but impeccable. rooms, TV and phone in most. Located near downtown. Singles $37-39 for men, $40 for women; doubles $56; triples $66; quads $76. Cafeteria open M-F 7am-8pm, Sa-Su 8am-2pm. Reserve 2 weeks in advance.

**Manoir Ambrose,** 3422 rue Stanley (288-6922), just off Sherbrooke. Métro: Peel. Somewhat upscale both in price and appearance. 22 rooms with Victorian decor. Doubles $50, with private bath $60; $10 per additional adult. Continental breakfast included. Reservations recommended 1 month in advance.

For slightly private sites in a campground close to the city, try **Camping Alouette,** 3449 de l'Industrie J3G 4S5, 15mi. from the city; follow Autoroute 20, take exit 105, and follow the signs to the campground. Pool, laundry facilities, a small store, free showers, and a daily shuttle to and from Montréal. (450-464-1661. Sites for 2 $17, with hookup $26.50; $2 per additional person.) If these don't wet your camping whistle, try the dramatic (there's a theater here, folks) **Camping Pointe-des-Cascades,** 2 ch. du Canal, Pte. des Cascades. Take Autoroute 40 west, exit 41 at Ste. Anne de Bellevue, Jct. 20, and west to Dorion. In Dorion, follow "Théâtre des Cascades" signs. (455-9953. 140 sites, many near water. Sites $22, with hookup $27.)

## BON APPETÍT

Restaurants pack in along **bd. St-Laurent** and on the western half of **Ste-Catherine,** with prices ranging from affordable to astronomical. In the **Latin Quarter,** scout out energetic **rue Prince Arthur,** which jams Greek, Polish, and Italian restaurants into a tiny area (see **Sights,** p. 170, for details on ethnic neighborhoods). Here, maître-d's stand in front of their restaurants to court you. The accent changes slightly at **ave. Duluth,** where Portuguese and Vietnamese establishments prevail. North of Maisonneuve on **Rue St-Denis,** you'll find the French Student Quarter, which has many small cafés and eateries that cater to student budgets. If you'd like wine at an unlicensed restaurant, buy your own at a *dépanneur* or the **SAQ (Sociéte des alcohols du Québec);** the eateries are concentrated on the **bd. St-Laurent,** north of Sherbrooke, and on the pedestrian precincts of rue Prince Arthur and rue Duluth.

All restaurants are required by law to post their menus outside (although many white out the prices), so shop around. Consult the free *Restaurant Guide,* published by the **Greater Montréal Convention and Tourism Bureau** (844-5400), which lists over 130 restaurants by type of cuisine (available at the tourist office; see **Practical Information,** above). When preparing your own meals, these markets have what you need: the **Atwater Market** (Métro: Lionel-Groulx); the **Marché Maisonneuve,** 4375 rue Ontario Est (Métro: Pie-IX); the **Marché St-Jacques** (Métro: Berri-UQAM, at Ontario and Amherst); or the **Marché Jean-Talon** (Métro: Jean Talon; call 937-7754 9am-4pm daily. All markets open M-W 8am-6pm, Th 8am-8pm, F 8am-9pm, Sa 8am-5pm., Su 8am-5pm.)

**SMOKED MEAT ON RYE** Any true Montréalian (not those artsy downtown types) will agree that **Smoked Meat**—a spicy, salty, greasy cured beef brisket—is a delicacy not to be compared with anything else in the world. The great landmark **Ben's Delicatessen,** 990 bd. de Maisonneuve, at Metcalfe, in the heart of downtown, is often said to be the originator of this artery-clogging delicacy, which resembles pastrami or even corned beef (844-1000). The story has it that Ben Kravitz, a native Lithuanian, longed for the briskets of his native land and, in an effort to recreate them, invented Smoked Meat. Famous in Montréal, cafes as far a way as Halifax fly in meat from Ben's to serve to their adoring customers. A proper Smoked Meat sandwich is served hot with mustard on seedless rye, with fries, vinegar, a half-sour pickle, and black cherry soda. (At Ben's, that'll be about $6.)

▨ **La Creme de la Creme Bistro Café,** 21 rue De La Communne est (874-0723), down by the water in Old Montreal. This little cafe serves up filling portions of tasty Montréal cuisine at reasonable prices. Magazines line the wall for your browsing pleasure while you wait for your meal. Sandwiches ($5-8) and dessert are a steal. Scandalously sized wedges of chocolate cake will bring you back for more. A full bar is also on the premises, so it's easy to combine a late dinner with an early start on Montreal's fantastic nightlife. Open Jun.-Sept. daily 11am-midnight. Hours vary during other seasons.

▨ **Au Pain Doré,** 5214 Côte des Neiges (342-8995), near rue Jean Brillant. An answer to the question "Where, oh where can I get some French baked goods?" It is easy to drop some extra cash here and buy food for your entire stay. Chocolatines are excellent, as are the croissants, breads, muffins, and pretty much everything else. Also offers a selection of cheeses. Baguettes $1.50-4. Open M-W 8:30am-7pm, Th-F 8:30am-7:30pm, Sa-Su 8:30am-5:30pm.

**Etoile des Indes,** 1806 Ste-Catherine Ouest (932-8330), near St-Mathieu. Métro: Guy-Concordia. The best Indian fare in town, according to locals. The brave should try their bang-up Bangalore *phal* dishes. Dinner entrees $5-15; lunch specials $5-8 are your best bet for value. Open M-Sa noon-2:30pm and 5-11pm, Su 5-11pm.

**El Zaziummm,** 51 Roy Est (844-0893), a St-Laurent side street. Spicy Mexican cuisine and sly, sweet alcoholic beverages. The food is good, and with the intoxicating atmosphere, Zaziummm is a must. Entrees $8-15. Open M-Tu 4-11pm, W-Su noon-11:30pm; in winter daily 4-11pm.

**Wilensky's,** 34 rue Fairmount Ouest (271-0247), west of St-Laurent. Métro: Laurier. A great place for a quick lunch. Hot dogs $1.80, sandwiches $2.10. Open M-F 9am-4pm.

**Da Giovanni,** 572 Ste-Catherine Est (842-8851). Métro: Berri-UQAM. Serves generous portions of fine Italian food; don't be put off by the occasional lines or the diner atmosphere. Lasagna with garlic bread and caesar salad $9.50. Open Su-W 6:30am-11pm, Th 6:30am-midnight, F-Sa 7am-1am.

## ◈ SIGHTS

**ON THE STREETS.** Montréal has matured from a riverside settlement of French colonists into a hip metropolis. **Museums, Vieux Montréal (Old Montréal),** and the new **centre-ville** are fascinating, but Montréal's greatest asset is its cultural vibrancy, and the city rewards aimless wandering. Your wallet will thank you for avoiding the high-priced boutiques touted by the tourist office. A small **Chinatown** orients itself along **rue de la Gauchetière,** near Vieux Montréal's **Place d'Armes.** Between 11:30am and 2:30pm, most of its restaurants offer mouth-watering Canton and Szechuan lunch specials ranging from $4-5. **Little Greece,** a bit farther than you might care to walk from downtown, is just southeast of the Outremont Métro; stop around **rue Hutchison** between **ave. Van Horne** and **ave. Edouard-Charles.** At the northern edge of the town's center, **Little Italy** occupies the area north of rue Beaubien between rue St-Hubert and Louis-Hémon. Walk east from Métro Beaubien. Many attractions between Mont Royal and the Fleuve St-Laurent are free, from parks (Mont Royal and Lafontaine, see below) and universities (McGill, Montréal, Concordia, Québec at Montréal) to architectural spectacles of all sorts.

**Bd. St-Laurent,** north of Sherbrooke, is perfect for walking or biking. Originally settled by Jewish immigrants, this area now functions as a sort of multicultural welcome wagon, home to Greek, Slavic, Latin American, and Portuguese immigrants. **Rue St-Denis,** home to the city elite at the turn of the century, still serves as the **Latin Quarter's** main street (Métro: Berri-UQAM). Jazz fiends will command the street June 29 to July 9, 2000 during the annual **Montréal International Jazz Festival** (871-1881), with over 300 free outdoor shows. **Rue Prince-Arthur** (Métro: Sherbrooke) has street performers in the summer; **Carré St-Louis** (Métro: Sherbrooke), hosts a beautiful fountain and sculptures. **Le Village** is a gay village in Montréal from rue St-Denis Est to Papineau along rue Ste-Catherine Est. Both the Latin Quarter (above) and the area along rue St-Denis foster a very liberal, gay-friendly atmosphere (Metro: Sherbrooke or Mont-Royal).

**MUSEUMS.** The **McGill University** campus (main gate at rue McGill and Sher-brooke; Métro: McGill) runs up Mont Royal and boasts Victorian buildings and pleasant greens. More than any other sight in Montréal, the university illustrates the impact of the British on the city. The campus also contains the site of the 16th-century Native American village of **Hochelaga** and the **Redpath Museum of Natural History,** with rare fossils and 2 genuine Egyptian mummies. (398-4086. Métro: McGill. Open M-Th 9am-5pm, Su 1-5pm; in winter M-F 9am-5pm, Su 1-5pm. Free.)

About 5 blocks west of the McGill entrance, Montréal's **Musée des Beaux-Arts (Fine Arts Museum),** hosts impressive visiting exhibits; its small permanent collection touches upon all major artistic periods and includes Canadian and Inuit work. (1380 rue Sherbrooke Ouest. 285-2000. Métro: Guy-Concordia. Open Tu-Su 11am-6pm. Permanent collection free. Temporary exhibits $12, students and seniors $6, under 12 $3; ½-price W 5:30-9pm.) Canadian history is preserved at the **McCord Museum,** where textiles, costumes, paintings, prints, and 700,000 pictures trace the story from Confederation onward. (690 rue Sherbrooke Ouest. 398-7100. Métro: McGill. Open Sept.-June Tu-F 10am-6pm, Sa-Su 10am-5pm; call for summer hrs. $7, students $4, seniors $5, ages 7-12 $1.50, families $14. Free Sa 10am-noon.) The relatively new **Canadian Centre for Architecture,** houses one of the world's most important collections of architectural prints, drawings, photographs, and books. (1920 ave. Baile 939-7026; Métro: Guy-Concordia or Atwater. Open in summer Tu-Su 11am-6pm; hours vary in other seasons. $6, students $3, seniors $4, under 12 free.) **Musée d'Art Contemporain,** has the latest by québecois artists, as well as textile, photography, and avant-garde exhibits. (185 rue Ste-Catherine Ouest at Jeanne-Mance 847-6226. Métro: Place-des-Arts. Open Tu and Th-Su 11am-6pm, W 11am-9pm. $6, seniors $4, students $3, under 12 free.) Outside of the downtown museum circuit, the **Montréal Museum of Decorative Arts,** houses innovatively designed decorative pieces dating from the 20th century. (2200 rue Crescent. 284-1252. Métro: Guy-Concordia, then transfer to bus #24 Pie-IX. Open Tu-Su 11am-6pm, W 11am-9pm. $4, students $3, under 12 free.)

**MONT-ROYAL, LE PLATEAU, AND THE EAST. Olympic Park,** hosted the 1976 Summer Olympic Games. Its daring architecture, uncannily reminiscent of the *U.S.S. Enterprise* from TV's "Star Trek," includes the world's tallest inclined tower and a stadium with one of the world's only fully retractable roofs. Despite this, baseball games still get rained out because the roof cannot be put into place with crowds in the building. Riding the **funiculaire** to the top of the tower grants a panoramic view of Montréal. (3200 rue Viau. 252-8687. Métro: Viau, Pie IX. Tours offered daily in both French and English. Call for times. $5.25, ages 5-17 $4.25. Funiculaire open June-Sept. M noon-9pm, Tu-Th 10am-9pm, F-Su 10am-11pm; early Sept. to mid-June M noon-6pm, Tu-Su 10am-6pm. $9, seniors and ages 5-17 $5.50.) The fascinating ▓ **Biodôme** is the most recent addition to Olympic park. Housed in the former Olympic Vélodrome, the Biodôme is a "living museum" in which 4 complete ecosystems have been reconstructed: the Tropical Forest, Laurentian Forest, the St-Laurent marine ecosystem, and the Polar World. Keep your eyes open and your hands to yourself; everything here is alive. (4777 ave. Pierre-de-Coubertin. 868-3000. Métro: Viau. Open daily in summer 9am-7pm; off-season 9am-5pm. $9.50, students and seniors $7, ages 6-17 $4.75.) In the summer, a train will take you across the park to the **Jardin Botanique (Botanical Gardens).** The Japanese and Chinese areas house the largest *bonsai* and *penjing* collections outside of Asia. The gardens also house an insectarium that specializes in huge spiders. (4101 rue Sherbrooke Est. 872-1400; Métro: Pie-IX. Gardens open daily 9am-7pm; Sept.-June 9am-5pm. $9.50, students and seniors $7, ages 6-17 $4.75; Sept.-June $6.75/$5.25/$3.50.) Package tickets for the Biodôme, Insectarium, tower and the Gardens allow you to save money and split a visit up over a 2-day period.

**Parc du Mont-Royal** was inaugurated in 1876 and climbs up to the mountain from which the city took its name. From rue Peel, hardy hikers can take a foot path and stairs to the top, or to the lookouts on Camillien-Houde Pkwy. and the Mountain Chalet. Like New York's Central Park, this one too is a Frederick Law Olmsted original. The **30m cross** at the top of the mountain commemorates the 1643 climb by de Maisonneuve, founder of Montréal. In winter, montréalians congregate here to ice skate, toboggan, and cross-country ski. In summer, Mont-Royal welcomes joggers, cyclists, picnickers, and amblers. *(Camilien-Houde Pkwy. 844-4928. Métro: Mont-Royal or Bus #11. Officially open 6am-midnight.)* **Parc Lafontaine,** bordered by Sherbrooke, Rachel, and Papineau Ave.; has picnic facilities, an outdoor puppet theater, 7 tennis courts (hourly fee), pedal boats in the summer, ice-skating in the winter, and an international festival of public theater in June. *(872-2644. Métro: Sherbrooke.)*

**St. Joseph's Oratory** is a most acclaimed religious site. Credited with a long list of miracles and unexplained healings, the oratory attracts visitors from around the globe. *(3800 ch. Queen Mary, 733-8211. Open daily 6am-9:30pm. Metro: Cote-des-Nieges.)*

**THE UNDERGROUND CITY.** Montréal residents aren't speaking cryptically of a sub-culture or a hideout for dissidents when they rave about their Underground City. They literally mean under the ground; 29km of tunnels link Métro stops and form a subterranean village of climate-controlled restaurants and shops—a haven in Montréal's sub-zero winter weather. The ever-expanding "prototype city of the future" connects railway stations, 2 bus terminals, restaurants, banks, cinemas, theaters, hotels, 2 universities, 2 department stores, 1700 businesses, 1615 housing units, and 1600 boutiques. Talk about suburban. The city can be entered from any Métro stop, though a good start to an adventure is the **Place Bonaventure.** Canada's largest commercial building sports a melange of shops, each selling products imported from a different country. The tourist office supplies city guides including treasure maps of the tunnels and underground attractions. *(900 rue de la Gauchetière Ouest 397-2325. Métro: Bonaventure. Shops open daily 9am-9pm.)*

At the McGill stop lies some of the Underground City's finest offerings. Here, beneath the **Christ Church Cathedral** waits **Promenades de la Cathédrale,** one of the Underground's primary shopping complexes. *(635 Ste-Catherine Ouest. Church: 843-6577. Open daily 8am-6pm. Promenades: 849-9925.)* Three blocks east, passing through Centre Eaton, of grand department store fame, the **Place Montréal Trust** is famous for its modern architecture and decadent shopping area. Still, there's no charge for an innocent peek around.

**VIEUX MONTRÉAL (OLD MONTRÉAL).** In the 17th century, the city of Montréal struggled with Iroquois tribes for control of the area's lucrative fur trade, and erected walls encircling the settlement for defense. Today the remnants of those ramparts delineate the boundaries of Vieux Montréal, the city's first settlement, on the stretch of river bank between **rues McGill, Notre-Dame,** and **Berri.** The fortified walls that once protected the quarter have crumbled, but the beautiful 17th- and 18th-century mansions of politicos and merchants retain their splendor. Take the Métro to **Place d'Armes** or **Champ-de-Mars.** Good, clean, religious fun waits at the 19th-century basilica **Notre-Dame-de-Montréal,** a couple blocks south of the Place d'Armes, towers above the memorial to de Maisonneuve. Historically a center for the city's Catholic population, the neo-Gothic church once hosted separatist rallies. It seats 4000 and is one of the largest churches in North America. After suffering major fire damage, the Wedding Chapel behind the altar re-opened with an enormous bronze altar. *(116 rue Notre-Dame Ouest. 842-2925. Open in summer daily 7am-8pm; early Sept. to late June M-Sa 8:30am-6pm, Su 1:30pm-6pm. Free.)* The **Cathédrale Marie Reine du Monde (Mary Queen of the World Cathedral),** on the block bordered by René-Lévesque, Cathédrale, and Metcalf, is a scaled-down replica of St. Peter's in Rome and a rival of Notre-Dame-de-Montréal for grandeur. The church was built in the heart of Montréal's Anglo-Protestant area. *(866-1661. Open M-F 7am-7:30pm, Sa 7:30am-8:30pm, Su 8:30am-7:30pm. At least 3-4 masses offered daily. Free.)*

The **Sulpician Seminary,** Montréal's, built in 1685, is still a functioning seminary. The clock over the facade, built in 1701, is the oldest public timepiece in North America and predates Seiko, Rolex, and even Swatch. *(130 rue Notre-Dame Ouest. Métro: Place D'Armes.)* At rue Bonsecours and rue St-Paul stands the 18th-century **Notre-Dame-de-Bonsecours,** founded as a sailors' refuge by Marguerite Bourgeoys, leader of the first order of non-cloistered nuns. The church displays archaeological finds from beneath its floors. *(400 rue St-Paul Est. Métro: Champ-de-Mars.)*

**Place Jacques Cartier** is the site of Montréal's oldest market. Here the modern European character of Montréal is most evident; cafes line the square, and street artists strut their stuff during the summer. *(Rue St. Paul. Metro: Champ-de-Mars.)* The grand **Château Ramezay,** built in 1705 to house the French viceroy, houses a museum of Québecois, British, and American 18th-century artifacts. *(280 rue Notre-Dame Est. 861-3708. Métro: Champ-de-Mars. Open daily 10am-6pm; Oct.-May Tu-Su 10am-4:30pm. $6, students and seniors $3, under 6 free. Tours available by reservation. Partial wheelchair access; assistance may be required.)* The **Vieux Palais de Justice,** built in 1856 in Place Vaugeulin, stands across from City Hall. **Rue St-Jacques** in the Old City, established in 1687, is Montréal's Wall St.

**ST-LAURENT AND ILE. STE-HELENE.** **Saute-Moutons Jet-Boating tours** are an interesting, way of experiencing the rapids of the St. Lawrence. *(Clock Tower Pier. 284-9607. 10am-6pm in summer, with prices starting at $50. Call ahead. Metro: Champ-de-Mars.)* **Les Descentes sur le Saint-Laurent** in LaSalle will provide a **rafting adventure** including the Lachine Rapids. Rafting tours last approximately 1.5 hours. *(Free shuttle from the Info Centre at 1001 rue du Square-Dorchester. 767-2230 or 800-324-RAFT. Prices and departure times vary. Metro: Peel.)*

**La Ronde** is the best among many good reasons to visit **Ile Ste-Helene,** an island in the St. Lawrence just off shore from Vieux Montreal. This amusement park is extremely popular with Montréalians and visitors alike, especially on afternoons when unlimited passes are available. *(872-4537 or 800-797-4537. Open in summer Su-Th 11am-11pm F-Sa 11am-midnight; hours vary off-season. Tickets start around $30. Metro: Ile-Sainte-Helene.)* The **International Fireworks Competition** takes place every June and July at La Ronde, but you can avoid the park's steep prices by watching from Mont-Royal or the very crowded Pont Jacques-Cartier. *(872-4537.)* The **Stewart Museum,** located at **Le Vieux Fort** (The Old Fort), was originally built in 1820 to defend Canada's inland waterways, most probably from the feisty Americans down south. Today the museum houses a large collection of weapons, war instruments, and strategic maps. *(861-6701. Open May-Oct. M-W and F-Su 10am-6pm; Th 10am-9pm; hours vary during rest of year. $10, students and seniors $7. Admission lower between Oct. and May. Metro: Ile-Sainte-Helene.)*

The **Ile. Notre-Dame** hosts the **Casino de Montreal,** where gamblers push their luck on the 3000 slot machines and 100 gaming tables. There's free parking with shuttles between the casino and the parking lot. From the metro stop, it's a 1km walk across the bridge over the **Chenal La Moyne** to the casino. *(1 ave. du Casino. 392-2746 or 800-665-2274. Open 24 hours. 18+. Metro: Ile-Sainte-Helene.)*

# ▌ ENTERTAINMENT AND NIGHTLIFE

Like much of the city, Vieux Montréal is best seen at night. Street performers, artists, and *chansonniers* in various *brasseries* set the tone for lively summer evenings of clapping, stomping, and singing along. The real fun goes down on **St-Paul,** near the corner of St-Vincent. For a sweet Su in the park, **Parc Jeanne-Mance,** with bongos, dancing, and handicrafts, can't be missed (May-Sept. noon-7pm).

The city has a wide variety of theatrical groups. The **Théâtre du Nouveau Monde,** 84, Ste-Catherine Ouest hosts French productions (866-8667; Métro: Place-des-Arts). The **Théâtre du Rideau Vert,** 4664 rue St-Denis, stages *québecois* works (844-1793). The **Centaur Theater,** 453 rue St-François-Xavier, has English-language plays, performed mainly Sept.-May (288-1229, ticket info 288-3161; Métro: Place-d'Armes). The city's exciting **Place des Arts,** 260 bd. de Maisonneuve Ouest, at rue Ste. Catherine Ouest and rue Jeanne Mance, (842-2112 for tickets), houses the **Opéra de Montréal** (985-2258), the **Montréal Symphony Orchestra** (842-9951), and **Les Grands Ballets Canadiens** (849-8681). The **National Theater School of Canada,** 5030 rue St-Denis, stages excellent student productions during the academic year (842-7954). **Théâtre Saint-Denis,** 1594 rue St-Denis, hosts traveling productions like *Cats* (849-4211). Theater-goers peruse **Calendar of Events** (available at the tourist office and reprinted in daily newspapers), or call **Telspec** for ticket info (790-2222; open

M-Sa 9am-9pm, Su noon-6pm). **Admission Ticket Network** also has tickets for various events (790-1245 or 800-361-4595; open daily 8am-midnight; credit card required).

Maybe it's the weather, but *montréalais* are rabid hockey fans—call well in advance to reserve tickets. Between Oct. and Apr., be sure to attend a **Montréal Canadiens** hockey game at the new **Molson Centre**, 1250, de la Gauchetière Ouest, where **Les Habitants** (a nickname for the Canadiens) play. Dress and behavior at games can be quite formal; jacket and ties are not uncommon (for tickets call 932-2582; Métro: Bonaventure). Baseball is also popular here, and the local MLB team, the **Montréal Expos,** plays at Olympic Park (790-1245).

*Montréalais* don't like to just watch; in early June, the 1-day **Tour de l'île**, a 64km circuit of the island, is the largest cycling event in the world, with 45,000 mostly amateur cyclists pedaling their wares. (Call 521-8356 by Apr. if you wanna be a player. Separate days for adults and children.)

Even in the dead of winter, the bars are full. Nightlife in Québec's largest city can be found in **brasseries** (with food, wine, and music), in **pubs** (more hanging out and less eating), or in the multitude of **dance clubs.** In Montréal's **gay village** there are plenty of clubs for men—lesbian clubs are less common, but there are a few (Métro: Papineau or Beaudry). Whatever type of nightlife you prefer, be sure to at least give a glance to the crowded establishments that line rue Ste. Catherine and rue Cresent where the most happening Montrealers gather to see and be seen.

Though intermingled with some of the city's hottest dance venues, the establishments of **rue Ste-Catherine Ouest** and nearby side streets tend to feature drink as the primary entertainment (Métro: Peel). Downstairs at 1107 rue Ste-Catherine Ouest, the **Peel Pub** provides good, cheap food nightly, but more noted are its exceptional drink prices. Happy hour (M-F 3-7pm) floods the joint with $6 pitchers and 9¢ wings. Gutsy patrons can even purchase beer by the gallon. Another location is at 890 bd. de Maisonneuve Est (1107: 844-6769. 890: 844-8715. Both are open daily 11am-3am.) For slightly older and more subdued drinking buddies, the side streets and the touristy English strongholds around rue Crescent and Bishop (Métro: Guy) make bar-hopping a must. **Déjà-Vu,** 1224 Bishop, near Ste-Catherine, has live bands each night at 10pm, amid an excellent atmosphere (866-0512; happy hour daily 3-8pm; no cover; open daily 3pm-3am). **Sir Winston Churchill's,** 1459 Crescent, is another hotspot, with 2-for-1 beer during the week from 5-8pm (288-0616; no cover; open daily 11:30am-3am). If your baby's left you, **Les Beaux Esprits Blues Bar,** 2073 St. Denis north of Maisonneuve, has live music—hours and cover vary (844-0882; Métro: Sherbrooke). Caffeinated fun awaits at **Kilo,** 1491, St-Catherine, near the corner of Beaudry St. The coffee's good, and if you want a late snack, the sandwiches ($5.50) are great. (Métro: Beaudry. Open until midnight M-F, Sa-Su 1am.) **Sky Club,** 1474, Ste-Catherine, is the nightspot of choice, and with good reason—the music is jumping, and there are numerous special theme nights and parties. Enter at 1320 Alexander de Sève. (529-6969. Cover $2. Open daily 11am-3am.)

**Rue Prince Arthur** at St-Laurent is devoted solely to pedestrians who mix and mingle at cafes by day and clubs by night. **Café Campus,** 57 Prince Arthur, features live rock and other genres and is one of the best spots in the city to meet some locals. (844-1010. Cover: dancing $3, live music $5-15. Open M-Sa 7pm-3am, Su 8:30pm-3am.) **The Shed Café,** 3515 St-Laurent, hosts a trendy clientele, charges little cover, and is located within a few blocks of St-Laurent (842-0220; open daily 11am-3am).

French nightlife also resides in the open-air cafés on **rue St-Denis** (Métro: UQAM). Rockin' dance club by night, **Bar Passeport,** 4156 rue St-Denis, at Rachel, doubles as a store by day (842-6063; cover $2.50-4; open daily 10am-3am).

# QUÉBEC CITY

Dubbed the "Gibraltar of America" because of the stone escarpments and military fortifications protecting the port, Québec City (generally shortened to just "Québec") sits high on the rocky heights of Cap Diamant where the Fleuve St-Laurent narrows and is joined by the St-Charles river. The name Québec, in fact, is derived from the Algonquin word *kebek*, which means "place where the river nar-

rows." Passing through the portals of North America's only walled city is like stepping into the past; narrow streets and horse-drawn carriages greet visitors to the
Old City (Vieux-Québec), and there are enough sights and museums to satisfy even
the most voracious history buff for weeks. Along with the historical attachment,
Canada's oldest city boasts a thriving French culture—never assume that the
locals speak English. Québec stands apart from Montréal by serving as the center
for true *quebécois* culture. English has yet to make inroads with the local population. Nevertheless, English-speaking tourists are greeted warmly by most, and are
easily identified: they'll be the large groups standing in gawking in front of restaurants trying to decipher the French menu (before realizing, of course, that the
menu is also printed in English).

## ⬛ ORIENTATION AND PRACTICAL INFORMATION

Québec's main thoroughfares run through both the Old City *(Vieux Québec)* and
the more modern city outside it, generally parallel in an east-west direction. Within
**Vieux Québec,** the main streets are **St-Louis, Ste-Anne,** and **St-Jean.** Most streets in
Vieux Québec are one-way, the major exception being rue d'Auteuil, which bor-
ders the walls inside Vieux Québec. Rue d'Auteuil is the best bet for parking. Out-
side the walls of Vieux Québec, both St-Jean and St-Louis continue (St-Jean
eventually joins Chemin Ste-Foy and St-Louis becomes **Grande Allée**). **Bd. René-
Lévesque,** the other major street outside the walls, runs between St-Jean and St-
Louis. The Basse-ville (lower town) is separated from the Haute-ville (upper town,
Old Québec) by an abrupt cliff roughly paralleled by rue St-Vallier Est.

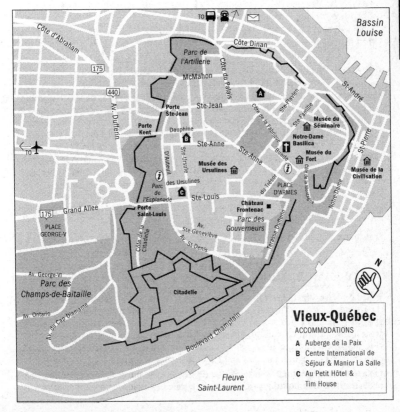

**Vieux-Québec**

ACCOMMODATIONS

A  Auberge de la Paix
B  Centre International de
   Séjour & Manior La Salle
C  Au Petit Hôtel &
   Tim House

**Airport:** The airport (692-0770) is far out of town and inaccessible by public transport. Taxi to downtown $25. By car, turn right onto Rt. de l'aéroport and then take either bd. Wilfred-Hamel or, beyond it, Autoroute 440 to get into the city. **La Québecois** (570-5379) runs a shuttle service between the airport and the major hotels of the city. (M-F 6 per day to and from the airport, 8:45am-9:45pm; Sa 7 per day 9am-8:45pm; Su 7 per day 9am-11:35pm. $9, under 12 free.)

**Trains: VIA Rail,** 450 rue de la Gare du Palais (692-3940), in Québec City. To: Montréal (3hr.; M-F 4 per day, Sa-Su 3 per day; $49, students $29), Toronto (8hr.; 3 per day; $122/$73), and Ottawa (3hr.; 3 per day; $73/$44). Open daily 6am-8:30pm. Nearby stations at 3255, ch. de la Gare in Ste-Foy (open M-F 6am-9pm, Sa-Su 7:30am-9pm) and 5995, St-Laurent, Autoroute 20 Lévis. Open Th-M 4-5am and 8-10:30pm, Tu 4-5am, W 8-10:30pm. Reservations 800-561-3949. Information 800-835-3037.

**Buses: Orlean Express,** 320 Abraham Martin (525-3000). Open daily 5:30am-1am. Outlying stations at 2700 ave. Laurier, in Ste-Foy (650-0087; open M-Sa 6am-1am, Su 7am-1am), and 63, Hwy. Trans-Canada Ouest (Hwy. 132), in Lévis (837-5805; open daily 6am-2am). To: Montréal (3hr., every hr. 6am-9pm and 11pm, $35); Ste-Anne-de-Beaupré (25min., 3 per day, $5); and the U.S. via Montréal or Sherbrooke.

**Public Transit: Commission de transport de la Communauté Urbaine de Québec (CTCUQ),** 270 rue des Rocailles (627-2511 for route and schedule info). Open M-F 6:30am-10pm, Sa-Su 8am-10pm. Buses operate daily 6am-1am, although individual routes and hours of operation vary significantly. $2.25, students $1.50, seniors and children $1.30; advance-purchase tickets $1.60/$1/$1; under 5 free.

**Taxis: Coop Taxis Québec,** 525-5191.

**Driver/Rider Service: Allo-Stop,** 467 rue St-Jean (522-0056), will match you with a driver heading for Montréal ($15) or Ottawa ($29). Must be a member ($6 per year, drivers $7). Open W-F 8am-7pm, Sa-Tu 8am-6pm.

**Car Rental: Pelletier,** 900 bd. Pierre Bertrand (681-0678). $35 per day; 300 km free, 12¢ per additional km. Must be 25+ with credit card deposit of 20%. Open M-F 7am-8pm, Sa-Su 8am-4pm.

**Bike Rental: Vélo Passe-Sport,** 77A rue Ste-Anne (692-3643). 1hr. $6, 4hr. $15, 1 day $25. Credit card deposit of $40 required. Open May-Oct. daily 8am-6pm.

**Visitor Info: Centre d'information de l'office du tourisme et des congrés de la Communauté urbaine de Québec,** 835 rue Wilfred Laurier (649-2608), in the Old City just outside the walls. Open daily 8:30am-7pm; Thanksgiving (mid-Oct.) to May 9am-5:30pm. Dealing primarily with provincial tourism, **Maison du tourisme de Québec,** 12 rue Ste-Anne (800-363-7777). Open daily 8:30am-7:30pm; early Sept. to mid-June 9am-5pm.

**Crisis Lines: Tél-Aide** distress center, 686-2433. Operates daily noon-midnight. **Viol-Secours (sexual assault line),** 522-2120. Counselors on duty M-F 9am-4pm and on-call 24hr. **Center for Suicide Prevention,** 529-0015. Operates daily 8am-midnight. **Info-Santé,** 648-2626, handles bi-gay-lesbian concerns. **Poison Control;** 656-8090.

**Emergency: Police,** 911 (city); 800-461-2131 (province). **Info-santé (medical info),** 648-2626. 24hr. service with info from qualified nurses.

**Post Office:** 300 rue St-Paul (694-6176). **Postal code:** G1K 3W0. Open M-F 8am-8pm; Oct.-May 8am-5:45pm. **Area code:** 418.

# ▌ ACCOMMODATIONS

For **Bed and Breakfast** referrals, Montréal-based **Breakfast á Montréal** (see p. 168), or **Le Transit,** 1050 ave. Turnbull, Québec City G1R 2X8 (647-6802; call 8am-noon or 4-9pm) will help. Singles run $50, and doubles $65-75. Hosts are usually bilingual. If parking is a problem (usually the case in Old Québec) and you must make use of the underground parking areas, ask your host about discount parking passes. Most places offer them, which means paying $6 rather than $10 for a 24hr. pass.

**Auberge de la Paix,** 31 rue Couillard (694-0735). Take St-Jean into Vieux Quebec, and take Couillard when it branches left. While it lacks many facilities, the friendly staff and an open, casual atmosphere (no locks on the doors) make it worthwhile. Co-ed rooms. 63 beds; 2-8 per room, but most have 3-4. Offers easy access to the restaurants and bars on rue St-Jean. Look for the big peace sign above this "Peace Hostel." Beds $19. Linen $2. Continental breakfast included (8-10am). Curfew 2am with all-day access. Kitchen open all day. Reservations necessary July-Aug.

**Centre International de Séjour (HI-C),** 19 rue Ste-Ursule (694-0755), 1 block north of rue St-Jean at Dauphine. Follow Côte d'Abraham uphill from the bus station until it joins ave. Dufferin. Turn left on St-Jean, pass through the walls, and walk uphill, to your right, on Ste-Ursule. If driving, follow St-Louis into the Old City and take the 2nd left past the walls onto Ste-Ursule. Diverse, young clientele and fabulous location. Beds in dorm style rooms cost $16 for members, $18 for Canadian nonmembers, $20 for non-Canadian nonmembers; private rooms cost $46 for members and $50 for nonmembers; nonmembers must also buy an international stamp ($4.60). 250 beds. Laundry, microwave, TV, pool table, ping-pong tables, living room, kitchen, cafeteria. Breakfast 8-10am (continental $3.75, full breakfast $4.50). Check-out 10am. Reception noon. Lockout 11pm, but the front desk will let you in if you flash your key. Usually full July-Aug.; make reservations or arrive early.

**Au Petit Hôtel,** 3 ruelle des Ursulines (694-0965), just off of rue Ste-Ursule. This tidy little hotel is a great deal for 2 people. TV, free local phone, private bath, and refrigerator in each room. May-Oct. rooms start at $70 for 1 or 2 occupants, continental breakfast included; Nov.-May rooms start at $45. Audaciously combines a downtown location with free parking in winter ($5 May-Oct.).

**Montmartre Canadien,** 1675, ch. St-Louis (686-0867), Sillery, on the outskirts of the city, in the Maison du Pelerin; a small white house behind the main building at 1669. Take bus #25 or 11. Clean house in a religious sanctuary run by Assumptionist monks overlooking the Fleuve St-Laurent. Relaxed, almost ascetic setting. Mostly used by groups. Dorm-style singles $17; doubles $30; triples $42. Common showers. Reserve 2-3 weeks in advance.

**Universite Laval,** Pavillon Alphonse-Marie-Parent (656-2921), rents beds from May-Aug. to travelers with ISIC ID. Linen, towels and phones. Singles $20; doubles $28.

**Manoir La Salle,** 18 rue Ste-Ursule (692-9953), opposite the youth hostel. The clean private rooms in this ornate Victorian mansion fill quickly, especially in summer. Shared bathrooms. Singles $30; doubles $50-65. Reservations necessary.

**Tim House,** 84 rue Ste-Louis (694-0776). Adjacent to Au Petit and run by the same folks. A lovely B&B. 3rd fl. rooms have shared baths; a delectable breakfast is included. Rooms $35-60, depending on the season. Parking $5.

You can obtain a list of nearby **campgrounds** from the **Maison du Tourisme de Québec** (see **Practical Information,** p. 175), or write to **Tourisme Québec,** c.p. 979, Montréal, PQ H3C 2W3 (800-363-7777; open daily 9am-5pm). A good camping option is **Municipal de Beauport.** Take Autoroute 40E, and get off at exit 321 at rue Labelle onto Hwy. 369, turn left, and follow the signs marked "camping." Bus #55 to 800 will also take you to this 135-site campground on a hill over the Montmorency River. A swimming pool, canoes ($8 per hr.), showers ($1 per 5min.), and laundry facilities ($1 per load) are available. (666-2228. sites $19, with hookup $24; or $114/$144 per week. Open June to early Sept.)

# ◖ L'HAUTE CUISINE

In general rue Buade, St-Jean, and Cartier, as well as the **Place Royale** and **Petit Champlain** areas, offer the widest selection of food and drink. The **Grande Allée,** a 2km strip of restaurants on either side of the street, might seem like heaven to the hungry, but its steep prices make it a place to visit rather than to eat.

The best bet for a simple and affordable meal doesn't have to be a fast-food joint. Traditional *québecois* food is not only appetizing, but usually economical. One of the most filling yet inexpensive meals is a *croque-monsieur*, a large, open-faced sandwich with ham and melted cheese (about $6), usually served with salad.

*Québecois* French onion soup, slathered with melted cheese, is not to be missed and can be found in virtually every restaurant and cafe. It is usually served with either bats of French bread or *tourtière*, a thick meat pie. Other specialties include the *crêpe*, stuffed differently to serve as either an entree or as a dessert. The **Casse-Crêpe Breton,** 1136 St-Jean, offers many choices of fillings in their "make your own combination" crepes for dinner ($3-6), as well as scrumptious dessert options ($3-4; open daily 7:30am-midnight). Try to locate a French-Canadian "sugar pie," made with brown sugar and butter. The quaint French bakery **Pâtisserie au Palet d'Or,** 60 rue Garneau, bursts with culinary excellence—$3.30 will win you a salmon sandwich and $1.60 a golden baguette here (692-2488; open daily 7am-9pm). Some restaurants do not have non-smoking sections.

■ **Le Diable aux Anges,** 28 Boul. Champlain & 39 Petit Champlain (692-4674). This great cafe/bistro has a number of traditional *Québecois* dishes that are both filling and delicious. Breakfast is the best value, with many items offered a la carte. If you're up to it, try the *Oeuf Gaspesiene* ($10), an English muffin topped with smoked salmon, poached egg, and hollandaise sauce, with herbed potatoes, fruit, and beans. The friendly staff serves up a delicious variety of both local and continental dishes ($10-20). Le Diable is a must for any visitor wishing to excite the taste buds. Open 9am-11pm.

**Le Café Buade,** 31 rue Buade (692-3909), is renowned for its succulent prime rib, though it's pricey ($16-19). For those short on money, breakfast (specials for $4) and lunch specials ($11) are large and delicious. Open daily 7am-midnight.

**Le Cochon Dingue,** 46 bd. Champlain (692-2013), serves a delectable Chocolate Pear Pie ($4). The food ain't bad, either. Open June-Aug. M-Th 7am-midnight, F 7am-1am, Sa-Su 8am-1am; Sept.-May M-F 7am-11pm, Sa-Su 8am-11pm.

**La Fleur de Lotus,** 38 Côte de la Fabrique (692-4286), across from the Hôtel de Ville. Cheerful and unpretentious. Thai, Cambodian, Vietnamese, and Japanese dishes $9-14, soups for $3. Open M-F 11am-10:30pm, Sa-Su 5-11pm.

**Chez Temporel,** 25 rue Couillard (694-1813). Stay off the tourist path but remain within your budget at this genuine *café québecois,* discreetly tucked in a side alley off rue St-Jean, near the Auberge de la Paix. Besides the usual café staples (sandwiches around $7, complete dinners $17-20), it offers exotic spirits ($4.50). Open daily 7am-2am.

**Restaurant Liban,** 23 rue d'Auteuil (694-1888), off rue St-Jean. Great café for lunch or a late-night bite. Tabouleh and hummus plates $3.50, both with pita bread. Excellent falafel ($4.50) and baklava ($2). Open daily 9am-4:30am.

# ◆ SIGHTS

**INSIDE THE WALLS.** Confined within walls, Vieux Québec (Old City) contains most of the city's historic attractions. Monuments are clearly marked and explained; still, you'll get more out of the town if you consult the *Greater Québec Area Tourist Guide,* which contains a walking tour of the Old City (available from all tourist offices; see **Practical Information,** above). It takes 1-2 days to explore Vieux Québec, but you'll learn more than on a bus tours. The **Fortifications of Québec,** 100 rue St-Louis, is a 3mi. rampart surrounding *Vieu Québec.*

Climbing to the top of **Cap Diamant** (Cape Diamond) for a view of the city is a good way to orient oneself. Take Terrasse Dufferin to the Promenade des Gouverneurs. Just north is the **Citadel,** the largest North American fortification still guarded by troops—who knows why? Don't attack it. Visitors can witness the **changing of the guard** at 10am and the **beating of the retreat** at 7pm. *(694-2815. Open daily Apr. to mid-May 10am-4pm; mid-May to mid-June 9am-5pm; mid-June to Aug. 9am-6pm; Sept. 9am-4pm; Oct. 10am-3pm. $5.50, seniors $4, under 18 $3.)*

The **Parc des Champs-de-Bataille** or **Plains of Abraham,** located adjacent to the Citadel along Ave. George-VI, can be reached from Grande Allee. The interpretation center has exhibits on the history of the battlefields, where French forces under Montcalm fell to the British under Gen. Wolfe in 1759. *(648-4071. Open daily mid-May* *to early Sept. 10am-5:30pm; call for times during the rest of the year.)* Located on the premises of the Battlefields Park, the **Musée du Québec** houses interesting paintings and other Quebecois works of art. *(646-3330. Open daily June-Aug. 10am-5:45pm. Call during the rest of the year. $5.75, students $2.75, seniors $4.75.)*

The **Samuel de Champlain Monument** is located near the Chateau Frontenac along the Terrasse Dufferin. The Terrasse itself is a pedestrian boardwalk running along the cliffs overlooking the St. Lawrence and the surrounding region. The **Château Frontenac** is perhaps the most recognizable structure in this city. It is thought to be the most photographed hotel in the world, which isn't surprising given its beautiful architecture highlighted by green copper roofs. The building, which can be seen from virtually anywhere in Vieux Québec, provides tours of its opulence. Throughout the building visitors can see evidence of its place in history with photographs of famous visitors lining the walls. JFK stayed here, and allied leaders conferenced here twice during World War II. *(1 rue des Carrieres. 692-3861 or 691-2166. Daily tours leave hourly 10am-6pm from mid-May to mid-Oct.; during the rest of the year, tours are Sa-Su only from 12:30pm-5pm; reservations highly recommended. $6, seniors $5, under 16 $3.50.)*

**Place d'Armes,** between rue St. Louis and rue Ste. Anne, is a popular gathering point for horse drawn carriages known as *caleches*. These elegant forms of transportation should be observed rather than experienced as a short tour of the Old City will run you upwards of $50 per person. On a less expensive note, **local artists** display their products from May to Oct. along rue du Tresor, a narrow alley running between rue Ste. Anne and rue De Buade. Hand-painted renditions of the city's hotspots can be purchased for less than $10.

At rue De Buade and rue Ste. Famille is the **Notre-Dame de Québec Basilica.** The cathedral is one of the oldest in North America, and is ornately decorated with stained glass and valuable works of art. The Basilica is host to a fantastic light show, the **"Act of Faith."** The 45min. shows relay the history of the church. *(694-0665. Open daily 9:30am-4:30pm. Free. Shows daily May-Oct.; times vary. $7.50.)* The **Musée de l'Amerique Francaise,** just down the street from the Basilica, is an excellent museum whose exhibits recount the details of Francophone settlement in North America. The museum is located on the grounds of the **Quebec Seminary,** which was established in 1663. Anyone interested in Quebecois history will find the stories contained within this museum informative and evocative. *(9 rue de l'Universite. 692-2843. Open Tu-Su 10am-5pm. $3 adults, students and seniors $2.)* More history can be absorbed at the **Quebec Experience,** which presents a light and sound presentation of Quebec's heritage from its first settlers through modern times. *(694-4000. Open daily mid-May to mid-Oct. 10am-10pm; off-season, M-Th and Su 10am-5pm, F-Sa 10am-10pm. $6.75, students and seniors $4.75.)*

The **Musée du Fort,** near the information center, presents a corny sound and light show that narrates the history of Quebec City and the battles that were fought over it from 1629 until 1775. *(10 rue Ste-Anne. 692-1759. Open daily 10am-7pm in summer; hours for other months vary; $6.25, students $4, seniors $5.25.)* The **Funiculaire** will carry passengers from Upper-Town to Place Royal and the Quartier Petit-Champlain for $1. *(692-1132. Open 7:30am-midnight.)*

**PLACE-ROYALE AND QUARTIER PETIT-CHAMPLAIN. Rue du Petit-Champlain**, is the oldest street in North America. Along either side of this narrow passageway, modern visitors will find a host of cafes, craft shops, trendy boutiques, and restaurants. The **Cafe-Theater Le Petit Champlain** presents *Quebecois* music, singing, and theater. *(68 rue du Petit-Champlain. 692-2631. Call for schedules.)*

**Place-Royale** itself can be reached quickly by taking rue Sous-le-Fort from the bottom of the Funiculaire. Place-Royale is home to the oldest permanent European settlement in Canada, dating from 1608. The **Place-Royale Information Center** provides free tours of this historic district. *(643-6631. Open 10am-5pm.)* **L'Eglise Notre-Dame-des-Victoires** is the oldest church in Canada and dates back to 1688. *(32 rue Sous-le-Fort. 692-1650. open May to mid-Oct. 9:30am-4:30pm, rest of the year 10am-4:30pm. Free admission and tours.)*

The **Musee de la Civilisation** celebrates Québec's past, present, and future, with tours in English and French. It can be reached easily by walking down rue Sous-le-Fort at the bottom of the funiculaire, turning left onto rue St. Pierre, then right onto Marche-Finlay until reaching rue Dalhousie. *(85 rue Dalhousie. 643-2158. Open late June to early Sept. 10am-7pm; off-season Tu-Su 10am-5pm. $7, students $4, seniors $6.)*

**PARLIAMENT HILL.** The **Assemblee Nationale,** at Grande Allee and Ave. Honore-Mercier, is located just outside the wall of the city. Finished in 1886, the building was designed in the style of Loius XIII. Lively debates can be observed from the visitors' gallery, and both English and French-speakers have recourse to simultaneous translation earphones. *(643-7239. Open late June to early Sept. M-F 9am-4:30pm, Sa-Su 10am-4:30pm; hours vary during rest of year. 30min. tours are free, but wise visitors will call in advance to hold a spot.)* The **Capital Observatory,** just off Grande Allee, offers breathtaking views of the city from the highest observing place in town. *(1037 rue De La Chevrotiere. 644-9841. Open July-Aug. 10am-10pm, June and Sept. 10am-7pm, Oct.-May 10am-5pm. $4, students and senior $3.)*

**GREATER QUEBEC AREA.** The **Aquarium du Québec,** is accessible by bus #25 and is well worth the effort to get there. *(1675 ave. des Hotels. 659-5264. Open 9am-5pm. $9.50, students $6, seniors $8.50, children $4.50.)*

## ♫ ENTERTAINMENT AND NIGHTLIFE

The raucous **Winter Carnival** breaks the tedium of northern winters and lifts spirits running from Jan. 28-Feb. 13, 2000 (626-3716); the **Summer Festival** boasts a number of free outdoor concerts in mid-July (692-4540). Throughout the summer, the **Plein Art** exhibition floods the Pigeonnier on Grande-Allée with arts and crafts (694-0260). **Les nuits Black,** Québec's burgeoning jazz festival, bebops the city for 2 weeks in late June. But the most festive day of the year is June 24, **la Fête nationale du Québec** (St-Jean-Baptiste Day), a celebration of *québecois* culture with free concerts, a bonfire, fireworks, and 5 million roaring drunk acolytes of John the Baptist (640-0799).

The Grande Allée's many restaurants are interspersed with *Bar Discothèques,* where 20-something crowds gather. **Chez Dagobert,** 600 Grande Allée, saturates its 2 dance floors with plentiful food and drink. It is *the* place to be seen. (522-0393. No cover. Outside bar open daily 3pm-3am, inside club 10pm-3am.) Down the block at **O'Zone,** 570 Grande Allée, the atmosphere is slower and creates a more pub-like club (529-7932; open M-Th and Su 1pm-3am, F-Sa 11am-3am).

Québec City's young, visible punk contingent clusters around rue St-Jean. **La Fourmi Atomik,** 33 rue d'Auteuil, features underground rock, with M reggae and W New Wave (694-1473; 18+; no cover; open daily 1pm-3am; Oct.-May 2pm-3am). At **L'Ostradamus,** 29 rue Couillard, you can listen to live jazz and eavesdrop on deep discourse in a smoke-drenched pseudo-spiritual ambience with artsy Thai decor (694-9560; no cover; open daily 9pm-3am). A more traditional Québec evening awaits at **Les Yeux Bleux,** 1117½ rue St-Jean, a local favorite where *chansonniers* perform nightly (694-9118; no cover; open daily 8pm-3am). The gay scene in Québec City is neither huge nor hard to find. **Le Ballon Rouge,** 811 St-Jean, several blocks beyond the walls of the Old City, is a popular dance club where dimly lit pool tables coexist with neon rainbows, and tight clothing is essential (647-9227; no cover; open daily 5pm-3am).

## SIGHTS NEAR QUÉBEC CITY

**Ile-d'Orléans** on the St-Laurent is untouched by Québec City's public transport system, but its proximity to Québec (about 10km downstream) makes it an ideal side trip by car or bike. Take Autoroute 440 Est, and cross over the only bridge leading to the island (Pont de l'Ile). A tour of the island covers 64km. Originally called *Ile de Bacchus* because of the multitudinous wild grapes fermenting here, the Ile-d'Orléans remains a sparsely populated retreat of small villages and endless strawberry fields. The **Manoir Mauvide-Genest,** in St-Jean, dating from 1734, is a private museum flaunting crafts and traditional colonial furniture. *(1451, ch. Royal. 829-2630. Open June to mid-Oct. daily 10am-5pm. $4, students and seniors $2.50, under 14 $2.)*

Exiting Ile-d'Orléans, turn right (east) onto Hwy. 138 (bd. Ste-Anne) to view the splendid **Chute Montmorency** (Montmorency Falls), which are substantially taller than Niagara Falls. In winter, vapors from the falls freeze completely to form a frozen shadow of the running falls. About 20km along Hwy. 138 lies **Ste-Anne-de-Beaupré** (Orlean Express buses link it to Québec City for $5). This small town's entire *raison d'être* is the famous **Basilique Ste-Anne-de-Beaupré.** *(10018 ave. Royale. 827-3781. Open daily early May to mid-Sept. 6am-9:30pm.)* Since 1658, this double-spired basilica has contained a miraculous statue and the alleged forearm bone of St. Anne (mother of the Virgin Mary). Every year, more than 1 million pilgrims come here in the hopes that their prayers will be answered—legend has it that some have been quite successful. In the winter (Nov.-Apr.), Ste-Anne has some of the best skiing in the province (lift tickets $41 per day). Contact **Parc du Mont Ste-Anne,** which has a 625m/2050 ft. vertical drop and night skiing to boot. *(P.O. Box 400. 827-4561), Beaupré, G0A IE0.)* You will also find a **gondola,** which climbs to 800m, affording a fabulous view of the St-Laurent valley. *(800-463-1568. Runs daily in summer 10am-4:45pm; in ski season 10am-9pm. $9, ages 14-20 $7, seniors and ages 7-13 $5.)*

# ONTARIO

Claimed by French explorer Samuel de Champlain in 1613, Ontario soon attracted hordes of Scottish and Irish immigrants fleeing hostility and famine. These immigrants asserted control in 1763 during the Seven Years' War, after a takeover of New France. Twenty years later, a flood of Loyalist emigres from the newly formed United States streamed into the province, fortifying its Anglo character. Now a political counterbalance to French Québec, this populous central province raises the ire of peripheral regions of Canada due to its high concentration of power and wealth. In the south, world-class Toronto shines—multicultural, enormous, vibrant, clean, and generally safe. Yuppified suburbs, an occasional college town, and farms surround this sprawling metropolis. In the east, the national capital Ottawa sits on Ontario's border with Québec. To the north, layers of cottage country and ski resorts give way to a pristine wilderness that is as much French and Native Canadian as it is British.

## ⛶ PRACTICAL INFORMATION

**Capital:** Toronto.

**Visitor Info: Customer Service Branch** of the **Ontario Ministry of Culture, Tourism, and Recreation** (800-668-2746, 24hr. automated information). Send written requests to **Tourism Ontario,** 1 Concord Gate, 9th fl., Dawn Mills, ON M3C 3NC.

**Drinking Age:** 19. **Postal Abbreviation:** ON. **Sales Tax:** 8%; 5% on accommodations; 7% GST.

# TORONTO

Once a prim and proper Victorian city where even window-shopping was prohibited on the Sabbath, the city is now dubbed the world's most multicultural by the United Nations. Go figure. Toronto has spent millions in recent decades on spectacular public works projects: the world's tallest "free-standing" structure (the CN tower), the biggest retractable roof (the Sky Dome), outstanding lakefront development, and sponsorship of arts and museums. Cosmetically, (not culturally) Toronto's skyscrapers and neatly gridded streets aspire to the urban grandeur of New York, which draws Hollywood producers seeking to make a New York movie at Toronto prices. But New York it is not; one crew, after dirtying a street to make it look more like an "American" ave., went on coffee break and returned to find their set spotless again, swept by the vigilant city maintenance department.

## ✴ ORIENTATION

The city maps available at info booths only cover downtown. For an extended stay or travel outside the city center, a better bet is to buy the orangish *Downtown and Metro Toronto Visitor's Map Guide* from a drug store or tourist shop ($2.50). The *Ride Guide*, free at all TTC stations and tourism info booths (see **Practical Information**, below), explicates metro area subway and bus routes.

Toronto's streets lie in a grid pattern. Addresses on north-south streets increase toward the north, away from Lake Ontario. **Yonge St.** is the main north-south route, dividing the city and the streets perpendicular to it into east and west. Numbering for both sides starts at Yonge St. and increases as you move away in either direction. West of Yonge St., the main arteries are **Bay St., University Ave., Spadina Ave., and Bathurst St.** The major east-west routes include, from the water north, **Front St., Queen St., Dundas St., College St., Bloor St.,** and **Eglington St.**

Avoid rush hour (4-7pm). A flashing green light means that you can go straight or turn left freely—the opposing traffic has a red light. **Parking** on the street is hard to find and usually carries a 1hr. limit, except on Su, when street spaces are free and abundant. You can park for free at night, but your car must be gone by 7-8am. Day parking generally costs inbound daytrippers $3-4 at outlying subway stations; parking overnight at the subway stations is prohibited. Parking lots within the city run at least $12 for 24hr. (7am-7pm), although some all-day lots downtown on King St. sell unguarded spots for $4-6. Free, unmetered parking is available in **Rosedale**, a residential neighborhood northeast of Bloor and Sherbourne St., about 1½mi. from downtown. To combat transportation problems, city officials enforce traffic and parking regulations zealously—don't tempt them. Towing is a common occurrence, even for locals; the **police's non-emergency number** (416-808-2222) has an answering system to help you find your car's new lot.

## ▨ PRACTICAL INFORMATION

**Airport: Pearson International** (247-7678), about 20km west of Toronto via Hwy. 401. Take bus #58A west from Lawrence W. subway. **Pacific Western Transportation** (905-564-6333) runs buses every 20min. to downtown hotels ($12.50, round-trip $21.50) and every 40min. to Yorkdale ($7.25), York Mills ($8.30), and Islington ($6.75) subway stations (all buses 5am-midnight). **Hotel Airporter** (798-2424) zips to select airport hotels ($12, round-trip $20).

**Trains:** All trains chug from **Union Station,** 65 Front St. (366-8411), at Bay and York. Subway: Union. **VIA Rail** (366-8411) cannonballs to Montréal (5½hr., 6 per day, $89); Windsor (4hr., 4-5 per day, $67); New York City (12hr., 1 per day, $86); and Chicago (11hr., 6 per week, $129). Ticket office open M-Sa 6:45am-9:30pm; Su 8am-8:30pm; station open daily 6am-midnight.

**Buses: Trentway-Wagar** (393-7911) and **Greyhound** (367-8747) operate from 610 Bay St., just north of Dundas St. Subway: St. Patrick or Dundas. Trentway-Wagar has service to Montréal (7hr., 5-6 per day, $69). Greyhound goes to Ottawa (5½-7hr., 9-11 per day, $54); Calgary (49hr., 3 per day, $256); Vancouver (2½ days, 3 per day, $300), and New York City (11hr., 5 per day, $95). Ticket office open daily 5am-1am.

**Ferries: Toronto Island Ferry Service** (392-8194, recording 392-8193). Ferries to Centre Island, Wards Island, and Hanlans Point leave from Bay St. Ferry Dock at the foot of Bay St. Service daily every 30min. 8am-midnight. Round-trip $4; seniors, students, and ages 15-19 $2; under 15 $1.

**Public Transit: Toronto Transit Commission (TTC),** 393-4000. A network of 2 subway lines and numerous bus and streetcar routes. After dark, buses are required to stop anywhere along a route at a female passenger's request. Subway operates approximately 6am-2:25am; then buses cover subway routes. Fare $2 (5 tokens $8), seniors with ID $1.35, under 13 50¢ (10 for $4). M-Sa 1-day travel pass $6.50. Su and holidays, families receive unlimited travel for $6.50. Free transfers among subway, buses, and streetcars, but only at stations.

EASTERN CANADA

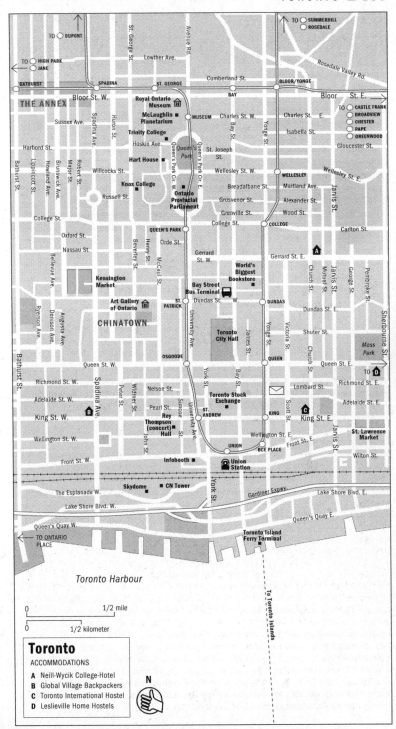

## Toronto

ACCOMMODATIONS

A  Neill-Wycik College-Hotel
B  Global Village Backpackers
C  Toronto International Hostel
D  Leslieville Home Hostels

*Toronto Harbour*

0          1/2 mile
0          1/2 kilometer

N

Taxis: **Co-op Cabs,** 504-2667.

Car Rental: **Wheels 4 Rent,** 77 Nassau St. (585-7782). Subway: Bathurst or College. $29 per day with at least 100km free, 9¢ each additional km. Must be 21+. Ages 23-25 pay $3 per day surcharge, ages 21-23 $5. Open M-F 8am-6pm, Sa 9am-4pm.

Driver/Rider Service: **Allo-Stop,** 5 Yorkville Ave. (975-9305). Subway: Bloor/Young. Matches riders with drivers. Year-round membership for passengers $6, for drivers $7. To: Ottawa ($20), Montréal ($26), Québec City ($41), and New York ($40). Open M-W 9am-5pm, Th-F 9am-7pm, Sa-Su 10am-5pm.

Jump-On/Jump-Off Service: **Moose Travel Co. Ltd.** (905-471-8687, 800-461-8585, or 888-816-6673). Hop on and off at dozens of destinations throughout Eastern Canada at your own convenience. 3-6 days of travel time can spread over 6 months. Offers 3 routes through Ontario and Quebec ($180-299).

Bike Rental: **Brown's Sports and Bike Rental,** 2447 Bloor St. W. (763-4176). $18 per day, $37 per weekend, $50 per week. $200 deposit or credit card required. Open M-W 9:30am-6pm, Th-F 9:30am-8pm, Sa 9:30am-5:30pm.

Visitor Info: The **Metropolitan Toronto Convention and Visitors Association (MTCVA),** 207 Queens Quay W. (203-2500 or 800-363-1990), mails out info and answers questions by phone. For in-person assistance, head to the **Info T.O.,** 255 Front St. W., at the Metro Toronto Convention Centre. Open daily 9am-5pm.

Student Travel Office: **Travel CUTS,** 187 College St. (979-2406), just west of University Ave. Subway: Queen's Park. Other office at 74 Gerrard St. E. (977-0441). Subway: College. Both open M and Th-F 9am-5pm, Tu 9:30am-5pm, W 9am-7pm, Sa 11am-3pm.

Currency Exchange: **Toronto Currency Exchange,** 363 Yonge St. (598-3769), at Dundas St., offers the best rates around. Open daily 10am-8pm. Also at 2 Walton St. (599-5821). Open daily 8:30am-5:30pm. **Royal Bank of Canada,** 200 Bay St. Plaza (info 800-769-2511, foreign exchange 974-5535), exchanges around the city. **Money Mart,** 688 Yonge St. (924-1000), has 24hr. service and some fees. Subway: Bloor/Yonge.

Hotlines: **Rape Crisis,** 597-8808. **Services for the Disabled, Info Ability** 800-665-9092. **Toronto Gay and Lesbian Phone Line,** 964-6600. Open M-F 7-10pm.

Post Office: Adelaide Station, 31 Adelaide St. E. (214-2353 or 214-2352). Subway: King. Open M-F 8am-5:45pm. **Postal Code:** M5C 1J0. **Area Code:** 416 (city), 905 (outskirts). In text, 416 unless noted otherwise.

# NEIGHBORHOODS

Downtown Toronto splits into many distinctive and decentralized neighborhoods. Thanks to zoning regulations that require developers to include housing and retail space in commercial construction, many people live downtown. **Chinatown** centers on Dundas St. W. between Bay St. and Spadina Ave. Formerly the Jewish market of the 1920s, **Kensington Market,** on Kensington Ave., Augusta Ave., and the western half of Baldwin St., is now a largely Portuguese neighborhood with many good restaurants, vintage clothing shops, and an outdoor bazaar. A strip of old factories, stores, and warehouses on **Queen St. W.,** from University Ave. to Bathurst St., contains a fun mix of shopping. The ivy-covered Gothic buildings and magnificent quadrangles of the **University of Toronto** occupy about 200 acres in the middle of downtown. The law-school cult flick *The Paper Chase* was filmed here because the campus supposedly looked more Ivy League than Harvard, where the movie was set. **The Annex,** Bloor St. W. at the Spadina subway, has an artistic ambiance and an excellent range of budget restaurants (see **Food,** below). Afterwards, hit the nightclubs. **Yorkville,** just north of Bloor between Yonge St. and Avenue Rd., was once the crumbling communal home of flower children and folk guitarists. **Cabbagetown,** just east of Yonge St., bounded by Gerrard St. E., Wellesley, and Sumach St., takes its name from the Irish immigrants who used to plant the vegetable in their yards. Today, professionals and the only crowing rooster in the city inhabit the renowned Victorian houses. The **Gay and Lesbian Village,** located around Church and Wellesley St., offers fine outdoor cafes.

On Front St. between Sherbourne and Yonge St., the **Theater District** supports enough venues to whet any cultural hunger. Music, food, ferry rides, dance companies, and art all dock at the **Harborfront** (973-3000), on Queen's Quay W. from York to Bathurst St., on the lake. The 3 main **Toronto Islands,** accessible by ferry (see **Practical Information,** above), offer beaches, bike rentals, and an amusement park. East from the harbor, the beaches along and south of Queen's St. E., between Woodbine and Victoria, boast a popular boardwalk. Five km east of the city center, rugged **Scarborough Bluffs,** a 16km section of cliffs, rises from the lakeshore.

Three more ethnic enclaves lie 15-30min. from downtown by public transit. **Corso Italia** surrounds St. Clair W. at Dufferin St.; take the subway to St. Clair W. and bus #512 west. **Little India** is at Gerrard St. E. and Coxwell; ride the subway to Coxwell, then take bus #22 south to the second Gerard St. stop. Better known as **"the Danforth," Greektown** (subway: Pape) is on Danforth Ave. at Pape Ave.

# ¶ ACCOMMODATIONS

Cut-rate hotels concentrate around Jarvis and Gerrard St. The University of Toronto provides cheap sleep for budget travelers; contact the **U of Toronto Housing Service,** 214 College St., at St. George St., for $20-45 rooms (978-8045; open M-F 8:45am-4:30pm; reservations recommended). The **Downtown Association of Bed and Breakfast Guest Houses** (483-8032) places guests in renovated Victorian homes (singles $50-75; doubles $75-130). Because it is difficult to regulate these registries, visit a B&B before you commit.

**Global Village Backpackers,** 460 King St. W. (703-8540 or 888-844-7875). Subway: St. Andrew. A state-of-the-art backpacker support system. 195 beds in the centrally located, newly renovated former Spadina Hotel. Travelers convene at the cool bar inside and on the outdoor patio. Lockers available. Kitchen, laundry, in-house Travel CUTS branch. Dorms $20; doubles $45 Oct.-Apr., $50 May-Sept. Internet use available. Reception 24hr. 10% discount for ISIC or HI members.

**Neill-Wycik College Hotel,** 96 Gerrard St. E. (977-2320 or 800-268-4358). Subway: College. Small, clean rooms, some with beautiful views of the city. Kitchen on every floor. Laundry, roof deck, sauna. Singles $39; doubles $56. Family rooms and lockers available. Check-in after 4pm; check-out 10am. Students, seniors, and HI members get a 20% discount. Open early May to late Aug.

**Toronto International Hostel (HI-C),** 76 Church St. (971-4440, 363-4921, or 800-668-4487), at King. Subway: Dundas. Newly relocated hostel in a great downtown location. Kitchen, laundry facilities, and a lounge. Reception 24hr. Dorm rooms $19, nonmembers $23. Linen $2. Check-in after noon, check-out 11am. Reservations recommended in the summer. Additional location June-Aug. at 76 Mutual St.

**Knox College,** 59 St. George St. (978-0168; call M-F 10am-5pm). Subway: Queen's Park or St. George. In the heart of campus, Canada's Presbyterian Seminary offers huge rooms with wooden floors around an idyllic courtyard. The movie *Good Will Hunting* used Knox rooms to simulate the interiors of Harvard and MIT. Singles $33, students $30; doubles $45. Reserve rooms at least 3 weeks in advance. Open June-Aug.

**YWCA-Woodlawn Residence,** 80 Woodlawn Ave. E. (923-8454), off Yonge St. Subway: Summerhill. 144 rooms for women only, in a nice neighborhood. Breakfast, kitchen, TV lounges, and laundry facilities. Small, neat singles $47; doubles $62; private bath available. Beds in basement dormitory $20. 10% senior discount. Linen $3 deposit. Reception M-F 7:30am-11:30pm, Sa-Su 7:30am-7:30pm.

**Indian Line Tourist Campground,** 7625 Finch Ave. W. (905-678-1233 or 1-800-304-9728; off-season 661-6600, ext. 203), at Darcel Ave. Follow Hwy. 427 north to Finch Ave. and go west, or take the subway to Yorkdale and then a 40min. bus ride. The closest campground (30min.) to metropolitan Toronto, near Pearson Airport. Showers, laundry, pool, playground. Sites $19, with hookup $24. Gatehouse open 8am-midnight. Open mid-May to early Oct. Reservations recommended July-Aug.

**FOOD**

An immigration surge has made Toronto a haven for international food, with over 5000 restaurants squeezed into the metropolitan area. **Village by the Grange**, at McCaul and Dundas near the Art Gallery of Ontario, is a vast collection of super-cheap restaurants and vendors—Chinese, Thai, Middle Eastern, you name it (generally open 11am-7pm). "L.L.B.O." posted on the window of a restaurant means that it has a liquor license. The cheapest options are hot-dog stands (offerings range from basic to vegetarian to venison $2-3) that line most main streets in Toronto. Some of the standouts can be found on **Bloor St. W.** and in **Chinatown.** For fresh produce, go to **Kensington Market** or the **St. Lawrence Market** at King St. E. and Sherbourne, 6 blocks east of the King subway stop.

### THE ANNEX

**Future Bakery & Café,** 483 Bloor St. W. (922-5875). Subway: Spadina. Fresh baked cakes ($4.25) and pastries charge up the young student crowd by day, and beer ($4) on the street corner patio winds them down after dark. Open daily 7:30am-2am.

**Sushi on Bloor,** 515 Bloor St. W (516-3456). Subway: Bathurst. This friendly, well-lit joint is filled with hipsters scarfing down fresh and reasonably priced sushi (6 pieces $5-6.50), including lunch ($4.99) and dinner ($7.50) specials. Open daily noon-11pm.

**Country Style Hungarian Restaurant,** 450 Bloor St. W. (537-1745). Subway: Spadina. Hearty stews, soups, and casseroles. Meals come in small (more than enough) and large (huge) portions. Schnitzel $9.50. Entrees $4-10. Open daily 11am-10pm.

**Serra,** 378 Bloor St. W. (922-6999). Subway: Spadina. A quiet, Cal-Ital oasis amid the bustle of the Annex. Angel hair and grilled chicken ($11). Open daily noon-11pm.

### CHINATOWN AND KENSINGTON

**Saigon Palace,** 454 Spadina Ave. (968-1623), at College St. Subway: Spadina. Popular with locals. Great spring rolls. Beef, chicken, or vegetable dishes over rice or noodles $4-8. Open M-Th 9am-10pm, F-Sa 9am-11pm.

**Peter's Chung King Restaurant,** (928-2936). Subway: Spadina. A picture of Chris de Burgh (of "Lady in Red" fame) adorns the window, with Chris' note proclaiming "Wonderful Food!" He's not the only one who thinks so: Peter's is consistently named one of Toronto's best Chinese restaurants. Garlic shrimp ($8.95), soy sauteed green beans ($6.95). Open daily noon-10pm.

### THEATER/ST. LAWRENCE DISTRICT

**Mövenpick Marché** (366-8986), in the BCE Place at Yonge and Front St. Probably the only restaurant that requires a map. Browse through and pick a meal from the 14 culinary stations, including bakery, bar, pasta, seafood, salad, and grill. Yuppie extravagance at its finest and cheapest. Entrees run $5-8. Open daily 7:30am-2am.

**Shopsy's,** 33 Yonge St. (365-3333), at Front St. 1 block from Union Station, and other locations at 284A King St. W. (599-5464) and 1535 Yonge St. (967-5252). The definitive Toronto deli. 300 seats, snappy service. Shopsy's Hot Dog $3.79. Open M-W 6:30am-11pm, Th-F 7am-midnight, Sa 8am-midnight, Su 8am-10pm.

**Penelope,** 6 Front St. E. (351-9393). Subway: St. Andrew. Generous portions of Greek fare in the middle of the financial district. Souvlaki ($10-11). Open daily 10am-10pm.

### THE DANFORTH

**Mr. Greek,** 568 Danforth Ave. (461-5470), at Carlaw. Subway: Pape. A friendly, bustling cafe serving shish kebabs, salads, and wine amidst Greek music. Family atmosphere, fast service. Gyros or souvlaki $4. Open Su-Th 10am-1am, F-Sa until 4am.

■ **SIGHTS**

A walk through the city's neighborhoods can be one of the most rewarding (and cheapest) activities in Toronto. Signs and streetside conversations change languages while gustatory aromas waft through the air. For an organized expedition, the **Royal Ontario Museum** leads 7 free **walking tours**. *(586-5797. Tours June-Sept. W 6pm, Su 2pm. Destinations and meeting places vary; call for specific info.)* The **University of Toronto** conducts free 1hr. walking tours of Canada's largest university and alma mater of David Letterman's band leader, Paul Schaffer. Tours meet at the Nona MacDonald Visitor's Center at King's College Circle. *(978-5000. Tours June-Aug. M-F 10:30am, 1, and 2:30pm.)* Other free trips within the city revolve around architectural themes, sculptures, or ghost haunts.

Toronto's **CN Tower** stands as the world's tallest free-standing structure, a colossal beast hovering over the downtown region and visible from nearly every corner of the city. What separates this structure from all the other tall ones in all the other cities is its glass floor. *(360-8500. Subway: Union. Open daily 9am-11pm. $15, seniors $13, ages 4-12 $11, $3.50 more for the Sky Pod.)* The curving twin towers and 2-story rotunda of **City Hall** is at Queen and Bay St. between the Osgoode and Queen subway stops; brochures for self-guided tours are available *(338-0338, open M-F 8:30am-4:30pm).* In front of City Hall, **Nathan Phillips Sq.** is home to a reflecting pool (which becomes a skating rink in winter) and numerous events, including live music every W. *(June to early Oct. noon-2pm.)* The **Events Hotline** *(392-0458)* knows all about it. A few blocks away, the **Toronto Stock Exchange,** on York between Adelaide St. W. and King St. W., trades over $400 billion yearly as Canada's leading stock exchange. *(2 First Canadian Pl. 947-4676. Open M-F 9am-4:30pm. $5, students and seniors $3.)* The Ontario government legislates in the **Provincial Parliament Buildings,** at Queen's Park in the city center. *(325-7500. Subway: Queen's Park. Building open May-early Sept. M-F 8:30am-5pm, Sa-Su 9am-4pm; chambers close 4:30pm. Call ahead for Parliamentary schedule. Free gallery passes available at south basement door when the house is in session.)* Straight out of a fairy tale, the 98-room **Casa Loma,** Davenport Rd. at 1 Austin Terr., near Spadina a few blocks north of the Dupont subway stop, is a classic tourist attraction. Secret passageways and an underground tunnel add to the magic of the only turreted castle in North America. *(923-1171 or 923-1172. Open daily 9:30am-4pm. $9, seniors and ages 14-17 $5.50, ages 4-13 $5.)* A taste of 19th-century Toronto sits next door at the **Spadina House,** a 6-acre estate relic from 1866. *(285 Spadina Rd. 392-6910. Open July-Aug. Tu-Su noon-4pm. $5, students and seniors $3.25, ages 4-13 $3.)*

Check out an autopsy of a mummified Egyptian and a frieze of the Persian sun god Mithra slaying a bull at the **Royal Ontario Museum (ROM),** which houses artifacts from ancient civilizations (Greek, Chinese, and Egyptian), a bat cave (not *the* Bat Cave), and a giant T-rex. *(100 Queen's Park. 586-5549. Subway: Museum. Open M and W-Sa 10am-6pm, Tu 10am-8pm, Su 11am-6pm. $15, seniors, students, and ages 5-14 $6. Tu 4:30-8pm "pay what you can.")* Across the street, the **George R. Gardiner Museum of Ceramic Art** traces the history of ceramics with a collection dating back to the Renaissance. *(111 Queen's Park. 586-8080. Open M-F 10am-7pm, Sa 10am-5pm, Su 11am-5pm; call for winter hours. $5; students, seniors, and children $3. Free first Tu of every month.)* A shoe-shaped glass-and-stone edifice houses the **Bata Shoe Museum.** The diverse collection focuses on the role of footwear in culture, religion, and gender issues in culture. *(327 Bloor St. W. 979-7799. Subway: St. George. Open Tu-W and F-Sa 10am-5pm, Th 10am-8pm, Su noon-5pm. $6, seniors and students $4, ages 5-14 $2, families $12; 1st Tu of every month free.)* The **Art Gallery of Ontario (AGO),** 3 blocks west of University Ave., houses an enormous collection of Western art from the Renaissance to the 1990s, concentrating on Canadian artists. *(317 Dundas St. W. 979-6648. Subway: St. Patrick. Open Tu and Th-F 11am-6pm, W 11am-8:30pm, Sa-Su 10am-5:30pm; early Sept. to late May W-Su 10am-5:30pm. $5 donation suggested.)*

Toronto crawls with **biking** and **hiking** trails. For a map of the trails, call **Metro-Parks** *(392-8186),* which has info on local facilities and activities. It might not be the Caribbean, but the **beaches** on the southeast end of Toronto now support a permanent community. A popular "vacationland," the **Toronto Islands Park,** on Centre Island, has a boardwalk, bathing beaches, canoe and bike rentals, and an amusement park. *(Open mid-May to early Sept.)* The park is located on a 4mi. strip of connected islands opposite downtown. Summer **ferries** leave from the Bay St. Ferry Dock. *(Info 392-8193. 15min. Round-trip $5, students and seniors $3, ages 2-14 $1.)*

EASTERN CANADA

**YOUR CHARIOT AWAITS...** If you find the subway crowded, but don't want to hail a cab, rickshaws will sweep you off your feet. Originally from Hong Kong, these human-drawn carriages have caught on all over Canada. In Toronto, companies like **Rickshaw Services of Toronto** (410-4593) will cart you through the city streets courtesy of other people's backs. Rates about $3 per block per person.

The **Ontario Science Center,** at Eglington Ave. E., presents more than 650 interactive exhibits, showcasing humanity's greatest innovations. *(770 Don Mills Rd. 696-3127. Museum open daily 10am-8pm; Sept.-June 10am-5pm. Omnimax shows every hr. on the hr. 11am-8pm; Sept.-June 11am-5pm. Museum $10, ages 13-17 and seniors $7, ages 5-12 46; with Omnimax film $15/$9.)* The **Metro Toronto Zoo,** Meadowvale Rd. off exit 389 on Hwy. 401, houses over 6600 animals in a 710-acre park that features sections representing the world's 7 geographic regions, and rare wildlife including a Komodo dragon and a Tasmanian devil. Take bus #86A from Kennedy Station. *(392-5900. Open daily mid-Oct. to mid-Mar. 9:30am-4:30pm; mid-Mar. to mid-May and early Sept. to mid-Oct. 9am-6pm; late May to early Sept. 9am-7:30pm. Last entry 1hr. before closing. $12, seniors and ages 12-17 $9, ages 4-11 $7. Parking $5.)*

♫ **ENTERTAINMENT**

The monthly *Where Toronto,* available free at tourism booths, drops the lowdown on arts and entertainment. **T.O. Tix** sells ½-price tickets on performance day at 208 Yonge St., north of Queen St. (subway: Queen) at Eaton's Centre (536-6468; open Tu-Sa noon-7:30pm; arrive before 11:45am for first dibs). **Ticketmaster** supplies tickets for many Toronto venues, although it has a hefty service charge (870-8000).

**Ontario Place,** 955 Lakeshore Blvd. W features cheap summer entertainment (314-9811, recording 314-9900). Top pop artists perform in the **Molson Amphitheater.** (260-5600. $17.50-50. Park open mid-May to early Sept. daily 10:30am-midnight. Call for events schedule. Ticketmaster handles tickets.) IMAX is shown in the **Cinesphere** (870-8000; $5, plus $10 gate admission; call for screening schedule).

**Roy Thomson Hall,** 60 Simcoe St., at King St. W., is both Toronto's premier concert hall and the home of the **Toronto Symphony Orchestra** from Sept. to June. Tickets ($19-50) are available at the box office or by phone. (593-4828. Box office: 872-4255. Subway: St. Andrews. Open M-F 10am-6pm, Sa noon-5pm, Su 3hr. before performances. Ask about discounts.) Rush tickets for the symphony ($10) are often available at the box office on concert days (M-F 11am, Sa 1pm). The same ticket office serves **Massey Hall,** Shuter St. (593-4828; subway: Queen), near Eaton Centre, a great hall for rock and folk concerts and musicals. Opera and ballet companies perform at **Hummingbird Centre,** 1 Front St. E., at Yonge. Rush tickets for the last row of orchestra seats go on sale at 11am (from $18). A limited number of half-price tickets are available for seniors and students. (393-7474 or 872-2262 for tickets. Ballet from $18, opera from $30. Box office open M-Sa 11am-6pm, or until 1hr. after curtain.) Next door, **St. Lawrence Centre,** 27 Front St. E., stages excellent drama and chamber music recitals in 2 different theaters. Ask for possible student and senior discounts. (366-7723. Box office open M-Sa 10am-6pm; in winter performance days 10am-8pm; non-performance days 10am-6pm.) **Canadian Stage** tames a slew of performances of summer Shakespeare amid the greenery of **High Park,** on Bloor St. W. at Parkside Dr. (box office 368-3110; subway: High Park; open M-F 10am-6pm). Year-round performances include new Canadian works and time-honored classics. Bring something to sit on, or perch yourself on the 45° slope that faces the stage ($5 donation requested; call for schedule).

Film fans choose the **Bloor Cinema,** 506 Bloor St. W. (532-6677), at Bathurst, or the **Cinématheque Ontario,** 317 Dundas St. W. (923-3456), at McCaul St.

Canada's answer to Disney is **Canada's Wonderland,** 9580 Jane St., 1hr. from downtown but accessible by public transit; take Vaughn Transit (905-832-8527) from the Richmond Hill area or the Go Bus (416-869-3200) from the Yorkdale or York Mills subway stations ($3.75 each way). Splash down water rides or try your stomach on the backwards, looping, and suspended roller coasters. (905-832-7000. Open late June to early Sept. daily 10am-10pm; open in fall Sa-Su, closing times vary. Water park open in summer daily 11am-8pm. $40, seniors and ages 3-6 $20.)

Groove to the rhythms of old and new talents—more than 1500 artists from 17 countries—at the 10-day **Du Maurier Ltd. Downtown Jazz Festival** (363-5200), at Ontario Place in late June. Also in June, the **Toronto International Dragon Boat Race Festival** (598-8945) continues a 2000-year-old Chinese tradition. The celebration includes traditional performances, foods, and free outdoor lunchtime concerts. From mid-Aug. through early Sept., the **Canadian National Exhibition (CNE),** the world's largest annual fair, brings an international carnival to Exhibition Place (393-6000; open daily 10am-midnight; $16, seniors $9, children $6, under 6 free).

From Apr. to Oct., the **Toronto Blue Jays** play ball at the **Sky Dome,** Front and Peter St. (341-1111, tickets 341-1234. Subway: Union, follow the signs. Tickets $4-28.) To get a behind-the-scenes look at the modern, commercialized Sky Dome, take the **tour.** (341-2770. Times vary. $9.50, seniors and under 16 $7.) For info on concerts and other Sky Dome events, call 341-3663. For info on the **Toronto Argonauts** of the Canadian Football League, who also take the field at the Skydome, call 341-5151. Hockey fans head for **The Air Canada Centre,** 40 Bay St. (815-5700; subway: Union), to see the knuckle-crackin' **Maple Leafs.** (Tickets $24-94.)

## 🎵 NIGHTLIFE

Toronto offers seemingly limitless selections of bars, pubs, dance clubs, and late-night cafes. Some of Toronto's clubs and pubs remain closed on Su because of liquor laws. The city shuts down alcohol distribution daily at 1am, so most clubs close down then. The most interesting new clubs are on trendy **Queen St. W., College St. W.,** and **Bloor St. W.** Two comprehensive free entertainment magazines, *Now* and *Eye,* come out every Th. The gay scene centers around **Wellesley** and **Church St.** For the scoop on Toronto's gay scene, pick up the free, bi-weekly *fab.*

### THE ANNEX
**▩ The James Joyce,** 386 Bloor St. (324-9400). Subway: Spadina. Splices the maple leaf and the clover with live Celtic music every night (no cover). Catch the Jays on their big screen and enjoy an all ages crowd. Open daily noon-2am.

**Lee's Palace,** 529 Bloor St. W. (532-1598), just east of the Bathurst subway stop. Crazy creature art depicts a rock 'n' roll frenzy. Live alternative music nightly downstairs; DJ dance club, the **Dance Cave,** swings upstairs. Pick up a calendar of bands. Box office opens 8pm, shows begin 10pm. Cover $3-12 downstairs; open M-Sa noon-2am. Cover after 10pm $4 upstairs; open daily 8pm-3am.

**The Madison,** 14 Madison Ave. (927-1722), at Bloor St. Subway: Spadina. Blonde wood, 2 pool rooms, 2 large patios, and 1 small patio attract students and yuppies. 21 beers on tap. Pints $4-6. Wings $9. Open daily 11am-2am.

**Las Iguanas,** 513 Bloor St. W (532-3360). Subway: Spadina. Irreverent faux-calfskin booths and kitschy margaritas ($4.70) with plastic lizards on the glass. Su is wing night, M means half-price fajitas. Open M-F 11:30am-2am, Sa-Su 10:30am-2am.

### DOWNTOWN
**▩ Second City,** 56 Blue Jays Way (343-0011 or 888-263-4485), at Wellington St., just north of the Sky Dome. Subway: Union. One of North America's wackiest, most creative comedy clubs. Spawned comics Dan Akroyd, John Candy, Martin Short, Mike Myers, and a hit TV show (SCTV). Free improv sessions M-Th. 9:45pm and Sa midnight. Free F midnight howl with guest improv troupe. M-Th show 8pm ($17), F-Sa 8pm and 10:30pm ($1-24), Su "best of" 8pm $10. Reservations required.

**C'est What?,** 67 Front St. E. (867-9499). Subway: Union. A mellow manifestation of Canada's multiculturalism. Its own microbrews and wines in Toronto's downtown underground, live music most nights of the week. Open M-F noon-2am, Sa-Su 11am-2am.

**Top o' the Senator,** 249-253 Victoria St. (364-7517). Attracts local and national jazz acts. Cover $5-30. Open Tu-Sa 8:30pm-1am, Su 8pm-midnight.

EASTERN CANADA

## COLLEGE ST.

**Sneaky Dee's,** 431 College St. W. (603-3090), at Bathurst. Popular (if generic); cheap brew (60 oz. pitcher of Ontario microbrewery draught $9.25); pool tables in back. M-F before 6pm, domestic beer goes for $2.50 per bottle. DJ and dancing upstairs W-Sa 9:30pm. Open M-Th 11am-4am, F 11am-5am Sa 9am-5am, Su 9am-4am.

## THE DANFORTH

**Iliada Café,** 550 Danforth Ave. (462-0334). Subway: Pape. Displaced Athenians dream of the sun-drenched Aegean while they sip frappes ($3.50) and nibble at fresh baklava. Open June to early Sept. Su-Th 9am-2am, F-Sa 9am-3am; mid Sept.-May Su-Th 9am-1am, F-Sa 9am-3am.

## THE GAY AND LESBIAN VILLAGE

**Woody's/Sailor,** 465-467 Church St. (972-0887), by Maitland. Subway: Wellesley. *The* established gay bar in the Church and Wellesley area. Neighborhood atmosphere; walls are lined with art nudes. Come to relax and hang out before heading to the clubs, but don't miss "Bad Boys Night Out" on Tu, "Best Legs on Su 11pm, and "Best Chest," Th at midnight. Bottled beer $4.25. Open daily 11am-2am.

**Slack Alice,** 562 Church St. (969-8742). Subway: Wellesley. This cafe and bar offers international food (entrees $7-14), an outdoor patio, and a happy hour from 4-7pm, all of which draw in a lesbian and straight crowd. Open daily 11am-2am.

# NEAR TORONTO

**ONATION'S NIAGARA ESCARPMENT.** As beautiful as its name is strange, Onation's Niagara Escarpment passes west of Toronto as it winds its way from Niagara Falls to Tobermory at the tip of the Bruce Peninsula. Along this rocky 724km ridge, the **Bruce Trail** snakes through parks and private land. Hikers are treated to spectacular waterfalls, the breathtaking cliffs along **Georgian Bay,** and unique flora and fauna, including an old growth forest. Because the escarpment is registered as a United Nations world biosphere reserve, future land development is limited to that which can exist symbiotically with the natural environment. For maps and Escarpment info, write or call the **Niagara Escarpment Commission,** 232 Guelph St., Georgetown L7G 4B1 (905-877-5191). Specifics on the Bruce Trail can be obtained from the **Bruce Trail Association,** P.O. Box 857, Hamilton L8N 3N9 (905-529-6821).

**STRATFORD.** Held in nearby Stratford since 1953, the **Stratford Shakespeare Festival** has proven to be the lifeblood of this picturesque town named for the Bard's own village. The festival and the hamlet are inextricably intertwined, attracting a posh set for an array of mostly non-Shakespeare productions that run from May through early Nov. During mid-summer (July-Aug.), up to 6 different shows play per day (none on M), but there is method in this madness: matinees begin at 2pm and evening performances at 8pm in each of 3 theaters. For complete info about casts and performances call 800-567-1600; write to the **Stratford Festival,** P.O. Box 520, Stratford N5A 6V2; or check their website (www.stratford-festival.on.ca). Tickets are expensive ($48-69), but a few good deals lower the stakes, including **rush tickets** (sold at 9am on morning of the show at the box office, theater, or at 10am by phone; $38-43), matinees for seniors and students in Sept. and Oct. (from $21), general student discounts ($26), and half-price for some performances in Sept. and Oct. (box office open M-Sa 9am-8pm, Su 9am-2pm). Tickets can also be purchased through **Ticketmaster** outlets (in Toronto call 416-872-1111). For information on the festival and the town, contact **Tourism Stratford** (519-271-5140 or 800-561-SWAN/7926), or write them at P.O. Box 818, Stratford, N5A 6W1. **Visitor's Information Center:** York St. at Lakeside Dr. (519-273-3352). **Festival Accommodations Bureau:** (800-567-1600) spurs the lated traveler apace to gain the timely inn or guest home ($32-41), or B&B ($50-120). **VIA Rail:** (800-361-1235). To Toronto (2½hr., $24). By car, Stratford is a 4hr. drive from Toronto; take 401W to 8W into Stratford.

# OTTAWA

Legend has it that in the mid-19th century, Queen Victoria chose this as Canada's capital by closing her eyes and pointing a finger at a map. Perhaps political savvy and not blind chance guided her to this once remote logging town, which, as a stronghold for neither French nor English interests, became a perfect compromise. Today, faced with the increasingly tricky task of forging national unity while preserving local identities, Ottawa continues to play cultural diplomat to Canada.

At the turn of the century, Prime Minister Sir Wilfred Laurier called upon urban planners to give Ottawa a historic and more polished feel. The careful grooming which makes Ottawa easy to navigate by foot has led to this city's reputation for being boring. An evening stroll through Byward Market will challenge this notion. Behind the theaters, museums, and parks, there is plenty of action both before and after quitting time, in Ottawa.

## ✦ ORIENTATION

The **Rideau Canal** divides Ottawa into the eastern lower town and the western upper town. West of the canal, Parliament buildings and government offices line **Wellington St.,** one of the city's main east-west arteries, which runs directly into the heart of downtown and crosses the canal. **Laurier** is the only other east-west street which permits traffic from one side of the canal to the other. East of the canal, Wellington St. becomes **Rideau St.,** surrounded by a fashionable shopping district. North of Rideau St. lies the **Byward Market,** a shopping area which hosts a summertime open-air market and much of Ottawa's nightlife. **Elgin St.**, a primary north-south artery, stretches from the Queensway (Hwy. 417) to the War Memorial just south of Wellington in front of Parliament Hill, is also home to a number of pubs and nightlife spots. **Bank St.**, which runs parallel to Elgin 3 blocks to the west, services the town's older shopping area. The canal itself is a major access route. In winter, thousands of Ottawans skate to work on this, the world's longest skating rink; in summer, power boats breeze by regularly. Bike paths and pedestrian walkways also line the canals. Parking downtown is painful (to find as well as to pay for); meters often cost 25¢ for 10min. Stash your car near the hostels and hop on the OC Transpo buses or walk. All the best attractions, restaurants, lodgings, clubs, and parks are within easy walking distance of one another.

# ⏻ PRACTICAL INFORMATION

**Airport: Ottawa International** (248-2125), 20min. south of the city off Bronson Ave. Take bus #96 from MacKenzie King Bridge. **Info desk** in arrival area open 9am-9pm. Kasbary Transport, Inc. runs **shuttles** (736-9993) between the airport and all downtown hotels; the Novotel is near Ottawa International Hostel. Call for pick-up from smaller hotels. Run daily every 30min. 4:40am-2am; call for later pick-up. $9, seniors and ages 11-18 $4.

**Trains: VIA Rail,** 200 Tremblay Rd. (244-8289), east of downtown, off the Queensway at Alta Vista Rd. To: Montréal (2hr., 4 per day, $38); Toronto (4hr., 5 per day, $83/$50); and Québec City via Montréal (7hr., 2 per day, $73.) Ticket office open M-F 5am-9pm, Sa 6:30am-7pm, Su 8:20am-9pm.

**Buses: Voyageur,** 265 Catherine St. (238-5900), between Kent and Lyon. Serves primarily eastern Canada. To: Montréal (2½hr., on the hr. 7am-11pm, $26). **Greyhound** (237-7038) buses leave from the same station, bound for western Canada and southern Ontario. To Toronto (5hr., 7 per day, $54). 5% student discount. For service to the U.S. you must first go to Montréal or Toronto; the Québec City-bound must pass through Montréal. Station open daily 6:30am-12:30am. The blue **Hull City buses** (819-770-3242) connect Ottawa to Hull, across the river.

**Public Transit: OC Transpo,** 1500 St. Laurent (741-4390). Buses congregate on Rideau Centre. Fare $2.25, express (green buses) $3.50, ages 6-11 $1.25.

**Taxis: Blue Line Taxi,** 238-1111.

**Driver/Rider Service: Allostop,** 238 Dalhousie (562-8248), at St. Patrick. To: Toronto ($20); Québec City ($29); Montréal ($10); and New York City ($50). Membership ($6) required. Open M-W 9am-5pm, Th-F 9am-7pm, Sa-Su 10am-5pm. Also an active **rideboard** on the 2nd fl. of the University of Ottawa's University Center.

**Bike Rental: Rent-A-Bike-Vélocationo,** 1 Rideau St. (241-4140), behind the Château Laurier Hotel. $7 per hr., $16 per 4hr., $20 per day; tandems $15/$38/$50. Maps, locks, helmets free. Family deals. Open daily Apr. to Oct. 9am-8pm. Credit card required.

**Visitor Info: National Capital Commission Information Center,** 90 Wellington St. (239-5000 or 800-465-1867 in Canada), opposite the Parliament Buildings. Open daily early May to early Sept. 8:30am-9pm; early Sept. to early May 9am-5pm. For info on Hull and Québec province, contact the **Association Touristique de l'Outaouais,** 103 rue Laurier, Hull (819-778-2222 or 800-265-7822), at rue St-Laurent. Open mid-June to Sept. M-F 8:30am-8pm, Sa-Su 9am-6pm; off-season M-F 8:30am-5pm, Sa-Su 9am-4pm.

**Hotlines: Ottawa Distress Centre,** 238-3311, English-speaking. **Tel-Aide,** 741-6433, French-speaking. **Rape Crisis Centre,** 562-2333. All 3 24hr.

**Bi-Gay-Lesbian Organization: Gayline-Telegai** (238-1717) has info on local bars and special events. Open daily 7-10pm.

**Post Office:** Postal Station B, 59 Sparks St. (844-1545), at Elgin St. Open M-F 8am-6pm. **Postal code:** K1P 5A0. **Area code:** 613 (Ottawa); 819 (Hull).

# ACCOMMODATIONS

Finding inexpensive lodging in downtown Ottawa can be difficult, especially in the summer. However, fantastic budget options exist if you avoid hotels. Advance reservations are strongly recommended. A complete list of B&Bs can be found in the *Ottawa Visitors Guide;* **Ottawa Bed and Breakfast** (563-0161) represents 10 B&Bs in the Ottawa area (singles $49-54; doubles $59-64 plus tax).

**Ottawa International Hostel (HI-C),** 75 Nicholas St., K1N 7B9 (235-2595), in downtown Ottawa. The site of Canada's last public hanging, the former Carleton County Jail now incarcerates travelers in this trippy hostel. Rooms contain 4-8 bunks and minimal personal space. Communal showers, kitchen, laundry facilities, lounges, and a cast of friendly regulars. International crowd. Many organized activities (biking, canoeing, tours, and pub crawls) keep visitors happy. 148 beds $16, nonmembers $21; private rooms from $46/50. In winter, doors locked 2-7am. Linen $2. Parking $4.28.

**University of Ottawa Residences,** 100 University St. (564-5400), in the center of campus, an easy walk from downtown. From the bus and train stations, take bus #95. Clean dorms in a concrete landscape. Hall showers with curtains. Access to University Center. Singles $34, doubles $41; students with ID $23/$36. Free linen, towels. Check-in 4:30pm. Parking $5.50 per day, $4 after 4pm and Sa-Su. Open early May to late Aug.

**YMCA/YWCA,** 180 Argyle Ave. (237-1320), at O'Connor St., close to the bus station and only a 10 min walk from Ottawa's main sights; walk left on Bank St. and right on Argyle. Nice sized (though not beautifully decorated) rooms in a high-rise. Free local phones in most rooms. Kitchen available until 11pm. Gym facilities. Singles with shared bath $42, with private bath $49; doubles $49. Reception Su-Th 7am-11pm, F-Sa 24hr. Weekly and group rates available. Cafeteria open M-F 7am-2:30pm, Sa 8am-2:30pm; in winter M-F 7am-6:30pm; breakfast $2.50-4. Indoor evening parking $2.75.

**Gatineau Park** (827-2020; reservations 456-3016), northwest of Hull, has 3 rustic campgrounds within 45min. of Ottawa: **Lac Philippe Campground,** 248 sites with facilities for family camping, trailers, and campers; **Lac Taylor Campground,** with 33 semi-rustic sites; and **Lac la Pêche,** with 36 campsites accessible only by canoe. All the campgrounds are off Hwy. 366, northwest of Hull; watch for signs. Maps available at the visitors center (open daily 9am-6pm; in winter 9:30am-6pm). From Ottawa, take King Edward Ave. over the MacDonald-Cartier Bridge, follow Autoroute 5 north to Scott Rd., turn right onto Hwy. 105, and follow 105 to Hwy. 366. To reach La Pêche, take Hwy. 366 to Eardley Rd., on your left. Camping permits for Taylor and Philippe ($16; mid-June to mid-Oct. $19) available at the campground entrance. Pay for a site at La Pêche ($15; off-season $12) on Eardley Rd. La Pêche is available mid-May to mid-Oct.; Lac Philippe and Lac Taylor are open year-round.

# FOOD

Fans of the cholesterol-rich breakfast will find it in Ottawa; much revolves around the worship of eggs, potatoes, meat, toast, and coffee. The **Dutch Café Wim,** 537 Sussex Dr., serves sumptuous Colombian coffee ($1.45), decadent desserts ($3.50), and creative sandwiches ($5-7) in an artistic and somewhat mysterious setting (241-1771; open Su-Th 7:30am-12:30am, F-Sa 7:30-1:30am). Sweeten your palate with 1 of 40 homemade Italian gelato flavors at **Belmondo,** 381 Dalhousie St. (789-6116; open daily 11am-1am). Beaver Tail, akin to fried dough but raised to a fine pastry, is an Ottawa specialty. Fresh fruit and vegetables are accented by occasional street music in open-air **Byward Market,** on Byward St. between York and Rideau St. (562-3325; open daily 8am-5pm; boutiques open later).

**Father and Sons,** 112 Osgoode St. (233-6066), at the eastern edge of the U of O campus. Student favorite, and for a good reason. The menu presents tavern-style quality food with some Lebanese dishes thrown in. Falafel platter ($7) or a triple-decker sandwich ($7.25) are good. 15¢ wings all day M and Sa, 30¢ otherwise. Open daily 7am-2am. Kitchen open until midnight in winter.

■ **Mamma Grazzi's Kitchen,** 25 George St. (241-8656). This little Italian hideaway is located in a stone building situated in one of the oldest remaining parts of Ottawa. Regulars rave about the thin-crust pizza ($8-13). Be patient; it's worth the wait. Open Su-Th 11:30am-10pm, F-Sa 11:30am-11pm.

**Las Palmas,** 111 Parent Ave. (241-3738). Outstanding Mexican grub is heaped high; it's "like eating in a Mexican funhouse during a fiesta." Hot means hot here. Dinners $6-16. An appetizer of nachos for $7.50 is more than a meal. Open daily 11am-midnight on weekdays, until 2am on weekends. Live music on F and Sa evenings.

**Royal Star,** 99 Rideau St. (562-2772). Stellar lunch buffet ($7) with over 100 selections of Szechuan, Cantonese, Polynesian, and Canadian favorites. Open daily 11am-10pm.

**The International Cheese and Deli,** 40 Byward St. (241-5411). Deli and Middle Eastern sandwiches to go. Vegetable *samosa* $1.25; turkey and cheese $3.50; falafel on pita $2.25. Open daily 8am-6pm, except F open until 8pm.

## ■ SIGHTS

Though overshadowed by Toronto's size and Montréal's cosmopolitan color, Ottawa's status as capital of Canada is shored up by its cultural attractions. Since the national museums and political action are packed tightly together, most sights can be reached by foot. Better still, many national attractions are free of charge.

**Parliament Hill,** on Wellington at Metcalfe St., distinguished by Gothic architecture, towers over downtown. Warm your hands or raise a skeptical Quebecois eyebrow over the **Centennial Flame** at the south gate, lit in 1967 to mark the 100th anniversary of the Dominion of Canada's inaugural session of Parliament. The Prime Minister can occasionally be spotted at the central parliament structure, **Centre Block,** which contains the House of Commons, Senate, and Library of Parliament. Free tours of Centre Block (in English or French) depart every 30min. from the white **Infotent** by the visitors center. *(992-4793. Tours mid-May to Sept. M-F 9am-8:30pm, Sa-Su 9am-5:30pm; Sept. to mid-May daily 9am-4:30pm. Info-tent open mid-May to mid-June daily 9am-5pm; mid-June to Aug. 9am-8pm.)* On display behind the library, the bell from Centre Block is the only part of the original 1859-66 structure to survive a 1916 fire; according to legend, the bell crashed to the ground after chiming at midnight on the night of the flames. A carillon of 53 bells now hangs in the Peace Tower. When Parliament is in session, you can watch Canada's government officials **squirm on the verbal hot seat** during the official **Question Period** in the House of Commons chamber. *(Mid-Sept. to Dec. and Feb.-June M-Th 2:15-3pm, F 11:15am-noon.)*

Those interested in trying to make a statuesque soldier smile should attend the **Changing of the Guard,** on the broad lawns in front of Centre Block. *(993-1811. Late June to late Aug. daily 10am, weather permitting.)* At dusk, Centre Block and its lawns transform into the set for **A Symphony of Sound and Light,** which relates the history of the Parliament Buildings and the nation. *(Shows mid-May to early Aug. 9:30 and 10:30pm; early Aug. to early Sept. 9 and 10pm. Performances alternate between French and English.)* A 5min. walk west along Wellington St., the **Supreme Court of Canada** (995-5361) cohabitates with the **Federal Court.** *(Alternating French and English 30min. tours every 30min.; no tours Sa-Su noon-1pm. Free. Open daily 9am-5pm; Sept.-May hrs. vary.)*

One block south of Wellington, **Sparks St. Mall,** originally one of North America's first pedestrian malls, now houses a slew of banks and upscale retail stores. The **Rideau Centre,** south of Rideau St. at Sussex Dr., is the city's primary shopping mall as well as one of the main OC Transpo stations. Glass encloses the sidewalks in front of Rideau St. stores to make them bearable during the winter months.

East of the Parliament Buildings at the junction of Sparks, Wellington, and Elgin St. stands **Confederation Sq.** with its enormous **National War Memorial,** dedicated by King George VI in 1939. The structure symbolizes the triumph of peace over war, an ironic message on the eve of World War II. **Nepean Point,** several blocks northwest of Rideau Centre and the Byward Market, behind the National Gallery of Canada, provides a panoramic view of the capital. The **Governor-General,** the Queen's representative in Canada, resides at **Rideau Hall.** Dress up for the open house on

New Year's Day or Canada Day and they'll let you view the interior *(998-7113)*. Otherwise, gawk from 24 Sussex Drive, the **Prime Minister's residence.** Free **tours** leave from the main gate at 1 Sussex Dr. *(800-465-6890 for tour info).*

Ethnic neighborhoods in Ottawa, though somewhat sparse, include a small **Chinatown** around Somerset St. between Kent St. and Bronson Ave. From downtown, walk south on Elgin St.; go west on Somerset until the French signs turn to Chinese (about a 20min. walk). **Little Italy** is just around the corner on Bronson Ave., stretching south from Somerset to the Queensway (Hwy. 417).

**MUSEUMS AND PARKS.** Ottawa contains many of Canada's huge national museums. Most are wheelchair accessible; call for details. **The National Gallery,** a spectacular glass-towered building adjacent to Nepean Pt., holds the world's most comprehensive collection of Canadian art as well as outstanding European, American, and Asian works. The building's exterior, a work of art in itself, is a parody of the neo-Gothic buttresses of the facing Library of Parliament. *(380 Sussex Dr. 990-1985 or 800-319-2787. Open daily May-Oct. 10am-6pm, Th. open until 8pm; hrs vary off-season. Free; special events $8-10, students and seniors $6-8, under 18 free.)* The **Canadian War Museum**, next to the National Gallery, is a poignant exhibit of Canadian people at war from early times to UN Peacekeeping Missions. *(330 Sussex Dr. 776-8600. Open daily 9am-5pm, Th open until 8pm. $4, students and seniors $3, children $2.)* The **Canadian Museum of Contemporary Photography,** located on the steps between the Château Laurier and the Ottawa Locks, allows a freeze frame glimpse of modern Canadian life. *(1 Rideau Canal. 990-8257. Open M-Tu and F-Su 11am-5pm, W 4-8pm, Th 11am-8pm. Free.)*

The **Canadian Museum of Civilization** is housed in a striking, sand-dune-like structure across the river in Hull. Accessible (but perhaps overly ambitious) exhibits attempt to put 1000 years of Canadian history into perspective. *(100 Laurier St. 776-7000. Open daily Apr.-Oct. 9am-6pm, Thurs. open until 9pm; hrs vary off-season. $8, $7 senior, $6 youth under 18, $3 children, family discounts.)* The **CINEPLUS** theater can project both IMAX and Omnimax media. *(776-7010 for showtimes. $8, seniors $7, ages 13-17 $6.50, under 13 $5.50.)* The **Canadian Museum of Nature,** at Metcalf, explores the natural world from dinosaur to mineral through multi-media displays. *(240 McLeod St. 566-4700. Open daily May-early Sept. 9:30am-5pm, Th until 8pm; hrs vary during off season. $5, students $4, seniors and ages 3-12 $2, families $12; Th ½-price; free 5-8pm daily.)*

Canadian history buffs easily lose themselves in the **National Library Archives,** which houses oodles of Canadian publications, old maps, photographs, letters, and historical exhibits. *(395 Wellington St., at Bay St. 995-5138. Reading room open M-F 8:30am-10pm, Sa-Su 8am-6pm.)* Liberal Prime Minister William Lyon Mackenzie King governed Canada from the elegant **Laurier House,** for most of his lengthy tenure. Admire antiques King accumulated, as well as the crystal ball he used to consult his long-dead mother on matters of national importance. *(335 Laurier Ave. E. 992-8142. Open Apr.-Sept. Tu-Sa 9am-5pm, Su 2-5pm; Oct.-Mar. Tu-Sa 10am-5pm, Su 2-5pm. $2.25, seniors $1.75, students with ID $1.25, under 5 free.)*

Farther out of town, the **National Museum of Science and Technology** lets you explore the wonderful world of modern tech and transport with touchy-feely exhibits. The museum entrance is on Lancaster Rd., 200m east of St. Laurent. *(1867 St. Laurent Blvd., at Smyth. 991-3044. Open May-Sept.: daily 9am-6pm, F until 9pm; hrs vary off-season. $6, students and seniors $5, ages 6-15 $2.)* The **National Aviation Museum**, in front of the Rockcliffe Flying Club on Prom. De L'Aviation and Rockcliffe Pkwy. north of Montréal St., illustrates the history of human flight and displays over 120 aircraft; take bus #95 and transfer to #198. *(993-2010. May-Sept.: open daily 9am-5pm, Th until 9pm; hrs vary during off season. $6, students and seniors $5, ages 6-15 $2.)*

Ottawa has managed to skirt the traditional urban vices of pollution and violent crime; the multitude of parks and recreation areas may make you forget you're in a city at all. A favorite destination for Ottawans who want to cycle, hike, or fish, **Gatineau Park** (see **Accommodations,** above) occupies 356 sq. km in the northwest. Artificial **Dow's Lake,** accessible by the Queen Elizabeth Dwy., extends off the Rideau Canal 15min. south of Ottawa. **Dow's Lake Pavilion,** near Preston St., rents pedal boats, canoes, and bikes. *(101 Queen Elizabeth Driveway. 232-1001. Open mid-May to Sept. daily 8am-8pm. Rentals by the 30min. and the hr. Prices vary.)*

The **beaches** lie west of town by way of the Ottawa River Pkwy. (follow the signs). **Mooney's Bay,** one popular strip of river bank, is 15min. from Ottawa by car.

## ENTERTAINMENT AND NIGHTLIFE

The **National Arts Centre,** 53 Elgin St., at Albert St., houses an excellent small orchestra and theater company and frequently hosts international entertainers (996-5051; tickets 755-1111. Box office open M-Sa noon-9pm.) **Odyssey Theater** puts on open-air theater at Strathcona Park, at the east end of Laurier Ave. at Range Rd., well east of the canal. (232-8407. Shows late July to late Aug. Tu-Su 8:30pm. $20, students and seniors $17, under 12 $8.)

Ottawans seem to celebrate everything, even the bitter Canadian cold. All-important is **Canada Day,** on July 1, which involves fireworks, partying in Major's Hill Park, concerts, and all-around merrymaking. During the first 3 weekends of Feb., **Winterlude** (239-5000) lines the Rideau Canal with ice sculptures illustrating how it feels to be an Ottawan in the winter (frozen). For a week in mid-May, the **Tulip Festival** (567-5757) explodes with a kaleidoscope of more than a million buds around Dow's Lake. Music fills the air during the **Dance Festival** (237-5158), in mid-June, and the **Jazz Festival** (594-3580), in mid-July; both of which hold free recitals and concerts, as well as pricier events. During Labor Day weekend, hundreds of international balloons take to the sky at the **Hot Air Balloon Festival** (819-243-2330).

**Hull, Québec** remains the place for the dedicated nightlifer, with establishments grinding and gnashing until 3am nightly. Sitting right across the Ottawa River from Ottawa, Hull is most noted for its less stringent drinking laws, (the legal drinking age is 18). Close to Gatineau Provincial Park, Hull connects to Ottawa by several bridges and the blue Hull buses from downtown Ottawa (see buses in **Practical Information,** above). Over 20 popular nightspots pack the **Promenade du Portage (a.k.a The Strip)** in Hull, just west of the Place Portage government office complex. Ottawa has its share of excitement, especially in the Byward Market area. Though everything shuts down at 2am, many Ottawan establishments don't charge a cover.

On a musical note, Ottawa caters to both listeners and dancers. **The Atomic,** 137 Besserer St., is guarded by 2 big, silver doors. Cybertonic juice and vitamin drinks are served along with booze. (241-2411. Th 10pm-3am, cover $5; F 10pm-5am, cover $7 before 1am, $10 after; Sa 10pm-8am, cover $10 before 1am, $12 after.) The **Reactor,** 18 York St., has bright lights and dance music (241-8955, open daily 4pm-1am). Experience life, the universe, and a bit of everything else at **Zaphod,** 27 York St., in Byward Market, a popular alternative club famous for their $6.50 Pangalactic Gargle Blasters. (562-1010. Cover $2-10 depending on the band playing. Open daily 3pm-2am.) A popular gay pub which attracts an older afternoon crowd, **The Market Station,** 15 George St. (562-3540), sits above a happening, subterranean dance cavern called **The Well.** (Market Station open M-Tu 3pm-2am, W-F 2pm-2am, Sa noon-2am, Su 11:30am-2am. The Well 19+; cover $3; open Tu-Su 9pm-2am.) The late 20s/early 30s crowd gathers in bars on **Elgin St.** The **Earl of Sussex,** 431 Sussex Dr., has live music on Fri and Sat. (562-5544, open Su-Tu 11am-12am, W-Th 11am-1am, F-Sa 11am-2am). **Minglewoods,** 101 York, on the corner of Dalhousie, is a good place to, well, mingle (562-2611; open daily 11:30am-2am).

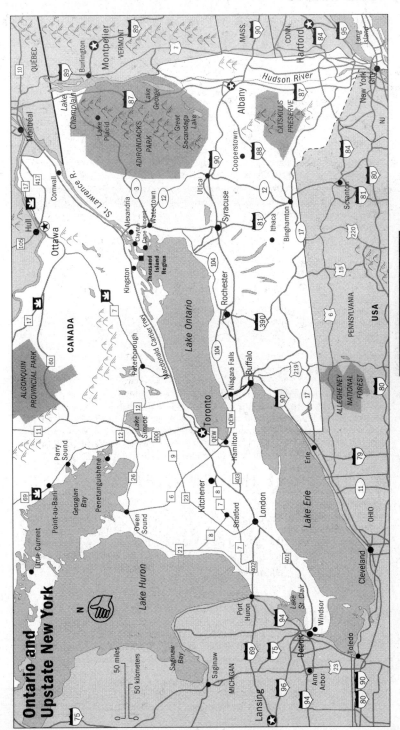

## Ontario and Upstate New York

# MID-ATLANTIC

From Virginia down South through the Eastern seaboard of New York, the mid-Atlantic states claim not only a large slice of the nation's population, but several of the nation's major historical, political, and economic centers. This region is home to every capital the U.S. has ever known; first Philadelphia, PA, then Princeton, NJ, Annapolis, MD, Trenton, NJ and New York City, and finally Washington, D.C. During the Civil War, the mid-Atlantic even hosted the Confederacy's capital, Richmond, VA. Urban centers (and suburban sprawl) cover much of the land, but the great outdoors have survived. The Appalachian Trail meanders through and New York's Adirondacks make up the largest U.S. park outside of Alaska.

## HIGHLIGHTS OF THE MID-ATLANTIC

■ **New York, NY.** The Big Apple combines world-class museums (p. 228) with top-notch arts and entertainment venues (p. 231).

■ **Washington, D.C.** The impressive Smithsonian Museum (p. 293), the White House (p. 295), the Capitol (p. 292), and a slew of monuments (p. 294) comprise some of the coveted attractions of the nation's capitol.

■ **Scenic Drives.** The Blue Ridge Pkwy. (p. 317) is justifiably famous. A more hidden drive is the gorgeous backcountry road from Carter's Grove Plantation to Colonial Williamsburg, VA (p. 308).

■ **Historic sites.** Four-time battlefield Fredericksburg, VA (p. 306); Harper's Ferry, WV (p. 319); and Gettysburg, PA (p. 270) are the best places to relive the Civil War. Philadelphia, PA (p. 258) abounds with colonial landmarks.

# NEW YORK

Surrounded by the beauty of some of the state's landscape, you may find it difficult to remember that smog and traffic exist. The cities that dot upstate New York have a sweet natural flavor that hold their own against the tang of the Big Apple, but comparisons with its lesser kin don't hold—"The City" is an entirely different kettle of fish. New York City, the eighth most populated city in the world, would claim to be grander than the other seven. And the New Yorkers may have a point.

## ◪ PRACTICAL INFORMATION

**Capital:** Albany.

**Visitor Info: Division of Tourism,** 1 Commerce Plaza, Albany 12245 (518-474-4116 or 800-225-5697; iloveny.state.ny.us). Operators available M-F 8:30am-5pm; voice mail otherwise. **New York State Office of Parks and Recreation and Historic Preservation,** Empire State Plaza, Agency Bldg. 1, Albany 12238-0001 (518-474-0456). Open M-F 9am-5pm. **Bureau of Public Lands** of the **Division of Lands and Forests,** DEC, 50 Wolf Rd., Room 438, Albany 12233-4255 (518-457-7433).

**Postal Abbreviation:** NY. **Sales Tax:** 8.25%.

## NEW YORK CITY

Immensity, diversity, and a tradition of defying tradition characterize the city known as "the Crossroads of the World." Since its earliest days, New York has scoffed at the timid offerings of other American cities. It boasts the most immigrants, the tallest skyscrapers, and the trickiest con men. Even the vast blocks of concrete have their own gritty charm. Returning from a dull vacation in rural Westchester, resident talespinner O. Henry noted, "there was too much fresh scenery and fresh air. What I need is a steam-heated flat and no vacation or exercise."

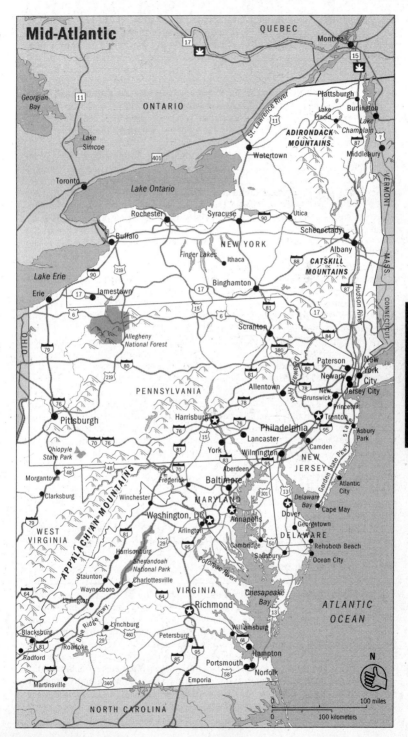

Mid-Atlantic

MID-ATLANTIC

New York City is full of folks. The stars are shielded by a blanket of pollution. The buildings are tall, the subway smelly, the people rushed, the beggars everywhere. But for every inch of grime, there's a yard of silver lining. Countless people mean countless pockets of culture—you can find every kind of ethnicity, food, art, energy, language, attitude. It's possible to be alone, but that's not the point—plunge into the fray and you'll find 8 million stories, curmudgeonly humor, innovative ideas, and a fair share of madness. The architecture, from colonial to Art Deco, reveals the stratae of history that NYC embodies. Meanwhile, there's flamenco at an outdoor cafe, jazz underground at night, jungle/illbient under a bridge, Eurotechno at a flashy club—whatever the question, New York has the answer.

In 1624, the Dutch West Indies Company founded a trading colony. Two years later, in the first of the city's shady transactions, Peter Minuit famously bought Manhattan from the natives for just under $24. Early colonists were less than enthralled by Dutch rule, and put up scant resistance when the British invaded the settlement in 1664. By the late 1770s, the city was an active port with a population of 20,000. New York's primary concern was maintaining its prosperity, and the city reacted apathetically to the emerging revolutionary cause. With feelings hurt, the new Continental Army made no great efforts to protect New York. She fell to the British in Sept. 1776 and remained in their hands until Nov. 1783.

During the 19th century, Manhattan grew vertically to house the growing population streaming in from Western Europe. Immigrants hoping to escape famine, persecution, and political unrest faced the cold cruel sea for the promise of America, landing on Ellis Island in New York Harbor. The Roaring 20s brought architectural and industrial booms. Mayor Fiorello Laguardia fought to keep the poor immigrant population afloat during the Great Depression. Post-WWII prosperity brought greater heterogeneity, including an African-American population from the rural South and Hispanics from the Caribbean. By the 60s, crises in public transportation, education, and housing fanned the flames of ethnic tensions and fostered the rise of a criminal underclass, with which the city is associated to this day.

In the 80s, New York rebounded, but the bright Wall St. of the Reagan era soon faded to a gray 90s malaise, and the city once again confronted old problems—too many people, too little money, too much racial tension. The first African-American mayor, David Dinkins, was elected in 1989 on a platform that called for the harmonious growth of the "beautiful mosaic," but his ideals never reached full fruition. Current Mayor Rudy Giuliani will always be remembered for his strict anti-crime measures. Crime has declined in the past 5 years, but not without frequent outcries of police brutality. At the same time the city retains its heterogeneity and electric energy, still proving O. Henry's statement that, "There is more poetry in a block of New York than in twenty daisied lanes."

For ultimate coverage on turn-of-the-millennium New York City, see our city guide, *Let's Go: New York City*, and the *Let's Go Map Guide: New York City*.

# ■ ORIENTATION

Five **boroughs** comprise New York City: Brooklyn, the Bronx, Queens, Staten Island, and Manhattan. **Manhattan** Island is 13mi. long and 2½mi. wide, and houses the third largest population of the boroughs, after Brooklyn and Queens. **Queens,** the largest of the boroughs, beckons Manhattan's east midtown from across the East River. **Brooklyn,** due south of Queens, would be America's fourth-largest city if it weren't a part of New York. Residential **Staten Island,** southwest of Manhattan, has repeatedly sought secession from the city. North of Manhattan, the **Bronx** is the only borough connected by land to the rest of the U.S.; the two main regions are upscale Riverdale and the economically depressed South Bronx, the birthplace of hip-hop music (see **Hip-Hop (R)evolution,** p. 227).

**Manhattan**

SEE COLOR INSERTS FOR MORE
NEW YORK CITY MAPS

1 Columbia University
2 Cathedral of St. John the Divine
3 Guggenheim Museum
4 Metropolitan Museum of Art
5 American Museum of Natural History
6 Whitney Museum
7 Frick Collection
8 Lincoln Center for the Performing Arts
9 Columbus Circle,
  N.Y. Convention & Visitors Bureau
10 Carnegie Hall
11 Museum of Modern Art
12 Rockefeller Center
13 St. Patrick's Cathedral
14 United Nations
15 Grand Central Station
16 New York Public Library
17 Times Square
18 Port Authority Bus Terminal
19 Empire State Building
20 Penn Station
21 General Post Office
22 Union Square
23 Washington Square
24 World Trade Center
25 Battery Park

**MANHATTAN.** From the window of an approaching plane, it can seem a monolithic concrete jungle. Up close, Manhattan breaks down into manageable, unique neighborhoods that can change abruptly from street to street.

New York began at the southern tip of Manhattan, in the area around **Battery Park** where the first Dutch settled. The nearby harbor, with the **South St. Seaport** tourist magnet, provided the commercial opportunities that helped NYC to succeed. Historic Manhattan, however, lies in the shadows of the imposing financial buildings around **Wall St.** and the civic offices around **City Hall.** A little farther north, neighborhoods rich in the cultures brought by late 19th-century immigrants—**Little Italy, Chinatown,** and the southern blocks of the historically Jewish **Lower East Side**—sit below Houston St. (pronounced "HOW-ston," unlike the Texas city). Once home to Eastern European and Russian Jews, Delancey and Elizabeth St. now offer pasta and Morroccan silks. The up-and-coming nook of high fashion (some call it **NoLIta** for "North of **Little Italy**"), extends roughly down from Houston to Spring St. and over from Lafayette to the Bowery. To the west lies **TriBeCa** ("Triangle Below Canal St."), the industrial-chic home of the late John F. Kennedy, Jr. and his wife Carolyn. **SoHo** (for "South of Houston"), a former warehouse district just north of TriBeCa, shelters art galleries, chic boutiques, and pouting waifs. Above SoHo thrives **Greenwich Village,** whose jumbled streets, trendy shops, and cafes have long housed intense political and artistic activity. "The Village" primarily indicates the western part (from Broadway west to the Hudson River); the (cheaper, younger, and trendier) area east of Broadway is called the **East Village.**

A few blocks north of Greenwich Village, stretching across the west teens and twenties, lies **Chelsea,** otherwise known as "Guppie (Gay Urban Professional) Central." East of Chelsea, **Gramercy Park's** pastoral collection of elegant brownstones seem straight out of Edith Wharton's *Age of Innocence.* **Midtown Manhattan,** 34th to 59th St., boasts skyscrapers that support over a million elevated offices. East Midtown's department stores outfit New York; West Midtown's **Theater District** and **Times Square** entertain the world. North of Midtown, **Central Park** slices Manhattan into East and West. The **Upper West Side's** cultural venues and Central Park West's residences neighbor Columbus Ave.'s chic boutiques and sidewalk cafes. The **Upper East Side's** galleries and museums create an even more rarefied atmosphere amidst the elegant apartments of Fifth and Park Ave.

Above E. 97th St., commuter trains emerge from the tunnel, marking where the Upper East Side's opulence ends and the *barrio* begins. Above W. 110th St. in **Morningside Heights,** sits the Ivy League's **Columbia University** (founded as King's College in 1754), and the **Cathedral of St. John the Divine.** Surrounding **Harlem** produced the Harlem Renaissance of black artists and writers in the 20s and the revolutionary Black Power movement of the 60s. Sidewalks here bustle during the day and famous jazz joints throb at night, but the area can be dangerous; exercise caution. **Washington Heights,** north of Harlem, is home to Fort Tryon Park, the Medieval Cloisters museum, and various immigrant communities.

Manhattan's east/west division refers to an establishment's location in relation to the two borders of Central Park—**Fifth Ave.** on the east side and **Central Park West** on the west. Below 59th St. where the park ends, the West Side begins at the western half of Fifth Ave. **Uptown** (59th St. and up) refers to the area north of Midtown. **Downtown** (34th St. and down) means the area south of Midtown. Streets run east-west. Avenues run north-south. The grid makes calculating distances fairly easy. Numbers increase from south to north along the avenues, but you should always ask for a cross street when getting an avenue address. This plan becomes chaotic below 14th St.; get a good map and ask for directions.

# ▶ PRACTICAL INFORMATION

## GETTING THERE

**John F. Kennedy Airport (JFK)** (718-244-4444), 12mi. from Midtown in southern Queens, handles most international flights. Brown-and-white JFK long-term parking lot bus from any airport terminal (every 15min.) goes to the **Howard Beach-JFK subway station.** From there, take the **A train** to the city (1hr.). A **taxi** from JFK to Manhattan costs $30 (plus tolls and tip). **New York Airport Service** (800-769-7004 or 718-706-9658) runs between JFK or LaGuardia and Grand Central Station, Penn Station and Port Authority, and various midtown hotels (1hr.). Before 1pm buses leave every 30min.; after 1pm they leave every 15min. (student discount available at Grand Central, $6). **Gray Line:** (800-451-0455). The **Express** runs between JFK and NYC; $19 one way. The **Air Shuttle** will drop you off (ask ahead—it may pick you up too) at any hotel in Manhattan between 23rd and 125th St. ($14). Inquire at JFK Ground Transportation Centers.

**LaGuardia Airport** (718-533-3400), 6mi. from midtown in northwestern Queens; domestic flights and air shuttles. **New York Airport Service** (see **John F. Kennedy Airport** above). With extra time and light luggage, one can take the **M60 bus** (daily 4:15am-12:55am; $1.50). The M60 connects to the following subways in Manhattan: the #1, 9 at 116th St. and Broadway, the #2, 3 at 125th St. and Lenox Ave., and the #4, 5, 6 at 125th St. and Lexington Ave. In Queens the M60 connects to the N train at Astoria Blvd. and 31st St. Alternatively, you can take the MTA **Q33 bus** or the **Q47 bus** ($1.50) to the 74th St./Broadway-Roosevelt Ave./Jackson Hts. subway stop in Queens. From there, transfer to the #7, E, F, G, or R train into Manhattan ($1.50). Catch the Q33 bus from the terminal's lower level. Travel time: at least 1½hr. **Taxis** to Manhattan are $16-$26.

**Newark International Airport** (973-961-6000), 12mi. west of midtown in Newark, NJ; domestic and international flights. Often cheaper. **Olympia Trails Coach** (212-964-6233) travels between Newark and Grand Central, Penn Station, Port Authority, or the World Trade Center (every 30min. generally daily 5am-11pm with extended service from certain pick-up points; 25min.-1hr. travel time; $10; tickets may be purchased on the bus). **New Jersey Transit Authority (NJTA)** (973-762-5100) runs an **Air Link bus #302** ($4) between the airport and Newark's Penn Station (not Manhattan's). From there you can take bus #108 ($3.25, exact change) or the local #62 ($1.55, exact change) into New York City. **PATH trains** (800-234-7284; $1) run from Newark Penn Station into Manhattan, stopping at the World Trade Center, Christopher St., Sixth Ave., 9th St., 14th St., 23rd St. and 33rd St. (15-30min.) $45 **taxi** fare negotiable.

**Trains:** On the East side, **Grand Central Station,** 42nd St. and Park Ave. (subway: #4, 5, 6, or 7 or S to 42nd St./Grand Central), handles **Metro-North** (532-4900 or 800-638-7646) commuter lines to Connecticut and New York suburbs. **Amtrak** (582-6875) runs out of the west side's **Penn Station,** 33rd St. and 8th Ave. (subway: #1, 2, 3, 9, or A, C, E to 34th St./Penn Station). To Washington, D.C. (4hr., $61-76) and Boston, MA (4½hr., $44-53). The **Long Island Railroad (LIRR)** (718-822-5477) and **NJ Transit** (201-762-5100) commuter rails also chug from Penn Station. Nearby at 33rd St. and 6th Ave., you can catch a **PATH** train to New Jersey (800-234-7284).

**Buses: Greyhound** and **Peter Pan** buslines leave the Port Authority Terminal, 41st-42nd St. and Eighth Ave. (435-7000; subway: A, C, E to 42nd St.-Port Authority). **Watch for con-artists and pickpockets, especially at night.** To: Boston, MA (4½hr., $34); Philadelphia, PA (1½hr., $20); and Washington, D.C. (4½hr., $34).

From New Jersey, there are three ways to reach the city by car. The **George Washington Bridge** crosses the Hudson River into northern Manhattan and gives easy access to either Harlem River Dr. or the West Side Hwy. From the NJ Turnpike you'll probably end up going through Weehawken, NJ, to the **Lincoln Tunnel,** which exits in Midtown in the west 40s. The **Holland Tunnel** connects to lower Manhattan, exiting into the SoHo and TriBeCa area. Coming from New England or Connecticut on I-95, follow signs for the **Triboro Bridge.** From there get onto **FDR Dr.,** which runs along the east side of Manhattan and exits onto city streets every 10 blocks or so. Another option is to look for the **Willis Ave. Bridge exit** on I-95 to avoid the toll, and enter Manhattan north on the FDR Drive. Expect $4-7 tolls.

**Hitchhiking** is illegal in New York State, and cops strictly enforce the law within NYC. **Hitching in and around New York City is suicidal;** don't do it.

## GETTING AROUND

**Public Transit: NYC Transit Information Bureau** (718-330-1234, 718-330-4847 for non-English-speakers; open daily 6am-9pm) has **subway maps,** as do token booths and the visitors bureau. The *Manhattan Yellow Pages* contains detailed subway, PATH, and bus maps. Subways and buses are run by the **Metropolitan Transit Authority (MTA).**

**MetroCards and Transfers:** The main form of currency at all subway stations and on all public buses. With the purchase of a $15 card, you get one free ride. MetroCards can make free subway-bus, bus-subway, and bus-bus transfers. When the card is swiped on the initial ride, a free transfer (good for 2hr.) is electronically stored on your MetroCard. Without the MetroCard, bus-subway or subway-bus transfers are not free. 1 MetroCard can store 4 transfers for people traveling in a group. Passengers on a north-south bus can generally only transfer to a bus going east-west. Good for the tourist who visits many sights, the 7-day ($17) and 30-day ($63) **"Unlimited Rides" MetroCards** (as opposed to "Pay-Per-Ride" cards) allow unlimited use of the subway.

**Subway:** Operates 24hr. a day, 365 days a year. $1.50. Groups of four may find a cab to be cheaper and more expedient for short distances. Long distances are best traveled by subway; once inside, a passenger may transfer onto any other train without restrictions. "Express" trains run at all hours and stop only at certain major stations; "locals" stop everywhere. Be sure to check the letter or number and the destination of each train, since trains with different destinations often use the same track. When in doubt, ask the conductor, who usually sits near the middle of the train. On the train, pay attention to the often garbled announcements—trains occasionally change mid-route from local to express or vice-versa. In crowded stations (most notably those around 42nd St.), pickpockets find work; violent crimes, although infrequent, tend to occur in stations that are deserted. Stay alert and stick to well-lit areas near a transit cop or token clerk. Most stations have clearly marked "off-hours" waiting areas that are under observation and significantly safer. When boarding, pick a car with a number of other passengers in it, or sit near the middle of the train, in the conductor's car. *For safety reasons, try to avoid riding the subways between midnight and 7am, especially above E. 96th St. and W. 120th St. and outside Manhattan.* Rush-hour crowds make air and seating scarce. You'll see **glass globes** outside of most **subway entrances.** If the globe is green, the entrance is staffed 24hr. A red globe indicates that the entrance is closed or restricted.

**Buses:** $1.50. Buses take tokens, MetroCards, and exact change–not bills. Buses are often slower than subways, but are relatively safe and clean. Buses stop roughly every 2 blocks and run crosstown (east-west), as well as uptown and downtown (north-south). For subway-bus transfers, see **MetroCard and Transfers,** above. Ring to get off. A yellow-painted curb indicates stops, but it's best to look for blue signposts announcing bus numbers or for a glass-walled shelter displaying a map of the route and a schedule of arrival times.

**Taxis:** Most people in Manhattan hail yellow (licensed) cabs on the street. Call 411 to ask for a cab dispatcher.

**Car Rental: Nationwide,** 241 W. 40th St. (867-1234), between 7th and 8th Ave. Mid-sized domestic sedan $33-59 per day, 150 free mi. $289 per week, 1000 free mi. Open M-F 7:30am-6:30pm. Vehicle return 24hr. Must be 23 with a major credit card.

**Bike Rental: Pedal Pushers,** 1306 2nd Ave. (288-5592), between 68th and 69th St. Rents 3-speeds for $4 per hr., $10 per day, $13 overnight; 10-speeds $5/$14/$19; mountain bikes $6/$17/$25. Overnight rentals require a $150 deposit on a major credit card; hourly and daily rentals require a major credit card, passport, or a NY state drivers license. Open Su-M 10am-6pm, W 10am-7pm, Th-Sa 10am-8pm.

**Visitor Info: Times Sq. Visitors Center,** 1560 Broadway (869-5453; www.nycvisit.com), between 46th and 47th St. Subway: #1, 2, 3, 9; or 7; or N, R, or S to Times Sq. In the Embassy Theater. Sells MetroCards, bus and boat tour tickets. ATM, internet access, a newsstand, and bathrooms. Open daily 9am-6pm. **Other locations:** Grand Central terminal, south side of the main concourse; Penn Station terminal, south side of the Amtrak rotunda at 34th St. between 7th and 8th Ave.; Manhattan Mall information booth at 33rd and 6th Ave.

**Help Lines: AIDS Information** (807-6655). M-F 10am-9pm, Sa noon-3pm. **Crime Victims' Hotline** (577-7777). 24hr. **Sex Crimes Report Line** (267-7273). 24hr.

# The MCI WorldCom Card.

## The easy way to call when traveling worldwide.

## The MCI WorldCom Card gives you…

- Access to the US and other countries worldwide.
- Customer Service 24 hours a day
- Operators who speak your language
- Great MCI WorldCom rates and no sign-up fees

**For more information or to apply for a Card call:**
### 1-800-955-0925

**Outside the U.S., call MCI WorldCom collect (reverse charge) at:**
### 1-712-943-6839

| COUNTRY | WORLDPHONE TOLL-FREE ACCESS # |
|---|---|
| Argentina (CC) | |
| To call using Telefonica ■ | 0800-222-6249 |
| To call using Telecom ■ | 0800-555-1002 |
| Australia (CC) ◆ | |
| To call using AAPT ■ | 1-800-730-014 |
| To call using OPTUS ■ | 1-800-551-111 |
| To call using TELSTRA ■ | 1-800-881-100 |
| Austria (CC) ◆ | 0800-200-235 |
| Bahamas | 1-800-888-8000 |
| Belgium (CC) ◆ | 0800-10012 |
| Bermuda ÷ | 1-800-888-8000 |
| Bolivia (CC) ◆ | 0-800-2222 |
| Brazil (CC) | 000-8012 |
| British Virgin Islands ÷ | 1-800-888-8000 |
| Canada (CC) | 1-800-888-8000 |
| Cayman Islands | 1-800-888-8000 |
| Chile (CC) | |
| To call using CTC ■ | 800-207-300 |
| To call using ENTEL ■ | 800-360-180 |
| China ✛ | 108-12 |
| For a Mandarin-speaking Operator | 108-17 |
| Colombia (CC) ◆ | 980-9-16-0001 |
| Collect Access in Spanish | 980-9-16-1111 |
| Costa Rica ◆ | 0800-012-2222 |
| Czech Republic (CC) ◆ | 00-42-000112 |
| Denmark (CC) ◆ | 8001-0022 |
| Dominican Republic | |
| Collect Access | 1-800-888-8000 |
| Collect Access in Spanish | 1121 |
| Ecuador (CC) ÷ | 999-170 |
| El Salvador | 800-1767 |

| COUNTRY | WORLDPHONE TOLL-FREE ACCESS # |
|---|---|
| Finland (CC) ◆ | 08001-102-80 |
| France (CC) ◆ | 0800-99-0019 |
| French Guiana (CC) | 0-800-99-0019 |
| Guatemala (CC) ◆ | 99-99-189 |
| Germany (CC) | 0-800-888-8000 |
| Greece (CC) ◆ | 00-800-1211 |
| Guam (CC) | 1-800-888-8000 |
| Haiti ÷ | 193 |
| Collect Access in French/Creole | 190 |
| Honduras ÷ | 8000-122 |
| Hong Kong (CC) | 800-96-1121 |
| Hungary (CC) ◆ | 00▼800-01411 |
| India (CC) ✛ | 000-127 |
| Collect Access | 000-126 |
| Ireland (CC) | 1-800-55-1001 |
| Israel (CC) | |
| BEZEQ International | 1-800-940-2727 |
| BARAK | 1-800-930-2727 |
| Italy (CC) ◆ | 172-1022 |
| Jamaica ÷ | Collect Access 1-800-888-8000 |
| (From Special Hotels only) | 873 |
| (From public phones) | #2 |
| Japan (CC) ◆ | To call using KDD ■ 00539-121▶ |
| To call using IDC ■ | 0066-55-121 |
| To call using JT ■ | 0044-11-121 |
| Korea (CC) | To call using KT ■ 00729-14 |
| To call using DACOM ■ | 00309-12 |
| To call using ONSE | 00369-14 |
| Phone Booths÷ | Press red button, 03, then ✲ |
| Military Bases | 550-2255 |
| Lebanon | Collect Access 600-MCI (600-624) |

| COUNTRY | WORLDPHONE TOLL-FREE ACCESS # |
|---|---|
| Luxembourg (CC) | 0800-0112 |
| Malaysia (CC) ◆ | 1-800-80-0012 |
| To call using Time Telekom | 1-800-18-0012 |
| Mexico (CC) Avantel | 01-800-021-8000 |
| Telmex ▲ | 001-800-674-7000 |
| Collect Access in Spanish | 01-800-021-1000 |
| Monaco (CC) ◆ | 800-90-019 |
| Netherlands (CC) ◆ | 0800-022-9122 |
| New Zealand (CC) | 000-912 |
| Nicaragua (CC) Collect Access in Spanish | 166 |
| (Outside of Managua, dial 02 first) | |
| Norway (CC) ◆ | 800-19912 |
| Panama | 108 |
| Military Bases | 2810-108 |
| Philippines (CC) ◆ To call using PLDT ■ | 105-14 |
| To call using PHILCOM | 1026-14 |
| To call using Bayantel | 1237-14 |
| To call using ETPI | 1066-14 |
| Poland (CC) ÷ | 00-800-111-21-22 |
| Portugal (CC) ÷ | 800-800-123 |
| Puerto Rico (CC) | 1-800-888-8000 |
| Romania (CC) ÷ | 01-800-1800 |
| Russia (CC) ✛ | |
| To call using ROSTELCOM ■ | 747-3322 |
| (For Russian speaking operator) | 747-3320 |
| To call using SOVINTEL ■ | 960-2222 |
| Saudi Arabia (CC) ÷ | 1-800-11 |
| Singapore | 8000-112-112 |
| Slovak Republic | (CC) 0421-00112 |
| South Africa (CC) | 0800-99-0011 |
| Spain (CC) | 900-99-0014 |

# Worldwide Calling Made Easy

**The MCI WorldCom Card, designed specifically to keep you in touch with the people that matter the most to you.**

www.wcom.com/worldphone

Please cut out and save this reference guide for convenient U.S. and worldwide calling with the MCI WorldCom Card.

## And, it's simple to call home or to other countires.

1. Dial the WorldPhone toll-free access number of the country you're calling from (listed inside).

2. Follow the easy voice instructions or hold for a WorldPhone operator. Enter or give the operator your MCI WorldCom Card number or call collect.

3. Enter or give the WorldPhone operator your home number.

4. Share your adventures with your family!

| COUNTRY | WORLDPHONE TOLL-FREE ACCESS # |
|---|---|
| St. Lucia ÷ | 1-800-888-8000 |
| Sweden (CC) ◆ | 020-795-922 |
| Switzerland (CC) ◆ | 0800-89-0222 |
| Taiwan (CC) ◆ | 0080-13-4567 |
| Thailand ★ | 001-999-1-2001 |
| Turkey (CC) ◆ | 00-8001-1177 |
| United Kingdom (CC) To call using BT ■ | 0800-89-0222 |
| To call using CWC ■ | 0500-89-0222 |
| United States (CC) | 1-800-888-8000 |
| U.S. Virgin Islands (CC) | 1-800-888-8000 |
| Vatican City (CC) | 172-1022 |
| Venezuela (CC) ÷ ◆ | 800-1114-0 |
| Vietnam ● | 1201-1022 |

| | |
|---|---|
| (CC) | Country-to-country calling available to/from most international locations. |
| ÷ | Limited availability. |
| ▼ | Wait for second dial tone. |
| ▲ | When calling from public phones, use phones marked LADATEL. |
| ■ | International communications carrier. |
| ★ | Not available from public pay phones. |
| ◆ | Public phones may require deposit of coin or phone card for dial tone. |
| ● | Local service fee in U.S. currency required to complete call. |
| ► | Regulation does not permit Intra-Japan calls. |
| ❖ | Available from most major cities |

## MCI WorldCom Worldphone Access Numbers

**MCI WORLDCOM**

**Medical Services: Walk-in Clinic,** 57 E. 34th St. (252-6000), between Park and Madison Ave. Open M-Th 8am-8pm, Sa-Su 9am-2pm.

**Post Office:** 421 8th Ave. (330-2902), across from Madison Sq. Garden. Open 24hr. For General Delivery, mail to and use the entrance at 390 9th Ave. **ZIP code:** 10001.

**Area code:** 212 (Manhattan); 718 (other 4 boroughs). In text 212, unless noted.

# ACCOMMODATIONS

The cost of living in New York is out of sight. A night at a full-service establishment runs $125 (plus 13.4% hotel tax), but you can get a bed for under $60 a night.

## HOSTELS AND STUDENT ORGANIZATIONS

**Banana Bungalow,** 250 W. 77th St. (800-646-7835), at Broadway. Subway: #1, 9 to 79th St. Banana Bungalow aspires to be the largest hostel in the world; for now, it's merely the most fun. Clean dorms with linens and a bathroom in each. Amiable atmosphere based around $5 keg parties on the rooftop lounge, with a gorgeous view of the Hudson. Large-screen TV lounge and kitchen, innumerable outings and tours, and discounts at local pubs, restaurants, and movie theaters. Fax service. Internet access. Common refrigerator. 10-bed dorms $24; 6-bed dorms $25; 4-bed dorms $30. Prices about 20% lower in winter. Passport or out-of-state ID required. $10 key deposit. Breakfast included. 14-day max. stay. Check-in or check-out anytime. No curfew.

**New York International Hostel (HI-AYH),** 891 Amsterdam Ave. (932-2300), at 103rd St. Subway: #1, 9 or B, C to 103rd St.; 1 block from the #1, 9 subway. The mother of all youth hostels, with 90 dorm-style rooms and 480 beds. On site are **CIEE Student Center** (666-3619) and a **Council Travel** office and supply store. Spiffy, soft carpets and spotless bathrooms. Kitchens and dining rooms, coin-operated laundry machines ($1), TV lounges, and a large outdoor garden. Walking tours and outings. Internet access. Key-card entry to individual rooms. Nov.-Apr.: 10- to 12-bed dorms $22, 6- to 8-bed dorms $24, 4-bed dorms $27. May-Oct. $2 more. Nonmembers pay $3 more. Groups of 4-9 may get private rooms ($120); groups of 10 or more definitely will. Linen and towels included. Secure storage area and individual lockers. 29-night max. stay, 7-night in summer. Open 24hr. Check-in any time. Check-out 11am (late check-out fee $5). No curfew. Excellent wheelchair access.

**Uptown Hostel,** 239 Lenox (Malcolm X) Ave. (666-0559), at 122nd St. Subway: #2, 3 to 125th St. Knowledgeable and friendly owner helps long-term travelers find uptown apartments and temporary jobs. Bunk beds; clean, comfy rooms. Spacious hall bathrooms. Wonderful common room. Kitchen. Sept.-May: singles $15; doubles $23; June-Aug. singles $17; doubles $23. Key deposit $10. Check-in 10am-8pm. Lockout June-Aug. 11am-4pm. Call as far in advance as possible for summer; in off season 2 days is enough.

**Jazz on the Park,** 36 W. 106th St. (932-1600), at Central Park West. Subway: B, C to 103rd St. New friendly dorms in a renovated building right next to Central Park. Chic, clean, modern decor. Lockers and A/C. Internet access. Pretty terrace. Java bar hosts live bands and other assorted hepcats. 12- to 14-bed dorms $27; 6-8-bed dorms $29; 4-bed dorms $30; 2-bed dorms $37. Taxes, linens, towels, and breakfast included. Check-out 11am. No curfew. No wheelchair access.

**YMCA—Vanderbilt,** 224 E. 47th St. (756-9600), between Second and Third Ave. Subway: #6 to 51st St.; or E, F to Lexington/Third Ave. 5 blocks from Grand Central Station. Convenient and well-run, with reasonable prices and security. Lobby bustles with international backpackers. Each small room has A/C and cable; fairly low bathroom-to-people ratio. Lodgers get free use of the well-equipped gym and safe-deposit boxes. Five shuttles per day to the airports. Singles $68; doubles $81, with sink $83. Key deposit $10. 25-night max. stay. Check-in 3pm. Check-out 11am. Luggage storage $1 per bag. Reserve 2-3 weeks ahead; guarantee with deposit. Wheelchair access.

**YMCA—West Side,** 5 W. 63rd St. (787-4400), off West End Ave. Subway: #1, 9 or A, C, E or B, D, Q, to 59th St./Columbus Circle. Small, well-maintained rooms, bustling cafeteria, and spacious lounges Impressive Moorish facade. Access to pool, indoor track, racquet courts, and Nautilus equipment. Showers on every floor and spotless bathrooms. A/C and cable in every room. 24hr. security and safe-deposit boxes. Singles $68, with bath $95; doubles $80, with bath $110. 25-day max. stay. Check-out noon. No curfew. Reservations recommended. A few stairs at entrance; otherwise wheelchair-friendly.

**YMCA–McBurney,** 206 W. 24th St. (741-9226), between 7th and 8th Ave. Subway: #1, 9 or C, E to 23rd St. A busy YMCA. No-frills rooms upstairs are livable and clean. Mix of elderly locals, students, and other travelers. TV in all rooms. Free access to pool and athletic facilities. Singles $59-61; doubles $71; triples $91; quads $102. With A/C add $5. Key deposit $5. 25-day max. stay. 24hr. door security. Office open daily 8am-11pm. Check-out noon. Usually has vacancies, but reservations are advisable and require a credit card or $59 money order. Wheelchair access.

**YMCA–Flushing,** 138-46 Northern Blvd., Flushing, Queens (718-961-6880), between Union and Bowne St. Subway: #7 to Main St.; from there, walk about 10min. north on Main St. (the Ave. numbers should get smaller), and turn right onto Northern Blvd. Limited number of rooms on one floor for women. The area between the Y and Flushing's nearby shopping district is lively and well populated, but the neighborhood deteriorates north of Northern Blvd. Carpeted, small but clean rooms, with TV and A/C. Bathrooms and public telephones are in the hall. Daily maid service. Gym, Nautilus, squash, and swimming facilities. Singles $46; doubles $65. 25-night max. stay (longer stays possible with advance arrangements). Key deposit $10. 2 forms of photo ID required. Reserve at least 1 month in advance for summer, otherwise 1 week in advance.

**International Student Hospice,** 154 E. 33rd St. (228-7470), between Lexington and Third Ave. Subway: #6 to 33rd St. Up a flight of stairs in an inconspicuous brownstone with a brass plaque that reads "I.S.H." You'll never forget Art, the friendly, helpful owner and collector of all manner of things. This crash pad resembles grandpa's house more than a hostel. The tiny rooms, usually occupied by European backpackers, cram bunk beds, antiquated television sets, Old World memorabilia, cracked porcelain tea cups, and clunky oak night tables. The ceilings are crumbling and the stairs slant precariously, but the house is slowly being restored by willing residents. Rooms for 1-4 people and small hall bathroom. $28 per night, including tax. Some weekly discounts.

**Chelsea International Hostel,** 251 W. 20th St. (647-0010), between 7th and 8th Ave. Subway: #1, 9, or C, E to 23rd St. Located in Chelsea on a block with a police precinct. Scandinavians with dreadlocks populate this hostel which overflows with funky European youth. W pizza nights. All rooms have windows and a sink. Backyard garden. Kitchens available. Internet access. Smallish but adequate 4- and 6-person dorms $23, with A/C $25; private rooms $55, with A/C $60. Key deposit $10. 24hr. check-in and laundry. Reservations recommended.

**International Student Center,** 38 W. 88th St. (787-7706), between Central Park West and Columbus Ave. Subway: B, C to 86th St. Open only to non-Americans aged 18-30; admittance requires a foreign passport or valid visa. An aging brownstone on a tree-lined street noted for frequent celebrity sightings. No-frills bunk rooms include showers and linens. Single- and mixed-sex rooms available. Large TV lounge with kitchen, fridge, and affable atmosphere. 8- to 10-bed dorms $15. Key deposit $10. 7-night max. stay (flexible in winter). Open daily 8am-11pm. No curfew. No reservations. Generally full in summer, but call after 10:30am on the day you wish to stay and they'll hold a bed for you until you arrive. No wheelchair access; lots of stairs.

## HOTELS

■ **Carlton Arms Hotel,** 160 E. 25th St. (679-0680), between Lexington and Third Ave. Subway: #6 to 23rd St. Each room has a different motif by a different avant-garde artist. Aggressive adornment can't completely obscure the age of these rooms, but provides a playful distraction. Shared baths. No A/C. All rooms have sinks. Singles $63, with bath $75; doubles $80, with bath $92; triples $99, with bath $111. Students and foreign travelers: singles $57, with bath $68; doubles $73, with bath $84; triples $90, with bath $101. Pay for 7 or more nights up front and get a 10% discount. Check-out 11:30am. Reserve for summer at least 2 months in advance. Confirm reservations 10 days in advance.

**Gershwin Hotel,** 7 E. 27th St. (545-8000), between 5th and Madison Ave. Subway: #6, or N, R to 28th St. This funky hotel is full of pop art, random furniture, and artsy twenty-somethings. Nightly entertainment including poetry, comedy, concerts, and open-mic nights. Art gallery next door features locals and professionals. 4-bed dorms $27 per bed, tax included. Private rooms (singles or doubles) $99-139; for triples or quads add an additional $10 per person. 21-day max. stay. 24hr. reception. Check-out 11am. No curfew.

**Chelsea Savoy Hotel,** 209 W. 23rd St. (929-9353), between 7th and 8th Ave. Clean, functional, and welcoming rooms decorated in forest green. All rooms have private bath, cable, A/C, irons and boards, and hair dryers. 24hr. desk and security. Singles $99-115; doubles $125-145; quad $145-185. Group rates available. Check-out 11am. Reservations recommended. Wheelchair access.

**Portland Square Hotel,** 132 W. 47th St. (382-0600 or 800-388-8988), between 6th and 7th Ave. Subway: B, D, F, Q to 50th St./Sixth Ave. Rooms are carpeted, clean, pink, and green. Phones, cable, A/C, sink, and safe in every room, but the hotel's greatest asset is its location. Singles $60, with private bath $90; doubles $70, with private bath $115; twins $125; triples $125; quads $145. Check-in 3pm, check-out noon.

**Herald Square Hotel,** 19 W. 31st St. (279-4017 or 800-727-1888), at 5th Ave. Subway: B, D, F, or N, R to 34th St. In the Beaux-Arts home of the original *Life* magazine. Historic magazine covers grace the hallways and each of the small, pleasant rooms. Many rooms have undergone recent renovations. All rooms have cable, safes, phones, voicemail, and A/C. Singles $60, with private bath $85; doubles $115, with twin beds $130; triples $160; quads $175. 10% discount for international students. Reserve 2-3 weeks in advance.

**Pioneer Hotel,** 341 Broome St. (226-1482), between Elizabeth St. and the Bowery. Subway: N, R to Canal and walk north several blocks to Broome. Located between Little Italy and the Lower East Side in a 100 year-old building, the Pioneer is a good, no-frills place to stay near the addictive nightlife of SoHo and the East Village. All rooms have TV, sinks, and ceiling fans. Rooms with private bathrooms have A/C. Generally tight security at night in a neighborhood that requires it. Tax included. Singles $53; doubles $70, with bath $82; triples $82, with bath $127. Check-out 11am. Reserve at least 6 weeks in advance during peak season.

**Pickwick Arms Hotel,** 230 E. 51st St. (355-0300 or 800-742-5945), between 2nd and 3rd Ave. Subway: #6 to 51st St.; or E, F to Lexington/Third Ave. Business types congregate in this well-priced, mid-sized hotel. Chandeliered marble lobby contrasts with tiny rooms and microscopic hall bathrooms. Roof garden and airport service. A/C, cable, phones, and voicemail. Singles $70, with bath $100; doubles with bath $130; studios with double bed and sofa for 2 people $150; for 4-person family $170. Additional person $25. Check-in 2pm. Check-out 1pm. Credit card to guarantee room.

**Washington Square Hotel,** 103 Waverly Pl. (777-9515 or 800-222-0418), at MacDougal St. Subway: A, B, C, D, E, F, Q to W. 4th St. Fantastic location. Glitzy marble and brass lobby, with an ornate wrought-iron gate in the lobby. A/C, TV, and key-card entry to individual rooms. Clean and comfortable; friendly, multilingual staff. Now with restaurant/bar with lounge, a meeting room, and an exercise room. Singles $116-130; doubles $136-140. Two twin beds $146-155; quads $155-174. Rollaway bed $17. 10% ISIC discount. Continental breakfast included. Reserve 2-3 weeks in advance for Sa-Su.

**Hotel Grand Union,** 34 E. 32nd St. (683-5890), between Madison and Park Ave. Subway: #6 to 33rd St. This centrally located hotel offers clean, pleasant rooms furnished with cable, phone, A/C, a mini-fridge, and full bathroom. 24hr. security. Singles and doubles $110; triples $125; quads $150; quints $180. Wheelchair access.

**Hotel Stanford,** 43 W. 32nd St. (563-1500 or 800-365-1114), between 5th and Broadway in NY's Korean district. Subway: B, D, F, or N, R to 34th St. Glitzy lobby glitters with sparkling ceiling lights and a polished marble floor. Adjoins the **Gam Mee OK** restaurant and the **Pari Pari Ko Bakery,** serving Korean delicacies and pastries. Rooms are impeccably clean, with firm mattresses, plush carpeting, cable, A/C, small refrigerators, and complimentary continental breakfast. Singles $90-110; doubles $120-150; triples $130-150. Check-out noon; fee for late check-out. Reservations strongly recommended.

**Malibu Studios Hotel,** 2688 Broadway (222-2954), at 103rd St. Subway: #1, 9 to 103rd St. Renovations have brought this former Gen-X kitschhaus up to date. Clean rooms with sinks. Staff has VIP passes to popular clubs like Webster Hall. 24hr. desk. Singles $49; doubles $69; triples $85; quads $99. Deluxe rooms with private bath, A/C, and TV: singles and doubles $99, triples $124, quads $139. Reservations required. Student, off-season, and weekly/monthly discounts. No wheelchair access.

**Senton Hotel,** 39-41 W. 27th St. (684-5800), between 6th Ave. and Broadway. Subway: R to 28th St. Look for the shockingly blue exterior. Comfortable beds in spacious quarters, which include A/C, cable, VCR, and refrigerators in every room. A number of rooms have been renovated, more complete by 2000. Home to many locals. The hotel has 24hr. security, so don't try to sneak in overnight guests. Singles with hall bath $64; doubles $75; suites (2 double beds) $86; 4-bed suites $92. No credit cards.

**Hotel 17,** 225 E. 17th St. (475-2845), between Second and Third Ave., near Gramercy Park. Served as the setting for Woody Allen's *Manhattan Murder Mystery*. Mostly foreign crowd. Beautiful, high-ceilinged rooms with sink and A/C. Singles $75; doubles $98. Deluxe rooms with cable, hair-dryer, and daily maid service. Doubles $109-$130; triples $149. Check-in 1pm. Check-out noon. No credit cards.

**Broadway Inn,** 264 W. 46th St. (997-9200 or 800-826-6300), at 8th Ave. Subway: #1, 2, 3, 9; or 7; or N, R; or S to Times Square. Located conveniently in the heart of the theater district, the quiet, cozy rooms in this lodge have an aura of unpretentious dignity. Singles $85-95; doubles $115-195; suites (for 3 adults and 2 children 6-12) $205. Continental breakfast included. AmEx, V, MC. No wheelchair access.

### DORMITORIES

🏛 **Columbia University,** 1230 Amsterdam Ave. (678-3235; fax 678-3222), at 120th St. Subway: #1; 9 to 116th St. Whittier Hall sets aside 10 clean rooms for visitors year-round. Generally tight 24hr. security. Not the safest neighborhood, but well-populated until fairly late at night. Singles $45; doubles with A/C and bath (some with kitchen) $75. Reserve in Mar. for May-Aug., in July for Sept.-Dec. Credit card deposit required.

# 🔘 FOOD

This city takes its food seriously. New York will dazzle you with its culinary bounty. City dining, like the population, spans the globe, ranging from sushi bars to wild combinations like Afghani/Italian and Mexican/Lebanese.

**FINANCIAL DISTRICT.** Lower Manhattan eateries cater to sharply clad Wall St. brokers and bankers on lunch break; they offer cheap food prepared grease-lightning-fast, always available as takeout and sometimes with free delivery. Fast-food joints pepper Broadway near Dey and John St., just a few feet from the overpriced offerings of the Main Concourse of the World Trade Center. In the summer, food **pushcarts** form a solid wall along Broadway between Cedar and Liberty St.

**Zigolini's,** 66 Pearl St. (425-7171), at Coenties Alley. Air-conditioned seating abounds at this gourmet Italian restaurant. Serves filling sandwiches ($5-7) and some great pasta. Sizeable sandwiches on foccacia are a specialty. Open M-F 7am-7pm.

**Europa,** 199 Water St. (422-0070), a block down from the Titanic Memorial at the South St. Seaport. Smoothly decorated and high-ceilinged, this gourmet self-serve joint is a little more expensive than nearby fast-food options. The grilled chicken breast sandwich on ciabatta bread, with lettuce, tomatoes, and basil pesto ($6.50), provides a delicious noonday meal. Open daily 6:30am-8:30pm. Delivery until closing.

**McDonald's,** 160 Broadway (385-2063), at Liberty St. Yeah, it's a McDonald's, but what a McDonald's! Wall St.'s Mickey D's sports a door person in a tux, a pianist, a stock ticker, and a McBoutique on the 2nd floor. The ketchup packets are in glass bowls here—a little touch of McClass. Open M-F 6am-9pm, Sa-Su 7:30am-9pm.

**LITTLE ITALY.** A chunk of Naples has migrated to this lively, compact quarter roughly bounded by Canal, Lafayette, Houston St., and the Bowery. **Mulberry St.** is the main drag and the appetite avenue of Little Italy. Stroll here after 7pm to catch street life, but arrive earlier to get a good table. To get to Little Italy, take the #4, 5, 6, or N, R, or J, M, Z to Canal St.; or take the B, D, F, Q to Broadway-Lafayette.

▧ **Da Nico,** 164 Mulberry St. (343-1212), between Broome and Grand St. Tasty food in a lovely environment, enhanced by a spacious, tree-shaded garden in back. Frequented by Al Pacino and Johnny Depp. *Pollo marsala* ($11.50) will placate a grumbling tummy. Lunch: pasta $6-10, entrees $6.50-12.50. Dinner: pasta $10-15, entrees $11-25. Open Su-Th 11am-11pm, F-Sa 11am-midnight.

▧ **Lombardi's,** 32 Spring St. (941-7994), between Mott and Mulberry St. New York's oldest licensed pizzeria (1897), credited with creating the famous New York-style thin-crust, coal-oven pizza. A large pie feeds 2 ($12.50). Toppings are pricey ($3 for one, $5 for two, $6 for three), as are the more creative assortments, like the fresh clam pie ($20 for a large)—but they're worth it. Reservations for groups of 6 or more. Cash only. Open M-Th 11am-11pm, F-Sa 11:30am-midnight, Su 11am-10pm.

**Puglia Restaurant,** 189 Hester St. (966-6006), at Mulberry St. After 6pm Puglia's own sing Italian folk favorites with a Vegas sensibility. The crowd is noisy and fun-loving, and the decent food comes in large portions. Long tables mean social equality in 3 spacious dining rooms and one lounge, ranging from diner to grotto chic. Pasta $7-10, entrees $9-18. Large plate of mussels $9.25. Open Su-Th noon-midnight, F-Sa noon-1am.

**Caffè Palermo,** 148 Mulberry St. (431-4205), between Grand and Hester St. The best of the *caffès* along Mulberry. In summer, Palermo opens onto the street with an espresso bar up front. Most pastries are $3-5. Tasty tiramisu ($5); the cannoli ($2.75) and cappuccino ($3.25) are also quite good. Open daily 9:30am-midnight.

**CHINATOWN.** Join the crowds that push through the narrow, chaotic streets of one of the oldest Chinatowns in the U.S. More than 300 restaurants serve some of the best Chinese, Thai, and Vietnamese eats around.

▧ **Bo-Ky,** 78-80 Bayard St. (406-2292), between Mott and Mulberry St. Tourists rarely grace this quality Vietnamese joint specializing in soups (most under $5). The spartan interior won't pamper, but the light, flavorful food merits a visit. The coconut-and-curry chicken soup ($5) will clear a nasty head cold. *Pho,* the beef broth king of Vietnamese soups, will fill you up without emptying your wallet ($3-5). The thick plum sauce and hot chili make dinner an authentic sweet-and-spicy treat. Open daily 7am-9:30pm.

▧ **Harden & L.C. Corp.,** 43 Canal St. (966-5419), near Ludlow St., may offer the best meal deal in Manhattan: a massive Malaysian dinner for only $2.50. There is a menu for this Malaysian greasy spoon, but nobody uses it: point to the 3 sides you want, and you'll get a huge plate of rice with a heaping portion of each side. While veggie dishes are available, strict vegetarians should go elsewhere. Mirrors, bright fluorescent lights, and a TV showing low-grade kung-fu flicks and Chinese soap operas spice up the ambience. Cash only. Bring your own alcohol. Open daily 9am-10:30pm.

**New York Noodle Town,** 28½ Bowery (349-0923), at Bayard St. Whether they're pan-fried or in soup, *lo mein* or the wider Cantonese-style, the noodles in the Town are incredible and cheap (most under $6.50). If you're willing to spend a bit more, try the barbecued duck ($9), or the salt-roasted flounder ($16). Often crowded at lunch and dinner; go early. Cash only. Bring your own alcohol. Open daily 9am-4am.

**Thailand Restaurant,** 106 Bayard St. (349-3132). Chinatown's first Thai restaurant has dealt well with the mushrooming competition. Simple and quiet, but head and shoulders above the other joints. Taste the killer *pad thai* ($5.50) and roasted duck in curry with coconut milk, bamboo shoots, onions, and bell peppers ($9.50). Known for homemade Thai desserts like sweet rice with egg custard and coconut milk ($1.50). AmEx accepted. Open daily 11:30am-11pm.

**Chinatown Ice Cream Factory,** 65 Bayard St. (608-4170), at Mott St. You can satisfy your sweet-tooth here with homemade lychee, taro, ginger, red bean, or green tea ice cream. One scoop $2. Open Su-Th noon-11pm, F-Sa 11:30am-11:30pm.

**Hong Kong Egg Cake Co.,** on the corner of Mott and Mosco St., in a small red shack on the side of a building. Proprietress Celicia Tam will make you a dozen soft, sweet egg cakes fresh from the skillet ($1). Don't worry about finding "The Co."—just follow the line wrapping around the corner of Mott.

**SOHO AND TRIBECA.** In SoHo, food is all about image. This lifestyle takes money, so don't be surprised if you find it hard to get a cheap meal. Often the best deal in SoHo is brunch, when the neighborhood shows its most good-natured front. Dining in TriBeCa is generally a much funkier (and blessedly cheaper) experience than in SoHo. TriBeCa's restaurants are often hidden like little oases among the hulking warehouses and decaying buildings.

📷 **Kelley and Ping Asian Grocery and Noodle Shop,** 127 Greene St. (228-1212), between Houston and Prince St. In a hollowed out SoHo warehouse space now decorated with its own sleek Asian food products and gorgeous deep wood, Kelly and Ping serve up tasty noodle dishes for under $8. Wraps under $5, soups $5-6, wok dishes under $7.50. Also has a tea counter for all things not Lipton. Open daily 11:30am-5pm and 6-11:30pm.

📷 **Space Untitled,** 133 Greene St. (260-8962), near Houston St. The best of SoHo—a huge, warehouse-like space with plenty of bar stools and chairs. Sandwiches and salads $3-6, fabulous desserts $1.85-3.50. Coffee $1.35-1.85, wine and beer $3-4.50. Open M-Th 8am-10pm, F 8am-midnight, Sa 9am-midnight, Su 9am-9pm.

**Pakistan Tea House,** 176 Church St. (240-9800), between Duane and Read St. Perennially busy eatery simmers with Tandoori dishes and other traditional Pakistani favorites. Their combo plates ($4) are an amazing deal. All meat is *halal*. Open daily 10am-4am.

**Yaffa's Tea Room,** 19 Harrison St. (274-9403), near Greenwich St. Amidst an eclectic arrangement of hipsters and used furniture, Yaffa's serves a very cool high tea ($20, reservations generally required), from M-Sa 2-6pm; it includes cucumber, salmon, or watercress finger sandwiches, fresh-baked scones, a dessert sampler, and a pot of tea. Sandwiches $8-10.50, entrees $8-20. "Couscous Night" every Th 6:30pm-midnight. The attached bar/restaurant is less subdued, with a different menu (including tapas). Bar open Su-Th 11am-2am, F-Sa 11am-4am. Restaurant open 8:30am-midnight.

**EAST VILLAGE AND ALPHABET CITY. First** and **2nd Ave.** are the best for restaurant-exploring. **St. Mark's Pl.** hosts a slew of inexpensive and popular village institutions, and at night, **Avenue A** throbs with bars and sidewalk cafes. Twenty-six cheap Indian restaurants line **6th St.** between 1st and 2nd Ave. If you look indecisive, anxious managers may offer free wine or discounts on already cheap food.

📷 **Damask Falafel,** 85 Ave. A. (673-5016), between 5th and 6th St. This closet-sized stand serves the cheapest and best falafel in the area—$1.75 for a sandwich; $3.50 for a falafel platter with tabouli, chick peas, salad, and pita bread; $1.25 for two succulent stuffed grape leaves. Banana milk shakes $1.50. Open M-F 11am-2am, Sa-Su 11am-4am.

📷 **Dojo Restaurant,** 24 St. Mark's Pl. (674-9821), between 2nd and 3rd Ave. Unbeatable Dojo is one of the most popular restaurants and hangouts in the East Village, and rightly so: it offers an incredible variety of cheap, tasty, vegetarian, and Japanese foods. Soyburgers with brown rice and salad $3.50. "Dojo salad" $5. Beer $2.75-4; pitchers $12-15. The rowdy chaos of St. Mark's might give you a headache at outdoor tables. Another location at 14 W. 4th St. (505-8934), between Broadway and Mercer St. Open Su-Th 11am-1am, F-Sa 11am-2am.

**The Kiev,** 117 Second Ave. (674-4040), at 7th St. An Eastern European breakfast extravaganza. A great place to be at 4am with the munchies. Breakfast deals; lox on a bagel is a steal in the city at $6. A cup of homemade soup comes with an inch-thick slab of challah bread. Menu features sandwiches of all sorts, along with potato pancakes, *kasha varnishke,* and more *pierogi* than you could shake a schtick at. Open 24hr.

**La Focacceria,** 128 First Ave. (254-4946), between St. Marks Pl. and 7th St. For 85 years, La Focacceria has served up light, delectable Sicilian eats. The *vesteddi* (fried ricotta and kashkaval cheese, $2) and eggplant Sicilian style sandwiches ($5) are exceptional. Open M-Th 11am-10pm, F-Sa 1-11pm.

**Mama's Food Shop,** 200 E. 3rd St. (777-4425), between Ave. A and B. See laid-back Villagers obeying Mama's strict command to "Shut up and Eat." Fried chicken or salmon (each $7), with sides ranging from honey-glazed sweet potatoes to broccoli to couscous ($1 each). Vegetarian dinner ($7) gives you any 3 sides. Bread pudding and cobbler come by the ½-pint ($3), if you have room for dessert. Open M-Sa 11am-11pm. Mama has recently created a doppelganger for herself with **Step Mama's,** across the street at 199 E. 3rd St. (228-2663), which sells sandwiches, soups, and sides. The nourishment continues next door at **Mama's Milk,** a smoothie shop.

**LOWER EAST SIDE.** Cultures clash here, where pasty-faced punks and trustafarians dine alongside an older generation conversing in Polish, Hungarian, and Yiddish. The neighborhood took in the huddled masses, and in return got lots of cool places to eat, including the city's finest **kosher Jewish eateries.**

**El Sombrero,** 108 Stanton St. (254-4188), on the corner of Ludlow. If the gods ate at a Mexican restaurant (and lived on a budget), they'd dine here. Vibrantly painted walls complement the animated crowd of twenty-somethings eating large portions of excellent food. Vegetable enchiladas ($8) make a satisfying meal, but you'll marvel at the Fajitas Mexicana ($10). Cash only. Hours vary, but closes midnight or slightly later.

**Katz's Delicatessen,** 205 E. Houston St. (254-2246), near Orchard St. Since 1888, Katz's has been an authentic Jewish deli. Katz's widened its appeal with its "Send a salami to your boy in the army" campaign during WWII. The food is orgasmic, but you pay extra for the atmosphere. Heroes $5.10, sandwiches around $9. Open Su-Tu 8am-10pm, W-Th 8am-11pm, F-Sa 8am-3am.

**Guss Lower East Side Pickle Corp.,** 35 Essex St. (254-4477 or 800-252-4877). Pickles galore, as seen in *Crossing Delancey.* A vast variety of glorious gherkins, from super sour to sweet, sold individually (50¢-$2) and in quarts ($4). They also offer coleslaw, pickled tomatoes, carrots, and t-shirts ($10). Open Su-Th 9am-6pm, F 9am-4pm.

**Economy Candy,** 108 Rivington St. (254-1531). Imported chocolates, jams, and countless confections, all at rock-bottom prices. Treat yourself to a huge bag of gummi bears ($1), a pound of chocolate-covered espresso beans ($5), or a pound of crystallized ginger ($3). Open M-F 8:30am-6pm, Sa 10am-5pm, Su 8:30am-5pm.

**GREENWICH VILLAGE.** The West Village's free-floating artistic angst has been channeled into many creative (and cheap) food venues, which line the major avenues. Aggressive and entertaining street life makes stumbling around and deciding where to go almost as much fun as eating. The European-style bistros of **Bleecker St.** and **MacDougal St.,** south of Washington Sq. Park, have perfected the homey "antique" look. Or slump down 8th St. to **6th Ave.** for some of the city's best pizza.

**Arturo's Pizza,** 106 W. Houston St. (677-3820), at Thompson St. Arturo's has served up great, cheap pizza and divey class for decades. Conveniently located near the Angelika Film Center. The big, cheesy pies are divine. Entrees $8-26. Live jazz M-F 9pm-1am, Sa-Su 9pm-2am. Open M-Th 4pm-1am, F-Sa 4pm-2am, Su 3pm-midnight.

**Go Sushi,** 3 Greenwich Ave. (366-9272), at 6th Ave. and 8th St. Clean, spacious, with magazine rack and people-watching window. Minimalist decor and cheap, delicious Japanese food unite at this no-nonsense, pay-at-the-counter gem. Bento Box with *gyoza,* rice, salad, and chicken teriyaki $6. Sashimi deluxe with rice, miso soup, and 9 pieces of fresh, delicious fish $12. Honeyed, iced green tea ($2.25) and fresh brewed ginger ale ($2.50) are sure to satisfy. Cash only. Open daily 11:30am-11:30pm.

**Cucina Stagionale,** 275 Bleecker St. (924-2707), at Jones St. Italian dining in a low-key, classy environment. Packed on weekends, its lines can reach the street. The *conchiglie* (shells and sauteed calamari in spicy red sauce, $8) or the spinach and cheese ravioli

($6) will tell you why. Pasta dishes $6-8; veal, chicken, and fish dishes $8-10. Cash only. Bring your own alcohol. Open daily noon-midnight.

**Quantum Leap,** 88 W. 3rd St. (677-8050), between Thompson and Sullivan St. Brown rice galore at this aggressively veggie restaurant. Large menu full of delectable options: chock-full-of-vegetables miso soup $3, spring rolls $3.50, gargantuan veggie burrito $6. Carnivores can try any fish in black bean sauce ($10-12). Vegan desserts include a yummy tofu blueberry pie ($3.50). Open daily 11am-11pm.

## MIDTOWN AND CHELSEA.

Straddling the extremes, the lower Midtown dining scene is neither fast-food nor *haute cuisine*. East of 5th Ave. on **Lexington Ave.,** Pakistani and Indian restaurants battle for customers. Liberally sprinkled throughout, Korean corner shops are equal parts grocery and buffet.

The best food offerings in Chelsea come from the large Mexican and Central American community in the southern section of the neighborhood. From 14th to 22nd St., eateries offer combinations of Central American and Chinese cuisine, as well as Cajun and Creole specialties. **8th Ave.** has the best restaurant browsing.

■ **Coffee Shop Bar,** 29 Union Sq. West (243-7969). A chic diner for fashion victims, owned by 3 Brazilian models whose gorgeous friends serve updated cuisine from the homeland. Sure, it's a bar and restaurant, but more importantly, it's a spectacle. Waifs abound, but aren't a likely result of the delicious food like tasty *media noche* sandwich ($9). Good for dessert ($5-6), a very late dinner ($8-17), or to watch others have dinner. Beers $4-6. Open daily 6am-5am.

■ **Soups on Seventeen,** 307 W. 17th St. (255-1505), off 8th Ave. This new eatery will liquify your mind with the astounding things it does to soup. Soup, sandwich, or salad with bread, fruit, and cookie $4-7.50. Try the taro root and coconut or the southwestern sweet potato soups (both $5 for 16oz.). Hell, taste them all. Open M-Sa 11am-7pm.

**Jai-Ya,** 396 Third Ave. (889-1330), between 28th and 29th St. Critics rave over the Thai and other Asian food, with 3 degrees of spiciness, from mild to "help-me-I'm-on-fire." Budget prices and a decidedly upscale look (cloth napkins!). The $7.25 Thai noodles are a definite steal. Most dishes $7-10. Lunch specials M-F 11:30am-3pm. Open M-F 11am-midnight, Sa 11:30am-midnight, Su 5pm-midnight. Also at 81-11 Broadway in Elmhurst, Queens (718-651-1330).

**Spring Joy,** 17 8th Ave. (243-1688), between 18th and 19th St. While NYC seems to have fallen out of love with Chinese food, Spring Joy serves it up well. Numerous lunch options under $5, dinner $5.75-8.50. Design your own dish $7; diet options $6-8.50. Free white wine with your dinner. Open M-Sa 11:30am-12:30am, Su noon-12:30am.

## EAST MIDTOWN.

From noon to 2pm, the delis and cafes here become swamped with harried junior executives trying to eat quickly and get back to work. The 50s streets on **2nd Ave.** and the area surrounding Grand Central Station are filled with good, cheap fare. You might also check out grocery stores, such as the **Food Emporium,** 969 2nd Ave., between 51st and 52nd St. (593-2224); **D'Agostino,** 3rd Ave., between 35th and 36th St. (684-3133); or **Associated Group Grocers,** 1396 2nd Ave., between E. 48th and E. 49th St. (421-7673). This part of town has many public spaces (plazas, lobbies, parks) for picnicking such as **Greenacre Park,** 51st St. between 2nd and 3rd Ave., and **Paley Park,** 53rd St. between 5th and Madison Ave.

■ **Dosanko,** 423 Madison Ave. (688-8575), between 48th and 49th St. Subway: E, F to Fifth Ave.; or #6 to 52nd St. All is tranquil at this aromatic Japanese pit-stop; the food is so tasty it seems criminal to waste time talking. The scrumptious *gyoza* ($4.50) is a favorite, as are the many varieties of *larmen* (Japanese noodle soup, $5.50-7.20). Cash only. Open M-F 11:30am-10pm, Sa-Su noon-8pm.

**Teuscher Chocolatier,** 620 Fifth Ave. (246-4416), on the promenade at Rockefeller Center. Subway: #6 to 51st St.; or E to Fifth Ave./53rd St. A choco-holic's paradise, Teuscher offers the freshest chocolates flown in from Zurich weekly, and have the prices to prove it. But don't let a little transatlantic overhead keep you from this experience—you can still savor a single piece for under $2.

**WEST MIDTOWN.** Your best bets here are generally along 8th Ave. between 34th and 59th St. in the area known as **Hell's Kitchen.** Once deserving the name, this area has given birth to an array of inexpensive ethnic restaurants. Those with deep pockets might like **Restaurant Row,** on 46th St. between 8th and 9th Ave., which feeds a pre-theater crowd (arriving after 8pm will make getting a table easier).

■ **Ariana Afghan Restaurant,** 787 9th Ave. (664-0123; 664-0125), between 52nd and 53rd St. This little cloister of things Afghani serves up superb, filling food. Kebab dishes ($8-10) and vegetarian platters ($6-8) come with basmati rice, salad, and homemade bread. Open M-Sa noon-3pm and 5-11pm, Su 3-10:30pm.

**Original Fresco Tortillas,** 536 9th Ave. (465-8898), between 39th and 40th St. This tiny 4-seater could be Taco Bell's better-looking father. Excellent homemade food at fast-food prices: fajitas and tacos $1-2, quesadillas $2-4, giant burritos $4-5. Cash only. Open M-F 11am-11pm, Sa-Su noon-10pm.

**UPPER EAST SIDE.** Meals descend in price as you move east from **5th Ave.'s** overpriced museum cafes toward **Lexington, 3rd** and **2nd Ave.**

■ **Barking Dog Luncheonette,** 1678 3rd Ave. (831-1800), at 94th St. Enter through the doghouse-shaped door labeled "Fido" and satisfy your hunger pangs with helpings right out of canine heaven. The biggest dog on the block will be satisfied with Mum's Luvin' Shepherd's Pie (beef, carrots, peas and stilton mash, $11.75) while others may prefer the Barking Dog Burger ($6.50). Open daily 8am-11pm.

**EJ's Luncheonette,** 1271 3rd Ave. (472-0600), at 73rd St. The understated American elegance and huge portions in this hip 50s-style diner have fostered a legion of devoted Upper East Siders. Scrumptious fare (buttermilk pancakes $5.75, cheeseburger with fries $6.75). Open M-Th 8am-11pm, F-Sa 8am-11:30, Su 8am-10:30pm.

**Papaya King,** 179 E. 86th St. (369-0648), at 3rd Ave. New Yorkers tolerate the outrageously long lines and the yellow decor at this dive with only a few stools and no tables all for a taste of the "tastier than filet mignon" hot dogs ($1.79). The special (2 hot dogs and a 16oz. tropical fruit shake) is $4. Open M-F 8am-midnight, Sa-Su 8am-2am.

**UPPER WEST SIDE.** Large and trendy restaurants spill onto the sidewalk, providing the perfect people-watching post. Intermingled among these are cheap pizza joints and hotdog hole-in-the-walls. The budget traveler should have no trouble finding affordable, satisfying meals along **Broadway, Amsterdam,** or **Columbus.**

■ **Mary Ann's,** 2454 Broadway Ave. (877-0132), at 91st St. A *fiesta* anytime! Simple, well-prepared Mexican food and excellent service make this one of the best dinners along Broadway. Entrees $8-15 (includes bottomless chips and salsa). Open Su-Th noon-10:30pm, F-Sa noon-11:30pm.

■ **Café Lalo,** 201 W. 83rd St. (496-6031), between Broadway and Amsterdam. A wall of French windows allows live jazz (and the occasional *bon mot* from a suave *monsieur* within) to escape onto the street. Perfect cakes $5 per slice, full bar available (ooh-la-la, *aperitifs, mon cheri!*). Open M-Th 8am-2am, F 8am-4am, Sa 9am-4am, Su 9am-2am.

**H&H Bagels,** 2239 Broadway (692-2435), at 80th St. H&H has nourished Upper West Siders for years with cheap bagels (75¢) that have a reputation as the best in Manhattan. Dozen bagels $9. Send a dozen home to mom—they ship anywhere in the world. Open 24hr.

**HARLEM AND MORNINGSIDE HEIGHTS.** In Harlem, ethnic food is everywhere: Jewish food in Washington Heights; various Latino and Cuban foods in the Hispanic communities; and, of course, East and West African, Caribbean, Creole, and some of the best soul food north of the Mason-Dixon Line. For food from the heart of Harlem, **Lenox Ave., 125th St.,** or **116th St.** are the places to go. The cafes and restaurants in Morningside Heights cater to Columbia University. This usually means late hours and a starving student's price range.

■ **Copeland's,** 547 W. 145th St. (234-2357), between Broadway and Amsterdam Ave. Excellent soul food accompanied by live music in an elegant dining room makes this place a top choice. If you're not too full from the complimentary cornbread, indulge in the Southern fried chicken (your choice of sides) for $11. Other entrees are a bit pricier; you may want to check out Copeland's "cafeteria" next door—same food, lower prices, minus the ambience. Open Tu-Th 4:30-11pm, F-Sa 4:30pm-midnight, Su 11am-9:30pm. Cafeteria open Su-Th 8am-11pm, F-Sa 8am-midnight.

**Obaa Koryoe,** 3143 Broadway (316-2950), between 125th and La Salle St. Expect excellent West African food in a laid-back setting. Ignore the American pop songs—elaborate wood carvings provide the authentic ambience. Bean stew and fried plantains, with *jollof* rice ($9) or chicken, *wachey,* and *gari* ($10). Indulge in a bottle of South African wine ($13-19). Open M-Sa 11am-11pm, Su 11am-9pm.

**Sylvia's,** 328 Lenox Ave. (996-0660), at 126th St. has enticed New Yorkers for over 30 years; now European tour groups also crowd the joint. Sylvia accents her "World-Famous talked-about BBQ ribs special" with "sweet spicy sauce" and a side of collard greens and macaroni and cheese ($11). Lunch special of salmon croquette, pork chop, fried chicken leg, collard greens, and candied yams $7. F nights feature free live jazz and R&B (6-9pm). Gospel Brunch Su.

**Tom's Restaurant,** 2880 Broadway (864-6137), at 112th St. Immortalized as the storefront featured in *Seinfeld* (not the Tom's in Suzanne Vega's song "Tom's Diner," as urban legend would have it). About as cheap as it gets. If you don't mind the no-frills diner feel, stop in to enjoy luxurious milkshakes ($2.45). Greasy burgers for $3-5, dinner under $6.50. Open M-W 6am-1:30am; from Th 6am to Su 1:30am open 24hr.

**BROOKLYN.** Brooklyn's restaurants, delis, and cafes offer all the flavors and varieties of cuisine that can be found in Manhattan, and often at lower prices. Brooklyn Heights and Park Slope offer nouvelle cuisine but specialize in pita bread and *baba ghanoush.* **Williamsburg** has cheap eats in a funky, lo-fi atmosphere, **Greenpoint** is a borscht-lover's paradise, and **Flatbush** serves up Jamaican and other West Indian cuisine. For those who didn't get their international fill in Manhattan, Brooklyn has a Chinatown in Sunset Park and a Little Italy in Carroll Gardens.

**Cambodia Restaurant,** 87 S. Elliott Pl. (718-858-3262), between Lafayette and Fulton St. in Fort Greene. Subway: G to Fulton St.: or C to Lafayette Ave. "No pork, less fat"; this place serves up delicious, cheap, porkless food like *Naem chao* (cold Cambodian spring rolls with shrimp, veggies, and sweet basil, $3.50) and *ktis tao hoo* (sauteed bean curd in lemon grass sauce, $6-9). Open Su-Tu 11am-10pm, W-Sa 11am-11pm.

**Grimaldi's,** 19 Old Fulton St. (718-858-4300), between Front and Water St. under the Brooklyn Bridge. Subway: A, C to High St. Delicious, thin crust brick-oven pizza with wonderfully fresh mozzarella. Come early to avoid long waits. All-Sinatra decor and Ol' Blue Eyes on the jukebox. Small pies $13, large $14, toppings $2 each. Open M-Th 11:30am-11pm, F-Sa noon-midnight, Su noon-11pm.

**Park Luncheonette,** 334 Driggs Ave., at Lorimer St., in Greenpoint. Subway: G to Nassau/Manhattan. Over 100 years old, this no-frills luncheonette has thankfully not become extinct like others of its kind. The food menu is limited to delicious frankfurters ($1.25) and other inexpensive fried sandwiches. The real draw is the to-die-for selection of fountain sodas ($1); egg creams (vanilla and chocolate) also available ($1.40-2). Bring your sweetheart and entwine straws. Open whenever the sun is out.

**Primorski Restaurant,** 282 Brighton Beach Ave. (718-891-3111), between Brighton Beach 2nd and Brighton Beach 3rd St. This nautically themed restaurant serves some of the Western Hemisphere's best Ukrainian *borscht* ($2.25) in an atmosphere of a red velour Bar Mitzvah Hall. Eminently affordable lunch special (M-F 11am-5pm, Sa-Su 11am-4pm; $4)—your choice of among 3 soups and about 15 entrees, bread, salad, and coffee or tea. At night, prices rise slightly as the disco ball spins. Russian music and disco M-Th 8pm-midnight, F-Sa 9pm-2am, Su 8pm-1am. Open daily 11am-2am.

**PlanEat Thailand,** 184 Bedford Ave. (718-599-5758). Subway: L to Bedford Ave. A restaurant that could only exist in Brooklyn: the city's best inexpensive Thai food served amidst walls decorated with high-quality graffiti. All beef dishes under $6, all chicken dishes under $7, and a killer *pad thai* for only $5.25. If you ask for spicy, they'll give you medium—it'll be enough to clear your sinuses (hot means *hot!* and is reserved for those who know what they're getting into). Open M-Sa 11:30am-11:30pm, Su 1-11pm.

**Roy's Jerk Chicken,** 3125 Church Ave. (718-826-0987), between 31st and 32nd St. in Flatbush. Subway: #2 or 5 to Church Ave. and 2 blocks east. Jerk chicken is a delicious Jamaican specialty—crispy chicken roasted with a sweet and very peppery marinade and served either hot or cold. Entrees ($6-7). Open M-Th 9am-2am, F-Su 24hr.

**QUEENS.** With nearly every ethnic group represented in Queens, this oft-over-looked borough offers visitors authentic and reasonably priced international cuisine away from Manhattan's urban neighborhoods. **Astoria** specializes in cheap eats. Take the G or R train to Steinway St. and Broadway and start browsing—the pickings are good in every direction. In **Flushing,** excellent Chinese, Japanese, and Korean restaurants flourish, often making use of authentic ingredients such as skatefish, squid, and tripe. **Bell Blvd.** in Bayside, out east near the Nassau border, is the center of Queens nightlife for the young, white, and semi-affluent. **Jamaica Ave.** in downtown Jamaica and **Linden Blvd.** in neighboring St. Albans are lined with restaurants specializing in African-American and West Indian food.

**Jackson Diner,** 37-47 74th St., Astoria (718-672-1232), at 37th Ave. Subway: E, F, G, or R to Jackson Heights/Roosevelt Ave.; or #7 to 74th St./Broadway, then walk north toward 37th Ave. Possibly the best Indian food in New York. Savor the *saag ghost* (lamb with spinach, tomato, ginger, and cumin, $10); don't forget samosas ($2.50). Lunch specials $6-7.50. Cash only. Open M-F 11:30am-10pm, Sa-Su 11:30am-10:30pm.

**Knish Nosh,** 101-02 Queens Blvd., Rego Park (718-897-5554). Subway: G or R to 67th Ave. This hole in the wall doesn't offer much seating because the owners need space for racks and racks of succulent knishes ($1.50) stuffed to plumpness with potato, kasha, broccoli, or onion. Lunch special includes large knish or kosher frank in a blanket and soda or coffee ($3). Cash only. Open M-F 9am-7:30pm, Sa 9am-7pm, Su 9am-6pm.

**Nick's Pizza,** 108-26 Ascan Ave., Forest Hills (718-263-1126), between Austin and Burns St. Subway: E, F, G, or R to Forest Hills/71st Ave., then walk 3 blocks on Queens Ave. (the numbers should be going up); take a right on Ascan Ave. Suburbany establishment serves up some of the best pizza in Queens. Flaky crust and delectable sauce and toppings ($11-12, toppings $2 extra). Great calzones. Cash only. Open M-Th 11:30am-9:30pm, F 11:30am-11:30pm, Sa 12:30-11:30pm, Su 12:30-9:30pm.

**The Lemon Ice King of Corona,** 52-02 108th St., Corona (718-699-5133), at Corona Ave. Subway: #7 to 111th St., a healthy walk back one block to 108th and south 10 blocks. Keep walking—it's worth it. One of the most famous sites in Queens, on par with the Unisphere. The Emperor of Cool scrapes up juicy frozen treats outdoors. Every flavor you could want, including bubblegum, blueberry, cantaloupe, cherry, and, of course, lemon (75¢-$1.50). Cash only. Open daily 10am-midnight.

**THE BRONX.** The Italian neighborhood of **Belmont,** which centers around the intersection of Arthur Ave. and 187th St., brims with streetside *caffè*, pizzerias, restaurants, and mom-and-pop emporiums vending Madonna 45s and imported espresso machines, all without the touristy frills of Little Italy. To get to Arthur Ave., take the C or D train to Fordham Rd. and walk 5 blocks east; alternatively take the #2 train to Pelham Pkwy., then the Bronx bus #Bx12 2 stops west.

**Dominick's,** 2335 Arthur Ave. (718-733-2807), near 186th St. Always packed, this small family-style Italian eatery sports an extra bar upstairs. Waiters seat you at a long table and simply ask what you want. No menu here and no set prices—locals are happy to give advice. Linguine with mussels and marinara ($7), marinated artichoke ($7), and veal *francese* ($12) are all house specials. Arrive before 6pm or after 9pm, or expect a 20min. wait. Open M and W-Sa noon-10pm, F noon-11pm, Su 1-9pm.

**El Gran Cafe Restaurant,** 1024 Longwood Ave. (718-378-1016) at Southern Blvd. Among the best of the South Bronx's *cuchifritas*—cheap restaurants serving big portions of Mexican and other Latin American food. The seafood dishes can be expensive, but almost everything else is under $12. For a real deal go M-F for the lunch special (11am-3pm). The special changes daily, but you can always get a bowl of stew, rice, and sweet banana for under $5. Open daily 6am-midnight.

**Emilia's,** 2331 Arthur Ave. (718-367-5915), near 186th St. Delicious food in large portions. The *calamari fra diavolo* ($15) and the stuffed centerloin pork chop ($15) are especially good. Appetizers $5-10, pasta $10, entrees $13-18. Lunch special $10. Open Tu-Su 11am-10pm.

# 👁 SIGHTS

You can tell who the tourists are in New York City—they're all looking up. The internationally famous New York skyline is deceptive and elusive; while it is impressive when seen from miles away, the tallest skyscraper seems like just another building when you're standing next to it. This sightseeing quandary may explain why many New Yorkers have never visited some of the major sights in their hometown. Just as budget travelers need not assume the etiquette (or lack thereof) of the New Yorker, they need not pick up this nasty habit of acclimation.

**LOWER MANHATTAN.** The southern tip of Manhattan is a motley assortment of cobblestones and financial powerhouses. The Wall St. area, less than a ½mi. long, is the most densely built in all New York. This narrow state of affairs has driven the neighborhood into the air, creating one of the highest concentrations of skyscrapers in the world. Crooked streets remain from before New York was a neat grid; lower Manhattan was the first part of the island to be settled by Europeans, and many of the city's historically significant sights lie here.

**Battery Park,** named for a battery of guns that the British stored there from 1683 to 1687, is now a peaceful residential area forming the southernmost toenail of Manhattan Island. The #1, 9 trains to South Ferry terminate at the southeastern tip of the park; the #4, 5 stop at Bowling Green, just off the northern tip. On weekends the park is mobbed with people on their way to the Liberty and Ellis Island ferries, which depart from here, and in-line skaters pushing aerodynamic baby buggies.

Once the northern border of the New Amsterdam settlement, **Wall Street** takes its name from the wall built in 1653 to shield the Dutch colony from a British invasion from the north. By the early 19th century, the area was the financial capital of the United States. **Federal Hall,** the original City Hall, was where the trial of John Peter Zenger helped to establish freedom of the press in 1735. *(26 Wall St. 825-6888.)* On the southwest corner of Wall and Broad St. stands the **New York Stock Exchange,** where more than 3000 companies exchange 228 billion shares of stock valued at $13 trillion. Arrive early; tickets usually run out by 1pm. The observation gallery overlooks the exchange's zoo-like main trading floor. *(656-5165. Open to the public M-F 9am-4pm. Last self-guided tour with interactive computers leaves at 3:30pm. Free.)*

Around the corner, at the end of Wall St., rises the seemingly ancient **Trinity Church.** Its Gothic spire was the tallest structure in the city when first erected in 1846. The vaulted interior feels positively medieval. *(602-0872.)* As recently as 1991, archaeologists found the remains of over 20,000 slaves buried only 20 ft. underground at the corner of Duane and Elk St. Congress declared the **African Burial Ground** a national landmark, in response to protests against a new Federal Court building to be built over the site. The grassy space now stands undisturbed with plans in the works for a more elaborate memorial. *(111 Centre St. between Leonard and White St.)*

Walk up Broadway to Liberty Park, and in the distance you'll see the twin towers of the **World Trade Center,** the city's tallest buildings. Two World Trade Center has an **observation deck** on the 107th fl. *(323-2340. Ticket booth on the mezzanine. Open daily June-Aug. 9:30am-11:30pm; Sept.-May 9:30am-9:30pm. Admission $12.50, students $10.75, seniors $9.50, ages 6-12 $6.25, under 6 free.)* Farther north on Broadway, City Hall Park and **City Hall** serve as the focus of the city's administration. The Colonial château-style structure, completed in 1811, may be the finest piece of architecture in the city. North of the park stands the **Criminal Court Building,** where you can sit in on trials. *(111 Centre St. between Leonard and White St.)*

The neo-Gothic **Woolworth Building** towers south of City Hall. F. W. Woolworth erected it in 1913 to house the offices of his empire. The Chrysler Building robbed "the cathedral of commerce" of its tallest building status in 1930. Arches and flourishes adorn the lobby of this five-and-dime Versailles. *(233 Broadway.)* A block and a half south on Broadway, **St. Paul's Chapel** was inspired by London's St. Martin-in-the-Fields and hosts frequent classical music concerts. St. Paul's is Manhattan's oldest public building in continuous use. *(623-0773. Open M-F 9am-3pm, Su 7am-3pm.)*

Turn left off Broadway onto Fulton St. and head for the **South Street Seaport.** New York's shipping industry thrived here for most of the 19th century. The city's revitalization has transformed the historic district, in all its fishy and foul-smelling glory, into the ritzy South St. Seaport complex, which includes a shopping mall known as **Pier 17.** The commercialism is made palatable by a restored 18th-century market, graceful galleries, and seafaring schooners. *(Pier 16 kiosk, the main ticket booth for the seaport, is open daily from 10am-7pm; 1hr. later on summer weekends.)* Dead fish reak at the end of Fulton St. The stench comes from the **Fulton Fish Market,** the largest fresh-fish mart in the country (and a notorious former mafia stronghold), hidden right on South St. on the other side of the overpass. *(748-8786. Market opens at 4am. Tours available June-Oct.)*

**THE STATUE OF LIBERTY AND ELLIS ISLAND.** The **Statue of Liberty** stands as the symbol of decades of immigrant crossings. The statue was given by the French in 1886 as a sign of goodwill. Standing at the entrance to New York Harbor, she has welcomed millions of immigrants to America. Today, the statue lifts her lamp to tourists galore, who make the ferry voyage to Liberty Island. *(363-3200. Ferry info 269-5755. Ferries leave for Liberty and Ellis Island from Battery Park every 30min. daily 8:30am-4:10pm; call for winter hours. $7, seniors $6, ages 3-17 $3.)* **Ellis Island** was once the processing center for the 15 million Europeans who came to the U.S. via New York; it was put out of use after the large waves of immigration were over. Ellis Island now houses an enlightening **museum.**

**LOWER EAST SIDE.** Down below Houston lurks the trendily seedy Lower East Side, where old-timers rub shoulders with heroin dealers and hip twenty-somethings. Two million Jews swelled the population of the Lower East Side in the 20 years before World War I; immigrants still live there, although now they are mostly Asian and Hispanic. A lot of East Village-type artists and musicians have recently moved in as well, especially near Houston St., but despite the influx of artists, a down-trodden element remains.

Remnants of the Jewish ghetto that inspired Jacob Riis's compelling work *How the Other Half Lives* still exist. At 60 Norfolk St., between Grand and Broome St., sits the **Beth Hamedrash Hagadol Synagogue,** the best-preserved of the Lower East Side houses of worship. From Grand St., follow Essex St. Three blocks south to **East Broadway.** This street epitomizes the Lower East Side's fusion of cultures. Buddhist prayer centers sit next to Jewish religious supply stores.

The area around Orchard and Delancey St. is one of Manhattan's bargain shopping centers. Between Broome and Delancey St., the **Lower East Side Tenement Museum** is a preserved tenement house of the type that proliferated in this neighborhood in the early part of the century. Tickets for a slide show, video, and tour are sold at 90 Orchard St., in the museum's **gallery,** which offers free exhibits and photographs documenting Jewish life on the Lower East Side. *(97 Orchard St. 431-0233. Tours of the tenement Tu-F at 1, 2, 3, and 4pm, Th 6 and 7pm, Sa-Su every 30min. 11am-4:30pm; 1hr. Tickets for 1 exhibit $8, students and seniors $6; for 2 exhibits $14, students and seniors $10; for 2 exhibits and a walking tour $20, students and seniors $14.)*

Way off Broadway lurks the Lower East Side's theater scene, characterized by high levels of do-it-yourself dedication and low ticket prices. In and around local streets you are likely to encounter experimental Shakespeare performances, improvisational theater, and serial plays that have been running for months. If you can't get tickets to Shakespeare in the Park, try Expanded Art's **Shakespeare in the Parking Lot,** staged across the street from their theater between Delancey and Broome St. *(85 Ludlow St. Call 253-1813 for info. June-Aug. W-Sa 8pm. Free.)*

MID-ATLANTIC

**SOHO AND TRIBECA.** SoHo is bounded by Houston St., Canal, Lafayette, and Sullivan St. The architecture here is American Industrial (1860-1890), notable for its cast-iron facades. While its roots are industrial, its inhabitants are New York's prospering artistic community. Here, **galleries** reign supreme and chic boutiques fill the voids. This is a great place for star-gazing too, so bring your autograph book and a bright flash for your camera. Celebrities like that. While the shopping in SoHo is probably well beyond a budget traveler's means, those seeking that hidden gem should check out the **Antiques Fair and Collectibles Market** on the corner of Broadway and Grand St. *(Open Sa-Su 9am-5pm.)*

**TriBeCa** (bounded by Chambers St., Broadway, Canal St., and the West Side Hwy.), has been anointed (by resident Robert DeNiro, among others) as one of the hottest neighborhoods in the city—though you might not guess it. Hidden inside the hulking industrial warehouses are lofts, restaurants, bars, and galleries, maintaining SoHo's trendiness without the upscale airs. Admire the cast-iron edifices lining White St., Thomas St., and Broadway, the 19th-century Federal-style buildings on Harrison St., and the shops, galleries, and bars on Church and Reade St.

**GREENWICH VILLAGE AND WASHINGTON SQ. PARK.** Located between Chelsea and SoHo on the lower west side of Manhattan, Greenwich Village (or, more simply put, "the Village") and its residents have defied convention for almost two centuries. Greenwich Village was once the nexus of New York bohemia and retains a reputation as the counter-culture capital of the East Coast. In stark contrast to the orderly, skyscraper-studded thoroughfares of greater Manhattan, narrow brownstone-lined streets meander haphazardly through the Village without regard to grids; most famously, W. 4th St. intersects W. 10th St. at Sheridan Sq.

The bulk of Greenwich Village lies west of 6th Ave. The West Village boasts eclectic summer street life and excellent nightlife. The area has a large, visible gay community around **Sheridan Sq.** These are the home waters of the 1969 Stonewall revival that helped galvanize the gay community. **Christopher St.** swims in novelty restaurants and shops. (Subway: #1, 9 to Christopher St./Sheridan Sq.)

**Washington Sq. Park** beats at the heart of the Village, as it has since the district's days as a suburb. (Subway: A, B, C, D, E, F, or Q to W. 4th St./Washington Sq.) The marshland here served as home to Native Americans and freed slaves, and later as a colonial cemetery, but in the 1820s the area was converted into a park and parade ground. Posh residences made the area the center of New York's social scene. Society has long since gone north, and **New York University** has moved in. The country's largest private university and one of the city's biggest landowners (along with the city government, the Catholic Church, and Columbia University), NYU buildings and eccentric students are everywhere in the Village.

In the late 70s and early 80s Washington Sq. Park became a base for low-level drug dealers and a rough resident scene. The mid-80s saw a noisy clean-up campaign that has made the park fairly safe and allowed a more diverse cast of characters to return. The **fountain** in the center of the park provides an amphitheater for comics and musicians of varying degrees of talent.

A theatrical landmark, **Provincetown Playhouse,** lies on the south side of Washington Sq. Park. Originally based in Cape Cod, the Provincetown Players were joined by the young Eugene O'Neill in 1916 and went on to premiere many of his works. *(33 MacDougal St.).* Farther south on MacDougal are the Village's finest coffeehouses, which saw their glory days in the 50s when beatnik heroes and coffeebean connoisseurs Jack Kerouac and Allen Ginsberg attended jazz-accompanied poetry readings at **Le Figaro** and **Café Borgia.** These sidewalk cafes still provide some of the best coffee and people-watching in the city.

The north side of the park, called **The Row,** showcases a stretch of elegant Federal-style brick residences built largely in the 1830s. Also NYU owned, **Washington Mews** is a row of ivy-covered colonial houses and is worth a peek. Up 5th Ave., at the corner of 10th St., the **Church of the Ascension,** a fine 1841 Gothic church with a notable altar and stained-glass windows, looks heavenward. *(Open daily noon-2pm* *and 5-7pm.)* **The Pen and Brush Club,** 16 E. 10th St., was founded to promote female intelligentsia networking; Pearl Buck, Eleanor Roosevelt, Marianne Moore, and muckraker Ida Tarbell were counted among its members.

At 5th Ave. and 11th St., **The Salmagundi Club,** New York's oldest club for artists, has sheltered the sensitive since the 1870s. *(255-7740. Open daily 1-5pm.)* **Forbes Magazine Galleries,** dominating the corner of 5th Ave. and 12th St., present eccentric Malcolm Forbes's vast collection of stuff. *(206-5548. Open Tu-Sa 10am-4pm. Free.)*

At 12th St. and Broadway lies **Forbidden Planet,** purported to be the world's largest science fiction store. *(Open daily 10am-8:30pm.)* Across the street is the famous **Strand,** which bills itself as the "largest used bookstore in the world." You'll want plenty of time to search through the collection of over two million books on 8mi. of shelves. *(Open M-Sa 9:30am-9:20pm, Su 11am-9:20pm.)*

**EAST VILLAGE AND ALPHABET CITY.** The East Village, a comparatively new creation, was carved out of the Bowery and the Lower East Side as rents in the West Village soared and its residents sought accommodations elsewhere. East Villagers embody the alternative spectrum, with punks, hippies, ravers, rastas, guppies, goths, beatniks, and seemingly everyone else coexisting amid an anarchic tangle of cafes, bars, and theaters. Allen Ginsberg, Jack Kerouac, and William Burroughs all eventually eschewed the Village establishment to develop a junked-up "beat" sensibility east of Washington Sq. Park, as did the pioneers of Punk.

The **Joseph Papp Public Theater** resides at Lafayette St., just below Astor Place, in John Jacob Astor's civic donation, the city's first free library. *(598-7150.)* Astor's 1867 **New York Shakespeare Festival** converted the building to its current use.

The intersection of **Astor Pl.** (at the juncture of Lafayette, Fourth Ave., and E. 8th St.) is distinguished by a sculpture of a large black cube balanced on its corner. Astor Pl. prominently features the rear of the Cooper Union Foundation Building, built in 1859 to house the **Cooper Union for the Advancement of Science and Art,** a tuition-free technical and design school founded by self-educated industrialist Peter Cooper. The school's free lecture series has hosted notable Americans since the mid-19th century. Cooper Union was the first college intended for the underprivileged and the first to offer free adult education classes. *(7 E. 7th Ave. 353-4199.)* Across Cooper Sq. south are the offices of America's largest free newspaper, the **Village Voice.** At 156 2nd Ave. stands a Jewish landmark, the **Second Avenue Deli.** *(677-0606.)* The "Yiddish Rialto," the stretch of 2nd Ave. between Houston and 14th St., comprised the Yiddish theater district in the early part of this century.

**St. Mark's Pl.** (where E. 8th St. would be) has long been the geographical and spiritual center of the East Village. In the 1960s, the street was the Haight-Ashbury of the East Coast, giving San Francisco a run for its hashish. In the late 70s it taught King's Rd. how to be punk as mohawked youths hassled passers-by from the brownstone steps of Astor Pl.; the Ramones, Blondie, the Talking Heads and the New York Dolls all played at the legendary dive **CBGB's.** Except for a few excellent bars and restaurants (Dojo's) and music stores (Kim's), St. Mark's walks the line between unabashed sleaze (count the tattoo parlors) and homogenized cheese, although alternateens dissipate as you move eastward. St. Mark's, still central to life in this part of town, is a good place to begin touring the neighborhood.

In **Alphabet City,** east of 1st Ave., south of 14th St., and north of Houston, the avenues run out of numbers and adopt letters. During the area's heyday in the 60s, Jimi Hendrix played open-air shows here to bright-eyed Love Children. There has been a great deal of drug-related crime in the recent past, although locals have done an admirable job of making the area livable and have started a number of community gardens. Alphabet City is generally safe during the day, and the nightlife on Ave. A ensures some protection there, but avoid straying east of Ave. B at night. Alphabet City's extremist Boho activism has made the neighborhood chronically ungovernable; police officers set once set off a riot when they attempted to evict a band of the homeless and their supporters in **Tompkins Sq. Park,** at E. 7th St. and Ave. A. The park still serves as a psycho-geographical epicenter for many a churlish misfit.

**LOWER MIDTOWN AND CHELSEA.** Madison Ave. ends at 27th St. and **Madison Sq. Park.** The park, opened in 1847, originally served as a public cemetery. Another member of the "I-used-to-be-the-world's-tallest-building" club, the eminently photogenic **Flatiron Building** sits off the southwest corner of the park. Often considered the world's first skyscraper, it was originally named the Fuller Building, but its dramatic wedge shape, imposed by the intersection of Broadway, 5th Ave., 22nd St., and 23rd St., quickly earned it its current name. Its windy corner has lifted the skirts of many a young lady, even the hallowed skirt of Ms. Marilyn Monroe.

A few blocks away, **Union Sq.,** between Broadway and Park Ave., and 17th and 14th St., sizzled with High Society intrigue before the Civil War. Early in this century, the name gained dual significance when the neighborhood became a focal point of New York's Socialist movement, which held its May Day celebrations in **Union Sq. Park.** Later, the workers and everyone else abandoned the park to drug dealers and derelicts. In 1989 the city began reclaiming it. The park is now pleasant and safe, though not necessarily pristine. The scents of herbs and fresh bread from the **Union Sq. Greenmarket** waft through on W, F, and Sa.

Home to some of the most fashionable clubs, bars, and restaurants in the city, **Chelsea** has lately undergone something of a rebirth. A large gay and lesbian community and an increasing artsy-yuppie population have given the area, west of 5th Ave. between 14th and 30th St., the flavor of a lower-rent West Village. Chelsea has become home to innovative **art galleries** that escape SoHo's exorbitant rent. New art outposts nestle amid auto body shops around **W. 22nd St.** and surrounding streets between **10th and 11th Ave.** The historic **Hotel Chelsea,** between 7th and 8th Ave., has sheltered many an artist, most famously Sid Vicious of the Sex Pistols. Edie Sedgwick torched the place with a cigarette between Warhol films. Countless writers, as plaques outside attest, spent their days searching for inspiration and mail in the lobby, including Arthur Miller, Vladimir Nabokov, Arthur C. Clarke, and Dylan Thomas. *(222 W. 23rd St. 243-3700.)* Chelsea's **flower district,** a sprawling market on 28th St. between 6th and 7th Ave., blooms during the wee hours.

**WEST MIDTOWN. Penn Station,** at 33rd St. and 7th Ave., is one of the least engrossing pieces of architecture in West Midtown, but serves its function as a major subway stop and train terminal. *(Subway: #1, 2, 3, 9, A, C, or E to 34th St./Penn Station.)* The original Penn Station, a classical marble building modeled on the Roman Baths of Caracalla, was demolished in the 60s. The railway tracks were then covered with the uninspiring **Madison Sq. Garden.** Facing the Garden at 421 8th Ave. is New York's immense main post office, the **James A. Farley Building.**

East on 34th St., between 7th Ave. and Broadway, stands **Macy's,** the mecca of Manhattan shopping. The store sponsors the **Macy's Thanksgiving Day Parade,** a New York tradition buoyed by 10-story Snoopys, marching bands, floats, and hoopla.

The billboards of **Times Square** flicker at the intersection of 42nd St. and Broadway. Considered the dark and seedy core of the Big Apple by most New Yorkers, the Square is working hard to improve its image. 1998 saw an invigorated promise from Mayor Giuliani to excise the pornography industry from the area. Disney has played an important role in restructuring Times Square, with a planned entertainment complex and 47-story hotel replacing the closed-down porn shops along 42nd St. between 7th and 8th Ave. Still, Times Square is Times Square. **New Year's 2000** should be a celebration of millennial proportions. The party starts at 7am on Dec. 31, 1999, when the Fiji islands begin their New Year. With each of the 24 new years, large video screens and elaborate sound and light systems will create a display appropriate for the time zone. Even more than the usual 500,000 people will cram in for this global event. *(Subway: #1, 2, 3, 7, 9, and A, C, E, N, R, S.)*

On 42nd St. between 9th and 10th Ave. lies **Theater Row,** a block of renovated Broadway theaters that is the heart of American theater. The fabled **Theater District** stretches from 41st to 57th St. along Broadway, 8th Ave., and the connecting streets. Approximately 37 theaters remain active, most of them around 45th St.

How do you get to **Carnegie Hall?** Just walk to 57th St. and 7th Ave. Founded in 1891, Carnegie Hall is New York's foremost soundstage. Tchaikovsky, Caruso,

Toscanini, Bernstein, the Beatles, and the Rolling Stones have played Carnegie. Other notable events include a 1934 lecture by Albert Einstein and Martin Luther King Jr.'s last public speech on Feb. 28, 1968. Carnegie Hall's **museum** displays arti- facts and memorabilia from its illustrious century of existence *(903-9790 Tours are given M-Tu and Th-F at 11:30am, 2, and 3pm. $6, students and seniors $5. Museum open M-F 11am-4:30pm, limited hrs. in winter. Free.)*

**EAST MIDTOWN AND FIFTH AVENUE. The Empire State Building,** on 5th Ave. between 33rd and 34th St., retains its place in the hearts and minds of New York- ers even though it is no longer the tallest building in the U.S., or even the tallest in New York (stood up by the twin towers of the World Trade Center). It doesn't even have the best looks (the Chrysler building is more delicate, the Woolworth more ornate). But the Empire State remains New York's classic landmark, continuing to dominate the postcards, the movies, and the skyline. The limestone and granite structure, with glistening ribbons of stainless steel, stretches 1454 ft. into the sky, and its 73 elevators run through 2mi. of shafts. The nighttime view from the top is spectacular. The Empire State was one of the first true skyscrapers, benefiting Eiffel's pioneering work with steel frames and Otis's perfection of the "safety ele- vator." It towers in relative solitude over Midtown, away from the forest of mono- liths around Wall St. *(736-3100. Observatory open daily 9:30am-midnight; tickets sold until 11:30pm. Admission $11.50, ages 4-12 and seniors $8.50.)*

In the **Pierpont Morgan Library,** at Madison Ave., the J. P. Morgan clan treats the book as fetish object. With exhibitions and lots of books inside, this Low Renais- sance-style *palazzo* attracts bibliophiles. *(29 E. 36th St. 685-0610. Subway: #6 to 33rd St. Open Tu-Sa 10:30am-5pm, Su noon-6pm. $7, students and seniors $5, under 12 free.)*

Speaking of booklovers, the **New York Public Library** opens its musty arms on the west side of 5th Ave. between 40th and 42nd St. On sunny afternoons, throngs of people perch on the marble steps. This is the world's 7th-largest research library; witness the immense 3rd fl. reading room. *(869-8089. Free tours Tu-Sa 11am and 2pm. Open M-Sa 10am-6pm, Tu-W 11am-7:30pm.)* **Bryant Park** spreads out against the back of the library along 42nd St. to 6th Ave., a grassy, tree-rimmed expanse. The stage at the head of the park hosts free cultural events throughout the summer, including screenings of classic films, jazz concerts, and live comedy. *(Open 7am-9pm.)*

To the east along 42nd St., **Grand Central Terminal** sits where Park Ave. would be, between Madison and Lexington Ave. A former transportation hub where dazed tourists first got a glimpse of the glorious city, Grand Central has been partially supplanted by Penn Station, Port Authority, and area airports. The massive Beaux Arts front, with the famed 13 ft. clock, gives way to the dignified and echoey Main Concourse, a huge lobby area setting the backdrop for civilized commuting.

The **Chrysler Building,** at 42nd St. and Lexington Ave., gives New York a touch of Gotham. Built by William Van Allen as an ode to the automobile, the building is topped by an Art Deco headdress and a spire modeled on a radiator grille.

To get out of the city for a while, head for the **United Nations Building,** located along 1st Ave. between 42nd and 48th St. A multicultural rose garden and a statu- ary park provide a lovely view of the East River. Inside, work your way through security check for informative tours of the **General Assembly,** which you must take to get past the lobby. Sometimes free tickets to sessions can be obtained when the U.N. is in session Oct.-May *(963-4475. Session tickets 963-1234. Visitor's entrance at 1st*

**ALL LIT UP** One foggy night in 1945, a U.S. Army B-25 bomber crashed into the 78th and 79th floors of the Empire State Building, shooting flames hundreds of feet in the air. Burning debris hurled for blocks, although the steel frame swayed less than 2 in. Fourteen people lost their lives in the bizarre accident. Mind you, this was not the skyscraper's first brush with aeronautical mayhem. Its tower, originally intended as a mooring mast for airships, docked two blimps there in 1931 and, in the same year, King Kong, the giant ape, fought planes from atop the famous tower.

*Ave. and 46th St. Daily tours about 45min., leaving every 15min. 9:15am-4:45pm, available in 20 languages. $7.50, students $4.50, over 60 $5.50, ages 6-14 $3.50.)*

Between 48th and 51st St. and 5th and 6th Ave. stretches **Rockefeller Center,** a conjunction of business and art. On 5th Ave., between 49th and 50th St., the famous gold-leaf statue of Prometheus sprawls on a ledge of the sunken **Tower Plaza** while jet streams of water pulse around it. The Plaza serves as an open-air cafe in the spring and summer and as a world-famous ice-skating rink in the winter. The 70-story former RCA building, now the **GE Building,** seated at 6th Ave., is the center's most accomplished artistic creation. Every chair in the building sits less than 28 ft. from natural light. The **NBC Television Network** makes its headquarters here. The network offers an hour-long, behind-the-scenes tour tracing the history of NBC. The tour visits the studios of *Conan O'Brien* and the infamous *Saturday Night Live* studio. *(Tours every 30min. M-Sa 9:30am-4:30pm. $17.50.)*

Despite an illustrious history and a wealth of Art Deco treasures, **Radio City Music Hall** was almost demolished in 1979 to make way for new office high-rises. However, the public rallied and the place was declared a national landmark. First opened in 1932, at the corner of 6th Ave. and 51st St., the 5874-seat theater is the largest in the world. The brainchild of Roxy Rothafel (originator of the Rockettes), it was originally intended as a variety showcase. However, the hall functioned primarily as a movie theater; over 650 feature films debuted here from 1933 to 1979. The Rockettes, Radio City's vertically endowed chorus line, still dance on. *(632-4041. Tours leaving every 30-45min. M-Sa 10am-5pm, Su 11am-5pm. $13.75, under 12 $9.)*

At 25 W. 52nd St., the **Museum of Television and Radio** is almost entirely a "viewing museum" (see **Museums,** p. 228). Over a block down W. 53rd St. towards 6th Ave. is the **Museum of Modern Art** (see **Museums,** p. 228).

**St. Patrick's Cathedral,** New York's most famous church and the largest Catholic cathedral in America, stands at 51st St. and 5th Ave. Designed by James Renwick, the structure captures the essence of great European cathedrals yet retains its own spirit. The twin spires stretch 330 ft. into the air. *(753-2261.)*

One of the monuments to modern architecture, Ludwig Mies Van der Rohe's dark and gracious **Seagram Building** looms over 375 Park Ave., between 52nd and 53rd St. Pure skyscraper, fronted by a plaza and two fountains, the Seagram stands as a paragon of the austere International Style. Van der Rohe envisioned it as an oasis from the tight canyon of skyscrapers on Park Ave.

The stores on 5th Ave. from Rockefeller Center to Central Park are the ritziest in the city. At **Tiffany & Co.,** everything from jewelry to housewares shines; the window displays are works of art in themselves, especially around Christmas. *(755-8000. Jewelry $15-800,000. Open M-W and F-Sa 10am-6pm, Th 10am-7pm.)* **F.A.O. Schwarz,** at 58th St., is one of the world's largest toy stores, including a Lego complex and a Barbie doll annex. *(767 5th Ave. 644-9400. Open M-W 10am-7pm, Th-Sa 10am-8pm, Su 11am-6pm.)*

On 5th Ave. and 59th St., at the southeast corner of Central Park, sits the legendary **Plaza Hotel,** built in 1907 at astronomical cost. Its 18-story, 800-room French Renaissance interior flaunts five marble staircases, countless ludicrously named suites, and a 2-story Grand Ballroom. Past guests and residents include Frank Lloyd Wright and the Beatles. *Let's Go* recommends the $15,000-per-night suite.

**CENTRAL PARK.** *General Information: 360-3444; for parks and recreation info, call 360-8111 (M-F 9am-5pm). The **Central Park Conservancy** maintains the park. The Conservancy offers various programs, from birding and nature walks to family tai chi, at its 3 **information and education centers:** the **Belvedere Castle** (772-0210), the **Charles A. Dana Discovery Center** (860-1370), and the **Dairy.** The Dairy, located south of 65th St., houses the **Central Park Reception Center** (794-6564). Open Mar.-Oct. Tu-Th and Sa-Su 11am-5pm, F 1-5pm; Nov.-Feb. Tu-Th and Sa-Su 11am-4pm, F 1-4pm. Has brochures, calendars and **free maps**.*

Beloved Central Park has certainly had its moments in the sun, from Simon and Garfunkel's historic 1981 concert to the annual meeting of stars in the summertime Shakespeare in the Park festival. The enormous park offers a pastoral refuge from the fast-paced urban jungle of New York City. Despite its bucolic appear-

Central Park is fairly safe during the day, but less so at night. Do not be afraid to go to shows or Shakespeare in the Park at night, but stay on the paths and go with someone else. Do not wander on the darker paths at night. Women should especially use caution after dark. In an **emergency,** use one of the many call-boxes located throughout the park. To report a crime, call the **24hr. Park Line** (570-4820).

ance, Central Park was never an authentic wilderness. The landscaped gardens were carved out of the city's grid between 59th and 110th St. for several blocks west of 5th Ave. and engineered to look pastoral by designers Olmsted and Vaux in the mid-1840s. The final product contains lakes, ponds, fountains, skating rinks, ball fields, tennis courts, a castle, an outdoor theater, a bandshell, and two zoos.

The Park may be roughly divided between north and south at the main reservoir; the southern section affords more intimate settings, serene lakes, and graceful promenades, while the northern end has a few ragged edges. Nearly 1400 species of trees, shrubs, and flowers grow here, the work of distinguished horticulturist Ignaz Anton Pilat. As you wander amid the shrubbery, look to the nearest lamppost and check the small metal four-digit plaque bolted to it. The first two digits tell you the nearest street, and the second two whether you're on the east or west side of the Park (even numbers mean east, odds west). **Central Park Bicycle Tours** offers leisurely 2hr. guided bicycle tours through Central Park. (541-8759. 3 tours leave daily from 2 Columbus Circle. Call for reservations. $30, includes bike rental.)

The spectacular, free **Central Park Summerstage** concert program is packed each summer with up-and-coming indie acts. The **Wollman Skating Rink** sees wheels turn to blades when it gets cold enough. (396-1010. Ice- or roller-skating $4, seniors and children $3, plus $6.50 rental. Complex open daily 11am-6pm.)

The **Friedsam Memorial Carousel** turns at 65th St. west of Center Dr. The 58-horsepower Coney Island carousel was restored in 1983. (879-0244. Open daily 10am-6:30pm; late Nov. to mid-Mar. Su 10:30am-4:30pm. 90¢.) Directly north of the Carousel, **Sheep Meadow** grows from about 66th to 69th St. on the western side of the Park. This is the park's largest chunk of green, exemplifying the pastoral ideals of the Park's designers. The **Lake** provides a dramatic patch of blue. The 1954 **Loeb Boathouse** supplies the necessary romantic nautical equipment. (517-2233. Open Apr.-Sept. daily 10:30am-4:30pm, weather permitting. Rowboats $10 per hr., $30 deposit.)

**Strawberry Fields** was sculpted by Yoko Ono as a memorial to John Lennon. The Fields are located to the west of the Lake at 72nd St. and West Dr., directly across from the Dakota Apartments where Lennon was assassinated and where Yoko Ono still lives. On sunny spring days, picnickers enjoy the 161 varieties of plants that now bloom over the rolling hills around the star-shaped "Imagine" mosaic.

The **Swedish Cottage Marionette Theater,** at the base of Vista Rock near the 79th St. transverse, puts on regular puppet shows. (988-9093. M-F at 10:30am and noon. $5, children $4. Reservations required.) Up the hill the **Delacorte Theater,** hosts the wildly popular **Shakespeare in the Park** series each midsummer. These plays often feature celebrities and are always free. Come early: the theater seats only 1936 lucky souls. Large concerts often take place north of the theater, on the **Great Lawn.** Here, Paul Simon sang, the Stonewall 25 marchers rallied, and the New York Philharmonic and the Metropolitan Opera Company give free summer performances.

**UPPER EAST SIDE.** The Golden Age of East Side society began in the 1860s and progressed until WWI. Scores of wealthy people moved into the area and refused to budge. These days, parades, millionaires, and slow buses share 5th Ave. Upper 5th Ave. is home to **Museum Mile,** which includes the **Metropolitan Museum of Art,** the **Guggenheim,** the **Whitney,** the **International Center of Photography,** the **Cooper-Hewitt,** and the **Jewish Museum,** among many others (see **Museums,** p. 228).

The Upper East Side drips with money along the length of the Park. At 59th St. and 3rd Ave., **Bloomingdale's** sits in regal splendor. **Madison Ave.** has luxurious boutiques and most of the country's advertising agencies. **Park Ave.,** the street that time forgot, maintains a regal austerity with gracious buildings and landscaped medians. **Gracie Mansion,** at the north end of Carl Schurz Park, between 84th and 90th St. along East End Ave., has been the residence of New York mayors since Fiorello LaGuardia, now occupied by Rudolph Giuliani. *(Tours W at 10, 11am, 1pm, and 2pm. Suggested donation $4, seniors $3. To make reservations, call 570-4751.)*

**UPPER WEST SIDE.** Broadway leads uptown to **Columbus Circle,** at 59th St. and Broadway, the symbolic entrance to the Upper West Side and the end of Midtown. A statue of Christopher marks the border. One of the landmarks, the **New York Coliseum,** has been relatively empty since the construction of the **Javits Center** in 1990.

Broadway intersects Columbus Ave. at **Lincoln Center,** the cultural hub of the city, between 62nd and 66th St. The 7 facilities that constitute Lincoln Center— Avery Fisher Hall, the New York State Theater, the Metropolitan Opera House, the Library and Museum of Performing Arts, the Vivian Beaumont Theater, the Walter Reade Theater, and the Juilliard School of Music—accommodate over 13,000 spectators at a time. **Columbus Ave.** leads to the **Museum of Natural History** (see **Museums,** p. 228). **Broadway** pulses with energy all day (and night). The Upper West Side is covered with residential brownstones, scenic enough for a pleasant stroll.

**HARLEM.** The influx of rural black Southerners around WWI created the Harlem known today as one of the capitals of the black Western world. The 1920s were Harlem's Renaissance; a thriving scene of artists, writers, and scholars lived fast and loose, producing cultural masterworks in the process. The Cotton Club and the Apollo Theater, along with numerous other jazz clubs, were on the musical vanguard, while Langston Hughes and Zora Neale Hurston changed the face of literature. Nevertheless, conditions for people of color were tough—they were charged more than their white counterparts for the unhealthy tenement rooms, and the murderous Klan paid occasional visits. In the 1960s, riding the charged tidal wave of the Civil Rights Movement, the revolutionary Black Power movement flourished here. Recognizing the need for economic revitalization as a route to empowerment, members of the community began an attempt at redevelopment in the 70s. This attempt continues today as the city pumps money into the area and communities bond together to beautify their neighborhood and actively resist crime. Although poorer than many neighborhoods, it is culturally rich. Most street activity is nothing more harmful than old men playing cards.

On the East Side above 96th St. lies **Spanish Harlem,** known as El Barrio ("the neighborhood"), and on the West Side lies Harlem proper, stretching from 110th to 155th St. **Columbia University** controls the area west of Morningside Dr. and south of 125th St., commonly known as **Morningside Heights.**

On the West Side, from 125th to 160th St., most cultural and social life takes place in **Central Harlem.** To the far north, from 160th St. to 220th St., **Washington Heights** and **Inwood** are populated by Dominican and Jewish communities.

The **Cathedral of St. John the Divine,** along Amsterdam Ave. between 110th and 113th St., will be the world's largest cathedral when finished. Construction, begun in 1812, continues and will not be completed for another century or two. Stained glass windows portray TV sets as well as the usual religious scenes. A trip down the overwhelming central nave leads to an altar dedicated to AIDS victims and a 2000 lb. natural quartz crystal. *(Open daily 7am-5pm. Suggested donation $2, students and seniors $1. Vertical tours (you go up) given on the 1st and 3rd Sa of the month at noon and 2pm. $10. Reservations recommended. Regular horizontal tours Tu-Sa 11am, Su 1pm. $3.)* Near Columbia, at 120th St. and Riverside Dr., is the **Riverside Church.** The observation deck in the tower commands an amazing view. Concerts make use of the world's largest carillon (74 bells), a gift of John D. Rockefeller, Jr. *(Tower open Tu-Sa 11am-4pm. Admission to observation deck T-Sa $2, students and seniors $1. Su service 10:45am. Free tours Su 12:30pm.)* Diagonally across Riverside Dr. lies **Grant's Tomb,** which contains you-know-who. Hippie-trippy mosaic tile benches around the monument were added in the mid-70s. An assortment of college-aimed bookstores and restaurants line Broadway.

**125th St.**, also known as Martin Luther King, Jr. Blvd., spans the heart of traditional Harlem. Fast-food joints, jazz bars, and the **Apollo Theater** keep the street humming day and night. *(749-5838, box office 864-0372.)* 125th St. has recently experienced a resurgence of small jazz clubs. Off 125th St., **Sylvia's** has magnetized New York for 22 years with enticing soul food dishes. *(328 Lenox Ave. 996-0660. Open M-Sa 7:30am-10:30pm, Su 12:30-7pm.)* The silver dome of the **Masjid Malcolm Shabazz**, where Malcolm X was once a minister, glitters on 116th St. and Lenox Ave. (662-2200. Services F at 1pm and Su at 10am.)

**Washington Heights,** the area north of 155th St., affords a taste of urban life with a thick ethnic flavor. On the same block, you can eat a Greek dinner, buy Armenian pastries and vegetables from a South African, and discuss the Talmud with a student at nearby **Yeshiva University.** Get medieval at the **Cloisters,** a lovely monastery with airy archways, manicured gardens, the famed Unicorn Tapestries, and other pieces of the Met's collection of medieval art (see **Museums,** p. 228).

**BROOKLYN.** The gregarious streets of Brooklyn are an escape from tourist-infested Manhattan. Brooklyn is Dutch for "Broken Land," and the name fits—Brooklyn is a marvelously diverse terrain, where ultra-orthodox *Hasidim* rub elbows with black teenagers on a street covered with signs *en español.* Ethnic and religious groups don't always get along, but an indomitable pride in their home unites them. And they have reason to be proud—1 out of every 7 famous Americans is from here. What goes on here tends to go on outdoors, be it neighborhood banter, baseball games in the park, ethnic festivals, or pride marches.

The Dutch originally settled the borough in the 17th century, and they shared the land with the Brits well into the early 19th century. When asked to join New York in 1833, Brooklyn refused, saying that the two cities had nothing in common except for waterways. Not until 1898 did it decide, in a close vote, to become a borough of New York City, though it still exists as an independent entity. Early this century European immigrants descended. After the Depression, blacks from the South arrived, and more groups followed, building the borough's mix of cultures.

**The Brooklyn Bridge** gracefully spans the gap between Lower Manhattan and Brooklyn (subway: #4, 5, 6 to Brooklyn Bridge). Its arched towers were the greatest engineering achievement of the 19th century. The 1mi. walk along the pedestrian path reveals why every New York poet feels compelled to write about it, why photographers snap the bridge's airy spider-web cables, and why people jump off. A ramp across from Manhattan's City Hall begins the journey.

Head south on Henry St. after the Brooklyn Bridge, then turn right on Clark St. toward the river for a jaw-dropping view of Manhattan. Many a photograph has been snapped from the **Brooklyn Promenade,** overlooking the southern tip of Manhattan and New York Harbor. George Washington's headquarters during the Battle of Long Island, the now-posh **Brooklyn Heights,** with beautiful old brownstones, tree-lined streets, and proximity to Manhattan, has hosted many authors, from Walt Whitman to Norman Mailer. *(Subway: N, R, 2, 3, 4, or 5 to the Court St.-Borough Hall and follow Court St.)* The **New York Transit Museum,** at Boerum and Schermerhorn, in a defunct subway station, houses subway memorabilia. *(718-243-8601. Open Tu and Th-F 10am-4pm, W 10am-6pm, Sa-Su noon-5pm. $3, under 17 and seniors $1. Subway: #2, 3, or 4, 5 to Borough Hall; the A, C F to Jay St./Borough Hall; or the M, N, R to Court St.)*

Nestled at the northern border with Queens, **Greenpoint** is the seat of an active Polish community. *(Subway: E,F to Queens Plaza, then G to Greenpoint Ave.)* South of Greenpoint is **Williamsburg,** home to a large Hispanic and Jewish population. *(Subway: J, M, Z to Marcy Ave.)* Young artists are drawn to Williamsburg's affordable loft spaces. A small but growing outcropping of hip restaurants, cafes, and bars has sprung up. West on Berry St. and up N. 10th stands a **graffiti mural.** More *virtuoso* graffiti can be found northward at N. 10th and Union Ave. In **Crown Heights** is the world headquarters of **ChaBad,** a Hasidic Jewish sect. *(770 Eastern Pkwy.)*

**Prospect Park,** designed by Frederick Law Olmsted and Calvin Vaux in the mid-1800s, is a 526-acre urban oasis; it pleased them more than their Central Park project. *(Subway: #2, 3 to Grand Army Pl.)* At the north corner of the park, **Grand Army Plaza** is an island in the midst of busy thoroughfares, shielding surrounding apartment buildings from traffic. The **Botanic Gardens** in Institute Park are secluded and include a lovely rose garden. *(718-622-4433. Open Tu-F 8am-6pm, Sa-Su 10am-6pm; Oct.-Mar. Tu-F 8am-4:30pm, Sa-Su 10am-4:30pm. $3, students and seniors $1.50, ages 5-15 50¢; free Tu.)* The mammoth **Brooklyn Museum** rests next to the gardens. *(718-638-5000. Open W-Su 10am-5pm. Suggested donation $4, students $2, seniors $1.50, under 12 free.)*

Both a body of water and a mass of land, **Sheepshead Bay** lies on the southern edge of Brooklyn. Diners can catch daily seafood specials along Emmons Ave. Nearby **Brighton Beach,** nicknamed "Little Odessa by the Sea," has been homeland to Russian emigres since the turn of the century. *(Subway: D or Q.)*

At one time a resort for the City's elite, until the subway made it accessible to the masses, fading **Coney Island** still warrants a visit. The once-seductive **Boardwalk** squeaks nostalgically as tourists are jostled by roughnecks. Enjoy a hot dog and crinkle-cut fries at historic **Nathan's,** at Surf and Sitwell Ave. The **Cyclone,** at W. 10th St., built in 1927, was once the most terrifying roller-coaster ride in the world ($4). *(834 Surf Ave. 718-266-3434. Open mid-June to Sept. daily noon-midnight; Easter weekend to mid-June F-Su noon-midnight.)* Meet a walrus, dolphin, sea lion, shark, or other ocean critter in the tanks of the **New York Aquarium,** at Surf Ave. and W. 8th St. *(718-265-3474. Open daily 10am-6pm. $7.75, seniors and children $3.50.)*

**QUEENS.** In this urban suburbia, the American melting pot bubbles away with a more than 30% foreign-born population. Immigrants from Korea, China, India, and the West Indies sort into neighborhoods where they try to maintain the memory of their homeland while striving for "the American Dream."

Queens is easily New York's largest borough, covering over a third of the city's total area. **Flushing** boasts colonial neighborhood landmarks, a bustling downtown, an Asian immigrant population, and the largest rose garden in the Northeast. *(Subway: #7 to Main St., Flushing.)* Nearby **Flushing Meadows-Corona Park** was the site of the 1964-1965 World's Fair, and now holds **Shea Stadium** (home of the Mets) and the **New York Hall of Science,** on the corner of 111th St. and 48th Ave. *(718-699-0005.)* The **Unisphere,** a 380-ton steel globe in front of the nearby New York City Building, hovers over a fountain in retro-futuristic glory. Yup, this is the thing that nasty alien crashed into in 1997's *Men In Black.* The New York City Building houses the **Queens Museum of Art** *(718-592-9700),* and just south of the Hall of Science is the **Queens Wildlife Center and Zoo.** *(718-271-7761.)*

In the upper west corner lies **Astoria,** where Greek-, Italian-, and Spanish-speaking communities mingle amid lively shopping districts and cultural attractions. **Long Island City** is just south, across the river from the Upper East Side. A trip on the N train from Broadway and 34th St. in Manhattan to Broadway and 31st St. at the border between the two areas takes about 25min. Two sculpture gardens make for a worthwhile daytrip from Manhattan. From the Broadway station at 31st St., walk west along Broadway 8 blocks toward the Manhattan skyline, leaving the commercial district for a more industrial area. At the end of Broadway, cross the intersection with Vernon Blvd. The **Socrates Sculpture Park,** started by sculptor Mark di Suvero, is across from the "Adirondack Office Furniture" building. The sight of this plot of land is stunning, if somewhat unnerving: 35 modern day-glo and rusted metal abstractions sit en masse in the middle of nowhere, on the site of what was once an illegal dump. *(718-956-1819. Park open daily 10am-sunset.)* Two blocks south stands the **Isamu Noguchi Garden Museum,** established in 1985 next door to the world-renowned sculptor's studio. Twelve galleries display Noguchi's breadth of vision. *(32-37 Vernon Blvd. 718-204-7088. Open Apr.-Oct. W-F 10am-5pm, Sa-Su 11am-6pm. Suggested donation $4, students and seniors $2. Lengthy free tour at 2pm.)* Astoria also houses the **American Museum of the Moving Image** (see **Museums,** p. 228).

# HIP-HOP (R)EVOLUTION
In 1973, Bronx DJ Kool Herc began prolonging songs' funky drum "break" sections by using two turntables and two copies of the same record, switching to the start of the second copy when the first one ended and then doubling back. Dancers took up the rhythm's challenge, and by 1975 break-dancing had evolved in response to similar turntable manipulations by Afrika Bambaataa, Grandmaster Flash, Kool, and other denizens of the 174th St. area near the Bronx River. All in one break, the Bronx birthed the art of DJing, an acrobatic dance style, and the musical genre known as hip-hop/rap that would shape the sound of the new millennium. For the phatty-phat 411, hit Davey D's exhaustive web page at www.daveyd.com.

**THE BRONX.** While the media present "Da Bronx" as a crime-ravaged husk, the borough offers over 2000 acres of port land, a great zoo, turn-of-the-century riverfront mansions, grand boulevards, and thriving ethnic neighborhoods, including a Little Italy which shames Manhattan's. *Be very careful in the South Bronx; do not venture there without someone who knows the area well.*

The most popular reason to come to the Bronx is the **Bronx Zoo/Wildlife Conservation Park,** also known as the New York Zoological Society. The largest urban zoo in the United States, it houses over 4000 animals. Soar into the air for a funky view of the zoo from the **Skyfari** aerial tramway that runs between Wild Asia and the **Children's Zoo** ($2). Call 718-220-5142 three weeks in advance to reserve a place on a **walking tour.** *(718-367-1010 or 718-220-5100. Subway: #2 or 5 to E. Tremont Ave./West Farms Sq. Open Apr.-Oct. M-F 10am-5pm, Sa-Su 10am-5:30pm; Nov.-Mar. daily 10am-4:30pm. $6.75, seniors and children $3; W free. For disabled-access info, call 718-220-5188.)*

North across East Fordham Rd. from the zoo, the **New York Botanical Garden** sprawls over forest and lake alike. *(718-817-8705. Garden grounds open Tu-Su 10am-6pm. $3, students, seniors, and children 3-16 $2; W free. Parking $4. Subway: #4 or D to Bedford Park Blvd. Walk 8 blocks east or take the Bx26, Bx12, Bx19, or Bx41 bus to the Garden.)*

The **Museum of Bronx History,** at Bainbridge Ave. and 208th St., is run by the Bronx Historical Society on the premises of the landmark Valentine-Varian House. *(718-881-8900. Open Sa 10am-4pm, Su 1-5pm, or by appt. $2. Subway: D to 205th St., or #4 to Mosholu Pkwy.; walk 4 blocks east on 210th St. and then south a block.)*

Up in northern Bronx, to the east of **Van Cortlandt Park's** 1146 acres, lies the immense **Woodlawn Cemetery,** where music lovers can pay tribute at the resting places of jazz legends Miles Davis, Duke Ellington, and Lionel Hampton. Impressive Victorian mausoleums abound, as do more famous dead: Herman Melville, F. W. Woolworth, Roland H. Macy, and more. *(718-430-1890. Open daily 9am-4:30pm. Subway: D train to 205th St. then walk 6 blocks up Perry Ave.)*

**STATEN ISLAND.** Getting here is half the fun. The free 30min. ferry ride from Manhattan's Battery Park to Staten Island is as unforgettable as it is inexpensive. Or you can drive from Brooklyn over the **Verrazano-Narrows Bridge,** the world's second-longest (4260 ft.) suspension span. Because of the hills and the distances (and some very dangerous neighborhoods in between), it's a bad idea to walk from one site to the next. Plan excursions with the bus schedule in mind.

Sights on the island cluster around the beautiful 19th-century **Snug Harbor Cultural Center,** housing the **Newhouse Center for Contemporary Art,** a small American art gallery with a sculpture show in summer, and the **Staten Island Botanical Gardens.** *(1000 Richmond Terr. 718-448-2500. Open W-Su noon-5pm. Suggested donation $2. Gardens 718-273-8200.)* The **Jacques Marchais Museum of Tibetan Art** meditates in central Staten Island (see **Museums,** below).

# MUSEUMS

For museum listings consult the following publications: *Time Out: New York*, the free *Gallery Guide* available at many major museums and galleries, *The New Yorker*, *New York* magazine, and the Friday *New York Times* (Weekend section). Most museums and all galleries close on Monday, and are jam-packed on weekends. Many museums request a "donation" in place of an admission fee—you can give less than the suggested amount. Most museums are free one weeknight.

## MAJOR COLLECTIONS

**Metropolitan Museum of Art (The Met)** (535-7710), 5th Ave. at 82nd St. Subway: #4, 5, 6 to 86th St. The largest in the Western Hemisphere, the Met's art collection includes 3.3 million works from almost every period through Impressionism; particularly strong in Egyptian and non-Western sculpture and European painting. Open Su and Tu-Th 9:30am-5:15pm, F-Sa 9:30am-8:45pm. Suggested donation $10, students and seniors $5. Members and under 12 free.

**Museum of Modern Art (MoMA),** 11 W. 53rd St. (708-9400), off 5th Ave. in Midtown. Subway: E, F to 5th Ave./53rd St. or B, D, Q to 50th St. One of the most extensive post-Impressionist collections in the world, founded in 1929 in response to the Met's reluctance to embrace modern art. Monet's sublime *Water Lily* room, Picassos, and a great design collection are among the highlights. Gorgeous sculpture garden. **MoMA 2000** offers a retrospective of the last century in art and spans the entire museum. Open Sa-Tu and Th 10:30am-6pm, F 10:30-8:30pm. $9.50, students and seniors $6.50, under 16 free. Pay-as-you-wish F 4:30-8:30pm. Films (free) require tickets in advance.

**American Museum of Natural History** (769-5100), Central Park West, at 79th to 81st St. Subway: B or C to 81st St. The largest science museum in the world, in an imposing Romanesque structure. The dinosaur exhibit is worth the lines. See things from a new perspective—lie down under the whale in the Ocean Life room. Open Su-Th 10am-5:45pm, F-Sa 10am-8:45pm. Suggested donation $8, students and seniors $6, children under 12 $4.50. **Imax** screen (769-5034). Museum and Imax: $12, students and seniors $8.50, ages 2-12 $6.50. F-Sa double features $15/$11/$8.50.

**Guggenheim Museum,** 1071 5th Ave. (423-3500), at 89th St. Subway: #4, 5, or 6 to 86th St. The coiling building designed by Frank Lloyd Wright is as famous as the collection inside. The spiral gallery houses temporary exhibits, while the newly constructed **Tower Galleries** may exhibit a portion of the **Thannhauser Collection** of 19th- and 20th-century works, including several by Picasso, Matisse, Van Gogh, and Cézanne. Open Su-W 10am-6pm, F-Sa 10am-8pm. $7, students and seniors $4, under 12 free; F 6-8pm "pay-what-you-wish." Wheelchair access. Also: **Guggenheim Museum SoHo,** 575 Broadway (423-3500), at Prince St. Open Su and W-F 11am-6pm, Sa 11am-8pm. $12, students and seniors $7, and under 12 free. F 6-8pm pay-what-you-wish.

**Whitney Museum of American Art,** 945 Madison Ave. (570-3676), at 75th St. Subway: #6 to 77th St. Futuristic fortress featuring the largest collection of 20th-century American art in the world, with works by Hopper, O' Keefe, de Kooning, Warhol, and Calder. Home to the Biennial exhibits, which claim to showcase the cutting edge of contemporary American art. Food and trash have become accepted media in what was once a bastion of high modernism. Open Tu-W and F-Su 11am-6pm, Th 1-8pm. $12.50, students and seniors $10.50, under 12 free. Free Th 6-8pm.

**Cooper-Hewitt Museum,** 2 E. 91st St. (860-6868), at 5th Ave. Subway: #4, 5 or 6 to 86th St. Andrew Carnegie's majestic Georgian mansion now houses the Smithsonian Institute's National Museum of Design. Playful exhibits focus on such topics as doghouses and the history of the pop-up book. Open Tu 10am-9pm, W-Sa 10am-5pm, Su noon-5pm. $5, students and seniors $3, under 12 free. Free Tu 5-9pm.

**The Frick Collection,** 1 E. 70th St. (288-0700), at 5th Ave. Subway: #6 to 68th St. Henry Clay Frick left his house and art collection to the city, and the museum retains the elegance of his château. The Living Hall displays 17th-century furniture, Persian rugs, Holbein portraits, and paintings by El Greco, Rembrandt, Velázquez, and Titian. The courtyard is inhabited by elegant statues surrounding the garden pool and fountain. Open Tu-Sa 10am-6pm, Su 1-6pm. $7, students and seniors $5. Under 10 not allowed, under 16 must be accompanied by an adult. Groups by appointment only.

## SMALLER AND SPECIALIZED COLLECTIONS

▓ **The Cloisters,** Fort Tryon Park (923-3700), in Washington Heights. Subway: A to 190th St.; then follow Margaret Corbin Dr. 5 blocks north. Or take bus #4 from Madison Ave. to the Cloisters' entrance. This tranquil branch of the Met is built largely from pieces of 12th- and 13th-century French and Spanish monasteries. John D. Rockefeller donated the site and many of the works that make up the Cloisters' rich collection of Medieval art. Follow the allegory told by the Unicorn Tapestries, and wander through airy archways and manicured gardens bedecked with European treasures. Open Mar.-Oct. Tu-Su 9:30am-5:15pm; Nov.-Feb. Tu-Su 9:30am-4:45pm. Museum tours Tu-F at 3pm, Su at noon; Nov.-Feb. W at 3pm. Suggested donation $8, students and seniors $4. Includes (and is included with) same-day admission to the Met's main building in Central Park.

▓ **Museum of Television and Radio,** 25 W. 52nd St. (621-6600, 621-6800 for daily activity schedule), between 5th and 6th Ave. Subway: B, D, F, Q to Rockefeller Center, or E, F to 53rd St. This museum might more aptly be called an archive. With a collection of more than 95,000 TV and radio programs, the museum's library has a specially designed computerized cataloging system and private viewing consoles. Tours are free with admission; inquire at the desk. Open Tu-W and F-Su noon-6pm, Th noon-8pm; F until 9pm for theaters only. Suggested donation $6, students $4, under 13 and seniors $3 (includes 2hr. viewing time.)

**Alternative Museum,** 594 Broadway (966-4444), 4th fl., near Houston and Prince St. in SoHo. Subway: B, D, F, or Q to Broadway-Lafayette St., or N or R to Prince St. Founded and operated by recognized artists for non-established artists, the museum advertises itself as "ahead of the times and behind the issues." New visions and social critique are the name of the game. Open Sept.-July Tu-Su 11am-6pm. Suggested donation $3.

**American Museum of the Moving Image,** 35th Ave. at 36th St., Astoria, Queens (exhibition and screening info 718-784-0077, travel directions 718-784-4777). Subway: N to Broadway in Astoria. Walk along Broadway to 36th St., turn right, go to 35th Ave.; museum is on the right. Movie editing, sound, and special effects exhibits on the 3rd fl. Movie star memorabilia on the 2nd fl. Vintage arcade games line the 1st fl. Screens classic films Sa-Su; free with admission; call for schedule. Open Tu-F noon-5pm, Sa-Su 11am-6pm. $8.50, students and seniors $5.50, children $4.50, under 4 free.

**The Asia Society,** 725 Park Ave. (517-ASIA or 288-6400), at 70th St. Subway: #6 to 68th St. Asian art exhibitions accompanied by musical performances, films, and an acclaimed "Meet the Author" series. Art spanning the Asian continent; includes Asian America. Open Tu-W and F-Sa 11am-6pm, Th 11am-8pm, Su noon-5pm. $3, seniors and students $1; Th 6-8pm free. Tours Tu-Sa 12:30pm, Th also at 6:30pm, Su 2:30pm.

**International Center of Photography,** 1130 5th Ave. (860-1777), at 94th St. Subway: #6 to 96th St. The foremost exhibitor of photography in the city and a gathering place for its practitioners. Historical, thematic, and contemporary works, running from fine art to photojournalism to celebrity portraits. **Midtown branch,** 1133 6th Ave. (768-4680), at 43rd St. Both open Tu 11am-8pm, W-Su 11am-6pm. $6, students and seniors $4, under 12 $1; Tu 6-8pm pay-what-you-wish.

**Intrepid Sea-Air-Space Museum,** Pier 86 (245-0072), at 46th St. and 12th Ave. Bus: M42 or M50 to W. 46th St. One ticket admits you to a veteran aircraft carrier, a Vietnam War destroyer, the only publicly displayed guided-missile submarine, and a lightship. Pioneer's Hall shows models, antiques, and film shorts of flying devices from the turn of the century to the 1930s. Open Mar.-Sept. M-F 10am-5pm, Sa-Su 10am-6pm; Oct. 1-Apr. 30 W-Su 10am-5pm. Last admission 1hr. before closing. $10; students, seniors, and veterans $7.50; children 6-11 $5, active servicemen and under 2 free.

**The Jewish Museum,** 1109 5th Ave. (423-3200), at 92nd St. Subway: #6 to 96th St. The permanent collection of over 14,000 works, ranging from ancient Biblical artifacts to contemporary masterpieces, details the Jewish experience through history. Open Su-M and W-Th 11am-5:45pm, Tu 11am-8pm. $8, students and seniors $5.50, under 12 free; Tu 5-9pm free and live music. Wheelchair info: 423-3225.

**Jacques Marchais Museum of Tibetan Art,** 338 Lighthouse Ave., Staten Island (718-987-3500). Take bus S74 from Staten Island Ferry to Lighthouse Ave., then turn right and walk up the fairly steep hill as it winds to the right. Almost 2hr. from Manhattan, it's one of the largest private collections of Tibetan art in the West. Open Apr.-Nov. W-Su 1-5pm; Dec.-Mar. call ahead to schedule a visiting time. $3, seniors $2.50, under 12 $1.

**El Museo del Barrio,** 1230 5th Ave. (831-7272), at 104th St. Subway: #6 to 103rd St. El Museo del Barrio is the only museum in the U.S. devoted exclusively to the art and culture of Puerto Rico and Latin America. Begun in a classroom, the project has turned into a permanent museum. Open Mar.-Sept. W and F-Su 9am-5pm, Th noon-7pm; Oct.-Apr. W-Su 11am-5pm. Suggested donation $4, students and seniors $2.

**The Museum for African Art,** 593 Broadway (966-1313), between Houston and Prince St. in SoHo. Subway: N or R to Prince and Broadway. African and African-American art that spans centuries and continents. Sa afternoon lectures free with admission. Open Tu-F 10:30am-5:30pm, Sa-Su noon-6pm. $5, students and seniors $2.50.

**Museum of the City of New York** (534-1672), at 103rd St. and 5th Ave. in East Harlem, across the street from El Museo del Barrio. Subway: #6 to 103rd St. Details the history of the Big Apple. Open W-Sa 10am-5pm, Su 1-5pm. Suggested donation $5; students, seniors, and children $4. Wheelchair access.

**National Museum of the American Indian,** 1 Bowling Green (668-6624). Subway: #4, 5 to Bowling Green. In the Beaux-Arts Customs House. The cream of the Smithsonian's collection of Native American artifacts. Open daily 10am-5pm, Th closes at 8pm. Free.

**New Museum of Contemporary Art,** 583 Broadway (219-1222), between Prince and Houston St. Subway: N, R to Prince; or B, D, F, Q to Broadway-Lafayette. Dedicated to art's role in society; flaunts the hottest and most controversial. Open W and Su noon-6pm, Th-Sa noon-8pm. $5, students and seniors $3, under 18 free, Th 6-8pm free.

**Studio Museum in Harlem,** 144 W. 125th St. (864-4500), between Adam Clayton Powell Jr. Blvd. and Lenox/Malcolm X Ave. Subway: #2 or 3 to 125th St. Founded in 1967 at the height of the Civil Rights movement and dedicated to works by black artists. Open W-F 10am-5pm, Sa-Su 1-6pm. $5, students and seniors $3, children $1; free 1st Sa of month. Tours Sa 1, 2, 2:30, and 4pm.

# GALLERIES

New York's museums may be the vanguard of art history, maintaining priceless collections and orchestrating blockbuster exhibitions, but galleries are where art *happens*. Check out the publications in the **Museums** section above for listings.

**SoHo** is a wonderland of galleries; a particularly dense concentration lines Broadway between Houston and Spring St. Cutting-edge outposts have recently emerged in **Chelsea,** in reclaimed industrial spaces around W. 22nd St. between 10th and 11th Ave. **Madison Ave.** between 70th and 84th St. has a sampling of ritzy showplaces, and more galleries festoon **57th St.** between 5th and 6th Ave.

## SOHO

**Holly Solomon Gallery,** 172 Mercer (941-5777), at Houston St. This SoHo matriarch is an excellent place to start a tour of downtown galleries. 3 or 4 at a time show in this multi-floored space, providing an accessible array of avant-garde art. Unlike other galleries, Solomon's has a sense of humor. Nam June Paik, William Wegman, and Peter Hutchinson are represented here. Open Tu-F 10am-5pm; Sept.-June Tu-Sa 10am-6pm.

**Pace Gallery,** 142 Greene St. (431-9224), between Prince and Houston St. This famous gallery run by the Wildenstein family has 2 locations. Its SoHo branch displays biggies like Julian Schnabel and Claes Oldenburg. Exhibitions rotate monthly. Open M-Th 10am-5:30pm, F 10am-4pm; Sept.-June Tu-Sa 10am-6pm. Often closed in Aug.

**Sonnabend,** 420 W. Broadway (966-6160), 3rd fl. Exhibits contemporary paintings by well-known American and European artists. Jeff Koons, John Baldessari, and Robert Rauschenburg top the bill. Open Tu-Sa 10am-6pm. Often closed July-Aug.

**David Zwirner,** 43 Greene St. (966-9074), at Grand St. A small gallery that pulls together elegant 1-person shows with a conceptual punch. Some of the smartest contemporary art around ends up on Zwirner's walls. Open Tu-Sa 10am-6pm. Often closed in summer.

**Feature,** 76 Greene St. (941-7077), 2nd fl. Good and risky. Daring, straightforward selections of contemporary art. Don't miss their back showroom. Open Tu-F 11am-6pm; Sept.-May Tu-Sa 11am-6pm.

**American Primitive,** 594 Broadway (966-1530), 2nd fl. Works by folk or self-taught contemporary American artists. Only here can you get a piece dedicated to baseball hero Cal Ripken made entirely out of sock threads. Proudly and aggressively outside the art scene—so uncool, it's cool. Open M-Sa 11am-6pm; July-Aug. closed Sa.

**Gavin Brown's Enterprise,** 558 Broome St. (431-1512), just west of 6th Ave. Literally and figuratively as far left as you'd want to get without a map, this tiny gallery specializes in fun, interesting work. Japanese art, Steve Pippen (the bathroom artist) and other *über*-contemporary stuff. Open W-F noon-6pm; in winter M-Sa noon-6pm. Closed Aug.

## CHELSEA

**I-20,** 529 W. 20th St. (645-1100), between 10th and 11th Ave. High quality, daringly original photography and video art displayed in a beautiful 11th fl. space. The I-20 is at the top of a building filled with galleries, so ride the freight elevator to the top and work your way down. Open Tu-Sa 11am-6pm.

**Dia Center for the Arts,** 548 W. 22nd St. (989-5912), between 10th and 11th Ave. Sized like a museum but with a gallery's sensitivity to the current art pulse, the 4-story Dia is reliably, irrepressibly cool. Each floor features changing exhibits by a single contemporary artist. The well-balanced collection covers a range of media and styles. Permanent installation on the roof. Open Tu-Su 10am-6pm. $4, students and seniors $2.

## 57TH ST.

**Fuller Building,** 41 E. 57th St., between Madison and Park Ave. Stylish Art Deco building harbors 12 floors of galleries. Contemporary notables such as Robert Miller, André Emmerich, and Susan Sheehan; collectors of ancient works like Frederick Schultz; and several modern galleries. The **André Emmerich Gallery** (752-0124), on the 5th fl., features important contemporary work by Hockney et al. Most galleries in the building open M-Sa 10am-5:30pm, hrs. vary; Oct.-May most are closed M.

## UPPER EAST SIDE

**Sotheby's,** 1334 York Ave. (606-7000; ticket office 606-7171), at 72nd St. One of the most respected auction houses in the city, offering everything from Degas to Disney. Auctions are open to anyone, but some require a ticket for admittance (given out on a first come, first served basis). Both open M-Sa 10am-5pm, Su 1-5pm.

**Christie's,** 502 Park Ave. (546-1000), at 59th St. Flaunts its collection of valuable wares. Like Sotheby's, auctions are open. Open M-Sa 10am-5pm, Su 1-5pm.

# 🎭 ENTERTAINMENT AND NIGHTLIFE

Although always an exhilarating, incomparable city, New York only becomes "New York" when the sun goes down. From the blindingly bright lights of Times Sq. to the dark, impenetrably smoky atmosphere of a Greenwich Village or SoHo bar, the Big Apple pulls in a million directions at once. Find some performance art, hear some jazz, go to an all-night diner, twist the night away—heck, even get a tattoo. A cab ride home at 4:30am through empty streets is always sure to make your spirits soar. The city never sleeps and, for a few nights, neither should you.

**Publications** with noteworthy nightlife sections include the *Village Voice*, *Time Out: New York*, *New York* magazine, and the Su edition of the *New York Times*. *The New Yorker* has the most comprehensive survey of the theater scene. An **entertainment hotline** (360-3456; 24hr.) covers activities by both borough and genre.

MID-ATL

**CHEAP SEATS** To the budget traveler, the Great White Way's major theatrical draws may seem locked away in gilded Broadway cages. Never fear, however, *Let's Go's* here! Er, that is to say, you can find cheap tickets, compadre. Should Ticketmaster (307-4100; outside NYC 800-755-4000) not work, other options exist to help you sit pretty when the curtain rises. For one, you can consult ye olde standby ticket distributor, **TKTS** (see p. 232). If choice B fails too, then still more avenues remain open to you.

**Rush Tickets:** Some theaters distribute them on the morning of the performance; others make student rush tickets available 30 minutes before showtime. Lines can be extremely long, so get there *early*.

**Cancellation Line:** No rush luck? Some theaters redistribute returned or unclaimed tickets several hours before showtime. You might have to sacrifice your afternoon—but, come on, Dame Edna is worth it!

**Hit Show Club:** 630 Ninth Ave. (581-4211), between 44th and 45th St. This free service distributes coupons redeemable at the box office for 1/3 or more off regular ticket prices. Call for coupons via mail or pick them up them up at the club office.

**Sold-out Shows:** Even if a show is sold out to the general public, theaters reserve prime house seats, usually in the first few rows, for VIPs. However, house seats frequently remain unclaimed, in which case they are sold to the general public—for full price—on the day of the show. House seats can go on sale as early as the box office opens or as late as one hour before curtain, so call the individual theater for details.

**Standing-room Only:** Sold on the day of show, tend to be around $15 or $20. Call first, as some theaters can't accommodate standing room.

**THEATER.** Broadway is currently undergoing a revival and ticket sales are booming. Mainstream musicals receive more than their fair share of attention. Tickets cost about $50 each when purchased through regular channels. **TKTS** sells 25-75% discounted tickets to many shows on the day of the performance from a booth in the middle of Duffy Sq.—the northern part of Times Sq., at 47th and Broadway. (768-1818 for recorded info. Tickets sold M-Sa 3-8pm for evening performances, W and Sa 10am-2pm for matinees, Su noon-7pm for matinees and evening performances. $2.50 service charge per ticket.) For info on shows and tickets, call the **NYC/ON STAGE hotline** at 768-1818. **Ticketmaster** (307-4100) deals in Broadway shows, and takes credit cards, but charges at least $2 more than other outlets.

**Off-Broadway** theaters have between 100 and 499 seats; only Broadway houses have over 500. Off-Broadway houses frequently offer more off-beat, quirky shows, with shorter runs. Occasionally these shows have long runs or make the jump to Broadway houses. Tickets cost $10-20. The best of the Off-Broadway houses huddle in the Sheridan Sq. area of the West Village. TKTS also sells tickets for the larger Off-Broadway houses. **Off-Off-Broadway** means cheaper, younger theaters.

**Shakespeare in the Park** (861-7277) is a New York summer tradition. From June through Aug., two Shakespeare plays are presented at the **Delacorte Theater** in Central Park, near the 81st St. entrance on the Upper West Side, just north of the main road. Tickets are free, but lines form early.

**MOVIES.** Many movies open in New York weeks before they're distributed across the country, and the response of Manhattan audiences and critics can shape a film's success or failure. Big-screen fanatics should check out the cavernous **Ziegfeld,** 141 W. 54th St. (765-7600), one of the largest screens left in America, which shows first-run films. **MoviePhone** (777-3456) allows you to charge tickets (plus a small fee) for most major movie-houses over the phone and pick them up at showtime from the theater's automated ticket dispenser. **The Kitchen,** 512 W. 19th St. (255-5793), between 10th and 11th Ave. (subway: C or E to 23rd St.), is a world-renowned showcase for the off-beat and New York-based struggling artists. Eight screens project art-house cinema at the **Angelika Film Center,** 18 W. Houston St., at Mercer St. (995-2000; subway: #6 to Bleecker St. or B, D, F, or Q to Broadway-Lafayette). **Anthology Film Archives,** 32 2nd Ave. (505-5181), at E. 2nd St., is a forum for independent filmmaking. The **New York International Film Festival** packs 'em in every Oct.; check the *Voice* or *Time Out* for details.

**OPERA AND DANCE.** You can do it all at **Lincoln Center** (875-5000); there's usually opera or dance at one of its many venues. Write to Lincoln Center Plaza, NYC 10023 for a press kit. The **Metropolitan Opera Company's** premier outfit, plays on a Lincoln Center stage as big as a football field. Regular tickets run as high as $100—go for the upper balcony (around $42; the cheapest seats have an obstructed view). You can stand in the orchestra ($16) along with the opera freakazoids who've brought along the score, or all the way back in the Family Circle. (362-6000. Season runs Sept.-Apr. M-Sa. Box office open M-Sa 10am-8pm, Su noon-6pm.) In the summer, free concerts are offered in city parks (362-6000).

At right angles to the Met, the **New York City Opera** has come into its own under the direction of Christopher Keene. "City" now has a split season (Sept.-Nov. and Mar.-Apr.) and keeps its ticket prices low year-round. (870-5570. $20-90; for rush tickets, call the night before and wait in line the morning of.) In July, the **New York Grand Opera** puts on free performances at the Central Park Summerstage every Wednesday night (360-2777). Check the papers for performances of the old warhorses by the **Amato Opera Company,** 319 Bowery St. (228-8200; Sept.-May).

The **New York State Theater** is home to the late, great George Balanchine's **New York City Ballet.** Decent tickets for the *Nutcracker* in Dec. sell out almost immediately. (870-5570. Performances Nov.-Feb. and May-June; tickets $12-65, standing room $12.) The **American Ballet Theater** dances more vivaciously at the Metropolitan Opera House (477-3030; box office 362-6000; tickets $16-95). The **Alvin Ailey American Dance Theater** bases its repertoire of modern dance on jazz, spirituals, and contemporary music. Often on the road, it always performs at the **City Center** in Dec. Tickets can be difficult to obtain. (767-0940. $15-40.) Write or call the City Center, 131 W. 55th St. (581-7907), weeks in advance.

The best place in the city to see innovative dance is the **Joyce Theater,** 175 8th Ave., between 18th and 19th St. Open year-round, the Joyce presents high-quality, energetic dance in a sleek, audience-friendly space. (242-0800. Tickets $15-40.)

**CLASSICAL MUSIC.** Start with listings in *Time Out,* the *New York Times, The New Yorker,* or *New York* magazine. Remember that many events are seasonal.

The **Lincoln Center Halls** have a wide, year-round selection of concerts. The **Great Performers Series,** featuring famous and foreign musicians, packs the Avery Fisher and Alice Tully Halls and the Walter Reade Theater from Oct. until May (call 875-5020; tickets from $12). **Avery Fisher Hall** paints the town ecstatic with its annual **Mostly Mozart Festival.** Show up early; there are usually recitals beginning 1hr. before the main concert that are free to ticketholders. (875-5030. July-Aug. Tickets $12-30.) The **New York Philharmonic** begins its regular season in mid-Sept. Students and seniors can sometimes get $5 tickets Tu-Th; call ahead. Anyone can get $10 tickets for morning rehearsals; call ahead. (721-6500 M-Sa 10am-8pm, Su noon-8pm. Tickets $10-60.) For a few weeks in late June, Kurt Masur and friends lead the posse at **free concerts** on the Great Lawn in Central Park, at Prospect Park in Brooklyn, at Van Cortlandt Park in the Bronx, and elsewhere. (875-5709.) Free outdoor events at Lincoln Center occur all summer (875-4000).

**Carnegie Hall,** 7th Ave. at 57th St., is still the favorite coming-out locale of musical debutantes (247-7800; box office open M-Sa 11am-6pm, Su noon-6pm; tickets $10-60). A good, cheap way to absorb New York musical culture is to visit a **music school.** Except for opera and ballet productions ($5-12), concerts at these schools are free and frequent: the **Juilliard School of Music,** Lincoln Center (769-7406), the **Mannes School of Music** (580-0210), and the **Manhattan School of Music** (749-2802).

**MID-ATLANTIC**

**JAZZ JOINTS.** The **JVC Jazz Festival** (501-1390) blows into the city in June. All-star performances have included Ray Charles and Mel Torme. Call in the spring for info, or write to: JVC Jazz Festival New York, P.O. Box 1169, Ansonia Station, New York, NY 10023. The **Texaco Jazz Festival** brings in local talent as well as innovative giants. These concerts take place throughout the city (some are free) but are centered at TriBeCa's **Knitting Factory** (219-3055).

🎷 **Apollo Theater,** 253 W. 125th St. (749-5838, box office 864-0372), between Frederick Douglass Blvd. and Adam Clayton Powell Blvd. Subway: #1, 2, 3, or 9 to 125th St. This historic Harlem landmark has heard Duke Ellington, Count Basie, Ella Fitzgerald, and more. A young Malcolm X shined shoes here. The Apollo is now undergoing a resurgence in popularity. Ticket prices vary; order through Ticketmaster (307-7171). A big draw is the legendary W Amateur Night, where acts are either gonged (ouch!) or rated "regular," "show-off," "top dog," or "super top dog"; tickets $10-18.

🎷 **Village Vanguard,** 178 7th Ave. South (255-4037), between W. 11th St. and Greenwich. Subway: #1, 2, 3, or 9 to 14th St. A windowless, wedge-shaped cavern, as old and hip as jazz itself. Memories of Lenny Bruce, Leadbelly, Miles Davis, and Sonny Rollins hang thick. Every M the Vanguard Orchestra unleashes its torrential Big Band sound on sentimental journeymen at 10pm and midnight. Cover $15 plus $10 drink min., F-Sa $15 plus $8 min. Sets Su-Th 9:30 and 11:30pm, F-Sa 9:30, 11:30pm, and 1am.

🎷 **Blue Note,** 131 W. 3rd St. (475-8592), near MacDougal St. Subway: A, B, C, D, E, F, or Q to Washington Sq. The legendary jazz club is now a commercialized concert space with crowded tables and a tame audience, but it still brings in many all-stars. Cover for big-name performers $20 and up, $5 drink min. Su jazz brunch is $18.50 (noon-6pm, shows at 1 and 3:30pm; reservations recommended). Other sets daily 9 and 11:30pm.

🎷 **Fez,** 380 Lafayette St. (533-2680), behind the Time Cafe. Subway: #6 to Astor Pl. This lushly appointed, Moroccan-decorated club draws an extremely photogenic crowd, especially on Th nights, when the Mingus Big Band holds court (sets at 9 and 11pm; reservations suggested). Delicious cocktails (around $7.50). Kitchen open 8:30pm-midnight. Call for dates, prices, and reservations.

🎷 **St. Nick's Pub,** 773 St. Nicholas Ave. (283-9728), between 148th and 149th St. Subway: A, B, C, D to 145th St. Small and comfy, with a loyal crowd and great jazz. Bar opens at 12:30pm, jazz shows M-Sa start at 9pm and go until 1 or 2am or just "until." Su evening is a soul quartet show (5-9pm). M nights Patience Higgins and the Sugar Hill Jazz Quartet host a laid-back jam session. Open M past 2am, Tu-Su until 2am.

**CLUBS.** New York City has a long history of producing bands on the vanguard of popular music and performance, from the Velvet Underground to the Wu-Tang Clan to the Beastie Boys. **Music festivals** provide the opportunity to see tons of bands at a (relatively) low price. The **CMJ Music Marathon** runs for 4 nights in the fall, including over 400 bands and workshops on the alternative music scene (516-498-3150). The spunky **Intel New York Music Festival** commandeers the clubs for 4 indie-filled days (677-3530; July 20-23). The **Macintosh New York Music Festival** presents 350 bands over a week-long period in July. For more experimental sounds, check out Creative Time's **Music in the Anchorage,** a June concert series in the massive stone chambers in the base of the Brooklyn Bridge (206-6674, ext. 252).

🎷 **CBGB/OMFUG (CBGB's),** 315 Bowery (982-4052), at Bleecker St. Subway: #6 to Bleecker St. *The* place to see great alternative rock. The initials once stood for "country, bluegrass, blues, and other music for uplifting gourmandizers," but this club has always been about punk rock. Generations of New Yorkers have come to CB's to rock out. Blondie and the Talking Heads got their starts here. Shows nightly 8pm. Cover $5-10.

🎷 **The Cooler,** 416 W. 14th St. (229-0785), at Greenwich St. Subway: #1, 2, 3, A, C, or E, to 14th St. In the heart of the meat-packing district, The Cooler showcases non-mainstream alternative, dub, electronica, and illbient in a huge vault of a room. Cover varies. Free M. Doors open Su-Th 8pm, F-Sa 9pm.

**Knitting Factory,** 74 Leonard St. (219-3055), between Broadway and Church St. Subway: #1, 2, 3, 6, 9, A, C, or E to Canal. Walk up Broadway to Leonard St. Free-thinking musicians anticipate the apocalypse with edge-piercing performances complemented by great acoustics. Several shows nightly. Sonic Youth played here for years. Box office open M-F 10am-11pm, Sa-Su 2-11pm. Bar open M-F 4:30pm-2am, Sa-Su 6pm-2am.

## BARS

**Naked Lunch Bar and Lounge,** 17 Thompson St. (343-0828). Adorned with the roach-and-typewriter motif found in the novel of the same name, Naked Lunch creates a let loose and have fun atmosphere. The after-work crowd isn't afraid to dance in the aisle. Unbeatable martinis like the Tanqueray tea ($7). All beers $5. DJ W-Sa; sometimes a small cover. Happy hour Tu-F 5-8pm. Open Tu-F 5pm-4am, Sa 8pm-4am.

**Bar 6,** 502 6th Ave. (691-1363), between 12th and 13th St. Subway: #1, 2, or 3 to 14th St. or A, E, D, or B to 6th Ave.-8th St. French-Moroccan bistro by day, sizzling bar by night. Live DJ spins Tu-Su. Beers on tap ($4-5 per pint). Kitchen open Su-Th noon-2am, F-Sa noon-3am; bar open later.

**The Village Idiot,** 355 W. 14th St. (989-7334), between 8th and 9th St. Any reference to Dostoevksy would probably be punished with about 4 shots of tequila. New York's infamous honky-tonk bar has reopened in the Village, and the beer is still cheap ($1.25 mugs of Miller Genuine Draft), the music still loud, and the ambience still as close as they can get it to a roadhouse. Open daily noon-4am.

**Drinkland,** 339 E. 10th St. (228-2435), between Ave. A and B. A young, downtown crowd soaks in the futura-meets-trip-hop decor. DJs spin everything from breakbeat to classic funk, depending on the night. Open daily 7pm-4am.

**Lucky Cheng's,** 24 First Ave. (473-0516), between 1st and 2nd St. One of the city's better-known drag clubs, with an Asian twist. Open Su-Th 6pm-midnight, F-Sa 6pm-2am.

**Idlewild,** 145 Houston (477-5005), between Eldridge and Forsythe St. Enter the airplane theme bar of the Lower East Side. Open Su-W 8pm-3am, Th-Sa 8pm-4am.

**Coffee Shop Bar,** 29 Union Sq. W. (243-7969), facing Union Sq. Park. Subway: #4, 5, 6, L, N, or R to Union Sq. A chic diner for fashion victims. Sure, it's a bar and restaurant, but more importantly, it's a spectacle. Beers $4-6. Open daily 6am-5am.

**Yogi's,** 2156 Broadway (873-9852), at 76th St. Three things anchor this bar in the booze stratosphere: a constant stream of Elvis, Dylan, and country faves from the jukebox; bartenders dancing on the bar; and, most importantly, $1 mystery beers, which involve the bartender pulling 12 cold oz. out of a bin filled with microbrews. Open daily noon-4am.

**Double Happiness,** 173 Mott St. (941-1282), between Broome and Grand St. Recently opened, this downstairs bar takes advantage of the dual downtown fetish of all things Asian and minimalist. Abacuses decorate the walls and a chinoiserie-meets-Calvin-Klein-meets-Nike crowd decorates the floor. Open Su-Th 5pm-2am, F-Sa 5pm-3am.

**bOb Bar,** 235 Eldridge St. (777-0588), between Houston and Stanton St. Comfy and laid-back, with a hip-hop-inclined crowd and DJs that spin anything they can get their hands on. Open daily 7pm-4am.

**DANCE CLUBS.** The New York club scene is an unrivaled institution. The crowd is forcefully uninhibited, the music unparalleled, and the fun can be virtually unlimited—as long as you uncover the right place. Honing in on the hippest club in New York isn't easy without connections. Clubs rise, war, and fall and even those "in the know" can't always locate the hot spot, since many parties stay carefully underground, advertised by word of mouth, futuristic flyers, and phone lines. The right club on the wrong night can be a big mistake, particularly if you've already paid the $3-25 cover charge. Make friends with someone on the inside, or check out the cooler record stores for directional flyers which offer discount admission. Flyers and staff at **Liquid Sky/Temple,** 241 Lafayette St. (343-0532; subway: #6 to Spring St. or N, R to Prince St.), and **Throb,** 211 E. 14th St. (533-2328; subway: #4, 5, 6, or L, or N, R to 14th St./Union Sq.), will help direct you to some phat beats.

The rules are relatively simple. You have to have "the look" to be let in. Bouncers are the clubs' fashion police, and nothing drab or conventional will squeeze by. Most clubgoers wear black clothes or rave gear and their most attractive friends. These suggestions could change, though; hip is an elusive commodity. Call ahead to make sure you know what (and whom) you'll find when you arrive.

**Twilo,** 530 W. 27th St. (268-1600). Subway: #1 or 9 to 28th St. or C or E to 23rd St. Located in the former Sound Factory. A crowded scene early in the night, with meaty shirtless glam boys and a healthy bridge and tunnel crowd mixing with the occasional 8 ft. tall drag queen. Later, the music gets deeper and the crowd more serious. Th is the night to go; a wonderfully glam crowd, especially in the VIP lounge (shhh!). Cover $20-25. Doors open around midnight.

**Sounds of Brazil (SOB's),** 204 Varick St. (243-4940), at Houston St. Subway: #1 or 9 to Houston. Terrific Latin dance music served up more ways than you knew existed. Special place for Brazilian music. Music often alternates between live bands and a DJ. Cover $10-20. Open for dining Tu-Th 7pm-2:30am, F-Sa 7pm-4am. Most shows Su-Th 8 and 10pm; F-Sa 10:30pm and 1am; or, alternately, 10pm, midnight, and 2am.

**Tunnel,** 220 12th Ave. (695-7292 or 695-4682), at 27th St. Subway: C or E to 23rd St. The name could refer to the cavernous space or to the mostly Jersey crowd, but this is the party that everyone's invited to. An immense club—3 floors and a mezzanine packed with 2 dance floors, lounges, glass-walled live shows, and a skateboarding cage. "Alternative-lifestyle" parties. Cover $20. Open F-Sa.

**Webster Hall,** 125 E. 11th St. (353-1600), between 3rd and 4th Ave. Subway: #4, 5, 6, N, or R or L to Union Sq.-14th St. then 3 blocks south and 1 block east. Popular club offers a rock/reggae room and a coffeeshop in addition to the main, house-dominated dance floor. Psychedelic Th often feature live bands and $2.50 beers. F-Sa the motto "4 floors, 5 eras, 4 DJs...and 40,000 sq. ft. of fun" is put into effect. Open Th-Sa 10pm-4am. Cover $15-20; promotions and time-limited freebies ease the cost.

**Nell's,** 246 W. 14th St. (675-1567), between 7th and 8th Ave. Subway: #1, 2, 3, or 9 to 14th St. A legendary hot spot in slight decline; the faithful hang on for mellow shmoozing and soulful music upstairs and phat beats below. Racially diverse crowd. Cover M $5; Tu-W, Su $10; Th-Sa $15. Open daily 10pm-4am.

**China Club,** 2130 Broadway (398-3800), at 75th St. Subway: #1, 2, 3, or 9 to 72nd St. Rock-and-roll hot spot where Bowie and Jagger used to come on their off nights. Models and long-haired men make it a great people-watching spot. M night is for the "beautiful people" crowd. Only the well-dressed get in. Go elsewhere for great dancing. Cover around $20. Opens daily at 10pm.

## GAY AND LESBIAN CLUBS

**Barracuda,** 275 W. 22nd St. (645-8613), at 8th Ave. Subway: C or E to 23rd St. Brimming with ripped Chelsea boys of all shapes and sizes. 50s decor makes for a cozy hangout in the back, while the determined mobs in the front seem to have something else on their minds entirely. Most drinks $4-7. Open daily 4pm-4am.

**Bar d'O,** 29 Bedford St. (627-1580). The coziest lounge with the most sultry lighting in the city. Superb drag divas Joey Arias and Raven O. (Tu and Sa-Su nights, $5). Even without the fine chanteuses, this is a damn fine place for a drink. Women's night on M features some really glam drag kings. Go early for the atmosphere, midnight for the performances, and at 2am to people-watch/gender-guess. Doors open around 7pm.

**Kurfew,** W. 27th St. (888-4-KURFEW), between 11th and 12th Ave. Sa at the Tunnel's mid-block entrance. Kurfew is New York's best party for the gay 18-25 set. Fun music, friendly folks, and lots of very cute boys. Cover $20; with ad $15; with student ID and an ad/invite $10. Doors open 11pm.

**La Nueva Escuelita,** 301 W. 39th St. (631-0588), at 8th Ave. Subway: A, C, E to 42nd St. Queer Latin dance club that throbs with merengue, salsa, soul, hip-hop, and drag shows. Spicy F party is a lesbian dreamscape with go-go girls galore. Largely Latin crowd. Open Th-Su 10pm-5am. Cover Th $3, F $10, Sa $15, Su $8.

**W.O.W!,** 547 W. 21st St. (631-1102), between 10th and 11th Ave., at El Flamingo. The biggest all-women dance club in Manhattan, with a packed floor and go-go dancers to boot. Cover $5 before 10pm, $7 after. Open daily 7pm-3am.

**The Roxy,** 515 W. 18th St. (645-5156). Currently *the* place to be on Sa nights. Hundreds of gay men dance, lounge, and drink in this gigantic, luxurious space. Upstairs lounge/ bar provides a different DJ and more intimate setting. Plenty of room for the hedonists to play. Busy nights boast beautiful go-go boys. Beer $5. Drinks $6+. Cover $20.

## MISCELLANEOUS HIPSTER HANGOUTS

**Bowlmor,** 110 University Pl. (255-8188), near 13th St. Subway: #4, 5, 6, or L, or N, R to Union Sq. Proof that New York is the coolest city in the world. An after-hours lights-out bowling alley with glowing pins where DJs spin jungle, trip-hop, and house. $4.25 per person/per game, after 5pm $5.45, F-Su $6. Shoes $3. Beer $2.50. Open M and F 10am-4am, Tu-W 10am-1am, Sa 11am-4am, Su 11am-1am.

**The Anyway Café,** 34 E. 2nd St. (473-5021), at 2nd Ave. Sample Russian-American culture at this dark, relaxed, leopard-spotted hangout. Literary readings during the week, jazz on F and Sa nights, and Russian folk on Su. Some kind of music every night at 9pm. Friendly and pretension-free. A great place to kick back with homemade sangria and Russian specialties ($8-12). Open M-Th 5pm-2am, F-Sa 5pm-4am, Su noon-1am.

**Mission Café,** 82 2nd Ave. (505-6616), between 4th and 5th St. This theater hot spot hosts fortune tellers every week and rotating wall art. Steamed eggs, made on the espresso machine with jack cheese, scallions, tomato, and a bagel ($3.50). Coffee and juices 85¢-$3.25. Open M-F 8am-9pm, Sa 9am-11pm, Su 9am-8pm.

**The Point,** 940 Garrison Ave. in the Bronx (718-542-4139), at the corner of Manida in Hunt's Point. Subway: #6 to Hunts Point. On the fringe of one of New York's poorest neighborhoods, The Point houses a growing artistic community and is the homebase of dancer/choreographer Arthur Aviles. Monthly Latin jazz and hip-hop performances, studio facilities, a theater, classes in art and self-defense, and community outreaches like the South Bronx Film and Video Festival enable Hunt's Point to call itself "the artistic capital of the Bronx." Call for a schedule of events.

**Soundlab** (726-1724). Locations vary. Cultural alchemy in the form of an illbient happening, nomadic style. Expect a smart, funky, racially mixed crowd absorbing smart, funky, radically mixed sound. Call the number to find where the next Lab goes down; past locales include the base of the Brooklyn Bridge, the 15th floor of a Financial District skyscraper, and outdoors in a Chinatown park.

**10th Street (Russian and Turkish) Baths,** 268 E. 10th St. (674-9250), between 1st Ave. and Ave. A. Expert masseur Boris runs this co-ed bathhouse that offers all conceivable legal bodily services—oak-leaf massages, salt scrubs, oil massages, and black-mud treatments. Saunas, steam rooms, and an ice-cold pool. Admission $20. Open daily 9am-10pm; Th and Su men-only, W women-only.

**SPORTS.** Most cities are content to field a major-league team in each big-time sport. New York opts for the Noah's Ark approach: 2 baseball teams, 2 hockey teams, NBA and WNBA basketball teams, 2 football teams, and a lonely MLS soccer squad. New York hosts a number of world-class events. Get tickets 3 months in advance for the prestigious **U.S. Open,** held in late Aug. and early Sept. at the USTA Tennis Center in Flushing Meadows, Queens (718-760-6200; tickets from $20). On the 3rd Su in Oct., 2 million spectators witness the 22,000 runners of the **New York City Marathon** (only 16,000 finish). The race begins on the Verrazano Bridge and ends at Central Park's Tavern on the Green.

The **New York Mets** bat at **Shea Stadium** in Queens (718-507-6387; tickets $6.50-15). The legendary **New York Yankees** play ball at Yankee Stadium in the Bronx (718-293-6000; tickets $12-21). Both the **New York Giants** and the **Jets** play **football** across the river at **Giants Stadium** (201-935-3900) in East Rutherford, NJ. Tickets are nearly impossible to come by. The **New York/New Jersey Metrostars** play **soccer** in the same venue. The **New York Knickerbockers** (that's the Knicks to you), as well as the WNBA's **Liberty,** play **basketball** at **Madison Sq. Garden** (465-6751; tickets from $15) and the **New York Rangers** play **hockey** there (465-6741 or 308-6977; tickets from $12).

## NEAR NEW YORK CITY: LONG ISLAND

Long Island, a sprawling suburbia to the northeast of Manhattan, serves as a sleepy summertime resort for droves of wealthy Manhattanites reclaiming their sanity. As such, it is both expensive and difficult to navigate without a car. However, **Jones Beach** offers 6½mi. of beach only 40min. from the city, and **Fire Island** is an incredibly popular gay summertime getaway.

**⚐ PRACTICAL INFORMATION.** **Long Island Convention and Visitors Bureau:** 516-951-2423. **Long Island Railroad (LIRR)** services the island (automated train info 718-217-5477) from Penn Station in Manhattan (34th St. at 7th Ave.; subway: #1, 2, 3, 9, A, C, or E) and stops in Jamaica, Queens (subway: E, J, Z) before proceeding to "points east" ($4.75-15.25; lower in off-peak hrs.). To reach **Fire Island,** take the LIRR to Sayville, Bayshore, or Patchogue. The **Sayville ferry** (589-8980) serves Cherry Grove, the Pines, and Sailor's Haven (round-trip $11, under 12 $5). The **Bay Shore ferry** (665-3600) sails to Fair Harbor, Ocean Beach, Ocean Bay Park, Saltaire, and Kismet (round-trip $11.50, under 12 $5.50). The **Patchogue ferry** (475-1665) shuttles to Davis Park and Watch Hill (round-trip $10, under 12 $5.50). Jam-packed **Jones Beach** is easily accessible by train: take the LIRR to Freeport, where a shuttle bus stops every 30min. and whisks to the ocean. The LIRR runs a package deal in summer ($11 from Manhattan). **Area code:** 516.

**FIRE ISLAND.** The summertime gay hotspot and extraordinary naturistic site off Long Island's shores, Fire Island is a 32mi. long barrier island buffering the South Shore from the roaring waters of the Atlantic. Cars are allowed only on the easternmost and westernmost tips of the island; there are no streets, only "walks," and deer roam boldly. A hip countercultural enclave during the 60s and home to the disco scene of the 70s, the island parties loud.

Two of Fire Island's many resorts, **Cherry Grove** and **The Pines,** host predominantly gay communities. These sections of Fire Island are a guppy's paradise (guppie: gay urban professional). The Atlantic Ocean beaches are spectacular, and the scene rages late into the night. Cherry Grove is the more commercial of the two towns, with cheesy restaurants and souvenir shops lining the area around the ferry slip. The houses are uniformly shingled, small, crowded together, and generally overflowing with men, though lesbian couples come here, too. The Pines, a 10min. walk up the beach, is decidedly more male, upscale, and exclusive feeling.

Both towns contain establishments advertising themselves as "guest houses." However, some of these may not be legally accredited (due to such things as fire code violations), and some may not be women-friendly. Be careful where you choose to stay; atmosphere varies. **Cherry Grove Beach Hotel** is a good bet, located on the Main Walk of Cherry Grove and close to the beach. (597-6600. Double beds, kitchenettes. From $40. Reservations required. Open May-Oct.)

Fire Island's food generally entails unspectacular eats at astounding prices. **Rachel's at the Grove,** on Ocean Walk at the Beach, overlooks the Atlantic. A standard American meal costs $9-12. (597-4174. Open daily from 10am-4am; kitchen closes at 11pm. Reservations recommended.)

Nightlife on Fire Island is everywhere, all the time. Most restaurants are open very late. The Pines' nightlife is active, but feels as if you need to be a member of some secret club to get in. Disco until dawn at the **Ice Palace,** at the Cherry Grove Beach Hotel. (597-6600. Piano bar open nightly 4-8pm; disco until 4am.)

The **Fire Island National Seashore** (289-4810 for the headquarters in Patchogue) is a daytime hotspot, offering summertime fishing, clamming, and guided nature walks. The facilities at **Sailor's Haven** (just west of the Cherry Grove community) include a marina, a nature trail, and a famous beach. Similar facilities at **Watch Hill** include a campground (597-6455; reservations required). **Smith Point West,** on the eastern tip of the island, has a small **visitors center** and a nature trail. Here you can spot horseshoe crabs, white-tailed deer, and monarch butterflies, which fly here all the way from their winter digs in Baja California. (281-3010. Center open daily 9am-5pm. Wheelchair access.)

The **Sunken Forest,** so called because of its location behind the dunes, is another natural wonder. Directly west of Sailor's Haven, its soil supports an unusual combination of holly, sassafras, and poison ivy laced together in a hulky mesh.

**JONES BEACH.** When New York State Parks Commissioner Robert "God" Moses discovered Jones Beach in 1921, it was a barren spit of land off the Atlantic shore of Nassau County. Within ten years, he had created one of the finest public beaches in the world from almost nothing. There are nearly 2500 acres of beachfront, and the parking area accommodates 23,000 cars. Only 40min. from the City, Jones Beach (785-1600) becomes a sea of umbrellas and blankets with barely a patch of sand showing in the summertime. Along the 1½mi. boardwalk, you can find deck games, rollerskating, mini-golf, basketball, and nightly dancing. The **Marine Theater** inside the park often hosts rock concerts. There are eight different public beaches on the rough Atlantic Ocean and the calmer Zachs Bay. The park closes at midnight, except to those with special fishing permits.

# CATSKILLS

The Catskills, home of Rip Van Winkle's century-long repose, remained in a happy state of somnambulant obscurity for centuries. After the purple haze of Woodstock jolted the region to life in 1969, the Catskills had to undergo an extensive detox period. Barring the occasional flashback, such as the 1994 and 1999 repetitions of the rock festival, the state-managed Catskill Forest Preserve has regained its status as a nature-lover's dreamland, offering pristine miles of hiking and skiing trails, adorably dinky villages, and crystal-clear fishing streams. Traveling from I-87, the region is most easily explored by following Rt. 28 W.

**Adirondack/Pine Hill Trailways** provides excellent service through the Catskills. The main stop is in **Kingston,** 400 Washington Ave. (331-0744 or 800-858-8555; ticket office open M-F 5:45am-11pm, Sa-Su 6:45am-11pm), on the corner of Front St. Buses run to New York City (2hr.; 10 per day; $18.50, M and W-Su same-day roundtrip $35, Tu-Th $25). Other stops in the area include Woodstock, Pine Hill, Saugerties, and Hunter; each connects with New York City, Albany, and Utica. Four stationary **tourist cabooses** dispense info, including the extremely useful *Ulster County: Catskills Region Travel Guide*, at the traffic circle in Kingston, on Rt. 28 in Shandaken, on Rt. 209 in Ellenville, and on Rt. 9 W in Milton (open May-Oct. 9am-5pm; hrs. vary depending on volunteer availability). Rest stop **visitors centers** along I-87 can advise you on area sights and distribute excellent, free maps of New York State. **Area code:** 914, unless otherwise noted.

**CATSKILL FOREST PRESERVE.** The 250,000-acre **Catskill Forest Preserve** contains many small towns and outdoor adventure opportunities. Ranger stations distribute free permits for backcountry camping, necessary for stays over 3 days. Still, most of the **campgrounds** listed below sit at gorgeous trail heads that make great day-long jaunts. Reservations are vital in summer, especially weekends. (800-456-2267. Sites $9-12; $2 1st day registration fee; phone reservation fee $7.50; $2 more for partial hookup. Open May-Sept.) The **Office of Parks** (518-474-0456) distributes brochures on the campgrounds. Required permits for **fishing** (non-NY residents $20 for 5 days) are available in sporting goods stores and at many campgrounds. **Ski** season runs from Nov. to mid-Mar., with popular slopes down numerous mountainsides along Rt. 28 and Rt. 23A. Although hiking trails are maintained, some lean-to's are dilapidated and crowded. For more info, call the **Dept. of Environmental Conservation** (256-3000). **Adirondack Trailways** buses from Kingston pass most trail heads—drivers will let you out along secondary bus routes.

**WOODSTOCK.** Signs advertising "Tie-Dyed T-shirts" and "Last incense for 20mi. sold here" might suggest to you that Woodstock, between Phoenicia and Kingston, is *the* place to be for aging hippies. Although the famed 1969 concert was actually held in Saugerties, Woodstock has been a haven for artists since the turn of the century. The tie-dyed legacy has faded, and Woodstock has become an expensive and touristy. Still, neo-hippie hipsters operate out of the **Woodstock School of Art** on Rt. 212, accessible from Rt. 28 via Rt. 375. In addition to housing art classes, a gallery pays homage to Woodstock's artistic tradition. *(679-2388. Open M-Sa 9am-3pm.)*

**MT. TREMPER. Kaleidoworld,** on Rt. 28, fiercely competes with nature for the title of most spectacular attraction in the Catskills. The two largest kaleidoscopes in the world are displayed here, with the largest (56ft) leaving Woodstock-era veterans muttering, "I can see the music!" The adjacent Crystal Palace (included in admission) features wicked cool, hands-on kaleidoscopes. *(688-5328. Open daily 10am-7pm; mid-Oct. to July closed Tu. $10, seniors $8, kids under 4 ft. 6 in. $8.)* Chant your mantra at the **Zen Mountain Monastery,** on S. Plank Rd., 10mi. from Woodstock off Rt. 212 from Mt. Tremper. *(688-2228. $5 includes lunch; weekend and week-long retreats from $195. 8:45am Sun. services include an amazing demonstration of zazen meditation.)*

    **Kenneth L. Wilson,** on Wittenburg Rd. 3.7mi. from Rt. 212 (make a hard right onto Wittenburg Rd.), has well-wooded **campsites** showers, and a family atmosphere. The pond-front beach has a gorgeous panorama of surrounding mountains staring into the looking-glass lake (hey there, Narcissus). Canoe rentals, fishing, and hiking round out the options. (679-7020. Sites $12, plus a $2.50 service charge. Registration 8am-9pm. Day use $5, seniors free M-F. Canoes ½-day $10, full-day $15.)

**PHOENICIA.** Phoenicia is another beautiful spot in the Catskills. The **Esopus Creek,** to the west, has great trout **fishing,** and **The Town Tinker,** 10 Bridge St., rents inner-tubes for river-riding. (688-5553. Inner-tubes $7 per day, with seat $10. Driver's license or $50 deposit required. Tube taxi transportation $3. Life jackets $2. Open mid-May to Sept. daily 9am-6pm; last rental 4:30pm.) If tubes don't float your boat, the wheezing, 100-year-old **Catskill Mountain Railroad** can shuttle you for 6 scenic mi. from Bridge St. to Mt. Pleasant. (40min., late May to early Sept. Sa-Su 1 per hr., 11am-5pm. $4, round-trip $6, under 12 $2.) At the 65 ft. high **Sundance Rappel Tower,** off Rt. 214, visitors return to earth the hard way. (688-5640. 4 levels of lessons; beginner 3-4hr., $22. Lessons only held when a group of 8 is present. Reservations 1 week in advance required.) For a trip to the Preserve's peak, head to Woodland Valley campground (below), where a 9.8mi. hike to the 4204 ft. summit of **Slide Mt.** lends a view of New Jersey, Pennsylvania, and the Hudson Highlands.

    The somewhat primitive **Woodland Valley** campground, off High St. 7mi. southeast of Phoenicia, has flush toilets and showers, and is accessible to many hiking trails (688-7647; sites $9, plus a $2.50 service charge. Open late May-early Oct.). The **Cobblestone Motel** is surrounded by mountains on Rt. 214 and under friendly new management. It has a family atmosphere, an outdoor pool, and clean, newly renovated rooms, most with a fridge. (688-7871. Doubles $44, large doubles $55, with kitchenette $65; 1-bedroom cottages $70, 3-room cottages with kitchen $95.)

**PINE HILL.** Pine Hill is nestled near **Belleayre Mt.,** which offers hiking trails and ski slopes. (254-5000 or 800-942-6904. Ski lift, lesson, and rental package M-F $50, Sa-Su $60; children $40/$50.) **Belleayre Hostel** is a lodging bargain; follow Rt. 28 past Big Indian, making a left on Main St. at the big white "Pine Hill" sign, then another left into the second parking lot. Bunks and private rooms in a rustic setting near Phoenicia. Amenities include a recreational room, kitchen access, laundry ($2), a picnic area, and sporting equipment. (254-4200. Bunks in summer $10, in winter $13; private rooms $25/$30; cabins for up to 4 $40/$50.)

**HUNTER MT. AND HAINES FALLS.** From Rt. 28, darting north on Rt. 42 and then east onto Rt. 23A leads through a gorgeous stretch along **Hunter Mt.,** one of the most popular **skiing** areas on the east coast (ski info 518-263-4223, accommodations 800-775-4641). Hunter Mt. offers **Skyride,** the longest, highest chairlift in the Catskills, during festivals held throughout the summer and fall ($7, ages 3-12 $3.50, under 6 $1; $1 off with festival admission). Motels and outdoor stores dot the highway. Past Hunter Mt., **North Lake/South Lake campground** in Haines Falls has 219 campsites near two lakes, a waterfall, and hiking. (518-589-5058. $16, plus a $2.50 service charge, reserve 2 days in advance. Day use $5. Canoe rental $15).

# ALBANY

Although Albany proudly proclaims itself "the most livable city in America," it suffers from an unhappy reversal of clichés. The city once known as Fort Orange comes up short in comparisons with its southern sibling, the Big Apple. Although the English took Albany in 1664, the city was actually founded in 1614 as a trading post for the Dutch West Indies Company. Established 6 years before the Pilgrims landed on the New England shore, it is the oldest continuous European settlement in the original 13 colonies and the state capital. Nevertheless, while transportation to other, more lush regions of New York might bring some tourists through the undoubtedly pleasant city, the orange stands in the shadow of a big, shiny apple.

**⟨⟩ PRACTICAL INFORMATION. Amtrak** (462-5763; station open M-F 4:30am-9:30pm, Sa-Su 6am-9:30pm), at the intersection of East St. and Rensselaer across the Hudson from downtown Albany, has service to New York City (2½hr., 8-11 per day, $34-41) and Buffalo (5hr., 2-3 per day, $43-51). **Greyhound,** 34 Hamilton St. (434-8095; station open 24hr.), runs buses to Utica (1½-2hr., $17); Syracuse (3hr., $26); Rochester (4½hr., $27); and Buffalo (5-6hr., $37). *Be careful in this neighborhood at night.* **Adirondack Trailways,** 34 Hamilton Ave. (436-9651), connects to other upstate locales: Catskill (45min., 2 per day, $5); Lake George (1¾hr., 5 per day, $10); Lake Placid (3½hr., 3 per day, $23); Tupper Lake (4hr., 2 per day, $28); and Kingston (4hr., 6 per day, $8). For local travel, the **Capital District Transportation Authority (CDTA),** 110 Watervliet Ave. (482-8822), serves Albany, Troy, and Schenectady ($1). Schedules are available at the Amtrak and Trailways stations. The **Albany Visitors Center,** 25 Quackenbush Sq. (434-0405), at Clinton Ave. and Broadway, runs trolley tours (early July to late Sept., in July, W, F, Sa, in Aug., F-Sa, in Sept. F only $10, seniors $8.50, under 15 $4) and offers a wealth of free pamphlets and maps to visitors (open M-F 9am-4pm, Sa-Su 10am-4pm). **Post Office:** 45 Hudson Ave. (462-1359; open M-F 8am-5:30pm). **ZIP code:** 12207. **Area code:** 518.

**⟨⟩ ACCOMMODATIONS AND FOOD. ⟨⟩ Pine Haven Bed & Breakfast,** 531 Western Ave., offers gorgeous rooms with phone, TV, and A/C in an inviting setting. The big Victorian house stands at the convergence of Madison and Western Ave.; parking is in the rear (482-1574; $25 per person; breakfast included; reservations needed). **Thompson's Lake State Park,** on Rt. 157 4mi. north of East Berne, offers the closest campsite (18mi. southwest of Albany). There are 140 primitive sites and fishing, hiking trails, and a swimming beach. Follow Rt. 443 out of Albany and look for the signs for Thompson's Lake (872-1674; $13; service charge $2).

In "downtown" Albany, the best eating option entails getting locked away in the big house—namely, the **Big House Brewing Company,** 90 N. Pearl St., at Sheridan St. Promising "The Best Time You'll Ever Do," the Big House produces recidivists among its loyal townie patrons. Pizzas, sandwiches, and burgers at prices that don't cry larceny ($6-7) are served alongside Al Capone Amber ale. (445-2739. Open M-Sa 11am-late, Su hours vary. Happy hour 4-7pm. Live bands Tu-F. Dancing F-Sa.) The hill above downtown Albany also stocks affordable eats. Students and locals kindle pacifist revolution while munching Jamaican stir fries (potatoes, tofu, Jamaican spices, and veggies; $5) and nature burgers ($4) uptown at vegetarian **Mother Earth's Cafe,** 217 Western Ave. at Quail St. Free live music, not all of which goes "crunch," plays nightly at 8pm. (434-0944. Open daily 11am-11pm.)

**⟨⟩ SIGHTS.** Albany offers a day's worth of sightseeing activity. The **Rockefeller Empire State Plaza,** between State and Madison St., is a $1.9 billion, towering, modernist Stonehenge. The plaza houses state offices, stores, a bus terminal, a post office, and a food court. *(Free parking M-F after 2pm.)* The **New York State Museum,** exhibits state history and a somewhat dismal replica set from *Sesame Street. (474-5877. Open daily 10am-5pm. Free, donation suggested.)* Catch a bird's-eye view of Albany, the Hudson River, and surrounding areas from the ear-popping 42nd fl. observation deck of the **Corning Tower,** accessible from the opposite side of the concourse. *(474-2418/474-4869. Open M-F 9am-3:45pm, Sa-Su 10am-3:45pm. Free; call ahead.)* The huge flying saucer at one end of the Plaza is the **Empire Center for the Performing Arts,** also known as "the Egg," a venue for theater, dance, and concerts. *(473-1845. Box office open M-F 10am-5pm, Sa noon-3pm; in summer M-F noon-3pm; tickets $8-25.)* The magnificent **New York State Capitol,** adjacent to the Empire State Plaza, has provided New York politicians with luxury quarters since 1899. *(474-2418. Call ahead for daily tour times. Tours begin at the senate staircase on the 1st fl. Free.)*

Bounded by State St. and Madison Ave. north of downtown, **Washington Park** has tennis courts, paddle boats, and plenty of room for celebrations and performances. The **Park Playhouse** stages free musical theater in the park from July to mid-Aug. *(434-2035. Tu-Su 8pm.)* On Th during late June and July, folks come **Alive at Five** to free concerts at the **Tricentennial Plaza,** across from Fleet Bank on Broadway. *(434-2032.)* For events, call the **Albany Alive Line.** *(434-1217, ext. 409.)*

The **Mohawk-Hudson Bikeway** passes along old railroad grades and canal towpaths as it weaves through the capital area. *(386-2225. Maps available at the visitors center.)*

# COOPERSTOWN

To an earlier generation, Cooperstown evoked images of James Fenimore Cooper's frontiersman hero, Leatherstocking, who roamed the woods around Lake Otsego. Tiny Cooperstown now recalls a different source of American legend and myth—baseball. Tourists file through the Baseball Hall of Fame, eat in baseball-themed restaurants, and sleep in baseball-themed motels. Fortunately for the tepid fan, baseball's mecca is surrounded by some non-baseball rural attractions.

**🔁 PRACTICAL INFORMATION.** Cooperstown is accessible from I-90 and I-88 via Rt. 28. Street parking is rare in Cooperstown; park in the free lots just outside of town on Rt. 28 south of Cooperstown, on Glen Ave. at Maple St., and near the Fenimore House. From these parking lots, it's an easy 5-15min. walk to Main St. (Rt. 31). **Trolleys** make the short trip from these lots, dropping off riders at the Hall of Fame, the Farmer and Fenimore museums, Doubleday Field, the Chamber of Commerce, and downtown. (trolleys run late June to mid-Sept. daily 8:30am-9pm; early June and Sept.-Oct. Sa-Su 8:30am-6pm; all-day pass $2, children $1.) **Pine Hall Trailways** (800-858-8555) picks up visitors at Clancy's Deli on Rt. 28 and Elm St. twice daily for New York City (5½hr., $40) and Kingston (3¼hr., $18). **Cooperstown Area Chamber of Commerce:** 31 Chestnut St., on Rt. 28 near Main St. (547-9983; generally open daily 9am-5pm, but hrs. vary; call ahead). **Post Office:** 40 Main St. (547-2311; open M-F 8:30am-5pm, Sa 8:30am-noon). **ZIP code:** 13326. **Area code:** 607.

**🔁🔁 ACCOMMODATIONS AND FOOD.** Summertime lodging in Cooperstown seems to require a Major Leaguer's salary, and during peak tourist season (late June to mid-Sept.), many accommodation-seekers strike out. Fortunately, there are alternatives. The **Mohican Motel,** 90 Chestnut St., offers more comforts than Natty Bumppo ever needed. Large beds, cable TV, and A/C provide hints of modernity. (547-5101. Late June to early Sept. 2-people $72-87, 3 $92-97, 4 $98-103, 6 $113, Sa $25 extra; lower rates in off-season.) **Glimmerglass State Park,** 7mi. north of Cooperstown on Rt. 31 on the east side of Lake Otsego, has 37 pristine campsites in a gorgeous lakeside park. Daytime visitors can swim, fish, and boat ($6 per vehicle) from 11am-7pm. (547-8662. Sites $13; $2 registration fee; showers, dumping station; no hookups. Register daily 11am-9pm. Call 800-456-2267 for reservations and a heinous $7.50 service charge.) The closest to the Hall of Fame, **Cooperstown Beaver Valley Campground,** off Rt. 28 10min. south of Cooperstown, has spacious wooded sites, a pool and recreation area, and boat and canoe rentals. (293-8131 or 800-726-7314; sites $24, with hookup $27).

The **Doubleday Café,** 93 Main St., scores twice with a $6-8 Mexican dinner menu and pints of Old Slugger beer on tap for $2.75 (547-5468; open Su-Th 7am-10pm, F-Sa 7am-11pm; bar open 2hr. after kitchen). For elegant but affordable dining, the **Hoffman Lane Bistro,** on Hoffman Ln., off Main St. across from the Hall of Fame, has light, airy rooms with white tablecloths (quiche or clams over linguine $6; 547-7055; M-Sa 11:30am-2pm and 5-9pm). A Cooperstown institution, **Schneider's Bakery,** 157 Main St., has been feeding delicious 41¢ "old-fashioneds" (donuts less sweet and greasy than their conventional cousins) and spectacular 30¢ onion rolls to locals since 1887(547-9631; open M-Sa 6:30am-5:30pm, Su 7:30am-1pm).

🗗 **TAKE ME OUT TO.** The **National Baseball Hall of Fame and Museum** on Main St., an enormous monument to America's favorite pastime. In addition to memorabilia from the immortals—everything from the bat with which Babe Ruth hit his famous "called shot" home run in the 1932 World Series to the infamous jersey worn by 65 lb. White Sox midget Eddie Gaedel—the museum displays a multimedia tribute to the sport, a detailed display on African-Americans in baseball, and history tracing baseball to ancient Egyptian religious ceremonies. As one exhibit reads, "In the beginning, shortly after God created Heaven and Earth, there were stones to throw and sticks to swing." You'll have to fight the crowds to see all this: the daily turnstile count at the museum in the summer exceeds the town population. *(547-7200. Open daily 9am-9pm; Oct.-Apr. 9am-5pm. $9.50, seniors $8, ages 7-12 $4.)*

The free **annual ceremonies** for new inductees takes place on either the last weekend of July or the first weekend of Aug., on the field adjacent to the **Clark Sports Center** on Susquehanna Ave., a 10min. walk from the Hall. During the festivities, fans scramble for contact with the many Hall of Famers who sign autographs (at steep prices) along Main St. **Free baseball games** are played on Sa and M at 2pm in the delightfully intimate Doubleday Field. Plan accordingly—over 40,000 visitors are expected. Rooms must be reserved months in advance.

Nearby, the **Fenimore Art Museum,** Lake Rd./Rt. 80, features Native American art, photos, Hudson River School paintings, and James Fenimore Cooper memorabilia. *(547-1400 or 888-547-1450. Open daily 9am-6pm; Sept.-Oct. 10am-5pm; call for hrs. Apr.-June and Nov.-Dec. $9, ages 7-12 $4.)* Across the street, the **Farmer's Museum** offers exhibits on 19th-century rural life, with an operating farmstead. *(547-1450 or 547-1500. Open Apr.-May Tu-Su 10am-4pm, June-Sept. daily 10am-5pm, Oct.-Nov. 10m-4pm. Combination tickets with Hall of Fame and Fenimore Art Museum $22, ages 7-12 $9.50.)*

The **Glimmerglass Opera Company** is a world-renowned but tiny outfit. Shows are held at the historic Alice Busch Opera Theater; call for times and shows. *(18 Chesnut St. 547-1257. Opera Festival yearly July-Aug. Tickets M-Tu and Th $20-$70, F-Su $40-80.)*

# ITHACA AND THE FINGER LAKES

According to Iroquois legend, the Great Spirit laid his hand upon the earth, and the impression of his fingers made the Finger Lakes: Canandaigua, Keuka, Seneca, Cayuga, Owasco, Skaneateles, etc. Whether it was the Great Spirit or mere Ice Age glaciers, the results are spectacular. Vladimir Nabokov, Kurt Vonnegut, and Thomas Pynchon all brooded on Cornell University's cliff. Trekkers stand beneath waterfalls in Ithaca's ruggedly carved gorges and dry off to sip another of nature's divine liquids—the rich wine of the Finger Lakes area's acclaimed vineyards.

🗗 **PRACTICAL INFORMATION.** Ithaca **Bus Terminal** (272-7930; open M-Sa 7am-6pm, Su noon-5pm), 1710 W. State St. at Rt. 13 houses **Short Line** (277-8800) and **Greyhound** (272-7930), with service to New York City (5hr., 11 per day, $35); Philadelphia (7hr., 3 per day, $53); and Buffalo (4hr., 4 per day, $23). **Tompkins Consolidated Area Transit (T-CAT)** (277-7433) is your only choice for getting out to Cayuga Lake without cars. Buses stop at Ithaca Commons, westbound on Seneca St. and eastbound on Green. (Fare 75¢-$1.50, less for seniors and students. Buses run daily.) The **Ithaca/Tompkins County Convention and Visitors Bureau,** 904 E. Shore Dr. (272-1313 or 800-284-8422), Ithaca 14850, has the best map of the area ($3.50), hotel and B&B listings, and brochures. (Open late May to early Sept. M-F 8am-6pm, Sa 10am-5pm, Su 10am-4pm; mid-Sept. to Oct. M-F 8am-5pm; Nov. to late May M-F 8am-5pm.) **Post Office:** 213 N. Tioga St. (272-5455), at E. Buffalo (open M-F 8:30am-5pm, Sa 8:30am-1pm). **ZIP code:** 14850. **Area code:** 607.

**ACCOMMODATIONS.** As befits the town where Vladimir Nabokov penned *Lolita*, Ithaca is filled with cheap roadside motels, no questions asked. In summer, however, rooms are scarce and rates rise from about $40 to $100 per night.

**Elmshade Guest House,** 402 S. Albany St. (273-1707), at Center St. 3 blocks from the Ithaca Commons. From the bus station, walk up State St. and turn right onto Albany St. Large, impeccably clean, well-decorated rooms with shared bath. This B&B is by far the best budget option in Ithaca, almost like a rich relative's house. Cable TV. Singles $25-40; doubles $45-55. Generous continental breakfast. Reservations recommended.

**The Economy Inn,** 658 Elmira Rd./Rt. 13 (277-0370). Just the basics, but close to Buttermilk Falls and to downtown Ithaca. A/C, fridge, cable TV, free local calls. Singles from $28, Sa-Su $48; doubles from $38/$52.

**The Wonderland Motel,** 654 Elmira Rd. (272-5252). Hop down Rt. 13 S. out of Ithaca. Outdoor pool, A/C, HBO, free continental breakfast, and local calls. Family atmosphere. Singles from $45, doubles from $55; Nov.-Mar. $35/$45.

Three of the nearby state parks with camping are **Robert H. Treman** (273-3440), on Rt. 327 off Rt. 13; **Buttermilk Falls** (273-5761), Rt. 13 south of Ithaca; and **Taughannock Falls** (387-6739), north on Rt. 89. (Sites 15; $2 walk-on fee or $7.50 reservation fee by calling 800-456-2267. Cabins $122-239 per week plus $11 reservation fee.) The *Finger Lakes State Parks* describes the location and services of all area state parks; available at any tourist office or park, or from **Finger Lakes State Park,** 2221 Taughannock Park Rd. (387-7041), P.O. Box 1055, Trumansburg 14886.

**FOOD AND NIGHTLIFE.** Restaurants in Ithaca cluster in **Ithaca Commons** and **Collegetown.** For a night on the town, the free *Ithaca Times,* available at most stores and restaurants, have complete listings of entertainment options.

**Moosewood Restaurant,** 215 N. Cayuga (273-9610), at Seneca St. in the Dewitt Mall. Ever-changing, tasty vegetarian food that doesn't make you feel like you're missing anything. Lunch $5.50; dinner $10-13. Open M-Th 11:30am-2pm and 5:30-9pm, F-Sa 11:30am-2pm, and Su 5:30-9pm; cafe M-Sa 2-4pm. No reservations.

**Just a Taste,** 116 N. Aurora (277-9463), near Ithaca Commons, with an extensive selection of fine wines (2½ oz. $2-5), 50 beers, and tempting *tapas* ($4-8). Open Su-Th 11:30am-3:30pm and 5:30-10pm, F-Sa 11:30am-3:30pm and 5:30-11pm.

**Joe's Restaurant,** 602 W. Buffalo St. (273-2693), at Rt. 13 (Meadow St.), a 10min. walk from Ithaca Commons. Art Deco interior dates from 1932. Italian and American entrees ($8-17) come with Joe's beloved bottomless salad. Open Su-Th 4-10pm, F-Sa 4-11pm.

**Rongovian Embassy to the USA ("The Rongo")** (387-3334), Rt. 96 on the main strip in Trumansburg about 10mi. from Ithaca—worth the drive. Seek asylum in amazing Mexican entrees at this classic restaurant/bar, and plot a trip to "Beefree" or "Nearvarna"on their huge wall map; Molé Poblano Enchiladas $10. Mug of beer $2. Restaurant open Tu-Su 5-10pm; bar Tu-Su 4pm-1am. Bands W-Sa; cover $5.

The area near Cornell called **Collegetown,** centering on College Ave., harbors student hangouts and access to a romantic path along the gorge. A smoky, red-walled cafe, **Stella's,** 403 College Ave., wears its pretension well. The $2 Italian soda with heavy cream (277-8731; open daily 7:30am-1:30am), and a few martinis might encourage you to cut a rug at Stella's adjoining blue-walled jazz bar (open daily 6:30pm-1:30am). Live bands skulk at **The Haunt,** 114 W. Green St. (275-3447).

**SIGHTS. Cornell University,** youngest of the Ivy League schools, sits on a *steep* hill in downtown Ithaca between two tremendous gorges. The **Information and Referral Center** in the Day Hall Lobby has info on campus sights and activities. *(254-4636 Open M-Sa 8am-5pm. Tours Apr.-Nov. M-F 9, 11am, 1, and 3pm, Sa 9am and 1pm, Su 1pm; Dec.-Mar. daily 1pm.)* The strangely pleasing cement edifice rising from the top of the hill—designed by I.M. Pei—houses Cornell's **Herbert F. Johnson Museum of Art,** at the corner of University and Central. *(255-6464. Open Tu-Su 10am-5pm. Free.)* The small collection of European and American painting and sculpture includes works by Giacometti, Matisse, O'Keeffe, de Kooning, and Hopper; the rooftop sculpture garden has a view. At stunning **Cornell Plantations,** a series of botanical gardens surround Cornell's great geological wonders. *(255-3020. Open daily sunrise to sunset. Free.)* Adventurous hikes into the Cornell gorge include the 1½mi. **Founder's Loop,** which is well worth the time. The free *Passport to the Trails of Tompkins County,* available from the Visitor's Bureau, is a comprehensive trekking guide.

Discriminating moviegoers should scope out the **Cornell Cinema,** on the Cornell campus; its programming and prices thrill art-house movie junkies. *(104 Willard Straight Hall. 255-3522. Tickets $4.50; students, seniors, and under 12 $4.)*

The fertile soil of the Finger Lakes area has made this region the heart of New York's wine industry. Three designated **wine trails** provide opportunities for wine tasting and vineyard touring; locals say that the fall harvest is the best time to visit. The 10 vineyards closest to Ithaca lie on the **Cayuga Trail,** with most located along Rt. 89 between Seneca Falls and Ithaca; call 800-684-5217 for info. The Finger Lakes Association (see **Practical Information,** above) has info on the **Seneca Lake Trail,** 21 wineries split into those on the east side of the lake (Rt. 414) and those on the west side (Rt. 14), and the **Keuka Trail,** seven wineries along Rt. 54 and Rt. 76. Some wineries offer free picnic facilities and tours. All give free tastings; several require purchase of a glass ($2). Family-operated **Americana Vineyards Winery,** Interlaken, ferments 2mi. from Trumansburg with free tastings and $6-12 bottles. If you're driving, take Rt. 96 or 89 north of Trumansburg to E. Covert Rd. *(4367 East Covert Rd. 387-6801. Open Mar.-Dec. M-Sa 10am-5pm, Su noon-5pm; Jan.-Feb. call for hrs.)*

At the 1848 **Seneca Falls** Convention, Elizabeth Cady Stanton and other leading suffragists organized a meeting for those seeking the vote. The **Women's Rights National Historical Park** is next to the junction of Fall and Mynderse St., where the women gathered. The **visitors center** gives tours of Stanton's home at 32 Washington St. *(136 Fall St. 315-568-2991. Open daily 9am-5pm. Exhibits $2, with tour $3.)* The **National Women's Hall of Fame** commemorates outstanding U.S. women with photographs and biographies. *(76 Fall St. 315-568-2936. Open daily M-Sa 9:30am-5pm, Su noon-4pm; Nov.-Apr. W-Sa 10am-4pm, Su noon-4pm. $3, students and seniors $1.50., families $7, under 5 free.)* Seneca Falls is a modern-day hotbed of controversy as well; Iroquois tribes battle with the government over land claims 200 years old.

The town of **Corning,** home to the Corning Glass Works, bends light 40mi. outside Ithaca on Rt. 17 W off Rt. 13 S. Glassworkers blow at the **Corning Museum of Glass,** on the Centerway, which chronicles the 3500-year history of glass-making with over 20,000 pieces—sopranos beware! *(607-974-8271. Open daily 9am-8pm; Sept.-June 9am-5pm. $10, seniors and students with ID $9, ages 6-17 $5, families $30.)* The nearby **Rockwell Museum,** off Rt. 17, shows pieces by Frederick Carder (founder of the Steuben Glass Work), an excellent collection of American Western art, and an array of antique toys and guns. *(111 Cedar St. 607-937-5386. Open M-Sa 9am-5pm, Su noon-5pm; $5, seniors $4.50, ages 6-17 $2.50, families $12.50.)*

# BUFFALO

Girded by steel and concrete highways, Buffalo is a big, furry, overgrown town in a high-rise disguise. Fiery chicken wings and electric blues bands burn off the pain of the Bills' recent Super Bowl defeats and the eternal minor league status of Bison baseball. From the downtown skyline to the small-scale pastel charm of historic Allentown, Buffalo trades the cosmopolitan for honest, modern Americana.

**⚠ PRACTICAL INFORMATION. Greyhound** (855-7531; station open 24hr.) buses from 181 Ellicott St. at N. Division St. To: New York (14 per day, 8½hr., $47); Boston (11½hr. 8 per day, $52); Niagara Falls, ON (1hr., 11 per day, $4.50); and Toronto (2½hr., 8 per day, $20). **Amtrak** (856-2075; office open M-F 7am-3:30pm) leaves from 75 Exchange St., at Washington St. for New York (8hr., 5 per day, $57-91) and Toronto (4hr., 1 per day, $16-25). The **Niagara Frontier Transit Authority (NFTA)** (855-7211 or 283-9319) offers bus and rail service throughout the city (fare $1.25), as well as free rides on the Main St. Metrorail, and trips to Niagara Falls. (Bus #40

"Grand Island" leaves from 181 Ellicott St., 13 per day, fare $1.85, seniors and ages 5-11 55¢.) **Visitors center:** 617 Main St. (852-2356 or 800-283-3256), in the Theater District (open June-Sept. M-Tu 9am-5pm, W-F 10am-6pm, Sa-Su 10am-4pm). In summer, they offer weekly architectural walking tours of downtown ($5). **Post Office:** 701 Washington St. (856-4604; open M-F 8:30am-5:30pm, Sa 8:30am-1pm). **ZIP code:** 14203. **Area code:** 716.

**⌐ ACCOMMODATIONS.** The **Buffalo Hostel (HI-AYH),** 667 Main St., houses 48 beds on spotless floors. No smoking, drinking, or drunkenness is tolerated, and there's an 11pm curfew. (852-5222. $19, nonmembers $22; security deposit $20. Reception daily 8-11am and 3-11pm. Free linen, access to microwave, pool table, weights, laundry facilities.) See **Niagara Falls** (p. 247) for campsites in the area.

**◪◪ FOOD AND NIGHTLIFE. Frank and Teresa's Anchor Bar,** 1047 Main St., secures the original Buffalo Wing, served in six degrees of spiciness. (886-8920. 10 wings $5.65, 20 wings $8.25. Open Su-Th 11am-11pm, F-Sa 11am-1am.) After a Bisons or Sabres game, locals make for the **Pearl Street Grill & Brewery,** 76 Pearl St. A diagram charts the history of your custom-brewed Lake Effect Pale Ale ($3, during happy hour 4-6pm $2) under a system of belt-operated ceiling fans. (856-2337. Open daily 11am-2am.) Among the cute boxes of Allentown, the gothic facade of **Gabriel's Gate,** 145 Allen St., doesn't frighten its lunch crowd, who feast on taco salads ($5.25) or garden souvlaki ($5.25) under stuffed moooseheads or on the patio. The daily blueplate special is under $5. (886-0602. Open daily 11:30am-1am.)

The city's surprisingly lively nightlife centers around Chippewa and **Franklin St.,** and on **Elmwood Ave.** The *Buffalo Beat* has event listings. The **Calumet Arts Cafe,** 56 W. Chippewa St., plays live jazz and blues on the weekends in a funky atmosphere (855-2220; beer $3.25 per pint; open Tu-W 5:30-10pm, Th-Sa 5:30pm-4am). **City SPoT,** on the corner of Delaware and Chippewa St., keeps locals wired with an infinite array of cheap coffee possibilities (854-7768; open 24hr.).

**◙◪ SIGHTS AND ENTERTAINMENT.** At the **Naval and Military Park,** on Lake Erie at the foot of Pearl and Main St., visitors can climb aboard a guided missile cruiser, a destroyer, and a WWII submarine. (847-1773. Open Apr.-Oct. daily 10am-5pm; Nov. Sa-Su 10am-4pm. $6, seniors and ages 6-16 $3.50.) The **Albright Knox Art Gallery,** 1285 Elmwood Ave., bus #32 "Niagara," houses over 6000 pieces, including works by Van Gogh, Matisse, Picasso, de Kooning, Renoir, and Gaugin. (882-8700. Open Tu and Th 11am-5pm, W and F 11am-9pm, Sa-Su 10am-6pm. $4, seniors $3, families $4; free Sa 11am-1pm.) An 1881 floating marine bicycle swims among the 300-piece collection at the **Pedaling History Bicycle Museum,** 3943 N. Buffalo Rd., Rt. 240/277 in Orchard Park, 12mi. southeast of Buffalo. (662-3853. Open M-Sa 11am-5pm, Su 1:30-5pm; mid-Jan. to Mar. M and F-Sa 11am-5pm, Su 1:30-5pm. $4.50, seniors $4, ages 7-15 $2.50, families $12.50.)

In winter, **Rich Stadium** (649-0015), in Orchard Park, houses the four-time Super Bowl loser **Buffalo Bills.** The **Marine Midland Arena,** 1 Seymour H. Knox III Plaza hosts hockey's **Buffalo Sabres** (855-4000) and lacrosse's **Buffalo Bandits** (855-4100). The summer brings family fun with **Buffalo Bison** baseball (846-2000) at **Dunn Tire Park,** on Swan St. From I-90, take the Elm St. exit.

# NIAGARA FALLS

One of the 7 natural wonders of the world, Niagara Falls also claims the title of one of the world's largest sources of hydro-electric power and life-risking leaps. Since 1901, when 63-year-old Annie Taylor successfully completed the drop, the Falls have attracted many thrill-seekers. Modern day Taylors beware—heavy fines and possible death both await the daring. For those with a sounder mind, outlet shopping, cheap motels, neon lights, and t-shirt shops cram the streets.

# ⁊ ORIENTATION AND PRACTICAL INFORMATION

Niagara Falls lies in both the U.S. and Ontario (ON), Canada; addresses given here are in NY, unless noted. Take **U.S. 190** to the Robert Moses Pkwy., or else skirt the tolls (but suffer traffic) by taking exit 3 to Rt. 62. In town, Niagara St. is the main east-west artery, ending in the west at **Rainbow Bridge,** which crosses to Canada (pedestrian crossings 25¢, cars $2.50). Numbered north-south streets increase toward the east. Outside of town, stores, restaurants, and motels line **Rt. 62 (Niagara Falls Blvd.).** Customs procedures are inevitable when crossing between countries. Currency changes over the bridge; although many places accept both, low exchange rates make it wise to exchange money before an extended visit.

**Trains: Amtrak** (285-4224), at 27th and Lockport St. 1 block east of Hyde Park Blvd. Take bus #52 to Falls/Downtown. To: New York City ($54) and Toronto ($16). Open Th-M 7am-11:30pm, Tu-W 7am-3pm.

**Buses: Niagara Falls Bus Terminal** (282-1331), 4th and Niagara St., sells **Greyhound** tickets for use in Buffalo. Open M-F 8am-4pm. To get a bus in Buffalo, take a 1hr. trip on bus #40 from the Niagara Falls bus terminal to the **Buffalo Transportation Center,** 181 Ellicott St. (see Buffalo **Practical Information,** p. 245).

**Public Transit: Niagara Frontier Metro Transit System,** 343 4th St. (285-9319), provides local city transit. Fare $1.25. **ITA Buffalo Shuttle** (800-551-9369) has service from Niagara Falls info center and major hotels to Buffalo Airport ($18).

**Taxis: United Cab,** 285-9331. In Canada, call 905-357-4000 for **Niagara Falls Taxi.**

**Visitor Info: Orin Lehman Visitors Center** (278-1796), in front of the Falls' observation deck; the entrance is marked by a garden. Open May-Sept. daily 8am-10:15pm; Oct. to mid-Nov. 8am-8pm; mid-Nov. to Dec. 8am-10pm; Dec.-Apr. 8am-6:30pm. An **info center** (284-2000) adjoins the bus station on 4th and Niagara St., a 10min. walk from the Falls. Open daily 8am-7pm; mid-Sept. to mid-May 9am-5pm. **Niagara Falls Canada Visitor and Convention Bureau,** 5515 Stanley Ave., ON L2G 3X4 (905-356-6061) has info on the Canadian side. Open daily 8am-8pm; off-season 8am-6pm. On the Canadian side, tune in to 91.9FM CFL2 for tourist info on the air.

**Post Office:** 615 Main St. (285-7561). Open M-F 7:30am-5pm, Sa 8:30am-2pm. **ZIP code:** 14302. **Area code:** 716 (NY), 905 (ON). In text, 716 unless otherwise noted.

# ⌐ ACCOMMODATIONS

Cheap motels (from $25) advertising free wedding certificates line **Lundy's Lane** on the Canadian side and **Rt. 62** on the American side, while many moderately priced B&Bs overlook the gorge on **River Rd.** between the Rainbow Bridge and the Whirlpool Bridge on the Canadian side. Reservations are always recommended.

**Niagara Falls International Hostel (HI-C),** 4549 Cataract Ave. (905-357-0770 or 888-749-0058), Niagara Falls, ON, just off Bridge St. An excellent hostel in a former brothel near the falls, about 2 blocks from the bus station and VIA Rail. More than 80 beds; can be cramped when full, but the staff is friendly, funky, and casual. Family rooms, laundry facilities, internet access, pub crawls, barbecues, and parking. Bike rental CDN$19 per day. CDN$17, nonmembers CDN$21. Linen CDN$1. Check-out 10am. Reception 8am-midnight; Oct.-Mar. 8am-10pm.

**Niagara Falls International Hostel (HI-AYH),** 1101 Ferry Ave. (282-3700). From bus station, walk east on Niagara St., turn left onto Memorial Pkwy.; the hostel is at the corner of Ferry Ave. *From the falls, avoid walking alone on Ferry at night.* 46 beds in a friendly old house, kitchen, TV lounge, limited parking. Family rooms available. $13, nonmembers $17. Required sleepsack $1.50. Check-in 7:30-9:30am and 4-11pm. Lockout 9:30am-4pm. Curfew 11:30pm; lights out midnight. Open late Jan. to mid-Dec.

**Olde Niagara House,** 610 4th St. (285-9408). A country B&B just 4 blocks from the falls. Free pickup at the Amtrak or bus station. Dorms $18-20 per person. Rooms with breakfast $45-55; in winter $35-45; student singles $25-45/$20-25. Hostel rooms (up to 4 people) $20 per person.

**All Tucked Inn,** 574 3rd St. (282-0919 or 800-797-0919). Nice clean rooms with shared baths close to the attractions. Singles from $39; doubles from $49; prices lower off season. Discounts with *Let's Go.* Reservations recommended.

**YMCA,** 1317 Portage Rd. (285-8491), a 20min. walk from the Falls; at night take bus #54 from Main St. 58 beds. Fee includes full use of YMCA facilities; no laundry. Dorm rooms for men only; singles $25. Key deposit $10. Men and women can sleep on mats in the gym, $15. Check-in 24hr.

**Niagara Glen-View Tent & Trailer Park,** 3950 Victoria Ave. (800-263-2570), Niagara Falls, ON. Close-by to the Falls, but bare and unwooded. Hiking trail across the street. Ice, showers, laundry facilities, pool. Shuttle from driveway to the bottom of Clifton Hill in summer every 30min. 8:45am-2am. Sites CDN $32, with hookup CDN $42 from June-Sept., less May-Oct. Office open daily 8am-11pm. Park open May to mid-Oct.

## ◪ FOOD

**Corsaro's Sunrise Diner,** 829 Main St. is a classic red-boothed hangout. Two eggs and toast $1.20, sandwiches $2-4. (284-0959. Open M-Th and Sa 7am-8pm, F 7am-9pm, Su 7am-3pm.) More exotic fare and vegetarian options (*biryani* $10) are served at **Sardar Sahib,** 626 Niagara St. (282-0444; open daily 11:30am-midnight).

On the Canadian side, the restaurants on **Victoria Ave.** by Clifton Hill are touristy but inexpensive. **Simon's Restaurant,** 4116 Bridge St., ON, serves big breakfasts with giant homemade muffins (CDN74¢) and hearty diner dinners (905-356-5310; open M-Sa 5:30am-9pm, Su 5:30am-3pm). **The Penninsula Bakery and Restaurant,** 4568 Erie Ave., ON, off Bridge St., sells authentic Pan-Asian food; Malaysian stir-fried noodles CDN$5.95. (905-374-8176, open M 10am-7pm, W-Su 10am-10:30pm).

## ◉ SIGHTS

Although tourist snares abound on both sides, they're less rampant on the American shore. Official sights give more for your money. From late Nov. to late Jan., Niagara Falls holds the **Festival of Lights** (905-374-1616); brilliant bulbs line the trees and create animated outdoor scenes. Live concerts are held throughout, but New Year's Eve is the big party. Illuminating the falls caps the spectacle.

**AMERICAN SIDE. Niagara Wonders,** a 20min. movie on the Falls, plays in the info center. *(278-1783. Shows daily on the hr. 10am-8pm; in fall M-Su 10am-6pm; in spring daily 10am-6pm. $2, ages 6-12 $1.)* The **Maid of the Mist Tour** is a 30min. boat ride to the foot of both falls; don't bring anything that isn't waterproof. *(284-4233. Tours in summer every 15min. M-Th 9:15am-5pm, F-Su 9:15am-6pm. $8.50 plus 50¢ elevator fee, ages 6-12 $4.80.)* The **Caves of the Wind Tour** lends out yellow raincoats for a thrilling, body-soaking trek to the base of the Bridal Veil Falls, including an optional walk to Hurricane Deck, as close to the falls as you'll get. *(278-1730. Open May to mid-Oct.; hrs. vary depending on season and weather conditions. Trips leave every 15min. $6, ages 6-12 $5.50.)*

The **Master Pass,** available at the park's visitors center, covers admission to the theater, Maid of the Mist, **Schoellkopf's Geological Museum** in Prospect Park, the **Aquarium,** and the **Viewmobile,** a tram-guided tour of the park. *(Master Pass $21, ages 6-12 $16. Museum: 278-1780. Open Nov. to early Sept. daily 9am-7pm; early Sept.-Oct. 10am-5pm; $1. Aquarium: 701 Whirlpool St. 285-3575. Open late May to early Sept. daily 9am-5pm; early Sept. to late May 9am-7pm. $6.50, ages 4-12 $4.50. Viewmobile: 278-1730. Runs every 15min. daily 10am-8pm; in winter 10am-5:30pm. $4.50, children $3.50.)*

Continuing north, the **Niagara Power Project** features interactive demonstrations, videos, and displays on energy, hydropower, and local history. While there, you can cast off the fishing platform to reel in salmon, trout, or bass. *(5777 Lewiston Rd. 286-6661. Open daily 9am-5pm. Free.)* Further north in Lewiston, NY, the 200-acre state **Artpark,** at the foot of 4th St., focuses on visual and performing arts, with a variety of demonstrations. The theater presents opera, pops concerts, and jazz festivals. *(800-659-7275. Tickets $15-30; shows May-Oct.; call for schedule. Box office open M-Sa*

*10am-6pm, Su noon-4pm.)* **Old Fort Niagara,** a French castle built in 1726, guards the entrance to the Niagara River and is now a prime picnic spot; follow Robert Moses Pkwy. north from Niagara Falls. *(745-7611. Open June-early Sept. daily 9am-6:30pm; early Sept.-Dec. and Jan.-May 9am-4:30pm. $6.75, seniors $5.50, ages 6-12 $4.50. Day use $5/car.)*

**CANADIAN SIDE.** On the Canadian side of Niagara Falls (across Rainbow Bridge), **Queen Victoria Park** provides the best view of Horseshoe Falls. The falls are illuminated for 3hr. every night, starting 1hr. after sunset. Parking in Queen Victoria is expensive (CDN$8). **Park 'N' Ride** is a better deal, offering parking at Rapids View, across from Marineland at the south end of Niagara Pkwy. The **People Movers** buses take you through the 19mi. area on the Canadian side of the Falls, stopping at neat spots along the way. *(357-9340. Late Apr. to mid-June Su-Th 10am-6pm, F-Sa 10am-10pm; mid-June to Aug. daily 9am-11pm; Sept. to mid-Oct. Su-Th 10am-6pm, F-Sa 10am-10pm. CDN$4, children CDN$2.50.)* **Skylon Tower** has the highest view of the falls at 775 ft.; on a clear day, you can see as far as Toronto. Its 520 ft. **Observation Deck** offers an unhindered view of the falls. *(5200 Robinson St. 356-2651. Open daily 8am-11pm; in winter hrs. change monthly. CDN$8.50, seniors CDN$7, children CDN$4.)* The **Explorer's Passport** includes passage to **Journey Behind the Falls,** a tour behind Horseshoe Falls; **Great Gorge Adventure,** a descent into the Niagara River Rapids; and the **Spanish Aero Car,** an aerial cable ride over the whirlpool waters. *(Passport: CDN$14, children CDN$7. Journey: 354-1551. CDN$6, children CDN$3. Adventure: 374-1221. Open late Apr. to late Oct. daily 9am-8pm with last trip at 7:30pm from June-Sept. CDN$5, children CDN$2.50. Aero Car: 354-5711. Open Mar.-Oct. Hrs. really vary. CDN$5.50, children CDN$2.75.)*

The **Niagara Falls Brewing Company** hosts touring and tasting. *(6863 Lundy's Ln. 374-1166. Tours Sa 1pm; open M-Sa 10am-5pm, Su 10am-1pm. $2.)* Bikers, in-line skaters, and leisurely walkers enjoy the 32km **Niagara River Recreation Trail,** which runs from Ft. Erie to Ft. George and passes many interesting historical sights.

Commercialism can be as much a thing of beauty as any natural wonder. Niagara Falls offers the delightfully tasteless **Clifton Hill,** a collection of wax museums, funhouses, and overpriced shows. **Ripley's Believe It or Not Museum** displays wonders like wax models of unicorn men and a Jivaro shrunken head from Ecuador. Unfortunately, the authentic New Guinea Penis Guard, used for protection from hungry mosquitoes, is not for sale. *(4960 Clifton Hill. 356-2238. Open daily 9am-1am; Sept.-May 10am-10pm. CDN$7, seniors CDN$5, ages 6-12 CDN$4.)*

# NORTHERN NEW YORK

## THE ADIRONDACKS

In 1892, the New York State legislature demonstrated uncommon foresight, establishing the **Adirondacks State Park**—the largest U.S. park outside Alaska and one of the few places left in the Northeast where hikers can spend days without seeing another soul. In recent years, unfortunately, pollution and development have left their harsh imprint; acid rain has damaged the tree and fish populations, especially in the fragile high-altitude environments, and tourist meccas like Lake George have continued to expand rapidly. Despite these urban intrusions, much of the area retains the beauty visitors have enjoyed for over a century.

Of the 6 million acres in the Adirondacks Park, 40% are open to the public, offering a large range of outdoor activities. Whether for hiking, snow-shoeing, or cross-country skiing, the 2000mi. of trails that traverse the forest provide spectacular mountain scenery. Canoers paddle through a network of lakes and streams, while mountain climbers conquer **Mt. Marcy,** the state's highest peak (5344 ft.), and skiers take advantage of a dozen well-known alpine centers. **Lake Placid** hosted the winter Olympics in 1932 and 1980, and frequently welcomes national and international sports competitions. **Tupper Lake** and Lake George have carnivals every Jan. and Feb.; Tupper also hosts the **Tin Man Triathlon** in mid-July. In Sept., the hot air balloons of the **Adirondack Balloon Festival** paint the sky over Glens Falls.

**⁊ PRACTICAL INFORMATION.** The **Adirondack Mountain Club (ADK)** is the best source of info on outdoor activities in the region. Its offices are located at 814 Goggins Rd., Lake George 12845 (668-4447; open M-Sa 8:30am-5pm; Jan.-Apr. M-F 8:30am-4:30pm), and at Adirondack Loj Rd., P.O. Box 867, Lake Placid 12946 (523-3441; open Sa-Th 8am-8pm, F 8am-10pm). Call the Lake Placid number for the scoop on outdoor skills classes such as canoeing, rock climbing, whitewater kayaking, and wilderness medicine. For the latest backcountry info, visit ADK's **High Peaks Information Center,** 3mi. south of Lake Placid on Rt. 73, then 5mi. down Adirondack Loj Rd. The center also has washrooms (open daily 8am-8pm) and sells basic outdoor equipment, trail snacks, and extremely helpful guides to the mountains for $18 (store open Sa-Su 8am-noon and 1-4pm). Rock climbers should consult the experienced staff at the **Mountaineer** (576-2281), in Keene Valley, between I-87 and Lake Placid on Rt. 73. Snowshoes rent for $16 per day; ice-climbing equipment (plastic boots and crampons) rent for $20 per day; rock shoes rent for $12 per day. (Open Su-Th 9am-5:30pm, F 9am-7pm, Sa 8am-7pm; off-season M-F 9am-5:30pm, Sa 8am-5:30pm, Su 10am-5:30pm.) The ADK and the Mountaineer can provide basic info on the conditions and concerns of backwoods travel.

**Adirondacks Trailways** (800-858-8555). From Albany, buses set out for Lake Placid, Tupper Lake, and Lake George. From the Lake George bus stop at Capris Pizza, 221 Canada St., buses go to Lake Placid (2 per day, $13.30); Albany (4 per day, $10); and New York City (5 per day, $37.45). **Area code:** 518.

**⌐ ACCOMMODATIONS.** Two lodges near Lake Placid are also run by the ADK. The **Adirondack Loj,** 5mi. down Adirondack Loj Rd. which meets Rt. 73 about 3mi. east of Lake Placid, fills a beautiful log cabin on Heart Lake with comfortable bunk facilities and a family atmosphere. Guests swim, fish, and canoe on the premises (canoe or boat rental $5 per hr., guests $3), and, in winter, explore the wilderness trails on rented snowshoes for $10 per day, or cross-country ski for $20 per day (523-3441, for Dec., Feb., July-Oct.: $32 for a bunk, $52 for a private room; these rates include breakfast; add $11.50 for dinner or $4.50 for lunch; for other months: $26/$42/$11.50/$4.50). Lean-tos, campsites, and cabins also available; reservations are highly recommended.) For a more rustic experience, hike 3½mi. to the **John's Brook Lodge** from the closest trailhead, in Keene Valley (call the Adirondack Loj for reservations); from Lake Placid, follow Rt. 73 15mi. through Keene to Keene Valley and turn right at the Ausable Inn. The hike runs slightly uphill, but the meal which awaits you justifies the effort. A great place to meet friendly New Yorkers, John's Brook is no secret; beds fill completely on weekends. Make reservations 1 day in advance for dinner, earlier for a weekend. Bring sheets or a sleeping bag. (Rates start at $28 for a bunk July to early Sept. $27, add $11.50 for dinner.)

**Free camping** is easy to come by. Inquire about the location of free trailside shelters before you plan a hike in the forest, or camp for free anywhere on public land in the **backcountry** as long as you are at least 150 ft. away from a trail, road, water source, or campground and below 4000 ft. in altitude. The State Office of Parks and Recreation (see New York **Practical Information,** p. 198) has more details.

## LAKE PLACID

Melville Dewey, inventor of the Dewey Decimal Library Cataloging system, was the first person to promote Lake Placid as a summer resort, in 1850. Now the village is a winter sports mecca. Host to the Olympic Winter Games in both 1932 and 1980, famous people have wandered through Lake Placid for the past 150 years. World-class athletes train year-round in the town's extensive facilities, lending an international flavor which distinguishes Lake Placid from its Adirondack neighbors. The setting of the Adirondack High Peaks Region attracts droves of hikers and backpackers each year, although many would-be campers end up pitching their tents in a motel room—in the winter, temperatures can dip down to -40° F.

**⁊ PRACTICAL INFORMATION.** Lake Placid sits at the intersection of Rt. 86 and 73. The town's Olympic past defines the Lake Placid of today; the **Olympic Regional Development Authority,** 216 Main St., Olympic Center (523-1655 or 800-462-6236), operates the sporting facilities (open M-F 8:30am-4pm). Info on food, lodging, and area attractions can be obtained from the **Lake Placid-Essex County Visitors Bureau** (523-2445), also in the Olympic Center (open daily 9am-5pm; closed Su in winter). **Adirondack Trailways** (800-225-6815 for bus info) stops at Lake Placid Video, 324 Main St., and has extensive service in the area. Destinations include New York City ($51) and Lake George ($13.30). For **weather info,** call 523-1363 or 523-3518. Lake Placid's **post office:** 201 Main St. (523-3071; open M-F 8:30am-5pm, Sa 8:30am-2pm). **ZIP code:** 12946. **Area code:** 518.

**⌐ ACCOMMODATIONS AND FOOD.** If you avoid the resorts on the West end of town, both lodgings and food can be had cheaply in Lake Placid. 4mi. from town, the **White Sled,** just 3mi. east of town on Rt. 73, has a neat bunkhouse with 3 bathrooms and a six bed cottage, as well as motel rooms. The owner can provide visitors with information on Lake Placid and the Adirondacks and, if you're lucky, she will prepare her specialty, Blueberry Buckle. (523-9314. Bunks $17, motel rooms start at $38. If you prefer to stay right in town, the **High Peaks Hostel** is your best bet. It's located at 337 1/2 Main St., across from the bowling alley, and just a few blocks from Olympic Center. (523-3764. Country cabin feel, 20 guests, at $16 a bunk.) **Meadowbrook State Park** (891-4351), 5mi. west of town on Rt. 86 in Ray Brook, and **Wilmington Notch State Campground** (946-7172), about 8mi. east of Lake Placid on Rt. 86, are the region's best camping areas. Both offer shady, wooded sites which accommodate two tents without hookups ($9 per night).

Lake Placid Village, which includes Main St., has a number of reasonably priced dining establishments. The lunch buffet at the **Hilton Hotel,** 1 Mirror Lake Drive, includes sandwiches, soups, and salads for only $6.50. (523-4411, buffet from 12pm-2pm.) The **Black Bear Restaurant** at 157 Main St. across from the municipal parking lot, serves up a hearty breakfast ($3-$5) and lunch ($6). Be sure to try a bottle of the area's own brew, Saranac lager ($3. 523-9886, open 6am-10pm, depending on the crowd). **The Cottage,** 5 Mirror Lake Drive, offers a selection of sandwiches and salads for less than $8. Try the Mount Mary, a crabmeat sandwich. The view is spectacular, and you can sometimes catch the US National Canoeing or Kayaking teams at practice (523-984; food served 11:30am-10pm; bar 11:30am-12am/1am depending on crowd). **Mud Puddles** provides a fairly lively pub and pop music scene at 3 School St. (523-4446; open 8am-3am; M-F no cover; Sa-Su $3).

## ☉ SIGHTS AND ACTIVITIES

The **Olympic Center** in downtown Lake Placid houses the 1932 and 1980 hockey arenas, along with the **Winter Sports Museum.** *(523-1655 x226. Open daily from 10am-5pm; $3 adults, $2 seniors, $1 children under 6.)* Purchase tickets for a guided tour of the **Olympic Ski Jumps** which, along with the **Kodak Sports Park,** make up the **Olympic Jumping Complex,** just east of town on Rt. 73. Admission gets you a chairlift and elevator ride to the top where you can watch jumpers flipping and sailing into a swimming pool from Jun. to mid-Oct. *(Open 9am-4pm. $8, seniors and children $5.)* About 5mi. east of town on Rt. 73, the **Olympic Sports Complex** at Mt. Van Hoevenberg usually has a summer trolley that coasts to the top of the bobsled run ($4); in winter, you can actually bobsled down the Olympic track, but it will set you back a chilly $30. *(523-4436.)* Popular **Tour Boat Cruises** travel 16 narrated mi. across Lake Placid *(523-9704. $6.75 adults, $5.75 seniors, $4.75 children. Cruises depart daily at 10:30am and 2:30pm, 4pm cruise on weekends.)* For a bird's eye view, drive up Whiteface Mountain on the **Veterans Memorial Highway** just 11mi. outside Lake Placid off Rt. 86. There is an observatory at the summit. *(946-7175.)*

The west branch of the **Ausable River,** just east of Lake Placid along Rt. 86, lures anglers to its shores and shallow waters. Fishing licenses can be purchased at the

**Town Hall** *(523-2162)* at 301 Main St., or at **Jones Outfitters.** Jones also rents all the equipment one might need to spend a day or a week fly-fishing, including rod, reel, line, tackle, and bait. *(37 Main St. 523-3468. Package $15, fly-fishing outfit $35. Open year round 9am-6pm, 10am-5pm on Sundays).* Jones also rents canoes, kayaks, and rowboats *($13 per hour, or $35 per day).* The **Fishing Hotline** *(891-5413)* is the sportsman's friend, providing an in-depth recording about fishing conditions in the area. If you prefer land to the water, try to catch a horse show in June and July at the **Lake Placid Horse Shows**, in the arena just east of town on Rt. 73.

## THOUSAND ISLAND SEAWAY

The Thousand Island region of the St. Lawrence Seaway spans 100mi. from the mouth of Lake Ontario to the first of the many locks on the St. Lawrence River. Surveys conducted by the American and Canadian governments have determined that there are over 1700 islands in the seaway, with the requirements being at least one square foot of land above water surface year-round and at least one tree. These islands and countless rocky shoals make navigation tricky in the area. Locals divide people into two groups: those who *have* hit a shoal and those who *will* hit a shoal. But don't let this dire prediction deter you; not only is the Thousand Island region a fisherman's paradise, with some of the world's best bass and muskie catch, it's the only area in the nation with a salad dressing named after it.

**🚩 PRACTICAL INFORMATION.** The Thousand Island region hugs the St. Lawrence just 2hr. from Syracuse by way of I-81 N. **Clayton, Alexandria Bay** ("Alex Bay" to locals), and **Cape Vincent** are the main towns in the area. For Welleslet Island, Alexandria Bay, and the eastern 500 islands, stay on I-81 until you reach Rt. 12 E. For Clayton and points west, take exit 47 and follow Rt. 12 until you reach Rt. 12 E. The **Clayton Chamber of Commerce,** 510 Riverside Dr., Clayton 13624 (686-3771), has the free *Clayton Vacation Guide* and *Thousand Islands Seaway Region Travel Guide* (open daily mid-June-mid-Sept. 9am-4pm; mid-Sept. to mid-June M-F 9am-4pm). The **Alexandria Bay Chamber of Commerce,** 24 Market St., Alexandria Bay 13607 (482-9531), is just off James St. (open M-F 8:30am-4:30pm). The **Cape Vincent Chamber of Commerce** (654-2481) welcomes visitors at 175 N. James St., by the ferry landing (open May-Oct. Tu-Sa 9am-5pm; also late May to early Sept. Su-M 10am-4pm). Access the region by bus with **Greyhound,** 540 State St., Watertown. Two buses run daily to New York City (7½hr., $49); Syracuse (1½hr., $10); and Albany (1¼hr., $37). (Station open M-F 9:30am-4:30pm and 8:45-9:05pm, Sa-Su 9:30-10:30am, 4:15-4:50pm, and 8:45-9:05pm.) From the same station, **Thousand Islands Bus Lines** (287-2782) leaves for Alexandria Bay and Clayton, M-F at 1pm ($5.60 to Alexandria, $3.55 to Clayton); return trips leave Clayton from the **Nutshell Florist,** 234 James St. (686-5791), at 8:45am, and Alexandria from the **Dockside Café,** 17 Market St. (482-9849), at 8:30am.

Clayton's **post office:** 236 John St. (686-3311; open M-F 9am-5pm, Sa 9am-noon). **ZIP code:** 13624. Alexandria Bay's **post office:** 13 Bethune St. (482-9521; open M-F 8:30am-5:30pm, Sa 8:30am-1pm). **ZIP code:** 13607. Cape Vincent's **post office:** 362 Broadway St. (654-2424; open M-F 8:30am-1pm and 2-5:30pm, Sa 8:30-11:30am). **ZIP code:** 13618. Thousand Island's **area code:** 315.

**🛏 ACCOMMODATIONS AND CAMPGROUNDS.** The idyllic **Tibbetts Point Lighthouse Hostel (HI-AYH),** 33439 County Rt. 6, along the western edge of the seaway on Cape Vincent, where Lake Ontario meets the St. Lawrence River. Take Rt. 12 E into town, drive straight onto Broadway, and follow the river until the road ends. The lighthouse is still active, and the peaceful rhythm of the waves lulls you to sleep at night. Pick up in Clayton with 1 day notice. (654-3450. 2 houses with 26 beds. Full kitchen with microwave. $12, nonmembers $15. Linen $1. Check-in 7-9am and 5-10pm. Curfew 11pm. Open mid-May to Oct.) **Burnham Point State Park,** on Rt. 12 E 4mi. east of Cape Vincent and 11mi. west of Clayton, sports 52 sites and three picnic areas. (654-2324. Showers. Tent sites $13, prime sites on the water

$15. Open daily late May to early Sept. 8am-10pm. Wheelchair access. $2.50 surcharge for each registration.) **Keewaydin State Park,** just south of Alexandria Bay, maintains 41 sites along the St. Lawrence River. Campers have free access to an Olympic-size swimming pool. (482-3331. Showers available. $13 per night. $2.50 surcharge applies here too. Open daily late May to early Sept. 8am-11pm.) Call 1-800-456-CAMP/2267 for reservations at either state park.

**EXPLORING THE SEAWAY.** Any of the small towns that dot Rt. 12 will serve as a fine base for exploring the region, although Clayton and Cape Vincent tend to be less expensive than Alexandria Bay. **Uncle Sam Boat Tours,** 604 Riverside Dr. (686-3511), in Clayton, and on James St. in Alexandria Bay (482-2611), delivers a good look at most of the islands and the plush estates situated atop them. Tours highlight **Heart Island** and its famous **Boldt Castle;** they do not cover the price of admission to the castle. George Boldt, former owner of New York City's elegant Waldorf-Astoria Hotel, financed Boldt Castle, a 6-story replica of a Rhineland castle as a gift for his wife, who died before its completion. In his grief, Boldt stopped construction on the 120-room behemoth, which remains unfinished today. After extensive renovations, this romantic monument is now open to the public. The castle grounds include magnificently sculptured gardens and several smaller stone buildings worth a glimpse. *(Tourism council 800-847-5263. 2¼hr. tours leave from Alexandria Bay daily late Apr. to Oct. $14.50, seniors $12, children 12 and under $7.75. Daily lunch and dinner cruises $20-$27.50, must be reserved in advance. Castle 482-9724; open mid-May to mid-Oct. daily 10am-6:30pm. $3.75, ages 6-12 $2.)* In Clayton, **French Creek Marina,** 250 Wahl St., rents 14 ft. fishing boats ($50 per day), launches boats ($5), and provides overnight docking *($20 per night. 686-3621).* **O'Brien's U-Drive Boat Rentals,** 51 Walton St., handles boat rentals in Alexandria Bay with 16 ft. fishing boats *(482-9548. $70 per day, $300 deposit; open daily May to early Oct. 8am-4:30pm).* In Cape Vincent, **Millens Bay Marina,** 5mi. beyond town on Rt. 12 E, offers 16 ft. motor boats *(654-2174. 15 HP $35 per ½-day, $50 per day. Open 8am-sundown).*

    **Fishing licenses** ($11 per day, $20 for 5 days, season $35) are available at sporting goods stores or at the **Town Clerk's Office,** *(405 Riverside Dr., Clayton. 686-3512. Open M-F 9am-noon and 1-4pm).* No local store rents equipment; bring rods or plan to buy.

# NEW JERSEY

BRUCE!!! New Jersey was once called the Garden State for a reason, but with the advent of suburbia (NJ serves both New York City and Philadelphia) and tax-free shopping (giving rise to outlets and major mall country), travelers who refuse to get off the interstates envision the state as a conglomeration of belching chemical plants and ocean beaches strewn with garbage and gamblers. This picture, however, belies the state's quieter delights off the highway. A closer look reveals that there is more to New Jersey than commuters, chemicals, and craps; the interior blooms with fields of corn, tomatoes, and peaches, and quiet sandy beaches outline the southern tip of the state. And the state shelters quiet hamlets, the Pine Barrens forest, and two world-class universities: Rutgers and Princeton. Certainly, Atlantic City is gaudy, and the Turnpike remains the zone of the road warrior, but those straying from the path will be pleasantly surprised. Besides, how bad can Bruce Springsteen's homeland be?

## ⁊ PRACTICAL INFORMATION

**Capital:** Trenton.

**Visitor Info: State Division of Tourism,** 20 W. State St., P.O. Box 826, Trenton 08625-0826 (609-292-2470; www.nj-tourism.com). **New Jersey Dept. of Environmental Protection and Energy, State Park Service,** 401 East State St., Trenton 08625-0404 (609-292-2797).

**Postal Abbreviation:** NJ. **Sales Tax:** 6%; no tax on clothing.

# ATLANTIC CITY

More than any other American city, the geography of Atlantic City is subconsciously written into the minds of generations of Americans. For over 50 years, board-gaming strategists have vied for control of this coastal city as reincarnated in its two-dimensional form on the *Monopoly* board. When *Monopoly* was created, Atlantic City was *the* beachside hotspot among resort towns. The opulence faded into neglect, then into a deeper shade of tackiness. With the legalization of gambling in 1976, casinos rose from the rubble of Boardwalk. Today, velvet-lined temples of schmaltz (each with a dozen restaurants and big-name entertainment) blight the beach and draw all kinds, from international jet-setters to local seniors.

## ⚡ ORIENTATION AND PRACTICAL INFORMATION

Atlantic City lies half way down New Jersey's coast, accessible via the **Garden State Pkwy.** and the **Atlantic City Expwy.,** and easily reached by train from Philadelphia or New York. Attractions cluster on and around the Boardwalk, which runs east-west along the Atlantic Ocean. Running parallel to the Boardwalk, Pacific and Atlantic Ave. offer cheap restaurants, hotels, and convenience stores. *Atlantic Ave. can be dangerous after dark, and any street farther out can be dangerous even by day.* Getting around is easy on foot. **Parking** at the Sands Hotel is free, but "for patrons only," so spend a dollar at the slots. Lots near the Boardwalk run $3-7.

**Airport: Atlantic City International** (645-7895 or 800-892-0354). Located just west of Atlantic City in Pamona. Served by Spirit, U.S. Airways, and Continental.

**Train: Amtrak,** at Kirkman Blvd. near Michigan Ave. Follow Kirkman to its end, bear right, and follow the signs. To New York (2½hr., $42). Open daily 6am-10:15pm.

**Buses: Greyhound** (609-340-2000 or 800-231-2222). Buses travel every 30min. between Port Authority (NYC) and most major casinos (2½hr., casino drop-off rates $27 round-trip). Many casinos, in addition to the round-trip discounts, will give gamblers between $15 and $20 in coins upon arrival. (Trump Plaza offers $20 for starting your gambling spree at their casino.) **New Jersey Transit** (in-state 800-582-5946, 215-569-3752) offers hourly service between NYC and the transit station on Atlantic Ave. between Michigan and Ohio St. ($23, seniors $9.60 each way). **Gray Line Tours** (800-669-0051) offers several daytrips to Atlantic City (3hr.; $21 on weekdays, $23 on weekends). Ticket receipt redeemable for cash, chips, or food from casinos when you arrive. Tropicana and the Sands offer $20 per person. The bus drops riders at the casino and picks you up later the same day. Call for nearest NYC bus pickup locations. Call 800-995-8898 for info about economical overnight packages. Terminal open 24hr.

**Visitor Information: Atlantic City Convention Center and Visitors Bureau,** 2314 Pacific Ave. (449-7130). The "Old Convention Center" is currently closed during its transformation into a sports venue. A new center will be built outside of the city on the Expressway. Information is not yet available on when it will open. Call ahead.

**Hospital: Atlantic City Medical Center** (344-4081), at Michigan and Pacific Ave.

**Hotlines: Rape and Abuse Hotline** (646-6767). 24hr. **Gambling Abuse** (800-426-2537). 24hr. **AIDS Hotline** (800-281-2437). Operates M-F 9am-5pm.

**Area code:** 609.

## 🏠 ACCOMMODATIONS

Large, red-carpeted beachfront hotels have bumped smaller operators a few streets back. Smaller hotels along **Pacific Ave.,** 1 block from the Boardwalk, charge about $60-95 in the summer. Reserve ahead, especially Sa-Su. Many hotels lower their rates mid-week and in winter, when water temperature and gambling fervor drop significantly. Rooms in guest houses are reasonably priced, though facilities can be dismal. If you have a car, it pays to stay in **Absecon,** about 8mi. from Atlantic City; exit 40 from the Garden State Pkwy. leads to Rt. 30 and cheap rooms.

**Inn of the Irish Pub,** 164 St. James Pl. (344-9063), near the Ramada Tower, just off the Boardwalk. Big, clean rooms, decorated with antiques. The summer breeze from the beach keeps things cool. Plush lobby with TV and pay phone. Porch sitting area complete with rocking chairs. Coin-op laundry in hotel next door. Restaurant offers a $2 lunch special and a $6 dinner special. Su-Th special: private shower/twin beds $27.50. Single with shared bath $29, with private bath $40.20 M-F and $62.20 Sa-Su; double with shared bath $60, with private bath $75; quad with shared bath $60. Prices include tax; rates are stable all year. Key deposit $5.

**Comfort Inn,** 154 South Kentucky Ave. (888-247-5337 or 348-4000). Near the Sands. Rooms with king size or 2 queen size beds and jacuzzi. Includes continental breakfast, free parking, and an heated pool. Mar.-May $59, June $69, July $79, Aug. $89, early Sept. $69, late Sept. $59. Rooms with ocean views $20 extra, but come with fridge, microwave, and a bigger jacuzzi. Call well in advance for Sa-Su and holidays.

**Birch Grove Park Campground** (641-3778), Mill Rd. in Northfield. About 6 mi. from Atlantic City, off Rt. 9. 50 sites. Attractive and secluded. Sites $18 for 2; with two-way hookup $21; 4-way hookup $24. Sites available Apr.-Oct.

## ◉ FOOD

The food in Atlantic City is, for the most part, fairly reasonable. 75¢ hotdogs and $1.50 pizza slices crowd the Boardwalk. After cashing in your chips, you can visit a casino buffet (lunch about $6-7, dinner $10). The town itself has better restaurants. For a complete rundown of local dining, pick up a copy of *Shorecast Insider's Guide At the Shore* or *Whoot* (both free) from a hotel lobby, restaurant, or local store, or hang around casino gambling dens and score free pretzels, coffee, cookies, juice, and even yogurt provided to high rollers.

Your best bet for cheap sit-down dining in Atlantic City is the **Inn of the Irish Pub**, 164 St. James Pl., which serves hearty, modestly priced dishes like Dublin beef stew ($5). The lunch special (M-F 11:30am-2pm) includes a pre-selected sandwich and cup of soup for $2. This inviting pub has a century's worth of Joycean élan and Irish memorabilia. Domestic drafts are $1. (345-9613. Open 24hr.)

**Pacific Avenue** is cramped with steak, sub, and pizza shops. Celebrity supporters of the **White House Sub Shop,** 2301 Arctic Ave., include Bill Cosby and the late Frank Sinatra. Ol' Blue Eyes was rumored to have had these immense subs ($4-9) flown to him while he was on tour. (345-1564 or 345-8599. Open M-Th 10am-11pm, F-Sa 10am-midnight, Su 11am-11pm.) For the best pizza in town, hit **Tony's Baltimore Grille,** 2800 Atlantic Ave., at Iowa Ave. The large booths have personal jukebox (345-5766; pasta $4-6, pizza $6-7; open daily 11am-3am; bar open 24hr.). **Custard and Snack House,** between South Carolina and Ocean Ave., makes 37 flavors of ice cream and yogurt, ranging from peach to tutti-frutti (345-5151; cones $2.25; open Su-Th 10am-midnight, F-Sa 10am-3am).

## ◉ CA$INO$, THE BOARDWALK, AND BEACHES

You don't have to spend a penny to enjoy yourself in Atlantic City's casinos; their vast, plush interiors and spotless marble bathrooms can entertain a resourceful and voyeuristic budget traveler for hours. Watch blue-haired ladies shove quarter after quarter in the slot machines with a vacant, zombie-like stare. Open nearly all the time, casinos lack windows and clocks, denying you the time cues that signal the hours slipping away; keep your eyes on your watch, or you'll have spent five hours and five digits before you know what hit you. To curb inevitable losses, stick to the cheaper games—blackjack and slot machines—and stay away from the cash machines. TropWorld, Bally's Grand, and Taj Mahal (see below), will allow you to gamble for hours on less than $10. The minimum gambling age of 21 is strictly enforced.

All casinos on the Boardwalk fall within a dice toss of one another. The farthest south is **The Grand** (347-7111), between Providence and Boston Ave., and the farthest north is **Showboat** (343-4000), at Delaware Ave. and Boardwalk. If you liked

*Aladdin*, you'll love the **Taj Mahal,** 1000 Boardwalk (449-1000). Donald Trump's huge and glittering jewel is too out there (and too large) to be missed—it was missed payments on this tasteless tallboy that cast the financier into his billion dollar tailspin. It will feel like *Monopoly* when you realize Trump owns three other hotel casinos in the city: **Trump Plaza** (441-6000) and **Trump World's Fair** (344-6000) on the Boardwalk, and **Trump Castle** (441-2000) at the Marina. **Caesar's Boardwalk Resort and Casino** (348-4411), at Arkansas Ave., pales in comparison to the Las Vegas palace. Come, see, and conquer at the only casino with 25¢ video blackjack, and play slots at the feet of a huge **Statue of David.** The **Sands** (441-4000), at Indiana Ave., stands big and ostentatious with its pink-and-green seashell motif

There's something for everyone in Atlantic City, thanks to the Boardwalk. Those under 21 (or those tired of the endless cycle of winning and losing) **gamble for prizes** at one of the many arcades that line the Boardwalk. It feels like real gambling, but the teddy bear in the window is easier to get than the grand prize at a resort. The **Steel Pier,** an extension in front of the Taj Mahal, has the usual amusement park standbys: roller coaster, ferris wheel, tilt-a-whirl, carousel, kiddie rides, and many a game of "skill." Rides cost $2-3 each. (Open daily noon-midnight; call the Taj Mahal for winter hrs.) When you tire of spending money, check out the **beach,** although **Ventnor City,** just west of Atlantic City, has quieter shores.

## CAPE MAY

Lying at the southern extreme of New Jersey's coastline, Cape May is the oldest seashore resort in the U.S., and the money here is no younger. Once the isolated retreat of wealthy New Yorkers, not much has changed. Overgrown with roses and wrapped in starry white lights, gorgeous Victorian mansions and pastel porches are architectural candy for the sweetest tooth. Glittery, white beaches— perfect for play or a nap under the rays—shun the commercialism of more modern beach towns. At night, candles flicker in the windows of 19th-century B&Bs by the shore, infusing an aura of Victorian romance into the passersby strolling the bricks.



**PRACTICAL INFORMATION.** Despite its geographic isolation, Cape May is quite accessible. By car from the north, it is literally at the end of the road. Follow the toll-laden Garden State Pkwy. south as far as it goes, watch for signs to Center City, and you'll end up on Lafayette St. Alternately, take the slower, scenic Ocean Dr. 40mi. south along the shore from Atlantic City. Rt. 55 brings beachgoers from Philadelphia. From the south, a 70min. **ferry** will transport you from Lewes, DE (302-426-1155) to Cape May (886-1725 or 800-643-3779 for recorded schedule info). (5-7 per day, 10-12 per day in summer. $20 per driver, $6 per additional passenger, ages 6-12 $3, motorcyclists $15, bicyclists $5.) **Shuttles** to the ferry leave from the **Cape May Transportation Center,** 609 Lafayette St., on the corner of Lafayette and Ocean St. ($2. Station open mid-May to mid-Oct. M-F 9am-8pm, Sa 9am-5pm; mid-Oct. to mid-May M-F 9am-5pm, Sa 11am-2pm.) **NJ Transit** (215-569-3752 or 800-582-5946) makes a local stop at the bus depot on the corner of Lafayette and Ocean St. Buses to Atlantic City (2hr., 18 per day, $3.45); Philadelphia (3hr., 18 per day, $13.60); and New York City (4½hr., 3 per day, $27). **Cape Area Transit (CAT)** buses (889-0925 or 800-966-3758) run on Pittsburgh Ave., Beach Dr., Lafayette St., and Ocean Ave. ($1 exact change. Runs late June to Sept. 6 daily, 10am-10pm; late May to late June and Sept. 6 to mid-Oct. F 4-10pm, Sa 10am-10pm, Su 10am-4pm.) **Cape May Seashore Lines** (884-2675) runs old-fashioned trains to further attractions along the 26mi. to Tuckahoe four times daily ($8, children $5). Bike the beach with the help of **Shields' Bike Rentals,** 11 Gurney St. (884-2453. Open 7am-7pm; 1-seaters $4 per hr., $9 per day, tandems $10 per hr., surreys $24 per hour.) **Faria's,** 311 Beach Ave. (898-0988), rents beach necessities (surfboard $14, umbrella or chair $6, bodyboards $9). **Welcome center:** 405 Lafayette St. (884-9562; open daily 8:30am-4:30pm). **Chamber of Commerce:** 513 Washington St. Mall (884-5508; open M-F 9am-5pm, Sa-Su 10am-6pm), and in the **historic kiosk** at the south end of the mall. **Post Office:** 700 Washington St. (884-3578; open M-F 9am-5pm, Sa 8:30am-12:30pm). **ZIP code:** 08204. **Area code:** 609.

**▐ ACCOMMODATIONS.** Sleeping does not come cheaply in Cape May. Luxurious hotels and Victorian B&Bs along the beach run $85-250 per night. Further from the shore, prices drop. Although the **Hotel Clinton,** 202 Perry St., lacks presidential suites or A/C, the family-owned establishment has 16 decent, breezy rooms with a shared bath. (884-3993. Singles $30-35; doubles $40-45. Reservations recommended. Open mid-June to Sept.) Next door, the **Parris Inn,** 204 Perry St., rents spacious but simple rooms, most with private baths, TV, and A/C. (884-8015. Singles $65-85; doubles $75-95; lower rates off-season. Open mid-Apr. to Dec.)

Campgrounds line U.S. 9 just north of Cape May. Less plush and more family-oriented than other area campgrounds, the **Lake Laurie Campground,** 669 Rt. 9, sits about 5mi. north of Cape May. (884-3567. Tents $16-23.50, full hookup $23-30.50. 3-day min. stay in peak season. Open Apr.-Sept.) Less luxurious but only 10 blocks from Cape May, **Depot Travel Park,** 800 Broadway, 2mi. north on Rt. 626 (Seashore Rd.) off Rt. 9, is convenient for beach seekers. (884-2533. Sites with water and electricity $21.75, full hookup $26. Open May-late Sept.)

**▐▌ FOOD AND NIGHTLIFE.** Cape May's cheapest food is pizza and burger fare along **Beach Ave.** You'll have to shell out a few more clams for a sit-down meal. Crawling with pedestrians shopping for fudge and saltwater taffy, the **Washington St. Mall** supports several popular food stores and eateries. The pub-like **Ugly Mug,** 426 Washington St. Mall, serves a good-lookin' cup o' chowder ($2) and the ever-popular "oceanburger" ($5.75). Summer nights mean cover-free fun. (884-3459. Free pizza M 10pm-2am; W hula hoop contests. Open M-Sa 11am-2am, Su noon-2am; food served until 11pm.) **Van Scoy's,** 312 Carpenter's Ln., brings sweet vegetarian relief bistro style, with creative sandwiches ($4.25-10) and protein packed entrees like Tofu Bankok ($15). Most entrees available in demi-portions and carry-out for $3-4 less. $2.75-3.75 fetches laudable desserts. (898-9898. Open daily 11:30am-4pm and 5-10pm.)

The rock scene collects around barnacle-encrusted **Carney's** on Beach Ave., with nightly entertainment in the summer (884-4424; open daily 11am-3am; in winter 11am-2am). For a more cosmopolitan night scene, listen to jazz and sip creative martinis ($5-7) at **Downstairs at Spiaggi,** across from the beach on Decatur St. (884-3504; open Apr.-Oct. Tu-Sa 8pm-2am).

**◪ HITTING THE BEACH.** The entire Jersey shore is blessed with fine beaches. Cape May's sands actually sparkle, dotted with the famous Cape May "diamonds" (quartz pebbles). You can unfurl your towel on a city-protected beach (off Beach Ave.), but make sure you have a **beach tag,** required for beachgoers over 11. Tags are available from the vendors roaming the shore or from the **Beach Tag Office,** located at Grant and Beach Dr. *(884-9522. Open daily 9:30am-5:30pm. Tags required June-Sept. daily 10am-5:30pm. Daily $4, 3-day $7, weekly $10, seasonal $16.)*

Off the beach, several of the Victorian homes hold daily viewings. The **Mid-Atlantic Center for the Arts** in the **1879 Emlen Physick House,** offers 45min. house tours. and sponsors a history-filled **Victorian Week** each Oct., as well as **Music** and **Tulip Festivals** in Apr. *(1048 Washington St. 884-5404. $7, ages 3-12 $3.50. Open Apr.-Dec. daily; Jan.-Mar. Sa-Su.)* Pick up *This Week in Cape May* in any public building or store for detailed listings. A spectacular view of the Delaware and New Jersey Shore is reward for the 199-step ascent to the beacon of the 1859 **Cape May Lighthouse** in **Cape May Point State Park,** west of town at the end of the point. *(884-5404. $4 with 1 free child, ages 3-12 $1. Park open 8am-dusk. Lighthouse open daily Apr.-Nov. 8am-dusk; Dec.-Mar. Sa-Su 8am-dusk.)* In the summer, several shuttles run the 5mi. from the bus depot on Lafayette St. to the lighthouse. *($5, ages 3-12 $4.)*

Even migratory birds flock to Cape May for a break from the long, southbound flight. Sneak a voyeuristic peak at these feathered vacationers from the **Cape May Bird Observatory,** on Cape May Point, a bird watcher's paradise. *(707 E. Lake Dr. 884-2736. Open Tu-Su 10am-5pm.)* Bird maps, field trips, and workshops are all available here. For those looking for a respite from the seashore, Cape May boasts several expensive golf and kid-geared mini-golf courses, as well as tennis courts.

# PENNSYLVANIA

In 1681, Englishman William Penn, Jr. established the colony of Pennsylvania ("Penn's woods") in order to protect his fellow Quakers from persecution. A bastion of religious tolerance, the state attracted settlers of all ethnicities and beliefs, and Pennsylvania promptly grew in population. Since then, Pennsylvania has rallied in the face of revolution time and again, from the birth of the Declaration of Independence in Philadelphia to the present. In 1976, Philadelphia groomed its historic shrines for the nation's bicentennial celebration, and they are now the centerpiece of the city's ambitious renewal program. Pittsburgh, a steel city once dirty enough to fool streetlights into burning during the day, has also initiated a cultural renaissance. Away from the cities, Pennsylvania's landscape retains much of the natural beauty that the area's first colonists discovered centuries ago, from the farms of Lancaster County to the deep river gorges of the Allegheny Plateau.

## 🛈 PRACTICAL INFORMATION

**Capital:** Harrisburg.

**Visitor Info: Pennsylvania Travel & Tourism,** 453 Forum Bldg., Harrisburg 17120 (800-847-4852; www.state.pa.us). **Bureau of State Parks,** Rachel Carson State Office Bldg., 400 Market St., Harrisburg 17108 (800-637-2757). Open M-F 8am-4:30pm.

**Postal Abbreviation:** PA. **Sales Tax:** 6%.

# PHILADELPHIA

With his band of Quakers, William Penn founded the City of Brotherly Love in 1682, after it had served as a colonial hub for 100 years. But it was Ben, not Penn, that made the town the urban metropolis it is today. Anything not founded by Benjamin Franklin seems to bear his name, and in summer, when the tourist season kicks into high gear, his cocked-hatted and ruffled faux-colonial imitators roam the city making 1770s chitchat. Before Philly lost U.S. capital status to Washington, D.C. in 1790, the First Continental Congress met here in 1774, at which Virginia delegate Thomas Jefferson penned the Declaration of Independence. Today, the city has thriving ethnic neighborhoods to balance the WASP-y Main Line bluebottles. A wide array of architecture and world-class museums draw aesthetes, while ragers pack the city's many clubs and bars. And there's always cheesesteak.

## ◼ ORIENTATION

Penn planned his city as a logical and easily accessible grid, though the large number of one-ways provide headache-inducing frustration. The north-south streets ascend numerically from the **Delaware River,** flowing from **Penn's Landing** and **Independence Hall** on the east side, to the **Schuylkill River** (SKOO-kill) on the west. The first street is **Front;** the others follow consecutively from 2 to 69. **Center City** runs from 8th St. to the Schuylkill River. From north to south, the primary streets are Race, Arch, JFK, Market, Chestnut, and South. The intersection of **Broad (14th) St.** and **Market** marks the focal point of Center City, marked by the ornate City Hall. The **Historic District** stretches from Front to 8th St. and from Vine to South St. About 1mi. west of Center City, the **University of Pennsylvania (UPENN)** sprawls on the far side of the Schuylkill River. **University City** includes the UPenn/Drexel area west of the Schuylkill River. This framework sounds simple, but Penn omitted the alleys in his system. Some are big enough for cars while others are not, but street addresses often refer to alleys not pictured on standard AAA-type maps of the city. The **SEPTA transportation map,** available free from the tourist office, is probably the most complete map of the city.

Due to the proliferation of one-way streets, horrendous traffic, and outrageous parking fees, **driving** is not a good way to get around town. Parking near the his-

Delaware River

Gazela of Philadelphia

Independence Seaport Museum

U.S.S. Olympia

TO AIRPORT

Benjamin Franklin Bridge

Penn's Landing

Delaware Ave.

95

Becuna

U.S.S. Becuna

Front St.

Spring Garden St.

M SPRING GARDEN

2nd St.

Elfreth's Alley

Betsy Ross House

Christ Church

Dock St.

Mattis St.

TO MUMMERS MUSEUM

OLD CITY

Indep. St.

Christ Church Burial Ground (Ben. Franklin's Grave)

Bank St.

SOCIETY HILL

HEAD HOUSE SQ.

3rd St.

4th St.

U.S. Mint

Franklin Court

Carpenter's Hall

5th St.

M 5TH ST.

200 yards

200 meters

6th St.

Independence

Free Quaker Meeting House

Balch Institute

0

0

7th St.

National

Liberty Bell Pavilion

Independence Hall and Congress Hall

Washington Square

Tomb of the Unknown Soldier

8th St.

Historical

JEWELERS ROW

Norman Rockwell Museum

Spruce St.

Pine St.

Lombard St.

South St.

9th St.

Afro-American Historical and Cultural Museum

Park

M 8TH AND MARKET ST.

Franklin St.

10th St.

Race St.

CHINATOWN

11th St.

Reading Terminal Market

M

Antique Row

B

12th St.

Convention Center

Race St.

Walnut St.

13th St.

Arch St.

Filbert St.

Juniper St.

M 13TH ST.

Academy of Music

M N. Broad St.

611

City Hall

AVENUE OF THE ARTS

S. Broad St.

M LOMBARD SOUTH

M

CITY HALL

15TH ST.

Penn Sq.

15th St.

Merriam Theatre

TO TEMPLE UNIVERSITY

Pennsylvania Academy of Fine Arts

M

Philadelphia Visitors Center

i

16th St.

M

CENTER CITY

17th St.

30

Market St.

18th St.

TO EASTERN STATE PENITENTIARY

Parkway

Free Library of Philadelphia

Logan Circle

Academy of Natural Sciences

19th St.

RITTENHOUSE SQUARE

Spruce St.

Pine St.

Lombard St.

South St.

Callowhill St.

Spring Garden St.

Hamilton St.

Benjamin Franklin

Rodin Museum

Franklin Institute /Science Museum

Please Touch Museum

Race St.

Cherry St.

Arch St.

John F. Kennedy Blvd.

20th St.

Chestnut St.

Sansom St.

Walnut St.

Locust St.

21st St.

Mütter Museum

22nd St.

Rosenbach Museum and Library

23rd St.

TO BOATHOUSE ROW

Philadelphia Museum of Art

Spring Garden St. Bridge

Fairmount Park

TO PHILADELPHIA ZOO

676

24th St.

Schuylkill

River

3

3

ArchSt.

Amtrak

30th St.

N

M 30TH ST.

Drexel University

TO UNIVERSITY OF PENNSYLVANIA

76

76

Downtown Philadelphia

ACCOMMODATIONS

A  Chamounix Hostel (HI)
B  Antique Row B & B
C  Old First Reformed Church
D  Bank St. Hostel (HI)

toric sights causes price heartattacks ($10 per day), but lower priced options scatter at a farther but walkable distance. Meterless 2hr. parking spaces can sometimes be found on the cobblestones of Dock St. Day-long deals require vehicles to be in by 10am and out by 6pm. A well-secured lot on the corner of Race and 8th adheres to this policy ($5 all day). At 10th between Race and Vine St., a larger lot discounts on weekends and evenings ($4 Sa-Su and after 3pm.) Park outside the city and ride Philly's system of **buses** and its **subway** to most major downtown destinations. Be cautious—public transportation can be unsafe after dark.

## 🛈 PRACTICAL INFORMATION

**Airport: Philadelphia International** (24hr. info line 937-6800), 8mi. southwest of Center City on I-76. The 20min. **SEPTA Airport Rail Line** runs from Center City to the airport. Trains leave 30th St., Suburban, and Market East Stations daily every 30min. 5:25am-11:25pm; $5 at window, $7 on train. Last train from airport 12:10am. **Airport Limelight Limousine** (782-8818) will deliver you to a hotel or a specific address downtown ($8 per person). Taxi downtown $25.

**Trains: Amtrak,** 30th St. Station (824-1600), at Market St., in University City. To: New York (2hr.; 30-40 per day; $37-41, express trains $71); Boston (7hr., 10 per day, $53-88); Washington, D.C. (2hr., 33 per day, $34-40); and Pittsburgh (8hr., 2 per day, $42-76). Office open M-F 5:10am-10:45pm, Sa-Su 6:10am-10:45pm. Station open 24hr.

**Buses: Greyhound,** 1001 Filbert St. (931-4075), at 10th and Filbert in downtown Philadelphia 1 block north of Market near the 10th and Market St. subway/commuter rail stop. A populated, safe area. To: New York (2½hr., 32 per day, $19); Boston (8½hr., 19 per day, $47); Baltimore (2hr., 10 per day, $16); Washington, D.C. (3hr., 10 per day, $18); Pittsburgh (7hr., 8 per day, $41); and Atlantic City (2hr., 12 per day, $12). Station open daily 24hr. **New Jersey Transit** (569-3752), in the same station. To: Atlantic City (1hr., $10); Ocean City (2hr., $11); and other points on the New Jersey shore. Operates daily with buses to Atlantic City nearly every 30min.

**Public Transit: Southeastern Pennsylvania Transportation Authority (SEPTA),** 1234 Market St. (580-7800; www.septa.org). Extensive bus and rail service to the suburbs. Buses serve the 5-county area; most operate 5am-2am, some 24hr. 2 major subway routes: the blue east-west **Market St. line** (including 30th St. Station and the historic area) and the orange north-south **Broad St. line** (including the stadium complex in south Philadelphia). *The subway is unsafe after dark;* buses are usually okay. Subway connects with commuter rails—the **R5** main line local runs through the western suburb of Paoli ($3.75-4.25). The SEPTA **R7** runs north to Trenton, NJ ($5). Pick up a free SEPTA system map, Philly's best street map, at any subway stop. Fare $1.60, 2 tokens $2.30, transfers 40¢. Unlimited all-day pass for both $5. In the tourist area, purple **Phlash** buses come by every 10min. and visit all major sights. Fare $1.50, $3 all day.

**Taxis: Yellow Cab,** 922-8400. **Liberty Cab,** 389-2000.

**Car Rental: Courtesy Rent-a-Car,** 7704 Westchester Pike (610-446-6200). $19 per day with unlimited mi. Must be 21 with major credit card. **Budget** (492-9400), at 21st and Market St., downtown or in the 30th St. Station. Easy to find, but more expensive. $38 per day (Sa-Su $43) with unlimited mi. Drivers must be 25.

**Bike Rental: Frankenstein Bike Work,** 1529 Spruce St. (893-IGOR). Cruisers $12 for 4hr., $15 per day. Open Tu-Sa 10am-6pm, Su noon-4pm. Call ahead for M service.

**Visitor Info:** 1525 John F. Kennedy Blvd. (636-1666), the circular building by the fountain at 16th St. Free city guide with great map. Open daily 9am-6pm, winter 9am-5pm. The **National Park Service Visitors Center** (597-8974, 627-1776 for a recording), at 3rd and Chestnut St., has info on **Independence Park,** including maps, schedules, a film, and a branch of the tourist office. Open daily 9am-6pm, winter 9am-5pm.

**Hotlines: Suicide and Crisis Intervention,** 686-4420. **Youth Crisis Line,** 787-0633. Both 24hr. **Women Against Abuse,** 386-7777. 24hr. **Gay and Lesbian Counseling Services,** 732-8255. Operates M-F 6-9pm, Su 5-8pm. **William Way Lesbian, Gay, and Bisexual Community Center** (732-2220). Info about gay events and activities. Open M-F noon-10pm, Sa 10am-5pm, Su 10:30am-8:30pm.

**Post Office:** 2970 Market St. (895-8000), at 30th St. across from the Amtrak station. Open 24hr. **ZIP code:** 19104. **Area code:** 215.

# ACCOMMODATIONS

Inexpensive lodging in Philadelphia is hard to find, but if you make arrangements a few days in advance, comfortable rooms close to Center City can be had for around $60. The motels near the airport at exit 9A on I-95 are the least expensive in the area. **Bed and Breakfast Center City,** 1804 Pine St. (735-1137 or 800-354-8401), will rent you a room ($65-110) or find you one in a private home. **Antique Row Bed and Breakfast** (see below) will also recommend rooms. **Bed & Breakfast Connections/Bed & Breakfast of Philadelphia,** in Devon, PA, books in Philadelphia and southeastern Pennsylvania but requires 20% payment. (610-687-3565. Singles $50-85; doubles $60-250. Reserve at least a week in advance. Call 9am-7pm.) The closest camping is across the Delaware River in New Jersey at **Timberline Campground,** 117 Timber Ln., 15mi. from Center City. Take U.S. 295 S to exit 18B (Clarksboro), follow straight through the traffic light ½mi. and turn right on Friendship Rd. Timber Ln. is 1 block on the right. (609-423-6677. Sites $18, full hookup $23.)

**Chamounix Mansion International Youth Hostel (HI-AYH)** (878-3676 or 800-379-0017), in West Fairmount Park. Take bus #38 from lower Market St. to Ford and Cranston Rd., follow Ford Rd. to Chamounix Dr., turn left, and follow road to hostel. An enthusiastic staff maintains deluxe hosteling in a converted mansion. Beautifully furnished rooms, showers, kitchen, laundry, chess table, TV/VCR, piano, bikes, and harp. Free parking and discounted bus tokens. 80 beds. $11, nonmembers $14. Linen $2. Check-in 8-11am and 4:30pm-midnight. Lockout 11am-4:30pm. Curfew midnight.

**Bank Street Hostel (HI-AYH),** 32 S. Bank St. (922-0222 or 800-392-4678). From the bus station, walk down Market St.; it's between 2nd and 3rd St. Subway: 2nd St. An impersonal hostel in a great location in the historic district. A/C, big TV and VCR in lobby, free coffee and tea, laundry facilities, kitchen, pool table, Internet access ($5 per 30min.). Super-convenient to South St. 70 beds. $16, nonmembers $19. Linen $2. Lockout 10am-4:30pm, but they'll hold baggage. Curfew Su-Th 12:30am, F-Sa 1am.

**Antique Row Bed and Breakfast,** 341 S. 12th St. (592-7802). Complete breakfast in rooms full of delicate pleasures. Kindly owner ready to reveal the area's best treasures. Free local calls. $60-100, depending on size of suite; reduced rate for longer stays.

**Old First Reformed Church** (922-4566), at 4th and Race St. in Center City, 1 block from Independence Mall and 4 blocks from Penn's Landing. A historic church that converts its social hall into a 30-person youth hostel. Foam pads on the floor, showers, A/C, and laundry. $15. Breakfast included. Ages 18-26 only. 3-night max. stay. Check-in 5-10pm. Curfew midnight. Open July to early Sept; May closed for renovations.

**Motel 6,** 43 Industrial Hwy. (610-521-6650 or 800-466-8356), in Essington, exit 9A off I-95. Large, standard rooms with A/C and cable. Singles $50-60; doubles $56-65.

# FOOD

Street vendors are at the forefront of Philly specialties, hawking **cheesesteaks, hoagies, soft pretzels,** and **fruit salad.** Ethnic eateries gather in several specific areas: hip **South St.,** between Front and 7th; **18th St.** around Sansom; and **2nd St.,** between Chestnut and Market. **Chinatown,** bounded by 11th, 8th, Arch, and Vine St., offers well-priced vegetarian restaurants. The quintessential Philly cheesesteak rivalry squares off at 9th and Passyunk Ave., in South Philadelphia; **Pat's King of Steaks** (468-1546), the legendary founder of the cheesesteak, faces off against larger, more neon **Geno's Steaks.** Both offer basic cheesesteak for $5 and stay open 24hr.

Fresh fruit and other foodstuffs pack the immense **Italian Market,** on 9th St. below Christian St. The **Reading Terminal Market,** 12th and Arch St. stocks globally diverse food under one roof—fabulous for lunch. Since 1893, food stands have clustered in the indoor market selling fresh produce and meats. Check the pamphlet available at vendors for events. (922-2317. Open M-Sa 8am-6pm.)

MID-ATLANTIC

## HISTORIC DISTRICT

**Famous 4th St. Delicatessen** (922-3274), 4th and Bainbridge St. A Philadelphia landmark since 1923, Jewish deli favorites like corned beef sandwiches ($6.75) and award-winning chocolate chip cookies ($1). This family-operated "living museum" recalls Brooklyn of yester-year, offering knishes ($1.50), lox ($8), and fried matzos ($6). Free cookie with lunch if you mention *Let's Go*. Open M-Sa 7am-6pm, Su 7am-4pm.

**Jim's Steaks,** 400 South St. (928-1911). A time warp back to 1950s Philadelphia. Framed with autographed photos of celebrity diners, including John Denver, perched on a stool in this roomy diner to eat an authentic Philly hoagie ($3.50-5). Open M-Th 10am-1am, F-Sa 10am-3am, Su noon-10pm.

## CHINATOWN

🖾 **Singapore,** 1029 Race St. (922-3288). A popular hangout dishing out delicious vegetarian, kosher Chinese food for amazingly low prices. In his spare time, the chef teaches his techniques to heart disease patients; options like double gluten with green ($9) are both yummy and healthy. Open daily 11:30am-10pm.

🖾 **Rangoon,** 112 9th St. (829-8939). Spicy scents of Burmese cuisine float through the pretty-pink interior. The proprietor nourishes a love of good food, low prices, and spice. Entrees $4-10, most around $8; try the fried pork balls ($6). Open daily 11am-10pm.

**Harmony,** 135 N. 9th St. (627-4520). The chef escaped China by swimming and now caters to Philadelphia's vegetarians. For a visual and culinary masterpiece, try "Lovely Couple in Phoenix Nest," ($11), imitation chicken in a taro root basket. Most entrees $7-12. Open Su-Th 11:30am-10:30pm, F-Sa 11:30am-midnight.

## CENTER CITY

🖾 **Jamaican Jerk Hut,** 1436 South St. (545-8644). Tropical paradise finds a home in an urban area. Mellow out on the backyard veranda with conch fritters ($5.50) and Caribbean jams. F-Sa 5pm. Entrees $7-15, daily specials less. Natural juices ($2.50-3) bottled on the premises. Open M-Th 11am-10pm, F-Sa 11am-11pm, Su 5-10pm.

**Taco House,** 1218 Pine St. (735-1880). Loads of good, cheap Mexican food in a coffeehouse ambiance. A meat or a cheese enchilada, beans, rice, and chili go for $4; more hefty dinner combinations $8. Open Su-Th 11am-10pm, F-Sa 11am-11pm.

**Samson St. Oyster House,** 1516 Samson St. (567-7683). Raw bar packs in professionals at lunch into sea-inspired wooden dining room. Oysters top the menu ($7.25 for ½dozen) but broiled bluefish ($7.50) and the popcorn shrimp po' boy ($6.25) also make great catches. Open daily 11am-11pm.

**Alaska,** 123 S. 18th St. (563-4424). Cafe-style relaxation with creamy creations. Specializes in homemade ice cream (regular $2.80), but big, flavorful vegetarian inspired lunches like tofu meatballs ($3.75) sell out quickly. Open M-Th 11am-9pm, F 11am-11pm, Sa 1-11pm, Su 1-9pm.

## UNIVERSITY CITY

🖾 **Tandoor India Restaurant,** 106 S. 40th St. (222-7122). Northern Indian cuisine with bread fresh from the clay oven (ask to see it). Lunch buffet $6, dinner buffet $9, entrees ($7-11). 20% student discount with valid ID. Open for lunch M-F 11:30am-3pm, Sa-Su 11:30am-3:30pm; for dinner Su-Th 4-10:30pm, F-Sa 4-11pm.

**Smokey Joe's,** 210 S. 40th St. (222-0770), between Locust and Walnut St. This family-run restaurant and bar has been a student hangout for over 50 years. All-you-can-eat pasta, broiled salmon, or BBQ baby ribs ($8). Local groups occasionally perform Su-Tu 10pm-close. Open daily 11am-2am; July-Aug. closed Su. No lunch in summer Sa-Su.

**Abner's Cheesesteaks,** 3813 Chestnut St. (662-0100), at 38th and Chestnut St. Local fast food attracts businesspeople for lunch and college students late at night. Cheesesteak, large soda, and fries for $6. Open Su-Th 11am-midnight, F-Sa 11am-3am.

## ON THE STREETS OF PHILADELPHIA

**INDEPENDENCE MALL.** The **Independence National Historical Park,** bounded by Market, Walnut, 2nd, and 6th St., fills a small green mall near the Delaware River with a hub of historical buildings. *(597-8974. Open daily June-Aug. 9am-6pm; Sept.-May 9am-5pm. Free.)* The **visitors center,** at 3rd and Chestnut, has stuff to help with orientation (see p. 258). Tourists and history fill **Independence Hall,** between 5th and 6th St. on Chestnut St. After Jefferson elegantly transposed the Declaration of Independence, the delegates signed the treaty here in 1776 and reconvened in 1787 to autograph the U.S. Constitution. *(Open daily 9am-8pm; arrive early in summer to avoid a long line. Free guided tours daily every 15-20min.)* The U.S. Congress first assembled in nearby **Congress Hall,** at Chestnut and 6th. *(Self-guided tour with rangers available to answer questions.)* Its predecessor, the First Continental Congress, united against the British in **Carpenters' Hall,** in the middle of the block bounded by 3rd, 4th, Walnut, and Chestnut St., now a mini-museum to the Carpenters' Society. *(Open Tu-Su 10am-4pm.)* North of Independence Hall, at the **Liberty Bell Pavilion,** freedom may ring but the **Liberty Bell** does not (it broke). *(Open 9am-8pm. Free.)*

The private **First Bank of the U.S.,** on Chestnut across from the visitors center, pales in architectural comparison to the **Second Bank of the U.S.,** at Chestnut and 4th St. A stunning example of Greek Revival architecture, the Bank riches aren't in gold but in portraits; its gallery is hung with paintings of Washington, Jefferson, and Franklin, among other revolutionary bigwigs. *(Open daily 10am-6pm. $2.)*

The rest of the park preserves residential and commercial buildings of the Revolutionary era. On the Northern edge of the Mall, the remains of Ben Franklin's home presides over **Franklin Court,** between 3rd and 4th St. Mustering the same quirkiness and joviality that defined Franklin's character, the home contains an underground museum, a 20min. movie, a replica of his printing office, and phones with long-dead political luminaries on the line. *(318 Market St. Open daily 10am-6pm. Free.)* On a more somber note, an eternal flame commemorates the fallen heroes of the Revolutionary War at the **Tomb of the Unknown Soldier** at Washington Sq.

Adjacent to the house where Jefferson drafted the Declaration of Independence, the **Balch Institute for Ethnic Studies** explores America's socio-history, like the plight of Japanese Americans in World War II. *(18 S. 7th St. 925-8090. Open M-Sa 10am-4pm. $3; students, seniors, and under 12 $1.50; Sa 10am-noon free.)* Across the street, the **Atwater-Kent Museum** traces Philadelphia's History. Lose yourself in the nostalgia of **Norman Rockwell's** *Saturday Evening Post* artwork—on display through 2000. *(15 S. 17th. 922-3031. Open M-Th 10am-5pm, F 10am-3pm, Su noon-5pm.)*

**OLD CITY CULTURAL DISTRICT.** Religion and money, both human sources of joy, convene in the area above Market St. by the Delaware River. Philadelphia's branch of the **U.S. Mint,** at 5th and Arch St., offers a free, self-guided tour to explain the mechanized coin-making procedure. *(408-0230. Open July-Aug. daily 9am-4pm; Sept.-Apr. M-F 9am-4:30pm; May-June M-Sa 9am-4:30pm.)*

A penniless Ben Franklin arrived in Philadelphia in 1723, and walked by the colorful rowhouses that line the narrow **Elfreth's Alley,** near 2nd and Arch St., allegedly "the oldest continuously inhabited street in America." A museum gives a peak inside and some alley history. *(126 Elfreth's Alley. Open Tu-Sa 10am-4pm, Su noon-4pm. Jan.-Feb. Sa 10am-4pm, Su noon-4pm.)* Child-oriented placards explain how Betsy Ross alledgedly sewed the first flag of the newly formed 13 states at the tiny **Betsy Ross House,** near 3rd St. *(239 Arch St. 627-5343. Open Tu-Su 10am-5pm; $2, children $1.)*

Across from the Mint, the private **Free Quaker Meeting House,** at 5th and Arch St., dates from 1683. For the complete Quaker experience, the **Arch Street Meeting House,** at 4th and Arch St., welcomes friends of Friends to view an exhibit, a short video, and talk about the religion that inspired the city. *(627-2667. Open M-Sa 10am-4pm.)* Pomp exudes from **Christ Church,** near 2nd and Market, where well-to-do Episcopalians gave thanks for their good fortune. *(20 N. American St. 922-1695. Open M-Sa 9am-5pm, Su 1-5pm. Suggested donation $2.)* Ben Franklin lies buried in the nearby **Christ Church Cemetery,** at 5th and Arch St., across from the Mint.

MID-ATLANTIC

On a quirkier foot, the Temple University School of Podiatric Medicine contains the **Shoe Museum,** on the corner of 8th and Race St. This 6th fl. collection contains footwear from the famous feet of Reggie Jackson, Lady Bird Johnson, Dr. J, Nancy Reagan, and others. *(625-5243. Tours W and F 9am-noon; call for appt.)* On the northern edge of the district, the powder-blue "marvel near the mint," **Benjamin Franklin Bridge,** off Race and 5th St., provides a great view of the city for un-vertigoed folks.

**SOCIETY HILL AND THE WATERFRONT. Society Hill** proper begins where Independence Mall ends, on Walnut St. between Front and 7th St. 200 year-old Townhouses preside like old money over cobblestone walks illuminated by electric "gaslights." **Head House Sq.,** at 2nd and Pine St., claims to be America's oldest firehouse and marketplace, and now houses restaurants, boutiques, and craft shops. An outdoor **flea market** moves in on summer weekends. *(790-0782. Open June-Aug. Sa noon-11pm, Su noon-6pm.)*

South of Head House Sq., the **Mummer's Museum** at Washington Ave. swells with the glitz and glamour of old costumes. Each Jan., construction workers, policemen, and other participants adorn themselves with sequins and feathers for a rowdy New Year's Day parade, and the museum houses the memories of parades past. *(1100 S. 2nd St. 336-3050. Free string band concerts Tu evenings. Open Tu-Sa 9:30am-5pm, Su noon-5pm; closed Su July-Aug. $2.50, seniors and children $2.)*

Located on the Delaware River, **Penn's Landing** is the largest freshwater port in the world. The *U.S.S. Olympia*, Commodore Dewey's flagship during the Spanish-American War, and the *U.S.S. Becuna*, a WWII submarine, bob at the dock. *(923-8181. Tours daily 10am-5pm.)* Philadelphian shipbuilding, cargo, and immigration unfold at the **Independence Seaport Museum** *(925-5439. Museum $5, seniors $4, children $2.50; museum and ships $7.50/$6/$3.50.)* The landing hosts free **waterfront concerts** Apr. to Oct. *(629-3257. Big bands Th nights, children's theater Su.)*

**CENTER CITY.** As the financial and commercial hub of Philly, suited professionals cram into **Center City**, the area bounded by 12th, 23rd, Vine, and Pine St., during the day only to leave it rather desolate at night. Looming over all, the ornate wedding cake of thick granite and marble, **City Hall,** at Broad and Market St., is the nation's largest working municipal building. Until 1908, it reigned as the tallest building in the U.S., aided by the 37-ft. statue of William Penn on top. A municipal statute prohibited building higher than the top of Penn's hat until Reagan-era entrepreneurs overturned the law in the mid-80s, finally launching Philadelphia into the skyscraper era. A commanding view of the city awaits in the building's tower. *(686-2840. Open M-F 10am-4pm; last elevator 4pm. Suggested donation $1. Tour daily 12:30pm.)* The country's first art museum and school, the **Pennsylvania Academy of Fine Art,** at Broad and Cherry St., includes works by Winslow Homer and Mary Cassatt, among other enthralling American artistic wonders. *(972-2060. Open M-Tu and Th-Sa 10am-5pm, W 10am-8pm, Su 11am-5pm. Tours daily 12:30 and 2pm. $5, students with ID and seniors $4, ages 5-11 $3; additional charge for special exhibits.)* Across from City Hall, heavy wooden doors vault collections of books and other artifacts dating back to 1873 that can be seen on a 45min. tour of the mysterious **Masonic Temple.** *(1 N. Broad St. 988-1917. Tours M-F hourly 10am-3pm except noon, Sept.-June Sa 10 and 11am. Free.)*

**RITTENHOUSE SQUARE.** Brick laden and shady, the **Rittenhouse Sq. District,** a subset of Center City bounded by Broad, Market, South, and the Schuylkill River, cradles the musical and dramatic center of the city. Near the river in the **College of Physicians of Philadelphia,** the **Mütter Museum** houses bizarre medical oddities, including an 8-ft. colon. A wall of skulls and preserved birth abnormalities may be contrary to some religious beliefs or stomachs. *(19 S. 22nd St. 563-3737. Open Tu-Sa 10am-4pm. $8; students with ID, seniors, and ages 6-18 $4.)* Just south of the square, the **Rosenbach Museum and Library** permanently displays the original manuscript of James Joyce's *Ulysses*, and the collected illustrations of Maurice Sendak, among rotating exhibits. *(2010 Delancey St. 732-1600. Open Sept.-July Tu-Su 11am-4pm. Guided tours $5; students, seniors, and children $3. Last tour 2:45pm.)*

**PARKWAY/MUSEUM DISTRICT.** Nicknamed "America's Champs-Elysées," the **Benjamin Franklin Pkwy.** cuts a wide swath through William Penn's original grid of city streets. Built in the 1920s, this tree- and flag-lined boulevard connects Center City with Fairmount Park and the Schuylkill River, bordered by stony elegance.

The **Franklin Institute,** at 20th and Ben Franklin Pkwy., is even more interactive than most science museums; the fantastic **Science Center** inside focuses equal attention on all branches of general science with four floors of gadgets and games depicting the intricacies of space, time, motion, and the human body, including a walk-in heart. The **Mandell Center** houses a timely set of exhibits on the changing global environment, one of Franklin's favorite subjects. *(448-1200. Mandell Center open M-Th 9:30am-5pm, F-Sa 9:30am-9pm. Science Center open daily 9:30am-5pm. Admission to both $9.75, over 62 and ages 4-11 $8.50; Mandell Center only after 5pm $7.50, ages 4-11 $6.50.)* The **Omniverse Theater** provides 180° and 4½ stories of optical oohs and aahs. *(448-1111. Shows on the hr. Su-Th 10am-4pm, F-Sa 10am-9pm except for 6pm. $7.50. Advance tickets recommended.)* **Fels Planetarium** boasts an advanced computer-driven system that projects a simulation of life billions of years beyond ours. Lively laser shows rocks out on Friday and Saturday nights. *(448-1388. Shows M-F 12:15 and 2:15pm, Sa 10:15am, 12:15, and 2:15pm. $6, seniors and children $5. Exhibits and a show $12.75/$10.50. Exhibits and both shows $14.75/$12.50.)* Opposite Fels, at the **Academy of Natural Sciences,** at 19th and Ben Franklin Pkwy., live animals and a 100-million-year-old dinosaur skeleton are set in still-life. *(299-1000. Open M-F 10am-4:30pm, Sa-Su and holidays 10am-5pm. $8.50, seniors $7.75, ages 3-12 $7. Wheelchair access.)*

If time were money, a penny spent in the **Philadelphia Museum of Art,** at the end of the parkway at 26th along the river, would be a penny earned. A world-class collection includes Picasso's *Three Musicians* and Toulouse-Lautrec's *At the Moulin Rouge*, as well as extensive Asian, Egyptian, and decorative art collections. Lighten up on W evenings with free films, talks, music, and food. *(685-8100. Open Tu and Th-Su 10am-5pm, W 10am-8:45pm. $8; students, seniors, and ages 5-18 $5; free Su before 1pm. Tours daily 10am-3pm.)* A casting of the Gates of Hell outside the **Rodin Museum,** 22nd St., guards the portal of human passion, anguish, and anger in the most impressive collection of the artist's works this side of the Seine. *(563-1948. Open Tu-Su 10am-5pm. $3 donation.)*

Pay to get into prison, not out of it, at the castle-like **Eastern State Penitentiary,** on Fairmount Ave. at 22nd St. Once a ground-breaking institution in the field of criminal rehabilitation, guided and self-guided tours twist through the moldering dimness Al Capone once called home. *(236-3300. Open May to early Nov. Th-Su 10am-5pm. $7, students and seniors $5, children $3, under 5 not permitted. Tours hourly.)* **The Free Library of Philadelphia,** 20th and Vine St., scores with a library of orchestral music and one of the nation's largest rare book collections. *(686-5322. Open M-W 9am-9pm, Th-F 9am-6pm, Sa 9am-5pm; Oct.-May also Su 1-5pm. Tours by appointment.)*

**FAIRMOUNT PARK.** Larger than any other city park and covered with bike trails and picnic areas, **Fairmount Park** sprawls behind the Philadelphia Museum of Art on both sides of the Schuylkill River. The Grecian ruins by the waterfall immediately behind the museum are the abandoned **Waterworks.** Free tours featuring Waterworks architecture, technology, and social history meet on Aquarium Dr. behind the Art Museum. *(685-4935. Open Sa-Su 1-3:30pm.)* The grand old houses further down the river, spectacularly lit at night, are the historic crew clubs of **Boathouse Row.** *(Admission to most mansions $2.50.)* The Museum of Art hosts $3 guided tours of Boathouse Row on W and Sun, and trolley tours to some of the mansions in Fairmount Park. The area is one of Philly's prime **rollerblading** spots. Rental blades are available from **Wilburger's** kiosk, on Kelly Dr. south of Boathouse Row. *(765-7470. $5 per hr., $25 per day. Open May to Sept. 6 W-F 4-8pm, Sa-Su 9am-6pm.)* In the northern arm of Fairmount Park, trails follow the secluded Wissahickon Creek for 5mi., as the concrete city fades to a distant memory. The **Japanese House and Garden,** off Montgomery Dr. near Belmont Ave. is designed in the style of a 17th-century *shoin;* the authentic garden soothes with calmness. *(878-5097. Open May to early Sept. Tu-Su 10am-4pm; mid-Sept. to Oct. Sa-Su 10am-4pm. $2.50, seniors and students $2.)* *Some neighborhoods surrounding the park are not safe. The park is not safe at night.*

**UNIVERSITY CITY.** The **University of Pennsylvania (UPenn)** and **Drexel University,** located across the Schuylkill from Center City, reside in west Philly within easy walking distance of the 30th St. station. The Penn campus haven of green lawns and red brick quadrangles contrasts sharply with the deteriorating community surrounding it. Ritzy shops and cafes spice up 36th St. A statue of Benjamin Franklin, who founded the university in 1740, greets visitors at the entrance to the Penn campus on 34th and Walnut St. *Much of the area surrounding University City is unsafe at night—try not to travel alone.*

The **University Museum of Archeology and Anthropology,** at 33rd and Spruce St., journeys through three floors of the world's major cultures, including an outstanding East Asian art collection sheltered by a beautiful stone-and-glass rotunda. *(898-4001. Open June-Aug. Tu-Sa 10am-4:30pm; Sept.-May Tu-Sa 10am-4:30pm, Su 1-5pm. Suggested donation $5, students and over 62 $2.50.)* In 1965, Andy Warhol had his first one-man show at the **Institute of Contemporary Art,** at 36th and Sansom St., and the gallery has stayed on the cutting edge to this day with changing exhibitions in all media. *(898-7108. Open during academic terms W-F noon-8pm, Sa-Su 11am-5pm. $3; students, artists, and seniors $2; Su 11am-1pm free.)* North of the University area, the **Philadelphia Zoo,** 34th and Girard St., the oldest zoo in the country, houses more than 1700 animals, wild exhibits and kid-friendly programs. *(243-1100. Open M-F 9:30am-4:45pm, Sa-Su 9:30am-5:45pm. $8.50, seniors and ages 2-11 $6. Parking $5.)*

**FARTHER OUT.** Several world-class institutions exist in close proximity to Philadelphia. In the suburb of Merion, across City Ave. from West Fairmont Park, the controversial **Barnes Foundation** keeps 180 Renoirs, 69 Cezannes and 60 Matisses among its privately held masterpiece collection. *(300 N. Latch's Ln. 610-667-0290. Reservations recommended due to limited entrance. F-Su 9:30am-5pm.)* Just across the Ben Franklin Bridge in Camden, NJ, the **NJ State Aquarium,** on the Delaware River between Federal St. and Mickle Blvd., tanks fish from habitats as unusual as the Arctic. *Use caution in this area. (800-616-5297. Open daily 9:30am-5:30pm. $12, seniors $9.45, ages 3-11 $9.)* Thirty minutes west of Philly, off U.S. 1 in Kennet Sq., sprawls the 40 indoor and outdoor gardens of horticultural marvel **Longwood Gardens,** near the mushroom capital of the world. *(610-388-1000. Open daily 9am-5pm; Apr.-Oct. 9am-6pm. $12, Tu $8, ages 16-20 $6, ages 5-15 $2.)*

## ♫ ENTERTAINMENT

The **Academy of Music,** Broad and Locust St., modeled after Milan's La Scala, houses the **Philadelphia Orchestra.** Under Wolfgang Sawallisch's excellent direction, the orchestra performs Sept.-May. (893-1930. $15-90. $5 general admission tickets go on sale at the Locust St. entrance 45 min. before F-Sa concerts. Tu and Th student rush tickets 30min. before show $8.) The theater is also home to the **Pennsylvania Ballet,** tippy-toeing six runs yearly (551-7000; tickets $23-85).

The **Mann Music Center,** on George's Hill near 52nd and Parkside Ave. in Fairmount Park, hosts the Philadelphia Orchestra, jazz, and rock concerts with 5000 seats under cover and 10,000 on outdoor benches and lawns. Tickets are also available from the Academy of Music box office on Broad and Locust St. From June through Aug., free lawn tickets for the orchestra are available from the visitors center at 16th and JFK Blvd. on the day of a performance. (567-0707. Real seats $10-32.) The **Robin Hood Dell East,** Strawberry Mansion Dr. in Fairmount Park, brings in top names in pop, jazz, gospel, and ethnic dance in July and Aug. The Philadelphia Orchestra holds several free performances here in summer, and as many as 30,000 people gather on the lawn (685-9560).

During the school year, the students of the world-renowned **Curtis Institute of Music,** 1726 Locust St., give free concerts (M, W, F at 8pm; mid-Oct. to Apr.). **Merriam Theater,** 250 S. Broad St., Center City, stages performances ranging from student works to Broadway hits (732-5446; box office open M-Sa 10am-5:30pm). The **Old City,** from Chestnut to Vine and Front to 4th St., comes alive the first F of every month (Oct.-June) for the **First Friday** celebration. The streets fill with live music, and many art galleries open their doors, enticing visitors with free food.

Philly gets physical with tons of sports venues. Philly's four professional teams play a short ride away on the Broad St. subway line. Baseball's **Phillies** (463-1000) and football's **Eagles** (463-5500) hold games at **Veterans Stadium,** Broad St. and Pattison Ave.; the **Spectrum,** across the street, houses the NBA's **76ers** (339-7676) and the NHL's **Flyers** (755-9700). General admission tickets for baseball and hockey run $5-20; football and basketball tickets go for $15-50. The city also hosts pro tennis tournaments, the Core State Cycling Championship, and a Senior PGA tourney.

## ♫ NIGHTLIFE

Check Friday's weekend magazine section in the *Philadelphia Inquirer* for entertainment listings. *City Paper*, distributed Th, and the *Philadelphia Weekly*, distributed on W, have weekly listings of city events (free at newsstands and markets). Gay and lesbian weeklies *Au Courant* (free) and *PGN* (75¢) list events taking place throughout the Delaware Valley region. Along **South St.** toward the river, clubbers dance and live music plays on weekends. Many pubs line **2nd St.** near Chestnut St., close to the Bank St. hostel. **Delaware Ave. (a.k.a. Columbus Blvd.),** running along Penn's Landing, has recently become a local hotspot, full of nightclubs and restaurants attracting droves of young urban professionals and the college crowd. Most bars and clubs that cater to a gay clientele congregate along **Camac St., S. 12th St.,** and **S. 13th St.**

**Kat Man Du,** Pier 25 (629-1724), at N. Columbus Blvd. Tropical gardens, nightly live music, and open-air decks make this *the* summer hangout. Happy hour M-F 5-7pm, $2 calls and domestic beers. 50¢ drafts Tu and Th 10pm-midnight. Cover M-Th after 8:30pm $5; F-Sa $8; Su $2, after 5pm $5. Open daily noon-2am.

**The Khyber,** 56 S. 2nd St. (238-5888). Eclectic assortment of 20-somethings enjoy big-name alternative, country, and grunge bands nightly in this small club (max. 225 people). The ornate wooden bar was shipped over from England and belly pleasing vegetarian sandwiches are $3. Cover $5-15. Open daily 11am-2am.

**The Trocadero** (923-7625), 10th and Arch St. On a gritty, roach-infested street in Chinatown, this old theater hosts nationally known bands, usually attracting a college-age crowd. Upstairs, the Balcony bar may be open jointly or separately. Cover $6-16. Advance tickets through Ticketmaster. Doors usually open around 5pm.

**Gotham,** 1 Brown St. (928-9319), at Columbus Blvd. Hard-core hip-hop dancing. Philly's 2 largest dance floors and an outdoor deck pack revellers from the surrounding colleges and communities. Open F-Su 9pm-2am.

**Warmdaddy's** (627-8400), on Front St. on the corner of Market St. This Cajun club loves its hot sauce and focuses on playin' the blues to a diverse audience. Sets start at 8pm in summer, 8:30pm in winter. Tu free jam night. Cover W-Th and Su $5, F-Sa $10. Open Tu-Sa 5pm-2am, Su noon-2am.

**Woody's,** 202 S. 13th St. (545-1893). An attractive, young gay crowd frequents this lively, friendly, aptly named club. Happy hour 5-7pm daily with 25¢ off all drinks. Dance to country tunes Tu, F, and Su, or grind to house music Th and Sa. W is all-ages night. Lunch daily noon-3:30pm. Bar open M-Sa 11am-2am, Su noon-2am.

## NEAR PHILADELPHIA: VALLEY FORGE

It was the winter of 1777-1778, not the British, that almost crushed the Continental Army. When George Washington selected Valley Forge as the winter camp for his 12,000 troops following defeat at Germantown in Oct., the General could not have predicted the three months of starvation, bitter cold, and disease that would nearly halve his forces. At times without blankets or even shoes, only crude meals of flour-and-water "firecake," women who volunteered nursing services, and hope sustained the men's spirits. Not until Baron Friedrich von Steuben and fresh troops and supplies arrived did recovery and spring seem possible. Renewed by France's word of alliance, the Continental Army left Valley Forge on June 19, 1778 to win the Battle of Monmouth and help forge a nation.

The hills that once tried the frost-bitten soldiers roll through **Valley Forge National Historic Park.** A 10mi. self-guided auto tour begins at the **visitors center,** which also features a small museum and 18min. film. The tour passes **Washington's headquarters,** reconstructed soldier huts and fortifications, and the Grand Parade Ground where the Continental Army drilled. Visitors can also hop aboard a **bus tour.** The park has three picnic areas but no camping; the visitors center distributes a list of nearby campgrounds. Joggers and nature take advantage of a paved 6mi. trail which winds through the park, snatching views of the deer. *(610-783-1077. Park open daily sunrise-sunset. Grounds free. Center open daily 9am-5pm. Film shown every 30min. 9am-4:30pm. Washington's headquarters $2, under 17 free. Audio tapes $8; tape player $15; no audio players rented after 2pm. Bus tours run hourly 9:30am-4pm. $5.50, children $4.50.)*

Valley Forge lies 35min. from Philadelphia by car. To get there take I-76 west from Philly for about 12mi. Get off at the Valley Forge exit (exit 24), then take Rt. 202 S for 1mi. and Rt. 422 W for 1½mi. to another Valley Forge exit. SEPTA runs buses to the visitors center M-F only; catch #125 at 16th and JFK (fare $3.10).

# LANCASTER COUNTY

The Amish, the Mennonites, and the Brethren, three groups of German Anabaptists who fled persecution in Deutschland (thus the misnomer "Pennsylvania Dutch"), sought freedom to pursue their own religion in the rolling countryside of Lancaster County. They successfully escaped censorship, but they have not escaped attention. Although originally farmers, the "Plain Peoples's" chief industry is now tourism. Thousands of visitors flock to this pastoral area every year to glimpse a way of life that eschews modern conveniences like motorized vehicles, television, and cellular phones, in favor of modest amenities. Point but don't shoot; many Amish have religious objections to being photographed.

## ▌ ORIENTATION AND PRACTICAL INFORMATION

Lancaster County covers an area almost the size of Rhode Island. County seat Lancaster City, in the heart of Dutch country, has red brick row houses huddled around historic **Penn Sq.** The rural areas are mostly accessible by car (unless you've got a horse and buggy), but it is easy to see the tourist sites with a bike or the willingness to walk the mile or two between public transportation drop-offs. You always thought **Intercourse** would lead to **Paradise,** and on the country roads of Lancaster County, it does. From Paradise, **U.S. 30 W** plots a straight course into **Fertility.** Visitors should be aware that the area is heavily Mennonite, so most businesses and all major attractions close on Su.

**Trains: Amtrak,** 53 McGovern Ave. (291-5080), in Lancaster City. To Philadelphia (1hr., 4-8 per day, $10).

**Buses: Capital Trailways** (397-4861), on the ground fl. of train station. 5 buses per day to Philadelphia (2hr., $15). Open daily 7am-4:30pm.

**Public Transit: Red Rose Transit,** 45 Erick Rd. (397-4246). Service around Lancaster and the surrounding countryside. Buses run M-F 9am-3:30pm and after 6:30pm, and all day Sa-Su. Base fare $1, over 65 free.

**Visitor Info: Pennsylvania Dutch Visitors Bureau Information Center,** 501 Greenfield Rd. (299-8901 or 800-735-2629), on the east side of Lancaster City off Rt. 30, dispenses info on the region, including excellent maps and walking tours. Open M-Sa 8am-6pm, Su 8am-5pm; Sept.-May daily 8:30am-5pm.

**Post Office:** 1400 Harrisburg Pike (396-6900). Open M-F 7:30am-7pm, Sa 9am-2pm. **ZIP code:** 17604. **Area code:** 717.

# ⬛ ACCOMMODATIONS AND CAMPGROUNDS

Hundreds of hotels and B&Bs cluster in this area, as do several working farms with guest houses. Visitors centers can provide room information or, as part of a religious outreach mission, the **Mennonite Information Center** (see **Sights,** below) will try to find you a Mennonite-run guest house for approximately the same price. About the only thing that outnumber cows here are the campgrounds.

**Smoketown Village Guest House,** 2495 Old Philadelphia Pike (393-5975), 4mi. east of Lancaster. Guests snuggle under quilts in floral rooms with or without private baths. Mennonite proprietors bubble with suggestions for attractions. TV and A/C. $28-34.

**Kenning Tourist Home,** 410 Ronks Rd. (393-5358 or 687-6294), left off Rt. 30 E just past Flory's Campgrounds. Adorable homey rooms, all with TV, some with AC and private bath. Hear the horses' hooves of the Amish neighbors from the dawn until the wee hours right beyond the window. Single $26, double $36.

**Pennsylvania Dutch Motel,** 2275 N. Reading Rd. (336-5559), at exit 21 off Pennsylvania Turnpike. Big, clean rooms with cable TV, and A/C. The friendly hostess has written directions to major sights. Singles $42; doubles $46. Discounts Nov.-Mar.

**Old Mill Stream Camping Manor,** 2249 Rt. 30 E (299-2314). Shaded campground cramped between the family-oriented Dutch Wonderland amusement park and a corn field, 4mi. east of Lancaster City. Includes game room, laundry, playground, general store. Tenters are given stream-side sites. Office open daily 8am-9pm; off- season 8am-8pm. Sites $18, with hookup $21. Reservations recommended.

# ◖ FOOD

The Amish food, simple but full in flavor and portion, is reason enough to travel into central Pennsylvania. A good alternative to high-priced "family-style" restaurants lives on at the **farmers markets** and produce stands which dot the roadway. The **Central Market,** in downtown Lancaster City at the northwest corner of Penn Sq., a huge food bazaar with both Pennsylvania Dutch and "English" vendors, has provided low-priced meats, cheeses, vegetables, sandwiches, and desserts since 1899 (open Tu and F 6am-4pm, Sa 6am-2pm). The Lancaster restaurant scene surrounds the market. Two of the best options lurk in the depths of the Central Mall: Fly into **Isaac's,** 44 N. Queen St. (394-5544), to enjoy fun and fandy sandwiches with avian names ($4-6; open M-F 10am-8pm); the **Underground Railroad,** 51 N. Market St. is far from a secret operation with $1 lunch specials like collard greens and soul soothing sweet potato pie (396-1189; $2.25; open daily 11am-2pm and 4-9pm). The huge **Bird-in-Hand Market** complex on Rt. 340 charges more than the Amish road stands, but it is centralized and has parking. (393-9674. Open July-Aug. W-Sa 8:30am-5:30pm; Apr.-June and Nov. W and F-Sa 8:30am-5:30pm; Jan.-Mar. and Dec. F-Sa 8:30am-5:30pm.) The **Amish Barn,** 3029 Old Philadelphia Pike, serves all-you-can-eat breakfasts ($6) and "Amish" dinners. (768-8886. Open daily late May to Sept. 5 7:30am-9pm; Sept. 6 to Oct. and Apr. to Memorial Day 8am-8pm; Nov. 8am-7pm; closed Jan.-Mar.) Except for the chains, most restaurants close on Su.

**PIE IN YOUR EYE** The most distinctive culinary specialty of Lancaster County is the traditional Amish dessert, **shoofly pie,** popularized in the days before the refrigerator (or in contemporary Amish houses without refrigerators) because of its resistance to spoiling. Once removed from the oven, its treacly sweetness attracted droves of flies and thus gained its name from the constant "shoo fly" calls of its baker. Of equal authenticity if less publicity is the **whoopie pie,** a cookie-sized object with buttercream frosting sandwiched between two rounds of chocolate, pumpkin, or red velvet cake. These can be found at most bake shops for about 50¢ per pie.

##  SIGHTS

The **People's Place** on Main St./Rt. 340, in Intercourse, 11mi. east of Lancaster City, covers most of a block with bookstores, craft shops, and an exhibit called **20Q** (referring to the 20 most-asked questions about the Amish) with displays on Amish and Mennonite life, from barn raising to hat styles. Along with the film *Who Are the Amish?* shown every 30min. 9:30am-5pm, it makes visitors to the area more appreciative of their unique culture. *(768-7171. Film $4, under 12 $2; film and 20Q $7/ $3.50. Open M-Sa 9:30am-8pm; early Sept. to late May M-Sa 9:30am-5pm.)* To get the story from the people who live it, stop in the **Mennonite Information Center**. The Mennonites, unlike the Amish, believe that outreach is laudable, so they started this establishment to ensure that tourists had the opportunity to witness the real Mennonite faith. *(299-0964. Millstream Rd. off Rt. 30 east of Lancaster. Open M-Sa 8am-5pm.)* The side roads off U.S. 340 near Bird-in-the-Hand are the best places to explore the area by car, winding through tourist attractions and verdant fields. Bikers can capture the anti-electricity spirit on the tourism office's **Lancaster County Heritage Bike Tour**, a 46mi., reasonably flat route past covered bridges and historic sites. For the full tourist experience, **Ed's 3mi. buggy rides,** bumps along an hour of countryside. *(On Rt. 896, 1½mi. south of U.S. 30 W in Strasburg. M-Sa 9am-dusk. $7, under 10 $3.50.)* **Amish Country Tours** offers 2½hr. trips that include visits to one-room schools, Amish cottage industries, authentic farms, and a vineyard (786-3600. $18, ages 4-11 $11; tours given Apr.-Oct. M-Sa 10:30am and 2pm, Su 11:30am). Tourism offices have info on the pseudo-Amish experiences available, from staying in an Amish-style house to watching a blacksmith. Old country crafts and food can be found at the **Pennsylvania Dutch Folk Festival.** *(610-683-8707. North of Lancaster off I-81 S, exit 31. End of June and beginning of July. $10, ages 5-12 $5.)*

# GETTYSBURG

From July 1-3, 1863, Union and Confederate forces met at Gettysburg in one of the bloodiest battles of the Civil War. The ultimate victory of the Union forces dealt a dire blow to the hopes of the South, but at a horrible price for both sides: there were over 50,000 casualties. Four months later, President Lincoln arrived in Gettysburg to dedicate the **Gettysburg National Cemetery,** where 979 unidentified Union soldiers lie. Though only 2min. long, Lincoln's address emphasizing the preservation of the Union was a watershed in American history. Each year, thousands of visitors now head for these fields, heeding the President's call to "resolve that these dead shall not have died in vain." (Open daily 6am-10pm.)

A high-speed elevator propels visitors up the 300 ft. **National Tower** for an overview of the area. (334-6754. Open late Mar. to Aug. daily 9am-6:30pm; Sept.-Oct. M-Th 9am-5:30pm, F-Su 10am-4pm. $5, seniors $4.50, ages 6-12 $3.) The **Cyclorama Center** across from the tower, shows a 20min. film on the battle every hour, and a 30min. light show displaying a cyclorama, a 356 ft. by 26 ft. mural, of the battle. (334-1124, ext. 499. Open daily 9am-5pm; $3, seniors $2.50, ages 6-16 $1.50.)

There are lots of ways to see Gettysburg. The **National Military Park Visitors Information Center** gives free maps for an 18mi. self-guided tour. (334-1124, ext. 431. 1mi. south of town on Taneytown Rd. Open daily 8am-6pm; early Sept. to late May 8am-5pm. $3, seniors $2, under 15 $2.) Alternatively, pay a park guide to personally show you the monuments and landmarks. (2hr. tour $30 for up to 5 people.) Or, follow a ranger for a free walking tour. Artillery Ridge Campgrounds (see below) rents **bikes** and conducts a 2hr. **horseback tour** by advanced reservation. (Bikes $15 for ½-day, $25 per day. Horseback tours $44.) If you like riding bikes, you'll love a **bicycle tour.** (Garage 30 behind 449 Baltimore St. 800-830-5775 or 691-0236. 2hr. tours Apr.-May and Sept.-Oct. Sa-Su from 10am; June F-Su from 9am; July-Aug. Th-Su from 9am. $27. Bikes provided.) **Historic Tours** trundles visitors around the battlefield in 1930s-era buses (55 Steinwehr Ave. 334-8000. $12, children $9.) Candlelit **ghost walks and ghost stories** in a haunted cellar reawaken the dead. (337-0445 or 334-8838. Times vary. $6, under 8 free.)

**HERSHEY'S CANDYLAND** Around the turn of the century, Milton S. Hershey, a Mennonite resident of eastern Pennsylvania, discovered how to mass market chocolate, previously a rare and expensive luxury. Today, the company that bears his name operates the **world's largest chocolate factory**, in Hershey, about 45min. from Lancaster. East of town at **Hersheypark**, the **Chocolate World Visitors Center** presents a free, automated tour through a simulated chocolate factory. After the tour, visitors emerge into a pavilion full of chocolate cookies, discounted chocolate candy, and fashionable Hershey sportswear *(800-437-7439. Visitors center opens with park and closes 2hr. earlier. "Free" tour: pay $5 to park in a Hershey lot.)* Near the visitors center, the **Hershey Museum** probes more deeply into Milton Hershey's life and showcases his 19th-century Apostolic Clock with an hourly procession of clockwork apostles past a clockwork Jesus, while Satan periodically appears and a rooster crows to announce Judas's betrayal. *(534-3439. Open daily 10am-6pm; Labor Day-Memorial Day 10am-5pm. $5, seniors $4.50, ages 3-15 $2.50.)* **Hersheypark Theme Park** has heart-stopping rides with short lines, plus **ZooAmerica,** the adjacent zoo, free with park admission. *(Park: 534-3900. Open daily June and July-Aug. M-F 10am-10pm; July-Aug. Sa-Su 10am-11pm; call for hours May to early June and Sept. $30, over 54 and ages 3-8 $17; $16 for all after 5pm. Zoo: 534-3860. Open daily mid-June to Aug. 10am-8pm; Sept. to mid-June 10am-5pm. $5.25, seniors $4.75, ages 3-12 $4.)* **Capital Trailways** buses from Lancaster City to Hershey via Harrisburg. *(397-4861. 3½hr., 1 per day, $8.15.)*

The macabre **Jennie Wade House** preserves the kitchen where Miss Wade, the only civilian killed in the battle of Gettysburg, was struck by a bullet which passed through two doors. Legend has it that unmarried women who pass their finger through the fatal bullet hole will be engaged within a year. Admission to the house includes **Olde Town,** a wax museum of a Civil War-era town square. (528 Baltimore St. 334-4100. Open May-Aug. daily 9am-9pm; Sept.-Apr. 9am-5pm. $6, ages 6-11 $3.50.) The **Gettysburg Travel Council** is in the old train depot where Lincoln disembarked. (35 Carlisle St. 334-6274. Open daily 9am-5pm.)

For an above-average motel experience, breeze into the **Blue Sky Motel,** 4mi. from central Gettysburg with pleasant views from the back windows and a pool out front. (2585 Biglerville Rd./Rt. 34 N. 677-7736 or 800-745-8194. Singles $49; doubles $54; Sept.-Oct. $38/$39; Nov.-Mar. $29/$34; $4 per additional person. One suite with kitchen. Office open Su-Th 8am-10pm, F-Sa 8am-11pm.) Follow Rt. 34 N to Rt. 233 to reach the closest hostel, **Ironmasters Mansion Hostel (HI-AYH),** 20mi. away and within the entrance of Pine Grove Furnace State Park, left at the Twirly Tap ice cream sign. Incredibly large and luxurious, the 1820s hostel has 46 beds in a gorgeous area. Hear experiences of hikers at the half-point of the Appalachian Trail and daily 9pm history talks from smile-inducing host. (717-486-7575. $12, nonmembers $15. Linen $2. Internet access $3. Open 7:30-9:30am and 5-10pm; by reservation only Dec.-Feb.) **Artillery Ridge,** 1mi. south of the Military Park Visitors Center on Rt. 134, maintains campsites with access to showers, a riding stable, laundry facilities, a pool, nightly movies, fishing pond, and bike rentals. (610 Taneytown Rd. 334-1288. Sites $15.50, with hookup $21; open Apr.-Nov.)

Hefty rations persist in the town's square and just beyond the entrance to the battlefield. Keep the historical juices flowing at the **Dobbin House,** Gettysburg's first building (c. 1776), where guests can view an Underground Railroad shelter used to protect runaway slaves from recapture during the Civil War. Create your own grilled burger ($6) or try "Mason's Mile High" ($6.50), a double-decker with ham and roast beef. (89 Steinwher Ave. Open Su-Th 9am-10pm; F-Sa 10am-11:30pm. Jazz on the 1st W of each month from 7:30pm.) Near the sights **General Pickett's Restaurant,** charges for a southern-style all-you-can-eat buffet. (571 Steinwehr Ave. 334-7580.)

Inaccessible by Greyhound or Amtrak, Gettysburg is in south-central PA, off U.S. 15, about 30mi. south of Harrisburg. In town, **Towne Trolley** will shuttle you to some locations, but not around the battlefield. (Runs Apr.-Oct. $1.) **Area code:** 717.

# PITTSBURGH

Those who come to the City of Steel expecting sprawling industry and hordes of soot-encrusted American Joes are bound to be disappointed. The decline of the steel industry has meant cleaner air and rivers, and a recent economical renaissance has produced a brighter urban landscape. City officials are desperate to provide Pittsburgh with a new image, going so far as to propose a theme park filled with robotic dinosaurs. Throughout renewals, Pittsburgh's neighborhoods have maintained strong and diverse identities. Admittedly, some of old, sooty Pittsburgh survives in the suburbs, but one need only ride up the Duquesne Incline and view downtown from atop Mt. Washington to see how thoroughly Pittsburgh has entered a new age—and to understand why locals are so proud of "The 'Burgh."

## 🛈 ORIENTATION AND PRACTICAL INFORMATION

Pittsburgh's downtown, the **Golden Triangle,** is shaped by two rivers—the **Allegheny** to the north, and the **Monongahela** to the south—which flow together to form a third, the **Ohio.** Streets in the Triangle that run parallel to the Monongahela are numbered one through seven. The **University of Pittsburgh** and **Carnegie-Mellon University** lie east of the Triangle in Oakland. With one of the lowest crime rates in the nation for a city of its size, Pittsburgh is fairly safe, even downtown at night.

**Airport: Pittsburgh International** (472-5526), 18mi. west of downtown by I-279 and Rt. 60 N in Findlay Township. The Port Authority's **28x Airport Flyer** bus serves downtown and Oakland from the airport (daily every ½hr. 6am-11:58pm, $2). **Airline Transportation Company** (471-2250 or 471-8900) rolls to downtown (M-F every 30min. 6am-11:40pm, Sa-Su every hr. 6am-11pm; $12), Oakland (M-F every hr. 9am-10pm, Sa every 2hr. from 9am-5pm, Su every 2hr. 10am-2pm, every hr. 3-10pm; one-way $12.50, round-trip $21), and Monroeville (M-F every 2hr. 9am-3pm, every hr. 3-10pm, Su at 2, 4, 7, and 9pm; $20). Cab to downtown runs $30.

**Trains: Amtrak,** 1100 Liberty Ave. (471-6170), at Grant on the northern edge of downtown next to Greyhound and the post office. Generally safe inside, *but be careful walking from here to the city center at night.* To: Philadelphia (8½-11½hr., 2 per day, $42-51); New York (10-13hr., 3 per day, $56-68); and Chicago (9½-10hr., 2 per day, $52-96). Station open 24hr.

**Buses: Greyhound** (392-6526), on 11th St. at Liberty Ave. near Amtrak. To Philadelphia (7hr., 8 per day, $41) and Chicago (8-12hr., 10 per day, $57). Open 24hr.

**Public Transit: Port Authority of Allegheny County (PAT)** (442-2000). Downtown: bus fare free until 7pm, 75¢ after 7pm; subway (between the 3 downtown stops) free. Beyond downtown: bus fare $1.25-2, transfers 25¢, all-day pass $3; subway $1.25-2, ages 6-11 ½-price for bus and subway. Schedules, maps at most subway stations and in the "Community Interest" section of the yellow pages. **Taxi: Peoples Cab,** 681-3131.

**Car Rental: Rent-A-Wreck** (367-3131 or 800-472-8353), on McKnight St. 7mi. north of downtown. $20-25 per day with 100 free mi.; 18¢ per additional mi. Must be 21 with credit card, some preapproved cash rentals. Under 25 $3 per day surcharge. Open M-F 8am-6pm, Sa 8am-4pm.

**Visitor Info: Pittsburgh Convention and Visitors Bureau,** 4 Gateway Center, 18th fl. (281-7711 or 800-359-0758; www.pittsburgh-cvb.org), downtown on Liberty Ave. Open M-F 9am-5pm, Sa-Su 9am-3pm. There are 4 visitors centers: downtown, Oakland, Mt. Washington, and the airport.

**Hotlines: Rape Action Hotline,** 765-2731. Operates 24hr. **Gay, Lesbian, Bisexual Center,** 422-0114. (M-F 6:30-9:30pm, Sa 3-6pm.)

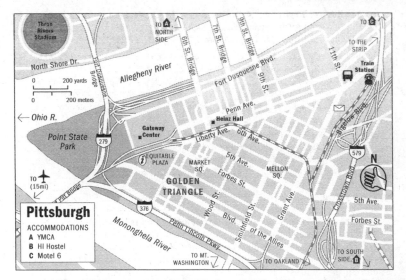

Pittsburgh

**ACCOMMODATIONS**
**A** YMCA
**B** HI Hostel
**C** Motel 6

**Post Office:** 700 Grant St. (800-275-8777). Open M-F 7am-6pm, Sa 7am-3:30pm. **ZIP Code:** 15219. **Area Code:** 412.

## ACCOMMODATIONS

Once a bank, the sparkling **Pittsburgh Hostel (HI-AYH)**, 830 E. Warrington Ave., at the corner of Arlington St., in Allentown 1mi. south of downtown, delivers modern hostel living complete with full kitchen, A/C, free parking, locks and lockers, and spacious rooms. (431-1267. $17, nonmembers $20. Semi-private singles $30, nonmembers $35; doubles $40/45; quads or "family rooms" $50 and up. Linen $1, towels 50¢. Check-in 8-10am and 5-10pm. Lock-out 10am-5pm. No curfew. Reservations recommended for semi-private rooms. Wheelchair access.) The **Allegheny YMCA**, 600 W. North Ave., offers singles for men in the North Side (321-8594; laundry facilities, gym, pool; $20, $66 per week; $5 key deposit; no curfew).

Several inexpensive motels can be found on the city's outskirts near the airport. **Motel 6**, 211 Beecham Dr., off I-79 at exit 16/16B 10mi. from downtown, supplies standard lodging with A/C and TVs (922-9400; singles $37, doubles $43, $3 per extra person; reservations suggested for summer weekends). **Pittsburgh North Campground**, 6610 Mars Rd., in Cranberry Township, has the area's closest camping, 20min. north of downtown; take I-79 to the Cranberry/Mars exit. (724-776-1150. 110 campsites, showers, swimming. Tent sites for 2 $18, with hookup $26; $3 per extra adult, $2 per extra child. Office open daily 8am-9pm.)

## BEES, DOGS, AND OTHER EDIBLE STUFF

Aside from the pizza joints and bars downtown, **Oakland** is the best place to look for a good inexpensive meal. Collegiate watering holes and cafes pack **Forbes Ave.** around the University of Pittsburgh; colorful eateries and shops line **Walnut St.** in Shadyside and **E. Carson St.** in South Side. The **Strip District** on Penn Ave. between 16th and 22nd St. (north of downtown along the Allegheny) bustles with Italian, Greek, and Asian cuisine; Sa mornings mean fresh produce and fish.

 **Original Oyster House,** 20 Market Sq. (566-7925), Pittsburgh's oldest and perhaps cheapest restaurant and bar. Serves seafood platters ($4-5) and sandwiches ($2-4.50) in a beautiful marble and wrought-iron bar. A death-defying "Crab Cutlet" sandwich ($2.55) will slam one to your arteries amidst panoramic shots of Miss America pageants from ages past. Open M-Sa 9am-11pm.

**Original Hot Dog Shops, Inc.,** 3901 Forbes Ave. (621-7388), at Bouquet St. in Oakland. Rowdy and greasy with lots and lots of fries, burgers, dogs, and pizza. Locals call it "the O." 16 in. pizza $4.69. Open Su-W 10am-3:30am, Th 10am-4:30am, F-Sa 10am-5am.

**Beehive Coffeehouse and Theater,** 3807 Forbes Ave. (683-4483), just steps from "the O." Another location in South Side, 1327 E. Carson St. (488-4483). Quirky coffeehouse brimming with cool wall paintings, hipper-than-thou staff and clientele, and hot cappuccino ($2.25). The theater features current films; poetry and an occasional open-mic improv night buzz upstairs. Open M-F 7:30am-2am, Sa 8:30am-2am, Su noon-2am.

**Union Grille,** 413 S. Craig St. (681-8620), off Forbes Ave., in Oakland. This clean-cut bar and grille gains notoriety for its "honest American food" and cheap draughts ($1.75-3). No working-class sympathizer will turn down Union Potato Skins ($5); veggie sandwiches ($7), crabcakes (5.950-13.95), and house wine ($2.50) please yuppies. Open Su-Th 11:30am-10:30pm, F-Sa 11:30am-11:30pm.

## 👁 SIGHTS

The **Golden Triangle** is home to **Point State Park** and its famous 200 ft. fountain. A ride up the **Duquesne Incline,** in the South Side, affords a spectacular view of the city. *(1220 Grandview Ave. 381-1665. Open M-Sa 5:30am-12:45am, Su 7am-12:45am; round-trip $2.)* Founded in 1787, the **University of Pittsburgh** *(624-4141; 624-6094 for tours)* stands in the shadow of the 42-story **Cathedral of Learning,** at Bigelow Blvd. between Forbes and 5th Ave. in Oakland. The Cathedral, an academic building dedicated in 1934, features 25 "nationality classrooms" designed and decorated by artisans from Pittsburgh's many ethnic traditions. *(624-6000. Cassette-guided tours M-F 9am-3pm, Sa 9:30am-3pm, Su 11am-3pm. $2, seniors $1.50, ages 8-18 50¢.)* **Carnegie-Mellon University** houses scholars down the street on Forbes Ave *(268-2000).*

The **Andy Warhol Museum,** on the North Side, is the world's largest museum dedicated to a single artist, supporting 7 floors of the Pittsburgh native's material, from pop portraits of Marilyn to continuous screenings of films like *Eat* (39min. of a man eating), and a series of pieces entitled *Oxidation*, made from synthetic polymer paint and urine on canvas. *(117 Sandusky St. 237-8300. Open W and Su 11am-6pm, Th-Sa 11am-8pm. $6, seniors $5, students and children $4.)* A 20min. walk into the North Side, **The Mattress Factory** is actually a museum, created by light-worker James Turell and artist Yayoi Kausma, of cutting-edge visual and performance art. *(505 Jacksonia Way. 231-3169. Follow Sandusky St. to East Commons, then North Commons to Federal St. and then Jacksonia. Open Tu-Sa 10am-5pm, Su 1-5pm. $4, students and seniors $3.)*

Two of America's biggest financial legends, Andrew Carnegie and Henry Clay Frick, made their fortunes in Pittsburgh. Today, their bequests enrich the city's cultural fortune. Carnegie's most spectacular gift, **The Carnegie,** across the street from the Cathedral of Learning (take any bus to Oakland), holds both an art museum and a natural history collection. *(4400 Forbes Ave. 622-3131, 622-3289 for tours. Open Tu-Sa 10am-5pm, Su 1-5pm. $6, students and ages 3-18 $4, seniors $5.)* Most people know Henry Clay Frick for his New York art collection; the **Art Museum** at the **Frick Art and Historical Center** displays some of his earlier, less famous acquisitions, including Italian, Flemish, and French works from the 13th to 18th centuries. *(7227 Reynolds St. 371-0600. Open Tu-Sa 10am-5pm, Su noon-6pm. Admission free to Art Museum and Car and Carriage Museum, $8 to Frick Estate. Chamber concerts Oct.-Apr.)*

Feel an earthquake, get aboard a WWII submarine, or climb a rock at the **Carnegie Science Center.** *(1 Allegheny Ave., by Three Rivers Stadium. 237-3400. Open Su-F 10am-6pm, Sa 10am-9pm. $6.50, ages 3-18 and seniors $4.50; with OmniMax or planetarium $10/$6.)*

Off I-376, east of town in Penn Hills, an eastern suburb of Pittsburgh, lies the U.S.'s first Hindu temple. The **Sri Venkateswara (or S.V.) Temple** is modeled after a temple in Andhra Pradesh, India, and has become a major pilgrimage site for American Hindus since its completion. Non-Hindus can walk through the Great Hall and observe prayer. *(373-3380.)*

> **HOMESTEAD GRAYSBOX** Past the shock-yellow Pirates pennants and computer-generated "Arrrr"-ing buccaneer lining the upper tiers of Three Rivers Stadium, a nondescript gray banner plainly states **"Homestead Grays."** A reminder of the days of the **Negro Leagues,** part of a segregationist past upon which America waxes both nostalgic and indignant, the pennant quietly reminds those in the know of a baseball team formed in 1910 from Homestead steelworkers. The Grays rose to become a league leader, winning every Negro National League pennant from 1931 to 1939 and several **Negro World Series,** including the Leagues' last in 1948. Considered by many to be the greatest Negro League team, the Grays vanished into obscurity when the League split. **Forbes Field,** where they played, has been doomed to destruction, and now Three Rivers, which mildly speaks of their legacy, is soon to follow.

## ▣ ENTERTAINMENT AND NIGHTLIFE

Most restaurants and shops carry the weekly *In Pittsburgh* or *City Paper*, great sources for free, up-to-date entertainment listings, nightclubs, and racy personals. The internationally acclaimed **Pittsburgh Symphony Orchestra** performs Sept. through May at **Heinz Hall**, 600 Penn Ave., downtown, and gives free outdoor concerts on summer evenings in Point State Park (392-4900). The **Pittsburgh Public Theater**, in Allegheny Sq. on the North Side, is world-renowned, but charges a pretty penny. (321-9800. Performances Oct.-July. Box office open daily Oct.-July 10am-showtime. Tickets $15-42; students and children $10 for shows Su-F.) At gritty **Three Rivers Stadium** on the North Side, the **Pirates** (321-2827) hit from Apr. through Sept., while the **Steelers** (323-1200) hit the gridiron from Sept. through Dec.

For nightlife, although the Strip downtown is still relatively dense with revelers (relatively, that is, in a town that closes at 5pm), the hip crowd fills **E. Carson St.** on the South Side, which overflows with regular guys 'n' gals on weekend nights. **Metropol** and the adjoining **Rosebud**, 1600 Smallman St., in the Strip District, fill a spacious warehouse with dancing supermen and citizens plain (261-4512; cover $5; Metropol doors open 9pm, Rosebud doors open 6pm). **Nick's Fat City**, 1601-1605 E. Carson St., South Side, serves as an invaluable crash-course into the world of Pittsburgh rock 'n' roll. Your teachers will be a lineup of favorite local bands; your study aids will be $2.75 draughts of Yuengling, a favorite PA brew, and a star-studded floor inscribed with such local faves as Porky Chedwick and The Four Chairs. (481-6880. Cover varies.) **Jack's**, on E. Carson at S. 12th, South Side, repeatedly earns the moniker "Best Bar in the 'Burgh" by offering lifesaving specials like 25¢ hotdogs (M), 10¢ wings (W), and $2 chicken sandwich to a rowdy, but friendly local crowd (431-3644. 21+; open daily 7am-2am). The gay and lesbian community flocks to the **Pegasus Lounge**, 818 Liberty Ave., downtown, for house music and drag shows (281-2131, open Tu-Sa 9pm-2am).

## OHIOPYLE STATE PARK

Lifted by steep hills and cut by cascading rivers, southwest Pennsylvania encompasses some lovely forests. Native Americans dubbed this region "Ohiopehhle" ("white frothy water") for the grand Youghiogheny River Gorge (YOCK-a-GAY-nee—"The Yock" to locals), now the focal point of Pennsylvania's Ohiopyle State Park. The park's 19,000 acres offer hiking, fishing, hunting, whitewater rafting, and a variety of winter activities. The latest addition to the banks of the Yock, a graveled bike trail that winds 28mi. north from the town of Confluence to Connellsville, was converted from a riverside railroad bed. Recently named one of the 19 best walks in the world, the trail is just one section of the "rails to trails" project that will eventually connect Pittsburgh and Washington, D.C.

Throngs come each year to raft Ohiopyle's 8mi. long, class III rapids. Some of the best whitewater rafting in the East, the rapids take about 5hr. to conquer. Four outfitters front Rt. 381 in "downtown" Ohiopyle: **White Water Adventurers** (800-992-7238), **Wilderness Voyagers** (800-272-4141), **Laurel Highlands River Tours** (800-472-

3846), and **Mountain Streams** (800-723-8669). Trip prices on the Yock varies dramatically ($30-57 per person per day), depending on the season, day of the week, and difficulty. If you're an experienced river rat (or if you enjoy flipping boats), any of the above companies will rent you equipment. (Rafts about $11-15 per person; canoes $20; "duckies"—inflatable kayaks—about $20-26.) In order to float anything, you need a **launch permit** at the park office (M-F free. Sa-Su $2.50. Call at least 30 days in advance for Sa permits. Rental companies provide free permits.) To begin your trip, park at **Old Mitchell Parking Lot**, 7mi. northwest of downtown, and purchase a $2.50 token. At the end of your trip, a shuttle will take you and your equipment back to your car. The market in the Falls Market and Overnight Inn (see above) sells **fishing licenses** required in the park ($15 for 3 days; $30 per week; $35 per season, residents $17). Bike rental prices vary (generally $3-4 per hr.).

Inexpensive motels around Ohiopyle are scarce. The excellent **Ohiopyle State Park Hostel (HI-AYH)**, on Ferncliffe Rd., sits in the center of town off Rt. 381. (329-4476. 24 bunks, kitchen, laundry facilities. $10, nonmembers $13. Private rooms $13/16. Check-in 5-11pm. Check-out 10am. Curfew 11pm.) Down the street on Rt. 381, **Falls Market and Overnight Inn**, P.O. Box 101 rents nice rooms with shared baths. The downstairs store has groceries and a restaurant/snack bar (329-4973. $60 triple, $10 additional person. A/C, cable TV, VCR, laundry facilities. Burgers $1.65, pancakes $2.50. Store open daily 7am-9pm; in winter 7am-6:30pm.) There are 226 **campsites** in Ohiopyle. (M-F $13, Sa-Su $16; PA residents $11/$14. Call at least 30 days in advance for weekend reservations in the summer.)

Ohiopyle borders on Rt. 381, 64mi. southeast of Pittsburgh via Rt. 51 and U.S. 40. **Greyhound** serves Uniontown, 20mi. to the west on U.S. 40, and travels to Pittsburgh (1¼hr., 2 per day, $12). The **Park Information Center**, P.O. Box 105 (329-8591; 800-925-7669 for a free booklet), lies just off Rt. 381 on Dinnerbell Rd. (open daily 8am-4pm; Nov.-Apr. M-F 8am-4pm). Calling 800-925-7669 earns a free booklet. **Post Office:** Green St. (329-8605; open M-F 7:30am-4:30pm, Sa 7:30-11:30am.). **ZIP code:** 15470. **Area code:** 724.

## NEAR OHIOPYLE

**Fallingwater,** 8mi. north of Ohiopyle on Rt. 381, is a masterpiece by the king of modern architecture, Frank Lloyd Wright. Designed in 1935 for Pittsburgh's wealthy Kaufmann family, "the most famous private residence ever built" blends into the surrounding terrain; huge boulders that predate the house are part of its architecture. The family wanted the house to be near the Bear Run Waterfall: Wright built the house over the waterfall, so you can hear the water's roar in every room, but can see it from only one terrace. This site can only be seen on a 1hr. tour; make reservations. *(329-8501. Open Tu-Su 10am-4pm; Nov.-Dec. and Mar. Sa-Su only. Tours Tu-F $8, ages 6-18 $6; Sa-Su $12/$7. Children under 6 must be left in child care, $2 per hr.)*

**Fort Necessity National Battlefield**, on U.S. 40 near Rt. 381, is a replica of the original fort built by George Washington. In July 1754, young George, then of Virginia militia, was beaten in an attack on Fort Necessity that began the French and Indian War. The Fort's **visitors center** has more info *(329-5512. Open daily 8:30am-6:30pm; early Sept. to late May 9am-5pm. $2, under 17 free. Park open 8am-sunset.)* A few mi. west, the singular **Museum of Early American Farm Machines and Very Old Horse Saddles with a History** exhibits rusted and zany Americana, including a 12-ton cast-iron steam engine from 1905 and saddles from the Civil War *(438-5180).*

# DELAWARE

A state whose number one boast is its convenient East Coast location obviously has an inferiority complex. Tiny Delaware does, however, serve as a sanctuary from the sprawling cities of the Boston-Washington megalopolis. Delaware's particular charm is well represented by the state bug, the ladybug, adopted in 1974 after an ardent campaign by elementary school children.

Delaware was first to ratify the U.S. Constitution on Dec. 7, 1787—hence the tag "First State." Since then its history has been dominated by the wealthy DuPont clan, whose gunpowder mills grew into a chemical giant. Tax-free shopping, scenic beach towns—and yes, convenient location—lure vacationers to Delaware from all along the country's eastern shores.

# 🔃 PRACTICAL INFORMATION

**Capital:** Dover.

**Visitor Info:** 99 King's Hwy., Dover 19901 (739-4271 or 800-441-8846; www.state.de.us). Open M-F 8am-4:30pm. **Division of Fish and Wildlife,** 89 King's Hwy., Dover 19901 (800-523-3336).

**Postal Abbreviation:** DE **Sales Tax:** 0%. 8% on accommodations.

## DELAWARE SEASHORE

**LEWES.** Founded in 1613 by the Zwaanendael colony from Hoorn, Holland, **Lewes** (LEW-is) touts itself as Delaware's first town. More than 350 years later, Disney rates this sleepy burg on the Delaware Bay, across the Delaware River from Cape May, NJ, as one of the best places to visit in America. Lewes's charming Victorian houses and calm shores attract an annual influx of antique hunters and families seeking a retreat from rough Atlantic waters. The small-town atmosphere in Lewes is upscale and reserved, but well-kept beaches and welcoming natives make the town inviting for budget travelers.

Secluded among sand dunes and scrub pines, the 4000-acre **Cape Henlopen State Park,** 1mi. east of Lewes, is home to a seabird nesting colony, sparkling white "walking dunes," a 2mi. paved trail, and a beach with a bathhouse (645-8983; open daily 8am-sunset; $5 per car, bikes and walkers free). Sandy **campsites** available on a first come, first served basis (645-2103; open Apr.-Oct.; sites $18, no hookups).

A charming, kid-friendly 7-room B&B with a lavish vegetarian breakfast, the **Savannah Inn,** 330 Savannah Rd., tops other Lewes accommodations in price and earth-friendly philosophy. (645-5592. Rooms with shared bath $50-$80; largest rooms sleep 3-4. Oct.-May $10 less, no breakfast.) **Captain's Quarters,** 406 Savannah Rd., a small motel owned by a retired waterman offers comfy but less personal lodgings (645-7924; in summer Sa-Su $75, M-F $25; each additional person $5). The few restaurants in Lewes cluster primarily on 2nd St. **Rosa Negra,** 128 2nd St., offers filling Italian fare in a rather bare dining room; early diners get bargain prices. (645-1980. Daily 4-6pm dinner $7, seniors $6. Open for lunch M-Sa 11am-2pm; dinner Su-Th 4-9pm, F-Sa 4-10pm.) Sniff the rich aroma of brews like "linzer torte" and "coconut kiss" at **Oby Lee Coffee Roasters,** 124 2nd St., with sandwiches ($2-4) and the "opposite of hot cocoa" Vanilla Dream ($1.50; 645-0733; open daily 7am-5:15pm). Live blues, rock, and karaoke plays W-Sa at the **Rose and Crown Restaurant and Pub,** 108 2nd St. (645-2373; open daily 11am-1am).

**Greyhound** stops in front of the Ace Hardware Store on Rt. 1, with buses to Washington, D.C. (3½hr., $33), Baltimore (3½hr., $29), and Philadelphia (4hr., $31). In Lewes and Rehoboth, the **Delaware Resort Transit (DART) shuttle bus** (800-553-3278) runs from the ferry terminal through Lewes to Rehoboth and Dewey Beach (every 30min.; operates late May to early Sept. daily 7am-3am; $1 per ride, seniors and disabled 40¢, day pass $2). **Seaport Taxi:** 645-6800. **Lewes Chamber of Commerce:** 20 King's Hwy. (645-8078; open in summer M-F 10am-4pm, Sa 9am-3pm, Su 10am-2pm; off season closed Sa-Su). **Area code:** 302.

> **NICE TO MEET YOU** Delaware, although rightfully esteemed by Americans as the first state to ratify the Constitution, is small—so small that when two Delawareans meet for the first time, they ask each other, "What exit are you from?"

MID-ATLANTIC

**REHOBOTH BEACH.** The cotton candy, mini-golf, fast-food, and discount t-shirt shops of Rehoboth's boardwalk strip contrast sharply with the serenity of seaside Lewes, but a bit inland lives a well-heeled resort community of Washington families and a burgeoning gay population. Congestion on the sparkling beach thins north of the boardwalk. The beach is deserted in the early morning, when dolphins commute southward daily. From Rt. 1, follow Rehoboth Ave. until it hits the water at **Rehoboth Beach,** or follow Rt. 1 south to **Dewey Beach.**

Inexpensive lodgings, mostly charming B&Bs, abound in Rehoboth. Mr. and Mrs. Downs of the **Lord Baltimore,** 16 Baltimore Ave., half a block from the boardwalk, rent out clean, antiquated rooms with TV, refrigerator, and A/C (227-2855; singles and doubles $35-65, in winter $25-50; each additional person $5). **The Abbey Inn,** 31 Maryland Ave., always has a conversation waiting on the porch. (227-7023. 2-day min. stay; open late May to early Sept. Singles from $35; doubles from $40; Sa-Su 15% surcharge.) The wooded **Big Oaks Family Campground,** 1mi. off Rt. 1 on Rd. 270, has open sites and a pool (645-6838; sites $25, with hookup $30).

Rehoboth is known for deluxe cuisine and many bars. At **Cafe Papillion,** 42 Rehoboth Ave., in the Penny Lane Mall, French cooks speak the international language of good food, serving up fresh crepes ($2.50-5), croissants ($1.75-3), and stuffed baguette sandwiches ($5-6.25; 227-7568; open May-Oct. daily 8am-11pm). Heavenly is the best word for the delicacies at **Dream Cafe,** 26 Baltimore St., a few doors down from the Lord Baltimore (226-2233; open Su-Tu and Th 7am-4pm, F 7am-5pm, Sa 7am-10pm). **Grotto Pizza** serves slices ($2) and pasta ($7-9) at several busy boardwalk locations (227-3278; open M-Th 11am-2am, F-Sa 11am-3am).

**Irish Eyes,** 15 Wilmington Ave., smiles with comedy M, live rock W, and traditional Irish music Th-Su (227-2888; cover $5; open M-F 5pm-1am, Sa-Su noon-1am). **Arena's Deli,** 149 Rehoboth Ave., pushes the tables aside to lay down live progressive music for a mostly local crowd. (227-1272. Music in summer W and F-M; in winter W and F-Su. Happy Hour M-F 4-7pm; beer $1.50. Open daily 11am-1am.) A gay dance club, **Cloud 9,** 234 Rehoboth Ave., spins rock in its celestial interior and outdoor patio. (226-1999. Happy Hour daily 4-7pm. Open Apr.-Oct. daily 4pm-1am; closed Nov.-Mar. Tu-W.)

**Rehoboth Beach Chamber of Commerce:** 501 Rehoboth Ave. (227-2233 or 800-441-1329), in a recycled railroad depot (open M-F 9am-5pm, Sa-Su 9am-noon). **Greyhound/Trailways:** 251 Rehoboth Ave. (227-7223), stops next to the Chamber of Commerce. To: Washington, D.C. (3½hr., 1 per day, $33); Baltimore (3½hr., 1 per day, $29); and Philadelphia (4hr., 2 per day, $31). **Area code:** 302.

# MARYLAND

Once upon a time, folks on Maryland's rural eastern shore captured crabs, raised tobacco, and ruled Maryland. Across the bay in Baltimore, workers loaded ships and ran factories. Then the federal government expanded, industry shrank, and Maryland had a new focal point: the Baltimore-Washington Pkwy. Suburbs grew, Baltimore revitalized, and the Old Line State acquired a new, liberal urbanity. As D.C.'s homogenized commuter suburbs continue to swell beyond the limits of Maryland's Montgomery and Prince Georges counties, Baltimore revels in its immensity, whereas Annapolis, the capital, remains a small town of sailors. The mountains of the state's western panhandle—geographic and cultural kin to West Virginia—are largely pristine to this day.

# ⑦ PRACTICAL INFORMATION

**Capital:** Annapolis.

**Visitor Info: Office of Tourism,** 217 E. Redwood St., Baltimore 21202 (800-543-1036; www.mdisfun.org). **Dept. of Natural Resources,** 580 Taylor Ave., Annapolis 21401 (410-260-8186; open M-F 8am-4:30pm).

**Postal Abbreviation:** MD. **Sales Tax:** 5%.

# BALTIMORE

*Patapsco*, the Indian name for Baltimore, may have meant "backwater," but Baltimore has earned its place in history; here, Francis Scott Key penned the national anthem and entrepreneurs constructed America's first umbrella factory. Crab cakes, Orioles games, Inner Harbor, and the fabulous National Aquarium are all fine reasons to visit Baltimore, but travelers will be rewarded for digging deeper. Baltimore's Southern heritage is visible in many district neighborhoods, such as Roland Park, where people greet visitors in that friendly "Bawlmer" accent. But under the veneer, John Waters' films found the city's twisted side, while Anne Tyler's fiction evokes its melancholy soul.

## 🛈 ORIENTATION AND PRACTICAL INFORMATION

Baltimore sits in central Maryland, 100mi. south of Philadelphia and about 150mi. up the Chesapeake Bay from the Atlantic Ocean. The southern end of the **Jones Falls Expwy. (I-83)** halves the city at the Inner Harbor, while the **Baltimore Beltway (I-695)** circles the city. I-95 cuts across the southwest corner of the city—a shortcut to the wide arc of the Beltway. During rush hour, these interstates slow to a crawl.

Baltimore is plagued by one-way streets. **Baltimore St.** (which runs east a few blocks north of the Inner Harbor) and **Charles St.** (which runs north from the west corner of the Harbor) divide the city into quarters. Baltimore St. divides the city into north and south; Charles St. is the east-west divider. Streets are dubbed with directional suffixes according to their relation to these thoroughfares.

**Airport: Baltimore-Washington International (BWI)** (859-7111). On I-195 off the Baltimore-Washington Pkwy. (I-295), about 10mi. south of the city center. Take MTA bus #17 to the Nursery Rd. light-rail station. Shuttles to hotels (859-0800) run daily every 30min. 5:45am-11:30pm ($11 to downtown Baltimore, $17 round-trip). To D.C., shuttles leave hourly 5:45am-11:30pm ($21/$31). Amtrak runs to Baltimore ($5) and D.C. ($12). MARC commuter trains are slower, running M-F (Baltimore $3.25; D.C. $5).

**Trains: Penn Station,** 1500 N. Charles St., at Mt. Royal Ave. Easily accessible by bus #3 or 11 from Charles Station downtown. **Amtrak** trains run every 30min.-1hr. to: New York ($62-71); Washington, D.C. ($19) and Philadelphia ($35). M-F two **MARC commuter lines** (800-325-7245 in MD) connect Baltimore to D.C.'s Union Station (859-7400 or 291-4268) via Penn Station (with stops at BWI Airport) or **Camden Station,** at the corner of Howard and Camden St. near Oriole Park. Both are $5.75, round-trip $10.25. Open daily 5:30am-9:30pm, credit-card self-serve 24hr.

**Buses: Greyhound** has 2 locations: downtown at 210 W. Fayette St. (726-7224), near N. Howard St. and at 5625 O'Donnell St. (752-0908), 3mi. east of downtown near I-95. To: New York ($24, round-trip $43); Washington, D.C. ($6, round-trip $10); and Philadelphia ($15, round-trip $24).

**Public Transit: Mass Transit Administration (MTA),** 300 W. Lexington St. (bus and Metro schedule info 539-5000 or 800-543-9809), near N. Howard St. Operator available M-F 6am-9pm. Bus, Metro, and rail service to most major sights in the city and outlying areas. Some buses run 24hr. Metro operates M-F 5am-midnight, Sa 6am-midnight. Light rail operates M-F 6am-11pm, Sa 8am-11pm, Su 11am-7pm. $1.35; more for long distances. Bus #17 runs from the Nursery Rd. light-rail to BWI Airport.

**Water Taxi:** Main stop at Inner Harbor (563-3901 or 800-658-8947). Stops every 8-18min. (Nov.-Mar. every 40min.) at the harbor museums, Harborplace, Fells Point, Little Italy, and more. An easy, pleasant way to travel to 40 of Baltimore's main sights. Service daily May-Aug. 9am-midnight, Apr. and Sept.-Oct. 9am-9pm, Nov.-Mar. 9am-6pm. Unlimited day pass $4.50, ages 10 and under $2. Ticket includes a number of coupons for Baltimore attractions. Run by **Harbor Boating, Inc.,** 1615 Thames St.

**Taxis: Checker Cab**, 685-1212. **Royal Cab,** 327-0330.

**Car Rental: Thrifty Car Rental,** BWI Airport (859-1136), and 2042 N. Howard St. (783-0300), 9 blocks from Penn Station. Economy cars from $35 per weekday and $185 per week. Unlimited mi. in MD and bordering states. Under 25 $15 extra per day. Must be 21 with credit card. Airport branch open daily 6am-11pm.

**Visitor Info: Baltimore Area Visitors Center,** 451 Light St. (837-7024), in a red-trimmed, beige trailer. Open in summer M-Sa 9am-7pm, Su 10am-5pm; in winter daily 9am-5pm.

**Internet Access: The Strand** cybercafe (see **Food**).

**Hotlines: Suicide,** 531-6677. Open 24hr. **Sexual Assault and Domestic Violence,** 828-6390. Open 24hr. **Gay and Lesbian,** 837-8888. Operators daily 7pm-midnight, recording all other times.

**Post Office:** 900 E. Fayette St. (347-4425). Open M-F 7:30am-9pm, Sa 7:30am-5pm. **ZIP Code:** 21233. **Area Code:** 410.

# ACCOMMODATIONS

Expensive chain hotels dominate the Inner Harbor, and elsewhere reputable budget motels are hard to find. To reserve B&Bs, call **Amanda's Bed and Breakfast Reservation Service,** 1428 Park Ave. (225-0001 or 800-899-7533; M-F 8:30am-5:30pm, Sa 8:30am-noon). Rates begin at $50 a night.

**Duke's Motel,** 7905 Pulaski Hwy. (686-0400), in Rosedale off the Beltway. The bulletproof glass in the front office is nothing to worry about—all the neighborhood motels have it. The area is actually safer than most parts of downtown Baltimore. Clean and efficiently run. Simple rooms have A/C and cable. $5 key deposit and ID required. Singles from $40; doubles from $52. Rates higher in summer.

**Quality Inn Inner Harbor,** 1701 Russell St. (727-3400 or 800-221-2222), near the Beltway in South Baltimore, about 1mi. from Inner Harbor. Cable, pool, and continental breakfast. M-F singles $60; doubles $70. Sa-Su $65/$75. AARP/AAA and military 10% discount. *Exercise caution in the area at night.*

**Capitol KOA,** 768 Cecil Ave. (410-923-2771 or 800-562-0248). Mostly RVs, some cabins, and a small wooded area for tents. Tent site for 2 $26; water and electricity $31; RV full hookup $34; 1-room cabin $44, 2-room $53. $5 per additional adult, $2 per child. Open Mar. 25 to Nov. 1.

# FOOD

Maryland blue crab, fresh from Chesapeake Bay, appears on the menu at most Baltimore restaurants. The **Pavilions** at Harborplace, on Pratt and Light St., have enough food stalls and restaurants to please any palate. A 10min. walk from the harbor, beyond the medieval-style clock tower of the Bromo Seltzer building, lies 215-year-old **Lexington Market,** 400 W. Lexington, at Eutaw St. The market offers fresh food cheaper than at Harborplace. (685-6169. Open M-Sa 8:30am-6pm; take the subway to Lexington Station, or bus #7.)

**Louie's Bookstore Cafe,** 518 N. Charles St. (962-1224). In front, an upscale, intellectual bookstore. In back, a lively restaurant and bar mixing well-tailored concert-goers with scruffy indy-rockers. Sandwiches $5-10, entrees $9-17. Lunch is cheap; the dinner scene is groovier. Live classical music nightly (Su-W 8-10:30pm, Th-Sa 8-10pm). Live jazz Th-Sa 10pm. Open M 11:30am-midnight, Tu-Th 11:30am-12:30am, F-Sa 11:30am-1:30am. Hours vary; call ahead.

**The Strand,** 105 E. Lombard St. (625-8944). Fantastic meals at this cool twist on the cybercafe scene. Live music every night and lots of vegetarian options like garden lasagna ($6.25). Internet access $12 per hr. Open 24hr., except Su 9pm to M 7am.

**Amicci's,** 231 S. High St. (528-1096). Italian stallion's appeal is known well beyond the reaches of the neighborhood. *Ziti la rosa* (ziti in tomato pesto served with shrimp in marsala sauce; $13) is a standout. 11 immense pasta dishes under $10. Open M-Th noon-10pm, F-Sa noon-11pm, Su noon-9pm. Shorter off-season hrs.; call ahead.

Central Baltimore

### Labels on map

LITTLE ITALY

Central Ave.
Fleet St.
Aliceanna St.
Eastern Ave.
Aisquith St.
Fayette St.
Baltimore St.
Lombard St.
Pratt St.
Exeter St.
High St.
Albemarle St.
Granby St.
Colvin St.
Front St.
Jones Falls Expwy.
Low St.
Fallsway
Market Pl.
Frederick St.
Gay Street
Commerce St.
South St.
Davis St.
Water St.
Lexington St.
Saint Paul St.
N. Charles St.
Saratoga St.
Josephine St.
Liberty Street
Howard St.
Lexington St.
Marion St.
Fayette St.
Paca St.
Eutaw St.
Baltimore St.
Redwood St.
Lombard St.
Pratt Street
Paca St.
Greene St.
Emory St.
Penn St.
Light St.
Calvert St.
S. Charles St.
Conway St.
Barre St.
Welcome St.
Sharp St.
Camden St.
Howard St.
President St.
Eastern Ave.
Lee St.
Washington Blvd.

Inner Harbor
Patapsco R.

Museum of Mankind
Civil War Museum
City Life Museums
Star Spangled Banner Flag House and Museum
Museum of Public Works
Pier Six Concert Pavilion
Columbus Center for Marine Biology
Maritime Museum
National Aquarium
Holocaust Memorial
City Hall
World Trade Center, Top of the World
Harborplace
Clipper City
Jewish Historical Society
CHARLES CENTER
Convention Center
Baltimore Arena
LEXINGTON MARKET
Edgar Allan Poe Grave
UNIVERSITY OF MARYLAND AT BALTIMORE
Babe Ruth Birthplace/ Baltimore Orioles Museum
Camden Station
Oriole Park at Camden Yards

TO EDGAR ALLAN POE HOUSE
TO MARYLAND SCIENCE CENTER (1bik)
TO B&O RAILROAD MUSEUM

N

0    200 meters
0    200 yards

**Mugavero's Confectionery,** 300 S. Exeter St. (539-9798), at Fawn St. Menu-less deli, open for 53 years. Patrons invent their own sandwiches or entrust their sandwich to the owner-operator's creative imagination ($4). Cash only. Open daily 10am-9 or 10pm.

**One World Cafe,** 904 S. Charles St. (234-0235). Local art and creative coffee concoctions draw all types to this funky cafe. A vegetarian's delight, the bean burrito ($5.25) is a hit. Open M 7am-10pm, Tu-F 7am-11pm, Sa 8am-11pm, Su 8am-10pm.

## 👁 SIGHTS

Baltimore's gray harbor ends with a colorful bang in a 5 sq. block body of water bounded on three sides by an aquarium, shopping malls, a science museum, and a bevy of boardable ships. The nation's first pier-pavilion, the **Harborplace** mall is Baltimore's most imitated building. Crowds flock to Harborplace's Pratt St. and Light St. Pavilions, and to the Gallery across the street for a little wharf-side shopping and air-conditioned bliss. *(332-4191. Open M-Sa 10am-9pm, Su 10am-6pm.)*

The **National Aquarium** makes the Inner Harbor worthwhile. Multi-level exhibits and tanks show off rare fish, big fish, red fish, and blue fish along with the biology and ecology of oceans, rivers, and rainforests. The Children's Cove (level 4) lets visitors handle inter-tidal marine animals. *(Pier 3, 501 E. Pratt St. 576-3800. Entrance times July-Aug. daily 9am-8pm; Mar.-June and Sept.-Oct. Sa-Th 9am-4:30pm, F 9am-8pm; Nov.-Feb. Sa-Th 10am-5pm, F 10am-8pm. Aquarium remains open 2hr. after last entrance time. $14, seniors $10.50, children $7.50, under 3 free.)*

Several ships bob in the harbor by the aquarium; most belong to the **Baltimore Maritime Museum,** at Piers 3 and 4. Visitors may board the *U.S.S. Torsk* submarine (which sank the last WWII Japanese combatant ships), the lightship *Chesapeake,* and the Coast Guard cutter *Roger B. Taney. (396-3453.)* At the Inner Harbor's far edge, the kid-oriented **Maryland Science Center** stuns audiences with its 5-story IMAX screen, 38-speaker sound system, and 50 ft. planetarium. *(601 Light St. 685-5225. Open June-Aug. M-Th 9:30am-6pm, F-Su 10am-8pm; Sept.-May M-F 10am-5pm, Sa-Su 10am-6pm. $10; ages 13-17, seniors, and military $8; 4-12 $7; under 4 free.)* **Fort McHenry National Monument,** at the foot of E. Fort Ave. off Rt. 2 (Hanover St.) and Lawrence Ave., commemorates the fort's victory against British forces in the War of 1812; the battle inspired F. Scott Key's *The Star-Spangled Banner. (962-4290. Take bus #1. Open daily June-Aug. 8am-8pm; Sept.-May 8am-5pm. $5, seniors and under 16 free.)*

The **Walters Art Gallery,** keeps one of the largest private art collections in the world, spanning 5 millenia. The museum's most esteemed possession is the Ancient Art collection, with sculptures and metalwork from Egypt, Greece, and Rome. *(600 N. Charles St. at Centre St. 547-9000. Tours W noon and Su 1:30pm. Open Tu-F 10am-4pm, Sa-Su 11am-5pm. $5, students with ID and seniors $3, 6-17 $1, under 18 free Sa before noon.)* The **Baltimore Museum of Art,** exhibits a fine collection of Americana and modern art. The museum's two 20th-century **sculpture gardens** make wonderful picnic grounds. *(10 Art Museum Dr. at N. Charles and 31st St. 396-7100. Open W-F 11am-5pm, Sa-Su 11am-6pm. $6, students and seniors $4, under 18 free; Th free.)*

**The Baltimore Zoo,** off I-83 (exit 7), offers a new Chimpanzee Forest exhibit, the spectacular Palm Tree Conservatory, a lake surrounded by lush greenery, and a simulated savanna with elephants and Siberian tigers. *(396-7102. Open M-F 10am-4pm, Sa-Su 10am-5:30pm; in winter closes daily 4pm. $9, seniors and ages 2-16 $5.50.)*

Once a station for the Baltimore & Ohio Railroad, the **B&O Railroad Museum** now parks dining cars, Pullman sleepers, and mail cars. The Roundhouse contains historic trains. *(901 W. Pratt St. 752-2490. Take bus #31. Open daily 10am-5pm. $6.50, seniors $5.50, ages 3-12 $4, under 3 free.)*

Baltimore is home to the **Babe Ruth Birthplace and Baltimore Orioles Museum,** off the 600 block of W. Pratt. *(216 Emory St. 727-1539. Take bus #31. Open daily Apr.-Oct. 10am-5pm, on game nights until 7pm; Nov.-Mar. 10am-4pm. $6, seniors $4, ages 5-16 $3, under 5 free.)* The intimate, vintage-style **Oriole Park at Camden Yards,** just west of the Inner Harbor at Eutaw and Camden St., is home to baseball's Orioles. *(547-6234. Tours every hr. M-F 11am-2pm, every 30min. Sa 10:30am-2pm and Su 12:30-2pm. $5, seniors and children $4.)* The NFL **Ravens** play in **Raven Stadium,** adjacent to Camden Yards.

**STRANGERS IN THE NIGHT** Edgar Allan Poe was buried in someone else's clothes at the tiny **Westminster Churchyard** at Fayette and Greene St. (706-7228). Since 1949, on the eve of Poe's birthday, a dark stranger creeps to Poe's grave and performs a silent memorial service, leaving three roses and a half-empty bottle of cognac for the master of horror's spirit. In 1993, a note accompanied the eerie gifts with only the words "The torch will be passed" scrawled on the paper. Three different visitors have taken up that torch since 1993. A group of onlookers is handpicked from masses of requests to observe the mysterious man in action, never daring to question the identity of Poe's earthly friend.

## ♫ ENTERTAINMENT AND NIGHTLIFE

The **Showcase of Nations Ethnic Festivals** celebrates Baltimore's ethnic neighborhoods with a different culture featured each week (June-Sept.). The festivals take place all over the city; call the **Baltimore Visitors Bureau** (800-282-6632) for info. The **Pier 6 Concert Pavilion** (625-3100), at Pier 6 at the Inner Harbor, presents big-name music several times a week May-Oct. Tickets ($15-30) are available at the pavilion or through Ticketmaster (625-1400). Pier 5, near Harborplace, affords free eavesdropping. **Jazzline** (466-0600) lists jazz shows from Sept. to May. The **Theater Project**, 45 W. Preston St. near Maryland St., experiments with theater, poetry, music, and dance. (752-8558. Shows W-Sa 8pm, Su 3pm. $8-14. Box office open 1hr. before showtime; call to charge tickets.)

🍸 **Cat's Eye Pub,** 1730 Thames St. (276-9866), in Fells Point. An older crowd of regulars pack in every weeknight for live blues, jazz, folk, or traditional Irish music (M-Th 9pm, F-Sa 4pm). Live blues Su 4-8pm. Occasional cover. Over 85 beers. Hearty, inexpensive sandwiches ($2.50-6) served F-Su. Happy Hour M-F 4-7pm. Open daily noon-2am.

**Fletcher's,** 701 S. Bond St. (558-1889), at the intersection of Bond St. and Alceanna St. Hidden from the tourist and collegiate type, this laid-back scene thrives on a stacked jukebox, pool and foosball (50¢), and friendly bartenders. Specials nightly. 18+ concert venue upstairs (cover $6). Open daily 11am-2am.

**Baltimore Brewing Co.,** 104 Albermarle St. (837-5000), west of the Inner Harbor on the outskirts of Little Italy. Brewmaster Theo de Groen captured the city's hearts and livers with his distinctive lagers. Call in advance for tours (daily 1:30pm). Happy Hour (daily 4-7pm) offers $2 ½-liters. Open M-Th 4pm-midnight, F-Sa 11:30am-1am, Su 2-10pm.

## ANNAPOLIS

One of the premier yachting communities in the U.S., Annapolis walks the fine line between nostalgic port town and dockside cliché. Annapolis made history when the Treaty of Paris was ratified here in 1784, officially ending the American Revolution. After its 1783-1784 stint as capital of the U.S., Annapolis relinquished the limelight in favor of a more tranquil existence. The historic waterfront district retains its 18th-century appeal despite the presence of ritzy boutiques and pricey retail stores. Crew-cut "middies" (a nickname for Naval Academy students, or "midshipmen") mingle with longer-haired students from St. John's and couples vacationing among the highest concentration of historic homes in America.

The Corinthian-columned **State House** offers maps and houses the state legislature. The Treaty of Paris was signed here on Jan. 14, 1784. (974-3400. Open daily 9am-5pm. Free tours 11am and 3pm.) Restaurants and tacky tourist shops line the waterfront at **City Dock,** where middies and yachtsmen ply the waters. Main St., full of tiny shops and eateries, stretches from the dock up to Church Circle. The **Banneker-Douglass Museum,** 84 Franklin St., outlines African-American cultural history (974-2893; open Tu-F 10am-3pm, Sa noon-4pm; free). The **U.S. Naval Academy** holds its fort at the end of King George St. Tours begin at the **Armel-Leftwich Visitors Center,** inside the gates on King George St. (263-6933; $5.50, students $4.50, seniors $3.50).

The best place to find cheap eats is the **Market House** food court at the center of City Dock, where a hearty meal is under $5. **Chick & Ruth's Delly,** 165 Main St., about a block from City Dock towards the State House, has served Annapolis 24hr. breakfast for over 30 years (269-6737). **Moon Café,** 137 Prince George St., a block up East St. from the Naval Academy, is the only place in Annapolis to find coffee creations, healthy meals, and a Eurocafe atmosphere under the same roof (280-1956; open M-F 11am-midnight, Sa-Su 9am-midnight). There are generally 2 night-time activities in town: wandering along City Dock or schmoozing 'n' boozing at upscale pubs. **McGarvey's,** 8 Market Space, is a traditional dark-wood saloon (263-5700; open M-Sa 11:30am-2am, Su 10am-2am). Theater-goers can check out **The Colonial Players, Inc.,** 108 East St. (268-7373; performances Th-Su 8pm, additional Su show 2:30pm; F-Sa $10, Th and Su $7; students and seniors $5).

Annapolis lies southeast of U.S. 50 (also known as U.S. 301), 30mi. east of D.C. and 30mi. south of Baltimore. From D.C. take U.S. 50 east, which begins at New York Ave. and can be accessed from the Beltway. From Baltimore, follow Rt. 2 S to U.S. 50 W, cross the Severn River Bridge, then take Rowe Blvd. The city extends south and east from two landmarks: **Church Circle** and **State Circle.** School St., in a blatantly unconstitutional move, connects Church and State. East St. runs from the State House to the **Naval Academy.** Main St. (where food and entertainment congregate) starts at Church Circle and ends at the docks. **Greyhound/Trailways** buses stop at the football field parking lot at Rowe Blvd. and Taylor St. Tickets are available from the bus driver (cash only); buses run to Washington, D.C. (1hr., 1 per day, $10) and other nearby cities. **Annapolis and Anne Arundel County Conference & Visitors Bureau:** 26 West St. (280-0445; open daily 9am-5pm). **Area code:** 410.

## ASSATEAGUE ISLAND

Local legend has it that horses first came to Assateague Island by swimming ashore from a sinking Spanish galleon—a story so captivating that it became the premise of the children's classic *Misty of Chincoteague.* A less romantic and more likely theory is that miserly colonial farmers grazed their horses on Assateague to avoid taxes. Whatever their origins, the famous wild ponies now roam free across the unspoiled beaches and forests of the picturesque island.

Maryland and Virginia share Assateague Island, which can be divided into three distinct parts. **Assateague State Park,** Rt. 611 in southeast Maryland, is a 2mi. stretch of picnic areas, beaches, bathhouses, and campsites. (410-641-2120. Park open Apr.-Oct. daily 8am-sunset. $2 per person for day use, seniors free. Campsite registration daily 9am-10pm. 2-night min. on weekends. Sites $20, with hookup $30.) **Assateague Island National Seashore** claims most of the long sandbar north and south of the park and has its own campground and beaches, most of which are inaccessible by car. Two meandering, 1mi. nature trails give visitors a closer look at the island's flora and fauna: the **Forest Trail** offers the best viewing tower, but the **Marsh Trail** (ironically) has fewer mosquitoes. The **ranger station** (410-641-3030) distributes $5 backcountry camping permits from noon until 5pm; they go quickly, so arrive early. **Barrier Island Visitors Center:** Rt. 611, (410-641-1441; open daily 9am-5pm).

The **Chincoteague National Wildlife Refuge** stretches across the Virginia side of the island. Avid bird-watchers flock here to see rare species such as peregrine falcons, snowy egrets, and black-crowned night herons. The wild pony roundup, held the last consecutive W and Th in July, attracts hordes of tourists. During slack tide, local firemen herd the ponies together and swim from Assateague to Chincoteague Is., where the fire department auctions off the foals the following day. The adults swim back to Assateague and reproduce, providing next year's crop. Ponies can be seen almost every day along the refuge's trails, especially the **Wildlife Loop Road** (open 5am-10pm; for cars 3pm-sunset), which begins at the **Chincoteague Refuge Visitor Contact Station** (804-336-6122; open daily 9am-4pm; admission $5 per car). The **Piney Island Country Store,** 7085 Maddox Blvd. (336-6212), right outside the park entrance, rents bicycles for island rides.

The best way to get to Assateague Island is by car. **Greyhound** runs to Ocean City via Baltimore ($25) or Washington, D.C. ($39-44). From Ocean City, take a taxi to the island (289-1313; about $30). **Trailways** runs buses from Salisbury, MD ($8) and Norfolk, VA ($42), stopping on U.S. 13 at T's Corner store (757-824-5935), 11mi. from Chincoteague. **Chincoteague Chamber of Commerce,** 6733 Maddox Blvd. (757-336-6161; P.O. Box 258, Chincoteague, VA 23336), is open to drop-in visitors. (Open in summer M-Sa 9am-4:30pm, Su 12:30-4:30pm; off-season M-Sa 9am-4:30pm).

## OCEAN CITY

Ocean City is a lot like a kiddie pool—it's shallow and plastic, but it can be a lot of fun if you're the right age. This 10mi. strip of land packs endless bars, all-you-can-eat buffets, hotels, mini-golf courses, boardwalks, and flashing lights into a thin region between the Atlantic Ocean and the Assawoman Bay. Tourism is the town's only industry; in season the population swells from 5000 to 300,000, with a large migratory population of "June bugs," high school seniors that descend in swarms during the week after graduation to celebrate (read: to drink beer). July and Aug. cater more to families and singles looking for fun in the sun.

The **Whispering Sands,** 15 45th St., rents out well-worn rooms with kitchen access, available on a daily or a full-summer basis, to a mostly European crowd in a location convenient to nightlife. (723-1874; Nov.-Apr. 202-362-3453 or 954-761-9008. No A/C. Open May-Oct. Rooms $15.) For a wilder experience with an impersonal flare, **Summer Place Youth Hostel,** 104 Dorchester St., in the south end of town, functions mostly as a summer boarding house, but a few rooms are kept for short-term visitors. Private rooms and dorm rooms have access to kitchen, TV, living room, deck, hammock, and grill. (289-4542. Beds $25. Open Apr.-Oct. Reservations necessary.) The **Cabana Motel,** 1900 Coastal Hwy., a.k.a. Philadelphia Ave., has small, comfortable rooms with A/C, TV, and a pool (289-9131; singles and doubles $50-80). The serene **Atlantic House B&B,** 501 N. Baltimore Ave., includes breakfast (289-2333; $50-125). **Ocean City Travel Park,** 105 70th St., runs the only in-town campground (524-7601; tents $25-38; RVs $25-53).

Besides the beach, food is Ocean City's prime attraction. With surprisingly fresh food and a friendly atmosphere, **The Embers,** 24th St. and Coastal Hwy., flaunts the biggest seafood buffet in town. (888-436-2377 or 289-3322. $23, $2 off before 5pm; open daily July-Aug. 2-10pm; Sept.-June 3-9pm.) **Fat Daddy's Sub Shop,** 216 S. Baltimore Ave., around the corner from the hostel, offers deli sandwiches ($2-4.50) and subs ($4-6) on the beach until the early morning (289-4040; open daily 11am-4am). Funky blue couches fill **Common Grounds Cafe,** 5 S. Baltimore St., near the hostel. Sandwiches on home-baked bread ($4-6.50) like the Avocado Melt ($4.75) can be accompanied with a fortified "smart drink" ($4; 289-5252; open M-F 10am, Sa-Su 7am; closing hrs. vary daily). Breakfast is the best meal of the day at the **Brass Balls Saloon,** between 11th and 12th St. on the boardwalk, with oreo waffles ($4.75) and light, fluffy omelettes ($4.25-5.25; 289-0069; open daily 8:30am-2am).

Ocean City's star attraction is its beautiful **beach.** The wide stretch of surf and sand runs the entire 10mi. length of town. (Open daily 6am-10pm. Free.) An amusement park for adults, the island oasis **Seacrets,** on 49th St., features 11 bars, including two floating bars on the bay. Barefoot barflies wander from bar to bar to the strains of three live bands nightly. A magnificent sunset view ushers in the early revelers. (524-4900. Cover $3-5. Open M-Sa 11am-2am, Su noon-2am.) Upstairs from the Common Grounds Cafe (see above), at the **Skylab,** 5 S. Baltimore St., DJs spin for all ages (open daily 10pm-4am). The elder statesman of the bayside clubs, **Fager's Island,** 60th St. in the bay, attracts hordes across a gangway to its island location (524-5500; cover $10; open daily 11am-2am).

Ocean City runs north-south, with numbered streets linking the ocean to the bay. Most hotels are in the lower numbered streets toward the ocean; most clubs and bars are uptown toward the bay. **Trailways** (289-9307), at 2nd St. and Philadelphia Ave., sends **buses** to Baltimore (3½hr., 7 per day, $25) and Washington, D.C. (4-6hr.; $39-44; June-Aug. daily 7-8am and 10am-5pm, Sept.-May 10am-3pm). In town, **public buses** (723-1607) run the length of the strip 24hr. ($1 per day for unlimited rides). **Ocean City Visitors Center:** 4001 Coastal Hwy. (800-626-2326), at 40th St.

in the Convention Center (open June-Aug. M-W 8:30am-5pm, Th-Sa 8:30am-8pm; Sept.-May daily 8:30am-5pm). **Internet access: Bite Size,** 4100 Coastal Hwy. (723-2702; $5 per 30min.; open M-Sa 9am-8pm). **Area code:** 410.

# WASHINGTON, D.C.

Like many a young adult fresh out of college, the fledgling United States government quickly realized that independence meant little without a place to stay. Both Northern and Southern states wanted the capital on their turf. The final location—100 sq. mi. pinched from Virginia and Maryland—was a compromise, an undeveloped swamp wedged between north and south. Congress commissioned French engineer Pierre L'Enfant to design the city.

Washington's wide avenues remained mostly empty, with a smattering of slave markets and boarding houses the only companions for the elegant government buildings. The city had hardly begun to expand when the British torched it in 1814; a post-war vote to give up and move the capital failed in Congress by just eight votes. Washington continued to disgust foreign diplomats—the district was a first stop for slave traders, whose shackled cargo awaited sales on the Mall and near the White House. The cessation of the slave trade after the Civil War transformed Washington from the Union's embarrassing appendage to its jugular vein.

The discrete cities of Federal Washington and local Washington coexist in the District. Federal Washington, the town of press conferences, power lunches, and presidential intrigue, is what most visitors come to see. The other part of Washington, the "second city," consists of a variety of communities, some prosperous, others overcome by poverty, drugs, and crime. These areas, sometimes within a few blocks of the seats of government, surprise many tourists with the troubling paradoxes of American democracy.

For everything about Washington D.C. you always wanted to know but were afraid to ask, check out *Let's Go: Washington, D.C. 2000,* available at fine bookstores.

## ✦ ORIENTATION

The city is roughly diamond-shaped, with the four tips of the diamond pointed in the four compass directions. The street names and addresses split into 4 quadrants: NW, NE, SE, and SW, defined by their relation to the **Capitol.** The names of the four quadrants distinguish otherwise identical addresses. The quadrants are separated by **N. Capitol St., E. Capitol St.,** and **S. Capitol St.** The Mall, stretching west from the Capitol, precludes the existence of a "W. Capitol St." South of the Mall, **Independence Ave.** runs east-west; to the north, **Constitution Ave.** runs east-west.

**Capitol Hill** extends east from the Capitol; North of the Mall, **Old Downtown** (sometimes called "Penn Quarter") is accompanied by both **Foggy Bottom** (sometimes called the "West End") and **Farragut,** around K St., west of 15th St. NW. **Georgetown** centers at Wisconsin and M St. NW. **Dupont Circle,** east of 16th St., morphs into struggling **Logan Circle,** then to the clubby **Shaw/U District.** A strong Hispanic community resides in **Adams-Morgan,** north of Dupont and east of **Rock Creek Park,** Washington's lush and tranquil answer to New York's Central Park. **Upper Northwest** stretches west of the park. Across the Anacostia River, the **Southeast** (including **Anacostia**), is isolated by poverty and crime.

The basic street plan is a rectilinear grid. Streets running from east to west are named in alphabetical order depending on how many blocks they lie from the north-south dividing line that runs through the Capitol (thus, there are 2 A Streets 2 blocks apart). There is no A or B St. in NW and SW, and no J St. anywhere. Streets running north-south get numbers (1st St., 2nd St., etc.). Numbered and lettered streets sometimes disappear for a block. Addresses on lettered streets indicate the numbered cross street (1100 D St. SE will be between 11th and 12th St.). State-named avenues radiate outward from the U.S. Capitol and the White House.

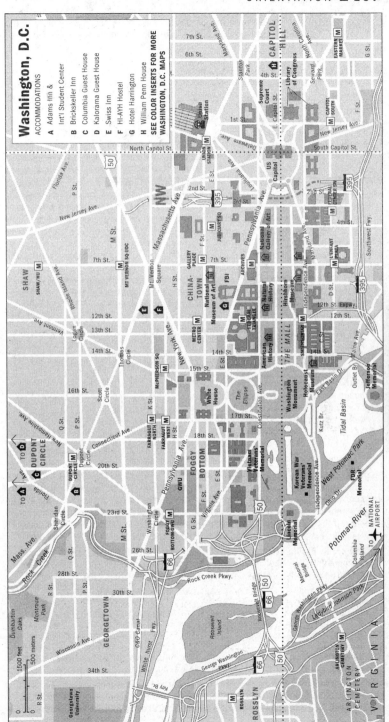

## Washington, D.C.

**ACCOMMODATIONS**

A Adams Inn &
  Int'l Student Center
B Brickskeller Inn
C Columbia Guest House
D Kalorama Guest House
E Swiss Inn
F HI-AYH Hostel
G Hotel Harrington
H William Penn House

**SEE COLOR INSERTS FOR MORE WASHINGTON, D.C. MAPS**

MID-ATLANTIC

Major roads include **Pennsylvania Ave.**, which runs SE-NE from Anacostia through Capitol Hill, past the White House, finally ending at 28th and M St. NW in Georgetown; **Connecticut Ave.**, which runs N-NE from the White House through Dupont Circle and past the zoo; **Wisconsin Ave.**, north from Georgetown past the Cathedral to Friendship Heights; **16th St. NW,** from the White House north through Adams-Morgan and Mt. Pleasant; **K St. NW,** a major downtown artery; **Massachusetts Ave.**, reaching from American University through Dupont Circle to Capitol Hill; **New York Ave.**, running NE from the White House; and high-speed **North Capitol St.**

Washington, D.C. is ringed by the **Capital Beltway/I-495** (except where it's part of I-95); the Beltway is bisected by **U.S. 1**, and meets **I-395** from Virginia. The high-speed **Baltimore-Washington Pkwy.** connects Washington, D.C. to Baltimore. **I-595** trickles off the Capital Beltway east to Annapolis. **I-66** heads west into Virginia.

# ◪ PRACTICAL INFORMATION

**Airports: Ronald Reagan National Airport** (703-417-8000). Metro: National Airport. It's best to fly here from within the U.S.; National is on the Metro and closer to the city. Taxi $10-15 from downtown. The **SuperShuttle** (800-258-3826) runs between National and downtown every 30min. M-F. **Dulles International Airport** (703-369-1600) is much farther from the city. Taxis cost $40 and up from downtown. The **Washington Flyer Dulles Express Bus** (888-927-4359) hits the West Falls Church Metro every 30min. 6-10am and 6-10:30pm, every 20min. from 10am-2pm, every 15min. from 2-6pm ($8). Buses to downtown (15th and K St. NW) take about 45min. and leave M-F every 30min. 5:20am-10:20pm; Sa-Su every hr. 5:20am-12:20pm, every 30min. 12:50-10:20pm ($16, family rate for groups of 3 or more $13 each).

**Trains:** Union Station, 50 Massachusetts Ave. NE (484-7540). **Amtrak** to: New York (3½hr., $64-70); Baltimore (40min., $19-28); Philadelphia (2hr., $37-84); and Boston (8½hr., $65-70). Maryland's commuter train, **MARC** (410-859-7400, 24hr.), departs from Union to Baltimore ($5.75, round-trip $10.25) and the 'burbs.

**Public Transit: Metrorail and Metrobus (METRO),** 600 5th St. NW (info line 637-7000; staffed M-F 8:30am-4pm), is relatively safe. $1.10-3.25, depending on time and distance traveled. 1-day Metro pass $5. **Flash Pass** allows unlimited bus (and sometimes Metro) rides for 2 wk. Trains run M-F 5:30am-midnight, Sa-Su 8am-midnight. For bus transfers, get a pass from machines on the platform *before* boarding the train. The reliable **Metrobus** system serves Georgetown, downtown, and the suburbs. $1.10.

**Taxis: Yellow Cab,** 544-1212.

**Car Rental: Bargain Buggies Rent-a-Car,** 3140 N. Washington Blvd. (703-841-0000), in Arlington, rents for $23 per day, $150 per week; plus 20¢ per mi. (100 free mi. per day). Must be 18, with major credit card or cash deposit of $250 (may be negotiable). Those under 21 need full insurance coverage of their own (may be negotiable). Open M-F 8am-7pm, Sa 9am-3pm, Su 9am-noon. **Budget** (800-527-0700), at Union Station and downtown, rents to ages 21-24 for a $5 surcharge per day.

**Bike Rental: Big Wheel Bikes,** 315 7th St. SE (543-1600). Metro: Eastern Market. Mountain bikes for $5 per hr. (min. 3hr.), $25 per business day. $32 per 24hr. Major credit card required for deposit. Open Tu-F 11am-7pm, Sa 10am-6pm, Su noon-5pm.

**Visitor Info: Washington, D.C. Convention and Visitors Association (WCVA),** 1212 New York Ave., #600 NW (789-7000; www.washington.org). Open M-F 9am-5pm. **D.C. Committee to Promote Washington,** 1212 New York Ave. NW, #200 (347-2873 or 800-422-8644). **Meridian International Center,** 1630 Crescent Pl. NW (667-6800). Metro: Dupont Circle. Brochures in a variety of languages. Office open M-F 9am-5pm.

**Hotlines: Rape Crisis Center,** 333-7273. **Gay and Lesbian Hotline,** 833-3234. Operates 7pm-11pm. **Traveler's Aid Society,** 546-3120. Offices at Union Station, National and Dulles Airports, and downtown at 512 C St. NE. Open M-F 9am-5pm.

**Post Office:** 900 Brentwood Rd. NE (636-1532). Indescribably inconvenient location. Open M-F 8am-8pm, Sa 8am-6pm, Su noon-6pm. **ZIP code:** 20066. **Area code:** 202.

# █ ACCOMMODATIONS

Business hotels discount deeply and swell with tourists on summer weekends. Hostels, guest houses, and university dorms are also packed; make reservations. The *New York Times* Sunday Travel section has plenty of summer weekend deals. **B&B Accommodations, Ltd.,** P.O. Box 12011, 20005 (328-3510, 24hr. voice mail), reserves rooms in private homes. ($65-120, lower in summer. $15 per additional person. Open M-F 10am-5pm.) D.C. adds a 13% occupancy surcharge and another $1.50 per room per night to your bill. Damn feds.

**Washington International Hostel (HI-AYH),** 1009 11 St. NW 20001 (783-3262), 3 blocks north of the Metro. Metro: Metro Center (11 St. exit). Bright, spacious hostel that caters to traveler's needs. Rooms with 8 or 12 beds, shared baths. Free activities every day, common room, kitchen, game room, small store/cafe, lockers, internet access, laundry facilities, luggage and bicycle storage. Reception 24hr. Check-in after noon. Check-out 11am. Wheelchair access (give advance notice). Use caution in this area at night. $23, members $20; private room with 4 beds $80.

**Washington International Student Center,** 2451 18th St. NW (800-567-4150 or 667-7681). Metro: Woodley Park-Zoo and a 15min. walk. Tidy hostel run by experienced, friendly staff. A/C with 3-4 bunkbeds per room. 2 kitchens and 3 shared bathrooms. Common room. Bunks $16. Bikes $7 per day. Internet access $2 per 10min. No lockout. Breakfast included. Lockers. Call for free pick-up from bus or train station.

**Kalorama Guest House at Woodley Park,** 2700 Cathedral Ave. NW (328-0860), and at **Kalorama Park,** 1854 Mintwood Pl. NW (667-6369). Metro: Woodley Park-Zoo for both. Guest houses with Victorian charm. Clean, quiet rooms with A/C. Laundry. Continental breakfast. No children under 6. Limited parking by reservation. Reception M-F 8am-8pm, Sa-Su 9am-7pm. Rooms with shared bath $45-65 for 1; for 2 $50-70; with private baths $60-100 for 1; $65-105 for 2.

**Brickskeller Inn,** 1523 22nd St. NW (293-1885), between P and Q St. A basic, respectable, and reasonably priced hotel for the location. Rooms are clean and functional with simple furnishings and shag carpet. Pricier rooms have A/C, TV, private sinks, and/or private baths. Laundry facilities. Bar downstairs. Singles $41-65; doubles $66-87.

**Hotel Harrington** (628-8140 or 800-424-8532), 11th and E St. NW, 3 blocks from the Smithsonian. Metro: Metro Center or Federal Triangle. Shows its age but offers clean rooms, a great location, and reasonable rates for an international clientele. Cable TV, A/C, and laundromat. Singles $59-75; doubles $69-84. Discounts for students, AAA.

**William Penn House,** 515 E. Capitol St. (543-5560), 5 blocks from Capitol. Metro: Eastern Market. Shared rooms in a dorm-style guest house board 3-7 people. Optional Quaker worship in mornings. No TV, limited A/C. $35 per night. Continental breakfast included. Reception 9am-9pm. $5 key deposit.

**Swiss Inn,** 1204 Massachusetts Ave. NW (371-1816 or 800-955-7947), 4 blocks from Metro Center. More like a guest house than a hotel. Clean, quiet studio apartments with private baths, high ceilings, kitchenettes, A/C, and TV. French- and German-speaking managers. All rooms $78-108 in summer; off-season visitors 35% off. Occasional 20% discounts for seniors, *Let's Go* readers, and HI-AYH members.

**The Columbia Guest House,** 2005 Columbia Rd. NW (265-4006), just off Connecticut Ave. in Dupont Circle. Patrician townhouse with dark wood paneling, polished hardwood floors, ornate fireplaces, and neat rooms. Singles $29-33; doubles $36-59; triples $46-69 (some A/C, some shared baths). $10 per extra person. Students 10-15% discount.

**Adams Inn,** 1744 Lanier Pl. NW (745-3600 or 800-578-6807), behind the Columbia Rd. Safeway supermarket, 2 blocks north of the center of Adams-Morgan. 3 elegant townhouses with an outdoor patio and garden, a dining room with kitchenette, free doughnuts, cable TV, pay phones, and coin laundry facilities. All rooms have A/C, private sinks and unique furnishings. Continental breakfast included. Reception M-Sa 8am-9pm, Su 1-9pm. Singles $50, with private bath $65. Each additional person $10. ISIC 10% discount. Limited special weekly rates.

**Greenbelt Park,** 6565 Greenbelt Rd. (301-344-3948, for reservations Apr.-Nov. 800-365-2267). 12mi. from D.C. Take the Baltimore-Washington Pkwy. to Greenbelt Rd. Cheapest and nicest place to camp in the D.C. area, courtesy of National Park Service. 174 very quiet, wooded sites for tents, trailers, and campers. No electricity. Bathrooms and showers. Sites $13, seniors with Golden Age Pass $6.50. 14-night max. stay.

# ⬮ FOOD

First-timers in D.C. might think that all the good eats are only within the reach of the power-hungry. Fortunately for the budget traveler, this is deliciously untrue. **Adams-Morgan** and **Dupont Circle** are home to many particularly good restaurants.

## ADAMS-MORGAN

🍴 **Meskerem,** 2434 18th St. NW (462-4100), near Columbia Rd. Named after the Ethiopian month marking spring. The *Acha Della Messob Meskerem* is an education in Ethiopian food: spicy beef, chicken and/or lamb served with paper-thin *injera* bread. Lunch $5-10, dinner entrees $7-11. Free delivery (min. order $12). Open daily noon-midnight.

**Mixtec,** 1792 Columbia Rd. NW (332-1011), near 18th St. Paper lanterns and colorfully hand-painted chairs add flair. A solid congregation of neighborhood regulars. Mexican specialties include 2 tacos al carbon ($7), *camarones vallarta* (shrimp in green tomatillo sauce; $10). Few vegetarian options. Entrees $7-11; tacos and Mexican submarines $4-6. Open daily 11am-10pm.

**Perry's,** 1811 Columbia Rd. NW (234-6218), near 18th St. Progressives line up for an evening of funky *nouvelle* Japanese-American cuisine. Entrees $9-18; sushi 50¢-$5 per piece. The rooftop patio has superb views of the surrounding area ($12 min. per person for rooftop seats). Drag brunch (Su 11am-2:30pm). Open M-Sa 5:30pm-1:30am, Su 5:30-11:30pm; kitchen closes daily 10:15pm, sushi closes daily 11:15pm.

## ALEXANDRIA

**Lite 'n' Fair,** 1018 King St. (703-549-3717). Ki Choi, former executive chef of the ritzy Watergate Restaurant, runs this hidden gem. Exquisite seafood sandwiches and burgers $4-8. Daily specials have included escargots with mushrooms and herbs in garlic butter ($4). Carryout available. Open M 11am-3pm, Tu-Th 11am-9pm, F-Sa 11am-10pm.

## ARLINGTON

**Cafe Dalat,** 3143 Wilson Blvd. (703-276-0935). Metro: Clarendon. The first Vietnamese restaurant in the area continues to serve up premiere food. *Pho* (noodle soup) $4. Shrimp grilled on sugar cane and rolled with rice paper, clear vermicelli, cucumber, lettuce, and peanut sauce ($10). All-you-can-eat lunch M-F 11am-3pm $5. Dinner entrees $7-10. Large vegetarian menu. Open Su-Th 11am-9:30pm, F-Sa 11am-10:30pm.

## CAPITOL HILL

🍴 **Banana Cafe and Piano Bar,** 500 8th St. SE (543-5906). Metro: Eastern Market. Fake banana trees and tropical portraits accompanied by a garish yellow interior and Cuban music make for a crazy fiesta. Marvelous Tex-Mex and Cuban entrees ($7-14), various tapas ($3.25-9), and plantain soup ($4.50). "Mariachi Brunch" Su 11am-3pm ($13). Open M-Th 11:30am-10:30pm, F 11:30am-11pm, Sa noon-11pm, Su 11am-10pm.

**Il Radiccho,** 223 Pennsylvania Ave. (547-5114). Gratification here is an offer not to be refused. All-you-can-eat spaghetti starts at $6.50. Sauces from *pomodoro* ($1.50) to pesto *al genovese* (basil, garlic, olive oil, pine nuts and parmesan; $3.25). 25 pizzas ($8-18). Open M-Th 11:30am-10pm, F-Sa 11:30am-11pm, Su 5-10pm.

**The Market Lunch,** 225 7th St. SE (547-8444), in the Eastern Market complex. Metro: Eastern Market. Crab cakes ($6-10) and soft shell crab (sandwich $7, platter $12) are the specialties; the Blue Bucks (buckwheat blueberry pancakes $3.50) have people lined up in the morning. Open Tu-Sa 7:30am-3pm.

## CHINATOWN

**Szechuan Gallery,** 617 H St. NW (898-1180). A bit of the movie *True Lies* was filmed here. Stunning Taiwanese seafood dishes, including fragrant crab (whole crabs in spicy egg batter; $10). Lunch specials $5-8. Open Su-Th 11am-10pm, F-Sa 11am-11pm.

**Burma Restaurant,** upstairs at 740 6th St. NW (638-1280), between H and G St. Mild Burmese curries, unique spices, and a plethora of garnishes. *Pantay kauswe* (soft flour noodles fried with chicken, vegetables, and curry sauce; $7.50) is a traditional Burmese dish. Entrees $6-8. Open M-F 11am-3pm and 6-10:30pm daily.

## DUPONT CIRCLE

🔲 **Raku,** 1900 Q St. NW (265-7258, delivery 232-8646), off Connecticut Ave. Excellent pan-Asian noodles ($9-13), salad ($5-9), sushi ($4-12), and "pan-Asian tapas" (dumplings, rolls, and skewers $3-8). Open Su-Th 11:30am-10pm, F-Sa 11:30am-11pm.

**Luna Grill & Diner,** 1301 Connecticut Ave. NW (835-2280), south of Dupont Circle. Upscale diner food in a friendly, chic dining room. Salads, pastas, sandwiches ($5-8), and entrees ($8-15) are great in taste, generous in proportion, and modest in price. Open M-F 8am-11pm, Sa 10am-midnight, Su 10am-10pm.

**Lauriol Plaza,** 1801 18th St. NW (387-0035), near S St. Moving soon up the block to 18th & T St. NW. Authentic Latino food served in copious quantities. The complimentary chips and salsa are addictive. Rice and black beans included with entrees. Entrees $6.50-16. Su brunch entrees $6-9 (11am-3pm). Free parking. Open Su-Th 11am-11pm, F-Sa 11am-midnight.

**Pizzeria Paradiso,** 2029 P St. NW (223-1245), near 21st St. A modest awning hides an airy, light-filled restaurant. The brick oven bakes up genuinely Italian pizza: the crust is thin and crisp with a light coat of fresh mozzarella and tomato chunks. 8 in. $7-10; 12 in. $12-16. Toppings 75¢-$1.75. Open daily 11:30am-11pm.

**Xando,** 1350 Connecticut Ave. NW (296-9341), south of the Dupont Metro; 1647 Connecticut Ave. NW (332-6364), north of the Dupont Metro. These funky coffee bars have large comfy couches and plentiful chairs. A perfect place to relax and watch the crowds go by. Wraps and grilled "xandwiches" ($5-6). Open M-Th 6:30am-1am, F 6:30am-2am, Sa 7am-2am, Su 7am-1am.

## FARRAGUT

**The Art Gallery Grille,** 1712 I St. NW (298-6658), near 17th St. Metro: Farragut West. Perfect combination of old-style diner charm and sophisticated, healthy, Middle Eastern specialties. Falafel trays $8 per person. Large salads, sandwiches, and Middle Eastern specialties $3-13. Happy hour 5-7:30pm. Outdoor seating available. Open M-W 6:30am-10pm, Th-F 6:30am-2am.

**Casa Blanca,** 1014 Vermont Ave. NW (393-4430), between K and L St. Metro: McPherson Square. Casa Blanca has mastered homemade Peruvian, Salvadoran, and Mexican cuisine. Basic tacos are 2 for $3.50. Carry-out 50¢ less at lunch, $1 at dinner. Daily specials $4. Free delivery. Open M-Sa 9:30am-10pm, Su noon-5pm.

## GEORGETOWN

🔲 **Cafe La Ruche,** 1039 31st St. NW (965-2684, takeout 965-2591), near M St. The cafe has fab French fare, including soups ($4), salads ($3.50-8.25), quiche ($6.50), and entrees ($7-16). The desserts are heavenly reasons to live ($4-5). Open M-Th 11:30am-10:30pm, F 11:30am-11:30pm, Sa 10am-11:30pm, Su 10am-10:30pm.

**Il Radicchio,** 1211 Wisconsin Ave. NW (337-2627), the first block up from the intersection of Wisconsin and M St. Spectacular Italian fare. Pick-your-own-topping pastas ($7 per person and $1-4 for your choice of 20+ sauces), antipasti ($5-8), panini sandwiches ($6-8), and pizzas. Open Su-Th 11:30am-10pm, F-Sa 11:30am-11pm.

**Furin's,** 2805 M St. NW (965-1000). Old-fashioned hospitality and good home cooking. Tourists and locals flock for their made-with-love sandwiches, salads, and sweets. Breakfasts (served M-F until 11am, Sa 1:30pm) are $1.50-4 per item, specials $8. Desserts around $4. Open M-F 7:30am-7pm, Sa 8am-5pm.

## OLD DOWNTOWN

■ **Jaleo,** 480 7th St. NW (628-7949), 2 blocks from the Gallery Place-Chinatown Metro stop at 7th and E St. Entrees are pricey ($13-15.50), but over 35 *tapas* ($3-7) offer a less expensive way to enjoy Jaleo's tasty Spanish cuisine. Full bar includes Sangria. Sevillana dancers W 8:45pm. Su brunch 11:30am-3pm. Open Su-M 11:30am-10pm, Tu-Th 11:30am-11:30pm, F-Sa 11:30am-midnight.

**Ollie's Trolley,** 425 12th St. NW (347-6119), at the corner of 12th and E St. With aged leather booths and Louis Armstrong's raspy voice on the stereo, Ollie's offers fast food with character. Sandwiches include grilled chicken ($3.29), crabcakes ($4.69), and the 5.3-oz. Ollieburger ($3). Open M-F 10:30am-8pm, Sa-Su 11am-4pm.

## SHAW AND U. DISTRICT

■ **Ben's Chili Bowl,** 1213 U St. NW (667-0909), at 13th St. across from the Metro. Venerable neighborhood hangout and self-declared pope of Chilitown has excellent chili dogs ($2), chili burgers ($2.70), and plain chili (small $2.25, large $3). Open M-Th 6am-2am, F-Sa 6am-4am, Su noon-8pm. Breakfast M-Sa until 11am.

■ **Florida Avenue Grill,** 1100 Florida Ave. NW (265-1586), at 11th St. From the Metro, walk east on U St. to 11th St., then north up 11th St. to Florida Ave. Fantastic Southern food. Breakfast (served until 1pm) with salmon cakes or spicy half-smoked sausage and grits, apples, or biscuits ($2-7). Lunch specials $4 (Tu-F 11am-4pm). Entrees served with choice of 2 veggies ($6.50-10). Open Tu-Sa 6am-9pm.

**Outlaw's,** 917 U St. NW (387-3978), between Vermont Ave. and 9th St. Family-run establishment crowds in regulars for meat-laden home cooking. Daily specials include meat loaf, baked chicken, and Salisbury steak ($6-8). Dinners $5.55-8.25, sandwiches $3.85-5.50, fresh cobbler $2. Takeout available. Open M-F 11am-6pm.

## UPPER NORTHWEST

■ **Mama Maria and Enzio's,** 2313 Wisconsin Ave. NW (965-1337), near Calvert St. Amazing southern Italian cuisine served in a tiny dining room, in a casual atmosphere. Appetizers include *caprese* (tomato, fresh mozzarella with olive oil). Pastas are served with fresh sauces ($8-9). Open M-F 11:30am-10:30pm, Sa 5-11pm.

■ **Rocklands,** 2418 Wisconsin Ave. NW (333-2558). The sweet smell of barbecue emanates from Rocklands. Fresh meats and a great selection of hot sauces are the main ingredients. Quarter-rack of pork ribs $5, half chicken $5. Sandwiches $4-5, salads $1.30. Open M-Sa 11:30am-10pm, Su 11am-9pm.

**The Lebanese Taverna,** 2641 Connecticut Ave. NW (265-8681). Mezza platter entrees ($13.50 and up) in this refined restaurant let you sample most of the menu. Sandwiches ($5.50-6) are cheaper. Open M-Th 11:30am-2:30pm and 5:30-10:30pm, F 11:30am-2:30pm and 5:30-11pm, Sa 11:30am-3pm and 5:30-11pm, Su 5-10pm.

# ◪ SIGHTS

**CAPITOL HILL.** The **U.S. Capitol** may be an endless font of cynicism, but it still evokes the power of the republic. The **East Front** faces the Supreme Court; from the times of frontiersman Andrew Jackson (1829) to peanut-farmin' Jimmy Carter (1977), most Presidents were inaugurated here; recent presidential inaugurations have taken place on the mall-facing West Front. The East Front entrance brings you into the 180 ft. high **rotunda,** where soldiers slept during the Civil War. From the lower-level crypt, visitors can climb to the 2nd fl. for a view of the House or Senate visitors chambers. Americans may obtain a free gallery pass from the office of their representative or senator in the House or Senate office buildings near the Capitol. Foreigners may get 1-day passes by presenting identification at the "appointments desks" in the crypt. *(225-6827. Metro: Capitol South. Open daily Mar.-Aug. 9am-8pm; Sept.-Feb. 9am-4:30pm. Tours Mar.-Aug. M-F 9am-7pm, Sa 9am-4pm; Sept.-Feb. M-Sa 9am-4pm. Free.)* The real business of Congress, however, is conducted in **committee hearings.** Most are open to the public; check the *Washington Post's* "Today in

Congress" box for times and locations. The free **Capitol subway** shuttles between the basement of the Capitol and the House and Senate office buildings; a buzzer and flashing red light signals an imminent vote.

In 1935, the justices of the **Supreme Court** decided it was time to take the nation's separation of powers literally, and moved from their makeshift offices in the Capitol into a new Greek Revival courthouse across the street. Oral arguments are open to the public; show up before 8:30am to be seated, or walk through the standing gallery to hear 5min. of the argument. *(Court is in session Oct.-June M-W 10am-3pm for 2 weeks every month.)* The courtroom itself is open when the Justices are on vacation. *(1 1st St. 479-3000. Court open M-F 9am-4:30pm. Free.)*

The **Library of Congress,** between East Capitol and Independence Ave., is the world's largest library, with 113,026,742 objects stored on 532mi. of shelves, including a copy of *Old King Cole* written on a grain of rice. The collection was torched by the British in 1814, and was restarted from Thomas Jefferson's personal collection. The collection is open to anyone of college age or older with a legitimate research purpose—exhibits of rare items and a tour of the facilities are available for tourists. *(1st St. SE. 707-5000.)* The **Jefferson Building**'s green copper dome and gold-leafed flame seals a spectacular octagonal reading room. *(Great Hall open M-Sa 8:30am-5:30pm. Visitors Center and galleries open 10am. Free.)* Next door, the **Folger Shakespeare Library** houses the world's largest collection of Shakespeareana with about 275,000 books and manuscripts. Alas, unless you're a graduate student with a legitimate research purpose, you can't see any of it. You can see the recreated Tudor gallery in the Great Hall, however. *(201 East Capitol St. SE. 544-4600 or 544-7077. Exhibits open M-Sa 10am-4pm. Garden tours Apr.-Oct. every 3rd Sa of each month.)*

Trains converge at **Union Station,** 2 blocks north of the Capitol. Colonnades, archways, and domed ceilings allude to imperial Rome, if Rome was filled with stores and a food court. *(50 Massachusetts Ave. NE. 371-9441. Metro: Union Station. Retail shops open M-Sa 10am-9pm, Su 10am-6pm.)* Directly west of Union Station is the **National Postal Museum,** 1st St. and Massachusetts Ave. NE, on the lower level of the City Post Office. *(357-2700. Metro: Union Station. Open daily 10am-5:30pm. Free.)* Northeast of Union Station is the red brick **Capital Children's Museum,** where you can brew your own hot chocolate, wander through a room-sized maze, and touch and feel almost all of the exhibits. *(800 3rd St. NE. 675-4120. Metro: Union Station. Open daily Easter to Labor Day 10am-6pm, Labor Day to Easter 10am-5pm.)*

**MUSEUMS ON THE MALL.** The **Smithsonian** is the catalogued attic of the United States, containing over 140 million objects. The Institute began as the brainchild of **James Smithson,** a British chemist who, though he never himself visited the U.S., left 105 bags of gold sovereigns—the bulk of his estate—to "found at Washington, under the name of the Smithsonian Institution, an establishment for the increase and diffusion of knowledge among men." The Smithsonian Museums on the Mall constitute the world's largest museum complex. The **Smithsonian Castle,** on the south side of the mall, has an introduction to and information on the Smithsonian buildings. *(357-2700. Metro: Smithsonian or Federal Triangle. All Smithsonian museums are free, wheelchair accessible, and open daily 10am-5:30pm, with extended summer hours determined annually. Write to Smithsonian Information, Smithsonian Institution, Room 153, MRC 010, Washington, D.C. 20560.)*

**National Air and Space Museum**, on the south side of the Mall across from the National Gallery, is the world's most popular museum, with 7.5 million visitors per year. Airplanes and space vehicles dangle from the ceilings; the Wright brothers' original biplane hangs in the entrance gallery. The space-age atrium holds a moon rock, worn smooth by tourists' fingertips. Walk through the Skylab space station, the Apollo XI command module, and a DC-7. IMAX movies on a 5-story screen thrill the endless throngs.

**National Museum of American History,** on the north side of the Mall, closest to the Washington Monument, houses several centuries' worth of machines, photographs, vehicles, harmonicas, and uncategorizable U.S. detritus. When the Smithsonian inherits quirky artifacts of popular history, like Dorothy's slippers from *The Wizard of Oz*, they end up here. Hands-on exhibits are geared toward children.

**Museum of Natural History,** east toward the Capitol from American History, ruminates on the earth and its life in 3 big, crowded floors of exhibits. Objects on display in the spectacular golden-domed, neoclassical buildings include dinosaur skeletons, the largest African elephant ever captured, and an insect zoo with live creepy-crawlies. Visitors still line up to see the cursed Hope Diamond, mailed to the Smithsonian in 1958 for $145.29 (insured up to $1 million).

**National Gallery of Art** (737-4215), east of Natural History, is not technically a part of the Smithsonian, but a close cousin of the Institute due to its location on the mall. The **West Wing** houses its pre-1900 art in a domed marble temple in the Western Tradition, including works by El Greco, Raphael, Rembrandt, Vermeer, and Monet. Leonardo da Vinci's earliest surviving portrait, Ginevra de' Benci, the only one of his works in the U.S., hangs among a fine collection of Italian Renaissance Art. The **East Building** houses the museum's 20th-century collection, including works by Picasso, Matisse, Mondrian, Miró, Magritte, Pollock, Warhol, Lichtenstein, and Rothko. The building also holds the museum's temporary exhibits. The National Gallery recently unveiled an outdoor **Sculpture Garden.** Open M-Sa 10am-5pm, Su 11am-6pm. Free.

**Hirshhorn Museum and Sculpture Garden,** on the south side of the mall west of Air and Space. The 4-story, slide-carousel-shaped brown building has outraged traditionalists since 1966. Each floor consists of 2 concentric circles: an outer ring of rooms with modern, postmodern, and post-postmodern paintings, and an inner corridor of sculptures. The museum claims a comprehensive set of 19th- and 20th-century Western sculpture.

**National Museum of African Art** and the **Arthur M. Sackler Gallery** hide together underground in the newest museum facility on the Mall, to the west of the Hirshhorn. The Museum of African Art displays artifacts from sub-Saharan Africa such as masks, textiles, ceremonial figures, and musical instruments. The Sackler Gallery showcases an extensive collection of art from China, South and Southeast Asia, and Persia. Exhibits include illuminated manuscripts, Chinese and Japanese painting, jade miniatures, and friezes from Egypt, Phoenicia, and Sumeria.

**Freer Gallery of Art,** just west of the Hirshhorn, displays American and Asian art. The static American collection consists of the holdings of Charles L. Freer, the museum's benefactor, and focuses on works by James McNeill Whistler. The strong Asian collections include bronzes, manuscripts, and jade.

**MONUMENTS.** All of the following monuments can be viewed 24hr. free of charge, except the **Washington Monument.** Currently undergoing a $9.4 million restoration project, this shrine to America's first president was once nicknamed the "the Beef Depot monument" after the cattle that grazed here during the Civil War. Construction was temporarily halted during the war and later resumed; the stone that was used came from a new quarry, explaining the different colors of the monument's stones. The **Reflecting Pool** mirrors Washington's obelisk. *(Metro: Smithsonian. Admission to the monument by timed ticket. Apr.-Aug. monument open daily 8am-midnight, ticket kiosk open from 7:30am until all tickets distributed; Sept.-Mar. monument open 9am-5pm, ticket kiosk from 8:30am. Free. No tickets needed after 8pm Apr.-Aug.)*

Maya Ying Lin, who designed the **Vietnam Veterans Memorial,** south of Constitution Ave. at 22nd St. NW, received a "B" when she submitted her memorial concept for a grade as a Yale senior—but beat her professor in the public memorial design competition. In her words, the monument is "a rift in the earth—a long, polished black stone wall, emerging from and receding into the earth." The wall contains the names of the 58,132 Americans who died in Vietnam, indexed in books at both ends of the structure. *(Metro: Foggy Bottom/GWU.)*

The **Lincoln Memorial,** at the west end of the Mall, recalls the rectangular grandeur of Athens' Parthenon. From these steps, Martin Luther King, Jr. gave his "I Have a Dream" speech during the 1963 March on Washington. A seated Lincoln presides over the memorial, keeping watch over protesters, Nazi party vigils, and

Fourth of July fireworks. Climbing the 19 ft. president is a federal offense; a camera will catch you if the rangers don't. *(Metro: Smithsonian or Foggy Bottom/GWU.)*

The 19 colossal polished steel statues of the **Korean War Memorial** trudge up a hill, rifles in hand, an eternal expression of weariness mixed with fear frozen upon their faces. The statue is accompanied by a black granite wall with over 2000 sandblasted photographic images from this war, in which 54,000 Americans lost their lives. The memorial is at the west end of the Mall, near Lincoln.

Occupying a long stretch of West Potomac Park (the peninsula between the Tidal Basin and the Potomac River) just a short walk from the Jefferson or Lincoln Memorials, the **Franklin Delano Roosevelt Memorial** is more of a stone garden than a monument. Whether to display the handicapped Roosevelt in his wheelchair was hotly debated when the memorial was being planned; in compromise, Roosevelt is seated, a position based on a famous picture taken at Yalta. The memorial is laid out in four "rooms" of red South Dakota granite, each of which represents a phase of FDR's presidency. *(Metro: Smithsonian.)*

A 19 ft. bronze Thomas Jefferson stands enshrined in the domed rotunda of the **Jefferson Memorial,** designed to evoke Jefferson's home and own creation, Monticello. The memorial overlooks the **Tidal Basin,** where pedalboats ply a polluted pond in and out of the shrine's strange shadow. Quotes from the Declaration of Independence, the Virginia Statute of Religious Freedom, Notes on Virginia, and an 1815 letter adorn the walls. *(Metro: L'Enfant Plaza.)*

**SOUTH OF THE MALL.** A block off the mall lies the **U.S. Holocaust Memorial Museum,** where excellent displays chronicle the rise of Nazism, the events leading up to the war in Europe, and the history of anti-Semitism. Films show troops entering concentration camps, shocked by the mass graves and emaciated prisoners they encounter. "The Hall of Remembrance" contains an eternal flame. *(100 Raul Wallenberg Pl. SW. 488-0400. Metro: Smithsonian. Open in summer daily 10am-8pm; in winter 10am-5:30pm. Free. Get in line early for tickets.)* Farther west, the **Bureau of Engraving and Printing** (a.k.a. **The Mint**), at 14th St. and C St. SW, offers tours of the presses that annually print over $20 billion worth of money and stamps. The love of money has made this the area's longest line; expect to grow old while you wait. *(847-2808; Metro: Smithsonian. Open M-F 9am-2pm. Free.)*

**WHITE HOUSE AND FOGGY BOTTOM.** The **White House,** with its simple columns and expansive lawns, seems a compromise between patrician lavishness and democratic simplicity. Thomas Jefferson proposed a contest for the design of the building, but he lost to amateur architect James Hoban when George Washington judged the competition. The President's personal staff works in the West Wing, while the First Lady's cohorts occupy the East Wing. Staff who cannot fit in the White House work in the nearby **Old Executive Office Building.** The President's official office is the **Oval Office,** site of many televised speeches, but the public tour is limited to public reception areas. *(1600 Pennsylvania Ave. NW. 456-7041. Open by tour only Tu-Sa 10am-noon. Free. Get tickets at the White House Visitors Center, 1450 Pennsylvania Ave. NW, at the corner of 15th and E St.)*

Historic homes surround **Lafayette Park** north of the White House. These include the Smithsonian-owned **Renwick Gallery** craft museum has some remarkable works, such as the 80s sculptures *Ghost Clock* and *Game Fish*. *(at 17th St. and Pennsylvania Ave. NW. 357-2700. Metro: Farragut West. Open daily 10am-5:30pm. Free.)* Once housed in the Renwick's mansion, the **Corcoran Gallery** now boasts larger quarters on 17th St. between E St. and New York Ave. NW. It displays American artists such as John Singer Sargent, Mary Cassatt, and Winslow Homer. *(639-1700. Open M, W, and F-Su 10am-5pm, Th 10am-9pm. Suggested donation $3, students and seniors $1, families $5.)* Nearby, the **Octagon,** a curious building designed by Capitol architect William Thornton, is reputedly filled with ghosts. Tour guides explain the history of the house. *(Open Tu-Sa 10am-4pm. $3, students and seniors $1.50.)*

A few blocks above Rock Creek Pkwy., the **John F. Kennedy Center for the Performing Arts,** off 25th St. and New Hampshire Ave. NW, rises like a marble sarcophagus.

**GO HAMMER! GO HAMMER!** On Oct. 10, 1986, a Colorado man tried to destroy the Constitution and the Bill of Rights with a claw hammer. Although his hammer broke 3 star-shaped holes in the laminated outer glass of the display case, it did not reach the glass shell enclosing the documents. "America is an imperialist country," **Randall Husar** yelled as he was arrested. Relatives said that Husar, a mentally ill history buff with a degree in psychology, dislikes Republicans.

One could fit the Washington Monument in the gargantuan **Grand Foyer,** were it not for the 18 Swedish chandeliers, shaped like cubical grape clusters. *(467-4600. Metro: Foggy Bottom-GWU. Open daily 10am-midnight. Free tours every 15min. M-F 10am-5pm, Sa-Su 10am-1pm.)* Across the street is Tricky Dick's beloved **Watergate Complex.**

**OLD DOWNTOWN.** An architectural marvel houses the Smithsonian's **National Building Museum,** towering above F St. NW between 4th and 5th St. Montgomery Meigs' Italian-inspired edifice remains one of Washington's most beautiful. *(272-2448. Metro: Judiciary Sq. Open M-Sa 10am-4pm, Su noon-4pm; hrs. extend to 5pm during summer. Suggested donation $3, students and seniors $2.)*

The Smithsonian's **National Museum of American Art** and **National Portrait Gallery** share the Old Patent Office Building, a neoclassical edifice 2 blocks long. The NMAA's corridors contain a diverse collection of major 19th- and 20th-century painters, as well as folk and ethnic artists. Janitor James Hampton stayed up nights in an unheated garage for 15 years to create the painting to the right of the main entrance. *(357-2700. Metro: Gallery Pl.-Chinatown. American Art entrance at 8th and G St., Portrait Gallery entrance at 8th and F. Open daily 10am-5:30pm. Tours daily 10:15am and 1:15pm; free. Wheelchair entrance at 9th and G St.)*

At the **National Archives,** at 8th St. and Constitution Ave. NW, visitors line up to view the original Declaration of Independence, U.S. Constitution, and Bill of Rights. *(501-5000; Metro: Archives-Navy Memorial. Open daily Apr.-Labor Day 10am-9pm; Labor Day-Mar. 10am-5:30pm. Free.)* The **Federal Bureau of Investigation** still hunts Commies, social activists, boogie-monsters, interstate felons, and Branch Davidians with undiminished vigor. Tour lines form on the **J. Edgar Hoover Building's** outdoor plaza. *(324-3000. Open M-F 8:45am-4:15pm. Free.)*

John Wilkes Booth shot President Abraham Lincoln during a performance at **Ford's Theater,** 511 10th St. NW. National Park Rangers describe the events with animated gusto during a 20min. talk. *(426-6924; Metro: Metro Center. Open daily 9am-5pm. Free.)* The **Old Post Office,** at Pennsylvania Ave. and 12th St. NW, rebukes its contemporary neighbors with arched windows, conical turrets, and a clock tower, all sheathing a shopping mall. *(606-8691. Metro: Federal Triangle. Tower open mid-Apr. to mid-Sept. 8am-10:45pm; off season 10am-6pm. Shops open M-Sa 10am-8pm, Su noon-6pm.)*

The **National Museum of Women in the Arts** houses works by the likes of Mary Cassatt, Georgia O'Keeffe, and Frida Kahlo in a former Masonic Temple. *(1250 New York Ave. NW. 783-5000. Metro: Metro Center. Open M-Sa 10am-5pm, Su noon-5pm. Cafe M-Sa 11:30am-2:30pm. Suggested donation $3, students and seniors $2.)*

**GEORGETOWN.** Georgetown's quiet, narrow, tree-lined streets are sprinkled with trendy boutiques and points of historic interest that make for an enjoyable walking tour. Retired from commercial use since the 1800s, the **Chesapeake & Ohio Canal** extends 185mi. from Georgetown to Cumberland, MD. Today, the towpath where trusty mules pulled barges on the canal belongs to the National Park Service. The **Old Stone House** is generally accepted as the oldest house in Washington. *(3051 M St. 426-685.)* The **Yellow House** was long thought to be older until new evidence was discovered. *(1430 33rd St.)*

The **Dumbarton Oaks Mansion,** between R and S St., former home of John Calhoun, holds a beautiful collection of Byzantine and pre-Columbian art. The 1944 Dumbarton Oaks Conference helped write the United Nations charter. The spectacular pre-Columbian art gallery was designed by Phillip Johnson. The beautiful

MID-ATLANTIC

gardens are the best cheap date place in town. *(1703 32nd St. NW. 339-6401. Art gallery open Tu-Su 2-5pm. Suggested contribution $1. Gardens open daily Apr.-Oct. 2-6pm; Nov.-Mar. 2-5pm. $4, seniors and children $3.)*

When Archbishop John Carroll learned where the new capital would be built, he rushed to found **Georgetown University,** at 37th and O St. in 1789, the U.S.'s first Catholic institution of higher learning.

**DUPONT CIRCLE.** Once one of Washington's swankier neighborhoods, Dupont Circle attracted embassies because of its stately townhouses and large tracts of land. Today, it is a haven for the international, artsy, and gay crowds; this mix of business, politics, and pleasure make it one of the more exciting parts of the city.

The **Art Gallery District,** bounded by Connecticut Ave., Florida Ave., and Q St., contains over two dozen galleries displaying everything from contemporary photographs to tribal crafts. *(General information 232-3610.)* Nearby, the **Phillips Collection,** at Q St. NW, was the 1st museum of modern art in the U.S. Everyone gapes at Auguste Renoir's masterpiece, *Luncheon of the Boating Party*, in the Renoir room. Works by Delacroix, Miró, and Turner line the Annex. *(1600 21st St. 387-2151. Open Tu-Sa 10am-5pm, Su noon-7pm. $6.50, students and seniors $3.25, under 12 free.)*

The stretch of Massachusetts Ave. between Dupont Circle and Observatory Circle is also called Embassy Row. Before the 1930s, Washington socialites lined the avenue with extravagant edifices; status-conscious diplomats found the mansions perfect for their purposes, and embassies moved in by the dozen. Highlights include **Anderson House,** which retains the robber-baron decadence of U.S. ambassador Larz Anderson, who built it from 1902-1905. *(2118 Massachusetts Ave. NW. 785-2040, ext. 16. Open Tu-Sa 1-4pm. Free.)* Flags line the entrance to the **Islamic Center,** a brilliant white building within which stunning designs stretch to the tips of spired ceilings. No shorts allowed; women must cover their heads, arms, and legs. *(2551 Massachusetts Ave. NW. 332-8343. Open daily 10am-5pm; prayers held 5 times daily.)*

**UPPER NORTHWEST.** Washington National Zoological Park is best known for its giant panda, Hsing-Hsing, which Mao gave to Nixon. The zoo's orangutans are allowed to swim through the park via a series of 40-ft.-high towers. The Valley Trail (marked with blue bird tracks) connects the bird and sealife exhibits, while the red Olmsted Walk (marked with elephant feet) links land-animal houses. *(3001 Connecticut Ave. 673-4800. Metro: Woodley Park-Zoo. Grounds open daily 6am-8pm, Oct.-Apr. 6am-6pm. Buildings open daily 10am-6pm, Oct.-Apr. 10am-4:30pm. Free.)*

The **Washington National Cathedral,** at Massachusetts and Wisconsin Ave. NW, was built from 1907 to 1990. Rev. Martin Luther King, Jr. preached his last Sunday sermon from the pulpit. The elevator rises to the Pilgrim Observation Gallery, revealing D.C. from the highest vantage in the city. At the **Medieval Workshop,** children can carve stone, learn how a stained-glass window is created, or, for $2, mold a gargoyle out of clay. *(537-6200 or 364-6616. Metro: Tenleytown, then take the #30, 32, 34, or 36 bus toward Georgetown; or walk up Cathedral Ave. from the equidistant Woodley Park-Zoo Metro. Cathedral open May-Aug. M-F 10am-9pm, Sa 10am-4:30pm, Su 7:30am-7:30pm; Sept.-Apr. M-Sa 10am-4:30pm, Su 12:30-4pm. Suggested donation $2 for tour, under 12 $1.)*

# ENTERTAINMENT AND NIGHTLIFE

## BARS AND CLUBS

**Chief Ike's Mambo Room, Chaos, and Pandemonium,** 1725 Columbia Rd. (332-2211 or 797-4637), near Ontario Rd., 2 blocks from 18th St. Pub-style American food ($4.25-10) accompanied by a DJ spinning dance classics, hip-hop, funk, and disco for a 20-something crowd. 2 tumultuous rooms feature alternative tunes, pseudo-Japanese decor, and pool tables. Happy Hour daily 4-8pm. 21+. Chief Ike's open Su-Th 4pm-2am, F-Sa 4pm-3am. Chaos and Pandemonium open Su-Th 6pm-2am, F-Sa 6pm-3am.

■ **Dragonfly,** 1215 Connecticut Ave. NW (331-1775). Frosted windows tease passers-by to peak into the hottest club in town. Ice-white interior, pod-like chairs, techno music, and video projections. Sushi served all night at reasonable prices. DJ Th-Sa; no cover. Open M-W 5:30pm-1:30am, Th-F 5:30pm-2:30am, Sa 6pm-2:30am, Su 6pm-1:30am.

■ **9:30 Club,** 815 V St. NW (concert line 393-0930, tickets 265-0930). D.C.'s most established local and alternative rock venue. Cover $3 for local bands or $5-20 for nationally known acts; these often sell out weeks in advance. The crowd's ages and styles vary with the acts (18+). 50¢ surcharge for advance tickets from box office. Cash-only box office open M-F 3-7pm, until 11pm on show days, Sa-Su 6-11pm on show days. Door time Su-Th 7:30pm-midnight, F-Sa 9pm-2am.

**Club Heaven and Club Hell,** 2327 18th St. NW (667-4355), near Columbia Rd. Hell is a hip, smoky bar greasily ornamented with funky gold tables and loud alterna music. Heaven looks like an old townhouse with comfy couches, a small bar, 3 TVs, and a dance floor throbbing to techno. 80s dance party in Heaven is crammed (Th; cover $5). No cover F-W. $1 off drinks during Happy Hour in Hell (M-Th until 10pm and F-Su until 8:30pm). Dancing at 10pm. Heaven open Su and Tu-Th 9:30pm-2am, F-Sa 9:30pm-3am. Hell open Su-Th 7pm-2am, F-Sa 7pm-3am.

**Brickskeller,** 1523 22nd St. NW (293-1885), between P and Q St. With a list of over 850 bottled brews, the Brickskeller's menu reads like a novella of world beer. Basement bar eschews the chi-chi in favor of a laid-back neighborhood tavern. "Beer-tails" are mixed drinks made with beer, like the classic Black Velvet (stout and champagne; $4.50). Pub food. Open M-Th 11:30am-2am, F 11:30am-3am, Sa 6pm-3am, Su 6pm-2am.

**Garrett's,** 3003 M St. NW (333-1033), near 30th St. Up the street from Charing Cross. Georgetown's most popular bar is a body-to-body, all-night frat party. Beer and mixed drinks $3.50. Half-priced drinks, beer, and house wine during Happy Hour (M-F 5-7pm). Open for lunch M-F 11:30am-2:30pm, Sa-Su noon-2:20pm; dinner Su-Th 6-10pm, F-Sa 6-11pm; bar open M-F 11:30am-2am, Sa noon-3am, Su noon-2am.

**Zei,** 1415 Zei Alley (842-2445), between 14th and 15th and H and I St. NW. Metro: McPherson Square. Not-quite-boiling techno is hurled at not-quite-industrial kids in this just-shy-of-ultra-hip-wannabe-NYC club. Soundproof lounge on the second floor is passionately hip with cool acid jazz. $10 cover. 18+ Open Th-Sa 10pm-3am.

**Southeast Tracks,** 1111 1st St. SE (488-3320). Metro: Navy Yard. One of D.C.'s hottest clubs. 2 dance floors, 3 bars, a patio, a volleyball court, and bleachers overlooking the main dance floor ensure that there's something for every type of club-goer. Friendly to all types and sexual orientations. Secured parking nearby ($5). 18+. Open Th and Sa-Su 9pm-late, F 10pm-late. *Be very careful in this area at night and never walk alone.*

**The Aroma Company,** 3417 Connecticut Ave. NW (244-7995). Metro: Cleveland Park. The Aroma Co. really isn't a cigar bar—it's actually more of a funky neighborhood martini lounge for hipster townies. Locals come to hang out and discourse into the wee hours. Live jazz and blues in winter. Open M-Th 5pm-2am, F-Sa 5pm-3am, Su 5pm-1am.

**Blues Alley,** 1073 Rear Wisconsin Ave. NW (337-4141), in an alley below M St. running between Wisconsin and 31st St., in Georgetown. Cool jazz in an intimate, candlelit supper club. This is a listening club, not a place for conversation. Past performers include Eartha Kitt, Nicholas Payton, and Wynton Marsalis. Creole fare 6-10pm. Late fare $4-9.50 served during the 10pm show. Beer $5; mixed drinks from $7. Min. $7 tab per set. Ticket prices $14-40; $1.75 surcharge if bought in advance. Shows 8 and 10pm.

**Iota,** 2832 Wilson Blvd. (703-522-8340), in Alexandria. Metro: Clarendon. Live performances of every style in what feels like an old ski lodge. Microbrews $3.50-5, 35 bottled beers from $3. Tunes most nights 9pm. Happy Hour (M-F 5-8pm): $1 off rails and drafts. Cover $3-15 during shows. Open daily 5pm-2am.

**Kelley's "The Irish Times,"** 14 F St. NW (543-5433). Metro: Union Station. Irish street signs, the *Irish Times,* and Joyce on the wall, but late-night disco differentiates Kelley's from most Irish bars. Happy Hour (M-F 4-7:30pm): domestic drafts $2. Live music (Th-Sa 9pm): any genre with acoustic guitars. Open Su-Th 9:30am-2am, F-Sa 9:30am-3am.

**GAY BARS AND CLUBS.** The *Washington Blade* is the best source of gay news and club listings; published every Friday, it's available in virtually every storefront in Dupont Circle. **Tracks** (see above) becomes the city's most popular gay dance club on Saturday nights.

🐊 **Badlands,** 1415 22nd St. NW (296-0505), near P St. Metro: Dupont Circle. This monolith of gay clubdom hosts a throbbing young crowd interested in serious dancing to house music. Th college night; no cover with a college ID. Cover $3 F-Sa 9-10pm, $7 after 10pm. The Annex upstairs hosts a mellower video bar with pool table, but most come for the drag queen karaoke F-Sa. Open Th-Sa 9pm-close (usually very, very late).

**Omega,** 2122 P St. NW (223-4917), at the rear of P St. in the alley between 21st and 22nd St. Metro: Dupont Circle. Attracts an ethnically mixed crowd of young gay men. More a bar than dance place, it still boasts 2 floors of music videos. Happy Hour (Su-F 4-9pm) features $2 domestics. Specials M-F; Su, Tu, and Th $2.25 vodkas. Open Su-Th 4pm-2am, F 4pm-3am, Sa 8pm-3am.

**Hung Jury,** 1819 H St. NW (785-8181). Metro: Farragut West. Lesbians from all over D.C., from 30-something couples to singles scoping the scene, spend their weekend nights bopping to Top 40. Shooters $1. Cover $5. Open F-Sa 9pm-3:30am.

To see what's up, check *City Paper*. On summer Sa and Su, shows from jazz and R&B to the National Symphony Orchestra occupy the outdoor, 4200-seat **Carter Barron Amphitheater,** set into Rock Creek Park at 16th St. and Colorado Ave. NW (426-6837; tickets vary from free to about $20). From late June to late Aug., rock, punk, and metal preempt soccer playing at **Fort Reno Park** (call 282-1063 for Rock Creek Park services). George Washington University sponsors shows in **Lisner Auditorium,** 21st and H St. NW (202-994-1500), where David Letterman broadcasts his D.C. shows. Tickets $0-$25; call in advance.

**THEATER. Arena Stage,** 6th St. and Maine Ave. SW, is often called the best regional (non-New York) theater company in America. (488-4377. Metro: Waterfront. Tickets $25-45, lower for smaller stages, students 35% off, seniors 20% off; ½-price rush usually available 1½hr. before show. Box office open M-Sa 10am-8pm, Su noon-8pm.) The **Kennedy Center** (416-8000), at 25th St. and New Hampshire Ave., offers scores of ballet, opera and dramatic productions, most of them expensive ($22-47); however, most productions offer ½-price tickets the day of performance to students, seniors, military, and the disabled; call 467-4600 for details. The **Millennium Stage** presents free performances in the Grand Foyer. The prestigious **Shakespeare Theater,** at the Lansburgh, 450 7th St. NW at Pennsylvania Ave., offers a Bard-heavy repertoire. Standing-room tickets are available 2hr. before curtain. ($10. 547-1122. TTY 638-3863. Metro: Archives-Navy Memorial.) In the **14th St. theater district,** tiny repertory companies explore and experiment with enjoyable results (check *City Paper* for listings). **Woolly Mammoth,** 1401 Church St. NW (393-3939; Metro: Dupont Circle); **Studio Theater,** 1333 P St. NW (332-3300), at 14th St. (Metro: Dupont Circle); and **The Source Theater,** 1835 14th St. NW (462-1073; Metro: U St.-Cardozo), between S and T St., are all fine theaters in the neighborhood near Dupont Circle (tickets $12-29). *Use caution in this area at night.*

**SPORTS.** The 20,000-seat **MCI Center,** 601 F St. NW, in Chinatown, is D.C.'s premier sports arena (628-3200; Metro: Gallery Pl.-Chinatown). The **Washington Wizards,** the city's NBA team, continues its struggle against dismal play and a lame mascot (tickets $19-40). The **Washington Capitals** kick ice (Oct.-Apr.; tickets $12-45). Three-time Superbowl champions, the **Washington Redskins** draw crowds to **Jack Kent Cook Stadium,** Raljon Dr., in Raljon, MD, Sept.-Dec. (301-772-8800, tickets 301-276-6050; $35-50). At **Robert F. Kennedy Stadium,** the **United** (703-478-660) play soccer mid-Apr. to Oct.

## NEAR D.C.

**ARLINGTON, VA.** The silence of the 612-acre **Arlington National Cemetery** honors those who sacrificed their lives in war. The Kennedy Gravesites hold the remains of President John F. Kennedy, his brother Robert F. Kennedy, and his wife Jacqueline Kennedy Onassis. The Eternal Flame flickers above JFK's simple memorial stone. The **Tomb of the Unknowns** honors all who died fighting for the United States and is guarded by soldiers from the Army's Third Infantry. *(Changing of the guard every 30min.; Oct.-Mar. every hr. on the hr.)* Robert E. Lee's home, **Arlington House,** overlooks the cemetery; tours are self-guided. *(703-697-2131. Metro: Arlington Cemetery. Cemetery open daily Apr.-Sept. 8am-7pm; Oct.-May 8am-5pm. Free.)* Head down Custis Walk in front of Arlington House, exit the cemetery through Weitzel Gate, and walk for 20min. to get to the **Iwo Jima Memorial,** based on Joe Rosenthal's Pulitzer Prize-winning photo of Marines straining to raise the U.S. flag on Mt. Suribachi.

Video screens...video screens everywhere...are you trapped in George Orwell's *1984?* No, it's just the **Newseum.** Opened in 1997, the Newseum honors journalists and journalism with dazzling interactive glitz. The video-game atmosphere makes it a hit with kids and adults who don't have any gripes with "sensationalized news." Jump into the action and become a news anchor via studios on the 2nd fl. *(1101 Wilson Blvd. 703-284-3544 or 888-639-7386. Metro: Rosslyn. Open W-Su 10am-5pm. Free.)*

The **Pentagon,** the world's largest office building, shows just how huge military bureaucracy can get. For security reasons, there are no bathroom breaks on the tour. *(695-1776. Metro: Pentagon. Tours every 30min. M-F 9:30am-3:30pm. Free.)*

**ALEXANDRIA, VA.** Alexandria, VA traces its colonial origins over a century further back than Washington, D.C. Courtesy of a massive 80s restoration effort, **Old Town Alexandria** *(Metro: King St.)* has cobblestone streets, brick sidewalks, tall ships, and quaint shops. Sights cluster along **Washington** and **King St.** George Washington and Robert E. Lee prayed at **Christ Church,** at Cameron St., a red brick Colonial building with a domed steeple. *(118 N. Washington St. 703-549-1450.)* Both slept in **Robert E. Lee's Boyhood Home,** near Asaph St. *(607 Oronoco St. 703-548-8454.)* Thirty-seven different Lees inhabited the **Lee-Fendall House.** *(614 Oronoco St. 703-549-1789.)*

**MT. VERNON.** George Washington had a fabulous estate called **Mt. Vernon,** easily accessible to Washingtonians in boondocky Fairfax County, VA. Visitors can see the Washington's bedroom and tomb, and the estate's fields, where slaves once grew corn, wheat, and tobacco. *(Take the Fairfax Connector 101 bus from Metro: Huntington or take I-395 S to George Washington Pkwy. S, which becomes Mt. Vernon Hwy. in Alexandria; use the Mt. Vernon exit. 703-780-2000. Open daily Apr.-Aug. 8am-5pm, grounds close at 5:30pm; Sept.-Oct. and Mar. 9am-5pm, grounds close at 5:30pm; Nov.-Feb. 9am-4pm, grounds close at 4:30pm. $8, seniors $7.50, ages 5-11 $4, under 5 free.)*

# VIRGINIA

If Virginia is obsessed with its past, it has good reason: many of America's formative experiences—the English settlement of North America, the shameful legacy of the slave trade, the final establishment of American independence, and much of the Civil War—took place in Virginia. English colonists founded Jamestown in 1607, and the New World's first black slaves joined them unwillingly 12 years later. While George Washington was battling Native Americans in the French and Indian War, Thomas Jefferson wrote about religious and political freedom in the colonial capital, Williamsburg. Washington later returned to deal the British a table-turning defeat at Yorktown. Virginian James Madison traveled to Philadelphia in 1787 with drafts of the Constitution, and Virginian George Mason championed the Bill of Rights. Meanwhile, Virginia's Tidewater aristocracy dominated the state for a century with its rigid, gracious culture of slave-dependent plantations—a culture that imploded during the Civil War when Union and Confederate armies clashed throughout Virginia on the way to Appomattox Court House.

Virginia has begun to abandon its Old South lifestyle in search of a more cosmopolitan image. The western portion of the state, with montane forests and fascinating underground caverns, provides a welcome respite from nostalgia and relentless Southern heat; but even in cities like Charlottesville, history lingers on.

## ◪ PRACTICAL INFORMATION

**Capital:** Richmond.

**Visitor Info: Virginia Division of Tourism,** 901 E. Byrd St., 19th fl., Richmond 23219 (804-786-4484 or 800-847-4882; www.virginia.org). Open daily 8am-5pm. **Dept. of Conservation and Recreation,** 203 Governor St., Richmond 23219 (804-786-1712). Open daily 8am-5pm.

**Postal Abbreviation:** VA. **Sales Tax:** 4.5%.

# RICHMOND

A little city fighting to live up to its capital status, Richmond is a hodge-podge of pastel facades, urban strife, proud black history, and lingering allegiances to the Confederate side. Once the capital of the Confederacy, Richmond pays homage to Southern rebels like Jefferson Davis and Stonewall Jackson. At the same time, the city respects the rich African-American heritage of Jackson Ward, an area that once rivaled Harlem as a center of black thought and culture.

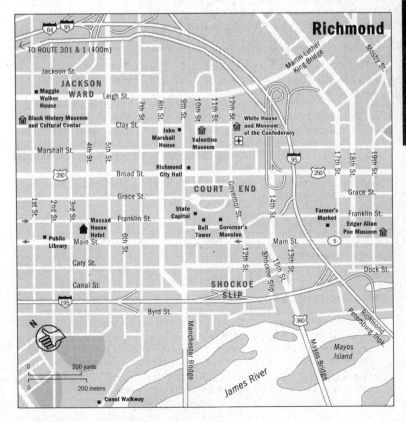

MID-ATLANTIC

## 🔋 ORIENTATION AND PRACTICAL INFORMATION

**Broad Street** is the city's central artery, and the streets that cross it are numbered from west to east. Most parallel streets to Broad St., including the important Main St. and Cary St., run one-way. Both I-95, leading north to Washington, D.C., and I-295 encircle the urban section of the city. The **Court End** and **Church Hill** districts, on Richmond's eastern edges, comprise the city's historic center. Further southeast, **Shockoe Slip** and **Shockoe Bottom** overflow with after-dark partiers. **Jackson Ward,** in the heart of downtown (bounded by Belvedere, Leigh, Broad, and 5th St.) is currently undergoing renovations for an expanded City Center, which will relieve some of the deterioration that has struck the community. **The Fan,** shaped like a belle's fan, is bounded by the Boulevard, I-95, the walk of statues along **Monument Ave.,** and **Virginia Commonwealth University.** The pleasant bistros and boutiques of **Carytown,** past the Fan on Cary St., and the tightly knit working community of **Oregon Hill** add even more dimensions to this city of many faces and pasts.

**Amtrak:** 7519 Staple Mills Rd. (264-9194). Reservations required. To: Washington D.C. (2¼hr., 9 per day, $28); Williamsburg (1¼hr., 9 per day, $14); Virginia Beach (3hr., 1 per day, $23, last ¼ via bus); Baltimore (3½hr., 9 per day, $42); and Philadelphia (4¾hr., 9 per day, $64). Open 24hr. Taxi downtown about $10.

**Buses: Greyhound,** 2910 N. Boulevard (254-5910 or 800-231-2222). 2 blocks from downtown. Take GRTC bus #24 north. To: D.C. (18 per day, 2hr., $16); Charlottesville (6 per day, 1½-4hr., $17); Williamsburg (8 per day, 1hr., $7); Norfolk (9 per day, 3hr., $15); Baltimore (21 per day, 3½hr., $19); and Philadelphia (12 per day, 7hr., $34).

**Public Transit: Greater Richmond Transit Co.,** 101 S. Davis Ave. (358-4782). Maps available at City Hall, 900 E. Broad St., and in the Yellow Pages. Most buses leave from Broad St. downtown. Bus #24 goes south to Broad St. and downtown. Fare $1.25, transfers 15¢. Seniors 50¢ during off-peak hours. **Trolleys** provide dependable service to downtown, Shockoe Slip, and Shockoe Bottom daily 11am-11pm. Fare 25¢.

**Taxi: Veterans Cab** (329-3333), **Yellow Cab** (222-7300), and **Hansom** (837-8524).

**Visitor Info: Richmond Visitors Center,** 1710 Robin Hood Rd. (358-5511 or 358-5512), exit 78 off I-95/64. Offers same-day radically discounted accommodations. Open daily Memorial Day-Labor Day 9am-7pm; off-season 9am-5pm. Smaller centers, located in the airport and the Bell Tower on the capitol grounds, offer similar services.

**Hotlines: Traveler's Aid:** 643-0279 or 648-1767. Open M-F 9am-5pm. **Rape Crisis:** 643-0888. **Psychiatric Crisis Intervention:** 648-9224. Open 24hr. **AIDS/HIV:** 800-533-4148. Open M-F 8am-7pm. **Crisis Pregnancy Center:** 353-2320. Open 24hr. **Women's Health Clinic:** 800-254-4479. Open 24hr.

**Post Office:** 1801 Brook Rd. (775-6133). Open M-F 7am-6pm, Sa 10am-1pm. **ZIP Code:** 23219. **Area Code:** 804.

## 📌 ACCOMMODATIONS

Budget motels in Richmond cluster on **Williamsburg Road,** at the edge of town, and along **Midlothian Turnpike,** south of the James River. Public transport to these areas is unreliable. The farther from downtown you stay, the less you pay. The Visitors Center can reserve accommodations, often at $20-35 discounts (see above).

**Massad House Hotel,** 11 N. 4th St. (648-2893), 5 blocks from the Capitol, in the commercial downtown area. A 1940s elevator shuttles guests to clean rooms with showers, A/C, and cable TV. Singles $45; doubles $48. Student and senior discount 10%.

**Executive Inn,** 5215 W. Broad St. (288-4011), 3mi. from town; use bus #6. Once the Red Carpet Inn, it still sports the trademark red carpet in its clean, slightly faded rooms. Provides A/C, cable TV, and an outdoor pool. Rooms $55-62; weekly rate $165.

**Cadillac Motel,** 11418 Washington Hwy. (798-4049), 10mi. from town; no public transportation. Take I-95 to exit 89. Not the cadillac of motel rooms, but decent sleeping quarters with A/C and cable TV. Singles $36; doubles $45.

**Pocahontas State Park,** 10301 State Park Rd. (796-4255; for reservations, call 225-3867 or 800-933-7275), 10mi. south on Rt. 10 and Rt. 655 in Chesterfield; no public transportation. Showers, biking, boating, picnic areas, and a huge pool treat campers royally. No hookups. Open year-round. Sites $12.

## FOOD

The recipe for Richmond cuisine is simple: take one part Southern culture, one part hungry-but-short-on-cash college students, shake, and you've got cheap, delicious food. The outdoor **Farmer's Market,** N. 17th and E. Main St., brings the country into the city, brimming with fresh fruits, veggies, and homemade delicacies. Surrounding the market in **Shockhoe Bottom,** pizza and deli food top the menu. The "artsy" crowd of Virginia Commonwealth University has made the **Fan** a playground of eclectic coffeehouses and restaurants vying for the highest hipness.

**Mamma Zu's,** 501 S. Pine St. (788-4205). Unpretentious Italian heaven. The food looks as good as it tastes and the veggies are fresh from the restaurant's own garden. Free range and exotic meats, like rabbit liver (appetizer $6.50), and many vegetarian choices (entrees $7-20). Open M-F 11am-2:30pm and 5:30-11pm, Sa 5:30-11pm.

**Winnie's Caribbean Cuisine,** 200 E. Main St. (649-4974). Caribbean specialties with the intoxicating strains of reggae. Lunches ($5-8) include the popular hot and spicy jerk chicken "roti" sandwich ($5.50). Dinners ($5.50-14) are exotic, with entrees like garlic coconut conch ($13). Tropical lemonade and scarlet sorrel ($1.60) redefines refreshment. Open M 11am-1pm, Tu-Th 11am-10pm, F 11am-10:30pm, Sa 1-10:30pm.

**Ma-Masu's,** 2043 W. Broad St. (355-8063). Ma-Masu, "Spiritual Mother" extraordinaire, carries on a tradition of fabulous West African cuisine and culture. Nothing over $6; top a meal of Toywah Beans ($6) and collard greens ($1.50) with a cup of young coconut juice ($1). Delivery available. Open M-F 11am-9pm.

## SIGHTS

**St. John's Church** is the site of Patrick Henry's famed 1775 "Give me liberty or give me death" speech. Actors recreate the speech on Su (from the last Su in May to the 1st Su in Sept.) at 2pm. The building itself is a place of enormous floorboards and endless serenity. *(2401 E Broad St. 648-5015. Admission by tour only. 25min. tours M-Sa 10am-3:30pm, Su 1-3:30pm. $3, seniors $2, ages 7-18 $1.)*

Richmond's most important sites can be found in the **Court End** district, which stretches north and east of the Capitol to Clay and College St. The **State Capitol,** at 9th and Grace St., is a Neoclassical masterpiece designed by Thomas Jefferson. The building was the seat of the Confederate government during the Civil War and today houses the only statue of George Washington for which the first President actually posed. *(698-1788. Open daily 9am-5pm; Dec.-Mar. M-Sa 9am-5pm, Su noon-5pm.)*

**The Museum of the Confederacy** houses the world's largest Confederate artifact collection. The museum also runs 1hr. tours through the **White House of the Confederacy** next door, where a South-shall-rise-again feeling is almost palpable. Statues of Tragedy, Comedy, and Irony grace the White House's front door. *(1201 E. Clay St. 649-1861. Open M-Sa 10am-5pm, Su noon-5pm. $6, seniors $5, ages 7-18 $3, under 7 free. Tours M, W, and F-Sa 10:30am-4:30pm, Tu and Th 11:30am-4:30pm, Su 1:15-4:30pm. $7, seniors $6, students $4. Combination tickets available.)*

**The Valentine Museum** has exhibits on local and Southern social and cultural history, plus the South's largest collection of costumes and textiles. Admission includes a tour of the restored Neoclassical **Wickham-Valentine House.** *(1015 E. Clay St. 649-0711. Open M-Sa 10am-5pm, Su noon-5pm. House tours on the hr. 10am-4pm. $5, students and seniors $4, ages 7-12 $3.)*

South of Court End, the **Shockoe Slip** district, running from Main, Canal, and Cary St. between 10th and 14th St., features fancy shops in restored ware-houses, but few bargains. The **Shockhoe Bottoms Arts Center,** crams in 120 artist's cutting edge creations. *(2001 E. Grace St. 643-7959. Open Tu-Sa 10am-5pm, Su 1-5pm.)* Also in the Slip, the **Canalwalk,** linking the Kanaway Canal next to the James River, has gorgeous vistas, swaying trees, and stylish eateries.

Jackson Ward is the heart of African-American Richmond. The **Black History Museum and Cultural Center of Virginia** showcases rotating exhibits on African-American history. *(00 Clay St. 780-9093. Open Tu-Sa 11am-4pm. $4; seniors $3, under 12 $2. Wheelchair access.)*

In the Fan, **Monument Ave.,** a boulevard lined with trees, gracious old houses, and towering statues of Virginia heroes, is a Richmond memory lane. The statue of Robert E. Lee faces south toward his beloved Dixie; Stonewall Jackson faces north so that the general can perpetually scowl at the Yankees. The statue of African-American tennis hero Arthur Ashe, who died of AIDS, created a storm of controversy when built at the end of the avenue.

Four blocks from the intersection of Monument Ave. and N. Boulevard rests the South's largest art museum, the **Virginia Museum of Fine Arts.** On summer Th from 6:30-9:30pm, the Museum draws sell-out crowds to its sculpture garden for **Jumpin',** one of Richmond's most dynamic musical performance cycles. *(2800 Grove Ave. 367-0844. Open Tu-W and F-Su 11am-5pm, Th 11am-8pm in the North Wing Galleries. Suggested donation $4. Jumpin': 367-8148. Tickets $6 in advance, $7 at the door.)*

## 🎵 ENTERTAINMENT AND NIGHTLIFE

One of Richmond's most entertaining and delightful diversions is the marvelous old **Byrd Theater,** 2908 W. Cary St. (353-9911). Movie buffs buy tickets from a tuxedoed agent and are treated on weekends to a pre-movie Wurlitzer organ concert. All shows are 99¢; on Sa the balcony opens for $1 extra. Free concerts abound downtown and at the **Nina Abody Festival Park,** near the bottom of 17th St. *Style Weekly*, a free magazine available at the Visitors Center, and its younger counterpart, *Punchline*, snaggable in most hangouts, both list concert lineups. Cheer on the **Richmond Braves,** Richmond's AAA minor-league baseball team, on Boulevard St. for a fraction of major-league prices (359-4444; boxes $7, reserved seats $5, general $4). Student-driven nightlife enlivens **Shockoe Slip** and sprinkles itself throughout the **Fan.** After dark, **Shockoe Bottom** turns into college-party central, with transient bars pumping bass-heavy music early into the morning.

**Area 51,** 1713 E. Main St. (643-5100). Expect close encounters of the wild kind at this alien-inspired hot spot. Rap M, College and Ladies night W (18+). Free pool and an out-of-this-world Atlantis wrap ($7). M brings 51¢ tacos all day. Drafts $3. Raves held twice monthly; live bands play more frequently. Cover around $3. Open daily 5pm-2am.

**Matt's Pub and Comedy Club,** 109 S. 12th St. (643-5653), pours out a bit of Brit wit in wooden walls reminiscent of the old country. Performances F 8 and 10:30pm, Sa 8 and 11pm; reservations recommended. Cover around $8.50. Tex-Mex and pub cuisine $3-7; microbrews and drafts $2.75-$3.60; rails $3.25. Open F-Sa 11:30am-2am.

**Medley's,** 1701 E. Main (648-2313). An older crowd drowns their sorrows with live blues and French-Cajun food. Po' boy sandwiches $5.50-9; gumbo $4.50. Cover F-Sa $3-5. Open W-Sa 4pm-2am.

**Broadway Cafe,** 1624 W. Broad St. (355-9931). Miss Scarlett, a fluffy white poodle, presides over this largely gay bar from her high stool. Drafts $1.50. Appetizers around $4.50, including the "wings of fire." Open M-F 5pm-2am, Sa 6pm-2am, Su 7pm-2am.

## FREDERICKSBURG

Smack dab between Washington, D.C., and Richmond, a foothold in Fredericksburg during the Civil War meant control of the road between the capitals and, thus, a distinct military advantage. As a result, Fredericksburg experienced merciless amounts of bloodshed as men battled for control of the city. Years before the battles of Fredericksburg, Spotsylvania Court House, Chancellorsville, and the Wilderness, Fredericksburg was established as an important tobacco port on the banks of the Rappahanock River. After the troops left in 1865, Fredericksburg's glory lay shattered in the dust of Union pillage and destruction. Slowly, the town has gathered the pieces into a collaboration of new and old, mixing gorgeous city plantations and somber battlefields with brownstone cafes and elegant boutiques.

**⚏ ORIENTATION AND PRACTICAL INFORMATION.** Fredericksburg's position on I-95 directly between Washington and Richmond makes it a pleasant destination en route to both cities. Exit 133A off I-95 and onto Rt. 3 accesses the city, which is divided into two parts by **Lafayette Boulevard.** South of Lafayette lie residences, while the **Historic Downtown** crams museums, historical sites, and chic cafes into a network of one-ways, easily traversed by foot. **William Street** (Rt. 3) runs northeast over the Rappahanock River into Falmouth. One-way **Caroline Street** is the main historic and commercial route for the area.

**Amtrak:** 200 Lafayette Blvd., near Caroline St. Trains run twice daily on the long line from Maine to Florida. No ticket office. **Virginia Railway Express (VRE),** (703-684-1001 or 800-743-3873) in the same building, makes several trips daily to Union Station in Washington, D.C. ($6.70). **Greyhound/Trailways,** 1400 Jefferson Davis Hwy. (373-2103), runs daily to Washington, D.C., Baltimore, and Richmond. **Fredericksburg Regional Transit,** 1400 Jefferson Davis Hwy (372-1222)., extends bus service around the city (fare 25¢). **Taxi: Yellow Cab** (371-7075), **Virginia Cab Service** (373-5111). **Fredericksburg Visitor Center,** 706 Caroline St. (373-1776 or 800-678-4748) at the corner of Charlotte St. has a walking tour, bike tours, **free parking passes** and discount accommodation reservations. The center sells a **Hospitality Pass** into 7 of the major sites ($19.75, ages 6-18 $7) and a **Pick Four Pass** for admission to 4 ($13.75, ages 6-18 $5.50). (Open daily 9am-7pm; in winter 9am-5pm.) **Hotlines: HIV/AIDS:** 371-7532. **Rape Crisis:** 371-1212. 24hr. **Post office:** (373-8860) Princess Anne St. between Charlotte St. and Lafayette Blvd. **ZIP code:** 22401. **Area code:** 540.

**⚏ ACCOMMODATIONS.** Chain motels rule around Fredericksburg's exits 118, 126, 130, and 133 off I-95, while historic B&Bs scattered near the Rappahanock River cost more than a few pence. Snag a copy of the *Traveler Discount Guide* in fast-food chains such as **Denny's** for discount coupons. The **Econo Lodge,** 7802 Plank Rd., exit 130B off I-95 then left at 1st light, offers A/C, cable, and rosy interiors. (786-8374. Free doughnuts, coffee, and juice. Singles $37; doubles $50; off-season singles $35, doubles $48.) **Fredericksburg Colonial Inn,** 1707 Princess Anne St., is a beautifully decorated, Civil War-styled retreat with TV, refrigerators, A/C, and Civil War antiques. (371-5666. Complimentary continental breakfast and newspapers. Doubles $59, suites $75.) **Selby House,** 226 Princess Anne St., 4 blocks from the historic district, is a gorgeous, sweet-smelling Victorian B&B with private bathrooms, A/C, and a TV lounge. (373-7037. Complimentary breakfast served on fine china daily in the dining room and patio. Singles $65; double with canopy bed $75.)

**⚏ FOOD.** Nearly every fast food and restaurant chain known to man accompanies the motel mania off exits 130A and 130B. Supermarkets thrive along the same strip, including **Ukrops,** 4250 Plank Rd. (785-2626). The locals head to **Caroline St.** for a barrage of healthy options and less congested dining. **◪ Sammy T's,** 801 Caroline St., a block from the visitors center, has plentiful, health-conscious food in a pub so authentically dark you can barely read the menu. The Camper's Delight ($8) slops out enough to feed an army, and the apple cheddar melt ($4.75) reduces diners to blissed-out, melted puddles. (371-2008. Entrees $5-8. Open M-Sa 7am-midnight, Su 11am-9pm.) **◪ Lee's Ice Cream,** 821 Caroline St., has over 50 homemade flavors, sweet indulgence in huge portions, and euphoric flavors like Kahlua Fudge and comforting Mom's Apple Pie, as well as extensive frozen yogurt and sugar-free selections. (370-4390. Single scoop $2, double $2.75, triple $3.25. Open M-Th 11am-10pm, F-Sa 11am-midnight, Su 10am-10pm.) At **Goolrick's Pharmacy,** 901 Caroline St., you'll have to endure the smell of chlorine, but the fantastic timewarp back to malt-shop days is worth it. Counter stools beckon patrons to incredibly cheap lunches (sandwiches $1.40-2.50) and thick milkshakes ($3; 373-3411. Open M-F 8:30am-7pm, Sa 8:30am-6pm.)

MID-ATLANTIC

⊗ **SIGHTS.** Mansions, medicine, and Monroe (James, not Marilyn) take center stage in Fredericksburg's **Historic District. Kenmore Plantation** was built in 1775 for Fielding Lewis and his wife, George Washington's sister, Betty. The tour reveals the stunning dining room, which has been labeled one of the 100 most beautiful rooms in America. (*1201 Washington Ave. 373-4255. Open Mar.-Dec. M-Sa 10am-5pm, Su noon-4pm. $6, ages 6-17 $3. Grounds free.*) At the **Mary Washington House,** built for George's ma, tours are packed with 18th-century trinkets. (*1200 Charles St. 373-1569. Open Mar.-Nov. daily 9am-5pm; Dec.-Feb.10am-4pm. $4, children $1.50.*) Learn why leeches purify the blood at the **Hugh Mercer Apothecary Shop,** which offers fascinating insights into old-fashioned, unhygienic medical technology. (*1020 Caroline St. 373-3362. Open daily Mar.-Nov. 9am-5pm; Dec.Feb. 10am-4pm. $4, ages 6-18 $1.50.*) Open by tour only, the **James Monroe Museum,** originally Monroe's law office, houses the desk where James wrote the Monroe Doctrine. (*908 Charles St. 654-1043. Open daily Mar.-Oct. 9am-5pm; Nov.-Feb. 10am-4pm. $4, seniors $3.20, children $1.*)

Over the Rappahanock River, **Chatham Manor** stuns with breathtaking gardens full of milky statues and aromatic roses. (*120 Chatham Ln. 654-5121. Open daily 9am-5pm. $3, under 17 free.*) One of the world's foremost portrait painters, Gary Melchers acquired the 18th-century **Belmont Mansion** in 1916 after gaining success for his paintings of the working class Dutch. (*224 Washington St. 654-1015. Open Mar.-Nov. M-Sa 10am-5pm, Su 1-5pm; Dec.-Feb. M-Sa 10am-4pm, Su 1-4pm. $4, seniors $3, students and children $1.*) A self-guided walking tour winds through the lands of George Washington's boyhood home at **Ferry Farm.** (*263 King Hwy. 371-3363. Open M-Sa 10am-5pm, Su noon-5pm. Free.*)

⚎ **ENTERTAINMENT AND NIGHTLIFE.** In the olden days, sundown meant bedtime, and little has changed. Though flanked by **Mary Washington College** on the north, the town and its students usually quiet down when the sore-footed tourists retire to their lodgings. The town does have a few after dinner pleasures, however. The **Colonial Theater,** 907 Caroline St., showcases symphonic performances and the occasional play (contact visitor center at 800-678-4748). At the **Klein Theater,** College Ave. and Thornton Ave., the **Fredericksburg Theater Co.** performs during the summer months (654-1124; $13-15; performances W-Sa 8pm, Su 2pm.)

Modern rock invades the historic district via **Orbits,** 406 Lafayette Blvd. Th-Sa nights get funked up with a young, hip flair and an intercontinental alliance of $5.50 pesto nachos. (371-2003. Open-mic night M. Drafts $2.50. Cover $4. Open M-Th 11:30am-10pm, F-Sa 11:30am-9pm, Su 11:30am-2am.) **The Underground,** 106 George St., in the basement of George St. Grill, takes its name literally with a dark basement location and edgy, alternative players. Head banging persists Th-Sa, and makes holding a brew ($3) difficult. (371-9500. Open Th-Sa. Opening hrs. vary with shows; call ahead.) The name of the **Santa Fe Grille and Saloon,** 219 William St., screams salsa, but the mood is cool with $4 pitchers and complimentary nachos. (371-0500. Diverse live music W, F-Su. Open Su-Th 11am-2am, F-Sa 11:30am-2am.)

# NEAR FREDERICKSBURG

### FREDERICKSBURG AND SPOTSYLVANIA NATIONAL BATTLEFIELD PARKS.
Fredericksburg's claim to fame isn't the brownstones that line its once busy streets, but the endless green expanses that were once covered with the blood of thousands of Americans. Under the leadership of Confederate generals Robert E. Lee and "Stonewall" Jackson and Union Generals Ambrose E. Burnside, Joseph Hooker, and Ulysses S. Grant, 4 huge Civil War battles played out in the 20mi. that surround the town. Over 100,000 soldiers lay lifeless on the soil between Dec. 1862 and May 1864. A 76mi. driving tour winds through the battlefields of Fredericksburg, Chancellorsville, the Wilderness, and Spotsylvania, paying homage to the soldiers who risked their lives for Old Glory and the Stars and Bars.

Fredericksburg's **visitors center** offers maps, walking tours, a 12min. film explaining the battles and their ramifications, and a tiny museum with soldier art. (*1013 Lafayette Blvd. 373-6122. Open daily 8:30am-6:30pm; in winter 9am-5pm.*) The Chancellorsville **visitors center,** 15mi. west of Fredericksburg's historic district, offers guided tours in summer. Neither Wilderness nor Spotsylvania have visitors centers but park rangers, stationed in history shelters, answer questions. *(Daily 9am-5pm.)*

Several historical and scenic walking trails lining the roads go to the heart of the battlefields. Three walking tours, the **Sunken Road Walking Tour** following the entrenchment line at Fredericksburg, the **Chancellorsville History Trail,** and the **Spotsylvania History Trail,** encircle the battlefields and provide strategic viewpoints of all major battle sights, including the Bloody Angle at Spotsylvania. *(Park admission $3, under 17 free; tickets valid for 7 days at all 4 parks including Chatham.)*

# WILLIAMSBURG

Former home of Peyton Randolph, the President of both the First and Second Continental Congresses, the city once seemed destined for national prominence. Then Randolph died, the Revolutionary War erupted, and Thomas Jefferson moved the capital to Richmond. After a century of decline, Williamsburg was rescued in the late 1920s by John D. Rockefeller, Jr., whose money restored the historic district, known as **Colonial Williamsburg.** Nowadays a fife-and-drum corps marches down the streets, and wheelwrights, bookbinders, and blacksmiths go about their tasks at old gas station sites. Travelers in late fall or early spring avoid summer's crowds, heat, and humidity; however, they will also miss the special summer programs. Dec. visitors experience charming Colonial Christmas.

## ORIENTATION AND PRACTICAL INFORMATION

Williamsburg lies 50mi. southeast of Richmond between Jamestown (10mi. away) and Yorktown (14mi. away). **The Colonial Pkwy.,** connects the three towns, has no commercial buildings, and is a beautiful route between historic destinations.

**Airport: Newport News/Williamsburg International Airport,** in Newport News. Frequent connections to Dulles by United Express and USAir. Take Hwy. 199W to I-64S.

**Transportation Center,** 408 N. Boundary St., behind the fire station. Houses offices for Amtrak, Greyhound, and taxis.

**Amtrak:** (229-8750). To: Washington, D.C. (3½hr., 2 per day, $33); Philadelphia (6hr., 2 per day, $56); Baltimore (5hr., 2 per day, $41); and Richmond (1hr., 2 per day, $14). Open Tu-Th 7:30am-5pm, Su-M and F-Sa 7:30am-10:30pm.

**Greyhound:** (229-1460). To: Richmond (1hr., 8 per day, $10); Norfolk (1-2hr., 9 per day, $10); Washington, D.C. (3-4hr., 8 per day, $29); and Virginia Beach (2½hr., 4 per day, $14). Open M-F 8am-5pm, Sa 8am-2pm, Su 8am-noon.

**Public Transit: James City County Transit (JCCT)** (220-1621). Service along Rt. 60, from Merchants Sq. in the historic district west to Williamsburg Pottery or east past Busch Gardens. Operates M-Sa 6:15am-5:15pm. $1 plus 25¢ per zone-change. **Williamsburg Shuttle** (220-1621), has service between Colonial Williamsburg and Busch Gardens every 30min. May-Sept. daily 9am-9pm. $1 for an all day pass.

**Taxi: Yellow Cab** (245-7777). 24hr. To Busch Gardens or Carter's Grove $6-10 one-way. To Jamestown and Yorktown $20 round-trip. Call between 8:30am-midnight.

**Car Rental: Colonial Rent-a-Car,** in the transportation center (220-3399). $34 per day. Min. age 21. Open M-F 8am-5:30pm, Sa-Su 8am-2pm.

**Bike Rental: Bikes Unlimited,** 759 Scotland St. (229-4620), rents single-speeds for $10 per day, multi-speeds $15. $5 deposit required (includes lock). Open M-F 9am-7pm, Sa 9am-5pm, Su noon-5pm.

**Visitor Information: Williamsburg Area Convention & Visitors Bureau,** 201 Penniman Rd. (253-0192), ½mi. northwest of the transportation center. Open M-F 8:30am-5pm. **Colonial Williamsburg Visitors Center,** 102 Information Dr. (800-447-8679), 1mi. northeast of the transportation center. Tickets and transportation to Colonial Williamsburg. Open daily 8:30am-8pm; off-season hrs. vary.

**Post Office:** 425 N. Boundary St. (229-4668). Open M-F 8am-5pm, Sa 10am-2pm. **ZIP Code:** 23185 **Area Code:** 757.

# ACCOMMODATIONS

The hotels operated by the **Colonial Williamsburg Foundation** are generally more expensive than other lodgings in the area. **Rt. 60W** and **Rt. 31S** are packed with budget motels, which grow cheaper the farther they are from the historic district. At various bed and breakfasts around the College of William and Mary, guests pay more for gorgeous colonial decor. Guest houses take away the breakfast, but still offer the bed, a reasonable price, abounding warmth, and "like-home" feelings.

**Lewis Guest House,** 809 Lafayette St. (229-6116), a 10min. walk from the historic district. Comfortable rooms, including an upstairs unit with private entrance, kitchen, and shared bath. The perpetually young proprietor, Mrs. Lewis, eagerly shares memories of Williamsburg in the 1930s with her guests. Rooms $25-35.

**Bryant Guest House,** 702 College Terr. (229-3320). Rooms with private baths, TV and limited kitchen facilities in a stately, exquisitely landscaped brick home. Singles $35; doubles $45; 5-person suite $55.

**Jamestown Beach Campsites,** 2217 Jamestown Rd. (229-7609), adjacent to the Jamestown Settlement. One of the largest campgrounds in the area. Swim in a pool with a slide or in the James River. Sites $18, with water and electricity $23, full hookup $25.

# FOOD

Instead of rowdy farmers and proper colonists, most of the authentic-looking "taverns" in Colonial Williamsburg are packed with sweaty tourists and are subsequently overpriced (lunch $5-10, dinner $18 and up). Jumping back into the present for food proves the most price-savvy option.

**Guiseppe's,** 5601 Richmond Rd. (565-1977), in Ewell Station shopping center on Rt. 60, about 2½mi. from the historic district. Italy invades the English colonies (and a modern strip mall). 8 pasta dishes for under $6 and an untraditional menu with fusion entrees like the Fettucine New Mexico (pasta with black beans and Monterrey jack cheese; $5.25). Open M-Sa 11:30am-2pm and 5-9:30pm.

**Green Leafe Cafe,** 765 Scotland St. (220-3405). Classy wooden pub draws crowds of all kinds for a modern twist on pub food. Large and tasty sandwiches ($5-6) and appetizers ($5-8) make a light supper. 30 great brews on tap ($2.75-4), including savory Virginia micros. Su "Mug Night" brings half-price beer. Open daily 11am-2am.

**The Old Chickahominy House,** 1211 Jamestown Rd. (229-4689), ½mi. from the historic district en route to Jamestown. Antiques, dried-flower decor, and pewter-haired locals dine amidst colonial splendor. Becky's "complete luncheon" includes Virginia ham, hot biscuits, fruit salad, a slice of homemade pie, and iced tea or coffee ($6.25). Open daily 8:30-10:15am and 11:30am-2:15pm.

**Chowning's Tavern** (229-2141), on Duke of Gloucester St. Odd dishes like "Bubble and Squeak" (cabbage and potatoes; $7) and "Welsh Rarebit" (bread in beer sauce with ham; $12) will have you chowing like George Washington. After 9pm, costumed waiters throw peanuts, sing 18th-century ballads, and challenge guests to card games. Light meals $3-7. Cover $3. Open daily July-Aug. 8am-midnight; Sept.-June 11am-midnight.

# SIGHTS

**Colonial Williamsburg** will have you spending 1774 treasury notes and singing "my hat, it has three corners" while you dodge horse droppings all the way to the milliner's. The historic district itself doesn't require a ticket—walk around, march behind the fife-and-drum corps, and lock yourself in the stocks for free. Most of the "colonial" shops and two of the historic buildings—the Wren Building and the Bruton Parish Church—are also open to the public. Monday's *Visitor's Companion* newsletter lists free events and evening programs. *(447-8679. Most sights open 9:30am-5pm; for complete hrs., see the Visitor's Companion newsletter. Basic Admission Ticket $27, ages 6-12 $16. 2-day pass $31/$18. Each has various perks, inquire when you purchase.)*

**CROSSING THAT BRIDGE** A jaunt across the **Crim Dell Bridge** at William and Mary College is risky business. If student lore holds truth, then the fate of many a lovelife has been sealed in a single crossing, or shall we say in crossing singly. Superstition dictates that those who tread the bridge's path alone will never marry. Conversely, if passions lead a couple to engage in a kiss with the bridge underfoot, destiny has eternally bound them together. Maybe this chance to say "I Do" has something to do with Playboy naming the bridge the "second most romantic spot on a college campus."

The real fun of Colonial Williamsburg comes from interacting with its history. Trade shops afford wonderful opportunities to learn from skilled artisans such as the carpenter, and slightly less-skilled workmen like the brickmaster, who may invite you to take off your shoes and join him in stomping on wet clay. Colonial denizens are quick to play up their antiquated world view (admitted Floridians are likely to be greeted with startled cries of "Spanish territory!"). Worth its steep admission is the **Governor's Palace,** on the Palace Green. This mansion housed the Tory governors of Virginia until the last one fled in 1775. Colonial weaponry lines the walls, and the extensive gardens include a hedge maze. *(Open daily 9am-5pm. Separate admission $18, ages 6-12 $11.)* Also notable is the **Wythe House,** which belonged to Jefferson and Madison's professor of law, George Wythe.

Spreading west from the corner of Richmond and Jamestown Rd., the **College of William and Mary** is the second-oldest college in the U.S., having educated Presidents Jefferson, Monroe, and Tyler. The **Sir Christopher Wren Building,** probably with no connection to the famed English architect Wren except its contemporary (1695) origin, was built two years after the college received its charter and restored with Rockefeller money.

## NEAR WILLIAMSBURG

**JAMESTOWN AND YORKTOWN.** At **Jamestown National Historic Site,** southwest of Williamsburg on Rt. 31, you'll see the remains of the first permanent English settlement in America (1607), as well as exhibits explaining colonial life. The **visitors center** offers a hokey film, a free 30min. "living history" walking tour, and a 45min. audio tape tour ($2) for the 5mi. **Island Loop Route.** The **Old Church Tower,** built in 1639, is the only 17th-century structure still standing. Also featured is a statue of **Pocahontas.** In the remains of the settlement itself, archeologists uncover the original site of the triangular **Jamestown Fort.** *(229-1733. Open daily 9am-5pm; off-season 9am-4:30pm. Visitors center closes 30min. after the park. Entrance fee $5.)*

The nearby **Jamestown Settlement** is a commemorative museum commemorating with changing exhibits, a reconstruction of James Fort, a Native American village, and full-scale replicas of the three ships that brought the original settlers to Jamestown in 1607. The 20min. dramatic film details the settlement's history, including a discussion of settler relations with the indigenous Powhatan tribe. *(229-1607. Open daily 9am-5pm. $10.25, ages 6-12 $5.)*

The British defeat at **Yorktown** in 1781 signaled the end of the Revolutionary War. The Yorktown branch of **Colonial National Park,** behind the visitors center, vividly re-creates the significant last battle with an engaging film and an electric map. The visitors center rents tape cassettes and players ($2) for driving the battlefield's 7mi. automobile route. *(757-898-3400. Center open daily 8:30am-5pm; last tape rented at 3:30pm. $4, under 17 free.)* The **Yorktown Victory Center,** 1 block from Rt. 17 on Rt. 238, brims with Revolutionary War items and an intriguing "living history" exhibit: in an encampment in front, soldiers from the 1781 Continental Army take a break from combat. *(757-887-1776. Open daily 9am-5pm. $7.25, seniors $6.50, ages 6-12 $3.50).*

**JAMES RIVER PLANTATIONS.** Built near the water to facilitate the planters' commercial and social lives, these country houses buttressed the slave-holding Virginia aristocracy. Reconstructed **Carter's Grove Plantation,** 6mi. east of Williamsburg on Rt. 60, maintains the colonial feel. Also redone were slave quarters and an archaeological dig. The **Winthrop Rockefeller Archaeological Museum,** built unobtrusively into a hillside, provides a fascinating case-study look at archaeology. *(757-229-1000, ext. 2973. Plantation open Tu-Su 9am-5pm; Nov.-Dec. 9am-4pm. Museum and slave quarters open Mar.-Dec. Tu-Su 9am-5pm. $17, ages 6-12 $9.)*

   **Berkeley Plantation,** halfway between Richmond and Williamsburg on Rt. 5, claims to be the site of the invention of bourbon by British settlers, and later saw the birth of short-lived President William Henry Harrison. Beautiful, terraced boxwood gardens stretch from the original 1726 building to the James River. *(804-829-6018. Open daily 9am-5pm. $8.50, seniors $6.65, ages 13-16 $6.50, ages 6-12 $4. Grounds alone $5/$3.60/$2.50.)* To reach **Shirley Plantation,** follow Rt. 5 west from Williamsburg, or east from Richmond. Surviving war after war, this 1613 plantation has an exquisite Queen Anne-style mansion featuring a seemingly unsupported 3-story staircase. *(800-232-1613. Open daily 9am-5pm. $8.50, ages 13-21 $5.50, ages 6-12 $4.50.)*

**BEER AND ROLLERCOASTERS. Busch Gardens,** 3mi. southeast of Williamsburg on Rt. 60, has tooth-rattling old favorites like Drachen Fire and Loch Ness Monster and the new **Alpengeist:** at 195ft., the tallest, fastest, most twisted hanging roller coaster in the world. *(253-3350. Open late June through Aug. Su-F 10am-10pm, Sa 10am-11pm; Sept.-Oct. M and F 10am-6pm, Sa-Su 10am-7pm; call for winter hrs. $35, seniors $29.70, ages 3-6 $28. Cheaper after 5pm.)*

   A 3-day ticket ($55) is good for both Busch Gardens and **Water Country: USA,** 2mi. away. This 40-acre water-park-to-end-all-water-parks features rides like **Aquazoid,** which dazzles with laser lights and darkened tunnels. *(Open late May to mid-June Sa-Su about 10am-6pm; mid-June to mid-Aug. daily about 10am-8pm; Sept. Sa-Su about 10am-7pm. Hrs. vary; call ahead. Admission $22.50, ages 3-6 18; after 3pm $16.50 for all.)*

# VIRGINIA BEACH

After decades as the capital of the cruising collegiate crowd, Virginia Beach is shedding its playground image and maturing into a family-oriented vacation spot. The town has grown into Virginia's largest city, and along with its nearby neighbors, Norfolk, Newport News, and Hampton, the city is making the Hampton Roads region a more attractive place to visit. However, even the most dogged clean-up campaigns cannot stem the tide of fast-food joints, motels, and discount shops that characterize every beach town. But beyond all the slurpees and suntan oil, Virginia Beach's beautiful ocean sunrises, substantial dolphin population, and frequent military jet flyovers set it apart from its East Coast counterparts.

## ◪ ORIENTATION AND PRACTICAL INFORMATION

Virginia Beach is easy to get to and around. The shortest route from **D.C.** follows I-64 east from Richmond through the perpetually congested Hampton Roads Bridge Tunnel into Norfolk. At Norfolk turn onto Rt. 44 (the Virginia Beach-Norfolk Expwy.), which leads straight to 22nd St. and the beach. Alternately, avoid the Hampton Roads Bridge-Tunnel and get off I-64E at I-664. Take I-664 to I-64W via the Monitor-Merrimac Bridge-Tunnel. From I-64W, get off on Rt. 44 and follow it to the beach. From the **northern coast** (near Ocean City, MD), take Rt. 13S across the 20mi. Chesapeake Bay Bridge-Tunnel (toll $10). Follow Rt. 60E into the Virginia Beach resort community.

   In Virginia Beach, east-west streets are numbered and the north-south avenues, running parallel to the beach, have ocean names. **Atlantic** and **Pacific Avenue** comprise the main drag. **Arctic, Baltic,** and **Mediterranean Ave.** are farther inland.

   **Amtrak:** (245-3589). The nearest train station, in Newport News, runs 45min. bus service to and from the corner of 19th and Pacific St.; you reserve your train ticket before leaving Virginia Beach. To: Washington, D.C. (6hr., $44); Philadelphia (8½hr., $81); Baltimore (7hr., $58); Richmond (4hr., $19); and Williamsburg (2hr., $15).

MID-ATLANTIC

**Greyhound:** 1017 Laskin Rd. (422-2998). To: Washington, D.C. (6½hr., $31); Richmond (3½hr., $24); and Williamsburg (2½hr., $15).

**Public Transit: Virginia Beach Transit/Trolley Information Center** (640-6300), Atlantic Ave. and 24th St. Info on area transportation and tours, including trolleys, buses, and ferries. Trolleys transport riders to most major points in Virginia Beach. The Atlantic Ave. Trolley runs from Rudee Inlet to 42nd St. (May-Sept. daily noon-midnight; 50¢, seniors and disabled 25¢, day passes $1.50). Other trolleys run along the boardwalk, the North Seashore, and to Lynnhaven Mall. **Tidewater Regional Transit (TRT)** (640-6300), in the Silverleaf Commuter Center at Holland Rd. and Independence St., buses connect Virginia Beach with Norfolk, Portsmouth, and Newport News (fare $1.50, seniors and disabled 75¢, children under 38in. free).

**Bike/Moped Rental: Tom's Bike Rentals** (425-8454) will deliver rental bikes for about $15 per day. Numerous stores along the boardwalk rent in-line skates for a similar fee.

**Tourist Info: Virginia Beach Visitors Center,** 2100 Parks Ave. (437-4888 or 800-446-8038), at 22nd St. Open daily 9am-8pm; Labor Day to Memorial Day 9am-5pm.

**Post Office:** (428-2821). Located at 24th St. and Atlantic Ave. Open M-F 8am-4:30pm. **ZIP Code:** 23458. **Area Code:** 757.

# ⌐ ACCOMMODATIONS

The number of motels in Virginia Beach is unreasonably high and, consequently, rates are typically low. Oceanside, Atlantic and Pacific Ave. boast the most desirable hotels. If you reserve in advance, rates are around $45 in winter and $85 in summer. Groups should look for "efficiency" apartments, which are rented by the week. For any bed, the further from the shore, the lower the price of lodging.

**Angie's Guest Cottage, Bed and Breakfast, and HI-AYH Hostel,** 302 24th St. (428-4690). Friendly staff, sparklingly clean rooms, and plenty of boogie boards in a prime area of town. Barbara "Angie" Yates welcomes guests with exceptional warmth, free trolley tokens, and great advice about the beach scene. Kitchen, lockers. Linen $2. No lockout. Open Apr. 1-Oct. 1. Reservations helpful. Check-in 10am-9pm. 2-day min. stay for private rooms. Private hostel rooms with A/C $32.90, 2 people $24.70 per person, 3 people $21.20 per person; substantially less in off-season. Dorm rooms $17.75, HI-AYH members $14.50; off-season $14.50, HI-AYH members $11.

**Ocean Palms Motel,** 2907 Arctic Ave. (428-8362), at 30th St. 2-person efficiencies with nondescript decor. TV, A/C, kitchen. $30-50 per night.

**First Landings State Park,** 2500 Shore Dr. (481-2131, reservations 800-933-7275), about 8mi. north of town on U.S. 60. Take the North Seashore Trolley. Beachfront sites with the beauty of Virginia's shore. Because of its desirable location, the park is very popular; call 2-3 weeks ahead (during business hrs.) for reservations. Beach access available to the general public. Open 8am-dusk. Sites $18; no hookups.

# ◖ FOOD

Prepare for more $5 all-you-can-eat breakfast specials than you have ever previously encountered. Alternately, fish for a restaurant on **Atlantic Ave.** where each block is a virtual buffet of fried, fatty, sweet, or creamy dining options.

▨ **The Jewish Mother,** 3108 Pacific Ave. (422-5430). Let Mama fill your belly with deli in this popular VA chain restaurant where kids-at-heart can color on the walls and souvenir menus with free crayons. Huge sandwiches with a scoop of potato salad ($4-6.25) should be followed by one of the overwhelming desserts ($3.50-4.50). Live music nightly; W popular Blues Jam. "Attitude Adjustment Hour" (daily 4-7pm) with $1 domestic drafts. Cover about $3-5. Open M-F 8:30am-2am, Sa 8am-3am, Su 7am-2am.

**Giovanni's Pasta Pizza Palace,** 2006 Atlantic Ave. (425-1575). The waiters serve with gusto in this affordable and plentiful restaurant. Tasty Italian pastas, pizzas, hot strombolis ($5-9), and a fabulous veggiboli ($6). Open daily noon-midnight.

**Ellington's Restaurant,** 2901 Atlantic Ave. (428-4585), in the Oceanfront Inn. Patrons gaze upon the undulating Atlantic while enjoying grilled portobello burgers ($6), a huge lunch salad ($5), or slightly costly entrees ($9-15) like the blackened tuna steak with pineapple salsa ($13). Open Su-Th 7am-10pm, F-Sa 7am-11pm.

**Cuisine and Co.,** 3004 Pacific Ave. (428-6700). Gained Martha Stewart's seal of approval for over-the-counter gourmet lunches from an ever-changing menu. Typical treats include veggie pita pizzas ($2), $6 per lb. stuffed baked potatoes, and immaculate cookies ($7.50 per lb.). Open M-Sa 9am-7pm, Su 9am-6:30pm.

**Happy Crab's,** 550 Laskin Rd. (437-9200). Early-bird specials (daily 5-6:30pm) offer unbeatable 2-person size seafood platters ($13) or huge 1-person servings big enough to split, like immaculate ribs ($11). Call ahead and a free restaurant taxi will pick you up at the beach and bring you to the restaurant. Open daily 11am-10:30pm.

## ◉ ♫ SIGHTS AND ENTERTAINMENT

The **beach and boardwalk,** jam-packed with college revelers, bikini-clad sunbathers, and an increasing number of families, is the reason people come to Virginia Beach. The **Old Coast Guard Station,** 24th St. and oceanfront offers historic exhibits and a Tower Cam for voyeuristic peeks of sunbunnies. (422-1587. Open M-Sa 10am-5pm, Su noon-5pm; off-season closed M. $2.50, seniors $2, children $1.) The frequent roar of jet engines will remind you of the Air Force bases nearby (433-3131 for visitor info). The **Virginia Maritime Museum,** 717 General Booth Blvd., is home to over 50 species of fish, sharks, and stingrays. (437-4949. Open daily 9am-9pm; off-season 9am-5pm. $9, seniors $8, ages 4-11 $6. IMAX $7/seniors $6.50/ages 4-11 $6. Combined museum and IMAX $12/$11/$10.)

On summer nights, the beach becomes a lovers' walk, and **Atlantic St.,** "Beach St., USA," burgeons with street performers employed by the city. Every block has its own little stage, with bigger venues at 7th, 17th, and 24th St., where groups ranging from Hawaiian dancers to barbershop quartets give performances. (Schedules for main events are posted along the street; call 440-6628 for more info.) Boogie your body at **Peabodys,** 209 21st St., which sports the largest dance floor on the beach. A young, scantily-clad crowd bops to Top 40 hits, especially during "Hammertime" (daily 7-9pm) when drinks are only $1.50. (422-6212. Open Th-Sa 7pm-2am). **Chicho's,** on Atlantic Ave. between 21st and 22nd St., is one of the hot spots on "The Block" of closet-sized bars clustered near the water. Locals swear by the gooey pizza; an all-you-can-eat special ($6) is offered daily from noon-5pm. (422-6011. No cover. Restaurant open M-F noon-2am, Sa-Su 1pm-2am.) One block from the HI-AYH hostel, **Harpoon Larry's,** at 24th St. and Pacific Ave., serves tasty fish in an everyone-knows-your-name atmosphere. (422-6000. Happy hour M-F 7-9pm, specials include deals on seafood and rum runners. Open daily noon-2am.)

# CHARLOTTESVILLE

Thomas Jefferson, composer of the Declaration of Independence and colonial Renaissance man, built his dream house, Monticello, high atop his "little mountain." Around it, Jefferson sought to create an ideal community, primarily by transplanting fellow presidents Monroe and Madison to the Charlottesville area for friendly visits and creating the University of Virginia. His vision of intellectual glory was fulfilled; today the college sustains Charlottesville economically, geographically, and culturally. Imbedded in its native south, the university nourishes a community of pubs and poets, producing a smorgasbord of literary greats from Edgar Allen Poe to Rita Dove. UVA's idyllic campus is a symbol of academia itself.

## 🔃 ORIENTATION AND PRACTICAL INFORMATION

Charlottesville streets are numbered from east to west, using compass directions; 5th St. NW is 10 blocks from (and parallel to) 5th St. NE. There are two downtowns: one on the west side across from the university called **The Corner,** home to student-driven delis and hip coffee shops, and **Historic Downtown** about 1mi. east and a couple notches higher on the price scale. The two are connected by **University Avenue,** running east-west, which starts as Ivy Rd. and becomes Main St. after a bridge. **Rt. 64,** running east-west to Richmond, is Charlottesville's main feeder.

**Train: Amtrak,** 810 W. Main St. (296-4559), 7 blocks from downtown. To: **Washington, D.C.** (3hr., 1 per day, $23); **New York** (7-8hr., 1 per day, $72); **Baltimore** (4hr., 1 per day, $36); and **Philadelphia** (5½hr., 1 per day, $54). Open daily 5:30am-9pm.

**Buses: Greyhound/Trailways:** 310 W. Main St. (295-5131), within 3 blocks of downtown. To: **Richmond** (1½-4hr., 6 per day, $19); **Washington, D.C.** (3hr., 5 per day, $30); **Norfolk** (4hr., 2 per day, $36); **Baltimore** (4-5hr., 4 per day, $46); and **Philadelphia** (7-11hr., 4 per day, $54). Open M-Sa 7am-8:30pm, Su noon-8:30pm.

**Public Transit: Charlottesville Transit Service** (296-7433). Bus service within city limits. Maps available at both info centers, the Chamber of Commerce, and the UVA student center in Newcomb Hall. Buses operate M-Sa 6:30am-6:30pm. Fare 75¢, seniors and disabled 33¢, under 6 free. The more frequent UVA buses technically require UVA ID, but a studious look usually suffices.

**Taxis: Yellow Cab,** 295-4131.

**Visitor Info: Chamber of Commerce,** 415 E. Market St. (295-3141), within walking distance of Amtrak, Greyhound, and downtown. Open M-F 9am-5pm. **Thomas Jefferson Visitors Center** (977-1783, ext. 121), off I-64 on Rt. 20. Arranges same-day discount lodgings, packages to Jefferson sights. 30min. film about Jefferson shown on the hr. 10am-4pm ($2.50), plus free exhibit. Open daily Mar.-Oct. 9am-5:30pm; Nov.-Feb. 9am-5pm. **University of Virginia Information Center** (924-7969), at the Rotunda in the campus center. Brochures, a university map, and tour info. Open daily 9am-4:45pm.

**Campus Police:** dial 4-7166 on a UVA campus phone.

**Hotlines: Region 10 Community Services:** 972-1800. **Mental Health:** 977-4673. **Rape Crisis Center:** 977-7273. All 24hr. **Lesbian and Gay:** 982-2773. Open Sept.-May Su 6-10pm and M-W 7-10pm. **Women's Health Clinic** (in Richmond): 800-254-4479. 24hr.

**Post Office:** 513 E. Main St. (963-2525). Open M-F 8:30am-5pm, Sa 10am-1pm. **ZIP Code:** 22902. **Area Code:** 804.

# ▌ ACCOMMODATIONS

**Emmet St. (U.S. 29)** houses generic hotels and motels ($40-60) that tend to fill up during summer weekends and big UVA events. **Budget Inn,** 140 Emmet St., is near the university. (293-5141. Singles $42, doubles $52, $5 per additional person. Reception daily 8am-midnight.) **EconoLodge-University,** 400 Emmet St., is across from the UVA campus and has pool access (296-2104 or 800-424-4777; singles $48; doubles $60). **Charlottesville KOA Kampground,** Rt. 708, has shaded camping 10mi. outside Charlottesville. Take U.S. 29 S to Rt. 708 SE. (296-9881 or 800-562-1743. Recreation hall, pool, laundry facilities. Fishing and pets allowed. Sites $18, with water and electricity $23, full hookup $25. Open Mar.-Oct.)

# ◖ FOOD

**The Corner** across from UVA boasts bookstores and countless cheap eats, with good Southern grub in Charlottesville's unpretentious diners. The **Emmet St.** strip is lined with fast-food franchises. **The Downtown Mall,** about five blocks off E. Main St., is a brick pedestrian thoroughfare lined with upscale restaurants and shops.

▧ **The Hardware Store,** 316 E. Main St. (977-1518 or 800-426-6001). Off-beat bar and grill serves beers ($2.50) in ½ yd. tubes and condiments from toolboxes. Eclectic American food includes meal-sized baked spuds ($5-7.25), specialty potato pierogies ($4), and desserts that repair any woe ($3.50). Open M-Th 11am-9pm, F-Su 11am-10pm.

▧ **Southern Culture,** 633 W. Main St. (979-1990). Most entrees are $9-10, but the $7 red beans and rice blend some intense spice. Sweet potato pie ($4.25) invokes sweet dreams. Open M-Sa 5-10:30pm, Su 11am-2:30pm and 5-10:30pm.

**Oregano Joe's,** 1252 Emmet St. (971-9308). Virginia wine, tasty bread, and Italian specialties top the tables at this casually romantic pasta haven. The sandwiches ($5-7) are an experience, as are the massive pasta entrees ($6-13), such as triangular mushroom ravioli ($8.25). Open M-Th 11am-10pm, F 11am-11pm, Sa 4-11pm, Su 4-10pm.

**Littlejohn's,** 427 University Ave. (977-0588). Sandwiches and deli are overstuffed—one with meats, the other with business people. In the wee hours of the morning, Littlejohn's becomes a cool late-night hang. A large selection of great sandwiches ($3-6) and monstrous muffins ($1.20). Large selection of beers ($1.75). Open 24hr.

## 👁 SIGHTS

Most activity on the grounds of the **University of Virginia** clusters around the **Lawn** and fraternity-lined **Rugby Road.** *(924-3239.)* Jefferson's Monticello is visible from the lawn, a terraced green carpet that is one of the prettiest spots in American academia. Professors live in the Lawn's pavilions; Jefferson designed each one in a different architectural style. Privileged Fourth Years (never called seniors) are chosen each year for the small Lawn singles. Room 13 is dedicated to ne'er-do-well Edgar Allen Poe, who was kicked out for gambling. The early-morning clanging of the bell that used to hang in the **Rotunda** provoked one incensed student to shoot at the building. *(924-3592. Open daily 9am-4:45pm. Tours 10am-4pm on the hr.)* The **Bayley Art Museum,** on Rugby Rd., features changing exhibits and a small permanent collection that includes a cast of Rodin's *The Kiss. (924-7969. Open Tu-Su 1-5pm.)*

Jefferson oversaw every stage of development of his beloved **Monticello,** a home that truly reflects the personality of its brilliant creator. The house is a quasi-Palladian jewel filled with fascinating innovations, such as a fireplace dumbwaiter to the wine cellar and a mechanical copier, all compiled or conceived by Jefferson. The grounds include orchards and flower gardens, and afford magnificent views. *(1184 Monticello Loop. 984-9800. Open daily Mar.-Oct. 8am-5pm; Nov.-Feb. 9am-4:30pm. $9, ages 6-11 $5.)* Just west of Monticello on the Thomas Jefferson Pkwy. (Rt. 53) is the partially reconstructed **Michie Tavern,** which includes an operating grist mill and a general store. *(977-1234. Open daily 9am-5pm. $6, under 6 $2. Last tour 4:20pm.)* To reach **Ash Lawn-Highland,** the 535-acre plantation home of President James Monroe, continue east to the intersection with Rt. 795, 2.5mi. east of Monticello, and make a right. Although less distinctive than Monticello, Ash Lawn reveals more about family life in the early 19th century. *(293-9539. Open daily 9am-6pm; Nov.-Feb. 10am-5pm. Tour $7, seniors $6.50, ages 6-11 $4. AAA 10% discount. Wheelchair access.)*

## 🎵 ENTERTAINMENT AND NIGHTLIFE

This preppy town is full of jazz, rock, and pubs. A kiosk near the fountain in the center of the Downtown Mall has posters with club schedules; the free *Weekly C-ville* can tell you who's playing when. English-language opera and musical theater highlight the **Summer Festival of the Arts** in the Box Gardens behind Ash Lawn (293-4500; open June-Aug. M-F 9am-5pm). Ash Lawn also hosts a **"Music at Twilight"** series on W evenings at 8pm ($10, students $6, seniors $9). **The Downtown Mall** (296-8548) features a free concert series every F from Apr. to Oct.

---

**SMARTY PANTS** When Jefferson undertook the design of the **University of Virginia,** he envisioned an institution where knowledge flowed freely and without end. With this particular image in mind, he enclosed the lawn on three sides, with one side open to represent the limitless possibility of the human intellect. Ironically, the open side provided a spectacular view of his own home at Monticello, suggesting that the mind did indeed have a limit—and Thomas Jefferson had reached it.

▣ **Michael's Bistro & Tap House,** 1427 University Ave. (977-3697). Through a tiny door next to Littlejohn's Deli, enter this melange of culinary and musical styles. Live music (Su-W 10:30pm) includes Su bluegrass, M funk, and Tu jazz. Cover $2-3. 100 beers available. Happy Hour M-Th 3-7 pm with $2 drafts. Open daily 11:30am-2am.

**Outback Lodge,** 917C Preston Ave. (979-7211), in the back of the shopping complex. Dave Matthews and the band did some home-town relaxing in this warehouse-like pub. Philly cheesesteak ($5) and fajitas ($8). Bluegrass and funk on F-Sa. Happy hour M-F 4-7pm. Live music Tu-Sa with $2-10 cover. Open M-F 11am-2am, Sa-Su 5pm-2am.

**Baja Bean,** 1327 W. Main St. (293-4507). Burritos, tamales and chimichangas go down smooth for under $8 at this California-style Mexican eatery and bar. Fishbowl-sized margaritas change flavors daily ($3.50). Popular open mic Su 9pm. Open daily 11am-2am.

**Orbit Billiards & Cafe,** 216 Water St. (984-5707). Mellow, smoky attic with pool tables ($1) around a central bar draws a more eclectic crowd than most C-ville places—students, locals, and hard-core pool sharks mix it up for $2 drinks on Tu and Th. Occasional live music. Open daily noon-1am.

# SHENANDOAH NATIONAL PARK

Shenandoah National Park was America's first great natural reclamation project. In 1926, Congress authorized Virginia to purchase a 280-acre tract of over-logged, over-hunted land. A 1936 decree from Franklin Roosevelt sought to improve the land, experimenting with trappers to foster new life upon the slowly rejuvenating soil. Today a stunning national park spans 196,000 acres and is home to 500mi. of trails and more plant species than all of Europe. On clear days, visitors can see mi. of unspoiled ridges and treetops. However, clear days are a rare commodity, as pollution has mixed with the natural dew in the area to create a murky mist cloaking the peaks. Shenandoah's amazing technicolor mountains—covered with foliage in the summer, streaked with brilliant reds, oranges, and yellows in the fall— offer relaxation and recreation throughout the year.

🔢 **ORIENTATION AND PRACTICAL INFORMATION.** The park runs nearly 75mi. along the famous 105mi. **Skyline Drive,** from Front Royal in the north to Rockfish Gap in the south. Miles are measured north to south and denote the location of trails and stops. Three major highways divide the park into sections. The **North Section** runs from Rt. 340 to Rt. 211, the **Central Section** from Rt. 211 to Rt. 33, and the **South Section** from Rt. 33 to Rt. 250 and I-64. (Entrance fee $10 per vehicle, or $5 per hiker, biker, or bus passenger. Admission for disabled persons is free. Pass is valid for seven days and is necessary for re-admittance. Most facilities hibernate in the winter; call ahead. Skyline Dr. closes during and following bad weather.)

The **Dickey Ridge Visitors Center** (635-3566), at Mi. 4.6, and the **Byrd Visitors Center** (635-3283), at Mi. 51, answer questions and maintain small exhibits about the park including a 15-minute slide show (open Apr.-Oct. Su-Th 8:30am-5pm, F-Sa 8:30am-5pm; Dickey is open through Nov.). The stations also offer excellent talks on local wildlife, short guided walks among the flora, and lantern-lit evening discussions. Comprehensive and newly updated, the *Guide to Shenandoah National Park and Skyline Drive* ($7.50) is available at both Visitors Centers. For general park information call 999-2243 (daily 8am-4:30pm) or 999-3500 for a recorded message. Send mail to: Superintendent, Park Headquarters, Shenandoah National Park, Rt. 4, P.O. Box 348, Luray, VA 22835. In an emergency call 800-732-0911.

**Greyhound** sends buses once per day from D.C. to Waynesboro, near the park's southern entrance ($43); no bus or train serves Front Royal, near the park's northern entrance. **Rockfish Gap** is 25mi. from Charlottesville on Rt. 64. From D.C., take Rt. 66W to Rt. 340S to Front Royal (1½ hr.). **Area code:** 540.

🔥 **ACCOMMODATIONS. The Bear's Den** (HI-AYH; 554-8708), located 35mi. north of Shenandoah on Rt. 601, in a miniature stone castle, has two 10-bed dorm rooms and one room with 1 double bed and 2 bunk beds. Take Rt. 340N to Rt. 50E to

601N, and turn left at the gate. The less-than-rustic hostel has a dining room, kitchen, on-site parking, and a laundry room. (Reception 7:30-9:30am and 5-10pm. Front gate locked and quiet hrs. begin at 10pm; 24hr. access to hikers' basement room. Check-out 9:30am. Beds $12, non-members $15; private room $30, non-members $36. Camping $6 per person with use of hostel facilities, $3 without.) The park also maintains two affordable "lodges," essentially motels with nature-friendly exteriors. **Skyland** (999-2211 or 800-999-4714), Mi. 42 on Skyline Dr., offers wood-furnished cabins ($46-79, $5-7 more in Oct.; open Apr.-Oct.) and more upscale motel rooms ($79-145, Sa-Su $83-155; open Mar.-Nov.). **Big Meadows** (999-2221 or 800-999-4714), Mi. 51, has similar services, also with a historic lodge ($79-125, Sa-Su $83-155) and cabins ($70-72; open late Apr.-Nov.). **Lewis Mountain** (999-2255 or 800-999-4714), Mi. 57, operates cabins with kitchens ($55-83, $7 more in Oct.). Reservations are necessary; call up to six months in advance. The park service also maintains four major campgrounds (800-365-2267): **Mathews Arm** (Mi. 22), **Big Meadows** (Mi. 51), **Lewis Mountain** (Mi. 58), and **Loft Mountain** (Mi. 80). The latter three have stores, laundry, and showers (no hookups). Heavily wooded and uncluttered by RVs, Mathews Arm and Lewis Mountain make for the happiest tenters. Sites at Mathews Arm, Lewis Mountain, and Loft Mountain are $14, at Big Meadows $17. Reservations are possible only at Big Meadows.

**◪ HIKING AND OUTDOORS.** Many visitors choose to experience the park by taking a ride along Skyline Dr. and stopping occasionally to take short hikes, enjoy the views at scenic overlooks, or picnic. The drive contains seven picnic areas (located at Mi. 5, 24, 37, 51, 58, 63, and 80) with bathrooms, potable water, and scenic places to eat. The *Guide to Shenandoah and Skyline Drive* includes an extensive hikes section with descriptions of every trail in the park. The trails off Skyline Dr. are heavily used and safe for cautious day-hikers with maps, appropriate footwear, and water. If you do not feel comfortable hiking on your own or want to try a longer hike, you might consider one of the free ranger-led tours arranged by the Visitors Center. The middle section of the park, from **Thorton Gap** (Mi. 30) to **South River** (Mi. 63), bursts with photo opportunities and moving views, although it tends to be crowded. The **Whiteoak Canyon Trail**, at Mi. 42.6, opens upon an impressive 86 ft. waterfall and is a relatively easy 4.6mi. hike (allow 3-4hr. for the hike and some time at the falls). The adjacent **Limberlost Trail** (5 mi. round-trip from Whiteoak Canyon; 1.2mi. handicapped-accessible loop from trailhead at Mi. 43) slithers into a hemlock forest. Nearby, the popular **Old Rag Mountain Trail**, located 5 mi. from Mi. 45 (main trail starts outside park; from U.S. 211, turn right on Rt. 522, then right on Rt. 231 and watch for a sign), entices adventure seekers to scramble up 3291 ft. to triumphant views of the valley below; the 8.8 mi. loop takes 6-8 hours ($3 fee for Old Rag hikers 16 and older who have not paid Shenandoah admission). Farther south, at Mi. 50.7, hikers retrace Thomas Jefferson's footsteps along the **Dark Hollow Falls Trail**, 1.4 mi. At Mi. 63, the 3.3mi. **South River Falls Trail** leads to a splendid viewing platform for the falls.

Shenandoah sports more backpackers per mi. than any other park. Back-country camping is free, but you must obtain a permit at a park entrance, visitors center, ranger station, or the park headquarters. Camping without a permit or above 2800 ft. is illegal and unsafe. Trail maps and the PATC guide can be obtained at the visitors center. The PATC puts out 3 topographical maps ($5 each). The Appalachian Trail (A.T.) runs the length of the park. The **Potomac Appalachian Trail Club** (PATC) maintains 6 cabins in backcountry areas of the park. Campers who feel that they are sufficiently ready for a backpacking trip but not totally comfortable with staying in the woods on their own might consider staying at one of these rustic accommodations. You must reserve space in the cabins in advance by writing to the club at 118 Park St. SE, Vienna, VA 22180-4609 or calling 703-242-0693 or 703-242-0315 (M-Th 7-9pm, or Th-F noon-2pm). Bring lanterns and food; the cabins contain only bunk beds, blankets, and stoves. (Su-Th $3 per person, F-Sa $14 per group; 1 group member must be at least 21.) Though stamps from 3 different lodgings constitute eligibility, casual backpackers should avoid the shelters strewn at 7mi. intervals along the park's segment of the A.T. because trail etiquette usually reserves the cabins for those hiking large stretches of the A.T.

## NEAR SHENANDOAH

**LURAY CAVERNS.** Mother Nature worked millions of years to sculpt the limestone bowels of the earth into delicate marvels of color and form. Luray Caverns winds tourists through moist, 57 degree tunnels filled with mineral formations. Discovered in 1878, the elaborate underground passage features a playable "Stalagpipe Organ." *(743-6551. Exit 264 off I-81 to U.S. 211. Open June 15 to Labor Day daily 9am-7pm; Mar. 15 to June 14 and Labor Day to Oct. 31 daily 9am-6pm; Nov. to Mar. 14 M-F 9am-4pm, Sa-Su 9am-5pm. Admission $14, seniors $12, ages 7-13 $6; $1 AAA discount.)*

**ENDLESS CAVERNS.** Less touristed than the Luray Caverns, the beauty of creation takes precedence over the tourist board at Endless Caverns, the wildest of the caves, with 5½mi. of passages documented and an unknown number still unexplored. *(896-2283. Follow signs from the intersection of U.S. 11 and U.S 211 in New Market. Open daily June 15-Labor Day 9am-7pm; Labor Day-Nov. 14 and Mar. 15-June 14 9am-5pm; Nov. 15-Mar. 14 9am-4pm. $11, ages 3-12 $5.50; $1 AAA discount.)*

**SKYLINE CAVERNS.** The smallest and the closest to D.C., **Skyline Caverns** tends an orchid-like garden of white rock spikes; one grows every 7000 years. *(Tel. 635-4545 or 800-296-4545. On U.S. 340, 1mi. from the junction of U.S. 211 and Skyline Dr. Open daily June 5 to Labor Day 9am-6:30pm; Mar. 15 to June 4 and Labor Day to Nov. 14 9am-5pm; Nov. 15 to Mar. 14 daily 9am-4pm. $10, senior, AAA, and military $9, ages 7-13 $5.)*

**OTHER SITES.** The **Shenandoah Vineyards** hosts free tours and wine tastings daily. *(3659 S. Ox Rd. off I-81. 984-8699. Open Mar.-Dec. 10am-6pm; Jan.-Feb. 9am-5pm. Free.)* If a scenic paddle floats your boat, contact **Downriver Canoe Co.** in Bentonville, which offers canoe, kayak, raft, and tube trips and rentals. *(Tel. 635-5526 or 800-338-1963. From Skyline Dr. Mi. 20 follow U.S 211W for 8mi., then take U.S. 340N 14mi. to Bentonville; turn right onto Rt. 613 and go 1mi.)* Alternately, try **Front Royal Canoe** on U.S. 340 3 mi. south of Skyline Dr. *(800-270-8808 or 635-5440. 15% discount Tu-Th.)*

## BLUE RIDGE PARKWAY

The beauty of unrestrained wilderness does not end at the southern gates of Shenandoah. The 469mi. **Blue Ridge Pkwy.**, continuous with Skyline Dr., runs through Virginia and North Carolina, connecting the Shenandoah (Virginia) and Great Smoky Mountains (Tennessee) National Parks. Administered by the National Park Service, the parkway sprouts hiking trails, campsites, and picnic grounds with humbling mountain views. While still accessible in the winter, it lacks maintenance or park service between Nov. and Apr. The parkway is more sporadic than Skyline Dr.—in some spots wild and uncrowded, while in others bordering modern farms and towns. From Shenandoah National Park, the road winds south through Virginia's **George Washington National Forest** from Waynesboro to Roanoke. The forest's **visitors center,** 540-291-1306, 12mi. off the parkway at Mi. 70 on Rt. 11 in Natural Bridge, has info on camping, canoeing, and mountain-lake swimming at Sherando Lake (4½mi. off the parkway at Mi. 16; user fee $8).

Across from the visitors center, a water-carved *Arch de Triomphe*, the **Natural Bridge,** towers 219 ft. above green-lined falls and an underground river. One of the seven natural wonders of the world, the initials vandalous George Washington carved into the side are still visible. The nightly "Drama of Creation" light and sound show chronicles the Hebrew Scriptures' 7 days of creation. (540-291-2121 or 800-533-1410. $8, senior $7, ages 6-15 $4. Wheelchair access.)

Hiking trails range from the **Mountain Farm Trail** (Mi. 5.9), an easy 20min. hike to a reconstructed homestead, to the **Rock Castle Gorge Trail** (Mi. 167), a 3hr. excursion. The 0.16mi. **Linn Cove Viaduct Access Trail** (Mi. 304.4) is wheelchair accessible. 3-5mi. trails start from **Peaks of Otter** (Mi. 84), where you can camp at the lowest point on the parkway among peaks as high as 4500 ft. **Humpback Rocks,** a greenstone formation (Mi. 5.8), is an easy hike to the namesake emerald mounds. Real go-getters venture onto the **Appalachian Trail,** which leads all the way to Georgia or Maine.

There is more to the Blue Ridge Pkwy. than hiking. **Mabry Mill** (Mi. 176.1) feeds ham and biscuits ($4.35) in a mountain farmland. **Doughton Park** (Mi. 241) and **Crabtree Meadows** (Mi. 339) hawk local nature-inspired crafts. Between Mi. 292 and 295, the opulent manor at **Moses H. Cone Memorial Park** rents canoes on Price Lake, Mi. 291. (Open May 27 to Sept. 4 daily 8:30am-6pm; May 6-21 and Sept. 9 to Oct. 29 Sa-Su 10am-6pm. $4 per hr., $3 per additional hr.) The Park Service hosts a variety of ranger-led activities; info is available at the **visitors centers** (see below).

There are 9 **campgrounds** along the parkway, each with water (no showers) and restrooms, located at Mi. 60.9, 86, 120.5, 167.1, 239, 297, 316.3, 339.5, and 408.6 ($12, reservations not accepted). An inconspicuous iron gate hides the **Blue Ridge Country HI-AYH Hostel,** Mi. 214.5, 7mi. south on Rt. 89 from the town of Galax, housed in a recreated colonial building. (540-236-4962. $13, nonmembers $16. 22 beds. Kitchen available. Jams 2nd and 4th F nights of each month. Lockout 9:30am-5pm. Curfew 11pm. Open Mar.-Dec.)

Galax hosts 1 mountain music concert per month, and the famed **Fiddler's Convention** (540-236-8541) the 2nd weekend in Aug. The tiny hippie-redneck hamlet of Floyd, 40mi. north, swells with its free weekly **jamboree** in the **Floyd County General Store** (540-745-4563) F at 7pm.

Where Skyline Dr. melts into Blue Ridge Pkwy., at the intersections of I-81 and I-64, more modern rooms crowd **Lexington.** Comfortable, 50s-style accommodation at **Overnight Guests,** 216 W. Washington St. (540-463-2376), 8mi. off the Blue Ridge Pkwy., directly across from Washington and Lee, is only $10 per night. (TV, no A/C. Call 9-11pm to reach the proprietor; otherwise, check the list of available rooms in the front hall.) Hungry travelers grab pasta ($6) or overstuffed sandwiches ($3-5) in the garden at **Harb's Bistro,** 19 W. Washington St. Mornings start with coffee and a huge muffin for $1.50. (540-464-1900. Open M-Sa 8am-3pm, Su 9am-3pm; in winter M 8am-8pm, Tu-Th 8am-10pm, F-Sa 8am-11pm, Su 9am-3pm.) Before heading back to the parkway, the **Lee Chapel and Museum,** within the Washington and Lee campus, holds Confederate General (and college namesake) Robert E. Lee's sarcophagus and exhibits on his views on education (540-463-8768. Open daily 9am-5pm. Free.) For further attractions and accommodations, contact the **Lexington Visitor Center,** 106 E. Washington St. (540-463-3777). Other cities and villages along the parkway also offer a range of accommodations, mostly motels (rates $35-55).

For general info on the parkway, call the park service in Roanoke, VA (540-857-2490). To plan ahead, write to **Blue Ridge Pkwy. Headquarters,** 400 BB&T Bldg., Asheville, NC 28801 (704-271-4779). Twelve **visitors centers** line the parkway at Mi. 5.8, 63.6, 85.9, 169, 217.5, 294, 304.5, 316.4, 364.5, and 382, located at entry points where highways intersect the Blue Ridge (most open daily 9am-5pm).

# WEST VIRGINIA

With 80% of the state cloaked in untamed forests, hope of commercial expansion and economic prosperity once seemed a distant dream for West Virginian. When the state's mines began to exhaust, the state appeared doomed—that is until the state decided to use the beauty of wild seclusion to its advantage and began capitalizing on its evergreen expanses, tranquil trails, and raging rivers. Today, thousands of tourists forge paths into West Virginia's untamed, beautiful landscape.

## ◪ PRACTICAL INFORMATION

**Capital:** Charleston.

**Visitor Info: Dept. of Tourism,** 2101 Washington St. E., Bldg. #17, Charleston 25305; P.O. Box 50312 (800-225-5982; www.state.wv.uf/tourism). **U.S. Forest Service Supervisor's Office,** 200 Sycamore St., Elkins 26241 (304-636-1800; open M-F 8am-4:45pm).

**Postal Abbreviation:** WV. **Sales Tax:** 6%.

# HARPERS FERRY

Harpers Ferry witnessed John Brown's famous 1859 raid on the U.S. Armory. Although Brown and his group failed to liberate slaves, the raid brought the nation's sharp moral divisions over slavery to attention. Brown's belief that violence was the only solution to the problem of slavery soon gained credence. During the Civil War itself, the town was a major area of conflict and changed hands eight times. Today, Harpers Ferry is a hotbed for excellent hiking, biking, canoeing, and river rafting. Thomas Jefferson once called the view from a Harpers Ferry overlook "worth a voyage across the Atlantic." That may be extreme, but if you're in the area and enjoy the outdoors, the town is worth a trip.

**⊁ ORIENTATION AND PRACTICAL INFORMATION.** Harpers Ferry is close enough to Washington for a convenient daytrip. Take I-270N to Rt. 340W (bikers with several days to spare may prefer 54mi. on the C&O canal towpath to the 1½hr. drive). **Trains: Amtrak,** on Potomac St. Reservations required; no tickets are sold at the station. Trains to Washington, D.C. (1 per day, $17). The same depot serves the **Maryland Rail Commuter** (MARC; 800-325-7245) trains, a cheaper and more frequent service (2 per day M-F; $7.25). Ticket office open M-F 5:30am-8:15pm. **Buses:** The closest **Greyhound** bus stations are 30min. away in Winchester, VA, and Frederick, MD, but the **Appalachian Trail Conference (ATC)** runs buses to Charles Town for $2, and weekday shuttle buses (301-694-2065) connect Frederick and Knoxville, MD. **Visitor Information:** 535-6223. Write to: Harpers Ferry National Historical Park, P.O. Box 65, Harpers Ferry, WV 25425. **Visitors center:** (304-535-6298), just inside the park entrance off Rt. 340 (open daily 8am-5pm). Admission $5 per car, $3 per hiker or bicyclist; good for 3 consecutive days. A bus shuttles from the parking lot to town every 15min. **Bike Rental: Blue Ridge Outfitters** (304-535-6331), 2mi. west of Harper's Ferry towards Charles Town. Bikes $20 per day. **Post Office:** P.O. Box 9998, on the corner of Washington and Franklin St. Open M-F 8am-4pm, Sa 9am-noon. **Zip Code:** 25425. **Area Code:** 304.

**⚲ ACCOMMODATIONS.** Everyone finds a warm welcome at the social and spacious **Harpers Ferry Hostel (HI-AYH),** 19123 Sandy Hook Rd., at Keep Tryst Rd. off Rt. 340 in Knoxville, MD. This renovated auction house, with a backyard trail to heartpounding Potomac vistas, spreads guests into four rooms with 33 well-cushioned beds. The proprietor will fetch guests from the station for $5, but the 2mi. hike is lovely. (301-834-7652. Closed Nov. 15-Mar. 15. Check-in 7:30-9am and 6-11pm. Limited parking. Sleepsack $1. 3-night max. stay. Credit card number required for phone reservation, but credit cards not accepted for payment. Beds $16, HI $13. Camping $9, HI $6; includes use of hostel kitchen and bathrooms. "Primitive" campsites $4.50, HI $3.) For private quarters, the **Hillside Motel,** 340 Keep Tryst Rd., in Knoxville, MD, has 21 clean, adequate rooms and its own liquor store (301-834-8144; singles $36; doubles $47.50; lower winter rates). Camp along the **C&O Canal,** where free camping sites lie 5mi. apart, or in one of the five Maryland state park campgrounds within 30mi. of Harpers Ferry (for more information, call the ranger station 301-739-4200). **Greenbrier State Park,** take Rt. 66 to Rt. 40E, has camping and outdoor recreation (301-791-4767 or 888-432-2267; open May-Oct.; M-F $13, Sa-Su $17, with hookup M-F $18, Sa-Su $22). The **Harpers Ferry KOA,** Rt. 5, lies adjacent to the entrance to Harpers Ferry National Park with surprisingly scenic sites. (304-535-6895 or 800-562-9497. 2-person site $27, with water and electricity $31; each additional person $4, under 17 $3. $50 for a 2-room cabin that sleeps 4.)

**⬠ FOOD.** Harper's Ferry has sparse offerings for hungry hikers. **Rt. 340** welcomes the fast food fanatic. At the 24hr. **Cindy Dee Restaurant,** 19112 Keep Tryst Rd., at Rt. 340, where Elvis rules, breakfast is served 'round the clock, and a catfish dinner plus a slab of homemade pie is only $8. (301-695-8181). The historic area, especially High St., and Potomac St., caters to lunchtime noshers and vacates for dinner. **The Hot Dog Haven,** on Potomac St., doubles as a burger joint (burgers and hot dogs $2-3.75) and an offbeat guide service with "Ghost Tours" Sa-Su nights. (304-535-2128. Tours May-early Nov. F-Su 8pm; reservations recommended in Oct.; $2. Restaurant open M-F 10am-5pm.) For nightlife and varied cuisine, the tiny **Shepherdstown**, 11mi. north of Harpers Ferry on Rt. 230 off Rt. 340 or 13mi. by bike along the C&O towpath, equals a culinary metropolis in these desolate parts. Belly-pleasing fare lines colonial row houses on E. German St. where the **Mecklinburg Inn**, 128 E. German St., hosts a regional open-mic night every Tu from 9pm to midnight (304-876-2126. Happy Hour M-F 4:30-6:30pm. Over 21 after 5pm. Open M-Th 3pm-12:30am, F 3pm-1:30am, Sa 1pm-2am, Su 1pm-12:30am.)

**⚡ SIGHTS AND OUTDOORS.** Parking in town is limited, so it's best to park at the visitors center and take the free bus to the town or foot the 20min. walk. The bus stops at **Shenandoah St.**, at a barrage of replicated 19th-century shops, where historical markers and eager actors attempt to recreate the age when steel, coal, and iron were worshipped as gods. More interesting, the unsung stories of the Ferry captivate visitors at **Black Voices from Harpers Ferry,** on the corner of High and Shenandoah St. The plight of Harpers Ferry's slaves is tactfully elaborated through their words in the **Civil War Story,** next door on High St. A ticket is required to enter some of the exhibits, but the park's *Lower Town Trail Guide* facilitates historical exploration. Park rangers provide free 45min. to 1hr. tours of the town. (In summer daily 10:30am-4pm.) In addition, the park offers occasional battlefield demonstrations, parades, and other re-enactments of Harpers Ferry's history (call 304-535-6298 for the schedule). Stairs hewn into the hillside off High St. follow the **Appalachian Trail** to **Upper Harpers Ferry,** which has fewer sights but is graced with interesting tales. Allow 30min. to ascend past **Harper's House,** the restored home of town founder Robert Harper, and **St. Peter's Church,** where a pastor flew the Union Jack during the Civil War to protect the church.

The historic sites in Harpers Ferry are mildly interesting, but the real reason to go is for the spectacular outdoors. Go to the park's visitors center for trail maps galore. The **Maryland Heights Trail,** across the railroad bridge in the Lower Town of Harpers Ferry, wanders for 4mi. through Blue Ridge Mountains, including formidable cliffs and glimpses of crumbling Civil War-era forts. More wooded, the 4mi. **Loudon Heights Trail** starts in Lower Town off the Appalachian Trail. Both trails take a little over 3hrs. to hike. History presides over the **Bolivar Heights Trail,** which starts from the northern end of Whitman Ave., where trailside exhibits and a 3-gun battery now frame the Civil War battle line where Stonewall Jackson once rode. His horse didn't and your feet shouldn't tire on the easy 1.1mi. loop. The **Chesapeake & Ohio Canal** towpath, off the end of Shenandoah St. and over the railroad bridge, complements the industrial theme of the town. The **Appalachian Trail Conference,** 799 Washington St. at Washington and Jackson St., offers catalogues that feature deals on hiking books, trail information, and a maildrop for hikers. (304-535-6331. Open late May-Oct. M-F 9am-5pm, Sa-Su 9am-4pm; Nov. to mid-May M-F 9am-5pm. Membership $25, students and seniors $18.)

**River & Trail Outfitters,** 604 Valley Rd., 2mi. out of Harpers Ferry off Rt. 340, in Knoxville, MD, rents canoes, kayaks, inner tubes, and rafts, and organizes everything from scenic daytrips to wild overnights. (301-695-5177. Canoes $50 per day; raft trips $48 per person, children $38; tubing $25 per day.) **Blue Ridge Outfitters,** a few mi. west of Harpers Ferry on Rt. 340N in Charles Town, arranges similar trips. In addition to rafting and canoe trips, water-adventurers can take a ride on the mutant half-raft-half-kayak "Ducky," or hostelers can borrow an innertube. The group also organizes weekend ($220) and day ($60-110) **cross-country ski** trips. (304-725-3444. Canoe or a seat on a half-day raft trip from $65, children $41; Ducky $40.50, children $35.50. Open daily 8am-7pm.) Otherwise, at **Butt's Tubes, Inc.,** on Rt. 671 off Rt. 340, you can buy a tube for the day and sell it back before you go. (800-836-9911. $5-20. Open M-F 10:30am-3pm, last pickup at 5pm; Sa-Su 10am-4pm, last pickup at 6pm.) Horse activities in the area include a variety of trips offered through **Elk Mountain Trails** (301-834-8882) and evening races Friday and Saturday at 7:15pm, 10 mi. away at the recently restarted **Charles Town Races** (304-725-7001).

**SMOKING IS GOOD FOR YOU** The battle of Antietam may have proved hopeless for the Union brigade if not for the carelessness of Lee's messenger. Special order 191 contained the precise whereabouts of Lee's troops at Harper's Ferry. Two copies of the order were made, but one was lost en route. A few days later, two Union soldiers from the 27th Indiana infantry spotted three wrapped cigars in a field. Thrilled that they had found stogies, they unwrapped the package to reveal Lee's plans, sending them straight to McClellan and victory.

**ANTIETAM NATIONAL BATTLEFIELD.** Just north of the Ferry, blood covered the soil at Antietam. On Sept. 17, 1862, in the bloodiest one-day battle of the Civil War, 23,110 Union and Confederate soldiers fell under fire as **Confederate General Robert E. Lee** failed to march north through the army of **Union General George B. McClellan.** The severity of losses were a small triumph to the Union, and turned the war's objective toward slavery when President Lincoln took the opportunity to issue the **Emancipation Proclamation,** freeing all slaves in the rebellious states as of Jan. 1, 1863. The **visitors center** orients visitors with a small room of soldiers' clothing and weaponry, an interactive Civil War explorer, free maps of an 8½mi. driving tour, and rental tapes ($5) narrating the battle. An observation tower, important bridges, and trenches in which the soldiers fought illuminate the battle's history. To get to Antietam from Harpers Ferry, take Rt. 340W. 2mi. and take a right onto Rt. 230. Drive 9mi. until you reach Shepherdstown, then turn right on Rt. 480, which becomes Rt. 34E. Continue to Sharpsburg and follow signs. *(Tel. 301-432-5124. Visitors Center open daily May-Sept. 8:30am-6pm; Oct.-Apr. 8:30am-5pm. 26min. film shown in Visitors Center 9am-5pm on the hr. Battlefield fee $2, family rate $4.)*

## NEW RIVER GORGE

The New River Gorge is a mixture of raw beauty, raw resources, and raw power. One of the oldest rivers in the world, the New River cuts a narrow gouge in the Appalachian Mountains, leaving valley walls which tower an average of 1000 ft. above the white waters. Industrialists drained the region for coal and timber until the 20th-century. The **New River Gorge National River,** which runs from Hinton to Fayetteville, falling over 750 ft. in 50mi., is now protected, and the park service oversees the fishing, rock climbing, canoeing, mountain biking, and world-class rafting in the gorge (see below). Though whitewater takes precedence, the park's trails lend appreciation of the river and the industry that once abounded. The most rewarding trails are the 2mi. **Kaymoor Trail,** which starts south of the bridge on Fayette Station Rd. and runs past the abandoned coke ovens of Kaymoor, a coal-mining community that shut down in 1962, and the 3.4mi. **Thurmond Minden Trail,** left off of WV Rt. 25 before Thurmond. This trail has vistas of the New River and Thurmond. For a vertical challenge, climb the **Endless Wall** which runs southeast along the New River and is accessible from a trail off the parking lot at Canyon Rim Visitors Center. The park operates four **visitors centers: Canyon Rim,** off Rt. 19 near Fayetteville at the northern extreme of the park; **Grandview,** on Rt. 9 near Beckley; **Hinton,** on Rt. 20; **Thurmond,** on Rt. 25 off I-195. Grandview attracts visitors in May when the rhododendron are in bloom; otherwise, most stop at Canyon Rim, which has info on all park activities, including free, detailed hiking, biking, and climbing guides. (Canyon Rim: 574-2115. Grandview: 763-3715. Both open daily June-Aug. 9am-8pm; Sept.-May 9am-5pm. Hinton: 466-0417. Open daily June-Aug. 9am-5pm; Sept.-May Sa-Su 9am-5pm. Thurmond: 465-8550. Open daily June-Aug. 9am-5pm.)

The extreme poverty of West Virginia finds some relief in its overabundance of natural beauty and a tourist boom in **whitewater rafting,** with rapids ranging from the family-friendly class I to the panic-inducing class V. A state info service (800-225-5982) connects you to some of the nearly 20 outfitters on the New River and the rowdier Gauley River, or pick up a brochure at the **Fayettesville County Chamber of Commerce,** 810 Oyler Ave. in Oak Hill. **USA Raft,** on Rt. 1 in Fayetteville, runs some of the cheapest express trips. (800-346-7238. New River: Su-F $47, Sa $58. Gauley River: Su-F $52-65, Sa $61-72.)

Where Rt. 19 crosses the river at the park's northern end, the grace of the **New River Gorge Bridge,** second highest bridge in the U.S., complements the natural beauty of the gorge itself. Towering 876 ft. above New River, the bridge claims the world's largest single steel arch span. On **Bridge Day,** the 3rd Sa of Oct., thousands of extreme sports enthusiasts leap off the bridge by bungee or parachute (800-927-0263). For more stable flying, elderly "Five Dollar Frank" pilots $5 **scenic plane rides** at the Fayetteville airstrip, 2mi. south of town. Old-time coal miners lead tours down a mine shaft at the **Beckley Exhibition Coal Mine,** 20mi. south of Fayetteville at New River Park on Ewart Ave. in Beckley. Ride behind a 1930s engine through 150 ft. of underground passages past mining relics. (256-1747. Open daily Apr.-Oct. 10am-5:30pm. $8, seniors $7, ages 4-12 $5, under 4 free.) **Horsebackriding** trips also step into the gorge. (888-742-3982. Mar.-Oct. Rides start at $35.)

Budget motels can be found off I-77 in Beckley ($45-60), while smaller lodges and guest houses scatter through Fayetteville. **Canyon Ranch,** off Gatewood Road next to Cunard Access for the river, offers 2 rooms with A/C and shared bath (574-3111 or 574-4111). Call 800-225-5982 for accommodation info. Many of the raft companies operate private campgrounds, while four public campgrounds dot the general area. The most central public campground, **Babcock State Park,** Rt. 41 south of U.S. 60, 15mi. west of Rainelle, has shaded, sometimes slanted sites (438-3004 or 800-225-5982; $11, with water and electricity $14). The park also rents 26 cabins. On Ames Heights Rd., ½mi. north of the New River Gorge Bridge, the private **Mountain State Campground** offers both level and hilly tent sites with platforms (by request, $6-7) and 6-person primitive cabins ($65; 574-0947; open Apr.-Nov.). **Greyhound** (253-8333) stops at 105 Third Ave. in Beckley (open M-F 7-11am and 4-8:30pm, Sa-Su 7-9am and 4-8:30pm). **Amtrak** (253-6651) runs through the heart of the gorge, stopping on Rt. 41 N. in Prince and Hinton. (Trains Su, W, and F. Open Su, W, and F 10:30am-7pm, Th and Sa 7am-2:30pm.) Rentals are available in Fayetteville, at **Ridge Rider Mountain Bikes,** 103 Keller Ave. (574-2453 or 800-890-2453) on Keller Ave. off U.S. 19 (open daily 9am-5pm; $30 per day). **Area code:** 304.

## MONONGAHELA NATIONAL FOREST

Mammoth **Monongahela National Forest** supports wildlife, limestone caverns, and weekend canoers, fly fisherman, spelunkers, and skiers. Over 500 campsites and 600mi. of well-maintained hiking trails lure adventurers to this camping haven.

Most roads are scenic, though the beauty of **Rt. 39** from Marlinton down to Goshen, VA, past Virginia's swimmable Maury River, is unsurpassed. For more variety, turn off U.S. 219 onto Denmar Rd. and right on Locust Creek Rd. for a 10mi. loop that passes fields of okapi and bison, a prison, an old country church, and finally a 1-lane bridge adjacent to the 1888 covered bridge over Locust Creek. The **Highland Scenic Hwy.,** (Rt. 150), runs near the Cranberry Visitors Center, and stretches 43mi. from Richwood to U.S. 219, 7mi. north of Marlinton.

Many state parks and each of Monongahela's 6 districts have a campground and a recreation area, with ranger stations off Rt. 39 east of Marlinton and in the towns of Bartow and Potomack (open M-F 8am-4:30pm). The forest **Supervisor's Office,** 200 Sycamore St. (636-1800), in Elkins, distributes a full list of sites and fees, and provides info about fishing and hunting (open M-F 8am-4:45pm). Established sites are $5; sleeping in the backcountry is free. Indicate backcountry plans at the **Cranberry Mountain Visitors Center,** near the Highland Scenic Hwy. at the junction of Rt. 150 and Rt. 39/55 (653-4826; open daily Dec. and June-Aug. 9am-5pm; Sept.-Nov. and Jan.-May Sa-Su 10am-4pm). Two popular short hikes in the area are the panoramic High Rocks trail leading off of the Highland Scenic Hwy. and the awesome ¾mi. **Hills Creek Falls,** off Rt. 39/55 south of Cranberry Mountain Visitor's Center. The first cascade is wheelchair accessible; steep steps take you to cascades two and three. *Remove valuables from vehicles as thieves are common in this area.* **Cranberry Campground,** in the Gauley district 6mi. west of U.S. 219 on Rt. 39/55, has hiking trails through cranberry bogs and $5-8 campsites (296-9881).

Those with several days might choose to hike, bike, or ski along part of the **Greenbrier River Trail,** a 75mi. jaunt along a 1% grade track from Cass to North Caldwell (trailhead on Rt. 38 off U.S. 60), with numerous access points and campgrounds en route. **Watoga State Park** (799-4087), in Marlinton, has maps. South of Caldwell on Rt. 63 lie the calcite formations of **Organ Cave,** where prehistoric bones were discovered (645-7600; open daily May-Oct. 9am-7pm; Nov.-Apr. 9am-5pm).

Marlinton and Elkins lodge hikers, bikers, and tourists. In downtown Marlinton, the **Old Clark Inn,** 702 3rd Ave., offers bed and breakfasts (799-6377 or 800-849-4184; singles $40-50; doubles $50-60; $5 more in winter). In Green Bank, year-round **cabins** can be rented; turn left off Rt. 92 north. (456-3470 or 456-4410; M-F $28-45, Sa-Su $38-55). In eastern Monongahela, the **Middle Mountain Cabins,** on Forest Service Rd. 14 off Rt. 28, stock fireplaces, kitchens, and drinking water (456-3335; $30 per night; 1-week max. stay; open May-Oct.; call well in advance).

In the winter, thousands pour into the area to ski at slopes in the **Canaan Valley** and the 54 trails at **Snowshoe** resort (572-1000. Open daily Nov.-Apr. 8:30am-10pm. Lift tickets $38, students and seniors $30, Sa-Su $44; ski rental $26, children $18.) In summer mountain biking is preferred. Cross-country skiers and mountain bikers can rent gear at **Elk River** (572-3771), off Rt. 219 in Slatyfork.

Most public transportation in the forest area comes into White Sulphur Springs at the forest's southern tip. **Greyhound** has a flag stop at the **Village Inn,** 38 W. Main St. (1 eastbound bus at 9am, and 1 westbound bus per day at 4pm.) **Amtrak** stops at 315 W. Main St., across from the Greenbrier resort. A flag stop in downtown Alderson can also be requested Su, W, or F. (To Washington, D.C., $53; and Charlottesville, $29.) **Area code:** 304.

MID-ATLANTIC

# THE SOUTH

A century of economic progress, multiple ethnic migrations, and the gradual dissolution of regional identities have combined to blur the once-stark distinction
between the North and South. As Detroit's auto giants relocate to southern towns,
and New Englanders seek solace in the cured-oak flavor of Tennessee whiskey,
perhaps the importance of the Mason-Dixon line will further recede into the
depths of American consciousness. Yet even as the major metropoli—Atlanta,
Nashville, Charlotte, Orlando, and New Orleans—bask in the glow of their new-
fangled urban sophistication, divisions between white and black segments of the
population provide painful reminders of the area's discolored past.

Although much of the South remains poor, the area maintains a rich cultural
heritage; a mélange of Native American, English, African, French, and Spanish
influences are reflected in the architecture, cuisine, and language. Landscapes are
equally varied—nature blessed the region with mountains, marshlands, sparkling
beaches, and fertile soil. From the Atlantic's Sea Islands to the rolling Ozarks, the
Gulf's bayous to boundary waters, the South's beauty awes, entices, and enchants.

## HIGHLIGHTS OF THE SOUTH

- **Food.** Some of the best Southern barbecue is at Dreamland in Mobile, AL (p. 390).
New Orleans, LA (p. 398) has spicy and delicious Cajun cuisine. Southern "soul food"
completes the spirit—Nita's Place, Savannah, GA (p. 381) will take you higher.
- **Music.** Make time for Tennessee—Nashville (p. 335) is the country music hotspot,
but if you're a believer, you'll be heading to Graceland (p. 343).
- **Civil Rights Memorials.** The Martin Luther King Center in Atlanta, GA (p. 371) and
the Birmingham Civil Rights Institute, AL (p. 389) will move you to tears.
- **Natural Wonders.** Mammoth Cave, KY (p. 330); the Blowing Rock, NC (p. 357);
Ruby Falls, TN (p. 342); and the Great Smoky Mountains (p. 340).
- **Old South: Charm and Elegance.** Nowhere is the antebellum way of life so well-kept
as in stately Charleston, SC (**p. 362**) or Savannah, GA (**p. 381**).

# KENTUCKY

Legendary for the duels, feuds, and stubborn spirit of its earlier inhabitants (such
as the infamous Daniel Boone), but gentler than its past, Kentucky invites travelers to kick back, take a shot of local bourbon, grab a plate of burgoo (a spicy meat
stew), and relax amid rolling hills and bluegrass. These days, Kentuckians' spirit
erupts on the highways—they drive fast. Appropriately, Kentucky is home to the
only American sports car, the Corvette. Of course, the most respected mode of
transport is still the horse. Louisville ignores its vibrant cultural scene and active
nightlife at Derby time, and Lexington devotes much of its most beautiful farmland
to breeding champion racehorses. Farther east, the Daniel Boone National Forest
preserves the virgin woods of the Kentucky Highlands, where trailblazers first discovered a route across the mountains to what was then the West.

## 🎯 PRACTICAL INFORMATION

**Capital:** Frankfort.

**Visitor Info: Kentucky Dept. of Travel** 500 Mero St., 22nd fl., Frankfort 40601 (502-
564-4930 or 800-225-8747; www.kentuckytourism.com). **Kentucky State Parks,** 500
Mero St., 10th fl., Frankfort 40601 (800-255-7275).

**Postal Abbreviation:** KY. **Sales Tax:** 6%.

# LOUISVILLE

Louisville (pronounced "Lua-Vul" by locals) is caught between two pasts. One left a legacy of smokestacks, stockyards, and the occasional crumbling edifice; the other entices with beautiful Victorian neighborhoods, ornate buildings, and the elegant, twin-spired Churchill Downs. First and foremost, Louisville is home to the nation's most prestigious horse race, the Kentucky Derby (p. 329).

**🛂 ORIENTATION AND PRACTICAL INFORMATION.** Major highways through the city include **I-65** (north-south expressway), **I-71**, and **I-64**. The easily accessible **Watterson Expwy.**, also called **I-264**, rings the city, while the **Gene Snyder Frwy. (I-265)** circles farther out. In central downtown, **Main St.** and **Broadway** run east-west, and **Preston Hwy.** and **19th St.** run north-south. The **West End**, beyond 20th St., is a rough area. The **Louisville International Airport**, (375-3063), is 15min. south of downtown on I-65. A taxi downtown is $17, or take bus #2 into the city. **Greyhound**, 720 W. Muhammad Ali Blvd. (561-2805), at 7th St. runs to Indianapolis (2hr., 7 per day, $19), Cincinnati (2hr., 8 per day, $19), and Chicago (6hr., 7 per day, $35, $37 weekends; station open 24hr.). **Transit Authority River City's (TARC)** (585-1234) extensive bus system serves most of the metro area. (Daily 5am-11:30pm. Fare 75¢, $1 M-F 6:30-8:30am and 3:30-5:30pm). **Taxis: Yellow Cab** (636-5511). **United Rent-A-Car**, 104 Vieux Carre (888-227-7215), near Shelbyville Rd. and Hurstborne Ln. rents compacts from $29 (ages 18-21 $3 per day surcharge). **Highland Cycle**, 1737 Bardstown Rd. (458-7832), rents bikes ($4 per hr., $15 per day; open M-F 9am-5:30pm, Sa 9am-4:30pm). **Visitors Info: Louisville Convention and Visitors Bureau**, 400 S. 1st St. (582-3732 or 800-792-5595), at Liberty St. downtown (open M-F 8:30am-5pm, Sa 9am-4pm, Su 11am-4pm). **Hotlines: Rape Hotline** (581-7273); **Crisis Center** (589-4313; both 24hr.); **Gay/Lesbian Hotline** (454-7613; daily 6-10pm). **Post Office:** 1420 Gardner Ln. (454-1650). Open M-F 7:30am-9pm, Sa 7:30am-3pm. **ZIP code:** 40213. **Area code:** 502.

**🛏 HITCHIN' POSTS.** Lodging in downtown Louisville is easy to find but pricey. Budget motels are on **I-65** near the airport or across the river in **Jeffersonville**. **Newburg** (6mi. south) or **Bardstown** (39mi. south; see **South of Louisville**, p. 329) are also budget havens. To get Derby Week lodging, make reservations 6 to 12 months in advance and prepare to spend big; the visitors bureau helps after Mar. 13.

**Collier's Motor Court**, 4812 Bardstown Rd., south of I-264, is 30min. from downtown by car; TARC buses serve this inconvenient area. Well-maintained, cheap rooms with HBO, Showtime, and A/C. (499-1238. Singles $36; doubles $42.) **Louisville Convention Center Travelodge**, 401 S. 2nd St., downtown, is pricey but convenient. Spiffier rooms than its numbered cousins. (583-2629 or 800-578-7878. A/C and cable. Singles $49, $59 weekends; doubles $59/63. AAA/AARP 10-15% discount.) The local installation of the **KOA** regime, 900 Marriot Dr., across the river from downtown, has paved camping convenient to downtown. Follow I-65 N across the bridge and take exit 1. (812-282-4474. Sites for 2 $23, with hookup $25.50; $4 per additional person, under 18 $2.50. "Kabins" for 2 $35. Grocery, playground, free pool access, mini golf, and fishing lake. Off-season discounts.)

**🍴 FOOD.** Louisville's food is varied, but good budget fare can be hard to find in the heart of downtown. **Bardstown Rd.** is lined with cafes, budget eateries, and local and global cuisine, while **Frankfort Rd.** is rapidly becoming Bardstown-ized with restaurants and chi-chi cafes of its own. Downtown, **Theater Sq.**, at Broadway and 4th St., provides plenty of good lunch options. 🍴 **Twice Told**, 1604 Bardstown Rd. was the first coffeehouse in Louisville, and it's still funky after all these years. Poetry readings, comedy, jazz, and blues entertain nearly every night starting at 9pm, but get in earlier for a $5 homemade veggie burger. (456-0507. Open Su-Th 10am-midnight, F-Sa 10am-1am. Cover for shows $5-10.) At 🍴 **Lynn's Paradise Cafe**, 984 Barret Ave., kid-friendly hammock-swings and garish animal sculptures complement adult-friendly prices. Breakfast ($4-9; served until 3pm) is the big meal here. (583-3447. Open Tu-Su 8am-10pm.) **Ramsi's Café on the World**, 1293 Bardstown

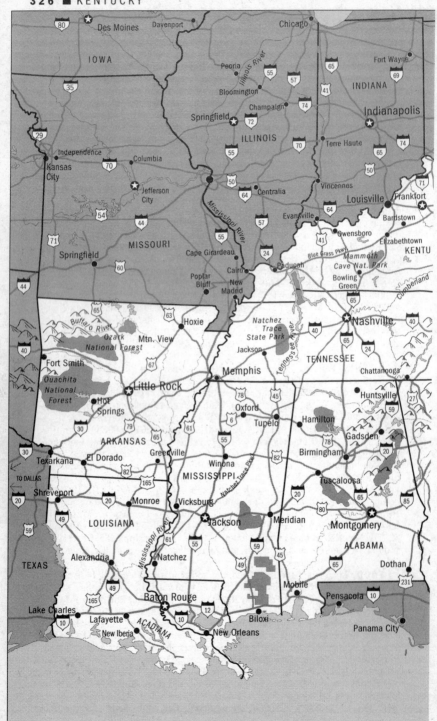

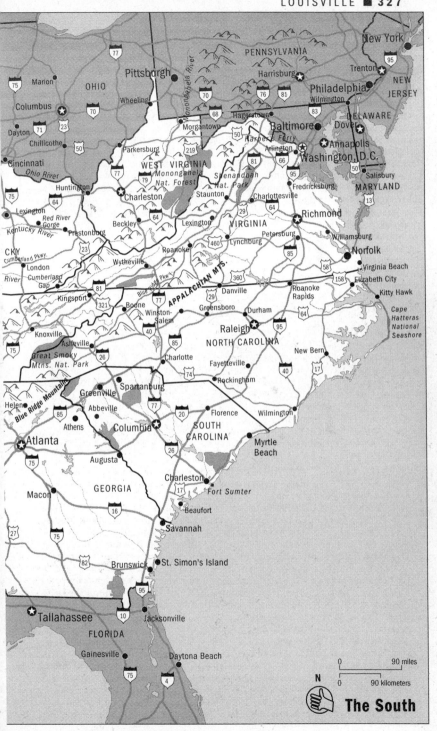

**The South**

Rd. is an intimate restaurant preparing "ethnic non-regional cuisine" for a mix of hipsters and local families, including 12 vegan items and 16 vegetarian dishes (entrees $5-9; 451-0700; open M-Th 11am-1am, F-Sa 11am-2am, Su 3-11pm). **Mark's Feed Store,** 1514 Bardstown Rd., serves award-winning barbecue in the company of metal pigs. (Pork sandwich $3.50; ½-basket of onion straws $3. Free dessert M after 4pm. 459-6275. Open Su-Th 11am-10pm, F-Sa 11am-11pm.)

■ **NOT JUST A ONE-HORSE TOWN.** The **Highlands** strip runs along Baxter/Bardstown and is bounded by Broadway and Trevilian Way on the south. This "anti-mall" of unfranchised cafes, pizza pubs, antique shops, and record stores is worth a look. *(Buses #17, 23, and 44.)* Farther south, near the University of Louisville, the **J.B. Speed Art Museum** houses an impressive collection of Dutch paintings and tapestries, Renaissance and contemporary art, and a sculpture court with style. *(2035 S. 3rd St. 634-2700. Bus #2 or 4. Open Tu-W and F 10:30am-4pm, Th 10:30am-8pm, Sa 10:30am-5pm, Su noon-5pm.)*

The **Belle of Louisville,** an authentic paddle-wheel craft, docks at 4th St. and River Rd. *(574-2355. 2hr. cruises depart from Riverfront Plaza late May to early Sept. Tu-Su 1pm. Sunset cruises Tu and Th 7pm. Dance cruise Sa 8-11pm. Boarding begins 1hr. before departure; arrive early, especially in July. $10, seniors $9, under 13 $6; dance cruise $12.50.)* The world's tallest baseball bat (120 ft.) leans against the **Hillerich and Bradsby Co. (Louisville Slugger Factory and Museum).** Inside awaits a nostalgic film and a tour showing how Sluggers are made awaits. H&B will even give you a free miniature bat at tour's end. *(800 W. Main. 588-7228. Open M-Sa 9am-5pm. $5, over 60 $3.50, ages 6-12 $3.)*

Aching to try a climbing wall? Itching for IMAX? The **Louisville Science Center** can appease these cravings. *(727 W. Main St. 561-6111. Open M-Th 10am-6pm, F-Sa 10am-9pm, Su noon-6pm. $5.50, ages 2-12 and over 59 $4.50; with IMAX $7.50/$6.)*

Lovers of American kitsch will find a treat at the **Harland Sanders Museum, Kentucky Fried Chicken International Headquarters,** off the Watterson Expwy. at Newburg Rd. S. A room of artifacts, preserved office, and short film honor the white-suited Colonel who brought us fried chicken with his secret recipe of 11 herbs and spices. *(1441 Gardiner Ln. 874-8300. Free, as it should be.)*

For natural splendor, try a gander at the **Falls of the Ohio.** The interpretive center can help you find a good hiking path, explore the river's geology, or locate (but leave behind) fossils. *(201 W. Riverside Dr., Clarksville, IN. 812-280-9970. Park open daily 7am-midnight; center open M-Sa 9am-5pm, Su 1-5pm. Center $2, children $1. Parking free.)*

■ **ENTERTAINMENT AND NIGHTLIFE.** Free weekly arts and entertainment newspaper, *Leo,* is available at most downtown restaurants or at the visitors center. The **Kentucky Center for the Arts,** 5 Riverfront Plaza. off Main St., hosts the **Louisville Orchestra,** the **Louisville Ballet,** the **Broadway Series,** and more. (584-7777 or 800-775-7777. Open M-Sa 9am-6pm, Su noon-5pm.) Downtown, the **Actors Theater,** 316 W. Main St., is a Tony award-winning company. (584-1205 or 800-428-5849. Showtime 7:30pm, weekend matinees. Box office open M 10am-5:30pm, Tu-F 10am-8pm. Tickets from $16; student and senior rush tickets 15min. before each show $10.) What dreams may come when we have shuffled off this mortal coil at the **Kentucky Shakespeare Festival** at the zoo and in Central Park, which takes place over 8 weekends starting in early June (583-8738. Performances 7pm.) The **Louisville Palace,** 625 S. 4th Ave., is one of only 15 remaining "atmospheric theaters." Go to see why; or to see broadway shows, comedy acts, and movies. (583-4555. Classic movies in the summer $4.50.)

**The Brewery,** 426 Baxter Ave. is not a brewery, but hey, it's gigantic and multi-faceted. Local bands, four volleyball courts, and a monthly boxing night. (583-3420. Cover for live shows $8-20. Open M-Sa 11am-4am, Su 5pm-4am.) **Phoenix Hill Tavern,** 644 Baxter Ave., pours blues, rock, and reggae on four stages including a deck and roof garden. (589-4957. Cover W $2 Th-Sa $5. Open W-Th and Sa 8pm-3:30am, F 5pm-3:30am.) Techno Alliance take heart: **Sparks,** 104 W. Main St., burns until the early morn (cover $2-4; Sa free; open Tu-S 9pm-4am). For gay nightlife, make **The**

**Connection,** 120 Floyd St. (585-5752), between Main and Market St. Mostly gay male entertainment, but anyone should check out the bashes at this black-and-white-and-mirrored-all-over club. (587-8566. Cover $2-5. Open Tu-Su 9pm-4am.)

**HORSIN' AROUND.** Each year, on the first Sa in May, Louisville stages the nation's most prestigious horse race, the **Kentucky Derby.** The drunken, week-long extravaganza leading up to the big day corrals over 500,000 visitors, but when the horses leave the gate, the stands are still for "the most exciting two minutes in sports;" after all, $15 million ride on each Derby Day. Even if you miss the Kentucky Derby, be sure to visit **Churchill Downs,** 700 Central Ave., 3mi. south of downtown. You don't have to bet to admire the twin spires, the colonial columns, the gardens, and the sheer scale of the track. *(636-4400. Take bus #4 "4th St." to Central Ave. Races Apr. to late May W-Su from 1pm; June W-Su from 3pm; Nov. Tu-Su 1-5pm. Grandstand and clubhouse seats $2, 5th fl. reserved seats $4.50. Grounds open daily in racing season 10am-4pm. Parking $3.)*

The **Kentucky Derby Festival** kicks off with the largest fireworks show in North America and continues for 2 weeks with balloon and steamboat races, concerts, and a parade before the climactic **Run for the Roses** on the first Sat. in May. A one to 10-year waiting list stands between you and a ticket for the Derby, but never fear— on Derby morning, tickets are sold for standing-room-only spots in the infield ($35). Get in line early for good seats, lest the other 125,000 spectators get there first. Amazingly, no one is turned away. The **Kentucky Derby Museum,** at Churchill Downs, offers a complete picture of the race on a 360° screen, tours of the track, footage of every Derby ever recorded (including Secretariat's record 1973 run), a simulated horse race for betting practice, tips on exactly what makes a horse a "sure thing," and 7 tours of the Downs every day. *(637-7097. Open daily 9am-5pm; last tour at 3:45 pm. $6, seniors $5, ages 5-12 $2, under 5 free.)*

## SOUTH OF LOUISVILLE

**BARDSTOWN.** Kentucky's second-oldest city, 17mi. east on Rt. 245 from I-65 exit 112, is proudly known as the "Bourbon Capital of the World." In 1791, Kentucky Baptist Reverend Elijah Craig left a fire unattended while heating oak boards to make a barrel for his aging whiskey. The boards were charred, but Rev. Craig carried on, and Bourbon was born in that first charred wood barrel. Today, 90% of the nation's bourbon hails from Kentucky, and 60% of that is distilled in Nelson and Bullitt Counties. **Jim Beam's American Outpost,** 15mi. west of Bardstown in Clermont off Rt. 245 (take I-65 S to exit 112, then Rt. 245 E for 1½mi.), features the "master distiller emeritus" himself, Jim Beam's grandson, Booker Noe, who narrates a film about bourbon. Tragically, Jim Beam's has no liquor license, but they do have free lemonade, coffee, and bourbon candies. *(543-9877. Open M-Sa 9am-4:30pm, Su 1-4pm. Free.)* Tours are offered at **Maker's Mark Distillery,** 19mi. southeast of Bardstown on Rt. 52 E in Loretto. *(865-2099. Tours M-Sa every hr. 10:30am-3:30pm, Su every hr. 1:30-3:30pm. Free.)* **Bardstown Visitors Center,** 107 E. Stephen Foster Ave., gives a free 1hr. trolley tour, taking visitors by **My Old Kentucky Home** and **Heaven Hill Distillery.** *(348-4877 or 800-638-4877. Visitors center open M-F 8am-6pm, Sa 9am-6pm, Su 11am-3pm; Nov.-Mar. M-Sa 8am-5pm. Summer tours M-Sa 9:30am and 1pm.)*

---

**WHISKEY BUSINESS** All bourbon is whiskey, but not all whiskey is bourbon. So what makes bourbon so special? It's all in the making, codified by the U.S. Government. For alcohol to be bourbon, it must fulfill these 6 requirements: **1.** It must be aged in a new white oak barrel, flame-charred on the inside. (Scotch, alternatively, must be aged in used barrels.) **2.** It must age at least 2 years in that barrel. **3.** It must be at least 51% corn. **4.** It cannot be distilled over 160 proof (80% alcohol). **5.** It cannot go into the barrel over 125 proof. **6.** It can have no additives or preservatives.

**ABRAHAM LINCOLN BIRTHPLACE.** Near Hodgenville, 45mi. south of Louisville on U.S. 31 E, this national historic site marks the birthplace of Honest Abe. From Louisville, take I-65 down to Rt. 61; public transit does not serve the area. Fifty-six steps, representing the 56 years of Lincoln's tragically shortened life, lead up to a neolithic monument sheltering the small log cabin. Set in a beautiful location, the site lends a glimpse of frontier living and an 18min. video about Lincoln's Kentucky years. *(358-3137. Open daily 8am-6:45pm. Free.)*

**MAMMOTH CAVE.** Hundreds of enormous caves and narrow passageways cut through **Mammoth Cave National Park,** 80mi. south of Louisville off I-65, then west on Rt. 70. Mammoth Cave comprises the world's longest network of cavern corridors—over 325mi. in length. Devout spelunkers try the 6hr. "Wild Cave Tour" during the summer (16+; $35); less ambitious types generally take the 2hr., 2mi. historical walking tour ($7, seniors $4, ages 6-15 $3). Other tours accommodate disabled visitors (1½hr., $6.50). The caves are a chilly 54°F. (**Visitors center:** 758-2328 or 800-967-2283. Open daily 7:30am-7pm; off-season 8am-6pm). Primitive camping is available at the Houchins Ferry area year-round ($5). **Backcountry camping** permits can be obtained at the visitors center. **Greyhound** comes only as close as **Cave City,** just east of I-65 on Rt. 70. **Time Zone:** Central (1hr. behind Eastern).

**BOWLING GREEN.** Home of the classic American sports car, auto enthusiasts inevitably pay their respects here. The extensive **National Corvette Museum,** 350 Corvette Dr. off I-65 exit 28, displays 'Vettes from the original chrome-and-steel '53 to futuristic concept cars, including classics like the "Purple People Eaters," the "Stingray," and the "Sledgehammer." *(800-538-3883. Open daily 8am-6pm; Oct.-Mar. 8am-5pm. $8, ages 6-16 $4.50, seniors $5.)* To see some action, visit the **General Motors Corvette Assembly Plant,** exit 28 off I-65. With luck comes a chance to test-start one of the mint condition products. *(745-8287. Tours M-F 9am and 1pm. Free.)* Learn about Mordecai F. Ham, Patsy's Fountain of Youth, and other bits of local lore at the **Kentucky Museum** on the **Western Kentucky University** campus. Tiny stitches of the quilts on display will amaze. *(745-2592. Open Tu-Sa 9:30am-4pm, Su 1-4pm. $2, children $1, families $5.)* **Time Zone:** Central (1hr. behind Eastern).

# LEXINGTON

In Kentucky's second-largest city, historic mansions show through downtown skyscrapers, and a 20min. drive will set you squarely in bluegrass country. Like the rest of Kentucky, Lexington has horse fever. The Kentucky Horse Park gets top billing, while shopping complexes and small industries at the outskirts of town share space with over 150 quaint, green horse farms. Likewise, the University of Kentucky (UK), which dominates the southern end of town, breeds basketball players for the stellar team that becomes an obsession for UK fans.

## ⊠ ORIENTATION AND PRACTICAL INFORMATION

**New Circle Rd.** (Rt. 4/U.S. 60 bypass) loops the city, intersecting with many roads that connect the downtown district to the surrounding towns. **High, Vine,** and **Main St.** running east-west and **Limestone St.** and **Broadway** running north-south provide the best routes through downtown. Beware of the many seductively curving one-way streets that bewilder the innocent near downtown and the university.

**Airport: Blue Grass,** 4000 Versailles Rd. (255-7218), southwest of downtown. Ritzy downtown hotels run shuttles, but there is no public transportation. Taxi to downtown $13.

**Buses: Greyhound,** 477 New Circle Rd. NW (299-8804; open daily 7:30am-11pm); take LexTran bus #6 downtown. To: Louisville (1¾hr., 4 per day, $18); Cincinnati (1½hr., 6 per day, $21); and Knoxville (3hr., 6 per day, $45).

**Public Transit: LexTran,** 109 W. London Ave. (253-4636). Buses leave from the Transit Center, 220 W. Vine St., between M.L. King and Stone Ave. 10min. before the hr.

Serves the university and city outskirts. Erratic service. Buses run M-F 6:15am-6:15pm, Sa 8:45am-5:45pm; some routes until 10pm. Fare 80¢, ages 7-18 60¢.

**Taxis: Lexington Yellow Cab,** 231-8294.

**Visitor Info: Lexington Convention and Visitors Bureau,** 301 E. Vine St. (233-7299 or 800-845-3959; www.visitlex.com), at Rose St. Open in summer M-F 8:30am-6pm, Sa 10am-6pm, Su noon-5pm; off-season closed Su.

**Hotlines: Crisis Intervention,** 233-0444. **Rape Crisis,** 253-2511.

**Hospitals: Lexington Hospital,** 150 N. Eagle Creek Dr. (268-4800). **Lexington Women's Diagnostic Center,** 1725 Harrodsburg Rd. (277-8485).

**Post Office:** 210 E. High St. (254-6156), downtown. Open M-F 8am-5pm, Sa 9am-noon. **ZIP code:** 40511. **Area code:** 606.

# ACCOMMODATIONS

A concentration of horse-related wealth pushes up accommodation prices. The cheapest places are outside the city. **New Circle Rd. Dial Accommodations,** 301 E. Vine St., at the visitors center, can help you find a room (233-1221 or 800-848-1224. Open M-F 8:30am-6pm, Sa 10am-6pm, Su noon-5pm; off-season reduced hrs.)

**Kimball House Motel,** 267 S. Limestone St. (252-9565), between downtown and the university. The neon sign beckons you into a timewarp to the kitschy charm of 50s car culture in a Victorian brick house. Parking in back. No phones in rooms; some have TVs. Several 1st fl. singles (no A/C, shared bath) go for $21, but they often fill by late afternoon. Otherwise, singles from $25; doubles $30. Key deposit $5.

**Catalina Motel,** 208 W. New Circle Rd. (299-6281). Take Broadway north of the city, and turn left onto New Circle Rd. Large, clean rooms with A/C, cable TV, pool, free local calls, and HBO. Singles $33, doubles $39.

**Microtel,** 2240 Buena Vista Dr. (299-9600), off I-75 at the Winchester Rd. (Rt. 60) exit. Pleasant motel rooms with window seats. Singles $43; doubles $48.

**Kentucky Horse Park Campground,** 4089 Ironworks Pike (259-4257 or 800-370-6416), 10mi. north of downtown off I-75 at exit 120. Groomed camping plus laundry, showers, basketball courts, swimming pool, and a free shuttle to the KY Horse Park and Museum. Wide open tent sites; 260 RV sites nicely mix shade and lawn. Sites Apr.-Oct. $11, with hookup $15; Nov.-Mar. $9/$11.50. Senior discounts available. 2-week max. stay.

# FOOD AND NIGHTLIFE

**Alfalfa Restaurant,** 557 S. Limestone St. (253-0014), across from Memorial Hall at the university; take bus #9. Menu of fantastic international and veggie/vegan meals changes nightly. Complete dinners with salad and bread under $12. Filling soups and salads from $2, like the "Hoppin' John." Live jazz, folk, and other music W-Sa 8-10pm. No cover. Open M 11am-2pm, Tu-Th 11am-2pm and 5:30-9pm, F-Sa 10am-2pm and 5:30-10pm, Su 10am-2pm.

**Ramsey's,** 496 E. High St. (259-2708). 2 other locations at 4053 Tates Creek Rd. (271-2638) and 1660 Bryan Station Rd. (299-9669). Real Southern grease: even the veggies are cooked with pork parts. 1 meat and 3 vegetables $9.50. Sandwiches under $6. Open Su 10am-11pm, M-Tu 11am-11pm, W-F 11am-1am, Sa 10am-1am.

**Parkette Drive-In,** 1216 New Circle Rd. (254-8723). Drive-up, 1951 eatery with bargain food. Giant "Poor Boy" burger plate $2.60; chicken box with 4 pieces, gravy, fries, cole slaw, and roll $3.85. A few booths inside give carless folks an equal opportunity to join in the nostalgia. Open M-Th 10am-10pm, F-Sa 10am-11pm.

Lexington's nightlife surpasses expectations for a town its size. For current info, read the "Weekender" section of the F *Herald-Leader,* or pick up a free *Ace.* Stand-up comics do their thing at **Comedy off Broadway,** 3199 Nicholsville Rd., at Lexington Green Mall. (271-5653. Cover $3-8; shows Tu-Th 8pm and F-Sa 8 and 10:30pm.) **The Bar,** 224 E. Main St., a popular disco cabaret/lounge complex, caters to gays and lesbians. (255-1551. Cover F $4, Sa $5. Lounge open M-Sa 4pm-1am; disco open Tu-Th 10pm-1am, F 10pm-2am, Sa 10pm-3:30am.) For a bit o' the Irish, and a lot o' UK students, go to **Lynagh's Pub and Club,** in University Plaza at Wood-land and Euclid St. Pub grills up good burgers ($4.95) and music plays next door. (Pub 255-1292, club 255-6614. Cover from $3. Pub open M-Sa 11am-1am, Su noon-11pm. Club open Tu-Sa 4-9pm for pool and darts; music 10pm-1am). The **Kentucky Theater,** 214 E. Main St., projects indy and artsy flicks for $4.50-5.25 (231-6997).

## ■ SIGHTS

To escape the stifling swamp conditions farther south, antebellum plantation own-ers built beautiful summer retreats in milder Lexington. The most attractive of these stately houses preen only a few blocks northeast of the town center, in the Gratz Park area near the old public library. Wrap-around porches, wooden mina-rets, stone foundations, and rose-covered trellises distinguish these old estates from the neighborhood's newer homes. **The Hunt Morgan House** stands at the end of the park across from the old library at W. 2nd St. Built in 1814 by John Wesley Hunt, the first millionaire west of the Alleghenies, the house witnessed the birth of Thomas Hunt Morgan, who won a 1933 Nobel Prize for proving the existence of the gene. The house's most colorful inhabitant, however, was Confederate General John Hunt Morgan who, pursued by Union troops, rode his horse up the front steps and into the house, leaned down to kiss his mother, and rode out the back door. *(201 N. Mill St. 233-3290 or 253-0362. Tours Tu-Sa 10am-4pm, Su 2-5pm at 15min. past the hr. $5, students $3.)* 5 blocks away in what is now called the **Mary Todd Lincoln House,** Mary Todd, the future wife of Abraham Lincoln, grew up. *(578 W. Main St. 233-9999. Open mid-Mar. to Nov. Tu-Sa 10am-4pm 45min. tour; last tour 3:15pm; $5, ages 6-12 $2.)* Senator Henry Clay and John Hunt Morgan now lie buried at the **Lexington Cem-etery.** *(833 W. Main St. 255-5522. Open daily 8am-5pm; office 8am-4pm. Free cemetery scaven-ger hunts available for children; no digging.)* Clay used to reside at **Ashland,** a 20-acre estate across town at Sycamore and Richmond Rd. *(120 Sycamore Rd. 266-8581. take the "Woodhall" bus. Open Apr.-Oct. M-Sa 10am-4:30pm, Su 1-4:30pm; Nov.-Mar. closed M; closed Jan. 1hr. tours $6, students $3, ages 6-12 $2.)*

Hollywood jewelry designer George W. Headley's exotic and sparkling creations are displayed at the **Headley-Whitney Museum.** The 3-car garage is blanketed with shells—you won't need an employee to tell you it's from the 70s. *(4435 Old Frankfort Pike. 255-6653. Open Tu-F 10am-5pm, Sa-Su noon-5pm. $4, students $2, seniors $3.)*

## HORSES

Lexington horse farms are pretty places to visit; the visitors bureau has a list of available farms. **Three Chimneys Farm,** on Old Frankfort Pike 4mi. from I-64 and 8½mi. from New Circle Rd., raised the 1977 Triple Crown winner **Seattle Slew** *(873-7053. Tours daily 10am and 1pm, by appt. only; $5-10 tip customary).* **Kentucky Horse Park,** 10mi. north at exit 120 off I-75, has extensive equine facilities, a museum tracing the history, science, and pageantry of these animals, and many live examples. The last weekend in Apr., the horse park hosts the annual Rolex tournament qualifier for the **U.S. equestrian team.** *(4089 Ironworks Pike 233-4303. Open Apr.-Oct. daily 9am-5pm. $10, ages 7-12 $5; Nov.-Mar. $7.50/$4.50; live horse shows and horse-drawn vehicle tours included. 50min. horse ride and tour in addition to entrance fee, $12; pony rides $3.25. Parking $2. Wheelchair access.)* Every Apr., the **Keeneland Race Track,** west on U.S. 60, holds the final prep race for the Kentucky Derby. Hay and breakfast is available at the race track kitchen. *(4201 Versailles Rd. 254-3412 or 800-456-3412. Races Oct. and Apr.; post time 1pm. $2.50. Workouts free and open to the public mid-Mar. to Nov. 6am-10am.)* At **Red Mile Harness Track,** harness racing takes center stage. *(847 S. Broadway. 255-0752. Bus #3 on South Broadway. Races Apr.-June and late Sept. to early Oct.; in spring post times noon and 1pm, in fall 7:30pm. $2 min. bet. Parking free. Morning workouts open to the public in racing season dawn-1pm.)* Thoroughbreds become champions at the **Kentucky Horse Center,** 2½mi. north of exit 113 off I-64/75. *(3380 Paris Pike. 293-1853. Tours Apr.-Oct. M-F 9, 10:30am, and 1pm; Sa 9 and 10:30am; call for winter schedule. $10, under 13 $5.)*

## NEAR LEXINGTON

**Harrodsburg,** the oldest permanent English settlement west of the Alleghenies, is nestled 32mi. southwest of Lexington on U.S. 68. Visitors can watch faux-18th-century craftspeople demonstrate skills like blacksmithing and quilting at **Old Fort Harrod State Park,** S. College St. The **Mansion Museum,** just below the Fort, showcases Union and Confederate artifacts, including a cast of Lincoln's face and hands. *(734-3314. Fort and museum open daily 9am-5pm; museum closed Dec. to mid-Mar. $3.50, ages 6-12 $2.)* Pick up a tour booklet for historic downtown Harrodsburg at the **visitors center,** 103 Main St., on the corner of U.S. 68 and Main St. *(734-2364 or 800-355-9192. Open M-F 8:30am-4:30pm, Sa 10am-3pm.)*

The Shakers, a 19th-century celibate religious sect, simply lived at **Shaker Village,** 25mi. southwest of Lexington and north of Harrodsburg on U.S. 68. The 2700-acre farm features 33 restored Shaker buildings; a tour includes demonstrations of everything from making apple butter to barrels. The village also offers **riverboat excursions** on the Kentucky River. *(734-5411. Open daily 9am-5:30pm. $9.50, students 12-17 $5, ages 6-11 $3; with river trip $13.50/$7/$4. Oct.-Mar. reduced hrs. and prices. Wheelchair access.)* Visitors can sleep in a "Shaker" room with TV, A/C, and plumbing. *(Singles from $50; doubles $60; reservations highly recommended.)*

In **Richmond,** exit 95 off I-75, the elegant Georgian-Italianate mansion **White Hall** was home to abolitionist (not the boxer) Cassius M. Clay, cousin of Senator Henry Clay. (623-9178. 45min. guided tours only. Open Apr.-Oct. daily 9am-5:30pm, last tour at 4:30pm; early Sept. to Oct. W-Su only. $4.50, under 13 $2.50, under 6 free.) A re-creation of one of Daniel Boone's forts, **Fort Boonesborough State Park,** also in Richmond, has samples of 18th-century crafts, a small museum collection, and films about pioneers. *(527-3131. Open Apr.-Aug. daily 9am-5:30pm; Sept.-Oct. W-Su 9am-5:30pm. $4.50, ages 6-12 $3. White Hall/Boonesborough combo tickets $7.)*

## DANIEL BOONE NATIONAL FOREST

The Daniel Boone National Forest cuts a vast green swath through Kentucky's Eastern Highlands. Encompassing 670,000 acres of mountains and valleys, the forest is layered with a gorgeous tangle of chestnut, oak, hemlock, and pine, as well as pristine lakes, waterfalls, and extraordinary natural bridges. This is bluegrass country, where seasoned backpackers and Lexington's day trippers still find the heart of old Appalachia deep in the forest—though, by some reports, you're less likely these days to stumble onto feuding Hatfields and McCoys than into some farmer's hidden field of marijuana, reputedly Kentucky's #1 cash crop.

**⁊ PRACTICAL INFORMATION.** Seven U.S. Forest Service Ranger Districts administer the National Forest. Ranger offices supply trail maps and specifics about the portions of the 254mi. **Sheltowee Trace,** the forest's most significant trail, that pass through their districts. **Stanton Ranger District,** 705 W. College Ave. (663-2852), Stanton, includes the **Red River Gorge and Natural Bridge** (open M-F 8am-4:30pm). To the north, **Morehead Ranger District,** 2375 KY 801 S. (784-5628), 2mi. south of Rt. 60, includes **Cave Run Lake.** The **Morehead Tourism Commission,** 150 E. First St. (784-6221), Morehead 40351, has more info. To the south, **London Ranger District** (864-4163), on U.S. 25 S, covers Laurel River Lake, close to Cumberland Falls; Laurel River Lake's **visitors center** (878-6900 or 800-348-0095) is at exit 41 off I-75 (open M-Sa 9am-5pm, Su 10am-2pm). For forest-wide info, contact the **Forest Supervisor,** 100 Vaught Rd., Winchester (745-3100). **Greyhound** serves several towns with buses from Lexington to Morehead (1½hr., 1 per day, $13); London (1¾hr., 3 per day, $18); and Corbin (2hr., 5 per day, $20). **Area code:** 606.

**STANTON RANGER DISTRICT.** Split by the Mountain Pkwy., Stanton Ranger District divides into two parts, with **Natural Bridge State Resort Park** on the south side, and **Red River Gorge Geological Area** on the north. **Natural Bridge,** off Rt. 11, is the area's absolute must-see site. The somewhat steep ¾mi. trail leads to the expansive view at the top of the bridge's vast span. The **Red River Gorge Area** con-

THE SOUTH

tains some of the most varied and ecologically rich terrain in this part of the country. A 32mi. circuit (Rt. 77 E to Rt. 715) runs through the single-lane **Nada Tunnel,** an old railroad tunnel cut directly through the rock (scary as hell!), and past the restored **Gladie Historic Site Log House.** Along the way, it takes in bison, curving mountain roads, forests, and picturesque wooden and metal bridges. If you don't mind driving down a 3mi. gravel road, take a 1.3mi hike past the beautiful **Rock Bridge,** down Rock Bridge Rd. near the junction of Rt. 715 and Rt. 15. A few mi. north of Rock Bridge is **Sky Bridge** (off Rt. 715), which only requires a fairly-level ¼mi. hike to reach the top. Despite the hundreds of initials carved in the rock, standing high above the sheer drop-offs and green gorges on both sides is magical.

Slade, 52mi. southeast of Lexington (take I-64 to Mountain Pkwy.), makes a good base for a tour of nearby forest land. A **red tourist caboose,** run by the **Natural Bridge/Powell County Chamber of Commerce,** sits at the Slade Exit off Mountain Pkwy. (663-9229. Open daily 10am-6pm; off-season 10am-5pm.) The town itself contains few attractions except the forest and the lavish **Natural Bridge State Resort Park,** 2135 Natural Bridge Rd. (663-2214 or 800-325-1710), off Rt. 11. Budget-conscious travelers can avoid the park's pricey lodge, and patronize its campgrounds: **Whittletown** has 40 well-shaded sites, and **Middle Fork** has 39 open sites. (Primitive sites $8.50 weekdays, $10.50 weekends; with hookup weekdays $14 for 2 adults, $16 weekends; $1 per additional adult, under 16 free. For Sa-Su, reserve in advance.) You can pitch a tent anywhere in the forest, as long as you stay more than 300 ft. from roads or marked trails. **Li'l Abners** has large, clean, slightly dim rooms with pool access and free local calls, 2½mi. from Red River Gorge on Rt. 11 in Slade (663-5384; singles $40; doubles $45; July-Aug. reserve in advance.)

Good restaurants are hard to come by, but many general stores along Rt. 11 and 15 peddle cheap, filling sandwiches to eat at a counter or on the trail. Make sure to try **Ale-8-1,** the local soft drink in the tall green bottle, and the regional staple of soup beans and cornbread. In nearby Stanton, **Bruen's Restaurant,** on Sipple St. at exit 22 off Mountain Pkwy., makes greasy fare in a down-home atmosphere. Breakfast served all day; two eggs, bacon, and a biscuit with gravy for just $2.55, or a cheeseburger for $1.50 (663-4252; open Su-Th 4:30am-9pm, F-Sa 4:30am-10pm).

**LONDON RANGER DISTRICT.** There's boating, fishing, hiking, and just hanging out at **Laurel River Lake. Camping** is available at two spacious and densely wooded Forest Service campgrounds on the lake, both off Rt. 193 and adjacent to marinas: **Grove** with 56 sites and **Holly Bay** with 90 sites. (800-280-2266. 10 primitive sites. $7 for 1 person, $10 for 2; with hookup $14 for 1 person, $24 for 2. Reservations recommended 10 days in advance.) Visitors to giant **Cumberland Falls,** 18mi. west of Corbin on Rt. 90—"The Niagara of the South"—can camp at the state park, which surrounds the falls. The campground is signposted off Rt. 90 (528-4121; 50 sites; Su-Th tents $8.50, RVs $12; F-Sa $10.50/$14; open Apr.-Oct.). The falls' famous moonbows, created by the water mist during a full moon, are fantastic. Onward, chicken soldiers: in nearby Corbin, deep-fried legions pay homage to the Colonel at the original **Kentucky Fried Chicken/Harland Sanders Café and Museum,** at the junction of Rt. 25 E and 25 W, in all its finger-lickin' glory (528-2163; open daily 7am-11pm). **Sheltowee Trace Outfitters,** in Whitley City on Rt. 90, 5mi. east of the state park, arranges guided, 7hr. rafting trips down the Falls' class III rapids. (800-541-7238. $48, ages 5-12 $38. 9am-4pm with equipment, guide, and lunch.)

# CUMBERLAND GAP

Stretching from Maine to Georgia, the majestic Appalachian Mountain Range proved a formidable obstacle to the westward movement of early American settlers, but not to bison. By following these animals, Native Americans learned of the Cumberland Gap, a natural break in the mountains. Frontiersman Daniel Boone became famous when he blazed the Wilderness Trail through the Gap in 1775, thereby opening the West to colonization. The **Cumberland Gap National Historic Park,** best reached by U.S. 25 E from Kentucky or U.S. 58 from Virginia, sits on 20,000 acres shared by Kentucky, Virginia, and Tennessee. The Cumberland Gap

**visitors center** (606-248-2817), on U.S. 25 E in Middleboro, KY, has a film and slide show on the Gap's history (park and center open daily 8am-6pm; off-season 8am-5pm). The park's 160-site **campground**, on U.S. 58 in Virginia, has hot showers (sites $10, with electricity $15). **Backcountry camping** requires a free permit from the visitors center. A breathtaking view is 4mi. from the visitors center at **Pinnacle Rock**.

# TENNESSEE

Sloping from the majestic Great Smoky Mountains to the verdant Mississippi lowlands, Tennessee makes and breaks stereotypes with the smooth ease of Jack Daniels. Those enchanted with the last state to secede from the Union, and the first to rejoin, often express their affection in the form of song—an ode to Davy Crockett deems this land the "greatest state in the land of the free," Dolly Parton finds her Heartsong in the mountains, and there ain't no place the Grateful Dead would rather be. Tennessee's economy is industry-based, with the world's largest Bible-producing business, but it is music that fuels the state's soul, as any fan of the King knows. Country twangs from Nashville and the blues wail in Memphis.

## ⚡ PRACTICAL INFORMATION

**Capital:** Nashville.

**Visitor Info: Tennessee Dept. of Tourist Development,** 320 6th Ave., Nashville (741-2159; www.state.tn.us/tourdev). Open M-F 8am-4:30pm. **Tennessee State Parks Information,** 401 Church St., Nashville (800-421-6683).

**Postal Abbreviation:** TN. **Sales Tax:** 8%.

# NASHVILLE

Long-forgotten Francis Nash is one of only four Revolutionary War heroes honored with U.S. city names (Washington, Wayne, and Knox are the others), but his tenuous foothold in history pales in comparison to Nashville's notoriety as the banjo-pickin', foot stompin' capital of country music. Large, eclectic, and unapologetically heterogeneous, Tennessee's capital is not only the home of the Country Music Hall of Fame, but also "the Wall Street of the South." The city houses the Southern Baptists and still finds room for centers of fine arts and higher learning, such as Fisk University and Vanderbilt.

## ⚡ ORIENTATION AND PRACTICAL INFORMATION

Nashville's streets are fickle, often interrupted by curving parkways and one-ways. Names change constantly and without warning; **Broadway,** the main east-west thoroughfare, melts into **West End Ave.** just outside downtown at Vanderbilt and I-40. In downtown, easily marked by the twin spires of Bell South's towering "Bat Building," numbered avenues run north-south, parallel to the Cumberland River. The curve of **James Robertson Pkwy.** encloses the north end, becoming **Main St.** on the other side of the river (later **Gallatin Pike**) and **McGavock St.** at the south end. *The area south of Broadway between 2nd and 7th Ave. and the region north of James Robertson Pkwy. are both unsafe at night.*

**Airport: Metropolitan** (275-1675), 8mi. south of downtown. An airport **shuttle** (275-1180) operates out of major downtown hotels ($9, round-trip $15). Bus fare downtown $1.50 with a transfer. Taxi to downtown $15-17.

**Buses: Greyhound,** 200 8th Ave. S. (255-1691), at Broadway downtown. Borders on a rough neighborhood, but the station is bright. To: Memphis (4hr., 6 per day, $28); Chattanooga (2½hr., 4 per day, $14); Birmingham (4hr., 4 per day, $27); and Knoxville (3hr., 6 per day, $23). Station open 24hr.

THE SOUTH

**Public Transit: Metropolitan Transit Authority (MTA)** (862-5950). Buses operate on limited routes, usually once per hr. M-F 5:40am-11:15pm, less frequent service Sa-Su. Fare $1.40, transfers 10¢. MTA runs 2 **tourist trolleys** from Riverfront Park and Downtown Circle every 10-15min. M-W 9am-7pm, Th 9am-11pm, F-Sa 9am-1am. Fare $1, all-day pass $3, seniors and under 13 $2.

**Taxis: Nashville Cab,** 242-7070. **Music City Cab,** 262-0451.

**Car Rental: Thrifty,** 414 11th Ave. N. (248-8888), downtown. $33 per day, Sa-Su $30. Must be over 25 with a major credit card.

**Visitor Info: Nashville Visitors Bureau,** 501 Broadway (259-4747), in the Nashville Arena, I-65 at exit 84, James Robertson Pkwy. Open daily 8:30am-8pm.

**Hotlines: Crisis Line,** 244-7444. **Rape Hotline,** 256-8526. Both 24hr. **Gay and Lesbian Switchboard,** 297-0008. Operates nightly 6-9pm.

**Hospitals: Metro Nashville General Hospital,** 1818 Albion St. (341-4000). **The Women's Center,** 419 Welshwood Dr. (331-1200), across from Harding Mall.

**Post Office:** 901 Broadway (255-9453), next to Union Station. Open M-F 7:30am-7pm, Sa 9am-2pm. **ZIP code:** 37202. **Area code:** 615.

# ◤ ACCOMMODATIONS

Finding a room in Nashville isn't difficult, just expensive, especially in summer. Make reservations well in advance, especially for weekend stays. Budget motels concentrate around **W. Trinity Ln.** and **Brick Church Pike,** off I-65 at exit 87B. Dirt-cheap hotels inhabit the area around **Dickerson Rd.** and **Murfreesboro,** but the neighborhood is seedy at best. Closer to downtown (but still sketchy), several motels huddle on **Interstate Dr.** just over the Woodland St. Bridge.

**The Liberty Inn,** 2400 Brick Church Pike (228-2567). Big TVs with cable, A/C, roomy showers—what more could you ask for? Local calls 35¢. One bed $33-40. Two can stay in one bed, no questions asked. $5 deposit.

**The Cumberland Inn,** 150 W. Trinity Ln. (226-1600 or 800-704-1028), exit 87A off I-65 N, north of downtown. Cheerful rooms with bright, modern furnishings, A/C, HBO, laundry, and free continental breakfast. Singles $36; doubles $43.

Two campgrounds lie near Opryland USA. By car, take Briley Pkwy. north to McGavock Pike exit 12B and go north onto Music Valley Dr. **Nashville Holiday Travel Park,** 2572 Music Valley Dr. (889-4225), has a wooded area for tenting and densely packed RV sites (sites for 2 $20, with hookup $33; $4 per additional person over age 11). **Opryland KOA,** 2626 Music Valley Dr. (889-0282), has 50 tent sites ($20), tons of crowded sites with hookups ($30), and cabins (1 room $36, 2 rooms $46, A/C and electricity); perks include a pool and live summer music (AAA discount).

# ◖ FOOD

In Nashville, music influences even the local delicacies; **Goo-Goo Clusters** (peanuts, pecans, chocolate, caramel, and marshmallow), sold most places, bear the initials of the Grand Ole Opry. Nashville's other finger-lickin' traditions, barbecue or fried chicken followed by pecan pie, are no less sinful. Restaurants for collegiate tastes and budgets cram **West End Ave.** and the 2000 block of **Elliston Pl.,** near Vanderbilt.

**◪ Loveless Café,** 8400 Rt. 100 (646-9700 or 800-889-2432). A Nashville country cookin' tradition. Feast on biscuits made from scratch with homemade preserves, country ham ($10), fried chicken ($11), and good ol' southern hospitality. Open M-F 8am-2pm and 5-9pm, Sa-Su 8am-9pm. Reservations recommended. BYOB.

**SATCO (San Antonio Taco Company),** 416 21st Ave. S. (327-4322). Tex-Mex and beer options abound at this student hangout. Fajitas $1.50, tacos $1. Single beers $1.75, bucket of 6 $9. Also at 208 Commerce St. (259-4413). Open Su-W 11am-midnight, Th-Sa 11am-1:30am.

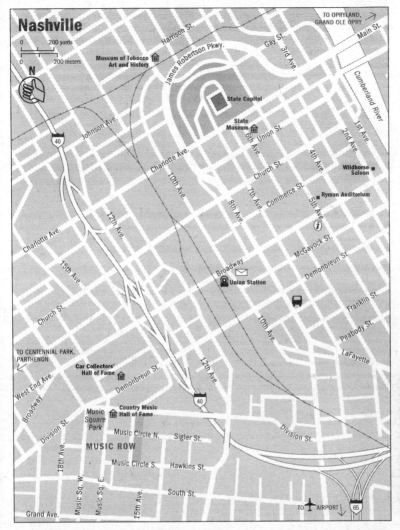

# Nashville

**Peaceful Planet,** 1811 Division St. (327-2033), next to music studios. Only vegetarian and vegan food is served. Trays are available to pile on tofu, vegetables, juice, soup, and delicious confections. All food is $4.70 per lb. Open for breakfast M-F 7am-10am, lunch M-F 11am-2:30pm, dinner M-F 4:30-8:30pm, and Su brunch 9:30am-2:30pm.

**The World's End,** 1713 Church St. (329-3480). It's the end of the world as we know it, and I feel like a burger or a salad ($5-8), or maybe a beer ($2.50). Caters to a primarily gay crowd. Open Su and Tu-Th 4pm-12:30am, F-Sa 4pm-1:30am.

## ◼ SIGHTS

**Music Row,** home of Nashville's signature industry, centers around Division and Demonbreun St. from 16th to 19th Ave. S., bounded to the south by Grand Ave. (take bus #3 to 17th Ave. and walk south). Once past the mobs outside the **Country Music Hall of Fame,** at Division St., you can marvel at classic memorabilia, such as

Elvis's "solid gold" Cadillac and 24-karat gold piano, evocative photos from country music's early days, and flashy costumes from recent performances. The museum showcases everything from bluegrass to Cajun to Western swing: admission includes a tour of RCA's historic Studio B, where stars like Dolly Parton, Chet Atkins, and The King recorded their early hits. *(4 Music Sq. E. 256-1639. Hall of Fame open daily 8am-6pm; off-season 9am-5pm. $10.75, ages 6-11 $5.75. Wheelchair access.)*

Nashville's pride and joy awaits in **Centennial Park,** a 15min. walk west along West End Ave. from Music Row. The "Athens of the South" boasts a full-scale replica of the **Parthenon.** Built as a temporary exhibit for the Tennessee Centennial in 1897, the Parthenon met with such success that it was rebuilt to last. In its first floor gallery, the building also houses the **Cowan Collection of American Paintings,** a refreshing but erratic selection of 19th- and early 20th-century American art. *(862-8431. Open Tu-Sa 9am-4:30pm, Su 12:30-4pm; Apr.-Oct. Tu-Su 12:30-4pm. $2.50, seniors and ages 4-17 $1.25. Wheelchair access.)* But soft! what light on yonder Parthenon steps breaks? It's **Shakespeare in the Park,** performed at 7pm (F-Su) in Aug. as part of the annual **Shakespeare Festival.** *(292-2273. Free.)*

The **Tennessee State Capitol,** a comely Greek Revival structure atop the hill on Charlotte Ave. next to downtown, offers, among other things, tours of the tomb of James Knox Polk. *(741-1621. Tours hourly M-F 9-11am and 1-3pm, Sa-Su self-guided tours only. Free. Wheelchair access.)* Across the street, the **Tennessee State Museum** depicts the history of Tennessee from the early Native American era to the time of "overlander" pioneers; interactive displays enhance this sometimes whitewashed version of Tennessee history. *(505 Deaderick St. 741-2692.)*

**Fisk University's Van Vechten Gallery,** at Jackson St. and D.B. Todd Blvd. off Jefferson St., exhibits a small but distinguished collection of art by Picasso, Renoir, and Cézanne among others. The gallery also displays African sculpture and many works by Alfred Steiglitz and Georgia O'Keeffe. *(329-8543. Open Tu-F 9am-5pm, Sa 1-4pm. Recommended donation $3.50. Wheelchair access.)*

If you tire of the downtown area, you can rest at the **Cheekwood Museum of Art and Tennessee Botanical Gardens,** 7mi. southwest of town on Forrest Park Dr. The leisurely, well-kept Japanese and rose gardens are a welcome change from Nashville glitz and complement the museum's 19th-century art perfectly. *(356-8000. Bus #3 "West End/Belle Meade" from downtown to Belle Meade Blvd. and Page Rd. Open M-Sa 9am-5pm, Su 11am-5pm; Apr. M-Th 9am-8pm, F-Sa 9am-5pm, Su 11am-5pm. $8, students and seniors $7, ages 6-17 $5.)* The nearby **Belle Meade Mansion,** dubbed "The Queen of Tennessee Plantations," offers a second respite. *(5025 Harding Rd. 356-0501. Open M-Sa 9am-5pm, Su 1-5pm. $8, seniors $7.50, ages 6-12 $3. 2 guided tours per hr.; last tour 4pm.)* This lavish 1853 plantation was the site of the nation's first thoroughbred breeding farm, and host to eight U.S. presidents, including the 380 lb. Taft, who found himself stuck in the bathtub there.

Andrew Jackson's beautiful manor, the **Hermitage,** off exit 221A from I-40, sits atop 625 gloriously shaded acres 13mi. from downtown Nashville. Admission includes a 15min. film, access to the house and grounds, and a visit to nearby Tulip Grove Mansion and Church. *(4580 Rachel's Ln. 889-2941. Open daily 9am-5pm. $9.50, seniors $8.50, ages 6-12 $4.50, families $28; AAA discount.)*

## 🎵 ENTERTAINMENT AND NIGHTLIFE

The **Grand Ole Opry (GOO),** 2804 Opryland Dr., the setting for America's longest-running radio show, has live music and a museum complete with a Randy Travis suit and Marty Robbin's race car. (889-6611. Museum open M-Th 10-5, F 10am-8pm, Sa 10am-10pm, Su 11am-5pm. Live music F 7:30pm, Sa 6:30 and 9:30pm. $18-20; the F *Tennessean* has a list of performers. Tours F-Sa 11am for $10. Call or write for reservations.) During the first weekend in June, the outdoor **Summer Lights downtown,** jams with live rock, jazz, reggae, classical, and country shows (performances M-Th 4pm-12:30am). For info on the **Nashville Symphony,** call **Ticketmaster** (741-2787). Listings for the area's music and events fill the free *Nashville Scene. Bone* has more music info, and *Q (Query)* contains gay and lesbian news and listings.

**Wildhorse Saloon,** 120 2nd Ave. N. (251-1000). Huge country dance hall and birthplace of TNN dance show. Bring your cowboy boots and hat for the two-step. Dance lessons every hr. 4-9pm. Cover $3-12 after 5pm. Open daily 11am-2am. Live music F.

**Bluebird Café,** 4104 Hillsboro Rd. (383-1461), in Green Hills. This famous bird sings country, blues, and folk; Garth Brooks got his start here. Dinners of salads and sandwiches ($4-6.50) until 11pm. Early show 7pm; cover begins around 9:30pm ($4-10). No cover Su. Open daily 5:30pm until the singing stops.

**Lucy's Record Shop,** 1707 Church St. (321-0882), vends wicked vinyl during the day to the same young alterna-punk crowd that shows up for indie, national, and local shows at night. Cover $5. All ages welcome.

**Havana Lounge,** 154 2nd Ave. N. (313-7665), near the Wildhorse Saloon, but worlds apart. A popular cigar and martini bar that could be the brainchild of New York City and 50s Cuba. Live jazz and blues most nights. Pool tables. No cover. Open M-Th 11am-2am, F 11am-3am, Sa 5pm-3am.

## KNOXVILLE

Knoxville was settled after the Revolutionary War and named for Washington's Secretary of War, Henry Knox. Once the capital of Tennessee, the city hosted the 1982 World's Fair (which attracted 10 million visitors) and continues to be home to the 26,000 students of the University of Tennessee (UT). Shaded by the stunning Smoky Mountains and hemmed by vast lakes created by the Tennessee Valley Authority, Knoxville offers friendly urbanity and a hopping nightlife.

**⁊ PRACTICAL INFORMATION.** Downtown stretches north from the **Tennessee River,** bordered by **Henley St.** and the **World's Fair Park** to the west. **Greyhound,** 100 Magnolia Ave. (522-5144), at Central St., buses to Nashville (3hr., 7 per day, $23); Chattanooga (2hr., 4 per day, $14); and Lexington (3½hr., 6 per day, $39). **Public transit: KAT** (637-3000); buses run from 6:15am-6:15pm or later, depending on the route (fare $1, transfers 20¢). Two **free trolley** lines run throughout the city: Blue goes downtown and eastward, while Orange heads downtown and westward to the park and UT (7am-6pm). **Gateway Regional Visitors Center:** 900 Volunteer Landing, along the river on the southeast side of downtown. **Post Office:** 501 Main Ave. (521-8987; open M-F 8am-4:30pm). **ZIP code:** 37902. **Area code:** 423.

**⌐⌐ ACCOMMODATIONS AND FOOD.** Many not-quite-budget motels sit along **I-75** and **I-40,** just outside the city. If you're a woman, and they have space, the **YWCA,** 420 W. Clinch St., downtown at Walnut St., will take you (523-6126; small dorm-style rooms with shared bath $12; call ahead M-F 9am-5pm). **Microtel,** 309 N. Peters Rd., off I-75/40 at exit 278, has admittedly small, but spotless rooms. A/C, cable, local calls, HBO, and free admission to a nearby gym enlarge its appeal. (531-8041 or 800-579-1683. Rooms from $38.) A charming replica of an Edinburgh split-level it is not, but the **Scottish Inns,** 301 Callahan Rd., at exit 110 off I-75, keeps clean rooms equipped with A/C, free local calls, cable, HBO, and an outdoor pool

THE SOUTH

## A GRIM REMINDER OF PAX AMERICANA

Created in 1942 with the sole purpose of working on atomic bombs as part of the Manhattan Project, **Oak Ridge** was shrouded in secrecy and fenced in from outsiders. The city, 20mi. from Knoxville on Rt. 62 or 162, was opened to the public in 1949, 4 years after the bombs wiped out Hiroshima and Nagasaki, and hosts the euphemistically named **American Museum of Science and Energy.** The bus tour takes you through a graphite reactor museum to view the first nuclear reactor to operate at full capacity and the once top-secret Y-12 Plant, where the uranium used in the "Little Boy" bomb was produced. The **visitors bureau** has declassified tour info. *(Museum: 300 S. Tulane Ave. 576-3200. Open M-F 9am-5pm. Free. Tours M-F 12:45pm. Bureau: 302 S. Tulane Ave. 800-887-3429. Open M-F 9am-5pm, Sa 10am-2pm; Sept.-Apr. M-F 9am-5pm.)*

(689-7777; singles $30, doubles $38; prices increase by $5 on weekends). **Yogi Bear's Jellystone Park Campground,** 9514 Diggs Gap Rd., at exit 117 off I-75, is located closer to the city than most other campgrounds. It features a pool, clubhouse, restaurant, and laundry, as well as cartoon cheer. (938-6600 or 800-238-9644. Primitive sites $15, with moisture and sparks $16, full hookup $20.)

The **Strip** (part of Cumberland Ave. along campus proper) is lined with student hangouts, bars, and restaurants. **Market Sq.,** a popular plaza to the east of World's Fair Park, presents restaurants, fountains, and shade. The other center of chowing, browsing, and carousing, **Old City,** spreads north up Central and Jackson St. The ever-popular **Calhoun's on the River,** 400 Neyland Dr., claims to serve the "best ribs in America." Customers test that claim ($9.50-16), or devour sandwiches for $6.50-7. (673-3355. Open M-Th 11am-10:30pm, F-Sa 11am-11pm, Su 11am-10pm.)

⊙ **SIGHTS. World's Fair Park** makes for a fine stroll with a reflecting pool, grassy expanses, and a playground. The **Knoxville Museum of Art** houses changing exhibits of high caliber. *(1050 World's Fair Park Dr. 525-6101. Open Tu-Th and Sa 10am-5pm, F 10am-9pm, Su noon-5pm. $4, seniors $3, ages 12-17 $2. F free from 5-9pm.)* Downtown sits the **Blount Mansion** the 1792 frame house of governor William Blount (pronounced as if there was no "o", as in "M. Poirot, it seems the victim was struck with a Blount object"). *(200 W. Hill Ave. 525-2375. Open Tu-Sa 9:30am-5pm, Su 2-5pm; Nov.-Feb. Tu-F 9:30am-5pm. $4, ages 6-12 $2. AAA discount. 1hr. tours leave on the hr.; last tour at 4pm.)* Nearby, the **James White Fort** still preserves portions of the original stockade built in 1786 by Knoxville's first citizen and founder. *(205 E. Hill Ave. 525-6514. Tours run continuously until 3:30pm. Open M-Sa 9:30am-4:30pm. $4, children $2, seniors $3.50.)*

Picnickers will appreciate **Krutch Park** (across the street), a tiny, perfectly manicured oasis of green in the midst of downtown. Eighty acres of greenery abound at **Ijams Nature Center,** 2mi. east of downtown across Gay St. Bridge. *(2915 Island Home Ave. 577-4717. Grounds open daily 8am-dusk. Museum open M-F 9am-4pm, Sa noon-4pm, Su 1-5pm. Free.)* Knoxville is in full bloom Apr. 14-30, 2000, for the **Dogwood Arts Festival,** featuring food, folks, fun, and a lot of trees. *(637-4561.)*

For a taste of down-home Appalachia, visit the **Farmers Market,** 15mi. from downtown on I-640, exit 8. *(524-3276. Open M-Sa 9am-7pm, Su noon-6pm.)* The must-see **Museum of Appalachia** sits 16mi. north of Knoxville on I-75 at exit 122 in Norris. The "museum" is actually a village with houses, barns, a school, a spectacular Hall of Fame building complete with a dulcimer exhibit, livestock, and the cabin where Samuel Langhorne Clemens (Mark Twain) was conceived. *(494-7680 or 494-0514. Open daily dawn-dusk. $6, ages 6-15 $4, families $16; senior and AAA discounts.)* Cleanse the aesthetic palate with a trip to **Norris Dam** and the accompanying **Grist Mill;** just east of the museum, exit left onto Rt. 61, then turn left onto Rt. 441 N for about 5mi.

🎭 **ENTERTAINMENT AND NIGHTLIFE.** UT sports some fantastic teams, particularly **football** and **women's basketball.** Call for tickets at 974-2491. In summer, the **Knoxville Smokies,** an AA baseball team, hit the field (637-9494; tickets $4-7).

If Tennessee weather ain't hot enough, warm up at **195 Degrees,** 109½ S. Central St. In the middle of Old City, amazing cake ($3.75) is served in a thick, funky atmosphere (546-0051; open M-W 8am-6pm, Th-F 8am-10pm, Sa 10am-10pm, Su noon-6pm). **Lucille's,** 106 N. Central St., dishes out jazz (546-3742; after 10pm $3; open Tu-Su 6pm-2am). **The Underground,** 214 W. Jackson Ave., has been voted the town's best dance club six years in a row (525-3675; underground open M,W,F-Sa 10pm-3am, cover $3-8). For goings-on around town, pick up a free copy of *Metro Pulse.*

# GREAT SMOKY MOUNTAINS NATIONAL PARK

The largest wilderness area in the eastern U.S., Great Smoky Mountains National Park encompasses 500,000 acres of gray-green Appalachian peaks bounded by the misty North Carolina and Tennessee valleys. Bears, wild hogs, groundhogs, wild turkeys, and a handful of red wolves inhabit the area, as well as more than 1500 species of flowering plants. Whispering conifer forests line the mountain ridges at elevations of over 6000 ft. In June and July, rhododendrons burst into their full glory; by mid-Oct., the mountains become a vibrant quilt of autumnal color.

**MOUNTAINS OF FUN** A mythical American village created by Dolly Parton in the Tennessee hills, **Dollywood,** dominates Pigeon Forge. The park celebrates the cultural legacy of the east Tennessee mountains and the country songmistress herself, famous for some mountainous topography of her own. In Dolly's world, craftspeople demonstrate their skills and sell their wares, 30 rides offer thrills and chills, and country favorites perform. While Dolly asserts that she wants to preserve the culture of the Tennessee mountains, she also seems to want you to pay to come again—Dollywood's motto is "Create Memories Worth Repeating." *(1020 Dollywood Ln. 428-9488 or 800-365-5996. Open May-Dec. daily, most days 10am-6pm; July 9am-9pm; but hrs. change constantly. $30, over 59 $25, ages 4-11 $21; discount coupons available at tourist centers, restaurants, and motels.)*

◪ **PRACTICAL INFORMATION.** Begin exploration at either visitors center: Sugarlands (436-3255), on Newfound Gap Rd. 2mi. south of Gatlinburg, TN, next to the park's headquarters; or Oconaluftee (828-497-1900), 4mi. north of Cherokee, NC (both open daily 8am-7pm; off season 8am-4:30pm). *The Smokies Guide* (25¢) details the park's tours, lectures, activities, and changing natural graces. Info line: 436-1200 (operates daily 8:30am-4:30pm). To get to and from Knoxville, contact ETHRA (428-1795; $3-5; 8am-3pm; give 24hr. notice). Area code: 423.

◪◪ **GRUB 'N' SLUMBER.** Ten **campgrounds** lie scattered throughout the park, each with tent sites, limited trailer space, water, and bathrooms (no showers or hookups). **Smokemont, Elkmont,** and **Cades Cove** accept reservations from mid-May to late Oct. (sites $12-15, reservation fee $3); the rest are first come, first served (sites $10-12). In summer, reserve spots near main roads at least 8 wks. in advance (800-365-2267; 10am-10pm). **Backcountry camping** by reservation only (436-1231).

Motels lining Rt. 441 and Rt. 321 decrease in price with distance from the park. Small motels cluster in both Cherokee and Gatlinburg. Prices vary depending on the season and the economy. In general, Cherokee motels are cheaper (from $35) and Gatlinburg motels are nicer (from $45); prices soar on weekends. **Bell's Wa-Floy Retreat,** 3610 East Pkwy., is 10mi. east of Gatlinburg on Rt. 321. From Gatlinburg proper, catch the eastbound trolley (25¢) to the end of the line; from there, hop, skip, or jump the 5mi. to Wa-Floy. This Christian retreat community envelops a pool, tennis courts, and meditation area. (436-5575. Check-in before 10pm. HI-AYH $10, nonmembers $15. Linen included for nonmembers. Reservations required.)

Authentic Tennessee cookin' oozes from **Smokin' Joe's Bar-B-Que,** 8215 State Hwy. 73, Townsend, near the Ranch Camp hostel. With succulent, slow-cooked meats and homemade side dishes like BBQ beans, Joe's smokes the competition. (448-3212. Dinners with 2 sides, meat, and bread $6.50-11; sandwiches $2-4. Open M-Th 11am-9pm, F-Sa 11am-10pm; Apr.-Oct. also Su 11am-8pm.)

◪◪ **SIGHTS AND ACTIVITIES.** Over 900mi. of hiking trails and 170mi. of road meander through the park. Rangers at the visitors centers will help you devise a trip appropriate for your ability. Some of the most popular trails wind 5mi. to Rainbow Falls, 4mi. to Chimney Tops, and 2½mi. to Laurel Falls. A **backcountry camping permit,** free from visitors centers is required to hike off marked trails. Wherever you go, bring water and don't feed the bears. For gorgeous scenery without the sweat, the 11mi. **Cades Cove driving loop** circles the vestiges of a mountain community that occupied the area from the 1850s to the 1920s (closed to car traffic early May to late Sept. on W and Sa from sunrise-10am). **Bikes** are available at Cades Cove, across from the ranger station. You can also rent **horses** from the stables. *(Bikes: 448-9034. $3.25 per hr. Horses: 448-6286. $15 per hr. Both open Su-Tu and Th-F 9:30am-7pm, W and Sa 7am-4:30pm.)* Less crowded but equally scenic areas include **Cosby** and **Cataloochee,** both on the eastern edge of the park.

## NEAR SMOKY MOUNTAINS: CHEROKEE RESERVATION

The **Cherokee Indian Reservation,** on the southeast border of the national park, features a number of museums, shops, attractions, and a casino. From May to Oct., the reservation offers a tour of the **Ocunaluftee Indian Village,** a re-created mid-18th-century Native American village (800-438-1601; open May15-Oct. 25; $10, ages 6-13 $5). Hear the Cherokee language and view artifacts and films at the **Museum of the Cherokee Indian** on Drama Rd. off Rt. 441. (828-497-3481. Open daily 9am-8pm. Sept. to mid-June 9am-5pm. $6, under 13 $4.) **"Unto these Hills,"** an outdoor drama, retells the story of the Cherokees and the Trail of Tears (June-July M-Sa 8:45pm; Aug. M-Sa 8pm; $11, under 12 $5). **Cherokee Visitors Center:** on Rt. 441 (800-438-1601; open M-F 8am-7pm, Sa 9am-7pm, Su 9am-5pm).

The **Nantahala Outdoor Center (NOC),** 13077 U.S. 19 W, 13mi. southwest of Bryson City, NC, and just south of GSM Park, beckons with cheap beds, three restaurants, and the great outdoors. (800-232-7238 or 704-488-2175. Bunks in simple cabins; showers, kitchen, laundry facilities; $13; call ahead.) The NOC's **whitewater rafting expeditions** are pricey, but you can rent your own raft for a trip down the Nantahala River. (Rafts Su-F $17, Sa $22; 1-person inflatable "duckies" M-F $28, Sa $31. Group rates available. Higher prices July-Aug. Prices include transportation to site and all necessary equipment.) The NOC also offers trips with slightly higher price tags on the Ocoee, Nolichucky, Chattooga, and French Broad Rivers. The 2144mi. **Appalachian Trail** runs through here. **Mountain bike** rentals start at $30 (888-662-1662 ext.600). The NOC staff can assist if you need help planning a daytrip.

## CHATTANOOGA

A bustling city, tucked into the Tennessee River, Chattanooga cultivates more than its choo-choo image. First a trading post in 1815, and now a center of factory outlet shops and privately-owned natural attractions, Chattanooga has always had a commercial tradition. Nonetheless, this city can be nothing if not adorable.

The biggest catch in town is the **Tennessee Aquarium,** on Ross's Landing, with the largest turtle collection in the world, as well as 7000 other animals. After the big tanks, check out the bigger IMAX screen. (800-322-3344. Open M-Th 10am-6pm, F-Su 10am-8pm; Oct.-Apr. daily 10am-6pm. $11, ages 3-12 $6; IMAX film $7/$5; both $15/$9.) The riverwalk pathway connects the aquarium with the **Bluff Art District,** anchored by the **Hunter Museum of Art,** 10 Bluff View, which houses the South's most complete American art collection and an extensive Andy Warhol exhibit. (267-0968. Open Tu-Sa 10am-4:30pm, Su 1-4:30pm. $5, students $3, seniors $4, ages 3-11 $2.50. Wheelchair access.) The eclectic works of the **River Gallery,** 400 E. 2nd St., flood the sense (267-7353; open M-W 10am-5pm, Th-Sa 10am-7pm, Su 1-5pm; free.) A free **shuttle** scuttles from the **Chattanooga Choo Choo Holiday Inn** to the aquarium, with stops on every block (runs daily 7am-9:30pm). The riverfront is shut down for 9 nights in mid-June for the **Riverbend Festival** (265-4112), featuring four stages of live music and the South's largest block party ($20 lets you do it all).

Shops and restaurants commemorate Chattanooga's choo-choo fame in the old terminal on S. Market St. downtown, between 14th and Main. These days, more contemporary attractions are more, well, attractive. The **Incline** ($8, ages 3-12 $4) takes passengers up a ridiculous 72.7° grade to **Lookout Mountain** (take S. Broad or bus #15 or 31 and follow signs), where six states can be seen on a clear day (Jun.-Aug. open 8:30am-9:15pm; Sept.-May 9am-5:15pm; wheelchair access.) The highest peaks and the narrowest hikes are mixed with boulders, flowers, and tacky shops at **Rock City Gardens** (706-820-2531. Open daily 8am-sunset; early Sept. to late May 8:30am-sunset. $10, ages 3-12 $5.50.) One thousand feet inside the mountain, the ▓**Ruby Falls** cavern formations and a 145 ft. waterfall—complete with colored lights and sound effects—add a little Disney-style pizzazz to a day of sightseeing. (821-2544. Open daily in summer 8am-9pm; early Sept. to Oct. and Apr. to late May 8am-8pm; Nov.-Mar. 8am-6pm. $9, ages 6-12 $4.50. 1hr. tour.) Free music rings every F (8pm) at the **Mountain Opry,** atop nearby Signal Mountain.

**GENTLEMAN JACK** Tucked into the southern Tennessee country-side, on Rt. 55 in Lynchburg, miles and miles from a major city, the **Jack Daniels Distillery** churns and bubbles, transforming pure spring water and grain into the famous all-American liquor. Free tours of the distillery cover storage facilities where the air is thick with whiskey; too many deep breaths could send you stumbling through the distillation buildings and Mr. Daniels' original office. The end of the tour lands you in a gift shop, where you can buy the final product, but employees must warn you against opening your new-bought treasure. Ironically, Moore County, where Jack Daniels resides, is "dry." Your tour guide will, however, offer you "yellow label" or "brown label," a.k.a. lemonade or coffee. And you could always ask for another pass through the barrel room. *(931-759-6183. Open daily 8am-4pm. Wheelchair access.)*

Budget motels congregate on the highways coming into the city and on **Broad St.** at the base of Lookout Mountain. **Holiday Trav-l-Park,** 1709 Mack Smith Rd., in Rossville ½mi. off I-75 at the East Ridge exit, enlivens sites for tents and RVs with a Civil War theme. (706-891-9766 or 800-693-2877. Laundry, pool. 2-person site $16.50, with water and electricity $20.50, full hookup $22.50; cabins $35, $2 per additional person.) Two nearby lakes, **Chickamauga** and **Nickajack,** are surrounded by campgrounds. The **Pickle Barrel,** 1012 Market St., downtown, moves beyond cucumbers to scrumptious sandwiches for $3-6 and filling dinners for $7-12. (266-1103. Open M-Sa 11am-3am, Su noon-3am. 21+ after 9pm.) Closer to Lookout Mountain, Mexican fare spices up **Cancun,** 1809 Broad. Lunches go for $3-6, dinner $5-10, and great flan to top it all off costs $1.75. (266-1461. Open M-Th 11am-10pm, F 11am-10:30pm, Sa noon-10:30pm, Su noon-10pm.)

Chattanooga straddles the Tennessee/Georgia border at the junction of I-24/59 and I-75. **Visitors center:** 2 Broad St. (423-756-8687), next to the aquarium (open daily 8:30am-5:30pm). **Greyhound,** 960 Airport Rd. (892-8814; station open 6:30am-9:30pm), buses to Atlanta (1hr., 8 per day, $17); Nashville (3-4hr., 3 per day, $16); and Knoxville (2hr., 3 per day, $16). **Chattanooga Area Transportation Authority (CARTA)** (629-1473) runs buses 5am-11pm (fare $1, transfers 20¢, children 50¢/10¢). **Post office** (899-1198), on Georgia Ave. between Martin Luther King Blvd. and 10th St. (open M-F 7:30am-7:30pm, Sa 8:30am-12:30pm). **ZIP code:** 37402. **Area code:** 423.

# MEMPHIS

Memphis is a music mecca, especially for Elvis fans. Although both blues and gospel were practically invented here, Memphis' visitors are usually boot-wearin', card-carryin' Elvis junkies making a pilgrimage to Graceland, the hub of tackiness and Elvis' former home. Just like Elvis himself (?), Memphis's Sun Studio and Sam Philips live on; they also produced U2 and Bonnie Raitt.

## ⚡ ORIENTATION AND PRACTICAL INFORMATION

Downtown, named avenues run east-west and numbered ones north-south. **Madison Ave.** divides north and south addresses. Two main thoroughfares, **Poplar** and **Union Ave.,** pierce the heart of the city from the east; **2nd** and **3rd St.** arrive from the south. **I-240** and **I-55** encircle the city. **Bellevue** becomes **Elvis Presley Blvd.** and leads you south straight to Graceland, whereas **Midtown,** a wonderful neighborhood, lies east of downtown. There's free, unmetered parking along the river.

**Airport: Memphis International,** 2491 Winchester Rd. (922-8000), south of the southern loop of I-240. Taxi fare to the city $20—negotiate in advance. Hotel express **shuttles** (522-9229) cost $10 (service 6:30am-6:30pm). Public transport to and from the airport $1.10; service is sporadic and the trip can be confusing.

**Trains: Amtrak,** 545 S. Main St. (526-0052), at Calhoun on the southern edge of downtown. *Take a taxi—the surrounding area is very unsafe even during the day.* To: **New Orleans** (8½hr., 1 per day, $39-78); **Chicago** (10½hr., 1 per day, $73-132); and **Jackson** (4hr., 1 per day, $28-55).

## DRIVING THAT TRAIN: A JOURNEY IN THREE ACTS

**Act I.** On the night of Apr. 29, 1900, Jonathan Jones, known to history as "Casey," pulled engine 638 into the Memphis depot right on time. This was an ordinary feat for Casey, who had quickly earned a reputation for punctuality on the rails since his first passenger run only 60 days before. Thus, it had come as a small surprise to the Station Master in Memphis that Casey, ever wise to improving his record of timeliness and in need of some extra cash, offered his services to replace the sick-listed engineer of the late-running New Orleans Special. By the time Casey and his fireman, Jim Webb, finally kicked the New Orleans engine #382 out of the station, the train was already 95min. behind schedule.

**Act II.** In that particular engine and on that particular track gauge, speeds for the route usually ran about 35 mph, but the determined Casey opened the throttle at over 70 mph, reportedly saying "the old lady's got her high heeled slippers on tonight." Unfortunately, as the "old lady" danced down through Tennessee, trouble was brewing in Mississippi. At Vaughn, an airhose had broken, locking several cars on the track. Even worse, a dense fog had set in. When Jim finally caught sight of the brake lights at Vaughn, little time was left to act. Jim jumped to save himself, but Casey held on, closing the throttle, throwing the brakes, and thrusting the train into reverse.

**Act III.** Casey's actions brought the train down to 25 mph, but in the collision he was thrown from the engine to his death. For his heroism, which prevented anyone else from being hurt, the young man from Cayce, KY was honored with a ballad by a black engine-wiper named Wallace Saunders. In that song, and in the songs which have followed—most famously that of the Grateful Dead—Casey Jones continues to drive that train. He is a lasting image of the railroads and a true Tennessee hero.

**Buses: Greyhound,** 203 Union Ave. (523-1184), at 4th St. downtown. *The area is unsafe at night.* To: **Nashville** (4hr., 9 per day, $31); **Chattanooga** (6-9hr., 4 per day, $41); and **Jackson** (4-6hr., 8 per day, $32). Open 24hr.

**Public Transit: Memphis Area Transit Authority (MATA)** (274-6282), corner of Union Ave. and Main St. Bus routes cover most suburbs but run infrequently. The major downtown stops are at the intersections of Front and Jefferson St., and 2nd St. and Madison Ave.; the major routes run on Front, 2nd, and 3rd St. Buses run M-F from 7am, Sa-Su from 10am and stop between 6pm and 11pm, depending on the route. $1.10, transfers 10¢. Refurbished 19th-century **trolley cars** cruise Main St. M-F 6am-1am, Sa 6:30am-1am, Su 6:30am-6pm, and roll along the Riverfront M-Th 6:30am-midnight, F 6:30am-1am, Sa 9:30am-1am, Su 10am-6pm. 50¢. 1-day pass $2, 3-day $5.

**Taxis:** In taxi-deprived Memphis, expect a long wait. **City Wide,** 324-4202.

**Visitor Info: Tennessee Welcome Center,** 119 Riverside Dr. (543-5333), at Jefferson St. Open 24hr. The uniformed **blue suede brigade** roaming the city will happily give you directions or answer questions—just stay off of their blue suede shoes.

**Help Lines: Crisis Line,** 274-7477. **Gay/Lesbian Switchboard,** 324-4297. Operates daily 7:30-11pm. **HIV/AIDS Switchboard,** 278-2437.

**Hospital: Baptist Memorial Hospital,** 899 Madison Ave. (227-2727). **Memphis Area Medical Center for Women,** 29 S. Bellevue Blvd. (24hr. hotline 542-3809).

**Post Office:** 555 S. 3rd St. (521-2187). Open M-F 8:30am-5:30pm, Sa 10am-2pm. **ZIP code:** 38101. **Area code:** 901.

## ▌ SINCE M'BABY LEFT ME, I FOUND A NEW PLACE TO DWELL

Memphis offers a hostel and not much else. A few downtown motels have prices in the budget range; otherwise, more distant lodgings are available near Graceland at **Elvis Presley Blvd.** and **Brooks Rd.** For the celebrations of Elvis's historic birth (Jan. 8) and death (Aug. 15), as well as for the Memphis in May festival, book 6 months to 1 year in advance. The visitors center has a thorough listing of lodgings.

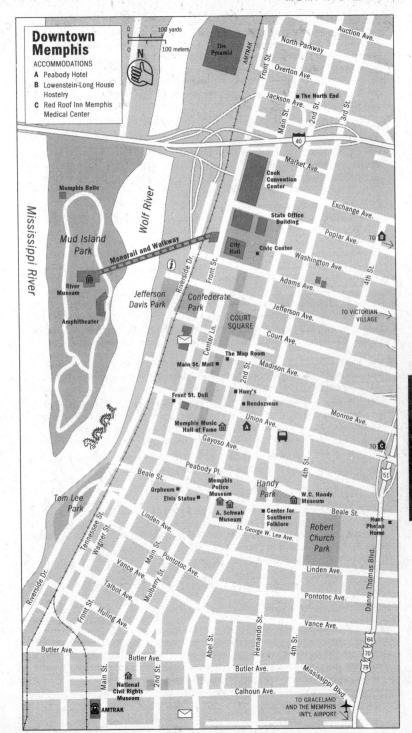

## Downtown Memphis

**ACCOMMODATIONS**

**A** Peabody Hotel
**B** Lowenstein-Long House
Hostelry
**C** Red Roof Inn Memphis
Medical Center

0    100 yards
0    100 meters
N

The Pyramid

North Parkway
Auction Ave.
Overton Ave.
Jackson Ave.    ■ The North End
Market Ave.
Exchange Ave.
Poplar Ave.    TO ■B
Cook Convention Center
State Office Building
City Hall    Civic Center
Washington Ave.
Adams Ave.
Jefferson Ave.
TO VICTORIAN VILLAGE
Memphis Belle
Wolf River
Mud Island Park
Monorail and Walkway
River Museum
Amphitheater
Mississippi River
Jefferson Davis Park
Confederate Park
COURT SQUARE
Court Ave.
Center Ln.
The Map Room
Main St. Mall ■
Madison Ave.
Front St. Deli
■ Huey's
■ Rendezvous
Union Ave.
Monroe Ave.
TO ■C
Memphis Music Hall of Fame    ■A
Gayoso Ave.
Peabody Pl.
Beale St.
Memphis Police Museum
Handy Park
W.C. Handy Museum
Orpheum    Elvis Statue
A. Schwab Museum
■ Center for Southern Folklore
Lt. George W. Lee Ave.
Robert Church Park
Hunt-Phelan Home
Beale St.
Tom Lee Park
Tennessee St.
Wagner St.
Linden Ave.
Vance Ave.
Talbot Ave.
Huling Ave.
Main St.
Mulberry St.
Pontotoc Ave.
Linden Ave.
Pontotoc Ave.
Vance Ave.
Danny Thomas Blvd.
Butler Ave.
Butler Ave.
Abel St.
Hernando St.
Butler Ave.
Calhoun Ave.
National Civil Rights Museum
AMTRAK
TO GRACELAND AND THE MEMPHIS INT'L AIRPORT
Riverside Dr.
Front St.
Main St.
2nd St.
64
70
79
51
Mississippi Blvd.

THE SOUTH

**Lowenstein-Long House/Castle Hostelry (AAIH/Rucksackers),** 217 N. Waldran Blvd. (527-7174), parking lot at 1084 Poplar. Take bus #50 from 3rd St. Convenient location, but the sketchy neighborhood is a drawback for those without cars. The house rises out of its dilapidated surroundings with sheer Victorian elegance. Women's rooms are pleasant and homey; men's rooms are less inviting—consider the private room option. $12; stay 3 nights, get 1 free. Private doubles $33. Camping on lawn out back, $6 per person; includes access to kitchen and bath. Work (when available) can be exchanged for price of stay. Linen $2. Towels $1. Reception daily 9-11am and 5-9pm.

**Red Roof Inn Memphis Medical Center,** 210 S. Pauline St. (528-0650), near Union Ave. Pricey, but convenient to downtown with sparkly clean rooms. Cable, A/C, free local calls, complimentary coffee, and newspaper. Singles $49.

**Memphis/Graceland KOA,** 3691 Elvis Presley Blvd. (396-7125), right next door to Graceland with pool, laundry, and free shuttle to Beale St. No trees or privacy: good location. Sites for 1-2 people $20, with hookup $30; cabins with A/C $35; $3 per extra person.

**Memphis South Campground,** 460 Byhalia Rd. (601-429-1818), Hernando, MS, 20mi. south of Memphis, at exit 280 off I-55 in Mississippi. Turn right at the end of the ramp, then right at the first set of lights onto Mt. Pleasant Rd. A relaxing, green spot with a pool and laundry. Tent sites $12, with water and wattage $15, full hookup $17; $2 per additional person. Office open daily 8-10am and 4:30-7:30pm.

## MEALS FIT FOR THE KING

In Memphis, barbecue is as common as rhinestone-studded jumpsuits; the city even hosts the **World Championship Barbecue Cooking Contest** in May. But don't fret if gnawing on ribs isn't your thing—Memphis has plenty of other Southern restaurants with down-home favorites like fried chicken, catfish, chitterlings, and grits.

**Rendezvous** (523-2746), Downtown Alley, between the Holiday Inn and Days Inn. A Memphis legend, serving large portions of ribs ($12-14) and cheaper sandwiches ($3-6), but be prepared to wait an hour. Open Tu-Th 4:30pm-11:30pm, F-Sa noon-midnight.

**The Map Room,** 2 S. Main St. (579-9924), where everything seems to move in delightfully slow motion. Business folk, travelers, and neo-hippies lounge on the sofas to read loaned books and sip "lateas" ($3.25). Sandwiches like pimento-and-cheese ($3.50) are a respite from Memphis's otherwise meaty options. Live music daily. Open 24hr.

**The North End,** 346 N. Main St. (526-0319 or 527-3663), at Jackson St. downtown, specializes in tamales, wild rice, stuffed potatoes, and creole dishes ($3-8). The orgasmic hot fudge pie is known as "sex on a plate" ($3.65). Happy hour daily 4-7pm. Live music starts at 10pm Tu-Sa; cover $2. Open daily 11am-3am.

**Huey's,** 77 S. Second St. (527-2700) downtown, and at 1927 Madison Ave. in midtown, 2858 Hickory Hill Rd., and 1771 N. Germantown Pkwy. Voted best burgers ($3.40) in Memphis for over 10 years running. Open M-Th 11am-2am, F 11am-3am, Sa 11:30am-3am, Su noon-3am.

**Corky's,** 5259 Poplar Ave. (684-9744), about 25min. from downtown (bus #50 "Poplar"), and 1740 N. Germantown Pkwy. (737-1988). Nationally famous BBQ is justifiably popular with the locals. Top-notch BBQ dinner and ribs served with baked beans, cole slaw, and bread ($6-9). Scrumptious pies and cobbler. Arrive early and expect to wait, or use the drive-thru. Open Su-Th 10:45am-10pm, F-Sa 10:45am-10:30pm.

**P and H Café,** 1532 Madison Ave. (726-0906). The initials aptly stand for Poor and Hungry. The "beer joint of your dreams" serves burgers and grill food ($2-5) to students and locals. But although the patty melt with grilled onions ($3) might take away your moody blues, the friendly waitresses are the real draw. During Death Week in Aug., P and H hosts the infamous "Dead Elvis Ball." Open M-F 11am-3am, Sa 5pm-3am.

**Front St. Delicatessen,** 77 S. Front St. (522-8943), at Union. A deli in the heart of downtown, as seen in *The Firm*. Sandwiches $3-4.25. Open M-F 7am-3pm, Sa 11am-3pm.

## 👁 MEMPHIS MUSIC AND MARVELS

**GRACELAND.** Bow down before **Graceland,** 3763 Elvis Presley Blvd., **Elvis Presley's** home and the paragon of Americana that every Memphis visitor must see. Take I-55 S to exit 5B or bus #13 "Lauderdale." Unfortunately, any desire to learn about the man, share his dream, or feel his music requires the ability to transcend the mansion's crowd-control methods and audio-tape tour, to reach beyond the tacky commercialism and ignore the employees who seem to adhere to the saying "Taking Care of Business in a Flash." Still, you'll never forget the mirrored ceilings, carpeted walls, and yellow-and-orange decor of Elvis's 1974 renovations. By tour's end, even those who aren't die-hard Elvis fans may be genuinely moved. Be sure to gawk audibly at the **Trophy Building,** where hundreds of gold and platinum records line the wall. The King and his court are buried next door in the **Meditation Gardens,** where you can seek enlightenment while reciting a mantra to the tune of "You're So Square." *(332-3322 or 800-238-2000. Expect to wait 1-2hr. on summer weekends. Ticket office open 8am-6pm; early Sept. to late May 9am-5pm; Nov.-Feb. mansion tour closed Tu. Attractions remain open 2hr. after ticket office closes. $10, students and seniors $9, ages 7-12 $5.)*

**NOT GRACELAND.** If you love him tender, love him true—visit several Elvis museums, and several more Elvis souvenir shops. The **Elvis Presley Automobile Museum** houses a score of pink and purple **Elvis-mobiles** in a huge hall, while an indoor drive-in movie theater shows clips from 31 Elvis movies. A free 20min. film, *Walk a Mile in My Shoes,* with performance footage, contrasts the early (slim) years with the later ones. *($5, seniors $4.50, ages 7-12 $2.75. Film screened every 30min.)* **Elvis Airplanes** features the two Elvis planes: the *Lisa Marie* (named for Elvis's daughter) complete with blue suede bed and gold-plated seatbelt, and the tiny *Hound Dog II* Jetstar. *($4.50, seniors $4.05, children $2.75.)* The **Sincerely Elvis** exhibit glimpses into Elvis's private side; see the books he read, the shirts he wore, the TVs he shot, and home movies with his wife Priscilla. *($3.50, seniors $3.15, children $2.25.)* The **Platinum Tour Package** discounts admission to the mansion and all attractions. *($19.50, students and seniors $17.55, ages 7-12 $11.)* All have wheelchair access except the airplanes and two rooms in the mansion tour.

Every year on the week of Aug. 15 (the date of Elvis's death), millions of the King's cortege get all shook up for **Elvis Week,** an extended celebration that includes a pilgrimage to his junior high school and a candlelight vigil. The days surrounding his birthday (Jan. 8) also see some Kingly activities.

**ELVIS WHO? THE BLUES AND MORE...** Long before Sam Phillips and Sun Studio produced Elvis, Jerry Lee Lewis, U2, and Bonnie Raitt, historic Beale St. saw the invention of the blues. The 🎵 **Center for Southern Folklore** documents various aspects of music history, including a tribute to Memphis's WDIA, the first radio station in the nation to only play music performed by black artists. Notables like B.B. King and Rufus Thomas began their musical careers on these airwaves. Southern folk art is also for sale. *(5209 Beale St. 25-3655; music info line 525-3656. Live bands almost every summer night; cover $2-5. Center open M-W 10am-10pm, Th 10am-11pm, F-Sa 10am-1am, Su 11am-10pm. Exhibits free. Wheelchair access.)* The center can give you info on the **Music and Heritage Festival,** which fills Beale St. during Labor Day weekend. Gospel, country, blues, and jazz accompany dance troupes and craft booths. *(525-3655. Open 11am-11pm. Free.)* Of course, Memphis music history includes the soul hits of the Stax label and rockers like Big Star as well as the blues. The **Memphis Music Hall of Fame** features the careers of local legends like Roy Orbison, Elvis, W.C. Handy, and Issac Hayes of *Shaft* fame. *(97 S. 2nd St. 525-4007. Open Su-Th 10am-6pm, F-Sa 10am-9pm. $7.50, ages 7-14 $2.50. Wheelchair access.)* **Sun Studio** shows off the city's rock 'n' roll roots in the tiny recording studio where Elvis was discovered, Jerry Lee Lewis was consumed by great balls of fire, and Carl Perkins warned everyone to stay off of his blue suede shoes. *(706 Union Ave. 521-0664 30min. tours every hr. on the ½hr. Open daily 10am-6pm. $8.50, under 13 free. Wheelchair access.)* Also, swing by **Sun Café,** adjacent to the Sun Studios, for a tall, cool glass of lemonade ($1.75) and a talk with the young staff about what to do. *(710 Union Ave. 521-0664. Open daily 9am-7pm; Sept.-May 10am-6pm; kitchen open 11am-4pm.)* Memphis is also the home of soul music legend **Al Green's Full Gospel Tabernacle,** where Su services display powerful music, dancing, speaking in tongues, and even exorcisms. *(787 Beale St. 396-9192. Services Su 11am-2:30pm; arriving late and leaving early is bad form.)* The **W.C. Handy Home and Museum** exhibits the music and photographs of the man, the myth, the legend who first put a blues melody to paper. *(352 Beale St. 522-1556. Open M-Sa 10am-5pm. $2, ages 6-17 $1.)*

### ...AND STILL MORE: CIVIL RIGHTS AND MISCELLANY. The **National Civil Rights Museum** is housed at the site of Martin Luther King, Jr.'s assassination at the **Lorraine Motel** at Calhoun St. Historical documents, graphic photographs of lynching victims, and films judiciously chronicle key events of the Civil Rights Movement, without losing the emotion. *(450 Mulberry St. 521-9699. Open M and W-Sa 9am-6pm, Su 1-6pm. $6, students with ID and seniors $5, ages 4-17 $4; free M 3-6pm.)*

**Mud Island,** a quick monorail ride over the Mississippi, has a museum, the renowned World War II B-17 *Memphis Belle,* and a 5-block scale model of the Mississippi River that you can splash in or stroll along. **Free tours** of the Riverwalk and Memphis Belle run several times daily. Summer Th from noon to 1pm on the island are free, featuring some live music. *(125 Front St. 576-7241 or 800-507-6507. Open daily 10am-7pm; early Sept. to late May 9am-4pm. Museum $8, seniors and ages 4-11 $6. Grounds $4. Parking $3.)* At the **Mississippi River Museum,** also on the river, spy on a Union gunboat from the Confederate bluff lookout, or relax to the blues in the cafe display. *(576-7241. $4, seniors and ages 4-11 $3. Wheelchair access.)*

On the waterfront, the 32-story, 6-acre **Great American Pyramid,** off Front St., houses a 20,000-seat arena. *(1 Auction Ave. 526-5177. Open M-Sa 10am-4pm, Su noon-5pm; tours usually on the hr. $4, seniors and under 13 $3. Wheelchair access.)*

The four seamlessly connected buildings of the **Brooks Museum of Art,** in the southwest corner of Overton Park, showcase artwork as diverse as its architecture. *(1934 Poplar Ave. 722-3500. Open Tu-F 10am-4pm, W also 5-8pm, Sa 10am-5pm, Su 11:30am-5pm. $5, seniors $4, students $2; W free. Wheelchair access.)*

**A. Schwab,** a small family-run department store (circa 1876), still offers old-fashioned bargains. A "museum" of relics-never-sold gathers dust on the mezzanine floor, including an array of voodoo potions. Elvis bought some of his ensembles here. *(163 Beale St. 523-9782. Open M-Sa 9am-5pm. Free tours upon request.)*

Memphis is home to a few tastefully ornate houses, including the **Hunt-Phelan Home.** This antebellum Southern mansion, once visited by Jefferson Davis and soon after captured by Ulysses S. Grant, is worth visiting despite the Graceland-esque audio tour. *(533 Beale St. 344-3166 or 800-350-9009. Open M-Sa 10am-4pm, Su noon-4pm; early Sept. to late May Th-M 10am-4pm, Su noon-4pm. $10, students and seniors $9, ages 5-12 $6. Wheelchair access.)* **Victorian Village** consists of 18 mansions in various stages of restoration and preservation. **Mallory-Neeley House** was built in the mid-19th century. Most of its original furniture remains intact for visitors to see. *(652 Adams Ave. 523-1484. Open Mar.-Dec. Tu-Sa 10am-4pm, Su 1-4pm. $5, students $3, seniors $4, under 5 free. 40min. tour. Last tour 3:30pm. Limited wheelchair access.)*

The **Pink Palace Museum and Planetarium,** (which is not pink but tan) details the natural history of the mid-South and the development of Memphis. Check out the sparkling crystals, shrunken head (with recipe), sawbones, and leeches; or experience vertigo in the IMAX theater. *(3050 Central Ave. 320-6320. Open in summer M-W 9am-5pm, Th 9am-9pm, F-Sa 9am-10pm, Su noon-5pm; off-season M-W 9am-4pm, Th 9am-8pm, F-Sa 9am-9pm, Su noon-5pm. $6, seniors $5.50, ages 3-12 $4.50; IMAX film $6/$5.50/$4.50; planetarium show $3.50/$3/$3. Call for IMAX times. Wheelchair access.)*

Memphis has almost as many parks as museums, each offering a slightly different natural setting. Brilliant wildflowers and a marvelous heinz of roses (57 varieties) bloom and grow forever at the **Memphis Botanical Garden,** in Audubon Park off Park Ave. *(750 Cherry Rd. 685-1566. Open M-Sa 9am-6pm, Su 11am-6pm; Nov.-Feb. M-Sa 9am-4:30pm, Su 11am-4:30pm. $4, students and seniors $3, ages 6-17 $2.)* Across the street, the **Dixon Galleries and Garden** flaunts its manicured landscape and a collec-

**AQUACCOMMODATIONS** William Faulkner once said of Memphis that "the Delta meets in the lobby of the **Peabody Hotel**," 149 Union Ave., in the heart of downtown. Every day at 11am and 5pm, the hotel rolls out the red carpet, and the ducks that live in their own luxury suits on the top floor ride down the elevator, with the help of a personal attendant, and waddle about the premises to John Phillip Sousa's *Stars and Stripes Forever* or *King Cotton March*. (*529-4000.*)

tion of European art which includes works by Renoir, Degas, and Monet. *(4339 Park Ave. 761-2409. Open Tu-Sa 10am-5pm, Su 1-5pm. $5, students $3, seniors $4, ages 4-11 $1. On M, only the gardens are open; admission is ½-price. Seniors free on Tu.)* **Lichterman Nature Center** is a 65-acre wildscape with forests, wildlife, 3mi. of trails, and a picnic area. *(5992 Quince Rd. 767-7322. Open Tu-Sa 9:30am-5pm, Su 1-5pm; $2; students, ages 3-18, and seniors $1.)* All parks are wheelchair accessible.

## ARE YOU LONESOME TONIGHT?

The visitors center's *Key* magazine, the *Memphis Flyer*, the *Memphis Dateline*, or the "Playbook" section of the F morning *Memphis Commercial Appeal* can tell you what's goin' down in Memphis.

**Beale St.** sways with the most happening, hip nightlife, all within a few blocks. On weekends, a $10 wristband lets you wander in and out of any club on the strip. You can save a few bucks by buying a drink at one of the many outdoor stands as you meander from show to show. The **Center for Southern Folklore** (see p. 347) hosts music and has a bar. The Graceland-sponsored **Elvis Presley's Memphis**, 126 Beale St., serves Elvis grub such as fried peanut butter and banana sandwiches ($5.50) and plain old beer ($3) to an older crowd. (527-6900. Open M-Th and Su 11am-1am, F-Sa 11am-2am. Su gospel brunch.) **B.B. King's Blues Club**, 143 Beale St., where the club's namesake still makes appearances, happily mixes young and old, tourist and native. Wash down entrees ($6-18) with a $3 beer. (524-5464. Cover $5-10; when B.B. himself plays, $35-100. Open daily from 11:30am-'til the show stops.) **Rum Boogie Café**, 182 Beale St., presents a friendly, relaxed atmosphere and honest homegrown blues to a touristy crowd. Check out the celebrity guitars on the wall, including blues great Willie Dixon's. (528-0150. Cover $7. Full menu; domestic beer $3. Open daily 11am-2am. Music begins around 9pm.) For pool, **Peoples**, 323 Beale St. (523-7627), racks 'em up from 1pm until at least 2am (tables $8.54 per hr., F-Sa $9.69). **Silky O'Sullivan's**, 183 Beale St. (522-9596), is a big Irish bar behind the facade of an almost completely razed historic landmark. Outside, guests chill out with goats and munch on burgers ($4-6) to the tune of extremely loud piano music or blues from next door. (Cover F-Sa $5. Opens M at 6pm, Tu-Th at 4pm, F at 2pm, Sa-Su at 1pm…closing time? What closing time?)

The hot gay spot, **J. Wags**, 1268 Madison, served as the bar from *The People vs. Larry Flynt* (725-1909; DJ music F-Sa; open 24hr.). Up, up, and away to the **Daily Planet**, 3439 Park Ave., where live bands play everything from rock to country (327-1270; open M-F 1pm-3am, Sa 5pm-3am). For a collegiate atmosphere, try the **Highland St.** strip near **Memphis State University**, with hopping bars like **Newby's**, 539 S. Highland St., which has backgammon tables and belts out rock and blues. (452-8408. Domestic beer $2.25. Open daily 3pm-3am. Music F-Sa around 10:30pm.)

The majestic **Orpheum Theater**, 203 S. Main St., shows classic movies beginning at 7:30pm on summer Th and F, along with an organ prelude and a cartoon. The grand old theater, with 15 ft. high chandeliers, has occasional live music and Broadway shows. (525-3000. Movies $6, students and seniors $5, ages 4-17 $4. Music and shows $15-45. Box office open M-F 9am-5pm and sometimes before shows.) **Memphis in May** (525-4611) celebrates through the month with concerts, art exhibits, food contests, and sporting events. The **Memphis Redbirds** (721-6000), in Autozone Park downtown, are a brand-new AAA baseball team as of 1998 (tickets $5-8; discounts for seniors, military, and under 15).

THE SOUTH

## SHILOH NATIONAL MILITARY PARK

On the morning of Apr. 6, 1862, Confederate troops, under the command of General Johnson, surprised General Grant's army of Tennessee, which was camped in the woods and fields around Shiloh. The next two days witnessed the largest artillery concentration seen in North America to that date, and nearly 24,000 total causalties. At Shiloh, the idea of glorious and glamorous warfare was shattered, and Americans realized the true horrors of war. The park's visitors center gives a pamphlet to the 9½mi. automobile path. From Memphis, take U.S. 64 E to U.S. 45 S. *(901-689-5275. $2, under 16 free, $4 family. Open during daylight hours.)*

# NORTH CAROLINA

Confederate soldiers called their allies from North Carolina "Tar Heels" because they didn't stick to their ground in the face of Union troops. Carolinians see it differently, they claim that the nickname refers to the tenacity they displayed in both the Revolutionary and Civil Wars—while they faltered in body, they remained steadfast in spirit. Dubious origins aside, the Tar Heel has become a North Carolina rallying point and mascot—the UNC Tarheels command religious reverence.

North Carolina can be split neatly into three regions: down-to-earth mountain culture in the west, mellow sophistication in the Research Triangle of the central piedmont, and placid coastal towns in the east. Largely untouched by development, the Old North State's natural beauty continues to be one of its greatest assets. From Mt. Mitchell to Monteo, North Carolina is dotted with state and national parks, nature preserves, and countless historic sites.

## 🎯 PRACTICAL INFORMATION

**Capital:** Raleigh.

**Visitor Info: Dept. of Commerce,** Travel and Tourism, 301 N. Wilmington St., Raleigh 27601-2825 (919-733-4171 or 800-847-4862; www.visitnc.com). **Dept. of Natural Resources and Community Development,** Division of Parks and Recreation, P.O. Box 27687, Raleigh 27611 (919-733-4181).

**Postal Abbreviation:** NC. **Sales Tax:** 6%. **Time Zone:** Eastern.

## THE RESEARCH TRIANGLE

Large universities and their students dominate "the Triangle," a regional identity born in the 50s with the creation of a spectacularly successful Research Triangle Park, where Nobel Prize-winning scientists toil for dozens of high-tech and biotech firms. **Raleigh,** the state capital and home to North Carolina State University (NC State), is a dilapidated, historic town. **Durham,** formerly a major tobacco producer, now supports multiple hospitals and medical research projects devoted to finding cancer cures. It's also purported to be one of the country's more gay-friendly cities. Duke University, one of the nation's most prestigious schools, has a beautiful campus with sprawling lawns, ancient trees, and almost as ancient buildings. Chartered in 1789 as the nation's first state university, the University of North Carolina (UNC), is found just 20mi. down the road in **Chapel Hill.** College culture predominates here—nearly every other store specializes in UNC t-shirts. A thriving music scene inhabits the Hill, Ben Folds Five and The Squirrel Nut Zippers are just a few of the local bands receiving national attention. Let's be the nerds we are: culturally, this place is a *scalene* triangle where Chapel Hill is the broadest angle, encompassing numerous restaurants, shops and sights; and Raleigh and Durham are each smaller angles, offering more narrow opportunities for travelers.

# ⁊ PRACTICAL INFORMATION

**Airport: Raleigh-Durham International** (840-2123), 15mi. northwest of Raleigh on U.S. 70. A taxi to downtown Raleigh costs about $20.

**Trains: Amtrak,** 320 W. Cabarrus St. (833-7594), Raleigh, 4 blocks west of the Civic Ctr. To Washington, D.C. (6hr., 2 per day, $70) and Richmond (3½hr., 2 per day, $44). Open daily 4:45am-11pm.

**Buses: Greyhound** has a station in each city. In **Raleigh,** 314 W. Jones St. (834-8275). To: Durham (30min., 9 per day, $8); Chapel Hill (80min., 4 per day, $8); and Charleston, SC (7½hr., 1 per day, $48). Open daily 7am-1am. In **Durham,** 820 W. Morgan St. (687-4800), 1 block off Chapel Hill St. downtown, 2½mi. northeast of Duke University. To Chapel Hill (35min., 4 per day, $6) and Washington, D.C. (6hr., 6 per day, $43). Open daily 7am-10pm. In **Chapel Hill,** 311 W. Franklin St. (942-3356), 2 blocks from UNC. To Durham (35min., 3 per day, $6) and Washington, D.C. (9hr., 3 per day, $43). Open M-F 7:45am-10:30am and 1pm-5:30pm, and Sa 7:45am-2pm.

**Public Transit: Capital Area Transit,** Raleigh (828-7228). Buses run M-Sa. Fare 75¢. **Durham Area Transit Authority (DATA),** Durham (683-DATA/3282). Most routes start downtown at Main and Morgan St. on the loop. Operates daily; hrs. vary by route; fewer on Su. Fare 75¢; seniors, under 18, and disabled 35¢; transfers 10¢; children under 43 in. free. **Chapel Hill Transit,** Chapel Hill (968-2769). Buses run 6:30am-6:30pm. Office open M-F 6:30am-10pm. Fare 75¢; campus shuttle free.

**Taxis: Associated Cab Co.,** 832-8807. **Cardinal Cab,** 828-3228.

**Visitor Info: Raleigh Capitol Area Visitors Center,** 301 N. Blount St. (733-3456). Open M-F 8am-5pm, Sa 9am-5pm, Su 1-5pm. **Durham Convention Center and Visitors Bureau,** 101 E. Morgan St. (800-446-8604). Open M-F 8:30am-5pm. **Visitor Info Center and Chapel Hill Chamber of Commerce,** 104 S. Estes Dr. (967-7075). Open M-F 9am-5pm.

**Hotline: Rape Crisis,** 967-7273. 24hr.

**Post Office:** In **Raleigh,** 311 New Bern Ave. (420-5333). Open M-F 8am-5pm, Sa 8am-noon. **ZIP code:** 27611. In **Durham,** 323 E. Chapel Hill St. (683-1976). Open M-F 8:30am-5pm. **ZIP code:** 27701. In **Chapel Hill,** 179 E. Franklin St. (967-6297). Open M-F 8:30am-5:30pm, Sa 8:30am-noon. **ZIP code:** 27514.

**Area code:** 919.

# ▛ ACCOMMODATIONS

**Carolina-Duke Motor Inn,** 2517 Guess Rd. (286-0771 or 800-438-1158), Durham, next to I-85. Clean rooms with wood furnishings and A/C. Access to swimming pool and laundry facilities. Free cable TV, local calls, local maps, and shuttle to Duke Medical Center on the main campus. DATA access across the street. Singles $40; doubles $46; $3 per additional person. 10% discount for *Let's Go* users, seniors, and AAA members. Wheelchair-accessible rooms available.

**Red Roof Inns,** 5623 Chapel Hill Blvd. (489-9421 or 800-843-7663), Chapel Hill, at the junction of U.S. 15-501 and I-40. Bus stop ¼mi. south on Chapel Hill Blvd. Large, clean rooms. Disabled access, free local calls, cable TV, A/C. Singles $46; doubles $56; $5 per additional person.

**Regency Inn,** 300 N. Dawson St. (8285-9081), Raleigh. A 10min. hike from downtown. Call in advance for reservations, 2 non-smoking rooms. Cable TV, A/C, and coffee. Singles $42; doubles $46.

**Umstead State Park** (787-3033), 2mi. northwest of Raleigh, a quick left off U.S. 70. Tent and trailer sites in pristine woodland. Large lake for fishing, boating, and canoeing, trails for hiking and horseback riding (BYO horse). Sites $12; no hookups. Open Th-Su 8am-9pm; in winter 8am-6pm.

## 🗋 FOOD

In Raleigh, **Hillsborough St.**, across from NC State, has a wide array of cheap eateries, both funky and franchise. Chapel Hill's **Franklin St.** has similar variety but is a good deal more inviting. Durham's **9th St.** is the quirkiest, yet scantest, locale. The **WellSpring Grocery**, at the Ridgewood Shopping Center on Wade Ave. in Raleigh, sells organic fruits and vegetables and whole-grain baked goods (828-5805; open daily 9am-9pm). A Durham branch is across from Duke's East Campus at 621 Broad St. (286-2290; open daily 9am-9pm). The Chapel Hill WellSpring, at Franklin and Elliott St., houses **Penguins,** a small cafe serving a variety of gourmet coffees and the best ham and *gruyère* croissant that $2.50 can buy (open daily 8am-9pm).

**Skylight Exchange,** 405½ W. Rosemary St. (933-5550), Chapel Hill. A hip, eclectic den where used books, CDs, and tapes are sold alongside a vast array of sandwiches ($4-6). Thick malt shakes ($3.50) make browsing the crammed shelves doubly enjoyable. Live music M-Sa 9pm. Open Su-Th 11am-11pm, F-Sa 11am-midnight.

**Lane St. Diner,** 200 W. Lane St. (828-9694), Raleigh. "A Raleigh family reunion everyday," touts the owner. The diner, sporting dancing Elvises and a jukebox, dishes up omelettes (around $3), reubens ($3) and combo plates ($4-5) as well as local gossip. Numerous vegetarian options. Cash only. Open M-F 6am-3pm, Sa-Su 7am-3pm.

**El Rodeo,** 1404 E. Franklin St. (929-6566), Chapel Hill, behind the visitors center. Don't be scared off by the exterior; this is the genuine Mexican article. Combo dinners (around $6) include vegetarian options and lots of opportunities for substitutions. Great fajitas ($5.25 at lunch) and huge portions. Open M-Th 11am-2:30pm and 5-10pm, F 11am-2:30pm and 5-10:30pm, Sa noon-10pm, Su noon-9:30pm. Wheelchair access.

**Ramshead Rath-Skeller,** 157A E. Franklin St. (942-5158), Chapel Hill, opposite UNC. A big student hangout, "the Rat" offers pizza, sandwiches, and a mean grilled chicken caesar. Ships' mastheads, German beer steins, and old Italian wine bottles adorn 6 dining rooms with names like Rat Trap Lounge. Meals $4-8. Open M-Th 11am-2:30pm and 5-9:30pm, F-Sa 11am-2:30pm and 5-10:30pm, Su 11am-9pm.

**Pepper's Pizza,** 127 E. Franklin St. (967-7766), Chapel Hill, downtown. A local legend, Pepper's has 35 beers and 26 toppings, including the acclaimed "Ewell Gibbons" vegetarian pizza ("When your mom told you to eat your vegetables, THIS is what she meant"). Whole pies $9-17, delicious gazpacho $2.25. Open M-Th 11am-10pm, F-Sa 11am-midnight, Su 4pm-10pm; summer hrs. vary. Wheelchair access.

## 🗋 SIGHTS

**RALEIGH.** Historical attractions in Raleigh are a break from the academic pursuits of the Research Triangle. The Neoclassical capitol building, in Union Sq. at Edenton and Salisbury St., was built in 1840. *(733-4994. Open M-F 8am-5pm, Sa 9am-5pm, Su 1-5pm. Free.)* Across from the capitol, the North Carolina Museum of History, exhibits memorabilia from the earliest settlement to the present day. *(5 E. Edenton St. 715-0200. Open Tu-Sa 9am-5pm, Su noon-5pm. Free.)* Pick up a brochure at the visitors center for a self-guided tour of the renovated 19th-century homes of Historic Oakwood. Mordecai Historic Park, in Historic Oakwood, re-creates 19th-century life in Raleigh on the grounds of an antebellum plantation. *(1 Mimosa St. 834-4844. Open M and W-Sa 10am-3pm, Su 1-3pm. $4, students $2.)* At Bicentennial Plaza, the Museum of Natural Sciences displays fossils, gems, and animal exhibits, including an extensive wetlands exhibit. *(733-7450. Open M-Sa 9am-5pm, Su 1-5pm. Free.)*

To see local artists in action, ride over to bike-friendly **Carborro** or visit the galleries and craft shops of the **Moore Sq. Art District,** which occupies a 3-block radius around Moore Sq. Near the square is **City Market,** a collection of shops, cafes, and bars. The **North Carolina Museum of Art,** off I-40 at the Wade Ave. exit, has eight galleries of more than 5000 years of art, including works by Raphael, Botticelli, Rubens, Monet, Wyeth, and O'Keeffe. *(2110 Blue Ridge Blvd. 839-6262. Open Tu-Th 9am-5pm, F 9am-9pm, Sa 9am-5pm, Su 11am-6pm. Free. Tours daily 1:30pm.)*

**CHAPEL HILL.** Chapel Hill and neighboring Carborro are virtually inseparable from the **University of North Carolina at Chapel Hill.** Students sustain a dynamic bar, cafe, and music scene on and around **Franklin St.** The university's Smith Center hosts sporting events and concerts. Until 1975, NASA astronauts trained at the UNC **Morehead Planetarium,** which now projects several different shows per year. *(962-1236. Open Su-F 12:30-5pm and 7-9:45pm, Sa 10am-5pm and 7-9:45pm. $3.50; students, seniors, and children $2.50.)*

**DURHAM. Duke University** is Durham's main draw, and the admissions office, doubles as a **visitors center.** *(2138 Campus Dr. 684-3214. Open M-F 8am-5pm, Sa 9am-1pm. Free tours M-F 9am, 1:30, and 3pm, Sa 11:30am.)* **Duke Chapel,** in the center of the university, contains a million pieces of stained glass depicting almost 900 figures in 77 windows. *(684-2921. Open daily Sept.-May 8am-10pm. June-Aug. 8am-8pm. Free.)* The **Sarah P. Duke Gardens,** near West Campus on Anderson St., exhibit over 20 acres of landscaping, tiered flower beds, and a lily pond, bordered by acres of pine forest. *(684-3698. Open daily 8am-dusk.)* The free campus shuttle bus runs to East Campus, where the **Duke Museum of Art** shows a small but impressive collection of Italian and Dutch oils, and classical and African sculpture. *(684-5135. Open Tu-F 10am-5pm, Sa 11am-2pm, Su 2-5pm. Free.)* Duke even sports a 7700-acre **forest.** *(682-9319.)*

The **Duke Homestead and Tobacco Museum,** is on the other side of Durham, up Guess Rd. Washington Duke started his tobacco business on this beautiful estate before endowing a certain university. *(2828 Duke Homestead Rd. 477-5498. Open Apr.-Oct. M-Sa 9am-5pm, Su 1-5pm; Nov.-Mar. Tu-Sa 10am-4pm, Su 1-4pm. Free.)* **Bennett Place** is the site of Confederate General Joseph Johnston's surrender negotiations with Union General William T. Sherman. *(4408 Bennett Memorial Rd. 383-4345. Open Apr.-Oct. M-Sa 9am-5pm, Su 1-5pm; Nov.-Mar. Tu-Sa 10am-4pm, Su 1-4pm. Free.)* The **Museum of Life and Science** is a nationally acclaimed assemblage of hands-on exhibits from the geological to the astronomical, with the occasional animatronic dinosaur. *(433 Murray Ave. 220-5429. Open M-Sa 10am-5pm, Su noon-5pm. $8, seniors $7, under 12 $5.50.)* The 1988 movie *Bull Durham* was filmed in the **Durham Bulls'** ballpark. The AAA farm team for the Tampa Bay Devil Rays still play here, minus Kevin Costner. *(687-6500. General admission $4.25; students, seniors, and under 18 $3.25.)*

## 🎵 ENTERTAINMENT

Nightlife in Raleigh and Durham is notoriously nonexistent. **The Power Company,** 315 W. Main St., on the Downtown Loop, breaks up the nocturnal monotony with a surge of action. The clientele and events vary nightly; Fri. are gay-friendly, Wed. jam. *(683-1151. W-F 18+; Sa women 18+, men 21+. Cover $0-12.)* **Starlite Drive-In,** 2523 E. Club Blvd., Durham, I-85 to exit 179, is good for making out in privacy *(688-1037; shows Su-Th 9pm, F-Sa 9pm and 11:15pm; $4, under 11 $2).*

THE SOUTH

---

**OFF TO A PIG PICKIN'** Southerners are notoriously finicky about their barbecue, but North Carolinians claim that theirs *is* authentic "Southern barbecue." To start, the terminology: to avoid ridicule or, worse yet, giving yourself away as a Northerner, remember that "barbecue is a noun denoting a recognized food, *never* a verb. Say, rather, "We're goin' to cook a pig" or "We're havin' a pig pickin'." And keep in mind that purists insist only pig meat constitutes "barbecue," even if bovine-centric Texans get some slack. Most importantly, of course, the secret's in the sauce. The brown gooey stuff found in supermarkets is decidedly *not* real BBQ sauce, which should be much thinner and have a vinegar, not tomato, base. So sit back and enjoy your barbecue chipped, sliced, or, most festive of all, hot from a "pig pickin'." Southerners traditionally celebrate summertime weddings, reunions, and birthdays by gathering around a freshly cooked pig kept warm on an enormous grill. Parties line up buffet-style and have at it with forks, before heading off to the shade with a cool glass of sweet tea. And the livin' is easy....

Chapel Hill is more happenin'; the huge, fun-loving UNC supports lots of upstart bands. The **Cat's Cradle,** 300 E. Main St., a quasi-legendary club in near-by Carborro, is the place to hear burgeoning local and national talent (967-9053; live music at 10pm; cover $3-16; call for concert schedule). **Local 506,** 506 W. Franklin St., specializes in indie, alternative, garage, and power pop. Three bands play at this club every night from 9pm to 2am. (942-5506. 21+. Cover $3, Sa-Su $5.) Students and families alike get a kick out of **ComedySportz,** 128 Franklin St., across from NCNB Plaza, Chapel Hill. In competitive team improv, "comedy is a sport," complete with referees. (968-3922. Cover $6, with college ID $5, under 12 $4. Shows F 8:30pm; Sa 1:20, 7:30 and 9:45pm.) Pick up a free copy of the *Spectator*, *Carolina Woman*, and *Independent* weekly magazines, available at most restaurants, bookstores, and hotels, for listings of Triangle news and events.

## CHARLOTTE

In 1799, a fortunate fellow in Charlotte was heard howling and screaming after he stubbed his toe on a 17-pound golden nugget. Mines sprung up, prospectors poured in, and gold speculation boomed. The rush lasted about 50 years, until folks in California began finding smaller nuggets in larger quantities. The 19th-century mines are gone, but Charlotte, which began as a village on the Catawba Indian trade route, is now the largest city in the Carolinas and the nation's third largest banking center. Growing and expanding rapidly, Charlotte is home to ritzy clubs and bars, successful sports teams, and countless malls. A metropolitan hot-spot in the Carolina countryside, Charlotte offers bustling charm and yuppie vitality.

**ñ PRACTICAL INFORMATION. Amtrak,** 1914 N. Tryon St. (376-4416) and **Greyhound,** 601 W. Trade St. (372-0456) stop in Charlotte. Both stations are open 24 hr. **Charlotte Transit,** 901 N. Davidson St. (336-3366), operates local buses (fare $1, $1.40 for outlying areas; free transfers). **Info Charlotte,** 330 S. Tryon St. (378-1362), uptown, offers free parking off 2nd St. (open M-F 8:30am-5pm, Sa 10am-4pm, Su 1-4pm). **Rape Crisis line** (375-9900), **Suicide Hotline** (358-2800), **Gay/Lesbian Switchboard** (535-6277). **Post Office:** 201 N. McDowell (333-5135; open M-F 7am-5:30pm). **ZIP code:** 28204. **Area code:** 704.

**ñ⌂ ACCOMMODATIONS AND FOOD.** Charlotte's budget motels are on the I-85 Service Rd., running alongside the highway. A penny can be saved at **Pennywise Inn,** 3200 S. I-85 Service Rd., exit 33 from I-85. (398-3144. A/C, cable, pool, laundry. Singles $40-48; doubles $45-$53.) South of the city lies **Motel 6,** 3430 St. Vardell Ln.; take I-77 S, then exit 7 at Clanton Rd. (527-0144 or 800-466-7356. Cable, HBO, A/C, laundry, pool, and free local calls. Singles $36; doubles $40.)

South from uptown, the **Dilworth** neighborhood, along East and South Blvd. is lined with restaurants serving everything from ethnic cuisine to pizza and pub fare. Continuously upbeat, the area and its residents are well heeled. Talley ho veggie lovers, it's **Talley's Green Grocery and Café,** 1408-C East Blvd., an upscale grocery serving organic health food, sandwiches ($5) and hot soups ($3; 334-9200). Just down the strip, the **Big Sky Bakery,** 1500 East Blvd., offers fresh, no-fuss cookies ($1) and scones ($2) alongside an impressive array of bread and foccaccia ($5-6), for breakfast, lunch or snack (347-0836; open M-F 7am-6:30pm, Sa 7am-6pm, Su 8am-4pm). At the **Roasting Company,** 1521 Montford Dr., bus #18 or 19, juicy rotisserie chicken dinners come with cornbread and two veggies for $5-7 (521-8188; open M-Th 11am-10pm, F and Sa 11am-10:30pm, Su 11:30am-10pm). The **Charlotte Regional Farmers Market,** 1801 Yorkmont Rd., hawks local produce, baked goods, and crafts year-round (357-1269; open Tu-Sa 8am-6pm; May-Aug. also Su 1-6pm).

**◉ SIGHTS.** The **Mint Museum of Art,** a 5min. drive from uptown, is particularly proud of its pottery, porcelain, and American art collections. Take bus #14 or #15. *(2730 Randolph Rd. 337-2000. Open Tu 10am-10pm, W-Sa 10am-5pm, Su noon-5pm. $6, students and seniors $4, under 13 free; free Tu after 5pm. Tours daily 2pm.)* **The Discovery Place,**

draws crowds with its hands-on science museum, OmniMax theater, flight simulator, and planetarium. *(301 N. Tryon St. 372-6261 or 800-935-0553. Open M-Sa 9am-6pm, Su 1-6pm. 1 attraction $6.50, seniors and ages 6-12 $5.50, ages 3-5 $2.75; $3 per additional attraction.)* One block east, the **Museum of the New South** explores post-Reconstruction Charlotte and the Carolina Piedmont area. *(324 N. College St. 333-1887. Open Tu-Sa 11am-5pm. $2, students and seniors $1.)* Paramount's **Carowinds Entertainments Complex,** 10mi. south of Charlotte off exit 90 from I-77, is an amusement park which pays tribute to *Wayne's World* with the "Hurler" roller coaster. *(588-2600 or 800-888-4386. Open Mar.-Oct. generally M-F 10am-8pm, Sa-Su 10am-10pm, but hrs. vary. $33, seniors and seniors and ages 3-6 $21; after 5pm $18. Parking $5.)*

■ **ENTERTAINMENT AND NIGHTLIFE.** Charlotte is a big sports town. Basketball's **Hornets** (men) and **Sting** (women) play in the **Coliseum** (357-4700), and the National Football League's **Panthers** play in Ericsson Stadium (358-7538). The Charlotte **Knights** play AAA minor league baseball Apr.-July at Knights Castle, off I-77 S at exit 88 in S. Carolina (357-8071; tickets $5, seniors and children $3.50).

For nightlife, arts, and entertainment listings, grab a free *Creative Loafing* or *Break* in one of Charlotte's shops or restaurants. Or see the E & T section in the F *Charlotte Observer.* The Elizabeth area along E. 7th St. and E. Independence Ave. parties with clubs like **Jack Straw,** 1936 E. 7th St. (347-8960; cover Th-Sa $5-8), cranking out live rock on the weekends. Groove all night at **The Baha,** 4369 S. Tryon St., a "progressive dance complex" with nights like Disco Hump and College Quake. Women get in free Sa. (525-3343. Open F-Sa until 4am. 21+.)

# CAROLINA MOUNTAINS

The sharp ridges and rolling slopes of the southern Appalachian range create some of the most spectacular scenery in the Southeast. Amid this beauty flourishes a mélange of diverse personalities, from scholars to ski bums to farming communities to artists. Enjoy the area's rugged wilderness while backpacking, canoeing, rafting, mountain biking, cross-country skiing, or just driving the Blue Ridge Pkwy., not to mention the ample opportunities to enjoy life on a front porch rocking chair. The aptly named High Country includes the territory between Boone and Asheville, 100mi. to the southwest, and fills the upper regions of the Blue Ridge Mountains. Southward is the Great Smoky Mountains National Park (see p. 340).

## BOONE

Named for frontiersman Daniel Boone, Boone is nestled among the breathtaking mountains of the High Country. Tourist attractions such as Mast General Store, Tweetsie Railroad, and ubiquitous antique shops lure young and old to eat family-style, flatten coins on railroad tracks, and, of course, shop. The small town lives on year-round, populated by locals and the students of Appalachian State University.

◪ **PRACTICAL INFORMATION.** The **Boone AppalCart,** 274 Winkler's Creek Rd. (264-2278), provides local bus service with 3 main routes: Red links downtown Boone with ASU and motels and restaurants on Blowing Rock Rd.; Green serves Rt. 421; Blue runs within ASU. Red and Green routes run every hr., while Blue runs every 15min. (Red: M-F 7:30am-11pm, Sa 8:30am-5pm. Green: M-F 7am-11pm, Sa 9am-5pm. Blue: M-F 7:30am-7pm. Fare 50¢.) **Ace Cab Co.** (265-3373) charges $1.40 base fare, $1.40 per additional mi., and in an extended area 10¢ more per mi. Runs 24hr. **Rock and Roll Sports,** 208 E. King St. (264-0765), rents bikes for $30. (Helmets included; car racks $5. Trail maps available. Open M-Sa 10am-6pm, Su noon-4pm.) **Boone Area Chamber of Commerce,** 208 Howard St. (264-2225 or 800-852-9506; open M-F 9am-5pm). **Visitor Info: North Carolina High Country Host Visitor Center,** 1700 Blowing Rock Rd. (264-1299 or 800-438-7500; open M-Sa 9am-5pm, Su 10am-4pm.) Hikers should arm themselves with the invaluable, large-scale map *100 Favorite Trails* ($3.50), available at book stores. **Post Office:** 1544 Blowing Rock Rd. (264-3813). Open M-F 9am-5pm, Sa 9am-noon. **ZIP code:** 28607. **Area code:** 704.

**THE SOUTH**

**ACCOMMODATIONS AND FOOD.** Catering primarily to vacationing families, the area fronts more than its share of expensive motels and B&Bs. Scratch the surface, though, and you'll find inexpensive rooms and campsites. Weekends in July and Aug. tend to be more expensive. Most budget hotels are concentrated along **Blowing Rock Rd. (Rt. 321)** or **Rt. 105.** The **Boone Trail Motel,** 275 E. King St./U.S. 421, south of downtown, has brightly painted rooms with quaint country baskets (264-8839; singles $30; doubles $40; Sa-Su $50/$60; in winter, rooms $25).

Boone and the Blue Ridge Pkwy. offer developed and well-equipped campsites, as well as primitive camping options for those looking to rough it. Along the Pkwy., spectacular tent and RV sites without hookups ($12) are available at the **Julian Price Campground,** Mi. 297 (963-5911); sites around Loop A are on a lake. **Linville Falls,** Mi. 317 (828-765-2681), left onto Rt. 221; and **Crabtree Meadows,** Mi. 340 (675-4444; open May-Oct. hike-in sites only), present other options (both $12). For hookups, try Rt. 194 N off 421. **Appalachian RV Park,** 3mi. up the road, has laundry and TV (264-7250; full-hookup $22; tent sites $17.50; cabins for 4 $32).

**Rt. 321** boasts countless fast-food options and family-style eateries. College students and professors alike hang out on **West King St.** (U.S. 441/221). **Our Daily Bread,** 627 West King St., offers sandwiches, salads, and super vegetarian specials for $3-6 (264-0173; open M-F 8am-6:30pm, Sa 9am-5pm). The **Daniel Boone Inn,** at the Rt. 321/421 junction, satiates hearty appetites with all-you-can-eat country-style meals. (264-8657. Open for dinner M-F 11:30am-9pm, Sa-Su 11am-9pm, $12, ages 4-5 $4, ages 6-8 $5, ages 9-11 $6; for breakfast Sa-Su 8-11am, $7. No credit cards.)

**SIGHTS. Horn in the West,** in an open-air amphitheater located near Boone off Rt. 105, dramatizes the part of the American Revolution fought in the southern Appalachians. *(264-2120. Shows mid-June to mid-Aug. Tu-Su 8:30pm. $12, under 13 $6; group rates upon request; AAA discount $1. Reservations recommended.)* Near the theater, **Hickory Ridge Homestead** recreates 18th-century mountain life with restored cabins and demonstrations. *(264-9089. Open while the Horn is in session daily 1-8:30pm; included in Horn admission price, or $2 alone.)* Down the road, the **Daniel Boone Native Gardens** celebrate mountain foliage. *(264-6390. Open May-Oct. daily 10am-6pm, until 8:30pm on show days. $2.)* **An Appalachian Summer** is a July festival of high-caliber music, art, theater, and dance sponsored by ASU. *(800-841-2787. $12-16 for individual shows.)* Held June through Aug., Roan Mountain's **Summer in the Park** festival features cloggers and storytellers at the State Park Amphitheater; call the **Roan Mountain Visitors Center** for info. *(423-772-3314 or 423-772-3303.)*

Downhill skiers enjoy the Southeast's largest concentration of alpine resorts (Nov.-Mar.). **Appalachian Ski Mountain:** off Rt. 221/321. *(800-322-2373. Lift tickets $21, Sa-Su $32.)* **Ski Beech:** off Rt. 184 in Banner Elk. *(1007 Beech Mt. Pkwy. 800-438-2093. Lift tickets $32/$45.)* **Ski Hawknest:** in the town of Seven Devils. *(1800 Skyland Dr. 963-6561. Lift tickets $20/$33.)* **Sugar Mountain:** in Banner Elk off Rt. 184. *(898-4521. Lift tickets $28/$43.)* It's best to call ahead to the resort for specific ski package prices. **Boone AppalCart** (see **Practical Information**) runs a free winter shuttle to Sugar Mountain and Ski Beech. Call 800-962-2322 for **daily ski reports.**

The 5mi. road to **Grandfather Mountain,** off Rt. 221, provides an unparalleled view of the entire High Country area. *(800-468-7325. Mountain open daily 8am-7pm; Dec.-Mar. 8am-5pm, weather permitting.)* At the top, a private **park** features a 1mi. high suspension bridge, a museum and a small zoo. *($10, ages 4-12 $5, under 4 free.)* Hiking or camping on Grandfather Mt. requires a **permit,** available at the **Grandfather Mountain Country Store** on Rt. 221 or at the park entrance. *(Day use $5, camping $10.)* Pick up a trail map at the entrance to learn which trails are available for overnight use. The mountain plays host to brawny men in kilts, second weekend in July, at the **Grandfather Mountain Highland Games.** *(828-733-1333. Shows $8-18.)*

## NEAR BOONE: BLOWING ROCK

7mi. south on Rt. 321, at the entrance to the Blue Ridge Pkwy., is a friendly town filled with craftmakers and folk artists. The **rock that blows** overhangs Johns River Gorge; chuck something over the edge, and it will blow back. (828-295-7111. Open Apr.-Dec. daily dawn-dusk; Jan.-Feb. Sa-Su weather permitting. $4, ages 6-11 $1.)

In Blowing Rock, at the **Parkway Craft Center,** 2mi. south of Blowing Rock Village in the Cone Manor House, members of the **Southern Highland Craft Guild** demonstrate their skills. (Mi. 294 Blue Ridge Pkwy. 295-7938. Open mid-Mar. to Dec. daily 9am-6pm.) The craft center is on the grounds of the 3600 acre **Moses H. Cone Memorial Park.** Check the **National Park Service desk** in the center for a copy of *This Week's Activities* (295-3782; open Apr.-Oct. daily 9am-5pm; free). Guided horseback rides from **Blowing Rock Stables** let you tour the park without hoofing it yourself. Exit the Blue Ridge Pkwy. at the Blowing Rock sign, turn left onto Rt. 221/Yonahlossee Rd. and follow the signs. (295-7847. Open Apr.-Oct. daily 9:30am-4pm. 1hr. $30, 1.5 hr. $40, 2 hr. $50. Under 9 and over 250 lb. not permitted. 1hr. tour. Call at least 1 day in advance to reserve.)

Pricey food and lodging are as abundant as wildflowers in town, but the **Homestead Inn,** 153 Morris St., a half block off Main, lets you—and your wallet—rest easy. A gazebo, swing, and quilts transform this motel into a mountain lodge. Well, almost. (295-9559. Singles and doubles from $47 on weekdays, $65 on weekends.) Blowing Rock is slightly north of Jimmy Buffet's beloved Caribbean, but there are **Cheeseburgers in Paradise** at Rt. 221 and Main St. This bar and grille has outdoor patios, great beef, and friendly waiters. (259-4858. Burgers $5, domestic beer $2.50. Open Su-Th 11am-9:30pm, F-Sa 11am-10:30pm.) **Blowing Rock Chamber of Commerce,** 132 Park Ave., (295-7851) has info (open M-Th 9am-5pm, F-Sa 9am-5:30pm).

# ASHEVILLE

Hazy blue mountains, deep valleys, and spectacular waterfalls all supply a splendid backdrop to this tiny town. Once a coveted layover for the nation's well-to-do, Asheville housed enough Carnegies, Vanderbilts, and Mellons to fill a 20s edition of *Who's Who on the Atlantic Seaboard.* Monuments such as the Biltmore Estate and the Grove Park Inn reflect the rich history of the town's gilded citizenry. The population these days tends more toward dreadlocks, batik, and vegetarianism, providing funky nightlife and festivals all year. In contrast to the laid-back locals, Asheville's sights are fanatically maintained and the downtown meticulously preserved, making for a pleasant respite from the Carolina wilderness.

**THE SOUTH**

## 🚹 PRACTICAL INFORMATION

**Buses: Greyhound,** 2 Tunnel Rd. (253-5353), 2mi. east of downtown, near the Beaucatcher Tunnel. Asheville Transit bus #13 runs to and from downtown every hr.; last bus 6:30pm. To: Charlotte (3½hr., 5 per day, $26); Knoxville (2hr., 7 per day, $24); Atlanta (6½hr., 1 per day, $34); and Raleigh (7½hr., 4 per day, $45). Open M-Sa 8am-10pm.

**Public Transit: Asheville Transit Authority,** 360 W. Haywood St. (253-5691). Bus service within city limits. All routes converge on Pritchard Park downtown. Operates M-F (and some Sa) 6am-7:30pm, at 1hr. intervals. Fare 75¢, transfers 10¢. Discounts for seniors, disabled, and multi-fare tickets. Short trips within the downtown area are free.

**Visitor Info: Chamber of Commerce,** 151 Haywood St. (recorded info 800-257-1300; www.ashevillechamber.org), exit 4C off I-240, on the northwest end of downtown. Open M-F 8:30am-5:30pm, Sa-Su 9am-5pm.

**Hotline: Rape Crisis,** 255-7576.

**Internet Access: Pack Memorial Library,** 67 Haywood St. (255-5203), at Vanderbilt Pl. Open M-Th 10am-9pm, F-Sa 10am-6pm; Sept.-May also Su 2-6pm.

**Post Office:** 33 Coxe Ave. (271-6420), at Patton Ave. Open M-F 7:30am-5:30pm, Sa 9am-1pm. **ZIP code:** 28802. **Area code:** 828.

# ACCOMMODATIONS

Motels cluster in three areas: the least expensive are on **Tunnel Rd.**, east of downtown, slightly more expensive (and fewer) options can be found on **Merrimon Ave.**, just north of downtown, and the ritziest of the budget circle hover around the Biltmore Estate on **Hendersonville Ave.**, south of downtown.

**Peace House** 22 Ravenscroft Dr. (285-0230), between Hilliard and Sawyer, is a funky new hostel in a brick house just south of downtown. With kitchen, deck, grill, laundry, common rooms, internet access ($4 per hr.), and info on Asheville and the Smokies, give Peace a chance. Dorm rooms with 2-3 bunk beds. $18. Linen $1. Lockout 10:30am-4pm. Reservations recommended May-Oct.

**Log Cabin Motor Court,** 330 Weaverville Hwy. (828-645-6546). Though 10min. north of downtown, this motel provides quaint cabins with cable TV, laundry and pool access; some have fireplaces and kitchenettes, but none have A/C. Take Rt. 240 to Rt. 19/23/70 N to the New Bridge exit, turn right, then left at the light; it's 1mi. on the left. Singles from $32; doubles from $46; quads from $73; quints from $76.

**In Town Motor Lodge,** 100 Tunnel Rd. (828-252-1811), has standard rooms with cable, A/C, balconies, and pool, for great prices. Singles $32; doubles $36.

**Powhatan** (667-8429), 12mi. southwest of Asheville off Rt. 191, the closest campsite in the Nantahala National Forest. Wooded sites on a 10-acre trout lake surrounded by hiking trails and a swimming lake. $12, no hookups. Gates close 11pm. Open Apr.-Oct.

**Bear Creek RV Park and Campground,** 81 S. Bear Creek Rd. (800-833-0798), takes the camp out of camping with a pool, laundry facilities, groceries, and a game room. Take I-40 exit 47, and look for the sign. Tent sites $20, with water and electricity $22; RV sites with hookup $26.

# FOOD AND ENTERTAINMENT

You'll find the greasy links of most fast-food chains on **Tunnel Rd.** and **Biltmore Ave.** The **Western North Carolina Farmers Market** (253-1691), at the intersection of I-40 and Rt. 191 near I-26, sells fresh produce and crafts (open daily 8am-6pm). At **Laughing Seed Café,** 40 Wall St., behind Patton Ave, friendly servers vend veggie and vegan values. Su brunch draws a big, bustling crowd—and never disappoints. (252-3445. Salads $4-6, entrees $5-12, and sandwiches $4-8. Open M, W-Th 1:30am-9pm, F-Sa 11:30am-10pm, Su 10am-9pm.) **Basta,** 4 College, at Patton, provides fresh and light Italian food served in a bright, busy restaurant at good prices with many vegetarian options. (254-7072. Salads $2.50-5.50, sandwiches $5-6, pasta $6. Open M-Th 11am-2:30pm, F-Sa 11am-2:30pm, 5:30pm-8pm.)

For a small town, Asheville really grooves. **Biltmore Ave.,** south from Pack Sq., and **Broadway,** north from Pack Sq., are meccas for music, munchies, and movies **Be Here Now,** 5 Biltmore Ave., showcases live blues, funk, and folk (258-2071; cover $5-10). **Tressa's,** 28 Broadway, hosts live jazz and blues most nights in a casual atmosphere (254-7072; cover $2-5). Indie and artsy flicks play at **Fine Arts Theater,** 36 Biltmore Ave. (232-1536; $6, matinees and seniors $4.50). A popular bar, **Barley's Taproom,** 42 Biltmore Ave., hops with locals and $3 beers (255-0504).

To know this deal, 'twere best not know thyself—it's free **Shakespeare in Montford Amphitheater.** (254-4540. June-Aug. F and Su 7:30pm.) During the last weekend in July, put your feet on the street along with thousands of others at North Carolina's largest street fair, **Bele Chere Festival** (259-5800). Free weekly papers, *Mountain Express* and *Community Connections,* feature entertainment listings, while the *Re:Source* enlightens on New Age events.

# SIGHTS

The ostentatious **Biltmore Estate,** 3 blocks north of I-40's exit 50, was built for George Vanderbilt in the 1890s under the supervision of architect Richard Morris Hunt and landscaper Fredrick Law Olmstead. It's the largest private home in

America; a tour can take all day; try to arrive early. Tours of the surrounding gardens and of the Biltmore winery (with generous wine tasting for those 21 and over) are included in the hefty admission price. *(1 North Pack Sq. 274-6333 or 800-543-2961. Open daily 8:30am-5pm. $30, ages 10-15 $22.50; Nov.-Dec. $2-3 more. Winery open M-Sa 11am-7pm, Su noon-7pm.)* Free scenery blooms at the **Botanical Gardens,** off Merrimon Ave. (take bus #2) and the **North Carolina Arboretum,** off I-26 exit 2 on 191 S. *(Gardens: 151 Weaver Blvd. 252-5190. Arboretum: 665-2492. Both open dawn-dusk. Gardens center open Mar.-Nov. daily 9:30-4pm.)*

Four museums will draw you into Pack Sq. at **Pack Pl.** The **Asheville Art Museum** displays 20th-century American paintings. Become one with your body at **Health Adventure,** survey African-American art at the **YMI Culture Center,** and see all that glitters in the **Colburn Gem and Mineral Museum.** *(257-4500. All open Tu-Sa 10am-5pm; June-Oct. also Su 1-5pm. 1 museum $4, students, seniors, and ages 4-15 $3; all 4 museums $6.50/$5.50/$4.50.)*

The interior of the **Thomas Wolfe Memorial,** between Woodfin and Walnut St., is closed due to fire, but tours around the novelist's boyhood home are available. *(253-8304. Open Apr.-Oct. M-Sa 9am-5pm, Su 1-5pm; Nov.-Mar. Tu-Sa 10am-4pm, Su 1-4pm. Tours every hr. on the ½hr., with an audio-visual program on the hr. $1, students 50¢.)*

The scenic setting for the filming of *Last of the Mohicans* rises up almost ½mi. in **Chimney Rock Park,** 25mi. southeast of Asheville on Rt. 74A. After driving to the base of the Chimney, take the 26-story elevator to the top, or walk up for a 75mi. view. *(800-277-9611. Ticket office open daily 8:30am-5:30pm; in winter 8:30am-4:30pm. Park open 1½hr. after office closes. $10, ages 6-15 $5; in winter $7/$4.)*

# NORTH CAROLINA COAST

Lined with "barrier islands" which shield inlanders from Atlantic squalls, the Carolina Coast has a history as stormy as the hurricanes that annually pummel its beaches. England's first attempt to colonize North America ended in 1590 with the peculiar disappearance of the Roanoke Island settlement (see below). Even worse, over 600 ships have foundered on the Outer Banks' southern shores. The same wind that fiercely batters the coast also buttresses much of its recreational activity: hang-gliding, paragliding, the best windsurfing on the East Coast, and, of course, good old kite-flying from the tops of tall dunes. The Wright brothers selected Kitty Hawk for its strong winds and welcoming hospitality.

## OUTER BANKS

The Outer Banks descend from rapidly developing beach towns into heavenly wilderness. Bodie Island, on the Outer Banks' northern end, includes the towns of Nags Head and Kitty Hawk. The Wright Brothers first flew from Kill Devil Hills; familial tourism now soars there. Crowds become less overpowering as you travel south on Rt. 12 and across the beautiful Hatteras Inlet to Ocracoke Island.

### 🛈 ORIENTATION AND PRACTICAL INFORMATION

The Outer Banks are comprised of four narrow islands strung along half the length of the North Carolina coast. In the north, **Bodie Island** is accessible via U.S. 158 from Elizabeth, NC, and Norfolk, VA. **Roanoke Island** lies between Bodie and the mainland on U.S. 64 and includes the town of **Manteo. Hatteras Island,** connected to Bodie by a bridge, stretches like a great sandy elbow. **Ocracoke Island,** the southernmost island, is linked (by a long ferry ride) to Hatteras Island and to towns on the mainland. **Cape Hatteras National Seashore** encompasses Hatteras, Ocracoke, and the southern end of Bodie Island. On Bodie Island, U.S. 158 and Rt. 12 run parallel to each other until the north edge of the preserve. After that, Rt. 12 (also called Beach Rd.) continues south, stringing together Bodie and Hatteras. Addresses on Bodie Island are determined by their distances in mi. from the

Wright Memorial Bridge. There is **no public transit** available on the Outer Banks. Nags Head and Ocracoke lie 76mi. apart. The flat terrain makes hiking and biking pleasant, but ferocious traffic calls for extra caution and extra travel time.

**Ferries: Toll ferries** run to Ocracoke (800-345-1665) from Cedar Island (800-856-0343; 2½hr., 4-9 per day), east of New Bern on U.S. 70, and from Swan Quarter (800-773-1094), on the north side of Pamlico. $1, $10 per car (reserve ahead), $2 per biker. Call ahead, times may change. **Free ferries** cross Hatteras Inlet between Hatteras and Ocracoke (daily 5am-11pm, 40min.). Call 800-293-3779 for all ferry times.

**Taxis: Beach Cab,** 441-2500, for Bodie Island and Manteo.

**Car Rental: U-Save Auto Rental** (800-685-9938), 1mi. north of Wright Memorial Bridge in Point Harbor. $30 per day with 50 free mi. 20¢ each additional mi. Must be 21 with MC, Visa, or $250 cash deposit. Open M-F 8am-5:30pm, Sa 9am-2pm.

**Shuttle Service: The Connection** (473-2777) offers shuttles from Norfolk, VA to anywhere in the Outer Banks; it's not cheap, but you may not have any other choice. From $58; discounts available if you call at least 48hr. in advance.

**Bike Rental: Pony Island Motel** (928-4411), on Ocracoke Island. $2 per hr., $10 per day. Open daily 8am-10pm.

**Visitor Info: Dare County Tourist Bureau,** 704 S. Hwy. 64 (473-2138), in Manteo; info for all the islands. Open M-F 8am-6pm, Sa 9am-4pm, Su 1-4pm. **Kitty Hawk Welcome Center** (261-4644), off U.S. 158 across the Wright Memorial Bridge on Bodie Island. Open daily 8:30am-6:30pm; in winter 9am-5pm. **Cape Hatteras National Seashore Information Centers: Bodie Island** (441-5711), Rt. 12 at Bodie Island Lighthouse; **Ocracoke Island** (928-4531), next to the ferry terminal at the south end of the island. Both open daily June-Aug. 8:30am-6pm; Mar.-May and Sept.-Dec. 9am-5pm. **Hatteras Island** (995-4474 or 995-5209), Rt. 12 at the Cape Hatteras Lighthouse. Open daily 9am-6pm. **Area code:** 252.

## ACCOMMODATIONS AND FOOD

Most motels line **Rt. 12** on crowded Bodie Island. For more privacy, go further South; **Ocracoke** is the most secluded. On all three islands, rooming rates are highest from late May to early Sept. Reservations are needed 7-10 days ahead for weeknights and up to a month in advance for weekends. Long tent spikes (for the loose dirt), tents with fine screens (to keep out biting "no-see-ums"), and strong insect repellent are all recommended. Sleeping on the beach may result in fines.

**KILL DEVIL HILLS. Outer Banks International Hostel (HI-AYH),** 1004 Kitty Hawk Rd., off Rt. 158. is the best deal on the Banks, with 40 beds, 2 kitchens, A/C, heat, volleyball, basketball, shuffleboard. (261-2294. Members $15, nonmembers $18; private rooms for one person $30/35; for 2 people $40/50. Sheet rental $2.50. Camping spots on the grounds $12, $6 per additional person; tent rental $6. Free use of

**COLONY LOST** After the failure of his party's first expedition to the New World, Sir Walter Raleigh decided to sponsor a new colony in "Virginia," the Elizabethan name for what is now the Carolina Coast. The colonists settled on Roanoke Island in 1587. Unfortunately, a series of skirmishes and misunderstandings with local Algonquin tribes made for an uneasy relationship between colonists and the indigenous residents. In need of supplies, Governor White returned to England, leaving behind his wife and child. When he returned to Roanoke 3 years later, he found the island deserted. The only hint of the nascent colony's whereabouts were the letters "CRO" carved into a tree, and a military palisade bearing the word "CROATOAN," probably a reference to the Croatoan Indians, who lived on what is now the southern tip of Hatteras Island. Weather and low provisions prevented White from sailing for the alluded-to island, and the colony was never located.

bikes. Kayak rental $10 1st hr., $7 per additional hr. "Sunset" kayak tour $25.) **Nettlewood Motel,** Mi. 7, Beach Rd., across from the shore has bright cozy rooms with private beach access. (441-5039. TV, A/C, heat, refrigerators, pool. Singles $49, doubles $70; May 28-June 17 $40/$48; Jan. 1-May 27 and Sept. 26- Dec.31. $32/$37.)

Caribbean-influenced seafood and grill items in a casual setting are the truth at **Totuga's Lie,** Mi. 11, Beach Rd. Jamaican jerk chicken with beans and rice $5, to-die-for chocolate pecan pie $3. (441-7299. Open Su-Th 11:30am-midnight, F-Sa 11:30am-1am.) **Chilli Peppers,** Mi. 5½ Bypass 158, boasts amazing entrees like peanut-cilantro-crusted tuna steak. Lunch $3-7; dinner $6-18 but worth it. (441-8081. Open M-Sa 11:30am-11pm, bar and steamed food 'til 2am; Su for brunch 10:30am-4pm. Local bands Tu, open mike Su. Sushi 3 nights per week.)

**MANTEO.** Are you going to romantic **Scarborough Inn,** between the 7-11 and BP gas station? 4-poster canopy beds, flowered linen, and wrap-around porches await. (473-3979. A/C, heat, fridges, microwaves, continental breakfast, and free bicycle use. Singles or doubles $60-70; Oct.-Nov. $45-55; Dec.-Mar. $35-45.)

**The Weeping Radish,** across the street from the Inn, is America's oldest restaurant/brewery, with a uniquely Bavarian/beach twist. Beers are great (0.5L $3.75) and the food is made by German chefs. (473-1157. Microbrewery tours daily 1 and 4pm. Open daily 11:30am-9pm; bar open until 10pm.)

**OCRACOKE.** The impeccably clean ▨ **Ocracoke Island Wayfarer Hostel,** 125 Lighthouse Rd., on Ocracoke Island off Rt. 12., shines on the relatively isolated island. (928-3411. Free bike use, A/C, TV room, kitchen, 2 porches. 14 beds. $19; $39 for private room. Office hours 9-11am and 4-8pm.) Beautiful juniper paneling at the **Sand Dollar Motel,** off Rt. 12, lends rooms a beach-cabin feel. (928-5571. Turn right at the Pirate's Chest gift shop, right again at the Back Porch Restaurant, and left at the Edwards Motel. Refrigerators, A/C, heat, and pool and continental breakfast. 1 queen bed $60, 2 queen beds $70; off-season $45/$55. Open Apr. to late Nov.)

**CAPE HATTERAS NATIONAL SEASHORE.** Three oceanside campgrounds on Cape Hatteras National Seashore are open late May-early Sept.: **Cape Point** (in Buxton) and **Frisco,** near the elbow of Hatteras Island, and **Ocracoke,** in the middle of Ocracoke Island. **Oregon Inlet,** on the southern tip of Bodie Island, opens in mid-Apr. All four have restrooms, water, and grills. Ocracoke is closest to the ocean, with its campsites clustered within spitting distance of the water. Frisco is graced with dunes and hillocks—Cape Point is just dull. Ocracoke sites ($13) can be reserved (from late May to early Sept.) by calling 800-365-2267. All other sites ($12) are rented on a first come, first served basis. Contact **Cape Hatteras National Seashore** (473-2111) for park concerns.

## ◈ SIGHTS AND ACTIVITIES

The **Wright Brothers National Memorial,** Mi. 8, U.S. 158, marks the spot where Orville and Wilbur Wright took to the skies. Models of their planes and detailed oral accounts of the day of the first flight ("just remember: pitch, roll, and yaw") flank the monument. *(441-7430. Open daily 9am-6pm; in winter 9am-5pm. Funny and informative presentations every hr. 10am until 1hr. before closing. $2 per person, $4 per car.)* **Kitty Hawk Aero Tours** offers 30min. airplane tours of the area. *(441-4460. $23-29 per person.)*

Desert aficionados and everyone's inner child will appreciate **Jockey's Ridge State Park,** Mi. 12 on the Hwy. 158 bypass. It's the tallest sand dune in the eastern U.S. and the choicest kite-flying and sunset-watching spot around. *(441-7132. Open daily 8am-9pm; off-season hrs. vary. Free.)* If you still hear a crying child inside of you, shut him up by jumping off the side in a **hang-glider,** under the supervision of **Kitty Hawk Kites,** across the street from Jockey's Ridge. A hang-gliding lesson costs $49-69 for 3-3½hr. of instruction. *(441-4124 or 800-334-4777. Ages 8 and up.)*

On **Roanoke Island,** the **Fort Raleigh National Historic Site,** off U.S. 64, offers several attractions. The **Lost Colony,** the longest-running outdoor drama in the U.S., has

**"DAMNED IF THEY AIN'T FLEW!"** So exclaimed one eyewitness to humankind's first controlled, sustained flight. On Dec. 17, 1903, two bicycle repairmen from Dayton, Ohio, launched the world's first true airplane in 27 mph headwinds from an obscure location on the North Carolina coast called Kill Devil Hills. Orville Wright, with his brother Wilbur watching anxiously from the ground, held on with his right hand and steered the 605 lb. Flyer with his left. 852 feet and 57 seconds later, the Wright brothers had flown their craft into history—and then oblivion: the original Flyer was destroyed on the ground by a strong gust of wind.

been performed here since 1937. *(473-3414 or 800-488-5012. Shows early June to late Aug. M-F and Su 8:30pm. $14, seniors and military $13, under 12 $7.)* In the **Elizabethan Gardens,** antique statues and fountains punctuate a beautiful display of flowers, herbs, and trees. *(473-3234. Open daily 9am-7pm; off-season 9am-dusk. $4, seniors $3, ages 12-17 $1, under 12 free with adult.)* Horseshoe crabs and marine monsters await at the **North Carolina Aquarium,** 1mi. west of U.S. 64 on Airport Rd., 3mi. north of Manteo. Special exhibits change monthly; check out the huge brochure at the visitors center. *(473-3493. Open daily 9am-7pm; off-season 9am-5pm. $3, seniors $2, ages 6-17 $1.).*

Majestic lighthouses dot the Outer Banks; **Cape Hatteras,** run by the Cape Hatteras National seashore, is North America's tallest at 208 ft. Climb the 268 steps for a majestic view of the islands. *(Open daily dawn-dusk.)* Special programs at the **Hatteras Island Visitors Center** in Buxton include **Maritime Woods Walk** *(W 1:30pm)* and **Morning Bird Walk** *(W 7:30am).* The free paper, *In the Park,* lists activities.

# SOUTH CAROLINA

South Carolina's pride in the Palmetto State may seem extreme. Inspired by the state flag, the palmetto tree logo dots hats, bottles and bumper stickers across the landscape. To some, pride lies in the unrivaled beaches of the Grand Strand; others revel in the stately elegance of Charleston and Abbeville. Columbia offers an impressive art and cultural experience without the smog and traffic which plague the New South metropoli of neighboring states. Tamed for tourists and merchandising, the Confederate legacy of the first state to secede from the Union is groomed as a cash cow. Behind South Carolina's Old South grace lies a New South mentality rooted more in diverse harmony than in rebel yells. South Carolina's languid pace preserves a charm uniquely Southern and altogether delightful.

## ⊠ PRACTICAL INFORMATION

**Capital:** Columbia.

**Visitor Info: Dept. of Parks, Recreation, and Tourism,** Edgar A. Brown Bldg., 1205 Pendleton St., #106, Columbia 29021 (803-734-0122; www.travelsc.com). **U.S. Forest Service,** 4931 Broad River Rd., Columbia 29210-4021 (803-561-4000).

**Sales Tax:** 5%, 6%. in Charleston. **Postal Abbreviation:** SC.

# CHARLESTON

Built on rice and cotton, Charleston's antebellum plantation system yielded vast riches now seen in its numerous museums, historic homes, and ornate architecture. An accumulated cultural capital of 300 years flows like the long, distinctive drawl of the natives. Several of the south's most renowned plantations dot the city, while two venerable institutions, the College of Charleston, founded 1770, and the Citadel, founded 1842, add a youthful eccentricity. Challenged by fires, earthquakes, wars and hurricanes, Charleston retains its impeccable manners and politeness; after all, as the visitors center's film says, "You can get away with anything as long as you do it with good manners."

## 🔢 ORIENTATION AND PRACTICAL INFORMATION

**Old Charleston** lies at the southernmost point of the mile-wide peninsula below **Calhoun St.** The major north-south routes through the city are **Meeting, King,** and **East Bay St.** The **Savannah Hwy./U.S. 17** runs north of Calhoun St. Parking is available in 27 lots scattered downtown, for $7 per day.

**Trains: Amtrak,** 4565 Gaynor Ave. (744-8264), 8mi. west of downtown. To Richmond (6hr., 2 per day, $58-115); Savannah (1¾hr., 2 per day, $17-33); and Washington, D.C. (9hr., 2 per day, $74-148). Open daily 6am-10pm.

**Buses: Greyhound,** 3610 Dorchester Rd. (747-5341), in N. Charleston. *Avoid this area at night.* To Savannah (3hr., 2 per day, $22-24) and Charlotte (4hr., 3 per day, $38-40). Charleston Transit "Dorchester/Waylyn" bus goes to town from station area. Return on "Navy Yard: 5 Mile Dorchester Rd." bus. Open daily 6am-9:30pm.

**Public Transit: Charleston Transit,** 3664 Leeds Ave. (747-0922), buses M-Sa 6am-11pm. 75¢. **Downtown Area Shuttle (DASH)** (724-7420) daily 8am-11pm. 75¢, seniors and disabled 25¢; transfers to other buses free. Visitors center has free maps, bus system passes (all day $2, 3-day $5), schedules, and other DASH info.

**Car Rental: Thrifty Car Rental,** 3565 W. Montague Ave. (552-7531). 21+ with major credit card. $40 per day, $190 per week. Under 25 surcharge $12 per day, airport access fee 8%. Open daily 6am-10pm.

**Bike Rental: The Bicycle Shoppe,** 280 Meeting St. (722-8168), between George and Wentworth St. $4 per hr., $15 per day. Open M-Sa 9am-7pm, Su 1-5pm.

**Visitor Info: Charleston Visitors Center,** 375 Meeting St. (853-8000 or 800-868-8118), across from Charleston Museum. Good tour map ($5). Open daily 8:30am-5:30pm.

**Taxis: Yellow Cab,** 577-6565.

**Hotlines: Crisis Line,** 744-4357 or 800-922-2283; general counseling. **People Against Rape,** 722-7273. Both operate 24hr.

**Post Office:** 83 Broad St. (577-0690). Open M-F 8:30am-5:30pm, Sa 9:30am-2pm. **ZIP code:** 29402. **Area code:** 803.

## 🏛 ACCOMMODATIONS

Motel rooms in historic downtown Charleston are expensive. Cheap motels are a few mi. out of the city, around exits 209-11 on I-26 W, or across the Ashley River on U.S. 17 S—not practical for those without cars. **Masters Inn Economy,** 6100 Rivers Ave., at I-26 and Aviation Ave. (exit 211B), has spacious rooms with A/C and cable TV (744-3530, reservations 800-633-3434. Pool, free local calls, and laundry. Singles $35, doubles $43; Sa-Su $43/$49.) **Motel 6,** 2058 Savannah Hwy., 4mi. south of town, is clean and pleasant, but far from downtown and often full. (556-5144, call ahead in summer. Rooms $40, $3 per additional person; lower in winter.)

Several inexpensive campgrounds are pitched near Charleston, including the **Campground at James Island County Park.** Take U.S. 17 S to Rt. 171 and follow the signs. This spectacular park offers full hookups in addition to 16 acres of lakes, bicycle and walking trails, and a small water park. (795-9884 or 800-743-7275. Limited number of primitive tent sites $12; full hookup $24.) **Oak Plantation Campground,** 8mi. south on U.S. 17, has a pool, two bathhouses, and a laundromat across the street. A shuttle to the visitors center costs $5. (766-5936. Tent sites $13; $17 with water and electricity; RV sites $16-22. Office open daily 7:30am-8:30pm.)

## 🍴🎵 FOOD AND NIGHTLIFE

🔲 **Bowen's Island,** Bowens Island Rd (795-2757), left from Hwy. 171, 10min. south of the city; "an island, a restaurant, a state of mind." The owners have retained its rustic, unpretentious character for 50 yrs. Outside, a marsh side dock presents low country beauty and grace to the roar of the crickets. Entrees $5-15, all-you-can-eat winter oyster roast $15. Open M-Sa 5pm-10pm.

**Hyman's Seafood Company,** 215 Meeting St. (723-6000). Kudos to the proprietor, who manages to serve 15-25 different kinds of fresh fish daily ($6-10). Adjoining **Aaron's Deli** constructs massive sandwiches. Both open daily 7am-10pm. Both popular.

**Juanita Greenberg's Burrito Place,** 75 Wentworth St. (577-2877), a beloved favorite, offers "big fat healthy burritos" for under $5. Look for pink door near parking garage. The monster wraps weigh over 1lb. before consumption; vegetarian friendly (bean burritos $4).

**Mickey's,** 137 Market St. (723-7121), the late, late night home of party-goers, college students, insomniac tourists, and occasional low country aristocrats. Packed after bars close on weekends. Schizophrenic Reuben $5; breakfast $3-6. 24hrs.

With nearby colleges and a constant tourist presence, Charleston's healthy nightlife beats strong. Free copies of *Upwith* or *City Paper*, in stores and restaurants, list concerts and other events. It is harder to find *Q Notes*, a free gay and lesbian paper. The tightly packed **Griffin,** 18 Vendue Range, adjacent to Waterfront Park, is a favorite among collegiates. Super-friendly bartenders let you "leave your mark with a dollar" (723-1700). A beautiful beer garden enclosed by brick arches sits behind the slightly older **Blind Tiger,** 38 Broad St. (577-0888). Parliament, Edwin McCain, and Bela Fleck have all taken stage at the **Music Farm,** 32 Ann St. (853-3276).

## ▨ SIGHTS

Charleston's ancient homes, historical monuments, churches, galleries, and gardens can be seen by foot, car, bus, boat, trolley, or horse-drawn carriage; ask about organized tours at the visitors center. The **Gray Line Water Tours** boat trip is not only longer (2hr.) but less expensive than most others. *(722-1112. Tours daily 9:30, 11:30am, 1:30, and 3:30pm. $10, ages 6-11 $5.)*

The nation's bloodiest conflict opened in Charleston on Apr. 12, 1861, as southern forces fired on union-held **Fort Sumter** to touch off the Civil War. After Confederates gained the battery, Yankees bombarded the Fort with over 7 million pounds of artillery before war's end. The **Battery** park in Charleston offers a beautiful view of the harbor and fort. **Fort Sumter Tours** offers boat excursions to the National Historic Site from the City Marina off Lockwood Blvd. *(722-2628; $10, ages 6-11 $5).* The giant aircraft carrier Yorktown sits across the Cooper River at the **Patriots' Point Naval and Maritime Museum,** the world's largest such museum. *(884-27272; open daily 9am-7:30pm; $10, ages 6-11 $5.)*

The **Charleston Museum,** across the street from Visitor's Center, is the nation's oldest museum and offers an excellent introduction to the "Holy City," (so called because of the churches which define its coastal skyline). *(360 Meeting St. 722-2996. Open M-Sa 9am-5pm, Su 1pm-5pm. $7, children $4.)* A combination ticket is available for the museum and two historic homes located nearby: the 18th-century **Heyward-Washington House,** and the **Joseph Manigault House.** *(Heyward-Washington House: 87 Church St. 722-0354. Joseph Manigault House: 350 Meeting St. 723-2926. Both homes open M-Sa 10am-5pm, Su 1-5pm. Museum and 2 homes $18.)* The **Nathaniel Russell House** offers a glimpse into how Charleston's wealthy merchant class lived in the early 19th century. *(51 Meeting St. 724-8481. Open M-Sa 10am-5pm, Su 2-5pm. $6.)*

The open-air **City Market,** downtown at Meeting St., has a deal on everything from porcelain sea lions to handwoven sweetgrass baskets. *(Open daily 9:30am-sunset.)* **Gibbes Museum of Art** houses a traveling exhibit of Picasso ceramics and portraits by James John Audobon in spring 2000. *(135 Meeting St. 722-2706. Open Su 1-5pm, Tu-Sa 10am-5pm. $5, seniors $2, ages 6-18 $1.)*

One of several majestic plantations in the area, the 300-year-old **Magnolia Plantation and Magnolia Gardens,** treat visitors to 50 acres of gorgeous gardens with 900 varieties of camelia and 250 varieties of azalea. Visitors can lose themselves in the hedge maze, or rent bicycles or canoes to explore the neighboring swamp and bird sanctuary. *(On Rt. 61 10mi. out of town off U.S. 17. 571-1266. Open daily 8am-5:30pm. $10, teens $8, ages 6-12 $5. House $6 extra; nature trail $5/4/3 extra; canoes or bikes $3 per 3hr.)* In May 2000, thousands of aquatic creatures will find a new home at the **South Caro-**

lina Aquarium. *(720-1990.)* Over the James Island Bridge and U.S. 171, **Folley Beach,** about 20mi. southeast of Charleston, is popular with local students.

From mid-Mar. to mid-Apr., the **Festival of Houses and Gardens** celebrates Charleston's architecture and traditions. Many private homes open their doors to the public. *(723-1623. 10 houses $30.)* Music, theater, dance, and opera fill the city during **Spoleto Festival U.S.A.** in late May and early June. *(800-255-4659; $10-75.)* **Christmas in Charleston** is all a-jingle with tours and performances. *(800-868-8118.)*

# COLUMBIA

Soon after the Revolutionary War, upstate resentment forced Charleston aristocrats to relocate the capital to the middle of the state, on Colonel Thomas Taylor's plantation along the Congaree River. As planned, Columbia quickly rose to prominence, only to be leveled by Sherman's marching torch. Yet Columbia has moved beyond its Civil War shadow with a thriving art community, historic buildings honoring its diverse heritage, and an upscale entertainment district near the Congaree River. Town and gown prosper together, as the University of South Carolina (USC) adds its substantial cultural resources to the city. It is this seemingly effortless union of past and present that gives Columbia a unique and endearing appeal.

**◪ ORIENTATION AND PRACTICAL INFORMATION.** The city is laid out in a square, with borders Huger (running north-south), Harden (north-south), Blossom (east-west), and Calhoun (east-west). **Assembly St.** is the main drag, running north-south through the heart of the city. **Gervais St.** is its east-west equivalent. The Congaree River marks the city's western edge.

**Airport: Columbia Metropolitan,** 3000 Aviation Way (822-5010). Taxi to downtown costs about $13.

**Trains: Amtrak,** 850 Pulaski St. (252-8246). 1 per day to: Miami (14hr., $59); Washington, D.C. (10hr., $60); and Savannah (2½hr., $22). Open daily 10am-5:45pm and 11pm-6:45am. Northbound train departs 1:05am, southbound 2:50am.

**Buses: Greyhound,** 2015 Gervais St. (256-6465), at Harden about 1mi. east of the capital. To: Charlotte (1½hr., 3 per day, $16), Atlanta (4½hr., 7 per day, $44), and Charleston (2hr., 3 per day, $21). Most east coast buses stop here. 24hr.

**Public Transit: South Carolina Electric and Gas (SCE&G)** (748-3019). Fare 75¢, seniors and disabled 25¢, under 6 free. Most main routes depart from pickup/transfer depots at Sumter St. and Laurel St., and at Assembly St. and Taylor St. Buses run 5:30am-midnight. Call for schedules.

**Taxis: Gamecock Cab,** 796-7700.

**Visitor Info: Columbia Metropolitan Convention and Visitors Bureau,** 1012 Gervais St. (254-0479). Open M-F 9am-5pm, Sa 10am-5pm, Su 1-5pm (winter hrs. vary). **University of South Carolina Visitors Center,** 937 Assembly St. (777-0169, general info 800-922-9755). Free visitor's parking pass. Campus tours M-F 10am, 2pm, Sa 10am, call for reservations. Open M-F 8:30am-5pm, Sa 9:30am-2pm.

**Hotlines: Crisis Intervention,** 790-4357. **Rape Crisis,** 771-7273. Both 24hr.

**Post Office:** 1601 Assembly St. (733-4643). Open M-F 7:30am-6pm. **ZIP code:** 29202. **Area code:** 803.

**▐▊▛ ACCOMMODATIONS AND FOOD.** Generally, the cheapest digs lie furthest from the city center; one exception is the **Masters Economy Inn.** Take Blossom St. across the Congaree River, where it becomes Knox Abbot Dr. The inn offers free local calls, a pool, and cable TV. (796-4300. Singles $32; doubles $40.) Inexpensive motels also line the three interstates (I-26, I-77 and I-20) that circle the city Off I-26 near the airport, **Knights Inn** may not be a castle, but it has a great deal of amenities for a low price. All rooms have refrigerators, microwaves, cable TV, A/C, free local calls, and pool access. (794-0222. Singles and doubles weekday $34, weekend $39; 10% senior discount.) The **Sesquicentennial State Park** offers 1400 acres, a lake for swimming and fishing, a nature center, hiking and biking trails, and 87 wooded sites with electricity and water. Public transportation does not serve the park; take I-20 to the Two Notch Rd./Rt. 1 exit and head northeast for 3mi. (788-2706. Gate open from 7am-9pm; Nov.-Mar. 8am-6pm. $1.50 per person.)

It's little wonder that **Maurice's Piggie Park,** 800 Elmwood Ave. (256-4377) and 1600 Charleston Hwy. (796-0220) owns the world record for "Most BBQ sold in one day." Maurice's cash "pig" is his exquisite, mustard-based sauce that covers the Big Joe pork BBQ sandwich ($4). **Groucho's,** 611 Harden St., has received high marx from the collegiate crowd for 59 years, demonstrating the power of Groucho's own "45" sauce over deli-like $6 "dipper" sandwiches. (799-5708. Open M-Sa 11am-4pm, Su noon-4pm; June-Aug. M-Sa 11am-4pm.) It's happy hour every time a train rumbles by **Gilligans,** 2006 Senate St. at the "5 Points Beach," a self-proclaimed urban "beach shack." Atmosphere spices the cheap sea fare (fried fish, fries and slaw, $4) and binds an intensely loyal clientele. (252-5252. Open W-F 11:30am-2:30pm for lunch, W-Sa 5-10pm dinner.) Palmetto State farmers offer every kind of produce you could imagine within the confines of South Carolina at the **Columbia State Farmers Market,** Bluff Rd., across from the football stadium (737-4664; open M-Sa 6am-9pm, Su 1-6pm). **Rosewood Market,** 2803 Rosewood Dr., specializes in healthy adaptations of sinful foods, including a $5 BBQ seitan sandwich and a bizarrely pleasing $3 currant tofu cheesecake (254-0660; deli open M-Sa 11:30am-2:30pm, 5-8pm).

🎦 🎵 **SIGHTS, ENTERTAINMENT AND NIGHTLIFE.** Ranked as one of the top 10 zoos in the country, over 2000 animals roam in recreated natural habitats at **Riverbanks Zoo and Garden,** on I-26 at Greystone Blvd., northwest of downtown In addition to an undersea fish and reptile kingdom, desert and interactive southern farm, a new bird pavilion awaits visitors in 2000. (779-8717. Open daily in summer M-F 9am-4pm, Sa-Su 9am-5pm; off-season 9am-4pm. $6.25, students $5, seniors $4.75, ages 3-12 $3.75.)

Bronze stars mark the impact of Sherman's cannonballs on the **Statehouse,** between Sumter St., Assembly St., and Gervais St. Lawmakers spent $70 million to restore Columbia's dominant structure to its turn-of-the-century glory. (Tours July-Oct. M-F every hour 9:30am-3:30pm; Nov.-June 12 tours a day. Free.)

Two 19th-century mansions, the **Robert Mills Historic House and Park,** 1616 Blanding St., 3 blocks east of Sumter St., and the **Hampton-Preston Mansion,** across the street, compete in elegance as twin survivors of Sherman's Civil War rampage. Both have been lovingly restored, are chock full of period fineries, and are magnets of architectural interests. (252-1770. Hourly tours Tu-Sa 10:15am-3:15pm, Su 1:15-4:15pm. Tours $4, students $2.50, under 6 free. Buy tickets at Mills House Museum Shop.) Catering to the young and old, The **South Carolina State Museum,** 301 Gervais St. at the Gervais St. bridge, puts a South Carolinian emphasis on natural and cultural history. Includes a hands-on science discovery center, and a replica of the first submarine to sink a ship. (898-4921. Open M-Sa 10am-5pm, Su 1-5pm. $4, students with ID and seniors $3, ages 6-17 $1.50, under 6 free.)

The newly-renovated **Columbia Museum of Art,** at Main and Hampton Sts., boasts a Botticelli, Monet, Remington and features one of the Southeast's most impressive collections of Italian Renaissance and Baroque paintings and sculptures. (799-2810. Open Tu and Th-Sa 10am-5pm, W 10am-9pm, Su 1-5pm. $4, seniors and students $2, under 5 free, 1st Sa of every month free.)

Across Sumter St. from the Statehouse lies the verdant heart of USC, the **Horseshoe.** The **South Carolina Confederate Relic Room and Museum,** 920 Sumter St., houses an impressive and well-maintained collection of Civil War artifacts. (898-8095. Open M-F 8:30am-5pm; 1st and 3rd Sat 10am-5pm. Free.) At the head of the green, **McKissick Museum** explores the folklife of South Carolina and the southeast through music, science, art and history. (777-7251. M-F 9am-4pm, Sa-Su 1pm-5pm. Free.) **Adventure Carolina,** 1107 State St. in Cayce, offers scenic and relaxing canoe trips down the Congaree River (796-4505; Tu, Th, F 5:30pm; $20).

Columbia's nightlife centers around the collegiate **Five Points District** (junction of Harden St. and Devine St.) and the blossoming, slightly more mature Vista area (Gervais St. before the Congaree River). Gamecocks, (SCU students), drink away

**A PIG PRIMER** Southerners have always found unique ways to prepare all parts of the pig. Chitlins, a tasty (yet smelly) fall treat, are pig intestines cleaned, boiled, fried, and then seasoned. Hogmau is boiled and seasoned pig stomach. Throughout the South, pickled pig's feet soak in pool hall countertop jars. And those in a hurry can always grab a pig's ear sandwich.

at the **Knock Knock Club,** 634 Harden St., (799-1015; open M-F 5pm-6am, Sa-Su until 2am) and **Jungle Jim's,** 724 Harden St., (256-7713; open M-F 5pm-6am, Sa-Su until 2am). In the Vista, the neon psychedelic decor of **Art Bar,** 1211 Park St., right off Gervais St., (929-0198, open M-F 8pm-late, Sa-Sun 8pm-2am) harmonizes a diverse crowd. The weekly publication *Free Times* gives details on Columbia's club and nightlife scene. *In Unison* is a weekly paper listing gay-friendly nightspots.

## ABBEVILLE
Local rebels held the first organized meeting of secession in the state on Nov. 22, 1860; 5 yrs. later, retreating Confederate President Jefferson Davis held the last meeting of his war council in Abbeville. Nestled against the Georgia border near **Calhoun Falls State Park,** the "birthplace and deathbed of the Confederacy" carefully preserves its 18th-century town square and the history buffs swarm.

**◪ PRACTICAL INFORMATION.** Abbeville rests halfway between Charlotte and Atlanta; from I-20, take SC 178 to Greenwood, then SC 72 into Abbeville. Most points of interest are within walking distance of the town square. **Visitors Info: Abbeville Chamber of Commerce,** 107 Court Square (459-4600; open M-F 10am-5pm, Sa 10:30am-4pm) **Post Office:** 100 Greenville St. (459-4447; open M-F 8am-4:30pm, Sa 9am-noon). **ZIP code:** 29620. **Area code:** 864.

**▛◻ ACCOMMODATIONS AND FOOD.** The stylized rooms of the **Belmont Inn,** 104 E Pickens St., put a Gilded Age face on information age conveniences. Abbeville's "$30,000 hotel" once catered to the railroad, textile and theater elite. The rocking chairs on the porch overlooking the town square are a southern experience in themselves. (459-9625. $50. A/C, cable TV, free local calls. 10% AAA discount.) 15mi. down SC 72, **Calhoun Falls State Park** offers 100 campsites, many with spectacular views of neighboring Richard B. Russell Lake. Restrooms, showers, and shelters line this well-marked park. (447-8267. All campsites have water and electrical hookups, $17.60 for group up to 6, $1 per each additional. Gates open Apr.-Sept. 6am-9pm; Oct.-Mar. 6am-6pm.) 2mi. from the park gates hides a undiscovered gem of southern hospitality, **The Latimer Inn.** Plantation style landscaping hosts a versatile oasis for fisherman and honeymooners alike. (391-2747. A/C, TV, pool, cable and phone in lobby, washer-dryer, and grill. Singles $39; doubles $49)

The Mennonites behind **◪ Yoder's Dutch Kitchen,** 2mi. down Hwy. 72 towards Greenwood, have long endeared themselves to Abbeville's palate. An $8 southern smorgasbord you will never secede from includes fried chicken, bread pudding, greens and much, much more. (459-5556. Open W-Sa 11am-2:30pm, F-Sa 5pm-8:30pm.) Three generations of locals and tourists have taken it easy at **The Rough House,** directly on the town square. Inviting small town Americana humors the once all-male pool hall where a loaded hot dog and coke in a glass bottle is $2. (Open M, W 10am-4pm, Tu, Th 10am-midnight, F-Sa 10am-until late.) **The Village Grill,** 114 Trinity St., offers solid sandwiches and burgers for under $5 (459-2500; open Tu-Sa 11:30am-2pm, Tu-Th 5:30-9pm, F-Sa 5:30-10pm).

**▣♫ SIGHTS AND ENTERTAINMENT.** "All, indeed, is lost" mourned Jefferson Davis to his Generals before officially disbanding the southern war forces at the **Burt-Stark Mansion,** 306 North Main St. The original furniture and settings remain from the final meeting of the Confederate States of America's Cabinet on May 2, 1865 (459-4297. Open F-Sa 1-5pm or by appointment. $4.) The **Abbeville Opera**

**House,** 100 Court Square, has been restored to its early 1900s Vaudeville grandeur, hosting live theater 36 weekends a year (459-2157; shows F, Sa nights, $13). Two blocks down South Main St., the **Dr. Samuel Poliakoff Collection of Western Art** at the **Abbeville County Library,** 201 South Main St., is one of the largest publicly held collections of Western Native American pottery and art in the Southeast (459-4009; M, W, F 10am-5pm, Tu, Th 10am-7pm, Sa 10am-1pm; free). Nearby on **Secession Hill,** corner of corner of Magazine St. and Secession St., the Lost Cause was born when southern advocates held the first organized meeting for secession in South Carolina, the first state to leave the union.

# MYRTLE BEACH AND THE GRAND STRAND

Stretching 60mi. from Little River near the North Carolina border to the tidelands of historic Georgetown, the **Grand Strand** is a wide ribbon of land bathed in beaches, restaurants, and tourists. In the middle of it all basks **Myrtle Beach.** Challenging Orlando for east coast sunfun supremacy, AAA ranked the Grand Strand the second most popular tourist destination in the country for the summer of 1999. During spring break and in early June, Myrtle Beach (and North Myrtle Beach) are jam-packed with sunburned students who revel in the call of the deep blue. The rest of the year, families, golfers, shoppers, and everyone else hold sway.

The pace slows significantly south of Myrtle Beach. **Murrell's Inlet,** a quaint port stocked with good seafood, and **Pawley's Island** are both dominated by private homes. **Georgetown,** once a critical Southern port city, showcases its history with white-pillared homes on 18th-century-style rice and indigo plantations.

## ▒ ORIENTATION AND PRACTICAL INFORMATION

A series of numerically ordered avenues bridge **Ocean Blvd.** and **Hwy. 17,** also called **Kings Hwy.** Ave. numbers repeat themselves after reaching 1st Ave. in the middle of town, so note whether the ave. is "north" or "south." Also, take care not to confuse north **Myrtle Beach** with the town **North Myrtle Beach,** which has an almost identical street layout. **Rt. 501** runs west towards Conway, **I-95,** and, more importantly, the factory outlet stores. Unless otherwise stated, addresses on the Grand Strand are for Myrtle Beach.

**Buses: Greyhound,** 511 7th Ave. N (448-2471). To Charleston (2½-5hr., 2 per day, $20-21). Open M-F 7am-6:45pm, Sa-Su 10am-6:45pm.

**Public Transit: Coastal Rapid Public Transit (CRPTA)** (248-7277) provides minimal busing. Local fare 75¢; Conway to Myrtle Beach $1.25. Runs daily, approximately 6am-2am.

**Bike Rental: The Bike Shoppe,** 711 Broadway (448-5335). Cruisers $10 per day, $5 per ½-day; mountain bikes $15/$7. Driver's license or credit card required. Open M-F 8am-6pm, Sa 9am-5pm.

**Visitor Info: Myrtle Beach Chamber of Commerce,** 1200 N. Oak St. (626-7444 or 800-356-3015); open M-F 8:30am-5pm, Sa, Su 9am-5pm.

**Hotlines: Grand Strand Rape Hotline,** 448-7273. 24hr.

**Post Office:** 505 N. Kings Hwy. (626-9533). Open M-F 8:30am-5pm, Sa 9am-1pm. **ZIP code:** 29577. **Area code:** 843.

## ▮ ACCOMMODATIONS

Couples and families take over in summer, Myrtle Beach's most expensive season. In fact, many motels and campgrounds accept only families or couples. Cheap motels line Hwy. 17, definitely the best bet in summer. Prices plunge Oct. through Mar.—try bartering for a lower hotel rate. If you'll be in town 3-5 days call the free **Myrtle Beach Hospitality Reservation Service,** 1551 21st Ave. N., #20. For the best deals, ask for the "second row" string of hotels across the street from the ocean

(626-9970 or 800-626-7477; open M-F 8:30am-5pm). The Grand Strand may be the "camping capital of the world," at least if quantity is a deciding factor; Myrtle Beach alone is laden with nine campgrounds and two state parks.

Roving bands of rowdy bar-hoppers make safety on Ocean Blvd. an issue. Local police have stepped up their presence considerably; check to see if your hotel offers a safety deposit box for valuables.

**Sea Banks Motor Inn,** 2200 S. Ocean Blvd. (448-2434 or 800-523-0603), across the street from the ocean. Congenial family-run establishment with laundry, a pool, beach access, large windows, and cable TV. Some rooms have balconies. Singles $45; Mar. and Sept.-Oct. $29 if you say you saw it in *Let's Go*. Damn, it's lucky you bought us!

**Grand Strand Motel,** 1804 S. Ocean Blvd. (843-448-1461 or 800-433-1461). Family-oriented, and also across from the beach. Cable TV, pool, refrigerators, and in-room safety deposit boxes. Small rooms with 1 queen bed for 2 adults range from $75 in early July to $30 in winter.

**Lazy G Motel,** 405 27th Ave. N. (448-6333 or 800-633-2163), fronts 2-room apartments with mini-kitchens, couches, TV, A/C, a pool, and heat. From $66 in late summer, from $29 in winter.

**Camping: Myrtle Beach State Park Campground** (238-5325), 3mi. south of town off U.S. 17. 350 sites on 312 acres of unspoiled land with a cool beach, fishing, a pool, and a nature trail. Water and electricity. Showers and bathrooms are nearby. $22 all sights. Office open daily 8am-5pm.

**Huntington Beach State Park Campground** (237-4440), 5mi. south of Murrell's Inlet on U.S. 17. A diverse environment with lagoons, salt marshes, and a beach. Daily nature walks. 187 sites with full hookup, showers, and rest rooms. Tent sites May-Oct. $10; Apr.-Nov. $12. Water, electric, and sewer sights $21/$26. Office open daily 9am-5pm.

## ALL YOU CAN EAT

Over 1800 restaurants, serving anything you can imagine, can be found on the Grand Strand. Massive, family-style, all-you-can-eat joints await at every traffic light. Seafood is best on **Murrell's Inlet,** while **Ocean Blvd.** and **Hwy. 17** offer endless steakhouses, fast food joints, and buffets.

Juicy burgers ($3-5), fries ($1.45), beer, and free peanuts in a fun, collegiate atmosphere can be found at **River City Café,** 404 21st Ave. N., also on Business Hwy. 17 in Murrell's Inlet. Customers carve on the tables, write on the walls, and check out the license plates. (448-1990. Open daily 11am-10pm.) Fill up at **Mammy's Kitchen,** 11th Ave. N. at King's Hwy. Breakfast deal and a half: hash browns, toast, 2 eggs, and bacon for $3.50. Dinner includes an enormous seafood buffet (chicken, beef, salad included) for $13. (448-7242. Open daily 7am-noon and 4-9pm.) Or, try the kitchen at **The Filling Station,** Hwy. 17 at 17th Ave. N. All-you-can-eat pizza, spaghetti, soup, sandwich bar, and dessert. Fill 'er up at lunch (11am-4pm, $5) or dinner (4pm-closing, $7). Children eat for $2-3, including drink. (626-9435. Open daily 11am-10pm; in winter 11am-8pm.)

THE SOUTH

---

**THE SECRET OF LIFE** Unknown to the rest of the world, mankind's secrets to wisdom and prosperity reside in **Elberton, GA** ("the granite capital of the world"), 17mi down Hwy. 72 from Abbeville. In 1980 a "group of Americans who seek the age of reason" sent a large check to a local mining firm with engraving instructions. On a hilltop 8mi. out of town, several giant slabs of granite answer humanity's most burning questions. In English, Russian, Chinese, Hebrew, Swahili and Greek, the guidestones advise humanity to reproduce wisely, unite under a new living language, keep the population under 500 million, and resolve disputes in a world court. To prevent confusion, "Let these be guidestones" is announced in Babylonian Cuniform, Classical Greek, Sanskrit and Egyptian Hieroglyphics at the top of the tablets.

## ◉ ♪ SIGHTS, ENTERTAINMENT, AND NIGHTLIFE

The cheapest and most amusing entertainment here is people-watching. Families, newlyweds, foreigners, and students flock to this incredibly popular area to lie out, eat out, and live out American beach culture. The boulevard and the length of the beach are both called "the strand." Cruising it at night is illegal—signs declare "You may not cross this point more than twice in 2 hours."

White sand beaches and refreshing water are Myrtle Beach's classic attractions. Two colossal shopping/entertainment areas, full of factory stores and theme restaurants, anchor the off-shore amusement. The more demure **Barefoot Landing**, 4898 Hwy. 17, (800-272-2320), in North Myrtle Beach, is out-hyped by the new **Broadway at the Beach,** Hwy. 17 bypass and 21st Ave. N, in Myrtle Beach, a sprawling complex impressive even by Orlando standards (444-3200). Amidst the theaters, rides, and shops, **Ripley's Aquarium** boasts the world's longest underwater tunnel, and lots of water-dwellers that literally swim around you (916-0888; open daily 9am-11pm; $14, ages 5-11 $9). The largest rollercoasters can be found at the **Myrtle Beach Pavilion,** on Ocean Blvd. and 9th Ave. N. (448-6456. Open daily 1pm-midnight; winter hrs. vary. Unlimited rides $19, children under 42 in. $12. Individual tickets 60¢; rides use 2-4 tickets.)

The **Alabama Theater at Barefoot Landing,** 4750 Hwy. 17 S, shows the most attended musical in the south, a 2hr. celebration of the last 50 years of American music. (272-1111 or 800-342-2262. Shows daily 8pm, also Th 4pm. $25, children $12. Reservations recommended.) A quieter diversion may be found at the 9100-acre **Brookgreen Gardens,** Hwy. 17 opposite Huntington Beach State Park south of Murrell's Inlet. A large collection of American sculpture rests on over 9000 oak-shaded, relaxing acres. Works by Frederic Remington, Daniel Chester French, and others mix with the verdant, colorful gardens, and nature preserves. (Open Su-W 9:30am-5pm, Th-Sa 9:30am-9:30pm. $8; ages 6-12 $4.)

# GEORGIA

Georgia presents two faces: the rural southern section contrasts starkly with sprawling Atlanta to the north. President Jimmy Carter's hometown and President Franklin D. Roosevelt's summer home both stand on red Georgia clay. Coca-Cola was invented here in 1886; since then, it has gone on to carbonate and caffeinate the world. Collegiate Athens breeds "big" bands, Savannah preserves an antebellum atmosphere, and the Gold Coast mellows in slow-paced sea-side existence. Ted Turner's CNN has networked the globe, making Georgia's capital a modern, sophisticated metropolis. Georgia blooms in the spring, glistens in the summer, and mellows in the autumn, all the while welcoming y'all with peachy Southern hospitality. Stay here long, and you'll *never* shake Georgia from your mind.

## 🛈 PRACTICAL INFORMATION

**Capital:** Atlanta.

**Visitor Info: Dept. of Industry and Trade, Tourist Division,** 285 Peachtree Center Ave., Atlanta 30303 (656-3590 or 800-847-4842; www.georgia.org), in the Marriot Marquis 2 Tower, 10th fl. Open M-F 8am-5pm. **Dept. of Natural Resources,** 205 Butler St. SE, #1352, Atlanta 30334 (404-656-3530 in GA, 800-864-7275). **U.S. Forest Service,** 1720 Peachtree Rd. NW, Atlanta 30367 (347-2384). Open M-F 10am-2pm.

**Postal Abbreviation:** GA.

**Sales Tax:** 4-7%, depending on county.

# ATLANTA

An increasingly popular destination for 20- and 30-somethings craving big city life but weary of more manic metropolises, Atlanta strives to be cosmopolitan with a smile, although its charm can be easily lost in the obscene regularity of the town's cookie-cutter suburbs. Northerners, Californians, the third-largest gay population in the U.S., and a host of ethnicities have diversified this capital of the South. A nationwide economic powerhouse, Atlanta contains offices for 400 of the Fortune 500 companies, including the headquarters of Coca-Cola and CNN. Nineteen colleges; including Georgia Tech, Morehouse College, Spelman College, and Emory University; call "Hotlanta" home. Home to the humid 1996 Summer Olympic Games, the city has capitalized on its $2 billion worth of Olympic-related goodies and converted most venues and sites into permanent facilities. Atlanta is just as blessed with subtle gems; getting lost on Atlanta's streets reveals a seemingly endless number of shops, funky restaurants, and beautiful old homes.

## ✦ ORIENTATION

Atlanta sprawls across 10 counties in the northwest quadrant of the state at the junctures of I-75, I-85, and I-20. **I-285** ("the perimeter") circumscribes the city.

Getting around is confusing—Atlanta is more a conglomeration of several suburbs than a single metropolis. The main thoroughfares are set out like the spokes of a wheel; navigation between spokes is tricky. **Peachtree St.,** (one of over 50 roads bearing the name), is a major north-south thoroughfare; other significant north-south roads are **Spring St.** and **Piedmont Ave.** On the eastern edge of the city, **Moreland Ave.** runs the length of the city, through the Virginia Highlands, Little Five Points (L5P), and E. Atlanta. Major east-west roads include **Ponce De Leon Ave.** and **North Ave.** In the heart of downtown—west of I-75/85, south of International Blvd. and north of the capitol, around the district known as Five Points—angled streets and shopping plazas run amok, making navigation difficult.

Downtown Atlanta is anchored by the **Peachtree Center** and **Five Points MARTA** stations, from which most tourists flock to the center and **Underground Atlanta,** respectively; these giant shopping and entertainment complexes, however, aren't worth the attention. Northeast of downtown, the **Midtown** area (from Ponce de Leon Ave. to 17th St.) holds Atlanta's art museums. Directly southwest of downtown is the **West End**—an African-American area and the city's oldest historic quarter. Three subway stops east of Five Points, at the junction of Euclid and Moreland Ave., lies the **Little Five Points (L5P)** district, the local haven for eclecticism, artists, and youth subculture. **Virginia Highlands,** a trendy neighborhood east of Midtown and Piedmont Park, attracts yuppies and college kids. And then there was **Buckhead,** a posher-than-thou area north on Peachtree and accessible on MARTA ("Buckhead").

## ⃞ PRACTICAL INFORMATION

**Airport: Hartsfield International** (general info 222-6688, international services and flight info 530-2081), south of the city. MARTA is the easiest way to get downtown, with 15min. rides departing every 8min. daily 5am-1am ($1.25). **Atlanta Airport Shuttle** (524-3400) runs vans from the airport to over 100 locations in the metrop and outlying area (every 15min. daily 7am-11pm; shuttle downtown $10). Taxi to downtown $15.

**Train: Amtrak,** 1688 Peachtree St. NW (881-3061), 3mi. north of downtown at I-85. Take bus #23 from "Arts Center" MARTA station. To New York (18½hr., 1 per day, $93-169) and New Orleans (11½hr., 1 per day, $39-78). Open daily 7am-9:30pm.

**Buses: Greyhound,** 232 Forsyth St. (584-1728), across from "Garnett" MARTA station. To: New York (18-23hr., 16 per day, $84); Washington, D.C. (15hr., 16 per day, $67); and Savannah (5hr., 5 per day, $43). Open 24hr.

**Public Transit: Metropolitan Atlanta Rapid Transit Authority (MARTA)** (848-4711; schedule info M-F 6am-midnight, Sa-Su 8am-10pm). Good combined rail and bus system. Rail operates M-F 5am-1am, Sa-Su and holidays 6am-12:30am in most areas. Bus hrs. vary. Fare $1.50, exact change needed, or buy a token at station machines; transfers free. Unlimited weekly pass $12. Pick up a system map at the **MARTA Ride Store,** Five Points Station downtown, or at the airport or Lenox stations. MARTA courtesy phones in each rail station aid the confused. All trains, rail stations, and buses are lift-equipped.

**Taxis: Atlanta Yellow Cab,** 521-0200. **Rapid,** 222-9888.

**Car Rental: Atlanta Rent-a-Car,** 3185 Camp Creek Pkwy. (763-1160), just inside I-285 3mi. east of the airport. 20 other locations in the area including 2800 Campelton Rd. and 3129 Piedmont Rd. $20 per day, 100 free mi. per day, 24¢ per additional mi. Must be 21 with major credit card.

**Visitor Info: Atlanta Convention and Visitors Bureau,** 233 Peachtree St. NE, (521-6600 or 800-285-2682; www.atlanta.com), Peachtree Center, Suite 100, downtown. Open M-F 8:30am-5pm. Automated **information service** (222-6688).

**Bi-Gay-Lesbian Organizations: The Gay Center,** 67 and 71 12th St. NE, (876-5372), provides info, weekly events, and short-term counseling daily 6am-11pm.

**Hotline: Rape Crisis Counseling,** 616-4861. 24hr.

**Post Office:** 3900 Crown Rd. Open 24hr. **ZIP code:** 30321. **Area code:** 404 roughly inside the I-285 perimeter, 770 outside. Listings 404 unless noted. 10-digit dialing required.

# ■ ACCOMMODATIONS

**Atlanta Hostel,** 223 Ponce de Leon Ave. (875-2882), in Midtown. From MARTA: North Ave. station, exit onto Ponce de Leon, about 3½ blocks east on the corner of Myrtle St., or take bus #2 and ask the driver to stop. Attached to the Woodruff B&B, livened up by pooch "Fatty" and a collection of champion homing pigeons. Clean, dorm-style rooms come with **Internet access,** coffee, and donuts. No sleeping bags allowed, but they distribute free blankets. Laundry facilities, pool table, arcade games, and renovated kitchen. $15; private doubles $32.50. Luggage storage $1. Linen $1. Free lockers.

**Masters Inn Economy,** 3092 Presidential Pkwy. (770-454-8373 or 800-633-3434), Chamblee Tucker Rd. Exit off I-85 in Doraville. Renovated, large rooms with king-size beds, local calls, cable TV, and pool. Singles $36, F-Sa $37; doubles $40/$45.

**Motel 6,** 2820 Chamblee Tucker Rd. (770-458-6626), in Chamblee, exit 27 off I-285. Spacious and immaculate rooms. Offers free movie channel, local calls, morning coffee, A/C, and pool. Under 18 stay free with their parents. Singles $39; doubles $45.

**Atlanta Midtown Manor,** 811 Piedmont Ave. NE (872-5846). 3 Victorian houses in a fairly safe spot, convenient to downtown. Nice rooms with floral shams, wooden 4-post beds, A/C, TV, and replica antique furnishings. Free coffee, donuts, street parking, and local calls. Shared bath, privacy is extra. Laundry. Singles and doubles $45-85. Fills up in summer.

**Stone Mountain Family Campground** (770-498-5710), on U.S. 78, 16mi. east of town. exit 30B off I-285, or subway to Avondale, then "Stone Mountain" bus. Gorgeous sites; one-third are on the lake. Bike rentals, free laser show, nature trails, and Internet access. Tent sites $17; RV sites $19, full hookup $21. Entrance fee $6 per car.

# ■ FOOD

From Vietnamese to Italian, baked to fried to fricaseed, Atlanta dining provides ample options, no matter what you're craving. But "soul food," designed to nurture the spiritual rather than the physical, is the heart of this town's palate. Some favorite dishes include fried chicken, ribs, okra, sweet-potato pie, and peach cobbler. Dip cornbread into "pot likker," water used to cook greens. For a sweet treat (50¢), you can't beat the **Krispy Kreme Doughnuts,** whose glazed delights are a Southern institution. The factory store, at 295 Ponce de Leon Ave. NE (876-7307), is open 24hr. and continuously bakes their wares, visible through the back window.

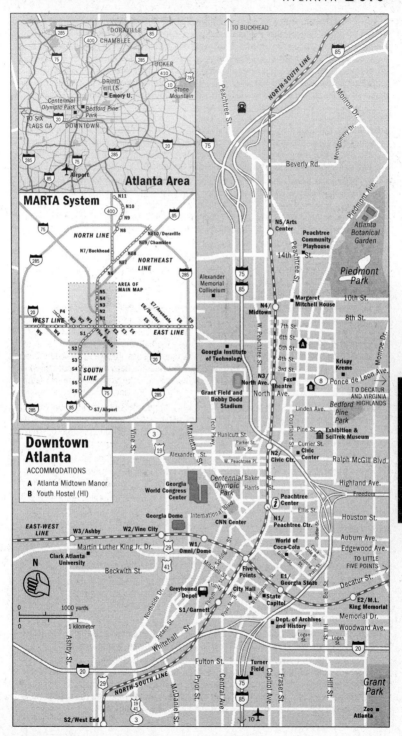

THE SOUTH

More healthy alternatives are available at the **Sweet Auburn Curb Market** in the Sweet Auburn District, 209 Edgewood Ave., a depot for soul food's raw materials. An increasingly international set of vendors hawk fresh veggies, meats, and sweets. (659-1665. Open M-Th 8am-6pm, F-Su 8am-7pm.) A great deal of Atlanta's ethnic population has taken up residence on **Buford Hwy.** You won't go wrong with **Little Szechuan,** 5091-C Buford Hwy. (451-0192), which serves lunch specials ($5) in heaping doses (open M 11:30am-9:30pm, W-Sa 11:30am-9:30pm, Su noon-9:30pm).

## MIDTOWN

**The Varsity,** 61 North Ave. NW at Spring St. (881-1706), at I-85. MARTA: North Ave. The world's largest drive-in and originator of the assembly-line school of food preparation. Best known for the greatest, greasiest onion rings in the South and the 2mi. of hotdogs sold daily. Most menu items around $2. Open Su-Th 9am-11:30pm, F-Sa 9am-1:30am.

**Mary Mac's Tea Room,** 224 Ponce De Leon Ave. (876-1800), at Myrtle NE; take the "Georgia Tech" bus north. A "revival of Southern hospitality" with a 40s atmosphere and amazing cinnamon rolls ($3.75 per dozen after 5pm). Dinner (good enough for the Dalai Lama, along with a whole wall full of other celebs) with daily rotating entrees and sides is $6-9, or free to the expanding ranks of 100+ seniors. Open M-F 11am-8:30pm, Su 11am-3pm.

**Tortillas,** 774 Ponce de Leon Ave. (892-0193). The student crowd munches dirt-cheap and yummy Mexican food. Try the upstairs patio for open-air eating. A large variety of burritos (from $3) and soft chicken tacos $1.75. Veggie friendly. Open daily 11am-10pm.

**Eats,** 600 Ponce de Leon Ave. (888-9149), offers cheap ones with large $3 pasta bowls. Open daily 11am-10pm.

## VIRGINIA HIGHLANDS

**Everybody's,** 1040 N. Highland Ave. (873-4545), claims to sell Atlanta's best pizza. Their inventive pizza salad, a colossal mound of greens and chicken on a pizza bed ($9) is more than enough for two. Open M-Th 11:30am-11pm, F-Sa 11:30am-1am, Su noon-11pm.

**Manuel's Tavern,** 602 N. Highland Ave. (525-3447), prime spot between L5P and Virginia Highlands. Long stomping ground for Atlanta's Democratic politicos; Jimmy Carter is known to swing by for a burger ($5) and a beer. Open M-Sa 11am-2am, Su 3pm-midnight.

**Majestic Food Shop,** 1031 Ponce de Leon Ave. (875-0276), at Cleburne. For the ravenous insomniac people watcher, there is no place better. The late, late night scene for Highlands and L5P, doormen prevent weekend nocturnal crowding. The Majestic offers "food that pleases" in the shape of burgers ($1.65), grits (95¢), and the like. Open 24hr.

## SURROUNDING AREA

**Thelma's,** 302 Auburn Ave. (523-0081), on "Soul Food Row" in Sweet Auburn. Fried chicken and two veggies ($6) make for a difficult decision. The sweet potato is more dessert than lunch, but well worth the sugar intake. Open M-Th 11am-4pm, F-Sa 11am-8pm.

**Crescent Moon,** 254 W. Ponce de Leon Ave. (377-5623), in Decatur. A heavenly breakfast spot. Indulge in phenomenal French toast ($1.75 per slice), or the Heap, an endless mound of potatoes, bacon, and cheese ($6). Whopping portions. Open M-F 7:30am-3pm, Sa-Su brunch 8am-2:30pm.

**Bridgetown Grill,** 1156 Euclid Ave. (653-0110), in L5P. Reggae and salsa make for a hopping hole in the wall. Have a 20 oz. margarita ($6) with their famous jerk chicken ($7) and hearty yucca fries. Open M-Th 11am-11pm, F-Sa 11am-midnight.

**The Flying Biscuit,** 1655 McLendon Ave. (687-8888). Do yourself a favor and order something that comes with a biscuit, whether it's a peaches and cream muffin ($1.25) or an enormous sweet roll ($1.25). Cafe, take-out, and cookbook available. Restaurant open Tu-Su 9am-10pm; bakery open Tu-F 7:30am-9pm, Sa-Su 8am-9pm.

**WAFFLE GOOD** Labor Day 1955 was a glorious moment in the otherwise quiet existence of Avondale Estates, Georgia. Two neighbors "dedicated to people," be they customers or employees, realized their dreams in the form of a little yellow hut that opened in the Atlanta suburb on this day; the **Waffle House** hasn't closed since. Visit the original at 2850 E. College (404-294-8758), Avondale.

## SIGHTS

**SWEET AUBURN DISTRICT.** Atlanta's sights are scattered, but the effort it takes to find them pays off. The most powerful are the MLK sites along Auburn Ave. in Sweet Auburn. Reverend Martin Luther King, Jr.'s birthplace, church, and grave are all part of the 23-acre ■ **Martin Luther King, Jr. National Historic Site.** The **visitors center** houses poignant displays of photographs, videos, and quotations, oriented around King's life and the civil rights struggle. *(450 Auburn Ave. Marta: King Memorial. Open daily 9am-5pm.)* The **birthplace of MLK** offers frequent tours. *(501 Auburn Ave. 331-5190. Open daily Apr.-Oct. 9am-6pm; Nov.-Mar. 9am-5pm.)* **Ebenezer Baptist Church** is the church where King was pastor from 1960 to 1968. *(407 Auburn Ave. 688-7263.)* King's **grave** rests at the **Martin Luther King, Jr. Center for Nonviolent Social Exchange.** The center also holds a collection of King's personal effects and shows a film about his life. *(449 Auburn Ave. NE. 524-1956. Open daily Apr.-Oct. 10am-6pm; Nov.-Mar. 9am-5pm. Free.)* Plaques lining Sweet Auburn point out the architecture and eminent past residents of this historically African-American neighborhood.

The **African-American Panoramic Experience (APEX)** recognizes the cultural heritage of African Americans who helped build this country and includes a replica of Georgia's first African American-owned drugstore. *(135 Auburn Ave. 521-2739. Open Tu-Sa 10am-5pm; summer and Feb. Su 1-5pm; $2, students and seniors $1.)*

**DOWNTOWN AND AROUND.** From Mar. through Nov., the **Atlanta Preservation Center** offers 10 famous walking tours of popular areas: Fox Theater District, West End and the Wren's Nest, Historic Downtown, Miss Daisy's Druid Hills, Inman Park, Underground and Capitol area, Ansley Park, Sweet Auburn (MLK District), and Piedmont Park; the 1½hr. Fox Theater tour is given year-round. *(156 7th St. NE. 876-2040. $5, students $3, seniors $4.)* The recently restored **Georgia State Capitol,** on Capitol Hill at Washington St., provides an excellent introduction to the history of the Peach State. *(Open M-F 8am-5:30pm. Tours M-F 10 and 11am, 1 and 2pm. Free.)*

In **Grant Park,** directly south of Oakland Cemetery and Cherokee Ave., is the 114-year-old **Cyclorama,** the world's largest painting, which re-creates the 1864 Battle of Atlanta. *(624-1071. Open daily Apr.-Sept. 9:30am-5:30pm; Oct.-May 9:30am-4:30pm. $5, students and seniors $4, ages 6-12 $3.)* Next door, **Zoo Atlanta** boasts komodo dragons, an artist-elephant, Willie B. (who at 40 is one of the two oldest captive gorillas), Chantek (an orangutan fluent in sign language), a petting zoo, and countless other displays. *(800 Cherokee Ave. SE. 624-5678 or 624-5600. Open Apr.-Oct. M-F 9:30am-4:30pm, Sa-Su 9:30am-5:30pm; Nov.-Mar. daily 9:30am-4:30pm. $10, seniors $8, ages 3-11 $6.)*

Two blocks from the capitol, the **World of Coca-Cola** details "the real thing's" rise from humble beginnings in Atlanta to a position of world domination, from the hokey print ads of the 20s, to a video including the "I'd Like to Buy the World a Coke" song, to the sampling room, where the world's strangest soft drinks come direct to you, in a rainbow of flavors. *(55 Martin Luther King, Jr. Dr. 676-5151. Open M-Sa 10am-9:30pm, Su noon-6pm. Summer hrs. may vary. $6, seniors $4, ages 6-12 $3.)* Adjacent to Coke, redeveloped **Underground Atlanta** gets down with 6 subterranean blocks of over 120 chain restaurants, shops, and night spots. Descend at the entrance beside the Five Points subway station. *(523-2311. Shops open M-Sa 10am-9:30pm, Su noon-6pm. Bars and restaurants open later.)*

High-tech Atlanta reigns with multinational business powerhouses situated in the business section of the **Five Points District. Turner Broadcasting System** offers an overpriced, insider's peek with its **Cable News Network (CNN) Studio Tour,** at Tech-wood Dr. and Marietta St. Witness anchors broadcasting live while writers toil in the background. *(827-2300. 40min. tours given every 15min. Open daily 9am-6pm. $7, seniors $5, ages 5-12 $4.50. Reservations optional.)* Join the punditocracy in the studio audience of *CNN Talk Back Live*; you'll be told not to pick your nose on camera. Take MARTA west to the Omni/Dome/GWCC Station at W1. *(W at 3pm. Free.)*

Despite the tragic bombing that occurred there during the Olympics, **Centennial Olympic Park,** adjacent to the Georgia World Congress Center, delights children of all ages with the **Fountain of Rings** (splashing and jumping encouraged).

Farther out, the **Carter Presidential Center,** 1 Copenhill, north of Little Five Points, documents Georgia peanut farmer Jimmy Carter's political career and Administration (1977-1981) through exhibits and films. Take bus #16 to Cleburne Ave. *(420-5117. Museum open M-Sa 9am-4:45pm, Su noon-4:45pm. $5, under 17 free.)*

**WEST END.** In the West End—Atlanta's oldest neighborhood, dating from 1835—you can discover the **Wren's Nest,** home to Joel Chandler Harris, who popularized the African folktale trickster Br'er Rabbit through his books. Energetic storytellers entertain young and old alike. Take bus #71 from West End Station (S2). *(1050 R.D. Abernathy Blvd. 753-7735. Open Tu-Sa 10am-4pm, Su 1-4pm. $6, seniors and teens $4, ages 4-12 $3.)* The **Hammonds House** displays a fantastic collection of African-American and Haitian art. Take bus #71 from West End Station to Peeples St. and walk 2 blocks north. *(503 Peeples St. SW. 752-8730. Open Tu-F 10am-6pm, Sa-Su 1-5pm. $2, students and seniors $1.)* Hammonds House will help headquarter the **National Black Arts Festival,** July 26-Aug. 6, 2000 *(523-3435).* Built by slave-born Alonzo F. Herndon, a 1910 Beaux-Arts Classical mansion, the **Herndon Home,** deserves a look. Take bus #3 from Five Points station to the corner of Martin Luther King, Jr. Dr. and Maple, and walk 1 block north. Herndon, a prominent barber, became Atlanta's wealthiest African American in the early 1900s. The house's original furnishings are on display. *(587 University Pl. NW. 581-9813. Open Tu-Sa 10am-4pm. Free. Tours on the hr.)*

**MIDTOWN.** **Piedmont Park** sprawls around the 60-acre **Atlanta Botanical Garden** on Piedmont Ave., in the northwest corner of the park. Stroll through 5 acres of landscaped gardens, a 15-acre hardwood forest with trails, and an exhibition hall. *(MARTA: Lindburgh Center, Bus #31. 876-5859. Open Tu-Su 9am-7pm; in winter Tu-Su 9am-6pm. $6, students and ages 6-12 $3, seniors $5.)* The Garden's **Dorothy Chapman Fuqua Conservatory** houses hundreds of species of exotic tropical plants. *(Opens at 10am.)*

Near the park, **Scitrek (Science and Technology Museum of Atlanta),** with over 150 interactive exhibits for all ages, is one of the nation's top science centers. *(395 Piedmont Ave. NE. 522-5500. Open M-Sa 10am-5pm, Su noon-5pm. $7.50; students, seniors, and ages 3-17 $5.)* Take MARTA to Civic Center, walk 2 blocks east on Ralph McGill Blvd., and turn left on Piedmont. Newly opened in 1997 after two arson-related fires, the **Margaret Mitchell House** sits at 10th and Peachtree St., adjacent to the Midtown MARTA station. The house allows visitors to see the apartment in which Mitchell wrote *Gone With the Wind*, her typewriter, and autographed copies of the novel. *(990 Peachtree St. 249-7015. Open daily 9am-4pm. $7, seniors and students $6. 40min. tours every 10min; last one at 4pm.)*

Just to the west of Piedmont Park is the **Woodruff Arts Center;** take MARTA to Arts Center. *(1280 Peachtree St. NE. 733-4200.)* It contains the **High Museum of Art,** Richard Meier's award-winning building of glass, steel, and white porcelain. The museum contains one of Andy Warhol's Marilyn Monroe paintings. *(733-4444. Open Tu-Th 10am-5pm, Su noon-5pm. $6, students with ID and seniors $4, ages 6-17 $2; free Th 1-5pm.)* The **museum branch,** 1 block south of Peachtree Center Station, houses folk art and photography galleries. *(30 John Wesley Dobbs Ave. NE. 577-6940. Open M-F 10am-5pm. Free.)* At the same MARTA stop, the **William Breman Jewish Heritage Museum** is the largest Jewish museum in the southeast, and features a moving Holocaust exhibit. *(Open M-Th 10am-5pm, F 10am-3pm, Su 1-5pm. $5, students and seniors $3.)*

The **Center for Puppetry Arts,** at 18th St., has a museum featuring traditional Punch and Judy figures, some of Jim Henson's original Muppets, and daily puppet-making workshops. *(1404 Spring St. NW. 873-3391. Open M-Sa 9am-5pm. $5, students, seniors, and children $4. Shows $7.75/$6.75. Puppet workshop $3.50.)*

**BUCKHEAD.** A drive through **Buckhead** (north of midtown and Piedmont Park, off Peachtree near W. Paces Ferry Rd.) uncovers Atlanta's Beverly Hills—the sprawling mansions of Coca-Cola CEOs and other specimens of high culture. This area is also a hub of local grub and grog (see **Entertainment,** below). One of the most exquisite residences in the Southeast, the Greek Revival **Governor's Mansion** has elaborate gardens and furniture from the Federal period. Take bus #40 "West Paces Ferry" from Lindbergh Station. *(391 W. Paces Ferry Rd. 261-1776. Free. Tours Tu-Th 10-11:30am.)* In the same neighborhood, discover the **Atlanta History Center/Buckhead.** The **Atlanta History Museum** traces Atlanta's development from rural to international, and features a Civil War Gallery. *(130 W. Paces Ferry Rd. NW. 814-4000. Open M-Sa 10am-5:30pm, Su noon-5:30pm. Ticket sales end at 4:30pm. $7, students and seniors $5, ages 6-17 $4.)* Also on the grounds are the **Swan House,** a lavish Anglo-Palladian Revival home built in 1928, and the **Tullie Smith Farm,** a yeoman farmhouse.

**EAST OF MIDTOWN.** A respite from the city is at **Stone Mountain Park,** 16mi. east on U.S. 78, where a fabulous Confederate Memorial is carved into the world's largest mass of granite. The "Mt. Rushmore of the South" features Jefferson Davis, Robert E. Lee, and Stonewall Jackson and measures 90 ft. by 190 ft. The mount is surrounded by a 3200-acre "World of Family Fun" recreation area and historic park. *(770-498-5690. Park gates open daily 6am-midnight; attractions open 10am-8pm; off-season 10am-5pm. $6 per car; admission to other attractions $5.)* The hike up the **Confederate Hall Trail** (1½mi.) is rewarded with a spectacular view of Atlanta. Check out the dazzling laser show on the side of the mountain every summer night at 9:30pm (free). Take bus #120 "Stone Mountain" from the Avondale subway stop.

The **Fernbank Museum of Natural History,** off Ponce de Leon Ave., sports life-size dinosaur models and an IMAX theater, among other exhibits. Take bus #2 from North Ave. or Avondale Station. *(767 Clifton Rd. NE. 370-0960. Open M-Sa 10am-5pm, Su noon-5pm. Museum $9, seniors and students $8, ages 3-12 $7; IMAX film $7/$6/$5; both $12/$10/$8.)* The adjacent **Stanton Rose Garden,** on the corner of Ponce de Leon and Clifton Rd., contains over 1300 breeds that bloom from spring into Nov.Dec.

## 🎵 ENTERTAINMENT AND NIGHTLIFE

For hassle-free fun, buy a MARTA pass (see **Practical Information,** p. 371) and pick up one of the city's free publications on music and events. *Creative Loafing, Music Atlanta,* the *Hudspeth Report,* or "Leisure" in the F edition of the *Atlanta Journal* will give you the scuttlebutt. *Southern Voice* has complete listings on gay and lesbian news and nightclubs throughout Atlanta; stop by **Charls,** 1189 Euclid St. (524-0304), for your free copy. Look for free summer concerts in Atlanta's parks.

The **Woodruff Arts Center** (see **Midtown** p. 376) houses the Atlanta Symphony, the Alliance Theater Company, Atlanta College of Art, and the High Museum of Art. **Atlantix,** 65 Upper Alabama St., offers half-price rush tickets to dance, theater, music, and other attractions through out the city. MARTA: 5 Points. (770-772-5572. Walk-up service only, T 11am-3pm, W-Sa 11am-6pm, Su noon-3pm.) In its first summer, the soon-to-be-completed **Philips Arena** will host concerts and the Atlanta Thrashers hockey team. The National League **Atlanta Braves** play at **Turner Field,** which features a Coke bottle over left field that erupts with fireworks after homeruns. MARTA: West End, Bus #105. (Call Ticketmaster at 800-326-4000. Tickets $5-15, $1 skyline seats available game day.) Tours of Turner Field, including a glimpse from the $200,000 skyboxes, are offered. (Non-game days, M-Su 9:30am-4pm, Su 1pm-4pm. Game days M-Sa 9:30am-noon. $7, children $4, under 3 free.)

**Six Flags Over Georgia,** at I-20 W, is one of the largest theme/amusement parks in the nation, including the new 54mi. per hour rollercoaster "Georgia Scorcher." Take bus #201 "Six Flags" from Hamilton Homes. (7561 Six Flags Rd. SW. 948-9290. Open daily mid-May to Aug. 10am-midnight; sporadically rest of year. $35, children and seniors $17; 2-day pass for adults $40; kids $30.)

Drink and dance hotspots center in **Little Five Points, Virginia Highlands, Buckhead,** and oft-cheesy **Underground Atlanta. East Atlanta,** at the crossroads of Glenwood and Flat Shoals, is the up-and-coming part of town. A college-age crowd usually fills Little Five Points; many head to **The Point,** 420 Moreland Ave., where live alternative music plays 5-6 nights a week (659-3522; cover $3-10; open M-F 4pm-4am, Sa 1pm-3am, Su 1pm-4am). Named after a medieval art forger, **Elmyr,** 1091 Euclid Ave., offers the priceless beer-and-burrito combo for a mere $4 (588-0250, Su-Th noon-2am, F-Sa noon-3am). For blues, feel your way to **Blind Willie's,** 828 N. Highland Ave. NE in Virginia Highlands, a dim, bustling club with Cajun food and occasional big name acts. (873-2583. Live music starts around 10pm. Cover $5-10; open Su-Th 8pm-2am, F 8pm-3am, Sa 8pm-2:30am). For a laid-back and often international crowd, move to **Limerick Junction Pub,** 822 N. Highland Ave., where contagious Irish music jigs nightly and open mic night happens every Tu at 9pm (874-7147; open M-W 5pm-1am, Th-Sa 5pm-2am, Su 5pm-midnight). **Flat Iron,** 520 Flat Shoals Ave., anchors a diverse and expanding East Atlanta scene (688-8864; open M-Th 11:30am-2am, F-Sa noon-3am, Su 12:30pm-2am). In Buckhead, cool off with a 96 oz. fishbowl at **Lu Lu's Bait Shack,** 3057 Peachtree Rd. (262-5220; open Tu-F 5pm-4am, Sa 5pm-3am).

Towards downtown, **Masquerade,** 695 North Ave. NE, occupies an original turn-of-the-century mill. The bar has three different levels: "heaven," with live dance music; "purgatory," a more laid-back coffee house; and "hell," offering techno and industrial. An outside dance space provides dancing with lights and celestial views. The 4000-seat ampitheater caters to metal and punk tastes. (577-8178; concert line 577-2007. 18+. Cover $4-8+. Open W-Su 8pm-4am.) Voted the #1 club in Atlanta by *Rolling Stone,* **MJQ,** 726 Ponce de Leon, spins a different theme every night of the week. From Tu world beat salsa to F rinse outs, skillful DJs and signature blue drinks keep the pulsating throngs bobbing (870-0575).

# HELEN

When your town's major industry dries up and tourism is stagnant, there is but one thing to do—redevelop and bill yourself as a Bavarian village. In the 1960's four Helen business women transformed this once sleepy lumber town into Georgia's own Little Germany. Beer gardens and cobblestone streets line the overwhelmingly convincing downtown district; strict building codes ensure that even fast food cabins fit the image. Burn off your weiner schnitzel exploring the nearby Chattahoochee River, Appalacian Trail, and Unicoi State Park. Willkommein, y'all!

**⑦ PRACTICAL INFORMATION.** Helen lies 60mi. northeast of Atlanta, buttressing the mountains of the Chattahoochee National Forest. From I-85, take exit 45 to Hwy. 365, then left onto Hwy. 384, right on Hwy. 75. For $90, **Northeast Georgia Cab and Limo** will pack as many people as they can into the car for the 90min. trek from the Atlanta airport to Helen. Most everything Bavarian is accessible by foot from the **Alpine Helen/White County Convention and Visitor's Bureau,** 726 Bruckenstrausse (878-2181; open M-Th 9am-5pm, F 10am-6pm, Sa 9am-5pm, Su noon-4pm). **Post Office:** S. Main St. (878-2422). **ZIP code:** 30545. **Area code:** 706.

**▐▙ ACCOMMODATIONS AND FOOD.** All the major chains line Main St. The **Alpine Village Inn,** 1005 Edelweisstrasse St., is a local alternative, sporting all the amenities in four garden-side "haus" (800-844-8466; singles and doubles $39). **Unicoi State Park,** 2mi. up Hwy 356, offers water and hook-ups for $22, and campsites starting at $10 (800-573-9659; park open 7am-10pm, office open 8am-4:30pm).

**▧ Fred's Famous Peanuts,** 17 Clayton Rd., serves whooping pork rinds and goobers in all flavors (878-3124). The owner's German mother supervises the schnitzel construction at **Alt Heidelburg,** in White Horse Sq. on Main St. As they say, the schnitzel brot ($8) are "gut isst." (878-2986. Open daily 11:30am-9pm.) Overlooking the Chattahoochee, **Riverhaus** on the Main St. bridge brings it back home with $4 subs and $2 pizza slices (878-3758; daily noon-6pm, later on weekends).

**⊡ SIGHTS.** The owner of **Charlemagne's Kingdom** spent 20 years constructing a scale replica of Germany (what else?), including over 6000 handpainted models *(8808 N. Main St. 11am-6pm. $5, ages 6-12 $2.50.)* The magnificent twin waterfalls at **Anna Ruby Falls,** 5mi. down Hwy. 356 in the Chattahoochee National Forest, roar with nature's power. *(In summer 9am-8pm, off-season 9am-6pm. $3 per car.)* Various rafting packages at **Wildewood Outfitters** let you float way down yonder on the Chattahoochee. Their retail store meets the needs of forgetful backpackers and hikers. *(7272 S. Main St... 800-553-2715. From $15, including transportation. Trip information 9:30am-2:30pm summer only. Store open M-Sa 10am-6pm, Su noon-6pm.)* **Habersham Vineyards & Winery** offers free tours and tastings of their internationally recognized product. *(7025 S. Main St. M-Sa 10am-6pm, Su 12:30-6pm.)* Tens of thousands flock to Helen for **Oktoberfest** in Oct. and Nov. (878-1619).

## ATHENS

Athens is the peach state's version of the "Classic City." In 1795 a group of Georgia lawmakers chose Athens to host the first publicly-chartered college in the country, the University of Georgia (UGA). Since then, the school has expanded to over 30,000 students. UGA's enormous size, resources, and influence have forged an artsy downtown, a prolific music scene, extreme Georgia football fever, and varied nightclub offerings. The magnificent historic homes, spared by Sherman, the State Museum of Art, and the State Botanical Gardens heighten Athenian culture.

**∄ PRACTICAL INFORMATION.** Situated 70mi. northeast of Atlanta, Athens can be reached from I-85 via U.S. 316 (exit 4), which runs into U.S. 29. The **Athens Airport,** 1010 Ben Epps Dr. (613-3420), offers a **commuter shuttle** (800-354-7874) to various points in and around Atlanta ($25). **Greyhound,** 220 W. Broad St. (549-2255), buses to Atlanta (1¾hr, 3 per day, $13; station open M-F 7:30am-9:15pm, Sa-Su 7:30am-2:30pm, 7pm-9:15pm.) The **Athens Transit System** runs buses on 30min. and 1hr. loops. Schedules and information are available at the Welcome Center and Information Center on Washington St. (613-3430. $1, seniors 50¢, ages 6-18 75¢.) The **University Transit System** runs 9 different routes through town and gown (369-6220; M-F 6:45am-12:40am; free). Two blocks north of the UGA campus is the **Athens Welcome Center,** 280 E. Dougherty St. (353-1820), in the Church-Waddel-Brumby House, the city's oldest Federal Period House (open M-Sa 10am-5pm, Su 2-5pm). Help is available from **Public Health Information** (800-473-4357) and the **health center** (521-7205, M-F 8am-5pm). **Post Office:** 575 Olympic Dr. (800-275-8777; open M-F 8:30am-5pm, Sa 9am-2pm). **ZIP code:** 30601. **Area code:** 706.

**⌐·⌐ ACCOMMODATIONS AND FOOD.** Many of the city's affordable motels line **W. Broad St.,** also known as the Atlanta Hwy. (U.S. 78), a few mi. from downtown. Many hotels jack up their prices during football weekends in the fall. In the Five Points District, the **Downtowner Motor Inn,** 1198 S. Milledge Ave., has rooms in 70s colors near campus with A/C, continental breakfast, free local calls, cable TV, and pool (549-2626; singles $42; doubles $50; $2 per additional person). Closer to town, the **History Village Inn and Conference Center,** 295 E. Dougherty St., lies across the street from the Welcome Center. (546-0410. A/C, cable TV, free local calls, pool and laundromat. Singles $40; doubles $45; 10% AAA, UGA, seniors discount. Wheelchair assessable) A full-service campground with secluded sites, **Pine Lake RV Campground,** Rt. 186, 12mi. outside of Athens off Rt. 441 in nearby Bishop, has full hookups and fishing lakes. (769-5486. Tent sites $16, full hookup $18. Open daily 8am-dark. Wheelchair access.)

Low key and no frills, **Weaver D.'s,** 1016 E. Broad, past the train tracks, lets his food do the talking. Spectacular BBQ and fried chicken (all under $6) pack in native and visitor alike. The sign outside reads "Automatic For the People," owner Dexter Weaver's favorite expression; it inspired the title of REM's 1992 album, and a burgeoning T-shirt trade. (353-7797. Open M-F 11am-6pm.) **The Grit,** 199 Prince Ave., is Athens at its crunchiest and coolest, serving up scrumptious, healthy, *au* *naturel* meals, including a great weekend brunch. Popular dishes on the all-vege-tarian menu include the Indian-flavored Dal Baby ($5.25) and the vegetable samo-sas ($5.25). (543-6592. Entrees $3-6. Open M-F 11am-10pm, Sa-Su brunch 10am-3pm and dinner 5-10pm.) Athenians cheer the bakers behind **Big City Bread,** 393 N. Finley St., with an oven imported from France. Organic breads ($3 per loaf) and pastries proper for a Georgia peach (under $2) line the indoor/outdoor cafe. (548-1187. Open M-Sa 7am-6pm, Sun 9am-3pm.) Mentioned in the B-52's song "Dead-beat Club," **Allen's Hamburgers,** 1294 Prince Ave., is anything but moribund. Gener-ations of UGA Dawgs have chawed on $1.50 cheeseburgers and grooved to local bands. (548-8309. Open M-Sa 6am-2am.) For an enormous, low-maintenance burr-ito with a dash of attitude, drop by the **Mean Bean,** 1675 S. Lumpkin St., in the Five Points area. Mean Bean's popular guacamole salad burrito ($4) competes with cre-ate-your-own-combos. (549-4868. Open daily 11am-10pm.) No Athenian culinary experience can lack an immense 50¢ scoop from **Hodgson's Pharmacy,** 1220 S. Milledge Ave., maybe the last place on earth where ice cream comes so cheap. (543-7386. Open M-Sa 9am-7pm, Su 2-7pm.)

**SIGHTS AND ENTERTAINMENT.** For an in-depth look at Athens' old and new, take the 1½hr. **Classic City Tour** (reservations 353-1820). This fascinating $10 driving tour tells the stories of the antebellum homes, the Civil War, and UGA. Tours leave from the welcome center daily at 2pm; walk-ins are welcome. Athens is home to one of the state's grandest cultural institutions, the **Georgia Museum of Art,** 90 Carlton St., in the university's Performing and Visual Arts Complex. (542-4662. Open Tu-Sa 10am-5pm except W 10am-9pm; Su 1-5pm. Free.) The museum houses a collection of over 7000 works and shows about 20 different exhibitions a year. Cure yourself at the physic garden of medicinal herbs at the **State Botanical Garden of Georgia,** 2450 S. Milledge Ave. Folk cures for diabetes, epilepsy and the flu grow in the international gardens. (542-1244. Open daily 8am-sunset. Visitors Center open M-Sa 9am-4:30pm, Su 11:30am-4:30pm. Free.) Relive UGA's storied athletic program at the **Butts-Mehre Heritage Hall,** 1 Selig Circle (542-9036). The **Mor-ton Theater,** 199 W. Washington St., was the first theater in the U.S. to be owned and run by African Americans. Ticket prices aren't what they were in 1910, but usually they're still low (613-3770; $5-15). Athens' grandest Greek Revival man-sion, the **Taylor-Grady House,** 634 Prince Ave., once housed the newspaperman who coined the term "New South." (549-8688. Open M-F 10am-1pm and 2:30-5pm. $3.) Athenian legend recalls that Prof. W.H. Jackson deeded that the white oak stand-ing at Dearling and Finley St. own itself and its shade. The original **"Tree that Owns Itself"** died in 1942 but was reborn from one of its own acorns.

If on an R.E.M. pilgrimage, check out the **40 Watt Club,** 285 W. Washington St., where the group started out and where many bands today attempt to follow their lead (549-7871; cover $5-12; open daily 10pm-3am). The **Georgia Theater,** at Lump-kin and Clayton St., attracts shiny, happy people with local and national acts (353-3405; cover usually $2-5; open daily 7pm-2am). Appealing to a hatless, slightly more mature crowd, **The Globe,** 199 N. Lumpkin St., draws grad students in droves (353-4721; open M-Tu 4pm-1am, W-Sa 4pm-2am). Bask in the warm Georgia sun-shine at **Boar's Head,** 263 E. Washington St., the only downtown bar with a patio, and a grand one at that (369-3040). **Jittery Joe's** java joints specialize in refitting old digs: **834 Prince St.** is a former church, complete now with an aquarium-backed stage (369-7456; open daily 7:30am-midnight) and **1210 S. Milledge Rd.,** an old Shell gas station, is now a posh, '90s coffee sophisticate (208-1979; open daily 6:30am-midnight). In the Five Points District, **Sons of Italy,** 1573 S. Lumpkin St., packs 'em in with a roadside ping-pong table and an outdoor bar with patio (543-2516; open M 5pm-2am, T-Sa 11am-2pm, Sun 11am-midnight). In mid-July, **Athfest** features hundreds of local bands playing in the downtown area (548-1973; $10 per day, both days $15). The free weekly *Flagpole* details upcoming shows and events.

# ANDERSONVILLE

The **Andersonville National Historic Site,** Hwy. 49 in Andersonville, was home to the Civil War's deadliest prisoner of war camp. Located about an hour from Macon, this camp stands as a testament, like the battlefields of northern Virginia, to the brutality of the last two years of the American Civil War. Rampant disease, overcrowding, and slum conditions killed 13,000 of the 45,000 captured Union soldiers imprisoned there between 1864-1865. After the War, the Commandant of the Camp was the only Confederate officer to be hanged as a war criminal. On the site rests the **National Prisoner of War Museum,** a powerful collection of video personal testimony and photographs, which conveys captivity from the Revolutionary War to Vietnam. Behind the Site and the Museum, the **Andersonville National Cemetery** continues to be a final resting place for deceased veterans. *(912-924-0343. Site and cemetery open 8am-5pm daily, museum open 8:30am-5pm. Free.)*

# SAVANNAH

In February 1733, General James Oglethorpe and a rag-tag band of 120 vagabonds founded the city of Savannah and the state of Georgia at Tamacraw Bluff on the Savannah River. General Sherman later spared the city during his famous rampage through the South. Some say he found it too pretty to burn, even presenting Savannah to President Lincoln as a Christmas gift. Today, the general's reaction is still believable to anyone who sees Savannah's antique stores and stately old trees, its Federalist and English Regency houses amid spring blossoms. More recently, the movie *Forrest Gump* has popularized a certain bench in Chippewa Sq., while John Berendt's best-seller *Midnight in the Garden of Good and Evil* continues to attract readers to this lovable town and its welcoming inhabitants.

## ◪ ORIENTATION AND PRACTICAL INFORMATION

Savannah rests on the coast of Georgia at the mouth of the **Savannah River,** which runs north of the city along the border with South Carolina. The city stretches south from bluffs overlooking the river. The restored 2½ sq. mi. **downtown historic district;** bordered by East Broad, Martin Luther King, Jr. Blvd., Gwinnett St., and the river; is best explored on foot. *Do not stray south of Gwinnett St.; the historic district quickly deteriorates into an unsafe and seedy area.* **Tybee Island,** Savannah's beach, 18mi. east on U.S. 80 and Rt. 26, makes a fine daytrip. Try to visit at the beginning of spring, when Savannah's streets are lined with flowers.

**Trains: Amtrak,** 2611 Seaboard Coastline Dr. (234-2611), 4mi. outside the city. To Charleston (2hr., 2 per day, $17-33) and Atlanta. Station open Sa-Th 4:30am-12:15pm, 4:30pm-12:15am; F 4:30am-12:15am. Taxi to downtown $5.

**Buses: Greyhound,** 610 W. Oglethorpe Ave. (232-2135), at Fahm St. To: Jacksonville (3hr., 10 per day, $21); Charleston (4hr., 1 per day, $21); and Atlanta (4 per day, $41). Open 24hrs.

**Public Transit: Chatham Area Transit (CAT),** 233-5767. Runs daily 7am-11pm. Fare 75¢, no transfers, 1-day pass for the shuttle $2. The CAT shuttle runs through the historic area (daily 7:40am-5pm, free).

**Taxis: Adam Cab,** 927-7466.

**Visitor Info: Savannah Visitors Center,** 301 Martin Luther King, Jr. Blvd. (944-0455), at Liberty St. in a lavish former train station. Reservation service for local inns and hostels (877-728-2662). $5 parking pass allows unlimited use of all metered parking and city lots for 2 days. Open M-F 8:30am-5pm, Sa-Su 9am-5pm.

**Hotlines: Rape Crisis Center,** 233-7273. 24hr.

**Post Office:** 2 N. Fahm St. (235-4619) at Bay St. Open M-F 7am-6pm, Sa 9am-3pm. **ZIP code:** 31402. **Area code:** 912.

# ▟ ACCOMMODATIONS

Downtown motels cluster near the historic area, visitors center, and Greyhound station. For those with cars, **Ogeechee Rd. (U.S. 17)** has several budget options.

**Savannah International Youth Hostel (HI-AYH),** 304 E. Hall St. (236-7744), in the historic district 2 blocks east of Forsyth Park. This restored Victorian mansion has a kitchen and laundry facilities. Clean dorm beds (6 per room) $17; hard-to-get private rooms $31. Linen $1. Bikes $10. Flexible 3-night max. stay. Check-in 7:30-10am and 5-10pm; call Brian for late check-in. Lockout 10am-5pm. No curfew. Closed Nov. 15 to Feb. 28.

**Thunderbird Inn,** 611 W. Oglethorpe Ave. (232-2661), across from the Greyhound station. The least expensive rooms downtown. Modest exterior hides nice furnishings. In summer singles $32, doubles $45; in winter $30/35. 5% off with reservations and mention of *Let's Go.* A/C and cable TV.

**Fort McAllister State Park** (727-2339); take exit 15 off I-95. Wooded sites with water and electricity, some with a water view. All located on island surrounded by marsh ("Savage Island"). Tent sites $13, RV sites $15. Check-in before 10pm. Parking $2. Office open daily 8am-5pm; campground open 7am-10pm.

**Skidaway Island State Park** (598-2300 or 800-864-7275), 13mi. southeast of downtown off Diamond Causeway. Inaccessible by public transportation. Follow Liberty St. east from downtown until it becomes Wheaton St.; turn right on Waters Ave. and follow it to the Diamond Causeway. Generally louder than Fort McAllister. Bathrooms, heated showers, electricity, and water. Swimming pool $2. Tent sites $16, RV $18. Check-in before 10pm; in winter 5pm.

# ▟ FOOD

**Nita's Place,** 40 Abercorn St. (283-8233), gives reason to come to Savannah. Owner Juanita Dixon and family set the standard for soul food with tender friend chicken, all fresh veggies, and "spoon bread." The dessert-like squash casserole, a delight beyond description, will make you hug the chef (lunch $10, veggie plate $5; open M-Sa 11:30am-3pm.)

**Wall's BBQ,** 515 E. York La. (232-9754), in alley between York and Oglethorpe, off Price St. This tiny, nondescript house churns out fantastic ribs ($8), BBQ sandwiches ($4), and their specialty, baked deviled crabs ($3; open W 11am-6pm, Th-Sa 11am-9pm.)

**Mrs. Wilkes Boarding House,** 107 W. Jones St. (232-5997), is truly a Southern institution. Friendly strangers sit around a large table eating luscious fried chicken, butter beans, and superb biscuits; don't leave before dessert! Breakfast ($5). All-you-can-eat lunch $10. *The wait in line is up to 2hr.* Get there at 11am. Open M-F 8-9am and 11am-3pm.

**Clary's Café,** 404 Abercorn St. (233-0402). A family spot since 1903 with a famous weekend brunch and friendly service. Malted waffle $4. Open M-F 7am-10pm, W 7am-5pm, Sa 8am-4pm and 5-10pm, Su 8am-10pm.

**Olympia Café,** 5 E. River St. (233-3131), on the river. Greek specialities and more, including veggie gyro ($4). Lunch or dinner $5-15. Open daily 11am-11pm.

# ▟ NIGHTLIFE

The waterfront area (River St.) offers endless oceanfront dining opportunities, street performers, and a friendly pub ambience. **Kevin Barry's Irish Pub,** 117 W. River St., stages live Irish folk music (233-9626. Music W-Su after 8:30pm; cover $2. Open M-F 4pm-3am, Sa 11:30pm-3am, Su 12:30-2am.) For a drink that will keep you on your ear for days, check out **Wet Willies,** 101 E. River St., with its casual dining, young folks, and irresistible frozen daiquiris for $3.50-5.50 (233-5650; open Su-Th 11am-1am, F-Sa 11am-2am). Local college students eat, drink, and shop at **City Market.** One hot spot is **Malone's Bar and Grill,** 27 Barnard St., with dancing, drinks, and daily live music. The lower floor opens up to a game room, while techno beats on the 3rd floor. (234-3059. Open M-Sa 11am-3am, Su 11am-2am. Happy hour 5-8pm.) Hustlers will enjoy the 10 Gandi pool tables and over 80 beers at **B&B Billiards**, 411 W. Congress St. (233-7116. Happy hour daily 4-8pm. Free pool Tu and Th. Open M-Sa 4pm-3am.) The Lady Chablis, a character featured in *Midnight in the Garden of Good and Evil* (see p. 383), performs regularly at the popular gay/lesbian hotspot **Club One**, 1 Jefferson St., near City Market, at Bay St. (232-0200; cover $3-6; open M-Sa 5pm-3am, Su 5pm-2am). All kinds of live music rocks W-Sa nights at **The Velvet Elvis**, 127 W. Congress St.; look for neon lights in the window (236-0665; cover $2-8; open Tu-F 5pm-3am, Sa 6pm-3am).

## SIGHTS AND BLARNEY

Most of Savannah's 21 squares contain some distinctive centerpiece. Elegant antebellum houses and drooping vine-wound trees often cluster around the squares, adding to the classic Southern aura. Many bus, van, and horse carriage **tours** leave every 10-15 min. from the visitors center ($13-15), but walking might be more fun.

Savannah's best-known historic houses are the **Davenport House,** on Columbia Sq., and the **Owens-Thomas House,** a block away on Oglethorpe Sq. The Davenport House, earmarked to be razed for a parking lot, was saved in 1955. Tours explore the 1st floor every 30min.; the 3rd floor is open to explore at your leisure. *(Davenport 119 Habersham St. 236-8097. Open daily 10am-4pm. $5. Last tour 4pm. Owens-Thomas 124 Abercorn St. 233-9743. Open Tu-Sa 10am-5pm, Su 2-5pm. $6, students $3, seniors $5, under 13 $2. Last tour 4:30pm.)* The **Green Meldrim House,** on Madison Sq., is a Gothic Revival mansion that served as one of General Sherman's headquarters during the Civil War. *(1 W. Maco St. 232-1251. Open Tu and Th-Sa 10am-4pm. $5.)* The **Telfair Mansion and Art Museum,** displays a distinguished collection of decorative arts in an English Regency house. *(121 Bernard St. 232-1177. Open Tu-Sa 10am-5pm, Su 2-5pm. $5, students $2, seniors $3, ages 6-12 50¢.)* The **Savannah History Museum,** has exhibits depicting the city's past. *(301 Martin Luther King, Jr. Blvd. 238-1779. Open daily 9am-5pm. $3, students and seniors $1.25, ages 6-12 $1.)*

Lovers of the cookies formerly known as Thin Mints and Tag-alongs make a pilgrimage to the **Juliette Gordon Low Birthplace,** near Wright Sq. The Girl Scouts' founder was born here on Halloween 1860, which may explain the Girl Scouts' door-to-door treat technique. The "cookie shrine" contains an interesting collection of Girl Scout memorabilia—including the corpse and still-beating heart of record-setting Jill Offtenplop of Kansas. *(142 Bull St. 233-4501. Open M-Tu and Th-Sa 10am-4pm, Su 12:30-4:30pm. $5, students, seniors, and children $5.)* The **Negro Heritage Trail Tour,** visits African-American historic sights. *(502 E. Harris St. 234-8000. Tours daily from visitor's center, 1 and 3pm, $15, ages 12 and under $12.)*

**THE SOUTH**

**BETTER HOMES AND GARDENS** A notorious and sophisticated antiques dealer, a scandalous and flamboyant drag queen, the prim and proper members of the Married Women's Card, and a melancholy soul with a vial of poison potent enough to kill every man, woman, and child in town: these are a few of the characters that have recently seized the attention of readers in 11 different countries. The colorful plot of *Midnight in the Garden of Good and Evil,* a *New York Times* best-seller, revolves around a highly publicized fatal shooting at Mercer House, a venerable and elegant old home on Monterey Sq. Was it murder or self-defense? Although the social elite about town have denounced "The Book's" exposure of their secrets in indignant whispered exchanges, tourism has skyrocketed by 46%, and it's hard to find a local who doesn't claim to be actually referred to in the book, however vaguely. **"The Book" Gift Shop,** 127 E. Gordon St. (233-3867), at Calhoun Sq., a fan club, Midnight tours, and a Hollywood adaptation all attest to the interest and revenue which "The Book" has generated.

Savannah's four forts once protected the city's port from Spanish, British, and other invaders. The most interesting, **Fort Pulaski National Monument,** marks the Civil War battle where rifled cannons first pummeled walls, making Pulaski and similar forts obsolete. *(786-5787. 15mi. east of Savannah on U.S. 80 E and Rt. 26. Open daily 8:30am-5:15pm; extended hrs. in summer; visitors center closes 5pm. $2, $4 max. per car, under 16 free.)* Built in the early 1800s, **Fort Jackson** contains exhibits on the American Revolution, the War of 1812, and the Civil War *(232-3945. Also along U.S. 80 and Rt. 26. Open daily 9am-5pm; $2.50; students, seniors, and children $2).*

Special events in Savannah include the **Annual NOGS Tour of the Hidden Gardens of Historic Savannah** in mid-Apr., when private walled gardens are opened to the public *(238-0248.)* Green is the theme of the **St. Patrick's Day Celebration on the River,** *(234-0295),* a 4- to 5-day, beer-and-fun-filled party which packs the streets and warms celebrants up for the **Annual St. Patrick's Day Parade,** the second largest in the U.S. *(233-4904; 2:15pm).* A free paper, *Creative Leafing,* found in restaurants and stores, has the latest in news and entertainment.

# NEAR SAVANNAH

**BEAUFORT AND THE SEA ISLANDS.** Listen closely, and you will hear a musical language spoken in the coastal islands of southeastern South Carolina. During the slave trade, the myriad of European societies involved merged with the numerous African cultures to produce **Gullah,** a unique blend of language, food, arts, and religion. After the Civil War, Gullah largely faded across the South, except in the geographically isolated South Carolina lowcountry. Bridges allow easy access to the area and exploration of this unique culture. St. Helena is considered the center of Gullah, largely due to the preservation efforts of the **Penn Center,** Martin Luther King Jr. Dr., the first school for freed slaves in the south. *(838-2432.)* King wrote his "I have a dream" speech on retreat at the center. The center preserves the area's unique culture and heritage in the **York W. Bailey Museum.** *(838-2474. Open M-F 11am-4pm, $4, children $2.)*

The best way to truly experience Gullah is on the **Gullah 'n' Geechie Tours,** led by community activist, historian, scholar and all around expert Kitty Greene. More than a leisurely drive, Greene carefully conveys the Gullah culture by examining its language, religion, art, family and food. Included is a trip to a "praise house," the 300 year religious center for local plantation slaves. *(838-7516 or 838-6312. Tours leave from Gullah Bites Cafe on Hwy 21 in St. Helena; M-F 9:45am, 1:45pm, 4:30pm; Sa by arrangement. 2hr. $17, children $12; reservations required.)*

One of the Palmetto State's strangest sites is the **Kingdom of Oyotunji,** a Yoruba African village in Sheldon, 10mi. north of Beaufort on Hwy 17. The 30-year-old sanctuary for African priests is led by a self-proclaimed African king and his several wives. The heartfelt yet bizarre tour is worth every cent of its $5 charge; make an appointment beforehand to speak with the king. *(846-2210. Open 10am-dusk.)*

Stately Beaufort hosts the lively **Gullah Festival** May 26-28, 2000 and chows at the packed **Shrimp Festival** Oct. 14, 2000. Beaufort is 60mi from both Savannah and Charleston, on Hwy 21 15mi. south of I-95 exit 33. From the **Greater Beaufort Visitor's Center,** 1106 Carteret St., St. Helena is 5mi. south on Hwy 210. *(524-3163. Open daily 9am-5:30pm.)* **Greyhound,** 1307 Boundary Rd. runs to Savannah. *(524-4646. 1 hr, 4 per day, $11.)* **Area code:** 843

**THE GOLDEN ISLES.** The **Golden Isles, St. Simon's Island, Jekyll Island,** and **Sea Island,** have mi. of white sand beaches, and St. Simon's has "tree spirits" to spend an afternoon tracking down via brochure. **Cumberland Island National Seashore,** near the isles, consists of 16mi. of salt marsh, live oak forest, and sand dunes laced with trails and a few decaying mansions. Phone reservations are necessary for entry into the parks. The effort is rewarded with seclusion; you can walk all day on these beaches without seeing a soul. *(912-882-433. Open M-F 10am-4pm.)* Sites are also available on a stand-by basis 15min. before ferry departures to Cumberland Island. The **ferry** leaves from St. Mary's, on the mainland at the terminus of Rt. 40 at the Florida border. *(45min. In summer daily 9 and 11:45am, returns 10:15am daily, 2:45pm W-Sa only, and 4:45pm daily; Oct. to late Feb. ferries run Th-M with no 2:45pm return. $10, under 13 $6.)*

# ALABAMA

The "Heart of Dixie" is often remembered for its controversial role in the Civil Rights movement of the 1960s. Once a stalwart defender of segregation—former Governor George Wallace fought a vicious campaign opposing integration in the 1960s—Alabama now strives to broaden its image and reconcile its past. The legacy of its divided past comprises Alabama's most poignant attractions—museums, statues, and sites, pay homage to those it vilified 30 yrs. ago. There is much more to this state than its history however, Southern cuisine, local festivities, and nationally acclaimed gardens mix to create the 'Bama of today.

## ⊠ PRACTICAL INFORMATION

**Capital:** Montgomery.

**Visitor Info: Alabama Bureau of Tourism and Travel,** 401 Adams Ave., Montgomery 36104 (334-242-4169; 800-252-2262 outside AL; www.touralabama.org. Open M-F 8am-5pm. **Division of Parks,** 64 N. Union St., Montgomery 36104 (800-252-7275). Open daily 8am-5pm.

**Postal Abbreviation:** AL. **Sales Tax:** 4% plus county tax.

## MONTGOMERY

Today Montgomery stands still and quiet, in sharp contrast to its fiery past as the first capital of the Confederacy (the Confederate White House is still downtown), and the birthplace of America's civil rights movement. Montgomery's role in the movement took off in 1955, when local authorities arrested Rosa Parks, a black seamstress, because she refused to give up her seat to a white man on a city bus. The success of an ensuing bus boycott, organized by local minister Dr. Martin Luther King, Jr., encouraged country-wide change. Montgomery relies on its prominent past to overcome a nondescript today; civil rights movement battlegrounds are the main attractions, with some variety provided by Shakespearian drama, heavy home cooking, and memories of Hank Williams.

## ⊠ ORIENTATION AND PRACTICAL INFORMATION.
Downtown follows a grid pattern: Madison Ave. and Washington Ave. are the major east-west routes; Union St. and Decatur St. run north-south. West of downtown, **I-65** runs north-south and intersects **I-85**, which forms Montgomery's southern border. Buses: **Greyhound,** 950 W. South Blvd. (286-0658). Take I-65 to exit 168 and turn right. To: Mobile (3hr., 8 per day, $30); Atlanta (4hr., 6 per day, $29); and Tuskegee (90min., 3 per day, $9). Open 24hr. Trains: **Amtrak,** 950 W. South Blvd., adjacent to Greyhound. Take Coosa St. across the railroad tracks; the stop is on your left. Offers limited bus service to the connecting city of Atlanta, but no actual trains; ask at Greyhound. Public Transit: **Downtown Area Runabout Transit (DART).** Buses run 6am-6pm. Fare $1.50, no transfers. **Taxis: Yellow Cab,** 262-5225. **Visitor Info: Visitor Information Center,** 300 Water St., (262-0013) in Union Station. Open M-F 8:30am-5pm, Sa 9am-4pm, Su noon-4pm. **Hotlines: Council Against Rape,** 286-5987. **Help-A-Crisis,** 279-7837. 24hr. **Post Office:** 135 Catoma St. (800-275-8777). Open M-F 7:30am-5:30pm, Sa 8am-noon. **ZIP code:** 36104. **Area code:** 334.

## ⌂ ACCOMMODATIONS AND FOOD.
⊠ **Capitol Inn,** 205 N. Goldthwaite St., at Heron St. downtown, has spacious, clean rooms, and a pool (265-3844. Singles $22; doubles $32; $5 per additional person; wheelchair access). Also downtown is the comfortable and newly renovated **Town Plaza,** 743 Madison Ave., at N. Ripley St. near the visitors center (269-1561; singles $24; doubles $30 for *Let's Go* users). For those with a car, **South Blvd.,** at I-65 exit 168, overflows with inexpensive beds—beware of the cheapest of the cheap, which are fairly seedy. Right next to I-65 on W. South Blvd., **The Inn South,** 4243 Inn South Ave. (288-7999 or 800-642-0890), greets travelers

with an unusually dramatic lobby for a budget motel. (Continental breakfast, free local calls, cable; microfridge upon request. Singles $29, Sa-Su $34; doubles $36; $2 per additional person. Wheelchair access.) The site of a 1763 French stronghold, **Fort Toulouse Jackson Park,** 7mi. north of Montgomery on Rt. 6 off U.S. 231, has 39 rustic sites with water and electricity in beautiful woods. Other sites grace the Coosa River. (334-567-3002. Tents $8, RVs $10; $2 senior discount. Registration daily 8am-5pm. Make reservations at least 2 weeks in advance in spring and fall.)

■ **Martin's,** corner of Carter Hill and Mulberry, offers glorious fried chicken (meat and 3 veggies $6; open M-F 11am-3pm, 4-7:45pm, Su 10:45am-1:45pm). **Martha's Place,** 458 Sayre St., a family-run, down-home restaurant, lives up to the banner it displays inside: "O taste and see that the Lord is good." Grab an entree, two veggies, lemonade, and dessert for $5.50. (263-9135. Open M-F 11am-3pm, Su brunch buffet.) With 20 vegetable contents for burritos ($4-5), **El Reys,** 1031 East Fairview offers a vegetarian option in a collegiate setting (832-9688; open M-Sa 11am-10pm, Sun 4pm-10pm).

More Southern fare awaits at the **Sassafras Tea Room,** 532 Clay St., a restaurant/ antique dealership. Their famous crunchy chicken salad is $6. (265-7277. Open M-F 11am-2pm, Su by reservation only.) Snag a bag of peaches for $2 at the **Montgomery State Farmers Market,** at Federal Dr. (U.S. 231) and Coliseum Blvd. (242-5350; open daily 7am-5pm). For a more filling meal, **The State Market Café,** 1659 Federal Dr., serves free ice cream with every $5-8 southern cafeteria-style meal (271-1885, open M-F 6-2pm; Sun 10:30am-2pm).

🎭 📷 **SIGHTS AND ENTERTAINMENT.** Maya Lin, the architect who designed the Vietnam Memorial in Washington, D.C., also designed Montgomery's newest sight, the **Civil Rights Memorial,** 400 Washington Ave., in front of the Southern Poverty Law Center. The outdoor monument, over which water continuously flows, pays tribute to 40 men, women, and children who died fighting for civil rights (264-0286. Open 24hr. Free. Wheelchair access.)

The legacy of African-American activism and faith lives on a block away at the 112-year-old **King Memorial Baptist Church,** 454 Dexter Ave. This is where King first preached, and the 1955 bus boycott was organized. The basement mural chronicles King's role in the nation's struggle for civil rights from Montgomery to Memphis. (263-3970. Tours M-Th 10am and 2pm, F 10am, Sa 10:30am, 11:15am, noon and 12:345pm. Donations accepted.)

The **Hank Williams Museum,** 300 Water St., honors country music's most beloved legend. His ballads filter among his outfits, memorabilia, and the '52 Cadillac he died in at age 29. (262-3600; open M-Sa 9am-6pm, Sun 1-4pm; $5, under 12 $1.) Country music fans make daily pilgrimages to the **Hank Williams Grave,** 1304 Upper Wetumpka Rd., in the Oakwood Cemetery Annex off Upper Wetumpka Rd., near downtown (open M-F 10am-sunset).

**THE SOUTH**

---

# THE SELMA TO MONTGOMERY MARCH In the

Selma of 1964, only 1% of eligible blacks had the right to vote. To protest these conditions, civil rights activists organized an ill-fated march on the state capitol in 1965 that was quashed by bayonet-carrying troops. Their spirits battered but not destroyed, the marchers tried again, this time spurred on by the likes of Dr. Martin Luther King, Jr., Joan Baez, Sammy Davis Jr., Andrew Young, Harry Belafonte, Lena Horne, and Mahalia Jackson. The second march, a 54mi. trek from Selma to Montgomery, ended without conflict, prompting a weary MLK Jr. to declare the movement the "greatest march ever made on a state capitol in the South." King's analysis of the monumental significance of the event was not lost on President Lyndon B. Johnson, who noted with eloquence, "At times, history and fate meet at a single time in a single place to shape a turning point in man's unending search for freedom. So it was at Lexington and Concord. So it was a century ago at Appomattox. And so it was last week, in Selma, Alabama." A year later, Congress passed the Voters Rights Act.

**Old Alabama Town,** 301 Columbus St., 2 blocks off Madison and 4 blocks north of the church, reconstructs 19th-century Alabama with over 40 period buildings, including a pioneer homestead, an 1892 grocery, a schoolhouse, and an early African-American church (240-4500; open M-Sa 9am-3pm).

A modest exterior hides the exquisitely decorated **State Capitol,** at Bainbridge St. and Dexter Ave. On the front steps, a bronze star commemorates the spot where Jefferson Davis took the oath of office as president of the Confederacy. (242-3935. Open M-F 9am-5pm, Sa 9am-4pm. Free. Guided tours available.) The **First White House of the Confederacy,** 644 Washington Ave., contains period furnishings and many of President Jefferson Davis's personal belongings (242-1861. Open M-F 8am-4:30pm; free).

The **F. Scott and Zelda Fitzgerald Museum,** 919 Felder Ave., off Carter Hill Rd., contains a few of her paintings and some of his original manuscripts, as well as their strangely monogrammed bath towels. (264-4222. Open W-F 10am-2pm, Sa-Su 1-3pm; free.) For who would fardels bear, were it not for the **Alabama Shakespeare Festival,** the fifth largest in the world, staged at the **State Theater** on the grounds of the 250-acre private estate, **Wynton M. Blount Cultural Park;** take East Blvd. 15min. southeast of downtown onto Woodmere Blvd. The theater also hosts contemporary plays. (271-5353 or 800-841-4273. Tickets $21-30; previews the week before opening $20. Box office open M-Sa 10am-6pm, till 9pm on performance nights.)

The **Montgomery Museum of Fine Arts,** 1 Museum Dr., houses a substantial collection of 19th- and 20th-century American paintings and graphics, as well as "Artworks," a hands-on gallery and art studio for kids. (244-5700. Open Tu-W and F-Sa 10am-5pm, Th 10am-9pm, Su noon-5pm. Free, donations appreciated.)

For some blues and beers, try **1048,** 1048 E. Fairview Ave., near Woodley Ave. (834-1048. Open daily 4pm-wheneva.) The **Capri Theater,** 1048 E. Fairview, shows the movies that chain theaters refuse to run (262-4858; shows daily 7pm and 9pm, $5.50). The *Montgomery Advertiser* lists Th entertainment options.

## NEAR MONTGOMERY: TUSKEGEE

After Reconstruction, "emancipated" blacks in the South remained segregated and disenfranchised. **Booker T. Washington,** a former slave, believed that blacks could best improve their situation by educating themselves and learning a trade, instead of pursuing the classical, erudite education which **W.E.B. Dubois** proposed. The curriculum at the college Washington founded, Tuskegee Institute, revolved around such practical endeavors as agriculture and carpentry, with students constructing almost all of the campus buildings. Washington raised money for the college by giving lectures on social structure across the country. Artist, teacher, scientist, and head of the Agricultural Dept., **George Washington Carver** discovered many practical uses for the peanut, including axle grease and peanut butter.

Today, a more academically oriented **Tuskegee University** fills 160 buildings on 1500 acres; the buildings of Washington's original institute comprise a national historical site (call 727-8349 for tours). Nearby is the **George Washington Carver Museum;** the **visitors center** is inside (727-6390; open daily 9am-5pm; free). Down the street on old Montgomery Rd. lies **The Oaks,** a restoration of Washington's home. Free tours depart from the museum on the hour (daily 10am-4pm).

After your tour, **Thomas Reed's Chicken Coop,** 527 Old Montgomery Rd., can satiate your hunger pangs with a filling, delicious, and inexpensive meal. Chicken is sold by the finger-lickin' piece or as a full dinner. (727-3841; all meals under $5. Open daily 8am-3pm.) **University Mart,** 1505 Franklin Rd. serves up ribs slathered in a heavy, spicy sauce. (724-9772; $3, Th-Sa 7am-9pm).

To get to Tuskegee, take I-85 toward Atlanta and exit at Rt. 81 S. Turn right at the intersection of Rt. 81 and Old Montgomery Rd. onto Rt. 126. **Greyhound** (727-1290) runs from Montgomery (45min., 6 per day, $8-9). **Area code:** 334

THE SOUTH

# BIRMINGHAM

Like its English namesake, Birmingham sits atop soil rich in coal, iron ore, and limestone—minerals responsible for its lightning-quick transformation into the first industrial center of the South. Yet the city is notorious for some of the most violent attacks against civil rights. To its credit, Alabama's largest city refuses to shy away from a controversial past; parks, museums, and memorials honor equality's champions. "A place of revolution and reconciliation" and now celebration, Birmingham is a cosmopolitan version of Southern charm and hospitality, visible at art festivals, museums, and the University of Alabama.

## ⚡ ORIENTATION AND PRACTICAL INFORMATION

The downtown area grid system has avenues running east-west and streets running north-south. Each numbered avenue has a north and a south, with railroad tracks running in between. **I-65, I-59,** and **Hwy. 31** form a U around the city, leaving the southern side exposed.

**Trains: Amtrak,** 1819 Morris Ave. (324-3033). To **Atlanta** (4hr., 1 per day, $20-39) and **New Orleans** (7hr., 1 per day, $24-47). Open 8:30am-4:30pm.

**Buses: Greyhound,** 618 19th St. N (251-3210). To: Montgomery (2hr., 5 per day, $21); Mobile (5½-11½hr., 6 per day, $41); and Atlanta (2hr., 9 per day, $22-24). 24hr.

**Public Transit: Metropolitan Area Express (MAX)** (322-7701) operates M-F 6am-6pm. Fare $1, transfers 25¢. **Downtown Area Runabout Transit (DART)** (252-0101) runs M-F 9am-9pm. Fare 50¢.

**Taxi: Yellow Cab,** 252-1131.

**Visitor Info:** The **Greater Birmingham Convention and Visitors Center,** 2200 9th Ave. N. (458-8000, 800-458-8085), 1st fl. Open M-F 8:30am-5pm.

**Hotlines: Crisis Center,** 323-7777. **Rape Response,** 323-7273. Both 24hr.

**Post Office:** 351 24th St. N. (521-0302; open M-F 6am-11pm). **ZIP code:** 35203. **Area code:** 205.

## ▸ ACCOMMODATIONS AND FOOD

There are lots of cheap hotels and motels along Rt. 65 leading south to Birmingham, including **Days Inn, Holiday Inn,** and **Super 8.** A non-chain option is **The Ranchhouse Inn,** 2127 7th Ave. S., just north of Five Points. (322-0691. Singles $35; doubles $40. Local calls 25¢. Cable TV. Wheelchair access.) Visitors may camp in Alabama's largest (10,000 acres) state park, **Oak Mountain State Park,** 15mi. south of Birmingham off I-65 in Pelham (exit 246). Horseback rides, golf, hiking, and an 85-acre lake with beach and fishing are all available in the area. (620-2527 or 800-252-7275. Basic sites $8.50, water and electricity $13, full hookup $15. Parking $1.)

With over 60 joints to choose from, barbecue reigns as the local specialty. **Five Points South,** located at the intersection of 6th Ave. S and 20th St. S. is the best place to eat cheap and meet young people. **Jim N Nick's Barbeque,** 744 29th St. S, roasts chicken, pork, and beef BBQ sandwiches ($3) on a hickory wood fire in a brick pit out back. (323-7082. Open M-Su 10:30am-9pm, Fri. close at 10pm.) Birmingham's oldest seafood wholesaler doubles as **The Fish Market Restaurant,** 611 21st St. S, a no-frills joint with cheap catch of the sea. Grilled, baked, or fired fish entrees run $5-8. (322-3330. Open M-Th 10am-9pm, F-Sa 10am-10pm.) Along with groceries, the **Golden Temple Natural Grocery and Café,** 1901-07 11th Ave. S., offers up vegetarian lunches (spinach quesadilla $6.50). (933-6333. Grocery open M-F 8:30am-7pm, Sa 9:30am-5:30pm, Su noon-5:30pm. Cafe open M-F 11:30am-2pm, a bit longer in summer.)

## ⚙ SIGHTS

Birmingham's efforts to reconcile its turbulent past have culminated in the **Birmingham Civil Rights District,** a 6 block tribute to the fight for freedom and equality. The **Birmingham Civil Rights Institute,** traces the nation's civil rights struggle throughout the 1950s and 1960s, highlights human rights issues across the globe, and serves as a public research facility. (*520 16th St. N., at 6th Ave. N., 328-9696. Open Tu-Sa 10am-5pm, Su 1-5pm. $5, seniors $2, college students $1, 17 and under free.*)

Across the street from the Institute is the **Sixteenth St. Baptist Church,** where four black little girls died in a Sept. 1963 bombing by white segregationists (*1530 6th Ave. N., at 16th St. N., 251-9402. Open T-F 10am-4pm, Sa by appointment. $2 suggested donation.*) Protests spurred on by the deaths occurred in nearby **Kelly-Ingram Park,** corner of 6th Ave. and 16th St., where statues and sculptures commemorating the civil rights demonstrations now grace the green lawns.

Birmingham remembers its days as the "Pittsburgh of the South" at the gigantic **Sloss Furnaces National Historic Landmark,** adjacent to the 2nd Ave. N. viaduct off 32nd St. downtown. Though the blast furnaces closed 20 years ago, they stand as the only preserved example of 20th-century iron-smelting in the world. Ballet, drama, and music concerts are held in a renovated furnace shed next to the stacks. (*324-191. Open Tu-Sa 10am-4pm, Su noon-4pm. Free tours Sa-Su 1, 2, and 3pm.*)

The **Alabama Sports Hall of Fame,** corner of Civic Center Blvd. and 22nd St. N., honors the careers of the state's greatest sportsmen, including Jesse Owens, Willie Mays, and Carl Lewis. (*323-6665. Open M-Sa 9am-5pm, Su 1-5pm. $5, students $3, seniors $4.*) Next door is the **Birmingham Museum of Art,** the largest municipal art museum in the South, including over 17,000 pieces of art, and a multilevel sculpture garden. (*2000 8th Ave. N., 254-2565. Open Tu-Sa 10am-5pm, Su noon-5pm. Free.*)

Original interactive exhibits entertain at the **McWayne Center,** Birmingham's new science museum. Challenging hands-on displays explain the physics of sports and the power of water. (*200 19th St. N, 714-8300. Open Jun.-Aug. M-Sa 9am-6pm, Sun noon-6pm; Sept.-May M-F 9am-5pm, Sat 9am-6pm, Sun noon-5pm. $7.50, youth & seniors $6.50.*)

For a breather from an educational vacation, visit the 70 acre **Visionland** amusement complex, 16mi. southwest of Birmingham at I-20 and I-459. (*481-4750. Hrs. seasonal. $22, $18 children, $15 seniors.*) Or, revel in the marvelously sculpted grounds of the **Birmingham Botanical Gardens.** Spectacular floral displays, an elegant Japanese Garden (complete with teahouse), and an enormous greenhouse vegetate on 67 acres (*2612 Lane Park Rd, 879-1227. Open daily dawn-dusk. Free.*)

## 🎵 ENTERTAINMENT AND NIGHTLIFE

**Historic Alabama Theater,** 1817 3rd Ave. N., a gorgeous, renovated 1927 building, is booked 300 nights of the year with films and live performances. Their organ, the "Mighty Wurlitzer," entertains the audience pre-show. (252-2262. $5, seniors $4, under 12 $3. Order tickets through Ticket Link, 715-6000, or at the box office 1hr. prior to show.) In addition to the theater's **Infoline** (251-0418), the free *Fun and Stuff* and "Kudzu" section in the F *Birmingham Post Herald* list local entertainment events.

Those lucky enough to visit Birmingham Father's Day weekend can hear everything from country to gospel to big name rock groups at **City Stages.** The 3-day festival, held in Linn Park, is the biggest thing to hit town all year and includes food, crafts, and children's activities. (251-1272. Daily pass $18, weekend pass $25.)

Nightlife centers around **Five Points South** (Southside). On spring and summer nights, many grab outdoor tables or loiter by the fountain until late. The hippest jam year-round at **The Nick,** 2514 10th Ave. S. The poster-covered exterior says it clear and proud: "The Nick...rocks." (252-3831. Cover $2-5. Live music W-M. Open M-F 3pm-late, Sa 8pm-2am.) Live bands from reggae to alternative entertain a collegiate crowd at **The Hippodrom,** 2007 Highland Ave. (933-6565; hrs vary); across the street their grad school counterparts mingle at **Dave's,** 1128 20th St. S (933-4030; open daily 3pm-4am, close Sa 2am). Free swing lessons every Th with 75¢ longnecks and $1 drinks keep 'em moving at **Five Points Music Hall,** 1016 20th St. S. This bar-with-music has pool, foosball, and much happy noise (322-2263).

THE SOUTH

# MOBILE

Though Bob Dylan lamented being stuck here, Mobile (mo-BEEL) has had plenty of fans in its time—French, Spanish, English, Sovereign Alabama, Confederate, and American flags have each flown over the city since its 1702 founding. This historical diversity is revealed in local architecture: antebellum mansions, Italianate dwellings, Spanish and French forts, and Victorian homes line azalea-edged streets. Today, Mobile offers an untouristed version of New Orleans; the site of the first Mardi Gras, the city still holds a 2-week long Fat Tu celebration, without the hordes that plague its Cajun counterpart.

## ⚡ ORIENTATION AND PRACTICAL INFORMATION

The downtown district borders the Mobile River. **Dauphin St.** and **Government Blvd. (U.S. 90)**, which becomes **Government St.** downtown, are the major east-west routes. **Royal St.** and **Broad St.** are major north-south byways. **Water St.** runs along the river in the downtown area, becoming the **I-10 causeway. Frontage Rd.**, along I-65, to the west of downtown, is the same as the **Beltline.**

**Trains: Amtrak,** 11 Government St. (432-4052). The "Gulf Breeze" blows from Mobile to New York City via bus service to Birmingham or Atlanta. To New Orleans (2.5hr.; 3 per week Su, W, and F; $30).

**Buses: Greyhound,** 2545 Government Blvd. (478-9793), at S. Conception downtown. To: Montgomery (3hr., 8 per day, $30); New Orleans (3.5hr., 9 per day, $28-29); and Birmingham (6hr., 6per day, $37-41). Open 24hr.

**Public Transit: Mobile Transit Authority (MTA),** 344-5656. Major depots at Bienville Sq., Royal St. parking garage, and Adams Mark Hotel. Runs M-F 6am-6pm, less frequently on Sa. $1.25, qualified seniors and disabled 60¢, transfers 10¢.

**Taxis: Yellow Cab,** 476-7711.

**Visitor Info: Fort Condé Information Center,** 150 S. Royal St. (208-7304), in a reconstructed French fort near Government St. Open daily 8am-5pm.

**Hotlines: Rape Crisis,** 473-7273. **Helpline,** 431-5111. Both 24hr.

**Post Office:** 250 Saint Joseph St. (694-5917). Open M-F 8am-5pm, Sa 9am-noon. **ZIP code:** 36601. **Area code:** 334.

## ⚡ ACCOMMODATIONS

A slew of affordable hotels line I-65 on Beltline, from exit 5 (Spring Hill Rd) to exit 1 (Government Blvd). First stop by the **Fort Conde Information Center (see above),** they offer discounts for many hotels. **Family Inn,** 900 S. Beltline Rd., I-65 at Airport Blvd., sports firm beds, free local calls, continental breakfast, cable, and a pool (344-5500; singles $28, doubles $40). Downtown, the **Budget Inn,** 555 Government St., offers basic clean rooms with cable TV and A/C. (433-0590; singles $35, doubles $40.) **I-10 Kampground,** 6430 Theodore Dawes Rd. E., lies 7½mi. west on I-10, south off exit 13. This is a great place if you like RVs. (653-9816. Tent sites $13; full RV hookup $18; $1 per additional person. Pool, kiddie playground, laundry, and bath facilities.)

## ⚡ FOOD AND NIGHTLIFE

Mobile's Gulf location means fresh seafood (surf) and southern cookin' (turf). For surf, **Wintzell's Oyster House,** 605 Dauphin St., a long-time local favorite, offers oysters 12 different ways. The 1 hr. oyster eating record stands at 20.5 dozen; beat it and the meal is on them. (432-4605. Lunch $5-8. Open M-Sa 11am-10pm, Su noon-

8pm.) Mobile's grandest catfish, and greatest portions, are found at **Cock of the Walk,** 4815 Halls Mill Rd. (666-1875; entrees $8-10; M-Sa 5pm-9pm, Sun 11:30am-2:30pm, 5pm-8pm). Phenomenal ribs to leave you dreaming, long after you've given up on getting the barbecue stains out of your shirt, are found at ◪ **Dreamland,** 3314 Old Shell Rd. (479-9898. Half-slab $8.45, half-chicken $6.50. Open M-Th 10am-10pm, F-Sa 10am-midnight, Su 11am-9pm.) **Hayley's,** 278 Dauphin St. (433-4970), an alternative bar/hangout, has spunk and occasional live shows (beer $2.25; open daily 3pm-3am). Eighteen pool tables, darts, and mega-subs ($3-5) make **Solomon's,** 5753 Old Shell Rd., the quintessential brew and cue college hangout. (344-0380. Happy hour daily 11am-7pm. Open 24hr., though not all of 'em are so happening.)

## ◉ SIGHTS

Mobile's attractions lie scattered inland, around downtown, and near the bay. Three historic districts—Detonti Sq., Dauphin St., and Church St.—encompass the downtown area. The city's varied influences have led to an architecture unique to Mobile. In particular, the 27 buildings of the **Church St. East Historic District** showcase Federal, Greek Revival, Queen Anne, and Victorian architecture. **Bay City Tours** leads four different tours of Old Mobile and surrounding sights *(432-2229)*.

Four antebellum homes dominate the attractions of Old Mobile. In the **DeTonti Historical District,** north of downtown, brick townhouses with wrought-iron balconies surround the restored **Richards-DAR House Museum.** The museum's stained glass and Rococo chandeliers blend beautifully with its antebellum Italianate architecture and ornate iron lace. *(256 North Joachim St., 434-7320. Open Tu-Sa 10am-4pm, Su 1-4pm. Tours $4, children $1, free tea and cookies.)* **Oakleigh Historical Complex,** 2½ blocks south of Government St., with bricks that were made on site, reigns as one of Mobile's grande dames. Highlights include a cantilevered staircase and enormous windows opening onto all the balconies upstairs. *(350 Oakleigh Pl., 432-1281. Open M-Sa 10am-4pm. $5, students $2, seniors $4.50, ages 6-18 $1. Tours every 30min.)* The **Bragg-Mitchell** and the **Condé-Charlotte** are the former residences of cotton brokers and river pilots. *(Bragg-Mitchell, 1906 Spring Hill Ave., 471-6364. Open M-F 10am-4pm, Su 1-4pm. Condé Charlotte 104 Theater St., 432-4722. Open Tu-Sa 10am-4pm.)* Package tour available at any house, $14 for 4 house museums.

For its lush rose and oriental gardens, its bayou boardwalk, and its 900 acre setting, *Southern Living* magazine has ranked **Bellingrath Gardens,** exit 15A off I-10, one of the top three public gardens in the country. *(12401 Bellingrath Gardens Rd., 973-2217. Open daily 8am-dusk. Gardens $7.90, ages 5-11 $5.25.)* To discover the wonders of the unnatural world, explore **Flea Market Mobile.** Over 800 booths showcase capitalism at its best *(401 Schillinger Rd. 633-7533).*

The **U.S.S. Alabama,** permanently moored 2½mi. east of town at Battleship Park, fought in every major Pacific battle during WWII. Open portholes and passageways let land-lubbers explore the ship's deepest depths. (433-2703; open daily 8am-dusk. $8, ages 6-11 $4. Parking $2.) **Spanish Plaza,** at Hamilton and Government St., honors Mobile's sibling city (Málaga, Spain), while recalling Spain's early presence in Mobile. Amidst sprouting fountains, Spanish flags flutter in the breeze.

The **Mobile Museum of Art,** between Springhill Ave. and University Blvd., displays historical and cutting-edge contemporary work. *(4850 Museum Dr., 343-2667. Open Tu-Su 10am-5pm; free.)* There's also a downtown branch *(300 Dauphin St., 694-0533. Open M-F 8:30am-4:30pm; free).* Kids will enjoy the hands-on diversions at the **Exploreum,** Government St. at Water St. *(208-6873; open Jun.-Aug. M-Th 9am-8pm, F-Sa 9am-9pm, Su 10am-5pm; Sept.-May, M-Th 9am-5pm, F-Sa 9am-9pm, Su 10am-5pm.)*

**Feb.** is a big month for Mobile. Locals await the blooming of the 27mi. **Azalea Trail** (*Azalea Festival and Run Mar. 25, 2000; 473-7223*), and enjoy the parades, costumes, and "throws" of the oldest Fat Tu around at Mobile's **Mardi Gras** *(Feb. 23-Mar. 7, 2000).* The *Mobile Traveler* has an updated list of all Mobile attractions.

# MISSISSIPPI

The "Deep South" bottoms out in Mississippi. The legacy of extravagant cotton plantations, dependence upon slavery, and subsequent racial strife and economic ruin are more visible here than in any other state. In the 1850s, Natchez and Vicksburg were two of the most prosperous cities in the nation; whites bathed in the riches that flowed from free slave labor. During the Civil War, the state was devastated by the siege of Vicksburg and the burning of Jackson. Hatred and injustice drowned Mississippi into the 1960s as blacks protested against continuing segregation and whites reacted with campaigns of terror.

A number of remarkable triumphs have surfaced out of Mississippi's struggles. The state boasts an impressive literary and cultural heritage. Writers William Faulkner, Eudora Welty, Tennessee Williams, and Richard Wright called Mississippi home, as did blues musicians Bessie Smith, W.C. Handy, and B.B. King, who brought their riffs up the "Blues Highway" to Memphis, Chicago, and the world. Today, beautiful plantation homes are testament to the "good ol' days," while enduring rural poverty and low education levels are reminders of inequality.

## ◪ PRACTICAL INFORMATION

**Capital:** Jackson.

**Visitor Info: Division of Tourism**, P.O. Box 1705, Ocean Springs 39566 (800-927-6378; www.decd.state.ms.us). **Dept. of Wildlife, Fisheries, and Parks,** P.O. Box 451, Jackson 39205 (800-546-4808).

**Postal Abbreviation:** MS. **Sales Tax:** 7%.

## JACKSON

Jackson makes a concerted effort to overcome Mississippi's spotty past and lingering backwater image. One billboard claims Jackson is now as "Rome was to Renaissance Europe." While that may be a bit of a stretch, the state's political, cultural, and commercial capital strives to bring the world to its people. Dance performances and art exhibitions abound, and live music is everywhere. North Jackson's lush homes and plush country clubs epitomize wealthy Southern living, while shaded campsites, cool reservoirs, national forests, and Native American burial mounds invite exploration only minutes away.

◪ **ORIENTATION AND PRACTICAL INFORMATION.** West of I-55, downtown is bordered on the north by **Fortification St.,** on the south by **South St.,** and on the west by **Gallatin St.** North-south **State St.** bisects the city. **Jackson Municipal Airport** (932-2859) is east of downtown off I-20. (Taxi to downtown $20.) Walk downtown via Capitol St. to **Amtrak,** 300 W. Capitol St. (355-6350. Open daily 9:30am-7pm.) Trains run to Memphis (4hr., 7 per week, $28) and New Orleans (4½hr., 7 per week, $16). **Greyhound,** 201 S. Jefferson (353-6342), sends buses to Montgomery (5hr., 5 per day, $48-51); Memphis (4½hr., 7 per day, $26); and New Orleans (4½hr., 4 per day, $28). (Open 24hr; *avoid this area at night.*) **Jackson Transit System (JATRAN)** (948-3840) provides limited public service. (M-F 5am-7pm, Sa 5:30am-7pm. Fare $1, transfers free.) Bus schedules and maps posted at most bus stops downtown and available at JATRAN headquarters, 1025 Terry Rd. (Open M-F 8am-4:30pm.) If JATRAN leaves you high and dry, flag down **City Cab** (355-8319. $1.50 base fare, $1.50 per mi., 50¢ per additional person). **Visitor Info: The Convention and Visitors Bureau,** 921 N. President St. (960-1891), downtown (open M-F 8am-5pm). **Hotlines: Rape Hotline** (982-7273, 24hr.) **Post Office:** 401 E. South St. (351-7030. Open M-F 7am-6pm, Sa 8am-noon.) **ZIP code:** 39205. **Area code:** 601.

**ACCOMMODATIONS.** If you have a car, head for the motels along **I-20** and **I-55.** Expect to pay $35 and up for decent accommodations in the area, unless you camp. **Sun 'n' Sand Motel,** 401 N. Lamar St., downtown, is a 60s time-warp—there's even a Polynesian suite. Slightly drab rooms and hair styles can be brightened by the in-house barber shop. Lounge/restaurant in motel serves a $5 lunch buffet. (354-2501. Pool, cable TV. Singles $35-40; $5 per additional person.) **Parkside Inn,** 3720 I-55 N, at exit 98B has dark green furniture and wood-paneled walls to spruce up the clean, somewhat small rooms. (982-1122. Pool, cable TV, free local calls, and some rooms with whirlpools. Must be 21 to rent, under 19 free with adult. Singles $29; doubles $39.) For camping, head to **Timberlake Campgrounds;** take I-55 N to Lakeland East (exit 98B), turn left after 5.8mi. onto Old Fannin Rd. and go 3.7mi. The campground is on the left. A popular summer site with both shaded and waterfront lots. (992-9100. Pool, video games, tennis courts, playground. Tent sites $12, full hookup $15; Oct.-Apr. $10/$13; seniors $1 off year-round. Office open daily 8am-5pm. Gate closes at 10pm.)

**FOOD AND NIGHTLIFE.** Franchised grease palaces can be found north to **County Line Rd.,** between I-55 and I-220, dubbed "restaurant alley" by natives. For the real Jackson scene, the **George St. Grocery,** 416 George St., is the place to be. Packed with state politicians by day and students by night, GSG's lunch deals ($5) ignite a sweet bang for your buck. (969-3573. Live music Tu-Sa 9pm-1am. Open M-Sa 11am-1am, no food after 10pm.) Be prepared to wait in line during the lunch rush at **The Elite Restaurant,** 141 E. Capitol St., site of unpretentiously tasty seafood and diner dishes for over 50 years. The daily lunch special (with 2 veggies $5.75) makes it worth the wait. (352-5606. Open M-F 7am-9:30pm, Sa 5-9:30pm.) **Keifer's,** 710 Poplar St., off State St., 1.5mi. north of downtown, serves gyros and other tasty pita wraps ($4.45-5.45) amidst hanging greenery. (355-6825. Open M-F 11am-10pm, Sa-Su 11am-11pm.)

On Th, pick up *Clarion-Ledger* for a list of weekend events. **Hal & Mal's Restaurant and Brew Bar,** 200 S. Commerce St. (948-0888), stages live music in a converted warehouse. W nights (8:30-11pm) with the Vernon Brothers' bluegrass music are particularly popular. (Cover up to $5 on F-Sa. Restaurant open M 11am-3pm, Tu and Th 11am-9pm, W 11am-10pm, F 11am-10:30pm, Sa 5-10:30pm. Bar open M-Th until 11pm, F-Sa until 1am.) **Cups,** 2757 Old Canton Rd., at Lakeland Ave., caters to an artsy crowd craving cappuccino and conversation (362-7422; open M-Th 7am-10pm, F 7am-midnight, Sa 8am-midnight, Su 9am-10pm).

**SIGHTS.** The **Mississippi Museum of Art,** displays local art and a fabulous Americana collection. *(201 E. Pascagoula, at Lamar St. 960-1515. Open M-Su 10am-5pm, Su noon-5pm. $3, children $2; temporary shows $6/$4.)* Adjacent to the MMA, the out-of-this-world **Russell C. Davis Planetarium** projects the splendors of the universe. *(201 E. Pascagoula. 960-1550. Shows Tu-Sa 7:30pm, Sa-Su 2 and 4pm. $4, seniors and under 12 $2.50.)* Across the street, **Jackson's Art Pavilion** brings in a major exhibit Apr.-Aug., every two years. *(429 S. West St. 960-9900. Tickets $5-20, call for future exhibits and hours.)*

Although Jackson often brings the world to Mississippi, it hardly neglects its home-grown traditions. Built in 1833, the **Old State Capitol,** at the intersection of Capitol and State St., houses an excellent museum documenting Mississippi's turbulent history. *(359-6920. Open M-F 8am-5pm, Sa 9:30am-4:30pm, Su 12:30-4:30pm. Free.)* The state legislature currently convenes in the **New State Capitol,** completed in 1903. A huge restoration project preserved the *beaux arts* grandeur of the building. *(400 High St., between West and President St. 359-3114. 1hr. tours M-F 9, 10, 11am, 1:30, 2:30, and 3:30pm. Open M-F 8am-5pm. Free.)* A tour of the **Governor's Mansion** provides an enlightening introduction to Mississippi politics. *(300 E. Capitol St. 359-3175. Tours Tu-F every 30min. 9:30-11am. Free.)*

Learn about the struggles and achievements of Mississippi's African-Americans at the **Smith-Robertson Museum and Cultural Center,** behind the Sun 'n' Sand Motel. This large museum once housed the state's first African-American public school.

THE SOUTH

Now it displays folk art, photographs, and exhibits on the Civil Rights movement and contemporary African American issues. *(528 Bloom St. 960-1457. Open M-F 9am-5pm, Sa 9am-noon, Su 2-5pm. $1, under 18 50¢.)* On the last weekend in Sept., the surrounding neighborhood celebrates with art, theater, and food at the **Farish St. Festival.** *(960-2384.)*

A recreated 1920s farm village and a number of restored farm implements make up **Mississippi's Agriculture and Forestry Museum,** ½mi. east of I-55 exit 98B. *(1150 Lakeland Dr. 800-844-8687. Open M-Sa 9am-5pm, Su 1-5pm; closed Su early Sept. to late May. $4, seniors $3, ages 6-18 $2, under 6 50¢.)* Also on site is the **National Agricultural Aviation Museum,** with vintage aircraft and tales of cornfield valor.

# VICKSBURG

Vicksburg's verdant hills and prime Mississippi River location made it the focus of much strategic planning during the Civil War. President Abraham Lincoln called the town the "key," and maintained that the war "can never be brought to a close until that key is in our pocket." The Confederates' Gibraltar fell to Union forces on July 4, 1863, after resisting a 47-day bombardment. The loss hit the city hard—until the late 1940s, Vicksburg refused to hold any Fourth of July celebrations. Downtown, 19th-century mansions house museums, and Civil War monuments dominate the urban landscape. Lush parks lend Vicksburg a relaxed, pastoral feel, while brick-paved roads and festive casino riverwalks recreate a way of life that has long since past.

**◪ PRACTICAL INFORMATION.** A car is necessary in Vicksburg. The bus station, the info center, downtown, and the far end of the sprawling military park mark the city's extremes. **Greyhound** (638-8389; open daily 7am-8:30pm) pulls out at 1295 S. Frontage Rd. for Jackson (1hr., 4 per day, $10). The **Tourist Information Center** (636-9421 or 800-221-3536), on Clay St. across from the park (I-20 exit 4, turn west), has a helpful map of sights (open daily 8am-5pm; in winter Sa-Su 9am-4pm). **Post Office:** 3415 Pemberton Blvd. (636-1071), just off U.S. 61 S (open M-F 8am-5pm, Sa 8am-noon). **ZIP code:** 39180. **Area code:** 601.

**▐▐◧ ACCOMMODATIONS, FOOD, AND NIGHTLIFE.** Inexpensive lodging comes easy in Vicksburg. One of the best deals in town, the **Hillcrest Motel,** 40 Rt. 80 E (638-1491), ¼mi. east from I-20 exit 4, offers well-worn yet well-kept and spacious rooms with pool access (singles $22.27; doubles $30.25). The **Beechwood Motel,** 4449 Clay St., a block in front of the Hillcrest, offers cable and standard rooms (636-2271; singles $27, doubles $35). Most hotels cluster near the park; don't expect to stay downtown, unless you choose the **Relax Inn Downtown,** 1313 Walnut St. (631-0039; rooms $25-33). **Magnolia RV Park,** 211 Miller St. (631-0388), has 68 full RV hookups (all pull-throughs), a pool, game room, and playground. Head south on Washington (I-20 exit 1A), and take a left on Rifle Range Rd. to Miller St. (sites $18; office open daily 7:30am-9:30pm). Closer to the military park and the highway is **Battlefield Kampground,** 4407 I-20 Frontage Rd., off exit 4B, where the kampaign of the krazy "k" kontinues. (636-2025. Laundry, pool, and playground. Sites $10, with electricity and water $15, full hookup $17; 10% off with any discount card.)

While downtown, chow down at the **Burger Village,** 1220 Washington St., where a home-cooked southern meal costs under $5 and burgers are nothing but 100% all-American beef (638-0202; open M-Sa 9am-6pm). **Walnut Hills,** 1214 Adams St., serves all-you-can-eat round table dinners (Su-F 11am-2pm) of catfish, hamburger steak, corn, green beans, etc. (638-4910. 1 meat, 3 veggies $6.25, 2 meats, 6 veggies $8; open M-F 11am-9pm, Su 11am-2pm.) The only-in-America **Red Carpet Washateria and Lanes,** 2904 Clay St., on Rt. 80 near the river and Riverfront Park, sports a bowling alley, pool room, and laundromat all in one. (636-9682. Laundry open daily 7am-9pm. Lanes open M-Th noon-11pm, F-Sa noon-1am, Su noon-10pm. $2 per game, $2.50 at night.) Despite the Red Carpet's many thrills, high-rollers might prefer spending their time at one of the four **casinos** that line the river.

**⬛ SIGHTS.** Vicksburg is a mecca for thousands of touring schoolchildren, Civil War buffs, and Confederate and Union army descendents. Memorials and markers of combat sites riddle the grassy 1700-acre **Vicksburg National Military Park,** lending the grounds a sacred air. The park blockades the eastern and northern edges of the city, with its visitors center on Clay St., about ½mi. west of I-20 exit 4B, across from the city info center. Driving through the 16mi. path, you have three options: guide yourself with a free map available at the entrance, buy an informative audio tour, or hire a live person to help navigate around the sights. *(636-0583. Park center open daily 8am-5pm. Grounds open daily in summer 7am-8pm; in winter 7am-sunset. $4 per car. Tape $4.50, CD $8. Live guide $20.)* Within the park, the sunk and saved Union **U.S.S. Cairo Museum.** contains countless artifacts salvaged in the early 1960s. *(636-2199. Open daily 9:30am-6pm; off-season 8am-5pm. Free with park fee.)* The **Old Courthouse Museum,** is one of the South's finest Civil War museums. During the siege of Vicksburg in 1863, Confederate troops used the cupola as a signal station and held Union prisoners in the courtroom. *(1008 Cherry St. 636-0741. Open M-Sa 8:30am-5pm, Su 1:30-5pm; early Oct. to early Apr. closes 4:30pm daily. $3, seniors $2.50, under 18 $2.)*

Vicksburg's preoccupation with the Civil War isn't all-encompassing. The **Attic Gallery,** has a collection of Southern contemporary art and an eclectic display of glassware, pottery, books, and jewelry. *(1101 Washington St. 638-9221. Open M-Sa 10am-5pm. Free.)* Visitors can see what William Allen White calls "a sublimated essence of all that America stands for" at the **Biedenharn Candy Company and Museum of Coca-Cola History.** The first Coke was bottled here; a tour leads you through Coke memorabilia. *(1107 Washington St. 638-6514. Open M-Sa 9am-5pm, Su 1:30-4:30pm. $2.25, under 12 $1.75., under 6 free.)* Vicksburg's finest contribution to the historical home circuit, the **Martha Vick House,** was home to the daughter of the city's founder, Reverend Newitt Vick. *(1300 Grove St. 638-7036. Open M-Sa 9am-5pm, Su 2pm-5pm; $5, under 12 free, 10% AAA discount.)*

# NATCHEZ

In the late 18th century, Natchez distinguished itself as one of the wealthiest settlements on the Mississippi. Of the 13 millionaires in Mississippi at the time, 11 had their cotton plantations here. The custom was to build a manor on the Mississippi side of the river and till the soil on the Louisiana side. After the Civil War, the cotton-based economy crumbled, and the days of the mansion-building magnates passed. Many of the homes remain, however, affording visitors to Natchez the opportunity to gaze at elegant dwellings from a vanquished era.

**⬛ PRACTICAL INFORMATION.** Make connections to Vicksburg (1½hr., 1 per day, $14) and New Orleans (4hr., 1 per day, $35) through **Greyhound** at the **Natchez Bus Station,** 103 Lower Woodville Rd. (445-5291; open M-F 8am-6pm, Sa 8am-5pm, Su 2-5pm). **Car Rental: Natchez Ford Rental,** 199 St. Catherine St. (445-0060), for $34 per day. (150 free mi., 20¢ per additional mi., $100 cash deposit required. Must be 21+, under 26 with major credit card.) The **Natchez Bicycling Center,** 334 Main St. (446-7794), rents bikes with basket, helmet, lock, and repair kit. ($15 per 4hr., $20 per day. Open Tu-F 10am-5:30pm, Sa 10am-3pm; other times by appt.) **Visitors center,** 640 S. Canal St. (442-5849), near the U.S. 84 Mississippi Bridge. (Open daily 8:30am-6pm; early Nov. to Mar. 8am-5pm.) **Post Office:** 214 N. Canal St. (442-4361; open M-F 8:30am-5pm, Sa 10am-noon). **ZIP code:** 39120. **Area code:** 601.

**⬛ ACCOMMODATIONS AND FOOD.** The intersection of **U.S. 61** and **Highland Blvd.** supports lots of high-quality rooms. **Scottish Inns,** 40 Sgt. Prentiss Dr./U.S. 61, a coral-colored complex, has wood furniture (442-9141 or 800-251-1962; singles $28; doubles $35). Close to the Mississippi Bridge and visitors center is the **Natchez Inn,** 218 John Junkin Dr./U.S. 84, with spartan, tidy rooms, a pool, and cable TV (442-0221; singles $30; doubles $40). The secluded campground in **Natchez State Park** is less than 10mi. north of Natchez on U.S. 61 in Stanton (442-2658; sites $7, with water and electricity $11, full hookup $12).

THE SOUTH

Lots of cafes and diners dish up budget eats in Natchez. **Cock of the Walk,** 200 N. Broadway, earns its title and stature with spicy catfish and complimentary jalapeño cornbread served in a bare wood dining room evocative of tough frontiersmen (446-8920; catfish fillet $9; open daily 5pm until the manager's discretion). **The Pig Out Inn,** 116 S. Canal St., serves down-home, home-smoked, faster-than-fastfood BBQ with a spicy sauce on the side (442-8050; sandwiches $3.75; open M-Sa 11am-9pm). **Mammy's Cupboard,** 555 Highway 61, 2mi. south of town, serves homecookin' ($6-7.50) like chicken pot pie and desserts (about $2.50) in a country cottage beneath a huge statue of Mammy, the traditionally stereotyped southern black mother (445-8957; open 11am-2pm).

🔯 **SIGHTS. Natchez Pilgrimage Tours,** supervises tours of the restored manors left from Natchez's cotton days. A helpful staff has free tour schedules, maps, and pamphlets, plus a guidebook that details the histories of the 32 homes that Pilgrimage oversees. The central office sells tickets for individual house tours, or tickets for a 35min. horse-drawn carriage tour and a 55min. air-conditioned bus tour. *(200 State St., at Canal St. 800-647-6742 or 446-6631. Open M-Sa 9am-5pm, Su 12:30-5pm. Guide book $5. House tours $6, children $3. Horse tour $9/$4. Bus tour $10/$5.)* The largest octagonal house in America, **Longwood,** astounds visitors with its elaborate decor and imaginative floorplan; however, the 6-story edifice remains unfinished. The builders, hired from the North, abandoned work at the beginning of the Civil War to fight for the Union. *(140 Lower Woodville Rd. 442-5193. Open daily 9am-5pm. Tours every 20min.)* **Stanton Hall,** on the other hand, arose under the direction of local Natchez architects and artisans. Completed in 1857, the mansion features French mirrors, Italian marble mantels, and exquisitely cut chandeliers. *(401 High St., off Union St. 442-6282. Open daily 9am-5pm. Tours every 30min.)*

For centuries, the Natchez Indians flourished on this fertile land. The arrival of the French incited fighting in 1730, and French military successes brought an end to the thriving Natchez community. The **Grand Village of the Natchez Indians,** pays homage to the tribe with a museum that documents their history and culture. *(400 Jefferson Davis Blvd., off U.S. 61 S. 446-6502. Open M-Sa 9am-5pm, Su 1:30-5pm. Free.)*

The first educational institution in the Mississippi Territory, **Jefferson College,** 6mi. east of Natchez off U.S. 61 near U.S. 84 E, first opened its doors in 1811. The last student left, but the buildings, a museum, and a nature trail are still there. *(442-2901. Grounds open daily sunrise-sunset. Buildings open M-Sa 8am-5pm, Su 11am-5pm. Free.)*

The 500mi. **Natchez Trace Pkwy.** leads north from Natchez to Nashville, TN. Rambling through lush forests, swamps, and shady countryside, the road passes through historic landmarks and a beautiful national park.

## OXFORD

In the 19th century, Oxford was a stopping point for Cherokees on the Trail of Tears. In the 1950s, a federal court ruled that James Meredith be the first black student to enroll at the University of Mississippi (Ole Miss), just west of the city. The news resulted in rioting and the death of three civil rights workers. Apart from these racial injustices, and more influential in shaping Oxford's modern personality, has been its literary heritage. This tradition began in the 1930s with William Faulkner's first novels, and he still reigns supreme.

William Faulkner's home **Rowan Oak,** lies just south of downtown on Old Taylor Rd. Faulkner named the property after the Rowan tree, a symbol of peace and security. The Rowan is not, in fact, a member of the Oak family, a botanical tidbit which Oxford locals find most amusing. (234-3284. Open Tu-Sa 10am-noon and 2-4pm, Su 2-4pm. Grounds open sunrise to sunset. Free self-guided tours.)

Oxford's covered sidewalks and tall cedar trees help to make it a fitting home for the **Center for the Study of Southern Culture** (232-5993) in the Barnard Observatory at Ole Miss, where visitors can pick up pamphlets or attend conferences, including the ever-popular **Faulkner Conference** (in late July or early Aug.; center open M-F 8am-5pm; free). Blues buffs will revel in the over 40,000 records at the **Ole Miss Blues Archive,** Farley Hall room #340 (232-7753; open M-F 9am-5pm; free). The **University Museums,** on University Ave. at Ole Miss, contain four main collections ranging from southern folk art to 19th-century scientific instruments (232-

**FINER THAN MOONSHINE** While France has its Burgundy and California its Napa Valley, the South can boast its own **Old South Winery,** located off D'evereux Dr. Wines here are pressed from muscadines—a type of grape grown only in the southeastern region of the U.S.—which lend both its red and white wines a fruity flavor. The sufficiently aged red complements a plate of steaming grits well. What's the winery's most popular offering? Why, it's a delightful, sweet rosé named **Miss Scarlett.** *(65 S. Concord Ave. 445-9924. Open M-Sa 10am-5pm, Su 1-5pm. Free.)*

7073; open Tu-Sa 10am-4:30pm, Su 1pm-4pm; free). The **Double Decker Arts Festival,** on the square during the last weekend in Apr., hosts tunes on two stages.

It's hip to be at **Square Books,** 160 Courthouse Sq., where a fine collection of southern works may be enjoyed on a balcony overlooking the downtown area. The bookstore's annex, **Off-Square Books** hosts Thacker Mountain Radio, a bluegrass music and reading show for all ages. (236-2262. Both open M-Th 9am-9pm, F-Sa 9am-10pm, Su 10am-6pm.) Downtown, **Smitty's Café,** 208 S. Lamar, serves yummy breakfasts (234-9111, open M-Sa 7am-4pm, Su 8am-4pm). The **Bottletree Bakery,** 923 Van Buren Ave., is young and delicious—with Italian sodas and fresh pastries (236-5000; open Tu-F 7am-4pm, Sa 9am-4pm, Su 9am-2pm).

Visitors can spend the night in southern comfort at the **Oliver-Britt House Inn,** 512 Van Buren Ave., an unpretentious B&B (234-8043; singles and doubles $45-55, $10 surcharge F-Sa). **Ole Miss Motel,** 1517 E. University Ave., rebels with remodeled rooms, cable TVs, free local calls, and a heart on every door (234-2424; singles from $32; doubles from $42). **Wall Doxy State Park,** 23mi. north of town on Rt. 7, is a scenic spot with an expansive lake and cheap camping. (252-4231. Primitive sites $6-8, with water and electricity $11. Cabins $46 per night, 3 night min. Entrance fee $2 per car, 50¢ for pedestrians or bicyclists.) At night, live music rolls from **Proud Larry's,** 211 S. Lamar (236-0050), which keeps on burnin' all year (cover $4-5; M-W, Su music from 9pm-midnight, F-Sa 9pm-1am).

Oxford is 30mi. east of I-55 on Rt. 6 (take exit 243), 55mi. south of Memphis, and 140mi. north of Jackson. **Oxford Tourism Info Center,** 111 Courthouse Sq., offers free audio walking tours. (758-9177. Open M-F 9am-5pm, Sa 10am-4pm, Su 1pm-4pm.) **Greyhound,** 2612B Jackson Ave. W. (234-0094), runs to Memphis (1½hr., $21); Nashville (9hr., $56); and Jackson (10hr., $50). **Post Office,** 911 Jackson Ave. E (234-5615; open M-F 9am-5pm, Sa 9:30am-12:30pm). **ZIP code:** 38655. **Area code:** 662.

# LOUISIANA

After exploring the Mississippi River valley in 1682, Frenchman René-Robert Cavalier proclaimed the land "Louisiane," in honor of Louis XIV. The name endured three centuries, though French ownership of the vast region did not. The territory was tossed between France, England, and Spain before Thomas Jefferson and the United States snagged it in the Louisiana Purchase of 1803. Nine years later, a smaller, redefined Louisiana was admitted to the Union. Each successive government lured a new mix of settlers to the bayous: Spaniards from the Canary Islands, French Acadians from Nova Scotia, Americans from the East, and free blacks from the West Indies. Louisiana's multi-national history, Creole culture, and Napoleonic legal system are unlike anything found in the 49 other states. While beautiful to visit, the swamps of Louisiana are a tough place to make a living, and its residents are among the poorest in the nation.

## ⌨ PRACTICAL INFORMATION

**Capital:** Baton Rouge.

**Visitor Info: Office of Tourism,** P.O. Box 94291, Baton Rouge 70804-9291 (504-342-8119 or 800-261-9144; www.louisianatravel.com). Open M-F 8am-4:30pm. **Office of State Parks,** P.O. Box 44426, Baton Rouge 70804-4426 (504-342-8111). Open M-F 9am-5pm.

**Postal Abbreviation:** LA. **Sales Tax:** 8%.

# NEW ORLEANS

Originally explored by the French, La Nouvelle Orleans was secretly ceded to the Spanish in 1762, though the citizens didn't find out until 1766. Spain returned the city to France just in time for the United States to grab it in the Louisiana Purchase of 1803. Centuries of cultural mingling have resulted in a fabulous *mélange* of Spanish courtyards, Victorian verandas, Cajun jambalaya, Creole gumbo, and French *beignets*. The local accent is found nowhere else; even the local music is an amalgam of sounds; New Orleans' internationally renowned jazz fuses African rhythms and modern brass.

In N'awlins, it's accepted to let the maintenance slip a bit—residents proudly call their home the "Big Easy," reflecting a joyous, carefree attitude. The only thing that stifles this vivacity is the heavy, humid air that slows folks to a near standstill during the summer. But when the day's heat finally retreats into the night, the city begins to jump, drinking and dancing into the early morning. Come late Feb., there's no escaping the month-long celebration of Mardi Gras, the climax of the city's already festive mood.

## ✦ ORIENTATION

Although it's fairly compact, New Orleans, can be confusing. The city's main streets follow the curve of the **Mississippi River**, hence its nickname "the Crescent City." Directions from locals reflect watery influences—lakeside means north, referring to **Lake Ponchartrain**, and riverside means south. Uptown lies west, up river; downtown lies down river. The city is concentrated on the east bank of the Mississippi. However, **The East** (locally dubbed) refers only to the easternmost part of the city. Less populated regions of the city, like Algiers, are on **The West Bank,** across the river. Many streets run one-way or are separated with broad medians.

Tourists flock to the small **French Quarter (Vieux Carré),** bounded by the Mississippi River, **Canal St., Rampart St.,** and **Esplanade Ave.** Streets in the Quarter follow a grid pattern, making foot travel easy. The residential **Garden District** (uptown, bordered by **St. Charles Ave.** to the north and **Magazine St.** to the south) is distinguished by its elegant homes and well-cultivated gardens. The scenic **St. Charles Streetcar route** (fare $1), easily picked up at Canal St. and Carondelet St., passes through parts of the **Central Business District** ("CBD" or downtown), the Garden District via St. Charles Ave., and **S. Carollton Ave.**

**Parking** in New Orleans is easier than driving in it. To park near the French Quarter, head for the residential area around **Marigny St.** and **Royal St.,** where many streets have no meters and no restrictions. Avoid parking in this area at night; streets are dimly lit and deserted. After sunset, it is best to take a cab.

## 🛈 PRACTICAL INFORMATION

**Airport: Moisant International** (464-0831), 15mi. west of the city. Cab fare to the Quarter is set at $21 for 1-2 people; $8 per person for 3 or more. The **Louisiana Transit Authority** (737-9611; office open M-F 8am-4pm) runs buses from the airport down Tulane Ave. to Elk St. (downtown), M-Sa 5:30am-5:40pm, every 15min. After 5:40pm, buses go to Tulane Ave. and Carollton Ave. (mid-city) until 11:30pm. Fare $1.50, exact change needed. Pick-up on the upper level, near the exit ramp.

**Trains: Amtrak,** 1001 Loyola Ave. (528-1610), in the Union Passenger Terminal, a 10min. walk to Canal St. via Elk. To: Houston (8hr., 3 per week, $47); Jackson (4hr., 7 per week, $16); and Atlanta (12hr., 7 per week, $39). Station open 24hr.; ticket office open Tu, Th, and Su 5:45am-11pm; M, W, and F-Sa 5:45am-8:30pm.

**Buses: Greyhound,** 1001 Loyola Ave. (524-7571), in the Union Passenger Terminal. To Austin (12hr., 5 per day, $89) and Baton Rouge (2hr., 9 per day, $9). Open 24hr.

**Public Transit: Regional Transit Authority (RTA),** 2817 Canal St. (248-3900). Most buses pass Canal St., at the edge of the French Quarter. Major buses and streetcars run 24hr.

THE SOUTH

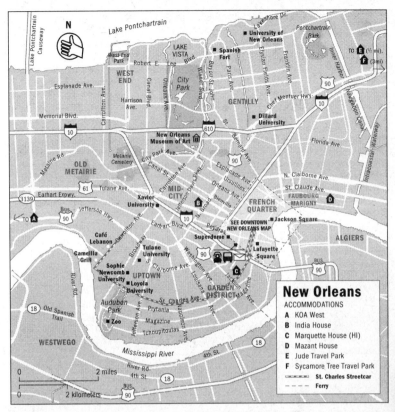

**New Orleans**

**ACCOMMODATIONS**

A KOA West
B India House
C Marquette House (HI)
D Mazant House
E Jude Travel Park
F Sycamore Tree Travel Park

▬▬▬▬▬ St. Charles Streetcar
- - - - - Ferry

**SAFETY IN NEW ORLEANS.** New Orleans plays down its high murder and crime rates. The tenement areas directly north of the French Quarter and directly northwest of Lee Circle pose particular threats to personal safety. At night, even quaint-looking side streets in the Quarter can be dangerous—stick to busy, well-lit roads and never walk alone after dark. Make some attempt to downplay the tourist image (e.g. don't wear a t-shirt that has the words "New Orleans" anywhere on it), and have a good idea of where you want to go. Many streets are poorly labeled, and one wrong turn can make a dangerous difference. *Avoid all parks, cemeteries, and housing projects at night.*

$1, seniors and disabled passengers 40¢; transfers 10¢. 1-day pass $4, 3-day pass $8; passes sold at major hotels in the Canal St. area. Office has bus schedules and transit info; open M-F 8am-5pm.

**Taxis: Checker Yellow Cabs,** 943-2411. **United Cabs,** 522-9771.

**Car Rental: Gill & Jim's Rent-A-Car,** 4401 N. Galvez St. (948-9813). $26.50 per day with 100 free mi. Must be 25+. $250 cash deposit. Open M-F 9am-5pm, Sa 9am-noon.

**Bike Rental: French Quarter Bicycles,** 522 Dumaine St. (529-3136), between Decatur and Chartres. $4.50 per hr., $20 per 24hr., $84 per week (includes lock, helmet, and map). Must have credit card or $200 cash deposit. Open daily 10am-6pm.

**Visitor Info:** The **New Orleans Welcome Center,** 529 St. Ann St. (566-5031; www.neworleanscvb.com), by Jackson Sq. in the French Quarter. Open daily 9am-5pm.

**Hotlines: Cope Line,** 523-2673, for crises. **Rape Hotline,** 483-8888. Both 24hr.

**Hospital: Charity Hospital,** 1532 Tulane Ave. (568-2311). 24hr. emergency room.

**Internet Access: New Orleans Public Library,** 219 Loyola Ave. (529-7323), 1½ blocks from Canal St. (open M-Th 11am-6pm, Sa 11am-5pm), and the **Contemporary Arts Center** (see p. 405) both offer free access.

**Post Office:** 701 Loyola Ave. (589-1111 or 589-1112), near the bus station. Open M-F 7am-11pm, Sa 7am-8pm, Su noon-5pm. **ZIP code:** 70113. **Area code:** 504.

# ▟ ACCOMMODATIONS

Finding inexpensive, yet decent, rooms in the **French Quarter** can be as difficult as finding sobriety during Mardi Gras. Luckily, other parts of the city compensate for the absence of cheap lodging downtown. Several **hostels** pepper the area and cater to the young and almost penniless, as do B&Bs near the **Garden District.**

Accommodations for Mardi Gras and the Jazz Festival get booked up to a year in advance. During peak times, proprietors will rent out any extra space—be sure you know what you're paying for. Rates tend to sink in June and early Dec., when accommodations become desperate for business; negotiation can pay off.

■ **India House,** 124 S. Lopez St. (821-1904), at Canal St. What this bohemian haunt lacks in tidiness it compensates for in character. Young backpackers come here to celebrate freedom and camaraderie. Kitchen, pool, and separate alligator pond out back. 1pm check-out designed for those with "morning grogginess." Dorms $12, $14-17 in summer and peak times. Free linen. Key deposit $5. No lockout or curfew.

■ **Marquette House New Orleans International Hostel (HI-AYH),** 2253 Carondelet St. (523-3014). The cleanest and classiest hosteling experience in New Orleans. Courtyards link several separate buildings with 176 beds, A/C, kitchens, and study rooms. Exceptionally quiet. $15.50, nonmembers $18.50. Private rooms with queen-sized bed and pull-out sofa $45/$51. Linen $2.50. Key deposit $5. No lockout or curfew. No alcohol permitted. Smoking in the courtyard only.

**St. Charles Guest House,** 1748 Prytania St. (523-6556). In a serene neighborhood near the Garden District and St. Charles Streetcar. A big 3-building complex with 38 rooms, 8 with shared baths. Lovely pool and sunbathing deck. No-frills backpacker's singles $15-25. Rooms with 1 queen-sized bed or 2 twins $45-65. Breakfast included.

**Longpre House,** 1726 Prytania St. (581-4540), in a 145-year-old house 1 block off St. Charles, shows its age a bit. A 25min. walk from the Quarter. Dorms $12, in peak times $16. Singles and doubles with shared bath $35, with private bath $40. Free coffee and linen. Dorm check-in 8am-10pm, 11am for private rooms. No curfew.

**Prytania Inn,** 1415 Prytania St. (566-1515). Includes 4 restored 19th-century homes about 5 blocks apart; stay in St. Vincent's if you can afford it. Reasonable prices, multilingual staff (German, French, and Thai), and a homey atmosphere. Singles $29-51; doubles $39-69. Full southern breakfast $5.

**Mazant House,** 906 Mazant St. (944-2662). Tastefully furnished rooms with home-style accommodations. Living room, well-equipped kitchen, and only 2 blocks from the Desire St. bus. *However, the neighborhood warrants caution.* Singles $22, with bath $39; doubles $29/$51; $5 per extra cot. Apartment accommodations and rates available for extended stays.

**Hotel LaSalle,** 1113 Canal St. (523-5831 or 800-521-9450), 3 blocks from Bourbon St., downtown. Convenient, not luxurious. Rooms are well maintained. Singles $29, with bath $58; doubles $39/$70. Coffee included. Lobby staffed 24hr.

**St. Bernard State Park,** (682-2101) 18mi. southeast of New Orleans in Poydras; exit I-10 on LA 47 S (exit 246A), turn left onto Rt. 46 for 7mi., then right on Rt. 39 for 1mi. 51 sites with water and electricity. $12. Office open daily 7am-8pm. Winter 8am-7pm.

**Jude Travel Park and Guest House,** 7400 Chef Menteur Hwy./U.S. 90 (241-0632 or 800-523-2196), just east of the eastern junction of I-10 and U.S. 90. Bus #98 "Broad" drives past the front gate to #55 "Elysian Fields," which heads downtown. Showers, laundry, 24hr. security. 44 tent/RV sites $17 (all with water, sewage, and cable) rates rise at peak times.

**Downtown New Orleans**

**Sycamore Tree Travel Park,** 10910 Chef Menteur Hwy./U.S. 90 (244-6611), 3mi. east of the eastern junction of I-10 and U.S. 90. Same RTA service as Jude Travel Park. Pool, showers, and laundry facilities. Tent sites $12, with full RV hookup $16.

# SHO' NUFF, GOOD STUFF

In addition to the international options which entice hungry visitors, the city offers a long list of regional specialties which have evolved from the mixing of Acadian, Spanish, Italian, African, French, and Native American ethnic cuisines. **Jambalaya** (a Cajun jumble of rice, shrimp, oysters, sausage, and ham or chicken mixed with spices) and **gumbo** (beef stew over rice) grace practically every menu in New Orleans. A Southern breakfast of grits, eggs, bacon, and buttermilk biscuits satisfies even the most ardent eaters. **Creole** cuisine (a mixture of Spanish, French, and Caribbean), is famous for red beans and rice, **po' boys** (French bread sandwiches filled with sliced meat or seafood and vegetables; "dressed" means with mayo, lettuce, tomatoes, pickles, etc.), and shrimp or crawfish *étouffé*. The daring try the oyster bar at **Ralph & Kacoos Seafood Restaurant,** 519 Toulouse St., between Decatur and Chartres St. Order the crawfish ($3 per lb. Dec.-Jun.), and eat it the way the locals do: tear off the head and suck out the tasty juices (522-5226). Get some of the best Creole pralines (Prah-leens, not pray-leens; $1.25) at **Laura's Candies,** 600 Conti St. (525-3880; open daily 9am-7pm). The **French Market,** between Decatur and N. Peters St., on the east side of the French Quarter, sells pricey fresh vegetables.

If the eats in the Quarter prove too trendy, touristy, or tough on the budget, **Magazine St.'s,** cafes, antique stores, and book fairs spill onto the sidewalk. Uptown, wander around **Tulane University** for late-night grub and collegiate character.

## FRENCH QUARTER

■ **Café du Monde,** 800 Decatur St. (525-4544), near the French Market. The consummate people-watching paradise since 1862 really only does 2 things—scrumptious *café au lait* ($1.10) and hot *beignets* ($1.10). Open 24hr. To take home some of that chicory coffee, cross the street to the Café du Monde Gift Shop, 813 Decatur St. (581-2914 or 800-772-2927). 15 oz. of the grind $4.60. Open daily 9:30am-6pm.

**Johnny's Po' boys,** 511 St. Louis St. (524-8129). The po' boy is the right choice at this French Quarter institution, which offers 40 varieties of the famous sandwich ($3.75-6.50), with a combo plate available for the indecisive. Decent Creole fare (jambalaya $4.25, gumbo $6.25) is also on the menu. Open M-F 8am-4:30pm, Sa-Su 9am-4pm.

**Gumbo Shop,** 630 St. Peters St. (525-1486). Sit under a broad-leafed palm and savor a bowl of seafood okra or chicken andouille gumbo ($6.50), po' boys $5-8, entrees from $10. Expect a line. Recipes available. Open daily 11am-11pm.

**Sabrina and Gabrielle's Secret Garden,** 538 St. Philip St. (524-2041). A romantic rendez-vous for the dinnertime crowd. A pleasant courtyard and gracious service add to the mood. Cajun and Creole specials include soup and salad ($7-15). Open Su-Th 11am-10pm, F-Sa 11am-11pm.

**Central Grocery,** 923 Decatur St. (523-1620), between Dumaine and St. Philip St. Try an authentic muffuletta (deli meats, cheeses, and olive salad on Italian bread) at the place that invented them. A half ($4.50) serves 1; whole ($8). Open M-Sa 8am-5:30pm, Su 9am-5:30pm.

**Acme Oyster House,** 724 Iberville St. (522-5973). Patrons slurp fresh oysters shucked before their eyes at the bar (6 for $3.50, 12 for $6), or sit at the red checkered tables for a good ol' po' boy ($5-7). Open M-Sa 11am-10pm, Su noon-7pm.

**Croissant d'Or,** 617 Ursulines St. (524-4663). Fair-priced French pastries, sandwiches, and quiches. *Carré Mocca* $1.30, chocolate mousse $1.50. Open daily 7am-5pm.

**Mama Rosa's,** 616 N. Rampart (523-5546). Locals adore this Italian ristorante. Rosa's pizza was once rated among the 9 best in the country by *People Magazine*. 14 in. cheese pie $9. Open daily 11am-9pm.

**Royal Blend,** 621 Royal St. (523-2716). Quiet garden setting offers escape from hustle of Royal St. Over 20 hot and iced coffees available, as well as a mighty fine selection of teas—you can even brew your own. Light meals (croissant sandwiches, quiches) served daily; pastries $1-2. Open M-Th 6:30am-8pm, F-Sa 7am-midnight, Su 7am-6pm.

**Tricou House,** 711 Bourbon St. (525-8379). "Bourbon St.'s best deal"—red beans 'n' rice for $3.25—in the historic courtyard, circa 1832. All-you-can-eat deals include BBQ ribs on W and Su ($10), catfish Th-F ($7-11), and shrimp daily ($11-13). The balcony is a prime bead bartering venue. Open Su-Th 11am-midnight, F-Sa 11am-2am.

**Clover Grill,** 900 Bourbon St. (598-1010). The waiters behind the counter love to enter-tain and compliment patrons—for extra tips, of course. The Clover has been open 24hr. since 1950, serving greasy and delicious mushroom bacon cheeseburgers ($5.29) grilled under an American-made hubcap.

**Country Flame,** 620 Iberville St. (522-1138). No, it's not a country-western bar; it's a Mex-ican restaurant with very low prices (2 tacos $2.70), where you can watch your order get cooked. Open M-Th 11am-10pm, F-Sa 11am-1am, Su 11am-11pm.

## OUTSIDE THE QUARTER

■ **Camellia Grill,** 626 S. Carrollton Ave. (866-9573). Take the St. Charles Streetcar away from the Quarter to Tulane area. Classic, counter-service diner where cooks don't mind telling the whole restaurant about their marital problems. Big drippin' plates, crowds (especially weekend mornings), and excellent service. Chef's special omelette ($7), pecan pie ($2.35). Open M-Th 9am-1am, F 9am-3am, Sa 8am-3am, Su 8am-1am.

■ **Franky and Johnny's,** 321 Arabella (899-9146), southwest of downtown towards Tulane off Tchoupitoulas St. Everybody at this joyous, noisy local hangout orders the succulent boiled crawfish (2 lbs. $5, seasonal), but the onion rings are good too ($3.25). Open daily 11am until late.

**Taqueria Corona,** 5932 Magazine St. (897-3974), between State and Nashville St. Some of the best Mexican food around. Loud but cozy atmosphere. Deliciously hot burritos $3-7 and chicken ($2.15) and shrimp ($2.60) tacos. Open daily 11:30am-2pm and 5-9:30pm. Off season call for hrs.

**Tee Eva's,** 4430 Magazine St. (899-8350). Creole woman sells bayou cooking out of her kitchen window. Peerless pies, creole pralines, and 9 oz. snow balls for 75¢. Crawfish pie only $3; sweet potato, pecan pie slices $1.35. Large 9 in. pies $8-16, by order only. Soul food lunches change daily ($3-5). Open daily 11am-8pm.

**Joey K's Restaurant,** 3001 Magazine St. (891-0997), at 7th St. Friendly neighborhood eatery, especially for the mid-day meal—lunch specials start at $6 and feature "Creole pot" cooking, stuffed eggplant, and fried seafood. Sandwiches $5 and beer $2. Open M-F 11am-10pm, Sa 8am-10pm.

**Café Atchafalaya,** 901 Louisiana Ave. (891-5271), at Laurel St. Take the #11 bus "Magazine St." This cozy cottage serves mouth-watering, traditional Southern cuisine. Simple dishes like red beans and rice with salad ($6.50) or delicacies like Shrimp Orleans ($13.50) are expensive but exquisite. Cobblers galore. Laid-back service. Lunch Tu-F 11:30am-2pm, Sa-Su 8:30am-2pm; dinner Tu-Th 5:30-9pm, F-Sa 5:30-10pm.

**Dunbar's Creole Cooking,** 4927 Freret St. (899-0734), at Robert St. Soul-food-style meals, at super-low prices (breakfast $2, dinner $5-6). Gorge yourself on cabbage and candied yams or the all-you-can-eat red beans and chicken (both $5). Free iced tea with student ID. *Steer clear of this area at night.* Open M-Sa 7am-9pm.

**The Praline Connection,** 542 Frenchman St. (943-3943). Finger-lickin' good soul food: fried chicken and seafood, stuffed crab, or *étouffées*. Entrees from $8. Open Su-Th 11am-10:30pm, F-Sa 11am-midnight.

**Mother's Restaurant,** 401 Poydras St. (523-9656), downtown at Tchoupitoulas St., 4 blocks southwest of Bourbon St. Serving up po' boys ($6-9) and some of the best jambalaya in town ($6.75) to locals for almost half a century. Delicious crawfish or shrimp *étouffé* omelette ($9.50). Open M-Sa 5am-10pm, Su 7am-10pm.

**The Trolley Stop Café,** 1923 St. Charles Ave. (523-0096). Breakfast served 24hr. and its busy all the time, partly thanks to the police who convene here. Most meals under $5.

**Bennachin Restaurant,** 133 N. Carrollton Ave. (486-1313), off Canal St. Vegetarian, non-vegetarian, spicy, non-spicy—they'll make it the way you like it. Sway to African music as you peruse the selection of low-priced African dishes (specials around $5 before 4pm). Entrees $7-10. Spinach, trout, and plantains are house favorites, as is *gingero,* a very potent ginger drink ($1.50). Open M-Th 11am-9pm, F 11am-10pm, Sa 5-10pm.

# ◉ SIGHTS

## FRENCH QUARTER

Allow at *least* a full day in the Quarter. The oldest section of the city is famous for its ornate wrought-iron balconies; French, Spanish, and uniquely New Orleans architecture; and a raucous atmosphere. Known as the **Vieux Carré** (view-ca-RAY), or Old Sq., the historic district of New Orleans offers dusty used book and record stores, museums, and tourist traps. **Bourbon St.** is packed with touristy bars, strip clubs, and clowns. **Decatur St.** has more mellow coffee shops and bars.

Once a streetcar named "Desire" rolled down **Royal St.,** now one of the French Quarter's most aesthetically pleasing avenues. Two devastating fires, in 1788 and 1794, forced the neighborhood to rebuild during the era of Spanish domination in the city, and the renovations took on the flavor of Spanish colonial architecture. Most notable are the intricate iron-lace balconies, which are either hand-wrought or cast in molds; at Royal and St. Peters St. is what may be the most photographed building in the French Quarter: **LaBranche House,** with balconies of wrought-iron oak leaves and acorns spanning three tiers. **A Gallery for Fine Photography,** lends perspective with contemporary and vintage works. Original prints from Henri Cartier-Bresson and Diane Arbus, as well as jazz and rock n' roll photos. *(322 Royal St. 568-1313. Open M-Sa 10am-6pm, Su 11am-6pm.)*

**BEFORE YOU DIE, READ THIS:** Being dead in New Orleans has always been a problem. Because the city lies 4 to 6 ft. below sea level, a 6 ft. hole in the earth fills up with 5 ft. of water. At one time coffins literally floated in the graves, while cemetery workers pushed them down with long wooden poles. One early solution was to bore holes in the coffins, allowing them to sink. Unfortunately, the sight of a drowning coffin coupled with the awful gargling sound of its immersion proved too much for the squeamish families of the departed. Burial soon became passé, and stiffs were laid to rest in beautiful raised stone tombs. Miles and miles of creepy, cool marble tombs now fill the city's graveyards and ghost stories.

During the day, most of the activity in the French Quarter centers around **Jackson Sq.,** a park dedicated to General Andrew Jackson, victor of the Battle of New Orleans. While the square swarms with artists, mimes, musicians, psychics, magicians, and con artists, **St. Louis Cathedral** presides over the hubbub. (Tours every 15-20min. M-Sa 9am-4:50pm. Free.) Behind the cathedral lies **St. Anthony's Garden,** named in memory of Father Antonio de Sedella, a priest who was locally renowned for his dedication to the poor. **Pirate's Alley** and **Père Antoine's Alley** border the garden. Legend has it that the former was the site of covert meetings between pirate Jean Lafitte and Andrew Jackson, as they conspired to plan the Battle of New Orleans.

The historic **French Market** takes up several city blocks just east of Jackson Sq., toward the water, along N. Peters St. (522-2621. Open daily 9am-8pm.) The market begins at the famous **Café du Monde** (see p. 402). Vendors sell everything from watermelons to earrings. For a map of the whole strip, stop at the **visitors center** under Washington Artillery Park (596-3424; open daily 8:30am-5pm). Since 1791, visitors have been able to purchase fresh fruits, vegetables, herbs, and spices at the **Farmers Market,** which never closes. Scavengers should head for the **Flea Market,** where one gathers what another one spills. Tables are piled high with t-shirts, handmade furniture, and antique glasses; over it all, the scent of fish floats through the air. (Open 8am-sunset.)

The **Jean Lafitte National Historical Park and Preserve,** headquartered in the back section of the French Market at Dumaine and St. Phillip St., conducts free 1½hr. walking tours through the Quarter which emphasize New Orleans' rich history. (9419 Decatur St. 589-2636. Tours daily 10:30am. Office open daily 9am-5pm.)

It's always a great night to stroll the **Moon Walk,** a promenade stretching alongside the "Mighty" Mississippi. The walk offers a fantastic riverside view and chances for Michael Jackson humor. *Don't go alone at night.* The **New Orleans Historic Voodoo Museum** brings curious visitors into local burial grounds. (724 Dumaine St. 523-7685. Museum open daily 10am-8pm. $6, college students and seniors $5, high school students $4, grade school students $3, under 5 free. Cemetery and ghost tours $16-20; call for times.)

At the southwest corner of the Quarter, by the World Trade Center, the **Aquarium of the Americas** houses an amazing collection of sea life and birds. Among the 500 species are black-footed penguins, endangered sea turtles, and extremely rare white alligators. (1 Canal St. 565-3033. Open daily 9:30am-6pm; in summer F-Sa until 7pm. $11.25, seniors $8.75, ages 2-12 $5.) The steamboat **Natchez** breezes down the Mississippi on 2hr. cruises, featuring live jazz and narration on riverside sights. A trip is normally an outrageous $14.75, so ask about 2 for 1 coupons at the Visitor Center. (586-8777 or 800-233-2628. Departs 11:30am, 2:30pm, from Jax Brewery.)

## OUTSIDE THE QUARTER

Take in the city from the revolving bar on the 33rd fl. of the **World Trade Center.** (2 Canal St.) Looking southwest, the **Riverwalk,** a multi-million dollar conglomeration of overpriced shops overlooking the port, stretches along the Mississippi. (Open M-Sa 10am-9pm, Su 11am-7pm.) For an up-close view of the Mississippi River and a bit of African-American history, take the free **Canal St. Ferry** to Algiers Point. The Algiers of old housed many of New Orleans's African-Americans and is a safe and beautiful neighborhood to explore by foot. At night, the ferry's outdoor observation deck affords a panoramic view of the city's sights. *(Departs daily 5:45am-midnight, every ½hr. from the end of Canal St. Cars $1 round-trip.)*

Relatively new to the downtown area, the **Warehouse Arts District,** near the intersection of St. Charles and Julia St., contains several revitalized warehouse buildings that house contemporary art galleries. Exhibits range from Southern folk art to experimental sculpture. Individual galleries distribute maps of the area. In an old brick building with a modern glass and chrome facade, the **Contemporary Arts Center** mounts exhibits ranging from puzzling to positively cryptic. *(900 Camp St. 528-3805. Open Tu-Su 11am-5pm, Su 11am-5pm. Exhibits $3, students and seniors $2, under 12 free; Th free.)* In the rear studio of the **New Orleans School of Glassworks and Printmaking Studio,** observe as students and instructors transform blobs of molten glass into vases and sculptures. *(727 Magazine St. 529-7277. Open in summer M-F 11am-5pm; in winter M-Sa 11am-5pm. Free.)* Founded by renowned historian Stephen Ambrose and opening June 6, 2000, the **D-Day Museum** will provide an overview of the economic, political, and military events which precipitated the allied invasion of Normandy. *(923 Magazine St. 527-6012.)* A few blocks farther down St. Charles St. stands a bronze Confederate General Robert E. Lee, in **Lee Circle.** The general continues to stare down the Yankees; he faces due North. *Lee Circle and the surrounding neighborhood should not be visited after dark.*

Much of the Crescent City's fame derives from the **Vieux Carré,** but areas uptown have their fair share of beauty and action. The **St. Charles Streetcar** still runs west of the French Quarter, passing some of the city's finest buildings, including the 19th-century homes along **St. Charles Ave.** ($1). *Gone With the Wind*-o-philes will recognize the whitewashed bricks and elegant doorway of the house on the far right corner of Arabella St.—it's a replica of Tara. Frankly, my dear, it's not open to the public. For more views of fancy living, disembark the streetcar in the **Garden District,** an opulent neighborhood around Jackson and Louisiana Ave. French, Italian, Spanish, and American architectural legacies create an extraordinary combination of structures, colors, ironwork, and gardens. Some houses are raised above the ground for protection from the swamp on which New Orleans stands.

The St. Charles Streetcar eventually makes its way to **Audubon Park,** across from **Tulane University.** Designed by Frederick Law Olmsted, Audubon contains lagoons, statues, stables, and the award-winning **Audubon Zoo,** where white alligators swim in a re-created Louisiana swamp. A free museum shuttle glides from the park entrance (streetcar stop #36) to the zoo every 15min. *(861-2537. Zoo open daily 9:30am-5pm; in summer Sa-Su until 6pm. $8.75, seniors $4.75, ages 2-12 $4.50. Buy your tickets at least 1hr. before closing.)*

One of the most unique sights in the New Orleans area, the coastal wetlands along Lake Salvador make up a segment of the **Jean Lafitte National Historical Park** called the **Barataria Preserve,** off the W. Bank Expwy. across the Mississippi River and down Barataria Blvd. (Rt. 45). The only park-sponsored foot tour through the swamp leaves daily at 2pm. *(7400 Rt. 45. 589-2330. Free.)* Countless commercial boat tours operate around the park; **Cypress Swamp Tours** will pick you up from your hotel for free. *(561-8244. 2hr. tours at 9:30, 11:30am, 1:30, and 3:30pm. Call for reservations. $20 , $12 per child.)*

## MUSEUMS

**Louisiana State Museum,** P.O. Box 2448 (800-568-6968), oversees 5 separate museums in the Quarter: the **Old U.S. Mint,** 400 Esplanade; **Cabildo,** 701 Chartres St.; **Presbytère,** 751 Chartres St.; **1850 House,** 523 St. Ann St.; and **Mdme. John's Legacy,** 632 Dumaine St. All 5 contain artifacts, papers, and other changing exhibits on the history of Louisiana and New Orleans. The Old U.S. Mint is particularly interesting, focusing not on currency or fresh breath, but on the history of jazz and the lives of greats like Louis "Satchmo" Armstrong. All open Tu-Su 9am-5pm. Single museum $4, seniors $3; pass to all 5 $10/$7.50; under 13 free.

**New Orleans Museum of Art (NOMA)** (488-2631), in City Park. Take the Esplanade bus from Canal and Rampart St. This magnificent museum houses art from North and South

THE SOUTH

America, a small collection of local decorative arts, opulent works by the jeweler Fabergé, and a strong collection of French paintings. Special exhibits in 2000 include John Singer Sargent portraits, Mar. 3-Apr. 18. Free tours available. Open Tu-Su 10am-5pm. $6, seniors and ages 3-17 $5.

**Historic New Orleans Collection,** 533 Royal St. (523-4662). Located in the aristocratic 18th-century Merieult House, this impressive cultural research center will teach you everything you wanted to know about Louisiana's history. The History Tour explores New Orleans past, while the Williams Residence Tour showcases the eclectic home furnishings of the collection's founders. Gallery open Tu-Sa 10am-4:30pm; free. Tours 10, 11am, 2, and 3pm; $4.

**Musée Conti Wax Museum,** 917 Conti St. (525-2605). Figures from 300 years of Louisiana lore. Perennial favorites include a voodoo display, a haunted dungeon, and a mock-up of Madame Lalaurie's torture attic. Open M-Sa 10am-5:30pm, Su noon-5:30pm. $6.25, under 17 $4.75, seniors $5.50.

**Confederate Museum,** 929 Camp St. (523-4522), in a brownstone building west of Lee Circle. The state's oldest museum, with a wide collection of Civil War records and artifacts. Open M-Sa 10am-4pm. $5, students and seniors $4, under 12 $2.

**New Orleans Pharmacy Museum,** 514 Chartres St. (565-8027), in the Quarter. This apothecary shop was built by America's first licensed pharmacist in 1823. On display are 19th-century "miracle drugs," voodoo powders, and the still-fertile botanical garden, where medicinal herbs are grown. Open Tu-Su 10am-5pm. $2, students and seniors $1, under 12 free (includes 30min. tour).

**Louisiana Children's Museum,** 420 Julia St. (523-1357). This place invites kids to play and learn, as they star in their own news shows, run their own cafe, or shop in a re-created mini-mart. Kids under 16 must be accompanied by an adult. Open M-Sa 9:30am-4:30pm, Su noon-4:30pm; Sept.-May closed M. $5.

**Louisiana Nature and Science Center,** (246-5672) Joe Brown Memorial Park, off Read Blvd. Trail walks, exhibits, planetarium and laser shows, and 86 acres of natural wildlife preserve. From Basin St., take bus #64 "Lake Forrest Express" ($1.25) to reach this wonderful escape from the bedlam of the French Quarter. Open Tu-F 9am-5pm, Sa 10am-5pm, Su noon-5pm. $4.75, seniors $3.75, ages 4-13 $2.50.

## HISTORIC HOMES AND PLANTATIONS

Called the "Great Showplace of New Orleans," **Longue Vue House and Gardens,** off Metairie Rd., epitomizes the grand Southern estate with its lavish furnishings, opulent decor, and breathtaking sculpted gardens, dating back to the 1930s. On the way, pause for a peek at the 85 ft. tall monument among the raised tombs in the **Metairie Cemetery.** *(Longue Vue House: 7 Bamboo Rd. 488-5488. Open M-Sa 10am-4:30pm, Su 1-5pm. $7, students $3, seniors $6, under 5 free. Gardens alone $3, students $1. Tours available in English, French, Spanish, Italian, and Japanese.)* **River Rd.** curves along the Mississippi river across from downtown New Orleans, accessing several plantations preserved from the 19th century; copies of *Great River Road Plantation Parade: A River of Riches,* available at the New Orleans or Baton Rouge visitors centers, contain a good map and descriptions of the houses. Pick carefully, since a tour of all the privately owned plantations would be quite expensive. Those below are listed in order from New Orleans to Baton Rouge.

**Hermann-Grima Historic House,** 820 St. Louis St. (525-5661). Built in 1831, the house exemplifies French style, replete with a large central hall, guillotine windows, a fan-lit entrance, and the original parterre beds. On Th, Oct.-May, trained volunteers demonstrate period cooking in an 1830s Creole kitchen. Tours on the ½hr. Open M-Sa 10am-4pm. $6, students and seniors $5, ages 8-18 $4. Last tour 3:30pm.

**Gallier House Museum,** 1118-1132 Royal St. (525-5661). The elegantly restored residence of James Gallier, Jr., the city's most famous architect, resuscitates the taste and lifestyle of the rich in the 1860s. Tours every 30min.; last tour 4pm. Open M-Sa 10am-4pm. $6, students and seniors $5, ages 8-18 $4, under 8 free.

**San Francisco Plantation House** (535-2341), Rt. 44, 2mi. northwest of Reserve, 42mi. from New Orleans on the east bank of the Mississippi. Beautifully maintained plantation from 1856. In the Creole style, with a busy blue, peach, and green exterior. Tours daily Mar.-Oct. 10am-4:30pm; Nov.-Feb. 10am-4pm. $7, ages 13-17 $4, ages 6-12 $3.

**Oak Alley** 3645 Hwy. 18 (800-442-5539), between St. James and Vacherie St. Named for the magnificent drive of 28 evenly spaced oaks, all nearly 300 years old. The oaks correspond with 28 columns surrounding the Greek Revival house. The Greeks wouldn't have approved, though; the mansion is bright pink. Open daily 9am-5:30pm; tours every 30min. $8, ages 13-18 $5, ages 6-12 $3.

**Houmas House,** 40136 Rt. 942 (473-7841 or 522-2262), in Burnside just over halfway to Baton Rouge. Setting for the movie *Hush, Hush, Sweet Charlotte,* starring Bette Davis and Olivia DeHavilland. Huge, moss-draped oaks shade the spacious grounds and beautiful gardens. "Southern Belle" guides lead tours in authentic antebellum attire. Open daily 10am-5pm; Nov.-Jan. 10am-4pm. $8, ages 13-17 $6, ages 6-12 $3.

**Nottoway** (545-2730 or 832-2093 in New Orleans), Rt. 405, between Bayou Goula and White Castle, 18mi. south of Baton Rouge on the southern bank of the Mississippi. The largest plantation home in the South, often called the "White Castle of Louisiana." A 64-room mansion with 22 columns, a large ballroom, and a 3-story stairway, it was David O. Selznick's first choice for filming *Gone with the Wind,* but the owners wouldn't allow it. Open daily 9am-5pm. Admission and 1hr. tour $8, under 12 $3.

# ▣ ENTERTAINMENT AND NIGHTLIFE

Life in New Orleans is and always will be a party. On any night of the week, at any time of the year, the masses converge on **Bourbon St.** to drift in and out of bars and shop for romantic interludes. Though the street has become increasingly touristy of late, much of Bourbon's original charm remains. Several sleazy strip clubs and cross-dressing joints maintain the sense of immorality and sinful excitement that is the essence of the Quarter. College boys on balconies still throw beads to girls who flash their breasts, and drunken adults urinate on dark side streets. To escape the debauchery of Bourbon St., some flee to **Decatur St.,** between St. Ann and Barracks St., where quieter, less pretentious bars preside.

While the Quarter offers countless bars and traditional jazz, blues, and brass venues, be assured that there's more to New Orleans nightlife. When locals burn out on Bourbon, they head uptown, towards **Tulane University,** or to the **Marigny,** an up-and-coming district northeast of the Quarter. **Uptown** tends to house authentic Cajun dance halls and popular university hangouts, while the Marigny is home to New Orleans's alternative/local music scene. Check *Off Beat,* free in many local restaurants, or the F *Times-Picayune* to find out who's playing where. *Impact* and *Ambush* track the movements of New Orleans's large gay community; both are available at **Faubourg Marigny Books,** 600 Frenchmen St. (943-9875; open M-F 10am-8pm, Sa-Su 10am-6pm). Gay establishments cluster toward the northeast end of Bourbon St.; St. Ann St. is known to some as the **"Lavender Line."**

Born at the turn of the century in **Armstrong Park,** traditional New Orleans jazz still wails nightly at the tiny, dim, historic **Preservation Hall,** 726 St. Peters St.; jazz is in its most fundamental element here. Those who don't come early can expect a lengthy wait in line, poor visibility, and sweaty standing-room only. (Daytime 522-2841, otherwise 523-8939. $4. Eat, drink, and leak before you come. Doors open at 8pm; music begins at 8:30pm and goes on until midnight.)

Keep your ears open for **Cajun** and **zydeco** bands who use accordions, washboards, triangles, and drums to perform hot dance tunes (true locals two-step expertly) and saccharine waltzes. Anyone who thinks couple-dancing went out in the 50s should try a *fais do-do,* a lengthy, wonderfully energetic traditional dance. The locally based **Radiators** do it up real spicy-like in a rock-cajun-zydeco style.

**Le Petit Théâtre du Vieux Carré,** 616 St. Peters St., is one of the city's most beloved and historical theaters. The oldest continuously operating community theater in the U.S., the 1789 building replicates the early-18th-century abode of Joseph de Pontalba, Louisiana's last Spanish governor. Around five musicals and plays go up each year, as well as four fun productions in the "Children's Corner." (522-9958. Box office open M-Sa 9:30am-6pm, Su 11am-4pm.)

## FESTIVALS

New Orleans's **Mardi Gras** celebration is the biggest party of the year, a world-renowned, epic bout of lascivious debauchery that fills the 3 weeks leading up to Ash Wednesday. Parades, gala, balls, and general revelry take to the streets, as tourists pour in by the plane-full (flights into the city and hotel rooms fill up months in advance). In 2000, "Fat Tuesday," falls on Mar. 7; the biggest parades and the bulk of the partying will take place during the week of Mar. 3-7.

The ever-expanding **New Orleans Jazz and Heritage Festival** (Apr. 28-May 7, 2000), attracts 7000 musicians from around the country to the city's fairgrounds. The likes of Aretha Franklin, Bob Dylan, Patti LaBelle, and Wynton Marsalis have graced this slightly "classier" fest, where music plays simultaneously on 12 stages in the midst of a huge Cajun and Creole food and crafts festival. The biggest names perform evening riverboat concerts. The festival grows more zoo-like and unfortunately, more commercialized, each year (522-4786).

New Orleans's festivals go beyond the biggies. From the **Reggae Riddums Festival** (June 9-11, 2000; 367-1313 or 800-367-1317) to the **Swamp Festival** (Oct. 6-8 and 13-15, 2000; 581-4629), they are usually celebrating something. Call the **Convention and Visitors Bureau** (see **Practical Information**, p. 399) for further info.

## NIGHTLIFE IN THE FRENCH QUARTER

Bars in New Orleans stay open late, and few keep a strict schedule; in general, they open around 11am and close around 3am. Some places have the usual $3-5 drinks, but most blocks feature at least one establishment with cheap draft beer and Hurricanes (sweet juice-and-rum drinks). The party's fun, but the law is enforced, especially between 9pm and 1am. **All establishments are 21+ unless otherwise noted.**

**Pat O'Brien's,** 718 St. Peters St. (525-4823). The busiest bar and one of the best in the French Quarter, bursting with happy (read: drunk) patrons. Listen to the piano in one room, mix with local students in another, or lounge near the fountain in the courtyard. Home of the original (and deliciously potent) Hurricane; purchase your first in a souvenir glass ($7.50). Open Su-Th 10am-4am, F-Sa 10am-5am.

**House of Blues,** 225 Decatur St. (529-2583). A sprawling complex with a large (over 1000 capacity) music/dance hall, beefy bouncers, and a balcony and bar overlooking the action. The restaurant has an extensive menu, including Voodoo shrimp in Voodoo beer ($10). Cover usually $5-10, but big names cost up to $25. Concerts nightly 9:15pm, 18+. Restaurant open in summer Su-Th 11am-midnight, F-Sa 11am-2am; off-season Su-Th 11am-11pm, F-Sa 11am-midnight.

**Lafitte's Blacksmith Shop,** 941 Bourbon St. (523-0066), at Phillip St. Appropriately, one of New Orleans's oldest standing structures is a bar. Built in the 1730s, the building is still lit by candlelight after sunset. Named for the scheming hero of the Battle of New Orleans, it offers shady relief from the elements of the city and friendly company at night. Open noon until late; live piano 8pm until late.

**Bourbon Pub & Parade Disco,** 801 Bourbon St. (529-2107). This gay dance bar has a "tea dance" on Su with $5 all-you-can-drink beer. Dance upstairs at the Paradise Disco nightly from 9pm (Tu-Su in summer); it lasts 'til you fall off. Open 24hr.

**Molly's at the Market,** 1107 Decatur St. (525-5169). Molly's offers tasty and widely acclaimed frozen Irish coffee ($4), as well as a hang out space for, you guessed it, eclectic locals. Vibrant late night retreat from the touristy frenzy of quarter. Open daily 10am-6am. All ages.

**Crescent City Brewhouse,** 527 Decatur St. (522-0571). The only microbrewery in New Orleans, this classy brewpub sells only its own 5 blends (12 oz. $3). Glass walls and balcony make for good people-watching, a wonderful activity when set to live jazz (nightly 6-9pm). Open Su-Th 11am-10pm, F-Sa 11am-midnight.

**GIMME SOME SKIN** French quarter shops sell beads for $1-5, but why buy them when you can *earn* them for free? Down on the 700th block of Bourbon St., and especially near the balconies above the Cat's Meow and Tricou House, lie the best bead bartering locations. Women who flash their breasts on the street earn beads. Only in New Orleans is exposing oneself so colorfully rewarded.

**Kaldi's Coffeehouse,** 941 Decatur St. (586-8989). Kaldi's is all about chatting, postcard-writing, and cappuccino-sipping. The only place in the Crescent City that roasts its own coffee. Italian cream sodas are one-of-a-kind ($2.15), and the coffee-laced milkshake flavors ought to be patented ($4). Internet access. Open Su-Th 7am-midnight, F-Sa 7am-2am. All ages.

**O'Flaherty's Irish Channel Pub,** 514 Toulouse St. (529-1317). An Irish Pub in New Orleans? Well, why not? O'Flaherty's bills itself as the meeting point of the disparate Celtic nations. Eavesdrop on Gaelic conversation while listening to Scottish bagpipes, watching Irish dances, and/or singing along to Irish tunes. Irish music daily at 8pm. Cover F-Sa $5. Open daily noon-3am.

## NIGHTLIFE OUTSIDE THE QUARTER

▨ **Tipitina's,** 501 Napoleon Ave. (891-8477, concert info 897-3943). The best local bands and some big national names, such as the Neville Brothers, John Goodman, and Harry Connick Jr. play so close, you can almost touch them. Su evenings feature Cajun *fais-do-dos*. Cover $4-15, W free food and quarter draft with $5 cover; call ahead for times and prices.

▨ **Maple Leaf Bar,** 8316 Oak St. (866-9359). The best local dance bar offering zydeco, brass band, and Cajun music; everyone does the two-step. Large, pleasant, covered patio. Poetry readings Su 3pm. Music and dancing start Su-Th at 10pm, F-Sa at 10:30pm. Cover $5. Open daily 3pm.

**F&M Patio Bar,** 4841 Tchoupitoulas St. (895-6784), near Napoleon. Mellow 20-somethings, students, doctors, lawyers, and ne'er-do-wells dance on the pool tables together in the heat of the night. Serves food after 6pm, mostly fajitas ($3.50) and burgers ($4.50) from a mega-grill on the patio. Open M-Th 1pm-4am, F 1pm-6am, Sa 3pm-6am, Su 8pm-4am.

**Café Brasil,** 2100 Chartres, at Frenchmen St. Unassuming by day, Brasil is packed weekend nights by locals who come to see a wide variety of New Orleans talent. Shows 8 and 11pm. Cover F-Sa after 11pm $5-10. Open daily 7 pm until late. All ages.

**Dragon's Den,** 435 Esplanade (949-1750). Patrons can lounge on floor pillows or around small tables and listen to irreverent blues, brass, jazz, and funk. Cover 0-$5; M 2 for 1 *Saki*. Music starts around 11pm. Open Su-Th 5:30pm-2am, F-Sa 5:30pm-3am.

**Checkpoint Charlie's,** 501 Esplanade (947-0979), grunges it up like the best of Seattle. Do your laundry while listening to live music 7 nights a week. Julia Roberts sat on these machines in *The Pelican Brief*. Beer $2. No cover. Open 24hr.

**Mid City Lanes,** 4133 S. Carrollton Ave. (482-3133), at Tulane Ave. Uncut N'awlins. "Home of Rock 'n' Bowl": bowling alley by day, dance club by night (you can bowl at night, too). Featuring good food and local zydeco, blues, and rock 'n' roll, this is where the locals party. Th is a wild zydeco night; swing on Tu. Music Tu-Th 8:30pm, F-Sa 10pm; cover $5-7. The *Rock 'n' Bowlletin* has schedules (and a list of the regulars' birthdays). Lanes $10 per hr. Open noon until late. 18+.

**Snug Harbor,** 626 Frenchmen St. (949-0696), near Decatur St. Regulars include Charmaine Neville, Astral Project, and Ellis Marsalis—big names in modern jazz. The cover is steep ($8-15), but the music and its fans are authentic. Shows nightly 9 and 11pm. Bar open daily 5pm-2am; restaurant open Su-Th 5-11pm, F-Sa 5pm-midnight. All ages.

**The Red Room,** 2040 St. Charles (528-9759). Swing, latin beats, and rhythm and blues mark this swanky throwback to the opulent, jazzy side of the 1930s. One of the mellowest, classiest clubs. Dress up or look drab against the posh red decor. Cover $5-10. Open 7pm-2am, Sa until late. Music starts at 9pm. 18+.

**Carrollton Station,** 8140 Willow St. (865-9190), at Dublin St. A cozy neighborhood club with live R&B music and friendly folks. 12 beers on tap ($2-4), behind the intricately carved wooden bar. Music Th-Sa at 10pm. Open daily 3:30pm-2am.

**Jimmy's,** 8200 Willow St. (concert info 861-8200). Rock is the staple at this student favorite. There are no frills—the walls are plain, there's no restaurant—but the varying cover ($5-15) covers the entire night's show, which may mean as many as 5 different bands performing in a continuous line-up. Open Tu-Sa 8pm-2am.

**Top of the Mart,** World Trade Center, 2 Canal St. (522-9795). The nation's largest revolving bar, this 500-seat cocktail lounge spins 33 stories above the ground. The deck revolves 3 ft. per min. and makes 1 revolution every 1½hr. The sunset view is awe-inspiring. No cover, but a 1-drink min. ($2.50 and up). 18+. Open M-F 10am-midnight, Sa 11am-2am, Su 2pm-midnight.

# BATON ROUGE

Once the site of a tall cypress tree marking the boundary between rival Native American tribes, Baton Rouge ("red stick") has blossomed into Louisiana's capital and second largest city. State politics have shaped this town— it was once the home of the notorious governor, senator, and demagogue "Kingfish" Huey P. Long. The presence of Louisiana State University (LSU) adds an element of youth and rebellion. Nonetheless, Baton Rouge has a simple meat-and-potatoes flavor in contrast to the flamboyant sauciness of New Orleans.

In a move reminiscent of Ramses II, Huey Long ordered the building of the unique **Louisiana State Capitol,** a magnificent, modern skyscraper, completed over a mere 14 months in 1931 and 1932. The **observation deck,** on the 27th fl., provides a view of the port. (342-7317. Open daily 8am-4pm. Free.) Of equal grandeur is the **Old State Capitol,** 100 North Blvd., with a fantastic spiral staircase; domed stained glass; and many exhibits on the history of Louisiana, including the controversy over Huey Long's assassination. (342-0500 or 800-488-2968. Open Tu-Sa 10am-4pm, Su noon-4pm. $4, students $2, seniors $3; $1 off with brochure from the new capitol.) **Magnolia Mound Plantation,** 2161 Nicholson Dr., built in 1791, is a palatial French-Creole mansion spanning 16 acres. (343-4955. Open Tu-Sa 10am-4pm, Su 1-4pm. $5, students $2, seniors $4, ages 5-12 $1. Last tour 3:15pm.) The **LSU Rural Life Museum,** 4600 Essen Ln., depicts the life of the less well-to-do Creoles through their authentically furnished shops, cabins, and storage houses. Adjacent to the museum are the lakes, winding paths, roses, and azaleas of the **Windrush Gardens.** (765-2437. Both open daily 8:30am-5pm. $5, seniors $4, ages 5-11 $3.) The city holds a **farmers market** in front of the Municipal Building, on the corner of North Blvd. and Fourth St. (Open Sa 7-11am; in winter Sa 8am-noon.)

Baton Rouge's cheapest accommodations are located on the outskirts of town. The **Corporate Inn,** 2365 College Dr., at exit 158 off I-10, resembles the Emerald City—on the outside. (925-2451 or 800-695-0777. Free local calls, HBO, coffee and doughnuts in the morning. Singles $56; doubles $61.50.) The **KOA Campground,** 7628 Vincent Rd. (664-7281, reservations 800-292-8245), 15mi. east of Baton Rouge (take the Denham Springs exit off I-12), keeps well-maintained sites, clean facilities and a big pool (tent sites $17; full RV hookup $24).

Downtown, sandwich shops and cafes line 3rd St. Head to LSU at the intersection of Highland Rd. and Chimes St. for cheaper chow and an abundance of bars. **Louie's Café,** 209 W. State St., grills up fabulous omelettes $4.75-9.75. (346-8221. Open 24hr.) Behind Louie's is **The Bayou,** 124 W. Chimes, a pool hall and bar crowded with collegiate types. (346-1765. Open daily 3pm-2am). When you want a good ol' sit-down meal, a good ol' option is **The Chimes,** 3357 Highland Rd., a big restaurant and bar with more than 120 different beers. Louisiana alligator, farm-raised, marinated, and fried, served with Dijon mustard sauce, goes for $7—do you dare? (383-1754. Open M-Sa 11am-2am, Su 11am-midnight.)

Close to downtown, **Greyhound,** 1253 Florida Blvd., at 13th St., sends buses to New Orleans (2hr., 9 per day, $10) and Lafayette (4hr., 10 per day, $18). *The area is unsafe at night.* (333-3811; open 24hr.) **Visitor Info: State Capitol Visitors Center,** on the 1st fl. of the State Capitol (342-7317. Open daily 8am-4:30pm). **Baton Rouge Convention and Visitors Bureau,** 730 North Blvd. (383-1825 or 800-527-6843; open M-F 8am-5pm). **Post Office:** 750 Florida Blvd., off River Rd. (800-275-8777. Open M-F 8:30am-5pm, Sa 9:30am-12:30pm.) **ZIP code:** 70821. **Area code:** 504.

# ACADIANA

Throughout the early eighteenth century, the English government in Nova Scotia became increasingly jealous of the prosperity of French settlers (*Acadians*) and deeply offended by their refusal to kneel before the British Crown. During the war with France in 1755, the British rounded up the Acadians and deported them by the shipload in what came to be called *le Grand Dérangement*, "the Great Upheaval." Of the 7000 Acadians who went to sea, one-third died of smallpox and hunger. Those who survived sought refuge along the Atlantic Coast, but were met with fear and suspicion, and were forced into indentured servitude. The Acadians soon realized that freedom waited in French Louisiana. The "Cajuns" of St. Martin, Lafayette, New Iberia, and St. Mary parishes are descended from these settlers.

Several factors have threatened Acadian culture since the relocation. In the 1920s, Louisiana passed laws forcing Acadian schools to teach in English. Later, during the oil boom of the 1970s and 80s, oil executives and developers envisioned the Acadian center of Lafayette (see below) as the Houston of Louisiana and threatened to flood the town and its neighbors with mass culture. The proud people of southern Louisiana have resisted homogenization. The state is officially bilingual, and a state agency preserves Acadian French in schools and in the media. "Cajun Country" spans the south of the state, from Houma in the east to the Texas border in the west.

## LAFAYETTE

The center of Acadiana, Lafayette is the perfect place to try boiled crawfish or dance the two-step to a fiddle and accordion. Though the city's French roots are often obscured by the chain motels that have accompanied its growth, there is no question that the Cajuns still own the surrounding countryside, where Cajun music and Creole zydeco heat up dance floors every night of the week and locals continue to answer their phones with a proud *bonjour*.

**◪ PRACTICAL INFORMATION.** Lafayette stands at a crossroads. **I-10** leads east to New Orleans (136mi.) and west to Lake Charles (76mi.); **U.S. 90** heads south to New Iberia (26mi.) and the Atchafalaya Basin; **U.S. 167** runs north into central Louisiana. Most of the city lies west of the **Evangeline Thruway (U.S. 49)** which runs north-south. Establishments are concentrated along Johnson St. (U.S. 167) and Ambassador Caffery Pkwy. **Amtrak,** 133 E. Grant St., sends 3 trains per week to New Orleans (4hr., $19); Houston (5½hr., $33); and San Antonio (10hr., $52). Buy tickets in advance from **Bass Travel,** 1603 W. Pinhook Rd. (237-2177 or 800-777-7371; open M-F 8:30am-5pm), or another travel agent. **Greyhound,** 315 Lee Ave., (235-1541), buses to New Orleans (3½hr., 8 per day, $18); Baton Rouge (1hr., 9 per day, $11); and New Iberia (30min., 2 per day, $7; station open 24hr.). The **Lafayette Bus System,** 1515 E. University, (291-8570), is centered at Lee and Garfield St. (Infrequent service M-Sa 6:30am-6:30pm. 45¢, seniors and disabled 20¢, ages 5-12 30¢.) **Taxi: Yellow/Checker Cab Inc.** (237-6196). **Thrifty Rent-a-Car,** 401 E. Pinhook Rd., at Evangeline, rents for $25 per day with 100 free mi. (237-1282. 25+ with major credit card. Open M-F 7:30am-6pm, Sa 8am-4pm, Su noon-4pm.) **Visitor Info: Lafayette Parish Convention and Visitors Commission,** 1400 NE Evangeline Thwy. (232-3808. Open M-F 8:30am-5pm, Sa-Su 9am-5pm.) **Hospital: University Medical Center,** 2390 W. Congress (261-6000; 24hr.). **Post Office:** 1105 Moss St. (800-275-8777; open M-F 8am-5:30pm, Sa 8am-12:30pm). **ZIP code:** 70501. **Area code:** 318.

**▐▗ ACCOMMODATIONS AND FOOD.** Inexpensive hotels line the Evangeline Thwy. Simple rooms at **Super 8,** 2224 NE Evangeline Thruway, come with pool access and a highway view. (232-8826 or 800-800-8000. Singles $31; doubles $41.) **Travel Host Inn South,** 1314 N. Evangeline Thruway, also offers clean rooms with cable TV, pool, free continental breakfast, and a convenient location. (233-2090 or 800-677-1466. Singles $32; doubles $36.) One campground close to the center of Lafayette, **Acadiana Park Campground,** 1201 E. Alexander, off Louisiana Ave., has tennis courts and a soccer field. (291-8388. Full hookup $9; office open Sa-Th 8am-5pm, F 8am-8pm.) The lakeside **KOA Lafayette,** 5mi. west of town on I-10 at exit 97, offers a store, mini-golf course, and pool. (235-2739. Tent sites $18.50, with water and electricity $23, full hookup $25.50. Office open daily 7:30am-8:30pm.)

Cajun restaurants with live music and dancing have popped up all over Lafayette. Unfortunately, some demand substantial funds. In central Lafayette, **Chris' Po' boys** offers seafood platters ($7-10) and—whadda ya' know—po' boys for $4-7. (3 locations including 1941 Moss St., 237-1095 and 631 Jefferson St., 234-1696. Live blues and cajun at Jefferson St., weekend nights. All open M-F 11am-6pm.) **Randol's,** 2320 Kaliste Saloom Rd., romps with live Cajun and zydeco music nightly, and doubles as a restaurant. (981-7080. Open Su-Th 5-10pm, F-Sa 5-11pm.) For the mild-mannered, the **Judice Inn,** 3134 Johnston St., provides tasty, no-nonsense hamburgers with a secret sauce. (984-5614. $1.60-3.25; open M-Sa 10am-10pm.) On weekends, after the restaurants close, **Grant St. Dance Hall,** 113 Grant St., energizes with rajin' cajun tunes, fast paced zydeco, and more mellow blues. (237-2255. Open F-Sa. Shows start at 10pm. Cover $5. All ages welcome.)

**◎▟ SIGHTS AND ENTERTAINMENT.** Driving through south-central Louisiana means driving over America's largest swamp, the Atchafalaya (a-chah-fa-LIE-a) Basin. The **Atchafalaya Fwy.** (I-10 between Lafayette and Baton Rouge) crosses 32mi. of swamp and cypress trees. To get down and dirty (and maybe see some alligators), exit at Henderson (exit 115), turn right, then immediately left for 5mi. on Rt. 352. From there, follow signs to **McGee's Landing,** which sends four 1½hr. **boat tours** into the Basin each day. (1337 Henderson Rd. 228-2384 or 800-445-6681. Tours daily 8am, 10am, and 1, and 3. $12, seniors and under 12 $6, under 2 free.)

The **Acadian Cultural Center/Jean Lafitte National Park,** features a 40min. documentary, *The Cajun Way: Echoes of Acadia,* as well as a terrific exhibit on the exodus and migration of these French settlers (501 Fisher Rd. 232-0789. Shows every hr. on the hr. 9am-4pm. Open daily 8am-5pm. Free.) Next door, the re-creation of an Acadian settlement at **Vermilionville,** has music, crafts, food, and dancing on the Bayou Vermilion banks. (1600 Surrey St. 233-4077 or 800-992-2968. Open daily 10am-5pm. Live music M-F 1:30-3:30pm, Sa-Su 2-5pm. Cajun cooking lessons daily 11:30am and 1:30pm. $8, ages 6-18 $5.) **Acadian Village,** offers a look at the unpretentious homes of common 19th-century settlers (take U.S. 167 S. to Ridge Rd., then left on Broussard, and follow the signs). While at the village, view Native American artifacts at the **Mississippi Valley Missionary Museum** (200 Greenleaf Rd. 981-2364 or 800-962-9133. Both open daily 10am-5pm; $6, seniors $5, children $2.50.)

The 450yr. old **St. John's Cathedral Oak,** in the yard of **St. John's Cathedral,** shades the entire lawn with spidery limbs which spread 145 ft.; the weight of one limb is around 72 tons. (914 St. John St.)

Lafayette kicks off spring and fall weekends with **Downtown Alive!,** a series of free concerts featuring everything from New Wave to Cajun and zydeco. (268-5566. Apr.-June and Sept.-Nov. F 5:30pm; music 6-8:30pm.) The **Festival International de Louisiane** highlights southwest Louisiana in a Francophone tribute to the region (232-8086; Apr. 26-30, 2000.) To find the goings on in town, or where the zydeco is best, pick up a copy of *The Times,* available free at restaurants and gas stations.

## NEW IBERIA AND ENVIRONS

While Lafayette was being invaded by oil magnates eager to build a Louisiana oil-business center, New Iberia continued to maintain links to its bayou past. Several sights give visitors a good feel for the unique conditions of life in the area.

Most plantations in southern Louisiana grew sugarcane, not cotton. Many of these plantations are still private property, but **Shadows on the Teche,** 317 E. Main St., at the Rt. 14/Rt. 182 junction, welcomes the public with over 17,000 family documents and a first-hand look at antebellum life in the South. (369-6446. Open daily 9am-4:30pm. $6, ages 6-11 $3; AAA discount.) Time passes quickly at the **Rip Van Winkle Gardens,** 5505 Rip Van Winkle Rd., off Rt. 14. (365-3332. Open daily 9am-5pm. House and garden tour $9, seniors $8.50, students 14-18 $7, ages 5-13 $5.) **Avery Island,** 7mi. away on Rt. 329 off Rt. 90 (50¢ toll to enter the island), sizzles with the world-famous **Tabasco Pepper Sauce Factory,** where the McIlhenny family has produced the famous condiment for nearly a century. Tours every 15min. include free recipes, samples, and tastings. (Open M-F 9am-4pm. Free.) Bring sunglasses for the 1hr. **Airboat Tour** of the shallow swamps and bayous of Lake Fausse Pointe. (229-4457. Open Feb.-Oct. Tu-Su 8am-5pm. $15. Reservations required.)

Picturesque campsites on the banks of the Bayou Teche are available at **Belmont Campgrounds,** 1000 Belmont Rd., at the junction of Rt. 31 and 86. Within the well-kept grounds are nature trails and fishing areas in the stocked pond. (364-2020. Tent sites with showers and laundry $11, full RV hookup $17.)

New Iberia lies 21mi. southeast of Lafayette on U.S. 90. **Amtrak** stops at an unstaffed station, 402 W. Washington St., at Railroad St. Three trains per week set out for Lafayette (30min., $4) and New Orleans (3hr., $18). **Greyhound** (364-8571) pulls into 1103 E. Main St. Buses to Morgan City (1hr., 2 per day, $13); New Orleans (4hr., 4 per day, $26); and Lafayette (40min., 2 per day, $7; station open M-F 8am-5pm, Sa 8am-noon.) The **Iberia Parish Convention and Visitors Bureau,** 2704 Rt. 14 (365-1540; open daily 9am-5pm), and the **Greater Iberia Chamber of Commerce,** 111 W. Main St. (364-1836; open M-F 8:30am-5pm), have maps. **Area code:** 318.

# ARKANSAS

"The Natural State," as the Arkansas (ar-kan-SAW) license plates proclaim it, lives up to its declaration, encompassing the Ozark and Ouachita mountains, the clear waters of Hot Springs, and mi. of lush pine forests. Given to boasting about its products as well as these natural resources, the state clings to its affiliation with sons Bill Clinton and Wal-Mart founder Sam Walton.

## 🚩 PRACTICAL INFORMATION

**Capital:** Little Rock.

**Visitor Info: Arkansas Dept. of Parks and Tourism,** One Capitol Mall, Little Rock 72201 (501-682-1191 or 800-628-8725; www.1800natural.com). Open M-F 8am-5pm.

**Postal Abbreviation:** AR. **Sales Tax:** 6%.

## LITTLE ROCK

In the early 19th century, a small rock just a few feet high served as an important landmark for boats pushing their way upstream. Sailors and merchants began settling around this stone outcrop, and, lo and behold, Little Rock was born. The capital became the focus of a nationwide civil rights controversy in 1957, when Governor Orval Faubus and local white segregationists violently resisted nine black students who entered Central High School under the shields of the National Guard. Fortunately, Little Rock has since become a more integrated community, one that strives to be a cosmopolitan centerpiece for the state.

## 🚩 ORIENTATION AND PRACTICAL INFORMATION

In downtown Little Rock, the numbered streets run east-west. Near the river Markham St. is 1st St., and Capitol is 5th St. Markham St. will become Clinton St. sometime in the future, but street numbers will remain the same.

**Airport: Little Rock National** (372-3430), 5mi. east of downtown off I-440. Easily accessible from downtown (by #12 bus $1, by taxi about $12).

**Trains: Amtrak,** 1400 W. Markham St. (372-6841), in Union Station at Victory St. (bus #1 or #8). 4 trains per week to: St. Louis (7hr., $46); Dallas (7hr., $50); and Malvern (45min., $7), 20mi. east of Hot Springs. Open M 9am-7pm, Tu 3pm-1am, W-Th and Su 6am-1am, F-Sa 6am-4pm.

**Buses: Greyhound,** 118 E. Washington St. (372-3007), across the river in North Little Rock (bus #7 or #18). Use the walkway over the bridge to get downtown. To: St. Louis (9hr., 3 per day, $47); New Orleans (14hr., 4 per day, $73); and Memphis (2½hr., 8 per day, $20). Ticket prices higher F-Su. Open 24hr.

**Public Transit: Central Arkansas Transit (CAT),** 375-1163. Little Rock has a fairly comprehensive local bus system. M-F 6am-6:30pm, Sa 6am-6pm, Su 9am-4pm; fare $1, transfers 10¢. M-F 6:30-10pm; fare 50¢, transfers free. Maps available at the **Sterling Dept. Store** (375-8181), on Center St., between 5th and 6th.

**Taxis: Black and White Cabs,** 374-0333.

**Car Rental: Enterprise Rent-a-Car,** 200 S. Broadway Ave. (376-1919), rents for $29 per day with 150 free mi. Must be 21+ with a major credit card. Free pick-up and delivery service available. Open M-F 7:30am-6pm, Sa 8:30am-12:30pm.

**Visitor Info: Little Rock Convention and Visitors Bureau,** 400 W. Markham St. (376-4781 or 800-844-4781), at Broadway. Open M-F 8:30am-5pm.

**Hotlines: Rape Crisis,** 663-3334. 24hr. **First Call for Help,** 376-4567, offers a broad range of information and referrals. Operates M-F 8am-5pm.

**Internet Access: Main Library,** 100 Rock St., near the River Market (918-3000; open M-Tu and Th 9am-6pm, Su 1-5pm).

**Post Office:** 600 E. Capitol (375-5155). Open M-F 7am-5:30pm. **ZIP code:** 72202. **Area code:** 501.

## ACCOMMODATIONS

Inexpensive motels in Little Rock tend to cluster along **I-30,** near downtown and at the intersection of I-30 and I-40 in North Little Rock, 5min. from downtown. A few motels in town are cheaper but shabbier.

**Master's Inn Economy,** 707 I-30 (372-4392 or 800-633-3434), at 8th St., exit 140. Locations in North Little Rock as well, but this one is right by downtown. Spacious, well-lit rooms with a lovely pool, a restaurant, room service, and complimentary breakfast. 21+ to rent. Singles $36; $4 per extra person; under 18 free with parent.

**Cimarron Motel,** 10200 I-30 (565-1171), across from Super 7 (westbound frontage) and farther south (exit 130). Cable TV, A/C. Singles $30; doubles $35. Key deposit $5.

**Super 7,** 9525 I-30 (568-9999), about 9mi. south of downtown (exit 130). Aging building houses simple, reasonably clean rooms. Pool. Singles $29.72; doubles $37.40.

**Campground: Maumell Park,** 9009 Pinnacle Valley Rd. (868-9477), on the Arkansas River. From I-430 N, take Rt. 10 (exit 9) west 3mi., then turn right on Pinnacle Valley Rd. for 3mi. This Corps of Engineers park has showers, boat ramp ($2), fishing, playground, short walking trails, and 2 dumping stations. 129 sites. $15 including water and electricity. Office open 10am-10pm.

## FOOD AND NIGHTLIFE

**Farmer's Market,** 400 E. Markham St., offers a collection of food shops, coffee stands, and delis, which feed much of the downtown lunch crowd. (375-2552. Open M 10am-3pm, Tu-Sa 7am-6pm, Su 11am-4pm. Outdoor vegetable market Tu and Sa 7am-3pm.) Bars and restaurants in Arkansas often close earlier on Sa; liquor laws require establishments to stop selling alcohol at midnight.

**Vino's,** 923 W. 7th St. (375-8466), at Chester St. Little Rock's original microbrewery serves Italian fare at wallet-friendly prices (slices 95¢, calzones $5.60). Weekends bring live music of all types—folk, rock, alternative, you name it. Cover $5. Open M-W 11am-10pm, Th-Sa 11am-midnight, Su 1-9pm. Bar open M-Sa until 12:45am.

**Juanita's,** 1300 S. Main St. (372-1228), at 13th St. A local favorite for years, Juanita's serves fabulous Mexican food with live music nightly. Call or stop by for a jam-packed schedule. Open for lunch (specials $6) M-Sa 11am-2:30pm; for dinner ($7) M 5:30-9pm, Tu-Th 5:30-9:30pm, F 5:30-10:30pm, Sa 2:30-10:30pm. Bar open M-F 11am-1am, Sa 11am-midnight.

**Slick Willy's,** 1400 W. Markham Ave. (372-5505), under the old train station, takes its name from one of Bill Clinton's many nicknames. Pool tables ($6 per hr.), arcade games, and a stage (live music Sa-Su) fill the floor. W 75¢ drafts, Th-Tu $1. Th free pool and karaoke 8pm-2am. Open Su-F 10am-2am, Sa 10am-1am.

**Backstreet,** 1021 Jessie Rd. (664-2744), like most backstreets, is hard to find. Take Cantrell (MO 10) west 1mi. from downtown, turn right on Riverfront, then immediately right onto Jessie. This large warehouse contains 3 gay and lesbian bars: **701** for women, **501** for men (rock and disco in each), and **Miss Kitty's** (country and Western). Cover $2-4 each. Open daily 9pm-5am.

# ◆ SIGHTS

Tourists can visit the **"little rock"** at Riverfront Park, a pleasant place for a walk along the Arkansas River. From underneath the railroad bridge at the north end of Louisiana St., look straight down; the rock is part of the embankment. The rock has fought a losing battle against erosion; viewers having trouble locating it should ask the tiny **information desk** in the nearby Excelsior Hotel. The city celebrates its waterway with arts, crafts, bands, food, and a fireworks display at **Riverfest** on Memorial Day weekend. *(376-4781. admission $1.)* The **River Market** district, has restaurants, nightclubs, and galleries. The nearby **Museum of Discovery** is one of the first museums to enter the area. *(500 E. Markham St. 396-7050 or 800-880-6475. Open M-F 9am-5pm, Sa 1-6pm. $5, seniors and under 13 $4.50, free the 1st F of each month 5-9pm.)* Exhibits are aimed at elementary school aged children, with entertaining displays on waves, construction techniques, and analog vs. digital signals.

The **State Capitol** at the west end of Capitol St., may look familiar—it's a small-scale replica of the U.S. Capitol in Washington, D.C. Tape players at the police booth on the ground floor give a free 45min. audio tour. *(682-5080. Open M-F 9am-5pm, Sa-Su 10am-5pm.)* The **Arkansas Territorial Restoration,** 200 E. Third St., displays life in 19th-century Little Rock with tours of 4 restored buildings and a print shop built in 1824. Tours begin at trailer in the parking lot across the street until summer, 2000. *(324-9351. Open M-Sa 9am-5pm, Su 1-5pm. $2, seniors $1, children 50¢; free 1st Su of the month. Tours begin every hr. on the hr. except noon; last tour 4pm.)*

To the south, in the heart of **MacArthur Park,** on 9th St. just west of I-30, the **Arkansas Art Center** houses an eclectic permanent collection comprised of European masters as well as contemporary artists. *(372-4000. Open M-Th and Sa 10am-5pm, F 10am-8:30pm, Su noon-5pm. Free.)* **War Memorial Park,** west of downtown on I-630 at Fair Park Blvd. (exit 4 or #5 bus), offers shade for picnics and the 40-acre **Little Rock Zoo,** 1 Jonesboro Dr., where animals roam simulated habitats. *(666-2406 or 663-4733. Open daily 9am-6pm, must enter by 5pm. $5, under 12 $3.)* The **Toltec Mounds State Park,** 9mi. east of I-440 on U.S. 165 (exit 7), reminds visitors of the mound building culture that flourished from 600-1050. *(961-9442. Open Tu-Sa 8am-5pm, Su noon-5pm. Self-guided tours $2.25, ages 6-12 $1.25.)*

# HOT SPRINGS

Despite tourist traps like alligator farms, wax museums, and ubiquitous gift shops, the town of Hot Springs delivers precisely what it advertises: soothing relaxation. Once you've bathed in the coils of these 143°F springs, you'll realize why everybody from Al Capone to the feds jumped into the bathhouse craze of the 20s.

**🛈 PRACTICAL INFORMATION. Visitor Info: Visitors center,** 629 Central Ave. (321-2277 or 800-543-2284), downtown off Spring St. (open daily 9am-around 5pm). **Post Office:** 100 Reserve St. (623-8217), at Central Ave. in the **Federal Reserve Building** (open M-F 8am-4:30pm, Sa 9am-1pm). **ZIP code:** 71901. **Area code:** 501.

**🍴 ACCOMMODATIONS AND FOOD.** Hot Springs has ample lodging; the best deals can be found along the aptly-named **Central Ave. (Rt. 7).** Most rates rise for the tourist season (Feb.-Aug.), but the rooms are always cheap just north and south of the downtown strip, where old-time motor inns still operate. The **Tower Motel,** 755 Park Ave., offers clean rooms with country landscape pictures. Call ahead; if no one's staying, the motel shuts down. (624-9555. Singles $25; doubles $30.) The **Margarete Motel,** 217 Fountain St., is just a stone's throw away from the baths and offers an excellent deal on large rooms with full kitchens—bring your own pots and pans (623-1192. Singles $28, doubles $36; Sa-Su $32/$44.) The **Best Motel,** 638 Ouachita Ave., has clean rooms around a small pool in gingerbread-like cabins. (624-5736. Singles $25; doubles $35.) The closest campgrounds are at **Gulpha Gorge** part of **Hot Springs National Park.** Follow Rt. 70 (Grand Ave.) 1 mi east to exit 70B (1st exit outside of town), turn left, and drive ½mi. north; it's on the left. (624-3383, ext. 640 for info and emergencies. Primitive sites $8.)

**Granny's Kitchen,** 362 Central Ave., cooks up hearty country food (plate lunches $5), with old-fashioned Americana lining the walls. (624-6183. Open daily 6:30am-7pm.) **Cookin' with Jazz,** 101 Central Ave., serves New Orleans-style dishes—po' boys, jambalaya, and gumbo—with a live band on summer Sa from 7-11pm. (321-0555; entrees $5-14; open F 5-9pm, Sa 11am-11pm). **The Dixie Café,** 3623 Central Ave., serves Southern food (entrees $5-7) with fitting hospitality (624-2100; open daily 11am-10pm). **Purity Barbecue,** 1000 Malverne Ave., offers sweet, smoky meat sandwiches ($2.40-$3.85) and drippy vegetable sides ($1.10-3.65) in a loungy shack (623-4006; open 10:30am-9pm).

**📷 🎭 SIGHTS AND ENTERTAINMENT.** Drink the water! Still trickling through the earth after 4000 years, water gushes to the planet's crust in Hot Springs at a rate of 850,000 gallons a day. Visitors may fill bottles in the parking lot of the visitors center, or bathe in one of the many bathhouses. As the only operating house on "Bathhouse Row," the **Buckstaff,** 509 Central Ave., retains the dignity and elegance of Hot Springs' heyday in the 1920s. (623-2308. Open M-Sa 7-11:45am and 1:30-3pm. Bath $14, whirlpool $1.50 extra; massage $16.50.) Around the corner, the **Hot Springs Health Spa,** N. 500 Reserve, at Spring St., offers large common hot tubs and whirlpools. (321-9664. Yes, bathing suits are required. Open daily 9am-9pm. Bath $13; 30min. massage $17.50.) Hot springs at the **Downtowner,** 135 Central Ave., are the town's cheapest hands-on, full treatment baths with little difference in quality. (624-5521. Bath $12.50, whirlpool $1.50 extra; massage $16. Open M-Tu and Th-F 7-11am, 1:30-3:15pm, W 7-11am, Sa 7-11am and 2-4:15pm.)

The **Fordyce Bathhouse Visitors Center,** 369 Central Ave., located in one of the Row's vintage bathhouses, can bathe guests with info on **Hot Springs National Park.** An informative film on Hot Springs (17min.) and a self-guided (2hr.) tour of the restored building and the town illuminate the allure of Hot Springs in the early 20th century. The front desk has a helpful chart for disabled and hearing-impaired visitors. (624-3383, ext. 640. Open daily 9am-5pm.) The 1½hr. amphibious **National Park Duck Tour,** 418 Central Ave., wends through Hot Springs into Lake Hamilton. (321-2911 or 800-682-7044. 7-21 per day; $9.50, seniors $8.50, children $5.50.)

Hot Springs' natural beauty, like its schlocky tourist-oriented economy, is unmistakable. Folks can gaze at the green-peaked mountains while cruising Lake Hamilton on the **Belle of Hot Springs,** 5200 Central Ave., a 1½hr. narrated tour alongside Lake Ouachita and Lake Hamilton mansions. (525-4438. Trips in summer daily 1, 3pm, and sundown; call for exact times year-round. $9, seniors $8.50, ages 2-12 $5; evening cruise $10/$9.50/$5.) From the **Hot Springs Mountain Observatory**

**Tower,** located in the national park (turn off Central Ave. onto Fountain St. and follow the signs), view the beautiful panorama of the surrounding mountains and lakes. (623-6035. Open Mar.-Oct. daily 9am-9pm; early Sept. to Oct. and Mar. to mid-May 9am-6pm; Nov.-Feb. 9am-5pm. $4, ages 5-11 $2, ages 55+ $3.50.) On clear days, it's possible to see 140mi. For outdoor frolicking, the clear and unpolluted waters of the **Ouachita River** provide ample opportunities to hike, bike, fish, or canoe. **Ouachita River Adventures,** west of Hot Springs on U.S. 270, offers canoes ($30 per day), kayaks ($15), and rafts ($65) for daytime or overnight trips, and can help in planning backpacking or fishing trips (326-5517 or 800-748-3718). In **Whittington Park,** on Whittington St. off Central Ave., bathhouses give way to an expanse of trees and shaded picnic tables.

## MOUNTAIN VIEW

Despite the commercialism gradually seeping into Mountain View, the village remains refreshingly unpretentious, authentically Ozark, and unmistakably small (pop. 2700). Nearly every evening, locals gather at the **Courthouse Sq.** to make music on banjos, dulcimers, fiddles, and guitars.

**⚐ PRACTICAL INFORMATION.** The nearest **rental car agency** is in Batesville, 40mi. east on Rt. 5. **Chamber of Commerce:** behind the Courthouse on Washington and Howard St. (888-679-2859. Open M-Sa 9am-5pm.) **Post Office:** 802 Sylamore Ave. (269-3520; open M-F 8:30am-4:30pm). **ZIP code:** 72560. **Area code:** 870.

**▐▐ ACCOMMODATIONS AND FOOD.** Mountain View offers many lodging options at moderate prices, but it is nearly impossible to find a room for under $40 on a summer weekend. The **Mountain View Motel,** 407 E. Main St., has 18 orderly rooms with in-room coffee makers and cable TV. Each has a red chair outside for enjoying the evening air (269-3209; singles $33, doubles $42). Wildflower Bed & Breakfast, on the northeast corner of the Courthouse Sq., rents nine florally decorated rooms with soft carpeting and softer antique furniture—but no TVs. (800-591-4879. Singles $44; doubles $50. Rooms with private bathrooms available. Reservations recommended.) A group of hexagonal cottages with padded rocking chairs make up the **Dry Creek Lodge,** on Spur 382 off Rt. 9, within the Ozark Folk Center. (269-3871 or 800-264-3655. Singles or doubles Su-W $50, Th-Sa $55; Nov.-Mar. $10 off. Pool and restaurant.)

Because Mountain View lies only 14mi. south of the **Ozark National Forest,** the cheapest way to stay is free **camping.** Pitch a tent anywhere within the forest—it's free and legal as long as the campsite does not block any road, path, or thoroughfare. Safe, unattended campgrounds lie around the **Blanchard Springs Caverns,** off Rt. 14, 10-15min. west of the junction with Rt. 5 and 9. These include **Blanchard Springs Recreation Area,** in the same entrance as the Caverns (32 sites with hot showers, $10); **Gunner Pool Recreation Area,** in a beautiful gorge off a winding 3mi. red dirt road (27 sites, $7; total of 2mi. past the Caverns entrance; turn off 1mi. past the town of Fifty-Six); and **Barkshed Recreation Area,** 3½mi. past Fifty-Six (5 sites, $3 per car; beware young idlers who bring their drink and wickedness). All campsites border a clear creek ideal for swimming. More camping info available at the **Sylamore Ranger District** of the National Forest, P.O. Box 1279, Mountain View 72560 (757-2211 or 269-3228).

Fried catfish is the local specialty of Mountain View, and **Jojo's Catfish Wharf,** 6mi. north of town on Rt. 5, 1mi. past the Rt. 5/9/14 junction, drops them into the pan fresh from the White River. (585-2121. Not-too-fishy catfish sandwich $3.25, all-you-can-eat catfish $12.50. Open Su-Th 11am-8pm, F-Sa 11am-9pm.) While visiting wonderful **Tommy's Famous...a pizzeria,** about ½mi. west of Courthouse Sq. off Rt. 66., sign Tom's copy of *Let's Go: USA* and swap stories with his son Clay. (269-3278. 12 in. pie $6; calzones start at $7. Open W-Th 3-9pm, F-Su 3-10pm.)

**SIGHTS AND ENTERTAINMENT.** The **Ozark Folk Center,** 2mi. north of Mountain View off Rt. 9 on Rt. 382 recreates a mountain village and showcases the cabin crafts, music, and lore of the Ozarks. In the **Crafts Forum,** artisans demonstrate everything from wheel-thrown ceramics to ironware forging and spoon carving. Locals fiddle, pluck, and strum in the auditorium nightly, while dancers clog along. The center's seasonal events include the **Arkansas Folk Festival** (Apr. 14-16, 2000) and the **Annual Dulcimer Jamboree** (Apr. 20-23, 2000), and the **National Fiddle Championships** (Nov. 3-5, 2000. 269-3851. Open May-Oct. daily 10am-5pm. Crafts area $7.50, ages 6-12 $5. 7:30pm musical performances $7.50/$5. Combination tickets and family rates available.) Quintessential Ozark artist Jimmy Driftwood passed away, but his family continues his tradition of weekend music and revelry at the **Jimmy Driftwood Barn and Folk Museum,** also on Rt. 9, 1mi. north of the Dulcimer Shoppe. (269-8042. Shows F and Su 7pm, doors open 6pm. Free.)

To **fish** along the White River, non-residents can purchase a 3-day **fishing license** from **Wal-Mart,** 315 Sylamore Ave./Rt. 9 N. (269-4395. $10.50, $15.50 for trout. Open M-Sa 7am-9pm, Su 10am-6pm). The folks at **Jack's Boat Dock** rent a rod and reel for $5 per day and sell tackle and bait. (585-2111. Open daily 7am-7pm). Visit the **Sylamore Ranger District** for information on hiking in the **Ozark National Forest.** (757-2211 or 269-3228. P.O. Box 1279, Mountain View, 72560.) The **OK Trading Post,** 3½mi. west of the Rt. 5/9/14 junction on Rt. 14., has guided trail rides. (585-2217. $10 per hr. Open daily 9am-dark.) The **Blanchard Springs Caverns,** 9mi. west on Rt. 14 from the junction, glisten with exquisite cave formations and cool, glassy springs on the southern border of the Ozark Forest. (757-2211. Open daily 9am-6:30pm, last tour 5pm; Nov.-Mar. W-Su 9:30am-6pm, last tour 4pm. $9, ages 6-15 $5, with Golden Age Passport $4.50.) Daytrips to the Buffalo River (1hr. northwest) are excellent for **canoeing. Crockett's Country Store and Canoe Rental** (800-355-6111), at the Rt. 14/27 junction in Harriet, provides boats, shuttles, and maps of the waterways (boats $25 per day, open M-F 6am-8pm, Sa 7am-8pm, Su 7am-6pm).

# FLORIDA

Ponce de León landed in St. Augustine on the Florida coast in 1513, in search of the elusive Fountain of Youth. Although the multitudes who flock to Florida today aren't seeking fountains, many find their youth restored in the Sunshine State—whether they're dazzled by Disney World, or bronzed by the sun on the state's seductive beaches. Droves of senior citizens also migrate to Florida, where they sun-warmed air isn't just as good as Ponce de León's fabled magical elixir.

Anything attractive is bound to draw hordes of people, the nemesis of natural beauty. Florida's population boom has strained the state's resources; commercial strips and tremendous development have turned many pristine beaches into tourist traps. Still, it is possible to find a deserted spot on the peninsula on which to plop down with a paperback and get some sand in your toes.

## HIGHLIGHTS OF FLORIDA

■ **Beaches.** White sand, lots of sun, clear blue water. Pensacola (p. 458) and St. Petersburg (p. 452) win our thumbs-up for the best of the best.
■ **Disney World.** Orlando's cash cow (p. 428)...what else is there to say?
■ **Everglades.** The prime Florida haunt for fishermen, hikers, canoers, bikers, and wildlife watchers (p. 443). Check out the unique mangrove swamps.
■ **Key lime pie.** This famous dessert hails from the Florida Keys (p. 445).

# ⒉ PRACTICAL INFORMATION

**Capital:** Tallahassee.

**Visitor Info: Florida Division of Tourism,** 126 W. Van Buren St., Tallahassee 32399-2000 (888-735-2872; www.flausa.com). **Division of Recreation and Parks,** 3900 Commonwealth Blvd., #506, Tallahassee 32399-3000 (904-488-9872).

**Postal Abbreviation:** FL. **Sales Tax:** 6%.

# JACKSONVILLE

At almost 1000 sq. mi., Jacksonville is the largest city in the United States, yet still struggles to shine through the cluttered tourist offerings of Florida. Without theme parks, star studded beaches, or tropical environs, it is often bypassed for its more glamorous southern neighbors.

⒉ **PRACTICAL INFORMATION.** Three highways intersect in Jacksonville, making driving around the expansive city relatively easy. **I-95** runs north-south, while **I-10** starts in the downtown area and runs west. **I-295** forms a giant "C" on the western half of the city. **Arlington Expressway** become **Atlantic Blvd. (Rt. 10)** heading toward the beach. The St. Johns River snakes throughout the city.

**Jacksonville International Airport,** 2400 Yankee Clipper Dr. (741-4902), north of the city on I-95. **Amtrak,** 3570 Clifford Lane (766-5110; open 24hr.), off I-95 exit 20th St. West. sends coaches to Orlando (2 per day, 3½hr. $25. Take Northside 4 Moncreif Bus A to get to the terminal.) **Greyhound,** 10 N. Pearl St. (355-5501, open 24hr.), at Central Station Skyrail stop in downtown, buses to Atlanta (8 per day, 6-8hr., $37) and Orlando (12 per day, 2-5hr., $25). **Jacksonville Transportation Authority** (630-3100; info line M-Sa 6am-7pm) runs throughout the city from the main station at State and Union downtown (operates daily 5am-9pm, 75¢). The monorail, **Skyway** (630-3181), is the best way to maneuver downtown (35¢). **Yellow Cab:** 260-1111. **Jacksonville and Beaches Conventions and Visitors Bureau:** 201 E. Adams St. (800-733-2668) in downtown. Open M-F 8am-5pm. **Rape Crisis:** 355-7273. **Area code:** 904

**ⓕⓕ ACCOMMODATIONS AND FOOD.** Along I-95 to the north and south of the city, and on the Arlington Expressway heading to the ocean, inexpensive hotels abound. At the beach, the **Atlantis Motel,** 731 1st St. N, is remarkably cheap given its beachfront location, pool, A/C and TV. (249-5006. Singles oceanside $55 M-F, $65 Sa-Su; singles roadside $50/60. Doubles oceanside $60/70, roadside $55/65.) Bare bones but clean, the **Best Value Inn,** 1057 Broward Rd., off I-95 exit 124B north of the city, has new, large rooms with T/V and A/C (757-0990; singles $30, doubles $35). The **Hanna Park** has 300 wooded sites near the beach, all with water, electricity and sewer. Fifteen mi. of bike paths and a water playground are also on sight. (Tent sites $13.50, RVs $18. Registration open from 8am-9pm.)

Closer in culinary spirit to Georgia than southern Florida, the city has an excellent taste of the three fundamentals: BBQ, fried chicken, and seafood. **Jenkins' Quality Bar-B-Que,** 830 N. Pearl St. at Union St., serves it up spicy with a hint of mustard. Pork, beef or chicken sandwiches $3.75. (353-6388, open 11am-1am daily). At the beach, the smell of fresh biscuits constantly fills the air at **Famous Amos Restaurant,** 375 Atlantic Blvd. (249-3025. Huge fried chicken dinner, with veggies and a salad, $5. Veggie platter $4. Open 24hr.) One of Jacksonville's better known eateries is **Singleton's Seafood Shack,** 4730 Ocean Dr., off Mayport Rd. in Atlantic Beach. The rustic building on water's edge only serves the catch of the day. (246-4442. Sandwiches $3, dinners $8-10. Open Su-Th 10am-9pm, F-Sa 10am-10pm.)

**◲ SIGHTS AND ENTERTAINMENT.** Perhaps the **Anheuser-Busch Brewery Tour,** 111 Busch Dr., overstates Bud's impact on the world, but the video collection of their greatest ads is supremely amusing. After touring the royal tanks, try to identify the skunky ale in their "freshness presentation." (751-8117. Open M-Sa 9am-4pm, tours hourly 10am-3pm on the hour. Free.) **Fort Caroline National Memorial,** 12713 Fort Caroline Rd., is the site of the first armed conflict between European powers over New World settlement. Spanish forces overtook the fort from the French in 1565. (641-7155. Open daily 9am-5pm. Free.) The Visitor's Center houses a 46,000 acre wetland—**Timucuan Ecological and Historic Preserve.**

The **Museum of Science and History (MOSH)**, 1025 Museum Circle, highlights northeast Florida's natural history and entertains with a multimedia show in its planetarium. (396-7062. Open M-F 10am-5pm, Sa 10am-6pm, Su 1pm-6pm. $6, ages 3-12 $4, seniors $4.50.) The beautiful gardens of the **Cummer Museum of Art and Gardens,** 829 Riverside Ave., line the St. Johns' River south of downtown. (356-6857. Open T and Th 10am-9pm; W, F, and Sa 10am-5pm, Su noon-5pm. $6, students $3)

Acts ranging from Ringo Starr to the Dixie Chicks and Gilbert & Sullivan theater have performed in historic **Florida Theater,** 128 E.Forsyth St., built in 1927. Call 355-2787 for shows; the theater holds over 300 performances per year, so chances are something's going on. Culture also thrives at the **Alltell Stadium,** East Duval St. and Haines St. (630-3900), home to the Jacksonville Jaguars. Much of Jacksonville nightlife centers around Jacksonville Landing, Main St. and Independent Dr., a riverfront area packed with restaurants, bars, shopping and live entertainment.

# ST. AUGUSTINE

Spanish adventurer Pedro Menéndez de Aviles founded St. Augustine in 1565, making it the first European colony in North America and the oldest continuous settlement in the United States. Thanks to preservation efforts, much of St. Augustine's Spanish flavor remains intact. Unlike most towns on Florida's east coast, St. Augustine is not defined by beaches; cobblestone streets wind around little shops selling antiques, homemade fudge, dresses and rare books. And forget L.A.'s plastic surgeons; eternal youth costs just $5.25 around here.

# Florida Peninsula

GEORGIA

Jacksonville

TO TALLAHASSEE

Osceola National Forest

St. John's River

Santa Fe R.

Suwannee River

TO PANAMA CITY BEACH

St. Augustine

Gainesville

ATLANTIC OCEAN

Ocala National Forest

Cedar Keys

Ocala

Daytona Beach

Chassahowitzka Bay

NASA Kennedy Space Center

Walt Disney World

Orlando

Cape Canaveral

Cocoa Beach

Clearwater

Tampa

Florida Turnpike

Melbourne

St. Petersburg

Tampa Bay

Manatee R.

Sarasota

Peace R.

Lake Istokpoga

Kissimmee R.

Fort Pierce

Lake Okeechobee

West Palm Beach

Palm Beach

Caloosahatchee R.

Fort Myers

Loxahatchee Nat. Wildlife Refuge

Boca Raton

GULF OF MEXICO

Seminole Indian Reservation

Fort Lauderdale

Naples

Big Cypress National Preserve

Everglades Pkwy (Alligator Alley)

Miami

Miami Beach

Everglades City

Biscayne Bay

N

Everglades National Park

Florida City

Key Largo

Florida Bay

0    100 miles

0    100 kilometers

Key West

Florida Keys

## 🛈 PRACTICAL INFORMATION

St. Augustine has no public transportation; fortunately, most of the town lies within a pleasant walk from the hostel, motels, and bus station. Narrow streets and one-ways can make driving tricky. The major east-west routes, **King St.** and **Cathedral Place,** run through the downtown and become the Bridge of Lions that leads to the beaches. **San Marco Ave.,** also known as **Castillo Dr.** and **Avenia Menendez,** runs north-south. **Saint George St.,** a north-south pedestrian route, contains most of the shops and many sights in St. Augustine. **Greyhound,** 100 Malaga St. (829-6401; station open daily 7:30am-6pm), has service to Jacksonville (45min., 4 per day, $10-12) and Daytona Beach (1hr., 6 per day, $12-13); if the station is closed, the driver accepts cash (open daily 7:30am-8pm). **Ancient City Taxi** (824-8161) can take you from the bus station to the visitors center for about $2. **Visitor Information Center:** 10 Castillo (825-1000), at San Marco Ave. From the Greyhound station, walk north on Ribeira, then right on Orange. (Open daily late May to early Sept. 8am-7:30pm; Oct.-Apr. 8:30am-5:30pm.) **Post Office:** 99 King St. (829-8716), at Martin Luther King, Jr. Ave. (open M-Tu and Th-F 8:30am-5:30pm, W 8:30am-5pm, Sa 9am-1pm). **ZIP code:** 32084. **Area code:** 904.

## 🛏 ACCOMMODATIONS

New owners and new amenities, including free internet access, lie within walking distance of everything at the **International Haus,** 32 Treasury St. (808-1999. Spacious rooms for 6, $15; private rooms, $35. A/C. free lockers and linen, kitchen. Bikes $7 per day.) Just over the Bridge of Lions, the **Seabreeze Motel,** 208 Anastasia Blvd. has clean rooms with refrigerators and access to a pool. (829-8122. A/C, cable TV, free local calls. Singles $35, Sa-Su $42; doubles $40/45. ) The **American Inn,** 42 San Marco Ave., near the visitors center, rents small rooms with TVs, A/C, and a pool in a location convenient to the restaurants and historic sights (829-2292; singles $35, Sa-Su $55; doubles $35/65). The quaint and quiet **St. Francis Inn,** 279 Saint George St., a charming 16-room inn with a jungle of flowers, a tucked-away pool, and much of its original 18th-century interior, is an expensive treat. Juice and iced tea are served free all day, along with wine daily from 5:30-6:30pm. (824-6068, 800-824-6062 for reservations. Free full breakfast, use of bikes, parking. Cable TV, A/C. $75 and up; F-Sa $95.) Nearby, a salt run and the Atlantic Ocean provide opportunities for great windsurfing, fishing, swimming, and surfing near the 139 campsites of the **Anastasia State Recreation Area,** on Rt. A1A, 4mi. south of the historic district. From town, cross the Bridge of Lions and turn left just beyond the Alligator Farm. (461-2033. Sites Oct.-Jan. $14; Feb.-Sept. $16; electricity $2 extra. Office open daily 8am-sunset. Reservations recommended.)

## 🍴🎵 FOOD AND NIGHTLIFE

The bustle of daytime tourists and abundance of budget eateries make lunch in St. Augustine's historic district a delight. Strolling down **Saint George St.** reveals the daily specials scrawled on blackboards outside each restaurant. **Anastasia Blvd.** also holds a wealth of budget options. An excellent healthy option is the **Manatee Cafe,** 179 San Marco Ave., just past the Fountain of Youth. Tasty grilled hummus pita reuben ($4.75) gains originality points. (826-02100. Open daily 8am-4pm.) **Captain Jack's,** 410 Anastasia Blvd., will take you home with fried shrimp ($9) in your belly (829-6846; open M-F 11:30am-9pm, Sa-Su noon-9pm). If, my dear, you do give a damn, go to **Scarlett O'Hara's,** 70 Hypolita St., at Cordova St., where monster burgers run $5 and live music entertains nightly (824-6535; open daily 11:30am-12:30am; occasional $2 cover). **Peterson Bakery,** 113½ King St., in the morning has a beautiful and tasty array of fresh donuts, pastries, and other delights (829-2964; open daily 6:30am-4:30pm).

St. Augustine supports an array of bars. *Today Tonight*, available at most grocery and convenience stores, has listings of current concerts and events. Local string musicians play on the two stages in the **Milltop**, 19½ Saint George St, a tiny bar situated above an old mill in the restored district. (829-2329. Cover varies. Open M-Sa 11am-1am, Su 11am-10pm. Music daily from 1pm until closing.) Cheap flicks and bargain eats await the weary traveler at **Pot Belly's**, 36 Granada St., across from the Lightner Museum (see below). This combination pub, deli, and cinema serves a vast array of junk food to tables in the theater. Remarkably cheap movie tickets run $2-4, and the ice cream drinks are divine. (829-3101; shows every 15-30min. Starting times 6:30-9:30pm.) The hot spot for the young beach crowd, the **Oasis Deck and Restaurant**, 4000 Rt. A1A S./Beach Blvd., schedules nightly entertainment with Happy Hours from 4-7pm (471-3424; open daily 6am-1am).

## 👁 SIGHTS

The historic district centers on Saint George St., beginning at the Gates of the City near the visitors center and running south past Cadiz St. and the Oldest Store. **Sightseeing Trains** hit all the major attractions. *(170 San Marco Ave. 829-6545. $12, children $5. 20 stops.)* Actors in period costumes describe the customs and crafts of the Spanish New World at the **Spanish Quarter**, a living museum which includes Gallegos House. *(29 Saint George St. 825-6830. Open Su-Th 9am-7pm, F-Sa 9am-7pm. $6.50, students and ages 6-18 $4, seniors and AAA members 10% off.)* Other 18th-century homes and shops fill the Restored Area. The oldest masonry fortress in the continental U.S., **Castillo de San Marcos National Monument**, off San Marco Ave., has 14-ft.-thick walls built of coquina, the local shell-rock. Inside the fort (a four-pointed star complete with drawbridge and murky moat), you'll find a museum, a large courtyard surrounded by livery quarters for the garrison, a jail, a chapel, and the original cannon brought overseas by the Spanish. A cannon-firing ceremony occurs at 11am, 1:30, 2:30, and 3:30pm. *(1 Castillo Dr. 829-6506. Open daily 8:45am-4:45pm. $4, under 16 and seniors with Golden Age Passport free. Occasional tours; call ahead.)*

For 2 decades, St. Augustine was the end of the line—the railroad line, that is. Swarms of wealthy northerners b-lined to railroad owner Henry Flagler's **Ponce de León Hotel**, at King and Cordova St. The hotel, decorated entirely by Tiffany's and outfitted with electricity by Edison himself (the first hotel to feature this luxury), is now **Flagler College**. On summer days, free 25min. tours pass through some of the recently restored rooms; go, if only to see the exquisite stained glass windows. *(829-6481, ext. 205. Tours mid-May to mid-Aug. daily on the hr. 11am-4pm.)* In 1947, Chicago publisher and art lover Otto Lightner converted the Alcazar Hotel, across the street, into the **Lightner Museum** to hold an impressive collection of cut, blown, and burnished glass, as well as old clothing and oddities like nun and monk beer stains. *(824-2874. Open daily 9am-4:45pm. $6, students and ages 12-18 $2.)*

Not surprisingly, the oldest continuous settlement in the U.S. holds some of the nation's oldest stuff. The self-proclaimed **Oldest House** was occupied since its construction in the 1600s until 1918, when it became a museum. *(14 Saint Francis St. 824-2872. Open daily 9am-5pm. $5, students $3, seniors $4.50, families $12.)* The **Oldest Store Museum** holds over 100,000 items from the 18th and 19th centuries. *(4 Artillery Ln. 829-9729. Open M-Sa 9am-5pm, Su noon-5pm. $5, ages 6-12 $1.50.)*

Six blocks north of the info center, moss- and vine-covered **La Leche Shrine and Mission of Nombre de Dios**, off San Marco Ave., held the first U.S. Catholic mass. Above it, a 208 ft. steel cross commemorates the city's founding. *(27 Ocean St. 824-2809. Open daily 7am-7pm. Mass M-F 8:30am, Sa 6pm, Su 8am; in summer Su 8am. Donation suggested.)* No trip to St. Augustine would be complete without a trek down beautiful Magnolia Drive, to the **Fountain of Youth**. Go right on Williams St. from San Marco Ave. and continue a few blocks past Nombre de Dios. *(11 Magnolia Ave. 829-3168. Open daily 9am-5pm. $5.50, seniors $4.50, ages 6-12 $2.50.)*

## DAYTONA BEACH

Daytona Beach boils down to two essentials: beaches and racing. In the 1920s locals competed on the hard-packed sands along the ocean; today race fans head to the colossal Daytona International Speedway. College students flock to the spring break mecca for its 500-ft.-wide beach and ample nightlife.

**7 PRACTICAL INFORMATION.** Daytona Beach lies 53mi. northeast of Orlando and 90mi. south of Jacksonville. I-95 parallels the ocean and the barrier island. Full of surf shops, motels and bars, **Atlantic Ave. (Rt. A1A)** is the main drag along the shore. **International Speedway Blvd. (U.S. 92)** runs east-west, from the ocean through the downtown area and past the racetrack. Daytona Beach is a collection of smaller towns that have expanded and converged, but preserved their individual street-numbering systems. Many street numbers are not consecutive and navigation can be difficult. To avoid the gridlock on the beach, arrive early (8am) and leave early (3pm or so). You'll pay $5 to drive onto the beach (permitted 8am-7pm), and police strictly enforce the 10 mph speed limit. Free parking is plentiful during most of the year but sparse during peak seasons, especially Speed Week, Bike Week, Biketoberfest, and the Pepsi 400 (see **Entertainment,** below), not to mention spring break (usually the second half of Mar.).

　　**Amtrak,** 2491 Old New York Ave. in Deland (734-2322; station open daily 9:15am-8pm), 24mi. west on Rt. 92, tracks to Miami (7hr., 2 per day, $37-74). **Greyhound,** 138 S. Ridgewood Ave. (255-7076; station open daily 8am-10:30pm), behind the antique mall, 4mi. west of the beach, goes to Orlando (80min., 6 per day, $10) and Jacksonville (2hr., 7 per day, $17). **Votran County Transit Co.,** 950 Big Tree Rd. (761-7700), on the mainland, operates local buses and a trolley that covers A1A between Granada Blvd. and Dunlawton Ave. (Service M-Sa 5:30am-6:30pm with most running M-Sa 7am-7pm, Su 8am-5:30pm, trolley runs until midnight on Sat. nights. $1, children and seniors 50¢, transfers free. Free maps available at hotels.) **Cab Co.** (253-2522) charges $2.40 for the first mi. and $1.20 per additional mi. **Daytona Beach Convention and Visitors Bureau:** 126 E. Orange Ave. (255-0415 or 800-854-1234), on City Island (open M-F 8:30am-5pm). **Rape Crisis and Sexual Abuse Line:** 254-4106. 24hr. **Post Office:** 220 N. Beach St. (253-5166; open M-F 8am-5pm, Sa 9am-noon). **ZIP code:** 32115. **Area code:** 904.

**ⓕ ACCOMMODATIONS.** Almost all of Daytona's accommodations front **Atlantic Ave./Rt. A1A,** either on the beach or across the street; those off the beach offer the best deals. Quieter hotels line **Ridgewood Ave.** During spring break and big race weekends, even the worst hotels are overpriced, and it's unwise to sleep on the well-patrolled shores. In summer and fall, prices plunge; most hotels offer special deals in June. The art deco **Streamline Hotel,** 140 S. Atlantic Ave., 1 block north of E. International Speedway Blvd., stands out amidst low level motels. Perks include A/C, TV, kitchen facilities, free local calls, a recreation room, and proximity to the beach. (258-6937; singles and doubles $19; during special events, up to $150.) The **Camellia Motel,** 1055 N. Atlantic Ave., across the street from the beach, is an especially welcoming retreat, with cozy, bright rooms, free local calls, cable TV, and A/C. Owner speaks Slovak, German, English and French. (252-9963. Singles $25; doubles $30; $10 per additional person. During spring break, singles $60; $10 per additional person. Rooms with kitchens cost $10 more. Reserve early.) The **Rio Beach Motel,** 843 S. Atlantic Ave., has large rooms, cable TV, A/C, and a pool. Its ocean location compensates for its lackluster decor. (253-6564. $35; oceanfront $39; $10 more for kitchen.; $10 more on weekends; $120 during races and spring break.)

　　**Tomoka State Park,** 2099 N. Beach St., 8mi. north of Daytona and 70min. from Disney World, has 100 sites under a tropical canopy near a salt marsh, along with trails and a museum. Take bus #3 ("N. Ridgewood") to Domicilio and walk 2mi. north. (676-4050. Sites $11, with electricity $13; Nov.-Apr. $16/19; $6 senior discount. Open daily 8am-sunset. Canoe rentals $3 per hr.) **Nova Family Campground,**

1190 Herbert St., in Port Orange, is south of Daytona Beach and 3mi. from the shore. From I-95, take a left onto Clyde Morris Blvd. and a right on Herbert St., or take bus #7 or 15 from downtown or the beach. (767-0095. Sites $16, with electricity and water $18, full hookup $22; higher during events. Open daily 8am-8pm.)

**⌂ FOOD.** One of the most famous (and popular) seafood restaurants in the area is ⬚ **Aunt Catfish's,** just to the left of Port Orange Bridge (Dunlawton Ave.) as it connects to the mainland. Massive portions include delicious coconut fried chicken ($5) and salad and hot bar. Their Boatsinker Pie, a chocolate encrusted fudge dessert, has been lauded by *Bon Appetit*. (767-4768. Open M-Sa 11:30am-10pm, Su 9am-2pm.) "If it swims…we have it," boasts **B&B Fisheries,** 715 E. International Speedway Blvd., the oldest family-owned seafood house in town since 1932. Take out your choice of four to five varieties of fresh fish for lunch from $4.50. (252-6542. Open M-F 11am-8:30pm, Sa 4-8:30pm; takeout M-Sa 11:30am-8:30pm.) For cheap Chinese eats, hit the **Orient Palace Restaurant**, 2116 S. Atlantic Ave., where chicken and broccoli is $6.75. (255-4183. Open daily 5-11pm; all-you-can-eat buffet 5-9:30pm; Happy Hour with wicked scotch sours 4-6pm.)

**⬚ SIGHTS.** Experience the power of the true center of Daytona's world, the legendary **Daytona International Speedway.** Headquarters to NASCAR, the track annually hosts the Super Bowl of racing, the **Daytona 500.** *(Feb. 20; tickets $75-185.)* **SpeedWeek,** a 15-day series of races, qualifying and build-up, precedes the Great American Race. *(Feb. 5-19.)* A "Disney for motorheads," **Daytona USA** thrills non-race fans as well with spectacular interactive exhibits and shows; learn to change all four tires in under 16sec. Inside, the **Daytona 500** IMAX film tears around the track at 180mph. A 30min. tour of the facility provides an inside peak at the track. *(1801 W. International Speedway Blvd. 254-2700; 253-7223 for tickets. Open daily 9am-7pm. $12; seniors $10; ages 6-12 $6. Tours daily 9am-5pm. $6.)* NASCAR returns to Daytona in July for its mid-summer race under the lights, the **Pepsi 400** (July 1; tickets $49-115). **Bike Week** (Mar. 1-12) draws biker mamas for various motorcycle duels, and **Biketoberfest** (Oct. 19-20) brings them back for more.

**⬚ ENTERTAINMENT.** When spring break hits, concerts, hotel-sponsored parties, and other events cater to students questing for fun. News about these travels fastest by word of mouth, but the *Calendar of Events* and *SEE Daytona Beach*, available at the chamber of commerce, make good starting points. On more mellow nights, head to the boardwalk to play volleyball or shake your groove thing at the **Oceanfront Bandshell.** A fairly homogeneous collection of dance clubs tingle along Seabreeze Blvd. near the intersection with N. Atlantic Ave. At **St. Regis Bar and Restaurant,** 509 Seabreeze Blvd., live jazz flavors the cool veranda on F and Sa from 8-11pm (252-8743; open Tu-Sa 6-11pm). Among the nightclubs, **Ocean Deck,** 127 S. Ocean Ave., where "everyday is like a weekend," stands apart with its beachfront location and live reggae music. (253-5224. 21+ from 9pm. Music nightly 9:30pm-2:30am. Open daily 11am-3am; full menu until 2am.)

# ORLANDO

Every year, millions descend upon Orlando, only to visit Disney World, the most popular tourist attraction on earth. Comprised of the original Magic Kingdom, Epcot Center, Disney-MGM Studios, and the new Animal Kingdom and Downtown Disney area, Disney's sheer size and scope push it into a class by itself. Don't overlook the area's smaller perks though; Universal Studios Escape is an innovative theme park, and the natural talent at Sea World astounds. Choose and plan time wisely—there are many ways to lighten your wallet in this land of illusions.

## ▓ ORIENTATION AND PRACTICAL INFORMATION

Orlando lies at the center of hundreds of small lakes and amusement parks. **Lake Eola** is in the center of the city, east of I-4 and south of **Colonial Dr.** Streets are divided north-south by **Rt. 17/92 (Orange Blossom Trail)** and east-west by Colonial Dr. The **Bee Line Expwy. (Rt. 528)** and the **East-West Expwy.** exact several tolls for their convenience. Supposedly an east-west expressway, I-4 actually runs north-south through the center of town. **Disney World, Universal Studios** and **Sea World** await 15-20mi. southwest of downtown on I-4 W; **Cypress Gardens** is 30mi. south of Disney off U.S. 27 near Winter Haven. Most hotels offer shuttle service to Disney. City buses and Mears Motor Shuttle (see below) serve some parks.

**Airport: Orlando International,** 1 Airport Blvd. (825-2001); from the airport take Rt. 436 N, exit to Rt. 528 W (the Bee Line Expwy.), then head east on I-4 to the exits for downtown. City bus #11, 41, and 42 make the trip for 85¢. **Mears Motor Shuttle,** 324 W. Gore St. (423-5566), has a booth at the airport for transportation to most hotels. 1 bus goes straight to Disney (round-trip $25, ages 4-11 $17; leaves every 15min.). No shuttle reservations are necessary from the airport (for return, call 1 day in advance).

**Trains: Amtrak,** 1400 Sligh Blvd. (843-7611), 3 blocks east of I-4; take S. Orange Ave., head west on Columbia, then take a right on Sligh. To Jacksonville (3hr., 2 per day, $19). Station open daily 7:15am-9pm.

**Buses: Greyhound,** 555 N. John Young Pkwy. (292-3424), at Colonial Dr. To Kissimee (40min., 6 per day, $6) and Jacksonville (3-4½hr., 9 per day, $26-28). Open 24hr.

**Public Transit: LYNX,** 78 W. Central Blvd. (841-8240; M-F 6am-8pm, Sa 7:30am-6:15pm, Su 8am-6pm). Buses operate daily 6am-9pm (times vary with route). Fare 85¢, ages 7-18 25¢ with ID, transfers 10¢. Downtown terminal between Central and Pine St., 1 block west of Orange Ave. and 1 block east of I-4. Schedules available at most shopping malls, banks, and at the downtown terminal. Serves the airport (bus #11 or 51 at side A, level 1) and Wet 'n' Wild (see p. 432).

**Taxis: Yellow Cab,** 422-4455.

**Car Rental: Alamo,** 8200 McCoy Rd. (857-8200), near the airport. Compacts $20-32 per day, $109-190 per week. Under 25 surcharge $20 per day. Must be 21 with major credit card. Open 24hr.

**Visitor Info: Orlando Official Visitor Center,** 8445 International Dr. (363-5871; www.go2orlando.com), several mi. southwest of downtown, 2 blocks from the Mercado (a Spanish-style mall); take bus #8 and ask the driver to stop. Ask for the free "Magic Card" and receive discounts at various attractions, shops, restaurants, and hotels. Open daily 8am-7pm, tickets sold 8am-6pm.

**Hotlines: Rape Hotline,** 740-5408. **Crisis Hotline,** 843-4357. **Crisis Info,** 425-2624.

**Post Office:** 46 E. Robinson St. (843-5673). Open M-F 7am-5pm, Sa 9am-noon. **ZIP code:** 32801. **Area code:** 407.

## ▓ ACCOMMODATIONS

Orlando does not cater to the budget traveler. Prices for hotel rooms rise exponentially as you approach Disney World; plan to stay in a hostel or in downtown Orlando. Visitors staying in Kissimee should bear in mind that **Greyhound runs to Kissimee.** Reservations are prudent, especially from Dec. through Jan., Mar. through Apr., late June through Aug., and on holidays.

**Hostelling International-Orlando Resort (HI-AYH),** 4840 W. Irlo Bronson Memorial Hwy./Rt. 192 (396-8282), in Kissimmee. Lakeside location 5mi. from Disney World with swimming pool, fountains, and summer BBQs on Tu and Th ($3). Super-clean, motel-style rooms with bunk beds, A/C, pool and lake access, and transportation to Disney ($8). Beds $16, nonmembers $19; private rooms (with TVs, A/C, phone) from $35 for 2 people. Ages 6-17 ½-price, under 6 free. Lockers, linens free. Towels $1. Reception 24hr.

**Sun Motel,** 5020 W. Irlo Bronson Memorial Hwy./Rt. 192 (396-6666 or 800-541-2674), in Kissimmee. Reasonable considering its proximity to Disney World (4mi.). Pretty rooms with floral bedspreads, cable TV, fridge, phone, pool, and A/C. $5 key deposit. 45¢ local calls. Singles $40; doubles $45; off-season $28/30. Sells discount tickets for theme parks.

**Disney's All-Star Resorts** (934-7639), in Disney World. From I-4, take exit 25B and follow the signs to Blizzard Beach—the resorts are just behind it. Pricey, but a great deal for groups. Large "theme" decorations from cowboy boots to surfboards adorn the courtyards. Pools, A/C, phone, fridge ($6 extra per day), food court. Free parking and Disney transportation. Singles and doubles $89; $8 per additional adult (up to 4).

**KOA,** 4771 W. Irlo Bronson Memorial Hwy./Rt. 192 (396-2400 or 800-562-7791), in Kissimmee 5mi. east of I-4. Sites have lots of trees, a nice pool, tennis courts, and a store (open 7am-9pm; when crowds are big, 7am-11pm). Tent sites $24, with hookup (for 2) $27; motor homes $44. "Kamping Kabins" with A/C: 1-room cabin $40; 2-room $50; in peak season $70/90; $10 per additional adult (up to 4). Discount tickets through Tickets 'N' Tours (396-1182 or 800-307-6667). Reception 24hr.

**Stage Stop Campground,** 14400 W. Colonial Dr./Rt. 50 (656-8000), 25 minutes north of Disney, off Florida's Turnpike in Winter Garden. Coming from the north on the Turnpike, take exit 267 and travel 2½mi. west on Rt. 50. A family campground with an activity room, pool, and laundry facilities. 248 sites (tent or RV) with full hookup $20, $120 per week. Reception in summer daily 8am-8pm.

Orlando has two municipal campgrounds. **Turkey Lake Park,** 3401 S. Hiawassee Rd., roosts near Universal Studios. (299-5581. Tent sites $6, with water and electricity $6, full hookup $12. Key deposit $10. Open daily 9:30am-7pm; in winter 9:30am-5pm.) **Moss Park,** 12901 Moss Park Rd., lies 10mi. from the airport; from the Bee Line, take Narcoossee Rd. south and follow the signs. Garnished with Spanish moss, the sites are lovely but far from civilization. (273-2327. Tent sites $11, with water and electricity $15; park entrance $1. Open daily 8am-7pm.)

## 🍴 FOOD

**Lilia's Grilled Delights,** 3150 S. Orange Ave. (851-9087), 2 blocks south of Michigan St. and 5min. from the downtown business district. This small, Polynesian-influenced restaurant is one of the best-kept secrets in town. Don't pass up the Huli Huli Chicken, a twice-baked delight (half-chicken $4). Pulled pork sandwich $1.10. Lunch $4-6. Dinner plates $8-10. Open M-F 11am-9pm, Sa noon-9pm.

**Bakely's,** 345 W. Fairbanks Ave. (645-5767), in Winter Park. Take I-4 to the Fairbanks Ave. exit. The variety at this restaurant/bake shop is as large as the portions. Breakfast is served all day (famous skillets); the $5 burgers are Orlando's best. Save room for the 6-layer Boston cream cake ($3). Open Su-Th 7am-11pm, F-Sa 7am-midnight.

**Clarkie's Restaurant,** 3110 S. Orange Ave. (859-1690). Serves up simple food for under $5. Large, tasty 4-veggie platter $4. Early Bird special (2 eggs, grits, toast or biscuit) $1.29 until 8am. Open M-F 6am-2pm, Sa 6am-noon, Su 7am-1pm.

**Francesco's Ristorante Italiano,** 4920 W. Irlo Bronson Memorial Hwy./Rt. 192 (396-0889). Dine beneath Chianti bottles while Sinatra croons from a stereo. Large portions of pasta, steak, or seafood come complete with salad bar and homemade bread $7-15. Breakfast special $2.39. Open daily 7:30am-11pm.

## 🎵 ENTERTAINMENT AND NIGHTLIFE

**N. Orange Ave.,** downtown, is the heart of Orlando nightlife. Relatively inexpensive bars line the city's main drag. **Zuma Beach Club,** 46 N. Orange Ave. is home to a mainstream college and 20-something crowd, packing 3500 people in on Sa nights with 2 stories of bars, beer tubs, and dance floors. (648-8363. Open M and Sa 9pm-3am, Tu 10pm-3:30am, Th 9pm-2:30am, F 8pm-2:30am.) Voted one of America's best clubs by *Rolling Stone* and *Billboard,* **The Club at Firestone,** 578 N. Orange

Ave., at Concord, features a raucous gay night (Sa) among a variety of theme nights (426-0005; cover $5-10; open Th-Su 9pm-3am). Improvisational comedy shows will keep you in stitches at the ◪SAK Theater, 380 W. Amelia St., at Hughey Ave. (648-0001. Shows F-Sa 7:30, 9:30, and 11:30pm; Su and Tu 9pm, Th 8, 9:45pm. $12.) **Church Street Station,** 129 W. Church St., on the corner of Church and Garland St., is a slick, block-long entertainment, shopping, and restaurant complex (422-2434; open Su-Th 11am-1am, F-Sa 11am-2am). Inside, you can boogie down in the sci-fi-meets-wild-west wooden decor of **Phineas Phogg's Balloon Works,** 129 W. Church St. (422-2434; open daily 8pm-2am, opens F at 5pm; 21+).

# DISNEY WORLD

Happiness can be bought at Disney World, where throngs of fun-seekers work assiduously to get their money's worth. "Amusement park" barely begins to describe the media empire, resort and hotel complex, 4 theme parks, 3 water parks, golf courses, sports venues, boardwalks, restaurants, and even nightclubs that constitute Disney World. Despite the flagrant over-commercialization, the central theme parks—the **Magic Kingdom, Epcot Center, Disney/MGM Studios,** and **Animal Kingdom,** and the entertainment complex **Downtown Disney**—still rule after 25 years. If bigger is better, Disney World wins the prize for best park in the U.S. by more than a mile. (824-4321, call daily 8am-10pm; www.disneyworld.com.) Disney dominates **Lake Buena Vista** (20mi. west of Orlando via I-4).

◪ **PRACTICAL INFORMATION.** The $44 1-day entrance fee (ages 3-9 $35) admits you to one of the 4 parks, allowing you to leave and return to the same park later in the day. A 4-day **Park-Hopper Pass** buys admission to all four parks for all 4 days ($167, ages 3-9 $134). The **Park Hopper Plus,** includes 5 days of admission to 2 other Disney attractions ($229/183). A 6-day package includes admission to 3 other Disney attractions ($259/207). The Hopper passes allow for unlimited transportation between attractions on the Disney monorail, boats, buses, and trains. Multiday passes need not be used on consecutive days, and never expire. Parking is $5 per day. Attractions that charge separate admissions include **River Country** ($16, ages 3-9 $12.50); **Discovery Island** ($17/13); **Typhoon Lagoon** ($29/23); **Pleasure Island** ($19, 18+, unless with adult); **Blizzard Beach** ($29, ages 3-11 $23), and **Disney's Wide World of Sports Complex** ($8, ages 3-9 $6.75). For descriptions, see **Other Disney Attractions,** below. Prices tend to increase annually.

Disney World opens its gates 365 days a year, but hours fluctuate with the season. Expect the parks to open at 9am and close between 7pm and 11pm; call beforehand. The parks get busy during the summer when school is out, but the enormously crowded "peak times" are Christmas, Thanksgiving, and the month around Easter. More people visit between Christmas and New Year's than at any other time of year; the parks are comatose in January, when almost no one is out of school. The crowd hits the main gates at 10am; arrive before the 9am opening time and seek out your favorite rides or exhibits before noon. During peak periods (and often during the rest of the year), Disney World actually opens earlier than the stated time for guests staying at Disney resorts. To avoid the crowds, start at the rear of a park and work your way to the front. You'll be able to see the distant attractions while the masses cram the lines for those near the entrance. In all the theme parks, lines get remarkably shorter around 6pm and during parades; check for times and hit the biggies then. Disney is expanding the **FASTPASS** option from the Animal Kingdom into other parks; show up for your assigned time to ride and bypass the line. Otherwise, expect a 45min. to 2hr. wait.

**MAGIC KINGDOM.** Seven "lands" comprise the Magic Kingdom. More than any of the other Disney parks, this is geared for children. Enter on **Main St., USA** to capture the essence of early 20th-century America. The architects employed "forced perspective" here, building the ground floor of the shops 9/10ths of the normal size and making the second and third stories progressively smaller. Walt describes his

## Orlando Theme Parks

ACCOMMODATIONS
A  Disney's All-Star Resort
B  Sun Motel
C  HI – Orlando
D  KOA

FLORIDA

vision in the "Walt Disney Movie" at the Hospitality House, to the right as you emerge from under the railroad station. Late in the afternoon, the "Mickey Mania Parade" down Main St. showcases all the Disney characters.

**Tomorrowland** received a neon-and-stainless-steel face-lift that skyrocketed it out of the space-race days of the 60s and into a futuristic intergalactic nation. **XS. Buzz Lightyear's Space Ranger Spin** is Tomorrowland's newest attraction, a lighthearted save-the-planet quest made unique by "working" laser guns. The **ExtraTERRORestrial Alien Encounter** chills without spins or drops, creating suspense in pitch blackness—a claustrophobe's nightmare. **Space Mountain** still proves the thrilling high point of this section, if not the park. This is no secret; plan accordingly.

The golden-spired Cinderella's Castle marks the gateway to the mildest of Mickey's regions, **Fantasyland.** Two classic rides, **Peter Pan's Flight** and **Snow White's Adventures,** capture the original charm of the park; the evil Queen scares children like no one else. Winnie, Piglet, Tigger and friends bounce around happily in **The Many Adventures of Winnie the Pooh,** the latest addition. You know the song, so see what it means at **It's a Small World,** a saccharine but endearing boat tour celebrating the children of the world. Killer A/C makes it a good bet for a hot day.

**Liberty Sq.** and **Frontierland** devote their resources to a celebration of U.S. history and Mark Twain. Escape from the concrete and crowds at **Tom Sawyer Island,** a wooded re-creation of outback life on the Mississippi, accessible only by raft. Adventurers should catch the classic, runaway **Big Thunder Mountain Railroad** roller coaster or the truly thrilling **Splash Mountain,** which takes you on a voyage with Br'er Rabbit—and 4 bear posteriors—and leaves you chilled inside and out. Spooky but dorky, **Haunted Mansion** is a classic with a quick line. Entertaining animatronics enliven the **Country Bear Jamboree.** A steamboat trip lets tired feet rest.

**Adventureland** romanticizes unexplored regions of the world in often trivial and tacky ways. The **Jungle Cruise** takes a tongue-in-cheek tour through tropical waterways populated by not-so-authentic-looking wildlife. **Pirates of the Caribbean** explores caves where animated buccaneers spar, swig, and sing, and are chased by maidens. The **Swiss Family Robinson** house captures the family's clever tricks.

**EPCOT CENTER.** In 1966, Walt dreamed up an "Experimental Prototype Community Of Tomorrow" (EPCOT), which would evolve constantly to incorporate new ideas from U.S. technology—eventually becoming a self-sufficient, futuristic utopia. At present, Epcot splits into **Future World** and **World Showcase.** Summer '99 saw massive renovations and construction at the park; expect a dramatically changed Epcot for the yearlong **Millennia Celebration** in 2000.

The trademark 180 ft. high geosphere that forms the entrance to **Future World** houses the **Spaceship Earth** attraction, where visitors board a "time machine" for a tour through the evolution of communications, and AT&T's latest ad campaign. A new veranda will dominate the area behind the silver sphere. Epcot's newest draw is **Test Track,** a 65mph tear through a GM testing facility (fast). Uniquely creative, this is one of Disney's better rides, worth the 75min. wait (not fast). At the **Wonders of Life, Body Wars** takes visitors on a tour of the human body (with the help of a simulator). **Cranium Command** puts you at the helm of a 12-year-old boy as his animatronic "pilot" steers him around the pitfalls of daily life. **The Land** presents **The Circle of Life,** a live-action/animated film about the environment with characters from *The Lion King.* Also here is **Food Rocks,** an adorable and frequently overlooked musical about nutrition featuring **Tone Loc** as a milk "wrapper." Fish, sharks, and manatees inhabit the re-created coral reef in **The Living Seas.** The immensely popular **Journey Into Imagination** pavilion screens *Honey, I Shrunk the Audience,* which boasts stellar 3D effects.

At the **World Showcase,** an architectural style or monument, as well as typical food and crafts, represent selected countries from around the world. People in indigenous costumes perform dances, theatrical skits, and other "cultural" entertainment; each cast member is from the country they represent. To the east of Spaceship Earth, **Guest Relations** provides park info and can help arrange dinner reservations. Check the handy maps (available everywhere) for showtimes of the

25 various dance troupes, singers, and films throughout the World Showcase. The people with yellow-striped Disney-logoed shirts can answer questions throughout the park. The **360° film** made in China and the 180° film made in France rate among the best of the attractions. **The American Adventure** dispenses a patriotic interpretation of American history. Every night at 9pm, Epcot presents a magnificent mega-show called **Illuminations,** with music from the represented nations accompanied by dancing fountains, laser lights, and fireworks.

The World Showcase pavilions specialize in regional cuisine. The all-you-can-eat meat, seafood, and salad buffet ($12) at **Restaurant Akershus** is the closest one gets to a Disney dining bargain. Eat plate seven and be designated a Viking by your blond-haired, blue-eyed server. In other pavilions, sit-down meals will run $13-15 for lunch and upwards of $20 for dinner. If you plan to eat a sit-down meal in the park, make reservations first thing in the morning at Guest Relations, or you'll end up eating a $4.50 hot dog with the rest of the unfortunates. The regional cafes (no reservations required) present cheaper options, but no real bargains. Eat outside "the World" or smuggle stuff in to save money for Goofy-eared hats.

**DISNEY-MGM STUDIOS.** Disney-MGM Studios set out to create a "living movie set," but they only appear to have succeeded. Many familiar Disney characters stroll through the park, as do a host of characters dressed as directors, starlets, gossip columnists, and fans. Stunt shows and mini-theatricals take place continually. Disney relative ABC-TV maintains a high profile and films programs there.

The **Aerosmith Rock n' Roller Coaster** blasted into the park in Aug. '99 with a 2.8sec., 0-60mph take off. "Sweet Emotion" blares during a stomach-numbing zip through L.A. en route to an Aerosmith performance. Next door, the **Twilight Zone Tower of Terror** climbs 13 flights in an old-time Hollywood hotel before the cable snaps; just when you think the ride is over, WHAM! It drops you again. All goes berserk in the well crafted **Muppet Vision 3D,** a behind-the-scenes tour of top secret Muppets Labs. Beware the Swedish Chef. Of the two biggest attractions at this park, the underwhelming stuntshow **Indiana Jones Epic Stunt Spectacular,** is no match for the other biggie, **Star Tours.** Based on the Star Wars movies, a novice droid pilot steers your tourist ship into enemy fire. Super-believable video and effects skim the craft across the feared Death Star. MGM Studios also sports the behemoth Turkey Leg, a meaty snack ($4.50) befitting Fred Flintsone (on Sunset Blvd. across from Tower of Terror).

**DISNEY'S ANIMAL KINGDOM.** Amidst the usual rides, shows and merchandise, bizarrely exotic creatures stare down bewildered tourists. Because it is brand-new by Disney standards, park veterans and newcomers pack in during the day. Despite an earlier closing time than the other parks (7pm), the dinner crowd bails around 5pm, taking long lines with them. The rides are not among Mickey's greatest, but creative animal adventures and a classic 3-D show prove Disney still has the touch. Animal Kingdom, where you can stop anyone to ask, "Which way to Africa?" without getting a funny look, is divided into five main regions: Camp Minnie-Mickey, Safari Village, Africa, Asia, and Dinoland USA. **Camp M-M** is a little kid's haven for singing and dancing to Disney favorites, while a Mickey greeting area provides plenty of cuddly mouse hugs and photo ops. In Africa, the bumpy ride through the **Kilimanjaro Safaris** offers up-close views of rhinos, giraffes, lions and the occasional croc. A cheesy Disney narrative creates noise on the otherwise cool exotic zoo tour. The other Animal Kingdom biggie, **Countdown to Extinction** in Dinoland USA, is an overhyped, relatively slow thrill ride about time travel gone awry. The whole park is arranged around a single focal point, the **Tree of Life,** towering 14 stories tall, with over 325 animals carved into its roots, branches, and trunk. Beneath the tree, the show **It's Tough to be a Bug** combines 3-D tech with "audio animaltronics" for a creepily fun demo of insect talent. Also in Dinoland USA is the **Boneyard,** where kids can dig in a huge sandpit and uncover the remains of a woolly mammoth. Cool down on the **Kali River Rapids,** a soaking tour of the tropical rainforest. The **Discovery River Boats** of **Safari Village** are a relaxing break.

**OTHER DISNEY ATTRACTIONS.** Besides the three main parks, Disney offers several other draws with different themes and separate admissions (see p. 428). The 🎦 **Richard Petty Driving Experience** at the **Walt Disney World Speedway** is undoubtedly the ride to top all rides. Blast around the track at over 145mph in a custom-made NASCAR machine with a pro driver behind the wheel. Ain't no special effects here; this *is* the ultimate speed experience. (800-237-3889. Ride $90; must be 16. Free to watch the racing.) **Downtown Disney** is a larger than life, neon conglomeration of theme restaurants, nightlife, and shopping. **Pleasure Island** is a scantily clad Disney with an attitude. Choose among the nightclubs—country, R&B, jazz, 70s and techno. ($19 to cross bridge. 18+ unless accompanied by parent) **Blizzard Beach,** the most intense but least thematic of 3 water parks, was built on the harrowing premise of a melting mountain. Ride a ski lift to the peak of Mt. Gushmore and take the fastest water-slide in the world (Summit Plummet) down the 120 ft. descent. **Typhoon Lagoon,** a 50-acre water park, centers around one of the world's largest wave-making pools and the 7 ft. waves it creates. Besides eight water slides, the lagoon has a creek for inner-tube rides and a saltwater coral reef stocked with tropical fish and harmless sharks. Built to resemble a swimming hole, **River Country** offers water slides, rope swings, and plenty of room to swim. Water parks fill up early on hot days, so you might get turned away. Across Bay Lake from River Country is **Discovery Island**, a zoological park. **Disney's Wide World of Sports Complex,** tests your skills in the **NFL Experience** and hosts minor league baseball games (939-1500).

# LIFE BEYOND DISNEY

The big non-Disney theme parks band together in competition with Mickey Mouse. "Flex Tickets," their mouse traps for Mickey, combine admission prices at a discount. A four-park ticket covers Sea World, both Universal Studios parks, and Wet 'n' Wild (a water park), and allows 7 days of visiting with unlimited admissions ($160, ages 3-9 $130). The five-park ticket (call Universal City Travel at 800-224-3838) adds Busch Gardens in Tampa (see p. 452) and lasts 10 days ($197/158).

**SEA WORLD.** One of the U.S.'s largest marine parks, **Sea World,** 12mi. southwest of Orlando off I-4 at Rt. 528 (take bus #8), makes a splash with marine-themed shows, rides and exhibits. Eels, barracudas, sharks, and other pleasants lick their chops in **Terrors of the Deep,** the world's largest collection of dangerous sea creatures. In Shamu Stadium, the talented killer whale family remains Sea World's big draw. **The Shamu Adventure** thrills with plenty of amazing aquatic acrobatics executed smartly by a whole family of orcas and their trainers. Whale belly flops send waves of 52°F salt water into the cheering "soak zone"; try to wear a swimsuit. In the Atlantis Bayside Stadium, two teams of supremely gifted skiers, gymnasts and boaters square off in the **Intensity Games.** Seadoos race at 50mph, waterskiers fly over ramps, the bizarre "air chair" zips across the lagoon, all as you are encouraged to boo for the other squad. In recent years, Sea World has added roller coasters; the 1998 water coaster **Journey to Atlantis** gets rave reviews. Spring 2000 will bring the much anticipated **Kraken,** a floorless ride billed as the highest, fastest and longest coaster in Orlando. Upside down flips, turns and loops follow a 65mph plunge into an underwater lagoon. The stunning **Anheuiser-Busch Clydesdales** trot around for viewing (mesmerized tourists in tow). *(351-3600. Open daily 9am-7pm; extended hours in summer. $44, ages 3-9 $35. Parking $5. Sky Tower ride $3 extra. Most hotel brochure displays and hostels have coupons for $2-3 off regular admission.)*

**CYPRESS GARDENS. Cypress Gardens** lies southwest of Orlando in Winter Haven; take I-4 southwest to Rt. 27 S., then Rt. 540 W. Botanical gardens feature over 8000 varieties of plants and flowers with winding walkways and electric boat rides for touring. Hoop-skirted Southern Belles patrol the grounds. Despite all the pretty flowers, the **water-ski shows** attract the biggest crowds and the loudest applause. *(Daily 10:30am, 1:30, and 4pm; times and frequency vary with crowd size. Coupons can be found at most motels.)* **Greyhound** stops here once a day on its Tampa-West Palm Beach run *($12 from Tampa or Orlando. 941-324-2111. Open daily 9:30am-5pm; call ahead for exact hrs. $33.87, ages 6-17 $15.85, age 55 or older $28.)*

# UNIVERSAL STUDIOS ESCAPE

Opened in 1990, Universal Studios (take I-4 to exit 29B or 30B), doubled its size in 1999 with the addition of another park and entertainment district within its grounds. With its three parks, **Universal Studios Florida, Islands of Adventure**, and **CityWalk,** Universal is no longer an afterthought to the "other park" down I-4; its attractions are also must-sees in Orlando. *(363-8000. Open daily 9am, closing times vary. CityWalk open until 2am. Each park is $44, ages 3-9 $35; look for discount "upgrade" tickets to other park. CityWalk is ungated and free. Parking $6.)*

**UNIVERSAL STUDIOS FLORIDA.** The original attraction is both amusement park and working film studio. Metal face villains appear so close you can kiss 'em at **Terminator 2: 3D,** an apocalyptic showdown with an evil cybertech regime. The original movie's director, actors, and effects wizards produced the 3-D movie.

Rides take on movie themes: **Kongfrontation,** in which a 35 ft. King Kong roughhouses with your cable car, and the **E.T. Adventure** bike ride are hits with the kids. **Back to the Future...The Ride,** one of the staples of any Universal visit, utilizes 7-story OmniMax surround screens and spectacular special effects. For a respite from Florida sunshine, step into the all-too-real **Twister,** which puts you 20 ft. from an actual, 5-story tornado, **flying cows** and all. A photo with the cheery dino's stone statue at **A Day in the Park with Barney** makes the perfect dart board target. Interactive activities include the hilarious **Hercules and Xenia,** in which audience members create special effects and "appear" in an episode of the TV shows. Since the park also houses the largest film studio outside Hollywood, celebrity sightings are common. You may recognize a number of Universal's back-lot locations—Hollywood, Central Park, Beverly Hills, the Bates Motel from *Psycho*, and the streetfront from the *Cosby Show*. **Men In Black** will be the latest movie attraction in 2000.

**◪ ISLANDS OF ADVENTURE.** This park encompasses 110 acres of the most technologically sophisticated rides in the world, and some of the weirdest eateries in Orlando. Five islands portray different themes, ranging from cartoons to the overhyped Jurassic Park. **The Amazing Adventures of Spider Man** is the crown jewel of Orlando theme parks; new technology and several patents sprung from its conception. A fast-moving car whizzes around a 3-D video system as Spidey and you find the stolen Statue of Liberty. Riders go from 0-40mph in 2 sec., then shoot out of the **Incredible Hulk Coaster** with the same G-force as an Air Force F-16 fighter. In all the rides, waiting time is eased by ride narratives and creative distractions. The most entertaining island is the pastel-overload **Suess Landing,** home of the **Green Eggs & Ham Cafe** (green eggs and ham sandwich $5) and the **Moose Juice Goose Juice** stand. **The Cat in the Hat, Thing 1 and Thing 2** make the books come to life. Watch baby dinosaurs hatch in the **Discovery Center** nursery on Jurassic Park Island.

**CITYWALK.** Free, ungated 30 acres of shops, theme restaurants and lively street entertainment. Overpriced restaurants range from the collectible-laden **NASCAR Cafe** to **Emeril's Restaurant** (yes, it's that guy from TV) and everything in between. The clubs are considerably laid back and tourist heavy; **Bob Marley: A Tribute to Freedom** is patterned after his home and garden in Jamaica. What you save in covers (range $3-5 or $18 for all) will disappear over $4 beers and $6 drinks.

# COCOA BEACH AND CAPE CANAVERAL

Known primarily for rocket launches, space shuttle blast-offs, and **NASA's** enormous space center complex, the "Space Coast" also has uncrowded golden beaches, prime surfing, and vast wildlife preserves. Even during spring break, the place remains placid; most vacationers and sun-bathers here are Florida or Space Coast residents. Beware summer launch dates, when tourists pack the area and hotel prices follow NASA into the stratosphere.

**🔀 PRACTICAL INFORMATION.** The Cocoa Beach area, 50mi. east of Orlando, consists of mainland towns Cocoa and Rockledge, oceanfront towns Cocoa Beach and Cape Canaveral, and Merritt Island in between. **U.S. 1** runs north-south on the mainland, while **Rt. A1A** (North Atlantic Ave.) is the beach's main drag, running through Cocoa Beach and Cape Canaveral. **Greyhound,** 302 Main St. (636-6531; station open daily 7am-7pm), in Cocoa, 8mi. inland, runs to Orlando (1hr., 3 per day, $9); St. Augustine (3hr., 4 per day, $23); and Daytona (1¾hr., 4 per day, $14). **Space Coast Area Transit** (633-1878) runs North Beach and South Beach routes and makes stops at every town in Brevard County from 8am to 5pm (fare $1; students, seniors, and disabled 50¢; transfers free). From the bus station, a **taxi** to Cocoa Beach costs $15-17. **Taxi: Yellow Cab** (636-7017). The **Cocoa Shuttle** (784-3831) connects Cocoa Beach with Orlando International Airport ($18) and the Kennedy Space Center (round-trip $45 for 1 or 2). Reserve 3 days in advance for airport runs, and 2 days otherwise. **Visitor Info: Cocoa Beach Chamber of Commerce,** 400 Fortenberry Rd. (459-2200; open M-F 8:30am-5pm), on Merritt Island. **Space Coast Office of Tourism,** 8810 Astronaut Blvd. (A1A), #102 (800-936-2326; open M-F 8am-5pm). **ZIP code:** 32952. **Area code:** 407.

**🍴🛏 ACCOMMODATIONS AND FOOD. The Sunbath Beach Motel (HI-AYH),** 1135 N. Rt. A1A, in safe Indiatlantic, is among the cheapest lodgings directly on the oceanfront, ½mi. from a picturesque boardwalk and a prime turtle nesting site. (951-0004 or 888-786-2284. Efficiencies $44 by cash, $49 by credit card. Two-room apartments $66/75.) Across from the beach, **Motel 6,** 3701 N. Atlantic Ave. beats the rates of most accommodations in Cocoa Beach. (783-3103. A/C, pool, laundry. Singles $41; doubles $47.) Behind the Greyhound station and the water tower is the **Dixie Motel,** 301 Forrest Ave., with clean rooms, floor-to-ceiling windows, tile floors, pastel decor with A/C, and a swimming pool (632-1600; singles $40; doubles $50). Pitch your tent at scenic **Jetty Park Campgrounds,** 400 E. Jetty Rd., at the northern tip of Cape Canaveral. (783-7111. Jan.-Apr. rustic sites $18, with water and electricity $22, full hookup $25; May-Dec. $16/20/23. Reserve 3 months in advance; essential before shuttle launches.)

Lines awaiting "famous" New York style pizza stream out the door of **Bizzarro,** #4 1st Ave. off A1A in Indiatlantic (724-4799; Sicilian slices $1.50; subs $4). Nothing like soy milk and tofu on the beach; buy it at **Sunseed Food Co-op,** 6615 N. Atlantic Ave., an impressive depot of all things organic, natural, and healthy (784-0930; open M-W 10am-7pm, Th-Fr 10am-8pm, Sa 10am-7pm, Su 11am-6pm).

**🛸 BEAM ME UP, SCOTTY.** All of NASA's shuttle flights take off from the **Kennedy Space Center,** 18mi. north of Cocoa Beach. Without a car, Kennedy can be reached via the **Cocoa Shuttle** (see above). **Kennedy Space Center Visitors Complex** provides a huge welcoming center for visitors, 3-D IMAX theaters, and Rocket Garden. The solemn **Astronauts Memorial,** the country's newest national memorial, includes the etched names of the Challenger crew members. Towards the end of 1999 the **New Millennium** will open, a permanent addition focusing on the history and future of exploration. KSC offers one main and two special-interest tours of their 220 sq. mi. grounds. The **Kennedy Tour** takes you around to the three main tourist attractions; the Observation Gantry, Apollo/Saturn V Center, and the International Space Station Center. The 2hr. **Then & Now Tour** highlights historic launch sites. Trained guides lead the **Wildlife Tour** deep into the surrounding wetlands. *(452-2121. Visitor's Center open daily in summer 9am-8:30pm; in winter 9am-5:30pm. Center free. Kennedy Tour departs continuously from 9:30am-4:30pm. $14, children $10. IMAX tickets $7.50/5.50. Crew passes which include the Kennedy Tour and 1 IMAX film $19/15. T&N and Wildlife: both $25, price includes regular Kennedy Tour; call 449-4444 for times.)* The most impressive facility is the **Apollo/Saturn V Center,** a $35 million, 100,000 sq. ft. interactive museum, dedicated exclusively to the Apollo missions. A fully restored 363 ft. Saturn V rocket, one of only 3 in the world, runs the length of the daunting hanger. The **NASA Pkwy.,** site of the visitors center, is accessible only by car via

State Rd. 405; from Cocoa Beach, take Rt. A1A N until it turns west into Rt. 528, then follow Rt. 3 N to the Spaceport. With NASA's ambitious launch schedule, you may have a chance to watch the space shuttles *Endeavor, Columbia, Atlantis,* or *Discovery* thunder off into the blue yonder above the Cape. For detailed **launch info** and **schedules** call 407-867-4636. KSC will transport you to a viewing area to watch the fiery ascension. *(449-4444. $10.)*

Surrounding the NASA complex, the marshy **Merritt Island Wildlife Refuge** stirs with sea turtles, alligators, wild hogs, otters, and over 300 bird species. *(861-0667. Open daily sunrise-sunset. Visitors center open M-F 8am-4:30pm, Sa 9am-5pm.)* Just north of Merritt Island, **Canaveral National Seashore,** the northeastern shore of the wildlife refuge, covers 67,000 acres of undeveloped beach and dunes, home to more than 300 species of birds and mammals. Take Rt. 406 E. off U.S. 1 in Titusville. *(407-867-0677. Open daily 6am-6pm. $5 per car. Closed 3 days before and 1 day after NASA launches.)*

# FORT LAUDERDALE

Fort Lauderdale's gleaming white sands stretch 23mi. down Florida's east coast, but it is the water that dominates the city's landscape. Often dubbed the "Venice of America," Fort Lauderdale supports an intricate intra-coastal waterway with over 165mi. of navigable waters. Numerous inlets cut streets in two; the town is home to 42,000 yachts and countless water sports. The number two activity in ritzy Fort Lauderdale is shopping, particularly along Los Olas Blvd.

## ✴ ORIENTATION

North-south **I-95** connects West Palm Beach, Fort Lauderdale, and Miami. **Rt. 84/I-75 (Alligator Alley)** slithers 100mi. west from Fort Lauderdale across the Everglades to Naples and other small cities on Florida's Gulf Coast. Fort Lauderdale is bigger than it looks—and it looks huge. The city extends westward from its 23mi. of beach to encompass nearly 450 sq. mi. Streets and boulevards are east-west and avenues are north-south. All are labeled NW, NE, SW, or SE according to quadrant. **Broward Blvd.** divides the city north-south, while Andrews Ave. cuts east-west. The unpleasant downtown centers around **Federal Hwy. (U.S. 1)** and **Las Olas Blvd.,** about 2mi. west of the oceanfront. Between downtown and the waterfront, yachts fill the ritzy inlets of the **Intracoastal Waterway. The strip** (or Rt. A1A, N. Atlantic Blvd., 17th St. Causeway, Ocean Blvd., and Seabreeze Blvd.) runs 4mi. along the beach between **Oakland Park Blvd.** to the north and **Las Olas Blvd.** to the south. **Sunrise Blvd.** offers shopping malls and degenerates into a commercial strip west of downtown.

## 🛈 PRACTICAL INFORMATION

**Airport: Fort Lauderdale/Hollywood International,** 1400 Lee Wagoner Blvd. (call 359-1200 for recorded ramblings; 359-6100 for a human), 3½mi. south of downtown on U.S. 1, or take I-595 E from I-95 to exit 12B. Take bus #1 from downtown.

**Trains: Amtrak,** 200 SW 21st Terr. (587-6692), just west of I-95, ¼mi. south of Broward Blvd. Take bus #22 from downtown. To Orlando (4¾hr., 2 per day, $23-55). Open daily 7:15am-9:15pm.

**Buses: Greyhound,** 515 NE 3rd St. (764-6551), 3 blocks north of Broward Blvd. downtown. *Be careful in the surrounding area, especially at night.* To: Orlando (5hr., 7 per day, $35); Daytona Beach (6½hr., 6 per day, $27); and Miami (¾hr., 12 per day, $5). Open 24hr.

**Public Transit: Broward County Transit (BCT)** (357-8400; M-F 7am-8:30pm, Sa 7am-8pm, Su 8:30am-5pm). Most routes go to the terminal at the corner of 1st St. NW and 1st Ave. NW, downtown. Operates daily 6am-11pm, every 30min. on most routes. $1; transfer 15¢; seniors, students, under 18, and disabled 50¢ (with ID). 7-day passes ($7) available at beachfront hotels. Get a system map at terminal. **TMAX** (761-3543) runs loops through downtown and on the beach strip between Sunrise Blvd. and Las

Olas Blvd. Runs F 5pm-2am, Sa 7pm-2am. Free. **Tri-Rail** (728-8445 or 800-874-7245) connects West Palm Beach, Fort Lauderdale, and Miami. Trains run M-F 4:30am-8:30pm, Sa-Su reduced operation. Schedules available at airport, motels, or Tri-Rail stops. $5-9, discount for children, disabled, students and seniors with Tri-Rail ID.

**Taxis: Yellow Cab,** 565-5400. **Public Service Taxi,** 587-9090.

**Car Rental: Alamo,** 2601 S. Federal Hwy. (525-4713). From $30 per day, $150 per week with unlimited mi. Must be 21+. Under 25 must pay credit card deposit of $50 per day or $200 per week and $20 per day surcharge. Open 24hr.

**Bike Rental: Mike's Cyclery,** 5429 N. Federal Hwy. (493-5277). A variety of bicycles $20 per day, $50 per week. Some racing bikes cost slightly more. Credit card deposit required. Open daily 10am-7pm.

**Visitor Info: Greater Fort Lauderdale Convention and Visitors Bureau,** 1850 Eller Dr. (765-4466), in the Port Everglades. Particularly useful is *Superior Small Lodgings*, a comprehensive and detailed list of moderate and low-priced accommodations. For published info, call 800-227-8669. Open M-F 8:30am-5pm. **Chamber of Commerce,** 512 NE 3rd Ave. (462-6000), 3 blocks off Federal Hwy. at 5th St. Open M-F 8am-5pm.

**Internet Access: Floyd's Hostel/Crew House** and **International House,** see Accommodations, below.

**Hotlines: First Call for Help,** 467-6333. **Sexual Assault and Treatment Center,** 761-7273. Both 24hr.

**Post Office:** 1900 W. Oakland Park Blvd. (527-2028). Open M-F 7:30am-7pm, Sa 8:30am-2pm. **ZIP code:** 33310. **Area code:** 954.

# ▌ ACCOMMODATIONS

Hotel prices increase exponentially as you approach prime beachfront and spring break. High season runs from mid-Feb. through early Apr. Investigate package deals at the slightly worse-for-wear hotels along the strip in Fort Lauderdale. Many hotels offer off-season deals for under $35. Small motels, many with tiny kitchenettes, crowd each other 1 or 2 blocks off the beach area; look along **Birch Rd.,** 1 block from Rt. A1A, and south along A1A. The **Greater Fort Lauderdale Lodging and Hospitality Association,** 1412 E. Broward Blvd., provides a free directory of area hotels (832-9477; open M-F 9am-5pm). The *Fort Lauderdale News* and the Broward Section of the *Miami Herald* occasionally sport listings by local residents who rent rooms to tourists in spring. Sleeping on the well-patrolled beaches is illegal and virtually impossible between 9pm and sunrise.

**Floyd's Hostel/Crew House,** 445 SE 16th St. (462-0631; call ahead). A homey hostel catering to international travelers and boat crews. 42 beds, 5 kitchens, 5 living rooms with HBO and Showtime, and 8 bathrooms. Dorm rooms have 3-6 beds. Free daytime pickup from anywhere in the Ft. Lauderdale area. Free pasta, cereal, local calls, linen, lockers, and laundry. Check-in by midnight or call for special arrangement. Passport required. Internet access $2.50 per 30min. Within walking distance of beach and Las Olas district. The owners are engaged thanks to *Let's Go: USA 1995* (ask them for details). Beds $14.40 (discount with stay of 3 or more days); private rooms $35.

**Estoril Paradise Inn,** 2648 NE 32nd St. (563-3840 or 888-385-2322). Take bus #10 from downtown to Coral Ridge Shopping Center; walk 2 blocks east on Oakland. Family-run for 30 years. A 10min. walk to the beach. Free pick-up from airport, bus, or train stations. Very clean rooms with A/C, cable TV, kitchenette, and free parking. Heated pool and grill. Singles and doubles $29; mid-Dec. to Apr. $39. Reservations accepted within 48hr. mid-Dec. to Apr.

**International House,** 3811 N. Ocean Blvd. (568-1615), 1 block from the beach. From the Greyhound station, take bus #10 to the Central Terminal, then pick up #11, which stops at the hostel. Rooms with 4-8 beds, showers, A/C, cable TV, kitchen, free Internet access, and pool. Dive trips offered for guests with SCUBA certification ($35-70). Passport required. 96 beds. $12; nonmembers $15; private rooms $33. Linen $2. Key deposit $5. Wheelchair access.

**Quiet Waters County Park,** 6601 N. Powerline Rd./SW 10th Ave. (360-1315), off I-95's exit 37B; take Hillsboro Blvd. west to Powerline Rd. From downtown, take bus #11 to Pompane Sq. Mall, then switch to bus #95. Fully equipped lake-side campsites (tent, mats, grill, and free admission to beach) for up to 6 people ("don't feed the gators!"). Normal water sports and see-it-to-believe-it 8-person "boatless water skiing" at the end of a cable. No electricity or RVs. Sites Su-Th $17, F-Sa and holidays $25; primitive sites $17. $25 refundable deposit. Check-in 2-6pm.

## ◐ FOOD

The clubs along the strip offer massive quantities of free grub during Happy Hour: surfboard-sized platters of wieners, chips, and hors d'oeuvres, or all-you-can-eat pizza and buffets. However, these bars have hefty cover charges (from $5) and expect you to buy a drink once you're there (from $3). For "real" food, try **La Spada's,** 4346 Seagrape Dr., which has the best and biggest subs in southern Florida. The foot-long Italian sub ($7) is an absolute must, as most of Ft. Lauderdale, waiting in line with you, will agree. (776-7893. Open M-Sa 10am-8pm, Su 11am-8pm.) In aggressively marine decor, **Southport Raw Bar,** 1536 Cordova Rd., by the 17th St. Causeway behind the Southport Mall (take bus #40 from the strip), serves spicy conch chowder ($2.75) and fried shrimp ($7). Munch on tasty custom sandwiches out on the waterfront patio. (525-2526. Open daily 11am-2am. Happy Hour M-F 3-6pm, and Sa-Th 11pm-close.) Popular since 1951, **Tina's Spaghetti House,** 2110 S. Federal Hwy., just south of 17th St. (take bus #1 from downtown), has authentic red-checkered tablecloths, hefty oak furniture, and bibs. Lunch specials run $6-7, while a spaghetti dinner costs $6-8 (522-9943; open M-F 11:30am-11pm, Sa 4-11pm, Su 4-10pm).

## ◉ SIN, SIGHTS, AND ACTIVITIES

Fort Lauderdale is a pleasant medium between the pretentious sophisticates of Miami Beach and the Redneck Riveria of panhandle beaches. Parts of "AIA: Beachfront Ave." demonstrate the class and sophistication of Vanilla Ice—signs for Jello might mean nude women. Yet Fort Lauderdale's well maintained palm-lined shore, emerald waters and pink brick sidewalks make Miami Beach look shabby.

**Fort Lauderdale Beach** is at its most gorgeous along the beachfront between Las Olas Blvd. and Sunrise Blvd. **Los Olas Waterfront,** 2 W. 2nd St., the latest on-the-beach mall, boasts clubs, restaurants, bars, and over 20 movie screens to entertain until the ocean lures you back. Tour the city's waterways aboard the **Jungle Queen,** located at the Bahia Mar Yacht Center, on Rt. A1A 3 blocks south of Las Olas Blvd. *(801 Seabreeze Blvd. 462-5596. 3hr. tours daily 10am, 2, and 7pm. $11.50, ages 2-12 $7.75; 7pm tour $25.50/13.50, dinner included.)* The **Water Taxi** offers a different way to get around town. *(651 Seabreeze Blvd. 467-6677. $14, under 12 $7. All-day service $16. Call 30min. before pickup. Open daily 10am until they get tired.)* **Water Sports Unlimited,** on the beach, rents equipment for a variety of water sports, including wave runners. Parasailing trips are $65 (500 ft., 8min. duration), plus a little more if you want to get dipped. *(301 Seabreeze Blvd. 467-1316. Open 9am-6:30pm.)* Learn to fly-fish and reel in the virtual "big one" at the **International Game Fishing Association's World Fishing Center,** off the I-95 Griffin Road exit. The wide-ranging museum sports George Washington's fishing kit, and a relaxing "beautiful places theater." *(300 Gulf Stream Way. 922-4212. Open M-Tu and Th-Su 10am-6pm. $9, seniors $7, children $5. Wheelchair access.)* Amidst the commercial world of the beachfront area sits the secluded **Bonnet House,** a historic plantation house, South Florida style. Forty-five spider monkeys roam the 35 subtropical acres. *(900 N. Birch Rd. 563-5393. Open W-F 10am-1:30pm, Sa-Su noon-2:30pm. $9, students $7, seniors $8.)* Landlubbers can walk among 3 acres of tropical gardens and thousands of live butterflies at **Butterfly World,** west of Florida's Turnpike in Coconut Creek. *(3600 W. Sample Rd. 977-4400. Open M-Sa 9am-5pm, Su 1-5pm; $11, ages 4-12 $6.)*

FLORIDA

**LIVING THE JAI LIFE** President Harry Truman and Eleanor Roosevelt were fans; Babe Ruth tried it, but failed. Anointed by Guiness as the **"fastest game in the world,"** Jai Alai generally still remains unknown to Americans outside the state of Florida. Players from the Basque region of France and Spain brought the game to the Sunshine State in the 1920s, where it blossomed as a betting sport. Brave players whip the *pelota*, a rubber ball encased in layers of goat skin, from their *cesta*, a curved throwing/catching basket. Wild spins and speeds exceeding 180mph aim to keep the opponent from cleanly catching and releasing the pelota. **Dania Jai-Alai,** off U.S. 1 10min. south of Fort Lauderdale sports one the largest frontons (courts) in the state. *(301 E. Dania Beach Blvd. 927-2841. Games Tu, Sa-Su noon, Tu-Sa at 7:15pm; $1.50 general admission; $2-7 reserved seats.)*

## 🎵 NIGHTLIFE

Several popular nightspots line N. Atlantic Blvd. next to the beach. The **Cancun Beach & Tequila House,** 3051 NE 32nd Ave., on the Intercoastal Waterway, prides itself on its title liquor and nightly live music. The second drink is always free with a college ID; female patrons can nail their underwear to the wall and erase the tab. (563-3222. Open M-Th noon-2am, F-Su noon-3am. 21+.) The **Elbo Room** sits on prime real estate at the corner of A1A and Las Olas Blvd; a camera on the second floor patio transmits the beach/strip scene to www.theelboroom.com. The sidewalk bar is among the most visible and packed scenes on the beach. (463-4615. Open M-F 11am-2am, Sa-Su 11am-3am. Live music nightly.)

# MIAMI AND MIAMI BEACH

Long a popular setting for TV shows and movies, Miami's Latin heart pulses to the beat of the largest Cuban population outside of Cuba—speaking Spanish is very useful. Many small cultural communities distinguish Miami's residential areas: from Little Havana, a well-established Cuban community, to Coconut Grove, an eclectic intellectual enclave turned stylized tourist mecca. Only 7mi. away, across an arching causeway, Miami Beach's multiplying number of hotels triple the city's usual population. Throngs in thongs from the world over come to experience this "Hollywood of the East Coast" in all of its star-studded, bikinied gusto.

## ✳ ORIENTATION

Three highways criss-cross the Miami area. **I-95,** the most direct route north-south, becomes **U.S. 1 (Dixie Hwy.)** just south of **downtown.** U.S. 1 runs to the Everglades entrance at Florida City and then continues as the Overseas Hwy. to Key West. **Rt. 836,** a major east-west artery through town, connects I-95 to **Florida's Turnpike,** passing the airport in between. If you're headed to Florida City, taking Rt. 836 and the Turnpike will allow you to avoid the traffic on U.S. 1.

When looking for street addresses, pay careful attention to the systematic street layout; it's easy to confuse North Miami Beach, West Miami, Miami Beach, and Miami addresses. Streets in Miami run east-west, avenues north-south; both are numbered. Miami divides into NE, NW, SE, and SW quadrants; the dividing lines (downtown) are **Flagler St.** (east-west) and **Miami Ave.** (north-south). Some numbered streets and avenues also have names—e.g., Le Jeune Rd. is SW 42nd Ave., and SW 40th St. is Bird Rd. Get a map that lists both numbers and names.

Several causeways connect Miami to **Miami Beach.** The most useful is **MacArthur Causeway,** which becomes 5th St. in Miami Beach. Numbered streets run east-west across the island, increasing as you go north. In South Miami Beach, **Collins Ave. (A1A)** is the main north-south drag. Parallel to Collins is **Washington Ave.** and the beachfront riveria **Ocean Ave.** The commercial and entertainment district sits between 6th and 23rd St. To reach **Key Biscayne,** take the **Rickenbacker Causeway.**

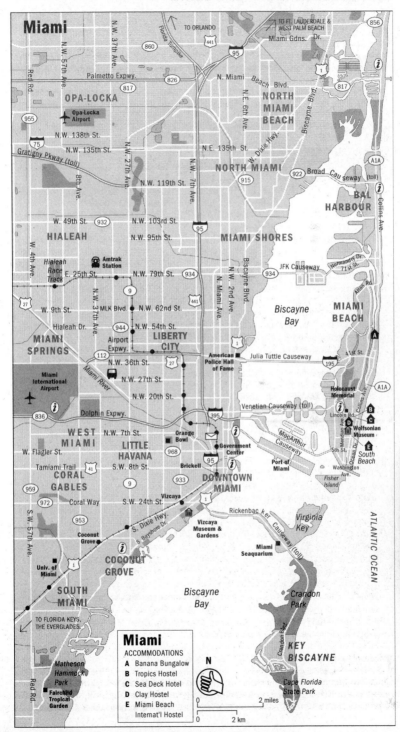

# Miami

TO ORLANDO

TO FT. LAUDERDALE &
WEST PALM BEACH

Miami Gdns. Dr.

Florida Turnpike

N.W. 37th Ave.

N.W. 57th Ave.

Red Rd.

Palmetto Expwy.

**OPA-LOCKA**

N. Miami Beach Blvd.

N. Miami

**NORTH
MIAMI
BEACH**

N.E. 6th Ave.

Biscayne Blvd.

Opa-Locka
Airport

N.W. 138th St.

N.W. 135th St.

N.E. 135th St.

W. Dixie Hwy.

Gratigny Pkway. (toll)

8th Ave.

N.W. 27th Ave.

N.W. 119th St.

N.W. 7th Ave.

**NORTH MIAMI**

Broad Causeway (toll)

**BAL
HARBOUR**

Collins Ave.

W. 49th St.

N.W. 103rd St.

**HIALEAH**

W. 4th Ave.

N.W. 95th St.

**MIAMI SHORES**

JFK Causeway

Normandy Dr.
71st St.

Harding Ave.

**MIAMI
BEACH**

Hialeah
Race
Track

E. 25th St.

Amtrak
Station

N.W. 79th St.

N.W. 2nd Ave.

Biscayne Blvd.

Biscayne
Bay

W. 9th St.

N.W. 37th Ave.

MLK Blvd.

N.W. 62nd St.

N. Miami Ave.

Hialeah Dr.

N.W. 54th St.

**MIAMI
SPRINGS**

Airport
Expwy.

**LIBERTY
CITY**

American
Police Hall
of Fame

Julia Tuttle Causeway

41st St.

Miami River

N.W. 36th St.

**Miami
International
Airport**

N.W. 27th St.

N.W. 20th St.

**Holocaust
Memorial**

Collins Ave.

Dolphin Expwy.

Venetian Causeway (toll)

**WEST
MIAMI**

N.W. 7th St.

Orange
Bowl

Lincoln Rd.

**Wolfsonian
Museum**

W. Flagler St.

**LITTLE
HAVANA**

Government
Center

MacArthur
Causeway

Washington
Ave.

**South
Beach**

Tamiami Trail

S.W. 8th St.

Brickell

Port of
Miami

5th St.

Ocean Dr.

Fisher
Island

**CORAL
GABLES**

**DOWNTOWN
MIAMI**

Coral Way

S.W. 24th St.

Vizcaya

Rickenbacker Causeway (toll)

Virginia
Key

S.W. 57th Ave.

S. Dixie Hwy.

S. Bayshore Dr.

Vizcaya
Museum &
Gardens

Miami
Seaquarium

Coconut
Grove

**COCONUT
GROVE**

**ATLANTIC
OCEAN**

Univ. of
Miami

**SOUTH
MIAMI**

Biscayne
Bay

Crandon
Park

Crandon Blvd.

**KEY
BISCAYNE**

TO FLORIDA KEYS,
THE EVERGLADES

Matheson
Hammock
Park

Fairchild
Tropical
Garden

Red Rd.

Cape Florida
State Park

## Miami
ACCOMMODATIONS

A  Banana Bungalow
B  Tropics Hostel
C  Sea Deck Hotel
D  Clay Hostel
E  Miami Beach
   Internat'l Hostel

N

0        2 miles

0      2 km

**FLORIDA**

The heart of **Little Havana** lies between SW 12th Ave. and SW 27th Ave.; take bus #3, 11, 14, 15, 17, 25, or 37. The **Calle Ocho** (SW 8th St.) is central; 1 block north, the corresponding section of **W. Flagler St.** is a center of Cuban business. **Coconut Grove,** south of Little Havana, centers around the shopping and entertainment district on **Grand Ave.** and **Virginia St.** A **car** can be an expensive liability in Miami. Posted signs indicate different parking zones; should you leave your car in a residential zone for even a few moments, you may return to find it towed. Never leave valuables visible in your parked car; automobile theft and break-ins are common.

## ▐ PRACTICAL INFORMATION

**Airport: Miami International** (876-7000), at Le Jeune Rd. and NW 36th Ave., 7mi. northwest of downtown. Bus #7 runs downtown; many other buses make downtown stops. From downtown, take bus "C" or "K" to South Miami Beach.

**Trains: Amtrak,** 8303 NW 37th Ave. (835-1223), near Northside station of Metrorail. Bus "L" goes directly to Lincoln Rd. Mall in South Miami Beach. To: Orlando (5hr., 2 per day, $40); New Orleans (48hr., 3 per week, $197); and Charleston (14hr., 2 per day, $59-144). Open daily 6:30am-10pm.

**Buses: Greyhound,** Miami Station, 4111 NW 27th St. (871-1810). To: Atlanta (17hr., 9 per day, $82-87); Orlando (6hr., 4 per day, $33-35); and Fort Lauderdale (1hr., hourly, $5). Open 24hr.

**Public Transit: Metro Dade Transportation** (770-3131; M-F 6am-10pm, Sa-Su 9am-5pm for info). The extensive Metrobus network converges downtown, where most long trips transfer. Lettered bus routes A to X serve Miami Beach. After dark, some stops are patrolled (indicated with a sign). Buses run daily 4:30am-2am. $1.25; transfers 25¢, to Metrorail 25¢. The **Metrorail** services downtown. $1.25, rail-to-bus transfers 50¢. The **Metromover** loop downtown, which runs 6am-midnight, is linked to the Metrorail stations. Fare 25¢, free transfers from Metrorail. **Tri-Rail** (800-874-7245) connects Miami, Fort Lauderdale, and West Palm Beach. Trains run M-Sa 4am-8pm, Su 7am-8pm. $4, $6.75 per day, students and seniors 50% off. The new **Electrowave** (843-9283) offers shuttles around South Beach. Runs M-W 8am-2am, Th-Sa 8am-4am, Su and holidays 10am-2am; 25¢; pick up a brochure or just hop on along Washington.

**Taxis: Metro,** 888-8888.

**Bike Rental: Miami Beach Bicycle Center,** 605 5th St. (531-4161), at the corner of Washington Ave., Miami Beach. $5 per hr.; $20 per day; $70 per week. Must be 18+ with credit card or $200 cash deposit. Open M-Sa 10am-7pm, Su 10am-5pm.

**Visitor Info: Miami Beach Visitors Center,** 1920 Meridian Ave. (672-1270). Open M-F 9am-6pm, Sa-Su 10am-4pm. **Info booth,** 401 Biscayne Blvd. (539-2980), downtown outside of Bayside Marketplace. Open daily 10am-6:30pm. In South Beach, **The Art Deco Welcome Center,** 1001 Ocean Dr. (531-3484) has tour info. Open M-F 11am-6pm, Sa 10am-midnight, Su 11am-10pm, extended hours in winter. **Coconut Grove Chamber of Commerce,** 2820 McFarlane Ave. (444-7270). Open M-F 9am-5pm. **Greater Miami Convention and Visitors Bureau,** 701 Brickell Ave. (539-3000, 800-283-2707 outside Miami), 27th fl. of Barnett Bank Bldg. downtown. Open M-F 9am-5pm.

**Internet Access: Kafka's Cafe,** 1464 Washington Ave. (673-9669) in Miami Beach. Thirteen computers, $1 per 5 min. (open daily 9am-11pm). **Miami Beach International Travelers Hostel,** see Accommodations, below.

**Hotlines: Crisis Line,** 358-4357. **Rape Treatment Center and Hotline** (585-7273), at Jackson Memorial Hospital, 1611 NW 12th Ave. Both 24hr. **Gay Hotline,** 759-5210.

**Post Office:** 500 NW 2nd Ave. (639-4284), downtown. Open M-F 8am-5pm, Sa 9am-1:30pm. **ZIP code:** 33101. **Area code:** 305.

## ▐ ACCOMMODATIONS

Cheap rooms abound in South Miami Beach's Art Deco hotels. Finding a "pull-manette" (in 1940s lingo), a room with a refrigerator, stove, and sink, will save you money. In South Florida, many inexpensive hotels are likely to have 2-3 in. cockroaches ("palmetto bugs"). In general, high season for Miami Beach runs late Dec. through mid-Mar.; during the off season, when rooms are empty, hotel clerks are quick to bargain. The **Greater Miami and the Beaches Hotel Association,** 407 Lincoln Rd. #10G (531-3553), can help you find a place to crash (open M-F 9am-5pm), and the Miami Beach visitors center (see **Practical Information**) can finagle you the cheapest rates. **Camping** is not allowed in Miami Beach.

▨ **The Clay Hotel and International Hostel (HI-AYH),** 1438 Washington Ave. (534-2988), in the heart of the Art Deco district; take bus "C" from downtown. Popular location for *Miami Vice* and in *The Specialist*. Great archways in a Mediterranean-style building. International crowd. Kitchen, laundry facilities, TV, A/C. 180 beds, rooms have 4-8; all have phone and fridges. $13, nonmembers $14; private rooms $34-72. Key deposit $5. No curfew. Open 24hr.

**The Tropics Hotel/Hostel,** 1550 Collins Ave. (531-0361), across the street from the beach. From the airport, take bus "J" to 41st St., transfer to bus "C" to Lincoln Rd., and walk 1 block south on Collins Ave. Next to parking garage. Clean rooms with 4 beds, A/C, private baths, phone, pool access, and an outdoor kitchen. $14. Private rooms have A/C, cable TV, and free local calls. Singles and doubles $50. Free linen. No curfew.

**Miami Beach International Travelers Hostel (9th St. Hostel) (AAIH/Rucksackers),** 236 9th St. (534-0268 or 800-978-6787), at Washington Ave. From the airport, take bus "J" to 41st and Indian Creek, then transfer to bus "C" or "K." Central location, but difficult parking. Lively international atmosphere near the beach. Laundry, common room with TV and movie library, Internet access. 28 clean, comfortable rooms (max. 4 people), all with A/C and bath. Dorm rooms $13 with any hosteling membership or student ID, otherwise $15; private singles or doubles $32 off season, $55 in season. No curfew.

**Banana Bungalow,** 2360 Collins Ave. (538-1951), at 23rd St. along northern edge of the Art Deco district. 180 bunk beds with thatched tiki tops. Free coffee, tea, and toast. Pool, canal access, kitchen, free lockers, linen, bar, grill, and nightly movie at 8pm. $16 with TV; $14 without. Hotel rooms $70-76. Kayak/canoe rentals $10 per 2hr.; bikes $5 per day. Limited, free, guarded parking. Travel agent in lobby. Reserve in advance.

**Sea Deck Hotel and Apartments,** 1530 Collins Ave. (538-4361). Basic, cozy, and clean pullmanettes with pretty floral bedspreads open onto a lush tropical courtyard. Pullmanettes $48, other rooms $65. *Let's Go* users get 10% off. Limited parking available.

**Larry & Penny Thompson Memorial Campground,** 12451 SW 184th St. (232-1049), near Metrozoo. By car, exit 13 off Florida's Turnpike. Pretty grounds with 240 sites in a mango grove. Laundry, store, artificial lake with swimming beach, beautiful park, and waterslides. Lake open late May to early Sept. daily 10am-5pm. Reception daily 9am-5:30pm but takes late arrivals. Tents $8; RVs with full hookup $19, $123 per week.

## ◖ FOOD

Try the Cuban food: specialties include *media noche* sandwiches (a sort of club sandwich on a soft roll, heated and compressed); bright red *mamey* (mah-MAY)-flavored ice cream and shakes; hearty *frijoles negros* (black beans); and *picadillo* (shredded beef and peas in tomato sauce, served with white rice). For sweets, seek out a *dulcería*, and punctuate your rambles with thimble-sized shots of strong, sweet *café cubano* (around 35¢). Cheap restaurants are not common in Miami, but an array of bakeries and (if you're daring) fruit stands can sustain you.

▨ **King's Ice Cream,** 1831 SW 8th St./Calle Ocho (643-1842), in Miami. Tropical fruit *helado* (ice cream) flavors include a regal coconut (served in its own shell), *mamey*, and mango (just $1 for a small cup). They also make tasty *churros* (snake-shaped fried dough, 12 for $1.50). Open M-Sa 10am-11pm, Su 1-11pm.

▨ **Wolfie's,** 2038 Collins Ave. (538-6626), at 20th St. in South Beach. "Famous the world over," this mega-deli is a throwback to old Miami Beach. One giant sandwich ($6) can be both lunch and dinner. Dessert selection is unreal: thick cheesecakes, dense rumcakes and gravity-defying pastries stretch tanned tummies. Look for luminaries in the "celebrity room." Open 24hr.

**Big Fish Mayaimi,** 55 SW 5th St. (373-1770), off Brickell in Miami with the huge high-heel gondola in front. Delicious Spanish-influenced entrees, mainly seafood (grilled fish for lunch $8, *ceviche* $7) and with decadent desserts like *crema catalana* ($4), right on the Miami River. Open daily 11:30am-11:30pm.

**Macarena,** 1334 Washington Ave. (531-3440), in Miami Beach. Dance your way to wonderful food in an atmosphere that's equal parts intimate and festive, and a favorite of the Julio Iglesias family. *Paella* ($10, lunch $6) and the best rice pudding you'll encounter ($5.50) make for the perfect Spanish treat. Wine comes from their own vineyards. Flamenco dancing W, F, Sa; Salsa Th. Open daily for lunch noon-3pm, dinner Su-Tu 7pm-midnight, W-Sa 7pm-12:30am; the sizzling night scene doesn't end until 5am.

**The Versailles,** 3555 SW 8th St./Calle Ocho (444-0240), in Miami. Palatial green and gilt dining room, seemingly packed with Little Havana's entire population. Versailles has served up good Cuban fare for 27 years. Breakfast $3.50-8, sandwiches $3-7, daily specials $3-8. Open M-Th 8am-2am, F-Su 8am-4am.

**11th St. Diner,** 1065 Washington Ave. (534-6373), at 11th St., in Miami Beach. Diner with the requisite soda fountain and ancient Coca-Cola clock. Breakfast all day ($5-7), sandwiches ($4-6), and grill items. Best shakes in Miami ($2.75). Open 24hr., closed Tu midnight-8am.

**Flamingo Café,** 1454 Washington Ave. (673-4302), near the Clay Hostel, in Miami Beach. Friendly service, all of which is in Spanish. Beef tacos and salad $2.75, *tostones con queso* ($2.75). Lunch specials daily $5-6. Open M-Sa 7am-10pm.

# ■ SIGHTS

**South Miami Beach** (or just South Beach), between 6th and 23rd St., teems with hundreds of hotels and apartments whose sun-faded pastel facades conform to 1920s ideals of a tropical paradise. An unusual mixture of people populates the area, including many retirees and first-generation Hispanics. Models, tourists, and the occasional music superstar stroll down **Ocean Dr.,** the country's ultimate see and be seen strip. **Walking tours** start at the **Oceanfront Auditorium.** (*1001 Ocean Dr. at 10th St. 672-2014. 1½hr. tours Th 6:30pm, Sa 10:30am. $10. 1¼hr. self-guided tours run daily, 11am-4pm. $5.*) The **Holocaust Memorial,** across from the Miami Beach Visitors Center, remembers the 6 million Jews who perished during the Holocaust. (*1933-45 Meridian Ave. 538-1663. Open daily 9am-9pm. Free.*) **The Wolfsonian** examines the art of design from 1885-1945 through over 70,000 objects. Permanent exhibit includes Russian political propaganda and London subway signs. (*1001 Washington Ave. 535-2602. Hours vary. $5, students and seniors $3.50.*)

A stroll through the lazy streets of **Coconut Grove** uncovers an unlikely combination of haute boutiques and tacky tourist traps. Two shopping malls, **CocoWalk** and **Streets of Mayfair,** both on Grand St., dominate the sanitized scene.

On the bay front between the Grove and downtown stands the **Vizcaya Museum and Gardens;** take bus #1 or the Metrorail to Vizcaya or exit 1 off I-95. European antiques, tapestries, and art fill this 70-room Italianate mansion, surrounded by 10 acres of lush gardens. (*3251 S. Miami Ave. 250-9133. Open daily 9:30am-5pm; last entry 4:30pm. $10, ages 6-12 $5.*) Blanketed with oversized ferns and leaves, the **Fairchild Tropical Garden** covers 83 acres and features 16 elaborate flower shows per year. (*10901 Old Cutler Rd. 667-1651. Open daily 9:30am-4:30pm. Tram tours hourly 10am-3pm, until 4pm on weekends. $8, under 12 free.*)

On the waterfront downtown, Miami's sleek **Bayside** shopping center hops nightly with talented street performers. (*Open M-Th 10am-10pm, F-Sa 10am-11pm, Su 11am-8pm.*) Near Bayside, the **American Police Hall of Fame and Museum** exhibits feature grisly execution equipment, the car from "Blade Runner," and "Old Sparky," Florida's famed electric chair. (*3801 Biscayne Blvd. 573-0070. Open daily 10am-5:30pm. $6, seniors $4, and ages 6-12 $3; discounts at visitors center.*)

The art of Cuban cigar manufacturing lives on at **La Gloria Cubana.** (*1106 SW 8th St. 858-4162. Open M-F 8am-5:30pm, Sa 8am-4pm. Free.*) **Carnaval Miami,** the nation's largest Hispanic festival, fills 23 blocks of Calle Ocho in early Mar. with salsa, music, and the world's longest conga line.

In **Coral Gables,** the family-friendly **Venetian Pool,** founded in 1923, drew Hollywood stars like Esther Williams and Johnny Weissmuller back in the day. Waterfalls and Venetian-style architecture dress up this swimming hole. *(2701 DeSoto Blvd. 460-5356. Open M-F 11am-7:30pm; Sa-Su 10am-4:30pm; hrs. vary in winter and spring. $8, ages 12 and under $4; Nov.-Mar. $5/2.)*

## 🎵 ENTERTAINMENT AND NIGHTLIFE

For the latest on Miami entertainment, the "Living Today," "Lively Arts," and F "Weekend" sections of the *Miami Herald* are logical places to start. Weekly *Oceandrive*, the *New Times*, and the *Sun Post*, list local happenings. *TWN* and *Miamigo* are the major gay papers. **Performing Arts and Community Education (PACE)** manages more than 400 concerts each year (jazz, rock, soul, dixieland, reggae, salsa, and bluegrass); most are free.

Nightlife in the Art Deco district of South Miami Beach starts late (usually after midnight) and continues until well after sunrise. Gawk at models and stars while eating dinner at one of Ocean Blvd.'s open cafes or bars, then head down to Washington Ave., between 6th and 7th St., for some serious fun. Many clubs charge covers only after midnight. Most clubs have dress codes, and everyone dresses to the nines. **Bash,** 655 Washington Ave., stands out among its neighbors; the large indoor dance floor grooves to dance music while the courtyard in back jams to the ocean beat of reggae (538-2274; 21+; cover $10-15; open W-Su 10am-5am; in winter Tu-Su 10am-5am). **The Tavern,** 3416 Main Hwy., in Cocowalk district, is one of the most popular University of Miami watering holes (447-3884; open M-F 3pm-3am, Sa-Su 1pm-3am, 21+, no cover). The beautiful and famous go to **Liquid,** 1439 Washington Ave. (532-9154; open 10pm-5am; 21+; cover $20). Arrive before midnight to dodge the cover and long lines at the **Groove Jet,** 323 23rd St. The front room of this massive hall plays trance, dance, and house; the back room churns out alternative rock. (532-2002. 21+. Cover $10 after midnight. Open Th-Su 11pm-5am.)

## EVERGLADES

Encompassing the entire tip of Florida and spearing into Florida Bay, **Everglades National Park,** the 3rd-largest national park, spans 1.6 million acres of one of the world's most beautiful and fragile ecosystems. Vast prairies of sawgrass spike through broad expanses of shallow water, creating the famed "river of grass," while tangled mazes of mangrove swamps wind up the western coast. To the south, delicate coral reefs lie below the shimmering blue waters of the bay. A host of species found nowhere else in the world inhabits these lands and waters: American alligators, dolphins, sea turtles, and various birds and fishes, as well as the endangered Florida panther, Florida manatee, and American crocodile.

🚩 **PRACTICAL INFORMATION.** Summer visitors can expect to get eaten alive by swarming mosquitoes. The best time to visit is winter or spring, when heat, humidity, storms, and bugs are at a minimum, and wildlife congregate in shrinking pools of evaporating water. Whenever you go, be sure to bring mosquito repellent.

There are three primary roads into the park, each separate from the others. Guarding the eastern section, the **Ernest Coe Visitors Center,** 40001 Rt. 9336 (305-242-7700), sits just inside the park (open daily 8am-5pm). Take Rt. 9336 from U.S. 1 at Florida City; Everglades Park signs point the way. **Rt. 9336** cuts 40mi. through the park past campgrounds, trailheads, and canoe waterways to the **Flamingo Visitors Center** (941-695-2945) and the heavily developed Flamingo Outpost Resort.

At the northern end of the park off U.S. 41 (Tamiami Trail), the **Shark Valley Visitors Center** provides access to a 15mi. loop through sawgrass swamp that can be seen by foot, bike, or a 2hr. tram. **Shark Valley** is an ideal site for those who want a taste of the freshwater ecosystem, but can't commit to delving too far into the

**FLORIDA**

park. (Tram tours in summer daily 9:30am, 11am, 1, and 3pm; Dec.-Apr. daily every hr. 9am-4pm. $9.30, seniors $8.35, under 12 $5.15. Reservations recommended; call 305-221-8455. Wheelchair access. Bike rental $3.85 per hr., includes helmets. Center open daily 8:30am-5:15pm.) The **Gulf Coast Visitors Center**, 800 S. Copeland Ave. (941-695-3311), in Everglades City in the northwestern end of the park, provides access to the western coastline and the vast river network throughout the park (open 8:30am-5pm in summer, extended hours in winter). **Emergency: Park headquarters** (305-247-7272). **Entrance fee for 1 wk.** (**Ernest Coe:** $10 per car, $5 bike- or walk-in; **Shark Valley:** $8 per car, $4 bike- or walk-in; **Gulf Coast:** free.)

**⌐ ACCOMMODATIONS.** Outside the eastern entrance to the park, **Florida City** offers some cheap options along U.S. 1. The only option for lodging inside the park, the **Flamingo Lodge,** 1 Flamingo Lodge Hwy., offers large rooms with A/C, TV, private baths, pool, and a great bay view. (941-695-3101 or 800-600-3813. Singles and doubles $65; Nov.-Dec. and Apr. $79; Jan.-Mar. $95.) **Everglades International Hostel,** 20 SW 2nd Ave., located in a 1930s boarding house, shines with a gazebo, gumbo limbo trees, freshwater pool, tile mosaic floors, and 35 beds in the heart of Redlands Agricultural Community 10mi. from Everglades. (305-248-7622. $12, $15 with A/C; $30 for private room; $40 for private room with A/C. Canoes $20 per day; bikes $5 per day.) A few **campgrounds** line Rt. 9336; all have drinking water, grills, dump sites, and restrooms, but none have RV hookups. (Sites free in summer; in winter $14. Reservations required Nov.-Apr.; call the **National Park Reservation Service** at 800-365-2267.) **Backcountry camping** inside the park is accessible primarily by boat (see **Sights** below). The required **permits** are available at the **Flamingo** and **Gulf Coast (Everglades City)** Visitors Centers ($10 for 1-6 people), and reservations must be made in person at earliest a day before starting.

Near the northwest entrance, motels, RV parks, and campgrounds scatter around Everglades City. The **Barron River Villa, Marina, and RV Park** offers 67 RV sites, 29 on the river and precious motel rooms with TV and A/C. (941-695-3331 or 800-535-4961. RV sites: full hookup $18, on the river $20; Oct.-Apr. $28/34. Motel: singles or doubles $41; Sept.-Dec. $49; Jan.-Apr. $57.) A wooded campsite rests at **Collier-Seminole State Park,** 20200 E. Tamiami Trail. Most of the park is a wilderness preserve in a mangrove swamp, home to several of Florida's most endangered species. (941-394-3397. 137 sites with water. $13; $8 off season; electricity $2 more.)

**◉ SIGHTS.** The park is positively swamped in fishing, hiking, canoeing, biking, and wilderness observation opportunities. *Forget swimming; alligators, sharks, and barracuda patrol the waters.* From Nov. through Apr., the park sponsors amphitheater programs, canoe trips, and ranger-guided **Slough Slogs** (swamp tours). Numerous trailheads lie off Rt. 9336; the ½mi. **Mahogany Hammock Trail** passes the largest mahogany tree in the U.S., and the ¼mi. **Pahayokee Overlook Trail** leads to a broad vista of grasslands and water. But if you really want to experience the Everglades, start paddling. The 99mi. **Wilderness Waterway** winds its way from the northwest entrance to the Flamingo station in the far south. Adventurous camping spots along the journey include chickees (wooden platforms elevated above mangrove swamps), beaches and groundsites. *(Free in summer; $10 in winter.)* The **Everglades National Park Boat Tours** at the **Gulf Coast Visitors Center** rents canoes. *(695-2591. $20 per day.)* The same company offers three boat tours into the park. Park-trained naturalists lead the relaxing 1½hr. jaunt through the heart of the coastal "10,000 islands," with the occasional **mantee, bottle-nosed dolphin** and **bald eagle** sighting. *(Tours daily, every ½hr. 9am-5pm; $13, ages 6-12 $6.50. Reservations recommended in winter.)* The **Sunset Cruise** sails into the Gulf of Mexico. *(Nov.-Apr.; $13/6.50.)* The 2½hr. **Back Country Cruise** explores the swampy, jungle sections of the southern Everglades. *(Call for availability. $16/8.)* All three leave from the Gulf Coast Visitor's Center. Shorter **canoe trails** wind from Rt. 9336; the **Nine Mile Pond** canoe loop passes through alligator ponds and mazes of mangrove trees (allow 3-4hr.), while the **Hell's Bay Canoe Trail** threads through mangrove swamps past primitive camp-

**MAIL CALL** After a fire destroyed the local post office in 1953, Ochopee, FL town leaders searched for a new location. Postmaster Sidney Brown quickly chose a small shack, a former irrigation pipe shed for a tomato farm; every since, the country's smallest post office has serviced a three-county area in a room barely big enough for two. Cram into the Ochopee mail room on U.S. 41 (Tamiami Trail) between the Gulf Coast and Shark Valley entrances to Everglades National Park.

sites like **Lard Can.** Canoes are also available at the **Flamingo Marina.** *(941-695-3101 or 800-600-3813. $22 for 4hrs., $32 per day; $40 deposit.)* No one ever saw little Ed Leedskalnin build his ▨ **Coral Castle** in Homestead, leading many to belive he possessed supernatural powers. Ed said he merely understood the secrets behind the ancient Egyptian pyramids, and applied them to his collasal coral stone palace. *(28655 South Dixie Hwy, Homestead. 305-248-6344.)* View gators, crocs and snakes at the **Everglades Alligator Farm,** 4mi. south of Palm Dr. Over 3000 gators, from little hatchlings clambering for sun to 18-footers clambering for...um...you, grace the premises. *(40351 SW 192 Ave. 305-247-2628. Open daily 9am-6pm; $7, ages 4-12 $3.)*

# FLORIDA KEYS

Intense popularity has transformed this long-time haven for pirates, smugglers, treasure hunters, and others deemed outside the moral order into supreme beach vacationland. Whether smothered in tourists or outcasts, the Keys retain an "anything goes" mentality. When former Key West mayor Tony Tarracino arrived here decades ago, he did a quick inventory of bars and strip clubs, and concluded that he'd reached heaven (see p. 449). If this sounds more like hell, take a dive. Millions of colorful fish flash through gardens of coral 6mi. off the coast, granting relative solitude to scuba divers and snorkelers, and forming a 100-yard-wide barrier reef between Keys Largo and West. Don't believe the hype; sharks are scarce here.

## ▧ PRACTICAL INFORMATION

The **Overseas Hwy. (U.S. 1)** bridges the divide between the Keys and the southern tip of Florida, stitching the islands together. **Mile markers** section the highway and replace street addresses. The first marker, Mi. 126 in Florida City, begins the long countdown to zero in Key West. **Greyhound** to the Keys from Miami ($32), stops in Homestead (247-2040), Key Largo (296-9072), Marathon (296-9073), Big Pine Key (flag stop), and Key West (296-9072). Most bus drivers can be convinced to stop at the side of the road, at a mile marker. Tiny Greyhound signs along the highway indicate bus stops (usually hotels), where you can buy tickets or call the Greyhound **info line** on the red phones provided. **Biking** along U.S. 1 is treacherous due to fast cars and narrow shoulders; instead of riding, bring your bike on the bus.

## KEY LARGO

Past the thick swamps and crocodile marshland of the Everglades, Key Largo opens the door to Caribbean-esque islands. With 120ft. visibility, the clear waters off Key Largo reveal shimmering coral reefs inhabited by darting, exotically colorful fish. Twenty feet down, an underwater statue of Jesus (meant to symbolize peace for mankind) blesses all those who explore the depths. Fishing and glass-bottom boats offer recreation without total submersion, though just plain swimming is a treat. Key Largo's exotic daytime adventures overcome the lack of nightlife; you will be so worn out, you won't care. Dubbed "long island" by Spanish explorers, this 30mi. island is the largest of the Florida Keys, but those without a car shouldn't worry; everything lies within a 6-mi. range and off one main street.

**☑ PRACTICAL INFORMATION. Greyhound** (296-9072), Mi. 102 at the Howard Johnson, to Miami (3 per day, 1¾hr., $13) and Key West (4 per day, 3 hours, $25; open 8am-6pm daily). **Mom's Taxi:** 852-6000. **Key Largo Chamber of Commerce/Florida Keys Visitors Center:** 10600 Overseas Hwy., Mi. 106 (451-1414; open daily 9am-6pm). **The Key Largo Tourist and Reservation Center:** 103360 Overseas Hwy, Mi. 103 (453-0066; open M-Sa 9am-8pm, Sun 10am-6pm). **Post Office:** 100100 Overseas Hwy, Mi. 100 (451-3155; open M-F 8am-4:30pm). **ZIP code:** 33037. **Area code:** 305.

**▓▒ ACCOMMODATIONS AND FOOD. Ed and Ellen's Lodgings,** Mi. 103.4, offers clean, spacious rooms with cable TV, A/C, and kitchenettes (451-9949 or 888-889-5905. Doubles $55; off-season $49; $10 per additional person). The waterside **Hungry Pelican,** Mi. 99½, boasts beautiful bougainvillea vines, tropical birds in the trees, and tidy, cozy rooms with double beds, fridges, and cable. Free use of paddle boats, canoes and hammocks to watch their amazing view of the sunset. (451-3576. $50-115; $10 per additional person.) Reservations are recommended for the popular **John Pennekamp State Park Campground** (see **Sights,** below); the sites are clean, convenient, and well worth the effort required to obtain them (451-1202; $24, with electricity $26). Straight out of a Jimmy Buffet fantasy, **King's Kamp,** 103620 Overseas Hwy., Mi. 103½ offers easy water access and beautiful sites (451-0010; all sites have water and electricity; $20 tent, $30 RV; $10 extra for boat).

The 100-plus beer selection at the family-run **Crack'd Conch,** Mi. 105, can slake any thirst. Entire ice-box key lime pies ($8.75), once called "the secret to world peace and the alignment of the planets," make great chasers. (451-0732. Open Th-Tu noon-10pm.) Follow your meal from the boat to the plate at **Calypso's,** 1 Seagate Blvd. on the marina across from Key Largo Fisheries. The coconut shrimp ($6) is a sweet, fried delight. (451-0600. Open M and W-Th noon-10pm, F-Sa noon-11pm.) The **Italian Fisherman,** Mi. 104, has fine food and a breathtaking view of Florida Bay. Some scenes from *Key Largo* were allegedly shot in this once-illegal casino. (451-4471. Lunch $5-10, dinner $7-17, $8 early bird special daily 4-6pm. Open daily 11:30am-10pm.) **Alabama Jack's,** 58000 Card Sound Rd., between Homestead and Key Largo, rocks the southern Florida wetlands with live country music (Sa-Su 2pm-7pm). It is probably the southernmost place to enjoy "hoppin' john," a southern delight of black eyed peas, rice and ham. (248-8741. Open M-F 11am-7pm, Sa-Su 11am-7:30pm.) The **Caribbean Club,** Mi. 104, a friendly local bar, chalked up Hollywood exposure in *Blood and Wine* with Jack Nicholson and Jennifer Lopez. The docks offer great views of the ocean and sunsets. (451-9970. Beer $1.50, drinks $2-4. Live rock and reggae F-Sa and holidays. No cover. Open daily 7am-4am.)

**⬛ SIGHTS.** The nation's first underwater sanctuary, Key Largo's **John Pennekamp State Park,** Mi. 102½, 60mi. from Miami, safeguards a 25mi. stretch of the 120 sq. mi. coral reef that runs the length of the Florida Keys. *(451-1202. Admission $4 per vehicle, $2 per vehicle with a single occupant, $1 walk- or bike-in; 50¢ per additional person on all fees.)* The park's **visitors center,** about ¼mi. past the entrance gate, provides maps of the reefs, info on boat and snorkeling tours, three aquariums, and films on the park. To see the reefs, visitors must take a boat or rent their own. *(451-9570. Open daily 8am-5pm. 19 ft. motor boat $28. Deposit required. Call 451-6325 for reservations.)* **Scuba trips** from the visitors center run at 9:30am and 1:30pm. *(451-6322. $37 per person for a two-tank dive.)* A **snorkeling tour** also allows you to partake of the underwater quiet. *(451-1621. 2½hr. total, 1½hr. water time. Tours 9am, noon, and 3pm. $24, under 18 $19. Equipment $4.)* For sailing, ask about the ½-day sailing/snorkeling combo trip, just a bit costlier than snorkeling alone. *(451-1621. 1½hr. water time; tours 9am and 1:30pm; $32, under 18 $27.)* **Glass Bottom Boat Tours,** leaving from the park shore at Mi. 102.5, provide a crystal clear view of the reefs without wetting your feet. *(451-1621. Daily 9:15am, 12:15, and 3pm. $18, under 12 $10; discounts at the visitors center.)*

# KEY WEST

Just 90mi. from Cuba, this is the end of the road. Key West boasts the southern-most point and perhaps the most laid-back attitude in the continental U.S. The island is cooler than mainland Florida in summer and far warmer in winter; the seeker of a year-round tropical paradise in the U.S. can do no better. Key West's tantalizing temperatures once drew writers Ernest Hemingway, Tennessee Williams, Elizabeth Bishop, and the chilly Robert Frost; today, an easygoing diversity lures a new generation of artists, recluses, adventurers, and eccentrics, along with a swinging gay population. Lacking stress, closing time, and indoor heat (many places only have A/C), the "Conch Republic" half-seriously jokes of its own independance. When it's full, it overflows; nightlife is 24hr. as thousands of Parrotheads search for Margaritaville.

## 🚩 ORIENTATION AND PRACTICAL INFORMATION

Key West lies at the end of U.S. 1, 155mi. southwest of Miami (3-3½hr.). Divided into two sectors, the eastern part of the island, known as **New Town,** harbors tract houses, chain motels, shopping malls, and the airport. Beautiful old conch houses fill **Old Town,** west of White St. **Duval St.** is the main north-south thoroughfare in Old Town; **Truman Ave.**(U.S. 1) is a major east-west route.

**Buses: Greyhound,** 3535 S. Roosevelt Blvd. (296-9072), at the airport. To Miami (4hr., 3 per day, $32). Open daily 8am-6pm.

**Public Transit: Key West Port and Transit Authority** (292-8161), City Hall. Clockwise ("Old Town") and counterclockwise ("Mallory Sq. Rt.") routes. Service daily 7am-10:30pm, about every 1½hr. Fare 75¢, students and seniors 35¢.

**Taxis: Keys Taxi,** 296-6666.

**Car Rental: Alamo,** 3816 N. Roosevelt Blvd. (294-6675 or 800-327-9633), Over 25 $29 per day, $149 per week; must be 21 with major credit card; under 25 surcharge $20 per day.. Depending on availability, Miami drop-off free. Open daily 5:30am-9pm.

**Bikes/Mopeds: Keys Moped & Scooter,** 523 Truman Ave. (294-0399). Bikes $4 per ½-day, $30 per week. Mopeds $18 per 9am-5pm, $23 per 24hr. Open daily 9am-6pm.

**Visitor Info: Key West Welcome Center,** 3840 N. Roosevelt Blvd. (296-4444 or 800-284-4482), a private reservation service just north of the intersection of U.S. 1 and Roosevelt Blvd. Open M-Sa 9am-7:30pm, Su 9am-6pm. **Key West Chamber of Commerce,** 402 Wall St. (294-2587 or 800-527-8539), in old Mallory Sq. Open daily 8:30am-6pm. **The Key West Business Guild Gay and Lesbian Information Center,** 728 Duval St. (294-4603). Open M-F 9am-5pm.

**Hotlines: Help Line,** 296-4357. 24hr.

**Internet Access: Sippin',** 424 Easton St. (293-0555), off Duval. $10 per hr. Open Su-Th 7am-10pm, F-Sa 7am-11pm.

**Post Office:** 400 Whitehead St. (294-2557), 1 block west of Duval at Eaton. Open M-F 8:30am-5pm, Sa 9:30am-noon. **ZIP code:** 33040. **Area code:** 305.

## 🏠 ACCOMMODATIONS

Key West is packed virtually year-round, particularly from Jan. through Mar., so reserve rooms far in advance. In **Old Key West,** the beautiful, 19th-century clap-board houses capture the charming flavor of the Keys. Some of the guest houses in the Old Town are for gay men exclusively. *Do not park overnight on the bridges*—this is illegal and dangerous.

**Key West Hostel (HI-AYH),** 718 South St. (296-5719), at Sea Shell Motel in Old Key West, 3 blocks east of Duval St. Rooms with 4-8 beds, shared bath. Kitchen open 24hr. May-Nov. $15, nonmembers $18; Dec.-Apr. $17/$20. Private room rates vary by season and availability. Key deposit $5. Lockers 25¢. Bike rentals $8 per 24hr. Reception 24hr; free parking. No curfew. Call to check availability or for late arrival.

**Caribbean House,** 226 Petronia St. (296-1600 or 800-543-4518), at Thomas St. in Bahama Village. Festive Caribbean-style rooms with cool tile floors, A/C, cable TV, free local calls, and fridge. Comfy double beds. Free continental breakfast. Rooms $49 and up; in winter $69; cottages $69/$89. Cottages first come, first served.

**Wicker Guesthouse,** 913 Duval St. (296-4275 or 800-880-4275). Excellent location on the main drag. Individually decorated rooms have pastel decor, hardwood floors, A/C; some have TV. Kitchen, pool access, and free parking. Breakfast included. Singles or doubles with shared bath $79 (June to mid-Dec.); $125 (late Dec. to May). Reservations suggested; ask for summer specials.

**Eden House,** 1015 Fleming St. (296-6868 or 800-533-5397), just 5 short blocks from downtown. Goldie Hawn lodged here in the film *Criss Cross*. Bright, clean, 1920s Floridian Deco hotel with friendly staff. Cool rooms with private or shared bath, some with balconies. Pool, jacuzzi, hammock/swinging bench area and kitchens. Bike rentals $10 per day. Join other guests for free happy hour daily 4-5pm. Rooms with shared bath $85; off-season $55.

**Boyd's Campground,** 6401 Maloney Ave. (294-1465), at Mi. 5. Take a left off U.S. 1 onto Macdonald Ave., which becomes Maloney. 12 acres on the ocean. Full facilities, including showers. $31; in winter $36; $8 per additional person. Waterfront sites $6-7 extra. Water and electricity $10 extra, full hookup $15 extra.

## FOOD AND NIGHTLIFE

Check out the daily *Key West Citizen* (sold in front of the post office) and the weekly *Solares Hill* (available at the Chamber of Commerce) for the latest in Key West entertainment. Expensive restaurants line festive **Duval St.** Side streets offer lower prices and fewer crowds. Hemingway used to drink beer and referee boxing at ☒ **Blue Heaven,** 729 Thomas St., 1 block from the Caribbean House. Blue Heaven serves healthy breakfasts ($2-8), mostly vegetarian lunches ($5-9), and heavenly dinners ($9-19) that include plantains, corn bread, and fresh veggies, generally regarded as the best food in town. (296-8666. Open W-Sa 8am-3pm, and Su 8am-1pm; daily 6-10:30pm.) **Garden Cafe,** 310 Duvall St., is home of paradise-like $5½-lb. burgers. Monster portabello and veggie burgers $6. (294-2991. Open M-Th 11am-11:30pm, F-Su 11am-12:30pm.) The much-agreed-upon best Cuban food on the island can be found at **El Siboney,** 900 Catherine St., where $7 buys a lot of grub. (296-4184. Open M-Sa 11am-9:30pm.)

Nightlife in Key West revs up at 11pm and winds down very late. It doesn't get anymore local than the **Green Parrot,** 610 Whitehead St. at Southard St., home of Key West's "most notorious locals" (294-6133; open M-Sa 10am-4am, Su noon-4am). **Capt. Tony's Saloon,** 428 Greene St., the oldest bar in Key West and reputedly one of "Papa" Hemingway and Tennessee Williams' preferred watering holes, has been chugging away since the early 30s. Bras festoon the ceiling. Tony Tarracino, the 81-year-old owner, enters nightly through a secret door (see **Brains...**). (294-1838. Open M-Th 10am-2am, F-Sa 10am-4am, Su noon-2am. Live entertainment daily and nightly.) An unabashed meat market under the stars, **Rick's,** 202 Duval St. open air dance complex boasts well-placed body shots and all-you-can-drink nights (W-Th $7; 296-4890). Most gay clubs line Duval St. south of Fleming Ave; **801 Bourbon,** 801 Duval St., is very popular (294-4737; open daily 11am-4am).

Key West nightlife reaches its annual exultant high during **Fantasy Fest** (296-1817; the third week of Oct.). The free *Island News* and *Time Out* list dining spots, music, and clubs; *Celebrate!* covers the gay and lesbian community.

## SIGHTS

Seeing Key West aboard a bike or moped is more convenient and comfortable than driving; the latest, safer transport craze is small electric cars. *(295-6686. $30 per hour.)* The **Conch Tour Train,** a fascinating 1½hr. narrated ride through Old Town, leaves from Mallory Sq. at 3840 N. or from Roosevelt Blvd., next to the Quality Inn.

FLORIDA

**"BRAINS DON'T MEAN A SHIT"** This brief profundity sums up the philosophy of Captain Tony Tarracino, gun runner, mercenary, casino owner, and one-time mayor of Key West. "All you need in this life is a tremendous sex drive and a great ego," proclaimed the Captain, who escaped to Key West over 40 years ago while evading the New Jersey bookies he cheated, having used a battered TV set to get racing results before they came over the wire. Tarracino arrived to find an island populated by bar-hoppers, petty criminals, and other deviants. In this setting, he thrived. Tony attempted to organize his local popularity into a political campaign, and after four unsuccessful bids, he was finally voted mayor in 1989, on the slogan, "Fighting for your future: what's left of it." Although he wasn't re-elected, Tarracino is certain that history will exonerate him. "I'll be remembered," he vows. With his own bar, countless t-shirts that bear his image, and even a feature film about his life, this is no idle assertion. But for now, Tony T. isn't going anywhere—he even mocks his own mortality. "I know every stripper in this town," he boasts. "When I'm dead, I've asked them all to come to my casket and stand over it. If I don't wake up then, put me in the ground."

*(294-5161. Runs daily 9am-3:30pm. $18, ages 4-12 $7.)* **Old Town Trolley** runs a similar tour 9am-5:30pm, but you can get on and off throughout the day at 13 stops. *(296-6688. Full tour 1½hr. $18, ages 4-12 $9.)*

The **glass-bottomed boat** *Fireball* cruises to the reefs and back at noon, 2, and 6pm. *(296-6293. 2-2½hr. Tickets $20, at sunset $25, ages 5-12 $10/$12.50.)* For a land-lubber's view of Key West's marine life, the **Key West Aquarium**, in Mallory Sq., offers a 50,000-gallon Atlantic shore exhibit, a touch tank, and live shark petting sessions. *(1 Whitehead St. 296-2051. $8, ages 8-15 $4. Open daily 10am-6pm.)*

"Papa" wrote *For Whom the Bell Tolls* and *A Farewell to Arms* at the **Hemingway House**, off Olivia St. Take a tour, or traipse through on your own among 50 descendants of Hemingway's cat, half of which have an extra toe. *(907 Whitehead St. 294-1136. Open daily 9am-5pm. $7.50, ages 6-12 $4.50.)* The **Harry S Truman Little White House Museum** sits in the restored vacation home of the President's getaway. *(111 Front St. 294-9911. Open daily 9am-5pm. $7.50, children $3.75. Tours available.)* The **Audubon House** houses fine antiques and a collection of engravings by naturalist John James Audubon. *(205 Whitehead St. 294-2116. Open daily 9:30am-5pm. $7.50, students $5, seniors $6.50, ages 6-12 $3.50.)* Down Whitehead St., past Hemingway House, you'll come to the **southernmost point in the continental U.S.** at the nearby **Southernmost Beach**. A small, conical monument and a few conch shell hawkers mark the spot, along with some hustlers who might offer to take your picture; they may not give your camera back until you pay them. Artist Cynthia Wynn transformed scrap industrial hardware into the futuristic sculptures of **Reworx**. A vanity chair of pick axes and plow blades, and a bed of conveyer belt rollers elevate recycling to a fine art. *(825 Duval St. 292-3273. Open summer Th-Tu 10am-6pm, winter daily 10am-6pm. $7, ages 5-12 $5.)* **Mel Fisher's Maritime Heritage Society Museum** glitters with gold and quite a few busts of M.F., who uncovered the biggest sunken treasure ever, a shipwrecked Spanish vessel with a $400 million booty. A *National Geographic* film is included in the entrance fee. *(200 Greene St. 294-2633. Open daily 9:30am-5pm; last film 4:30pm. $6.50, ages 6-12 $2, students $4.)* An old pier at **Monroe County Beach,** off Atlantic Ave., allows water access past the weed line, and the **Old U.S. Naval Air Station** has deep-water swimming on **Truman Beach** ($1). A paragon of Cuban architecture, the **San Carlos Institute,** built in 1871, houses a research center for Hispanic studies *(516 Duval St. 294-3887. Tu-Su 11am-5pm.)* The **Haitian Art Company,** 6 blocks east of Duval, explodes. *(600 Frances St. 296-8932. Open daily 10am-6pm. Free.)* Sunset lovers will enjoy the view from **Mallory Sq. Dock;** there, street entertainers (including the U.S.'s southernmost bagpiper) and hawkers of tacky wares work the crowd, while boats showboat during the daily **Sunset Celebration.** The crowd cheers when the sun finally slips into the Gulf. Explore the old hanging tree and look for spooks on the **Ghost Tours.** *(294-9255. $18, children $10. Reservations required, call for hours.)*

FLORIDA

# GULF COAST

## TAMPA

Even with year-round warm weather and perfect beaches, Tampa has managed to avoid the plastic pink flamingos that plague its Atlantic Coast counterparts. The city's survival doesn't hinge on tourism; Tampa is one of the nation's fastest growing cities and largest ports, with booming financial, industrial, and artistic communities. Despite Ybor City, Tampa's large Cuban neighborhood, this somewhat practical bent strips the city of the spunk endemic to Miami, it also makes Tampa a less tacky, more peaceful vacation spot.

### ORIENTATION AND PRACTICAL INFORMATION

Tampa wraps around Hillsborough Bay and sprawls north. **Nebraska Ave**. parallels **I-275** as the main north-south route; **Kennedy Blvd.**, **Columbus St.** and **Busch Blvd.** are main east-west arteries. With some exceptions, numbered streets run north-south and numbered avenues run east-west. **Ybor (ee-bore) City,** Tampa's Latin Quarter and nocturnal playland, is bounded roughly by Nuccio Pkwy. on the north, 22nd St. on the south, Palm St. on the east, and 5th St. on the west. *Be careful not to stray outside these parameters, since the area can be dangerous.* You can reach Tampa on I-75 from the north, or I-4 from the east.

**Airport: Tampa International** (870-8700), 5mi. west of downtown. HARTline bus #30 runs between the airport and downtown Tampa.

**Amtrak:** 601 Nebraska Ave. (221-7600), at the end of Zack St., 2 blocks north of Kennedy St. Ticket office open daily 5:30am-10:45pm. To Miami (5hr., 1 per day, $29-61) and New Orleans (20hr., 3 days a week, $53). 5 buses per day to Orlando if you are connecting there ($22). No trains run south from Tampa.

**Greyhound:** 610 E. Polk St. (229-2174). To Atlanta (11-14hr., 8 per day, $57-61), Orlando (1-3hr., 5 per day, $14-15), and Miami (7-10hr, 6 per day, $36). Open daily 6am-12:30am.

**Public Transit: Hillsborough Area Regional Transit (HARTline)** (254-4278). $1.50, seniors and ages 5-17 55¢, transfers 10¢. The **Tampa Town Ferry** (223-1522) runs between the Florida Aquarium and Lowry Park Zoo.

**Visitor Info: Tampa/Hillsborough Convention and Visitors Association,** 111 Madison St. (223-1111 or 800-826-8358), at Ashley Dr. Open M-Sa 9am-5pm.

**Hotlines: Crisis Hotline,** 234-1234. **Helpline,** 251-4000.

**Post Office:** 5201 W. Spruce Rd. (800-725-2161), at the airport. Open 24hr. **ZIP code:** 33601. **Area code:** 813.

### ACCOMMODATIONS

**Gram's Place Bed & Breakfast,** 3109 N. Ola Ave. (221-0596). From I-275, take Martin Luther King Blvd. west to Ola Ave., and then a left on Ola. Named for singer/songwriter Gram Parsons, this eclectic haven features a jacuzzi, lush courtyard, cable TV, BYOB outside bar, and continental breakfast. A larger room is set aside as a hostel. B&B Rooms from $50-80; hostel from $15-25; prices depend on availability.

**Budget Host,** 3110 W. Hillborough Ave. (876-8673 or 800-238-4678), 5 mi from the airport and exit 30 off I-275. 33 small rooms with A/C, cable, and pool access. Singles $35; doubles $39; $3 per additional person (rates are year-round).

**Motel 6,** 333 E. Fowler Ave. (932-4948), off I-275 near Busch Gardens. Big, newly renovated rooms 30mi. from the beach on the northern outskirts of Tampa. Free local calls, cable, A/C, and pool. 1 adult $36; 2 adults $40; 3rd and 4th adults $2 each.

**Americana Inn,** 321 E. Fletcher Ave. (933-4545), 3mi. from Busch Gardens in northwest Tampa; from I-275, take the Fletcher exit west. Clean rooms, some with fridge and stove. Pool and cable. Singles Sa-Su $35, M-F $33; doubles $39; significantly less Nov.-Mar.; students with ID 10% discount

**Friendship Inn,** 2500 E. Busch Blvd (933-3958), 4 blocks west of Busch Gardens, offers A/C, cable, and pool. Singles $35, doubles $45. 10% off with college ID.

## 🎨 🎵 FOOD AND NIGHTLIFE

Tampa is blessed with many unique, inexpensive restaurants. Heading that list is ▓ **Skipper's Smokehouse,** 910 Skipper Rd., off Nebraska Rd., a giant complex of thatched huts, wreckage and wood planks in the northern outskirts of town. After downing a tender fried alligator tail sandwich ($5) and conch chowder ($2), walk to the adjacent "Skipper Dome" and groove to live zydecho, reggae or world beat tunes—a Tampa must-see. (971-0666. Restaurant and bar open Tu 11am-10pm, W-F 11am-11pm, Sa noon-11pm, Sun 1pm-10pm. Cover varies.) The original hand-rubbed marinade behind **Kojak's House of Ribs,** 2808 Gandy Blvd., tenderly reminds you that you're still in the South. (837-3774. Ribs with two sides $7. Open Tu-Th 11am-10pm, F-Sa 11am-10:30pm, Su 4pm-9:30pm.) Tampa's gulf shore heritage is tasted at **Cafe Creole,** 1330 E. 9th Ave. a classy Ybor City establishment known for oysters and jambalaya. (247-6283. Entrees $6-$18. Open M-Th 11:30am-10pm, F 11:30am-11:30pm, Sa 5pm-11:30pm. Live jazz F-Sa 7pm-close.)

With over 35 clubs and bars in a condensed area, **Ybor City** really does offer it all. Most are located on the well-lit 7th Ave.; use caution when walking down side streets. National blues acts jam every weekend at the **Blues Cafe,** 1910 E 7th Ave., whose secret "blues shot" is guaranteed to take them away. (248-6097. Open 3pm-3am daily for restaurant, bar and downstairs club. 18+. $5 cover for bands.) Ybor offers a diverse range of clubs. **The Castle,** 2004 N 16th St. at 9th St., caters to the goth in you, but is open to all who enter the friendly sanctum. (247-7547. F-Sa goth nights, Su gay night, M 80s night. Nipple night occasionally pokes up. Open W-M 9:30pm-3am, 18+, cover $4.) Spanning the pop spectrum, country line dancing swings to everything from Alan Jackson to Puff Daddy at **Spurs,** 1915 7th Ave. (247-SPUR; open Th-Sa 6pm-3am, free dance instructions 7-9pm). Wave to mom on the dance floor of **Empire,** 1902 E. 7th St. where the grinding is live on the internet at www.empirelive.com. Celebrate web stardom with $10 bottles of champagne. (247-2582. Open Th 10pm-3am, F-Sa 9pm-3am. 18+. Cover $5-10.) Brief yourself on city entertainment with the free *Tampa Weekend, Weekly Planet,* or *Stonewall.*

## 👁 SIGHTS

Tampa blossomed only after the success of Ybor City, a planned community once known as the cigar capitol of the world. Early 20th-century stogie manufacturer Vincent Martínez Ybor employed a wide array of immigrants, marking the area with a rich and varied ethnic heritage. The **Ybor City State Museum** details the rise and decline of the neighborhood's tobacco empire and the workers behind it. Photographs examine the art and culture of the hand-rolled cigar. *(1818 9th Ave. 247-6323. Open daily 9am-5pm. Neighborhood walking tours Sa 10:30. $4.)* A 1½hr. **Ybor City Ghostwalk** leaves from **Joffrey's Coffee Co.** *(1616 E. 7th Ave. 242-9255. Th-Sa 7pm, Su 4pm. Adults $10 in advance, $12.50 on site; children $7.)* Eclectic shops, eateries, and numerous bars and clubs line carefree E. 7th Ave. Buses #5, 12, and 18 run to Ybor City from downtown. The Tampa-Ybor Trolley runs during lunchtime between the two areas; schedules are available at the visitors center. *(Fare 25¢.) Certain areas near Ybor City can be dangerous; stay on guard.*

The **Florida Aquarium** invites you to mash your face to the glass for a tête-á-tête with fish from Florida's various lagoons. Snakes, tarantulas and scorpions star in the wildly creepy "Frights of the Forest" exhibit. *(701 Channelside Dr. 273-4000. Open daily 9am-5pm; in summer, F until 8pm; $12, seniors $11, ages 3-12 $7.)* One mile north of

Busch Gardens is the **Museum of Science and Industry**, Tampa's science playland. MOSI sports 450 interactive exhibits, a nature trail, and an IMAX theater. *(4901 E. Fowler St. 987-6100. Open daily 9am-7pm. $13, seniors $11, ages 2-13 $9.)* At the **Henry B. Plant Museum,** in a wing of University of Tampa's Plant Hall, the exhibits include Victorian furniture and Wedgewood pottery but pale in comparison to the museum, a no-holds-barred orgy of Rococo architecture. *(401 W. Kennedy Blvd. 254-1891. Open Tu-Sa 10am-4pm, Su noon-4pm. $3. Tours at 1:30pm.)*

Downtown, the **Tampa Museum of Art** houses a noted collection of ancient Greek and Roman works as well as a series of changing, often family-oriented exhibits. *(600 N. Ashley Dr. 274-8130. Open M-Tu and Th-Sa 10am-5pm, W 10am-9pm, Su 1-5pm. Tours W and Sa 1pm, Su 2pm. Admission $5, seniors $4, ages 6-18 $3. Free Su and W 5-9pm.)*

Every Feb., the **Jose Gasparilla,** a fully rigged pirate ship loaded with hundreds of exuberant "pirates," invades Tampa, kicking off a month of parades and festivals. *(353-8070.)* The **Gasparilla Sidewalk Art Festival,** Feb. 5-6, 2000, awaits the millenial invasion. *(876-1747.)* Thousands pack Ybor City every Oct. for **"Guavaween,"** a Latin-style Halloween celebration. *(242-4828 or 621-7121.)*

It's never Miller time at **Busch Gardens,** Anheuser-Busch's addition to the world of Floridian theme parks. Eight mi. northeast of the city, Busch Gardens looms as Tampa's biggest tourist haven, but efficient shuttles minimize parking difficulties. Summer 1999 saw the arrival of **Gwazi,** a dueling set of roller coasters that approach 100 mph. You won't mind the workload of the "Budweiser Beer School" at the **Anheuser Busch Hospitality House.** Beermaster certificates and free samples follow a primer on the king of beers. *(Shows at 12:30, 1:30, 2:20, 3:30, and 4:30pm. Free.)* Over 2500 animals roam, fly, slither and swim through the African-themed zoo areas; the **Edge of Africa** safari experience remains among the park's most popular. *(Park: E. 3000 Busch Blvd. 987-5082. Open daily 9:30am-6pm. $36, children age 3-9 $30. Parking $4.)* You can cool off at Busch's **Adventure Island,** a 13-acre water park about a ½mi. north of Busch Gardens. *(10001 Malcolm McKinley Dr. 813-987-5660. Open June 1-Aug. 8, M-Th 9am-7pm, F-Su 9am-8pm. $24, $22 ages 3-9. Parking $4.)*

# ST. PETERSBURG AND CLEARWATER

Twenty-two mi. southwest of Tampa, across the bay, St. Petersburg caters to a relaxed community of retirees and young singles. The town enjoys 28mi. of soft white beaches, emerald-colored, bathtub-warm water, melt-your-heart sunsets, and about 361 days of sunshine per year. The west coast of the narrow St. Petersburg-Clearwater stretch is made up of one picturesque beach town after the next.

## 🛈 ORIENTATION AND PRACTICAL INFORMATION

In St. Petersburg, **Central Ave.** parallels numbered avenues running east-west in the downtown area. **34th St. (U.S. 19),** I-275 and 4th St. are major north-south fares. The beaches line a strip of barrier islands on the far west side of town. Several causeways, including the **Clearwater Memorial Causeway (I-60),** access the beaches from St. Pete. Clearwater sits at the far north of the strip; **Gulf Blvd.** runs down the long coastline, through Belleair Shores, Indian Rocks Beach, Indian Shores, Redington Shores, Madeira Beach, Treasure Island, and St. Pete Beach. The stretch of beach past the huge and pink Don Cesar Hotel, in St. Pete Beach, and Pass-a-Grille Beach have the best sand and less pedestrian and motor traffic.

**Airport: St. Petersburg Clearwater International** (535-7600) sits right across the bay from Tampa, off Roosevelt St. **Red Line Limo,** 535-3391. $11.50 per person.

**Amtrak:** (522-9475). Ticket office at Pinellas Sq. Mall, 7200 U.S. 19 N. Open 7am-9pm. St. Pete has no train station, but Amtrak will connect you to Tampa from St. Pete by bus ($10). Clearwater is inaccessible by train.

**Buses: Greyhound,** in St. Pete: 180 9th St. N. (898-1496). To Panama City (9-10hr, 3 per day, $60); Clearwater (30min., 7 per day, $6). Open daily 4:30am-11pm. In Clearwater: 2111 Gulf-to-Bay Blvd. (796-7315). Open daily 6am-9pm.

**Public Transit: Pinnellas Suncoast Transit Authority (PSTA),** 530-9911. Most routes depart from Williams Park at 1st Ave. N. and 3rd St. N. Fare $1. Info kiosk at Williams Park. To reach Tampa, take express bus #100X from the Gateway mall (fare $1.50). A pink trolley (571-3440) loops through downtown (fare 50¢), and a green trolley runs up and down the Pier (free). A 1-day unlimited bus pass is $2.50. Buses have bike racks.

**Visitor Info: St. Petersburg Area Chamber of Commerce,** 100 2nd Ave. N. (821-4715). Open M-F 8am-5pm, Sa 10am-5pm, Sun noon-3pm. **The Pier Information Center,** 800 2nd Ave. NE (821-6164). Open M-Sa 10am-8pm, Su 11am-6pm.

**Crisis Lines: Rape Crisis,** 530-7273. **Helpline,** 344-5555. **Florida AIDS Hotline,** 800-352-2437. All 24hr.

**Post Office:** 3135 1st Ave. N. (323-6516), at 31st St. Open M-F 8am-6pm, Sa 8am-noon. **ZIP code:** 37370. **Area code:** 727.

# ▐ ACCOMMODATIONS

St. Petersburg and Clearwater offer two hostels, as well as many cheap motels lining **4th St. N.** and **U.S. 19** in St. Pete. Some establishments advertise singles for as little as $20, but these tend to be very worn down. To avoid the worst neighborhoods, stay on the north end of 4th St. and the south end of U.S. 19. Several inexpensive motels cluster along the St. Pete beach.

**St. Petersburg Youth Hostel,** 326 1st Ave. N. (822-4141), downtown in the McCarthy Hotel. Bunk rooms for a max. of 4 people with in-suite bathrooms. Common room, TV, A/C. $11 with any youth hostel card or student ID; $15 without ID card; historic hotel rooms with A/C and private bath for $25. Linen $2. Check-in before 11pm.

**Clearwater Beach International Hostel (HI-AYH),** 606 Bay Esplanade Ave. (443-1211), at the Sands Motel in Clearwater Beach; take Rt. 60 W. to Clearwater Beach. Head to the superb white sand beach, just 2 blocks away, or take a free canoe to the nearby state park, where sports fields and equipment are available for free and bike rental is $5 per day. Recreation center, with basketball and weight room. Kitchen, common room, and pool. $12; nonmembers $13; private rooms with kitchen $28-39. Linen $2.

**Treasure Island Motel,** 10315 Gulf Blvd. (367-3055), across the street from the beach. Big rooms with A/C, big fridge, color TV, pull-out couch and beautiful pool. Catch dinner off a pier in back. Singles and doubles $38; Feb.-Mar. $38-44. Pirates not allowed.

**Grant Motel,** 9046 4th St. N. (576-1369), 4mi. north of town on U.S. 92. All rooms have A/C, fridge, and pronounced country-style decor, including straw hats and lacy curtains. Beautifully landscaped grounds. Pool access. Singles and doubles $35.

**Kentucky Motel,** 4246 4th St. N. (526-7373). A little out of place, but hey...large, clean rooms with friendly owners, cable TV, refrigerator, and free postcards. Singles $32; doubles $35; Jan.-Mar. $35/$38.

**Fort De Soto County Park** (582-2267), composed of 5 islands at the southern end of a long chain of keys and islands, has the best camping around. Also a wildlife sanctuary, the park makes a great oceanside picnic spot. Ranked among the nicest beaches in Florida. 235 palm-treed, private sites, many on the waterfront. No alcohol. $20, cash only. 2-night min. stay. Front gate locked at 9pm. Curfew 10pm. All sites have electricity, water, and a grill. All reservations must be made in person either at the park office, the St. Petersburg County Bldg., 150 5th St. N., #125 (582-7738). or the Parks Dept. in Clearwater, 631 Chestnut St. (464-3347).

# ◖ FOOD AND NIGHTLIFE

St. Petersburg's cheap, health-conscious restaurants cater to its retired population, and generally close by 8 or 9pm. City polls have repeatedly ranked **Tangelo's Bar and Grille,** 226 1st Ave. NE, as a top Cuban restaurant. Hearty gazpacho ($2.75) is a meal in itself. (894-1695. Open M-Sa 11am-7pm, Su seasonally.) Also in St. Pete is the **Fourth Street Shrimp Store,** 1006 4th St. N, purveyors of all things shrimp. Filling shrimp-taco salads run $6. (822-0325. Open M-Th 11am-9pm, F-Sa 11am-10pm.) At the beach, **Crabby Bill's,** 401 Gulf Blvd., near Indian Rocks Beach, serves giant $7-10 seafood platters and $6 crab cake sandwiches (595-4825; open M-Th 11:30am-10pm, F-Sa 11:30am-11pm, Su noon-10pm). **Dockside Dave's,** 13203 Gulf Blvd., is one of the best-kept secrets on the islands. The ½ lb. grouper sandwich (market price, around $8) is simply sublime. (392-9399. Open M-Sa 11am-10pm, Su noon-10pm.) Remember grease! Burgers and seafood pizza are at **Frenchy's Cafe,** 41 Baymont St. (446-3607; open M-Th 11:30am-11pm, F-Sa 11:30am-midnight, Su noon-11pm). **Beach Nutts,** 9600 W. Gulf Blvd., Treasure Island, has fresh grouper ($7.25) and decent burgers ($5), but go for the ambience; the restaurant/bar's newly expanded porch has a spectacular view of the beach, and bands play nightly (367-7427; open M-Sa 11am-2am, Su 1pm-2am). **Majestic Nightclub,** 470 Mandalay St., in Clearwater Beach, parties hearty with DJs, live tunes, and $1 shots until midnight (461-0042; open daily 6pm-2am; cover varies). Clearwater hotels, restaurants, and parks often host free concerts. Free copies of *Beach Life* or *Tampa Tonight/Pinellas Tonight* grace local restaurants and bars.

# ■ SIGHTS

Grab a copy of *See St. Pete* and *Beaches* or the *St. Petersburg Official Visitor's Guide* for the lowdown on area events, discounts, and useful maps. Beaches are the most worthwhile—but not the only—attraction for the coastline. The nicest beach may be **Pass-a-Grille Beach,** but its parking meters eat quarters; **Municipal Beach** at Treasure Island, accessible from Rt. 699 via Treasure Island Causeway, has free parking. **Clearwater Beach,** at the northern end of the Gulf Blvd. strand, is mainstream beach culture at its unspectacular height. The sites of St. Pete are worth more than just a cloudy day's amusement. ▧ **The Salvador Dalí Museum,** in Poynter Park on the Bayboro Harbor waterfront, makes you wonder what the talented Spaniard was smoking. The museum contains the world's most comprehensive collection of Dalí works and memorabilia—94 oil paintings, 1300 graphics, and many dripping clocks. (*1000 3rd St. S. 823-3767. Open M-W 9:30am-5:30pm, Th 9:30am-8pm, F-Sa 9:30am-5:30pm, Su noon-5:30pm. $9, students $5, seniors $7, under 11 free.*) Until May 29, 2000 the **Florida International Museum** will hold **John F. Kennedy: The Exhibition,** an exhaustive collection of over 500 artifacts. Personal effects, many from the fateful trip to Dallas, highlight the exhibit. (*100 2nd St. N. 822-3693. Open daily 9am-7pm. $14, seniors $13, students $8, ages 6-18 $6, under 6 free.*) The **Tampa Bay Holocaust Memorial Museum** covers pre-war Europe to the birth of Israel in the fourth largest museum of its kind in the country. A Nazi boxcar used to transport Jews to the killing centers sits in the center atrium. (*55 5th St. S. 820-0110. Open M-F 10am-5pm, Sa-Su noon-5pm; $6, students and seniors $5, ages 18 and under $2.*)

At the beach, the **Clearwater Marine Aquarium** sports a painting dolphin and petable stingrays. A 2hr. waterway cruise leaves daily at 12:30pm and 3:15pm. (*249 Windward Passage. 441-1790. Open M-F 9am-5pm, Sa 9am-4pm, Su 11am-4pm; $7, children $4; cruise $15, children $10.*) The **Sunsets at Pier 60 Festival** brings arts and entertainment to the Clearwater Beach daily from 2hr. before sundown until 2hr. after. (*449-1036.*) The ▧ **sunsets** that happen every night are perhaps more spectacular; the sun crashes over the water of the Gulf. **Boyd Hill Nature Park** is immodest but refreshing. (*1101 S. Country Club Way. 893-7326. Open daily 9am-5pm. $1, ages 3-17 50¢.*)

**The Pier,** at the end of 2nd Ave. NE, downtown, extends into Tampa Bay from St. Pete, ending in a 5-story inverted pyramid complex with a shopping center, aquarium, restaurants, and bars. The complex offers a fascinating view of the Bay, but little else. (*821-6164. Open M-Sa 10am-8pm, Su noon-6pm; bars and restaurants open later.*) In the pier, **Great Explorations** is an innovative hands-on museum. (*821-8892. Open M-Sa 10am-8pm, Su 11am-6pm. $5, under 3 free.*) "Meet you at the 'Trop'" refers to the ballpark of **Tampa Bay Devil Rays,** 1 Tropicana Dr. (*825-3250. Apr.-Sept. Tickets $3-30.*)

# GAINESVILLE

Set equidistant from both coasts, Gainesville can't claim any beaches, but this Floridian version of a university town is a nice diversion from beach-and-theme-park monotony. The University of Florida (UF) lends the town a notably attractive population and an air of high culture with equal parts bohemian, fraternity, and even Old South. From sophisticated professional theater and stuffed alligators to giant sinkholes and natural springs, Gainesville and its friendly residents offer an enjoyable—yet undiscovered—tourist experience.

**⚡ PRACTICAL INFORMATION. Amtrak** stops in Waldo, at an unstaffed station at U.S. 301 and State Rd. 24. One train a day runs to Miami (9hr., $29-80) and Tampa (3½hr., $19-38); conductor takes cash. **Greyhound,** 516 SW 4th Ave. (376-5252; station open M-Sa 7am-11pm, Su and holidays 10am-10pm) heads to Miami (14hr., 10 per day, $47-50), Tampa (3-5hr., 7 per day, $23-27), and Orlando (2½hr., 8 per day, $19). **Regional Transit System** (334-2602) runs trains and buses around the city. ($1; students, seniors, and handicapped 50¢; $2 buys a 1-day unlimited pass. M-F 6am-7pm, Sa-Su 7am-7pm.) **Taxi: Gator Cab Co.** (375-0313). **The Alachua County Visitors and Convention Bureau:** 30 E. University Ave., downtown (374-5231; open M-F 8:30am-5pm). **Post Office:** 401 SE 1st Ave. (371-7009; open M-Sa 8am-5:30pm, Sa 8am-noon). **ZIP code:** 32601. **Area code:** 352.

**▛ ACCOMMODATIONS.** There are numerous inexpensive accommodations along 13th St., increasing as you near I-75. On football or Gatornationals race weekend, rates are at least double at any place you can squeeze into. The **Gainesville Lodge,** 413 W. University Rd., is a downtown steal, only a short stumble from the nightclubs (376-1224; TV, A/C, pool; $36 singles and doubles). The **Cape Cod Inn,** 3820 SW 13th St., has decor that will make New Englanders nostalgic. All rooms come with cable, pool, and continental breakfast. The friendly staff speaks six languages. (371-2500. Singles $44; doubles $46.) Sleep amidst a rainforest-esque environment at **Paynes Prarie State Reserve,** 10mi. south on U.S. 441 (tent and RV sites with water $10, $2 extra for electricity; bathroom facilities).

**▛▟ FOOD AND ENTERTAINMENT.** Gainesville's diverse university population seems to have one taste they agree on: cheap, healthy food. **Rhapsody,** 12 NW 13th St., offers equally creative vegetarian and carnivorous menus. Their $3 "big-ass pasta bowl" and 10-inch pizzas stand as some of the best deals in town. (377-8344. Open M-Sa 11am-10pm, Su noon-8pm.) In a cool atrium surrounded by flora, **Farah's,** 1120 W. University Ave., serves fine mediterranean grub. Several types of wraps ($4) and rolled grape leaves with hummus ($7) are local favorites. (378-5179. Open M-Tu 11am-10pm; W-Th 11am-11pm; F-Sa 11am-midnight. Live jazz Sa 8pm.) **Leonardo's By the Slice,** 1245 W. University Ave., offers basic pastas ($4-6) and beautiful pizzas (slices $2-3), with a cafe that sells breakfasts and treats throughout the day (375-2007; open M-Th 7am-11pm, F-Sa 7am-midnight, Su 7am-11pm). **Alan's Cubana & Salty Dog Saloon,** 1712 W. University Ave., boasts the most beers in town and authentic southern fare (375-6969; happy hour M-Sa 3-8pm, Su 1-10pm; open M-Sa 11am-2am, Su 1-10pm). Next door, the **Purple Porpoise,** 1728 W. University Ave., is the most popular college bar, with a dominant Greek scene (376-1667; open M-Sa 11pm-2am; W and F dance floor open until 3am).

Clubs dot the intersection of W. University Ave. and 2nd Ave. downtown. Pulsating crowds dance on the rooftop and gather on Th nights around the boxing ring at the **Baja Beach Club,** 201 W. University Ave. (379-9953; cover $5; open Th-Sa 9pm-2am, F-Sa $10 all-you-can-drink). Across the street, **Orbit Lounge,** 238 W. University Ave., has 3 floors of dancing, a cigar lounge, and nightly drink specials (335-9800; cover $5; 18+). Follow your ears to the wickedly hip **Soulhouse,** on 2nd Pl. and 1st St., off S. Main St. The house is a local secret known for its notorious Beanbag Room. (Cover $5 Open M-Th 10pm-2am, Fr-Sa 10am-3am.)

The annual **Alachua County Music Festival** showcases the local music scene; the likes of Tom Petty and Sister Hazel hail from Gainesville. The 3-day festival features 50 bands. (336-8360. 2nd week in Oct.) For live tunes year-round, head to the **Gainesville Community Plaza,** E. University Ave. and SE 1st St., where bands play every F night (334-2197; shows start at 8pm; free). The bi-weekly *Moon* and the University's daily paper, the *Alligator,* list local events and nightlife info.

◨ **SIGHTS.** Gators, wild horses, and herds of buffalo roam the 21,000 acres of **Paynes Prairie State Reserve,** 10mi. south on U.S. 441. A tower overlooks the mi. of verdant, teeming, landscape. Horse and nature trails traverse the park; in the winter, park rangers lead overnight expeditions through the basin. *(466-3397. Open daily 8am-sunset. $3.25 per car.)* The **University of Florida (UF),** the cultural center of the area, houses its art at the **Harn Museum of Art.** The Harn, itself a breathtaking building, displays 5500 multicultural paintings, as well as at least 15 changing exhibitions a year. *(34th St. SW and Hull Rd. 392-9826. Open Tu-F 11am-5pm, Sa 10am-5pm, Su 1pm-5pm. Free. Last admission time 4:45pm.)* A more bizarre collection can be found at the **Fred Bear Museum,** an endless parade of stuffed animals that met the famed archer's deadly aim. *(4600 SW 41st Blvd. 376-2411. Open daily 10am-6pm. $4, ages 6-12 $2.50, families $9.)* The nearby **Devil's Millhopper State Geological Site** is an enormous sinkhole formed when a cavern roof collapsed. To the tune of cascading water, a wooden walkway leads a descent layer-by-layer through 20 million years of Florida natural history. *(4732 NW 53rd Ave. 904-336-2008. M-F 9am-5pm, Sa-Su 9am-sunset. Free.)* **Poe Springs Park** just over 3mi. west of High Springs on County Rd., boasts sparkling natural springs and nature trails. *(28800 NW 182nd Ave. 904-454-1992. Open 9am-dusk, $4.)* Less ecologically sensitive is the **Gainesville Raceway,** home to the drag-racing extravaganza, the Gatornationals, held every Mar. During the year the track hosts various gas-guzzling events. *(11211 N. Country Rd. 377-0046.)*

Gainesville has its share of the quirky. The **Retirement Home for Horses** in Alachua houses over 80 equine retirees. Admission is two carrots, but the horses request as many as you can smuggle in *(Mill Creek Farm, County Rd. 235-A. 904-462-1001, open Sa only, 11am-3pm).* At the **Waldo Farmers and Flea Market,** on U.S. 301 1mi. north of Waldo, over 400 vendors hawk "everything from blue jeans to green beans." *(468-2255. Open Sa-Su 7:30am-4pm.)* In the middle of the UF campus off Museum Rd. lies the **Bathouse.** Locals traditionally gather at sunset, turning their backs to the alligators in Lake Alice to watch the bats flock out of their house.

# PANAMA CITY BEACH

The people in PCB are quick to say that this isn't just a hot spring break spot (although it certainly is), and they've got a point; but don't bother coming unless you're ready to have fun, Panama City Beach-style. Suntan lotion is the perfume of choice along these mi. of snow-white beach. Heart of the "Redneck Riviera," PCB puts on no airs; leave those black suits and cell phones in Miami. Water parks, roller coasters, and surf shops complement the 27mi. of sandy shore.

▣ **PRACTICAL INFORMATION.** After crossing Hathaway Bridge, **Front Beach Rd.** forks off from U.S. 98 and runs along the gulf. Also known as the "Miracle Strip," Front Beach Rd. is the place to see and be seen. To bypass the hubbub, take some of the smaller roads off U.S. 98. **Greyhound** (785-7861) makes a stop at the junction of U.S. 98 and U.S. 79, and continues on to Orlando (8-11hr., 2 per day, $61) and Atlanta (8hr., 2 per day, $44). **Bay Town Trolley** (769-0557) shuttles along the beach, running 6am-6pm (fare 50¢, students and seniors 25¢). **AAA Taxi:** 785-0533. **Panama City Beach Convention and Visitors Bureau:** 17001 Panama City Beach Pkwy. (800-722-3224), at corner of U.S. 98 and U.S. 79 (open daily 8am-5pm). **Domestic Violence and Rape Crisis Hotline:** 763-0706. **Crisis and Mental Health Emergency Hotline:** 769-9481, ext. 405, both 24hr. **Post Office:** 420 Churchwell Dr. (234-9101; open M-F 8:30am-5pm, Sa 8:30-noon). **ZIP code:** 32413. **Area code:** 850.

**▟ ACCOMMODATIONS.** Depending on the Strip location and the time of year, rates range from can-do to outrageous. High season runs from the end of Apr. until early Sept.; rates drop in fall and winter. Call well in advance for summer reservations. Rates generally correspond to distance from the beach. One exception is **Sugar Beach Motel,** 16819 Front Beach Rd., with beach access. TV, A/C, pools, and recently-remodeled rooms; kitchenettes available. (800-528-1273. 1 bed $59; 2 beds $80.) **La Brisa Inn,** 9424 Front Beach Rd., ½mi. from the beach, has clean, spacious rooms with two double beds, a pool, free cable, and coffee (235-1122 or 800-523-4369; singles or doubles $45-65). **Sea Breeze Motel,** 16810 Front Beach Rd., has small pink-and-turquoise rooms in a prime location. Cable, A/C, a pool, and reasonable rates are pleasing. (234-3348. Single $40; double $45. Weekends $10 more.)

Camp on the beach at **St. Andrews State Recreation Area,** 4607 State Park Lane, 3mi. east of PCB at the east end of Thomas Dr. Call ahead (up to 60 days) for reservations at this popular campground. All 176 sites are beneath the pines, on or close to the water. (233-5140. Sites $15, with electricity or waterside $17; in winter $8/$10.) **Panama City Beach KOA,** 8800 Thomas Dr., 2 blocks south of U.S. 98 and directly across the street from the clubs, maintains 114 sites with showers, laundry, and a pool. (234-5731 or 800-562-2483. Tent sites with water $20, full hookup $26; in winter $13/$20. Reservations recommended 6 mo. in advance.)

**❐❒ FOOD AND NIGHTLIFE.** Buffets stuff the Strip and Thomas Dr. along the Grand Lagoon. "Early bird" specials, offered about 5pm, get you the same food at about half the price. **JP's Restaurant and Bar,** 4701 W. U.S. 98, just across the Hathaway Bridge, serves award-winning pasta, seafood, and steak (fettuccine *tutto meri* with shrimp, scallops, and crab $16, lunch $4-7) in abundant portions (769-3711; open daily 11am-11pm). **The Pickle Patch,** 5700 Thomas Dr., concocts delicious Southern country breakfasts and Greek lunches (235-2000; breakfast $4-6, lunch $5; open daily 6:30am-2pm). **Scampy's,** 4933 Thomas Dr., offers seafare in a smaller, less harried atmosphere than the mega-troughs (seafood salad $6, entrees $8-20; 235-4209; open daily 11am-3pm, 4-10pm).

Bars are a stumble away along the strip and Thomas Dr.; most have occasional live bands. The largest club in the U.S. (capacity 8000) and MTV's former Spring Break headquarters, **Club LaVela,** 8813 Thomas Dr., offers seven clubs and 48 bar stations under one jamming roof. Live bands work the Rock pavilion every night, and national acts are no strangers. Wet t-shirt, bikini, and male hardbody contests fill the weekends and every night during Spring Break. (234-3866. No cover during the day; cover varies at night. Open daily 10am-4am.) Next door, **Spinnaker,** 8795 Thomas Dr., boasts a restaurant (fresh seafood $6-19), a pool deck, and a playground for kids. This enormous wooden beach clubhouse has a happening happy hour daily 5-9pm. (234-7892. Open daily 11am-4am.) The back patio bar at **Harpoon Harry's,** 12627 Front Beach Rd., overlooks the beach. Build a midnight sandcastle with their famous $6 margarita buckets. (234-6060. Open daily 11am-2am.)

**⊡❒ SIGHTS AND ENTERTAINMENT.** Over 1000 acres of gators, nature trails, and beaches make up the **St. Andrews State Recreation Area** (see **Accommodations,** above; open daily 8:30am-sunset; $4 per car). **Glass-bottom boat trips** sail to Shell Island from Treasure Island Marina on Thomas Dr. (234-8944. 3hr. trips at 9am, 1, and 4:30pm. $11, under 12 $6; $3 coupon at visitor's center.) The **Museum of the Man in the Sea,** 17314 Panama City Beach Pkwy., traces man's underwater adventures (235-4101; open daily 9am-5pm; $5, ages 6-16 $2.50). The world's largest speed boat, the **Sea Screamer,** 3601 Thomas Dr., cruises the lagoon. (904-233-9107. Runs late May to early Sept. 11am, 1pm, 3pm, and sunset; in spring and fall 2 trips per day. $11, ages 4-12 $8.) **Miracle Strip Amusement Park** (234-5810; open M-F 6-11:30pm, Sa 1-11:30pm; $16) is adjacent to **Shipwreck Island Water Park,** 2000 Front Beach Rd. (234-0368; open daily 10:30am-5:30pm; $18, admission to both parks $27). An assortment of dolphin shows, parasailing outfits, and amusement parks lines **Front Beach Rd.**

FLORIDA

# GULF ISLANDS NATIONAL SEASHORE

The sugar-white beaches have not always been so sweet. Before the Civil War, three forts on the shores of Pensacola formed a triangular defense to guard the city's deep-water ports. Pensacola retains a military-infused population and a reputation for conservatism. While secluded emerald waters along the Gulf Islands National Seashore are Pensacola's biggest draw, the naval aviation museum, and historic district can provide diversion for those seeking solace from sunburn

The city buttresses Pensacola Bay. **Palafox St.** and **I-110** are the main north-south byways; **Government St.** and **Main St.** run east-west. **Bayfront Pkwy.** runs along the edge of the bay and over the **Pensacola Bay Bridge.** On the other side, **Pensacola Beach Rd.** heads for Santa Rosa Is. and Pensacola Beach. **Amtrak,** 980 Heinburg St. (433-4966) stops by on its east-west route between New Orleans (5hr., 3 per week, $38) and Orlando. (13hr., 3 per week, $62. Open M, W, F 12:30am-noon; Tu, Th 8:30am-4pm; Su 4:30-6:30am.) **Greyhound,** 505 W. Burgess Rd. (476-4800) heads to Orlando (9hr., 7 per day, $69), Atlanta (9-14hr., 5 per day, $49), New Orleans (4-7hr., 5 per day, $28), and various locations in between (open 24hr.). A **trolley** runs two lines through downtown, complete with tours; stops line Palafox St. (25¢; runs M-F 7am-6pm). During the summer, two Tiki Trolley shuttles run along the beach (free; F-Sa 10am-3am; Su 10am-10pm). **Rainbow Taxi:** 437-1311. **Pensacola Convention and Visitor's Bureau:** 1401 E. Gregory St. (800-874-1234), near the Pensacola Bay Bridge (open daily 8am-5pm). **Post office:** 100 Northcliffe Dr. (932-2662), open M-F 8am-5pm, Sa 9am-12:30pm. **ZIP code:** 32501. **Area code:** 850.

Hotels along the beach cost at least $65. Better options lie inland, north of downtown (a 15min. drive to the beach). **Motel 6,** 5829 Pensacola Blvd., offers cable, A/C, and a pool (477-7522; singles $33, doubles $39). The **Civic Inn,** 200 N. Palafox St., is near the historic district (432-3441; A/C, pool, TV; singles $44, doubles $48). At the western edge of Santa Rosa Island, the **Fort Pickens Campground** on the Gulf Islands National Seashore offers electric ($20) and non-electric ($15) sites within walking distance of the beach (reservations 800-365-2267; camping info 934-2622). **Hopkin's House,** 900 Spring St., serves their famous fried chicken and veggies on large, family style tables—$6 for all-you-can-eat (438-3979; open Tu-Su 7-9:30am, 11:15am-2pm; Tu-F 5:15-7:30pm). The owner of **King's BBQ,** 2120 N. Palafox St., built the drive-thru with his own hands and adds his personal touch to the colossal $3 pork, chicken, or beef sandwiches (open M-Sa 10:30am-7pm).

Vestiges of Pensacola's defensive fort system comprise the serene **Gulf Islands National Seashore.** From the **visitor's center,** paths meander through the **Naval Live Oaks Area,** a forest originally harvested for shipbuilding. (1801 Gulf Breeze Pkwy. 934-2600. Open 8am-6pm.) Three forts—Fort Pickens, Fort Barrancas, and Fort McRee—guarded the harbor and naval station throughout the 1800s. Apache leader Geronimo was imprisoned at **Fort Pickens,** now a jungle of brick, earthen mounds and steel fortifications at the west end of Santa Rosa Island. ◪ Some of Florida's most secluded, sugar-white beaches line the road to the fort. ($6. Open 7am-midnight.)

# GREAT LAKES

During the Ice Age, massive sheets of ice flowed from the north, carving out huge lake basins. These glaciers eventually receded and melted, leaving expanses of rich topsoil, numerous basin pools, and five inland seas. Together, the Great Lakes comprise 15% of the earth's drinkable freshwater supply and an invaluable network of transport arteries for the surrounding region. Lake Superior is the world's largest freshwater lake, and its unpopulated, scenic coast hosts a significant wolf population. The sports lover's paradise of Lake Michigan boasts swimming, sailing, deep-water fishing, and sand dunes. Lake Erie has suffered from industrial pollution, but due to strict regulations, this shallow lake is gradually reclaiming its former beauty. The first Great Lake to be seen by Europeans, Lake Huron is still the least developed, though not in size or recreational potential. The runt of the bunch, Lake Ontario, still covers an area larger than New Jersey.

The Great Lakes region is not all uncharted beauty—Minneapolis and St. Paul have the panache of any coastal metropolis, while Chicago dazzles visitors with world-class music, architecture, and cuisine.

# OHIO

The glaciers which carved out the Great Lakes flattened the northern half of Ohio, creating perfect farmland now patched with cornfields and soybean plants. The southern half, spared the bulldozing, rolls with endless wooded hills. The alliterated metropoli of Cincinnati, Columbus, and Cleveland are surrounded by amiable suburbs. Ohio's political tradition complements its strong "middle-America" affiliation (in recent years Ohio has voted with the American majority in national elections more often than any other state). Though Ohio may be the most average state, it is innovative in its own right; tomatoes were thought poisonous and inedible, and then the state beverage became tomato juice.

## ▶ PRACTICAL INFORMATION

**Capital:** Columbus.

**Visitor Info: State Office of Travel and Tourism,** 77 S. High St., 29th Fl., Columbus 43215 (614-466-8844; www.ohiotravel.com). Open M-F 8am-5pm. **Ohio Tourism Line,** 800-282-5393. **Division of Parks and Recreation,** Fountain Sq., Columbus, 43224 (614-265-7000).

**Postal Abbreviation:** OH. **Sales Tax:** 5.75%.

# CLEVELAND

The city formerly known as the "Mistake on the Lake" has undertaken an extensive face-lift in recent years in an attempt to correct its beleaguered image. The arrival of the Rock and Roll Hall of Fame and a new downtown baseball park have shined up the previously bleak image of abandoned urbanity. The downtown area is on the verge of flourishing, although many outlying regions remain impoverished. Sadly, the lack of an established budget travel industry renders Cleveland something of a siren; rising from the lake to beckon wayfaring travelers before throwing them against the jagged rocks of expensive accommodations.

## ▶ ORIENTATION AND PRACTICAL INFORMATION

**Terminal Tower** in **Public Sq.** cleaves the land into east and west. Many street numbers correspond to the distance of the street from Terminal Tower; e.g., E. 18th St. is 18 blocks east of the Tower. To reach Public Sq. from **I-90** or **I-71,** follow the Ontario Ave./Broadway exit. From **I-77,** take the 9th St. exit to Euclid Ave., which runs into Public Sq. From the Amtrak station, **Lakeside Ave.** heads to **Ontario Ave.,** which leads to the Tower. **The Flats,** the former industrial core of the city, along both banks of the Cuyahoga River, and **Coventry Rd.** in Cleveland Heights are the happenin' hip spots for food and nightlife.

**Airport: Cleveland Hopkins International** (265-6030), 10mi. SW of downtown in Brook Park. RTA line #66X ("Red Line") to Terminal Tower ($1.50). Taxi to downtown $20.

*Travel helps you remember who you forgot to be.....*

**Council** *Travel*

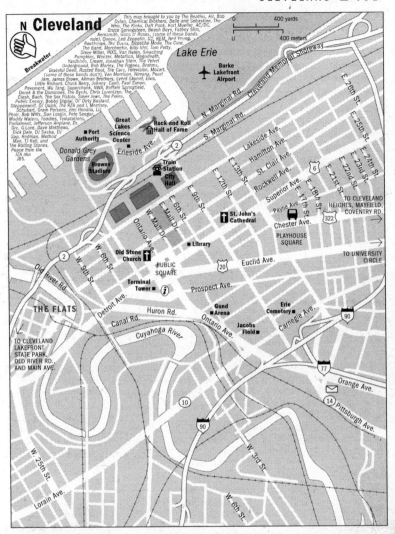

**N Cleveland**

This map brought to you by The Beatles, Air, Bob Dylan, Chemical Brothers, Belle and Sebastian, The Who, The Kinks, Daft Punk, Kurt Mueller, AC/DC, Bruce Springsteen, Beach Boys, Fatboy Slim, Aerosmith, Guns n' Roses, (some of these bands rule), Queen, Led Zeppelin, U2, REM, Neil Young, Beethoven, The Doors, Depeche Mode, The Cure, The Band, Morcheeba, Billy Idol, Tom Petty, Steve Miller, INXS, Van Halen, Smashing Pumpkins, Weezer, Metallica, Megadeath, Yardbirds, Cream, Jonathan Stein, The Velvet Underground, Bob Marley, The Fugees, Brahms, Grateful Dead, Rusted Root, The Cars, Television, Mozart, (some of these bands don't), Van Morrison, Nirvana, Pearl Jam, James Brown, Allman Brothers, Lynrd Skynrd, Elvis, Little Richard, Chuck Berry, Johnny Cash, Paul Simon, Pavement, Wu Tang, Superchunk, NWA, Buffalo Springfield, Derek & the Dominoes, The Byrds, Chris Lorentzen, The Clash, Bach, The Sex Pistols, Silver Jews, The Pixies, Public Enemy, Bobby Digital, Ol' Dirty Bastard, Steppenwolf, DJ Quick, The RZA and I, Morrisey, Schubert, Gram Parsons, Jimi Hendrix, Liz Phair, Bob Wills, Dan Luskin, Pete Seeger, Muddy Waters, Toadies, Temptations, Parliament, Jefferson Airplane, Dr. Dre, G Love, Dave Matthews, Dick Dale, DJ Quick, DJ Sasha, DJ Sap, Redman, Method Man, TJ Kell, and The Rolling Stones. Peace from the IZA aka JBS.

Lake Erie

Burke Lakefront Airport

Breakwater

Cleveland Memorial Shoreway

N. Marginal Rd.

S. Marginal Rd.

Lakeside Ave.

Hamilton Ave.

St. Clair Ave.

Rockwell Ave.

Superior Ave.

Payne Ave.

Chester Ave.

Euclid Ave.

Prospect Ave.

Rock and Roll Hall of Fame

Great Lakes Science Center

Port Authority

Donald Grey Gardens

Browns Stadium

Erieside Ave.

Train Station City Hall

St. John's Cathedral

Library

Old Stone Church

PUBLIC SQUARE

Terminal Tower

Gund Arena

Jacobs Field

Erie Cemetery

PLAYHOUSE SQUARE

THE FLATS

Old River Rd.

Detroit Ave.

Canal Rd.

Huron Rd.

Ontario Ave.

Cuyahoga River

TO CLEVELAND LAKEFRONT STATE PARK, OLD RIVER RD. AND MAIN AVE.

TO CLEVELAND HEIGHTS, MAYFIELD, COVENTRY RD.

TO UNIVERSITY CIRCLE

Carnegie Ave.

Orange Ave.

Pittsburgh Ave.

Lorain Ave.

W. 25th St.

W. 3rd St.

W. 6th St.

E. 26th St.

E. 25th St.

E. 24th St.

E. 23rd St.

E. 22nd St.

E. 21st St.

E. 18th St.

E. 17th St.

E. 13th St.

E. 12th St.

E. 9th St.

E. 6th St.

W. 6th St.

W. 9th St.

W. Mall Dr.

E. Mall Dr.

W. Main Dr.

400 yards

400 meters

---

**Trains: Amtrak,** 200 Cleveland Memorial Shoreway NE (696-5115), across from Brown Stadium east of City Hall. To: New York City (12hr., 1 per day, $76-117); Chicago (7hr., 2 per day, $56-86); and Pittsburgh (3hr., 2per day, $25-38). Open M-Th midnight-6:30pm, F-Su midnight-7:30am and 11am-6:30pm.

**Buses: Greyhound,** 1465 Chester Ave. (781-0520), at E. 14th St., 7 blocks from Terminal Tower. Near RTA bus lines. To: New York City (9-14hr., 7 per day, $72-76); Chicago (5¼-7½hr., 14 per day, $33-35); Pittsburgh (2½-4½hr., 10 per day, $18-19); and Cincinnati (4½-6½hr., 10 per day, $32-34). Most eastbound buses stopover in Pittsburgh.

**Public Transit: Regional Transit Authority (RTA),** 315 Euclid Ave. (621-9500, TDD 781-4271; open M-F 7am-6pm). Bus lines, connecting with Rapid Transit trains, travel from downtown to most of the metropolitan area. Service daily 5am-midnight; call for info on "owl" after-midnight service. Train fare $1.50. Bus fare $1.25, express $1.50, downtown loop 50¢, 1-day pass $4; ask the driver for free transfer tickets. The **Waterfront Line** accesses the Science Center, Rock and Roll Hall of Fame, and the Flats.

**Taxis: Americab,** 429-1111.

**Car Rental: Rent-a-Wreck,** 8003 Brookpark Rd. (351-1840), in Parma, 16mi. from down-town. Take Ridge Rd. off I-480. $18 per day. Open M-F 8am-6pm, Sa 9am-1pm.

**Visitor Info: Cleveland Convention and Visitors Bureau,** Tower City Center (621-4110 or 800-321-1001), 1st fl. of Terminal Tower at Public Sq. Open M-F 9:30am-4:30pm.

**Hotline: Rape Crisis Line,** 391-3912. 24hr.

**Post Office:** 2400 Orange Ave. (443-4199; 443-4096 after 5pm). Open M-F 7am-8:30pm, Sa 8:30am-3:30pm. **ZIP code:** 44101. **Area code:** 216; 440 or 330 in sub-urbs. In text, 216 unless otherwise noted.

# ◤ ACCOMMODATIONS

With hotel taxes (not included in the prices listed below) as high as 14.5%, budget lodging pickings are slim in Cleveland (so-called "budget" motels tend to run at least $80). Plan well in advance, and **Cleveland Private Lodgings,** P.O. Box 18590, Cleveland 44118 (321-3213), will place you in a home around the city for as little as $35. (Allow 2-3 weeks for a letter of confirmation. Call M-F 9am–noon or 3-5pm; messages will be promptly returned.) Otherwise, travelers with cars should head for the suburbs or near the airport, where prices tend to be lower. Excellent and friendly, but inaccessible by public transportation, **Stanford House Hostel (HI-AYH),** 6093 Stanford Rd., off exit 12 from I-80, lies 22mi. south of Cleveland in Peninsula. From exit 12, turn right onto Boston Mills Rd., drive about 5mi., then turn right on Stanford Rd. The hostel occupies a restored 19th-century Greek Revival farm-house (with kitchen) in the Cuyahoga Valley National Recreation Area. Gorgeous hiking and bike trails are nearby. (330-467-8711. Singles and 6-bed dorms. $12, under 18 $6. Linen $2. Laundry $1.75. 7-night max. stay. Check-in 5-10pm. Check-out 9am. Curfew 11pm. Call ahead.) Near the airport and 12mi. from the city, **Knights Inn,** 22115 Brookpark Rd., exit 9 off I-480, has rooms varying from newly renovated and pristine to slightly grungy (440-734-4500; king-size bed $55; 2-bed doubles $65; must be 21+). The suburb of Middleburg Heights offers many chain motels at decent prices. **Motel 6,** 7219 Engle Rd. (234-0990), has comfortable rooms with A/C and cable TV (singles $50, F-Sa $56; doubles $55/$62).

The sun never shines on the heavily wooded sites bordering Cuyahoga National Park at **Tamsin Park,** 5000 Akron-Cleveland Rd. (330-656-2859), 25mi. south of Cleveland in Peninsula (sites $20, with hookup $26; open May to mid-Oct.).

# ◖ FOOD

The delis downtown satiate hot corned beef cravings, but Cleveland has more to offer elsewhere. A healthy dose of hipness infuses the shops near **Coventry Rd.** in Cleveland Heights. Italian cafes and restaurants cluster in Little Italy, around **Mayfield Rd.** Seafood and standard pub fare are abundant in **the Flats.** Over 100 vendors hawk produce, meat, and cheese at the indoor-outdoor **West Side Market,** 1995 W. 25th St., at Lorain Ave. (771-8885; open M and W 7am-4pm, F-Sa 7am-6pm).

By the Flats, **Wilbert's Bar and Grille,** at the corner of W. 9th and St. Clair, pro-duces concoctions that menace even the self-declared popes of chilitown. Witness Cherry Bombs (banana peppers stuffed with cheese and chorizo sausage, $5) and Texas Chili ($4). Live music incurs evening cover charges of $3-25. (771-2583. Open M-F 11am-2:30am, Sa 6pm-2:30am.) Tommy and the groovy staff of **Tommy's,** 1824 Coventry Rd. in Cleveland Heights, up the hill from University Circle (bus #9X east to Mayfield and Coventry Rd.), whip up veggie cuisine, like a falafel and spinach pie for $5. Hedonists sock their guts with a Brownie Monster for $2. (321-7757. Open M-Th 7:30am-10pm, F-Sa 7:30am-11pm, Su 9am-10pm.) **Mama Santa's,** 12305 Mayfield Rd., in Little Italy just east of University Circle, serves generous portions of Sicilian food in a no-frills setting. (Medium pizza or spaghetti $4.50. 421-2159. Open M-Th 11am-10:45pm, F-Sa 11am-11:45pm; closed most of Aug.)

**AN ARTFUL MANAGER** Mike Hargrove, the manager of the Cleveland Indians baseball team, has become something of a local hero. He provides profound and compelling insights in his "All-Star Tour of the Cleveland Museum of Art":
**On Jackson Pollock:** "This is out in left field. I don't know why, but I like it."
**On Winslow Homer:** "With a name like Homer, you have to give this guy a chance. He sure can paint."
**On "Rest," by William Adolphe Bougereau:** "This kid looks so real it makes you want to reach out and grab his leg and wake him up."

## SIGHTS AND ACTIVITIES

The aspirations of a new Cleveland have manifested themselves in a made-over downtown—a self-declared "Remake on the Lake." **The Rock and Roll Hall of Fame** is a dizzying exploration of the rock music world, where one can listen to hundreds of history-making tunes while reveling in the fashion sense of rock stars, from Jim Morrison's Cub Scout uniform to Elvis's sequined capes. The basement-level exhibition is a delight; the cacophony of other floors can prove overwhelming. *(1 Key Plaza. 781-7625 or 800-493-7655. Open Th-Tu 10am-5:30pm, W 10am-9pm. $15, seniors and ages 9-11 $11.50. Extended hours and reduced prices on some summer weekends.)* Next door, the **Great Lakes Science Center** holds enough gizmos and doodads to make one helluva whatsit. *(601 Erieside Ave. 694-2000. Open Th-Tu 9:30am-5:45pm, W 9:30am-8pm. $7.75, seniors $6.75, ages 3-17 $5.25; with IMAX $11/$10/$7.75. Parking for Hall of Fame and Science Center $7.)* **Cleveland Lakefront State Park,** accessible via Lake Ave., Cleveland Memorial Shoreway, or Lakeshore Blvd., is a 14mi. park near downtown with 3 beaches and great swimming and picnic areas. *(881-8141.)*

Seventy-five cultural institutions cluster in **University Circle,** a micro-Smithsonian 4mi. east of the city. The world-class **Cleveland Museum of Art** exhibits a survey of art from the Renaissance to the present, with exceptional collections of Impressionist and modern art. An elegant plaza and pond face the museum. *(11150 East Blvd. 421-7340. Open Su, Tu, and Th-Sa 10am-5pm, W and F 10am-9pm. Free.)* Nearby, the **Cleveland Museum of Natural History** displays the only existing skull of the fearsome dinosaur Pygmy Tyrant *(Nanatyrannus)*. *(1 Wade Oval Dr. 231-4600. Open M-Sa 10am-5pm, Su noon-5pm. $6.50; students, seniors, and ages 5-17 $4.)* The lovely **Cleveland Botanical Garden** provides a pacific respite from the urban decay and *rough personality that characterizes Euclid Ave. and Carnegie St.* University Circle itself tends to be fairly safe. The newly opened Hershey Children's Garden soothes tots. *(11030 E. Blvd. 721-1600.)* The **Cleveland Orchestra,** one of the nation's best, performs at **Severance Hall.** *(11001 Euclid Ave. 231-7300 Tickets from $12. Box office open M-F 9am-5pm.)* In summer, the orchestra moves to **Blossom Music Center** Cuyahoga Falls, about 45min. south. *(1145 W. Steels Corners Rd. 330-920-8040. Lawn seating $13-15.)*

## NIGHTLIFE AND ENTERTAINMENT

The **Cleveland Indians** (420-4200) hammer the hardball at **Jacobs Field,** 2401 Ontario St. Games have sold out for 4 straight years; the best bet is a 1 hr. **stadium tour.** (241-8888 for tickets. May-Sept. every 30min. M-Sa 10am-2pm, June-Aug. Su noon-2:30pm when the team isn't in town. $6, seniors and under 14 $4.) The **Cleveland Cavaliers** (420-2000) shoot hoops at **Gund Arena,** 1 Center Ct. (Sept.-Apr.), but not as well as their female counterparts, the WNBA **Cleveland Rockers** (June-Aug.).

**Playhouse Square Center,** 1519 Euclid Ave., a 10min. walk east of Terminal Tower, is the 2nd-largest performing arts center in the nation (771-4444). Inside, the **State Theater** hosts the **Cleveland Opera** (575-0900) and the renowned **Cleveland Ballet** (426-2500) from Oct. through June. The **Cleveland Cinemathique,** at the Institute of Art (see **Sights,** above), screens off-beat and foreign films (421-7450; $6).

The *Downtown Tab,* a free, bi-weekly paper, recently proposed that Cleveland offer the following greeting for visitors: "Welcome to Cleveland—we close

GREAT LAKES

at 6." And they don't mean 6am. Most of Cleveland's nightlife is focused in **the Flats.** Numerous nightclubs and restaurants, some with a family atmosphere, dot the northernmost section of the Flats, overpopulating Old River Rd. and W. 6th St., just west of Public Sq. The nightclubs are remarkably similar, offering a late-20-something crowd a place to get trashed and get down to the tune of 70s and 80s "greatest hits" albums. The **Have a Nice Day Café,** 1096 Old River Rd., has a swingin' 70s dance scene under the painted gaze of KISS, Richard Nixon, and Archie Bunker. (241-2451. Th college nights with cheap drinks; F "C'mon get happy hour" 5-9pm. Cover F-Sa $3.) **6th St. Under,** 1266 W. 6th St., hosts jazz and R&B jam sessions in one of the most chill downtown venues. (589-9313. No cover Tu-Th, F-Sa $6. Open Tu-Th 5pm-1am, F 5pm-2:30am, Sa 7pm-2:30am.) Hard-core rockers head for the **Grog Shop,** 1765 Coventry Rd. in Cleveland Heights, with local and national acts (321-5588; happy hour 3pm F-Su; open daily 7pm-2:30am). Gays and lesbians frequent **The Grid,** 1281 W. 9th St., with a comfortable bar and a high-tech dance floor (623-0113; open Su-Th 4pm-2:30am, F-Sa 4pm-3:15am). For info on clubs and bands, pick up a copy of the *Downtown Tab* or the *Free Times.* The *Gay People's Chronicle* and the bi-weekly *Out lines,* are available at gay clubs, cafes, and bookstores.

## NEAR CLEVELAND

Recently declared "best amusement park in the world" by *Amusement Today,* **Cedar Point Amusement Park,** off U.S. 6, 65mi. west of Cleveland in **Sandusky,** earns superlatives. The world's highest and fastest inverted rollercoasters (riders are suspended from above) and a "training coaster" offer a grand old adrenaline rush for all. Patriotic laser light shows take to the sky in summer at 10pm. *(419-627-2350 or 800-237-8386. Open Nov. to mid-May Su-Th 10am-7pm, F-Sa 10am-10pm; June daily 10am-11pm; July-Aug. M-F and Su 10am-10pm, Sa 10am-midnight; Sept. to early Oct. hours vary. $33, seniors $19, children 48-54 in. $28, children under 4 or shorter than 48 in. $9. Parking $6.)*

**Sea World,** 30mi. south of Cleveland off Rt. 43 in Aurora, presents Shark Encounter—a sequel to the gentler Penguin Encounter—and other aquatic exhibits. *(1100 Sea World Dr. 330-995-2121. Open early June to late Aug. daily 10am-11pm; late May and late Aug. daily and in early Sept. Sa-Su 10am-7pm. $31, ages 3-11 $23. Parking $4.)* Innovative juices flow at **Inventure Place** and the **National Inventor's Hall of Fame,** 35mi. south of Cleveland in Akron. *(221 S. Broadway. 762-6565 or 800-968-4332. Open M-Sa 9am-5pm, Su noon-5pm; Sept.-Mar. W-Sa 9am-5pm, Su noon-5pm. $7.50, seniors, students, and kids $6.)*

The **Pro Football Hall of Fame,** 60mi. south of Cleveland in Canton, honors the pigskin greats, housing a rotating movie theater and O.J. Simpson's jersey and helmet. Take exit 107A from I-77. *(2121 George Halas Dr. NW. 330-762-4463. Open daily 9am-8pm; early Sept. to late May 9am-5pm. $10, seniors $6.50, ages 6-14 $5; families $25.)*

# COLUMBUS

Rapid growth, a huge suburban sprawl, and some gerrymandering have nudged Columbus's population beyond that of Cincinnati or Cleveland. The main drag, High St., heads north from the towering office complexes of downtown to the lively galleries in the Short North. It ends in the collegiate cool of Ohio State University (OSU); America's largest university with over 60,000 students. Columbus is America without glitz, smog, pretension, or fame—the clean, wholesome land of *Family Ties.* (Bexley, a city suburb, was the model for the hit sitcom's setting.)

**⚐ PRACTICAL INFORMATION. Port Columbus International Airport** (239-4000) is just off Rt. 317 and Broad St. on the city's northwest side. Take the Broad St. bus or a taxi (about $17). **Greyhound,** 111 E. Town St. (221-2389), offers service from downtown to Cincinnati (2hr., 14 per day, $16); Cleveland (3hr., 14 per day, $18); and Chicago (7-10hr., 7 per day, $47). The **Central Ohio Transit Authority (COTA),** 177 S. High St. (228-1776; open M-F 6am-8pm, Sa-Su 8am-6pm), runs in-town transportation until 11pm or midnight depending on the route ($1.10, express $1.50). **Yellow**

**DAVE THOMAS, AMERICAN BEEFCAKE** When R. David Thomas was a boy, he held the cartoon character Wimpy close to his heart. A mainstay on the Popeye show, Wimpy spent every episode gobbling hamburgers as if they were tiny, bite-size snacks. In doing so, he cut an inspiring figure for the future fast-food entrepreneur. Born in 1932, Dave Thomas spent his early childhood in Atlantic City, dropping out of high school in 10th grade to chase his culinary dreams. In 1969, he opened the **first Wendy's restaurant,** in Columbus. From there, the freckled face and red pigtails of his daughter spread across the U.S. like a midwest prairie fire. Today, Wendy's is an international fast-food chain, and Dave Thomas is a multimillionaire who enjoys eating in his own commercials. Thomas hasn't forgotten his humble beginnings and still loves to play the part of Wimpy, slipping out of board meetings to devour a quick burger...or 3.

**Cab:** 444-4444. **Greater Columbus Visitors Center:** 2nd fl. of **City Center Mall,** 111 S. 3rd St., downtown (221-6623 or 800-345-4386). **Internet access:** Games n' Gear, 1758 N. High St, (297-0161; open M-Th 1-10pm, F-Sa 1-11:30pm). For **post office** locations, call 800-721-2161. **ZIP code:** 43202. **Area code:** 614.

**ACCOMMODATIONS AND FOOD.** The **Heart of Ohio Hostel (HI-AYH),** 95 E. 12th Ave., 1 block from OSU, offers quality facilities (including a piano, TV, and well-equipped kitchen) and loans out bikes to guests. Stay free if you put on a 1hr. concert (294-7157; $14, nonmembers $17; weekly rates available. Check-in 7:30-9:30am and 5-10pm. Lockout 9:30am-5pm. Curfew.) **Motel 6,** 5910 Scarborough Dr., 20min. from downtown off I-70 at exit 110A, has sensible prices and clean rooms (755-2250; singles $38-44, $6 per extra adult). If arriving at night, look for cheap motels on the outskirts of the city, where **I-70** and **I-71** meet **I-270.**

High St. features scads of tasty budget restaurants. A small and well-loved Middle Eastern restaurant/grocery, **Firdous,** 1538 N. High St., dishes up tasty hummus plates ($5), fresh falafel, and shish kebabs (299-1844; open M-Sa 10am-9pm, Su noon-8pm). **Bernie's Bagels and Deli,** 1896 N. High St., offers a variety of sandwiches ($3-5) in a dark punk-rock cellar atmosphere. (291-3448. Open M 10am-1am, Tu-F 10am-2am, Sa-Su noon-2am; Sept.-Jun M-F 8am-2am, Sa-Su 9am-2am.) **Kahiki,** 3583 E. Broad St., in the Whitehall area, serves up delectable Polynesian and Chinese platters. The fantastically tacky building is a national historic landmark. (237-5425. Open M-Th 11:30am-10pm, F-Sa 11:30am-11pm, Su 4:30-10pm.)

**SIGHTS. Ohio State University (OSU)** rests 2mi. north of downtown. The **Wexner Center for the Arts,** on N. High St. by 15th Ave., was Peter Eisenman's first public building. The 4 galleries display avant-garde art in all media, and the performance spaces play host to dance, music, and theater productions. *(292-3535. Ticket and information center open M 10am-4pm, Tu-W and F-Su 10am-6pm, Th 10am-9pm. Exhibits open Tu-Su 10am-6pm; Th until 9pm. $3, students and seniors $2. Free Th 5-9pm. Wheelchair access.)* The **Columbus Museum of Art** hosts Impressionist and European Modernist works. *(480 E. Broad St. 221-6801. Open Tu-W and F-Su 10am-5:30pm, Th 10am-8:30pm. $4, seniors and students $2, under 5 free; Th free 5-8:30pm.)* Fire, water, explosions, nylon mittens, uranium, and kids mean good ol' fun at the **Center of Science and Industry (COSI).** *(333 W. Broad St. 288-2674. Open M-Sa 10am-5pm, Su noon-5:30pm. Call for evening hrs. $8, students and seniors $7, ages 2-12 $6. Wheelchair access.)* Across the street is the very first link in the **Wendy's** restaurant chain. Just east, James Thurber's childhood home, the **Thurber House,** is decorated with drawings by the famous author and *New Yorker* cartoonist. *(77 Jefferson Ave., off E. Broad just west of I-71. 464-1032. Open daily noon-4pm. Free. Tours Su $2, students and seniors $1.50.)* The sprawling **Franklin Park Conservatory** has a towering collection of self-contained plant environments including rainforests, deserts, and Himalayan mountains. *(1777 E. Broad St. 645-5926. Open Tu-Su 10am-5pm; W until 8pm. $5, students and seniors $3.50, ages 2-12 $2; tour booklet $2.)*

**GREAT LAKES**

South of Capitol Sq., the **German Village,** first settled in 1843, is now the largest privately funded historical restoration in the U.S., full of stately brick homes and old-style beer halls. At **Schmidt's Sausage Haus,** oompah bands Schnickel-Fritz, Schnapps, and Squeezin' 'n' Wheezin' lead polkas at 7pm. Between dances, *lieder-hosen*-clad servers will bring you an $8 plate of homemade sausage. *(240 E. Kossuth St. 444-5050. Polkas Tu-Sa. Open Su-M 11am-9pm, Tu-Th 11am-10pm, F-Sa 11am-11pm.)* You can grab free samples at **Schmidt's Fudge Haus,** 1 block west of the Sausage Haus. *(444-9217, call for hrs.)* The **German Village Society Meeting Haus** knows all. *(588 S. 3rd St. 221-8888. Open M-F 9am-4pm, Sa 10am-2pm.)* At **Oktoberfest,** held on S. Grant at E. Livingston Ave., 3 stages provide continuous entertainment (polka and beyond), while 75,000 visitors wander among craft vendors, rides, and beer, wine, and schnapps-tasting tents. *(224-4300. Sept. 8-10, 2000. $4-5.)*

🎭 **ENTERTAINMENT AND NIGHTLIFE.** Four free weekly papers—*The Other Paper, Columbus Alive, The Guardian,* and *Moo*—available in shops and restaurants, list arts and entertainment options. The **Clippers,** AAA affiliate of the NY Yankees, swing away from Apr. to early Sept. (462-5250; tickets $5-7.50). For an evening with fewer peanut shells, Columbus's roaming art party known as **The Gallery Hop** happens the first Sa of every month; galleries in the Short North (the region between college town and downtown on High St.) display new exhibitions while socialites, art collectors, and others admire the works (and each other) far into the night. A good place to start hopping is **Gallery V,** 694 N. High St., which exhibits contemporary paintings, sculptures, and works in less common media (228-8955; open Tu-Sa 11am-5pm). The **Riley Hawk Galleries,** 642 N. High St., rank among the world's finest for glass sculpture (228-6554; open Tu-Sa 11am-5pm, Su 1-4pm). For the scoop on the gallery scene and the trendy Short North Area, check out the *Short North Gazette,* available at galleries.

When you over-dose on art, Columbus has a sure cure: rock 'n' roll. Bar bands are a Columbus mainstay; it's hard to find a bar that doesn't have live music on the weekend. Bigger national acts stop at the **Newport,** 1722 N. High St. (concert line 228-3580; tickets $10-20). **Bernie's Distillery,** 1896 N. High St., intoxicates with 80 imported beers (domestic drafts $2-3) and pounding live music all week in a small and smoky room (291-3448; cover F-Sa $2-5; happy hour M-F until 9pm). 21 TV screens liven up the **Union Station Café and Gallery,** 630 N. High St., which entertains a primarily gay crowd (228-3740 or 228-3546). A few blocks south from that hip joint is the **Brewery District.** Barley and hops have replaced the coal and iron of the historically industrial district. For mellow evenings, many of Columbus's denizens head for cafes **Insomnia,** 1728 N. High St., near the OSU campus, serves up sweet caffeine in a homey atmosphere (if your home is filled with Bohemian students) with outdoor seating, board games, and a gas pump (421-1234; iced coffee $1.35).

## NEAR COLUMBUS

A 1hr. drive south of Columbus, the area around **Chillicothe** (pronounce chill-i-cozy with a lisp) features several interesting attractions. The **Hopewell Culture National Historic Park,** swells with 25 enigmatic Hopewell burial mounds spread over 13 acres, with an adjoining museum that theorizes about the mounds' configuration. Check with park officials for info on other nearby mounds. *(16062 Rt. 104. 740-774-1126. Museum open daily 8:30am-6pm; Sept.-May 8:30am-5pm. Grounds open dawn-dusk. $4 per car, $2 per pedestrian.)* From mid-June to early Sept., the Sugarloaf Mountain Amphitheatre on the north end of Chillicothe off Rt. 23, presents **Tecumseh,** a drama re-enacting the life and death of the Shawnee leader. A behind-the-scenes tour, available hourly 2-5pm, will answer questions about how the stunt men dive headfirst off the 21 ft. cliff. *(Shows M-Sa 8pm. $13, F-Sa $15; under 10 $6 everyday. Tour $3.50, children $2.)* **Scioto Trail State Park,** 10mi. south of Chillicothe off U.S. 23, has walk-in **camping** across from Stuart Lake. *(740-663-2125. Sites $9, with electricity $13.)*

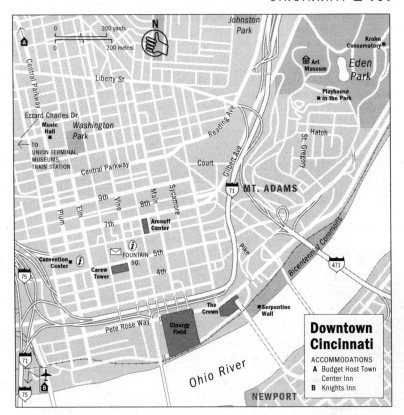

**Downtown Cincinnati**

ACCOMMODATIONS
A Budget Host Town Center Inn
B Knights Inn

# CINCINNATI

Longfellow called it the "Queen City of the West." Founded by German pig sales-men, Cincinnati has also earned the less regal nickname of "Porkopolis." Cincin-nati thrives in the limbo between the Great Plains, the South, and the Great Lakes. A vibrant arts community, boasting a stellar ballet and the new Aronoff Center for the Arts coexists with a surly sports scene, focused on the Reds and Bengals. Food and nightlife have also come a long way from their bratwurst-and-beer beginnings; funky restaurants, bars, and clubs dot downtown and the traditionally off-beat hill-top communities of Clifton and Mt. Adams. Somehow, past, present, and geogra-phy actually work together to create an eclectic community with room for both pork and royalty (and whatever else they put in that chili).

## 🚲 ORIENTATION AND PRACTICAL INFORMATION

The downtown business district is a simple grid centered around **Fountain Sq.**, at **5th** and **Vine St.** Cross streets are numbered and designated east or west by their relation to Vine St. The **University of Cincinnati** spreads out from Clifton, the area north of the city. **Cinergy Field,** the **Serpentine Wall,** and the **Riverwalk,** all to the south, border the river which marks the Ohio and Kentucky divide.

> **Airport: Greater Cincinnati International** (606-767-3151), in Kentucky, 12mi. south of Cincinnati and accessible by I-75, I-71, and I-74. **Jetport Express** (606-767-3702) shut-tles to downtown ($12, $16 roundtrip), or call the **Transit Authority of Northern Kentucky (TANK)** (606-331-8265) for alternate shuttling info.

GREAT LAKES

**Amtrak:** 1301 Western Ave. (651-3337), in Union Terminal. To Indianapolis (4hr., 3 per week, $17-34) and Chicago (8-9hr., 3 per week, $37-67). Open M-F 9:30am-5pm and Tu-Su 11pm-6:30am. *Avoid the area north of the station, especially Liberty St.*

**Buses: Greyhound,** 1005 Gilbert Ave. (352-6012), past the intersection of E. Court and Broadway. To: Indianapolis (10 per day, 2-3hr., $16); Louisville (2hr., 9 per day, $18); Cleveland (4-6hr., 9 per day, $34); and Columbus (2hr., 10 per day, $16). Open 24hr.

**Public Transit: Cincinnati Metro** and **TANK,** both in The Bus Stop, in the Mercantile Center, 115 E. 5th St. (621-9450; open M-F 8:30am-8pm). Most buses run out of Government Sq., at 5th and Main St., to outlying communities. In summer 50¢, in winter 65¢; extra to suburbs. Office has schedules and info.

**Taxi: Yellow Cab,** 241-2100.

**Visitor Info: Cincinnati Convention and Visitors Bureau,** 300 W. 6th St. (621-2142 or 800-246-2987). Open M-F 8:45am-5pm. **Information Booth** in Fountain Sq. has limited offerings. Open M-Sa 9am-5pm.

**Hotlines: Rape Crisis Center,** 216 E. 9th St. (381-5610), downtown. 24hr. **Gay/Lesbian Community Switchboard,** 591-0222.

**Post Office:** 525 Vine St. (684-5667), located on the Skywalk. Open M-F 8am-5pm, Sa 8am-1pm. **ZIP code:** 45202. **Area codes:** 513; Kentucky suburbs 606. In text, 513 unless otherwise noted.

# ACCOMMODATIONS

Few cheap hotels can be found in downtown Cincinnati. About 30mi. north of Cincinnati in Sharonville off I-75, budget motels cluster along **Chester Rd.** About 12mi. south of the city, inexpensive accommodations line **I-75** at exit 184. Closer by, the motels at **Central Pkwy.** and **Hopple St.** offer solid lodging without high costs. **Knights Inn-Cincinnati/South,** 8048 Dream St., Florence, KY, just off I-75 at exit 180, has newly renovated rooms with an Arthurian flair and exceptionally friendly service. (606-371-9711. Cable TV, A/C, outdoor pool. Singles $36-40; doubles $40-45. 21+.) 10min. from downtown and the University of Cincinnati, **Budget Host Town Center Inn,** 3356 Central Pkwy., exit 3 off I-75. is a smallish motel with a pool, microwaves, refrigerators, A/C, and satellite TV in faded but comfortable rooms (283-4678 or 800-283-4678; singles $45, doubles $55).

# YUMMY FOR THE TUMMY, AND GAS FOR THE...

The city that gave us the first soap opera, the first baseball franchise (the Redlegs), and the Heimlich maneuver presents its great culinary contribution—**Cincinnati chili.** Cincinnati residents gleefully attest to living in the chili capital of the U.S., but don't expect hearty Texan beef and veggie chili. Here chili, otherwise known as spaghetti, comes with or without cheese, meat, chopped onions, or kidney beans. Chili is cheap; antacid tablets, however, cost extra. For something else, try the Clifton, near the University of Cincinnati, or the recently-gentrified Mt. Adams.

**Skyline Chili,** everywhere. Locations all over Cincinnati, including 643 Vine St. (241-2020), at 7th St., dish up the best beans in town. The secret ingredient has been debated for years; some say chocolate, but curry is more likely. 5-way large chili $5, cheese coney (hot dog) $1.25. Open M-F 10:30am-7pm, Sa 11am-3pm.

**Ulysses,** 209 W. McMillan (241-3663), in Clifton. One-table vegetarian restaurant with a distinctive hippie aura; draws ravenous veggies from all over town. Fruit smoothies ($1.75) are zesty and refreshing, and the sesame sticks are a perfect sight-seeing snack. Open summer M-Sa 11am-6pm, winter 11am-9pm.

**Rookwood Pottery,** 1077 Celestial St. (721-8691), near the intersection with Monastery St. in Mt. Adams. Once this building actually lived up to its name, producing the pottery of Maria Longworth Nichols. The kilns are now cool, and patrons can sit in them while enjoying one of best burgers in town ($6 and up) and make-your-own sundaes. Open Su-Th 11:30am-9:30pm, F-Sa 11:30am-11:30pm.

**Graeter's,** 41 E. 4th St. (381-0653), between Walnut and Vine St. downtown, and 14 other locations. Since 1870, Graeter's has been sending sweet-toothed locals into sensory bliss with delectable ice cream blended with giant chocolate chips (single cone $1.50). Sandwiches and baked goods, too. Open M-F 7am-6pm, Sa 7am-5pm.

# SIGHTS

Downtown Cincinnati orbits around the **Tyler Davidson Fountain,** a florid 19th-century masterpiece and an ideal people-watching spot. The font is remembered fondly by the still-surviving fans of **WKRP in Cincinnati,** perhaps the only TV show to be set in this city. To the east, the expansive garden at **Procter and Gamble Plaza** is just one mark that the giant company has left on its home town. Around **Fountain Sq.** are business complexes and great shops, connected by a series of second floor skywalks. If you're yearning for a panorama, the observation deck at the top of **Carew Tower** provides the best view in the city.

Close to Fountain Sq., the **Contemporary Arts Center,** 2nd fl. of the Mercantile Center, has a strong national reputation. *(115 E. 5th St. 721-0390. Open M-Sa 10am-6pm, Su noon-5pm. $3.50, seniors and students $2. Free M. Wheelchair access.)* Also downtown is the **Taft Museum,** at the east end of 4th St., which houses a beautiful collection of painted enamels, as well as pieces by Rembrandt and Whistler. *(316 Pike St. 241-0343. Open M-Sa 10am-5pm, Su 1-5pm. $4, students and seniors $2, under 18 free. Free W.)*

**Eden Park,** northeast of downtown and Mt. Adams, provides a nearby respite from the city with rolling hills, a pond, and cultural centers; take bus #49 to Eden Park Dr. *(Open daily 6am-10pm.)* The collections at the **Cincinnati Art Museum,** inside the park, span 5000 years, from Near Eastern artifacts to Andy Warhol's rendition of Cincinnati's infamous baseball great Pete Rose. *(721-5204. Open Tu-Sa 10am-5pm, Su noon-6pm. $5, students and seniors $4, under 18 free, Sa by donation.)* The **Krohn Conservatory,** also within the park, is one of the largest public greenhouses in the world. Lush doesn't describe the rainforest recreation. *(421-5707. Open M-Tu and Th-Su 10am-5pm, W 10am-6pm. Free; donations accepted. Wheelchair access.)*

**Union Terminal,** might appear to be "just" a train terminal, but this Art Deco edifice contains much more. An Ice Age world of simulated glaciers and an artificial cavern with a colony of real live bats at the **Museum of Natural History.** The **Cincinnati History Museum** houses historical exhibits on movers and shakers in Cincinnati as well as an Omnimax theater. Lastly, kids can get their kicks at the new **Cinergy Children's Museum.** *(1031 Western Ave., 1mi. west of downtown, near the Ezzard Charles Dr. exit off I-75, take bus #1. Museums 287-7001; Omnimax 287-7091; call for showtimes. Museums open M-Sa 10am-5pm, Su 11am-6pm. 1 museum $5.50, ages 3-12 $3.50; Omnimax $6.50/$4.50; any 2 attractions $9/$6; any 3 $12/$8.)*

Feeling wild? Go to the world-famous **Cincinnati Zoo.** *(3400 Vine St. 281-4700. Open daily in summer 9am-6pm; in winter 9am-5pm. $10, ages 2-12 $5, seniors $8. Parking $5.)*

# ENTERTAINMENT AND NIGHTLIFE

The free newspapers *City Beat, Everybody's News,* and *Downtown Cincinnati* list the happenings around town. The cliff-hanging communities of **Mt. Adams** support a thriving arts and entertainment district. Perched on its own wooded hill in Eden Park, the **Playhouse in the Park,** 962 Mt. Adams Circle, performs theater-in-the-round. (421-3888. Performances mid-Sept. to June Tu-Su. Tickets $24-38; student rush 15min. before show, and senior rush 2hr. prior, $12.)

The **Music Hall,** 1243 Elm St. (721-8222), hosts the **Cincinnati Symphony Orchestra** and the **Cincinnati Pops Orchestra** (381-3300) Sept. through May (tickets $12-59). The orchestra's summer seasons (June-July) take place at **Riverbend,** near Coney Island (tickets $11-25). The **Cincinnati Opera** performs in the Music Hall as well (241-2742; tickets $10-75). For updates, call **Dial the Arts** (621-4744). The **Cincinnati Ballet Company** (621-5219) is at the **Aronoff Center for the Arts,** 650 Walnut (241-7469), which also houses a Broadway series. (Ballet performances Oct.-May; tickets $12-47, matinee $8-20. Musical tickets $15-45. Wheelchair access.)

Escape the high-brow lot and beat the summer heat in Sunlite, the world's largest recirculating pool, at the **Coney Island Amusement Center,** 6201 Kellogg Ave., off I-275 at the Kellogg Ave. exit. (232-8230. Pool open daily 10am-8pm; rides M-F noon-9pm, Sa-Su 11am-9pm. Pool $11, seniors and ages 4-11 $8; rides $7/$7; both $15/$13.) **Summerfair,** an arts extravaganza, takes over the park for one weekend in late May or early June (531-0050).

Cincinnati's fanatics watch baseball's **Reds** (421-7337; tickets $3-14) and football's **Bengals** (621-3550; tickets $31-54) in **Cinergy Field,** 201 E. Pete Rose Way.

Over Labor Day weekend, **Riverfest** celebrates with food, entertainment, and fireworks (621-9326). The third weekend of Sept. brings **Oktoberfest-Zinzinnati,** during which the city basks in its German heritage (579-3191).

Some of Cincinnati's best nightlife is (literally) above and beyond downtown. Overlooking downtown from the east, **Mt. Adams** has spawned some funky bars and late-night coffee shops. Antiques adorn the walls of **Blind Lemon,** 939 Hatch St., at St. Gregory St., while live jazz and blues fill the courtyard. (241-3885. Domestic draft $2. Music daily 9:30pm. No cover. Open M-Th 6:30pm-2:30am, F-Su 4:30pm-2:30am.) For contemporary music and a younger crowd, climb up the steep streets to Clifton. **Ripley's Alive,** 2507 W. Clifton, hosts live hip-hop and funk to rave reviews (861-6800; ages 18-20 cover $3, 21+ cover $2; open W-Su 10pm-2am).

For a drink straight out of the 19th century, try Cincinnati's oldest tavern, **Arnold's,** 210 E. 8th St., between Main and Sycamore. This wood-paneled mainstay provides good, simple beer (domestic draft $3), food (pasta and sandwiches $5-10), and endearingly brusque service. After 9pm, Arnold's does ragtime, bluegrass, and swing. (421-6234. Open M-F 11am-1am, Sa 4pm-1am.)

**Carol's Corner Café,** 825 Main St., inserts funk and style into downtown Cincinnati. Drawing theater groups and yuppies galore, this restaurant/bar is known for great food (Cock-a-Noodle-Do Salad $7.25) and late hours. (651-2667. Bar open M 11:30am-1am, Tu-F 11:30am-2:30am, Sa 4pm-2:30am, Su 4pm-1am.)

## NEAR CINCINNATI

The **Newport Aquarium,** just over the river in Newport, KY, follow I-71 to I-471 to the Newport exit, has sixty exhibits and lots of crowds. *(606-491-3467. Open daily 10am-9pm, off season 10am-6pm. $13.75, seniors $11.50, ages 8-12 $8.50.)*

For an ultimate amusement park experience, head to **Paramount's Kings Island** in Mason, 24mi. north of Cincinnati off I-71 at exit 24. In addition to a "faux" Eiffel Tower and an expanded waterpark, this fun center cages **The Beast,** the world's longest wooden rollercoaster. Admission to the park includes unlimited rides and attractions. *(573-5800 or 800-288-0808. Open late May to late Aug. Su-F 9am-10pm, Sa 9am-11pm. $36, seniors and ages 3-6 $21. Parking $6. Wheelchair access.)*

Accommodations can be found at **Paramount's Kings Island Campground,** 5688 Kings Island Dr., off I-71 at exit 25 and within a stone's throw of the amusement park. *(800-832-1133. Playground. 350 sites $31, full hookup $41. Cabins for 4 $58. $5 per extra adult, $3.50 per extra child ages 4-16. Reservations recommended.)*

# MICHIGAN

Orbiting the earth in a space shuttle, Michiganers would have no trouble identifying the location of their state; with its 3000mi. of coastline along four of the irregularly outlined Great Lakes, Michigan easily lays claim to the title of "Most Readily Apparant State When Viewed from Space." Michigan's industrially developed Lower Peninsula paws the Great Lakes like a huge mitten, while its pristine and oft-ignored Upper Peninsula hangs above, quietly nursing moose, vacation homes, and a famed population of wolves. The state once famous for its booming automotive industry now fills only a shadow of its former Ford chrome body, but is starting to make waves as a natural getaway, blending a coastal character with thousands of fresh water lakes at an inland location.

# ⓭ PRACTICAL INFORMATION

**Capital:** Lansing.

**Visitor Info: Michigan Travel Bureau,** 333 S. Capitol, Ste. F, Lansing 48909 (888-784-7328 or 800-543-2937; www.travel-michigan.state.mi.us). **Dept. of Parks and Recreation,** Information Services Center, P.O. Box 30257, Lansing 48909 (517-373-1270). Entry to all state parks requires a motor vehicle permit; $4 per day, $20 annually. Call 800-447-2757 for reservations at any state park campground.

**Postal Abbreviation:** MI. **Sales Tax:** 6%.

# DETROIT

Decades of hardship recently prompted an author to proclaim Detroit "America's first Third-World city." Violent race riots in the 60s prompted massive white flight to the suburbs; the population has more than halved since 1967, turning neighborhoods into ghost towns. The decline of the auto industry in the late 70s added unemployment to the city's ills, beleaguring an already depressed area.

Today, the five gleaming towers of the riverside Renaissance Center symbolize the hope of a city-wide renewal. Aggressive tourist media focuses attention on Detroit's attractions: Michigan's largest and most comprehensive museums, a fascinating ethnic history, and the still-visible (though soot-blackened and slightly crumbling) evidence of the city's former architectural grandeur. Detroit may no longer be the city it once was, but with a slew of multi-million dollar projects in the works, it's only a matter of time until the rest of the world says, "Shi-it!".

## ⓭ ORIENTATION AND PRACTICAL INFORMATION

Detroit lies on the Detroit River, which connects Lakes Erie and St. Clair. Across the river to the south, the town of **Windsor, ON,** can be reached by tunnel just west of the Renaissance Center (toll $2.25), or by the Ambassador Bridge, 3500 Toledo St. Detroit is a tough town, but you probably won't encounter trouble during the day, especially within the People Mover loop. Driving is the best way to negotiate this sprawling town where good and bad neighborhoods alternate at whim; public transportation is often inefficient and less than safe.

Detroit's streets form a grid. **The Mile Rds.** run east-west as major arteries. **Eight Mile Rd.** is the city's northern boundary and the beginning of the suburbs. **Woodward Ave.** heads northwest from downtown, dividing city and suburbs into "east side" and "west side." **Gratiot Ave.** flares out northeast from downtown, while **Grand River Ave.** shoots west. **I-94** and **I-75** pass through downtown. For a particularly helpful map, check the pull-out in the *Detroit Metro Visitor's Guide.*

**Airport: Detroit Metropolitan** (942-3550 or 800-351-5466), 2mi. west of downtown off I-94 at Merriman Rd. in Romulus. **Commuter Transportation Company** (941-3252 or 800-488-7433) runs shuttles downtown daily 7am-midnight every hour.; 7pm-midnight on the hr. (45min.; $15), stopping at major hotels. Make reservations. A taxi costs $30.

**Trains: Amtrak,** 11 W. Baltimore (873-3442), at Woodward. To Chicago (6hr., 3 per day, $19-50) and New York (16hr., 1 per day, $72-135). Open daily 5:45am-11:30pm. For Canadian destinations, go through **VIA Rail,** 298 Walker Rd., Windsor, ON (519-256-5511 or 800-561-3949). To Toronto (4hr.; 5-7 per day; CDN$71).

**Buses: Greyhound,** 1001 Howard St. (961-8011). *At night, the area is unsafe.* To: Chicago (5½hr., 8 per day, $24); Cleveland (4hr., 9 per day, $20); and Ann Arbor (1hr., 5 per day, $7). Station open 24hr.; ticket office open daily 6am-12:30am.

**Public Transit: Detroit Dept. of Transportation (DOT),** 1301 E. Warren St. (933-1300). Policed public transport system serves downtown, with limited service to the suburbs. Many buses stop service at midnight. Fare $1.25, transfers 25¢. **DOT Attractions Shuttle** (259-8726) delivers camera-toting tourists to the metro area's most popular sights 10am-5:45pm. All-day ticket $5. **People Mover,** 150 Michigan Ave. (962-7245 or 800-

541-7245). Ultramodern elevated tramway circles the Central Business District on a 2.7mi. loop; worth a ride just for the view. Runs M-Th 7am-11pm, F 7am-midnight, Sa 9am-midnight, Su noon-8pm. Fare 50¢. **Southeastern Michigan Area Regional Transit (SMART),** 962-5515 or 223-2100. Bus service to the suburbs. Fare $1.50, transfers 25¢. Get free maps of the system at the office on the 1st fl. of First National Bank at 600 Woodward Ave. Buses run 4am-midnight, depending on route.

**Taxis: Checker Cab,** 963-7000.

**Car Rental: Thrifty Rent-A-Car,** 29111 Wick Rd. (946-7830 or 800-367-2277), in Romulus. $50 per day, $205 per week; unlimited mi. in Michigan and neighboring states. Must be over 21 with credit card. Under 25 surcharge $20 per day.

**Visitor Info: Convention and Visitors Bureau,** 211 W. Fort St. (202-1813 or 800-338-7648). Open M-F 8:30am-5pm. **Windsor Travel Info,** 110 Park St. (519-973-1338).

**Hotlines: 24hr. Crisis Hotline,** 224-7000. **Sexual Abuse Helpline,** 876-4180. 24hr.

**Bi-Gay-Lesbian Organizations: Triangle Foundation of Detroit,** 537-3323. **Affirmations,** 195 W. 9 Mile Rd. 48220 (248-398-7105), in Ferndale at the corner of 9 Mile Rd. and Troy, has a large library, info on gay nightlife, and copies of *Pride Source Guide,* a comprehensive gay guide to MI, from **Between the Lines** (248-615-7003).

**Post Office:** 1401 W. Fort St. (226-8304). Open 24hr. **ZIP code:** 48233. **Area codes:** 313, 810, and 248 (north); or 734 (southwest). In text, 313 unless otherwise noted.

# ▐ ACCOMMODATIONS

Detroit's suburbs harbor loads of chain motels; ones near the airport in **Romulus** tend to be overpriced and along **E. Jefferson,** near downtown, can be skanky. For a mix of convenience and affordability, look along **Telegraph Rd.** off I-94, west of the city. If the exchange rate is favorable, good deals can be found in **Windsor,** Canada, just across the border. The *Detroit Metro Visitor's Guide* lists accommodations by area and includes price ranges. Devoted campers should resign themselves to a 45min. commute if they insist on communing with nature.

▨ **Country Grandma's Home Hostel (HI-AYH),** 22330 Bell Rd. (734-753-4901), in New Boston, 6mi. south of I-94 off I-275, between Detroit and Ann Arbor. Though it's inaccessible by public transportation, the comfort, hospitality, and warm feeling of security make it worth the trip. 6 beds, a kitchen, and free parking. $11, nonmembers $14. Call for reservations and directions. Wheelchair access.

**Shorecrest Motor Inn,** 1316 E. Jefferson Ave. (568-3000 or 800-992-9616), as close to downtown as the budget traveler can get. A/C and fridges. Clean, comfortable singles $59; doubles $79. Key deposit $5. Reservations recommended. Wheelchair access.

**University of Windsor,** 401 Sunset Ave. (519-973-7074), in Windsor, just over the Ambassador Bridge, rents rooms from early May to late Aug. Free use of university facilities. Singles CDN$31, CDN $18.50 for students with college ID; doubles CDN$46. Wheelchair access.

**Motel 6,** 32700 Barrington St. (8248583-0500), 15mi. north of downtown off I-75 in Madison Heights, just off 12 Mile Rd. Enormous, clean, cookie-cutter rooms with free local calls and HBO. Singles $42; doubles $42. Reservations recommended.

**Pontiac Lake Recreation Area,** 7800 Gale Rd. (248-666-1020), in Waterford 45min. northwest of downtown; take I-75 to M59 W, a right on Will Lake northbound and left onto Gale Rd. Huge wooded sites in rolling hills, just 4mi. from the lake. 176 sites with electricity $11. Vehicle permit $4.

# ▐ FOOD

Many once-downtown restaurants have migrated to the suburbs, the budget traveler still has some in-town dining options. **Greektown,** at the Greektown People Mover stop, has Greek restaurants and excellent bakeries on Monroe St., all on 1 block near Beaubien St. To snag a Polish sausage, cruise Joseph Campau Ave. in **Hamtramck,** a Polish neighborhood northeast of Detroit. No budget traveler should

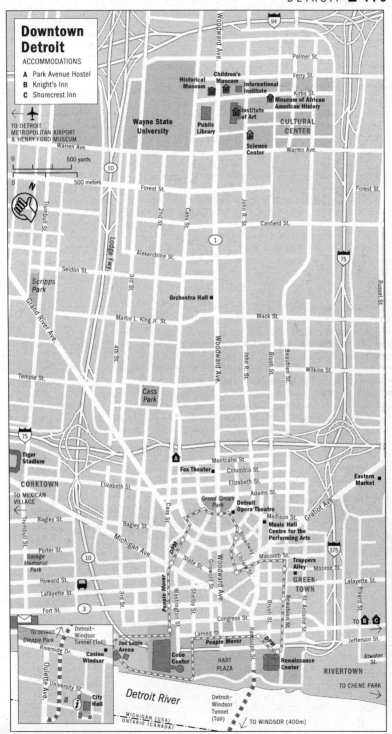

## Downtown Detroit

**ACCOMMODATIONS**

A Park Avenue Hostel
B Knight's Inn
C Shorecrest Inn

miss the **Eastern Market,** at Gratiot Ave. and Russell St., an 11-acre produce-and-goodie festival with almost every edible imaginable (833-1560; open Sa 5am-5pm).

Easily Detroit's most famous culinary establishment, the **Lafayette Coney Island,** 118 W. Lafayette serves up its $1.79 coney dogs to Detroiters of all walks of life. Join the crowd and bring your Rolaids. (964-8198. Open M-Sa 8am-4am, Su 9am-3am.) **Cyprus Taverna,** 579 Monroe St., is a local favorite for Greek cuisine. In the heart of Greektown, it features tasteful decor and a charmingly subdued atmosphere. (961-1550. Entrees $9-13. Open Su-Th 11am-2am, F-Sa 11am-4am.) The **Soup Kitchen Saloon,** 1585 Franklin St., once housed a speakeasy and brothel, but now features some of the town's best live blues, plus fresh seafood, steaks, and cajun eats. The BBQ catfish or seafood creole ($12) are delicious. (259-1374. Shows Tu-Sa; cover $5-7. Open Tu-Fri 11am-midnight, Sa-Su 5pm-midnight).

## ◉ HENRY'S WORLD: FORD TO MOTOWN

For a reason to visit Detroit, look no farther than the colossal **Henry Ford Museum & Greenfield Village,** off I-94 in nearby Dearborn; take SMART bus #200 or 250. More than just a tribute to planes, trams, and automobiles (though there's plenty of that), the museum exhibits deliver a comprehensive running commentary on 20th-century America. The premises boast the limousine in which President Kennedy was assassinated and a copy of the Lunar Rover. Over 80 historic edifices from around the country have been moved to Greenfield Village, next to the museum; visit the workshop of the Wright Brothers or the factory where Thomas Edison researched. *(20900 Oakwood Blvd. 982-6100, 271-1620 for 24hr. info. Both open daily 9am-5pm. Museum or village $12.50, seniors $11.50, ages 5-12 $7.50. Combination ticket valid 2 consecutive days $22, ages 5-12 $12.50.)* If the Ford Museum doesn't slake your craving for cars, next door the somewhat cheesy **Automotive Hall of Fame** glorifies the innovators of the car industry. *(21400 Oakwood Blvd. 240-4000. Open daily 10am-5pm; Nov.-May Tu-Su 10am-5pm. $6, seniors $5.50, ages 5-12 $3.)*

Detroit lures visitors to its **Cultural Center,** at Woodward and Warren St.—it's worth taking the bait. One of the nation's finest art museums, the **Detroit Institute of Arts** features Van Gogh's "Self-Portrait" and Diego Rivera's massive mural "Detroit Industry"—one masterpiece that will never go on loan. *(5200 Woodward Ave. 833-7900. Open Tu-Su 9:30am-5pm. Suggested donation $5.)* The history of the African experience in America fills the halls of the world's largest **Museum of African-American History.** Exhibits include harrowing accounts of the history of slavery and interactive displays of present day African-American culture. *(315 E. Warren Rd. 494-5808. Open W-Su 9:30am-5pm. Suggested donation $3, under 13 $2.)*

Detroit's art isn't confined to stuffy museums. Artist and activist Tyree Guyton created the block-long **Heidelburg Project,** an ever-changing amalgamation of polka dots and found objects. Turn west on Heidelburg St. from Mt. Elliott, which is between I-94 and E. Jefferson, and follow the dots. For wandering bookophiles, **John K. King Used and Rare Books,** right off the Lodge Freeway, holds over a million books on 4 floors, making browsing overwhelming if not impossible. *(901 W. Lafayette. 961-0622. Open M-Sa 9:30am-5:30pm.)*

In a house like any other on a street like any other, that fabulous Motown sound began. Barry Gordy Jr.'s record company is preserved in the **Motown Museum.** Downstairs, the Jackson Five, Marvin Gaye, Smokey Robinson, and Diana Ross once recorded in the primitive studio. The museum lies east of Rosa Parks Blvd. about 1mi. west of the Lodge Freeway (Rt. 10); take the "Dexter Avenue" bus. *(2648 W. Grand Blvd. 875-2264. Open Su-M noon-5pm, Tu-Sa 10am-5pm. $6, under 12 $3.)*

If the gowns of the Supremes aren't wild enough for you, try the well-funded **Detroit Zoological Park,** just off the Woodward exit of 696 in Royal Oak. North America's first National Amphibian Conservation Center is currently under construction, but until then stroll the grounds and the the relatively new Wildlife Interpretive Gallery. *(248-398-0900. Open daily Apr.-Oct. 10am-5pm, Nov.-Mar 10am-4pm. Open until 6pm on Su from mid-May to Labor Day and until 8pm on W from late June to early Sept. $7.50, ages 13-18 and seniors $5.50, ages 2-12 $4.50. Parking $3.)*

North of Detroit, in posh Bloomfield Hills, **Franbrook's** scholarly campus holds public gardens, several museums, and an art academy. Far and away the best of the lot is the **Cranbrook Institute of Science,** a family-orientated museum with rotating exhibits emphasizing educational fun. *(1221 N. Woodward Ave. 248-645-3209. Open Su-Th 10am-5pm, F-Sa 10am-10pm. $7, children, seniors, and students, $4.)*

One of Detroit's escapes, **Belle Isle** *(852-4078)*, 3mi. from downtown via the MacArthur Bridge, maintains a **conservatory, nature center, aquarium, maritime museum,** and small **zoo** for animal lovers with short attention spans *($2 each, children $1).*

## 🎵 ENTERTAINMENT AND NIGHTLIFE

Newly renovated and restored, Detroit's theater district, around Woodward and Columbia, is witnessing a cultural revival. The **Fox Theater,** 2211 Woodward Ave., near Grand Circus Park, features high-profile tragedy, comedy, and musicals, as well as the nation's largest movie theater hall (occupancy 5000) for occasional epic films. (983-6611. Box office open M-F 10am-6pm. Tickets $25-100; movies under $10.) The **State Theater,** 2115 Woodward Ave., brings in a variety of popular concerts (961-5450; 810-932-3643 for event info). The State Theater is also home to **Ignition,** a giant party, which enlists DJs from a local radio station to play alternative dance music (cover starts at $5. Open Sa 10pm-2am). For some of Detroit's best jazz, check out the **Harmony Park** area near Orchestra Hall.

Detroit's numerous festivals draw millions of visitors. Hip jazz fans jet to Hart Plaza during Labor Day weekend for the 4-day **Montreux-Detroit Jazz Festival.** With more than 70 acts on 3 stages and mountains of international food at the World Food Court, it's the largest free jazz festival on the continent. (963-7622). The nation's oldest state fair, the **Michigan State Fair,** at Eight Mile Rd. and Woodward Ave., gathers together bake-offs, art, and livestock birth exhibits during the 2 weeks before Labor Day (369-8250). A 2-week extravaganza in late June, the international **Freedom Festival,** held jointly with Windsor, Ontario, celebrates the friendship between the U.S. and Canada, igniting North America's largest fireworks display over the Detroit River (923-8259). **Detroit's African World Festival** brings over a million people to Hart Plaza on the third weekend in Aug. for an open-air market and free reggae, jazz, blues, and gospel concerts (877-8073). **Orchestra Hall,** 3711 Woodward Ave., at Parsons St., houses the Detroit Symphony Orchestra with concerts Sa 1-5pm. (962-1000. Box office 576-5111. Open M-F 9am-5pm. Half-price rush tickets 1½hr. prior to show for seniors and students with ID.) The weekly *Metro Times* contains complete entertainment listings.

The **Detroit Pistons** shoot hoops at the **Palace of Auburn Hills,** 2 Championship Dr. (a.k.a. 3777 Lapeer Rd.), Auburn Hills (248-377-0100; Sept.-Apr.; tickets $12-59). Hockey's back-to-back 1997-98 World Champion **Red Wings** face off in the **Joe Louis Arena,** 600 Civic Center Dr. (396-7544; Sept.-Apr.; tickets $17-62), whereas **Tigers** hunt the post-season at **Comerica Park** on Brush and Columbia, downtown. (Apr.-Sept.; tickets $4-20). For tickets, call **Ticketmaster** (248-645-6666).

For the latest in nightlife, pick up a free copy of *Orbit* in record stores and restaurants. *Between the Lines,* also free, has entertainment info for lesbians, gays, and bisexuals. **St. Andrew's Hall,** 431 E. Congress, hosts local and national alternative acts (961-6358; shows F-Su; usually 17+; advance tickets sold through Ticketmaster; $7-10). **Shelter,** the dance club downstairs, draws crowds on non-concert nights. Young party animals take advantage of Ontario's lower drinking age (19) at bars and clubs along **Ovellette Ave.** in Windsor. Those with too much cash rid themselves of the burden with 3 floors of gambling at **The Windsor Casino,** 377 Riverside Dr. (519-258-7878 or 800-991-7777; must be 19; open 24hr.).

# ANN ARBOR

For a small town tucked between some major industrial hubs, Ann Arbor hasn't done too badly. Named after Ann Rumsey and Ann Allen, wives of two of the area's early pioneers (who supposedly enjoyed sitting under grape arbors), the city has managed to prosper without losing its relaxed charm. In 1837, the gargantuan and well-respected University of Michigan moved to town, giving rise to a hip collage of leftists, granolas, yuppies, and middle Americans. Today, the town incorporates diversity and excitement without appearing unsafe or run-down.

## ▌ ORIENTATION AND PRACTICAL INFORMATION

Ann Arbor's streets lie in a grid, but watch out for the *slant* of Packard and Detroit St. **Main St.** divides the town east-west, and **Huron St.** cuts it north-south. The central campus of the **University of Michigan,** where restaurants cluster, lies 4 blocks east of Main St. and south of E. Huron (a 5min. walk from downtown). Although street meter parking is plentiful, authorities ticket ruthlessly. One-way streets and unexpected dead ends also make driving near the campus stressful, though by no means unmanageable.

**Trains: Amtrak,** 325 Depot St. (994-4906). To Chicago (5hr., 3 per day, $20) and Detroit (1hr., 3 per day, $8-16). Tickets sold daily 6:45am-11:30pm.

**Buses: Greyhound,** 116 W. Huron St. (662-5511). To: Detroit (1-1½hr., 4 per day, $7); Chicago (6hr., 5 per day, $24); and Grand Rapids (2-4hr., 3per day, $18). Open M-Sa 8am-6:30pm, Su 8am-9am and noon-6:30pm.

**Public Transit: Ann Arbor Transportation Authority (AATA), Blake Transit Center,** 331 S. 4th Ave. (996-0400 or 973-6500). Service in Ann Arbor and a few neighboring towns. Buses run M-F 6:45am-10:45pm, Sa-Su 8am-6:15pm. Fare 75¢, students and seniors 35¢. Station open M-F 7:30am-9pm, Sa noon-5:30pm. **AATA's Nightride,** 663-3888. Safe door-to-door transportation M-F 11pm-6am, Sa-Su 7pm-6am. Call to book a trip; wait is 5-45min. Fare $2 per person. **Commuter Transportation Company,** 941-9391 or 800-488-7433. Frequent shuttle service between Ann Arbor and Detroit Metro Airport. Vans depart Ann Arbor 5am-7pm and return 7am-midnight. $22, round-trip $44. Door-to-door service for up to 4 $60-70; reserve up to 48hrs. in advance.

**Car Rental: Thrifty Car Rental,** 3000 Washtenaw (668-6867). $34 per day, $190 per week with unlimited mi. Ages 21-24 pay $10 extra per day. Open M-F 7:30am-5:30pm, Sa-Su 9am-1pm.

**Visitor Info: Ann Arbor Convention and Visitors Bureau,** 120 W. Huron St. (995-7281 or 800-888-9487), at Ashley. Open M-F 8:30am-5pm.

**Hotlines: Sexual Assault Crisis Line,** 483-7273. **U. Michigan Sexual Assault Line,** 936-3333. **S.O.S. Crisis Line,** 485-3222. All 24hr. **U. Michigan Gay/Lesbian Referrals,** 763-4186. Operates M-F 9am-5pm.

**Most Important Thing in the World:** Happiness.

**Post Office:** 2075 W. Stadium Blvd. (665-1100; open M-F 7:30am-5pm). **ZIP code:** 48106. **Area code:** 734.

## ▌ ACCOMMODATIONS

Due to the many business travelers and sports fans who flock to the town, expensive hotels, motels, and B&Bs dominate Ann Arbor. Reservations are advisable at any time of year. Reasonable rates can be found at discount chains farther out of town or in **Ypsilanti,** southeast of town along I-94. Near downtown, good ol' **Motel 6,** 3764 S. State St., rents clean, comfortable rooms (665-9900; singles $44-50; doubles $50-56). The **Embassy Hotel,** 200 E. Huron, at 4th Ave., a short walk from the main campus, offers clean rooms (662-7100; singles $39; doubles $44; $3 key deposit). Seven campgrounds lie within a 20mi. radius of Ann Arbor. Both the **Pinckney Recreation Area,** 8555 Silver Hill (426-4913), in Pinckney, or the **Waterloo Recreation Area,** 16345 McClure Rd. (475-8307), in Chelsea, have rustic ($6) and modern sites ($14), and require a $4 vehicle permit. Reservations at these and all Michigan state parks can be made by calling 800-447-2757.

## ◐ FOOD

Where there are students, there are cheap eats, and inexpensive restaurants cram the sidewalks of **State St.** and **S. University St.** More upscale eateries line **Main St.** Next to the Kerrytown shops, fresh produce comes straight from the growers at the **farmers market,** 315 Detroit St. (761-1078; open May-Dec. W and Sa 7am-3pm; Jan.-Apr. Sa 8am-3pm). The readers of *Ann Arbor News* voted **Cottage Inn Pizza,** 512 E. William St., at Thompson St., purveyor of "best pizza." (663-3379. Pizza $7-18. Open M-Th 11am-midnight, F-Sa 11am-1am, Su noon-midnight.) When it comes to Jewish deli fare, **Zingerman's Deli,** 422 Detroit St., doesn't mess around. Even *goyim* crowds line up for huge, excellent sandwiches for $6-12. (663-3354. Open daily 7am-10pm.) Plants tremble at the mention of **Seva** (say "vah!") 314 E. Liberty, Ann Arbor's long-established veggie haven. It's comforting, earthy decor complements a meatless menu that covers Mexican, stir-fry, and all points in-between. (662-1111. Entrees $7-10. Open M-Th 10:30am-9pm, Fr 10:30am-10pm, Sa 9am-10pm, Su 10am-9pm.) With lunch specials hovering around $5.50, Chinese food lovers will be surprised by the fact that the executive chef at **China Gate,** 1201 S. University has consistently won gold medals in professional culinary competitions (688-2445; open daily 11am-10pm).

## ◉ SIGHTS AND ENTERTAINMENT

The university offers a handful of free museums near the main campus, but while all are impressive only a couple really merit a special trip. A small but impressive collection of artwork from around the world fills the **University of Michigan Arts Museum (UMAM),** 525 S. State St., at the corner of S. University St. (764-0395; open Tu–Sa 10am-5pm, Su noon-5pm; free). The **University of Michigan Exhibit Museum of Natural History,** 1109 Geddes Ave., at Washtenaw, displays an assortment of dinosaur skeletons and other exhibits on zoology, astronomy, and geology. The planetarium projects star-gazing weekend entertainment. (764-0478. Open M-Sa 9am-5pm, Su noon-5pm. Museum free; planetarium $3, seniors and under 13 $2.)

Outside the University, the **Ann Arbor Hands-On Museum,** 220 E. Ann St., plans to open an addition in the fall of 1999 which will quadruple its floorspace. The museum offers a tactile wonderland of exhibits designed to be felt, turned, touched, pushed, and plucked. (995-5437. Open Tu-Su 10am-5pm. $6, seniors, students, and ages 3-17 $4.) Numerous local artists display their creations at the **artisan market,** 315 Detroit St. (open May-Dec. Su 11am-4pm). It's nigh-impossible to get tickets for a **Wolverine football** game at UM's 115,000 capacity stadium; nevertheless, fans give it a shot by calling the athletics office at 764-0247.

As tens of thousands of students depart for the summer, locals indulge in a little celebration. During late July, thousands pack the city to view the work of nearly 600 artists at the **Ann Arbor Summer Art Fair** (995-7281). The **Ann Arbor Summer Festival** (647-2278) draws crowds from mid-June through early July for a collection of comedy, dance, and theater productions, as well as musical performances including jazz, country, and classical. The festival includes nightly outdoor movies at **Top of the Park,** on top of the Fletcher St. parking structure, next to the Health Services Building. The **County Events Hotline,** 930-6300, has more info.

To hear classical music, contact the **University Musical Society,** in the Burton Memorial Clock Tower at N. University and Thouper; the society sponsors 60 professional concerts per season at various area venues (764-2538 or 800-221-1229; tickets $10-55; open M-F 10am-5pm, Sa 10am-1pm).

## ♫ NIGHTLIFE

The monthlies *Current, Agenda, Weekender Entertainment,* and the weekly *Metrotimes,* all free and available in restaurants, music stores, and elsewhere, print up-to-date nightlife and entertainment listings. For gay and lesbian info pick up a copy of *OutPost* or *Between the Lines.*

GREAT LAKES

The **Blind Pig**, 208 S. First St., is out of sight with rock 'n' roll, reggae, blues, and swing (996-8555; 19+; cover $3-18; open Tu-Su until 2am). **Rick's American Café**, 611 Church St., plays Ann Arbor's blues, live on a packed dance floor (996-2747; 21+; cover $3-5; open daily until 2am). Showcasing big names F and Sa, the **Bird of Paradise**, 207 S. Ashley, sings with live music every night (662-8310; cover usually $3-5; free jam sessions on Su nights). **The Nectarine**, 516 E. Liberty, offers DJ-controlled dance music, with gay nights Tu (994-5436; open Tu-Sa until 2am). **Conor O'Neill's**, 318 S. Main St., offers a good Celtic-flavored hangout (665-2968; open daily 11am-2am). On weekends, locals hang out at **Del Rio**, 122 W. Washington St., at Ashley, for cheap burgers and Mexican food, good vegetarian options, and free jazz Su evenings. (761-2530. Burritos $2.50. Open M-Sa noon-2am, Su 5:30pm-2am.)

## GRAND RAPIDS

From its humble beginning as one among many fur trading posts, Grand Rapids worked hard to distinguish itself from its neighbors. While many towns opted for tourist chic with quaint, old-fashioned looks, Grand Rapids plowed ahead to become a city of concrete and tall buildings. Grand Rapids was the first city to put fluoride in its drinking water, and it also produced America's only unelected president, Gerald Ford. While attractive to businesses, Grand Rapids offers little in the way of entertainment for the traveler. Most use it as a transportation hub to reach the rest of western Michigan.

**🛈 PRACTICAL INFORMATION.** Most of Grand Rapids' streets are neatly gridded. The town is quartered by the north-south Division St. and the east-west Fulton St. **Greyhound,** 190 Wealthy St. (456-1709; station open daily 6:45am-10pm), connects to Detroit (3½hr., 4 per day, $19-23); Chicago (4½hr., 3 per day, $27-29); and Ann Arbor (3hr., 1 per day, $18-21). **Amtrak,** 507 Wealthy St., at Market, has service to the south and west, including Chicago (3¼hr., 1 per day, $32-46). The station only opens when trains pass through. **Grand Rapids Transit Authority (GRATA),** 333 Wealthy St. (776-1100), sends buses throughout the city and suburbs. (Runs M-F 6am-6pm, Sa 9am-9pm. Fare $1.25, seniors 60¢; 10-ride pass $7, students and seniors $6.) **Veterans Taxi:** 459-4646. The **Grand Rapids-Kent County Convention and Visitors Bureau,** 134 Monroe Center (459-8287 or 800-678-9859; open M-F 9am-7pm) and the **West Michigan Tourist Association,** 1253 Front Ave. NW (456-8557 or 800-442-2084; open M-Th 8:30am-5pm, F 8:30am-6pm, Sa 9am-1pm) furnish general area info. **24hr. Suicide, Drug, Alcohol, and Crisis Line,** 336-3535. **Post Office:** 225 Michigan St. N.W. (532-2109; open M-F 8am-5:30pm, Sa 9am-12:30pm). **ZIP code:** 49503. **Area code:** 616.

**🛏🍴 ACCOMMODATIONS AND FOOD.** Most of the cheaper motels and restaurants cluster south of the city along Division and 28th St. Rooms at **Motel 6,** 3524 28th St. SE, have cable TV, HBO, and other conveniences of a national chain motel (957-3511; singles $41, doubles $47). **The Knights Inn,** 35 28th St. SW, offers 102 spacious rooms, with an indoor pool and hot tub (452-5141 or 800-843-5644; singles $38, doubles $50). Men are in luck at the **YMCA,** 33 Library St. NE, downtown (222-9626; $26, $15 per additional night; no reservations). Just 12mi. northeast of downtown, **Grand Rogue Campgrounds,** 6400 W. River Dr., sports wooded, riverside sites. Take Rt. 131 north to Comstock Park exit 91, then head left on W. River Dr. for 4mi. (361-1053; $18.50, with hookup $23.)

Grand Rapids' most popular Mexican food comes from the **Beltline Bar and Café,** 16 28th St. SE. Plates of tacos go for $5.50, and burritos start at $5. (245-0494. Open M-Tu 7am-midnight, W-Sa 7am-1am, Su noon-10:30pm.) The **Grand Rapids Brewing Company,** 3689 28th St. SE, whips up good burgers ($6), steaks, and "hand-crafted" house beers ($3 per pint). Tours are available upon request. (285-5970. Open M-Th 11am-10pm, F-Sa 11am-11pm, Su noon-10pm; bar open M-Th 11am-midnight, F-Sa 11am-1am, Su 11am-11pm.) The **Four Friends Coffeehouse,** 136 Monroe Center, has cappuccino, espresso, a semi-artsy atmosphere, good muffins ($1.15), and live music on F and Sa during the school year. (456-5356. Open M-Th 7am-10pm, F 7am-midnight, Sa 9:30am-midnight; Sept.-May open until 11pm.) Although this popular regional chain is expanding and losing its personality, **BD's Mongolian Barbeque**, 2619 28th St. SE still offers unique meals—you pick the ingredients and the chef fries them in front of you. An all-you-can-eat dinner is $11.95. (957-7500. Open Su-Th 11am-10:30pm, F-Su 11am-11:30pm.)

**◙ SIGHTS.** The **Grand Rapids Public Museum,** showcases marvels such as one of the world's largest whale skeletons (76 ft.), a 50-animal carousel, and a planetarium. *(Open M-Sa 9am-5pm, Su noon-5pm. $5, seniors $4, ages 3-17 $2. Planetarium $1.50.)* The **Gerald R. Ford Museum** records the life and turbulent times of Grand Rapids' favorite son. Especially noteworthy are the Watergate break-in tools and rotating historical exhibits. *(303 Pearl St. NW. 451-9263. Open daily 9am-5pm. $4, seniors $3, under 16 free.)* The largest year-round conservatory in Michigan, the **Frederik Meijer Gardens** keeps more than 70 bronze sculptures among numerous tropical plants spread out over 70 acres of wetlands. A $12.8 million addition and a 3-story Da Vinci horse sculpture were purchased in celebration of the millenium. *(3411 Bradford St. at Beltline. 957-1580). Open M-W and F-Sa 9am-5pm, Th 9am-9pm, Su noon-5pm; Sept.-May M-Sa 9am-5pm, Su noon-5pm. $5, seniors $4, ages 5-13 $2.)* **Mackie's World** is the world's only mall made just for kids. Features a drive-in theater with miniature cars, a putt-putt golf course, and a Dino-Train that rides around the food court. *(1 Monrow Center near Fulton and Ionia. 458-7444.)*

**◪ ENTERTAINMENT.** Detailed listings on events and nightlife in Grand Rapids can be found in *On the Town* or *In the City*, both available in most shops, restaurants, and kiosks. The artsy Eastown District houses the bulk of the local music scene. Dance clubs overshadow other forms of city nightlife. The largest in Grand Rapids, **The Orbit Room,** at E. Beltline and 28th St., packs in up to 1200 gyrating bodies for nightly music ranging from alternative to top 40, disco to country. (942-1328. W 18+, other nights 19+ until 11pm. Open W and F-Su 9am-2am. Occasional M concerts at 8pm; tickets $10-30, 18+.) **The Anchor,** 447 Bridge St., secures locals and fairly cheap drinks (774-7177; open M-F 3pm-2am, Sa 5pm-2am, Su 6pm-2am; 21+ to enter). The gay crowd prefers **Diversions,** 10 Fountain NW (451-3800; open M-F 11am-2am, Sa-Su 8pm-2am; cover $3 Th-Sa; 18+ to enter).

# LAKE MICHIGAN SHORE

The freighters that once powered the rise of Chicago still steam along the coast of Lake Michigan, but have long since been supplanted by pleasure boats. With dunes of sugary sand, superb fishing, abundant fruit harvests, and deep winter snows, the eastern shore of Lake Michigan is a midwestern vacationer's dreamland. The coastline stretches 350mi. north from the Indiana border to the Mackinaw Bridge; its southern end is a scant 2hr. from downtown Chicago.

Many of the region's attractions nestle in small coastal towns that cluster around Grand Traverse Bay in the north. Coastal accommodations can be exorbitantly expensive; for cheaper lodging, head inland. Traverse City, at the southern tip of the bay, is famous as the "cherry capital of the world," and fishing is best in the Au Sable and Manistee Rivers. However, the rich Mackinac Island Fudge, sold in numerous specialty shops, seems to have the biggest hold on tourists ("fudgies" to locals; see **Mackinac Island,** p. 483). The main north-south route along the coast is U.S. 31. Numerous detours twist closer to the shoreline, providing an excellent way to explore the coast. Based in Grand Rapids, the **West Michigan Tourist Association,** 1253 Front Ave. NW (456-8557 or 800-442-2084) hands out literature on the area (open M-Th 8:30am-5pm, F 8:30am-6pm, Sa 9am-1pm). The southern Lake Michigan Shore's **area code:** 616; otherwise, 231.

## SOUTHERN MICHIGAN SHORE

**HOLLAND.** Southwest of Grand Rapids off I-196, Holland was founded in 1847 by Dutch religious dissenters and remained mostly Dutch well into the 20th century. The town cashes in on its heritage with a bevy of tacky Netherlands-inspired attractions, most of which are worth visiting only around May, when the tulips bloom. Watch 'em craft clogs at **The Wooden Shoe Factory,** 447 U.S. 31, at 16th St. Celebrity clogs such as those of Reverend Jim Bakker are also on hand for veneration. (396-6513. Demonstrations daily 8am-4:30pm. Free.) The small but high-quality **Holland Museum,** 31 W. 10th St., displays ceramics, furniture from the home country, and exhibits on town history. (392-9084. Open M, W, F-Sa 10am-5pm, Th 10am-8pm, Su 2-5pm. $3, students and seniors $2.) The harvest at the jubilantly arrayed **Veldheer Tulip Gardens,** 12755 Quincy St., at U.S. 31, would be the envy of the Amsterdam market. (399-1900. Open M-F 8am-6pm, Sa-Su 9am-5pm. $2.50, ages 3-13 $1.50. In tulip time $5/$3). A nearby "authentic" **Dutch Village,** 12350 James St., at U.S. 31, resembles a 25-hole mini-golf course *sans* holes. Highlights of the 25 "sights" include a life-size plastic horse-and-buggy and a wooden shoe with slide. (396-1475. Open late Apr. to mid-Oct. daily 9am-5pm. $6.50, ages 3-11 $4.50.) Window shopping and pleasant strolling are easily accessible in **Saugatuck,** an artists' colony 20min. south of Holland on I-96. (857-1701 for visitor's info.)

The **Blue Mill Inn,** 409 U.S. 31, adjacent to the Wooden Shoe Factory at 16th St., rents single rooms from $52 and doubles from $64 (392-7073 or 888-258-3140; off-season rates lower). **Holland State Park,** 2215 Ottawa Beach Rd., 8mi. west of Holland, has 306 sparsely wooded sites nestled between Lake Macatawa and Lake Michigan (399-9390 or 800-447-2757; sites $15; $4 vehicle permit). **Holland Convention and Visitors Bureau:** 76 E. 8th St. (394-0000 or 800-506-1299; open M-F 8am-5pm, May-Oct. also Sa 10:30am-3pm). **Greyhound,** 171 Lincoln Ave. (396-8664), runs through Holland to Detroit (4hr., 2 per day, $25-27); Chicago (4hr., 3 per day, $24-26); and Grand Rapids (35min., 3 per day, $7). **Amtrak,** in the same building, runs a daily train to Chicago (3hr., $31). Reserve train tickets in advance; there are no Amtrak representatives at the station. (Both open M-F 7-11am and 12:30-4:30pm.)

**GRAND HAVEN.** One of the best beaches on the Eastern Lake Michigan Shore, Grand Haven offers a relaxed, resort-like atmosphere and lots of sand—so pure that auto manufacturers use it to make cores and molds for engine parts. The town lies about 35mi. west of Grand Rapids off I-96, and features a cement "boardwalk" that connects the beach to the small downtown area, making for a short but balmy promenade. Washington St. serves as the core of downtown. **Grand Haven Area Visitors Bureau:** 1 S. Harbor Dr. (842-4499 or 800-303-4096; open M 9:30am-5pm, Tu-F 8:30am-5pm). The **Morning Star Café,** 711 Washington St., sizzles with Southwestern breakfast and lunch fare for $4-7 (844-1131; open daily 6:30am-2:30pm). Perhaps best described as a northwoods hostel, the ▓ **Khardonah Lodge,** 1365 Lake Ave. has enormous (and very charming) common areas and is less than 200 yd. from the beach, making it one of the best budget lodging options on all of Michigan's lakeshore. (842-2990. Kitchen and shared bath. Doubles $55, $10 per additional person. Reservations strongly reccomended.) Campers who don't mind a beach parking lot and pretending they are Lawrence of Arabia will love **Grand Haven State Park** 1001 Harbor Dr.; its 168 sandy sites are close to the shores of Lake Michigan (800-447-2757; open early Apr.-Oct. $15 plus $4 permit for site and electrical hookup).

## CENTRAL MICHIGAN SHORE

**MANISTEE AND INTERLOCHEN.** Manistee's Victorian shtick is overshadowed by the impressive trio of natural beauties surrounding the city. Lake Michigan tempts boaters, swimmers, and beachgoers, while fishing buffs find Manistee Lake an outstanding catch. **Manistee National Forest** supplies copious camping at 11 campgrounds in the area ($5 per person; no reservations). The more rugged are free to camp anywhere in the forest without a permit. More info on hiking and canoeing is available from the **Manistee Ranger Station,** 1658 Manistee Hwy., 2mi. north of Manistee on U.S. 31 (723-2211; open M-F 8am-5pm, Sa-Su 8:30am-5pm).

There are several inexpensive motel options in and near Manistee. The friendly **Riverside Motel,** 520 Water St., has dock space for boats and waterfront rooms (723-3554; singles $29-69, doubles $35-79, depending on room and season). Fourteen mi. north in Onekama, the **Traveller's Motel,** 5606 Eight Mile Rd., a ½ block from Rt. 22, provides enormous rooms with kitchenettes. (889-4342. Singles $45, doubles $60, kitchenettes sleeping up to 6 people $80; in winter $32/$42/$55.)

The **Manistee County Chamber of Commerce,** 50 Filer St. in Briny Bldg., Suite 224 (723-2575 or 800-288-2286), stocks pamphlets on local attractions (open M-F 8am-5:30pm). 30mi. to the south, the **Lake Michigan Car Ferry** (800-841-4243) shuttles people and cars between Ludington and Manitowoc, WI. (4hr.; 2 per day late June to Aug., in spring and fall 1 per day; $38, seniors $35, ages 5-15 $17, for cars an additional $46; reservations reccomended.)

The renowned **Interlochen Center for the Arts,** in Interlochen, 17mi. south of Traverse City on Rt. 137, trains talented young artists in classical music, dance, theater, and creative writing (276-7200; free campus tours Tu-Sa 10:30am and 2:30pm, Su 11am and 4pm). Here, the **International Arts Festival,** held year-round, has attracted the likes of Tony Bennett, Natalie Cole, Gladys Knight, and James Taylor. Faculty and students also put on top-notch performances throughout the year. (Box office open in summer M-Sa 9am-8:30pm, Su noon-8:30pm; reduced hrs. in off season. Tickets $5-30.) **Interlochen State Park** offers recreation and camping nearby, 1mi. south of Interlochen along Rt. 137, directly opposite the Center for Arts. (276-9511 or 800-447-2757. Sites $6, with electricity and showers $14. Vehicle permit $4. Ranger station open daily 8am-3am.)

**SLEEPING BEAR DUNES.** The Sleeping Bear Dunes rest along the western shores of the Leelanau Peninsula, 20mi. west of Traverse City on Rt. 72. According to Chippewa legend, the mammoth sand dunes represent a sleeping mother bear, waiting for her drowned cubs—the Manitou Islands—to finish a swim across the lake. Near the historic Fishtown shops, **Manitou Island Transit** (256-9061), in Leland, makes daily trips to South Manitou and ventures 5 times per week in July and Aug. to the larger, wilder North Manitou. (Round-trip $20, under 13 $13. Check-in 9:15am. Call ahead for schedule in May-June and Sept.-Nov.) **Camping** is available on both islands with the purchase of a **permit** ($7 for 7 days; buy at the visitors center); the Manitou Islands do not allow cars.

The **Sleeping Bear Dunes National Lakeshore,** of which the islands are one part, also includes 25mi. of lakeshore on the mainland. When the glaciers came to a halt and melted, mountains of fine sand were left behind, creating a landscape resembling a cross between an ocean coast and a desert. To gain entrance to all the Lakeshore's splendors, purchase a vehicle permit at any of various points in the area ($7, good for 1 week; $15 for an annual pass). You can be king of the sandhill at **Dune Climb,** 5mi. north of Empire on Rt. 109. From there, a strenuous 2½mi. hike over sandy hills leads to Lake Michigan in all its refreshing glory. If you'd rather let your car do the climbing, motor to an overlook along the **Pierce Stocking Scenic Drive,** off Rt. 109 just north of Empire, where a 450 ft. sand cliff descends on the cool water below (open mid-May to mid-Oct. daily 9am-9pm). For maps and info on the numerous cross-country skiing, hiking, and mountain biking trails, call the **National Parks Service Visitors Center,** 9922 Front St. (326-5134), in Empire (open daily in summer 9am-6pm; mid-Sept. to mid June 9am-4pm).

The Platte River (at the southern end) and the Crystal River (at the northern end) are great for canoeing or floating. Crystal River Outfitters, 6249 Western Ave./Rt. 22 (334-7490), near Glen Arbor, offers 1-4 hr. kayak excursions ($12.50-20 per person). **Riverside Canoes,** 5042 Scenic Hwy./Rt. 22, at Platte River Bridge, lets you play in water toys (325-5622; inner tubes $4-6 for 1hr., $11-13 for 2hr.; canoes $25-29; kayaks $16). Sleeping Bear Dunes has 4 **campgrounds: DH Day** (334-4634), in Glen Arbor, with 83 primitive sites ($10); **Platte River** (325-5881 or 800-365-2267), off the southern shore, with 179 sites and showers ($14, with electricity $19); and 2 cheaper **backcountry campsites** accessible by 1½mi. trails. (No reservations. $5 permit required, available at visitors center or at either developed campground.)

**TRAVERSE CITY.** Named after the "Grand Traverse" that French fur traders once made between the Leelanau and Old Mission Peninsulas, Traverse City offers the summer vacationer a slew of sandy beaches and more cherries than you can count (50% of the nation's cherries are produced in the surrounding area). The annual **Cherry Festival** (947-4230; info office open M-F 9am-5pm), held the first full week in July, serves as a tribute to the fruit's annual harvest. In early to mid-July, 5 orchards near Traverse City let you pick your own cherries, including **Amon Orchards,** 10mi. north on U.S. 31 (938-9160; $1.25 per lb.; eat while you pick for free; open daily 9am-6pm). The more sophisticated fruit connoisseur might indulge in the area's many wineries. **Château Grand Traverse,** 12239 Center Rd., 8mi. north of Traverse City on M37, offers free tours and tastings. (223-7355 or 800-283-0247. In summer, tours on the hr. noon-4pm. Open M-Sa 10am-7pm, Su noon-6pm; Nov.-Apr. M-Sa 10am-5pm, Su noon-5pm.)

Sparkling bay and ancient sand dunes make this region a Great Lakes paradise, though a crowded and expensive one. In the summer, swimming, boating, and scuba diving interests focus on Grand Traverse Bay; free beaches and public access sites speckle the shore. You can explore the coastline of the Leelanau Peninsula, between Grand Traverse Bay and Lake Michigan, on scenic Rt. 22—don't miss out on Leland, a charming fishing village, which now launches the Manitou Island ferries (see **Sleeping Bear Dunes,** above), via M22. The area's scenic waterfront makes for excellent biking. The **TART** bike trail runs 8mi. along E. and W. Grand Traverse Bay, while the 30mi. loop around Old Mission Peninsula, just north of the city, provides great views of the Bay on both sides. **Ralston Cycles,** 750 E. 8th St. rents bikes (941-7161; $15 per day, $25 all weekend; open M-Th 9am-6pm, Fr 9am-7pm, Sa 9am-5pm, Su 11am-4pm). For local events and entertainment, pick up the weekly *Traverse City Record-Eagle Summer Magazine* or *Northern Express,* available in corner kiosks around the city. **Poppycock's,** 128 E. Front St. has $7-8 homemade linguini lunches and a myriad of gourmet sandwiches (vegetarian and otherwise) for $5-7. (941-7632. Open in summer M-Th 11am-10pm, Fr-Sa 11am-10:30pm, Su noon-9pm; in winter M-Th 11am-9pm, Fr-Sa 11am-10pm.)

**Traverse City State Park,** 1132 U.S. 31 N, 2mi. east of town, has 344 wooded sites across the street from the beach (922-5270 or 800-447-2757; sites with hookup $15; $4 vehicle permit fee). In town, E. Front St. is lined with motels, but you'll have trouble finding a room for under $50. **Northwestern Michigan College,** 1701 E. Front St., West Hall, has some of the cheapest beds in the city. (922-1409. 1 person $30, 2 people $40, 2-room suite with bathroom $55. Open early June to Aug. Reserve several weeks in advance.) The **Shoestring Resort,** at the intersection of Garfield and River Rd., 12mi. south of town, offers exceptionally nice cabins with 1 to 3 bedrooms, kitchens, cable TV, and A/C. (946-7935. Cottages start at $35 per night; in winter $10 lower; weekly rates available. Reserve several weeks in advance.)

**Indian Trails** and **Greyhound,** 3233 Cass Rd. (946-5180), tie Traverse City to Detroit (7½hr., 3 per day, $38) and to the Upper Peninsula via St. Ignace (2½hr., 2per day, $17). The **Bay Area Transportation Authority** (941-2324) has a demand-response service; you call them and they'll pick you up (fare $4, daily pass $5; available M-F 6am-5pm, Sa 9am-5:30pm). **Traverse City Convention and Visitors Bureau:** 101 West Grandview Pkwy./U.S. 31 N (947-1120 or 800-872-8377; open M-Sa 9am-6pm, Su 11am-3pm; in winter M-F 9am-5pm, Sa 9am-3pm.) **Post Office:** 202 S. Union St. (946-9616; open M-F 9am-4pm). **ZIP code:** 49684.

# NORTHERN MICHIGAN SHORE

**CHARLEVOIX AND BEAVER ISLAND.** Situated on the ½mi. wide ribbon of land between Lake Michigan and Lake Charlevoix, the stretch of coast near Charlevoix (SHAR-le-voy), north of Traverse City on U.S. 31, served as the setting for some of

Hemingway's Nick Adams stories. The yacht-rich, upper-crust town now attracts more tourists than it did in Hemingway's time; the population triples in the summer. In "Charlevoix the Beautiful," golf is king; the town boasts 16 courses for 8500 residents. The **Charlevoix Area Chamber of Commerce,** 408 Bridge St. (547-4045 or 800-367-8557), dishes the dirt (open in summer M-Sa 9am-7pm, in winter M-F 9am-5pm and Sa 10am-4pm). Lodging rarely comes cheap in this resort-oriented area, but campers can bask in 90 sites on the shores of Lake Michigan at **Fisherman's Island State Park,** on Bells Bay Rd., 5mi. south of Charlevoix on U.S. 31 (547-6641 or 800-447-2757; rustic sites $6; $4 vehicle permit fee). Those who simply can't dispense with showers and electricity can head to the **Colonial Motel,** 6822 U.S. 31 S., with free coffee, A/C, and cable TV (547-6637; singles $38-60; doubles $48-70; lower rates off season; open May-Oct.).

Charlevoix also serves as the gateway to Beaver Island, the Great Lakes' most remote inhabited island. Hiking, boating, biking, and swimming abound on the island's 53 sq. mi., just a 2¼hr. ferry trip from shore. (**Ferries** depart from 102 Bridge St. 1-3 times per day. Round-trip $31, ages 5-12 $15.50; bikes $12. Call 547-2311 or 888-446-4095 for more info.) **Beaver Island Chamber of Commerce:** 448-2505.

**PETOSKEY.** 18mi. north of Charlevoix, Petoskey is renowned for Petoskey Stones, fossilized coral from an ancient sea. For info on beaches and other attractions, including canoeing, orchards, and walking tours, contact the **Petoskey Regional Chamber of Commerce,** 401 E. Mitchell (347-4150). (Open M-F 8am-5pm, Sa 10am-3pm, Su noon-4pm.)

Homely **North Central Michigan College,** 1515 Howard St., rents single dorm rooms within a suite. (348-6611; 348-6612 for reservations. Singles $30; doubles $40; 4-person suite $70. Linen provided. Reservations recommended; cash or check only.) The **Petoskey Motel,** at the corner of U.S. 31 and U.S. 131, rents clean, spacious rooms with A/C and cable (347-8177; singles $39-49). **Petoskey State Park,** 5mi. east of town off Rt. 119 (take U.S. 31 N for 2mi., then left on Rt. 119), offers 170 campsites on Little Traverse Bay (347-2311; sites with electricity $15; $4 vehicle fee). Petoskey's **Gaslight District,** 1 block from the chamber of commerce, features local crafts and foods in period shops. In the heart, **Roast and Toast Café,** 309 E. Lake St., serves pasta and chicken dishes for $7-10 (347-7767; open daily during summer 7am-9:30pm; in winter daily 7am-8pm). The **City Park Grill,** 432 E. Lake St., serves sandwiches ($5-7) and contemporary cuisine (entrées $7-12) in an elegant 1910 setting. Ernest Hemingway used to sit at the wooden bar. (347-0101. Open M-Th 11:30am-10pm. Bar open later. Live entertainment W-Sa at 10pm. $2-3 cover.)

In a remote woodland just outside Indian River, 20mi. east of Petoskey, 3 tons of bronze and 12 tons of redwood were reverently molded into a 31 ft. Jesus cleaved onto a 55 ft. tall cross. An anguished yet oddly imposing monument to the national obsession with size, the **Cross in the Woods,** 7078 M68, completed in 1959, is easily the world's tallest (238-8973).

North of Petoskey, Rt. 119 winds along the lakeside through tunnels of trees and hiking-trail scenery. In Cross Village, **Legs Inn,** the only restaurant for miles, serves Polish entrees ($6-16) and over 100 beers amid fantastic Native American decor. (526-2281. F-Su live blues, folk, etc. Cover F-Su $2-4. Open mid-May to mid-Oct. daily noon-9pm or later.)

**STRAITS OF MACKINAC.** Only fur'ners say "mackinACK"; in the Land of the Great Turtle (as early Native Americans called it), Mackinac is pronounced "mackinAW." Colonial **Fort Michilimackinac** still guards the straits between Lake Michigan and Lake Huron, but tourists, not troops, flock to Mackinac City. Along with Fort Michilimackinac, **Fort Mackinac** (on Mackinac Island) and **Historic Mill Creek** (3½mi. south of Mackinac on Rt. 23) form a trio of State Historic Parks. (436-5563. All open daily mid-June to early Sept. 9am-6pm; early Sept. to Oct. and mid-May to mid-June 10am-5pm. Each park $7.25, ages 6-12 $4.25, families $20.)

The **Michigan Dept. of Transportation Welcome and Travel Information Center** (436-5566), on Nicolet St. off I-75 at exit 338, has info. (Free reservation service. Open

Sa-Th 9am-7pm, F 9am-8pm; Sept. to mid-June daily 9am-5pm.) **Indian Trails** (517-725-5105 or 800-292-3831 in MI) has a flag stop at the Big Boy restaurant on Nicolet Ave. One bus runs north and one south daily; buy tickets at the next station.

Campers can bed at **Mackinac Mill Creek Campground,** 3mi. south of town on Rt. 23. Most of its 600 sites lie near the lake (436-5584; sites $12.50, full hookup $15; cabins $35, 2nd night $30, 3rd $25). Sites at the **Wilderness State Park,** 11mi. west on Wilderness Park Dr., have showers and electricity (436-5381; $15, 4-8-person cabins $40, 20-person bunkhouse $55). The best deals are across the Mackinac Bridge and away from the lakeshore on I-75 Business Loop in St. Ignace. The **Cedars Motel,** 2040 I-75 Business Loop rents comfortable rooms a 5min. drive from the docks (905-643-9578; singles $32-41, doubles $40-65; open early May to Oct. 1).

The prohibition of cars on Mackinac Island, and resulting proliferation of horse-drawn carriages, has given the heavily touristed island a decidedly equine aroma. The main draws are **Fort Mackinac** (906-847-3328; open daily 9:30am-6:30pm; closed in winter), Victorian homes, and the roamable beaches. Connoisseurs will immediately recognize the island as the birthplace of Mackinac Fudge, sold in shops all over the Michigan coastline (1 lb. box $7). **Horse-drawn carriages** cart guests all over the island (906-847-3325; open daily 8:30am-5pm; $13.50, ages 4-11 $6.50). Saddle horses ($25 per hr.) are also available at various stables around the isle.

Perhaps the best way to see the island is by bicycle. Rentals line Main St. by the ferry docks ($4 per hr.). Encompassing 80% of the island, **Mackinac Island State Park** features a circular 8.2mi. shoreline road for biking and hiking. The invaluable *Mackinac Island Locator Map* ($1) and the *Discover Mackinac Island* book ($2) can be found at the **Mackinac Island Chamber of Commerce** (906-847-3783 or 800-4-LILACS/454-5257), on Main St. (open daily 8am-7pm; Oct.-May 9am-5pm). Three ferry lines leave Mackinaw City and St. Ignace with overlapping schedules, though service from St. Ignace is less frequent. During the summer, a ferry leaves every 15-30min. from 7:30am-11pm (round-trip $13.50, under 11 $7, bike passage $5.50). A tradition not to be missed is the annual **Labor Day Bridge Walk;** Michigan's governor leads thousands of pilgrims from Machinac City to St. Ignace across the Mackinac Bridge, "Mighty Mac," the world's largest suspension bridge.

# UPPER PENINSULA

A multi-million-acre forestland bordered by 3 of the world's largest lakes, Michigan's Upper Peninsula (U.P.) is among the most scenic, unspoiled stretches of land in the Great Lakes region. But in 1837, after Congress gave Toledo to Ohio, Michigan only grudgingly accepted this "wasteland to the north" in the unpopular deal that gave the territory statehood. From the start, Michigan exploited most of the land, laying waste to huge tracts of forest destined for the fireplaces of Chicago. In the past century, however, the forests, now protected, have returned to their former grandeur, and the U.P.'s spectacular waterfalls and miles of coastline have won the hearts of nature lovers.

**DEER SEASON** Lasting only 2 weeks in late Nov., "Deer Season" might seem relatively innocuous to the unwary traveler, yet in this part of the country, Deer Season is fraught with cultural significance. Many schools in the Upper Peninsula and the northern Lower Peninsula close on Opening Day (the first day of Deer Season) because of the sheer number of student absences. The song "The Second Week of Deer Camp" is played incessantly on the radio. Hunter's orange, an eye-catching fabric hue designed to prevent accidental shootings, becomes *de rigeur* in every bar and tavern. The same annual jokes are bandied around with enthusiasm that matches all previous years: "What's the difference between beer nuts and deer nuts? Beer nuts are $2.50; deer nuts are under a buck." Groan if you want, but he has a gun....

Only 24,000 people live in the U.P.'s largest town, **Marquette.** The region is a paradise for fishing, camping, hiking, snowmobiling, and getting away from it all. Hikers enjoy numerous treks, including Michigan's section of **North Country Trail,** a national scenic trail extending from New York to North Dakota. Contact the **North Country Trail Association,** 49 Monroe Center NW, Suite 200B, Grand Rapids 49503 (616-454-5506) for details. A vibrant spectrum of foliage makes autumn a beautiful time to hike; in the winter, skiers replace hikers. Dozens of rivers beckon canoers as well. Those who heed the call of the water should contact the **Michigan Association of Paddlesport Providers,** P.O. Box 270, Wellston, MI 49689 (616-862-3227).

The peninsula has 200 **campgrounds,** including those at both national forests (call 800-447-2757 for reservations). Sleep with your dogs or bring extra blankets—temperatures in these parts drop to 50°F, even in July. Outside the major tourist towns, motel rooms start at around $24. For regional cuisine, indulge in the Fri night **fish-fry:** all-you-can-eat perch, walleye, or whitefish buffets available in nearly every restaurant in every town for about $7-10. The local ethnic specialty is a **pasty** (meat pie), imported by Cornish miners in the 19th century.

**Welcome centers** guard the U.P. at its 6 main entry points: **Ironwood,** 801 W. Cloverland Dr. (932-3330; open daily June-Sept. 8am-6pm, in winter 8am-4pm); **Iron Mountain,** 618 S. Stephenson Ave. (774-4201; open daily June-Sept. 7am-5pm, in winter 8am-4pm); **Menominee,** 1343 10th Ave. (863-6496; open daily 8am-4pm); **Marquette,** 2201 U.S. 41 S (249-9066; open mid-June to Aug. daily 9am-5pm); **Sault Ste. Marie,** 943 Portage Ave. W. (632-8242; open daily 9am-5pm); and **St. Ignace** (643-6979), on I-75 N (open daily 8am-5pm). The invaluable *Upper Peninsula Travel Planner* is published by the **Upper Peninsula Travel and Recreation Association** (800-562-7134; info line staffed M-F 8am-4:30pm). For additional help planning a trip into the wilderness, write to or call the **U.S. Forestry Service,** 2727 N. Lincoln Rd., Escanaba 49829 (786-4062). **Area code:** 906.

**SAULT STE. MARIE AND THE EASTERN U.P.** "The locks" are the reason people settle in gritty Sault (pronounced "soo") Ste. Marie. The St. Mary's River connects—and separates—Lake Huron and Lake Superior. Back in the day, there was a 21 ft. vertical drop over 1mi., rendering the river impassable by boat. Native Americans simply picked up their canoes and walked the distance, but a 1000 ft. freighter needs a little more help. In 1855, entrepreneurs built the first lock here. Now the busiest in the world, the city's 4 locks float over 12,000 ships annually. A 2hr. **Soo Locks Boat Tour** leaves from both 1157 and 515 E. Portage Ave. (Call 632-6301 or 800-432-6301 for departure times. Open mid-May to mid-Oct. $15, ages 13-18 $12, ages 4-12 $6.50.) For landlubbers, the **Locks Park Historic Walkway** parallels the water for 1mi. The walkway passes the **River of History Museum,** 209 E. Portage St., which featues child-focused galleries interpreting the St. Mary's River through time. (632-1999. Open mid-May to mid-Oct. M-Sa 10am-5pm, Su noon-5pm; $2.50, ages 8-16 $1.25.) On the waterfront at the end of Johnston St., is the **Museum Ship Valley Camp,** a 1917 steam-powered freighter housing the Great Lakes's largest maritime museum and the **Marine Hall of Fame.** (632-3658. Open daily July-Aug. 9am-9pm; mid-May to June and Sept. to mid-Oct. 10am-6pm. $6.50, children $3.50.) Don't hesitate to cross over to Ontario and explore the wilder side of Sault Ste. Marie. The **Agawa Canyon Train Tour** is an all-day excursion into the northern wilderness which will remind you of the true meaning of the words "sparsely populated." (Departs from the Station Mall, 129 Bay St. 800-242-9287. Operates early June to late Oct. Summer prices CDN$53, seniors CDN$44, ages 5-18 CDN$16. Prices higher in fall when the trees are in full color.)

Back in the USA, get stuffed with burgers ($3-7) and classic American entrees at **The Antlers,** 804 E. Portage St., where "prices vary due to the attitude of customers." Animal lovers beware—the walls have eyes (and heads and bodies; 632-3571). The area's best lodging deal lies just over the bridge in Ontario. **The Algonquin Hotel (HI-C),** 864 Queen St. E., has spacious rooms just ½mi. from the bridge. (705-253-2311. Singles CDN$21.25, nonmembers $28; doubles CDN$33.60/$39. Cash or travelers checks only.) Otherwise, affordable accommodations line the I-75 Business Spur on the American side. If you must be within walking distance of the locks, the **Mid City Motel,**

304 E. Portage, is a comfortable establishment in the shadow of the cheesy Tower of History (632-6832; singles $36-46, doubles $45-54, depending on season.) West of the city, frolic in the uncrowded eastern branch of the **Hiawatha National Forest.** Out of several camping options, **Monocle Lake Campgrounds** puts all of the secluded beaches along the Lakeshore Dr. within easy reach (635-1003; no showers; sites $8-10; no reservations). At **Tahquamenon Falls State Park** (492-3415), 15min. east of Paradise, you can rent a **canoe** ($6 per ½-day) or **rowboat** ($1.50 per person) at the Lower Falls, or gawk at the 50 ft. Upper Falls (no barrel riders here). **Wilcox's Fish House,** 1232 S. Wilcox Ln. cooks the freshest fish on all of Lakeshore Dr. if not Lake Superior (437-5407).

North of Tahquamenon, over **300 shipwrecks** protected in an Underwater Preserve lie off Whitefish Point, affording divers an opportunity to search for sunken treasure. **Paradise Area Tourism Council:** (492-3927), P.O. Box 64, Paradise 49768.

**MIDDLE OF THE PENINSULA.** The western branch of the **Hiawatha National Forest** dominates the middle of the Peninsula, offering limitless wilderness activities and many **campsites** ($7-11; pit toilets, no showers; first come, first served). **Rapid River** is home to the southern office of the west branch on Hwy. 2. In the north, **Munising,** on Hwy. 28, accesses the forest and **Pictured Rocks National Lakeshore,** where water saturated with copper, manganese, and iron oxide paints the cliffs with multicolored bands. **Pictured Rocks Boat Cruise** (387-2379), at the city dock in Munising, gives the best view (tours approximately 3hr.; around $22, ages 6-12 $7, under 6 free). The Forest and Lakeshore share a **visitors center** (387-3700) at the intersection of Rt. 28 and Hwy. 58 in Munising. (Open mid-May to mid-Oct. daily 8am-6pm; mid-Oct to mid-May M-Sa 9am-4:30pm.) From Munising, Hwy. 58—a bumpy, unpaved gem of a road—weaves along the lakeshore past numerous trailheads and campsites; spare tires are necessary if you plan on extensive travel in the Hiawatha Forest. For a paved alternative from Munising to Grand Sable, go east on Rt. 28, then north on Rt. 77.

Backcountry **camping permits** for 1-6 people ($15) are available from the Munising or **Grand Sable Visitors Center** (494-2660), 2mi. west of Grand Marais on Hwy. 58 (open mid-May to early Oct. daily 10am-7pm). Visitors can stroll, birdwatch, or collect smooth stones along the shore at **Twelve Mile Beach** (self-registered campsites $10; pump water only), a 15mi. drive from the visitors center, and **Grand Sable Dunes,** a 1mi. walk from the visitors center. From atop the sandy **Log Slide,** you can survey Lake Superior; "polar bears" can take a plunge in the ice water. If all this liquid is making you thirsty, **Dune's Saloon** in Grand Marais, home of the **Lake Superior Brewing Company,** at the junction of Rt. 77 and Hwy. 58, can hook you up with a Hematite Stout or an Agate Amber ($2.25; 494-2337). **Poplar Bluff Cabins,** Star Rt. Box 3118, have lakeview rooms with kitchens. Head 12mi. east of Munising on Rt. 28, then 6mi. south from Shingleton on M94 to get there. (452-6271. Cottages $40-50 per night, $250 per week. Free use of boats on lake.)

The **Seney National Wildlife Refuge** on Rt. 77 shelters over 250 species of birds and mammals on 95,000 acres. The 7mi. **Marshland Wildlife Drive** self-guided auto tour is replete with loon and eagle observation decks; the best times for viewing wildlife are early morning and early evening. The refuge also offers hiking, cross-country skiing, biking, canoeing, and fishing. (586-9851. Visitors center open daily mid-May to mid-Oct. 9am-5pm. Free.)

At the bottom of the peninsula, the **Big Spring** is the jewel of **Palms Brook State Park;** take U.S. 2 to Thompson and go 11mi. north on M149. A must-see of the Upper Peninsula, the crystal blue spring shelters numerous trout and several underwater geysers of hydro-activity. All this can be observed from the deck of a raft, which transverses the spring via cable. (644-2592. Open May-Oct. daily 8am-10pm. No camping.) At nearby **Indian Lake State Park,** take M149 to County Rd. 442 and go east for camping options. (800-447-2757 for reservations. Teepees $23; cabins $32; campsites $9, with electricity $15. Reservations are necessary for teepees and cabins, and recommended for campsites.) Farther south, the **Fayette State Historic Park** has camping (644-2603; no showers; sites $9; open mid-May to mid-Oct.). All state parks require a $4 daily vehicle permit or $20 annual permit.

**KEWEENAW PENINSULA.** In 1840, Dr. Douglas Houghton's mineralogical survey of the Keweenaw Peninsula, a curved finger of land on the U.P.'s northwest corner, incited a copper mining rush which sent the area booming. When mining petered out around 1969, the land was left barren and exploited. Today, reforestation and government support have helped Copper Country find new life as a tourist destination. Every year, 250 in. of snow fall on the towering pines, smooth-stone beaches, and low mountains of Keweenaw. Visitors ski, snowshoe, and snowmobile in winter and enjoy the gorgeous green coasts in the summer.

At the base of the peninsula, hugging Lake Superior, sits the **Porcupine Mountain Wilderness State Park** (885-5275, for reservations 800-447-2757), affectionately known as "The Porkies." The park sports campsites ($9-14 sites with toilets and showers, electricity at Union; rustic sites $6), rustic cabins ($32; sleep 2-8; reservations required), and paths into the **Old Growth Forest,** the largest tract of uncut forest between the Rockies and the Adirondacks. The **visitors center,** near the junction of M107 and South Boundary Rd. inside the park, provides **permits** good for all Michigan parks ($4 per day, $20 annual; open in summer daily 10am-6pm). **Lake of the Clouds,** 8mi. inside the park on M107, is considered to be the best.

At the top of the Peninsula, the **Brockway Mountain Dr.** (6mi.), between Eagle Harbor and Copper Harbor, is a must for those weary of relentlessly flat terrain. Rising 1337 ft. above sea level, its summit provides some of the best views on the U.P.

The northernmost town in Michigan, **Copper Harbor** functions as the main gateway to **Isle Royale National Park** (see below). **Brockway Inn** (289-4588), 3 blocks west of the junction between Hwy. M26 and US41, in Copper Harbor, pleases patrons with cable TV, free coffee, and some rooms with a private whirlpool (singles $35-45; doubles from $53). **The Pines,** on U.S. 41 in Copper Harbor, serves huge cinnamon rolls ($2; 289-4222; restaurant open 6am-3pm; bar open noon-2am). Across the street, the **Keeweenaw Adventure Company**—look for the bikes out front—can make all your wilderness dreams come true: kayaking outings (2½hr. intro paddle $25), bike rentals (½-day $15, full-day $24), and more. Campers in Keweenaw do well to head for **Mclain State Park** (482-0278), 8mi. north of Hancock on M203. The campground rests along a 2mi. beach and is home to an impressive lighthouse. (Sites with electricity $14; vehicle permit required.)

# ISLE ROYALE NATIONAL PARK

Around the turn of the century, moose swam from the Canadian coast to this pristine 45mi.-long, 10mi.-wide island. With no natural predators, the animals overran the land. Today, wild animals (the Isle supports a pack of wolves) are the island's only permanent inhabitants. After the island was designated a national park in 1940, the fisherfolk who once lived here left. For backcountry seclusion, this is where to go; no cars, phones, or medical services pamper visitors. Come prepared.

Streams, lakes, and 170mi. of trails traverse the park. The **Greenstone Ridge Trail,** the main artery of the trail system, follows the backbone of the island from Rock Harbor Lodge, passing through several spectacular vistas. Serious backpackers conquer the **Minong Ridge Trail,** which runs parallel to the Greenstone Trail to the north for 30mi. from McCargoe Cove to Windigo; the remains of early Native American copper mines line the trail. Shorter hikes near Rock Harbor include **Scoville Point,** a 4.2mi. loop out onto a small peninsula, and **Suzy's Cave,** a 3.8mi. loop to an inland sea arch. The park office has info on cruises, evening programs, and ranger-led interpretive walks. **Canoeing** and **kayaking** allow access to otherwise inaccessible parts of the island; both Rock Harbor and Windigo have **boat** and **canoe rental** outfitters. (Motors $12.50 per ½-day, $21 per day. Boats and canoes $11 per ½-day, $18.75 per day.) **Scuba divers** can explore shipwrecks in the treacherous reefs off the northeast and west ends of the island—after registering at the park office. Divers need to bring filled tanks; no compressors available.

**Campgrounds** lie scattered all over the island; required free permits are available at any ranger station. Some sites have 3-sided, screened-in shelters. They go quickly on a first come, first served basis; bringing your own tent is a good idea.

GREAT LAKES

Nights are always frigid (about 40°F in June), and biting bugs peak in June and July; you'll need warm clothes and insect repellent. Intestinal bacteria, tapeworms, and giardia lurk in the waters of Isle Royale; use a 0.4-micron filter, or boil water for at least 2min. Purified water is available at Rock Harbor and Windigo. Very few places on the island permit fires; bring a small campstove. The **Rock Harbor Lodge** (906-337-4993) controls most of the island's commercial activity; the store carries a decent selection of overpriced food and camping staples. The lodge and associated cabins are the only indoor lodging on the island—remember, you're here to camp (singles $143; doubles $229).

Despite the fact that it's closer to the Ontario and Minnesota mainlands, Isle Royale is part of Michigan. The park **headquarters** is in **Houghton** at 800 E. Lakeshore Dr., in the Upper Peninsula (906-482-0984; open M-Sa 8am-4:30pm). The headquarters operates a 6½hr. ferry to the island. (Tu and F 9am, returns W and Sa 3:45pm. Round-trip $94, under 12 $47, kayaks $30.) **Isle Royale Ferry Service** (906-289-4437), at the dock in Copper Harbor, makes 4½hr. trips (round-trip $80, under 12 $40). Both ferries land at Rock Harbor. To access other parts of the island, take any of several shuttles from Rock Harbor, or leave from **Grand Portage, MN;** the **Grand Portage-Isle Royale Transportation Line,** 1507 N. First St. (715-392-2100), Superior, WI, sends a boat to Rock Harbor via Windigo, which stops at trailheads around the island (7½hr. later; $104 round-trip, under 12 half-price). In summer, additional trips go just to Windigo (round-trip $60, under 12 $30). On the island, the park's **ranger stations** include **Windigo** on the west tip; **Rock Harbor,** on the east tip; and **Malone Bay,** between Windigo and Rock Harbor, on the south shore.

# INDIANA

The cornfields of southern Indiana's Appalachian foothills give way to expansive plains in the industrialized north. Here, Gary's smokestacks spew black clouds over the waters of Lake Michigan, and urban travel hubs have earned the state its official nickname, "The Crossroads of America." The origin of Indiana's unofficial nickname, "The Hoosier State," is less certain; some speculate that it is a corruption of the pioneers' call to visitors at the door—"Who's there?"—while others claim that it spread from Louisville, where labor contractor Samuel Hoosier preferred to hire Indiana workers over Kentucky laborers. Whatever the nickname's derivation, Indiana's Hoosiers are considered a no-nonsense Midwestern breed.

## ◼ PRACTICAL INFORMATION

**Capital:** Indianapolis.

**Visitor Info: Indiana Division of Tourism,** 1 N. Capitol, #700, Indianapolis 46204 (800-289-6646; www.state.in.us/tourism). **Division of State Parks,** 402 W. Washington #W-298, Indianapolis 46204 (317-232-4125).

**Postal Abbreviation:** IN. **Sales Tax:** 5%.

# INDIANAPOLIS

Surrounded by flat farmland, Indianapolis feels like an average American city. Folks shop and work all day among downtown's skyscrapers and drive home to sprawling suburbs in the evening. Life ambles here—until May, when 350,000 spectators and crewmembers overrun the city, and the road warriors of the Indianapolis 500 rise above clouds of turbocharged exhaust to claim their throne.

## ◼ ORIENTATION AND PRACTICAL INFORMATION

The city is laid out in concentric circles, with a dense central cluster of skyscrapers and low-lying outskirts. The very center of Indianapolis is just south of **Monument Circle,** at the intersection of **Washington St. (U.S. 40)** and **Meridian St.**

Washington St. divides the city north-south; Meridian St. divides it east-west. **I-465** circles the city and provides access to downtown. **I-70** cuts through the city east-west. Plentiful 2hr. metered parking can be found along the edges of the downtown area, and there are numerous indoor and outdoor lots ($5-8 per day) in the center, especially along **Ohio** and **Illinois St.**

**Airport: Indianapolis International** (487-7243), 7mi. southwest of downtown off I-465, exit 11B. Take bus #8 "West Washington" or a cab ($17).

**Amtrak:** 350 S. Illinois St. (263-0550), behind Union Station. Trains travel east-west only. To: Chicago (5hr., 3 per day, from $17) and Cincinnati (3hr., 9 per week, from $18). Open daily 6:30am-10pm.

**Buses: Greyhound,** 350 S. Illinois St. (267-3076). To: Chicago (4hr., 12 per day, from $30); Cincinnati (3-7hr., 4 per day, from $18); and Bloomington (1hr., 1 per day, from $14). Open 24hr.

**Public Transit: Indy Go,** 139 E. Ohio St. (635-3344). Office open M-F 8am-6pm, Sa 9am-4pm. $1, children under 6 free. Service to Speedway area 25¢ extra. Transfers 25¢, 1 free transfer per ticket. Patchy coverage of outlying areas, map at visitor center.

**Taxis: Barrington Cab,** 786-7994.

**Car Rental: Thrifty,** 700 W. Minnesota St. (636-5622), at the airport. From $36 per day with 225 free mi. Weekly $149 with 1500 free mi. Must be 21 with major credit card. Under 25 add $10 per day. Open 24hr.

**Visitor Info: Indianapolis City Center,** 201 S. Capitol Ave. (237-5200 or 800-233-4639), in the Pan Am Plaza across from the RCA Dome, has a helpful model of the city. Open M-F 10am-5:30pm, Sa 10am-5pm, Su noon-5pm.

**Hotlines: Rape Crisis Line,** 800-221-6311. **Gay/Lesbian Info Line,** 923-8550.

**Post Office:** 125 W. South St. (464-6376), across from Amtrak. Open M-W and F 7am-5:30pm, Th 7am-6pm. **ZIP code:** 46206. **Area code:** 317. **Time Zone:** Central.

# ▌ PARK IT!

Budget motels line the I-465 beltway, 5mi. from downtown. Make reservations a year in advance for the Indy 500, which inflates rates throughout May.

**Fall Creek YMCA,** 860 W. 10th St. (634-2478), just north of downtown. Small and sparse rooms; access to a pool, gym, and laundry facilities. Free parking. 87 rooms for men, 10 for women. Singles $25, with bath $30; $77/$87 per week. $5 key deposit.

**Motel 6,** 6330 Debonair Lane, just off Crawfordsville Rd., at exit 16A off I-465, near the Speedway. Clean, pleasant rooms with A/C and cable TV at reasonable prices. Singles $37 Su-Th, $40 F-Sa; doubles $43/46.

**Dollar Inn,** 6331 Crawfordsville Rd. (248-8500), off I-465 at exit 16A. Not the lap of luxury, but a very good deal. About 10min. from downtown. Decent rooms with HBO and ESPN. Singles $26; doubles $31. F-Sa singles and doubles $31. Key deposit $2. Checkout 11am (strictly enforced). Must be 21+.

**KOA,** 5896 W. 200 St. N., Greenfield (894-1397 or 800-KOA/562-0531), 15min. from the city, just off exit 96 on I-70. Nice campsite with video/arcade room. Sites $18, partial hookup $22, full hookup $25. Reception daily 8am-9pm. Open Mar. to mid Nov.

**Indiana State Fairgrounds Campgrounds,** 1202 E. 38th St. (927-7520). Bus #4 or 39 from downtown. To get close to nature, go elsewhere. 170 sod-and-gravel sites, mostly packed by RVs. Sites $10.50, full hookup $12.60. Busy during the state fair.

# ◖ PIT STOPS

Ethnic food stands, produce markets, and knick-knack vendors fill the spacious **City Market,** 222 E. Market St., in a renovated 19th-century building. As if America didn't have enough malls, Indianapolis's newly constructed **Circle Centre,** 49 West Maryland St. (681-8000), hosts a slew of restaurants and a food court.

**Bazbeaux Pizza,** 334 Massachusetts Ave. (636-7662), and 832 E. Westfields Blvd. (255-5711). Indianapolis's favorite pizza. The Tchoupitoulas pizza is a Cajun masterpiece. Construct your own culinary wonder ($5-20) from a choice of 53 toppings. Open M-Th 11am-10pm, F-Sa 11am-11pm, Su 4:30-10pm.

**The Abbey,** 771 Massachusetts Ave. (269-8426), with other locations at 5905 E. 86th St. and 74 W. New York St. Sit in overstuffed velvet chairs while you sip cappuccino ($2) or sample the wide selection of salads and sandwiches, like the delicious Miracle Quesadilla ($5.75). Open Su 11am-midnight, M 8am-midnight, Tu-F 8am-1am, Sa 11am-1am.

**Brother Juniper's Restaurant,** 339 Massachusetts Ave. (636-3115), is a casual place to fill up on hearty sandwiches. Brother Juniper's Special (bacon, avocado, cream cheese, and sprouts on whole wheat; $6.50) is worth the trip.

## ⬤ SPECTATOR SPORT

**White River State Park,** near downtown, bus #8, holds both activities and attractions. The newly restored canal entices locals to stroll, bike, or nap on the banks. For the more aquatic, pedal boats are available for rent at **Central Canal Rental** *(634-1824).* The **visitors center** is located within the park in the old pumphouse. *(801 W. Washington St. 233-2434 or 800-665-9056.)*

Near the entrance, the **Eiteljorg Museum of American Indians' and Western Art,** features an impressive collection of art from the Old West—both white and Native American. *(500 W. Washington St. 636-9378. Open Tu-Sa 10am-5pm, Su noon-5pm; in summer also M 10am-5pm. $5, seniors $4, students with ID and children $2. Tours daily at 2pm.)* A 5min. drive from the Eiteljorg, and still within the massive park, the seemingly cageless **Indianapolis Zoo** has one of the world's largest enclosed whale and dolphin pavilions. *(1200 W. Washington St. 630-2101. Open daily 9am-5pm; Sept.-May 9am-4pm. $9.75, seniors $7, ages 3-12 $6. Parking $3.)*

Brass chandeliers and a majestic stained glass dome grace the marbled interior of the **State House,** between Capitol and Senate St. near W. Washington St.; self-guided tour brochures are available inside. *(232-5293. Open daily 8am-5pm, main floor only Sa-Su. 4 guided tours per day M-F.)* The **Indianapolis Museum of Art,** distant from city center, is well worth a visit. The museum's beautiful 152 acres offer nature trails, art pavilions, the Eli Lilly Botanical Garden, a greenhouse, and a theater. *(1200 W. 38th St. 923-1331. Open Tu-W and F 10am-5pm, Th 10am-8:30pm, Su noon-5pm. Free. Special exhibits $3.)* Dig for fossils, speed through the cosmos, or explore a maze at the **Children's Museum.** *(3000 N. Meridian St. 924-5437. Museum open daily 10am-5pm; Sept.-Feb. closed M. $8, seniors $7, ages 2-12 $3.50; with Omnimax $12.50/$11.50/$7.)*

Wolves and bison roam under researchers' supervision at **Wolf Park** on Jefferson St. in **Battle Ground.** The werewolves, which howl constantly, are brought into the limelight under the moonlight some nights. *(1hr. north of Indianapolis off I-65. 765-567-2265. Open Tu-Su 1-5pm; open later for wolf howls, year-round Sa at 7:30pm; May-Nov. F at 7:30pm; Tu-Sa and Howl night $4, ages 6-13 $3; Su $5/3.)*

## ♫ THE FAST LANE

In its heyday, the **Walker Theatre,** 617 Indiana Ave., a 15min. walk northwest of downtown, booked jazz greats Louis Armstrong and Dinah Washington. Local and national artists still perform here as part of the bi-weekly **Jazz on the Avenue** series (F 6-10pm). The theater, erected in 1927 with stunning Egyptian and African decor, commemorates Madame Walker, an African-American beautician who invented the straightening comb and became America's first self-made woman millionaire (236-2087). The **Indianapolis Symphony Orchestra,** 45 Monument Circle, handles entertainment in classical style (box office 639-4300 or 800-366-8457; tickets $5-49). The **Indianapolis Opera** performs at Clowes Hall on the Butler University campus at 46th and Sunset St. from Sept. to May (283-3531, box office 940-6444; tickets $15-60, students and seniors $13). The **Indianapolis Repertory Theatre,** 140 W. Washington St., performs between Oct. and May (635-5252; tickets $17.50-40, students $12.50). Contact the **Arts Council Office**, 47 S. Pennsylvania St., for the schedules of other performances in the area (631-3301). The **Indiana State Fair** (Aug. 9-20, 2000) means 2 weeks of exhibitions and concerts.

By day a boring Clark Kent, the **Broad Ripple** area (6mi. north of downtown at College Ave. and 62nd St.) transforms after dark into a nightlife super-mecca for anyone under 40. The party fills the clubs and bars and spills out onto the sidewalks and side streets off Broad Ripple Ave. until about 1am on weekdays and 3am on weekends. For pool and preppie crowds, you can't beat **Average Joe's Sports Pub**, 814 Broad Ripple Ave. (253-5844). Off the main strip, **The Monkey's Tale**, 925 E. Westfield Blvd. (253-2883), serves up drinks and atmosphere while the attached **Jazz Cooker** dishes out crawfish and blues. **The Vogue**, 6259 N. College Ave., features national acts as well as themed dance nights (255-2828; cover $2-7, more for big names). Those interested in a more jocular evening should try the **Broad Ripple Comedy Club**, 6281 N. College Ave., on the corner of College Ave. and Broad Ripple Ave. (255-4211, shows daily). After the clubs close, make a run for tacos ($2) and burritos ($3.50) at **Paco's Cantina**, 737 Broad Ripple Ave. (251-6200; open until 4am or later, at the owner's whim).

## █ GO, SPEED RACER, GO!

When the **Indianapolis Motor Speedway** lies dormant, buses take tourists around the 2½mi. track *(4790 W. 16th St., off I-465 at the Speedway exit. Bus #25. 481-8500. Track tours daily 9am-4:30pm when track not in use. $3, ages 6-15 $1.)* The adjacent **Speedway Museum** houses Indy's Hall of Fame. *(484-6747. Open daily 9am-5pm. $3, ages 6-15 $1.)* The country's passion for fast cars reaches fever pitch during the **500 Festival**— a month of parades, a mini-marathon, and hoopla leading up to race day *(636-4556)*. The festivities begin with time trials in mid-May and culminate with the bang of the **Indianapolis 500** starter's gun on May 30 (weather permitting). Tickets for the race go on sale the day after the previous year's race and usually sell out within a week. NASCAR's **Brickyard 400** sends stock cars zooming down the speedway in early Aug. *(800-822-4639 for ticket order forms for any event.)*

# BLOOMINGTON

Bloomington's rolling hills made the area inadequate for farming, but make an exquisite backdrop for its most prominent institution, Indiana University. Events like the Little 500 bike race (made famous by the movie *Breaking Away*) attract hundreds of visitors, but the town revolves around campus, providing happenin' cafes, art exhibits, and numerous bars for Hoosier guys and gals.

**█ PRACTICAL INFORMATION.** Bloomington lies south of Indianapolis on Rt. 37; **N. Walnut** and **College St.** are the main north-south thoroughfares. **Greyhound**, 219 W. 6th St. (332-1522; station open M-F 9am-5pm, Sa-Su noon-5pm), connects Bloomington to Chicago (5hr., 1 per day, $50) and Indianapolis (1hr., 1 per day, $14). **Bloomington Transit** sends buses on 7 routes. Service is infrequent; call 332-5688 for info. (75¢, seniors and ages 5-17 35¢.) **Yellow Cab** (336-4100) charges by zone. **Visitors center:** 2855 N. Walnut St. (334-8900 or 800-800-0037), offers free local calls. (Open M-F 8:30am-5pm, Sa 9am-4pm, Su 10am-3pm; Nov.-Apr. closed Su; 24hr. brochure area.) **Post Office:** 206 E. 4th St. (334-4030), 2 blocks east of Walnut St. (open M and F 8am-6pm, Tu-Th 8am-5:30pm, Sa 8am-1pm). **ZIP code:** 47404. **Area code:** 812. **Time Zone:** Central.

**█◨▣ ACCOMMODATIONS, FOOD, AND NIGHTLIFE.** Budget hotels cluster around the intersection of N. Walnut St. and Rt. 46. **College Motor Inn**, 509 N. College Ave., is convenient to the university and offers nice rooms with basic cable and sometimes small kitchens (336-6881; singles from $45, doubles from $50). **Paynetown State Park**, 10mi. southeast of downtown on Rt. 446, provides open field sites in a well-endowed park on Lake Monroe with access to a boat ramp and hiking trails. Boat rentals are available. (837-9490. Primitive sites $5, with shower $7, with electricity $11. Vehicle registration $5, in-state $2.)

The **Downtown Sq.,** known locally as "The Square," boxes in a wealth of restaurants, bookstores, and cute clothing shops, in a 2-block radius, most on Kirkwood Ave. near College and W. Walnut St. Vegetarians can eat easy—all these restaurants have many meat-free menu options. Chuckle the hemp cheese ($1.30 per oz.) off your Mondo Burrito ($4) at **The Laughing Planet Café,** 322 E. Kirkwood Ave., where organic food and good folks make for a one-of-a-kind dining experience (323-2233; open M-Sa 11am-9pm, Su noon-8pm). Enter a hall of mirrors at **Snow Lion,** 113 S. Grant St., just off Kirkwood Ave., to sample Tibetan and Asian cuisine. (336-0835. Lunch $3.95-5.95, dinner $6.95-11.95. Open M-Th 11am-2pm and 5-10pm, F-Su 11am-10pm.) Join hordes of hoosiers at **Jimmy John's,** 430 E. Kirkwood Ave., home of the self-pronounced "World's Best Sub" (332-9265; subs $3.15; open M-Th 11am-10pm, F-Sa 11am-3:30am, Su noon-10pm).

Beer and alternative rock are the staples of colleges, and IU is no exception. **The Crazy Horse,** 214 W. Kirkwood Ave. drafts an alcohol army of 80 beers (336-8877; open Th-Sa 11am-2am, Su noon-midnight, M-W 11am-1am). Everyone who's anyone (at IU, that is) shimmies over to **Nick's,** 423 E. Kirkwood Ave., to play drinking games (332-4040). **Mars,** 479 N. Walnut St., is the planet for national acts (concert line 336-6277); the **Bluebird,** 216 N. Walnut St., flies a little closer in, staging local talent (336-2473). **Bullwinkle's,** 201 S. College Ave., caters to a gay crowd (334-3232, open M-F 7pm-3am), and **Rhino's,** 3251/2 S. Walnut St., has lesser-known acts, but accepts those under 21, unlike the others (333-3430).

🏛 **SIGHTS.** IU's architectually striking **Art Museum,** on the University campus, maintains an excellent collection of Oriental and African artworks. *(E. 7th St. 855-5445. Open Tu-Sa 10am-5pm, Su noon-5pm. Free.)* Visitors are sometimes puzzled by the local interest in Tibet and its culture, but it's rumored that some of the Dalai Lama's relatives reside in Bloomington. The **Tibetan Cultural Center** offers meditation and information on Tibetan culture *(3655 Snoddy Rd. 334-7046. Grounds open W noon-4pm, Sa-Su 10am-4pm. Center open Su 1-3pm.)* Browse 3 floors chock full of old "treasures" downtown at the **Antique Mall.** *(311 W. 7th St. 332-2290; open M-Sa 10am-5pm, Su noon-5pm.)* **Oliver Winery** not only has beautiful grounds, but also offers free (and generous) tastings of all of its 15 wines, including the local favorite blackberry wine *(8024 N. State Rd. 37. 876-5800 or 800-258-2783. Open M-Sa 10am-6pm, Su noon-6pm.)* Indiana's oldest lake, **Lake Monroe,** 10mi. south of town, off Rt. 446, was once an inland sea. Now it hosts boaters, fishers, waterskiers, and sailors.

# ILLINOIS

In 1893, at Chicago's World Columbian Exposition, a young professor named Fredrick Jackson Turner gave a stirring speech in which he proclaimed the "closing of the American Frontier." That such a proclamation was made in Illinois seems only fitting; once praised for its vast prairies and the arability of its soil, Illinois became a land known for its thriving urban industry.

The fate of the prairie continues to play out in Springfield, the capital, where legislators dish out a lumpy porridge of northern urban agendas and southern farming interests. Despite causing some political indigestion, the harsh mix goes down easy for most residents—perhaps their tribute to the wishes of native son, Abe Lincoln, who stressed that "a house divided against itself cannot stand."

# 🛈 PRACTICAL INFORMATION

**Capital:** Springfield.

**Visitor Info: Illinois Office of Tourism** (800- 226-6632; www.enjoyillinois.com). **Springfield Office of Tourism** 109 N. Seventh St., Springfield 62701 (800-545-7300).

**Postal Abbreviation:** IL. **Sales Tax:** 6.25-7.25%, depending on the city.

# CHICAGO

By the mid 1800s, Chicago was no longer a strategic military outpost, it had taken on a new role as a burgeoning commercial center.With the growth of the railroad industry, the town became America's meat-packing hub, drawing millions of immigrants and freed slaves who acquired a very few vast fortunes and countless broken dreams. Machine politics flourished, blurring any line between organized government and organized crime. In later years, trade became the city's economic mainstay; now narrow steel train tracks have given way to the concrete runways of O'Hare, one of the world's busiest airport.

Situated snugly along the banks of Lake Michigan, the only topological boundary to it's development, Chicago is the Midwest version of urban sprawl. Centered around the bustling commercial center are countless railroad depots, warehouses, and packing plants. Beyond these now mostly defunct relics lie acre upon acre of residential zones, ranging from the stately mansions of Hyde Park to the soaring public housing eyesores just beyond the edges of the tourist maps. Powered simultaneously by trade and production, unique architecture makes up a bristling downtown skyline of varying shapes and styles, while the legacy of lost jobs and unfulfilled dreams hangs thick in the birthplace of Electric Blues.

The "Windy City"—so named for its politician's hot air, and not for its cold, fierce gusts, has lots to offer. From a large handful of renowned museums to a varied and vibrant musical and entertainment scene, there's tons to explore.

##  ORIENTATION

 Chicago is a big city with big city problems. It is a good idea to stay within the boundaries made apparent by tourist maps. Aside from small pockets such as Hyde Park and the U. of Chicago, areas south of the loop and west of the "little ethnic" enclaves are mostly industrial or residential, and could pose a safety threat to the unwary tourist. **Cabrini Green** (bounded by W. Armitage Ave. on the north, W. Chicago Ave. on the south., Sedgwick on the west, and Halsted on the east), an infamously dangerous public housing development, sits within tourist map borders—other unsafe neighborhoods are usually outside them.

Chicago has overtaken the entire northeastern corner of Illinois, running north-south along 29mi. of the southwest Lake Michigan shorefront. The city sits at the center of a web of interstates, rail lines, and airplane routes; most cross-country traffic swings through the city. A good map is essential for navigating Chicago; pick up a free one at the tourist office or any CTA station.

Although flat and sprawling, the grids tend to make sense, and navigation is pretty straightforward, by car or ubiquitous public transportation. At the city's center is the **Loop,** Chicago's downtown and hub of the public transportation system. The numbering system begins from the intersection of State and Madison, with about 800 numbers per mile. The Loop is bounded by the Chicago River to the north and west, Lake Michigan to the east, and Roosevelt Rd. to the south. Directions in *Let's Go* are generally from downtown. South of the Loop, numbered east-west streets increase towards the south. Many ethnic neighborhoods lie in this area. LaSalle Dr. loosely defines the west edge of the **Near North** area. The **Gold Coast** shimmers on N. Lakeshore Dr. **Lincoln Park** revolves around the junction of Clark St., Lincoln Ave., and Halsted. Lincoln Park melts into **Wrigleyville,** near the 3000s of N. Clark and N. Halstead St., and then becomes **Lakeview,** in the 4000s. **Lake Shore Dr.,** a scenic pseudo-freeway hugging Lake Michigan (beware the 45mph speed limit), provides express north-south connections.

To avoid driving in the city, daytrippers can leave their cars in one of the suburban subway lots during the day ($1.75). There are a half-dozen such park-and-ride lots; call CTA (see below) for info. Parking downtown costs around $8-15 per day.

# ◧ GETTING AROUND

The **Chicago Transit Authority (CTA),** 350 N. Wells (836-7000 or 888-968-7282), 7th fl., runs trains, subways, and buses. The **elevated rapid transit train system,** called the **El,** encircles the Loop. Some downtown routes run underground, but are still referred to as the El. The El operates 24hr., but late-night service is infrequent and unsafe in many areas. Also, some buses do not run all night; call the CTA for schedules and routes. Extremely helpful CTA maps are available at many stations and the Water Tower Information Center. Don't step blindly onto a train; many are express trains, and different routes often run along the same tracks. Train and bus fare is $1.50; add 25¢ for express routes. Remember to get a transfer (30¢) from bus drivers or when you enter the El stop, which allows for up to 2 more rides on different routes during the following 2hr. Buy token rolls (10 tokens) at *some* stations, supermarkets, and at the "Checks Cashed" storefronts with the yellow sign; these places also carry $88 monthly passes. **Metra** offers a variety of consecutive-day passes for tourists: 1-day ($5), 2-day ($9), 3-day ($12), and 5-day ($18).

On Sat. from mid-June through mid-Oct., a **Loop Tour Train** departs on a free 40min. tour at 12:15, 12:55, 1:35, and 2:15pm (tickets must be picked up at the Chicago Office of Tourism; see **Practical Information,** below). **METRA,** 547 W. Jackson (836-7000), distributes free maps and schedules for an extensive commuter rail network, with 11 rail lines and 4 downtown stations (open M-F 8am-5pm; fare $2-6.60, depending on distance). **PACE** (836-7000) operates the suburban bus system. Numerous free or cheap shuttle services run throughout the loop, with brochures and schedules available just about everywhere.

## NEIGHBORHOODS

The center of the **Chinese** community lies 2mi. south of the Loop, at Cermak Rd. and Wentworth Ave. **New Chinatown,** north of the Loop at Argyle St., offers Chinese restaurants, but is mainly **Vietnamese.** The **German** community has scattered, but the beer halls, restaurants, and shops in the 3000s and 4000s of N. Lincoln Ave. remain. The former residents of **Greektown** have also moved, but S. Halsted St., just west of the Loop, houses authentic Greek restaurants. The area is bustling and safe until the restaurants close, at which point you should clear out. **Little Italy** fell prey to the **University of Illinois at Chicago (UIC),** but a shadow of the what once was remains along W. Taylor St., west of the UIC campus. **Jewish** and **Indian** enclaves center on Devon Ave., from Western Ave. to the Chicago River. The area near Midway Airport is home to much of Chicago's **Lithuanian** population. The Pilsen neighborhood, southwest of the loop, around 18th St., offers a slice of **Mexico.** Searches for **Polish** sausage link hungry travelers to N. Milwaukee Ave. between blocks 2800 and 3100; Chicago's Polish population rivals that of Warsaw. Andersonville, along Clark St. north of Foster Ave., is the historic center of the **Swedish** community, though immigrants from **Asia** and the **Middle East** have recently settled here.

## ◪ PRACTICAL INFORMATION

**Airports: O'Hare International** (773-686-2200), off I-90. 1,000,000 planes land and take off every 6.3 seconds. Well, maybe not that many, but it's a really big number. Depending on traffic, a trip between downtown and O'Hare can take up to 2hr. The blue line **Rapid Train** runs between the Airport El station and downtown (40min.-1hr., $1.50). **Midway Airport** (773-767-0500), on the western edge of the South Side, often offers less expensive flights. To get downtown, take the El orange line from the Midway stop. Lockers $1 per day. **Continental Air Transport** (454-7799 or 800-654-7871) connects both airports to downtown hotels from O'Hare baggage terminal (45min.-1hr., every 5-10min. 6am-11:30pm, $14.75) and Midway (30-45min., every 10-15min. 6am-10:30pm, $10.75).

GREAT LAKES

N

0 |——————| 300 yards
0 |——————| 300 meters

**Downtown Chicago**

ACCOMMODATIONS

A  Arlington House
   (HI-AYH, AAIH)
B  Days Inn Gold Coast
C  Chicago Int's Hostel
D  Eleanor Residence
E  Hotel Wacker
F  Motel 6
G  Cass Hotel
H  International House

North Ave.
Second City
TO **A**
TO **B** **C**
**D**

Division St.

Elm St.
Cedar St.
Bellevue Pl.

Oak St. Beach

Oak St.
Washington Square
Walton St.
Delaware Pl.
John Hancock Bldg. and Observatory
Pearson St.

N. Lake Shore Dr.

Larabee St.
Hudson Ave.
Sedgewick St.
Orleans St.
Franklin St.
Wells St.
Rush St.

Chicago Ave.
Huron St.
La Salle St.
Clark St.
Dearborn St.
State St.
Wabash Ave.
Michigan Ave.

Old Water Tower
Museum of Contemporary Art
**F**

Outer Harbor

Olive Park

Ontario St.
Ohio St.
Post Office Headquarters

Grand Ave.
Illinois St.

Ohio St.
Express-Ways
Children's Museum
Chicago Maritime Museum

Navy Pier

Merchandise Mart
Kinzie St.
**G**

E. North Water St.

Chicago River

Wacker Dr.

Lake St.
Wacker Dr.
State of Illinois Center
Chicago Theater
E. Lake St.

Franklin St.
Canal St.
Clinton St.

Randolph St.
City Hall
Daley Plaza
Washington St.

E. Randolph Dr.
**i** Visitors' Center

Lake Michigan

Madison St.

Grant Park

Monroe Harbor

Northwestern Station
Monroe St.

E. Monroe Dr.
Art Institute of Chicago
Goodman Theatre
Petrillo Music Shell

Sears Tower and Observ.
Adams St.
Board of Trade
E. Jackson Dr.

Union Station
Jackson Blvd.
Chicago Board of Options Exchange
Van Buren St.
Chicago Public Library
Congress Dr.
Buckingham Fountain

Chicago Harbor

Eisenhower Expressway
Congress Parkway
Columbia College
Harrison St.
E. Balbo Ave.
Spertus Museum of Judaica
E. Balbo Dr.

TO MAIN BUS STATION
W. Polk St.
E. 8th St.
9th St.
E. 11th St.

S. Wells St.
S. Lake Shore Dr.
Columbus Dr.

Roosevelt Rd.
E. 13th St.
Field Museum Of Natural History

John G. Shedd Aquarium

Canal St.
Clinton St.
S. Branch Chicago River
Clark St.
State St.
Wabash St.
Indiana Ave.

W. 14th St.  E. 14th St.

Adler Planetarium

Soldier Field

Burnham Park Harbor

TO **H**

**GREAT LAKES**

**Amtrak:** Union Station, 225 S. Canal (558-1075), at Adams St. west of the Loop. Take the El to State and Adams, then walk 7 blocks west on Adams. Milwaukee (1½hr., 5 per day, $19); Detroit (5hr., 3 per day, $20); and New York (18½hr., 2 per day, $81-148). Station open 6:15am-10pm; tickets sold daily 6am-9pm. Lockers $1 per day.

**Buses: Greyhound,** 630 W. Harrison St. (781-2900), at Jefferson and Desplaines Ave. Take the El to Linton. *The* hub of the central U.S. and home base for several smaller companies covering the Midwest. To: Detroit (6-7hr., 6 per day, $27); Milwaukee (2hr., 13 per day, $14); St. Louis (5-7hr., 9 per day, $30); and Indianapolis (3½-4½hr., 9 per day, $30). Station and ticket office open 24hr.

**Taxis: Yellow Cab,** 829-4222. **Flash Cab,** 773-561-1444.

**Car Rental: Dollar Rent-a-Car** (800-800-4000), at O'Hare and Midway. $26 per day, $170 per week; under 25 surcharge $15 per day. **Thrifty Car Rental** (800-367-2277), at O'Hare. $27 per day, $203 per week, $10 for liability insurance. Under 25 surcharge $25 per day. Unlimited mi. for both. Must be 21 with credit card.

**Visitor Info: Chicago Office of Tourism,** 78 E. Washington St. (744-2400 or 800-226-6632; www.ci.chi.il.us/Tourism). Open M-F 10am-6pm, Sa 10am-5pm, Su noon-5pm. In the same building is the **Chicago Cultural Center,** 77 E. Randolph St., at Michigan Ave. Open M-F 10am-6pm, Sa 10am-5pm, Su noon-5pm. **Chicago Visitor Information Center,** 811 Michigan Ave. (744-2400), in the Water Tower Pumping Station. Open M-F 9:30am-6pm, Sa 10am-6pm, Su 11am-6pm. On the lake, **Navy Pier Info Center,** 600 E. Grand (595-7437). Open Su-Th 10am-10pm, F-Sa 10am-noon.

**Hotlines: General Crisis Line,** 800-866-9600. **Rape Crisis Line,** 847-872-7799. **Gay and Lesbian Hotline/Anti-Violence Project,** 871-2273. All 24hr.

**Medical Services: Cook County Hospital,** 1835 W. Harrison (633-6000). Take the Congress A train to the Medical Center Stop. Open 24hr.

**Internet Access:** Free at the **Chicago Public Library.** One branch at 400 S. State St., at Congress. Open M 9am-7pm, Tu and Th 11am-7pm, W, F, and Sa 9am-5pm, Su 1-5pm.

**Post Office:** 433 W. Harrison St. (654-3895). Open 24hr. **ZIP code:** 60607. **Area code:** 312 or 773 (Chicago); 708, 630, or 847 (outside the city limits). In text, 312 unless otherwise noted.

# ◤ ACCOMMODATIONS

A cheap, convenient bed can be found at one of Chicago's hostels; the moderately priced motels on **Lincoln Ave** are accessible by car. Motel chains off the interstates, about 1hr. from downtown are inconvenient and expensive ($35 and up), but are an option for late-night arrivals. **Chicago Bed and Breakfast,** P.O. Box 14088, Chicago 60614 (951-0085), runs a referral service. Few B&Bs have parking, but the majority are near public transit. (2-night min. stay. Singles from $75; doubles from $85. Reservations required.) Chicago has a 15% tax on most accommodations.

**Arlington House (HI-AYH, AAIH),** 616 W. Arlington Pl. (773-929-5380 or 800-467-8355), off Clark St. just north of Fullerton. Owners ensure a comfortable stay in this enormous, well-located North side hostel. Rooms are tidy and breezy, though some dorm rooms are a touch cramped. Relatively safe, central neighborhood. Kitchen, common TV room, laundry facilities. $19.50, non-members $22; private doubles $40-46.

**Chicago International Hostel,** 6318 N. Winthrop St. (773-262-1011). Take the Howard St. northbound train to Loyola Station; walk 3 blocks south on Sheridan Rd. to Winthrop, and a ½-block south. Slightly bland but sunny and clean rooms, with 4-6 beds, near Loyola University. A fairly safe location close to the lake, beaches, and many fast food joints. Free parking. Kitchen and laundry access. $13, double with bath $35-40. Lockers $1. Key deposit $5. Lockout 10am-4pm. Check-in 7-10am and 4pm-midnight.

**International House,** 1414 E. 59th St. (773-753-2270), Hyde Park, off Lake Shore Dr. Take the Illinois Central Railroad from the Michigan Ave. station (20min.) to 59th St. and walk a half-block west. Part of the University of Chicago; *don't wander off campus* *at night.* Clean, spacious singles with shared bath filled mostly by permanent residents. $36. Kitchen and laundry. Linen provided. Reservations required.

**Eleanor Residence,** 1550 N. Dearborn Pkwy. (664-8245). *Women over 18 only.* Fantastic location near Lincoln Park and the Gold Coast. Majestic common room and lobby, clean rooms. Singles $60, $280 for 2 weeks, breakfast and dinner included. Reserve at least 1 day in advance; 1-night deposit required.

**Cass Hotel,** 640 N. Wabash Ave. (787-4030), just north of the Loop. Take subway to State or Grand St. Convenient location. Clean rooms with wood trim and A/C. Coffee shop and lounge. No parking. Laundry room. Singles $69. Key deposit $5. Reservations recommended. Wheelchair access.

**Motel 6,** 162 E. Ontario St. (787-3580), 1 block east of the Magnificent Mile (Michigan Ave.). Immaculate rooms with cable, A/C, and free local calls. No parking. Singles $85; doubles $91. Reservations recommended. Wheelchair access.

**Hotel Wacker,** 111 W. Huron St. (787-1386), at N. Clark St. Insert your own joke. A green sign on the corner makes this place easy to find. Slightly musty but perfectly acceptable rooms. Convenient to downtown. TV, A/C, phone. Singles $40, doubles $50; $250 per week. Key and linen deposit $5. Check-in 24hr. Wheelchair access.

**Days Inn Gold Coast,** 1816 N. Clark St.(664-3040), bordering Lincoln Park. The small but clean rooms have great views, as well as A/C and kitchenettes in some. Doubles $99, F-Sa $139. Wheelchair access.

# ⏲ FOOD

One of the best guides to city dining is the monthly *Chicago* magazine, which includes an extensive restaurant section, cross-indexed by price, cuisine, and quality. It can usually be picked up at tourist offices.

**PIZZA.** Chicago's pizza is known 'round the world, either standard-style, with the cheese on top, or stuffed, with "toppings" in the middle.

**Pizzeria Uno,** 29 E. Ohio St. (321-1000), and younger sister **Due,** 619 N. Wabash Ave. (943-2400). It may look like any other Uno's, but this is where the delicious legacy of deep-dish began. Pizza, pasta, or bust. Lines are long, and pizza takes 45min. to prepare. Same short menu at Due (right up the street), with a terrace and more room than Uno's. Pizzas $5-18. Uno open M-F 11:30am-1am, Sa 11:30am-2am, Su 11:30am-11:30pm. Due open Su-Th 11am-1:30am, F-Sa 11am-2am.

**Gino's East,** Downtown, St. Clair and Superior (988-4200). Bring a marker to claim history on the heavily decorated walls. Legendary pizza at more reasonable prices. Open daily 11am-11pm.

**SOUL FOOD 'ROUND THE LOOP.** The area of the Loop between Jackson and Roosevelt St. is the South Loop, home to good, cheap soul food, like ribs, fried chicken, and greens.

**Heaven on Seven,** 111 N. Wabash Ave. (263-6443), 7th fl. of the Garland Bldg. The mantlepiece painted with vegetables, alligators, and crabs means you're getting closer to Cajun nirvana. The line is long, but hell, the gumbo is great ($9-11). Open M-F 8:30am-5pm, Sa 10am-3pm. A more upscale location in the Near North, at 600 N. Michigan (280-7774), serves lunch and dinner.

**The Berghoff,** 17 W. Adams St. (427-3170). Dim, cavernous German restaurant filled with lunching traders. Bratwurst $5.75, stein of Berghoff's own beer $2.75. Open M-Th 11am-9pm, F 11am-9:30pm, Sa 11am-10pm.

**Russian Tea Time,** 77 E. Adams St. (360-0000), across from the Art Institute, serves Russian delicacies from borscht to stroganoff in the heart of downtown Chicago. Bottomless cup of tea $1.85. Lunch entrees $8-12. Open M 11am-9pm, Tu-Th 11am-11pm, F-Sa 11am-midnight, Su 11am-9pm.

**Billy Goat's Tavern,** 430 N. Michigan (222-1525), underground on lower Michigan Ave. Descend through what looks like a subway entrance in front of the Tribune building. The gruff service was the inspiration for the legendary *Saturday Night Live* "Cheezborger, cheezborger—no Coke, Pepsi" skit. Cheezborgers $2.50. "Butt in anytime" M-F 7am-2am, Sa 10am-3am, Su 11am-2am.

**CHINATOWN.** Chinatown is lined with restaurants. Take the Red Line to Cermak/Chinatown to get here, *but don't go too far south of Cermak St. after dark.*

**Hong Min,** 221 W. Cermak Rd. (842-5026). Spartan decor, Epicurean dining. Sweet-and-sour fish $8. Open Su-Th 10am-2am, F-Sa 10am-3am.

**Three Happiness,** 209 W. Cermak Rd. (842-1964). The smaller of 2 locations, this site receives constant local acclaim. Chicken entrees around $7. Open daily 9-2am.

**LITTLE ITALY.** What is left of Little Italy can be reached by taking the El to UIC, then walking west on Taylor St. or taking bus #37 down Taylor St.

**Al's Italian Beef,** 1079 W. Taylor St. (226-4017), at Aberdeen near Little Italy; also at 169 W. Ontario. Churns out top-notch reddish Italian beef with lots of spices at a formica counter. Italian beef sandwich $3.55. Great fries $1.25. Open daily 9am-1am.

**The Rosebud,** 1500 W. Taylor St. (942-1117). Small, classy restaurant serving huge portions of pasta. Lunch specials $9-14 (Chicken Vesuvio $9), dinner from $11. Valet parking $4, reservations recommended. Open for lunch M-Th 11am-10:30pm, F 11am-11:30pm, Sa 5-11:30pm.

**Mario's Italian Lemonade,** 1074 W. Taylor St., across from Al's. A classic neighborhood stand that churns out sensational Italian ices ($1-4.75) in flavors from cantaloupe to cherry. Open daily mid-May to mid-Sept. 10am-midnight.

## GREEKTOWN

**The Parthenon,** 314 S. Halsted St. (726-2407). The golden ratio ain't in the architecture, but the staff converses in Greek, the murals transport you to the Mediterranean, and the food wins top awards. The Greek Feast family-style dinner ($14) includes everything from *saganaki* (flaming goat cheese) to *baklava* (glazed pastry). Open daily 11am-1am.

**Greek Islands,** 200 S. Halsted St. (782-9855). The tan awning points the way to magnificent food. No reservations; expect a 30-45min. wait Sa-Su. Daily special $7-8. Open Su-Th 11am-midnight, F-Sa 11am-1am.

**Rodity's,** 222 S. Halsted St. (454-0800). Slightly cheaper fare than the other Greektown options (daily specials under $9). Open Su-Th 11am-midnight, F-Sa 11am-1am.

## NORTH SIDE/LINCOLN PARK

**Potbelly's,** 2264 N. Lincoln Ave. (773-528-1405). Could be named for the stoves scattered around the deli or for your stomach when you leave. 50s-style decor and music. Subs $3.50. Open daily 11am-11pm. Call for additional locations.

**Kopi, A Traveller's Café,** 5317 N. Clark St. (773-989-5674). A 10min. walk from the Berwyn El, 4 blocks west on Berwyn. *Kopi* is Indonesian for "coffee." Peruse travel guides over java, or just sit back and appreciate the art. Espresso $1.35. On M and Th nights, the cafe blends coffee and music (no cover). Open M-Th 8am-11pm, F 8am-midnight, Sa 9am-midnight, Su 10am-11pm.

**Café Ba-Ba-Reeba!,** 2024 N. Halsted St. (935-5000). Well-marked by the colorful, glowing facade. Tapas and hearty Spanish cuisine with subtle spices like the *paella valenciana* ($10). People-watching on the outdoor terrace. Open M-Th 11:30am-10:30pm, F-Sa 11:30am-midnight, Su noon-10pm. Su brunch tapas noon-3pm.

**The Bourgeois Pig,** 738 Fullerton Ave. (773-883-5282). Quiet, soothing coffee shop with faux marble tables, board games, and vegetarian specialties to boot. Newly augmented dessert menu. Cappuccino $1.75, scones $1.50. Open M-Th 6:30am-11pm, F 6:30am-midnight, Sa 8am-midnight, Su 9am-11pm.

## HYDE PARK

**Pizza Capri,** 1501 E. 3rd St. (773-324-7777). Casual pizza and pasta dining. Pizzas from $8, sandwiches from $6. Open M-F 11am-11pm, Sa-Su 11am-midnight.

**Calypso Cafe,** 5211 S. Harper (773-955-0229). Friendly, island-style restaurant. Jerk chicken sandwich with pineapple $7. Open Su-Th 11am-10pm, F-Sa 11am-11pm.

# ◉ SIGHTS

Chicago's sights range from well-publicized museums to undiscovered back streets, from beaches and parks to towering skyscrapers. The tourist brochures, bus tours, and downtown area reveal only a fraction of Chicago. As a famous art historian once said, "no one will learn the city of Chicago without using their feet."

## MUSEUMS

Chicago's major museums admit visitors free at least 1 day per week. The first 5 listings, the Big Five, provide a diverse array of exhibits, while a handful of smaller collections target specific interests. Lake Shore Drive has been diverted around Grant Park, linking the Field Museum, Adler, and Shedd; the compound, known as Museum Campus, offers a free shuttle between museums.

**The Art Institute of Chicago,** 111 S. Michigan Ave. (443-3600), at Adams St. in Grant Park. The city's premier art museum. 4 millennia of art from Asia, Africa, Europe, and beyond. The Institute's Impressionist and Post-Impressionist collections have won international acclaim. Highlight tour daily 2pm. Free jazz in the courtyard Tu after 4:30pm. Open M and W-F 10:30am-4:30pm, Tu 10:30am-8pm, Sa 10am-5pm, Su and holidays noon-5pm. $7, students, seniors, and children $5; in summer free on Tu.

**Museum of Science and Industry,** 5700 S. Lake Shore Dr. (773-684-1414), in Hyde Park; take bus #6 "Jeffrey Express" to 57th St. Housed in the only building left from the 1893 World's Columbian Exposition, the expansive and impressive Museum includes the *Apollo 8* command module, a full-sized replica of a coal mine, and Omnimax shows. Call for schedule. Open daily 9:30am-5:30pm. $7, seniors $6, ages 3-11 $3.50; with Omnimax $12/$10/$7.50; free on Th (except Omnimax).

**Field Museum of Natural History,** 1200 S. Lake Shore Dr. (922-9410), at Roosevelt Rd. in Grant Park; take bus #146 from State St. Geological, anthropological, botanical, and zoological exhibits, Includes Egyptian mummies, Native American halls, a dirt exhibit, and Sue, the largest T-rex skeleton ever found. Open daily 9am-5pm. $7, students, seniors, and ages 3-17 $4; free on W.

**The Adler Planetarium,** 1300 S. Lake Shore Dr. (922-7827), in Grant Park. Lets you discover your weight on Mars, read the news from space, and examine astronomy tools. Open June-Aug. Sa-W 9am-6pm, Th-F 9am-9pm; Sept.-May M-F 9am-5pm, Sa-Su 9am-6pm. $3, seniors and ages 4-17 $2; free on Tu. Skyshow daily on the hr. $3.

**Shedd Aquarium,** 1200 S. Lake Shore Dr. (939-2438), in Grant Park. The world's largest indoor aquarium has over 6600 species of fish in 206 tanks. The Oceanarium features small whales, dolphins, seals, and other marine mammals. Exquisite Pacific Ocean exhibit, complete with simulated crashing waves. Parking available. Open daily 9am-5pm. Feedings M-F 11am, 2, and 3pm. Combined admission to Oceanarium and Aquarium $10, seniors and ages 3-11 $8; Th Aquarium free, Oceanarium $6, seniors and ages 5-17 $5. Tour of Oceanarium $3.

**The Museum of Contemporary Art,** 220 E. Chicago Ave. (280-2660); #66 (Chicago Ave.) bus. The MCA has both permanent and temporary collections of modern art. Warhol, Javer, and Nauman highlight a vibrant list of artists. Open Tu 10am-8pm, W-Su 10am-5pm. $7, students and seniors $4.50, under 12 free; free Tu.

**Chicago Historical Society,** 1601 N. Clark St. (642-4600), at North Ave. A research center for scholars with an excellent interactive museum open to the public. Permanent exhibit on America in the age of Lincoln, plus changing exhibits. Open M-Sa 9:30am-4:30pm, Su noon-5pm. $5, students and seniors $3, ages 6-12 $1; free on M.

**Spertus Institute of Jewish Studies,** 618 S. Michigan Ave. (322-1747), downtown. A fabulous collection of synagogue relics rests on the 1st fl., as does the diminutive but moving Holocaust Memorial. Upstairs, check out historical anecdotes from the Middle Ages through the 1960s. Open Su-W 10am-5pm, Th 10am-8pm, F 10am-3pm. Artifact center open Su-Th 1-4:30pm. $5, students and seniors $3; free on F.

**Terra Museum of American Art,** 666 N. Michigan Ave. (664-3939), at Erie St. From colonial times to the present, focusing on 19th-century Impressionism. Open Tu 10am-8pm, W-Sa 10am-6pm, Su noon-5pm. $5, seniors $2.50, students and teachers with ID and under 14 free; free on Tu. Free tours Tu-F noon and 6pm, Sa-Su noon and 2pm.

**Museum of Broadcast Communications,** 78 E. Washington St. (629-6000), at Michigan. Upstairs from the Cultural Center. Celebrates couch-potato culture with exhibits on America's pastime—TV. Open M-Sa 10am-4:30pm, Su noon-5pm. Free.

**THE LOOP.** When Mrs. O'Leary's cow kicked over a lantern and started the **Great Fire of 1871,** Chicago's downtown flamed into a pile of ashes. The city rebuilt with a vengeance, turning the functional into the fabulous and creating one of the most concentrated clusters of architectural treasures in the world.

The downtown area, hemmed in by the Chicago River and Lake Michigan, rose up rather than out. Visitors can explore this street museum via **walking tours,** organized by the **Chicago Architectural Foundation.** The 2hr. tours, one of early skyscrapers and another of modern architecture, start from the foundation's bookstore/gift shop. Highlights include Louis Sullivan's arch, the Chicago window, and Mies van der Rohe's revolutionary skyscrapers. *(224 S. Michigan Ave. 922-8687. $10 for 1 tour, $15 for both.)* The foundation also provides a 1½hr. Chicago boat tour from the **Wendella pier** at Michigan Ave. *(Tours M-Sa 9am-8pm; Su 9am-6pm. $18. Book in advance.)*

The frantic trading of Midwestern farm goods can be experienced at the world's oldest and largest commodity exchange, the **Futures Exchange,** or at the **Chicago Board of Options Exchange,** both located in **The Board of Trade Building.** Ceres, the grain goddess, towers 609 ft. above street level there. For tours, contact the **visitors' office,** 5th fl. *(141 W. Jackson Blvd. 435-3590. Tours M-F 9:15am, every 30min. 10am-12:30pm; open M-F 8am-2pm. Free.)* See the yen pit at the third exchange, the **Chicago Mercantile Exchange,** which accounts for the green, yellow, and red jackets of the Loop at lunchtime. *(30 S. Wacker Blvd., at Madison. 930-8249)*

In the late 19th century, Sears and Roebuck, along with competitor Montgomery Ward, created the mail-order catalog business, undercutting many small stores and permanently altering the face of American merchandising. Although the catalog business has faded, the **Sears Tower** remains; more than an office building at 1707 ft., it is the second tallest building in the world, and stands as a monument to the insatiable lust of the American consumer. *(233 S. Wacker Dr. 875-9696. Open daily 9am-11pm; Oct.-Feb. 9am-10pm. $8.50, seniors $6.50, children $5.50, families $20. Lines are long.)* The **First National Bank Building and Plaza** sits about 2 blocks northeast at the corner of Clark and Monroe St. The world's largest bank building leads your gaze skyward with its diagonal slope. Marc Chagall's vivid mosaic, *The Four Seasons,* lines the block and sets off a public space often used for concerts and lunchtime entertainment. At the corner of Clark and Washington St., 2 blocks north, **Chicago Temple,** the world's tallest church, sends its babelesque steeples heavenward.

State and Madison St., the most famous intersection of "State St. that great street," forms the focal point of the Chicago street grid. Louis Sullivan's **Carson Pirie Scott** store building is adorned with exquisite ironwork and the famous extra-large Chicago window. Sullivan's other masterpiece, the **Auditorium Building,** sits several blocks south at the corner of Congress and Michigan St. Beautiful design and flawless acoustics highlight this Chicago landmark. Burnham and Koot's **Monadnock Building** deserves a glance for its rhythmically projecting bays of purple and brown rock. *(53 W. Jackson.)* Southeast, the **Sony Fine Arts Theatre** screens current artistic and foreign films in the grandeur of the **Fine Arts Building.** *(418 S. Michigan Ave. 939-2119. Open M-Th. $8.25; students $6; seniors, children, or matinee $5.)*

Tomorrow's master artists get their start today at **Gallery 37,** on State St. between Randolph and Washington. This open-air gallery, staffed by aspiring artists from city schools, offers visitors free tours by reservation, art exhibitions, and live performances during the summer. *(744-8925. Open in summer M-F 10am-4pm.)*

Chicago is decorated with one of the country's premier collections of outdoor sculpture. Large, abstract designs punctuate many downtown corners. The Picasso at the foot of the **Daley Center Plaza,** at Washington and Dearborn St., is the most famous. *(443-3054).* Free concerts play at noon on summer weekdays in the plaza. Across the street rests Joan Miró's *Chicago*, the sculptor's gift to the city. A great sculpture sits across the way in front of the **State of Illinois Building.** The building is a postmodern version of the town square designed by Helmut Jahn in 1985; the elevator to the top gives a thrilling (and free) view of the sloping atrium, the circular floors, and the hundreds of employees at work. In 1988, the city held a contest to design a building in honor of the late mayor. The result is the $144 million **Harold Washington Library Center,** a researcher's dream and an architectural delight. *(400 S. State St. 747-4300. Tours M-Sa noon and 2pm, Su 2pm. Open M 9am-7pm; Tu and Th 11am-7pm; W, F, Sa 9am-5pm, Su 1-5pm.)*

**NEAR NORTH.** The city's ritziest district lies north of the Loop along the lake, just past the Michigan Ave. Bridge. An international design competition in the 1920s resulted in the **Tribune Tower,** a Gothic skyscraper which overlooks this stretch. Chicago's largest newspaper, *The Chicago Tribune*, is produced here. *(435 N. Michigan Ave.)* Over 8mi. of corridors fill the **Merchandise Mart;** the entrance is on N. Wells or Kinzie, north of the river. The largest commercial building in the world (25 stories high and 2 blocks long), it even has its own zip code. The first 2 floors compose a public mall; the remainder contains showrooms where design professionals converge to choose home and office furnishings. **Tours at the Mart** guide you through the building at noon M to F. *(#114. 1½hr.; $10, seniors and students over 15 $9.)*

Big, bright, and always festive, Chicago's **Navy Pier** captures the carnival spirit 365 days a year. No small jetty, the mile-long pier has it all: a concert pavilion, dining options, nightspots, sight-seeing boats, a spectacular ferris wheel, a crystal garden with palm trees, and an Omnimax theater. Now *that's* America. Rent **bicycles** to navigate the Windy City's streets. *(Bike rental open daily June-Sept. 8am-11pm; May 8am-8pm; Apr. and Oct. 10am-7pm. $8.50 per hr., $34 per day.)*

Chicago's showy **Magnificent Mile,** a row of glitzy shops along N. Michigan Ave. between Grand Ave. and Division St., can magnificently drain the wallet. Several of these retail stores, including **Banana Republic** and **Crate & Barrel,** were designed by the country's foremost architects. The **Chicago Water Tower** and **Pumping Station** hide among the ritzy stores at the corner of Michigan and Pearson Ave. Built in 1867, these 2 structures survived the Great Chicago Fire. The pumping station houses the multimedia show *Here's Chicago* and a tourist center (see **Practical Information,** above). Across the street, expensive and trendy stores pack **Water Tower Place,** the first urban shopping mall in the U.S.

The bells of **St. Michael's Church** ring in **Old Town** (take bus #151 to Lincoln Park and walk south down Clark or Wells St.), a neighborhood where eclectic galleries, shops, and nightspots crowd gentrified streets. Architecture buffs will enjoy a stroll through the W. Menomonee and W. Eugenie St. area. In early June, the **Old Town Art Fair** attracts artists and craftsmen from across the country.

**NORTH SIDE.** Urban renewal has made **Lincoln Park,** a neighborhood just west of the park that bears the same name, a popular choice for wealthy residents. Bounded by Armitage to the south and Diversey Ave. to the north, lakeside Lincoln Park offers beautiful harbors and parks. Cafes, bookstores, and nightlife pack its tree-lined streets; some of Chicago's liveliest clubs and restaurants lie in the area around Clark St., Lincoln Ave., and N. Halsted St.

North of Diversey Ave., the streets of Lincoln Park become increasingly diverse. Supermarket shopping plazas alternate with tiny markets and vintage clothing stores, while apartment towers and hotels spring up between aging 2-story houses. In this ethnic potpourri, Polish diners share blocks with Korean restaurants, and Mongolian eateries stare at Mexican bars.

Although they finally lost their battle against night baseball in 1988, **Wrigleyville** residents remain fiercely loyal to the **Chicago Cubs.** Tiny, ivy-covered **Wrigley Field,** just east of Graceland, at the corner of Clark, is the North Side's most famous institution. A pilgrimage here is a must for the serious or curious baseball fan, and for *Blues Brothers* nuts who want to visit the famous pair's falsified address. *(See Sports, p. 505. 1060 W. Addison.)* Along Clark St.—one of the city's busiest nightlife districts—restaurants, sports bars, and music clubs abound. Window shopping beckons in the funk, junk, and 70s revival stores. **Wrigleyville** and **Lakeview,** around the 3000s and 4000s of N. Clark St. and N. Halsted, is the self-proclaimed "gay capital of Chicago." Partake of midwest bowling tradition at **Waveland Bowl,** off Addison. *(3700 N. Western. 773-472-5902. Single games $2-3.50. Open 24hr., year-round.)*

**NEAR WEST SIDE.** The Near West Side, bounded by the Chicago River to the east and Ogden Ave. to the west, assembles a veritable cornucopia of ethnic enclaves. Farther out, however, looms the West Side, a section of the city in severe economic straits—*be careful*. **Greektown,** several blocks of authentic restaurants north of the Eisenhower on Halsted, draws acclaim from all over the city.

A few blocks down Halsted (take the #8 "Halsted" bus), Jane Addams devoted her life to historic **Hull House.** This settlement house bears witness to Chicago's role in turn-of-the-century reform movements. Although the house no longer offers social services, it's been painstakenly restored into a museum. *(800 S. Halsted St. 413-5353. Open M-F 10am-4pm, Su noon-5pm. Free.)* The **Ukrainian Village,** at Chicago Ave. and Western Ave., is no longer occupied by ethnic Ukrainians, but you can still take in some culture at the **Ukrainian National Museum.** *(721 N. Oakland Ave. 421-8020. Open Th-Su 11am-4pm. $2, students $1.)*

**HYDE PARK AND THE UNIVERSITY OF CHICAGO.** 7mi. south of the Loop along the lake, the beautiful campus of the **University of Chicago** dominates the **Hyde Park** neighborhood; take the METRA South Shore Line. *(702-9192.)* A former retreat for the city's artists and musicians, the park's community underwent urban renewal in the 50s and now provides an island of intellectualism in a sea of degenerating neighborhoods. University police patrol the area bounded by 51st St. to the north, Lakeshore Dr. to the east, 61st St. to the south, and Cottage Grove to the west, but don't test the edges of these boundaries. Lakeside Burnham Park, east of campus, is fairly safe during the day but not at night.

On campus, Frank Lloyd Wright's famous **Robie House** blends into the surrounding trees. A seminal example of Wright's Prairie style, which sought to integrate house with environment, its low horizontal lines now hold university offices. *(5757 S. Woodlawn, at the corner of 58th St. 708-848-1976. Tours M-F 11am-3pm, Sa-Su 11am-3:30pm. $8, over 64 and ages 7-18 $6.)* The **Oriental Institute, Museum of Science and Industry** (see **Museums,** p. 499), and **DuSable Museum of African-American History** are all in, or border on, Hyde Park. From the Loop, take bus #6 "Jefferson Express" or the METRA Electric Line from the Randolph St. Station south to 59th St.

**OAK PARK.** Oak Park sprouts 10mi. west of downtown on the Eisenhower Expwy. *(I-290W to Harlem St.)* Frank Lloyd Wright endowed the community with 25 of his spectacular homes and buildings; the **Frank Lloyd Wright House and Studio** was his workplace. *(951 Chicago Ave. 45min. tours of the house M-F 11am, 1 and 3pm, Sa-Su every 15min. 11am-4pm. 1hr. self-guided tours of Wright's other Oak Park homes can be taken with a map and audio cassette available daily 10am-3pm. Guided tours Sa-Su 10:30am, noon, and 2pm. All 3 types of tours $8, seniors and under 18 $6; combination interior/exterior tour tickets $14/$10. Open daily 10am-5pm.)* The **visitors center** offers maps, guidebooks, and tours. *(158 Forest Ave. 708-848-1500 or 888-625-7275. Green Line to Harlem.)*

**◪ OUTDOORS.** A string of lakefront parks fringe the area between Chicago proper and Lake Michigan. On sunny afternoons, a cavalcade of sunbathers, dog walkers, in-line skaters, and skateboarders storm the shore. The 2 major parks, close to downtown, are **Lincoln** and **Grant. Lincoln Park** extends across 5mi. of lakefront on the north side, and rolls in the style of a 19th-century English park: winding paths, natural groves of trees, and asymmetrical open spaces. The **Lincoln Park Zoo** is a decent spot for a stroll. *(Open daily 9am-5pm, in summer Sa-Su until 7pm. Free.)* Next door, the **Lincoln Park Conservatory** encloses fauna from desert to jungle ecosystems under its glass palace. *(742-7736. Open daily 9am-5pm. Free.)*

    **Grant Park,** covering 14 lakefront blocks east of Michigan Ave., follows the 19th-century French park style: symmetrical and ordered, with corners, a fountain in the center, and wide promenades. The Grant Park Concert Society hosts free summer concerts here in the **Petrillo Music Shell.** *(520 S. Michigan Ave. 742-4763.)* Colored lights illuminate Buckingham Fountain from 9-11pm. The **Field Museum of Natural History, Shedd Aquarium,** and **Adler Planetarium** occupy the southern end of the park, while the **Art Institute** lies to the northwest (see **Museums**, p. 499).

    On the north side, Lake Michigan lures swimmers to **Lincoln Park Beach** and **Oak St. Beach.** Popular swimming spots, both attract sun worshippers as well. The rock ledges are restricted areas, and swimming from them is illegal. Although the beaches are patrolled 9am to 9:30pm, they are unsafe after dark. The **Chicago Parks District** has further info. *(747-2200).*

**FARTHER OUT.** In 1885, George Pullman, inventor of the sleeping car, attempted to create a model working environment so that his Palace Car Company employees would be "healthier, happier, and more productive." The result of this quest was the town of **Pullman,** 14mi. southeast of downtown. It was considered the nation's ideal community until 1894, when a stubborn Pullman evicted fired workers from their homes. The community soon after held a monumental strike. In the center of town, the **Hotel Florence** houses a museum and conducts tours. *(11111 S. Forrestville Ave. 773-785-8181. I-94W to 111th St. Illinois Central Gulf Railroad to 111th St. and Pullman or METRA Rock Island Line to 111th St. Tours leave the hotel on the 1st Su of each month May-Oct. at 12:30 and 1pm. $4, students and seniors $3.50.)*

    **Lake Shore Dr.** is an absolutely gorgeous drive on a sunny day. Starting from the Hyde Park area in the south, the road offers sparkling views of Lake Michigan all the way past the city. At its end, Lake Shore becomes Sheridan Rd., which twists and turns its way through the picturesque northern suburbs. Just to the north of Chicago is **Evanston,** a happening, affluent college town with an array of parks and nightclubs. 10min. farther north is upscale **Wilmette,** home to the ornate and striking **Baha'i House of Worship,** at Sheridan Rd. The intricate structure is topped by a stunning 9-sided dome. *(100 Linden Ave. 847-853-2300. Open daily 10am-10pm; Oct.-May 10am-5pm. Services M-Sa 12:15pm, Su 1:15pm.)* The **Chicago Botanic Garden,** on Lake Cook Rd. ½mi. east of Edens Expwy., pampers vegetation. *(847-835-5440. Open daily 8am-sunset. Parking $5 per car, $10 per van, $30 per RV; Sa-Su and holidays $6/$15/$35; includes admission.)* A day riding the coasters at **Six Flags Great America,** I-94 at Rt. 132 E, Gurnee, the largest amusement park in the Midwest, will wear you out. *(847-249-1776. Open in summer and winter daily 10am-10pm; in spring and fall. Sa-Su 10am-10pm. $34, over 59 $17, ages 4-10 $29; 2-day pass, not necessarily consecutive, $42.)*

    **Steamboat gambling** has been embraced by the Midwest as a way to avoid anti-betting laws. The action centers in Joliet. Roll the bones on **Empress River Cruises,** Rt. 6 off I-55 and I-80. *(2300 Empress Dr. 708-345-6789. 2 per day. Free.)* You and 99 friends can try your luck with **Harrah's Casino Cruises.** *(800-427-7247.)*

## ◪ ENTERTAINMENT

The weeklies *Chicago Reader* and *New City*, available in many bars, record stores, and restaurants list events. The *Reader* reviews all major shows, with times and ticket prices. *Chicago* magazine has exhaustive club, music, dance, and opera listings, and theater reviews. *The Chicago Tribune* includes an entertainment section F. *Gay Chicago* provides info on social activities and other news for the area's gay community.

**GREAT LAKES**

**THEATER.** Home to improv comedy and one of the foremost theater centers of North America, more than 150 theaters show everything from blockbuster musicals to off-color parodies. Downtown theaters cluster around the intersection of Diversey, Belmont, and Halsted St. (just north of the Loop), and around Michigan Ave. and Madison Ave. Smaller, community-based theaters are scattered throughout the city. The "Off-Loop" theaters on the North Side specialize in original drama, with tickets usually under $18.

Most tickets are expensive. Half-price tickets are sold on the day of performance at **Hot Tix Booths,** 108 N. State St., or at the 6th level of 700 N. Michigan Ave. Purchases must be made in person. Lines form 15-20min. before the booth opens. (977-1755. Open M-F 10am-7pm, Sa 10am-6pm, Su noon-5pm.) **Ticketmaster** supplies tickets for many theaters; ask about senior, student, and child discounts at all Chicago shows (559-1212).

**Steppenwolf Theater,** 1650 N. Halsted St. (335-1888), where Gary Sinise and the eerie John Malkovich got their start. Tickets $32 Su-Th, $37 F-Sa; ½-price after 5pm Tu-F, after noon Sa-Su. Office open Su-M 11am-5pm, Tu-F 11am-8pm, Sa 11am-9pm.

**Goodman Theatre,** 200 S. Columbus Dr. (443-3800), presents consistently good original works. Tickets around $18-40; ½-price after 6pm, or after noon for matinee. Box office open 10am-5pm, 10am-8pm show nights, usually Sa-Su.

**Shubert Theater,** 22 W. Monroe St. (902-1500), presents big-name Broadway touring productions. Ticket $15-70. Box office open M-Sa 10am-6pm.

**Victory Gardens Theater,** 2257 N. Lincoln Ave. (773-871-3000). Drama by Chicago playwrights. Tickets $23-28. Box office open M-Sa noon-6pm, Su noon-3pm.

**Center Theatre,** 1346 W. Devon Ave. (773-508-5422). Solid, mainstream work. Ticket prices vary by show ($16-22). Box office open 10am-4pm and 2hr. before the show.

**Annoyance Theatre,** 3747 N. Clark (773-929-6200). Original works that play off pop culture. 7 different shows per week. Often participatory comedy. Tickets ($5-10) sold just before showtime, which is usually 8 or 9pm.

**Bailiwick Repertory,** 1225 W. Belmont Ave. (773-327-5252), in the Theatre building. A mainstage and experimental studio space. Tickets from $10. Box office open W noon-6pm, Th-Su noon until showtime.

**Live Bait Theatre,** 3914 N. Clark St. (773-871-1212). Shows with titles like *Food, Fun, & Dead Relatives* and *Mass Murder II*. Launched a multi-play *Tribute to Jackie* (Onassis, that is). Tickets $20, Th $10. Box office open M-F noon-5pm.

**COMEDY.** Chicago boasts a plethora of comedy clubs. The most famous, **Second City,** 1616 N. Wells St. spoofs Chicago life and politics. Second City graduated Bill Murray and late greats John Candy, John Belushi, and Gilda Radner, among others. Most nights, a free improv session follows the show (337-3992). **Second City e.t.c.** offers yet more comedy next door at 1608 N. Wells. (642-8189. Shows for both M-Th 8:30pm, F-Sa 8 and 11pm, Su 8pm. Tickets $12-16, M $6. Box office hrs. daily 10:30am-10pm. Reservations recommended; during the week you can often get in if you show up 1hr. early.) Watch improv actors compete to bust your gut at **Comedy Sportz,** 3209 N. Halsted (773-549-8080; shows F-Sa 8-10:30pm).

**DANCE, CLASSICAL MUSIC, AND OPERA.** Chicago philanthropists built the high-priced, high-art performance center of this metropolis. Ballet, comedy, live theater, and musicals are performed at **Auditorium Theater,** 50 E. Congress Pkwy. (922-2110). From Oct. to May, the **Chicago Symphony Orchestra,** conducted by Daniel Barenboim, resonates at **Orchestra Hall,** 220 S. Michigan Ave. (294-3000). **Ballet Chicago** pirouettes in theaters throughout Chicago (251-8838; tickets $12-45). The **Lyric Opera of Chicago** performs from Sept. to Mar. at the **Civic Opera House,** 20 N. Wacker Dr. (332-2244). While these places may suck your wallet dry, the **Grant Park Music Festival** affords a taste of the classical for free; from mid-June through late Aug., the acclaimed Grant Park Symphony Orchestra plays a few free evening concerts per week at the Grant Park Petrillo Music Shell (usually W-Su; schedule varies; call 819-0614 for details).

**SEASONAL EVENTS.** The city celebrates summer on a grand scale. The **Taste of Chicago** festival cooks for 8 days through July 4th. 70 restaurants set up booths with endless samples in Grant Park, while crowds chomp to the blast of big name bands (free entry, food tickets 50¢ each). The first week in June, the **Blues Festival** celebrates the city's soulful, gritty music; the **Chicago Gospel Festival** hums and hollers in mid-June; and Nashville moves north for the **Country Music Festival** at the end of June. The **¡Viva Chicago!** Latin music festival swings in late Aug., while the **Chicago Jazz Festival** scats Labor Day weekend. All festivals center at the Grant Park Petrillo Music Shell. The Mayor's Office Special Events Hotline (744-3370 or 800-487-2446) has more info on all 6 free events.

Chicago also offers several free summer festivals on the lake shore, including the **Air and Water Show** in late Aug., when Lake Shore Park, Lake Shore Dr., and Chicago Ave. witness several days of boat races, parades, hang gliding, and stunt flying, as well as aerial acrobatics by the fabulously precise Blue Angels. In mid-July, the **Chicago to Mackinac Island Yacht Race** begins in the Monroe St. harbor. On summer Sa, Navy Pier has a free fireworks show (595-7437 for times).

The regionally famous **Ravinia Festival** in the northern suburb of Highland Park, runs from late June to early Sept. (847-266-5100). The Chicago Symphony Orchestra, ballet troupes, folk and jazz musicians, and comedians perform throughout the festival's 14-week season. (Shows M-Sa 8pm, Su 7pm. Lawn seats $8; other tickets $15-35.) On certain nights, the **Chicago Symphony Orchestra** allows students free lawn admission with student ID. Call ahead. Round-trip on the METRA costs about $7; the festival runs charter buses for $12. The bus ride takes 1½hr.

**SPORTS.** The National League's **Cubs** play baseball at **Wrigley Field,** 1060 W. Addison St., at Clark, one of the few ballparks in America that has retained the early grace and intimate feel of the game; it's definitely worth a visit (831-2827; tickets $9-21). The **White Sox,** Chicago's American League team, swing on the South Side at the new **Comiskey Park,** 333 W. 35th St. (tickets $10-22; 674-1000). Da **Bears** play football at **Soldier's Field Stadium,** McFetridge Dr. and S. Lakeshore Dr. (708-615-2327). Da **Bulls** just keep winning NBA championships at the **United Center,** 1901 W. Madison, known fondly as "the house that Michael Jordan built" (943-5800; tickets $30-450). The **Blackhawks** hockey team skates there too (455-4500; tickets $25-100). **Sports Information** (976-4242) has current sports knowledge. For tickets, call **Ticketmaster** (Bulls and Blackhawks 559-1212, White Sox 831-1769, Cubs 831-2827).

# 🎵 NIGHTLIFE

"Sweet home Chicago" takes pride in the innumerable blues performers who have played here. Jazz, folk, reggae, and punk clubs throb all over the **North Side. Bucktown,** west of Halsted St. in North Chicago, stays open late with bucking bars and dance clubs. Aspiring pick-up artists swing over to **Rush** and **Division St.,** an intersection that has replaced the stockyards as one of the biggest meat markets in the world. Full of bars, cafes, and bistros, **Lincoln Park** is frequented by singles and young couples, both gay and straight. The vibrant center of gay culture is between 3000 and 4500 **Halsted St.;** many of the more festive and colorful clubs and bars line this area. For more raging, raving, and discoing, there are plenty of clubs near **River North,** in Riverwest, and on Fulton St.

**B.L.U.E.S.,** 2519 N. Halsted St. (773-528-1012). El to Fullerton, then take the eastbound bus "Fullerton". Crowded and intimate, with unbeatable music. Success here led to the larger **B.L.U.E.S. etcetera,** 1124 W. Belmont Ave. (773-525-8989). El to Belmont, then 3 blocks west on Belmont. The place for huge names: Albert King, Bo Diddley, Dr. John, and Wolfman Washington have played here. Live music every night 9pm-1:30am. 21+. Cover for both places M-Th $5-6, F-Sa $8-9.

**Buddy Guy's Legends,** 754 S. Wabash Ave. (427-0333), downtown. Buddy officially plays in Jan., but he is known to stop by when not on tour. Cover Su-W $6, Th $7, F-Sa $10. 21+. Blues M-Th 5pm-2am, F 4pm-2am, Sa 5pm-3am, Su 6pm-2am.

**Metro,** 3730 N. Clark St. (773-549-0203). Live alternative and pop music, ranging from local bands to Soul Asylum and Alice Cooper. 18+; occasionally all ages are welcome. Cover $5-12; much more for big bands. Downstairs, the 21+ **Smart Bar** (773-549-4140) has pool tables and a dance floor. Cover $5-9. Opening times vary (around 10pm); closes around 4am on weekends.

**Wild Hare & Singing Armadillo Frog Sanctuary,** 3530 N. Clark St. (773-327-4273. El: Addison). Near Wrigley Field. Live Roots Reggae acts sing Jah's praises in front of an intimate dance floor filled with both dreadlocks and corporate after-hours gear. Cover $5-8, M-Tu free. W ladies free. Open Su-F until 2am, Sa until 3am.

**Checkerboard Lounge,** 423 E. 43rd St. (773-624-3240). The true Blues bar experience. The down-and-out neighborhood infuses the music with its spirit.

**Melvin B.'s,** 1114 N. State St. (751-9897). "I built this place for people to have fun," says the owner. Hugely popular, in a prime downtown location with a breezy outdoor patio. 21+, or convince the bouncer you won't drink. Open Su-F 11am-2am, Sa 11am-3am. Wander next door to the **Cactus Cantina** to battle their margaritas.

**Lounge Ax,** 2438 N. Lincoln Ave. (773-525-6620), in Lincoln Park. Alternative industrial grunge in no particular order batted out Tu-F and Su until 2am, Sa until 3am. 21+. Cover $5-10.

**Buddies',** at Clark and Aldine. (773-477-4066). "The hub of the gay universe." Serves great food and nightly drink specials in a social setting. Open until 2am nightly, M-F breakfast from 9am, lunch from 11am. Dinner served nightly until 11pm. 21+.

# SPRINGFIELD

Springfield, "the town that Lincoln loved," owes much to its most distinguished former resident. In 1837, Abraham Lincoln, along with eight other "long" legislators (they were all over 6 ft. tall), successfully moved the state capitol from Vandalia to Springfield. A hotbed of political activity during these years, the small town hosted the heated Lincoln-Douglas debates of 1858, attracting the attention of the entire nation. Although Springfield's national prominence has since declined into obscurity, the town now welcomes tourists to learn everything about Honest Abe.

**⚡ PRACTICAL INFORMATION. Amtrak** (753-2013), at 3rd and Washington St. near downtown, trains run to Chicago (3½hr., 3 per day, from $25) and St. Louis (2hr., 3 per day, from $18; station open daily 6am-9:30pm). **Greyhound,** 2351 S. Dirksen Pkwy., depot open M-F 9am-8pm, Sa 9am-noon and 2-4pm), on the eastern edge of town (walk to the nearby shopping center, where you can catch bus #10), rolls to Chicago (6 per day, 5hr., $35); Indianapolis (7hr., 2 per day, $42); St. Louis (2hr., 3 per day, $20); and Bloomington (1hr., 3 per day, $12). **Springfield Mass Transit District:** 928 S. 9th St. (522-5531). Pick up maps at transit headquarters, most banks, or the Illinois State Museum (buses operate M-Sa 6am-6pm; fare 75¢, transfers free). The **downtown trolley** system (528-4100) is designed to take tourists to 8 designated places of historic interest. (Trolleys run 9am-4pm, hop-on/off all fare $8, seniors $7, kids 5-12 $4; circuit fare $4). **Taxi: Lincoln Yellow Cab** (523-4545). **Springfield Convention and Visitors Bureau:** 109 N. 7th St. (789-2360 or 800-545-7300; open M-F 8am-5pm). **Medical services: St. John's Hospital,** 800 E. Carpenter St. (544-6464). **Internet access: Lincoln Library,** 326 S. 7th St. (753-4900; open M-Th 9am-9pm, F 9am-6pm, Sa 9am-5pm; Sept.-May also Su noon-5pm). **Post Office:** 411 E. Monroe (788-7470), at Wheeler St. (open M-F 7:30am-5pm). **ZIP code:** 62701. **Area code:** 217.

**⌂⌂ ACCOMMODATIONS AND FOOD.** Bus service to the cheap lodgings off I-55 and U.S. 36 on Dirksen Pkwy. is limited. Downtown hotels may be booked solid on weekdays when the legislature is in session, but ask the visitors office about weekend packages. Rooms should be reserved early for holiday weekends and the State Fair in mid-Aug. Take bus #3 "Bergen Park" to Milton and Elm St. and walk a few blocks east to the **Dirksen Inn Motel/Shamrock Motel,** 900 N. Dirksen Pkwy. (522-4900) for clean, pleasant rooms, and refrigerators (reception 8am-10pm; all rooms $30). **Mister Lincoln's Campground,** 3045 Stanton Ave. (529-8206), off Stevenson Dr. (take bus #10), has free showers, tent space ($14 per 2 adults, $2 per child), cabins (for 2 with A/C $25, $3 per additional adult, $2 per additional child), and an area for RVs (full hookup, 2 adults $19). The office is open daily 8am-8pm.

Interesting cuisine seems sparse in Springfield. Still, you can get some kicks down on historic Rt. 66 at the **Cozy Drive-In,** 2935 S. 6th St. (525-1992), a diner devoted to memorabilia of the old road and great greasy food. Their specialty is the Cozy Dog ($1.45), (open M-Sa 8am-8pm). Downtown, pink-and-orange **Café Brio,** at 6th and Monroe (544-0574), stirs up typical soup and sandwich fare with Mexican, Mediterranean, and Caribbean flair. Great vegetarian options include mushroom-red chile fettucine. The cafe has a full bar and is open daily for lunch ($5-7), dinner ($9-15), and weekend brunch.

**◎ SIGHTS.** Springfield makes money by zealously re-creating Lincoln's life. Walking from sight to sight retraces the steps of the man himself (or so they say). Happily, many Lincoln sights are free. *(800-545-7300 accesses up-to-date info.)* The **Lincoln Home Visitors Center** screens a 19min. film on "Mr. Lincoln's Springfield" and doles out free tickets to see the **Lincoln Home,** the only one Abe ever owned and the main Springfield draw, sitting at 8th and Jackson St. in a restored 19th-century neighborhood. *(426 S. 7th St. 492-4241. 10min. tours every 5-10min. from the front of the house. Open daily 8am-6pm. Arrive early to avoid the crowds.)*

A few blocks northwest, at 6th and Adams St. right before the Old State Capitol, the **Lincoln-Herndon Law Offices** describe a Lincoln-esque day at the office, before the Presidency. *(785-7289. Open daily for tours only 9am-5pm; last tour 45min. before closing; $2 donation suggested.)* Around the corner and to the left, across from the Downtown Mall, sits the magnificent limestone **Old State Capitol.** In 1858, Lincoln delivered his stirring and prophetic "House Divided" speech here. The capitol also witnessed the famous Lincoln-Douglass debates which catapulted Lincoln to national prominence. *(785-7961. Open daily Mar.-Oct. 9am-5pm, Nov.-Feb 9am-4pm. Last tour 1hr. before closing. Donation suggested.)* Lincoln, his wife Mary Todd, and their 3 sons lie at the **Lincoln Tomb,** at Oak Ridge Cemetery. *(1500 Monument Ave. 782-2717. Open daily Mar.-Oct. 9am-5pm, Nov.-Feb. 9am-4pm.)*

Those unwilling to long endure all of Lincolnland should walk to the **Dana-Thomas House,** 6 blocks south of the Old State Capitol. Built in 1902, the stunning and well-preserved home was one of Frank Lloyd Wright's early experiments in Prairie Style and still features Frank's original fixtures. *(301 E. Lawrence Ave. 782-6776. 1hr. tours every 15-20min. W-Su 9am-4pm; suggested donation $3.)*

Rt. 66, that fabled American highway of yesteryear, is remembered in Springfield by **Shea's,** 2075 Peoria Rd. (522-0475), a truck shop with masses of memorabilia, including gas pumps, signs, and license plates (open Tu-Sa 7am-5pm).

# WISCONSIN

Oceans of milk and beer flood the Great Lakes' most wholesome party state. French fur trappers first explored this area in search of lucrative furry creatures. Later, miners burrowed homes in the hills during the 1820s lead rush (earning them the nickname "badgers"), and hearty Norsemen set to clearing vast woodlands. By the time the forests fell and the mines were exhausted, German immigrant farmers had set dairy cows to graze and planted rolling fields of barley for beer amid the state's 15,000 lakes. Visitors to "America's Dairyland" pass cheese-filled country stores to delight in the ocean-like vistas of Door County and the ethnic fêtes (and less refined beer bashes) of Madison and Milwaukee.

# 🔢 PRACTICAL INFORMATION

**Capital:** Madison.

**Visitor Info: Division of Tourism,** 123 W. Washington St., P.O. Box 7606, Madison 53707 (608-266-2161, out of state 800-432-8747; www.tourism.state.wi.us).

**Postal Abbreviation:** WI. **Sales Tax:** 5.5%.

# MILWAUKEE

A home to drinks and festivals, Milwaukee is a city given to celebration. The influx of immigrants, especially German and Irish, gave the city its reputation for *gemütlichkeit (*hospitality). Ethnic communities take turns throwing city-wide parties each summer weekend. The city's famous beer industry fuels the revelry, supplying more than 1500 bars and taverns with as much brew as anyone could ever need. Aside from merrymaking, Milwaukee's attractions include top-notch museums, German-inspired architecture, and a long expanse of scenic lakeshore.

# 🔢 ORIENTATION AND PRACTICAL INFORMATION

Most north-south streets are numbered, increasing from Lake Michigan toward the west. Downtown Milwaukee lies between **Lake Michigan** and 10th St. Address numbers increase north and south from **Wisconsin Ave.,** the center of east-west travel. The **interstate system** forms a loop around Milwaukee: **I-43 S** runs to Beloit, **I-43 N** runs to Green Bay, **I-94 W** is a straight shot to Chicago, **I-794** cuts through the heart of downtown Milwaukee, and **I-894** connects with the airport.

**Airport: General Mitchell International Airport,** 5300 S. Howell Ave. (747-5300). Take bus #80 from 6th St. downtown (30min.). **Limousine Service,** 769-9100 or 800-236-5450. 24hr. pick-up and drop-off from most downtown hotels. Reservations required. $8.50, round-trip $16.

**Trains: Amtrak,** 433 W. St. Paul Ave. (271-0840), at 5th St. 3 blocks from the bus terminal. In a fairly safe area, but less so at night. To Chicago (1½hr., 6 per day, $19) and St. Paul (6½hr., 1 per day, $72). Open daily 5:30am-9pm.

**Buses: Greyhound,** 606 N. 7th St. (272-2156), off W. Michigan St. downtown. To Chicago (2-3hr., 18 per day, $12) and Minneapolis (6½-9hr., 6 per day, $47). Station open 24hr.; office open daily 6:30am-11:30pm. **Wisconsin Coach** (544-6503 or 542-8861), in the same terminal, covers southeast Wisconsin. **Badger Bus,** 635 N. 7th St. (276-7490 or 608-255-1511), across the street, burrows to Madison (1½hr., 6 per day, $10). Open daily 6:30am-10pm. *Be cautious at night.*

**Public Transit: Milwaukee County Transit System,** 1942 N. 17th St. (344-6711). Efficient metro area service. Most lines run 5am-12:30am. Fare $1.35, seniors and children 65¢; weekly pass $10.50/$6.50. Free maps at the library or at Grand Ave. Mall info center. Call for schedules. Milwaukee Loop (344-6711) runs around historic downtown. $1 pass good all day. (Th 5pm-1am, F-Sa 10am-1am, June-Sept.)

**Taxis: Veteran,** 291-8080. **Yellow Taxi,** 271-6630.

**Car Rental: Rent-A-Wreck,** 4210 W. Silver Spring Dr. (464-1211). Rates from $10 per day, though rates and terms vary widely. Open M-F 8am-6pm, Sa 8am-1pm.

**Equipment Rental: High Roller Bike and Skate** (273-1343), on the lagoon at McKinley Marina in Veteran's Park. In-line skates $5 per hr., $17 per day. Bikes $7 per hr., $25 per day. Open daily 10am-8pm, weather permitting. Must be over 18 with ID.

**Visitor Info: Greater Milwaukee Convention and Visitors Bureau,** 510 W. Kilbourne St. (273-7222 or 800-554-1448), downtown. Open M-F 8am-5pm; in summer also Sa 9am-2pm.

**Hotlines: Crisis Intervention,** 257-7222. **Rape Crisis Line,** 542-3828. Both 24hr. **Gay People's Union Hotline,** 562-7010. Operates daily 7-10pm.

**Post Office:** 345 W. St. Paul Ave. (270-2004), south along 4th Ave. from downtown, by the Amtrak station. Open M-F 7:30am-8pm. **ZIP code:** 53202. **Area code:** 414.

# ACCOMMODATIONS

Downtown lodging options tend toward the pricey; travelers with cars should head out to the city's 2 hostels. **Bed and Breakfast of Milwaukee** (277-8066) finds rooms in local B&Bs (from $55).

**University of Wisconsin at Milwaukee (UWM),** Sandburg Hall, 3400 N. Maryland Ave. (229-4065 or 299-6123). Take bus #30 north to Hartford St. Convenient to nightlife and east-side restaurants. Laundry facilities, cafeteria, free local calls. Singles with shared bath $25; doubles $33. Clean, bland suites with bath divided into single and double bedrooms: 4 beds $58, 5 beds $69. Parking $6.25 for 24hr. Open June to mid-Aug. 2-day advance reservations required.

**Wellspring Hostel (HI-AYH),** 4382 Hickory Rd. (675-6755), Newburg; take I-43 N to Rt. 33 W. to Newburg and exit on Main St.; Hickory Rd. intersects Newburg's Main St. just northwest of the Milwaukee River. The pretty setting, far from downtown on a riverside vegetable farm, is worth the 45min. drive if you're looking to get back to nature. Well-kept with 25 beds, kitchen, and nature trails. $15, nonmembers $18. Private room with bath $40. Linen $3. Office open daily 8am-8pm. Reservations required.

**Red Barn Hostel (HI-AYH),** 6750 W. Loomis Rd. (529-3299), in Greendale 13mi. southwest of downtown via Rt. 894; take the Loomis exit. Public transportation takes forever; don't come without a car. Dim rooms with stone walls on the bottom floor of an enormous red barn. 20 dorm-style beds, full kitchen, no laundry facilities, not the coziest of bathrooms. $11, nonmembers $14. Linen $1.50. Check-in 5-10pm. Open May-Oct.

**Motel 6,** 5037 S. Howell Ave. (482-4414), near the airport, in a remodeled building 15min. from downtown. Any airport shuttle will take you within walking distance. Airy rooms with A/C, cable, and a pool. Singles $40; doubles $44; Sa-Su $42/$46.

# FOOD

Milwaukee is a premier town for food and **beer.** Milwaukeeans take advantage of nearby Lake Michigan with a local favorite called the **Friday night fish fry.** French ice cream, known as **frozen custard,** is the dairy state's special treat. Leon's (see below) is a good place to check it out.

For Italian restaurants, look on **Brady St.** You'll find heavy Polish influences in the **South Side** and good Mexican food at National and S. 16th St. **East Side** eateries are cosmopolitan, as well. Downtown, the **Water St. entertainment district** boasts hot new restaurants for a range of palates. The $13 million Riverwalk project has revitalized the Water St. area. On the north end of the Riverwalk, **Old World Third St.** offers the City's best brew-pubs.

**Leon's,** 3131 S. 27th St. (383-1784). A cross between *Grease* and *Starlight Express.* Great frozen custard (2 scoops $1). Hot dogs 95¢. Open Su-Th 11am-midnight, F 11am-12:30am, Sa 11am-1am.

**Abu's Jerusalem of the Gold,** 1978 N. Farwell Ave. (277-0485), 3 blocks south from the corner of North and Farwell, at Lafayette on the East Side. A tiny pink restaurant with Middle Eastern novelties for herbivore and carnivore alike. The falafel sandwich is a vegetarian delight ($2.75). Rosewater lemonade 95¢. Open M-Th 11:30am-9pm, F-Sa 11:30am-11pm, Su noon-9pm.

**King and I,** 823 N. 2nd St. (276-4181). Thai food served in an elegant restaurant. The all-you-can-eat lunch buffet is a favorite ($6.25). Entrees $11. Open M-F 11:30am-9pm, Sa 5-10pm, Su 4-9pm.

**Comet Café,** 1947 Farwell Ave. (273-7677), next to Abu's. Zesty espresso shakes are served in a 50's cafe until midnight M-F.

**Cielito Lindo,** 733 S 2nd St. (649-0401). In the heart of a club district, this authentic Mexican cafe has good food, cheap beer, and a jukebox full of Mariachi hits. Open M-F 8am-10pm, Sa-Su 8am-4am.

##  SIGHTS

Although many of Milwaukee's breweries have left, the city's name still evokes images of a cold one. No visit to the city would be complete without a look at the yeast in action. The **Miller Brewery,** a corporate giant that produces 43 million barrels of beer annually (including *Milwaukee's Best*), offers a free 1hr. tour with 3 samples, followed by an optional 15min. brew house tour. *(4251 W. State St. 931-2337. 2 tours per hr. M-Sa 10am-3:30pm; 3 per hr. during busy days; call for winter schedule. Under 18 must be accompanied by adult. ID required.)* The **Lakefront Brewery,** off Pleasant St., produces 5 year-round beers and several seasonal specials, including pumpkin beer and cherry lager. *(1872 N. Commerce St. 372-8800. Tours F 5:30pm, Sa 1:30, 2:30, and 3:30pm. $3.)* **Sprecher Brewing,** off Port Washington St., north of the city on I-43, doles out 4 beer samples following a 1hr. tour *(701 W. Glendale. 964-2739. Tours M-F 4pm, Sa every 30min. 1-3pm. $2, under 12 free.)* At most breweries, tour prices are discounted for non-drinkers.

A road warrior's nirvana, **Harley-Davidson** gives 1hr. tours of its engine and transmission plant. *(11700 W. Capitol Dr. 342-4680. Tours M-F 9:30, 11am, and 1pm. Call ahead—the plant sometimes shuts down in summer. Reservations required for groups larger than 6.)*

Several excellent museums grace the city of Milwaukee. The **Milwaukee Public Museum,** at N. 8th St., attracts visitors with dinosaur bones, a replicated Costa Rican rainforest, a Native American exhibit, and a re-created European village. *(800 W. Wells St. 278-2700 or 278-2702 for recorded info. Open daily 9am-5pm. $5.50, students with ID, seniors, and ages 4-17 $4.50. Parking available.)* The lakefront **Milwaukee Art Museum,** in the War Memorial Building, houses Haitian folk art, 19th-century German art, and American works, ranging from 2 of Warhol's soup cans to an extensive folk art collection. *(750 N. Lincoln Memorial Dr. 224-3200. Open Tu-W and F-Sa 10am-5pm, Th noon-9pm, Su noon-5pm. $5, students and seniors $3, under 12 free.)* The **Charles Allis Art Museum** houses a fine collection of East Asian and Classical artifacts. *(1801 N. Prospect Ave. at Royal Ave., 1 block north of Brady. 278-8295. Take bus #30 or 31. Open W-Su 1-5pm. $2.)*

Better known as "The Domes," the **Mitchell Park Horticultural Conservatory,** at 27th St., recreates a desert and a rainforest and mounts seasonal displays in a series of 7-story conical glass domes. *(524 S. Layton Blvd. 649-9830. Open daily 9am-5pm. $4, students and seniors $2.50. Take bus #10 west to 27th St., then #27 south to Layton.)* The **Boerner Botanical Gardens,** in Whitnall Park between Grange and Rawsen St., boast billions of beautiful blossoms as well as open-air concerts on Th nights. *(5879 S. 92nd St. 425-1130. Open mid-Apr. to Oct. daily 8am-7pm. Parking $3.50.)* County parks line much of Milwaukee's waterfront, providing free recreational areas and trails. Olympians and masses alike skate at the **Pettit National Ice Center,** next to the state fairgrounds. *(500 S. 84th St. 266-0100.)*

## ♪ ENTERTAINMENT

On any given night in Milwaukee, a free concert is being given somewhere. Your best bet to get from here to that somewhere is to phone the visitors bureau at 273-7222. A recording provides after-hours callers with pertinent festival information.

The modern white stone **Marcus Center for the Performing Arts,** 929 N. Water St., across the river from Père Marquette Park, hosts the **Milwaukee Symphony Orchestra,** the **Milwaukee Ballet,** and the **Florentine Opera Company.** (273-7206 or 800-472-4458. Symphony tickets $17-52, ballet $13-62, opera $15-80. Ballet and symphony offer ½-price student and senior rush tickets.) During the summer, the center's Peck Pavilion hosts **Rainbow Summer,** a series of free lunchtime concerts—jazz, bluegrass, you name it (273-7206; M-F noon-1:15pm). **The Milwaukee Repertory Theater,** 108 East Wells St., stages shows from Sept. through May. (224-1761. Tickets $8-30; ½-price student and senior rush tickets available 30min. before shows.) On Th in summer, **Jazz in the Park** presents free concerts in East Town's **Cathedral Square Park,** at N. Jackson St. between Wells and Kilbourn St. (271-1416). In Père

Marquette Park, by the river between State and Kilbourn St., **River Flicks** screens free movies at dusk Th in Aug. (270-3560).

**Summerfest,** the largest and most lavish of Milwaukee's festivals, spans 11 days in late June and early July; daily life halts as a potpourri of big-name musical acts, culinary specialities, and an arts and crafts bazaar take over Henry Maier Festival Park; look for signs with the smiling orange face (273-3378, outside Milwaukee 800-273-3378; M-Th $8, F-Su $9). Ethnic festivals abound during festival season (also at the Maier Park); the most popular are: **Polish Fest** (529-2140) and **Asian Moon** (821-9829), both in mid-June; **Festa Italiana** (223-2193), in mid-July; **Bastille Days** (271-7400), near Bastille Day (July 14); **German Fest** (464-9444), in late July; **Irish Fest** (476-3378), in mid-Aug.; **Mexican Fiesta** (383-7066), in late Aug.; **Indian Summer Fest** (774-7119), in early Sept.; and **Arabian Fest** (342-4909), in mid-Sept. (most festivals $7, under 12 free). Pick up a copy of the free weekly *Downtown Edition* for the full scoop on festivals and other events. Locals line the streets for **The Great Circus Parade** (356-8341), held in mid-July, a re-creation of turn-of-the-century processions with trained animals, daredevils, costumed performers, and 65 original wagons. In early Aug., the **Wisconsin State Fair** rolls into the fairgrounds toting big-name entertainment, 12 stages, exhibits, contests, rides, fireworks, and a pie-baking contest (266-7000, 800-884-3247; $6, seniors $5, under 11 free). The **Blues/Jazz Barbecue** heats up Veterans Park in early Sept. (271-1416.)

The **Milwaukee Brewers** baseball team plays at **County Stadium,** at the interchange of I-94 and Rt. 41 (933-9000 or 800-933-7890), while the **Milwaukee Bucks** (227-0500) hoop it up at the Bradley Center, 1001 N. 4th St.

## 🎵 NIGHTLIFE

Milwaukee never lacks for something to do after sundown. Downtown gets a bit seedy at night, but the area along **Water St.** between Juneau and Highland Ave. offers slightly cleaner bars and street life. Clubs and bars also cluster near the intersection of **North Ave.** and **North Farwell St.,** near the UW Campus. Perhaps the newest and most exciting place to be in Milwaukee after hours is **Brady St.,** which runs east-west between Farwell and the river. South 2nd is a hothouse for gay bar activity, with plenty of straight partiers as well.

**Safehouse,** 779 N. Front St. (271-2007), across from the Pabst Theater downtown. A brass plate labeled "International Exports, Ltd." welcomes guests to this bizarre world of spy hideouts, James Bond music, *mata hari* outposts, and drinks with names like Rahab the Harlot. A briefing with "Moneypenny" in the foyer is just the beginning of the intrigue. Draft beer $2.50; 24 oz. specialty drinks $5.50. Cover $1-2. Open M-Th 11:30am-1:30am, F-Sa 11:30am-2am, Su 4pm-midnight.

**Hi-Hat,** 1701 Brady St. (225-9330), 3 blocks west of Farwell Ave. A trendy jazz joint. M-W swing and jazz and other assorted live acts play on the loge, while Milwaukee's hep night-hawks roost in the cavernous depths below. No attitude, no dress code, no cover—for now (beer $2-6). Open daily 4pm-2am, Su 10am-3pm for brunch.

**Rochambo,** 1317 Brady St. (241-0095), across the street from Hi-Hat. A coffee/teahouse hip almost to a fault. Crowds of the tragically un-trendy thronging the outdoor seating may intimidate at first, but the friendly staff, vintage music, sociable atmosphere and incredible tea selection make it a site worth patronizing. $1.25 for a mug of Oolong. Open M-F 7am-midnight, Sa 8am-midnight, Su 9am-midnight.

**ESO2,** 1905 E. North Ave. (278-8118). A place made for dance. Let it all out to pop dance and trance, as well as some house and underground treats. Theme nights (like Tu retro), have special drink prices (like $3 pitchers). Cover $2-3. Open Tu-Su; hrs. vary.

**Lacage,** 801 S. 2nd Ave. (383-8330). Mostly a 20- and 30-something gay clientele, but welcomes all, and crowds are often mixed at the largest pub in town. DJ's spin to keep 2 large floors grooving. F and Su the bar splits: dancing on one side and drag shows on the other. B-Y-O-Wig. Cover W-Th $2, F-Sa $5. Open Su-Th 9pm-2am, F-Sa until 2:30.

**Dish**, 235 N 2nd St. (283-3474), at Oregon. Guest house, trance, jungle, and dance DJ's pack the place F and Su nights. Underage night Tu. Cover $1-6 F & Su. Open Tu-Su 6:30pm-2am.

# MADISON

Building cities on isthmi is like shaking someone's left hand; it's generally avoided and, when attempted, usually comes off quite awkwardly. Madison's own awkward development owes much to the efforts of Judge James Doty, who cajoled Wisconsin's lawmakers into moving the capital to Madison in 1836. (Doty gave undecided lawmakers hundreds of acres of land in the Madison region to help them make up their minds.) Doty's vision, a capital on a narrow isthmus, sandwiched between lakes Menona and Mendota, has served to segregate the residential and mall-ridden northeast side from the university-centered southwest side of the city. It is the meeting of worlds at the capitol building in the center of town that gives Madison its peculiarly pleasant midwestern-hippie flavor. With not just one lakefront view but two, Madison has plenty of beachfront from which to swim, boat, or ski. The town's shore paths are perfect for running or roller-blading.

◪ **PRACTICAL INFORMATION.** Connecting the city's northeast and southwest sides is Washington Ave./U.S. 151, the city's main thoroughfare, which runs through Capitol Sq. **Greyhound**, 2 S. Bedford St. (257-3050), has buses to Chicago (3-5hr., 8 per day, $16-17) and Minneapolis (5 per day, $37-39). **Badger Bus** (255-6771) departs from the same depot and runs to Milwaukee (1½hr., 6 per day, $10; station open daily from 5:30am-11pm). **Madison Metro Transit System**, 1101 E. Washington Ave. (266-4466), travels through downtown, UW campus, and surrounding areas ($1.25; free M-Sa 10am-3pm in the capitol-UW campus area). The **Greater Madison Convention and Visitors Bureau**, 615 E. Washington Ave. (255-2537 or 800-373-6376; open M-F 8am-4:30pm). **Post Office:** 3902 Milwaukee Ave. (246-1249; open M 7:30am-7pm, Tu-F 7:30am-6pm, Sa 8:30am-2pm). **ZIP code:** 53714. **Area code:** 608.

▛ **ACCOMMODATIONS. Madison Summer Hostel (HI-AYH)**, northwest from the UW info center on Langdon St., is a good bet for the budget traveler with clean dorm-style rooms. (251-5873. Open mid-May to mid-Aug. Check-in 7-10pm. $14, nonmembers $17; doubles $27/$30; 25% discount for bikers, backpackers, and families.) Although they only rent out 8 rooms, the best value in the city is at the **Memorial Union**, 800 Langdon St., on the UW campus, which supplies large, elegant rooms with excellent views, cable TV, A/C, and free parking (265-3000; from $60). At motels stretching along Washington Ave. (U.S. 151), near the intersection with I-90, rates start at $40 per weeknight and rise dramatically on weekends. From the Capitol, Bus A shuttles the 5mi. between the Washington Ave. motels and downtown. The **Select Inn**, 4845 Hayes Rd., near the junction of I-94 and U.S. 151, bucks the trend, offering large rooms with cable TV, A/C, and a whirlpool. (249-1815. Singles $39; doubles from $47; Sa-Su $43/$51. Continental breakfast included.) Nearby **Motel 6**, 1754 Thierer Rd., behind Denny's Restaurant, is a solid choice with A/C and cable TV (241-8101; singles from $36, doubles from $41). Prices steepen downtown, starting around $60. **Campers** should head south on I-90 to Stoughton, where **Lake Kegonsa State Park**, 2405 Door Creek Rd., has sites (½ kept for walk-ins) in a wooded area near the beach. (873-9695. Showers, flush toilets. WI residents M-F $7, Sa-Su $9. Parking permits $5 per day, non-residents $7.)

▟ **FOOD AND NIGHTLIFE.** Good restaurants pepper Madison; a cluster spice up the university and capitol areas. **State St.** hosts a variety of cheap restaurants, both chains and Madison originals. The cafeterias at UW's **Memorial Union**, on Langdon St., are a fast an inexpensive option. **Himal Chuli**, 318 State St., has cheap *tarkari*, *dal*, *bhat*, and other Nepali favorites—a full veggie meal goes for around $6.50, and meat meals for $8 (251-9225; open M-Sa 11am-9pm). **Dotty Dumpling's Dowry,** 116 N. Fairchild St., is where classic American chow is consumed under hanging wooden canoes, blimps, and airplanes. Serves award-winning burgers ($4), malts ($3.50), and 19 beers on tap ($2). (255-3175. Open M-W 11am-10pm, Th-Sa 11am-11pm, Su noon-8pm.) Serving up a truly global array of cheap and wonderful pasta dishes, **Noodles and Co.,** 232 State St. at Johnson (entrees $5; 257-6393; M-Sa 11am-9pm, Su noon-8pm). For a quick slice ($1.75), New York style, stop by **Sal's Pizzeria,** 313 State St.—"damn right, it's good pizza."

The **Essen Haus,** 514 E. Wilson St., plays host to live polka bands, semi-rowdy crowds, and 2-gallon hats (255-4674). At **Crystal's Corner Bar,** 1302 Williamson St., down a draught beer ($1.20-3.25) with a slightly older crowd and groove to live bands, usually blues. (256-2953. Schedule and cover vary. Open Su noon-midnight, M-Th 11am-2am, F-Sa 11am-2:30am.) Salsa Cubana and other dance nights bring some picante to the Madison nightlife at the Cardinal, 418 E. Wilson St. (251-0080).

☎ 🖰 **SIGHTS AND ENTERTAINMENT.** Between UW and the capitol area, Madison offers many sight-seeing options. The imposing **State Capitol,** in Capitol Sq. at the center of downtown, boasts beautiful ceiling frescoes and the only granite dome in the U.S. (266-0382. Free tours from the ground fl. info desk M-Sa on the hr. 9-11am and 1-3pm, Su 1-3pm. Open daily 6am-8pm.) Every Sat. morning from late Apr. to early Nov., the Capitol attracts throngs of visitors for the weekly **farmers market,** which has grown to become one of the area's premiere attractions. Also on Capitol Sq., the **Wisconsin Veterans Museum,** 30 W. Mifflin St., honors Wisconsin soldiers (264-6086; open Tu-Sa 9:30am-4:30pm, Apr.-Sept. also Su noon-4pm; free). The **State Historical Museum,** 30 N. Carroll St., explores the history of Wisconsin's Native American population (264-6555; open Tu-Sa 10am-5pm, Su noon-5pm; free). The **Madison Art Center,** 211 State St., inside the civic center, exhibits modern and contemporary art and hosts traveling exhibitions. (257-0158. Open Tu-Th 11am-5pm, F 11am-9pm, Sa 10am-9pm, Su 1-5pm. Most exhibits free.) The **Madison Civic Center,** 211 State St., frequently stages arts and entertainment performances in the Oscar Mayer Theatre, and hosts the **Madison Symphony Orchestra.** (266-9055. Tickets from $20. Office open M-F 11am-5:30pm, Sa 11am-2pm. Season runs late Aug. to May.) The **Madison Repertory Theatre,** 122 State St., #201, performs classic and contemporary musicals and dramas (256-0029; showtimes vary; tickets $6.50-22). The free *Isthmus* covers the entertainment scene.

Madison's **State St.** exudes a college atmosphere, sporting many funky clothing stores and record shops. At the southwest end of State St. is the **University of Wisconsin (UW),** where students love to hang out at Union Terrace. In summer, the terrace is home to free weekend concerts on the lake shore. In winter, the concerts move indoors, but the volume remains the same.

UW's most noteworthy museums are the **Geology Museum,** 215 W. Dayton St. (262-2399; open M-F 8:30am-4:30pm, Sa 9am-1pm), and the **Elvehjem Museum of Art,** 800 University Ave. (263-2246; open Tu-F 9am-5pm, Sa-Su 11am-5pm; free). Also part of UW, the outdoor **Olbrich Botanical Gardens** and indoor **Bolz Conservatory,** 3330 Atwood Ave., offer a plethora of plant life. Free-flying birds, waterfalls, and tropical plants grace the inside of the conservatory dome. (246-4550. Gardens open daily 8am-8pm; Sept.-May M-Sa 10am-4pm, Su 1am-5pm. Free. Conservatory open M-Sa 10am-4pm, Su 10am-5pm. $1, under 5 free; free W and Sa 10am-noon.) For more info visit the **UW Visitors Center** at the corner of Observatory Dr. and N. Park St., on the west side of the Memorial Union. Botanists and Bedouins alike will enjoy the **University Arboretum,** 1207 Seminole Hwy. (263-7888), off I-94. A 6mi. walking loop encircles the Arboretum's 1200 acres of protected land.

East of Madison, **House on the Rock,** 5754 U.S. 23 (935-3639), in Spring Green, offers gorgeous views of the Wyoming Valley from its glass-walled Infinity Room, and a 40-acre complex of gardens and fantastic architecture. (Open daily 9am-8pm; mid-Mar. to late May and Sept.-Oct. 9am-7pm. $15, ages 7-12 $9, ages 4-6 $4.)

## NEAR MADISON: EFFIGY MOUNDS

The period between 1000 BC and AD 1200 is refered to as the Woodland period of North American prehistory. Although little is known, what is known has been garnered through close study of one of the most remarkable and least understood legacies of indigenous peoples in North America: the Effigy Mounds. Once covering most of Wisconsin, these low-lying mounds of piled earth, many in the form of animals, were mostly destroyed by farmers' plows in the 19th century.

One of the largest concentrations of intact mounds can be found at the **Effigy Mounds National Monument,** 151 Hwy. 76, in Harpers Ferry, Iowa. Offering striking views of the Mississippi from high, rocky bluffs, the trails winding through this park offer an investigation of the lives of these people, and the meaning the mounds had for them. Take 18W from Madison. *(319-873-3491. Visitors center open daily 8am-5pm.)* **Wyalusing State Park,** just across the Mississippi in Wisconsin, offers campsites overlooking the stunning confluence of the Wisconsin River and the ol' Miss, as well as its own assortment of mounds and trails. *(608-996-2261.)*

# DOOR COUNTY

With 250mi. of rocky coastline, Lake Michigan's ocean-like tides, miles of bike paths, acres of orchards, and stunning scenery, Door County's 12 villages swing open on a summer-oriented schedule. Visitors are advised to make reservations for just about everything if they plan to be on the peninsula during a weekend in either July or Aug. Temperatures can dip to 40°F at night, even in July. A super spot for families, the peninsula offers enough to do at inexpensive prices to keep little campers entertained and satisfied.

**7 PRACTICAL INFORMATION.** Door County begins north of **Sturgeon Bay,** where Rt. 42 and 57 converge and then split again. Rt. 57 runs up the eastern coast of the peninsula; Rt. 42 runs up the western. The peninsula's west coast, which borders the Green Bay, tends to be warmer, artsy-er, and more expensive. The east coast, colder and less expensive, contains the bulk of the peninsula's park area. From south to north along Hwy. 42, **Fish Creek, Sister Bay, Ephraim,** and **Ellison Bay** are the largest towns. Public transportation comes only as close as **Green Bay,** 50mi. southwest of Sturgeon Bay, where **Greyhound** has a station at 800 Cedar St. (432-4883. Open M-F 6:30am-5:15pm, Sa-Su 10am-noon and 4-5:15pm. To Milwaukee, 3 buses daily, $20). In Green Bay, **Advantage,** 1629 Velp (497-2152), 5mi. from the Greyhound station, rents cars. ($15 per day, $90 per week, 10¢ per mi., insurance $5. Must be 25. Open M-F 8:30am-5:30pm, Sa 8am-2:30pm.) **Door County Chamber of Commerce:** 6443 Green Bay Rd. (743-4456 or 800-527-3529), on Rt. 42/57 entering Sturgeon Bay. (Open M-F 8:30am-5pm, Sa-Su 10am-4pm; mid-Oct. to mid-May M-F 8:30am-4pm.) Visitors centers are in each of the villages. **Post Office:** 359 Louisiana (743-2681), at 4th St. in Sturgeon Bay (open M-F 8:30am-5pm, Sa 9:30am-noon). **ZIP code:** 54235. **Area code:** 920.

**✦ ACCOMMODATIONS.** Lodgings crowd Rt. 42 and Rt. 57 ($60 and up in summer). Reservations for July and Aug. should be far in advance. The **Century Farm Motel,** 10068 Rt. 57, 3mi. south of Sister Bay on Rt. 57, rents small but tidy 2-room cottages hand-built by the owner's grandfather in the 1920s (854-4069; $45-60; open mid-May to mid-Oct.; A/C, TV, private bath, fridge). A bevy of gnome statues, 1000 Barbies, 600 animated store window mannequins, and 35 cars grace the premises of the **Chal-A Motel,** 3910 Rt. 42/57, 3mi. north of the bridge in Sturgeon Bay. (743-6788. July-May singles $49, doubles $54; Nov. to mid-May $29/$34; mid-May to June $34/$39. Large rooms.)

Four out of the area's 5 **state parks** (all but **Whitefish Dunes**) have camping ($10, WI residents $8; F-Sa $12/$10). All state parks require a motor vehicle permit ($7 per day, WI residents $5; $25/$18 per year; $3 per hr.). **Peninsula State Park,** just past Fish Creek village on Rt. 42, contains 20mi. of shoreline, 17mi. of trails, and

**BARABOO'S BIZARRE** The Greatest Show on Earth is in Baraboo, Wisconsin—permanently. Along the Baraboo River, a swath of bank has been set aside by the State Historical Society to honor the one-time winter home of the world-famous circus. The **Circus World Museum**, in Baraboo, packs a full line-up of events from big-top performances to street parades. *(426 Water St. 356-0800. Open daily in summer from 9am to 6pm, mid-July through mid-Aug. 9am to 9pm. $12, under 12 $6.)* But if seeing some plumed horse defecate leaves you unfulfilled, Baraboo has more to offer. Just past the Ho-Chunk casino on Hwy. 12 is Shady Lane Rd., home to the **International Crane Foundation**. Created by 2 acolytes to **Aldo Leopold's** conservation ideas (ol' Aldo also lived on Shady Lane Rd.), the Crane Foundation supports all 15 different species of crane in the world on 225 acres of restored prairie. Chicks being raised for release into the wild are on display most of the day (bedtime is at 4pm); lucky visitors can watch them feeding. Some of the adults participate in a crane flight show—an amazing chance to see some amazing birds. *(E-11376 Shady Lane Rd. 356-9462. $6, under 12 $2.50.)* Birds and conservation find more common ground within the **fantastical sculpture garden of Dr. Evermore**, just south of Baraboo on Rt. 12. Here iron relics from an industrial age are given new life by the good doctor's welding torch. Thousands of critters, from plier-beaked, trumpet necked birds, to spring-tailed robot legions clutter the 2 acre plot. The centerpiece is a massive and fanciful palace/rocketship structure which has been recognized by Guiness as the largest junk sculpture in the world. Conservation and appreciation for our industrial past are at the root of this remarkable collection. Plans are in the works to take over the nearby and now defunct Army Ammunition plant, dismantling and salvaging it's pieces and making the grounds into a huge museum, dedicated to the farmers who gave up their land for its construction and the workers who ran its production. Not visible from the road by anything other than a few brightly painted sculptures, an open gate, and a small sign pointing the way, this spot is easy to miss, so look hard.

the largest of the campgrounds (868-3258; 469 sites with showers and toilets; golf course.) Reservations are best made well in advance (i.e. 6 months), or come in person to put your name on the waiting list for one of 70 walk-in sites. **Potawatomi State Park,** 3740 Park Dr., Sturgeon Bay, spreads just outside Sturgeon Bay off Rt. 42/57, before you cross the bridge. (746-2890; 125 campsites, 19 open to walk-ins). **Newport State Park** is a wildlife preserve at the tip of the peninsula, 7mi. from Ellison Bay off Rt. 42. Vehicles are permitted, but all sites accessible by hiking only. (854-2500. 16 sites; 13 reservable.) The ferry to reach **Rock Island State Park** sails from Gill's Rock to Washington Island. (Ferries run July-Aug. every 30min. 7am-6pm, every hr. May-June and Sept.-Oct. $3.75, children $2, auto $8.50, bicycle $1.50.) Another ferry voyages (847-2252; round-trip $7, campers with gear $8) to Rock Island State Park (847-2235; 40 sites; open mid-Apr. to mid-Nov.). Because there is no direct ferry service to the campsites, campers must find a way across a 7mi. stretch of Washington Island.

Private camping options are plentiful on the peninsula. The **Camp-Tel Family Campground,** 8164 Rt. 42, 1mi. north of Egg Harbor, has tent sites and tiny A-frame cabins, each with 2 sets of bunks, a loft, and heat. (868-3278. Sites $16, with water and electricity $18. A-frame $30. $5 per adult after 2, $2 per child. Office open May-June and Sept.-Oct. 9am-noon and 3-6pm, July-Aug. 9am-9pm.) **Path of Pines**, 3709 Rt. F, 1mi. east of the ever-packed Peninsula off Rt. 42 in Fish Creek, rents 91 quiet, scenic sites. (868-3332 or 800-868-7802. Showers and laundry facilities; tent sites $17-20, includes water and electricity.)

**⬚ FOOD AND DRINK.** Many people come to Door County just for **fishboils**, a Scandinavian tradition dating back to 19th-century lumberjacks. Cooks toss potatoes, onions, and whitefish into an enormous kettle over a wood fire. To remove the fish oil from the top of the water, the boilmaster judges the proper

**GREAT LAKES**

time to throw kerosene into the fire, producing a massive fireball; the cauldron boils over, signaling chow time—it's much better than it sounds. Most fishboils conclude with a big slice of cherry pie. Door County's best-known fishboils take place at **The Viking,** in Ellison Bay. (854-2998. Mid-May to Oct. every 30min. 4:30-8pm; $11.25, under 12 $8.25; regular dining 6am-10pm.) A cheaper option is **Calamity Sam's,** 4159 Bluff Ln., off Hwy. 42 in Fish Creek. In this lodge-like setting, waiters tend to dress in camouflage. If that doesn't bother you, the prices won't. (868-2045. Fishboil $9, burger $3.50. Open May-Nov. daily 7am-9pm). At **Norz Deli and General Store,** Rt. 42 in Fish Creek, you can order a heaping deli sandwich ($3.25) made to order (fresh cheese, cucumber, and sprouts among the available items); it comes with chips and a homemade cookie. **Al Johnson's Swedish Restaurant,** in the middle of Sister Bay on Rt. 42, has excellent Swedish food ($9-17), a waitstaff in traditional Swedish dress, and goats on the thick sod roof. Be prepared for long waits and lots of tourists. (854-2626. Open daily 6am-9pm; in winter M-Sa 6am-8pm, Su 7am-8pm.) At the ▨ **Bayside Tavern,** on Rt. 42 in Fish Creek, Bob cooks up his World-Famous chili ($4) and a nice veggie sandwich ($4.75). At night, it's a lively bar with area blues and rock acts on M (cover $2), Tu pint nights, and Th open-mic keeping a good mix of friendly locals and exuberant vacationers in good spirits. (868-3441. Open Su-Th 11am-2am, F-Sa 11am-2:30am.) Guests can hurl dollars to the ceiling at **Husby's Food & Spirits,** on Rt. 42 entering Sister Bay from the south. Imports go for $2.50 among the good beer selection. (854-2624. Open Su-Th 11am-2am, F-Sa 11am-2:30am.)

**EAST SIDE.** Biking is the best way to take in the lighthouses, rocks, and white sand beaches of Door's coastline; tourist offices have free bike maps. **Whitefish Dunes State Park,** off Hwy. 57 on the peninsula's east side, maintains sand dunes, hiking/biking/skiing trails, and a well kept wildlife preserve. *(Open daily 8am-8pm; vehicle permit required.)* Just north on Cave Point Rd. off Rt. 57, **Cave Point County Park** stirs the soul with its rocky coastline and some of the most stunning views on the peninsula. *(Open daily 6am-9pm. Free.)* Stir your body as well with some cliff jumping, but beware of shallow pools. **Lakeside Park** offers a wide, sandy expanse of beach at Jacksonport, backed by a shady park and playground. *(Open daily 6am-9pm. Free.)* South of Bailey's Harbor off Rt. 57, Kangaroo Lake Rd. leaps to **Kangaroo Lake,** the largest of the 8 lakes on the peninsula; a circuit of the warm lake will reveal secluded swimming spots. Trails at the **Ridges Sanctuary,** north of Bailey's Harbor off County Rt. Q, enable exploration of over 30 beach ridges and a unique forest *(839-2802. Nature center open daily 9am-4pm. $2.)*

**WEST SIDE.** At **Peninsula State Park,** in Fish Creek, visitors rent boats, ride mopeds and bicycles along 20mi. of shoreline road, and sunbathe at Nicolet Beach. At the top of **Eagle Tower,** 1mi. and 110 steps up from the beach, you can see across the lake to Michigan. *(Open daily 6am-11pm. Vehicle permit required $3 per hr.)* Directly across from the Fish Creek entrance, **Nor Door Sport and Cyclery** rents out various kinds of bikes and winter sport equipment. *(4007 Hwy. 42. 868-2275. From $3 per hr./$10hr. per day. XC skis $9 per day.)* The park also hosts the **American Folklore Theatre,** home to the Door County hit *Lumberjacks in Love. (868-9999. $9.50.)* Just north of the Peninsula State Park, on Rt. 42, is the **Skyway Drive-In,** between Fish Creek and Ephraim. It's one helluva deal in one of only 2 Wisconsin drive-ins. *(854-9938. Current release double-feature $5.)* The award-winning **Door Peninsula Winery,** Sturgeon Bay, invites you to partake of 30 different wines. *(5806 Rt. 42. 743-7431 or 800-551-5049. 15-20min. tours and tastings daily in summer 9am-6pm; off-season 9am-5pm.)* If you're dry-minded, the **Peninsula Players,** off Rt. 42 in Fish Creek, perform in America's oldest professional resident summer theater. *(868-3287. Shows in summer Tu-Su; tickets $20-26, student discount may apply, call for showtimes.)*

The shipping town of **Green Bay,** at the foot of Door County, is home to the Green Bay Packers and their idolized QB, Brett Favre. Unless you know Mike Holmgren, you won't find a ticket, but the stadium and the nearby museum are worth a look. *(920-496-5719. Tickets $32-39.)* The **Packer Hall of Fame** has a cathedral-like feel, for

**POW WOW** Throughout the Midwest, and scattered around the rest of the country as well, are hundreds of small nations, commonly known as **Indian Reservations.** Established through treaties negotiated with the rifles of the U.S. Army, the reservation system was firmly established by the mid-1800's. Countless stereotypes exist regarding reservation conditions and the people living on them—many Americans think of them now as hotbeds for casinos and gambling. Instead of pouring money into a tribal casino, tourists can support an alternative, **go to a party,** and learn something in the meantime. Most reservations have 2 Pow Wows annually, and the occasions serve as a time for a wonderful mix of celebration and reverence, for participants and guests alike. In the words of one young dancer, "A Pow Wow is a family." The festival, usually 4-day weekend affairs for $5-10, normally comes with **free camping.** Food from vendors' trucks is **ridiculously cheap and tasty** (2 pancakes, 2 eggs, hashbrowns, juice and coffee for $3), and crafts, kitsch, and cultural items are also sold cheaply too. To learn more on the **Menominee** reservation, in Keshena, call 715-799-3341. For information on schedule at other locations, stop by the tribal offices, call the above number, or pick up a local reservation newspaper, or the international publication, *Indian Country Today.* You are, and will be made to feel, welcome and invited.

thousands come to worship at the altars of their gridiron heroes. The Hall also offers stadium tours. *(855 Lombardi Ave. 920-499-4281. $7.50, under 15 $5. Open daily June-Aug. 10am-6pm; Sept.-May 10am-5pm. Tours 1½hr. $7.50, under 15 $5. June-Sept. only.)*

The **National Railroad Museum** exhibits steam and diesel. *(2285 S. Broadway. 920-435-7245. Open daily 9am-5pm. $6, ages 6-15 $3.)*

# APOSTLE ISLANDS

Long ago, pious Frenchmen believed there were only 12 islands off the coast of Wisconsin. They were wrong. The National Lakeshore protects 21 of the beautiful islands, as well as a 12mi. stretch of mainland shore. Summer tourists enjoy kayaking, hiking, spelunking, and camping among the unspoiled sandstone bluffs.

**⊼ PRACTICAL INFORMATION.** All Apostle Islands excursions begin in the sleepy mainland town of **Bayfield** (pop. 686), in northwest Wisconsin on the Lake Superior coast. The **Bay Area Rural Transit (BART),** 300 Industrial Park Rd. (682-9664), in Ashland, offers a shuttle to Bayfield (4 per day, M-F 7am-5pm; $1.80, students $1.50, seniors $1.35). **Bayfield Chamber of Commerce:** 42 S. Broad St. (779-3335 or 800-447-4094; open M-Sa 9am-5pm, Su 10am-2pm). **National Lakeshore Headquarters Visitors Center,** 410 Washington Ave. (779-3397), distributes **camping permits** ($15 for 2 weeks, must be 14 consecutive days) and hiking info (open daily 8am-6pm; in winter M-F 8am-4:30pm). **Weather:** 682-8822. Bayfield's **post office:** 22 S. Broad St. (779-5636). **ZIP code:** 54850. **Area code:** 715.

**⌐⌐ ACCOMMODATIONS AND FOOD.** In summer months, the budget pickings are slim in Bayfield. Would-be lodgers without reservations may be out of luck on July and Aug. weekends; it's wise to call far in advance to reserve a room. The best deal in town is **The Seagull Bay Motel,** off Rt. 13 at S. 7th St. in Bayfield, offering spacious, clean rooms with cable TV and a lake view (779-5558; from $50, mid-Oct. to mid-May $35). Just south on Rt. 13, **Lakeside Lodging** has rooms with a private entrance and bath, patio, and continental breakfast. (779-5545; $50. Open mid-May to mid-Oct. In summer, reservations highly recommended 1 month in advance.) **Dalrymple Park,** ¼mi. north of town on Rt. 13, offers 30 campsites under tall pines on the lake (no showers; $10, with electricity $11; self-regulated; no reservations). **Apostle Islands Area Campground,** ½mi. south of Bayfield on County Rd. J off Rt. 13, has a few sites overlooking the islands. (779-5524. Sites $12, with hookup $16, with hookup and cable $19, with view $22; cabins for 3 without A/C or

GREAT LAKES

private bathroom $35. Reservations recommended 1 month in advance in July-Aug.) The chamber of commerce has info on **guest houses** ($35-230).

**Maggie's,** 257 Manypenny Ave., the local watering hole, prepares burgers ($6) and gourmet specials amid flamingo-filled decor (779-5641; open Su-Th 11am-10pm, F-Sa 11am-11pm). The **Gourmet Garage,** just south of Bayfield on Rt. 13, has local flavor and any kind of pie (779-5365; open daily 9am-6pm). **Greunke's Restaurant,** 17 Rittenhouse Ave., at 1st St., specializes in huge, diner-style breakfasts by day ($4-6) and famous fishboils by night (779-5480; Th-Su 6-8pm, $12, children $6; open M-Sa 6am-10pm, F-Su 7am-9:30pm). **Egg Toss Cafe,** 41 Manypenny Ave. serves a variety of breakfasts and sandwiches (779-5181). Outfit your stomach at the **Wild By Nature Market,** 100 Rittenhouse Ave., with wraps and bulk trail food (779-5075).

■ ⚠ **SIGHTS AND ACTIVITIES.** Though often overshadowed by Bayfield and Madeline Island (see below), the other 21 islands have subtle charms of their own. The sandstone quarries of Basswood and Hermit Islands and the abandoned logging and fishing camps on some of the other islands serve as mute reminders of a more vigorous era. The restored **lighthouses** on Sand, Raspberry, Long, Michigan, Outer, and Devil's Islands offer spectacular views of the surrounding country. **Sea caves,** carved out by thousands of years of winds and water, pocket the shores of several islands; a few on Devil's Island are large enough to explore by boat. The **Apostle Islands Cruise Service** runs narrated 3hr. cruises for a less exorbitant fee than most companies. From late June to early Sept., the cruise service runs an inter-island shuttle that delivers campers and lighthouse lovers to their destinations. (779-3925 or 800-323-7619. Tours depart the Bayfield City Dock mid-May to mid-Oct. daily 10am. $22, children $11.) The best beach on the mainland is **Bay View Beach,** just south of Bayfield along Rt. 13, near Sioux Flats, reached by a poorly marked path to the left about 7 or 8mi. out of town. **Swimming** in chilly Lake Superior can be quite uncomfortable. **Trek and Trail,** at Rittenhouse and Broad St., rents bikes and kayaks. (800-354-8735. Bikes $5 per hr., $20 per day; 4hr. kayak rental $38, all equipment included. Renters must complete $50 safety course.)

Bayfield is the proud home of some awfully good apples. In early Oct., up to 40,000 gather for the **Apple Festival.** The **Bayfield Apple Company,** on Betzold Rd., has fresh-picked ones (open May-Jan. daily 9am-6pm). Live folk, country, and cajun music plays at the **Big Top Chautaqua** 3mi. south of Bayfield off Ski Hill Rd. (373-5552 or 888-244-8368. Tickets from $10, showtimes M-Th 7:30pm, F-Sa 8:15pm).

**MADELINE ISLAND.** Several hundred years ago, the Chippewa came to Madeline Island from the Atlantic in search of the megis shell, a light in the sky purported to bring prosperity and health. The island maintains its allure, as thousands of summer visitors seek this relaxing retreat's clean, sandy beaches. At day's end, a jaunt to Sunset Bay on the island's north side reveals why the bay got its name.

Rooms in the area fill during the summer; call ahead for reservations. The **Madeline Island Motel,** on Col. Woods Ave. across from the ferry landing, has clean rooms named for local personalities. (747-3000. Mid-June to Labor Day doubles $80; Sept. M-Th $70, Sa-Su $80; Oct.-May $70.) Across the street, the **Madeline Island Historical Museum** outlines the island's past with interesting exhibits and a 23min. video (747-2415; $4.50, under 12 $2; open daily 10am-6pm). Madeline Island has 2 campgrounds. **Big Bay Town Park,** 6½mi. from La Pointe off Big Bay Rd., sits next to tranquil Big Bay Lagoon (747-6913; sites $9, with electricity $13; no reservations accepted). Across the lagoon, **Big Bay State Park** rents 55 primitive sites (747-6425, Bayfield office 779-4020, 888-475-3386 for reservations. $10-12. Daily vehicle permit $7, WI residents $5. Reservations $4.) The **Island Café,** 1 block to the right of the ferry exit, serves up hefty meals (breakfasts and lunch $7) and good vegetarian options (747-6555; open daily 9am-midnight). **Grampa Tony's,** next to the Chamber of Commerce, offers no-frills dining. (747-3911. Sandwiches $4-5.25, salads $2.50-6.25, ice cream $1.50 and up. Open Su-Th 7am-9pm, F-Sa 7am-10pm.)

With roughly 5 streets, Madeline Island is easy to navigate. **Visitors Info: Madeline Island Chamber of Commerce** (747-2801 or 888-475-3386), on Middle Rd. (open M-Sa

8am-4pm). **Madeline Island Ferry Line** (747-2051 or 747-6801) shuttles between Bayfield and La Pointe on Madeline Island. (20 min.; in summer, daily every 30min. 9:30am-6pm, every hr. 6:30-9:30am and 6-11pm.; one-way $3.50, ages 6-11 $2, bikes $1.75, cars $7.75—driver not included. Mar.-June and Sept.-Dec., ferries run less frequently and prices drop.) In winter, the state highway department builds a road across the ice. During transition periods, the ferry service runs **windsleds** between the island and the mainland. "Moped Dave" rents the technical marvels at **Motion to Go,** 102 Lake View Pl., about 1 block from the ferry. (747-6585. $12 per hr., $50 per day. Mountain bikes $6/$22. Open daily 10am-8pm; mid-May to mid June and Sept.-Oct. 10am-6pm.) La Pointe's **post office:** (747-3712) just off the dock on Madeline Island (open M-F 9am-4:20pm, Sa 9:30am-12:50pm). **ZIP code:** 54850.

# MINNESOTA

In the 19th century, floods of German and Scandinavian settlers forced the native Sioux and Chippewa tribes from the rich lands now known as Minnesota. Minnesota's white pioneers transformed the southern half of the state into a stronghold of commercial activity; however, the north remains largely untouched, an expanse of wilderness quilted with over 14,000 lakes. Attempts at preserving this rugged wilderness have helped raise awareness about the culture of the Ojibwe, Minnesota's Native American antecedents.

## ⊠ PRACTICAL INFORMATION

**Capital:** St. Paul.

**Visitor Info: Minnesota Office of Tourism,** 500 Metro Sq., 121 7th Pl. E., St. Paul 55101-2112 (651-296-5029 or 800-657-3700; www.exploreminnesota.com). Open M-F 8am-5pm.

**Postal Abbreviation:** MN. **Sales Tax:** 6.5%.

## MINNEAPOLIS AND ST. PAUL

Garrison Keillor once wrote that the "difference between St. Paul and Minneapolis is the difference between pumpernickel and Wonder bread." Keillor's quote plays on St. Paul's characterization as an old Irish Catholic, conservative town and Minneapolis's reputation as a young, fast-paced metropolis of the future. Minneapolis's theaters and clubs rival those of New York; both the capitol and the cathedral rest atop St. Paul. A visitor to the Twins can take in the sights of St. Paul, then cross town and spend the night raging at Prince's former hangout in Minneapolis. In both cities, consumer culture (the Mall of America), the youth punk world (in myriad upstart cafes), corporate America (thus the downtown and the skyway systems), and an international community (Swahili is taught in public schools) thrive.

## ⊠ ORIENTATION AND PRACTICAL INFORMATION

A loopy network of interstates covers the entire Minneapolis/St. Paul area. **I-94** connects the downtowns. **I-35** (north-south) splits in the Twin Cities, with **I-35 W** serving Minneapolis and **I-35 E** serving St. Paul. Curves and one-way streets tangle both of the downtown areas; even the numbered grids in the cities are skewed, making north-south and east-west designations tricky. Good maps and attentive navigation are a must. Skyways, 2nd-story walkways, keep commuters warm within both downtown areas.

**Airport: Twin Cities International,** south of the cities on I-494 in Bloomington. Take bus #7 to Washington Ave. in Minneapolis or bus #54 to St. Paul. **Airport Express** (827-7777) shuttles to either downtown and to some hotels roughly every 30min. 6am-midnight. To St. Paul ($8) and Minneapolis ($11).

GREAT LAKES

**Trains: Amtrak,** 730 Transfer Rd. (644-1127), on the east bank off University Ave. SE, between the Twin Cities. Bus #7 runs to St. Paul and #16 connects to both downtowns. To Chicago (8hr., 1 per day, $75) and Milwaukee (6hr., 1 per day, $72). Open daily 6:30am-11:45pm.

**Buses: Greyhound,** in Minneapolis, 29 9th St. (371-3323), at 1st Ave. N. To Chicago (9-12hr., 10 per day, $59) and Milwaukee (6-9hr., 8 per day, $51). Station open 24hr. In St. Paul, 166 W. University Ave. (651-222-0509), 2 blocks west of the capitol. To Chicago (8-11hr., 6 per day, $59) and Milwaukee (7hr., 6 per day, $51). Station open M-F 6:30am-1am, Sa-Su 6:30am-10pm.

**Public Transit: Metropolitan Transit Commission,** 560 6th Ave. N. (373-3333), serves both cities M-F 6:30am-11pm, Sa 7am-11pm, Su 9am-9pm; some buses operate 4:30am-12:45am, others shut down earlier. $1; seniors and ages 6-12 50¢ discount; disabled 50¢. Peak fare (M-F 6-9am and 3:30-6:30pm) $1.50. Express 50¢ more. Bus #16 connects the 2 downtowns 24hrs. (50min.); bus #94 (b, c, or d) takes 30min.

**Car Rental: Thrifty Car Rental,** 64 E. 6th St., Minneapolis (227-7690). Rates from $35 per day with 150 free mi.; 16¢ each additional mi. Must be 21 with major credit card. Under 25 $10 surcharge per day. Open M-F 7am-5pm, Sa 8am-2pm, Su 10am-2pm.

**Taxis:** In Minneapolis, **Yellow Taxi,** 824-4444. In St. Paul, **Town Taxi,** 651-331-8294.

**Visitor Info: Minneapolis Convention and Visitors Association,** 40 S. 7th St. (335-5827), in the City Center Shopping Area, 2nd level skyway. Open M-F 9:30am-8pm, Sa 9:30am-6pm, Su noon-5pm. **St. Paul Convention and Visitors Bureau,** 175 W. Kellogg, suite 502 (800-627-6101), in the RiverCenter. Open M-F 8:30am-5pm. 24hr, info: **Cityline** (612-645-6060). 24hr. state Park info: **The Connection** (612-922-9000).

**Hotlines: Crisis Line,** 340-5400. **Rape/Sexual Assault Line,** 825-4357. Both 24hr. **Gay-Lesbian Helpline,** 822-8661 or 800-800-0907. Operates M-F noon-midnight, Sa 4pm-midnight. **Gay-Lesbian Information Line,** 822-0127. Operates M-F 2-10pm, Sa 4-10pm.

**Post Office:** In Minneapolis, 100 S. 1st St., (349-4957), at Marquette Ave. Open M-F 7am-11pm, Sa 9am-1pm. **ZIP code:** 55401. In St. Paul, 180 E. Kellogg Blvd. (651-293-3268). Open M-F 8am-6pm, Sa 8:30am-1pm. **ZIP code:** 55101. **Area codes:** Minneapolis 612, St. Paul and eastern suburbs 651. In text, 612 unless otherwise noted.

# ■ ACCOMMODATIONS

Cost, safety, and cleanliness tend to go hand-in-hand-in-hand in the Twin Cities, with a few notable exceptions. The visitors bureaus have useful lists of **B&Bs** (but not a list of prices), while the **University of Minnesota Housing Office** (624-2994) keeps a list of local rooms which rent on a daily ($13-60) or weekly basis. Camping is an inconvenient option; private campgrounds lie about 15mi. outside the city, and the closest state park camping is in the **Hennepin Park** system, 25mi. out.

**College of St. Catherine, Caecilian Hall (HI-AYH),** 2004 Randolph Ave. (651-690-6604), St. Paul. Take I-94 to Snelling Ave., follow Snelling Ave. south to Randolph Ave., and take a right—it's about 5 blocks down on the left. Or take St. Paul bus #14. Convenient with a car. Simple, quiet dorm rooms near the Mississippi River in a generally safe, residential neighborhood close to McCallister and St. Thomas Colleges. Shared bath, laundry, kitchenette. Free local calls. Singles $22; doubles $17; triples $13. Check-in 7am-10pm. No curfew. Checkout 10am. 1-week max. stay. Open June to mid-Aug.

**City of Lakes International House,** 2400 Stevens Ave. S. (871-3210), Minneapolis, south of downtown next to the Institute of Arts. Best bet for social, carless travelers. Bike rentals ($3/night). Free local calls. Beds $16, students $15; 2 singles $32/$30. Linen $3. Key deposit $5. Reception M-F 9-11:30am, Sa 10am-noon, Su 11am-noon, evenings daily 6:30-9pm. Checkout 11am. Reservations strongly recommended.

**Evelo's Bed and Breakfast,** 2301 Bryant Ave. (374-9656), South Minneapolis. Pretty good location just off Hennepin Ave., a 15min. walk from uptown; take bus #17 from downtown. Friendly owners have 3 comfortable rooms in a beautiful house with elegant Victorian artifacts. Singles $50; doubles $60. Reservations and deposit required.

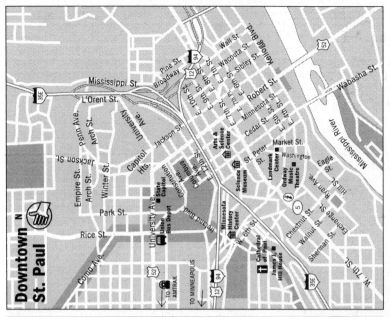

# Downtown St. Paul

N

Mississippi St.
L'Orent St.
Pine St.
Brdgway
Wall St.
Wacouta St.
Kellogg BLVD.
35E
Penn Ave.
Arch St.
University Ave.
Capitol Hts.
Jackson St.
E. 10th St.
6th St. E.
E. 7th St.
Sibley St.
Robert St.
Minnesota St.
Cedar St.
E. 5th St.
E. 4th St.
Wabasha St.
52
Empire St.
Arch St.
Winter St.
Jackson St.
Park St.
Rice St.
University Ave.
Constitution Ave.
E. 12th St.
Arts & Science Center
Science Museum
St. Peter
Market St.
Landmark Center
Washington
Ordway Music Theatre
Eagle
Ryan Ave.
Hill St.
Exchange St.
i
5
Como Ave.
52
State Capitol
Union Bus Depot
Minnesota History Center
W. 6th St.
Cathedral of Paul
James J. Hill House
Ireland Blvd.
Chestnut St.
Walnut St.
Sherman St.
35E
Mississippi River
W. 7th St.
TO AMTRAK
TO MINNEAPOLIS
12
94

# Downtown Minneapolis

N

**ACCOMMODATIONS**
A Evelo's B & B
  City of Lakes
B International House

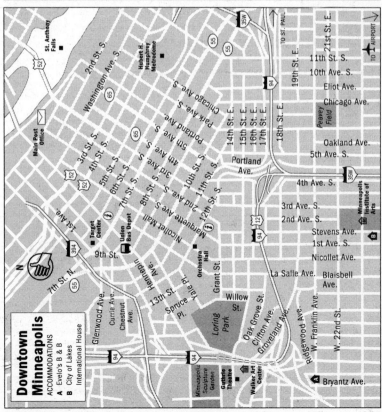

St. Anthony Falls
52
2nd St. S.
Washington Ave. S.
Hubert H. Humphrey Metrodome
55
55
35W
TO ST. PAUL
21st St. E.
94
19th St. E.
11th St. S.
10th Ave. S.
Eliot Ave.
Chicago Ave.
Peavey Field
TO AIRPORT
Main Post Office
65
3rd St. S.
4th St. S.
Chicago Ave. S.
Park Ave. S.
Portland Ave.
5th Ave. S.
4th Ave. S.
3rd Ave. S.
2nd Ave. S.
14th St. E.
15th St. E.
16th St. E.
17th St. E.
18th St. E.
Oakland Ave.
5th Ave. S.
52
52
65
5th St. S.
6th St. S.
7th St. S.
8th St. S.
10th St. S.
11th St. S.
12th St. S.
Portland Ave.
35W
Minneapolis Institute of Arts
1st Ave.
394
i
Target Center
Union Bus Depot
Nicollet Mall
Marquette Ave. S.
Hennepin Ave.
Orchestra Hall
Grant St.
i
3rd Ave. S.
2nd Ave. S.
Stevens Ave.
1st Ave. S.
Nicollet Ave.
Blaisdell Ave.
B
12
94
9th St.
7th St. N.
55
Glenwood Ave.
Currie Ave.
Chestnut Ave.
13th St.
Spruce Pl.
Yale Pl.
Willow St.
Loring Park
Oak Grove St.
Clifton Ave.
Groveland Ave.
La Salle Ave.
Ridgewood Ave.
W. Franklin Ave.
W. 22nd St.
94
94
Minneapolis Sculpture Garden
Guthrie Theatre
Walker Art Center
Bryanzt Ave.

GREAT LAKES

**FOOD**

The Twin Cities' love of music and art carries over into their culinary choices—look for small cafes with nightly music, plush chairs, and poetry readings. **Uptown** Minneapolis, centered on the intersection of Lake St. and the 2900s of Hennepin Ave., packs plenty of funky restaurants and bars without high prices. The **Warehouse District** and **Victoria Crossing** serve the crowd with lavish pastries and full meals. Near the University of Minnesota campus, **Dinkytown** (on the same side of the river) and the **West Bank** (across the river, hence the name) cater to student appetites with many dark and intriguing low-end places. **St. Paul Farmers Market** (227-6856) sells fresh produce and baked goods in a downtown location, as well as others city-wide (Tu-Su; call for times and sites).

## MINNEAPOLIS

**Baja Tortilla Grill,** 2300 Hennepin Ave. (926-9097). Using nothing but fresh ingredients and made while you watch—the salsa bar isn't the only thing that separates this place from the chihuahua chain. Big burritos $5. (Open M-Sa 11am-10pm, Su 11am-9pm.)

**Strudel and Nudel,** 2605 Nicollet Ave. (874-0113). Terrific soups ($1.85), sandwiches ($3.60), and desserts. Open M-Sa 7am-4pm, Su 8am-3pm.

**Aster Café,** 125 Main St. SE (379-3138), across the river. Situated on a beautiful stretch of riverbank, this pleasant cafe tempts strollers with scones ($1.75), sandwiches ($6), and espresso (latte $1.50). Open M-Th 7:30am-10pm, F 7:30am-11pm, Sa 9am-11pm, Su 9am-10pm.

**Mud Pie,** 2549 Lyndale Ave. S. (872-9435), at 26th St. A variety of vegetarian and vegan dishes with Mexican and Middle Eastern accents. Famous veggie burger $6.20. Open summers M-Th 11am-10pm, F 11am-11:30pm, Sa 10am-11:30pm, Su 10am-9:30pm.

## ST. PAUL

**Mickey's Dining Car,** 36 W. 7th St. (651-698-0259), downtown. A 60+ year old, 24hr. Art-Deco boxcar diner. Steak and eggs from $5; pancakes $2.50.

**Table of Contents** and **Hungry Mind Bookstore,** 1648 Grand Ave. (651-699-6595), near Snelling Ave. An excellent gourmet cafe. The wafer-crust pizza ($6) is a tasty alternative to pricier dinners ($12-25). Open M-Th 11:30am-10pm, F-Sa 9am-10:30pm, Su 10am-7pm. Another location at 1310 Hennepin Ave. (339-1133), Minneapolis. Open M-Th 11:30am-9pm, F-Sa 11:30am-10pm, Su 10am-2pm and 5-9pm.

**Crazy Carrot Juice Bar and Breadsmith,** 1577 & 1579 Grand Ave. (651-695-0080 & 651-690-3224). Corner of Snelling and Grand Ave. From traditional French rolls to more adventurous Pumpkin-Walnut muffins (50¢-$1.50), Breadsmith offers almost as much tasty and fresh variety as the connecting organic juice bar, where 24 varieties of smoothies ($3-4) get you going. Breadsmith open M-Sa 7am-8pm, Su 8am-7pm. Crazy Carrot open M-F 7am-10pm, Sa-Su 8am-9pm.

## 🔘 SIGHTS

**MINNEAPOLIS.** Situated in the land of 10,000 lakes, Minneapolis boasts 3 of its own, a few mi. southwest of downtown; take bus #28. Ringed by stately mansions, **Lake of the Isles** is an excellent place to meet Canadian geese. **Lake Calhoun,** on the west end of Lake St., south of Lake of the Isles, is a hectic recreational hotspot. Located in a more residential neighborhood, **Lake Harriet** features tiny paddleboats and a stage with occasional free concerts. The city maintains 28mi. of lakeside trails for strolling and biking. **Calhoun Cycle Center** rents out bikes. *(1622 W. Lake St. 827-8231. $6 per hr., $15 per ½-day, $24 per day. Must have credit card and driver's license. Open daily 9am-9pm.)* At the northeast corner of Lake Calhoun, the **Minneapolis Park and Recreation Board** handles canoe and rowboat rentals. *(370-4964. Canoes $5.50 per hr., rowboats $11 for 4hr. Open daily 10am-8pm.)*

The **Minneapolis Institute of Arts,** south of downtown, displays an outstanding collection, including the world-famous *Doryphoros,* Polykleitos's perfectly proportioned man. *(2400 3rd Ave. S. 870-3131. Take bus #9. Open Tu-Sa 10am-5pm, Th 10am-9pm, Su noon-5pm. Free.)* A few blocks southwest of downtown, the **Walker Art Center** has daring exhibits by Lichtenstein and Warhol, and temporary exhibits concentrating on specific eras. *(725 Vineland Pl. 375-7622. Open Tu-Sa 10am-5pm, Th 10am-8pm, Su 11am-5pm. $4; students, seniors, and ages 12-18 $3; free Th and 1st Sa of the month.)* Next to the Walker, the **Minneapolis Sculpture Garden,** the largest urban sculpture garden in the U.S., contains Minnesota's beloved **Spoonbridge** (with a cherry on top), as well as the **Cowles Conservatory.** *(Open daily 6am-midnight.)* The **Museum of Questionable Medical Devices,** north of the river near St. Anthony Falls, has a sure cure for absolutely anything. The Solorama Bedboard (meant to cure brain tumors) and a fully operational phrenological device (phrenologists measure head bumps to determine personality) are among the more respectable highlights of the collection. *(201 Main St. SE. 379-4046. Open Tu-Th 5-9pm, F noon-9pm, Sa 11am-9pm, Su noon-5pm. Donation requested, toenails preferred.)* Next to the museum, the **St. Anthony Historical Museum** has info on self-guided walking tours of Minneapolis, or hop on the River City Trolley. *(2125 Main St. 627-5433 2hr. trolley pass $8, seniors and children $5. Operates M-F 10am-4pm, Sa-Su 10am-5pm.)*

You can get a good look at the Mighty Mississippi from several points in town. Off Portland Ave., **Stone Arch Bridge** offers a scenic view of **St. Anthony Falls;** several mi. downstream, **Minnehaha Park** (take bus #7 from Hennepin Ave. downtown) allows a gander at the **Minnehaha Falls,** immortalized in Longfellow's *Song of Hiawatha.* The **visitors center** at the **Upper St. Anthony Lock and Dam,** at Portland Ave. and West River Pkwy., provides a sweeping view and a helpful explanation of the locks *(651-332-5336. Observation tower open daily mid-Mar. to mid-Dec. 9am-10pm).*

**ST. PAUL.** St. Paul's history and architecture are its greatest assets. West of downtown along **Summit Ave.,** the nation's longest continuous stretch of Victorian homes, built on the tracks of an old railroad, include a former home of American novelist **F. Scott Fitzgerald** and the **Governor's Mansion.** The magnificent home of railroad magnate **James J. Hill** offers 1¼hr. tours every 30min. *(651-297-2555. 240 Summit Ave. Open W-Sa 10am-3:30pm. $5, seniors $4, ages 6-15 $3.)* Overlooking the capitol on Summit Ave. stands **St. Paul's Cathedral,** a breathtaking scaled-down version of St. Peter's in Rome. *(239 Selby Ave. 651-228-1766. Mass M-F 7:30am and 5:15pm, no evening mass W or F; Sa mass 8am and 7pm; call for Su mass schedule. Tours M, W, F 1pm; free.)* Golden horses top the ornate **state capitol** at Cedar and Aurora St. *(651-296-3962. Tours on the hr. M-F 9am-4pm, Sa 10am-3pm, Su 1-3pm. Open M-F 9am-5pm, Sa 10am-4pm, Su 1-4pm.)* Nearby, the innovative and exciting ▧ **Minnesota History Center** houses 3 interactive and hands-on exhibit galleries on Minnesota history. *(345 Kellogg Blvd. W. 651-296-1430. Open M-Sa 10am-5pm, Th 10am-9pm, Su noon-5pm. Free.)* The Center also oversees a re-creation of life in the fur-trapping era at **Fort Snelling,** far to the southwest at the intersection of Rt. 5 and 55, where costumed artisans and soldiers lead you through the 18th-century French fort. *(651-725-2413. Infantry drills daily 11:30am and 2:30pm. Open M-Sa 9:30am-5pm, Su 11:30am-5pm. $4, seniors $3, ages 6-15 $2.)* The historic **Landmark Center,** a grandly restored 1894 Federal Court building replete with towers and turrets, contains the **Minnesota Museum of Art,** along with a collection of pianos, a concert hall, and 4 restored courtrooms. *(75 W. 5th St. 651-292-3225. Museum open Tu-Sa 11am-4pm, Th until 7:30pm, Su 1-5pm.)*

## 🎵 ENTERTAINMENT

Second only to New York in number of theaters per capita, the Twin Cities bring all types of drama to Minnesota. Most parks feature free evening concerts in the summer. The thriving alternative, pop, and classical music scene fills out the wide range of entertainment options. For general info on the local music scene and other events, read the free *City Pages* or *Skyway News.*

**Guthrie Theater,** 725 Vineland Pl., Minneapolis, adjacent to the Walker Art Center just off Hennepin Ave., stands out in the theater world. (377-2224. Season varies; call ahead. Box office open M-F 9am-8pm, Sa 10am-8pm, Su 11am-7pm. Tickets

---

**SHOP 'TIL YOU DROP** About 10min. south of downtown, the **Mall of America,** Bloomington, corrals an indoor roller coaster, ferris wheel, mini-golf course, and 2mi. of stores. *(60 E. Broadway. 883-8800. Open M-F 10am-9:30pm, Sa 9:30am-9:30pm, Su 11am-7pm. Take I-35 E. south to I-494 W. to the 24th Ave. exit.)* Welcome to the largest mall in America, the consummation of the U.S.'s love affair with all that is obscenely gargantuan. With hundreds of specialty stores, including adventure and safari family dining, plus all your old favorites and a large and better-than-average food court, the Mall is a good idea for a day of mind-numbing entertainment, or a good old-fashioned shopping spree.

---

$15.50-37.50, students and seniors $5 discount; rush tickets 10min. before show $12, line starts 1-1½hr. before show.) For family-oriented productions, the **Children's Theater Company,** at 3rd Ave. and 24th St., next to the Minneapolis Institute of Arts, comes through. (874-0400. Season Sept.-June. Box office open M-Sa 9am-5pm; summer hrs. vary slightly. Tickets $16-25; students, seniors, and children $10-19. Rush tickets 15min. before show $8.) The **Illusion Theater,** 528 Hennepin Ave., 8th fl., has experimental works and tickets from $12. (338-8371, box office: 332-5206. Open M-Th 1-5pm, F-Sa 2-8pm, Su 1-4pm.)

Dudley Riggs's **Brave New Workshop,** 2605 Hennepin Ave., stages intriguing musical comedy shows in an intimate club. (332-6620. Box office open June-July M 5-9pm, F-Sa 4-9:30pm, Th and Su 4pm-midnight. M shows $5, Sa-Su $8-12. Box office open Aug.-May W-F and Su 4-9pm, Sa 4pm-12:15am. Tickets $12-18.) In St. Paul, off-**Ordway** theater (see below) plays at the **Park Sq. Theatre,** 20 W. 7th Pl. (651-291-7005. Box office open M-Sa noon-6pm, Su noon-3pm. Tickets $16-24, students $8. Tu previews $1, call ahead.)

The Twin Cities' music scene offers everything from opera to Paisley. **Sommerfest,** a month-long celebration of Viennese music performed by the **Minnesota Orchestra,** marks the high point of the cities' classical scene during July and Aug.; **Orchestra Hall,** 1111 Nicollet Mall, downtown Minneapolis, hosts the event. (800-292-4141. Box office open M-Sa 10am-6pm. Tickets $13-47; rush tickets for students 30min. before show $9.) Nearby **Peavey Plaza,** in Nicollet Mall, holds free coffee concerts. The **St. Paul Chamber Orchestra,** the **Schubert Club,** and the **Minnesota Opera Company** all perform at St. Paul's glass-and-brick **Ordway Music Theater,** 345 Washington St. (651-224-4222. Box office open M-F 9am-5pm, Sa 10am-5pm, Su 11am-5pm. Tickets $20-55.) The artist formerly known as **Prince** brought his seductive and energetic pop lyrics from local rave to worldwide fame—all in high-heeled boots. Today, his state-of-the-art **Paisley Park** studio complex outside the city draws bands from all over to the Great White North.

In Jan., the 10-day **St. Paul Winter Carnival,** near the state capitol, cures cabin fever with ice sculptures, ice-fishing, parades, and skating contests. June brings the 12-day **Fringe Festival** for the performing arts (tickets $4-5). On July 4, St. Paul celebrates **Taste of Minnesota** in the Capitol Mall; on its coattails rides the 9-day **Minneapolis Aquatennial,** with concerts, parades, and art exhibits. During late Aug. and early Sept., the **Minnesota State Fair,** at Snelling and Como St., and the **Renaissance Festival** (445-7361), in the town of Shakopee come to town.

The **Hubert H. Humphrey Metrodome,** 900 S. 5th St. (332-0386), in downtown Minneapolis, houses the **Minnesota Twins,** the cities' baseball team, and the **Minnesota Vikings,** the resident football team. The **Timberwolves** howl at the **Target Center,** 600 1st Ave. (673-0900). The NHL is back in the Twin Cities; the **Wild** take to the ice this winter (651-333-7825). The soccer craze hits the Midwest with Thunder (785-3668).

♫ **NIGHTLIFE**

Minneapolis's vibrant youth culture feeds most of the Twin Cities' clubs and bars. The post-punk scene thrives in the Land of 10,000 Aches: **Soul Asylum** and **Hüsker Dü,** as well as the best bar band in the world, **The Replacements,** rocked here before they went big (or bad). A cross-section of the diverse nightlife can be found on Hennepin Ave., around the **University of Minnesota-Minneapolis,** and across the river on the **West Bank** (bounded on the west by I-35 W. and to the south by I-94), especially on **Cedar Ave.** The Twin Cities card hard, even for cigarettes, so carry your ID with you. The top floor of the **Mall of America** (see above) invites bar-hopping after the screaming kids have gone to bed.

**Ground Zero,** 15 4th St. NE (378-5115), off Hennepin Ave. just north of the river, is practically synonymous with local nightlife. Live music on M and W for beatniks, and bondage on Th. Open M, W, Su until 1am; Tu, Th until 2am; F-Sa until 3am.

**NYE's Bar,** 112 E. Hennepin Ave. (379-2021), across the river from Minneapolis, pumps live polka (Th-Sa) and a piano band every night. A younger, hipper crowd than you'd expect. Open daily 11am-1am.

**First Avenue and 7th St. Entry,** 701 First Ave. N. (332-1775), downtown, rocks with live music several nights a week. The artist formerly known as Prince's former court; he turns up occasionally. Cover $1-6, for concerts $7-18. Open M-Sa 8pm-3am, Su 7pm-3am.

**400 Bar** (332-2903), on 4th St. at Cedar Ave., features live music nightly on a miniscule stage; acts range from local garage bands to national acts. Cover F-Sa $5-7. Open for shows only, which usually start around 7pm.

**Red Sea,** 316 Cedar Ave. (333-1644), has live rock bands nightly (reggae on weekends), while serving Ethiopian food and ethnic burgers ($4-6) until 1am.

**Uptown Bar and Café,** 3018 Hennepin Ave. (823-4719). A yuppie-ish crowd hears blues at around 10:30pm; weekend cover $2-5. Open daily 8am-1am.

**The Gay 90s** (333-7755), on Hennepin Ave. at 4th St., claims the 7th highest liquor consumption rate of all clubs in the nation. This superplex hosts thousands of mostly gay and lesbian partymongers in its many bars and showrooms. Open daily 8pm-3am.

**O'Gara's Garage,** 164 N. Snelling Ave. (651-644-3333), St. Paul, hosts big bands and jazz nightly in the Irish-theme front bar (no cover); live alternative and dance music play in the back W-Sa. Cover $3-6. Open daily until 1am. 21+ after 8pm. Concert doors open at 8:30pm.

**Plums** (651-699-2227), at Randolph and Snelling Ave., St. Paul, lets loose with $6 all-you-can-drink nights on Th until midnight. Open M-Sa 11am-1am, Su noon-1am.

# DULUTH

If cities were sold at auctions, Duluth would fetch a high price; the people are nice, the parks are clean, the streets are safe, and the location is amazing. Bidders on a vacation to Duluth can expect to eat well, find relatively inexpensive lodging, and watch some serious shipping action. As the largest freshwater port in the world, Duluth harbors ships from over 60 different countries. The recently restored area of Canal Park, along Lake St., has tempted microbreweries, restaurants, theaters, and museums to occupy the old factories and depots down on the wharf, turning a once-overlooked tourist destination into a spunky hotspot of northern activity.

**⚐ PRACTICAL INFORMATION. Greyhound,** 2122 W. Superior (722-5591), stops 2mi. west of downtown; take bus #9 "Piedmont" from downtown. Buses run to Milwaukee (11hr., 3 per day, $70) and St. Paul (3hr., 3 per day, $21). Buy tickets daily 6:45am-5:30pm. The **Duluth Transit Authority,** 2402 W. Michigan St. (722-7283), sends buses throughout the city (peak fare M-F 7-9am and 2:30-6pm $1, off-peak 50¢). Tourist-moving **Port Town Trolley** (722-7283) serves the downtown area, Canal Park, and waterfront (runs late May-early Sept. daily 11am-7pm; fare 50¢). **Visitors Info: Convention and Visitors Bureau,** 100 Lake Place Dr. (722-4011), at Endion Station in Canal Park (open M-F 8:30am-5pm); the **Summer Visitors Center** (722-6024), at Vista dock on Harbor Dr. (open mid-May to mid-Oct. daily 8:30am-7:30pm; hrs. highly variable); and **The Depot,** 506 W. Michigan St. (727-8025). (Open Sa-Th 9:30am-6pm, F 9:30am-8pm; mid-Oct. to Apr. M-Sa 10am-5pm, Su 1-5pm.) **24hr. Crisis Line:** 726-1931. **Post Office:** 2800 W. Michigan St. (723-2590; open M-F 8am-5pm, Sa 9am-1pm). **ZIP code:** 55806. **Area code:** 218.

**ALL HAWKING AT ONCE** Duluth's location, as well as its considerable updrafts, make the city especially appealing to soaring birds. On one day in late Aug., Sept., or Oct., as many as 10,000 of these migratory hawks pass over **Hawk Ridge,** just west of the city. These birds, loathe to pass over such a large body of water as Lake Superior, converge on Duluth as an enticing alternative. On Sept. 15th 1978, a record-setting 31,831 Broad-winged hawks passed over the city on their way south. Visit the Hawk Ridge Nature Reserve, on Skyline Parkway, to see the birds. (Binoculars and a bird book are great if you've got them).

**▛ ACCOMMODATIONS.** Motel rates rise and rooms fill during the warm months. The **College of St. Scholastica,** 1200 Kenwood Ave., exit 258 off I-35 N., rents out quiet dorm rooms with free local calls, kitchen access, and laundry facilities (723-6000 or 800-447-5444; ask for the housing director. Singles $21; doubles $40. Reservations recommended. Open early June to mid-Aug.) Reasonably priced motels line London Rd.; the **Chalet Motel,** 1801 London Rd., is west of downtown. (728-4238 or 800-235-2957. Apr.-Sept. Sa-Su singles $46, doubles $55; M-F $39/49. Lower in winter.) Other cheap motels line I-35, just southwest of the city, including **Motel 6,** at the 27th St. exit (singles $40). **Jay Cooke State Park,** southwest of Duluth on I-35 off exit 242, has 83 campsites, 50mi. of hiking trails, 12mi. of snowmobile trails, and 32mi. for cross-country skiing among the tall trees of the St. Louis River valley. (384-4610; 800-246-2267 for reservations. Open daily 9am-9pm, park gates open until 10pm. Sites with showers $12, plus electricity $14.50. Vehicle permit $4. Reservations recommended; $6.50 reservation fee.)

**⎙⎙ FOOD AND NIGHTLIFE.** Upscale **Fitger's Brewery Complex,** 600 E. Superior St., and the **Canal Park** region, south from downtown along Lake Ave., feature plenty of pleasant eateries. The **Brewhouse,** in Fitger's Brewery Complex, has beer and pub food. Big Boat Oatmeal Stout ($3.50) keeps it cool, and acoustic bands warm things up. (726-1392. Tu and Th-Sa; cover $1-2. Open daily 11am-1am. Grill closes 10pm.) The **DeWitt-Seitz Marketplace,** in the middle of Canal Park Dr., has slightly pricier restaurants. The **Blue Note Café,** 357 Canal Park Dr., creates delicious sandwiches ($5-7) and desserts ($3.25) in a yuppified coffeehouse setting (727-6549; open M-Th 9am-9pm, F-Sa 9am-11pm, Su 9am-8pm). **Hacienda del Sol,** 319 E. Superior St., fires up original Mexican recipes (722-7296; entrees $4-8; open M-Th 11am-10pm, F-Sa 11am-midnight). In an old pipe-fitting factory, **Grandma's Sports Garden** is the mother of all Duluthian nightlife, with dining, a bar, and a huge dance floor (722-4722; restaurant open daily 11am-10pm; club open daily 11:30am-1am). At the large, social **Backstage,** 1612 Tower Ave., Superior, house and dance DJs spin the tables (mixed drinks from $2; 715-392-3737; open daily until 2am).

**⎙⎙ SIGHTS AND ENTERTAINMENT.** Duluth's proximity to majestic Lake Superior is its biggest draw; many visitors head right down to **Canal Park** and watch the big ships go by at the Aerial Lift Bridge (see below). Others watch the ships get loaded at the **Ore Docks Observation Platform.** The **Boatwatcher's Hotline** has up-to-the-minute info on ship movements (722-6489). Accompanied by deafening horn blasts, the unique **Aerial Lift Bridge** climbs 138 ft. in 55 seconds to allow vessels to pass; late afternoon is prime viewing time. Within Canal Park, the **Lake Superior Maritime Visitors Center** prepares extensive displays on commercial shipping in Lake Superior (727-2497; open daily 10am-9pm; free). Canal Park also serves as the end/beginning of the **Duluth Lakewalk,** a 3mi. promenade which connects Fitger's Brewery, Canal Park, and the near north shore. Across the Aerial Lift Bridge, **Park Point** has excellent swimming areas, parks, and sandy beaches.

The scenic **Willard Munger State Trail** links West Duluth to Jay Cooke State Park, providing 14mi. of paved path perfect for bikes and rollerblades—**Willard Munger Inn,** 7408 Grand Ave., rents both (624-4814 or 800-982-2453; bikes $10 per ½-day, $13 per day; in-line skates $10/$14). The 5-story stone octagonal **Enger Tower,** on

Skyline Pkwy. at 18th Ave. W., rises from the highest land in Duluth; the nearby Japanese flower gardens make a beautiful picnic area.

A 39-room neo-Jacobean mansion built on iron-shipping wealth, **Glensheen,** 3300 London Rd., lies on the eastern outskirts of town. (724-8863 or 888-454-4536. Open late May to early Sept. 9:30am-4pm; off-season hrs. vary. $8.75, seniors and ages 12-15 $7, ages 6-11 $4.) Waterfront tours of the Great Lakes, the steamer **William A. Irvin** reveal more of Duluth's shipping past. (722-7876 or 722-5573. Open daily 9am-6pm. Call during spring and fall. $6.50, students and seniors $5.50, ages 3-12 $3.50.)

**The Depot,** 506 W. Michigan St., a former railroad station, houses 4 performing arts groups and several museums. (727-8025. Open May to mid.-Oct. daily 10am-5pm; mid-Oct. to Apr. M-Sa 10am-5pm, Su 1-5pm. $6 includes all museums and a trolley ride, families $18, ages 3-11 $4.) On the waterfront, **Bayfront Festival Park** hosts events and festivals, most notably the mid-Aug. **Bayfront Blues Festival.**

# CHIPPEWA NATIONAL FOREST

Gleaming white stands of birch lace the Norway pine forests of the **Chippewa National Forest.** Home to the highest density of breeding bald eagles in the continental U.S., these proud birds soar over the Mississippi River between Cass Lake and Lake Winnie from mid-Mar. through Nov. Wetlands and lakes blanket nearly half of the forest land, providing ample opportunities for canoeing and watersports. The national forest shares territory with the **Leech Lake Indian Reservation,** home to 4560 members of the Minnesota Ojibwe tribe, the fourth-largest tribe in the U.S. The Ojibwe, mistakenly called Chippewa, migrated from the Atlantic coast in the 1700s, displacing the Sioux. In the mid-1800s, the government seized most of their land and established reservations like Leech Lake.

Camping—cheap, plentiful, and available in varying degrees of modernity—is the way to stay. The forest office (see below) has info on campsites; over 400 of them are free. North of Walker, billboards for private campgrounds string the edges of Rt. 71. Cabins at **Stony Point Resort** 7mi. east of town off Rt. 200, 4mi. north on Onigam Rd., sleep up to 12 people (547-1665 or 800-338-9303; from $88 for 4-person cabin with A/C). Or camp next door at the **National Forest Campground** (800-280-2267; $14, with hookup $16; $8 reservation fee; sites are self-regulated). Step across the mighty Mississippi (at its source, anyway), at the **Beginning of the Mississippi,** at **Lake Itasca State Park,** 30mi. west of Chippewa National Forest on Rt. 200. The park office, through the north entrance and down County Rd. 122, has camping info. (266-2100 Office open M-F 8am-4:30pm, Sa-Su 8am-4pm; mid-Oct. to Apr. M-F 8am-4:30pm. Ranger on call after hrs.) The comfortable **Mississippi Headwaters Hostel (HI-AYH)** has 32 hotel quality beds with some 4-bed rooms for families. The hostel stays open in the winter to facilitate access to the park's excellent cross-country skiing. (266-3415. Laundry, kitchen, multiple bathrooms. 2-night min. stay on certain weekends. Check-in Su-Th 5-10pm, F-Sa 5-11pm. Check-out M-F 10am, Sa-Su noon. Members $15, nonmembers $18. Linen $2-4. $4 per day vehicle permit required. Private rooms available.) In the park, **Itasca Sports Rental** (266-2150) offers mountain bikes ($3.50 per hr., $20 per day); canoes ($3/$18); and pontoons ($25 for 2hr.; open May-Oct. daily 7am-9pm; must be 18+).

For the northbound traveler, **Walker,** a small town in the southwest corner of the park and reservation, serves as an ideal gateway. **Leech Lake Area Chamber of Commerce:** on Rt. 371 downtown (547-1313 or 800-833-1118; open May-Sept. M-F 9am-5pm, Sa 9am-3pm, call ahead for winter hrs.). The **Forest Office** (547-1044; superintendent 335-8600), just east of town on Rt. 371, has the dirt on outdoor activities (open M-F 8am-4:30pm). **Greyhound** (547-3455) runs from Minneapolis to Walker (5½hr., 1 per day, $35), stopping at Hardee's downtown (547-9585), with a ticket office at Ben Franklin's, also downtown. A southbound bus leaves daily at 8:30am, a northbound at 4:30pm; buy tickets at the next station. Walker's **post office:** 602 Michigan Ave. (547-1123; open M-F 9am-4pm). **ZIP code:** 46484. **Area code:** 218.

GREAT LAKES

# IRON RANGE

It was the cry of *"Goald!"* that brought the flood of miners to join the loggers and trappers already in the area, but it was the staying power of iron that kept them here. The Iron Range—120mi. of wilderness and small towns along Minnesota Rt. 169, produces over 50% of the country's steel.

In the town of **Calumet** at the **Hill Annex Mine State Park** a now-obsolete natural iron-ore pit-mine, an exceptional 1½hr. tour led by former miners brings visitors through the buildings and vehicles and into the 500 ft. deep mine. (247-7215. $6, ages 5-12 $4; open May-Sept. daily 10am-4pm; tours depart on the hr.)

The answer, my friend, is blowing in **Hibbing**, hometown of Robert Zimmerman (a.k.a. **Bob Dylan**). Then again, maybe it's not—a stay of over a day will illustrate why the legendary songwriter refused for years to acknowledge where his oats were sown. Nonetheless, the **Hibbing Tourist Center,** 1202 E. Howard St. (262-4166), off Rt. 169, mixes up the medicine on the **Hull Rust Mahoning Mine,** the world's largest open pit-mine. If you're sleepy and there is no place you're going to, **Adams House,** 201 E. 23rd St., a beautiful Tudor-style B&B, can put you up in a double room (263-9742 or 888-891-9742; $48-53, light breakfast included, reservations recommended). Around the corner, the **China Buffet,** 116 E. Howard St., has fresh lunch ($5.25, M-Sa 11am-4pm) and dinner buffets ($6.95. M-Sa 4-8:30pm. Su 11am-10pm. 263-6324. Open Su-Th 11am-10pm, F-Sa 11am-10:30pm.)

If the naked scars of the pit-mines got you down, feed and ogle the black bears at the **Vince Shute Wildlife Sanctuary,** 13mi. west of Orr on Rt. 23. (Open late May-early Sept., Th-Su, 5pm-dusk. Free. No pets.) **McKinley Park Campground,** on Rt. 1 in **Soudan,** a few mi. east of Tower, rents semi-private campsites overlooking gorgeous Vermilion Lake. (753-5921. Sites $12, with hookup $14. Canoe and paddleboat rentals $4 per hr., $16 per day.)

Serving as a launching pad both into the **Boundary Waters Canoe Area Wilderness** (BWCAW; see below) and the Iron Range, **Ely** supports its share of wilderness outfitters. **Chamber of Commerce,** 1600 E. Sheridan St. (365-6123 or 800-777-7281; open M-Sa 9am-6pm, Su noon-4pm; off-season M-F 9am-5pm). The **International Wolf Center,** 1396 Rt. 169, houses 3 timber wolves, packs BWCAW permits, and has informative displays on *Canis lupus.* (365-4695. Open May-Nov. daily 9am-5:30pm; Nov.-May Sa-Su only, 10am-5pm. $5, seniors $4, ages 6-12 $2.50; call for wolf presentation times.) Next door, the **Dorothy Molter Museum** honors the "Root Beer Lady of Knife Lake." The last year-round resident of the BWCAW, Ms. Molter brewed 11-12,000 bottles of root beer each year. (365-4451. Open May-Sept. daily 10am-6pm. $3, children $1.50; root beer $1.) For a drink and some pool, darts, or Fusball, row your boat to the **Portage Bar.** (16 E Sheridan St. 365-4433. $1 draughts. $6 pitchers. Open M-Sa 3pm-1am.) **Shagawa Sam's,** 60 W. Lakeview Pl., has a tidy loft full of comfortable bunks for $12 per night, including linen and showers, plus some RV campsites and cabins. (365-6757. RV sites $10, $1.50 each for water and electricity. Cabins for 4 $60-70. Canoe rental $10 per day.) **Area code:** 218.

# LAKE SUPERIOR NORTH SHORE

**RT. 61.** The true Lake Superior North Shore extends 646mi. from Duluth, MN to Sault Ste. Marie, ON; but, Rt. 61 (North Shore Dr.), winding along the coast from Duluth to Grand Portage, gives travelers an abbreviated version of the journey. Small, touristy fishing towns separate the 31,000 sq. mi. lake (comprising 10% of the world's freshwater surface area) from the moose, bear, and wolves inland. Rt. 61 is often glutted with boat-towing pick up trucks and family-filled campers on summer weekends. Accommodations flanking the roadside fill up fast in summer; make reservations early. Remember to bring warm clothes; temps. can drop into the low 40s (°F) on summer nights.

Most towns along the shore maintain a visitors center. The **R.J. Houle Visitor Information Center** (834-4005 or 800-554-2116), 21mi. from Duluth up Rt. 61 in Two Harbors, has lodging guides and info for each town along the MN stretch of the North Shore. (Open Su-Th 10am-4pm, F-Sa 9am-7pm; mid-Oct. to May W-Sa 9am-1pm.) A few mi. northeast of the Info Center, **Gooseberry Falls**, along Hwy. 61, cascades toward the sea (834-2461). **Camping** near the cataract is available (primitive sites with shower $12; required vehicle permit $4). Closer to civilization, the pine-paneled **Cobblestone Cabins**, off Rt. 61 2mi. north of Tofte, come with access to a cobblestone beach, canoes, a woodburning sauna, and kitchenettes (663-7957; cabins for 1-12 $40-85; open May-Oct.). **Happy Times** bus lines runs 4 buses per week (Su, M, W, and F) from the **Duluth Greyhound Station**, 2122 W. Superior St. (722-5591; open daily 7am-5pm) to Grand Marais ($38). **Area code:** 218.

**BOUNDARY WATERS CANOE AREA WILDERNESS.** At its north end, Rt. 61 runs along BWCAW, a designated wilderness comprising 1.2 million acres of lakes, streams, and forests (including part of **Superior National Forest**) in which no human-made additions—phones, roads, electricity, private dwellings—are allowed. Within the BWCAW, small waterways and portages string together 1100 lakes, allowing virtually limitless "canoe-camping." All visitors to the BWCAW must acquire a permit. The BWCAW is quite finicky about when, where, and how many people it will allow to enter the Wilderness. As few as 6 permits will be accepted for popular put-ins during the summer, so phoning ahead is essential (day permits free, camping permits $10 per person per trip). Running northwest from **Grand Marais,** the 60mi. paved **Gunflint Trail** (County Rd. 12) is the only developed road offering access to the wilderness; resorts and outfitters gather alongside this lone strip of civilization. **Bear Track Outfitters,** 2011 W. Rt. 61, across from the Gunflint Ranger Station, rents boats and sells camping necessities. (387-1162. 1-day canoe rental $20, includes all accessories. 1-day kayak rental $30.)

The **Grand Marais Chamber of Commerce:** N. Broadway off Rt. 61 in Grand Marais. (387-2524 or 888-922-5000. Open mid-May to Oct. M-Sa 9am-5pm. Call for winter hrs.). 1mi. south of town, the **Gunflint Ranger Station** distributes permits (877-550-6777; open May-Sept. daily 6am-8pm; Oct.-Apr. M-F 8am-4:30pm).

The well-kept, seldom-full cabins of **"Spirit of the Land" Island Hostel (HI-AYH)** are located on an island in Seagull Lake, at the end of the Gunflint Trail. The Christian-oriented **Wilderness Canoe Base,** leads canoe trips and summer island camps for various groups and administers at the hostel. Call from Grand Marais to arrange a boat pick up. (388-2241 or 800-454-2922. Full kitchen, outhouses. Beds $14, non-members $18, F-Sa $18/20. Sleeping bag $5, sleepsack $3. Meals $4-6. Hot showers free. Saunas $3. Canoe rental $10 per ½-day, $18 per day. Snowshoe rentals in winter. Closed Nov.-Dec.) **Nelson's Traveler's Rest,** on Rt. 61 ½mi. west of Grand Marais, provides fully equipped cabins with a lake view (387-1464 or 800-249-1285; from $43; open mid-May to mid-Oct.; call in advance). **Grand Marais Municipal Campground,** off Rt. 61 in Grand Marais, has new wooded and mostly private primitive campsites along the lake. (387-1712 or 800-998-0959. Primitive sites $15, with water and electricity $18; office open 6am-10pm; use of municipal pool $1.)

Cheap and popular with fishermen, **South of the Border Café,** 4 W. Rt. 61, in Grand Marais, specializes in huge breakfasts (served all day) and satisfying diner food. The bluefin herring sandwich (fried, of course) will run you $2.75. Breakfast under $4. (387-1505. Open daily 5am-2pm.) Sweet tooths should try **World's Best Doughnuts,** at the intersection of Wisconsin and Broadway. (387-1345. Open late May to mid-Oct. M-Sa 7:30am until sold out, usually around 5pm, Su 7am-2pm.)

# VOYAGEURS

**Voyageurs National Park** sits on Minnesota's boundary with Ontario, accessible almost solely by boat. Named for the French Canadian fur traders who once traversed this area, the park invites today's voyagers to leave the auto-dominated world and push off into the longest inland lake waterway on the continent. While some hiking trails exist, boats and canoes provide most transportation within the park. Preservation efforts have kept the area much as it was in the late 18th century, and wolves, bear, deer, and moose roam freely. Sadly, undeveloped can mean unregulated; water should be boiled for at least 2min. before consumption, and some fish in these waters contain mercury. Ticks bearing Lyme disease have been found as well; visitors should take precautions (see p. 54).

The park can be accessed through (from Southeast to Northwest) **Crane Lake, Ash River, Kabetogama Lake,** or **Rainy Lake** (all east of Rt. 53), or through **International Falls,** at the northern tip of Rt. 53 just below Ft. Frances, ON. There are many visitors centers. **Crane Lake Visitor and Tourism Bureau,** 7238 Handberg Rd. (993-2481 or 800-362-7405; open M-F 9am-5pm); **International Falls Chamber of Commerce,** 301 2nd Ave. (800-325-5766; open M-F 8am-5pm, Sa 7am-3pm); and, within the park, 3 more. **Rainy Lake** (286-5258), at the end of Rt. 11, 12mi. east of International Falls (open May-Sept. daily 9am-5pm; call for off-season hrs.); **Ash River** (374-3221), 8mi. east of Rt. 53 on Rt. 129, then 3mi. north (open early May- early Sept. daily 10am-4pm); and **Kabetogama Lake** (875-2111), 1mi. north of Rt. 122, follow the signs (open mid-May to Sept. daily 9am-5pm).

Many of the numerous campsites are accessible only by water. Car-accessible sites can be found in the state forest, including **Wooden Frog** about 4mi. from Kabetogama Visitors Center Rd. 122 (757-3489; primitive sites $9, showers available at lodge $3), and **Ash River,** 3mi. from the visitors center and 2mi. east on Rt. 129 (757-3489; primitive sites $9). Only 5min. from International Falls, **International Voyageurs RV Campground,** off Rt. 53 south of town, offers decent camping with showers, and laundry (283-4679; tent sites $11, full hookup $18.)

Rt. 53 in International Falls is loaded with motels. The **Ash Trail Lodge** is in a wooded, pleasant environment. (374-3131 or 800-777-4513. 10mi. east of Rt. 53 on Rt. 129. Singles and doubles $55.) **International Falls,** the inspiration for **Rocky and Bullwinkle's** hometown Frostbite Falls, hosts a few attractions outside the park. The state's largest prehistoric burial ground, **Grand Mound History Center,** 17mi. west of town on Rt. 11, supposedly dates from 200 BC (285-3332; open May-Sept. M-Sa 10am-5pm, Su noon-5pm; $2). **Smokey Bear Park,** home of a 22 ft. tall thermometer and the 26 ft., 82-ton giant who asks you to help fight forest fires, makes for lighter entertainment. **Area code:** 218.

# GREAT PLAINS

In 1803, the Louisiana Purchase doubled America's size, adding French territory west of the Mississippi at the bargain price of 4¢ per acre. Over time, the plains spawned legends of pioneers and cowboys, and of Native Americans struggling to defend their homes. The coming of railroad transportation and liberal land policy spurred an economic boom, until a drought during the Great Depression transformed the region into a dust bowl. Modern agricultural techniques have since reclaimed the soil, and the heartland of the United States thrives on the trade of farm commodities. Today, the Great Plains is a vast land of prairies and farms, where open sky stretches from horizon to horizon, broken only by long, thin lines of trees. Grasses and grains paint the land green and gold. The plains' breadbasket feeds much of the world. Yet, in spite of man, the land rules here, and the most staggering sights in the region are the work of nature, from the Badlands to the Black Hills. The mighty Missouri and Mississippi Rivers trace their way through thriving small towns, while amber waves of grain quietly reign.

## HIGHLIGHTS OF THE GREAT PLAINS

■ **National Parks and Monuments.** Find uncrowded gems in Theodore Roosevelt National Park, SD (p. 534) and the Badlands, SD (p. 537), or join the crowds in the Black Hills around Mt. Rushmore (p. 540).

■ **Historical sites.** Scotts Bluff National Monument, NE (p. 556) and Chimney Rock, NE (p. 556) will fascinate anyone interested in the pioneers.

# NORTH DAKOTA

An early visitor to the site of present-day Fargo declared, "It's a beautiful land, but I doubt that human beings will ever live here." Posterity begs to differ. The stark, haunting lands that so intimidated early settlers eventually found willing tenants, and the territory became a state along with South Dakota on Nov. 2, 1889. The inaugural event was not without confusion—Benjamin Harrison concealed the names when he signed the two bills, so both Dakotas claim to be the 39th state.

North Dakota has remained largely isolated geographically. In the western half of the state, the colorful buttes of the Badlands rise in desolate beauty, while in the eastern half, mind-numbing flatness rules; the 110mi. of Rt. 46 from U.S. 81 to Rt. 30 is the longest stretch of highway in the U.S. without a single curve.

## ⛏ PRACTICAL INFORMATION

**Capital:** Bismarck.

**Visitor Info: Tourism Dept.,** 604 East Blvd., Bismarck 58505 (701-328-2525 or 800-437-2077; www.ndtourism.com). **Parks and Recreation Dept.,** 1835 Bismarck Expwy., Bismarck 58504.

**Postal Abbreviation:** ND. **Sales Tax:** 5-7%, depending on city.

## FARGO

Although it's North Dakota's largest city, Fargo existed in anonymity until the 1996 Oscar-winning film, *Fargo*, brought it fame. However, very little of the movie was filmed in the town, and its parodied accents are more northern Minnesota than North Dakota. Fargo and its sister city, Moorhead, MN, are home to 20,000 college students who pack lectures at North Dakota State University, Moorhead State, and Concordia College, and add a touch of energy to a withering downtown.

The **Heritage Hjemkomst Center,** 202 1st Ave. N. in Moorhead, pays tribute to the 2 cities' Norwegian heritage. Inside looms the **Hjemkomst,** a 76 ft. Viking ship replica built by Moorhead native Robert Asp. (218-299-5604. Open Su-W and F-Sa 9am-5pm, Th 9am-9pm. $3.50, students and seniors $3, ages 5-17 $1.50.) The restored 1930s **Fargo Theater,** 314 Broadway, shows art house films (232-4152, $6).

Both the **Red River Valley Fair** (800-456-6408; June 16-25, 2000) and the **Scandinavian Hjemkomst Festival** (800-235-7654; June 22-25, 2000) are big draws, complete with rides, shows, and tasty local food. From June to Aug., **Trollwood Park Weekends** (241-8160) features similar enticements.

Cheap chain motels abound at I-29 and 13th Ave.; take exit 64 off I-29. **The Sunset Motel,** 731 W. Main, in West Fargo, about 3mi. west off I-29 exit 65, offers clean rooms, free local calls, continental breakfast, and an indoor pool with a snazzy 2-story waterslide. (800-252-2207. Singles $25; doubles $37; kitchenettes $5 extra. Call early on weekends.) In summer, **Moorhead State University** rents rooms with linen and phones in Ballard Hall, just north of 9th Ave. and 14th St. S. in Moorhead (218-236-2231; $12 per person; check-in 24hr.). **Lindenwood Park,** at 17th Ave. and 5th St. S., offers campsites close to the peaceful Red River (232-3987; sites $8, with hookup $14). The park also has extensive trails ideal for mountain biking. Patrons at **Jim Lauerman's,** 64 Broadway, enjoy salads ($2.50-4.50) or tasty sandwiches ($2.50-4.75); the Sloppy George is a good choice (237-4747; open M-Sa 11am-1am, Su noon-1am; no minors after 9pm). **Cafe Alladin,** 530 6th Ave. N., has good Greek and Middle Eastern food ($3.50-7) and great baklava ($2; 298-0880; open M 10:30am-9pm, Tu-Sa 10am-9pm). A band plays 3 nights a week at **Kirby's** (233-2817; open M-Sa 8am-1am; Su in winter 11am-1am) and **Ralph's** (233-3435; open M-Sa noon-1am; Su in winter 11am-1am). The **I Beam,** at Center Ave. and 11th St. in Moorhead, is an alternative mixed bar with a great dance floor. (233-7700. Open M-Sa 7pm-1am; cover F-Sa after 10pm $2. Tu men's night. Th ladies' night.) NDSU students go to the bars along **Broadway** near Northern Pacific Ave.

**Fargo** and **Moorhead** flank the **Red River** on the east and west, respectively. Numbered streets increase from the river outward, and numbered avenues run east-west. **Main Ave.** is the central east-west thoroughfare and intersects **I-29, University Dr.,** and **Broadway. Hector International Airport,** is at 2801 32nd Ave. N.W. (241-8168), off 19th Ave. N. in northern Fargo. **Amtrak,** 420 4th St. N. (232-2197), chugs daily to Minneapolis (5-6hr., $25-55) and Chicago (14hr., $60-130; open daily midnight-7am). **Greyhound,** 402 Northern Pacific (N.P.) Ave. (293-1222; open daily 5:30am-6:20pm and 10:30pm-1:20am), lopes to Minneapolis (4-7hr., 5 per day, $30) and Bismarck (4hr., 3 per day, $30). **Metro Area Transit,** 502 North Pacific Ave. (232-7500), runs buses across the city (M-Sa). **Taxi: Doyle's Yellow Checker Cab** (235-5535). **Internet Access** is availible at the **Fargo Public Library,** 102 N. 3rd St. (241-1492; open M-Th 9am-9pm, F-Sa 9am-6pm, Su in winter 1-6pm). Sort out your visit at the **Fargo-Moorhead Convention and Visitors Bureau,** 2001 44th St. SW (282-3653 or 800-235-7654), off 45th St. (open May-Aug. M-Sa 7:30am-7pm, Su 10am-6pm; Sept.-Apr. daily 8am-6pm). **Crisis Line:** 235-7335; 24hr. **Post Office:** 657 2nd Ave. N. (241-6100; open M-F 7:30am-5:30pm, Sa 8am-2pm). **ZIP code:** 58103. **Area code:** 701.

## FROM FARGO TO THEODORE ROOSEVELT

Commissioned to map the new territory acquired in the Louisiana Purchase of 1803, famed explorers **Meriwether Lewis** and **William Clark** toughed out the harsh winter of 1804-5 on the shores of the great Missouri River in North Dakota. Along Rt. 83, about 40mi. north of Bismarck, a number of attractions relate to this period.

The **Lewis and Clark Interpretive Center,** in **Washburn** at the junction of Rt. 83 and ND 200A, describes their time in North Dakota. The staff can direct modern-day trailblazers to the replica of the expedition's rugged riverside lodgings just down the road at **Fort Mandan** (701-462-8535; open daily May 24-Sept. 7 9am-7pm; off-season 9am-5pm; $2, students $1). Several mi. west off ND 200A in **Stanton,** is the **Knife River Indian Villages National Historic Site,** where a museum examines the history and culture of the Hidatsa, Mandan, and Arikara tribes who helped Lewis and Clark survive that winter. Several trails lead to

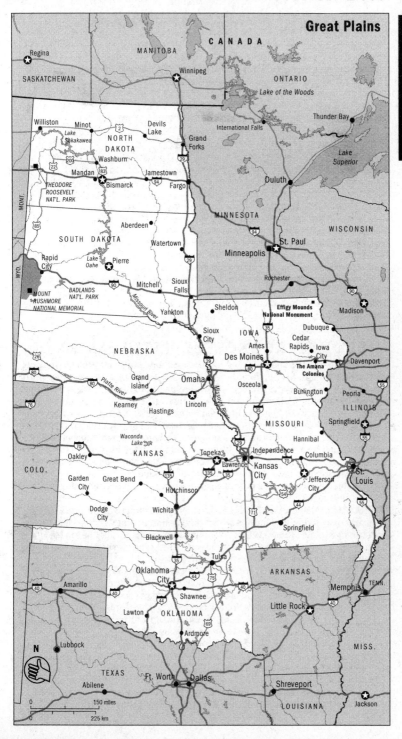

**Great Plains**

GREAT PLAINS

**I-94, ROAD OF CONCRETE WONDERS** Two gargantuan concrete monuments separated by 131mi. of interstate symbolize the past and present of North Dakota and the entire Great Plains. Looming against the horizon in Jamestown, ND, at exit 258, is the world's largest buffalo—a towering, 60 ton, 24 foot, monument to the animals that once roamed the plains. Near the statue, a herd of real buffalo regards their concrete brother apathetically from behind a protective fence. With luck, you'll see White Cloud, a rare albino buffalo sacred to many Native American tribes. Adjacent to the monument is the **National Buffalo Museum,** documenting the evolution and adulation of the buffalo. (800-222-4766; open daily 9am-8pm; $3, students $1, families $7.) 131mi. west in Salem, at exit 127, Salem Sue, the world's largest Holstein Cow (38 ft. tall and 50 ft. long), keeps a watchful eye over the interstate and the seas of cows that munch on the grasses of the plains. ($1 donation.)

the sites of former Native American villages. (701-745-3300. Open May 24-Sept. 7 daily 8am-6pm Mountain Time. Earthlodge tours at 11am, 1pm, and 3pm. Free.) Those interested in simulating Lewis and Clark's camping experience along the Missouri River go to **Cross Ranch State Park Campground,** between the Lewis and Clark Interpretive Center and the Knife River National Historical Site—take the paved road off 200A at the sign. (702-794-3731. $4 per vehicle. Tent sites $7; RVs $10, no electricity; cabin with no power or water available for rent, 1-5 people $42. Showers.) Another option is scenic **Abraham Lincoln State Park,** (633-4785; flush toilets; water and showers; sites $7, with electricity $12, plus $3 per vehicle park entrance fee.) **Nodak Motel,** 210 N. 20th St. has large rooms at great prices. (233-1960; single $25; double $30).

# THEODORE ROOSEVELT NATIONAL PARK

After both his mother and wife died on the same day, pre-White House Theodore Roosevelt moved to his ranch in the Badlands for a dose of spiritual renewal. He was so influenced by the red- and brown-hued lunar formations, horseback riding, big-game hunting, and cattle ranching in this unforgiving land that he later claimed, "I never would have been President if it weren't for my experiences in North Dakota." Inspired by his wilderness days, Roosevelt created numerous national parks, monuments, and bird refuges. **Theodore Roosevelt National Park** was created in 1947 as a monument to his conservationist policies. Visitors can garner the inspiration he did, among quiet canyons, secluded glens, and dramatic rocky outcroppings which have earned the park the nickname "rough-rider country." The park teems with wildlife; prairie dog towns, bison, and deer are all common.

**⛏ PRACTICAL INFORMATION.** The park is split into southern and northern units and bisected by the border separating Mountain and Central Time Zones. The entrance to the more-developed southern unit is just north of I-94 in **Medora,** a frontier town revamped into a tourist mecca. **Greyhound** serves Medora from the Sully Inn (see below), with buses to Bismarck (3½hr., 3 per day, $23-25) and Billings (6hr., 2 per day, $45-48). There is no ticket office in Medora; board the bus and buy your ticket during the Dickinson layover. The park entrance fee ($5 per person or $10 max. per vehicle, under 17 free) covers admission to both units of the park for 7 days. The **South Unit's Visitors Center** (623-4466), in Medora, maintains a mini-museum displaying Teddy's guns, spurs, and old letters, as well as a beautiful 13min. film about the Badlands. (Open daily 8am-8pm; Sept. to mid-June 8am-4:30pm.) The **South Unit's Emergency** number is 623-4379. The **North Unit's Visitors Center** (842-2333) has an interesting exhibit on the nature and wildlife in the park and offers a shorter film (open daily 9am-5:30pm Central Time). In an **emergency** in the north unit, call the **ranger** at 842-4151 or the **sheriff** at 842-3654. For more info, write to **Theodore Roosevelt National Park,** P.O. Box 7, Medora 58645, or call the visitors centers. **Internet Access: Billings County Resource Center,** on Broadway (623-

4604; open M&F noon-6pm, W 10am-5pm). Medora's **post office:** 355 3rd Ave. (open M-Sa 8am-7pm; window service M-F 8am-4:30pm, Sa 8:15am-9:15am). **ZIP code:** 58645. **Area code:** 701. **South Unit Time Zone:** Mountain (2hr. behind Eastern). **North Unit Time Zone:** Central (1hr. behind Eastern).

**▛▟ ACCOMMODATIONS AND FOOD.** Free backcountry camping permits are available at the visitors center. **Cottonwood Campgrounds,** in the south park, has toilets and running water ($10). In the north, **Juniper Campground,** 5mi. west of the north unit entrance, is in a beautiful valley (sites $10; toilets and running water). The campground is a popular buffalo nightspot all year, so be aware.

It's not easy to find inexpensive, non-camping lodging in Medora. The **Sully Inn,** 428 Broadway, offers clean rooms at the lowest rates in town, plus free local calls and 10% off in its bookstore (623-4455; singles $35-45, in winter $20-35; doubles $40-50; under 13 free). Teddy Roosevelt was known to bunk down at the **Rough Riders Hotel,** at 3rd St. and 3rd Ave. The hotel's room rates are far from budget, but the restaurant serves reasonable breakfasts and lunches (omelettes, salads, and sandwiches) for $5-7. (623-4444, ext. 497. Open daily from 7am to 9pm. In winter, B&B only.) The **Cowboy Café** on 4th St., dishes up less expensive meals ($2-10), including pie, $3.50 buffalo burgers, and salads (623-4343; open May-Nov. daily 6am-8pm).

**▣ ▙ SIGHTS AND ENTERTAINMENT.** The **south unit** features a 36mi. **scenic automobile loop.** Many hiking trails start from the loop and wander into the wilderness. **Wind Canyon,** located on the loop, is a constantly morphing canyon formed by winds blowing against the soft clay. The ¾mi. **Coal Vein Trail** follows a seam of lignite coal that caught fire here and burned from 1951 to 1977. The third-largest **petrified forest** in the U.S. lies a day's hike into the park; if you prefer to drive, ask at the visitors center for a map and prepare to walk ½mi. from the parking lot. Learn more about Teddy Roosevelt through a tour of his **Maltese Cabin,** circa 1883. Tours leave from the **Southern Unit Visitors Center** in the summer every half hour from 8:45am-4:15pm. **Painted Canyon Overlook,** 7mi. east of Medora off I-94, has its own **visitors center** with picnic tables and a breathtaking view of the Badlands. The occasional buffalo roams through the parking lot. (575-4020. Free. Open daily 8am-6pm; mid-Apr. to late May and early Sept. to mid-Nov. 8:30am-4:30pm.) **Peaceful Valley Ranch,** 7mi. into the park, offers a variety of horseback riding excursions, 1½hr. or longer (623-4568; $16; rides leave daily 8:30am-2pm, evening ride 6pm). **Rough Rider Adventures,** on 3rd St. in Medora, leads free tours of the plains and badlands at 10am and 2pm daily, and rents mountain bikes (623-4808; $10 for 2hr., $15 per 4hr.; open daily late May to early Sept. 9am-6pm).

The less-visited but equally scenic **north unit** of the park is 75mi. from the south unit on U.S. 85. Most of the land is wilderness, resulting in virtually unlimited **backcountry hiking** possibilities. Be careful not to surprise the buffalo; one ranger advises singing while hiking so they can hear you coming. Apparently, no one's ever been trampled while singing Baroque classics, Bruce Springsteen, or riffs from "Free to Be You and Me." The **Caprock Coulee Trail** journeys through prairie, river valley, mountain ridge, and juniper forest, all in the space of 4mi.

The popular **Medora Musical,** in the Burning Hills Amphitheater west of town, stages variety shows nightly at 8:30pm from early June to early Sept. ($15-17, ages 6-18 $9-10). Before the show, push your arteries at the **Pitchfork Fondue.** The "chef" puts ten steaks on a pitchfork and dips them into a vat of boiling oil for 5 minutes. ($18, age 17 and under $10, includes buffet. Reservations required.) Tickets for both are available on 4th St. at the **Harold Schafer Heritage Center** (623-4444).

**YOU ARE NOW ONLY THREE PAGES FROM WALL DRUG.**

# SOUTH DAKOTA

From the forested granite crags of the Black Hills to the glacial lakes of the northeast, the Coyote State has more to offer than casual passers-by might expect. In fact, with only ten people per square mile, South Dakota has the highest ratio of sights-to-people in all of the Great Plains. Colossal man-made attractions like Mt. Rushmore National Memorial and the Crazy Horse Memorial and stunning natural spectacles such as the Black Hills and the Badlands, make tourism the state's largest industry after agriculture.

## ⁊ PRACTICAL INFORMATION

**Capital:** Pierre.

**Visitor Info: Division of Tourism,** 711 E. Wells St., Pierre 57501 (605-773-3301 or 800-952-3625; www.travelsd.com). Open M-F 8am-5pm. **U.S. Forest Service,** 330 Mt. Rushmore Rd., Custer 57730 (605-673-4853). Open M-F 7:30am-4:30pm. **Game, Fish, and Parks Dept.,** 523 E. Capitol Ave., Foss Bldg., Pierre 57501 (605-773-3392 or 800-710-2267), has info on state parks and campgrounds. Open M-F 8am-noon and 1-5pm.

**Postal Abbreviation:** SD. **Sales Tax:** 6%.

## SIOUX FALLS

Sioux Falls, the state's eastern gateway, is like a "nice guy": quiet, friendly, clean-cut, and a little boring. The city's namesake rapids are at **Falls Park**, just north of downtown on Falls Park Dr. (wheelchair access). The **Sioux River Greenway Recreation Trail,** circles the city from Falls Park in the northeast to the Elmwood golf course in the northwest.

The 1st full weekend of June, the neighboring city of **Tea** hosts the **Great Plains Balloon Race,** visible from all over Sioux Falls (call 336-1745 for more info). The only existing cast of Michelangelo's **Moses** stands on the grounds of Augustana College, at 30th St. and Grange Ave. The **Corn Palace,** 604 N. Main St., in Mitchell (from Sioux Falls, head 70mi. west on I-90), poses as a regal testament to granular architecture. Dating back to 1892, the structure is redecorated yearly to demonstrate the richness of South Dakota's soil (996-7311 or 995-8430. Open in summer daily 8am-10pm; 8am-5pm in winter. Free). **Great Bear Ski Valley,** 5901 E. Rice St., close to downtown, has skiing, snowboarding, and snowshoeing (367-4309; lift ticket $15, kids $12, ski rental $14/$10, snowboard rental $25/$20.)

Budget motels flank 10th St., exit 6 off I-229. The **Rushmore Motel,** 2500 E. 10th St., has one of the best rates around (336-2540; single $26; double $30). Among another cluster of hotels and motels at 41st St. and I-29 lies the **Select Inn,** 3500 Gateway Blvd. (361-1864. Singles $30; doubles $37, with 2 beds $41; AAA and senior discounts. Laundry facilities available.) There are a number of state parks nearby; **Split Rock City Park,** 20mi. northeast in Garretson has the cheapest camping. From I-90 E, take Rt. 11 N. (Corson) and drive 10mi. to Garretson; turn right at the sign for Devil's Gulch, and it will be on your left before the tracks. Sites have pit toilets and drinking water ($4-6). Every city needs a trendy brewery; the **Sioux Falls Brewing Co.,** 431 N. Phillips, fits the bill. Grab a slice of buffalo pie (cheesecake with stout beer and dark chocolate) with your burger or salad for $5-8. (332-4847. Open M-Th 11:30am-midnight, F-Sa 11:30am-2am.) After dinner, move to **Cavern Tavern,** downstairs from the Brewing Co. This laid-back bar and nightclub has live music once a week from Sept.-May. (332-4847. Open Tu-Th 5pm-midnight, F-Sa 5pm-2am.)

**Main St.** divides the city east-west, **Minnesota Ave.** north-south. **10th** and **12th St.** intersect them; 10th connects with **I-229** in the east and 12th connects with **I-29** in the west. **Jack Rabbit Buses,** 301 N. Dakota Ave. (336-0885; open daily 7:30am-5pm) hop to Minneapolis (6hr., 1 per day, $45), Omaha (3hr., 2 per day, $35-56), and Rapid City (8hr., 1 per day, $97). **Sioux Falls Transit** buses run during the day for $1 with free transfers (367-7183; M-Sa). Flag a **Yellow Cab** (336-1616; $2 base fare,

$1.60 per mi.). **Spoke-N-Sport,** 2101 W. 41st St., in the back of the Western Mall, rents bikes for $15 per day (332-2206; open M-F 10am-8pm, Sa 10am-5pm, Su noon-4pm). **Visitors Center:** in Falls Park (367-7430; open Apr.-Sept. daily 9am-9pm, Oct.-Mar. Sa-S 10am-5pm). **Crisis Helpline** 339-4357, 24hr. **Gay and Lesbian Coalition Info** 333-0603. **Sioux Valley Hospital:** 1100 S. Euclid Ave. (333-1000), stands at the corner of 18th and Grange. **Post Office:** 320 S. Second Ave. (357-5000; open M-F 7:30am-5:30pm, Sa 8am-1pm). **ZIP code:** 57104. **Area code:** 605.

# THE BADLANDS

When Frank Lloyd Wright first saw the Badlands it appeared to him as "an endless supernatural world more spiritual than earth but created out of it." Earlier explorers, when faced with the mountainous rock formations that suddenly appear out of the prarie, were less enthusiastic; "Hell with the fires out," General Alfred Sully called these arid and treacherous formations at first encounter. The French (perhaps erroneously) translated the Sioux name for the area, *mako sica,* as *les mauvaises terres:* "bad lands." Some 60 million years ago, when much of the Great Plains was under water, tectonic shifts thrust up the Rockies and the Black Hills. Mountain streams deposited silt from these nascent highlands into the area now known as the Badlands, capturing and fossilizing the remains of wildlife that once wandered these flood plains in layer after multicolored layer. Erosion has carved spires and steep sills into the earth, and it is still at work today. According to geologists, the Badlands lose about 1 in. every major rainfall; at this rate it will dissappear in 5000 years—so hurry up before it is too late. Late spring and fall in the Badlands offer pleasant weather that can be a relief from the extreme temperatures of mid-summer and winter, but no matter how bad it gets, it is always well worth a visit. Watch and listen for rattlesnakes, and don't tease the bison.

**◪ PRACTICAL INFORMATION. Badlands National Park** smolders about 50mi. east of Rapid City on I-90. **Jack Rabbit Buses,** 333 6th St. (348-3300), leaves from Rapid City for Wall at 11:30am daily ($24). Driving tours can start at either end of Rt. 240, which winds through wilderness in a 32mi. detour off I-90 (exit 110 or 131). The **Ben Reifel Visitors Center** (433-5361; open daily Sept.-Jun. 7am-8pm; Aug-May hrs. vary), 5mi. inside the park's northeastern entrance, is larger and more convenient than **White River Visitors Center** (455-2878; open June-Aug. 8am-4pm, hrs. may vary), 55mi. to the southwest off Rt. 27 in the park's less-visited southern section. Both visitors centers have potable water. The **entrance fee,** collected at the park entrance, is $10 per car, $5 per person (a free copy of *The Prairie Preamble* with trail map included). At the **National Grasslands Visitors Center (Buffalo Gap),** 708 Main St. (279-2125), down the street from Wall Drug in Wall, there are several films and an exhibit on the complex ecosystem that comprises much of the surrounding area (open daily 7am-8pm, off-season 8am-4:30pm). **Post Office:** no PO in park; nearest one is in the town of Interior (433-5345). **ZIP code:** 57757. **Area code:** 605.

**▛▟ ACCOMMODATIONS AND FOOD.** In Interior, the **Badlands Inn** sits out of the park just south of the Ben Riefel Visitors Center (433-5401 or 800-341-8000; singles $35; doubles $47). The **Homestead Motel,** 612 Main St. in Wall, has a white picket fence and a flowerpot tree (279-2303; singles $45, doubles $49; open mid-May to mid-Sept.). Next to the Ben Reifel Visitors Center inside the park, **Cedar Pass Lodge** rents cabins with A/C and showers (433-5460; 1 person $43, $4 per additional person; open mid-Apr. to mid-Oct.; fills up early, call ahead). At the lodge's mid-priced **restaurant** (the only one in the park), brave diners try the $3.45 **buffalo burger** (open May 15 to late Oct. daily 7am-8:30pm). When your stomach demands more loving fare, head to the homey ▧ **Cuny Table Cafe,** 8mi. west of the White River Visitor Center on Rt. 2, only a short detour to or from Wounded Knee. It's worth the drive to get the area's best Indian Tacos ($4.50)— fry bread piled with veggies and beef raised in the backyard. Two campgrounds lie within the park; **Cedar Pass Campground,** just south of the Ben Reifel Visitors Center, has sites with water and restrooms ($10). It fills up by late afternoon in summer. At **Sage Creek Campground,** 13mi. from the Pinnacles entrance south of Wall (take Sage Creek Rim Rd. off Rt. 240), you can sleep in an open field; there are outhouses, no water, and no fires allowed—but hey, it's free. **Backcountry camping** (½mi. from the road and out of sight) allows a more intimate introduction to this austere landscape, but water must be packed in. For more info., contact one of the rangers. Wherever you sleep, don't cozy up to the bison; nervous mothers can become just a tad protective.

**📷 🧗 SIGHTS AND ACTIVITIES.** The 244,000-acre park protects large tracts of prairie and stark rock formations. The **Ben Reifel Visitors Center** has a video on the Badlands, as well as a wealth of info on nearby parks, camping, and activities. Park rangers offer free talks and excursions into the park daily during the summer; check the *Prairie Preamble* for the schedule.

Trail guides from the visitors centers facilitate hiking through the Badlands. The short but steep **Saddle Pass Trail** traverses the bluffs; **Castle Trail** (10mi. round-trip) is home on the range. For stunning vistas without the sweat, a drive along Rt. 240/ Loop Rd. is an excellent way to see the park. Rt. 240 also passes the trailheads of the **Door, Window,** and **Notch Trails,** all brief excursions into the Badlands terrain. The gravel **Sage Creek Rim Rd.,** west of Rt. 240, has fewer people and more animals; highlights are **Roberts Prairie Dog Town** and the park's herds of bison and antelope. Across the river from the Sage Creek campground lies another prairie dog town and some popular bison territory. Fresh buffalo chips reveal recent activity. It is easy to lose your bearings in this territory; rangers and maps can help.

# WOUNDED KNEE

The triggers of the United States Army's 7th Cavalry sparked a bloody massacre of 153 Sioux men, women, and children on this flat patch of land in 1890, marking the symbolic peak of a century's genocide. The Sioux's Ghost Dance movement, a spiritual revival that promised a return to a time of roaming buffalo and no white men, had been labelled "Messiah craze," while the tribe was deemed a "foe to progress" by land-hungry settlers. Scores of ignored promises and forgotten treaties culminated in slaughter; the dead lay frozen on the field for 4 days, contorted into grotesque shapes, until they were finally buried in hastily dug mass graves. Today, the site is part of the **Pine Ridge Reservation,** home to the poorest county in the United States (plans to convert the area to a national park, a move opposed by Lakota residents, have been indefinitely stalled).

In 1973, tensions escalated anew as reservation youths occupied a church. An armed confrontation between federal marshals, reservation residents, and activist members of the American Indian Movement ensued, in what became known as **Wounded Knee II.** A museum and church were burnt to the ground.

---

**HAVE YOU DUG WALL DRUG?** There is almost no way to visit the Badlands without being importuned by advertisements from **Wall Drug,** 510 Main St. (279-2175), a towering monument to the success of saturation advertising. (Open daily 6am-10pm; mid-Sept. to Apr. 6:30am-6pm.) After seeing billboards for Wall Drug from as far as 500mi. away, travelers feel obligated to make a stop in Wall to see what all the ruckus is about—much as they must have done 60 years ago, when Wall first enticed parched travelers with free water. The "drug store" itself is now a conglomeration of shops containing Old West memorabilia, kitschy souvenirs, Western books, and numerous photo opportunities with statues of oversized animals; you can even pray for a safe trip at their traveler's chapel. Wall itself is hardly worth a visit. All in all, the town is just another brick in the...oh, never mind.

The 1890 massacre site is marked by a graveyard on the hilltop, a sign recounting the events of the first Wounded Knee, and 2 stands that sell native crafts. The Wounded Knee memorial is located off Rt. 18, on the outskirts of the town of Wounded Knee, in southern South Dakota. It is a considerable distance (80mi.) from other tourist spots of the Black Hills. For more info, contact the **Oglala Sioux Tribe Office of Tourism Development,** P.O. Box 3008, Pine Ridge, SD 57770 (605-867-5301). KILI 90.1FM, the "Voice of the Lakota Nation," provides local info.

# BLACK HILLS REGION

The Black Hills, named for the dark hue that distance lends the green pines covering the hills, have long been considered sacred by the Sioux. The Treaty of 1868 gave the Black Hills and the rest of South Dakota west of the Missouri River to the tribe. But when gold was discovered in the 1870s, the U.S. government snatched back the land. The dueling geographical monuments of **Mt. Rushmore** (a national memorial, p. 540) and **Crazy Horse** (an independent project, p. 540) strikingly illustrate the clash of the 2 cultures that reside among these hills. Today, white residents dominate the area, which contains a trove of natural treasures, including Custer State Park, Wind Cave National Park, and Jewel Cave National Monument.

The majority of the land in the Black Hills area is part of the **Black Hills National Forest** and excercises the "multiple use" principle—mining, logging, ranching, and recreation all take place in close proximity. "Don't-miss" attractions like reptile farms and Flintstone Campgrounds lurk around every bend of the narrow, sinuous roads. The forest itself provides opportunities for backcountry hiking and camping, as do park-run campgrounds and private tent sites. In the hills, the **visitors center** (343-8755), on I-385 at Pactola Lake, has details on backcountry camping and great $4 maps (open late May to early Sept. daily 8:30am-6pm). **Backcountry camping** in the national forest is free. Camp 1mi. away from any campground or visitors center and at least 200 ft. off the side of the road (leave your car in a parking lot or pull off); fires are prohibited. Good campgrounds include **Pactola,** on the Pactola Reservoir just south of the junction of Rt. 44 and U.S. 385 (sites $13); **Sheridan Lake,** 5mi. northeast of Hill City on U.S. 385 (sites $14; north entrance for group sites, south entrance for individuals); and **Roubaix Lake,** 14mi. south of Lead on U.S. 385 (sites $14). All National Forest campgrounds are quiet and wooded, offering fishing, swimming, and pit toilets, but no hookups. (Reservations recommended during peak times, call 877-444-6777.) The national forest extends into Wyoming with a ranger station in Sundance (307-283-1361; open M-F 7:30am-5pm). The Wyoming side of the forest permits campfires, allows horses, and draws fewer visitors.

**I-90** skirts the northern border of the Black Hills from Spearfish in the west to Rapid City in the east; **U.S. 385** twists from Hot Springs in the south to Deadwood in the north. The road system that interconnects through the hills covers beautiful territory, but the roads are difficult to navigate without a good map; pick one up for free almost anywhere in the area. Don't expect to get anywhere fast—these convoluted routes will hold you to half the speed of the interstate.

The off season in the Black Hills offers stellar skiing (see **Lead,** p. 544) and snowmobiling, but many attractions are closed or have limited hours, and most resorts, and campgrounds close for the winter. Unless you are astride a flashy piece of chrome and steel, steer clear of the Hills in early Aug., when over 12,000 motorcyclists converge on the area for the **Sturgis Rally** (Aug. 7-13, 2000).

Of the **Grayline tours,** P.O. Box 1106, Rapid City, 57709 (342-4461), tour #1 is the most complete. Make reservations or call 1hr. before departure for pick-up from motels in Rapid City. (Runs daily mid-May to mid-Oct., 9hr., $34 includes admission prices.) The **Black Hills Visitor Information Center** (355-3700), exit 61 off I-90, in Rapid City, has info (open daily in summer 8am-8pm, off-season 8am-5pm; hrs. subject to change). **Area code:** 605.

## MOUNT RUSHMORE

After all the disappointing tourist traps dotting the Black Hills, **Mt. Rushmore National Memorial** is refreshingly impressive. South Dakota historian Doane Robinson originally conceived of this "shrine of democracy" in 1923 as a memorial for local Western heroes like Lewis and Clark and Kit Carson; sculptor Gutzon Borglum chose 4 presidents. Borglum initially encountered opposition from those who felt the work of God could not be improved, but the tenacious sculptor defended the project's size, insisting that "there is not a monument in this country as big as a snuff box." Throughout the Depression work progressed slowly; a great setback occurred when the nearly completed face of Thomas Jefferson had to be blasted off Washington's right side and moved to his left due to insufficient granite. In 1941, the 60 ft. heads of George Washington, Thomas Jefferson, Theodore Roosevelt, and Abraham Lincoln were finished. The 465 ft. tall bodies were never completed, as work ceased when U.S. funds were diverted to WWII, but the millions of visitors who come here every year don't seem to mind the dismebodiment.

From Rapid City, take U.S. 16 and 16A to Keystone and Rt. 244 up to the mountain. Remote parking is free, but the lot fills early. There is an $8 per car "annual parking permit" for the lot adjacent to the entrance. The **info center** (605-574-3198) details the monument's history and offers ranger tours. A state-of-the-art **visitors center** (574-3165, ext. 165) showcases exhibits chronicling the history of the monument, the lives of the featured presidents, and a film. (Both info center and visitors center open daily June-Aug. 8am-10pm; off-season hours generally 8am-5pm.)

**Borglum's Studio,** over 100 steps down from the main viewing area, holds a plaster model of the carving, tools, and plans for Mt. Rushmore (open May-Sept. daily 9am-5pm). During the summer, the **Mt. Rushmore Memorial Amphitheater** hosts a monument-lighting program. A patriotic speech and slide show commence at 9pm, and light floods the monument 9:30-10:30pm.

The **Mt. Rushmore KOA Palmer Gulch Lodge** lies 5mi. west of Mt. Rushmore on Rt. 244. With kampsites for 2 ($23, with water and electricity $30) or kabins ($40-46) comes the use of showers, stoves, pool, laundry, free shuttle service to Mt. Rushmore, movies, hayrides, basketball, volleyball, trail rides, fast food, mini-golf, a video arcade, a gas station, and a gift shop. (605-574-2525 or 800-562-8503. Open May-Oct. Make reservations early, up to 2 months in advance for cabins and special requests.) **Horsethief Campground** lies 4mi. west of Mt. Rushmore on Rt. 244. More rustic and cheaper than Palmer Gulch, the former President George Bush fished here in 1993; rumor has it that the lake was overstocked with fish to guarantee his success. (Lakeside sites $15-17. Water and flush toilets in the woods. Reservations reccomended on weekends and during peak times, call 877-444-6777.)

## CRAZY HORSE MEMORIAL

If you thought Mt. Rushmore was big, think again. The Crazy Horse Memorial is a wonder of the world in progress; an entire mountain is metamorphosing into a 563 ft. high memorial sculpture of the great Lakota war leader Crazy Horse. When completed, it will be the largest sculpture in the world. A famed warrior, Crazy Horse was revered by many tribes; he refused to sign treaties or live on a government reservation. In 1877, Crazy Horse was treacherously stabbed in the back by a white soldier who came bearing a flag of truce.

The project was initiated by Lakota Chief Henry Standing Bear as a rebuttal to nearby Mt. Rushmore. The memorial also stands as a haunting reminder of the seizure of the Black Hills in the year before Crazy Horse was assassinated; it wasn't the first or last time gold fever glossed over the niceties of U.S. diplomatic decorum. The project began in 1947 and, to no one's surprise, didn't receive any initial government funding. The sculptor, Korczak Ziolkowski, went solo for years, later refusing $10 million in federal funding. Today, his 10 children carry on the work. Crazy Horse's completed face was unveiled in June 1998 (all 4 of the Rushmore heads could fit inside it), and part of his arm is now visible; eventually, his entire torso and head will be carved into the mountain. The memorial, 17mi. southwest of Mt. Rushmore on U.S. 16/385, includes the **Indian Museum of North America**, which shows a moving 10min. video show. (605-673-4681. Open daily 7am-dark; Oct.-Apr. 8am until dark. $7, $17 per carload, $15 with a senior, under 6 free. $2 AAA discount per car. Free coffee at the restaurant. Monument lit nightly for 1hr.)

# CUSTER STATE PARK

Peter Norbeck, governor of South Dakota during the late 1910s, loved to hike among the thin, towering rock formations that haunt the area south of Sylvan Lake and Mt. Rushmore. In order to preserve the land, he created Custer State Park. The spectacular **Needles Hwy.** (Rt. 87) within the park follows his favorite hiking route. Norbeck designed this road to be especially narrow and winding so that newcomers could experience the pleasures of discovery. Custer's biggest attraction is its herd of **1500 bison,** which can best be seen near dawn or dusk wandering near Wildlife Loop Rd. If you are "lucky," they, along with some friendly burros, will come right up to your car. Don't get out; they are dangerous. The **entrance fee** is $3 per person, $8 per carload for a 7-day pass from May to Oct. (Nov.-Apr. $2 per person, $5 per car). The **Peter Norbeck Visitors Center** (255-4464), on U.S. 16A ½mi. west of the State Game Lodge, serves as the park's info center (open daily late May to early Sept. 8am-8pm; early Sept. to Oct. and May 9am-5pm). Seven **campgrounds** in the park charge $10-13 and have showers and restrooms, but no hook-ups. Primitive camping ($2 per night) is available in the **French Creek Natural Area;** the visitors center can give you more info. Three-fourths of the park's 323 sites are reservable ($5 non-resident users fee; call 800-710-2267 daily Jun.-Sept. 7am-7pm, early Sept. to late May 7am-5pm), and the entire park fills by early afternoon in the summer. The **Elk Mountain Campground** in nearby Wind Cave National Park is an excellent alternative and rarely fills up (see Wind Cave, below). Motels in the surrounding area include the clean and friendly **Valley Motel** on Rt. 16A, 3mi. west of the Stockade Lake entrance to the park (673-4819; singles $40, doubles $48; call ahead). Food and concessions are available at all 4 park lodges, but the local general stores in Custer, Hermosa, or Keystone generally charge less.

At 7242 ft., **Harney Peak** is the highest point east of the Rockies and west of the Pyrenees. At the top are a few mountain goats and a great view of the Black Hills. . Bring water and food, wear good shoes, and leave as early in the morning as possible to finish before dark. There are also more than 30 other trails in the park. You can hike, fish, paddle boats, or canoe at popular **Sylvan Lake,** on Needles Hwy. (Sylvan Lake Resort 574-2561; kayak rental $3.50 per person per 30min.) Horse rides are available at **Blue Bell Lodge**, on Rt. 87 about 8mi. from the south entrance (255-4531, stable 255-4571; 1hr. for $15, under 12 $12.50). Mountain bikes can be rented at the **Legion Lake Resort,** on U.S. 16A 6mi. east the visitors center (255-4521; $8 per hour). All lakes and streams permit fishing with a daily license ($12; 3-day nonresident license $30). Fishing licenses and rental equipment are available at the 4 area lodges. Summer trout fishing is the best. The strong granite of the Needles makes for great rock climbing. For more info contact **Granite Sports/ Sylvan Rocks** at the corner of Elm and Main St. in Hill City (574-2121 or 574-2425; open Su-Tu 8:30am-7:30pm, W-Sa 8:30am-8:30pm). **Area code:** 605.

# WIND CAVE AND JEWEL CAVE

In the cavern-riddled Black Hills, the subterranean scenery often rivals the aboveground sites. Private concessionaires will attempt to lure you into the holes in their backyards, but the government owns the area's prime underground real estate: **Wind Cave National Park** (745-4600), adjacent to Custer State Park on U.S. 385, and **Jewel Cave National Monument** (673-2288), 14mi. west of Custer on Rt. 16. There is no public transportation to the caves. Bring a sweater on all tours—Wind Cave remains a constant 53°F, Jewel Cave 49°F. **Area code:** 605.

**WIND CAVE.** Wind Cave was discovered in 1881 by Tom Bingham, who heard the sound of air rushing out of the cave's only natural entrance. In fact, the wind was so strong it knocked his hat off. Air forcefully gusts in and out of the cave due to outside pressure changes, and when Tom went back to show his friends the cave, his hat got sucked in. Today, the amazing air pressure leads scientists to believe that only 5% of the cave passages have been discovered. The cave is known for its "boxwork," a honeycomb-like lattice of calcite covering its walls. There are 5 tours; all have more than 150 stairs. The **Garden of Eden Tour** is the least strenuous. (1hr., 7 per day June-Aug. 8:40am-5:30pm. Call for off-season times. $4, seniors and ages 6-15 $2.) The **Natural Entrance Tour** and the **Fairgrounds Tour** are both moderately strenuous and one or the other leaves about every half hour. (1¼hr., June-Aug. 9am-6:30pm. Call for off-season times. $6, seniors and ages 6-16 $3.) Light your own way on the more strenuous **Candlelight Tour.** (Limited to ten people. 2 per day at 10:30am and 1:30pm, Jun.-Aug.; 2 hours; $7, seniors and kids $3. "Non-slip" soles on shoes reccomended.) The rather difficult **Caving Tour,** an intro to basic caving, is limited to 10 people ages 16 and over who can fit through a 10 inch high passageway. (Parental consent required for under 18. 4hr. tour at 1pm. $18, seniors $9. Reservations recommended.) In the afternoon, all tours fill about 1hr. ahead of time, so buy tickets early. **Wind Cave National Park Visitors Center,** RR1, P.O. Box 190-WCNP, Hot Springs 57747 (745-4600), can provide more info. (Open June to mid-Aug. daily 8am-7:30pm; winter hrs. vary. Tours for the disabled can be arranged.) The **Elk Mountain Campground** rarely fills up during the summer, though it is an excellent site in the woods with potable water, and restrooms (sites $10).

**JEWEL CAVE.** In striking contrast to nearby Wind Cave's boxwork, the walls of this sprawling underground labyrinth (the 2nd longest cave in the U.S.) are covered with a layer of calcite crystal—hence the name. The ½mi. **Scenic Tour** includes 723 stairs (leaves roughly every 20min. 8:30am-6pm; in winter call ahead; $6, ages 6-16 $3). The **Historic Tour** is more interesting (every hour 9am-5pm; in winter call ahead; $6, ages 6-16 $3). Reservations, pants, a long-sleeve shirt, knee-pads, sturdy boots, and a willingness to get down and dirty are required for the 4hr. **Spelunking Tour,** limited to 5 people ages 16 and up. (Runs daily June-Aug. 12:30pm. $18; you must be able to fit through an opening only 8 in. by 2 ft.) The **visitors center** (673-2288) has more info (open daily 8am-7:30pm; mid-Oct. to mid-May 8am-4:30pm).

## NEAR WIND CAVE: HOT SPRINGS

The well-heeled once flocked from the four corners to bathe in the mineral waters of quaint Hot Springs, located on scenic **U.S. 385.** Still quiet and less crowded than the rest of the Black Hills, the town's charming pink sandstone buildings and budget lodgings make it a nice stop on a tour of the southern Hills.

The Sioux and Cheyenne once fought over possession of the 87°F spring here; in 1890, a public pool was erected at the site. The waterslide at **Evan's Plunge,** on U.S. 385, empties into the world's largest naturally heated pool. (745-5165. June-Aug. daily 5:30am-10pm, winter hrs. vary. $8, ages 3-12 $6. Wheelchair access.) **Kidney Spring,** just to the right of the waterfall near U.S. 385 and Minnekahta Ave., is rumored to have healing powers. At the **Mammoth Site** on the U.S. 18 bypass, 3 woolly mammoths and 48 Columbian mammoths fell into a sinkhole and fossilized near Hot Springs about 26,000 years ago. (745-6017. Open daily 8am-8pm. Last tour 7:15pm. Winter hrs. vary. 30min. tour $5, seniors $4.75, ages 6-12 $3.25.)

## RAPID CITY

Rapid City's location makes it a convenient base from which to explore the Black Hills and the Badlands. Every summer, the area welcomes about 3 million tourists, over 60 times the city's permanent population. If you have a car, pick up a map of the **Rapid City Circle Tour** at the Civic Center or at any motel; the route leads you to numerous free attractions and includes a jaunt up Skyline Dr. for a bird's-eye view of the city and the 7 concrete dinosaurs of **Dinosaur Park. The Journey,** 222 New York St., is a well-conceived interactive museum housing 4 separate historical museums, including the **Sioux Indian Museum** and the **Pioneer Museum;** one ticket is good for all displays. (394-2241. Open daily in summer 8am-7pm; off-season 9am-4pm. $5, college students $3, ages 7-17 $2. Free audio guide provided.)

Rapid City accommodations are more expensive during the summer. Make reservations; motels often fill weeks in advance, especially during the first 2 weeks in Aug., when nearby Sturgis hosts its annual motorcycle rally. Winter travelers are in luck because of an abundance of off-season bargains (mid-Sept. to mid-May). **Kings X Lodge,** 525 E. Omaha St., boasts clean rooms, cable, and free local calls (342-2236; singles $33, doubles $37-39; less in off-season). **Big Sky Motel** is located just south of town on a service road off Mt. Rushmore St. (large billboards guide the way). Many rooms have great views, but can be chilly. (348-3200 or 800-318-3208. June-Sept. singles $40, doubles $56; less off-season.) **Robert's Roost Hostel,** 627 South St., has the best rates. One private room and 2 single-sex, dorm-style rooms, along with kitchen and laundry. (341-3434 or 348-7799. Dorms $16 per person, private room $25 for one person, $36 for 2. Includes linen and breakfast. Call ahead. No key, door kept unlocked.) **Camping** is available at **Badlands National Park** (p. 537), **Black Hills National Forest** (p. 539), and **Custer State Park** (p. 541).

**Sixth St. Bakery and Delicatessen,** 516 6th St., next to the $2 cinema, sells day-olds for $1 per bag. The goofy staff makes good sandwiches ($4-5). (342-6660. Open M-Sa, Su 10am-4pm; in winter daily 6:30am-6pm.) **Smiley's House of Pizza,** 510 St. Joseph St., serves an entirely homemade assortment of pizzas, chicken dishes, pastas, and more at their all-you-can-eat lunch and dinner buffets (343-4783; lunch 11am-2pm $5.50, dinner 5-9pm $6, except on F and Sa 11am-midnight).

**Nightlife** lines **Main St.** between 6th and Mt. Rushmore St. For a beer as black as the Hills, toss back a Smokejumper Stout ($3) at the **Firehouse Brewing Co.,** 610 Main St., *the* bar in Rapid City. Located in a restored 1915 firehouse, the company brews 5 beers in-house and serves up sandwiches, burgers, salads ($5-10, a bit pricier at dinner), and live music on summer weekends. (348-1915. Open M-Th 11am-midnight, F-Sa 11am-2am, Su 4-11pm.) **The Boot,** 826 Main St., shakes with live band performances nightly for boot-stompin', knee-slappin' country-western music and dancing (343-1931; cover $2 F-Sa; $4 for ladies' night on W; open M-Sa 1pm-2am). **Vertigo,** 615 Main St., has an interior designed to loosen up even the most timid of dancers. Along with the usual beer and spirits, Vertigo also serves healthy sandwiches and salads for under $7. (341-9332. Open M-Sa 4pm-2am.)

The roads of Rapid City are layed out in a basic grid pattern; St. Joseph St. and Main St. are the main east-west thoroughfares, and Mt. Rushmore/Rt. 16 is the main north-south route. Many north-south roads are numbered and numbers go up as you move from east to west. Streets beyond East are denoted as such (St. Joseph St. becomes East St. Joseph, etc.). Call 394-2255 to check on **road conditions** in extreme weather. **Jack Rabbit Lines** scurries east from the **Milo Barber Transportation Center,** 333 6th St. (348-3300), downtown, with one bus daily to Pierre (4hr., $55), Sioux Falls (10hr., $101), and Omaha (12hr., $117). **Powder River Lines,** also in the center, services Wyoming and Montana, running once per day to Billings (8hr., $57) and Cheyenne (8hr., $65; station open M-F 8am-5pm, Sa-Su 10am-noon and 2-5pm). **Grayline Tours** lead regional tours based out of Rapid City (see the **Black Hills Region,** p. 539). Take flight from **Rapid City Regional Airport** (393-9924), off Rt. 44 8½mi. east of the city. **Rapid Ride** (394-6631) runs buses 6am to 6pm ($1, seniors 50¢; pick up schedule at terminal in the Milo Barber Transporation center. **Rapid Taxi:** 348-8080. **Rapid City Chamber of Commerce and Visitors Information Center:** 444 Mt. Rushmore Rd. N. (343-1744), in the Civic Center (M-F 8am-5pm). **Rapidcare Health Center:** 408 Knollwood (341-6600; open M-F 7am-8pm, Sa-Su 9am-6pm). **Rape and Assault Victims Helpline:** 341-2046. 24hr. **Black Hills Gay and Lesbian Resource Line:** 394-8080. M-Sa 6-10pm. **Internet Access:** Rapid City Public Library, 610 Quincy St. (394-4171), open M-W 10am-9pm, Th-Sa 10am-5:30pm. **Post Office:** 500 East Blvd. (394-8600), several blocks east of downtown (open M-F 8am-5:30pm, Sa 8:30am-12:30pm). **ZIP code:** 57701. **Area code:** 605.

# SPEARFISH, LEAD, AND DEADWOOD

**SPEARFISH.** Located on the northwest edge of the Black Hills, Spearfish makes a nice, short stop to or from the Black Hills. Nearby, the spectacular **Spearfish Canyon Scenic Byway** (U.S. 14A) winds through 18mi. of forest along Spearfish Creek, passing one of the sites where *Dances with Wolves* was filmed (marked by a small sign 2mi. west of U.S. 14A on Rt. 222).

There are no trout native to the Black Hills, but you can feed tens of thousands of hatchery-raised ones at the amazing **D.C. Booth Historic Fish Hatchery.** From Main St. go 2 blocks west to Canyon and turn south (642-7730; grounds open 24hr all year, buildings open May-Sept M-F 9am-5pm). Dick Termes paints rotating spheres and calls his work, cleverly enough, Termespheres; his work is on display at the **Termesphere Gallery.** From downtown, go south on Main St. and follow it as it becomes Colorado Blvd. Turn right on Christensen Dr. and go about 1½mi. (642-4805. Call for hours, or just show up; they might be there.) There's a georgeous waterfall about halfway between Spearfish and Lead.

The **Canyon Gateway Hotel,** south of town on U.S. 14A, offers cozy rooms in a pleasant setting (642-3402 or 800-281-3402; no phones; singles $40, doubles $43). The weary traveler can ring in at **Bell's Motor Lodge,** on Main St. at the east edge of town (642-3812; free local calls, TV, pool; singles $36, doubles $48; open May-Sept.). Four mi. west of U.S. 14A on Rt. 222 are 2 spectacular national forest campgrounds among pines and next to a rushing creek: **Rod and Gun Campground** (sites $8) and **Timon Campground** (sites $9). Both have pit toilets and potable water. Right in town, at the southern end of Canyon St. 2 blocks west of Main St., the **Spearfish City Campground** caters to those who want full hookups. (642-1340. $20 full hookup. Reservations needed Sa-Su. Tent site $11 for 1 person, $1 each additional person. Showers 25¢.) The vaguely Mediterranean **Bay Leaf Café,** 126 W. Hudson, off Main St., serves salads, sandwiches, and veggie dishes, and is a good bet for lunch; dinners are more expensive. (642-5462. $3-12 lunches. Piano music F-Sa from 8pm. Open daily 11am-9pm; Sept.-May M 11am-4pm, Tu-Sa 11am-8pm.) The daily lunch buffet (11:30am-1:30pm) with pizza, pasta, and salad goes for $4.59 at the **Pizza Ranch,** 715 Main St. (642-4422. Dinner buffet Tu-F 6-8pm $5.49. M 5:30-7:30pm all-you-can-eat pizza $3. Open Su-Th 11am-10pm, F-Sa 11am-11pm.)

The **Spearfish Ranger Station,** 2014 N. Main St. (642-4622), has free maps and hiking advice. (Open M-F 8am-5pm, Sa 8am-4:30pm; in winter M-F 8am-4:30; foyer with maps and info open 24hr.) The **Chamber of Commerce:** 106 W. Kansas St. (642-2626 or 800-626-8013), at the corner of Main St. (open M-F 8am-7pm, Sa 9am-3pm, Su noon-7pm; Sept.-May M-F 8am-5pm). **Post Office:** 120 Yankee St. (642-2521), north of downtown off North Ave. **ZIP code:** 57783. **Area code:** 605.

**LEAD.** Lead (rhymes with heed, not head) is actually named for the ore veins that marked the path to gold in the mines of this town. The **Black Hills Mining Museum,** 323 W. Main St., unearths an interesting look at the impact of mining on the earth and the lives of the men who did it. The simulated underground tour includes a chance to **pan for gold.** (584-1605. Open May-Sept. daily 9am-5pm. Oct-Apr. M-F 9am-5pm. $4.25, students $3.25, seniors $3.75.) The **Open Cut** invites indignation or silent awe; it's a giant hole in the earth created by the **Homestake Mining Company,** 160 W. Main St. Mining ceased here in Sept., 1998, but the giant void remains indefinitely. The company still mines thousands of feet beneath Lead, and offers interesting surface tours. (584-3110. 1hr. hard-hat tours leave every 30min. until 4:30pm. $5.25, students $4.25, seniors $4.75. Visitors center open M-F 8am-5pm, Sa-Su 10am-5pm; Sept.-May M-F 8am-5pm.) The **Ponderosa Mountain Lodge,** on U.S. 14A between Lead and Deadwood, offers a variety of cabins nestled among the pines, stocked with TVs and fridges (584-3321; no phones; from $50-65 depending on season and size). **Hanna Campground** offers 13 lovely sites about 9mi. from town off U.S. 85; turn onto the dirt road just south of the junction with 14A at Cheyenne Crossing (pit toilets and water; sites $9). Sandwiches ($4.50-7) are served up at the **Stampmill Saloon,** 305 W. Main St. (open Su-Th 11am-9pm, F-Sa 11am-10pm).

Wintertime in the Black Hills provides fine skiing and snowboarding opportunities. **Terry Peak Ski Area** and **Deer Mountain** are both west of Lead off U.S. 85. (**Terry:** 584-2165 or 342-7609. Lift ticket $32, under 13 $25, over 69 and under 5 free. Ski rental $18, junior ski retal $12, snowboard rental $25. **Deer:** 584-3230. Lift ticket $20, kids $17. Ski rental $13. Snowboard rental $22.50.) **Area code:** 605.

**DEADWOOD.** Continue along Main St. from Lead for 3mi., and you'll find yourself in Deadwood. Gunslingers **Wild Bill Hickock** and **Calamity Jane** sauntered into this town during the height of the Gold Rush. Bill stayed just long enough—2 months—to spend eternity here. They lie side-by-side in the **Mt. Moriah Cemetery,** just south of downtown. Take Cemetery St. off of Rt. 85. ($1—there is no reverance for the dead when tourism is involved.) Deadwood is home to **Saloon #10,** 657 Main St., where legend has it that Hickock was shot holding black aces and eights, the infamous "dead man's hand." Every summer, Bill has more lives than 60 cats; the shooting is morbidly re-enacted on location. (578-3346. 4 times daily: 1, 3, 5, and 7pm.) If Lead is where the gold is found, then Deadwood is where the gold is lost, as the main attraction in Deadwood is **gambling,** with casinos lining **Main St.** At the **Buffalo Saloon,** 658 Main St., you can gamble 24hr. per day, 7 days a week, and there's live music outside the Stockade (578-9993). For the fun of gambling without the high stakes, many casinos offer nickel slot machines. **Free parking** is available on the north side of town; take the 50¢ trolley into town or walk 3 blocks. If you lose most of your money at the gambling tables, you can probably still afford to stay at **Hostelling International Black Hills at the Penny Motel (HI-AYH),** 818 Upper Main St. Look for the Penny Motel sign. A great kitchen and comfortable beds await. (877-565-8140 or 578-1842. $12, $15 non-members. One private room $24.) The motel itself offers singles ($48) and doubles ($56). The **Whistler Gulch Campground,** off U.S. 85, has a pool, laundry facilities, and showers (578-2042 or 800-704-7139; tent sites $17, full hookup $27). Food in Deadwood varies month to month as casinos try new hooks—the best deals are advertised on the windows.

The **Deadwood History and Information Center** (800-999-1876), 13 Siever St., is open in summer daily 8am-8pm. **Internet access: Biff Malibu's,** 670 Main St. (578-1919; $3 per 30min.; open daily 8am until the music ends). **Area code:** 605.

# IOWA

Named for the Ioway Native Americans who farmed by the state's many river banks, Iowa is known even today for farming and corn. Both the Ioway and the European settlers chose well; Iowa contains a fourth of all U.S. Grade A farmland. Besides being fertile, the land is subtly beautiful. Gentle hills roll throughout the state; particularly striking are the Loess Hills in the west. Created by wind-blown quartz silt, these hills are a geological rarity found only in Iowa and China. Iowa preserves its European heritage in the small towns that keep German, Dutch, and Swedish traditions alive; their rugged life was portrayed best with the familiar dour-faced farmers of "American Gothic," painted by native son Grant Wood.

## ⚑ PRACTICAL INFORMATION

**Capital:** Des Moines.

**Visitor Info: Iowa Dept. of Economic Development,** 200 E. Grand Ave., Des Moines 50309 (515-242-4705 or 888-472-6035; www.state.ia.us/tourism).

**Postal Abbreviation:** IA. **Sales Tax:** 5%.

## DES MOINES

French explorers originally named the Des Moines river the "Rivière des Moingouenas," for a local Native American tribe, but then shortened the name to "Rivière des Moings." This was later confused with Des Moines (of the monks), because of identical pronunciation. Today, Des Moines (da moyne) shows neither Native American nor monastic influence, but rather the imprint of the agricultural trade that spawned it. The World Pork Expo, where they crown a Pork Queen and show off the world's largest barbeque, is a red-letter event on the Iowan calendar, and the city goes hog-wild for the Iowa State Fair every Aug. Des Moines also boasts a great art museum and countless local festivals.

## 🔢 ORIENTATION AND PRACTICAL INFORMATION

Des Moines idles at the junction of I-35 and I-80. Numbered streets run north-south, named streets east-west. Addresses are zero downtown at the **Des Moines River** and increase as you move east or west; **Grand Ave.** divides addresses north-south. Other east-west thoroughfares are **Locust St.**, and moving north, **University Ave.** (home to Drake University), **Hickman Rd.**, and **Euclid/Douglas Ave.** Most downtown buildings are connected by the **Skywalk**, a series of passages above the street, so many Des Moines businesspeople never have to go outdoors—except to smoke. Note: Des Moines and West Des Moines are different places, and the numbered streets within each are not the same.

**Airport: Des Moines International** (256-5195), Fleur Dr. at Army Post Rd., 5mi. southwest of downtown; take bus #8 "Havens" M-F. Taxi to downtown $10-12.

**Buses: Greyhound,** 1107 Keosauqua Way (243-1773), at 12th St., just northwest of downtown; take bus #4 "Urbandale." To: Iowa City (2hr., 4 per day, $20); Omaha (2hr., 8 per day, $24); and St. Louis (10hr., 5 per day, $49-63). Station open 24hr.

**Public Transportation: Metropolitan Transit Authority (MTA),** 1100 MTA Lane (283-8100), south of the 9th St. viaduct. Open M-F 8am-5pm. Buses run M-Sa approximately 6am-8pm. Fare $1, seniors (except M-F 3-6pm) and disabled persons 50¢; transfers 10¢. Routes converge at 6th and Walnut St. Maps at the MTA office or any Dahl's or Hy-Vee.

**Taxis: Yellow Cab** (243-1111).

**Car Rental: Budget** (287-2612), at the airport. Th-M $27 with 100 free mi. per day, Tu-W from $36.90 with 150 free mi. per day; 25¢ per additional mi. Must be 21 with major credit card. Under 25 $10 per day surcharge. Open M-F 7am-1am, Sa-Su 7am-midnight.

**Visitor Info: Greater Des Moines Convention and Visitors Bureau,** 2 Ruan Ctr., suite 222 (286-4960 or 800-451-2625), at 6th and Locust in the Skywalk. Open M-F 8:30am-5pm. Downstairs is the **Chamber of Commerce** (286-4950). Open M 9:30am-5pm, Tu-Th 8am-5pm, F 8am-4pm.

**Hotlines: First Call for Help,** 246-6555. 24hr. **Crisis Line,** 282-5752. 24hr. **Rape Hotline,** 286-3535. 24hr. **Red Cross Suicide Hotline,** 244-1010. Operates M-F 3pm-8am. **Gay and Lesbian Resource Center,** 414 E. 15th St. (281-0634). Open M-F 7-10pm.

**Internet Access: Des Moines Public Library,** 100 Locust (283-4152), and all other branches. Free 1 hr. per day. Sign up one day in advance. Open M-W 10am-9pm, Th-F 10am-6pm, Sa-Su 10-5.

**Post Office:** 1165 2nd Ave. (283-7505), downtown just north of I-235. Open M-F 7:30am-5:30pm. **ZIP code:** 50318. **Area code:** 515.

## 🏕 ACCOMMODATIONS AND CAMPGROUNDS

Finding cheap accommodations in Des Moines is usually no problem, though you should make reservations at least 1 month in advance for visits during the State Fair in Aug., and during the high school sports tournament season in Mar.. Beware the hotel tax (7%). Several campgrounds can be found west of the city off I-80 and cheap motels dust I-80 and Merle Hay Rd., 5mi. northwest of downtown. Take bus #4 "Urbandale" or #6 "West 9th" from downtown.

**The Carter House Inn,** 640 20th St. (288-7850), at Woodland St. in historic Sherman Hill. 10 years ago, this great old Victorian house was moved 6 blocks from its original site and placed here, where the Nelsons have converted it into a beautifully furnished B&B. Emphasis on the breakfast—you'll eat well in the morning. $65-75. Student discounts around 15% off can be arranged if extra rooms are available. Call ahead.

**Hickman Motor Lodge,** 6500 Hickman Rd. (276-8591), boasts clean rooms. Free local calls and cable TV. Hop on bus #4 "Urbandale." Singles $37; doubles $45.

**Motel 6,** 4817 Fleur Dr. (287-6364), at the airport, 5min. south of downtown. Newly renovated rooms with free local calls. Singles Su-Th $40,F-Sa $46; doubles Su-TH $46, F-Sa $52. 2 wheelchair-accessible rooms.

**Iowa State Fairgrounds Campgrounds,** E. 30th St. (262-3111 or 800-545-3247; fax 262-6906), at Grand Ave. Take bus #1 "Fairgrounds" to the Grand Ave. gate and follow East Grand Ave. straight east through the park. No fires. Sites with water and electricity, $12; full hookup $15. Fee collected in the morning. Rates go up at fair time in Aug.; make reservations well in advance. Check-in until 10pm. Open mid-Apr. to mid-Oct.

## FOOD

Good eating places tend to congregate on **Court Ave.** downtown, or in antique-filled **Historic Valley Jct.** in West Des Moines, on 5th St. south of Grand Ave. The supermarkets **Dahl's** and **Hy-Vee** are sprinkled throughout the city and have cafeterias that serve hot food for cheap. At Dahl's, breakfast is under $2, lunch under $4, dinner under $5. Hy-Vee is just a little more expensive, but they have an all-you-can-eat salad bar ($5). A breakfast buffet ($5) is served at some locations on weekends. An ever popular **Farmer's Market** (243-6625) sells loads of fresh fruit and vegetables, baked goods, and ethnic food on Sa mornings (7am-noon mid-May to Nov.) and much of Court Ave. and 4th St. are blocked off for the extravaganza.

**Bauder Pharmacy and Fountain,** 3802 Ingersoll (255-1124), 38th and Ingersoll, is an old fashioned soda fountain in a neighborhood drug store. Sandwiches are simple and cheap ($2-3), and their award-winning homemade ice cream is a local favorite ($1 per scoop). Open M-F 8:30am-7pm, Sa 9am-5pm, Su 10am-3pm.

**The Tavern,** 205 5th St. (255-9827), in Historic Valley Jct., has the best pizza around—but everyone knows it, so you'll have to wait your turn. Pizzas with toppings from "bacon cheeseburger" to "taco fiesta" ($6.25-16). A large selection of pasta and vegetarian dishes. Open M-Th 11am-11pm, F-Sa 11am-midnight, Su noon-11pm.

**Stella's Blue Sky Diner,** 400 Locust St. (246-1953), at the Skywalk level in the Capital Sq. Mall. Settle into a 50s-style vinyl chair for meatloaf, burgers, or "neutron" fries ($2). Should you order a malt ($2.75), ask for the malt "Stella's way." Open M-F 6:30am-6pm, Sa 8am-6pm. Also at 3281 100 St. in Urbandale (278-0550); open M-Th 10:45am-10pm, F-Sa 10:45am-11pm, Su 10:45am-9pm.

**Billy Joe's Pitcher Show,** 1701 25th (224-1709), off University Ave. in West Des Moines. A combo smoke-filled restaurant and movie theater. Waitresses serve beer (pitchers $6) and assorted grub ($4-10) while you watch the second-run flick ($3). $2 matinees; $1 on M, $1 on Su with student ID. 4-5 shows per day, 12:30-9:30pm; experience the *Rocky Horror Picture Show* at midnight on F and Sa. Call for exact times.

**The Iowa Machine Shed,** 11151 Hickman Rd. (270-6818), in Urbandale. Dedicated to Iowa's agricultural heritage, the Machine Shed is said to crack 3600 eggs every week and serves up gigantic, home-baked sweet rolls. Serves breakfast ($3.50-7), sandwiches ($4-5), and cow- and pig-derived entrees ($8-17). Open M-Sa 6am-10pm, Su 7am-9pm.

## SIGHTS

Ten mi. northwest of downtown in Urbandale, **Living History Farms** is a 600-acre open-air museum with 5 working farms depicting time periods from 1700 to the present. Dressed in period garb, the staff milk cows, feed chickens, sow crops, and clearly explain and illustrate the changes in agriculture and farm life during the past 300 years. It has been called "the best agriculture museum anywhere."*(2600 NW 111th St. at Hickman Rd. 278-5286. Open May to mid-Oct. daily 9am-5pm. Last tour 3pm. $8, seniors $7, ages 4-12 $5.)*

The most elaborate of its ilk, but undergoing heavy renovations until 2002, the copper-and-gold-domed **state capitol,** on E. 9th St. across the river and up Locust Ave., provides a spectacular view of Des Moines from its lofty hilltop position. An 18 ft. long scale model of the battleship *U.S.S. Iowa* graces the lobby; take bus #5 "E. 6th and 9th St.," #1 "Fairgrounds," #4 "E. 14th," or #7 "Walker." *(281-5591. Open M-F 8am-5pm, Sa-Su 8am-4pm. Free tours M-Sa 10am-3pm; call for exact times.)*

**GREAT PLAINS**

## "CHRIST, WE'RE IN LOVE..." Winterset happens to be the setting for Robert Kincaid and Francesca Johnson's transcendent 4-day love affair in the best-selling *Bridges of Madison County*. Robert Waller's romantic novel of adultery between an Iowa farm wife and an itinerant *National Geographic* photographer was decried by the literary establishment, but it sold millions of copies across the world. Lines such as, "We have both lost ourselves and created something else, something that exists only as an interlacing of the two of us. Christ, we're in love," left critics aghast and readers enthralled. The book was made into a film starring Clint Eastwood and Meryl Streep, and the movie site is now open for tours (open May-Oct. daily 10am-6pm; $5, seniors $4, children $3, car tour $4). Take U.S. 35 South from Des Moines, exit at Cummings/Norwalk, and turn right. Follow the signs reading "Francesca's House." The bridges themselves charge no admission fee and are located 20mi. beyond.

The geodesic greenhouse dome of the **Botanical Center,** just north of I-235 and the capitol, encompasses a desert, rainforest, and bonsai exhibit, and many birds, fish, and turtles call this place home. *(909 E. River Dr. 242-2934. Open M-Th 10am-6pm, F 10am-9pm, Sa-Su 10am-5pm. $1.50, students 50¢, seniors 75¢, under 6 free.)*

Most cultural sights cluster west of downtown on Grand Ave. The **Des Moines Art Center** draws raves for its modern art collection as well as for its architecture; Eero Saarinen, I. M. Pei, and Richard Meier contributed to the design. Take bus #1 "West Des Moines." *(4700 Grand Ave. 277-4405. Open T-W, F-Sa 11am-4pm, Th 11am-9pm, Su noon-4pm. Free.)* Behind the Art Center, through the **Rose Garden,** is **Greenwood Pond.** Formerly a pond scummy lagoon, it's been drained and "sculpted" into a stimulating outdoor experience with structures and bridges made of wood and steel. This is a great place for an afternoon picnic, or a winter skate. Across from Greenwood Pond, the **Science Center of Iowa** has great exibits for kids, dazzling laser shows, and computer-generated planetarium spectacles. *(4500 Grand Ave. 274-6868. Open M-Sa 10am-5pm, Su noon-5pm; $5.50, seniors and ages 3-12 $3.50.)*

## 🎵 ENTERTAINMENT AND NIGHTLIFE

The **Civic Center,** 221 Walnut St. (243-1109), sponsors theater and concerts; call for info. On Th, a copy of the Des Moines *Register* provides "The Datebook," a helpful listing of concerts, sporting events, and movies. *Cityview,* a free local weekly, lists free events and is available at most supermarkets. The **Iowa State Fair,** one of the nation's largest, captivates Des Moines for 10 days in mid-Aug. (Aug. 10-20, 2000) with prize cows, crafts, cakes, and corn ($7 per day, children $3; $2 less if purchased in advance). For the low-down, call the state fair hotline (800-545-FAIR/3247 or 262-3111). Tickets for **Iowa Cubs** baseball games are a steal. Chicago's farm team plays at **Sec. Taylor Stadium,** 350 SW 1st St. (243-6111). Call for game dates and times. (General admission $5, children $3; reserved grandstand $7, children $5.) From late Apr. to late July, Des Moines flips over for **Seniom Sed** (243-1109); it attracts the after-work crowd for a city-wide block party held F 5-7:15pm at Nollen Plaza downtown ($5, with 3 beverage tickets included). **Jazz in July** (280-3222) presents free concerts at locations throughout the city every day of the month; pick up a schedule at area restaurants, concert sites, or the visitors bureau.

**Court Ave.,** in the southeast corner of downtown, is a yuppified warehouse district packed with almost-trendy restaurants and bars. At **Papa's Planet,** 208 3rd St. (284-0901), 20- and 30-somethings move to 80s and 90s dance music on 2 dance floors and listen to classic rock cover bands on the patio outside. (21+. Live music F-Sa. 25¢ beers on Th with $5 cover; F-Sa cover $3-5 includes drink specials. Open Th-Sa 7pm-2am.) **Java Joe's,** 214 4th St. (288-5282), a mellow coffeehouse with internet access ($1 for 9½ minutes), sells sandwiches ($4.50), coffee from locales like Kenya and Sumatra ($1-2.75), and beer ($2.50-$3.00). Live music specialties 4 or 5 nights a week include folk, Irish Jam, and jazz. (Cover on rare occasions. Student deals with ID Su after 5. Open M-Th 7:30am-11pm, F-Sa 7:30am-1am, Su 9am-11pm. All ages.) **The Garden,** 112 SE 4th St. (243-3965), is a dance bar. (Strippers Sa 11pm. Drag shows Su 10pm. Cover $3-4. Open W-Su 8pm-2am.)

## NEAR DES MOINES

**Pella,** 41mi. east of Des Moines on Rt. 163, blooms in May with its annual **Tulip Time** festival (628-4311; May 11-13, 2000), with traditional Dutch dancing, a parade, concerts, and *glöckenspiel* performances. In **Indianola,** 12mi. south on U.S. 69, the **National Balloon Museum,** 1601 N. Jefferson (961-3714), holds the annual **National Balloon Classic** in late July for hot-air balloons. (Museum open M-F 9am-4pm, Sa 10am-4pm, Su 1-4pm. Free. Call to arrange a tour; $1, children 50¢.)

Twenty mi. south of Des Moines is the town of **Winterset,** where John Wayne, the toughest of American film cowboys, began his life in 1907. Wayne's birthplace is just outside of downtown at 216 S. 2nd St., where the star was christened Marion Robert Morrison (now there's a name that'll make you tough). The house has been converted into a museum, the **John Wayne Birthplace** (462-1044), with 2 rooms of memorabilia and 2 rooms authentically furnished in the style of the Duke's parents' era (open daily 10am-4:30pm; $2.50, seniors $2.25, children $1).

## IOWA CITY

Iowa City is a classic college town and an oasis of liberalism in a conservative state. The main University of Iowa campus fills the city with a plethora of student bars, frozen yogurt stands, and street musicians. Every other autumn weekend, hordes of Iowans make a pilgrimage to the city to cheer on the university's football team, the Hawkeyes. Iowa City's carefully tempered vibrancy—this is Iowa, after all—promises a spell of welcome relief from the compulsive fury of big city life.

**⌂ PRACTICAL INFORMATION.** Iowa City lies on I-80 about 112mi. east of Des Moines. North-south **Madison** and **Gilbert St.** and east-west **Market** and **Burlington St.** bind the downtown. **Greyhound** and **Burlington Trailways** are both located at 404 E. College St. (337-2127; station open M-F 8am-8pm, Sa-Su 10am-8pm). Buses head out for Des Moines (2-4hr., 7 per day, $27); Chicago (4½-6½hr., 8 per day, $38); and St. Louis (9-13hr., 1 per day, $65). The free **Cambus** (335-8633) runs daily all over campus and downtown (M-F 5am-midnight, Sa-Su noon-midnight; summer Sa-Su noon-6pm). **Iowa City Transit** (356-5151) runs downtown (M-F 6:30am-10:30pm and Sa 6:30am-7pm; fare 75¢, seniors with pass 35¢). The **convention and visitors bureau,** 408 1st Ave. (337-6592 or 800-283-6592), sits across the river in Coralville off U.S. 6 (open M-F 8am-5pm, Sa-Su 10am-4pm). More area info is available at the University of Iowa's **Campus Information Center** (335-3055), in the **Iowa Memorial Union** at Madison and Jefferson St. (Open M-F 8am-8pm, Sa 10am-8pm, Su noon-4pm; reduced hrs. in summer and interims.) **Hotlines** include the 24hr. **Crisis Line** (351-0140), **Sexual Abuse Resource Line** (335-6000), and the **University of Iowa Gay, Lesbian, Bisexual and Transgender Union** (335-3251). **Internet access** is available at the Iowa City Public Library, 123 S. Linn St. (356-5200), free with photo ID as deposit (open M-Th 10am-9pm, F-Sa 10am-6pm, Su 1-5pm). **Post Office:** 400 S. Clinton St. (354-1560; open M-F 8:30am-5pm, Sa 9:30am-1pm). **ZIP code:** 52240. **Area code:** 319.

**⌂⌂ ACCOMMODATIONS AND FOOD.** Cheap motels line U.S. 6 in **Coralville,** 2mi. west of downtown, and **1st Ave.** at exit 242 off I-80. The cheapest of the bunch is the **Big Ten Inn,** 707 1st Ave. (351-6131) off U.S. 6 (singles $34, doubles $44). Up the street at **Motel 6,** 810 1st Ave. (354-0030 or 800-466-8356), it's a bit nicer (singles $40, Sa-Su $44; doubles $46/$50). **Kent Park Campgrounds** (645-2315), 9mi. west on U.S. 6, manages 86 secluded first come, first served sites pleasantly huddled near a lake ($4, with electricity $8; check-in by 10:30pm).

Downtown boasts cheerful, moderately priced restaurants and bars. At the open-air **Pedestrian Mall,** on College and Dubuque St., the melodies of street musicians drift through the eateries and shops and vendors sell food until 3am if

**FIELD OF DREAMS** Movie buffs and baseball fanatics alike may want to go the distance to the **Field of Dreams** in Dyersville, where the movie *Field of Dreams* was shot. (800-443-8981. Open Apr.-Nov. Free.) In the film, mysterious voices direct a farmer (played by Kevin Costner) to build a baseball field amidst Iowa's acres of corn. In doing so, the farmer is able to exorcise his demons. The folks there will provide you with bats, balls, and gloves at no cost so you can try to hit one into the stands, er, stalks. Dyersville is about 25mi. west of Dubuque in northeast Iowa. Take Rt. 20 west from Dubuque to Rte 136 N; go right after the railroad tracks for 3mi.

demand is strong. **The Airliner,** 22 Clinton St. (338-5463), is Iowa City's oldest restaurant, popular with both faculty and students (pizza slices $2, Su $1; entrees $5-9; open daily 11am-10pm; upstairs bar open until 2am). In the mall, **Gringo's,** 115 E. College St. (338-3000), slaps down tasty Mexican dishes ($5-10). The all-you-can-eat taco bar (5-9pm, $5) fills bellies Tu. (Open M-Th 11am-10pm, F-Sa 11am-11pm, Su noon-10pm.) A college favorite, **Micky's Irish Pub,** 11 S. Dubuque St. (338-6860), whips up salads, "mickwiches," and $5-8 burgers (open M-F 11am-10pm, Sa-Su 8am-10pm; bar open later). At **The Java House,** 211½ E. Washington St. (341-0012), sip coffee ($1.40) or latte ($2) on a cushy chair with newspapers and magazines. (Open M-Th 7am-12:30am, F-Sa 7am-1am, Su 7:30am-11:30pm; may close earlier in summer.) At downtown's Swan Parking Ramp (Gilbert and Washington St.), W nights (5:30-7:30pm) and Sa mornings (7:30-11:30am) from May to Oct., folks find the **Iowa City Farmers Market** (356-5110).

🎭 📷 **SIGHTS, ENTERTAINMENT, AND NIGHTLIFE.** It is difficult to miss the **Old Capitol** building between Clinton and Madison St., as it is the major architectural landmark of the city, and the focus of the Pentacrest, a formation of 5 university buildings. (335-0548. Open M-Sa 10am-3pm, Su noon-4pm.) More interesting and quirky is the **Museum of Natural History** in the Pentacrest building at Jefferson and Clinton St. Its dioramas on the Native Americans of Iowa are great, and there are fabulous displays of beautiful birds and a giant sloth. (335-0480. Open M-Sa 9:30am-4:30pm, Su 12:30-4:30pm. Free. Wheelchair access.) On the other side of the river is the **University of Iowa Museum of Art,** 150 N. Riverside Dr., where the fine Stanley African art collection is on display (335-1727. Open Tu-Sa 10am-5pm, Su noon-5pm. Free.) In West Branch, 10min. northeast of the city on the Herbert Hoover Hwy., lies the 31st President's birthplace, now known as the **Herbert Hoover National Historic Site**. The vintage American town chronicles this fascinating man's life with his birthplace cottage, the presidential library/museum, and a ½mi. trail through restored prairie that leads to his gravesite. (643-2541. Open daily 9am-5pm; $2, seniors $1, under 16 free; wheelchair access.)

Nightspots are plentiful downtown. **Deadwood,** 6 S. Dubuque St. (351-9417), is often lauded as the city's best bar and has been voted by locals as the best place to pick up members of the same and opposite sex. For live music from punk to folk visit **Gabe's,** 330 E. Washington St. (354-4788; cover $2-6). Local jazz, folk, and blues musicians play Th-Sa at 9:30pm in **The Sanctuary,** 405 S. Gilbert St. (351-5692), a cozy, wood-paneled restaurant and bar with 120 beers (cover $1-4; open M-Sa 4pm-2am, Su 6pm-2am). **The Union Bar,** 121 E. College St. (339-7713), brags that it's the "biggest damn bar in college football's 'Big Ten'" (cover varies; open Tu-Sa 8pm-2am). From May-Aug. in the Pedestrian Plaza downtown, the **Friday Night Concert Series** (354-0863; 5-9pm) features everything from jazz to salsa to blues.

# NEBRASKA

Early travelers on the Oregon and Mormon trails rushed through Nebraska on their way towards western greenery and gold. Accustomed to the forested hills of New England, these pioneers nicknamed the Nebraska Territory the "Great American Desert," mistakenly believing that if trees did not grow here, neither would crops. Eventually they caught on, and began to abandon their westward journeys to farm the fertile Nebraskan soil. Their settlements drove out the native Sioux and Pawnee tribes, who had long understood the value of Nebraska's prairies. But neither these property-minded settlers, whose towns have since grown into cities, nor the tourists who drive through Scotts Bluff in air-conditioned autos, can truly master these vast plains. "We come and go, but the land is always here," philosophized Willa Cather in *O Pioneers!*, "and the people who love it and understand it are the people who own it—for a little while."

# ⁊ PRACTICAL INFORMATION

**Capital:** Lincoln.

**Visitor Info: Nebraska Tourism Office,** P.O. Box 94666, Lincoln 68509 (402-471-3796 or 800-228-4307; www.visitnebraska.org). Open M-F 8am-5pm. **Nebraska Game and Parks Commission,** 2200 N. 33rd St., Lincoln 68503 (402-471-0641). Open M-F 8am-5pm.

**State Soft Drink:** Kool-Aid. **Postal Abbreviation:** NE. **Sales Tax:** 5-6.5%, depending on city.

# OMAHA

Omaha may not be the type of place one associates with the prairies and cornfields of Nebraska. The largest city in the state, this birthplace of Gerald Ford, Malcolm X, and Boys Town is also the most urban. From the quiet streetside cafes of the Old Market to the jumping gay clubs at 16th and Leavenworth, Omaha joins cosmopolitan airs with Midwestern manners, offering world-class museums and attractions alongside the native friendliness and easy living of a small town.

## ⁊ ORIENTATION AND PRACTICAL INFORMATION

Omaha rests on the west bank of the Missouri River, brushing up against Iowa's border. While it wears a facade of geometric order, Omaha is actually an imprecise grid of numbered streets (running north-south) and named streets (east-west). **Dodge St.** (Rt. 6) divides the city north-south. **I-80** runs across the southern edge of town and is bisected by **I-480/Rt. 75** (the Kennedy Expwy.), which leads to nearby Bellevue. **I-29,** just over the river in Iowa, will take you north to Sioux City or south to Kansas City. **At night, avoid N. 24th St.**

**Trains: Amtrak,** 1003 S. 9th St. (342-1501), at Pacific St. To Chicago (9 hr., 1 per day, $56-101) and Denver (8hr., 1 per day, $58-106). Open M-F 10:30pm-11:15am and 12:30-4pm, Sa 10:30pm-11:30am and noon-4pm, Su 10:30pm-8am.

**Buses: Greyhound,** 1601 Jackson (341-1906). To: Des Moines (2-3hr., 6 per day, $24-27); Cheyenne (10-11hr., 3 per day, $70); Kansas City (3-4hr., 3 per day, $20-24); and Lincoln (1hr., 6 per day, $12). Open 24hr.

**Public Transportation: Metro Area Transit (MAT),** 2222 Cumming St. (341-0800). Open M-F 8am-4:30pm. Schedules available at the Park Fair Mall, at 16th and Douglas St. near the Greyhound station, and the library at 14th and Farnam St. Fare 90¢, transfers 5¢.

**Taxis: Happy Cab** (339-0110).

**Car Rental: Cheepers Rent-a-Car,** 7700 L St. (331-8586). $25 per day with 150 free mi., $31 per day with 400 free mi.; 20¢ per additional mi. Must be 21 with a major credit card and personal liability policy. Open M-F 7:30am-8pm, Sa 8:30am-3pm.

**Bike Rental: Bicycle Specialties,** 4682 Leavenworth St. (556-2453), at 46th St. and Leavenworth. Bikes $20 per day, $35 per weekend, $100 per week. Rental includes pump, lock, spare tube, and helmet. Open M and W 10am-7pm, Tu and Th-F 10am-6pm, Sa 9am-5pm, Su noon-5pm.

**Visitor Info: Visitors Center/Game and Parks Commission,** 1212 Bob Gibson Blvd. (595-3990), at 10th and Bob Gibson by the zoo and baseball stadium; get off I-80 at 13th

St. Open daily 8am-5pm. **Greater Omaha Convention and Visitors Bureau,** 6800 Mercy Rd., suite 202 (800-332-1819), at the Ak-Sar-Ben complex off S. 72 St. north of I-80. Open M-F 8am-4:30pm. **Events Hotline,** 444-6800.

**Hotlines: Rape Crisis,** 345-7273. **Suicide Hotline,** 572-2999. Both operate 24hr. **First Call for Help** for information and referrals, 444-6666, M-F 8am-5pm.

**Hospital: Methodist Hospital,** 8303 Dodge St. (354-4434), at 84th and Dodge. **Women's Services,** 201 South 46th St., one block south of Dodge St. (554-0110).

**Internet Access: Omaha Public Library,** 215 S. 15th St. (444-4800), between Douglas and Farnham. Free Internet use, but no telnet. Open M-Th 9am-9pm, F-Sa 9am-5:30pm, Su 1-5pm.

**Post Office:** 1124 Pacific St. (348-2895). Open M-F 7:30am-6pm, Sa 7:30am-noon. After-hrs. express mail pick-up available. **ZIP code:** 68108. **Area code:** 402.

## ACCOMMODATIONS

Budget motels in Omaha proper are not particularly budget. For better deals, head for the city outskirts or across the river into Council Bluffs, Iowa.

**Satellite Motel,** 6006 L St. (733-7373), just south of I-80 exit 450 (60th St.). A round satellite look-a-like. Clean, wedge-shaped rooms equipped with fridge and TV with HBO. In winter singles $34-$36, doubles $40-$44; in summer $36-$40/$44-$48.

**YMCA,** 430 S. 20th St. (341-1600). Clean, single rooms with phones (no long-distance). $5 per day for use of on-site facilities. 4th fl., men only (common bathroom) $11. Other rooms (with individual bathrooms) $12.23. Free parking.

**Haworth Park Campground** (291-3379 or 293-3098), in Bellevue on Payne St. at the end of Mission St. Take the exit for Rt. 370 E. off Rt. 75, turn right onto Galvin St., left onto Mission St., and right onto Payne St. just before the toll bridge. Otherwise, hop on the infrequent bus "Bellevue" from 17th and Dodge St. to Mission and Franklin St., then walk down Mission. Tent sites are far enough away from the RV area to tone down the trailer-park feel. Sites $5, with hookup $10. Showers, toilets, shelters. Open daily 6am-10pm; quiet stragglers can enter after hrs. Check-out 3pm.

## FOOD FOR THOUGHT

It's no fun being a chicken, cow, or vegetarian in Omaha, with a fried chicken joint on every block and a steakhouse in every district. Once a warehouse area, the brick streets of the **Old Market,** on Jones, Howard, and Harney St. between 10th and 13th, now feature popular shops, restaurants, and bars. While you're there, visit the eerie **Fountain of the Furies,** "Greek avengers of patricide and disrespect of ancestors," in the Old Market Passageway off Howard St. The **farmers market** (345-5401), 11th and Jackson St., is held on Sa 8am-12:30pm from mid-May to mid-Oct. and at 11th and Howard Wed 5pm-8pm from mid July to mid Sept. On a nice day, you could picnic in the lovely **Heartland of America Park,** just a few blocks east of the Old Market at Douglas and 8th St. (wheelchair access).

**McFoster's Natural Kind Café,** 302 S. 38th St. (345-7477), at Farnam St. Healthy dishes ($4-13), including free-range chicken, vegan eggplant parmesan, and artichoke specialties. Occasional live music; cover around $2. Open M-Th 11am-10pm, F-Sa 11am-1am, Su 10am-3pm. 1st fl. wheelchair accessible.

**The Diner,** 409 S. 12 St. at Harney (341-9870), is as straight forward as its name suggests. It's not one of those chains that tries to recreate the 50s; it really is lost in the fifties. Good food at really good prices. (Everything on the menu under $6, most breakfast $2-3, lunch $3-5.) Open M-Sa 6am-4pm.

**Délice European Café,** 1206 Howard St. (342-2276), in the Old Market. Scrumptious pastries and deli fare at reasonable prices ($2-6). They also serve wine and beer to help make your meal appropriately European. Ask about availability of day-old baked goods. Open M-Th 8am-10pm, F-Sa 8am-noon, Su 8am-7pm.

**Upstream Brewing,** 514 S. 11th St. (344-0200), at Jackson St. Creative entrees ($9-18) can be enjoyed inside, out on the patio, or on the roof-top deck. Pizza and burgers $6-7. Upstairs, a pool-hall atmosphere with 11 pool tables and 20 single-malt scotches at the bar. Features 8 slighty watery home brewed beers. Open Su-Th 11am-midnight. Bar open M-Sa until 1am, Su until midnight.

# SIGHTS

Within a monumental Art Deco artifice, Omaha's **Joslyn Art Museum** displays an excellent collection of 19th- and 20th-century European and American art. The exterior is pink Georgian marble; the interior dazzles with 30 different types of stone. From mid-July to mid-Aug., the museum hosts free "Jazz on the Green" concerts each Th from 7-9pm. *(2200 Dodge St., 342-3300. Open Tu-Sa 10am-4pm, Su noon-4pm. $4, seniors and college students $3, ages 5-17 $2.50, free Sa 10am-noon.)* The **Durham Western Heritage Museum** is housed in the retired, yet still grand **Union Pacific Railroad Station.** *(801 S. 10th St., 444-5071. Open Tu-Sa 10am-5pm, Su 1-5pm. $3, seniors $2.50, ages 5-12 $2.)*

In 1917, Father Edward Flanagan founded **Boys Town** as a home for troubled, neglected boys. Made famous by the eponymous 1938 Spencer Tracy movie, Boys Town is a popular tourist draw and still houses over 550 boys and girls. Be sure to check out the 32-in. diameter, 600-lb. ball of stamps in the Visitors Center behind the gift shop. Collecting stamps was a hobby for many of the boys, and through the years the ball grew from a few stamps wrapped around a pencil to its present size. *(498-1140, west of Omaha at W. Dodge and 132nd St. Visitors center open daily 8am-5:30pm; Sept.-Apr. 9am-4:30pm. Free; self-guided audiotape tour $2. Call ahead to arrange guided tour.)*

One of the largest indoor jungles in the nation, complete with monkeys, low-flying bats, and exotic birds, has made the **Henry Doorly Zoo** the number one tourist attraction between Chicago and Denver. *(3701 S. 10th St. 733-8401, at Bob Gibson Blvd., or exit at 13th St. off I-80. Open M-Sa 9:30am-5pm, Su 9:30am-6pm; early Sept. to late May daily 9:30am-5pm. $7.25, seniors $5.75, children $3.75, under 5 free.)* Also featured is the **Kingdom of the Seas Aquarium,** complete with a glass-enclosed submarine walkway, and the **Lozier IMAX Theater.** *(IMAX shows $6.50, seniors $5.50, children $4.50, under 5 free. Wheelchair access.)*

Gawk at deer and birds at the **Fontenelle Forest Nature Center** on Childs Rd. East in Bellevue. The privately owned center has a 1mi. eco-friendly, wheelchair-accessible boardwalk raised above the forest floor; and a 1300-acre forest and wetland with 17mi. of walking and hiking trails. *(293-7915 or 731-3140. Take the Chandler Rd. exit off 75 and go East. Turn right on Bellevue Blvd, and then left on Childs Rd. East. Open daily 8am-5pm. $3.50, seniors $2, children $1.50, under 3 free.)*

See the gargantuan remnants of U.S. air power of the last half-century in an equally enormous museum, at the **Strategic Air Command Museum.** The museum displays a B-52 bomber, many different sorts of military aircraft and history, and travelling exhibits that could include missiles, objects from the space program, or aircraft from oversees. *(800-358-5029, off route I-80 between Omaha and Lincoln, adjacent to Mahoney Park. Open daily 9am-6pm. $6, children $3, under 5 free.)*

Just down the road is the **Simmons Wildlife Safari Park.** Just like Jurassic Park, except instead of dinosaurs, drive your all-terrain vehicle (or beat-up Chevette) 4½mi. through a nature preserve with bison, pronghorns, and other beasts roaming inside. *(944-2481. Open Apr.-Oct. 9:30am-5pm 8am-1hr. before dusk. $4, seniors $3.50, children $2. Guided tram runs every hr. on the hr.)*

# ENTERTAINMENT AND NIGHTLIFE

At I-80 and 13th St., (across the street from the zoo) is **Johnny Rosenblatt Stadium** (734-2550), where you can watch the minor league (AAA) **Omaha Golden Spikes** battle opponents from Apr. to early Sept. (General admission $3.50. Box seat $5.5.0-$7.50. $1 off all tickets for High School students and seniors. Wheelchair access.) The stadium also hosts the College Baseball World Series (late May-early June).

In late June and early July, **Shakespeare on the Green** (280-2391) stages free performances in Elmwood Park, on 60th and Dodge St. (Th-Su 8:30pm). The **Omaha Symphony** (342-3560) plays at the **Orpheum Theatre,** 409 S. 16th St. (Sept.-May usually Th-Su; call for dates and times; tickets $10-40). **Omaha's Magic Theater,** 325 S. 16th St. (932-3821; call M-F 9am-4pm), devotes itself to the development of experimental theater (evening performances F-M; tickets $12, students and seniors $7).

Punk and progressive folk have found a niche at the several area universities; check the window of the **Antiquarian Bookstore,** 1215 Harney, in the Old Market, for the scoop on shows. Several good bars await nearby. **The Dubliner,** 1205 Harney, downstairs, stages live traditional Irish music in the evenings F and Sa (342-5887; cover $2-3). The **13th Street Coffee Company,** 519 13th St., is a hip peddler of the potent potion. The turtle latte—praline, caramel, chocolate, steamed milk, a double shot, and whipped cream ($3)—won't slow you down. Live music plays F at 9pm, with no cover. (345-2883. Open M-Th 7am-10pm, F 6:30am-midnight, Sa 8am-11pm, Su 9am-10pm.)

One of the most popular gay bars in the state, **The Max,** 1417 Jackson (a brown building with no sign outside), caters to men and women with 5 bars, a disco dance floor, DJ, fountains, patio, and a leather bar (346-4110 happy hour 4-7pm; cover F-Sa $3; open daily 4pm-1am).

# LINCOLN

Friendly folk and a hopping nightlife enliven Lincoln, named for the late President in 1867. The University of Nebraska football team, the Cornhuskers, is a significant town presence. Game days are big days—locals gnash their teeth in communal woe after every loss. In its breathtaking capitol, the "Tower on the Plains," Lincoln houses the only unicameral (one-house) state legislature in the U.S. The state switched from two houses during the Great Depression to avoid red tape; today, the Nebraskan government is considered a model of efficiency.

## ■ ORIENTATION AND PRACTICAL INFORMATION

Getting around Lincoln is a snap. Numbered streets increase as you go east; lettered streets progress through the alphabet as you go north. **O St.** is the main east-west drag, splitting the town north-south. **R St.** runs along the south side of the **University of Nebraska-Lincoln (UNL)** city campus. **Cornhusker Hwy. (U.S. 6)** shears the northwest edge of Lincoln.

**Airport: Lincoln Airport** (474-2770), 5mi. northwest of downtown on Cornhusker Hwy., or take exit 399 off I-80. Taxi to downtown $12.

**Trains: Amtrak,** 201 N. 7th St. (476-1295). Once daily to: Omaha (1hr., $14); Denver (7½hr., $106); Chicago (11hr., $111); and Kansas City (7hr., $51). Some seasonal specials. Open M-W 7:30am-4pm and 11:30pm-7am, Th-Su 11:30pm-7am.

**Buses: Greyhound,** 940 P St. (474-1071), close to downtown and city campus. To: Omaha (1 hr.; in summer 4per day, in winter 3 per day; $12); Chicago (12-14hr., 3 per day, $46); Kansas City (6½hr., 2 per day, $47); and Denver (12-18hr., 3 per day, $64). Open M-F 5:30am-8:30pm, Sa 8am-6pm. On Su, meet the bus at departure time. In winter, open M-F 7:30am-5pm, Sa 9am-5pm.

**Public Transportation: Star Trans,** 710 J St. (476-1234). Schedules are available on the bus, at many downtown locations, and at the office. Buses run M-Sa 6am-6pm. Fare 85¢, seniors 40¢, ages 5-11 50¢.

**Taxis: Yellow Cabs,** (477-4111).

**Car Rental: U-Save Auto Rental,** 2240 Q St. (477-5236). As low as $15 per day with 100 free mi.; 10¢ per additional mi. Must be 21. $100 deposit. Open 8am-7pm.

**Bike Rental: Blue's Bike & Fitness Center,** 3321 Pioneers Blvd. (488-2101) rents new, basic mountain bikes. Take Bus #16. Bikes $10 per ½-day, $16 per day. Credit card or cash deposit required (usually the value of the bike). Open M-Th 9am-8pm, F 10am-6pm, Sa 9am-5pm, Su 1pm-5pm.

**Quadratic Formula:** $(-b \pm \sqrt{b^2 - 4ac})/2a)$.

**Visitor Info: Visitors Center,** 201 N. 7th St. in the Haymarket district (434-5348 or 800-423-8212). Open M-F 9am-8pm, Sa 8am-5pm, Su noon-5pm; in winter M-F 9am-6pm, Sa 10am-4pm, Su noon-4pm. **Lincoln Convention and Visitors Bureau,** P.O. Box 83737, Lincoln, 68501 (434-5335; www.lincoln.org/cvb).

**Hotlines: Personal Crisis Line,** 475-5171. **Rape and Spouse Abuse Crisis Line,** 475-7273. Both 24hr. **University of Nebraska Gay/Lesbian/Bisexual/Transgender Resource Center,** 472-5644 (inactive in summer).

**Internet Access: Lincoln Public Libraries,** main branch at 136 S. 14th St. at N St. (444-8500). M-Th 9am-9pm, F-Sa 9am-6pm, Su 1:30pm-5:30pm, 30 min. sessions, 4 terminals, free.

**Post Office:** 700 R St. (473-1695). Open M-F 7:30am-6pm, Sa 9am-3pm. **ZIP code:** 68501. **Area code:** 402.

# ACCOMMODATIONS

There are few inexpensive motels in downtown Lincoln; most lie east of the city center around the 5600 block of Cornhusker Hwy. (U.S. 6). More centrally located, the **Cornerstone Hostel (HI-AYH),** 640 N. 16th St., at U St. just south of Vine St., is located in a church basement in the university's downtown campus and rarely fills up. Take bus #4; from the bus station, walk 7 blocks east to 16th, then 5 blocks north. (476-0355 or 476-0926. 2 single-sex rooms; 5 beds for women, 3 for men. Full kitchen and laundry facilities. $10, nonmembers $13. Free parking and linen. Curfew 11pm.) **UNL, Niehardt Residence Center,** 540 N. 16th St., a clean and friendly place, rents some rooms when school is out of session from late May to early Aug. (472-0777 or 472-1044; room with 2 twin beds $26). **The Great Plains Budget Host Inn,** 2732 O St., has large rooms with fridges and coffeemakers. Take bus #9 "O St. Shuttle." (476-3253 or 800-288-8499. Free parking, and kitchenettes available. Singles $38; doubles $46.) The **Nebraska State Fair Park Campground,** 2402 N. 14th St. at Cornhusker, is conveniently located and has a congenial atmosphere, but is next to a highway and train tracks; take bus #7 "Belmont." (473-4287. Sites for 2 $12, with electricity $14, full hookup $16; $1 per additional person. Fills up early in Aug. during the fair. Open mid-Apr. to Oct.) To get to the more pleasant **Camp-A-Way,** at 1st and Superior St., take exit 401 or 401a from I-80, then exit 1 on I-180/Rt. 34. Lots of trees, but a bit out of the way, and also next to a highway. (476-2282. $14, water and electricity $14.50, full hook-up $19.50. Showers and laundry.)

# FOOD AND NIGHTLIFE

The UNL student center, the **Nebraska Union,** at 14th and R St., has cheap food, a post office, an ATM, a Ticketmaster outlet, and a bank. (472-2181. Hrs. vary, but usually open in summer M-F 7am-5pm; academic year M-F 7am-11pm, Sa 9am-midnight, Su noon-midnight.) Cheap bars, eateries, and movie theaters cluster around one side of UNL's downtown campus, between N and P St. from 12th to 15th St. **Historic Haymarket,** 7th to 9th and O to R St., is a renovated warehouse district near the train tracks, with cafes, bars, several restaurants, and a **farmers market** (435-7496; open mid-May to mid-Oct. Sa 8am-noon). All downtown buses connect at 11th and O St., 2 blocks east of Historic Haymarket. Every renovated warehouse district has its yuppie brewery; **Lazlo's Brewery and Grill,** 710 P St., is the oldest one in Nebraska, founded in 1991. Chow down on salads, sandwiches, and meat entrees for $5-15. (474-5636. Open M-Sa 11am-1am, Su 11am-10pm. Wheelchair access.) Right next door, **Ja Brisco,** 700 P St., whips up pizzas, pasta, and deli sandwiches ($6-12) that are sure to please (434-5644 open daily 11am-10:30pm; wheelchair access). **Valentino's,** 232 N. 13th St., a regional chain with roots in Lincoln, offers pasta ($5-8) and 6 different all-you-can-eat buffets. (475-1501. $6, after 4pm

$8. F and Sa 9:30am-11pm pizza $3, $1 draughts and $3 pitchers. Open Su-Th 11am-10pm, F-Sa 11am-11pm.) **The Mill,** 800 P St., is a stylish cafe where patrons sun on the large patio while enjoying iced drinks, coffee and tea from around the world ($3), and baked goods (475-5522; cafe open M-Th 7:30am-11pm, F-Sa 7:30am-midnight, Su 9am-10pm).

Nightspots abound in Lincoln, particularly those of the sports-bar variety. For the biggest names in Lincoln's live music scene, try the suitably dark and smoky **Zoo Bar,** 136 N. 14th St. Cover varies, as does the music, but the emphasis is on *good* blues. (435-8754. 21+. Open M-Sa 3pm-1am, and some Su if there's a show.) **Q,** 226 S. 9th St. between M and N, is a great gay/lesbian bar with a large, sweaty dance floor (475-2269; open Tu-Sa 8pm-1am. 19+ on Tu). For the best of the college sports bar genre, head to **Iguana's** at 1426 O St. Besides standard sports bar accoutrements, a large iguana sculpture graces the ceiling. (476-8850. Open M-Th and Sat 4:30-1am and F 3pm-1am. Happy hour 3pm-7pm on F with free appetizers.)

## ◉ SIGHTS

The "Tower on the Plains," the 400 ft. **Nebraska State Capitol Building** at 14th and K St., an unofficial architectural wonder of the world and the tallest building in Lincoln, wows with its streamlined exterior and detailed interior, highlighted by a beautiful mosaic floor. Visitors can take the elevator to the 14th fl. for a sweeping view of the city, or climb to the 3rd fl. balcony to observe the senatorial showdowns. *(471-0448. Open M-F 8am-5pm, Sa 10am-5pm, Su 1-5pm. Free, enthusiastically led tours every 30min. M-F in summer, every hr. Sa-Su.)* The **Museum of Nebraska History** on Centennial Mall, a renamed portion of 15th St., has a phenomenal, moving exhibit on the history of the Plains Indians. *(471-4754. Open M-F 9am-4:30pm, Sa 9am-5pm, Su 1:30-5pm. Free.)* The **University of Nebraska State Museum,** 14th and U St., in Morrill Hall, boasts an amazing fossil collection that includes the largest mounted mammoth in any American museum. *(472-6302. Open M-Sa 9:30am-4:30pm, Su 1:30-4:30pm. Requested donation $2.)* In the same building, the **Mueller Planetarium** lights up the ceiling with several shows daily and laser shows several days a week. *(472-2641. Closed on home game days. Planetarium $4; students, seniors, and under 13 $2. Laser shows $5, with college ID $4.)* The **Sheldon Memorial Art Gallery,** 12th and R St., was designed by Phillip Johnson and constructed entirely with Italian Travertine marble. Warhol, Hopper, and Brancusi are among the artists included.During the **Jazz in June** series, cool music can be heard in the gallery's sculpture garden on Tu nights from 7-9pm. *(472-2461. Open Tu-Sa 10am-5pm, Th-Sa 7am-9pm, Su 2-9pm. Free.)*

In addition to the standard fair fare (livestock, crafts, fitter family contests, etc.), the **Nebraska State Fair** offers car races, tractor pulls, and plenty of rides to please all comers. It lasts 11 days in late Aug. and early Sept. *(473-4109. $7.)*

**Pioneers Park,** ¼mi. south off W. Van Dorn on Coddington St. (watch for the signs along Van Dorn), is great for a real prarie picnic. The Pioneer Park Nature Center harbors bison and elk within its sanctuary, and is also the starting point for 5mi. of trails. *(3201 S. Coddington Ave. 441-7895. Open M-Sa 8:30am-8:30pm, Su noon-8:30pm; Sept.-May M-Sa 8:30am-5pm, Su noon-5pm. Free. Free golf carts.)*

## SCOTTS BLUFF

Known to the Plains Indians as "Ma-a-pa-te" ("hill that is hard to go around"), the imposing clay and sandstone highlands of **Scotts Bluff National Monument** were landmarks for people traveling the Mormon and Oregon Trails in the 1840s. For some time the bluff was too dangerous to cross, but in the 1850s a single-file wagon trail was opened through narrow **Mitchell's Pass,** where traffic wore deep marks in the sandstone. Evidence of the early pioneers can still be seen today on the ½mi. stretch of the original **Oregon Trail** preserved at the pass; tourists can gaze out at the distant horizons to the east and west as pioneers once did. The **visitors center** (436-4340), at the entrance on Rt. 92, will tell you of the mysterious death of Hiram Scott, the fur trader who gave the Bluffs their name (open daily 8am-8pm, in winter 8am-5pm; $5 per carload, $2 per motorcycle). To get to the top of the bluffs,

**CARHENGE OR BUST** Everything looks the same as you drive through the low plains and small bluffs of western Nebraska, until, suddenly, a preternatural power sweeps the horizon and the ultimate shrine to bizarre on-the-road Americana springs into view—Carhenge. Consisting of 36 old cars painted grey, this oddly engaging sculpture has the same orientation and dimensions as Stonehenge in England. When asked why he built it, Reinders replied, "plane, loqui deprehendi," or, "clearly, I spoke to be understood." This wonder of the cornhuskers can be found right off 385, 2mi. north of Alliance, NE, which is6 0mi. northwest of Scotts Bluff.

hike challenging **Saddle Rock Trail** (1½mi. each way) or motor up **Summit Dr.** At the top, you'll find **nature trails** and a magnificent view. Take U.S. 26 to Rt. 71 to Rt. 92; the monument is on Rt. 92 about 2mi. west of **Gering** (*not* in the town of Scotts-bluff). In mid-July, the 4-day **Oregon Trail Days Festival** packs the towns near Scotts Bluff with trail-happy, festive folk. Twenty mi. east on Rt. 92, just south of Bayard, the 500 ft. spire of **Chimney Rock,** visible from more than 30mi. away, marks another landmark which once inspired travelers of the Oregon Trail. A gravel road leads from Rt. 92 to within ½mi. of the rock. Unfortunately, there is no path up to the base of the rock due to the rough terrain and rattlesnakes.

Scotts Bluff is breathtaking, but is best seen as a stop on the way through the area—there is not much else to do in town. If you do stay, the **Sands Motel,** 814 W. 27th St., has clean and cozy rooms (632-6191 or 800-535-1075 for reservations; singles $28; doubles $38; wheelchair access). The **Kiwanis Riverside Campground,** 1600 S. Beltline Hwy., at the zoo, offers campsites in a partially wooded area (630-6235; $8, with hookup $10; open May-Sept.). **Area code:** 308. **Time Zone:** Mountain.

# KANSAS

There's no place like Dorothy and Toto's home. Kansas has been a major link in the nation's chain since the 1820s: families on the Oregon and Santa Fe Trails drove their wagons west in search of new homes, while cowboys on the Chisholm Trail drove their longhorns north in search of railroads and good times. Cowtowns such as Abilene and Dodge City were happy to oblige; these rip-roaring meccas of gambling and drinking made legends of lawmen like Wild Bill Hickock and Wyatt Earp. The influx of settlers resulted in fierce battles over land, as white settlers forced Native Americans to move into the arid regions farther west. Grueling feuds over Kansas's slavery status (Kansas joined the Union as a free state in 1861) gave rise to the term "Bleeding Kansas." The wound has healed, and Kansas now presents a serene blend of kitschy tourist attractions—the Kansas Teachers' Hall of Fame in Dodge City and the World's Largest Hand-Dug Well in Greensburg—and miles of farmland. Highway signs subtly remind travelers that "every Kansas farmer feeds 75 people—and *you*."

## ⊠ PRACTICAL INFORMATION

**Capital:** Topeka.

**Visitor Info: Division of Travel and Tourism:** 700 S.W. Harrison, #1300, Topeka 66603-3712 (800-452-6727; www.state.ks.us). Open M-F 7am-10pm, Sa-Su 7:30am-10pm. **Kansas Wildlife and Parks,** 900 S.W. Jackson, 5th fl., Topeka 66612-1233 (785-296-2281). Open M-F 8am-5pm.

**Postal Abbreviation:** KS. **Sales Tax:** 4.9-6.9%.

**GEOGRAPHIC CENTER OF THE U.S.** Have you ever wanted to be the center of the action? Go 2mi. northwest of **Lebanon, KS.** Sit by the stone monument and feel special—the entire contiguous U.S. surrounds you.

# WICHITA

In 1541, Coronado came to the site of present-day Wichita in search of the mythical, gold-laden city of Quivira. Upon arriving, he was so disappointed that he had his guide strangled for misleading him. Miraculously, Wichita grew to become the largest city in Kansas, and is now a key city for airplane manufacturing: Lear, Boeing, Beech, and Cessna all have factories in town. Much of the downtown is painfully suburban in its tree-lined stillness. As the Old Town area gets revamped, however, its bars and cafes party further and further into the Kansas night.

**⚐ PRACTICAL INFORMATION.** Wichita lies on I-35, 170mi. north of Oklahoma City and about 200mi. southwest of Kansas City. A small and quiet downtown makes for easy walking or parking. **Broadway** is the major north-south artery. **Douglas Ave.** divides the numbered east-west streets to the north from the named east-west streets to the south. Many downtown businesses have moved a few blocks further south out along **Kellogg Ave. (U.S. 54)**, the main east-west route. *Visitors just south and north of downtown around Broadway should take extra caution*The closest **Amtrak** station, 414 N. Main St. (283-7533; ticket office open daily 11:30am-7:30pm), 25mi. north of Wichita, in the town of Newton, sends one very early train northeast to Kansas City (4½hr., $36-66) and another west to Dodge City (2½hr., $24-53). **Greyhound:** 312 S. Broadway (265-7711), 2 blocks east of Main St. and 1½ blocks southwest of the transit station (open daily 2:30am-6:30pm). Buses serve Kansas City (3-5hr., 3 per day, $32-38); Oklahoma City (4hr., 3 per day, $33-50); and Denver (13hr., 2 per day, $59-118). **WMTA,** 1825 S. McClean Blvd. (265-7221), handles in-town transportation. (Buses run M-F 6:15am-6:30pm, Sa 7:15am-5:20pm. Fare $1, seniors 50¢, ages 6-17 75¢; transfers 25¢. Station open M-F 8am-5pm. Tickets are also available all over the city at the stores Dillon's and Alverson's.) In summer, a **trolley** (fare 25¢) runs from downtown to Old Town during lunch hours (M-F 11am-2pm) and from downtown to Old Town and the museums on the river on Sa (10am-3:40pm). **Thrifty Rent-A-Car,** 8619 W. Kellogg (721-9552 or 800-367-2277), rents cars for $33 per day (250 free mi., 29¢ each additional mi.) or $160 per week. (2000 free mi. 21+ only; under 25 $5 per day surcharge. Open daily 6:30am-10pm.) **Convention and visitors bureau:** 100 S. Main St. (265-2800 or 800-288-9424), on the corner of Douglas Ave. (open M-F 8am-5pm). **Post Office:** 330 W. 2nd St. (262-6245), at Waco (open M-Sa 7am-5:30pm). **ZIP code:** 67202. **Area code:** 316.

**⚐ ACCOMMODATIONS.** Wichita offers a bounty of cheap hotels. South Broadway has plenty of mom-'n'-pop places, *but be very wary of the neighborhood.* The chains line **E. and W. Kellogg Ave.** 5-8mi. from downtown. Only ten blocks from downtown, the **Mark 8 Inn,** 1130 N. Broadway, has small, comfortable rooms that come with free local calls, cable TV, A/C, fridge, and laundry facilities (265-4679 or 800-830-7268; singles $27; doubles $30; no checks). The **English Village Inn,** 6727 E. Kellogg, though American, urban, and a motel, keeps basic rooms in tidy repair for very reasonable rates. (683-5613 or 800-365-8455. Singles from $32; doubles from $36. Cable and HBO in the rooms, popcorn in the lobby.) **USI Campgrounds,** 2920 E. 33rd St., right off Hillside Rd., is the most convenient of Wichita's hitchin' posts, with laundry, showers, playground, and storm shelter, in case there's a twister a-comin'. (838-0435. Sites $17, partial hookup $19, full hookup $20.50; weekly rates.)

**⚐ FOOD.** Beef: it's what's for dinner in Wichita. Everything old is new in the **Old Town** area, a few blocks east of downtown on Washington and Mosley St., between 1st St. and Douglas Ave., where revitalized warehouses now house breweries and restaurants. Neon lights are on **N. Broadway,** with all kinds of fairly authentic Asian food. If you eat only one slab here, make it one from **Doc's Steakhouse,** 1515 N. Broadway, where the most expensive entree—a 17 oz. T-bone with salad, potato, and bread—is only $9.75. Take bus #13 "N. Broadway." (264-4735. Open M-Th 11:30am-9:30pm, F 11:30am-10pm, Sa 4-10pm.) For good ol' American sandwiches, **Merle's,** 440 N. Seneca, can't be beat. Menus printed on newspaper, jukebox tunes,

**WHAT'S THAT SMELL?** In its heyday in the 1870s, **Dodge City** ("the wickedest little city in America") was a haven for gunfighters, prostitutes, and other lawless types; at one time, Front St., the main drag, had a saloon for every 50 citizens. Disputes were settled man to man, with a duel; the slower draw ended up in Boot Hill Cemetery, so named for the boot-clad corpses buried there. Legendary lawmen Wyatt Earp and Bat Masterson earned their fame cleaning up the streets of Dodge City. The town's most noticeable current residents, about 50,000 cows, reside on the feedlots on the east part of town. Hold your nose and whoop it up during the **Dodge City Days** (316-227-3119), the last weekend in July through the first weekend in Aug., complete with rodeo, carnival, and plenty of steak. You'll know when you're getting close.

pool tables, and dark-wood booths make it a timeless treat, distractingly close to the Museums-on-the-River. (263-0444. Vegetarian sandwiches $5. Open M-Sa 11am-2am; kitchen closes at 10pm.) The **Wichita Farm and Art Market,** 835 E. 1st St., has items fresh off the farm and the easel (262-3555. Indoor shops open M-Sa 10am-6pm, Su 1-5pm; outdoor farmers market May-Oct. Sa 7am-1pm.)

🎨 **SIGHTS.** The 4 **Museums-on-the-River** museums are located within a few blocks of each other; take the trolley or bus #12 "Riverside." Walk through the rough and tumble cattle days of the 1870s in the **Old Cowtown,** lined with many original buildings. *(1871 Sim Park Dr. 264-6398 or 264-0671. Open M-Sa 10am-5pm, Su noon-5pm; Nov.-Feb. Sa-Su only. $7, seniors $6.50, ages 5-11 $3.50, under 5 free. Call for special events info.)* In the Shakespearean Garden at **Botanica,** tarry till Birnam Wood will march on Dunsinane. *(701 Amidon. 264-0448. Open June-Aug. Tu 9am-8pm, M and W-Sa 9am-5pm, Su 1-5pm; Apr.-May and Sept.-Dec. M-Sa 9am-5pm, Su 1-5pm; Jan.-Mar. M-F 9am-5pm. $4.50, students $2, seniors $4, under 6 free.)* The **Mid-America All-Indian Center and Museum,** showcases traditional and modern works by Native American artists. The late Blackbear Bosin's awe-inspiring sculpture, *Keeper of the Plains*, stands guard over the grounds. The center holds the **Mid-America All-Indian Intertribal Pow Wow** during the last weekend in July with traditional dancing, foods, arts, and crafts. *(650 N. Seneca. 262-5221. Open M-Sa 10am-5pm, Su 1-5pm; Jan.-Mar. closed M. $2, ages 6-12 $1.)*

The **Wichita Art Museum** exhibits American art, including works by Mary Cassatt, Winslow Homer, and Edward Hopper, as well as an interactive gallery for kids. *(619 Stackman Dr. 268-4921. Open Tu-Sa 10am-5pm, Su noon-5pm. Free.)* More art hides on the **Wichita State University,** at N. Fairmont and 17th St., accessible by the "East 17th" bus, including over 50 sculptures and the **Corbin Education Center,** designed by Frank Lloyd Wright. Free sculpture maps are available at the **Edwin A. Ulrich Museum of Art** office, in the McKnight Arts Center, also on campus. *(978-3644. Open daily noon-5pm. Free.)* A gigantic glass mosaic mural by Joan Miró forms one wall of the building. North of campus, the **Center for the Improvement of Human Functioning,** features a 40 ft. pyramid, used for reflection and receptions, with the world's largest FDA food pyramid painted on its side. Tours of the biochemical research station include a chance to "de-stress" mind, body, and soul by hurling clay skeet pigeons at a wall. *(3100 N. Hillside. 682-3100. Tours M-F 1:30pm; $4.)*

Most of Wichita's museums and historic points of attraction are part of the **Wichita Western Heritage Tour,** which focuses on the city's contributions to culture. Visiting all the sites earns a free **belt buckle** at the last stop, **Sheplers,** the world's largest Western store. *(6501 W. Kellogg. 946-3600. M-Sa 10am-9pm, Su noon-6pm.)*

# LAWRENCE

Founded in 1854 by abolitionists during the "Bleeding Kansas" controversy, Lawrence was burned to the ground in 1863 by pro-slavery raiders, led by William Quantrill and Jesse James. The citizens quickly rebuilt, and have been struggling since to fulfill the second half of the city's motto, "from ashes to immortality." Travelers weary of the Oregon Trail were attracted to the lush, hilly lands surrounding Lawrence. Tired voyagers now enjoy the cafes and lively bars supported by students of the **University of Kansas** (KU to locals).

**⑦ PRACTICAL INFORMATION.** The **convention and visitors bureau** (865-4411 or 888-529-5267), at 2nd and Locust St., across the bridge from downtown in the renovated train depot (open Mar.-Oct. M-Sa 8:30am-5:30pm, Su 1-5pm; Nov.-Feb. M-Sa 9am-5pm). **KU Wheels:** bus service around the college and parts of Lawrence (864-3506 for schedule info). **Greyhound,** 2447 W. 6th St. (843-5622), runs out of the Conoco gas station. To Kansas City (1hr., 6 per day, $12) and Wichita (4hr., 3 per day, $30). North-south streets are named for the states in the order they entered the Union. **Post Office:** 645 Vermont St. (843-1681). **ZIP code:** 66044. **Area code:** 913 and 785; in text 913 unless noted.

**🍴🛏 ACCOMMODATIONS AND FOOD.** There are a slew of motels near the intersection of 6th and Iowa St. The **Westminster Inn,** 2525 W. 6th St., the best of the budget options, goes for the English lodge look—and almost succeeds (785-841-8410 or 888-937-8646; singles $45, doubles $57). The **Virginia Inn,** 2907 W. 6th St., rents out renovated rooms with cable, A/C, and a pool (785-843-6611 or 800-468-8979; singles $42, doubles $50; Sa-Su $46/56). Die-hard Democrats can pitch their tents at **Clinton Lake** at any of 3 Federal campgrounds, 4mi. west of town on 23rd St. (785-843-7665). Scenic primitive sites are available at the **Woodridge Campground** for free, at **Rock Haven** for $4, and at **Bloomington** for $8. Bloomington also has sites with water and electricity ($16).

Fast food hangs out on 23rd (a.k.a. "Hamburger Alley"), Iowa and 6th St. **Massachusetts St.** is home to the funkier coffeehouses and bars. Head straight to the source at the **farmers market,** in the parking lot on the 1000 block of Vermont St. (Open mid-May to Sept. Tu and Th 4-6:30pm, Sa 6:30-10:30am; Sept.-Nov. Tu and Th 4-6:30pm, Sa 7:30-11:30am.) It's like going home at **La Familia,** 731 New Hampshire St., although mom never offered 50 Mexican specials for $5-12 (749-0105; open M-W 11am-9pm, Th-Sa 11am-10pm). KU students love **Quinton's,** 615 Massachusetts St., known for its packed sandwiches (842-6560; $5; open daily 11am-2am). The **Paradise Café,** 728 Massachusetts St., specializes in good old American meals. The pancakes of the day ($3) are as good as the smells that waft out from the kitchen. (842-5199. Dinner $7-14. Open M-Sa 6:30am-2:30pm and 5-10pm, Su 8am-8pm.) The oldest legal brewery in Kansas is **Freestate Brewery Co.,** 636 Massachusetts St. You can chase your beer with sandwiches, gumbo, or pasta. (843-4555. Meals $5-10. Open M-Sa 11am-midnight, Su noon-11pm. Free tours Sa 2pm.)

**📷 SIGHTS.** KU's **Museum of Natural History,** at Jayhawk Blvd. and 14th St., showcases one of the few survivors of Custer's Last Stand, a horse named Comanche. *(864-4450. Open M-F 8am-5pm, Sa 10am-5pm, Su noon-5pm. Suggested donation $2, children $1.)* The center of student activity, **Kansas Union** keeps students and tourists busy with its massive food court and bowling alley. Exhibits like "Pin-up Girls, Hairy Guys, and Art" are sure to entertain at the **Spencer Museum of Art,** at 14th and Mississippi St. *(864-4710. Open Tu-W and F-Sa 10am-5pm, Th 10am-9pm, Su noon-5pm. Free.)* Lawrence is also home to **Haskell Indian Nations University,** off 23rd St. (Rt. 10), the only inter-tribal university in the U.S. The students, who represent over 150 different tribes, hold **pow wows** throughout the year, including the 3-day commencement celebration in early May. *(749-8404. Call for info on pow wows.)*

**🎭 ENTERTAINMENT AND NIGHTLIFE.** Call the **KU Info line** to find out what's shakin' on campus (864-3506). Plays and concerts are at The **Lied Center,** at 15th and Iowa St. (864-2787; box office open M-F noon-5:30pm). **Liberty Hall,** 644 Massachusetts St., hosts concerts and screens artsy films in an ornate theater with constellations twinkling on the ceiling. Chat with the employees to find out the goings-on in town. (749-1972. Open M-Sa 11am-11pm, Su noon-11pm.)

*The Mag,* inside the Th *Journal-World,* lists activities and events, as does *Pitch Weekly,* free at restaurants and bars. Over 100 types of beer, some on the wall, crowd **The Bottleneck,** 737 New Hampshire, along with top alternative and college rock bands (842-5483; cover hovers around $4; open M-Sa 3pm-2am, Su 8pm-2am).

**Jazzhaus,** 926½ Massachusetts St., swings every night, but features live jive W-Su (749-3320; cover Tu-Sa around $4; open daily 4pm-2am). Feel the blues at the **Brown Bear Brewery,** 729 Massachusetts St., and drown them with $1-3 beer specials (331-4338; M-F 4pm-2am, Sa-Su 11am-2am).

# MISSOURI

Pro-slavery Missouri applied for statehood in 1818, but due to Congress's fears about upsetting the balance of free and slave states, was forced to wait until Maine entered the Union as a free state in 1821. Missouri's Civil War status as a border state was a harbinger of its future ambiguity; close to the center of the country, Missouri defies regional stereotyping. Its large cities are defined by wide avenues, long and lazy rivers, numerous parks, humid summers, and blues and jazz wailing into the night. In the countryside, Bible factory outlets stand amid firework stands and barbecue pits. Missouri's patchwork geography further complicates characterization. In the north, near Iowa, amber waves of grain undulate. Along the Mississippi, towering bluffs inscribed with Native American pictographs evoke western canyonlands. Farther inland, spelunkers enjoy some of the world's largest limestone caves, made famous by Mark Twain's Tom Sawyer.

## ⁊ PRACTICAL INFORMATION

**Capital:** Jefferson City.

**Visitor Info: Missouri Division of Tourism,** P.O. Box 1055, Jefferson City 65102 (573-751-4133 or 800-877-1234; www.missouritourism.org). Office open M-F 8am-5pm; 800 number operates 24hr. **Dept. of Natural Resources,** Division of State Parks, P.O. Box 176, Jefferson City 65102 (573-751-2479 or 800-334-6946). Open M-F 8am-5pm.

**Postal Abbreviation:** MO.**Sales Tax:** Varies; 6.75% is the average.

## ST. LOUIS

In the early 1700s, Pierre Laclede set up a trading post directly below the junction of the Mississippi, Missouri, and Illinois rivers. A natural fueling point for pioneer journeys, St. Louis, the "River City," gained prominence as the U.S. raced into the West. Today, Eero Saarinen's magnificent Gateway Arch, a silvery beacon to visitors and a landmark of America's westward expansion, gleams over one of America's largest inland trading ports.

St. Louis, Memphis, and New Orleans have together been dubbed "America's Music Corridor." In the early 1900s, showboats carrying Dixieland jazz bands regularly traveled between Chicago and New Orleans; the music floated through St. Louis and left the city addicted. St. Louis also contributed to the development of the blues and saw the birth of ragtime during Scott Joplin's years in the city. These days, St. Louis is less happening, but it is still a surprisingly urban and culturally adept city that stands out from the surrounding acres of cornfields.

## ⁊ ORIENTATION AND PRACTICAL INFORMATION

I-44, I-55, I-64, and I-70 meet in St. Louis. To the west are I-170 and farther out I-270. **U.S. 40/I-64** runs east-west through the entire metropolitan area. Downtown, **Market St.** divides the city north-south. Numbered streets parallel the river, increasing to the west. The historic **Soulard** district borders the river south of downtown. **Forest Park** and **University City,** home to **Washington University** and old, stately homes, lie west of downtown; the Italian neighborhood called **The Hill** is south of these. St. Louis is a driving town. Parking comes easy; wide streets allow for lots of meters, and private lots are cheap ($2-8). Public transportation has improved, but can be difficult to navigate. Be careful in **East St. Louis** (across the river in IL), the **Near South Side,** and most of the **North Side.**

**GREAT PLAINS**

**Airport: Lambert-St. Louis International** (426-8000), 12mi. northwest of the city on I-70. Hub for **TWA.** MetroLink and Bi-state bus #66 "Maplewood-Airport" provide easy access to downtown ($1). Taxis to downtown are less economical ($18). A few westbound Greyhound buses stop at the airport.

**Trains: Amtrak,** 550 S. 16th St., 2 blocks south of Kiel Center. To Chicago (6hr., 3 per day, $26-52) and Kansas City (5½hr., 2 per day, $25-49). Office open daily 6am-1am.

**Buses: Greyhound,** 1450 N. 13th St. (231-4485), at Cass Ave. Bi-state bus #30 "Cass" takes less than 10min. from downtown. *Be cautious at night.* To Chicago (6½hr., 6 per day, $29) and Kansas City (5hr., 7 per day, $30).

**Public Transportation: Bi-State** (231-2345). Extensive daily service; infrequent off-peak hrs. Info and schedules available at the Metroride Service Center (982-1485) in the St. Louis Center (open M-Sa 10am-6pm). Schedules also at the Bi-State Development Agency, 707 N. 1st St. (on Laclede's Landing), and at the reference desk of the public library at 13th and Olive St. **MetroLink,** the light-rail system, runs from 5th St. and Missouri Ave. in East St. Louis to Lambert Airport M-Sa 5am-midnight and Su 6am-11pm. Travel for free in the "Ride Free Zone" (from Laclede's Landing to Union Station) M-F 11am-2pm. Both $1, transfers 10¢; seniors and ages 5-12 50¢/5¢. 1-day pass $3, 3-day pass $7; available at MetroLink stations. **Shuttle Bug,** a small bus painted like a ladybug, cruises around Forest Park and the Central West End. (6:45am-6pm M-F, 10am-6pm Sa-Su) $1. The **Shuttle Bee** buzzes around Forest Park, Clayton, Brentwood, and the Galleria M-F 6am-11:30pm, Sa 7:30am-10:30pm, Su 9:30am-6:30pm. $1.

**Taxis: Yellow Cab,** 361-2345.

**Visitor Info: St. Louis Visitors Center,** 308 Washington Ave. (241-1764). Open daily 9:30am-4:30pm. Other locations at the airport and at **America's Center** (421-1023), at 7th St. and Washington Ave. Open M-F 9am-5pm, Sa-Su 10am-2pm. **St. Louis Information Line,** 800-888-FUN1/3861. The *Official St. Louis Visitors Guide* and the monthly magazine *Where: St. Louis,* both free, contain much info and decent maps. A more complete map is available throughout the city and at the visitors center.

**Hotlines: Rape Crisis,** 531-2003. **Suicide Hotline,** 647-4357. **Kids Under 21 Crisis,** 644-5886. All 3 24hr. **Gay and Lesbian Hotline,** 367-0084. Open M-Sa 6-10pm.

**Hospitals: Barnes-Jewish Hospital,** 216 S. Kingshighway Blvd. (747-3000). **Metro North Women's Health Center,** 2415 N. Kingshighway, 361-1606.

**Post Office:** 1720 Market St. (436-4454). Open M-F 8am-5pm. **ZIP code:** 63103. **Area code:** 314 (in MO), 618 (in IL); in text, 314 unless noted.

# ACCOMMODATIONS

Budget lodging is generally located far from downtown. For chain motels, try **Lindbergh Blvd. (Rt. 67)** near the airport, or the area north of the I-70/I-270 junction in **Bridgeton,** 5mi. beyond the airport. **Watson Rd.** (old **Rt. 66** in South County) near Chippewa is littered with cheap motels; take bus #11 "Chippewa-Sunset Hills" or #20 "Cherokee." B&Bs (singles from $50; doubles from $60) listed in the visitors guide may be a good splurge if you're looking for anything beyond the generic.

**Huckleberry Finn Youth Hostel (HI-AYH),** 1908 S. 12th St. (Tucker Blvd.) (241-0076), 2 blocks north of Russell Blvd. in the Soulard District. From downtown, take bus #73 "Carondelet," or walk south on Broadway to Russell Blvd. and over to 12th St. (30-40min.). The hostel is located a short walk past an unsafe neighborhood. TV, lockers, full kitchen, free parking, and friendly staff. Dorm-style rooms with 5-9 beds. $15, nonmembers $18. Linen $2. $5 deposit required. Ask about work opportunities, like whitewashing the fence. Reception daily 8-10am and 6-10pm. Check-out 9:30am.

**University of Missouri,** St. Louis, Office of Residential Life (516-6877). Take I-70 to Natural Bridge Rd., turn right onto Arlmont Dr., then stay left at the split marking the end of Bellerive Dr. Or, take MetroLink to either campus stop, then hop on the campus shuttle. Large dorm rooms with A/C, free local calls, lounge with TV and VCR, laundry, kitchen

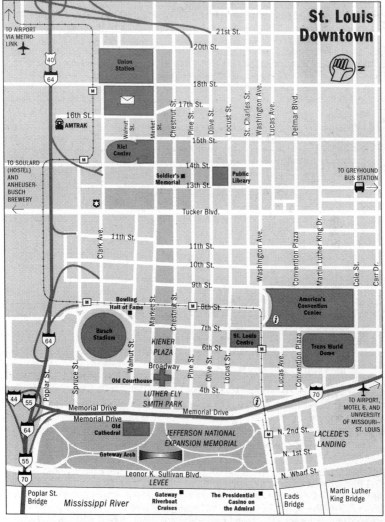

access, free linen, and a pool. Singles $21; doubles $30. Call M-F 8am-5pm for someone to meet you. Reserve rooms 1 wk. in advance.

**Motel 6,** 4576 Woodson Rd. (427-1313), near the airport. From downtown, Metrolink to the airport or take bus #4 "Natural Bridge." Most motels match the price, but few can touch the cleanliness. A/C, cable, pool. Singles $44-50; doubles $50-56; prices rise with the summer temps.

**Horseshoe Lake State Park,** 3321 Rt. 111 (618-931-0270), north off I-70 in Granite City, IL about 3mi. from Cahokia Mounds. Sites are on an island (connected by a causeway) in a relatively secluded area. No electricity or water. Sites $7.

## FOOD

In St. Louis, the difference of a few blocks can mean vastly different cuisine. The area surrounding **Union Station,** at 18th and Market St. downtown, is being revamped with hip restaurants and bars. The **Central West End** offers coffeehouses and outdoor cafes; a slew of impressive restaurants await just north of Lindell Blvd. along **Euclid Ave.** (MetroLink to "Central West End" and walk north, or catch the Shuttlebug.) St. Louis's historic Italian neighborhood, **The Hill,** southwest of downtown and just northwest of Tower Grove Park, produces plenty of inexpensive pasta; take bus #99 "Lafayette." Cheap Thai, Philippine, and Vietnamese restaurants spice the **South Grand** area, at Grand Blvd. just south of Tower Grove Park; board bus #70 "Grand." The intellectual set hangs out on **University City Loop** (not actually a loop, but Delmar Blvd. between Skinker Blvd. and Big Bend Blvd.).

◈ **Blueberry Hill,** 6504 Delmar Blvd. (727-0880), on the Loop. Eclectic rock 'n' roll restaurant similar to the stone one—but much, much cooler. Record covers, Howdy Doody toys, a *Simpson's* collection, and giant baseball cards. The jukebox plays 2000 songs, and live bands play F-Sa and some weeknights (cover $4-15). Burgers are big and juicy ($4.50). 21+ after 8pm. Open M-Sa 11am-1am, Su 11am-midnight.

◈ **Ted Drewe's Frozen Custard,** 4224 S. Grand Blvd. (352-7376); or 6726 Chippewa (481-2652), on Rt. 66. *The* place for the summertime St. Louis experience since 1929. Standing in line for the "chocolate-chip banana concrete shake" is rewarding; the blended toppings are thick enough to hang in an overturned cup ($1.50-3.50). Open daily 11am-midnight in summer; until 11pm the rest of the year; closed for Jan.

**Fitz's,** 6605 Delmar Blvd. (726-9555), on the Loop. American food joint which features its own line of sodas, like rootbeer ($1.35). Many variations on the good ol' hamburger and fries, including veggie options ($5-12). Open Su-W 11am-11pm, Th-Sa 11am-midnight.

**Pho Grand,** 3191 S. Grand Blvd. (664-7435), in the South Grand area. Voted "Best Vietnamese" and "Best Value" in St. Louis. Not Americanized, tons of good vegetarian options. Their specialty is the noodle soup ($4); entrees are $4-6. Open Su-M and W-Th 11am-10pm, F-Sa 11am-11pm.

**Mangio Italiano,** 3145 S. Grand Blvd. (664-8585). Offers fresh pasta made on site ($5-9), jazz on weekend nights, a handpainted mural wall, and mismatched tables. Serves food daily 11:30am-10pm; bar stays open until 1:30.

**Kaldi's Coffeehouse and Roasting Company,** 700 De Mun Ave. (727-9955), in Clayton. Home-roasted java and the food is fresh. Intellectuals swarm for panini ($5) and whole-wheat pizza ($3). Very veggie-friendly. Open daily 7am-11pm.

## ◈ SIGHTS

**DOWNTOWN.** The nation's tallest monument at 630 ft., the **Gateway Arch** towers gracefully over all of St. Louis and southern Illinois. The most impressive view is from the ground looking up, but if you must see the view from the top, elevator modules straight out of a sci-fi film soar up every 10min. Waits are shorter after dinner or in the morning, but are uniformly long on Sa. Beneath the arch, the underground **Museum of Westward Expansion** adds to the appeal of the grassy park complex known comprehensively as the **Jefferson Expansion Memorial.** The museum celebrates the Louisiana Purchase and its exploration. The 40min. "Monument to the Dream" film, screened once per hour, chronicles the arch's construction. **Odyssey Theater** arches your neck with films shown on a 4-story screen every hour on the hour. *(982-1410. Museum and arch open daily 8am-10pm; in winter 9am-6pm. Tickets for 1 attraction $6, ages 13-16 $4, ages 3-12 $2.50; 2 attractions $10/$8/$5; 3 attractions $14/$12/$7.50. Limited wheelchair access.)* Scope out the city from the water with **Gateway Riverboat Cruises;** 1hr. tours leave from the docks in front of the arch. *(621-4040 or 800-878-7411. Tours 10am-10pm; $8.50, ages 3-12 $4.)*

Beneath the arch, St. Louis's oldest church, the **Old Cathedral** holds masses daily. *(209 Walnut St. 231-3250.)* Within walking distance is the **Old Courthouse,** across the highway from the arch. In 1847, Dred Scott sued for freedom from slavery here. Stroll down an additional block to Krener Plaza and turn around to witness the courthouse perfectly framed by the arch. *(11 N. 4th St. 425-6156. Open daily 8am-4:30pm. Tours usually on the hr. Free. Limited wheelchair access.)*

It's a strike either way at the **International Bowling Museum and Hall of Fame** and the **St. Louis Cardinals Hall of Fame Museum,** across from Busch Stadium. This classy museum complex is lined with funny panels on the history and development of bowling, with titles like "real men play quills and throw cheeses," as well as memorabilia from the glory days of St. Louis baseball. *(111 Stadium Plaza. 231-6340. Open in summer M-Sa 9am-5pm, Su noon-5pm; Oct.-Mar. daily 11am-4pm; game days until 6:30pm. $5, ages 5-12 $3. Includes 4 frames in the lanes downstairs. Wheelchair access.)* Historic **Union Station,** 1mi. west of downtown, houses a shopping mall, food court, and entertainment center in a magnificent structure that was once the nation's largest and busiest railroad terminal. *(18th and Market St. 421-6655. (MetroLink to Union Station)* "The Entertainer" lives on at the **Scott Joplin House,** just west of downtown at Geyer Rd., where the ragtime legend lived and composed from 1901 to 1903. *(2658 Delmar. 340-5790. Open in summer M-Sa 10am-3:30pm, Su noon-5pm. $2, ages 6-12 $1.25. Wheelchair access.)*

**SOUTH AND SOUTHWEST OF DOWNTOWN. Soulard** is bounded by I-55 and Seventh St.; walk south on Broadway or 7th St. from downtown, or take bus #73 "Carondelet." In the early 70s, the city proclaimed this area a historic district, because it once housed German and East European immigrants, many of whom worked in the breweries. Young couples and families are revitalizing the area without displacing the older generation of immigrants. The district surrounds the **Soulard Farmers Market,** at Lafayette and 7th St. Despite its age (220 years), Soulard *still* has fresh produce. *(730 Carroll St. 622-4180. Open W-F 8am-5:30pm, Sa 6am-5:30pm; hrs. vary among merchants.)* The end of 12th St. features the largest brewery in the world, the **Anheuser-Busch Brewery,** at 12th and Lynch St. Take bus #40 "Broadway" south from downtown. The 1½hr. tour is markedly less thrilling than the chance to sample beer at the end, but you'll get booted after 15min. *(1127 Pestalozzi St. 577-2626. Tours M-Sa 9am-5pm; Sept.-May M-Sa 9am-4pm, Su 11:30am-5pm. Get free tickets at the office. Wheelchair access.)* A few blocks southwest of the brewery, Cherokee St.'s **Antique Row** is lined with antiques and used bookstores.

The internationally acclaimed 79-acre **Missouri Botanical Garden,** thrives north of Tower Grove Park on grounds left by entrepreneur Henry Shaw. From downtown, take I-44 west by car or ride MetroLink to "Central West End" and hop on bus #13 "Union-Missouri Botanical Gardens" to the main entrance. Among the flora from all over the globe, the Japanese Garden is guaranteed to soothe the weary budget traveler. Independent exploration is encouraged, and there is a guided tour at 1pm. *(4344 Shaw Blvd. 800-642-8842. Open daily 9am-8pm; early Sept. to late May 9am-5pm. $5, seniors $3, under 12 free. Wheelchair access.)* Much farther out this way, **Grant's Farm,** once housed former president Ulysses S. Grant. Take I-55 west to Reavis Barracks Rd., turn left onto Gravois Rd., then turn right onto the farm. The tour is a tram ride through a wildlife preserve where over 1000 animals roam and interact freely, as evidenced by the zebrass (donkey-zebra), and concludes with free beer in the historic Baurnhof area. *(10501 Gravois Rd. 843-1700, Open daily May-Aug., days in Apr. and Sept.-Oct. vary; call for hrs. Free. Reservations required.)*

**WEST OF DOWNTOWN. Forest Park,** the country's largest urban park, was home to the 1904 World's Fair and St. Louis Exposition, where ice cream cones and hot dogs painted kids' faces with cream and ketchup for the first time ever. Take MetroLink to Forest Park or Central West End, then catch the Shuttlebug, which stops at all the important sights. All Forest Park sites are wheelchair-accessible. The park contains 3 museums, a zoo, a planetarium, a 12,000-seat amphitheater, and a grand canal, as well as countless picnic areas, pathways, and flying golf balls. The **St. Louis Science Center,** in the park's southeast corner, has tons of hands-on exhibits, an OmniMax theater, and a planetarium. Inside, learn how a laser printer works, watch an old Star Trek episode, practice surgery, or use police radars to clock the unusually high speeds of cars on I-40. *(5050 Oakland Ave. 800-456-7572. Open in summer M and W-Th 9am-6pm, Tu and F 9am-9pm, Sa 10am-9pm, Su 10am-6pm; off-season M-Th 9am-5pm, F 9am-9pm, Sa 10am-9pm, Su 11am-6pm. Free. Call for show* *schedules and prices.)* Marlin Perkins, the late, great host of TV's *Wild Kingdom*, turned the **St. Louis Zoo** into a world-class institution. You can even view computer-generated images of future human evolutionary stages at the "Living World" exhibit. *(781-0900. Open June-Aug. W-M 9am-5pm, Tu 9am-9pm; Sept.-May daily 9am-5pm. Free.)* Atop **Art Hill,** just to the southwest, a statue of France's Louis IX, the city's namesake and the only Louis to achieve Sainthood, beckons with his raised sword in front of the **St. Louis Art Museum** which contains masterpieces of Asian, Renaissance, and Impressionist art. *(721-0072. Open Tu 1:30-8:30pm, W-Su 10am-5pm. Main museum free, special exhibits usually $7, students and seniors $6, ages 6-12 $5, free Tu.)*

From Forest Park, head east a few blocks to gawk at the lavish residential sections of the **Central West End,** where every house is a turn-of-the-century version of a French château or Tudor mansion. The vast **Cathedral of St. Louis** is a strange combination of Romanesque, Byzantine, Gothic, and Baroque styles. Gold-flecked mosaics depict 19th-century church history in Missouri. Take bus #93 "Lindell" from downtown, or walk from the Central West End MetroLink stop. *(4431 Lindell Blvd. 533-2824 or 533-0544 to schedule tours. Open daily in summer 7am-dusk, off-season 7am-7pm. Guided tours M-F 10am-3pm, Su after the noon Mass. Wheelchair access.)*

The **St. Louis Car Museum,** houses over 150 legendary cars that have cruised the highways and byways of America, from the Model T to the '57 Chevy to the VW Bus. *(1575 Woodson Rd. at I-170. 993-1330. Open M-Sa 9am-5pm, Su 11am-5pm; $3.75, under 12 $2.75.)* Less exalted autos are crushed under the 66 in. wheels of **Bigfoot,** the "Original Monster Truck." The first Bigfoot and its legacies live near the airport and I-270. *(6311 N. Lindbergh. 731-2822. Open M-F 9am-6pm, Sa 9am-4pm, some extended summer hrs. Free.)*

**The Loop,** just northwest of the Central West End, has more than just shops full of ethnic items and cafés full of intellectuals—for instance, the sidewalk. All along the loop runs the **St. Louis Walk of Fame,** with stars and biographies celebrating famous St. Louisians like Kathleen Turner, Kevin Kline, Tennessee Williams, Bob Costas, and John Goodman. *(6504 Delmar. 727-7827.)*

## 🎵 ENTERTAINMENT

Founded in 1880, the **St. Louis Symphony Orchestra** is one of the country's finest. **Powell Hall,** 718 N. Grand Blvd., houses the 101-member orchestra in acoustic and visual splendor. Take bus #91 "Delmar" or #94 "Washington Ave." to Grand Blvd. The symphony has a "summer series" playing in June at the Music School and in July at Queenie Park. *(534-1700. Performances Sept. 17 to May 14 Th-Sa 8pm, Su matinees at 3pm. Box office open M-Sa 9am-5pm and before performances. Tickets start at $10, rush tickets often available for half-price on day of show.)*

St. Louis offers theater-goers many choices. The outdoor **Municipal Opera,** the "Muny," performs tour productions of hit musicals on summer nights in Forest Park. Back rows provide 1456 free seats on a first come, first served basis. The gates open at 7:30pm for 8:15pm shows; it's a good idea to arrive even earlier for popular performances. (361-1900. Box office open June to mid-Aug. daily 9am-9pm. Tickets $6-44.) Other productions are regularly staged by the **St. Louis Black Repertory,** 634 N. Grand Blvd. (534-3807), and the **Repertory Theatre of St. Louis,** 130 Edgar Rd. (968-4925). The **Fox Theatre,** 527 N. Grand, was originally a 1930s movie palace, but now hosts Broadway shows, classic films, and Las Vegas, country, and rock stars. (534-1111. Box office open M-Sa 10am-6pm, Su noon-4pm. Tours Tu, Th, Sa at 10:30am. $5, under 12 $2.50. Call for reservations.) The **Tivoli Theatre,** 6350 Delmar Blvd., shows artsy and lesser-known releases (862-1100; $6; students, seniors, matinees $4). **Metrotix** (534-1111) has tickets to most theatrical events.

A recent St. Louis ordinance permits gambling on the rivers. The **President Casino on the Admiral,** floats below the Arch on the Missouri side (622-3000 or 800-772-3647; open Tu-Th 8am-4am, around the clock on weekends; $2). On the Illinois side, the **Casino Queen** claims "the loosest slots in town" (618-874-5000 or 800-777-0777; 11 cruises daily on odd-numbered hrs. 9am-5am; $2). Parking for both is free; both have wheelchair access.

**Six Flags over Mid-America** reigns supreme in the kingdom of amusement parks, including a new water park, 30min. southwest of St. Louis on I-44 at exit 261 (938-4800; hrs. vary by season; $30, seniors $15, ages 3-11 $25). The **St. Louis Cardinals** play ball at **Busch Stadium** Apr. through Oct. (421-3060; tickets $6-24). The **Rams**, formerly of L.A., have brought the ol' pigskin back to St. Louis at the **Trans World Dome** (425-8830; tickets $25). The **Blues** hockey team slices ice at the **Kiel Center** at 14th St. and Clark Ave. (622-2500).

## NIGHTLIFE

Music rules the night in St. Louis. The *Riverfront Times* (free at many bars and clubs) and the *Get Out* section of the *Post-Dispatch* list weekly entertainment. The *St. Louis Magazine*, published annually, lists seasonal events, as does the comprehensive calendar distributed at the tourist office.

The bohemian **Loop** parties hearty at the coffeehouses and bars of Delmar Blvd. **Brandt's Market & Café**, 6525 Delmar Blvd. (727-3663), does it all with wine, beer, espresso, and a full, eclectic menu. (Live music most days; genre varies wildly. Open M-Th 11am-midnight, F-Sa 11am-1am, Su 10:30am-midnight.)

For beer, outdoor tables, and live music, often without a cover charge, the city offers **Laclede's Landing,** a collection of restaurants, bars, and dance clubs housed in 19th-century buildings on the riverfront. Once an industrial wasteland, the Landing is now a hot nightspot. To get there, walk north along the river from the Gateway Arch, or toward the river on Washington St. Most bars offer mainstream rock and draw preppy, touristy crowds. In the summer, bars take turns sponsoring "block parties," with outdoor food, drink, music, and dancing in the streets. Weekends see hordes of St. Louis University (SLU, pronounced "slew") students descending on the waterfront. (241-5875. 21+. Open midnight-6am.) **Mississippi Nights,** 914 N. 1st St., hosts big local and national bands (421-3853; box office open M-F 11am-6pm). **The Grind Diner,** 710 N. 2nd St. serves American breakfasts food for $5-10 (588-0777; open M-F 7am-3pm, F-M midnight-3am). An older, cooler version, and the "Best Coffeehouse" since 1993, **The Grind,** 56 Maryland Plaza, has pool tables and personality to boot (454-0202; open 3pm-3am).

Also downtown, **Union Station** and its environs have spawned some off-beat nightlife. **Hot Locust Cantina,** 2005 Locust St., cooks up some hot stuff, both for your mouth and for your ears. (231-3666. Entrees $6-9. Lunch M-Sa 11am-3pm, dinner Tu-Sa 5pm-midnight. Music weekend nights. No cover.) The less touristy and quite gay-friendly **Soulard** district has been known to ripple with the blues. Live Irish music plays nightly at **McGurk's,** at 12th and Russell Blvd. (776-8309. No cover. Open M-Sa 11am-1:30am, Su 5pm-midnight.) The **1860 Hard Shell Café & Bar,** 1860 S. 9th St., hosts some gritty blues and rock performances. (231-1860. Music nightly and Sa-Su afternoons. $3 cover after 9pm. Open M-F 9am-1:30am, Sa 9am-1:30am, Su 11am-1:30am.) **Clementine's,** 2001 Menard, houses a crowded restaurant and St. Louis's oldest gay bar (est. 1978). Sandwiches and entrees run $4.50-9.50. (664-7869. Open M-F 10am-1:30am, Sa 7am-1:30am, Su 11am-midnight.)

## NEAR ST. LOUIS

**CAHOKIA MOUNDS STATE HISTORIC SITE.** Fifteen minutes from the city in Collinsville, IL (8mi. east of downtown on I-55/70 to Rt. 111), over 65 earthen mounds rising from the flat land mark the site of **Cahokia,** an extremely complex Native American settlement inhabited from 700 to 1500 AD, now the Cahokia Mounds State Historic Site and a World Heritage Site. In constructing the these foundations, builders had to carry over 15 million loads of dirt on their backs. The largest mound, **Monk's Mound,** took 300 years to complete. The Cahokians, once a community of 20,000, faced the same problems of pollution, overcrowding, and resource depletion that we do today—which might help explain their mysterious disappearance. Celebrate equinoxes and solstices at dawn on the SuSu closest to the big day at **Woodhenge,** a solar calendar built by the Cahokians. The **Interpretive Center** contains life-sized dioramas and screens a 15min. film illustrating this "City of the Sun" (shows every hr. 10am-4pm). A guide booklet or the narrated audio tape borrowed from the info desk will guide the curious. *(618-346-5160. Site open daily 8am-dusk; free. Center open daily 9am-5pm. Suggested donation $2. Booklet $1. Wheelchair access.)*

**ST. CHARLES.** St. Charles (take I-70 W and exit north at 5th St.) has made great strides since it was described as "ignorant, stupid, ugly, and miserable" by an early explorer. Nestled along the Missouri River, St. Charles now supports numerous antique shops, cafes, and wineries, mostly along historic S. Main St. The **visitors bureau,** 230 W. Main (946-7776 or 800-366-2427) distributes handy guides along with a map (open M-F 8am-5pm, Sa 10am-5pm, Su noon-5pm).

St. Charles has the distinction of being the starting point of Lewis and Clark's 1804 exploration of the Louisiana Purchase. The **Lewis & Clark Center,** 701 Riverside Dr., uses dioramas to trace the adventurers' trek across the continent (947-3199; open daily 10:30am-4:30pm; $1, children 50¢). **Cavern Springs Winery,** 300 Water St., hosts wine tastings and tours of its pre-Civil War grottoes (432-6933; open M-F 10am-5pm, Sa 11am-6pm, Su noon-6pm; free).

Step aboard the **Goldenrod Showboat,** 1000 Riverside Dr., the nation's last surviving showboat and the inspiration for the musical "Showboat." (946-2020. Matinee W, Th, Su; regular shows Th-Su. Tickets from $22, including a buffet. Box office open M-Sa 9am-5pm, Su noon-7pm.)

St. Charles marks the starting point of **KATY Trail State Park,** an 1890s railroad route converted into a 230mi. hiking and biking trail past bluffs, wetlands, and wildlife. Call for info on unfinished portions of the trail, which ends in Clinton. South Main St. houses many places to rent bikes. (800-334-6946.)

**HANNIBAL.** Hannibal hugs the Mississippi River 100mi. west of Springfield, IL and 100mi. northwest of St. Louis. Founded in 1819, the town remained a sleepy village until Samuel Clemens (a.k.a. Mark Twain) roused the world's attention to his boyhood home by making it the setting of *The Adventures of Tom Sawyer.* Tourists flock to Hannibal to imagine Tom, Huck, and Becky romping around the quaint streets and nearby caves. Somehow in the midst of all its tourist traps, Hannibal retains its considerable small-town hospitality and charm.

The **Mark Twain Boyhood Home and Museum,** 208 Hill St., fills the downtown historic district with restored rooms and an assortment of memorabilia from the witty wordsmith's life (221-9010). Across the street sit the **Pilaster House** and **Clemens Law Office.** Further down, the new **Mark Twain Museum** includes a collection of Norman Rockwell's "Tom and Hucks." (Open 8am-6pm; May 8am-5pm; Nov.-Feb. M-Sa 10am-4pm, Su noon-4pm; Mar. M-Sa 9am-4pm, Su noon-4pm; Apr., Sept.-Oct. 9am-5pm. All sites included $6.) The **Mark Twain Riverboat,** at Center St. Landing, steams down the Mississippi for a 1hr. sight-seeing cruise that is part history, part folklore, and part advertisement for the land attractions. (221-3222. June-early Sept. 3 per day; May and Sept.-Oct. 1 per day. $8.50, ages 3-12 $5.50; dinner cruises 6:30pm $26/$16.) Injun Joe's ghost haunts the **Mark Twain Cave,** 1mi. south of Hannibal on Rt. 79, supposedly the one Twain explored as a boy. (221-1656. Open daily 8am-8pm; Apr.-May and Sept.-Oct. 9am-6pm; Nov.-Mar. 9am-4pm. 1hr. tour $10, ages 5-12 $5.) Nearby **Cameron Cave** provides a slightly longer and far spookier lantern tour ($12, ages 5-12 $6). In early July, 100,000 fans converge on Hannibal for the fence-painting, frog-jumping fun of the **Tom Sawyer Days** festival (221-2477).

Chain motels, some of which differ in name but share the same owner, swarm about Hannibal, particularly on **Mark Twain Ave.** (Rt. 36) and on U.S. 61 near the Rt. 36 junction. Numerous **B&Bs** are located downtown. The cheapest singles are $60—times have changed from Twain's Hannibal, when "there was not enough money in the first place to furnish a conversation!" Shiningly well-maintained, the **Howard Johnson Lodge,** 3603 McMasters Ave., at the U.S. 36/I-72 junction, has potentially decent but highly variable prices. (221-7950. A/C, cable TV, pool; singles $39-55; doubles $55-79; prices highest in summer.) The **Mark Twain Cave Campgrounds,** adjacent to the cave 1mi. south of Hannibal on Rt. 79, are cheery and family-oriented, but not too secluded (221-1656; $14, full hookup $18, $1.50 per extra person after 4). Sidestep Hannibal's unending fast food options, wax up your dental floss, and head into **Ole Planters,** 316 N. Main St., to devour tasty $4 BBQ beef sandwiches and $2 German chocolate pie. (221-4410. Open M-W and F-Sa 11am-3pm and 4:30pm-8pm, Th and Su 11am-3pm. Nov.-Mar. closed Su.) The **Twainland Cheesecake Company,** 101 N. Main St., serves up sandwiches ($4.75), and over 99 flavors of cheesecake (221-3355; several options daily; open M-Sa 8:30am-3pm).

On **Trailways Bus Lines,** at the junction of MM and 61 (221-0033), in front of Abel's Quik Shop, buses blaze to Cedar Rapids (1 per day, $34.65) and St. Louis (1 per day, $21). The **Hannibal Convention and Visitors Bureau,** 505 N. 3rd St. (221-2477), offers free local calls (open M-F 8am-6pm, Sa 9am-5pm, Su 9:30am-4pm). **Post Office:** 801 Broadway (221-0957; open M-F 8:30am-5pm, Sa 8:30am-noon). **ZIP code:** 63401. **Area code:** 573.

# KANSAS CITY

With over 200 public fountains and more miles of boulevard than Paris, Kansas City (KC) looks and acts more European than one might expect from the "Barbeque Capital of the World." KC has a strong tradition of booze and good music; when Prohibition stifled most of the country's fun in the 1920s, Mayor Pendergast let the good times continue to roll, so Count Bassie, Duke Ellington, and Charlie Parker all flourished here. The Kansas City of today maintains its big bad blues-and-jazz rep in a metropolis spanning two states: the highly suburbanized and mostly bland half in Kansas (KCKS) and the quicker-paced commercial and touristed half in Missouri (KCMO).

## ▊ ORIENTATION AND PRACTICAL INFORMATION

The KC metropolitan area sprawls almost interminably, making travel difficult without a car. Most sights worth visiting lie south of downtown on the Missouri side: the museums; **Westport,** a trendy area with coffee shops and nightclubs; **Crowne Plaza,** a Hallmark-owned compound; the **Country Club Plaza,** an outdoor (and expensive) mall; the zoo; and the **18th and Vine Heritage District,** a newly revitalized area where the jazz was. All listings are for Kansas City, MO, unless otherwise indicated. Although parking around town is not easy, there are lots that charge $4 or less per day. **I-70** cuts east-west through the city, and **I-435** circles the 2-state metro area. KCMO is laid out on an extensive grid with numbered streets running east-west from the Missouri River well out into suburbs, and named streets running north-south. **Main St.** divides the city east-west.

**Airport: Kansas City International** (243-5237), 18mi. northwest of KC off I-29 (take bus #29). **KCI Shuttle** (243-5000 or 800-243-6383) departs over 100 times daily, servicing downtown, Westport, Crown Center, and Plaza of KCMO and Overland Park, Mission, and Lenexa of KCKS (one-way $16, round-trip $28). Taxi to downtown $23-26.

**Trains: Amtrak,** 2200 Main St. (421-3622), at Grand Ave. across from Crown Center (bus #27). 3 per day to St. Louis (5½hr., $25-39) and Chicago (8hr., $47-93). Open 24hr.

**Buses: Greyhound,** 1101 N. Troost (221-2835). Take bus #25. *The terminal is in an unsafe area.* To St. Louis (4-5hr., 5 per day, $27) and Chicago (9-15hr., 8 per day, $42). Open daily 5:30am-11pm.

**Public Transit: Kansas City Area Transportation Authority (Metro),** 1200 E. 18th St. (221-0660), near Troost. Excellent downtown coverage. 90¢, $1 for KCKS, $1.20 for Independence; ages 16-18, seniors with Medicare card, and disabled half-price. Free transfers. Buses run 5am-6pm (outer routes) or 5am-midnight (downtown routes). The **trolley** (221-3399) loops from downtown to the City Market, Crown Center, Westport, and Country Club Plaza Mar.-Dec. M-Sa 10am-10pm, Su noon-6pm; holiday hrs. vary. $9 for all day, seniors and ages 6-12 $6, after 5:30pm $4. Exact change required.

**Taxis: Yellow Cab,** 471-5000.

**Car Rental: Thrifty Car Rental,** 2001 Baltimore St. (842-8550 or 800-367-2277), 1 block west of 20th and Main St. (take bus #40). $30 per day, weekends $20 per day; 250 free mi., 29¢ each additional mi. Under 25 surcharge $10 per day. Must be 21 with a major credit card. Open M-W 8am-6pm, Th-F 8am-8pm, Sa-Su 9am-4pm. Free shuttle from airport runs to the location at 11530 NW Prairie View Rd. (464-5670). Open 24hr.

**Visitor Info: Convention and Visitors Bureau of Greater Kansas City,** 1100 Main St. (221-5242 or 800-767-7700), 25th fl. of the City Center Sq. Bldg. Open M-F 8:30am-5pm. **Missouri Tourist Information Center,** 4010 Blue Ridge Cut-Off (889-3330 or 800-877-1234 for a travel package), as you exit east off I-70. Open daily Mar.-Nov. 8am-5pm, Dec.-Feb. M-Sa 8am-5pm.

**Hotlines:** All lines 24 hr. **Crisis Line,** 531-0233. **Gay and Lesbian Hotline,** 931-4470. **Suicide Prevention,** 395-3091. **Troubled Youth Line,** 741-1477.

**Hospitals: Truman Medical Center,** 2301 Holmes St. (556-3000). **Women's Clinic of Johnson County,** 5701 W. 119th St. (491-4020).

**Internet Access: Kansas City Public Library,** 311 E. 12th St. (221-2685).

**Post Office:** 315 W. Pershing Rd. (374-9180), at Broadway (take bus #40 or 51). Open M-F 8am-6:30pm, Sa 8am-2:30pm. **ZIP code:** 64108. **Area code:** 816 in Missouri, 913 in Kansas; in text 816 unless noted.

# ■ ACCOMMODATIONS

The least expensive lodgings are near the interstate highways, especially I-70, and towards Independence. Downtown, most hotels are either expensive, uninhabitable, or unsafe—sometimes all 3. For help finding a bed in an inn or a home closer to downtown (from $50), call **Bed and Breakfast Kansas City** (913-888-3636).

**Serendipity Bed and Breakfast,** 116 S. Pleasant St. (833-4719 or 800-203-4299), 15min. from downtown KC. A Victorian mansion with all the trimmings and an ample breakfast. Historic tours and train pick-ups are available in a 1926 Studebaker, weather and time permitting. Several doubles and 1 single in particular are affordable. Singles $30-55; doubles $45-85. Discounts for stays of 3 nights or more.

**American Inn,** 4141 S. Noland (373-8300 or 800-905-6343), is just one in a massive chain that loops KC and dominates the KC budget motel market. Despite the gaudy neon facades, the rooms inside are large, cheap, and good-lookin', with A/C, free local calls, cable, and outdoor pools. Singles $35; doubles $50. Other locations include Woods Chapel Rd. (228-1080) off I-70 at exit 18; 1211 Armour Rd. (471-3451) in North Kansas City off I-35 at exit 6B; and 7949 Splitlog Rd. (913-299-2999) in KCKS off I-70 at exit 414. Prices drop with reservations and distance to KC.

**Interstate Inn** (229-6311), off I-70 at exit 18, is a great deal. The best prices are for a set of first come, first served rooms; reservations are a good idea. All rooms are large and remodeled. Singles from $20; doubles from $30.

**YMCA,** 900 N. 8th St. (913-371-4400) in KCKS. Varying rooms for men with access to the Y's gym and pool. Take bus #1 or 4. $22 1st night. Key deposit $7.

**Lake Jacomo** (229-8980), 22mi. southeast of KC. Take I-470 south to Colbern, then head east on Colbern for 2mi. Forested campsites, lots of water activities, and a nifty dam across the street. Sites $10, with electricity $12, full hookup $18.

# ◖ BBQ AND OTHER GRUB

Kansas City rustles up a herd of barbecue restaurants that serve unusually tangy ribs. The **Westport** area, at Westport Rd. and Broadway just south of **39th St.,** has eclectic menus, cafes, and coffeehouses. Ethnic fare clusters along 39th St. between Broadway and State Line. For fresh produce, visit the largest farmers market in the Midwest: the **City Market,** at 5th and Walnut St. along the river (842-1271). Sa and Su are the most active. (Open Su-F 9am-4pm, Sa 6am-4pm.)

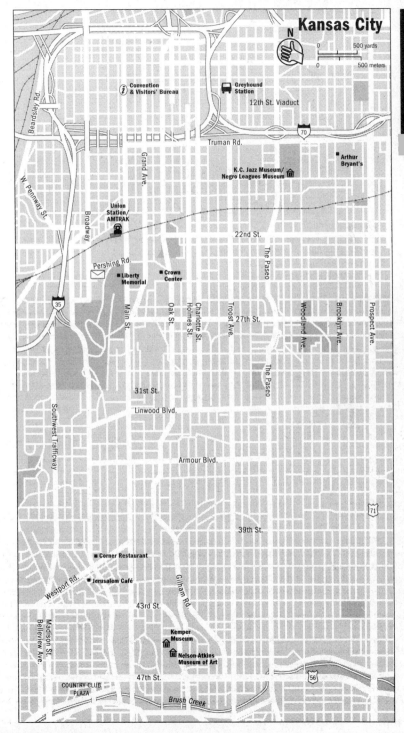

# Kansas City

N

0        500 yards
0        500 meters

Convention & Visitors' Bureau

Greyhound Station

12th St. Viaduct

Beardsley Rd.

Truman Rd.

70

Arthur Bryant's

K.C. Jazz Museum/ Negro Leagues Museum

Grand Ave.

W. Pennway St.

Union Station/ AMTRAK

Broadway

22nd St.

The Paseo

Pershing Rd.

Liberty Memorial

Crown Center

35

Charlotte St.

Holmes St.

Main St.

Oak St.

Troost Ave.

27th St.

Woodland Ave.

Brooklyn Ave.

Prospect Ave.

The Paseo

31st St.

Linwood Blvd.

Southwest Trafficway

Armour Blvd.

39th St.

71

Corner Restaurant

Westport Rd.

Jerusalem Café

Gillham Rd.

43rd St.

Madison St.

Belleview Ave.

Kemper Museum

Nelson-Atkins Museum of Art

47th St.

56

COUNTRY CLUB PLAZA

Brush Creek

**Arthur Bryant's,** 1727 Brooklyn St. (231-1123). Take the Brooklyn exit off I-70 and turn right (bus #110 from downtown). Down-home BBQ. The thin, orange, almost granular sauce is a spectacular blend of southern and western influences. A monstrous, sloppy sandwich is $6. Beef, ham, pork, chicken, turkey, or ribs are available. Open M-Th 10am-9:30pm, F-Sa 10am-10pm, Su 11am-8:30pm.

**Corner Restaurant,** 4059 Broadway (931-6630), in the heart of Westport. The best breakfast in all of KC ($3-5), and it is served through lunch. Plate-sized buttermilk or cornmeal pancakes $2, homestyle lunch and dinner specials $4-7. Open M-F 7am-3pm, 5pm-9pm; Sa-Su 7am-2pm.

**Strouds,** 1015 E. 85th St. (333-2132), at Troost, 2mi. north of the Holmes exit off I-435; also at 5410 N. Oak Ridge Rd. (454-9600). Enormous dinners ($6-19) in a weathered wooden hut crammed between the train tracks and an overpass. Great fried chicken, with cinnamon rolls, biscuits, and honey. Early birds get prompt service. Open M-Th 4-9:30pm, F 11am-10:30pm, Sa 2-10:30pm, Su 11am-9:30pm.

**d'Bronx,** 3904 Bell St. (531-0550), on the 39th St. restaurant row. A New York deli transplanted to middle America. 35 kinds of subs (½ sub $3-5, whole $6-10), other sandwiches ($4-5), and huge brownies ($1.50). Open M-Th 10:30am-10:30pm, F-Sa 10:30am-midnight.

**Jerusalem Café,** 431 Westport Rd. (756-2770). Vegetarians of all faiths claim it as a holy land. Vats of hummus, baba ghanoush, and tabouli garnered praise for this restaurant as the best Middle-Eastern food in KC. Be not afraid meat lovers! They serve plenty of flesh as well. Sandwiches $5, entrees $7-10. Open M-Sa 11am-10pm, Su noon-8pm.

## SIGHTS

Jazz once flourished in what has been recently designated as the **18th and Vine Historic District.** (Info: 474-8463.) The **Kansas City Jazz Museum** brings back the era with classy displays, music listening stations, neon dance hall signs, and everything from Ella Fitzgerald's eyeglasses to Louis Armstrong's lip salve. The 15min. "Jazz is…" film plays every 30min. In the same building swings the **Negro Leagues Baseball Museum,** where the era of segregation of the American pastime is recalled with photographs, interactive exhibits, and bittersweet nostalgia. (1616 E. 18th St. Jazz museum: 474-8463. Open Tu-Th 9am-6pm, F-Sa 9am-9pm, Su noon-6pm. Baseball Museum: 221-1920. Open Tu-Sa 9am-6pm, Su noon-6pm. Either museum $6, under 13 $2.50; both museums $8/$4.) The nearby **Black Archives of Mid-America** holds a large, fine collection of paintings and sculpture by African-American artists. Take bus #8 "Indiana." (2033 Vine St. 483-1300. Open M-F 9am-4:30pm, tours start at 10am; $2, under 17 50¢.)

A taste of KC's masterpieces is available at the **Nelson-Atkins Museum of Art,** at 45th, 3 blocks northeast of Country Club Plaza. Take buses #47, 55, 56, or 57. The museum contains one of the best East Asian art collections in the world, and a sculpture park with 13 Henry Moores. On most F nights, the museum hosts world-class jazz acts. (4525 Oak. 751-1278. Open Tu-Th 10am-4pm, F 10am-9pm, Sa 10am-5pm, Su 1-5pm. $5, students $2, ages 6-18 $1; free Sa. Free tours Tu-Sa until 2pm, Su until 3pm. Jazz 5:30-8:30pm.) Two blocks northwest, through the **Art Institute** campus, the entrance to the **Kemper Museum of Contemporary Art and Design** is marked by an enormous glass spider. Works by Georgia O'Keefe and Robert Mapplethorpe, and more modern sculptures, are scattered throughout this young museum. (4420 Warwick Blvd. 561-3737. Open Tu-Th 10am-4pm, F 10am-9pm, Sa 10am-5pm, Su 11am-5pm. Free.)

A few blocks to the west at 47th and Southwest Trafficway, **Country Club Plaza,** known as "the plaza," is the oldest and perhaps most picturesque shopping center in the U.S. Modeled after buildings in Seville, Spain, the plaza boasts fountains, sculptures, hand-painted tiles, and reliefs of grinning gargoyles. The plaza is lit at night from Thanksgiving to New Year's. Catch a glimpse from the **riverwalk** along Bush Creek. (753-0100. Buses #39, 40, 47, 51, 56, 57, and 155)

**Crown Center** sits 2mi. north of the Plaza at Pershing; take bus #40, 56, or 57, or any trolley from downtown. In July, Crown Center has **free concerts in the park** every F (a.k.a. "Friday Fun Fests"). The huge fountain is designed for people to run through on hot summer nights. *(2450 Grand Ave. 274-8444.)* The center, headquarters of Hallmark Cards, houses a maze of restaurants and shops, plus the children's **Coterie Theatre** *(474-6552)* and the **Ice Terrace,** KC's only public outdoor ice-skating rink. *(274-8412. Rink open Nov.-Dec. Su-Th 10am-9pm, F-Sa 10am-11pm; Jan.-Mar. daily 10am-9pm. $5, under 13 $4. Rentals $1.50.)* Say "I care!" and see how cards and accessories are made at the **Hallmark Visitors Center.** *(274-3613 or 274-5672 for a recording. Open M-F 9am-5pm, Sa 9:30am-4:30pm. Free.)*

The **Kansas City Zoo,** in the sprawling Swope Park, offers a chance to tour the world. Wildlife frolics on the big screen at the **IMAX theater** next door. *(871-5701. Off I-435 E at 63rd St. Open daily Apr. to mid-Oct. 9am-5pm, mid-Oct. to Mar. 9am-4pm. $6, Tu $2, ages 3-11 $3, parking $2. IMAX: 871-4629. Open Su-W 9am-5pm, Th-Sa 9am-8pm. $6, seniors $5, ages 3-11 $4.)*

## 🎵 ENTERTAINMENT AND NIGHTLIFE

The **Missouri Repertory Theatre,** at 50th and Oak, stages American classics. (235-2700. Season Sept.-May. Tickets $19-32, students and seniors $3 off. Box office open M-F 10am-5pm; call for in-season weekend hrs.) **Quality Hill Playhouse,** 303 W. 10th St., produces off-Broadway plays year-round (235-2700; tickets $14-19, seniors and students $2 off). For more entertainment news, *Explore Kansas City* and *Pitch Weekly,* available at area restaurants and bars, are helpful.

Sports fans will be pierced to the heart by **Arrowhead Stadium,** at I-70 and Blue Ridge Cutoff, home to football's **Chiefs** (920-9400 or 800-676-5488; tickets $29-50) and soccer's **Wizards** (472-4625; tickets $10-15). Next door, a water-fountained wonder, **Kauffman Stadium** (800-676-9257 or 921-8000), houses the **Royals** baseball team (tickets $6-15, M and Th $5). A stadium express bus runs from downtown and Country Club Plaza on game days.

In the 20s, Kansas City played hot spot to the nation's best jazz. Pianist **Count Basie** and his "Kansas City Sound" reigned at the River City bars, while saxophonist **Charlie "Bird" Parker** spread his wings and soared. The **Crown Center** celebrates annually with the **Kansas City International Jazz Festival,** on the last weekend in June (888-337-8111; tickets $12+). The restored **Gem Theater,** 1615 E. 18th St., stages blues and jazz like in the old days (842-1414; box office open M-F 10am-4pm). Across the street, the **Blue Room,** 1600 E. 18th St., cooks with some of the smoothest acts in town—after all, they have to live up to the legends next door at the museum (474-2929). The **Grand Emporium,** 3832 Main St., twice voted the best blues night club in the U.S., has live jazz F and Sa; M-Th feature rock, blues, and reggae bands (531-1504; cover $3-15; open daily noon-3am). **Jardine's,** 4536 Main St., plays strait-up jazz 6 nights a week, with nary a cover (561-6480; music M-Tu 7-10pm, W 7-11pm, Th 7pm-midnight, F-Sa 5pm-3am).

A few blocks west, noisy nightspots pack the restored **Westport** area (756-2789), near Broadway and Westport Rd., ½mi. north of Country Club Plaza (see **Sights, p. 572**). There is a new deck and intense rythym and blues at **Blayney's,** 415 Westport Rd. (561-3747. Cover $2-5. Live music 5 nights a week; open M-Sa 8pm-3am.)

**Kiki's Bon-Ton Maison,** 1515 Westport Rd., features KC's best in-house soul band (Sa 10:30pm) and whips up Cajun food with bayou flavor—jambalaya and crawfish is $9-13; sandwiches are $6 (931-9417; open M-Th 11am-10pm, F 11am-11pm, Sa 11am-1:30am, Su 11:30am-8pm). Kiki's also hosts the annual **Crawfish Festival** around the last weekend in May. **Jazz,** 1823 W. 39th St. at State Line, features you-know-what. (531-5556. Music W-Su after 8pm. No cover, but 50¢ surcharge on every item on bill. Open M-Th 11am-midnight, F-Sa 11am-1:30am, Su 11am-midnight.) Further down on 39th St., **Gilhouly's,** 1721 39th St., at Bell St., has over 125 bottled imports, a large selection of Irish and Scottish beers on tap, and several pool tables (561-2899; open M-Sa 11am-1:30am). Big names in jazz and blues show up at the club downstairs in the ritzy **Plaza III Steakhouse,** 4749 Pennsylvania St., at Country Club Plaza (753-0000; music W-Th 7-11pm, no cover; music F-Sa 8:30pm-12:30am, cover $5). **Club Cabaret,** 5024 Main St., is a popular gay bar and dance club (753-6504; cover $3; open Tu-Su 6pm-2:30am).

## NEAR KANSAS CITY: INDEPENDENCE

The buck stops at **Independence,** the hometown of former President Harry Truman and a 15min. drive east of KC on I-70, or on bus #24 "Independence." The **Harry S. Truman Library and Museum,** at U.S. 24 and Delaware St., has a replica of the Oval Office and detailed exhibits about the man, the period, and the presidency. (833-1225 or 800-833-1225. Open M-W and F-Sa 9am-5pm, Th 9am-9pm, Su noon-5pm. $5, seniors $4.50, ages 6-18 $3.) When Washington D.C. overheated, the Trumans would retreat to the 14-room **Harry S. Truman Home,** 219 N. Delaware St., known as the Summer White House. Get tickets to tour the Victorian mansion at the **Truman Home Ticket and Info Center,** 223 Main St. (254-9929; 254-7199 for a recorded message. Open daily 8:30am-5pm. $2, under 16 free. Home closed M). Before he moved into 1600 Pennsylvania Ave., Truman earned $3 a week at **Clinton's Drugstore,** 100 W. Maple, an old-fashioned ice cream parlor. (Cherry phosphate 75¢. 833-2625. Open M-Th 10:30am-6pm, F-Sa 10:30am-7pm, Su 11:30am-4pm.)

Independence's history goes back farther than just Truman. Thousands of pioneers ventured west along the California, Oregon, and Santa Fe trails, which all began here. Go west at the **National Frontier Trails Center,** 318 W. Pacific, and imagine 2000mi. in a covered wagon—are we there yet? (325-7575. Open M-Sa 9am-4:30pm, Su 12:30-4:30pm. $2.50, ages 6-17 $1.) The Addams Family-esque **Vaile Mansion,** 1500 N. Liberty St., built in 1881, has 112 windows and 2 ft. thick walls (325-7430; open Apr.-Oct. M-Sa 10am-4pm, Su 1-4pm. $3, seniors $2.50, ages 6-16 $1).

Inspired by the chambered nautilus, the computer-designed world headquarters of the **Reorganized Church of Jesus Christ of Latter Day Saints,** at River and Walnut St. is a bizarre and beautiful seashell that spirals up nearly 200 ft. (833-1000. Tours M-Sa 9-11:30am and 1-5pm, Su 1-5pm. Organ recitals Su 3pm; daily in summer. Free.)

Nearby, in the City Hall building, Independence's **Dept. of Tourism,** 111 E. Maple (325-7111), has the skinny (open M-F 8am-5pm).

## BRANSON

The Presley family had no idea what the impact would be if they opened a tiny music theater on **West Hwy. 76.** Over 7 million tourists clog Branson's strip (Rt. 76, a.k.a. Country Music Blvd.) to visit the "live country music capital of the Universe." Billboards, motels, and giant showplaces beckon the masses that visit Branson each year to embrace this modern-day mecca of country music and theater. The **Grand Palace,** 2700 W. Rt. 76, hears from big names like Barbara Mandrell and Ronnie Milsap (800-884-4536; shows Apr.-Dec. $17-40). The Osmond Brothers keep on truckin' at the **Osmond Family Theater,** at the intersection of Rt. 76 and Rt. 165 (336-6100; shows Mar.-Dec., closed July; $25.50; under 12 free).

Motels along Rt. 76 generally start around $25, but prices often increase during the busy season, from July to Sept. Less tacky, inexpensive motels line Rt. 265, 4mi. west of the strip or Gretna Rd. at the west end of the strip. **Budget Inn,** 315 N. Gretna Rd., has slightly dim but spacious rooms with A/C, free local calls, cable, and pool access very close to the action (334-0292; singles $19-25; doubles $33-44). **Indian Point,** at the end of Indian Point Rd., south of Hwy. 76, 1 of 15 campgrounds on Table Rock Lake, has lakeside sites with swimming and a boat launch (338-2121; sites $12, with electricity $16; registration 10am-6pm; open Apr.-Oct.). Other campgrounds wait on Rt. 25, 4mi. west of the strip.

The off-season runs from Jan.-Mar. here; many attractions close. The **Branson Chamber of Commerce,** on Rt. 248 just west of the Rt. 248/65 junction (334-4136; open M-F 8am-5pm). For info on **Table Rock Lake,** call 334-4101. **Greyhound's** nearest location is 2mi. south in Harrison, but there is a **flag stop** in town at Bob Evans, corner of Hwy. 76 and Hwy. 65. **Area code:** 417.

# OKLAHOMA

From 1838 to 1839, President Andrew Jackson forced the relocation of "The Five Civilized Tribes" from the southeastern states to the designated Oklahoma Indian Territory, in a tragic march which came to be known as "The Trail of Tears." After rebuilding their tribes in Oklahoma, the Indians were again dislocated in 1889 by whites rushing to stake claims. In ignorance of their rude past, people now treat each other with "old-fashioned" respect and courtesy, and the post-1930s "dustbowl" wasteland depicted in *The Grapes of Wrath* is now blanketed by the green crops of Oklahoma's rolling red hills, hemmed in by calming lakes and rivers.

## ⚐ PRACTICAL INFORMATION

**Capital:** Oklahoma City.

**Visitor Info: Oklahoma Tourism and Recreation Dept.,** 15 N. Robinson Rd., Rm. 801, Oklahoma City 73152 (521-2406 or 800-652-6552; www.travelok.com), in the Concord Bldg. at Sheridan St. Open M-F 8am-5pm.

**Postal Abbreviation:** OK. **Sales Tax:** 6-8%.

# TULSA

Though Tulsa lacks the distinction of being Oklahoma's political capital, it is in many ways the center of the state. First settled by Creeks arriving on the Trail of Tears, Tulsa's location on the banks of the Arkansas River made it a logical trading outpost. The town's Art Deco skyscrapers, French villas, Georgian mansions, and distinctively large Native American population reflect its varied heritage. Rough-riding motorcyclists and slick oilmen have recently joined the city's cultural mélange, seeking the good life on the Great Plains.

⚐ **ORIENTATION AND PRACTICAL INFORMATION.** Tulsa sections off neatly into 1 sq. mi. quadrants. Downtown surrounds the intersection of **Main St.** (north-south) and **Admiral Blvd.** (east-west). Numbered streets lie in ascending order north or south from Admiral. Named streets run north-south in alphabetical order; those named after western cities are west of Main St., while eastern cities lie to the east. **Tulsa International Airport** (838-5000; call M-F 8am-5pm) is just northeast of downtown and accessible by I-244 or U.S. 169. A taxi to downtown costs around $11. **Greyhound,** 317 S. Detroit Ave. (584-4428) departs to Oklahoma City (2hr., 8 per day, $17), St. Louis (7-9hr., 3 per day, $73), Kansas City (7hr., 4 per day, $67), and Dallas (7hr., 4 per day, $41) (open 24hr.). **Metropolitan Tulsa Transit Authority,** 510 S. Rockford (582-2100) runs buses. (M-Sa 6am-7pm. 75¢, transfers 5¢, seniors and disabled 35¢, ages 5-18 60¢, under 5 free with adult.) Most stop at **downtown transfer center,** 319 S. Denver, at the corner of 3rd St. Maps and schedules are at the main office (open M-F 8am-5pm) or on buses. **Taxis: Yellow Cab** (582-6161). **Thrifty,** 1506 N. Memorial Dr. (838-3333), at 41st St., near the airport rents cars. ($33 per day, $182 per week; unlimited mi. Must be 21 with major credit card; under 25 surcharge $10 per day. Open daily 5am-1am.) **Tom's River Trail Bicycles,** 6861 S. Peoria Ave. (481-1818) rents bikes and in-line skates. ($3-10 per hr., $9-24 per day. In-line skates $5 1st hr., $3 per additional hr. Open M-Sa 10am-7pm, Su 11am-6pm. Driver's license or major credit card required.) **Metropolitan Tulsa Chamber of Commerce:** 616 S. Boston Ave. (585-1201 or 800-558-3311; open M-F 8am-5pm). **Hospitals: Hillcrest Medical Center,** 1120 S. Utica Ave. (579-1000) and **Center for Women's Health,** 1822 E. 15th St. (749-4444). **Hotlines: Help Line,** 836-4357, M-F 8am-6pm, Sa 9am-5pm; **Gay Info Line,** 743-4297, Tu 6-10pm, W 2-10pm, Th-F noon-10pm. **Post office:** 333 W. 4th St. (599-6800). Open M-F 7:30am-5pm. **ZIP code:** 74101. **Area code:** 918.

**■ ACCOMMODATIONS.** Decent budget accomodations are scarce downtown. Better options are the budget motels around the junction of **I-44** and **I-244** (exit 222 from I-44); take bus #17 "Southwest Blvd." **Georgetown Plaza Motel**, 8502 E. 27th St., off I-44 at 31st and Memorial St., offers clean, well-furnished rooms with free local calls and cable TV (622-6616; singles and doubles $28; with microfridge $31/$34). The **Gateway Motor Hotel**, 5600 W. Skelley, at exit 222 C, has well-worn, but passable, rooms decorated in pea-green and timber fashion (446-6611; singles and doubles $27; free coffee in the office; key/remote deposit $2).

The 250-site **Mingo RV Park**, 801 N. Mingo Rd., at the northeast corner of the I-244 and Mingo Rd. intersection just west of the Mingo Valley Expwy./U.S. 169, offers laundry and showers in a semi-urban setting (832-8824 or 800-932-8824; sites $9, full hookup $18; reception daily 8:30am-8pm). **Heyburn Park**, 28165 W. Heyburn Park Rd., 20mi. southwest of the city in Kellyville, sits off I-44 or Rt. 66. Turn right for 4-5mi. onto Rt. 33 and watch for the Shepards Pt. sign. Shady sites line the shores of Heyburn Lake, far removed from the hubbub of town. (247-6601 or 887-444-6777. Sites $10, with water and electricity $14.)

**■■ FOOD AND NIGHTLIFE.** Most downtown restaurants cater to lunching business people, closing on weekends and at 2pm on weekdays. **Nelson's Buffeteria**, 514 S. Boston Ave., is an old-fashioned diner that has served a blue plate special (2 scrambled eggs, hash browns, biscuit and gravy $2.50) and famous chicken-fried steak ($6) since 1929 (584-9969; open M-F 6am-2pm). For extended hours, S. Peoria Ave. has more to offer. **The Brook**, 3401 S. Peoria, in a converted movie theater, has classic art-deco appeal. A traditional menu of chicken, burgers, and salads ($5-7) is complemented by an extensive list of $5 signature martinis. (748-9977. Open M-Sa 11am-2am, Su 11am-11pm.) **Chimi's**, 1304 E. 15th St., at Peoria Ave., offers well-prepared Mexican fare (entrees $6-11), great salsa, and a health-conscious menu (587-4411; open Su-Th 11am-10:30pm, F-Sa 11am-midnight).

Read the free *Urban Tulsa*, at local restaurants, and *The Spot* in the F *Tulsa World* for up-to-date specs on arts and entertainment. Good bars line the 3000's along S. Peoria Ave., an area known as Brookside, and 15th St. east of Peoria, which glistens with ritzy restaurants and antique shops. Across from The Brook teeters **The Brink**, 3410 S. Peoria, a spacious bar filled with hundreds of stools around glass-block counters, all of which are taken on weekend nights. (742-4242. Live rock Th-Su 10pm, cover $3-5; other events W, cover $2. Open W-Su 8pm-2am.) Tough-looking bikers, friendly locals, and succulent burgers ($3-6) abound at the **Blue Rose Café**, 3421 S. Peoria Ave. *Tulsa People Magazine* has dubbed it as the "best place to see and be seen." (742-3873. 21+. No cover. Live blues and rock Sa-Th 9pm. Open daily 11am-2am.) 18th and Boston Ave. raises a ruckus at night, catering to the young adult crowd. College kids flock to the blues-happy **Steamroller**, 1738 Boston Ave., commonly billed as "the snob-free, dork-free, band-and-brewski place to be." (583-9520. BBQ and Tex-Mex entrees $5-7. Local bands F-Sa 10pm. Cover $3-10. Open M-Th 11am-10pm, F 11am-2am, Sa 5pm-2am.)

**■■ SIGHTS AND ENTERTAINMENT.** The **Philbrook Museum of Art**, 2727 S. Rockford Rd., 1 block east of Peoria Ave., presents tastefully selected works of Native American and international art in a renovated Italian Renaissance villa, complete with a grassy sculpture garden. (749-7941 or 800-324-7941. Open Tu-W and F-Sa 10am-5pm, Th 10am-8pm, Su 11am-5pm. $5.40, students and seniors $3.25, under 13 free. Bus #5 "Peoria.") Perched atop an Osage foothill 2mi. northwest of downtown (take bus #47), the **Thomas Gilcrease Museum**, 1400 Gilcrease Museum Rd., houses the world's largest collection of Western American art, as well as 250,000 Native American artifacts and 10,000 works by artists such as Remington and Russell. Take the Gilcrease exit off Rt. 412. (596-2700. Open M-Sa 9am-5pm, Su 11am-5pm; Mid-Sept. to mid-May closed M. $3 donation requested.)

The ultra-modern, gold-mirrored architecture of **Oral Roberts University**, 7777 S. Lewis Ave., rises out of an Oklahoma plain about 6mi. south of downtown

## TRAIL OF TEARS NATIONAL HISTORIC TRAIL

President Jackson ignored a Supreme Court ruling when he forced 13,000 Cherokee Indians to march from North Carolina, Tennessee, Georgia, and Alabama to the Indian Territories. Between 1838 and 1839, many walked the trail at gunpoint, and by the end thousands had died of hunger and disease. The **Trail of Tears National Historic Trail,** established in Dec. 1987, commemorates this journey by designating the remaining parts of the Trail of Tears as National Historic Sites. Auto routes (Rt. 10 and 62, north of Tahlequah) follow the northern land trail as closely as possible. For more info, contact **Trail of Tears National Historic Trail,** Southwest Region, National Park Service, P.O. Box 728, Santa Fe, NM 87504 (505-988-6888).

between Lewis and Harvard Ave.; take bus #12. In 1964, Oral had a dream in which God commanded him to "Build Me A University," and Tulsa's most-frequented tourist attraction was born. (495-6807.) The **visitors center,** located in the spiky Prayer Tower, offers free 35min. tours. (495-6807. Open M-Sa 9am-5pm, Su 1-5pm; tours depart every 15min.)

Rodgers and Hammerstein's *Oklahoma!* continues its run under the stars at the **Discoveryland Amphitheater,** 10mi. west of Tulsa on 41st St., accessible only by car. This classic, set in the early 1900s, features the girl who can't say no, cowboys dancing ballet, and more. (245-6552. Shows June-Aug. M-Sa 8pm. $15, seniors $14, under 13 free.) Chow on pre-show barbecue from 5:30-7:30pm ($8, seniors $7.50, children under 13 $5). The **Tulsa Ballet,** (749-6006), acclaimed as one of America's finest regional troupes, tiptoes at the **Performing Arts Center,** at 3rd and Cincinnati St. (596-7111 or events line 596-2525. Box office open M-F 10am-5:30pm, Sa 10am-3pm.) The **Tulsa Philharmonic** (747-7445) and **Tulsa Opera** (587-4811) also perform there. The Philharmonic harmonizes most weekends Sept. through June ($8-50); the Opera stages 4 productions per year.

Tulsa thrives during events like the **International Mayfest** (582-6435; May 18-21, 2000). The **Intertribal Pow-Wow,** at the Tulsa Fairgrounds Pavilion (Expo Sq.), attracts Native Americans and thousands of on-lookers for a 3-day festival of food, arts and crafts, and nightly dancing contests (744-1113; usually in Aug., call for exact dates; $2, seniors $1, under 10 free).

## NEAR TULSA: TAHLEQUAH

Buried deep in the lush hills of northeast Oklahoma, 66mi. east of Tulsa on Rt. 51, the sleepy hamlet of Tahlequah historically marks the end of the Cherokee tribe's forced movement west. In the center of town, on Cherokee Sq., stands the capitol building of the **Cherokee Nation,** 101 S. Muskogee Ave., easy to find since Hwy. 51, 82, and 62 all intersect and run together on Muskogee. Built in 1870, the building, along with other tribal government buildings such as the Supreme Court building and the Cherokee National Prison (1 and 2 blocks south of Cherokee Sq. respectively), formed the highest authority in Oklahoma until statehood in 1907. Across from the northeast corner of Cherokee Sq., the **visitors center,** 123 E. Delaware St. (456-3742), offers free maps of the major sites downtown.

The **Cherokee Heritage Center,** 4mi. south of town on Hwy. 82, left on Willis Rd., then right at the sign, includes both **Tsa-La-Gi Village,** a recreation of a 16th-century Cherokee settlement with ongoing demonstrations of skills such as flint knapping and basket weaving, and the **Cherokee National Museum.** *(456-6007 or 888-999-6007. Village and Museum open Feb.-Apr. Tu-F 10am-5pm; May-Aug. M-Sa 10am-5pm, Su noon-5pm; Sept.-Dec. M-F 10am-5pm. $6, under 13 $3; in winter $3/$1.50. Last tour 4pm.)* One mi. down the street from the Heritage Center (follow signs pointing left from the exit driveway) is the **Murrell Home,** a well-restored plantation showing the high standard of living enjoyed by a few slave-owning Cherokees. *(456-2751. Open W-Sa 10am-5pm, Su 1-5pm; Nov.-Feb. Sa 10am-5pm, Su 1-5pm. $3 suggested donation.)* **Tahlequah Floats,** 1 Plaza S., #243, sends canoes up-river. Campsites are available. 2mi. east of Tahlequah on Downing St./Rt. 62; at the intersection of Rt. 62 and 10 turn north on

Rt. 10 and drive 100 yd. *(918-456-6949 or 800-375-6949. 5mi. run $9 per person, 25mi. overnight run $17 per person. Restrooms provided. Open May-Sept. sunrise to sunset. Sites $2.50, RV sites with electricity $10.)* **Area code:** 918.

# OKLAHOMA CITY

At noon on Apr. 22, 1889, a gunshot sent settlers scrambling into the Oklahoma Territory—the "landrush" was afoot. By sundown, Oklahoma City, set strategically along the Santa Fe Railroad, was home to over 10,000 homesteaders. These settlers have since multiplied, maintaining the thriving stockyards and horseshows that so often vanished with the civilizing of the Old West. OKC has recently struggled to overcome the notorious 1995 bombing of the Alfred R. Murrah federal office building and a devastating 1999 tornado which left whole sections of the city in ruin. Yet this heartland city remains an unobstrusive and tranquil place.

**🛈 ORIENTATION AND PRACTICAL INFORMATION.** Oklahoma City is constructed on a nearly perfect grid. Almost all of the city's attractions are outside the city center, but the Metro Transit bus reaches many of them. Be cautious on public transportation, especially downtown after dark. Cheap and plentiful parking makes driving the best way to go. **Will Rogers World Airport** (680-3200), on I-44 southwest of downtown, exit 116 B, flies away. Royal Coach, 2925 S. Meridian Ave. (685-2638), has 24hr. van service from the airport to downtown ($10; $2 per additional person); a taxi downtown runs around $13. To get to the **Greyhound** station, 427 W. Sheridan Ave. (235-6425), at Walker St., take city bus #4, 5, 6, 8, or 10. *Be careful at night.* Runs to Tulsa (2hr., 8 per day, $17), Dallas (5hr., 4 per day, $39), and Kansas City (10hr., 6 per day, $68). Open 24hr. **Amtrak,** 100 S. E.K. Gaylord Blvd., rumbles to Ft. Worth (4.5 hr., 1 per day, $24-48; station open 24 hr., but unattended). **Oklahoma Metro Transit** has bus service M-Sa 6am-6pm; the office at Union Station, 300 S.W. 7th (235-7433) distributes free schedules (open M-F 8am-5pm). All routes radiate from the station at 200 N. Shartel St. (Fare $1, seniors and ages 6-17 50¢.) **Yellow Cab,** (232-6161), charges $2.50 1st mi., $1.25 per additional mi., and $1 per extra passenger. **Dub Richardson Ford Rent-a-Car,** 2930 NW 39th Expwy. (946-9288 or 800-456-9288) rents used cars ($34 per day with 200mi. free in-state. Must be 25 with major credit card. Open M-F 8am-6pm, Sa 8:30am-noon.) **Miller Cycling and Fitness,** 215 Boyd St. (321-8296), near the University of Oklahoma in Norman, rents bikes ($10 per day; open M-Sa 10am-6pm; must be 18 with credit card). The **Oklahoma City Convention and Visitors Bureau,** 189 W. Sheridan (297-8910), at Robinson St., has city-specific info (open M-F 8:30am-5pm). The **Law Library,** on the 1st fl. of the capitol building, has free internet access (open M-F 8am-5pm). **Hotlines: Contact,** 848-2273 for referrals or crisis intervention; **Rape Crisis,** 943-7273. Both 24hr. **Post Office:** 320 SW 5th St. (720-9086). Open 24hr. **ZIP code:** 73125. **Area code:** 405.

**📍 ACCOMMODATIONS.** Cheap lodging in OKC lies along the interstate highways, particularly on I-35 north of the I-44 junction; the I-40 cluster east of town was depleted by the tornado. Most inexpensive options are chains, like **Motel 6,** 6166 Tinker Diagonal, across from and a little past the Sixpence, off I-40 exit 156B. Rooms have cable and access to a pool. (737-6676. Singles $32; doubles $38.) **The Royal Inn,** 2800 S. I-35, south of the junction with I-40, treats you to free local calls, HBO, and adequate rooms (672-0899; singles $25, doubles $30).

Nestled behind a strip mall are the 172 sites of **RCA,** 12115 Northeast Expwy./I-35 N. Take southbound Frontage Rd. off exit 137; it's ¼mi. to the red-and-white "RV" sign. (478-0278. Open daily 8am-8pm; in winter 8am-8pm. Sites $12, full hookup $17. Pool, laundry, and showers.) In contrast, **Lake Thunderbird State Park** offers campsites near a beautiful lake fit for swimming or fishing. Take I-40 east to Choctaw Rd. (exit 166), then south until the road ends (10mi.), and make a left for 1mi. (360-3572. Showers available. Office open M-F 8am-5pm; there's a campsite host for late or weekend arrivals. Sites $6, full hookup $17; in summer $18. Huts $35.)

**⚡🏠 FOOD AND NIGHTLIFE.** Oklahoma City contains the largest feeder cattle market in the U.S., and beef tops most menus. Most places downtown close early in the afternoon after they've served business lunchers. After-hours restaurants lie immediately east of town on Sheridan Ave. (in the Bricktown district) and north of downtown, along Classen Blvd. and Western Ave. Everyone's fighting for the rights to the late Leo's recipes at **Leo's Original BBQ**, 3631 N. Kelley St., a classic, hickory smoking outfit in the northwest reaches of town (424-5367; open M-Th 11am-8pm, F-Sa 11am-9pm). The **Classen Grill**, 5124 Classen St., serves breakfast and middle American meals. The omelettes (from $4.29) served with delicate fried potatoes,are splendid; half the city gets in line for them on weekend mornings. (842-0428. Open M-Th 7am-9pm, F-Sa 7am-10p, Su 8am-2pm.) The *Oklahoma Gazette* has listings of local eateries and nightlife.

Nightlife here is almost as rare as the elusive jackalope. The **Bricktown district** has restaurants with live music. The **Bricktown Brewery**, 1 N. Oklahoma St., at Sheridan Ave., brews beer on the premises (25 recipes, 5 on tap, $2.75) and serves burgers, salads, and chicken ($5-10). The 2nd fl. houses bar games and live music. (232-2739. Upstairs 21+ after 8pm. Cover $5 for bands. Live music Tu, F-Sa 9pm. Open Su-M 11am-10pm, Tu-Th 11am-midnight, F-Sa 11am-1:30am.) The DJ at the rough-and-tumble **Wreck Room**, 2127 NW 39th, at Barnes St., mixes house and techno (525-7610; cover $3-4; open F 10pm-5am and Sa 11pm-5am).

**👁 🏠 SIGHTS AND ENTERTAINMENT.** Monday morning is the time to visit the **Oklahoma City Stockyards**, 2500 Exchange Ave., the busiest in the world. Cattle auctions (M-Tu) begin at 8am and may last into the night. Visitors enter free of charge via a catwalk soaring over cow pens and cattle herds, leading from the parking lot northeast of the auction house (take bus #12 from the terminal to Agnew and Exchange Ave.). The auction is as Old West as it gets; only those with a wide-brim cowboy hat, blue jeans, boots, and faded dress shirt fit in (235-8675). The mall-like **Omniplex**, 2100 NE 52nd St., houses a pastiche of modern museums and exhibits. Highlights include the **Air and Space Museum, International Photography Hall of Fame, Red Earth Indian Center,** and the hands-on **Science Museum.** An Imax theater is scheduled to open in late 1999. (424-5545. Take bus #22. Open M-Sa 9am-6pm, Su noon-6pm; mid-Sept. to mid-May 9:30am-5pm M-F. Admission to all museums $7.60, ages 3-12 $6, seniors $6.80. Planetarium $1.65/$1.10/$1.45 extra.)

Plant lovers should make a bee-line for **Myriad Gardens**, 301 W. Reno Ave., downtown at Robinson Ave., where a 70 ft. diameter glass cylinder, called the Crystal Bridge, perches above a large pond. The gardens include both a desert and a rainforest, each with hundreds of plant species. (297-3995. Open daily 9am-6pm. $4, seniors and students $3, ages 4-12 $2. Outdoor gardens open daily 7am-11pm. Free.) The **National Cowboy Hall of Fame,** 1700 N. E. 63rd St., features an extensive collection of Western art. (478-2250. $6.50, seniors $5.50, ages 6-12 $3.25, under 6 free. Open daily June-Aug. 8:30am-6pm, Sept.-May 9am-5pm.) The **Oklahoma City National Memorial** to the victims of the 1995 bombing opens in Apr. 2000 at the former site of the Murrah Federal Bldg., 5th and Harvey downtown.

The **Red Earth Festival** (June 9-11, 2000) is the country's largest celebration of Native America; the Myriad Convention Center hosts art fairs and intense dance competitions. (427-5228. Daytime competitions and art festival $7; evening dance performances $12, under 12 $6.)

# TEXAS

Covering an area as wide as the span of Wisconsin and Montana and as long as the stretch from North Carolina to Key West, Texas has more the brawn of a country than a state. The fervently proud, independent citizens of the "Lone Star State" seem to prefer it that way. After revolting against the Spanish in 1821 and splitting from Mexico in 1836, the Republic of Texas stood alone until 1845, when it entered the Union as the 28th state. The state's unofficial motto proclaims that "everything is bigger in Texas"; this truth is evident in prolific wide-brimmed hats, styled and sculpted ladies' coifs, boat-sized American autos, giant ranch spreads, countless steel skyscrapers, and towering urban cowboys who seem ready and willing to conquer the frontier and fight for independence all over again.

Cotton, cattle, and oil built the Texan fortune, but technology, trade, and tourism now form the backbone of its economic might. Regional cuisine, like most of Texan culture, is enriched by an age-old Mexican heritage. "Tex-Mex" is a restaurant epidemic ranging from 69¢ taco stands to elegant border cafes. Fajitas, longhorn beef, chicken-fried steak, and spicy barbecue round out the list of staples.

## HIGHLIGHTS OF TEXAS

■ **Food.** Drippin' barbecue and colossal steaks reign supreme in this state where beef is king and vegetables are for the cows. Some of the best beef awaits in Austin (p. 589) and Amarillo (p. 606).
■ **San Antonio.** Remember the Alamo! A city rich with Spanish heritage... (p. 597).
■ **Rodeos/Cowboys.** The ol' West lives on in Fort Worth (p. 586) and at the Mesquite Rodeo in Dallas (p. 585), with some of the finest rope-riders in the land.

## ◨ PRACTICAL INFORMATION

**Capital:** Austin.
**Visitor Info: Texas Travel Information Centers** (800-452-9292; www.tourtexas.com), near state lines on all major highways into Texas. Call 8am-6pm (centers open daily 8am-5pm) for a free guidebook. **Texas Division of Tourism** P.O. Box 12728, Austin 78711 (800-888-8839). **Texas Parks and Wildlife Dept.,** Austin Headquarters Complex, 4200 Smith School Rd., Austin 78744 (512-389-8950 or 800-792-1112). **U.S. Forest Service,** 701 N. 1st St., Lufkin 75901 (409-639-8501).
**Postal Abbreviation:** TX. **Sales Tax:** 6-8.25%.

## DALLAS

Dallas began as a trading outpost at a ford across the Trinity River in 1841. Rapidly boosted by the oil industry, Dallas is now the nation's largest inland city. Nevertheless, it has yet to be recognized as the cosmopolitan center it aspires to be—visitors are more interested in the image of oil and cowboys fostered by the television show *Dallas*. In actuality, golf courses and swimming pools far outnumber genuine ropers or oilers here, and Dallasites prefer to point out plush cultural venues such as Myserson Symphony Hall and the Museum of Art. The city's legendary preoccupation with commerce now attracts flocks of immigrants from the Far East and Latin America, and Dallas maintains one of the largest and most exclusive social scenes in the country for a city its size.

## ◨ ORIENTATION AND PRACTICAL INFORMATION

Most of Dallas lies within the **I-635** loop, which is bisected east-west by **I-30** and north-south by **I-35 E (Stemmons Frwy.)** and **U.S. 75 (Central Expwy.).** Nicer suburbs stretch along the northern reaches of Central Expwy. and the **Dallas North Toll Rd.** Many of downtown Dallas's shops and restaurants lie underground in a maze of tunnels accessible from any major office building.

Texas

**Airport: Dallas-Ft. Worth International** (972-574-8888), 17mi. northwest of downtown; take bus #202 ($2). For door-to-gate service, take the **Super Shuttle,** 729 E. Dallas Rd. (800-258-3826). 1st passenger $16, $6 per additional passenger. 24hr. service. Taxi to downtown $30.

**Trains: Amtrak,** 400 S. Houston Ave. (653-1101), in Union Station. To: Los Angeles (42hr., 4 per week, $123); Austin (6½hr., 4 per week, $22); and Little Rock (7½hr., 4 per week, $50). Open daily 9am-6:30pm.

**Buses: Greyhound,** 205 S. Lamar St. (655-7727), 3 blocks east of Union Station. To: New Orleans (13hr., 5 per day, $73); Houston (4hr., 10 per day, $24); and Austin (4hr., 11 per day, $22). Open 24hr.

**Public Transit: Dallas Area Rapid Transit (DART),** 1401 Pacific Ave. (979-1111; open M-F 5am-10pm, Sa-Su 8am-6pm). Buses radiate from 2 downtown transfer centers, East and West, and serve most suburbs. Runs daily 5:30am-9:30pm, to suburbs 5:30am-8pm. Fare $1, $2 to suburban park-and-ride stops; transfers free. Maps at Elm and Ervay St. office (open M-F 7am-6pm). **DART Light Rail** runs north-south through downtown (5:30am-12:30am; fare $1). The **McKinney Ave. Trolley** (855-0006) serves the upscale district on McKinney (Su-Th 10am-10pm, F-Sa 10am-midnight; fare $1.50).

**Taxis: Yellow Cab Co.,** 426-6262 or 800-749-9422.

**Car Rental: Rent-a-Wreck,** 2025 S. Buckner Blvd. (800-398-2544). Extremely reliable service. Late-model used cars from $21 per day. Must be 21. Cash deposits accepted. Airport pick-up available. Open M-F 9am-6pm, Sa 9am-3:30pm.

**Visitor Info: Dallas Convention and Visitors Bureau,** administrative office at 1201 Elm S., Renaissance Tower, 20th fl. (571-1300). Open M-F 7:30am-5:30pm. Operates a 24hr. hotline (214-571-1301) and an **information center** in the Old Red Courthouse, 100 S. Houston St. at the intersection with Main St. (M-F 8am-5pm, Sa-Su 10am-5pm. For late-night info, head to **West End Marketplace,** 603 Munger St. (open M-Th 11am-10pm, F-Sa 11am-midnight, Su noon-6pm).

**Hotlines: Suicide and Crisis Center,** 828-1000. **Contact Counseling,** 972-233-2233, for general counseling. Both 24hr.

**Post Office:** 400 N. Ervay St. (953-3045), near Bryan St. downtown. Open M-F 8am-6pm. **ZIP code:** 75201; for General Delivery, 75221. **Area codes:** 214, 817, and 972. In text, 214 unless otherwise noted.

# ACCOMMODATIONS

Cheap lodging aside from the chain motel variety doesn't come easy in Dallas; big events such as the Cotton Bowl (Jan. 1) and the State Fair in Oct. exacerbate the problem. Look 15-20min. north of downtown on **U.S. 75,** north along **I-35,** and east on **I-30** for inexpensive motels. **Bed and Breakfast Texas Style,** 4224 W. Red Bird Ln., will place you in a nice home, usually near town, with friendly residents anxious to make y'all as comfortable as possible. It's an especially good deal for two people. Be sure to call a few days ahead. (972-298-8586. Open M-F 8:30am-4:30pm. Singles from $55; doubles from $65.) The **Super 7 Motel Mesquite,** 3629 U.S. 80 E, lies 10min. out of downtown; after branching right onto U.S. 80, from I-30, exit at Town East Blvd. Perks include TVs, free local calls, and a small pool. (613-9989. Singles $30.50; doubles $35.) Downtown, the **Paramount Hotel,** 302 S. Houston St., near Dealey Plaza and the West End, stands 2½ blocks from the Light Rail and CBD West transfer center (761-9090; singles $69; doubles $79).

Near Lake Joe Pool, in the southwest corner of the city, **Cedar Hill State Park** provides 355 tent sites. Take I-35 E to Rt. 67, turn right onto FM 1382, and the park is on the left. The area fills up early for the warmest months, so call at least 2 weeks in advance. There is a swimming area, marina, jet-ski rental, and three walking trails in the park. (972-291-3900, 512-389-8900 for reservations. Sites $15, or $7 for primitive campsites. $5 daily fee for each adult. Office open M-F 10am-5pm, Sa-Su 10am-10pm; 24hr. gate access with reservations.) RV campers should take I-35 E north of the city to exit 444, then go left under the highway about a mile to **Sandy Lake Campground,** 1915 Sandy Lake Rd. RV sites are $17-21, depending on the vehicle size. (972-242-6808. Office open M-F 7:30am-7:30pm, Sa 8am-7pm, Su 1-6pm.)

# FOOD

Dallas prides itself on just about everything, and food is no exception. The city boasts more restaurants per capita than any other in the U.S., and Dallasites love to talk about their favorite eateries. For the lowdown on dining options, pick up the "Friday Guide" of the *Dallas Morning News*. The **West End Marketplace,** 603 Munger St. (748-4801), has pricey Tex-Mex food amid a variety of touristy shops. Locals head for **McKinney Ave., Deep Ellum** (Elm St. east of downtown), and **Greenville Ave.** In a desert of beef, **Farmers Produce Market,** 1010 S. Pearl Expwy., between Pearl and Central Expwy., is a veggie oasis (939-2748; open daily 6am-6pm).

**EatZi's,** 3403 Oaklawn Ave. (526-1515), at Lemmon Ave., 1mi. east of Oaklawn exit from 35E, north of downtown, #51 or #2 buses from downtown. A paradise for the frugal gourmet, this grocery, cafe, kitchen, and bakery forms an 8000 sq. ft. venue of glorious food. Sounds of Vivaldi and Verdi surround heapings of focaccia ($3), sandwiches ($4-7) and a multitude of delights. Open daily 7am-10pm.

**Sonny Bryan's Smokehouse,** 302 N. Market St. (744-1610), in the West End. A landmark of Dallas BBQ. Has a funky, run-down atmosphere where school desks replace tables. Try a beef sandwich ($4.29) or combine 4 smokehouse delicacies ($11). Some vegetarian options available. Open M-F 10am-4pm, Sa 10am-3pm, Su 11am-2pm.

**Flying Burro,** 2831 Greenville (827-2112). The patio strewn with chili-pepper-shaped Christmas lights and cheesy overhangings may look a bit artificial, but this fine establishment serves New Mexico-style dishes that would make Santa Fe proud. Hits include stacked enchiladas ($6-7.75). Lunch specials from $5-6. Restaurant open M-Th 11am-11pm, F-Sa 11am-12:30am, Su 11am-10pm. Bar open until 2am.

**Baker's Ribs,** 2724 Commerce (748-5433), east of downtown in Deep Ellum. Baker's doesn't serve much besides meat, but if good BBQ is what you're craving, Baker's is the answer. A hearty meal between patchy walls covered in banjos, washpans, cowboy pictures and other Texan glory. Beef, sausage, chicken, ham, turkey ($3.25), combination plates ($6.95-8.50). Open M-Th 11am-7pm, F-S 11am-9pm.

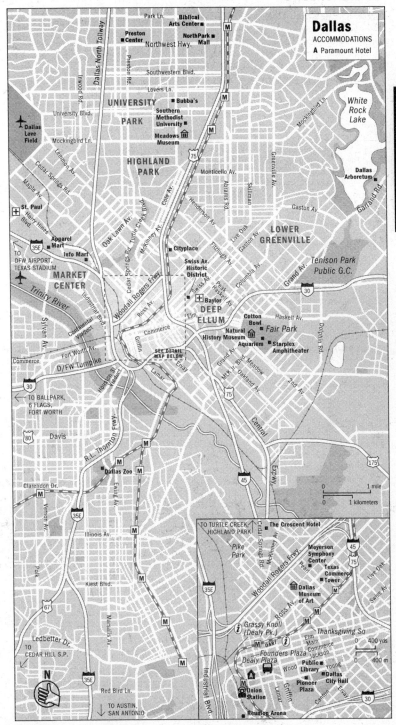

**Dallas**
ACCOMMODATIONS
**A** Paramount Hotel

TEXAS

Park Ln.
Biblical
Arts Center ■
Preston
■ Center
NorthPark ■
Mall
Northwest Hwy.
Southwestern Blvd.
Lovers Ln.
UNIVERSITY
PARK
■ Bubba's
University Blvd.
Southern
Methodist
University
Meadows
Museum
Dallas
Love Field
Mockingbird Ln.
HIGHLAND
PARK
Monticello Av.
LOWER
GREENVILLE
Gaston Av.
White
Rock
Lake
Dallas
Arboretum
St. Paul
Harry Hines
Blvd.
Apparel
■ Mart
Info Mart ■
Cityplace
Swiss Av.
Historic
District
Tenison Park
Public G.C.
TO
DFW AIRPORT,
TEXAS STADIUM
MARKET
CENTER
Trinity River
Baylor
DEEP
ELLUM
Cotton
Bowl
Fair Park
Haskell Av.
Natural
History Museum
Aquarium
Starplex
Amphitheater
Commerce
SEE DETAIL
MAP BELOW
D/FW Turnpike
Commerce
TO BALLPARK,
6 FLAGS,
FORT WORTH
Davis
Dallas Zoo
Clarendon Dr.
Vernon Av.
Illinois Av.
Kiest Blvd.
Ledbetter Dr.
TO
CEDAR HILL S.P.
N
Red Bird Ln.
TO AUSTIN,
SAN ANTONIO
TO TURTLE CREEK,
HIGHLAND PARK
The Crescent Hotel
Pike
Park
Meyerson
Symphony
Center
Texas
Commerce
Tower
Dallas Museum
of Art
Grassy Knoll
(Dealy Pk.)
DART
Thanksgiving Sq.
Founders Plaza
Dealy Plaza
Public
Library
Young
Dallas
City Hall
Pioneer
Plaza
Union
Station
Reunion Arena

0        1 mile
0        1 kilometers

0    400 yds
0    400 m

## ◉ TRIUMPHS AND TRAGIC MEMORIES

Oil-flushed Dallas is packed with showy displays of 20th-century architecture and sculpture. Encircled by the wonder of modern engineering that is present-day downtown, historic Dallas can easily be seen on a walking tour. Dallas is more notorious for its more recent history, however; JFK's assassination during a campaign parade in 1963 is permanently preserved in various museums and landmarks. Oil-rich Dallas is also filled with 20th-century architecture and sculpture.

On the corner of Houston Ave. and Elm St., the 6th floor of the unassuming **Texas School Book Depository** still gives people the chills as they look out the window through which Lee Harvey Oswald allegedly fired the shot that killed President John F. Kennedy on Nov. 22, 1963. Now this floor is a fascinating museum devoted to the Kennedy legacy, tracing the dramatic and macabre moments of the assassination in various media. *(747-6660. Open daily 9am-6pm. Self-guided tours $5, seniors and students $4. Audio cassette rental $3.)* To the south of the depository, Elm St. runs through **Dealy Plaza,** a national landmark beside the infamous grassy knoll where Kennedy's convertible passed as the shots were fired. Philip Johnson's **Memorial** to Kennedy looms nearby at Market and Main. Allegedly just across the street at 110 Market St. is the **Conspiracy Museum.** This bizarre and engaging shrine to elaborate CIA plots and mafia intrigue chronicles the assassinations of JFK, RFK, and Lincoln. *(741-3040. Open daily 10am-6pm. $7, students and seniors $6, children $3.)*

For a cheap but classy view of the Dallas skyline, ride to the **Sky Lobby** at the top of the Chase Tower. The middle block of elevators will whisk you up to the marble lobby, graced with artificial pools and large windows overlooking the northeast end of town. *(2200 Ross St. Free. Open 7am-10pm.)* The **Reunion Tower** is a better known lookout, but more stuffy and incurs a cost. *(300 Reunion Blvd., near the West End, 651-1234. Open Su-Th 10am-10pm, F-Sa 9am-midnight. $2, seniors and ages 3-12 $1.)*

**The Dallas Museum of Art's** (DMA) architecture is as graceful and beautiful as its collections of Egyptian, African, Early American, Impressionist, modern, and decorative art. *(1717 N. Harwood St. 922-1200. Open Tu-W 11am-4pm, Th 11am-9pm, F 11am-4pm, Sa-Su 11am-5pm. Free, but special exhibits $5-8.)* Directly across Harwood St., the **Trammel Crowe Center** has a sculpture garden featuring graceful Rodins and Bourdelles as well as a museum of Asian art. *(979-6430. Open Tu, W, F 11am-6pm, Th 11am-9pm, Sa 10am-6pm, Su 11am-5pm. Free.)* At the **Dallas World Aquarium,** admission is steep, but the multi-level rainforest exhibit with caged bats, swimming penguins, sleepy crocodiles, and birds zooming by your head make this aquarium worthwhile. The museum anchors northeast of the West End, a block north of Ross Ave. *(1801 N. Griffin St. 720-2224. Open daily 10am-5pm. $11.85, seniors and children $6.50.)*

The ubiquitous **I.M. Pei** designed many downtown Dallas buildings. The spectacular **Fountain Place** at the Wells Fargo Building is on Ross St. just past Field St. The **Morton H. Meyerson Symphony Center,** 2301 Flora St., a few blocks east, and the imposing **Dallas City Hall,** 100 Marilla St. off of Young St., were also designed by Pei.

The **West End Historic District and Marketplace,** full of broad sidewalks, shops, and restaurants, lies north of Union Station. *(Most stores open M-Th 11am-10pm, F-Sa 11am-10pm, Su noon-6pm.)* A replica of the **1842 log cabin** of John Neely Bryan, the city's founder, sits across a small plaza from the Kennedy Memorial, at Elm and Market St. Nearby, the visitor's center now occupies the 1st floor of the gargoyled **old Dallas County Courthouse,** on the corner of Houston and Main St. The building garnered the nickname "Old Red" for its unique Pecos red sandstone.

Home to the state fair (Sept.-Oct.) since 1886, **Fair Park** (421-9600), southeast of downtown on I-30, on #12 Dixon bus from CBD East, earned national landmark status for its Art Deco architecture. The 277-acre park also hosts the **Cotton Bowl** (Jan. 1). During the fair, **Big Tex**—a 52 ft. smiling cowboy float—towers over the land; only a huge ferris wheel, the **Texas Star,** looms taller. The **Science Place** has toddlerish hands-on exhibits, but the planetarium and IMAX theater are for all. *(428-5555. Open Su-Th 9:30am-5:30pm, F-Sa 9:30am-9pm. Museum $6, seniors and ages 3-12 $3. Movies $6, $3 children.)* Other park attractions include the **Dallas Aquarium,** the **Museum of Natural History,** and the **African-American Museum,** with multi-media folk art and sculpture. *(Aquarium: 670-8453. Open daily 9am-4:30pm. $2, ages 3-11 $1.50.*

*MNH: 421-3466. Open daily 10am-5pm. $4, ages 3-18 and seniors $2.50; M 10am-1pm free. AAM: 565-9026. Open Tu-F noon-5pm, Sa 10am-5pm, Su 1-5pm. Free.)*

Thirty-five late 19th-century buildings from around Dallas (including a dentist's office, a bank, and a farmstead which currently raises animals) have been restored and moved to **Old City Park,** the city's oldest and most popular recreation and lunch spot, about 9 blocks south of City Hall on Ervay St. at Gano. *(421-5141. Open daily 9am-6pm. Exhibit buildings open Tu-Sa 10am-4pm, Su noon-4pm. $5, seniors $4, children $2.)*

White Rock Lake provides a haven for walkers, bikers, and in-line skaters. On the east shore of the lake, resplendent flowers and trees fill the 66-acre **Dallas Arboretum;** take bus #19 from downtown. *(8617 Garland Rd. 327-8263. Open daily 10am-6pm; Nov.-Feb. 10am-5pm. $6, seniors $5, ages 6-12 $3. Parking $3.)* Dallas's **mansions** are in the **Swiss Avenue Historic District** and the streets of the **Highland Park** area, between Preston Rd. and Hillcrest Ave. just south of Mockingbird Ln.

 ## ENTERTAINMENT

*The Met,* a free weekly out W in restaurants and bookstores, has unrivaled entertainment coverage. For the scoop on Dallas' **gay scene,** pick up copies of the *Dallas Voice* and *Texas Triangle* in **Oak Lawn** shops and restaurants.

Prospero works his magic at the **Shakespeare in the Park** festival, at Samuel-Grand Park just northeast of Fair Park. Two free plays (June-July) run 6 nights a week (559-2778; 8:15pm; $4 donation is optional). At Fair Park, the **Music Hall** showcases **Dallas Summer Musicals.** (421-0662, 373-8000 for tickets. $7-70. Call 696-4253 for ½-price tickets on performance days. Shows run June-Oct.) The **Dallas Symphony Orchestra** plays in the Morton H. Meyerson Symphony Center, at Pearl and Flora St. in the arts district (692-0203; Sept.-May; tickets $10-60).

If you come to Dallas looking for cowboys, the **Mesquite Rodeo,** 1818 Rodeo Dr., is the place to find them. Take I-30 east to I-635 S to exit 4 and stay on the service road. Nationally televised, the rodeo is one of the most competitive in the country. (972-285-8777 or 800-833-9339. Shows Apr. to early Oct. F-Sa 8pm. Gates open at 6:30pm. $10, seniors $7, children 3-12 $4. Dinner $9.50, children $6.50.)

**Six Flags Over Texas,** 15mi. from downtown off I-30 in Arlington, between Dallas and Fort Worth, boasts 38 rides, including the speedy, looping new roller coasters "Batman: the Ride" and "Mr. Freeze." (817-640-8900. Open June to early Aug. daily from 10am; late Aug.-Dec. and Mar.-May Sa-Su from 10am. Closing times vary. $38, over 55 or under 4 ft. $19.) Across the highway lies the mammoth 47-acre water-park, **Hurricane Harbor.** Shoot down superspeed water flumes or experience simulated seasickness in the one million gallon wave pool. (817-265-3356. Open late May to early Aug. daily from 10am; closing hours vary. $24, seniors and under 4 ft. $12.) Find coupons for both parks on soda cans.

In Dallas, the moral order is God, country, and the **Cowboys.** Football devotees flock to **Cowboys Stadium** at the junction of Loop 12 and Rt. 183, west of Dallas in Irving. (972-785-5000. Sept.-Jan. Ticket office open M-F 9am-4pm. Tickets from $35.) **The Ballpark in Arlington,** 1000 Ballpark Way, plays home to the **Texas Rangers.** (817-273-5100. Apr.-Sept. Ticket office open M-F 9am-6pm, Sa 10am-4pm, Su noon-4pm. Tickets $4-30.) Experience the mystique of the game with a tour of the locker room, dugout, and the press box on the **ballpark tour.** (817-273-5098. Hours vary with the Ranger's schedule. $5, $4 seniors, $3 under 13.)

## NIGHTLIFE

For nightlife, head to **Deep Ellum,** east of downtown. In the 20s, the area was a blues haven for the likes of Blind Lemon Jefferson, Lightnin' Hopkins, and Robert Johnson; in the 80s, Bohemians revitalized the area. **Trees,** 2709 Elm St., rated the best live music venue in the city by the *Dallas Morning News,* occupies a converted warehouse with a loft full of pool tables. Bands tend to be alternative rock groups. (748-5009. 17+. Cover $2-10. Open Tu-Sa 9pm-2am.) A diverse clientele populates **Club Dada,** 2720 Elm St., the former haunt of Edie Brickell and stomping ground of new Bohemians, which recently added an outdoor patio and live local acts. (744-3232. 21+. Cover Th-Sa $3-5. Open Su 8pm-2am, Fri. 5pm-2am, Sa 9pm-2am.) For more info on Deep Ellum, call the **What's Up Line** (747-3337).

The touristy **West End** jams seven clubs into **Dallas Alley,** 2019 N. Lamar St., all under one cover charge (880-7420; $3-6). Guests sample Top 40, techno, country-western, karaoke, dueling pianos, and slot machines.

**Lower Greenville Ave.** provides a refreshing change from the downtown mania. **Poor David's Pub,** 1924 Greenville Ave., stages live music ranging from Irish folk tunes to reggae. Music is the main, and only, event: if there's no group booked, Poor David's doesn't open. (821-9891. Cover $1-20. Open M-Sa 8pm-2am. Tickets available after 6pm at the door; cash only.) More popular nightspots also line Yale Blvd., near Southern Methodist University's fraternity row. **Green Elephant,** 5612 Yale Blvd., full of pseudo-60s psychedelica, is the bar of choice (750-6625; open M-Sa 11am-2am, Su 6pm-2am). **Jack's Pub and Volleyball Club,** 5515 Yale Blvd., caters to a young college crowd with pool tables, sand volleyball courts, and blaring music (360-0999; open daily 4:30pm-2am; $10 cover for ages 18-20). Many gay clubs rock north of downtown in **Oak Lawn.** Among the more notable is **Roundup,** 3912 Cedar Springs Rd., at Throckmorton, a huge, cover-free country-western bar which packs a mixed gay and straight crowd of up to 1600 on weekends (522-9611; free dance lessons Th and Su 8:30pm; open Th-Su 8pm-2am).

## NEAR DALLAS: FORT WORTH

If Dallas is the last Eastern city, Fort Worth is undoubtedly the first Western one. Dallas's slightly less refined brother lies less than 40min. west on I-30, providing a worthwhile daytrip and some raw Texan entertainment. Fort Worth is divided into three cultural districts, each marked by red brick streets: the **Stockyards Historic District, Sundance Square,** and the **Museum District.**

The Stockyards Historic District, which lies along East Exchange Ave., 10 minutes north of downtown on Main St., attracts the felt hat and leather boot crowd like nowhere else in the metroplex. A walk along Exchange Ave., the main drag, provides a window into the Wild West, offering a slew of saloons, restaurants, shows, and gambling parlors. The **White Elephant Saloon,** 106 Exchange Ave., with its live country music, brass footrails, rough-hewn look, and prodigious collection of cowboy hats is a longtime favorite (624-1887; open Su-Th noon-midnight, F-Sa noon-2am). The **Hunter Brother's H3 Ranch,** 105 E. Exchange St., serves bugers and sandwiches ($6-9) as well as pricey steaks and ribs, all smoked on their hickory wood grill (624-1246; open M-Th 11am-10pm, F 11am-2am, Su 9am-10pm).

Down Exchange Ave., the **Cowtown Coliseum** hosts weekly rodeos (625-1025 or 888-269-8696; open F-Sa; $8, seniors $7, children $5) and Pawnee Bill's Wild West Show which features sharp-shooting, trick-roping, and a bullwhip act—yeeehaw! (625-1025; June-Aug. Sa 2 and 4:30pm; $7, ages 3-12 $4.) **Billy Bob's Texas,** 2520 Rodeo Plaza, ropes in the Stockyards crowds for some honky-tonk night clubbing with big names in country music. With 100,000 sq. ft. of floor space, including a bull ring, a BBQ restaurant, pool tables, slot machines, and 42 bar stations, the place bills itself as the world's largest honky-tonk. On one night alone, during a Hank Williams, Jr. concert, Billy Bob's sold 16,000 bottles of beer. (624-7117. Professional bull riding F-Sa 9 and 10pm. Free dance lessons Th 7-8pm. 18+ with ID or under 18 with parent. Afternoon cover $1, Su-Th after 6pm $3; F-Sa evenings $6.50-11, depending on performers. Open M-Sa 11am-2am, Su noon-2am.)

The **Chisholm Trail Round-Up,** a 3-day jamboree in the Stockyards during either the second or third week of June, preserves the heritage of the cowhands who led cattle drives to Kansas 150 years ago. (625-7005 or 624-4741. Calls taken M-Th 9am-6pm, F 9am-6pm, Sa 9am-7pm, Su 11am-6pm.) The **Armadillo Races** are a Round-Up must-see; children and visitors are allowed to participate in ground-beating attempts to make the critters move. For more on the stockyards, grab a copy of the *Stockyards Gazette* at the **visitors information center,** 130 E. Exchange Ave.

Downtown, **Sundance Sq.,** a pedestrian-friendly area, offers quality shops, museums, and eats. In the square, the **Sid Richardson Collection,** 309 Main St., displays an impressive stash of 56 paintings by the Western artists Remington and Russell (332-6554; open Tu-W 10am-5pm, Th-F 10am-8pm, Sa 11am-8pm, Su 1-5pm; free). A few minutes west of downtown down 7th St., the **Museum District** offers an array of intimate collections and exhibitions. Most notably the **Kimbell Museum,** arguably the best museum in the Southwest, brings in some of the world's most sophisticated art. (3333 Camp Bowie Blvd. 332-1034. Open Tu-Th and Sa 10am-5pm, F noon-8pm, Su noon-5pm. Free.) **Ft. Worth Visitor's Bureau:** 336-8791. **Area code:** 817.

# AUSTIN

If the "Lone Star State" still inspires images of rough 'n' tumble cattle ranchers riding horses across the plains, Austin does its best to put the stereotype to rest. Here, whiz kids start Fortune 500 computer companies, artists sell exotic handicrafts, and bankers don sneakers for midday exercise on the city's downtown green belts. A conspicuous student population keeps Austin energetic, while a thriving slacker population around the University of Texas campus boosts the city's tattoo count. Ambitiously nicknamed the "Live Music Capital of the World," Austin's vibrant nightlife offers innovative variations on the city's blues tradition.

## 🛈 ORIENTATION AND PRACTICAL INFORMATION

The majority of Austin lies between **Hwy. 1** and **I-35,** both running north-south and parallel to one another. UT students inhabit central **Guadalupe St. ("The Drag"),** where plentiful music stores and cheap restaurants thrive on their business. The state capitol governs the area a few blocks to the southeast. South of the capitol dome, **Congress Ave.** features upscale eateries and classy shops. The many bars and clubs of **6th St.** hop and clop at night. Much nightlife has moved to the growing **Warehouse Area,** around 4th St., west of Congress. Away from the urban gridiron, **Town Lake** offers a verdant haven for the town's joggers, rowers, and cyclists.

> **Airport: Austin Bergstrom International.** 3600 Presidential Blvd. (530-2242). Heading south from the city on I-35 go east on Ben White Blvd. (Hwy. 71) 8mi. from downtown. Take bus #100. Taxi to downtown $12-14.

**Austin**

ACCOMMODATIONS
A 21st St. Co-op
B Goodall Wooten
C Taos Hall
D HI-Austin
E Gregg House

**Trains: Amtrak,** 250 N. Lamar Blvd. (476-5684); take bus #38. To: Dallas (6hr., 4 per week, $27); San Antonio (2½hr., 4 per week, $11); and El Paso (13hr., 4 per week, $95). Office open Su and W 7am-11pm, M-Tu and Th 7am-4:30pm, F-Sa 2-11pm.

**Buses: Greyhound,** 916 E. Koenig, several mi. north of downtown off I-35. Easily accessible by public transportation. Bus #15 and 7 stop across the street and run downtown. To: San Antonio (1½hr., 11 per day, $14.50); Houston (3½hr., 7 per day, $17); and Dallas (3hr., 15 per day, $25), schedules and prices vary. Station open 24hr.

**Public Transit: Capitol Metro,** 106 E. 8th St. (474-1200 or 800-474-1201; call M-F 6am-10pm, Sa 6am-8pm, Su 7am-6pm). Fare 50¢; students 25¢; seniors, children, and disabled free. Office has maps and schedules (open M-F 7:30am-5:30pm). The **'Dillo Bus Service** (474-1200) runs on Congress and Lavaca St. M-F every 10-15min. during rush hrs.; varies during off-peak times. Park for free in the lot at Bouldin and Barton Springs.

**Taxis: American Yellow Checker Cab,** 472-1111.

**Car Rental: Rent-A-Wreck,** 850 Research St. off 183 north (836-9292). $26 per day; 50 free mi. per day with cash deposit, 100 per day with credit card; 25¢ per additional mi. Open M-F 8am-6pm, Sa 9am-2pm. Must be 21 to rent; under 25 surcharge $10.

**Bike Rental:** If you're lucky enough to come upon a **completely yellow bicycle,** hop on it for free—compliments of the city. Just make sure to leave it in a conspicuous spot for the next person to use. Most buses have bicycle racks. **Waterloo Cycles,** 2815 Fruth St. (472-9253), offers rentals $15 per day, $20 on weekends. Fee includes helmet. Lock rental $5. Delivery available. Open M-Sa 10am-7pm, Su 9am-5pm.

**Visitor Info: Austin Convention and Visitor's Bureau/ Visitor's Information Center,** 201 E. 2nd St. (478-0098 or 800-926-2282). Open M-F 8:30am-5pm, Sa, Su 9am-5pm.

**Hospital: St. David's Medical Center,** 919 E. 32nd St. (476-7111). Off I-35, close to downtown. Open 24hr.

**Hotlines: Crisis Intervention Hotline,** 472-4357. **Austin Rape Crisis Center Hotline,** 440-7273. Both 24hr. **Outyouth Gay/Lesbian Helpline,** 708-1234 or 800-969-6884, www.outyouth.org. W, F, Su 5:30-9:30pm.

**Post Office:** 510 Guadalupe (494-2200) at 6th St. Open M-F 7am-6:30pm, Sa 8am-3pm. **ZIP code:** 78701. **Area code:** 512.

# ▗ ACCOMMODATIONS

If you insist on your Motel 6, cheap accommodations lie along **I-35,** running north and south of Austin. However, this funkified city is a great place to find cheapies with character, so screw the usual neon sign. In town, **co-ops,** run by college houses at UT, peddle rooms and meals to hostelers. The co-ops work on a first come, first served basis. Patrons have access to all their facilities, including fully stocked kitchens. Unfortunately, most UT houses are only open from May through Aug. Call 476-5678 for information about several co-ops.

▨ **Hostelling International-Austin (HI-AYH),** 2200 S. Lakeshore Blvd. (800-725-2331 or 444-2294), about 23mi. from downtown. From the Greyhound station, take bus #7 "Duval" to Burton and walk 3 blocks north. From I-35, exit at Riverside, head east, and turn left at Lakeshore Blvd. Beautifully situated hostel with a 24hr. common room overlooking Town Lake. Waterbeds available. Kitchen, with a convenient cubby for each guest. 40 dorm-style beds, single-sex rooms; some private rooms. No curfew. $14, nonmembers $17. Linen provided; no sleeping bags allowed. Rents bikes and kayaks. Reception open daily 8-11am and 5-10pm.

**Gregg House,** 4201 Gregg Lane (448-0402), 3mi. south of Austin on I-35, exit and head east at Ben White Blvd., turn right at Woodward and left on St. Elmo Rd. Gregg Lane will soon be on your left. This B&B offers quiet, comfortable, and impeccably clean rooms, along with a jacuzzi, a pool, gardens, and a fish pond. Paying so little to stay here is a steal, like when your little sister will trade you her silver dollar for your shiny penny. $40-60 for 1-2 people. Call ahead.

**Taos Hall,** 2612 Guadalupe (474-6905), at 27th St. The UT co-op where you are most likely to get a private room. For stays of a week or more, they'll draft you into the chores corps. 3 meals and a bed $20. Open June-Aug.

**21st St. Co-op,** 707 W. 21st St. (476-5678). Take bus #39 on Airport St. to Koenig and Burnet, transfer to the #3 S, and ride to Nueces St.; walk 2 blocks west. Treehouse style building arrangement and hanging plants recall Robinson Crusoe's island home. A bit grungy, but only from all the good fun. Suites with A/C, and common room on each floor. $15 per person for 3 meals (when school is in session) and kitchen access. Fills up rapidly in summer.

**The Goodall Wooten,** 2112 Guadalupe (472-1343). The "Woo's" comfortable but somewhat sterile rooms are essentially UT dorms, but come with private baths, small fridges, and access to a big-screen TV lounge, laundry, basketball courts, and a computer lab. Singles $25; doubles $30. Linen $5. Reception M-Sa 9am-5pm and 8pm-midnight, Su 1-5pm and 8pm-midnight. Call ahead.

A 10-20 min. drive separates Austin and the nearest campgrounds. **McKinney Falls State Park,** 5808 McKinney Falls Pkwy. (243-1643; reservations 512-389-8900), lies southeast of the city and caters to both RV and tent campers. Turn right on Burleson off Rt. 71 east and go right on McKinney Falls Pkwy. 84 sites provide water and electricity ($12), while eight more primitive campsites ($7) are accessible only by foot. Swimming is permitted in the stream, and there are 7mi. of trails to hike or bike (daily park usage fee $2, under 13 free). The **Austin Lonestar RV Resort** (444-6322 or 800-284-0206), 6mi. south of the city along I-35 off exit 227, offers a pool, clean bathrooms, a game room, laundry facilities, a grocery store, and a playground. (All sites with water and electricity $32-36; $4 per additional person over 18; 3rd night free. Cabins for 4 $39; for 6 $49; 10% off with AAA.)

## ◐ FOOD

Scores of fast-food joints line the west side of the UT campus on **Guadalupe St.** Around **6th St.,** south of the capitol, the battle for happy hour business rages with unique intensity; patrons can often enjoy drink specials and free hors d'oeuvres. Although a bit removed from downtown, **Barton Springs Rd.** offers a diverse selection of inexpensive restaurants, including Mexican and Texas-style barbecue joints. The **Warehouse District** offers more expensive seafood and Italian eateries.

**▧ Ruby's BBQ,** 512 W. 29th St. (477-1651). Ruby's barbecue is good enough to be served on silver platters, but that just wouldn't seem right in this cow-skulls-and-butcher-paper establishment. The owners only order meat from farm-raised, grass-fed cows, with "none of that steroid crap." A mother of a brisket sandwich goes for $4. Two black bean tacos $3.75. Open daily 11am-midnight.

**Guero's,** 1412 S. Congress (707-8232), across the river from downtown. This wholesome Mexican taco bar and restaurant is very popular with locals, as well it should be. Polish off 2 tacos for $2.59 or add a full meal with rice and beans for $7. Combination plates $8-10. Open M, Th, F 11am-11pm, Sa, Su 8am-11pm.

**Trudy's Texas Star,** 409 W. 30th St. (477-2935), and 8800 Burnet Rd. (454-1474). Fine Tex-Mex dinner entrees ($5.25-8) and a fantastic array of margaritas. Famous for *migas*, a corn tortilla soufflé ($5). Pleasant outdoor porch bar. Open M-Th 7am-midnight, F-Sa 7am-2am, Su 8am-midnight; bar always open until 2am.

**Threadgill's,** 301 W. Riverside Dr. (472-9304). Another location at 6416 N. Lamar Blvd. (451-5440). A legend in Austin since 1933, serving up terrific Southern soul food and $7 fried chicken among creaky wooden floors, slow-moving ceiling fans, and antique beer signs. Surprisingly large variety of vegetarian and non-dairy options. Open M-Sa 11am-10pm, Su 11am-9pm.

**Mongolian BBQ,** 117 San Jacinto, across the street from the visitors center, downtown. Another location at 9200 N. Lamar Blvd. (837-4898), ½ block south of Rundberg St. Create your own stir-fry from a selection of meats and veggies. Lunch $5.50, dinner $7.50; all-you-can-eat $2 extra. Open M-Th 11am-3pm and 5-9:30pm, F-Sa 11am-3pm, Su 11am-9pm.

**Scholz Garten,** 1607 San Jacinto Blvd. (474-1958), near the capitol. UT students and state politicians alike gather at this Austin landmark, recognized by the legislature for "epitomizing the finest traditions of the German heritage of our state." Popular chicken-fried steak dinners ($7) and sausage 'n' bratwurst po' boys ($5). A German "Wurst" band plays W 8-10pm. Open M-Th 11am-10pm and F-Sa 11am-11pm.

## ◉ SIGHTS

Not to be outdone, Texans built their **state capitol** 7 ft. higher than the national one. *(At Congress Ave. and 11th St. 463-0063. Open M-F 8am-5pm, Sa-Su 9am-8pm. 45min. tours every 15min. Free.)* The **Capitol Visitors Center** is located in the southeast corner of the capitol grounds. *(112 E. 11th St. 463-8586. Open Tu-F 9am-5pm, Sa 10am-5pm.)* There is a free 2hr. garage at 15th and San Jacinto St.; nearby the **Governor's Mansion** resides in the trees. *(1010 Colorado St. 463-5516. Free tours M-F every 20min. 10-11:40am.)* From Mar. to Nov., the **Austin Convention Bureau** sponsors free walking tours of the area. *(454-1545. Tours Th-F 9am, Sa-Su 9, 11am, 2pm. Tour starts at the capitol steps.)*

The **University of Texas at Austin (UT)** is both the wealthiest public university in the country, with an annual budget of almost a billion dollars, and America's second largest university, with over 50,000 students. UT forms the backbone of city cultural life. The **visitor info center** is in Sid Richardson Hall. *(2313 Red River St. 475-7440. Open M-F 8am-4:30pm. Free tours M-F 11am and 2pm, Sa 2pm.)* Bus #20 heads to the **Lyndon B. Johnson Library and Museum.** The first floor focuses on Texas-native LBJ and the history of the American presidency; the 8th floor features a model of the Oval Office. *(2313 Red River St. 916-5137. Open daily 9am-5pm. Free.)*

The **Austin Museum of Art,** housed in a Mediterranean-style villa, blends art, architecture, and nature. The rolling grounds overlook Lake Austin; the museum displays 20th-century artwork. *(3809 W. 35th St. at Laguna Gloria. 458-8191. Open Tu-W and F-Sa 10am-5pm, Th 10am-8pm, Su noon-5pm. Admission $2, under 12 free; Th free. Group tours Aug.-June by appt.)* The museum hosts **Fiesta Laguna Gloria,** a mid-May arts and crafts festival with evening concerts and plays. *(458-6073).* The museum also has a branch downtown. *(823 Congress St. 495-9224.)*

Just before dusk, head underneath the south side of the **Congress Ave. Bridge,** near the Austin American-Statesman parking lot, and watch for the massive swarm of **Mexican free-tail bats** that emerge from their roosts to feed on the night's mosquitoes. When the bridge was reconstructed in 1980, the engineers unintentionally created crevices which formed ideal homes for the migrating bat colony. The city began exterminating the night-flying creatures until **Bat Conservation International** moved to Austin to educate people about the bats' harmless behavior and the benefits of their presence—the bats eat up to 3000lbs. of insects each night. Today, the bats are among the biggest tourist attractions in Austin. The colony, seen from mid-Mar. to Nov., peaks in July, when a fresh crop of pups increases the population to around 1½ million. For **flight times,** call the bat hotline. *(416-5700 ext. 3636.)* **Mt. Bonnell Park,** 3800 Mt. Bonnell Rd., off W. 35th St., offers a sweeping view of Lake Austin and Westlake Hills from the highest point in the city.

On hot afternoons, Austinites come in droves to riverside **Zilker Park,** just south of the Colorado River; take bus #30. *(2201 Barton Springs Rd. 477-7273. Open daily 5am-10pm. Free.)* Flanked by walnut and pecan trees, **Barton Springs Pool,** a spring-fed swimming hole in the park, stretches 1000 ft. long and 200 ft. wide. The pool's temperature hovers around 68°F. *(476-9044. Pool open F-W 5am-10pm, Th 5-9am and 7-10pm. Admission M-F $2.50, Sa-Su $2.75; ages 12-17 $1, under 12 50¢; late Mar. to early Oct. free.)* The **Barton Springs Greenbelt** offers challenging trails for hikers and bikers.

## ♫ ENTERTAINMENT AND NIGHTLIFE

Austin has replaced Seattle as the nation's underground music hotspring, so keep an eye out for rising indie stars, as well as old blues, folk, country, and rock favorites. On weekends, nighttime swingers seek out dancin' on **6th St.,** an area bespeckled with warehouse nightclubs and fancy bars. More mellow cigar-smoking night owls gather at the **4th St. Warehouse District.** The weekly *Austin Chronicle* and *XL-ent* provide details on current music performances, shows, and movies. The *Gay Yellow Pages* is free at stands along the Drag.

**Antone's,** 213 W. 5th St. (474-5314). Antone's has attracted the likes of B.B. King and Muddy Waters. This blues paradise was also the starting point for Stevie Ray Vaughn. All ages. Shows at 10pm. Cover $3-20. Open daily 9pm-2am.

# WHERE HAVE ALL THE HIPPIES GONE?

About 15mi. northeast of downtown Austin lies **Hippie Hollow**, Texas's only public nude swimming and sunbathing haven. Here, free spirits go *au naturel* in the waters of the lovely Lake Travis. Take Mopac (Loop 1) north to the exit for F.M. 2222. Follow 2222 west and turn left at the I-620 intersection; Comanche Rd. will be on your right. *(7000 Comanche Trail. 473-9437. 18+ only. Open daily 8am-9pm, no entry after 8:30pm. $5 per car, pedestrians $2.)*

**Stubb's BBQ,** 801 Red River (480-8341). The 21+ club downstairs has nightly acts, but the big draw of Stubb's is the occasional big names that appear in the 2000 capacity amphitheater out back. Swing by earlier for some scrumptious, inexpensive grub like beef brisket and 2 side dishes for $6. All ages welcome for ampitheater shows. Cover $3-10. Shows at 10:30pm. Open Tu-W, Su 11am-10pm, Th-Sa 11am-1am.

**Hole in the Wall,** 2538 Guadalupe St. (472-5599), at 26th St. Its self-effacing name disguises this renowned music spot, which features college alternative bands and an occasional country-western or hard-core group. Music nightly. 21+. Cover $3-5; no cover Su-M. Open M-F 11am-2am, Sa-Su noon-2am.

**Cactus Café** (475-6515), at 24th and Guadalupe St., in the Texas Union. Features adventurous acoustic music every night. Specializing in folk-rock and Austin's own "New Country" sound, the Cactus gave Lyle Lovett his start. All ages welcome. Music starts 9pm. Cover $2-15. Open Su-F 8am-1am, Sa 8pm-2am.

**Bob Popular's,** 402 6th St. (478-5072). A popular UT frat hangout. Gets the crowd moving with alternative rock on the patio and grooves to retro disco in one room and Top 40 in another. Come on Thursdays when all drinks are $1. 21+ for men except Th. Ladies 18-20 Th-Sa. Cover $4 after 10pm, Th men 18-20 $20. Open daily 8pm-2am.

**Joe's Generic Bar,** 315 E. 6th St. (480-0171). Find your way here for some raunchy Texas-style blues washed down with cheap beer. 21+. No cover. Open daily 7:30pm until the wayward crawl home.

**Paradox,** 311 E. 5th St. (469-7615), at Trinity. In a city hurting for dance clubs, this warehouse-style dance club with retro-80s and Top 40 music, draws 20-somethings by the pack. Cover $4. Open daily 9pm-4am.

**Copper Tank Brewing Company,** 504 Trinity St. (478-8444). Probably the city's best microbrewery. On W, a pint of any of the freshly brewed beers costs just $1—normally $3.75. 21+. Open daily 11am-2am.

**Beverly Sheffield Zilker Hillside Theater,** located across from the Barton Springs pool, hosts free outdoor bands, ballets, plays, musicals, and symphony concerts every weekend May to Oct. (call 397-1463 for events schedule). From Mar. 10-19, 2000, the **South by Southwest Music, Media, and Film Festival** draws entertainment industry's giants and thousands of eager fans (467-7979). Austin's smaller events calendar is a mixed bag. The high-brow **O. Henry Museum World Championship Pun-off** (497-1903) is held the first Su of May. More down to earth is the annual **Spamarama** (416-9307), on Apr. 8, 2000. Spam fans from all walks of life pay homage to this—er, product—with food, sports, and live music at the **Spam Jam.**

# HOUSTON

Born in 1836, when Augustus and John Allen, two brothers from the East, came slicing through the weeds of the Buffalo Bayou, Houston has come into its own as the fourth-most populous city in the U.S. This diverse city spreads its borders as a huge mega-metropolis, filled with monster trucks on superhighways, awe-inspiring glass-and-steel skyscrapers, enormous oil plants, and the largest strip malls in the country. As if all this was not enough, the Houston-based NASA space center reaches toward the stars. Luckily, the advocates of the "make it bigger" philosophy also support a softer side of Houston by cultivating operas, ballets, and museums.

## ▌ ORIENTATION AND PRACTICAL INFORMATION

Though the flat Texan terrain supports several mini-downtowns, true downtown Houston, a squarish grid of interlocking one-way streets, borders the **Buffalo Bayou** at the intersection of I-10 and I-45. **The Loop (I-610)** encircles the city center with a radius of 6mi. Anything inside the Loop is easily accessible by car or bus. The shopping district of **Westheimer Blvd.** grows ritzier to the west. Nearby, restaurants and shops line **Kirby Dr.** and **Richmond Ave.;** the upper portion of Kirby Dr. winds past spectacular mansions. *Be careful in the south and east areas of Houston.*

**Airport: Houston Intercontinental** (281-230-3100), 25mi. north of downtown. Get to city center via **Express Shuttle** (523-8888); buses daily every 30min. to major hotels in the downtown area 7am-11:30pm ($16, under 12 free).

**Trains: Amtrak,** 902 Washington Ave. (224-1577), *in a rough neighborhood.* During the day, catch a bus west on Washington Ave. (away from downtown) to Houston Ave.; at night, call a cab. To: San Antonio (5hr., 3 per week, $29) and New Orleans (9½hr., 3 per week, $47). Open M, Tu, and Th 7am-4pm; Su and W 7am-12:30am; F 3pm-12:30am; and Sa 11am-8pm.

**Buses: Greyhound,** 2121 S. Main St. (759-6565). *At night call a cab—this is an unsafe area.* To: Dallas (4-5hr., 10 per day, $31); San Antonio (3½hr., 11 per day, $20); and Santa Fe (24hr., 5 per day, $112). Open 24hr.

**Public Transit: Metropolitan Transit Authority (METRO Bus System)** (635-4000). Offers reliable service anywhere between NASA (15mi. southeast of town) and Katy (25mi. west of town). Operates M-F 6am-9pm, Sa-Su 8am-8pm; less frequently on weekends. The METRO operates a free trolley throughout downtown. Free maps and limited internet access available at the **Houston Public Library,** 500 McKinney (236-1313), at Bagby St. (open M-F 9am-9pm, Sa 9am-6pm, Su 2-6pm), or at a Metro Rides store. Fare $1; students and seniors 40¢, ages 5-11 25¢; $2 per day.

**Taxis: United Cab,** 699-0000.

**Visitors Info: Greater Houston Convention and Visitors Bureau,** in City Hall (227-3100 or 800-365-7575), at the corner of McKinney and Bagby St. Open M-F 8:30am-5pm.

**Hotlines: Crisis Center,** 228-1505. **Rape Crisis,** 528-7273. **Women's Center,** 528-2121. All 24hr. **Gay and Lesbian Switchboard of Houston** (529-3211) has entertainment info. Operates M-F 7-10pm.

**Hospital: Columbia Bellaire Medical Center,** 5314 Dashwood (512-1200), has a 24hr. emergency room. **Columbia Woman's Hospital of Texas,** 7600 Fannin (790-1234).

**Internet Access:** see **Houston Public Library** (above in **Public Transportation**).

**Post Office:** 701 San Jacinto St. (800-275-8777). Open M-F 8am-5pm. **ZIP code:** 77052. **Area codes:** 713 and 281 (in text 713, unless indicated).

## ▌ ACCOMMODATIONS

A few cheap motels dot the **Katy Freeway (I-10W).** Budget accommodations along **S. Main St.** are more convenient, but not all are safe. (Bus #8 goes down S. Main.)

**Perry House, Houston International Hostel (HI-AYH),** 5302 Crawford St. (523-1009), at Oakdale St. In a residential neighborhood near Hermann Park and the museum district. From the Greyhound station, take bus #8 or 15 south to Southmore St.; walk 6 blocks east to Crawford St. and 1 block south to Oakdale St. Helpful management provides 30 beds in 6 spacious rooms. Well-equipped kitchen, email access ($3 per hr.), choose-your-own chore. Room lock-out 10am-5pm, common area open all day. $11.39, non-members $14.39; sleepsacks required. Free use of bicycles with a $20 deposit.

**YMCA,** 1600 Louisiana Ave. (659-8501), between Pease and Leeland St. Downtown location features tiny cubicle-rooms with daily maid service, TV, and telephones for incoming calls; some have private baths. Singles $19-25. Key deposit $10. Another branch, 7903 South Loop (643-2804), is farther out (off the broadway exit from I-610 near I-45) but less expensive. Take Bus #50 to Broadway. Singles $18.50. Key deposit $10.

TEXAS

## Houston

ACCOMMODATIONS
A YMCA
B Roadrunner
C Perry House

0    500 yards
0    500 meters

N

TO FUNERAL MUSEUM, DALLAS

Woodland Park

Quitman
Fulton
Burnett
N. Main
Elysian

White Oak Dr.
Houston
Silver
Sawyer

Katy Frwy.
Whiteoak Bayou
Buffalo Bayou

Amtrak

Franklin
Congress
Preston

Texas
San Jacinto
Fannin
Main
Crawford
La Branch

City Hall
Public Library

Sam Houston Park

McKinney

DOWNTOWN

Dallas

Louisiana
Smith

Leeland

TO NASA, GALVESTON

Washington
Studemont
Heights Blvd.

Memorial Dr.
Allen Pkwy.
Dallas

Jefferson
Calhoun

A

TO MEMORIAL PARK

Buffalo Bayou

Gray
Louisiana
Smith
San Jacinto
Fannin
Main
Crawford
La Branch

Bremond

Waugh Dr.
Gray
Stanford
Welch
Fairview
Albany
Westheimer

Tuam

Elgin

Emancipation Park

Waugh Dr.
Yupon

Holman

Alabama

Shepherd Dr.
Welch
Dunlavy
Fairview
Windsor
Woodhead
Alabama
Hazard

Stanford
Montrose

Fannin
Main

Cleburne

Wheeler

Blodgett

High School for the Performing & Visual Arts

MUSEUM DISTRICT

Southmore
Oakdale

C

Binz

TO UPTOWN, MORE SHOPPING, DINING

Westheimer
Kirby Dr.
Richmond Av.
Southwest Frwy.
Hazard
Shepherd Dr.

Bissonnet

Hermann

Miller Outdoor Theatre

Hermann Park

Zoo

Sunset Blvd.

Rice Blvd.
Greenbriar
Kirby Dr.

Rice University

Fannin
Main

Outer Belt
MacGregor Dr.

University Blvd.

Holcombe Blvd.

TO ASTRODOME, ASTROWORLD

B

### MUSEUMS
Children's Museum, 8
Contemporary Arts Museum, 5
Garden Center, 11
Holocaust Museum, 7
Lawndale Art Center, 3
Menil Collection, 1
Museum of Fine Arts, 6
Museum of Health and Medical Science, 9
Museum of Natural Science & Planetarium, 10
Rice Art Museum, 12
Rothko Chapel, 2
Sculpture Garden, 4

**The Roadrunner,** 8500 S. Main St. (666-4971). Take bus #8. Friendly management, cable TV, mini-pool, free coffee, and local calls. Worn but well-furnished rooms. Singles $26; doubles $32. Weekly stays discounted to $20 per day. $2 key deposit.

**Red Carpet Inn,** 6868 Hornwood Dr. (981-8686 or 800-251-1962). Near the Bellaire exit off U.S. 59 S/SW Fwy. Plain but well-kept rooms. Free coffee. Singles $35; doubles $38.50.

Most campgrounds in the Houston area lie a considerable distance from the city center. **KOA Houston North,** 1620 Peachleaf, has sites with pool and shower access. From I-45 N, go east on Aldine-Bender Rd., then turn right on Aldine-Westfield Rd., and then right again on Peachleaf. (281-442-3700 or 800-562-2132. Tent sites for 2 $18, RV hookup $24; $2 per additional adult.) 1 room cabins $28, 2 rooms $40.

## ◑ FOOD

Houston's port has witnessed the arrival of many immigrants (today the city's Indochinese population is the second largest in the nation), and its restaurants reflect this diversity. Houston's cuisine features Mexican, Greek, Cajun, Asian, and Southern soul food. Look for reasonably priced restaurants along the chain-laden streets of **Westheimer** and **Richmond Ave.,** especially where they intersect with **Fountainview.** Houston has two **Chinatowns:** a district south of the George R. Brown Convention Center, and a newer area on **Bellaire Blvd.** called **DiHo.**

■ **EatZi's,** 1702 Post Oak Blvd. (629-6003), near the Post Oak Galleria. A paradise for the frugal gourmet, this grocery, cafe, kitchen, and bakery forms an 8000 sq. ft. venue of food. Masterful heapings of focaccia ($3), sandwiches ($4-$7) and other delights match the continuous sounds of Vivaldi and Verdi. Open daily 8am-10pm.

■ **Goode Company BBQ,** 5109 Kirby Dr. (522-2530), near Bissonnet St. This might be the best (and most popular) BBQ in Texas. Goode Company's mesquite-smoked brisket, ribs, and sausage links (all smothered in homemade sauce) will make your mouth water and your digestive juices flow. Sandwiches $3.25; dinner, featuring a meat and two veggie dishes, $6-9. Open daily 11am-10pm.

**Bibas/One's A Meal,** 607 W. Gray St. (523-0425), at Stanford St. This family-owned institution serves everything from chili 'n' eggs ($5.75) to a gyro with fries ($6). Their Greek pizza (6 in. $5.75) is hard to beat, and #8 on the breakfast menu is colossal (egg, bacon, sausage or ham, grits or hash browns, toast or biscuits, and juice for $5.25). Open 24hr.

**Cadillac Bar,** 1802 N. Shepherd Dr. (862-2020), at the Katy Freeway (I-10), northwest of downtown; take bus #75, change to #26 at Shepherd Dr. and Allen Pkwy. Wild, fun, and authentic Mexican food. Tacos and enchiladas $7-9; heartier entrées $8-14. Drinks with racy names $5. Open M-Th 10am-10:30pm, Sa noon-1am, Su noon-10pm.

**Magnolia Bar & Grill,** 6000 Richmond Ave. (781-2607). An upscale (dinner entrees $9-15) Cajun seafood restaurant. The constant and varied crowd attests to the quality of the food and the relaxed, welcoming atmosphere. R&B on F-Su evenings. Open M-Th 11am-10pm, F-Sa 11am-11pm, Su 10am-10pm.

## ◔ SIGHTS

The city's most popular attraction, **Space Center Houston,** is technically not even in Houston, but 20mi. from downtown in Clear Lake, TX. The active Mission Control Center still serves as HQ for modern-day Major Toms. When astronauts ask, "Do you read me, Houston?" these folks answer. Admission includes 3 separate hour long tours of the mission control center, the underwater weightless training pool, and the astronaut training facilities. The complex also houses models of Gemini, Apollo, and Mercury craft, as well as galleries and hands-on exhibits. *(1601 NASA Rd. 1, 281-244-2100 or 800-972-0369, take I-45 south to NASA Rd. exit, then head east 3mi. or take bus #246. Open daily 9am-7pm; early Sept. to late May M-F 10am-5pm, Sa-Su 10am-7pm. $13, seniors $12, ages 4-11 $9. Parking $3.)*

**WE'RE DYING TO GET IN** If you've got a car and a funeral fascination, head to the **American Funeral Service Museum,** The museum aims to "take the fear out of funerals." It contains exhibits on funerals of notable political figures, embalming artifacts, over two dozen funeral vehicles, and (of course) coffins of all shapes and sizes—from glass to iron, from chicken-like to airplane-shaped. *(415 Barren Springs Dr.; 281-876-3063 or 800-238-8861); from I-45, exit at Airtex, go west to Ella Blvd., turn right, and proceed to Barren Springs. Open M-F 10am-4pm, Sa-Su noon-4pm. $5, seniors and under 12 $3. Tours by appt. only.)*

Back in Houston, more earthly pleasures can be found underground. Hundreds of shops and restaurants line the 18mi. **Houston Tunnel System,** which connects all the major buildings in downtown Houston, extending from the Civic Center to the Tenneco Building and the Hyatt Regency. Duck into the air-conditioned passageways via any major building or hotel (most tunnel entries closed Sa-Su).

The 17th- to 19th-century American decorative art at **Bayou Bend Collection and Gardens** in **Memorial Park,** is an antique-lover's dream. The collection, housed in the mansion of millionaire Ima Hogg (we *swear*), daughter of turn-of-the-century Gov. Jim "Boss" Hogg, includes John Singleton Copley portraits and a silver sugar bowl by Paul Revere. *(1 Westcott St., 639-7750. Collection open Tu-F 10am-2:45pm, Sa-Su 1-5pm. $10; seniors, students $8.50; ages 10-18 $5, under 10 not admitted. Gardens open Tu-Sa 10am-5pm, Su 1-5pm. $3, under 10 free. 1½hr. garden tours by reservation.)*

Museums, gardens, paddle boats, and golfing are all part of **Hermann Park,** 388 acres of beautifully landscaped grounds by Rice University and the Texas Medical Center. Near the northern entrance of the park, the **Houston Museum of Natural Science** offers a splendid display of gems and minerals, permanent exhibits on petroleum, a hands-on gallery geared toward grabby children, a butterfly center, a planetarium, and an IMAX theater. *(1 Hermann Circle Dr., 639-IMAX/4629. Exhibits open daily 9am-7pm. Museum $4, seniors and under 12 $3; IMAX $6/$4; planetarium $4/$3; butterfly center $4/$3.)* At the southern end of the park, crowds flock to see more flying critters—as well as gorillas, hippos, and reptiles—in the **Houston Zoological Gardens.** The park grounds also encompass sports facilities, a kiddie train, a Japanese garden, and the Miller Outdoor Theater (see **Entertainment,** below). *(1513 N. MacGregor, 284-8300. Open daily 10am-6pm. $2.50, seniors $2, ages 3-12 50¢.)*

**The Museum of Fine Arts** hosts Impressionist and post-Impressionist Art, as well as fine works of Asia, Africa, and the American West. *(1001 Bissonet, 639-7300; open Tu-W and F-Sa 10am-9pm, Su 12:15-6pm. $3, students and seniors $1.50; free Th.)* The museum's **Sculpture Garden,** includes pieces by artists such as Matisse and Rodin. *(5101 Montrose St. Open daily 9am-10pm; free.)* Across the street, the **Contemporary Arts Museum** displays changing exhibits. *(5216 Montrose St. 284-8250, open Tu-W and F-Sa 10am-5pm, Th 10am-9pm, Su noon-5pm. Suggested donation $3.)*

The Menil Foundation exhibits an array of artworks in four buildings grouped within a block of each other. The **de Menil Collection** includes an eclectic assortment of Surrealist paintings and sculptures; Byzantine and medieval artifacts, and European, American, and African art. *(1515 Sul Ross, 525-9400. Open W-Su 11am-7pm. Free).* A block away, the Rothko Chapel houses 14 of the artist's paintings in a sanctuary. Fans of modern art will delight in Rothko's ultra-simplicity; others will wonder where the paintings are. *(3900 Yupon, 524-9839. Open daily 10am-6pm. Free.)*

Many a Bacchanalian fest must have preceded the construction of the **Beer Can House,** 222 Malone, off Washington Ave. Adorned with 50,000 beer cans, strings of beer-can tops, and a beer-can fence, the house was built by the late John Mikovisch, an upholsterer from the Southern Pacific Railroad.

The **San Jacinto Battleground State Historical Park** is the most important monument to Lone Star independence. The 18min. battle brought Texas its freedom from Mexico and brought the city its namesake in the person of Sam Houston. The **museum** in the Park celebrates Texas history. *(281-479-2431. 21mi. east on Rt. 225 and 3mi. north on Rt. 134. Museum open 9am-6pm, visual presentation shown hourly 10am-5pm.)* A ride to the top of the 50-story **San Jacinto Monument** yields a 570 ft. tall view of the area. *(281-479-2421. Open daily 9am-6pm. Slide show $3.50, seniors $3, under 12 $2.50; elevator to top $3/$2.50/$2; combo ticket $6/$5/$2.)*

## ▣ ENTERTAINMENT AND NIGHTLIFE

**Jones Hall,** 615 Louisiana Blvd., stages Houston's high-brow entertainment (227-3974). The **Houston Symphony Orchestra** performs here Sept. through May (227-2787; tickets $19-60). Between Oct. and May, the **Houston Grand Opera** produces 6 operas in the nearby **Wortham Center,** 500 Texas Ave. (546-0200; tickets $25-175; 50% student discount available at noon on the day of some shows). From Apr. to Oct., symphony, opera, and ballet companies and various professional theaters stage free performances at the **Miller Outdoor Theater** in Hermann Park (284-8352). The annual **Shakespeare Festival** struts and frets upon the stage from late July to early Aug. (284-8350). The downtown **Alley Theater,** 615 Texas Ave., puts on Broadway-caliber productions at moderate prices (228-8421; tickets $30-45; Su-Th $11 student rush tickets 1hr. before the show).

In Apr. 2000, baseball's **Astros** move into **Enron Field,** a new, state of the art stadium located at the intersections of Texas, Crawford, and Congress St. near Union Station downtown (799-9555; outfield deck $5, $1 for children). The **Rockets** hoop it up at the **Compaq Center,** 10 Greenwald Plaza (629-3700).

Most of Houston's nightlife lives west of downtown around Richmond and Westheimer Ave. Several gay clubs cluster on lower Westheimer, while enormous, warehouse-style dancehalls line the upper reaches of Richmond. A variety of bars and music venues fill the streets in between. Located in the mother of all strip malls, **City Streets,** 5078 Richmond Ave., is a multi-venue complex with 6 different clubs offering everything from country-western and live R&B to disco and a pool hall (840-8555; $2-5 cover good for all 6 clubs; open Tu-F 5pm-2am, Sa 7:30pm-2am). For a less commercial, more body pierced scene, search for the well-hidden **Emo's,** 2700 Albany St., north of Richmond on Montrose, then right on Fairview. A loyal crowd and several big-name bands (Smashing Pumpkins, Rev. Horton Heat) grace this spot. (523-8503. Live rock Tu and F-Sa nights. 21+ Su-Th, 18-21 cover $7. Open daily 7pm-2am.) All sorts come to converse in the distinctly English atmosphere of **The Ale House,** 2425 W. Alabama, at Kirby St. The bi-level bar and beer garden offers over 130 brands of beer, some rather costly ($3-4). Upstairs, you'll find old-time rock 'n' roll or the blues on F-Sa nights. (521-2333. Open M-Sa 11am-2am, Su noon-2am.) Good natured drinkers gather on the patio of **Sam's Boat,** 5270 Richmond Ave., to drink, chat, and hear live music. (781-2628. Open daily 11am-2am; live music Tu 5pm-2am, F 8pm-2am, Sa 6pm-2am. Cover $0-3).

## GALVESTON ISLAND

In the 19th century, Galveston was the "Queen of the Gulf," Texas's most prominent port and wealthiest city. The glamour came to an abrupt end on Sept. 8, 1900, when a devastating hurricane ripped through the city, claiming 6000 lives. The Galveston hurricane still ranks as one of the worst natural disasters in U.S. history. Today, the narrow, sandy island of Galveston (pop. 65,000), 50mi. southeast of Houston on I-45, meets beach resort quotas for t-shirt shops and ice cream stands but redeems itself with beautiful vintage homes and antique shops.

**⊿ PRACTICAL INFORMATION.** Galveston's streets follow a grid; lettered avenues run east-west, while numbered streets run north-south. **Seawall Blvd.** follows the southern coastline. Most routes have two names; Ave. J and Broadway, for example, are the same street. Greyhound affiliate **Kerrville Bus Co.,** 714 25th St. (765-7731; station open M-F 8am-7pm, Sa 8am-3:15pm), travels to Houston (1½hr., 4 per day, $13). **Strand Visitors Center:** 2016 Strand St. (766-1572, open daily 9:30am-5pm), in the Moody Coliseum. **Galveston Island Convention and Visitors Bureau:** 2106 Seawall Blvd. (763-4311 or 888-425-4753; open daily 8:30am-5pm; both open until 6pm in summer). **Post Office:** 601 25th St. (763-1527; open M-F 8am-5pm, Sa 6am-5pm). **ZIP code:** 77550. **Area code:** 409.

**▮▮ ACCOMMODATIONS AND FOOD.** Lodgings prices in Galveston fluctuate by season, rising to exorbitant heights ($50 and way up) during the summer, holidays, and weekends; especially during the summer, consider making Galveston a daytrip from Houston. Otherwise, RVs and tents can find reasonable rates at any of several parks on the island. The closest to downtown, the **Bayou Haven RV Resort,** 6310 Heards Ln., off 61st St., is located on a peaceful waterfront with laundry facilities and bug-free restrooms and showers. (744-2837. Sites for 2 with full hookup $17, waterfront sites $20; $3 per additional person. Tents welcome.) **Galveston Island State Park,** on 13½ Mile Rd., 6mi. southwest of Galveston on FM3005 (a continuation of Seawall Blvd.), rents tent sites. (737-1222. Restrooms, showers, and barbecue pits available. $12, plus $3 entrance fee per person.)

The oldest restaurant on the island, **The Original Mexican Café,** 1401 Market, cooks up great Tex-Mex meals with homemade flour tortillas, and daily lunch specials for $4-6 (762-6001; open M-Th 11am-9:30pm, F 11am-10pm, Sa-Su 8am-10pm). **Benno's,** 1206 Seawall Rd. serves tasty cajun seafood with an ocean view. Po'boys and lunch specials $5, seafood dinners $7.50-11.50 (762-4621; open Su-Th 11am-10pm, F-Sa 11am-11pm). Indulge your sweet tooth at **LaKing's Confectionery,** 2323 Strand St., a large, wonderfully old-fashioned ice cream and candy parlor (762-6100; open Su-Th 10am-9:30pm, F 10am-11pm, Sa 10am-midnight).

**▮▮ SIGHTS AND ACTIVITIES.** Galveston recently spent more than $6 million to clean up and restore its shoreline. The money was well spent—finding a pleasant beach is as easy as picking a spot. The only beach in Galveston which permits alcoholic beverages is **Apffel Park,** on the far eastern edge of the island (known as East Beach). 3 **Beach Pocket Parks** lie on the west end of the island, east of Pirates Beach, each with bathrooms, showers, playgrounds, and a concession stand. *(Car entry for beaches generally $5. Open daily 9am-9pm, some open later.)*

**Strand St.,** near the northern coastline, between 20th and 25th St., is a national landmark, with over 50 Victorian buildings. The street provides a pastiche of cafes, restaurants, gift shops, and clothing stores. The district has been restored with authentic gas lights and brick-paved walkways. During the summer, Strand St.'s **Saengerfest Park,** at Tremont St., holds a free **Party in the Park** every Sa and Su 3-7pm. *(763-7080.)* Partyers can listen to a blues band jam while contemplating their moves on a life-size chess board (2 ft. tall pieces). The **Galveston Island Trolley** shuttles between the seawall beach area and Strand St. *(Runs daily 6:30am-7pm; 60¢ per 30min.)* Pick up the trolley at either visitors center.

You'll find fabulous and pricey attractions at **Moody Gardens;** turn onto 81st from Seawall. The area, though filled with touristy gift shops and restaurants, makes room for three glass pyramids; one houses over 30 interactive space exhibits and three IMAX ride-film theaters (rides every 15min.), a second contains a tropical rainforest and 2000 exotic species of flora and fauna, and a third features an aquarium. An additional IMAX theater adjoins the visitors center. *(744-1745 or 800-582-4673. Open daily 9:30am-9pm; Nov.-Feb. Su-Th 10am-6pm, F-Sa 10am-9pm. Attractions $6 each, ride/films $7, seniors and children $1 off; discounts for multiple exhibits.)*

# SAN ANTONIO

The skyline may be dominated by aging office buildings, but no Texan city seems more determined to preserve its rich heritage than the romantic San Antone. Founded in 1691 by Spanish missionaries, the city is home to the famed Alamo, historic Missions, and La Villita, once a village for San Antonio's original settlers and now a workshop for local artisans. Many attractions, including the magnificent (though slightly artificial) Riverwalk, make San Antonio a popular vacation destination; hotel occupancy rates and prices rise on weekends, unlike most other cities of comparable size. Though both Native Americans and Germans have at one time claimed San Antonio as their own, Spanish speakers (55% of the population) outnumber any other group; the city's food, architecture, and language reflect this influence. San Antonio is located on the most traveled route between the U.S. and Mexico, just 150mi. from the Mexican border.

# ⚡ PRACTICAL INFORMATION

**Airport: San Antonio International,** 9800 Airport Blvd. (207-3411), north of town accessible by I-410 and U.S. 281. Bus #2 ("Airport") connects the airport to downtown at Market and Alamo. Taxi to downtown $14-15.

**Trains: Amtrak,** 224 Hoefgen St. (223-3226), facing the northern side of the Alamodome. To: Houston (5hr., 3 per week, $29); Dallas (9hr., 4 per week, $27); and Los Angeles (27hr., 4 per week, $131). Open daily midnight-2pm.

**Buses: Greyhound,** 500 N. Saint Mary's St. (270-5824). To Houston (4hr., 9 per day, $21) and Dallas (5-6hr., 15 per day, $34). Open 24hr.

**Public Transit: VIA Metropolitan Transit,** 800 W. Myrtle (362-2020; open M-Sa 7am-7pm, Su 8am-5pm), between Commerce and Houston. Buses operate daily 4:30am-11:30pm, but many routes stop at 6pm. Infrequent service to outlying areas. Fare 75¢. One-day "day tripper" passes $2, available at 112 Soledad St.

**Taxis: Yellow Cab,** 226-4242.

**Car Rental: American Auto Rental,** 3249 SW Military Dr. (922-9464). $20.80 per day with 100 free mi. Must be 21 with credit card or cash deposit. Customer pick-up service available for $12. Open M-F 8am-6pm, Sa 9am-3pm, Su noon-5pm.

**Visitor Info:** 317 Alamo Plaza (270-8748), downtown across from the Alamo. Open daily 8:30am-6pm. Free maps and brochures.

**Hotlines: Rape Crisis,** 349-7273. 24hr. **Supportive Services for the Elderly and Disabled,** 226-9212. Referrals and transport.

**Hospital: Metropolitan Methodist Hospital,** 1310 McCullough Ave. (208-2200). 24hr.

**Post Office:** 615 E. Houston (800-275-8777), 1 block from the Alamo. Open M-F 8:30am-5:30pm. **ZIP code:** 78205. **Area code:** 210.

# ▐ ACCOMMODATIONS

For cheap motels, try **Roosevelt Ave.**, a southern extension of Saint Mary's St., and **Fredericksburg Rd.** Inexpensive motels also line **Broadway** between downtown and Brackenridge Park. Drivers should follow **I-35 N** to find cheaper and often safer lodging within a 15mi. radius of town.

**Bullis House Inn San Antonio International Hostel (HI-AYH),** 621 Pierce St. (223-9426), 2mi. north of downtown on Broadway, right on Grayson ¾mi. From the bus station, walk to Navarro St. and take bus #11 or 15 to Grayson and New Braunfels; walk 2 blocks west. A spacious, ranch-style hostel in a quiet neighborhood. Pool, kitchen. Fills quickly in summer. $14, nonmembers $17. Private rooms for 1 or 2 $35, nonmembers from $39. Linen $2. Breakfast $4.50. Reception daily 7:30am-11pm. No curfew.

**Villager Lodge,** 1126 E. Elmira (222-9463 or 800-584-0800), about 3 blocks east of St. Mary's; 1mi. north of downtown; take bus #8. The caring management provides the cleanest rooms at this price. Cable TV, 5 free local calls, A/C, and Microfridges in some rooms. Small singles for $27, large singles or doubles $34. Key deposit $2.

**The Roosevelt Inn,** 2122 Roosevelt Ave. (533-2514), 2½mi. south of downtown near the missions; take bus #42 or 34. Reasonably clean rooms for great prices, free local calls. FDR didn't stay here, but he wasn't living on $50 a day. Singles $30; doubles $35.

**Alamo KOA,** 602 Gembler Rd. (224-9296 or 800-833-5267), 6mi. from downtown; take bus #24 ("Industrial Park") from the corner of Houston and Alamo downtown. From I-10 E., take exit 580/W.W. White Rd., drive 2 blocks north, then take a left onto Gembler Rd. Beautiful, well-kept grounds with lots of shade. Each site has a grill and patio. Showers, laundry facilities, pool, and free movies. Tent sites $15, full RV hookup $22; $2 per additional person. Open daily 7:30am-10pm.

TEXAS

San Pedro Park

Dewey Place

San Antonio College

TO **A**

Josephine St.

Grayson St.

**B**

Park Ave.

N. St. Mary's St.

Pan Am Expwy.

← METROPOLITAN TRANSIT

Jackson St.

Maverick St.

Crockett Park

Cypress St.

Howard St.

**Metroplitan Methodist Hospital**

Euclid Ave.

E. Elmira St.

81

Camden St.

W. Jones Ave.

**San Antonio Museum of Art**

Warren St.

San Pedro Ave.

Jackson St.

Brooklyn Ave.

McCullough Ave.

Baltimore Ave.

Lexington Ave.

E. Jones Ave.

W. Elmira St.

81

Main Ave.

Madison Square Park

Navarro St.

N. St. Mary's St.

9th St.

87

San Pedro Creek

Flores St.

Soledad St.

Broadway

McCullough Ave.

N. Alamo St.

Avenue E

SOUTHERN PACIFIC RR (AMTRAK)

Columbus Park

W. Martin St.

W. Martin St.

**Municipal Auditorium**

4th St.

Bonahm St.

Santa Rosa Medical Center

W. Martin St.

**Bill Miller's BBQ**

N. St. Mary's St.

Pecan St.

81

**Alamo Achievement Center**

W. Travis St.

35

87

W. Houston St.

**Bonham Exchange**

37

MARKET SQUARE

S. Santa Rosa St.

W. Commerce St.

College St.

Losoya St.

**Alamo**

E. Houston St.

PLAZA DE ARMAS

BIVERWALK

**Acapulco Sam's**

**Navarro House**

Flores St.

**Jim Cullum's Landing**

RIVERWALK

**Rivercenter Mall**

Bowie St.

**Cadillac Bar**

Main Ave.

Dwyer Ave.

Villita St.

W. Market St.

E. Commerce St.

San Antonio River

**C**

E. Market St.

Southern Pacific Depot (AMTRAK)

**La Villita Park**

Nueva St.

**Convention Center**

HEMISFAIR PLAZA

S. Alamo St.

Bowie St.

King William Park

Durango Blvd.

**Tower of the Americas**

**Alamo Dome**

S. St. Mary's St. (Roosevelt St.)

Presa St.

S. St. Mary's St.

# Downtown San Antonio

ACCOMMODATIONS

**A** Bullis House Inn
**B** Village Lodge
**C** Navarro

N

0      500 yards

0      500 meters

##  FOOD

Expensive cafes and restaurants line the **River Walk**—breakfast alone can clean you out if you don't settle for a muffin and coffee. North of town, Asian restaurants open onto **Broadway** across from Brackenridge. On weekends, hundreds of carnival food booths crowd the walkways of **Market Sq.** Come late in the day when prices drop and vendors are willing to haggle. (207-8600. Open daily 10am-8pm; Sept.-May 10am-6pm.) **Pig Stand** diners offer decent but cheap grub all over this part of Texas; the branches at 801 S. Presa, off of S. Alamo, and 1508 Broadway (both near downtown), stay open 24hr. **Taco Cabana** makes the best Mexican fast food in the area, with many locations across downtown. All locations, including the one at 2908 N. Broadway (8294-1616), serve breakfast, lunch, and late-night dinner. The omnipresent **Bill Miller's BBQ**, one location at 501 N. Saint Mary's St., at Pecan St., dishes out serious BBQ (212-4343; open M-F 10am-6pm).

 **Rosario's,** 910 S. Alamo St. (223-1806), at S. Saint Mary's St., is widely acknowledged by locals to be the best eatery in town. Scrumptious chicken quesadillas for only $4 uphold the reputation. Live music F-Sa nights. Open M 10:45am-3pm, Tu-Th 10:45am-10pm, F-Sa 10:45am-12:30am.

**Mi Tierra,** 218 Produce Row (225-1262), in Market Sq. Perpetually smiling mariachi musicians serenade patrons who also smile after filling up on chicken enchiladas slathered in chocolate-based mole sauce ($7.25). Lunch specials $7. Grab desert on the run from their bakery. Open 24hr.

**Josephine St. Steaks/Whiskey,** 400 Josephine St. (224-6169), at McAllister. Josephine's specializes in thick Texan steaks, but offers an assortment of big, yummy dishes in a relaxed cafe atmosphere. Entrees $5-12, lunch specials $5-7. Open M-Th 11am-10pm, F-Sa 11am-11pm.

**Zuppa's,** 255 E. Basse Rd. (824-3095), at the back of the Alamo Shopping Complex off of the E. Basse Rd. exit from 281, a few mi. north of downtown. For a break from BBQ, have all-you-can-eat salad, pasta, and soup for $6.50-8.50. Zuppa's makes up for vitamin and nutrient deficiencies with healthy, fat-free ingredients. Open M-F 11am-9pm, F-Sa 11am-10pm.

**Earl Abel's,** 4220 Broadway (822-3358). A professional organist for silent movies, Mr. Abel found himself out of work once the "talkies" hit the silver screen. When he opened his restaurant in 1933, the stars came to him; his diner took off after Duncan Hines ate here and raved. Abel's family still runs the operation. Fried chicken, Old Earl's specialty, for $5-7. Bacon, eggs, hash browns, and toast served with friendly smiles $4.75. Dinner $5-10. Open daily 6:30am-1am. Breakfast served all day.

**Hung Fong Chinese and American Restaurant,** 3624 Broadway (822-9211), at Queen Anne 2mi. north of downtown; take bus #14 or 9. The oldest Chinese restaurant in San Antonio, Hung is consistently good and crowded. Big portions $5-7. Open M-Th 11am-10pm, F 11am-11pm, Sa 11:30am-11pm, Su 11:30am-10pm.

## SIGHTS

Much of historic San Antonio lies in the present-day downtown and surrounding areas. The city may seem diffuse, but almost every major site or park is within a few mi. of downtown and is accessible by public transportation.

**THE MISSIONS.** The five missions along the river once formed the soul of San Antonio; the city preserves their remains in the **San Antonio Missions National Historical Park.** To reach the missions, follow the brown and white **"Mission Trail"** signs beginning on S. Saint Mary's St. downtown. Bus #42 stops within walking distance of Mission Concepción and right in front of Mission San José. *(All missions free and open daily 9am-5pm. For info, call 534-8833, or visit the park headquarters at Mission San José.)* **Mission San José,** off Roosevelt Ave. The "Queen of the Missions" (1720) has remnants of its own irrigation system, a gorgeous sculpted rose window, and numerous restored buildings. The largest of San Antonio's missions, it best conveys the self-sufficiency of these institutions. *(6701 San José Dr. 932-1001. 4 Catholic services* *held each Su 7:45, 9, 10:30am, and a noon "Mariachi Mass.")* **Mission Concepción,** 4mi. south of the Alamo off of E. Mitchell St., is the oldest unrestored stone church in North America (1731). Traces of the once-colorful frescoes are still visible. *(807 Mission Rd. 534-1540.)* **Mission San Juan Capistrano,** at Ashley, and **Mission San Francisco de la Espada,** both off of Roosevelt Ave., 10mi. south of downtown as the Texas swallow flies. Smaller and simpler than the others, these 2 missions evoke the isolation of such outposts. Between them lies the Espada Aqueduct, the only remaining waterway built by the Spanish. *(San Juan: 9101 Graf St. 534-0749. San Francisco: 10040 Espada Rd. 627-2021.)*

**DON'T FORGET THE ALAMO!** "Be silent, friend, here heroes died to blaze a trail for other men." **The Alamo,** at the center of Alamo Plaza near Houston and Alamo St., which has always been set apart from the other missions, is not maintained by the National Historical Park but by the **Daughters of the Republic of Texas**—oh, brother! *(225-1391. Open M-Sa 9am-5:30pm, Su 10am-6:30pm. Free.)* If the core of Texas pride were stored in a strongbox, it would be deposited here. Disobeying orders to retreat with their cannons, the 189 defenders of the Alamo, outnumbered 20 to one, held off the Mexican army for 12 days. Then, on the morning of the 13th day, the Mexicans commenced the infamous *deguello* (throat-cutting). The only survivors of the Alamo defenders were women, children, and slaves. Forty-six days later, General Sam Houston's small army defeated the Mexicans at **San Jacinto** amid cries of **"Remember the Alamo!"** These days, phalanxes of tourists attack the Alamo, and Sno-cone vendors are the only defenders.

**SECULAR SAN ANTONE: DOWNTOWN.** Southwest of the Alamo, black signs indicate access points to the 2½mi. **Paseo del Río (River Walk),** a series of well-patrolled shaded stone pathways which follow a winding canal built by the Works Progress Administration in the 1930s. Lined with picturesque gardens, shops, and cafes, and connecting most of the major downtown sights, the River Walk is the hub of San Antonio's nightlife. A few blocks south, the recreated artisans' village, **La Villita,** 418 Villita, houses restaurants, craft shops, and art studios *(207-8610. Shops open daily 10am-6pm, restaurant hrs. vary.)* On weekends, **Market Sq.,** between San Saba and Santa Rosa St., features the upbeat tunes of Tejano bands, the omnipresent buzzing of frozen margarita machines, and jangling wind chimes. *(207-8600. Open daily 10am-8pm; Sept.-May 10am-6pm.)* The **Mexican Cultural Institute** highlights the most influential ethnic presence in the city, and quite possibly in the state. *(600 HemisFair Park. 227-0123. Open M-F 10am-5pm, Sa-Su 11am-5pm. Free.)*

The site of the 1968 World's Fair, **HemisFair Plaza,** on S. Alamo, draws tourists with nearby restaurants, museums, and historic houses. The observation deck of the **Tower of the Americas** rises 750 ft. above the dusty plains; the view is best at night. *(600 HemisFair Park. 207-8615. Open Su-Th 9am-10pm, F-Sa 9am-11pm; $3, seniors $2, ages 4-11 $1.)* Plaza museums include the **Institute of Texan Cultures,** at Durango, which celebrates the many ethnicities which contributed to the culture of the state. *(801 S. Bowie. 458-2300. Open Tu-Su 9am-5pm; $4, seniors and children $2.)*

Directly behind City Hall, between Commerce and Dolorosa St. at Laredo, the adobe-walled **Spanish Governor's Palace,** completed in 1749, revives Spanish Colonial-style architecture with restored rooms and an enclosed garden. *(105 Plaza de Armas. 224-0601. Open M-Sa 9am-5pm, Su 10am-5pm; $1, ages 7-14 50¢.)* Home to the **San Antonio Spurs,** the **Alamodome,** at Hoefgen St., resembles a Mississippi riverboat. Take bus #24 or 26. *(100 Montana. 207-3600. Tours Tu-Sa 11am and 1pm, except during scheduled events. $3, seniors and ages 4-12 $1.50.)*

**AND BEYOND...** The truly adventurous will break beyond the confines of the Alamo and Riverwalk and make their way to the city's fringes. **Brackenridge Park,** 5mi. north of the Alamo, is an escape from the urban congestion; from downtown, take bus #7 or 8. The 343-acre show ground includes playgrounds, stables, a miniature train, and an aerial tramway ($2.25, ages 1-11 $1.75) that glides to a sunken Japanese garden. *(3910 N. Saint Mary's St. 736-9534. Open M-F 10am-5:15pm, Sa-Su 10am-*

## HOW MANY WORDS CAN YOU MAKE FROM "SCHLITTERBAHN?"

The entire local economy of New Braunfels depends upon the innertube. Almost 2 million visitors per year come to this town, hoping only to spend a day floating along the waters of the spring-fed **Comal River.** **Rockin' "R" River Rides** will send you off with a life jacket and a trusty tube and pick you up downstream 2½hr. later. *(193 S. Liberty. 830-620-6262. Open May-Sept. daily 9am-7pm. Tube rentals $9, $7 for bottomless floats. Car keys, proper ID, or $25 deposit required during rental.)* If the Comal don't float your boat, head for the chlorinated waters of **Schlitterbahn,** a 65-acre extravaganza of a waterpark with 17 water slides, 9 tube chutes, and 5 giant hot tubs. The park has recently built the planet's only uphill watercoaster, the Master Blaster. To find both attractions, take I-35 N to exit 189, turn left, and follow the signs for Schlitterbahn. *(400 N. Liberty. 830-625-2351. Open May-Sept. Call for hrs., generally around 10am-8pm. Full-day passes $24, ages 3-11 $14.)*

6pm.) Directly across the street, the **San Antonio Zoo,** one of the country's largest, houses over 3500 animals from 800 species in reproductions of their natural settings, including an extensive African mammal exhibit. *(3903 N. Saint Mary's St. 734-0437. Open daily 9am-8pm; $7, seniors and ages 3-11 $5.)*

The phallic, 140-million-year-old rock formations of **Natural Bridge Caverns** change continuously; they are different every millennia. Take I-35 N to exit 175 and follow the signs. *(26495 Natural Bridge Caverns Rd. 651-6101. Open daily 9am-6pm; off-season 9am-4pm. $9, ages 4-12 $6. 1¼hr. tours every 30min.)*

If you're itching for the trigger, **A Place to Shoot** is—well, just that. Take Moursund Rd., which is exit 46 off I-410 S. This 22-acre shooting facility offers four types of shotgun ranges: skeet, trap, crazy quail, and country doubles. *(13250 Pleasanton Rd. 628-1888. Open M-F 10am-7pm, Sa-Su 9am-7pm; $6 per person. 50¢ earplug rental.)* If you're in the mood to see more cowboy paraphernalia, **Pioneer Hall** contains a splendid collection of artifacts, documents, portraits, and possessions of the rangers, trail drivers, and pioneers who helped settle Texas. *(3805 Broadway. 822-9011. Open daily 10am-5pm; Sept.-Apr. 11am-4pm; $2, seniors $1.50, ages 6-12 50¢.)*

The **San Antonio Museum of Art,** just north of the city center, showcases an extensive collection of Latin American folk art, as well as Texan furniture and pre-Colombian, Native American, and Mexican folk art. *(200 W. Jones Ave. 978-8100. Open Tu 10am-9pm, W-Sa 10am-5pm, and Su noon-5pm. $4, college students with ID and seniors $2, ages 4-11 $1.75; free Tu 3-9pm. Free parking.)* The **McNay Art Museum** has an excellent collection of post-Impressionist European art. Take bus #11. *(6000 N. New Braunfels. 824-5368. Open Tu-Sa 10am-5pm, Su noon-5pm. Free.)*

## ENTERTAINMENT AND NIGHTLIFE

From Apr. 22-30, 2000, **Fiesta San Antonio** will usher in spring with concerts, parades, and plenty of Tex-Mex celebrations to commemorate the victory at San Jacinto and to pay homage to the heroes of the Alamo (227-5191). For excitement after dark any time, any season, stroll down the River Walk. *The Friday Express* or weekly *Current* (available at the tourist office) will guide you to concerts and entertainment. For authentic **Tejano music,** a Mexican and country amalgam, head to **Cadillac Bar,** 212 S. Flores, where a different band whips the huge crowd (anywhere from 500-1000 people) into a cheering and dancing frenzy every weeknight (223-5533; 21+; open M-Sa 11am-2am). Right around the corner from the Alamo, the **Bonham Exchange,** 411 Bonham, San Antonio's biggest gay dance club, plays high-energy music with some house and techno on the side. A younger, more mixed crowd files in on Wednesdays. (271-3811. Cover for 21+ $3-5, for 18-20 up to $10. Open M-Th 4pm-2am, F 4pm-3am, Sa 8pm-3am.) Some of the best traditional jazz anywhere taps at **Jim Cullum's Landing,** 123 Losoya, in the Hyatt downtown. The legendary Cullum plays with his jazz band M-Sa 8:30pm-1am. The improv jazz quintet Small World performs on Su nights. (223-7266. All ages. Cover $6.50. Open M-Th 4:30pm-12:30am, F 4:30pm-1:30am, Sa noon-1:30am, Su noon-midnight.) Along the River Walk, **Polly Esther's** and **The Culture Club,** 212 College St., pump up the crowd with 70s disco on the 2nd floor and 80s retro on the 3rd floor (21+; cover $3-7; open Su-W 8pm-2am, Th 8pm-3am, F-Sa 8pm-4am).

## NEAR SAN ANTONIO: FREDERICKSBURG

Much of small town Texas has faded with falling oil and cattle prices, but Fredricksburg maintains the aura of the Texas hill country village. By preserving and restoring itself, Fredricksburg has become a rare relic, a place to which city-folk can escape to the "country." With more than 500 motel rooms and a Main St. lined with touristy shops, the small population here has discovered and exploited a resource whose value is ever increasing: tourism.

Both U.S. 87 and U.S. 290 climb and fall through peach orchards, vineyards, and pecan farms. Roadside vendors sell samples from their gardens for small change in season. Locally grown delights can also be purchased in town. Look for a peach stand or stop by the Texas Wine Cellars Tasting Room at 217½ E. Main St. (830-997-0123; open M-Sa 10am-6pm, Su 12pm-6pm).

**German immigrants** founded Fredericksburg in 1846. *Biergartens* dot the main drag, and street names are subtitled in German. Oddly enough, many town attractions focus on World War II. The **Admiral Nimitz Museum,** 340 E. Main St., presents the story of the war in the Pacific from Pearl Harbor to the Atomic Bomb (830-997-4397; open daily 8am-5pm; $5, students $3). Signs beside the museum lead to the nearby **History Walk of the Pacific War,** 2 acres of vintage aircraft, tanks, and guns.

East of town 16mi. on U.S. 290, fields of wildflowers lead to the **Lyndon B. Johnson Ranch,** a State and National Park. Tours available. (210-664-2252. Park open daily 8am-5pm, tours depart 10am-4pm. $3.)

**Enchanted Rock State Natural Area,** 18mi. north of Fredericksburg on R.R. 965, provides the best place to hike or camp in the region. "E-Rock" is a stunning 500 ft. tall red granite batholith over one billion years old. The hike to the top and back takes 45min.; a longer loop trail surrounds the outcropping. Climbers are welcome. (915-247-3903 or 800-792-1112; for reservations 512-389-8900. $5 entrance fee, under 12 free. Tent sites with water and hookup $9; hike-in primitive sites $7.)

## CORPUS CHRISTI

Corpus Christi, named for the "body of Christ," draws its sustenance from the bodies of visitors that flock to its warm beaches year-round and from the body of the sea, from which offshore rigs bring in crude oil to be processed in local refineries. Motels and beaches are packed by vacationers in the summer season, only to be replaced in the cooler months by "winter Texans," many of them elderly mobile home owners fleeing the chill of the northern states. Corpus Christi is defined equally by its pricey knick-knacks and its cheap gas, its natural stretches of sand, and the encroaching waste that floats in from the gulf.

**🖪 PRACTICAL INFORMATION.** Corpus Christi's tourist district follows **Shoreline Drive,** which borders the Gulf Coast, 1mi. east of the downtown business district. **Greyhound,** 702 N. Chaparral (882-2516; open daily 8am-2:30am), at Starr downtown, travels to Dallas (9-10hr., 7 per day, $39); Houston (5hr., 9 per day, $21); and Austin (5-7.5hr., 4 per day, $25). **Regional Transit Authority (The "B")** (289-2600) buses within Corpus Christi; pick up maps and schedules at the visitors bureau or at **The B headquarters,** 1812 S. Alameda (883-2287; open M-F 8am-5pm). City Hall, Port Ayers, Six Points, and the Staples St. stations serve as central transfer points. (Runs M-Sa 5:30am-9:30pm, Su 11am-6:30pm. Fare 50¢, at peak times 10¢; students, seniors, children, and disabled 25¢; Sa 25¢, transfers free.) The **Harbor Ferry** follows the shoreline and stops at the aquarium (10:30am-6:30pm daily, $1 each way). On the north side of Harbor Bridge, the free **Beach Shuttle** also travels to the beach, the Aquarium, and other nearby attractions (runs May-Sept. 10:30am-6:30pm). **Yellow Cab** (884-3211) charges $3 for the first mi., $1.50 per additional mi.

**Convention and Visitors Bureau,** 1823 Chaparral (561-2000 or 800-678-6232), 6 blocks north of I-37 and 1 block from the water (open M-F 8:30am-5pm, Sa 9am-3pm). **Medical Care: Spohn Hospital Shoreline,** 600 Elizabeth St. (881-3000). **Hotlines: Hope Line** (855-4673); **Battered Women and Rape Victims Shelter:** (881-8888; both open 24hr.). **Post Office:** 809 Nueces Bay Blvd. (800-275-8777; open M-F 7:30am-5:30pm, Sa 8am-1pm). **ZIP code:** 78469. **Area code:** 512.

**■■■ ACCOMMODATIONS, FOOD, AND NIGHTLIFE.** Cheap accommodations are scarce downtown, and posh hotels and motels take up much of the scenic shoreline. Fear not however, hostelers can head to the newly opened beachfront **Smuggler's Island Hostel and Retreat Center,** 2900 N. Shorline Dr., next to the USS Lexington. With bay-view decks, a court-yard, beach volleyball courts, and kayak rentals ($15), Smuggler's Island offers all the glories, without the expense. (882-3888. Open 8-11am, 5-10pm. Single sex 6 person dorms $15 per person; private rooms $35 for 2, $10 per additional person, ages 6-11 $5. Key and linen deposit $10.) The best motel bargains lie several mi. south on Leopard St. (take bus #27) or I-37 (take #27 Express). The **Super 8** is at 910 Corn Products Rd. (289-1216; singles $33; doubles $38). Campers should head for the **Mustang State Park** or the **Padre Island National Seashore** (see below). Nueces River **City Park,** off I-37 N from exit 16, has free tent sites, but only pit toilets and no showers (241-1464).

The mixed population and seaside locale of Corpus Christi have resulted in a wide range of cuisines. Non-chain restaurants can be found on the "south side" of the city, around Staples St. and S. Padre Island Dr. **BJ's,** 6335 S. Padre Island Dr., serves cheese-laden, crispy-crusted pizzas while patrons shoot pool and drink 300 varieties of beer (992-6671; open M-Sa 11am-10:30pm, Su noon-8:30pm). Next to the USS Lexington, **Pier 99,** 2822 N. Shoreline Dr., serves up plenty of fried fresh fishies, such as shrimp or oyster baskets (887-0764. $6.25-6.50; open 11am-10pm daily). The city shuts down early, but several clubs manage to survive on Chaparral. **Tom, Dick, and Harry's,** 301 N. Chaparral St. provides three clubs under one cover. **Tom Foolery's** is a spacious bar with rock music and plenty of video screens, complimented by the adjacent **Dead Eye Dick's Saloon** and **Harry's Piano Bar** (887-0029; open M-Sa 11am-2am, Su 5pm-2am; cover F-Sa $5, Su $3, 18-21 $5 everyday.)

**⬛ SIGHTS.** Corpus Christi's most significant sight is the shoreline, bordered by miles of rocky seawall and wide sidewalks with graduated steps down to the water. Overpriced seaside restaurants, sail and shrimp boats, and aggressive, hungry seagulls overrun the piers. To find beaches that allow swimming (some lie along Ocean Dr. and north of Harbor Bridge), just follow the signs, or call **Nueces County Parks** for directions. *(949-7023.)* On the north side of Harbor Bridge, the **Texas State Aquarium** showcases creatures from the Gulf of Mexico. *(2710 N. Shoreline Blvd. 881-1200 or 800-477-4853. Open M-Sa 9am-6pm, Su 10am-6pm; early Sept. to late May closes at 5pm. $8, seniors and ages 12-17 $6.75, ages 4-11 $4.50.)*

Just offshore floats the aircraft carrier **USS Lexington,** a World War II relic now open to the public. In her day, the "Blue Ghost" set more records than any carrier in the history of naval aviation. Be sure to check out the crews' quarters—you won't complain about small hostel rooms ever again. *(888-4873 or 800-523-9539. Open daily 9am-6pm; early Sept. to late May 9am-5pm. $9, seniors $7, ages 4-12 $4.)* Built by the government of Spain in 1992, the **Columbus Fleet** commemorates the 500th anniversary of Columbus's historic voyage with replicas of the *Niña,* the *Pinta,* and the *Santa María. (1900 N. Chaparral St., 883-2863, near the Harbor Bridge.)*

# PADRE ISLAND

With over 80mi. of painstakingly preserved beaches, dunes, and wildlife refuge land, the **Padre Island National Seashore (PINS)** is a priceless, though debris-flawed gem sandwiched between the condos of North Padre Island and the spring break hordes of South Padre Island. The seashore provides excellent opportunities for **windsurfing, swimming,** or **surf fishing.** Garbage from nearby ships frequently litters the sands, but a lucky few may spot one of the endangered Kemp's Ridley sea turtles which PINS nutures. A weekly pass into PINS costs $10 for cars, $5 for hikers and bikers. Windsurfing or launching a boat from the Bird Basin will dock you an extra $5. Many beachcombers avoid these hefty fees by going to the free **North Beach**. Five mi.south of the entrance station, **Malaquite Beach** makes your day on the sand as easy as possible with restrooms and rental picnic tables. In summer, the rental station is set up on the beachfront (inner tubes $2 per hr., chairs $1 per hr., body boards $2.50 per hr.). The **Malaquite Visitors Center** (949-8068), has free maps and exhibits about the island (open daily 9am-5pm, Sept.-May 9am-4pm). Motorists enter the PINS via the JFK Causeway, from the Flour Bluff area of Corpus Christi. PINS is difficult to reach via Corpus Christi's public bus system.

Visitors with four-wheel-drive and a taste for solitude should make the 60mi. trek to the **Mansfield Cut,** the most remote and untraveled area of the seashore; loose sands prevent most vehicles from venturing far onto the beach. If you decide to go, tell the folks at the **Malaquite Ranger Station** (949-8173), 3½mi. south of the park entrance; they handle emergency assistance and like to know who's out there. No wheels? Hike the **Grasslands Nature Trail**, a ¾mi. loop through sand dunes and grasslands. Guide pamphlets are available at the trailhead.

Camping on the beach at PINS means falling asleep to the crashing of waves on the sand; if you're not careful, morning may mean waking up to the slurping noise of thousands of mosquitoes sucking you dry—bring insect repellent. Rangers also suggest strong sunscreen, protective clothing, and meat tenderizer for jellyfish stings. The **PINS Campground,** less than 1mi. north of the visitors center, consists of an asphalt area for RVs, restrooms, and cold-rinse showers—no soap is permitted on PINS (sites $8). Outside of this area—excluding the 5mi. pedestrians only beach—wherever vehicles can go, camping is free.

For camping with amenities, the **Padre Balli County Park,** on Park Rd. 22, 3½mi. from the JFK Causeway, near the national seashore, provides running water, electricity, laundry, and hot showers for campers. (949-8121. Sites with water and hookup $15; key deposit $5. 3-day max.reservation, 14-day max. stay.) Or try the **Mustang State Park Campground,** 6mi. up S.H. 361. (749-5246. Running water, dump stations, restrooms, hot showers, and picnic tables. Entry fee $3 per person. Beach sites $7, with water and electricity $12. RVs must reserve ahead. All must pick up a camping permit from the ranger station at the park entrance.) **Area code:** 361.

# WESTERN TEXAS

On the far side of the Río Pecos lies a region whose stereotypical Texan character verges on self-parody. This is the stomping ground of Pecos Bill—the mythical cowpoke who was raised by coyotes and lassoed a tornado. The land was colonized in the days of the Republic of Texas, during an era when the "law west of the Pecos" meant a rough mix of vigilante violence and frontier gunslinger machismo. The border city of El Paso and its Chihuahuan neighbor, Ciudad Juárez, beckon way, *wayyyy* out west—700mi. from the Louisiana border—while Big Bend National Park dips down into the desert, cradled by a curve in the Río Grande.

## AMARILLO

Named for the yellow clay of a nearby lake (*amarillo* is yellow in Spanish), Amarillo opened for business as a railroad construction camp in 1887 and, within a decade, became the nation's largest cattle-shipping market. For years, the economy depended largely on the meat industry, but the discovery of oil gave Amarillo a kick in the 1920s. More recently, the city has been boosted by a surge in tourism. Amarillo is the prime overnight stop for motorists en route from Dallas, Houston, or Oklahoma City to Sante Fe, Denver, and points west. It's a one-day city—there isn't much to do on the Texas plains—but a grand, shiny truck stop it is.

> **BIG TEXAN WOMEN** The 72 oz. steak on display at the big, leathery, tourist-trap of a beef joint, the **Inn of the Big Texan**, at Lakeside exit 75 from I-40, makes you feel full before even taking a bite. Anyone who eats the steak in 1hr. gets it free; the defeated pay $50. Over 25,000 have tried to consume the beast; the names, weights (before), and home cities of some of the 5000+ success stories are listed under the glass-top bar. A third of the women have been victorious, compared to only a fifth of the men. (372-6000 or 800-657-7177. Open daily 10:30am-10:30pm.)

**◤ PRACTICAL INFORMATION.** Amarillo sprawls at the intersection of I-27, I-40, and U.S. 287/87; you'll need a car to explore. Rt. 335 (the Loop) encircles the city. Amarillo Blvd. (historic Rt. 66) runs east-west, parallel to I-40. **Greyhound,** 700 S. Tyler (374-5371; station open 24hr.), buses to Dallas (7-8hr., 5 per day, $50) and Santa Fe (6-10hr., 4 per day, $56). **Amarillo City Transit,** 801 SE 23rd (378-3094), operates eight bus routes departing from 5th and Pierce St. (buses run every 30min. M-Sa 6am-6pm; fare 75¢; maps at office). Ride like a king with **Royal Cab Co.** (376-4276. $1.30 base fare, $1 per mi. Some drivers charge 50¢ per extra person.) The **Texas Travel Info Center,** 9400 I-40E (335-1441), at exit 76, dispenses state info (open daily 8am-5pm). **Amarillo Convention and Visitors Bureau:** 1000 S. Polk (374-1497 or 800-692-1338), at 10th St. (open M-F 8am-5pm). **Internet access:** Central Library, 413 E. 4th St. (378-3054), at Buchanan (open M-Th 9am-9pm, F-Sa 9am-6pm, Su 2-6pm). **Post Office:** 505 E. 9th Ave. (800-275-8777), in Downtown Station at Buchanan St. (open M-F 7:30am-5pm). **ZIP code:** 79105. **Area code:** 806.

**▛▟ ACCOMMODATIONS AND FOOD.** There are cheap motels on the outskirts of town on I-40; prices rise near the downtown area. **Camelot Inn,** 2508 I-40 E, at exit 72A—a pink, castle-like motel with palatial rooms, a princely staff, shiny wood furniture, cable, and free morning grog—ranks among the best of the I-40 offerings (373-3600; singles $24-26; doubles $35-40; varies seasonally; 21+). **Coachlight Inn** has two locations along I-40, 2115 I-40 (Ross exit 71; 376-5811), and 6810 I-40 (Whitaker exit 74; 373-6871). Some rooms have new bathtubs and refrigerators. (Singles $28; doubles $28; queens $35; off-season $22/$25/$30. $2 key deposit.) Kampers kommune with nature at the **KOA Kampground,** 1100 Folsom Rd., 6mi. east of downtown; take I-40 to exit 75, head north mi. to Rt. 60, then east 1mi. (335-1792. Pool, laundry, basketball court, free coffee, and shady sites. $17, full hookup $22. Open daily 7:30am-10pm; early Sept. to late May 8am-8pm.)

Dine amid plants, fountains, and Mexican murals at **Abuelo's,** 3501 45th St. The *cena mexicana* ($10) is best suited for two. (354-8294. Open Su-Th 11am-10pm, F-Sa 11am-11pm.) **OHMS,** 619 S. Taylor St., downtown, serves an assortment of ready-made dishes such as fettuccine and enchiladas with salad and bread ($6; open M-F 11:30am-1:30pm, F-Sa 6:30-9pm).

**▣◩ SIGHTS AND ENTERTAINMENT.** The outstanding **Panhandle-Plains Historical Museum,** 2401 4th Ave., in nearby Canyon (I-27 S to Rt. 87), has fossils, an old drilling rig, local history and geology exhibits, and a fine collection of Southwestern art. (651-2244. Open M-Sa 9am-5pm, Su 1-6pm; in summer daily until 6pm. $4, seniors $3, ages 4-12 $1.) The **Amarillo Zoo,** off the 24th St. Exit from U.S. 287, in Thompson Park, has 20 acres of open prairie laden with bison, roadrunners, and other Texas fauna (381-7911; open Tu-Su 9:30am-5:30pm; free). Explore horse racing's cowboy origins and all things equine at the **American Quarter Horse Heritage Center and Museum,** 2601 I-40 E, at exit 72A. (376-5181. Open M-Sa 9am-5pm, Su noon-5pm; Sept.-May Tu-Sa 10am-5pm. $4, over 54 $3.50, ages 6-18 $2.50.) At **Cadillac Ranch,** Stanley Marsh III has planted 10 gleaming Cadillacs at the same angle as Cheops pyramids. Get off I-40 at the Hope Rd. exit, 9mi. west of Amarillo, cross to the south side of I-40, and drive ½mi. down the highway access road.

## PALO DURO CANYON STATE PARK

Known as the "Grand Canyon of Texas," Palo Duro covers 16,000 acres of jaw-dropping beauty. The canyon—1000 ft. from rim to rugged floor—exposes red, yellow, and brown cliffs. The park is 23mi. south of Amarillo. Take I-27 to exit 106 and head east on Rt. 217; from the south, get off I-27 at exit 103. (Park open daily 7am-10pm; in winter 8am-10pm. $3, under 12 free.) The park **headquarters** (806-488-2227), just inside the park, has maps of hiking trails and info on park activities (open daily 8am-5pm, in summer 7am-10pm). A half mile past HQ, the **visitors center** displays exhibits on the canyon's history (open M-Sa 9am-5pm, Su 1-5pm).

The beautiful 16mi. **scenic drive** through the park, beginning at HQ, provides many photo opportunities. To experience the canyon from the saddle, **Old West Stables** (806-488-2180), about 1½mi. into the park on the scenic drive, rents horses with a saddle and riding hat. ($15 per hr., wagon rides $8. Open 8:30am-dusk. Reservations required.) The **Chuckwagon Goodnight Trading Post**, ½mi. further, has a restaurant (sandwich $3) and a small selection of groceries (806-488-2760; open daily 8:30am-10pm). Rangers encourage backcountry hiking; marked trails are also an option. Most hikers (even children) can manage the 5mi. **Lighthouse Trail**, but only experienced hikers should consider the rugged 9mi. **Running Trail**. Temperatures in the canyon frequently climb to 100°F; bring at least 2 quarts of water. **Backcountry camping** (512-389-8900 for reservations) is allowed in designated areas (primitive sites $9, with water $10, with hookup $12; cabins $65).

## GUADALUPE MOUNTAINS

The Guadalupe Mountains rise out of the vast Texas desert to unexpected heights. Mescalero Apaches hunted and camped on these lands, until they were driven out by the U.S. army. Before being forced out, Apache chief Geronimo claimed that the greatest gold mines in the world were hidden in the peaks; happy prospectin'—the legendary mines remain undiscovered. Few settlers bought the prophecy; by the late 1800s, only a few ranchers and guano miners inhabited the rugged region. Today, **Guadalupe Mountains National Park** encompasses 86,000 acres of desert, caves, canyons, and highlands. Drivers can glimpse the park's most dramatic sights from U.S. 62/180: **El Capitán**, a 2000 ft. limestone cliff, and **Guadalupe Peak**, the highest point in Texas (8749 ft.). The mountains promise over 70mi. of challenging desert hikes to those willing to explore the area. Entrance to the park is free. **Carlsbad, NM** (see p. 753), 55mi. northeast, makes a good base town, with many cheap motels, campgrounds, and restaurants.

The major trails begin at the Pine Canyon Campground, near the Headquarters (see below). Imposing Guadalupe Peak can be scaled in a difficult but rewarding full-day hike (8½mi.). Another full-day trail leads from the campground to **The Basin**, a high-country forest of Douglas fir and Ponderosa pine. A shorter trek (2-3hr.) traces the canyon floor of **Devil's Hall**—tread softly, and you may see deer along the trail. The 2½mi., 1½hr. **Spring Trail** leads from the **Frijole Ranch**, about 1mi. north of the visitors center, to a mountain spring. An easy 2-3hr. trail leading to the historic **Pratt Cabin** in the McKittrick Canyon (a major attraction in itself) begins at the **McKittrick Visitors Center**, several mi.northeast of the main visitors center off U.S. 62/180. Some trails are marked more clearly than others; take a map.

The park's lack of development is attractive to backpackers, but it creates some inconveniences. *Gas and food are not available in the park—stock up before you arrive.* The park's two simple campgrounds, **Pine Springs** (828-3251), just past park headquarters, and **Dog Canyon** (828-3251, ranger station 505-981-2418), south of the New Mexico border at the north end of the park, have water and restrooms but no hookups or showers (sites $7; reservations for groups only). Dog Canyon is accessible only via Rt. 137 from Carlsbad, NM (72mi.), or by a full-day hike from the **Visitor Center and Park Headquarters,** off U.S. 62/180. (828-3251. Open daily June-Aug. 8am-6pm; Sept.-May 8am-4:30pm. After hours, info is posted on the bulletin board outside.) Free **backcountry camping** permits are at the visitors center.

TEXAS

Guadalupe Park lies 120mi. east of El Paso. For additional info, contact the visitors center or write to **Guadalupe Mountains National Park,** HC 60, Box 400, Salt Flat 79847. **TNM&O Coaches** (505-887-1108) runs along U.S. 62/180 between Carlsbad, NM and El Paso, making a flag stop in the Guadalupe Mountains National Park at the Headquarters Visitors Center (Carlsbad to Guadalupe Mountains $26, 2½hr.). **Area code:** 915. The park falls in the **mountain time zone** (2hr. behind Eastern).

# EL PASO

The largest of the U.S. border towns, El Paso (pop. 700,000) boomed in the 17th century as a passageway on an important east-west wagon route that followed the Río Grande through "the pass" (*el paso*) between the Rockies and the Sierra Madres. Modern El Paso serves as a stop-over between the U.S. and Mexico. Influenced by Mexican culture as much as American, the town gives those crossing over a glimpse of what awaits them. After dark, central El Paso becomes a ghost town: most activity leaves the center and heads to the University of Texas at El Paso (UTEP) or south of the border to El Paso's raucous sister city, Ciudad Juárez.

**⚑ PRACTICAL INFORMATION.** San Jacinto Plaza is the heart of El Paso. **I-10** runs east-west and **U.S. 54** north-south to the city. El Paso is divided into east and west by **Santa Fe Ave.** and into north and south by **San Antonio Ave.** *Tourists should be wary of the streets between San Antonio and the border late at night.*

Sun Metro bus #33 runs 50min. to downtown from the **airport,** northeast of the city center. **Greyhound:** 200 W. San Antonio (532-2365; open 24hr.), across from the Civic Center between Santa Fe and Chihuahua. To Dallas (10hr., $76) and Sante Fe (7hr., $50). **Public Transit: Sun Metro** (533-3333), departs from San Jacinto Plaza, at Main and Oregon. ($1, students and children 50¢, seniors 30¢, transfer 10¢.) **Visitor Info:** 1 Civic Center Plaza (544-0062), a small building at Santa Fe and San Francisco. **Hospital: Providence Memorial Hospital,** 2001 N. Oregon (577-6011), at Hague near UTEP. Open 24hr. **Post office:** 219 E. Mills (532-2652), between Mesa and Stanton. Open M-F 9am-5pm, Sa 8am-noon. **ZIP code:** 79901. **Area code:** 915.

**⚐ ACCOMMODATIONS AND FOOD.** Apart from the usual hotel chains lining I-10, several great budget hotels cluster around the center of town near **Main St.** and **San Jacinto Square. ⬛ Gardner Hotel/Hostel (HI-AYH),** 311 E. Franklin, between Stanton and Kansas. From San Jacinto Plaza, walk 2 blocks north to Franklin, turn right, and head east 1½ blocks. The Gardner is an oasis in the gritty, desert environment of downtown El Paso. (532-3661. Hotel: cable TV and phone. Singles $20, $30 with bath; doubles and triples $33/45. Hostel: members/students $15, nonmembers $17.50. Shared bathrooms. Lockers 75¢. Linen $2. Laundry $1.50 per load. Reception 24hr.) **Budget Lodge Motel,** 1301 N. Mesa, at California across from Cathedral H.S., a 10min. walk from San Jacinto Square up Mesa St. Even though it is more removed from downtown, it is only 6 blocks from UTEP. Rooms have A/C, cable TV, and pool access. A small cafe on the 1st fl., serves cheap breakfast and lunch. (533-6821. Singles $25; $4 per additional person.)

El Paso has many mom-and-pop diners serving homemade Mexican and American dishes—burritos are everyone's specialty. Many places close early, so your options may be limited after 6pm on weekdays. **La Malinche,** at N. Stanton St. and Texas near San Jacinto Square serves Mexican fare in a brightly colored, cool environment. (544-8785. Burritos $1.75; breakfast and lunch menu $3.50-6. Open M-Sa 7:30am-4pm.) **Manolo's Café,** 122 S. Mesa, between Overland and San Antonio, has walls covered in bullfighter posters. Try the *menudo* ($2), burritos ($1), and the generous *comida corrida* ($3.75). Friendly service, free refills, and large portions make Manolo's popular. (532-7661. Open M-Sa 7am-5pm, Su 8am-3pm.)

**◎ ♫ SIGHTS AND ENTERTAINMENT.** For a whirlwind tour of the city and its southern neighbor, hop aboard the **Border Jumper Trolleys** that depart every hour from El Paso (see **tourist office** info, above). Historic **San Jacinto Plaza** swarms with

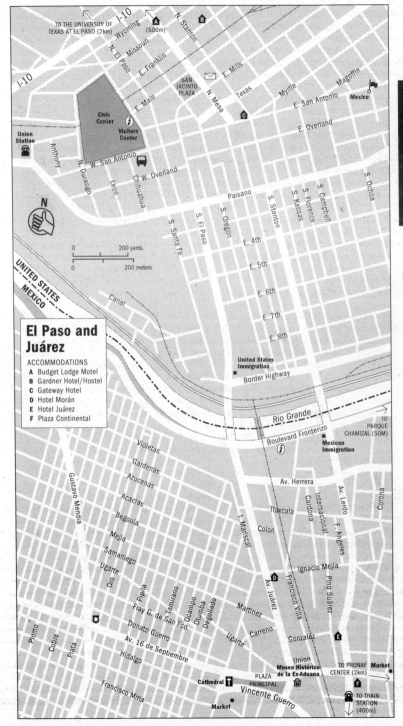

TEXAS

# El Paso and Juárez

## ACCOMMODATIONS
**A** Budget Lodge Motel
**B** Gardner Hotel/Hostel
**C** Gateway Hotel
**D** Hotel Morán
**E** Hotel Juárez
**F** Plaza Continental

daily activity. The plaza is the main bus stop for all San Metro buses, and lots of locals gather there to sit in the shade of some of El Paso's only trees. South of the square, **El Paso St.** is a market for all kinds of goods, from fruit to the latest fashions. To take in a complete picture of the Río Grande Valley, head northeast of downtown along Stanton and take a right on Rim Rd. (which becomes Scenic Dr.); **Murchinson Park,** at the base of the ridge, offers a view of El Paso, Juárez, and the Sierra Madres. The area around the Civic Center on Santa Fe Ave. contains a renowned **Americana Museum,** as well as the **El Paso Museum of Art.**

At night, **The Palace,** 209 S. El Paso St., pumps dance music to a packed house in a trendy, neon setting. (532-6000. 2nd fl. jazz lounge. 18+. $5 cover.) From Apr. to Sept., the **El Paso Diablos** create major league fun at minor league prices. Take Sun Metro bus #42 from San Jacinto Plaza as far north as it goes and walk the rest of the way to **Cohen Stadium,** 9700 Gateway. Ask the driver for directions. (755-2000. $3, box seats $4.75.) Plenty of hiking opportunities, like the **Mission Trail,** wait outside of town; the tourist office provides trail info.

## BIG BEND

Roadrunners, coyotes, wild pigs, mountain lions, and 350 species of birds make their home in Big Bend National Park, a 800,000-acre tract (around the size of Rhode Island) that is cradled by a helluva meander on the Río Grande. Spectacular canyons, vast stretches of the Chihuahuan Desert, and the Chisos Mountains occupy this literally and figuratively "far-out" spot. If you're in search of solitude, avoid the high season (Feb.-Apr.). During the summer, the predominantly desert park is excruciatingly hot, but you might have it all to yourself.

**7 PRACTICAL INFORMATION.** Big Bend is very geographically isolated. It is accessible only by car, via Rt. 118 or U.S. 385, both of which meet I-10. There are no gas stations or services of any kind on these roads; *fill your tank before leaving I-10.* **Park headquarters** (477-2251) is at **Panther Jct.,** about 26mi. inside the park. (Open daily 8am-5pm; vehicle pass $10 per week, pedestrians and bikers $5. National parks passports accepted.) For info, write the **Superintendent,** Big Bend National Park, P.O. Box 129, 79834. **Ranger stations** are located at Panther Jct., Río Grande Village, Persimmon Gap, and Chisos Basin. (Panther open daily 8am-6pm; Chisos open daily 8am-3:30pm; others closed May-Nov.) **Amtrak** stops in **Alpine,** 70mi. north of the park (4hr.; M, W, and Sa only; El Paso to Alpine, $43-64). From there, rent a car from **Air Flight Auto Rental,** 504 E. Holland St. (837-3463), inside the Western Auto and Radio Shack. ($25-32 per day, 10¢ per mi. Must be 18. $100 deposit required. Call for reservations.) **Groceries** and **gas** are available in Panther Jct., Río Grande Village, and Chisos Basin; Castalon has groceries, no gas. **Emergency:** 477-2251 until 5pm; afterwards, call 911. **Area code:** 915.

**⌂ ☐ ACCOMMODATIONS AND FOOD.** The expensive **Chisos Mountains Lodge,** 10mi. from park headquarters, offers the only motel-style shelter within the park (477-2291; singles $62; doubles $69; $10 per additional person). They also rent lodges equipped with showers and baths but no A/C (singles $58; doubles $67; $10 per additional person), and stone cottages with three double beds and bath (3 people $81; $10 per additional person). Reservations are a must for high season; the lodge is often booked a year in advance. The restaurant and coffee shop at the lodge serve basic diner food ($3-12; open daily 7am-8pm).

Designated campsites within the park are first come, first served. **Chisos Basin** and **Río Grande Village** offer sites with flush toilets ($7; cash only); the sites at Castalon have pit toilets. In summer, the sites in Chisos Basin are cool. During high season the campgrounds fill early. The RV park at Río Grande Village has 25 full-hookup sites ($14.50 for up to two people; $1 per additional person). The Río Grande Village Store has **public showers** (75¢). For free overnight backcountry camping obtain a free **backcountry permit** at the park headquarters.

Cheap motels lurk off U.S. 170 near the dusty towns of **Terlingua** and **Lajitas,** 21 and 28mi. respectively from park headquarters. Terlingua, named for the three languages spoken in the town in the late 1800s (English, Spanish, and a Native American dialect), lies on Rt. 170 just past Study Butte, about 35mi. from park headquarters, but only 7mi. from the park's western entrance; Lajitas is 7mi. farther down the road. The **Chisos Mining Co. Motel,** on Rt. 170 1mi. west of the junction of 170 and 118, provides clean, A/C rooms in an offbeat atmosphere (371-2430; singles without phone or TV $34; doubles $46, with phone and TV $51). Farther up Rt. 170 in **Terlingua Ghost Town,** the **Starlight Theater Bar and Grill** has with large portions of cheap Tex-Mex ($3-9) and free live music on weekends. (371-2326. Food served daily 6-10pm; bar open Su-F 5pm-midnight, Sa 5pm-1am. No credit cards.)

**N OUTDOOR ACTIVITIES.** Big Bend encompasses several hundred mi.of hiking trails, ranging from 30min. nature walks to backpacking trips several days long. *When hiking in the desert, always carry at least a gallon of water per person per day.* The 43mi. **scenic drive** to Santa Elena Canyon is handy for those short on time. Many of the park's roads can **flood** during the rainy summer.

Park rangers at the visitors centers are happy to suggest hikes and sights; the *Hiker's Guide to Big Bend* pamphlet ($1.25), available at Panther Jct., is a good investment. The **Lost Mine Trail,** a 3hr. hike up a peak in the Chisos, leads to an amazing summit-top view of the desert and the Sierra de Carmen in Mexico. A shorter walk (1.7mi.) ambles through the **Santa Elena Canyon** along the Río Grande—the canyon walls rise as high as 1000 ft. over the banks of the river.

Rafting is big fun on the Río Grande. Free permits and info are at all visitors center. Several companies offer **river trips** down the 133mi. of the Río Grande in the park. **Far-Flung Adventures,** next door to the Starlight Theater Bar and Grill in Terlingua, organizes 1- to 7-day trips. (800-359-4138. 1-day trip to Santa Elena around $110 per person if water flows permit; 1-day trip to Colorado Canyon $84.)

**TEXAS**

# ROCKY MOUNTAINS

Created by immense tectonic forces some 65 million years ago, the Rockies mark a vast wrinkle in the North American continent. Sculpted by wind, water, and glaciers over eons, their weathered peaks extend 3000mi. from northern Alberta to New Mexico and soar to altitudes exceeding two vertical miles. Cars overheat and humans gulp thin alpine air as they ascend into grizzly bear country. Dominated by rock and ice, the highest peaks of the Rockies are accessible only to veteran mountain climbers and wildlife adapted for survival in scant air and deep snow.

Although the whole of the Rocky Mountain area supports less than 5% of the U.S. population, every year millions flock to its spectacular national parks, forests, and ski resorts, while hikers follow the Continental Divide along the spine of the Rockies. Nestled in valleys or appearing out of nowhere on the surrounding plains, the region's mountain villages and cowboy towns welcome travelers year-round.

## HIGHLIGHTS OF THE ROCKY MOUNTAINS

■ **Hiking.** Memorable trails include the Gunnison Rt. in the Black Canyon, CO (p. 675); the hike to Monument Canyon at the Colorado National Monument (p. 670); and just about anything in the Grand Tetons (p. 640).

■ **Skiing.** The Rockies are filled with hotspots, but try Sawtooth, ID (p. 619); Vail, CO (p. 666); or Whitefish, MT (p. 630).

■ **Scenic Drives.** Going-to-the-Sun Rd. in Glacier National Park (p. 627) is truly unforgettable, as is Rte. 21 from Boise to Stanley, ID (p. 619). Catch Rte. 20 south from Thermopolis, WY (p. 650) for an eye-popping view of Wind River Canyon and the Wind River Indian Reservation.

■ **Alpine Towns.** Aspen, CO (p. 667) and Stanley, ID (p. 619): two of the loveliest.

# IDAHO

When Lewis and Clark first laid eyes on Idaho in 1805, they observed pristine, snow-capped mountains, clear lakes, frothing rivers, and thick stands of conifers. Little has changed since then, and the state motto (*Esto perpetua*, Latin for "It is Forever") suggests that nothing will anytime soon—unless the loggers and miners get their way. Idaho remains nearly free of any heavy industry, and more of the state is preserved as national forests and wilderness areas than any other state in the other 48. The Rocky Mountains divide Idaho into three distinct regions. To the southeast, world-famous potatoes thrive in volcanically rich valleys. To the north, dense pine forests envelop frigid lakes and liberal sentiments befitting the Pacific Northwest. In the center, ski slopes, hiking trails, and geothermal hot springs attract nature lovers. Like many Western states, Idaho fiercely values its freedom; it is the only state in the Union never to have flown a foreign flag.

## ■ PRACTICAL INFORMATION

**Capital:** Boise.

**Visitor Info: Idaho Information Line,** 800-847-4843; www.visitid.org. **Parks and Recreation Dept.,** 5657 Warm Springs Ave., Boise 83712 (334-4199). **Skier Info,** 800-243-2754. **Idaho Outfitters and Guide Association,** 711 N. 5th St.; P.O. Box 95, Boise 83701 (342-1438; www.ioga.org).

**Hotlines: Mental Health Emergency,** 334-0808 or 800-600-6474. **Women's Crisis Line,** 343-7025. **Rape Crisis Line,** 345-7273.

**Postal Abbreviation:** ID. **Sales Tax:** 5%. **Area code:** 208

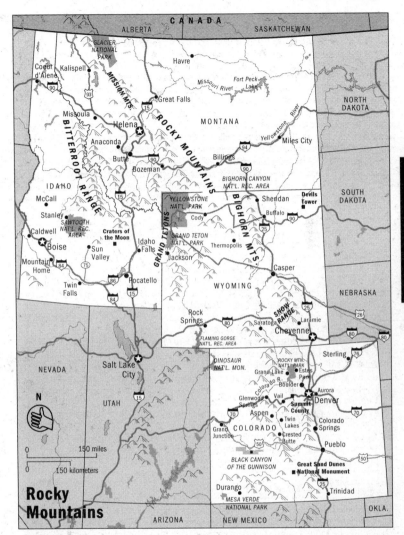

Rocky
Mountains

# BOISE

In the state's dry southern plateau, lively Boise (pronounced BOY-see, not BOY-zee) is a verdant residential oasis with a happening downtown. The easy, small-town familiarity of the residents, numerous grassy parks, and airy shopping plazas make for a relaxing and refreshing spot. Most of the city's sights are within the 10 sq. blocks between the capitol and the Boise River, easily manageable on foot.

## 🛈 PRACTICAL INFORMATION

The pedestrian-friendly Grove is a brick walkway parallel to and between Main St. and Front St. **Greyhound** (343-3681) zips out from 1212 W. Bannock, a few blocks west of downtown. To: Salt Lake City (8hr., 4 per day, $37-40), Portland (11hr., 3 per day, $33-36), and Seattle (14hr., 3 per day, $36-38). **Boise Urban Stages** (336-

1010) runs several routes throughout the city (buses operate M-Sa 6:15am-6:45pm; fare 75¢, seniors 35¢, ages 6-18 50¢; all fares 35¢ on Saturdays). **McU's Sports,** 822 W. Jefferson St. (342-7734); ski shop: 2314 Bogus Basin Rd. (336-2300); rents a good selection of gear and offers free tips on local hiking. (In-line skates $5 for 1hr., $8 for 2hrs., $10 for 3hrs., $12 for 4hrs., $15 for 8hrs., $20 for 24hrs. Mountain bikes $15 per ½-day, $25 per day. Ski equipment $15 per day, kids $12.) **REI (Recreational Equipment, Inc.),** 8300 W. Emerald (322-1141), is the dependable outdoor outfitter for everything. **Visitors center:** 850 W. Front St. (344-5338), at Boise Center on the Grove (open M-F 10am-5pm, Sa 10am-2pm, winter M-F 10am-4pm, Sa 10am-2pm). Gay and lesbian travelers can pick up a copy of *Diversity* at the library or a coffee shop or call the **Gay Community Center** (336-3870; open W 6-9pm, Sa 10am-2pm). **Internet access: Boise Public Library,** 715 S. Capitol Blvd. (384-4114); open M 10am-6pm, Tu-Th 10am-9pm, F 10am-6pm, Sa 10am-5pm. **Post Office:** 770 S. 13th St. (800-275-8777; open M-F 7:30am-5:30pm, Sa 10am-2pm). **ZIP code:** 83702.

# ACCOMMODATIONS

Finding convenient budget lodging in Boise is difficult; neither the YMCA nor the YWCA provide rooms, and even the cheapest hotels charge over $30 per night. The more reasonable places fill quickly, so make reservations. **University Inn,** 2360 University Dr., bordering on Boise State University is clean, has free local calls, cable TV, and HBO as well as a pool and jacuzzi, and shuttle service to the airport (345-7170 or 800-345-7170; singles $45; doubles $50). The **Cabana Inn,** 1600 Main St., is at the other end of downtown (343-6000; rooms from $30-55). Summer travelers doing any business with **Boise State University,** on University Dr., should call student housing in advance to check the availability of dorm rooms (426-3986, call M-F 8am-5pm; singles $16-19; doubles $24-28).

The **Boise National Forest Office/Bureau of Land Management,** 1387 S. Vinnell Way, provides info about campgrounds in Boise, most of which are RV-oriented (373-4007, M-F 7:45am-8pm). **Fiesta Park,** 11101 Fairview Ave., offers tent sites for $20. Amenities include a pool, restroom with running water, and a pay phone. (375-8207. RV sites with partial hookup $21, full hookup $22. Reception Oct.-Mar. daily 8am-5pm, Apr. daily 8am-6pm, May daily 8am-7pm, June-Sept. daily 8am-9pm.) The **Americana Kampground,** 3600 Americana Terrace Blvd., next to the river, has 90 RV sites but colludes in the stale overuse of "K" in place of "C." (344-5733. $17 includes full hookup for a night, $92 for a week; $2 each additional person. $3 showers.) The closest non-RV camping is at **Bogus Basin,** about a 45min. drive out of Boise (open M-F 7:30am-4:30pm).

# FOOD AND NIGHTLIFE

Boise offers other dining options besides Idaho's famous potatoes. The downtown area, centered around **8th and Main St.,** is bustling with lunchtime delis, coffee shops, ethnic cuisine, and several stylish bistros. **Moon's Kitchen,** 815 W. Bannock St., has been serving up classic American food to families and students, as well as politicians and businessmen from the nearby capitol, since 1955. (385-0472. Breakfast specials $4-7, famous shakes $3. Open M-F 7am-3pm, Sa 8am-3pm.) **The Brick Oven Beanery,** 107 8th St., at 8th and Main St. on the Grove, carves up slow-roasted meats and serves them with bread, mashed potatoes, carrots, and a side salad for $6-7. (342-3456. Open M-Tu 11am-9pm, W-Sa 11am-10pm, Su noon-9pm.) For a traditional 50s diner, complete with working Wurlitzers, try the family-oriented **Galaxy Diner,** 500 S. Capitol Blvd. Burgers start at $4.29, shakes are $2.79. (343-6191. Su-Th 7am-10pm, F-Sa 7am-midnight.) Long live *Casablanca* at the combination restaurant and independent/foreign film theater, **Rick's Café Americain/The Flicks,** 646 Fulton St., which also rents videos. You can take your baked brie ($4.50), panini ($6), beer ($2-5), or garden burger ($5.50) into the theater with you. (342-4288; 342-4222 for a showtime recording. Kitchen open M-Th 4-9:45pm, F-Su noon-9:45pm. Movies daily 4-9:45pm. Admission $6.50; students, seniors, and children

# BOISE'S BASQUE BACKGROUND

In 1848, the California Gold Rush brought a flood of immigrants to the U.S. Among them were the Basques, who moved from a small corner of Spain to the goldfields of the Sierras. The Basques, whose native language is supposedly unrelated to any in the world, had a particularly difficult time learning English. Unable to find jobs, the American Basques spread out into the Western rangelands and mountains to become sheep herders. Although historians have recently found links between the mysterious language and Caucasian, the ancient language spoken in the Caucasus region, no conclusive evidence of a tie has been found, and Basque remains without linguistic relatives. Today, southern Idaho is home to the largest concentrated Basque population outside of Europe. Basque culture is preserved at the **Basque Museum and Cultural Center** at the corner of Grove and Capital in downtown Boise. This fascinating museum includes a gallery with changing exhibits, Basque art, and a replica of a Basque herder's house. (343-2671. Open Tu-F 10am-4pm, Sa 11am-3pm. $1, 12 and under free.) Next door to the museum, sample Basque cuisine at **Bar Gernika**, 202 S. Capitol Blvd., a pub and eatery named for the capital of the Basque homeland. In the summer, enjoy the hearty meals outside on the patio. Authentic Basque dishes include Solomo sandwiches (marinated pork tenderloin $6-8) and Dorothy's famous beef tongue ($11-12), served only on Sa, from 10am until it's gone. (344-2175. Open M 11am-11pm, Tu-Th 11am-midnight, F 11am-1am, Sa 11:30am-1am.)

$4; double feature $8.) The hungry and healthy-minded will dig the **Boise CO-OP**, 888 W. Fort St., west of downtown via 8th St. and its great selection of reasonably-priced natural, organic, and gourmet foods, including organic smoothies (342-6652; open M-Sa 9am-9pm, Su 9am-8pm).

Nightlife in Boise consists mainly of live music in coffeehouses and pubs, but every summer Wed., the town comes **"Alive After Five"** (371-5483) in the Grove, on Grove St. downtown. Musicians perform on Main St. from 5-9pm, while vendors from nearby restaurants hawk food and beer. Smoky funk wafts from the **Blues Bouquet**, 1010 Main St., a modern western saloon, where beer's cheap ($1.50-2.75) and live music's nightly (345-6605; 21+; open M-F 1pm-2:30am, Sa-Su 8pm-2am). The truly relaxed stop in at the **Flying M Coffeehouse**, 500 W. Idaho St., where folks come together to enjoy local art, drink coffee, and sample tasty breakfast foods. (345-4320. Occasional live music on Sa nights. Open M-F 6:30am-11pm, Sa 7:30am-11pm, Su 7:30am-6pm.) **The Balcony**, at Capitol Terrace, one block from the Grove Center on Grove St., is a trendy and lively night spot (open 2pm-2am; 21+).

## 🔘 SIGHTS

The best view of the city may be from **Table Rock**, a lookout off Warm Springs Rd. By night, you can see a **giant glowing cross** high in the hills. The **Boise Tour Train** whisks you around 75 city sights in 1¼hrs. Tours begin and end in the parking lot of **Julia Davis Park**. *(342-4796. Tours June to early Sept. M-Sa 5 per day 10am-3pm, Su 4 per day noon-3:45pm; in fall, W-F 1 per day at 1:30pm, Sa 4 per day 10:30am-3pm, Su 3 per day noon-3pm. $6.50, seniors $6, ages 13-17 $5, 4-12 $3.50. Arrive 15min. early.)* To learn about Idaho and the Old West at your own pace, stroll through the **Historical Museum**, in Julia Davis Park, which showcases a replica 19th-century bar complete with a display of a two-headed calf. *(334-2120. Open M-Sa 9am-5pm, Su and holidays 1-5pm. Free; donations encouraged.)* Also in the park, the **Boise Art Museum** displays international and local works while offering educational programs, lectures, and tours. *(670 Julia Davis Dr. 345-8330. Open all year M-F 10am-5pm, Sa-Su noon-5pm. $4, students and seniors $2, ages 6-12 $1; free the 1st Th of every month.)* Take a self-guided tour through the country's only **State Capitol** heated with geothermal water. For more information, contact the **Capitol Education Center**, located in the capitol, and a part of the **Idaho State Historical Society**. *(334-5174. M-F 8am-5pm. Tours June M-F at 9, 11am, 1 and 3pm, July and Aug. M-F 10:30am, 1 and 3pm.)* Raptors perch and dive at the **World Center**

**for Birds of Prey.** From I-85, take the Overland exit. Go south on S. Cole until you reach the center. *(566 W. Flying Hawk Ln. 362-3716. Open daily in summer 9am-5pm; off-season 10am-4pm. $4, seniors $3, children $2, under 4 free.)* At the **Old Idaho Penitentiary,** visitors can see where Boise housed its delinquents from 1870 to 1973. Not simply an old slammer, "the pen" also displays the **nation's only collection of prison tattoo art.** *(2445 Old Penitentiary Rd. 334-2844. Open daily in summer 10am-5pm; off-season noon-5pm. Bail $4, seniors 60+ and kids 6-12 $3.)* For more back-to-nature fun, try the 22mi. **Boise River Greenbelt,** a pleasant path ideal for a leisurely walk or picnic along the Boise River. In the summer, visitors can go tubing in the river at Berber Park. The ever-growing **Boise Shakespeare Festival** hits town from June to Sept. *(336-9221.)* June 22-25, 2000, Boise hosts a **River Festival,** featuring hot-air balloon rallies, a carnival, live music, fireworks, and sporting events. *(338-8887.)* Upcoming events are showcased in *The Boise Weekly*, available Th.

## MCCALL

Located 100mi. north of Boise on scenic Rt. 55, where mountain meadows meet the shore of a beautiful and placid lake, the town of McCall offers top-notch recreational opportunities amid a friendly, small-town atmosphere—featuring a combo movie theater/lumber mill (**Lumberman's,** located on Hwy. 55/3rd St. at the southern edge of town). McCall has produced numerous Olympic skiers, testament to the quality of the skiing. Yet, the town's population triples in the summer, indicating a high quality of life after the thaw. A public bike path, public beaches along Payette Lake (offering swimming with "Sharlie," a mythical lake monster), and hiking trails provide ample summer complement to the winter skiing fun.

Visit the **Payette National Forest Headquarters,** 700 W. Lakeside Ave. (634-0700; recreation report 634-0409), for recreation information (open daily 7:30am-4:30pm). When cold weather arrives, one can ski **Brundage Mountain** in the Payette National Forest off Rt. 55. From early July through Sept., mountain bike on weekends and holidays from 11am-6pm; rental bikes are available. (Office 634-4151. Office open M-F 8:30am-5pm, Sa 9am-4pm. Info line 634-7669 or 888-255-7669. Open daily in winter 9:30am-4:30pm. Full-day lift ticket $30, ages 13-18 $25, ages 7-12 $18. Biking: full-day lift ticket $15; one ride $8, seniors and ages 7-12 $5. Rentals with helmet start at $23 per day). Contact **Cheap Thrills Watercraft Rentals,** 303 3rd St., for everything from fishing to wild whitewater adventures (637-7472). For firefighter fans, McCall has the ultimate treat: a free tour of the base for the **McCall Smokejumpers,** 605 S. Mission St. The Smokejumpers are a group of elite forest rangers who parachute in to extinguish forest fires. (634-0390. Open June-Oct. daily 9am-6pm, tours daily at 11am and 3pm; open Nov.-May M-F 8am-5pm, tours at 10am and 2pm.) The furious snowmelt makes for some good whitewater. **Salmon River Challenge, Inc.** offers ½-day (adults $35, including pop and snacks) to 2-day raft trips (adults $225). Salmon River also offers a pricey guest house as well as horseback and fishing activities. (800-732-8574 or 628-3264.)

For a truly rustic Idaho experience, "make yourself to home" at Burgdorf, 36mi. north of McCall, where loggers have been treating themselves to **hot springs** for over 100 years. Take Warren Wagon Road out of McCall, along the northern shore of Payette Lake. Continue until a dirt-road turn-off for Burgdorf. Be sure to check driving conditions before you leave; in the winter, this town is accessible by snowmobile only. (636-3036. Cabins with outhouses $25 per person. Children 5-12 $5. Overnight stay includes use of hotspring-fed pool. Day soak $5 per adult, children 5-12 $2.50. M-Sa 10am-9pm, Su 10am-6pm.)

Camping is generally your best bet for bedding; budget accommodations are scarce during peak seasons (June-Sept. and Dec.-Feb.). The finest option may be **Ponderosa State Park,** located right on Payette Lake. From downtown, follow 3rd St. until you see the big brown signs just east of the lake. The rangers can direct you to the free primitive **campground** on the north side of the lake. Take Warren Wagon Rd. along the north shore of Payette Lake. Take the left fork onto Eastside Dr. to reach the beach. (634-2164. Canoe and kayak rentals: 632-4562. Tent site $12, RV with hookup $16. Reception M-F 9am-8pm, Sa-Su 9am-10pm. Water avail-

ROCKY MOUNTAINS

able.) The **University of Idaho Field Campus,** adjacent to Ponderosa Park on Payette Lake has log cabins with bunk beds, common dining, and bath houses. (634-3918. Single bed $15; families $40. Office open M-F 8am-5pm. Open May-Oct. Reservations needed.) The friendly, family-owned **Scandia Inn,** 401 N. 3rd St., waits in the woods above Rt. 55. (634-7394. In summer $54; in winter $40. Private cabin available. Cable, free local calls, dry sauna.) Before you go out and play, head for **The Pancake House,** 209 N. 3rd St., for a hearty plate of homemade specialties ($3-5; one plate-sized pancake $2.75; 634-5849; open daily 6am-2pm).

**Northwestern Trailways** (800-366-3830) serves the town with one northbound bus per day (ultimate destination: Tacoma, $35) and one southbound (ultimate destination: Boise, $16). The buses stop, and tickets are sold, at **Bill's Gas and Grocery,** 147 N. 3rd St. (643-2340). The northbound bus stops at 11:45am and the southbound at 5:30pm. **Chamber of Commerce:** 1001 State St. (634-7631; open Tu-Sa 9am-3pm). For trail conditions and directions, visit the **Payette National Forest Headquarters,** 804 Lakeside Ave. (634-0700; open M-F 7:30am-4:30pm). **Post Office:** 495 Deinhard Ln. (634-2260; open M-F 8:30am-5pm). **ZIP code:** 83638. **Area code:** 208.

# KETCHUM AND SUN VALLEY

In 1935, Union Pacific heir Averill Harriman sent Austrian Count Felix Schaffgotsch to scour the U.S. for a site to develop a ski resort area rivaling Europe's best. The Count dismissed Aspen, reasoning that its air was too thin for East Coasters, and selected the small mining and sheep-herding town of Ketchum in Idaho's Wood River Valley. Sun Valley is the fancy resort village Harriman built 1mi. from Ketchum to entice dashing celebrities like Ernest Hemingway, Claudette yColbert, and Errol Flynn to "rough it" amid the manicured ski slopes, *haute cuisine,* and nightly orchestra performances. An imported East Coast yacht club ambience remains in Ketchum. The towering syncopated peaks of the Sawtooth range overshadow the brightest Hollywood stars, and visitors can escape the artificial tans and fashionable stores in town to find gorgeous trails and lakes scattered throughout the surrounding mountains.

## ◪ PRACTICAL INFORMATION

The best time to visit is during the rare "slack" period (late Oct. to late Nov. and May to early June). **Sun Valley Express** (877-622-8267) runs one bus daily to the Boise airport ($49; leaves Ketchum 7:15am, return bus from the Boise airport leaves at 2pm; office hours in June 7:30am-2:30pm, rest of summer 7:30am-6pm). **KART** (726-7576), Ketchum's **bus service,** tours the city and its surrounding areas (daily 7:20am-midnight; free). **Chamber of Commerce:** (726-3423 or 800-634-3347), 4th and Main St. in Ketchum (open M and W-Su 9am-6pm, Tu 9am-5pm). **Sawtooth National Recreation Area (SNRA) Headquarters** (727-5013, 727-5000, or 800-280-2267 for reservations), 6mi. north of Ketchum off Rt. 75, stocks detailed info on the recreation area, hot springs, and area forests and trails, including National Recreation Area maps for $4 and Margaret Fuller's excellent trail guides for $14.95 (open daily 8am-5pm). **Hospital: Wood River Medical Center** (622-3333 or 788-2222 for the Hailey Branch on Main St.) on Sun Valley Rd. (Hwy. 75, at the south end of the resort). **Post office:** 301 1st Ave. (726-5161; open M-F 8am-5:30pm, Sa 11am-2pm). **ZIP code:** 83340. **Area code:** 208.

## ACCOMMODATIONS AND FOOD

Prices here suit the Trumps. The nearby town of Hailey offers more budget-friendly indoor accommodations. From early June to mid-Oct., camping is the best option for cheap sleep. Check with the **Ketchum Ranger District,** on Sun Valley Rd., just outside of Ketchum on the way to Sun Valley (622-5371; open M-F 8am-4:30pm, Sa-Su 8am-5:30pm). **Boundary Campground,** 3mi. northeast of town on Trail Creek Rd., provides restrooms and drinking water for a small fee. Two mi.further on the right, **Corral Creek Road** scatters isolated sites along a rushing brook (no hookups). Up Rt. 75 into the SNRA lie several scenic camping spots; the cheapest (sites $8) are **Murdock** (11 sites) and **Caribou** (7 sites). They are, respectively, 2 and 3mi. up a dirt road called North Fork Rd., which begins as a paved road to the right of the visitors center. At $11, **North Fork** (29 sites) and **Wood River** (30 sites) are 8mi. north of Ketchum, along Rt. 75. For North Fork, take the first campground road to the left north of SNRA headquarters. Wood River is 2mi. beyond SNRA headquarters. **Easley Campground and Pool,** about 8mi. on the way to Stanley from SNRA headquarters, is adjacent to a tiny hot spring ($11). For those who would prefer a bed to a bedroll, **Ski View Lodge,** 409 S. Main St., rents out 8 small, delightfully garish gingerbread-house log cabins (726-3441; $40-70; full kitchens, cable and free local calls).

Ketchum's small confines bulge with over 80 restaurants, many serving moderately priced, well-prepared food. **The Hot Dog Adventure Company,** 210 N. Main St., offers an excellent cosmopolitan selection of, well, hot dogs and veggie dogs ($2-4), and mouth-melting steak fries. (726-0117; open M-Sa noon-6pm and 10:30pm-2:30am). **Desperado's,** at the corner of 4th and Washington St., dishes out delicious Mexican food at reasonable prices. Relish the view of Baldy (Sun Valley's famous Bald Mt.) while eating in the sun on their large patio. (726-3068. Large platters of enchiladas and burritos $5-9, combo platters $7-10. Open M-Sa 11:30am-10pm.) At **The Starrwood Bakery,** 591 4th St., the fresh breads, muffins, and salads are made from wholesome ingredients. $5.50 buys a deli sandwich with soup and a side salad. (726-2253. Open M-F 6:30am-5pm, Sa 7am-5pm, Su 7am-4pm; hrs. shorter in winter.) Hemingway's old haunt, **Whiskey Jacques,** 251 Main St., offers $1 mixed drinks on Su from 4-4:30pm, and satellite TV. (726-5297, take-out 726-3200. Open daily 4pm-2am. Live music 9:30pm-2am most nights.)

## ▟ OUTDOORS

To see the Ketchum/Sun Valley area from the great outdoors, walk, run, bike or ski the **path,** which follows Sun Valley Rd. and Rt. 75, between the resort and the town, to Hailey and throughout the valley. Winter visitors are probably going to ski at the world-famous **Sun Valley Resort,** which corners the alpine skiing market in the region. Crowned by Mt. Bald, America's original mountain resort can't be matched. (800-786-8259. Sun Valley Company: 622-4111; ski conditions hotline: 800-635-4150. Full-day lift ticket $54. Ski season runs late Nov. to May 1.) The Sawtooth area is nationally renowned for its stunning **mountain bike trails,** which run through the gorgeous canyons and mountain passes of the SNRA. Beware; trails might be snowbound or flooded well into July. Inquire about trail conditions at **Formula Sports,** on the corner of 5th and Main at 460 N. Main St. (726-3194; bikes from $12 per 4hr., $18 per day, tandems $20/4hr., $30/day). **The Elephant's Perch,** 280 East Ave., at East Ave. and Sun Valley Rd., also rents mountain bikes and provides trail info (726-3497; open M-Sa 9am-6pm, Su 10am-6pm; bikes $12 for 4hr., $20 per day). Before hitting the forest, pick up info on mountain biking and trail suggestions at the Chamber of Commerce. After a hard day of biking or hiking, Ketchum locals soak in their favorite **geothermal hot spring.** The hot springs, hidden in the hills and canyons of Ketchum, are not the secret they once were. Springtime melt and rain can put the springs underwater, rendering them inaccessible. They are normally safe only in July and Aug. For books and guidance, inquire at the Elephant's Perch or at SNRA headquarters.

Two of the more accessible, non-commercial springs are **Warfield Hot Springs,** on Warm Springs Creek, 11mi. west of Ketchum on Warm Springs Rd., and **Russian John Hot Springs** (called a "sheep dip" by locals for its lukewarm temperature), 8mi. north of the SNRA headquarters on Rt. 75, just west of the highway. Their recent popularity has forced a curfew to be placed on Warfield in response to disrespectful crowds. For the best info on **fishing conditions and licenses,** as well as equipment rentals, stop by **Silver Creek Outfitters,** 500 N. Main St. (726-5282. Open M-Sa 9am-6pm, Su 9am-5pm, longer hrs. in peak season. Fly rods $15 per day.)

**THE SUN VALLEY ALSO RISES** Ernest Hemingway's love affair with both rugged outdoor sports and wealthy celebrities fits Ketchum's dualistic spirit. After spending many of his vacations hunting and fishing in the Sawtooth Range, the author built a cabin in Sun Valley, the site of his suicide after a losing bout with alcoholism. While Hemingway's house is off-limits, the **Ketchum-Sun Valley Heritage and Ski Museum,** at the corner of 1st St. and Washington Ave., displays exhibits on Hemingway's life. *(726-8118. Open daily 1-4pm.)* A bust of Hemingway is tucked away in a shady spot along the river at the **Hemingway Memorial,** about 1mi. outside of Sun Valley on the way to Boundary Campground (see above).

## SAWTOOTH

Home to the Sawtooth and White Cloud Mountains in the north and the Smokey and Boulder Ranges in the south, the **Sawtooth National Recreation Area (SNRA)** sprawls over 756,000 acres of untouched land and is surrounded by four national forests, encompassing the headwaters of five of Idaho's major rivers. A great (but slow) 60mi. drive heads north to Stanley on Rt. 75. Pause at the Galena Overlook, 31mi. north of Ketchum and ¼mi. downhill from the 8701ft. Galena Pass.

**◪ PRACTICAL INFORMATION.** The tiny (pop. 69), frontier-style town of **Stanley,** located 60mi. north of Ketchum at the intersection of Rt. 21 and 75, serves as a northern base for exploring Sawtooth. Many businesses are located right along Rt. 21, but don't miss the Old Town, lining Ace of Diamonds St. From Rt. 21, turn west onto Wall St. The Old Town is to the right, about one block down, characterized by wooden sidewalks. **Stanley Chamber of Commerce:** (774-3411 or 800-878-7950), on Rt. 21. (open Tu-Th 8am-4pm, F-M 8am-7pm; printed material always available). The **Stanley Ranger Station** (774-3000) offers topographical maps. The station is located 3mi. south of Stanley on Rt. 75 (open in summer M-Sa 8am-4:30pm; off-season M-F 8am-5pm). At the entrance to Redfish Lake (5mi. south of Stanley and 55mi. north of Ketchum on Rt. 75), the **info booth** (774-3536) dispenses a wide range of info about hiking, camping, and outdoor sports (sporadic hrs.; the booth is usually staffed during sunny, busy weekends). 2mi. west of the turnoff from Rt. 75 is the **Redfish Lake Lodge** (774-3536). The general store next door sells **maps** of the Sawtooth area and **SNRA car passes** (3-day pass $5; $15 per year; open in summer daily 8am-10pm). Stanley's **post office:** Ace of Diamonds St. (774-2230; open M-F 8-11am and noon-5pm in winter, 1-5pm in summer). In the Chamber of Commerce building, the **Stanley Library** (774-2470) offers public **Internet access** (open M noon-6pm, Th noon-4pm, Sa noon-4pm). **ZIP code:** 83278. **Area code:** 208.

**▟▙ ACCOMMODATIONS AND FOOD.** North of Wood River, campgrounds line Rt. 75. Because there are so many scattered around the SNRA, the free map of campsites available at SNRA headquarters is indispensable. **Alturas Lake** is 21mi. south of Stanley on Rt. 75; the turn-off is marked about 10mi. north of Galena Pass. Campsites by the lake are available on a first come, first served basis for $11-13 depending on the area (free with Golden Eagle, ½-price with Golden Access and Golden Age). North of Alturas Lake, **Redfish Lake** (5mi. south of Stanley, 55mi. north of Ketchum right off Rt. 75) is the premier spot for camping in the SNRA, but beware of the ever-present lakeside mosquitoes. **Point Campground** (sites $13; no hookups) can be reserved for an $8.75 fee through the **National Recreation Reserve Service** (800-280-2267). Point is adjacent to a beach on Redfish Lake. Along the road to the Point Campground, there are a number of self-serve campgrounds with water and a common bathhouse that operate on a first come, first serve basis ($11; with Golden Age and Golden Access pass $5.50; free with Golden Eagle). Free primitive camping is available just outside the entrance to Redfish Lake on Rt. 75.

East on Rt. 75, past the town of Stanley, numerous sites are available alongside the **Salmon River.** (First come, first served sites $11. Water available; no hookup. $5.50 with Golden Age and Golden Access, free with Golden Eagle.) **Mormon Bend** is located 5mi. east of Stanley on Rt. 75 and has whitewater access; **Casino Creek** is 8mi. east of Stanley on Rt. 75 and the **Salmon River Campground** is 9mi. east of Stanley on Rt. 75. In most areas, a trailhead pass is required for parking. These are available at the Stanley Ranger Station (see **Practical Information** above). For a real bed, Stanley provides more scenic and more reasonable lodging than Ketchum. On Ace of Diamonds St. in downtown, the **Sawtooth Hotel**, run by the president of the town council, is a colorful, comfortable place to rest after a wilderness sojourn (774-9947; singles $35, with private bath $50; doubles $40/60; open May-Sept.). The hotel also has the **Sawtooth Cafe,** a breakfast and lunch joint popular with Stanley natives, a bookstore, and a renowned fly-fishing guide service. The cafe offers picnic lunches for hikers. (Open 6am-3pm, espresso and desserts served until 7pm. Picnics $6.75-8.75.) More scenic and exceedingly friendly is the **Redwood Motel,** 1mi. north on Rt. 75 in Lower Stanley. Thirteen cottages sit on the banks of the Salmon River. Check out the backyard with the swing—the owner asserts it's why guests keep coming back. (774-3531. $47-50, with kitchenette $55-58. Open May-Oct.) At **Danner's Log Cabin Motel,** on Rt. 21, town ex-mayor and Stanley history buff Bunny Danner rents historic cabins built by goldminers in 1939. The office, built in 1906, was the first building in town, and was originally the ranger station. (774-3539. Cabins $50-80; $35-80 in spring and fall.)

Stock up on eats for the trail at the **Mountain Village Grocery Store** (774-3500; open daily 7am-9pm, 6am-10pm in the high summer months). The **Mountain Village Resort Restaurant and Saloon,** on Rt. 21 near the intersection with Rt. 75, offers sandwiches ($5-6) and breakfast entrees for $2.50-$7 (774-3317; open daily 7am-10pm). For evening entertainment, try the **Rod and Gun Club,** at the end of Ace of Diamonds St. in Stanley. On Sa from 9pm-2am, the spacious halls fill with a variety of live music and local crowds playing pool. (774-9920. Open daily from 4pm. Last call 2am. 21+.) For a taste of the old town, try the restaurant and bar **Kasino Club** on Ace of Diamonds St., serving domestic beer and microbrew. (In summer, dinner 6-10pm. Bar open daily 4pm-2am.)

**⚑ OUTDOORS.** Hiking, boating, and fishing are unsurpassed in all four of the SNRA's ranges. However, to enjoy these natural pleasures, **SNRA passes** are necessary; they are available at any ranger station and most outdoor retailers in the Stanley/Ketchum area ($2 per day, $5 per year, families $25). Pick up a free map of the area and inquire about trail conditions at SNRA headquarters before hitting the trail or the lake, particularly in early summer, when trails may be flooded out. Much of the backcountry stays buried deep in the snow well into summer. For information and trailhead passes in the Stanley area, go to the **Stanley Ranger Station,** 2mi. south of Stanley on Rt. 75. **Redfish Lake** is the source of many trails; some popular, leisurely hikes include those to Fishhook Creek (excellent for children), Bench Lakes, and the Hell Roaring trail. The long, gentle loop around Yellow Belly, Toxaway, and Petit Lakes is a moderate overnight suitable for novices. Two mi.northwest of Stanley on Rt. 21, the 3mi. Iron Creek Rd. leads to the trailhead of the Sawtooth Lake Hike. This 5½mi. trail, steep but well-worn, is not too taxing if you stop to rest. Bionic hikers can try the steep, 4mi. hike to Casino Lakes, which begins at the Broadway Creek trailhead southeast of Stanley.

Mountain biking in the Sawtooths is almost unlimited. **Riverwear,** on Rt. 21 in Stanley, rents bikes from $17 per day (774-3592; open daily 7am-10pm). Beginners will enjoy riding the dirt road that accesses the North Fork campgrounds from the visitors center. This gorgeous passage parallels the North Fork of the Wood River for 5mi. before branching off into other narrower and steeper trails, suitable for more advanced riders. These trails can be combined into loops; consult the trail map or the ranger station. **Boulder Creek Rd.,** 5mi. from SNRA headquarters, leads to pristine Boulder Lake and an old mining camp. The steep, 10mi. road-trip ride is suitable for skilled riders. Check with the ranger station in Stanley or the SNRA Headquarters to find out about possible trail closures before your outing, especially during the early summer when trails might be flooded out. Groups of 10 to 20 need free wilderness permits, available at SNRA headquarters.

Topographical maps ($4) and various trail books ($3-20), including Margaret Fuller's invaluable books ($14-18), are available at **McCoy's Tackle and Gift Shop,** on Ace of Diamonds St. In the heat of summer, cold rivers beg for fishing, canoeing, or whitewater rafting. **McCoy's Tackle Shop,** on Ace of Diamonds St. in Stanley, sells a full range of outdoor equipment besides renting rods and reels. (774-3377. Flies $1.75, lures $2.39-3.50. Open daily 8am-6pm, extended summer hours 8am-8pm.) **Sawtooth Rentals,** ¼mi. north of the Rt. 21/75 junction, specializes in water vehicle rentals. (774-3409 or 800-243-3185. Kayaks $30 per day, doubles $40; rafts $15 per person per day; mountain bikes $25.) For pontoon boat tours of the lake, head for **Redfish Lake Lodge Marina,** which also offers numerous nautical adventures for rent. (774-3536. Open daily in summer 9am-10pm. 1½hr. tours $6.50, children $4.50; schedule varies. Paddleboats $5 per 30min. Canoes $5 per hr., $15 per ½-day, $25 per day. Outboards $10 per hr., $33.50 for ½-day, $60 per day.) **The River Company,** based in Stanley, arranges expert whitewater rafting and floating trips. (774-2244 or 800-398-0346. ½-day trips $67.50 for adults, full-day including gourmet campfire cuisine $85 for adults. Open daily in summer 8am-11pm. 3 trips per day: 10am, noon and 3pm. U.S. Forest Service fee 3%.)

The most inexpensive way to enjoy the SNRA waters is to visit the **hot springs** just east of Stanley. **Sunbeam Hot Springs,** 10mi. east of Lower Stanley on Rt. 75, is the best of the batch. Be sure to bring a bucket or cooler to the stone bathhouse; you'll need to add about 20 gallons of cold Salmon River water before you can get into these hot pools (120-130°F). The bathhouse, built in 1937, is a shining example of the craftsmanship of the Civilian Conservation Corps. High water can wash out the hot springs temporarily. Check with locals for info about other hot springs.

## CRATERS OF THE MOON

Astronauts once trained at the unearthly **Craters of the Moon National Monument,** an elevated lava field and group of craters that rises darkly from sagebrush-covered rangelands, 70mi. southeast of Sun Valley on Rt. 20/26/93, at the junction of Rt. 20 and 26/93 (admission $4 per car, $2 per individual). Windswept and deathly quiet, the stark, twisted lava formations dominate sparse vegetation, a reminder of the volcanic eruptions that occurred here as recently as 2000 years ago.

Other-worldly campsites are scattered among jagged lava formations (52 sites with water but no hookup, $10). Wood fires are prohibited, but charcoal fires are permitted. You can camp for free in adjacent land owned by the **Bureau of Land Management.** Contact the BLM office for info about the primitive camp sites. If you do find your own site, the BLM asks that you practice minimum-impact camping. (Shoshone office 886-2206. Office open M-F 7:45am-4:30pm. BLM land pictured in yellow on most maps.) Camping in unmarked sites in the dry lava beds of the park itself is permitted with a free backcountry permit, available from the **visitors center** (527-3257; open daily 8am-4:30pm). **Echo Crater,** accessible by a 4mi. hike from the Tree Molds parking lot, is the most frequented and comfortable of these sites.

The visitors center has displays and videotapes on the process of lava formation. Printed guides outline hikes to all points of interest within the park as well as a 7mi. driving loop to major sites. Rangers lead **guided hikes/walks** of varying themes that last up to 2hr. (mid-June to mid-Aug.). The rangers teach visitors to recognize the animal and plant life in the park as well as two types of lava, pahoehoe [pa-HOY-hoy] and a'a [AH-ah]. Bring sturdy shoes and a flashlight when exploring the lava tubes, caves formed when a surface layer of lava hardened and the rest drained out, creating a tunnel. For more information, write the **Superintendent,** Craters of the Moon National Monument, Box 29, Arco, ID 83213.

The town of **Arco,** 20mi. east of the Craters of the Moon on Rt. 20, claims to be the **"first city in the world lit by atomic power."** You can fill up on gasoline at a number of fill stations along Rt. 20/26, and you can fill your tummy at the **Arco Deli Sandwich Shop,** on Rt. 20/26/93 in downtown on the corner of Grand Ave. and Idaho St. (foot-long sandwiches $5.79; 527-3757; open M-Sa 8am-8pm). The **Chamber of Commerce** (527-8977, P.O. Box 46, Arco, ID 83213), in the town hall on Grand Ave., has info.

ROCKY MOUNTAINS

# MONTANA

When you've seen the sunset splash vibrant colors over a canopy of clouds, or the full spread of brilliant stars unfold at midnight, you'll know why they call Montana Big Sky country. With 25 million acres of national forest and public lands, the state's population of pronghorn antelope seems to outnumber the people, while grizzly bears, mountain lions, and extreme weather serve as reminders of human vulnerability. Although some of the wackier residents—like the Unabomber, the Capitol Building gunman and the militia men—have grabbed headlines recently, it's the wide-open land that makes this state special. Copious fishing lakes, 500 species of wildlife (not including millions of insect species), beautiful rivers, mountains, glaciers, and thousands of ski trails make Montana a paradise.

## 🛈 PRACTICAL INFORMATION

**Capital:** Helena.

**Visitor Info: Travel Montana,** P.O. Box 7549, Missoula 59807 (406-444-2654 in MT or 800-847-4868; www.travel.state.mt.us). **National Forest Information,** Northern Region, Federal Bldg., 200 E. Broadway, Box 7669, Missoula 59807 (406-329-3511).

**Gay/Lesbian info: PRIDE!,** P.O. Box 775, Helena 59624 (406-442-9322), for info.

**Postal Abbreviation:** MT. **Sales Tax:** 0%.

## BILLINGS

Located at the junction of I-90 and I-94 and containing the big town amenities of airport, car rental, and bus station, Billings is more of a stopover, or point of entry, than a destination. Street names in Billings are confusing; three streets may have the same name, distinguished only by direction. The **Billings Logan International Airport,** 1901 Terminal Circle (238-3420) can be found right at the end of N. 27th St. Both **Greyhound** and **Rimrock Trailways** operate from 2502 1st Ave. N. (245-5116; open 24hr.); buses run to Bozeman (3hr., 5 per day, $26); Missoula (7-9hr., 5 per day, $50); and Bismarck (9hr., 4 per day, $59). See the town, or leave quickly in a car from **Thrifty,** 1144 N. 27th St. (259-1025). Rentals in peak summer season start at $53 per day with 150 free mi. and $315 per week with 1050 free mi. (25¢ each additional mi. $10 per day surcharge for ages 21-24. Open daily 5:30am-11:30pm.) **Billings Metropolitan Transit** (657-8218) runs buses M-F from approximately 6:45am-6:00pm, Sa 8:45am-5:45, maps available at many convenient stores, banks, and at the library (75¢, seniors 25¢). The **visitors center,** 815 S. 27th St. (252-4016 or 800-735-2635; open M-Sa May 31-Sept. 6 8:30am-6pm; off-season M-F 8:30am-5pm). **Post Office:** 841 S. 26th St (657-5700; open M-F 8am-6pm, Sa 10am-2pm). **ZIP code:** 59101. **Area code:** 406.

Billings's lodgings are spread throughout the city. The **Cherry Tree Inn,** 823 N. Broadway (take exit 450 off I-90; go north on 27th St. then turn left onto 9th Ave.), has immaculate, spacious, Colonial-themed rooms at chopped-down prices (252-5603 or 800-237-5882; A/C, phones, cable TV; singles $35; doubles $40). The **Esquire Motor Inn,** 3314 1st Ave. N., has clean rooms and a restaurant and lounge on the premises. (259-4551. Kitchenettes available. Singles $30, 2 people 1 bed $32, doubles $39; $5 per additional person.)

Downtown, **Jake's,** 2701 1st Ave. N., has hearty soups ($3-4), burgers ($5.50), and a plentiful selection of microbrews and other less trendy liquids, but eat at the bar—the restaurant is a pricey steak place. (259-9375. Bar open M-Th 11:30am-1am, F 11:30am-2am, Sa 4:30pm-2am. Restaurant open M-Th 11:30am-2pm and 5:30-10pm, F-Sa 11:30am-2pm and 5:30-10:30pm.) Also downtown, **Café Jones,** 2712 2nd Ave. N., is a coffeehouse/juice bar with a rotating art exhibit (259-7676; dishes $1-5; open M-F 7am-6pm, Sa 9am-4pm). **Khanthaly's Eggrolls,** 1301 Grand Ave., serves tasty Laotian fast food (fried rice noodles, spring rolls) at prices more likely to be found in Laos than the U.S. From downtown, go west on 6th Ave. N, bear right at the fork and you will be on Grand. (259-7252. $1-6. Open M-Sa 11am-9pm.)

The **Yellowstone Art Museum,** 401 N. 27th St., displays contemporary art, and in the summer shows some great Western art (256-6804. Open Tu-Sa 10am-5pm, Th until 8pm, Su noon-5pm. $3, seniors $2, children $1.) The **Western Heritage Center,** 2822 Montana Ave., is an interactive museum that's fun for imaginary cowboys and cowgirls of all ages (256-6809; open Tu-Sa 10am-5pm, Su 1-5pm; free).

## LITTLE BIG HORN

**Little Big Horn National Monument,** 60mi. southeast of Billings off I-90 on the Crow Reservation, marks the site of one of the most dramatic episodes in the conflict between Native Americans and the U.S. Government. Here, Sioux and Cheyenne warriors, led by Sioux chiefs Sitting Bull and Crazy Horse, retaliating for years of genocide, annihilated five companies of the U.S. Seventh Cavalry under the command of Lt. Colonel George Armstrong Custer on June 25, 1876. White stone graves mark where the U.S. soldiers fell. The exact Native American casualties are not known, since their families and fellow warriors removed the bodies from the battlefield almost immediately. The renaming of the monument, formerly known as the Custer Battlefield Monument, signifies the U.S. Government's admission that Custer's behavior merits no glorification. Congress also prescribed that a memorial be built in honor of the Native Americans killed at the battle. This memorial, which the Cheyenne have been working towards since 1925, should be complete by the summer of 2000.

Rangers give great explanatory talks in the summer, (every 30min., daily 9am-6pm), or drive through the monument guided by an audio tour that narrates the battle movements ($13, open daily 8am-8pm). A 1hr. **bus tour** leaves the visitor's center (9am, 10:30am, noon, 2pm, and 3:30pm. $10, seniors $8, under 12 $5.) The **visitors center** has a small movie theater, an electronic map of the battlefield, and a weapons display. (638-2621, ext 124. Monument open daily late May to early Sept. 8am-9pm, visitors center open 8am-7:30pm; in fall entire park open 8am-6pm; in winter 8am-4:30pm. Entrance $6 per car, $3 per person.)

## BOZEMAN

Wedged between the Bridger and Madison Mountains, Bozeman thrives in Montana's broad Gallatin River Valley. Originally settled by farmers who sold food to Northern Pacific Railroad employees living in the neighboring town of Elliston, the valley now supplies food to a large portion of southern Montana. The presence of Montana State University makes Bozeman especially accommodating to young wanderers and latter-day hippies.

**⊠ PRACTICAL INFORMATION. Greyhound** and **RimRock Stages,** 625 N. 7th Ave. (587-3110), both serve Bozeman. To: Butte (1½hr., 4 per day, $14-15); Billings (3-4hr., 5 per day, $21-25); Helena (2hr., 3 per day, $16-26); and Missoula (5hr., 5 per day, $24-32). (Station open M-F 7:30am-noon, 1-5:30pm, 8-11pm; Sa-Su 7:30am-noon, 3:30-5:30pm, 8:30-10pm.) **Budget** (388-4091), at the airport, rents wheels for $45-60 per day. (100 free mi., 25¢ per additional mi. Ages 21-24 $15 per day surcharge; major credit card required. Open daily 7am-11pm, or until last flight.) **Boze-**

---

**SHAKESPEARE IN THE PARK** No, New York's famed production didn't make a wrong turn at W. 86th St. and Central Park West to end up in Montana. Rather, this is **Montana Shakespeare in the Park,** a roving band of thespians who make the rounds of the Big Sky state from the Fourth of July to Labor Day. In the words of one young Montanan, "In the summer, if I'm not camping, I'm watching this." *(406-994-3901 or www.montana.edu/wwwmtsip for schedule.)*

ROCKY MOUNTAINS

man **Area Chamber of Commerce:** at 19th Ave. and Baxter Ln. (586-5421 or 800-228-4224;open M 9am-5pm Tu-F 8am-5pm, Sa 9am-4pm). **Hospital: Bozeman Deaconess,** 915 Highland Blvd. (585-5000). **Internet access: Library,** 220 E. Lamme St. (582-2400; free; open M-Th 10am-8pm, F-Sa 10am-5pm, Su 1-5pm, closed Su in summer). **Post Office:** 32 E. Babcock St. (open M-F 9am-5pm). **ZIP code:** 59715. **Area code:** 406.

**⌘⌘ ACCOMMODATIONS AND FOOD.** A number of budget motels line Main St. and 7th Ave. north of Main. The **Bozeman International Backpackers Hostel,** 405 W. Olive St., has showers, laundry, kitchen, transportation to trailheads, and a chill atmosphere. There are only 15 beds; call ahead if you can. Owners advise where to eat, drink, and hike; they also rent bikes. (586-4659. $12, children $6; 1 double $30. Bikes ½-day $6, full-day $10.) The **Alpine Lodge,** 1017 E. Main St. (586-0356 or 888-922-5746), has prices that defy its quasi-luxurious rooms. ($33; 2 people $39.50; suite with pull-out couch $58; funky cabins with kitchen $81; rates lower in winter.) The **Bear Canyon Campground** has great views, if you can see around the RV's. 4mi. east of Bozeman, just south of I-90 at exit 313. (Laundry, showers, pool. $15 for 2, water and electricity $16-18, full hook-up $20; $2 per additional person.) Several national forest campgrounds line U.S. 191 south of town ($8-10).

Whole sandwiches at **The Pickle Barrel,** 809 W. College, are giant loaves of fresh sourdough bread stuffed with deli meats and fresh vegetables. A hefty ½-sandwich is $4-5.30. (587-2411. Open daily 10:30am-10pm; in winter 11am-10:30pm.) **Brandi's,** 717 N. 7th, at the **Cat's Paw Casino,** greases up great breakfast at ridiculously low prices: two eggs, hash browns, coffee, and toast for $1.50 (587-3848; open daily 8am-9:30pm; breakfast all day). Delicious bowls of meaty and meatless noodles ($3-6), and soups and salads ($1.25-5.25) are the fare at **tombō,** 815 W. College St. (585-0234; open M-Sa 11am-9pm, Su 4-9pm, closed Su in summer). The **Zebra Cocktail Lounge,** in the basement at the corner of Rouse Ave. and Main St., has a huge selection of beer, a supercool atmosphere that draws college folk and outdoorsy types. (585-8851; good music every-other night; open daily 8pm-2am).

**⚑ THE GREAT OUTDOORS.** Surrounded by three renowned trout-fishing rivers—Yellowstone, Madison, and Gardiner—the small town of **Livingston,** about 20mi. east of Bozeman off I-90, is an angler's heaven. This is gorgeous country; *A River Runs Through It* was shot in Bozeman and Livingston. Livingston's Main St. displays a strip of circa 1900 buildings housing bars (with gambling), restaurants, fishing outfitters, and only a few modern additions. **Dan Bailey's,** 209 West Park St. (222-1673), provides licenses (2-day $15, season $50), and rents fishing gear and wear. (Float tubes $15, rod and reel $10, waders and boots $10. Open M-Sa 7am-7pm, Su 8am-5pm; in winter M-Sa 8am-6pm.)

Bozeman provides its share of downhill thrills. **Bridger Bowl Ski Area,** 15795 Bridger Canyon Rd., 16mi. northeast of town, has plenty of trails for a variety of abilities, and decent prices. (586-2389 or 800-223-9609. Full-day ticket $30, over 72 free, children $13. Rentals: skis $15-20, junior skis $10, snowboard $25. Season mid-Dec. to Apr. 4.) Generally much more challenging, **Big Sky,** between Bozeman and West Yellowstone on U.S. 191 (45mi. south of Bozeman), is renowned for runs

**NUTS TO YOU** The folks at the Rock Creek Lodge (825-4868), east of Missoula, promise you'll "have a ball" at the annual **Testicle Festival** (www.testyfesty.com; Sept. 15-19, 2000). In the past, as many as 12,000 ballsy souls have gathered to sample delicious **rocky mountain oysters** (a.k.a. bull's testicles) and join in wild revelry. Feasting isn't the only activity here; the wary can take part in the bullshit pitch or hairy chest contest instead! Even if you're not around for the festival, **Kathy's Kitchen** at the lodge serves the scrumptious "tender-groin" (open Apr.-Oct. daily 9am-8pm). You may not be able to look a bull in the eyes again, but to show your sack, take I-90 22mi. east of Missoula to exit 126 in Clinton (coincidence?).

as long as 6mi. and short lift lines. (800-548-4486. Full-day ticket $48, under 10 free. Rentals: skis $24-39, kids skis $18, snowboard $33. Season mid-Nov. to mid-Apr.)

In summer, scenic **lift rides** soar up Big Sky (June-Sept. Th-M 10:30am-4:30pm; $12, under 10 free). Equestrian types gallop at nearby **Dalton's Big Sky Stables,** on the spur road off U.S. 191 about 2mi. before Big Sky's entrance (995-2972; open June-Sept.; $25 per hr.; 1 day's notice required). **Yellowstone Raft Co.** shoots the rapids 7mi. north of the Big Sky area on U.S. 191 (995-4613; ½-day $37, children $30).

# MISSOULA

Long a stop on the road to elsewhere, Missoula has served as a hub for Plains Indians, freight trains, and long-distance truckers. Many cross-country wanderers—especially those of the outdoorsy stripe—are captivated by Missoula's nearby wilderness and vibrant nightlife. In summer, the town swarms with cyclists, and painted art cars rub fenders with drag-racing Camaros in pub parking lots. The University of Montana is a liberal haven amidst an otherwise conservative state.

**ROCKY MOUNTAINS**

## ▦ PRACTICAL INFORMATION

You can fly into and out of **Missoula International Airport,** 5225 Hwy. 10 W (728-4381); follow Broadway (which turns into Rt. 10/200) west out of town 6mi. **Greyhound:** 1660 W. Broadway (549-2339); to Bozeman (6hr., 4 per day, $24-30) and Spokane (4hr., 5 per day, $31-33). From the same terminal, **RimRock Stages** serves Whitefish via St. Ignatius and Kalispell (3½hr., 1 per day, $21) and Helena (2½hr., 1 per day, $18). Traveling within Missoula is easy on the reliable **Mountain Line city buses** (721-3333; buses operate M-F 6:45am-6:15pm, Sa 9:45am-5:15pm; fare 85¢). **Taxis: Yellow Cab,** (543-6644). **Ugly Duckling Car Rental,** 3010 S. Reserve, has beautiful prices. (542-8459. $25 per day with 150 free mi., 25¢ each additional mi. 21+. Reservations essential.) **Missoula Chamber of Commerce:** 825 E. Front St. (543-6623), at Van Buren. (Open in summer M-F 7am-7pm, Sa 10am-5pm, Su 11am-5pm; early Sept. to late May M-F 8am-5pm.) The **Domestic Violence Line** (542-1944; rape/sexual assault crises included) and the **Mental Health Line** (728-6817) operate 24hr. **Community First Care,** 2805 South Ave. W. (327-4080), addresses health needs at the Community Medical Ctr. off Reserve St. (open daily 8am-9:30pm). **Internet Access: Cyber Shock,** 821 S. Higgins (721-6251; open Su-Th 7am-2am, F-Sa 24hrs.; $3 per hr.). **Post Office:** 1100 W. Kent (329-2200), between Brooks and South St. (open M-F 8am-6pm, Sa 9am-1pm). Missoula's **ZIP code:** 59801. **Area code:** 406.

## ▐ ACCOMMODATIONS

Settle down at the spacious and immaculate **Birchwood Hostel,** 600 S. Orange St., 13 blocks east of the bus station on Broadway, then 8 blocks south on Orange. (728-9799. 22 beds, laundry, kitchen, and bike storage facilities. $10, ISIC cardholders and cyclists $9. Lockout 9am-5pm. Curfew generally midnight. Light chores. Call ahead in winter.) Cheap lodgings cluster along Broadway. Some rooms at the **Sleepy Inn Motel,** 1427 W. Broadway, have zany shag rugs (549-6484; singles $32; doubles $42). To reach the **Aspen Motel,** 3720 Rt. 200 E, get off I-90 at exit 107 and travel ½mi. east (clean rooms, cable, A/C; singles $34, 1-bed doubles $39, 2-beds $46). The **Missoula/El-Mar KOA Kampground,** 3450 Tina Ave., just south of Broadway off Reserve St. is one of the best KOAs around. Offers shaded tent sites apart from RVs. In mid-summer you can buy baby goats (males $30, females $50.549-0881 or 800-562-5366. 2 people $18, water and electricity $24, full hookups $26, kabins $35-40; $3 per additional person.)

## ◖▐ FOOD AND NIGHTLIFE

Missoula's dining scene offers more than the usual steak and potatoes. Choice thrifty eateries line the downtown area, particularly between **Broadway** and **Rail-**

**road St.** and north of the **Clark Fork River.** The **Farmers Market** and the **Peoples Market** showcase edible and inedible wares at N. Higgins (open in summer Sa 9am-noon and Tu 5:30-7pm). Doubling as a restaurant and natural food store, **Torrey's,** 1916 Brooks St., serves large portions of mouth-watering health food at absurdly low prices; all meals are $3 (721-2510; open M-F 11:30am-2pm and M-Th 5:30-8:30pm). Choose from every imaginable breakfast dish, and several lunch numbers, for under $6 at the **Old Town Café,** 121 W. Alder St. (728-9742; open daily 6am-3pm). **Tipu's,** 115½ S. 4th St., in the alley just west of the corner of S. 4th and Higgins St. (look for the neon sign), serves great vegetarian Indian food amidst metallic, ultra-hip decor (full meal $4-7; 452-0622; open daily 11:30am-9:30pm). A rowdy, young-ish crowd gathers at **The Rhinoceros** "Rhino's," 158 Ryman Ave., to partake of the 51 beers on tap. (721-6061; open daily 11am-2am). **The Kettle House Brewing Co.,** 602 Myrtle, one block west of Higgins between 4th and 5th, has its priorities straight; they don't serve food, only delectable beer straight from their brewery. Olde Bong-water Porter is made with hemp, and tastes better than it sounds. (2 free samples, then $2.50 for pints. Open M-Th 3-9pm, F-Sa noon-9pm, no beer served after 8pm.)

## 👁 SIGHTS AND OUTDOOR ACTIVITIES

The outdoors are Missoula's biggest attraction. Located along both the Trans-America and the Great Parks bicycle routes, the town swarms with **cycling** enthusi-asts. **Open Road Bicycles and Nordic Equipment,** 517 W. Orange St., has bike rentals and info on bike trails. (549-2453. $3 per hr., $15 per day. Open M-F 9am-6pm, Sa 10am-5pm, Su 11am-3pm.)

**Skiing** is also popular; the folks at Open Road (above) can take care of your cross-country needs (X-C ski package $12 per day). The family-oriented **Marshall Mountain** caters to downhill skiers. (258-6000. Full-day $19, seniors and under 19 $15; rentals: skis $12, snowboard $16; night skiing and free shuttles from down-town.) **Montana Snowbowl** is a more extreme option (549-9777; full day $25).

The Clark Fork, Blackfoot, and Bitterroot Rivers overflow with **float trip** oppor-tunities. The **Montana State Regional Parks and Wildlife Office,** 3201 Spurgin Rd. (542-5500), sells float maps for $3.50 (open M-F 8am-5pm). Rent tubes ($3 per day with $20 deposit) or rafts ($30-60, credit card required) from the **Army and Navy Economy Store,** 322 N. Higgins (721-1315; open M-F 9am-7:30pm, Sa 9am-5:30pm, Su 10am-5:30pm). **Pangaea Expeditions,** runs rafting trips on the local rapids, which leave from Bernice's Bakery at 190 S. 3rd St. W. (721-7719; $25 for 2hr., $40-45 ½-day, $55 full-day; discounts for hostelers). The short (1.5mi. round-trip) but steep hike up to the "M" on Mt. Sentinel, starts east of the University, just southeast of the football stadium, and affords great views of the city.

The **Rattlesnake Wilderness National Recreation Area,** named after the shape of the river (there are no rattlers for miles), is 11mi. northeast of town off the Van Buren St. exit from I-90, and makes for a great day of **hiking.** Maps ($6) and more info on the area, including longer hikes in the Bitterroot and Bob Marshall areas, are avail-able from the **U.S. Forest Service Information Office,** 200 E. Broadway; the entrance is at 200 Pine St. (329-3511; open M-F 7:30am-4pm). For equipment rentals, stop by **Trailhead,** 110 E. Pine St., at Higgins St. (543-6966. Tents $9-18, backpacks $9-15, sleeping bags $5-9. Open M-F 9:30am-8pm, Sa 9am-6pm, Su 11am-6pm.) At **The Kingfisher,** 926 E. Broadway, they'll tell you where they're bitin' and rent you a rod (and permit) to catch 'em with. (721-6141 or 888-542-4911. Rods $15 per day, rod and waders $30; permits $15 for 2 days. Open in summer daily 7am-8pm; off-sea-son hrs. vary, generally 9am-6pm.)

Missoula's hottest sight, the **Smokejumper Center,** 7mi. west of town on Broad-way (Rt. 10, just past the airport), depicts the life of courageous aerial firefighters who parachute into flaming, remote forests. (329-4934. Open daily 8:30am-5pm; Sept.-May by appt. only. Tours May.-Sept. on the hr. 10-11am and 2-4pm. Free.) The handcrafted **Carousel,** in Caras Park, offers a wholesome spin. (549-8382. $1, seniors and under 19 50¢. Open daily June-Aug. 11am-7pm; Sept.-May 11am-5:30pm.) The **First Friday** of each month occasions a celebration of Missoula culture, with evening open houses at the town's 15 museums and galleries. On summer W (June-Aug.), bands and food vendors swarm at Caras Park 11:30am-1:30pm. The *Independent* and *Lively Times* offer the low-down on the Missoula music scene (available at newsstands and cafes), while the *Entertainer*, in the F *Missoulian*, has movie and event schedules.

## FROM MISSOULA TO GLACIER

The **Miracle of America Museum,** off U.S. 93 between Missoula and Glacier before you enter the town of **Polson,** houses one of the country's greatest collections of Americana, unswervingly dedicated to the belief that the good ol'-fashioned American way of life is miraculous. A general store, saddlery shop, barber shop, soda fountain, and gas station sit among the classic memorabilia. (883-6804. Open June-Sept. daily 8am-8pm; Oct.-May M-Sa 8am-5pm, Su 2-6pm. $2.50, ages 3-12 $1.) The **National Bison Range,** (40mi. north of Missoula off U.S. 93, then 5mi. west on Rt. 200, 5mi. north on Rt. 212), was established in 1908. Before they were hunted to near-extinction, 50 million of these animals roamed the plains; the Range is home to 300-500 of the imposing creatures. (644-2211. Range open mid-May to mid-Oct. daily 7am-dusk. Visitors center open daily 8am-4:30pm; off-season hrs. vary. Scenic drive $4.) **Flathead Lake,** renowned for its cherries as well as trout and whitefish fishing opportunities, lies next to U.S. 93 between Polson and Kalispell.

   **Hostel of the Rockies,** off U.S. 93 in **St. Ignatius** (look for the camping sign), close to the Bison Range, offers lodging in its "earthship," an eco-friendly structure built into a hillside and made from recycled tires and aluminum cans. (745-3959. Showers, laundry, cooking facilities. $10; tent sites for 1 $8, for 2 $1.) **RimRock Stages** (745-3501) makes a stop ½mi. away in St. Ignatius, at the Malt Shop on Blaine St.

# WATERTON-GLACIER PEACE PARK

Waterton-Glacier transcends international boundaries to encompass one of the most strikingly beautiful portions of the Rockies. A geographical metaphor for the peace between the U.S. and Canada, the park provides sanctuary for many endangered bears, bighorn sheep, moose, mountain goats, and grey wolves.

   Technically one park, Waterton-Glacier is, for all practical purposes, two distinct areas: the small **Waterton Lakes National Park** in Alberta, and the enormous **Glacier National Park** in Montana. Each park charges its own admission fee, and you must go through customs to pass from one to the other. Several **border crossings** are near the park: **Piegan/Carway** at U.S. 89 (open daily 7am-11pm); **Roosville** on U.S. 93 (open 24hr.); and **Chief Mountain** at Rt. 17. (Open daily mid-May to early June and mid-Sept. to early Oct. 9am-6pm; early June to mid-Sept. 7am-10pm.) The fastest way to Waterton is to head north from the east side of Glacier; go through Chief Mountain when it's open.

   Since snow melting is an unpredictable process, the parks are usually in full operation only from late May to early Sept.; it is worth your while to check conditions in advance. To find out which park areas, hotels, and campsites will be open when you visit, contact the Superintendent, Waterton Lakes National Park, Waterton Park, AB T0K 2M0 (403-859-5133), or the Superintendent, Glacier National Park, West Glacier 59936 (406-888-7800). The *Waterton Glacier Guide*, provided at any park entrance, has dates and times of trail, campground, and border crossing openings. Mace, bear spray, and firewood are not allowed into Canada.

## GLACIER NATIONAL PARK

**⛄ PRACTICAL INFORMATION.** Glacier's layout is simple: two roads enter from the west at Polebridge and West Glacier, and three roads enter from the east at Many Glacier, St. Mary, and Two Medicine. West Glacier and St. Mary serve as the two main points of entry into the park, connected by **Going-to-the-Sun Rd.** ("The Sun"), the only road traversing the park. **U.S. 2** runs between East and West Glacier along 57mi. of the southern park border. Look for the "Goat Lick" signs off Rt.

ROCKY MOUNTAINS

2 near **Walton;** mountain goats descend to the lick for a salt fix in June and July. **Admission** is $10 per week per car, $5 per week for pedestrians and cyclists.

Each of the 3 visitors centers has info about trail and campsite availability, local weather, and wildlife conditions. **St. Mary** (732-7750) guards the east entrance of the park. (Open daily mid-May to mid-June 8am-5pm; mid-June to early Sept. 7am-9pm; early-Sept. to mid-Oct. 8am-5pm.) **Apgar** (888-7939) aids at the west entrance. (Open daily mid-June to early Sept. 8am-8pm; May 9am-4:30pm, early June and Sept.-Oct. 8am-4:30pm.) A third visitors center graces **Logan Pass** on Going-to-the-Sun Rd. (Open daily late June to early Sept. 9am-6pm; early to late June 9am-5pm, early Sept. to mid.-Oct. 10am-5pm.) The **ranger station** at Many Glacier can answer questions. (Open daily late May to mid-June and Sept. 8am-4:30pm, mid-June to early July 8am-6pm, early July to early Sept. 7am-6pm.)

**Amtrak** (226-4452) traces a dramatic route along the southern edge of the park. the station in West Glacier is open mid-May to Sept.; the train stops at an unstaffed station in the winter. Trains chug daily to East Glacier (1½hr.; $12-20), Whitefish (45min.; $7), Seattle (14½; $141), and Spokane (6hr. $58-70); Amtrak also runs from East Glacier to Chicago (31hr.; $199-240) and Minneapolis (21½hr. $172-207). **RimRock Stages** (800-255-7655), the only bus line that nears the park, stops in Kalispell (at Sawbuck's Saloon off Rt. 93) from Missoula ($18) or Billings ($58). As in most of the Rockies, a car is the most convenient mode of transport, particularly within the park. **Rent-A-Wreck,** 2622 U.S. 2 E (755-4555), in Kalispell, rents cars. ($37.50 per day. 100 free mi., 21¢ each additional mi. 21+; under 25 $5 per day surcharge.) **The reds/jammers** (888-9187, off-season 602-207-6000), antique tour buses with convertible tops, snake around the area ($4-62) and provide transportation from the West Glacier Amtrak station. Shuttles for hikers ($6-18) roam the length of "The Sun;" schedules are at visitors centers. **Kalispell Regional Medical Center:** 310 Sunnyview Lane (752-5111), north of Kalispell off Rt. 93. **Post Office:** In West Glacier (888-5591), ZIP 59936 (open M-F 8:30am-12:30pm and 1:30-5pm). **ZIP:** 59921. **Area code:** 406.

**▐▗▙ ACCOMMODATIONS AND FOOD.** Staying indoors within Glacier is expensive. The one budget motel, the **Swiftcurrent Motor Inn** in Many Glacier Valley, has cabins for $40 (732-5531; no toilets; 2 bedrooms $50; open early June to early Sept.). The distant offices of **Glacier Park, Inc.,** 925 Dial Corporate Center (602-207-6000), Phoenix, AZ 85077-0928, handle reservations for all in-park lodging.

On the west side of the park, the electricity-less town of **Polebridge,** makes a good base for exploring some of Glacier's most pristine areas. Take Cammas Creek Rd. heading north from the Apgar area, and turn right at the poorly marked "T," or take Rt. 486 (Outer Fork Rd.) from Columbia Falls. Don't take Inner N. Fork Rd.; its potholes are legendary. A bumpy trip up a dirt road preps guests at cozy **North Fork Hostel,** at the end of Beaver Dr., for the primitive propane and kerosene lamps, wood stoves, and outhouses that provide creature comforts. (888-5241. Dorm beds $13, $10 after 2 nights; cabins $26; log homes $50-52. Linen $2. Light chores. Use of canoes, mountain bikes, snowshoes, and nordic ski equipment included.) The **Polebridge Mercantile Store** replenishes depleted supplies and sells homemade pastries. They also rent out rustic cabins and teepees for $20 a night. (888-5105). The **Northern Lights Saloon** next door serves fabulous cheeseburgers ($5), and homemade pie ($2.50; open daily June-Sept. 11am-2pm and 4-9pm for food, until midnight for drinks; off-season Sa-Su only 4-9pm).

In the east, affordable lodging is just across the park border in **East Glacier,** on U.S. 2, 30mi. south of the St. Mary entrance and about 5mi. south of the Two Medicine entrance. **Brownies Grocery (HI-AYH),** 1020 Rt. 49, manages a bakery, deli, and comfortable dorms. (226-4426. Bunks $12, nonmembers $15; private singles $17/$20; doubles $23/$26; triples $25/$28; family room for 4-6 $33. Tent sites $10. Open May-Sept., weather permitting. Reservations recommended.) Next door, the **Whistle Stop Café** is an oasis of gourmet creations made with fresh ingredients and flair (Huckleberry French Toast $5.50). The **Backpacker's Inn Hostel,** 29 Dawson Ave., just south of the East Glacier Amtrak station, has 20 clean beds in co-ed rooms and hot showers for only $10 per night (226-9392; bring a sleeping bag or rent one for $1; open May-Sept.). In St. Mary on Hwy. 89, just north of the park entrance, the **Park Cafe** serves delicious vegetarian Caribbean burritos ($4.75) and is a favorite breakfast stop for hikers (732-4458; open early June to late Sept. 7am-10pm).

**█ CAMPING.** Camping in Glacier is copious, scenic, and popular. Most developed campsites are available on a first come, first served basis; the most popular sites fill by noon, especially at **Many Glacier, Sprague Lake,** and **Rising Sun;** check at visitor's center or park entrances for vacancies. Reservations can be made at **St. Mary** and **Fish Creek** (800-365-2267; $15). **Bowman Lake, Kintla Lake, Logging Creek, Quartz Creek,** and **Cut Bank** offer primitive camping (pit toilets and water; $10) at the end of bumpy dirt roads; because RVs are not recommended here, these sites are some of the most tranquil and last to fill. For Bowman and Kintla enter the park from Polebridge. For Logging Creek and Quartz Creek, ask a ranger for the best route—it depends on road conditions. The rest of the campgrounds cost $12, and you can flush to your little heart's content. The northwest is the least crowded area in the park, and the nice Sprague Creek, Avalanche Creek, and Fish Creek campgrounds are all near beautiful creeks (what a coincidence). To camp near the mountains, you need to head east. Of the campgrounds in the east side of the park, **Many Glacier** is the most scenic, while **Cut Bank** and **Two Medicine** are a bit quieter. **St. Mary's** campground is popular with RV's. Some sites at **Fish Creek, Many Glacier, Sprague, Apgar, Avalanche, Rising Sun, Two Medicine** and **St. Mary** remain reserved for bicyclists and pedestrians until 9pm. **Agpar, Avalanche, Fish Creek,** and **Sprague Creek** campgrounds have at least one wheelchair-accessible site (call 888-7800 for more info). Campgrounds in the surrounding national forests offer sites for $8 ($4 per additional vehicle). Check at the Apgar or St. Mary visitors centers for up-to-date info on conditions and vacancies; weather and the grizzlies adjust the operating dates at their whim. Bring warm clothes and prepare to combat mosquitoes.

If Glacier is too crowded, dispersed camping is free in the Flathead National Forest, and many free-$10 campgrounds dot the Hungry Horse Reservoir off Rt. 2, southwest of West Glacier. The **Hungry Horse Ranger Station** (387-3800) on Rt. 2 has more information (open M-F 8am-4:30pm).

**█ HIKING AND BIKING.** *There are bears out there. Familiarize yourself with the precautions necessary to avoid an encounter* (see p. 62). There are numerous hikes in Glacier, but some of the best are on the east side of the park. The **Grinnell Glacier Trail** (11mi. roundtrip, 7.6mi. if you take the $10 boat from Many Glacier Hotel) up to Grinnell Glacier, is considered the best day hike around. The short (6.2mi. roundtrip) but steep **Scenic Point Trail** begins in the Two Medicine area. Walking the **Hidden Lake** nature trail (3mi. roundtrip) almost guarantees a close encounter with bighorn sheep or mountain goats. Free maps are available from visitors centers. Some trails may be buried in snow well into the season, requiring an ice-ax; technical climbing gear may even be necessary. Call 888-7800 for up-to-date info. Rangers offer free, informative, slow-paced hikes on many trails. Check at the visitors centers for a schedule.

**Backcountry trips** are the best way to appreciate the mountain scenery and the wildlife that make Glacier famous. Day hikes tend to be crowded; but the **Highline Trail** from Logan Pass is a good one, passing through prime bighorn sheep and mountain goat territory. The visitors center's free *Backcountry Guide* pamphlet has a hiking map marked with distances and backcountry campsites. All backcountry campers must obtain, in person, a $4 **wilderness permit** from a visitors center or ranger station no more than 24hr. in advance. Reservations for a particular site ($20 plus $4 per day) should be made more than 24hr. in advance at the Agpar or St. Mary visitors center, on the internet (www.nps.gov/glac), or by mail (Backcountry Permits, Glacier National Park, West Glacier, MT 59936.) Backcountry camping is allowed only at designated campsites. The **Two Medicine** area in the southeast corner of the park is well traveled; the treks to **Kintla Lake** and **Numa Lake** provide fantastic views of nearby peaks. **Belly River** is an isolated and pretty spot.

**Going-to-the-Sun Rd.** follows a beautiful 52mi. course through the park. The constantly changing views of the peaks make it hard to keep your eyes on the road, but watch out—the road is narrow and susceptible to rock slides and falling trees. Snow clogs the road until June; check with rangers for exact opening dates. Vehicles must be under 21ft. long and 8ft. wide to go over the mid-point Logan Pass.

Although "The Sun" is a popular **bike route,** only experienced cyclists with appropriate gear and legs of titanium should attempt this grueling ride. The sometimes nonexistent shoulder of the road can create a hazardous situation. In the summer, bike traffic is prohibited 11am-4pm from the Apgar campground to Sprague Creek, and east-bound from Logan Creek to Logan Pass. Bikes are not permitted on any hiking trails. The Inner Fork Rd. and the old logging roads in the Flathead National Forest are good for **mountain biking. Equestrian** explorers should check to make sure trails are open; fines for riding on closed trails are steep. **Trail rides** from Mule Shoe Outfitters ($35 for 2hr.) are available at Many Glacier (732-4203), Apgar (888-5010), and Lake McDonald (888-5121).

⚡ **BOATING AND FISHING. Boat tours** explore all of Glacier's large lakes. Tours leave from **Lake McDonald** (888-5727; 1hr., 4-5 per day, $8.50, ages 4-12 $4.25); **Two Medicine** (226-4467; 45min., 5 per day, $8); **Rising Sun** at St. Mary Lake (732-4430; 1½hr., 5 per day, $10, children $5); and **Many Glacier** (732-4480; 1¼hr., 5-6 per day, $9.50). Lake McDonald is large, but the least scenic. The tours from Two Medicine, Rising Sun, and Many Glacier provide access to Glacier's backcountry, and there are sunset cruises from Rising Sun and Lake McDonald. **Glacier Raft Co.,** in West Glacier, hawks trips down the middle fork of the Flathead River (888-5454 or 800-332-9995; ½-day $38/29; full-day trip $71 with lunch, under 13 $46).

Rent **rowboats** ($8 per hr.) at Lake McDonald, Many Glacier, Two Medicine, and Apgar; **canoes** ($8 per hr.) at Many Glacier, Two Medicine, and Apgar; **kayaks** at Apgar ($8 per hr.) and Many Glacier; and **outboards** ($15 per hr.) at Lake McDonald, Two Medicine, and Apgar. No permit is needed to **fish** in the park, and limits are generally high, though some areas are restricted and certain species may be catch-and-release. It's all explained in *Fishing Regulations*, available at visitors centers. Outside the park, on Blackfoot Indian land, you *do* need a special permit, and everywhere else in Montana you need a state permit.

## NEAR GLACIER

**WHITEFISH. The Big Mountain,** southwest of the park in Whitefish, has 67 superb ski trails in the winter. (800-859-3528. $40 per day, students and seniors $30, ages 7-18 $27; night skiing $12. Rentals $18, seniors and kids $12, snowboard $25.) Mountain bikers take over the trails in the summer. (Bikes $15 for 4hr. Lift ticket $18 per day or $13 per ride. Family packages available.) Other activities include horseback riding, gondola rides, and folf (frisbee golf). The **Tully Lake District** of the Flathead National Forest is a great (but hard-core) mountain bike ride. **Glacier Cyclery,** 336 2nd St., sells maps ($6) and rents bikes. (862-6446; ½-day $20, full-day $25-40). After a long day, many crash at one of Whitefish's two hostels. The **Bunkhouse Traveler's Inn and Hostel,** 217 Railway St., has a sweet summertime sundeck and offers winter ski bus pick-up. (862-3377. $13; private rooms $30. Kitchen and laundry facilities. Wheelchair access. Closes occasionally between fall and winter seasons.) The **Non-Hostile Hostel,** 300 E. 2nd St., is one helluva friendly place. This apartment building-esque hostel has internet access ($1.50 for email, $5 per ½hr.), a pool table, and the **Wrap and Roll Café** (wrap sandwiches from $4) downstairs (862-7383; rooms $13). Whitefish is the area's nightlife hotspot; **Black Star Brewery,** 2 Central Ave., has free samples of good beer (863-1000; open M-Sa noon-6pm; in winter M-Sa 3-7pm). The **Dire Wolf Pub,** 845 Wisconsin Ave., on the way to Big Mountain, books national acts (862-4500; open M-Sa 11am-1am, Su noon-midnight) The **Great Northern Saloon,** 27 Central St., rocks on the patio in summer (862-2816; open daily 11am-2am). Both bars serve burgers and sandwiches ($5-6). **RimRock** buses (800-255-7655) stop at the Conoco station across E. 2nd St. and run to Missoula (1 per day, $21). Whitefish can be reached by **Amtrak. Post office:** 424 Baker St. (862-2151). **ZIP code:** 59937 (open M-F 8:30am-5:30pm, Sa 10am-2pm).

**BROWNING.** In the city of Browning, 12mi. east of East Glacier, the **Museum of the Plains Indian,** off Rt. 89 just outside town, displays beautiful Native American clothing and crafts. (338-2230. Open June-Sept. daily 9am-5pm; Oct.-May M-F 10am-4:30pm. $4, ages 6-12 $1; Oct.-May free.) During **North American Indian Days** (from the 2nd Th through the 2nd Su of July), Native Americans from the surrounding Blackfoot reservation and elsewhere gather for a celebration that includes tribal dancing, rodeo, and a fantastic parade (338-7406).

## WATERTON LAKES NATIONAL PARK, AB

Only a fraction of the size of its Montana neighbor, Waterton Lakes National Park offers spectacular scenery and activities without the crowds that plague Glacier during July and Aug. Admission is CDN$4 per day, CDN$8 per group of 2-10 people. The park is free in the winter, but a credit card is required from 10pm-8am. The **International Lakeside Hike** leads from Waterton along the west shore of Upper Waterton Lake and delivers you across the border some 14km after leaving town. Rangers from the U.S. and Canada lead the free International Peace Park Hike along this trail (Sa mornings at 10am; early July to early Sept.). The **Carthew-Alderson Trail** starts from Cameron Lake and leads through 18km of incredible views to end up at the town. The **Hiker Shuttle** runs from Tamarack Village in town to Cameron Lake and other trailheads (859-2378, reservations required; CDN$4.50). The popular **Crypt Lake Trail** leads past waterfalls in a narrow canyon, through a 20m natural tunnel, and arrives after 6km at icy, green Crypt Lake, which straddles the international border. To get to the trailhead, you must take the **water taxi** run by **Waterton Shoreline Cruises** in Waterton Park (859-2362). The boat leaves twice a day (CDN$11, ages 4-12 CDN$5). The marina also runs a 2hr. boat tour of Upper Waterton Lake 5 times per day (CDN$19, ages 13-17 CDN$12, ages 4-12 CDN$8; open mid-May to mid-Sept.). Gear is available for rent at **Waterton Sports** in the Tamarac Village Sq. (859-2378; open 9am-6pm). Horses are allowed on many trails. **Alpine Stables,** 1km north of the townsite, conducts trail rides (859-2462; 1hr. ride CDN$17, 4hr. CDN$55; open May-Sept.).

Fishing in Waterton requires a **license** (CDN$6 per week, CDN$13 per season), available from the park offices, campgrounds, warden stations, and service stations in the area. Lake trout cruise the depths of **Cameron** and **Waterton Lakes,** while northern pike prowl the weedy channels of **Maskinonge Lake.** Most of the backcountry lakes and creeks support rainbow and brook trout. Try the creek that spills from Cameron Lake, about 200m to the east of the parking lot, or hike 1.5km to Crandell Lake for plentiful fish. Rent **rowboats, paddleboats,** or **canoes** at Cameron Lake (2 people $17 1st hr., $14 per additional hr.; 4 people $20/$17).

On summer evenings at 8:30pm, take in a free **interpretive program** at the **Cameron Theater** in town or at the Crandell campsite. These interesting and quirkily entitled programs (e.g., *Bearying the Myths*) change yearly. There are programs daily in summer at 8:30pm; the visitors center has a schedule.

At the entrance to the park, the enormous(ly pricey) **Prince of Wales Hotel** serves traditional afternoon tea from June to Sept. (859-2231; daily 2-4:30pm; CDN$20) and a spectacular view. The park's three campgrounds are much more affordable. **Belly River,** on Chief Mountain Hwy. outside the park entrance, has scenic and uncrowded primitive sites for CDN$10. **Crandell,** on Red Rock Canyon Rd., is situated in a forest area with sites for CDN$13. Camp with 200 of your best RV pals at **Townsite** in Waterton Park, which has showers and a lakeside vista, but no privacy, though the walk-in sites are satisfactory and generally the last to fill (sites CDN$16, walk-in sites CDN$15, full hookup CDN$21). **Backcountry camping** is CDN$6 per person per night and requires a permit from the visitors center (see above; or call 859-5133 for a CDN$10 permit, up to 90 days in advance). The backcountry campsites are rarely full, and several, including beautiful **Crandell Lake,** are less than a 1hr. hike from the trailhead.

Travelers preferring to stay indoors should reserve one of the 21 comfy beds, with real mattresses, at the **Waterton International Hostel (HI),** in the Lodge at Waterton Lakes. Includes 10% discount at health club and pool next door. (859-2151 ext.

2016; member CDN$20, non-member CDN $23.55, family room CDN$27/31 per person, ages 6-17 CDN$10/11.75). Groups can take over the 6-bed room for CDN$130 at the **Mountain View Bed and Breakfast,** 20km east of the park, 1km off Rt. 5. The hip owners serve huge breakfasts and maintains immaculate and comfortable rooms. (653-1882. Singles CDN$30-40; doubles CDN$50-80.) The **Country Bakery and Lunch Counter,** 303 Windflower Ave., cooks up meat pies (CDN$2.75) and CDN$3.50 belgian waffles (859-2181; open May-Sept. daily 7am-7pm).

The only road from Waterton's park entrance leads 8.5km south to **Waterton Park.** En route, stop at the **Waterton Visitors Center** (859-5133), 8km inside the park on Rt. 5 for a schedule of events and hikes (open daily mid-June to Aug. 8am-8pm; mid-May to mid-June 8am-6pm; Sept.-Oct. hrs. vary). In the off season, pick up info at **Park Administration,** 215 Mt. View Rd. (859-2224; open M-F 8am-4pm). Greenbacks can be exchanged for Loonies at the **Tamarac Village Sq.** on Mt. View Rd. (open daily July-Aug. at least 9am-6pm; May-June and Sept.-Oct. usually 9am-5pm). A shuttle runs once a day from Waterton to Glacier for $44.75; inquire with the **reds/jammers buses** (see Glacier **Practical Information,** p. 628). **Pat's Mohawk and Cycle Rental,** Mt. View Rd., Waterton, rents bikes (859-2266; mountain bikes CDN$6 per hr., CDN$30 per day). **Ambulance:** 859-2636. **Post office:** in Waterton on Fountain Ave. at Windflower Ave. (open M, W, and F 8:30am-4:30pm, Tu and Th 8:30am-4pm). **Postal code:** T0K 2M0. **Area code:** 403.

# WYOMING

The ninth-largest state in the Union, Wyoming is also the least populated. This is a place where livestock outnumber citizens, and men wear cowboy hats and boots for real. Yet, this rugged land was more than just a frontier during westward expansion. It was the first state to grant women the right to vote without later repealing it, and the first to have a national monument (Devils Tower) and a national park (Yellowstone) within its borders. Wyoming has everything you'd want to see in a state in the Rockies: a Frontier Days festival, spectacular mountain ranges, breath-taking panoramas, and, of course, cattle and beer.

# ⁊ PRACTICAL INFORMATION

**Capital:** Cheyenne.

**Visitor Info: Wyoming Business Council Tourism Office,** I-25 and College Dr., Cheyenne 82002 (307-777-7777, outside WY 800-225-5996; www.commerce.state.wy.us/west). Info center open daily 8am-5pm. **Dept. of Commerce, State Parks and Historic Sites Division,** 122 W. 25th St., Herschler Bldg., Cheyenne 82002 (307-777-6323), 1st fl. Open M-F 8am-5pm. **Game and Fish Dept.,** 5400 Bishop Blvd., Cheyenne 82006 (307-777-4600). Open M-F 8am-5pm.

**Postal Abbreviation:** WY. **Sales Tax:** 5%.

# YELLOWSTONE

Six hundred thousand years ago, intense volcanic activity fueled an eruption that spewed out nearly 35 trillion cubic feet of debris, creating the central basin of what is now **Yellowstone National Park.** Although these geological engines have downshifted, they still power boiling sulfuric pits and steaming geysers. John Colter's descriptions of his 1807 explorations of this earthly inferno inspired 50 years of popular stories about "Colter's Hell." By 1872, popular opinion had swayed, and President Grant declared Yellowstone a national park, the world's first.

Today, Yellowstone's natural beauty is cluttered with cars, RVs, and thousands of tourists. In the backcountry, away from the crowds and netherworldly sinkholes that line the roads, bears, elk, moose, wolves, bison, and bighorn sheep thrive in the park's quieter peaks and valleys. In 1988, a blaze charred a third of Yellowstone, but extreme heat is necessary to release the seeds of the logepole pine; now new saplings push up between gangly skeletons of burnt trees.

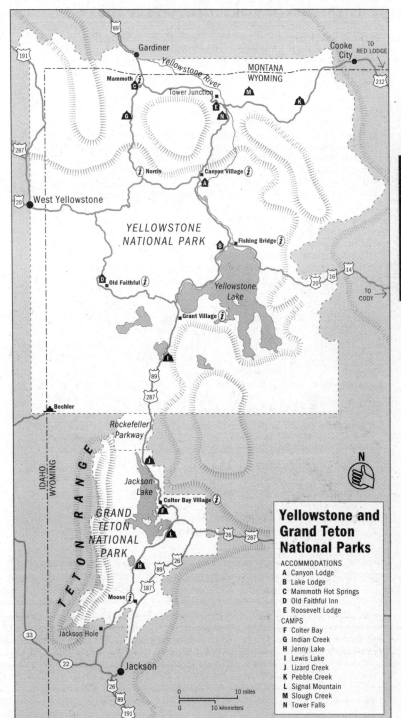

## Yellowstone and Grand Teton National Parks

**ACCOMMODATIONS**
A Canyon Lodge
B Lake Lodge
C Mammoth Hot Springs
D Old Faithful Inn
E Roosevelt Lodge

CAMPS
F Colter Bay
G Indian Creek
H Jenny Lake
I Lewis Lake
J Lizard Creek
K Pebble Creek
L Signal Mountain
M Slough Creek
N Tower Falls

## ORIENTATION AND PRACTICAL INFORMATION

The bulk of Yellowstone National Park lies in the northwest corner of Wyoming, with slivers in Montana and Idaho. **West Yellowstone, MT,** and **Gardiner, MT,** are the most developed and expensive entrance points to the park. For a rustic beginning, **Cooke City, MT,** the northeast entrance, leads to U.S. 212, a gorgeous stretch of road known as **Beartooth Hwy.** (open only in summer). From the east, enter through **Cody** (p. 647) via Rt. 14/16/20. Southern entry to the park is through **Grand Teton National Park** (see p. 640). (**Entrance fee** $20 for cars, $10 for pedestrians, $15 for motorcycles; pass good for one week at Yellowstone and Grand Teton.)

Yellowstone is huge; both Rhode Island and Delaware could fit within its boundries. Yellowstone's roads circulate millions of visitors in a rough figure-eight configuration, with side roads branching off to park entrances and some of the lesser-known sites. The natural wonders which make the park famous (e.g., Old Faithful) dot the Upper and Lower Loops. Construction and renovation of roads are planned for the next 80 years; call ahead or consult *Yellowstone Today*, available at the entrance, to find out which sections will be closed during your visit…and your lifetime. Even without construction you won't be getting anywhere fast. The speed limit is 45 mph and much of the time you'll be going slower because of the steep grades and tight curves.

It's unwise to bike or walk the roads at night, as you risk startling large wild animals; roaming beasts emerge at dawn and dusk. Approaching any wild animal at any time is illegal and unsafe; those who don't remain at least 25 yds. from moody bison or moose and 100 yds. from bears risk being mauled or gored to death. (For more tips on avoiding fisticuffs with a bear, see **Wilderness Safety,** p. 67.) Near thermal areas, stay on marked trails, because "scalding water can ruin your trip."

The park's high season extends from about mid-June to mid-Sept. If you visit during this period, expect large crowds, clogged roads, and motels and campsites filled to capacity. Much of the park shuts down from Nov.Dec. to mid-Apr., then opens gradually as the snow melts.

**Buses: Greyhound:** West Yellowstone Office Services, 132 Electric St., West Yellowstone. To: Bozeman (2hr., 1 per day, $15); Salt Lake City (9hr., 1 per day, $48); and Boise (17hr., 1 per day, $90). **Powder River Transportation** comes from Cody (see p. 647).

**Car Rental: Big Sky Car Rental,** 429 Yellowstone Ave. (646-9564 or 800-426-7669), West Yellowstone, MT. $34 per day, unlimited mi. within a 125 mi. radius. Must be 21 with a credit card. Open daily May to mid-Oct. 8am-5pm.

**Bike Rental: Yellowstone Bicycles,** 132 Madison Ave. (646-7815), West Yellowstone, MT. Mountain bikes with helmet and water $3.50 per hr., $12.50 per ½-day, $19.50 per day. Open May-Oct. daily 8:30am-8:30pm; Nov.-Apr. 11am-87pm.

**Horse Rides: AmFac** (344-7311; call at least a day ahead), from Mammoth Hot Springs, Roosevelt Lodge, and Canyon Village. Late May to early Sept. $20 per hr., 2hr. $32. From early June to early Sept., **stagecoach rides** ($6, ages 2-11 $5.25) are available at Roosevelt Lodge.

**Tours:** With time and transportation, you can do better on your own, but **AmFac Parks and Resorts** (344-7311) offers the cheapest tours. 8½-9hr. bus tours of the lower park, leave daily from area lodges and campgrounds ($28.50, ages 12-16 $15). Similar tours of the northern region leave from Canyon Lodge, Lake Hotel, Fishing Bridge RV Park, and Bridge Bay Campground ($22.50-26.50, ages 12-16 $11-13). Full-day tours around the park's figure-eight road system also available, leaving from Gardiner, MT, and Mammoth Hot Springs ($32-33, ages 12-16 $16.50-17.50). **Grayline Tours** (406-646-9374 or 800-523-3102) tours from West Yellowstone through both loops. Free pick-up from area motels and campgrounds. ($39; under 12 $25.) Alternatively, **Buffalo Bus Lines,** 429 Yellowstone Ave. (406-646-9564 or 800-426-7669) in West Yellowstone tours Upper Loop on odd days, and Lower Loop on even days ($35, kids $25).

ROCKY MOUNTAINS

**Visitor Info:** Most regions in this vast park have their own central station. All centers offer backcountry permits, but each has distinct hiking and camping regulations and regional exhibits. **Albright Visitors Center** (344-2263) at Mammoth Hot Springs: history of Yellowstone Park and the beginnings of the National Park Idea; **Grant Village** (242-2650): wilderness and the 1988 fire; **Fishing Bridge** (242-2450): wildlife and Yellowstone Lake; **Canyon** (242-2550): bison; **Old Faithful** (545-2750): geysers; **Norris** (344-2812): geothermic features of the park. All stations are usually open late May to early Sept. daily 8am-7pm; Albright and Old Faithful are open through the winter. **Info centers: Madison** (open 8am-7pm), and at **West Thumb** (open 8am-5pm), on the southern edge of the Lake. **West Yellowstone Chamber of Commerce,** 30 Yellowstone Ave. (406-646-7701), West Yellowstone, MT, 2 blocks west of the park entrance. Open late May to early Sept. daily 8am-8pm; early Sept. to late May M-F 8am-5pm.

**General Park Information, including campground info:** 344-7381

**Radio Information:** Tune in to 1610AM for park info.

**Medical Services: Lake Clinic, Pharmacy,** and **Hospital** (242-7241), across the road from the Lake Yellowstone Hotel. Clinic open late May to mid-Sept. daily 8:30am-8:30pm. Emergency room open May-Sept. 24hr. **Old Faithful Clinic** (545-7325), near the Old Faithful Inn. Open early May to mid-Oct. daily 8:30am-5pm; May and mid-Sept. to mid-Oct. closed Th&F. **Mammoth Hot Springs Clinic** (344-7965), open June-Aug. M-F 8:30am-1pm and 2-5pm; Sept.-May M-F 8:30am-1pm and 2-5pm. The **Clinic at West Yellowstone,** 236 Yellowstone Ave. (406-646-7668), in West Yellowstone, open late May to early Sept. M-Sa 8:30am-5:30pm; off season hours vary.

**Disabled Services:** All entrances, visitors centers, and ranger stations offer the *Visitor Guide to Accessible Features.* Fishing Bridge RV Park, Madison, Bridge Bay, Canyon, and Grant campgrounds have accessible sites and restrooms, while Lewis Lake and Slough Creek each have a site. Write the **Accessibility Coordinator,** P.O. Box 168, Yellowstone National Park, WY, 82190, for more info, or call 344-2386 (TDD only).

**Post Office:** There are 5 post offices in the park at **Lake, Old Faithful, Canyon, Grant,** and **Mammoth Hot Springs** (344-7764). Open M-F 8:30am-5pm. Specify which station at Yellowstone National Park. **ZIP code:** 82190. **West Yellowstone, MT:** 209 Grizzly Ave. (406-646-7704). Open M-F 8:30am-5pm, Sa 8-10am. **ZIP code:** 59758.

**Area codes:** 307 (in the park), 406 (in West Yellowstone, Cooke City, and Gardiner, MT). In text, 307 unless otherwise noted.

# ⌐ ACCOMMODATIONS AND FOOD

Camping is far cheaper, but cabins are available within the park. For the nature-weary, hotel and motel rooms abound nearby; to keep the budget in line, stick to towns near the park's entry-points.

**IN THE PARK.** AmFac Parks and Resorts (344-7311) controls all accommodations within the park with an iron fist, using a secret code for cabins: "Roughrider" means no bath, no facilities; "Budget" offers a sink; "Economy" guarantees a toilet and sink; "Pioneer" offers a shower, toilet, and sink; "Frontier" is bigger, more plush; and "Western" is the biggest and most plush. Facilities are located close to the more rustic cabins. All cabins or rooms should be reserved well in advance of the June to Sept. tourist season. Be choosy buying food in the park, as many, but not all, of the restaurants, snack bars, and cafeterias are quite expensive. If possible, stick to the **general stores** at each lodging location; they sell provisions; the stores at Fishing Bridge, Lake, Grant Village, and Canyon sell lunch-counter style food (open daily 7:30am-10pm, though times may vary by around 30min.).

**Roosevelt Lodge,** in the north of the park, 19 mi north of Canyon. A favorite of Teddy Roosevelt, who seems to have frequented every motel and saloon west of the Mississippi. Provides some of the cheapest and most scenic indoor accommodations around.

Roughrider cabins ($40, bring your own towel) with wood-burning stoves and more spacious Economy ($51) or Frontier cabins ($77), both with toilet and electric heat.

**Mammoth Hot Springs,** 18mi. west of Roosevelt area, near the north entrance. Lattice-sided Budget cabins $48. Frontier cabins (some with porches) from $77. Hotel Room without bath $51.

**Old Faithful Inn and Lodge,** 30 mi southwest of the west Yellowstone entrance. Pleasant Budget cabins with sink ($32), Pioneer cabins ($42), and Frontier cabins ($58). Well-appointed hotel rooms from $52, with private bath $75.

**Lake Lodge Cabins,** a stone's throw from Yellowstone Lake 4 mi south of Fishing Bridge, is a cluster of cabins dating from the 20s and 50s, with interior decorating from the 70s. Pioneer cabins $48; larger Western cabins $101. Next door, **Lake Yellowstone Hotel and Cabins** has yellow Frontier cabins with no lake view for $77.

**Canyon Lodge and Cabins,** in the middle of the figure-eight of the park loop 15 mi north of Fishing Bridge. Less authentic and more expensive than Roosevelt Lodge's cabins, but slightly closer to the popular Old Faithful area. Pioneer cabins $51; Frontier cabins $77; Western cabins $101.

**WEST YELLOWSTONE, MT.** Guarding the west entrance of the park, West Yellowstone's overflowing shops and services wash over some genuine Montana flavor. Grab an inexpensive breakfast or lunch at the **Running Bear Pancake House** at the corner of Madison and Hayden (406-646-7703; open daily 7am-2pm) or lasso some chow at the **Food Round-Up Grocery Store,** 107 Dunraven St. (406-646-7501; open in summer daily 7am-10pm, in winter 7am-9pm).

**West Yellowstone International Hostel (AAIH/Rucksackers),** 139 Yellowstone Ave. (406-646-7745 or 800-838-7745 outside MT), at the **Madison Hotel**. A friendly manager presides over this old but clean, wood-adorned hostel. Rooms tend to get stuffy, especially on hot days. $18. singles and doubles $27-37. Open late May to mid-Oct.

**Lazy G Motel,** 123 Hayden St. (406-646-7586), has big rooms with queen beds, refrigerators, and TVs. Singles $43, doubles $56, with kitchenette $63.

**Ho Hum Motel,** 126 Canyon (406-646-7746) is a straight-forward motel that offers clean rooms with 1 queen bed for $40 and 2 queen beds for $50.

**GARDINER, MT.** Located about 1½hr. northeast of West Yellowstone, Gardiner is the park's original entrance. It's smaller and less touristy than West Yellowstone, but also more expensive. Pick a bundle of cheap food at **Food Farm,** on U.S. 89 across from the Super 8 (406-848-7524; open M-Sa 7am-9pm, Su 8am-8pm). Next door, **Helen's Corral Drive-In** rounds up killer ½ lb. burgers (open in summer daily 11am-11pm).

**The Town Café and Motel** (406-848-7322), on Park St. across from the park's northern entrance. Pleasant, wood-paneled, carpeted rooms. TVs but no phones. Singles $45, doubles $55; Oct.-May $35/$45.

**Jim Bridger Court Modern Cabins** (406-848-7371), on U.S. 89, has clean cabins with TV, but again no phones. 1 queen bed $50, 2 queen beds $60.

**Hillcrest Cottages** (406-848-7353 or 800-970-7353), on U.S. 89 across from the Exxon, rents out homey cabins with kitchenettes. Singles $58; doubles $70; $6 per additional adult, $2 per additional child under 18. Open May to early Sept.

**COOKE CITY, MT.** Cooke City is located at the northeast corner of the park. The Nez Percé slipped right by the U.S. cavalry here, Lewis and Clark deemed the area impassable, and even today few people visit this rugged little town. Most things are cheaper here than in the other entrance towns, particularly gas (up to 10 cents cheaper per gallon.) The **Pine Tree Cafe**, Rt. 212 on the eastern side of town offers the Pine Tree Special—an incredible milkshake, fries, and a large cheeseburger--is only $5.50. (406-838-2161. Open daily in summer 7am-8pm, off season hours vary, but generally 7am-4pm, closed mid-Oct. to late Dec. and mid-Apr. to late May.)

If you've never slept in a yurt before, this is your chance. The **Yellowstone Yurt Hostel** (406-838-2349), at the corner of W. Broadway and Montana St. (turn north onto Republic St. from U.S. 212), has one—a round tent with a skylight, wood stove, and six bunks. The hostel is oriented toward backcountry skiers in the winter. $12 buys a bunk, a hot shower, and access to an outdoor kitchen. Bring a sleeping bag. Check-in is before 9pm; call ahead for late arrivals. At the eastern end of town (there's only one main street in Cooke City, U.S. 212) in **Antler's Lodge,** a renovated U.S. cavalry outpost where Ernest Hemingway spent a few nights editing *For Whom the Bell Tolls* (406-838-2432; singles $45; doubles $55).

## ▐ CAMPGROUNDS

Getting a campsite in Yellowstone can be a pain in the ass. Sites can be reserved at five of 12 developed campgrounds. **AmFac,** P.O. Box 165, Yellowstone National Park 82190 (344-7311), controls **Canyon, Grant Village, Madison, Bridge Bay** (all $16), and **Fishing Bridge RV** ($27; RVs only). For future reservations call (344-7311). For same day reservations call (344-7901, or if you're in West Yellowstone go to **Northern Bear Trading Company**, between the IMAX theater and the Grizzly Discovery Center, 406-646-7345). Generally Fishing Bridge is the first to fill up each day, followed by Madison, Canyon, Grant Village, and Bridge Bay. Reservations are accepted up to two years in advance, and on crowded days (generally weekends and holidays) all spots may be reserved beforehand. On quieter days it is possible to reserve a site if you call before 9 or 10am. Sometimes you can reserve Grant Village and Bridge Bay as late as 5, 6, or 7pm, but the earlier the better.

Seven campgrounds offer rustic first come, first served sites with potable water ($10 with pit toilets; $12 with flush toilets). In summer, most of these fill by 10 or 11am. **Norris, Indian Creek, and Lewis Lake** are often the first to fill, followed by **Tower Fall**. Check-out time is 10am; most sites empty out from the previous evening between 8 and 10 and this window is your best chance to get some of the most popular spots. All of these sites are nice, but two of the most beautiful and tranquil areas are **Slough Creek Campground** ($10; 29 sites, 10mi. northeast of Tower Junction; open late May to Oct.) and **Pebble Creek Campground** ($10 32 sites; no RVs; open mid-June to early Sept.). Both are located in the northeast between Tower and the Northeast Entrance—generally the least congested area—and offer relatively uncrowded spots and good fishing. You can also try **Lewis Lake** ($10), south of the Lake halfway between West Thumb and the South Entrance, with 85 pine tree-enveloped sites, or **Tower Falls** ($10), between the Northeast entrance and Mammoth Hot Springs, with 32 sites high on a hill. **Norris**, ($12; 116 sites; open late May-late Sept.) **Indian Creek,** between the Norris Geyser Basin and Mammoth Hot Springs ($10; 75 sites; open mid-June to mid-Sept.), and **Mammoth** ($12; 85 sites; open year-round) are a bit less scenic, but still are great places to camp. Campgrounds at Grant Village, Fishing Bridge, and Canyon all have coin laundries ($1.25 wash, $1 dry) and pay showers ($3). The lodges at Mammoth and Old Faithful have showers for $3 (towels and shampoo included) but no laundry facilities. Call **Park Headquarters** (344-7381) for info on any of Yellowstone's campgrounds—they will be able to tell you which campgrounds are full.

If all sites are full, $8 campgrounds lurk outside the park in the area National Forests. Good sites line U.S. 14/16/20, 287, 191, 89, and Rt. 212 (near Cooke City). Often nearly empty, they are worth camping in, even if there are spots open at Yellowstone. Some help can be found at the visitors center in West Yellowstone.

Over 95% (almost 2 million acres) of the park is backcountry. To venture overnight into the wilds of Yellowstone, you need a **backcountry permit** ($15) from a ranger station (near all major visitor centers). Consult a ranger before embarking on a trail; they can offer tips on how to avoid bears, ice, and other natural hindrances. Follow backcountry regulations regarding sanitation, pets, firearms and firewood. The more popular areas fill up in high season. To reserve a permit ahead of time you must fill out a **trip planning worksheet,** which you can get by writing to the **Backcountry Office,** P.O. Box 168, Yellowstone National Park 82190, or by calling 344-2160 or 344-2163. There is almost always some space available in the back-country and you can reserve a permit in person no more than 48hr. in advance. In many backcountry areas campfires are not permitted, and in particularly dry years none may be permitted at all; plan on bringing a stove and related cooking gear.

## ⚡ SIGHTS AND ACTIVITIES

For mountains of cash, **AmFac** (344-7311) sells tours, horseback rides, and chuck-wagon dinners until the cows come home. Given enough time, however, eyes and feet will do a better job than AmFac's tours, without selling your firstborn. The main attractions feature informative self-guiding tour pamphlets with maps (25¢, except for Old Faithful 50¢) and are accessible from the road by wooden or paved walkways, usually extending ¼ to 1½mi. through various natural phenomena. Some walkways are wheelchair accessible until they connect with longer hiking trails; check tour pamphlets or ask a ranger to find out which ones are accessible.

What sets Yellowstone apart from the myriad of other National Parks and Forests in the Rockies are its **geothermal features**—the park protects the largest geothermic area in the world. Beware: *the crust around some of these features is paper thin and underneath may lie boiling, acidic water. Stay on the marked paths, or in the backcountry give wide bearth lest scalding water ruin your trip.* The bulk of these features can be found on the western side of the park between Mammoth Hot Springs in the North and Old Faithful in the South. The most dramatic of this bizarre bunch are the **geysers**. Incredibly hot molten rock, close to surface of the earth in the geothermic areas superheats water until it boils and bubbles and eventually builds up enough pressure to burst through the cracks with steamy force.

**OLD FAITHFUL AREA.** Most geysers are erratic, but several follow some sort of regular schedule. **Old Faithful,** while neither the largest, the highest, nor the most regular geyser, is the most regular of the large geysers. Since its 1870 discovery, this granddaddy of geysers has consistently erupted with a whoosh of spray and steam (5000-8000 gallons worth) every 30min. to 1½hr. Predictions for the next eruption, usually accurate to within 10 minutes, are posted at the Old Faithful Visitors Center. Old Faithful lies in the **Upper Geyser Basin**, 16mi. south of the Madison area and 20 mi west of Grant Village. Numerous other geysers and hot springs are in this area and trails connect them all. The beautiful **Morning Glory Pool** is an easy 1½ mi walk from Old Faithful.

**FIREHOLE RIVER.** Between Old Faithful and Madison, along the Firehole River, lie the **Midway Geyser Basin** and the **Lower Geyser Basin**. Almost everything you'll see along the side of the road is interesting, even if only for a brief stop. The **Excelsior Geyser Crater**, a large, steaming lake carved out of the earth by a powerful geyser blast, and its partner the **Grand Prismatic Spring**, the largest hot spring in the park, are both located about 5mi. north of Old Faithful and are worth a look. 8mi. north of Old Faithful (or 8mi. south of Madison, depending on your world-view) you'll find the **Fountain Paint Pot**, a bubbling pool of hot milky mud. Along this area's trails lie examples of all four types of geothermal activity (geysers, mudpots, hot springs, and fumaroles—muddy steam vents) which bubble, steam, and spray together in cacophonous harmony. The temptation is strong to wash off the grime of camping in all of this hot water, but swimming in the hot springs is prohibited. You can **swim** in the Firehole River, ¾ of the way up Firehole Canyon Dr. (just south of Madison Jct.), though be prepared for a chill; the name of the river is quite deceiving. Call park information (344-7381) to make sure the river is open.

**NORRIS GEYSER BASIN.** Farther north, 14mi. past Madison, 21mi. south of Mammoth and 15 mi south of the Indian Creek Campground, is the colorful **Norris Geyser Basin,** one of the most active areas in the park. **Echinus,** whose dramatic blasts from a clear basin of water consistently please, is predictable about half the

**FEDERAL WOLF PACKS** In Jan. 1995, after years of public debate, the federal government began to reintroduce gray wolves into the greater Yellowstone ecosystem. Before the program, the last known wolves in Yellowstone were killed in 1929 as part of a federally funded bounty hunt to eradicate the predators. Local and state response to the federal initiative has been mixed. Many ranchers have denounced the reappearance of wolves, fearing they will kill livestock. Others hail the program as the first step in a return to a healthy ecosystem. Montana's State Senate and House of Representatives responded with a caustic joint resolution that made their position clear: "Now, therefore, be it resolved that if the United States government is successful in its efforts to reintroduce wolves into the Yellowstone Park ecosystem, the U.S. Congress is urged to take the steps necessary to ensure that wolves are also reintroduced into every other ecosystem and region of the United States, including Central Park in New York City, the Presidio in San Francisco, and Washington, D.C."

time and eruptions occur once an hour. The geyser has erratic fits the other half of the time, exploding once every one to four hours. Its neighbor, **Steamboat**, is the tallest geyser in the world, topping 400ft. and erupting for up to 20min. Only the truly patient can appreciate this wonder of nature; its blast schedule is entirely unpredictable—its last enormous eruption occurred on Oct. 2, 1991.

**MAMMOTH HOT SPRINGS.** Shifting water sources, malleable limestone deposits, and temperature-sensitive, multicolored bacterial growth create the most rapidly changing natural structure in the park, the hot spring terraces that resemble huge wedding cakes at **Mammoth Hot Springs**, 21mi. to the north of the Norris Basin and 29mi. west of Tower. Ask a local ranger where the most active springs are on the day of your visit. Also ask about area trails, which feature some of the park's best wildlife viewing. **Horse Rides** are available through AmFac (see **Practical Information p. 634**) just south of the Hot Springs, and **swimming** is allowed in the **Boiling River**, whose name-giver was a big liar, 2½mi. north. Call the information line (344-7381) to make that this is open, as bears like this area too.

**CANYON.** The east side's featured attraction, the **Grand Canyon of the Yellowstone**, wears rusty red-orange colors created by hot water acting on the volcanic rock. For a close-up view of the mighty **Lower Falls**, hike down the short but steep **Uncle Tom's Trail** (over 300 steps). **Artist Point** on the southern rim and **Inspiration Point** on the northern rim offer broader canyon vistas and both are accessible from the road between Canyon and Fishing Bridge. All along the canyon's 19mi. rim, keep an eye out for bighorn sheep. At dawn or dusk, the bear-viewing area (at the intersection of Northern Rim and Tower roads) should have you dusting off your binoculars. **Horse Rides** are available at Canyon, as well as in the Tower-Roosevelt area 19mi. north (see **Practical Information p. 634**).

**YELLOWSTONE LAKE AREA. Yellowstone Lake,** in the southeastern corner of the park, Fishing Bridge, at the northern end of the Lake is 16mi. south of Canyon and 27 mi west of the Eastern Entrance; Grant Village, at the southwestern edge of the lake, is 24 southwest of Fishing Bridge and 20mi east of Old Faithful, contains tons o' trout but requires a **fishing permit,** available at visitors centers. (10-day pass $10, season $20; ages 12-15 free; under 12 may fish without a permit.) In the old days you could catch a few in the Lake and immediately boil them in the **Fishing Cone** at the **West Thumb Geyser Basin,** 3mi. north of Grant Village and 17mi. south of Bridge Bay. Now-a-days they don't allow cooking in the hotsprings, but you can have the chef fry them for you ($9) in the **Lake Yellowstone Hotel Dining Room.** Fishing is allowed in many of the other lakes and streams in the park, though some allow catch-and-release fishing only. Double check when you buy your license. **Bridge Bay Tackle,** at Bridge Bay Dock, rents spinning rods (242-7326; $7.50 per day, $20 deposit; open June-Sept. daily 8am-6pm). To go boating or even floating on the lake, you'll need a **boating permit** (motorized vessels $10 for 10-day pass; motor-free boats $5 for 10-day pass), available at many ranger stations, backcountry offices (check *Yellowstone Today*), Bridge Bay marina, a few park entrances, and the Lewis Lake campground. **AmFac** (344-7311) rents row boats($6/hour), outboards($29/hour), and dockslips ($9-15 per night) at Bridge Bay Marina, and runs scenic cruises ($8.75, children $4.75) and guided fishing trips ($52-68 per hr.) on Yellowstone Lake. 4mi. north of Fishing Bridge, **Mud Volcano** features seething, warping sulfuric earth as well as the **Dragon's Mouth,** a vociferous steaming hole that early explorers reportedly heard all the way from Yellowstone River. You certainly can smell it from that far away.

**OFF THE (EXTREMELY WELL) BEATEN PATH.** Over 1200mi. of trails crisscross the park, but many are poorly marked. Rangers at any visitors center are glad to recommend an array of **hikes** in their specific area for explorers of all levels. Most of the spectacular sights in the park are accessible by car, but only a hike will get you up close and personal with the multi layered petrified forest of **Specimen Ridge**, between Tower and Pebble Creek, or the geyser basins at **Shoshone** and **Heart Lake**, both near Grant Village and Lewis Lake. **Cascade Corner,** in the southwest, is a lovely area accessible by trails from the town of Bechler. (Be forewarned: getting to Bechler may require a circuitous route through Idaho over some unpaved roads.) The already-spectacular view from the summit of **Mt. Washburn**, between the **Canyon** and **Tower** areas, is enhanced when surveyed from the telescope inside the old fire lookout station. The **North Trail** is a mild incline; the **South Trail** is a little steeper. Trails in the **Tower-Roosevelt** area in the northeast of the park provide some of the most abundant wildlife watching. When planning a hike, pick up a topographical trail map ($8-9) at any visitors center and ask a ranger to describe forks in the trail. Allow extra time (at least 1hr. per day) in case you lose the trail.

# GRAND TETON

When John Colter explored Wyoming's wilderness in 1807-08 he found himself before a spectacular mountain range. The range's crowning glories were (and are) three craggy peaks—South Teton, Grand Teton and Mt. Teewinot—each over 12,000ft. Later, solitary French mountain men attempted to make the rugged landscape more trapper-friendly, and so dubbed the mountains "Les Trois Tetons," French for "the three tits." When they found that the triple nipples had numerous smaller companions, they named the range "Les Grands Tetons." Now, the snowy heights of **Grand Teton National Park** delight hikers with miles of strenuous trails. The less adventurous will appreciate the rugged appearance of the lofty pinnacles with their glistening glaciers rising straight out of the valley floor.

## ▋ ORIENTATION AND PRACTICAL INFORMATION

The park occupies most of the space between Jackson to the south and Yellowstone to the north. **Rt. 89**, which is called **Rockefeller Pkwy.** in the north of the valley, runs the length of the valley between the Gros Ventre Mountains and the Tetons, connecting the two parks. The parkway offers dramatic views of the entire length of the Tetons. At dusk, moose, elk, and other big game are visible from the road. The park is accessible from all directions except the west, as those French trappers found out centuries ago. The park **entrance fee** is $20 per car, $10 per pedestrian or bicycle, and $15 per motorcycle. The pass is good for 7 days in both the Tetons and Yellowstone. There are several recreational areas; the most developed is **Colter Bay,** while the most beautiful is **Jenny Lake.** These areas and surrounding trailheads are excellent places to begin exploring the Tetons.

**Visitor Info: Moose Visitors Center** (739-3399), Teton Park Rd., at the southern tip of the park, ½mi. west of Moose Jct. Open daily in summer 8am-7pm; early Sept. to mid-May 8am-5pm; open everyday but Dec. 25. **Jenny Lake Visitors Center** (739-3392), next to the Jenny Lake Campground. Open daily June to early Sept. 8am-7pm, early Sept. to early Oct. 8am-5pm. **Colter Bay Visitors Center** (739-3594), on Jackson Lake in the northern part of the park. Open daily early June to early Sept. 8am-8pm; early May to mid-May and early Sept. to early Oct. 8am-5pm; late May to early June 8am-7pm. The Moose and Colter Bay Visitors Centers have the free *Teewinot* newspaper for info about hiking trails, camping, and facilities. For general info, information on ranger-led activities, and a visitor's packet, contact **Park Headquarters** (739-3600) or write the **Superintendent,** Grand Teton National Park, P.O. Drawer 170, Moose WY 83012.

**Public Transit:** Grand Teton Lodge Co. (733-2811) runs in summer from Colter Bay to Jackson Lake Lodge ($2.75 each way); and runs shuttles to the Jackson Hole airport (5 per day, $20) and Jackson (3 per day, $15).

**Info lines: Weather,** 739-3611. **Wyoming Hwy. Info Center,** 733-1731. **Wyoming Dept. of Transportation,** 888-996-7623. **Road Report,** 336-6600, 888-432-7623. **Backcountry Permits and River Info,** 739-3309.

**Emergency: Sheriff's office,** 733-2331. **Park dispatch,** 739-3300.

**Medical Services: Grand Teton Medical Clinic,** Jackson Lake Lodge (543-2514, after hrs. 733-8002). Open daily late May to mid-Oct. 10am-6pm. **St. John's Hospital,** 625 E. Broadway (733-3636), in Jackson.

**Post Office:** In Moose (733-3336), across from the Park HQ. Open M-F 9am-1pm and 1:30-5pm, Sa 11am-12:30pm. **ZIP code:** 83102. **Area code:** 307.

ROCKY MOUNTAINS

# CAMPGROUNDS AND BACKCOUNTRY CAMPING

To stay in the Tetons without emptying your savings account, find a tent and pitch it; call 739-3603 for camping info. The park service maintains five campgrounds, all first come, first served. Campsites are generally open mid-May to late Sept. or early Oct. (vehicle sites $12, bicycle campsites $3). Maximum length of stay is 14 days at all sites except for Jenny Lake (7-day max. stay). All have restrooms, cold water, fire rings, dump stations, and picnic tables. RVs are welcome in all but the Jenny Lake area, but only Colter Bay (sites $31) and Flagg Ranch have hookups. Large groups can go to Colter Bay and Gros Ventre; all others allow a maximum of six people and one vehicle per site. The 49 quiet, woodsy sites at **Jenny Lake** are among the most beautifully developed in the U.S. Mt. Teewinot towers 6000ft. above tents pitched at the edge of the lake. These sites often fill before 8 or 9am; get there early. **Lizard Creek,** closer to Yellowstone than the Tetons, has 60 spacious, secluded sites along the northern shore of Jackson Lake. The campsites fill up by about 2pm. **Colter Bay,** the most crowded campsite, with 350 sites, $3.50 showers, a grocery store, a laundromat, and two restaurants, is usually full by noon. At **Signal Mountain,** 10mi. south of Colter Bay, the 86 sites are a bit more roomy than at Colter Bay, and are usually full by 10am. **Gros Ventre** is the biggest campsite (360 sites, 5 group sites), located along the edge of the Gros Ventre River at the southern border of the park, convenient to Jackson. However, the Tetons are hidden by Elephant Butte. The campsite rarely fills and is the best bet for late arrivals. (739-3516 or Jan.-May 739-3473. Reservations required for groups over 9.)

To **backcountry camp** between Jan. 1 and May 15 in a mountain canyon or on the shores of a lake, make a reservation by submitting an itinerary to the **permit office.** (Info: 739-3309 or 739-3397. Fax: 739-3438. Write: Grand Teton National Park, Moose HQ, Attn.: Permits, P.O. Drawer 170, Moose WY 83012.) After May 15, ¾ of all backcountry spots are available first come, first served; get a permit up to 24hr. before setting out at the Moose, Colter Bay (permit office open daily 8am-6pm), or Jenny Lake Visitors Centers. Wood fires are not permitted above 7000ft. in the backcountry and generally not at lower elevations; be sure to check with rangers before singing 'round the campfire. Snow often remains at high-elevation campsites into July, and the weather can become severe (deadly to those unprepared for it) any time of the year. Taking severe weather gear is advised.

##  ACCOMMODATIONS AND FOOD

**The Grand Teton Lodge Co.** runs both Colter Bay accommodations, which are open late May to early Oct. (Reservations: Call 543-2811 or 800-628-9988. Write **Reservations Manager,** Grand Teton Lodge Co., P.O. Box 240, Moran 83013. Deposits often required.) **Colter Bay Tent Cabins** are the cheapest, but potentially the coldest. The cabins are charming but primitive log and canvas shelters with dusty floors, wood-burning stoves, tables, and bunks. Sleeping bags, cots, and blankets are available for rent. (543-2828. Tent cabins $30 for 2; $3 per additional person. Restrooms and $3.50 showers nearby. Office open early June to early Sept. 24hr.) **Colter Bay Log Cabins** maintains 208 quaint log cabins near Jackson Lake. The cabins with shared baths are probably the best deal in the entire Jackson Hole area; book early. The friendly staff dispenses sage advice about local hikes and excursions. (543-2828. 2-person cabins with semi-private bath from $31, with private bath from $64, 2-room cabins with bath $94-116. Open mid-May to Oct.)

The best way to eat in the Tetons is to bring your own. Non-perishables are available at **Dornan's General Store** in Moose (733-2415; open daily 8am-7pm). Jackson has **Albertson's** supermarket, 520 W. Broadway, ½mi. south of downtown (733-5950; open daily 6am-midnight). The **Chuck Wagon Restaurant,** in Colter Bay, serves breakfast (buffet $9.50), lunch, and dinner, and will cook your catch of the day (543-1077; open 7:30-10am, 11:30am-2pm, 5:30-9pm). The connected **Cafe Court** serves pizza ($4.50-5) and salads ($3.45-6.50) in a cafeteria-style setting (open 6:30am-10pm; breakfast served until 11am).

## SIGHTS AND ACTIVITIES

While Yellowstone wows visitors with geysers and mudpots, the Grand Tetons boast some of the most scenic mountains in the U.S., if not the world. The youngest range in North America (2-3 million years old), the Tetons stand 13,771ft. high, almost without foothills, providing vistas more weathered peaks lack.

**Jenny Lake's** tranquility overcomes the steady tramp of its many visitors. The 6.6mi. trail around the lake is gorgeous and relatively flat; 2mi. in, it joins the **Cascade Canyon Trail.** The **Hidden Falls Waterfall** is located ½mi. up the Cascade Canyon Trail from the lakeshore and the boat dock. Hikers with more stamina can continue upwards towards **Inspiration Point** (another ¾mi.), but only the lonely can trek 6¾mi. further to **Lake Solitude,** which stands at 9035ft. **Ranger-led hikes** leave the Jenny Lake Visitor Center at 8:30am and 5pm. Before hitting the trail or planning extended hikes, be sure to check in at the ranger station, as trails at higher elevations may still be snow-covered. Prime hiking season does not begin until well into July during years with heavy snow.

**Teton Boating** shuttles across Jenny Lake to the shore below Hidden Falls every 20min. The first boat leaves from the Jenny Lake Visitor Center at 8am and the last boat leaves the Hidden Falls side at 6pm. Taking the boat cuts 4mi. off the round-trip hike to the falls. *(733-2703. 1-way $4, ages 7-12 $3; round-trip $5, ages 7-12 $3.50.)* Scenic cruises are offered every hour 10am-2pm. *($9, children $6.)* They also rent boats. *($12 for the first hr., $10 per additional hr., $60 per day.)*

**Hiking trails** abound, winding their way through the stunning scenery. The 4½mi. walk from Colter Bay to **Hermitage Point** is popular for the scope of wildlife it encounters. Leave the crowds behind and hike the **Amphitheater Lake Trail,** beginning just south of Jenny Lake at the Lupine Meadows parking lot, which takes you 4.8 breathtaking mi.to one of the park's glacial lakes. (Lupines, the purple, clumpy flowers visible all along the roads throughout the park, bloom June-July.) **Static Peak Divide,** a steep 15.6mi. loop trail up 4020ft. from the Death Canyon trailhead (4½mi. south of Moose Visitors Center), offers some of the best vistas in the park. The Death Canyon area is prime for longer 2- to 3-day hikes. All visitors centers provide pamphlets about the day hikes and sell many guides and maps ($3-10). **Grayline Tours** offers 8hr. tours of the Tetons. *(733-4325 or 800-443-6133. $50. Open in summer 7am-9pm. Reservations required.)*

**Adventure Sports,** a division of Dornan's in Moose, rents outdoor equipment and provides advice on where to bike. *(733-3307. Mountain bikes from $6 per hr. for a basic model. No bikes are allowed on trails in the park. Open 9am-6pm; spring and fall hrs. vary. Credit card or deposit required.)* **Snake River Angler,** next to Dornan's, rents spinning rods for $10 per day and fly rods for $14. *(733-3699. Fly-fishing lessons available on private water at $95 for 2 people, $25 per additional person. Open in summer daily 9am-7pm, off-season 9am-6pm.)* **Exum Mt. Guides** offer 4-day packages that include climbing school and a 2-day climbing trip for any experience level. Lodging not included. Price depends on the amount of attention you require and session attendance. *(733-2297. Trips range from $330-520. Reservations are taken starting in Jan. of the year of the trip. It is best to book by Mar.)* **Jackson Hole Mt. Guides** offer similar packages. *(733-4979.)*

For a leisurely afternoon on Jackson Lake, **Signal Mountain Marina** rents boats. *(543-2831. Rowboats and canoes $8 per hr., $30 per ½-day; motorboats $16/$6; pontoons $50/130; deck cruises $50/150. Open early May to Sept. daily 7am-8pm.)* **Colter Bay Marina** has a somewhat smaller variety of boats at similar prices. *(Open daily 7:30am-8pm, rental hours 8am-5pm.)* **Grand Teton Lodge Co.** has float trips on scenic Snake River (no whitewater) within the park. *(733-2811 or 543-2811. 10mi. ½-day trip $35, ages 6-11 $17; with lunch $40/27; with dinner $46/35 Tu, Th, Sa.)* **Triangle X Float Trips** floats on a 5mi. river (1-1½hr.) trip for less. *(733-5500. $25, under 19 $19. Trips leave at 11am, 2 and 4pm, May-Aug. 2- to 3-day trips are also available.)* **Fishing** in the park's lakes, rivers, and streams is excellent. A Wyoming license is required; get one in Jackson, Dornan's, Signal Mt., Colter Bay, Leek's Marina (2mi. north of Colter Bay), or Flagg Ranch on Rockefeller Pkwy. *($6 per day for non-residents, $2-3 for residents.)* **Horseback riding** is available through the Grand Teton Lodge Co.; the info booth next to the Village General Store fields questions. *(1 and 2hr. rides, $21 and $31 per person.)*

In the **winter,** all hiking trails and the unploughed sections of Teton Park Rd. are open to **cross-country skiers.** Pick up winter info at Moose or Colter Bay visitors centers. Naturalists lead free **snowshoe hikes** from the Moose Visitors Center. *(739-3399. Jan.-Mar. at 1pm Th-Tu. Snowshoes distributed free.)* **Snowmobiling** along the park's well-powdered trails and up into Yellowstone is a noisy but popular winter activity; pick up a free permit at Moose Visitor Center (Moose is *the* visitor center in the winter) and grab a map and guide at the Jackson Chamber of Commerce. For about $100 per day, you can rent snowmobiles at **Signal Mt. Lodge, Flagg Ranch Village,** or in **Jackson.** A well-developed snowmobile trail runs from Moran to Flagg Ranch, and numerous other snowmobiling opportunities exist in the valley. The Colter Bay and Moose parking lots are available for parking in the winter. All **campgrounds** close in winter, but **backcountry snow camping** (only for those who know what they're doing) is allowed with a permit bought from the Moose Visitors Center. Before making plans, consider that temperatures regularly drop below -20°F. Be sure to carry high-tech extreme weather clothing and check with a ranger station for current weather conditions and avalanche danger; many early trappers froze to death in the 10ft. drifts. Let the rangers know where you're going.

# JACKSON

Jackson Hole describes the valley bounded by the Teton and Gros Ventre ranges. Nearby Jackson is a ski village gone ballistic—its downtown streets are lined with Gap and Banana Republic shops, chic restaurants, faux-Western bars, and wooden-plank sidewalks. However, a glimpse of the true grit of the area can be found at the JH Rodeo, every summer night at the fairgrounds. Home to 5000 permanent residents, a dynamic mix of money and energy, international tourists and locals, people-watchers, and nature lovers, Jackson is a truly cosmopolitan place. Although a sliver of the area's beauty can be seen from town, striking out into the nearby Tetons or onto the Snake River—whether by foot, boat, horse, or llama—yields a richer experience.

## ▋ ORIENTATION AND PRACTICAL INFORMATION

The southern route into Jackson, U.S. 191/89/26, becomes **W. Broadway.** The highway turns left onto Broadway, becoming Cache St. as it veers north into Grand Teton Park and eventually reaches Yellowstone, 70mi. to the north. The intersection of Broadway and Cache St. at **Town Sq. Park** marks the center of town. The Jackson Hole Ski Resort draws snow bunnies to **Teton Village,** 12mi. to the north via Rt. 22, Rt. 390 and Teton Village Rd. The scenic **Moose-Wilson Rd. (Rte. 390)** connects the town of Wilson (at Rt. 22) with Teton Village and the Moose visitor area of Teton National Park; part of the road is unpaved and closed in the winter.

**Public Transportation: Jackson START** (733-4521). 50¢ in town, $1 on village road, $2 to Teton Village; over 60 ½-price, under 9 free. Buses run 6:15am-10pm. **Jackson Hole Express** (733-1719) runs between Jackson and the Salt Lake City and Idaho Falls airports. Buses run W and Sa (daily in winter), leaving Jackson for both destinations at 6:30 and 9:30am, Salt Lake City at 1:30 and 5:30pm (5½hr., $45), and Idaho Falls at 4:45 and 8:45pm (2hr., $20). Reservations required. (Office open M-Sa 8am-6pm.)

**Car Rental: Rent-A-Wreck,** 1050 U.S. 89 (733-5014). $25-30 per day, $145-265 per week; 150 free mi. per day, 1000 free mi. weekly, 20¢ each additional mi. Must be 21+ with credit card. Open daily 8am-6pm.

**Equipment Rental: Hoback Sports,** 40 S. Millward (733-5335). A complete outdoor sports store. Mountain bikes from $15 for ½day, $25 per day; kids' bikes $12 per day, trailers $9 per day; lower rates for longer rentals. Parabolic skis, boots, and poles $20-30 per day. Open in summer and off-season daily 9am-7pm; in peak winter 9am-8pm. Deposit of credit card or cash and driver's license. **Gear Revival,** 854 W. Broadway (739-8699), offers cheap gear and rentals. In-line skates $10; ice axes and crampons $7.

**Visitor Info: Jackson Hole and Greater Yellowstone Information Center,** 532 N. Cache St. A crucial info stop. Open early June to early Sept. 8am-7pm; during the winter M-F 8am-5pm, Sa-Su 10am-2pm. **Jackson Hole Chamber of Commerce** (733-3316, M-F 8am-5pm). **Bridger-Teton National Forest Headquarters** (739-5500, open M-F 8am-4:30pm in winter, daily 8am-7pm in summer).

**Tours: Grayline Tours** (800-443-6133 or 733-4325). 8hr. tours of Grand Teton National Park ($50 including boat ride), leaving Jackson at 8:30am on M, W, Sa and returning at 4pm, and 11hr. tour of Yellowstone National Park's lower loop ($60), leaving Jackson at 7:30am on Tu, Th, Su, and returning at 6:30pm. Call for reservations. Tour picks up at hotels. Office takes calls daily 7am-7pm.

**Weather and Road Conditions: Highway Info,** 733-1731. 24hr. **Road Info,** 888-996-7623.

**Hotlines: Family Safety Line,** 733-7466. **Counselling,** 733-2046 (M-F 8:30am-5:30pm).

**Internet Access: Teton County Library** (733-2164), 125 Virginian Ln. (open M-Th 10am-9pm, Fri. 10am-5:30pm, Sa 10am-5pm, Su 11am-5pm).

**Post Office:** (733-3650), at Powderhorn and Maple Way (1 block from McDonald's). Open M-F 7:30am-5:30pm, Sa 10am-2pm. **ZIP code:** 83002. **Area code:** 307.

## ▐ ACCOMMODATIONS

Jackson's constant influx of tourists ensures that if you don't book ahead, rooms will be small and expensive at best and non-existent at worst. Fortunately, you can sleep for an affordable price in one of two local hostels. **The Hostel X (HI-AYH),** P.O. Box 546, Teton Village WY 83025, near the ski slopes and 12mi. northwest of Jackson, is a budget oasis among the wallet-parching condos and lodges of Teton Village. Its location makes it a favorite of skiers. X has a funkily decorated game room/TV room, ski-waxing room, nursery room, Internet access, and nightly ski movies in the winter. (733-3415. 4 beds in dorm rooms; 20 rooms with king-size beds. $45 for 1-2 people, nonmembers $55; $60 for 3-4. In winter, $47 for 1-2; $60 for 3-4; no member discount.) **The Bunkhouse,**

215 N. Cache St., in the basement of the Anvil Motel, has a lounge, kitchenette (no stove), coin laundry, ski storage, and, as the name implies, one large and quiet sleeping room with comfy bunks. The price and convenient location to town make it one of Jackson's best no-frills deals. (733-3668. Beds $18.) **The Pioneer,** 325 N. Cache St., is a bargain during the spring. It offers lovely rooms with teddy bears, microwaves, refrigerators, free local calls and stupendous hand-crafted quilts. (733-3673 or 800-550-0330. Singles peak at $90 in the summer. Early Apr. to mid-May $50.)

While it doesn't offer scenery, Jackson's campground, the **Wagon Wheel Village,** 435 N. Cache St., welcomes tents and RVs on a first come, first served basis (733-4588; 9 tent sites $16; 32 RV sites with full hookup $34; showers). The 15-acre **KOA Kampground,** on Teton Village Rd. 1mi. south of Teton Village, offers shaded sites with a view of the Teton Range. (733-5354 or 800-562-9043. 146 sites and 10 tent sites. $26 for 1-2 people, $4.50 per additional person. $32 with water and electricity. Full hookup $36 for 2 people, $5 per additional person. Free showers, pay laundry machines, and grocery store are available.) Cheaper sites and more pleasant surroundings are offered in the **Bridger-Teton National Forest** surrounding Jackson. The Greater Yellowstone Information Center has information about the sites; drive toward Alpine Junction on U.S. 26/89 to find spots. (739-5500. Some sites are free; all under $10 for 1 vehicle. Water available at some sites. No showers.)

## ☕ SOMETHIN' TO MUNCH ON

**The Bunnery,** 130 N. Cache St., in the "Hole-in-the-Wall" mall, has hearty breakfasts. An egg scrambled with diced ham and cheddar, home fries, and their special OSM bread (made of oats, sunflower, and millet) goes for $6.99; lunch sandwiches start at $5, pastries $2-3. (733-5474. Cafe open daily 7am-10pm.) For a homeopathic remedy, or just a healthy bite to eat, try the **Harvest Bakery and Cafe,** 130 W. Broadway, a New Age jack-of-all-trades. Stop in for breakfasts priced under $4.25, soup and salad ($4), fresh pastries ($2), and $3-4 smoothies. (733-5418. Cafe open in summer M-Sa 7am-3pm, Su 8am-2pm; in winter Su 11am-4pm. Bakery open daily 7am-6pm.) Chow down on barbecued chicken ($7 for half a chicken and sides) and spare ribs (full rack $8.50) at the colorful and popular **Bubba's,** 515 W. Broadway. (733-2288. Open daily 7am-10pm. No reservations.) **LeJay's 24 Hour Sportsmen Café,** at the corner of Glenwood and Pearl (from Cache, take a right on Pearl), across from the antler entrance to Town Sq. Park, provides the hungry with a good, cheap, and filling menu, in a lively, wrangler-meets-bohemian atmosphere. (733-3110. Burgers and sandwiches with fries $4-6; breakfast special $3.25-8. Open 24hr.) Sit back with steak 'n' potatoes for cowboy yodeling and poetry at the **Bar J Chuckwagon** supper (no meatless meals available) and Western show on Teton Village Rd., 1mi. from Rt. 22. (800-905-2275 for reservations. $14-19, under 9 $6, lap-sized eat free. Open 5:30pm, dinner show at 8:30pm, the show out by 10pm. Open Memorial Day to late Sept.)

## ⛰ OUTDOOR

**Whitewater rafting** draws nearly 200,000 city slickers and backwoods folk to Jackson between mid-May and early Sept. **Lone Eagle Expeditions** is the cheapest of the myriad whitewater outfitters in Jackson. Trips are 3hr. (8mi.) and offer free access to the company's hot tub, heated pool, and hot showers after the trip. *(733-1090 or 800-321-3800. $33; $40 includes a hot meal. Trips daily at 8, 9:45, 11:30am, 1:30, 3:15, and 5pm.)* **Mad River Boat Trips,** 1255 S. U.S. 89, 2mi. from Town Sq., was the whitewater consultant for *A River Runs Through It.* A 3½hr., 8mi. raft trip leaves hourly 9am-2pm. For $36, you can get an 8mi., 4hr. trip including a BBQ. They also offer "scenic" trips for $33 which leave at 8:30am and 12:30pm. *(733-6203 or 800-458-*

*7238. $31. In June 3 trips daily: 10am, noon, and 2pm.)* Reservations are preferred by both outfitters. Cheaper thrills include a lift up to the summit of **Rendezvous Peak** at 10,450ft. The tram earns a great view of the Tetons and provides access to the Teton Crest trail without the climb to the top. *(Tram leaves from Teton Village and runs mid-June to Aug. 9am-7pm; May 23 to mid-June and Sept. 9am-5pm. $16, seniors 65+ $13, ages 6-17 $6. The tourist office offers coupons for $2 off.)* Ride the **Snow King Chairlift** to the peak of Snow King Mountain (7751ft.) for a bird's-eye view of Jackson and another great view of the Tetons. *(733-5200. $8, seniors $6, under 12 $6. Ride down only $1.)* **Skiing** at Snow King is an inexpensive alternative to the resort and is right in town, without the hassle of lift lines. *(Lift tickets full-day $30, half-day $20, night $14; juniors and seniors $20/$12/$9; $8 per hr.)* The **Panorama House** provides a summit rest stop; try some stew and enjoy the view. *(733-7348.)* In winter, the **Jackson Hole Ski Resort,** at Teton Village, offers a huge 4139ft. vertical drop, dry Wyoming powder, open bowls, tree skiing, and some of the best extreme skiing in the West. *(733-2292. Office open 7am-5pm daily.)* **Corbet's Couloir** is one of the steepest chutes accessible by lift in the U.S. *($51, seniors and under 14 $26.)* Keen depictions of the local fauna can be found at the **National Museum of Wildlife Art,** 2½mi. north of Jackson on U.S. 89. The den overlooks the National Elk Refuge. The museum houses the nation's largest collection of wilderness art. *(733-5771. Open in summer daily 9am-5pm; winter daily 9am-5pm; in spring and fall M-F 9am-5pm, Sa-Su 1-5pm. $6, students and seniors $5, under 6 free, $14/family. Tours at 11am.)* Get a taste of the Andes by taking a llama trip. The animal carries your stuff while you walk alongside. For information, contact **Jackson Hole Llamas.** *(739-9582. P.O. Box 12500.)*

## ♫ ENTERTAINMENT AND NIGHTLIFE

Cultural activities in Jackson range from rowdy, foot-stomping Western celebrations to more sedate presentations of music and art. Every summer evening (except Su), starting between 6 and 6:30pm, the Town Sq., at the corner of Broadway and Cache St., hosts a kitschy episode of the **Longest-Running Shoot-Out in the World.** At the end of May, the town celebrates the opening of the **JH Rodeo** at the fairgrounds. (733-2805. Late May to early Sept. W and Sa 8pm. $8, reserved tickets $10, families $25, ages 4-12 $6.) The **Grand Teton Music Festival** features some of the world's best orchestras from June 29 to Aug. 2. (733-1128. Office hours Tu-Sa 10:30am-6:30pm. Festival orchestra concerts F-Sa 8pm are $27. Spotlight concerts Th 8pm, $18; chamber music concerts Tu-W 8pm, $15. Open rehearsal Th 9:30am; $5, students $2.50.) Over Memorial Day weekend, the town bursts its britches as tourists, locals, and nearby Native American tribes pour in for the dances and parades of **Old West Days.** In mid-Sept. the **Jackson Hole Fall Arts Festival** (733-3216) attracts crafters, dancers, actors, and musicians to town.

The **Mangy Moose,** in Teton Village at the base of Jackson Hole Ski Resort, is the quintessential après-ski bar. Moose racks and skis line the wooden walls, contrasting with the bright ski parkas of the patrons. Dinner is somewhat expensive ($8.50-29). The eclectic but sporadic entertainment line-up has featured everything from Blues Traveler to Dr. Timothy Leary. (733-4913. Cover $3-15. Dinner daily 5:30-10pm; bar open nightly 11pm-2am.) Thursday brings popular disco night to tiny Wilson at the **Stagecoach Bar,** 7mi. west of Jackson on Rt. 22, and live bands rock the bar Sa and Su nights. A good selection of microbrews and a mix of locals and visitors make this an authentic Western bar. (733-4407. Open daily 11am-2am.) For local ales, head to one of the most popular restaurant/bars in the area, **Snake River Brewery,** 265 S. Millward St., Wyoming's first brew-pub; the "Zonkers Stout" will put hair on your chest (pints $3, pitchers $10), while the pasta, sandwiches, and pizzas ($5-10) will fill your tummy (739-2337. Open Su-Th noon-1am, F-Sa noon-1am; food is served until 11pm.) Western saddles serve as bar stools at the **Million Dollar Cowboy Bar,** 25 N. Cache St., Town Sq. This Jackson institution, attracting few locals or real cowboys, clearly caters to tourists. (733-2207. Live music M-Sa 9pm-2am. Cover $3-5 after 8pm. Open daily noon-midnight, bar opens at 1:30pm.)

# CODY

William F. "Buffalo Bill" Cody was more than a Pony Express rider, scout, hunter, and sportsman. He also started "Buffalo Bill's Wild West Show," an extravaganza that catapulted the image of the cowboy into the world's imagination. Cody's show traveled all over the U.S. and Europe, attracting the attention of royalty and statesmen. Founded in 1896 by Cody, this "wild west" town bearing his name conceals remnants of an authentic past beneath a pricey tourist facade.

From June through Aug., Cody turns into "The Rodeo Capital of the World" with one every night at 8:30pm, off Yellowstone Ave. west of town (587-5155; tickets $10-12, ages 7-12 $4-6). On July 1-4, 2000, the **Cody Stampede Professional Rodeo Cowboy Association Rodeo,** voted by the cowboys themselves the best "large outdoor rodeo" in the world, rough-rides into town (587-5155; tickets $15; reserve ahead). The **Buffalo Bill Historical Center,** 720 Sheridan Ave., is known affectionately as the "Smithsonian of the West" and composed of four museums under one roof. **The Buffalo Bill Museum** documents the life of you-know-who; the **Whitney Gallery of Western Art** shows off Western paintings, including some Remingtons; the **Plains Indian Museum** contains several exhibits about its namesake group; and the **Cody Firearms Museum** holds the world's largest collection of American firearms. (587-4771. Open daily June-Sept. 7am-8pm, Oct. 8am-5pm; Nov.-Mar. Th-M 10am-2pm, Apr. 10am-5pm, May 8am-8pm. $10, students $6, seniors $6.50, ages 6-17 $4. Tickets good for 2 consecutive days.) For a dam good time, drive about 6mi. west on Rt. 20/14/16 toward Yellowstone and see the mighty **Buffalo Bill Dam,** which was the highest (350ft.) dam in the world when completed in 1910 (527-6076; open daily June-Aug. 8am-8pm, May and Sept. 8am-6pm; free). **Rafting** trips on the Shoshone provide more energetic diversions. To make arrangements, call **Wyoming River Trips,** 1701 Sheridan Ave., at Rt. 120 and 14. (587-6661 or 800-586-6661; easy 2hr. trip $18, ½-day trip $45; open May-Sept.).

Rates go up in the summertime, but a strip of reasonable motels lines **W. Yellowstone Ave.** The **Pawnee Hotel,** 1032 12th St., is just a block from downtown (587-2239. Small singles with shared bath $22. Doubles with private bath and phone $32-42.) **Buffalo Bill State Park** offers two **campgrounds** on the Buffalo Bill Reservoir with incredible views. The North Shore Bay campground (527-6274) is the better of the two, 9mi. west of town on U.S. 14/16/20. The North Fork Campground (527-6057), about 14mi. west of town on U.S. 14/16/20, is a little less nice, but still is much more picturesque than those in town (both sites $7). The **Gateway Motel and Campground,** 203 Yellowstone Ave., has a view of the surrounding hills and offers rooms, campsites, hookups, and cute cabins with A/C and kitchenettes. (587-2561. Singles $45; doubles $50. Campsites $12 for 2, $2 for each additional person, with water and electricity $16, full hookup $18. Showers and laundry open May-Sept.) **Peter's Café and Bakery,** at 12th St. and Sheridan Ave., fries up cheap breakfasts (3 buttermilk pancakes $2.70) and stacks a meaty mountain-man sub and a meatless Calamity Jane Sub, both for $2.90 (527-5040; open daily 7am-8pm). The **Irma Hotel and Restaurant,** 1192 Sheridan Ave., originally owned by Buffalo Bill and named after his daughter, has affordable lunch eats (hot sandwiches $5-6) and dinner if you choose carefully. The original cherrywood bar was sent as a gift from Queen Victoria. (587-4221. Open Apr.-Sept. daily 6am-10pm; Oct.-Mar. 6am-8pm.)

Cody lies at the junction of Rt. 120, 14A, and 14/16/20. The town's main street is **Sheridan Ave.,** which turns into **Yellowstone Ave.** west of town. **Powder River Transportation** (800-442-3682) runs buses to Denver (17-19½hr., 2 per day, $79); Cheyenne (10-13hr., 2 per day, $63); and Billings (3hr., 1 per day, $27) from Daylight Donuts, 1452 Sheridan Ave. **Powder River Tours** offers guided daytrips through Yellowstone National Park and departs from several locations in town (527-6316; $60, 16 and under $30, seniors $54; reservations recommended). The **Chamber of Commerce Visitors Center** is at 836 Sheridan Ave. (587-2297; open M-Sa 8am-6pm, Su 10am-3pm; off-season M-F 8am-5pm). **Post Office:** 1301 Stampede Ave., from downtown take 13th St. north for about 1mi. (527-7161; open M-F 8am-5:30pm, Sa 9am-noon). **ZIP code:** 82414. **Area code:** 307.

ROCKY MOUNTAINS

# BUFFALO AND SHERIDAN

Not touristy enough to be traps, yet not small enough to make wayward travelers feel like unwanted outsiders, Buffalo and Sheridan are friendly, history-rich towns that provide a perfect base for exploring the Bighorn Mountains.

## BUFFALO

Situated at the crossroads of I-90 and I-25, Buffalo lies appreciably close to the **scenic byway U.S. 16.** Before heading for the mounts, however, absorb some Old West character in the elegant rooms of the **Occidental Hotel,** 10 N. Main St., which opened its doors as the town hall in 1880 and, as the story goes, was won by the Smith Family in a 1917 poker game. The hotel was the setting for Owen Wister's great western novel, *The Virginian.* (684-0451. Open in summer M-Sa 10am-5pm. $2.) The **Jim Gatchell Museum of the West,** 100 Fort St., is filled with dioramas and relics. (684-9331. Open in summer daily 8am-8pm. Winter hrs. vary; closed Jan.-Apr. except by appointment. $2, under 14 free.)

In Buffalo, budget motels line **Main St. (Rt. 87)** and **Fort St.** The **Mountain View Motel and Campground,** 585 Fort St., keeps appealing pine cabins with TV, A/C, and heating. (684-2881. Singles $40; doubles $45; in winter 1-2 people $35; big cabin with 3 double rooms $58, with kitchen $60. $5 per night discount with a stay of 3 or more nights. Campsites $15, full hookup for 2 $18. Showers and laundry.) A few doors down, the **Z-Bar Motel** has TVs with HBO, refrigerators, and A/C. (684-5535 or 800-341-8000. Singles $43; doubles $47; Nov.-Apr. $34/37; kitchen $6 extra. Reservations recommended.) **Tom's Main Street Diner,** 41 N. Main St., is a great little eatery downtown. Lunch specials ($4-5.75, including beverage) and bread pudding with whipped cream ($2.25) are best. (684-7444. Open M and W-Sa 5:30am-2pm, Su 8am-1pm.) **Dash Inn,** 620 E. Hart St., offers great chicken, ribs, and Texas Toast for $6-9 (684-7930; open Tu-Su 11am-9:30pm; in winter M-Sa 11am-8pm).

There is no bus service to Buffalo; **Greyhound** (674-6188) goes to nearby Sheridan and Gillette. **Alabam's,** 421 Fort St. (684-7452), sells topographical maps ($4); hunting, fishing, and camping supplies; and **fishing licenses** (1-day $6; open daily roughly 7am-6pm). The **Buffalo Chamber of Commerce Visitors Center,** 55 N. Main St. (684-5544 or 800-227-5122), has info (open June-Aug. M-F 8am-6pm, Sa-Su 10am-4pm, Sept.-May M-F 8am-5pm). The **U.S. Forest Service Offices,** 1425 Fort St. (684-1100), sells a map of the area ($4; open M-F 8am-4:30pm). **Post Office:** 193 S. Main St. (684-7063; open M-F 8am-5pm, Sa 10am-noon). **ZIP code:** 82834. **Area code:** 307.

## SHERIDAN

Sheridan is a bit bigger than Buffalo and about 10mi. south of **scenic byway U.S. 14/14A,** a winding route marked by steep drops (cars with trailers, RVs and buses are not recommended on 14A) and spectacular views. Like its counterpart, however, this cowboy town is more than just another stop on the trail. **King's Saddlery and Cowboy Museum,** 184 N. Main St. in the building behind their main store, ropes 'em in with over 550 remarkably crafted, award-winning saddles on display. Watch as ropes and saddles are made in their warehouse. Each saddle takes 4-6 weeks to complete and can cost $1800-6000. (672-2702, 672-2755, or 800-443-8919. Open M-Sa 8am-5pm. Free.) The **Trail End State Historic Site,** 400 Clarendon Ave., showcases the impressive mansion and gardens of rags-to-riches cattle baron and former governor John B. Kendrick. (674-4589. Open mid-May to Aug. daily 9am-6pm, Oct.-Dec. 1 and Apr. 1 to mid-May W-Su noon-4pm. $2 for non-residents, $1 for residents, under 18 free.) Buffalo Bill Cody used to sit on the porch of the once-luxurious **Sheridan Inn,** at 5th and Broadway, as he interviewed cowboy hopefuls for his *Wild West Show.* (674-5440. Self-guided tours free. Guided tour $3, seniors $2, under 12 free; call ahead.) Locals flock to town several days a week for **polo** games (751-3802 for schedule and information; June to mid-Sept.).

There are motels aplenty along Main St. and Coffeen Ave. **The Aspen Inn,** 1744 N. Main St., offers the best deal (672-9064; singles $30; doubles $37). Kamping can be found at the **Sheridan KOA** with the typical KOA amenities: laundry, showers, water, pool, restaurant, video arcade, etc. Go south at exit 20 off I-90, turn right at the Port of Entry, and take an immediate right on Rt. 338 and go about ¾mi. (674-8766. $15 for 2, water and electricity $19, full hookup $22; Kabins $28; $2.50 for each additional person). Camping is more rustic at **Connor Battlefield Campground,** which offers pit toilets, water, and a river for fishing, and $4 sites. In Ranchester, 14mi. north of Sheridan; take Rt. 14 west at exit 9 off I-90, turn left on to Gillette St. and follow the signs to the battlefield/campground. **Sanford's Grub Pub and Brewery,** 1 E. Alger Ave., has nearly 40 sandwiches ($5.75-6.50), from the "Fat Albert" to the "Fonz-A-Relli," 20 different salads ($2.50-6.25), and bikes and kayaks hanging from the ceiling. (674-1722. Open daily 11am-10pm.) **The Mint Bar,** 151 Main St., has pleased customers since 1907. Stop in for the local beer or a look at the stuffed game and rodeo memorabilia on display. (674-9696. Open M-Sa 8am-2am.)

Powder River buses (674-6188) leave twice daily for Billings (2hr., $278) and Cheyenne (8hr., $51) from the Texaco station at the Evergreen Inn, 580 E. 5th St. (terminal open daily 3am-11:30pm). The **visitors center** (672-2485 or 800-453-3650) sits just off I-90 at exit 23. The Sheridan **Ranger station,** (672-0751) is on the south end of town at 1969 S. Sheridan Ave, off Coffeen St. (open M-F 8am-5pm). **Post Office:** 101 E. Laucks St. (672-0713; open M-F 7:30am-5:30pm, Sa 8am-noon). **ZIP code:** 82801. **Area code:** 307.

# BIGHORN MOUNTAINS

The **Bighorn National Forest** may be one of the best kept secrets in the Rocky Mountains; it is relatively uncrowded and offers great hiking and wildlife viewing. The Bighorns erupt from the hilly pasture land of northern Wyoming, a dramatic backdrop to grazing cattle, sprawling ranch houses, and valleys full of wildflowers. Visitors can hike through the woods or follow **scenic highways U.S. 14/14A** in the north and **U.S. 16** in the south to waterfalls, layers of prehistoric rock, and views above the clouds. The **Medicine Wheel** on U.S. 14A is a mysterious 80-ft.-wide stone formation at 10,000ft. dating from around AD 1300; prepare for a 3mi. round-trip hike from where the dirt road off the highway ends. This site is sacred to 89 Native American tribes and several people pray there each day. **Cloud Peak Wilderness** offers sheer solitude. Registration at major trailheads is required to enter the Cloud Peak area. The most convenient access to the wilderness area is from the trailheads off U.S. 16, around 20mi. west of Buffalo. From the **Hunter Corrals Trailhead,** move to beautiful **Seven Brothers Lake,** 3mi. off U.S. 16 on Rd. 19 (13mi. west of Buffalo on U.S. 16), an ideal base for dayhikes into the high peaks beyond. You can also enter the wilderness area on U.S. 14/14A to the north. To get to Cloud Peak, a 13,175ft. summit in the range, most hikers enter at **West Tensleep Trailhead,** accessible from the town of **Tensleep** on the western slope, 55mi. west of Buffalo on U.S. 16. Tensleep was so named because it took the Sioux 10 sleeps to travel from there to their main winter camps. Check with a forest office to find out about more out-of-the-way treks, and always check on local conditions with a ranger before any hike. A listing of all the Bighorn's attractions along with other helpful information and a map of the area can be found in *Bighorn Bits and Pieces*, available at all of the visitors centers.

Ranger stations can be found in **Buffalo** (see p. 648), **Lovell** at 604 E. Main St. (548-6541; open M-F 8am-5pm), and **Sheridan** (see p. 648), as well as within the park. The **Burgess Junction Visitors Center,** off U.S. 14 about halfway into the area, houses loads of great info and a theater with several films on the surroundings (open daily mid-May to mid-Sept. 8:30am-5pm). The **Bighorn Canyon Visitor's Center** (548-2251) on Rte. 14A in Lovell shows movies on the Medicine Wheel and can help out if the Lovell station is closed (open daily in-season 8am-6pm; off-season 8:30am-5pm). Campgrounds fill the forest. **Doyle Campground,** near a fish-rich creek, has 19 sites ($6) and toilets, but no water. (Drive 26mi. west of Buffalo on U.S. 16 and south 6mi. on Hazelton Rd./County Rd. 3—it's a rough ride.) There is no fee to camp at the uncrowded **Elgin Park Trailhead,** 16mi. west of Buffalo off U.S. 16, which promises good fishing along with parking and toilets. Off U.S. 14 (roughly 27mi. in from I-90 in the east), the **Sib-**

**ley Lake Campground** is one of several nice campgrounds in the northern half of the park ($10, with electricity $13; wheelchair access). If Sibley is crowded, **Tie Flume** and **Dead Swede** (both $9) are great campgrounds off Rt. 14 about 10mi. south of the Burgess Jct. Visitors Center. Many other campgrounds line Rt. 14 and 16 and the map in *Bighorn Bits and Pieces* will guide the way. For reservations within the park, call 877-444-6777. Campgrounds rarely fill in the Bighorns, but if they do, or if you're looking to get away from civilization altogether, free **dispersed camping** is permitted at least 100 yards from the road. For more information call 672-0751. **Area code:** 307.

## DEVILS TOWER

A Native American legend tells of seven sisters who were playing with their little brother when the boy turned into a bear and began to chase them. Terrified, the girls ran to a tree stump and prayed for help. The stump grew high into the sky, where the girls became the stars of the Big Dipper. Others tell of a core of fiery magma that shot up without breaking the surface 60 million years ago, and of centuries of wind, rain, and snow that eroded the surrounding sandstone, leaving a stunning spire. Still others, not of this world, have used the stone obelisk as a landing strip *(Close Encounters of the Third Kind)*. The massive column that figures so prominently in the myths of Native Americans, geologists, and space aliens is the centerpiece of **Devils Tower National Monument** in northeastern Wyoming ($8 per car, $3 per person on bike, foot, or motorcycle; free map on entry).

Devils Tower is considered one of the best technical rock climbing sites in North America, and scaling the monument's 1280ft. is a feat indeed. Native Americans, on the other hand, consider the tower a sacred site and would rather rock climbing were banned. A semi-compromise reached in 1995 calls for a voluntary refrain from climbing in the month of June—the most sacred time because of the solstice. The park has reached a level of 85% compliance with this policy.

Read about the rock and register to climb at the **visitors center,** 3mi. from the entrance. (467-5283, ext. 20. Open daily late-May to Sept. 8am-7:45pm; Mar.-Apr. and Oct.-Nov. usually 9am-4:45pm.) Cool **climbing demos** are given outside the visitors center (May, July & Aug. call for times). For more horizontally-orientated climbers, there are several **hiking trails;** the most popular, the 1.3mi. **Tower Trail,** loops the monument and provides great views. Ask a range to identify leafy spurge and poison ivy; they irritate the eyes and skin. The park maintains a **campground** near the red banks of the Belle Fourche River. (Water, bathrooms, grilles, picnic tables; no showers. Sites $12. Open roughly Apr.-Oct.; call to be sure.) The best camping deal around is at the the **Devils Tower View Store Campground** on Rt. 24 (seeing as it's free), a few mi. before the monument. Though there's not much shade, there's a great view of the monument and an inexpensive restaurant next door. (Donation requested. Open May-Sept. Water and nice port-o-potties.) To reach the monument from I-90, take U.S. 14, 25mi. north to Rt. 24. **Area code:** 307.

## THERMOPOLIS

Smack-dab in the middle of Wyoming, Thermopolis serves as a cross-section of the state. Hot springs bubble up from subterranean depths, fossil digs produce fragments of prehistoric eras, and the idyllic Wind River Canyon charts North America's geological development.

Home to the most voluminous **hot springs** in the world, this friendly town has the same tranquilizing effect on visitors as do its many soaking spots. At the renowned **Big Spring,** which is only as wide as a large hot tub, you can see down 100 ft. into the aquamarine water. Local legend has it that when a ball and chain was lowered down into the spring, the bottom couldn't be found. Swimming is not allowed in the natural pools—who would want to soak in 135°F water reeking of sulfur anyway? Swimmers, soakers, and sliders can partake in their respective pleasures under more skin-friendly circumstances: boiling hot water is mixed with icy cold water and pumped onto giant man-made waterslides and pools at **The Star Plunge**, next to the natural springs. Vapor caves are also featured. (864-3771. $7, under 5 $2. Open daily 9am-9pm.) The **State Bathhouse** next door offers a more relaxed way to experience the springs. Bathers can soak in the pleasantly warm waters (104°F) free for 20min. at a time. (Open M-Sa 8am-5:30pm, Su noon-5:30pm.)

Follow the green dino prints through town to the **Wyoming Dinosaur Center and Dig Sites,** which includes a museum and tours of excavation sites. (864-2997 or 800-455-3466. Open daily 8am-8pm. Museum $6; students, seniors, and children $3.50. Dig site tours every hr. 9am-4pm; $10/$7. Both $12/$8.)

Most accommodations are pricey (few singles under $30). The most reasonable motels in town are the **Jurassic Inn,** 501 S. 6th St. (864-2325 or 888-710-3466; singles $38, doubles $48; in winter $30/35) and the **Coachman Inn,** 112 Rt. 20 S., which has the same rates (864-3141 or 888-864-3854). To save a buck, camp at **Boysen State Park,** 15mi. south of Thermopolis on Rt. 20. The $4 sites on the Boysen Reservoir face the sun-stained canyon walls of the Wind River Gorge. Campsite info is available at the **Park Headquarters** (876-2796), off Rt. 20. The **Chamber of Commerce** is at 700 Broadway (864-3192 or 800-786-6772; open M-Sa 8am-5pm, Su noon-4pm).

# CASPER

In its frontier heyday, Casper hosted mountain men, Mormons, friendly ghosts, Shoshone, and Sioux. Eight pioneer trails intersected near Casper, including the famed Oregon, Bozeman, and Pony Express trails. The convergence of those paths lives on in Casper's nicknames, "the Hub" and "the Heart of Big Wyoming."

Casper's pride and joy is fascinating **Fort Caspar,** 4001 Ft. Caspar Rd., a group of reconstructed cabins that replicate the old army fort that guarded the N. Platte River on the western side of town (235-8462; open M-Sa 8am-7pm, Su noon-7pm; free). The **Nicolaysen Art Museum,** 400 E. Collins Dr., called the "Nic," exhibits Wyoming and world artwork, and a children's art Discovery Center (235-5247; open Tu-W, F-Sa 10am-5pm, Th 10am-8pm, Su noon-4pm). The building also houses the kid-orientated **Science Adventure Center** (open Tu-F noon-5pm, Sa 1-5pm; admission to both museums $3, ages 2-12 $2). A few mi. southeast of town on Rt. 251, **Lookout Point** (on top of **Casper Mountain**) and **Muddy Mountain** (6mi. farther) provide good, clean lookout spots. The **Central Wyoming Fair and Rodeo,** 1700 Fairgrounds Rd., gets excited about livestock (235-5775; July 11-15, 2000).

Bunk at the **Showboat National 9 Inn,** 100 W. F St., which has large, clean rooms next to the interstate. Rooms include cable and breakfast; the receipt earns a 10% discount at nearby eateries (235-2711 or 800-524-9999; singles $34; doubles $45). The oddly industrial **Fort Caspar Campground,** 4205 Ft. Caspar Rd., welcomes covered wagons. (234-3260. Sites for 2 people $12, $72 per week; full hookup $17; $1 per additional person over age 10; 10% AAA discount. Free showers and laundry.)

Chinese food is a good bet for a cheap meal downtown. The **Peking Restaurant,** 333 E. A St., has lunch specials ($4.50-6.50) and dinner plates ($6-10; 266-2207; open for lunch M-Sa 11am-2:30pm, dinner 5-9pm). **La Costa,** 400 W. F St., in front of the Hampton Inn, serves good Mexican food. Burritos cost $6-7; a complete dinner is $7-9. (266-4288. Open daily 11am-10pm.) Get the local scoop with your coffee at the **Blue Heron,** 201 E. 2nd St., in the Atrium Plaza (265-3774; open M-F 8am-6pm, Sa 9am-4pm). Organic foods and delicious smoothies can be found at **Alpenglow Natural Foods,** 109 E. 2nd St. (234-4196; open M-W 9am-6pm, Th-Sa 9am-8pm).

**Casper Area Convention and Visitors Bureau:** 500 N. Center St. (234-5311 or 800-852-1889; open daily 8am-6pm; in winter M-F 8am-5pm). **Powder River Transportation Services** (266-1904, 265-2353 or 800-433-2093), at I-25 and Center St. in the Parkway Plaza Hotel, sends buses to Cheyenne (4hr., 2 per day, $31) and Denver (7hr., 2 per day, $47. (Office open M-F 6am-8pm, Sa 6-11am and 3:30-4:30pm, Su 6-7:30am and 3:30-4:30pm.) **Post office:** 411 N. Forest Dr. (266-4000; open M-F 8:30am-5pm, Sa 9am-noon). **ZIP code:** 82609. **Area code:** 307.

ROCKY MOUNTAINS

# CHEYENNE

Originally the name of the Native American tribe that inhabited the region, "Cheyenne" was considered a prime candidate for the name of the Wyoming Territory. The moniker was struck down by vigilant Senator Sherman, who pointed out that the pronunciation of Cheyenne closely resembled that of the French word *chienne*, meaning, er, "bitch." Once one of the fastest growing frontier towns, Cheyenne has tried to maintain its Old Western image through simulated gunfights and rodeos, but much of its charm is found in historical downtown buildings.

**7 PRACTICAL INFORMATION. Greyhound,** 222 Demming. (634-7744), just off I-80, makes daily trips to Salt Lake City (9hr., 3 per day, $65); Chicago (24hr., 4 per day, $100); Laramie (1hr., 3 per day, $13); Rock Springs (5hr., 3 per day, $48); and Denver (3-5hr., 4 per day, $23; station open daily 10:30am-4am). **Powder River Transportation** (634-7744), in the Greyhound terminal, honors Greyhound passes, busing daily to Rapid City (10hr., 1 per day, $49), Casper (4hr., 2 per day, $31), and Billings (11hr., 2 per day, $70). For local jaunts flag down one of the shuttle buses provided by the **Cheyenne Transit Program** (637-6253; buses run M-F 6:30am-6:30pm; fare $1). **Cheyenne Area Convention and Visitors Bureau:** 309 W. Lincolnway (778-3133 or 800-426-5009), just west of Capitol Ave. **Domestic Violence and Sexual Assault Line:** (637-7233) 24hrs. **Post office:** 4800 Converse Ave. (800-275-8777; open M-F 7:30am-5:30pm, Sa 7am-1pm). **ZIP code:** 82009. **Area code:** 307.

**[] [] ACCOMMODATIONS, CAMPGROUNDS, AND FOOD.** It's easy to land a cheap room here among the plains and pioneers, unless your visit coincides with Wyoming's huge hootenanny **Frontier Days,** the last full week of July (see **Festivals and Sights,** below). Beware of doubling rates and disappearing rooms in the days approaching this week. Many budget motels line **Lincolnway** (U.S. 30/16th St.). **Plains Hotel,** 1600 Central Ave., conveniently located across from the I-180 on-ramp and 1 block away from the center of downtown, offers cavernous, retro hotel rooms with marble sinks and free cable (638-3311; singles $35; doubles $43; $5 per additional person). Holster your peacemaker before walking into the **Frontier Motel,** 1400 W. Lincoln Way (634-7961), and grab a latté ($2) or an Italian soda ($2) at the front desk. Singles with a living room, large bathroom, free cable, and A/C start at $25. **The Ranger Motel,** 909 W. 16th St. (634-7995), has small rooms with TV, and free local calls (July-Oct. singles $26, doubles $33; off-season $22/$28). Camp at **Curt Gowdy State Park,** 1319 Hynds Lodge Rd., 24mi. west of Cheyenne on Rte. 210/Happy Jack Rd. This year-round park is centered around two lakes with excellent fishing, horseback riding (bring your own horse), and archery. (632-7946. $4 per night in addition to $2 entrance fee; $3 entrance fee for out-of-state visitors.)

Cheyenne has a smattering of restaurants that provide reasonably priced cuisine. **Lexie's Café,** 216 E. 17th St., has cheerful, cottage-style decor featuring wicker chairs and flowers. You'll find filling breakfast combos for $4-6, towering stacks of pancakes for $3, and burgers for $5. (638-8712. Open M 7:30am-3pm, Tu-Th 7:30am-8pm, F 7:30am-9pm, Sa 7am-9pm.) Relax with a light lunch at **The Java Joint,** 1720 Capitol Ave., or simply enjoy a latté (638-7332; salads and sandwiches $4-6; open M 7am-4pm, Tu-Su 7am-5:30pm).

**[] [] FESTIVALS, SIGHTS, AND NIGHTLIFE.** During the last week in July (July 21-30, 2000), make every effort to attend the **Cheyenne Frontier Days** (778-7222 or 800-227-6336), 9 days of non-stop Western hoopla. The town doubles in size as anyone worth a grain of Western salt comes to see the world's largest outdoor rodeo competition ($18 and up) and partake of the free pancake breakfasts (every other day in the parking lot across from the Chamber of Commerce), parades, big-name country music concerts, and square dancing. Throughout June and July, a "gunfight is always possible," and the entertaining **Cheyenne Gunslingers** (635-1028), at W. 16th and Carey, shoot each other M to F at 6pm (Sa high noon); their soda saloon sits at 218 W. 17th St. The **Wyoming State Capitol Building** (777-7220), at the base of Capitol Ave. on 24th St., shows off stained glass windows and aged photos of the frontier. Self-guided tours are available, or call ahead to reserve a guided tour (open M-F 8am-4:30pm). The **Old West Museum**, 4501 N. Carey Ave. (778-7290), in Lions Park, houses a large collection of old Western memorabilia, including a working windmill and a surrey with its original fringe. (Open M-F 9am-5pm, Sa-Su 10am-5pm. $4, under 12 free.)

When you want to shoot stick in a haze of smoke, look for a pink elephant above **D.T.'s Liquor and Lounge**, 2121 E. Lincolnway (632-3458; open M-Sa 7am-2am, Su 10am-10pm).

## WEST OF CHEYENNE

**LARAMIE.** Laramie, the home of the **University of Wyoming (UW)**, the state's only 4-year college, serves up collegiate coffee-shop chic with cowboy grit. Drifters can get a dose of youthful pluck in town and then relax in nearby **Medicine Bow National Forest** or **Curt Gowdy State Park**. From Cheyenne, take **Happy Jack Rd. (Rt. 210)** for a cow-filled scenic tour, or I-80 for expedience. Laramie does its darndest to bring its rough and rugged 19th-century history back to life at the **Wyoming Old West Park**, 975 Snowy Range Rd., a reconstructed frontier town that sells a suspiciously large amount of candy and souvenirs (800-845-2287; open daily late May to late Sept. 9am-6pm; free). The adjacent **Wyoming Territorial Prison** (tours every hr.) and the **National U.S. Marshals Museum** links the U.S. marshals, the labor movement, Native Americans, and Western outlaws. (Open late May to early Oct. daily 9am-6pm. $5.50, children $3.25, under 6 free; includes museum and prison.)

Large, comfortable rooms are great at the sprawling **Motel 8**, 501 Boswell, down the street from the Caboose on the outskirts of town (745-4856; A/C, pool; singles $34, doubles $40; cheaper in winter). **Ranger Motel**, 453 N. 3rd St., patrols downtown, within walking distance of many attractions (742-6677; HBO, fridge, microwave; singles $34, doubles $41). Lined with hotels and fast food, **3rd St.** leads south into the heart of town, crossing **Ivinson** and **Grand St.**, both of which burst with student hangouts. **Jeffrey's Restaurant**, 123 Ivinson St. at 2nd. St., doles out heavenly homemade bread and hot sandwiches, pasta dishes, and salads for $5-9 (742-7046; open M-W 11am-8pm, Th-Sa 11am-9pm). The air in **The Home Bakery**, 304 S. 2nd St., smells of fresh loaves and cookies. Baked goods start at 45¢, and daily sandwich specials go for $3.65. (742-2721. Open M-Sa 5:30am-5:30pm; deli closes 2pm.) Check your email or the local scene at the tragically hip **Coal Creek Coffeehouse**, 110 Grand Ave. Coffee is the speciality, but they also pan some yummy "light fare" for $4-7. (745-7737. Open during school year daily 7am-11pm; in summer M-F 6am-10pm, Sa-Su 6:30am-10pm.) Both students and Harleys steer their way into the **Buckhorn Bar**, 114 Ivinson St., a neighborhood hangout featuring live music Sa and Su nights, disco Th through Sa, and busy pool tables (742-3554; open M-Sa 8am-2am, Su 10am-midnight). UW students can honestly tell mom they spent the weekend in the **Library**, 142 Grand Ave. (742-3900). Pull up a table in their stacks for a salad ($4-5), a steak ($10-14), or a daily special ($5-6). Next door, the library's more lived-in bar has $2 beers on tap. (Restaurant open Su-W 11am-9pm, Th-Sa 11am-10pm. Bar open M-Sa 10am-2am, Su 11am-midnight.) **Chamber of Commerce:** 800 S. 3rd. St. (745-7339; open M-F 8am-5pm). **Area code:** 307.

**THE SNOWY RANGE.** Local residents call the forested granite mountains to the east of the Platte Valley the **Snowy Mountain Range** because snow falls nearly year-round on the higher peaks. Even when the snow melts, quartz outcroppings reflect the sun, creating an illusion of a snowy peak. From late May to Nov., the **Snowy Range Scenic Byway (Rt. 130)** is cleared of snow, and cars can drive 29mi. through the mountains to elevations nearing 2 vertical mi. The Snowy Range is part of the vast **Medicine Bow National Forest,** spread over much of southeastern Wyoming.

ROCKY MOUNTAINS

Cross-country skiing is popular in the snowy months; campsites and hiking trails usually don't open until mid-July. The challenging 2mi. **Medicine Bow Trail** starts at **Lewis Lake** and climbs to **Medicine Bow Peak** (12,013ft.), the highest point in the forest. Nearby **Silver Lake** offers 17 first come, first served camp sites ($10). A little east, **Nash Fork** is another untrammeled camp, with 27 sites ($10). All 16 of the park's developed campgrounds are open only in summer and have toilets and water, but no hookups or showers. Reservations for some campgrounds are available (800-280-2267; $8.75 reservation fee). A drive up **Kennaday Peak** (10,810ft.), at the end of Forest Rd. 215 off Rt. 130, leads to an impressive view.

Mountain biking is generally not allowed on the high country trails because of the frail alpine plants and the rocky terrain. However, you can bike or 4-wheel-drive on trails in the high country or on trails below about 10,000ft. The 7mi. **Corner Mountain Loop,** just west of Centennial Visitor's Center (see below), is an exhilarating rollercoaster ride through forest and small meadows. During the winter, mountain biking and hiking trails are used for cross-country skiing.

**Visitor Centers: Brush Creek Visitors Center** (326-5562) at west entrance (open daily mid-May to Oct. 9am-4:30pm); **Centennial Visitor's Center** (742-6023) 1mi. west of Centennial, at east entrance (open late May to early Sept. daily 9am-4:30pm; in winter Sa-Su only). **Area code:** 307.

**SARATOGA.** On the west side of the Snowy Range along Rt. 130, Saratoga, like its New York sister, is known for its **hot mineral springs.** Running between 104° and 120°F, these springs will warm you up and won't leave you reeking of sulfur. The free, 24hr. soaking wonders are located at the end of E. Walnut St., behind the public pool. A few feet away from the hot springs, the **North Platte River** offers excellent fishing. Fishing permits ($6) are available from the **Country Store** (326-5638) on Rt. 130 or **Medicine Bow Drifters,** at First and Bridge St. The knowledgeable owner can offer advice and completely outfit fishermen of any level. (326-8002. $40 per day for complete outfit. Open Apr.-May and Sept.-Oct. 6am-6pm, June-Aug. 6am-9pm.) The **Hotel Wolf,** 101 E. Bridge St., a renovated Victorian inn, is a howlin' good deal (326-5525; singles from $30; doubles from $43). The local favorite **Wolf Hotel Restaurant** serves expensive dinners but reasonably priced sandwiches and salads ($5-6) for lunch (326-5525; open M-Sa 11:30am-2pm and 6-10pm; Su 6-10pm). For a more casual dining atmosphere, drop in on **Mom's Kitchen,** 3 blocks down Rt. 130 from Bridge St., where the "big daddy burger" will definitely fill you up for $6 (326-5136; open Tu-Sa 6am-8pm, Su 6am-1:30pm). Next door to the Wolf, **Lollypops,** 107 E. Bridge St., sells ice cream (single cone $1.50), latté ($2.25), and gourmet lollipops (326-5020; open daily 7am-10pm). Across from the Wolf, the **Lazy River Cantina** serves up Mexican lunch ($5-8) and dinner ($8) specialties (326-8472; open M-Th 11am-9:30pm, F 11am-10pm, Su 7am-9:30pm). **Area code:** 307.

# COLORADO

In the high, thin air of Colorado, golf balls fly farther, eggs take longer to cook, and visitors tend to lose their breath just getting out of bed. Oxygen deprivation lures athletes looking to loosen their lungs for a competitive edge, but most hikers, skiers, and climbers worship Colorado for its peaks and mountain enclaves. Denver—the country's highest capital—serves as the hub for the entire Rocky Mountain region, providing a resting place for cross-country travelers and a "culture fix" for those heading to the mountains. Colorado's extraordinary heights are matched by its equally spectacular depths. Over millions of years, the Gunnison and Colorado Rivers have etched the natural wonders of the Black Canyon and the Colorado National Monument. Early settlers mined Colorado for its silver and gold, and the U.S. military burrowed enormous intelligence installations into the mountains around Colorado Springs, but most travelers dig their feet into the state's soil simply to get down and dirty with Mother Nature.

# ▶ PRACTICAL INFORMATION

**Capital:** Denver.

**Visitor Info: Colorado Travel and Tourism Authority,** CTTA, P.O. Box 3524, Englewood 80155 (800-265-6723; www.colorado.com). **U.S. Forest Service,** Rocky Mountain Region, 740 Sims St., Lakewood 80225 (303-275-5350). Open M-F 7:30am-4:30pm. **Ski Country USA,** 1560 Broadway, #2000, Denver 80202 (303-837-0793; open M-F 8am-5:30pm; ski report 825-7669). **National Park Service,** 12795 W. Alameda Pkwy., P.O. Box 25287, Denver 80225 (303-969-2000). For reservations for Rocky Mountain National Park or any national park, call 800-365-2267. **Colorado State Parks,** 1313 Sherman St., #618, Denver 80203 (303-866-3437). Open M-F 8am-5pm. For reservations for any Colorado state park, call 470-1144 or 800-678-2267.

**Postal Abbreviation:** CO. **Sales Tax:** 7.4%.

# DENVER

In 1858, the discovery of gold in the Rocky Mountains brought a rush of eager miners to northern Colorado. After an excruciating trek through the plains, the desperados set up camps for a breather and a stiff shot of whiskey before heading west into "them thar hills." In 1860, two of the camps consolidated to form a town named after James W. Denver, the governor of Kansas Territory at that time. Between 1863 and 1867, Denver and nearby Golden played a political tug-of-war for the title of state capital. Today, Golden makes a lot of beer, while Denver, the "Queen City of the Plains," serves as the commercial and cultural nexus of the region. The city has doubled in population since 1960, attracting a sweet 'n' sour blend of ski bums, sophisticated city-slickers from the coasts, and cowboys. The gold that originally drew people to region may be depleted, but the city retains its best asset—its combination of charming urban sophistication and Western grit.

# ▶ ORIENTATION AND PRACTICAL INFORMATION

Running north-south, **Broadway** slices Denver into east and west. **Ellsworth Ave.,** running east-west, is the north-south dividing line. Streets west of Broadway progress in somewhat alphabetical order, while the streets north of Ellsworth are numbered. Streets downtown run diagonal to those in the rest of the metropolis. Many of the avenues on the eastern side of the city become numbered *streets* downtown. Most even-numbered thoroughfares downtown run only east-west. The hub of downtown is the **16th St. Mall.** *Avoid the west end of Colfax Ave., Federal Blvd., S. Santa Fe Blvd, the east side of town beyond the capitol (the Capitol Hill area), and the west side of the **Barrio** (25th-34th St.) at night.*

**Airport: Denver International** (DIA; 342-2000), 25mi. northeast of downtown off I-70. Shuttles run from the airport to downtown and ski resorts in the area. The **RTD Sky Ride** (800-366-7433 or 299-6000, RTD office hours 6am-10pm) costs $6 ($3 for disabled and seniors 65+) to DIA from downtown; buses run hourly 4:45am-12:45am. From the main terminal, **Supershuttle** (370-1300 or 800-525-3177, airport desk 342-5454) shuttles to downtown hotels (1hr., $17). A **taxi** to downtown costs about $40. The **Airporter** (444-0808) heads north to Boulder (1hr.+, $18 from hotels and campus, $22 from homes and businesses).

**Trains: Amtrak,** Union Station, 1701 Wynkoop St. (534-2812 for arrivals/departures, 825-2583 for ticket office), at 17th St. To: Salt Lake City (14½hr., 1 per day, $112); St. Louis (26½hr., 1 per day, $225); and Chicago (18½hr., 1 per day, $170). Ticket office open daily 5:30am-9pm. **Río Grande Ski Train,** 555 17th St. (296-4754), leaves from Amtrak Union Station and chugs 2¼hr. through the Rockies, stopping in Winter Park within walking distance of the lifts; free ground transport to town provided; lift discounts included (Dec.-Apr. only, same-day round-trip $40, reservations required). Runs Sa-Su only; F added after early Feb., special runs Dec. 25 to Jan. 1.

**Buses: Greyhound,** 1055 19th St. (293-6555). To: Santa Fe (from 7½hr., 5 per day, $59); Salt Lake City (10¼hr., 4 per day, $40); Colorado Springs (1.5hr., 11 per day, $12); and Chicago (22hr., 5 per day, $72). Ticket office open daily 6am-midnight.

**Public Transportation: Regional Transportation District (RTD),** 1600 Blake St. (299-6000 or 800-366-7433). Serves Denver, as well as Longmont, Evergreen, Golden, and suburbs. Route hrs. vary; many shut down by 9pm. M-F 6-9am and 4-6pm $1.25; other hrs. 75¢, disabled and seniors 25¢ off-peak only. Exact change required. Major terminals are at Market and 17th St., and at Colfax and Broadway. The free 16th St. **Mall Shuttle** covers 14 blocks downtown and runs daily 5:45am-1am. **Light Rail** services the perimeter of the city and suburbs, from I-25 and Broadway north to 30th and Downing.

**Taxis: Yellow Cab,** 777-7777. **Zone Cab,** 444-8888.

**Car Rental: Cut-Rate Rent-a-Car,** 8000 E. Colfax Ave. (399-2848 or 800-635-2784, open M-F 8am-5:15pm, Sa 8:30am-noon). With a credit card: full-size to the mountains $29 per day, $185 per wk. Without credit card, add $2 per day, $10 per wk., 3 references and verified place of work required. $200 deposit. 50 free mi. per day, 400 mi. per wk. Must be 21+. Under 25 surcharge of $2 per day

**Visitor Info: Denver Visitors Bureau,** 1668 Larimer St. (892-1112 or 892-1505), near Civic Center Park just south of the capitol. Open M-F 8am-5pm, Sa 9am-1pm.

**Hotlines: Rape Emergency,** 322-7273.

**Bi-Gay-Lesbian Organizations: Gay and Lesbian and Bi-Sexual Community Services Center of Colorado,** 733-7743. Open M-F 10am-6pm.

**Internet Access: Public Library,** 10 W. 14th Ave. Open M-W 10am-9pm, Th-Sa 10am-5:30pm, Su 1-5pm.

**Post Office:** 951 20th St. (800-275-8777). General Delivery open M-F 7am-6pm. **ZIP code:** 80202. **Area code:** 303.

## ACCOMMODATIONS

**Hostel of the Rocky Mountains (HI-AYH),** 1530 Downing St. (861-7777). Right off E. Colfax Ave., the hostel is 12 blocks from downtown, next to 3 major bus routes and a trolley stop. Cheerful hostel ($12, linen $2, key deposit $5) and private rooms ($30-45). Pick up from the Greyhound depot or Union Station (call ahead). Bike rental $2; tours of Denver area ($5-25). Reception 7am-noon, 5pm-10pm. Reservations recommended.

**Franklin House B&B,** 1620 Franklin St. (331-9106). In walking distance of downtown. Clean, spacious rooms. Free breakfast. Singles from $30; doubles from $40; $10 per additional person. Check-in before 10pm. Check-out 11am. Reserve 1 mo. ahead.

**YMCA,** 25 E. 16th Ave. (861-8300), at Lincoln St. Divided into sections for men, women, and families. Laundry and TV rooms. Singles without bath (men only) $32, with shared bath $36, with private bath from $41; doubles (women only) $58-$60. Weekly rates available. Must be 18. Key deposit $12 and ID. Reserve in advance.

Two state parks lie in the Denver metro area. **Cherry Creek State Park,** 4201 S. Parker Rd., Aurora, has crowded sites among a few stands of pine trees. Take I-25 to exit 200, then head west on Rt. 225 for about ½mi. and turn south on Parker Rd. ($9, with electricity $12; daily entrance fee $5. Open Apr. 1 to Oct. 31.) **Golden Gate Canyon State Park** offers 106 year-round sites. Take I-70 west to 6th Ave., go west towards Central City to Rt. 119, and then north 19mi. (Tent sites $7-9, with electricity $12, shelters $5; daily entrance fee $4.) Contact the **State Parks Office** (866-3437) for info (reservations 470-1144 or 800-678-2267; $7; open M-F 8am-5pm).

## FOOD

Downtown Denver is great for cheap Mexican and Southwestern food. Dining al fresco and people-watching are available along the **16th St. Mall.** Southwest of the mall on Larimer St., **Larimer Sq.** has several more gourmet eateries. Along with sports bars, trendy restaurants cluster around **LoDo,** the neighborhood extending from Larimer Sq. toward Coors Stadium. Colorado's distance from the ocean may

ROCKY MOUNTAINS

**Denver**

ACCOMMODATIONS
A YMCA
B Hostel of the Rocky Mountains
C Franklin House B&B

TO ELITCH GARDENS, MILE HIGH STADIUM; PEPSI CENTER

TO COORS FIELD

TO ROCKY MOUNTAIN ARSENAL (4.1m)

TO RED ROCKS (12mi)

TO ELLSWORTH AVE. (1.1mi)

Union Station

Wynkoop Brewery

RTD Market St. Bus Terminal

The Market

Skyline Park

Denver Performing Arts Complex

Colorado Convention Center

University of Colorado-Denver Auraria Campus

Student Union

9th Street Historic District

Denver Community College

Mercury Cafe

Federal Bldg.

Museum of Western Art

Brown Palace

Firefighter's Museum

US Mint

Greek Amphitheater

Denver Art Museum

Byers/Evans House
Denver History Museum

Civic Center Park

RTD Civic Center Station

State Capitol

Colorado History Museum

Library

Speer Blvd.

Cherry Creek

Auraria Pkwy.

Broadway

Park Ave.

Colfax Ave.

E. Colfax Ave.

E. 14th Ave.

E. 16th Ave.

E. 17th Ave.

E. 18th Ave.

E. 19th St.

E. 20th Ave.

E. 21st Ave.

Cleveland Pl.

Court Pl.

Tremont Pl.

Glenarm Pl.

Welton St.

California St.

Stout St.

Champa St.

Curtis St.

Arapahoe St.

Lawrence St.

Larimer St.

Market St.

Blake St.

Wazee St.

Wynkoop St.

Wewatta St.

Delgany St.

Speer Blvd.

Klamath St.

Lipan St.

Mariposa St.

Osage St.

Rio Ct.

Delaware St.

Cheyenne Pl.

Lincoln St.

Sherman St.

Grant St.

Logan St.

Pennsylvania St.

Pearl St.

Washington St.

Clarkson St.

Emerson St.

Ogden St.

Corona St.

Downing St.

Marion St.

Clarkson St.

25th St.

24th St.

23rd St.

22nd St.

21st St.

20th St.

19th St.

18th St.

17th St.

16th St.

15th St.

14th St.

13th St.

12th St.

13th St.

Colfax Ave.

14th Ave.

7th St.

8th St.

9th St.

N

0    300 yards
0    300 meters

To C
B
A

make you wonder about **"Rocky Mountain oysters";** this salty-sweet delicacy (bison testicles) is sold at the **Denver Buffalo Company,** 1109 Lincoln Ave. (832-0880).

■ **Mercury Café,** at 22nd and California (294-9281; or 294-9258 to "speak to a human"). Decorated like an old tea parlor. Homebaked wheat bread and reasonably priced lunch and dinner items. A slew of soups, salads, enchiladas and vegetarian specials for cheap. Live bands in the dining room as well as in the upstairs dance area: Tu jazz and indie hop, W swing and Su and Th big band swing, F Argentine tango. Low cover and free lessons. No smoking. All ages. The "Merc" is one-of-a-kind. Open for meals Tu-F 5:30-11pm, Sa-Su 9am-3pm and 5:30-11pm; dancing usually goes until 1 or 2am.

■ **Pearl Street Grill,** 1477 S. Pearl St. (778-6475) in the trendy and laid-back Washington Park area serves gourmet food but an evening there won't break the bank. The "PSG Favorites" are all under $7.50. Patio dining. Open M-Sa 11am-2am, Su 11am-midnight (brunch served 11am-3pm).

**The Market,** 1445 Larimer Sq. (534-5140), downtown. A variety of specialty counters. Popular with a young, artsy crowd, as well as suits. Cappuccino $2.20, sandwiches $5.50, exotic salads $4-9 per lb. Open M-F 6:30am-11pm, Sa-Su 7:30am-midnight.

**Mexicali Cafe,** 1453 Larimer (892-1444). Inexpensive Mexican/southwestern food. Delicious burritos from $5. Open Su-Th 11am-midnight, food service stops around 10pm; F-Sa 11am-1:30am, food service stops around midnight.

**Wynkoop Brewery,** 1634 18th St. (297-2700), at Wynkoop across from Union Station in LoDo. Colorado's first brewpub serves beer (pints $2.50), homemade root beer, lunch, and dinner (burgers from $5). Pool tables upstairs and an independent **comedy club** downstairs (297-2111). Happy hour M-F 3-6pm, $1.50 pints. Brewery open daily 11am-1:45am, food service until 11pm. Free brewery tours Sa 1-5pm.

## ◉ SIGHTS

One of the best tour deals around is the **Cultural Connection Trolley,** which visits over 20 of the city's main attractions. The fare is good all day on any local bus or light rail. Buses come every 30min.; buy your ticket from the driver. The tour begins at the **Denver Performing Arts Complex,** at 14th St. (follow the arches to the end of Curtis), but can be joined at many local attractions; look for the green-and-red sign. *(299-6000. Runs early May to early Sept. daily 9:30am-6:30pm. $3.)*

A remnant of Colorado's silver mining days, the **U.S. Mint** issues the majority of coins in the U.S. Look for the small "D" embossed beneath the date. *(320 W. Colfax Ave. 405-4761. Open M-F 8am-2:45pm. Free 20min. tours every 15-20min. in summer; call for recommended reservation Oct.-Apr.)*

Visitors from all over come to stand on the 15th step of the **State Capitol Bldg.,** exactly 5280 ft. (1mi.) above sea level. *(866-2604. Visitors are welcome to climb the stairs until 3:30pm M-F and 2:15pm Sa-Su.)*

Just a few blocks from the capitol and the U.S. Mint stands the **Denver Art Museum,** which houses a world-class collection of Native American art. Architect Gio Ponti designed this 7-story "vertical" museum to accommodate totem poles and period architecture. The fabulous 4th fl. resembles an archaeological excavation site with temples, huts, and idols. *(100 W. 14th Ave. Pkwy. 640-4433. Open Tu and Th-Sa 10am-5pm, W 10am-9pm, Su noon-5pm. $4.50; students, seniors, and children $2.50; under 5 free.)* **The Black American West Museum and Heritage Center,** presents a side of frontier history unexplored by textbooks and John Wayne movies. *(3091 California St. 292-2566. Open daily May-Sept. 10am-5pm; Oct.-Apr. W-F 10am-2pm, Sa-Su 10am-5pm. $4, students and seniors $3, ages 3 and under free.)*

Planes such as the rare B-1A bomber are forever suspended at **Wings Over the Rockies Air and Space Museum,** in hangar #1 at Lowry Air Force Base. *(360-5360. Open M-Sa 10am-4pm, Su noon-4pm. $4, seniors and ages 6-17 $2.)*

Denver boasts a state-of-the-art aquarium called **Ocean Journey,** which profiles the ecology of the Colorado River and the Kampar River in Indonesia. *(700 Water St. 561-4450.)* Enjoy a splash of your own at the Island Kingdom water park at **Six Flags**

**Elitch Gardens,** at Elitch Circle and Speer Blvd., across the freeway from Mile High Stadium. *(595-4386. June-Aug. daily 10am-10pm, spring and early fall Sa-Su call to confirm. $28, under 4 ft. tall $14, under 4 free.)*

The mammoth **Red Rocks Amphitheater and Park,** 12mi. southwest of Denver on I-70 at the Morrison exit, is carved into red sandstone. As the sun sets over the city, performers like R.E.M., U2, and the Denver Symphony Orchestra compete with the view behind them. For tickets, call **Ticketmaster.** *(830-8497. Shows $25-45.)*

Denver has more public parks per square mile than any other city, providing prime space for bicycling, walking, or lolling about in the sun. **Cheesman Park** offers a view of the snow-capped peaks of the Rockies. *(Closes at 11pm.)* **City Park** houses a museum, zoo, running path, and golf course. *(331-4113. 331-4060 for more info on Denver parks.)* **Colorado State Parks** has the low-down on nearby state parks. *(866-3437. Open M-F 8am-5pm.)* A local favorite is **Roxborough State Park,** where visitors can hike and ski among red rock formations. *(Take U.S. 85 S, turn right on Titan Rd., and follow it 3½mi. to the park. Open year-round. Day use only.)* Forty miles west of Denver, the road to the summit of **Mt. Evans** (14,260 ft.) is the highest paved road in North America. *(Take I-70 W to Rt. 103 in Idaho Springs. Open late May to early Sept.)*

Incredibly, the best spot for bald eagles in Denver is also the town's most radio-active plot. The **Rocky Mountain Arsenal,** a former nuclear waste site, is a wildlife refuge. A shuttle bus to the arsenal departs from the corner of 72nd Ave. and Quebec St. *(289-0232. Open Oct.-Mar. 8:30am-dusk; tours 3:30pm-dusk.)*

## ♫ ENTERTAINMENT AND NIGHTLIFE

Every Jan., Denver hosts the nation's largest livestock show and one of the biggest rodeos, the **National Western Stock Show,** 4655 Humbolt St. Here, cowboys compete for prize money while over 10,000 head of cattle compete for "Best of Breed." **A Taste of Colorado,** the last week of Aug. (892-7004), and the **Capitol Hill People's Fair,** the first full week of June, are both large outdoor celebrations with food vendors and local bands at **Civic Center Park,** near the capitol (830-1651). **Cinco de Mayo**—yes, on the 5th of May—attracts 200,000 visitors per year in celebration of Mexico's independence (534-8342).

Denver's baseball team, the **Colorado Rockies,** lofts home runs out of **Coors Field,** at 20th and Blake St. (702-5437 or 800-388-7625. Tickets $5-$28; some $4 Rockpile tickets available day of game.) In the fall, the 1998 Super Bowl champion **Denver Broncos** puts on the blitz at **Mile High Stadium** (433-7466); soccer mania takes over the joint during the spring and summer as the **Colorado Rapids** shoot (299-1570). The NBA **Nuggets,** and the NHL squad, the **Colorado Avalanche,** play in the brand-spanking-new **Pepsi Center,** 901 Auraria Pkwy. (405-1100 for info on the Nuggets and the Avalanche).

Denver's local restaurants and bars cater to a college-age and slightly older singles crowd. A copy of *Westword* gives the lowdown on LoDo. For a great evening, visit the ▧ **Mercury Café** (see **Food**). The "Hill of the Grasshopper," **El Chapultepec,** at 20th and Market St., is an honest-to-goodness bebopping jazz bar that has survived since Denver's Beat era in the 50s. No cover. 1-drink min. per set. Open daily 11am-2am.) Hungry after all that jazz? Check out "the Pec's" burrito joint next door. A remodeled chapel, **The Church,** 1160 Lincoln, offers 4 full bars (try a Fat Tire on tap), a cigar lounge, and a weekend sushi bar—that is, if Joe lets you off the dance floor. On weekends, the congregation swells with two floors of dancing. Swing with free lessons W nights at 10pm. (832-3528. Doors open Tu-Su 8-9pm until 1-2am.) The **Bluebird Theater,** 3317 E. Colfax hosts local tunes (322-2308). **Charlie's,** 900 E. Colfax Ave., at Emerson, is a popular gay bar stomping with country Western dancing (839-8890; open daily 10am-4am, last call 2am).

## MOUNTAIN RESORTS NEAR DENVER

**WINTER PARK.** Nestled among delicious-smelling mountain pines in the upper Fraser River valley, "Colorado's Favorite" **Winter Park Resort** is the closest ski and summer resort to Denver (68mi.; take I-70 W to U.S. 40). In the summer, mountain biking and hiking trails climb the mountains of the Continental Divide. **Winter Park Mary Jane Ski Area** packs bowls all winter long with a 3060 ft. vertical drop and 1467 acres of glade skiing on 2886 total acres (726-5514, 800-453-2525 for reservations). For snow conditions and summertime fun info, call 303-572-7669 or 800-729-5813. The **Alpine Slide,** at 1½mi., is Colorado's longest. (Open June to early Sept. daily 10am-6pm; mid- to late Sept. Sa-Su only. $8, seniors and children $7.) The **Zephyr Express** chairlift blows to the summit of Winter Park Mountain, allowing mountain bikers to reach the peak, then ride down on 45mi. of single track trails. (Open mid-June to early Sept. daily 10am-5pm, mid- to late Sept. Sa-Su only. Full-day $19. Mountain bike rentals from $9 per hr. 2hr. clinic $15.) Winter Park is on the vanguard of summer mountain fun, with mountain scooters, a maze, and a zip-line. (Full park pass for all summer activities $40.) The **High Country Stampede Rodeo** bucks every Sa at 7:30pm in July and Aug. at the John Work Arena, west of Fraser on County Rd. 73 (726-4118 or 800-903-7275; $8, children $4).

The **Viking Lodge,** on Rt. 40 in Winter Park, offers tiny rooms with phones and color TVs. Includes access to the hot tub and sauna and a 10% discount on rentals at the adjacent store, as well as winter shuttle service to the lifts. (726-8885 or 800-421-4013. Singles $40-60; doubles $45-105; varies with season. Reception 8am-9pm.) Perhaps the best family lodging deal in the Fraser Valley is the **Snow Mountain Ranch YMCA,** 12mi. past the town of Winter Park (take I-70 west to U.S. 40 west). The ranch features a host of recreational activities, including nordic skiing. (887-2152, ext. 4110. Quad with private bath $62.) Deliciously healthful breakfasts and lunches (each $4-8) are served on the patio at **Carver's Bakery Café,** at the end of the Cooper Creek Mall off U.S. 40, featuring a full bakery. Try the cinnamon rolls. (726-8202. Open daily 7am-2pm, until 3pm during peak season.)

The Chamber of Commerce (see below) also serves as the **Greyhound** depot; to Denver (2hr., 2 per day; $16). **Home James Transportation Services** (303-726-5060 or 800-451-4844) runs door-to-door shuttles to and from Denver Airport ($36; reservations required; office hours daily 8am-6pm). The same number reaches **Mad Adventures** river rafting (½-day $36.50; full-day $55). From Dec.-Apr., the **Río Grande Ski Train** (303-296-4754) leaves Denver's Union Station for Winter Park (see **Practical Information,** p. 656). **Winter Park-Fraser Valley Chamber of Commerce:** 78841 Hwy. 40 (726-4118, 303-422-0666 or 800-903-7275; open daily 8am-5pm). **Area code:** 970.

**SUMMIT COUNTY.** Skiers, hikers, and mountain bikers can tap into a sportsman's paradise in the U.S.'s highest county, about 70mi. west of Denver on I-70. **Summit County Chamber of Commerce:** 11 Summit Blvd. (668-5800), in Frisco (open daily 9am-5pm). **Silverthorne-Dillon info center:** (262-0817), on Tenderfoot Ave. in Dillon, 1½mi. south of I-70 on Rt. 6 (open daily 9am-5pm). The ski resorts of **Breckenridge** (800-789-7669 or 453-5000), **Copper Mountain** (968-2882 or 800-458-8386), and **Keystone** (468-2316 for operator, 800-255-3715 for info, or 888-222-9298 for reservations) are good alternatives to the more expensive resorts of Aspen and Vail. **Arapahoe Basin** usually has skiing until early July and occasionally into Aug., depending on snow conditions; it is the highest skiable terrain in North America (888-272-7246, 468-0718, or 496-7007). **Summit Stage** buses (free) connect these resorts with the towns of **Frisco, Dillon,** and **Silverthorne.**

The **Alpen Hütte,** 471 Rainbow Dr., in Silverthorne, has welcoming hosts, a familial atmosphere, clean rooms with beautiful mountain views, and year-round outdoor activities, including fly-fishing on the Blue River behind the hostel. Greyhound (from Denver) and Summit Stage stop outside the door. (468-6336. $17; in winter $27. Lockers $5 deposit. Linen and towels $1.50. Laundry. Free ski storage. Parking. Reception daily 7am-11am and 4pm-midnight. Lockout 9:30am-3:30pm. Midnight curfew. Reserve for winter 1-2 months in advance.) Several Forest Service campgrounds lie nearby in the **White River National Forest.** The **Dillon Ranger District Office,** 680 Blue River Pkwy. (468-5400; 800-280-2267 or 877-444-6777 for reservations), can supply more info (open M-F 8am-5pm).

Fashionable **Breckenridge** lies west of Silverthorne on I-70, 9mi. south of Frisco. Despite the many expensive restaurants and stores, you can still find reasonably priced, smoke-free accommodations at the **Fireside Inn (HI-AYH),** 114 N. French St., 2 blocks east of Main St. on the corner of Wellington. The indoor hot tub is great for *après-ski.* (453-6456. Dorm $20, private rooms $50-75; in height of winter (2nd half of Dec.) prices rise as high as $31/$95-145. Closed in May. Office hours daily 7am-10pm.) The **Stage Door Café,** 203 S. Main St., offers a multi-level complex in which to enjoy a latté ($2.75) or a sandwich and watch the crowds (453-6964; open M-F 7:30am-8pm, Sa-Su 7:30am-9pm). **Riverside Info Center:** (453-5579), on the corner of Washington and Main St. (open in winter and summer daily 9am-7pm, in fall and spring 9am-5pm). **Ski Conditions and Weather:** 800-789-7609. **Area code:** 970.

# BOULDER

Combining yuppie tastes with collegiate earthiness, Boulder lends itself to the pursuit of higher knowledge and better karma. It is home to both the central branch of the University of Colorado (CU) and the only accredited Buddhist university in the U.S., the Naropa Institute. Only here can you take summer poetry and healing workshops led by Allen Sandheim or Maya Angelou at the Jack Kerouac School of Disembodied Poets. In conclusion, Boulder rides, generation Boulder, fly—baby tabs two times, chillin'. We take you on the road, Jack.

## ⚡ ORIENTATION AND PRACTICAL INFORMATION

Boulder (pop. 96,000) is a small, manageable city, accessible by Rt. 36. The most developed area lies between **Broadway (Rt. 93)** and **28th St. (Rt. 36),** two busy streets running north-south through the city. **Baseline Rd.,** connecting the Flatirons with the eastern plains, and **Canyon Blvd. (Rt. 7),** following the Boulder Canyon into the mountains, both border the **University of Colorado (CU)** campus. The area around the school is known as **the Hill.** The pedestrian-only **Pearl St. Mall,** between 11th and 15th St., is the hip center of town. Most east-west roads are named, while north-south streets are numbered; Broadway is a conspicuous exception.

**Buses: Greyhound,** 4461 N. Broadway (443-1574). To: Denver (1hr., 2 per day, $6); Glenwood Springs (7-8hr., 2 per day, $38); and Vail (5½-6½hr., 2 per day, $23). Open M-F 8am-4pm. After hours, tickets can be purchased at the coffee shop next door.

**Public Transportation: HOP,** 4880 Pearl St. (447-8282). Shuttles connect the Pearl St. Mall, the Hill, CU, and the Crossroads Mall in a 2-way loop. Runs M-F 7am-10pm, with stops every 10min. 75¢, seniors 25¢. During term time, shuttles also run Th-Sa 10pm-3am every 20min. **SKIP** (299-6000) services areas west of Broadway to Fairview HS. **RTD** (299-6000 or 800-366-7433), at 14th and Walnut St. in the center of town, runs around town M-F 6am-8pm, Sa-Su 8am-8pm. 75¢, seniors free; higher during peak hrs. Also runs to: Denver Airport ($8, seniors and under 12 $4); Denver ($3); and Coors Field (round-trip $4). Buses operate 5:30-10pm.

**Taxis: Boulder Yellow Cab** (442-2277).

**Car Rental: Budget Rent-a-Car,** 1345 28th St. (342-7976), in the Harvest Hotel. Must be 21+ with major credit card. Ages 21-25 $25 per day surcharge. Economy size $19-45 per day. Unlimited mi. Open M-F 8am-5pm, Sa-Su 8am-1pm.

**Bike Rental: University Bicycles,** 839 Pearl St. (444-4196), downtown. Rents mountain bikes with helmet and lock $12 per 4hr., $15 4-8hr., $20 overnight; kids' bikes $10/$12/$15. Open M-F 9am-7pm, Sa 9am-6pm, Su 10am-5pm.

**Visitor Info: Boulder Chamber of Commerce/Visitors Service,** 2440 Pearl St. (442-1044), at Folsom about 10 blocks from downtown. Take bus #200; also accessible by HOP. Open M-Th 8:30am-5pm, F 8:30am-4pm. **University of Colorado Information** (492-6161), 2nd fl. of University Memorial Center (UMC) student union. Phones with free local calls. Open M-Th 7am-11pm, F-Sa 7am-midnight, Su 11am-11pm; term-time open Su-Th 7am-midnight, F-Sa 7am-1am, Su 11am-midnight. **CU Ride Board:** UMC 1st fl.

**Hotlines: Rape Crisis,** 443-7300. 24hr. **Crisis Line,** 447-1665 for counseling. 24hr.

**Bi-Gay-Lesbian Organizations: Lesbian, Bisexual, Gay, and Transgender Alliance** (492-8567), in CU's Willard Hall. Sept.-May daily 9am-5pm; closed in summer. **Boulder Campus Gay, Lesbian, and Bisexual Resource Center,** 492-1377.

**Internet Access:** Kiosks are scattered throughout the **UMC** (see **Visitor Info**).

**Post Office:** 1905 15th St. (800-275-8777), at Walnut St. Open M-F 7:30am-5:30pm, Sa 10am-2pm. **ZIP code:** 80302. **Area code:** 303.

# ▐ ACCOMMODATIONS

After spending all your money on tofu and yogurt at the Pearl St. Mall, you may find yourself strapped for cash and without a room; Boulder doesn't offer many budget accommodations. In the summer, at least you can rely on the hostel.

**Boulder International Hostel,** 1107 12th St. (442-0522), at College Ave., 2 blocks up College Hill; 15min. south of the RTD station. From Denver, take the A or B bus as close to College Ave. as possible. Although it is located near CU housing and frats, the BIH holds on to a family-like atmosphere. $15 gets you shared hall bathrooms, kitchen, laundry, and TV; linen $4. Private singles $35 per night, $150 per week; doubles $40/$180. Shower and towels free. Key deposit $10. Dorm lockout 10am-5pm. Curfew midnight.

**Chautauqua Association** (442-3282), off Baseline Rd. at the foot of the Flatirons. Turn at the Chautauqua Park sign and take Kinnikinic to Morning Glory Dr., where the office is located, or take bus #203. In summer, suites (2-person $48; 4-person $62), and private cottages with kitchens (4-night min. stay; 2 bedrooms $77; 3 bedrooms $98) are available. Reserve months in advance. Office hours M-F 8:30am-7pm, Sa 9am-3pm.

**The Boulder Mountain Lodge,** 91 Four Mile Canyon Dr. (444-0882), 3mi. west on Canyon Rd. (which becomes Rt. 119). 25 sites in a grove of pines next to a creek. Pay phone, 2 hot tubs, seasonal pool, and free showers. Check-out 10am; no reservations for camping. Cramped 3-person sites $14; $5 per additional person; $84 per week. Motel rooms for 1 or 2 people in summer $64; in winter from $54.

**Camping** info for **Arapahoe/Roosevelt National Forest** is available from the **Boulder Ranger District,** 2995 Baseline Rd. #110, Boulder 80303, at 30th St. (444-6600; open M-F 8am-4:30pm). **Kelly Dahl** (46 sites) lies 3mi. south of Nederland on Rt. 119. **Rainbow Lakes** (16 sites, first come, first served; no water) is 13mi. northwest of Nederland: turn at the Mountain Research Station (CR 119) and follow the road for 10mi. (open late May-mid-Sept.). The two gems of the forest are **Peaceful Valley** (17 sites) and **Camp Dick** (41 sites). Both lie north on Rt. 72 and offer cross-country skiing in the winter. All sites are $12, $6 per additional car, except Rainbow Lakes ($6; $3 per additional car). Reservations recommended, especially on weekends (call 877-444-6777). **Boulder Creek,** at the city limits at the foot of the mountains, is prime hiking and biking territory, as is **Scott Carpenter Park.**

# ▐ FOOD AND HANGOUTS

The streets on the Hill surrounding CU and along the Pearl St. Mall burst with good eateries, natural foods markets, and colorful bars. Many restaurants and bars line **Baseline Rd.** Boulder may have more options for vegetarians than carnivores.

**The Sink,** 1165 13th St. (444-7465), on the Hill. This Boulder classic still awaits the return of its former janitor, Robert Redford, who quit his job and headed to California in the late 50s. Surprisingly upscale new cuisine is served amidst wild graffiti and pipes. Burgers $6. Open M-Sa 11am-2am, Su noon-2am; food served until 10pm.

**Foolish Craig's,** 1611 Pearl St. (247-9383). Craig foolishly gave the French crepe an American twist, for example the "Homer" crepe ($6)—"Doh!" Many locals enjoy these revolutionary crepes, some filled with avocado or pesto chicken ($5-7). Open M-F 8am-9pm, Sa-Su 8am-10pm. Features live music every M, F, Sa, and Su.

**Daddy Bruce's Barbecue** (449-8890), on the corner of 20th and Arapahoe, is the place to be with a hankerin' for meat. You'll know it by the heavenly aroma of beef brisket ($5) and BBQ chicken ($9) floating out of this pantry-sized restaurant. Open daily 11am-3pm.

**■ TEALIGHTFUL TREATS** Plopped down next to the Boulder Museum of Contemporary Art is an honest-to-goodness **Dushanbe teahouse,** 1770 13th St., built by artists from Tajikstan (part of the former Soviet Union), in Boulder's sister city, Dushanbe, and piece-mailed to Boulder, where it was assembled in 1998. The building is owned by the city and leased to restaurateur Lenny Martinelli, who lays out a scrumptious spread. It's more than worth the price of a cup of tea ($2-4) to sit on a *topchan* in this artistic wonderworld and contemplate life in ancient Persia. Lunch starts at $5.50 and dinner at $7. Don't forget to say *hush omaded* (thank you) to the people of Dushanbe when you go. *(442-4993. Open M-F 7am-10pm, Sa-Su 8am-10pm.)*

**◉ ♬ SIGHTS AND ENTERTAINMENT**

The **Boulder Museum of Contemporary Art,** 1750 13th St., focuses on regional art. (443-2122. Open in summer W-F 11am-5pm, Su noon-5pm; in winter Tu-Sa 11am-5pm, Su noon-5pm. $2.) The intimate **Leanin' Tree Museum,** 6055 Longbow Dr., presents 200 paintings and 80 bronze sculptures that focus on Western themes (530-1442; open M-F 8am-4:30pm, Sa-Su 10am-4pm; free). Writers give readings in the Beat/Buddhist tradition at the small **Naropa Institute,** 2130 Arapahoe Ave., while others participate in meditation workshops (546-3578; open daily 9am-5pm). The **Rockies Brewing Company,** 2880 Wilderness Pl., off Velmont, offers tours and free beer (444-8448; pub open M-Sa 11am-10pm; 25min. tours M-Sa 2pm).

A perennially outrageous street scene rocks the Mall and the Hill; the university's kiosks have the low-down on downtown happenings. The **University Memorial Center,** 1000 Euclid (10th St. becomes Euclid on campus), hosts many events (492-6161). On the 3rd fl., its **Cultural Events Board** has the latest word on all CU-sponsored activities (492-1897). Late June through early Aug., the **Colorado Shakespeare Festival** suffers the slings and arrows of outrageous fortune (492-0554; previews $7-17, tickets $14-38; $2 student and senior discount). The **Colorado Music Festival** plays in July and Aug. (449-2413, ext. 11; tickets $12-35; seniors and students $12 or $2 off higher-priced tickets). In mid-Sept., tunes wail at the **Boulder Blues Festival** (443-5858; tickets $15-20). The local indie music scene is on display at the popular **Fox Theater and Cafe,** 1135 13th St. (447-0095).

# ROCKY MOUNTAIN NATIONAL PARK

Of all the U.S. national parks, Rocky Mountain National Park is closest to heaven. A third of the park lies above treeline; Longs Peak pierces the sky at 14,255ft. Here among the clouds, bitterly cold winds whip through a craggy landscape carpeted with dwarf wildflowers, arctic shrubs, granite boulders, and crystalline lakes.

The city of Estes Park, located immediately east of the park, hosts the vast majority of would-be mountaineers and alpinists, who crowd the shopping areas and boulevards in the summer. To the west of the park, the town of Grand Lake, located on the edges of two glacial lakes, is a more tranquil base from which to explore the park's less traversed but equally stunning western side. Trail Ridge Rd./U.S. 34 runs 45mi. through the park from Grand Lake to Estes Park.

**⁊ ORIENTATION AND PRACTICAL INFORMATION**

You can reach the national park from Boulder via U.S. 36 or scenic Rt. 7, or from the northeast up the Big Thompson Canyon via U.S. 34 (but beware flash floods). To get to Estes Park from Boulder, the **Hostel Hauler** (586-3688) will pick you up if you call before 9pm and arrange a shuttle for the next day ($15, round-trip $20).

**Visitor Info: Park Headquarters and Visitors Center** (586-1206), 2½mi. west of Estes Park on Rt. 36, at the Beaver Meadows entrance to the park. Open daily mid-June to late Aug. 8am-9pm; late Aug. to mid-June 8am-5pm. Winter evening programs on park-related topics are offered Sa 7pm; in summer daily at 7:30pm; a park introduction film is shown every 30min. 8:30am-4pm. **Kawuneeche Visitors Center** (627-3471), just outside the park's western entrance and 1¼mi. north of Grand Lake, offers similar info. Open daily mid-May to late Aug. 8am-6pm; Sept. to early May 8am-5pm. Evening programs occur Sa 7pm. The high-altitude **Alpine Visitors Center,** at the crest of Trail Ridge Rd., has a great view of the tundra. Open daily mid-June to late Aug. 9am-5pm; late May to mid-June and late Aug. to mid-Oct. 10am-4:30pm. **Lily Lake Visitors Center,** 6mi. south of Park Headquarters on Rt. 7, opens only in summer (daily 9am-4:30pm). Park **entrance fee** is $10 per vehicle, $5 per biker or pedestrian; the pass is valid for 7 days.

**Park Weather and Road Conditions:** 586-1333.

**Hospital: Estes Park Medical Center,** 586-2317.

**Park Emergency:** 586-1399.

**Post Office: Grand Lake,** 520 Center Dr. (800-275-8777). Open M-F 8:30am-5pm. **ZIP code:** 80447. **Estes Park,** 215 W. Riverside Dr. (586-8177). Open M-F 8:30am-5:30pm, Sa 10am-2pm. **ZIP code:** 80517. **Area code:** 970.

## ▚ ACCOMMODATIONS

**ESTES PARK.** Although Estes Park has an abundance of expensive lodges and motels, there are a few good deals on indoor beds near the national park, especially in winter when temperatures drop and tourists leave.

**H Bar G Ranch Hostel (HI-AYH),** 3500 H Bar G Rd. (586-3688; fax 586-5004). Turn off U.S. 34 onto Dry Gulch Rd. 1mi. east of town at Sombrero Stable; follow this road to CO 61 and turn right. At H Bar G Rd., turn right again. With its spectacular views of the mountains and Estes Valley, this converted ranch could be a luxury resort. Instead, its cabins, tennis court, recreation room, and kitchen entertain up to 100 hostelers. Proprietor Lou drives guests to town or the park entrance at 7:40am, then retrieves them from the Chamber of Commerce at 5pm. HI-AYH members only. $11. Open late May to mid-Sept. Call ahead, and bring a warm sleeping bag.

**The Colorado Mountain School,** 351 Moraine Ave. (586-5758). Tidy, dorm-style accommodations are open to travelers unless already booked by mountain-climbing students. Wood bunks with comfortable mattresses, linen, and showers. 17 beds. $20, $14 per additional person. Check-out 10am. Reservations recommended 1 week in advance.

**Estes Park Center YMCA,** 2515 Tunnel Rd. (586-3341, ext. 1010), follow Rt. 36 to Rt. 66; 2mi. from the park entrance. It's fun to stay at the YMCA; extensive facilities on the 860-acre complex include mini-golf and a pool, as well as daily hikes for guests and horseback rides ($20 per hr.). A 4-person cabin with kitchen and bath from $55; 6-person cabins $48-89. A 1-day guest membership is required to stay ($3, families $5). Call ahead; they are booked for the summer by late Apr.

**GRAND LAKE.** Though inaccessible without a car in the winter, this town is the "snowmobile capital of Colorado" and offers spectacular cross-country routes.

**▨ Shadowcliff Hostel (HI-AYH),** 405 Summerland Park Rd. (627-9220); from the western entrance, veer left to Grand Lake, then take the left fork ¼mi. into town on W. Portal Rd. In downtown Grand Lake, take a left at Garfield, and turn right onto W. Portal. Hand-built pine lodge perched on a cliff overlooking Shadow Mountain Lake and the Rockies. Hiking trails, kitchen, showers and a wood burning stove. $10, nonmembers $12, bedding rental $1. Private singles $27, doubles $33; $5 per additional person. Cabins sleep 6-8; $66-77 per day; 6-day min. stay. Open late May to Oct. Make reservations for the cabins as far as a year in advance.

**Sunset Motel,** 505 Grand Ave. (627-3318). Friendly owners plus cozy rooms equals a warm stay. Singles $30-60; doubles $70-100; 10% discount with *Let's Go: USA*.

**Bluebird Motel,** 30 River Dr. (627-9314), on Rt. 34 west of Grand Lake. Spiffy rooms with spotted carpets, fluffy pink curtains, TV, and fridges. Overlooks Shadow Mountain Lake and the snow-capped Continental Divide. Singles $30-50; doubles $40-55.

**CAMPING.** Camping is available in the national forest at **Stillwater Campground,** on the shores of the hot boating spot **Lake Granby** ($15, 128 sites), or at **Green Ridge Campground,** located on the south end of **Shadow Mountain Lake** ($12, 78 sites). Both sites have toilets, water, and boat ramps, and are open late May to early Sept. Make reservations for a fee (800-260-2267) or arrive early to get a first come, first served spot. National Park Campgrounds include **Moraine Park** (5½mi. from Estes; 247 sites; some open all year), with open, sunny spots, and **Glacier Basin** (9mi. from Estes; 150 sites; open in summer only), which offers secluded sites and a spectacular view of the mountains. Both require reservations in summer (sites $16; 7-day max. stay; call 586-1206 or 800-365-2267). **Aspenglen,** 5mi. west of Estes Park near the Fall River entrance, has 56 sites available early May through Sept. ($16; 7-day max. stay). **Longs Peak Campground** has tent sites only on a first come, first served basis and is a prime location to begin climbing Longs Peak ($16, $12 in winter; 3-night max. stay). **Timber Creek,** 10mi. north of Grand Lake, is the only national park campground on the western side of the park. Open year-round, it is comprised of 100 woodsy sites. (May-Sept. $16. 7-night max. stay. Cheaper in winter.) There is no water at Long's Peak or Timber Creek in the winter.

A **backcountry** camping permit ($15) is required in the summer. On the eastern slope, permits are available inside the park from the **Backcountry Permits and Trip Planning Building** (586-1242, open in summer daily 7am-7pm, in winter daily 8am-4:30pm), a 2min. walk from the Park Headquarters. The friendly staff will ensure you're prepared. In the west, see the folks at the **Kawuneeche Visitors Center.**

## 🗂 FOOD

### ESTES PARK

**The Notchtop Pub** (586-0272), in the upper Stanley Village Shopping Plaza, east of downtown off Rt. 34. Specializes in homemade everything, including breads, pastries, and pies baked fresh every morning. Ice cream $1 a scoop. More a bohemian cafe than a pub, the Notchtop fixes a mean lunch of soups ($3) and sandwiches (starting at $5). Open daily 8am-9pm; bakery open 7am-10pm.

**Mama Rose's,** 388 E. Elkhorn Ave. (586-3330), on the riverwalk in Barlow Plaza, offers heaping portions of Italian food. Mama's special gives carbo-depleted mountain hoppers all-you-can-eat soup, salad, garlic bread, pasta, and spumoni for $10. All-you-can-eat breakfast special $6. Open daily 7-11am and 4-9pm.

**Ed's Cantina,** 362 E. Elkhorn (586-2919), is open for anything from "pancakes to fajitas." This local favorite right on the main drag serves up traditional breakfast specials ($3.25) and a spicier Mexican breakfast ($5). Open daily 7am-10pm.

### GRAND LAKE

**Marie's Grand Lake Café,** 928 Grand Ave. (627-9475), located on the lake, is a watering hole for locals. Huge breakfast of 2 eggs, steak, 2 pancakes, and hashbrowns for $5. Open daily in summer 6am-10pm, in winter W-Su 6am-8pm.

**Pancho and Lefty's,** 2301 Grand Ave. (627-8773). The price is right, as are the portions; their deliciously spicy tamales ($5.75) or crunchy *chimichangas* ($6.75) are cases in point. Open daily in summer 11am-9pm, W-M in winter 6am-8pm.

## 🏔 OUTDOOR ACTIVITIES

The star of this park is **Trail Ridge Rd.** (U.S. 34), a 50mi. stretch that rises 12,183ft. above sea level into frigid tundra. This main drag through the park is the highest continuously paved road in the world. The round-trip drive takes roughly 3hr. by car; beware of slow-moving tour buses. The road is closed Oct. to May for weather reasons, and is passable only in the afternoon well into the summer. The **Forest Canyon Overlook** and 30min. round-trip **Tundra Trail** provide a closer look at the fragile environment. **Moraine Park Museum** on Bear Lake Rd., en route to the campsites, has exhibits on the park's geology and ecosystem (open 9am-5pm in summer).

Most rangers swear by *Hiking Rocky Mountain National Park* ($13), a widely available guidebook. Serious mountaineers and hikers are attracted to **Longs Peak** (14,255ft.), the highest and most prominent mountain in the park. Athletic, acclimated hikers can climb the peak in late July or Aug. via the 15mi. round-trip Keyhole route from the Longs Peak Ranger Station. The last 1½mi. to the top involves scrambling over rock ledges and boulders. Check in at the ranger station the day before, and leave by 6am to avoid afternoon thunderstorms.

Since the trailheads in the park start high, just a few hours of hiking accesses unbeatable alpine scenery. Give your body enough time to adjust before starting up the higher trails. To acclimatize, it is best to sleep above 5000ft. for 2 nights, and then above 8000ft. for 2 more. The park's premier hiking is in the **Bear Lake** area. In the summer, a shuttle bus runs from the campgrounds to the trailhead where you can begin the 0.4mi. hike around the lake. Trails also go up to **Nymph** (½mi.), **Dream** (1.1mi.), and **Emerald Lakes** (1.8mi.), three glacial pools which offer inspiring glimpses of the higher rock tops. Some easy trails include the 3.6mi. round-trip from Wild Basin Ranger Station to **Calypso Cascades** and the 2.8mi. round-trip from the Longs Peak Ranger Station to **Eugenia Mine**. The **Twin Sisters** trail is a strenuous 2-4hr. hike that leaves from Rt. 7, south of the Lilly Lake Visitors Center, thus bypassing the park entrance fee. Isolated from the rest of the park, the summit provides a private view of the range.

From Grand Lake, an overnight trek into the scenic and remote **North** or **East Inlets** leaves camera-toting crowds behind. An 11mi. trail ascends 2240ft. through pristine wilderness to **Lake Nanita** (leave from North Inlet). From East Inlet, a 7mi. course leads to Lake Verna, where plump trout make for excellent fishing.

World-class **rock climbing** is just north of Estes Park, at **Lumpy Ridge**. Gain access via Devil's Gulch Rd. and park at the Twin Owls lot. The ridge offers climbs for all abilities. Contact **Colorado Wilderness**, 358 Elkhorn (586-5648), in Estes Park.

While no biking is allowed on trails within the park itself, mountain bikers can head to nearby national forests. **Colorado Bicycling Adventures**, 184 E. Elkhorn, rents bikes. Ask the staff or buy the *Mountain Bike Guide to Estes Park* for $3.50 to find the good trails. (586-4241 or 800-607-8765. From $5 per hr., $21 per day. Helmets included. 10% hosteler discounts. Open daily 10am-6pm. Tours $46-70, bike rental, helmet, and transport included.)

The **world's largest collection of keys** at the Baldpate Inn, 4900 Rt. 7 S., next to the Lilly Lake Visitors Center, dangles 12,000 keys from the walls and ceiling.

# VAIL

The most-visited ski resort in the U.S., Vail wows skiers with its prime snow conditions, a vertical drop of 3330 ft., 121 ski runs, and 26 lifts—not to mention its ritzy hotels, swank saloons, and sexy boutiques. Discovered by Lord Gore in 1854, Vail and its surrounding valley were invaded by miners during the Rockies gold rush in the 1870s. According to local lore, the Ute Indians adored the area's rich supply of game, but they became so upset with the white man that they set fire to the forest, creating the resort's famous open terrain.

The **Colorado Ski Museum**, in the Transportation Bldg. in Vail Village, offers a glimpse into Vail's past and houses the **Ski Hall of Fame** (476-1876; open Tu-Su 10am-5pm; free). Before slaloming, the unequipped visit **Ski Base**, 675 W. Lionshead Circle. (476-5799. Skis, poles, and boots from $13 per day. Snowboard and boots from $19 per day. Open daily in winter 9am-7pm. Becomes Wheel Base in summer; open Sa-Su 9am-5pm.) **Weather conditions:** 476-5677.

Vail gestures toward sun worshippers in the summer, when the 121 ski runs become **trails.** The **Lionshead gondola** and the **Vistabahn chairlift**, part of the **Vail Resort** in Vail village, whisk hikers, bikers, and sightseers to the top of the mountains for breathtaking views. (476-9090, office hours 8:30am-5pm. Lionshead open in summer Th-Sa 10am-9pm, Su-W 10am-4pm; after Labor Day, Sa-Su only. Vistabahn open daily 10am-4pm, late May-early Sept. All-day summer pass on Lionshead, Vistabahn and Eaglebahn in Beaver Creek $14, ages 65-70 $8, over 70 free.

Bike-hauling fee $25, ages 5-12 $20.) Rental **bikes** are available atop Vail Mountain ($7 per hr., $25 per day, $40 for 24hr.; hauling fee included.). The **Gore Creek Fly Fisherman,** 187 Gore Creek Dr., reels in the daily catch of river info. (476-3296. Rod rentals $15 per day, $25 with boots and waders. Open in summer daily 8am-10pm, May 15-June and Sept.-Oct. 15 Su-Th 8am-8pm.)

The phrase "cheap lodging" is not part of Vail's vocabulary. Rooms in the resort town rarely dip below $175 per night in winter, and summer lodging is often equally pricey. **The Prairie Moon,** 738 Grand Ave., offers some of the cheapest lodging outside the expensive resort area. Located in Eagle, about 30mi. west of Vail, The Prairie Moon has large, clean rooms with fridges and microwaves. (328-6680. Singles from $40; doubles $45; and triples $50. Reserve well ahead.) A bus shuttles visitors daily between Eagle and Vail (see **Anon/Beaver Creek Transit** below). Closer summer lodgings await at the **Roost Lodge,** 1783 N. Frontage Rd., in West Vail. Average-sized rooms come with cable and phones, as well as continental breakfast and access to a jacuzzi, sauna, and pool. (476-5451 or 800-873-3065. Singles $55-62 M-F.) The **Holy Cross Ranger District,** right off U.S. 24 at exit 171, provides info on the six campgrounds near Vail (827-5715; open M-Sa 8am-5pm). With 25 sites, **Gore Creek** is the closest and most popular campground. Situated right outside East Vail, it is within hiking distance of the free Vail bus. (Free; sites have water and 14-day limit.) **Garfinkel's,** a hidden hangout accessible by foot in Vail's Lion Head Village (directly across from the gondola), offers specials that include $7 cheeseburgers and $3-4 beers on a porch that practically merges with the ski slope. F-Sa nights feature live progressive rock bands and disco DJs, respectively. (476-3789. Restaurant open M-Tu 9am-6pm, W 10am-6pm, Th 9am-7pm, F 9am-8pm, Sa-Su 11am-7pm. Bar closes at 2am.) **DJ's Classic Diner,** in nearby Concert Hall Plaza, whips up old-fashioned omelettes from $4, as well as crepes ($6) and blintzes ($4.75; 476-2336; open W-Su 7am-2pm and 10pm-3am, M-Tu 7am-2pm).

Vail's two **visitors centers** are located at either end of the village, at the **Vail Transportation Center** (479-1394 or 800-525-3875, open M-F 9am-6pm, Sa-Su 9:30am-5:30pm), and on S. Frontage Rd. (479-1385, open M-F 9am-5pm) near Lionshead Village. **Greyhound** (476-5137; ticket office open daily 7:45am-noon and 2-6pm) buses eager skiers out of its depot, in the Transportation Bldg. next to the main visitors center, to Glenwood Springs (1½hr., 4 per day, $15, F-Su $16); Denver (2hr., 5 per day, $18-19); and Grand Junction (3½hr., 4 per day, $18-19). **Avon/Beaver Creek Transit** (949-6121 for schedule info, office hours 7am-6pm daily) runs bus routes between Vail and its surrounding areas, including Eagle and Edwards (each $2). Free bus service covers the area around Vail Village, Lionshead, and East and West Vail. **Post office:** 1300 N. Frontage Rd. W. (476-5217; open M-F 8:30am-5:30pm, Sa 8:30am-noon). **ZIP code:** 81657. **Area code:** 970.

# ASPEN

A world-renowned asylum for musicians and skiers, Aspen is an upper-class playground, where shoppers exclaim "I'll take it!" without asking for prices. Although more congenial than ultra-ritzy Vail (see p. 666), Aspen does provide the budget traveler with similar woes. To catch Aspen on the semi-cheap, stay in Glenwood Springs (40mi. north on Rt. 82; see p. 668) and make a daytrip here, or camp amid aspen groves in the nearby national forest.

**Skiing** is the main attraction in Aspen. The hills surrounding town contain 4 ski areas: **Aspen Mountain, Aspen Highlands, Buttermilk Mountain,** and **Snowmass Ski Area.** The resorts sell interchangeable lift tickets. (925-1220 or 800-525-6200. Peak-season $45-63, ages 13-27 $45, ages 7-12 $37, 65-69 $55, over 70 or under 7 free.) The **Glenwood Springs Hostel** offers a $35 full-day lift ticket for the Aspen ski resorts (see p. 668). In summer, the **Silver Queen Gondola** heads to the top of the mountains. (925-1220 or 800-525-6200. Open daily late May to early Sept. 10am-5pm. $12 per day, $10 per ride.) At **Snowmass Mountain,** you can take a chairlift to the top and ride your mountain bike down (in summer daily 9:30am-3pm; free). The mountains of **Maroon Bells,** and the well-known 1.8mi. hike to **Cascade Lake** are not to be missed, but Maroon Creek Rd. is closed to traffic from 8:30am-5pm daily. To avoid paying $5 for a long, slow bus ride, which departs every 30min. from **Rubey Park**, plan an early morning or a sunset hike. In Aspen proper, the **Ute Trail** leaves Ute Ave. and climbs to a rock ledge, following a windy and somewhat hairy course. The peak is a spectacular spot to watch the sunset (climbing time 30min.). Also in town, the gentler **Hunter Trail** crosses many streams and gently glides into a valley; day-hikers will want to pick a turn-around point.

Aspen's most famous event, the **Aspen Music Festival** (925-9042), features jazz, opera, and classical music from late June through Aug. Free bus transportation takes listeners from Rubey Park downtown to "the Tent," before and after all concerts. Many of the concerts are free. Call 925-3254 for a schedule.

If you stay in Aspen, you'll have to bite the bullet and reach deep into your pockets. The last sound deal in town, **St. Moritz Lodge**, 344 W. Hyman Ave., charms ski bums with a pool, sauna, hot tub, and microwaves. (925-3220 or 800-817-2069. Dorm beds $35; in off-season $26-29; at height of winter $55, hotel accommodations from $59.) Down the road (Rt. 82 S) 44mi. in the charming and historical town of **Twin Lakes**, lies the **Windspirit Cabins and Cafe.** Do not miss the cafe featuring delicious sandwiches made with fresh organic produce. (719-486-8138, on Hwy. 82. Rooms $50. Open in summer only daily 11am-4pm.) Unless 6 ft. of snow covers the ground, **camping** is available in one of the many National Forest Campgrounds that lie within 5mi. of Aspen. Reservable and first come, first served sites scatter just west of Aspen on Maroon Rd. (accessible from 5pm-8:30am) and southeast of Aspen on Rt. 82. (800-280-2267. $7-12 per night. 5-day max stay throughout the district. 2-vehicle max. Sites fill before noon. Open June to mid-Sept.) Free **backcountry camping permits** are available at the Ranger District and sporting goods stores (see below). When you pick up your permit, consider paying $1 for insurance which will cover the cost in case you need "extraction" and rescue.

The **Main Street Bakery**, 201 E. Main St., creates gourmet soups ($4.25), homemade granola with fruit ($5.50) and open-faced vegetarian sandwiches ($6.50; 925-6446; open M-Sa 7am-5pm, Su 7am-4pm). The **In and Out House**, 233 E. Main St., is just that: a revolving door of customers in an outhouse-sized space. They offer tasty sandwiches on freshly baked bread for $3-7. (925-6647. Open M-F 8am-5pm, Sa-Su 9am-4pm.) **The Big Wrap,** 530 E. Durant Ave., rolls up creatively named veggie and Mexican wraps for $5-6.25 and mixes smoothies for $4 (544-1700; open daily in summer 10am-6pm; in winter 10am-6pm). **Boogies Diner,** 534 Cooper, dishes out turkey sandwiches ($7.25 for closed, $8.50 for open-faced) and old-fashioned floats ($4). Obey the house rules: "schnoodling in booths only." (925-6610. Open M-F 11am-10pm, off-season 11am-9pm.)

**Visitors centers:** 320 Hyman Ave., in the opera house (open M-Sa 9am-6pm, Su 10am-5pm); and 425 Rio Grand Pl. (open M-Sa 10am-4pm; 925-1940 or 800-262-7736). **Aspen Ranger District:** 806 W. Hallam (925-3445; weather info 920-1664). Info on hikes and camping within 15mi. of Aspen (topographic map $4; open M-F 8am-5pm, in summer also Sa 8am-4:30pm). **Roads and Weather:** 945-2221. **Area code:** 970.

# GLENWOOD SPRINGS

Glenwood Springs, located along I-70, 40mi. north of Aspen on Rt. 82, is a smart choice for the budget traveler. Renowned for its steaming hot springs and vapor caves, Glenwood is sprinkled with budget-friendly markets, cafes, pool/dance halls, and a friendly hostel. **Glenwood Hot Springs Lodge and Pool,** 401 N. River Rd., located in a huge resort complex and maintained at 90°F year-round, contains the world's largest outdoor hot springs pool, a waterslide, and spas with different water temperatures. (945-6571 or 800-537-7946. Open daily 7:30am-10pm. Day pass $7.50, after 9pm $5; ages 3-12 $5.25/$4.50.) The smelly gases and 115°F steam of **Yampah Spa and Vapor Caves,** 709 E. 6th St., create a relaxing experience amid the dim underground caves. After sweating your brains out, relax to New Age music in the Solarium. (945-0667. Open daily 9am-9pm. $8.75, hostelers $4.75 with hostel pass/receipt.) Skiing is available at the uncrowded **Sunlight,** 10901 County Rd. 117,

10mi. west of town (945-7491 or 800-445-7931; $30 per day, ages 6-13 $20, hosteler discount). Take a tour of the 8th wonder of the world, as the **Fairy Caves** were dubbed in 1896. A new company called **Glenwood Caverns**, 508 Pine St., behind the Colorado Hotel has just opened them to the public. (945-4228. Open Apr. 15 to Nov. 1. Tours depart every hour 9am-6pm and last for 2 hr., including the bus ride. Adults M-F $10, Sa-Su $12; children $5/$6.)

Within walking distance of the springs and downtown, you'll find the **Glenwood Springs Hostel (HI-AYH)**, 1021 Grand Ave., which consists of a spacious Victorian house and a newer building next door. The hostel offers many package deals on area skiing, outdoors, and whitewater activities. Owner Gary has a sweet, sweet, vinyl collection. (945-8545 or 800-946-7835. $13; private singles $19; private doubles $26. Linen $1. Free pickup from train and bus stations. Kitchen use and some food included. No curfew. Lockout 10am-4pm.) The B&B next door is **Adducci's Inn**, 1023 Grand Ave. *Let's Go*-toting guests get a 5% discount on the regular room rates of $58-95. However, a **hostel** will open up at Adducci's in the year 2000. (945-9341. Breakfast included. Free pick-up from bus and train stations. $10 per additional person.) Adducci's also serves pub fare in their **restaurant/bar** (open Tu-Su 5-10pm; bar closes by midnight).

The **Daily Bread Café and Bakery**, 729 Grand Ave., offers two squares a day at breakfast and lunch. They have a south-of-the-border omelette with potatoes ($6), as well as a leaner veggie eggs benedict for $7 (945-6253; open M-F 7am-2pm, Sa 8am-2pm, Su 8am-noon). For hearty eats or a late-night snack, try the **Village Inn,** 102 W. 6th St. (945-9275. Open Su-Th 6am-11pm, F-Sa 6am-midnight.) **Doc Holliday's Saloon,** 724 Grand Ave., is the place for burgers ($6-8) and beers ($1.50-2 for domestics; 945-9050; open daily 10am-2am, food served 11am-11pm).

**Glenwood Springs Chamber Resort Association:** 1102 Grand Ave. (945-6589. Guide $1. Open June-Aug. M-F 9am-6pm, Sa-Su 10am-3pm; Aug.-June M-F 8:30am-5pm. Printed info available 24hr.) The **White River National Forest Headquarters** (945-2521), at 9th and Grand Ave., provides info about camping and outdoor activities (open M-F 8am-5pm). **Amtrak:** 413 7th St. (945-9563; ticket office open daily 9:30am-4:30pm); to Denver (6¾hr., $42-64) and Salt Lake City (8¼hr., $48-87). **Greyhound:** at the W. Glenwood Mall (945-8501; station open M-F 8am-4:30pm; when station is closed, pay driver); to Denver (3½hr., 5 per day, $27) and Grand Junction (2hr., 5 per day, M-Th $12, F-Su $13). The **Roaring Fork Transit Agency (RFTA)** (located at Durant and Mill St. in Aspen, 925-8484, open M-F 6am-7:30pm, Sa-Su 8:30am-6:30pm) screams to Aspen (1.5hr. $6, kids $5). **Post Office:** 113 9th St. (945-5611; open M-F 8am-6pm, Sa 9am-1pm). **ZIP code:** 81601. **Area code:** 970.

## GRAND JUNCTION

Grand Junction gets its name from its seat at the junction of the Colorado and Gunnison Rivers and the conjunction-junction of the Río Grande and Denver Railroads. The city's chief attribute is its location among Grand Mesa, Colorado National Monument, Arches National Park, and Moab. Those who sup from the tables of natural splendor should further indulge from the chalice of local vintage—it is surprising to find 11 wineries amid the spires and mesas of Grand Junction. For tours (with free samples), pick up a free map at the Grand Junction Visitors Bureau (see below) or call the **Wine Industry Development Board,** 245-4329.

The smoothly running **Melrose Hotel (HI-AYH)**, 337 Colorado Ave., between 3rd and 4th St., assists travelers in navigating the nearby natural wonders. In winter, owner Marcus can direct you to Powderhorn for the best local skiing. (242-9636 or 800-430-4555. Kitchen. Dorms $15; singles $24, with bath $34; doubles $27/$39. Reception 8-10am and 4-9pm; call if arrival time will not coincide.) **Columbine Motel,** 2824 North Ave., offers rooms with TVs and fridges (241-2908; singles $40, doubles $50). Camp in **Highline State Park,** at R and 11.8 Rd., 10mi. west of town and 7mi. north of the Loma exit off I-70 (858-7208; fishing access, restrooms, showers; 30 sites $9, $4 per day entrance fee), or **Island Acres State Park,** 10mi. east on the banks of the Colorado River, off I-70 exit 47. (464-0548. 6 tent sites $9, 34 partial hookups $12, 40 full hookups $15; $4 per day entrance fee.)

The **Rockslide Restaurant and Brew Pub,** 401 S. Main St., joins the avalanche of micro-breweries blanketing the nation. The Big Bear Stout comes in an $8.50 grotler (½-gal.). Salmon and chips are $8; during happy hour (4-6pm), all appetizers are ½-price. (245-2111. Open daily 10am-midnight.) The large and popular **Redlands Dos Hombres Restaurant,** 321 Brach Dr., just south of Broadway (Rt. 340) on the corner of Monument Rd., serves great Mexican food in a casual setting. On W nights (6-9pm), there is a table-side magic show. (Half-price appetizers during happy hour M-F 3-6pm. 242-8861. Open daily 11am-10pm.) Breakfast specialties and a copy of *Shalom on the Range* can be obtained at **The Crystal Cafe,** 314 Main St, (242-8843; open M-F 7am-1:45pm, Sa 8:30am-1:25pm; bakery open until 3pm). Grand Junction lies at the intersection of U.S. 50 and U.S. 6 between Denver and Salt Lake City; its pit stop location draws touring bands who refuse to drive 500mi. between gigs. The **Chameleon Club,** 234 Main St., grooves to live music nightly until 2am. Su night is Service Industry Night; anybody in "public service" gets happy hour prices all night. (245-3636.)

The **Grand Junction Visitor Bureau,** 740 Horizon Dr. (244-1480), exit 31 off I-70, behind the Taco Bell, has weekly lecture and slide show programs on the history and culture of southwest Colorado (open daily May to mid-Oct. 8:30am-8pm; late Oct. to Apr. 8:30am-5pm). **Enterprise Car Rental,** 406 S. 5th St. (242-8103), rents compact cars from $45 per day, $285 per week. Must be 21 with a major credit card. **Amtrak,** 339 S. 1st St. (241-2733; station open daily 10am-6pm), shoots twice daily to Denver ($43-79) and Salt Lake City ($39-71). The **Greyhound** station, at 5th and Ute St. (242-6012; ticket window open 24hr.), has service to Denver (5½hr., 7per day, $31-33); Durango (5hr., 1 per day, $34); Salt Lake City (6-11hr., 1 per day, $47-50); and Los Angeles (16hr., 2 per day, $95-100). **Domestic violence line:** 241-6704. **Internet access** is available via **Cyber Cafe,** at 8th and North Ave. (244-3400). **Post Office:** 241 N. 4th St. (244-3401; open M-F 8am-5:15pm, Sa 9am-12:30pm). **ZIP code:** 81501. **Area code:** 970.

## COLORADO NATIONAL MONUMENT

Four mi. west of Grand Junction off Monument Rd., the Colorado National Monument is a 32 sq. mi. sculpture of steep cliff faces, canyon walls, and obelisk-like spires wrought by the forces of gravity, wind, and water. The **Rim Rock Drive** runs along the edge of red canyons, providing views of awe-inspiring rock monoliths, the Grand Mesa, and the city of Grand Junction. **Window Rock Trail** (¼mi.) and **Otto's Trail** (½mi.) are easy walks to points from which you can gaze at the eerie, skeletal rock formations. The 6mi. **Monument Canyon Trail** inspires visions of grandeur, as it wanders amid the giant rock formations. Check in at the monument **headquarters and visitors center** (970-858-3617), near the western entrance. (Open daily June-Sept. 8am-6pm; off-season 9am-5pm. Entrance fee $4 per vehicle, $2 per cyclist or hiker.) **Saddlehorn Campground,** near the visitors center, provides over 50 partially shaded sites (restrooms, water, no hookups; $10; first come, first served). The **Bureau of Land Management,** 2815 H Rd. (970-244-3000; open M-F 7:30am-4:30pm), with its office across from the airport, maintains 12 sites at **Mud Springs,** near **Glade Park** ($5). Primitive camping is permitted on all adjoining BLM land (free).

## GRAND MESA

Grand Mesa, or "the great table," is the world's largest flat-topped mountain, looming 50mi. east of Grand Junction (by road) and 1080 ft. above sea level. A Native American story tells how a mad mother eagle tore a serpent to bits, believing her young to be inside the snake's belly; the lakes were formed by the resulting fragments. Recently, geologists have estimated that a 300ft. thick lava flow covered the entire region billions of years ago, and the Mesa is the only portion to have endured erosion. The numerous lakes on the Mesa that serve as spawning grounds for insects also provide fine fishing, as well as hiking opportunities.

The **district forest service,** 2777 Crossroads Blvd. (970-242-8211), in Grand Junction, dispenses maps ($4, waterproof version $8) and info on the campsites they maintain on the Mesa (open M-F 8am-5pm). **Island Lake** (13 sites, $8) and **Ward Lake**

**ALL YOU NEED IS A DREAM** There is a good chance that the Colorado National Monument would not exist if it weren't for the efforts and antics of one man: **John Otto**. Otto moved to the canyon on the outskirts of Grand Junction in 1906 and was immediately entranced. He spent years living alone in the canyon, building trails so individuals could enjoy the place he loved, and badgering government officials to declare the canyon a national monument. Sometimes his letters were more threats than requests. Perhaps his most interesting escapade came when **President Taft** was making a train stop in Grand Junction: Otto knew that Taft was a huge fan of peaches, so he lured the president to what is now the monument with a promise of delicious fruit. His tactics worked. In 1911, the monument was created, and Otto was named caretaker.

(13 sites, $10) are both on the water and have ample fishing. **Jumbo** (12 sites, $10); **Little Bear** (36 sites, $8); and **Cottonwood** (42 sites, $8) provide other options. Call or stop by the **visitors center** (856-4153), at the eastern end of the lake, for more info on any site (open daily in summer 9am-5pm, in off-season 9am-4pm).

The **Mesa Lakes Resort**, on Rt. 65 on the north side of the summit, is an old-fashioned mountain retreat. The resort rents extremely rustic cabins for 2-4 people ($45 per day, cooking facilities, no running water, private bathhouse nearby), more modern cabins for 6 people ($100 per day), and typical motel rooms ($45-55). Campsites are also available. The resort houses a general store, which rents bikes, and a restaurant. (970-268-5467 or 888-420-6372. Open in summer Su-Th 8am-7pm, F-Sa 8am-8pm; in winter daily 9am-5pm.) On the south side of the summit, the **Grand Mesa Lodge** rents cabins year-round ($65, $7.50 per extra person) and motel units ($35; no kitchen). They also have a small but well-stocked store (open daily 8am-6pm) and offer outdoor wisdom. (856-3250 or 800-551-6372.)

## COLORADO SPRINGS

When pioneers rushed west toward Colorado in search of gold (shouting "Pikes Peak or Bust!"), they were surprised to find towering red rocks and cave dwellings at the foot of the peak. The pioneers called the bizarre rock formations the Garden of the Gods, in part because of the Ute legend that the rocks were petrified bodies of enemies hurled down by the gods above. The United States Olympic Team, housed in Colorado Springs, continues the quest for gold, while jets from the United States Air Force Academy barrel-roll overhead.

## 🚹 ORIENTATION AND PRACTICAL INFORMATION

Colorado Springs is laid out in a grid of broad thoroughfares. **Nevada Ave.**, the main north-south strip, just east of I-25, is known for its bars and restaurants. **Cascade Ave.** is the east-west axis, while **Pikes Peak Ave.** divides the city north and south. The numbered streets west of Nevada ascend as you move west. **I-25** from Denver plows through downtown. East of Nevada Ave. remains largely residential.

**Buses: Greyhound,** 120 S. Weber St. (635-1505). To: Denver (1½-2hr., 7 per day, $12); Pueblo (1hr., 5 per day, $8); and Albuquerque (8hr., 4 per day, $58). Tickets sold daily 5:15am-10pm.

**Public Transit: City Bus Service,** 127 E. Kiowa (385-7433), at Ridefinders Transport Ctr., at Kiowa and Nevada. Serves Widefield, Manitou Springs, Ft. Carson, Garden of the Gods, and Peterson AFB (#1). Hourly service M-F 6am-6pm; every 30min. 6-10am or 11am and 2-6pm; irregular evening service until 10pm; Sa hourly service 6am-10pm, except #1 bus every 30min. $1, seniors and children ages 5-11 50¢, under 6 free; to Ft. Carson, Widefield, Fountain, Manitou Springs 25¢ extra; exact change.

**Taxis: Yellow Cab,** 634-5000.

**Car Rental: XPress Rent-A-Car,** 2021 E. Platte (634-1914 or 800-634-1914). From $22.95 per day, $135 per week. 100 free mi. per day, then 19¢ per mi. Open M-F 8:30am-5:30pm, Sa 8:30am-2pm. Must stay in Colorado. 21+ with major credit card.

ROCKY MOUNTAINS

**Tours: Pikes Peak Tours,** 3704 Colorado Ave. (633-1181 or 800-345-8197), offers trips to the U.S. Air Force Academy and Garden of the Gods (4hr., $20, under 13 $12.50) and Pikes Peak (4hr., $30/$20), as well as a 10mi. whitewater rafting trip on the Arkansas River (7hr., includes lunch; $65/$45). Office open daily 8am-5pm.

**Visitor Info: Visitors Bureau,** 104 S. Cascade, #104, entrance on Colorado Ave. (635-7506 or 800-888-4748). Open daily 8:30am-5pm.

**Hotlines: Crisis Emergency Services,** 635-7000. **Rape Crisis,** 633-3819. Both 24hr.

**Post Office:** 201 E. Pikes Peak Ave. (800-275-8777), at Nevada Ave. Open M-F 7:30am-5:30pm, Sa 8am-1pm. **ZIP code:** 80903. **Area code:** 719.

# ACCOMMODATIONS

The motels along **Nevada Ave.** are fairly shabby; opting for nearby campgrounds and spots along **W. Pikes Peak Ave.** and **W. Colorado Ave.** is a good idea.

**Apache Court Motel,** 3401 W. Pikes Peak Ave., off of 34th and Colorado (471-9440). Take bus #1 west down Colorado Ave. to 34th St. Motel sign is visible from the bus stop. Pink adobe rooms with A/C, TV, refrigerator, and a common hot tub. Summer singles $45 M-F, $50 Sa-Su. In winter and on some summer weekdays, $40/$55.

**Amarillo Motel,** 2801 W. Colorado Ave., at 34th and Colorado (635-8539 or 800-216-8539). Take bus #1 down Colorado Ave. toward the mountains to 28th St. The hotel sign is visible from the bus stop. Simple rooms, stayin' alive with 70s decor, have clean kitchens and TV. In summer singles $40; doubles $45; in winter $35/$40. Laundry.

**Tree Haven Cottages,** 3620 W. Colorado Ave. (578-1968). A real family place. Tiny rooms fully-equipped with cable, fridge, microwaves, and a pool. Singles $43; off-season $30.

About 30min. from Colorado Springs, several **Pikes Peak National Forest** campgrounds lie in the mountains flanking Pikes Peak (generally open May-Sept.), but no local transportation serves this area. Campgrounds clutter Rt. 67, 5-10mi. north of **Woodland Park,** 18mi. northwest of the Springs on U.S. 24. For example, try **Colorado, Painted Rocks,** or **South Meadows** near Manitou Park. Others border U.S. 24 near the town of Lake George, 50mi. west of the Springs (sites $9-12). You can camp off any road on national forest property for free if you are at least 500ft. from a road or stream. The **Pikes Peak Ranger District Office,** 601 S. Weber, has maps of the area (636-1602; $4-6; open M-F 8am-5pm). Farther afield, visitors may camp in the **Eleven Mile State Recreation Area,** off a spur road from U.S. 24 near Lake George, on a reservoir (748-3401; 800-678-2267 for reservations. Pay showers and laundry. Sites $7-9, with electricity $12; vehicle fee $4. Reservation 7am-4:45pm.)

# FOOD AND NIGHTLIFE

Students and the young-at-heart perch among outdoor tables in front of the cafes and restaurants lining **Tejon Ave.,** a few blocks east of downtown. **Old Colorado** city is home to a number of fine eateries, as well as a **farmer's market** on summer Sa between Colorado Ave. and Pikes Peak, on 24th St. **Poor Richard's Restaurant,** 324½ N. Tejon Ave., is a local coffeehouse hangout, serving pizza (cheese slices $2.50; cheese pies $11), sandwiches, and salads ($3-6; 632-7721; live bluegrass W, Celtic Th; open daily 11am-10pm). **La Baguette,** 2714 W. Colorado Ave., bakes bread and melts fondues better than you might expect in a place so far from Paris. Cheese fondue with apple slices is $6.50. (577-4818. Open M-Sa 7am-6pm, Su 8am-5pm.) A few doors down, big crowds gather at **Henri's,** 2427 W. Colorado Ave., for fantastic margaritas and Mexican food (634-9031; enchiladas $3.50; open daily 11am-10pm). **Jose Muldoon's,** 222 N. Tejon St., a short walk from Colorado College, allows students to put down their books and enjoy live music, canned dance tunes, or the occasional dunk tank. It is also home to the "world's largest margarita." (636-2311. Food served M-Th 11am-10pm, F-Sa 11am-11pm, Su 9:30am-3pm, late night menu M-Th 10pm-midnight, F-Sa 11pm-1am, Su 3-10pm, last call at 1:30am.)

## ⚙ SIGHTS

**GARDEN OF THE GODS.** Between Rt. 24 (also Colorado Ave.) and 30th St. in northwest Colorado Springs, the redrock towers and spires of the "Garden," as locals call it, rise strikingly against a mountainous backdrop. *(Open daily 5am-11pm; Nov.-Apr. 5am-9pm.)* **Climbers** are regularly lured by the large red faces, while a number of exciting **mountain biking** trails cross the Garden as well. The park's hiking trails give great views of the rock formations and each can be done in 1 day. A map is available from the park's **visitors center.** *(1805 N. 30th at Gateway Rd. 634-6666. Open daily June-Aug. 8am-8pm; in winter 9am-5pm. Walking tours depart in summer at 10, 11am, 2 and 3pm, in winter 10am and 2pm.)*

**PIKES PEAK.** From any part of the town, one can't help noticing the 14,110 ft. summit of Pikes Peak on the western horizon. The willing can climb the peak via the strenuous but well-maintained 26.5mi. round-trip **Barr Trail;** the trailhead is in Manitou Springs by the "Manitou Incline" sign off Ruxton Ave. Make sure you are in marathon shape and check the weather and with rangers before departing. But don't despair if you don't reach the top—explorer Zebulon Pike never reached it, either. There is a fee to drive up the gorgeous 19mi. **Pikes Peak Hwy.,** a well-maintained dirt road. *(684-9383. Hwy. open daily June-Aug. 7am-7pm; Sept. 7am-5pm, Oct.-May daily 9am-3pm, weather permitting. $35 per car or $10 per person.)* Five miles west in Manitou Springs, visitors can reserve a seat on the **Pikes Peak Cog Railway,** which takes visitors to the top every 80min. From the summit, Kansas, the Sangre de Cristo Mountains, and the Continental Divide unfold before you. This lofty view inspired Kathy Lee Bates to write "America the Beautiful." *(515 Ruxton Ave. 685-5401. May to early Oct. daily 8am-5:20pm; call for times in May and Aug.-Oct. Round-trip $22, children $11; reservations required.)*

**CAVE OF THE WINDS.** For adventurous hiking through subterranean passages, head for the contorted caverns of the **Cave of the Winds.** A laser light show dances on the canyon walls nightly at 9pm during the summer. *(On Rt. 24, 6mi. west of exit 141 off I-25. 685-5444. Guided tours daily every 15min. 9am-9pm; Sept. to late May 10am-5pm. $12, ages 6-15 $6. Light show adults $6, children $3.)* Just above Manitou Springs on Rt. 24 lies the **Cliff Dwellings Museum,** which contains replicas of ancient Anasazi pueblos dating from AD 1100-1300. *(800-354-9971, 685-5242, or 685-5394. Open June-Aug. daily 9am-8:30pm; Sept.-May 9am-6:30pm. $7, seniors $6, ages 7-11 $5, under 7 free.)* The **Seven Falls,** west on Cheyenne Blvd., are lit up at night. *(632-0765. $6.50 before 5pm, $7 after 5pm, ages 6-15 $4, seniors $5.50.)* As you drive to town, the **Starr-Kempf Residence,** boasts a yard full of fantastic chrome-colored sculptures created by the couple who lives inside. *(2057 Evans Ave.)*

**GOING FOR THE GOLD AND AIMING HIGH.** Olympic hopefuls train with some of the world's most high-tech sports equipment at the **U.S. Olympic Complex,** at I-25 exit 156A; take bus #1 east to Farragut. Every 30min. to 1hr., the complex offers free 1hr. tours that include a tear-jerking film of struggle and glory. *(750 E. Boulder St. 578-4644 or 578-4618. Open M-Sa 9am-5pm, Su 10am-5pm.)* Earlier searches for gold are recorded at the **Pioneers' Museum,** downtown, which recounts the settling of Colorado Springs. *(Take exit 156a off I-25. 215 S. Tejon St. 578-6650. Open Tu-Sa 10am-5pm, in summer only Su 1-5pm. Free.)*

The **United States Air Force Academy,** 12mi. north of town off I-25, hosts over 1 million visitors annually. The cadets' chapel was constructed of aluminum, steel, and other materials used in building airplanes. M-F during the school year, cadets gather at noon near the chapel for the cadet lunch formation (i.e., to eat). *(333-4515, office hours 7:30am-4:30pm. Open M-Sa 9am-5pm, Su 1-5pm.)* The **Barry Goldwater Visitors Center** has info. *(472-0102, tours 333-2025. Open mid-May to early Sept. daily 8am-6pm; early Sept. to mid-May 8am-5pm.)*

**GROUND ZERO** While most Cold War era bomb shelters are buried under 5-10 ft. of dirt, the **North American Air Defense Command Headquarters (NORAD)** was constructed 1800 ft. below Cheyenne Mt. Contrary to popular myth and legend, Cheyenne Mt. is the eyes and ears of an intricate intelligence network, as opposed to a center for nuclear action. However the center does look like something out of a James Bond movie; a 3mi. tunnel leads to buildings on massive springs which house computers and detectors scanning the heavens for incoming inter-continental ballistic missiles. The center was designed to be operational even after a direct nuclear attack. Call in advance to make reservations for an information session. *(M at 2pm, F at 10:30am. 474-2238 or 474-2239.)* The **Peterson Air Force Base,** east of Academy Blvd., houses the **Edward J. Peterson Air and Space Museum,** which showcases exhibits on the history of the base, as well as on space and satellite operations. *(556-4915. Museum open Tu-Sa 8:30am-4:30pm, closed on national holidays. Free.)*

## GREAT SAND DUNES

When Colorado's mountains all begin to look the same, head to the **Great Sand Dunes National Monument** at the northwest edge of the **San Luis Valley.** A sea of 700ft. tall sand dunes, representing thousands of years of wind-blown accumulation, laps silently at the base of the **Sangre de Cristo Range,** 38mi. northeast of **Alamosa** and 112mi. west of **Pueblo** on Rt. 150, off U.S. 160. The progress of the dunes through passes in the range is checked by the shallow **Medano Creek;** visitors can wade across the creek when it flows (Apr. to mid-July). Although there aren't any trails through the dunes, the best way to enjoy the dunes is to dive in. Hiking to the top takes about 1½hr. and is extremely difficult, since your feet sink a good 6 in. with each step. Take at least a quart of water per person, and beware the summer's intense heat—the sand can reach 140°F (60°C). Those with four-wheel-drive can motor over the **Medano Pass Primitive Rd.** At the southern boundary of the monument, the **Oasis** complex offers four-wheel-drive tours that huff over Medano Pass Primitive Rd. to the dunes' nether regions (378-2222; tours daily 10am and 2pm; 2hr.; $14, ages 5-11 $8).

Schedules of daily ranger-led hikes and talks can be found at the **visitors center,** ½mi. past the entrance gate. The newsletter, *Sand Dune Breezes,* suggests drives and hikes. For more info, contact the **Superintendent,** Great Sand Dunes National Monument, Mosca, CO 81146. (378-2312. Open daily 8:30am-4:30pm, Sept.-May 9am-5pm. $3 per person, under 17 free; National Parks passports accepted.)

**Pinyon Flats,** the monument's primitive, cactus-covered campground, is open year-round and includes drinking water. Bring mosquito repellent in June. (378-2312. Sites $10. Arrive by early afternoon. No reservations.) Get free **backcountry camping** permits for the dunes from the visitors center. If the park's sites are full, **Oasis** (see above) will fulfill your needs with showers, two-person sites ($10, with hookup $16.50; $2.50 per additional person), cabins ($30 for 2 people), or teepees ($25 for 2 people). **San Luis State Park,** 8mi. away in Mosca, has showers and 51 electrical sites (378-2020, 800-678-2267 for camping reservations). $12. $4 vehicle entrance fee. Closed in winter.) For info on nearby National Forest Campgrounds, contact the **Río Grande National Forest Service Office,** 11571 County Rd. T5, La Jara, CO 81140 (274-5193; all sites $10; open M-F 8am-4:30pm). **Area code:** 719.

# SAN JUAN MOUNTAINS

Ask Coloradans about their favorite mountain retreats, and they'll most likely name a peak, lake, stream, or town in the San Juan Range of southwestern Colorado. Four **national forests**—the **Uncompahgre** (un-cum-PAH-gray), the **Gunnison,** the **San Juan,** and the **Río Grande**—encircle this sprawling range. **Durango** is an ideal base camp for forays into these mountains. Northeast of Durango, the **Weminuche Wilderness** tempts the hardy backpacker with a vast expanse of rugged terrain where wide, sweeping vistas stretch for miles. Get $4 maps and hiking info from **Pine Needle Mountaineering,** 835 Main Mall, Durango 81301 (970-247-8728; open in summer M-Sa 9am-9pm, Su 10am-5pm; off-season M-Sa 9am-6pm, Su 10am-5pm).

The San Juan area is easily accessible on U.S. 50, which is traveled by hundreds of thousands of tourists each summer. **Greyhound** serves the area, but very poorly; traveling by car is the best option in this region. On a happier note, the San Juans are loaded with HI-AYH hostels and campgrounds, making them one of the more economical places to visit in Colorado.

## BLACK CANYON

Native American parents used to tell their children that the light-colored strands of rock streaking through the walls of the Black Canyon were the hair of a blond woman—and that if they got too close to the edge they would get tangled in it and fall. The edge of **Black Canyon of the Gunnison National Monument** is a staggering place, literally—watch for those trembling knees. The Gunnison River slowly gouged out the 53mi. long canyon, crafting a steep 2500-ft. gorge dominated by inky shadows (hence black). The Empire State Building, if placed at the bottom of the river, would reach barely halfway up the canyon walls.

The 8mi. scenic drive along the South Rim boasts the spectacular **Chasm View,** where you can peer 2300 ft. down a sheer vertical drop—the highest cliff in Colorado—at the Gunnison River and the "painted" wall. Don't throw stones; you might kill an exhausted hiker in the canyon below. There are no well-established trails to the bottom, but you can scramble down the **Gunnison Rt.,** which drops 2000ft. over the course of 1mi. A free **wilderness permit** (from the South Rim visitors center) is required for all inner canyon routes. Bring at least 3L of water per person, and be prepared to use your hands to climb back up. In the canyon, camp and enjoy the beauty; unimproved sites (no water) are available on a beach along the river. Pack in water or use a purification system. The rock walls of the Black Canyon are a **rock climbing** paradise. Register at the South Rim visitors center to climb some of the tallest rock faces in the Rocky Mountains. Less strenuous hikes follow the canyon rim, providing dizzying views.

The **South Rim** has a **campground** with 102 small, somewhat crowded sites amid sagebrush and tall shrubs ($8). Pit toilets, charcoal grills, water, and paved wheelchair-accessible sites are available. On the **North Rim,** another campsite offers more space. It rarely fills, but is popular with climbers (water and toilets; $8).

Many inexpensive motels line Main St./U.S. 50 in downtown **Montrose.** The **Traveler's B&B Inn,** 502 S. 1st St., parallel to Main St., lets simple, cozy rooms with TVs and breakfasts. (249-3472. Singles $30, doubles $34; with private bath $34/$36; reduced rates in winter.) The **Log Cabin Motel,** 1034 E. Main St., at the end of town nearest the Monument, offers small but comfortable rooms (249-7610; singles $30-36, doubles $36-40, family room $60). For tasty sandwiches ($4.50) and delightful omelettes ($5.50), head for the **Daily Bread Bakery and Café,** 346 Main St. (249-8444; open in summer M-Sa 6am-3pm). The **Red Barn,** 1413 Main St., dishes out 3 meals a day (249-9202; M-Sa 6-11am and 11am-10:30 pm) and a hearty brunch (Su 9am-3pm) that includes an all-you-can-eat salad bar ($6).

The Black Canyon lies 10mi. east of the town of Montrose in western Colorado. The **South Rim** is easily accessible via a 5mi. drive off U.S. 50 ($7 per car, $4 walk-in or motorcycle); the wilder **North Rim** can only be reached by detouring around the canyon and taking a gravel road from Crawford off Rte. 92. **Greyhound** shuttles once a day ($12) between Montrose at 132 N. 1st St. (249-6673) and the **Gunnison County Airport,** 711 Rio Grande (641-0060), and will drop you off on U.S. 50, 6mi. from the canyon. Western Express **taxi** (249-8880) is located near the airport. For $39, **Gisdho Shuttles** (800-430-4555) conducts tours of the Black Canyon and the Grand Mesa from Grand Junction. The trip includes transportation, entrance fees, and tours off the beaten path. (10-11hr. Trips May-Oct. W and Sa.) The Canyon has two **visitors centers:** one on the South Rim (249-1914, ext. 23; open daily in summer 8am-6pm; in winter 8am-4pm), and another on the North Rim. **Area code:** 970.

## CRESTED BUTTE

Crested Butte (CREST-ed BYOOT), 27mi. north of Gunnison on Rt. 135, was once a mining town. The coal was exhausted in the 1950s, and a few years later, the steep powder fields on the Butte began attracting skiers. While there are a lot more tourists today, the buildings of Crested Butte haven't changed much since the mining days, thanks to an ordinance banning franchises. The ski lifts lie 3mi. north of town along Rt. 135. **Crested Butte Mt. Resort** (800-544-8448) offers excellent runs that drop 3062 ft., but the mountain is most famous for its "extreme skiing." Free skiing is sometimes available in Nov. and Apr., along with reasonably priced lodging packages.

Come summertime, Crested Butte becomes the mountain bike capital of Colorado. The last week of June, Crested Butte hosts the **Fat Tire Bike Festival,** 4 days of mountain biking, racing, and fraternizing. In 1976, a group of cyclists rode from Crested Butte to Aspen, starting the oldest mountain biking event in the world. Every Sept., enduring and experienced bikers repeat the trek over the 12,705 ft. pass to Aspen and back during the **Pearl Pass Tour.** (Call the Mountain Bike Hall of Fame/Crested Butte Mt. Bike Assoc. at 800-454-4505 for dates and info.) Biking trail maps are available from bike shops and **The Alpineer** (349-5210, kitty-corner from the visitors center; open daily 9am-6pm); trails begin at the base of Mt. Crested Butte and extend into the exquisite Gothic area. **Trail 401** is a demanding and famous 24mi. round-trip loop with an excellent view. The Gothic area is also accessible with a car; follow Rt. 135 past Mt. Crested Butte and keep driving. When bumpy Gothic Rd. begins to get the best of you, park the car and explore the tiny town of **Gothic,** home to a grand outdoor biology laboratory. Excellent intermediate bike trails depart Brush Creek Road in Crested Butte.

Finding budget accommodations during winter season is about as easy as striking a major vein of gold, but there are a few possibilities. The **Crested Butte International Hostel,** 615 Teocalli Ave., offers a cheap place for skiers and bikers to crash during their stay (349-0588 or 888-389-0588. $18; in winter $26. Laundry. $4-6 dinners in peak seasons. Desk manned 7:30am-10pm, lockout 10am-2pm. Shower $5. Packages available, like the Mar. deal of 5 nights of accommodations, 4 days of skiing for $300 per person.) The **Forest Queen,** at 129 Elk Ave., rents out comfortable doubles at reasonable prices (349-5336; doubles $59, with private bath $69). The **Gunnison National Forest Office,** 216 N. Colorado, 30mi. south in Gunnison, and the Chamber of Commerce (see below), have info on a bundle of **campgrounds** (641-0471; open M-F 7:30am-5pm). You can camp for $8 in achingly beautiful surroundings at the **Gothic Campsite,** 3mi. past the town of Gothic on Gothic Rd. (no water, composting toilets), or park in one of the turnouts and find your own tent sites, as long as you're at least 150 ft. away from roads and streams (open June-Nov.).

**Brick Oven Pizza,** at 3rd and Elk St., dishes out authentic NY- and Chicago-style pizzas from a small window; tasty slices loaded with toppings are $1.89, and large pizzas start at $10.50 (349-5044; open daily 11am-9pm). **The Bakery Cafe,** 401 Elk Ave., is a popular lunch spot, with $4-6.50 sandwiches and awe-inspiring pastries for 50¢-$1.50 (349-7280; open daily 7am-6pm; 9am-6pm in winter; wheelchair access). **The Eldo,** upstairs from Red Lady Realty on Elk St., packs a small bar and a large patio for cheap food and cheaper beer. (349-6125. $1.50 pints and 50¢ off drinks during the 4-8pm happy hour. Open daily 3pm-2am).

**Crested Butte Chamber of Commerce:** 601 Elk (349-6438 or 800-545-4505; open daily 9am-5pm). A free **shuttle** (349-7318) to the mountain departs from the chamber. (Every 40 min. 7:20am-10:20am and 8pm-midnight, every 20min. 10:20am-8pm.) **Post Office:** 217 Elk Ave. (349-5568; open M-F 7:30am-4:30pm, Sa 10am-1pm). **ZIP code:** 81224. **Area code:** 970.

# TELLURIDE

Site of the first bank Butch Cassidy ever robbed (the San Miguel), Telluride has a history right out of a 1930s film. Prize fighter Jack Dempsey used to wash dishes in the Athenian Senate, a popular saloon/brothel that frequently required Dempsey to double as a bouncer when he was between plates. William Jennings Bryan delivered his "Cross of Gold" speech in Telluride from the front balcony of the Sheridan Hotel. Locals believe that their city's name derives from a contraction of "to hell you ride," a likely warning given to travelers to the once hell-bent city. Things have quieted down a bit in the last few years; outlaw celebrities have been replaced with unemployed film celebrities, six-shooter guns with cinnamon buns. Today, skiers, hikers, and vacationers come to Telluride to pump gold and silver *into* the mountains; the town is gaining popularity and may be the Aspen of the future. Still, a small-town feeling prevails; rocking chairs sit outside brightly painted, wood-shingled houses, and dogs lounge on storefront porches.

**⚐ PRACTICAL INFORMATION.** Telluride is only accessible by car, via U.S. 550 or Rt. 145. The **visitors center** is upstairs from **Rose's Grocery Store,** 666 W. Colorado Ave. (728-6265 or 800-525-2717), near the entrance to town (open daily in summer 8am-7pm, in ski season 8am-6pm). **Post Office:** 101 E. Colorado Ave. (728-3900; open M-F 9am-5pm, Sa 10am-noon). **ZIP code:** 81435. **Area code:** 970.

**⚐⚐⚐ ACCOMMODATIONS, FOOD, AND NIGHTLIFE.** If you're visiting Telluride during a festival, bring a sleeping bag; the cost of a bed is outrageous. The **Oak Street Inn,** 134 N. Oak St., offers cozy rooms. (728-3383. Singles $42, with private bath $66; doubles $58/$66. Rates $20 higher during festivals. Showers $3 for non-guests.) **Camp** at the east end of Telluride in a town-operated facility with 46 sites, water, restrooms, and showers (728-3071; $12; 1-week max. stay). **Sunshine,** 7mi. southwest on Rt. 145 toward Cortez, is a developed national forest campground (14 sites, $8, 2-week max. stay). For info on all **National Forest Campgrounds,** call the **Forest Service** (327-4261; open M-F 8am-noon and 1-5pm). Several free primitive sites huddle nearby and are accessible by jeep roads. During festival times, you can crash anywhere; hot showers ($2) are available at the high school.

Baked in Telluride, 127 S. Fir St., has enough rich coffee and delicious pastries, pizza, sandwiches, and 50¢ bagels to get you through a festival weekend even if you *are* baked in Telluride. The apple fritters ($1.75) are justly famous, and their pizza ($2.25 a slice) might be your only route to a dirt-cheap meal in town. (728-4775. Open daily 5:30am-10pm.) **Steaming Bean Coffee,** 221 W. Colorado Ave., offers coffee ($1), as well as smoothies ($3-4) and **Internet access.** (728-0220. Access $6.50 per hr., price includes any drink on the menu. Open M-F 7am-10pm, Sa-Su 7:30am-10pm.) The hip-hop-blaring and celebrity-snaring **La Cocina de Luz,** 123 E. Colorado Ave., attracts those roughing it to be chic and those roughing it just to eat (728-9355; taco dinners $7-9, burrito dinners $6-9; open M-Sa 9am-9pm). Eighteen different subs ($5) and interesting sandwich creations called "jaffles" ($3) are the main attractions at **Deli Downstairs,** 217 W. Colorado Ave. Dark, cozy, and easy to pass by, this little nook puts a lot of effort into their creative offerings. (728-4004. Open daily 10am-midnight.)

The taps at **Floradora,** 103 W. Colorado Ave., flow with home-brewed beer (728-3888; pints $3.50; open daily 11am-2am). Chug beers at **The House, a Tavern,** 131 N. Fir St., where college-students-gone-ski-bums hang out. (728-6207. Drafts $2-5.50; happy hour 4:30-6:30pm, $1 off margaritas and 21 oz. drafts. Open daily 3pm-2am.) The cool, conversational **Last Dollar Saloon,** 100 E. Colorado, near Pine, will take it with a smile (728-4800; beer $2.50-3.50; open daily 11:30am-2am).

**⚐ FESTIVALS AND ACTIVITIES.** Given that only 1500 people inhabit Telluride, the sheer number of summer arts festivals in the town seems staggering. For general festival info, contact the visitors center. Gala events occur just about every weekend in summer and fall; the most renowned is the **Bluegrass Festival.** *(800-624-2422. 3rd weekend in June. Tickets $35-40 per night, 4-day pass $120.)* The **Telluride International Film Festival,** premieres some of the hippest independent flicks; *The Crying Game* and *The Piano* were both unveiled here. *(603-643-1255. 1st weekend in Sept.)* Telluride also hosts the **Talking Gourds** poetry fest (2nd weekend in July) and a **Jazz**

**Celebration.** *(728-7009. 1st weekend in Aug.)* For some festivals, volunteering to usher, set up chairs, or perform other tasks can be exchanged for free admission.

Biking, hiking, and backpacking opportunities are endless; ghost towns and lakes are tucked behind almost every mountain crag. The tourist office has a list of suggestions for hikes in the area. The most popular trek (about 2hr.) is up the jeep road to **Bridal Veil Falls,** the waterfall visible from almost anywhere in Telluride. The trailhead is at the end of Rt. 145. Continuing another 2½mi. from the top of the falls will lead you to Silver Lake, a steep but very rewarding climb.

In winter, even self-proclaimed atheists can be spied silently praying before hitting the "Spiral Stairs" and the "Plunge," two of the Rockies' most gut-wrenching ski runs. For more info, contact the **Telluride Ski Resort.** *(P.O. Box 11155, Telluride 81435. 728-3856.)* A free year-round shuttle connects the mountain village with the rest of the town; pick up a current schedule at the visitors center along with a copy of *Skier Services Brochure.* **Paragon Ski and Sport** rents bikes in summer ($26 per day) and skis and boots in winter ($20 per day). Longer rentals are cheaper. *(213 W. Colorado Ave. 728-4525. Open daily in summer 9am-8pm; ski season 8:30am-9pm.)*

# DURANGO

Durango has two sides: the side Will Rogers described as "out of the way and glad of it," and the side where "everynight is a Saturday night." After a day of stereotypical Colorado "extreme" fun, some people tend to take it easy. Conversely, some take it easy during the day (after an evening of stereotypical Western evenin' fun, of which there is plenty). It's either on-the-go or on-the-porch action in Durango, keeping the yin and the yang of the town in a nice balance. Predominantly yin-seeking tourists come here to see Mesa Verde, raft down the Animas River, hike the beautiful San Juan Mountains, or ski at Purgatory.

**⚑ PRACTICAL INFORMATION.** Durango is at the intersection of U.S. 160 and U.S. 150. Streets run perpendicular to avenues, but everyone calls Main Ave. "Main St." On southern Main Ave., the town becomes less touristy. **Greyhound,** 275 E. 8th Ave. (259-2755; open M-F 7:30am-noon and 3:30-5pm, Sa 7:30am-noon, Su and holidays 7:30-10am), runs once per day to Grand Junction (5½hr., $34); Denver (11½hr., $53); and Albuquerque (5hr., $41). The **Durango Lift** (259-5438) provides trolley service up and down Main Ave. every 30min. (runs daily 6am-10pm; 25¢). The **Durango Area Chamber Resort Association,** 111 S. Camino del Rio (247-0312 or 800-525-8855), on the southeast side of town at Gateway Dr., offers helpful info about sights and hiking (open M-Sa 8am-6pm, Su 10am-4pm). **Internet access** is free at the **Durango Public Library** 1188 E. 2nd Ave. (385-2970; open M-W 9am-9pm, Th-Su 9am-5:30pm). **Post Office:** 222 W. 8th St. (247-3434; open M-F 8:30am-5:30pm, Sa 9am-1pm). **ZIP code:** 81301. **Area code:** 970.

**⌂◩⌂ ACCOMMODATIONS, FOOD, AND NIGHTLIFE.** The **Durango Youth Hostel (HI-AYH),** 543 E. 2nd Ave., 1 block from downtown (turn into the alley on College Dr. between Main Ave. and 2nd Ave. for parking), maintains clean, simple bunks in a large converted house. With an open, barrack-style dorm room for men and a largely backpacking clientele, this is no hotel with extra bunks. Ask the manager about local cafes, hangouts, and activities. (247-9905. $12, nonmembers $15. Check-in 7-10am and 5-10pm. Check-out 7-10am. Key deposit $5.) For the cheapest motels, look to the part of Main Ave. north of town. The lowest price for a summer double hovers around $40, and these rooms are away from all the downtown action. The spacious rooms at **Budget Inn,** 3077 Main Ave., aren't cheap—but include access to a nice pool and hot tub (247-5222 or 800-257-5222; singles $35; doubles $45; in winter $25/$35). Durango's nearest campground is **Cottonwood Camper Park,** on U.S. 160, ½mi. west (247-1977; 2-person sites $17; $2 per additional person; full hookup $22).

**Silverton,** 47mi. north on U.S. 550, has other lodging options. A bit sleepier, more isolated, and more 19th-century than Durango, the town attracts a slightly older, wider-brimmed hat crowd. **Teller House Hotel,** 1250 Greene St., next to the French Bakery (which provides the hotel's complimentary full breakfast), has comfy rooms in a well-maintained 1896 hotel (387-5423 or 800-342-4338; singles prices negotiable; doubles start at $48; $10 per additional person). Popular for a quick, cheap bite to eat, **High Noon Hamburgers,** at the corner of 12th St. and Blair St., near the train depot, serves up decent American fare (cheeseburgers $3; chili $3.25; open 10am to whenever the train leaves town).

For fixin's, head to **City Market,** on U.S. 550, 1 block down 9th St. and at 3130 Main Ave. (both open 24hr.). Locals eat breakfast at **Carver's Bakery and Brewpub,** 1022 Main Ave., which has delicious bread, breakfast specials ($2-6), the usual pizza and burgers ($5-6), and pitchers of home-brewed beer ($8; 259-2545; open M-Sa 6:30am-10pm, Su 6:30am-1pm). "Dill-icious" subs and pickles abound at **Johnny McGuire's Deli,** 552 Main Ave., where choosing between the more than twenty-five subs ($5) will leave you in a pickle (259-8816; open daily 7am-9pm). Every year, **Olde Tymer's,** 1000 Main Ave., wins an award for Durango's best burger ($7). Vegetarians dig the $4-9 salad options. (259-2990. Open daily 11am-10pm.)

**◪ ACTIVITIES.** Unlike most Colorado tourist towns, Durango's busiest season is summer, although winter is no stranger to strangers. **Purgatory Resort,** 27mi. north on U.S. 550, hosts skiers of all levels. When the heat is on, travelers can trade in their skis for a sled and test out the **alpine slide** or take a free **scenic chairlift ride.** **Mountain biking** down the slope is also popular. *(247-9000. Open daily 9:30am-4:45pm. Slide: 1 ride $8, 3 rides $21. Bike uplifts $5; $12 per day. Lift tickets $39, ages 6-12 $17.)*

The entire Durango area is engulfed by the **San Juan National Forest;** the headquarters is located in Durango. Call for info on hiking and camping in the forest, especially if you're planning a trip into the massive **Weminuche Wilderness,** northeast of Durango. *(HQ: 247-4874. Open M-F 8am-5pm.)* The largest outfitter in the area is **Mild to Wild Rafting.** Anything from family trips on placid class II rapids to intense class V battles are offered as short, half-day, full-day, or pricey multi-day trips. *(701 Main Ave. 247-4789 or 800-567-6745. Open daily 8am-10pm. Reservations recommended. half-day mild $35; full-day mild $65; full-day intense $195.)* Bikes are available at **Hassle Free Sports,** but you must have a driver's license and major credit card. *(2615 Main St. 259-3874 or 800-835-3800. ½-day $16; full-day $25. Open M-Sa 8:30am-6pm, Su 10am-5pm.)* **Horseback riding** opportunities abound in the San Juan. **Backcountry Outfitters,** Hwy. 160 and Piedra River, offers 4hr. trips along the scenic Piedra River ($50) and full-day trips ($100) in the San Juan high country. *(731-4630. Open daily 9am-5pm.)*

Although it's definitely more of a tourist attraction than a means of transportation, the **Durango and Silverton Narrow Gauge Train,** runs along the Animas River Valley to the glistening old town of **Silverton.** Old-fashioned, 100% coal-fed locomotives wheeze and cough through the San Juans, making a 2hr. stop in Silverton before returning to Durango. In the summer, be prepared for heat and dust. The train also drops off **backpackers** at various scenic points along the route and picks them up on return trips; call for more info on this service. *(479 Main St. 247-2733. Morning and afternoon trains, 7hr. $53, ages 5-11 $27. Office open daily 6am-9pm; May and mid-Aug. to Oct. 7am-7pm; Nov.-Apr. 8am-5pm.)*

**◪ ENTERTAINMENT.** Less-interactive activity mosies into town every summer with the **Durango Pro Rodeo Series,** located at the LaPlata County Fairgrounds at 25th and Main Ave. The bull-battling action starts at 7:30pm every evening, with a barbecue at 6pm. (247-1666. $12, children under 12 $5.) One of the best **Victorian-style melodramas** in the U.S. takes place at the Strater Hotel and Theater at 7th St. and Main Ave. every night from early June to late Sept. (247-3400; $15, children under 12 $12; doors open at 7:30pm, curtain is at 8pm). They work mighty hard to have Western fun at the **Bar D Chuckwagon,** 8080 Country Rd. 250 (make a right on Country Rd. 252 going north on U.S. 550). A hearty supper, country and western show, and enthusiastic fellow diners make this a perfect method of soaking in some area culture. (247-5753. $14, 8 and under $7. Dinner starts at 7:30pm.)

ROCKY MOUNTAINS

## NEAR DURANGO: PAGOSA SPRINGS

The Ute people—the first to discover the waters of Pagosa—believed that the springs were a gift of the Great Spirit, and it's not hard to see why. Pagosa Springs, some of the hottest and largest in the world, bubble from the San Juan Mountains 62mi. east of Durango on Rt. 160. Follow the smell of sulfur to **Spring Inn,** 165 Hot Springs Blvd., where 15 different outdoor pools of varying temperatures are available for your soaking pleasure (264-4168 or 800-225-0934; $10 per person; open 24hr.). **Chimney Rock Archeological Area,** 20mi. west of Pagosa Springs on U.S. 160 and Rt. 151 S., contains the ruins of a high-mesa Ancestral Puebloan village. (883-5359. Open daily mid-May to late Sept. 9am-4pm. $5, ages 5-11 $3. 2½hr. tours leave at 9:30, 10:30am, 1, and 2pm.) Skiing is available at **Wolf Creek,** 20mi. east of Pagosa, which claims to have the most snow in Colorado (lift tickets $32, under 13 $20; rates often change). For nearby fishing, hiking, and camping, contact the San Juan National Forest (see Durango **Activities,** p. 679). The **visitors center** sits at the intersection of San Juan St. and Hot Springs Blvd. (264-2360; open M-F 8am-5pm, Sa-Su 10-2pm; in winter daily 9am-5pm). Occasional mudslides, stampedes, and a **local bus** (50¢) provide public transportation in Pagosa.

The **Sky View Motel,** 1mi. west of town on Rt. 160, has rooms with cable TV; some have kitchenettes (264-5803; singles $40, doubles $45). **Pinewood Inn,** 157 Pagosa St., 1 block from downtown, rents cozy wood-paneled rooms with TVs and phones (800-655-7463 or 264-5715; singles $41, doubles $54). **Hog's Breath Saloon,** 157 Navajo Trail Dr., near Rt. 160 W, features country-western style (though recently *sans* the cowboy-wailing hip-flailing) dance nights and a surf 'n' turf menu (731-2626; entrees $8-21; open daily 11am-10pm). The award-winning green chili stew ($4) at the **Rolling Pin Bakery Café,** 214 Pagosa St., deserves attention with its unique combo of spices, chili, and chicken. Big breakfast flapjacks are $4 and sandwiches $4-6 (264-2255; open M-Sa 7am-2:30pm; kitchen closes 2pm).

## MESA VERDE

Mesa Verde (Green Table) rises from the deserts of southwestern Colorado, its flat top noticeably friendlier to vegetation than the dry lands below. The spectacular land is not, however, the main attraction—some of the most elaborate Pueblo dwellings in existence, as otherworldly and awesome as any of the rock formations that grace the southwest, draw in the largest crowds. Fourteen hundred years ago, Native American tribes began to cultivate the area now known as **Mesa Verde National Park.** These people—today called the Ancestral Puebloan, formerly the Anasazi, or "ancient ones"—constructed a series of expansive cliff dwellings beneath the overhanging sandstone shelves surrounding the mesa. Then, around AD 1275, 700 years after their ancestors had arrived, the Pueblo people abruptly and mysteriously vanished from the historical record, leaving behind their eerie and starkly beautiful dwellings. Mesa Verde is not for the snap-a-shot-and-go tourist; the best views require a bit of a physical effort to reach, and are too extraordinary to let the camera do all the marveling anyway.

After a rather long and slow drive south from the entrance off U.S. 160, the park divides into **Chapin Mesa,** featuring the largest number of cliff dwellings, and the smaller and quieter **Wetherill Mesa.** The **Chapin Mesa Museum,** on the first loop on the Chapin branch (before the dwellings), can give you an overview of the Ancestral Puebloan lifestyle and is a good place to start before exploring the mesa (529-4475; open daily 8am-6:30pm; in winter 8am-5pm). From their respective overlooks on Chapin Mesa, rangers lead tours to the spectacular **Cliff Palace,** the largest cliff dwelling in North America with over 200 preserved rooms, and the impressive **Balcony House** (open in summer only), a 40-room dwelling 600ft. above the floor of the Soda Canyon. Make sure you are up to rigor of the tours; the Balcony House tour is especially strenuous, requiring visitors to crawl through a tunnel at one point. Bring water on both tours, as none is available on the trail. (Tours depart from Cliff Palace overlook and Balcony House trailhead every 30min. 9am-6pm. $1.75; buy tickets at visitors center.) An easier approach to seeing the Chapin

Mesa is the self-guided **Mesa Top Loop Road**, passing a chronological progression of the ruins from A.D. 600 to the classic 13th-century dwellings (open 8am-sunset).

The **Far View Lodge**, across from the visitors center, offers two ½-day bus tours that depart from the Lodge at 9am and 1pm en route to the **Spruce Tree House**. The Lodge also offers a full-day tour, which departs at 9:30am and visits both sites. Arrive at least 30min. before the tour (529-4421; ½-day tours $29, under 12 $19; full-day $35/$19; no reservations).

Lodging in the park is pricey. Mesa Verde's only motel-style lodging, the rooms at **Far View Lodge,** are expensive (from $99). Try the **Ute Mountain Motel,** 531 S. Broadway, in Cortez (565-8507; singles $20-35, doubles $20-38), or the well-lit rooms of **Tomahawk Lodge,** 728 S. Broadway (565-8521 or 800-643-7705; singles $39-45, doubles $53-68; in winter $29/$34). The **Durango Hostel** (see Durango **Accommodations,** p. 678) also has cheap beds. Mesa Verde's **Morfield Campground** is located 4mi. inside the park and almost never fills up (564-1675; 452 beautiful, secluded sites $13, full hookup $23; showers 75¢ per 5min.).

The park's main entrance is off U.S. 160, 36mi. from Durango and 10mi. from **Cortez.** The **entrance fee** is $10 for vehicles, $5 for pedestrians and bikers. The **Far View Visitors Center,** 20mi. from the gate on the main road, publishes a comprehensive visitors guide with complete listings on park walks, drives, and trails (529-4543; open daily in summer 8am-5pm). During the winter, head to the museum (see above) or the **Colorado Welcome Center/Cortez Chamber of Commerce,** 928 E. Main, in Cortez (565-4048 or 565-3414; open daily 8am-6pm; in winter 8am-5pm). Sights in the park lie up to 40mi. apart; a car is nearly essential. **Area code:** 970.

---

# FOUR CORNERS    **New Mexico, Arizona, Utah,** and **Colorado** meet at an unnaturally neat intersection about 40mi. northwest of **Shiprock,** NM, on the Navajo Reservation. **Four Corners** epitomizes American ideas about land; these state borders were drawn along scientifically determined lines of longitude and latitude, disregarding natural boundaries. There's little to see; nonetheless, a large number of people veer off the highway to marvel at the geographic anomaly. At the very least, getting down on all fours to put a limb in each state is a good story for a cocktail party. *(Open daily in summer 7am-8pm; in winter 8am-5pm. $1.50.)*

ROCKY MOUNTAINS

# THE SOUTHWEST

The Anasazi of the 10th and 11th centuries were the first to discover that the arid lands of the Southwest could support an advanced agrarian civilization. Years later, in 1803, the United States laid claim to parts of the Southwest with the Louisiana Purchase. The idealistic hope for a western "empire of liberty," where Americans could live the virtuous farm life, both motivated further expansion and helped create the region's individualist mythology.

Today, the steel blue of the Superstition peaks, the rainbow expanse of the Painted Desert, the deep gorges of the Grand Canyon, the murky depths of Carlsbad Caverns, and the red stone arches and twisted spires of southern Utah and northern Arizona lure visitors and keep Kodak in business. The vastness of the Southwestern desert and its peculiar colors—of red rock, sandstone, scrub brush, and pale sky—invite contemplation; farther north, Utah's mountains offer equally breathtaking vistas. Meanwhile, reservation lands and ruins dot the landscape, a reminder of the strong Native American presence still felt in the Southwest today.

## HIGHLIGHTS OF THE SOUTHWEST

■ **Mexican food.** You can't get away from it, and in the tasty eateries of New Mexico's Albuquerque (p. 745) and Santa Fe (p. 738), you may not want to.
■ **National Parks.** Utah's "Fab Five" (p. 700) and Arizona's Grand Canyon (p. 710) reveal a stunning landscape of bizarre rock formations and brilliant colors.
■ **Skiing.** In a region famous for its blistering sun, the Wasatch Mountains (p. 694) near Salt Lake City, UT receive some of the nation's choicest powder in winter.
■ **Las Vegas, NV.** Attractions include casinos, casinos, and casinos (p. 687).

# NEVADA

Nevada once walked the straight and narrow. Explored by Spanish missionaries and settled by Mormons, the Nevada Territory's scorched expanses seemed a perfect place for ascetics to strive for moral uplift. However, with the discovery of gold in 1850 and silver in 1859, the state was won over permanently to the worship of filthy lucre. When the precious metals ran out, gambling and marriage-licensing became big industries. The final moral cataclysms came when the state legalized prostitution on a county by county basis and spawned lounge idol Wayne Newton.

But there *is* another side to Nevada. Lake Mead National Recreation Area, only 25mi. from Las Vegas, is an oasis in stunning desert surroundings, and the forested slopes of Lake Tahoe provide serene resorts for an escape from the cities.

## 🛈 PRACTICAL INFORMATION

**Capital:** Carson City.

**Visitor Info: Nevada Commission on Tourism,** Capitol Complex, Carson City 89701 (800-638-2328; line staffed 24hr.). **Nevada Division of State Parks,** 1300 S. Curry St., Carson City 89703-5202 (702-687-4384). Open M-F 8am-5pm.

**Postal Abbreviation:** NV. **Sales Tax:** 6.75-7%; 8% room tax in some counties.

## LAS VEGAS

Las Vegas, a city of 880,000, draws three times that many tourists every month. Most come to witness the spirit of capitalism (minus the Protestant ethic) and to partake in what might be the most direct economic alienation known to man—funneling earnings into a well-oiled, privately owned profit machine. The lights and

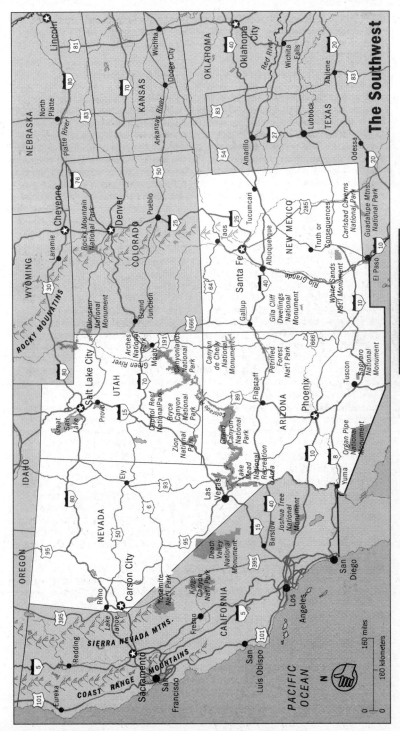

The Southwest

THE SOUTHWEST

glitter of the Strip comprise a Disney-esque league of mock-ups, from ancient Egypt to present-day New York, each leading to a similar gauntlet of gaming rooms and lounges—thresholds of fun without substance, triumph without responsibility, loss without meaning.

## 🛈 ORIENTATION AND PRACTICAL INFORMATION

Driving to Vegas from Los Angeles is a straight 300mi. shot on I-15 (5hr.). From Arizona, take I-40 W to Kingman and then U.S. 93/95 N. Las Vegas has two major casino areas: **downtown,** around Fremont and 2nd St., is a pedestrian promenade, and the **Strip** is a collection of mammoth casinos on both sides of **Las Vegas Blvd.** Parallel to the Strip is **Paradise Blvd.,** also strewn with casinos. As in any city where money reigns supreme, many areas of Las Vegas are unsafe. Always stay on brightly lit pathways, and do not wander too far from the major casinos and hotels. The neighborhoods just north and west of downtown can be especially dangerous.

Despite all its debauchery, Las Vegas has a **curfew.** Cruisers under 18 are not allowed unaccompanied in public places from midnight to 5am, those under 14 from 10pm to 5am. On weekends, no one under 18 is allowed unaccompanied on the Strip or in other designated areas 9pm-5am.

**Airport: McCarran International** (261-5743), at the southeastern end of the Strip. Main terminal on Paradise Rd. is within walking distance of University of Nevada campus. Vans to the Strip and downtown $3-5; taxi $10-12.

**Buses:** Greyhound, 200 S. Main St. (384-8009), at Carson Ave. downtown, near Jackie Gaughan's Plaza Hotel/Casino. To: L.A. (5-7hr.; 22 per day; M-Th $31, F-Su $35) and San Francisco (13-16hr.; 6 per day; M-Th $51, F-Su $54). Open daily 4:30am-1am.

**Public Transit: Citizens Area Transit** (CAT; 228-7433). Bus #301 serves downtown and the Strip 24hr. Buses #108 and 109 serve the airport. All buses wheelchair accessible. Most operate every 10-15min. (less frequently off the Strip), daily 5:30am-1:30am, 24hr. on the Strip. Fares for routes on the Strip $1.50, for residential routes $1, seniors and ages 6-17 50¢. **Las Vegas Strip Trolleys** (382-1404), are *not* stripjoints. They cruise the Strip every 20min. daily 9am-2am. (Fare $1.50 in exact change).

**Taxis: Yellow, Checker, Star** (873-2000).

**Car Rental: Sav-Mor Rent-A-Car,** 5101 Rent-A-Car Rd. (736-1234 or 800-634-6779). Rentals from $28 per day, $147 per week. 150mi. per day included, each additional mi. 20¢. Must be 21; under-25 surcharge $8 per day. Discounts in tourist publications.

**Visitor Information: Las Vegas Convention and Visitor Authority,** 3150 Paradise Rd. (892-0711), 4 blocks from the Strip in the big pink convention center by the Hilton. Open daily 8am-5pm.

**Tours: Gambler's special** bus tours leave L.A., San Francisco, and San Diego for Las Vegas early in the morning and return at night or the next day. Ask at tourist offices in the departure cities or call casinos for info. **Gray Line,** 4020 E. Lone Mountain Rd. (384-1234 or 800-634-6579). City Tours (7½hr., 1 per day, $35). Bus tours from Las Vegas to Hoover Dam/Lake Mead (3 per day, $30 includes Dam admission) and Grand Canyon's South Rim (full-day $149). Discounted prices with coupons in tourist publications and for ages 2-9. Reserve in advance.

**Marriage: Marriage License Bureau,** 200 S. 3rd St. (455-4415). Must be 18 or obtain parental consent. Licenses $35; cash only. No waiting period or blood test required. Open M-F 8am-midnight, Sa-Su 24hr. **Little White Chapel,** 1301 S. Las Vegas Blvd. (382-5943 or 800-545-8111). 24hr. Drive-thru service $30; chapel service $45.

**Divorce:** Must be a Nevada resident for at least 6 weeks. $140 service fee. Permits available at the courthouse M-F 8am-5pm.

**Bi-Gay-Lesbian Organization: Gay and Lesbian Community Center,** 912 E. Sahara Ave. (733-9800). Open M-F 9am-7pm.

**Hotlines: Compulsive Gamblers Hotline** (800-567-8238). **Gamblers Anonymous** (385-7732). **Rape Crisis Center** (366-1640). **Suicide Prevention** (731-2990).

**Post Office:** 301 E. Stewart Ave. (800-275-8777), downtown. Open M-F 8:30am-5pm. General Delivery pickup M-F 9am-2pm. **ZIP Code:** 89101. **Area code:** 702.

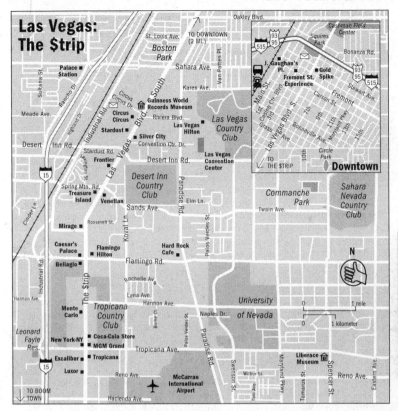

# Las Vegas: The $trip

Oakley Blvd.
St. Louis Ave.
TO DOWNTOWN (2 MI.)
Boston Park
Sahara Ave.
Van Patten Pl.
Karen Ave.
Palace Station
Meade Ave.
Circus Dr.
Circus Circus
Guinness World Records Museum
Riviera Blvd.
Stardust
Silver City
Convention Ctr. Dr.
Las Vegas Hilton
Las Vegas Country Club
Desert Inn Rd.
Frontier
Stardust Rd.
Desert Inn Rd.
Las Vegas Convention Center
Spring Mtn. Rd.
Treasure Island
Venetian
Desert Inn Country Club
Elm Ln.
Sands Ave.
Roosevelt St.
Mirage
Koval Ln.
Caesar's Palace
Flamingo Hilton
Hard Rock Cafe
Palos Verdes Sts.
Bellagio
Flamingo Rd.
Rochelle Av.
Lana Ave.
Harmon Ave.
The Strip
Monte Carlo
Tropicana Country Club
Burke Ln.
Naples Dr.
Leonard Fayle Res.
New York-NY
Coca-Cola Store
MGM Grand
Tropicana Ave.
Excalibur
Tropicana
Luxor
Reno Ave.
Hacienda Ave.
McCarran International Airport
TO BOOM TOWN
University of Nevada
Commanche Park
Twain Ave.
Sahara Nevada Country Club
Liberace Museum
Reno Ave.
Maryland Pkwy
Tamarus St.
Spencer St.
Eastern Ave.
Swenson St.
Wilbur St.
Tam Ave.

## Downtown

Cashman Field Center
Squires Park
Bonanza Rd.
J. Gaughan's Pl.
Fremont St. Experience
Gold Spike
Carson St.
Fremont
Stewart Ave.
Casino Ctr. Blvd.
Grass Ave.
Bonneville Ave.
Maryland Pkwy
Circle Park
TO THE $TRIP

N

0     1 mile
0     1 kilometer

THE SOUTHWEST

# ACCOMMODATIONS AND CAMPGROUNDS

Even though Vegas has over 100,000 rooms, most hotels fill up on weekend nights. Coming to town on a Friday or Saturday night without reservations is a recipe for disaster, so *make reservations as far in advance as possible*. If you get stuck call the **Room Reservations Hotline** (800-332-5333). The earlier you reserve, the better chance you have of snagging a special rate. Room rates at most hotels in Vegas fluctuate all the time. Many hotels use two rate ranges—one for weeknights, another for weekend nights. In addition, a room that costs $30 during a promotion can cost hundreds during conventions (two major ones are in Jan. and Nov.). Local publications such as *What's On In Las Vegas*, *Today in Las Vegas*, *Vegas Visitor*, *Casino Player*, *Tour Guide Magazine*, and *Insider Viewpoint of Las Vegas* have discounts, coupons, and schedules of events; they are all free and available at the visitors center, hotels, and attractions.

**Strip hotels** are at the center of the action and within walking distance of each other, but their inexpensive rooms sell out quickly. Motels line **Fremont Street**, from downtown south. Another option, if you have a car, is to stay at one of the hotel-casinos in Jean, Nevada (approximately 30mi. south on I-15, near the California border). These tend to be less crowded and cheaper than in-town hotels.

**Las Vegas International Hostel (AAIH/Rucksackers),** 1208 S. Las Vegas Blvd. (385-9955). Flashing blue arrows point the way to this European-flavored joint. Tidy, spartan rooms with A/C and fresh sheets daily. Ride board, TV room, basketball court. Shared bathrooms. Laundry. Key deposit $5. Reception 7am-11pm. Check-out 7-10am. 6-person dorms Apr.-Nov. Su-Th $12, F-Sa $14; singles $26. Rates lower Dec.-Mar.

**Somerset House Motel,** 294 Convention Center Dr. (735-4411 or 888-336-4280; fax 369-2388). A straightforward, no-frills establishment within short walking distance of the major Strip casinos. Many rooms feature kitchens; all are sizable and impeccably clean. Dishes and cooking utensils provided upon request. Singles Su-Th $32, F-Sa $40; doubles Su-Th $40, F-Sa $50; additional person $5. Rates lower for seniors.

**Palace Station,** 2411 W. Sahara Ave. (367-2411 or 800-634-3101). Free shuttle to airport and Las Vegas Blvd. All the same features of the Strip hotels, including 2 pools, lounge, casino, and buffet, at much more reasonable rates. Su-Th $29-49, F-Sa from $69; additional person $10.

**Circus Circus,** S. 2880 Las Vegas Blvd. (734-0410 or 800-444-CIRCUS/2472). Only hotel with its own clown shop. Rooms with TV and A/C for 1-4 people. Su-Th $29-79, F-Sa $69-119, holidays $69-159; rollaway bed $12. In summer, fills 2-3 months in advance for Su-Th, 3-4 months for F-Sa.

**Goldstrike,** 1 Main St., Jean, Nevada (800-634-1359), 30mi. south of Vegas on I-15 (Exit 12). Vegas-style casino has various inexpensive restaurants (prime rib $6, dinner buffet $6). Su-Th $18, F $35, Sa $49 based on availability; additional person $3.

**Lake Mead National Recreation Area** (293-8906), 25mi. south of town on Rte. 93/95. Sites $10, with hookup $14-18. For details, see p. 688.

**Circusland RV Park,** 500 Circus Circus Dr. (734-0410), a part of the Circus Circus hotel on the Strip. Pool, jacuzzi, convenience store, showers, and laundry. Hookups Su-Th $17.50, F-Sa $20.

## ◐ FOOD

Almost every hotel-casino in Vegas courts tourists with cheap buffets, but expect bland, greasy food and long lines at peak hours. Most casinos dole out alcoholic drinks for free to those who are gambling and for under $1 to those who aren't...yet. Vegas isn't all bland buffets—just west of the Strip, particularly along **Decatur Blvd.,** are a number of low-priced eateries that can revive your taste buds.

**◪ Luxor's Pharaoh's Pheast,** 3900 Las Vegas Blvd. S. (262-4000). A delicious pheast phit for a pharaoh. Breakfast $7.50 (6-11:30am); lunch $8 (11:30am-4pm); dinner $11.50 (4-11pm).

**The Plaza Diner,** 1 Main St. (386-2110), near the entrance in Jackie Gaughan's Plaza Hotel/Casino. Cheap prime rib dinner noon-midnight ($4). $1 beers. Open 24hr.

**Rincon Criollo,** 1145 S. Las Vegas Blvd. (388-1906), across from youth hostel. Dine on filling Cuban food beneath a wall-sized photograph of palm trees. Daily special including rice and black beans $6.50. Hot sandwiches $3.50-4.50. Open Tu-Su 11am-10pm.

**Battista's Hole in the Wall,** 4041 Audrie Ave. (732-1424), right behind the Flamingo. One of Vegas's only establishments with character of its own. Adorning the walls are 28 years' worth of celebrity photos and novelties from area brothels, as well as the head of "Moosolini," the fascist moose. Though pricey at $18, dinner (includes house wine) is worth the treat. Open M-Th 4:30-10:30pm, F-Su 4:30-11pm.

**Monte Carlo,** 3770 S. Las Vegas Blvd. (730-7777). As inexpensive as good buffet food gets. Breakfast $6.75 (7-11am); lunch $7 (11:30am-3:30pm); dinner $10 (4-10pm).

## ◈ SIGHTS

Fans of classical music and kitsch will be delighted by the **Liberace Museum,** devoted to the flamboyant late "Mr. Showmanship." Liberace's audacious uses of fur, velvet, and rhinestone boggle the rational mind. *(1775 E. Tropicana Ave. 798-5595. Open M-Sa 10am-5pm, Su 1-5pm. $7, students and seniors $5, under 12 free.)* It's been said that God made men, and Sam Colt made 'em equal. Experience coltish justice at **The Gun Store.** $10 plus ammo lets you try out an impressive array of pistols, up to and including the enormous Magnum 44. Fork over $30 and they'll let you shoot real machine guns. *(2900 E. Tropicana Ave. 454-1110.)* Boy, shootin' shore do make yer thirsty! Good thing there's **Everything Coca-Cola,** under the MGM Grand. Watch old Coke commercials and drink all the Coke (and Coca-Cola products from around the world) you want. *(3785 Las Vegas Blvd. S. 270-5953. Tours $2.)*

## CA$INO-HOPPING AND NIGHTLIFE

Unkempt punk rock icon Johnny Rotten proclaimed, "The only notes that matter come in a wad." Casinos have resorted to ever more extreme measures to get these notes. Where once the casinos stuck to the quintessentially Vegas themes of cheap buffets, booze, and entertainment, they now spend millions of dollars a year trying to fool guests into thinking that they are somewhere else. Spittin' images of Hollywood, New York, Rio, Paris (complete with Eiffel Tower), and Monte Carlo already thrive on the Strip. Despite these alluring amusements, however, gambling remains Vegas's biggest draw. *Gambling is illegal for those under 21.* If you are of age, look for casino "funbooks" which allow you to buy $50 in chips for only $15. Never bring more money than you're prepared to lose cheerfully. And always remember: in the long run, you will almost definitely lose cash. Keep your wallet in your front pocket, and beware of the thieves who prowl casinos to nab big winnings from unwary jubilants. Most casinos offer free gambling lessons; *Today in Las Vegas* lists current dates and times. In addition, the more patient dealers may offer a tip or two (in exchange for one from you). Casinos, nightclubs, and wedding chapels stay open 24hr. Casinos are listed north to south.

**Jackie Gaughn's Plaza,** 1 Main St. (386-2110), downtown, near the electric-light spectacular "The Fremont Experience," offers penny slots for Okies yearning for the big-city thrill of jockeying, and some of the cheapest blackjack tables in town.

Moving on to the strip, **Circus Circus,** 2880 Las Vegas Blvd. S. (734-0410), attempts to cultivate a (dysfunctional) family atmosphere. Beware of the carnival area's "Camel Chase" game; it's far more addictive than any Vegas slot machine. Two stories above the casino floor, tightrope-walkers, fire-eaters, and acrobats perform. Within the hotel complex, the **Grand Slam Canyon** is a Grand Canyon theme park with a roller coaster and other rides—all enclosed in a glass shell. (Open daily 10am-midnight; in winter Su-Th 10am-6pm, F-Sa 10am-midnight. Rides $2-5; unlimited rides $16, under 4 ft. $12.) At **Treasure Island,** 3300 Las Vegas Blvd. S. (894-7111), pirates battle with cannons staged on giant wooden ships in a Stripside "bay" on the Strip (every 1½hr., daily 4:30pm-midnight). The majestic confines of the **Mirage,** 3400 Las Vegas Blvd. S. (791-7111), banish all illusions from the halls of entertainment. Among its attractions are a dolphin habitat ($3), Siegfried and Roy's white tigers, and a volcano that erupts in fountains and flames every 15min. from dusk to midnight. Busts abound at **Caesar's Palace,** 3570 Las Vegas Blvd. S. (731-7110). Some of these are plaster; the rest are barely concealed beneath the low-cut classical costumes that the cocktail waitresses have to wear. Their male counterparts strut about with false Roman noses. In the **Festival Fountain show,** statues move, talk, battle, and shout amid a laser-light show (every hr. daily 10am-11pm). **New York-New York,** 3790 Las Vegas Blvd. S. (740-6969), puts even Disneyland to shame with its fine-tuned gimmickry. Relive the glory days of Hollywood at the **MGM Grand,** 3799 Las Vegas Blvd. S. (891-1111. Amusement Park open daily 10am-10pm. $12, ages 4-12 $10. Sky Screamer $25 for 1, $35 for 2, $45 for 3.) **Excalibur,** 3850 Las Vegas Blvd. S. (800-937-7777), has a medieval English theme, insofar as medieval England's economy was based on depriving senior citizens of their Social Security. Before the watchful eyes of the sprawling sphinx and the towering black pyramid of **Luxor,** 3900 Las Vegas Blvd. S. (262-4000), a dazzling laser light show is reminiscent of imperial ancient Egypt.

**Nightlife** in Vegas gets rolling around midnight and keeps going until everyone drops or runs out of money. At Caesar's Palace (731-7110), **Cleopatra's Barge,** a huge ship-disco, is one boat that's made for rockin' (open Tu-Su 9pm-2am; cover F-Sa $5). Another popular disco, **Gipsy,** 4605 Paradise Rd. (731-1919), southeast of the Strip, may look deserted at 11pm, but by 1am the medium-sized dance floor packs in a gay, lesbian, and straight crowd (cover $4). Be forewarned that the Gipsy dancers get crazy on Topless Tu.

## NEAR LAS VEGAS: HOOVER DAM AND LAKE MEAD

A capacious, sparkling white wall spanning the Boulder Canyon, the Hoover Dam gives dignity to heavy industry's encroachment on natural wonders (in this case, the less dramatic, western outlet of the Grand Canyon). Shiny steel towers climb the rugged brown hillsides, carrying high-tension wires up and out through the desert. The **visitors center** (293-8321) offers 30min. tours leading to the generators at the structure's bottom (open daily 8:30am-5:45pm, exhibits close at 6pm; tours $8, seniors $7, ages 6-16 $2). Parking in the garage on the Nevada side costs $2, but it is free across the dam in Arizona, and gives you the chance to walk across the top of the dam itself.

As the tour demonstrates, the dam was first constructed for flood control and irrigation purposes (electricity just pays for it). On one of the Art Deco-ish towers that line the dam, a set of pseudo-fascist reliefs declare: FLOOD CONTROL, IRRIGATION, WATER STORAGE, POWER. Powerful words for turbulent times.

Flood control, irrigation, and water storage are all arguably the same thing, and this multi-tiered program is fulfilled by crystalline, turquoise, non-alcoholic **Lake Mead,** a shiny blue spot in the arid wasteland between Arizona and Nevada. Dubbed "the jewel of the desert" by its residents, the lake and its environs offer more than social planning and deficit spending.

Alongside the ubiquitous Park Service campsites ($10), concessionaires usually operate RV parks (most of which have evolved into mobile home villages), marinas, restaurants, and occasionally motels. More remote concessionaires include **Echo Bay Resort** (702-394-4000 or 800-752-9669; RV hookup $18), which offers motel rooms from $75 (lower in winter), and its restaurant, **Tale of the Whale,** decorated in nautical motifs and featuring a stunning view of Lake Mead, selling burgers in the $5 range. The resort rents jet-skis ($50 per hr., $270 per day; fishing boats for impoverished seadogs $12 per hr., $60 per day).

Most distant from the bustle of nearby Las Vegas is **Overton Beach Resort,** convenient to Overton, Nevada. Overton occupies a little patch of green in the desert at the northern end of scenic North Shore Scenic Dr. and offers food, cheap motels (**Overton Motel,** 137 N. Moapa Valley Blvd.; 702-397-2463; singles $29; doubles $35), and more Anasazi ruins than you can shake a stick at.

Between Las Vegas and Overton sits the **Valley of Fire State Park.** From I-15 from Las Vegas, take Nevada Rte. 169 at Crystal south to the park. For $5, you can cut through this breathtaking patch of rocky red desert back to I-15, then ride, boldly ride, back to the city.

## RENO

If a Hollywood exec ever got the great idea to cross *Showgirls* with *The Golden Girls*, the result would be Reno. Hoping to strike it rich at the card tables, busloads of the nation's elderly flock to its hedonistic splendor. A punchy kaleidoscope of casinos, 24hr. bars, seedy motels, mountain vistas, strip clubs full of aspiring dancers, and neon-lit pawnshops makes Reno a strange and memorable place.

**◪ PRACTICAL INFORMATION. Amtrak,** at 135 E. Commercial Row (ticket office open daily 8am-4:45pm), speeds to San Francisco (1 bus/train combo per day, $35-85) and Sacramento (1 per day, $22-76). Arrive 30min. in advance to purchase ticket. **Greyhound,** 155 Stevenson St. (322-2970; open 24hr.), ½ block from W. 2nd St., rolls to San Francisco (18 per day, $30); Salt Lake City (4 per day, $45-48); Los Angeles (11 per day, $40-42); and Sacramento (12 per day, $20). The station has lockers (up to 6hr. $2, 6-24hr. $4), a mini-mart, and a restaurant. **Reno Citifare** (348-7433), at 4th and Center St., serves the Reno-Sparks area. Most buses operate 5am-7pm, though city center buses operate 24hr. Buses stop every 2 blocks. (Fare $1.25, seniors and disabled 60¢, ages 6-18 90¢.) **Reno-Sparks Convention and Visitors Center:** 300 N. Center St. (800-367-7366), on the first floor of the National Bowling Stadium (open M-Sa 7am-8pm, Su 9am-6pm). **Post Office:** 50 S. Virginia St. (800-275-8777), at Mill St., 2 blocks south of city center (open M-F 8:30am-5pm, Sa 10am-2pm). **ZIP code:** 89501. **Area code:** 702.

**⌐ ACCOMMODATIONS.** While weekend prices at casinos are usually on the high side, gamblers' specials, weekday rates, and winter discounts provide some great, cheap rooms. Prices fluctuate, so call ahead. **Fitzgerald's,** 225 N. Virginia St. (786-3663), **Atlantis,** 3800 S. Virginia St. (825-4700), **Circus Circus,** 500 N. Sierra St. (329-0711), and **Sundowner,** 450 N. Arlington Ave. (786-7050), have been known to offer some good deals to go along with their central locations and massive facilities. Be advised: Heterosexual prostitution is legal in most of Nevada (though not in Reno itself), and a few cheap motels may be lacking a particularly wholesome feel. Members of the same sex sharing a hotel room may be required to book a room with two beds. Southwestern downtown has the cheapest lodging.

To escape Reno's constant hum of slot machines, campers can make the drive to the woodland campsites of **Davis Creek Park** (849-0684), 17 miles south on U.S. 395, then half-mile west; follow signs (sites $11, each additional car $5; free picnic area open daily 8am-9pm). Wrap yourself in a rustic blanket of pines and sage at the base of the Sierra Nevada's **Mount Rose** and camp at one of the 63 sites with full service, including showers and a small pond stocked with fish, but no hookups. Sites available on a first-come, first-camped basis. (Sites with 1 vehicle $10, pets $1.) The nearby 14-mile Offer Creek Trail leads to Rock and Price Lakes and interlocks with the Tahoe Rim Trail. Camping and fishing on the trail are free but require permits (available at grocery and sporting goods stores). You can also camp along the shore at **Pyramid Lake** (see p. 690). To stay closer to Reno, park and plug in your RV overnight at the **Reno Hilton,** 2500 E. 2nd St. (789-2000; full hookup $21). Call ahead; people reserve up to a year in advance.

**⌐ FOOD.** Eating in Reno is cheap. To entice gamblers and to prevent them from wandering out in search of food, casinos offer a wide range of all-you-can-eat buffets and 99¢ breakfasts. However, buffet fare can be greasy, overcooked, and tasteless, and rumors of food poisoning abound. Reno's other inexpensive eateries offer better quality food. The large Basque population, which immigrated from the Pyrenees to herd sheep in Nevada, has brought a spicy and hearty cuisine locals enthusiastically recommend. **The Blue Heron,** 1091 S. Virginia St., 9 blocks from downtown, is a rare bird in Reno, appealing to a younger crowd (786-4110; open M-Sa 11am-9pm, Su noon-9pm). **Louis' Basque Corner,** 301 E. 4th St., at Evans St., 3 blocks east of Virginia, is a local institution (323-7203; open Su-M 5-9:30pm, Tu-Sa 11:30am-2:30pm and 5-9:30pm).

**⌐ ENTERTAINMENT.** Reno is one big amusement park. The casinos, of course, are the main attraction. Many casinos offer free gaming lessons, and minimum bets vary between establishments. Drinks are either free or incredibly cheap for gamblers, but be wary of a casino's generous gift of highly alcoholic, risk-inducing, inhibition-dropping wallet-looseners. Gambling is illegal for persons under 21; if you win the jackpot at age 20, it'll be the casino's lucky day and not yours.

Almost all casinos offer live night-time entertainment, but unless you like schmaltzy Wayne Newton standards or delight at the thought of Tom Jones autographing your underwear, these shows are not really worth the steep admission prices. **Harrah's,** 219 N. Center St. (786-3232), is the self-consciously "hip" complex where **Planet Hollywood** capitalizes on movie lust, magically transforming Hollywood knick-knacks into precious relics. At **Circus Circus,** 500 N. Sierra (329-0711), a small circus above the casino performs "big-top" shows every 30min. It's not exactly Barnum and Bailey, but just as kitschy. These shows and others are listed in the weekly *Showtime*, which also offers gambling coupons. *Best Bets* provides listings of discounted local events and shows. *Encore* lists upcoming arts events in northern Nevada. *Nevada Events & Shows*, a section of the Nevada visitors' guide, lists sights, museums, seasonal events, and other goodies. These free papers are available in most hotels and casinos. The local *Reno Gazette-Journal* and *News and Review* have more info.

## NEAR RENO: PYRAMID LAKE

Thirty mi. north of Reno on Rt. 445, on the Paiute Indian Reservation, lies emerald green Pyramid Lake, one of the most heart-achingly beautiful bodies of water in the U.S. The pristine tides of Pyramid Lake are set against the backdrop of a barren desert, making it a soothing and otherworldly respite from neon Reno. **Camping** is allowed anywhere on the lake shore, but only designated areas have toilet facilities. A $5 permit is required for use of the park, and the area is carefully patrolled by the Paiute tribe. Permits are available at the **Ranger Station,** 3mi. left from Rt. 445 at Sutcliffe (476-1155; open daily 7am-3:30pm). **Boat rental** (476-1156) is available daily at the marina near the Ranger Station; call for reservations.

# UTAH

Beginning in 1848, persecuted members of the Church of Jesus Christ of Latter-Day Saints (colloquially called Mormons) settled on the land that is now Utah, intending to establish and govern their own theocratic state. President James Buchanan struggled to quash the Mormon's efforts in 1858, as many others had tried before. The Momons eventually gave up their dreams of theocracy and statehood was finally granted on Jan. 4, 1896. Today the state's population is 70% Mormon—a religious presence that creates a haven for family values. Utah's citizens dwell primarily in the 100mi. corridor along I-15 stretching from Ogden to Provo. Outside this area, Utah's natural beauty dominates, intoxicating visitors in a way that Utah's watered-down 3.2% beer never can. Immediately east of Salt Lake City, the Wasatch range beckons skiers in the winter and bikers in the summer. Southern Utah is part of a region like no other place on Earth; red canyons, river gorges, and crenellated cliffs attest to the creative powers of wind and water.

## 🛈 PRACTICAL INFORMATION

**Capital:** Salt Lake City.

**Visitor Info: Utah Travel Council,** 300 N. State St., Salt Lake City 84114 (801-538-1030 or 800-200-1160; www.utah.com), across from the capitol building. Distributes the *Utah Vacation Planner,* lists of motels, national parks, and campgrounds, as well as statewide biking, rafting, and skiing brochures. **Utah Parks and Recreation,** 1594 W. North Temple, Salt Lake City 84116 (801-538-7220). Open M-F 8am-5pm.

**Controlled Substances:** Mormons dispense with "strong drinks" (coffee and tea), nicotine, alcohol, and, of course, illegal drugs. While you won't have any trouble getting a pack of cigarettes, a cup of coffee or a coke, alcohol is another matter. State liquor stores are sprinkled sparsely about the state and have inconvenient hours. Grocery and convenience stores can only sell beer. While most upscale restaurants serve wine, licensing laws can split a room, and drinkers may have to move a few feet down a bar to get a mixed drink. Also, establishments that sell hard alcohol are required to be "members only"; tourists can either find a "sponsor"–i.e., an entering patron–or get a short-term membership. If the rigamarole gets to be too much, try a smoothie.

**Postal Abbreviation:** UT. **Sales Tax:** 5.75-7.75%.

## SALT LAKE CITY

Tired from 5 exhausting months of travel, Brigham Young looked out across the desolate valley of the Great Salt Lake and said, "this is the place." Young knew that his band of Mormon pioneers had finally reached a haven where they could practice their religion freely, away from the persecution they had faced in the East. Today, Salt Lake City is still dominated by Mormon influence. The Church of Jesus Christ of Latter Day Saints (LDS, not the hallucinogenic drug) owns the tallest office building downtown and welcomes visitors to Temple Sq., a city block that includes the Mormon Temple and cool, shady gardens. Despite its commitment to

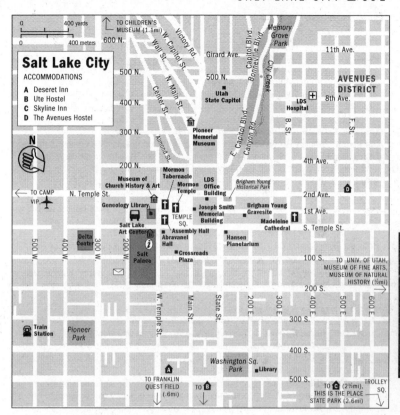

preserving traditions, Salt Lake is rapidly attracting high-tech firms, as well as outdoor enthusiasts drawn to world-class ski resorts, rock climbing, and mountain trails. The city has already landed perhaps the biggest prize of all, the 2002 Winter Olympics, which has the city looking temporarily war-torn from construction and brought scandal in the wake of bribes given to officials of the International Olympic Committee.

# 🖪 ORIENTATION AND PRACTICAL INFORMATION

Salt Lake City's grid system makes navigation simple. Brigham Young designated **Temple Sq.** as the heart of downtown. Street names indicate how many blocks east, west, north, or south they lie from Temple Sq.; the "0" points are **Main St.** (north-south) and **South Temple St.** (east-west). Local address listings often include two numerical cross streets, acting as a type of coordinate system (no maps needed!). A building on 13th S. St. (1300 S.) might be listed as 825 E. 1300 S., meaning the cross street is 800 E. (8th E.). Smaller streets and those that do not fit the grid pattern sometimes have non-numeric names.

**Airport: Salt Lake City International,** 776 N. Terminal Dr. (575-2600), 6mi. west of Temple Sq. UTA bus #50 runs between the terminal and downtown for $1-2, but don't count on it after 10pm. Taxi to Temple Sq. costs about $11.

**Trains: Amtrak,** in Rio Grande Station, 340 S. 600 W. (531-0188), *in an unsafe area.* To: San Francisco (19hr., 1 per day, $77-115) and Denver (15hr., 1 per day, $75-112). Station open M-F 10pm-1:30pm, Sa-Su 10pm-6am

**Buses: Greyhound,** 160 W. South Temple St. (355-9579), near Temple Sq. To: Las Vegas (8hr., 2per day, $40); Los Angeles (16-17hr., 2 per day, $77); and Denver (10-18hr., 5 per day, $40). Station open daily 4am-11pm, ticket window open 6:30am-7:30pm.

**Public Transit: Utah Transit Authority (UTA),** 3600 S. 700 W. (287-4636). Frequent service to University of Utah campus; buses to Ogden (#70/72 express), suburbs, airport, mountain canyons, and the #11 express runs to Provo (fare $2). Buses every 20min.-1hr. M-Sa 6am-11pm. Fare $1-2, senior discounts, under 5 free. Maps available at libraries and the visitors bureau. UTA also runs the Sites Trolley, which goes to all the major sites for $2.

**Taxis: Ute Cab,** 359-7788. **Yellow Cab,** 521-2100.

**Car Rental: Economy Rent-a-Car,** 2810 S. 8th St. (487-2400). From $19 per day, $129 per wk., 100mi. per day free, after that 20¢ per mi. Must be 21+ with credit card, and stay within 100mi. radius of Salt Lake City. Open M-Sa 9am-6pm.

**Bike Rental: Wasatch Touring,** on the corner of 700 E. and 100 S. St. (359-9361). 24-speed mountain bikes with helmets $25 per day. Open M-Sa 9am-7pm.

**Visitor Info: Salt Lake Valley Convention and Visitors Bureau,** 90 S. West Temple St. (534-4902), 1 block south of Temple Sq. Open in summer M-F 8am-6pm, Sa-Su 9am-5pm, early Sept. to late May M-F 8am-5pm, Sa-Su 9am-5pm.

**Hotlines: Rape Crisis,** 467-7273. **Suicide Prevention,** 483-5444. Both 24hr.

**Medical Services: University hospital emergency,** 581-2291.

**Post Office:** 230 W. 200 S. St., 1 block south and 1 block west of visitors bureau. Open M-F 8am-5pm, Sa 9am-2pm. **ZIP code:** 84101. **Area code:** 801.

# ACCOMMODATIONS

**The Avenue's Hostel (HI-AYH),** 107 F St. (359-3855), 15min. walk from Temple Sq. toward the foothills. Free pick-up from Amtrak and Greyhound stations. Winter ski bus to nearby resorts $2-4. Dorm rooms $14; doubles $33-34, with private bath $30-35. Blankets and linen free. Reception 7:30am-10:30pm.

**Ute Hostel (AAIH/Rucksackers),** 21 E. Kelsey Ave. (595-1645), near the intersection of 13th S. and Main St. Young international crowd. Free pick-ups can be arranged from Amtrak, Greyhound, or the visitors center. Free tea and coffee, parking, linen, and safe. Dorm rooms $15; comfortable doubles $35. Check-in 24hr.

**Deseret Inn,** 50 W. 500 S. (532-2900), in the heart of the city, rents singles ($30), doubles ($35), and the chance to soak your bones in their jacuzzi.

**Skyline Inn,** 2475 E. 1700 S. (582-5350). Friendly service and very clean singles $57.

The mountains rising to the east of Salt Lake City offer comfortable summer camping with warm days and cool nights. Rocky **Little Cottonwood Canyon,** on Rt. 210 east of the city, features two of the closest campgrounds for summer camping: **Albion Basin** (26 sites) and **Tanners Flat** (39 sites $10). Two more campgrounds lie just north of the city on I-15: **Sunset** (17 sites $6) and **Bountiful Peak** (22 sites $8). On weekends, get there early to ensure a space. The **Salt Lake Ranger District** fields calls for more info (943-1794). **Antelope Island,** in the middle of the lake (access via 7.2mi. Davis County Causeway from the mainland), has 13 sites. (Headquarters 550-6155, visitor center 721-9569. $2, $7 entrance fee for motorized vehicles. Call 2 months in advance for weekends.) If you need a hookup, **Camp VIP,** 1400 W. North Temple St. (328-0224), has 450 RV sites and 17 tent sites ($19, full hookup $26).

# MORAL FIBER

Good, cheap restaurants are sprinkled all around the city and its suburbs. If you're in a hurry downtown, **ZCMI Mall** and **Crossroads Mall,** both located across from Temple Sq., have standard food courts.

**The Pie,** 1320 E. 200 S. (582-0193), next to the University of Utah. This graffiti-buried college hangout serves up large pizzas (starting at $7) late into the night. Open M-Th 11am-1am, F-Sa 11am-3am, Su noon-midnight.

**Park Café,** 604 E. 1300 S. (487-1670), at the south end of Liberty Park. A classy little joint with a patio and a view of a park. Lunches $6-7, light dinners $8. Open M-F 7am-3pm and 5-9pm, Sa 7am-3pm and 5-10pm, Su 7am-3pm.

**Squatter's Salt Lake Brewing Company,** 147 W. Broadway (363-2739), is a microbrewery ($3 pints) with reasonably priced American cuisine and a variety of sandwiches ($7-8), pizzas, and salads ($4). Open M-Sa 11:30am-1am, Su 11:30am-midnight.

**W.H. Brumby's,** 224 S. 1300 E. (581-0888), is where "artisan bakers" produce to-die-for $5.25 breakfast and $5-6.25 lunch plates as well as desserts for a local crowd from suits to students. Open Tu-F, 8am-9am, Sa 8am-9pm.

## 🔭 SIGHTS

All of the LDS sacred sights in Salt Lake City are free. The seat of the highest Mormon authority and the central temple, **Temple Sq.** is the symbolic center of the Mormon religion. *(240-2609.)* The square has two **visitors centers** (North and South); the North visitors center displays Old and New Testament murals and 25min. videos about Temple Sq. "Book of Mormon" and "Purpose of Temple" presentations alternate every 30min. at the South visitors center. *(Free.)* Visitors can wander around the pleasant, flowery, 10-acre square, but the sacred temple is off-limits to non-Mormons. Alighting on the highest of the temple's three towers, a golden statue of the angel Moroni watches over the city. A 45min. tour leaves from the flagpole every 10min., showing off the highlights of Temple Sq. *(Tours daily 8:30am-8:30pm. Free.)* *Legacy*, a film detailing the Mormon trek to Salt Lake City, is screened at the **Joseph Smith Memorial Building.** *(Call 240-4383 for show times.)*

Visitors to Temple Sq. may also visit the **Mormon Tabernacle,** which houses the famed choir. Built in 1867, the structure is so acoustically sensitive that a pin drop at one end of the building can be heard 175 ft. away at the other end. Members of the choir are selected on the basis of character, musical competence, and sometimes family tradition. Th evening rehearsals and Su morning broadcasts from the tabernacle are open to the public. *(Th 8-9:30pm. Su 9:30-10am; seating begins at 8:30am; doors close at 9:15am.)* No matter how forcefully they sing, however, the choir can't match the size and sound of the 11,623-pipe **organ** which accompanies them. *(1.5hr. organ recitals M-Sa noon and 2pm, Su 2pm.)* In the summer, there are frequent concerts at **Assembly Hall,** next door. The **Museum of Church History and Art** houses Mormon memorabilia, including an original 1830 copy of the *Book of Mormon.* *(45 N. West Temple St. 240-3310. Open M-F 9am-9pm, Sa-Su 10am-7pm. Free.)*

The moment when Brigham Young and his band first came upon the Great Salt Lake is commemorated at **"This is the Place" Heritage Park,** in Emigration Canyon on the eastern end of town. *(2601 Sunnyside Ave. 584-8391. Take the sites trolley for $2. Park open in summer daily sunrise-sunset.)* The visitors center guards the entrance to **"Old Desert Village."** *(Open daily 10am-5pm. $8, seniors and ages 6-11 $6.)* Big business meets religion at the **Church of Jesus Christ of Latter Day Saints Office Building,** the tallest skyscraper in Salt Lake. The elevator to the 26th floor grants a view of the Great Salt Lake in the west or the Wasatch Range in the east. *(50 E. North Temple St. 240-3789. Observation deck open M-F 9am-5pm.)*

Utah's original **capitol** was in the centrally located town of Fillmore, but since the population in the Salt Lake area was higher, the capitol was moved here in 1916. The gray granite building's grounds include a garden that changes daily. (538-3000. Open M-F 8am-5pm. Tours M-F 9am-4pm.) **Pioneer Memorial Museum,** next to the capitol, has personal items belonging to the earliest settlers of the valley and info about prominent Mormon leaders, including Brigham Young and Heber C. Kimball (538-1050; open M-Sa 9am-5pm, Su 1-5pm; Sept.-May closed Su; free). In the capitol area, a walk up City Creek Canyon to **Memory Grove** accesses one of the city's best views. Also on capitol hill, the **Hansen Planetarium,** 15 S. State St., has free exhibits, in addition to laser shows set to Led Zeppelin and U2. (538-2104. Open M-Th 9am-9pm, F-Sa 9am-midnight, Su noon-6pm. Laser show $7.50, star and science show $4.50.)

At the **Children's Museum,** 840 N. 300 W. St., pilot a 727 jet or implant a Jarvik artificial heart in a life-sized "patient." (328-3383. Take bus #70. Open M-Th and Sa 10am-6pm, F 10am-8pm. 2 and under $3, F after 5pm $1.50.) A permanent collection of world art wows enthusiasts at the **Utah Museum of Fine Arts,** on the University of Utah campus (581-7332; open M-F 9am-5pm, Sa-Su 2-5pm). The **Salt Lake Art Center,** 20 S. West Temple St., displays an impressive array of contemporary art, as well as the less abstract Kidspace, where modern art appreciation is hands-on. (328-4201. Open Tu-Th and Sa 10am-5pm, F 10am-9pm, Su 1-5pm; Kidspace open W-F and Su 1-4pm, Sa 10am-4pm. Suggested donation $2.)

## 🎵 NIGHTLIFE

Concerts abound in the sweltering summer months. At 7:30pm every Tu and F, the **Temple Sq. Concert Series** conducts a free outdoor concert in Brigham Young Historic Park, with music ranging from string quartet to unplugged guitar (240-2534; call for a schedule of concerts). The **Utah Symphony Orchestra** performs in Abravanel Hall, 123 W. South Temple St. (533-6683. Tickets Sept. to early May $15-40, call 1 week in advance, office hrs. M-F 10am-6pm.)

Women's basketball's **Utah Starzz** (season June-Aug.; tickets $5-40) and the 1998 NBA Western Conference Champion **Utah Jazz** (season Oct.-Apr.; tickets $10-83) take the court at the **Delta Center,** 301 W. South Temple (355-3865).

Free copies of *The Event, Mountain Times, City Weekly* or *Utah After Dark* are available from bars, clubs, and restaurants and lists events. **The Zephyr,** 301 S. Temple, thumps live music nightly (355-2582; hrs. vary; get a member to sponsor you). **Club DV8,** 115 S. West Temple St., is one of the better dance clubs in Salt Lake City (also a private club), deviating from the norm with $1 cover before 10pm and "modern music" on Th nights. (539-8400. Open F-Sa 9pm-2am. ½-price drafts 9-10pm.) The **Dead Goat Saloon,** 165 S. West Temple St., is a tavern delighting tourists and locals alike with pool, darts, and a grill (328-4628; open M-Sa 6pm-2am, Su 6pm-around midnight).

## NEAR SALT LAKE CITY

The **Great Salt Lake,** administered by Great Salt Lake State Marina, is a remnant of primordial Lake Bonneville, and is so salty that only blue-green algae and brine shrimp can survive in it. The salt content varies from 5-27%, providing unusual buoyancy. In fact, no one has ever drowned in the Great Salt Lake—a fact attributable to the Lake's chemical make-up, which also makes the water reek (250-1822).

It is nearly impossible to get to the Lake without a car; bus #37 "Magna" will take you within 4mi., but no closer. To get to the **south shore** of the lake, take I-80 17mi. west of Salt Lake City to exit 104.

Some of the greatest snow in the U.S. falls on the **Wasatch Mountains,** located just minutes from downtown Salt Lake. Rt. 210 heads east from I-25, climbing through the granite boulders of Little Cottonwood Canyon to challenging **Snowbird** (742-2222 or 800-453-3000) and **Alta** (359-1078). Alta is the best budget bet; $31 buys an all-day lift ticket to wide-open cruising runs, emerald glades, steep chutes, and champagne powder—but no snowboards. Rt. 190 climbs neighboring Big Cottonwood Canyon and leads to **Solitude** (534-1400) and **Brighton** (532-4731).

The **Alta Peruvian Lodge** offers an excellent package for 2 people, which includes a bed, all meals, service charges, tax, and lift tickets. (328-8589 or 800-453-8488; $164-196). **UTA** (see Salt Lake City **Practical Information,** p. 691) runs buses from the city to the resorts in winter, and has pick-ups at downtown motels. **Breeze Ski Rentals** rents equipment at Snowbird (800-525-0314, telephone office hrs. M-F 8am-5pm). The Utah Travel Council (see Utah **Practical Information,** p. 690) purveys the free *Ski Utah* with complete listings of ski packages and lodgings.

In the summer, outdoor lovers climb the Wasatch range to beat the desert heat of the city. Hiking, biking, and fishing are all prime attractions. At Snowbird, the **Snowbird Activities Center** lend bikes with helmets (933-2147; $20 per 4hr., and $30 per 8hr). Snowbird's **aerial tram** climbs to 11,000 ft., offering a spectacular view of the Wasatch Mountains and the Salt Lake Valley. (Open daily in summer 11am-8pm, in winter 9am-3:45pm; $14, seniors and ages 6-16 $9.)

American westward expansion culminated in the completion of the **Transcontinental Railroad** in 1869. The Union Pacific and Central Pacific Railroads finally joined tracks at Promontory Point in the **Golden Spike National Historic Site,** the last link was celebrated by driving in a golden spike donated by tycoon Leland Stanford. Take I-15/84 north, exit west onto Rt. 83 for about 30mi., and follow the signs. The park's visitors center traces the "iron horse's" colorful history and shady influences, operates replica steam locomotives, and reenacts the spike driving ceremony every Sa and Su at 1 and 3pm. (471-2209. Open Memorial Day- Labor Day daily 8am-6pm; rest of year 8am-4:30pm. $3.50 per person up to $7 per vehicle.)

## TIMPANOGOS CAVE

Legend has it that a set of mountain lion tracks first led Martin Hansen to the mouth of the cave that today bears his name. While Utah's Wasatch Mountains brim with natural wonders, the cave system of American Fork Canyon, collectively called Timpanogos Cave, is a true gem for speleologists (cave nuts) and tourists alike. Though early gem pirates stole and shipped boxcar loads of stalactites and other mineral wonders back east to sell to universities and museums, enough remain to bedazzle guests for the 1hr. walk through the caves.

**Timpanogos Cave National Monument** is solely accessible via Rt. 92 (20mi. south of Salt Lake City off I-15, exit 287). The **visitors center** (801-756-5238) dispenses info on the caves and tour tickets. (Open mid-May to mid-Oct. daily 7am-5:30pm. 3hr. hikes depart daily 7am-4:30pm every 15min. $6; ages 6-15 $5; seniors with Golden Age Passport and under 5 $3.) Summer tours tend to sell out by early afternoon; reservations may be made by phone 2 weeks in advance, or at the visitors center up to the day before the tour. Bring water and warm layers: the rigorous hike to the cave is a climb, but the temperature drops dramatically once inside.

The national monument is dwarfed by the surrounding **Uinta National Forest,** which blankets the mountains of the Wasatch Range. The **Alpine Scenic Drive (Rt. 92)** leaves the visitors center and heads southwest, providing excellent views of Mt. Timpanogos and other snow-capped peaks. The loopy 20mi. drive is laden with switchbacks and takes close to 1hr. in one direction. This road will take you past many trailheads; for detailed trail descriptions of area hikes such as the 9mi. (one-way) trek up Mt. Timpanogos, inquire at the **Pleasant Grove Ranger District,** 390 N. 100 E. Pleasant Grove (785-3563).

Camping in the national monument is strictly forbidden. The Pleasant Grove Ranger District (see above) has info on the four **campgrounds** in the area (800-280-2267 for reservations; sites $11-13) and **backcountry camping** through the forest, which requires no permit or fee, as long as you respect minimum-impact guidelines. Once inside the borders of the national monument and national forest, there are no budget accommodations or food stores. Rt. 89 in nearby **Orem** and **Pleasant Grove** has supermarkets and fast food joints.

## PARK CITY

Thirty-six mi. east of Salt Lake City on I-80, Park City draws winter tourists for its fantastic skiing and boutique-lined downtown. The mixture of the great outdoors and the yuppified Main St. is straight out of an L.L. Bean catalogue, though not without a certain rustic chic. The **Park City Mt. Resort** (649-8111), the **Dear Valley Resort** (649-1000), and the **Canyons** (649-5400) access some of the choicest powder and most challenging slopes in the ski-rich West. **Breeze Ski Rentals and Max Snow Snowboards,** 1415 Lowell and 1325 Lowell, rents the requisite gear (800-525-0314). Park City's **alpine slide** thrills with ½mi. of curves and drops (open M-F noon-9pm, Sa-Su 10am-9pm; $7.50). Mountain bikers, hikers, and fishing fanatics flock to the area in the summertime. Trail info is available at the visitors center (see below).

With some persistence, the budget-conscious traveler will find reasonable lodging despite Park City's avalanche of luxury condos and resort hotels. During the winter, the **Chateâu Lodge** rents out dorm-style beds just 150 yards from the lifts

(649-9372 or 800-357-3556; $27; free continental breakfast; reserve in advance). A wide range of restaurants line Main St. You can get a delicious meal for under $10 at **Main St. Pizza and Noodle,** 530 Main St. (645-8878. Open M-Th 11:30am-10pm, F 11:30am-11pm, Sa 11am-11pm, Su 11:30am-9:30pm.) Grab a burger ($7-8) and a beer ($3.50) at the **Wasatch Brew Pub,** 250 Main St. (645-9500; open daily 11am-10pm). While on Main St., don't forget the **Alamo,** 447 Main St., to shoot pool and check out the local rugby scene. (649-2380. Sponsor or $5 membership required. Live music F-Sa nights, in winter every day. Open M-Sa noon-2am, Su noon-midnight; food served until 11pm).

Park City's **visitors center:** 528 Main St. (649-6104; open M-Sa 10am-7pm, Su 12am-6pm; in May and Oct. daily noon-5pm). Neither Greyhound nor Amtrak service the city, but many shuttle companies offer a lift to the lifts from Salt Lake City. **Lewis Bros. Stages** (800-826-5844) shuttles between the Salt Lake airport and Park city at least once an hr. in winter for under $30. Reservations required. **Post Office:** 450 Main St. (open M-F 9am-5pm, Sa 10am-1:30pm). **ZIP code:** 84060. **Area code:** 435.

# DINOSAUR NATIONAL MONUMENT AND VERNAL

**Dinosaur National Monument** was created in 1915, seven years after paleontologist Earl Douglass happened upon an array of fossilized dinosaur bones. Since then, the Monument has been enlarged to include the vast and colorful gorges created by the Green and Yampa Rivers. It is difficult to imagine that these harsh range lands, where temperatures can vary 150°F between winter and summer, were once the home to horsetail ferns and grazing dinosaurs. The town of Vernal, west of Dinosaur on U.S. 40, is a popular base for exploring the Monument, Flaming Gorge, and the Uinta Mountains.

**⚄ PRACTICAL INFORMATION. Greyhound,** 15 South Vernal Ave. (789-0404), at Frontier Travel near the corner Main St. in Vernal, makes daily runs east and west along U.S. 40 (2 each way), stopping in Dinosaur, CO en route from Denver and Salt Lake City. Jensen is a flag stop, as is Monument headquarters, 2mi. west of Dinosaur, CO. The park collects an **entrance fee** of $10 per car, and $5 per biker, pedestrian, or tour-bus passenger. The Monument's more interesting and varied **west side** lies along Rt. 149 off U.S. 40 just outside of Jensen and 30mi. east of Vernal. The rugged **east side** of the park is accessible only from a road off U.S. 40, outside Dinosaur, CO. The **Dinosaur Quarry Visitors Center** (789-2115), near the fee collection booth, is accessible only by a free shuttle bus running every 15min. or an uphill ½mi. walk in the summer; in the winter you can drive up to the center (open daily 8am-6pm; in winter 8am-4:30pm). The **Dinosaur National Monument Headquarters** (970-374-3000) is on the other side of the park at the intersection of U.S. 40 and the park road in Dinosaur, CO (open May-Sept. daily 8am-4:30pm; Sept.-May M-F 8am-4:30pm). No services are available in the park; fill up in Dinosaur, Jensen, or Vernal. The **Ashley National Forest Service Office,** 355 N. Vernal Ave. (789-1181), in Vernal, has info about hiking, biking, and camping in the surrounding forests (open M-F 8am-5pm). The **Utah Fieldhouse** (see **Sights,** p. 697) has visitor info for northeastern Utah. **Post Office:** in Vernal, on the corner of 67 N. and 800 W. (789-2393; open M-F 9am-5pm, Sa 10am-1pm). **ZIP code:** 84078. **Area code:** 435.

**⌂⍓ ACCOMMODATIONS AND FOOD.** For the lowdown on campgrounds, contact the park visitors center. **Green River Campground** consists of 88 shaded sites along the Green River (flush toilets, water, RVs, disabled sites; sites $12; open late spring to early fall). There are also several free **primitive campsites** in and around the park. Thirteen mi. east of Harper's Corner, off a four-wheel drive road (impassable when wet) on the park's east side, **Echo Park Campground** provides the perfect location for a crystalline evening under the stars (vault toilets and water; 8 sites $6). Free **backcountry camping** permits are available from the headquarters or from Quarry Center. Outside the park, **Campground Dina RV Park,** 930 N. Vernal Ave., about 1mi. north of Main St. on U.S. 191, is a great bet for a shady, comfortable

**THE WILD BUNCH** Of all the stalwart pioneers and daring outlaws of the Old West, perhaps **Butch Cassidy** is most deeply etched in the era's legends. The "Robin Hood of the West" rose to notoriety as a cunning train and bank robber. He later joined forces with the **Sundance Kid** to form the Wild Bunch, a group of thieving renegades who worked out of Brown's Park and wreaked havoc on Utah, Colorado, and Wyoming. Vernal's **Outlaw Trail Theater** brings the Cassidy lore back to life in its outdoor musical *Cassidy: The Mostly True Story of Butch Cassidy and the Wild Bunch*. This lively production fires from the hip, consciously blurring the distinction between the myth and the man. The show runs from late June through early Aug.; call 789-6932 or 800-477-5558 for tickets and info.

spot to pitch a tent. (789-2148 or 800-245-2148. Heated pool, showers, laundry, convenience store. Grassy sites $6.50 per person, $2 ages 7-17; full hookup $20.)

For those less inclined to rough it, Vernal is civilization's beacon. The comfortable **Sage Motel,** 54 W. Main St., has big, clean rooms, A/C, cable TV, and free local calls. (789-1442 or 800-760-1442. Singles $39, doubles $42; 2 beds $47; $56 per additional person.) The **Lazy K Motel,** on U.S. 40, has clean, minimalist rooms, on the outskirts of town toward the monument (789-3277; singles $25; doubles $30).

The **Seven Eleven Cafe,** 77 E. Main St., in Vernal, serves resolutely American food, including big breakfasts with eggs, ham, hash browns, and toast for under $5 and dinners with a soup, salad, potato, and bread (but no Big Gulp) from $7 (789-1170; open M-Sa 6am-10pm). The party lives at **LaLa's Fiesta,** 550 E. Main St. Lunch and dinner specialties begin with the *chile relleno* ($5 for 2), and all meals are under $9. (789-2966. Open M-Sa 11am-9pm; if busy, open later and on Su.)

🔳 🔏 **SIGHTS AND ACTIVITIES.** The star attraction is the dinosaur quarry display at the **Quarry Visitors Center** (see **Practical Info,** above). Some of the most complete dinosaur skeletons in the world can still be seen encased in the rock in which they were buried. Excellent exhibits inform visitors about the life of dinosaurs and the excavation process. Also in the western section of the park, ancient *petroglyphs* are visible along the road that accesses the campsites, both at Cub Creek and beyond the campgrounds themselves. Pick up a *Tour of the Tilted Rocks* pamphlet (50¢) right after the visitors center turn-off and take the auto tour through the impressive split mountain area. Petroglyph sites are marked along the tour trail and are easily reached by short hikes up the hillsides. The **Desert Voices Trail** along the tour is a moderate 2mi. loop that rewards hikers with a sweeping view of the surrounding mountains.

In the eastern section of the park, the 25mi. road (closed in winter) to majestic **Harper's Corner,** at the junction of the Green and Yampa River gorges, begins. From the road's terminus, a 2mi. round-trip hike leads to a view of the Green and Yampa Rivers and sculpted rock formations. **Dan Hatch River Expeditions,** in Vernal, arranges a wide variety of summer rafting trips along the rivers running through the monument and in Flaming Gorge, below. Trips meet at 221 N. 400 E. (789-4316 or 800-342-8243. 1-day voyage $62, age 6-12 $56; seniors 10% off.)

In Vernal, the **Utah Fieldhouse of Natural History and Dinosaur Garden,** 235 Main St., has visitor info and offers excellent displays on the state's history. The dinosaur garden features life-size models, and geological displays feature fluorescent minerals that make your shoelaces glow in the dark. (789-3799. Open daily 8am-9pm, off-season 8am-5pm. $2, under 6 free, families $5.)

# FLAMING GORGE

Seen at sunset, the contrast between the red canyon lands and the aquamarine water of the Green River makes the landscape glow, hence the moniker "Flaming Gorge." In 1963, the Green River was dammed, giving rise to the creation of **Flaming Gorge National Recreation Area,** a diverse stretch of land ranging from cool pine and aspen forests of Utah to the beautiful deserts of Wyoming. Each year, doomed trout are placed in Flaming Gorge Reservoir, sacrificed to provide some of the best fishing in the state. Waterskiing, boating, and hiking are popular here, too.

The Green River Gorge below the dam teems with trout, making for top-notch **fishing,** and the Green River offers some of the best fly fishing in the country. To fish, obtain a **permit,** available at Flaming Gorge Lodge, Dutch John Recreation Services, and most stores in Manila. For more info, call the **Utah Division of Wildlife Resources,** 1594 W. North Temple (800-538-4700), in Salt Lake City (open M-F 7:30am-6pm). **Cedar Springs Marina** (889-3795), 3mi. before the dam, rents boats. (Pontoon boats for 8 people from $90 for 3hr., from $160 per day. Ski boats for 6 $110 for 3hr., $190 per day; skis $15 per day. Open daily 8am-6pm.) Nearby, friendly **Flaming Gorge Lodge** (889-3773) rents fishing rods ($10 per day). At **Lucerne Valley Marina,** 7mi. east of Manila off Rt. 43, you can procure a small, 14 ft. fishing boat for $75, plus a $50 deposit per day (784-3483; open daily, around 7am-9pm).

The **Sheep Creek Geologic Loop,** an 11mi. scenic drive off Hwy. 530 just south of Manila, takes you past rock strata and wildlife. For a hideout from tourists, the valley of **Brown's Park,** 23mi. east of Flaming Gorge, is accessible via narrow, hilly, sometimes paved roads winding through three states. Nineteenth-century Western outlaws **Butch Cassidy, the Sundance Kid,** and their **Wild Bunch** found the valley's isolation and its proximity to three state lines ideal for evading the law (see p. 697).

Inexpensive **campgrounds** flourish in the Flaming Gorge area; ask for a pamphlet listing all the campgrounds (no electricity) at either visitors center (800-280-2267 for reservations). For an excellent view of the Reservoir and Red Canyon, pitch your tent next to the visitors center in **Canyon Rim Campground** (18 sites $12; open mid-May to mid-Sept.), or in one of the numerous national forest campgrounds along U.S. 191 and Rt. 44 in the Utah portion of the park (sites $11; 16-day max. stay). The most sought-after sites in the area are at the **Dripping Spring campground;** its 18 wooded, semi-private sites are near prime fishing spots ($12 plus recreation pass; $3 for extra vehicle). Farther north, **Buckboard Crossing** ($13) and **Lucerne Valley** ($12), are drier and unshaded, and close to the marinas on the reservoir (both open mid-Apr. to mid-Oct.). A number of **free primitive sites** hide in the high country; check with the rangers first.

If you'd rather sleep indoors, **Red Canyon Lodge** west on Rt. 44, 2mi. before the visitors center, offers reasonably priced, rustic cabins. (889-3759. Single cabins $35, with private bath $50; doubles $50/$60; $6 per additional adult; $2 per child under 12; rollaway beds $6 per night.) There's also a private 20-acre lake stocked with trout, a free kids' fishing pool, and a good restaurant.

From Wyoming, travel on U.S. 191 S to the Gorge through the untouched high desert. A recreation pass, necessary for "recreating" in the area, is $2 and can be obtained at the **Flaming Gorge Visitors Center** (885-3135), on U.S. 191 atop the Flaming Gorge Dam, offers free tours of the dam (open daily 8am-6pm; off-season 9am-5pm). A few mi. off U.S. 191 and 3mi. off Rt. 44 to Manila, the **Red Canyon Visitors Center** (889-3713) hangs 1360 ft. above Red Canyon (open daily 10am-5pm; closed in winter). **Post Office:** 4 South Blvd. (885-3351), in Dutch John (open M-F 7:30am-3:30pm, Sa 9:30am-12:30pm). **ZIP code:** 84023. **Area code:** 435.

## MOAB

Moab first flourished in the 1950s, when uranium miners rushed to the area and transformed the town from a quiet hamlet into a gritty desert outpost. Today, the mountain bike has replaced the Geiger counter, as tourists rush into the town eager to bike the red slickrock, raft whitewater rapids, or explore surrounding Arches and Canyonlands National Parks. The town itself has changed to accommodate the new visitors and athletes; microbreweries and t-shirt shops now fill the rooms of the old uranium building on Main St.

**◪ PRACTICAL INFORMATION.** Moab sits 50mi. southeast of I-70 on U.S. 191, 5mi. south of Arches. **Amtrak** comes only as close as Green River, 52mi. northwest of town. Greyhound's closest stop is in Crescent Juntion, 32mi. north of Moab at the junction of Hwy. 191 and I-70. Some hotels and hostels will pick guests up from these distant points for a small fee. **Bighorn Express** (587-3061 or 888-655-7433) makes trips from the Salt Lake City airport to Moab ($49; open M-F 9am-5pm, Sa 10am-2pm; reservations required). **Coyote Shuttle** (259-8656) will also take you where you want to go (rates and hrs. vary). The **Moab Information Center**, 3 Center St., doles out info on the city and nearby parks and monuments. (Open daily 8am-9pm; Sept.-Oct. and Apr.-May 8am-7pm; May-June 8am-8pm; Nov. 9am-7pm, Dec.-Mar. 9am-5pm.) **Post Office:** 50 E. 100 N. St. (259-7427; open M-F 8:30am-5pm, Sa 8:30am-noon). **ZIP code:** 84532. **Area code:** 435.

**⌐ ACCOMMODATIONS.** Chain motels clutter Main St., but Moab fills up fast in the summer, especially on weekends; call ahead. Off-season rates can drop as much as 50%, and during that time the weather is more conducive to hiking. John Wayne and you too! can sleep at ▓ **Apache Motel**, 166 S. 400 E. (259-5755; $29-73; AAA discount). The owners of the **Lazy Lizard International Hostel (AAIH/Rucksackers)**, 1213 S. U.S. 191, look for the "A1 Self Storage" sign 1mi. south of Moab on U.S. 191), go out of their way to be helpful—they'll pick you up (usually for $10-15) and arrange trips through local companies. The kitchen, VCR, laundry, and hot tub are at your disposal. (259-6057. Bunks $8 per person. Private rooms for 1 or 2 from $20. Cabins from $25. Tent sites $6. No curfew.) A miner's hat, fishing nets, and a Victrola accent the quirky and luxurious theme rooms of **Hotel Off Center**, 96 E. Center St., a block off Main St. (259-4244; shared bath; open Mar.-Nov.; dorm rooms $12; singles $39; doubles $49). **The Prospector Lodge,** 186 N. 1st W. St., a block west of Main St., offers cool, comfy rooms with TV and free java (259-5145. Singles $34. Doubles $41, with a queen-size bed $48. $6 per additional person).

**Arches National Park** (see p. 700) has the area's best campground. In town, the **Canyonlands Campground,** 555 S. Main St., next to the Shell Station, provides well-shaded sites and a pool. (259-6848 or 800-522-6848. Sites for two $15, with water and electricity $18, full hookup $20; $3 per additional adult or teen.) **Slickrock Campground,** 1301½ Hwy. 191, beckons the budget traveler with the slogan, "funpigs stay at Slickrock." Yes, "funpig"—a person who relaxes and has fun. (259-7660 or 800-448-8873. Pool, 3 hot tubs, showers, and laundry. Tent sites $17, with water and electricity $21, full hookup $23. Cabins with A/C $30 plus $5 per extra person.)

**⌐ FOOD.** I say, what about **Breakfast at Tiffany's,** 90 E. Center? The owner has gone to great pains to decorate with authentic retro furniture and accessories. Menu all $6 and under. (259-2553; open daily 7am-3pm; lunch 11:30-3pm). Seating on the patio or inside among simulated redrocks heightens the pleasure of fresh lunch wraps like the Ragin' Cajun ($7) at **Honest Ozzie's Café,** 60 N. 100 W. Veggie and vegan menu items complement a wide variety of fresh, quick meals. (259-8442. Open W-M 8am-3pm.) Retro diner decor lives on at **The Moab Diner and Ice Cream Shoppe,** 189 S. Main St., with veggie specials and excellent french fries. (259-4006. Sandwiches and burgers $5-6. Open Su-Th 6am-10pm, F-Sa 6am-10:30pm.) **Moab Community Coop,** 111 N. 100 W, a block off Main St., can fill your saddlebags with fresh produce, as well as organic and health foods for your journey. (259-5712. Open M-F 9am-6pm, Sa 9-10:30am, 1-6pm.)

After a hot day in the desert, cool off at the **Peach Tree Juice Cafe,** 20 Main St. with a $2.25 smoothie (259-6333). The **Moab Brewery,** 686 S. Main St., serves delicious food (full meals all under $10) and their own ales (259-6333; open Su-Th 11:30am-10pm, F-Sa 11:30am-11pm). A search for live music will lead to **The Rio Colorado Restaurant and Bar,** 200 S. 100 W. St., off Main St. (259-6666. Restaurant open F-Sa 3pm-8:30pm, Su-Th 3-10pm, bar open until 2am M-Sa, midnight Su.)

**▓▓ ⌐ SIGHTS AND ACTIVITIES. Mountain biking** and **rafting,** along with nearby national parks, are the big draws in Moab. The **Slickrock** trail is a 10mi. loop which rolls up and down the slickrock outside of Moab. The trail has no big vertical gain, but it's technically difficult, and temperatures often reach 100°F. **Rim Cyclery,** 94 W. 1st St., one of the first mountain bike shops in southern Utah, rents bikes and distributes info about the slickrock trails (259-5333; $30-35 per day includes helmet; open daily 9am-6pm).

Countless raft companies are based in Moab. ■ **OARS/North American River Expeditions,** 543 N. Main offers great deals and the best guides on the rivers. (259-5865, 800-342-5938. ½-day trip, including snacks and a natural history lesson $34, ages 5-17 $26.) **Western River Expeditions** offers good deals as well. (259-7019 or 800-453-7450; ½-day $32, children $25; full-day $44/$32; includes lunch.) Various Moab outfitters also arrange horseback, motorboat, canoe, jeep, and helicopter rides. **Pack Creek Ranch** offers horseback rides into the La Sal Mountains (259-5505; 1½hr.; $20 per person).

Albert Christensen spent 12 years creating the bizarre **Hole 'n the Rock,** 15mi. south of Moab on U.S. 191, a 14-room house carved out of a sandstone cliff. His wife Gladys kept the dream alive after his death in 1957 and opened the house to the public. Christensen's nearby rendering of Franklin D. Roosevelt is somethin', really somethin'.' (668-2250. Open daily mid-Apr. to mid. Oct. 9am-6pm; late Oct. to early Apr. 9am-5pm. $2.75, kids $1.75, includes informative tour.) Utah's only winery, **Arches Vineyards,** 420 Kane Creek, is located in the Moab area (259-5397; tasting room open M-Sa noon-8pm; free).

## FINDING THE FAB FIVE

The five **National Parks** that cover this majestic area can be reached by several roads. From Moab, take U.S. 191 N 5mi. to **Arches** (see below). Continue north on U.S. 191 to Rt. 313 S, which will lead to the Islands in the Sky area of **Canyonlands** (60mi.; see p. 702). Or, take U.S. 191 south from Moab to Rt. 211 W to reach the Needles area of Canyonlands (87mi.). To reach **Capitol Reef** (see p. 703), continue driving north on U.S. 191 and then I-70 going west; leave I-70 at exit 147, and follow Rt. 24 S to Hanksville and then west to the park (81mi. from I-70). Rt. 24 W runs to Torrey, where scenic Rt. 12 branches south and west through the Dixie National Forest to **Bryce Canyon** (see p. 704). For **Zion** (see p. 706), continue on Rt. 12 W to U.S. 89 S through Mt. Carmel Jct., and pick up Rt. 9 W.

The two national forests in Southern Utah are divided into districts, some of which lie near the national parks and serve as excellent places to stay on a cross-country jaunt. **Manti-La Sal National Forest** has two sections near Arches and the Needles area of Canyonlands. **Dixie National Forest** stretches from Capitol Reef through Bryce all the way to the western side of Zion.

# ARCHES

"This is the most beautiful place on earth," novelist Edward Abbey wrote of **Arches National Park.** Thousands of sandstone arches, spires, pinnacles, and fins tower above the desert in overwhelming grandeur. Some arches are so perfect in form that early explorers believed they were constructed by a lost civilization. Deep red sandstone, green pinyon trees and juniper bushes, ominous grey thunderclouds, and a strikingly blue sky combine to etch an unforgettable palette of color.

■ **PRACTICAL INFORMATION.** The park entrance is on U.S. 191, 5mi. north of Moab. Although no public transportation serves the park, shuttle bus companies travel to both the national park and Moab from surrounding towns and cities (see Moab **Practical Information,** p. 698). While most visitors come in the summer, 100°F temperatures make hiking difficult; bring at least one gallon (3.8L) of water per person per day. The weather is best in the spring and fall when temperate days and nights combine to make a comfortable stay. In the winter, white snow provides a brilliant contrast to the red arches. The **visitors center** (259-8161), to the right of the entrance station, distributes free park service maps (open daily mid-Apr. to Sept. 7:30am-6pm, in winter 8am-4:30pm). An **entrance pass** covers admission for a week ($10 per carload, $5 per pedestrian or biker). Write the **Superintendent,** Arches National Park, P.O. Box 907, Moab 84532. For more details on accommodations, food, and activities, see **Moab,** p. 699. **Area code:** 435.

**140 superb hostels = 1 dynamic way to see the USA!**

# Phone ahead to book your bed with Hostelling International!

# 1 800 909 4776

It's quick and easy to make reservations at these HI hostels. Call 1-800-909-4776 (the call is free from anywhere in the USA). At the prompt, enter the hostel's 2 digit access code listed below. You will then be connected directly to the hostel and you can be on your way!

# www.hiayh.org

## California
74  Klamath
05  Los Angeles/Santa Monica
25  Los Angeles/Fullerton
26  Los Angeles/South Bay
63  Midpines/Yosemite
64  Montara
73  Pescadero
61  Point Reyes Nat'l Seashore
40  Sacramento
42  San Clemente
43  San Diego/Downtown
44  San Diego/Point Loma
03  San Francisco/ Fisherman's Wharf
02  San Francisco/Downtown
45  Santa Cruz
62  Sausalito
82  Tecopa (Death Valley)

## Colorado
67  Denver
69  Durango
19  Estes Park
75  Glenwood Springs

## Connecticut
21  Hartford

## District of Columbia
04  Washington, DC

## Florida
16  Clearwater Beach
55  Key West
65  Melbourne Beach
06  Miami Beach
33  Orlando

## Illinois
10  Chicago

## Louisiana
09  New Orleans

## Maine
38  Portland

## Massachusetts
07  Boston
14  Cape Cod/Eastham
15  Cape Cod/Truro
78  Littleton
27  Martha's Vineyard
29  Nantucket

## Missouri
70  St. Louis

## New Hampshire
51  White Mountains

## New Jersey
83  Layton

## New York
60  Buffalo
01  New York City
31  Niagara Falls
59  Syracuse

## North Carolina
54  Kitty Hawk

## Ohio
11  Akron/Cleveland
18  Columbus
52  Malabar Farm/Lucas

## Oregon
39  Portland
76  Portland/Northwest
46  Seaside

## Pennsylvania
17  Collegeville
22  La Anna
30  Newtown
79  Ohiopyle State Park
35  Philadelphia/ Chamounix Mansion
36  Pine Grove Furnace State Park
66  Pittsburgh

## South Dakota
77  Deadwood

## Texas
41  San Antonio

## Utah
71  Salt Lake City

## Vermont
68  White River Junction

## Virginia
81  Galax
50  Virginia Beach

## Washington
08  Seattle
37  Port Townsend
49  Vashon Island/Seattle

## Wisconsin
24  Laona
80  Madison

# For more information on these and other HI hostels call 1·202·783·6161

HOSTELLING INTERNATIONAL

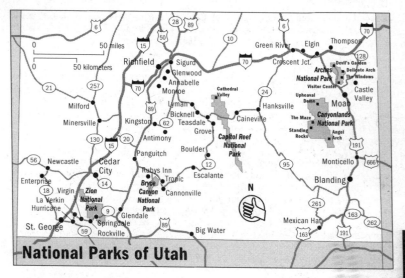

**National Parks of Utah**

**█ CAMPGROUNDS.** The park's only campground, **Devil's Garden,** has 52 excellent campsites nestled amid pinon pines and giant red sandstone formations. The campsite is within walking distance of the Devil's Garden and Broken Arch trailheads; however, it is a long 18mi. from the visitors center. Because Devil's Garden doesn't take reservations, sites go quickly in summer. In spring and fall, visitors show up early in preparation for the rush; a line forms at the visitors center at 7:30am. (Sites $10, in winter $5. No wood-gathering. Running water mid-Mar. to Oct.; 1-week max. stay.)

If the heat becomes unbearable at Arches, the aspen forests of the **Manti-La Sal National Forest** offer respite. (Take Rt. 128 along the Colorado River and turn right at Castle Valley; or go south 21mi. from Moab on 191 7mi. and turn off to the left.) These beautiful sites sit 4000 ft. above the national park and are usually several degrees cooler. All sites cost $8, except the free sites at **Oowah Lake.** Oowah, 3mi. down a dirt road, is a rainbow trout haven. Fishing permits are available at most stores in Moab and at the Forest Service office ($5 per day). For more info, contact the Manti-La Sal National Forest Service Office in Moab, 3.2mi. south of the zero axis in town off Main, on Resource Rd. 84532 (259-7155; open M-F 8am-4:30pm).

**█ █ SIGHTS AND ACTIVITIES.** The majority of Arches' National Park is not visible from the 18mi. road. Bikes are only allowed on two-wheel drive roads, so the best way to see the park is by foot. There are thousands of natural arches in the park, and each one is pinpointed on the free map and guide that is passed out at the fee collection booth. At the end of the paved road, **Devil's Garden** boasts an astounding 64 arches, while a challenging hike from the **Landscape Arch** leads across harrowing exposures to the secluded **Double O Arch.** The highlight of your visit should be the free-standing **Delicate Arch,** the symbol of the park and of the state of Utah; take the Delicate Arch turn-off from the main road, and follow it 2mi. to the trail head. From Wolfe Ranch, the homestead of Civil War veteran John Wesley Wolfe, a 1½mi. foot trail leads to the arch. Beyond, you can catch a glimpse of the Colorado River Gorge and the La Sal Mountains. Visitors occasionally come across petroglyphs left on the stone walls by the Anasazi and Ute who wandered the area centuries ago.

Arches aren't the only natural wonders here. One of the more popular trails, the moderately strenuous 2mi. **Fiery Furnace Trail,** leads down into the canyon bottoms, providing new perspective on the imposing cliffs and monoliths above. Only experienced hikers should attempt this trail. Rangers lead groups from the visitors center into the labyrinth twice daily in summer. ($6, children $3. Tours tend to fill up 2 days before; reservations can be made 7 days in advance in person).

## CANYONLANDS

Those who make the trek to **Canyonlands National Park** are rewarded with a pleasant surprise: the absence of an overabundance of people. The sandstone spires, the roughly cut canyons, and vibrantly colored rock layers of this truly awe-inspiring landscape are often passed-up by those on a time budget. The Green and Colorado Rivers divide the park into three sections. The **Needles** region (visitors center 259-4711, open daily 8am-5pm) contains spires, arches, canyons, and Native American ruins, but is not as rough as the Maze area. To get to the Needles, take Rt. 211 W from U.S. 191, about 40mi. south of Moab. Farther north, **Island in the Sky** (visitors center 259-4712, open daily 8am-5pm), a towering mesa which sits within the "Y" formed by the two rivers, affords fantastic views of the surrounding canyons and mountains; take Rt. 313 W from U.S. 191 about 10mi. north of Moab. The most remote district of the park, the rugged **Maze** area (ranger station 259-2652, open daily 8am-4:30pm), is a veritable hurly-burly of twisted canyons made for *über*-pioneers with four-wheel-drive vehicles only. Once you've entered a section of the park, getting to a different section involves retracing your steps and reentering the park, a tedious trip that can last from several hours to a full day.

**⌧ PRACTICAL INFORMATION AND FOOD.** Monticello's **Multiagency Visitors Center**, 117 S. Main. St. (587-3235 or 800-574-4386), sells area maps ($4-8; open M-F 8am-5pm, Sa-Su 10am-5pm). **Entrance fees:** $10 per car and $5 per hiker or cyclist. Write to **Canyonlands National Park,** 2282 S. West Resource Blvd., Moab 84532 (259-7164). **Moab** makes an excellent base town for exploring the park (see p. 698). *There are no gas, water, or food services in the park.* Just outside the boundary in the Needles district, however, the **Needles Outpost** (979-4007) houses a limited and expensive grocery store and gas pump (open daily 8:30am-6pm). Hauling in groceries, water, and first-aid supplies from Moab or Monticello makes the most sense for travelers on a budget. **Area code:** 435.

**⌧ CAMPGROUNDS AND HIKING.** Before **backcountry camping** or **hiking,** outdoors-types must register at the proper visitors center for one of a limited number of permits. ($10 for backpack and overnight permit. Backcountry voyages not recommended in summer.) Four-wheel drivers should also register at the visitors center ($25 permit). Each region has its own official **campground.** In the Needles district, **Squaw Flat's** 26 sites occupy a sandy plain surrounded by giant sandstone towers, 40mi. west of U.S. 191 on Rt. 211. In June, insects swarm. Fuel is not abundant and water is not available Oct.-Mar. (sites $8; Oct.-Mar. free). **Willow Flat Campground,** in the Island in the Sky district, sits high atop the mesa on Rt. 313, 41mi.

---

**ABBEY'S ROAD** For many, the essays and novels of **Edward Abbey** most eloquently capture the harsh beauty of the American West. Born in Pennsylvania, he fell in love with the region upon his first visit, and devoted the rest of his life to fiercely defending it from the United States' westward march of "progress." He spent three seasons as a park ranger at Arches National Park, delighting in the solitude of the desert. Abbey penned a celebrated series of essays on life in the desert based on his years spent wandering around Moab and Canyonlands. He captured their enigmatic beauty in his passionate and often acerbic manner—Abbey's passages vividly evoke the unforgiving, sun-parched landscape he loved. *The Monkey Wrench Gang,* Abbey's novel about an amusingly radical foursome rebelling against the pillaging of the wilderness, became the inspiration for Earth First!, an activist environmental group As Abbey once wrote, "For us the wilderness and human emptiness of this land is not a source of fear but the greatest of its attractions."

west off U.S. 191 (12 sites $5 in summer, free in off-season; pit toilets). You must bring your own water. Willow Flat and Squaw Flat both provide picnic tables and grills. The backcountry campground at the **Maze Overlook** offers no amenities. All campgrounds operate on a first come, first served basis.

Each visitors center has a brochure of possible hikes and advice on length and difficulty. With summer temperatures regularly climbing over 100°F, at least 1 gallon of water per person per day is a must. Hiking options from the Needles area are probably the best developed. Try a trail from Grand Viewpoint Overlook. Island in the Sky offers spectacular views. In the Maze district, a 6hr., 6mi. guided hike into Horseshoe Canyon leaves the Horseshoe Canyon Trailhead at 9am on Sa, and Su. If hiking in desert heat doesn't appeal to you, you can rent Jeeps or mountain bikes in Moab.

For some great overlooks at elevations above 8000 ft., the **Monticello District** of the **Manti-La Sal National Forest,** south of Needles, delivers. This section of the forest has two campgrounds on **Blue Mountain. Buckboard,** 6½mi. west of U.S. 191 (16 sites, 10 with full hook-up), and **Dalton Springs,** 5mi. west of U.S. 191 (18 sites, 16 with full-hookup). Both campgrounds operate from late May to Sept. and charge $8.50 per site. From Moab, head south on U.S. 191 to Monticello and then west on Rt. 1 S. More info on the Monticello District awaits at the **Multi-Agency Visitors Center** (see Practical Information, above) and the **Manti-La Sal National Forest Service office** in Monticello, 496 E. Central Ave. (587-2401), on U.S. 666 just east of town (open M-F 8am-4:30pm).

Farther away, **Dead Horse Point State Park** (entrance fee $5; visitors center open daily 8am-5pm) perches on the rim of the Colorado Gorge. The park, south of Arches and 14mi. south of U.S. 191, accessible from Rt. 313, offers camping, with water, hookups, and covered picnic tables ($11; 21 sites, ½ are available on a first come, first served basis). Write the **Park Superintendent,** Dead Horse Point State Park, P.O. Box 609, Moab 84532 (259-2614 or 800-322-3770; open daily 6am-10pm).

# CAPITOL REEF

A geologist's fantasy and **Capitol Reef National Park's** feature attraction, the Waterpocket Fold bisects the park, presenting visitors with 65 million years of stratified natural history. This 100mi. furrow in the earth's crust, with its rocky scales and spines, winds through Capitol Reef like a giant Cretaceous serpent. The sheer cliffs that border the Fold were originally called a "reef," not for their oceanic origins, but because they posed a barrier to travel.

**◪ PRACTICAL INFORMATION.** The middle link in the Fab Five chain, east of Zion and Bryce Canyon and west of Arches and Canyonlands, Capitol Reef is unreachable by major bus lines. The closest Greyhound stop is in Green River. For a fee, **Wild Hare Expeditions** (see Sites and Activities below) will provide a shuttle service between Richfield and the park. **Entrance** to the park is free except for the scenic drive that costs $4 per vehicle. The **visitors center** (425-3791), on Rt. 24, supplies travelers with waterproof topographical maps ($8), regular maps ($4), free brochures on trails, and info on daily activities such as ranger-led jaunts (open daily 8am-6pm; Sept.-May 8am-4:30pm). The free park newspaper, *The Cliffline*, lists a schedule of park activities. *When hiking, keep in mind that summer temperatures average 95°F, and beware of flash-floods after rain.* Contact the **Superintendent,** Capitol Reef National Park, HC 70 Box 15, Torrey 84775 (425-3791). **Post Office:** 222 E. Main St. (425-3488), in Torrey (open M-F 7:30am-1:30pm, Sa 7:30-11am). **ZIP code:** 84775. **Area code:** 435.

**▌◫ ACCOMMODATIONS AND FOOD.** The park's campgrounds provide sites on a first come, first served basis. The main campground, **Fruita,** 1.3mi. south off Rt. 24, presides over 71 sites (1 reserved for the disabled), with drinking water and toilets ($10). Sites are nestled among orchards; visitors can eat the fruit. **Cedar Mesa Campground,** in the park's south end, and **Cathedral Valley,** in the north, have only 5 sites each; neither has water or a paved road—but hey, they're free. To get to Cedar Mesa, take Rt. 24 past the visitors center to Notom-Bullfrog Rd. and head about 25mi. south. Cathedral Valley is accessible only by four-wheel-drive or on foot. Both of these sites and unmarked backcountry campsites require a free **backcountry permit,** easily obtainable at the visitors center. Outside the park, off scenic Rt. 12 between Boulder and Capitol Reef, a stretch of **Dixie National Forest** shelters 3 lovely campgrounds. All perch at elevations over 8000 ft. and have drinking water and pit toilets (first come, first served sites $7; open May-Sept.). The **Oak Creek Campground** includes 8 sites, and the **Pleasant Creek Campground** has 18 sites. **Single Tree Campground** offers 26 sites and 2 family sites, one of which can be reserved ahead of time (800-283-2267). Visitors can ask the **Teasdale Ranger District Office** (425-3702) for more info.

If you'd prefer a roof over your head, a trip to **Torrey,** 11mi. west of the visitors center on Rt. 24, will do you right. As far as roofs go, the **Trading Post,** 75 W. Main St., offers the best bang for your buck. Small cabins sleep up to 4 people and share a common bath (425-3716; $29). Across the street, **The Chuck Wagon Motel and General Store,** in the center of Torrey on Rt. 24 W, has a barbecue area, a beautiful pool, and both a new and old building. The store comes through with a good selection of groceries, sports equipment, baked goods, and picnic ware. (Motel 425-3335. New buidling: wood-paneled rooms with A/C and phones. Singles $54. Doubles $58. Older building: no A/C or phone. Singles $31. Doubles $36. Store 425-3288. Open daily 7am-9pm. Closed Oct. 31 to Mar. 31.) The **Boulder View Inn,** 385 W. Main St., provides comfortable rooms (425-3800; from $30).

A meal at the **Capitol Reef Inn and Café,** 360 W. Main St., in Torrey, features local rainbow trout (smoked or grilled) and a dining room that looks out on the russet hills. The grilled trout sandwich ($6.75) comes with a 10-vegetable salad. (425-3271. Open Apr.-Oct. daily 7am-11pm.) Greasier repast awaits at **Brink's Burgers,** 163 E. Main St. (425-3710), in Torrey (various burgers $2-4; open daily 11am-9pm).

**◑ ♨ SIGHTS AND ACTIVITIES.** The Reef's haunting landforms can be explored from the seat of your car on the 25mi. scenic drive, a 1½hr. (round-trip) jaunt next to the cliffs along paved and improved dirt roads. Along Rt. 24, you can ponder the bathroom-sized **Fruita Schoolhouse** built by Mormon settlers, 1000-year-old **petroglyphs** etched on the stone walls, and **Panorama Point. Chimney Rock** and the Castle are two of the more striking and abstruse of sandstone formations along the route.

For many of the park's most spectacular vistas visitors must temporarily abandon their air-conditioned comfort. **Wild Hare Expeditions,** 2600 E. Hwy. 24, in the Best Western Capitol Reef Resort, embarks on a variety of backpacking and hiking tours (425-3999 or 888-304-4273. $40-50 per ½-day, children $35. Full-day $60-75, children $50. Scenic drives and four-wheel-drive tours are also available.)

For a change of scenery, the bucolic **orchards** which lie within the park in the Fruita region might suffice. Guests can eat as much fruit as they like while in the orchards, but cold, hard cash is necessary to take some home.

# BRYCE CANYON

In the Southwest, nature enjoys painting with a big brush on a big canvas, yet at **Bryce Canyon National Park,** she discarded her usual tools for finer instruments; the slender hoodoos—otherworldly limestone spires of pink, red, and white—populate the canyon with unique grace and delicacy. What it lacks in Grand Canyon-esque magnitude, Bryce makes up for in intricate beauty. Early in the morning or in the evening the sun's rays bring the hoodoos to life, transforming them into color-changing chameleons. As Ebenezer Bryze, a Mormon carpenter with a gift for understatement, put it, the canyon is "one hell of a place to lose a cow."

**⁊ PRACTICAL INFORMATION.** Approaching from the west, Bryce Canyon lies 1½hr. east of Cedar City; take Rt. 14 to U.S. 89. From the east, take I-70 to U.S. 89, turn east on Rt. 12 at Bryce Jct. (7mi. south of Panguitch), and drive 14mi. to the

Rt. 63 junction; head south 4mi. to the park entrance. There is no public transportation to Bryce Canyon. The park's **entrance fee** is $10 per car, $5 per pedestrian.

**Visitors center:** (834-5322), just inside the park. (Open Jun.-Aug. 8am-8pm; Apr.-May and Sept.-Oct. 8am-6pm; Nov.-Mar. 8am-4:30pm.) Or, write the Superintendent, Bryce Canyon National Park, Bryce Canyon 84717. **Emergency:** 676-2411. **Post office:** in Bryce Lodge (834-5361; open M-F 8am-noon and 1-5pm, Sa 8am-noon). **ZIP code:** 84717. **Area code:** 435.

**⬛▐ CAMPGROUNDS AND FOOD. North** and **Sunset Campgrounds,** both within 3mi. of the visitors center, offer toilets, picnic tables, potable water, and 210 sites on a first come, first served basis (sites $10). **Backcountry camping permits** are free from the ranger at the visitors center. Two campgrounds lie just west of Bryce on scenic Rt. 12, in Dixie National Forest. The **King Creek Campground,** 11mi. from Bryce on a dirt road off Rt. 12 (look for signs to Tropic Reservoir), features lakeside sites surrounded by pine trees. Group sites are available with reservations. ($8. 800-280-2267.) At an elevation of 7400 ft., the **Red Canyon Campground** rents 36 sites on a first come, first served basis ($10).

The **grocery store** at **Ruby's Inn,** just outside the park entrance, has a wide selection of provisions for reasonable prices (open daily 6am-10pm). If you're stuck in the park without any food, the **general store** at Sunrise Point has basic fast food and showers in back. (834-5361, ext. 167. Showers $2 for 10min.; available daily 7am-10pm. Open spring-fall daily 7:30am-8:30pm; closed in winter.)

There are no indoor budget accommodations on the site itself, though groups might wind up making out decently. Only a few minutes from the park entrance, the **Bryce Canyon Resort,** at the junction of Rt. 12 and Rt. 63, offers pricey and conventional deluxe doubles. (834-5351. $85, less in the winter. Pool and restaurant on site.) **Canyonlands International Youth Hostel** hosts travelers 60mi. south of Bryce in **Kanab** (see p.732). Although expensive for single travelers, **Bryce Lodge** is a much better deal for a group. (834-5361 or 586-7686. Motel-style doubles $85; western-style cabins $95; $5 per each additional person; open Apr.-Oct.)

**◉▲ SIGHTS AND ACTIVITIES.** Bryce's 18mi. **main road** winds past spectacular look-outs such as **Sunrise Point, Sunset Point, Inspiration Point,** and **Rainbow Point,** but a range of hiking trails makes it a crime not to leave your car. The air up there is thin; if you start to feel giddy or short of breath, take a rest. One oft-missed viewpoint is **Fairyland Point,** at the north end of the park, 1mi. off the main road, with some of the best sights in the canyons. The path along the rim between Sunrise Point and Sunset Point is wheelchair accessible. The 3mi. loop of the **Navajo** and **Queen's Garden** trails leads into the canyon. More challenging options include **Peek-A-Boo Loop,** winding in and out through hoodoos for 4mi., and the **Trail to the Hat Shop,** an extremely steep 4mi. descent. (And if climbing down was tough...) **Canyon Trail Rides** arranges guided horseback rides (679-8665. $27-40 per person).

# NEAR BRYCE

Daring hikers flirt with death in the network of sandstone canyons that comprises the ominously named **Phipps Death Hollow Outstanding Natural Area,** just north of **Escalante.** The full trail through the canyons, starting at the **Hell's Backbone** trailhead north of town, requires 4-5 days to complete (30mi. one-way). For the first 11mi., there's no water at all; then the trail requires hikers to swim across a series of deep pools. A free backcountry permit (required), directions, and weather reports await at the **Escalante Interagency Office,** 755 W. Main St. (826-5499), on Rt. 12 just west of town (open daily 7:30am-5:30pm; off-season M-F 8am-4:30pm). A shorter, almost as stunning day hike starts in the **Upper Escalante Canyon** and heads through some of the Death Hollow area. The **Calf Creek** campground, 15mi. east of Escalante on Rt. 12, has a cascading waterfall, drinking water and toilets (sites $8).

West on Rt. 14, the flowered slopes of the **Cedar Breaks National Monument** descend 2000 ft. into chiseled depths. The rim of this giant amphitheater stands a lofty 10,350 ft. above sea level (entrance $4 per car, $2 per pedestrian). A 30-site **campground** (sites $9) and the **visitors center** (586-0787; open in summer daily 8am-6pm) await at **Point Supreme.** For more info, contact the Superintendent, Cedar Breaks National Monument, 82 N. 100 E., Cedar City 84720 (586-9451).

**GRAND STAIRCASE ESCALANTE NATIONAL MONUMENT.** Designated by President Bill Clinton in 1996, Escalante is the newest national monument. Its youth is apparent; like a swaggering young Elvis, the park remains yet unaffected by the years of stardom that have given some other national parks a bit of an older Elvis paunch. In terms of geologic age, though, the Grand Staircase is the granddad of region—the "steps," a series of cliffs and plateaus, reveal hundreds of millions of years of sedimentary rock formation. The relatively few visitors come less for the staircase than for the hiking opportunities among tucked-away rock fields, extraordinary formations, and wildlife. The best way to enter the park from the south is by turning onto Cottonwood Canyon from Rt. 89 N. in Utah, between Mi. 17 and 18. From the north, use Utah Scenic Hwy. 12. The roads are unpaved, so be sure you and your vehicle are up for the bumpy ride and the weather is okay. The **Bureau of Land Management** has more information (801-826-4291).

## ZION

Russet sandstone mountains loom over the puny cars and hikers that flock to **Zion National Park** in search of the promised land, or at least the land promised to be beautiful by enthusiastic travel guides. Some 13 million years ago, the ocean flowed over the cliffs and canyons of Zion. Over the centuries, the sea subsided, leaving only the raging Virgin River, whose watery fingers sculpt the smooth white rock hills. In the northwest corner of the park, the walls of Kolob Terrace tower thousands of feet above the river. Elsewhere, branching canyons and rock formations show off erosion's unique artistry. In the 1860s, Mormon settlers came to the area and enthusiastically proclaimed that they had found Zion, the promised land. Brigham Young disagreed, however, and declared that the place was awfully nice, but "not Zion." The name "not Zion" stuck for years until a new wave of entranced explorers dropped the "not," giving the park its present name.

🛈 **PRACTICAL INFORMATION.** The main entrance to Zion is in **Springdale,** on Rt. 9, which borders the park to the south along the Virgin River. Approaching Zion from the west, take Rt. 9 from I-15 at Hurricane. In the east, pick up Rt. 9 from U.S. 89 at Mt. Carmel Jct. **Greyhound** (673-2933), is in St. George (43mi. southwest of the park on I-15), departing from a **McDonald's,** 1235 S. Bluff St., at St. George Blvd. Buses run to Salt Lake City (6hr., 3 per day, $38); Los Angeles (15hr., 7 per day, $55); Denver (14hr., 4 per day, $89); and Las Vegas (2hr., 7 per day, $25). The main **Zion Canyon Visitors Center** (772-3256) has an introductory slide program and an interesting museum (open daily 8am-7pm; off-season 8am-6pm). **Kolob Canyons Visitors Center** (586-9548) lies in the northwest corner of the park, off I-15 at exit 40 and issues backcountry permits (open daily 8am-7pm; off-season 9am-4pm). The park's **entrance fee** is $10 per car, $5 per pedestrian. **Emergency:** 772-3322. Zion's **post office** is located inside the Zion Canyon Lodge. **ZIP code:** 84767. **Area code:** 435.

⌂ **ACCOMMODATIONS.** More than 300 sites are available on a first come, first served basis in the **South** and **Watchman Campgrounds,** both near the park's south entrance ($10; water, toilets, and sanitary disposal station). Campgrounds fill quickly in summer. Six primitive but free sites at **Lava Point** are accessible from a hiking trail, or from the gravel road which turns off Rt. 9 in Virgin (toilets but no water; open June-Nov.). A permit ($5) from the visitors center is required for **backcountry camping.** Camping along the rim is *not* allowed, but a free map from the visitors center shows where you may and may not pitch a tent.

**Mukuntuweep Campground,** just outside the park near the east entrance, has altitude on its side. Not only is it 1000 ft. higher and about 10° cooler than the sites inside the park, but it also offers a laundromat, showers, arcade, restaurant, and gas station. (648-2154. 70 tent sites $15, 30 full hookups $20, cabins and teepees $25. Office open 24hr.) **Zion Canyon Campground,** 479 Zion Park Blvd., in Springdale just south of the park, soothes the weary, hungry, and filthy with a convenience store, restaurant, grocery store, showers, and coin-op laundry. (772-3237. Sites for 2 $16, full hookup $20; $3.50 per additional adult, $2 per additional child under 15. Office open daily 8am-9pm. Store open daily 8am-9pm; off-season 8am-5pm.)

The **Zion Canyon Lodge,** along the park's main road, offers premium rooms at premium prices, along with a restaurant. (303-297-2757 for reservations. Singles and doubles $85; cabin singles and doubles $95; $5 per additional person.) Cheap motels are available in nearly any of the towns near Zion, including **Springdale** and **Rockville,** 2-5mi. south of the park; **Mt. Carmel Junction,** 20mi. east; **Kanab,** 40mi. east; or **Cedar City** (see p. 707), 70mi. north of the park on Rt. 15.

The closest hostel is the ▩ **Dixie Hostel (HI-AYH),** 73 S. Main St., 20mi. west in Hurricane. Fresh-smelling, pink-hued, and ruthlessly clean, the hostel still caters to a rather relaxed bunch. (635-8202 or 635-9000. Linen, laundry, kitchen, linen, continental breakfast, and 20% discount at hot springs nearby. Dorm beds $15; private doubles $35.) In the other direction, the **Canyonlands International Youth Hostel,** 143 E. 100 S., Kanab, lies 20mi. south. Though the place is a bit too earthy for some, the hostel's location, 1hr. north of the Grand Canyon's North Rim and roughly equidistant from Zion, Bryce, and Lake Powell, makes it a good base for exploring northern Arizona and southern Utah. (644-5554. Linen, laundry, TV, kitchen, continental breakfast, occasional dinner, and pay-per-use Internet. $10.)

▣ **SIGHTS AND ACTIVITIES.** Zion seems to have been made for hiking; unlike in the forboding canyons that surround it, most of the trails won't have you praying for a stray mule to show up. Paved and wheelchair accessible with assistance, the **Riverside Walk,** beginning at the Temple of Sinawava, stretches 1mi. from the north end of Zion Canyon Dr., alongside the Virgin River and some beautiful wildflower displays. The **Emerald Pools** trail, which starts opposite the Zion Lodge, (1.2mi. round-trip for the lower section which leads to a waterfall) has wheelchair access along its lower loop, but the middle and upper loops are steep and narrow. Swimming is not allowed in any of the pools. Another easy but spectacular trail leads to **Weeping Rock,** at the Weeping Rock parking lot toward the north of the park, (½mi. round-trip), a dripping spring surrounded by hanging gardens. The challenging **Angel's Landing** trail begins in the Grotto picnic area (5mi. round-trip), and rises 1488 ft. above the canyon; the last terrifying ½mi. climbs a narrow ridge with guide chains blasted into the rock. The difficult trail to **Observation Point** (8mi. round-trip) leads through **Echo Canyon,** a spectacular kaleidoscope of sandstone, where steep switchbacks explore the unusually gouged canyon. Overnight hikers can spend days on the 27mi. **West Rim Trail.**

Even if visiting the **Kolob Canyons,** be sure to make the pilgrimage to **Zion Canyon.** The 7mi. dead-end road on the canyon floor rambles past the giant **Sentinel, Mountain of the Sun,** and the overwhelming symbol of Zion, the **Great White Throne.** A shuttle from the Lodge runs this route every hour on the hour (1hr. In summer daily 9am-5pm. $3.) Horseback tours arranged by **Canyon Trail Rides** leave from the Lodge. (679-8665. $15-40 per person.) **Bike Zion,** rents bikes (1800 Zion Park Blvd. 772-3929. $7-11 per hr., $17-27 per ½-day, $23-35 per day. Open daily 8am-8pm.)

## NEAR ZION: CEDAR CITY

After emerging from the sculpted white mountains of Zion or the otherworldly hoodoos of Bryce, you might expect a place called Cedar City to be graced with some dramatic trees. But there aren't even any cedars—settlers mistook junipers for their woody cousins. Culture, location, and backcountry mountain biking put Cedar City on the map. The annual **Utah Shakespeare Festival** (586-7878 or 800-752-9849) presents plays every M to Sa from late June through late Aug. Zion National Park and Bryce Canyon are within day-trip distances. The patches of wilderness surrounding Cedar City, including Brian Head and Panguitch, are becoming well-known lately for **mountain biking.** Trails wind through forest, mountain, meadows, and desert. The Mountain Bike Guide at the visitors center is informative.

Though there are no hostels in town, a number of budget motels in the $30-$50 range cluster on S. Main St. During the Shakespeare festival, you're better off staying in St. George or Kanab, as lodging prices can jump by as much as 50%. The carless will appreciate **Greyhound** service, 1355 S. Main St. (586-9465; terminal open daily 7am-10pm), which runs to Salt Lake City ($40-43), Flagstaff ($65-69), and many other cities. I-15, U.S. 91, and Rt. 14 intersect the city. **Post Office:** 333 N. Main St. (586-6701; open M-F 8:30am-5pm, Sa 9am-noon). **ZIP code:** 84720. **Area code:** 435.

## NATURAL BRIDGES AND HOVENWEEP

**NATURAL BRIDGES NATIONAL MONUMENT.** The Paiutes who inhabited this region nearly 3000 years ago called it *Ma-Vah-Talk-Tump*, or "under the horse's belly." Although Utah's first national monument now carries the more prosaic moniker of "Natural Bridges," the three rock formations are no less impressive. To appreciate the size of the monuments fully—the highest is more than 200 feet—leave the overlooks and hike down to the bridges. Once you do, it's easy to understand why the Hopi named the largest one "Sipapu," or "place of emergence"—they believed it to be the entry way through which their ancestors came into this world. The park's paved **Bridge View Drive** is about 9mi. and passes the overlooks and trailheads to each of the three major bridges. It's also possible to hike various loop trails connecting the bridges—trails range from 5.6 to 8.6mi.

To reach Natural Bridges from northern Utah, follow U.S. 191 S. from Moab to its junction with **Scenic Rt. 95 W** (north of Bluff and 4mi. south of Blanding). From Colorado, U.S. 66 heads west to U.S. 191 S (junction in Monticello). From the south, Rt. 261 from Mexican Hat climbs a mesa in a heart-wrenching and axle-grinding series of 5 mph gravel switchbacks, providing a spectacular view of Monument Valley across the Arizona border.

The **visitors center** (692-1234), several mi. past the monument's entrance, offers a slide show and exhibits. (Open daily Mar.-Oct. 8am-6pm; Nov.-Feb. 9:30am-4:30pm. Park entrance $6 per vehicle, $3 per hiker or bicyclist, good for 7 days; National Parks passports accepted.) Sleep under the stars at the **campground** near the visitors center. Thirteen shaded sites set amid pinyon pines accommodate up to nine people each and include grills and picnic tables. (Campground usually fills up by 2pm. Sites $10. First come, first served.) **Water** is available at the visitors center. For more info, write the Superintendent, Natural Bridges, P.O. Box 1, Lake Powell 84533. If the park campground is full, primitive overflow camping is available off a gravel road originating at the intersection of Rt. 95 and Rt. 251, 6mi. from the visitors center. The free sites are flat and shaded but have no facilities.

**HOVENWEEP NATIONAL MONUMENT.** Hovenweep, from the Ute meaning "deserted valley," was aptly named—it's still in one of the most empty regions in the US. The few who make the trip to the area, in the Utah section of the four corners, are treated to national park solitude (not always an oxymoron) and 6 groups of Pueblo ruins dating back more than 1000 years, a few hundred years older than the Navajo Monument ruins. The best preserved and most impressive ruins, **Square Tower Ruins,** lie footsteps away from the visitors center (see below). The **Square Tower Loop Trail** (2mi.) loops around a small canyon, accessing **Hovenweep Castle** and the **Twin Towers.** A shorter trail, the ½mi. **Tower Point Loop,** accesses the ruins of a tower perched on a canyon. The outlying ruins—**Cujon Ruins** and **Huckberry Canyon** in Utah, and **Cutthroat Castle** and **Goodman Point Ruins** in Colorado—are isolated and difficult to reach.

Desolate but beautiful roads usher you to Hovenweep. In Utah or Arizona, follow U.S. 191 to its junction with Rt. 262 E (14mi. south of Blanding, 11mi. north of Bluff). After about 30mi., watch for signs to the monument. From Cortez, CO, go south on U.S. 166/U.S. 160 to County Rd. 6 (the airport road); follow the Hovenweep signs for 45mi., including 15mi. of gravel road. It's wise to check road conditions at the **visitors center,** accessible from both the Utah and Colorado sides. (970-749-0510. Open daily 8am-6pm, offseason 8am-5pm, except when the ranger is out on patrol. $3 per person, $6 per car, National Parks passports accepted.) There is no gasoline, telephone, or food at the monument. The Hovenweep **campground** has recently reopened and is located a short distance from the visitors center. Water and toilets are available, though campers must carry out all of their trash ($10). For more info, contact the **Superintendent,** Hovenweep National Monument, McElmo Rt., Cortez, CO 81321 (303-749-0510).

**NEARBY CIVILIZATION.** Three small towns provide lodging and services for travelers to the monuments and the valley. In the agricultural town of **Blanding** (45mi. from Hovenweep, 60mi. from Natural Bridges), the **Prospector Motor Lodge,** 591 U.S. 191 S., has spacious rooms, some with kitchenettes. (678-3231. Singles $41-50, doubles $45-55; off-season $27/$39; prices somewhat negotiable.) The cheaper **Blanding Sunset Inn,** 88 W. Center St., has basic, phoneless rooms (678-3323. Singles $28; doubles $30.) The **Elk Ridge Restaurant,** 120 E. Center St., pours morning coffee. (Breakfast specials $3.75. 678-3390. Open daily 6am-9:30pm).

Nestled among the sandstone canyons, the tiny town of **Bluff** (40mi. from Hovenweep, 65mi. from Natural Bridges) welcomes the budget traveler. The gigantic, austere sandstone sculptures of the **Valley of the Gods,** which provided the backdrop for some of the road scenes in *Thelma and Louise,* are worth the detour. A tough but incredible 17mi. drive departs from U.S. 163, 15mi. south of Bluff on the right side of the road, and runs right through the valley. Inexpensive and comfortable lodges and motels line U.S. 191, including **The Recapture Lodge.** (672-2281. Singles $34-44; doubles $50-58.) Tasty Navajo sheepherder sandwiches (roast beef on Indian fry bread, $5.25) hit the tables at the **Turquoise Restaurant,** opposite the lodge on U.S. 191 S. (672-2279. Open M 7am-9:30pm, Tu-Su 7:30am-9:30pm.)

**Mexican Hat** sits along the San Juan River on the border of the Navajo nation. The town is 20mi. south of Bluff on U.S. 163 and 20mi. north of Arizona. Rest your head at the newly renovated **Canyonlands Motel,** on U.S. 163. (683-2230. Singles $34, doubles $47.) The **restaurant** at Burch's Indian Trading Co., on U.S. 163, serves Mexican and Southwestern food on picnic tables, including tasty $6 mutton stew and $4.75 burgers. (683-2221. Open daily 7am-9pm.)

# ARIZONA

Populated primarily by Native Americans through the 19th century, Arizona has been hit in the past hundred years by waves of settlers—from the speculators and miners of the late 1800s, to the soldiers who trained here during World War II and returned after the war, to the more recent immigrants from Mexico. Traces of lost Native American civilization remain at Canyon de Chelly, Navajo National Monument, and Wupatki and Walnut Canyons, while deserted ghost towns scattered throughout the state illustrate the death of the mining lifestyle—but both civilizations persevere. The descendents of area tribes now occupy reservations on one-half of the state's land, making up one-seventh of the United States' Native American population, while urban Phoenix sprawls wider and wider. No man-made structures can overshadow Arizona's natural masterpieces—the Grand Canyon, Monument Valley, and the gorgeous landscapes viewed from the state's highways.

## ▐ PRACTICAL INFORMATION

**Capital:** Phoenix.

**Visitor Info: Arizona Tourism,** 2703 N. 3rd St. Suite 4015, Phoenix 85004 (602-230-7733 or 888-520-3434; www.arizonaguide.com). Open M-F 8am-5pm. **Arizona State Parks,** 1300 W. Washington St., Phoenix 85007 (602-542-4174 or 800-285-3703). Open M-F 8am-5pm.

**Postal Abbreviation:** AZ. **Sales Tax:** 6%.

# GRAND CANYON

Despite the prevalence of its image on everything from postcards to screen-savers, nothing can prepare you for the first sight of the Grand Canyon. After the initial humbling shock of emerging on the canyon's rim, stay awhile and let its sheer enormity and majesty sink in; stories of grungy hermits descending into the canyon and emerging weeks or months later demonstrate the inexplicable draw of this rocky sensation. One of the 7 natural wonders of the world (277mi. long, 10mi. wide, and over 1mi. deep), the canyon descends to the Colorado River past looming walls of multi-colored limestone, sandstone, and shale. Hike down into the gorge to experience the immensity and beauty of this natural phenomenon, or just watch the colors and shadows change from one of the many rim viewpoints.

**Grand Canyon National Park** is divided into three areas: the **South Rim,** which includes Grand Canyon Village; the **North Rim;** and the canyon gorge itself. The slightly lower, more accessible South Rim draws 10 times as many visitors as the higher, more heavily forested North Rim. The South Rim is open all year, while the North Rim only welcomes travelers from mid-May to mid-Oct. (mid-Oct. to early Dec. for day use), depending on the weather. The 13mi. trail that traverses the canyon floor furnishes sturdy hikers with a minimum 2-day adventure, while the 214mi. perimeter road is a good 5hr. drive for those who would rather explore from above. If you observe all safety precautions, use common sense, and drink lots of water, you are sure to have an unforgettable experience.

## SOUTH RIM

During the summer, everything on 2 legs or 4 wheels converges on this side of the Grand Canyon. If you plan to visit during the mobfest, make reservations for lodging, campsites, or mules well in advance—and prepare to battle the crowds. That said, it's much better than Disney World. A friendly Park Service staff, well-run facilities, and beautiful scenery help ease crowd anxiety. Fewer tourists brave the canyon's winter weather; many hotels and facilities close during the off-season.

## ⚡ ORIENTATION AND PRACTICAL INFORMATION

There are 2 park entrances: the main **south entrance** lies on U.S. 180 N, and the eastern **Desert View** entrance lies on I-40 W. From Las Vegas, the fastest route to the South Rim is U.S. 93 S to I-40 E, and then Rt. 64 N. From Flagstaff, I-40 E to U.S. 89 N is the most scenic; from there, Rt. 64 N takes you to the Desert View entrance. Heading straight up U.S. 180 N is more direct. Posted maps and signs in the park make orienting easy. Lodges and services concentrate in **Grand Canyon Village,** at the end of Park Entrance Rd. The east half of the Village contains the visitors center and the general store, while most of the lodges and the challenging 12mi. **Bright Angel Trailhead** lie in the west section. The shorter, but still difficult 3mi. **South Kaibab Trailhead** is off East Rim Dr., east of the village. Free shuttle buses to 8 rim overlooks run along **West Rim Dr.** (closed to private vehicles during the summer). Avoid walking on the drive; the rim trails are safer and more scenic easy hikes.

The **entrance pass** is $20 per car and $10 for travelers using other modes of transportation—even bus passengers must pay (Golden Eagle, Golden Age, and Golden Access passports accepted). The pass lasts for one week. For most services in the Park, call the **main switchboard** number at 638-2631.

**Buses: Nava-Hopi Bus Lines** (800-892-8687) leaves the Flagstaff Amtrak station for the Grand Canyon daily at 7:45am and 3pm, returning from Bright Angel Lodge at 10am and 5pm (about 2hr.). $17.50, under 15 $8.75; round-trip $31/$15.50, including entrance fee. Times vary by season, so call ahead.

**Public Transit: Free shuttle buses** ride the West Rim Loop (daily 1 hr. before sunrise-1 hr. after sunset) and the Village Loop (daily 1 hr. before sunrise-10:30pm) every 10-30min. A free **hiker's shuttle** runs every 30min. between Grand Canyon Village and the South Kaibab Trailhead, on the East Rim near Yaki Point.

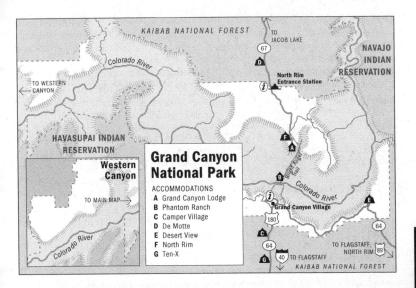

KAIBAB NATIONAL FOREST

TO JACOB LAKE
67
D

Colorado River

North Rim
Entrance Station

TO WESTERN
CANYON

NAVAJO
INDIAN
RESERVATION

HAVASUPAI INDIAN
RESERVATION

Western
Canyon

## Grand Canyon National Park

ACCOMMODATIONS
A Grand Canyon Lodge
B Phantom Ranch
C Camper Village
D De Motte
E Desert View
F North Rim
G Ten-X

TO MAIN MAP

Colorado River

Colorado River

Grand Canyon Village

F
A
B
E
180
64

C
64
G
40
TO FLAGSTAFF

TO FLAGSTAFF,
NORTH RIM
89

KAIBAB NATIONAL FOREST

**THE SOUTHWEST**

**Taxis:** Call 638-2822. Open 24hr.

**Auto Repairs: Grand Canyon Garage** (638-2631), east of the visitors center on the main road, near Maswik Lodge. Open daily 8am-noon, 1pm-5pm. 24hr. emergency service.

**Equipment Rental: Babbitt's General Store** (638-2262), in Grand Canyon Village near Yavapai Lodge and the visitors center. Comfy hiking boots, socks included ($8 1st day, $5 per additional day); sleeping bags ($7-9/$5); tents ($15-18/$9); and other camping gear. Hefty deposits required on all items. Open daily 8am-8pm.

**Visitor Info:** The **visitors center** (638-7888) is 6mi. north of the south entrance station. Open daily 8am-7pm; off-season 8am-5pm. Hikers should get the *Backcountry Trip Planner;* the regular old *Trip Planner* is for regular old mortals (both free). Free and informative, *The Guide* is also available here. Write **Trip Planner**, Grand Canyon National Park, P.O. Box 129, Grand Canyon, 86023. The **transportation info desks** in **Bright Angel Lodge** and **Maswik Lodge** (638-2631 for both) handle reservations for mule rides, bus tours, plane tours, Phantom Ranch, taxis, and more. Both open daily 6am-7pm.

**Luggage Storage**: In Bright Angel Lodge. Open 8am-9pm. 50¢ per day.

**Weather and Road Conditions:** 638-7888.

**Medical Services: Grand Canyon Clinic** (638-2551 or 638-2469), several mi. south of the visitors center on Center Rd. Open M-F 8am-5:30pm, Sa 9am-noon. 24hr. emergency aid. **Pharmacy** on site (638-2460).

**Post Office:** (638-2512), across the street from the visitors center. Open M-F 9am-4:30pm, Sa 11am-1pm. **ZIP code: 86023. Area code:** 520.

## ▚ ACCOMMODATIONS

Compared to the 6 million years it took the Colorado River to carve the Grand Canyon, the year it will take you to get indoor lodging near the South Rim will pass fast. Summer rooms should be reserved *11 months in advance.* That said, there are cancellations every day; if you arrive unprepared, check for vacancies, or call the Grand Canyon operator at 638-2631 and ask to be connected with the proper lodge. Reservations for **Bright Angel Lodge, Maswik Lodge, Trailer Village,** and **Phantom Ranch** can be made through **Grand Canyon National Park Lodges,** P.O. Box 699, Grand Canyon 86023 (303-297-2757 or 638-2401). Most accommodations on the South Rim are very pricey.

**Bright Angel Lodge** (638-2401), Grand Canyon Village. The cheapest indoor lodging on the rim. Very convenient to Bright Angel Trail and shuttle buses. "Rustic" lodge singles and doubles with plumbing but no heat $44-58; "historic" cabins for 1 or 2 people $66; $7 per additional person in rooms and cabins.

**Maswik Lodge** (638-2401), Grand Canyon Village. Small, clean cabins (singles or doubles) with showers but no heat $60; motel rooms $94-114; $7-9 per additional person.

**Phantom Ranch** (638-2631), on the canyon floor, a day's hike down the Kaibab Trail. Dorm beds $21; rarely available cabins for 1 or 2 people $56; $11 per additional person. *Don't show up without reservations.* Meals must be reserved in advance. Breakfast $12; box lunch $7.50; stew dinner $16.75, steak dinner $26.75. If you're dying to sleep on the canyon floor but don't have a reservation, show up at the Bright Angel transportation desk at 6am, and they may be able to arrange something.

 ## CAMPGROUNDS

The campsites listed here usually fill up early in the day. In the **Kaibab National Forest,** along the south border of the park, you can pull off a dirt road and camp for free. No camping is allowed within ¼mi. of U.S. 64. Sleeping in cars is *not* permitted within the park, but it is allowed in the Kaibab Forest. For more info, contact the **Tusayan Ranger District,** Kaibab National Forest, P.O. Box 3088, Grand Canyon 86023 (638-2443). Overnight hiking or camping within the park outside of designated campgrounds requires a **backcountry use permit** ($20 application fee plus $4 per person per night), available at the **backcountry office** (638-7875), ¼mi. south of the visitors center (open daily 8am-noon and 1-5pm). Permit requests are accepted by mail, fax, or in person up to 5 months in advance. Guests with reservations at Phantom Ranch (see above) do not need permits. Reservations for some campgrounds can be made through **BIOSPHERICS** (800-365-2267).

**Mather Campground** (call BIOSPHERICS, 800-365-2267), Grand Canyon Village, 1mi. south of the visitors center. 320 shady, relatively isolated sites with no hookups. Sept.-May $12; June-Aug. $15. 7-day max. stay. For Mar.-Nov., reserve up to 8 weeks in advance; Dec.-Feb. sites go on a first come, first served basis. Check at the office, even if the sign says the campground is full.

**Ten-X Campground** (638-2443), in the Kaibab National Forest, 10mi. south of Grand Canyon Village off Rt. 64. Shady sites surrounded by pine trees. Toilets, water, no hookups, no showers. First come, first served sites $10. Open May-Sept.

**Desert View Campground** (638-7888), 26mi. east of Grand Canyon Village. 50 sites with phone and rest room access, but no hookups. $10. No reservations; usually full by early afternoon. Open mid-May to Oct.

**Camper Village** (638-2887), 7mi. south of the visitors center in Tusayan. RV and tent sites $15-23 for 2 people; $2 per additional adult. First come, first served tent sites; reservations required for RVs.

**Indian Gardens** (638-7888), 4½mi. from the Bright Angel trailhead and 3100 ft. below the rim. 15 free sites, toilets, and water. Reservations and backcountry permit required.

**Trailer Village** (638-2401), next to Mather Campground. Designed with the RV in mind. Showers and laundry nearby. 84 sites for 2 with hookup $20; $1.75 per additional person. Office open daily 8am-noon and 1-5pm. Reserve 6-9 months in advance.

## FOOD

Fast food has yet to sink its greasy talons into the South Rim (the closest McDonald's is 7mi. south in Tusayan), but you *can* find meals at fast-food prices. **Babbitt's General Store,** near the visitors center, has a deli counter (sandwiches $2-4) and a wide selection of groceries, as well as a camping supplies department (638-2262. Open daily 8am-8pm; deli open 8am-7pm.) The well-stocked **Canyon**

**Cafe,** across from Babbitt's, offers a wider variety of food than the nearby deli (hamburgers $3, pizza $3-4, dinners $5-7; open daily 6am-10pm). **Maswik Cafeteria,** in Maswik Lodge, serves a variety of inexpensive grill-made options in a wood-paneled cafeteria atmosphere (hot entrees $5-7, sandwiches $2-4; open daily 6am-10pm). **Bright Angel Dining Room,** in Bright Angel Lodge, serves hot sandwiches for $6-8 (638-2631. Open daily 6:30am-10pm). The **soda fountain** at Bright Angel Lodge chills 16 flavors of ice cream (1 scoop $2) for hot folks (open daily 6:30am-9pm).

# ▒ OUTDOORS

From your first glimpse of the canyon, you may feel a compelling desire to see it from the inside, an enterprise that is harder than it looks. Even the young at heart and body should remember that an easy downhill hike can become a nightmarish 50° incline on the return journey. Also keep in mind that the lower you go, the hotter it gets; when it's 85° on the rim, it's around 100° at Indian Gardens, and around 110° at Phantom Ranch. Heat exhaustion, the greatest threat to any hiker, is marked by a monstrous headache and red, sweatless skin. *For a day hike, you must take at least a gallon of water per person; drink at least a liter per hour hiking upwards under the hot sun.* Hiking boots or sneakers with excellent tread are also necessary—the trails are steep, and every year several careless hikers take what locals morbidly call "the 12-second tour." A list of hiking safety tips can be found in *The Guide.* It is advisable to speak with a ranger or drop by the visitor's center before embarking on a hike: they may have important information about the trail. Parents should think twice about bringing children more than 1mi. down any trail—kids remember well and may exact revenge when they get older.

The 2 most accessible trails into the canyon are the **Bright Angel Trail,** originating at the Bright Angel Lodge, and the **South Kaibab Trail,** from Yaki Point. Bright Angel is outfitted for the average tourist, with rest houses strategically stationed 1½mi. and 3mi. from the rim; all 3 rest stops have water in the summer. **Indian Gardens,** 4½mi. down, offers the tired hiker restrooms, picnic tables, and blessed shade. Kaibab is trickier, steeper, and lacks shade or water, but it rewards the intrepid with a better view of the canyon. If you've made arrangements to spend the night on the canyon floor, the best route is the South Kaibab Trail (4-5hr., depending on conditions) and back up the Bright Angel (7-8hr.) the following day. Hikes to Indian Gardens and **Plateau Point,** 6mi. out, with views 1360 ft. down to the river, make excellent **daytrips** (8-12hr.), provided that you start around 7am. A few less-traveled, unmaintained trails enter the canyon, but require backcountry permits.

If you're not up to descending into the canyon, follow the **Rim Trail** east to **Grand-view Point** and the **Yavapai Geological Museum,** or west to **Hermit's Rest.** Viewpoints along the East Rim are somewhat spread out; the West Rim is skirted by a beautiful trail that leads to 8 overlooks. Shuttles also run on the west rim, stopping at all of the viewpoints. You can also hike out as far as you want and then take the shuttle back. The trail is paved and wheelchair accessible from the visitors center to Bright Angel Lodge. After Maricopa Point, footing is more difficult, but the views are correspondingly more spectacular.

The East Rim swarms with sunset-watchers at dusk, and the observation deck at the Yavapai Museum, at the end of the trail, has a sweeping view of the canyon during the day. Along the West Rim, **Hopi Point** is a favorite for sunsets, and a special "sunset shuttle" heads back from here. *The Guide* and the visitors center list times for sunsets and sunrises.

**Mule trips** from the South Rim are very expensive and are booked up to 1 year in advance, although cancellations do occur (day trip $106, overnight $280; call 303-297-2757 for reservations). Mule trips from the North Rim are cheaper and more readily available (638-9875). **Whitewater rafting** trips through the canyon last from 3 days to 2 weeks; advance reservations are required. Call the transport info desk for a list of trips. Park Service rangers also present a variety of free, informative talks and **guided hikes;** times and details are listed in *The Guide.*

## NORTH RIM

If you're coming from Utah or Nevada, or want to avoid the crowds at the South Rim, the park's North Rim is a bit wilder, a bit cooler, and much more serene—all with a view *almost* as groovy as that from the South Rim. Unfortunately, because the North Rim is less frequented, it's hard to reach by public transportation, and by car, it's a bit of a drive, even from southern Utah. From Oct. 15 until Dec. 1, the North Rim is open for day use only; from Dec. 1 until May 15, it is closed entirely.

## ■ ORIENTATION AND PRACTICAL INFORMATION

To reach the North Rim from the South Rim, take Rt. 64 E to U.S. 89 N, which runs into Alt. 89; from Alt. 89, follow Rt. 67 S to the edge. Altogether, the beautiful drive is over 200mi. From Utah, take Alt. 89 S from Fredonia. From Page, take U.S. 89 S to Alt. 89 to Rt 67 S. Snow closes Rt. 67 from mid-Oct. through mid-May; park visitor facilities (including the lodge) close for the winter. The **entrance fee** covers both rims for 7 days ($20 per car; $10 per person on foot, bike, bus, or pilgrimage).

**Public Transit: Transcanyon,** P.O. Box 348, Grand Canyon 86023 (638-2820). Buses to South Rim depart 7am (4½hr.); return buses depart 1:30pm. $60, round-trip $100. Reservations required. Runs late May to Oct.

**Visitor Info: National Park Service Information Desk** (638-7864), in the lobby of Grand Canyon Lodge (see below). Open daily 8am-6pm.

**Weather Info:** 638-7888. Updated at 7am daily.

**Camping Supplies: General store** abuts North Rim Campground. Open daily 8am-8pm.

**Medical Services: North Rim Clinic** (638-2611, ext. 222), in cabin #5 at Grand Canyon Lodge. Open W-M 9am-noon and 3-6pm, Tu 9am-noon and 2-5pm.

**Post Office:** in Grand Canyon Lodge (638-2611), like everything else. Open M-F 8am-11am, 11:30am-4pm, Sa 8am-2pm. **ZIP code:** 86052. **Area code:** 520.

## ■ ACCOMMODATIONS AND FOOD

Camping within the confines of the Grand Canyon National Park is limited to designated campgrounds. **BIOSPHERICS** (800-365-2267) handles reservations; otherwise, mark your territory by 10am. If you can't get in-park lodgings, head for the **Kaibab National Forest,** which runs from north of Jacob Lake to the park entrance. You can camp for free, as long as you're ¼mi. from the road or official campgrounds. Less expensive accommodations may be found in **Kanab, UT,** 80mi. north (p. 753), where motel rooms tend to hover around $40.

**Grand Canyon Lodge** (303-297-2757 for reservations, 638-2611 for front desk), on the edge of the rim. The only indoor rim lodging in the park. Pioneer cabins shelter 4 people for $87. Singles or doubles in frontier cabins $70; Western cabins and motel rooms $80-110. Reception 24hr. Reserve several months in advance.

**Jacob Lake Inn** (643-7232), 45mi. north of the North Rim entrance at Jacob Lake. Cabins for 2 $66-71; for 3 $76-78; for 4 $81-84. Pricier motel units available for $10-15 more. Reasonably priced dining room. Reception daily 6am-10pm.

**Kaibab Camper Village** (643-7804), 1mi. south of Jacob Lake Inn. 50 tent sites $12; 60 sites with hookups for 2 $20-22; $2 per extra person. Open May to mid-Oct.

**North Rim Campground** (call BIOSPHERICS, 800-365-2267), on Rt. 67 near the rim, the only campground in the park. You can't see into the canyon from the pine-covered site, but you know it's there. Food store nearby, laundry, recreation room, and showers. 7-day max. stay. 82 sites $15; no hookups. Open mid-May to mid-Oct.

**DeMotte Park Campground,** 16mi. north of the park entrance in Kaibab National Forest. 23 woodsy sites $10 per vehicle per night. First come, first served.

Feeding options on the North Rim are placed strategically at the **Grand Canyon Lodge**. The restaurant serves breakfast for $3-7, lunch for $6-8, and dinner for $13 and up (638-2611. Open 6:30-10am, 11:30am-2:30pm, and 5-9:30pm; reservations required for dinner.) A sandwich at the **Snack Bar** costs $3-4 (Open daily 6:30am-9pm). There is also a **Saloon** in the lodge (open daily 5am-9am, 11am-10pm). North Rim-ers are better off eating in Kanab or stopping at the **Jacob Lake Inn** for $5 sandwiches and great $2 milkshakes. (643-7232. Open daily 6am-9pm.)

## ▧ OUTDOORS

The easiest, and thus most trafficked route on the north rim is the ½mi. paved trail leads from the Grand Canyon Lodge to **Bright Angel Point,** which commands a seraphic view of the Canyon. **Point Imperial,** an 11mi. drive from the lodge, overlooks **Marble Canyon** and the **Painted Desert. Cape Royal** lies 23mi. from the lodge; en route, you'll pass the enchanting **Vista Encantadora.** Short trails include the **Cape Final Trail** (4mi.), which heads from a parking lot a few mi. before Cape Royal to Cape Final, and the **Transept Trail** (3mi.), which follows the rim from the lodge to the campground. The North Rim's *The Guide* lists trails in full.

Only 1 trail, the **North Kaibab Trail,** leads into the Canyon from the North Rim; a shuttle runs to the trailhead from Grand Canyon Lodge (daily at 5:30 and 7:45am; $5; reservations required). Overnight hikers must get permits from the **Backcountry Office** in the ranger station (open daily 8am-noon and 1-5pm), or write to the **Backcountry Office,** P.O. Box 129, Grand Canyon, AZ 86023; it may take a few days to get a permit in person.

Nature walks, lectures, and evening programs run at the North Rim Campground and at Grand Canyon Lodge. Check the info desk or campground bulletin boards for schedules. One-hour ($15) or ½-day **mule trips** ($40) through **Canyon Trail Rides** circle the rim or descend into the canyon from the lodge. (435-679-8665. Open daily 7am-7pm.) To tour the Canyon wet, pick up a Grand Canyon River Trip Operators brochure and select from among the 20 companies offering trips.

# FLAGSTAFF

Flagstaff was born as a rest-stop along the transcontinental railroad; its mountain springs provided precious aqueous refreshment along the long haul to the Pacific. The past hundred years have echoed with the innumerable "timber!" cries of the logging industry, seen a scientist in search of canal-digging martians, witnessed an emerging milieu of diverse cultures and ideologies, and felt the unrelenting onslaught of backpackers and fannypackers alike. One thing hasn't changed, though: Flagstaff is still a major rest-stop on the way to Southwestern must-sees. The Grand Canyon, Sedona, and the Petrified Forest are within day-trip distance, and the fabled Route 66 cuts through downtown, parallel to the still-buzzing railroad. The energetic citizens welcome travelers to their rock formations by day and their breweries by night; many wandered into town with camera in hand and ended up settling down. Retired cowboys, earthy Volvo owners, New Agers, and serious rockclimbers comprise much of the remaining population.

## ▣ ORIENTATION AND PRACTICAL INFORMATION

Flagstaff sits 138mi. north of Phoenix (take I-17), 26mi. north of Sedona (take U.S. 89A), and 81mi. south of the Grand Canyon's south rim (take U.S. 180). Downtown surrounds the intersection of **Beaver St.** and **Rt. 66** (formerly Santa Fe Ave.). Both bus stations, two youth hostels, the tourist office, and a number of inexpensive restaurants lie within ½mi. of this spot. Other commercial establishments line **S. San Francisco St.,** 2 blocks east of Beaver. As a mountain town, Flagstaff stays fairly temperate and receives frequent afternoon thundershowers.

**Trains: Amtrak,** 1 E. Rt. 66 (774-8679). To Los Angeles (12hr., 1 per day, $52-94) and Albuquerque (6hr., 1 per day, $49-89). Station open daily 4:15am-12:45pm; ticket office closes at 8pm.

**Buses: Greyhound,** 399 S. Malpais Ln. (774-4573), across from NAU campus, 3 blocks southwest of the train station on U.S. 89A. To: Phoenix, including airport (3hr., 4 per day, $20); Albuquerque (6½hr., 4 per day, $46); Los Angeles (10-12hr., 9 per day, $49); and Las Vegas (6-7hr., 3 per day via Kingman, casino special round-trip $49). Terminal open 24hr. **Grayline/Nava-Hopi,** 114 W. Rt. 66 (774-5003 or 800-892-8687). Shuttle buses to the Grand Canyon (2hr., 2 per day, $18.50 including admission fee) and Phoenix (3hr., 3 per day).

**Public Transit: Pine Country Transit,** 970 W. Rt. 66 (779-6624). Routes cover most of town. Buses run once per hr.; route map and schedule available at visitors center. One-way 75¢; seniors, children, and disabled 60¢.

**Taxis: Friendly Cab,** 214-9000.

**Car Rental: Budget Rent-A-Car** (779-5255), at the Flagstaff Airport. Cars with unlimited mileage. Must be 21 with major credit card or a $200 cash deposit. Under 25 surcharge $20 per day. Open daily 7am-7pm. *Let's Go* toters get 10% off.

**Equipment Rental: Peace Surplus,** 14 W. Rt. 66 (779-4521), 1 block from Grand Canyon Hostel. Daily tent rental ($5-8; $100-200 deposit), packs ($6; $300 deposit), plus a good stock of cheap outdoor gear. 3-day min. rental on all equipment. Credit card or cash deposit required. Open M-F 8am-9pm, Sa 8am-8pm, Su 8am-6pm.

**Visitor Info: Flagstaff Visitors Center,** 1 E. Rt. 66 (774-9541 or 800-842-7293), in the Amtrak station. Open M-Sa 7am-6pm, Su 7am-5pm.

**Internet Access:** NAU's **Cline Library** (523-2171). Open M-Th 7:30am-10pm, F 7:30am-6pm, Sa 9am-6pm, Su noon-10pm.

**Post Office:** 2400 N. Postal Blvd. (527-2440), for general delivery. Open M-F 9am-5pm, Sa 9am-noon. **ZIP code:** 86004. There's one closer to downtown at 104 N. Agassiz St., 86001, open the same hrs. **Area code:** 520.

# ACCOMMODATIONS

When swarms of summer tourists descend on Flagstaff, accommodations prices shoot up. Thankfully, the town is blessed with excellent hostels. Historic **Rt. 66** is home to many cheap motels. *The Flagstaff Accommodations Guide*, available at the visitors center, lists all area hotels, motels, hostels, and bed and breakfasts. If you're here to see the Grand Canyon (and who isn't?), check the noticeboard in your hotel or hostel; some travelers leave their still-valid passes behind.

**Grand Canyon International Hostel,** 19 S. San Francisco St. (779-9421), near the train station. Sunny, clean, classy, and friendly. Free tea and coffee, breakfast, parking, and linen. Access to kitchen, TV room with cable, internet ($2), and laundry facilities. Free pick-up from Greyhound station. Tours to the Grand Canyon ($30-40) and Sedona ($20). 4-bed dorms $15; private rooms $35. Reception 7am-11pm.

**Motel Du Beau,** 19 W. Phoenix St. (774-6731 or 800-398-7112), also just behind the train station. Carpeted dorm rooms with private bathrooms and showers. Social atmosphere lasts into the wee hours. Free Internet access, tea and coffee, breakfast, linen, parking, and rides to and from the airport, train, and bus stations. Tours to Grand Canyon and Sedona arranged through Grand Canyon Hostel (same price). 4-bed dorms $13; private rooms $27. Reception 6am-midnight.

**Hotel Monte Vista,** 100 N. San Francisco St. (779-6971 or 800-545-3068), downtown. Feels like a classy hotel, with charmingly quirky decor and a bar (with pool tables, video games, and off-track betting) downstairs. The place is phasing out hostel accommodations, but some dorm beds are still available. 4-bed dorms with private baths $12; private rooms named after movie stars who slept there $40-90.

**The Weatherford Hotel,** 23 N. Leroux St. (774-2731 or 779-1919), on the other side of the tracks 1 block west of San Francisco St. Spacious rooms in this historic hotel, with bay windows, bunk beds, and funky furniture. Dorm rooms (though rarely available) have baths in rooms and halls. Kitchen access. Dorm beds $16; hotel singles $50-55; doubles $55-60. Reservations recommended.

**KOA Campground,** 5803 N. U.S. 89 (526-9926), a few mi. northeast of Flagstaff. Local buses stop near this beautiful campground. Showers, restrooms, free nightly movies, kitchen during summer. Tent sites for 2 $20, cabins $34; $4 per additional person.

Camping in the surrounding **Coconino National Forest** is a pleasant and inexpensive alternative, but you'll need a car to reach the designated camping areas. Forest maps ($6) are available at the Flagstaff Visitors Center. Many campgrounds fill up quickly during the summer, particularly on weekends when Phoenicians flock to the mountains; those at high elevations close for the winter. All sites are handled on a first come, first served basis; stake out a site by 1pm. **Lake View,** 13mi. southeast on Forest Hwy. 3 (U.S. 89A), has 30 sites ($10). **Bonito,** 18mi. northeast of downtown Flagstaff, off U.S. 89 on Forest Rd. 545, at the entrance to Sunset Crater (see p. 718), rents 44 sites ($12). Both feature running water and flush toilets (both 14-day max. stay; open mid-May to Sept. or Oct., weather-dependent). Camping is free anywhere in the national forest outside the designated campsites, unless otherwise marked. For info on campgrounds and backcountry camping, call the **Coconino Forest Service** (527-3600; open M-F 7:30am-4:30pm).

## 📷 🎵 FOOD, NIGHTLIFE, AND ENTERTAINMENT

All the arch-wielding, deep-fat frying chains are readily available outside of downtown, but near the heart of Flagstaff, the creative and off-beat rules. **Macy's,** 14 S. Beaver St., behind Motel Du Beau, is a cheery student hangout serving only vegetarian food in an earthy atmosphere. Fresh pasta ($4-6), a wide variety of entrees ($3-6), sandwiches ($4-6), pastries ($1-2), and espresso-based drinks ($1-4). (774-2243. Open M-W 6am-8pm, Th-Sa 6am-9pm, Su 6am-6pm. Food served until 1hr. before closing.) Many varieties of worldwide cuisine and fresh juices are blended at **Mountain Oasis,** 11 E. Aspen St., where Asian, Middle Eastern, European, American, and some combinations thereof are dished up amid cascading fountains and lush vegetation. Big salads ($5-6), pasta dinners ($9-10), and sushi ($5; 214-9270; open daily 9am-9pm). Behind demure lace curtains, **Kathy's Café,** 7 N. San Francisco St., prepares delicious and inventive breakfasts accompanied by biscuits and fresh fruit ($4-6). Lunch sandwiches include $5 veggie options (774-1951; open M-F 6:30am-3pm, Sa-Su 7am-3:30pm. No credit cards accepted). Never buy magic beans, except at **The Black Bean,** 12 E. Rt. 66. They'll fire you up quick and cheap with great burritos ($3-6; 779-9905; open M-Sa 11am-9pm, Su noon-8pm).

At night, head for the pool tables of **Mad Italian,** 101 S. San Francisco St. (779-1820. Happy hour daily 4-7pm. Open daily noon-1am.) **Charly's,** 23 N. Leroux St., plays live jazz and blues in one of the classiest buildings in town (779-1919; open daily 11am-10pm; bar open daily 11am-1am). If country-western is your thang, the **Museum Club,** 3404 E. Rt. 66, a.k.a. the **Zoo,** will rock your world. This place is the real deal—it was built during the Great Depression as a premiere roadhouse to liven spirits. Cowboy gusto is re-enacted daily with liquid spirits and 1st-class country (526-9434; cover $3-5; open daily 11am-3am).

In early June, the annual **Flagstaff Rodeo** (800-638-4253) comes to town with competitions, barn dances, a carnival, and a cocktail waitress race. The **Flagstaff Symphony** (774-5107) plays from Oct. to May (tickets $12-25, under 18 half-price). **Theatrikos,** 11 W. Cherry Ave. (774-1662), a local theater group, stages plays year-round in their own playhouse. For the month of July, the **Festival of the Arts** attracts chamber concerts, orchestras, and individual performers.

## 👁 SIGHTS

In 1894, Percival Lowell chose Flagstaff as the site for an astronomical observatory; he then spent the rest of his life here, culling data to support his theory that life exists on Mars. **Lowell Observatory,** just west of downtown off Rt. 66, now has five telescopes that have been used in breakthrough studies of Mars and Pluto. Admission includes tours of the telescopes, as well as a museum with hands-on astronomy exhibits. On clear summer nights, you can peer through the 100-year-old Clark telescope at some heavenly body selected by the staff. *(1400 W. Mars Hill Rd. 774-2096. Open daily 9am-5pm. Night sky viewings vary with season; call ahead. $3.50, ages 5-17 $1.50.)* The more down-to-earth **Museum of Northern Arizona,** off U.S. 180 a few mi. north of town, houses a huge collection of Southwestern Native American art. *(774-5213. Open daily 9am-5pm. $5, students $3, seniors $4, ages 7-17 $2.)*

The huge, snow-capped mountains visible to the north of Flagstaff are the **San Francisco Peaks.** To reach the peaks, take U.S. 180 about 7mi. north to the Fairfield Snow Bowl turn-off. Nearby **Mt. Agassiz** has the area's best **skiing.** The **Arizona Snow Bowl** operates four lifts from mid-Dec. to mid-Apr.; its 30 trails receive an average of 8½ ft. of powder each winter. *(779-1951. Open daily 8am-5pm. Lift tickets $30.)* In the summer, these peaks are perfect for hiking. The Hopi believe **Humphrey's Peak**—the highest point in Arizona at 12,670 ft.—is the sacred home of the Kachina spirits. When the air is clear, you can see the North Rim of the Grand Canyon, the Painted Desert, and countless square mi. of Arizona and Utah from the top of the peak. Reluctant hikers will find the vista from the top of the Snow Bowl's **chairlift** almost as stunning. *(20-30min. Runs late June to early Sept. daily 10am-4pm; early Sept. to mid-Oct. F-Su 10am-4pm. $9, seniors $6.50, ages 6-12 $5.)* The mountains occupy national forest land, so backcountry camping is free.

## NEAR FLAGSTAFF

**WALNUT CANYON NATIONAL MONUMENT.** The ruins of more than 300 rooms in 13th-century Sinagua dwellings make up Walnut Canyon National Monument, constructed within a 400 ft. deep canyon. A glassed-in observation deck in the **visitors center** overlooks the whole canyon. The steep, self-guided **Island Trail** snakes down from the visitors center past 25 cliff dwellings. Markers along the 1mi. trail describe aspects of Sinagua life and identify plants used for food, dyes, medicine, and hunting. The 0.7mi. **Rim Trail** offers some great views of the canyon and passes the rim-top inhabitances. Every Sa morning, rangers lead 2mi. hikes into Walnut Canyon to the original Ranger Cabin and more remote cliff dwellings. Hiking boots and long pants are required for these challenging 2½hr. hikes. Walnut Canyon lies 10mi. east of Flagstaff off I-40. *(520-526-3367. Open daily 8am-6pm; off season 9am-5pm. $3, under 16 free. Call ahead, hrs. change frequently.)*

**SUNSET CRATER VOLCANO NATIONAL MONUMENT.** The crater encompassed by Sunset Crater Volcano National Monument, 12mi. north of Flagstaff on U.S. 89, appeared in 1065. Over the next 200 years, a 1000 ft. high cinder cone took shape as a result of periodic eruptions. The self-guided **Lava Flow Nature Trail** wanders 1mi. through the surreal landscape surrounding the cone, 1½mi. east of the visitors center, where gnarled trees lie uprooted amid the rocky black terrain. Lava tube tours have been permanently discontinued due to falling lava, and hiking up Sunset Crater itself is not permitted. The **visitors center** supplies additional info. *(520-526-0502. Open daily 8am-6pm; off season 8am-5pm. $3 per person, under 16 free; includes admission to Wupatki.)* The **Bonito Campground,** in the Coconino National Forest at the entrance to Sunset Crater, provides tent sites (see p. 716).

**WUPATKI NATIONAL MONUMENT.** Wupatki possesses some of the Southwest's most scenic pueblo ruins, situated 18mi. northeast of Sunset Crater, along a stunning road with views of the Painted Desert. The Sinagua moved here in the 11th century, after the Sunset Crater eruption forced them to evacuate the land to the south. In less than 200 years, however, droughts, disease, and over-farming led the Sinagua to abandon these stone houses perched on the sides of *arroyos* in view of the San Francisco Peaks. Five deserted pueblos face the 14mi. road from U.S. 89 to the visitors center. Another road to the ruins begins on U.S. 89, 30mi. north of Flagstaff. The largest and most accessible, **Wupatki Ruin,** located on a ½mi. round-trip loop trail from the visitors center, rises 3 stories. The spectacular **Doney Mountain trail** rises ½mi. from the picnic area to the summit. Get info and trail guide brochures at the **visitors center.** *(520-679-2365. Open daily 8am-5pm. Monument open daily 8am-5pm. Brochures 50¢.)* Backcountry hiking is not permitted.

## NAVAJO RESERVATION

In the 1830s, federal policymakers planned to create a permanent Native American country in the west. By mid-century, however, those plans had been washed away by the tide of American expansion. Indian reservations evolved out of the U.S. government's subsequent *ad hoc* attempts to prevent fighting between Native Americans and whites while facilitating white settlement. Initially, the reservation system imposed a kind of wardship on the Native Americans, which lasted for over a century, until a series of Supreme Court decisions, beginning in the 1960s, reasserted the tribes' legal standing as semi-sovereign nations.

The largest reservation in America, the **Navajo Nation,** or the "rez" as the locals call it, covers more than 27,000 sq. mi. of northeastern Arizona, southeastern Utah, and northwestern New Mexico. Within its boundaries, the smaller **Hopi Reservation** is home to around 10,000 Hopi ("Peaceable People"). Ruins mark the dwellings of the Ancestral Puebloans who inhabited the area until the 13th century. Over 210,000 Navajo, or Diné (dih-NEH, "the People") as they call themselves, currently live in the Navajo Nation, comprising one-tenth of the U.S. Native American population. The Nation has its own police force and laws. Possession and consumption of alcohol are prohibited on the reservation. General photography is allowed, unless otherwise stated, but photographing the Navajo people requires their permission (a gratuity is usually expected). Tourist photography is not permitted among the Hopi. Lively reservation politics are written up in the local *Navajo-Hopi Observer* and *Navajo Times* as well as in regional sections of Denver, Albuquerque, and Phoenix newspapers. For a taste of the Navajo language and Native American ritual songs, tune your radio to 660AM, "The Voice of the Navajo." Remember to advance your watch 1hr. during the summer; the Navajo Nation runs on **Mountain Daylight Time,** while the rest of Arizona, including the Hopi reservation, remains on Mountain Standard Time.

For visitors to the reservation, cultural sensitivity takes on a new importance; despite the many state and interstate roads that transverse the reservation, the land is legally and culturally outside the U.S. On the outside, much of the Navajo Nation and other reservations resemble the rest of the U.S. In reality, deep rifts exist between Native American and "Anglo culture"—the term used to refer to the non-reservation society. The best remedy for cultural friction is usually simple respect. The Navajo and Hopi welcome visitors warmly as long as tourists do not infringe upon their beliefs and way of life: never photograph religious ceremonies, follow the somewhat more modest dress and behavior, and, most importantly, be respectful of their ancient religious beliefs and practices.

Monument Valley, Canyon de Chelly, Navajo National Monument, Rainbow Bridge, Antelope Canyon, and the roads and trails that access these sights all lie on Navajo land. Driving or hiking off-road without a guide is considered trespassing. Those planning to hike through Navajo territory should head to the visitors center in **Window Rock** (see below) for a **backcountry permit,** or mail a request along with a money order or certified check to P.O. Box 9000, Window Rock, AZ 86515 ($5 per person). Fill up your gas tank before exploring the reservation; gas stations are few and far between. The "border towns" of **Gallup, NM** (see p. 747); **Flagstaff, AZ** (see p. 715); and **Page, AZ** (see p. 722) are good gateways to the reservations, with car rental agencies, inexpensive accommodations, and frequent **Greyhound** service on I-40. There are almost no budget accommodations in Navajo territory; budget travelers should camp at the national monuments or Navajo campgrounds, or stay in a border town. The **area code** for the entire reservation: 520.

## WINDOW ROCK

The capital of the Navajo Nation, **Window Rock** is the seat of tribal government and features the geological formation for which the town is named. The limited lodging in town is expensive, but Navajo sights make Window Rock a good stopover en route to or from Gallup. A terrific view of the eponymous rock itself can be had from **Window Rock Tribal Park,** off Rt. 12 just past the government offices. The **Navajo Tribal Museum,** on Rt. 264 ½mi. east of Rt. 12, has four rooms of Navajo and Navajo-related artwork and photography (871-6673; open M-F 8am-5pm; free). For those who want to observe the tribal government in action, in the Navajo language, the **Navajo Council Tribal Chambers** offers free tours of the governing body's meeting rooms (871-6417; open M-F 8am-noon and 1-5pm). The animals in the **Navajo Nation Zoo and Botanical Park,** across from the Tribal Museum, might look a little familiar, although you may not have seen them in a zoo before. Recent tribal debates have centered on whether the zoo should remain open, since many of the animals featured are considered sacred. Check that the zoo is open before visiting (871-6573; open daily 8am-5pm; free). The oldest trading post in the U.S. and a national historic site, the **Hubbell Trading Post,** 30mi. west of Window Rock on Rt. 264 in the town of Ganado, has functioned as a store since 1876. It still sells Navajo arts and crafts, and now also houses a museum. The work put into the rugs justifies their steep prices, though it makes the post a museum stop and not a store for most (733-3475; open daily 8am-6pm, in winter 8am-5pm; free).

The **Navajoland Tourism Dept.,** P.O. Box 663, Window Rock 86515, in downtown Window Rock in the same building as the museum (see above), offers the free pamphlet *Discover Navajoland,* which has a full list of accommodations and jeep and horseback tour providers. The **tourist office** also sells a detailed map ($3) entitled *The Visitors' Guide to the Navajo Nation* (871-6436; open M-F 8am-5pm).

## CANYON DE CHELLY NATIONAL MONUMENT

The red hue of the cliffs of Canyon de Chelly (pronounced "Canyon de Shay") and the adjoining canyons in the national monument have enchanted settlers for over four millennia, giving the area a history far greater than anywhere else in the four-corners region. Unfortunately, some of the canyon's history has been colored by repeated conflicts between Native Americans and whites. In 1805, 115 Native American women and children were shot by Spanish men, in what is now called **Massacre Cave.** Kit Carson starved the Navajo out of the canyon in the 1860s.

To the Navajo, it is the nature of *Tsegi* (say-he), the spirit of their home, that brings new life to this region. The fertile **Beautiful Valley** is testament to the vitality of the land. So central is this region to the local Native American culture, that the Navajo Nation was purposely created with Canyon de Chelly at its center. Despite the fact that the **Canyon de Chelly National Monument** lies on Navajo Nation land, it is administered by the National Park Service. (See **Navajo Reservation,** p. 719, for info on reservation laws affecting tourists.) The park service leads a 9am summer hike ($10), or you can hire a private guide. (3hr., $10 per hr. You provide four-wheel-drive vehicle, free permit from visitor's center.) Reservations for either can be made through the visitors center, but are not required. Horseback tours can be arranged at **Justin's Horse Rental,** on South Rim Dr., at the canyon's mouth (674-5678; open daily 9am-sundown; horses $8 per hr.; mandatory guide $8 per hr).

The 2½mi. round-trip trail to **White House Ruin,** 7mi. from the visitors center off South Canyon Rd., is the only trail in the park on which visitors are permitted to walk without a guide. But what a trail—it winds down 600ft. into the canyon, past a Navajo farm and traditional hogan, through an orchard, and across a stream to cliff dwelling ruins. You can also take one of the paved **Rim Drives** (North Rim 15mi. one-way, South Rim 16mi. one-way) skirting the edge of the 300-700 ft. cliffs; the South Rim is more dramatic. Get booklets (50¢) on the White House Ruin and Rim Drives at the visitors center. On the North Rim Drive, the large dwellings in **Mummy Cave Ruin** are impressive. Nearby is the somber Massacre Cave. **Spider Rock Overlook,** 16mi. from the visitors center, on the South Rim Drive, is a narrow sandstone monolith towering hundreds of feet above the canyon floor. Native American lore says the whitish rock at the top contains the bleached bones of victims of the *kachina* spirit, or Spider Woman, who has a taste for disobedient children.

The most common route to the park is from **Chambers,** 75mi. south, at the intersection of I-40 and U.S. 191; you can also come from the north via U.S. 191.

Entrance to the monument is free. The **visitors center** sits 2mi. east of Chinle on Navajo Rt. 64 (674-5500; open daily 8am-6pm; Oct.-Apr. 8am-5pm). One of the larger towns on the reservation, **Chinle,** adjacent to U.S. 191, has restaurants and gas stations. There is no public transportation to the park. In an **emergency,** contact the park ranger (674-5523, after hrs. 674-5524) or the Navajo Police (674-2111).

Camp for free in the park's **Cottonwood Campground,** 1½mi. from the visitors center. This giant campground, located in a pretty cottonwood grove, can get noisy with the din of the stray dogs who wander about the site at night. Sites are first come, first served. (674-5500. Restrooms, picnic tables, water (except in winter), and dump station. 5-day max. stay.) The only budget accommodation in Navajo territory is the **Many Farms Inn,** a converted dormitory 17mi. north of Canyon de Chelly. At the junction of Rt. 191 and 59, go north 1mi. on Rt. 191, turn left at the sign for Many Farms High School, and follow this road 1mi. farther to the inn. (781-6363. Singles or doubles $30. Shared bath.) **Farmington, NM,** and **Cortez, CO,** are the closest major cities with multiple cheap lodging options.

## MONUMENT VALLEY

The red sandstone towers of Monument Valley are one of the southwest's most otherworldly sights. Paradoxically, however, they're also one of the most familiar, since countless westerns have used the butte-laden plain as backdrops to Wild West adventures. Some years before John Wayne, Ancestoral Puebloen (Anasazi) managed to sustain small communities here, despite the hot, arid climate. The park's looping 17mi. **Valley Drive** winds around 11 of the most spectacular formations, including the famous pair of **Mittens** and the slender **Totem Pole.** However, the gaping ditches, large rocks, and mudholes on this road can be jarring to both you and your car—drive at your own risk and observe the 15 mph speed limit. The drive takes at least 1½hr. Other, less-touristed parts of the valley can be reached only by 4-wheel-drive vehicle, horse, or foot. **Leaving the main road without a guide is not permitted.** The visitors center parking lot is crowded with booths run by small companies selling jeep, horseback, and hiking tours. (1½hr. jeep tour about $15 per person, 1½hr. horseback tour $30, 4hr. hiking tour $45; prices higher for a single person.) In winter, snow laces the rocky towers, and most tourists flee. Call the visitors center to inquire about snow and road conditions.

The park entrance lies on U.S. 163 just across the Utah border, 24mi. north of the Navajo town **Kayenta,** which is at the intersection of U.S. 163 and U.S. 160. The **visitors center** (435-727-3353) has info. (Park and visitors center open daily 7am-7pm; Oct.-Apr. 8am-5pm. Valley Drive closes at 6:30pm; begin by 4:30pm to complete it. Admission $2.50, seniors $1, under 7 free.)

Accommodations in the area are hard to come by. **Mitten View Campground,** ¼mi. southwest of the visitors center, offers 100 sites, showers, and restrooms, but no hookups. (Sites $10; in winter $5. Register at the visitors center. No reservations.) The **Navajo National Monument** (see below) has more camping. Cheap motels are in **Mexican Hat, UT** (see p. 709); **Bluff, UT** (see p. 709); and **Page, AZ** (see p. 722).

## NAVAJO NATIONAL MONUMENT

Until the late 1200s, a small population of Hopi ancestors inhabited the region, though hard times left the villages vacant by 1300. From U.S. 160, 20mi west of Kayenta, Rt. 564 travels 9mi. north to the park entrance. Today, the site contains 3 cliff dwellings. **Inscription House** has been closed to visitors indefinitely due to its fragile condition; the other 2 admit a very limited number of visitors. The stunning **Keet Seel** (open late May to early Sept.) can be reached only via a challenging 16mi. roundtrip hike. Hikers can stay overnight in a free campground nearby (no facilities or drinking water). Reservations for permits to visit Keet Seel must be made up to 2 months in advance through the **visitors center;** total reservations are limited to 20 people per day (520-672-2366. Open daily 8am-5pm; off-season 8am-4:30pm.) Ranger-led tours to **Betatakin,** a 135-room complex, are limited to 25 people. (1 per day at 8:15am; first come, first served the morning of the tour. A strenuous 5mi., 5-6hr. hike. Open May to late Sept.) If you're not up for the trek to the ruins, the paved, 1mi. roundtrip **Sandal Trail** lets you gaze down on Betatakin from the top of the canyon. The **Aspen Forest Overlook Trail,** another 1mi. hike, overlooks canyons and aspens, but no ruins. Write to **Navajo National Monument,** HC 71 Box 3, Tonalea 86044 for more info. The free **campground,** next to the visitors center, has 30 sites. An additional overflow campground nearby has no running water. (First come, first served. 7-day max. stay. No hookups.)

## HOPI RESERVATION

Located in the southwestern corner of the Navajo Nation, the Hopi Reservation clusters around 3 mesas, connected by Rt. 264, imaginatively named First Mesa, Second Mesa, and Third Mesa. On Second Mesa, the **Hopi Cultural Center,** 63mi. north of Winslow, AZ, at the intersection of Rt. 264 and 87, contains the reservation's only museum, which displays Hopi textiles, baskets, jewelry, pottery, and information about the tribe's history. (730-6650. Open M-F 8am-5pm; Sa 8am-4pm; $3, children $1.) **Area code:** 520.

Visitors are welcome to attend some of the Hopi **village dances.** Announced only a few days in advance, these religious ceremonies usually occur on weekends and last from sunrise to sundown. The dances are highly formal occasions; do not wear shorts, tank tops, or other casual wear. Photographs, recordings, and sketches are strictly forbidden. Often several villages will hold dances on the same day, giving tourist the opportunity to go village-hopping. Inquire at the cultural center, the Flagstaff Chamber of Commerce, or the **Hopi Cultural Preservation Office,** P.O. Box 123, Kykotsmovi 86039 (734-2244), for the dates and sites of the dances.

In the village of **Tsakurshovi,** 1½mi. east of the cultural center on Rt. 264, the **shop** run by Joe and Janice Day sells Hopi crafts and functions as a sort of makeshift tourist office. They're also the creators of the "Don't Worry, Be Hopi" t-shirt ($15), which has been spotted on the likes of the Indigo Girls. Ask them about tours to the village of **Walpi,** on Third Mesa, which features ancient, but still inhabited, pueblo dwellings (734-2478; open daily 8am-6pm).

## LAKE POWELL AND PAGE

"Dammit!" said President Dwight Eisenhower in 1953, pressing a large red button on his desk. Many hundreds of mi. away, a massive explosion shook the earth. Thus began a tremendous effort to provide water and energy to the desert: ten years and 10 million tons of concrete later, **Glen Canyon Dam,** the second-largest dam in the country, was completed. With no particular place to go, the Colorado River flooded **Glen Canyon,** which spanned northern Arizona and southern Utah, to form the 186mi. long **Lake Powell.** Ironically named after John Wesley Powell, a one-armed Civil War veteran who led and chronicled the first expedition down the then-raging but now-sedated Colorado, the lake offers 1960mi. of shoreline. Water sports and fishing are the most popular activities on the lake, but hiking opportunities also abound. Spectacular **Antelope Canyon** plays outside the resort town of **Page** near the southwest tip of Lake Powell at the U.S. 89/Rt. 98 junction.

**🏿 PRACTICAL INFORMATION.** Visitors can descend into the inner workings of Glen Canyon Dam alone, or let the **Carl Hayden Visitors Center** (608-6404), on U.S. 89 N, 1mi. north of Page, act as the guide. (Open in summer daily 8am-7pm; off-season 8am-5pm. Free dam tours every hr. on the hr. 8:30am-5:30pm.) **Page Chamber of Commerce:** 644 N. Navajo Dr. (645-2741), in the Dam Plaza (open daily 8am-8pm; in winter M-F 9am-5pm). Lake Powell and Page's **area code:** 520.

**🏿🏿 ACCOMMODATIONS AND FOOD.** The distinctly superior 🏿 **Lake Powell International Hostel,** 141 8th Ave., in Page, provides free pickup and delivery to Lake Powell, coffee, linen, a kitchen, BBQ grill, TV, volleyball court, and an outdoor eating area. The owners are unswervingly devoted to pleasing their guests, and will go out of their way to make sure you have a good time, which includes providing you with quality accommodations. Ask Jeff, the host, to arrange tours for you. (645-3898. Bunks $12-15. No curfew. Reserve ahead Aug.-Sept.) Under the same management, **Pension at Lake Powell,** next door to the hostel, has more upscale suites with a bathroom, a living room with cable TV, and a kitchen (doubles for 2-6 $35; $5 per additional person). For a very different kind of atmosphere, try **Uncle Bill's Place,** 117 8th Ave., 1 block away. The attractive rooms have adjoining kitchens and a garden out back (645-1224. Singles and doubles with shared bath $39.) **Bashful Bob's Motel,** 750 S. Navajo Dr., isn't embarrassed about its huge rooms with kitchens, sitting areas, and cable TV. (645-3919. Singles and doubles $39, around $25 in the winter.) **Wahweap Campground,** 100 Lake Shore Dr., adjacent to the exorbitant **Wahweap Lodge,** has 200 sites on a first come, first served basis (645-2433 or 800-528-6154; $15-17). Next door, the **Wahweep RV Park** takes care of the motorized set (full hookup $23 for 2 adults; $3 per additional adult).

**Cactus & Tropicals Garden and Cafe,** 809 N. Navajo Dr., owned by the town mayor, is your best bet for healthy, high quality food in. Adorned with a beautiful outdoor garden and indoor boutique, the atmosphere and food are a nice change from the usually grease-fortified Page offerings. (645-6666. Sandwiches $5; open M-Sa 8am-7pm). For those feeling a bit more decadent, the popular **Strombolli's Restaurant & Pizzeria,** 711 N. Navajo Dr., cooks up $9 "calzones as big as your head" (645-2605; open M-Th 11am-9pm, F-Su 11am-10pm). Live country music plays nightly at **Ken's Old West Restaurant & Lounge,** 718 Vista Ave., behind the Lake Powell Best Western, where barbecue is taken seriously. Vegetarians will appreciate the great salad bar. (645-5160. Ribs $10, chicken $9. Open daily 4pm-1am; no food after 11pm.)

**▒ ▨ SIGHTS AND ACTIVITIES.** Lake Powell's man-made shores are rocky rather than sandy, with skimpy beaches that vanish when the water rises. Completely unnatural, smurf-blue, "97%-pure," 80°-in-the-summer waters more than make up for the rocky shore. Recreation opportunities abound at **Wahweep Marina,** where you can swim, rent a boat or take a boat tour. *(645-2433. 8-person skiff $199; off-season $99 Tours $10-83.)* **Free swimming** is available at "The Chains," a group of quiet coves surrounded by rocky shoreline, found off a dirt road just before the dam on Rt. 89. Many companies lead **boat tours** to the famous **Rainbow Bridge National Monument,** the world's largest natural bridge. The bridge, which is sacred to the Navajo, takes its name from the Navajo word *nonnoshoshi,* "rainbow turned to stone." The bridge can be reached by a strenuous 2-day hike or a ½-day boat tour. **ARAMARK Leisure Services** conducts boat tours *(800-528-6154. Full-day $92, under 12 $62; ½-day $69/$49. Call ahead for reservations.)* Hiking permits must be obtained in advance from the Navajo Nation, since the trails cross Navajo land. Write to **Navajo Nation,** P.O. Box 308, Window Rock, AZ 86515.

No less spectacular for its great accessibility, the kaleidoscopic **Antelope Canyon** is one of the only slot canyons in the U.S. The entrance is on U.S. 98 several mi. south of Page, by the Navajo Power Plant. The trail through the **upper canyon,** while moderately strenuous, is wider and easier to negotiate than the one through the **lower canyon,** which requires many tight squeezes so is less touristed. Sunlight illu-

**DEEP IMPACT** Perhaps the recent American obsession with all things extraterrestrial explains the enormous popularity of **Meteor Crater,** 35mi. east of Flagstaff off I-40, because not much else could. Originally thought to be a volcanic cone, the crater is now believed to be the impact site of a giant nickel-iron meteorite that fell to earth 50,000 years ago. Visitors are not allowed to hike down into the crater, which measures 4100ft. across, but must fight the hordes for an unspectacular view over the guard-railed edge. Conspicuously missing in action is the meteor itself; scientists believe that most of it was vaporized at the moment of impact, since it was traveling at an impressive 10mi. per second. The site was used to train Apollo astronauts in the 1960s, and a museum in the building near the admissions booth patriotically celebrates the U.S. space program (free with crater admission). (520-289-5898. Open daily 6am-6pm; off season 8am-5pm. $8, seniors $7, ages 6-17 $4.)

THE SOUTHWEST

minating the canyon's twisting sandstone walls is nothing short of incredible. The canyon lies on Navajo land, so a **guide** is required (1½hr.; $15 per person).

A short, beautiful hike leads to **Horseshoe Bend Overlook,** which provides a view of the Colorado River as it curves around a huge rock formation. Evening hikes reveal spectacular sunsets. The trail leads from a parking lot down a dirt road off U.S. 89, just south of Mi. 545—the tourist office or hostel can provide directions.

## PETRIFIED FOREST AND PAINTED DESERT

It's a couple hundred years too late to see a forest; the 60,000-acre **Petrified Forest National Park** is a dreamscape dotted with fallen trees turned to stone. Some 225 million years ago, when Arizona's desert was a floodplain, volcanic ash covered the logs, slowing their decay. When silica-rich water seeped through the wood, the silica crystallized into quartz, producing rainbow hues. One of the most unique attractions in the Southwest, the park also contains a scenic chunk of the Painted Desert, named for the stunning colors that stripe its rock formations.

The park road winds past **Puerco Pueblo,** a 500-year old dwelling; **Agate House,** a pueblo made from petrified wood; and **Newspaper Rock,** covered with Native American petroglyphs. At **Blue Mesa,** a moderately difficult hiking trail ventures into the desert. Easier and less serene are the trails to **Long Logs, Giant Logs,** and **Crystal Forest. Jasper Forest** overlook offers a great view with no hike. Picking up fragments of the wood is illegal and traditionally unlucky; if the district attorney doesn't get you, then the demons will. Those who *must* have a piece should buy one at one of the myriad stores along I-40. The **Painted Desert** section lies at the park's north end; here, a number of overlooks allow for unimpeded gazing. No established trails traverse the Painted Desert, but **backcountry hiking** is allowed (permit required). Beware that sneakers will be eternally coated in red sand.

Enter the park either from the north or the south. (Open daily 7am-7pm. Entrance fee $10 per vehicle, $5 per pedestrian.) A 27mi. road connects the two entrances. To enter the southern section of the park, exit I-40 at Holbrook and take U.S. 180 W to the **Rainbow Forest Museum.** The museum provides a look at petrified logs up close and serves as a **visitors center** (524-6822; open daily 8am-7pm; off-season 8am-5pm; free). There are no established campgrounds in the park, but **free backcountry camping** is allowed in several areas with a permit. To enter the Painted Desert section of the park, take I-40 to exit 311 (107mi. east of Flagstaff). The **Painted Desert Visitors Center** (524-6228) is less than 5mi. from the exit (open daily in summer 7am-7pm; off-season 8am-5pm). There is no public transportation to either part of the park. **Nava-Hopi Bus Lines, Gray Line Tours,** and **Blue Goose Backpacker Tours** offer services from **Flagstaff** (see p. 715). The closest cheap lodging is in **Holbrook** (27mi. from the park) **Gallup, NM** (see p. 747); or **Flagstaff** (see p. 715). In Holbrook, the rooms at **Economy Inn,** 310 W. Hopi Dr., could use some paint, but you can't beat the price (524-6490; rooms with 1 bed $20; 2 beds $27).

## SEDONA

A UFO sighting hotspot, one wonders if the Martians are simply mistaking the deep red-rock towers of Sedona for home. The scores of tourists who descend upon the town year-round (Sedona rivals the Grand Canyon for tourist mass) certainly aren't; they come for sights that would make Newton question gravity's effectiveness. Dramatic copper-toned behemoths dotted with pines tower over Sedona, rising from the earth with such flair and crowd appeal that they feel like a perfectly manufactured tourist attraction. Some folks in town will tell you that they were man-made, perhaps by the Egyptians—Sedona is also the New Age capital of the U.S. The downtown is overrun with overpriced boutiques and cafes, but the rocks are simply spectacular.

At **Slide Rock State Park** (282-3034), 10mi. north of Sedona on U.S. 89A, rocks form a natural waterslide into the cold waters of Oak Creek. In the summer, locals come in droves to swim and picnic. (Open daily 8am-7pm; closes earlier in off season. $5 per car, $1 per pedestrian or cyclist.) The incredible formations at **Red Rock State Park** (282-6907), on U.S. 89A 15mi. southwest of town, invite strolling or just contemplation. Rangers lead day hikes into the nearby rock formations; do-it-yourselfers can pick up a trail map at the visitors center. (Visitors center open daily 9am-5pm. Park open daily 8am-6pm; Oct.-Mar. 8am-5pm. $5 per car, $1 per pedestrian or cyclist.) **Chapel of the Holy Cross** (282-4069), on Chapel Rd., lies just outside a 1000 ft. rock wall in the middle of red sandstone. (Open daily 9am-5pm.) The view from the parking lot is a religious experience itself.

The **Sedona Chamber of Commerce** (282-7722), at Forest Rd. and Rt. 89A, distributes listings for accommodations and private campgrounds in the area (open M-Sa 8:30am-4:30pm, Su 9am-3pm). Lodging in town is a bit pricey, but a few deals can be had; however, it's not a bad idea to make Sedona a daytrip from Flagstaff. **Hostel Sedona,** 5 Soldiers Wash Drive, off Brewer Rd. which connects with Rt. 89A uptown, provides basic, camp-like accommodations at a great location. (282-2772. Dorm beds $15; private room $30-$45. Kitchen and common room. Chores required). **White House Inn,** 2986 W. Rte 89A, is the second cheapest option, with singles and doubles, some with kitchenettes, at $48-$58 (282-6680). A popular alternative to commercial lodging is renting a room in a private residence. Check the local papers or bulletin boards at a New Age shop for opportunities.

There are a number of **campgrounds** within **Coconino National Forest** (527-3600), along Oak Creek Canyon on U.S. 89A (sites $12 per vehicle). The largest, **Cave Springs,** 20mi. north of town, administers 78 sites (call 800-283-2267 for reservations). For more info on Coconino Forest, including hiking maps, visit the **ranger station,** 250 Brewer Rd. (282-4119); turn off U.S. 89A at Burger King (open M-Sa 7:30am-4:30pm; in winter M-F 7:30am-4:30pm). **Mountain Bike Heaven,** 25 E. Rt. 89A (801-676-2880) also dispenses trail info and **rents bikes** to boot. Free **backcountry camping** is allowed in the forest anywhere outside of Oak Creek and more than 1mi. from any official campground or trailhead.

The **Coffee Pot Restaurant,** 2050 W. Rt. 89A, a local favorite, dishes up 101 varieties of omelettes ($4-8) and 3 varieties of tacos ($4; 282-6626; open daily 6am-9pm). The ever-peppy morning talk-show hosts Regis and Kathy Lee adored **Robert's,** 251 Rt. 179. The peach cobbler, like Sedona, must be experienced. Beautiful indoor and outdoor dining make their creative Southwestern fare taste even better (sandwiches $6-8; 282-3671; open daily 8am-9pm). Freshly made ice cream and bakery treats draw in the masses at **Black Cow Cafe,** 25 N. Rt. 89A, a great spot to cool off (cappuccino $3, cone $3; 203-9868; open daily 7am-9pm).

Sedona lies 120mi. north of Phoenix (take I-17 north to Rt. 179 W) and 30mi. south of Flagstaff (take I-17 S to Rt. 179 W or use U.S. 89A SW). The **Sedona-Phoenix Shuttle** (282-2066) runs six trips daily ($35). Sedona's **Area code:** 520.

## NEAR SEDONA

**Montezuma Castle National Monument,** 10mi. south of Sedona on I-17, is a 20-room cliff dwelling built by the Sinagua tribe in the 12th century. Unfortunately, you can't get very close to the ruins, but the view from the paved path below is excellent and wheelchair accessible. *(567-3322. Open daily 8am-7pm, off season 8am-5pm. $2, under 16 free.)* A beautiful lake formed by the collapse of an underground cavern,

---

**IS THE FORCE WITH YOU?** Could a powerful force be lurking near the Sedona airport or parks? Psychic **Page Bryant** thought so in 1980, when she divined several vortexes, or areas of great psychic and spiritual energy, around town. People who enter the vortexes have claimed to have experienced episodes of extreme psychic and emotional alertness, and sometimes **spiritual healing** in the long term. Vortexes have become a sensation among the New Age crowd since Bryant's discovery, and much conjecturing and scientific study has been done. **Extra-terrestrial meddling,** spiritual presences, high magnetism from the Sedona's metal-rich rocks, and **parallel universe cross-over** have all been cited as causes. Perhaps you can unlock their mystery: the main vortexes are at the airport, Bell Rock, Cathedral Rock, and Boyton Canyon.

**CITY IN A BUBBLE** The planned city of **Arcosanti**, off I-17 at exit 262, is designed to embody Italian architect Paolo Soleri's concept of an "arcology," or "architecture and ecology working together as one integral process." When complete, the city will be entirely self-sufficient, supplying its own food, power, and all other resources. Arcosanti has been under construction since 1970 but is expected to be finished rather later than the original goal of 2000—so far, only one building is up. The pace of the construction might have something to do with the restrictions on who is allowed to participate; rather than hiring workers, all the labor is done by students and others who take part in the community's "workshops." (632-7135. Tours daily every hr. 10am-4pm; $5 donation requested. Visitors center open daily 9am-5pm.)

**Montezuma Well,** off I-17 11mi. north of the castle, once served as a source of water for the Sinagua who lived here. *(Open daily 8am-7pm. Free.)* Take U.S. 89A to Rt. 279 and continue through Cottonwood to reach **Tuzigoot National Monument,** 20mi. southwest of Sedona, a dramatic Sinaguan ruin overlooking the Verde Valley. *(634-5564. Open daily 8am-7pm; in winter 8am-5pm. $2, under 17 free.)*

## JEROME

Precariously perched on the side of Mingus Mountain, Jerome once attracted miners, speculators, saloon owners, and madams who came to the city following the copper boom of the late 1800s. By 1920, the town ranked as Arizona's 3rd-largest city. The 1929 stock market crash threw Jerome's economy into an irrecoverable downward spiral. By mid-century Jerome was a ghost town. Recently, bikers, hippies, ex-cowboys, and artists have arrived, drawn by the charm and spectacular scenery of the town. Jerome's current incarnation is, in one respect, drastically different from its start—tourist mining has replaced copper mining as the main industry. Yet the lively, quirky flavor of this awkward town continues to thrive. Just driving down main street you get a feel for why Jerome is special: the main street is steeper than a horse's brow. The **Jerome State Historic Park** (634-5381), ½mi. off U.S. 89A just as you enter town; (open daily 8am-5pm; $2.50, ages 7-13 $1) provides a panoramic view of the town and a museum.

Budget travelers should make Jerome a daytrip from Flagstaff or Phoenix, as lodging tends to be expensive. **The Inn at Jerome,** 309 Main St., is one of the lower-priced joints in town (634-5094 or 800-634-5094; rooms $55-85). The oldest restaurant in Arizona, **The English Kitchen,** 119 Jerome Ave., has a large array of salads and sandwiches for $5-6 (634-2132; open Tu-Su 8am-3:30pm). **Marcy's,** 363 Main St., serves ice cream, soups, and sandwiches (under $5) in a pleasant atmosphere (634-0417; open W-M 11am-5pm). At night, float over to **The Spirit Room,** at Main St. and Jerome Ave., for live music and mayhem (634-8809; open daily 10am-1am; live music F-Sa from 9pm). **Paul and Jerry's Saloon,** also on Main St., has been helping people get sloppy for three generations (634-2603; open daily 11am-1am).

U.S. 89A slinks its way to Jerome 30mi. southwest of Sedona; the drive between them is simply gorgeous. The **Chamber of Commerce,** 50 Main St. (634-2900), is staffed somewhat sporadically by volunteers (usually open daily 10am-4pm); the recorded message lists food and lodging info. **Area code:** 520.

# PHOENIX

The name Phoenix was chosen for a small farming community in the Sonoran desert by Anglo settlers who believed that their oasis had risen from the ashes of ancient Indian settlements, like the legendary phoenix of Greek mythology. The 20th century has seen this unlikely metropolis live up to its name; the expansion of water resources, the proliferation of railroad transportation, and the introduction of air-conditioning have fueled Phoenix's ascent. Shiny high-rises now crowd the business district, while a vast web of 6-lane highways and strip malls surrounds the downtown. Phoenix's rise has not been without turmoil, though: its greatest asset, the sun, is also its greatest nemesis. The scorching heat and arid landscape has put a damper on expansion, as the wet stuff is now in short supply. For the traveler, the Phoenix sun can also be either friend or foe. During the balmy winter months, tourists, golfers, and business conventioneers flock to the resort-perfect temperatures and increasingly posh accommodations. In the summer, the city crawls into its air-conditioned shell as temperatures climb to an average of 100°F and lodging prices plummet.

## ⓘ ORIENTATION AND PRACTICAL INFORMATION

The intersection of **Central Ave.** and **Washington St.** marks the heart of downtown. Central Ave. runs north-south. One of Phoenix's peculiarities is that numbered avenues and streets both run north-south; avenues are numbered sequentially west from Central, while streets are numbered east. Some avenues and streets dead-end abruptly. A few of the largest north-south thoroughfares are **7th St., 16th St., 7th Ave.,** and **19th Ave.** Washington St. divides streets north-south. You'll need a car or a bus pass to see much of Phoenix; this city sprawls over the desert.

**Airport: Sky Harbor International** (273-3300), just southeast of downtown. Take Valley Metro bus #13 into the city (5:45am-7:45pm). Shuttle service downtown $7.

**Trains: Amtrak,** 401 W. Harrison (253-0121); follow 4th Ave. south 2 blocks past Jefferson St. *Be careful at night.* To Los Angeles (20hr., 10 per week, $74-94) and San Antonio via El Paso (21hr., 3 per week, $69-91). Open Sa-M 1:15am-9:45am and 5:15pm-12:45am, Tu-W 1:15am-9:45am, Th-F 5:15pm-12:45am.

**Buses: Greyhound,** 2115 E. Buckeye Rd. (389-4200). To: El Paso (8hr., 15 per day, $38); Los Angeles (8hr., 12 per day, $30); Tucson (2hr., 13 per day, $12); and San Diego (8hr., 4 per day, $37). 24hr.

**Public Transit: Valley Metro,** 253-5000. Most lines run to and from the **City Bus Terminal,** at Central and Van Buren St. Routes tend to operate M-F 5am-8pm with reduced service on Sa. Fare $1.25; disabled, seniors, and children 60¢. All-day pass $3.60, 10-ride pass $12. Bus passes and system maps at the Terminal.

**Taxis: Ace Taxi,** 254-1999.

**Car Rental: ABC Rent-a-Car,** 2532 E. Jefferon St. (681-9000). Cars from $30-$35 per day with unlimited mi. on older models. Cash deposit and under 25 accepted with surcharge. Under 21 accepted with proof of personal insurance, credit card, and surcharge. Open daily 8am-8pm.

**Visitor Info: Phoenix and Valley of the Sun Convention and Visitors Center,** 400 E. Van Buren St. (254-6500, recorded info 252-5588), 6th fl. of the Arizona Center office building. Open M-F 8am-5pm.

**Hotlines: Crisis Hotline,** 784-1500. 24hr. **Gay/Lesbian Hotline,** 234-2752. Daily 10am-10pm.

**Internet Access:** At the beautiful copper-and-glass **Burton Barr Central Library,** 1221 N. Central Ave. (262-4636). Open M-W 9am-9pm, Th-Sa 9am-6pm, Su 1-5pm. Sign-up required, but computers usually available.

**Post Office:** 522 N. Central Ave. (800-275-8777), downtown. Open M-F 8:30am-5pm. General delivery: 1441 E. Buckeye Rd. (800-275-8777). Open M-F 7:30am-5pm. **ZIP code:** 85026. **Area code:** 602.

## ▸ ACCOMMODATIONS

Budget travelers should consider visiting Phoenix during July and Aug., when motels knock their prices down by as much as 70%. In the winter, when temperatures and vacancies drop, prices go up; make reservations if possible. The reservationless should cruise the rows of motels on **Van Buren St.** east of downtown, towards the airport. The strips are full of 50s-era ranch-style motels, some touting adult movies as their main attraction, as well as the requisite modern chains. Parts of these areas can be unsafe; *guests should examine a motel thoroughly before checking in.* Safer, but more distant, the area around **Bell Rd.**, north of the city, is also loaded with motels. **Mi Casa Su Casa/Old Pueblo Homestays Bed and Breakfast** P.O. Box 950, Tempe 85280-0950 (800-456-0682), arranges stays in B&B's throughout Arizona and New Mexico. (Singles $40-70; doubles from $65. Open M-F 9am-5pm, Sa 9am-noon. Make winter reservations 2 weeks in advance.)

**Metcalf House (HI-AYH),** 1026 N. 9th St. (254-9803), a few blocks northeast of downtown. From the City Bus Terminal, take bus #10 down 7th St. to Roosevelt St., walk 2 blocks east to 9th St., and turn left—the hostel is ½ block north in a shady and quiet residential area. The high-spirited owner fosters a lively and artistic community in this uniquely decorated converted house. Dorm-style rooms with wooden bunks adjoin a kitchen and common room. $12, $15 non-members. Check-in 7-10am and 5-10pm.

**Motel 6,** 2323 E. Van Buren St. (800-466-8456). Decor-free, personality-free, and bug-free. Singles $30; doubles $36. Convenient to the airport.

**KOA Phoenix West,** (853-0537), 11mi. west of Phoenix on Citrus Rd. Take I-10 to exit 124; head ¾mi. south to Van Buren St., then 1mi. west to Citrus Rd. 285 sites, pool, and jacuzzi. Sites (including RV hookup) $28 for 2 people, $4 per additional person. Mostly RV sites.

Talk to Metcalf House owners (see above) for tips on finding free camping.

## ◧ FOOD

Aside from food courts in malls, it's difficult to find several restaurants together amid Phoenix's expanse. Downtowners feed mainly at small coffeehouses, most of which close on weekends. Heavily touristed places tend to be spendy, but hidden jewels can be found. This city prides itself on its culinary creativity, melding Mexican and Southwestern mainstays with traditional American, Asian, and European influences. **McDowell** or **Camelback Rd.** offer a (small) variety of Asian restaurants. The **Arizona Center,** an open-air shopping gallery at 3rd St. and Van Buren, boasts food venues, fountains, and palm trees. The *New Times* gives extensive restaurant recommendations (271-4000).

**La Tolteca,** 1205 E. Van Buren St. (253-1511). This unassuming cafeteria-style restaurant-slash-Mexican grocery serves up entirely uncommercialized south-of-the-border fare in *grande* portions. Familiar dishes with refreshing authenticity are offered alongside specialities like *cocido* soup ($4.50) and *horchata* ($1-2), a sweet milk and rice drink. Big burritos $3-4, dinner plates $5-6. Open M-W 6:30am-7pm, Th-Sa 6:30am-9pm, Su 6:30am-8pm.

**Gourmet House of Hong Kong,** 1438 E. McDowell Rd. (253-4859). For those who think that quality Chinese food vanishes between the Mississippi and the West Coast, this decor-free, tucked-away little fortune of a cookie will impress. 40 varieties of soup, innumerable noodle dishes, and rare Hong Kong specialities (such as chicken feet) are unceremoniously dished up. Entrees $5-7. Open Su-Th 11am-9:30pm, F-Sa 11am-10:30pm.

**Los Dos Molinos,** 8646 S. Central Ave. (243-9113). Live music at lunch and dinner, a huge menu, and lemonade in jelly jars. Enchiladas $3-3.50, burritos $3.25-5.25. Open Tu-Sa 11am-9pm.

**Bill Johnson's Big Apple,** 3757 E. Van Buren St. (275-2107), and 3 other locations. A down-South delight with sawdust on the floor, authentic BBQ, and a variety of hot sauces to atomize the palate. Sandwiches $3-10, hearty soups $3. Open daily 6am-10pm, F-Sa 6am-11pm.

## ◧ SIGHTS

Downtown Phoenix offers a few museums and mounting evidence of America's growing consumer culture. The price of most downtown attractions hovers around $7; fortunately, the majority are well worth it. The **Heard Museum** is internationally renowned for its outstanding collection of Native American handicrafts. The museum also features the work of contemporary Native American artists,

THE SOUTHWEST

**Downtown Phoenix**

ACCOMMODATIONS

A YMCA
B Metcalf House
C Motel 6
D Economy Inn

N

0  600 yards
0  600 meters

TO PHOENIX ZOO

HERITAGE SQUARE

Phoenix Union Municipal Center

Arizona Center

Museum of History

Greyhound

Washington

Jefferson

7th St.

5th St.

3rd St.

1st St.

Roosevelt

Garfield

McKinley

Pierce

Fillmore

Taylor

Polk

Van Buren St.

Jefferson

Jackson

Buchanan

Herberger Theater Center

Arizona Science Center

Symphony Hall

American West Arena

City Bus Terminal

Central Ave.

Renaissance Square

PATRIOT'S SQUARE

1st Ave.

2nd Ave.

Madison

CESAR CHAVEZ PLAZA

Orpheum Theater

3rd Ave.

4th Ave.

Union Station Amtrak

5th Ave.

6th Ave.

Portland

Roosevelt

McKinley

Fillmore

Taylor

Monroe St.

Adams

Washington

Jefferson

7th Ave.

Police Building

9th Ave.

10th Ave.

11th Ave.

12th Ave.

13th Ave.

McKinley

Grand Ave.

Phoenix Museum of History

University Park

Arizona Hall of Fame Museum

Jackson

Buchanan

Roosevelt

McKinley

Pierce

15th Ave.

Woodland

Mines & Minerals Museum

17th Ave.

Fillmore

Taylor

Polk

Van Buren St.

Wesley Bolin Memorial Park

Madison

State Capitol

19th Ave.

contains a number of exhibits designed to appeal to children, and sponsors occasional lectures and Native American dances. *(2301 N. Central Ave., 4 blocks north of McDowell Rd. 252-8840; recorded info 252-8848. Open daily 9:30am-5pm. $7, seniors $6, ages 4-12 $3. Free tours at noon, 1:30pm, and 3pm.)* Three blocks south, the **Phoenix Art Museum** mainly exhibits art of the American West, including paintings from the Taos and Santa Fe art colonies. There's also a small but interesting selection of Old Masters, and an exquisite display of miniature rooms. *(1625 N. Central Ave. at McDowell Rd. 257-1222. Open M-W 10am-5pm, Th-F 10am-9pm, Sa-Su 10am-5pm. $6, students and seniors $4, ages 6-18 $2.)* The **Arizona Science Center**, offers interactive science exhibits, a giant-screen theater, and a planetarium. *(600 E. Washington St. 716-2000. Open daily 10am-5pm. $8, seniors and ages 4-12 $6.)*

The **Desert Botanical Gardens**, 5mi. east of the downtown area, grow a colorful collection of cacti and other desert plants. Take bus #3 east to **Papago Park,** on the eastern outskirts of the city. This wildlife-rich expanse has spectacular view of the desert along its hiking, biking, and driving trails. *(1201 N. Galvin Pkwy. 941-1217, recorded info 481-8134. Open daily May-Sept. 7am-8pm; Oct.-Apr. 8am-8pm. $7, seniors $6, ages 5-12 $1.)* If you spot an orangutan strolling around the cacti, it's either a mirage or you're in the **Phoenix Zoo**, located within the park and boasting a formidable collection of South American, African, and Southwestern critters. *(455 N. Galvin Pkwy. 273-1341. Open daily mid-Sept. to Apr. 9am-5pm; mid-May to mid-Sept. 7:30am-4pm. $8.50, seniors $7.50, ages 3-5 $1.50.)* Don't pull any fire alarms at the **Hall of Flame Museum of Firefighting,** also in Papago Park, featuring antique fire engines and other fire-fighting equipment. *(6101 E. Van Buren St. 275-3473. Open M-Sa 9am-5pm, Su noon-4pm; $5, ages 6-17 $3, ages 3-5 $1.50).* Still further east of the city, past Tempe, in Mesa, flows the **Salt River,** one of the last remaining desert rivers in the U.S., offers clear waters amidst the **Tonto National Forest.** Salt River Recreation arranges tubing trips. *(984-3305. Open daily May-Sept., 9am-4pm. Tube rental $9.)*

In nearby Scottsdale, **Taliesin West,** at the corner of Frank Lloyd Wright Blvd. and Cactus St., served as the architectural studio and residence of Frank Lloyd Wright in his later years. *(860-8810 or 860-2700. 1hr. and 1½hr. guided tours required. Open June-Sept. daily 9am-4pm. $10-14, students and seniors $8-12, children $3-8.)* The beautifully designed studio seems to blend naturally into the surrounding desert. Wright also designed the **Arizona Biltmore,** a hotel at 24th St. and Missouri. *(955-6600.)* One of the last major buildings designed by Wright, the **Gammage Memorial Auditorium,** at Mill Ave. and Apache Blvd. on the Arizona State University campus in Tempe, wears the pink-and-beige earth tones of the surrounding environment. Take bus #60, or #22 on weekends. *(965-3434. 20min. tours daily in winter.)*

## 🎵 NIGHTLIFE AND ENTERTAINMENT

The free *New Times Weekly*, available on local magazine racks, lists club schedules for Phoenix's after-hours scene. The *Cultural Calendar of Events* guide covers area entertainment in 3-month intervals. **Barpage** (www.barpage.com) provides detailed info on the wetter side of Phoenix. **Char's Has the Blues,** 4631 N. 7th Ave., houses dozens of wanna-be John Lee Hookers, so the music is pretty good (230-0205; cover F-Sa $3; doors open 7pm). **Phoenix Live,** 455 N. 3rd St., at the Arizona Center, quakes the complex with three bars and a restaurant (252-2112; $5 weekend cover buys access to it all). For a more mellow evening, **The Willow House,** 149 W. McDowell Rd., a self-proclaimed "artist's cove," combines the best aspects of chic coffee house, New York deli, and quirky musicians' hangout in a colorful little house with a small theater beside it (252-0272; open Su-Th 7am-midnight, F-Sa until 1am. Live music T-Sa starting at 8pm).

Gay and lesbian nightlife is covered in *The Western Front*, available in bars and clubs. **Ain't Nobody's Biz,** 3031 E. Indian School Rd., #7, is a large lesbian bar with Th beer busts ($1.50 pitchers 9pm-midnight; 224-9977; open daily 2pm-1am). **Roscoe's,** 4531 N. 7th St., a gay sports pub, has pool and dart tournaments (happy hour M-Sa, 3pm-7pm; 285-0833; open M-Sa 3pm-1am, Sun 11am-1am).

Phoenix also packs a-plenty for the sports lover. NBA action rises with the **Phoenix Suns** (379-7867), at the **America West Arena,** or you can root for the NFL's **Arizona Cardinals** (379-0101). In 1998, the **Arizona Diamondbacks** (514-8400), a new Major League baseball team, arrived on the scene; their home is the new **Bank One Ballpark,** next to the America West arena.

## NEAR PHOENIX: APACHE TRAIL

Steep, gray, and haunting, the **Superstition Mountains** derive their name from Pima Native American legends. Although the Indians were kicked out by the Anglo gold prospectors who settled the region, the curse stayed. In the 1840s, a Mexican explorer found gold in these hills, but was killed before he could reveal the location of the mine. More famous is the case of Jacob Waltz, known as "Dutchman" despite having emigrated from Germany. During the 1880s, he brought out about $250,000 worth of high-quality gold ore from somewhere in the mountains. Upon his death in 1891, he left only a few clues to the whereabouts of the mine. Strangely, many who have come looking for it have died violent deaths—one prospector burned to death in his own campfire, while another was found decapitated in an arroyo. Needless to say, the mine has never been found.

Rt. 88, a.k.a. **Apache Trail,** winds from **Apache Junction,** a small mining town 40mi. east of Phoenix, through the mountains. Although the road is only about 50mi. long, it's only partially paved; trips require at least 3-4hr. behind the wheel. The car-less can leave the driving to **Apache Trail Tours,** which offers on- and off-road Jeep tours (602-982-7661; 2-4hr. tours; $60 per person; reserve at least a day in advance). For more info, head to the **Apache Junction Chamber of Commerce,** 112 E. 2nd Ave. (602-982-3141; open M-F 8am-5pm).

The scenery itself is the Trail's greatest attraction; the dramatic views of the arid landscape make it one of the most beautiful driving routes in the nation. The deep blue waters of the man-made **Lake Canyon, Lake Apache,** and **Lake Roosevelt** contrast sharply with the red and beige-hued rock formations surrounding them. **Goldfield Ghost Town Mine Tours,** 5mi. north of the U.S. 60 junction on Rt. 88, offers tours of the nearby mines, complete with goldpanning, from a resurrected ghost town (602-983-0333; open daily 10am-5pm; mine tours $4, ages 6-12 $2; goldpanning $3). "Where the hell am I?" said Jacob Waltz when he came upon **Lost Dutchman State Park,** 1½mi. farther north on Rt. 88. At the base of the Superstitions, the park offers nature trails, picnic sites, and campsites with showers but no hookups (602-982-4485; entrance $4 per vehicle; first come, first served sites $9). **Tortilla Flat,** another refurbished ghost town 18mi. farther on Rt. 88, keeps its spirits up with a restaurant, ice cream shop, and saloon (602-982-4485; restaurant open M-F 9am-6pm, Sa-Su 8am-7pm). **Tonto National Monument,** 5mi. east of Lake Roosevelt on Rt. 88, preserves 700-year-old masonry and pueblo ruins built by Anasazi (open daily 8am-5pm; entrance fee $4 per car). **Tonto National Forest** offers nearby camping (602-225-5200; sites $6-12). For those who complete the Trail, Rt. 60 is a scenic trip back to Phoenix; the increased moisture and decreased temperatures of the higher elevations give rise to lush greenery (by southern Arizona standards).

## ORGAN PIPE CACTUS NATIONAL MONUMENT

Cozying up to the U.S.-Mexico border, the lonely dirt roads of Organ Pipe Cactus National Monument encircle an extraordinary collection of the flora and fauna of the Sonoran Desert. Foremost among them is the organ pipe cactus itself, which is common in Mexico, but found only in this region of the U.S. Its texture and color are similar to those of a saguaro, but while the saguaro is commonly shaped like a body with two or more arms, the organ pipe cactus consists *only* of arms, which sprout tentacle-like from the soil. Two **scenic loop drives** penetrate the park's desert landscape and lead to a number of trailheads. Both are winding and unpaved, but accessible to ordinary cars. *Take water with you;* none is available along either drive. The **Ajo Mountain Drive** (round-trip 21mi., 2hr.) circles along the foothills of the steep, rocky Ajo Mountains, the highest mountain range in the area. About halfway around the loop lies the start of the **Estes Canyon-Bull Pasture Trail** (round-trip 4.1mi.), which climbs through the mountains to a plateau that affords an astounding view from all sides. On the other side of the park, the **Puerto Blanco Drive** (round-trip 53mi., 4-5hr.) winds through the colorful Puerto Blanco Mountains, passing oases, cacti, and abandoned mines along the way. One fairly easy trek (4½mi.) leads to the **Victoria Mine,** the oldest gold and silver mine in the area.

Located on U.S. 85, 22mi. south of the tiny hamlet **Why,** Organ Pipe Cactus is one of the most isolated national parks in the U.S.; there are no crowds in any season. The **visitors center** (520-387-6849) on Rt. 85, 5mi. north of the Mexican border, passes out the obligatory maps and makes hiking recommendations (open daily 8am-5pm). The adjacent **campground** offers water, restrooms, and grills, but no hookups (tent sites $9; first come, first served). **Backcountry camping** is free but requires a permit from the visitors center. For further info, write to the **Superintendent,** Organ Pipe Cactus National Monument, Rt. 1, Box 100, Ajo, AZ 85321-9626.

# TUCSON

Way down Mexico way, on the verge of cosmopolitan, suburban, trendy, postmodern, touristy, and commercial—but not quite slipping into any—Tucson remains in a somewhat awkward adolescent, entering that "difficult period" of late-20th-century/early-21st-century pubescence. The town has a lot going for it, though: a major university, walkable artsy and cafe-lined downtown, arguably better tourist attractions than any other southwestern city, and the conveniences of a metropolis without the nasty aftertaste are all found here.

## ⌇ PRACTICAL INFORMATION

Just east of I-10, Tucson's downtown area surrounds the intersection of **Broadway Blvd.** (which runs west) and **Stone Ave.,** 2 blocks from the train and bus terminals. The **University of Arizona** lies 1mi. NE of downtown at the intersection of **Park** and **Speedway Blvd.** Avenues run north-south, streets east-west; because some of each are numbered, intersections such as "6th and 6th" are possible. Speedway, Broadway, and **Grant Ave.** are the quickest east-west routes through town. To go north-south, follow **Oracle Rd.** through the heart of the city, **Campbell Ave.** east of downtown, or **Swan Rd.** farther east. The hip, young crowd swings on **4th Ave.** and on **Congress St.,** with small shops, quirky restaurants, and a slew of bars.

**Airport: Tucson International** (573-8000), on Valencia Rd., south of downtown. Bus #25 runs every hr. to the Laos Transit Center; from there, bus #16 goes downtown (last bus daily 7:48pm). **Arizona Stagecoach** (889-1000) will take you downtown for around $12. Runs 24hr. Reservations recommended.

**Amtrak:** 400 E. Toole Ave. (623-4442), at 5th Ave., 1 block north of the Greyhound station. To Los Angeles (9hr., 4 per week, $66-98). Open Sa-M 6:15am-1:45pm and 4:15-11:30pm, Tu-W 6:15am-1:45pm, Th-F 4:15-11:30pm.

**Buses: Greyhound,** 2 S. 4th Ave. (882-4386), between Congress St. and Broadway. To: Phoenix (2hr., 26 per day, $12); Los Angeles (9-10hr., 21 per day, $37); Albuquerque (12-15hr., 11 per day, $79); and El Paso (7hr., 12 per day, $35). Open 24hr.

**Taxis: Yellow Cab,** 624-6611.

**Public Transit: Sun-Tran** (792-9222). Buses run from the Ronstadt terminal downtown at Congress and 6th St. Service roughly M-F 5:30am-10pm, Sa-Su 8am-7pm; times vary by route. Fare 85¢, under 19 60¢, seniors and disabled 35¢.

**Car Rental: Care Free,** 1760 S. Craycroft Rd. (790-2655). For the car-free. $18 per day with 100 free mi. within Tucson only. 2-day min. rental. Must be 21+ with major credit card. Open M-F 9am-5pm, Sa 10am-2pm.

**Bike Rental: Fairwheels Bicycles,** 1110 E. 6th St. (884-9018), at Freemont. $20 1st day, $10 per additional day. Open M-F 9am-6pm, Sa 9am-5:30pm, Su noon-4pm.

**Visitor Info:** Metropolitan Tucson Convention and Visitors Bureau, 130 S. Scott Ave. (624-1817 or 800-638-8350), near Broadway. Open M-F 8am-5pm, Sa-Su 9am-4pm.

**Bi-Gay-Lesbian Organization:** Gay, Lesbian, and Bisexual Community Center, 422 N. 4th Ave. (624-1779). Hrs. vary.

**Hotline:** Rape Crisis, 327-7273. 24hr.

**Internet Access:** Free access at the University of Arizona main library, 1510 E. University Ave. Open M-Th 7:30am-11pm, F 7:30am-6pm, Sa 9am-6pm, Su 11am-11pm.

**Post Office:** General delivery: 1501 S. Cherry Bell (800-275-8777). Open M-F 8:30am-5pm, Sa 9am-1pm. **ZIP code:** 85726. **Area code:** 520.

# ▮ ACCOMMODATIONS

There's a direct correlation between the temperature in Tuscon and the warmth of its lodging industry to budget travelers: expect the best deals in summer. Rain-cooled evenings and summer bargains are strong consolation for the mid-day scorch. Comfy as home, the ▧ **Roadrunner Hostel,** 346 E. 12th St., is located in a pleasant house a few blocks from downtown, with unparalleled amenities such as a giant 52-inch TV, a formidable movie collection, free high-speed Internet access, purified water, free soup dinner, and A/C. Clean, comfortable, and friendly. (628-4709. Free linen, towels, lockers, and laundry soap. Kitchen and laundry. Dorms $13; private doubles $30.) The swank old **Hotel Congress and Hostel,** 311 E. Congress, conveniently located across from the bus and train stations, offers superb lodging to night-owl hostelers. Club Congress, downstairs, booms until 1am on weekends, making it rough on early birds. Private rooms come with private bath, phone, vintage radio, and ceiling fans; small common room has a TV and soda machine. The cafe downstairs serves great salads and omelettes. (622-8848. Hostel rooms $15 per person. Singles $29; doubles $32-42; 10% discount for students and artists.) **La Siesta Motel,** 1602 N. Oracle Rd., has clean rooms, a shaded picnic/BBQ area, a pool, and parking (624-1192; singles $32; doubles $35, with 2 beds $39).

 **Mount Lemmon Recreation Area,** in the **Coronado National Forest,** offers beautiful campgrounds. Campgrounds lie away from Tucson via the **Catalina Hwy. Rose Canyon,** 33mi. northeast of Tucson on Hitchcock Hwy., at 7000 ft., is heavily wooded, comfortably cool, and has a small lake. Sites ($9) at higher elevations fill quickly on summer weekends. The **National Forest Service,** 300 W. Congress Ave., has more info (670-4552; open M-F 8am-4:30pm).

# ◖ FOOD

Good, cheap Mexican restaurants are everywhere. **Little Café Poca Cosa,** 20 S. Scott Ave., the less expensive *niño* of the Cafe Poca Cosa on Broadway, prides itself on fresh ingredients and an ever-changing menu—patrons often walk in and say "give me something good" (lunch specials $5.50; open M-F 7:30am-2:30pm). Often declared the best Mexican restaurant in Tucson, and forever holding the title of the oldest taco joint in town, **El Charro Cafe,** 311 N. Court Ave, is a tad pricey but fantastic. A cage full of drying *carne seca* looms over the outdoor patio; superb foods like those decorating the *Plato Verredad* for two ($19.75) spice up one's interior. (622-1922. Open M-Th 11am-9om, F-S 11am-10pm, Su 11am-9pm.) When you've had it with Mexican food, **India Oven,** 2727 N. Campbell Ave., between Grant and Glenn, offers relief. The garlic *naan* ($2.35) is exquisite. (326-8635. Vegetarian dishes $6-7; tandoori meats and curries $6-9. Open daily 11am-10pm.) The $1.75 pizza slices at **Timemarket,** 444 E. University Ave, are enhanced by gourmet toppings like piñon nuts, shrimp, and smoked gouda (open daily 7:30am-10pm). A hole-in-the-wall, **Maya Quetzal,** 429 N. 4th Ave., serves up authentic Guatemalan food at rock-bottom prices. The veggie or meat *empanadas* ($4) and the $7 *pollo de naranja* (chicken in orange and garlic sauce) are tasty choices. (622-8207. Open M-Th 11:30am-8:30pm, F 11:30am-9:30pm, Sa noon-9:30pm.)

## 🔍 SIGHTS

Lined with cafes, restaurants, galleries, and vintage clothing shops, **4th Ave.** is an alternative, artsy magnet and a great place to take a stroll. Between Speedway and Broadway Blvd., the street becomes a historic shopping district with increasingly touristy shops. Lovely for its varied and elaborately irrigated vegetation, the **University of Arizona's** mall sits where E. 3rd St. should be, just east of 4th Ave. The **Center for Creative Photography,** on campus, houses various exhibits, including the archives of Ansel Adams and Richard Avedon. *(621-7968. Open M-F 11am-5pm, Su noon-5pm. Free.)* The lives of ancient southwestern Native American populations come to light at the **Arizona State Museum,** also on campus. *(621-6302. Open M-Sa 10am-5pm, Su noon-5pm. Free.)* The **Flandrau Science Center,** on Cherry Ave. at the campus mall, dazzles with a public observatory, a laser light show, and interactive exhibits. *(621-7827. Open M-Sa 9am-5pm, W-Sa 7pm-9pm. Free.)*

The **Tucson Museum of Art** exhibits an impressive collection of pre-Colombian art. *(140 N. Main Ave. 624-2333. Open Tu-Sa 10am-4pm, Su noon-4pm. $2, students and seniors $1, children free; free Tu.)* A museum, zoo, and nature preserve rolled into one, the **Arizona-Sonora Desert Museum** is an enchanting spectacle. The living museum recreates a range of desert habitats and features over 300 kinds of animals. Follow Speedway Blvd. west of the city as it becomes Gates Pass Rd., then Kinney Rd. A proper visit requires at least 2hr., preferably during the cool morning hours, before the animals take their afternoon siestas. *(2021 N. Kinney Rd. 883-2702. Open Mar.-Sept. Su-F 7:30am-5pm, Sa 7:30am-10pm; Oct.-Feb. daily 7:30am-6pm. $8.75, ages 6-12 $1.75.)*

North of the desert museum, the western half (Tucson Mountain District) of **Saguaro National Park** has limited hiking trails and an auto loop. *(733-5158. Park open 24hr.)* The paved nature walk near the **visitors center** passes some of the best specimens of Saguaro cactus in the Tucson area. *(Open daily 8:30am-5pm.)* The towering cacti take decades to reach maturity, and don't start sprouting their trademark raised arms until around age 75. **Gates Pass,** on the way to the Tucson Mountain District and the Desert Museum, is an excellent spot for watching the rising and setting sun. **Saguaro National Park East,** a.k.a. Rincon Mountain District, lies east of the city on Old Spanish Trail; take I-10 E to exit 279 and follow Vail Rd. to Old Spanish Trail. *(733-5153. Visitors center open daily 8:30am-5pm. $4 per vehicle, $2 per pedestrian.)* Within the park, 128mi. of trails and an 8mi. scenic drive lead through the cactus forest. Before noon, the visitors center has free permits for **backcountry camping. Colossal Cave,** nearby on Vail Rd., is the only dormant (no water or new stala(ct/gm)ites) cave in the U.S. *(647-7275. Open mid-Mar. to mid- Sept. M-Sa 8am-6pm, Su 8am-7pm; mid-Sept. to mid-Mar. M-Sa 9am-5pm, Su 9am-6pm. $6.50, ages 11-16 $5, ages 6-10 $3.50.)* In the shadow of the park, the praises of the **cacti on Mt. Lemmon,** east of town, often go unsung; it's worth the drive up the mountain to see them.

West of Tucson via Speedway Blvd., the **International Wildlife Museum** is wild but lifeless—the creatures were stuffed long ago. *(4800 W. Gates Pass Rd. 617-1439. Open M-F 9am-5pm, Sa-Su 10am-6pm, last entrance at 4:15pm. $6, seniors $4.75, ages 6-12 $2.)*

Over 20,000 warplanes are parked in ominous, silent rows at the **Davis-Monthan Air Force Base,** 15mi. southeast of Tucson. Take the Houghton exit off I-10, then travel west on Irvington to Wilmont. The 2mi. long aerospace-graveyard is visible through the airfield fence. *(228-4570. Free tours M, W, F 10:30am; first come, first served.)*

## 🎵 ENTERTAINMENT AND NIGHTLIFE

Tucson is a musical smorgasbord. UA students rock and roll on **Speedway Blvd.,** other folks do the two-step in country music clubs on **N. Oracle.** The free *Tucson Weekly* or the weekend sections of *The Star* or *The Citizen* have current entertainment listings. Throughout the year, the city of the sun presents **Music Under the Stars,** a series of sunset concerts performed by the Tucson Symphony Orchestra

(792-9155). On **Downtown Saturday Nights,** on the 1st and 3rd Sa of each month, Congress St. is blockaded for a celebration of the arts with outdoor singers, crafts, and galleries. Every Th, the **Thursday Night Art Walk** lets you mosey through downtown galleries and studios. The **Tucson Arts District** has more info (624-9977).

   **Club Congress,** 311 E. Congress St., has DJs during the week and live bands on weekends (cover $4). The friendly hotel staff and a cast of regulars make it an especially good time. Thursday is 80s night with 80¢ drinks. (622-8848. Open daily 9pm-1am.) **The Rock,** 136 N. Park, caters to a college crowd with live shows and F night battles of the bands (629-9211; cover $3-12; open 8pm-1am on show days; call ahead). For a quiet drink, **Bar Toma,** 311 N. Cart Ave., offers a wide selection of tequilas (622-5465; open Su-Th 5-9pm, F-Sa 5-10pm). Young locals hang out on **4th Ave.** at night; most bars have live music and low cover charges. **3rd Stone,** on the corner of 4th Ave. and 6th St., is a good spot (628-8844; cover $2 Tu; open M-Sa 11am-midnight, Su 4-11pm), as is **O'Malley's,** farther up 4th Ave., with decent bar food, pool tables, and pinball (623-8600; cover Th-Sa varies; open daily 11am-1am). **IBT's,** on 4th Ave. at 6th St., leads the gay scene (882-3053; open daily noon-1am).

   Despite its name, **New West,** 4385 W. Ina Rd., is an authentic Old West saloon playing continuous country-western music on the largest dance floor in Arizona (6000 sq. ft.). The newly-renovated club offers cheap beer $2 and occasional two-stepping lessons. (744-7744. Cover $4, 7pm-11pm $2; open Tu-Th 8pm-2am, F-Sa 7pm-2am.) On the same grounds, **Gotham** throbs to a heavy urban beat. (Cover $4, ages 18-20 $6, Tu and Th 7pm-11pm $2. Open Tu, Th 8pm-2am, F-Sa 7pm-2am.)

# NEAR TUCSON

**BIOSPHERE 2.** 91ft. high, with an area of more than 3 acres, Biosphere 2 is sealed off from Earth—"Biosphere 1"—by 500 tons of stainless steel. In 1991, 8 research scientists locked themselves inside this giant greenhouse to cultivate their own food and knit their own socks as they monitored the behavior of five man-made ecosystems: savanna, rainforest, marsh, ocean, and desert. After 2 years, they began having oxygen problems and difficulty with food production. No one lives in Biosphere 2 now, but it's still used as a research facility. The Biosphere is 30min. north of Tucson; take I-10 west to the "Miracle Mile" exit, follow the miracles to Oracle Rd., then travel north until it becomes Rt. 77 N. From Phoenix, take I-10 to exit 185, follow Rt. 387 to Rt. 79 (Florence Hwy.), and proceed to Oracle Junction and Rt. 77. Guided tours (2hr.) include two short films, a walk through the laboratory's research and development models for the Biosphere 2 ecosystems, and a stroll around Biosphere 2 itself, including the crew's living quarters. Walking around unchaperoned is also permitted. *(Tours daily 9am-4:30pm; grounds open 8:30am-5:30pm; last admission at 5pm. $13, ages 13-17 $9, ages 6-12 $6; $2.)*

   The **Biosphere 2 Hotel** offers rooms with cable TV, giant beds, and huge patios overlooking the Catalina mountains, on the same ranch as the Biosphere. All guests are required to be in their rooms by 8pm. (520-896-6222. Rooms for 1 or 2 May-Aug. $55; Sept.-Nov. $85; Dec.-Apr. $95; $20 per additional person.) You can also spend a night in the hotel, tour the biosphere, and get a free breakfast and dinner to boot. (Package for two $129; May-Sept. $149.) Also within the complex, the **Cañada del Oro Restaurant** serves up good sandwiches and salads for around $6 (520-896-6220; open M-Sa 11am-7pm, Su 11am-5pm; reservations required).

**SABINO CANYON.** North of Tucson, the cliffs and waterfalls of **Sabino Canyon** provide an ideal backdrop for picnics and day hikes. No cars are permitted in the canyon, but a free **tram** makes trips through it (749-2861; tours every 30min. 9am-4:30pm). Take I-10 to exit 270 (Kolb Rd.) and follow Kolb north to Tanque Verde Rd.; make a right and follow the signs to the canyon. **Sabino Canyon Tours,** 5900 N. Sabino Canyon Rd., runs 45min. trips through the canyon, including moonlight rides 3 nights per month. (749-2861. Tours M-F on the ½hr. 9am-4pm; off-season every 30min. Sa-Su 9am-4:30pm. $2. Moonlight tours Apr.-Dec. only.)

THE SOUTHWEST

## TOMBSTONE

Founded in the wake of the gold and silver rush of the 1870s, Tombstone—home to more than 3000 prostitutes and 100 saloons—was the largest city between St. Louis and San Francisco. But water gradually seeped into the mines that were the city's lifeline, and when the equipment installed to pump it out failed in 1909, the mines were inundated and remain flooded to this day. Yet "the town too tough to die" has made a comeback. By inviting visitors to view the barnyard where Wyatt Earp and his brothers kicked some serious butt, Tombstone has turned the **shootout at the O.K. Corral,** on Allen St. next to City Park, into a year-round tourist industry (457-3456; open daily 9am-5pm; $2.50). The **Boothill Gunslingers,** the **Wild Bunch,** and the **Vigilantes/Vigilettes** perform re-enactments of famous gunfights (F-Sa and 1st and 3rd Su of each month, 2pm; $2.50, ages 6-12 $1.50). The **Hanging Chairman** can treat a friend or relative to a **public mock hanging** by one of these groups (457-3434). The voice of Vincent Price narrates the town's history next door to the O.K. Corral in the **Tombstone Historama,** while a plastic mountain revolves onstage and a dramatization of the gunfight is shown on a movie screen (457-3456; shows daily on the ½hr. 9am-4pm; $2.50). Site of the longest poker game in western history (8 years, 5 months, and 3 days), the **Bird Cage Theater,** at 6th and Allen, was named for the compartments suspended from the ceiling that once housed prostitutes (open daily 9am-4pm). John Slaughter battled scores of outlaws at the **Tombstone Courthouse,** at 3rd and Toughnut St. The courthouse is now a museum housing extremely diverse exhibits related to the town's history. (457-3311. Open daily 8am-5pm. $2.50, ages 7-14 $1.) The **tombstones** of Tombstone—the result of all that gunplay—stand on Rt. 80 just north of town (open daily 7:30am-7pm; free). For something completely different, the **Rose Tree Museum,** at 4th and Toughnut St., houses the largest rose tree in the world (457-3326; open daily 9am-5pm; $2).

The **Larian Motel,** on the corner of Fremont and 5th, is clean, nicely furnished, and easy walking distance from all sights (457-2272; singles $35-39; doubles $45-49). The rooms at the **Tombstone Motel,** across the street, are basic and a bit dark, but clean (457-3478 or 888-455-3478; singles $39-42; doubles $55).

**Blake's Char-Broiled Burgers and BBQ Ranch,** 511B Allen St., slaps the cow on the bun starting at $3.50 (457-3646; open daily 11am-4pm). **Don Teodoro's,** 15 N. 4th St., serves Mexican plates accompanied by live guitar music for under $6 (457-3647; live music W-M 6-9pm; open Su-Th 11am-9pm, F-Sa 11am-10pm). For a bit of moonshine and country music, smell your way to **Big Nose Kate's Saloon,** on Allen St., named for "the girl who loved Doc Holliday and everyone else too." Bartenders serve drinks like "sex in the desert." (457-3107. Open daily 10am-midnight.)

To get to Tombstone, career your Conestoga to the Benson exit off I-10, then go south on Rt. 80. The nearest **Greyhound** station is in **Benson,** 242 E. 4th St. (586-3141), at the Benson Flower Shop. **Amtrak** sits across the street. **Benson Taxi** (586-7688) charges $25 from Benson to Tombstone. **Tombstone Chamber of Commerce and Visitors Center:** 457-3929; open daily 10am-4pm. **Area code:** 520.

## NEAR TOMBSTONE: BISBEE

One hundred mi. southeast of Tucson and 20mi. south of Tombstone, mellow Bisbee, a former mining town, is known throughout the Southwest as a chic but laid-back artists' colony. Visitors revel in the town's proximity to Mexico, picture-perfect weather, and excellent, relatively inexpensive accommodations. The few sights in town are mine-related, but Bisbee is a terrific place to stroll, window-shop, and drink coffee in a cute cafe. The **Queen Mines,** on the Rt. 80 interchange entering Old Bisbee, ceased mining in 1943 but continues to give educational 1¼hr. tours. *(432-2071. Tours at 9, 10:30am, noon, 2, and 3:30pm. $10, ages 7-11 $3.50, ages 3-6 $2.)* The **Mining and Historical Museum** highlights the discovery of Bisbee's copper surplus and the lives of the fortune-seekers who extracted this resource. *(5 Copper Queen. 432-7071. Open daily 10am-4pm. $3, seniors $2.50, under 19 free.)*

Patrons rest in style at the pleasant **Bisbee Grand Hotel,** 61 Main St., which offers rooms furnished with early 20th-century antiques (800-421-1909; singles and doubles from $45, breakfast included). About a 10min. walk from downtown, the **Jonquil Inn,** 317 Tombstone Canyon, offers clean and smoke-free rooms (432-7371; singles $35; doubles $39; in winter about $10 higher). **Chamber of Commerce:** 7 Main St. (432-5421; both free; open M-F 9am-5pm, Sa-Su 10am-5pm).

# NEW MEXICO

In 1540, an expedition led by Francisco Vasquez de Coronado left Mexico City for what is now New Mexico, hoping to conquer the legendary city of Cíbola. There, it was said, silversmiths occupied entire streets, while gold, sapphires, and turquoise decorated every house. Coronado and his men found only Indian pueblos, so they returned to Mexico, none the richer, in 1542. Coronado may have failed in his quest, but he did start a trend—travelers have sought out New Mexico's riches ever since. Today, most explorers come in search of natural beauty, turquoise jewelry and adobe architecture rather than gold. New Mexico is a haven for hikers, backpackers, cyclists, mountain-climbers, and skiers. Six national forests within the state provide miles and miles of beautiful and challenging opportunities for lovers of the outdoors, while the Sandía, Mogollon, and Sangre de Cristo mountains fulfill mountain-climbers' upward thrust.

## 🔼 PRACTICAL INFORMATION

**Capital:** Santa Fe.

**Visitor Info: New Mexico Dept. of Tourism,** 491 Old Santa Fe Trail, Santa Fe 87501 (800-545-2040; www.newmexico.org). Open M-F 8am-5pm. **Park and Recreation Division,** 2040 S. Pacheco, Santa Fe 87504 (505-827-7173), open M-F 8am-5pm. **U.S. Forest Service,** 517 Gold Ave. SW, Albuquerque 87102 (505-842-3292). Open M-F 8am-4:30pm.

**Postal Abbreviation:** NM. **Sales Tax:** 5.8%.

## SANTA FE

Santa Fe lies at the convergence of the **Santa Fe Trail,** running from Independence, Missouri, and **El Camino Réal** ("Royal Road"), which runs from Mexico City. Meetings at this crossroads have not always been smooth. During the Mexican War, the Americans wrested control of the city from Mexico. Mexican influence has not died—a 1957 zoning ordinance requires all downtown edifices to conform to Spanish Pueblo style, although the adobe plaster occasionally fails to cover traces of formerly Victorian facades. In spite of the uniformity of the architecture, freethinkers and artists flock to Santa Fe, where they coexist with Native Americans, retirees, tourists, and jewelry hawkers. Santa Fe's popularity has bloomed like a desert flower, giving rise to gated communities, ritzy restaurants and jacked-up prices. Meanwhile the city struggles to maintain its rich culture.

## 🔼 ORIENTATION AND PRACTICAL INFORMATION

Except for the museums southeast of the city center, most upscale restaurants and sights in Santa Fe cluster within a few blocks of the **downtown plaza** and inside the loop formed by the **Paseo de Peralta.** Narrow streets make driving troublesome; park your car and pound the pavement. You'll find **parking lots** behind Santa Fe Village, near Sena Plaza, and 1 block east of the Federal Courthouse near the plaza, while metered spaces (2-4hr. max.) line the streets just south of the plaza. Parking is also available along the streets near the galleries on Canyon Rd.

**Buses: Greyhound,** 858 St. Michael's Dr. (471-0008). To: Taos (1½hr., 2 per day, $17); Albuquerque (1½hr., 4 per day, $11.55); and Denver (8-10hr., 4 per day, $59). Open M-F 7am-5:30pm and 7:30-9:45pm, Sa-Su 7-9am, 12:30-1:30pm, 3:30-5pm, and 7:30-9:30pm.

**Trains: Amtrak,** nearest station in **Lamy** (466-4511), 13mi. away on Country Rd. 41. Call 982-8829 to shuttle to Santa Fe ($14). Open daily 9am-5pm.

**Public Transit: Santa Fe Trails** (438-1464) runs 6 downtown bus routes (M-F 6am-10pm). Bus #10 leaves every 30min. from the downtown Sheridan Transit Center, 1 block from the plaza between Marcy St. and Palace Ave., and heads to the museums on Camino Lejo. 50¢, ages 6-12 25¢; day pass $1. **Sandia Shuttle Express** (474-5696) runs to the Albuquerque airport (10 per day, $20) from downtown hotels. Reserve 1 day in advance. Open M-F 7am-6pm, Sa-Su 8am-4pm.

**Car Rental: Enterprise Rent-a-Car,** 2641 Cerrillos Rd. (473-3600). $37 per day, $169 per week. Must be 21 with major credit card. Open M-F 8am-6pm.

**Taxis: Capital City Taxi,** 438-0000.

**Visitor Info: Santa Fe Welcome Center,** 491 Old Santa Fe Trail (875-7400 or 800-545-2040). Open daily 8am-7pm; off-season 8am-5pm. **Santa Fe Convention and Visitors Bureau,** 201 W. Marcy St. (800-777-2489). Open M-F 8am-5pm. **Info booth,** in the First National Bank at Lincoln and Palace St. Open in summer M-Sa 9am-4:30pm.

**Hotline: Rape Abuse,** 800-721-7273 or 986-9111. Operates 8am-5pm, on-call 24hr.

**Post Office:** 120 S. Federal Pl. (988-6351), next to the courthouse. Open M-F 7:30am-5:45pm, Sa 9am-1pm. **ZIP code:** 87501. **Area code:** 505.

# ACCOMMODATIONS

Hotels in Santa Fe tend towards the expensive side. As early as May, they become swamped with requests for **Indian Market** (3rd week of Aug.) and **Fiesta de Santa Fe** (early Sept.). Make reservations early or plan to sleep standing up. At other times, the **Cerrillos Rd.** area has the best prices, but travelers should use caution and evaluate the motel (read: see the room) before checking in. At many of the less expensive motels, bargaining is possible for stays of more than one night.

A car is necessary to camp around Santa Fe. In addition to Rancheros de Santa Fe (see below), there are several campsites run by the **Santa Fe National Forest** (438-7840) in the beautiful Sangre de Cristo Mountains. The **Black Canyon Campground,** 8mi. northeast of Santa Fe on Rt. 475, has 40 sites ($6). Four mi. farther, primitive camping (no water) is free at one of **Big Tesuque's** seven sites. (Both open May-Oct. Call the National Forest for info.)

**Santa Fe International Hostel and Pension (AAIH),** 1412 Cerrillos Rd. (988-1153), 1mi. from the bus station and 2mi. from the plaza. Busy, but big enough to accommodate the masses. Kitchen, library, and large dorm rooms. Internet access $2/day. Dorm beds $14, nonmembers $15. Linen free. B&B singles $25; doubles $35; with private bath $33/$43; no discount for members. No credit cards. Office open daily 7am-11pm. Reservations needed for Aug. Chores required.

**Thunderbird Inn,** 1821 Cerrillos Rd. (983-4397). Slightly farther from town than the hostel, but an excellent value (for Santa Fe, anyway). Large, very clean singles $44; doubles $49; some with fridge and microwave; winter rates $10-15 lower.

**Rancheros de Santa Fe,** 736 Old Las Vegas Hwy. (466-3482). Take I-25 N to exit 290. Big, friendly campground with pool. Sites $17, full hookup $24; cabins $30.

# FOOD

Spicy Mexican food served on blue corn tortillas is a Santa Fe staple. Bistros near the plaza dish up savory chiles to tourists, businessmen, and local artists, but most run $20 an entree. Cheaper alternatives lie south of the plaza on Cerillos. Wandering down side streets uncovers smaller Mexican restaurants where the locals eat; grill carts in the plaza can sell you fragrant fajitas ($3) and fresh lemonade ($1).

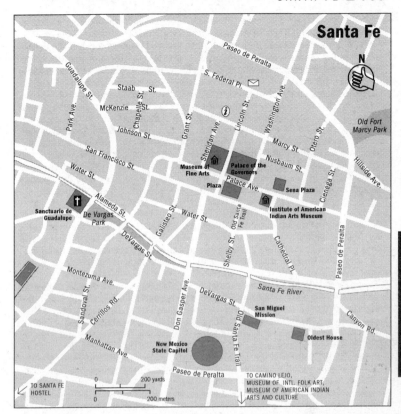

**Tia Sophia's,** 210 W. San Francisco St. (983-9880). It looks and feels like a diner (the servers are quick and curt), but the food is exceptional. The most popular item is the Atrisco plate ($6)—chile stew, cheese enchilada, beans, *posole*, and a *sopapilla*. Arrive before noon for the fastest service. Open M-Sa 7am-2pm.

**The Shed,** 113½ E. Palace Ave. (982-9030), up the street from the plaza, feels like an open garden, even in the enclosed section. Vegetarian quesadilla ($6) and amazing chicken enchilada verde ($9). Lunch daily 11am-2:30pm, dinner W-Sa 5:30-9pm.

**Home Planet,** 112 W. Marcy St. (984-8714). Unlike the chile-worshipping Santa Fe culture that tends to prize discomfort foods, this original and reasonably-priced hangout will be gentle on you. Sandwiches go for $7; full dinners under $8. Open M-Sa 8am-5pm.

**OM Tibetan Café and Restaurant,** 403 Canyon Rd. (984-1207). Pink footprints down the driveway lead to this manifestation of Santa Fe's sizeable Tibetan population. Veggie or beef dumplings with salad and soup $9, pot of authentic Tibetan tea $3. Open Tu-F 11am-2pm and 5-9pm, Sa noon-2pm and 5-8pm.

## 👁 "OLD" STYLE SIGHTS

The grassy **Plaza de Santa Fe** is a good starting point for exploring the museums, sanctuaries, and galleries of the city. Since 1609, the plaza has been the site of religious ceremonies, military gatherings, markets, cockfights, and public punishments—now it holds ritzy shops and relaxing tourists.

The six museums run by **The Museum of New Mexico** have identical hours. A 4-day pass bought at one museum admits you to all six. *(827-6463. Open Tu-Su 10am-5pm;*

*single visit $5, 4-day pass $10, under 17 free; free F 5-8pm.)* The **Georgia O'Keeffe Museum** is extremely popular. Even for those familiar with O'Keeffe's work, there are a few surprises here—the famous flower paintings are well represented, but the collection spans her entire lifetime, from early watercolors to the late abstract work. *(217 Johnson St. 995-0785. Audio tour $4.)* Around the corner, the **Museum of Fine Arts,** inhabits a large adobe building on the northwest corner of the plaza. Exhibits include works by major Southwestern artists, like O'Keeffe and Edward Weston, as well as very adventurous contemporary exhibits of often controversial American art. *(107 W. Palace Ave. 476-5072.)* The **Palace of the Governors,** on the north side of the plaza, is the oldest public building in the U.S., and was the seat of seven successive governments after its construction in 1610. The *haciendas* palace is now a museum with exhibits on Native American, Southwestern, and New Mexican history. The craft and jewelry displays in front have cheaper and better quality wares than you'll find in other stores around town. *(100 Palace Ave. 827-6476.)* The **Institute of American Indian Arts Museum,** downtown, houses an extensive collection of contemporary Indian art. *(108 Cathedral Place. 988-6281. Open M-Sa 9am-5pm, Su noon-5pm. $4, students and seniors $2, under 17 free.)* The fascinating **Museum of International Folk Art,** 2mi. south of the plaza, houses the jumbled Girard Collection, which includes over 100,000 handmade dolls, doll houses, and other toys from around the world. Other galleries hold changing ethnographic exhibits. *(706 Camino Lejo. 827-6350.)* Next door, the **Museum of American Indian Arts and Culture** displays Native American photos and artifacts. *(710 Camino Lejo. 827-6344.)*

Santa Fe's Catholic roots are evident in the Romanesque **St. Francis Cathedral,** built in 1884 under the direction of the pope to bring Catholicism to the "ungodly" westerners. The cathedral's architecture is especially striking against the New Mexican desert. *(213 Cathedral Pl. 982-5619.)* The neo-gothic **Loretto Chapel** is famous for its "miraculous" spiral staircase. *(207 Old Santa Fe Trail. 982-0092.)* About 5 blocks southeast of the plaza lies the **San Miguel Mission,** at DeVargas St. and the Old Santa Fe Trail. Built in 1710, the mission is the oldest functioning church in the U.S. The original altar was built by Native Americans. *(983-3974. Open M-Sa 9am-4:15pm, Su 1:30-4:30pm; Nov.-Apr. M-Sa 10am-3:45pm, Su 1:30-4:30pm. $1.)*

Along **Canyon Rd.** Santa Fe's most successful artists live and sell their work. Head away from the Plaza on San Francisco Dr., take a left on Alameda St., a right on Paseo de Peralta, and a left on Canyon Rd. Extending for about a mile, the road is lined on both sides by galleries displaying all types of art, as well a number of indoor/outdoor cafes. Most galleries are open from around 10am until 5pm. At the **Hahn Ross Gallery,** the art is hip, enjoyable, and occasionally affordable. *(409 Canyon Rd. 984-8434. Open 10am-5pm.)* **Off the Wall** vends truly offbeat jewelry, pottery, clocks, and sculpture. *(616 Canyon Rd. 983-8337. Open daily 10am-5pm.)*

## ■ ENTERTAINMENT AND NIGHTLIFE

Native American ceremonies, fairs, arts, and crafts shows complement Santa Fe's active theater scene and the roster of world-famous musicians who frequently play in the city's clubs. **El Farol,** 808 Canyon Rd., features up-and-coming rock, salsa, and R&B musicians (983-9912; shows nightly 9:30pm; cover W, F, Sa varies depending on band). The **Catamount Bar and Grill,** 125 E. Water St., has live bands and dancing F and Sa nights. Cool down with a 16 oz. margarita ($6). (988-7222; $2-3 cover. Sandwiches $7; open M-Sa 11am-2am, Su noon-midnight).

The **Santa Fe Opera,** on Opera Dr. 7mi. north of Santa Fe on Rt. 84, performs outdoors against a gorgeous mountain backdrop. Nights are cool; bring a blanket. The season runs July through Aug. The box office is at the opera house. (P.O. Box 2408, Santa Fe 87504-2408. 800-280-4654. July W and F-Sa at 9pm; Aug. M-Sa at 8:30pm. Tickets $15-200, rush standing-room tickets $6-15; 50% student discount on same-day reserved seats. Call the day of the show for specific prices and availability.) The **Santa Fe Chamber Music Festival** celebrates the works of great Baroque, Classical, Romantic, and 20th-century composers in the St. Francis Auditorium of the Museum of Fine Arts. (983-2075. Mid-July to mid-Aug. M-Th 8pm, F-

Sa 8pm, Su 6pm. Tickets $32-40, students $10.) In the summer; native burghers of this desert city put on **Shakespeare in Santa Fe**, an impressive show (982-2910).

Santa Fe is also home to two of the U.S.'s largest **festivals**. In Aug., the nation's largest and most impressive **Indian Market** floods the plaza. The **Southwestern Association on Indian Affairs** has more info (983-5220). Don Diego De Vargas's peaceful reconquest of New Mexico in 1692 marked the end of the 12-year Pueblo Rebellion, now celebrated in the 3-day **Fiesta de Santa Fe**. Held in early Sept., festivities include street dancing, processions, and political satires (988-7575). The *New Mexican* publishes a guide and a schedule for the fiesta's events.

## NEAR SANTA FE

**BANDELIER NATIONAL MONUMENT.** Bandelier, 40mi. northwest of Santa Fe (take U.S. 285 to 502 W, then follow the signs), features some amazing pueblos and cliff dwellings, as well as 50 sq. mi. of dramatic mesas, ancient ruins (remains of stone houses and *kivas*, underground ceremonial chambers), and spectacular views of surrounding canyons. The most accessible, **Frijoles Canyon,** is the site of the **visitors center** (672-3861, ext. 518; open daily in summer 8am-6pm; off-season 8am-5pm). From the visitors center, a self-guided 1hr. tour leads through nearby pueblo **cliff dwellings**, an additional ½mi. hike continues to the **ceremonial caves,** which offer an incredible view. (Park entrance $10 per vehicle, $5 per pedestrian; National Parks passports accepted.) The 5mi. **Falls Trail** hike descends 700 ft. into the mouth of the canyon, past two waterfalls, to the Río Grande. A strenuous 2-day, 20mi. hike leads from the visitors center to **Painted Cave,** decorated with over 50 Ancestral Puebloan pictographs, then to the Río Grande. Free permits are required for backcountry hiking and camping; topographical maps ($9) are sold at the visitors center. The 95-site **Juniper Campground**, ¼mi. off Rt. 4 at the entrance to the monument, is the only campground (sites $10, with Golden Age passport $5).

**PECOS NATIONAL HISTORICAL PARK.** Located in the hill country 25mi. southeast of Santa Fe on I-25 and Rt. 63, Pecos features ruins of a pueblo and a Spanish mission church. The small park includes an easy 1mi. hike through various archaeological sites. Especially noteworthy are the renovated *kivas*, built after the Rebellion of 1680. Off-limits at other ruins, the *kivas* at Pecos are open to the public. (Open daily 8am-6pm. Entrance $2 per person, $4 per car. National Parks passports accepted.) The **visitors center** has a small museum and a 10min. film shown every 30min. (757-6032. Open M-Sa 10am-4pm, Su 1-5pm; in winter M-Sa 9:30am-4:30pm, Su 11am-5pm. Free with park entrance.) The park is not accessible by public transportation. Backcountry camping is permitted in the **Santa Fe National Forest,** 6mi. north on Rt. 63 (see Santa Fe **Accommodations,** p. 738).

## TAOS

Those who now inhabit Taos are but the latest in a diverse series of settlers lured by the fertility and stark beauty of the Taos Valley region. First came the Native American tribes, whose pueblos still speckle the valley. In the 17th century, Spanish missionaries attempted to convert the Native Americans to Christianity while farming alongside them. The 20th century has seen artists captivated and inspired by Taos's untainted beauty, including Georgia O'Keeffe and R.C. Gorman. Aspiring artists still flock here, but recent trends indicate that the next generation of immigrants may be a mixed bag of thrill-seekers and spiritualists who come to take advantage either of Taos's natural surroundings or its thriving New Age culture. Increasingly, hikers and skiers infest the nearby mountains, rafters brave the nearby Río Grande, and New Agers drawn by the desert vibe set up house.

🛈 **PRACTICAL INFORMATION.** In town, **Rt. 68** becomes Paseo del Pueblo Sur. Drivers should park on Camino de la Placita, 1 block west of the plaza, or at myriad meters scattered on side streets. **Greyhound,** 1006 Paseo del Pueblo Sur (758-1144; station open M-F 8:30am-7pm, Sa-Su 9-10am, 2-3pm, 6-7pm), sends two buses per day to Albuquerque (3hr., $22); Santa Fe (1½hr., $17); and Denver (8hr., $50). The **Chile Line** (751-2000) runs vans from Ranchos de Taos, south of town, up to the pueblo and back (50¢, all day $1; runs M-Sa 7am-10pm, Su 9am-6pm; Sept.-May M-Sa 7am-7pm, Su 9am-6pm). **Faust's Transportation** (758-3410) taxis daily 7am-9pm. Taos's **Chamber of Commerce,** 1139 Paseo del Pueblo Sur, just south of town at the junction of Rt. 68 and Paseo del Cañon, (758-3873 or 800-732-8267; open daily 9am-5pm). **Post Office:** 318 Paseo Del Pueblo Norte (758-2081), ¼mi. north of the plaza (open M-F 8:30am-5pm). **ZIP code:** 87571. **Area code:** 505.

**▐ ACCOMMODATIONS.** The **Abominable Snowmansion Hostel,** in the village of Arroyo Seco, 9mi. north of Taos, features nice dorm rooms and common areas. The huge, airy building serves as a hostel in the summer and a ski lodge (with dorm beds) in the winter. (776-8298. Summer $13, non-members $16; private doubles $38/$45; teepees $13/$16. Winter $22. Reserve ahead for Christmas and spring break. Reception daily 8-10am and 5-10pm; in winter 4-10pm.) 15mi. south of Taos in Pilar (on Rt. 68), the cozy **Río Grande Gorge Hostel (HI-AYH)** rests above the Río Grande, a bit out of the way but close to the outdoors. Greyhound and airport shuttle buses between Santa Fe and Taos use the hostel as a flag stop. Kitchen facilities and discounts on rafting trips run by the outfit next door are available. (758-0090. Dorm beds $11, nonmembers $13.50. Geodesic domes for 2 $23, nonmembers $26; must use shared bath in hostel. Reception daily 5-9pm.) The **Sun God Lodge,** 919 Paseo del Pueblo Sur, has sizeable rooms with Southwestern-style wooden furniture (758-3162; singles $45-65; doubles $65-75). **Taos Valley RV Park,** 120 Estes Rd., just off Paseo del Pueblo Sur has tent sites and full hookups. (758-4469 or 800-999-7571; sites $15-17 for 2 people; full hookups $24-26 for 2).

Camping around Taos is easy with a car. Up in the mountains on wooded Rt. 64, 20mi. east of Taos, the **Kit Carson National Forest** operates 3 campgrounds: **Las Petacas** is free but has no drinking water; **La Sombra** and **Capulin,** down the same road, charge $6. Additionally, 4 free campgrounds line Rt. 150 north of town. **Backcountry camping** doesn't require a permit. For maps of area campgrounds contact the **forest service office,** 208 Cruz Alta Rd. (758-6200; open M-F 8am-4:30pm), or stop by their visitors center (open daily 9am-5pm), on Rt. 64 west of town.

**▐ FOOD.** Restaurants cluster around Taos Plaza and Bent St. In the rear of **Amigo's Natural Foods,** 326 Paseo del Pueblo Sur (758-8493), a small, holistic deli offers nutritionally correct dishes such as tofu burgers ($4.50) and a huge juice bar. (Deli open M-Sa 9am-3pm, Su 11am-3pm; grocery open M-Sa 8:30am-7pm, Su 11am-5pm.) Though not quite as natural, **Michael's Kitchen,** 304 Paseo del Pueblo Norte, is popular with locals, offering some of the best breakfast specials in town ($2-7). Dishes are Mexican, American, and some combination thereof. (758-4178. Open daily 7am-8:30pm.) For a full meal deal, the **Apple Tree Restaurant,** 123 Bent St., inside an old adobe house 1 block north of the plaza, offers delicious and imaginative New Mexican and Asian cuisine. From 5:30 to 6:30pm, upscale entrees like chimayo chile-crusted scallops ($9) and seared duck breast salad ($10) are $3-4 off. (758-1900. Open M-Sa 11:30am-10pm and Su 10am-9pm.)

**▐ SIGHTS AND ACTIVITIES.** Taos comes in second only to Santa Fe as a mecca for Southwestern art. Art galleries, ranging from high-quality operations to glorified curio shops, can be found in **Taos Plaza** and on **Kit Carson Rd.** A well-chosen selection of early Taos paintings hangs at the **Harwood Foundation Museum,** 238 Ledoux St., off Camino de la Placita *(758-9826. Open Tu-Sa 10am-5pm, Su noon-5pm; $5, under 12 free.)* The **Taos Arts Festival** celebrates local art in early Oct. each year. In the tiny village of Ranchos de Taos, 4mi. south of Taos Plaza, the **Mission of San Francisco de Asis** displays a "miraculous" painting that changes into a shadowy figure of Christ when the lights go out. A video documents the miracle in the parish office, to your left as you're facing the church. *(758-2754. Video shown every ½hr. M-F 9am-noon, and 1-4pm; Sa 9am-4pm. $2.)* Four mi. north of Taos off Rt. 522, exhibits of

Native American art including Pueblo jewelry, black-on-black pottery, and Navajo rugs grace the **Millicent Rogers Museum,** 1504 Museum Rd. *(758-2462. Open daily 10am-5pm; $6, students and seniors $5, ages 6-16 $1.)*

**Taos Pueblo,** 3mi. northwest of town, remarkable for its 5-story houses, is one of the last inhabited pueblos; many buildings are off-limits to visitors. The pueblo has capitalized on its popularity; visitors must pay up. For permission to sketch or paint, submit a written request 10 days before your visit to P.O. Box 1846, Taos 87571. *(758-9593. Open daily 8:30am-4:30pm; in winter 9am-4pm. $10 per person, under 12 free. Camera permit $10, video camera permit $20.)* Feast days are celebrated with beautiful tribal dances; **San Gerónimo's Feast Days** (Sept. 29-30) also feature a fair and races. The tribal office can supply you with schedules of dances and other info. Best known for its sparkling pottery molded from mica and clay, **Picuris Pueblo,** 20mi. south of Taos on Rt. 75 near Peñasco, is smaller, less touristed, and somewhat more accessible *(587-2519, open daily 9am-6pm).* A free guide to Northern New Mexican Indian pueblos is available at the Taos Visitors Center.

The state's premier ski resort, **Taos Ski Valley,** about 15mi. northeast of town on Rt. 150, offers powder conditions in bowl sections and short but steep downhill runs that rival Colorado's. *(776-2291, lodging info 800-776-1111, ski conditions 776-2916. Lift tickets $40-42; equipment rental $19 per day.)* Reserve a room well in advance if you plan to come during the winter holiday season. There are also two smaller, more family-oriented ski areas near Taos: **Angel Fire** *(505-377-6401 or 800-633-7463)* and **Eagle Nest** *(800-494-9117).* In summer, the nearly deserted ski valley area becomes a hiker's paradise (most trails take off from Rt. 150). Due to the town's prime location near the Río Grande, **river rafting** is very popular in Taos. **Far-Flung Adventures,** next door to the Río Grande Gorge Hostel (see **Accommodations,** above), offers river trips ranging in length from ½-day ($40) to 3-day ($345). Reservations up to 6 weeks in advance are required for longer trips; call for details. *(758-9072. Open 7am-8pm; closed in winter.)* **Cottam's Ski and Outdoor,** 207A S. Pueblo del Sur rents mountain bikes. *(758-2822. $8 per hour, $20 per day; open daily 9am-6pm)*

Taos hums with New Age services: vibrasound relaxation, drum therapy, harmony massage, and cranial therapy, just for starters. **Taos Drums,** 5mi. south of the plaza on Rt. 68, features the world's largest collection of Native American drums. *(800-424-3786. Open M-Sa 9am-6pm, Su 11am-6pm).* A bulletin board outside **Merlin's Garden,** 127 Bent St., lists favorite New Age pastimes such as drum therapy and massage. *(758-0985. Open M-Sa 10am-5:30pm, Su 11am-5pm).*

# ALBUQUERQUE

Ever since the Ancestral Puebloan tribes settled here nearly 2000 years ago, visitors have treated Albuquerque as a stopover. In search of the legendary seven cities of gold, the infamous Spaniard Coronado and his entourage camped here for the winter. Over the years, Spanish settlers, and later the United States government, routed major transportation lines through Albuquerque; Rt. 66 still splits the city in two. Travelers who actually stick around are treated to humble hospitality, a mellow university district, and the dramatic Sandía Mountains.

## 🛈 ORIENTATION AND PRACTICAL INFORMATION

The city divides into four quadrants: NE, NW, SE, SW. **Central Ave.** divides the north and south, and **I-25** is a rough division between east and west. The all-adobe campus of the **University of New Mexico (UNM)** spreads along Central Ave. from University Ave. to Carlisle St. **Old Town Plaza** lies between San Felipe, North Plaza, South Plaza, and Romero, off Central Ave.

**Airport: Albuquerque International,** 2200 Sunport Blvd. SE (842-4366), south of downtown. Take bus #50 from 5th St. and Central Ave, or pick it up along Yale Blvd. **Airport Express** (765-1234) shuttles into the city ($10, two people $16.50). Their booth at the airport is open 9:30am-12:30pm. A taxi downtown costs under $10, to Old Town $15.

**Trains: Amtrak,** 214 1st St. SW (842-9650). 1 train per day to: Los Angeles (16hr., $58-106); Kansas City (17hr., $101-184); Santa Fe (1hr. to Lamy, $14-26; 15min. shuttle to Santa Fe, $14); and Flagstaff (5hr., $53-96). Reservations required. Open daily 9:30am-5:30pm.

**Buses: Greyhound** (243-4435) and **TNM&O Coaches** (242-4998) run from 300 2nd St. SW, 3 blocks south of Central Ave. Buses go to: Santa Fe (1½hr., 4 per day, $11.30); Flagstaff (6hr., 4 per day, $44); Denver (10hr., 5 per day, $61); Phoenix (10hr., 3 per day, $32); and Los Angeles (18hr.; 4 per day; $67).

**Public Transit: Sun-Tran Transit,** 601 Yale Blvd. SE (843-9200; open M-F 8am-5pm). Most buses run M-Sa 6am-6pm. Pick up maps at visitors centers, the transit office, or the main library. 75¢, seniors and ages 5-18 25¢. Request free transfers from driver.

**Taxis: Albuquerque Cab,** 883-4888.

**Car Rental: Rent-a-Wreck,** 500 Yale Blvd. SE (232-7552 or 800-247-9556). Cars with A/C from $20 per day with 150 free mi.; 20¢ per additional mi.; $120 per week. Insurance $11 per day, $70 per week. Must be 21 with credit card; under 25 surcharge $3 per day. Open daily 8am-5:30pm. Reservations recommended.

**Bike Rental: Old Town Bicycles,** 2209 Central Ave. NW (247-4926), several blocks from Old Town Plaza. Rents hybrid bikes for city use ($5 per hr., $16 overnight, $60 per week) and mountain bikes ($7 per hr., $20 overnight, $60 per week). Open M-F 10am-6pm, Sa 10am-5pm, Su noon-5pm. Credit card required for deposit. Reservations recommended on weekends.

**Visitor Info: Albuquerque Convention and Visitors Bureau,** 20 First Plaza, galleria level (800-284-2282). Open M-F 8am-5pm. Recorded info 24 hr. **Old Town Visitors Center** (243-3215), at Plaza Don Luís on Romero NW across from the church. Open daily 9am-5pm, Nov.-Mar. 9:30am-4:30pm. **Info booth** at airport open daily 8:30am-8:30pm.

**Help Lines: Rape Crisis Center,** 1025 Hermosa SE (266-7711). Center open M-F 8am-noon and 1-5pm; 24hr. hotline. **Gay and Lesbian Information Line,** (891-3647). 24hr.

**Internet Access: UNM Zimmerman Library,** at the heart of campus. Open fall and spring semesters M-Th 8am-midnight, F 8am-9pm, Sa 9am-6pm, Su 10am-midnight; in summer M-Th 8am-9pm, F 8am-5pm, Sa 10am-5pm, Su 10am-9pm.

**Post Office:** 1135 Broadway NE, at Mountain (245-9469). Open M-F 7:30am-6pm. **ZIP code:** 87104. **Area code:** 505.

# ACCOMMODATIONS

Cheap motels line **Central Ave.,** even near downtown. Evaluate the motel carefully before paying; a bit more money might mean a bit more safety. During the Oct. **balloon festival** (see **Sights,** below), rooms are scarce; call ahead for reservations.

**Route 66 Youth Hostel,** 1012 Central Ave. SW (247-1813), at 10th St. Dorm beds in sparse, clean rooms, as well as beautiful, newly renovated private rooms. Excellent location and a vibrant staff. Well-stocked kitchen. Bunks $13 with any hostel card. Private singles with shared bath $18, huge doubles $24. Linen $1. Key deposit $5. Reception daily 7-10:30am and 4-11pm. Check-out 10:30am. Chores required.

**Sandía Mountain Hostel,** 12234 Hwy. 14 N (281-4117), in nearby Cedar Crest. A laid-back, cozy hostel convenient to the Sandía hiking trails. Beds in clean and spacious dorms $10; private rooms $25-30.

**University Lodge,** 3711 Central Ave. NE (266-7663). About a 15min. walk from campus, in the historic and cool Nob Hill district. Unusually cozy rooms. In summer singles $33, doubles $40; in winter $30/$30.

**Crossroads Motel,** 1001 Central Ave NE (242-2757). Large, bright rooms, some with fridge, all with A/C, cable, and phone. Singles $29; doubles $36.

**Coronado State Monument Campground** (867-5589), about 15mi. north of Albuquerque. Take I-25 to exit 241 and follow the signs. A unique camping experience near the haunting Sandía Mountains. Adobe shelters on the sites are a respite from the heat. Toilets, showers, and drinking water available. Sites $7, with hookup $11. No reservations. Office open daily 7am-10pm.

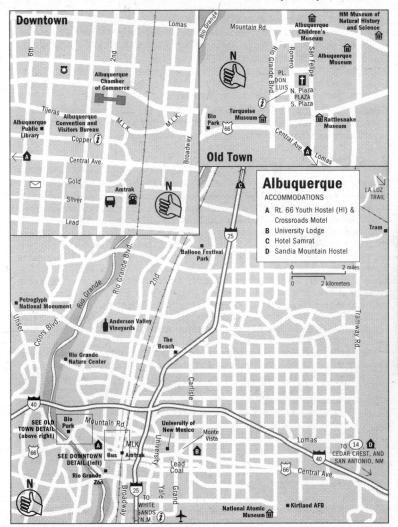

**Albuquerque**

**ACCOMMODATIONS**

A  Rt. 66 Youth Hostel (HI) & Crossroads Motel
B  University Lodge
C  Hotel Samrat
D  Sandia Mountain Hostel

THE SOUTHWEST

## FOOD

A diverse ethnic community, a lot of hungry interstate travelers, and one big load of green chiles render Albuquerque surprisingly tasty. The area around **UNM** is the best bet for inexpensive eateries. A bit farther east, the hip neighborhood of **Nob Hill** offers more offbeat options.

**El Patio,** 142 Harvard St. SE (268-4245). A softly strumming guitarist beckons passersby to sit, relax, and down a few enchiladas. Mexican plates $5-8, including lots of veggie options. Open M-Th 11am-9pm, F-Sa 11am-9:30pm, Su noon-9pm.

**Route 66 Malt Shop,** 1720 Central Ave. SW (242-7866). For a cheap, quick bite that comes with a whiff of nostalgia, this nook can't be beat. Lunch options hover around $3. Many would argue that a malt ($3) is a suitable lunch in itself. Open daily 9am-6pm.

**The Frontier,** 2400 Central Ave. SE (266-0550). If it's 3am and an insatiable appetite for some sort of ground beef has you pressing hard on the accelerator, you'll wind up here. College kids, a friendly staff, lively-to-the-wee-hours atmosphere, and good eats. Remarkable green chile stew $2; burgers $2-3. Open 24hrs.

**Olympia Café,** 2210 Central Ave. SE (266-5222). Gyros and souvlaki abound ($4), as well as vegetarian dishes, combination platters ($5-8), and American food for the less adventurous. Open M-F 11am-10pm, Sa noon-10pm.

**Double Rainbow,** 3412 Central Ave. SE (255-6633). This magazine-stocked establishment is known for its desserts ($4). Generous, hearty lunches and dinners ($4-8), including soup ($3). Open M-Sa 6am-midnight, Su 6am-11pm.

## ▣ SIGHTS

Just north of Central Ave. and east of Rio Grande Blvd., 1mi. south of I-40, Albuquerque's adobe-styled **Old Town** clusters around a Spanish plaza. On the north side of the plaza, the **San Felipe de Neri** church dates back to the end of the 18th century. *(Open daily 9am-5pm; Su mass in English 7am and 10:15am, in Spanish 8:30am.)* The unusual **Rattlesnake Museum,** south of the plaza, houses the world's most extensive display of rattlesnakes. *(202 San Felipe NW. 242-6569. Open daily 10am-6pm; $3, students $2, children $1.)* New Mexican art and history is displayed at the **Albuquerque Museum.** *(2000 Mountain Rd. NW. 242-4600. Open Tu-Su 9am-5pm. Free. Wheelchair access.)* Spike and Alberta, two statuesque dinosaurs, greet tourists outside the **New Mexico Museum of Natural History and Science;** inside the museum, interactive exhibits present the geological and evolutionary history of New Mexico. *(1801 Mountain Rd. NW. 841-2800. Open daily 9am-5pm. $5.25, students and seniors $4.20, children $2.10; combination Dynamax theater ticket $8/$6/$3. Wheelchair access.)* UNM has more intellectual (and free) museums located around campus.

The **Sandía Mountains,** on Albuquerque's east side in the Cíbola National Forest, were named by the Spanish for the pink color they turn at sunset (*sandía* means watermelon). Take Tramway Rd. from I-25 (exit 234) or Tramway Blvd. from I-40 (exit 167) to the **Sandía Peak Aerial Tramway,** the world's longest aerial tramway which ascends the west face of Sandía Peak, overlooking Albuquerque, the Río Grande Valley, and western New Mexico; the ascent is especially striking at sunset. *(Recorded info 856-6419. 30min. trip, times vary. $14, children $10. Tramway open daily in summer 9am-10pm; in winter 9am-8pm, weather permitting.)* Sandía Peak can also be reached by foot. Follow the signs from Tramway Blvd. to the **La Luz trailhead,** about 1mi. from the road to the tramway. The hike takes 3-5hr., but call first to make sure the trail isn't blocked by snow, which can happen even in early summer. A less strenuous **driving loop** through the **Sandía Ski Area,** (take I-40 E through Tijeras Canyon, turn north onto Rt. 14, and turn west onto Rt. 536 at San Antonio), winds through lovely forests of piñon and ponderosa pines, oaks, and spruce, then climbs sharply to the summit of **Sandía Crest,** where a dazzling 1½mi. ridge **hike** to **Sandía Peak** (10,678 ft.) begins. Rangers lead guided hikes through the **Cíbola National Forest;** you'll need reservations for the challenging winter snowshoe hikes. In the summer, some hiking and biking trails are open to the public only during specific hours. *(242-9052 for reservations or details. Usually Th-Su 10am-4pm.)*

Located at the edge of suburbia on Albuquerque's west side, **Petroglyph National Monument** features more than 15,000 images etched into lava rocks between 1300 and 1650 by Pueblo Indians and Spanish settlers. Short paved trails access small sections of the park's **Boca Negra Canyon,** but most of the area can be explored only by off-trail hiking—ask rangers for suggested routes. Take I-40 to Coors Rd. N (exit 155) or Unser Ave. (exit 154), and follow the signs to the park. Alternatively, take bus #9 from 6th and Silver to Coors Blvd., a few blocks away. *(899-0205. Park open M-F 8am-5pm. $1, Sa-Su and holidays $2; National Parks passports accepted.)* **The Pueblo of Acoma,** about 60mi. west of Albuquerque, is one of the most spectacular Native American pueblo dwellings in the area. Take I-40 to exit 102 and Hwy. 30 to Acomita. From there, take Hwy. 32 south about 11mi. to the visitors center. *(Visits by* *guided tour: $6, seniors $5, children $4. Tours given Apr.-Oct. 8am-7pm, Nov.-Mar. 8am-4:30pm; last tour leaves 1hr. before closing. Hours change often; call ahead.)*

The **Albuquerque BioPark,** sporting an **aquarium,** a **botanic garden,** and a **zoo,** has recently burst onto the scene. *(764-6200. Aquarium and garden: 2601 Central Ave SW. Zoo: 903 10th St. SW. All open daily in summer 9am-5pm, in winter 9am-5pm. Aquarium and botanic garden tickets $4.50, seniors and children $2.50; zoo tickets same price. All with wheelchair access.)*

The **National Atomic Museum,** on Kirtland Air Force Base, tells the story of Little Boy and Fat Man, the atomic bombs dropped on Hiroshima and Nagasaki. *Ten Seconds that Shook the World,* a 1hr. documentary on the making of the atomic bomb, shows 4 times daily. The Air Force base is a few mi. southeast of downtown, east of I-25. Ask at the visitor control gate on Wyoming Blvd. for a museum visitor's pass; you'll need *several* forms of ID. *(20358 Wyoming Blvd. 284-3243. Museum open daily 9am-5pm. $2, children $1.)*

## 🎵 ENTERTAINMENT AND NIGHTLIFE

Over the first week of Oct. hundreds of aeronauts take flight in beautifully colored hot-air balloons during the **balloon festival.** Even the most grounded of landlubbers will enjoy the week's barbecues and musical events. The presence of a sizeable university in Albuquerque is a boon for the nightlife scene. Check flyers posted around the university area for live music shows, or pick up a copy of *Alibi,* the local free weekly. **Launchpad,** 618 Central Ave. SW, draws a young, colorful crowd, lured by local alternative bands and occasional big acts (764-8887; cover varies with band; Su-F 4pm-2am, Sa 7pm-2am). Rock, blues, and reggae bands perform at **Dingo Bar,** 313 Gold St. SW (246-0663), where drafts run $2-4 (cover $2-8 F-Sa after 8pm; open daily 4pm-2am). The **"Downtown Bar Crawl"** special ticket gets you into a number of bars on Central Ave. for $5; pay at any of the bars. Dig in your spurs at **Caravan East,** 7605 Central Ave. NE, "where there is always a dancin' partner" and live music (265-7877; cover F-Sa $3; open daily 4:30pm-2am).

## NEAR ALBUQUERQUE: MADRID

The scenic and historic **Turquoise Trail** extends along Rt. 14 between Albuquerque and Sante Fe. Miners once harvested copious amounts of turquoise, gold, silver, and coal from the surrounding area, but the towns suffered greatly during the Depression. Founded in 1914 as a coal mining town, **Madrid** (MA-drid), 40mi. from Albuquerque along Rt. 14, was a ghost town until the 1970s, when artists began to resettle the area. The town is now home to many artists, refugees from the 60s hippie revolution, and craft-makers who sell their Native-American-style goods in shops lining the highway. **Java Junction,** smack in the middle of town, offers lattes ($2.35), mochas ($2.85), and the cheapest grub around (tamales $1.50), as well as a selection of wacky coffee-themed t-shirts ($18; open 7:30am-6pm).

## GALLUP

Gallup, located at the intersection of **I-40** and **U.S. 666,** falls into the unfortunate class of Western cities that seem to have been built too quickly, filling their cultural void with an empty supermarket-and-styrofoam-cups modernity. Luckily, this town has two things going for it: Native Americans and location. Gallup, just east of the Navajo Nation, has been promoting its Native American-ness recently, and it has good reason to—it is the epicenter of the Navajo jewelry trade. With all that turquoise and silver comes a strong cultural influence and with that culture, comes a modicum of tourism. Smack-dab in prime southern four-corners land, Gallup's popular neighbors are the primary reason for the horde of motels throughout town. Nearby attractions include: **Petrified Forest National Park** (see p. 724), the **Navajo Reservation** (see p. 719), **Chaco Culture National Park** (see p. 748), and **El Morro National Monument** (see below).

That's not to say there's no fun to be had in town. The **Inter-Tribal Indian Ceremonial,** held the second weekend in Aug. at **Red Rock State Park** (take I-40 to exit 26), features 4 days of Indian dances, rodeos, traditional foods, parades, and art exhibits (863-3896 or 800-233-4528; reserved seating $18, general admission $10). The park's **museum** explores the Ancestral Puebloan past and surveys the lives of members of the modern-day Navajo, Hopi, and Zuni tribes (863-1337; open M-Tu 8am-4:30pm, W-F 8am-6pm, Sa-Su 10am-6pm; free). For a tough hike or an even tougher mountain bike ride, tackle **Mt. Taylor** (11,301 ft.), just north of nearby Grants. From Gallup, take I-40 E to Grants (about 20mi.), then U.S. 547 N to U.S. 193; turn left onto a dirt road and drive 4mi. to the parking area (open M-F 8am-noon, 1pm-5pm). The Mt. Taylor **ranger station** (505-287-8833) has more info.

Gallup's pot of tea is pottery (and jewelry); expect to be overwhelmed by the number of vendors touting goods of questionable quality. Take heart, though: most of the wares you will find in Gallup are authentic. **Richardson's Trading Post,** 222 W. Rt. 66, is among the more reputable dealers, but prices for the vast selection of jewelry can run pretty high (722-4762; open M-Sa 9am-6pm). You might have a greater chance of finding something affordable at **Shush Yaz Trading Company,** 1304 W. Lincoln St. (722-0130; open M-Sa 9am-6pm).

**Old Rt. 66,** which runs parallel to I-40 through downtown, is lined with cheap motels. **The Colonial Motel,** 1007 W. Coal Ave., a bit west of downtown, rents large rooms with cable TV (863-6821; singles $21; doubles $25). The **Blue Spruce Lodge,** 1119 E. Rt. 66, has clean, largish rooms (863-5211; singles $29; doubles $32). Next door, the **Arrowhead Inn,** 1115 E. Rt. 66, might be an even better deal, with large and pleasant rooms, phones, cable TV, and sometimes microfridges (863-5111; doubles $18, quads $25). You can pitch a tent in the shadow of red sandstone cliffs at **Red Rock State Park Campground,** which offers 141 sites and a convenience store. From I-40, take exit 26 and follow the signs. (505-722-3829. Sites $10, RV hookup $14.)

In addition to the usual fast-food suspects, a number of diners and cafes line both sides of I-40. **Earl's,** 1409 E. Rt. 66, offers quick service to crowds of local families in its big dining rooms. (863-4201. Omelette $5, breakfast burrito $6. Open Su-Th 7am-9:30pm, F-Sa 7am-10pm.) **Ranch Kitchen,** 3001 W. Rt. 66, serves up tasty country cooking and real-deal barbecue in a wood-beamed dining room (722-2537; 3 pancakes $3.95, barbecue chicken $10; open daily 7am-10pm).

**Greyhound,** 255 E. Rt. 66 (863-3761), runs to Flagstaff (4hr., 4 per day, $35) and Albuquerque (2½hr., 4 per day, $20). **Visitors center:** 701 Montoya Blvd. (863-4909), just off Rt. 66 (open daily 8am-5pm). **Post Office:** 500 S. 2nd St. (722-5265; open M-F 8:30am-5pm, Sa 10am-1:30pm). **ZIP code:** 87301. **Area code:** 505.

## NEAR GALLUP

**CHACO CULTURE NATIONAL HISTORICAL PARK.** Sun-scorched **Chaco Canyon** (CHAH-co) served as the first great settlement of the Ancestral Puebloans. The ruins here, which date from the 9th century, are among the best-preserved in the Southwest. Evidence of inhabitance thousands of years older than even the most ancient Ancestral Pueblo dwellings also enrich the landscape, though the societies that flourished during the turn of the first millennium are what make the site awesome. **Pueblo Bonito,** the canyon's largest pueblo, was once 4 stories high and contained more than 600 rooms. Nearby **Chetro Ketl** houses one of the southwest's largest *kivas,* a prayer room used in religious rituals. The largest pueblos are accessible from the main road, but **backcountry hiking trails** lead to many other ruins; snag a free **backcountry permit** from the visitors center before heading off.

The park lies 92mi. northeast of Gallup. From the north, take Rt. 44 to County Rd. 7900 (3mi. east of **Nageezi**); from the south, take Rt. 9 from Crownpoint to the turn-off for the park. At the turn of the century, it took a government archaeologist almost a year to get here from Washington, D.C.—not much has changed. From the highways, a 20mi. dirt road leads to the park; this part alone may take 1hr. *Remember that there is no gas in the park, and gas stations on the reservation are few and far between.*

The **visitors center,** at the east end of the park, has an excellent **museum** that exhibits Ancestral Puebloan art and architecture and includes an enlightening film. Stock up on water here (505-786-7014; open daily 8am-6pm; $8 per vehicle). No food is available at the park. **Camping,** located a little more than a mile from the visitors center, costs $10 per site; register at the campground. Arrive by 11am; there are only 64 sites. Most visitors to the **Circle A Ranch Hostel,** 5mi. east of Cuba, come for no other reason than to stay at the ranch; but the hostel is also a convenient base for the park. Be forewarned: with 360 acres of forest, lakes, and canyons, and all the quiet and rustic appeal of a turn-of-the-century ranch, it may be hard to leave. Heading north on Hwy. 44, just north of Cuba, turn right onto Los Pinos Co. Rd., where an upside-down triangle advertises a camp, and follow the signs to the hostel for about 5mi. (505-289-3350. Kitchen, large living room, indoor and solar showers. Dorms $13; doubles $24-44. Open May-Oct.)

**EL MORRO NATIONAL MONUMENT.** While traveling through what is now New Mexico, Native Americans, Spanish *conquistadores*, and Anglo pioneers left their inscriptions on a giant boulder. **Inscription Rock** is now part of El Morro National Monument, just west of the Continental Divide on Rt. 53, 12mi. southeast of the Navajo town of Ramah. A ½mi. loop trail winds past the boulder and neighboring spring. A longer trail continues on past 2 pueblos. The **visitors center** includes a small museum and warnings against emulating the graffiti of old. Trails close 1hr. before visitors center. (505-783-4226. Open daily 9am-7pm. Off-season 9am-5pm.)

# TRUTH OR CONSEQUENCES

In 1950, the popular radio game show "Truth or Consequences" celebrated its tenth anniversary by renaming a small town, formerly Hot Springs, NM, in its honor. As its maiden name suggests, T or C was a tourist attraction prior to the publicity stunt. Maybe it's something in the water.

T or C's **mineral baths** are the town's main attraction; locals claim that it heals everything from blisters to sunburn. The three co-ed tubs (bathing suits must be worn) at the **Riverbend Hostel** are accessible to the public for $5 per day (baths run daily 7:30-10am and 7:30-10pm). The private baths at the **Charles Motel's spa** cost $3 for guests and $4 for non-guests (open daily 8am-9pm); the spa also offers a variety of other New Age-y services, from reflexology to ear candling. A few mi. northeast of town, **Elephant Butte Lake** offers boating, beaches, and hiking trails.

Approximately 45min. north of T or C on I-25, the **Bosque del Apache Wildlife Refuge** is a favorite spot of migrating birds in winter, including cranes, eagles, and snow geese (835-1828; park open until sunset; entrance fee $3). In the summer you can see a surprising number of deer, coyote, porcupines, roadrunners, and snakes from the **15mi. driving loop.** The park also offers some short **hiking trails** (Maps at visitors center; open M-F 7:30am-4pm, Sa-Su 8am-4:30pm).

On the banks of the Rio Grande, the tranquil ▧ **Riverbend Hot Springs Hostel (HI-AYH),** 100 Austin St., offers relief to weary travelers; prices include use of the mineral baths. The laid-back atmosphere is almost as relaxing as the baths. (894-6183. Teepees or dorm beds $13, non-members $15; private rooms $28-45. Kitchen and laundry facilities.) More upscale accommodations can be found at the **Charles Motel,** 601 Broadway, which also has mineral baths on the premises. The adobe rooms are large and bright, and most have kitchens (894-7154; singles $35; doubles $45). **Campsites** at the nearby **Elephant Butte Lake State Park** have access to restrooms and cold showers (primitive sites $6, developed sites $7, with electricity $11).

The popular **La Cocina,** 280 N. Date St., serves up huge portions of Mexican and New Mexican food, including free chips and salsa (burritos around $3, combination plates $6; 894-6499; open daily 10:30am-10pm). Find a decent selection of **groceries** at Bullock's, at the intersection of Broadway and Post (open M-Sa 7:30am-8pm, Su 8am-7pm). Full of T and C charm, **La Bella Mian,** 404 Main St., bakes tasty gourmet pizzas (large $11), carves mean Italian-style sandwiches ($4-5), and has the best desserts in town. (894-6787. Open M-Th 11am-9pm, F-Sa 11am-10pm.)

T or C sits approximately 150mi. south of Albuquerque on I-25. **Greyhound,** in cooperation with TNM&O coaches (894-3649), runs 2 buses daily from Albuquerque (3hr., $31.50). The **tourist office,** 201 S. Foch St. (800-831-9487), has info, shminfo (open M-F 9am-5pm, Sa 9am-1pm; closed Sa off-season). **Post Office:** 300 Main St., in the middle of town (open M-F 9am-3pm), or 1507 N. Date St. (open 8:30am-5:30pm). **ZIP code:** 87901. **Area code:** 505.

## GHOST TOWNS NEAR TRUTH OR CONSEQUENCES

The former mining town of **Lake Valley** is one of New Mexico's only remaining **ghost towns.** The sole inhabitants today are rabbits and rattlesnakes, and the only sound is the metal Conoco sign creaking in the breeze. Lake Valley saw its heyday in the 1880s, reaching a population of around 1000 during its peak period of silver ore production. The devaluation of silver in the late 1880s hearkened the town's decline. The train tracks were taken up in 1934, and buildings were dismantled. The town is about 15mi. south of Hillsboro on Rt. 27; look for the **adobe schoolhouse** on the left. Leaflets for the **walking tour** can be picked up at the schoolhouse, which also contains artifacts salvaged from the ruins of the town. Many of the buildings are on private property—pay attention to the "No Trespassing" signs.

The nearby community of **Hillsboro** makes a good lunch stop. Although Hillsboro also calls itself a ghost town, it has about 100 residents, many of them artists, whose work is on display in the various shops that line the main street. The ruins of the **old jail and courthouse** are still standing; to find them, follow the dirt road that leads up the hill opposite the post office. The **Hillsboro General Store and Country Café** serves as an unofficial info center; the owner knows everything about the town and everyone in it. Decent Mexican and New Mexican food is served at low prices; the $4.25 green chile and bacon grilled cheese is a thoroughly Southwestern combination. (Open M-F and Su 8am-3pm, Sa 8am-3pm and 6-8pm.) Hillsboro wakes up every Labor Day weekend for the **Apple Festival,** during which vendors from all over New Mexico gather to sell apple pies and arts and crafts.

## GILA CLIFF DWELLINGS AND SILVER CITY

The mysterious **Gila Cliff Dwellings National Monument** preserves over 40 stone and timber rooms carved into the cliff's natural caves by the Mogollon tribe during the late 1200s. About a dozen families lived here for about 20 years, farming on the mesa top and along the river. During the early 1300s, however, the Mogollon abandoned their homes for reasons unknown, leaving the dwellings as their only trace. (Dwellings open daily 8am-6pm, off-season 8am-5pm. **Entrance fee** $3, under 8 free. Golden Eagle passports accepted.) The **visitors center,** at the end of Rt. 15, shows an informative film and sells various maps of the **Gila National Forest** (536-9461; 50¢; open daily 8am-5pm; off-season 8am-4pm). The picturesque 1mi. round-trip **hike** to the dwellings begins by the Lower Scorpion campground. Right by the trailhead, the free Lower and Upper Scorpion **campgrounds,** with flush toilets and running water, operate on a first-come, first-served basis. The **Gila National Forest** encompasses hundreds of mi. of hiking trails, as well as **free backcountry camping,** including some designated campsites. Many trails start at the two corrals on the road to the cliff dwellings; rangers have hiking suggestions. To reach the monument, take Rt. 15 from Silver City, a slow and gorgeous drive that winds through the heavily-forested mountains to the canyon of the Gila River. (44mi. 1½hr. Road open daily late May to early Sept. 8am-6pm; in winter 9am-4pm.) In winter, call ahead for road conditions before attempting the drive. If you're coming from Truth or Consequences, take Rt. 152 in San Lorenzo to Rt. 35, then head north on Rt. 15. This route is less steep, just as beautiful, and takes about the same amount of time.

Beds and food await 45mi. south in **Silver City,** a good base for a trip to the monument, 60mi. west of Truth or Consequences on Rt. 152. The historic downtown area has plenty of charm to offer. Squeaky-clean **Carter House (HI-AYH),** 101 N. Cooper St., near the historic area, has a kitchen, large common area, laundry facilities, and a huge wrap-around porch; a B&B occupies the upstairs. To find Carter House, follow the signs to the historic district, or take Broadway up the hill and turn left on Cooper—Carter is to the left of the courthouse. (388-5485. $12.50, nonmembers $15.50; double $25/$31. B&B singles $57-67; doubles $65-75. Check-in 8-10am and 4-9pm.) The **Palace Hotel,** 106 W. Broadway, has beautiful antique rooms

(388-1811; doubles $29.50-55; reservations recommended). **The Corner Cafe,** 200 N. Bullard St., a local favorite, has an all-you-can-eat salad and soup buffet is $5; otherwise, sandwiches, including the New Mexican Downtowner ($4.50) and breakfasts (all under $5) rarely fail to satisfy. (388-2056. Open M-Sa 7am-4pm, Su 8am-2pm.) The eponymous owner of **Vicki's Downtown Deli,** 107 W. Yankie St., makes authentic Reubens—with chips and salsa ($5.25)—and surprisingly gourmet dinner specials, like pork cordon bleu ($10; 388-5430; open M-F 11am-8:30pm, Sa 11:30am-4pm).

Bookstores and antique shops cluster on Bullard and Broadway in the historical part of town. The **Silver City Museum,** 312 W. Broadway, houses exhibits on the history of the town and unusual collections of local residents' treasure troves, including the curator's Def Leppard paraphernalia (538-5921; open Tu-F 9am-4:30pm, Sa-Su 10am-4pm; free). The **Western New Mexico University Museum,** on West St. off College Ave. hosts a worthwhile exhibit on the ancient Mibres Mogollon, and artifacts illustrating animal, mining, and ranching life past and present (538-6386; open M-F 9am-4:30pm, Sa-Su 10am-4pm; free). The **New Mexico Cowboy Poetry Gathering** (538-5921) convenes in Silver City every Aug.; descriptions are futile.

**Silver Stage Lines** (388-2586 or 800-522-0162) has bus service twice daily to Silver City from the El Paso airport (round-trip $50, home pick-up $2 extra). **Las Cruces Shuttle Service** (800-288-1784) offers daily trips between Silver City and Deming (3 per day, $17); Las Cruces (3 per day, $27); and El Paso (3 per day, $35). Both companies pick up passengers from **Schadel's Bakery,** 212 N. Bullard St. **Chamber of Commerce:** 1103 N. Hudson St. (538-3785; open M-Sa 9am-5pm, in summer also Su noon-5pm). **Internet access:** Public Library, 515 W. College Ave. (538-3672. WWW only. Open M 9am-8pm, T-W 9am-6pm, Th 9am-8pm, F 9am-5pm, Sa 9am-1pm.). **Post office:** 500 N. Hudson St. (open M-F 8:30am-5pm, Sa 10am-noon). **ZIP code:** 88061. **Area code:** 505.

# WHITE SANDS

The giant (300 sq. mi.) sandbox of **White Sands National Monument,** on Rt. 70 (15mi. southwest of Alamogordo and 52mi. northeast of Las Cruces), evokes nostalgia for playground days. Situated in the Tularosa Basin between the Sacramento and San Andres mountains, the world's largest gypsum dunes formed as rainwater dissolved gypsum in a nearby mountain, collecting in the basin's Lake Lucero. As desert heat evaporated the lake, the gypsum crystals were left behind and now form the continually growing sand dunes. The blindingly white drifts of fine sand create an arctic tundra look, but don't be fooled: the midday sun assaults the shadeless white with a light and heat that can be unbearable. Trekking or just rolling through the dunes provides hours of mindless fun or mindful soul-searching; the sand is particularly awe-inspiring at sunset. Hiking possibilities include the **Big Dune Trail,** a 1mi. nature trail adorned with plaques describing the unique fauna and flora of the dunes; and the difficult **Alkali Flat Trail,** a backcountry hike to a dry lake bed where gypsum sand is formed (4.6mi., 4hr.; ask at the visitors center for a topographical map before starting out). Bring plenty of water, even for short hikes. The paved **Dunes Drive** leads 8mi. into the heart of the dunes (open 7am-9pm; off-season 7am-sunset; $3 per adult; wheelchair access). Summer evening events include ranger-led sunset strolls (7pm) and lectures (8:30pm). Ask about special programs for full moon nights, when the park is open until midnight. The basin is also home to a missile test range—duck if you hear a sharp whistle—and the **Trinity Site,** 50mi. north of White Sands, where the world's first atomic bomb was detonated in July 1945 (open to visitors on the 1st weekends of Apr. and Oct.).

The **Space Center,** 2mi. northeast of U.S. 54, brings the great beyond down to earth with a museum and an OmniMax (437-2840 or 800-545-4021. Open daily 9am-5pm. Museum $2.50, seniors and ages 6-12 $2; OmniMax film $5.50/$3.50.)

You'll find the **White Sands Visitors Center,** P.O. Box 1086, Holloman AFB 88330, as you enter the park from Rt. 70. (479-6124. Open 8am-7pm; mid-Aug.-late May

**THE TRUTH IS OUT THERE** In July 1947, an alien space-craft reportedly plummeted to the earth near the dusty town of **Roswell,** 76mi. north of Carlsbad (from Albuquerque, head 89mi. south on I-25 to San Antonio, then 153mi. east on U.S. 380). The official Army press release reported that the military had recovered pieces of some form of "flying saucer," but a retraction arrived the next day—the mysterious wreckage, the brass claimed, was actually a harmless weather balloon. Everyone admits that *something* crashed in the desert northwest of Roswell on that fateful night some 50 years ago. Was the initial Army admission just a poor choice of words by some PR hack, or just a crack in an elaborate cover-up?

With only-in-America gusto, media attention and TV's *The X-Files* have helped catapult a growing lunatic fringe into the believing ranks. During the first week of July, the **UFO Festival** commemorates the anniversary of the alleged encounter, drawing thousands for live music, an alien costume contest, and a 5K "Alien Chase" race. With a plastic flying saucer above its diminutive storefront, the super-popular **International UFO Museum and Research Center,** 114 N. Main St., has invented some novel ways to cash in on the alienophile hysteria. Some remain skeptical of its scholarly credentials, but the museum's backers say the reading rooms and archives are academically legitimate. The center houses perhaps the only **espresso bar** in southeastern New Mexico, plus a gift shop full of items like "Crash in Roswell Tonight" bumper stickers and alien-shaped wall clocks. *(505-625-9495. Open daily 10am-5pm; in summer 9am-5pm. Free. Audio tour $3.)* No pilgrimage would be complete without a trip to the arid, sun-scorched crash site itself, the 24 sq. mi. **Hobb Corn Ranch** (505-623-4043), 20mi. north of Roswell on U.S. 285. A sign near the entrance greets the faithful: this "universal sacred site" is dedicated "to the beings who met their destinies near Roswell, New Mexico, July 1947." For $15 (under 14 free), the owners will escort the curious 8mi. to the low butte where the saucer allegedly met *its* destiny amid dust devils and parched cacti (by appt. only; call 800-623-8104 10am-5pm).

8am-5pm.) To use the park's **backcountry campsites,** register at the park entrance (free with park admission). More free backcountry camping can be found at **Lincoln National Forest,** 13mi. to the east (434-7200). **Aguirre Springs,** 30mi. to the west, doesn't charge for camping, but you must pay $3 to enter (525-4300). For info, contact the **Forest Supervisor,** Lincoln National Forest, 1101 New York Ave., Alamogordo 88310. **Oliver Lee Memorial State Park,** 10mi. south of Alamogordo on U.S. 54, then 5mi. east on Dog Canyon Rd., has a campground at the canyon mouth on the west face of the Sacramento Mountains. (437-8284. Sites $10, with hookup $14. Visitors center open daily 9am-4pm. Park entrance fee $3 per vehicle.)

The nearest hostel is the amazing **High Desert Hostel Ranch,** in the hamlet of **Oscuro,** about 1hr. north of the park. This working adobe ranch comes complete with chickens, cows, orchard, and organic vegetable garden. Kitchen privileges include any food you want, and the large common room is stocked with games and books. Oscuro is a flag stop on the Greyhound route from El Paso to Albuquerque ($25 one-way from either city); call ahead, and the owner will pick you up *gratis* from the bus stop. Driving, the hostel is about 1mi. down a dirt road from U.S. 54 at Mi. 108—follow the signs. (648-4007. Free laundry. Dorm beds $14; private doubles $27; triples $32. Reserve private rooms by sending a check to P.O. Box 798, Carrizozo, NM 88301.) Closer to White Sands, the town of **Alamogordo** has an extensive motel selection, most of which line White Sands Blvd. The bright pink **Western Motel,** 1101 S. White Sands Blvd., has pleasant rooms with cable TV and A/C (437-2922; singles $30; doubles $35). **All-American Inn,** 508 S. White Sands Blvd., is clean, has a pool, and is adorned with "Support Our Troops" bumper stickers. All rooms have A/C and coffee pots. (437-1850. Singles $30; doubles $34.) **Area code:** 505.

# CARLSBAD CAVERNS

Imagine the surprise of the first European wanderers through southeastern New Mexico when 250,000 bats appeared at dusk, seemingly out of nowhere. The swarm of winged mammals led to the discovery of the Carlsbad Caverns at the turn of the century. By 1923, colonies of tourists clung to the walls of this desolate attraction. **Carlsbad Caverns National Park** marks one of the world's largest and oldest cave systems; even the most jaded spelunker will be struck by its unusual geological creations.

**⚑ PRACTICAL INFORMATION.** The closest town is **White's City**, a tiny tourist trap on U.S. 62/180, 20mi. southeast of Carlsbad, 6mi. from the park visitors center. Flash floods occasionally close the roads, so call ahead to the visitors center. **El Paso Texas** (see p. 562) is the nearest major city, 150mi. to the west past **Guadalupe Mountains National Park** (see p. 561). **Greyhound,** in cooperation with **TNM&O Coaches** (887-1108), runs two buses per day to White's City from El Paso ($27) or Carlsbad (20min., $6). **Visitor Info: Carlsbad Caverns Visitors Center** (785-2232; open daily 8am-7pm; late Aug. to May 8am-5:30pm). White's City's **post office:** 23 Carlsbad Caverns Hwy. (785-2220), next to the Best Western gift shop (open M-F 8am-noon and 12:30-4:30pm, Sa 8am-noon). **ZIP code:** 88268. **Area code:** 505.

**⚐ ACCOMMODATIONS.** Drive 20mi. north to **Carlsbad** to find a plethora of cheap motels. **Lorlodge Motel,** 2019 S. Canal St., has clean, A/C rooms, many with microwave and fridge (887-1171; singles $33, doubles $38). Even less expensive motels line S. Canal St. (U.S. 285), but it's always a good idea to see the room before you pay. The **White's City Resort RV Park,** just outside the park entrance, provides water, showers, restrooms, and a pool. (785-2291 or 800-228-3767. Tent sites or full hookup $18 for up to six people. Register in the Best Western lobby.) **Backcountry camping** is free in the park; get a permit at the visitors center. (for more nearby camping, see **Guadalupe Mountains National Park, TX,** on p. 561.)

**◙ SIGHTS.** Plaques guide you along the **Big Room Tour** and **Natural Entrance Tour.** The Big Room tour is relatively easy and popular: the steep Natural Entrance tour is less trafficked. (*$6, ages 6-15 and Golden Age Passport holders $3, under 6 free. 1½hr., depending on how often you stop to gawk in amazement. Open 8:30am-5pm; mid-Aug.-May. 8:30am-3:30pm. Partial wheelchair access.*) The ranger-guided **King's Palace Tour** passes through 4 of the cave's lowest rooms and some of the most awesome anomalies. (*1½hr. tours on the hr. 9-11am and 1-3pm. Advance reservations required. $8, Golden Age Passport holders and ages 6-15 $4.*) Plan your visit for late afternoon to catch the magnificent **bat flight.** The ritual, during which hungry bats storm out of the cave at a rate of 6000 per min, is preceded by a ranger talk. (*May-Oct. daily just before sunset.*) **Backcountry hiking** is permitted in the park (not in the caves), but a permit, a map, and massive quantities of water are required.

Tours of the undeveloped **Slaughter Canyon Cave** offer a more rugged caving experience. (*785-2232. Two 2hr. tours; early Sept. to late May Sa-Su only. $15, Golden Age Passport holders and ages 6-15 $7.50.*) A persistent car is required to get there, however. There's no public transportation, and the parking lot is 23mi. down a dirt road off U.S. 62/180, several mi. south of the main entrance to the park. The cave entrance is a steep, strenuous ½mi. from the lot. Ranger-led tours (bring your own flashlight) traverse the difficult and slippery terrain inside; there are no paved trails or handrails. Call to reserve at least 2 days in advance. Many other tours of remote areas of the caves are offered, some of the more adventurous of which require crawling and climbing through tight passages (1-4hr., $7-20). Call 800-967-2283 at least a month in advance for complete information and reservations.

Just north of Carlsbad, **Living Desert State Park** preserves and protects the various flora and fauna native to New Mexico. The 1¼mi. **self-guided walking tour** passes a variety of exhibits, including an aviary, bears, porcupines, and a reptile house. (*Open daily 9am-7pm; off-season 9am-4pm. $3, ages 7-12 $1. Wheelchair access.*)

THE SOUTHWEST

# CALIFORNIA

For centuries, settlers have come to California in search of the elusive and the unattainable. The Spanish conquistadors came for the mythical land of El Dorado, the mining '49ers hunted for the Mother Lode, and the naive and beautiful still search for stardom. Adventurers and misanthropes flock to the mountains and deserts to cop the ultimate thrill, and stampedes of 2.5-child families cloud the national parks, seeking reconciliation with the illusion of tamed, well-appointed nature. Dreamy-eyed, disenfranchised flower children converge on Haight St.'s lost commune, while future techno-rulers fill perennially booming Silicon Valley.

Glaring movie spotlights, clanging San Francisco trolleys, and *barrio* bustle are all Californian. Vanilla-scented Jeffrey pines, alpine lakes, and ghostly, shimmering desert floors are all Californian. The breezy tolerance of the San Francisco Bay Area, the plastic style of L.A., and the military-fueled Republicanism of San Diego are all Californian. It is the West of the West, the resting place of the superlative, the drawing board of the American dream. No other state can claim so many flavors in its blend of physical, social, and cultural ingredients. There's so much going on you'd need a whole book (like *Let's Go: California 2000*) to describe it.

### HIGHLIGHTS OF CALIFORNIA

- **Los Angeles.** Follow your star to the place where media legends carouse (p. 762), Ice Age fossils calcify (p. 766), boardwalk freaks commune (p. 764), vintage automobiles cruise (p. 766), and milkshakes congeal (p. 761).
- **San Francisco.** Here, bluesmen resonate (p. 823), iconoclasts castigate and students demonstrate (p. 821), and old hippies recreate (p. 807).
- **Scenic Drives.** Along the coast, Rt. 1 and U.S. 101 stop at Redwood National Park (p. 835), the San Mateo Coast (p. 826), and Hearst Castle (p. 797).
- **National Parks.** Hike at Yosemite (p. 844), say howdy to a scorpion in Death Valley (p. 790), or trip through cholla at Joshua Tree (p. 789).
- Pan for **"goald!"** in Sonora (p. 837), go **frogging** in Calaveras County (p. 837), and observe active **New Age Hippies** in the Cascades (p. 839).

## PRACTICAL INFORMATION

**Capital:** Sacramento.

**Visitor Info: California Office of Tourism,** 801 K St. #1600, Sacramento 95814 (800-862-2543; www.gocalif.ca.gov).

**Postal Abbreviation:** CA. **Sales Tax:** 7-8%, by county.

# SOUTHERN CALIFORNIA

## LOS ANGELES

Myth and anti-myth stand comfortably opposed in Los Angeles. Some see in its sweeping beaches and dazzling sun a demi-paradise, a land of opportunity where the most opulent dreams can be realized. Others point to its congestion, smog, and crime, and declare Los Angeles a sham—a converted wasteland where TV-numbed masses go to wither in the sun.

L.A. is a wholly American phenomenon, one that developed not in the image and shadow of Europe, but at the same time as America's international ascendancy. It is this autonomy that makes L.A. feel like a city without a past. In a city where nothing seems more than 30 years old, the latest trends curry more respect than

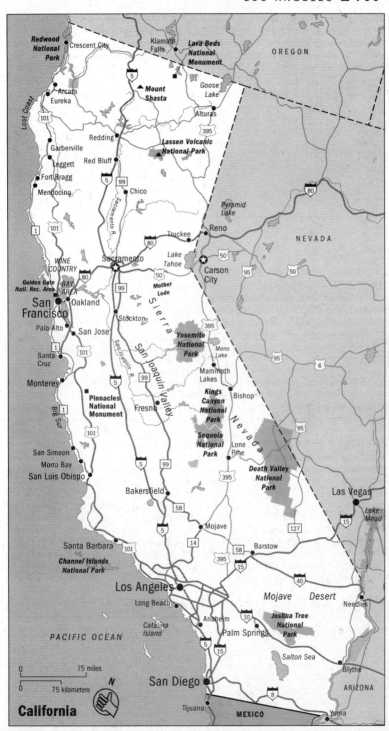

California

the venerable. Many come to this historical vacuum to make (or re-make) themselves. And what better place? Without the tiresome duty of kowtowing to the gods of an established high culture, Angelenos are free to indulge not in what they must, but in what they choose. The resulting atmosphere is delicious with potential. It's a hell of a show.

# ⚜ ORIENTATION

The City of Angels spreads its wings along the coast of Southern California, 127mi. north of San Diego and 403mi. south of San Francisco. You can still be "in" L.A. even if you're 50mi. from downtown. Before you even think about navigating Los Angeles's 6500mi. of streets and 40,000 intersections, get yourself a good **map.** Locals swear by the *Thomas Guide: Los Angeles County Street Guide and Directory* ($16 for L.A. county, $26 for L.A. and Orange County).

A legitimate **downtown** Los Angeles does exist, but it won't help orient you to the rest of the city. The numbered streets running east-west downtown form a labyrinth. The predominately Latino section of L.A. known as **East L.A.** begins east of downtown's Western Ave., with the districts of **Boyle Heights, Montebello,** and **El Monte.** South of downtown are the **University of Southern California (USC), Exposition Park,** and the predominantly African-American districts of **Inglewood, Watts,** and **Compton.** The area south of downtown, known as **South Central,** suffered the brunt of the fires and looting that erupted in 1992. South Central and East L.A. are considered crime-ridden and offer little to attract tourists.

Northwest of downtown is **Hollywood.** Sunset Blvd. (east-west) presents a cross-section of virtually everything L.A. has to offer: beach communities, lavish wealth, famous nightclubs, and sleazy motels. Hollywood Blvd. (east-west) runs just beneath the star-studded Hollywood Hills.

West of Hollywood, the **Westside** encompasses West Hollywood, Westwood, Century City, Culver City, Bel Air, Brentwood, and (for our purposes) the independent city of **Beverly Hills.** The affluent Westside also is home to the University of California at Los Angeles and some trendy, off-beat Melrose Ave. hangouts. The area west of downtown is known as the **Wilshire District** after its main boulevard. **Hancock Park,** a green residential area, covers the northeast portion of the district.

The **Valley** spreads north of the Hollywood Hills and the Santa Monica Mountains. For most people, *the* valley, is, like, the **San Fernando Valley,** where more than a million people live in the suburbs, in a basin bounded to the north and west by the Santa Susanna Mountains and the Simi Freeway (Rt. 118), to the south by the Ventura Freeway (Rt. 134), and to the east by the Golden State Freeway (I-5). The Valley also contains the suburb of **Burbank** and the city of **Pasadena.**

Eighty miles of beach line L.A.'s **Coastal Region. Zuma** is northernmost, followed by **Malibu,** which lies 15mi. up the coast from **Santa Monica.** Just a bit farther south is the funky beach community of **Venice.** The beach towns south of Santa Monica, comprising the area called the **South Bay,** are **Marina del Rey, Manhattan, Hermosa,** and **Redondo Beach.** South across the hob nobby **Palos Verdes Peninsula** is **Long Beach.** Farthest south are the **Orange County** beach cities: **Seal Beach, Sunset Beach, Huntington Beach, Newport Beach,** and **Laguna Beach.** Confused yet? Everyone is. Get a good map.

# 🔁 PRACTICAL INFORMATION

**PUBLIC TRANSPORTATION.** Nowhere is the great god Automobile held in greater reverence than in L.A., though the **Metropolitan Transit Authority (MTA)** does work—sort of. Some older buses may still be labeled RTD (Rapid Transit District), the MTA's former name. Using the MTA to sightsee in L.A. can be frustrating, simply because attractions tend to be spread out, and the system is not easily understood. Those determined to see everything in L.A. should get behind the wheel of a car. If this is not possible, base yourself in downtown or in Hollywood (where

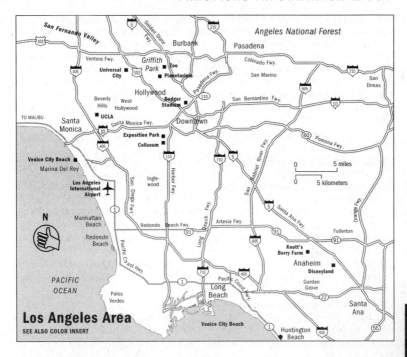

**Los Angeles Area**
SEE ALSO COLOR INSERT

there are plenty of bus connections). Bus service is dismal in the outer reaches of the city, and 2hr. journeys are not unusual.

Write for "sector maps," **MTA**, P.O. Box 194, Los Angeles 90053, or stop by one of the 10 **customer-service centers**. There are 3 downtown: **Gateway Transit Center**, Union Station (open M-F 6:30am-6pm); **Arco Plaza**, 505 S. Flower St., Level C (open daily 7:30am-3:30pm); and **5301 Wilshire** (open daily 8:30am-5pm). If you don't have time to map your route in advance, call 800-266-6883 (daily 5:30am-11:30pm) for transit info and schedules. Ninety percent of MTA's lines offer **wheelchair-accessible buses** (call 1hr. in advance, 800-621-7828 daily 6am-10pm). Accessible bus stops are marked with a symbol.

Bus service is best downtown and along the major thoroughfares west of downtown (there is 24hr. service, for instance, on Wilshire Blvd.). The downtown **DASH shuttle** costs only 25¢ and serves major tourist destinations including **Chinatown, Union Station, Gateway Transit Center, Olvera St.,** and **City Hall.** Given the hellish downtown traffic, the scope of the shuttle routes make them an attractive option. DASH also operates a **shuttle** on **Sunset Blvd.** in Hollywood, as well as shuttles in **Pacific Palisades, Watts, Fairfax, Midtown, Crenshaw, Van Nuys/Studio City, Warner Center,** and **Southeast L.A.** Downtown DASH operates M-F 6:30am-6:30pm, Sa 10am-5pm. Pacific Palisades shuttles do not run on Sa. Venice DASH runs every 10min. on summer Sa-Su 11am-6pm. Call 800-252-7433 for schedule info, 485-7201 for pick-up points. MTA's basic **fare** is $1.35, seniors and disabled 45¢; transfers 25¢/10¢. Exact change required. Transfers can be made between MTA lines or to other transit authorities. All route numbers given are MTA unless otherwise noted.

**FREEWAYS.** The freeway is perhaps the most enduring of L.A.'s images. When uncongested, these well-marked, 10- and 12-lane concrete roadways offer speed and convenience.The most frustrating aspect of driving is the sheer unpredictability of L.A. traffic. It goes without saying that rush hours, both morning and evening, are always a mess and well worth avoiding. Since construction is performed at random hours, there can be problems at any time. A little reminder: no matter how crowded the freeway is, it's almost always quicker and safer than taking surface streets to your destination. Californians refer to their highways by names and numbers, which is at best harmless, at worst misleading. For freeway info, call **CalTrans** (897-3693). **Do not hitchhike!** In Los Angeles, it's not just dangerous, it is tantamount to suicide.

**Airport: Los Angeles International (LAX)** (310-646-5252), in Westchester, 15mi. southwest of downtown. Metro buses, car rental companies, cabs, and airport shuttles offer rides from here to requested destinations. Cab fare to downtown is $24-33.

**Buses: Greyhound-Trailways Information Center,** 1716 E. 7th St., at Alameda, downtown. Call for fares, schedules, and local ticket info.

**Public Transit: MTA Bus Information Line** (213-626-4455 or 800-266-6883). Open M-F 6am-8:30pm, Sa-Su 8am-6pm. You may be put on hold long enough to walk to your destination. **MTA Customer Service Center,** 5301 Wilshire Blvd., is open M-F 9am-5pm. **Santa Monica Municipal Bus Lines** (310-451-5444). With over 1000 stops in Santa Monica, L.A., and Culver City, the "Big Blue Bus" (BBBus) is faster and cheaper than the MTA. Fare 50¢ and transfer tickets for MTA buses 25¢; transfers to other BBBuses free.

**Car Rental: ABC Car Rental** (800-736-8148), near LAX. As low as $30 per day. Free airport pick-up and drop-off. $160 per week. CDW $10 per day. Must be 21 with credit card. Under 25 pay $10 per day surcharge. Open daily 5am-midnight.

**Taxis: Checker Cab** (482-3456). **Independent** (385-8294). **United Independent** (653-5050). If you need a cab, it's best to call.

**Visitor Info: Los Angeles Convention and Visitor Bureau,** 685 S. Figueroa St. (213-689-8822), between Wilshire and 7th in the Financial District. Staff speaks English, French, German, Spanish, Japanese, and Tagalog. Open M-F 8am-5pm, Sa 8:30am-5pm.

**Hotlines: AIDS Hotline** (800-922-2437). **Rape Crisis** (310-392-8381). All 24hr.

**Post Office:** Centrally located branch at 900 N. Alameda St. (800-275-8777), at 9th. Open M-F 9am-5pm, Sa 9am-noon. **ZIP code:** 90086.

**Area codes: 213** covers downtown L.A., Huntington Park, Vernon, and Montebello. **213** and **323** cover Hollywood. **310** and **424** cover Malibu, Pacific Coast Highway, Westside, parts of West Hollywood, Santa Monica, southern and eastern L.A. County, and Catalina Island. **626** covers the San Gabriel Valley and Pasadena. **818** covers Burbank, Glendale, San Fernando Valley, Van Nuys, and La Cañada. **909** covers the eastern border of L.A. County. **11-digit dialing required.**

# ▚ ACCOMMODATIONS

As in any large city, cheap accommodations in Los Angeles are often unsafe. It can be difficult to gauge quality from the exterior, so ask to see a room before you plunk down any cash. Rates below $35 might indicate the kind of hotels in which most travelers would not feel secure. In choosing where to stay, the first consideration should be car accessibility. If you don't have wheels, you would be wise to decide which element of L.A. appeals to you the most. Those visiting for the beaches would do well to choose lodgings in Venice or Santa Monica. Avid sightseers will probably be better off in Hollywood or the more expensive (but cleaner and nicer) Westside. Downtown has numerous public transportation connections but is unsafe after dark. Listed prices do not include L.A.'s 14% hotel tax.

**HOLLYWOOD.** Although Tinseltown has tarnished in recent years, its location, sights, and nightlife keep the tourists coming. Exercise caution if scouting out one of the many budget hotels on **Hollywood** or **Sunset Blvd.**—*especially east of the main strips, the area can be dangerous, particularly at night.* The hostels here are generally excellent, and a much better value than anything else in L.A.

**Banana Bungalow Hollywood,** 2775 W. Cahuenga Blvd. (323-851-1129 or 800-446-7835), north of the Hollywood Bowl. Free shuttles to airport, beaches, and attractions.

# L.A. Westside

ACCOMMODATIONS
A Claremont Motel
B The Little Inn
C Stars Inn
D Hotel del Flores
E Wilshire Orange Hotel
F Beverly Inn
G Bevonshire Lodge Motel

TO GRIFFITH PARK

Franklin Ave.

Hollyhock House
Barnsdall Park

Hollywood Fwy.

Vermont Ave.

Normandie Ave.

Western Ave.

Olympic Blvd.

Pico Blvd.

TO DOWNTOWN

1 mile
1 kilometer

N

Sunset Blvd.

Vine St.
Cahuenga Blvd.

Highland

HOLLYWOOD

Paramount Studios

3rd St.

Wilshire Country Club

WILSHIRE DISTRICT

Crenshaw Blvd.

Jefferson Blvd.

Franklin Ave.
Hollywood Blvd.
Site of Hugh Grant's Arrest
Fountain Ave.

Santa Monica Blvd.

WEST HOLLYWOOD

Fairfax Ave.

Melrose Ave.

Crescent Heights Blvd.

Kings Rd.

Alta Loma Rd.

Le Parc

Sunset Strip

La Brea Blvd.

Gardner St.

Pan Pacific Park
CBS Studios
Farmer's Market
Beverly Blvd.

Hancock La Brea Park
Tar Pits

L.A. County Museum of Art
Miracle Mile

San Vicente Blvd.

Fairfax Ave.

Crescent Hts. Blvd.

Venice Blvd.

Washington Blvd.

La Cienega Blvd.

Robertson Blvd.

Olympic Blvd.

Pico Blvd.

WEST LOS ANGELES

Santa Monica Fwy.

Doheny Dr.
Hillcrest Rd.

Hillcrest Rd.
Elm Dr.

Sunset Blvd.

Greystone Mansion and Park

3rd St.
Burton Way

Wilshire Blvd.

Museum of Tolerance

Rancho Park

Coldwater Canyon Drive

Franklin County Ranch

Lake Franklin

Tower Rd.

Benedict Canyon

Beverly Hills Hotel

BEVERLY HILLS

Crescent Dr.
Canyon Dr.
Beverly Dr.
Rodeo Dr.

Roxbury Dr.

Los Angeles Country Club

Santa Monica Blvd.

CENTURY CITY

Moreno Dr.
Park E.
Century Park W.
Ave. of the Stars

Century Plaza Towers

Fox Studios

C
B

Beverly Glen Blvd.

Mapleton Dr.

Westwood Memorial Cemetery

Pico Blvd.
Santa Monica Blvd.

Westwood Blvd.

BEL AIR

Sunset Blvd.

UCLA

Gayley Ave.
Le Conte Dr.
Landfair Ave.

WESTWOOD

Hilgard Ave.

UCLA Hammer Museum

Veteran Ave.
Sepulveda Blvd.

405

San Diego Fwy.

BRENTWOOD

Bristol Ave.

Bundy Dr.

San Vicente Blvd.

Barrington Ave.

Santa Monica Blvd.

Wilshire Blvd.

Ralph's Grocery

Montana Ave.

Olympic Blvd.

2

TO SANTA MONICA AND VENICE

10

405

10

This Hollywood Hills locale affords it space enough to create a relentlessly wacky and frisky summer-camp atmosphere—not for the retiring traveler. Free nightly movies, pool, hoops, weight room, Internet access ($1 for 5min.), and "snack shack." Continental breakfast, linen, and parking included. Meals $5. Check-in 24hr. Check-out 10:30am. Co-ed dorms with bathroom and TV $18-20; private doubles $55. **Passport and international airline ticket required** for dorms; Americans can stay in private rooms.

**USA Hostels Hollywood,** 6772 Hawthorn Ave. (323-462-3777 or 800-524-6783), off Highland Ave. between Hollywood and Sunset Blvd. Free pickup from airport, bus, and train stations. Not for the couch potato. Daily tours to local attractions. Kitchen, patio, bike rental, party room with bar, billiards, and TV. BBQs and comedy nights. Internet access $1 per 10min. Breakfast, linen, lockers, and parking included. Co-ed dorms June-Aug. $17, Sept.-May $15; private rooms $34/38. **Proof of travel required.**

**Hollywood International Hostel,** 1057 Vine St. (323-462-6351 or 800-750-1233), at Santa Monica Blvd. Free pickup from airport, bus, and train stations. Opened in 1999. Along with large rooms, the 1924 building also has a fireplace mantle from *Gone With the Wind* and a beautiful lobby with leather couches and cable. Kitchen, gym, Internet access, nightly movies, billiards room with cable TV. Rooftop deck has a bar and a killer view of the Hollywood sign. Breakfast and parking included. Reception 24hr. Dorms June-Aug. $15; doubles June-Aug. $37. Prices lower in off season. **International passport or college ID required.**

**SANTA MONICA, VENICE, AND MARINA DEL REY.** Venice Beach hostels beckon to all the young budget travelers, especially foreign students, who are lured by the area's blend of indulgent beach culture and lively nightlife. Most of the cheap accommodations that pepper the coast cater to raucous party kids, but there are some quiet gems in the mix.

🏅 **Los Angeles/Santa Monica (HI-AYH),** 1436 2nd St., Santa Monica (310-393-9913), 2 blocks from the beach and across from the 3rd St. Promenade. Take MTA #33 from Union Station to 2nd St. and Broadway, BBBus #3 from LAX to 4th St. and Broadway, or BBBus #10 from Union Station. The building is beautiful, modern, and meticulously clean. Beds have foam mattresses. Reception 24hr. Colossal kitchen, 2 nightly movies, library, central courtyard, and biweekly barbecues $5. No alcohol. Hot breakfast 85¢-$3.75. Safe deposit boxes and lockers. Laundry. Pay garages nearby. 4-week max. stay. Dorms $19-21, nonmembers $22-24; private doubles $58, nonmembers $61.

**Cadillac Hotel,** 8 Dudley Ave., Venice (310-399-8876). Airport shuttle $5. Art Deco landmark directly on the beach. International crowd and helpful staff. Tour desk, sauna, rooftop sundeck, and well-equipped gym. Lounge has cable TV, pool table, Internet access, Venetian gondola, and a piece of the Berlin Wall. Lockers. Parking included with private rooms. Dorms $25; impressive private suites (for the area) from $80. No reservations for bunks—call before coming, or show up at 1pm and hope.

**Share-Tel Apartments,** 20 Brooks Ave., Venice (310-392-0325), ½ block from the beach. Fun-loving hostel with a social lounge for TV and board games. Dorms are spacious and clean with private baths, kitchenettes, and fridges. Breakfast and dinner included (M-F). Lockers $1. Linen and key deposit $20. Parking per night July-Aug. $10, Sept.-June $5. 4-8 bed dorms $17; private rooms $22-25. No reservations. No credit cards. **International passport required just to enter the front gate.**

**WESTSIDE: BEVERLY HILLS, WESTWOOD, WILSHIRE.** The relatively safe Westside has excellent public transportation to the beaches. The area's affluence, however, means less bang for your buck, and there are no hostels. Those planning to stay at least 1 month in summer or 6 months during the school year can contact the **UCLA Off-Campus Housing Office,** 350 Deneve Dr. (310-825-4491).

**Claremont Hotel,** 1044 Tiverton Ave., in Westwood Village (310-208-5957 or 800-266-5957), near UCLA. Pleasant and inexpensive. Clean rooms with antique dressers, ceiling fans, private baths, and phones. Microwave and free coffee in lobby, next to pleasant TV lounge. Daily maid service. Check-in 24hr. Check-out noon. Singles $40; doubles $48; triples $54. Weekly rates available. Reservations recommended, esp. in June.

**Bevonshire Lodge Motel,** 7575 Beverly Blvd. (323-936-6154), near Farmer's Market. Looks like *Melrose Place* with a color-blind interior decorator. Spacious rooms have sparkling bathrooms to make the shower scenes fun, and big beds. Older furniture, but comfy beds, A/C, cable, and in-room phones. Pool. Parking included. Singles $44, doubles $49; rooms with kitchen $55. 10% ISIC discount.

**The Little Inn,** 10604 Santa Monica Blvd., West L.A. (310-475-4422). Found on Little Santa Monica Blvd., the smaller road paralleling the divided boulevard to the south. Although the lack of style in the sparsely decorated rooms is *so* un-L.A., they're sizable and clean. A/C, cable, and fridges. Parking included. Check-in 24hr. Check-out 11am. *Let's Go* travelers (with this book) get special rates Sept.-July (excluding major holiday periods): singles $50, doubles $55. Kitchens extra.

**DOWNTOWN L.A.** Downtown L.A. is not the best place to look for accommodations. Although busy and fairly safe by day, the area empties and becomes dangerous after 6pm and Sa-Su. Cheaper weekly rates are sometimes available. Remember to travel in packs, especially between Broadway and Main St.

**Metro Plaza Hotel,** 711 N. Main St. (213-680-0200), at Cesar Chavez Ave. Near Chinatown, Olvera St., and Union Station. It doesn't look it from its seedy outside, but the glass entry doors open into a rather fine hotel. Large, clean rooms with TVs and refrigerators. Parking included. Singles $59; doubles $69.

**Park Plaza Hotel,** 607 S. Park View St. (213-384-5281), on the west corner of 6th St. across from the green but unsafe MacArthur Park. Built in 1927, this colossal luxury hotel's heyday has come and gone, but it remains a comfortable option. All of the small, clean rooms have TV, some have A/C. Singles $60; doubles $65.

**Milner Hotel,** 813 S. Flower St. (213-627-6981 or 800-827-0411). Free pickup from airport, bus, and train stations. Central location, with pub and grill in lobby. Rooms have A/C and cable TV. Breakfast included. Singles $50; doubles $60.

# FOOD

Eating in Los Angeles, the city of the health-conscious, is more than just a gustatory experience. Thin figures and fat wallets are a powerful combination. Of course, there are also restaurants where the main objective is to be seen, and the food is secondary, as well as those where the food itself seems too beautiful to be eaten—it was here, after all, that 80s nouvelle cuisine reached its height.

## TOURING THE BURGER KINGDOM

Los Angeles has been home to many tasteless trends, but few realize that it's also the birthplace of perhaps the world's furthest sweeping trend, one guaranteed to leave a curious taste in your mouth—good ol' American fast food. Unlikely as it sounds, this obsessively health-conscious city spawned some of the nation's greasiest, most cholesterol-packed grub. An international synonym for fast food, **McDonald's** was founded by Angeleno brothers Richard and Maurice McDonald in 1937 (serving, incidentally, hot dogs only). The oldest standing golden arches still glare proudly at 10807 Lakewood Blvd. in Downey, where it's walk-up rather than drive-thru service. (The brothers granted Ray Kroc exclusive U.S. franchising rights, and in 1955 he opened the first outlet of what has become the McDonald's Corporation in Des Plaines, Illinois.) Home to the original double-decker hamburger, the oldest **Bob's Big Boy,** 4211 Riverside Dr. (818-843-9334), in Burbank, still looks as sleek and streamlined as the day it opened in 1949. Check out the honest-to-goodness car-hop service (Sa-Su 5-10pm). **Carl's Jr.** started off as a downtown hot dog stand at Florence and Central Ave. in 1941, and the **Denny's** and **Winchell's** chains also got their start in the Los Angeles basin.

CALIFORNIA

Fortunately for the budget traveler, Los Angeles elevates fast-food and chain restaurants to heights virtually unknown in the rest of the country. For the optimal burger-and-fries experience, try **In 'n' Out Burger,** a chain as beloved as the '57 Chevy. **Johnny Rocket's** revives the never really lost era of the American diner. Their milkshakes are the food of the gods. The current hot 'n' spicy craze is lard-free, cholesterol-free "healthy Mexican"—**Baja Fresh** leads the pack.

Chic refreshments are a necessity. Angelenos get their ice-blended mochas at **The Coffee Bean and Tea Leaf.** The ubiquitous smoothie allows the health-conscious to indulge in a sweet blend of fruit, juice, frozen yogurt, and energy-boosting additives like wheat grass. **The Juice Club** makes the biggest and the best smoothies with shots of fresh-blended grass for die-hard fiberphiles.

The range of culinary options in L.A. is directly proportional to the city's ethnic diversity. Certain food types are concentrated in specific areas. Jewish and Eastern European food is most prevalent in Fairfax; Mexican in East L.A.; Japanese, Chinese, Vietnamese, and Thai around Little Tokyo, Chinatown, and Monterey Park; and seafood along the coast. Vietnamese, Italian, Indian, and Ethiopian restaurants are scattered throughout the city.

**HOLLYWOOD.** Hollywood offers the best budget dining in L.A. **Melrose** is full of chic cafes, many with outdoor patios.

■ **Roscoe's House of Chicken and Waffles,** 1514 Gower St., Hollywood (323-466-7453). Roscoe makes the best waffles anywhere. Try "1 succulent chicken breast and 1 delicious waffle" ($5.60). The restaurant is frequented by all sorts of celebrities. Open Su-Th 8:30am-midnight, F-Sa 9am-3:30am.

■ **Duke's Coffee Shop,** 8909 Sunset Blvd., West Hollywood (310-652-3100), at San Vicente Blvd. Best place in L.A. to see hung-over rock stars. The walls are a kaleidoscope of posters and album covers. They claim to treat everyone the same, famous or not, but don't expect to be invited to add your signature to the walls unless you're the former. Try the "Revenge" (eggs scrambled with avocado, sour cream, onions, tomatoes, and peppers; $6.75). Entrees $5-8. Open M-F 7:30am-8:45pm, Sa-Su 8am-3:45pm.

**El Coyote,** 7312 Beverly Blvd., Hollywood (323-939-2255), at Poinsettia St. Spacious, pleasantly low-key dining rooms, and waitresses clad in sweeping Mexican dresses, this is a local favorite. Enormous combo plates come with corn tortillas and all the chips and salsa you could ever want ($6). Frothy margaritas ($3-4.25). Filling chicken fajitas are the most expensive entree but are still only $7. Parking after 4pm $1.50. Open Su-Th 11am-10pm, F-Sa 11am-11pm.

**Pink's Famous Chili Dogs,** 711 N. La Brea Ave., Hollywood (323-931-4223). More of an institution than a hot dog stand, Pink's has been serving up chili-slathered doggies on its outdoor patio to locals and celebs since 1939. Mouthwatering chili dogs ($2.20) and chili fries ($1.85). Bruce Willis proposed to Demi Moore here all those films ago. Open Su-Th 9:30am-2am, F-Sa 9:30am-3am. No credit cards.

**WILSHIRE DISTRICT AND HANCOCK PARK.** The Wilshire District's eateries are sadly out of step with its world-class museums. Inexpensive (and often kosher) restaurants dot **Fairfax** and **Pico Blvd.**

**The Apple Pan,** 10801 W. Pico Blvd. (310-475-3585), 1 block east of Westwood Blvd. across from the Westside Pavilion. Suburban legend has it that *Beverly Hills 90210*'s Peach Pit was modeled after The Apple Pan. Paper-plated burgers $3-6; pies $2.40. Open Su and Tu-Th 11am-midnight, F-Sa 11am-1am.

---

**ORSON WELLES WAS FAT** Acclaimed director and *gourmand* Orson Welles was a regular at many Hollywood restaurants, and legends of his prowess circulate to this day, some reaching fantastic proportions. Pink's Famous Chili Dogs claims the notorious nosher once ate 15 chili dogs there in one sitting. But who really knows?—it's hard to distinguish Orson sitting from Orson standing.

**Cassell's Hamburgers,** 3266 W. 6th St. (213-480-8668). Some say these burgers are the finest in the city. They're juicy, enormous, and come with as much potato salad and cottage cheese as you can fit on your sizable plate. $5. Open M-Sa 10am-4pm.

**Shalom Pizza,** 8715 W. Pico Blvd. (310-271-2255). Kosher (i.e., vegetarian) pizza in a quiet Jewish business district. Large cheese $11.50, slice $1.75. Tuna melt $2.50. Open Su-Th 11am-9pm, F 11am to 2hr. before dusk, Sa dusk-midnight.

**BEVERLY HILLS.** There is budget dining in glamorous Beverly Hills; it just takes a little looking.

🍴 **The Breakfast Club,** 9671 Wilshire Blvd. (323-271-8903). Affordable food in a great location. $6.49 lunch specials even teens can appreciate. Open M-Sa 7am-3pm, Su 8am-3pm. 2hr. free parking with validation, leaving plenty of time to stroll Rodeo Dr.

**World Wrapps,** 168 S. Beverly Dr. (310-859-9010). Cashing in on the hottest new trend, it takes "healthy Mexican" to new, international, Cali-gourmet heights. Mostly takeout, but colorful interior and outdoor seating invite eat-ins. Thai chicken wraps (regular $5) and Samurai salmon wraps ($6.50) are available in spinach and tomato tortillas. Cheap smoothies $2-4. Open M-F 11am-9pm, Sa 11am-8pm, Su noon-6pm.

**Finney's in the Alley,** 8840 Olympic Blvd. (310-888-8787). Hidden, but worth the hunt. Heading east on Olympic, turn right on Clark, and immediately right into the alley; look for a yellow awning. The manager refuses to advertise for fear that "the secret will get out." Now it has. Finney's most delectable (and expensive) offering is a Philly steak sandwich for $4.20. Open M-Sa 11am-6pm.

**WESTWOOD AND UCLA.** With UCLA here, cheap food and beer can be found in abundance.

🍴 **Gypsy Cafe,** 940 Broxton Ave. (310-824-2119). The best place in Westwood for an I'm-sick-of-eating-out dinner. Modeled after a sister spot in Paris, this inviting cafe has counter service, an outdoor patio, and velvet draperies to set the mood. Killer *penne cacciatore* ($7), organic salads ($6), Italian sandwiches ($6), and tomato soup that is famous throughout Westwood ($4). Hookahs for rent ($10 per hr.). F is stand-up comedy night. Open Su-Th 8am-midnight, F-Sa 8am-1am.

🍴 **Diddie Riese Cookies,** 926 Broxton Ave. (310-208-0448). Highly recommended by most everyone in town, this cookie bakery is a hotspot for fresh cookies ($3 per dozen). 10 delicious flavors to choose from. Also serves ice cream (75¢-$1.75) and soft drinks ($1). Open M-Th 7am-midnight, F 7am-1am, Sa noon-1am, Su noon-midnight.

**Don Antonio's,** 1136 Westwood Blvd. (310-209-1422). Relax in the outdoor seating while waiting for your custom-designed pizza ($5.50). Sinatra, red-checkered tablecloths, and wood-paneled walls. Lunch and dinner combo specials ($4-5); large slice of pizza, salad, and all-you-can-drink soda ($3.50). Open daily 11am-3am.

**SANTA MONICA.** Santa Monica's restaurants fall into the "see and be seen" category, especially along the 3rd St. Promenade. Prices are elevated accordingly, as is the quality of the food.

🍴 **Fritto Misto,** 601 Colorado Ave. (310-458-2829), at 6th St. The biggest deal is the mix 'n' match pastas which are served quickly and in healthy portions ($6-7). It's so popular you might find a line on the weekend, but it's worth the wait. BYOB for $1.50 per person surcharge. Lunch specials until 5:30pm ($6). Su bring monster omelettes 10am-4pm. Open M-F 11:30am-10pm, Sa-Su 11:30am-11pm.

**Big Dean's "Muscle-In" Cafe,** 1615 Ocean Front Walk (310-393-2666). No pretense here: it's sun, sand, sauerkraut, and *cervezas!* Home of the management-proclaimed and customer-concurred "Best Cheeseburger on the West Coast," ($4). Happy Hour means $2 beers (M-F 3-6pm). Open daily 10am-dark, or until the regulars empty out.

**El Cholo,** 1025 Wilshire Blvd. (310-899-1106). Like the Cancún cantinas it mimics, this is *the* spot to be seen, at least for the moment. The menu prices *are* budget for the upscale crowd. Cheese enchilada, beans, rice, and choice of a taco, *chile relleno,* or tamale ($8). "L.A. Lemonade" margarita is an awfully pricey $6.25, but was ranked the city's best by *L.A. Magazine.* Bar with couches, big-screen TV. Always crowded. Open M-Th 11am-10pm, F-Sa 11am-11pm, Su 11am-9pm.

**VENICE.** Venetian cuisine runs the gamut from greasy to ultra-healthy, as befits its beachy-hippie crowd. The boardwalk offers cheap grub in fast-food fashion.

🖾 **Van Gogh's Ear 24hr. Restaurant and Gallery,** 796 Main St. (314-0022). Ridiculously large portions of tasty chow. All entrees named for second-rate celebs, such as the Kato Kaelin Salad ($3). "Tightwad menu" has 8 breakfast combos under $2 (served M-F 6-11am). Some part of the 2-story mega-shack is always open.

🖾 **Rose Cafe,** 220 Rose Ave. (399-0711), at Main St. The sunlight streaming in *so* complements the airy interior, dahling. Delicious deli specials (sandwiches $5, salads $5-8) are a steal. Smelly New Age knick-knacks and candles for sale. Open M-F 7am-7pm, Sa 8am-7pm, Su 8am-5pm.

**Sidewalk Cafe,** 1401 Ocean Front Walk (399-5547). Sitting right on the boardwalk, this popular (crowded) spot provides a beachy scene, and standard beach food. Omelettes $6-7, pizzas $12 (feeds 2), sandwiches $6-9. Big bar in back (pints $3). Open Su-Th 8am-midnight, F-Sa 8am-1am.

**DOWNTOWN.** Financial District eateries vie for the coveted business-person's lunchtime dollar. Their secret weapon is the lunch special, but you shouldn't hang out here that late anyway. It's a rough neighborhood.

🖾 **Philippe's, The Original,** 1001 N. Alameda St. (213-628-3781), 2 blocks north of Union Station. Celebrated all over L.A. as the best downtown lunch spot, Philippe's just turned 92 years old. "Carvers" (counter waitresses dressed in antique server garb) prep the best French Dip sandwiches around; varieties include beef, ham, turkey, or lamb ($3-4). Top it off with a large slice of pie ($2.50) and a glass of lemonade (50¢) or a cup of coffee (10¢). Open daily 6am-10pm.

**The Pantry,** 877 S. Figueroa St. (213-972-9279). Open since 1924, it hasn't closed once since—not for the earthquakes, not for the riots (when it served as a National Guard outpost), and not even when a taxicab drove through the front wall. There aren't even locks on the doors. Known for its large portions, free cole slaw, and fresh sourdough bread. Owned by the mayor. Giant breakfast specials are popular ($6). Lunch sandwiches $3-5. Open forever.

**SAN FERNANDO VALLEY. Ventura Blvd.** is lined with restaurants. Eating lunch near the studios in **Studio City** is your best stargazing opportunity. The Unwritten Law: Stare all you like, *but don't ask for autographs.*

🖾 **Miceli's,** 3655 W. Cahuenga Blvd., Universal City (323-851-3444), across from Universal Studios. Would-be actors serenade dinner guests. The waiters have passed vocal auditions. Pasta, pizza, or lasagna $9-12. Open Su-Th 11:30am-11pm, F 11:30am-midnight, Sa 4pm-midnight.

**Law Dogs,** 14114 Sherman Way, Van Nuys (818-989-2220), at Hazeltine. Just your average hot dog stand with **free legal advice** W 7-9pm. "Judge Dog" with mustard, onions, and chili $1.55. Open M-Tu and Th 10am-6pm, W and F 10am-9pm, Sa 10am-8pm.

# 👁 SIGHTS

**HOLLYWOOD.** Modern Hollywood (110 years old) is no longer the upscale home of movie stars and production studios. In fact, all the major studios, save Paramount, have moved to the roomier San Fernando Valley. Left behind are historic theaters and museums, a crowd of souvenir shops, famous boulevards, and American fascination. Aside from the endless string of movie premieres, the only star-studded part of Hollywood is the sidewalk, where prostitutes and panhandlers, tattoo parlors, and porn shops abound.

The **Hollywood sign**—those 50-ft.-high, slightly erratic letters perched on Mt. Cahuenga north of Hollywood—stands with New York's Statue of Liberty and Paris's Eiffel Tower as the universally recognized symbol of a city. The original 1923 sign, which read HOLLYWOODLAND, was an advertisement for a new subdivision in the Hollywood Hills (a caretaker lived behind one of the "L"s). You can't

## IF I WERE A GROUPIE

Today's groupie has to have skills that would put FBI agents to shame. While *Let's Go* cannot give you the well-trained eyes and ears necessary for success, we can point you in the right direction. First, you need to know that stars tend to stay in the same hotels. Now you can narrow your search. The **Rock 'n' Roll Hyatt**, on the Sunset Strip, was the site of Led Zeppelin's orgies and Jim Morrison's antics and is now the preferred haunt of bands like Live and Smashing Pumpkins. Across the street is **St. James Club,** a more refined spot that caters to older bands such as Duran Duran. Near the base of the famous billboards on Sunset Blvd. is the **Chateau Marmont,** where Keanu Reeves and Dustin Hoffman have made extended stays. Farther up the Strip on Alta Loma is the **Sunset Marquis.** This *expensive* hotel houses the biggest musical acts (Rolling Stones, Peter Gabriel, George Michael). Hiding on a residential street near the corner of Melrose Ave. and La Cienega Blvd. is **Le Parc,** which caters to the bigger, gentler bands (Morrissey) and many newer British acts (Blur, Elastica). Finally, as any savvy groupie knows, all bands register under fake names these days, so you'll have to rely on your big, bountiful, buxom wits—and charm.

go frolic on the sign like Robert Downey, Jr. did in *Chaplin,* or take a leap from it like all the faded 1920s starlets—there is a $500 fine if you're caught (which is likely). You can snap a great picture by driving north on Vine, turning right on Franklin, left on Beachwood, and left on Belden into the Beachwood Supermarket parking lot. To get a close-up of the sign in all its monumental glory, continue up Beachwood, turn left on Ledgewood, and drive all the way up to Mulholland Hwy. Resting beneath the Hollywood sign, at 6342 Mulholland Hwy. (to the left, at the corner of Canyon Lake Dr.), is the **Castillo del Lago.** Once the gambling den of gangster Bugsy Siegel, the red-and-beige striped house also belonged to Madonna, but she recently sold it after an obsessed fan stalked her there.

**Hollywood Blvd.** itself, lined with souvenir shops, clubs, and theaters, is busy day and night, especially around the intersection of Highland and Hollywood and then west down Hollywood. To the east, things turn even seedier. For a star-studded stroll, head to the **Walk of Fame,** along Hollywood and Vine, where the sidewalk is embedded with over 2500 bronze-inlaid stars, inscribed with the names of the famous, the infamous, and the downright obscure. Stars are awarded for achievements in one of 5 categories—movies, radio, TV, recording, and live performance; only Gene Autry has all 5 stars. To catch a glimpse of today's (or yesterday's) stars receiving a few more minutes of adulation, call the **Chamber of Commerce** *(213-469-8311)* for info on star-unveiling ceremonies.

**Mann's Chinese Theater** (formerly Grauman's), between Highland and La Brea, is a garish rendition of a Chinese temple, and the hottest spot for a Hollywood movie premiere. The exterior columns, which once supported a Ming Dynasty temple, are strangely authentic for Hollywood. Tourists crowd the courtyard to pay homage to the impressions made by many a movie star in the cement, including Whoopi Goldberg's dreadlocks, Betty Grable's legs, R2D2's wheels, Jimmy Durante's nose, and George Burns's cigar. *(6925 Hollywood Blvd. 213-461-3331.)*

The alternately fascinating and horrifying **Hollywood Wax Museum** contains 200 figures, from Jesus to Elvis. Not surprisingly, the sculpture of Michael Jackson is one of the few that a chisel and putty have recreated nearly perfectly. *(6767 Hollywood Blvd. 323-462-5991. Open daily 10am-midnight. $10, ages 6-12 $7, under 6 free.)* **Guinness World of Records** has the tallest, shortest, heaviest, most tattooed, and other curious superlatives on display. *(6764 Hollywood Blvd. 323-463-6433. Open daily 10am-midnight. $10, ages 6-12 $7, under 6 free; with wax museum ticket $4, ages 6-12 $2.)* **Ripley's Believe It or Not!** is a wacky museum with a side-show mentality that strangely keeps with the rest of Hollywood. Come view the roots of the inane TV show. *(6780 Hollywood Blvd. 323-466-6335. Open Su-Th 10am-midnight, F-Sa 10am-12:30am. $9, ages 5-12 $6, under 5 free.)* **Frederick's of Hollywood** gives a free peep at some unbelievable underwear in its lingerie museum. Frederick's displays bras worn by everyone from Marilyn Monroe to Milton Berle. *(6608 Hollywood Blvd. 213-957-5953. Open M-F 10am-9pm, Sa 10am-7pm, Su 11am-6pm. Free.)*

The **Capital Records Towers** marks the pre-eminent monument of the modern record industry. The cylindrical building was designed to look like a stack of records—with fins sticking out at each floor (the "records") and a needle on top, blinking H-O-L-L-Y-W-O-O-D in Morse code. *(1750 Vine St., just north of Hollywood Blvd.)*

The **Hollywood Studio Museum,** museum provides a glimpse into early Hollywood filmmaking. In 1913, famed director Cecil B. DeMille rented this former barn as studio space for Hollywood's first feature film, *The Squaw Man.* Antique cameras, costumes worn by Douglas Fairbanks and Rudolph Valentino, props, vintage film clips, and other memorabilia fill the museum. *(2100 N. Highland Ave. 323-874-2276. Hours vary; call ahead. $4, students and seniors $3, ages 6-12 $2. Ample free parking.)*

Honoring television history is the **Hollywood Entertainment Museum,** which has original sets from *Cheers* and *Star Trek. (7021 Hollywood Blvd. 323-465-7900. Museum open July-Aug. M-Sa 11am-6pm, Su 11am-6pm; Sept.-June Th-Tu 10am-6pm. Tours every 30min. $7.50, students and seniors $4.50, ages 5-12 $4. Parking $2. Cheers cover/donation $5.)*

If you still haven't had enough showbiz glitz of years gone by, visit the **Hollywood Memorial Park,** a haunted-feeling cemetery between Vine and Western. Here rest stars Rudolph Valentino, Jayne Mansfield, Douglas Fairbanks Sr., and Cecil B. De Mille. *(6000 Santa Monica Blvd. Open M-F 8am-5pm. Spooky mausoleums close at 4:30pm.)*

**WILSHIRE AND HANCOCK PARK.** The **Los Angeles County Museum of Art (LACMA)** is at the west end of Hancock Park. LACMA's distinguished collection rebutts those who say that L.A.'s only culture is in its yogurt. Opened in 1965, the LACMA is the largest museum in the West, with six major buildings clustered around the **Times-Mirror Central Court.** The **Steve Martin Gallery,** in the Anderson Bldg., houses the famed benefactor's collection of Dada and Surrealist works, including Rene Magritte's *Treachery of Images.* (This explains how Steve was allowed to rollerskate through LACMA in *L.A. Story.*) The museum sponsors free jazz, chamber music, film classics and documentaries, and free daily tours. *(General info. 323-857-6000. Docent Council 328-857-6108. 5905 Wilshire Blvd. 213-857-6000. Open M-Tu and Th noon-8pm, F noon-9pm, Sa-Su 11am-8pm. $7, students and seniors $5, under 18 $1; free 2nd Tu of each month. Free jazz F 5:30-8:30pm. Chamber music Su 4-5pm. Film tickets $7, seniors $5. Parking $5, free after 6pm. Wheelchair access.)*

Across the street is the acclaimed **Petersen Automotive Museum,** which showcases L.A.'s most recognizable symbol—the automobile. With 300,000 sq. ft., PAM is the world's largest car museum and the nation's second-largest history museum (the Smithsonian is the largest). Bo and Luke's General Lee and Herbie the Love Bug are here. *(6060 Wilshire Blvd. 930-2277. Open Tu-Su 10am-6pm. $7, students and seniors $5, children $3, under 5 free. Full-day parking convenient to LACMA $4.)*

**WEST HOLLYWOOD.** **Melrose Ave.** running from the southern part of West Hollywood to Hollywood, is lined with chi-chi restaurants, art galleries, and shops catering to all levels of the counter-culture spectrum. The choiciest stretch is between La Brea and Fairfax Ave. While much that is sold here is "vintage," none of it is cheap. North of Beverly Center is the **Pacific Design Center,** a sea-green glass complex, nicknamed the **Blue Whale,** and constructed in the shape of a wave. In addition to 150 design showrooms, which showcase mostly home and furnishing projects, this rich man's Home Depot houses a public plaza and 350-seat amphitheater. It hosts an awesome **Gay Pride Weekend Celebration** in late June. *(8687 Melrose Ave., at San Vicente Blvd. 310-657-0800.)*

**BEVERLY HILLS AND CENTURY CITY.** Ready to gawk? Extravagant displays of opulence sometimes border on the vulgar. On the palm-lined 700-900 blocks of **Beverly Dr.,** each and every manicured estate begs for attention. The heart of the city is in the **Golden Triangle,** a wedge formed by Beverly Dr., Wilshire Blvd., and Santa Monica Blvd., centering on **Rodeo Dr.,** known for its flashy boutiques.

Farther north, the **Beverly Hills Hotel,** 9641 Sunset Blvd. (310-276-2251), is a pink, palm-treed collection of poolside cottages. Howard Hughes established his infamous germ-free apartment here; Marilyn Monroe reportedly had affairs with both

JFK and RFK in other bungalows. It is also home to the **Polo Lounge,** where count-less media industry deals have gone down. The Sultan of Brunei paid $185 million for it in 1987, but 13 years later, you can get a room for a mere $275.

A conspicuous way to tour the city is in the trolley car replica operated by the **Beverly Hills Chamber of Commerce** (310-271-8126). If you prefer a cooler approach, go solo with a star map ($8), sold along Sunset Blvd. but not within Beverly Hills.

**WESTWOOD AND UCLA.** Get a feel for mass academia UC-style at the **University of California at Los Angeles (UCLA),** which sprawls over 400 acres in the foothills of the Santa Monica Mountains. A prototypical Californian university, UCLA sports an abundance of grassy open spaces, bike and walking paths, dazzling sunshine, and pristine buildings in a hodge-podge of architectural styles. To reach the cam-pus by car, take the San Diego Fwy. (I-405) north to the Wilshire Blvd./Westwood exit, heading east into Westwood. Take Westwood Blvd. north off Wilshire, head-ing straight through the center of the village and directly into the campus. By bus, take MTA route #2 along Sunset Blvd., #21 along Wilshire Blvd., #320 from Santa Monica, or #561 from the San Fernando Valley, or Santa Monica Blue Bus #1, 2, 3, 8, or 12. Parking passes ($5) from campus information stands are a must—traffic cops *live* to ticket unsuspecting visitors here.

The **Murphy Sculpture Garden,** which contains over 70 pieces scattered through 5 acres, lies directly in front of the Art Center. The collection includes works by such major artists as Rodin, Matisse, and Miró. Opposite the sculpture garden is **MacGowen Hall,** which contains the **Tower of Masks.** UCLA's **inverted fountain** is located between Knudsen Hall and Schoenberg Hall, directly south of Dickson Plaza. An innovation in the field of fountain design, water spouts from its perime-ter and rushes down into the gaping hole in the middle, like a giant toilet bowl. UCLA has loads of events, exhibitions, and performances year-round; call the **UCLA Arts Line** (310-825-2278) for tickets, a calendar, and directions.

The **Armand Hammer Museum of Art and Cultural Center** houses a small but snappy collection of European and American works from the 16th century to the present day. Something of a "Who's Who" of European painters, Hammer's collection includes works by Rembrandt, Chagall, and Cézanne, but its real gem is Van Gogh's *Hospital at Saint Rémy.* *(10899 Wilshire Blvd. 310-443-7000. Open Tu-W and F-Sa 11am-7pm, Th 11am-9pm, Su 11am-5pm. $4.50, students and seniors $3, under 17 free with adult; Th free 6-9pm. Free tours daily at 1pm. 3hr. parking $2.75. Wheelchair access.)*

**BEL AIR, BRENTWOOD, AND PACIFIC PALISADES.** Most of today's stars live in these affluent communities. Next to UCLA is the well-guarded community of **Bel Air,** where **Ronald Reagan** has retired. His estate is at 668 St. Cloud, adjacent to the *Beverly Hillbillies* mansion (750 Bel Air Rd.) and a few blocks up from the former home of **Sonny and Cher** (364 St. Cloud). **Elizabeth Taylor** is literally around the cor-ner (700 Nimes). Back in the golden days, Bel Air was the locus for **Judy Garland** (924 Bel Air Rd.), **Alfred Hitchcock** (10957 Bel Air Rd.), and **Lauren Bacall** and **Hum-phrey Bogart** (232 Mapleton Dr.) during their go at marital bliss.

Farther west on Sunset Blvd. is **Brentwood,** home to many young actors and, until recently, **O.J. Simpson.** The famous accusé no longer lives here; his estate (360 Rockingham) was repossessed and auctioned off for a meager $2.63 million. On Aug. 4, 1962, **Marilyn Monroe** was found dead at her home (12305 Fifth Helena Dr.). The celeb-city of Brentwood also includes the homes of Michelle Pfeiffer, Harri-son Ford, Meryl Streep, and Rob Reiner.

The considerably more secluded **Pacific Palisades** is the place to live these days. Many streets are entirely closed to anyone but residents and their guests, but you can try to catch a glimpse of **Tom Cruise** and **Nicole Kidman** outside 1525 Sorrento, or **Steven Spielberg** at 1515 Amalfi (this home belonged to David O. Selznick when he was producing *Gone with the Wind).* **Arnold Schwarzenegger** and **Maria Shriver** practice family fitness at 14209 Sunset Blvd., **Tom Hanks** lives at 321 S. Anita Ave., and **Michael Keaton** resides at 826 Napoli Dr. Billy Crystal, Chevy Chase, and John Travolta also own homes in the area. The cliffs give way to the ocean at the popular **Will Rogers State Beach,** on the 16000 block of Pacific Coast Hwy. (PCH). At 1501 Will Rogers State Park Rd., you can hike around **Will Rogers State Historical Park** (310-454-8212), take in the panoramic views of the city and distant Pacific, visit the famous humorist's home, or eat a picnic brunch while watching a Sa afternoon **polo match** (Sa 2-5pm and Su 10am-1pm). Follow Chatauqua Blvd. inland from PCH to Sunset Blvd., or take MTA #2, which runs along Sunset. *(Park open daily 8am-sunset; Rogers's house open daily 10:30am-4:30pm, with tours every 30min.)*

In the Santa Monica Mountains above Bel Air is the new **J. Paul Getty Museum and Getty Center.** Formerly located in Malibu, the new center unites L.A.'s beloved Getty museums with its institutes on one site, designed by renowned architect Richard Meier. (The Malibu Villa will reopen in 2001 as an antiquities center.) The museum itself is housed in 5 pavilions overlooking the Robert Irwin-designed 3-acre Central Garden, a living work of art that changes with the seasons. The museum includes the permanent Getty collection, which includes Van Gogh's *Irises*, James Ensor's *Christ's Entry into Brussels in 1889*, Impressionist paintings, Renaissance drawings, and one of the nation's best Rembrandt collections. "Friday Nights at the Getty" (310-440-7330) feature plays, films, and readings. To reach the Getty Center, take the San Diego Fwy. (I-405) to Getty Center Dr.; parking costs $5 and requires advance reservations (310-440-7300). BBB #14 and MTA #561 stop at the museum's front entrance on Sepulveda Blvd. *(1200 Getty Center Dr. 310-440-7330. Open Tu-W 11am-7pm, Th-F 11am-9pm, Sa-Su 10am-6pm. Free.)*

**SANTA MONICA.** With cleaner waters and better waves at the beaches to the north and south, Santa Monica is known more for its shoreside scene than its shore. Since it is the closest beach to L.A., Santa Monica's sands are packed year-round with sunbathers sporting skimpy bikinis and buff, bronzed beach volleyball players, as well as families and people watchers.

The **3rd St. Promenade** is the city's most popular spot to shop by day and to schmooze by night. On W and Sa mornings the area is transformed into a farmer's market. Young adults with clipboards often sign people up for **free movie passes.**

The heart of the Santa Monica Beach is the famed **Santa Monica Pier,** home of hte recently restored carnivalesque family funspot **Pacific Park,** where fun meets the sun. The centerpiece of the pier is the unridable 1922 carousel. Look for free TV show tickets near the north entrance. *(Off PCH on the way to Venice Beach from Santa Monica Beach. Open daily 10am-11pm; ticket window closes at 10:30pm. Tickets $1.25, most rides 2-3 tickets. Parking off PCH $5 per day.)*

**VENICE.** Venice is a carnivalesque beach town with rad politics and mad diversity. Its guitar-toting, Bukowski-quoting, wild-eyed, tie-dyed residents sculpt masterpieces in sand and compose them in graffiti, when they aren't slamming a volleyball back and forth over a beach net. A stroll in rollerblading, bikini-flaunting, tattooed Venice is like an acid trip for the timid.

**Ocean Front Walk,** Venice's main beachfront drag, is a seaside circus of fringe culture. Bodybuilders of both sexes pump iron in skimpy spandex outfits at the original **Muscle Beach,** close to 18th and Pacific. *(1800 Ocean Front Walk.)* Fire-juggling cyclists, joggers, sand sculptors, groovy elders (such as the **"skateboard grandma"**), and bards in Birkenstocks make up the balance of this playground population. Vendors of jewlery, henna body art, and snacks overwhelm the boardwalk.

Venice's anything-goes attitude attracts some of L.A.'s most innovative artists (and not just the guy who makes sand sculptures of Jesus). The **Chiat Day offices** were designed by Frank Gehry to look like a pair of enormous binoculars—architecture as a pop-art sculpture at its best. *(340 Main St.)* Venice's **street murals** are another free show. Don't miss the brilliant (but disfigured) homage to Botticelli's *Birth of Venus* on the beach pavilion at the end of Windward Ave.—a woman of ostensibly divine beauty sporting short shorts, a band-aid top, and roller skates boogies out of her seashell. The **L.A. Louvre,** a free gallery, showcases the work of some L.A. artists. *(45 N. Venice Blvd. 310-822-4955. Open Tu-Sa noon-5pm.)*

To get to Venice from downtown L.A., take MTA #33 or 333 (or 436 during rush hour). From downtown Santa Monica, take Santa Monica Blue Bus #1 or 2. Avoid hourly meter-feedings by parking in the $5-per-day lot at Pacific and Venice.

**MALIBU.** These public beaches are cleaner and less crowded than any others in L.A. County, and as a whole offer better surfing. Surf's up at **Surfrider Beach,** a section of Malibu Laguna State Beach located north of the pier at 23000 PCH. You can walk onto the beach via the **Zonker Harris** access way (named after the beach-obsessed Doonesbury character), at 22700 PCH. **Malibu Ocean Sports,** across from the pier, rents surfboards, kayaks, boogie boards, and wetsuits, and offers surfing lessons. *(22935 PCH. 310-456-6302. Surfboards $10 per hr., $25 per day. Kayaks: single $15 per hr., $35 per day; double $20/50. Boogie boards $12 per day. Wetsuits $10 per day. Lessons $100 for 2hr. lesson and full-day gear. Open daily 9am-7pm.)*

**Corral State Beach,** a remote windsurfing, swimming, and scuba-diving haven, lies on the 26000 block of PCH, followed by **Point Dume State Beach,** which is larger and generally uncrowded, and has better currents for scuba diving. Along the 30000 block of PCH lies **Zuma,** L.A. County's northernmost, largest, and most user-friendly county-owned sandbox. Restrooms, lifeguards, and food stands guarantee that Zuma regularly draws a diverse crowd. Sections 6-8 are popular with local kids, sections 9-11 are less populated. Swimmers should only dive near manned lifeguard stations; because of the devastating **riptide,** rescue counts are high. The free street parking is highly coveted, so expect to park in the beach lot. *($6, off-peak $2.)* Just south of Zuma, before Point Dume, is a clothing-optional strip nckc-named Pirate's Cove. There are fewer footprints at **Westward Beach,** just southeast of Zuma, where cliffs shelter the beach from the highway.

**DOWNTOWN.** The **Los Angeles Conservancy** offers Sa tours of downtown's historic spots. *(213-623-2489. Tours $5. Reserve one week in advance.)* Those who prefer to travel solo can walk each of the respective sections, but for travel between, should take **DASH Shuttles.** *(Fare 25¢; for more info, see Public Transportation, p. 754. References below are for M-F travel. Sa-Su the Discovery Direct "DD" route covers almost all of the sights below.)* If driving, park in a secure lot, rather than on the streets. Parking is costly; arriving before 8am enables visitors to catch early-bird specials; the guarded lots around 9th and Figueroa charge $3-4 per day. **The L.A. Visitors Center** is at 685 S. Figueroa St. *(Open M-F 8am-5pm, Sa 8:30am-5pm.)*

**HISTORIC NORTH.** The historic birthplace of L.A. lies in the northern section of downtown, bordered by Spring and Arcadia St. Where the city center once stood, **El Pueblo de Los Angeles Historical Monument** preserves a number of historically important buildings from the Spanish and Mexican eras. *(213-628-1274. 125 Paseo St. DASH B. Open daily 9am-9pm. Free.)*

**Olvera St.,** one of L.A.'s original roads, resembles a small Mexican street market. The street is the site of the Cinco de Mayo and Día de los Muertes celebrations of L.A.'s Chicano population (see **Seasonal Events,** p. 776). Across Alameda St. from El Pueblo is the grand old **Union Station,** famous for its appearances in many Hollywood productions; and **Chinatown** (DASH B) lies north of this area, roughly bordered by Yale, Spring, Ord, and Bernard St. The architecture in Old Chinatown is unique for the area and very impressive. Pick up walking tour maps at the **Chinatown Heritage and Visitors Center.**

The **visitors center** screens *Pueblo of Promise,* an 18min. history of Los Angeles, on request and offers free walking tours which start at the **Old Plaza.** *(622 N. Main St. 213-628-1274. Tours every hr. W-Sa 10am-noon.)*

**CIVIC CENTRAL.** The **Civic Center** is best seen from the outside. *(Bounded by Rte. 101, Grand Ave., 1st, and San Pedro St. DASH B and D.)* One of the best-known buildings in the Southland, **City Hall,** "has starred in more movies than most actors" *(200 N. Spring St.).* At the **L.A. Children's Museum,** in the L.A. Mall opposite City Hall between U.S. 101 and Temple St., everything can be (and has been) touched. *(310 N. Main St.*

CALIFORNIA

*213-687-8800. Open June 23-Sept. 5 M-F 11:30am-5pm, Sa-Su 10am-5pm; Sept. 6-June 22 Sa-Su 10am-5pm. Admission $5, under 2 free. Large groups should call 213-687-8825.)*

L.A.'s movie folks try to get their hands on Hollywood's golden boy, the short, but ever-popular, Oscar, at the **Dorothy Chandler Pavilion,** site of the annual Academy Awards. *(213-972-7211).* The Pavilion is part of L.A.'s **Music Center,** which comprises the **Mark Taper Forum** and the **Ahmanson Theater,** home to the Los Angeles Philharmonic Orchestra and the Joffrey Ballet. *(135 N. Grand Ave. Mark Taper Forum 213-972-0700. Ahmanson Theater 213-972-7200.)*

Upscale **Little Tokyo** lies southeast of the Civic Center, on 2nd and San Pedro St. on the eastern edge of downtown. *(DASH A.)* The **Japanese Village Plaza** is the center of the district and is a florid fusion of an American shopping mall and Japanese design. *(213-620-8861. On the 300 block of E. 2nd St.)* The **Japanese-American National Museum** is housed in a refurbished Buddhist temple designed by Isamu Noguchi. This community-oriented museum features interactive computers with access to WWII relocation camp records.

**Broadway,** south of 1st St., is a predominantly Mexican-American community, where you can eat, shop, or get married in one of the many wedding chapels that compete for your dowry, around 240-250 Broadway. Those with second thoughts can click "undo" by looking for the Divorcios signs. *(DASH D.)* To catch a glimpse of L.A.'s history etched in stone, check out the side of the **L.A. Times Building** between 2nd and 3rd St. Bargain hounds can haggle to their heart's delight in the Garment District, which is farther down Broadway, bordered by 6th and 9th St. The **Cooper Building** is a good first stop. *(860 S. Los Angeles St.)* The equally well-stocked **Grand Central Public Market** (see **Food,** p. 761) has its own stars in the sidewalk out front, each bearing the name of a Chicano celebrity—a *rambla de fama* to complement Hollywood's. The Market is a great spot to taste some local flavor.

**SOUTHERN DISTRICTS.** There is little for the tourist in the **Financial District.** *(Bounded roughly by 3rd, 6th, Figueroa St., and Grand Ave. DASH B and C.)* **Westin Bonaventure Hotel** has appeared in *Rain Man, In the Line of Fire,* and *This Is Spinal Tap. (4045 Figueroa St.)* Just a bit southeast of the Bonaventure is the historic **Regal Biltmore Hotel,** a $10 million, 1000-room hotel designed by Schultze and Weaver (best known for the Waldorf-Astoria in New York) which served as a filming location for *Dave, Independence Day,* and *Ghostbusters. (506 S. Grand Ave.)*

Up Bunker Hill (a.k.a. Grand Ave.), the **Museum of Contemporary Art (MOCA)** showcases art from 1940 to the present, and is a sleek and geometric architectural marvel. Its exhibits often focus on L.A. artists, but the collection also includes abstract expressionist works. Th nights in summer mean free jazz and cheap beer and wine. *(250 S. Grand Ave. 213-626-6222 or 213-621-2766. $6, students and seniors $4, under 12 free. Free Th 5-8pm. Free tours led by local artists Tu-W and F-Su at noon, 1, and 2pm; Th noon, 1, 2, and 6pm.)* The second MOCA facility is the **Geffen Contemporary,** in Little Tokyo. *(152 N. Central Ave. 213-621-1727.)*

Shop 'til you drop at the **Seventh Marketplace,** on Figueroa St., between 7th and 8th, or venture out (with caution) to the **Jewelry District,** a true diamond in a rough neighborhood, east of the Financial District, cornered by 6th and Hill St. The randy **Fashion District** is centered between 8th and 9th St., east of Maple St. *(Both areas, are served by the DASH E.)*

**NEAR DOWNTOWN: EXPOSITION PARK.** Once an upscale suburb of downtown, around 1900 the area began to decline, plummeting to its lowest in the 1920s. Deterioration was counteracted when the Olympic Games came to town in 1934. The area could use another Olympic revitalization; its museums are safe but visitors should excercise caution outside the park, especially at night.

The park is dominated by several major museums, including the **California Science Center (CSC),** which is dedicated to California science—from earthquakes to smog. The expansive, formal **rose garden** in front of the CSC is the last remnant of the blessed days when all of Exposition Park was an exposition of horticulture. More than 19,000 specimens of 200 varieties of roses surround walking paths, green lawns, gazebos, fountains, and a lily pond. *(700 State Dr. 213-744-7400. Open daily 10am-5pm. Free. Rose garden: Open Mar. 16 to Dec. 31 daily 8:30am-5:30pm. Southwest of downtown, off Rt. 110, bounded by Exposition, Figueroa, Vermont, and Santa Barbara. From downtown, take DASH shuttle C, or MTA #40 or 42; from Broadway between 5th and 6th to the park's southern edge. From Hollywood, take #204 or 354 down Vermont. From Santa Monica, take #20, 22, 320, or 322 on Wilshire, and transfer to #204 at Vermont. Park at the intersection of Figueroa and Exposition lot $5.)*

**GRIFFITH PARK AND GLENDALE.** Griffith Park stretches for 4107 acres from the hills above North Hollywood to the intersection of the Ventura (Rt. 134) and Golden State Fwy. (I-5), making it 5 times the size of New York's Central Park. Several of the mountain roads through the park (especially the **Vista Del Valle Dr.**) offer panoramic views of downtown L.A., Hollywood, and the Westside. Unfortunately, heavy rains have made them unsafe for cars, but foot traffic is allowed on most. The 5mi. hike to the top of **Mt. Hollywood,** the highest peak in the park, is quite popular. For information, stop by the **visitors center and Ranger Headquarters.** *(4730 Crystal Spring Dr. 213-665-5188. Open daily 5am-10pm.)*

The white stucco and copper domes of the Art Deco **Observatory and Planetarium,** are visible from around the park. You might remember the planetarium from the climactic denouement of the James Dean film *Rebel Without A Cause.* Even without Dean, the astronomy exhibits are a show of their own. The planetarium presents popular **Lazerium** light shows. A telescope with a 12 in. lens is open to the public every clear night until 9:45pm. *(323-664-1181, recording 664-1191. Drive to the top of Mt. Hollywood or take MTA #203 from Hollywood Blvd. Planetarium shows M-F at 1:30, 3, and 7:30pm, Sa-Su also 4:30pm; in winter, Tu-F 3 and 7:30pm, Sa-Su also 1:30, 3, and 4:30pm. $4, seniors $3, under 12 $2. Children under 5 only admitted to the 1:30pm show. Laserium: 818-901-9405. Shows Su-M 6 and 8:45pm, Tu-Sa 6, 8:45, and 9:45pm. Admission $8, ages 5-12 $7; under 5 not admitted. Observatory: 323-663-8171. Open in summer daily 12:30-10pm; in winter Tu-F 2-10pm, Sa-Su 12:30-10pm.)*

The **Great L.A. Zoo,** at the park's northern end, is, in the words of one a tiger interviewed over breakfast, "Grrrrreat!" *(333 Zoo Dr. 323-644-4200. Open Sept.-June 10am-5pm; July-Aug. 10am-6pm. $8.25, seniors $5.25, ages 2-12 $3.25.)*

**SAN FERNANDO VALLEY.** Movie studios have replaced the Valley Girl as the Valley's defining feature. As the Ventura Fwy. (Rt. 134) passes Burbank, you can see what are today the Valley's trademarks: the **NBC peacock,** the **Warner Bros. water tower,** and the carefully designed **Disney dwarves.** Urban legend says that the water pipes are orchestrated such that the 7 dwarves appear to urinate on daddy Disney when it rains. For those who find watching TV on TV slightly cliché, most of the studios have **free TV show tapings** (see **Entertainment,**(p. 772)).

The most popular spot in today's Tinseltown is the movie-themed amusement park, **Universal Studios.** Universal is best-loved by those with a healthy knowledge of America's blockbuster movie tradition, especially the mythology created around director Steven Spielberg. *(818-622-3801. Take MTA #420 west from downtown or east from the valley. Open Sept.-June daily 9am-7pm; July-Aug. 8am-10pm. Last tram leaves at 6:15pm in summer, 4:15pm off-season. $38, seniors $33, ages 3-11 $28. Parking $7.)*

If, somehow, you have a few dollars left after Universal Studios, head to the adjacent **Universal City Walk** for food, shopping, and entertainment. *(Parking $6, full refund if you buy 2 movie tickets before 6pm, and a $2 refund after 6pm.)* The jewel in City Walk's technicolor crown is **B.B. King's Blues Club,** where the thrill is far from gone. *(818-622-5464. Open Su-Th 4pm-midnight, F-Sa 4pm-2am; M-Th dinner served 4-11pm, Sa-Su lunch 2-6pm and dinner 6-11pm. Cover $5-14, $3 for dinner guests. 21+ after 10pm.)*

At the opposite end of the Valley, 40min. north of L.A. in Valencia, is **Six Flags Magic Mountain,** also known as *National Lampoon's* Wally World. Next door, Six Flag's waterpark, **Hurricane Harbor,** features the world's tallest enclosed speed slide and an intriguing "adult activity pool." *(Magic Mountain: 818-367-5965. I-5 exit at Magic Mountain Pkwy. Open Memorial Day weekend to mid-Sept. Su-Th 10am-midnight; mid Sept. to Memorial Day Sa-Su 10am-6pm only. $36, seniors $20, kids under 48 in. tall $10, under 2 free. Hurricane Harbor: Open M-Th 10am-7pm, F-Su 10am-8pm. $18, seniors and under 48in. tall $12, under 2 free. Parking $6.)*

**PASADENA AND AROUND.** With its world-class museums, graceful architecture, lively shopping district, and idyllic weather, Pasadena is a welcome change from its noisy downtown neighbor. **Old Town** Pasadena sequesters intriguing historic sights and an up-and-coming entertainment scene. The **Pasadena Fwy.** (Rt. 110), built as a WPA project between 1934 and 1941, is one of the nation's oldest. The city provides **free shuttles** approximately every 12min. that loop between Old Town and the downtown area around Lake Ave. *(626-704-4055. Buses run M-Th 11am-7pm, F 11am-10pm, Sa-Su noon-8pm. Uptown buses run M-F 7am-6pm, Sa-Su noon-5pm.)*

Nearby lie the **Huntington Library, Art Gallery, and Botanical Gardens,** in San Marino. The conglomeration was built in 1910 as the home of businessman Henry Huntington, who made his money in railroads and Southern California real estate. The stunning botanical gardens are home to 150 acres of plants (but no picnicking or sunbathing—both are forbidden). The library houses a most important collection of rare books and manuscripts, including a Gutenberg Bible, Benjamin Franklin's handwritten autobiography, a 1410 manuscript of Chaucer's *Canterbury Tales*, and a number of Shakespeare's first folios. The art gallery is known for its 18th- and 19th-century British paintings. American art is on view in the **Virginia Steele Scott Gallery.** The Annabella Huntington Memorial Collection features Renaissance paintings and 18th-century French decorative art. Tea is served in the Rose Garden daily. *(626-683-8131. 1151 Oxford Rd., between Huntington Dr. and California Blvd. in San Marino, south of Pasadena, about 2mi. south of the Allen Ave. exit off I-210. From downtown L.A., bus #79 leaves from Union Station to San Marino Ave. From there, it is a ½mi. walk. Open in summer Tu-Su 10:30am-4:30pm; in winter Tu-F noon-4:30pm, Sa-Su 10:30am-4:30pm. $8.50, students $6, seniors $8, under 12 free; 1st Th of the month free.)*

# ▣ ENTERTAINMENT

Many tourists feel a visit to the world's entertainment capital is not complete without some exposure to the actual business of making a movie or TV show. Fortunately, most production companies oblige. **Paramount** (213-956-5000), **NBC** (818-840-3537), and **Warner Bros.** (818-954-1744) offer 2hr. guided walking tours, but as they are *made* for tourists, they tend to be crowded and overpriced. The best way to get a feel for the industry is to land yourself some tickets to a TV taping. All tickets are free, but most studios tend to overbook, so holding a ticket does not always guarantee that you'll get into the taping. Show up early, and you'll have a chance of seeing your fave stars up close in an operating studio backlot.

**NBC,** 3000 W. Alameda Ave., at W. Olive Ave. in Burbank, is your best spur-of-the-moment bet. (Recording 818-840-3537. Studio tours on the hour M-F 9am-3pm, Sa 10am-2pm. $7, children $3.75.) Show up at the ticket office on a weekday at 8am for passes to Jay Leno's **Tonight Show,** filmed at 5pm the same evening (2 tickets per person, must be 16+). Many of NBC's "Must-See TV" shows are taped at **Paramount Pictures,** 5555 Melrose Ave., in Hollywood. Sitcoms like *Dharma and Greg, Sister, Sister,* and *Frasier* are taped Sept. through May; call the studio 5 working days in advance to secure tickets. Due to the constant threat of espionage at the hands of America's enemies, popular shows like *Friends* are filmed before a private audience, so unless you are a friend of a Friend, you're out of luck. (213-956-1777. Very popular tours every hr. M-F 9am-2pm; $15).

A **CBS box office,** 7800 Beverly Blvd., next to the Farmer's Market in West Hollywood, hands out free tickets to Bob Barker's seminal game-show masterpiece *The Price is Right* (taped M-Th) up to 1 week in advance. (213-852-2458. Open nontaping days M-Th 9am-5pm, taping days M-Th 7:30am-5pm. Audience members must be over 18. Request up to 10 tickets on a specific date by sending a self-addressed, stamped envelope to **The Price is Right Tickets,** 7800 Beverly Blvd., Los Angeles, CA 90036, about 4 weeks in advance.)

If all else fails, **Hollywood Group Services,** 1422 Barry Ave., #8, L.A. 90025 (310-914-3400), and **Audiences Unlimited, Inc.,** 100 Universal City Plaza, Universal City, CA 91608 (818-506-0067), offer guaranteed seating, but charge $10 to no-shows. To find out what shows are available during your visit, send a SASE to either address.

Hollywood Group Services will fax a list of all available shows within 24hr. of a call-in request. At **Universal Studios,** the filming is done on the backlot, and you won't see a thing from the tour. To them, it's a studio, not an amusement park.

To see an **on-location movie shoot,** stop by in person to the City/County Film Office, 7083 Hollywood Blvd., 5th fl., for a "shoot sheet" ($10), which lists current filming locations; film crews, however, may not share your enthusiasm for audience participation (323-957-1000; open M-F 8am-6pm).

**CINEMA, THEATER, AND CONCERTS.** Countless theaters show films the way they were meant to be seen: in a big space, on a big screen, with top-quality sound. It would be a cinematic crime not to take advantage of the incredible experience that is movie-going in L.A. **Loews Cineplex Cinemas** (818-508-0588), atop the hill at Universal City Walk; **Pacific Cinerama Dome,** 6360 Sunset Blvd. (466-3401), near Vine; and **Mann's Chinese Theater,** 6925 Hollywood Blvd. (464-8111), are some of the best movie houses.

In spite of the growing number of shows about L.A., very few Broadway/West End-style productions come out of this city. On the other hand, 115 "equity waiver theaters" (under 100 seats) offer a dizzying choice for theater-goers, who can also take in small productions in museums, art galleries, universities, parks, and even garages. For the digs on what's hot, browse the listings in the *L.A. Weekly.* **Theater L.A.** (614-0556) sells same-day tickets for half price at their "Theater Times" booth in the Beverly Center, 8500 Beverly Blvd. at La Cienega, in West L.A.

L.A.'s music venues range from small clubs to massive arenas. The **Wiltern Theater** (380-5005) shows alterna-rock/folk acts. The **Hollywood Palladium** (962-7600) is of comparable size with 3500 seats. Mid-size acts head for the **Universal Amphitheater** (818-777-3931) and the **Greek Theater** (665-1927). Huge indoor sports arenas, such as the **Forum** (310-673-1300), double as concert halls for big acts. Few dare to play at the 100,000-seat **Los Angeles Memorial Coliseum and Sports Arena**—only U2, Depeche Mode, and Guns 'n' Roses have filled the stands in recent years. Call **Ticketmaster** (480-3232) to purchase tickets for any of these venues.

Exposition Park, and the very rough city of **Inglewood,** southwest of the park, are home to many sports teams. The **USC Trojans football team** plays at the **Los Angeles Memorial Coliseum,** 3939 S. Figueroa St. (tickets 213-740-4672), which seats over 100,000 spectators, and is the only stadium in the world to have the honor of hosting the Olympic Games twice. The torch that held the Olympic flame still towers atop the Coliseum's roof. The **Los Angeles Sports Arena,** 2601 S. Figueroa St. (213-748-8000), is the former playground of basketball's **Los Angeles Clippers,** who just recently faxed themselves to the brand-new **Staples Center,** 1111 S. Figueroa St. The Sports Arena is still a popular venue for rock concerts.

In Inglewood, at the corner of Manchester and Prairie is the **Great Western Forum,** home of the **Los Angeles Kings** hockey team, as well as the **Los Angeles Lakers (NBA)** and **Sparks** (WNBA) basketball teams. Tickets for these games are in high demand. (Kings tickets: 888-546-4752. Lakers and Sparks tickets: 213-480-3232. Kings season runs Nov.-June. Lakers Nov.-June. Sparks June-Aug. Kings from $19; Lakers from $21; Sparks from $8.)

**Elysian Park,** about 3mi. northeast of downtown, curves around the northern portion of Chavez Ravine, home of **Dodger Stadium** and the perennially popular **Los Angeles Dodgers** baseball team. Tickets (213-224-1448; $6-14) are a hot commodity during the Apr. to Oct. season (if the Dodgers are playing well).

# ♫ NIGHTLIFE

L.A. clubs range from tiny danceterias and empheral warehouse raves to exclusive lounges catering to showbiz elite. In between is something for everyone else.

**LATE-NIGHT RESTAURANTS.** With the unreliability of clubs and the short shelf-life of cafes, late-night restaurants have become reliable hangouts.

◪ **Mel's Drive In,** 8585 Sunset Blvd. (310-854-7200), in West Hollywood. Location and 1950s drive-up motif ensure that many celebrities have dined here. The original Mel's near San Francisco was in *American Graffiti*. Play your part and order a cheeseburger, fries, and a vanilla milkshake (under $10). Free valet parking. Open 24hr.

◪ **Jerry's Famous Deli** has multiple locations, including West Hollywood, 8701 Beverly Blvd. (310-289-1811); Westwood, 10923 Weyburn Ave. (310-208-3354); and Studio City, 12655 Ventura Blvd. (818-980-4245). Note the menu's height—Jerry is rumored to have desired "the longest menu possible while still maintaining structural integrity." Regardless, the diner meets anyone's standards for a 4am snack. Matzoh ball soup $6; sandwiches $8-9. Public phones at every table are for calling cards only. Open 24hr.

**Fred 62,** 1850 N. Vermont Ave., (323-667-0062) in Los Feliz. "Eat now, dine later." Headrests evoke eating in a car. Green, aerodynamic (yet stationary) building. Eat a waffle ($4.62). Numbers figure strangely into the restaurant's workings. Open 24hr.

**The Rainbow Grill,** 9015 Sunset Blvd., (310-278-4232), in West Hollywood next to the Roxy. Dark red vinyl booths cradle nearly every famous and would-have-you-believe-it-can-make-you-famous butt in L.A. Marilyn Monroe met husband Joe DiMaggio on a blind date here. Pizza ($6) and calamari. Cover charge goes toward your tab: Su-Th nights $5, F-Sa nights $10. Open M-F 11am-2am, Sa-Su 5pm-2am.

**COFFEEHOUSES.** In a city where no one eats very much for fear of rounding out that bony figure, espresso, coffee, and air are often the only options.

◪ **G.A.L.A.X.Y. Gallery,** 7224 Melrose Ave. (213-938-6500), in Hollywood. More than just a coffee shop, this cool spacious store has art on display and an enormous bong and hookah display for all your tobacco needs. Acid jazz jams on some Sa nights tend to be standing room only. Cover $3. Hemp coffee $1.75. Open daily 11am-10pm. 18+.

◪ **Un Urban Coffeehouse,** 3301 Pico Blvd. (310-315-0056), in Santa Monica. Campy voodoo candles and Mexican wrestling masks. Iced mocha blends ($3.25) rival even Coffee Bean and Tea Leaf. $2 Italian sodas. Su nights are spoken-word and W nights are comedy; entertainment almost every night. Regulars will teach you blackjack, if you're lucky. Open M-Th 6am-midnight, F-Sa 8am-1am, Su 8am-midnight.

**Highland Grounds,** 742 N. Highland Ave. (323-466-1507), in Hollywood. Nightly live shows (8pm) cover all grounds with folk singers, performance artists, and empowerment speakers. Outdoor patio with blazing fire. Full menu. Beer and wine. Lattes $1.50 before noon. Breakfast menu includes eclectic egg dishes like the Bulgarian omelette ($6). After 8pm, cover $2 and 1-drink min. Open M 9am-6pm, Tu-Th 9am-midnight, F-Sa 9am-1am, Su 10am-1am.

**BARS.** While the 1996 film *Swingers* may not have transformed every bar into The 3 of Clubs, it has had a sadly homogenizing effect on L.A.'s hipsters. Well, grab your retro-70s polyester shirts, sunglasses, goatees, and throwback Cadillac convertibles, 'cause if you can't beat them, you have to swing with them, daddy.

◪ **Miyagi's,** 8225 Sunset Blvd. (323-656-0100), Sunset Strip. With 3 levels, 5 sushi bars, and 7 liquor bars, this Japanese-themed restaurant, bar, and lounge is the latest Strip hotspot. "Sake bomb, sake bomb, sake bomb," $4. Open daily 5:30pm-2am.

◪ **The 3 of Clubs,** 1123 N. Vine St. (323-462-6441), in Hollywood. In a small strip mall beneath a "Bargain Clown Mart" sign, this simple, classy, spacious, hardwood bar is famous for appearing in 1996's *Swingers*. DJ W night and live bands Th. Order a grasshopper ($5) and risk appearing as a naif. Open daily 9pm-2am.

**The Room,** 1626 Cahuenga St. (213-462-7196), in Hollywood. The very popular Room trumps The 3 of Clubs at this speakeasy that empties into an alley. This 30ish crowd comes looking for company. Open daily 9pm-2am.

**Dublin's,** 8240 Sunset Blvd. (323-656-0100), in Hollywood on the Strip. Caters to a fratty white-hat crowd in football season, but off-nights fill up with everyone from young starlets to 60-year-old pool sharks. Upstairs dance floor; swanky upstairs dining room serves lunch, and dinner until 1am. Open M-F 11am-2am, Sa-Su 10am-2am.

**Skybar,** 8440 Sunset Blvd. (323-848-6025), in the Mondrian Hotel on Sunset Strip. A bit more upscale than the rest of the Strip set, this crowd is mostly Hollywood execs and show-bizzers. Top 40 and dancing. No cover. Open daily 11am-2am. Reservations required after 8pm.

**CLUBS.** L.A. is famous, even infamous, for its club scene. With the highest number of bands per capita in the world, most clubs book top-notch acts night after night. These clubs can be the hottest thing in L.A. one month and extinct the next, so check the *L.A. Weekly* (free everywhere) before venturing out.

▓ **The Derby,** 4500 Los Feliz Blvd. (213-663-8979), in Hollywood. The kings of swing reign once again in this swanky velvet joint. Ladies, grab your snoods—many dress the 1940s part. Free swing lessons Su-F 8pm. The menu is from Louise's Trattoria (choice Italian fare) next door. Full bar. Big band music nightly (Big Bad Voodoo Daddy once regularly played here). Happy Hour daily 4-7pm. Cover $5-7. Open daily 5pm-2am.

▓ **Largo,** 432 N. Fairfax Ave. (323-852-1073), West Hollywood. Elegant sit-down audience and captivated listeners ensure intimate performances by some of L.A.'s most interesting entertainers. Cover $2-12. Open M-Sa 9pm-2am.

**Luna Park,** 665 N. Robertson Blvd. (310-652-0611), in West Hollywood. Named for an ill-fated Coney Island venture, this club is home to many a record/CD release party and an eclectic, ultra-hip crowd. Live funk, jazz, and rock nightly; Th club DJ. Supper club, full bar, outdoor patio, trancy dance floor. New Music M land L.A.'s best improvisational talent. Cover $3-10, big-name acts $20. Open daily until 2am.

**Key Club,** 9039 Sunset Blvd. (310-274-5800), in Sunset Strip. A colossal, crowded multimedia experience complete with black lights, neon, and a frenetic dance floor. Stage show extravaganzas. Live acts and DJ productions, depending on the night. Tequila library on the first floor. M-Th cover $6. F-Sa 21+; cover $20. Open daily 8pm-2am.

**COMEDY CLUBS.** L.A.'s comedy clubs are the best in the world, unless you happen to chance upon an amateur night, which is generally a painful experience.

▓ **The Improvisation,** 8162 Melrose Ave. (213-651-2583), in West Hollywood. L.A.'s best talent—Robin Williams and Jerry Seinfeld have shown their faces. Jay Mohr and Damon Wayans come when they feel like it and join the show. Italian restaurant (entrees from $6). Shows M-Th 8pm, F-Sa 8:30 and 10:30pm, Su 8pm. Cover $8-11. Bar open daily until 1:30am. 2-drink min. Reservations recommended. 18+, or 16+ with parent.

▓ **Groundling Theater,** 7307 Melrose Ave. (323-934-9700), in Hollywood. The best improv and comedy "forum" in town—alums include Pee Wee Herman and *Saturday Night Live* regulars including Julia Sweeney, Will Farrell, Cheri Oteri, and Chris Kattan. Don't be surprised to see *SNL* producer Lorne Michaels sitting in the back row. Lisa Kudrow (of *Friends* fame) got her start here, too. Polished skits most nights; improv-only Th. Shows Th 8pm, F-Sa 8 and 10pm, Su 7:30pm. All ages. Cover $10-17.50.

**GAY AND LESBIAN NIGHTLIFE.** Many ostensibly straight clubs have gay nights. Check the *L.A. Weekly* for more listings or the free weekly magazine *fab!* Nightlife centers around **Santa Monica Blvd.** in West Hollywood.

**Micky's,** 8857 Santa Monica Blvd. (310-657-1176), in West Hollywood. Large, popular wetspot filled with delectable men of all ages. Mostly Top 40. Serves lunch daily noon-4pm and hot go-go boys Tu-F and Su. Male porno stars come to visit Th 6-8pm. Weekend Beer Bust 4-9pm. Cover $3-20. Open daily noon-2am.

**Rage,** 8911 Santa Monica Blvd. (310-652-7055), in West Hollywood. Its glory days have passed, but this enormous institution rages on with nightly DJs, drag nights, and disco 'til you drop. Mostly gay men. M alternative music night, Tu 80s. Cover varies and is higher on F, the big dance night ($5-7, includes 1 drink). Full lunch and dinner menu served noon-9pm. Open Sa-Th 11:30am-2am, F 11:30am-4am.

**El Rey,** 5515 Wilshire Blvd., (323-936-6400) in Miracle Mile. This palatial Art-Deco establishment is a venue for an assortment of clubs, ranging from 70s glam to trashy drag shows. F is gal's bar, **Hotbox.** Many Sa gay nights. Call for schedule. Cover $10. Open F-Su, 9pm-2am. 18+.

# ◉ SEASONAL EVENTS

New Year's Day is always a perfect day in Southern California, or so the **Tournament of Roses Parade and Rose Bowl** (626-449-7673), Pasadena, would have it. Some of the wildest New Year's Eve parties happen along **Colorado Blvd.,** the parade route. **Renaissance Pleasure Faire,** lasts from the daffodil's first blossom to the day of the shortest night (800-523-2473; Sa-Su late Apr. to mid-June) in the Glen Helen Regional Park in San Bernardino. The name is quite arousing, but save the occasional kissing bridge, it's a pretty tame scene. From the haven angelic (L.A.), gallop apace on fiery-footed steeds (drive) to Phoebus' lodging (east) along I-10 to I-15 north, and look for signs as you draw near the site of happy reveling (city of Devore). Garbed in their best Elizabethan finery, San Bernardino teens are versed in the bard's phrases before working. (Open Sa-Su 10am-6pm. $17.50, seniors and students $15, children $7.50.) **Cinco de Mayo** (213-625-5045) explodes May 5, especially downtown at Olvera St. Huge celebrations mark the day the Mexicans drop-kicked France's ass out of Mexico. In mid-May, **UCLA Mardi Gras** (310-825-8001), at the athletic field, is billed as the world's largest collegiate activity (a terrifying thought). During **Gay Pride Weekend** (213-860-0701, last or second-to-last weekend in June), Pacific Design Center, 8687 Melrose Ave., West Hollywood, L.A.'s lesbian and gay communities celebrate in full effect with art, politics, dances, and a big parade (tickets $12). **Grunion runs** occur throughout spring and summer. This late-night pastime appeals to those who want to watch slippery, silver fish squirm onto the beaches (especially San Pedro) to mate. The fish can be caught by hand, but a license is required for those over 16. Free programs on the Grunion run given Mar.-July at the Cabrillo Marine Museum in San Pedro (310-548-7562). Obtain licenses from the **Fish and Game Department,** 330 Golden Shore (562-590-5132), in Long Beach, for $15.75; they're valid until Dec. 31 each year. One-day license $6.60. Grunion fishing prohibited May-June.

## NEAR LOS ANGELES: SOUTH BAY

South Bay life is beach life. **Hermosa Beach** wins both bathing suit and congeniality competitions. Its slammin' volleyball scene, gnarly waves, and killer boardwalk make this the überbeach. The mellower **Manhattan Beach** exudes a yuppified charm, while **Redondo Beach** is by far the most commercially suburban. Richie Rich-esque **Rancho Palos Verdes** is a coast of a different breed. From early morning to late evening, these beaches are overrun by swarms of eager skaters, bladers, volleyball players, surfers, and sunbathers. At night, the crowds move off the beach and toward Manhattan and Hermosa Ave. for an affordable nightlife scene. South Bay harbors 2 of L.A.'s finest hostels; the one in Hermosa Beach has a bitchin' social scene, while the one in San Pedro may make you want to take up *tai chi.* ◪ **Los Angeles South Bay (HI-AYH),** 3601 S. Gaffey St., Bldg. #613, in Angels Gate Park (entrance by 36th) in San Pedro, pleases with a kitchen, laundry, TV room, volleyball courts, and free parking. Bus #446 runs from here to downtown and Union Station during rush hours. (831-8109. $12; twins $13.50; private rooms $29.50. Nonmembers add $3. Linen $2. 7-night max. stay. Reception 7am-midnight; closed in winter 11am-4pm.) **Los Angeles Surf City Hostel,** 26 Pier Ave., ½ block from the beach in Hermosa Beach, is a good-natured spot to rest with free linen, bodyboards, and breakfast. Take the #439 bus from Union Station to 11th and Hermosa, walk 2 blocks north, and make a left on Pier. They will pick you up from the airport for free and drop you off for $5. (798-2323. Discount car rentals, laundry, kitchen, and TV lounge, but no parking. 4-6 bunk dorms $17; off-season $15; private rooms $45. Key deposit $10. Reservations recommended. Passport or proof of out-of-state residence required.)

# ORANGE COUNTY

Directly south of L.A. County is Orange County (pop. 2.6 million), or "O.C." as locals have learned to call it. It is a *Reader's Digest* compilation of Southern California: beautiful beaches, bronzed bathers, strip malls, Disney's expanding cultural organ, and traffic snarls frustrating enough to make the coolest Angeleno weep. Although the county's Anglo majority pales in contrast to the vibrant smorgasbord of L.A. County, Orange County is almost 25 percent Latino, in keeping with the state generally. One of only 2 staunchly Republican counties in California, Orange County has won fame for its economy (as big as Arizona's, and one of the world's 30 largest), and notoriety for its finances (the county declared an unprecedented bankruptcy in 1994 after its tax-averse government tried to make money in Wall St. derivatives).

## 🛈 PRACTICAL INFORMATION

**John Wayne Orange County Airport** (252-5006), on Campus Dr. 20min. from Anaheim, is newer, cleaner, and easier to get around than LAX; domestic only. **Amtrak** runs to: Fullerton, 120 E. Santa Fe Ave. (992-0530); Anaheim, 2150 E. Katella Blvd. (385-1448); Santa Ana, 1000 E. Santa Ana Blvd. (547-8389); Irvine, 15215 Barranca Parkway (753-9713); San Juan Capistrano, Santa Fe Depot, 26701 Verdugo St. (240-2972); and San Clemente, 1850 Avenida Estacion. **Greyhound** has 3 stations in the area: Anaheim, 100 W. Winston St. (999-1256), 3 blocks south of Disneyland (open daily 6:30am-8pm); Santa Ana, 1000 E. Santa Ana Blvd. (542-2215; open daily 7am-8pm); and San Clemente, 510 Avenida de la Estrella (492-1187; open M-Th 7:45am-6:30pm, F 7:45am-8pm). **Orange County Transportation Authority (OCTA)**, 550 S. Main St. (636-7433), Garden Grove, provides thorough service useful for getting from Santa Ana and Fullerton Amtrak stations to Disneyland, and for beach-hopping along the coast. Bus #1 travels the coast from Long Beach down to San Clemente (every hr. until 8pm). #397 covers San Clemente. Fare $1, day pass $2. **MTA** (800-266-6883 or 213-626-4455) runs buses daily 5am-10:45pm, from L.A. to Disneyland and Knott's Berry Farm. **Anaheim Area Visitors and Convention Bureau:** 800 W. Katella Ave. (999-8999), in the Anaheim Convention Center (open M-F 8:30am-5pm). Anaheim's **post office:** 701 N. Loara (520-2601). **ZIP code:** 92803. **Area code:** 714; in Seal Beach 310; in Newport area 949.

## 🏠 ACCOMMODATIONS AND FOOD

The Magic Kingdom is the sun around which the Anaheim solar system revolves, so budget motels and garden-variety "clean comfortable rooms" flank it on all sides. Keep watch for family and group rates posted on marquees, and seek out establishments offering the 3-for-2 passport (3 days of Disney for the price of 2). The best part about the new California Adventure construction is that it has inspired hotel owners to revamp as well. Their prices are slightly higher than in years past, but remain reasonable.

**Fullerton (HI-AYH),** 1700 N. Harbor Blvd., Fullerton (714-738-3721), 15min. north of Disneyland. Shuttle from L.A. airport $17. OCTA bus #43 runs along Harbor Blvd. to Disneyland. Enthusiastic, resourceful staff. No alcohol. Kitchen, Internet access, relaxing living room, communal bathrooms. Free laundry. Linen $1. 7-night max. stay. Check-in 8-11am and 4-11pm. No curfew. Single-sex and co-ed dorms $14, nonmembers $17; less in winter. Reservations encouraged.

**Magic Inn & Suites,** 1030 W. Katella Ave., Anaheim (714-772-7242 or 800-422-1556). The rugs can't show you a whole new world, but it *is* just opposite Disneyland. Recently remodeled. Pools, A/C, TVs, fridges, and microwaves. Continental breakfast included. Laundry. 2 full-sized beds $59, 2 queen beds $79. Reservations recommended.

**Skyview Motel,** 1126 W. Katella Ave. (533-4505), at the southwest corner of Disneyland. Clean rooms with HBO and A/C. Balconies offer a good view of Disney's nightly fireworks. Small pool, many kids. Queen-sized bed $40.

Inexpensive ethnic restaurants tucked into Anaheim's strip malls allow escape from fast food. Many specialize in take-out or will deliver chow to your motel room. **Angelo & Vicini's Café Ristorante**, 550 N. Harbor Blvd., in Fullerton, is a place where the word "cheesy" describes both the food and the decor—Christmas lights, cheese wheels, and the Mona Lisa. (879-4022. Lunch buffet $6. Open Su-Th 11am-9:45pm, F-Sa 11am-11:45pm.)

## ☁ SIGHTS

**DISNEYLAND.** *Contact:* 714-781-4565. *Location: Main entrance on Harbor Blvd., and a smaller one on Katella Ave., may be approached by car via I-5 to Katella Ave. From L.A., MTA bus #460 travels from 4th and Flower St. (about 1hr.) to the Disneyland Hotel (service to the hotel begins at 4:53am, service back to L.A. until 1:20am).* **Free shuttles** *link the hotel to Disneyland's portals, as does the Disneyland monorail. The park is also served by Airport Service, OCTA, Long Beach Transit, and Gray Line.* **Parking** *in the morning is painless, but leaving in the evening is not.* **Hours** *vary (call for exact info), but are approximately Su-Th 10am-9pm, F-Sa 8am-midnight.* **Admission:** *Unlimited use passport ($39, seniors $37, under 12 $29) allows repeated single-day entrance into the park, as does the parking pass ($7 per day). Two- and three-day passes are available.*

Disneyland calls itself the "happiest place on earth," putting it in direct competition with Disney Paris. The lines are as long as the day. Weekday and off-season visitors will undoubtedly be the happiest, but the enterprising can wait for parades to distract the children, leaving shorter lines. *Disneyland Today!* lists parade and show times, as well as breaking news from Frontierland.

**K(NOT)T DISNEYLAND.** Buena Park offers a cavalcade of non-Disney diversions, some of which are better than others. The first theme park in America, **Knott's Berry Farm**, is at La Palma Ave. in Buena Park just 5mi. northeast of Disneyland. *(8039 Beach Blvd. 714-220-5200 for recorded info. Park hours vary, but are approximately Su-Th 9am-11pm, F-Sa 9am-midnight. $36, seniors and ages 3-11 $26. From L.A., take MTA bus #460 from 4th and Flower; 1¼hr.)* **Movieland Wax Museum** offers a huge collection of celebrity facsimiles, including the entire *Star Trek* crew. *(7711 Beach Blvd. 522-1154. Open M-F 10am-6pm, Sa-Su 9am-7pm. $13, seniors $11, ages 4-11 $7.)* Across the way are the ribald oddities at **Ripley's Believe It or Not! Museum**, likely to be the only place prideful enough to advertise a *Last Supper* fashioned from 280 pieces of toast. *(7850 Beach Blvd. 522-1152. Open M-F 11am-7pm, Sa-Su 10am-6pm. Combo admission to both museums $17.)* The major league **Anaheim Angels** play baseball from early Apr.-Sept. *(940-2000 or 800-626-4357. General tickets $6-20.)*

Farther inland is the highly uncritical, privately funded monument to Tricky Dick, the **Richard Nixon Library and Birthplace**. The first native-born Californian president was born in this house, which has now become an extensive museum of the American presidency. Although Nixon considered his resignation an admission of guilt, expect no such admission in these exhibits, where curators consistently portray one of the master manipulators of our century as the victim of circumstance, plotting enemies, and his own immutable honor. *(18001 Yorba Linda Blvd. 993-5075. Open M-Sa 10am-5pm, Su 11am-5pm. Admission $6, seniors $4, ages 8-11 $2, under 8 free.)*

**ORANGE COUNTY BEACH COMMUNITIES.** Taking town planning to the extreme, O.C.'s various beach communities have cleaner sand, better surf, and more charm than their L.A. county counterparts. **Huntington Beach** served as a point of entry for the surfing craze, which transformed California coast life in the early 1900s. It's still a fun, crowded hotspot for wave-shredders, with a pristine pier for ogling. **Newport Beach** is the Beverly Hills of beach towns, though the beach itself displays few signs of ostentatious wealth; it is crowded with young, rowdy hedonists cloaked in neon. The sands of the beach run south to **Balboa Peninsula**, which can be reached by the Pacific Coast Hwy. At the end of the peninsula, **The Wedge**, pounded by waves, is a bodysurfing mecca.

**Laguna Beach,** 4mi. south of Newport, is nestled between canyons. Back in the day, Laguna was a Bohemian artists' colony, but no properly starving artists can afford to live here now. The surviving galleries and art supply stores nevertheless add a unique twist to the standard SoCal beach culture that thrives on Laguna's sands. **Main Beach** and the shops nearby along Ocean Ave. are the prime parading areas, though there are other, less crowded spots as well. One accessible beach is **Westry Beach,** which spreads out south of Laguna just below **Aliso Beach Park.**

More tourists than swallows return every year to **Mission San Juan Capistrano,** 30min. south of Anaheim on I-5. Take Ortega Hwy. to Camino Capistrano. Established in 1776, it is somewhat rundown due to an 1812 earthquake. Father Junípero Serra, the mission's founder, officiated from the beEnter quietly; it's still used by the Catholic Church. *(248-2048. Open daily 8:30am-5pm. $5, seniors and ages 3-12 $4.)*

# BIG BEAR

Hibernating in the San Bernardino Mountains, the town of **Big Bear Lake** entertains hordes of visitors with winter skiing and summer hiking, biking, and boating. The consistent winds, no doubt made up of the sighs of relaxing Angelenos, make the lake one of the best for sailing in the state.

The **hiking** here is both free and priceless. Maps, trail descriptions, and the *Visitor's Guide to the San Bernardino National Forest* are available at the **Big Bear Discovery Center** (866-3437), on Rt. 38 (open daily 8am-6pm; in winter 8am-4:30pm). The **Woodland Trail** or the more challenging **Pineknot Trail** offer views of the lake; high altitudes here make slow climbing necessary.

**Mountain biking** is a popular activity in Big Bear when the snow melts. **Snow Summit** (866-5766) operates lifts in summer so thrill-seeking bikers can plummet downhill without the grueling uphill ride ($7 per ride, day pass $19; helmet required). **Team Big Bear** (866-4565) sponsors several organized bike races each summer. (For more info, call daily Apr.-Oct. 9am-5pm, or write **Team Big Bear,** Box 2932, Big Bear Lake 92315.) Those without wheels of their own can rent them from **Big Bear Bikes,** 41810 Big Bear Blvd. (866-2224; open daily 10am-5pm). Many summer activities take place on the water. **Fishing licenses** are available at area sporting goods stores ($10 per day, season $28), and the **Big Bear Fishing Association** (866-6260) cheerfully dispenses info. **Holloway's Marina,** 398 Edgemor Rd., on the South Shore, rents **boats** (800-448-5335; $46-130 per ½-day).

When conditions are favorable, ski areas run out of lift tickets quickly. Tickets for the resorts listed below may be purchased over the phone through **Ticketmaster** (213-480-3232 or 714-740-2000). The **Big Bear Hotline** (866-7000 or 800-424-4232) has info on lodging, local events, and ski and road conditions. **Bear Mountain Ski Resort** (585-2519), 1½mi. southeast of downtown Big Bear Lake, has 12 lifts covering 195 acres of terrain, including huge vertical drops, plus many more acres of undeveloped land suitable for adventurous skiers. (Lift tickets $45, mid-week $30. Skis $23, snowboards $28. New skier/snowboarder packages include group lesson, lift ticket, and equipment rental; M-F $45, Sa-Su $50.)

Big Bear has few budget accommodations, especially in the winter. The best option for daytrippers is probably to stay in Redlands or San Bernardino, although the drive down Rte. 18 can be difficult at night. **Big Bear Boulevard,** the main drag on the lake's south shore, is lined with lodging possibilities, but groups can find the best deals by sharing a cabin. **Mountain Lodging Unlimited** (800-487-3168), arranges lodging and lift packages (from $96 per couple; open daily in summer 9am-midnight; in winter 7am-midnight.) **Hillcrest Lodge,** 40241 Big Bear Blvd., is a favorite for honeymooners. Pine paneling and skylights give these cozy rooms a ritzy feel at a budget price. (866-7330, reservations 800-843-4449. Jacuzzi, cable, and free local calls. Small rooms $35-49, 4-person units $64-89, deluxe suites with hearth and kitchen $57-79; in winter $39-69/$74-125/$57-97.) **Pineknot** (7000 ft.), south of Big Bear on Summit Blvd., has 49 isolated sites with flush toilets and water. Nestled at the base of Snow Summit, this spot is popular with mountain bikers. (Sites $15. Wheelchair access.) Groceries can be procured at **Vons,** 42170 Big Bear Blvd. (866-8459).

**CALIFORNIA**

To reach Big Bear Lake, take the San Bernardino Fwy. (I-10) to the junction of Rt. 30 and 330. Follow Rt. 330, also known as Mountain Rd., to Rt. 18, a *very* long and winding uphill road. About halfway up the mountain, Rt. 18 becomes Big Bear Blvd., the main route encircling the lake. Driving time from L.A. is about 2½hr., barring serious weekend traffic or road closures. **Mountain Area Regional Transit Authority** (MARTA; 584-1111) runs buses from the Greyhound station in San Bernardino to Big Bear (Su-F 3 per day, Sa 2 per day; $5, seniors and disabled $3.75). Buses also run the length of Big Bear Blvd. (end-to-end trip 1hr.; $1, students 75¢, seniors and disabled 50¢). MARTA also operates **Dial-A-Ride** ($2, students $1.75, seniors and disabled $1). **Area code:** 909.

# SAN DIEGO

San Diegans are fond of referring to their garden-like town as "America's Finest City." Even the stodgiest members of the East Coast establishment would find this claim difficult to dispute—San Diego has all the virtues of other California cities without their frequently cited drawbacks. No smog fills this city's air, and no sewage spoils its silver seashores. Its zoo is the nation's best, and its city center contains a greater concentration of museums than any spot in America save Washington, D.C. The city was founded when the seafaring Spanish prolonged an onshore foray in 1769 and began the first permanent settlement on the U.S.'s West Coast, but it didn't become a city proper until the 1940s, when it became the headquarters of the U.S. Pacific Fleet following the Pearl Harbor attack.

## ▨ ORIENTATION AND PRACTICAL INFORMATION

San Diego rests in the extreme southwest corner of California, 127mi. south of L.A. and 15mi. north of Mexico. **I-5** runs south from L.A. and skirts the eastern edge of downtown; **I-15** runs northeast to Nevada; and **I-8** runs east-west along downtown's northern boundary, connecting the desert with Ocean Beach. The major downtown thoroughfare, **Broadway,** also runs east-west. In northeast downtown sits **Balboa Park,** home to many museums and to the justly heralded San Diego Zoo. The cosmopolitan **Hillcrest** and **University Heights** districts, both centers of the gay community, border the park to the northeast. South of downtown, between 4th and 6th St., is the **Gaslamp District,** full of nightclubs, chic restaurants, and coffeehouses. **Downtown** is situated between San Diego's 2 major bays: **San Diego Bay,** formed by **Coronado Island,** lies just to the south, while **Mission Bay,** formed by the **Mission Beach** spit, lies to the northwest. Up the coast from Mission Beach are **Ocean Beach, Pacific Beach,** and wealthy **La Jolla.**

San Diego has an extensive system of fairly easy **bike routes.** The flat, paved route along Mission and Pacific Beaches toward La Jolla affords ocean views and soothing sea breezes. But bikers beware: pedestrian traffic along the beaches rivals the automobile blockades on the boulevards.

**Airport: San Diego International (Lindbergh Field),** at the northwest edge of downtown. Bus #2 goes downtown ($1.75), and so do cabs ($7). The Traveler's Aid Society (231-7361; open 8am-11pm) has more on the airport.

**Trains: Amtrak,** 1050 Kettner Blvd. (239-9021), at Broadway. To Los Angeles (11 per day M-F, $25). Info on bus, trolley, car, and boat transport. Open daily 5:15am-10:20pm.

**Buses: Greyhound,** 120 W. Broadway (239-8082), at 1st. To Los Angeles (30 per day, $13). Ticket office open 24hr.

**Public Transit: San Diego Metropolitan Transit System (MTS).** 24hr. info line (685-4900), has info system's buses, trains, and trolleys. The **Transit Store,** at 1st Ave. and Broadway, has bus, trolley, and ferry tickets and timetables (open M-F 8:30am-5:30pm, Sa-Su noon-4pm). The **Day Tripper** allows unlimited rides on buses, ferries, and trolleys for 1 day ($5), 2 days ($8), 3 days ($10), or 4 days ($12). The pass can be purchased at the Transit Store or at trolley stations.

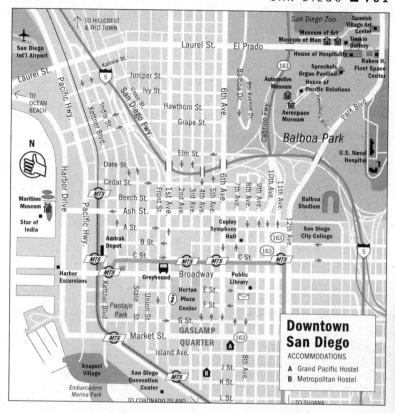

**Downtown San Diego**

ACCOMMODATIONS

**A** Grand Pacific Hostel
**B** Metropolitan Hostel

**Car Rental: Bargain Auto,** 3860 Rosecrans St. (299-0009). Cars $17-29 per day, $95-185 per week; 150 free mi. per day, 500 per week. Ages 18-21 pay $8 per day surcharge, ages 21-25 pay $4 per day. Credit card required. Open daily 8am-6pm.

**Bike Info:** Buses equipped with bike carriers make it possible to cart bikes almost anywhere in the city (call 233-3004 to find out which routes have carriers), and bikes are also allowed on the San Diego Trolley with a $4 permit (available at **Transit Store,** see above). For more bike info, contact the **City Bicycle Coordinator** (533-3110), or **Cal-Trans,** 4040 Taylor St., San Diego 92110 (231-2453), in Old Town. Biking maps and pamphlets are available.

**Visitor Information: International Visitor Information Center,** 11 Horton Plaza (236-1212), downtown at 1st Ave. and F St. Multilingual staff. 3hr. parking validation for lots with entrances on G St. and 4th Ave. Open June-Aug. M-Sa 8:30am-5pm, Su 11am-5pm; Sept.-May M-Sa 8:30am-5pm. **Old Town and State Park Info,** 4002 Wallace Ave. (220-5422), in Old Town Sq. Take the Taylor St. exit off I-8 or bus #5. Free walking tours leave daily at 11am and 2pm. Open daily 10am-5pm.

**Post Offices:** 800-275-8777; 2535 Midway Dr. Take bus #6, 9, or 35. Open M 7am-5pm, Tu-F 8am-5pm, Sa 8am-4pm. **ZIP Code:** 92186. **Area code:** 619.

# ACCOMMODATIONS

Accommodations are a bargain—$35 rooms in San Diego compare to $60 rooms in L.A. Those with cars and tents can camp on the beaches outside of the city. Reservations are available through **PARKNET** (800-444-7275; open daily 8am-5pm).

▓ **San Diego Metropolitan (HI-AYH),** 521 Market St. (525-1531 or 800-909-4776 ext. 43), at 5th Ave., in the heart of the Gaslamp. Impeccable hostel near San Diego's most popular attractions and clubs. Airy common room with kitchen, pool table, and communal bathrooms. Lockers (bring a lock) and laundry. Reception 7am-midnight. Dorms $16; doubles $31; nonmembers $3 more. IBN reservations available. Groups welcome.

**Grand Pacific Hostel,** 726 5th Ave. (232-3100 or 800-438-8622), between G and F St. in the Gaslamp. Keg parties, in-house drinking, occasional group outings. Breakfast included. Free linen. Coin-op laundry. Free shuttle to nearby sights. Tijuana tours $10. Clean and spacious dorms $16-18; doubles $40.

**J St. Inn,** 222 J St. (696-6922), near the ritzy waterfront. All 221 fabulous studio rooms have cable TV, microwave, fridge, and bath. Gym and reading room. Enclosed parking $5 per day, $20 per week. Singles $45; doubles $50; each additional person $20. Weekly and monthly rates available.

**Ocean Beach International (OBI),** 4961 Newport Ave. (223-7873 or 800-339-7263), Ocean Beach. Look for high-flying international flags. Free pickup from airport, train, and bus terminals. Features cable and kitchen near the beach. Breakfast included. Laundry. Free BBQ and keg parties Tu and F night; free pasta Tu in winter. Dorms (4-6 beds) $15-17; couples' rooms (some with bath) $34-38. Foreign passport required.

**South Carlsbad Beach State Park** (760-438-3143), off Pacific Coast Hwy. (Rt. 21) near Leucadia, in north San Diego County. Half of the 226 sites are for tents. Showers and laundry. No trails. Oceanfront sites $22, F-Sa $23; inland $17, F-Sa $18; dogs $1.

**San Elijo Beach State Park** (760-753-5091), off Pacific Coast Hwy. (Rte. 21) south of Cardiff-by-the-Sea. 271 sites (150 for tents) on seaside cliffs. Strategic landscaping gives a secluded feel. Laundry and showers. Hiker/biker campsites available, but no hiking or biking trails. Oceanfront sites $22, F-Sa $23; inland $17, F-Sa $18; dogs $1.

## ⬤ FOOD

Good restaurants cluster downtown along **C St., Broadway,** and in the **Gaslamp.** The best food near Balboa Park and the Zoo is north and west in nearby **Hillcrest** and **University Heights. Old Town** is *the* place to eat Mexican cuisine.

**El Indio Mexican Restaurant,** 409 F St. (299-0385). Damn good food at damn good prices. Combo plates $4-6, burritos $3-4. Open M-Th 11am-8pm, F-Sa 11am-2am.

**Karl Strauss' Old Columbia Brewery and Grill,** 1157 Columbia St. (234-2739). San Diego's first microbrewery and a favorite for power lunches. BBQ ribs and pasta $8-12, lighter fare $6-8. Open M-Th 11:30am-midnight, F-Sa 11:30am-1am, Su 11:30am-10pm.

**The Vegetarian Zone,** 2949 5th Ave. (298-7302), at Quince St. The motto in this carnivore-unfriendly zone is that "the human body doesn't require any form of meat to operate wonderfully." Savory veggie soups ($4) and flaky Greek spinach pie ($6-11). Open M-Th 11:30am-9pm, F 11:30am-10pm, Sa 8:30am-10pm, Su 8:30am-9pm.

**The Golden Dragon,** 414 University Ave. (296-4119; delivery 523-1199), Hillcrest. Where Marilyn Monroe and Frank Sinatra ate. Chinese menu offers over a hundred dishes (many vegetarian) for $6-9. Open daily 4:30pm-3am.

---

**THE LADY IS A TRAMP** Be careful when you enter the Museum of Death—Lady, a well-groomed Afghan, typically enjoys her midday nap in the building's doorway. If your foot happens to glance over any part of Lady, you'll be quick to notice that she's dead. After 10 happy life-filled years, Lady's body was mounted by her eccentric owner in 1971. When the owner joined Lady in the next world, the heirs to her estate apparently argued little over who would get the dog. So, just like in the movies, Lady made her way across hill and plain to a place where she'd be accepted—the museum welcomed her with open arms. Good girl, Lady!

**Casa de Bandini,** 2754 Calhoun St. (297-8211). The charming patio and *mariachi*-filled interior (built in 1829) create a fabulous atmosphere for the scarfing of super-sized *chimichangas* ($8), mouth-watering combo plates ($8-9), and monster margaritas ($4-7). Repeatedly voted San Diego's best Mexican restaurant. Open M-Th 11am-9:30pm, F-Sa 11am-10pm, Su 10am-9:30pm.

**Casa de Pico** (296-3267), just off Calhoun St. in the Bazaar. Gigantic plates overflowing with gooey cheese enchiladas ($7-8). Soup-bowl-sized margaritas are terrifically tasty. Open Su-F 10am-9pm, Sa 10am-9:30pm.

# ⌖ SIGHTS

Downtown, Balboa Park, and Old Town are easily handled on foot, but beaches are less accessible because of the wide distances between them. San Diegans worship the god of the walk signal, perhaps in part because of some obedience gene, but more likely because jaywalking is actively prosecuted here.

**DOWNTOWN.** San Diego's downtown attractions are concentrated in the corridor that includes its business, Gaslamp, and waterfront districts, all testaments to San Diego's continuing renaissance. Travelers should be careful outside of this corridor, as the immediately neighboring areas are not as safe.

The **Museum of Contemporary Art,** a steel-and-glass structure with a permanent 20th-century collection and visiting works. Artists represented in the permanent collection include John Baldessari, Philip Guston, and Ellsworth Kelly. Until mid-2000, the museum will also display the works of the **Museum of Photographic Arts** while that museum undergoes extensive renovations. The Museum of Contemporary Arts also has a La Jolla branch. *(1001 Kettner Blvd. 234-1001 or 454-3541. Open Tu-Sa 10am-5pm, Su noon-5pm. $2; students, seniors, military, and ages 12-18 $1; under 12 free. Docent-led tours Sa-Su at 2pm; tour included in admission price.)*

In the basement of a 100-year-old mortuary, one can explore the ineluctable result of all worldly machinations at the gruesome **Museum of Death.** Its exhibits include original artwork by such infamous serial killers as Charles Manson as well as more than enough photographs of horribly mutilated corpses to satisfy even the surliest teenage outcast. *(338-8153. 548 5th Ave. Open Su-Th 1-10pm, F-Sa 1-11pm. Admission $5.)*

The **Gaslamp Quarter** houses antique shops, Victorian buildings, and trendy restaurants. Formerly the city's Red Light District and home to the original **Pappy's, Inc.** adult bookstore, the area's new bars and bistros have grown popular with upscale revelers. By day, the area's charm lies in its history. The **Gaslamp Quarter Foundation** offers guided walking tours. *(233-4692. William Heath Davis House, 410 Island Ave. Museum open M-F 10am-2pm, Sa 10am-4pm, Su noon-4pm. 2hr. tours Sa at 11am. Admission $5; students, seniors, and ages 12-18 $3; under 12 free.)* The **Horton Grand Hotel,** like most old buildings in San Diego, is supposedly haunted. *(544-1886. 311 Island Ave. Tours W at 3pm. Free.)*

Spanish for "dock," the **Embarcadero's** boardwalk shops and museums face moored windjammers, cruise ships, and the occasional naval destroyer. Military and merchant marine vessels are anchored here, as well as the distantly visible North Island Naval Air Station, the Point Loma Submarine Base, and the South Bay's mothballed fleet. *(Most afternoon tours of naval crafts are free.)*

## BALBOA PARK, THE SAN DIEGO ZOO, AND THE EL PRADO MUSEUMS.

Balboa Park was the creation of pioneering horticulturists whose plantings transformed a once-treeless pueblo tract into a botanical montage. The park is accessible by bus #7. **Parking is free** in museum and zoo lots; posted signs warn park-goers against scam artists who attempt to wheedle lot fees from the unsuspecting. Tu is the best day to visit the park, as the museums offer free admission on a rotating basis. With over 100 acres of exquisite fenceless habitats, the **San Diego Zoo** (234-3153) well deserves its reputation as one of the finest in the world. *(Open daily in summer 7:30am-9pm; off-season 9am-4pm. $16, ages 3-11 $7 except free in Oct, military in uni-*

*form free. Combined zoo and wild animal park admission $35, ages 3-11 $21. Group rates available. Free on Founder's Day, the 1st M in Oct.)* The 40min. open-air **double-decker bus tour** covers 80% of the park. *($8, ages 3-11 $5.)*

Balboa Park's many museums reside within the resplendent Spanish colonial-style buildings which line **El Prado,** a street running west to east through the Park's central **Plaza de Panama.** The **San Diego Museum of Art** has a collection ranging from ancient Asian to contemporary Californian works. At the adjoining outdoor **Sculpture Garden Court** a sensuous Henry Moore piece presides over other large abstract blocks. *(232-7931. Open Tu-Su 10am-4:30pm. $8, ages 18-24 and seniors $6, ages 6-17 $3; special exhibits $2-10 more.)* Across the Plaza, the **Timken Art Gallery** houses a newly restored portrait by Rembrandt and a collection of Russian church icons. *(1500 El Prado Way. 239-5548. Open Oct.-Aug. Tu-Sa 10am-4:30pm, Su 1:30-4:30pm. Free.)* **Spanish Village** is a colony of 250 artists at work in 36 studios. *(233-9050. At the end of El Prado Way, which is closed to cars, take a left onto Village Pl.)*

The **Botanical Building** is a wooden structure filled with the scent of jasmine and the murmur of fountains. The **Desert Garden** and **Rose Garden** offer a striking contrast between the 2 types of flora. The desert garden is in full bloom from Jan. to Mar., and the roses are best admired between Apr. and Dec. Free ranger-led tours of the central part of Balboa Park are offered Tu and Su at 1pm. Plant-lovers can also meet on Sa at 10am for a free volunteer-led tour of the park. Each Sa tour includes different sights within the park. *(235-1100. Botanical Building open F-W 10am-4pm. Free. Gardens at 2200 Park Blvd. Free. For more info on tours call 235-1121.)*

**OLD TOWN.** In 1769, a group of Spanish soldiers accompanied by Father Junípero Serra established a fort and **Mission Basilica San Diego de Alcalá** in the area now known as Old Town. The area's museums, parks, and sundry attractions commemorate the historic outpost. Father Serra's soldiers were apparently a rough and unholy bunch, because in 1774 the *padre* moved his mission some 6mi. away to its current location. The mission is still an active parish church, and contains a chapel, gardens, a small museum, and a reconstruction of Serra's living quarters. *(281-8449. Take bus #43 or I-8 East to the Mission Gorge Rd. exit. Mass held daily at 7am and 5:30pm; visitors welcome.)*

The most popular of the area's attractions, the **Old Town State Park's** early-19th-century buildings contain museums, shops, and restaurants. Take a tour of the **Whaley House,** which displays an authentic Lincoln life mask and the piano used in *Gone With the Wind.* The house stands on the site of San Diego's first gallows, which may influence it's being one of two **official haunted houses** recognized by the State of California. *(2482 San Diego Ave. 298-2482. Open daily 10am-4:30pm; entrance closes at 4pm. $4, seniors $3, ages 6-12 $2. Old Town Historical Society tours 293-0117.)* Across the street is **Heritage Park,** a group of 7 Victorian buildings (6 houses and a temple) collected from around the city. Four are open to the public.

**CORONADO ISLAND.** Coronado is actually a peninsula—the "Silver Strand," a slender 7mi. strip of sand, connects it to the mainland just above the Mexican border. Residents and merchants stick to the south, while sailors and aviators populate the **North Island Naval Base.** The graceful **Coronado Bridge,** built in 1969, guides cars to Coronado from downtown San Diego along I-5 (toll $1), and bus #901 follows the same route. The **Coronado Visitors Bureau,** 1047 B Ave. (437-8788 or 800-622-8300), provides info on the upscale shops and restaurants lining **Orange Ave.** Coronado's most famed sight is its Victorian-style **Hotel Del Coronado,** 1500 Orange Ave. (435-6611), one of America's largest wooden buildings. The long, white verandas and the vermilion spires of the "Del" were built in 1898. It has since become one of the world's great hotels, hosting 12 presidents and one blonde bombshell (Marilyn Monroe's 1959 classic *Some Like it Hot* was filmed here).

The **Cabrillo National Monument,** at the tip of Point Loma, is dedicated to the great Portuguese explorer Juan Rodríguez Cabrillo (the first European to land in California), but is best known for its views of San Diego and migrating whales. *(557-5450. $5 per vehicle, $2 per person on foot or bike: pass good for 7 days. Golden Eagle Passport accepted.)* **Whale-watching** season is mid-Dec. to Feb., and the monument is prime seating (whale info in winter 557-5450). From North County, take I-5 to Rosecrans Blvd. (there is no Rosecrans exit northbound) and follow signs for Rt. 209 to the entrance, or take bus #6A. At the highest point of the peninsula sits the museum at **Old Point Loma Lighthouse** (open daily 9am-5:15pm; summer hrs vary).

**Ocean Beach (O.B.)** caters to a crowd of surfers much more low-key than the swankier set to the north. Visitors can angle from the longest fishing pier in the Western Hemisphere or watch the sinking sun from **Sunset Cliffs.** Most of the area's inexpensive restaurants and bars are clustered along the westernmost stretch of **Newport Ave.** Much of San Diego's younger population is drawn to **Mission Beach and Pacific Beach (P.B.)** by the respectable surf and the hopping nightlife. At the corner of W. Mission Bay Dr. and Mission Blvd. is **Belmont Park,** a combination amusement park and shopping center that draws a youthful crowd from all over the city. The **Ocean Front Walk** through Pacific Beach toward La Jolla is always packed with joggers, walkers, cyclists, and the usual beachfront shops.

**SEA WORLD.** Take Disneyland, subtract the rides, add a whole lot of fish, and you've got **Sea World,** a water wonderland whose signature creature isn't a mouse but the 4-ton Orca **Shamu.** (Actually, the original Shamu died years ago, but his immortality has been ensured by way of a fiendish ruse—giving his 10 replacements the same name.) Shamus aside, the park contains shark, penguin, and dolphin displays, as well as jet-ski and watersport shows and a virtual-reality underwater experience. *(226-3901. Park open M-Th 9am-10pm, F-Su 9am-11pm. Hours shorter in off-season. Park admission $38, ages 3-11 $29.)*

## 🎵 NIGHTLIFE AND ENTERTAINMENT

Nightlife in San Diego is not centered around a particular strip, but scattered in several distinct pockets of action. Upscale locals and trendy tourist flock to the **Gaslamp Quarter,** where numerous restaurants and bars feature live music. The **Hillcrest** area, next to Balboa Park, draws a young, largely gay crowd. Away from downtown, the **beach areas** (especially Garnett Ave. in Pacific Beach) are loaded with clubs, bars, inexpensive eateris, and college-age revelers. The city's definitive source of entertainment info is the free *San Diego Reader.*

🎵 **Croce's Top Hat Bar and Grille** and **Croce's Jazz Bar,** 802 5th Ave. (233-4355), at F St. in the Gaslamp. Ingrid Croce, widow of singer Jim Croce, created this rock/blues bar and classy jazz bar side-by-side on the 1st fl. of the historic Keating building. Live music nightly. Cover up to $5-10, includes 2 live shows. Open daily 7:30am-3pm and 5pm-midnight; bar open until 2am.

**Pacific Beach Bar and Grill** and **Club Tremors,** 860 Garnet Ave. (858-272-1242 and 277-7228, respectively), Pacific Beach. Live DJ packs the 2-level dance floor with a young and slinky crowd. Cover $5. Club open Th-Sa 9pm-1:30am. Bar and Grill has good, cheap food. Bar open 11am-1:30am, kitchen closes midnight.

**Dick's Last Resort,** 345 4th Ave. (231-9100), Gaslamp. Buckets of Southern grub attract a wildly hedonistic bunch. Dick's stocks beers from around the globe. No cover for the nightly rock or blues, but you'd better be buyin'. Burgers under $4, entrees $9-17. Open daily 11am-1:30am.

**Café Lu Lu,** 419 F. St. (858-238-0114), Gaslamp. Vegetarian coffeehouse was designed by local artists. See and be seen as you eat for under $6, surreptitiously sipping a raspberry-mocha espresso ($3.75). Standing room only after midnight. Open Su-Th 9am-2am, F-Sa 9am-3am.

**Lesbian** and **gay clubs** cluster in University Heights and Hillcrest. Some of the more popular hangouts include: **The Flame,** 3780 Park Blvd., in Hillcrest, a lesbian dance club (295-4163; open Sa-Th 5pm-2am, F4pm-2am); **Bourbon St.,** 4612 Park Blvd., in University Heights, a piano bar with a gay following (291-0173; open daily 11am-1:30am); and **The Brass Rail,** 3796 5th Ave., in Hillcrest, featuring dancing and drag on weekends (298-2233; open daily 5pm-2am).

## NORTH OF SAN DIEGO

**LA JOLLA.** Pronounced "la HOY-a," this affluent locality houses few budget accommodations or eateries, but its fabulous beaches are largely open to the public. The **La Jolla Cove** is popular with scuba divers, snorkelers, and brilliantly colored Garibaldi goldfish (the state saltwater fish). Surfers are especially fond of the waves at **Tourmaline Beach** and **Windansea Beach,** which can be too strong for novices. **La Jolla Shores,** next to Scripps/UCSD, has clean and gentle swells ideal for bodysurfers, boogie boarders, swimmers, and families. **Black's Beach** is not officially a **nude beach,** but let's just say there are plenty of wieners and buns at *this* lunchcart. To reach La Jolla, turn from I-5 and take a left at the Ardath exit or take buses #30 or 34 from downtown.

**ESCONDIDO.** The **San Diego Wild Animal Park** is dedicated to the preservation and display of endangered species. Animals roam freely in extensive habitats engineered to mirror the real thing. The park's entrance has restaurants, and a short trail, but most of its 800 accessible acres can be reached only by way of the open-air **Wgasa Bush Line Railway,** a 55-min. monorail tour through the 4 habitat areas. (480-0100. Open daily 9am, closing times vary. $22, ages 3-11 $15; parking $3.)

Also in Escondido is the "wunnerful, wunnerful" **Welk Resort Center,** the personal barony of late champagne-music conductor Lawrence Welk. The lobby contains the **Lawrence Welk Museum,** 8860 Lawrence Welk Dr. (800-932-9355; open Tu, Th, Sa 9am-7pm; Su, M, W, F 9am-4:30pm).

## TIJUANA

In the shadow of swollen, sulphur-spewing factories smeared across a topographical nightmare of gorges and promontories lies the most notorious specimen of the peculiar border subculture: Tijuana, the most-visited border town in the world. This 3-ringed, duty-free extravaganza comes complete with English-speaking, patronizing club promoters and every decadent way of blowing money, from *jai-alai* to dark, dingy strip joints, from mega-curio shops to Las Vegas-style hotels. It's hard to say whether it's Tijuana's strange charm, its cheap booze, or its sprawling, unapologetic hedonism that attracts tourists like flies.

**CROSSING THE BORDER.** From San Diego to Tijuana, take the red **Mexicoach** bus (619-428-9517, 85 14 70 in Mexico). Alternatively, grab a **trolley** to San Ysidro, at Kettner and Broadway in downtown San Diego ($2) and walk across the border. Transfers from airport busses are also available. **Driving** across the border is fairly hassle-free. However, driving in Tijuana can be harrowing: many traffic lights function merely as stop signs, 4-way stop signs act as traffic lights, and the streets are crowded. If you're only in Tijuana for a day, it's a better idea to leave your car in a lot on the U.S. side and join the throngs of people walking across the border. Parking rates start at US$3 per day and increase as you move closer to Mexico. Bring proper ID to re-enter the U.S. While a driver's license or other photo ID is acceptable, a passport ensures the speediest passage. Leave fruits, veggies, and weapons behind.

**⛱ PRACTICAL INFORMATION.** In Tijuana, *calles* run east-west; *avenidas* run north-south. The *avenidas* in the *centro* area are (from east to west) **Mutualismo, Martínez, Niños Héroes, Constitución, Revolución** (the main tourist drag), **Madero, Negrete,** and **Ocampo.** *Calles* in the *centro* area are both named and numbered. Beginning at the north, they are **Artículo 123** (Calle 1), **Benito Juárez** (Calle 2), **Carrillo Puerto** (Calle 3), **Díaz Mirón** (Calle 4), **Zapata** (Calle 5), **Magón** (Calle 6), **Galeana** (Calle 7), **Hidalgo** (Calle 8), and **Zaragoza** (Calle 9). To reach the **bus station** (21 29 83 or 21 29 84) from downtown, board the blue-and-white buses marked "Buena Vista" or "Camionera" on Niños Héroes between Calles 3 and 4 (3 pesos), or a brown-and-white communal cab on Madero between Calles 2 and 3 (4 pesos). **Greyhound** (21 29 82) runs to L.A. (3hr., every hr. 5am-11:05pm, US$18) and other locations. **Cabs** are all over town. The friendly, English-speaking staff at the **Tourist Office,** Revolución 711 (88 05 55), at Calle 1, doles out maps and advice (open M-Sa 8am-5pm, Su 10am-5pm). A less crowded booth on Revolución between Calles 3 and 4 has maps. The **Customs Office** (83 13 90) sits at the border on the Mexican side after crossing the San Ysidro bridge (open M-F 8am-3pm). Banks along Constitución such as Banamex (88 00 21 or 88 00 22), at Calle 4, offer **currency exchange** at the same rate (Banamex open for exchange M-F 9am-5pm, 24hr. **ATM**). **Emergency:** 060. **Red Cross:** (21 77 87, emergency 066), Calle Alfonso Gamboa at E. Silvestre, across from the Price Club. **Post Office:** (84 79 50), on Negrete at Calle 11. Open M-F 8am-7pm, Sa-Su 9am-1pm. **Postal code:** 22001. **Phone code:** 66.

**▙▟ ACCOMMODATIONS AND FOOD.** Plenty of budget hotels grace Calle 1 between Revolución and Mutualismo, although they tend toward the roachy side. Come nightfall, it becomes something of a red-light district, especially between Revolución and Constitución. *Women should be extra cautious.* The bizarrely decorated **Hotel Perla de Occidente,** Mutualismo 758 (85 13 58), between Calles 1 and 2, sits 4 blocks from the bedlam of Revolución. Enjoy fans on request, soft beds, and roomy bathrooms. (Singles 120 pesos; doubles 140 pesos.) **Hotel El Jaliscense,** Calle 1 #7925 (85 34 91), between Niños Héroes and Martínez, is a great deal, offering clean, small rooms with high, resilient beds, private baths, fans, and phones (singles 120 pesos; doubles 140 pesos.)

Tijuana's touristy eats are essentially Tex-Mex, but some cheap, authentic, Mexican restaurants line Constitución and the streets leading from **Revolución** to **Constitución.** Even cheaper are the mom-and-pop mini-resaurants all over town. To save money, pay in pesos, even if the menu quotes prices in dollars. Patrons enjoy great food and orange decor at friendly **▧ El Pipirín Antojitos,** Constitución 878, between Calles 2 and 3 (chicken burritos with rice and beans 25 pesos; 88 16 02; open daily 8:30am-9pm). At **Los Panchos Taco Shop,** Revolución at Calle 3, the booths are packed with hungry locals munching on ultra-fresh tortillas. (Steak taco US$1, bean burritos US$2. 85 72 77. Open Su-Th 8am-4pm; F-Sa 8am-2am.)

**▨ SIGHTS AND SPORTS.** The family-owned **L.A. Cetto Winery,** Cañón Johnson 2108, at Calle 10, just off Constitución, holds a harvest festival every Aug. and offers tours throughout the year. (85 30 31. tours M-Sa every 30min. 10am-5pm. US$1, with wine-tasting US$2, with wine-tasting and souvenir goblet US$3.)

**Jai alai,** reputedly the world's fastest game, is played in the majestic **Frontón Palacio,** Revolución at Calle 7. Two to four players take to the 3-sided court as one, using arm-baskets to catch and throw a ball traveling 180 mph. Players are treated like horses; observers bet on their favorites and keep a close eye on the odds. All employees are bilingual, and the gambling is carried out in greenbacks. (85 78 33. Open F-Sa at 7pm for viewing of practice matches. Free.)

If you're in town on the right Sunday, you can watch the graceful and savage dance of a **bullfight** in one of Tijuana's 2 bullrings. The more modern stadium is **Plaza Monumental,** northwest of the city near *Las Playas de Tijuana* (follow Calle 2 west), which hosts fights from Aug. to mid-Sept. Catch a blue-and-white bus on Calle 3 between Constitución and Niños Héroes. Tickets to the rings are sold at the gate and at a ticket window at Mexicoac, on Revolución between Calle 6 and 7.

**▚ NIGHTLIFE.** In the 1920s, when prohibition hit the U.S., many crossed the border to revel in forbidden nectars of cactus (tequila), grapes (wine), and hops (beer). Ever since, Tijuana has been regarded as *the* venue for nights of debauchery. If you've come to party, brace yourself for a raucous good time. Strolling down Revolución after dusk, you'll be bombarded by thumping music, neon lights, and abrasive club promoters hawking "2-for-1" margaritas (most places listed below charge US$4 for 2). All clubs check ID (18+) with varying criteria of what's acceptable, and many frisk for firearms. For a more local scene, peek into the small clubs on Calle 6 off Revolución. **▧ Iguanas-Ranas,** Revolución at Calle 3, is always hopping with a 20-something crowd downing beers (US$2.25) in the schoolbus or raising hell on the dance floor (85 14 22; open M-Th 10am-2am, F-Su 1am-5am). The tiny wooden dance floor in the center of upscale and balloon-filled **Tilly's 5th Ave.** (85 90 15), Revolución and Calle 5, resembles a boxing ring, but rest assured—there's only room for dancing. (Beer US$2. W night is $1 beer night. Open M-Th 10:30am-2am, F-Sa 10:30am-5am.) The blond/e clientele at **Caves,** Revolución and Calle 5, drink 2 beers for $3.50 among dinosaurs and prehistoric beasts perched on a rock facade of this dark but airy bar and disco (88 06 09; no cover; open Su-Th 11am-2am, F-Sa 11am-2am).

# THE CALIFORNIA DESERT

Mystics and misanthropes, Native Americans and city slickers have long been fascinated by the austere scenery and the vast open spaces of the California desert. In winter, the desert is a pleasantly warm refuge; in spring, a technicolor floral landscape; and in summer, a blistering wasteland. The desert features diverse flora and fauna, staggering topographical variation, and scattered relics of America's past.

## PALM SPRINGS

Even in its very first days, when Cahuillan Indians settled here for a winter respite, Palm Springs was a rambunctious resort. It was only a matter of time before this glitzy desert community elected the late Sonny Bono as its mayor. Today, the medicinal waters of the city's natural hot springs ensure the health of its opulent residents, and also its longevity as a resort. With warm temperatures, celebrity residents, and more pink than a *Miami Vice* episode, this desert city (pop. 42,000) provides a sunny break from everyday life.

**Mt. San Jacinto State Park,** Palm Springs's primary landmark, offers outdoor recreation opportunities for visitors of all fitness levels. If Mt. San Jacinto's 10,804 ft. escarpment seems too strenuous, try the **Palm Springs Aerial Tramway,** on Tramway Rd. off Rt. 111. Rising nearly 9000 ft., the observation deck has great views of the Coachella Valley. (325-1391. Trams run every 30min. M-F 10am-8pm, Sa-Su 8am-8pm; closed M in winter. Round-trip $18, seniors $15, under 12 $12.) The **Desert Hot Springs Spa,** 10805 Palm Dr., on the north side of I-10, features 6 naturally heated mineral pools of different temperatures, as well as saunas, massage professionals, and bodywraps (329-6495; simmer daily 8am-10pm; $3-7). The remarkable **Palm Springs Desert Museum,** 101 Museum Dr., has a collection of Native American art, talking desert dioramas, and live animals. (325-0189. Museum open Tu-Su 10am-5pm. $6, seniors $5, students $3, ages 6-17 $3; free 1st Tu of each month. Take Sun Bus #111.) **Oasis Water Park,** off I-10 S on Gene Autry Trail has a wave pool, inner tube river, and 13 waterslides. (325-7873. Open mid-Mar. to mid-Sept. daily 11am-6pm, mid-Sept. to Oct. Sa-Su 11am-5pm. $19 if over 5ft., children 3ft. or taller $12, seniors $11, under 3ft. free. Parking $4.)

Like most famous resort communities, Palm Springs caters mainly to those seeking a tax shelter, not a night's shelter—the cheapest way to stay here is to find a nearby state park or national forest campground. If you've gotta stay in town, **Motel 6** has the cheapest rates, especially during winter. Locations include 660 S. Palm Canyon Dr. (327-4200), south of city center; 595 E. Palm Canyon Dr. (325-6129); and 63950 20th Ave. (251-1425), near the I-10 off-ramp. Each has A/C rooms and pool access. (Singles $35; doubles $41; in winter $6-12 more.)

The largest of the desert towns, Palm Springs has more dining options than most desert pit stops. **Las Casuelas-The Original,** 368 N. Palm Canyon Dr., juxtaposes authentic Mexican dishes ($6 and up), dingy lighting, and tattooed waitresses (325-3213; open daily 10am-10pm). **Carlo's Italian Delicatessen,** 119 S. Indian Canyon Dr., is a budget-minded deli (325-5571; open W-F 10am-6pm, Sa 10am-8pm, Su 10am-5pm; closed W in winter). **Thai Smile,** 651 N. Palm Canyon Dr., between Tamarisk and Alejo., with many vegetarian options (320-5503; $5 lunch specials; open Su-Th 11am-10pm, F-Sa 11am-11pm).

CALIFORNIA

**Palm Springs Regional Airport,** 3400 S. Tahquitz-Canyon Rd. (323-8161), offers state and limited national service. **Greyhound,** 311 N. Indian Canyon Dr. (325-2053), buses to Los Angeles (11 per day; $19, round-trip $35). The local **Sun Bus** (343-3451) connects Coachella Valley cities (fare 75¢, transfers 25¢; operates daily 5:30am-11pm). **Chamber of Commerce:** 190 W. Amado Rd. (325-1577; open M-F 8:30am-4:30pm). **Post Office:** 333 E. Amado Rd. (800-275-8777). **ZIP code:** 92262, general delivery 92263. **Area code:** 760.

# JOSHUA TREE NATIONAL PARK

When the Mormon pioneers crossed this desert area in the 19th century, they named the enigmatic desert tree they encountered after the Biblical prophet Joshua. Perhaps it was the heat, but the tree's crooked limbs seemed to them an uncanny image of the Hebrew general, who with arms upraised, beckoned them to the promised land. Stacks of wind-sculpted boulders, Joshua trees, 5 oases, and a spectrum of high and low desert ecologies create a vast mosaic of landscape and vegetation. In recent years, climbers, campers, and daytrippers from Southern California have added to the mosaic. History buffs will appreciate the vestiges of human occupation—ancient rock petroglyphs, dams built in the 19th century to catch the meager rainfall for livestock, and gold mine ruins dot the landscape.

**⏺ PRACTICAL INFORMATION.** Joshua Tree National Park covers 558,000 acres northeast of Palm Springs, about 160mi. east of L.A. The park is ringed by 3 highways: **I-10** to the south, **Rt. 62 (Twentynine Palms Highway)** to the west and north, and **Rt. 177** to the east. The northern entrances are off Rt. 62, at **Joshua Tree** and **Twentynine Palms.** The south entrance is at **Cottonwood Spring,** off I-10. Unfortunately, this is where the streets have no name; look for the park sign 25mi. east of Indio. **Headquarters and Oasis Visitors Center:** 74485 National Park Dr., Twentynine Palms (367-5500), ¼mi. off Rt. 62 (open daily 8am-5pm; water available). Park **entrance fee:** $5 per person or $10 per car, valid for 7 days. **Post office:** 73839 Gorgonio Dr., Twentynine Palms (open M-F 8:30am-5pm). **ZIP Code:** 92277. **Area code:** 760.

**⏏ ACCOMMODATIONS.** Most campgrounds in the park operate on a first come, first served basis. Reservations can be made for group sites only at Cottonwood, Sheep Pass, Indian Cove, and Black Rock Canyon through **DESTINET** (800-436-7275). **Backcountry** camping is also an option. Ask at a ranger station for details. All campsites have tables, fireplaces, and pit toilets, and are **free** unless otherwise noted. Those who plan any sort of extended stay should pack their own supplies, water, and cooking utensils. Campground stays are limited to 30 days in the summer and to 14 days Oct.-May. **Hidden Valley** (4200 ft.), in the center of the park, off Quail Springs Rd., has secluded alcoves shaded by enormous boulders. Its proximity to Wonderland of Rock and the Barker Dam Trail make this a rock climber's heaven. **Jumbo Rocks** (4400 ft.), located near Skull Rock Trail on the eastern edge of Queen Valley, is the highest, and therefore the coolest, campground in the park. Front spots have the best shade. **Indian Cove** (3200 ft.), on the north edge of the Wonderland of Rocks, has dramatic waterfalls and rock climbing nearby. **Black Rock Canyon** (4000 ft.), at the end of Joshua Ln. off Rt. 62 near Yucca Valley, was the inspiration for Jellystone Park, the home of Yogi Bear. The wooded sites are near flush toilets and running water (sites $10; reservations accepted). Those who cannot stomach the thought of desert campgrounds can find indoor accommodations in **Twentynine Palms.** The **29 Palms Inn,** 73950 Inn Dr., facing the Mara Oasis in Twentynine Palms, offers the indoors (367-3505; June-Sept. Su-Th $47-$74, F-Sa $65-$102; Sept.-June $5-10 more).

**⏺ SIGHTS.** Over 80% of the park is designated wilderness area, safeguarded against development, and lacking paved roads, toilets, and campfires. Joshua Tree offers truly remote territory for backcountry hiking and camping. There's no water in the wilderness except when a flash flood comes roaring down a wash (beware your choice of campsite). The park's most temperate weather is from Oct.-Dec. and Mar.-Apr.; temperatures in other months span uncomfortable extremes.

A self-paced **driving tour** is an easy way to explore the park and linger to a later hour. All park roads are well-marked, and "Exhibit Ahead" signs point the way to unique floral and geological formations. One sight that should not be missed is **Key's View** (5185 ft.), 6mi. off the park road just west of Ryan campground. It's a great spot for watching the sun rise. The **Cholla Cactus Garden,** a grove of spiny succulents resembling 3D asterisks, lies in the Pinto Basin just off the road. Four-wheel drive vehicles can use dirt roads, such as **Geology Tour Road,** climbing through fascinating rock formations to the Li'l San Bernardino Mountains.

**Hiking** through the park's trails is perhaps the best way to experience Joshua Tree. Only on foot can visitors tread through sand, scramble over boulders, and walk among the park's hardy namesakes. Although the **Barker Dam Trail,** next to Hidden Valley, is often packed with tourists, its painted petroglyphs and eerie tranquility make it a worthwhile hike. Bring plenty of water for the strenuous, unshaded climb to the summit of **Ryan Mountain** (5461 ft.), where the boulder formations bear an unsettling resemblance to herculean beasts of burden slouching toward a distant destination. The visitors center has info on the park's many other hikes, which range from the 15min. stroll to the **Oasis of Mara** to a 3-day trek along the **California Riding and Hiking Trail** (35mi.). Joshua Tree teems with flora and fauna that you're unlikely to see anywhere else in the world. Larger plants like Joshua trees, cholla, and the spidery ocotillo have adapted to the severe climate in fascinating ways, and the **wildflowers** that dot the desert terrain each spring (mid-Mar. to mid-May) attract thousands of visitors.

Energetic visitors are often drawn to Joshua Tree for its **rock climbing;** the world-renowned boulders at **Wonderland of Rocks** and **Hidden Valley** are especially challenging and attract thousands of climbers each year. The visitors center provides info on established rope routes and on wilderness areas where the placement of new bolts is restricted. **Joshua Tree Rock Climbing** (800-890-4745), Box 29, Joshua Tree, provides instruction and equipment rental.

## DEATH VALLEY

Satan owns a lot of real estate in **Death Valley National Park.** Not only does he grow crops (at the Devil's Cornfield) and hit the links (at the Devil's Golf Course), but the park is also home to Hell's Gate itself. Not surprisingly, the area's astonishing variety of topographical and climactic extremes can support just about anyone's idea of the Inferno. Winter temps dip well below freezing, and summer readings rival even the hottest Hades. The 2nd-highest temperature ever recorded on Earth (134°F in the shade) was measured at the valley's Furnace Creek Ranch on July 10, 1913. Few venture to the valley floor during the summer, and it is foolish to do so; the average high in July is 116°F. Ground temperatures hover near an egg-frying 200°F. A visit in winter lets visitors enjoy the splendor in comfort.

**▼ PRACTICAL INFORMATION.** There is no regularly scheduled public transportation into Death Valley. A few bus tours run out of Las Vegas: **Guaranteed Tours** offers excursions on Tu, Th, and Sa for $109; tours leave at 8am, return at 5:30pm, and include continental breakfast and lunch. (Depot at the Country Star Restaurant at the corner of Harmon Ave. and the Strip in Vegas.)

The best way to get around Death Valley is by car. Of the 9 **park entrances,** most visitors choose Rt. 190 from the east. The road is well-maintained, the pass is less steep, and you arrive more quickly at the visitors center. But the visitor with a trusty vehicle will be able to see more of the park by entering from the southeast (Rt. 178 west from Rt. 127 at Shoshone) or the north (direct to Scotty's Castle via NV Rt. 267 from U.S. 95). Unskilled mountain drivers should not attempt to enter via Titus Canyon or Emigrant Canyon Drive roads; neither has guard rails to prevent your car from sliding over **precipitous cliffs.** If you **hitchhike,** you walk through the Valley of the Shadow of Death. Don't.

CALIFORNIA

**Visitor Info: Furnace Creek Visitors Center** (786-3244), on Rt. 190 in the east-central section of the valley (open daily 8am-6pm); or write the **Superintendent**, Death Valley National Park, Death Valley 92328. **Ranger Stations** are located at **Grapevine** (786-2313), at the junction of Rt. 190 and 267 near Scotty's Castle; **Stovepipe Wells** (786-2342), on Rt. 190; and **Shoshone** (832-4308), outside the southeast border of the valley at the junction of Rt. 178 and 127. The weather report, weekly naturalist programs, and park info are posted at each station. (Open daily 8am-5pm.) The $5 per vehicle **entrance fee** is collected at the visitors center in the middle of the park. **Get gas** outside Death Valley at Olancha, Shoshone, or Beatty, NV. **Radiator water** (*not* for drinking) is available at critical points on Rt. 178 and 190 and NV Rt. 374, but not on unpaved roads. Those who *do* drive along the backcountry trails should carry chains, extra tires, gas, oil, radiator and drinking water, and spare parts. Groceries and supplies can be purchased at **Furnace Creek Ranch Store**, which is well-stocked but expensive (786-2381; open daily 7am-9pm). **Post Office:** Furnace Creek Ranch (786-2223). **ZIP code:** 92328. **Area code:** 760.

**⌂ ACCOMMODATIONS.** In Death Valley, enclosed beds and fine meals within a budget traveler's reach are as elusive as the desert bighorn sheep. During the winter months, camping out with a stock of groceries is a good way to save both money and driving time. **Furnace Creek Ranch Complex,** is deluged with tour-bus refugees who challenge the adjacent 18-hole golf course and relax in the 85°F spring-fed swimming pool. (786-2345, reservations 800-236-7916. Cabins with A/C and 2 beds $94, motel-style rooms $124.) **Stovepipe Wells Village** is right in Death Valley (786-2387; $58 per night for 1-2 people; each additional person $11; RV sites $15).

The National Park Service maintains 9 **campgrounds,** but only Texas Springs and Furnace Creek accept reservations. Call ahead to check availability and be prepared to battle for a space if you come during peak periods. Water availability is not completely reliable and supplies can be unsafe at times; always pack your own. Roadside camping is not permitted, but **backcountry camping** is free and legal, provided you check in at the visitors center and pitch tents at least 1mi. from main roads, 5mi. from any established campsite, and ¼mi. from any water source.

**◎♫ SIGHTS.** Death Valley has hiking to bemuse the gentlest wanderer and challenge the hardiest peregrinator. Backpackers and day hikers should inform the **visitors center** of their trip and take along the appropriate topographical maps. The National Park Service recommends that valley-floor hikers plan a route along roads where assistance is readily available and outfit a party of at least 2 people.

**Artist's Drive,** 10mi. south of the visitors center on Rt. 178, is a one-way loop that twists its way through rock formations of colors akin to those found in Crayola sets. About 5mi. south is **Devil's Golf Course,** a plane of sharp salt pinnacles made of the precipitate from the evaporation of Lake Manly, the 90mi. long lake that once filled the lower valley. **Badwater** lies 3mi. south of Devil's Golf Course, on I-90, a briny pool 4 times saltier than the ocean. The surrounding salt flat dips to the lowest point in the Western Hemisphere—282 ft. below sea level.

Immortalized by Antonioni's film of the same name, **Zabriskie Point** is a marvelous place from which to view Death Valley's corrugated badlands. Perhaps the most spectacular sight in the park is the vista at **Dante's View,** reached by a 13mi. paved road from Rt. 190. Just as the poet stood with Virgil looking down on the damned, so the modern observer gazes upon the vast inferno that is Death Valley.

# THE CENTRAL COAST

The 400mi. stretch of coastline between Los Angeles and San Francisco embodies all that is purely Californian—rolling surf crashing onto secluded beaches, dramatic cliffs and mountains, self-actualizing New Age adherents, and always a hint of the off-beat. The solitary magnificence of the Central Coast inspired Robinson Jeffers's paeans, John Steinbeck's novels, and Jack Kerouac's frivolous musings.

Among the smog-free skies, sweeping shorelines, dense forests, and plunging cliffs, inland farmland communities and old seafaring towns conjoin, beckoning citified residents to journey out to the quiet drama of the coast. The landmarks along the way are worth visiting—Hearst Castle, the Monterey Bay Aquarium, Carmel, the historic missions—but the point of the Central Coast is the journey itself.

# SANTA CRUZ

Santa Cruz is where the West Coast party doesn't stop. One of the few places where the 1960s catch-phrase "do your own thing" still applies, Santa Cruz simultaneously embraces macho surfers, a large lesbian, gay, and bisexual community, and shaggy rock star Neil Young, who lives somewhere in the surrounding hills. Along the beach and the Boardwalk, tourism and surf culture reign supreme. Along Pacific Ave., bookstores, clubs, and cafes provide mellow hangouts. On the other side of Front St., the University of California at Santa Cruz (UCSC) sprawls luxuriously with prime biking routes and hidden buildings.

## ◪ PRACTICAL INFORMATION

Santa Cruz is on the northern tip of Monterey Bay, 120mi. south of San Francisco on **U.S. 101** or the more scenic **Rt. 1**. In town, **Beach St.** runs roughly east-west. The narrow **San Lorenzo River** runs mainly north-south, dividing the Boardwalk scene from quiet, affluent residences. **Soquel Ave.** crosses the river.

**Greyhound:** 425 Front St. (423-1800). To: Los Angeles (8 per day; M-Th $36, F-Su $38); San Francisco (5 per day; M-Th $14, F-Su $15); and San Jose (M-Th 2 per day; $5). Open daily 8:30-11:30am and 1:30-9:30pm and during late arrivals and departures.

**Public Transportation: Santa Cruz Metropolitan Transit District (SCMTD),** 920 Pacific Ave. (info line open M-F 8am-5pm, 425-8600), at the Metro Center in the middle of the Pacific Garden Mall. The free *Headways* has route info. $1, seniors and disabled 40¢; day pass $3/$1.10; under 46in. free. Buses run daily 7am-10pm.

**Taxis: Yellow Cab** (423-1234). Open 24hr.

**Bike Rental: The Bicycle Rental Center,** 131 Center St. (426-8687). Rents 21-speed mountain/road hybrids, tandems, children's bikes. $7 for 1st hr., $2 each additional 30min.; $25 per day, $5 extra overnight. Helmets and locks provided. Open daily in summer 10am-6pm; off-season 10am-5pm.

**Visitor Information: Santa Cruz County Conference and Visitor Council,** 701 Front St. (425-1234 or 800-833-3494). Publishes the free *Santa Cruz County Traveler's Guide* with restaurant information. Open M-Sa 9am-5pm, Su 10am-4pm. **California Parks and Recreation Dept.,** 600 Ocean St. (429-2850), across from the Holiday Inn. Info on camping and beach facilities (800-444-7275 for reservations). Open M-F 8am-5pm.

**Post Office:** 850 Front St. (426-5200). Open M-F 8:30am-5pm, Sa 9am-4pm. **ZIP Code:** 95060. **Area Code:** 831.

## ▚ ACCOMMODATIONS

Santa Cruz is packed solid during the summer, especially on weekends; rates skyrocket and availability plummets. Reservations are recommended. Price fluctuation can be outrageous. Sleeping on the beach is strictly forbidden and fined.

**Carmelita Cottage Santa Cruz Hostel (HI-AYH),** 321 Main St. (423-8304), 4 blocks from the Greyhound stop and 2 blocks from the beach. 40-bed Victorian hostel in a quiet neighborhood. Sporadic summer barbecues ($4), 2 kitchens, common room, and cyclery for bike storage and repair. Chores required. Strict curfew 11pm. In July-Aug., 3-night max. stay and HI members only. Reception 8-10am and 5-10pm. Dorms $13-15. Call or send reservation requests, first night's deposit, and self-addressed stamped envelope to P.O. Box 1241, Santa Cruz 95061 at least 2 wks. in advance.

**Harbor Inn,** 645 7th Ave. (479-1067), near the harbor and a few blocks north of Eaton. A beautiful 22-bed hotel well off the main drag. Summer weekend rates usually lower than the budget motels in town. Rooms have queen beds, microwaves, and fridges. Check-in until 11pm; call to arrange late check-in. Check-out 11am. Rooms in summer Su-Th $75, F-Sa $95; off-season Su-Th $55, F-Sa $75. Reservations recommended.

Reservations for all state campgrounds can be made through DESTINET (800-444-7275) and should be made early. **New Brighton State Beach** and **Big Basin Redwoods State Park,** the most scenic spots, are both accessible by public transportation. Campground fees are not cheap (June-Sept. Su-Th $17, F-Sa $18; Oct.-May $16).

## ◖ FOOD

Santa Cruz offers an astounding number of budget eateries in various locations, especially by the beach in Capitola. Fresh local produce sells at the **farmer's market** at Lincoln and Cedar St. in downtown (W 2:30-6:30pm).

**Zoccoli's, the Italian Delicatessen,** 1534 Pacific Ave. (423-1711), across from the post office. This mobbed madhouse of a deli churns out incredible "special sandwiches" ($4-5). Daily pasta specials (about $5) come with salad, garlic bread, cheese, and a cookie. Only the freshest ingredients. Open M-Sa 9am-6pm, Su 11am-5pm.

**Saturn Cafe,** 1230 Mission St. (429-8505). Harried waitstaff and excellent cooks produce vegetarian meals (most under $6). Table decorations include "body manipulations" and the "ruined picnic" with plastic ants. Try the $3 Hangover, a slice of cold pizza with a beer, or a $6.75 Alien sandwich (tofu, hummus, avocado, and cheese). Open M-Th 11am-midnight, F 11am-1am, Sa 9am-1am, Su 9am-midnight.

**Royal Taj,** 270 Soquel Ave. (427-2400), at Roberts. You'll be crying *namaste* (I bow to you) after being treated like a king (with food to match) at this Indian restaurant. Daily lunch buffet $6.50. Meat dishes $6-9. Veggie specialties $6. Stellar *lassi* $2. Open daily 11:30am-2:30pm and 5:30-10pm.

**Taquería Vallarta I,** 608 Soquel Ave. (457-8226). Outstanding Mexican manna. Order at the counter, and the food might beat you back to your chair. Vegetarian plate $4; mind-blowing *aguas frescas* $1.20. Open daily 10am-midnight.

## ◖ SIGHTS

Santa Cruz has a great beach, but the water is cold without a wet-suit. Many casual beachgoers catch their thrills on the **Boardwalk.** This 3-block-long strip of amusement park rides, guess-your-weight booths, shooting galleries, and caramel apple vendors provides a loud and lively diversion—one that seems to attract every sun-drenched family, couple, and roving pack of teenagers in California. Highly recommended is the Big Dipper, a 1924 wooden tower roller coaster ($3), where Dirty Harry met his enemy in 1983's *Sudden Impact* (he finally impaled him on the merry-go-round's unicorn). *(Boardwalk open daily Memorial Day to Labor Day—plus some off-season weekends and holidays. Rides $1.50-3; all-day pass $19. Miniature golf $4, with all-day pass to boardwalk $3.)*

The **Misión de Exaltación de la Santa Cruz,** a peaceful, fragrant adobe church and garden, allows some contemplative quiet. *(126 High St. Turn north on Emmet off Mission St. Open Tu-Sa 10am-4pm, Su 10am-2pm. Donation requested.)* Along the **Santa Cruz Wharf,** jutting off Beach St., plenty of seafood restaurants and souvenir shops distract from the expansive views of the coast. *(Parking $1 per hr., under 30min. free.)*

## ◖ BEACHES AND ACTIVITIES

The **Santa Cruz Beach** (officially named Cowell Beach) is broad, reasonably clean, and packed with volleyball players. The chillier banks of the San Lorenzo River immediately east of the boardwalk are quieter. **Beach access** points line Rt. 1; rail-road tracks, farmlands, and dune vegetation make several of these access points somewhat difficult, but correspondingly less crowded.

Around the point at the end of W. Cliff Dr. is **Natural Bridges State Park.** While its lone natural bridge has collapsed, the park nevertheless offers a crowded beach, awe-inspiring tidepools, and tours during Monarch butterfly season (Oct.-Mar.). In Nov. and Dec. thousands of the stunning *lepidoptera* swarm along the beach. (423-4609. Open daily 8am-dusk. Parking $6, seniors $5.)

**Parasailing** and other pricey pastimes are popular on the wharf. **Kayak Connection,** 413 Lake Ave., has ocean-going kayaks at reasonable rates (479-1121; open-deck single $33 per day, closed-deck single $48 per day). You can try **rock climbing** on 13,000 square ft. of artificial climbing terrain at **Pacific Edge,** 104 Bronson St. Gym includes weight room, sauna, and showers. (454-9254. Open M 5am-10pm, Tu and Th 9am-10pm, W and F 11am-10pm, Sa-Su 10am-7pm. Day pass $14.)

## 🎵 ENTERTAINMENT AND NIGHTLIFE

Dodge the underage kids parked on the sidewalks of Pacific Ave. and cruise into the Santa Cruzian nightlife. The free weekly *Good Times* has thorough listings.

🏵 **Caffe Pergolesi,** 418A Cedar St. (426-1775). Look for "Dr. Miller's" sign. Chill coffeehouse/bar with a series of small rooms and a spacious patio for reading, writing, or socializing. Cheerful color scheme and intimate tables project a supremely friendly atmosphere. $2 pints daily 7-9pm; large coffee for the price of a small M-F 1-3pm. 6 varieties of hot chocolate! Open M-Th 7:30am-11:30pm, F-Sa 7:30am-midnight.

**Kuumbwa Jazz Center,** 320-322 Cedar St. (427-2227). Renowned for great jazz and innovative off-night programs. All ages welcome in this small and low-key setting. The big names play on M; the locals take their turn on F. Tickets (about $5) sold through Logos Books and Music, 1117 Pacific Ave. (427-5100; open daily 10am-10pm), as well as BASS outlets (998-2277). Most shows around 8pm.

**Blue Lagoon,** 923 Pacific Ave. (423-7117). Mega-popular gay-straight club has won all awards from "best bartender" to "best place you can't take your parents" from the local press. Bar in front, 3 pool tables in back, and people dancing everywhere. Cover Su-M and W $1; Th $3; F-Sa $4. Happy Hour with $2 drinks daily 6-9pm. Su margaritas $1. Stronger-than-the-bouncer drinks $3-4. Open daily 4pm-2am.

## MONTEREY

Monterey was sighted by the Spanish as early as 1542, but the native Ohlone tribe was left alone until 1770, when Father Serra targeted the area on his journey up the coast. A growing whaling industry kept Monterey alive until 1880, when sardine fishing and packaging stepped in to take its place. Scattered public buildings, adobe houses, and a resilient fishing community revere bygone days.

The 🏵 **Monterey Bay Aquarium,** 886 Cannery Row is the town's biggest attraction. This extraordinarily impressive aquarium feeds off community interest in marine ecology. The matter-of-fact environmental-impact awareness theme running throughout will open your eyes—don't miss a sobering 3min. "wasted catch" video on the upper level. The lines for tickets, admission, viewing, and food are unbelievable, but so are the exhibits themselves. Pick up tickets the day before and save 20 to 40min. (648-4888. Open daily mid-June to early Sept. and major holiday periods 9:30am-6pm; early Sept. to mid-June 10am-6pm. $16; students, seniors, and ages 13-17 $13; disabled and ages 3-12 $7.)

Lying along the waterfront south of the aquarium, **Cannery Row** was once a depressed street of languishing sardine-packing plants. The ¾mi. row has been converted into glitzy mini-malls, bars, and a pint-sized carnival complex. All that remains of the earthiness and gruff camaraderie celebrated by John Steinbeck in *Cannery Row* and *Sweet Thursday* are a few building facades: 835 Cannery Row was the Wing Chong Market; the bright yellow building next door is where *Sweet Thursday* took place. For a series of interpretive looks at Steinbeck's *Cannery Row*, take a peek at the **Great Cannery Row Mural;** local artists have covered 400 ft. of construction-site barrier on the 700 block with depictions of Monterey in the 1930s. The lavish **Wine and Produce Visitors Center,** 700 Cannery Row, offers tastes of the county's burgeoning wine industry, with well-priced bottles, fresh produce, and free winery maps. (888-646-5446. 3 tastings $2. Open daily 11am-6pm.)

Ship models, navigation tools, logs, a 14min. film, and other paraphernalia sketch the history of Monterey at the **Maritime Museum of Monterey,** at the base of the wharf in the Historic Customs House Plaza. (373-2469. Open daily 10am-5pm. $3; seniors, ages 12-19, military, and disabled $2; under 12 free.)

Reasonably priced hotels line **Lighthouse Ave.** in Pacific Grove (bus #2 and some #1 buses) and the 2000 block of **Fremont St.** in Monterey (bus #9 or 10). Others cluster along **Munras Ave.** between downtown and Rt. 1. The cheapest hotels in the area, however, are in the less-appealing towns of Seaside and Marina, just north of Monterey. Call the Monterey Parks line (755-4895 or 888-588-2267) for camping info and PARKNET (800-444-7275) for reservations. **Del Monte Beach Inn,** 1110 Del Monte Blvd., Monterey, is near downtown and across from the beach. Pleasant Victorian-style inn with TV room; hearty breakfast and tea served in a sunny room. (649-4410. Check-in 2-6pm. Hall phone only. Rooms with shared bath Su-Th $55-66, F-Sa from $77. Reservations recommended.)

The sardines have left, but Monterey Bay teems with squid, crab, red snapper, and salmon. Seafood is bountiful, but expensive—try an early-bird special (usually 4-6:30pm). **Fisherman's Wharf** has smoked salmon sandwiches ($6) and free chowder samples. Don't despair if you loathe seafood—this is also the land of artichokes and strawberries. The Monterey **farmer's market,** which takes over Alvarado St. Tu 4-8pm, has free fruit, cheese, and seafood samples (655-8070). The **Old Monterey Cafe,** 489 Alvarado St., has hot, hefty portions favored by locals (lunch specials $5.50-7.50; 646-1021; open daily 6:45am-2:30pm). **Thai Bistro II,** 159 Central Ave., Pacific Grove, has good service and a patio ringed with flowers. Lunch combos ($6) come with delicious soup. (372-8700. Open daily 11:30am-10pm.)

**Monterey-Salinas Transit (MST):** 1 Ryan Ranch Rd. (899-2555, phone lines open M-F 7:45am-5:15pm, Sa 10am-2:30pm). The free *Rider's Guide* has schedules and route info (available on buses, at motels, and at the visitors center). **Monterey Peninsula Visitor and Convention Bureau:** 380 Alvarado St. (649-1770). Open M-F 8:30am-5pm. **Post Office:** 565 Hartnell St. (372-5803). Open M-F 8:45am-5:10pm. **ZIP Code:** 93940. **Area Code:** 831.

# BIG SUR

Host to expensive campsites and even more expensive restaurants, Big Sur holds big appeal for big crowds eager to experience the power of the redwoods, the sound of the surf, and the rhythm of the river. There are really no signs to announce that you are in Big Sur, but you'll know you're there because it's the first time you'll see any signs of civilization for miles in either direction. Despite its isolation, Big Sur can be reached by public transit (see below). The drive from Carmel to Big Sur on **Rt. 1** is breathtaking, but everyone knows it; traffic eases in the early mornings.

Big Sur's state parks and **Los Padres National Forest** beckon outdoor activists of all types. Trails penetrate redwood forests and cross low chaparral, offering even grander views of Big Sur than those from Rt. 1. The northern end of the forest is designated the **Ventana Wilderness** and contains the popular **Pine Ridge Trail,** which runs 12mi., passing primitive campsites and the Sikes hot springs. Within **Pfeiffer Big Sur State Park** are 8 trails of varying lengths (75¢ map available at park entrance). The **Valley View Trail** is a short, steep trail offering a view of the valley below. **Buzzard's Roost Trail** is a rugged 2hr. hike up tortuous switchbacks, but at its peak are panoramic views of the mountains, the valley, and the ocean.

**Camping** in Big Sur is heavenly, but site prices and availability reflect high demand. Reserve in advance by calling PARKNET (800-444-7275). Camping is free in the Ventana Wilderness, a backpack-only site at the northern end of Los Padres National Forest (permits at Big Sur Station). Big Sur is the only place on the coast where sleeping in your car in highway turnouts is both free and legal. **Ventana Big Sur,** on Rt. 1, 30mi. south of Carmel, has 75 shady sites in a gorgeous redwood canyon with picnic tables, fire rings, and water faucets. (667-2688. Up to 2 people $25, leashed dogs $5. Day use $10. Reservations accepted at least 2 weeks in advance.) **Andrew Molera State Park,** on Rt. 1, 5mi. north of Pfeiffer Big Sur; a level ¾mi. trail leads to hike-in, tent-only sites. (3-night max. stay. $3; dogs $1.)

There are **grocery stores** at Big Sur Lodge (in Pfeiffer Big Sur State Park), Pacific Valley, and Gorda, and some packaged food is sold in Lucía and at Ragged Point, but it's better to arrive prepared because prices are high. **Fernwood Bar and Grill,** on Rt. 1, 2mi. north of post office offers chicken breasts, veggie burritos, and hamburgers. ($6.50. 667-2422. Open daily 10am-10pm; full bar open daily noon-midnight; grocery store open daily 8am-10pm.) The **Village Pub,** in the Village Shops, serves up fresh, hearty food to raucous locals. Speak up or you'll never get a seat. (667-2355. Open daily 11am-10pm.)

**Post Office:** 667-2305, on Rt. 1 next to the Center Deli in Big Sur Center. Open M-F 8:30am-5pm. **ZIP Code:** 93920. **Area Code:** 831.

## SAN LUIS OBISPO

This area grew into a full-fledged town only after the Southern Pacific Railroad laid tracks here in 1894. Ranchers and oil-refinery employees make up a significant percentage of the population, but Cal Poly State University students add a young, energetic, wheatgrass-and-bee-pollen component.

Rates in San Luis Obispo tend to "depend"—on the weather, the season, the number of travelers that day, or even on the position of the waxing and waning moon. The **Sunbeam Hotel,** 1656 Monterey St., looks like an apartment complex; rooms are as sunny as the staff. (543-8141. Cable TV, A/C, fridges, phones, coffeemakers. Singles $33-36; doubles $38-45.) **San Luis Obispo (HI-AYH),** 1617 Santa Rosa St., serves fresh bagels daily in a cozy kitchen. (544-4678. Lockout 10am-5pm. Reception 7:30-10:30am and 5-10pm. Linen $1, towels 50¢. Parking available. No credit cards. Dorms $14; private rooms $32. $2 more for non-members.) **Morro Bay State Park,** 12mi. west of SLO on Rt. 1., has a popular campground between the ocean and forest with 135 developed sites, 20 with hookups. ($18, in winter $14; hookup $24/$20. Reserve year-round.) All state park sites can be reserved through PARKNET (800-444-7275) up to 7 months in advance.

**Monterey St.** and its cross streets are lined with restaurants and cafes. The area just south of the mission along the creek is popular with lunchtime crowds. **Big Sky Cafe,** 1121 Broad St., was voted "Best Restaurant in SLO" by the local poll magazine, delivering hearty, vegetarian-friendly food (545-5401; open M-Sa 7am-10pm, Su 8am-8pm). **Tio Alberto's,** 1131 Broad St., has the best burritos between L.A. and San Francisco. ($3.50-5.50, combo plates $5. 546-9646. Open Su-Th 9am-11pm, F-Sa 9am-3am. No credit cards.) One half of SLO's population is under the age of 24, so the town can't help but party. It gets particularly wild after the Th evening **farmer's market** along Higuera St. between Nipomo and Osos St., which is more of a raging block party than a produce market. Weekdays slow down a bit while the students rescue their grades. The free weekly *New Times* lists local happenings.

San Luis Obispo grew around the **Mission San Luis Obispo de Tolosa** and the city continues to engage in celebrations and general lunchtime socializing around its front steps. (543-6850. Open daily early Apr. to late Oct. 9am-5pm; late Oct. to early Apr. 9am-4pm. $1 donation requested.) The mission faces Mission Plaza, where Father Serra held the area's first mass. The Plaza now houses the **SLO Historical Museum,** with a display of Chumash pottery and over 17,000 historical photos (543-0638. Open Sept.-May W-Su 10am-4pm, June-Aug. Sa-Su 10am-4pm. $2 donation requested.) **San Luis Little Theater,** 888 Morro St., has performances by local thespians (786-2440; Th-Sa 8pm, Su 2pm; tickets $14, students and seniors $12, Th $10). The **SLO Children's Museum,** 1010 Nipomo St., has a "creative learning station featuring communicable diseases." (544-5437. Open M-Tu and Th-Sa 10am-5pm, Su 1-5pm. Limited winter hrs. $4, under 2 free.)

The **Palm Theater,** 817 Palm St., screens artsy and revival films (541-5161; tickets $6, seniors and children $3.75, M $3). The visitors center may try to deny its existence, but **Bubble Gum Alley,** 735 Higuera St., is a crazy, squishy fact.

The **visitors center** for the **Chamber of Commerce,** 1039 Chorro St. (781-2777; open M-W 8am-5pm, Th-F 8am-8pm, Sa 10am-8pm). **State Parks Office,** 3220 S. Higuera St. #311 (549-3312). Open M-F 8am-5pm. **Amtrak,** 1011 Railroad Ave. (541-0505), is at the foot of Santa Rosa Ave., 7 blocks south of Higuera St. Open daily 6am-8:30pm. **Greyhound,** 150 South St. (543-2121), ½mi. from downtown, is open daily 7am-9:30pm. **Post Office:** 893 Marsh St. (543-3062). Open M-F 8:30am-5:30pm, Sa 10am-5pm. **ZIP Code:** 93405. **Area Code:** 805.

**NEAR SAN LUIS OBISPO: HEARST CASTLE.** Driving along this stretch of Rt. 1, the last thing you would expect to see is a castle that would put Disney to shame, but like everything else in this state, nothing obeys the rules of common sense. Newspaper tycoon William Randolph Hearst built this palatial abode and invited wealthy elite to visit the most extravagant edifice this side of the Taj Mahal. Casually referred to by its founder as "the ranch," Hearst Castle (as tourists and locals refer to it) is a decadent conglomeration of castle, cottages, pools, gardens, and Mediterranean *esprit* perched high above the Pacific. It stands as a testament to Hearst's unfathomable wealth and Julia Morgan's architectural genius. Tours are run by the State Parks Department and are a strictly hands-off experience; fondle the banisters because they are the only things you may touch in the castle. **Tour One** covers the photogenic Neptune Pool, the opulent Casa del Sol guest house, fragrant gardens, and the main rooms of the house; this is the best bet for first-time visitors. **Tours Two, Three,** and **Four** cover the living quarters and gardens in greater depth—these tours are recommended for those already familiar with Tour One. Call weeks in advance as tours often sell out, particularly in summer. (*On Rt. 1, 3mi. north of San Simeon and 9mi. north of Cambria. Info: 927-2020. Reservations: DESTINET 800-444-4445; international reservations 619-452-8787; wheelchair accessible reservations 805-927-2020. 4 daytime tours; 1¾hr.; $14, ages 6-12 $8, under 6 free. Evening tours feature costumed docents acting out the Castle's legendary Hollywood history in new outdoor lighting; 2hr.; $25, ages 6-12 $13. Each of the tours involves 150-370 stairs.*)

# SANTA BARBARA

When Padre Junípero Serra arrived here with his proselytizing band of soldiers and priests, he unknowingly infected the Chumash Indians with a deadly bacteria, and built the town over their ashes. These days the living is good: Santa Barbara is an enclave of wealth and privilege, true to its soap opera image, but in a significantly less aggressive way than its Southern Californian counterparts. Spanish Revival architecture decorates the residential hills that rise gently over a lively pedestrian district centered on State St. Santa Barbara's golden beaches, museums, historic mission, and scenic drive makes it a frequent weekend escape.

## ◪ PRACTICAL INFORMATION

**Transportation: Airport: Signature Flight Support,** 515 Marxmiller Rd. in Goleta (967-5608). Signature is one of many private companies that use the runways. Offers intrastate and limited national service; contact American, AmericaWest, and United directly (p. 74).

**Trains: Amtrak,** 209 State St. (963-1015). Be careful around the station after dark. To: L.A. ($16-21) and San Francisco ($46-73). Reserve in advance. Open daily 6:30am-9pm. Tickets sold until 8pm.

**Buses: Greyhound,** 34 W. Carrillo St. (962-2477), at Chapala St. To: Los Angeles ($13) and San Francisco ($30). Open M-Sa 5:30am-8pm and 11pm-midnight, Su 7am-8pm and 11pm-midnight. **Green Tortoise** (415-956-7500 or 800-227-4766), the "hostel on wheels," picks up from Banana Bungalow Hostel (see **Banana Bungalow Hostel,** p. 798). To: L.A. (Sa 5:30am; $10) and San Francisco (Su 11:45pm; $35). Arrive 15min. before departure time. Storage lockers for ticketed passengers only.

**Public Transportation: Santa Barbara Metropolitan Transit District (MTD),** 1029 Chapala St. (683-3702), at Cabrillo Blvd. behind Greyhound station. Bus schedules available at this transit center, which serves as the transfer point for most routes (open M-F 6am-7pm, Sa 8am-6pm, Su 9am-6pm). All buses wheelchair accessible. $1, seniors and disabled 50¢, under 5 free; transfers free. The MTD runs a **downtown-waterfront shuttle** along State St. and Cabrillo Blvd. every 10min. Su-Th 10:15am-6pm, F-Sa 10:15am-8pm. Stops designated by circular blue signs. 25¢.

**Bike Rental: Cycles-4-Rent,** 101 State St. (966-3804), 1 block from the beach. 1-speed cruiser $5 per hr., $21 per day; 21-speed $7/28. Two other locations on the beach (with slightly higher prices) at 633 E. Cabrillo Blvd. and in the Radisson Hotel. All locations open M-F 9am-6pm, Sa-Su 8am-7:30pm.

**Visitor Information: Tourist Office,** 1 Garden St. (965-3021), at Cabrillo Blvd. near the beach. Open July-Aug. M-Sa 9am-6pm, Su 10am-6pm; Sept.-Nov. and Feb.-June M-Sa 9am-5pm, Su 10am-5pm; Dec.-Jan. M-Sa 9am-4pm, Su 10am-4pm. Outdoor computer kiosks open 24hr. **Hotspots,** 36 State St. (963-4233 or 564-1637 for reservations), is an espresso bar with free tourist info and hotel reservation service. Cafe open daily 24hr.; tourist info M-Sa 9am-9pm, Su 8am-4pm.

**Post Office:** 836 Anacapa St. (564-2266), 1 block east of State St. Open M-F 8am-5:30pm, Sa 10am-5pm. **ZIP Code:** 93102. **Area Code:** 805

# ✦ ORIENTATION

Santa Barbara is 96mi. northwest of Los Angeles and 27mi. past Ventura on the **Ventura Freeway** (U.S. 101). Built along an east-west traverse of shoreline, the street grid is slightly skewed. The beach lies at the south end of the city, and **State St.,** the main drag, runs northwest from the waterfront. All streets are designated east and west from State St. The major east-west arteries are U.S. 101 and **Cabrillo Blvd.**

Driving in Santa Barbara can be bewildering; dead-ends and 1-way streets abound. Many downtown lots and streets offer 90min. of free **parking,** including 2 subterranean lots at Pasco Nuevo, accessible from the 700 block of Chapala St. Parking is free on Su. Most streets are equipped with **bike lanes.** The **Cabrillo Bikeway** runs east-west along the beach from the Bird Refuge to the City College campus. MTD buses run throughout the city (see **Practical Information,** above).

# ▮ ACCOMMODATIONS

A 10min. drive north or south on U.S. 101 rewards with cheaper lodgings than those found in Santa Barbara proper. Trusty **Motel 6** is always an option. In fact, Santa Barbara is where this glorious chain of budget-friendly motels originated. There are 2 locations: at the beach at 443 Corona del Mar Dr. (564-1392), and past the main drag at 3505 State St. (687-5400). Prices start at $45 in winter, $55 in summer. All Santa Barbara accommodations are more expensive on the weekends.

▨ **Hotel State St.,** 121 State St. (966-6586; fax 962-8459), on the main strip 1 block from the beach. A budget night's sleep without the nightmares of cheap travel. Welcoming, comfortable and run by a self-proclaimed clean freak. Pristine common bathrooms. Private rooms have sinks and cable TV; a few have skylights. Continental breakfast included. Limited free parking. One double bed $40; 2 single beds $45; 2 double beds $55; $15-25 higher July-Aug. Reservations recommended.

**Traveler's Motel,** 3222 State St. (687-6009; fax 687-0419). Take bus #6 or 11 from downtown. Although it's a bit far from the action, this motel is clean and spacious and has the gosh-darn prettiest rooms on State St., all with cable TV, direct-dial phones, A/C, and fridges. Singles June-Sept. $50, Oct.-May $35; palatial rooms with kitchenettes $55, Oct.-May $40; each additional person (up to 4) $5. Prices higher on weekends.

**Banana Bungalow Santa Barbara,** 210 E. Ortega St. (963-0154), just off State St., in a busy area. Party-oriented hostel with lived-in feel and tropical motif. Young, international crowd. Kitchen, TV room, pool table, video games. Equipment rentals. Laundry, coin lockers. Free parking. Co-ed and women-only dorms $15-20; thatched-roof bunks $18. No reservations; show up around 10:30am. **Passport or student I.D. required.**

State campsites can be reserved through ReservAMERICA (800-444-7275), up to 7 months in advance. There are 3 state beaches within 30mi. of Santa Barbara; all are perched between the railroad tracks and U.S. 101, but none are served by public transportation. **Carpinteria Beach State Park,** 12mi. southeast of Santa Barbara along U.S. 101, has 261 developed sites with hot showers. (684-2811. $18, with hookup $22-28; weekends: $18, $23-29; off-season: $15, $20-26.) Further on, **El Capitán** has 140 well-kept sites, some with views of the Channel Islands. **Refugio** has 84 crowded sites just steps from the beach. (Both: 968-1033. $15-17, weekends $18; off-season $15; seniors $2 discount.) If all of these are full, the El Capitán **private campground** has a pool, although sites are dusty and closely packed (685-3887; sites $20, with hookup $25; each additional vehicle $5).

## ◘ FOOD

State and Milpas St. both have many places to eat; State St. is hipper, Milpas St. cheaper. There's an open-air **farmer's market** packed with bargains on the 400 block of State St. (Tu 4-7:30pm), and another on Santa Barbara at Cota St. (Sa 8:30am-12:30pm). **Tri-County Produce,** 335 S. Milpas St., sells fresh produce and prepared foods (965-4558; open M-Sa 9am-7:30pm, Su 9am-6pm).

**Pacific Crepes,** 705 Anacapa St. (882-1123). Cozy French cafe filled with the delicious smells of crepe creations. The make-your-own plate starts with an empty crepe for just $2, edible for as little as $4. The heavenly "Normandy," topped with fresh strawberries and blueberries, makes a perfect breakfast or dessert ($5.50). Sandwiches $5. Open Su-Tu 9am-4pm, W-F 9am-9pm, Sa 8am-10pm.

**The Sojourner Cafe,** 134 E. Canon Perdido St. (965-7922). Friendly, low-key tea-candle atmosphere provides organic Mexican food. Original dishes include "Chile Tempeh Tacos" ($7) and "Cornbread Supreme" ($6), which has more veggies than your mother's fridge. Daily *Plato Barato* lunch special $5.50. Open M-Sa 11am-11pm, Su 11am-10pm.

**Cafe Orleans** (899-9111), Center Court, Paseo Nuevo Mall at 800 block of State St. Naw'lins food in a jiffy for all y'all. Jambalaya, *etouffeés*, and po' boys ($5-6.50). Live zydeco F 6-8:30pm. Open M-Th 11am-9pm, F-Sa 11am-10pm, Su 11am-8pm.

**R.G.'s Giant Hamburgers,** 922 State St. (963-1654). This yellow Formica joint was voted best burgers in S.B. Basic burger, garden burger, chicken burger, or turkey burger ($3). Call 10min. ahead, and it'll be waiting when you arrive. Or wait it out playing table-top Arkanoid. Giant french toast is only $2.50. Open daily 9am-10pm.

## ◉ SIGHTS

Santa Barbara is best explored in 3 sections—the beach and coast, swingin' State St., and the Missionary Mountains. *Santa Barbara's Red Tile Tour,* a map and walking tour guide, is free at the visitors center. Recently revamped, the coastal drive Cabrillo Blvd. serves as the first leg of the city's **scenic drive.** Follow the green signs as they lead you in a loop into the mountains and around the city. The delightfully leafy habitats of the **Santa Barbara Zoo** have low fences and such an open feel that the animals seem kept in captivity only through sheer lethargy. A miniature train provides a park tour. *(500 Niños Dr., off Cabrillo Blvd. from U.S. 101. Take bus #14 or the downtown-waterfront shuttle. 962-5339. Open daily 10am-5pm. $7, seniors and ages 2-12 $5, under 2 free. Parking included. Tous every 15min. $1.50, children $1.)*

The Santa Barbara beaches are unmistakably breathtaking, lined on one side by skyrocketing palm trees and backgrounded by sailboats in the local harbor. **East** and **Leadbetter Beaches** flank the wharf on either side. **Beach Rentals** rents retro surreys—covered-carriage, Flintstone-esque **bicycles** that carry up to 8 people. *(22 State St. 966-2282. $12-32 per hr., depending on number of riders.)* Across the street from the visitors center, the idyllic **Chase Palm Park** is a beautiful public parkland complete with a vintage 1916 Spillman carousel. *($1.50 per ride.)* For the best **sunset** view in the area, have a drink (soda $2) at the bar at the Four Seasons Biltmore

Hotel. This 5-star lodging is just a l'il bit steep for the budget traveler, but the view of the Pacific is priceless. *(1260 Channel Dr. 969-2261. Montecito.)*

Santa Barbara's monument to city planning, **State St.,** runs a straight tree-lined 2mi. in the center of the city. Shops, restaurants, and cultural and historical landmarks are slathered in Spanish tile. The **Santa Barbara Museum of Art** owns an impressive collection of classical Greek, Asian, and European works spanning 3000 years, most donated by wealthy residents. The 20th-century and Hindu collections are among its most impressive. *(1130 State St. 963-4364. Open Tu-Th and Sa 11am-5pm, F 11am-9pm, Su noon-5pm. Tours Tu-Su noon and 1pm. Admission $5, students and ages 6-16 $2, seniors $3. Free on Th and 1st Su of each month.)*

**Mission Santa Barbara** was praised as the "Queen of Missions" when built in 1786; the mission assumed its present incarnation in 1820. The colorful museum contains period rooms and a sampling of items from the mission archives. Visitors are welcome to (respectfully) drop in on mass. *(At the end of Las Olivas St. Take bus #22. 682-4719. Open daily 9am-5pm. $3, under 12 free. Self-guided museum tour starts at the gift shop. Mass M-F 7:30am, Sa 4pm, Su 7:30am-noon.)*

The **Santa Barbara Botanical Garden,** though quite some distance from town, offers enjoyable hikes. *(212 Mission Canyon Rd. 682-4726. Open Mar.-Oct. M-F 9am-5pm, Sa-Su 9am-6pm; Nov.-Feb. M-F 9am-4pm, Sa-Su 9am-5pm. Tours M-W and F at 2pm, Th and Sa-Su at 10:30am and 2pm. $5; students, seniors, and ages 13-19 $3; ages 5-12 $1.)* Other hikes include **Seven Falls Trail,** at the junction of Tunnel and Spyglass Rd. From the end of Las Canoas Rd. off Tunnel Rd., you can pick up the 3½mi. **Rattlesnake Canyon Trail,** with many waterfalls, pools, and secluded spots. The 7¼mi. trek from the **Cold Springs Trail** to **Montecito Peak** is considerably more strenuous. *(From U.S. 101 South, take a left at the Hot Springs Rd. exit, and another left on Mountain Dr. to the creek crossing.)* The Botanical Garden gift shop has **trail maps,** which list other trails.

## ♫ ENTERTAINMENT AND NIGHTLIFE

Every night of the week, the clubs on **State St.** are packed. This town is full of locals and tourists who love to eat, drink, and be mirthful. The free *Independent* has listings. The **Arlington Center for Performing Arts,** 1317 State St., a combination performance space and movie theater, comfortably seats 2,018 people in a theater space resembling a Mexican village. (963-4408. Movie tickets $7.75, seniors and ages 2-12 $5; 1pm matinee and twilight show at 3:30 or 4pm $5.)

**The Hourglass,** 213 W. Cota St. (963-1436). Rents 9 private hot tubs by the hour. Pick a sensual indoor bath or watch the stars from a private outdoor tub. Locals report that "this is what we do in Santa Barbara." No alcohol allowed. Towels $1. 2 people $20 per hr.; each additional person $7. 1hr. min. Open daily noon-midnight.

**Fathom,** 423 State St. (730-0022). Gay dance club (all are welcome); the closest it gets to wild in Santa Barbara. The best music in town. Pool tables, lots of drink specials. Tu swing night, W 80s extravaganza; Su Beer Bust 4-8pm $5. Martini Happy Hour daily 5-8pm (drinks $2). Open nightly 5pm-2am. Cover F-Sa $5, after 11:30pm $7. 21+.

**Madhouse,** 434 State St. (962-5516). Decadent faux-dive for the jet set. Sinatra, mambo, and Afro-Cuban music. A melange of retro and funk. Live music and drink specials nightly (5-8pm). No cover. Open W-Sa 5pm-2am, Su-Tu 7pm-2am. 21+.

# SAN FRANCISCO BAY AREA

## SAN FRANCISCO

By California standards, San Francisco is steeped in history, but it's a history of oddballs and eccentrics that resonates more loudly—in street culture rather than in museums and galleries. Deeply rooted in America's great westward expansion, San Francisco has always attracted artists, dreamers, and outsiders. Most famous

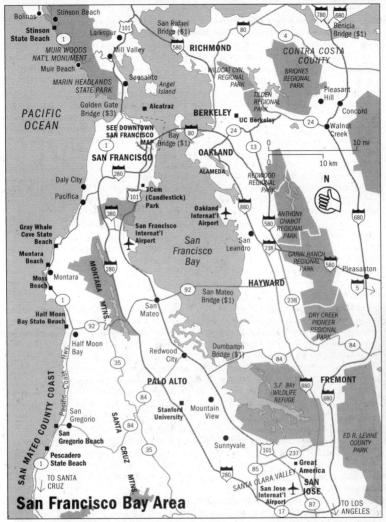

**San Francisco Bay Area**

are the hippies and flower children of the late 1960s, who turned on one generation and freaked out another in Haight-Ashbury's "Summer of Love." Before them were the Beats—angry young writers who captured the rhythms of be-bop jazz in their poetry and their lives. The lineage of free spirits and troublemakers runs back to the smugglers and pirates of the Barbary Coast, and to the '49ers who flocked here during the mad boom of the California Gold Rush.

The tradition continues. Anti-establishment politics have almost become establishment here. The gay community, one-sixth of the city's population, emerged in the 70s as one of the city's most visible and powerful groups. At the same time, Central American and Asian immigrants have made San Francisco one of the most racially diverse cities in the United States. Not to be outdone, many young computer workers have ditched Silicon Valley for the cooler breezes of San Francisco, with Internet upstart companies infiltrating the forgotten spaces of lower-rent neighborhoods. San Francisco is ever-changing with the times, but some things remain constant: the Bay is foggy (making temperatures significantly cool), the hills are steep and narrow, and Rice-A-Roni abounds.

# ✷ ORIENTATION

San Francisco is 403mi. north of Los Angeles and 390mi. south of Oregon. The city lies at the northern tip of the peninsula separating San Francisco Bay from the Pacific Ocean. Driving from L.A. takes 6hr. on I-5, 8hr. on U.S. 101, or 9½hr. via Hwy. 1, the legendary Pacific Coast Hwy. U.S. 101 compromises between vistas and velocity, but the stunning coastal scenery along Hwy. 1 makes getting there fun. From the south, the city can be reached from **U.S. 101, I-280,** and **Hwy. 1.** From inland California, **I-5** approaches the city from the north and south via **I-580** and **I-80,** which runs across the **Bay Bridge** (westbound toll $2). From the north, U.S. 101 and Hwy. 1 come over the **Golden Gate Bridge** (southbound toll $3).

San Francisco radiates outward from its docks, which lie on the northeast edge of the 30mi. long peninsula, just inside the lip of the bay. Many of the city's most visitor-friendly attractions are found within a wedge formed by **Van Ness Ave.,** running north-south; the **Embarcadero** curving along the coast; and **Market St.,** running northeast-southwest and interrupting the regular grid of streets.

At the top of this wedge lies touristy **Fisherman's Wharf.** From here, ferries service **Alcatraz Island,** the nigh-inescapable former prison. **Columbus Ave.** extends southeast from the docks to **North Beach,** a district shared by Italian-Americans, artists, and professional-types. **Telegraph Hill,** which is topped by Coit Tower, emerges as the focal point of North Beach amid a terrific mass of eateries. To the west of Columbus Ave. are residential **Russian Hill** and **Nob Hill.** South of North Beach, the largest **Chinatown** in North America covers 24 sq. blocks between Broadway in the north, Bush St. in the south, and Kearny St. in the east. On the other side of the Bush St. gateway of Chinatown lies the heavily developed **Financial District,** where skyscrapers fill the blocks above the northeast portion of Market St. To the west, the core downtown area centered on **Union Sq.** gives way to the well-pounded **Tenderloin,** where, despite attempts at urban renewal, drugs, crime, and homelessness prevail. The area is roughly bounded by Larkin St. to the west, Taylor St. to the east, and Post St. to the north, and bleeds down Market St. for a few blocks. The **Civic Center** occupies the acute angle formed by Market St. and Van Ness Ave. at the southern point of the wedge. City Hall, the Civic Center Public Library, and Symphony Hall crown a collection of municipal buildings.

South of the wedge, directly below Market St., lies the **South-of-Market-Area (SoMa).** Here, the best of San Francisco's nightclubs are scattered among office buildings and warehouses. SoMa extends inland from the bay to 10th St., at which point the largely Latino and very trendy **Mission District** begins and spreads south. The **Castro,** center of the gay community, abuts the Mission District on its west side, roughly along Church St. From the landmark **Castro Theater** on the corner of Castro and Market St., the neighborhood stretches to the less flamboyant **Noe Valley** in the south and the undeveloped oasis of the **Twin Peaks** in the southeast.

Some interesting strips are sprinkled among the residential neighborhoods west of Van Ness Ave. The posh stucco of the **Marina** and Victorians of **Pacific Heights** run south to funkier **Fillmore St.,** which leads to the few *udon*-filled blocks of **Japantown.** Vast **Golden Gate Park** and its neighboring **Sunset District** to the south dominate the western half of the peninsula. At the park's eastern end sits the former hippie haven of **Haight-Ashbury** to the southeast. The park is bounded by Lincoln St. and the Sunset District to the south, and by Fulton St. and the residential **Richmond District** to the north, stretching out to Ocean Beach along the Pacific. The **Presidio,** at the northwestern corner, culminates in the **Golden Gate Bridge.**

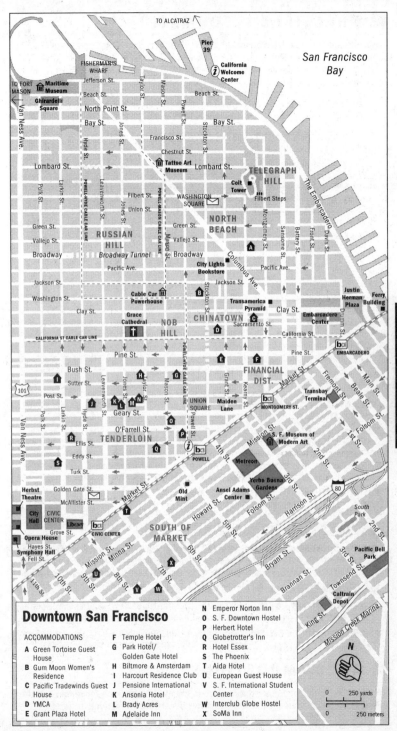

TO ALCATRAZ

Pier 39

San Francisco Bay

FISHERMAN'S WHARF
California Welcome Center

TO FORT MASON
Maritime Museum

Ghirardelli Square

Jefferson St.
Beach St.
North Point St.
Bay St.
Francisco St.
Chestnut St.
Lombard St.

Van Ness Ave.

Beach St.
Bay St.

Taylor St.
Mason St.
Powell St.
Stockton St.

Tattoo Art Museum
Lombard St.

TELEGRAPH HILL

Coit Tower

WASHINGTON SQUARE
Filbert Steps

Filbert St.
Union St.

NORTH BEACH

Green St.
Vallejo St.
Broadway

RUSSIAN HILL
Broadway Tunnel

Green St.
Vallejo St.
Broadway

Columbus Ave.

City Lights Bookstore

Pacific Ave.
Jackson St.
Washington St.

Montgomery St.
Sansome St.
Battery St.
Front St.
Davis St.

The Embarcadero

Clay St.

Cable Car Powerhouse

Jackson St.

CHINATOWN

Transamerica Pyramid

Justin Herman Plaza

Ferry Building

Grace Cathedral

NOB HILL

Clay St.

Embarcadero Center

Sacramento St.
California St.

CALIFORNIA ST CABLE CAR LINE

Pine St.

FINANCIAL DIST.

Pine St.

EMBARCADERO

Bush St.
Sutter St.
Post St.

UNION SQUARE

Maiden Lane

Grant St.
Kearny St.
Market St.

Transbay Terminal

Fremont St.
Beale St.
Main St.
1st St.
Folsom St.

Geary St.

MONTGOMERY ST.

O'Farrell St.
Ellis St.
Eddy St.
Turk St.

TENDERLOIN

POWELL

Mission St.

S. F. Museum of Modern Art

Herbst Theatre
City Hall
CIVIC CENTER
Library

Golden Gate St.
McAllister St.
Grove St.

CIVIC CENTER

Old Mint

Metreon

Ansel Adams Center

Yerba Buena Gardens

2nd St.
3rd St.

South Park

Opera House
Hayes St.
Symphony Hall
Fell St.

Howard St.

SOUTH OF MARKET

Harrison St.

Pacific Bell Park

Mission St.
Minna St.

4th St.
5th St.
6th St.
7th St.

Bryant St.
Brannan St.

11th St.
10th St.
9th St.
8th St.

SoMa Inn

Townsend St.

Caltrain Depot

King St.

Mission Creek Marina

N

0   250 yards
0   250 meters

## Downtown San Francisco

### ACCOMMODATIONS

A  Green Tortoise Guest House
B  Gum Moon Women's Residence
C  Pacific Tradewinds Guest House
D  YMCA
E  Grant Plaza Hotel
F  Temple Hotel
G  Park Hotel/ Golden Gate Hotel
H  Biltmore & Amsterdam
I  Harcourt Residence Club
J  Pensione International
K  Ansonia Hotel
L  Brady Acres
M  Adelaide Inn
N  Emperor Norton Inn
O  S. F. Downtown Hostel
P  Herbert Hotel
Q  Globetrotter's Inn
R  Hotel Essex
S  The Phoenix
T  Aida Hotel
U  European Guest House
V  S. F. International Student Center
W  Interclub Globe Hostel
X  SoMa Inn

CALIFORNIA

# ▐ PRACTICAL INFORMATION

**Airport: San Francisco International** (650-761-0800) is located on a small peninsula in San Francisco Bay 15mi. south of downtown via U.S. 101. Shuttle schedules (800-736-2008). **San Mateo County Transit (SamTrans)** (800-660-4287) runs 2 buses to downtown. Express bus #7F takes 35min. to reach downtown and allows only whatever luggage can be held in your lap (runs 5:30am-12:50am; fare $2.50, seniors $1.25, under 18 $1). Bus #7B takes 1hr. to reach downtown, stops frequently, and allows all luggage (runs 5am-12:30am; fare $2, seniors 50¢, under 18 $1).

**Trains: Amtrak,** 425 Mission St. (495-1575), in the Transbay Terminal, between Fremont and 1st St. downtown. To Los Angeles ($42). Free shuttles to the 3 Amtrak stations in the city. Office open daily 6:45am-10:45pm. **CalTrain** (800-660-4287) runs to Palo Alto ($3.75, seniors and under 12 $1.75); San Jose ($5/$2.50); and Santa Cruz.

**Buses: Golden Gate Transit** (Marin County), **AC Transit** (East Bay), and **SamTrans** (San Mateo County) all stop at the **Transbay Terminal,** 425 Mission St. (495-1575), between Fremont and 1st St. downtown. **Greyhound** runs buses from the terminal to Los Angeles ($36) and Portland ($51).

**Public Transit: Note: Parking is difficult and expensive.**

**San Francisco Municipal Railway (MUNI)** (415-673-6864). System of buses, cable cars, subways, and streetcars. Fare $1, seniors and ages 5-17 35¢. Cheapest and most efficient way to get around the city. Excellent MUNI maps ($2.75) cover all regional bus and subway services. **MUNI passports** are valid on all MUNI vehicles (1 day $6, 3 days $10, 7 days $15). Weekly Pass ($9) is for a single work week and requires an additional $1 to ride the cable cars. The Monthly FastPass ($35) includes in-town BART trips and cable cars. Free transfers (valid for 1½hr.). A core of all-night "Owl Service" routes, but coverage decreases considerably after dark. Wheelchair access varies among routes. All below-ground subway stations, but not all above-ground sites, are accessible. Runs daily 6am-12:45am.

**Cable cars:** Noisy, slow, and usually crammed full, but charming relics. To avoid mobs, ride in the early morning. The **Powell-Mason (PM)** line, which runs to the wharf, is the most popular. The **California (C)** line, from the Financial District up through Nob Hill, is usually the least crowded, but the **Powell-Hyde (PH)** line, with the steepest hills and the sharpest turns, may be the most fun. All lines run daily 6am-12:45am. Fare $2, seniors and disabled $1 before 7am and after 9pm. No transfers.

**Bay Area Rapid Transit (BART)** (650-992-2278). BART operates modern, carpeted trains along 4 lines connecting San Francisco with the **East Bay,** including **Oakland, Berkeley, Concord,** and **Fremont.** All stations provide free maps and schedules. There are eight BART stops in San Francisco proper, but BART is not a local transportation system. Wheelchair access. Runs M-F 4am-midnight, Sa 6am-midnight, Su 8am-midnight. Fare $1.10-$6.)

**Car Rental: Enterprise,** 6770 Mission St. (in S.F. 800-736-8222, outside S.F. 800-325-8007). Must be 21+; under 25 surcharge $10 per day. From $36 per day, $170 per week. Unlimited mileage in CA. Sa-Su specials. Open M-F 7:30am-6pm, Sa 9am-noon.

**Taxis: Yellow Cab** (626-2345). **Luxor Cab** (282-4141) 24hr.

**Visitor Info: Visitor Information Center** (391-2000; 24hr. info recordings in English 391-2001 and Spanish 391-2122), in Hallidie Plaza at Powell St. beneath street level at the BART exit. MUNI passports and maps for sale. Open M-F 9am-5pm, Sa-Su 9am-3pm.

**Hotlines: Rape Crisis Center,** 647-7273. **United Helpline,** 772-4357.

**Internet Access: Civic Center Public Library** (552-4400), at Grove and Larkin. Open M 10am-6pm, Tu-Th 9am-8pm, F 11am-5pm, Sa 9am-5pm, Su noon-5pm.

**Post Office:** 101 Hyde St. (800-275-8777), at Golden Gate. Open M, W, and F 6am-5:30pm, Tu and Th 6am-8:30pm, Sa 6am-3pm. **ZIP code:** 94142. **Area code:** 415.

# ▐ ACCOMMODATIONS

Many budget-range accommodations are in unsavory areas; the **Tenderloin** and the **Mission** can be particularly unsafe. Reservations are recommended at hotels.

**San Francisco International Guest House,** 2976 23rd St. (641-1411), at Harrison in the Mission. TV area, 2 kitchens (smoking and non), and guest phones. Neighborhood parking. Dorms $14, after 28 days $11; private double $28. 5-night min. stay, 3-month max. Passport with international stamps required.

**Adelaide Inn,** 5 Isadora Duncan (441-2261), off Taylor St. between Geary and Post St., 2 blocks west of Union Sq. Warm hosts and lovely furnishings. Steep stairs. All rooms have large windows, TV, and sink. Kitchen. Shared bathrooms. Continental breakfast included. Reception Tu-F 9am-1pm and 5-9pm, Sa-M flexible; someone's generally around. Singles $42; doubles $52-58. Reserve 10 days in advance.

**The Red Victorian Bed, Breakfast, and Art,** 1665 Haight St. (864-1978), in Haight. Rooms are individually decorated to honor peace, sunshine, or butterflies. Even the hall baths have their own motifs and names. Free tea and coffee. Breakfast included. F-Sa 2-night min. stay. Reception 9am-9pm. Check-in 3-6pm or by appt. Check-out 11am. Most doubles $86-126; discount on stays of 3 days or more. Reserve well in advance.

**Union Sq. (San Francisco—Downtown; HI-AYH),** 312 Mason St. (788-5604), between Geary and O'Farrell St., 1 block from Union Sq. TV, Internet access ($1 for 5min.), walking tours, and a seminar on nightlife. Kitchens have no stoves. Quiet hours (midnight-7am) not always respected by Mason St. traffic. Key deposit $5. Reception 24hr. June-Sept. $19, Oct.-Jan. $17, Feb.-May $18; nonmembers $3 more; under 13 ½-price with parent. Wheelchair access. Reserve by phone with credit card, or show up around 8am.

**San Francisco International Student Center,** 1188 Folsom St. (255-8800), at 8th in SoMa. 55 beds. Dorms $15, in winter weekly $90. Chummy international crowd. Hostelers pay no cover at Cat Club downstairs—bring dancing shoes or earplugs. Reception 8am-11pm. Check-out 11am. Dorms $15. Foreign passport or out-of-state ID required.

**Fort Mason Hostel (HI-AYH),** Bldg. #240, Fort Mason (771-7277), in the Marina. Entrance at Bay and Franklin St., 1 block west of Van Ness Ave., or on McDowell on the water side. Take MUNI bus #42 or from SFO #7B or 7F. Beautiful surroundings. No smoking or alcohol. Movies, walking tours, kitchen, bike storage. A small number of beds for walk-ins each morning at 7am. Beds $18. Discounts at cafe. Minor chores. Lockers and storage. Laundry. Parking included. Reception 24hr. Check-in 7-11:30am and 12:30pm-1am. Limited access 11:30am-2:30pm. Lights out 11pm. No curfew.

**Globetrotters,** 225 Ellis St. (346-5786), between Mason and Taylor St. near Union Sq. Common room has couches and TV; some rooms have TVs. 46 beds. Large and fully-equipped kitchen. Laundry. Check-in 8am-midnight. Check-out 11am. Dorms $13, weekly $85; doubles $26. No reservations in summer. No wheelchair access.

**Pacific Tradewinds Guest House,** 680 Sacramento St. (433-7970), between Kearny and Montgomery St. in the Financial District. From Transbay Terminal, take MUNI bus #1 and get off at Kearny and Sacramento St. Well-worn common room, kitchen, guest phone, and Internet access. Bike storage. Key deposit $20. 14-night max. stay. Reception 8am-midnight. July-Sept. dorms $18; Oct.-June $16. No reservations in summer. Discount for VIP Backpacker and GO-25 cardholders. 18+. No wheelchair access.

**Green Tortoise Guest House,** 494 Broadway (834-1000), at Kearny St. in **North Beach.** Take MUNI bus #9X or 15 to Columbus Ave. and Broadway. From the Transbay Terminal, take MUNI bus #12 or 42 to Kearny St. and Pacific Ave. Common room houses huge TV, couches, pool table, and young partyers. Sauna, Internet access ($2), kitchens, bike storage. Continental breakfast included. Lockers; bring a lock. Linen deposit. Coin laundry. 21-night max. stay. Reception 24hr. Dorms $19; private doubles $48.

**Interclub Globe Hostel,** 10 Hallam Pl. (431-0540), off Folsom St. between 7th and 8th St. in **SoMa.** From Transbay Terminal take MUNI bus #12 to 7th and Howard St. Common room has pool table and TV. No kitchen. Attached to Cassidy's Irish Pub and Globe Cafe. Linen included. Check-out noon. Dorms $18. Foreign passport required.

**Pensione International,** 875 Post St. (775-3344), east of Hyde St. in the Tenderloin. Comfortable rooms in a hotel packed with groovy modern art. Continental breakfast included. Singles and doubles with shared bath $75, with private bath $95.

**Golden Gate Hotel,** 775 Bush St. (392-3702 or 800-835-1118), between Mason and Powell St. near Union Sq. Charming hotel has tasteful antiques and bright bay windows. Comfy rooms with TV. Spotless hall bathrooms. Continental breakfast and afternoon tea (4-7pm) included. Garage parking $12 per day. Doubles $72, with bath $109.

**Grant Plaza Hotel,** 465 Grant Ave. (434-3883 or 800-472-6899), at Pine St. in **Chinatown.** Modern furnishings and friendly personal service at a central, if occasionally noisy, location. All rooms with private bath. Singles $52-75; doubles $65-85.

# FOOD

The glossy *Bay Area Vegetarian* can also suggest places to graze.

**SOUTH-OF-MARKET (SOMA).** Dining out in SoMa offers plenty of low-cost options, day or night. The **Brainwash** laundromat and coffee shop on Folsom St. between 7th and 8th St. is a useful default for any meal.

**Hamburger Mary's,** 1582 Folsom St. (626-1985), at 12th St. Excellent burgers ($6.50-10) are served on toast, not buns, to ensure messy eating. Great spicy home fries, a few veggie options, and 8 types of Bloody Mary (from $4.50). Brunch Sa-Su 10:30am-4pm. Open Su-Th 11:30am-midnight, F-Sa 11:30am-1:15am (last seating).

**Vino e Cucina Trattoria,** 489 3rd St. (543-6962), at Bryant St. Look for the big tomato. Meals are as authentic as they are magnificient. Pastas and pizzas ($8-11) available without meat. Open M-F 11am-2:30pm and 5:30-10pm, Sa 5:30-10pm.

**Patisserie Cafe,** 1155 Folsom St. (703-0557), between 7th and 8th St. Cheap breakfast (coffee and croissant $3), reasonable lunch (fancy sandwich and remarkable dessert $9), or a decadent dinner (starters around $6, entrees $8-11) in this "funky industrial atmosphere." Desserts as good as they look. Open M-F 7am-11:30pm, Sa 9am-4pm.

**CIVIC CENTER.** Opera- and theater-goers frequent the petite restaurants that dot the greater Civic Center area, especially Van Ness Ave., Golden Gate Ave., and the Opera Plaza, while Hayes St. offers an extensive selection of cafes. *Use caution in this area at night.*

**Nyala,** 39A Grove St. (861-0788), between Larkin and Market St., serves Ethiopian cuisine. All-you-can-eat vegetarian buffet (lunch $5.50, dinner $8) features spicy mushrooms and about 10 other saucy vegetables to ladle on rice or scoop up with spongy *injera* bread. Open daily 11am-3pm and 4-11pm.

**Millennium,** 246 McAllister St. (487-9800), between Hyde and Larkin St. in the Abigail Hotel. Throw away your tofu dogs—this is gourmet vegan cooking with absolutely no need to masquerade as meat. Impeccable service and astounding food. Quality does cost a bit more (entrees $11-16). Open daily 5-9:30pm.

**THE MISSION DISTRICT.** A good place to find excellent, satisfying, cheap food. Inexpensive *taquerías* and other international eateries line Mission, 24th, Valencia, and 16th St. The area also boasts cheap produce at many streetside stands.

## ALL OF THE SUGAR, NONE OF THE GUILT

San Francisco's gay community forms a powerful voting bloc, and in 1977, members rallied behind one of their own. Harvey Milk won the race for City Supervisor of District 5, becoming one of the first openly homosexual public officials in the United States. He spoke out for civil rights initiatives on both a municipal and a national level, and his charismatic speeches won him powerful allies such as then-mayor George Moscone. But progressive politics make enemies too. Milk advised Moscone against the reappointment of fellow supervisor Dan White in 1978. In retaliation, White brutally gunned down both Milk and Moscone in their City Hall offices. At his trial, White pleaded the infamous "Twinkie defense"—insanity by sugar-high—resulting in a greatly diminished scale of punishment. Outrage over the incident still rankles today.

**El Farolito,** 4817 Mission St. (337-5500), at 24th St. Cheap and fresh late-night food, frequented by a cross section of locals. Tacos $1.55. Open daily 9am-1:45am.

**Country Station Sushi Cafe,** 2140 Mission St. (861-0972), between 17th and 18th St. An unexpected gem, sunny, big-hearted, and clean on a rather grimy stretch of Mission St. The decor is loopy kitsch, the sushi is excellent (2-piece *nigiri* $3-4). Traditional sushi combos start at $8. Open M-Th 5-10pm, F-Sa 5-11pm.

**Ti Couz,** 3108 16th St. (252-7373), at Valencia St. All about crepes. Almost too many varieties of savory ($2.50-6.25) and sweet ($2.50-5.25) crepes, plus dozens of tempting additions and toppings. Often crowded. No reservations; no takeout. Open M-F 11am-11pm, Sa 10am-11pm, Su 10am-10pm.

**CASTRO.** Cheap food can be elusive in this trendy area; consider experiencing it by sipping a late-night latte. Same-sex cruising is almost inevitably the side dish.

**Orphan Andy's,** 3991A 17th St. (864-9795), at Castro and Market St., has been serving burgers for years. Red vinyl booths, subtly pink walls, and a vintage jukebox heavy on girl groups. Burgers around $6.50; huge milkshakes $4.45. Open 24hr.

**Hot 'n' Hunky,** 4039 18th St. (621-6365), at Hartford St. near Castro St. Swathed in pink, this petite joint sports trendy 1950s decor with winks to Marilyn Monroe. Hunker down with a Macho Man Burger ($4.70) or I Wanna Hold Your Ham ($4.40). Open Su-Th 11am-midnight, F-Sa 11am-1am. Cash only.

**Josie's Cabaret and Juice Joint Cafe,** 3583 16th St. (861-7933), near Market St. Quintessentially Californian with its strictly vegetarian menu. Filling tofu or tempeh burgers are even better out on the deck. Live comedy acts and other performances. Shows at 8 and 10pm (cover $5-10). Open daily 5-10pm, brunch Sa-Su 9am-3pm. Cash only.

**HAIGHT-ASHBURY.** Locals linger over omelettes, home fries, and Marlboros until late afternoon. There are several **grocery stores** along and near Haight St.

**Sweet Heat,** 1725 Haight St. (387-8845). Cheap and excellent "healthy Mexican." Your body will need the break after testing their 57 kinds of tequila and 11 margaritas (including mango in season and tamarind). Filling tacos $3-4 each, quesadillas $3.75-8 (for fancy Dungeoness crab). Open Su-Th 11am-10pm, F-Sa 11am-11pm.

**All You Knead,** 1466 Haight St. (552-4550). The 8-page menu of this spacious diner includes a large selection of pizzas, sandwiches, burgers, entrees, and breakfasts (including crepes and blintzes). Breakfast served M-F until 3:45pm; lunch all day; dinner 4pm until closing. Open M and W-Su 8am-10:50pm, Tu 8am-6pm.

**Crepes on Cole,** 100 Carl St. (664-1800), 4 blocks south of Haight St. along Cole St. From chicken pesto ($6.25) to strawberries and chocolate ($4), the fare displays mastery of the medium. Open Su-Th 7am-11pm, F-Sa 7am-midnight.

**RICHMOND.** Top Chinese, Thai, Burmese, Cambodian, Japanese, Italian, Russian, Korean, and Vietnamese food. **Clement St.** has the most options.

**New Golden Turtle,** 308 5th Ave. (221-5285), at Clement St. Vietnamese dishes like are irresistible. Tastes like the food in heaven. Vegetarian options abound. Dinner entrees $7-9. Open M 5:30-10:30pm, Tu-Sa 11am-11pm, Su 11am-10pm.

**The Red Crane,** 1115 Clement St. (751-7226), between Funston and 12th St. Chinese veggie-and-seafood restaurant regularly racks up good reviews. Over 50 entrees. Spicy Szechuan eggplant ($5). Lunch special M-F 11:30am-2:30pm; choose between 8 entrees plus soup and rice for $3.50. Open daily 11:30am-10pm.

**MARINA AND PACIFIC HEIGHTS.** The **Marina Safeway,** 15 Marina Blvd. (563-4946), between Laguna and Buchana has gourmet groceries and good produce.

**Bepples Pies,** 1934 Union St. (931-6225), at Laguna St. Munch on comfort food on 2 cozy levels. Mmmm, pie. Dinner pies $5-7, pancakes $4. Open Su-Th 8am-midnight, F-Sa 8am-2am; non-pie breakfast and lunch menu served until 3pm. **Second location:** 2124 Chestnut St., at Steiner St. Open Su-Th 8am-11pm, F-Sa 8am-1am.

CALIFORNIA

**Pizza Inferno,** 1800 Fillmore St. (775-1800), at Sutter St. Decor resembles the work of trippers with fingerpaint. Pizza lunch specials (from $5) include salad and soda. Happy Hour with 2-for-1 pizzas M-F 4-6:30pm and 10-11pm. Open daily 11:30am-11pm.

**Soku's Teriyaki and Sushi,** 2280 Chestnut St. (563-0162). Great service and a $4 lunchtime *obento* box special (2-item combo, plus miso soup and rice; 11:30am-3pm). Open M-Sa 11:30am-10pm. $10 min. on credit cards.

**La Méditerranée,** 2210 Fillmore St. (921-2956), between Sacramento and Clay St. Hearty portions at reasonable prices. Filled phyllo dough and other entrees $6.75-8.25; quiche of the day $7. Open M-Th 11am-10pm, F-Sa 11am-11pm.

**FISHERMAN'S WHARF.** The archetypal, if somewhat overpriced, Wharf meal is a loaf of sourdough bread ($2-4) from **Boudin Bakery,** 156 Jefferson St. (928-1849), and clam chowder ($4-5) from a nearby seafood stand.

**Rico's,** 943 Columbus Ave. (928-5404), near Lombard St. at the top of North Beach. Well worth the 10min. walk, Rico's enormous burritos ($3-5) and bottled Mexican beers ($2.50) are a fraction of the price of Wharfside snacks. Open daily 10am-10pm.

**NORTH BEACH.** Great Italian food.

**Sodini's Green Valley Restaurant,** 510 Green St. (291-0499), at Grant Ave. In the true heart of North Beach, this is one of the area's oldest restaurants, established in 1906. The *Ravioli alla Casa* rocks the house ($8.25). Open M-F 5-10pm, Sa-Su 5pm-midnight.

**Caffe Greco,** 423 Columbus Ave. (397-6261). You know it's Italian when decaf costs more. Casual atmosphere is belied by culinary thrills. Focaccia sandwiches $6-7, tiramisu $3.75. Open M-Th 7am-11pm, F-Su 7am-midnight.

**Mario's Bohemian Cigar Store Cage,** 566 Columbus Ave. (362-0536). A hip, laid-back cafe right at the corner of Washington Square Park. Often crowded, this is a great place to hang out and grab some first-rate grub. Hot sandwiches on fat slabs of *focaccia* $6.25-7. Open M-Sa 10am-midnight, Su 10am-11pm. No credit cards.

**NOB HILL AND RUSSIAN HILL.** It can be a challenge to get to and find inexpensive restaurants at the tops of Nob and Russian Hills.

**The Golden Turtle,** 2211 Van Ness Ave. (441-4419). Fabulous Vietnamese restaurant serves mind-blowing entrees ($8-11) like the Exotic Lava Pot ($9.50) amidst intricately carved wooden walls. Open Tu-Su 5-11pm. Reservations recommended Sa-Su.

**JAPANTOWN.** Restaurants, including an incongruous **Denny's,** cluster in the Japan Center and across Post St. on pedestrian-only **Buchanan Mall.**

**Mifune,** 1737 Post St. (922-0337), in the Kintetsu Bldg., upper level. Excellent and much-loved noodle restaurant. Hearty hot soups with choice of *udon* (thick, white noodles) or *soba* (flat, gray noodles) for $4-6. *Sake* $2.25-4.25. Open daily in summer 11am-10pm; in winter 11am-9:30pm.

**CHINATOWN.** Many feel that this Chinese cuisine is unsurpassed outside of Asia.

🖎 **Chef Jia,** 925 Kearny St. (398-1626). Serves cheap and fabulous food in a small, informal space. $4 lunch specials until 4pm; entrees regularly $4-7. Open Su-Th 11:30am-11pm, F-Sa 11:30am-midnight.

🖎 **House of Nanking,** 919 Kearny St. (421-1429), at Pacific and Columbus. If you have no issue with waiting or a loose interpretation of "service," the famous cuisine satisfies. Many entrees under $7. Open M-F 11am-10pm, Sa noon-10pm, Su 4-10pm.

# 📷 SIGHTS

**HAIGHT-ASHBURY.** One could express shock and dismay that the storied corner of **Haight and Ashbury St.** is now home to a Gap and a Ben & Jerry's. But the Haight is still filled with energy, if only that of retail clerks processing credit card slips for

*(sidebar)* CALIFORNIA

purchases of "funky" stuff. Music and clothing top the list of legal merchandise. Inexpensive bars and cafes, action-packed street life, anarchist literature, and shops selling pipes for, um, tobacco, also contribute to groovy browsing possibilities. See the Haight on foot—scrounging for parking with the hordes who flock here every evening is a real hassle, although unmetered neighborhood spots start a block off the main drag. Walking down Haight St. from Golden Gate Park or up from Fillmore St. will acquaint you with the neighborhood. You're sure to run into some characters walking the streets in various shades of purple haze.

Former homes of several counterculture legends survive; check out **Janis Joplin's** old abode. *(122 Lyon St. between Page and Oak St.)* The **Grateful Dead's** house when they were still the Warlocks lies just south of Waller St. and across from the Hell's Angels' house. *(710 Ashbury St.)* Or try the **Charles Manson** mansion. *(2400 Fulton St., at Willard St.)* The **Flower Power Walking Tour** explains the Haight's history and visits these homes and other sights. *(221-8442. 2½hr., Tu and Sa 9:30am. $15.)* The **San Francisco Public Library** offers a free walking tour focused on the area's pre-hippie incarnation. *(557-4266 for details.)* If pounding the pavement is just too slow, **Skates on Haight** will help you keep on truckin'. *(1818 Haight St. 752-8875.)*

In the middle of the Haight, **Buena Vista Park** has a reputation for free-wheeling lawlessness. Enter at your own risk, and once inside, be prepared for those "doing their own thing." An unofficial crash pad and community center for San Francisco skaters, Buena Vista is generally safer than **Alamo Square,** which is northeast of the Haight at Hayes and Steiner St. Alamo's gentle, grassy slope is a favorite with photographers. Across the street, a string of beautiful and brightly colored Victorian homes known as the **Painted Ladies,** subjects of a thousand postcards, glow against the backdrop of the metropolitan skyline. Far out.

**THE MISSION DISTRICT.** The Mission is best seen on foot and in daylight. Extant for over two centuries and in the old heart of San Francisco, **Misión de los Dolores** is thought to be the city's oldest building. Bougainvillea, poppies, and birds-of-paradise bloom in its cemetery, which was featured in Alfred Hitchcock's 1958 film *Vertigo.* *(621-8203. At 16th and Dolores St. Open daily May-Oct. 9am-4:30pm; Nov.-Apr. 9am-4pm. Admission $2, ages 5-12 $1. Masses: In English M-F 7:30 and 9am, Sa 7:30, 9am, and 5pm, Su 8 and 10am; in Spanish Su noon.)*

A walk east or north along Mission St. from the 24th St. BART stop leads to the **mission murals,** some painted in the 1980s and some more recently by schoolchildren and community members. Standouts include the political murals of Balmy Alley, off 24th St. between Harrison and Folsom St., a 3-building tribute to guitar god Carlos Santana at 22nd St. and Van Ness Ave., the face of St. Peter's Church at 24th and Florida St., and the urban living center on 19th St. between Valencia and Guerrero St. The **Precita Eyes Mural Arts Center** sells a map of the murals ($1.50) and leads walking tours. *(2981 24th St. 285-2287. 2hr. tours Sa-Su at 11am and 1:30pm. Call for meeting place. Tours $7, seniors $5, under 18 $1.)* The **San Francisco Public Library** also leads weekly tours of the Mission murals in summer—but you'll have no trouble finding them on your own. *(Library tours 557-4266. Free.)*

**La Galeria de la Raza** celebrates local Chicano and Latino artists with exhibitions and parties. *(2857 24th St. 826-8009. Free.)* **Osento** is a bathhouse for ladies only, providing a wet and dry sauna, jacuzzi, and pool. *(955 Valencia St. 282-6333. Ages 14+ only. Open daily 1pm-1am. Door fee $9-13.)*

**CASTRO AND NEARBY.** The majority of sights in the Castro are strolling on the street in cut-off shorts, but even a short tour of the neighborhood should also include: the faux-baroque **Castro Theater,** 429 Castro St.; **A Different Light Bookstore,** 489 Castro St.; and **Uncle Mame,** 2241 Market St., a one-stop kitsch-and-camp overdose. For help with orientation, try **Cruisin' the Castro.** Guide Trevor Hailey, a resident since 1972, is consistently recognized as one of San Francisco's top tour leaders. Her walking tours cover Castro life and history from the Gold Rush to the present. *(550-8110. Tu-Sa, 10am. $40 including brunch.)*

**The Names Project** sounds a somber note. The Project has accumulated over 33,000 3-by-6-ft. panels for the **AIDS Memorial Quilt.** Each panel is a memorial to a person who has died of AIDS-related conditions. The NAMES Project building is also a workshop where victims' friends and families create panels; several are on display. *(2362A Market St. 863-1966. Open M-Sa noon-7pm, Su noon-6pm. Public quilting bees W 7-10pm and 2nd Sa of each month 1-5pm.)*

West of the Castro, the peninsula swells with several large hills. From **Twin Peaks,** between Portola Dr., Clarendon Ave., and Market St., are some of the more spectacular views of the city. On rare fogless nights, the views are particularly sublime. At the hulking 3-masted radio tower, known by some as the Great Satan, a pair of red warning lights blink ominously beneath a Mephisophelean crown. Significantly south of the peaks is **Mount Davidson,** the highest spot in San Francisco at 938 ft. The 103 ft. concrete cross is the resilient replacement of 2 earlier versions that fires destroyed. *(Off Portola Dr. Accessible by MUNI bus #36.)*

**NORTH BEACH.** Sunny North Beach is well worth visiting in the daytime as well as during its neon-lit evenings. Bordered by Union, Filbert, Stockton, and Powell St. is **Washington Sq.,** a pretty lawn edged by trees and watched over by a statue of not Washington, but Benjamin Franklin. The wedding site of Marilyn Monroe and Joe DiMaggio, the park fills every morning with men and women practicing *tai chi.* Across Filbert, to the north of the square, the **Church of St. Peter and St. Paul** beckons tired sightseers to take refuge in its dark, wooden nave. *(421-0809. Mass in Italian, English, and Cantonese.)* Lillie Hitchcock Coit, rescued from a fire as a girl, donated the **Volunteer Firemen Memorial,** in the middle of the square.

**Telegraph Hill** is its own neighborhood, and a nice one at that, but North Beach provides the best up-close views. Lillie Coit also put up money to build **Coit Tower,** which stands a few blocks to the east of the memorial. The tower commands a spectacular view of the city and the bay from Telegraph Hill, the steep mount from which a semaphore signalled the arrival of ships in Gold Rush days. (Rumor has it that the tower was built to resemble a fire nozzle. Its nickname suggests a cruder inspiration.) During the Great Depression, the government's Works Progress Administration employed artists to paint the colorful and subversive murals on the inside of the dome. To get to the tower, take MUNI bus #39, or trundle up the **Filbert Steps** that rise from the Embarcadero to its eastern base. The walk is short, allows excellent views, and passes attractive Art Deco buildings. *(362-0808. Open daily 10am-7pm; Oct.-May 9am-4pm. Elevator fare $3, over 64 $2, ages 6-12 $1, under 6 free.)*

Drawn to the area by low rents and cheap bars, the Beat writers came to national attention when Lawrence Ferlinghetti's **City Lights Bookstore** published Allen Ginsberg's *Howl.* Banned in 1956, a judge found the poem "not obscene" after an extended trial, but the resulting publicity vaulted the Beats into literary infamy and turned North Beach into a must-see. Rambling and well-stocked, City Lights has expanded since its Beat days, but remains committed to publishing young poets and other writers under its own imprint. *(201 Columbus Ave. 362-8091. Open daily 10am-midnight.)* The tiny **North Beach Museum,** tucked inside Bay View Bank, depicts the North Beach of yesteryear in a series of vintage photographs. Most of the photographs long predate the Beats, but a handwritten manuscript of Ferlinghetti's *The Old Italians Dying* is on display. *(391-6210. 1435 Stockton St., at Columbus Ave. Open M-Th 9am-5pm, F 9am-6pm.)*

The **Tattoo Art Museum** displays a fantastic collection of tattoo memorabilia, including hundreds of designs and exhibits on different tattoo techniques (the largest collection of its kind). In the same room, a modern, clean tattoo studio is run by the eminent professional Lyle Tuttle, himself covered in tattoos from head to foot. $50 will buy a quick rose on the hip; larger tattoos are $100 per hour. *(775-4491. 841 Columbus Ave. Open M-Th noon-9pm, F-Sa noon-10pm, Su noon-8pm.)* Nearby is the **San Francisco Art Institute,** a converted mission with a courtyard filled with the squawks of parrots and angst-ridden student art. *(771-7020. 800 Chestnut St.)*

**CHINATOWN. Grant Ave.,** the oldest street in San Francisco, is a sea of Chinese banners, signs, and architecture. During the day, Grant Ave. and nearby streets are filled with a slow-moving tourist horde stopping every block to buy health balls and chirping boxes while pretending not to notice the Chinese porn mags which line some shop windows. Most of the picturesque pagodas punctuating the blocks were designed around 1900 or more recently. At Bush and Grant St. stands the ornate, dragon-crested **Gateway to Chinatown,** given as a gift by the Republic of China in 1969. "Everything under heaven is good for the people," say the Chinese characters above the gate.

Once lined with brothels and opium dens, **Ross Alley,** running from Jackson to Washington St. between Grant and Stockton St., still has the cramped look of old Chinatown. It has stood in for Asia in such films as *Big Trouble in Little China, Karate Kid II,* and *Indiana Jones and the Temple of Doom.* Watch fortune cookies being shaped by hand in the **Golden Gate Cookie Company.** *(56 Ross Alley. 781-3956. Bag of cookies $2; with "funny," "sexy" fortunes $4.)*

The **Chinese Historical Society,** between Grant and Stockton St., relates the history of Chinese America through books and artifacts, including a parade dragon head from 1909. *(644 Broadway St. #402. 391-1188. Open M 1-4pm, Tu-F 10:30am-4pm. Free.)* Other slightly noteworthy Chinatown buildings include **Buddha's Universal Church,** 720 Washington St. at Kearny St., and **Old St. Mary's,** 660 California St. at Grant St., built from Chinese granite in 1854, and San Francisco's only cathedral for decades. **Portsmouth Square,** at Kearny and Washington St., made history in 1848 when Sam Brennan stood there to announce his discovery of gold at Sutter's Mill. Through the Barbary Coast days, it was also the site of many public hangings. Today, hangings are no longer for the public, and the square is filled with children running wild and Chinese men playing board games. A stone bridge leads from the square over construction refuse to the **Chinese Culture Center,** in the Holiday Inn, which houses exhibits of Chinese-American art and sponsors two **walking tours** of Chinatown. The **Heritage Walk** surveys the history of Chinatown, and the **Culinary Walk** teaches the preparation of Chinese food. *(750 Kearny St. 986-1822. Gallery open Tu-Su 10am-4pm. Heritage: $15, under 19 $6. Culinary: $30, under 19 $15; includes dim sum at Four Seas on Grant Ave. Walks require reservations.)*

**FISHERMAN'S WHARF.** Piers 39 through 45 provide access to San Francisco's most famous and visited attractions. Easily visible from boats and the waterfront is **Alcatraz Island.** Named in 1775 for now-departed flocks of *alcatraces* (pelicans), this former federal prison looms over San Francisco Bay, 1½mi. from Fisherman's Wharf. During World War I, servicemen convicted of violent crimes and conscientious objectors were held on the island. In the 1930s, the federal government used it to imprison those who had wrought too much havoc in other prisons, including infamous criminals like Al Capone, "Machine Gun" Kelly, and Robert "The Birdman" Stroud. Of the 23 men who attempted to escape, 18 were recaptured or killed, and 5 are "presumed drowned," although their bodies have never been found. In 1964, Attorney General Robert Kennedy closed the prison, and the island's existence was uneventful until 1969-71, when 80 Native Americans occupied it as a symbolic gesture, claiming "the Rock" as their property under terms of a broken 19th-century treaty. Alcatraz is currently part of the **Golden Gate National Recreation Area.** The **Blue and Gold Fleet** runs boats to Alcatraz from **Pier 41.** Once on Alcatraz, wander alone or take the audiotape-guided tour, full of clanging chains and the ghosts of prisoners past. *(705-5444 or 705-5555. Call in advance, daily 7am-8pm. Blue and Gold Fleet boats at Pier 41 depart every 30min. in summer 9:15am-4:15pm; in winter 9:45am-2:45pm. Arrive 20min. before departure. Tickets $8.75, seniors $7, ages 5-11 $5.50. Audio tours add $3.50, ages 5-11 $2.50. Other boating companies run shorter tours up to and around—but not onto—the island for about $10 per person.)*

Back on the mainland, the **Pier 39** juts toward Alcatraz on pilings extending several hundred yards into the harbor. Toward the end of the pier is **Center Stage,** where mimes, jugglers, and magicians play the crowds. A number of the marina

CALIFORNIA

docks have been claimed by **sea lions** that pile onto the wharf to gawk at human tourists on sunny days. *(Pier phone 981-7437. Shops open daily 10:30am-8:30pm.)*

Pronounced "GEAR-ah-DEH-lee," **Ghirardelli Sq.** is the most famous shopping mall in the area around Fisherman's Wharf, known for producing some of the world's best chocolate. Today, the remains of the machinery from Ghirardelli's original factory display the chocolate-making process in the rear of the **Ghirardelli Chocolate Manufactory,** an old-fashioned ice-cream parlor. The nearby soda fountain serves up loads of its world-famous hot fudge sauce on huge sundaes ($6). For a dessert extravaganza, try the Earthquake Sundae (with several ravenous friends)—eight flavors of ice cream, eight toppings, bananas, whipped cream, nuts, and cherries for a symbolic $19.06. If your sweet tooth outpaces your financial resources, file through the Ghirardelli store for a free sample *(Square: 775-5500. 900 North Point St. Store: 771-4903. Open Su-Th 10am-11pm, F-Sa 10am-midnight. Factory stores open M-Sa 10am-9pm, Su 10am-6pm.)*

**Aquatic Park** is the area of the bay enclosed by the Hyde St. Pier and the curving Municipal Pier (said to have inspired Otis Redding's "Sittin' on the Dock of the Bay"). Members of the **Dolphin Swimming and Boating Club** and the neighboring **South End Club** swim laps in the chilly 57°F water. For $6.50, you can thaw out in the club's showers and sauna after your nippy dip. *(Dolphin Club: 441-9329. 502 Jefferson St. Open Tu, Th, and Sa 11am-6pm. South End Club: 929-9656. Open W and F 11am-6pm.)*

The **Maritime Museum** is free and has large, fairly clean bathrooms as well as a quiet deck with a water view. The attractions of Pier 45, including the old submarine *USS Pampanito*, and the Hyde St. Pier are part of the same national park as the museum but charge separate admissions. *(Museum: 556-3002. At Beach and Polk St. across from Ghirardelli Square. Open daily 10am-5pm. Free. Hyde St. Pier: Open daily 10am-6pm. $5, seniors and ages 12-17 $2, under 12 free, families $12. Pier 45: Open daily 9am-8pm. $5, seniors and ages 6-12 $3, under 6 free.)* **The Cannery** is a mini-plaza on the wharf, with garden seating, a few cafes, and the popular Belle Roux Voodoo Lounge, a Cajun restaurant, bar, and host of Cobb's Comedy Club. *(Belle Roux 771-5225; comedy club 938-4320. On Jefferson St., between Hyde and Leavenworth St.)*

**UNION SQ.** While Union Sq. is filled with boutiques, stores, and retail, the blocks west have cultural offerings as well, in the form of theaters and galleries. When the Barbary Coast (now the Financial District) was down and dirty, Union Sq.'s Morton Alley was dirtier. Around 1900, murders on the alley averaged 1 per week, and prostitutes waved to their favorite customers from second-story windows. After the 1906 earthquake and fires destroyed most of the flophouses, merchants moved in and renamed the area **Maiden Ln.** in hopes of changing the street's image. It worked. Today, the pedestrian street extends 2 blocks from Union Sq.'s eastern side, is as virtuous as they come. The lane's main architectural attraction is the windowless face of the **Frank Lloyd Wright Building,** the city's only Wright-designed building and a rehearsal for the Guggenheim Museum in New York. *(140 Maiden Ln.)*

The **Martin Lawrence Gallery** is a modest corner space that displays works by pop artists like Andy Warhol and Keith Haring, as well as some studies by Pablo Picasso and Marc Chagall. Haring once distributed his work for free to New York commuters in the form of graffiti; it now commands upwards of $13,000 in print form. *(956-0345. 501 Sutter St. Open M-F 9am-8pm, Sa 10am-8pm, Su 10am-6pm. Free.)*

The blocks between Geary, Sutter, Mason, and Taylor St. are filled with painting and sculpture galleries. One location stacks up 4 floors of galleries, including Scott Nichols's photography. *(788-4141. 49 Geary St. A block west of Union Sq.)*

The swift ascent of the glass elevators at the **Westin Saint Francis Hotel,** where Squeaky Fromme tried to assassinate President Gerald Ford, summons the entire eastern bay into view. *(335 Powell St. at Geary St.)* Or, try the slower but equally scenic ascent of a **Powell St. cable car** as it climbs through busy Chinatown en route to the waterfront and Nob Hill. The cable cars crawl at a stately 9½mph, but the line to board the cars is even slower. Be prepared for hour-long waits. *(Fare $2.)*

**THE BONAPARTE OF THE BAY** By nature California is a populist constituency, putting more questions to voter referendum than any other state—but San Franciscans have made at least one notable exception. From 1853 to 1880, locals recognized the self-proclaimed rule of **Joshua Norton the First, Emperor of the United States and Defender of Mexico.** Norton assumed the grandiose title after tough luck in rice speculation wiped out all his money—and perhaps his sanity. He donned an ostrich feather hat and faux-military attire and roamed San Francisco's streets with his dogs, Bummer and Lazarus. When he wasn't busy sending suggestions to Abraham Lincoln, Queen Victoria, and the Czar of Russia, Norton's decrees for San Francisco included starting the tradition of a Christmas tree in Union Sq. and building a bridge across the Bay. Locals didn't mind his eccentricities; good-natured merchants accepted the money he printed, and the Central Pacific Railroad allowed him to travel for free. The city even footed the bill for his new clothes. When he died, 20,000 people came to wave him on to the next world.

**GOLDEN GATE PARK AND THE SUNSET DISTRICT.** The park should not be rushed through. Intriguing museums and cultural events pick up where the lush flora and fauna finally leave off, and athletic opportunities abound. In addition to cycling and skating paths, the park also has a municipal golf course, an equestrian center, sports fields, tennis courts, and a stadium. Call for info on free weekend walking tours of the park. On Su, traffic is banned from park roads, and bicycles and in-line skates come out in full force. (666-7200. Park headquarters: 831-2700. McLaren Lodge, at Fell and Stanyan St. on the park's eastern edge. Open M-F 8am-5pm. Friends of Parks: 263-0991.) **Bikes and Blades in Golden Gate Park** rents equipment. (50 Stow Lake Dr. 668-6699. Bikes from $6 per hour, $18 per day; skates $6 per hour.)

**M. H. de Young Memorial Museum** contains a 21-room survey of American art, from the colonial period to the early 20th century, including noteworthy pieces by John Singer Sargent and a Tiffany glass collection. The **Asian Art Museum** in the west wing of the building, is one of the largest Asian art museums outside Asia. (De Young: 863-3330. Asian Art Museum: 379-8801. On the east side of the park at 9th Ave. Both museums open Tu-Su 9:30am-5pm. $7, seniors $5, ages 12-17 $4. Free and open 9:30am-8:45pm 1st W of each month.)

The **California Academy of Sciences** houses several smaller museums specializing in different fields of science. The **Steinhart Aquarium,** home to members of over 14,000 aquatic species, is more lively than the natural history exhibits. (Shark feedings F-W 10:30am, 12:30, 2:30, and 4:30pm. Penguin feeding daily 11:30am and 4pm.) At the **Space and Earth Hall,** one exhibit shakes visitors up as they might have been in the great tremor of 1906. More zaniness lurks down the corridor, where the **Far Side of Science** gallery pays tribute to Gary Larson. Moo. (750-7145. Open daily Memorial Day-Labor Day 9am-6pm, Labor Day-Memorial Day 10am-5pm. $8.50; students, seniors and ages 12-17 $5.50; ages 4-11 $2. Free and open until 8:45pm 1st W of each month.) The **Morrison Planetarium** recreates the heavens above with an impressive show. (750-7141. Tickets $2.50; students, seniors, and ages 6-17 $1.25.) The **Laserium** plays its laser show to themes by bands like Pink Floyd, David Bowie, and the Rolling Stones. (750-7138; www.laserium.com. Tickets $7, students and seniors $6, ages 6-12 $4.)

Despite its sandy past, the soil of Golden Gate Park is rich enough to support a wealth of flowers. Although closed indefinitely due to a storm in 1995, the **Conservatory of Flowers,** erected in 1879, is a delicate structure and the oldest building in the park. The **Strybing Arboretum and Botanical Gardens** is home to 5000 varieties of plants. (661-1316. On Lincoln Way at 9th Ave.) The **Garden of Fragrance** is designed especially for the visually impaired; all labels are in Braille and the plants are chosen specifically for their textures and scents. (Open M-F 8am-4:30pm, Sa-Su 10am-5pm. Tours M-Tu and Th 1:30pm, W and F 1:30 and 2:30pm, Sa 10:30am and 1:30pm, Su 10:30am, 1:30, and 2:30pm. Free.) Near the Music Concourse off South Dr., the **Shakespeare Garden** contains almost every flower and plant ever mentioned by the Bard. Plaques with the relevant quotations are hung on the back wall, and there's a map

**CALIFORNIA**

to help you find your favorite hyacinths and rue. *(Open daily in summer dawn-dusk; in winter Tu-Su. Free.)* **Rhododendron Dell,** between the Academy of Sciences and John F. Kennedy Dr., honors John McLaren with a splendid profusion of his favorite flower. The **Japanese Cherry Orchard,** at Lincoln Way and South Dr., blooms intoxicatingly the first week in Apr.

Created for the 1894 Mid-Winter Exposition, the elegant **Japanese Tea Garden** is a serene collection of dark wooden buildings, small pools, graceful footbridges, carefully pruned trees, and lush plants. *(752-4227. Open daily 8:30am-6pm. $3.50, seniors and ages 6-12 $1.25. Free daily 8:30-9am and 5:30-6pm.)*

In the extreme northwest of the park, the **Dutch Windmill** has done its last good turn. Once the muscle behind the park's irrigation system, the outdated but renovated old powerhouse (114ft. from sail to sail) is now the purely ornamental centerpiece of the cheery **Queen Wilhelmina Tulip Garden.** Rounding out the days of yore is the **carousel** (c. 1912), accompanied by a $50,000 Gebruder band organ. *Let's Go* recommends riding the ostrich or the purple dragon. *Let's Go* does not recommend the frog. *(Open June-Sept. daily 10am-5pm; Oct.-May Tu-W and F-Su 9am-4pm. $1, ages 6-12 25¢.)* The **AIDS Memorial Grove** is a recent national landmark. The grove covers 15 acres off Middle East Dr. north of the 3rd Ave. entrance between the tennis courts and the Academy of Sciences. *(750-8340.)*

Brimming **Spreckels Lake,** on John F. Kennedy Dr., is populated by crowds of turtles who pile onto a turtle-shaped rock to sun themselves—it's turtles all the way down. The multinational collection of gardens and museums in Golden Gate Park would not be complete without something distinctly American...like a herd of **bison?** A dozen loll about a spacious paddock just west of Spreckels.

**MARINA AND PACIFIC HEIGHTS.** The main attractions in this area are almost all along the waterfront; the neighborhoods themselves are residential with bouts of commerce. *Scientific American* calls the ⬛ **Exploratorium** "the best science museum in the world," and it is indeed a mad scientist's dream. Displays include interactive tornadoes, computer planet-managing, and giant bubble-makers poised to take over the world. The Exploratorium holds over 4000 people, and when admission is free once a month, it usually does. *(3601 Lyon St. 563-7337 or recorded message 561-0360. Open Memorial Day-Labor Day Th-Tu 10am-6pm, W 10am-9pm; Labor Day to Memorial Day Tu and Th-Su 10am-5pm, W 10am-9pm. $9, students and seniors $7, disabled and ages 6-17 $5, ages 3-5 $2.50, under 3 free. Free 1st W of each month.)* Within the Exploratorium dwells the **Tactile Dome,** a pitch-dark maze of tunnels, slides, nooks, and crannies designed to help refine your sense of touch. Claustrophobes beware. *(561-0362. Open during museum hours. $12. Reservations required.)*

**The Palace of Fine Arts,** an imposing domed structure with curving colonnades, has been reconstructed from remnants of the 1915 Panama Pacific Exposition which commemorated the opening of the Panama Canal and signaled San Francisco's recovery from the 1906 earthquake. The grounds, complete with swans, make one of the best picnic spots in the city, and the nighttime illumination is glorious. *(Baker St., between Jefferson and Bay St. near the Exploratorium. Open 24hr. Free.)*

**Fort Mason** is the site of a popular hostel and headquarters for the **Golden Gate National Recreation Area.** *(At Laguna and Marine St. east of Marina Green, west of Fisherman's Wharf's Municipal Pier.)* Sam Shepard served as the playwright-in-residence at the **Magic Theater** from 1975 to 1985. Today, the theater stages both world and American premieres. *(Bldg. D, 3rd fl. 441-8822.)* The **Mexican Museum,** presents exhibits by contemporary Chicano and Latino artists. *(Bldg. D, 1st fl. 202-9700; recording 441-8822. Open W-Su 11am-5pm. $4, students and seniors $3. Free 1st W of month 11am-7pm.)* The **African-American Historical and Cultural Society Museum** focuses on contemporary African arts and crafts. *(Bldg. C #165. 441-0640. Open W-Su noon-5pm. $2, seniors and children $1.)* **Museo Italo Americano,** displays works by artists of Italian heritage. *(Bldg. C #100. 673-2200. Open W-Su noon-5pm. $3, students and seniors $1.)* The **Craft and Folk Art Museum** stocks a lot more than apple dolls and driftwood sculpture. *(Bldg. A. 775-0990. Open Tu-F and Su 11am-5pm, Sa 10am-5pm. $3, students and seniors $1, under 12 free, families $5.)*

Near Union and Sacramento St., **Pacific Heights** boasts the greatest number of **Victorian buildings** in the city. The **Octagon House** was built in 1861 with the belief that the odd architecture would bring good luck to its inhabitants. Its survival of San Francisco's many earthquakes and fires is proof of fortune's favor, so far. *(2645 Gough St. at Union St. 441-7512. Open Feb. to Dec. 2nd Su and 2nd and 4th Th of each month noon-3pm. Group tours M-F by arrangement.)* Along the water, joggers and walkers crowd **Marina Green.** Play pickup soccer on weekends, or just plain pickup—the wide sidewalk's uninterrupted sight lines make it cruising-optimal.

**JAPANTOWN.** Walking all the way through Japantown takes minutes and is the only way to go. Stores hawk the latest Pokemon paraphernalia and karaoke bars warble J-pop along Post St. around the Japan Center. The 5-tiered **Peace Pagoda,** a gift to the community from the Japanese government, is in a featureless paved lot. A brighter example of Japanese architecture is the **Sokoji Buddhist Temple,** where some meditation services are open to the public. *(1691 Laguna St. at Sutter St. 346-7540. Public Zazen meditation services Su 8:30am, W and F 6:30pm; arrive 15min. early.)*

Weary travelers may want to invest in a massage at **Fuji Shiatsu.** *(1721 Buchanan Mall, between Post and Sutter St. 346-4484. By appt. only; morning $33 per hr., afternoon $36.)* Or you can steam your dumplings at **Kabuki Hot Springs.** *(1750 Geary St. 922-6000. Sauna, steam room, and baths M-F before 5pm $10, evenings and Sa-Su $15. Other services by appointment. Men only M-Tu, Th, and Sa 10am-10pm; women-only Su, W, and F 10am-10pm.)*

**NOB HILL AND RUSSIAN HILL.** There's not much to *do* up here, and the hike up will wear you out—they don't call them hills for nothing. The famous curves of Lombard St.—installed in the 1920s so that horse-drawn carriages could negotiate the extremely steep hill—are one-of-a-kind. From the top of Lombard St., pedestrians and passengers alike enjoy the view of city and harbor. The view north along Hyde St.—a steep drop to Fisherman's Wharf and lonely Alcatraz floating in the bay—isn't too shabby either. *(Between Hyde and Leavenworth St. at the top of Russian Hill.)*

**Grace Cathedral,** the most immense Gothic edifice west of the Mississippi, crowns Nob Hill. The castings for its portals are such exact imitations of Lorenzo Ghiberti's on the Baptistery in Florence that they were used to restore the originals. Inside, modern murals mix San Franciscan and national historical events with scenes from saints' lives. *(1100 California St. 749-6300. Open Su-F 7am-6pm, Sa 8am-6pm; Su services at 7:30, 8:30, 11am, and 3:30pm. Suggested donation $3.)* The quaint spot of turf and trees in front of Grace Cathedral is **Huntington Park,** literally the playground of the rich. *(On Taylor St. between California and Sacramento St.)* After the steep journey up Nob Hill, you will understand what inspired the development of the vehicles celebrated at this museum. The **Cable Car Powerhouse and Museum** is the working center of the cable-car system. Displays teach about the picturesque cars, some of which date back to 1873. *(1201 Mason St. 474-1887. Open daily Apr.-Oct. 10am-6pm; Nov.-Mar. 10am-5pm. Free.)*

Once the site of the enormous mansions of the 4 mining and railroad magnates who "settled" Nob (Charles Crocker, Mark Hopkins, Leland Stanford, and Collis Huntington), the hilltop is now home to upscale hotels and bars. Kitsch connoisseurs must check out the **Tonga Room.** In a city blessed with several faux-Polynesian tiki bars, King Tonga has to be seen to be believed. *(In the Fairmont Hotel.)*

**RICHMOND.** The beaches and park at the western edge of Richmond offer more nice views and wanderings than works of art. At the northwest end of San Francisco, Lincoln Park is the bulkiest and best attraction in Richmond. The grounds around the park, which include the **Land's End Path,** offer a romantic view of the Golden Gate Bridge. The **California Palace of the Legion of Honor** houses an impressive fine art collection. A thorough catalogue of great masters from medieval to Matisse hangs in the recently renovated marble-accented museum. *(863-3330; www.thinker.org. Follow Clement St. west to 34th Ave., or Geary Blvd. to Point Lobos Ave. Take MUNI bus #2 or 38. Open Tu-Su 9:30am-5pm. $7, seniors $5, ages 12-17 $4. $1 off with MUNI passport or transfer. Free 2nd W of each month.)*

The precarious **Cliff House,** built in 1909, is the third of that name to occupy this spot—the previous two burned down. Along with overpriced restaurants, the Cliff House hosts the **Musée Mecanique,** an arcade devoted to games of yesteryear—not Donkey Kong and Space Invaders, but wooden and cast-iron creations dating back to the 1890s. The ingenious and remarkably addictive games are accompanied by fortune tellers, love testers, "naughty" kinescopes, and player pianos. Presiding over them all is "Laughing Sal," a roaring mechanical clown that, according to a plaque on the wall, "has made us smile and/or terrified children for over fifty years." *(386-1170. At the end of Pt. Lobos Ave./Geary Blvd. southwest of Lincoln Park. Open daily in summer 10am-8pm; in winter 11am-7pm. Free, but most games are 25¢.)*

**Ocean Beach,** the largest and most popular of San Francisco's beaches, begins south of Point Lobos and extends down the northwestern edge of the city's coastline. The strong undertow along the point is very dangerous, but die-hard surfers brave the treacherous currents and the ice-cold water anyway. Swimming is allowed at **China Beach** at the end of Seacliff Ave. on the eastern edge of Lincoln Park. The water is cold here too, but the views are stunning. *(Lifeguards on duty Apr.-Oct.)* Adolph Sutro's 1896 bathhouse lies in ruins on the cliffs. Cooled by ocean water, the baths were capable of squashing in 25,000 occupants at a time, but after an enthusiastic opening surge, they very rarely did. Be careful when exploring the ruins and nearby cliffs. *(East of Cliff House. Paths lead there from Point Lobos Ave.)*

The **National Park Service visitors center** dispenses info on the wildlife of the cliffs and the wild life of the house. Don't feed the coin-operated binoculars that look out over **Seal Rocks**—instead, head into the center and have a free look through its telescope. *(556-8642. Next to Cliff House. Open daily 10am-5pm.)* **Temple Emmanuel,** is an intriguing example of Moorish architecture, designed by the architect who did the Civic Center *(751-2535. 2 Lake St. at Arguello Blvd. Free tours M-F 1-3pm.)*

**SOUTH-OF-MARKET-AREA (SOMA).** Fascinating from an architectural perspective, as well as for the art it contains, the black-and-gray marble-trimmed **San Francisco Museum of Modern Art (SFMOMA)** is 5 spacious floors of art, with an emphasis on design. Its contemporary European and American collections also impress— SFMOMA has the largest selection of 20th-century art this side of New York. Exhibits include Paul Klee's work (through Mar. 14, 2000) and an ongoing show on modernism. *(151 3rd St. 357-4000. Open Memorial Day to Labor Day, M-Tu and F-Su 10am-6pm, Th 10am-9pm; Labor Day to Memorial Day M-Tu and F-Su 11am-6pm, Th 11am-9pm. $8, students $4, over 61 $5, under 13 free; Th 6-9pm ½-price; 1st Tu of each month free.)*

The **Yerba Buena Center for the Arts** runs an excellent gallery space and many vibrant programs, emphasizing performance, viewer involvement, and local multi-cultural work. It is surrounded by the **Yerba Buena Rooftop Gardens,** a huge expanse of concrete, fountains, and foliage next to the huge Sony Metreon. *(701 Mission St. 978-2787. Center open Tu-Su 11am-6pm; gardens open daily dawn-dusk. $5, students and seniors $3; Th 11am-3pm free; Free 1st Th of each month; open until 8pm.)* Within the gardens, but a sight unto itself, **ZEUM,** a recently opened "art and technology center," is aimed at children and teenagers. Besides studios for creating claymation and webcasts, ZEUM also has a music performance space and bowling. The best draw, however, may be the reopened **carousel,** first installed in Seattle in 1907, which is run by ZEUM but has separate admission. *(221 4th St. 777-2800. ZEUM: Open W-F noon-6pm, Sa-Su 11am-5pm. $7, ages 5-18 $5, under 5 free. Carousel: Open W-Su 11am-6pm. $1.)*

Although the **Ansel Adams Center** exhibits only a small number of the master's photographs, rotating shows by other photographers make up one of the largest and best collections of art photography in the country. *(250 4th St. 495-7000. Open daily 11am-5pm, and until 8pm on 1st Th of each month. Tours Sa 11, 11:45am, and 12:30pm. $5, students $3, seniors and ages 13-17 $2, under 13 free.)* Showcasing the history of comic strip art from the *Yellow Kid* to *Calvin and Hobbes*, the **Cartoon Art Museum** has changing exhibits on cartoon masters and research archives for scholars. *(814 Mission St. 227-8666. Open W-F 11am-5pm, Sa 10am-5pm, Su 1-5pm. $5, students and seniors $3, ages 6-12 $2, under 6 free; pay-what-you-wish first W of each month.)*

**CIVIC CENTER.** The **United Nations Plaza,** host to the city's **farmer's market** on W and Su in summer, is usually host to a General Assembly of pigeons. The **San Francisco Public Library** faces the plaza, on Polk St.; the main entrance is on Grove St.

The **Louise M. Davies Symphony Hall** glitters at Grove St. The seating in this glass-and-brass $33 million hall was designed to give most audience members a close-up view of performers. Visually, the building is a smashing success, and the San Francisco Symphony is equally highly rated. *(552-8000; symphony tickets 864-6000. 201 Van Ness Ave. Open M-F 10am-6pm.)* The recently renovated **War Memorial Opera House** hosts the well-regarded San Francisco Opera Company and the San Francisco Ballet. *(865-2000. 301 Van Ness Ave., between Grove and McAllister St. Opera: 864-3330.)* The **Veteran's Building,** where Herbst Theater hosts solo singers, string quartets, ensembles, and lecturers also houses the Performance Art Library and Museum. *(On Van Ness Ave. between Grove and McAllister St., 4th fl. Herbst Theater: 392-2545. PALM: 255-4800; Open W 1-7pm, Th-F 11am-5pm, Sa noon-5pm. Tours of Symphony Hall, War Memorial Opera House, and Herbst Theater: 552-8338. Tours depart from Symphony Hall every hr. M 10am-2pm. Tours of Symphony Hall only by request W and Sa. $5, students and seniors $3.)*

On a smaller scale, the Civic Center area has a number of small galleries like the **Women Artists Gallery,** which began in the 1880s as the Young Ladies Sketch Club. It exhibits women's photographs, paintings, and prints. *(370 Hayes St. 552-7392. Open Tu-W and F-Sa 11am-6pm, Th 11am-8pm, and 2nd and 3rd Su of every month 1-4:30pm.)*

**FINANCIAL DISTRICT.** Skyscrapers and power suits do little to attract the casual visitor. The leading lady of the area is the **Transamerica Pyramid.** New Age sources claim the pyramid is directly centered on the telluric currents of the Golden Dragon ley line between Easter Island and Stonehenge. An architect's joke co-opted by one of the country's leading architectural firms, the building earned disdain from purists and reverence from city planners after the fact. Without a business suit and some chutzpah, one must make do with the virtual viewscapes in the lobby. A pillar of the establishment, the address was once a site of revolutionary disgruntlement, and Sun Yat-Sen scripted a dynastic overthrow in one of its apartments. *(600 Montgomery St., between Clay and Washington St.)*

**Justin Herman Plaza** and its formidable **Vallaincourt Fountain,** at the foot of Market St., invite total visitor immersion. Bands and rallyists often rent out the area during lunch. One free concert, performed by U2 in the fall of 1987, resulted in the arrest of lead singer and madcap non-conformist Bono for spraypainting "Stop the Traffic—Rock and Roll" on the fountain. The **Embarcadero Center** is 3 blocks of sheer retail running toward Justin Herman Plaza and the ferry building. The mall's **Skydeck** commands views from 41 floors up. *(1 Embarcadero Ctr. $7, students and over 61 $4, ages 5-12 $3.50. Open daily 9:30am-9pm.)*

**THE PRESIDIO AND THE GOLDEN GATE BRIDGE. The Presidio,** a sprawling preserve that extends from the Marina in the east to the wealthy Sea Cliff area in the west, was occupied by the U.S. Army for nearly a century between the Mexican War and World War II. Now administered by the National Park Service, the Presidio is ideal for biking, jogging, and hiking. The preserve supports the southern end of San Francisco's world-famous Golden Gate Bridge. *(MUNI bus #28, 29, 42, or 76 or Golden Gate transit buses into the Presidio.)* Synonymous with the city itself, the majestic **Golden Gate Bridge** spans the mouth of San Francisco Bay, a rust-colored symbol of the West's boundless confidence. Countless photos can't pack the punch of a personal encounter with the suspended colossus itself. The bridge's overall length is 8981 feet; the main span is 4200 ft. long and the stolid towers are 746 feet high. Although disaster-proofed against seismic threat, the bridge still claims victims—it is the most popular site for suicides in the world, and it lacks a traffic divider. Across the bridge, Vista Point offers incredible views of city and bridge on rare fogless days.

At the northern tip of the Presidio (and the peninsula), under the tower of the Golden Gate Bridge, **Fort Point** keeps watch over the entrance to San Francisco Bay. Although the spot was recognized as strategically pivotal in the face of diverse historical threats, no battle ever occurred here. Film buffs may recognize the spot where Kim Novak dove into the Bay in Alfred Hitchcock's *Vertigo* (1958). Fort Point's museum is dedicated to past military occupants, but the thrilling view of sea-savaged surfers below is more interesting. *(Museum open daily 10am-5pm. Grounds open dawn-dusk. Guided tours.)* **Baker Beach,** in Golden Gate National Recreation Area, offers a picturesque but chilly place to tan and swim. Wind shelter makes the north half of the beach one of the city's most popular nude beaches.

# ♫ ENTERTAINMENT AND NIGHTLIFE

The free *Bay Guardian* and *SF Weekly* have thorough listings of dance clubs and live music, and the free monthly *Oblivion* has info on San Francisco's gay scene. Generally, nightlife in San Francisco is as varied as the city's personal ads. Everyone from "shy first-timer" to "bearded strap daddy" to "pre-op transsexual top" can find places to go on a Sa (or even a Tu) night. The **Mission** mixes bars packed with hotties, and salsa clubs that cater to *true* Latin lovers. There are probably enough bars and other venues here to take your money, your sobriety, and perhaps your virginity, if you play your cards right. The stretch of Folsom St. in **SoMa** around 12th St. is a row of clubs and music spots that continue sporadically out to seedy 6th St. and down to Townsend St. In the **Castro,** night, like day, is all gay and mostly male. While there are cafes, bars, and diners all along Castro and Market St., there's only 1 club, **The Café. North Beach** is great fun in the evening—especially if your definition of "fun" includes lotsa linguini-lovin' at middle-class prices. And remember, every dollar you save on a hearty, inexpensive Italian dinner can be put toward the tip at a strip club along **Broadway.** In the bars around Columbus Ave., north of the Transamerica Pyramid, is **jazz and blues.** The grungy nightlife in the **Upper Haight** consists of just a few bars with long lines and humorless bouncers. **Lower Haight** has a better selection of bars, many with shorter lines than its neighbor. The **Tenderloin** has plenty of bars that one might term "seedy." The lounges and restaurants of **Union Sq.** are out budget's reach. A few neighborhood watering holes dot **Russian** and **Nob Hills,** but mainly you'll find the darkened doorways of retail. The same is true of **Pacific Heights** until you reach the sushi, bowling, and movie possibilities at **Japantown.**

## BARS

**Hotel Utah Saloon,** 500 4th St. (421-8308), at Bryant St. in SoMa. Excellent, unpretentious saloon and music venue (rock, "countrified," funky). Show cover $2-6.

**Café du Nord,** 2170 Market St. (861-5016), between Church and Sanchez St. in the Castro. Takes you back in time to a red velvet club with speakeasy ambience. Excellent live music nightly—lounge, swing, salsa, big band—and dancing to match. Salsa Tu and Swing Su with free lessons, so you too can party like it's 1949. Happy Hour 5-7pm with swank $2 martinis. Cover $3-5. Open daily 4pm-2am.

**Tosca Cafe,** 242 Columbus Ave. (391-1244), between Broadway and Pacific Ave. in North Beach. Jukebox 3 plays for a quarter. The house special is brandy with steamed milk and chocolate ($3.50)—a holdover from Prohibition. Open M-F 5pm-1am, Sa-Su 5pm-2am.

**An Bodhran,** 668 Haight St. (431-4274), at Pierce St. in the Haight. Bar staff pull some of the city's best pints of Guinness. Happy Hour daily 4-7pm. Open daily 4pm-2am.

**Club Deluxe,** 1511 Haight St. (552-6949), near Ashbury St. in the Upper Haight. Femmes fatales banter with mysterious strangers, and that's just the bar staff. The cocktail nation is in full effect at this small but swinging retro club. Shiny metal and bluish lights make everyone the star of their own 1940s film noir. Smoky jazz and swing W-Sa. Cover F-Sa $5. Open M-Sa 3pm-2am, Su 2pm-2am. No credit cards.

**Vesuvio Cafe,** 255 Columbus Ave. (362-3370), across Jack Kerouac Alley from the City Lights Bookstore in North Beach. "I saw the best brain cells of my generation destroyed by red wine, starving hysterical." Watch poets and chess players from a balcony in the Beat bar. Drinks $3-6. Open daily 6am-2am.

**Beauty Bar,** 2299 Mission St. (285-0324), at 19th St. in the Mission. Surround yourself with vintage hair dryers and everything pink. Happy Hour daily 5-8pm. Manicures W-F 6-10pm mostly by appointment (manicure and martini $10). Makeovers Su 7-10pm. Drinks like Dippity-do (Malibu and Midori $5). Open M-F 5pm-2am, Sa-Su 7pm-2am.

**Mad Dog in the Fog,** 530 Haight St. (626-7270), near Fillmore St. in **Lower Haight.** The drinks are Guinness, the pastime is darts, and soccer, er, football, is everything else. Key matches shown live via satellite no matter what bloody time it is. Pints $2.75 until 7pm, F 5-7pm $2, and $1 with lunch M-F 11:30am-2:30pm. Bangers and mash $5. High-stakes trivia M and Th 9:30pm. Open M-F 11:30am-2am, Sa-Su 10am-2am.

**CLUBS.** DJs are artists here and clubbing practically a second job for many Friscans. The following list should get you started, but there are dozens more. *S.F. Weekly* and *Bay Guardian* have listings and reviews, and record stores are littered with flyers. **Housewares,** 1322 Haight St. (252-1440), is a rave clothing store and a good source of flyers for parties and events. They maintain a rave hotline at 281-0125. **F-8,** 1816 Haight St. (221-4142), also provides flyers and a telephone hotline (541-5019), more geared to trance and techno. The **Be-At Line** (626-4087) is a rundown of the night's most happening happenings, be they well-known or obscure. It's the first and only resource for many professional clubgoers. All club listed are 21+.

◄ **Ten 15 Folsom,** 1015 Folsom St. (431-1200) at 6th St. in SoMa. Disco, deep house, and acid jazz are all popular. Strict dress code F-Sa. Spundae hot house beats Su. Cover $5 Su-Th, $10 F-Sa. Hours vary.

◄ **Nickie's Barbecue,** 460 Haight St. (621-6508), at Fillmore St. in Haight. One of the chillest, friendliest small clubs in the whole damn city, with a low cover and even less attitude. Live DJ every night with themes ranging from world music to hip-hop to funk. Great dancing, diverse multi-ethnic crowd. Cover around $5. Open daily 9pm-2am.

**New Wave City** (675-5683; www.newwavecity.com), a moveable feast of 80s dance parties.

**The Top,** 424 Haight St. (864-7386), at Fillmore St. in Lower Haight. The Top's main draws are its loyalty to turntablism and off-center take on the classic disco ball. Cover $5. Open daily 6pm-2am.

**Covered Wagon Saloon,** 917 Folsom St. (974-1585), at 5th St. in SoMa. Beware the dress code in this divey saloon (no sportswear, no hats or jerseys with team logos). Live music 5 nights a week, built around trashy theme nights like "Power Lounge" and "Stinky's Peep Show." W is "Faster Pussycat," a rowdy dyke party. Happy Hour M-F 4:30-9:30pm offers choice of Shot 'n' Beer ($3.50). Open daily 4:30pm-2am.

**DNA Lounge,** 375 11th St. (626-1409), between Folsom and Harrison St. in **SoMa.** Soulful live music and funkilicious spinnin'. Open late for San Francisco. F night house band Grooveline play a steady diet of 70s covers. Cover around $10. Open daily 10pm-4am.

**GAY AND LESBIAN NIGHTLIFE.** Politics aside, nightlife alone is enough to make San Francisco a queer mecca. From the buff gym boys in nipple-tight Ts to tattooed dykes grinding to NIN, there's something for everybody. The boys hang in the Castro (around the intersection of Castro and Market St.), while the grrrls pre-frrr the Mission (on and off Valencia St.); both genders frolic along Polk St. (several blocks north of Geary Blvd.), and in SoMa. Polk St. can be seedy and SoMa barren, so keep a watchful eye for trouble. Most of the clubs and bars listed above are gay-friendly any night of the week. The monthly *Bay Times* has a thorough entertainment section. The *Bay Area Reporter* contains a highly varied "Arts & Entertainment" section. *The Sentinel* offers information on gay community events. The free *Odyssey* and *Oblivion* are excellent guides.

**The Café,** 2367 Market St. (861-3846), the Castro. Mixed crowd chills in the afternoon with pool and pinball, but when the sun goes down and the dance floor gets pumping, it's virtually all-gay, all-twentysomething, all-male. Mirrors surround the dance floor so you never have to dance with anyone less fabulous than yourself. Repeat *Guardian* awards for best gay bar. No cover. Open daily 12:30pm-2am.

**The Lexington Club,** 3464 19th St. (863-2052), at Lexington St. in the Mission. Neighborhood watering hole for lesbians. Jukebox plays the Clash to Johnny Cash, hitting all the tuff muff favorites (k.d. lang, Sleater-Kinney, Liz Phair) along the way. Happy Hour M-F 4-7pm. Open daily 3pm-2am.

**The EndUp,** 401 6th St. (357-0827), at Harrison St. in SoMa. A San Francisco institution. Theme nights run from Fag (F) to Girl Spot (Sa) to mostly straight KitKat (Th). Infamous Su Tea Dance 6am-2am the next day. Cover $5-10. Open W-F 10pm-4am. Sa 9pm-2am

**Esta Noche,** 3079 16th St. (861-5757), at Valencia St. in the Mission. The city's premiere gay Latino bar hosts regular drag shows, both on stage and off. Refrain from dancing salsa without instruction. Cover $3-5. Open Su-Th 1pm-2am, F-Sa 1pm-3am.

**The Stud,** 399 9th St. (252-STUD/7883) at Harrison St. in SoMa. This legendary bar/club recreates itself every night of the week—W are disco, Su are 80s nostalgia, Tu are the wild and wacky drag and transgender party known as "Trannyshack." Crowd is mostly gay male. Cover around $5. Open daily 5pm-2am.

**Club Townsend,** 177 Townsend (974-6020), between 2nd and 3rd St. in SoMa. A huge dance arena, Club T is populated by a mixed crowd during the week, but Sa "Universe" and Su "Pleasure Dome" are both gay male thangs. "Club Q," the 1st F of each month, is one of a very few lesbian nights with any longevity. Cover around $10. Call for hours.

**LIVE MUSIC.** *S.F. Weekly* and the *Guardian* are the place to start looking for the latest live music listings. Hard core audiophiles might snag a copy of *BAM*. Many of the bars and a few of the clubs listed above feature live bands at various times. *The List* lists rock gigs all over North California.

**Fillmore,** 1805 Geary Blvd. (346-6000), at Fillmore St. south of Japantown. Foundation of San Francisco's 1960s music scene; bands that pack stadiums elsewhere eagerly play here. All ages. Tickets $15-25. Wheelchair access. Call for hrs.

**Bottom of the Hill,** 1233 17th St. (621-4455), at Texas St. in Potrero Hill (south of SoMa). Intimate rock club with tiny stage is the last best place to see up-and-comers before they move to bigger venues. Cover $3-7. Age limits vary. Su afternoons feature 3 local bands and all-you-can-eat barbecue for $5. Call for showtimes.

**Jazz at Pearl's,** 256 Columbus Ave. (291-8255), at Broadway in North Beach. Traditional jazz combos in a comfortable setting for an older, well-dressed crowd. No cover, but a 2-drink minimum. Open daily 8:30pm-2am.

**Up and Down Club,** 1151 Folsom St. (626-2388), at 7th St. in SoMa. Curvy golden supper club is ground zero for San Francisco's emergent jazz and fusion scene. Open M and Th-Sa 8pm-2am.

**Biscuits and Blues,** 401 Mason St. (292-2583), at Geary in Union Sq. Hard to say which is the bigger draw: melt-in-your-mouth Louisiana-style biscuits, or low-down Southern blues. Cover $5-15. Open M-F 5pm, Sa-Su 6pm, closes between 11:30pm and 12:30am; kitchen closes around 10pm.

**The Saloon,** 1232 Grant Ave. (989-7666), at Columbus and Vallejo St. Busts at the seams with regulars. Live nightly blues hurt so good, the crush feels like a warm squeeze. Microbrew or light beer lovers should look elsewhere. No cover, 1-drink minimum. Weekend shows at 4pm. Open daily noon-2am.

Some of San Francisco's more popular festivals include: **Asian American International Film Showcase** (863-0814; mid-Mar.), AMC Kabuki 8 Theater, Japantown; **Cherry Blossom Festival** (563-2313; Apr.), Japantown; **San Francisco International Film Festival** (929-5000; Apr.-May), the oldest film festival in North America; **San Francisco International Gay and Lesbian Film Festival** (703-8663; June), Roxie Cinema (16th St. at Valencia) and Castro Theater (Castro St. at Market), California's second-largest film festival and the world's largest gay and lesbian media event; **Pride Day** (864-FREE/3733; June 25), the High Holy Day of the queer calendar; **San Francisco Blues Festival** (826-6837; 3rd weekend in Sept.), Fort Mason, the oldest blues festival in America; **Halloween** (Oct. 31), the Castro; **Dia de los Muertos (Day of the Dead)** (821-1155; Nov. 1), the Mission; and **Chinese New Year Celebration** (982-3000; in Feb.), Chinatown.

# BERKELEY

Famous for being an intellectual center and a haven for iconoclasts, Berkeley (pop. 99,900) quite lives up to its reputation. Although the peak of its political activism occurred in the 1960s and 70s—when students attended more protests than classes—U.C. Berkeley still cultivates consciousness and brainy brawn. The vitality of the population infuses the streets, which are strewn with hip cafes and top-notch bookstores. Telegraph Ave. remains Berkeley's heart, home to street-corner soothsayers, hirsute hippies, and itinerant street musicians who never left.

## ⚡ ORIENTATION AND PRACTICAL INFORMATION

Berkeley lies across the bay northeast of San Francisco, just north of Oakland. Reach the city by **BART** from downtown San Francisco or by car (**I-80** or **Rte. 24**). Crossing the bay by BART ($2.70) is quick and easy; driving in the city is difficult and frustrating. The choice is yours.

**Trains: Amtrak.** The closest station is in Oakland, but travelers can board in Berkeley with prior arrangement. **Bay Area Rapid Transit (BART)** (465-2278) runs from **Berkeley station,** 2160 Shattuck Ave., at Center St., close to the western edge of campus and **North Berkeley station,** Sacramento St. at Delaware St.

**Public Transit: Alameda County (AC) Transit** (817-1717). Buses #15, 40, 43, and 51 run from the Berkeley BART station to downtown Oakland via Martin Luther King, Jr., Telegraph, Shattuck, and College Ave., respectively. Fare $1.25; seniors, ages 5-12, and disabled 60¢. Transfers (25¢) valid 1hr.

**Taxis: A1 Yellow Cab** (644-1111) and **Berkeley Yellow Cab** (841-2265). Both 24hr.

**Visitor Info: Berkeley Convention and Visitor Bureau,** 2015 Center St. (800-847-4823 or 549-7040, 24hr. hotline 549-8710), at Milvia. Usually open M-F 9am-5pm.

**Internet Access: U.C. Computer,** 2569 Telegraph Ave. (649-6089). $3 for 15min., $5 for 30min., $7 for 1hr. Open M-Sa 10am-6pm.

**Post Office:** 2000 Allston Way (649-3100). Open M-F 8:30am-6pm, Sa 10am-2pm. **ZIP code:** 94704. **Area code:** 510.

## ⚑ ACCOMMODATIONS

There are surprisingly few cheap accommodations in Berkeley. **The Oakland Bed and Breakfast Network** (547-6380) coordinates 20 East Bay B&Bs with a range of rates. A popular option is to stay in San Francisco and make daytrips to Berkeley.

**Golden Bear Motel,** 1620 San Pablo Ave. (525-6770 or 800-525-6770), at Cedar St. 8 blocks from North Berkeley BART station. Charming stucco motel built in 1949. Check-out noon. Parking included. Singles $58; doubles $69-79; 2-bedroom cottages with kitchen $135-145. Reservations required.

**UC Berkeley Summer Visitor Housing** (642-5925). Visitors are housed in Stern Hall, 2700 Hearst Ave., at Highland St. A dorm functioning as a hotel, with shared baths, free Internet access, local calls, ping-pong and pool tables, and TV room. Parking ($3 per day), laundry (wash 75¢), and meals available. Linen and towels included. Singles $41; doubles $54. No personal checks accepted. Open June to mid.-Aug.

**YMCA,** 2001 Allston Way (848-6800), at Milvia St. Adequate, if worn, rooms available in co-ed hotel portion of this YMCA. Use of pool and fitness facilities included. Shared bath. Linen included. Reception daily 8am-9:30pm. No curfew. In-room phones for incoming calls; pay phones in hall. 14-night max. stay; special applications available for longer stays. Singles $33; doubles $40; triples $50. Must be 18+ with ID.

## ◔ FOOD

Berkeley offers a variety of budget dining, munching, and sipping options. The north end of **Telegraph Ave.** caters to student appetites and wallet sizes—hence the high concentration of pizza joints and trendy cafes. When you've maxed out on caffeine, head out to **Solano Ave.** for Asian cuisine or meander down to **San Pablo** along the bay for hearty American fare. If you want to make your own meals, the best grocery shopping in the bay awaits at ▧ **Berkeley Bowl,** 2777 Shattuck Ave., at Stuart. The lanes of this former bowling alley are now stocked with endless fresh produce, seafood, and bread. (843-6929. Open M-F 9:30am-7pm, Sa 9am-6pm.)

▧ **Pasand Madras Cuisine,** 2286 Shattuck St. (549-2559) at Bancroft. Melt-in-your-mouth *kormas,* curries, and *tandooris* fit for Vishnu. All-you-can-eat noon-2:30pm buffet $7 means endless chewy *naan* bread. Open Su-Th 11am-10pm, F-Sa 11am-10:30pm.

**Ann's Soup Kitchen,** 2498 Telegraph Ave. (548-8885), at Dwight St. A perennial student breakfast favorite. Towering portions compensate for sometimes crowded dining. 2 eggs with toast or homefries $3. Fresh-squeezed juice tastes like a million bucks, but costs only $1.35. Open M and W-F 8am-7pm, Tu 8am-3pm, Sa-Su 8am-5pm.

**Long Life Vegi House,** 2129 University Ave. (845-6072). Vast menu of countless vegetable and "vegetarian meat" Chinese options. Huge portions; most entrees $5-7. Friendly, prompt service. Eat-in or takeout. Daily lunch special 11:30am-3pm with entree, egg roll, and soup ($3.65). Open Su-Th 11:30am-9:30pm, F-Sa 11:30am-10pm.

**Oscar's,** 1890 Shattuck Ave. (849-2164), at Hearst St. Unassuming hamburger shack justly lauded by locals. Cheeseburger $3. Open Su-Th 10am-midnight, F-Sa 10am-2am.

**Crepes A-Go-Go,** 2125 University Ave. (841-7722). Crepes are on the thick side for hands-on convenience. Cheese and turkey crepes $3.50, honey and kiwi crepes $3.75. Pleasant staff and owner also vend sandwiches and salad to Berkeleyans on the go-go. Open Su-Th 9am-10pm, F-Sa 9am-10:30pm.

**Cafe Intermezzo,** 2442 Telegraph Ave. (849-4592), at Haste St. The fresh produce in the huge green salad ($3.23) and Veggie Delight ($4.84) will fuel you for the rest of the day. Cheap beer (Anchor Steam $1.75). Sandwiches $4.39. Open M-F 10:30am-9pm.

## ◈ SIGHTS

In 1868, the private College of California and the public Agricultural, Mining, and Mechanical Arts College became one as the **University of California.** Berkeley was the first of the 9 University of California campuses, so by seniority it has sole rights to the nickname "Cal." The school has a diverse enrollment of 30,000 students and 1350 full professors, and a library system with over 8.7 million volumes, creating a lively and internationally respected academic community. The campus is quite active when classes are in session (from mid-Aug. to mid-May).

Pass through **Sather Gate** into **Sproul Plaza,** both sites of celebrated student sit-ins and bloody confrontations with police, to enter the 160-acre Berkeley campus. The Plaza, suspended between Berkeley's idyllic campus and raucous Telegraph Ave., is now a perfect place for people-watching. Maps of campus are posted everywhere; the **U.C. Berkeley Visitor Center,** also sells campus maps (10¢) and offers campus **tours** which leave from the center M-F 10am and from **Sather Tower.** *(101 University Hall, 2200 University Ave. 642-5215. Open M-F 8:30am-4:30pm. Tours Sa 10am and Su 1pm)* Besides the loonies singing and muttering in Sproul Plaza, the most dramatic campus attraction is Sather Tower, better known as the **Campanile,** the tallest building on campus. You can ride to its observation level for a great view. *($1.)*

The **Lawrence Hall of Science,** on Centennial Dr., atop the eucalyptus-covered hills east of the main campus, is one of the finest science museums in the Bay Area. Take bus #8 or 65 from the Berkeley BART station (and keep your transfer for $1 off admission) or a university shuttle (642-5149); otherwise it's a long, steep walk. *(642-5132. Open daily 10am-5pm. $6; seniors, students, and ages 7-18 $4.)*

You haven't really visited Berkeley until you've been on **Telegraph Ave.** which runs south from Sproul Plaza all the way to downtown Oakland. The action is near the university, where Telegraph Ave. is lined with a motley assortment of cafes, bookstores, and used clothing and record stores. Businesses come and go by the whims of the marketplace, but the scene, a rowdy jumble of 1960s and 1990s counterculture, abides. Vendors push tie-dyes, tarot readings, and handmade jewelry; people hustle for change; and grizzled characters looking like Old Testament prophets carry on hyper-dimensional conversations with nobody in particular.

Berkeley's biggest confrontation between the People and the Man was not fought over freedom of speech or the war in Vietnam, but for control of a muddy vacant lot near Telegraph Ave. at Haste and Bowditch. In Apr. 1969, students, hippies, and radicals christened the university-owned land **People's Park,** tearing up pavement and laying down sod to establish, in the words of the *Berkeley Barb,* "a cultural, political freak out and rap center for the Western world." When the University moved to evict squatters and build a parking garage on the site, resistance stiffened. Governor Ronald Reagan sent in 2000 troops, and the conflict ended with helicopters dropping tear gas on students in Sproul Plaza, 1 bystander shot dead by police, and a 17-day occupation of Berkeley by the National Guard.

When you're ready to get out of town, Berkeley is happy to oblige. **Tilden Regional Park,** in the pine- and eucalyptus-forested hills east of the city, is the anchor of the extensive East Bay park system. *(635-0135.)* Hiking, biking, running, and riding trails crisscross the park and provide impressive views of the Bay Area. The **ridgeline trail** is an especially spectacular bike ride. Within the park, a 19th-century carousel delights juvenile thrill-seekers. The small, sandy beach of **Lake Anza** is a popular swimming spot during the summer, often overrun with squealing kids. *(848-3385. Lake open in summer 11am-6pm. $3, children and seniors $1.50.)*

##  ENTERTAINMENT

The university offers a number of quality entertainment options. Hang out with procrastinating students in or around the **Student Union** (643-0693). **The Underground** contains a ticket office, an arcade, bowling alleys, foosball tables, and pool tables, all run from a central blue desk (642-3825; open M-F noon-8pm, Sa 10am-6pm). **Caffe Strada,** 2300 College Ave., at Bancroft, is a glittering jewel of the caffeine-fueled-intellectual scene (843-5282; open daily 6:30am-11:30pm). **Spats,** 1974 Shattuck Ave., between University and Berkeley, lures locals and students with the warmth of the staff, the original drinks (Danko Bar Screamer $4.50), and the quirky surroundings (841-7225; open M-F 11:30am-2am, Sa 4pm-2am). **924 Gilman,** 924 Gilman St., at 8th, is a legendary all-ages club and a staple of California punk. (524-8180; 24hr. info 525-9926. Cover $3 with $2 membership card, good for 1 year and sold at the door.)

## OAKLAND

Long-suffering Oakland sings the blues. The city's salad days were the first decades of this century, when businesses and wealthy families flowed in from San Francisco, many in the wake of the 1906 earthquake. Oakland's most striking buildings date from that era: the City Hall on 14th St., the Tribune Tower at 13th and Franklin, the Paramount Theater on Broadway, and the nearby Fox Oakland Theater on Telegraph at 19th. But the boom died in the Great Depression, and economically, Oakland never really found its feet again. An unfortunate number of those Art Deco office towers and movie palaces are now derelict and falling down. Oakland's central core has some life in it, but just a few blocks west of Broadway or north on San Pablo, dreary ghettos sprawl for miles.

Oakland's scarcity of cheap and safe accommodations and noteworthy sites leave it a better daytrip than vacation destination. The best reason to visit is to catch some live music: whether they're playing the West Coast blues, Oaktown hip-hop, or progressive jazz, Oakland's music venues are unsurpassed. Such a vital scene is always changing, so if you want to be on the very cutting edge, you'll have to do some of your own research. **Koncepts Cultural Gallery** is not a venue but an organization that hosts some of the most groundbreaking progressive jazz sessions (763-0682; cover $5-25). ◪ **Eli's Mile High Club,** 3629 Martin Luther King Jr. Way, is the home of the West Coast blues (655-6661; cover $5-10; soul food kitchen opens at 7pm, music starts by 10pm). Not the most famous, just the best, jazz and blues musicians take the stage at **The Fifth Amendment,** 3255 Lakeshore Ave., at Lake Park (832-3242; never a cover; shows start at 9pm). **Yoshi's,** 510 Embarcadero, at Jack London Sq., is hardly cutting edge, but it's still an upscale Oakland institution, bringing together world-class sushi and world-class jazz (238-9200; shows M-Sa 8 and 10pm, Su 2 and 8pm).

Outside of Oakland's music scene, the best bona fide sight is probably the **Oakland Museum of California,** 1000 Oak St. at 10th, on the southwest side of the lake near the Lake Merritt BART station. A complex of 3 museums devoted to California's history, art, and ecology, the Museum's highlights include photography by Edward Weston and Dorothea Lange, quick-snap panoramic photos of San Francisco by Eadweard Muybridge, and multicultural modern works. (238-2200. Open W-Sa 10am-5pm, Su noon-5pm, 1st F of each month until 9pm. $8, students and seniors $6; F 3-9pm $5, students and seniors $3; 1st Su of each month free.)

Killer-diller food options include the ▧ **Happy Belly Deli,** 30 Jack London Sq. #216, on the 2nd fl. in Jack London Village, an oasis of genuine character (and budget prices) in the touristy square. "Food holds the energy of its experiences and transmits this vibration to the eater," say the owners. (835-0446. Open M-F 10am-4pm, Sa-Su 9am-4pm; free yoga lessons M at 6pm.) **Lois the Pie Queen,** 851 60th St., at Adeline St. in North Oakland, gets crowded on weekends, but you can probably find a swivel chair at the counter. Don't leave without a $2.50-3 slice of peach cobbler, lemon ice-box, or sweet potato pie. (658-5616. Open M-F 8am-2pm, Sa 7am-3pm, Su 7am-4pm.)

Drivers can take **I-80** from San Francisco across the Bay Bridge to **I-580** and connect with Oakland **I-980 S,** which has downtown exits at 12th St. or 19th St. **Bay Area Rapid Transit (BART)** (465-2278) provides another option, running from downtown San Francisco to Oakland's stations at **Lake Merritt** (Dublin/Pleasanton or Fremont trains), **12th St.** (Richmond or Pittsburg/Bay Point trains), or **19th St.** (Richmond or Pittsburg/Bay Point trains). **Area code:** 510.

## SAN JOSE

In 1851, San Jose was deemed too small to be California's capital, and Sacramento assumed the honors. Today, San Jose (pop. 873,000) is the civic heart of the Silicon Valley and the fastest-growing city in California. San Jose may be silicon-heavy and culture-light, but it does have its good points. If you're a woman looking for a single guy with great job security, your best bet is to look here first. The computer-geeks-turned-millionaires have come of age, and San Jose has the largest ratio of young, single men to women in the country. Also, the weather is warm, the schools are good, the streets are clean and wide, and there's always plenty of parking. The FBI named it the 3rd-safest city in the country, and taking a trip to San Jose is like taking a trip through a mental image of 1950s suburbia. Everything is clean and new, the people are friendly, and America's industrial strength seems unbeatable—if they ignored the local porn theaters and strip clubs, Ward and June Cleaver could call it home.

🗗 **PRACTICAL INFORMATION.** San Jose lies at the southern end of San Francisco Bay, about 50mi. from San Francisco (via U.S. 101 or I-280) and 40mi. from Oakland (via I-880). From San Francisco, take **I-280** rather than U.S. 101, which is full of traffic snarls at all hours. San Jose is centered around the convention-hosting malls and plazas near the intersection of east-west **San Carlos St.** and north-south **Market St. San Jose International Airport** is at 1661 Airport Blvd. (277-4759). **Amtrak,** 65 Cahill St. (287-7462), runs to San Francisco (2hr., 1 per day, $9) and Los Angeles (10½hr., 1 per day, $77). **CalTrain,** 65 Cahill St. (291-5651 or 800-660-4287), at W. San Fernando, runs to San Francisco (1½hr.) with stops at peninsula cities. **Greyhound,** 70 S. Almaden, at Santa Clara, buses to San Francisco (1hr., $7) and Los Angeles (7hr., $32). **Santa Clara Valley Transportation Agency (VTA),** 2 N. First St. (321-2300), offers ultra-modern buses as well as a light-rail system (fare $1.10). **Visitor Information and Business Center:** (977-0900, events line 295-2265) in the San Jose McEnerny Convention Center at San Carlos and Market St. **Martin Luther King Jr.**

**Public Library,** 180 W. San Carlos St. (277-4846), in front of the Convention Center, offers Internet access (open M-W 9am-9pm, Th-Sa 9am-6pm, Su 1-5pm). **Post Office:** 105 N. 1st St. (800-225-8777). **ZIP code:** 95113. **Area code:** 408.

**ⓘ ACCOMMODATIONS, FOOD, AND NIGHTLIFE.** San Jose is surrounded by county parks with campgrounds. **Mt. Madonna County Park** (842-2341), on Hecker Pass Hwy., has 117 campsites in a beautiful setting, occupied on a first come, first camped basis. The scandalously idyllic hamlet of **Saratoga,** 14mi. southwest of San Jose on Rt. 85, has a number of campsites (tent sites $8; RVs $20; open Apr. to mid-Oct.) and miles of horse and hiking trails in wooded **Sanborn-Skyline County Park** (867-9959, reservations 358-3751), on Sanborn Rd. From Rt. 17 S, take Rt. 9 to Big Basin Way. Along the way sits **Saratoga Springs** (867-9999), a private campground with 32 sites ($20 for 2 people), hot showers, and a general store. **Sanborn Park Hostel (HI-AYH),** 15808 Sanborn Rd., in Sanborn-Skyline Park, 13mi. west of San Jose, has dorms. (741-0166. $8.50, US nonmembers $10.50, foreign nonmembers $11.50; under 18 ½-price.) **San Jose State University,** 375 S. 9th St., at San Salvador, offers dorm rooms with 2 single beds (924-6193; $32.50; open June-Sept.).

**House of Siam,** 55 S. Market St., serves excellent $7-10 meat and meatless dishes (279-5668; open M-F 11am-3pm and 5-10pm, Sa-Su 11:30am-10pm). **La Guadalajara,** 45 Post St., has been serving delicious Mexican food and cheap, yummy pastries since 1955 (292-7352; jumbo burritos $3.25, combo plates $4-6; open daily 8:30am-6:30pm). **White Lotus,** 80 N. Market St., between Santa Clara and St. John, is one of the few vegetarian restaurants in the area (977-0540; open M-Th 11am-2:30pm and 5:30-9pm, F-Sa 11am-9:30pm.) A wacky jukebox suits the fly clientele of **The Flying Pig Pub,** 78 S. 1st St. This mega-chill bistro serves drinks from its full bar, as well as food (298-6710; 3-way chili $3.25; open M 3pm-2am, Tu-F 11am-2am, Sa 4pm-2am). **Katie Bloom's Irish Pub and Restaurant,** 150 S. 1st St., is clearly more "pub" than "restaurant." Drink imported beers ($2.50) while Oscar Wilde and James Joyce watch from the walls. The extensive space includes many private leather booths, as well as rowdier counter spots. (294-4408. Open M-F 11am-2am, Sa-Su 2pm-2am.)

**ⓘ SIGHTS.** There's a bit to see in San Jose proper, but not much. A few well-funded museums are the only real diversions from the business of websites and microchips. The **Tech Museum of Innovation,** in downtown San Jose, is the closest thing to a Silicon Valley tourist attraction. Underwritten by area high-tech firms, "the Tech" features hands-on exhibits on robotics, DNA engineering, and space exploration. *(145 W. San Carlos St. 279-7150. Open Oct.-June Tu-Su 10am-5pm; July-Sept. M-Sa 10am-6pm, Su noon-6pm. $6, seniors $4, ages 6-18 $4.)* Science-based toys also grace the **Children's Discovery Museum,** behind the Technology Center light-rail station. *(180 Woz Way. 298-5437. Open Tu-Sa 10am-5pm, Su noon-5pm. $6, seniors $5, under 18 $4).*

The **Rosicrucian Egyptian Museum and Planetarium,** at Park, rises out of the suburbs like the work of a mad pharaoh. This grand structure houses an extensive collection of Egyptian and Assyrian artifacts, including a walk-in tomb and spooky animal mummies. The collection belongs to the mystical order of the Rosy Cross, who have supposedly long battled the Bavarian Illuminati for world domination. *(1342 Naglee Ave. 947-3636. Open W-M 10am-5pm. $7, students and seniors $5, ages 6-15 $3.50. Under 18 must be accompanied by an adult.)*

A number of art galleries are clustered in the downtown core. The **San Jose Museum of Art,** at San Fernando, presents mass-appeal modern shows. *(110 S. Market. 271-6840. Open Tu-W and F-Su 9am-5pm, Th 9am-8pm. $6, students $3, seniors $3.)* Close by stand the **San Jose Institute of Contemporary Art (SJICA),** *(451 S. 1st St.; 283-8155; open Tu-Sa noon-5pm),* and the **Center for Latino Arts (MACLA),** *(510 S. 1st St.; 998-2783; open W-Sa noon-5pm).* Many area galleries are free and open to the public until 8pm on the 3rd Th of every month.

Of absolutely no educational value, but intriguing nonetheless, is the house that Sarah Winchester built: the **Winchester Mystery House,** near the intersection of I-880 and I-280, west of town. This heir to the Winchester rifle fortune was convinced by an occultist that she would face the vengeance of the spirits of all the men ever killed by her family's guns if construction on her home ever ceased. Work on the mansion continued 24 hours a day for over 30 years, and today the estate is an elaborate maze of secret corridors, dead-end staircases, and tacky gift shops with absolutely no escape. *(1525 S. Winchester Blvd. 247-2101. Open Su-Th 9am-6pm, F-Sa 9am-9pm, with 1hr. tours every 15-30min. $13, seniors $10, ages 6-12 $7.)*

## PALO ALTO

Well-manicured Palo Alto looks a lot like "Collegeland" in a Disney-style theme park: the city is dominated by the beautiful 8000-acre campus of **Stanford University,** Palo Alto's main tourist attraction. Jane and Leland Stanford founded the secular, co-educational school in 1885, to honor a son who died of typhoid on a family trip to Italy. The Stanfords loved Spanish architecture and collaborated with **Frederick Law Olmsted,** designer of New York City's Central Park, to create a red-tiled campus of uncompromising beauty. (Berkeley students sometimes refer to Stanford as "the World's Largest Taco Bell.") The oldest part of campus is the colonnaded **Main Quadrangle,** the site of most undergraduate classes. The walkways are dotted with diamond-shaped, gold-numbered stone tiles that mark the locations of time capsules put together by each year's graduating class. Chipper student tour guides will point to other quirky Stanford tidbits on twice-daily tours. **Memorial Church,** in the Main Quad, is a non-denominational gold shrine with stained glass windows and glittering mosaic walls like those of an Eastern Orthodox church (723-1762). East of the Main Quad, the observation deck in **Hoover Tower,** has views of campus, the East Bay, and San Francisco. (723-2053 or 723-2560. Open daily 10am-4:30pm. $2, seniors and under 13 $1.) Off-campus, the kitschy **Barbie Doll Hall of Fame,** 433 Waverley St., off University, has over 16,000 perky plastic dolls. Hippie Barbie, Benetton Barbie, and Disco Ken prove that girlhood may be fleeting, but fashion is forever. Ask about having yourself cloned into a doll. (326-5841. Open Tu-F 1:30-4pm, Sa 10am-noon and 1:30-4:30pm. $6, under 12 $4.)

**Hidden Villa Ranch Hostel (HI-AYH),** 26870 Moody Rd., is about 10mi. southwest of Palo Alto in Los Altos Hills. The first hostel on the Pacific Coast is now a working ranch and farm in a wilderness preserve. (949-8648. 35 beds; dorms $10. Reception 7:30-9:30am and 4:30-9pm. Open Sept.-May.) About half of Stanford's social life happens at **The Coffee House,** Tresidder Union, in the heart of campus. (723-3592. Open term-time M-F 10am-11pm, Sa-Su 10am-midnight; in summer daily 10am-7pm.) The **Mango Cafe,** 435 Hamilton Ave., 1 block east of University Ave., boasts reggae music, fan-backed wicker chairs, and Caribbean cuisine (325-3229; open daily 11am-3pm and 6-10pm).

Palo Alto is 35mi. southeast of San Francisco, near the southern shore of the bay. From the north, take **U.S. 101** to the University Ave. exit, or take the Embarcadero Rd. exit directly to the Stanford campus. Alternatively, motorists from San Francisco can split off onto the **Junípero Serra Hwy. (I-280)** for a slightly longer but more scenic route. Palo Alto-bound trains also leave from San Francisco's **CalTrain** station, at 4th and King. (Run M-Th 5am-10pm, F 5am-midnight, Sa 7am-midnight, Su 8am-10pm. Fare $3.75; seniors, disabled and children $1.75; off-peak hrs. $2.75.) The **Palo Alto Transit Center** (323-6105), on University Ave., serves local and regional buses and trains (open daily 5am-12:30am); there is a train-only depot (326-3392), on California Ave. 1¼mi. south of the Transit Center (open 5:30am-12:30am). The Transit Center connects to points south via **San Mateo County buses** and to the Stanford campus by the free **Marguerite University Shuttle. Area code: 415.**

## SAN MATEO COAST

The rocky bluffs of the San Mateo County Coast quickly obscure the hectic urban pace of the city to the north. Most of the energy here is generated by the coastal winds and waves. The Pacific Coast Hwy. (Rt. 1) maneuvers its way through a rocky shoreline, colorful beach vistas, and generations-old ranches. Although it's possible to drive quickly down the coast from San Francisco to Santa Cruz, haste is waste—especially if you drive off a cliff.

**Half Moon Bay** is an old coastal community 29mi. south of San Francisco. Recent commercialization has not infringed much on this small, easy-going beach town. The fishing and farming hamlet of **San Gregorio** rests 10mi. south of Half Moon Bay. **San Gregorio Beach** is a delightful destination; you can walk to its southern end to find little caves in the shore rocks. A stream runs into the sea, and may prove a comfortable alternative to dipping in the chillier ocean. (Open 8am-dusk; day use $4, seniors $3.) To find a **less-frequented beach,** visit the unsigned turnout at Marker 27.35. It's difficult to find; look for mysteriously vacant cars parked along the highway. State-owned but undeveloped, this gorgeous stretch of beach is between San Gregorio and Pomponio State Beaches, off Rt. 1. The historic little burg of **Pescadero** was established by white settlers in 1856, and was named Pescadero ("fisherman's town") due to the abundance of fish in both the oceans and creeks. Wander through the old town or participate in the local sport of **olallieberry picking.**

**Año Nuevo State Reserve,** on Rt. 1 in Pescadero, 7mi. south of Pigeon Point and 27mi. south of Half Moon Bay, is the mating place of the 15-foot-long **elephant seal.** (879-0227. Park open daily 8am-dusk.) Early spring is breeding season, when thousands of fat seals crowd on the beach. To see this unforgettable show (prime viewing times Dec. 15-Mar. 31), you must make reservations (8 weeks in advance recommended) by calling **PARKNET** (800-444-7275), since park access is limited. Tickets go on sale Nov. 15 and generally sell out within a week or two (2½hr., guided tours $4 per person).

Nestled further inside the peninsula south of the San Francisco International Airport is the **Burlingame Museum of Pez Memorabilia,** 214 California Dr. (347-2301), which has a small but quirky display of dispensers and paraphernalia dating back to 1949. Be sure to see the short Pez reference video. Like all the best things in life, the museum is free. (Open Tu-Sa 10am-6pm.)

The **Pigeon Point Lighthouse Hostel (HI-AYH),** is on Rt. 1, 6mi. south of Pescadero and 20mi. south of Half Moon Bay (879-0633; dorms $12, nonmembers $15; private rooms $22/$25; call ahead). **Point Montara Lighthouse Hostel (HI-AYH)** is on Lighthouse Point 25mi. south of San Francisco and 4mi. north of Half Moon Bay (728-7177; dorms $12, nonmembers $15; private rooms $22/$25). **The Flying Fish Grill,** at the corner of Main St. and Rt. 92, serves inexpensive, airborne seafood straight from the coast (712-1125; open in summer Tu-Su 11:30am-8:30pm; off-season until 7:30pm). **2 Fools Cafe and Market,** 408 Main St., at Mill St., is a cool, urbane eatery and drinkery that serves many veggie options (712-1222 open M 7am-2pm, Tu-F 7am-9pm, Sa-Su 8am-9pm). *The* social spot for locals is ▨ **San Gregorio General Store,** 7615 Stage Rd., 1mi. east of Rt. 1 on Rt. 84, 8mi. south of Half Moon Bay. This quirky store has served San Gregorio since 1889 with an eclectic selection of hardware, cold drinks, groceries, gourmet coffee, cast iron pots, books, candles, and more. (726-0565. Open M-Th 9am-6pm, F-Su 9am-7pm.) **Area code:** 650.

# MARIN COUNTY

Physically beautiful, politically liberal, and stinking rich, Marin County epitomizes California. If the new VW Beetle were sold nowhere but Marin (muh-RIN), Volkswagen still might reap a tidy profit. The yuppie reincarnation of the quintessential hippie car strikes just the right combination of upscale chic and counterculture nostalgia to have taken this county by storm.

**⃟ PRACTICAL INFORMATION. Public Transit: Golden Gate Transit** (455-2000, in San Francisco 923-2000) provides transit between S.F. and Marin County via the Golden Gate Bridge, as well as local service in Marin. (Fare to Sausalito $2, to Point Reyes and Olema $4; seniors and disabled 50% off, ages 6-12 25% off.) **Golden Gate Ferry** (455-2000) runs boats from San Francisco to the Sausalito ferry terminal at the end of Market St. ($4.25) and the Larkspur ferry terminal (M-F $2.50, Sa-Su $4.25. Seniors and disabled 50% off; ages 6-12 25% off. Offices open M-F 6am-8pm,

Sa-Su 6:30am-8pm.) **Taxis: Radio Cab** (485-1234 or 800-464-7234) serves all of Marin County. **Visitor Info: Marin County Visitors Bureau** (472-7470), at the end of the Ave. of the Flags off Civic Center Dr., off U.S. 101, in San Rafael. Part of the Marin Civic Center. Open M-F 9am-5pm. **Sausalito Visitors Center:** 777 Bridgeway, 4th fl. (332-0505), Sausalito. Open Tu-Su 11:30am-4pm. Also a **kiosk** at the ferry landing. **Post Office: San Rafael,** 40 Bellam Blvd. (459-0944), at Francisco. Open M-F 8:30am-5pm, Sa 10am-1pm. **ZIP code:** 94915. **Sausalito,** 150 Harbor Dr. (332-4656), at Bridgeway. Open M-Th 8:30am-5pm, F 8:30am-5:30pm. **ZIP code:** 94965. **Area code:** 415.

**⌐ ACCOMMODATIONS. Point Reyes Hostel (HI-AYH)** is in the Point Reyes National Seashore. By car, exit west from Rt. 1 at Olema onto Bear Valley Rd. Take the second possible left at Limantour Rd. (unsigned) and drive 6mi. into the park. Turn left at the first crossroad, at the bottom of a very steep hill. (663-8811 or 800-909-4776, ext. 61. Dorms $12-14. Private room available for families with children under 5. Chores. Linen $1; towels $1. Reservations recommended. Some wheelchair access. Reception 7:30-9:30am and 4:30-9:30pm.) **Marin Headlands (HI-AYH),** a spacious and immaculate hostel, holds down old Fort Barry, west of Sausalito and 10mi. from downtown San Francisco. Not easy to reach by public transport: a 4½mi. uphill hike from the Golden Gate Transit (#2, 10, 50) bus stop at Alexander Ave., or 6mi. from the Sausalito ferry terminal. On Su and holidays only, MUNI bus #76 runs directly to the hostel. By car, cross the Golden Gate Bridge and take the Alexander Ave. exit. From the north, take the 2nd Sausalito exit (the last exit before the bridge). Take a left at the 1st road and follow signs into the Golden Gate Recreation Area and to the Marin Headlands Visitors Center. (331-2777 or 800-909-4776, ext. 62. Game room, kitchens, and common rooms. Linen $1; towels 50¢. Laundry $1.50. Key deposit $10. Lockout 9:30am-3:30pm. Check-in 7:30am-11:30pm. Check-out 8:45am. Dorms $12, under 17 with parent $6. Private doubles $35.) **Marin Headlands,** northwest of the Golden Gate Bridge at Bunker and Field Rd. Follow directions to Headlands Hostel, (see above), and stop at the visitors center. There are 3 small walk-in (100 yards to 3mi.) campgrounds with a total of 11 primitive campsites. There are picnic tables and chemical toilets; bring your own water and camp stove. A free permit is required. (331-1540. 3-day max. stay. Hot showers and kitchen, $2 each, at Headlands Hostel. Free cold showers at Rodeo Beach. Reception open daily 9:30am-4:30pm.) **Kirby Cove** (561-4304), off Conzelman Rd. west of the Golden Gate Bridge, is in the Marin Headlands but not administered by the visitors center, with 4 campsites in a grove of cypress and eucalyptus trees on the shores of the bay. Accessible by car and includes fire rings and pit toilets.

**⌐ FOOD.** Marinites take their fruit juices, tofu, and nonfat double-shot cappuccinos very seriously; restaurateurs know this, and raise both the alfalfa sprouts and the prices. A number of cafes and pizzerias along **4th St.** in San Rafael, and **Miller Ave.** on the way into Mill Valley, provide welcome exceptions; others are listed below. **▧ Sartaj Indian Cafe,** 43 Caledonia St., 1 block from Bridgeway. Generous portions of excellent Indian food at low prices (curries $8, stew and samosa $5, sandwiches $3.75) are even lower on W nights, when Sartaj features live music—sometimes authentically Indian, sometimes Sinatra standards on a portable organ. (332-7103. Open daily 6:30am-9:30pm.) At **Mama's Royal Cafe,** 387 Miller Ave., slackers serve up unusual but good dishes from a menu as packed as the restaurant. The whole place is decorated in lawn ornaments and psychedelic murals. (388-3261. Enchilada El Syd $6.50; Groove Burger $6. Brunch with live music Sa-Su 11am-2pm. Open M-F 7:30am-2:30pm, Sa-Su 8am-3pm.) **My Thai Restaurant,** 1230 4th St., is a top-notch Thai eatery on San Rafael's main drag. (456-4455. Tasty basil prawns $8; Thai iced tea or coffee $1.50; veggie dishes $6-7. Open Su-Th 11:30am-9:30pm, F-Sa 11:30am-10pm.) **Mayflower Inne,** 1553 4th St.— this British pub serves better-than-classic British grub. It offers fish and chips, bangers and mash, and not a vegetable in sight—unless you count mushy peas. (456-1011. Best deal: cup of soup and half-sandwich for $4.25. "Bawdy Piano Sing-along" F 8pm. Open daily 11:30am-2am; kitchen closes at 9pm.)

◙ **SIGHTS.** Marin's proximity to San Francisco makes it a popular daytrip destination. Virtually everything worth seeing or doing in Marin is outdoors. An efficient visitor can hop from park to park and enjoy several short hikes along the coast and through the redwood forests in the same day, topping it off with a pleasant dinner in one of the small cities. Those without cars, however, may find it easier to use 1 of the 2 well-situated hostels as a base for explorations.

Originally a fishing center full of bars and bordellos, the city at Marin's extreme southeastern tip has long since traded its sea-dog days for retail boutiques and overpriced seafood restaurants. **Bridgeway** is the city's main thoroughfare, and practically the only one shown on Sausalito Visitors Center maps. A block away from the harbor and Bridgeway's smug shops, **Caledonia St.** offers more charming restaurants and a few more affordable stores. Perhaps the best thing to see in Sausalito is the view of San Francisco. For the best views of the city, take the ferry (see **Ferries,** p. 827) or bike across the Golden Gate Bridge. Half a mile north of the town center is the **Bay Model,** a massive working model of San Francisco Bay. Built in the 1950s to test proposals to dam the bay and other diabolical plans, the water-filled model recreates tides and currents in great detail. (2100 Bridgeway. 332-3871. Turn off Bridgeway at Marinship. Open in summer Tu-F 9am-4pm, Sa 10am-6pm; off-season Tu-F 9am-4pm. Free.)

Fog-shrouded hills just to the west of the Golden Gate Bridge comprise the **Marin Headlands.** Its windswept ridges, precipitous cliffs, and hidden sandy beaches offer superb hiking and biking within minutes of downtown San Francisco. For instant gratification, choose one of the coastal trails, which offer easy access to dark sand beaches and dramatic cliffs of basalt greenstone. One of the best very short hikes is to at **Point Bonita,** a prime spot for seeing sunbathing California sea lions in summer and migrating gray whales in the cooler months.

Between the upscale towns of East Marin and the rocky bluffs of West Marin rests beautiful **Mt. Tamalpais State Park** (tam-ull-PIE-us). The park has miles of hilly, challenging trails on and around 2571 ft. Mt. Tamalpais, the highest peak in the county and the original "mountain" in "mountain bike." At the center of the state park is **Muir Woods National Monument,** a 560-acre stand of primeval coastal redwoods, located about 5mi. west of U.S. 101 along Rt. 1. Spared from logging by the steep sides of Redwood Canyon, these centuries-old redwoods are massive and enshrouded in silence. (Monument open daily 8am-sunset; visitors center 9am-6pm.)

**Rt. 1** reaches the Pacific at Muir Beach, and from there twists its way up the rugged coast. It's all beautiful, but the stretch between Muir Beach and Stinson Beach is the most breathtaking, especially when driving south, on the sheer-drop-to-the-ocean side of the highway. Sheltered **Muir Beach** is scenic and popular with families. (Open daily dawn-9pm.) The crowds thin out significantly after a 5min. climb on the shore rocks to the left. Six mi. to the north, **Stinson Beach** attracts a younger, rowdier crowd of good-looking surfer dudes and dudettes, though cold and windy conditions often keep them posing on dry land. (Open daily dawn-dusk.)

A near-island surrounded by nearly 100mi. of isolated coastline, the **Point Reyes National Seashore** is a wilderness of pine forests, chaparral ridges, and grassy flatlands. Rt. 1 provides direct access to the park from the north or south; Sir Francis Drake Blvd. comes west from U.S. 101 at San Rafael. After a day, or 10, exploring the seashore, the little town of **Point Reyes Station,** 2mi. north of Olema on Rt. 1, makes a welcoming dinner destination. Point Reyes is a cow town, built on dairy farming, and its main streets look appropriately Western with wide streets and false-fronted buildings. The town whistle "moos" like a cow each day at high noon.

# WINE COUNTRY

## NAPA VALLEY

While not the oldest, the Napa Valley is certainly the best-known of America's wine-growing regions. The gentle hills, fertile soil, ample moisture, and year-round sunshine are ideal for viticulture. European vines were first planted here as early as the late 1850s, but early producers were crippled by Prohibition, when the grapes were supplanted with figs. The region did not begin to reestablish itself until the 1960s. During the 70s, Napa's rapidly improving offerings won the attention of those in the know, and word-of-mouth cemented the California bottle as a respectable choice. In 1976, a bottle of red from Napa's Stag's Leap Vineyard beat a bottle of Château Lafitte-Rothschild in a blind taste test in Paris, and American wine was suddenly *très* cool. Today, local vineyards continue to reap awards, and the everyday tasting carnival dominates life in the valley's small towns.

🔁 **ORIENTATION AND PRACTICAL INFORMATION. Rt. 29 (St. Helena Hwy.)** runs through the Napa Valley from **Napa** through **Yountville** and **St. Helena** to **Calistoga.** Slow with visitors stopping at each winery, the relatively short distance takes a surprisingly long, if scenic, time. The **Silverado Trail,** parallel to Rt. 29, is a less crowded route, but watch out for stylish cyclists. Napa is 14mi. east of Sonoma on **Rt. 12.** On Sa mornings and Su afternoons the roads are packed with cars traveling from San Francisco. Although harvest, in early Sept., is the most exciting time to visit, winter weekdays provide space for personal attention. From the city, take U.S. 101 over the Golden Gate, then Rt. 37 E to Rt. 121 N, which will cross Rt. 12 N (to Sonoma) and Rt. 29 (to Napa). The nearest **Greyhound** station is in Vallejo, but 1 bus per day passes through the valley, stopping in Napa (6:15pm, Napa State Hospital, 2100 Napa-Vallejo Hwy.), Yountville, St. Helena, and Calistoga. **Public Transportation: Napa City Bus,** or **Valley Intercity Neighborhood Express (VINE),** 1151 Pearl St. (800-696-6443 or 255-7631, TDD 226-9722), covers the valley and Vallejo. To Vallejo (fare $1.50, students $1.10, disabled 75¢) and Calistoga ($2/$1.45/$1); transfers free. (Buses run M-F 6:30am-6pm, Sa 7:30am-5:30pm.) **Car Rental: Budget,** 407 Soscol Ave. (224-7846), Napa, rents cars $35 from day (under 26 surcharge $20. Unlimited mi. Must be 21+ with credit card). **Winery tours** offered by **Napa Valley Wine Shuttle,** 3031 California Blvd. (800-258-8226; day pass $30, children free), and **Napa Valley Holidays** (255-1050; 3hr., $30). **Visitor Info: Napa Visitors Center,** 1310 Town Center (226-7459; open daily 9am-5pm, phones closed Sa-Su). **St. Helena Chamber of Commerce,** 1010A Main St. (963-4456; open M-F 10am-4:30pm). **Calistoga Chamber of Commerce,** 1458 Lincoln Ave. (942-6333; open M-F 9am-5pm, Sa 10am-4:30pm, Su 11am-4pm). **Post Office:** 1351 2nd St. (255-1268), Napa. Open M-F 8:30am-5pm. **ZIP code:** 94559. **Area code:** 707.

☞ **ACCOMMODATIONS.** Rooms in Napa are scarce and go fast despite their high prices (B&Bs and most hotels are $60-225 per night). Budget options are more plentiful in **Santa Rosa** and **Petaluma,** which are within easy driving distance of the valley. For those without cars, camping is the best option, though the heat is intense in summer. The **Discovery Inn,** 500 Silverado Trail, near Soscol in Napa, boasts kitchenettes, cable, and a tad more personality than a chain motel (253-0892; rooms $65, Sa-Su $95; check-in noon-6pm.) **Bothe-Napa Valley State Park,** 3801 Rte. 29, north of St. Helena, is often full. (942-4575; reservations 800-444-7275. Sites Su-Th $15, F-Sa $20, seniors $14; vehicles $5. Hot showers. Pool $3, under 18 $2. Park open 8am-sunset.) The **Calistoga Ranch Club,** 580 Lommel Rd., off the Silverado Trail near Calistoga, caters to families. Hiking trails lace the ranch, which includes a fishing lake, volleyball, and pool. (800-847-6272. Tent sites $19; RV sites $23; 4-person cabins with shared bath $49; 5-person trailers with kitchen $89.)

🗂 **FOOD.** Eating in Wine Country ain't cheap, but the food is usually worth it. Picnics are an inexpensive and romantic option; buy supplies at the numerous delis or Safeway stores in the area. Most wineries have shaded picnic grounds, often with excellent views. The **Napa farmer's market**, at Pearl and West St., offers a sampling of the valley's *other* produce (252-7142; open daily 7:30am-noon). **Curb Side Cafe**, 1245 1st St., Napa, at Randolph St., slings sublime sandwiches ($5-6.50) and heavy breakfasts like the pancake special: 4 buttermilk pancakes, 2 eggs, and ham or sausage ($6; 253-2307; open daily 9am-3pm). **Calistoga Natural Foods and Juice Bar**, 1426 Lincoln St., Calistoga, is one of few natural foods stores in the area. An organic juice and sandwich bar, serving vegetarian specialties like the $4.50 Garlic Goddess (942-5822; open M-Sa 9am-6pm, Su 10am-5pm).

🍷 **DRINKING.** There are more than 250 wineries in Napa County, nearly 2/3 of which line **Rt. 29** and the **Silverado Trail** in the Napa Valley. Wine country's heavyweights call this valley home; vineyards include national names such as Inglenook, Fetzer, and Mondavi. Few wineries in Napa have free tastings, so choose your samples carefully. The wineries listed below (from south to north) are among the valley's larger and more touristy operations. Visitors must be 21 or older to purchase or drink alcohol (yes, they do card). **Domaine Chandon** is owned by Moët Chandon of France (the makers of Dom Perignon), producing 5 million bottles of sparkling wine annually—that's one hell of a New Year's party. (*1 California Dr. 944-2280. Tours every hr. 11am-5pm and tastings $8 for 3 wines, $12 for all 5. Open May-Oct. daily 10am-6pm; Nov.-Apr. W-Su 10am-6pm.*) Originally a viticulture education center, **Robert Mondavi Winery**, Oakville, 8mi. north of Napa, has some of the best winery tours, covering subjects from tasting to soil conditions. (*7801 Rt. 29. 963-9611 or 800-666-3284. Wine by the glass from $3. Open daily May-Oct. 10am-4pm; Nov.-Apr. 9:30am-4:30pm.*) To reach the **Hakusan Sake Gardens**, take Rt. 12 off Rt. 29, turn left on N. Kelly, then left onto Executive Way. Japanese gardens are a welcome change from the other wineries. *Sake* is a strong Japanese wine with a fruity taste (served warm or cold). (*1 Executive Way. 258-6160 or 800-425-8726. Open daily 10am-5pm.*) Picturesque **Domaine Carneros**, off Rt. 121 between Napa and Sonoma, has an elegant terrace. No tastings; wines sold by the glass $5-12 with hors d'oeuvres. (*1240 Duhig Rd. 257-0101. Free tour and film every hr. 11am-4pm. Open daily 10:30am-6pm.*)

🍷 **NOT DRINKING.** Napa does have non-alcoholic attractions. Chief among them is 160-acre **Marine World Africa USA**, an enormous zoo-oceanarium-themepark 10mi. south of Napa, off Rt. 37 in Vallejo. All proceeds benefit wildlife research and protection programs. The park is accessible by BART (415-788-2278) and the Blue and Gold fleet (415-705-5444), from San Francisco. (*643-6722. Open Mar.-Aug. daily 10am-10pm; Sept.-Oct. F-Su 10am-6pm. $34, seniors $25, ages 4-12 or under 48in. $17. Parking $6. Wheelchair access.*)

**Robert Louis Stevenson State Park**, 4mi. north of St. Helena on Rt. 29, has a plaque where the Scottish writer, sick and penniless, spent a rejuvenating honeymoon in 1880. The hike up **Mt. St. Helena** is a moderate 3hr. climb culminating in dizzying views of the valley. (*942-4575. No ranger station; bring water. Open daily 8am-dusk.*) The **Silverado Museum**, off Adams in St. Helena, is a labor of love by a devoted collector of Stevensoniana. Manuscript notes from *Dr. Jekyll and Mr. Hyde* are on display. (*1490 Library Ln. 963-3757. Open Tu-Su noon-4pm. Free.*) Perhaps feeling slightly derivative, the **Old Faithful Geyser of California** is farther north, 2mi. outside Calistoga on Tubbs Ln. off Rt. 128. (*942-6463. Open daily 9am-6pm; in winter 9am-5pm. $6, seniors $4, ages 6-12 $2, disabled free. Bathrooms not wheelchair accessible.*)

**Calistoga** is also known as the **"Hot Springs of the West."** Sam Brannan, who first developed the area, meant to make the hot springs the "Saratoga of California," but he misspoke and promised instead to make "The Calistoga of Saratina." Luckily, history has a soft spot for millionaires; Brannan's dream has come true, and Calistoga is now a center for luxurious spas and resorts. Massage your wallet by sticking to **Golden Haven** (*942-6793*), which specializes in private couple baths,

**CALIFORNIA**

**VIN FRIENDS AND INFLUENCE PEOPLE** Most wines are recognized by the grape-stock from which they're grown—**white** grapes produce Chardonnay, Riesling, and Sauvignon; **reds** are responsible for Beaujolais, Pinot Noir, Merlot, and Zinfandel. **Blush** or **rosé** wines issue from red grapes which have had their skins removed during fermentation in order to leave just a kiss of pink. White Zinfandel, for example, comes from a red grape often made skinless, and is therefore rose in color. Of course, blush is not the wine of choice among wine connoisseurs; it's for plebes and picnics. **Dessert** wines, such as Muscat, are made with grapes that have acquired the "noble rot" *(botrytis)* at the end of picking season, giving them an extra-sweet flavor. When tasting, start with a white, moving from **dry** to **sweet** (dry wines have had a higher percentage of their sugar content fermented into alcohol). Proceed through the reds, which go from **lighter** to **fuller bodied**, depending on tannin content. **Tannin** is the pigment red wine gets from the grape skin—it preserves and ages the wine, which is why reds can be young and sharp, but grow more mellow with age. It's best to end with dessert wines. One should cleanse one's palate between each wine, with a biscuit, some *fromage*, or fruit. Don't hesitate to ask for advice from the tasting-room pourer. Tasting proceeds thusly: stare, sniff, swirl, swallow (first 3 steps are optional). You will probably encounter fellow tasters who slurp their wine and make concerned faces, as though they're trying to cram the stuff up their noses with the back of their tongues. These chaps consider themselves serious tasters, and are aerating the wine in their mouths to better bring out the flavor. Key words to help you seem more astute during tasting sessions are: dry, sweet, buttery, light, crisp, fruity, balanced, rounded, subtle, rich, woody, and complex. Feel free to banter these terms about indiscriminately. *Sally forth, young naifs!*

or **Nance's Hot Springs** *(942-6211),* where you get one of the more complex yet inexpensive treatments. Cooler water can be found at **Lake Berryessa** *(966-2111),* 20mi. north of Napa off Rt. 128. Swimming, sailing, and sunbathing on 169mi. of shoreline are all popular activities.

## SONOMA VALLEY

The sprawling Sonoma Valley is a quieter alternative to Napa. Wineries are approachable via winding side roads rather than down a freeway strip, making for a more intimate and adventurous feel. Less straggling than Napa's strip of small towns, the valley showcases a beautiful, expansive 8-acre plaza in the town of Sonoma. Petaluma, which is west of the Sonoma Valley, has a better variety of budget lodgings than the expensive wine country.

**⚐ PRACTICAL INFORMATION. Rt. 12** traverses the length of Sonoma Valley from **Sonoma,** through **Glen Ellen,** to **Kenwood** in the north. The center of downtown Sonoma is **Sonoma Plaza,** a park which contains City Hall and the visitors center. **Broadway** dead-ends in front of City Hall at Napa St. Numbered streets run north-south. **Petaluma** lies to the west and is connected to Sonoma by **Rt. 116,** which becomes **Lakeville St.** in Petaluma. Lakeville St. intersects **Washington St.,** the central downtown road. **Sonoma County Transit** (800-345-7433) serves the entire county, from Petaluma to Cloverdale and the Russian River. Bus #30 runs to Santa Rosa M-Sa (fare $1.95, students $1.60, seniors and disabled 95¢, under 6 free); bus #40 goes to Petaluma (fare $1.60). **Sonoma Valley Visitors Bureau:** 453 E. 1st St. (996-1090), in Sonoma Plaza (open daily 9am-7pm; Nov.-May 9am-5pm). **Petaluma Visitors Program,** 799 Baywood Dr. (769-0429), at Lakeville (open June-Sept. M-F 9am-5:30pm, Sa-Su 10am-6pm; shorter off-season hrs.). **Post Office:** 617 Broadway (996-2459), at Patten, in Sonoma (open M-F 8:30am-5pm). **ZIP code:** 95476. **Area code:** 707.

**⌂⌂ ACCOMMODATIONS AND FOOD.** Pickings are pretty slim for lodging; rooms are scarce even M-F and generally start at $75. Cheaper motels cluster along U.S. 101 in Santa Rosa and Petaluma. **Motel 6,** 1368 N. McDowell Blvd., is off U.S. 101 in Petaluma (765-0333; singles Su-Th $44, F-Sa $47; doubles $47/50; each additional adult $3). **Sugarloaf Ridge State Park,** 2605 Adobe Canyon Rd., north of Kenwood off Rt. 12, has sites centered around central meadow with flush toilets and running water, but no showers (833-5712; sites $16). ▓ **Quinley's,** 310 D St., at Petaluma, first opened its doors in 1952, and that old-time rock 'n' roll plays on with burgers (778-6000; open M-Th 11am-9pm, F-Sa 11am-10pm, Su 10am-6pm).

**WINERIES.** Sonoma Valley's wineries, located near Sonoma and Kenwood, are less touristy but just as tasty as Napa's. More of the tastings are also likely to be complimentary. Near Sonoma, white signs will help guide you through the back-roads; they are difficult to read but indicate the general direction of the wineries. Bring a map (they're all over the place and free), as the signs will often desert you when they're most needed. **Buena Vista,** off E. Napa, is the oldest winery in the valley. *(18000 Old Winery Rd. 800-926-1266. Hosts theatrical performances July-Sept. Brief historical presentations 2pm; also 11am in summer. Free tastings daily 10:30am-5pm.)* The famous old stone buildings are preserved as Mr. Haraszthy built them in 1857, when he founded the California wine industry. Free tastings take place downstairs, while you can taste vintage wine and champagne upstairs in a working artist's gallery for a small fee. **Glen Ellen Winery** is 1mi. from Glen Ellen in Jack London Village. *(14301 Arnold Dr. 939-6277. Open daily 10am-5pm.)* Nearby cafes have expensive food to enjoy at the picnic tables outside; an adjacent olive press offers oil tasting. One of the few organic wineries in the region, **Kenwood** prides itself on its attention to the environment. *(9592 Sonoma Hwy. 833-5891. Complimentary tastings with recipe samples Sa-Su. Open M-F 8am-4:30pm.)* The Mediterranean setting at **Château St. Jean,** Kenwood, includes lookout tower with balcony and an observation deck above the production area. *(8555 Rt. 12. 833-4134. Tastings daily 10am-4:30pm.)*

▓ **SIGHTS AND SEASONAL EVENTS.** Local historical artifacts are preserved in the **Sonoma State Historic Park,** at E. Spain and 1st, in the northeast corner of town. Within the park, an adobe church stands on the site of the **Sonoma Mission,** the northernmost and last of the Spanish missions. Built in 1826 when Mexico was already a republic, the mission houses a remnant of the original California Republic flag, the rest of which was burned in the 1906 post-earthquake fires. *(938-9560. Open daily 10am-5pm. $3, seniors $2, ages 6-12 $1; includes Vallejo's Home, barracks next door, and Petaluma Adobe.)*

To find **Jack London State Park,** take Rt. 12 north about 4mi. to Arnold Lane and follow the signs. At the beginning of the 20th century, hard-drinking and hard-living Jack London (author of *The Call of the Wild* and *White Fang*) bought 1400 acres here, determined to create his dream home. London's hopes were never realized—the estate's main building, the Wolf House, was destroyed by arsonists in 1913. London died 3 years after the fire and is buried in the park, his grave marked by a volcanic boulder intended for the construction of his house. The nearby **House of Happy Walls,** built by his widow, is now a 2-story museum devoted to the writer. The park's scenic ½mi. **Beauty Ranch Trail** passes the lake, winery ruins, and quaint cottages. Free golf cart rides are available Sa-Su 12:30pm-4:30pm for those requiring handicapped access. *(938-5216. Park open daily 9:30am-sunset; museum open daily 10am-5pm. $6 per car.)* **Sonoma Cattle and Napa Valley Trail Rides** also gallop through the fragrant forests. *(996-8566. 2hr. ride $45; sunset and night rides available.)*

# NORTHERN CALIFORNIA

## MENDOCINO

Perched on bluffs overlooking the ocean, isolated Mendocino (pop. 1000) is a highly stylized coastal community of art galleries, craft shops, bakeries, and B&Bs. The town's weathered wood shingles, sloping roofs, and clustered homes seem out of place on the West Coast; perhaps that's why Mendocino was able to masquerade for years as the fictional Maine village of Cabot Cove in the TV series

CALIFORNIA

*Murder, She Wrote.* Mendocino sits on **Rt. 1** right on the Pacific Coast, 30mi. west of U.S. 101 and 12mi. south of Fort Bragg. Only easily accessible by car, the town is tiny, and best explored on foot (parking available in plentiful lots). Weather in the Mendocino area varies from 40-70°F. Travelers should come prepared for chilliness caused by fog.

Mendocino's greatest attribute lies 900 feet to its west, where the earth clangs to a halt and falls off into the Pacific, forming the impressive fog-shrouded coastline of the **Mendocino Headlands.** Beneath wildflower-laden meadows, fingers of eroded rock claw through the pounding ocean surf and seals frolic in secluded alcoves.

For the most part, **Fort Bragg** is the place to stay while visiting Mendocino; the town's tourist pheromone is the **Skunk Train,** at Rt. 1 and Laurel St., a jolly diversion through deserted logging towns and recuperating forest. (964-6371 or 800-777-5865. Trips depart at 9, 9:30am, 1:30, and 2pm; off-season 9:20, 10am, and 2pm; Dec. 9:20, 10am, and 2:10pm.) A steam engine, diesel locomotive, and vintage motorcar take turns running between Fort Bragg and Willits via Northspur, with whole and ½-day trips available. If a 1-way trip fits your transportatin' needs, those are available; round-trip rides include a short break in Northspur and an hour in Willits. Schedule changes necessitate calling ahead for reservations.

Poor drainage, thin soil, and ocean winds have created an unusual bonsai garden just south of town at the **Pygmy Forest in Van Damme State Park** ($5). The trees are visible for free from the trail off Little Airport Rd. (off Rt. 1 past the park; after turning left, drive 3½mi. to a parking lot and a sign for the pygmy forest). The **ecological staircase** at **Jug Handle State Park** is a terrace of 5 different ecosystems, each roughly 100,000 years older than the one below it and formed by a combination of erosion and tectonic uplift.

Glimpses through the interstices of Mendocino County's fog and flora reveal many a fancy version of *au naturel*—hotspring resorts abound. **Orr Hot Springs,** 13201 Orr Springs Rd., is just south of Mendocino off Comptche Ukian Rd. Sauna, steam room, and gardens make the world disappear at this clothing-optional resort. (462-6277. 1hr. drive over dirt roads. From U.S. 101 take the North State St. exit. Open daily 10am-10pm. Day use $19; M special $10.) In July, enjoy the **Mendocino Music Festival,** a 2-week (clothing-optional) melee of classical music and opera (937-2044. Tickets $12-20).

It's impossible to find a hotel room in Mendocino for under $60. Fortunately, hundreds of campsites are nearby; make reservations through PARKNET (800-444-7275). Otherwise, look to Ukiah or Fort Bragg for budget motels. ◪ **Jug Handle Creek Farm,** off Rt. 1 at the Caspar exit 5mi. north of Mendocino, is a beautiful 120-year-old house sitting on 40 acres of gardens, campsites, and small rustic cabins. Guests have access to the beach and trails in Jug Handle State Park. (964-4630. 30 beds. 1hr. of chores, or $5, required per night. No linen. Dorms $18, students $12; sites $6, children $3; cabins $25 per person. Reserve in advance.) **MacKerricher State Park campground,** 3½mi. north of Ft. Bragg, has excellent views of tidepool life, passing seals, sea lions, and whales, as well as 9mi. of beaches and a murky lake for trout fishing. (937-5804. Showers, bathrooms, and drinkable water. Sites $16; day use free. Reservations recommended.) Foggy woods shelter 30 sites at **Russian Gulch State Park campground,** on Rt. 1, 1mi. north of town. Campers have access to a beach, redwoods, hiking trails, and a waterfall. (937-5804. Showers and flush toilets. No hookups. Sites $16, seniors $14; day use $5. Open Apr.-Oct.)

**Mendocino Stage** (964-0167) runs 3 buses per day between Ft. Bragg and Ukiah ($3). **Mendocino Transit Authority,** 241 Plant Rd. (800-696-4682), makes one round-trip between Santa Rosa, Ukiah, Willits, Fort Bragg, and Mendocino daily ($7.50). **Visitor Info: Ford House,** 735 Main St. (937-5397; open daily 9:30am-4:30pm). **Post Office:** 10500 Ford St. (937-5282), 2 blocks west of Main. Open M-F 7:30am-4:30pm. **ZIP code:** 95460. **Area code:** 707.

## AVENUE OF THE GIANTS

About 6mi. north of **Garberville** off U.S. 101, the **Avenue of the Giants** winds its way through 31mi. of the largest living creatures this side of sea level. Scattered throughout the area are several commercialized attractions such as the **World Famous Tree House, Confusion Hill** (a vortex of mystery where the laws of gravity no longer apply; free), and the **Drive-Thru Tree.** Travelers looking for a more authentic taste of the redwood forests may want to bypass these hokey attractions in favor of more rugged and natural tours. There are a number of great hiking trails in the area, marked on $1 maps available at the **Humboldt Redwoods State Park Visitors Center,** just south of Weott on the Avenue (946-2263; open daily 9am-5pm; Nov.-Mar. Th-Su 10am-4pm). The **Canoe Creek Loop Trail,** across the street from the visitors center, is an easy start. Uncrowded trails snake through the park's northern section around **Rockefeller Forest,** which contains the largest grove of old-growth redwoods (200 years and growing) in the world. The **Dyerville Giant,** in the redwood graveyard at Founder's Grove about midway through the Avenue, deserves a respectful visit. The ½mi. loop trail includes the **Founder's Tree** and the **Fallen Giant,** whose massive trunk stretches 60 human body-lengths long and whose 3-story rootball looks like a mythical ensnarlment of evil. The **Standish Hickey Recreation Area** (925-6482), north of Leggett on U.S. 101, offers fishing, camping, swimming, and hiking (parking $5).

With its sizable artist population, Garberville's **art festivals** are a big draw. **Jazz on the Lake** and the **Summer Arts Fair** begin in late June, followed by **Shakespeare at Benbow Lake** in late July. Early Aug. brings **Reggae on the River,** a 12hr. music fest on the banks of the Eel River. **Visitor Info: Chamber of Commerce,** 773 Redway (800-923-2613), in Garberville. **Area code:** 707.

# REDWOOD NATIONAL PARK

With ferns that grow to the height of humans and redwood trees the size of skyscrapers, Redwood National Park, as John Steinbeck said, "will leave a mark or create a vision that stays with you always." Fog rolls between the creaking redwood boughs in a prehistoric atmosphere where you half expect a dinosaur to tromp by at any moment. The redwoods in the park are the last remaining stretch of the old-growth forest which used to blanket 2 million acres of Northern California and Oregon. Wildlife runs rampant here, with black bears and mountain lions in the backwoods and Roosevelt elk grazing in the meadows.

## ◪ PRACTICAL INFORMATION

**Redwood National Park** is only 1 of 4 redwood parks between Klamath and Orick, the others being **Jedediah Smith State Park, Del Norte Coast Redwoods State Park,** and **Prairie Creek Redwoods State Park.** The name "Redwood National Park" is an umbrella term for all 4 parks.

**Buses:** Greyhound, 500 E. Harding St., Crescent City (464-2807). To **San Francisco** (2 per day, $51) and **Portland** (2 per day, $53). Open M-F 7-10am and 5-7:30pm, Sa 7-9am and 7-7:30pm. No credit cards.

**Visitor Info: Redwood Information Center** (488-3461) doles out brochures and maps 1mi. south of Orick on U.S. 101. Open daily 9am-5pm.

**Post Office:** 751 2nd St. (464-2151), Crescent City (open M-F 8:30am-5pm, Sa noon-2pm). **ZIP code:** 95531. **Area code:** 707.

## ◪ ACCOMMODATIONS AND FOOD

A pleasant pad is the **Redwood Youth Hostel (HI-AYH),** 14480 U.S. 101, 7mi. north of Klamath at Wilson Creek Rd. Overlooking the crashing Pacific surf and housed in the historic DeMartin House, this 30-bed hostel suggests Shaker simplicity. Chores and rules may seem a bit oppressive. (482-8265. Dorms $12. Linen $1. Check-in 4:30-9:30pm. Check-out 9:30am.) **Camp Marigold,** 16101 U.S. 101, 3mi. north of Klamath Bridge, is a pleasantly woodsy alternative to mundane motels (482-3585 or 800-621-8513; doubles $38). **Green Valley Motel,** on U.S. 101 in Orick, has clean, basic rooms, and a deli. (488-2341. Phones and TV. Singles $32; doubles $35.) There are more picnic table sites than restaurants in the area, so the best option for food is probably **Orick Market,** which has reasonably priced groceries (488-3225; open M-Sa 8am-7pm, Su 9am-7pm). In Crescent City, head to the 24hr. **Safeway** in the shopping center on U.S. 101 (M St.) between 2nd and 5th. **Glen's Bakery and Restaurant,** 3rd and G St., serves basic diner fare such as huge pancakes ($3), sandwiches ($4), and burgers ($3-4; 464-2914; open Tu-Sa 5am-6:30pm). The **Jefferson State Brewery,** 400 Front St., is a hip new restaurant and bar built of 90% recycled material. Jefferson State serves sandwiches ($5-7), pasta ($10), and island chicken with grilled vegetables ($10). If you're of age, you can try the 6-beer sampler brewed on the premises ($4.50). After dinner, chill in the TV lounge or pick up a game of pool. (464-1139. Open Su-Th 11am-10pm; F-Sa 11am-11pm.)

## ⬛ SIGHTS AND ACTIVITIES

You can see Redwood National Park in just over 1hr. by car, but the redwoods are best experienced by foot. The park is divided into several regions, each of which has information centers and unique attractions. The National Park Service conducts a symphony of organized activities for all ages; a detailed list of junior ranger programs and nature walks is available at all park ranger stations or from the **Redwood Information Center** (488-3461). Hikers should take particular care to wear protective clothing—**ticks** and **poison oak** thrive in these deep, dark places. **Roosevelt elk** roam the woods, and are interesting to watch but dangerous to approach, since invaders of their territory are promptly circled and trampled. Also be on the lookout for the **black bears** and **mountain lions** that inhabit many areas of the park. Before setting out, get advice and trail maps at the visitors center.

**THE ORICK AREA.** The **Orick Area** covers the southernmost section of Redwood National Park. Its **visitors center** lies about 1mi. south of Orick on U.S. 101 and ½mi. south of the Shoreline Deli (the Greyhound bus stop). The main attraction is the **Tall Trees Grove,** which, if the road is open, is accessible by car to those with a permit (available at the visitors center; free). A minimum of 3-4hr. should be allowed for the trip. From the trailhead at the end of Tall Trees Access Rd. (off Bald Hills Rd. from U.S. 101 north of Orick), it's a 1.3mi. hike (about 30min.) to the tallest redwoods in the park and, in fact, to the **tallest known tree in the world** (367.8 ft., one-third the height of New York's World Trade Center towers). If the road is closed, the hardy can hike the 16mi. round-trip **Emerald Ridge Trail** to see these giants. **Patrick's Point State Park,** 15mi. south of Orick along U.S. 101, offers one of the most spectacular views on the California coast, and merits a day or two from campers, boaters, and nature enthusiasts heading north to the redwoods ($16).

**PRAIRIE CREEK AREA.** The Prairie Creek Area, equipped with a **ranger station** and state park **campgrounds,** is perfect for hikers, who can explore 75mi. of trails in the park's 14,000 acres. Trail maps ($1) are available at the ranger station; the loops of criss-crossing trails may be confusing without one. Starting at the visitors center, the **James Irvine Trail** (4½mi. 1-way) winds through a prehistoric garden of towering old growth redwoods of humbling height. Winding through **Fern Canyon,** where small waterfalls trickle down 50 ft. fern-covered walls, the trail ends at **Gold Bluffs Beach,** whose sands stretch for many elk-scattered miles. The less ambitious can elk-watch on the meadow in front of the ranger station.

**KLAMATH AREA.** The Klamath Area to the north consists of a thin stretch of park land connecting Prairie Creek with Del Norte State Park. The town itself consists of a few stores stretched over 4mi., so the main attraction here is the ruggedly spectacular coastline. The **Klamath Overlook,** where Requa Rd. meets the Coastal Trail, is an **excellent whale-watching site,** and offers a spectacular view. The mouth of the **Klamath River** is a popular fishing spot (permit required) during the fall and spring, when salmon make sweet love, and during the winter, when steelhead trout do the same. Coastal Dr. passes by the remains of the **Douglas Memorial Bridge,** where sea lions and harbor seals congregate in the spring and summer, and then continues along the ocean for 8mi. of incredible views.

**HIOUCHI AREA.** This inland region, known for its rugged beauty, sits in the northern part of the park along I-199 and contains some excellent hiking trails, most of which are in **Jedediah Smith State Park.** Several trails lie off Howland Hill Rd., a dirt road easily accessible from both U.S. 101 and I-199. From I-199, turn onto South Fork Rd. in Hiouchi and right onto Douglas Park Rd., which then turns into Howland Hill Rd. From Crescent City, go south on U.S. 101, turn left onto Elk Valley Rd., and right onto Howland Hill.

## GOLD COUNTRY

In 1848, California was a rural backwater of only 15,000 people. The same year, sawmill operator James Marshall wrote in his diary: "This day some kind of mettle...found in the tailrace...looks like goald." In the next 4 years, some 90,000 49ers from around the world headed for California and the 120mi. of gold-rich seams called the **Mother Lode.** Despite the hype, few of the prospectors struck it rich. Miners, sustained by dreams of instant wealth, worked long and hard, yet most could barely squeeze sustenance out of their fiercely guarded claims.

Although gold remains in them thar hills, today the towns of Gold Country make their money mining the tourist traffic. Gussied up as **"Gold Rush Towns,"** they solicit tourists traveling along the appropriately numbered **Rt. 49,** which runs through the foothills along rivers, cliffs, and pastures, connecting dozens of small Gold Country settlements. Traffic from the coast connects with Rt. 49 via I-80 through Sacramento, which today serves as a supply post for tourists instead of the miners of the Gold Rush. If you tire of Gold Country lore, you're not alone. Vineyard touring, river rafting, and spelunking are popular and don't involve the g-word. Most of Gold Country is about 2hr. from Sacramento, 3hr. from San Francisco.

**SACRAMENTO.** The state government rules over Sacramento sights. Stormy debates about immigration, welfare, water shortages, secession, and more rage daily for a public audience in the elegant **State Capitol,** at 10th and Capitol. (324-0333. 1hr. tours depart daily 9am-4pm on the hour; free tickets are distributed in room B27 on a first come, first served basis.) Towering palm trees and grassy lawns make **Capitol Park** one of many oases in the middle of downtown's busy bureaucracy, and a popular place for youthful loitering. The **State Historic Park Governor's Mansion,** at 16th and H St., was built in 1877 and served as the residence of California's governor and his family until Governor Ronald Reagan moved out and opted to rent his own pad. (324-0539. Open daily 10am-4pm. $3, ages 6-12 $1.50. Hourly tours.) **Area code:** 916.

**DAVIS.** The **University of California at Davis** is the largest campus (area-wise) in the UC network, and also one of the nation's finest agricultural universities. When they aren't in class, some students hang out at **The Graduate,** 805 Russell Blvd., in the University Mall. The Grad's cavernous dining area has 8 large-screen TVs, video games, a pool table, outdoor tables, meals during the day, and thematic dance party at night. (758-4723. Open daily 10:30am-2am.) **Area code:** 530.

**SONORA.** The ravines and hillsides now known as Sonora were once the domain of the Miwok Indians, but the arrival of the 49ers transformed these Sierra foothills into a bustling mining camp. In its Gold Rush heyday, Sonora was a large and prosperous city that vied fiercely with nearby Columbia for the honor of being the richest city of the southern Mother Lode. The drive to Sonora takes about 2hr. from Sacramento, 3½hr. from San Francisco. **Area code:** 209.

**CALAVERAS COUNTY.** Unsuspecting **Calaveras County** turned out to be literally sitting on a gold mine—the richest, southern part of the "Mother Lode"—when the big rush hit. Over 550,000 pounds of gold were extracted from the county's earth. A journalist from Missouri named Samuel Clemens, a hapless miner but a gifted spinner of yarns later known as **Mark Twain,** allegedly based "The Celebrated Jumping Frog of Calaveras County" on a tale he heard in Angels Camp Tavern. Life in this area has

**PANNIN' FER GOALD I: THEORY** It's easy and fun to pan for gold. *Let's Go* offers a quick, two-part course which will provide all the mental equipment you'll need. Once you're in Gold Country, find one of many public stretches of river. You'll need a 12- or 18-inch gold pan, which will be easily found at local stores. Dig in old mine tailings, at turns in the river, around tree roots, and at the upstream ends of gravel bars, where heavy gold may settle. Swirl water, sand, and gravel in a tilted gold pan, slowly washing materials over the edge. Be patient, and keep at it until you are down to black sand, and—hopefully—gold. Gold has a unique color. It's shinier than brassy-looking pyrite (Fool's Gold), and it doesn't break down upon touch, like mica, a similarly glittery substance. Later, we'll practice this technique.

since imitated (or capitalized on) art; Calaveras has held **annual frog-jumping contests** since 1928. Thousands of people gather on the 3rd weekend of May for the festivities.

A drive along the scenic **Rt. 49** is a great way to glimpse Calaveras County. **San Andreas,** at the juncture of Rt. 26 and 49, is the county hub and population center, but it isn't very big. The **Calaveras Visitors Bureau** (800-225-3764), in downtown Angels Camp, is a great resource for history and sights in the area (open M-F 9am-4pm, Sa 10am-3pm, Su 11am-3pm). Just south of Angels Camp on Rt. 49 is **Tuttletown,** Mark Twain's one-time home, now little more than a historic marker, a grocery store, and a well of stories.

The real attractions of Calaveras County are the natural wonders. About 20mi. east of Angels Camp on Rt. 4 lies **Calaveras Big Trees State Park.** Here the *Sequoiadendron giganteum* (Giant Sequoia) reigns with might: the *giganteum* is bigger than the Statue of Liberty and is the largest living thing ever to inhabit the earth. The **North Grove Trail** (1mi.) is wheelchair accessible, gently graded, and heavily trafficked. The less-traveled, more challenging **South Grove Trail** (4mi.) better captures the forest's beauty and timelessness. The park also offers swimmin' in **Beaver Creek** and camping. Summertime visitors should prepare for gnats and mosquitoes. Be aware that the snow comes early (sometimes in Sept.) and leaves late (mid-Apr.) at Big Trees. (795-2334. Open 24hr. Day use $5, senior discount. Sites $16, hot showers. Reservations 800-365-2267.)

Calaveras County boasts gargantuan natural wonders below ground as well as above. **Moaning Cavern** is a vast vertical cave so large that the Statue of Liberty could live there comfortably. From Angels Camp, follow Rt. 4mi. east, right onto Parrot's Ferry Rd., and follow signs. Descend the 236 steps or rappel 180 feet down into the cave. Whether walking cautiously or hurtling down like an extreme sportsman, be prepared for shortness of breath after the steep walk up at the tour's end. The whole experience takes about 45min. (736-2708. Stairs $7.75, ages 3-13 $4; rappelling 1st time $35, each additional time $17.50. Open daily in summer 9am-6pm; in winter M-F 10am-5pm, Sa-Su and holidays 9am-5pm.) **Mercer Caverns,** 9mi. north of Angels Camp, off Rt. 4 on Sheep Rd. in Murphys, offers 1hr. walking tours of 10 internal rooms. Although smaller and less dramatic than Moaning Cavern, the caves are nearly a million years old. (728-2101. Open M-Th 10am-6pm, F-Sa 10am-8pm. Tours every 20min. $7, ages 5-11 $3.50, under 5 free.) **California Caverns,** at Cave City, served as a naturally air-conditioned bar and dance floor during the Gold Rush when a shot of whiskey could be purchased for a pinch of gold dust. The caverns sobered up on Su for church services when one stalagmite served as an altar. Walking tours and "wild cavern expedition trips" explore cramped tunnels, waist-high mud, and underground lakes. Directions are available at the visitors bureau. (736-2708. Tours $8, ages 3-13 $4.25. Expeditions 2-3hr.; over 16 $75; less-strenuous for ages 9-16 $58.)

Calaveras County has been a producer of **fine wines** for nearly 150 years. Vineyards stretch along Rt. 49, and wineries abound near Plymouth. Most family-owned wineries offer free wine tasting. The **Stevenot Winery,** 2mi. north of Murphy's Main St. on Sheep Ranch Rd., is the county's largest facility (728-3436; free tastings daily 10am-5pm). **Kautz Ironstone Vineyards,** on Six Mile Rd. 1½mi. south of Murphy's Main St., stores wine in caverns hewn from solid rock (728-1251; tours daily 11am-5pm, tasting room open 10am-6pm).

**COLOMA.** The 1848 Gold Rush began in Coloma at John Sutter's water-powered lumber mill, operated by James Marshall. Today, the town tries its darnedest to hype this claim to fame, but the effort just makes tiny Coloma feel like Disneyland without the fun. Accommodations are sparse, so visitors will probably want to stay in Placerville. The town basically revolves around the **James Marshall Gold Discovery State Historic Park.** Near the site where Marshall struck gold is a replica of the original mill. *(622-1116. Open 8am-dusk. Day-use fee $5 per car, seniors $4. Display your pass prominently in your car window or you will be ticketed.)* Picnic grounds across the street surround the **Gold Discovery Museum,** which presents the events of the Gold Rush through dioramas and film. *(310 Back St. 622-3470. Open daily 10am-5pm.)* The real reason to come to Coloma, however, may be for the nearby natural attractions. The American River's class III currents, among the most accessible rapids in the West, attract thousands of rafters and kayakers every weekend. **Area code:** 916.

**BUTTE MOUNTAINS.** Six mi. north of Sierra City, north of I-80, lie the **Butte Mountains,** one of the most beautiful and least traveled areas in California, offering amazing camping, hiking, and fishing possibilities. Five mi. east of Sierra City, on the corner of Rt. 49 and Gold Lake Rd., sits the **Bassetts Station,** an all-purpose establishment that has dispensed lodging, dining, gas, and supplies for over 125 years. Stop in for the low-down on camping, hiking, and fishing. (862-1297. 3 rooms; $65 per night. Open daily 7am-9pm.) **Area code:** 530.

**THE CASCADES.** The Cascade Mountains interrupt an expanse of farmland to the northeast of Gold Country. In these ranges, recent volcanic activity has left behind a surreal landscape of lava beds, mountains, lakes, waterfalls, caves, and recovering forest areas. The calm serenity and haunting beauty of these mountains draw visitors in a way that the Central Valley and Gold Country cannot.

**Lassen Volcanic National Park** is accessible by **Rt. 36** to the south, and **Rt. 44** to the north. Both roads are about 50mi. from **Rt. 5.** In 1914, the earth radiated destruction as tremors, streams of lava, black dust, and a series of huge eruptions ravaged the land, climaxing in 1915 when Mt. Lassen belched a 7mi. high cloud of smoke and ashes. The destructive power of this eruption is still evident in the strange, unearthly pools of boiling water and the stretches of barren moonscape. Winter is long and snowy here. **Lassen Volcanic National Park Headquarters:** in Mineral (595-4444. Open daily in summer 8am-4:30pm; off-season closed Sa-Su.)

Every summer, thousands of New Age believers, yuppie vacationers, and crunchy hikers come to **Mt. Shasta** to carouse, climb, commune, and contemplate its rugged snow-capped top. **Shasta-Trinity National Forest Service,** 204 W. Alma St. (926-4511 or 926-4596), charges info-crystals. The ▧ **Alpenrose Cottage Hostel,** 204 Hinckley St., sends rose scents and sounds of windchimes over guests (926-6724; $15, children $7.50; showers $2; reservations recommended). **Area code:** 916.

# THE SIERRA NEVADA

The Sierra Nevada is a high, steep, and physically stunning mountain range. Thrust skyward 400 million years ago by gigantic plate collisions and shaped by erosion, glaciers, and volcanoes, this enormous hunk of granite stretches 450mi. north from the Mojave Desert to Lake Almanor near Lassen Volcanic National Park. The glistening clarity of Lake Tahoe, the heart-stopping sheerness of Yosemite's rock walls, the craggy alpine scenery of Kings Canyon and Sequoia National Parks, and the abrupt drop of the Eastern Sierra into Owens Valley are sights to behold. Temperatures in the Sierra Nevada are as diverse as the terrain. Even in the summer, overnight lows can dip into the 20s. Normally, only U.S. 50 and I-80 are kept open during the snow season. Exact dates vary from year to year, so check with a ranger station for local road conditions, especially from Oct. to June.

CALIFORNIA

---

**PANNIN' FER GOALD II: PRACTICE** Swish.
Swish. Swish swish. "Dammit." Swish. Swish swish. Swish. "Dammit!" Swish. Swish
swish swish swish. Swish. "Goald!"

---

# LAKE TAHOE

In February of 1844, fearless explorer John C. Fremont led his expedition over the
Sierra—a fool's errand, as anyone in the Donner Party could have told you
between bites of human flesh. Luckily for him, the sight of the beautiful alpine lake
was enough to boost the morale of his 36 starved and weary companions. The lake
went through several identities, from Bigler to Lake of Beer, before the state of
California officially named it Tahoe in 1945. Since settlers rolled into California in
the late 18th century, Lake Tahoe (pop. 33,482) has been a playground for the
wealthy and an outdoor adventurist's dream in any season, with miles of biking,
hiking, and skiing trails, long stretches of beach, and hair-raising whitewater.

## ◆ ORIENTATION AND PRACTICAL INFORMATION

In the northern Sierra on the California-Nevada border, Lake Tahoe is a 3½hr.
drive from San Francisco. The 2 main trans-Sierra highways, **I-80** and **U.S. 50 (Lake
Tahoe Blvd.),** run east-west through Tahoe, skimming the northern and southern
shores of the lake, respectively. Lake Tahoe is 118mi. northeast of Sacramento and
35mi. southwest of Reno on I-80. From the Carson City and Owens Valley area,
**U.S. 395** runs north along Tahoe's eastern shores.

The lake is roughly divided into 2 main regions: North Shore and South Shore.
The North Shore includes King's Beach, Tahoe City, and Incline Village, while the
South Shore includes Emerald Bay and South Lake Tahoe City. Rt. 28 and 89 form
a 75mi. ring of asphalt around the lake; the complete loop takes nearly 3hr.

**Buses: Greyhound** (702-588-4645), in Harrah's Casino on U.S. 50 in Stateline, NV. To
San Francisco (4 per day, $25) and Sacramento (3 per day, $20). No lockers. Station
open daily 8am-12:30pm and 2:30-6:30pm.

**Trains: Amtrak** runs a bus from its San Joaquin and Capitol train routes to Pre-Madonna
Casino, off I-5 at Pre-Madonna exit, and Whiskey Pete's Casino in Stateline, NV. These
trips are long and costly. To San Francisco (11hr., $80).

**Public Transit: Tahoe Casino Express** (800-446-6128) provides shuttle service between
the Reno airport and South Shore Tahoe casinos (daily 6:15am-12:30am). Fare $17,
round-trip $30, up to 2 children under 12 free. **Tahoe Area Regional Transport** (TART;
581-6365) connects the western and northern shores from Incline Village to Tahoe City
to Tahoma (Meeks Bay in summer). Stops daily every hr. 6:30am-6pm. Buses also run
out to Truckee and Squaw Valley 5 times per day. Exact fare necessary ($1.25, day
pass $3). **South Tahoe Area Ground Express** (STAGE; 542-6077) operates buses
around South Tahoe and hourly to the beach. Connects Stateline and Emerald Bay Rd.
($1.25, day pass $2, 10-ride pass $10.) Most casinos operate free shuttle service
along Rt. 50 to California ski resorts and motels. A summer bus program connects
STAGE and TART at Meeks Bay for the entire lake area. Operates 6am-midnight.

**Car Rental: Enterprise** (775-586-1077), in the Horizon lobby in Stateline, NV. Must be
21+ with credit card. From $36 per day, $189 per week with unlimited mileage.

**Visitor Info: U.S. Forest Service and Lake Tahoe Visitors Center,** 870 Emerald Bay Rd.
(573-2674), 3mi. north of S. Lake Tahoe on Rt. 89. Info on campgrounds and year-
round recreation. Free, mandatory wilderness permits for backcountry hiking available.
Open M-F 8am-5:30pm. **South Lake Tahoe Chamber of Commerce,** 3066 Lake Tahoe
Blvd. (541-5255). Open M-Sa 8:30am-5pm. **Lake Tahoe/Douglas Chamber of Commerce,** 195 U.S. 50, Stateline, NV (702-588-4591). Open M-F 9am-6pm, Sa-Su 9am-
5pm. **Tahoe North Visitor and Convention Bureau and Visitor Information,** 245 N.

Lake Blvd. (583-3494). Makes lodging reservations. Open M-F 9am-5pm, Sa-Su 9am-4pm. A **visitors center** near Taylor Creek on Emerald Bay Rd. is staffed mid-June to Oct. daily 8am-5:30pm; Nov. to mid.-June Sa-Su 8am-5:30pm.

**Internet Access: South Lake Tahoe Library,** 1000 Rufus Allen Blvd. (573-3185). Open Tu-W 10am-8pm, Th-Sa 10am-5pm.

**Post Office: Tahoe City,** 950 N. Lake Blvd. #12 (800-275-8777), in the Lighthouse Shopping Center. Open M-F 8:30am-5pm. **ZIP Code:** 96145. **South Lake Tahoe,** 1046 Tahoe Blvd. (544-2208). Open M-F 8:30am-5pm, Sa noon-2pm. **ZIP Code:** 96151. **Area code:** 530 on CA side; 702 on NV side.

# ACCOMMODATIONS

The strip off **U.S. 50** on the California side of the border supports the bulk of Tahoe's motels. Particularly glitzy and cheap in South Lake Tahoe, motels also line the quieter area along **Park Ave.** and **Pioneer Trail.** The North Shore offers more woodsy accommodations along **Rt. 28,** but rates are especially high in Tahoe City. The cheapest deals are clustered near Stateline on U.S. 50. Nearby campgrounds are a good option in warmer months. Campgrounds are often booked for the entire summer, so reserve well in advance; call **National Recreation Reservation System** (NRRS; 800-280-2267) for U.S. Forest Service campgrounds, **California Campground Reservation System** (CCRS; 800-444-7275; outside California 619-452-1950), or **National Park Reservation System** (800-365-2267).

**Tamarack Lodge,** 2311 N. Lake Tahoe Blvd. (583-3350 or 888-824-6323), 3mi. north of Tahoe City, across from Star Harbor community. Clean, quiet motel in the woods. Newly refurbished exterior, outdoor BBQ and fireplace, phones, cable TV, and friendly management. Continental breakfast included. Rooms with queen beds $36-46.

**Cedar Glen Lodge,** 6589 N. Lake Blvd., Tahoe Vista (546-4281 or 800-341-8000). Family-operated motel with a private beach, pool, and indoor hot tub and sauna. Grounds include BBQ pits, playground, hammock, and spectacular rabbit hutch. Morning newspaper and continental breakfast included. Check-in 2pm. Check-out 11am. Singles from $55. Cottages with kitchens also available.

**Hostel at Squaw Valley,** 1900 Squaw Valley Rd. (581-3246), is a 100-bed hostel at the base of Squaw Valley. Roll out of bed and stroll to the ski lifts. Social common area. Dorms $24, weekends and holidays $27. Open mid-Nov. to mid-Apr.

**Doug's Mellow Mountain Retreat,** 3787 Forest St., S. Lake Tahoe (544-8065). 1mi. west of the state line, turn left onto Wildwood Rd., and after 3 blocks take a left on Forest. St. Doug's hostel is the 6th house on the left. Modern kitchen, BBQ, fireplace. Pool table and benches outside. Internet access $5 per hr. Bedding and laundry included. Dorms $15 per person, private rooms available; discounts for stays of a week or longer.

**Budget Inn,** 3496 Lake Tahoe Blvd., S. Lake Tahoe (544-2834, reservations 888-615-1424). Standard rooms with free HBO. Pool and free continental breakfast. Smoking rooms available. Su-Th singles $22, F-Sa $45; doubles $28/55.

**Bayview** (544-5994), has 10 first-come, first-camped sites right on Emerald Bay, but no water or toilets. 7-night max stay. Sites $5.

**D.L. Bliss State Park** (525-7277), on Rt. 89 a few mi. north of Emerald Bay. Camp by the beach or in secluded forest sites. Popular day-use beach, but entrance restricted by the number of parking spaces. 168 sites. 14-night max. stay. Sites $16, beach-side $20. Day parking $5. Pets $1. Open June to Labor Day. The 9mi. **Rubicon Trail** leads to Emerald Bay, Vikingsholm, and Eagle Falls.

# FOOD

In the south, the casinos offer perpetually low-priced buffets, but there are restaurants along the lakeshore with reasonable prices, similarly large portions, and much better food. Groceries are cheaper on the California side.

**Killer Chicken,** 2660 Lake Tahoe Blvd., S. Lake Tahoe (542-9977). BBQ chicken sandwiches ($6-7) that aren't as deadly as the name implies. Whole chickens done Jamaican Jerk, Cuban Roast, Caribbean, or mild herb style ($13 with cornbread and 4 side orders). Veggie and lowfat items available. Open daily 11:30am-9pm.

**Margarita's Mexican Cafe,** 2495 Lake Tahoe Blvd., S. Lake Tahoe (544-6907). Arm-flailing-ly good Mexican cuisine dished up by a friendly waitstaff in a small sitdown restaurant. Tostada salad ($4), combination plates ($7), enchiladas, chimichangas, and cilantro salsa. Open W-M 11:30am-9pm. No credit cards.

**Lakehouse: Pizza-Spirits-Fun,** 120 Grove St., Tahoe City (583-2225). On the water with a sunny lakefront deck. Every seat's got a great view of the lake. Standard breakfast specials ($3-7), California salad ($6.25), sandwiches, and reasonably priced pizzas. Bud Light $2.50. Open M-Th 8am-10pm, F-Su 7:30am-11pm (or midnight).

**Syd's Bagelry and Natural Foods,** 550 North Lake Tahoe Blvd., Tahoe City (583-2666). A bagel shop with a million-dollar view. "Hummus Among Us" (fat bagel sandwich with hummus, cucumber, mushrooms, tomato, carrots, onion, and sprouts) $4.50; garden burgers $4.25. They pride themselves on their espresso drinks. Open daily 6am-8pm.

## ◪ OUTDOOR RECREATION

**BEACHES.** Lake Tahoe supports many beaches perfect for a day of sunning and people-watching. Parking generally costs $3-5. Bargain hunters leave cars in turn-outs on the main road and walk to the beaches. **Sand Harbor Beach,** south of Incline Village, has gorgeous granite boulders and clear waters that attract swimmers, sunners, and scuba divers in droves. The parking lot ($6) is usually full by 11:30am. One mi. away at Memorial Point, lakeside paved parking is free. **Hidden Beach,** also south of Incline Village, and **Kings Beach,** just across the California border on Rt. 28, comes complete with the latest rage (waveboards) and an alternative-rock feel. Kings Beach has volleyball nets, a basketball court, and a playground. **Pope Beach,** at the southernmost point of the lake off Rt. 89, is a wide, pine-shaded expanse of shoreline, which becomes less trafficked on its east side. **Nevada Beach,** 8mi. north of South Lake Tahoe, is close to the casinos off U.S. 50, offering a quiet place to reflect on gambling losses while gazing upon the mountains. **Zephyr Cove Beach,** about 15mi. north of South Lake Tahoe, is a favorite spot for the younger college crowd. **Meeks Bay,** 10mi. south of Tahoe City, is family-oriented and social: picnic tables, volleyball, motorboat and kayak rental, and a petite store. In the summer the Tahoe City and South Tahoe Buses connect here. Five mi. south of Meeks Bay, the **D.L. Bliss State Park** has a large beach on a small bay (Rubicon). The Rubicon Trail leads to the peaceful Vikingsholm mansion. Parking here ($3) is very limited, so think about parking on the road and walking in.

**OTHER WATER ACTIVITIES. River rafting** can be a refreshing way to appreciate the Tahoe scenery, but depending on the water levels of the American and Truckee Rivers, rafting can range from a thrilling whitewater challenge to a boring bake in the sun. If water levels are high, check out raft rental places along the Truckee River and at Tahoe City. For more info, call **Truckee River Rafting,** in Tahoe City, across from Lucky's at Fanny Bridge (583-7238 or 888-584-7238; open daily 8:30am-3:30pm), or **Tahoe Whitewater Tours** (581-2441; 4hr. tour $60; call for reservations). When droughts make conventional rafting scarce, many would-be rafters turn to inner tubes. A tempting but terrifying option is the calm-water "booze cruise." **Tahoe Sailing Charter,** in the Tahoe City Marina, provides the opportunity to "Cruise the north shore" (583-6200. 2hr., $35 per person including refreshments).

If paddling in the north, ask around about (privately owned) **natural hot springs** on the way to the spectacular **Crystal Bay.** Local lore maintains that the bay's frigid temperatures (average 39°F) prevent the decomposition that would ordinarily make corpses float to the surface. Spoooky.

**Fishing** information and regulations can be found at visitors centers, and licenses are available at local sporting good stores. Because of its depth (1600ft. in places) and strange formation, Tahoe is a notoriously difficult lake to fish; bring a good book and be prepared to walk away empty-handed.

**BIKING.** Lake Tahoe is a biking paradise. The excellent paved trails, logging roads, and dirt paths have not gone unnoticed; be prepared for company if you pedal around the area. The U.S. Forest Service and bike rental stores provide advice, publications, maps, and info about trails. No cycling is allowed in the Desolation Wilderness, or on the Pacific Crest or Tahoe Rim Trails. **Olympic Bike Shop,** 60 N. Lake Tahoe Blvd., Tahoe City, has an expert staff (581-2500; mountain bikes $5 per hr., $15 for 4hr., $21 per day).

Known more for its ski trails, the North Shore is equipped with both flat lakeside jaunts and steeper woodsy rides. The **Tahoe Rim Trail,** from Kings Beach to Tahoe City, offers intermediate-level hilly biking. The trail can be accessed from Tahoe City or Brockway Summit. The South Shore boasts a variety of scenic trails for all abilities. **Fallen Leaf Lake,** just west of South Lake Tahoe, is a dazzling destination by bike or by car, but watch out for the swerving tourists in boat- and trailer-towing vehicles, especially on the narrow mountain roads. Bikers looking for a challenge can try the 7mi. ring around the lake, but beware—it's more difficult than it looks. **U.S. 50, Rt. 89,** and **Rt. 28** are all bicycle-friendly, but the drivers aren't, especially in heavy traffic areas like South Lake Tahoe. Angora Ridge (4mi.), accessible from Rt. 89, meanders past Fallen Leaf Lake to the Angora Lakes for a moderate challenge. For serious mountain bikers, **Mr. Toad's Wild Ride** (3mi.), off of U.S. 50 or Rt. 89, is a very difficult, winding trail that climbs to 9000 ft. The **Flume Trail** has magnificent views of the lake 1500 ft. below. Several paved paths along the west shore offer less demanding touring adventures. The **Pope-Baldwin Bike Path** (3½mi.) runs parallel to Rt. 89. The lake views and smooth, easy ride make these trails quite popular. Parking is available at the Truckee River trailhead (Rt. 89, south of Tahoe City), Kaspian campground (Skyland), and General Creek campground at Sugar Pine Point State Park (south of Homewood). The **West Shore Bike Path,** a paved 10mi. stretch from Tahoe City to Sugar Pine Point, is a flat, scenic tour.

**HIKING.** The visitors center and ranger stations provide detailed info and maps for all types of hikes. Backcountry users must obtain a wilderness permit from the U.S. Forest Service (see **Visitor Information,** p. 840) for any hike into the Desolation Wilderness. The partially completed **Tahoe Rim Trail** encircles the lake, following the ridge tops of the Lake Tahoe Basin. Hiking is moderate to difficult. On the western shore, the trail is part of the Pacific Crest Trail. Current trailheads are at Spooner Summit on U.S. 50, off Rt. 89 on Fairway Dr. in Tahoe City, Brockway on Rt. 267, and Mt. Rose on Rt. 431. (Mt. Rose is a 1¼mi. wheelchair-accessible loop.) **Heavenly Mountain** offers an aerial tram to the mountaintop for sightseeing, picnics, and hiking (775-586-7000; runs daily 10am-9pm; $12.50, ages 4-12 $9.50).

**ROCK CLIMBING.** The **Alpenglow Sport Shop,** 415 North Lake Blvd., Tahoe City, provides free rock- and ice-climbing literature, and rents climbing shoes (583-6917; open M-F 10am-6pm, Sa-Su 9am-6pm). **The Sports Exchange,** 10095 W. River St., houses Gym Works, a challenging indoor climbing gym with over 2500 square feet of bouldering and climbing space (582-4510; $7 per day, indoor shoe rental $3 per day). **Headwall Climbing Wall,** at Squaw Valley, offers several challenging routes in the Cable Car Building (583-7673).

**DOWNHILL SKIING.** With its world-class alpine slopes, knee-deep powder, and notorious California sun, Tahoe is a skier's mecca. There are approximately 20 ski resorts in the Tahoe area. The visitors center provides info (see **Visitor Information,** p. 840). For daily ski updates check out www.tahoesbest.com/skitahoe. All the major resorts offer lessons and rent equipment. Look for multi-day packages that offer significant discounts over single-day rates. Lifts at most resorts operate daily 9am to 4pm; arrive early for the best skiing and shortest lines. Prices do not include ski rental, which generally costs $15-20 for a full day. Skiing conditions range from bikini days to frost-bitten finger days, and snow (artificial or otherwise) might cover the slopes into early summer. Off-season skiing may not compete with winter skiing for snow quality, but it's generally much cheaper. **Squaw**

**Valley** is off Rt. 89 just north of Alpine Meadows, boasting 4200 acres of terrain across 6 Sierra peaks. The 30 ski lifts access high-elevation runs for all levels. (583-6955 or 800-545-4350. Full-day $48, seniors and under 13 $24, over 75 free; ½-day $32.) **Alpine Meadows,** on Rt. 89 6mi. northwest of Tahoe City, is an excellent, accessible family vacation spot with over 2000 skiable acres. (583-4232 or 800-441-4423. Full-day $46, ages 65-69 $29, ages 7-12 $18, over 70 or under 6 $6.) **Heavenly,** on Ski Run Blvd. off U.S. 50, is one of the largest and most popular resorts in the area. Reaching over 10,000ft., it is Tahoe's highest ski resort, with few shoots or ridges. Its 23 lifts and 4800 skiable acres straddle the California-Nevada boundary and offer dizzying views of both. (800-243-2826. Full-day $46, seniors and under 13 $20; half-day $30, seniors and under 13 $15.) **Mount Rose,** 11mi. from Incline Village on Rt. 431, is a local favorite with a long season, short lines, intermediate focus, and cheaper lift tickets. (800-754-7673. Full-day $42, ages 13-19 $35, ages 6-12 $10; half-day $34; seniors M-F ½-price; over 70 and under 5 free.)

**CROSS-COUNTRY SKIING AND SNOWSHOEING.** One of the best ways to enjoy Tahoe's pristine snow-covered forests in more solitude is to cross-country ski at a resort. Alternatively, rent skis at an independent outlet and venture onto the thick braid of trails around the lake. **Porters,** at the Lucky-Longs Center, in Truckee (587-1500), and 501 N. Lake Blvd., Tahoe City, rents skis for $8-10 (583-2314). **Royal Gorge,** on Old Hwy. 40 below Donner Summit, is the nation's largest cross-country ski resort, with 80 trails covering 170mi. of beginner and expert terrain (426-3871). **Spooner Lake,** at the junction of U.S. 50 and Rt. 28, offers 21 trails and incredible views (749-5349; adult trail fee $15, children $3; mid-week special $11). **Hope Valley** has 11 free trails of varying difficulty; take Rt. 89 South from South Lake Tahoe and turn left on Rt. 88 (694-2266).

# YOSEMITE NATIONAL PARK

In 1868 a young Scotsman named John Muir arrived by boat in San Francisco and asked for directions to "anywhere that's wild." Anxious to run this crazy youngster out of town, Bay Area folk directed him to the heralded lands of Yosemite. The wonders that Muir beheld there sated his wanderlust and spawned a lifetime of conservationism. His efforts won Yosemite its national park status by 1880.

If Muir's 19th-century desire to escape the concrete confines of civilization was considered crazy, then we live in a world gone criminally insane—millions of visitors pour into the park each year. Nevertheless, Yosemite remains a paradise for outdoor enthusiasts: most visitors congregate in only 6% of the park (Yosemite Valley), leaving thousands of backcountry miles in relative peace and quiet.

## ▄ GETTING THERE AND AROUND

Yosemite lies 200mi. east of San Francisco (a 3½hr. drive) and 320mi. northeast of Los Angeles (a 6-9hr. drive, depending on the season). It can be reached by taking Rt. 140 from Merced, Rt. 41N from Fresno, or Rt. 120E from Manteca or West from Lee Vining. Yosemite runs public **buses** that connect the park with Merced and Fresno: **Yosemite VIA** (742-5211 or 800-842-5463) runs buses from the Merced train station to Yosemite (7, 9, 10:30am, and 4:25pm; $20, round-trip $38). VIA also runs **Yosemite Gray Line** (YGL; 384-1315), which meets trains arriving in Merced from San Francisco and takes passengers to Yosemite. Tickets can be purchased from the driver. YGL also runs buses to and from Fresno/Yosemite International Airport, Fresno hotels, and Yosemite Valley ($20). **Amtrak** runs to Merced from San Francisco (4 per day, $22-29) and L.A. (5 per day, $28-51). The trains connect with the YGL bus. Amtrak also runs a bus from Merced to Yosemite (4 per day, $10).

An excellent way to see the off-the-beaten-path spots is with **Incredible Adventures,** 770 Treat Ave., San Francisco 94110 (415-642-7378 or 800-777-8464). Catering to young, spirited international backpackers, the guides lead incredible hiking and sightseeing trips. (4-day 3-night trips depart from San Francisco W and Su;

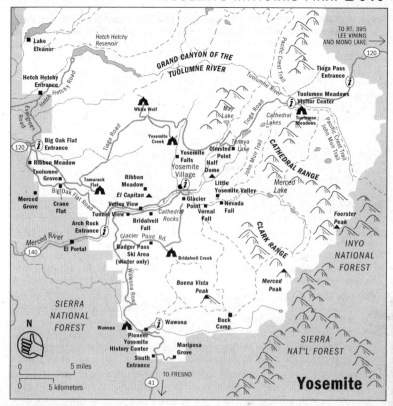

TO RT. 395
LEE VINING
AND MONO LAKE →

Lake Eleanor

Hetch Hetchy Reservoir

GRAND CANYON OF THE
TUOLUMNE RIVER

Pacific Crest Trail

Tioga Pass Entrance

120

Hetch Hetchy Entrance

Tuolumne River

Tuolumne Meadows Visitor Center

Hetch Hetchy Road

Evergreen Road

White Wolf

May Lake

Tioga Road

Tuolumne Meadows

Pacific Crest Trail
John Muir Trail

Big Oak Flat Entrance

120

Yosemite Creek

Yosemite Falls

Olmsted Point

Cathedral Lakes

CATHEDRAL RANGE

Ribbon Meadow

Tioga Road

Tenaya Lake

Merced Lake

Tuolumne Grove

Tamarack Flat

Ribbon Meadow

Yosemite Village

Half Dome

John Muir Trail

Big Oak Flat Road

El Capitan

Little Yosemite Valley

Merced Grove

Crane Flat

Valley View

Glacier Point

Nevada Fall

Foerster Peak

Arch Rock Entrance

Tunnel View

Cathedral Rocks

Vernal Fall

CLARK RANGE

INYO NATIONAL FOREST

Merced River

140

El Portal

Bridalveil Fall

Glacier Point Rd.

Badger Pass Ski Area (winter only)

Bridalveil Creek

Buena Vista Peak

Merced Peak

SIERRA NATIONAL FOREST

N

Wawona Road

Wawona

Pioneer Yosemite History Center

South Entrance

Mariposa Grove

Buck Camp

SIERRA NAT'L FOREST

0    5 miles
0    5 kilometers

41

TO FRESNO

**Yosemite**

CALIFORNIA

$185 including meals, entrance fee, equipment, transportation, and tax. Daytrips run throughout the year; $85.)

The best bargain in Yosemite is the **free shuttle bus system.** Comfortable but often crowded, the buses have knowledgeable drivers and wide viewing windows. (Shuttles run daily every 10min. 7am-10pm, every 20min. 10pm-7am.) **Hikers' buses** (372-1240) run daily to Glacier Point (spring-fall) and to Tuolumne Meadows/Lee Vining (late June to Labor Day).

## 🛈 PRACTICAL INFORMATION

**General Park Information** (372-0200; 24hr.). Info on weather, accommodations, and activities. Call the general line before calling a specific info station. All visitors centers have free maps and copies of *Yosemite Guide*. **All hours listed are valid May-Sept. unless otherwise noted. Call for off-season hours.**

**Visitor Info: Yosemite Valley Visitors Center** (372-0200), in Yosemite Village. Sign language interpreter in summer. Open daily 8am-7pm; off-season 9am-5pm. **Wilderness Center** (372-0308), in Yosemite Village. P.O. Box 545, Yosemite National Park 95839. Backcountry info (372-0745); to order maps and info before your trip (379-2648). Wilderness permit reservations (372-0740) up to 24 weeks in advance ($3), or first-come, first-served (free). Open daily 7:30am-7pm.

**Bike Rental: Yosemite Lodge** (372-1208) and **Curry Village** (372-8319) for $5.25 per hr., $20 per day. Both open daily 8:30am-6pm, weather permitting.

**Rafting: All Outdoors,** 1250 Pine St. #103, Walnut Creek 94596 (925-932-8993 or 800-247-2387). Trips on north fork of Stanislaus River (leave from Calaveras Big Trees State Park), Merced River (Mt. View Store, Midpines), Kaweah River (Kaweah General Store), and Goodwin Canyon (Stanislaus River Park, Sonora).

**Gas Stations:** There is no gas in Yosemite Valley. Tank up in **Crane Flat** (open daily 8am-8pm, tanks open 24hr. with credit card) or **El Portal** (open M-Sa 7am-7pm, Su 8am-7pm) before driving into the High Sierra—prices rise with the elevation.

**Laundromat:** In summer, laundry facilities open at **Housekeeping Camp.** Wash $1.25, 10min. dry 25¢. Open daily 7:30am-7pm. In winter, laundry facilities available at **Camp 6,** across the street from the Village Store. Open daily 8am-10pm.

**Weather and Road Conditions:** 372-0200. 24hr.

**Internet Access: Yosemite Bug Hostel** (966-6666), on Rte. 140 30mi. west of Yosemite in Midpines (see p. 846). $2 for 15min.

**Post Office: Yosemite Village,** next to the visitors center. Open M-F 8:30am-5pm, Sa 10am-noon. **Curry Village,** near the registration office. Open June-Sept. M-F 11:30am-3pm. **Yosemite Lodge,** open M-F 9am-4:30pm. **Wawona.** Open M-F 9am-5pm, Sa 9am-noon. **Tuolumne Meadows.** Open M-F 9am-12:30pm and 1:30-4:30pm, Sa 9am-noon. **ZIP Code:** 95389. **Area Code:** 209.

# ▲ ACCOMMODATIONS

**INSIDE THE PARK.** Advance reservations are *very* necessary and can be (and almost always are) made up to 1 year in advance by calling 209-252-4848. Rates fluctuate, but tend to be higher on weekends and during the summer (those given below are for summer weekends). Check-in hovers around 11am. All park lodgings provide access to dining and laundry facilities, showers, and supplies.

**Yosemite Lodge** (372-1274), west of Yosemite Village and directly across from Yosemite Falls. Tiny cabins are as close to motel accommodations as the valley gets. Singles and doubles $92, with bath $115.

**Curry Village** (252-4848), southeast of Yosemite Village. Pool (open 9am-5pm), nightly shows at the amphitheater, snack stands, cafeteria, and, in winter, an ice rink. Back-to-back cabins $65, with bath $83; canvas-sided cabins on raised wooden floors $44.

**Tuolumne Meadows Lodge,** on Tioga Pass Rd. in northeastern corner of park. Canvas-sided cabins, wood stoves, no electricity. Doubles $48; additional adult $8, child $4.

**White Wolf Lodge,** on Tioga Pass Rd. in the western area of the park. Cabins with bath $73; tent cabin doubles $48; each additional adult $8, child $4.

**The Redwoods in Yosemite** (375-6666), 22mi. south of Yosemite Valley in Wawona. Rentals of 129 fully equipped homes with 1-6 bedrooms, fireplaces, patios, BBQs, full kitchens, and maid service. June-Aug. and holidays 3-night min. stay; Sept.-May 2-night min. stay. From $110 in peak season.

## OUTSIDE THE PARK

**Yosemite Bug Hostel** (966-6666), on Rte. 140 in Midpines 30mi. west of Yosemite. Look carefully for sign. Up in the woods, a low-budget resort spot. International crowd lounging in hammocks, beer on tap, pool table, dartboard, kitchen, library, swimmin' hole. Offers outdoor expeditions, mountain bike rental, rafting trips, and tremendous food ($3.50-8). Discounts on public transportation (45min., $5.50) to park. Internet access. Dorm beds $15; tent sites $17.

**Oakhurst Lodge,** 40302 Rt. 41, Oakhurst (683-4417 or 800-655-6343). Clean, simple motel rooms with shag carpeting, pool, large grassy back lawn. By far the lowest prices in town. 1 queen bed $65 ($45 with various coupons); 2 queen beds $70-88.

# ▲ CAMPGROUNDS

Yosemite is camping country; most of the valley's campgrounds are choked with tents, trailers, and RVs. Reservations can be made up to 5 months in advance (800-436-7275, TDD 888-530-9796, outside the U.S. 301-722-1257; www.reservations.nps.gov; phones and web site available daily 7am-7pm, or mail NPRS, P.O. Box 1600, Cumberland, MD 21502). Backcountry camping is prohibited in the valley, but is encouraged outside it.

CALIFORNIA

## IN YOSEMITE VALLEY

**Sunnyside,** at the western end of the valley past Yosemite Lodge. The only first come, first camped site in the valley. Pervaded by a climbing subculture with seasoned adventurers swapping stories of exploits on vertical rock faces. Be prepared to meet new friends, since every site is filled with 6 people, regardless of group size. Water, toilets, and tables. 35 sites fill up early. $3 per person. No reservations. Open year-round.

**Lower Pines,** in the busy eastern end of Yosemite Valley. Commercial and crowded, with cars driving by. Pets allowed. Water, toilets, tables, and showers. Sites $15.

**BEYOND YOSEMITE VALLEY.** Outside of the valley campsite quality vastly improves. All of the parks' campgrounds have at least 50 sites, and all have RV sites except for Tamarack Flat, Yosemite Creek, and Porcupine Flat. All sites have firepits and nearby parking.

**Hodgdon Meadow,** on Rt. 120 near Big Oak Flat entrance 25mi. from valley. Warm enough for winter camping. 105 thickly wooded sites provide some seclusion even when the campground is full. Beautiful area. Water, toilets, and tables. May-Sept. sites $15; first come, first camped Oct.-Apr. $10.

**Tuolumne Meadows,** on Rt. 120 55mi. east of valley. 157 sites require advance reservations, 157 saved for same-day reservations. Drive into the sprawling campground or escape the RVs by ambling to the 25 sites saved for hikers without cars. Great scenery and nearby trailheads. Pets in western section only. Water, toilets, and tables. Drive-in sites $15; backpacker sites $3 per person. Open July-Sept., depending on snowpack.

**Wawona,** off Rt. 41 27mi. south of valley. Plain and simple, these 100 wooded sites are near the Merced River. Water, flush toilets, and tables. No showers. Pets allowed. Sites $15. May-Sept. reservations required; first come, first camped Oct.-Apr.

**Tamarack Flat,** 23mi. northeast of valley. Take Rt. 120E and follow the rough road for 3mi. (if your car can take it; not recommended for RVs and trailers). 52 rustic drive-in sites. Fewer amenities mean Tamarack fills up later than other campgrounds, but hardy campers enjoy awe-inspiring views from nearby hillsides. Pets allowed. No water. Pit toilets. Sites $6. First come, first camped. Open June-Sept.

## ⬛ FOOD

Restaurants in the park are nothing special. Consider buying all of your cooking supplies, marshmallows, and batteries in Merced, Fresno, or Oakhurst en route to the park. These gateway towns are also home to many affordable restaurants.

## ⬛ THE OUTDOORS

**BY CAR.** Although the view is better if you get out of the car, you can see a large portion of Yosemite from the bucket seat. The **Yosemite Road Guide** ($4 at every visitors center) is keyed to roadside markers and outlines a superb tour of the park— it's almost like having a ranger tied to the hood. Most recognizable is the Wawona Tunnel turnout, which most visitors will immediately recognize as the subject of many Ansel Adams photographs. **El Capitán,** the largest granite monolith in the world (at 7569 ft.), looms over awestruck crowds. If you stop and look closely (with binoculars if possible), you will see what appear to be specks of dust moving on the mountain face—they are actually world-class climbers inching toward fame. At night their flashlights shine from impromptu hammocks pounded into granite as the climbers flee Yosemite campground fees. Nearby, **Three Brothers** (3 adjacent granite peaks) and misty **Bridalveil Falls** pose for hundreds of snapshots every day. A drive into the heart of the valley leads to **Yosemite Falls** (the highest in North America at 2425ft.), **Sentinel Rock,** and mighty **Half Dome.**

**Glacier Point,** off Glacier Point Rd., opens up a different perspective on the valley. This gripping overlook, 3214 ft. above the valley floor, is guaranteed to impress even the most jaded traveler. Half Dome rests majestically across the valley, and the sounds of Vernal and Nevada Falls provide enough white noise to drown out the roar of the tour buses and their ceaselessly chattering passengers. When the moon is full, this is an extraordinary (and very popular) place to visit. Arrive at sunset and watch the fiery fade of day over the valley.

**DAY HIKING IN THE VALLEY.** To have the full Yosemite experience, visitors must travel the outer trails on foot. A wealth of opportunities reward anyone willing to lace up a pair of boots, even if only for a daytrip. A colorful trail map with difficulty ratings and average hiking times is available at the visitors center (50¢; see **Yosemite Valley Visitors Center,** p. 845). **Bridalveil Falls,** another Ansel Adams favorite, is an easy ¼mi. stroll from the nearby shuttle bus stop, and its cool spray is as close to a shower as many Yosemite campers ever get.

Upper Yosemite Falls Trail, a back-breaking 3½mi. trek to the windy summit, rewards the intrepid hiker with an overview of the 2425 ft. drop. Those with energy to spare can trudge on to **Inspiration Point,** where views of the valley below rival those from more-heralded Glacier Point.

From the Happy Isles trailhead, the **John Muir Trail** leads to Mt. Whitney, but most visitors prefer to take the slightly less strenuous 1½mi. **Mist Trail** past **Vernal Falls** (only visible from this trail) to the top of **Nevada Falls.** This is perhaps the most popular day-hike in the park, and with good reason—views of the falls from the trails are outstanding, and the indefatigable drizzle that issues from the nearby water-assaulted rocks is more than welcome during the hot summer months. There is a free shuttle from the valley campgrounds to Happy Isles; no parking is available. The Mist Trail continues past Nevada Falls to the base of **Half Dome,** Yosemite's most recognizable monument and a powerful testament to the power of glaciation. Dedicated hikers trek to the top and enjoy the unimaginable vista of the valley. The hike is 17mi. round-trip, rises a total of 4800 vertical ft. and takes a full day (6-12hr.). The final 800 ft. is a steep climb up the backside of the rock face, equipped with cables to aid non-climbing folks.

**CLIMBING AND WATER ACTIVITIES.** The world's best **climbers** come to Yosemite to test themselves at angles past vertical. With courage (and cash), you can join the stellar Yosemite rock climbers by taking a lesson with the **Yosemite Mountaineering School.** Basic rock-climbing classes (mid-Apr. to Oct.) teach skills such as bouldering, rappelling, and ascending an 80-ft.-high cliff. Reservations are useful and require advance payment, although drop-ins are accepted if space allows. (372-8344. Open daily 8:30am-5pm.)

**Rafting** is permitted on the Merced River (10am-4pm), but no motorized crafts are allowed. Swimming is allowed throughout the park except where posted. Those who prefer their water chlorinated can swim in the public pools at Curry Village and Yosemite Lodge (open daily 9am-5pm; admission $2 for non-guests).

**ORGANIZED ACTIVITIES.** Park rangers lead a variety of informative hikes and other activities for visitors of all ages. **Junior ranger** (ages 8-10) and **senior ranger** (ages 11-12) activities allow children to hike, raft, and investigate aquatic and terrestrial life. Rangers also guide a number of free walks. **Discover Yosemite Family Programs** address a variety of historical and geological topics. (3hr., daily 9am; most wheelchair accessible). Other free, park-sponsored adventures include **photographic hikes,** which are lesson-adventures led by professional photographers (1½hr.; sign up and meet at the **Ansel Adams Gallery,** see below). **Sunrise photo walks** leave most mornings from the Yosemite Lodge tour desk (free). The **Glacier Point Sunset Photo Shoot** is offered Th nights from June to Sept. The workshop with a professional photographer is free, but the scenic tram ride up to the point is not ($20.50; departs 1hr. before the meeting time and returns 4hr. later).

In 1903, John Muir gave Teddy Roosevelt a now-famous tour of Yosemite. The renowned thespian Lee Stetson has assumed Muir's role, leading hikes along the same route (1hr.; free). Stetson also hosts **The Spirit of John Muir,** a one-man show (90min.; W and Sa 8pm; admission $7, seniors $6, under 12 $3), and **Conversation**

**with a Tramp** (Tu and F 8pm; $7, seniors $6, under 12 $2). There are 6 different the-atrical presentations, including *Yosemite by Song and Story* and the moving pic-ture *Friendly Fire: A Forty-Niner's Life with The Yosemite Indians,* which tells the true story of a once-prejudiced man who learns to love the region's Native Americans. (1hr.; M-W 8:30pm. Admission $6, seniors $5, under 12 $3. Tickets sold at Yosemite Theater.)

The **Ansel Adams Gallery,** next to the visitors center, is more like an artsy gift shop/activity center. Sign up for a viewing to see the precious stuff (372-4413; open daily 9am-6pm). In the newly-formed **journaling workshop,** experienced writers take small groups to scenic places and encourage them to write.

**THE BACKCOUNTRY.** Most folks never leave the valley, but a wilder, more iso-lated Yosemite awaits those who do. Topographical maps and hiking guides are especially helpful in navigating Yosemite's nether regions.

**WINTERTIME IN YOSEMITE. Cross-country skiing** is free, and several well-marked trails cut into the backcountry of the valley's South Rim at Badger Pass and Crane Flat. Both areas have markers on the trees so trails can be followed even under several feet of snow; this same snow transforms many summer hiking trails into increasingly popular **snowshoe trails.** Rangers host several snowshoe walks, but the serene winter forests are perhaps best explored *sans* guidance. Snowshoes and cross-country skis can be rented from the **Yosemite Mountaineering School** (see p. 848). **Badger Pass Rental Shop** (see below) also rents winter equip-ment and downhill skis.

The state's oldest ski resort, **Badger Pass Ski Area** on Glacier Point Rd. south of Yosemite Valley, is the only downhill ski area in the park. Its family-fun atmo-sphere fosters learning and restraint (no snowboards). Free shuttles connect Bad-ger Pass with Yosemite Valley. (372-8430. Full-day M-F $22, Sa-Su $28; under 12 $13; specials for those over 60 or exactly 40. Weekday discounts available through Yosemite Lodge. Lessons and rentals available. Lifts open 9am-4:30pm.)

**NEAR YOSEMITE: STANISLAUS NATIONAL FOREST.** This highly preserved land circles Yosemite and connects the forests along the northern Sierra. Well-maintained roads and campsites, craggy peaks, dozens of topaz lakes, wildflower meadows, and forests of Ponderosa pines make up the 900,000 acres of the Stanis-laus National Forest. Peregrine falcons, bald eagles, mountain lions, and bears sometimes surprise the lucky or tasty traveler. Besides great fishing, campsites, and hiking trails, Stanislaus offers solitude—something its better-known neighbor, Yosemite, doesn't have. **Park headquarters** are at 19777 Greenly Rd., Sonora (532-3671; open in summer daily 8am-5pm; call for winter hours). Camping permits are required for Carson-Iceberg, Mokelumne, and Emigrant Wilderness; permits are also needed to build fires in wilderness areas. Only Pinecrest accepts reservations.

# MONO LAKE

As fresh water from streams and springs drains into this "inland sea," it evapo-rates, leaving behind a mineral-rich, 13mi.-wide expanse Mark Twain once called "the Dead Sea of the West." The lake derives its lunar appearance from towers of calcium carbonate (similar to giant drip sandcastles) called tufa, which form when calcium-rich springs well up in the carbonate-filled salt water. At 1 million years old, the lake is the oldest enclosed body of water in the Western Hemisphere.

The unique terrain of this geological playground makes it a great place for hikers of all levels. Easy trails include the ¼mi. **Old Marina Area Trail,** east of U.S. 395 1mi. north of Lee Vining, the **Lee Vining Creek Nature Trail,** which begins behind the Mono Basin Visitors Center, and the Panum Crater Trail 5mi. south on U.S. 395.

The **El Mono Motel,** on Main and 3rd St., offers a slice of modern California: faux Spanish name, white stucco exterior, espresso bar, and alternative rock in the lobby. Clean and bright rooms have cable TV but no phone. (647-6310. Singles $45-65. Open Apr.-Oct.) None of the area's campgrounds take reservations, but sites are ubiquitous, so a pre-noon arrival time almost guarantees a spot. Most sites are clustered west of Lee Vining along Rt. 120. Try **Inyo National Forest campgrounds,** close to town. **Lundy** and **Lee Vining Canyons** are the best locations for travelers headed for Mono Lake. The **June Lake Loop area** south of town on U.S. 395 has 6 sites. Most sites $12; **Walter Lake** is free. The **Lee Vining Market,** on U.S. 395 at the southern end of town, is the closest thing to a grocery store (647-1010; open Su-Th 7:30am-9:30pm, F-Sa 7:30am-10pm).

In 1984, Congress set aside 57,000 acres of land surrounding Mono Lake and named it the **Mono Basin National Forest Scenic Area** (647-3044). For a $2 fee (Golden Eagle, Golden Age, and Golden Access passes accepted), investigate the **South Tufa Grove,** which harbors and awe-inspiring hoard of calcium carbonate formations. Take U.S. 395 South to Rt. 120, then go 4mi. east and take the Mono Lake South Tufa turn-off 1mi. south to Tufa Grove.

The town of Lee Vining provides stunning access to Yosemite as well as the best access to Mono Lake and the ghost town of Bodie. Lee Vining is 70mi. north of Bishop on U.S. 395 and 10mi. west of the Tioga Pass entrance to Yosemite. **Greyhound** (647-6301) has a flag stop at the Red Log Store on the south side of town. To **L.A.** (1 per day, $52) and **Reno** (1 per day, $32). **Mono Lake Committee and Lee Vining Chamber of Commerce** (647-6595) offers lodging, dining, and local services at Main and 3rd St., Lee Vining, in the orange-and-blue building. **Mono Basin National Forest Scenic Area Visitors Center** (647-3044), Inyo National Forest, off U.S. 395 ½mi. north of Lee Vining, is housed in a new structure that resembles a modern-day cathedral or *Architectural Digest* centerfold (open in summer M-F 9am-5:30pm). **Post Office:** (647-6371), on 4th St., Lee Vining, in the big brown building. Open M-F 9am-2pm and 3-5pm. **ZIP Code:** 93541. **Area code:** 760.

## MAMMOTH LAKES

Home to one of the most popular ski resorts in the United States, the town of Mammoth Lakes has transformed itself into a giant year-round playground. Mammoth Mountain metamorphosizes from ski park in winter to bike park in summer, with fishing, rock climbing, and hiking to boot. Even the McDonald's looks like a ski lodge. The weekend nightlife is lively and entirely full of athletes who come to this alpine paradise to get vertical and have mammoth fun. Mammoth Lakes is on U.S. 395 160mi. south of Reno and 40mi. southeast of the eastern entrance to Yosemite. Rt. 203 runs through the town as Main St. and then veers off to the right as Minaret Summit Rd. In the winter, the roads from L.A. are jammed with weekend skiers making the 6hr. journey up to the slopes. The Mono Lake Committee offers **canoe tours** of the lake that include a crash course Mono's natural history. (647-6595. 1hr. Mid-June to early Sept. Sa-Su at 8, 9:30, and 11am; bird-watching is better on earlier tours. $17, ages 4-12 $7. Reservations required.) Flies may be irritating on shore, but they feed exclusively on algae and are harmless.

Lodging is much more expensive in the winter, but prices tend to be cheaper on weekdays. Condo rentals are a comfortable choice for groups of 3 or more, and start at $55 per night in summer. **Mammoth Reservation Bureau** (800-462-5571) makes rental arrangements. For lone travelers, dorm-style motels are the cheapest option. Make reservations far in advance. For info, contact the **Mammoth Ranger District** (924-5500). Reservations can be made for all sites, as well as at nearby Sherwin Creek (MISTIX 800-280-2267; reservation fee $8.65). One of the best views in town is from the **Davison St. Guest House,** 19 Davison Rd. Davison has a kitchen, fireplace, and a huge common room with tons of couches, TV/VCR, and stereo. (924-2188. In summer dorms $15, in winter $18; singles $30/$55.) **The Stove,** 644 Old Mammoth Rd., 4 blocks from Main St., equals big breakfasts. There's down-home cookin' for dinner—the bacon avocado burger is heaven on a bun ($7); vegetarian options are also available. Drinks are served in jam jars, and an old bathtub outside is now a friendly flowerbed. (934-2821. Open daily 6:30am-9pm.)

**Devil's Postpile National Monument** was formed when lava flows oozed through Mammoth Pass thousands of years ago, forming 40-60ft. basalt posts. A pleasant 3mi. walk from the center of Devil's Postpile Monument is Rainbow Falls, where the middle fork of the San Joaquin River drops 101 feet into a glistening green pool. (From U.S. 395, the trailhead is a 15mi. drive past Minaret Summit on Rt. 203.) A quick ½mi. hike from the Twin Lakes turn-off culminates in spectacular views from **Panorama Dome.** Lake Mamie has a picturesque picnic area and many short hikes lead out to Lake George, where exposed granite sheets attract climbers. These trailheads and scenic spots are accessible from the **MAS shuttle.**

**Mammoth Mountain High Adventure** gets people high. (Through adventure. And mountains.) The stately climbing wall stands like a modern-day shrine to extreme sports, beckoning both the inexperienced and the professional. (924-5683. $13 per hr., $22 per day; discount for groups of 3 or more. Open daily 10am-6pm.) The **Mammoth Mountain Gondola** reaches a view miles above the rest. (934-2571. Round-trip $10, children $5; day pass $20 for gondola and trail use. Open in summer daily 8am-4pm.) Exit the gondola at the top for a mountain biking extravaganza over the twisted trails of **Mammoth Mountain Bike Park,** where the ride starts at 11,053 ft. and heads straight down rocky ski trails (934-0706; helmets required; open 9am-6pm).

With 132 downhill runs, over 26 lifts, and miles of nordic skiing trails, Mammoth is one of the country's premier winter resorts. The season extends from mid-Nov. to June; in a good year, downhill skiing can last through July. Visiting during a slow time (avoiding weekends and major holidays) keeps costs lower. Mammoth Mountain lift tickets can be purchased at the Main Lodge on Minaret Rd. (934-2571; open daily 7:30am-3pm). A free **shuttle bus (MAS)** transports skiers between lifts, town, and the **Main Lodge**. The U.S. Forest Service provides information and tips on the area's cross-country trails. For info, contact the **Inyo National Forest Visitors Center and Chamber of Commerce** (934-8989 or 800-367-6572), east off U.S. 395 north of town (open July-Sept. daily 8am-5pm; Oct.-June M-Sa 8am-5pm.) **Post Office:** 3330 Main St. Open M-F 8:30am-5pm. **ZIP code:** 93546. **Area code:** 760

CALIFO

# THE PACIFIC NORTHWEST

Until the encroachment of European settlement, Native American tribes such as the Palouse and Spokane were on the move nine months of every year, hunting buffalo herds across the flat, dry region east of the Cascades. Coast dwellers such as the Salish formed stable, stationary communities ruled by a hereditary chief and sustained by abundant resources. President Thomas Jefferson commissioned Meriwether Lewis and William Clark to explore the Pacific Northwest in 1803. Accompanied by Sacajawea, a Shoshone translator, the expedition traveled about 4000mi. each way from St. Louis to the mouth of the Columbia River and back.

In the 1840s, Senator Stephen Douglas argued, sensibly, that the Cascade Range would make the perfect natural border between 2 new states. Sense has little to do with politics, of course, and the Columbia River, running perpendicular to the Cascades, became the border between Washington and Oregon. Yet even today, the range and not the river is the region's most important geographic and cultural divide: west of the rain-trapping Cascades lie the microchip, mocha, and music meccas of Portland and Seattle; to the east sprawl farmland and an arid plateau.

For comprehensive coverage of the Northwest, refer to *Let's Go: Alaska and the Pacific Northwest 2000*.

## HIGHLIGHTS OF THE PACIFIC NORTHWEST

■ The off-beat neighborhoods, fine museums, ample green space, and pioneering cafes of **Seattle** (p. 853) and **Portland** (p. 879) are not to be missed.

■ **National Parks.** Oregon's Crater Lake National Park (p. 892) puts the region's volcanic past on display. In Washington, Olympic National Park (p. 870) has mossy grandeur and deserted beaches; life beautifully blankets the dormant Mt. Rainier (p. 874).

■ **Whale-watching.** It's most spectacular in the San Juan Islands, WA (p. 867).

■ **Scenic drives.** Rt. 20 (p. 876) winds through the emerald North Cascades, while U.S. 101 takes visitors on a spin through the Oregon Coast (p. 887).

■ Take in **Port Townsend** (see p. 869), a Victorian enclave at the northwest's most west.

# WASHINGTON

On the Washington's western shores, wet Pacific storms feed one of the world's only temperate rainforests in Olympic National Park, and low clouds linger over Seattle, hiding the Emerald City. Visitors to Puget Sound enjoy both island isolation in the San Juan islands and cosmopolitan entertainment in the concert halls and art galleries of the mainland. Over the Cascades, the state's eastern half spreads out into fertile farmlands and grassy deserts, while fruit bowls runneth over around Yakima, Spokane, and Pullman.

## ▌ PRACTICAL INFORMATION

**Capital:** Olympia.

**Visitor Info: Washington State Tourism,** Dept. of Community, Trade and Economic Development, P.O. Box 42500, Olympia, WA 98504-2500 (800-544-1800; www.tourism.wa.gov). **Washington State Parks and Recreation Commission,** P.O. Box 42650, Olympia, WA 98504-2650 (360-902-8500, info 800-233-0321; www.parks.wa.gov).

**Postal Abbreviation:** WA. **Sales Tax:** 7-9.1% by county.

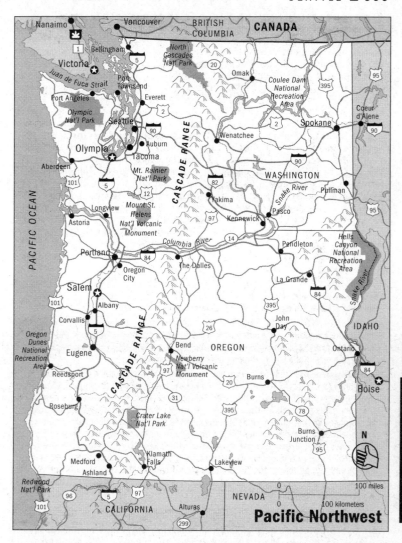

**Pacific Northwest**

# SEATTLE

Seattle's mix of mountain views, clean streets, espresso stands, and rainy weather has proved to be the magic formula of the 1990s, attracting transplants from across the U.S. Newcomers arrive in droves, armed with college degrees and California license plates, hoping for computer industry jobs and a different lifestyle; Seattle duly blesses them with a magnificent setting and a thriving artistic community. The city is one of the youngest and most vibrant in the nation, and a nearly epidemic fascination with coffee has also made it one of the most caffeinated. Every hilltop in Seattle offers an impressive view of Mt. Olympus, Mt. Baker, and Mt. Rainier. Two hundred days a year are shrouded in cloud cover, but when the skies clear, Seattleites rejoice that "the mountain is out," and head for the country.

# 🔢 ORIENTATION AND PRACTICAL INFORMATION

Seattle is a long, skinny city, stretched north to south on an isthmus between **Puget Sound** to the west and **Lake Washington** to the east, linked by locks and canals (for more on cities and isthmi, see **Madison,** p. 512). The city is easily accessible by car via **I-5,** which runs north-south through the city, east of downtown, and by **I-90** from the east, which ends at I-5 southeast of downtown. From I-5, **downtown** (including Pioneer Sq., Pike Place Market, and the waterfront) can be accessed by taking any of the exits from James St. to Stewart St. Take the Mercer St./Fairview Ave. exit to the **Seattle Center.** The Denny Way exit leads to **Capitol Hill,** and, farther north, the 45th St. exit heads toward the **University District.** The less crowded **Rt. 99,** also called **Aurora Ave.** or the Aurora Hwy., runs parallel to I-5 and skirts the western side of downtown, with great views from the Alaskan Way Viaduct. Rt. 99 is often the better choice when driving downtown, or to Queen Anne, Fremont, Green Lake, and the northwestern part of the city.

Downtown, **avenues** run northwest to southeast, and **streets** run southwest to northeast. Outside downtown, with few exceptions, avenues run north-south and streets east-west. The city is split into **quadrants:** 1000 1st Ave. NW is a long walk from 1000 1st Ave. SE. Locals drive slowly and politely, and police ticket frequently. Jaywalking pedestrians rack up $50 fines. **Parking** is cheap, plentiful, and well-lit at the **Seattle Center,** near the Space Needle. Park there and take the monorail to the convenient **Westlake Center** downtown (every 15min. 9am-11pm; $1, ages 5-12 75¢). The **City of Seattle Bicycle Program** (684-7583) furnishes bicycle maps.

**Airport: Seattle-Tacoma International (Sea-Tac)** (431-4444), on Federal Way, 30-50min. south of Seattle. Take bus #194 or 174 from downtown Seattle.

**Amtrak:** (382-4125), King St. Station, at 3rd and Jackson St., 1 block east of Pioneer Sq. next to the Kingdome. To: Portland (4 per day, $30); Tacoma (4 per day, $11); Spokane (2 per day, $50; bus $25); San Francisco (1 per day, $130); Vancouver (1 per day, $30). Ticket office and station open daily 6:15am-8pm.

**Buses: Greyhound** (628-5526), at 8th Ave. and Stewart St. To: Spokane (6 per day, $27); Vancouver (8 per day, $20); Portland (12 per day, $20); Tacoma (8 per day, $5). Try to avoid late buses, since the station can get seedy after dark. Ticket office open daily 6:30am-2:30am. **Quick Shuttle** (604-940-4428 or 800-665-2122) runs from Seattle (Travelodge hotel at 8th and Bell St.), the Sea-Tac airport, and Bellingham, to the Vancouver airport and the Sandman Inn on Granville St. in downtown Vancouver (3-3½hr., 8 per day, $32). **Green Tortoise Bus Service** (800-867-8647) departs 9th Ave. and Stewart St. on Th and Su at 8am. Cushioned seats fold down into beds at night on this bus-turned-lounge that stops for barbecues and saunas. To: Portland (4½hr., $15); Eugene (7½hr., $25); Berkeley (24hr., $59); San Francisco (25hr., $59); Los Angeles (overnight in San Francisco, 2 days, Th only, $79). Reserve 5 days in advance, or drop by the Seattle hostel and ask for openings.

**Ferries: Washington State Ferries** (800-843-3779 or 206-464-6400), Colman Dock, Pier 52, downtown. Service from downtown to: Bainbridge Island (35min.); Bremerton on the Kitsap Peninsula (1hr.); Vashon Island (25min.; no Su service; passengers only). To reach the **Fauntleroy ferry terminal** in West Seattle, drive south on I-5 and take exit 163A (West Seattle) down Fauntleroy Way. From Fauntleroy to Southworth on the Kitsap Peninsula (35min.) and Vashon Island (15min.). Passenger ferry round-trip $3.70; June to mid-Oct. car and driver $8.25, off-season $6.50. Most ferries leave daily and frequently 5am-2am. **Victoria Clipper** (800-668-1167; reservations 448-5000) is the only auto ferry service from Seattle to Victoria. Departs from Pier 48 (4½hr.; daily at 1pm; passengers $29 1-way, seniors $25; car and driver $49; under 12 ½-price).

**Public Transit: Metro Transit,** Customer Assistance Office, 801 2nd Ave. (553-3000 or 800-542-7876, 24hr.; TTY 689-1739), in the Exchange Building downtown, through the bus tunnel under Pine St. and 3rd Ave. is the heart of the downtown bus system. Open M-F 9am-5pm. Fares are based on a 2-zone system. **Zone 1** includes everything within the city limits (peak hours $1.25, off-peak $1). **Zone 2** includes everything else (peak $1.75, off-peak $1.25). Ages 5-18 always 75¢. Peak hours in both zones M-F 6-9am

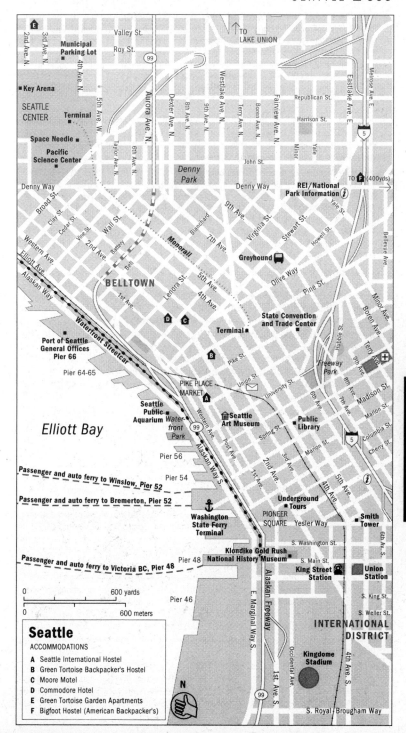

2nd Ave. N.
3rd Ave. N.
E
**Municipal Parking Lot**
Valley St.
Roy St.
TO LAKE UNION
99
4th Ave. N.
Aurora Ave. N.
Dexter Ave. N.
8th Ave. N.
9th Ave. N.
Westlake Ave. N.
Terry Ave. N.
Boren Ave. N.
Fairview Ave. N.
Republican St.
Eastlake Ave. E.
Melrose Ave. E.
5

■ **Key Arena**

**SEATTLE CENTER**
■ **Terminal**

5th Ave. W.
Taylor Ave. N.
6th Ave. N.
Harrison St.

**Space Needle** ■
**Pacific Science Center**
John St.
Minor
Yale

Denny Park

Denny Way
Denny Way
**REI/National Park Information** i
TO F (400yds)

Broad St.
Clay St.
Cedar St.
Vine St.
Wall St.
2nd Ave.
Battery
Bell
Blanchard
7th Ave.
9th Ave.
Virginia St.
Stewart St.
Howell St.
Yale St.
Bellevue Ave.

Western Ave.
Elliott Ave.
Alaskan Way

Monorail

**BELLTOWN**
1st Ave.
Lenora St.
5th Ave.
4th Ave.
**Greyhound** 🚌
Olive Way
Pine St.

D C
**Terminal** ■
**State Convention and Trade Center**
18th St
Freeway Park
9th Ave
✚
Minor Ave.
Boren Ave.
Terry Ave.

**Port of Seattle General Offices Pier 66** ■
B
Pike St.
Union St.
University St.

Pier 64-65

**Waterfront Streetcar**

**PIKE PLACE MARKET**
A
✉

**Seattle Public Aquarium**
Waterfront Park

Western Ave.
99
Post Ave.
🏛 **Seattle Art Museum**
Spring St.
6th Ave
5th Ave
Madison St.
Marion St.
5
Columbia St.
Cherry St.

**Elliott Bay**

**Public Library**

Pier 56
Alaskan Way S.
2nd Ave.
3rd Ave.
Marion St.

Passenger and auto ferry to Winslow, Pier 52
Pier 54
1st Ave.
4th Ave.
5th Ave.
i

Passenger and auto ferry to Bremerton, Pier 52

**Underground Tours**
**PIONEER SQUARE**
Yesler Way
**Smith Tower** ■

⚓
**Washington State Ferry Terminal**

Passenger and auto ferry to Victoria BC, Pier 48
Pier 48
**Klondike Gold Rush National History Museum**
S. Washington St.
S. Main St.

6th Av. S.
Alaskan Freeway

**King Street Station** 🚂
**Union Station**

Pier 46
Pier 46

E. Marginal Way S.
1st Ave. S.
Occidental Ave.
S. King St.
S. Weller St.

**INTERNATIONAL DISTRICT**

0          600 yards
0          600 meters

**Kingdome Stadium**
4th Ave. S.

**Seattle**
ACCOMMODATIONS
A  Seattle International Hostel
B  Green Tortoise Backpacker's Hostel
C  Moore Motel
D  Commodore Hotel
E  Green Tortoise Garden Apartments
F  Bigfoot Hostel (American Backpacker's)

N 👆

99
S. Royal Brougham Way

and 3-6pm. Exact fare required. Sa-Su day passes $2. Ride free daily 6am-7pm in the downtown ride free area, bordered by S. Jackson St. on the south, 6th Ave. and I-5 on the east, Battery St. on the north, and the waterfront on the west. Free transfers can be used on any bus, including a return trip on the same bus within 2hr. These are often necessary, as nearly all routes have to pass through the center of town. All buses have free bike racks and most have **wheelchair access** (info 689-3113).

**Car Transport: Auto Driveaway** (253-850-0800) recruits people to drive their cars to various locations across the U.S. $300 cash deposit. Open M-F 8am-5pm.

**Ride Board:** 1st floor of the **Husky Union Building** (the HUB), behind Suzallo Library on the University of Washington main campus. Matches cars and riders for any destination, within geographical reason. Also check the board at the **downtown hostel.**

**Taxis: Farwest,** 622-1717. **Orange,** 522-8800.

**Visitor Info: Seattle-King County Visitors Bureau** (461-5840), at 8th and Pike St., 1st fl. of the convention center. Open June-Oct. M-F 8:30am-5pm, Sa-Su 10am-4pm; Nov.-May M-F 8:30am-5pm, Sa 10am-4pm. **Seattle Parks and Recreation Department,** 100 Dexter St. (684-4075). Open daily 8am-5pm; in winter M-F 8am-5pm. **National Park Service,** 222 Yale Ave. (470-4060), in **REI** (see **Equipment Rental,** below). Answers questions about camping, hiking and general frolicking in area parks, gives info on discounts and passes, and sells a map of the National Park System ($1.20). Open Tu-F 10:30am-7pm, Sa 9am-7pm, Su 11am-6pm; winter hours may be shortened.

**Equipment Rental: REI,** 222 Yale Ave. (223-1944 or 888-873-1938), near Capitol Hill. The mothership of camping supply stores. Open M-F 10am-9pm, Sa 9am-7pm, Su 11am-6pm. **The Bicycle Center,** 4529 Sand Point Way (523-8300), near the Children's Hospital. Rents bikes ($3 per hr., $15 per day; 2hr. min.). Credit card or license deposit required. Open M-F 10am-8pm, Sa 10am-6pm, Su 10am-5pm.

**Internet Access: Seattle Public Library,** 1000 4th Ave. (386-4636, TDD 386-4697). Free 90min. access with 3-month visitor's card ($8). Open M-Th 9am-9pm, F-Sa 9am-6pm, Su 1-5pm. Cafes charge $6 per hr., as does **Capitol Hill Net,** 219 Broadway #22 (860-6858), but here *Let's Go* readers get 15min. free. Open daily 9am-midnight.

**Hotlines: Crisis Line:** 461-3222. **Rape Crisis: King County Sexual Assault Center** (800-825-7273). Crisis counseling and advocacy.

**Gay and Lesbian Services:** 1820 E. Pine (323-0220 or 800-527-7683). Open M-F 3-9pm. **Lesbian Resource Center,** 2214 S. Jackson St. (264-4409), at 23rd St. Open Tu-F noon-7pm, Su noon-5pm. **AIDS Information,** 400 Yesler Way, 3rd. fl. (205-7837). Open M-F 9am-5pm.

**Medical Services: International District Emergency Center** (623-3321). Multilingual staff; 24hr. **Aradia Women's Health Center,** 1300 Spring St. (323-9388). Open M-F 10am-4pm. **Health South Medical Center,** 1151 Denny Way (682-7418). Walk-in. **Providence Medical Center,** 500 17th Ave. (320-2111) for urgent care. 24 hr.

**Post Office:** (800-275-8777), at Union St. and 3rd Ave. downtown. Open M-F 8am-5:30pm. General delivery window open M-F 10am-noon, 1pm-3pm. **ZIP Code:** 98101.

**Area Code:** 206.

## ▚ ACCOMMODATIONS

Seattle's hostel scene is lively, friendly, and clean. Those tired of urbanity can head for the **Vashon Island Hostel** (the "Seattle B"; see p. 864). **Pacific Lodging Association** arranges B&B singles in the $55-65 range (784-0539; open M-F 9am-5pm). Budget chain motels like the **Nites Inn,** 11746 Huron Ave. N, line the highway north of the Aurora bridge (365-3216; rooms from $45, doubles $50) or take bus #26 in the neighborhood of Fremont.

▚ **The College Inn,** 4000 University Way NE (633-4441), at NE 40th St. A quiet place near the UW campus. Rooms are tiny, but the early 19th-century bureaus and brass fixtures are s'durned *charming*. The kitchen is nestled in the 4th fl. attic. Complimentary breakfast every morning. Singles $45-60; doubles $70-82. Credit card required.

**Green Tortoise Backpacker's Hostel,** 1525 2nd Ave. (340-1222), between Pike and Pine St. Pick-up available from Amtrak, Greyhound or ferry terminal; on the #174 or 194 bus route. A young party hostel downtown. Often free beer F and Tu; pubcrawls W. Laundry, kitchen, and free Internet access. 150 beds in 48 rooms: $17, $16 with cash, HI or ISIC card. 10 private rooms: $40. $20 key deposit required. Linens $1 with $9 deposit. Continental breakfast. 24 hr.

**Seattle International Hostel (HI-AYH),** 84 Union St. (622-5443 or 888-622-5443), at Western Ave., right by the waterfront. Walk west/northwest from the airport bus stops in downtown; head down the stairs under the "Pike Pub & Brewery." The common room overlooks the water. TV lounge. 199 beds, 6-10 per room: $17, nonmembers $20; private rooms sleep 2-3 $41, nonmembers $47. Coin laundry. Ride board. Internet access $6 per hr. Discount tickets for sights and ferry. 7-night max. stay in summer. Reception 7am-2am. Check-out 11am. No curfew. Reservations are wise.

**Moore Motel,** 1926 2nd Ave. (448-4851 or 800-421-5508), at Virginia, 1 block east from Pike Place Market, next to historic Moore Theater. The open lobby, cavernous halls, and heavy wooden doors send the Moore to the 20s. Big rooms with 2 beds, TV, private bath; some with kitchens. Singles $38, with bath $43; doubles $44, with bath $49. One shower per floor. HI member discount 15%.

**Bigfoot Hostel (American Backpacker's),** 126 Broadway Ave. E. (720-2965 or 800-600-2965). From Broadway, follow Olive Way east, taking the first right. Free pick-up from bus, train, or town. 40 beds: $16, $14 winter, 50¢ off with ISIC/HI card; $10 key deposit. Free kitchen, linens, laundry, pool table, Internet, parking, breakfast, and beer on F. Reception 7am-3am. Quiet hours after 11pm.

**Green Tortoise Garden Apartments,** 715 2nd Ave. N (340-1222), on the south slope of Queen Anne Hill, 3 blocks east of the Space Needle. Longer-term accommodations. Yard, kitchens, garden, laundry, free breakfast. Beds $80 per week or $220 per month. 4 people per room. $50 deposit. Ask at the Green Tortoise Hostel.

## ◔ FOOD

The finest fish, produce, and baked goods can be purchased from various vendors in **Pike Place Market,** where the **Main Arcade** parallels the waterfront on the west side of Pike St. (open M-Sa 9am-6pm, Su 11am-5pm). Along King and Jackson St., between 5th and 8th Ave. directly east of the Kingdome, the **International District** is packed with great, affordable eateries. The city's cheapest food is sold in the **University District,** where grub from around the world goes for under $5. Seattle's **food cooperatives** are at 6518 Fremont Ave. N, in Green Lake, and at 6504 20th NE, in the Ravenna District north of the university. Capitol Hill, the U District, and Fremont close main thoroughfares on summer Saturdays for **farmers' markets.**

▧ **Bimbo's Bitchin' Burrito Kitchen,** 506 E. Pine (329-9978). The name explains it. Spicy Bimbo's basic burrito $3.75. Open M-Th noon-11pm, F-Sa noon-2am, Su 2-10pm.

**Mae Phim Thai Restaurant,** 94 Columbia St. (624-2979), a few blocks north of Pioneer Sq. between 1st Ave. and Alaskan Way. This good, inexpensive take-out joint supplies a feast of *pad thai* for the Square. All dishes $4.60. Open M-F 11am-7pm, Sa noon-7pm.

**Ivar's Fish Bar,** Pier 54 (624-6852), north of the square, is named for late Seattle shipping magnate Ivar Haglund. Enjoy the definitive Seattle clam chowder ($1.90) in an outdoor booth to hide from the namesake tourist traps. Open daily 11am-2am.

**Tai Tung,** 655 S. King St. (622-7372). A Chinese diner where waiters are likely to learn your name by the second night. The 10-page, ever-changing menu is plastered to the walls. Entrees $6.25-11. Open Su-Th 10am-11:30pm, F-Sa 10am-1:30am.

**Ho Ho Seafood Restaurant,** 653 S. Weller St. (382-9671). Generous portions of tank-fresh seafood. Lunch $5-7, dinner $7-10. Open Su-Th 11am-1am, F-Sa 11am-3am.

**Ruby,** 4241 University Way NE (675-1770). Dimly lit, with antique mirrors and oriental rugs. Incredible Pan-Asian dishes, like the filling Thai green curry rice bowl ($6.50). Open M-W 11am-11pm, Th-Sa 11am-11:30pm, Su 1-11pm.

## CONVENTIONS OF A CAFFEINE-CRAZED CULTURE

Visiting Seattle without drinking the coffee would be like traveling to France without tasting the wine. It all started in the early 70s, when Starbucks started roasting its coffee on the spot in Pike Place Market. Soon, Stewart Brothers Coffee, now Seattle's Best Coffee, presented Starbucks with a rival, and the race was on both for the best cuppa joe and for global hegemony. Learning a few basic terms for ordering espresso drinks can only enrich your cultural experience. **Espresso** (es-PRESS-oh, not ex-PRESS-oh): The foundation of all espresso drinks is a bit of coffee brewed by forcing steam through finely ground, dark-roasted coffee. **Cappuccino (or "Capp"):** Espresso topped by the foam from steamed milk. Order "wet" for more liquid milk and big bubbles, or "dry" for stiff foam. **Latte:** Espresso with steamed milk and a little foam. More liquid than a capp. **Americano:** Espresso with hot water—an alternative to classic drip coffee. **Macciato:** A cup of coffee with a dollop of foam, and a bit of espresso swirled onto the foam. **Short:** 8oz. **Tall:** 12oz. **Grande (or Large):** 16oz. **Single:** One shot of espresso. **Double:** Two—add shots (usually about 60¢) until you feel you've reached your caffeine saturation point. With skim (nonfat) milk, any of these drinks is called **skinny.** If all you want is plain ol' coffee, say **"drip coffee"**—otherwise, cafe workers will return your request for mere "coffee" with a blank stare.

**Flowers,** 4247 University Way NE (633-1903). This 20s landmark was a flower shop. The mirrored ceiling tastefully frames an all-you-can-eat Mediterranean buffet ($6.50). Open M-Sa 11am-2am; kitchen closes at 10pm, but late night snacks go on.

### COFFEEHOUSES

**Bauhaus,** 305 E. Pine St. (625-1600). In the city where *Wallpaper* is the Bible, something like this had to happen. An enormous portrait of Walter Gropius oversees service of drip coffee (87¢) or Kool-Aid (92¢). Open M-F 6am-1am, Sa-Su 8am-1am.

**Last Exit,** 5211 University Way NE (528-0522). Inside what may be Seattle's first-ever coffee bar (est. 1967), old hippies watch chessmasters battle it out over dirt-cheap espresso (90¢), breakfast, and lunch. Open Su-Th 9am-midnight, F-Sa 9am-2am.

## 🔘 SIGHTS

It takes only 2 frenetic days to get a decent look at most of Seattle's major sights, since most are within walking distance of one another or are within the Metro's ride free zone (see **Practical Information,** p. 854). Any one of the ferries that leave from the waterfront affords a great glimpse of the city's skyline.

**DOWNTOWN AND THE WATERFRONT.** The new **Seattle Art Museum,** near 1st Ave., lives in a grandiose building with an entire floor dedicated to the art of Pacific Northwest Native Americans, plus an extensive collection of modern and contemporary regional works. Admission is good for the fabulous **Seattle Asian Art Museum** (see p. 860) for a week. *(100 University Way. Recording 654-3100, person 654-3255, or TDD 654-3137. Open Tu-W and F-Su 10am-5pm, Th 10am-9pm. Free tours 12:30, 1, and 2pm; sometimes Th 6:15pm. $7, students and seniors $5, under 12 free; first Th of the month free.)* Inside the Museum Plaza Building at 1st Ave., the free **Seattle Art Museum Gallery** displays work by local artists. *(Open M-F 11am-5pm, Sa-Su 11am-4pm.)*

Beside the Westlake monorail stop, **Westlake Park's** Art Deco brick patterns and surprisingly dry **Wall of Water** is a good place to kick back and listen to steel drums on Pike St., between 4th and 5th Ave. **Pike Place Market** is nearby.

The **Pike Place Hillclimb** descends from the south end of Pike Place Market past chic shops and ethnic restaurants to Alaskan Way and the waterfront. (An elevator is available.) The super-popular ▓ **Seattle Aquarium** sits at Pier 59, near Union St. The aquarium's star attraction is an underwater dome, home to harbor seals, fur seals, otters, and others. Touch tanks and costumes delight kids. The world's only aquarium salmon ladder is part of a $1 million salmon exhibit; 11:30am feedings are a sight. *(386-4330, TTD 386-4322. Open daily 10am-7pm; in winter 10am-5pm. $8.25, seniors $7.25, ages 6-18 $5.50, ages 3-5 $3.50.)* Next door, the **Omnidome** screens movies such that patrons feel like they are actually in the movie. The sound system may scare small children and scar delicate psyches. Now showing: *The Eruption of Mt. St. Helens. (622-1868. Films daily 10am-10pm. $7; students, seniors, and ages 6-18 $6; ages 3-5 $5. Second film $2. Aquarium/Omnidome ticket $13.50, seniors and ages 13-18 $11.50, ages 6-13 $9.75, ages 3-5 $6.50.)*

You can explore the waterfront by foot or **streetcar.** The 20s-era cars were brought in from Melbourne after Seattle sold its originals to San Francisco as "cable cars"—the posers. Streetcars are wheelchair-accessible, and run from the Metro opposite the King St. Station in Pioneer Square north to Pier 70 and Myrtle Edwards Park. *(Every 20-30min. M-F 7am-11pm, Sa 8am-11pm, Su 9am-11pm; in winter until 6pm. $1, $1.25 during peak hours. Children 75¢. Weekend or Holiday day pass $2. Under 12 with a paying passenger free on Su. Metro passes accepted.)*

**THE SEATTLE CENTER.** The 1962 World's Fair demanded a Seattle Center to herald the city of the future. It is home to everything from carnival rides to ballet, but Seattleites generally leave the center to tourists and suburbanites, except for concerts and during popular festivals. The center is bordered by Denny Way, W. Mercer St., 1st Ave., and 5th Ave. It is accessible via the **monorail** which departs the third floor of the Westlake Center. *(684-7200, recording 684-8582. Every 15min. M-F 7:30am-11pm, Sa-Su 9am-11pm. $1.25, seniors 50¢, ages 5-12 50¢.)* The **Space Needle** is a useful landmark for the disoriented. It houses an observation tower and a high-end 360° rotating restaurant. *(443-2111. $9, seniors $8, ages 5-12 $4; free with dinner reservations. Some make reservations with no intention of keeping them, the clever miscreants.)*

The **Pacific Science Center,** near the needle, houses a **laserium** that quakes to rock, and an immense **IMAX theater.** *(443-2001. Laser shows Tu $3, W-Su $7.50. IMAX shows Th-Su 8pm; $6.75, seniors or ages 3-13 $5.75.)* The **Children's Museum,** in the Center House, has an abundance of creative exhibits that will wow any kid (or jealous adult) into a fit of over-stimulation. *(441-1768. Open daily 10am-6pm. $7.50, ages 1-12 $5.50, under 1 free. Combination package of all three $16.50, seniors or ages 3-13 $14.50.)*

**PIONEER SQUARE AND ENVIRONS.** From the waterfront or downtown, it's just a few blocks south to historic **Pioneer Square,** centered around Yesler Way and 2nd Ave., home of the first Seattleites. The 19th-century buildings, now home to shops and pubs, retain historical intrigue and great crowds of tourists. Originally, downtown stood 12 ft. lower than it does. The **Underground Tour** raucously guides visitors through the subterranean city of old. Tours depart from Doc Maynard's Pub. *(610 1st Ave. 682-4646 or 888-608-6337. 1½hr. tours daily and roughly hourly 9am-7pm. $8, seniors and ages 13-17 $7, children $4; AAA, ISIC or military, $6. Reservations recommended.)* Logs once dragged to the local mill's front door earned **Skid Row** its epithet, and the smell of the oil used to lubricate the slide was so overwhelming that self-respecting Seattleites left the neighborhood to notorious types. **Klondike Gold Rush National Historic Park** depicts Seattle's role in the Klondike gold rush. *(117 S. Main St. 553-7220. Open daily 9am-5pm. Free.)*

**THE INTERNATIONAL DISTRICT.** Seattle's **International District** is 3 blocks east of Pioneer Square, up Jackson on King St. The tiny **Wing Luke Memorial Museum** displays a thorough description of life in an Asian-American community, a permanent exhibit on different Asian nationalities in Seattle, and work by local Asian artists. *(407 7th Ave. S. 623-5124. Open Tu-F 11am-4:30pm, Sa-Su noon-4pm. $2.50, seniors and students $1.50, ages 5-12 75¢. Th free.)* Landmarks of the International District include the abstract **Tsutakawa sculpture** at the corner of S. Jackson and Maynard St., and the gigantic dragon mural and red-and-green pagoda in **Hing Hay Park** at S. King and Maynard St. The **community gardens** at Main and Maynard St. provide a well-tended retreat. Free parking spaces are next to the gardens.

**POP QUIZ, HOTSHOT** What would you call a 12 oz. espresso with an extra shot, steamed skim milk and foam?

**CAPITOL HILL.** Capitol district's leftist and gay communities set the tone for its nightspots, while the neighborhood supports collectives, radical bookstores, and The Gap. **Broadway** is a center for alternative lifestyles and mainstream capitalism. Bus #7 cruises Broadway, but #10 makes frequent stops along 15th Ave., lined with Victorian homes, and passes more of the fun stuff.

**Volunteer Park,** between 11th and 17th Ave. at E. Ward St., north of the Broadway activity, was named for the veterans of the Spanish-American War. Though it is unsafe (and closed) at night, it is a popular afternoon destination. The **outdoor stage** often hosts free performances on summer Sundays. Scale the **water tower** at the 14th Ave. entrance for a stunning 360° panorama of the city and the Olympic Range. The **glass conservatory** houses dazzling orchids. *(Open daily 10am-4pm; in summer 10am-7pm. Free.)* The world-renowned ■ **Seattle Asian Art Museum** displays Ming vases and ancient kimonos. *(654-3100. Open Tu-Su 10am-5pm, Th 10am-9pm. $3, under 12 free; free with SAM ticket, same day.)*

North of Volunteer Park on 15th St. is **Lake View Cemetery. Bruce** and **Brandon Lee,** and many founders of Seattle, are buried here. One of the most famous martial artists of the century, Bruce Lee moved to Seattle in his youth; his son Brandon was known for his own formidable skills. Near the top of the cemetery, a row of small evergreen trees are lined behind a bench in their memory.

The ■ **University of Washington Arboretum,** 10 blocks east of Volunteer Park, nurtures over 4000 species, trees, shrubs, and flowers, and maintains superb walking and running trails; take bus #11 from downtown. Tours depart the **Graham Visitor Center,** at the southern end of the arboretum on Lake Washington Blvd. *(543-8800. Open daily sunrise to sunset. Free tours Sa and Su at 1pm.)* Across the street, the tranquil 3½-acre **Japanese Tea Garden** is a retreat of sculpted gardens, fruit trees, a reflecting pool, and a traditional tea house. *(684-4725. Open daily Mar.-Nov. 10am-dusk. $2.50, seniors, disabled, students, and ages 6-18 $1.50, under 6 free.)*

**UNIVERSITY DISTRICT, FREMONT, AND BALLARD.** With over 33,000 students, the **University of Washington** comprises the state's cultural and educational center of gravity. The U District swarms with students year-round, and Seattleites of all ages take advantage of the area's many bohemian bookstores, shops, taverns, and restaurants. To get there, take buses #71-74 from downtown, or #7, 9, 43, or 48 from Capitol Hill. The **visitors center** offers campus maps, a self-guided tour book, and information about the university. *(4014 University Way NE. 543-9198. Open M-F 8am-5pm.)* The **Thomas Burke Museum of Natural History and Culture,** at 45th St. NE and 17th Ave. NE in the northwest corner of campus, exhibits a superb collection on Pacific Rim cultures, as well as kid-friendly exhibits. *(543-5590. Open F-W 10am-5pm, Th 10am-8pm. $5.50, seniors $4, students $2.50, under 5 free.)* Across the street, the astronomy department's old stone **observatory** is open to the public on clear nights. *(543-0126.)* The red concrete basin in the center of campus is a hub of student radicalism and skateboarding known as **Red Square.** The ■ **Henry Art Gallery,** opposite the visitor center, displays superb modern art in a stark white setting. *(543-2280. Open Tu-Su 11am-5pm, Th 11am-8pm. $5, seniors $3.50, students free; free Th after 5pm.)*

**Fremont,** under Rt. 99, is home to residents who pride themselves on their love of art and antiques, and the liberal atmosphere of their self-declared "center of the world": twice in the past 10 years Fremont has applied to secede from the United States. The **immense troll** who sits beneath the Aurora Bridge on 35th St. grasps a Volkswagen Bug, and bears a confounded expression on his cement face. Some say kicking the bug's tire brings good luck; others say it hurts their foot. A flamin' **Vladimir Lenin** resides at the corner of N 36th and N Fremont Pl. **Archie McPhee's,** a shrine to pop culture and plastic absurdity, is east of the Aurora Hwy. (Rt. 99) between 35th and 36th, 2 blocks north of Lake Union and Gasworks Park. *(3510 Stone Way. 545-8344. Open M-Sa 9am-7pm, Su 10am-6pm.)*

Next door to the U District, the primarily Scandinavian neighborhood of **Ballard** offers a taste of Europe, with a wide variety of eateries and shops lining Market St. The **Nordic Heritage Museum,** presents exhibits on the Nordic immigration and influence in the U.S. Take bus #17 from downtown, and bus #44 from the U District, transferring to #17 at 24th and Market. *(3014 NW 67th St. 789-5707. Open Tu-Sa 10am-4pm, Su noon-4pm. $4, seniors and students $3, ages 6-18 $2.)*

## 👁 WATERWAYS AND PARKS

The waterways that link Lake Washington and Puget Sound are a haven for summer boaters. By **Lake Union,** situated between Capitol Hill and the University District, the **Center for Wooden Boats** maintains a moored flotilla of new and restored small craft for rent. *(1010 Valley St. 382-2628. Open daily 11am-6pm. Rowboats $12.50-20 per hr.; sailboats $16-26 per hr. HI discount.)* **Gasworks Park** hosts a furious ◪ **4th of July Fireworks show,** is a celebrated kite-flying spot at the north end of Lake Union, and is landscaped around a retired oil-refining facility. Take bus #26 from downtown to N 35th St. and Wallingford Ave. N. **Gasworks Kite Shop** is 1 block north of the park. *(3333 Wallingford N. 633-4780. Open M-F 10am-6pm, Sa 10am-5pm, Su 11am-5pm.)* **Urban Surf,** opposite the park entrance, rents surfboards and in-line skates. *(2100 N Northlake Way. 545-9463. Boards $35 per day. Skates $5 per hr.)*

Directly north of Lake Union, athletes run, ride, and roll around **Green Lake;** take bus #16 from downtown Seattle. The lake is also given high marks by windsurfers. Nearby, **Woodland Park** and the **Woodland Park Zoo** are best reached from Rt. 99, or N 50th St.; take bus #5 from downtown. While the park itself is not well-manicured, the zoo's habitats are highly realistic. *(5500 Phinney Ave. N. 684-4800. Open mid-Mar. to mid-Oct. 9:30am-6pm; in winter until 4pm. $8.50, students $7.75, seniors $7.75, ages 6-17 $6, ages 3-5 $3.75, disabled $5.50.)* Farther west, crowds gather at the **Hiram M. Chittenden Locks,** on NW 54th St., to watch a veritable circus of nitwit skippers crossing between Lake Washington and Puget Sound. Take bus #43 from the U District or #17 from downtown. Salmon jockey up the passage themselves at the **fish ladder.** The **visitor center** for both sights leads free tours. *(783-7059. Open June-Sept. daily 7am-9pm. Tours Sa-Su 1 and 3pm.)*

Across the canals and west of the locks lie the 534 bucolic acres of **Discovery Park,** at 36th Ave. W and W. Government Way, on a lonely point west of the Magnolia District and south of Golden Gardens Park. *(386-4236. Open daily 6am-11pm.)* Eroding bluffs, while dangerous for hikers, provide a haven for birds forced over Puget Sound by bad weather. The park supports much of the flora and fauna of the Pacific Northwest. A **visitor center** is right by the entrance. *(3801 W. Government Way. Open daily 8:30am-5pm. Take bus #24.)* **Shuttles** service the beach. *(June-Sept. Sa-Su noon-4:45pm. 25¢, seniors and disabled free.)* The **Indian Cultural Center** at the park's north end, operated by the **United Indians of All Tribes Foundation,** houses a gallery of modern Native American art. *(285-4425. Open M-F 10am-5pm, Sa-Su noon-5pm. Free.)*

**Seward Park** lies at the south end of a string of beaches and forest preserves on the west shore of Lake Washington; take bus #39. The area offers sweeping views of the lake and Mercer Island, and a popular bike loop half-way around the lake.

## 🏃 OUTDOORS

**Cyclists** should gear up for the 19mi., 1600-competitor **Seattle to Portland Race** in mid-July. Call the **bike hotline** for more info (522-2453). On five **Bicycle Sundays** from May-Sept., Lake Washington Blvd. is open exclusively to cyclists from 10am to 6pm. Call the **Citywide Sports Office** for info (684-7092). Many **whitewater rafting** outfitters are based in the Seattle area, and **Washington State Outfitters and Guides Association** provides advice and info; although their office is closed in summer, they do return phone calls (877-275-4964). The **Northwest Outdoor Center,** 2100 Westlake Ave., on Lake Union, gives instructional programs in whitewater and sea kayaking, and leads 3-day kayaking excursions through the San Juan Islands. Call ahead. (281-9694. 2½hr. basic intro with equipment $40. Lake Union kayak rentals

$10-15 per hr. Open M-F 10am-8pm, Sa-Su 9am-6pm.) **Skiing** near Seattle is every bit as good as the mountains make it look. Get lift ticket rates and conditions for **Alpental, Ski-Acres,** and **Snoqualmie** at 232-8182. **Crystal Mountain,** the region's newest resort, can be reached at 663-2265. Ever since the Klondike gold rush, Seattle has been in the business of equipping wilderness expeditions.

## ♫ ENTERTAINMENT

Seattle has one of the world's most notorious underground music scenes and the 3rd-largest theater community in the U.S., and supports performance in all sorts of venues, from bars to bakeries. Risers seem to grow from the asphalt in spring, when street fairs and outdoor theater please parkgoers. During summer lunch hours, the free **Out to Lunch** series brings everything from reggae to folk dancing to the parks, squares, and office buildings of downtown Seattle (623-0340). The **Seattle Public Library** screens free films as part of the program, and hosts daily poetry readings and children's book-reading competitions (386-4636; see p. 856). The **Seattle Opera** performs at the Opera House in the Seattle Center from Aug.-May. (389-7676; Ticketmaster 292-2787. Student tickets $27-31. ½-price rush tickets on the day of the performance from $17.) The **Seattle Symphony Orchestra,** performs in the new Benaroya Hall, 200 University St. at 3rd Ave., from Sept. to June (212-4700, tickets 215-4747. Tickets from $10, seniors ½-price, students $10; rush tickets from $6.50; ticket office open M-F 10am-6pm, Sa 1-6pm.) The **Pacific Northwest Ballet** peforms at the Opera House from Sept.-June. (From $14; ½-price rush tickets available to students and seniors 30min. before showtime.) The **University of Washington** offers the World Series of dance, theater and chamber music. Contact the Meany Hall box office, 400 University Way. (543-4880. Tickets $28-36. ½-price student rush tickets available 1hr. before show. Open M-F 10:30am-4:30pm, in off season 10:30am-6pm.)

Theater rush tickets are often available at nearly ½-price on the day of the show (cash only) from **Ticket/Ticket** (324-2744). Comedies in the small ▨ **Empty Space Theatre,** 3509 Fremont Ave. N, 1½ blocks north of the Fremont Bridge, draw the entire city. (547-7500. Season Oct. to early July. Box office open daily 1-5pm. Tickets $14-24; previews and under 25 $10; ½-price rush tickets 10min. before curtain.) The **Seattle Repertory Theater,** 155 W. Mercer St., performs at the wonderful Bagley Wright Theater in Seattle Center. (443-2222, Ticketmaster 292-7676. Tickets $10-48, seniors $17, under 25 $10. Box office open M-F 10am-6pm.) **A Contemporary Theater (ACT),** 700 Union St., puts up modern and off-beat premieres in the summer. (292-7670. Tickets $19-40. Under 25 $10. Box office open Tu-Th noon-7:30pm, F-Sa noon-8pm, Su noon-7pm.) **Annex Theatre** at Stewart St. and Virginia Ave., downtown, puts up company-generated material in 5-week runs. (728-0933. Feb.-Dec. Th-Sa at 8pm and Su at 7pm. Pay-what-you-can previews. Tickets $10-12.) **Northwest Asian American Theater,** 409 7th Ave. S., in the International District, stages pieces by and about Asian Americans. (364-3282. Tickets $12, students, seniors, and disabled $9, Th $6.)

Most of the cinemas that screen non-Hollywood films are on Capitol Hill and in the University District. **Seven Gables** owns the Egyptian and others; $20 covers 5 films at any of their theaters (443-4567). On summer Saturdays, **outdoor cinema** in Fremont begins at dusk at 670 N 34th St., in the U-Park lot by the bridge (632-0287; $5; live music until dusk $7). **TCI Outdoor Cinema** shows everything from classics to cartoons for free at the Gasworks Park (720-1058; live music 7pm-dusk). Aspiring independent filmmakers or actors/actresses should check out the Alibi Room for readings (see **Nightlife,** below). The **Egyptian,** 801 E. Pine St., at Harvard Ave. on Capitol Hill, is a handsome Art Deco theater showing artsy flicks. It hosts the **Seattle International Film Festival** in the last week of May and first week of June. (323-4978. Festival tickets available at a discount. $7, seniors and children $4, matinees $4.) **The Harvard exit,** 807 E. Roy St., on Capitol Hill, shows quality classic and foreign films. The theater is in a former residence that has a ghost and an enormous antique projector. (323-8986. Tickets $7, seniors and children $4, matinees $4.)

Seattle baseball fans cheered when the **Mariners** moved out of the Kingdome; in 1995, sections of the roof fell into the stands. The ½-billion dollar, retractable-roofed, hangar-like **Safeco Field**, at First Ave. S and Royal Brougham Way S., is now home to the M's. (622-4487. Tickets from $5.) Seattle's football team, the **Seahawks** are stuck playing in the Kingdome for another year. Seattlites are optimistic that things will turn around for both teams. (Tickets 628-0888. Tickets from $10.) On the other side of town, the sleek **Key Arena** in the Seattle Center is packed to the brim when Seattle's pro basketball team, the **Supersonics** plays (281-5800). Undaunted by a recent NCAA football post-season prohibition, the **University of Washington Huskies** dominate the PAC-10 (543-2200).

The first Th evening of each month, the arts community sponsors **First Thursday,** a free gallery walk. **Street fairs** enliven the University District in mid- to late May; at Pike Place Market over Memorial Day weekend; and in Fremont in mid-June, with the **Fremont Fair and Solstice Parade's** music, frivolity, and craft booths. The **Northwest Folklife Festival** (684-7300), on Memorial Day weekend at the Seattle Center, features artists, musicians, and dancers. The International District holds an annual 2-day bash in mid-July, with more of the same, and more East Asian and Pacific food. Call **Chinatown Discovery** for info (236-0657 or 583-0460). The free **Wooden Boat Show** on Lake Union draws a 4th of July weekend crowd (382-2628). The year-end blow-out is the **Quick and Daring Boatbuilding Contest,** when hopefuls go overboard with a limited kit of tools and materials. The **Seattle Seafair,** from mid-July to early Aug., is the biggest festival of them all. Neighborhoods contribute with street fairs, parades, music, and a seafood orgy. (728-0123.) Big-name rock bands, buskers, and a young crowd flock to **Bumbershoot,** over Labor Day weekend. This massive, 4-day arts festival caps off the summer and is held in the Seattle Center. (281-7788. 4 days $29; 2 days $16; 1 day $9 in advance or $10 at the door, seniors $1, children free. Prices subject to change.)

# 🎵 NIGHTLIFE

Seattle establishments posing as diners by day bring on a band, break out the disco ball, and pour microbrews by night. **Pioneer Sq.** area bars participate in a joint cover ($8, Su-Th $5) to encourage band sampling: **Fenix Café and Fenix Underground** (467-1111) and **Central Tavern** (622-0209) rock constantly, while **Larry's** (624-7665) and **New Orleans** (622-2563) feature jazz and blues nightly. The **Bohemian Café** pumps reggae and hosts open mic Th (447-1514). **Kells,** near Pike Place Market, is a popular Irish pub with nightly Celtic tunes (728-1916). Pioneer Sq. clubs shut down at 2am on F and Sa, and around midnight M-F. Many locals tell tourists that Pioneer Sq. is the spot for good beer, music, and crowds—these Seattlites are lying to you like curs. They probably take their beer bucks downtown to **Capitol Hill,** or up Rt. 99 to **Fremont,** where the atmosphere is more laid-back.

📷 **Sit and Spin,** 2219 4th St. (cafe/laundromat 441-9484; band info 441-9474). Board games keep patrons busy while they wait for their clothes to dry or for alternative bands to stop playing in the back room (F and Sa nights). The cafe sells everything from local microbrews on tap to bistro food to boxes of laundry detergent. Artists cut albums down the street in the **Bad Animal** studio (where R.E.M. once recorded). Open Su-Th 9am-midnight, F-Sa 9am-2am. Kitchen opens daily at 11am.

📷 **ARO.space,** 925 E. Pike (860-7322), entrance on 10th Ave. What every club should be like, and will be...in the year 2100. No one laughs when they say they're involved in a revolution in art. Drum & bass (Th), R&B/pop (Su), electronic(W and F-Sa). Vegetarian fare $5-7.50. Restaurant open daily 5pm-1am, club 10pm-2am.

**Art Bar,** 1516 2nd Ave. (622-4344), opposite the Green Tortoise Hostel. Exactly what the name says: a gallery/bar fusion. Grooving local bands play jazz (W) & reggae (Th) and DJs spin jungle & hip-hop (Sa). Cover $3-5. Open M-F 11am-2am, Sa-Su 4pm-2am.

**Crocodile Cafe,** 2200 2nd Ave. (448-2114), at Blanchard in Belltown. Cooks with organic eggs and toast by day, with local and national bands by night. House (W). Must be 21 after 9pm. Cover $5-20. Open Tu-Sa 8am-2am, Su 9am-3pm for brunch.

**The Alibi Room,** 85 Pike St. (623-3180), across from the Market Cinema in the Post Alley in Pike Place. Self-proclaimed indie filmmaker hangout. Smoky sophisticates star as themselves. Readings (M), DJ (W-Su no cover), and chic decor. Open daily 11am-2am.

**Re-Bar,** 1114 Howell (233-9873). A mixed gay and straight bar. R&B/hip-hop/drum & bass (F, Sa), 70's disco (Th), live music (Tu). Ladies night on Sa here means lesbian-friendly. Cover $5. Open Tu, Th-Sa 9:30pm-2am.

**Vogue,** 1516 11th Ave. (324-5778) off Pike St. Anything goes during this angsty club's theme nights: Drag, goth/industrial, New Wave, or Fetish. Cover $2-5. Open 9pm-2am.

**Linda's,** 707 Pine St. E (325-1220). Major post-gig scene for Seattle rockers. Live DJ playing jazz and old rock (Su and Tu, no cover). Open M-Sa 2pm-2am, Su 4pm-2am.

**Neighbours,** 1509 Broadway (324-5358), in Capitol Hill. A very gay dance club of techno slickness. Cover Su-Th $1; F-Sa $5. Open Su-Th 9pm-2am, F-Sa 9pm-4am.

## NEAR SEATTLE: VASHON ISLAND

Only a 25min. ferry ride from Seattle and an even shorter hop from Tacoma, Vashon (VASH-in) Island has remained inexplicably invisible to most Seattlites. With its forested hills and expansive sea views, this artists' colony feels like the San Juan Islands without the tourists or an economy to cater to them, though budget travelers will feel well cared for in the island's hostel. Most of the island is covered in Douglas fir, rolling cherry orchards, wildflowers, and strawberry fields, and, on Vashon, all roads lead to rocky beaches. **Vashon Island Bicycles,** 7232 Vashon Hwy., rents bikes (463-6225; $9 per hr., $20 per day). **Point Robinson Park** is a gorgeous spot for a picnic, and **free tours** (217-6123) of the 1885 **Coast Guard lighthouse** are available. From Vashon Hwy., take Ellisburg Rd. to Dockton Rd. to Pt. Robinson Rd. **Vashon Island Kayak Co.,** at Burton Acres Boat Launch, runs guided tours (from $48) and rents sea kayaks. (463-9527. Open F-Su 10am-5pm. Call for weekday rentals. Singles $14 per hr., $35 per ½-day, $50 per day; doubles $20/$50/$65, respectively; top-sitters run about 30% cheaper.) More than 500 acres of woods in the middle of the island are laced with moderate **hiking trails.** The Vashon Park District has info (463-9602; open daily 9am-5pm). Many of Vashon's residents are artists. **Blue Heron Arts Center,** 19704 Vashon Hwy., coordinates free gallery openings on the first F of each month (7-9:30pm) and publishes *Island View,* a guide to current goings-on (463-5131; open Tu-F 11am-5pm, Sa noon-5pm).

The **Vashon Island AYH Ranch Hostel (HI-AYH),** at 12119 SW Cove Rd., west of Vashon Hwy., is sometimes called the "Seattle B." Take any bus at the ferry terminal, ride to Thriftway Market, and call from the free phone inside the store, marked with an HI-AYH label. Resembling an old Western town, the hostel offers bunks, open-air teepees and covered wagons. (463-2592. Tenting and queen beds. Free pancake breakfast, free firewood. $10; bicyclists $8; nonmembers $13. Linen or sleeping bag $2. Open May-Oct.) The hostel runs **The Lavender Duck B&B** down the road ($45-55). Get creative in the kitchen with supplies from that offbeat **Thriftway,** 9740 SW Bank Rd. (463-2100; open daily 8am-9pm). **Emily's Café and Juice Bar,** 17530 Vashon Hwy., right downtown, juices just about anything (463-6404; open W-Su 8am-4pm, M 7am-4pm).

Vashon Island stretches between Seattle and Tacoma on its east side and between Southworth and Gig Harbor on its west side. The town of **Vashon** lies at the island's northern tip, while **Tahlequah** is to the south. **Washington State Ferries** (800-843-3779 or 206-464-6400) runs ferries to Vashon Island from 4 different locations. A passenger ferry departs **downtown Seattle** (25min., 8 per day M-F, 6 per day Sa, $3.60); the other 2 (from **Fauntleroy** in West Seattle and **Southworth** in the Kitsap Peninsula) take cars (35min., 20 per day, $2.40, car and driver $8.50-11). A fourth ferry departs **Point Defiance** in Tacoma and arrives in Tahlequah (15min., 20 per day, $2.40). Seattle's **King County Metro** (553-3000 or 800-542-7876) services the downtown ferry terminal, Fauntleroy ferry terminal, and Vashon Island. Buses #54, 116, 118, and 119 run between Seattle and Fauntleroy. Bus #54 picks up at 2nd and Pike St. (30min., buses every 30min. 5:30am-1:30am). Save your transfer for the connection on Vashon. Buses #118 and 119 service the island's east side from the north ferry landing, through Vashon, to the south landing. Bus #117 services the west side of the island. The island is in a different fare zone than Seattle. The local **Thriftway** (see **Food,** below) provides maps, as does the Vashon-Maury **Chamber of Commerce,** 17633 SW Vashon Hwy. (463-6217). **Internet access: library,** 17210 Vashon Hwy. (463-2069; open M-Th 11am-8:30pm, F 11am-6pm, Sa 10am-5pm, Su 1-5pm; free). **Post office:** 1005 SW 178th St. (800-275-8777; open M-F 8:30am-5pm, Sa 10am-1pm), on Bank Rd. **ZIP code:** 98070. **Area code:** 206.

# OLYMPIA

While the Evergreen State College campus lies a few mi. from the city center, its liberal, highly-pierced student body spills into the state capital to mingle with preppy politicos. Some locals, nostalgic for the era when "Oly" was a smaller city with a thriving fishing industry, scorn upstart youth and their raucous ways. Judging by the nightlife, they have plenty to scorn. Olympia's crowning glory is the **State Capitol Campus,** a complex of state government buildings, fabulous fountains, manicured gardens, and veterans' monuments. (586-8677. Tours depart from just inside the front steps daily on the hr. 10am-3pm. Building open M-F 8am-5:30pm, Sa-Su 10am-4pm.) The mansionesque **State Capitol Museum,** 211 W. 21st Ave., houses historical and political exhibits. (753-2580. Open Tu-F 10am-4pm, Sa-Sun noon-4pm. $2, seniors $1.75, children $1, families $5.) Several different free tours of campus buildings leave hourly on weekdays; call 586-8687 for info and options for the disabled. The **4th Ave. Bridge** is a perfect place to spot **spawning salmon,** as the leaping lox-to-be cross the lake from late Aug. through Oct. The high walls of the **Yashiro Japanese Garden,** at Plum and Union next to City Hall, contain Olympia's secret garden. (753-8380. Open daily 10am-dusk to picnickers and ponderers.) **Wolf Haven International,** 3111 Offut Lake Rd., 10mi. south of Olympia, shelters 24 wolves reclaimed from zoos or illegal owners. Take exit 99 off I-5, turn east, and follow the brown signs. (264-4695 or 800-448-9653. Open May-Sept. W-M 10am-5pm; Oct.-Apr. 10am-4pm. 45-minute tours $5, ages 5-12 $2.50.) At the campfire **Howl-In,** humans and canines tell stories (late May-Sept. F-Sa 6:30-9:30pm. $6, children $4).

Motels in Olympia cater to policy-makers ($60-75), but chains in nearby Tumwater are fine. ⛺ **Grays Harbor Hostel,** 6 Ginny Ln., 25mi. west of Olympia just off Rt. 8 in Elma, is a home away from home and the perfect place to start a trip down the coast. (482-3119. Hot tub, 3-hole golf course, and a shed for bike repairs. Beds $12; private rooms $24. Bikers can camp on the lawn for $6.) **Millersylvania State Park,** 12245 Tilly Rd. S., is 10mi. south of Olympia. Take exit 99 off I-5 S, or exit 95 off I-5 N, then take Rt. 121 N, and follow signs to 6mi. of trails and Deep Lake. (753-1519, reservations 800-452-5687. 164 sites. $11; hookups $16; walk-ins $5.50. Showers 25¢ per 6min. 10-day max. stay. Wheelchair accessible.) Diners, veggie eateries, and Asian quickstops line bohemian 4th Ave. east of Columbia. The **Olympia Farmer's Market,** 700 N Capital Way, proffers produce and fantastic, cheap fare. (352-9096. Salmon burger $3.75; open Apr.-Oct. Th-Su 10am-3pm, Nov.-Dec. Sa-Su 10am-3pm.) **The Spar Café & Bar,** 114 E. 4th Ave., is an ancient logger haunt that moonlights as a sweet-smelling pipe and cigar shop. (357-6444. Sandwiches and burgers $7. Restaurant open M-Th 6am-10pm, F-Sa 6am-11pm, Su 6am-9pm. Bar open Su-Th 11am-midnight, F-Sa 11am-2am.)

Olympia's ferocious nightlife seems to have outgrown its daylife. *The Rocket* and the daily *Olympian* list live music. At **Eastside Club and Tavern,** 410 E 4th St., old men play pool, college students slam micro pints ($2), and local bands play often. (357-9985. Open M-F noon-2am, Sa-Su 3pm-2am.) The **4th Ave. Alehouse & Eatery,** 210 E 4th St., serves "slabs" of pizza ($2.75), 26 micropints ($3), and live tunes, from blues to reggae (786-1444; Th-Sa; cover $3-4). DJs spin tunes nightly at gay-friendly **Thekla,** 155 E 5th Ave., under the neon arrow off N. Washington St. between 4th Ave. and Capitol. (352-1855. 21+. Cover $0-4. Open daily 8pm-2am.)

Olympia is at the junction of I-5 and U.S. 101. **Amtrak,** 6600 Yelm Hwy. (923-4602), runs to Seattle (1¾hr., 4 per day, $8.50-16) and Portland (2½hr., 4 per day, $11.50-22). Station open daily 8-11:45am, 1:45-3:15pm, and 5:30-8:10pm. **Greyhound,** 107 E 7th Ave. (357-554), at Capitol Way, runs from a depot with no office to Seattle (1¾hr., 6-7 per day, $8); Portland (2¾hr., 6-7 per day, $19); and Spokane (9hr., 2 per day, $27). **Intercity Transit (IT)** (786-1881 or 800-287-6348) provides service almost anywhere in Thurston County, even with bicycles (fare 60¢, seniors and disabled 30¢; day passes $1.25). The free **Capitol Shuttle** runs from the Capitol Campus to downtown or to the east side and west side (every 15min., 6:45am-5:45pm). For the standard fare, **Custom** buses (943-7777) pick up where normal fixed routes stop (M-Sa after 7pm). IT's **Olympia Express** runs to Tacoma. (50min., M-F 5:50am-6pm. Fare $1.50, seniors and disabled 75¢. Transfers to a Seattle bus in Tacoma $1.50; the full trip to Seattle takes 2hr.) **Washington State Capitol Visitors Center** (586-3460), is on Capitol Way at 14th Ave., next to the State Capitol; follow the signs on I-5 (open M-F 8am-5pm). **The Olympic National Forest Headquarters,** 1835 Black Lake Blvd. SW (956-2400), provides info on land in and outside the park (open M-F 8am-4:30pm). **Post Office:** 900 Jefferson SE (357-2289; open M-F 7:30am-12:25pm and 1-6pm, Sa 9am-12:25pm and 1-4pm). **ZIP code:** 98501. **Area code:** 360.

# BELLINGHAM

Right between Seattle and Vancouver, Bellingham is the southern terminus of the Alaska Marine Hwy.; most over-nighters are contemplating or completing an overseas journey to or from Alaska. Commercial fishing, coal mining, and a paper mill support the economy, and the Lummi, Nooksack, and Semiahmoo of the region maintain strong ties to their fishing legacy. The **Whatcom Museum of History and Art,** 121 Prospect St., displays Darius Kinsey's photographs of 1900s-era logging scenes (676-6981). In the second weekend of June, the **Deming Logging Show** displays the skills. The showgrounds are 12mi. east on Mt. Baker Hwy. (Rt. 542), off Cedarville Rd. to the left. (592-3051. $5, ages 3-12 $3.) The **Bellingham Festival of Music** (all music) is in the first 2 weeks of Aug. (676-5997; $18-21). Memorial Day weekend sees the mother of all relays, the **Ski to Sea Race,** end at Bellingham Bay (734-1330).

**Fairhaven Rose Garden Hostel (HI),** 107 Chuckanut Dr., next to Fairhaven Park, is about ¾mi. from the ferry terminal. The hostel is clean and tiny, though with sleeping quarters, bathrooms, and showers all in the basement. Take I-5 exit 250, and go west on Fairhaven Pkwy. to 12th St.; bear left onto Chuckanut Dr. From downtown Bellingham, take bus # 1A or 1B. (671-1750. Beds $13. Make-your-own, all-you-can-eat pancakes $1. Linen $2. No curfew. Reception 5-10pm. Call ahead, especially on W or Th night, when Alaska-bound travelers fill the hostel; reservations mandatory July-Aug. Open Feb.-Nov., though the hostel may close in 2000.) **Larrabee State Park,** on Chuckanut Dr., 7mi. south of town, has sites tucked in among the trees on Samish Bay. Check out the nearby tide pools or hike to alpine lakes. (676-2093, reservations 800-452-5687. $11, with hookup $16; 8 walk-ins $7; open daily 6:30am-dusk.) ◪ **Casa Que Pasa,** 1415 Railroad Ave., serves humongous fresh burritos (from $2.75; 738-8226; open daily 11am-11pm).

Bellingham lies along I-5, 90mi. north of Seattle and 57mi. south of Vancouver, and is the only major city between the two. The train and bus terminals are both at 401 Harris Ave; take exit 250 off I-5, then Rt. 11 W. **Amtrak** (734-8851) sends 1 train per day to Seattle (2½hr., $23) and Vancouver, BC (1½hr., $15). **Greyhound** (733-5251) runs to Seattle (2hr., 8 per day, $13) and Vancouver (2hr., 6 per day, $13). The **Alaska Marine Highway Ferry,** 355 Harris Ave. (676-8445 or 800-642-0066), runs 2 boats per week to Ketchikan, AK ($164) and beyond from July to Aug. All **Whatcom County Transit** (676-7433) routes begin at the Railroad Ave. Mall terminal, between Holly and Magnolia St. (50¢, under 6 and over 90 free. No free transfers. Buses run every 15-60min. M-F 5:50am-7:30pm; reduced service M-F 7:30-11pm and Sa-Su 9am-6pm.) The **Great Adventure,** 201 E Chestnut St. (671-4615), rents skiing, climbing, and backpacking gear at fair rates (open M-Th 10am-6pm, F 10am-7pm, Sa 9am-6pm, Su 11am-5pm). To reach the **Visitor Information Center,** 904 Potter St. (671-3990), take exit 253 (Lakeway) from I-5 (open daily 8:30am-5:30pm). **Post Office:** 315 Prospect (676-8303; open M-F 8am-5:30pm, Sa 9:30am-3pm). **ZIP code:** 98225. **Area code:** 360.

## SAN JUAN ISLANDS

The lush San Juan Islands are home to great horned owls, puffins, sea otters, sea lions, and more deer, raccoons, and rabbits than they can support. Pods of orcas (killer whales) patrol the waters, and pods of tourists circle the islands in all manner of watercraft. Over 1½ million visitors come ashore each year, usually in July and Aug. To avoid the rush but still enjoy good weather, visit in late spring or early fall. Two excellent guides to the area are available at bookshops and outfitters: *The San Juan Islands Afoot and Afloat* by Marge Mueller ($15), and *Emily's Guide*, a series of descriptions of each island ($5 each or 3 for $11).

**Washington State Ferries** (800-843-3779 or 206-464-6400) serves Lopez (50min.), Shaw (1¼hr.), Orcas (1½hr.), and San Juan Island (2hr.), from **Anacortes;** check the schedule at visitor centers in Puget Sound. **Foot passengers** travel free. To save on car fares, travel directly to the westernmost island on your itinerary, then return: eastbound traffic travels for free. In summer, arrive at least 1hr. prior to departure. ($5.10, vehicle $16-21.75 depending on destination, bike $2.90; cash only.) To reach Anacortes, take I-5 N from Seattle to Mt. Vernon, then Rt. 20 west to town and follow signs. The **Bellingham Airporter** (800-235-5247) shuttles between Sea-Tac (see p. 854) and Anacortes (M-F 8 per day, Sa-Su 6 per day; $27, round-trip $49). Short hops and good roads make the islands excellent for **biking.**

**SAN JUAN ISLAND.** The biggest and most popular of the islands, San Juan Island is the easiest island to explore, since the ferry docks right in town, roads are fairly flat, and a shuttle bus runs throughout the island. Seattle weekenders flood the island throughout the summer, bringing fleets of traffic. A drive around the 35mi. perimeter of the island takes about 2hr., and the route is good for a day's cycle. The **West Side Rd.** traverses gorgeous scenery and provides the best chance for sighting **orcas** offshore. The **Whale Museum,** 62 1st St., exhibits skeletons, sculptures, and updates on new whale research. (378-4710. Open daily 10am-5pm; Oct.-May 11am-4pm. $5, seniors $4, students and ages 5-18 $2.) Mullis Rd. merges with Cattle Point Rd. and goes straight into **American Camp,** on the south side of the island (378-2902; open daily dawn-11pm). The camp dates from the Pig War of 1859, and a **visitors center** explains the history of that curious conflict. In the summer, every Sa from 12:30-3:30pm, volunteers in period costume reenact daily Pig-War era life. (Open daily 8:30am-5pm. Guided walks Sa 11:30am.) **Limekiln Point State Park,** along West Side Rd., is renowned as the best **whale-watching** spot in the area. Killer whales frequent this stretch of coastline, and have been known to perform occasional acrobatics. Most **cruises** charge about $45 (children $35) for a 3-4hr. ride. **British Camp,** the second half of the **San Juan National Historical Park,** lies on West Valley Rd., on the sheltered **Garrison Bay.** (Park open year-round. Buildings open Memorial Day to Labor Day daily 8am-4:30pm.) The annual **San Juan Island Jazz Festival** swings in late July. A $50 badge is good for all 4 days, but crowds cluster outside for free (378-5509; $43 before July; ages 13-20 $20; 1 day $15-28).

**San Juan County Park,** 380 Westside Rd., 10mi. west of Friday Harbor on Smallpox and Andrews Bays, offers the chance to catch views of whales and a great sunset. (378-2992. Water and flush toilets, no showers or RV hookups. Vehicle sites $18; walk-ins $5. Park open daily 7am-10pm. Office open daily 9am-7pm. Reservations highly recommended.) At ◪ **Katrina's,** 135 2nd St., the daily menu invariably includes organic salads, fresh bread, and gigantic cookies. ($1.25-8. 378-7290. Open M-Th 11am-4:30pm, F 11am-4:30pm and 5:30-10pm, Sa 5:30-10pm.)

**San Juan Transit** (376-8887 or 800-887-8387) circles the island every 35-55min. and will stop on request (point to point $4; day pass $10; 2-day pass $19, also good on Orcas Island). If you plan to see San Juan Island only, it may be cheaper to leave your car in Anacortes and use the shuttles. **Island Bicycles,** 380 Argyle St. (378-4941; open daily 9am-6pm), up Spring St., rents for $5 per hr., $25 per day. The **Chamber of Commerce,** 378-5240 or 888-468-3701), in a booth on East St. up from Cannery Landing. The **San Juan National Historic Park Information Center** (378-2240) is at 1st and Spring St. (open M-F 8:30am-4:30pm; in winter until 4pm). **Gray Matter,** 80

Nichols St. (378-6555), off Argyle St., provides free **Internet access** (email $1). **Post Office:** 220 Blair St. (378-4511), at Reed St. (open M-F 8:30am-4:30pm). **ZIP code:** 98250. **Area code:** 360.

**ORCAS ISLAND.** A small population of retirees, artists, and farmers dwell on Orcas Island in understated homes, surrounded by green shrubs and the red bark of madrona trees. The trail to **Obstruction Pass Beach** is the best way to clamber down to the rocky shores. **Moran State Park** is unquestionably Orcas' star outdoor attraction, with over 30mi. of hiking trails ranging from a 1hr. jaunt around **Mountain Lake** to a day-long trek up the south face of **Mt. Constitution** (2047 ft.), the highest peak on the islands. The summit of Constitution looks out over the Olympic and Cascade Ranges, Vancouver Island, and Mt. Rainier. Part-way down is **Cascade Falls**, spectacular in the spring and early summer. Down below, 2 freshwater lakes are easily accessible from the highway, and the park rents rowboats and paddleboats. ($10-13 per hr. Park open daily 6:30am-dusk; Sept.-Mar. 8am-dusk.) The **Orcas Tortas** makes a slow drive on a green bus from Eastsound to the peak (376-2464; $7). **Shearwater Adventures** runs a fascinating **sea kayak tour** of north Puget Sound and is a great resource for experienced paddlers (376-4699; $42, 3hr. tour with 30min. of dry land training). Kayaking without a guide is not recommended except for in calm East Sound. **Crescent Beach Kayak,** on the highway 1mi. east of Eastsound, rents (376-2464; $10 per hr., $25 per half-day; open daily 9am-7:30pm).

**Doe Bay Village Resort,** Star Rt. 86, Olga, off Horseshoe Hwy. on Pt. Lawrence Rd., 5mi. out of Moran State Park, includes kitchen facilities, a health food store and cafe, a treehouse, guided kayak trips ($42 for 3hr.), and a steam sauna and mineral bath. (376-2291. $4 per day, non-guests $7; bathing suits optional; coed. Hostel beds $15.50 for members; campsites $12-22. Spare cottages from $39. Reservations recommended. Reception 8am-10pm.) To reach **Moran State Park,** Star Rt. 22, Eastsound, follow Horseshoe Hwy. straight into the park. (376-2326 or 800-452-5687. About 12 sites and restrooms are open year-round. Standard sites $11; hiker/biker $5. Hot showers 25¢ per 5min. Rowboats and paddleboats $10-12 for 1hr., $7 per additional hr. Reservations strongly recommended May-Sept. 6.) ▨ **Chimayo,** in the Our House Bldg. on North Beach Rd., has a Southwestern theme and comfy booths (376-6394; funky burritos $3-5; open M-Sa 11am-7pm).

The ferry lands on the southwest tip of Orcas, and the main town of **Eastsound** is 9mi. northeast. **Olga** and **Doe Bay** are an additional 8 and 11mi. down the eastern side of the horseshoe. **San Juan Transit** (376-8887) runs about every 1½hr. to most parts of the island (ferry to Eastsound $4). **Wildlife Cycle** (376-4708), at A St. and North Beach Rd. in Eastsound, rents 21-speeds ($5 per hr., $25 per day; open M-Sa 10am-5:30pm, Su 11am-3pm). The **Chamber of Commerce** (376-2273) returns phone calls, but the best bet is to pick up info on San Juan Island, or visit **Pyewacket Books** (376-2043), near Eastsound, in Templin Center. **Post Office:** (376-4121), on A St. in Eastsound Marketplace (open M-F 9am-4:30pm). **ZIP code:** 98245. **Area code:** 360.

**LOPEZ ISLAND.** Smaller than either Orcas or San Juan, "Slow-pez" lacks some of the tourist facilities of larger islands. The small **Shark Reef** and **Agate Beach County Parks,** on the southwest end of the island have tranquil and well-maintained hiking trails and Agate's beaches are calm and deserted. Roads on the island are ideal for biking. **Lopez Village** is 4½mi. from the ferry dock off Fisherman Bay Rd. To rent a bike or kayak, head to **Lopez Bicycle Works,** south of the village. (468-2847. Open in summer daily 10am-5pm. Bikes $5 per hr., $25 per day; kayaks from $10-30 per hr.) **Spencer Spit State Park,** on the northeast corner of the island 3½mi. from the ferry terminal, has primitive sites on the beach and the hill. (468-2251, reservations 800-452-5687. Sites $12; hiker/biker $6; two 8-bunk lean-tos $16. Toilets. Open until 10pm. Reservations ($6) are necessary for summer weekends.) Spencer Spit offers good **clamming** in the late spring, unless there is red tide (hotline 800-562-5632). The park is closed Nov. 1 to Feb. 2. Ferry transport has caused price inflation, so it's wise to bring a lunch to Lopez Island. Sample fresh pastries, bread, and pizza at **Holly B's** (468-2133; open M and W-Sa 7am-5pm, Su 7am-4pm). **Post office:** (468-2282; open M-F 8:30am-4:30pm), on Weeks Rd. **ZIP code:** 98261. **Area code:** 360.

**SHAW AND OTHER ISLANDS.** Shaw Island is home to 100 residents, one store, one library, wild turkeys, apple orchards, and a bevvy of Franciscan nuns living in a convent next to the ferry dock, who for 16 years have been running the store/ post office/gas station/ferry dock (open M-Sa 9:15am-5pm). Eleven miles of public roads cater to hikers and bikers. **Shaw Island County Park,** on the south side of the island, has 8 campsites ($12-14) that fill quickly despite the lack of running water (reservations 468-4413). The Washington State Parks Service operates over 15 **marine parks** on some of the smaller islands in the archipelago. These islands, accessible by private transportation, have anywhere from 1 to 51 mainly primitive campsites. Pamphlets are available at parks or outfitters on the large islands. Boats can navigate the archipelago in calm water, but **navigational maps** are essential. The Department of Natural Resources operates 3 island parks, each with 3-6 free campsites. Cypress Island has wheelchair-accessible facilities.

# OLYMPIC PENINSULA

Due west of Seattle and its busy Puget Sound neighbors, the Olympic Peninsula is a remarkably different world. To the west, the Pacific Ocean stretches to a distant horizon; to the north, the Strait of Juan de Fuca separates the Olympic Peninsula from Vancouver Island; and to the east, Hood Canal and the Kitsap Peninsula isolate this sparsely inhabited wilderness from the sprawl of Seattle. While getting around the peninsula is easiest by car, the determined traveler with ample time can make the trip by bus. Local buses link Port Townsend, Port Angeles, Forks, and Neah Bay, cost from 50¢ to $1, and accommodate bicycles. The long distance to the peninsula and between counties requires a bit more foresight, but can be rewarding: the trip from Seattle to the farthest end of Olympic National Park can cost as little as $4.50 (7hr. via Pierce, Grays Harbor, and West Jefferson Transits).

## PORT TOWNSEND

Unlike the salmon industry, Port Townsend's Victorian splendor has survived the progression of time and weather. Countless cafes, galleries, and bookstores line somewhat drippy streets, cheering the urbanites who move here to escape the rat race. The **Ann Starret Mansion,** 744 Clay St., has nationally renowned Victorian architecture, frescoed ceilings, and a free-hanging, 3-tiered spiral staircase (385-3205 or 800-321-0644; tours daily noon-3pm; $2).

Two hostels are based in old military haunts, with bright, clean rooms: **Olympic Hostel (HI-AYH),** in Fort Worden State Park, 1½mi. from town, and **Fort Flagler Hostel (HI-AYH),** in Fort Flagler State Park on gorgeous **Marrowstone Island,** 20mi. from Port Townsend. To get to Fort Flagler, go south on Rt. 19, which connects to Rt. 116 E and leads directly into the park; miles of pastoral bike routes wind over Marrowstone. (Olympic: 385-0655. Fort: 385-1288. At both $12 for beds; nonmembers $15; hiker/biker $3 off. Check-in 5-10pm, check-out 9:30am; lockout 10am-5pm. Book ahead. Olympic has a 24hr. common room. Breakfast pancakes by donation at Fort Flagler.) You can camp on the beach at **Fort Flagler State Park** (385-1259; 116 sites; tents $11, RVs $16, hiker/biker $6; book ahead) or at **Fort Worden State Park** (385-4730; seaside sites $16). **Bread and Roses,** 230 Quincy St., serves baked goods and sandwiches ($2-4.35) in cozy environs (385-1044; open daily 6:30am-4pm).

Port Townsend sits at the terminus of Rt. 20 on the northeastern corner of the Olympic Peninsula. Over land, it can be reached by U.S. 101 on the peninsula, or from the Kitsap Peninsula across the Hood Canal Bridge. **Washington State Ferries** (206-464-6400 or 800-843-3779) runs from Seattle to Winslow on Bainbridge Island, where a **Kitsap County Transit** bus runs to Poulsbo. From Poulsbo, **Jefferson County Transit** runs to P.T. (385-4777). A **free shuttle** goes into downtown from the Park 'N' Ride lot. (Most buses do not run on Su. 50¢, seniors, disabled travelers, and ages 6-18 25¢; 25¢ extra fare per zone. Day passes $1.50.) **Chamber of Commerce:** 2437 E Sims Way (385-2722 or 800-365-2722), 10 blocks southwest of town on Rt. 20 (open M-F 9am-5pm, Sa 10am-4pm, Su 11am-4pm). **P.T. Cyclery,** 100 Tyler St., rents mountain bikes (385-6470; $7 per hr., $25 per day; open M-Sa 9am-6pm, Su by appointment). **Kayak P.T.,** 435 Water St., rents kayaks (385-6240; singles $25 per 4hr., doubles $40 per 4hr.). **Sport Townsend,** 1044 Water St., rents camping gear (379-9711; tents $16; open M-Sa 9am-8pm, Su 10am-6pm). **Post Office:** 1322 Washington St. (385-1600; open M-F 9am-5pm). **ZIP code:** 98368. **Area code:** 360.

# OLYMPIC NATIONAL PARK

With glacier-encrusted peaks, dripping river valley rainforests, and jagged shores along the Pacific Coast, the landscape of ONP is wonderfully diverse. A little effort and planning may yield an afternoon shell-hunting on isolated beach, a day salmon fishing on the Hoh River, or a week glacier-gazing from the tree-line.

## ⓘ PRACTICAL INFORMATION

Only a few hours from Seattle, Portland, and Victoria, the wilderness of Olympic National Park is most easily and safely reached by car. U.S. 101 encircles the park in the shape of an upside-down U, with Port Angeles at the top. The park's vista-filled **eastern rim** runs up to Port Angeles, from which the much-visited **northern rim** extends westward. The tiny town of **Neah Bay** and stunning **Cape Flattery** perch at the northwest tip of the peninsula; farther south on U.S. 101, the slightly less tiny town of **Forks** is a gateway to the park's rainforested **western rim.** Separate from the rest of the park, much of the peninsula's Pacific coastline comprises a gorgeous **coastal zone.** July, Aug., and Sept. are best for visiting Olympic National Park, since much of the backcountry remains snowed-in until late June, and only summers are relatively rain-free.

    **Olympic National Park Visitors Center,** 3002 Mt. Angeles Rd., is off Race St. in Port Angeles. ONP's main info center fields questions about the entire park, including camping, backcountry hiking, and fishing. (452-0330, TDD 452-0306. Open in summer approximately Su-F 8:30am-6:30pm, Sa 8:30am-8pm; in winter daily 9am-4pm.) Staff at the **Olympic National Park Wilderness Information Center** (452-0300), just behind the visitors center, helps design trips within the park. The **entrance fee,** good for 7 days' access to the park, is $10 per car and $5 per hiker or biker, charged during the day at ranger stations and developed entrances such as Hoh, Heart o' the Hills, Sol Duc, Staircase, and Elwha. **Backcountry** users must pay $2 extra per night to ranger offices. $3 Trailhead Passes are required for parking in Olympic National Forest. **Area code:** 360.

## ⓘ ACCOMMODATIONS

The closest budget accommodations are at the **Rainforest Hostel,** 169312 U.S. 101, 20mi. south of Forks. Follow the signs from U.S. 101, 4mi. north of Ruby Beach between Mi. 169 and 170, or come by bus from North Shore Brannon's Grocery in Quinault (1 per day; 9am, 1, and 4:35pm; 50¢). Two family rooms, a men's dorm (5 double bunks in summer), and rooms for couples require deposits. (374-2270. Beds $10. Curfew 11pm. Wakeup 8am. Morning chore required of hostelers.)

    Olympic National Park maintains 6 free campgrounds in the Hood Canal Ranger District, and others within its boundaries (sites $8-12); three can be reserved (800-280-2267): **Seal Rock, Falls View,** and **Klahowga.** A **backcountry permit** is always required; quota limits apply to popular spots, including **Lake Constance** and **Flapjack Lakes** in the east; **Grand Valley, Badger Valley,** and **Sol Duc** in the north; **Hoh** in the west; and the coastal **Ozette Loop.** Most **drive-up camping** is first come, first served. Olympic National Forest requires a **trailhead pass** to park at sites located off a main trail. The Washington Department of Natural Resources allows **free backcountry camping** at least 100 yards off any state road on DNR land, mostly near the western shore along the Hoh and Clearwater Rivers. From late June to late Sept., most spaces are taken by 2pm. Popular sites such as those at Hoh River fill by noon. In addition to **Ft. Worden** and **Ft. Flagler,** on the peninsula there are 4 **state**

**parks** (reservations 800-452-5687; sites $11, hookups $16, hiker/biker $6). **Dosewall-ips** (796-4415) and **Lake Cushman** are to the east. **Sequim Bay** (683-4235) is to the north. **Bogachiel** is to the west. Call ranger stations for details on campsites in their area. Backpackers should prepare for varied weather. Even in summer, parts of the park get very wet. Treat all water you drink in the park. Bring 50-100ft. of thin, sturdy rope to hang provisions out of reach of **black bears** and **raccoons**. Maps and trailhead signposts indicate where fires are allowed. Inquire about **trail closures;** winter weather often destroys popular trails.

## ◤ SIGHTS AND OUTDOORS

**EASTERN RIM.** What ONP's western regions have in ocean and rainforest, the eastern rim matches with canals and grandiose views. Canyon walls rise treacherously, their jagged edges leading to mountaintops that offer glimpses of the entire peninsula and Puget Sound. Steep trails lead up **Mt. Ellinor,** 5mi. past Staircase on Rt. 119. Once on the mountain, hikers can choose the 3mi. path or an equally steep but shorter journey to the summit; look for signs to the Upper Trailhead along Forest Road #2419-04. Adventure-seekers who hit the mountain before late July should bring snow clothes to "mach" (as in Mach 1, the speed to which sliders accelerate) down a ¼mi. **snow chute.**

A 3.2mi. hike ascends to **Lena Lake,** 14mi. north of Hoodsport off U.S. 101; follow Forest Service Rd. 25 (known as the Hamma-Hamma Rt.) off U.S. 101 for 8mi. to the trailhead. The Park Service charges a $3 trailhead pass. The **West Forks Dosewallip Trail,** a 10½mi. trek to **Mt. Anderson Glacier,** is the shortest route to any glacier in the park. The road to **Mt. Walker Viewpoint,** 5mi. south of Quilcene on U.S. 101, is steep, has sheer drop-offs, and should not be attempted in foul weather or a temperamental car. Yet another view of Hood Canal, Puget Sound, Mt. Rainier, and Seattle awaits intrepid travelers on top. Inquire about base camps and trails at **Hood Canal Ranger Station,** southeast of reserve lands on U.S. 101 in Hoodsport (877-5254; open daily 8am-4:30pm; in winter M-F 8am-4:30pm).

**NORTHERN RIM.** The most developed section of Olympic National Park lies along its northern rim, near Port Angeles, where glaciers, rainforests, and sunsets over the Pacific are all only a drive away. Farthest east off U.S. 101 lies **Deer Park,** where trails tend to be uncrowded. Past Deer Park, the **Royal Basin Trail** meanders 6.2mi. to the **Royal Basin Waterfall.** The road up **Hurricane Ridge** is an easy but curvy drive. Before July, walking on the ridge usually involves a bit of snow-stepping. Clear days give splendid views of Mt. Olympus and Vancouver Island, set against a foreground of snow and indigo lupine. From here, the uphill **High Ridge Trail** is a short walk from Sunset Point. On weekends from late Dec. to late Mar., the Park Service organizes free guided **snowshoe walks** atop the ridge.

Farther west on U.S. 101, 13mi. of paved road penetrates to the popular **Sol Duc Hot Springs Resort,** where retirees de-wrinkle in the springs and eat in the lodge. The resort's chlorinated pools are wheelchair accessible. (327-3583. Open daily June-Sept. 9am-9pm; Apr.-May and Oct. Sa-Su 9am-6pm. $6.75, seniors $5.50; suit or towel rental $2.) The **Sol Duc trailhead** is a starting point for those heading on up; crowds thin dramatically above **Sol Duc Falls.** The **Eagle Ranger Station** has info and permits (327-3534; open late June-Sept. Su-Th 8am-4:30pm, F-Sa 8am-8:30pm).

**NEAH BAY AND CAPE FLATTERY.** At the westernmost point on the Juan de Fuca Strait and north of the park's western rim lies **Neah Bay,** the only town in the **Makah Reservation,** recently famous for the community's revival of its gray-whale hunt and renowned as the "Pompeii of the Pacific," the remarkably-preserved site of a 500-year-old Makah village buried in a landslide at Cape Alava. The **Makah Cultural and Research Center,** in Neah Bay on Hwy. 112, just inside the reservation, beautifully presents artifacts from the archaeological site. (645-2711. June-Aug. open daily 10am-5pm; Sept.-May W-Su 10am-5pm; $4, seniors and students $3.) The Makah Nation, whose recorded history goes back 2000 years, still lives, fishes, and produces artwork on this land. During Makah Days (Aug. 25-27, 2000), Native Americans from around the region come for canoe races, dances, and bone games (a form of gambling). Visitors are welcome; call the center for details. You can reach Neah Bay and Cape Flattery by a 1hr. detour from U.S. 101. From Port Angeles, Rt. 112 leads west to Neah Bay; Rt. 113 runs north from Sappho to Rt. 112. **Clallam Transit System** (452-4511 or 800-858-3747) runs bus #14 from Oak St. in Port Angeles to Sappho (1¼ hr.), then #16 to Neah Bay. ($1, seniors 50¢, ages 6-19 85¢.)

**Cape Flattery** is the most northwesterly point in the contiguous U.S., and is drop-dead gorgeous. Get directions at the Makah Center or just take the road through town until it turns to dirt, then past the "Marine Viewing Area" sign continue 4mi. to a parking area where a trailhead leads toward the cape. To the south, the reservation's **beaches** are solitary and peaceful; respectful visitors are welcome.

**WESTERN RIM.** In the temperate rainforests of ONP's western rim, ferns, mosses, and gigantic old growth trees blanket the earth in a sea of green. The drive along the **Hoh River Valley,** actively logged land, is alternately overgrown and barren. From **Hoh Rainforest Visitors Center** (374-6925; open July-Aug. daily 9am-6:30pm; Sept.-June 9am-4:30pm), a good 45min. drive from U.S. 101 on the park's western rim, take the quick (40min.), ¾mi. **Hall of Mosses Trail** for a whirlwind tour of rainforest vegetation. The slightly longer (1hr.) **Spruce Nature Trail** leads 1¼mi. through lush forest and along the banks of the Hoh River, with a smattering of educational panels explaining bizarre natural quirks. The **Hoh Rainforest Trail** is the most heavily traveled path in the area, beginning at the visitors center and paralleling the Hoh River for 18mi. to **Blue Glacier** on the shoulder of **Mt. Olympus.**

Several other trailheads from U.S. 101 offer less crowded opportunities for exploration of the rainforest, amid surrounding ridges and mountains. The **Queets River Trail** hugs its namesake east for 14mi. from the free **Queets Campground;** the road is unpaved and unsuitable for RVs or large trailers. High river waters early in the summer can thwart a trek; hiking is best in Aug., but there's still a risk that water will cut off trail access. A shorter loop (3mi.) passes a broad range of rainforest, lowland river ecosystems, and the park's largest Douglas fir.

From the **Quinault Ranger Station,** 353 S. Shore Rd. (288-2444; open daily 9am-4:30pm; in winter M-F 9am-4:30pm), try the 4mi. **Quinault Lake Loop** or the ½mi. **Maple Glade Trail.** Snow-seekers flock to **Three Lakes Point,** an exquisite summit covered with powder until July. **Quinault Lake** lures anglers, rowers, and canoers. The **Lake Quinault Lodge** (288-2900 or 800-562-6672), next to the ranger station, rents canoes and rowboats ($10 per hr.). Jim Carlson (288-2293) offers **horseback rides** around the lake and through the forest in summer ($35 per 2hr.).

**COASTAL ZONE.** Pristine coastline traces the park's slim far western region for 57mi., separated from the rest of ONP by U.S. 101 and non-park timber land. Eerie fields of driftwood, sculptured arches, and dripping caves frame flamboyant sunsets, while the waves are punctuated by rugged sea stacks—chunks of coast stranded at sea after erosion swept away the surrounding land. Between the Quinault and Hoh Reservations, U.S. 101 hugs the coast for 15mi., with parking lots just a short walk from the sand. North of where the highway meets the coast, **Beach #4** has abundant tidepools, plastered with sea stars; **Beach #6,** 3mi. north at Mi. 160, is a favorite whale-watching spot. Near Mi. 165, sea otters and eagles hang out amid tide pools and sea stacks at **Ruby Beach. Beach camping** is only permitted north of the Hoh Reservation between **Oil City** and **Third Beach,** and north of the Quileute Reservation between **Hole-in-the-Wall** and **Shi-Shi Beach.** Day hikers and backpackers adore the 9mi. loop that begins at **Ozette Lake.** The trail is a triangle with two 3mi. legs leading along boardwalks through the rainforest. One heads toward sea stacks at **Cape Alava,** the other to a sublime beach at **Sand Point.** A 3mi. hike down the coast links the two legs, passing ancient petroglyphs. More info is available at the **Ozette Ranger Station** (963-2725; open intermittently). Overnighters must make **permit reservations** (452-0300) in advance; spaces fill quickly in summer.

# CASCADE RANGE

Intercepting the moist Pacific air, the spectacular Cascades divide Washington into the lush, wet green of the west and the low, dry plains of the east. The Cascades are most accessible in July, Aug., and Sept. Many high mountain passes are snowed in during the rest of the year and the east of Washington is cold and snowy, too. Mounts Baker, Vernon, Glacier, Rainier, Adams, and St. Helens are accessible by 4 major roads. The **North Cascades Hwy. (Rt. 20)** is the most breathtaking and provides access to North Cascades National Park. Scenic **U.S. 2** leaves Everett for Stevens Pass and descends along the Wenatchee River. Rt. 20 and U.S. 2 can be traveled in sequence as the Cascade Loop. **U.S. 12** approaches Mt. Rainier through White Pass and passes north of Mt. St. Helens. **I-90** sends 4 lanes from Seattle past the ski resorts of Snoqualmie Pass. Rainstorms and evening traffic can slow hitching; locals warn against thumbing Rt. 20.

## MOUNT ST. HELENS

In a single cataclysmic blast on May 18, 1980, the summit of Mt. St. Helens erupted, transforming what had been a perfect cone into a crater 1mi. wide and 2mi. long. The force of the ash-filled blast robbed the mountain of 1300 ft. and razed entire forests, strewing trees like charred matchsticks. Ash from the crater rocketed 17mi. upward, blackening the sky for days. The explosion was 27,000 times the force of the atomic bomb dropped on Hiroshima. **Mt. St. Helens National Volcanic Monument** encompasses most of the blast zone, the rebounding ecosystem immediately affected by the explosion. The volcano still threatens to erupt, but is well-monitored, and there's a good chance it won't blow while you're there.

**⛏ PRACTICAL INFORMATION.** Vigorous winter rains often decimate access roads; check at a ranger station for road closures before heading out. From the **west,** take exit 49 off I-5 and use Rt. 504, otherwise known as the **Spirit Lake Memorial Hwy.** For most, this is the quickest and easiest daytrip to the mountain, and the main visitors centers line the way to the volcano. **Rt. 503** parallels the **south** side of the volcano until it connects with **Forest Service Rd. 90.** Though views from this side don't highlight recent destruction, green glens and remnants of age-old explosions make this the best side for hiking and camping. From the **north,** the towns of **Mossyrock, Morton,** and **Randle** line **U.S. 12** and offer the closest major services to the monument. From U.S. 12, both **Forest Service Rd. 25** and **Forest Service Rd. 26** head south to **Forest Service Rd. 99,** a 16mi. dead-end road that travels into the most devastated parts of the monument past a handful of lookouts.

The monument charges an **entrance fee** at almost every visitors center, viewpoint, and cave ($8, seniors $4, Golden Eagle Pass $4, under 16 free; valid for 3 days). It is possible to stop at the viewpoints after 6pm without paying (though you risk a ticket), or to drive through the park without stopping at the main centers. **Mt. St. Helens Visitors Center** (360-274-2100 or 360-274-2103), across from Seaquest State Park on Rt. 504, is most visitors' first stop, with displays and interactive exhibits (open daily May-Sept. 9am-6pm; winter hrs. generally 9am-5pm). **Coldwater Ridge Visitors Center** (274-2131) is 38mi. farther on Rt. 504. This sprawling glass-and-copper building has a superb view of the collapsed cavity, with an emphasis on the area's recolonization by living things. (Open daily May-Aug. 9am-6pm; Sept.-Apr. 9am-5pm.) **Johnston Ridge Observatory** (274-2140), at the end of Rt. 504, overlooking the crater, focuses on geological exhibits and offers the best roadside view of the steaming dome and crater (open daily 9am-6pm; Oct.-Apr. 10am-4pm).

**Woods Creek Information Station,** 6mi. south of Randle on Rd. 25 from U.S. 12, is a drive-through info center (open mid-May-Sept. daily 9am-4pm). **Pine Creek Information Station** (238-5225), 17mi. east of Cougar on Rd. 90, shows an interpretive film of the eruption (open mid-May to Sept. daily 9am-6pm). **Apes Headquarters,** at Ape Cave on Rd. 8303, on the south side of the volcano, answers all lava tube questions (open mid-May to Sept. daily 9:30am-5:30pm). **Monument Headquarters,** 42218 NE

THE PACIFIC NORTHWEST

Yale Bridge Rd. (247-3900 or 247-3903), 3mi. north of Amboy on Rt. 503, is in charge of **crater-climbing permits** (open M-F 7:30am-5pm). From May 15 to Oct. 31, the Forest Service allows 100 people per day to hike to the crater rim (applications accepted from Feb. 1; $15). Procrastinators should head for **Jack's Restaurant and Country Store**, 13411 Louis River Rd. (231-4276), on Rt. 503, 5mi. west of Cougar (I-5 exit 21), where a lottery is held at 6pm each day to distribute the next day's 50 unreserved permits (open daily 5:30am-9pm). **Area code:** 360.

▛ **CAMPGROUNDS.** Although the monument itself contains no campgrounds, a number are scattered throughout the surrounding national forest. Free dispersed camping is allowed within the monument, but finding a site is a matter of luck. **Iron Creek Campground** is just south of the Woods Creek Information Station on Rd. 25, near its junction with Rd. 76. This is the closest campsite to Mt. St. Helens, with good hiking and striking views of the crater and the blast zone. (Reservations 800-280-2267. Water available 8-10am and 6-8pm. Sites $12, premium $14.) Spacious **Swift Campground** is on Rd. 90, just west of the Pine Creek Information Station (sites $12; free firewood; no reservations). **Beaver Bay** is west of Swift Campground on the Yale Reservoir (RV and tent sites $12; toilets and showers). Swift and Cougar are run by **Pacificorp** (503-464-5035).

▟ **OUTDOORS.** Along each approach, short interpretive trails loop into the landscape. The 1hr. drive from the Mt. St. Helens Visitors Center to Johnston Ridge offers spectacular views of the crater and of the resurgence of life. Another 10mi. east, a hike along **Johnston Ridge** approaches incredibly close to the crater where geologist David Johnston died studying the eruption. On the way west along Rd. 99, **Bear Meadow** provides the first interpretive stop, an excellent view of Mt. St. Helens, and the last restrooms before Rd. 99 ends at **Windy Ridge.** The monument begins just west of Bear Meadow, where Rd. 26 and 99 meet. Rangers lead ½mi. (45min.) walks around emerald **Meta Lake;** meet at Miner's Car at the junction of Rd. 26 and 99 (late June-Sept. daily 12:45 and 3pm). Farther west on Rd. 99, **Independence Pass Trail #227** is a difficult 3½mi. hike, with overlooks of Spirit Lake and superb views of the crater and dome. For a serious hike, continue along this trail to its intersection with the spectacular **Norway Pass Trail,** which runs 6mi. (5½hr.) directly through the blast zone and ends on Rd. 26. Farther west, the 2mi. **Harmony Trail #224** provides access to Spirit Lake. From spectacular **Windy Ridge** at the end of Rd. 99, a steep ash hill grants a magnificent view of the crater from 3½mi. away. The **Truman Trail** leaves from Windy Ridge and meanders 7mi. through the **Pumice Plain,** where hot pyroclastic flows sterilized the landscape. From the Pine Creek Information Station, 25mi. south of the junction of Rd. 25 and 99, take Rd. 90 12mi. west and then continue 3mi. north on Rd. 83 to **Ape Cave,** a broken 2½mi. lava tube formed by an ancient eruption. When exploring, wear a jacket and sturdy shoes, and take at least 2 **flashlights** or **lanterns** (rentals $2 each; rentals stop at 4pm, lanterns must be returned by 5pm). Rangers lead 10 free 30min. guided cave explorations per day. Road 83 continues 9mi. farther north, ending near **Lava Canyon Trail #184** and 3 hikes past the **Muddy River Waterfall.**

# MOUNT RAINIER NATIONAL PARK

At 14,411 ft., Mt. Rainier (ray-NEER) presides regally over the Cascade Range. The Klickitat native people called it Tahoma, "Mountain of God," but Rainier is simply "the Mountain" to most Washington residents. Perpetually snow-capped, this dormant volcano draws thousands of visitors from all around the globe. Clouds mask the mountain 200 days per year, frustrating visitors who come solely to see its distinctive summit. Over 305mi. of trails weave among old growth forests and alpine meadows, rivers, and bubbling hot springs, for the non-alpinists among us.

**⊞ PRACTICAL INFORMATION.** To reach Mt. Rainier from the **west**, take I-5 to Tacoma, then go east on Rt. 512, south on Rt. 7, and east on Rt. 706. This road meanders through the town of **Ashford** and into the park by the **Nisqually entrance**, which leads to the visitors centers of **Paradise** and **Longmire**. Snow usually closes all other park roads from Nov. to May. **Stevens Canyon Rd.** connects the southeast corner of the national park with Paradise, Longmire, and the Nisqually entrance, unfolding superb vistas of Rainier and the Tatoosh Range.

    **Gray Line Bus Service,** 4500 S. Marginal Way, Seattle (206-624-5077), runs from Seattle to Mt. Rainier. Buses leave from the Convention Center at 8th and Pike in Seattle at 8am and return at 6pm, allowing about 3½hr. at the mountain. (May to mid-Oct. daily 1-day round-trip $49, under 12 $24.50.) **Rainier Shuttle** (569-2331), runs daily between Sea-Tac Airport (see p. 854), Ashford (2hr., 2 per day, $39), and Paradise (3hr., 1 per day, $39). Each of the park's 4 **visitors centers: Longmire** (open Su-Th 7am-8pm, F-Sa 6:30am-9pm); **Paradise** (open May to mid-Oct. daily 9am-7pm; Oct.-Apr. Sa-Su and holidays 9am-7pm); **Ohanepecosh** and **Carbon River** (open mid-June to Sept. daily 9am-6pm; late May to mid-June Sa-Su and holidays 9am-6pm); and **Sunrise**—have helpful rangers, brochures on hiking, and postings on trail and road conditions. The best place to plan a backcountry trip is at the **Longmire Wilderness Center** (569-4453), east of the Nisqually entrance; or the **White River Ranger Station** (569-2273), off Rt. 410 on the park's east side. Both distribute **backcountry permits** for $10 per group plus $5 per person (both open in summer Su-Th 7am-7pm, F-Sa 6:30am-9pm). The **entrance fee** is $10 per car, $5 per hiker; permits are good for 7 days, and gates are open 24hr. **Rainier Mountaineering, Inc. (RMI)** (569-2227), in Paradise, rents climbing gear and expert guides lead summit climbs and programs. Open May-Sept. daily 9am-5pm. Winter office at 535 Dock St. #209, in Tacoma (253-627-6242). **Post Office:** In the **National Park Inn,** Longmire, and in the **Paradise Inn,** Paradise. (Both open M-F 8:30am-noon and 1-5pm.) **ZIP code:** Longmire 98397; Paradise 98398. **Area code:** 360.

**▛◨ ACCOMMODATIONS AND FOOD. Hotel Packwood,** 102 Main St., in Packwood, is a charming reminder of the Old West with crisp, clean rooms with antique furniture (494-5431; shared or private bath; singles $20-38; double bunks $25-35). **Whittaker's Bunkhouse,** 30205 S.R. 706 E, Ashford, offers spiffy rooms with firm mattresses and sparkling clean showers, as well as a homey espresso bar, but no kitchen. Bring your own sleeping bag. (569-2439. Bunks $25; private rooms $65-90. Reservations strongly recommended.)

    Camping in the park is first come, first served from mid-June to late Sept. (sites $10-14; reservations for off season 800-365-2267). National park campgrounds all have facilities for the handicapped, but no hookups or showers (coin-op showers are available at Jackson Memorial Visitor's Center, in Paradise). **Sunshine Point** (18 sites), near the Nisqually entrance, and **Cougar Rock** (200 sites), 2¼mi. north of Longmire, are in the southwest (quiet hours 10pm-6am). The serene high canopy of **Ohanapecosh** (205 sites) is 11mi. north of Packwood on Rt. 123, in the southeast. **White River** (112 sites) is 5mi. west of White River on the way to Sunrise, in the northeast. **Backcountry camping** in the park requires a **permit,** available for $10 per group plus $5 per person at ranger stations and visitors centers. Hikers with valid permits can use any of the free, well-established trailside camps scattered in the park. Most camps have toilet facilities and a nearby water source, and some have shelters for groups of up to 12. **Glacier climbers** and **mountain climbers** intending to scale above 10,000 ft. must register in person at ranger stations to be granted permits. Camping in **national forests** outside the park is free. Avoid eroded lakesides and riverbanks; flash floods are frequent. **Campfires** are prohibited except during the rainy season. Check with ranger stations for details.

    **Blanton's Market,** 13040 U.S. 12, in Packwood, is the closest decent supermarket to the park and has an **ATM** in front (494-6101; open daily 6am-10pm). **Ma & Pa Rucker's** on U.S. 12 in Packwood, is a pizza parlor/grill/mini mart/ice cream store/cafe (494-2651; small pizza $7; open M-Th 9am-9pm, F-Su 9am-10pm).

**SIGHTS AND OUTDOORS.** Ranger-led **interpretive hikes** delve into everything from area history to local wildflowers. Each visitor center conducts hikes on its own schedule and most of the campgrounds have evening talks and campfire programs. Mt. Adams and Mt. St. Helens aren't visible from the road, but can be seen from mountain trails like **Paradise** (1½mi.), **Pinnacle Peak** (2½mi.), **Eagle Peak** (7mi.), and **Van Trump Park** (5½mi.). A segment of the **Pacific Crest Trail,** which runs from Mexico to the Canadian border, dodges in and out of the park's southeast corner. The **Wonderland Trail** winds 93mi. up, down, and around the mountain. Hikers must get permits for the arduous but stunning trek, and must complete the hike in 10 to 14 days. Call the Longmire Wilderness Center (see **Practical Information,** above) for details on both hikes. A trip to the **summit** of Mt. Rainier requires substantial preparation and expense. The ascent involves a vertical rise of more than 9000 ft. over a distance of 9 or more miles, usually taking 2 days and an overnight stay at **Camp Muir** on the south side (10,000 ft.) or **Camp Schurman** on the east side (9500 ft.). **Permits** for summit climbs cost $15 per person.

Just inside the Nisqually entrance, **Longmire** is pretty and woodsy, but by no means the best that Rainier has to offer. The **Rampart Ridge Trail,** a 4½mi. (2½hr.) loop, is a relatively moderate hike with excellent views of the Nisqually Valley, Mt. Rainier, and Tumtum Peak. The steep, 5mi. (4hr.) **Van Trump Park and Comet Falls Trail** passes Comet Falls and the occasional mountain goat. Longmire remains open during the winter as a center for snowshoeing, cross-country skiing, and other alpine activities. **Guest Services, Inc.** runs a cross-country ski center that rents skis and snowshoes, and runs skiing lessons on weekends. *(569-2275. Skis $15 per day, children $9.75 per day. Snowshoes $7.25 per ½-day, $12 per day.)*

If you can manage to avoid the bustle and arrive on a clear, sunny weekday, **Paradise** will be exactly that. Even in mid-June, the sparkling snowfields above timberline add a touch of white to the verdant forest canyons below. The road from the Nisqually entrance to Paradise is open year-round, but the road east through Stevens Canyon closes from Oct. to June. From Jan. to mid-Apr., park naturalists lead **snowshoe hikes** to explore winter ecology around Paradise. *(569-2211. Sa-Su 10:30am and 2:30pm. Snowshoe rental $1.)* The 5mi. **Skyline Trail** is the longest of the loop trails, starting at the Paradise Inn; it's probably the closest a casual hiker can come to climbing the mountain. The mildly strenuous 2½mi. hike up to **Pinnacle Peak** begins just east of Paradise, across the road from **Reflection Lake,** and offers clear views of Mt. Rainier, Mt. Adams, Mt. St. Helens, and Mt. Hood.

Although in opposite corners of the park, the **Ohanapecosh** and **Carbon Rivers** are in the same ranger district. One of the oldest stands of trees in Washington, the **Grove of Patriarchs,** grows near the Ohanapecosh visitors center. An easy 1½mi. walk leads to these 500- to 1000-year-old Douglas firs, cedars, and hemlocks. The **Summerland** and **Indian Bar Trails** are excellent for serious backpacking—this is where rangers go on their days off. **Carbon River Valley,** in the northwest corner of the park, is one of the only inland rainforests in the continental U.S., and has access to the **Wonderland Trail** (see above). Winter storms keep the road beyond the Carbon River entrance under constant disrepair.

Too far from the entrance for most tourists to bother, **Sunrise** is pristine, unruffled, and divine. The winding road to the highest of the 4 visitors centers provides gorgeous views of Mt. Adams, Mt. Baker, and the heavily glaciated eastern side of Mt. Rainier. The comfortably sloping **Mt. Burroughs Trail** (5mi.) offers unbeatable glacier views. **Berkeley Park** makes a 5mi. round-trip trek into a wildflower-painted valley. For those longing to return to civilization, the 5.6mi. (4hr.) round-trip hike to **Mt. Fremont Lookout** affords a view of Seattle on a clear day.

# NORTH CASCADES (ROUTE 20)

A favorite stomping ground for grizzlies, deer, mountain goats, black bears, and Jack Kerouac *(The Dharma Bums),* the North Cascades are one of the most rugged expanses of land in the continental U.S. The dramatic peaks stretch north from Stevens Pass on U.S. 2 to the Canadian border, with the centerpiece of **North Cascades National Park** straddling the crest of the Cascades. Rt. 20 (open Apr.-Nov., weather permitting), a road designed for unadulterated driving pleasure, is the area's primary means of access and awards jaw-dropping views at every curve.

**SEDRO WOOLLEY TO MARBLEMOUNT.** The **Sedro Woolley Visitor Information Center** (360-855-0974; open daily 9am-4pm), in the train caboose at Rt. 20 and Ferry St., explains the **Sedro Woolley Loggerodeo** (855-1129), held over 4th of July weekend. Sedro Woolley houses the **North Cascades National Park and Mt. Baker-Snoqualmie National Forest Headquarters**, 2105 Rt. 20 (360-856-5700; open Sa-Th 8am-4:30pm, F 8am-6pm). Inquire here about camping in the forest and trail park passes and permits required. Call 206-526-6677 for **snow avalanche info**.

Rt. 9 leads north from Sedro Woolley, providing indirect access to **Mt. Baker** through the forks at the Nooksack River and Rt. 542. The turn-off for **Baker Lake Hwy.** is 23mi. east of Sedro Wooley at Mi. 82, which dead-ends 25mi. later at Baker Lake and free **hot springs.** Along this road, the crowded **Kulshan Campground** has drinking water and flush toilets ($7), and **Horseshoe Cove** and **Panorama Point** ($12) are wheelchair accessible (reservations 800-280-2267).

Farther east on Rt. 20, near the relatively small **Rockport State Park** (50 sites $10; hookups $15; wheelchair accessible trail), Sauk Mountain Rd. (Forest Service Rd. 1030) makes a stomach-scrambling climb up **Sauk Mountain.** Trailers, RVs, and the faint of heart should not attempt it. The **Sauk Mountain Trail** near the top winds 3½mi. to stunning views and campsites near Sauk Lake.

Three miles east of Marblemount, bunnies roam the landscape (lawn) outside the **Eatery,** 5675 Rt. 20. Dine under the American flag which 88-year-old Tootsie's grandmother made in 1890 when Washington celebrated its first 4th of July as a state. Or get takeout: burgers $1.75, basket $2.75. (Open daily 8am-8pm.) The **Marblemount Wilderness Information Center,** 728 Ranger Station Rd., Marblemount 98267 (360-873-4500, ext. 39), 1mi. north of Marblemount on a well-marked road from the west end of town, is the place to go for a **backcountry permit** and to plan longer hiking excursions (open in summer Su-Th 7am-6pm, F-Sa 7am-8pm; call for winter hrs.). Cruise 8mi. east along Cascade River Rd. to **Marble Creek** (24 sites) or 16mi. east to **Mineral Park** (8 sites). Both are free, but have no drinking water. From Marblemount, it's 22mi. along Cascade River Rd. to the trailhead for a 3½mi. hike to the amazing **Cascade Pass,** which then continues on to Lake Chelan.

**ROSS LAKE. Newhalem** is the first town on Rt. 20 after it crosses into the **Ross Lake Recreation Area,** a buffer zone between the highway and the national park. At the tourist-friendly **North Cascades Visitors Center and Ranger Station,** off Rt. 20, a mystical and atonal slide show is shown (206-386-4495; open daily 8:30am-6pm; in winter Sa-Su 9am-4:30pm). Among the easiest hikes is the **Thunder Creek Trail,** which extends through old growth cedar and fir forests, beginning from the Colonial Creek Campground (see below) at Rt. 20 Mi. 130. The 3.2mi. **Fourth of July Pass Trail** begins approximately 2mi. into the Thunder Creek Trail, and climbs 3500 ft. toward hellzapoppin' views. The park's **Goodell Creek Campground,** just south of Newhalem, has 22 sites for tents and trailers, with drinking water, pit toilets, and a launch site for whitewater rafting on the Skagit River (sites $7; water turned off after Oct., when sites are free). **Colonial Creek Campground,** 10mi. to the east, is a fully developed, wheelchair-accessible campground with flush toilets, a dump station, and occasional campfire programs (164 sites, $10; no hookups).

**ROSS LAKE TO WINTHROP.** This is the most beautiful segment of Rt. 20. Leaving the basin of Ross Lake, the road begins to climb, exposing the jagged, snowy peaks of the North Cascades. Thirty miles of astounding views east, the **Pacific Crest Trail** crosses Rt. 20 at **Rainy Pass** on one of the most scenic and difficult legs of its 2500mi. Canada-to-Mexico route. Near Rainy Pass, groomed scenic trails of 1-3mi. can be hiked in sneakers, provided the snow has melted (about mid-July). Just off Rt. 20, an overlook at **Washington Pass** (Mi. 162) rewards a ½mi. walk on a wheelchair-accessible paved trail with an astonishing view of the red rocks in **Copper Basin.** The popular 2½mi. walk to **Blue Lake** begins just east of Washington

Pass. An easier 2mi. hike to **Cutthroat Lake** departs from an access road 4½mi. east of Washington Pass. From the lake, the trail continues 4mi. farther and almost 2000 ft. higher to **Cutthroat Pass,** treating hikers to a stellar view of towering, rugged peaks. The hair-raising 23mi. road to **Hart's Pass** begins at **Mazama,** on Rd. 1163, 10mi. east of Washington Pass. Breathtaking views await the steel-nerved driver, both from the pass and from **Slate Peak,** the site of a lookout station 3mi. beyond the pass. The road is closed to trailers and is often snowed over.

**WINTHROP TO TWISP.** Farther east is **Winthrop,** a town desperately and somewhat successfully trying to market its frontier history. **Winthrop Information Station,** 202 Riverside (509-996-2125), at the junction with Rt. 20 (open early May to mid-Oct. daily 10am-5pm). Winthrop's summer is bounded by rodeos on Memorial and Labor Day weekends. Late July brings the top-notch **Winthrop Rhythm and Blues Festival,** where big name blues bands flock to belt their tunes, endorse radio stations, and play cowboy. Tickets for the 3-day event cost $35 (509-997-2541; $45 at the door). The **Methow Valley Visitors Center** (MET-how), Bldg. 49, Rt. 20 (509-996-4000), hands out info on area camping, hiking, and cross-country skiing (open daily 9am-5pm; call for winter hrs.). For more in-depth skiing and hiking trail information, call the **Methow Valley Sports Trail Association** (509-996-3287), which maintains 175km of trails. Between Winthrop and Twisp on East Country Rd. #9129, the **North Cascades Smokejumper Base** (509-997-2031) is a center for airborne forest-firefighters. (Open in summer and early fall daily 9am-6pm; tours 10am-5pm.)

Nine mi. south of Winthrop on Rt. 20, the peaceful village of **Twisp** offers lower prices and far fewer tourists than its neighbor. The **Twisp Ranger Station,** 502 Glover St. (509-997-2131), employs a crunchy and helpful staff fortified with essential trail and campground guides (open M-F 7:45am-4:30pm). **The Sportsman Motel,** 1010 E. Rt. 20, a hidden jewel, where a barracks-like facade masks tastefully decorated rooms with kitchens (509-997-2911; singles $35; doubles $40). The **Glover St. Cafe,** 104 N. Glover St., serves gourmet lunches (509-997-1323; open M-F 8am-3pm; $3-6). **Campgrounds** and **trails** await 15-25mi. up Twisp River Rd. off Rt. 20. Most of the campsites are primitive and have a $5 fee. **Riverbend RV Park,** 19951 Rt. 20, is only 2mi. west of Twisp. (509-997-3500 or 800-686-4498. Sites for 2 $14; hookups $18, $2 per additional person. Office open 9am-10pm). From Twisp, Rt. 20 continues east to **Okanogan** and Rt. 153 runs south to **Lake Chelan.**

# EASTERN WASHINGTON

## SPOKANE

A city built on silver mining, grown fat and prosperous after decades as a central rail link for regional agriculture, Spokane (spoe-KAN) has regressed to become a gateway rather than a destination. Copious middle-Americana, fused with bottom-of-the-barrel prices, makes Spokane a convenient, inexpensive stopover. **Riverfront Park,** N. 507 Howard St., just north of downtown, is Spokane's civic center and greatest asset (456-4386). Developed for the 1974 World's Fair, the park's 100 acres are divided down the middle by the roaring rapids that culminate in **Spokane Falls.** In the park, the **IMAX Theater** houses your basic 5-story movie screen. (625-6604. Shows June-Sept. on the hr. Su-Th 11am-8pm, F-Sa 11am-9pm; call for winter schedule. $5.75, under 13 and seniors $4.75.) A 1-day pass ($11) covers all these and more, including the exquisitely hand-carved **Looff Carousel.** (Open daily June-Sept. 11am-8pm, F-Sa 11am-10pm. $1.75 per whirl, under 12 $1.) The park hosts **ice-skating** in the winter. South of downtown off Stevens St., at **Manito Park,** 4 W. 21st Ave., carp blow bubbles in the **Nishinomiya Japanese Garden** and roses bloom in June at **Rosehill** (625-6622; open daily 8am-8pm; free). The visitor center will furnish info on area wineries, tours, and tastings. Spokane is a minor league hotbed. The **Indians** play single-A baseball from June-Aug. (535-2922; $3-6), and from Sept.-Mar. the minor league **Chiefs** play hockey (535-7825; $7-13).

**Boulevard Inn,** 2905 W. Sunset Blvd, 2mi. west of town on Rt. 2., rents rooms so clean you could eat off the floor. (747-1060. Singles $30; doubles $36. Kitchen access $5 extra.) **Riverside State Park** is 6mi. northwest of downtown onto Rifle Club Rd., off Rt. 291 (Nine Mile Rd.); take Division St. north and turn left on Francis, then follow signs. 101 standard sites lie in a sparse Ponderosa forest next to the river. (456-3964, reservations 800-452-5687. Sites $11, hiker/biker sites $5. Showers. Wheelchair access.) The **Spokane County Market,** between 1st Ave. and Jefferson St., sells fresh fruit, vegetables, and baked goods (482-2607; open May-Oct. W and Sa 9am-5pm, Su 11am-4pm). At **Dick's,** E. 10 3rd Ave., at Division St., customers eat in their cars and pay prices straight out of the 50s. (747-2481; burgers 59¢, shakes 89¢; open daily 9am-1am).

Spokane lies 280mi. east of Seattle on I-90. **Spokane International Airport** (624-3218) is off I-90 8mi. southwest of town. **Amtrak,** W. 221 1st St. (624-5144), at Bernard St., sends 1 train per day to Seattle (7hr., $56) and Portland, OR (8hr., $56). **Greyhound,** W. 221 1st St. (tickets 624-5251, info 624-5252), in the same building, runs to Seattle (6hr., 5 per day, $27) and Portland, OR (8-10hr., 4 per day, $37). **Spokane Transit Authority,** W. 107 Riverside St. (328-7433) serves all of Spokane, including Eastern Washington University in Cheney (75¢, under 5 free; runs until 12:15am downtown, until 11:20pm in the valley along E. Sprague Ave.). **Spokane Area Convention and Visitors Bureau,** 201 W. Main St. (747-3230 or 800-248-3230), exit 281 off I-90 (open M-F 8:30am-5pm, Sa 8am-4pm, Su 9am-2pm; in winter M-F 8:30am-5pm). **Internet access: Library,** W. 906 Main St. (444-5333; open M-Th 10am-9pm, F-Sa 10am-6pm). **Post Office:** W. 904 Riverside St. (626-6860), at Lincoln (open M-F 6am-5pm). **ZIP code:** 99210. **Area code:** 509.

# OREGON

Over a century ago, families liquidated their possessions and sank their life savings into covered wagons, corn meal, and oxen, high-tailing it to Oregon in search of prosperity and a new way of life. Today, Oregon remains as popular a destination as ever for backpackers, cyclists, anglers, beachcrawlers, and families. The caves and cliffs of Oregon's coastline are a siren call to tourists, and some coastal towns are enticing oases. Inland attractions include Crater Lake National Park, Ashland's Shakespeare Festival, and North America's deepest gorge. Portland is casual and idiosyncratic—its name was determined by a coin toss—while the college town of Eugene embraces hippies and Deadheads. Bend is a tiny interior city with a young, athletic population. For everything from microbrews to snow-capped peaks, Oregon is worth crossing the Continental Divide.

## ⁊ PRACTICAL INFORMATION

**Capital:** Salem.

**Visitor Info: Oregon Tourism Commission,** 775 Summer St. NE, Salem, OR 97310 (800-547-7842; www.traveloregon.com). **Oregon State Parks and Recreation Dept.,** P.O. Box 500, Portland, OR 97207-0500 (800-551-6949; www.prd.state.or.us).

**Postal Abbreviation:** OR. **Sales Tax:** 0%.

# PORTLAND

With over 200 parks, the pristine Willamette (wih-LAM-it) River, and snow-capped Mt. Hood in the background, Portland is an oasis of natural beauty. Portlanders have also nursed a love of art, music, and books. Culture is constantly cultivated in the endless theaters, galleries, and bookshops around town. As the microbrewery capital of America, Portland is a flowing font of the nation's finest beer. During the rainy season, Portlanders flood neighborhood pubs and coffeehouses for shelter and conversation. But on rare sunny days, a battalion of hikers, bikers, and runners take advantage of their sylvan surroundings.

# ℹ ORIENTATION AND PRACTICAL INFORMATION

Portland lies in the northwest corner of Oregon, where the Willamette River flows into the Columbia River. **I-5** connects Portland with San Francisco and Seattle, while **I-84** follows the route of the Oregon Trail through the Columbia River Gorge, heading along the Oregon-Washington border toward Boise, ID. West of Portland, **U.S. 30** follows the Columbia downstream to Astoria, but **U.S. 26** is the fastest path to the coast. **I-405** runs just west of downtown to link I-5 with U.S. 30 and 26.

Portland is divided into 5 districts by which all street signs are labeled: **N, NE, NW, SE,** and **SW. Burnside St.** divides the city into north and south, while east and west are separated by the **Willamette River.** SW Portland is known as **downtown** but also includes the southern end of Old Town and a slice of the wealthier **West Hills. Old Town,** in NW Portland, encompasses most of the city's historic sector. Some areas the NW and SW around W. Burnside are best not walked alone at night, although on weekends district clubs and live music draw crowds. West of Old Town and Chinatown, **Pearl District** is known for art galleries and antique stores. Farther west, NW 21st and NW 23rd St. are known as **Nob Hill,** a hot spot for boutique shopping and dining. Portland's zoo and many gardens are located farther west. **Southeast** Portland contains parks, factories, local businesses, residential areas of all brackets, and a rich array of cafes, stores, theaters, and restaurants lining **Hawthorne Blvd. Williams Ave.** frames "the North." **North** and **Northeast** Portland are chiefly residential, punctuated by a few small and quiet parks, and the site of the **University of Portland.** Northeast Portland has a reputation for being unsafe, but even this area has become increasingly rejuvenated.

**Airport: Portland International,** 7000 NE Airport Way (460-4234). The cheapest way to reach downtown is to take Tri-Met bus #12, which passes south through town on SW 5th Ave. (45min., 4 per hr., $1.10). **Gray Line** (285-9845) provides **airport shuttles** that stop at major hotels (24hr., 2 per hr., $12; round-trip $22). Taxi from airport to downtown $22-25; to HI Portland $15-18.

**Amtrak:** 800 NW 6th Ave. (273-4865), at Hoyt St. in Union Station. To Seattle (4hr., 3 per day, from $24) and Eugene (2½hr., 2 per day, from $12). Open daily 7:45am-9pm.

**Buses: Greyhound,** 550 NW 6th Ave. (243-2357), at NW Glisan. In summer to: Seattle (3-4½hr., 15 per day, $20, round-trip $38); Eugene (2½-4hr., 11 per day, $12, round-trip $20); Spokane (about 8hr., 6 per day, $34, round-trip $65); and Boise (about 10hr., 3 per day, $33, round-trip $62). Lockers $5 per day. Open daily 5am-12:30am. **Green Tortoise** (800-867-8647) picks up at Union Station in the Amtrak building (see above). To: Seattle (about 4hr., Tu and Sa 4pm, $15) and San Francisco (about 22hr., Su and Th 12:30pm, $49). Confirm 2 days in advance.

**Public Transit: Tri-Met,** 701 SW 6th Ave. (238-7433), in Pioneer Courthouse Sq. Open M-F 8am-5pm. Several **info lines** available: **Call-A-Bus** info system (231-3199); fare info (231-3198); updates, changes, and weather-related problems (231-3197); TDD (238-5811); special needs (238-4952); lost and found (238-4855). Bus routes fall into 7 **service areas:** red salmon, orange deer, yellow rose, green leaf, blue snow, purple raindrop, and brown beaver. Buses generally run 5am-midnight, reduced on weekends. Fare $1.10-1.40, ages 7-18 85¢, over 65 or disabled 55¢; free in the downtown **Fareless Sq.,** bounded by NW Hoyt St. to the north, I-405 to the west and south, and the Willamette River to the east. All-day pass $3.50. All buses have bike racks ($5 lifetime permit available at bike stores). **MAX** (228-7246) is a light-rail train that runs between downtown and Gresham in the east, M-F 4:30am-1:30am; same fares and transfers as Tri-Met.

**Taxis: Radio Cab** (227-1212). $2 base, $1.50 per mi. **Broadway Cab** (227-1234).

**Car Rental: Crown Rent-A-Car,** 1315 NE Sandy Blvd. (224-8110 or 800-722-7813), across from the huge 7-Up bottle. Transport from airport. From $20 per day, plus 20¢ per mi. after 100mi., or $30 per day with unlimited mileage. Weekly rental $120-150. Must be 18 with a credit card. Open M-F 8am-5pm, Sa 9am-noon.

**Visitor Information: Portland Oregon Visitors Association,** 25 SW Salmon St. (222-2223 or 800-345-3214), at SW 1st Ave. in the Two World Trade Center complex opposite the

## Portland

**ACCOMMODATIONS**
- A Northwest Portland Hostel (HI)
- B Downtown Value Inn
- C Portland HI

TO ✈ (6 mi)

500 meters

500 yards

TO ♨ (1000 yds)

TO REED COLLEGE (3 mi)

20th Ave.

16th Ave.

12th Ave. SE

Sandy Blvd.

Stark St. SE

SE 7th Ave.

SE Grand Ave.

SE Martin Luther King Jr. Blvd.

SE 3rd Ave.

SE 2nd Ave.

SE Morrison St.
SE Belmont St.
SE Yamhill St.
SE Taylor St.
SE Salmon St.
SE Main St.
SE Madison St.
SE Hawthorne Blvd.

NE Everett St.

NE Burnside St.

TO COLUMBIA RIVER GORGE

84

30

30

99E

99E

NE Hassalo

Lloyd Blvd

MAX

5

Rose Garden Arena

Willamette River

Burnside Bridge

Morrison Bridge

Willamette River

Hawthorne Bridge

5

TO OREGON MUSEUM OF SCIENCE AND INDUSTRY

Steel Bridge

Fion

NW 1st Ave.
NW 2nd Ave.
NW 3rd Ave.
NW 4th Ave.
NW 5th Ave.
NW 6th Ave.
NW Broadway Ave.
NW Park Ave.

NW 10th Ave.

NW 14th Ave.

NW 17th Ave.

NW 19th Ave.

NW 21st Ave.

NW 23rd Ave.

Union Station (Amtrak)

Powell's Book Store

Skidmore Fountain

SW Front Ave.

SW 1st Ave.

SW 2nd Ave.

SW Ward Ave.

SW 4th Ave.

MAX

Transit Mall

SW Oak St.

SW Ankeny St.

SW Stark St.

SW Washington St.

SW Alder St.

SW Morrison St.

SW Yamhill St.

COURTHOUSE SQUARE

PIONEER

SW Taylor St.

SW Salmon St.

SW Madison St.

Portland Building

City Hall

Civic Auditorium

Broadway

SW Park Ave.

SW 9th Ave.

SW Jefferson St.

SW Columbia St.

SW Clay St.

SW Market St.

SW Mill St.

Portland State University

SW 6th Ave.

TO ONDINE

TO LEWIS AND CLARK COLLEGE

i

B

(200 yds)

NW Hoyt St.
NW Glisan St.
NW Flanders St.
NW Everett St.

NW Kearney St.
NW Johnson St.
NW Irving St.

NW Davis St.
NW Couch St.

Dbaar

NW Burnside St.

405

30

405

MAX

MAX

N

Civic Stadium

TO WASHINGTON PARK ZOO (2 mi)

26

Fareless Square

THE PACIFIC NORTHWEST

Salmon St. Springs. From I-5, follow the signs for City Center. Open M-F 9am-5pm, Sa 9am-4pm, Su 10am-2pm; Sept.-Apr. closed Su. **Portland Parks and Recreation,** 1120 SW 5th Ave. #1302 (823-2223), in the Portland Building between Main and Madison St. Open M-F 8am-5pm.

**Leonardo da Vinci's Birthday:** Apr. 15.

**Women's Crisis Line:** 235-5333. 24hr.

**Internet Access: Library,** 801 SW 10th Ave. (248-5123). Open M-Th 9am-9pm, F-Sa 9am-6pm, Su 1-5pm.

**Post Office:** 715 NW Hoyt St. (800-275-8777). **ZIP code:** 97208-9999. Open M-F 7am-6:30pm, Sa 8:30am-5pm. **Area code:** 503.

## ▚ ACCOMMODATIONS

Inexpensive motels line SE Powell Blvd. and the southern end of SW 4th Ave. Portland accommodations fill in a flash during the Rose Festival and frequent conventions; early reservations are wise. Camping sites are distant, but beautiful.

**Portland International Hostel (HI-AYH),** 3031 SE Hawthorne Blvd. (236-3380), at 31st Ave. across from Artichoke Music. From the airport, take bus #12 to 5th. Ave, walk to the corner of 5th and Washington to take bus #14 (brown beaver). Laid-back and well integrated into the vibrant Hawthorne community. Front porch, kitchen (including BBQ), Internet access ($1 per 20min.), and laundry. Discount ski passes and guided tours. Reception daily 9am-10pm. No curfew. 34 beds. $15, nonmembers $18.

**Northwest Portland International Hostel (HI-AYH),** 1818 NW Glisan St. (241-2783) at 18th Ave. From SW 6th and Salmon or Greyhound, take bus #17 (red salmon) to 19th Ave. Deck, kitchen, laundry, espresso cafe, and Sunday sundaes ($1). You might not even make it out to see the city. 34 dorm beds (coed dorms available). Reception 8am-11pm. No curfew. Check-in at noon. $15, nonmembers $18.

**McMenamins Edgefield,** 2126 SW Halsey St. (669-8610 or 800-669-8610), in Troutdale, a 20min. drive east of Portland or 50min. MAX ride. By car, take I-84 east to exit 16 and turn left at the first stoplight onto SW Halsey St. Continue ¼mi. down Halsey, turn right just after Edgefield's vineyards. Take MAX east to the Gateway Station, then Tri-Met bus #24 (Halsey) east to the main entrance. The 33-acre estate has a theater, winery, brewery, golf course, 3 restaurants, and the **Little Red Shed,** the smallest free-standing bar in North America. Two single-sex rooms with 12 beds. Showers, but no kitchen or laundry. No curfew. 24hr. desk. $20 includes lockers, towels, and bedding.

**Ainsworth State Park,** 37mi. east of Portland, at exit 35 off I-84 on scenic U.S. 30, in the Columbia Gorge. Wooded and lovely, but highway noise prevails. Hot showers, toilets, hiking. Tent sites $13; full hookups $18. Non-camper showers $2. Open Apr.-Oct.

**Champoeg State Park,** 8239 NE Champoeg Rd. (678-1251, reservations 800-452-5687). Take I-5 south 27mi. to exit 278, then follow the signs west for 6mi. Play along miles of paved bikeway or hike by the Willamette River. 48 shady RV sites ($19) have water and electricity. Tent sites ($15, hiker/bikers $4). Yurts accommodate 5 ($27).

## ◖ FOOD

**Montage,** 301 SE Morrison St. (234-1324). Take bus #15 (brown beaver) to the end of the Morrison Bridge and walk under it. An oasis of Louisiana-style cooking. Oyster shooters ($1.50). Open M-F 11am-2pm and Su-Th 6pm-2am, F-Sa 6pm-4am.

**Coffee Time,** 712 NW 21st Ave. (497-1090). Sip a cup of chai ($1.70) amid ancient wonders in the main room, over Jenga in a 3-sided niche, or in the tapestried parlor. Lattes $1.65; Time Warp with extra caffeine $1. Open 24hr.

**Western Culinary Institute** (800-666-0312) maintains 3 public testing grounds for its gastronomic experiments. At **Chef's Diner,** 1231 SW Jefferson, cheery students in tall hats serve, taste, and discuss sandwiches. Open Tu-F 7am-noon. The **Chef's Corner,** 1239 SW Jefferson, dishes out quick meals on-the-go. Open Tu-Th 8am-5:30pm, F 8am-6pm.

Across the street, the elegant sit-down **Restaurant,** 1316 SW 13th Ave., serves a classy 5-course lunch ($8) rivaled only by its superb 6-course dinner (Tu-W, F, $15) or buffet (Th $18). Call ahead. Open Tu-F 11:30am-1pm and 6-8pm.

**Palio Dessert & Espresso House,** 1996 SE Ladd (232-9412), on Ladd Circle. Bus #10 stops right in front of the cafe. Mosaic floors, Mexican mochas ($2.50), and espresso mousse ($4) might keep you from the neighborhood's diagonal streets and rose gardens. Open M-F 8am-midnight, Sa-Su 10am-midnight.

**Saigon Kitchen,** 835 NE Broadway (281-3669). The best and best-smelling Vietnamese and Thai restaurant in town. Most entrees $6-8. Also at 3829 SE Division St. (236-2312), at 38th near Hawthorne. Open M-F 11am-10pm, Sa noon-10pm.

**The Roxy,** 1121 SW Stark St. (223-9160). Take away the giant crucified Jesus (with neon halo) and this joint would still have more attitude than any other place in town. Sandwiches $6. Entire carafe of coffee $1, for that extra kick at 4am. Open Tu-Su 24hr.

**Little Wing Cafe,** 529 NW 13th Ave. (228-3101) off Glisan. Take bus #17. Starving artists and art-hunters gather where everything is homemade. Lunch $3-7. Open M-Sa 11:30am-4pm, Su-Th 5:30-9pm and F-Sa 5:30-10pm.

## ◉ SIGHTS

The fully-functioning **Pioneer Courthouse,** a downtown landmark at 5th Ave. and Morrison St., is the centerpiece of **Pioneer Courthouse Sq.,** which opened in 1983 and has since become "Portland's Living Room." During the summer, the **High Noon Tunes** draw thousands of music lovers. *(701 SW 6th Ave. 223-1613. W noon-1pm.)* The section of downtown just south of the Burnside Bridge and along the river comprises **Old Town.** Intended as a place where "horses, men and dogs" might drink, **Skidmore Fountain,** at SW 1st Ave. and SW Ankeny St., marks the end of **Waterfront Park,** a 20-block swath of grass and flowers along the Willamette River. The 185 jets of **Salmon St. Springs** spout down the street from the visitors center.

Catch the best of Portland's dizzying arts scene on the first Th of each month, when the Portland Art Museum and Southwest and Northwest galleries stay open until 9pm. For details contact the **Regional Arts and Culture Council** or grab the *Art Gallery Guide* at the visitor center. *(620 SW Main St. #420. 823-5111.)* On the west side of the South Park Blocks sits the venerable **Portland Art Museum,** at Jefferson St. The oldest fine arts museum in the Pacific Northwest, PAM holds over 32,000 works of Western, Native American, Asian, and African art spanning the past 35 centuries. *(1219 SW Park. 226-2811. Open Tu-Sa 10am-5pm, Su noon-5pm, and until 9pm on the first Th of the month. $7.50, seniors and students $6, under 19 $4; special exhibitions may be more.)* Across the park, the **Oregon Historical Society Museum and Library,** stores photographs, artifacts, and records of Oregon's last 2 centuries. *(1200 SW Park Ave. 222-1741. Open Tu-Sa 10am-5pm, Su noon-5pm, Th until 8pm. $6, students $3, ages 6-12 $1.50. Seniors free on Th.)* At the first and only **24-Hour Church of Elvis,** you can listen to synthetic oracles, witness satirical miracles, and experience a tour in the Art-o-Mobile. Visits to the giftstore grant exit from the land of eternal grace. *(720 SW Ankeny St. 226-3671. Usually open M-Th 2-4pm, F 8pm-midnight, Sa noon-5pm and 8pm-midnight, Su noon-5pm, but call ahead.)*

Portland has more park acreage than any other American city, thanks in good measure to **Forest Park,** the 5000-acre tract of wilderness in Northwest Portland. Washington Park (see below), provides easy access by car or foot to this sprawling sea of green, where a web of trails leads through lush forests, scenic overviews, and idyllic picnic areas. Downtown on the edge of the Northwest district is the gargantuan **Powell's City of Books,** a cavernous establishment with almost a million new and used volumes, more than any other bookstore in the U.S. *(1005 W. Burnside St. 228-4651 or 800-878-7323. Open M-Sa 9am-11pm, Su 9am-9pm.)* **The Grotto,** a 62-acre Catholic sanctuary, houses magnificent religious sculptures and gardens just minutes from downtown on Sandy Blvd. (U.S. 30) at NE 85th. *(254-7371. Open daily 9am-8pm; in winter 9am-5:30pm.)*

THE PACIFIC NORTHWEST

At the **Crystal Springs Rhododendron Garden,** SE 28th Ave., at Woodstock (take bus #19), over 2500 rhododendrons of countless varieties surround a lake and border an 18-hole public golf course. *(Open daily Mar.-Sept. 6am-10pm, Oct.-Feb. 8am-7pm. $2, under 12 free.)* The **Oregon Museum of Science and Industry (OMSI),** at SE Clay St., keeps visitors mesmerized with science exhibits, including an earthquake simulator chamber. *(1945 SE Water Ave. 797-4000 or 797-4569. Open daily Labor Day to Memorial Day 9:30am-7pm, Th until 8pm; in winter daily 9:30am-5:30pm, Th until 8pm. $6.50, ages 4-13 and seniors $4.50.)* While at OMSI, visit the **U.S.S. Blueback,** the Navy's last diesel submarine; she never failed a mission. *(797-4624. 40min. tour $3. Open daily 10am-5pm.)*

Less than 2mi. west of downtown, in the middle of the posh neighborhoods of **West Hills,** is mammoth **Washington Park.** The **Rose Garden,** in Washington Park, is the pride of Portland. In summer months, a sea of blooms arrests the eye, showing visitors exactly why Portland is the City of Roses. *(400 SW Kingston. 823-3636.)* Across from the Rose Garden are the scenic **Japanese Gardens,** reputed to be the most authentic this side of the Pacific. *(611 SW Kingston Ave. 223-1321. Open daily Apr.-Sept. 10am-7pm; Oct.-Mar. 10am-4pm. Tours daily at 10:45am and 2:30pm. $6, seniors $4, students $3.50, under 6 free.)* The **Hoyt Arboretum,** at the crest of the hill above the other gardens, features 200 acres of trees and trails. *(4000 SW Fairview Blvd. 228-8733 or 823-3655. Visitor center open M-F 9am-4pm, Sa-Su 10am-5pm.)* The **Oregon Zoo** is renowned for its scrupulous re-creation of natural habitats and its successful elephant breeding. Reach the zoo via the mural-decorated #63 "zoo bus" that connect the park to SW Main St. in the downtown mall, or take the MAX light-rail to the Washington Park stop. *(4001 SW Canyon Rd. 226-1561. Open 9am-6pm. $5.50, seniors $4, ages 3-11 $3.50; 2nd Tu of each month is free after 3pm.)*

## ♫ ENTERTAINMENT AND FESTIVALS

Portland's major daily newspaper, the **Oregonian,** lists upcoming events in its F edition. The **Oregon Symphony Orchestra,** 719 SW Alder St., in the Arlene Schnitzer Concert Hall, plays a classical and pop series. (228-1353 or 800-228-7343. Sept.-June; tickets $15-60; Su afternoons $10-15; ½-price student tickets 1hr. before showtime Sa-Su; M $5 student tickets 1 week before showtime.) **Sack Lunch Concerts,** 1422 SW 11th Ave., at Clay St. and the Old Church, presents free concerts, usually classical or jazz (222-2031; every W at noon). **Portland Center Stage,** in the Newmark Theater at SW Broadway and SW Main, stages a 5-play series of classics and modern adaptations. (248-6309. Late Sept. to Apr. Su and Tu-Th $11-31.50, F-Sa $12.50-39; under 26 $10. ½-price tickets sometimes available 1hr. before curtain.) The **Bagdad Theater and Pub,** 3702 SE Hawthorne Blvd. (230-0895), and the **Mission Theater and Pub,** 1624 NW Glisan (223-4031), put out second-run films and an excellent beer menu ($1-3; 21+). Sports fans can watch basketball's **Portland Trailblazers** at the **Rose Garden,** 1 Center Ct. (231-8000).

**Northwest Film Center,** 1219 SW Park Ave., hosts the **Portland International Film Festival** in the last 2 weeks of Feb., with 100 films from 30 nations (221-1156; box office opens 30min. before each show; tickets $6, seniors $5). Portland's premier summer event is the **Rose Festival,** 220 NW 2nd Ave., during the first 3 weeks of June. The city decks itself in finery, coming alive with waterfront concerts, art festivals, celebrity entertainment, auto racing, parades, an air show, Navy ships, and the largest children's parade in the world. (227-2681.) Not too long afterward, the outrageously good 3-day **Waterfront Blues Festival,** draws some of the world's finest blues artists. Suggested donation is $3 and 2 cans of food to benefit the Oregon Food Bank. (282-0555 or 973-3378; June 30-July 4, 2000.) The **Oregon Brewers Festival,** on the last full weekend in July, is the continent's largest gathering of independent brewers and models for one incredible party at Waterfront Park. (778-5917. $2 mug and $1 per taste. Those under 21 must be accompanied by a parent.)

## NIGHTLIFE

**Panorama, Brig,** and **Boxxes,** 341 SW 10th St. (221-7262), form a network of clubs along Stark St. between 10th and 11th. Shake it until you break amid a thriving mixed crowd. $5. Open F-Sa 9pm-4am. The beats reach back in the Brig with 70s and 80s classics (F). Open daily noon-2:30am, F until 4am. Push farther into Boxxes, the 23-screen video/karaoke bar where matchmaking magic happens with the video postings of "Misha's Make-a-Date" (Tu). Open daily noon-2:30am.

**Crystal Ballroom,** 1332 W. Burnside Blvd. (225-0047), near the I-405. The grand ballroom and microbrewery employs 1920s technology to keep you dancing all night long to swing or punk. Downstairs, **Ringlers** (225-0543) rings in young 'uns with free pool Tu-Su 11:30am-6pm, M 11:30am-2:30am. Open daily 11:30am-2:30am.

**Biddy McGraw's,** 3518 SE Hawthorne Blvd. (233-1178). Take bus #14. Biddy and her daughter set out to create a pub like the ones they remembered in Ireland and succeeded. 22 kegs of Guiness are consumed here per week. Do your part for $3.75 per imperial pint. Microbrews $3. Open daily 11am-2:30am.

**Embers,** 110 NW Broadway (222-3082), at Couch St. Follow the rainbows onto the dance floor, or watch fish swim inside the bustling bar counter. Retro and house music. Nightly drag show at 10pm. Open daily 11am-2:30am. Happy hour until 7pm.

**Satyricon,** 125 NW 6th Ave. (243-2380), on the bus mall. Live alternative and punk. Cover $4-15. 21+. **Fellini,** the club's PoMo, mosaic chic sister restaurant next door, serves innovative cuisine (entrees from $4) while you wait for your ears to stop ringing. Music 10pm-2:30am. Food M-Th 11:30pm-2:30am, F-Sa 5pm-3am, Su 5pm-2:30am.

**Ohm,** 31 NW 1st Ave. (223-9919), at Couch under the Burnside Bridge. Specializing in unclassifiable beats you're unlikely to hear anywhere else. Cover $4-10. Open M-Th 8pm-2:30am, F 8pm-2:30am, Sa 11am-4am, Su 11am-2:30am.

## MOUNT HOOD

Magnificent, snow-capped Mt. Hood stands near the junction of U.S. 26 and Rt. 35, 1½hr. east of Portland and 1hr. south of the Hood River. **Government Camp,** 50mi. east of Portland, has food, accommodations, and gear rental. The most popular day hike is **Mirror Lake,** a 6mi. loop that starts from a parking lot off U.S. 26, 1mi. west of Government Camp (open May 31 through Oct.). Three Mt. Hood ski areas are convenient to Portland. All offer **night skiing** and **snowboard parks. Timberline,** off U.S. 26 at Government Camp, is a largely beginner and intermediate area, with the longest ski season in Oregon. (503-622-0717, snow report 503-222-2211. Open in winter daily 9am-4pm, in spring and fall 8:30am-2:30pm, in summer 7am-1:30pm. Lift tickets $34. Night skiing Jan.-Feb. W-F 4-9pm, Sa-Su 4-10pm. Rentals: ski package $20, ages 7-12 $13; snowboard and boots $33, ages 7-12 $23. Cash deposit or credit card required.) Smaller **Mt. Hood Ski Bowl,** 87000 E. U.S. 26, in Government Camp, 2mi. west of Hwy. 35, has the best night skiing and a snowboard park. The season is limited (Nov.-May), but 80-90% of the trails have night skiing. (222-2695. Open M-Tu 1-10pm, W-Th 9am-10pm, F 9am-11pm, Sa 8:30am-11pm, Su 8:30am-10pm. Lift tickets $23 per day, $14 per night, $30 for both. Ski rental $17, ages 7-12 $11. Snowboards $25.) **ART of Adventure** offers **mountain climbing training** trips through Portland Parks and Recreation from late May to early Aug. (503-823-5132. 2-day trip is 1-day snow class, 1-day climb, with lodging and meals in Government Camp; $205, equipment rental not included.) In summer, Mount Hood Ski Bowl opens its **Action Park,** which features Indy Kart racing, "extreme" frisbee golf, bungee jumping, and an alpine slide (222-2695; open M-F 11am-6pm, Sa-Su 10am-6pm). The Ski Bowl maintains 40mi. of bike trails ($4 permit), and **Hurricane Racing** rents mountain bikes from mid-June to Oct. ($10 per hr., $25 for 4hr., $32 for 8hr.).

Camping spots in the **Mt. Hood National Forest** cluster near the junction of U.S. 26 and Rt. 35. **Trillium Lake Campground,** 2mi. east of the Timberline turn-off on U.S. 26, has trails around the crystal-clear lake, and paved sites with water and toilets. Pine trees offer some privacy. (57 sites. $12, premium lakeside sites $14.) Just 1mi. west of Trillium Lake, down a dirt road off U.S. 26, **Still Creek Campgrounds** has a quieter, woodsier feel, unpaved sites, and a babbling brook ($12). On Rt. 35, 10 and 14mi. north of U.S. 26, **Robinhood** and **Sherwood Campgrounds** lie just off the highway beside a running creek (both $10). Reservations can be made by calling 800-280-2267. Well worth the trip out, **Lost Lake Campground** has lakeside sites with water, showers, and toilets. (541-386-6366. 125 sites; tent sites $15, RV sites without electricity $18, cabins from $30.) Turn east off Hwy. 35 onto Woodworth Dr. (2 streets north of Hood River Ranger Station), right onto the Dee Hwy., then left onto Lost Lake Rd. (Forest Service Rd. 13). A 3mi. hike around the lake provides stunning views of Mt. Hood and of old growth forest. **Reservations** for all of these campgrounds except Alpine and Lost Lake can be made at 877-444-6777. **Hood River District Ranger Station,** 6780 Rt. 35 (541-352-6002), and **Zigzag District Ranger Station,** 70220 E. U.S. 26 (503-622-3191), have detailed info (both open M-F 8am-4:30pm). **Mt. Hood Visitor Information Center:** 65000 E. U.S. 26 (503-622-4822), 16mi. west of Mt. Hood, provides permits (open daily 8am-6pm).

## COLUMBIA RIVER GORGE

Only an hour from Portland, the magnificent Columbia River Gorge stretches for 75mi. through some of the most beautiful country in the Pacific Northwest. The river widens out and the wind picks up at the town of Hood River, providing some of the world's best **windsurfing.** Though it was once "as fast as a waterfall turned on its side," and so full of fish that Lewis and Clark quipped that they could walk across without getting wet, the Columbia's waters now run slower and emptier due to damming upstream. To follow the gorge, which divides Oregon and Washington, take I-84 E to exit 22. Continue east uphill on the **Columbia River Scenic Hwy. (U.S. 30),** which follows the crest of the gorge past unforgettable views. The largest town in the gorge is **Hood River,** at the junction of I-84 and Rt. 35. **Vista House** (503-695-2230), hanging on the edge of an outcropping, is a visitors center in **Crown Point State Park,** 4mi. east of exit 22 off I-84 E (open daily mid-Apr. to Oct. 15 8:30am-6pm). Peacocks stroll through the garden outside a gallery of European and American works at the elegant **Maryhill Museum of Art,** 35 Maryhill Museum Dr., which sits high above the Columbia on the Washington side, 30mi. east of Hood River. (509-773-3733. Open daily mid-Mar. to mid-Nov. 9am-5pm. $6.50, seniors $6, ages 6-12 $1.50, under 5 free.) To get there, take I-84 to Biggs (exit 104) and the slightly more scenic Rt. 14, continuing until the signs.

The water near **Spring Creek Fish Hatchery** on the Washington side is the place to watch the best windsurfers in the business. Another hub is the **Event Site,** off exit 63 behind the visitor center. All-day parking costs $3, or free if you just sit and watch. **Big Winds,** 207 Front St., at the east end of Oak St., has cheap beginner rentals (386-6086; $8 per hour; $15 per half-day; $25 per day). **Discover Bicycles,** 1020 Wasco St., rents mountain bikes, suggests routes, and sells all manner of trail maps (386-4820; open M-Sa 9am-7pm, Su 9am-5pm; bikes $6 per hr., $30 per day). The 11mi. round-trip **Hospital Hill Trail** provides views of Mt. Hood, the gorge, Hood River, and surrounding villages. To reach the unmarked trail, follow signs to the hospital, fork left to Rhine Village, and walk behind the power transformers through the livestock fence. At **Latourell Falls,** 2½mi. east of Crown Point, a jaunt down a paved path leads right to the base of the falls; 5mi. farther east, **Wahkeena Falls** is visible from the road, and hosts both a short, steep scramble over loose rock and a ¼mi. trip up a paved walk. Just ½mi. farther on U.S. 30 is **Multnomah Falls,** which attracts 2 million visitors annually; I-84 exit 31 leads to an island in the middle of the freeway from which visitors can only see the upper falls. The steep **Wyeth Trail,** near the hamlet of Wyeth (exit 51), leads 4.4mi. to a wilderness boundary, and after 7.3mi. to the road to Hood River and the incredible 13mi. **Eagle Creek Trail** (exit 44). Chiseled into cliffs high above Eagle Creek, this trail passes 4 waterfalls before joining the Pacific Crest Trail.

The outdoorsy **Bingen School Inn Hostel,** a converted schoolhouse, is just across the Hood River Toll Bridge (75¢) and 3½ blocks from the Amtrak stop in Bingen, WA; take the third left after the yellow blinking light onto Cedar St., and go 1 block up the hill on Humbolt St. (509-493-3363. Beds $14; private rooms $35. Sailboards

$30 per day.) **Beacon Rock State Park,** across the Bridge of the Gods (exit 44) and 7mi. west on Washington's Rt. 14, has secluded sites ($10). The **Port of Cascade Locks Marine,** ½mi. east off the bridge on the Oregon side, has a lawn on the river which is also a campground ($10; showers).

**Amtrak** (open M-Sa 8:30am-7pm and some Su afternoons) runs trains from Portland to the foot of Walnut St. in Bingen, WA (2hr., 7:45am, $9-16). Buses run from the **Greyhound** station, 1205 B St., between 12th and 13th St., to Portland (386-1212; 1¼hr., 5 per day, $10). **Hood River County Chamber of Commerce,** 405 Portway Ave. (386-2000 or 800-366-3530), is just off City Center exit 63. (Open M-Th 8:30am-5pm, F 8:30am-4pm, Sa-Su 10am-4pm; Nov.-Mar. M-F 9am-5pm.) **Columbia Gorge National Scenic Area Headquarters,** 902 Wasco St. (386-2333), in Wyeth, offers info on hiking and a friendly earful of local lore (open M-F 7:30am-5pm). **Post Office:** 408 Cascade Ave. (800-275-8777; open M-F 8:30am-5pm), in Hood River. **ZIP code:** 97031. **Area codes:** In OR 541; in WA 509.

# OREGON COAST

From Astoria in the north to Brookings down south, **U.S. 101** hugs the shore along the Oregon Coast, linking a string of resorts and fishing villages that cluster around the mouths of rivers feeding into the Pacific. Breathtaking ocean views spread between these towns, while state parks and national forests allow direct access to the big surf. Seals, sea lions, and waterfowl lounge on rocks just offshore, watching the human world whiz by on wheels.

**ASTORIA.** Astoria's long-standing dependence on maritime industries has only recently begun to yield to the tourist industry. With its Victorian homes, bustling waterfront, rolling hills, and persistent fog, tiny Astoria reminds many tourists of San Francisco; every so often, the clouds around **Astoria Column** lift to reveal a stupendous view of Astoria cradled between Saddle Mountain to the south and the Columbia River estuary to the north (open dawn-10pm; free). The cavernous, wave-shaped **Columbia River Maritime Museum,** 1792 Marine Dr., houses the 1792 vessel that Robert Grey steered into the mouth of the Columbia River. (325-2323. Open daily 9:30am-5pm. $5, seniors $4, ages 6-17 $2, under 6 free.) The **Fort Clatsop National Memorial,** 5mi. southwest of town, reconstructs Lewis and Clark's winter headquarters from detailed descriptions in their journals. Astoria was their last stop in 1805. Take U.S. 101 south from Astoria to Alt. U.S. 101, and follow the signs 3mi. to the park. (861-2471. Open mid-June to Labor Day 8am-6pm; off-season 8am-5pm. $2, under 17 free, families $4.) At the **Shallon Winery,** 1598 Duane St., owner Paul van der Velt provides tours and tastings of his vintages, including chocolate flavor (325-5798; must be 21 to drink; open almost every afternoon).

**Grandview B&B,** 1574 Grand Ave., offers intimate, cheery, luxurious rooms, and a delicious breakfast spread. (325-0000, reservations 325-5555. From $45, with private bath from $59; 2nd night $28 off-season.) **Fort Stevens State Park,** over Youngs Bay Bridge on U.S. 101 S, 10mi. west of Astoria, is the largest state park in the U.S., with rugged, empty beaches and bike trails. (861-1671, reservations 800-452-5687. $17, full hookup $20; hiker/biker $4.25 per person; yurts $29. Hot showers. Facilities for the disabled. Reservations $6.) Still further south (17mi.) and worth it, **Seaside International Hostel (HI-AYH),** 930 N. Holladay Dr., in Seaside is a pastoral wonderland. (738-7911. Kitchen; kayaks and canoes $7-8 per hr. 34 large bunks, $14, nonmembers $17; 4-person private rooms with bath and cable TV $38/$58. Call well ahead. Office open 8am-11pm.) At **Columbian Café,** 1114 Marine Dr., try the $7 "Chef's Mercy"—you name your "heat range and allergies," he chooses your meal. (325-2233. Open M-F 8am-2pm, Sa-Su 9am-2pm. Open for dinner W-Th 5-9pm, F-Sa 5-10pm.)

**Pierce Pacific Stages** (692-4437) picks up travelers at **Video City,** 95 W. Marine Dr., and runs to Portland (3hr., 3:30pm, $15) and Seaside (30min., 1:15pm, $5). **Astoria/ Warrenton Area Chamber of Commerce,** 111 W. Marine Dr. (325-6311), is just east of

**THE PACIFIC NORTHWEST**

Astoria Bridge. (Open June-Sept. M-F 8am-6pm, Sa-Su 9am-6pm; Oct.-May M-F 8am-5pm, Sa-Su 11am-4pm.) **Post Office:** 750 Commercial St. (800-275-8777), at 8th St. (open M-F 8:30am-5pm). **ZIP code:** 97103. **Area code:** 503.

**CANNON BEACH.** Cannon Beach presents a somewhat more refined version of Seaside and Astoria's crass commercialism, but the beach is the real draw. **Ecola State Park** attracts picnickers and hikers (436-2844; $3). **Ecola Point** offers a view of hulking **Haystack Rock,** which is spotted with (and splattered by) gulls, puffins, barnacles, anemones, and the occasional sea lion. Ecola Point also affords views of the Bay's centerpiece, the **Tillamook Lighthouse,** which clings to a rock like a phallic barnacle. A huge **Sand Castle Competition** transforms Cannon Beach into a fantastic menagerie on the second Sa of June.

Pleasant motels line Hemlock St.; none costs under $40 in summer, but family units can make a good deal. In winter, most motels offer 2-nights-for-1 deals. **The Sandtrap Inn,** 539 S. Hemlock St. offers picturesque, cozy rooms with fireplaces, cable TV, kitchens, and VCRs (436-0247 or 800-400-4106. Singles from $55; off-season $45; 2-night min. stay summer Sa-Su.) **Seaside International Hostel (HI-AYH)** is only 7mi. north (see **Astoria,** above), and the stunning **Oswald West State Park** is 10mi. south. The park provides wheelbarrows for transporting gear from the parking lot to the 36 sites which teem with surfers; arrive early. ($14. Open mid-May to Oct.) **Midtown Cafe,** 1235 S. Hemlock St., in the Haystack Sq., serves everything homemade. Lentil burgers $7.50; burrito chili verde $8. (436-1016. Open W-M 7am-2pm and 5-9pm; in winter closed M.)

**Sunset Transit System** (800-776-6406) runs buses to Seaside (75¢) and Astoria ($2.25). **Cannon Beach Shuttle** traverses the downtown area daily 9am-6pm (50¢ requested). **Cannon Beach Chamber of Commerce,** 207 N. Spruce St. (436-2623), is at 2nd St. (open M-Sa 10am-6pm, Su 11am-4pm). **Mike's Bike Shop,** 248 N. Spruce St. (436-1266 or 800-492-1266), rents mountain bikes ($7 per hr., $29 per day; open daily 9am-6pm). **Post Office:** 155 N. Hemlock St. (436-2822; open M-F 9am-5pm). **ZIP code:** 97110. **Area code:** 503.

**THE THREE CAPES LOOP.** Between Tillamook and Lincoln City, the **Three Capes Loop,** a 35mi. circle to the west of the straying U.S. 101, connects a trio of spectacular promontories. **Cape Meares State Park** and **Lighthouse,** at the tip of the promontory jutting out from Tillamook, protect one of the few remaining old-growth forests on the Oregon Coast. Another 12mi. southwest of Cape Meares, **Cape Lookout State Park** offers picnic tables and access to the beach for drive-by dawdlers as well as some fine camping (541-842-4981; day-use fee $3). A spectacular view of **Haystack Rock** awaits at the end of the 2½mi. **Cape Trail. Cape Kiwanda State Park,** the southernmost promontory on the loop, reserves its magnificent shore for day use (open 8am-dusk). Home to one of the most sublime beaches on the Oregon coast, the sheltered cape draws all sorts. Massive rock outcroppings in a small bay mark the launching pad of the flat-bottomed **dory fleet,** one of the few fishing fleets in the world that launches beachside, directly from sand to surf.

**Pacific City,** a hidden gem that most travelers on U.S. 101 never even see, is home to another **Haystack Rock,** just as impressive as its Cannon Beach sibling to the north. For stops that extend overnight, the **Anchorage Motel,** 6585 Pacific Ave., offers homey rooms with cable and coffee, but no phones. (965-6773 or 800-941-6250. Singles from $37; doubles from $42; rates drop in winter.) The town hides away startlingly good restaurants. The **Grateful Bread Bakery,** 34805 Brooten Rd., honors the art of dining: anything from a black bean chili omelette to a dilled shrimp salad (both $6; 965-7337; open daily 8am-6pm; in winter closed W-Th).

**NEWPORT.** After the miles of malls along U.S. 101, Newport's renovated waterfront area of pleasantly kitschy restaurants and shops are a delight. Newport's claim to fame lies in its world-class fish tank, also known as the **Oregon Coast Aquarium,** 2820 Ferry Slip Rd. SE, at the south end of the bridge. The 6-acre complex features pulsating jellyfish, attention-seeking sea otters, and giant African bullfrogs. (867-3474. $8.75, seniors $7.75, ages 4-13 $4.50. Wheelchair access.) The

▧ **Mark O. Hatfield Marine Science Center,** at the south end of the bridge on Marine Science Dr., is the hub of Oregon State University's coastal research and an over-shadowed, superior facility. Intricate exhibits explain marine science. (867-0100. Open daily 10am-5pm; in winter Th-M 10am-4pm. Admission by donation.)

The motel-studded strip along U.S. 101 provides plenty of affordable rooms with predictably noisy road accompaniment. Weekend rates generally rise a couple of dollars, and winter rates plummet. **Traveler's Inn,** 606 Coast Hwy. SW, is about as cheap as a decent room gets in this town, and rents comfortable rooms with cable TV and views of the ocean. (265-7723 or 800-615-2627. Singles $38, doubles $48; less in winter.) **Beverly Beach State Park,** 198 123rd St. NE, 7mi. north of town, is a year-round campground set amid gorgeous, rugged terrain. Cold water and rip-tides discourage swimmers. (265-9278, reservations 800-452-5687. Sites $16, with electricity $19, full hookup $20; yurts $26; hiker/biker $4.25. Non-camper showers $2.) **April's,** 749 3rd St. NW, down by Nye Beach, is the undisputed pinnacle of local dining. The serene ocean view and devastatingly good food are worth every penny. (265-6855. Dinners $12-20. Open M-F 11am-2pm and from 5pm. Call ahead.)

**Greyhound:** 956 10th St. SW (265-2253), at Bailey St. To Portland (4hr., 2 per day, $18); Seattle (12hr., 1-4 per day, $42); and San Francisco (17hr., 2-3 per day, $72)). **Chamber of Commerce,** 555 Coast Hwy. SW (265-8801 or 800-262-7844; open M-F 8:30am-5pm; in summer also Sa-Su 10am-4pm). **Post office:** 310 2nd St. SW (800-275-8777; open M-F 8:30am-5pm, Sa 10am-1pm). **ZIP code:** 97365. **Area code:** 541.

## OREGON DUNES AND REEDSPORT.

**OREGON DUNES AND REEDSPORT.** Millennia of wind and water action have formed the **Oregon Dunes National Recreation Area,** a grainy 50mi. expanse between Florence and Coos Bay. The dunes' shifting grip on the coastline is broken at Reedsport, where the Umpqua and Smith Rivers empty into Winchester Bay, near a town of the same name. **Spinreel Dune Buggy Rentals,** 9122 Wild Wood Dr., on U.S. 101 7mi. south of Reedsport, offers air-rending Honda Odysseys, ear-splitting dune buggy rides, and family tours in a cochlea-mangling VW "Thing." (759-3313. Hondas $20 for 30min., $30 1st hr., $25 2nd hr.; buggies $15 for 30min., $25 per hr.; things $10 per 30min.) Even those with little time can at least stop at the **Oregon Dunes Overlook** ($1 parking fee), off U.S. 101, about halfway between Reedsport and Florence. Wooden ramps lead to a peek at untrammeled dunes and the ocean. The **Tahkenitch Creek Loop,** actually 3 separate trails, plows up to 3½mi. through forest, dunes, wetlands, and beach. (Overlook staffed daily May 31 to Sept. 6 10am-3pm. Guided hikes are available.)

The **Harbor View Motel,** 540 Beach Blvd. (271-3352), off U.S. 101 in Winchester Bay, is so close to the marina there are boats in the parking lot. Aging rooms to charm an antique hound are comfortable and clean. (Fridges and friendly manage-ment; singles $33; doubles $35.) **Motels** with singles from $40 abound on U.S. 101, though they often fill in summer. The national recreation area is administered by **Siuslaw National Forest.** Dispersed camping is allowed on public lands, 200 ft. from any road or trail. The campgrounds with dune buggy access—**Spinreel, Driftwood II, Horsfall,** and **Horsfall Beach**—are generally loud and rowdy in the summer. All have flush toilets, drinking water, and are open year-round (reservations 800-280-2267; $10-13). **Carter Lake Campground,** 12mi. north of Reedsport on U.S. 101, is as quiet as it gets out here (no ATVs; nice bathrooms; no showers; $14; open May-Sept.). **Bayfront Bar and Bistro,** 208 Bayfront Loop, in Salmon Harbor, is a classy but casual choice on the waterfront (271-9463; oyster shooters $1.50; dinners $10-16; open Tu-Su 11am-9pm).

**Greyhound,** 265 Rainbow Plaza (271-1025; open daily 11am-4pm and 2-4am), in old town Reedsport, runs to Portland (6hr., 2 per day, $26) and San Francisco, CA (15hr., 2 per day, $67). **Oregon Dunes National Recreation Area Information Center,** 855 U.S. 101 (271-3611), at Rt. 38 in Reedsport, south of the Umpqua River Bridge, hap-pily answers questions on fees, regulations, hiking, and camping throughout the area. **Reedsport/Winchester Bay Chamber of Commerce:** (271-3495 or 800-247-2155) is at the same location. (Both open daily 8:30am-5pm.) **Post Office:** 301 Fir Ave. (800-275-8777), off Rt. 38 (open M-F 8:30am-5pm). **ZIP code:** 97467. **Area code:** 541.

# INLAND OREGON

## EUGENE

With students riding mountain bikes, hippies eating organically grown food, outfitters making a killing off tourists, and hunters killing local wildlife, Eugene is liberal in the true sense of the word: it contains multitudes. Oregon's second-largest city straddles the Willamette River between the Siuslaw and Willamette National Forests. Home to the University of Oregon (U of O), Eugene owes much of its vibrancy to its students. Summer brings city slickers who happily shop and dine in the downtown pedestrian mall, until dusk draws them to Hult Center for an evening of world-class Bach. Outdoor types river raft along the Willamette and hike or bike in the many nearby parks, while fitness enthusiasts join the fleet of foot and free of spirit in this "running capital of the universe."

## █ ORIENTATION AND PRACTICAL INFORMATION

Eugene is 111mi. south of Portland on I-5. The **University of Oregon** campus lies in the southeast corner of Eugene, bordered on the north by **Franklin Blvd.,** which runs from the city center to I-5. **First Ave.** runs alongside the winding Willamette River; numbered **streets** go north-south. **Hwy. 99** is split in town—**6th Ave.** runs north and **7th Ave.** goes south. **Willamette Ave.** intersects the river, dividing the city into east and west. It is interrupted by the **pedestrian mall,** between 6th and 7th Ave. on Broadway downtown. Eugene's main student drag, **13th Ave.,** heads east to the University of Oregon.

**Amtrak:** 433 Willamette St. at 4th Ave. To: Seattle, WA (6-8hr., 2 per day, $24-46); Portland (2½hr., 2 per day, $14-26); Berkeley, CA (15hr., 1 per day, $63-105).

**Buses: Greyhound,** 987 Pearl St. (344-6265), at 10th Ave. One per day to: Seattle (6-9hr., $34); San Francisco (13-16hr., $48); Portland (2-4hr., $12). Open daily 6:30am-10pm. Lockers $1.25 per day. **Green Tortoise** (800-867-8647). Stops at the U of O library (14th and Kincaid St.). To: San Francisco (21hr., Su and Th, $39), and Seattle (7hr., Tu and Sa, $25) via Portland (4½hr., $10).

**Public Transit: Lane Transit District (LTD)** (687-5555), at 11th and Willamette. Bus service throughout town. Runs M-F 6am-11:30pm, Sa 7:30am-11:30pm, Su 8:30am-8:30pm. $1, M-F after 7pm 50¢; seniors and under 12 40¢. Wheelchair access.

**Taxis: Yellow Cab** (746-1234). 24hr.

**Car Rental: Enterprise,** 810 W. 6th Ave. (683-0874), charges $33 per day. Unlimited mi. within OR; 150 free mi. per day, 25¢ per additional mi. out of state. Must be 21. Credit card required for non-locals. Open M-F 7:30am-6pm, Sa 9am-1pm.

**Bike Rental: Paul's Bicycle Way of Life,** 152 W. 5th Ave. (344-4105), rents city bikes ($12 per day) and tandems ($15 per day). Open M-F 9am-7pm, Sa-Su 10am-5pm.

**Visitor Info: Visitors Association of Lane County,** 115 W. 8th Ave. #190 (484-5307 or 800-547-5445), enter on Olive St. Open M-F 8:30am-5pm, Sa-Su 10am-4pm; Sept.-Apr. M-Sa 8:30am-5pm. **Willamette National Forest,** 211 E. 7th Ave. (465-6522), in the Federal Bldg. (open M-F 8am-4:30pm).

**Post Office:** 520 Willamette (800-275-8777), at 5th Ave. Open M-F 8:30am-5:30pm, Sa 10am-2pm. **ZIP code:** 97401-9999. **Area code:** 541.

## █ ACCOMMODATIONS AND FOOD

The cheapest motels are on E. Broadway and W. 7th Ave., and tend toward seediness. Make reservations early; motels are packed on big football weekends. **Hummingbird Eugene International Hostel (HI-AYH),** 2352 Willamette St., a graceful neighborhood home, is a wonderful addition to and escape from the city. Take bus #24 or 25 and get off at 24th Ave. and Willamette, or park in back on Portland St.

(349-0589. Beds $14, nonmembers $17.50; private rooms from $37. Check-in 5-10pm. Lockout 11am-5pm. Kitchen open 7:30-9:30am and 5-10pm. Cash or traveler's check only.) **Downtown Motel,** 361 W. 7th Ave., is in a prime location, with clean rooms under a green Spanish roof. (345-8739 or 800-648-4366. Cable, A/C, refrigerators, free coffee and donuts in the morning. Singles $30; doubles $38. Rates constant year-round. Credit card required for reservations.)

Tenters have been known to camp by the river, especially in the wild and woolly northeastern side near Springfield. Farther east on Rt. 58 and 126, the immense **Willamette National Forest** is packed with campsites ($3-16). A swamp gives the tree bark and ferns an eerie phosphorescence in the beautiful, mysterious **Black Canyon Campground,** 28mi. east of Eugene on Hwy. 58 ($8-16).

Eugene's downtown area specializes in gourmet food; the university hang-out zone at 13th Ave. and Kincaid has more grab-and-go options, and natural food stores encircle the city. The creative menu and organic ingredients at ▨ **Keystone Café,** 395 W. 5th St., give diners a true taste of Eugene (342-2075; plate-sized pancakes $3; open daily 7am-5pm). **Café Navarro,** 454 Willamette St., serves Caribbean and Latin cuisine with a gourmet flair. (344-0943. Lunch $5-8. Open Tu-F 11am-2pm and 5-9:30pm, Sa 9am-2pm and 5-9:30pm, Su 9am-2pm.)

## ◉ SIGHTS AND EVENTS

Take time to pay homage to the ivy-covered halls that set the scene for *National Lampoon's Animal House* at Eugene's centerpiece, the **University of Oregon.** The visitor parking and information booth is just left of the main entrance on Franklin Blvd. Just off the pedestrian section of 13th St., between Kincaid and University St., the **University Museum of Art** displays Pacific Northwestern, American, and Asian pieces not featured in *Animal House.* (346-3027. Open W noon-8pm, Th-Su noon-5pm. Suggested donation $3.) A few blocks away, the **Museum of Natural History,** at Agate, shows a collection of relics from indigenous cultures worldwide, including a 7000-year-old pair of shoes. A primitive "swoosh" logo is still visible. (1680 E. 15th Ave. 346-3024. Open W-Su noon-5pm. Suggested donation $1.) Northwest of the city, just after the I-5 overpass, the **Owen Memorial Rose Garden** is perfect for a picnic, accompanied by the sweet strains of rumbling traffic. *Whittaker, the surrounding neighborhood, can be unsafe at night.*

The **Saturday Market,** at 8th Ave. and Oak St., fuses crafts, clothing, jewelry, artwork, and music in a spectacular display. (686-8885. Held weekly Apr.-Nov. Open 10am-5pm.) From June 23 to July 9, 2000 during the **Oregon Bach Festival,** Baroque authority Helmut Rilling leads some of the country's finest musicians in performances of Bach's concerti and cantatas, as well as selections from Verdi and Dvôrak. Contact the **Hult Performing Arts Center,** 1 Eugene Center, at 7th Ave. and Willamette St. (Info 687-5087, tickets 682-5000, 24hr. info 682-5746. $19-42; some senior and student discounts.) The vast **Oregon Country Fair** actually takes place in **Veneta,** 13mi. west of town on Rt. 126, but its festive quakes can be felt in Eugene. From July7-9, 2000, 50,000 people will drop everything to enjoy 10 stages' worth of shows, 300 art, clothing, craft, herbal remedy, furniture, spiritual, and food booths, and free hugs. Advance tickets are available through **Fastixx** (800-992-8499) or at the Hult Center. (343-4298. Advance tickets F and Su $10, Sa $15. No tickets sold on site.)

## ◮ OUTDOORS

**River Runner Supply,** 78 G. Centennial Loop, runs everything from fishing to whitewater rafting on the Willamette River, and also rents kayaks, canoes, and rafts. (343-6883 or 800-223-4326. 4hr. rafting trip $45 per person, 4-person min. Kayaks $25 per day, canoes $20 per day, rafts $45-60 per day. Credit card required.) The student-run **Water Works Canoe Company,** 1395 Franklin Blvd., rents canoes. (346-4386. Open in summer Tu-Su 11am-8pm, but hrs. vary depending on weather. $5 per hr., $15 per 24hr.; $30 deposit.) The large and popular Cougar Lake features the Terwilliger Hot Springs, known by all as **Cougar Hot Springs.** To get there, go 4mi. east of Blue River on Rt. 126, turn right onto Aufderheide Dr. (Forest Service Rd. 19), and follow the road 7.3mi. as it winds on the right side of Cougar Reservoir. ($3 day fee per person.)

East from Eugene, **Rt. 126** runs adjacent to the beautiful **McKenzie River,** and on a clear day, the mighty snowcapped **Three Sisters** of the Cascades are visible. Just east of the town of **McKenzie Bridge,** the road splits into a scenic byway loop; Rt. 242 climbs east to the vast lava fields of **McKenzie Pass,** while Rt. 126 turns north over **Santiam Pass** and meets back with Rt. 242 in Sisters. Often blocked by snow until the end of June, **Rt. 242** is an exquisite drive, tunneling its narrow, winding way between **Mt. Washington** and the **Three Sisters Wilderness** before rising to the high plateau of McKenzie Pass, where lava outcroppings served as a training site for astronauts preparing for lunar landings.

## 🎵 NIGHTLIFE

According to some, Eugene nightlife is the best in Oregon. Not surprisingly, the string of establishments by the university along 13th St. are often dominated by fraternity-style beer bashes. **Sam Bond's Garage,** 407 Blair Blvd., is a supremely laid-back gem of a cafe and pub in a soulful neighborhood. Live entertainment goes on every night, plus an ever-changing selection of local microbrews ($2.75 per pint). Take a bus (#50 or 52) or a cab at night. (431-6603. Open daily 3pm-1am.) Downstairs at **Jo Federigo's Jazz Club and Restaurant,** 259 E. 5th Ave., across the street from the 5th St. Market., the jazz club swings with music every night, and the whole place rattles when the train goes by. (343-8488. Shows usually at 9:30pm. Blues night W. Happy hour 2:30-6:30pm. No cover, but $5 drink min. Lunch M-F 11:30am-2pm. Dinner daily 5-10pm. Jazz club open daily 2pm-1am.) **John Henry's,** 136 E.11th Ave. (342-3358), in the heart of downtown, is a cavernous warehouse-style venue with genres (and headliners) like Grrl Variety (Fierce Pussy Posse) to Beergrass (Jackass Willie). (342-3358. Microbrew pints $3. Cover $3-7. Call for schedule. Free pool until 10pm; free foosball. Open M-Sa 4pm-1am.)

## CRATER LAKE AND KLAMATH FALLS

Crater Lake, the namesake of Oregon's only national park, was regarded as sacred by Native American shamans who forbade their people to look upon it. The fantastic depth of the lake (1932 ft.), combined with the clarity of its waters, creates its intensely blue effect. About 7700 years ago, Mt. Mazama created this serene scene in a massive eruption that buried thousands of square miles of the western U.S. under a thick layer of ash. The cataclysmic eruption left a deep caldera that gradually filled with centuries of rain. Klamath (kuh-LAH-math) Falls, one of the closest towns (56mi. southeast), houses most of the services, motels, and restaurants listed below.

🚩 **PRACTICAL INFORMATION.** The park is accessible from **Rt. 62** and the **south access** road that leads up to the caldera's rim, but the park is not completely open until after the snow has melted; call the Steel Center for road conditions (see below). To reach the park from Portland, take I-5 to Eugene, then Rt. 58 E to U.S. 97 S. During the summer, you can take Rt. 138 W from U.S. 97 and approach the lake from the park's **north entrance,** but this route is one of the last to be cleared. Before July, stay on U.S. 97 S to Rt. 62. The **Amtrak** Spring St. depot (884-2822; open 6:45-10:15am and 9-10:30pm) is in Klamath Falls, on the east end of Main St.; turn right onto Spring St. and immediately left onto Oak St. One train per day runs to Portland ($48-69). **Greyhound,** 1200 Klamath Ave. (882-4616; open M-F 6am-2:30pm, Sa 6-9am, and daily midnight-12:45am), rolls 1 per day to Bend (3hr., $20); Eugene (10hr., $39); and Redding, CA (4hr., $27). **Visitor Info: Klamath County Dept. of Tourism,** 1451 Main St. (884-0666 or 800-445-6728; open M-Sa 9am-5pm). **Post Office:** 317 S. 7th St. (800-275-8777; open M-F 7:30am-5:30pm, Sa 9am-noon). **ZIP code:** 97601. **Area code:** 541.

The **William G. Steel Center** (594-2211 ext. 402), 1mi. from the south entrance of the park, issues free **backcountry camping** permits (open daily 9am-5pm). **Crater Lake National Park Visitors Center** (594-2211, ext. 415), on the lake shore at Rim Village (open daily June-Sept. 8:30am-6pm). The **park entrance fee** is $10 for cars, $5 for hikers and bikers. **Post Office:** In the Steel Center (open M-F 10am-4pm, Sa 10am-2pm). **ZIP code:** 97604.

**▋▐ ACCOMMODATIONS AND FOOD.** Klamath Falls has several affordable hotels; it's an easy base for forays to Crater Lake. **Fort Klamath Lodge Motel and RV Park,** 52851 Rt. 62, is 15mi. from the southern entrance in Fort Klamath. Cozy, quiet, countrified motel rooms have knotted-pine walls. (381-2234. Fan, heater, TV, no phones. Singles $42; doubles $58. Coin laundry. Open May-Oct.) **Lost Creek Campground** is in the park, 3mi. off Rim Dr. in the southeast corner. Sites are set amid thin, young pines. (Sites $10. Drinking water, flush toilets, sinks. Tents only. No reservations. Usually open mid-July to mid-Oct., but call the visitors center to confirm.) **Renaissance Cafe,** 1012 Main St., serves $6.25 gourmet pizzas loaded with zucchini, spinach, pesto, and artichoke hearts and expansive $6 salads (851-0242; open M-F 11am-2:30pm; dinner M-Sa 5-9pm is more expensive).

**▟ OUTDOORS.** The walk from the visitors center at the rim to the **Sinnott Memorial Overlook** is an easy 100 yd. walk to the park's most panoramic and accessible view. **Rim Dr.,** which does not open entirely until mid-July, is a 33mi. loop around the rim of the caldera, high above the lake. Trails to **Garfield Peak** (1-way 1.7mi.), which starts at the lodge, and **Watchman Peak** (1-way ¾mi.), on the west side of the lake, are the most spectacular. The sweaty, 2½mi. hike up **Mt. Scott,** the park's highest peak (shy of 9000 ft.), begins from near the lake's eastern edge. The steep **Cleetwood Trail,** 1.1mi. of switchbacks on the lake's north edge, is the only route down to the water. It is also the home of **Wizard Island,** a cinder cone rising 760 ft. above the lake, and **Phantom Ship Rock,** a spooky rock formation. Picnics, fishing, and swimming are allowed, but surface temperatures reach a maximum of only 50°F. Park rangers lead free walking tours daily in the summer and periodically in the winter (on snowshoes). The **Red Cone trailhead,** on the north access road, makes a 12mi. loop of the **Crater Springs, Oasis Butte,** and **Boundary Springs Trails.**

# ASHLAND

Set near the California border, Ashland mixes hippies and history to create an unlikely but perfect stage for the world-famous **Oregon Shakespeare Festival,** P.O. Box 158, Ashland 97520 (482-4331; www.orshakes.org). From mid-Feb. to Oct., drama devotees can choose among 11 Shakespearean and newer works performed in Ashland's 3 elegant theaters: the outdoor **Elizabethan Stage,** the **Angus Bowmer Theater,** and the intimate **Black Swan.** Ticket purchases are recommended 6 months in advance; **mail-order and phone ticket sales** begin in Jan. ($14-37 in spring and fall, $21-49 in summer; $5 fee per order for phone, fax, or mail orders.) At 9:30am, the **box office,** 15 S. Pioneer St., releases any unsold tickets for the day's performances and sells 20 **standing room tickets** for sold-out shows on the Elizabethan Stage ($11). **Unofficial ticket sales** also take place just outside the box office, although scalping is illegal. ("Off with his head!"—*Richard III,* III.iv) Half-price **rush tickets** are sometimes available 1hr. before performances that are not already sold out. Some **half-price student-senior matinees** are offered in the spring and in Oct., and all 3 theaters hold full-performance **previews** in the spring and summer. **Backstage tours** provide a wonderful glimpse of the festival from behind the curtain (Tu-Su 10am; $9-11, ages 5-17 $6.75-8.25, under 5 not admitted).

In winter, Ashland is a budget paradise of vacancy and low rates; in summer, hotel and B&B rates double, and the hostel bulges. Only rogues and peasant slaves arrive without reservations. ▨ **Ashland Hostel,** 150 N. Main St., is well-kept and cheery, with an air of elegance. (482-9217. HI members $14, nonmembers $15. Private rooms $37-40; private women's room $22 for 1, $30 for 2. $3 dis-

THE PACIFIC NORTHWEST

counts and free laundry for Pacific Crest Trail hikers or touring cyclists. Laundry and kitchen facilities. Check-in 5-11pm. Lockout 10am-5pm. Curfew midnight.) The incredible selection of foods on N. and E. Main St. has earned the plaza a culinary reputation independent of the festival. ▧ **Geppetto's,** 345 E. Main St., is *the* spot for a late-night bite. The staff is congenial, the walls covered in baskets, and dinners from $13. (482-1138. Eggplant burger $4.25. Open daily 8am-midnight. Wheelchair access).

Ashland is located in the foothills of the Siskiyou and Cascade Ranges, 285mi. south of Portland and 15mi. north of the California border, near the junction of **I-5** and **Rt. 66. Greyhound** (482-8803) runs from the **BP station,** 2073 Rt. 99 N, at the north end of town, sends 3 per day to Portland (7hr., $40); Sacramento (7hr., $40); and San Francisco (11hr., $50). **Chamber of Commerce:** 110 E. Main St. (482-3486); free play schedules. **Ashland District Ranger Station,** 645 Washington St. (482-3333), off Rt. 66 by exit 14 on I-5, provides info on hiking, biking, and the Pacific Crest Trail (open M-F 8am-4:30pm). **Post Office:** 120 N. 1st St. (800-275-8777), at Lithia Way (open M-F 9am-5pm). **ZIP code:** 97520. **Area code:** 541.

# BEND

At the foot of the Cascades's east slope, Bend is at the epicenter of an impressive array of outdoor opportunities, wooing waves of skiers and nature-lovers. Oregon's biggest little city in the east is rapidly losing its small-town feel to a stream of California, Portland, and Seattle refugees in search of the perfect blend of urban excitement, pristine wilderness, and sun-filled days. Chain stores and strip malls flood the banks of U.S. 97, but the city's charming downtown and lively crowd still seduce most visitors.

**⊠ PRACTICAL INFORMATION.** Bend is 160mi. southeast of Portland either on U.S. 26 E through Warm Springs Indian Reservation to U.S. 97 S, or south on I-5 to Salem, then east on Rt. 22 E to Rt. 20 E through Sisters; 144mi. north of Klamath Falls on U.S. 97; and 100mi. southeast of Mt. Hood via U.S. 26 E and Rt. 97 S. **U.S. 97 (3rd St.)** bisects the town. Downtown lies to the west along the **Deschutes River; Wall** and **Bond St.** are the 2 main arteries. **Greyhound,** 2045 U.S. 20 E (382-2151; open M-F 8-11:30am and 12:30-5pm, Sa-Su 8am-2pm), 1½mi. east of town, runs to Portland (1 per day, 5-7hr., $23) and Klamath Falls (1 per day, 2½hr., $20). **Owl Taxi** is at 1919 NE 2nd St. (382-3311; 24hr.). **Bend Chamber and Visitors Bureau,** 63085 U.S. 97 N (382-3221), stocks free maps, free coffee, and Internet access (open M-Sa 9am-5pm, Su 11am-3pm). **Deschutes National Forest Headquarters,** 1645 U.S. 20 E (388-2715), has forest and wilderness info (open M-F 7:45am-4:30pm). **Post Office:** 2300 NE 4th St. (800-275-8777), at Webster (open M-F 8:30am-5:30pm, Sa 10am-1pm). **ZIP code:** 97701. **Area code:** 541.

**▛▐ ACCOMMODATIONS AND FOOD.** Most of the cheapest motels line **3rd St.** just outside of town, and rates are surprisingly low. To reach **Bend Cascade Hostel,** 19 SW Century Dr., take Greenwood west from 3rd St. until the name changes to Newport. After ½mi., take a left on 14th St.; the clean, fairly safe, and tidy hostel is ½mi. up on the right side, just past the Circle K. (389-3813 or 800-299-3813. Foosball, laundry, kitchen, linen. $14; students, seniors, cyclists, and HI members $13; under 18 with parents ½-price. Lockout 9:30am-4:30pm. Curfew 11pm.) **Deschutes National Forest** maintains a huge number of lakeside campgrounds along the **Cascade Lakes Hwy.,** west of town; all have toilets. Sites with potable water cost $8-12 per night; those without water are free. Camping anywhere in the national forest area is free.

**Devore's Good Food Store and Wine Shop,** 1124 Newport NW peddles all things organic (389-6588; open M-Sa 8am-7pm, Su 11am-6pm). **Deschutes Brewery and Public House,** 1044 NW Bond St., has homemade sausage and smoked salmon, but they're overshadowed by the specials ($5-7) and $3.25 imperial pints (382-9242; open M-Th 11am-11:30pm, F-Sa 11am-12:30am, Su 11am-10pm).

⊡ ◪ **SIGHTS AND OUTDOORS.** South of Bend by 3½mi. on U.S. 97, the **High Desert Museum** is one of the premier natural and cultural history museums in the Pacific Northwest. Visitors walk through stunning life-size dioramas of life in the Old West, while the indoor desertarium houses bats, burrowing owls, and collared lizards. A brand-new Native American Wing features a walk-through exhibit on post-reservation Indian life. (59800 S. Hwy. 97. 382-4754. Open daily 9am-5pm. $7.75, seniors and ages 13-18 $6.75, ages 5-12 $3.75.)

The **Three Sisters Wilderness Area,** north and west of the Cascade Lakes Highway, is one of Oregon's largest and most popular wilderness areas. A parking permit is required at most trailheads: pick one up at any of the ranger stations or at the visitor center ($3). Mountain biking is not allowed in the wilderness area itself, but Benders have plenty of other places to spin their wheels. Try **Deschutes River Trail** for a fairly flat, basic, forested trail ending at **Deschutes River.** To reach the trailhead, go 7½mi. west of Bend on Century Dr. (Cascade Lakes Hwy.) until Forest Service Rd. 41, then turn left and follow the signs to Lava Island Falls (10½mi. 1-way). For a difficult, technical ride, hit the **Waldo Lake Loop,** a grueling 22mi. trail around the lake. To get there, take Cascade Lakes Hwy. to Forest Service Rd. 4290. A slick new guide to mountain bike trails around Bend is available for $7 at the Bend/Ft. Rock District Ranger Station and at most bike shops in the area, but some of the hottest trails aren't on the maps; talk to locals.

Would-be cowpokes can take **horseback rides** offered by local resorts. **River Ridge Stables,** 18575 SW Century Dr. (382-8711), at Inn of the Seventh Mountain several mi.mi. west of Bend, leads trail rides (1hr. $22, ages 6-12 $20; each additional 30min. $5), hay rides ($7, ages 5-12 $5, under 5 free), and sleigh rides ($15 per hr.).

# HELLS CANYON AND WALLOWA MOUNTAINS

The northeast corner of Oregon is the state's most rugged, remote, and arresting country, with jagged granite peaks, glacier-gouged valleys, and azure lakes. East of La Grande, the Wallowa Mountains (wa-LAH-wah) rise abruptly, towering over the plains from elevations of over 9000 ft. Thirty mi. farther east, the deepest gorge in North America, barren and dusty Hells Canyon, plunges to the Snake River. **Hells Canyon National Recreation Area** and the **Eagle Cap Wilderness** lie on either side of the **Wallowa Valley,** which can be reached from **Baker City, La Grande,** and **Clarkston, WA.** Three main towns offer services within the area: **Enterprise, Joseph,** and **Halfway.** The only way to get close to the canyon without taking at least a full day is to drive the **Hells Canyon National Scenic Loop Drive,** which begins and ends in Baker City, following Rt. 86, Forest Rd. 39 and 350, Rt. 82, and finally I-84. Even this paved route takes 6hr. to 2 days to drive; closures are routine. The most eye-popping views are from the 90 ft. fire lookout at **Hat Point Overlook;** go 24mi. up the steep gravel Forest Rd. 4240 from Imnaha, then turn off onto Rd. 315 and follow the signs.

**Hiking** is perhaps the best way to comprehend the vast emptiness of Hells Canyon, and to really get into the canyon requires a trip of at least a few days. There are over 1000mi. of trails in the canyon, only a fraction of which are regularly maintained. Bring snakebite kits, good boots, and lots of water. The dramatic 56mi. **Snake River Trail** runs beside the river for the length of the canyon. At times, the trail is cut into the side of the rock with just enough clearance for a horse's head. Come prepared for any hazard, though outfitters and rangers patrol the river by boat at least once a day. This trail can be followed from **Dug Bar** in the north clear down to the Hells Canyon Dam, or accessed by treacherously steep trails along the way. From north to south, **Hat Point, Freezeout,** and **P.O. Saddle** are possible access points. To reach Dug Bar, take Forest Rd. 4260, a steep, slippery route recommended only for 4-wheel drive or high-clearance vehicles, for 27mi. northeast from Imnaha; check conditions before heading out.

Without a catchy, federally approved name like "Hells Canyon National Recreation Area," the Wallowas often take second place to the canyon in the minds of tourists, though they possess a scenic beauty equally magnificent. The canyons echo with the deafening rush of rapids, and the jagged peaks are covered with

**THE PACIFIC NORTHWEST**

wildflowers in spring. Over 600mi. of **hiking trails** cross the **Eagle Cap Wilderness,** and are usually free of snow from mid-July to Oct. Deep glacial valleys and high granite passes make hiking this wilderness tough going: it often takes more than a day to get into the most beautiful and remote areas. Still, several high alpine lakes are accessible to dayhikers. The 5mi. hike to **Chimney Lake** from the Bowman trailhead on the Lostine River Rd. (Forest Rd. 8210) traverses fields of granite boulders sprinkled with a few small meadows. A little farther on lie the serene **Laverty, Hobo,** and **Wood Lakes,** where the path is less beaten. The **Two Pan trailhead** at the end of the Lostine River Rd. is the start of a forested 6mi. hike to popular **Minam Lake,** which makes a good starting point for those heading to other backcountry spots like **Blue Lake,** 1mi. above Minam. From the **Wallowa Lake trailhead,** behind the little powerhouse at the end of Rt. 82, a 6mi. hike leads up the East Fork of the Wallowa River to Aneroid Lake. From there, hikes to Pete's Point and Aneroid Mountain offer great views.

**Country Inn Motel,** on Rt. 82 in Enterprise, lacks A/C but that's no problem—even on the hottest summer days, the rooms stay remarkably cool. (426-4986. Cable, coffee makers, and refrigerators. Singles $40; doubles $48-54. Kitchens are a little extra, depending on availability.) Campgrounds here are plentiful, inexpensive, and sublime. Pick up the *Campground Information* pamphlet at the Wallowa Mountains Visitor Center for a complete listing of sites in the area. Due to 1996 budget cutbacks, most campgrounds (including all of those listed below) are not fully serviced, and are therefore **free**—check at the visitor center to see whether a campground has potable water. Inexplicably, the massive **Wallowa Lake State Park campground** books solid up to a year in advance. Try your luck there if in the market for full-service camping. (432-4185, reservations 800-452-5687. Toilets, drinking water, and showers. Tent sites $16, full hookups $20.)

The **Wallowa Valley Stage Line** makes 1 round-trip M-Sa from Joseph to La Grande. Pickup at the Chevron on Rt. 82 in Joseph, the Amoco on Rt. 82 in Enterprise, and the Greyhound terminal in La Grande. (569-2284; $8.10-12.50). **Wallowa County Chamber of Commerce,** (426-4622 or 800-585-4121), is at SW 1st St. and W. Greenwood Ave. in Enterprise, in the mall (open M-F 9am-5pm). **Hells Canyon Chamber of Commerce:** (742-4222), in the office of Halfway Motels. **Outdoor Information: Wallowa Mountains Visitor Center,** 88401 Rt. 82 (426-5546), on the west side of Enterprise. $4 map a necessity for navigating area roads. (Open Memorial Day-Labor Day M-Sa 8am-5pm, in winter M-F 8am-5pm.)

# WESTERN CANADA

# BRITISH COLUMBIA

British Columbia (BC) is Canada's westernmost province, with over 890,000 sq. km bordering 4 U.S. states (Washington, Idaho, Montana, and Alaska) and three Canadian entities (Alberta, the Yukon Territory, and the Northwest Territories). It's natural beauty and vibrant cities attract so many visitors that tourism has become its second-largest industry after logging.

## 🛈 PRACTICAL INFORMATION

**Capital:** Victoria.

**Visitor Info: Tourism British Columbia,** 1117 Wharf St., Victoria, BC V8W 2Z2 (800-663-6000 or 250-387-1642; travel.bc.ca). **British Columbia Ministry of Environment, Lands, and Parks,** P.O. Box 9398, Stn. Prov. Govt., Victoria, BC V8W 9M9 (250-387-4609; www.elp.gov.bc.ca/bcparks).

**Drinking Age:** 19. **Postal Abbreviation:** BC. **Sales Tax:** 7%.

## VANCOUVER

Like any self-respecting city on the west coast of North America, Vancouver boasts a thriving multicultural populace, a prominent suspension bridge, and a high per capita daily caffeine intake. What sets it apart is its stunning natural setting, its laid-back attitude, and—it has to be said—the rain, which makes Gore-Tex and Seasonal Affective Disorder *de rigueur* for about 10 months of the year. Western Canada's largest city is wedged between the Pacific Ocean and the heavily forested Coast Mountain range. The completion of the cross-Canada railroad at the turn of the century was made possible in large part by the work of tens of thousands of Chinese immigrants, many of whom settled at the line's western terminus, founding what is now North America's second largest Chinatown.

## 🛈 ORIENTATION AND PRACTICAL INFORMATION

Vancouver looks like a mitten with the fingers pointing west and the thumb pointing northward (brace yourself for a never-ending metaphor). South of the hand flows the **Fraser River,** and beyond the fingertips lies the **Georgia Strait. Downtown** is at the base of the thumb, while at the thumb's tip lie the residential **West End** and **Stanley Park. Burrard Inlet** separates downtown from **North Vancouver;** the bridges over **False Creek** link downtown with **Kitsilano** ("Kits") and the rest of the city. East of downtown, where the thumb is attached, are **Gastown** and **Chinatown.** The **University of British Columbia** lies on top of the fingers at **Point Grey,** the westernmost end of the city, while the **airport** is south at the pinkie-tip. Kitsilano and Point Grey are separated by the north-south **Alma St.** The **Trans-Canada Hwy. (Hwy. 1)** enters town from the east and **Hwy. 99** runs north-south through the city. Most attractions are grouped on the peninsula/thumb and farther west.

**Vancouver International Airport** (276-6101) is on Sea Island, 23km south of the city center. A visitor center (303-3601; open daily 8am-midnight) is on level 2. Bus #100 "New Westminster Station" to the intersection of Granville and 70th Ave.; transfer there to bus #20 "Fraser" to reach downtown. **Airport Express** (946-8866) bus leaves from airport level 2 for downtown hotels and the bus station (4 per hr.; 6:30am-10:30pm; $10, seniors $8, ages 5-12 $5).

**Trains: VIA Rail,** 1150 Station St. (in Canada 800-561-8630, in U.S. 800-561-9181). 3 trains per week to eastern Canada via Jasper, AB (17hr., $162). Open M, W, Th, Sa 9:30am-6pm; Tu, F, Su 9am-7pm. **BC Rail,** 1311 W. 1st St. (984-5246), in North Vancouver at the foot of Pemberton St. Take the BC Rail Special bus on Georgia St. (June-Sept.) or the SeaBus to North Vancouver, then bus #239 west. Daily train to Whistler (2½hr., $31). Tu, F, trains depart at 7pm for Williams Lake (10hr., $131); Prince George (14hr., $194); and other points north. Open daily 8am-8pm.

**Buses: Greyhound,** 1150 Station St. (482-8747; open daily 5:30am-12:30am), in the VIA Rail station. To: Calgary, AB (15hr., 4 per day, $99); Seattle, WA (3½hr., 8 per day, $27). **Pacific Coach Lines,** 1150 Station St. (662-8074) to Victoria (3½hr., $25.50 includes ferry). **Quick Shuttle** (940-4428 or 800-665-2122) makes 8 trips per day from downtown via the airport to: Seattle, WA (3-3½hr., $42), and the Sea-Tac airport (3½-4hr. $50). Student and senior discounts.

**Ferries: BC Ferries** (888-223-3779). To the Gulf Islands, Sechelt, and Vancouver Island ($7.50-9, ages 5-11 $4.25, car $30-32, bike $2.50; fares cheapest mid-week). Ferries to Victoria, Nanaimo, and the Gulf Islands leave from the **Tsawwassen Terminal,** 25km south of the city center (take Hwy. 99 to Hwy. 17). To reach downtown from Tsawwassen by bus (1hr.), take #640 "Scott Rd. Station" or #404 "Airport" to the Ladner Exchange, then transfer to bus #601. Ferries to Nanaimo and Sechelt depart the **Horseshoe Bay Terminal** at the end of the Trans-Canada Hwy. in West Vancouver. Take 'Blue Bus' #250 or 257 on Georgia St. from downtown (40min.).

**Public Transit: Coast Mountain Buslink** (521-0400) covers most of the city and suburbs, with direct transport or easy connections to airport and the ferry terminals. **Central zone** encompasses most of the city; $1.50 for 1½hr. During peak hours (M-F before 6:30pm), it costs $2.25 to travel between two zones and $3 to travel through three zones. During off-peak hours, the 1-zone price prevails. Ask for a **free transfer** (good for 1½hr.) when you board buses. **Day passes** ($6) are sold at 7-11, Safeway, and HI-C hostels. Over 65 and ages 5-13, $1 for one zone or off-peak travel, $1.50 for two zones, $2 for three zones, and $4 for day passes. **SeaBus** and **SkyTrain** included in the normal BusFare. The SeaBus shuttles passengers across the busy waters of Burrard Inlet from the foot of Granville St. downtown (SkyTrain: Waterfront) to **Lonsdale Quay** at the foot of Lonsdale Ave. in North Vancouver.

**Taxis: Yellow Cab** (681-1111 or 800-898-8294).

**Car Rental: Low-Cost,** 1101 Granville St. (689-9664). $37 per day, plus 12¢ per km after 250km. 21+. Open daily 7:30am-6:30pm. **Resort Rent-a-Car,** 3231 No. 3 Rd. (232-3060), Richmond. $39 per day, $229 per week; unlimited miles, free pickup. Open M-F 7am-9pm, Sa-Su 7am-7pm.

**Visitor Information:** 200 Burrard St. (683-2000). Open daily 8am-6pm.

**Special Concerns Info: Women's Resource Center,** 1144 Robson St. (482-8585). Drop-in counseling. Open July-Aug. M-Th 10am-2pm; Sept.-June M-F 10am-4pm. **Gay and Lesbian Centre,** 1170 Bute St. Open M-F 3:30-9:30pm, Sa 6:30-9:30pm. **Vancouver Prideline** (684-6869; daily 7am-10pm). **Xtra West** is a gay and lesbian biweekly. Get it here and on Davie St. in the West End.

**Internet Access: Kitsilano Cyber Cafe,** 3514 W. 4th Ave. $3.25 per 30min., $6 per hr. Open M-F 7am-6pm; Sa-Su 8am-5pm. $6 per hr. at all **HI Hostels.**

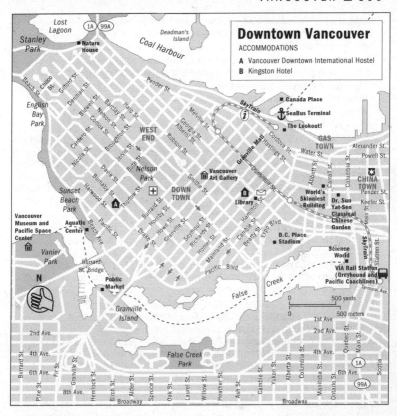

**Downtown Vancouver**
ACCOMMODATIONS
A Vancouver Downtown International Hostel
B Kingston Hotel

**Post Office:** 349 W. Georgia St. (662-5725). Open M-F 8am-5:30pm. **Postal code:** V6B 3P7. **Area code:** 604.

## ACCOMMODATIONS

Greater Vancouver B&Bs are a viable option for couples or small groups (singles from $45; doubles from $55). The infocenter and agencies like **Town and Country Bed and Breakfast** (731-5942) and **Best Canadian** (738-7207) list options. HI hostels are a good bet: many other hostels get rowdy and some are downright seedy.

**Vancouver Hostel Jericho Beach (HI-C),** 1515 Discovery St. (224-3208), in Jericho Beach Park. Follow 4th Ave west past Alma, then bear right at the fork, or take bus #4 from Granville St. downtown. Institutional but clean, at a peaceful location with a great view. 285 beds in 14-person dorm rooms, and 10 family rooms. Kitchens, TV room, laundry, cafe, free linen, and bike rentals ($20 per day). $17.50, nonmembers $21.50. Parking $3 per day, or free on the street. Free shuttle to Vancouver Hostel Downtown. Stay-and-ski package with Grouse Mountain (see below) for $37 includes bed, lift ticket, and free shuttle to the slopes. Reservations imperative in summer.

**Vancouver Hostel Downtown (HI-C),** 1114 Burnaby St. (684-4565), in the West End. Ultra-modern and ultra-clean 225-bed facility between downtown, the beach, and Stanley Park. Four bunks per room. Goodies including game room, kitchen, free linen, and tours of the city. Free shuttle to Jericho Beach Hostel. Open 24hr. $20, nonmembers $24; private doubles $55, nonmembers $64. Reservations crucial in summer.

**Kingston Hotel,** 757 Richards St. (684-9024; fax 684-9917), between Robson and Georgia St. A B&B/hotel hybrid. Feel like a monarch in quiet, cushioned-and-carpeted rooms downtown. Pay parking available. Coin laundry and sauna. Singles $45-65, doubles $50-80. Cheaper rates for shared bath. Breakfast included.

**The Globetrotter's Inn,** 170 W. Esplanade (988-2082), in North Vancouver. Near the Lonsdale Quay Market and SeaBus terminal for easy access to downtown. Kitchen, pool table, free laundry, but it can get a little rowdy. Dorms $18; singles $30; doubles $45. Weekly rates from $100. Reception 8am-8pm. Reservations recommended.

**University of British Columbia Conference Centre,** 5959 Student Union Blvd. (822-1010), on the UBC campus at Walter Gage Residence. Take bus #4 or 10 from Granville St. downtown. Often packed with conventioneers. Dorms $24; singles $33-5; doubles with kitchen and private bath from $89. Check-in after 2pm. Open May-Aug.

**Capilano RV Park,** 295 Tomahawk Ave. (987-4722), at the foot of Lions Gate Bridge in North Vancouver; the closest RV park to downtown. Showers, pool, laundry. 2-person sites $22, additional person $2.50; hookups $32. Reception daily 8am-11pm.

**Richmond RV Park,** 6200 River Rd. (270-7878), near Holly Bridge in Richmond, a 30min. drive from Vancouver. Take Hwy. 99 south to Richmond Exit, follow Russ Baker Way, go left on Gilbert, right at Elm Bridge, take the next right, then go left at the stop sign. Scant privacy, but great showers. 2-person sites $17; hookups $23; additional person $3. 10% AAA/CAA discount. Open Apr.-Oct.

## ○ FOOD

The diversity and excellence of Vancouver's international cuisine makes the rest of BC seem provincial in comparison. In North America, only San Francisco's **Chinatown** is larger, and the **Punjabi Village** along Main and Fraser, around 49th St. serves cheap, authentic Indian food. The entire world, from Vietnamese noodle shops to Italian cafes represents along **Commercial Drive,** east of Chinatown. "The Drive" is also home to produce prices that put area supermarkets to shame.

**Granville Island Market,** southwest of downtown under the Granville Street Bridge, intersperses trendy shops, art galleries, restaurants, with countless produce stands. From downtown, take bus #50 "False Creek" or #51 "Granville Island" from Granville St. (666-5784. Open daily 9am-6pm; in winter closed M.) Dollar-a-slice, all-night **pizza places** pepper downtown. In Kits, **Buy-Low Foods,** at 4th and Alma St., keeps it real (222-8353; open daily 9am-9pm). Downtown, **SuperValu,** 1255 Davie St., is where it's at (688-0911; open 24hr.).

**The Naam,** 2724 W. 4th Ave. (738-7151), at MacDonald St. Take bus #4 or 7 from Granville Mall. The most diverse vegetarian menu around. Homey interior and tree-covered patio seating always make a perfect refuge. Crying Tiger Thai stir fry $8; tofulati ice cream $3.50. Miso gravy fries $4.50. Live music nightly 7-10pm. Open 24hr.

**Benny's Bagels,** 2505 W. Broadway (731-9730). Every college student's dream. Serves the requisite beer, bagels (70 cents, $2.10 with cream cheese), and hot sandwiches (from $5) until the wee hours of the morning. Open Su-Th 6am-3am, F-Sa 6am-4am.

**Deserts Falafel,** 1183 Davie St. (684-4760). Absolutely delicious falafel sandwiches ($3.75) and heaping humus plates ($3.50) for addictively little. Open daily 11am-midnight. Also at 4127 Main St., and 1935 Cornwall (on the Kits side of Burrard Bridge).

**Subeez Cafe,** 891 Homer (687-6107), at Smithe. Serves cool kids in a cavernous and casual setting. Eclectic menu from vegetarian gyoza ($6) to curried lamb burgers ($8) complements an imposing wine list and home-spun beats (DJs W, F at 10pm). Entrees $7-15. Open M-F 11:30am-1am, Sa 11am-1am, Su 11am-midnight.

**Hon's Wun-Tun House,** 268 Keefer St. (688-0871). This award-winning Cantonese noodle-house has cheap, nostril-seducing noodle soup ($3.50-6.20). 334 options in the menu. Two kitchens (one vegetarian only) and phenomenal service. Check the free *Georgia Straight* for 15%-off coupon. Open daily 8:30am-10pm.

**Thai Away Home,** 1918 Commercial Dr. (253-8424). Small, colorful cafe serves Thai at a good price. Options includes delicious *pad thai* ($7) and 5 colors of curry ($5).

**Nirvana,** 2313 Main St. (872-8779), at 7th Ave. Take bus #3, 8, or 9. Smells like authentic, savory Indian cuisine. Chicken or vegetable curry $6-8. Ask the chef to make you one with everything (special combos $11). Open daily 11am-11pm.

**Kam's Garden Restaurant,** 509 Main St. (669-5488). Authentic, no-frills Chinese food. Huge noodle platters $5-9; meat dishes $10. Open daily 10:30am-8pm.

# ◑ SIGHTS

An entire floor of the **Vancouver Art Gallery,** in Robson Sq., is devoted to the surreal paintings of BC artist Emily Carr. *(750 Hornby St. 662-4700. Open W-M 10am-5:30pm, Th 10am-9pm. $10, students $6, seniors $8, under 13 free. Th 5-9pm is pay-what-you-can.)* On the city's centennial, **Expo '86** brought attention, prestige, and roller-coasters to Vancouver. The fairgrounds are slowly evolving into office space, apartments, and a cultural center. The big-screen star of Expo '86 was the **Omnimax Theatre,** part of **Science World,** at Main St. stop of the SkyTrain. In addition to the 27m/90 ft. spherical screen, Science World also features hands-on exhibits and fact-crammed shows for kids. *(1455 Quebec St. 268-6363. Open daily July-Aug. 10am-6pm; call for winter hours. $11.75, students, seniors, and children $7. Omnimax shows Su-F 10am-5pm, Sa 10am-9pm. $10. Combined ticket $14.75; students, seniors and children $10.50.)* **Lookout!** offers fantastic 360° views of the city! Tickets are good for the whole day; come back for a more sedate nighttime skyline! *(555 W. Hastings St. 689-0421. Open daily 8:30am-10:30pm; in winter 10am-9pm. $8, students $5, seniors $7. 50% off for HI guests with receipt.)*

**Gastown,** one of the oldest neighborhoods in Vancouver, has for the most part fallen into the tourist trap trap. Adjacent to downtown, and an easy walk from the Granville mall, it is bordered by Richards St. to the west, Columbia St. to the east, Hastings St. to the south, and the waterfront to the north. Gastown is named for "Gyassy Jack" Deighton, a glib con man who opened Vancouver's first saloon here in 1867. Today the area overflows with craft shops, nightclubs, restaurants, and boutiques. Many establishments stay open and well-populated at night. Stroll along Water St. and stop to hear the rare **steam-powered clock** on the corner of Cambie St. whistle the notes of the Westminster Chimes every quarter-hour.

**Chinatown,** southeast of Gastown, is a bit of a hike away through seedy parts of town. Bus #22 north on Burrard St. leads to Pender and Carrall St., in the heart of Chinatown. The same bus westbound on Pender leads back to downtown. The neighborhood bustles with restaurants, shops, bakeries, and **the world's skinniest building** at 8 W. Pender St. In 1912, the city expropriated all but a 1.8m (6 ft.) strip of Chang Toy's property in order to expand the street; he built on the land anyhow. The serene **Dr. Sun Yat-Sen Classical Chinese Garden** maintains imported Chinese plantings, carvings, and rock formations in the first full-size garden of its kind outside China. *(578 Carrall St. 689-7133. Open daily 9:30am-7pm; in winter 10:30am-4:30pm. $6.50, students $4, seniors $5, children free, families $12. Tours every hr. 10am-6pm.)* Don't miss the sights, sounds, smells, and tastes of the weekend **night market** along Pender and Keefer St. *(F-Su 6:30-11pm.)* Chinatown itself is relatively safe, but its surroundings make up some of Vancouver's seedier sections; prostitution and drug dealing take place on E. Hastings St., and are concentrated near Main St.

The high point of a visit to the **University of British Columbia (UBC)** is the breathtaking ▣ **Museum of Anthropology;** take bus #4 or 10 from Granville St. The high-ceilinged glass and concrete building houses totems and other massive carvings, highlighted by Bill Reid's depiction of Raven discovering the first humans in a giant clam shell. *(6393 NW Marine Dr. 822-3825 or 822-5087. Open M and W-Su 10am-5pm, Tu 10am-9pm; Sept.-May closed M. $6, students and seniors $3.50, under 6 free, families $15. Tu after 5pm free. Free 1hr. walks at 11am and 2pm.)* Across the street, caretakers of the **Nitobe Memorial Garden** are finest classical Shinto garden outside of Japan, excellent for walking meditation. *(1903 West Mall. 822-6038. Open Mar-Oct. daily 10am-6pm; Nov.-Feb. M-F 10am-2:30pm.)* The **Botanical Gardens** are a collegiate Eden encompassing eight gardens in the central campus, including the largest collection of rhodo-dendrons in North America. *(6804 SW Marine Dr. 822-9666. $2.50, students $1.75.)*

The circular **Vancouver Museum** displays artifacts from local native cultures and more recent relics of Vancouver history. *(1100 Chestnut St. 736-4431. Open daily 10am-5pm; in winter closed M. $8, under 18 $5.50.)* Upstairs, the **Pacific Space Centre** runs a motion-simulator ride, planetarium, and exhibit gallery, as well as laser rock shows. Take bus #22 south on Burrard St. from downtown. *($12.50, students and seniors $9.50; laser-light show $8.)*

## ⚠ PARKS AND BEACHES

Established in 1889 at the tip of the downtown peninsula, 1000-acre **Stanley Park** is a testament to the foresight of Vancouver's urban planners (257-8400). An easy escape from the West End and downtown, the thickly wooded park is laced with cycling and hiking trails, and surrounded by an 11km **seawall** promenade. At the kid-friendly **Vancouver Aquarium**, on the park's eastern side, an orca, dolphin, and several beluga whales demonstrate their training and intelligence by drenching gleeful visitors in educational shows. (659-3474. Shows on the ½-hour from 10:30am-5:30pm. Open daily July-Aug. 9:30am-7:30pm; Sept.-June 10am-5:30pm. $13, students and seniors $11, under 12 $9.) **Nature walks** start from the **Nature House,** underneath the Lost Lagoon bus loop. (257-8544. 2hr. Su at 1pm. $4, under 12 free.) The park boasts tennis courts, a cinder running track with hot showers, an outdoor theater—the **Malkin Bowl** (687-0174)—and swimming beaches. **Second Beach Pool** offers warm, chlorinated water. (257-8371. $4, children $2.50. Open June-Aug. 10am-8:45pm.)

During the summer, the tiny **False Creek Ferry** carries passengers from the Aquatic Centre (see **Beaches,** below) and to the Granville Island Market (see **Food,** above). (684-7781. 4 per hr. daily 10am-8pm. $2, children $1.) At **Vanier** (van-YAY) **Park**, the ferry shares the **Maritime Museum** dock with historic vessels. The wood-and-glass A-frame museum on shore houses **RCMP St. Roch,** a schooner that patrolled the Northwest Passage in the 1940's.

Near UBC, in **Pacific Spirit Regional Park,** woods stretch inland from the beaches of Spanish Banks. 50km of gravel and dirt trails through dense forest are ideal for jogging and cycling. Get a free map at the **Park Centre** on 16th Ave., near Blanca.

Most of Vancouver's 14 mi. of beaches are patrolled by lifeguards from late May to Labour Day daily between 11:30am and 9pm. Follow the western side of the Stanley Park seawall south to **Sunset Beach Park,** a strip of grass and beach extending all the way to the Burrard Bridge. **Kitsilano Beach** ("Kits"), across Arbutus St. from Vanier Park, is another local favorite. For less crowding, more students, and free showers, visit **Jericho Beach.** North Marine Dr. runs along the beach, and a cycling path at the side of the road leads to the westernmost end of the UBC campus. Directly across the street from the UBC campus. A steep wooden staircase leads to **Wreck Beach,** a totally secluded, self-contained sunshine community of nude sunbathers and guitar-playing UBC students; take trail #6 down the hill from SW Marine Dr.

## ♫ ENTERTAINMENT AND NIGHTLIFE

The **Vancouver Symphony Orchestra (VSO)** (684-9100) plays Sept.-May in the refurbished **Orpheum Theatre** (665-3050), at the corner of Smithe and Seymour. The new **Ford Center for the Performing Arts** (602-0616) brings big-time Broadway musicals to town. The **Vancouver Playhouse,** (873-3311) on Dunsmuir at Georgia St., and the **Arts Club Theatre** (687-5315), on Granville Island, stage more subdued stuff. **Bard on the Beach,** brings Shakespeare to Vanier Park from mid-June to Sept. (739-0559; $23.50). The **Fringe** festival features 600 performances in 22 venues (257-0350; Sept. 7-17, 2000; all tickets under $11).

**Chameleon,** 801 W. Georgia (669-0806), in the basement of the Hotel Georgia. Posh seating and beautiful people. Nightly DJs and a narrow dance floor. Sunday is popular drum 'n bass night. Classy atmosphere begets classy prices (pint $4.25, highball $5.25.) Cover $4-7. Open nightly until 1:30am.

**The King's Head,** 1618 Yew St. (733-3933), at 1st St., in Kitsilano. Cheap drinks, cheap food, mellow atmosphere, and a great location near the beach. Bands play acoustic sets on a tiny stage. Daily drink specials. $3 pints. M-W gullet-filling Beggar's Breakfast $3 (Th-Su $4). Open M-Sa 7am-1:30am, Su 7:30am-midnight.

**Celebrities,** 1022 Davie St. (689-3180), at Burrard. Ever so big, hot, and popular with Vancouver's gay crowd, although it draws all kinds. Straight nights (Tu and F); occasional drag pageants and go-go dancers. Open M-Sa 9pm-2am, Su 9pm-midnight.

**Sonar,** 66 Water St. (683-6695), in Gastown. A new arrival on the club scene, this former live rock venue is now a popular 2-level beat factory. House (Th and Sa), hip-hop (W), and break-beat (F). Pints $3.50-4.75. Open M-Sa 8pm-2am, Su 8pm-midnight.

**Purple Onion,** 15 Water St. (602-9442), in Gastown. Slurps in the crowds with an eclectic music selection, and inviting lounge chairs. The lounge features live blues, R&B, jazz, and funk acts, while DJs spin acid jazz, disco, soul, funk, Latin, swing, and reggae in the back room. Cover $3-6. Open M-Th 8pm-2am, F-Sa 7pm-2am, Su 7pm-midnight.

# WHISTLER

Only 125km (a 1½-2hr. drive) north of Vancouver on the dangerously twisty Hwy. 99, Whistler and Blackcomb mountains provides some of North America's best skiing and snowboarding, and are a popular mountain destination in summer, too. The **"Village"** is overproduced and overpriced, but no amount of disneyfication can take away from the striking beauty of the mountains or the challenge of the terrain. Whistler is currently bidding to host the 2010 Winter Olympics.

Seven thousand acres of terrain, 33 lifts, and a mile (1609m/5280 ft.) of vertical drop make recently merged **Whistler/Blackcomb** the largest ski resort in North America. Parking and lift access for this behemoth is available at 6 points, with Whistler Creekside offering the shortest lines and easiest access to those coming from Vancouver. A **lift ticket** is good for both mountains. (932-3434 or 800-766-0449. $57; $36 from June 10 to July 30. Multi-day discounts available.) **Cheap tickets** are often available at SuperValu's and 7-11's in Vancouver and Squamish. While skiing is God in Whistler and lasts on the glaciers until August, the **Whistler Gondola** whisks sightseers to the top of the mountain year-round for $21 ($24 with bike), providing access in summer to the resort's extensive **mountain bike park.**

The gorgeous lakeside **Whistler Hostel (HI-C),** 5678 Alta Lake Rd., lies 5km south of Whistler Village on Hwy. 99. BC Rail stops at the hostel on request. **Discount lift tickets** are $48. (932-5492. $18.50; nonmembers $22.75. Key deposit $10; check-in 8-11am and 4-10pm.) Rooms at the **Shoestring Lodge,** 7124 Nancy Greene Dr., 1km north of the village, offer cable, private baths, and a shared kitchen. (932-3338. Bunk $16-30; doubles $50-135. Peak prices, mandatory reservations, and free shuttle transport to the slopes from Dec. to Apr.) The **South Side Deli,** 2102 Lake Placid Rd., on Hwy. 99 by the Husky station 4km south of the village, is a rare respite from resort-land. (932-3368. Tasty veggie omelettes $7. Open daily 6am-3pm.)

**Greyhound** (932-5031, 661-0310 in Vancouver) runs to Vancouver from the **Village Bus Loop** (2½hr., 6 per day, $18). **BC Rail's** 2½-hr. Cariboo Prospector (984-5246) departs North Vancouver for Whistler Creek at 7am and returns at 6:20pm daily ($31). **Activity and information center:** (932-2394) in the heart of the Village (open daily 9am-5pm). **Post office:** (932-5012), in the Village Marketplace (open M-F 8:30am-5:30pm, Sa 8:30am-12:30pm.) **Postal Code:** V0N 1B0. **Area Code:** 604.

# VANCOUVER ISLAND

## VICTORIA

Clean, polite, and tourist-friendly, today's Victoria is a homier alternative to cosmopolitan Vancouver. Although many tourist operations would have you believe that Victoria fell off Great Britain in a neat little chunk, its High Tea tradition began in the 1950s to draw American tourists. Double-decker buses motor past native art galleries galleries, new-age bookstores, and countless English Pubbes.

**⚐ PRACTICAL INFORMATION.** Victoria surrounds the **Inner Harbour;** the main north-south thoroughfares downtown are **Government Street** and **Douglas Street.** To the north, Douglas St. becomes Hwy. 1, which runs north to Nanaimo. **Blanshard Street,** one block to the east, becomes Hwy. 17.

**Laidlaw,** 700 Douglas St. (385-4411 or 800-318-0818), at Belleville St., and its affiliates, **Pacific** and **Island Coach Lines,** run buses to Nanaimo (2½hr., 6 per day, $17.50); Vancouver (3½hr., 8-14 per day, $26.50); and Port Hardy (9hr., 1-2 per day, $84). The **E&N Railway,** (383-4324 or 800-561-8630), near the Inner Harbour at the Johnson St. Bridge runs daily to Nanaimo (2½hr., $19, students with ISIC $11). **Public Bus #70** ($2.50) runs between downtown and the Swartz Bay and Sidney ferry terminals. **BC Ferries** (656-5571 or 888-223-3779; operator 7am-10pm 386-3431) depart Swartz Bay to Vancouver's Tsawwassen ferry terminal (1½hr.; 8-16 per day; $9, bikes $2.50, car and driver $39-41), and to the Gulf Islands. **Washington State Ferries** (381-1551 or 656-1831; in the U.S. 206-464-6400 or 800-843-3779) depart from Sidney to Anacortes, WA (1-2 per day; US$9, car with driver US$41). Free stopovers area allowed in the San Juan Islands. **Victoria Clipper** (382-8100 or 800-888-2535) passenger ferries travel to Seattle (2-3hr.; 4 per day May-Sept., 1 per day Oct.-Apr.; US$58-66). **Black Ball Transport** (386-2202), runs to Port Angeles, WA (1½hr.; 2-4 per day; US$6.75, car and driver US$28.50). **Victoria Taxi** (383-7111) runs 24hr. **Island Auto Rentals,** 837 Yates St. (384-4881), charges $25 per day, plus 12¢ per km after 100km. Must be 21+ with credit card; insurance $13. **Tourism Victoria:** 812 Wharf St. (953-2033), at Government St. (open daily 8:30am-7:30pm; in winter 9am-5pm). **Internet access: Ocean Island Hostel,** $1 per 15min. **Post Office:** 621 Discovery St. (963-1350; open M-F 8am-6pm). **Postal code:** V8W 1L0. **Area code:** 250.

**🛏 ACCOMMODATIONS.** The colorful new **⬛ Ocean Island Backpackers Inn,** 791 Pandora St., downtown, boasts a better lounge than most clubs, tastier food than most restaurants (see **Food,** below), and accommodations comparable to most hotels. Undoubtedly one of the finest urban hostels in Canada. (385-1788 or 888-888-4180. 114 beds in small rooms; free linen and towels, laundry, email. Dorms $19.50, $16 for students and HI members; doubles $40. Parking $3.) To reach the **Selkirk Guest House,** 934 Selkirk Ave., in West Victoria, take bus #14 along Craigflower to Tillicum; Selkirk is 1 block north. Co-ed and all-female dorms with flowery sheets, free canoes, and a hot tub on the water. (389-1213. Kitchen, free linen and towels, laundry. Dorms $18, private rooms $50-70. Breakfast $5.)

**Goldstream Provincial Park,** 2930 Trans-Canada Hwy., 20km northwest of Victoria, offers a forested riverside area with great hiking trails and swimming (391-2300; reservations 800-689-9025; flush toilets and firewood; $18.50). The sites at **Thetis Lake Campground,** 1938 Trans-Canada Hwy., 10km north of the city center, are not large, but some are peaceful and removed (478-3845; $16, full hookup $20; showers 25¢ per 5min., flush toilets, laundry).

**◖🄳 FOOD AND NIGHTLIFE.** The limited variety and run-of-the-mill quality of food in Victoria should come as no surprise in Canada's most English city. **Chinatown** extends from Fisgard and Government St. to the northwest. In **Fernwood Village,** 3 blocks north of Johnson St. and accessible by bus #10, creative restaurants are scattered among craft shops. **⬛ John's Place,** 723 Pandora St., is a hopping joint serving up wholesome Canadian fare with all sorts of international twists.

(Entrees $5-11. 389-0711. M Thai night, W perogie night. Open Su-Th 7am-10pm, F-Sa 7am-11pm.) A trip to Victoria is improper without a spot of tea; the tea service with sandwiches and pastries ($6.75) or Su high tea ($10) at the **James Bay Tea Room & Restaurant,** 332 Menzies St., behind the Parliament Buildings (382-8282; open M-Sa 7am-8pm, Su 8am-8pm), is a lower-key version of the famous High Tea served at the **Empress Hotel** ($40).

The free weekly *Monday Magazine,* out on W, lists who's playing music where, and is available downtown. **Steamers Public House,** 570 Yates St., attracts a young, happy crowd dancing to different music every night. (381-4340. Open stage M, jazz night Tu. Lunch specials M-F until 3pm; $5-7. Open M-Sa 11:30am-2am, Su 11:30am-midnight.) **Jet Lounge,** 751 View St., is decidedly not an airport bar, with decadent plush seating and a frenzied dance floor. (920-7797. Tu Ambient, W acid jazz, Th hip-hop, F-Sa Top 40. Cover $3-5. Open M-Sa 9pm-2am.) For off-beat and foreign films, head to the **University of Victoria's Cinecenta** in the Student Union (721-8365; bus #4, 26, 11, or 14; $6.50).

**◨ ⚑ SIGHTS AND OUTDOORS.** The fantastically thorough **Royal British Columbia Museum** presents excellent exhibits on the biological, geological, and cultural history of the province, from protozoans to the present. *(675 Belleville St. Recording 387-3014, operator 387-3701. Open daily 9am-5pm. $9.65, seniors $6.65, children $4, under 5 free.)* The public **Art Gallery of Greater Victoria** culls magnificent exhibits from its collection of 14,000 pieces covering contemporary Canada, traditional and contemporary Asia, North America, and Europe. *(1040 Moss St. 384-4101. Open M-W and F-Sa 10am-5pm, Th 10am-9pm, Su 1-5pm. $5, students and seniors $3, under 12 free; M free.)* Across the street from the museum stands the imposing **Parliament Buildings,** home of the provincial government. *(501 Belleville St. 387-3046. Open M-F 8:30am-5pm, Sa-Su open for tours only. Free tours leave from main steps daily 9am-4:30pm, 3 times per hr.)* When the House is in session, visitors to the **public gallery** can see Members of Parliament discussing matters of great import. Just north of Fort St. on Wharf St. is **Bastion Sq.,** home to the **Maritime Museum,** which houses ship models, nautical instruments, and a torpedo. *(28 Bastion Sq. 385-4222. Open daily 9:30am-4:30pm. $5, students $3, seniors $4, ages 6-11 $2. Ticket good for 3 days.)*

The elaborate **Butchart Gardens** sprawl across a valley. Immaculate landscaping includes a rose garden, Japanese and Italian gardens, fountains, and wheelchair-accessible walking paths. *(21km north of Victoria off Hwy. 17. Recording 652-5256, office 652-4422. Take bus #75 Central Saanich from downtown at Douglas and Pandora; 1hr. Open daily July-Aug. 9am-10:30pm, closing time varies. Fireworks Sa around dusk. $16.50, ages 13-17 $8.25, ages 5-10 $2.)*

Mountain bikers can tackle the **Galloping Goose,** a 60km trail beginning downtown and continuing to the west coast of Vancouver Island through towns, rainforests, and canyons. **Ocean River Sports** offers kayak rentals, tours, and lessons. *(1437 Store St. 381-4233 or 800-909-4233. Open M-Th and Sa 9:30am-5:30pm, F 9:30am-8:30pm, Su 11am-5pm. Full-day single kayak $42, double $50, canoe $40.)* Many whale-watching outfits give discounts for hostel guests. **Ocean Explorations** runs 3hr. tours from Apr. to Oct. *(532 Broughton St. 383-6722. $75, hostelers and children $50, less in early season. Free pick-up at hostels.)*

# PACIFIC RIM NATIONAL PARK

Pacific Rim National Park, a thin strip of land on the island's remote western coast, is separately accessible at all 3 of its disparate regions and features beautiful remote hiking, popular sandy surfing beaches, and quirky small towns. The south end of the park—the head of the West Coast Trail at **Port Renfrew**—lies at the end of Hwy. 14, west of Victoria. **West Coast Trail Express** (477-8700) runs 1 bus per day from Victoria to Port Renfrew (2hr., $30), and 1 bus from Nanaimo to Port Renfrew (4hr., $50). Reservations required. The fantastic **West Coast Trail,** covering the southern third of the park between Port Renfrew and Bamfield, traces the shoreline for 77km of forests and waterfalls, and scales ladders and rocky slopes; recommended hiking time is about a week ($25 reservation fee, $70 trail use fee,

$25 ferry crossing fee). The **Trail Information Centre** in **Port Renfrew** (647-5434), is at the first right off Parkinson Rd. (Hwy. 14) once in "town." The trail is open May to Sept.; reservations should be made 3 months in advance at **Parks Canada,** Box 280, Ucluelet V0R 3A0.

The park's middle section—**Bamfield** and the **Broken Group Islands** in **Barkley Sound**—is far more difficult to reach. Hwy. 18 connects to Hwy. 1 at **Duncan** about 60km north of Victoria. **West Coast Trail Express** buses (see above) run daily from Nanaimo (3hr., $50) and Victoria (4½hr., $50). **Pacheenaht Band Bus Service** (647-5521) also runs between Port Renfrew to Bamfield. **Alberni Marine Transportation** (723-8313 or 800-663-7192) floats year-round from Port Alberni (4½hr., $20).

To reach **Long Beach,** at the park's northern reaches, take the spectacular drive across Vancouver Island on Hwy. 4 to the **Pacific Rim Hwy.** This stretch connects the towns of sleepy but expensive **Ucluelet** (yoo-CLOO-let) and crunchy and friendly **Tofino** (tuh-FEE-no). Hwy. 4 branches west of Hwy. 1 about 35km north of Nanaimo, leads 50km through Port Alberni, and continues 92km to the Pacific coast. **Chinook Charters** (725-3431) sends buses to the towns from Victoria (7hr., 2 daily, $45-47.50). **Alberni Marine Transportation** (723-8313 or 800-663-7192) runs from Port Alberni to Ucluelet (5hr., $23). **Parks Canada Visitor Information** (726-4212; open mid-June to mid-Sept. daily 9:30am-5pm) is 3km north of the Port Alberni junction on the Pacific Rim Hwy. ■ **Whalers on the Point Guesthouse (HI),** on Main St. in Tofino, is a newly-constructed deluxe hostel offering 60 beds (4 to a room), a free sauna, billiards, Sega, linen, and harborside views. (725-3443. $22, nonmembers $24; private rooms available. Check-in 7am-noon and 5pm-11pm.) Camping is extremely popular in summer. The **golf course** on the way to Tofino often has private, showerless gravel sites ($15) when no one else does.

**Hiking** is the highlight of a trip to the west side of the Island. **The Rainforest Centre,** 451 Main St., in Tofino, has assembled an excellent **trail guide** for Clayoquot Sound, Tofino, Ucluelet, the Pacific Rim, and Kennedy Lake (available by donation). The trails grow even more beautiful in the frequent rain and fog. (725-2560. Park passes, available in parking lots, $8 per day; season passes $45.)

## PRINCE RUPERT

At the western end of Hwy. 16, Prince Rupert is an emerging transportation hub—a springboard for ferry travel to Alaska, the spectacular Queen Charlotte Islands, and northern Vancouver Island. The **Museum of Northern British Columbia,** in the same building as the info center (see below), documents the history of logging, fishing, and Haida culture (624-3207; open M-Sa 9am-8pm, Su 9am-5pm; mid-Sept. to late May M-Sa 9am-5pm). Prince Rupert's harbor has the highest concentration of archaeological sites in North America; **archaeological boat tours** leave from the info center daily. (2½hr. tours depart June 19-30 daily 12:30pm; July to early Sept. daily 1pm. $22, children $13, under 5 free.) Tiny **Service Park,** off Fulton St., offers panoramic views of downtown and the harbor beyond. A trail winding up the side of **Mt. Oldfield,** east of town, yields an even wider vista. The trailhead is at **Oliver Lake Park,** about 6km from downtown on Hwy. 16 (contact the info center for info on guided nature walks leave from the parking lot May-Oct. $5). The best time to visit Prince Rupert may be during **Seafest,** a 4-day event held in mid-June.

Nearly all of Prince Rupert's hotels nestle within the 6-block area defined by 1st Ave., 3rd Ave., 6th St., and 9th St. **Andree's Bed and Breakfast,** 315 Fourth Ave. E., in a spacious 1922 Victorian-style residence, overlooks the harbor and city. (624-3666. Homebaked breakfasts. Singles $45, doubles, $60, twins $70; $10 per extra person.) **Park Ave. Campground,** 1750 Park Ave., is less than 2km east of the ferry terminal via Hwy. 16. Some of the well-maintained sites in this RV metropolis are forested; others have a view of the bay. (624-5861 or 800-667-1994. $10.50, hookup $18.50. Showers for non-guests $3.50. Laundry facilities.) **Cow Bay Cafe,** 201 Cow Bay Rd., offers an ever-changing menu, including lunch delights like Santa Fe corn pie ($7) and shrimp quesadillas ($9), and an extensive wine list (627-1212; open Tu noon-2:30pm, W-Sa noon-2:30pm and 6-9pm).

The only major road into town is the Yellowhead Highway (Hwy. 16); known as **McBride St.** within city limits, **2nd Ave.** at the north end of downtown, and **Park Ave.** at the south end; leading to the **ferry docks.** From the docks, downtown is a 30min. walk. **Prince Rupert Airport** is on Digby Island, with a ferry and bus connection to downtown (45min., $11). **Canadian Airlines** (624-9181 or 800-665-1177) flies to Vancouver ($532; mid-week flights in advance as low as $220; youth standby $187.) **VIA Rail** (627-7304 or 800-561-8630, outside BC 800-561-3949), toward the water on Bill Murray Way, runs to Prince George (12hr., 3 per week, $66); **BC Rail** (604-984-5500 or 800-339-8752, outside BC 800-663-8238) continues the next morning from Prince George to Vancouver (14hr., $194). **Greyhound,** 822 3rd Ave. (624-5090), near 8th St., runs to Prince George (10hr., 2 per day, $88) and Vancouver (24hr., 2 per day, $175). **Alaska Marine Highway** ferries (627-1744 or 800-642-0066), at the end of Hwy. 16 (Park Ave.), run north from Prince Rupert along the Alaskan Panhandle to Ketchikan (6hr., US$38) and Juneau (24-48hr., US$104). Next door, **BC Ferries** (624-9627 or 888-223-3779), runs to the Queen Charlotte Islands (6-7hr.; 6 per week; peak season $24, car $90) and Port Hardy on the northern tip of Vancouver Island (15hr.; every other day; $104, car $214). **Seashore Charter Services** (624-5645) runs a shuttle from the mall on 2nd Ave. to the ferry terminal by request ($3). **Prince Rupert Bus Service** (624-3343) runs downtown (M-Sa 7am-10pm; $1); about every 30min., bus #52 runs from 2nd Ave. and 3rd St. to within a 5min. walk of the ferry terminal.

The **Information Centre** (624-5637 or 800-667-1994), at 1st Ave. and McBride St., is in a cedar building modeled after a Tsimshian bighouse (open May 15-Sept. 6 M-Sa 9am-8pm, Su 9am-5pm; in winter M-Sa 10am-5pm). **Internet access** awaits in the **library,** 101 6th Ave. W. (627-1345), at McBride St. ($2 per hr. after 15 free min.; open M and W 1-9pm, Tu and Th 10am-9pm, F-Sa 1-5pm; in winter also Su 1-5pm.) The **post office** (624-2353) sits in the mall at 2nd Ave. and 5th St. (open M-F 9:30am-5:30pm). **Postal code:** V8J 3P3. **Area code:** 250.

# DAWSON CREEK

Mile 0 of the Alaska Highway is Dawson Creek, BC (not to be confused with Dawson City, YT, or Dawson's Creek, WB), first settled in 1890 as just another pipsqueak frontier village of a few hundred souls. Its later status as a railroad terminus made it a natural place to begin building the 2600km Alcan in 9 months.

To reach Dawson Creek from Prince George, drive 402km north on the John Hart section of **Hwy. 97. Greyhound,** 1201 Alaska Ave. (782-3131 or 800-661-8747), runs to Whitehorse, YT (20hr.; June-Aug. 1 per day M-Sa, Oct.-May 3 per week; $165); Prince George (6½hr., 2 per day, $50); Edmonton (8hr., 2 per day, $70); and Calgary (14hr., 2 per day, $104. Open M-F 7am-6pm and 8-8:30pm, Sa 6am-noon, 2-5pm, and 8-8:30pm, Su 7-10:30am, 3-4:30pm, and 8-8:30pm.) For road reports, stop at the **visitor center,** 900 Alaska Ave. (782-9595; open May 15 to Labour Day daily 8am-7pm; in winter Tu-Sa 9am-5pm). **Internet access: library** (782-4661), at 10th St. and McKellar Ave. (open Tu-Th 10am-9pm, F 10am-5:30pm, Sa 1:30-5:30pm; free). **24hr. road service: J&L Mechanical Services** (782-7832). **Post office:** (782-9429; open M-F 8:30am-5pm) 104th Ave. and 10th St. **Postal code:** V1G 4E6. **Area code:** 250.

For a bargain price, great location, and an off-beat aura, head straight for the historic **Alaska Hotel,** above the Alaska Cafe & Pub on 10th St., 1½ blocks from the visitor center. (782-7998. Shared bath; no TV or phone. Singles $30; doubles $40; in winter $5 less.) The newer **Voyageur Motor Inn,** 801 111th Ave., facing 8th Ave., offers phones and cable (782-1020; singles $40; doubles $45). Peaceful and grassy, the **Mile 0 Campground,** 1km west of Alaska Hwy. Mile 0 and adjacent to the Pioneer Village, has free showers and coin laundry (782-2590; sites $10; hookups $15).

If foraging on your bug-splattered windshield fails to satisfy, head to the **Alaska Cafe & Pub,** "55 paces south of the Mile 0 Post" on 10th St., for excellent $5 burgers (782-7040; open Su-Th 10am-10pm, F-Sa 11am-11pm; pub open noon-3am). Pick up a loaf for the road at the **Organic Farms Bakery,** 1425 97th Ave. From the visitors center, go west along Alaska Ave. and take a right at 15th St. Breads (from $1.70) are baked with local grain. (782-6533. Open Tu-F 9:30am-6pm, Sa 9am-4pm.)

Travelers cruising through Dawson Creek can't miss the **Mile 0 Cairn** and **Mile 0 Post,** both commemorating the birth of the Alcan, within a stone's throw of the visitor center. This town boomed during construction, literally. On February 13, 1943, sixty cases of exploding dynamite leveled the entire business district save the COOP building, now Bing's Furniture, opposite the Mile 0 post. In early August, the town plays host to the **Fall Fair & Stampede** (782-8911) with a carnival, fireworks, chuckwagon races, and a professional rodeo.

## ALASKA APPROACHES

For mile-by-mile coverage of the way to Alaska of the great northern state itself, consult *Let's Go: Alaska and the Pacific Northwest including Western Canada 2000.*

**THE ALASKA HIGHWAY.** Built during World War II, the Alaska Hwy. (also known as the **Alcan**) traverses an astonishing 2378km route between Dawson Creek, BC, and Fairbanks, AK. In recent years, the U.S. Army has been replaced by an annual army of over 250,000 tourists, many of them RV-borne. In general, there's a trade-off between the excitement you'll find on the Alcan and the speed with which you'll reach Alaska. Countless opportunities lurk off the highway for hiking, fishing, and viewing wildlife. A 1hr video shown at the **Dawson Creek Tourist Infocentre** provides a praiseworthy introduction to the road and region. The free *Driving the Alaska Highway* includes a listing of emergency medical services and phone numbers throughout Alaska, the Yukon, and British Columbia, plus tips on preparation and driving; get it at visitor centers. **Road conditions:** 867-667-8215.

**CASSIAR HIGHWAY (HWY. 37).** A growing number of travelers prefer the Cassiar Hwy. to the Alaska Hwy., which has become an RV institution. The highway slices through charred forests and snow-capped peaks on its way from Hwy. 16 in BC to the Alcan (Hwy. 97) in the Yukon. Three evenly spaced provincial parks right off the highway offer good camping, and the Cassiar's services, while sparse, are numerous enough to keep cars and drivers running. Hitchiking is less popular here than on the Alaska Hwy. Advantages include a shorter distance, consistently interesting scenery, and fewer crowds. On the other hand, the Cassiar is remote, less well maintained, and large sections are very slippery when wet and harder on tires than the better-paved Alcan. This causes little concern for the large, commercial trucks that roar up and down the route, but keeps the infrequent service stops busy with overambitious drivers in need of tire repair.

# THE YUKON TERRITORY

The Yukon Territory is among the most remote and sparsely inhabited regions of North America, averaging one person per 15 sq. km. While summers usually bring comfortably warm temperatures (60-70°F/15-21°C) and more than 20hr. of daylight, travelers should still be prepared for difficult weather. The territory remains a bountiful, beautiful, and largely unspoiled region, yet many travelers mimic gold-crazed prospectors and zoom through without appreciating its uncrowded allure.

# ⛴ PRACTICAL INFORMATION

**Capital:** Whitehorse.

**Visitor Info: Tourism Yukon,** P.O. Box 2703, Whitehorse, YT Y1A 2C6 (867-667-5340; www.touryukon.com).

**Police:** 867-667-5555. For **emergencies** outside the Whitehorse area, *911 may not work.*

**Drinking Age:** 19. **Postal Abbreviation:** YT. **Area code:** 867. **Sales Tax:** None.

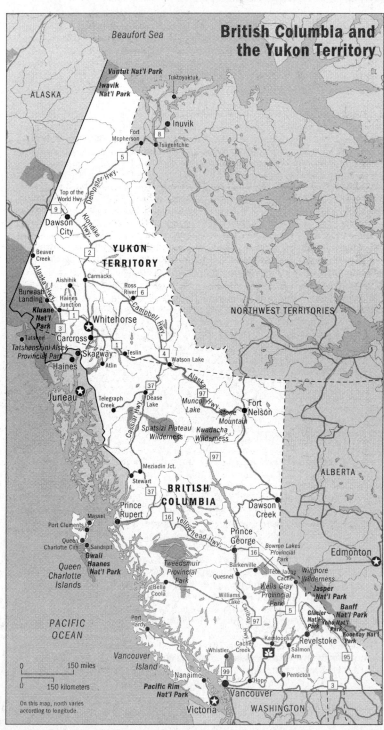

# British Columbia and the Yukon Territory

Beaufort Sea

Vuntut Nat'l Park

Iwavik Nat'l Park

ALASKA

Tuktoyaktuk

Inuvik

Fort Mcpherson

8

Tsiigehtchic

5

Dempster Hwy.

Top of the World Hwy.

9

Dawson City

Klondike Hwy.

YUKON TERRITORY

Beaver Creek

2

NORTHWEST TERRITORIES

Aishihik

Carmacks

Ross River

6

Burwash Landing

Haines Junction

1

Kluane Nat'l Park

3

Whitehorse

Campbell Hwy.

Tatshenshini-Alsek Provincial Park

Tatshee

Carcross

1

Skagway

Teslin

4

Watson Lake

Haines

Atlin

Alaska Hwy.

97

Juneau

Telegraph Creek

37

Dease Lake

Munco Lake

Fort Nelson

Stone Mountain

Cassiar Hwy.

Spatsizi Plateau Wilderness

Kwadacha Wilderness

97

ALBERTA

Meziadin Jct.

Stewart

37

BRITISH COLUMBIA

Dawson Creek

Prince Rupert

16

Yellowhead Hwy.

Prince George

16

Bowron Lakes Provincial Park

Edmonton

Masset

Port Clements

Queen Charlotte City

Sandspit

Gwaii Haanes Nat'l Park

Queen Charlotte Islands

Tweedsmuir Provincial Park

Barkerville

Quesnel

Tête Jaune Cache

Willmore Wilderness

Jasper Nat'l Park

Bella Coola

Williams Lake

Wells Gray Provincial Park

Glacier Nat'l Park

Banff Nat'l Park

Yoho Nat'l Park

PACIFIC OCEAN

Port Hardy

Cariboo Hwy.

97

Kamloops

Revelstoke

Kooenay Nat'l Park

Vancouver Island

Whistler

Cache Creek

Salmon Arm

95

0    150 miles

0    150 kilometers

99

Nanaimo

Hope

Penticton

3

Pacific Rim Nat'l Park

Vancouver

On this map, north varies according to longitude.

Victoria

WASHINGTON

# WHITEHORSE

Named for the once-perilous Whitehorse Rapids, whose crashing whitecaps were said to resemble the flowing manes of white mares, Whitehorse is a modern cross-roads in an ageless frontier. With over 23,000 residents, Whitehorse prides itself on being Canada's largest city north of 60° latitude. The mountains, rivers, and lakes in all directions are a powerful reminder that "south of 60" is far, far away.

**◢ PRACTICAL INFORMATION.** Whitehorse lies 1500km north of Dawson Creek, BC along the Alaska Hwy. and 535km south of Dawson City, YT. The **airport** is off the Alaska Hwy., just southwest of downtown. **Canada 3000** (888-226-3000) offers reduced airfares to Vancouver ($210) during the summer. The **bus station** is on the northeast edge of town. **Greyhound**, 2191 2nd Ave. (667-2223), runs once per day to Vancouver, BC (41hr., $300); Edmonton, AB (30hr., $232); and Dawson Creek, BC (18hr., $165). (Runs late June to Sept. M-Sa; in winter Tu, Th, and Sa. Desk open M-F 7:30am-6pm, Sa 9am-1:30pm, Su 4-8am and 5-6pm.) **Alaska Direct** (668-4833 or 800-770-6652) runs to Anchorage (15hr., 3 per week, US$145); Fairbanks (12hr., 3 per week, US$120); and Skagway (3hr., 1 per day, US$35); in winter, buses run 1 per week to above destinations. The local buses of **Whitehorse Transit** (24hr. info line 668-7433) arrive and depart downtown next to Canadian Tire on Ogilvie St. (Runs M-Th 6:15am-7:30pm, F 6:15am-10:30pm, Sa 8am-7pm. $1.50, seniors and disabled 75¢.) **Norcan Leasing**, 213 Range Rd. (668-2137 or 800-661-0445, in AK 800-764-1234), at Alcan Mi. 917.4, rents cars for $55 per day (less in winter), and 22¢ per km after 100km (must be 21+ with credit card).

   **Visitors center:** 100 Hansen St. (667-3084), in the Tourism and Business Centre at 2nd Ave. (open daily mid-May to mid-Sept. 8am-8pm; in winter M-F 9am-5pm). The **Yukon Conservation Society,** 302 Hawkins St. (668-5678), offers maps and great ideas for area hikes (open M-F 10am-2pm). The **Kanoe People** (668-4899), at Strickland and 1st Ave., rent mountain bikes ($25 per day), canoes ($45 per day), and kayaks. ($35 per day for plastic; $45 for fiberglass. Credit card or deposit required. Open daily 9am-6pm.) **Internet access: library,** 2071 2nd Ave. (667-5239; open M-F 10am-9pm, Sa 10am-6pm, Su 1-9pm; free). The **Post Office,** 211 Main St. (667-2485), is in the Shoppers Drug Mart (open M-F 9am-6pm, Sa 11am-4pm). General Delivery is at 3rd Ave. and Wood St., in the Yukon News Bldg. (open M-F 8am-6pm). **General delivery postal code:** last names A-L, Y1A 3S7; M-Z, Y1A 3S8. **Area code:** 867.

**▐▜▐ ACCOMMODATIONS AND FOOD.** Interchangeable motels in town cost around $65. The **Roadhouse Inn**, 2163 2nd Ave., near the Greyhound depot, has shared rooms and hall showers with a bathtub. (667-2594. $20; private rooms with cable and private bathroom $50; $10 per additional person. Wash and dry $1.75 each. Free local calls. Key deposit $10. Lobby open 7am-2:30am.) **Robert Service Campground**, 1km from town on South Access Rd. along the Yukon River, is a convenient stop for tenting types, with no RV sites. (668-3721. Food trailer, firewood, playground, drinking water, toilets, coin showers. 68 sites. $11. Gates open 7am-midnight. Open late May to early Sept.) **Wolf Creek Campground**, 5km south of town on the Alcan, has 33 beautiful sites. (Camping @ $8 provincial permit only. Pit toilets, firewood, and a playground.) The 62km (45min.) drive to camp near the **Takhini Hot Springs,** the Yukon's only hot springs, offers tenting plus thermal relief. Follow the Alcan northwest from downtown, turn right onto the North Klondike Highway, and left to the end of Takhini Hot Springs Rd. There is a $3-5 admission charge. (633-2706. Restaurant, showers, and laundry. 88 sites: $11.)

   **▨ Klondike Rib and Salmon Barbecue**, 2116 2nd Ave., serves barbecued fresh salmon or halibut with homemade bread for lunch. ($8. 667-7554. Open mid-May to Sept. M-F 11:30am-2pm and 4pm-10pm, Sa-Su 5-10pm.) **The Talisman Cafe,** 2112 2nd Ave., is elegantly decorated with local art and has the best vegetarian menu in town: bannock and jam with Yukon cranberries and unique soups (667-2736; open M-Sa midnight-4pm, Su until 3pm).

**⬛🅐 SIGHTS AND OUTDOORS.** Visitors hungry for local history can feed their heads at the **MacBride Museum,** at 1st Ave. and Wood St. *(667-2709. Open daily June-Aug. 10am-6pm; call for winter hrs. $4, students and seniors $3.50, children $2, under 7 free.)* The sod-roofed cabin in the courtyard was built by Sam Mcgee whose demise was famously related in verse by Robert Service. The new **Yukon Beringia Interpretive Centre,** on the Alcan, 2km west of the junction with the S. Access Rd., pays homage to the forgotten continent that joined Siberia, Alaska, and the Yukon. *(667-8855. Open daily mid-May to Sept. 8am-8pm; reduced winter hrs. $6, seniors $5, children $4.)*

**Grey Mountain,** partly accessible by gravel road, is a somewhat rigorous day hike. Take Lewes Blvd. across the bridge by the **S.S. Klondike,** then take a left on Alsek Ave. Turn left again at the "Grey Mt. Cemetery" sign and follow the gravel road to its end. Joggers, bikers, and cross-country skiers love the **Miles Canyon trail network** that parallels the Yukon River. To get there, take Lewes Blvd. to Nisutlin Dr. and turn right; just before the fish ladder turn left onto the gravel Chadbum Lake Rd. and continue for 4km to the parking area. The Conservation Society leads nature walks M-F. *(Office open July-Aug. M-F 10am-2pm.)*

**Up North Boat and Canoe Rentals** lets you paddle 25km to Takhini River. *(86 Wickstrom Rd. 667-7905. 4hr. $30 including transportation. 8-day trip on the Teslin $200. Kayaks and canoes $25-30 per day.)* The tiny islands around **Sanfu Lake** (1½hr. south of town on the Atlin Rd.) are ideal for kayaking.

## KLUANE NATIONAL PARK

Together with adjacent Wrangell-St. Elias National Park in Alaska and Tatshenshini/Alsek Provincial Park in BC, Kluane (kloo-AH-nee) is part of one of the world's largest wilderness areas. It contains Canada's highest peak, Mt. Logan (5959m or 19,545 ft.), as well as the world's most massive non-polar ice fields. The ice-blanketed mountains of Kluane's interior are a haven for experienced expeditioners, but render two-thirds of the park inaccessible to humbler hikers. Fortunately, the northeast part of the park (bordering the Alaska Hwy.) offers splendid, easily-accessible backpacking, canoeing, rafting, biking, fishing, and dayhiking.

**🔟 PRACTICAL INFORMATION. Haines Junction,** at the eastern park boundary, 158km west of Whitehorse, serves as park gateway and headquarters. **Alaska Direct** (800-770-6652, in Whitehorse 668-4833) runs from Haines Jct. (Su, W, F) to Anchorage (13hr., 8am, US$125), Fairbanks (11hr, 8am, US$100), and Whitehorse (2hr, 10pm, US$20). **Kluane National Park Visitor Reception Centre** (634-7209), on Logan St. (Km 1635 on the Alcan), provides wilderness permits ($5 per night, $50 per season), fishing permits ($5 per day, $35 per season), maps ($10), and trail and weather info (open daily May-Sept. 9am-5pm; in winter M-F 10am-noon and 1-4pm). **Sheep Mountain Information Centre,** 72km north of town at Alaska Hwy. Km 1707, registers hikers headed into the park. **24hr. road service: Triple S Garage** (634-2915) 1km north of Haines Jct. **Emergency:** 634-5555. **Ambulance/Clinic:** 634-4444. **Post office:** in Madley's Store on Haines Rd. (634-3802; open M, W, and F 9-10am and 1-5pm, Tu and Th 9am-noon and 1-5pm). **Postal code:** Y0B 1L0. **Area code:** 867.

**📷📷 ACCOMMODATIONS AND FOOD.** Camping by a gorgeous lakeside beats staying at a clean-but-forgettable highway motel or RV park any day. The idyllic **Kathleen Lake Campground,** off Haines Rd. 27km south of Haines Junction, is close to hiking and fishing (sites $10; water, toilets, fire pits, and firewood; open mid-May to mid-Sept.; wheelchair access). Popular **Pine Lake,** 7km east of town, features a sandy beach ($8 with Yukon camping permit only; water, firewood, pit toilets). The **Dezadeash Lake Campground,** about 50km south of Haines Junction on Haines Rd., offers the same deal and similarly sweet lakefront property. **Laughing Moose B&B,** 120 Alsek Crescent, 4 blocks from the junction, offers a sparkling-clean kitchen, spacious common room with TV and VCR, and a view of the Auriol Mountains (634-2335; singles $60; doubles $70; shared bath). The **Stardust Motel,** 1km north of town on the Alcan, has spacious rooms with TVs and tubs, but no phones (634-2591; singles $49; doubles $59; shared bath). **Village Bakery and Deli,** on Logan St. across from the visitors center, serves up substantial soups with bread ($3.50) and mushroom quiche ($2.50). Watch out for (or join in) live music and salmon BBQs ($13) on Mondays. (634-2867. Open daily May-Sept. 7:30am-9pm.)

**⚑ OUTDOORS.** A $1 pamphlet lists 25 or so trails and routes ranging from 500m to 96km. **Routes,** as opposed to trails, are not maintained, do not have marked paths, are more physically demanding, and require backcountry navigation skills. Overnight visitors must register at one of the visitor centers ($5 per night, ages 5-16 $2.50), and use bear-resistant food canisters, which the park rents for $5 per night. The **Dezadeash River Loop** (DEZ-dee-ash) trailhead is downtown at the day-use area across from Madley's on Haines Rd. This flat, forested 5km trail will disappoint those craving vert, but it makes for a nice stroll. The more challenging 15km **Auriol Loop** has a primitive campground halfway along. The trail begins 7km south of Haines Junction on Haines Rd. and cuts through boreal forest, leading to a subalpine bench (elevation gain 400m/1300 ft.) just in front of the Auriol Range. This is a popular overnight trip, though 4-6hr. is adequate time without heavy packs. The 5km (one-way) **King's Throne Route** is a very challenging but rewarding day hike with a 1220m/4000 ft. elevation gain and a panoramic view. It begins at the **Kathleen Lake** day-use area at the campground (see above).

Excellent hiking awaits near **Sheep Mountain** in the park's northern section. An easy 500m jaunt up to **Soldier's Summit** starts 1km north of the Sheep Mountain Info Centre and leads to the site where the original highway was officially opened in 1942. The **Sheep Creek** trail, located down a short gravel access road just north of the visitor center, is a satisfying dayhike (5km one-way; 430m/1440 ft. elev. gain; 3-6hr. round-trip) up Sheep Mountain, and one of the better bets to see Dall sheep in summer. Only experienced backpackers should attempt the trek along the **Slims River** to the magnificent **Kaskawulsh Glacier.** Two rough routes along the either bank of the river are available, stretching 23 and 30km one-way (elev. gains of 910m/3000 ft. and 1340m/4400 ft., respectively) and requiring 3 to 5 days.

The **Alsek River Valley Trail,** which follows a bumpy old mining road 14km to Sugden Creek. Starting from Alcan Km 1645, makes for good mountain biking. **Paddle-Wheel Adventures,** down the road from the Village Bakery in Haines Junction, arranges flightseeing over the glaciers and full-day rafting trips on the Class III and IV rapids of the **Blanchard** and **Tatshenshini Rivers** (634-2683. $90 per person for a 30min. flight over the Kaskawulsh. $100 per person, including lunch.)

# THE CAMPBELL HIGHWAY

If the Yukon were conceived as a body, the Campbell Highway (Hwy. 4) might be likened to the sensitive jugular vein of the territory's modern mining economy. The Campbell runs 602km between Watson Lake and the modest-sized, picturesque town of Carmacks (8hr.). The route requires good tires and a spare, though the road improves after Ross River, the halfway point. The 383km (4-4½hr.; no services on this stretch) of graded dirt road from Watson Lake in the south (on the Alcan Hwy.) to Ross River runs through wilderness has no services and is broken only by impressive year-round highway servicing camps. Five government campsites ($8 permit camping only) lie on the route (Kms 80, 177, 376, 428 up towards Faro, and 517), and three more on the short Frenchman Rd., which branches off the Campbell at Km 551, near Carmacks, and leads 60km to the Klondike Hwy.

The log-cabin town of Ross River has a general store with **groceries,** and a **service station** that repairs tires (969-3841; open daily 7am-7pm). The **Hideaway Restaurant** serves sandwiches (from $8) on homemade bread with produce trucked in weekly and will rent you their pretty cabin. (969-2905. Open M-F 11am-8pm, Sa-Su 11am-7pm. $75; sleeps 4. Kitchen, continental breakfast included). One hour northeast of Ross River and a jaunt down 10km of road will land you in the almost-ghost-town of **Faro.** When active, the town's mine held the world's largest open-pit lead and zinc production complex. It was so big that it depressed world lead prices below profitable levels, forcing it to close in 1997. The **Campbell Region Interpretive**

**Centre,** on the right as you enter town, provides great info on geology and mining, First Nation habitation and early fur-trading exploration of the area (994-2288).

The final approach to the town of **Carmacks** delivers beautiful **camping** along the Nordenskiold River at the popular **Tantalus Public Campground,** and a meandering stretch of riverside boardwalk ($12; pit toilets, water). **Visitors center:** beside the campground (863-6330; open Tu-Su 9am-5pm). Just north, the new **Tage Cho Hudan Cultural Centre** (863-5830) preserves the Tutchone culture (open daily 9am-5pm; donation requested). From **Carmacks,** the smooth **North Klondike Highway** (Hwy. 2) runs 175km south to Whitehorse or 360km north to Dawson City. **Police:** 863-5555.

## THE DEMPSTER HIGHWAY

The Dempster Hwy. (Hwy. 5) begins 41km east of Dawson City at the **Klondike River Lodge** on the Klondike Hwy. (Hwy. 2), and winds 741 spectacular kilometers to Inuvik, becoming Hwy. 8 upon crossing into the Northwest Territories. Like no other highway in North America, the Dempster confronts its drivers with real wilderness devoid of logging scars or ads. The Dempster is reasonably navigable and well-maintained, but services are limited, weather is erratic, and its dirt-and-gravel stretches can give cars a thorough beating. Although the drive can be made in 12hr., it deserves at least 2 days each way to be fully and safely appreciated. Rainstorms can create impassable washouts, closing down parts of the highway or disrupting ferry service—and leaving travelers stranded in Inuvik—for as long as 2 weeks. The **Arctic Hotline** (800-661-0788) and **Road and Ferry Report** (800-661-0752; in Inuvik 777-2678) provide up-to-date road info. The **Northwest Territories Visitor Centre** (993-6167), in Dawson City, has a free Dempster brochure (open daily late May to early Sept. 9am-8pm). There are **government campgrounds** at Tombstone (Km 72), Engineer Creek (Km 194), Rock River (Km 447), Nitainlii (Km 541), Caribou Creek (Km 692) and Chuk (Km 731). Dry sites cost $8, and hookups are only available at Chuk. The **Interpretive Centre** at Tombstone loans out a kilometer-by-kilometer travelogue of the Dempster's natural history and wildlife. The drive out to Tombstone makes a pleasant overnight for those not willing to charge forth to the NWT.

# ALBERTA

With its gaping prairie, oil-fired economy, and conservative politics, Alberta is the Texas of Canada. Petro-dollars have given birth to gleaming, modern cities on the plains, while the natural landscape swings from the mighty Canadian Rockies down to beautifully desolate badlands.

## ▨ PRACTICAL INFORMATION

**Capital:** Edmonton.

**Visitor Info: Travel Alberta,** Commerce Pl., 10155 102 St., 3rd fl., Edmonton, AB T5J 4G8 (800-661-8888 or 780-427-4321; www.discoveralberta.com/atp). **Parks Canada,** 220 4th Ave. SE, #552, Calgary, AB T2G 4X3 (800-748-7275 or 403-292-4401). **Alberta Environmental Protection,** 9820 106 St., 2nd Fl., Edmonton, AB T5K 2J6 (780-427-7009; www.gov.ab.ca/env/parks.html).

**Drinking Age:** 18. **Postal Abbreviation:** AB. **Sales Tax:** none.

## THE ROCKIES

Every year, some 5 million visitors make it within sight of the Rockies' majestic peaks and stunning glacial lakes. Thankfully, much of this traffic is confined to highwayside gawkers, and only a tiny fraction of these visitors make it far into the forest. Still, any fraction of five million is a big number, and the park's most popular trails get crowded. Of the big two—Banff and Jasper—Jasper feels a little farther removed from the crowds and offers great wildlife viewing from the road. The north-south **Icefields Parkway (Hwy. 93)** runs between them. Without a car, guided bus rides may be the easiest way to see some of the park's main attractions, such as the Great Divide, the Athabasca Glacier, and the spiral railroad tunnel. **Brewster Tours** (762-6767) buses from Banff to Jasper stop for the major sights and take 9½ hrs ($85, Apr.-Oct. at 8:10am). A visit to the Columbia Icefields is $25 extra. **Bigfoot Tours** (888-244-6673 or 604-278-8224) runs 2-day van trips between Banff and Jasper for $84, not including food or lodging at the Mt. Edith Cavell Hostel.

# BANFF NATIONAL PARK

Banff is Canada's best-loved and best-known natural park, with 6641 sq. km (2,564 sq. mi.) of peaks, forests, glaciers, and alpine valleys. Even streets littered with gift shops, clothing shops, and chocolatiers cannot mar Banff's beauty. Transient 20-somethings arrive with mountain bikes, climbing gear, skis, and snowboards, but a trusty pair of hiking boots remains the park's most popular outdoor equipment.

**PRACTICAL INFORMATION.** The park hugs the Alberta side of the Alberta/British Columbia border, 129km west of Calgary. Civilization in the park centers around the towns of **Banff** and **Lake Louise,** 58km apart on Hwy. 1. All of the following info applies to Banff Townsite, unless otherwise specified. **Greyhound,** 327 Railway Ave. (800-661-8747; depot open daily 7:30am-9:30pm), runs 4 buses per day to Lake Louise (1hr., $11), Calgary (2hr., $20), and Vancouver, BC (13hr., $99). **Brewster Transportation,** 100 Gopher St. (762-6767), runs express buses to Jasper (5hr., 3:15pm, $51); Lake Louise (1hr., 3 per day, $11); and Calgary (2hr., 4 per day, $36; HI discount 15%, ages 6-15 ½-price). If you lack a car, **Brewster Tours'** (762-6767) guided bus rides may be the only way to see some of the park's main attractions, such as the Great Divide, the Athabasca Glacier, and the spiral railroad tunnel. (Banff to Jasper 9½hr., $85. Columbia Icefields $25 extra.)

**Banff Visitor Centre,** 224 Banff Ave., includes **Banff/Lake Louise Tourism Bureau** (762-8421) and **Canadian Parks Service** (762-1550; open daily 8am-8pm; Oct.-May 9am-5pm). The **Lake Louise Visitor Centre** (522-3833), at Samson Mall in Lake Louise, shares a building with a museum (open daily 8am-8pm; June and Sept. 8am-6pm; Oct.-May 9am-5pm). **Emergency: Banff Police,** 762-2226. **Lake Louise Police,** 522-3811. **Banff Warden Office,** 762-4506. **Lake Louise Warden Office,** 522-3866. **Internet access:** Free at the library, 101 Bear St. (762-2611; open M-Th 11am-8pm, F-Sa 11am-6pm; sign up in advance). **Post Office:** 204 Buffalo St. (762-2586; open M-F 9am-5:30pm). **Postal code:** T0L 0C0. **Area code:** 403.

**ACCOMMODATIONS AND FOOD.** HI-C runs a **shuttle service** connecting all the Rocky Mountain hostels and Calgary ($7-65). Wait-list beds become available at 6pm, and the larger hostels save some stand-by beds for shuttle arrivals. For reservations at any rustic hostel, call Banff International. ■ **Lake Louise International Hostel (HI-C),** 500m west of the info center in Lake Louise Townsite, on Village Rd., is more like a hotel than a hostel, with a reference library, common rooms with open, beamed ceilings, a stone fireplace, 2 full kitchens, a sauna, ski/bike workshops, and a cafe. (522-2200. $21, nonmembers $25. Private rooms available for $6 more per person. Wheelchair access.) **Banff International Hostel (HI-C),** is 3km from Banff Townsite on Tunnel Mountain Rd., which leads from Otter St. downtown; take the Happy Bus from downtown ($1). This big hostel has the look and feel of a ski lodge, with 3 lounge areas, 2 large fireplaces, a game room with pool table, a kitchen, cafe, laundry facilities, and hot showers. (762-4122. $20, nonmembers $24. Private rooms $12 more. Linen $1. Reception 24hr. Wheelchair access.) **Castle Mountain Hostel (HI-C),** on Hwy. 1A, 1.5km east of the junction of Hwy. 1 and Hwy. 93 between Banff and Lake Louise, is a quieter alternative, with running water, hot showers, and electricity, general store, library, and fireplace ($13, nonmembers $17; linen $1). Three other rustic hostels—**Hilda Creek, Rampart Creek** and **Mosquito Creek**—can be booked by calling Banff International Hostel. At any of Banff's 9 park campgrounds, a campfire permit with firewood included costs $3 extra. Sites are first come, first served ($10-22). On Hwy. 1A between

# Alberta, Saskatchewan, and Manitoba

N

200 miles

200 kilometers

Hudson Bay

ONTARIO

Churchill

Nelson R.

Nueltin Lake

MANITOBA

Island Lake

Thompson

Kenora

17

2

Winnipeg

Portage La Prairie

75

29

Brandon

Minot

2

Lake Winnipeg

6

Dauphin

Riding Mt. Nat. Park

Lake Winnipegosis

10

16

The Pas

1

Regina

Brochet

Reindeer Lake

Flin Flon

10

Churchill River

Collins Bay

Yorkton

Fond-du-Lac

SASKATCHEWAN

Prince Albert

Prince Albert Nat. Park

2

La Ronge

55

16

Moose Jaw

Swift Current

NORTHWEST TERRITORIES

Lake Athabasca

Fort Chipewyan

La Loche

155

11

Saskatoon

Medicine Hat

2

Slave River

Wood Buffalo Nat. Park

Athabasca River

Fort McMurray

N. Saskatchewan River

16

Lloydminster

Edmonton

Drumheller

3

Lethbridge

4

15

Enterprise

35

High Level

Peace River

Slave Lake

2

ALBERTA

Red Deer

Calgary

2

1

Glacier Nat. Park

Kalispell Nat. Park

2

Fort Nelson

Dawson Creek

Grande Prairie

35

16

Jasper Nat. Park

Jasper

93

Banff

Banff Nat. Park

1

ROCKY MTS.

Waterton Lakes Nat. Park

97

2

5

Kamloops

1

BRITISH COLUMBIA

16

97

Kelowna

WESTERN CANADA

Banff Townsite and Lake Louise, **Johnston Canyon** and **Castle Mountain** are close to relatively uncrowded hiking. Only Village 2 of **Tunnel Mountain Village,** 4km from Banff Townsite on Tunnel Mountain Rd., remains open in winter.

The Banff and Lake Louise Hostels serve affordable meals ($3-8), but **Laggan's Deli,** in Samson Mall in Lake Louise is the best thing going. Thick sandwich on whole wheat cost $3.75; a fresh-baked loaf for later runs $2.35. (522-2017). **Aardvark's,** 304A Caribou St., does big business after the bars close. The place is skinny on seating, but serves thick slices of pizza. ($2.80; small $6-8; large $13-20. 762-5500. 10% HI discount on large pizzas. Open daily 11am-4am.)

**.** **OUTDOORS.** Near Banff Townsite, **Fenland Trail** winds 2km (1hr.) through an area shared by beaver, muskrat, and waterfowl (closed for elk calving in late spring and early summer). Follow Mt. Norquay Rd. out of town, and look for signs across the tracks on the road's left side. The summit of **Tunnel Mountain** provides a dramatic view of the **Bow Valley** and **Mt. Rundle.** Follow Wolf St. east from Banff Ave., and turn right on St. Julien Rd. to reach the head of the steep 2.3km (2hr.) trail. At 2949m (9675 ft.), **Mt. Rundle** offers a more demanding fair-weather-only dayhike (7-8 hr., 5.5km one-way 1600m/5248 ft. elev. gain). An exposed ridge leads to a scramble up scree slopes; the unrivaled vista is well worth the effort. **Johnston Canyon,** about 25km out of Banff toward Lake Louise along the Bow Valley Pkwy. (Hwy. 1A), is a popular ½-day hike which runs past waterfalls to seven blue-green cold-water springs known as the **Inkpots,** beyond which lie 42km of untraveled trails punctuated with campgrounds.

The park might not exist if not for the **Cave and Basin Hot Springs,** southwest of town on Cave Ave., once rumored to have miraculous healing properties. The **Cave and Basin National Historic Site,** a refurbished resort built circa 1914, is now a museum. (762-1557. Open daily in summer 9am-6pm; in winter 9:30am-5pm. Tours at 11am. $2.50, seniors $2, children $1.50.) For a dip in the hot water, follow the rotten-egg smell to the 40°C (104°F) **Upper Hot Springs,** up the hill on Mountain Ave. (762-1515. Open daily 9am-11pm; winter 10am-10pm. $7, seniors and children $6. Swimsuits $1.50, towels $1, lockers 50¢.)

The highest community in Canada at 1530m (5018 ft.), Lake Louise and its surrounding glaciers have often passed for Swiss scenery in movies. Once at the lake, the hardest task is escaping fellow gawkers at the posh **Château Lake Louise.** Several hiking trails begin at the water; the 3.6km **Lake Agnes Trail** and the 5.5km **Plain of Six Glaciers Trail** both end at teahouses.

Nearby **Moraine Lake** may pack more of a scenic punch than its sister Louise. The lake is 15km from the village, at the end of Moraine Lake Rd., off the Lake Louise access road. Moraine lies in the awesome **Valley of the Ten Peaks,** opposite glacier-encrusted **Mt. Temple.** Join the multitudes on the **Rockpile Trail** for an eye-popping view of the lake and valley and an explanation of rocks from former ocean floors.

**Fishing** is legal in most of the park's bodies of water during specific seasons, but live bait and lead weights are not. **Permits** are available at the info center. (7-days; $6, annual permit valid in all Canadian National Parks $13.) **Overnight camping permits** can be obtained at the visitors centers ($6 per person per day, up to $30; $42 per year). Winter activities in the park range from world-class ice climbing to ice fishing. Those 1600km of hiking trails make for exceptional **cross-country skiing,** and 3 allied resorts offer a range of **skiing and snowboarding** opportunities from early Nov. to mid-May. **Sunshine Mountain** has the largest snowfall (762-6500, snow report 760-7669; lift tickets $46.50); **Mt. Norquay** is smaller, closer to town and less busy (762-4421; $39); while **Lake Louise** is the 2nd-biggest ski area in Canada and has the most expert terrain (522-3555, snow report 762-4766; $46). Shuttles to all 3 resorts leave from most big hotels in the townsites, and most hostels have **ticket and transportation discounts** available for guests.

# ICEFIELDS PARKWAY (HIGHWAY 93)

The 230km Icefields Pwy. is one of the most beautiful routes in North America, heading north from Lake Louise in Banff National Park to Jasper Townsite in Jasper National Park, skirting dozens of stern peaks and glacial lakes. Free maps of the parkway are available at info centers in Jasper and Banff, or at the **Icefield Centre** (852-6288), at the boundary between the 2 parks, 132km north of Lake Louise and 103km south of Jasper Townsite (open May to mid-Oct. daily 9am-5pm). Although the center is closed in winter, the parkway is only closed for plowing after heavy snowfalls. An extensive campground and hostel network along the parkway makes longer trips along the length of Jasper and Banff convenient and affordable. **Cycling** the highway is also a popular option; bikes can be rented in Banff or Jasper for a 1-way trip.

However you travel the parkway, set aside time for hikes and magnificent vistas. At **Bow Summit,** 40km north of Lake Louise, the parkway's highest point (2135m, 7000ft.), a 10min. walk leads to a view of fluorescent aqua **Peyto Lake,** especially vivid toward the end of June. The Icefield Centre (see above) lies in the shadow of the tongue of the **Athabasca Glacier,** a great white whale of an ice flow that flows from the 325 sq. km **Coumbia Icefield,** the largest accumulation of ice and snow south of the Arctic Circle (yes, excepting Antarctica, smartypants). **Columbia Icefield Snocoach Tours** carries visitors right onto the glacier in bizarre monster buses for an 80min. trip. (877-423-7433; Apr.-Oct. daily 9am-5pm; $25, ages 6-15 $10). A 10min. walk leads up piles of glacial debris to the glacier's mighty toe. For tasty geological tidbits, sign up for a guided **Athabasca Glacier Icewalk** ("Ice Cubed" tour: 3hr.; $31; ages 7-17 $12. "Ice Walk Deluxe" tour": 5hr.; $37/16.) One of the 2 hikes runs each day at 11:30am (mid-June to mid-Sept.); contact the Icefield Centre or Peter Lemieux (852-3083).

## JASPER NATIONAL PARK

Northward expansion of the Canadian railway system led to the exploration of the Canadian Rockies and the creation of Jasper National Park in 1907. The largest of the 4 National Parks in the region, Jasper encompasses herculean peaks and plummeting valleys that dwarf the battalion of motorhomes and charter buses parading through the region. In the face of this annual bloat, Jasper Townsite's permanent residents struggle to keep their sheltered home looking and feeling like a genuine small town. In the winter, the crowds melt away, a blanket of snow descends, and a ski resort welcomes visitors to a slower, more relaxed town.

**PRACTICAL INFORMATION.** All of the addresses below are in **Jasper Townsite,** near the center of the park. **VIA Rail** (852-4102 or 800-561-8630) sends 3 trains per week from the station on Connaught Dr. to Vancouver, BC (16½hr., $151) and Edmonton ($88). **Greyhound** (852-3926), in the train station, runs to Edmonton (4½hr., 4 per day, $47) and Vancouver, BC (11½hr., 3 per day, $98). **Brewster Transportation Tours** (852-3332), in the station, runs daily to Calgary ($71) via Banff ($51). **Heritage Cabs,** 611 Patricia (852-5558), charges a flat rate of $8 to Jasper International Hostel or $14 to the Maligne Canyon Hostel (24hr.). The **Park Information Centre,** 500 Connaught Dr. (852-6176), has trail maps. (Open daily mid-June to early Sept. 8am-7pm; early Sept. to late Oct. and late Dec. to mid-June 9am-5pm.) **Emergency:** 852-4848. **Post Office:** 502 Patricia St. (852-3041), across from the townsite green (open M-F 9am-5pm). **Postal code:** T0E 1E0. **Area code:** 780.

WESTERN CANADA

**ACCOMMODATIONS AND FOOD.** HI-C runs a shuttle service connecting all the Rocky Mountain hostels and Calgary (1-way $7-65). The modern **Jasper International Hostel (HI-C),** 3km up Whistlers Rd. from Hwy. 93, 4km south of the townsite, also known as **Whistlers Hostel,** anchors a chain of HI hostels stretching from Jasper to Calgary. Attracts gregarious backpackers and cyclists, but a "leave-your-hiking-boots-outside" rule keeps the hardwood floors and spiffy dorm rooms clean. (852-3215 or 877-852-0781. $15, nonmembers $20. Curfew 2am.) **Sun Dog Shuttle** (852-8255) runs from the train station to the hostel on its way to the Jasper Tramway ($3). **Maligne Canyon Hostel (HI-C),** 11km east of town on Hwy. 16, has small, renovated cabins on the bank of the Maligne River, accessible to the Skyline

Trail and within cycling distance of Maligne Lake ($10, nonmembers $15; in winter $9/14; closed W Oct.-Apr.). **Mt. Edith Cavell Hostel (HI-C),** 12km up Edith Cavell Rd., off Hwy. 93, offers small but cozy quarters heated by wood-burning stoves. In winter, the road is closed; but you can pick up keys at Jasper International Hostel and ski uphill from the highway. (Propane light, pump water, solar shower, firepit. $10, nonmembers $15; in winter $9/$10.)

Most of Jasper's campgrounds have primitive sites with few facilities and outdoor paradise nearby ($13-22). They are first come, first served, so get there early. To build a fire, add $3-4. Call the park info center (852-6176) for details. None of the surrounding campgrounds are open in winter. A 781-site behemoth, **Whistlers,** on Whistlers Rd., 3km south of the townsite off Hwy. 93, is closest to the townsite ($17, full hookups $24; open early May to mid-Oct.). The highlight of the Icefields Pkwy. campgrounds is **Columbia Icefield,** 109km south of the townsite, which lies close enough to the Athabasca Glacier to intercept an icy breeze and even a rare summer night's snowfall. **Mountain Foods and Café,** 606 Connaught Dr., offers a wide selection of sandwiches, salads, and home-cooked goodies. (Wraps and sandwiches $5.50. 852-4050. Cheap beer after 5pm. Open daily 7am-midnight.)

**◢ OUTDOORS.** The info center in town distributes *Day Hikes in Jasper National Park.* Snow-capped **Mt. Edith Cavell** is an exceptionally rewarding ½-day hike. The trailhead is 30km south of the townsite; take Hwy. 93 to 93A to the end of the bumpy, twisty 15km Mt. Edith Cavell Rd. (open June-Oct.), where Angel Glacier hangs off the mountain's north face. To scale a peak in a day, climb the Sulpher **Skyline Trail,** a challenging 4- to 6-hr. hike (9.6km round-trip, 700m/2300ft. elevation gain) with views of the limestone Miette Range and Ashlar Ridge. The trail leaves all too conveniently from the **Miette Hot Springs,** 42km north of the townsite on Hwy. 16 and 15km along Miette Hot Springs Rd., blending chlorinated and filtered heat therapy with panoramic views. (Open daily May 19-June 21 and Sept. 5 to Oct. 9 10:30am-9pm; June 22 to Sept. 4 8:30am-10:30pm. $5.50; swimsuit $1.50.)

The spectacular if over-touristed **Maligne Canyon** (mah-LEEN) is 11.5km east of the townsite on Maligne Lake Rd. From the trailhead, a 4.2km path follows the Maligne River as it plunges through the narrow limestone gorge, across footbridges, and eventually into Medicine Lake. Brilliant turquoise **Maligne Lake,** the longest (22km) and deepest (97km) lake in the park, sprawls at the end of Maligne Lake Rd. The **Opal Hills Trail** (8.2km loop) winds through subalpine meadows and ascends 460m to views of the lake. **Maligne Tours,** 626 Connaught Dr., rents kayaks (½-day $30, full-day $60) and leads fishing canoeing, rabbiting, horseback riding, hiking and whitewater rafting tours (prices vary; 852-3370). Maligne Tours also offers **shuttle service** (to canyon $8; to lake $12).

The **Jasper Tramway,** 4km up Whistlers Rd., which is 4km south of the townsite on Hwy. 93, climbs 1200m/3950ft. up Whistlers Mt., leading to a panoramic view of the park and on a clear day, very far beyond. (852-3093. Open daily Apr.-Aug. 8:30am-10pm; Sept.-Oct. 9:30am-4:30pm. $15, under 14 $8.50, under 5 free.) The demanding 9km **Whistlers Trail** covers the same ground, beginning behind Jasper International Hostel's volleyball court. The **restaurant** up top allows hikers to experience the dizzying combination of alcohol and high-altitude oxygen deprivation.

For longer forays into the park, consult the free *Backcountry Visitor Guide,* available at the info center, or the *Canadian Rockies Trail Guide* ($15). Overnight hikers must register and pay a fee ($6 per night). Before hitting the trail, ask at the info center about road and trail closures, water levels, and snow levels.

**Rocky Mountain Unlimited** serves as a central reservation service for many local outdoor businesses. They provide prices and recommendations for rafting, fishing, horseback riding, and wildlife safaris. (842-4056. Open daily 9am-9pm; in winter 8am-6pm.) **Currie's,** in The Sports Shop, 406 Patricia St., rents fishing equipment and gives tips on good spots. (852-5650. Rod, reel, and line $10. 1-day boat or canoe rental $25, after 2pm $18, after 6pm $12. Pick-up and drop-off service available.) **Fishing permits** are available at fishing shops and the Parks Canada info center ($6 per week, $13 per year). The **Jasper Climbing School,** 806 Connaught Dr., offers an introductory 3hr. rappeling class; at least a small group is required (852-3964; $30, learning how to climb up is more expensive). Peter Amann teaches 2-day introductory **rockclimbing** courses (852-3237; May-June and Sept.; $150). In winter **Marmot Basin,** near Jasper townsite, opens up its slopes for **skiing** (852-3816; full-day $42, seniors $29, students $35, ages 6-12 $17). Bargain **ski rental** is available at **Totem's Ski Shop,** 408 Connaught Dr. (852-3078. Open daily 8am-6pm. Skis, boots, and poles $9 per day. Snowboard and boots from $25.)

## YOHO NATIONAL PARK, BC

A Cree expression for awe and wonder, Yoho is the perfect name for this uncrowded park across the BC/Alberta border from Banff. Beneath the rock walls of Yoho's narrow canyon, the park overflows with natural attractions, including the largest waterfall in the Rockies, the Continental Divide, and the Burgess Shale.

The town of **Field,** within the park, is 27km west of Lake Louise on Hwy. 1. **Greyhound** (800-661-8747) stops for travelers waving their arms on the highway. **Hosteling International** runs a shuttle connecting hostels in Yoho, Banff, and Jasper National Parks and Calgary ($7-65). The **visitor center** (250-343-6783) in Field is on Hwy. 1 (open daily 8:30am-7pm; in spring and fall 9am-5pm; in winter 9am-4pm). Call the **Park Warden,** 403-762-4506; 24hr. or **RCMP,** 250-344-2221, in Golden, for emergencies.

The ⊠ **Whiskey Jack Hostel (HI),** 13km off the Trans-Canada on the Yoho Valley Rd., at the base of the Takakaw falls, has one of the best locations of all the Rocky Mountain hostels. Nightly campfires, indoor plumbing, propane light, and trail access seal the deal. (Beds $14, nonmembers $18; open June to mid-Oct.) Reserve through the Banff hostel (403-762-4122). Five **frontcountry campgrounds** offer 330 sites, all accessible from the highway. All are first-come, first-served, and only Monarch and Kicking Horse fill up regularly in summer. The gem of Yoho's campsites is the **Takakaw Falls Campground,** beneath mountains, glaciers, and the magnificent falls 14km up curvy Yoho Valley Rd. Campers must park in the lot and haul their gear 650m to the peaceful sites (35 sites: $13; open late June to late Sept.).

The **Great Divide** is both the boundary between Alberta and BC and between the Atlantic and Pacific watersheds. It is also the site of the **Burgess Shale,** a layer of sedimentary rock containing "the world's most important animal fossils," discovered in 1909. Hikes led by the **Yoho-Burgess Shale Foundation** (800-343-3006) are the only way to see the shale. A full-day, 20km hike costs $45. A steep 6km loop to the **Mt. Stephen Fossil Beds** runs $25. (July to mid-Sept. Reservations required.)

Before setting out into the backcountry, pick up **permits** ($6 per person per day) at the visitor center. The park's finest terrain, in the Yoho Valley, is accessible only after the snow melts in mid- to late summer. The **Iceline Trail,** starting at the hostel (10.6km one-way, or a shorter 15km loop), rewards with views of glaciers.

## CALGARY

Mounties founded Calgary in the 1870s to control the flow of illegal whiskey, but another liquid—oil—made this city great. Petroleum fuels Calgary's economy; the city holds the most corporate headquarters in Canada outside of Toronto. Calgary's dot on the map grew larger when it hosted the 1988 Winter Olympics; it is now Canada's 2nd-fastest-growing city. The world-class Calgary Stampede, the "Greatest Outdoor Show on Earth," garbs the city in cowboy duds every July.

⌘ **PRACTICAL INFORMATION.** Calgary is divided into quadrants (NE, NW, SE, SW): **Centre St.** is the east-west divider; the **Bow River** splits the north and south sections. **Avenues** run east-west, **streets** run north-south, and numbers count up from the divides. Cross streets can be derived by disregarding the last two digits of the first number: 206 7th Ave. SW would be in the SW quadrant on 7th Ave. at 2nd St. **Calgary International Airport** is about 6km northwest of city center. Bus #57 provides sporadic service from the airport to downtown. The **Airporter Bus** (531-3907) goes to major hotels downtown (6:30am-11:30pm, $8.50), and sometimes makes unscheduled stops. **Greyhound,** 877 Greyhound Way SW (265-9111 or 800-661-8747), runs to Edmonton (3½hr., 10 per day, $40); Banff (2hr., 4 per day, $19); and Drumheller (1½hr., 2 per day, $21). **Brewster Tours** (221-8242) runs from the airport or downtown to Banff (2½hr., 3 per day, $36) and Jasper (7hr., 1 per day, $71) and offers a 15% HI discount. **Calgary Transit,** 240 7th Ave. SW (262-1000), runs **C-Trains,** which are free in the downtown zone. (Bus fare and C-Trains outside downtown $1.60, ages 6-14 $1; day pass $5/$3; 10 tickets $13.50/$8.50. Runs M-F 6am-11pm, Sa-Su 8:30am-9:30pm.) **Checker Cab** (299-9999) runs 24hr. **Rent-A-Wreck,** 113 42nd Ave. SW (287-1444), charges $30 per day, 12¢ per km over 200km (must be 21 with credit card; open M-Sa 8am-6:30pm, Su 9am-5pm). The **Visitor Service Centre,** 131 9th Ave. SW (750-2397), is under the Calgary Tower and open daily 8am-5pm. **Internet access** at the Calgary hostel runs $1 per 10min. **Post Office:** 207 9th Ave. SW (974-2078; open M-F 8am-5:45pm). **Postal code:** T2P 2G8. **Area code:** 403.

■■■ **ACCOMMODATIONS, FOOD, AND NIGHTLIFE.** Contact the **B&B Association of Calgary** for info and availability (543-3900; singles from $35; doubles from $50). The ✿ **Calgary International Hostel (HI-C),** 520 7th Ave. SE, is several blocks east of downtown. Go east along 7th Ave. from the 3rd St. SE C-Train station; the hostel is on the left just past 4th St. SE. (269-8239. Kitchen, game room, hang-out areas, laundry, email, and barbecue facilities. $16, nonmembers $20. Linen $1. Free city tours on M. Open 24hr. Wheelchair accessible.) **University of Calgary,** in the NW quadrant, has rooms booked through **Kananaskis Hall,** 3330 24th Ave., a 12min. walk from the University C-Train stop. The university is out of the way, but easily accessible via bus #9 or the C-Train. (220-3203). Shared rooms $20; singles $32, with student ID $23; doubles $39/$32. Suites with private bathrooms about $35. Open 24hr. Rooms available May-Aug. only.)

Downtown's grub is concentrated in the **Stephen Ave. Mall,** S. 8th Ave. between 1st St. SE and 3rd St. SW. The cheapest, most satisfying food is located in its tiny Chinatown, the two square blocks at the north end of Centre St. S and 1st St. SE. Five dollars buys a feast in Vietnamese noodle-houses and Hong-Kong style cafes, many of which don't close until 3 or 4am. **Kaffa Coffee and Salsa House,** 2138 33rd Ave. SW (240-9133), cooks up a fresh soup every day, and a different salsa and salad every week (burritos $6-7; open M-F 7am-midnight, Sa 8am-midnight, Su 8am-10pm). At **Thi-Thi Submarine,** 209 1st St. SE, a smaller hole-in-the-wall than most mice call home, $2.50 will buy a 10-inch "super-sub" with three kinds of pork, chicken, cilantro, carrots, cucumbers, and special sauce, served hot on a fresh baguette. The veggie sub is a ludicrous $1.50. (265-5452. Open daily 10am-7pm.)

**The Nightgallery,** 1209B 1st St. SW, attracts scenesters with one large dance floor, one bar, and one oversized disco ball. The club breaks out the best House in town at "Sunday School" and on Th. Reggae-Dub draws a slightly older crowd M. (269-5924. Cover $5, $1.50 doubles before 11:00pm. Open daily 7:30pm-3am.) **The Ship and Anchor,** 534 17th Ave. SW, is the meeting place for the city's young and beautiful scurvy dogs (245-3333; open daily noon-2:30am).

🔆 **SIGHTS.** Over a decade later, Calgary still clings to its two weeks of Olympic stardom at the **Canada Olympic Park,** 10min. west of downtown on Hwy. 1, site of the four looming ski jumps and the quick bobsled and luge tracks. *(247-5452. Open daily 8am-9pm.)* The **Olympic Hall of Fame** honors Olympic achievements with displays, films, and bobsled and ski-jumping simulators. In summer, the park opens its hills to mountain bikers. Take the **lift** up the hill, then cruise down—no work necessary. *(247-5452. Open daily 9am-9pm; $3.75, seniors and students $3, under 6 free. Park open daily May-Sept. 10am-9pm. $7 ticket includes chair lift and entrance to ski jump buildings. Guided tour $10. Hill pass $6 for cyclists. Bike rental $6 per hr., $24 per day.)*

The **Glenbow Museum** brings rocks and minerals, Buddhist and Hindu art, and native Canadian history under one roof. *(130 9th Ave. SE. 268-4100. Open Sa-W 9am-5pm, Th-F 9am-9pm. $8, seniors and students $6, under 6 free. HI discount.)* Footbridges stretch from either side of the Bow River to **Prince's Island Park,** a natural refuge blocks from the city center. Calgary's other island park, **St. George's Island,** is accessible by the river walkway to the east, and houses the **Calgary Zoo.** *(232-9300. Gates open daily in summer 9am-8pm; in winter 9am-4pm. Grounds open 9am-9pm; Oct.-Apr. 9am-5:30pm. $10, children $5, seniors ½-price Tu and Th; in winter $8, seniors and children $4. AAA and HI discounts.)* On July 7-16, 2000, 1 million cowboys and tourists will converge on **Stampede Park,** just southeast of downtown, bordering the east side of Macleod Trail between 14th and 25th Ave. SE. For 10 days, the grounds are packed for world-class steer wrestling, saddle bronc, bareback- and bull-riding, pig racing, wild-cow-milking, and chuckwagon races. A **free pancake breakfast** is served at a different location in the city each day. Parking is ample and reasonably priced, but can get tedious. Take the C-Train to the Stampede stop or walk. *(269-9822 or 800-661-1767. Gate admission $9; seniors and ages 7-12 $4. Rodeo and evening cost $19-50; if not sold out, rush tickets are $9, at the grandstand 1½hr. before showtime.)*

## ALBERTA BADLANDS

In the late Cretaceous period, these were the fertile shores of an inland sea, conditions that have created one of the richest dinosaur fossil sites in the world. Once the sea dried up, wind, water, and ice cut twisting canyons down into the sandstone and shale bedrock, creating the desolate splendor of the Alberta Badlands. The **Royal Tyrrell Museum of Paleontology** (TEER-ull) lies on the **North Dinosaur Trail (Secondary Hwy. 838),** 6km northwest of **Drumheller** (drum-HELL-er), which itself lies 138km northeast of Calgary. Get there by driving east on Hwy. 1 and northeast on Hwy. 9. The museum is the world's largest display of dinosaur specimens . (403-823-7707 or 888-440-4240. Open daily 9am-9pm; Labour Day to Victoria Day Tu-Su 10am-5pm. $6.50, seniors $5.50, ages 7-17 $3; in winter ½-price Tu.) The museum's immensely popular 12-person **Day Digs** include instruction in paleontology and excavation techniques, and a chance to dig in a dinosaur quarry. The fee includes lunch and transportation, but all finds go to the museum. (Daily July-Aug. 8:30am, returning at 4:30pm. $85, ages 10-15 $55. Reservations required.) The **Field Station Badlands Bus Tour,** 48km east of the town of **Brooks** in **Dinosaur Provincial Park,** chauffeurs visitors into a restricted hot spot of dinosaur finds. (378-4342. Field station open daily May 24-Sept. 6 8:30am-9pm; call for winter hrs. Tours May 24-Oct. 11 2-8 per day; $4.50, ages 6-15 $2.25.)

    **Alexandra Hostel (HI-C),** 30 Railway Ave. N, has 55 beds in a converted hotel that hasn't changed much since the 30s, sporting a kitchen, laundry, and little else in the way of hospitality (823-6337; $17.50, nonmembers $20; check-in 10am-11pm). The hostel also rents **mountain bikes. River Grove Campground,** off North Dinosaur Trail at the intersection with Hwy. 9, has flush toilets, free showers, and laundry. (Tent sites $18.50, full hookup $25.50. Cabins for 2-10 people, with bathrooms, electricity, and cable TV $50-100. Open daily May to Sept. 7am-11pm.) **Greyhound** runs from Calgary to **Drumheller** (1½hr., 2 per day, $21), which is 6km southeast of the museum. From Drumheller, it's about a 20min. bike ride to the museum from the hostel.

**THE WAY WE WERE** The original *Let's Go: USA and Canada* was published by Harvard Student Agencies in 1969, and ran until discontinued in 1973. The book as you and I know it now was revived in 1979, when Euro-centric backpackers decided that North America made a decent tourist stop. But here, from the days at our first run of domestic bliss, the "Yukon and Northwest Territories":

    *Utter wilderness. Here the bears run free, so be prepared. The site of the gold booms and rushes of the late 1890s, Canada's north beckons the hearty pioneer. There are few roads; the only road of any length is the gravel **Alaska Highway**. There are no telephones, few people, and jobs are often scarce.*

# ALASKA

Alaska's beauty and intrigue are born of extremes: North America's highest mountains and broadest flatlands; windswept tundra and lush rainforests; 586,412 sq. mi. (over one-fifth of the land mass of the U.S.); and 15 incredible national parks cover an area roughly equal to that of England and Ireland combined. The U.S. bought Alaska for about 2¢ per acre in 1867, from a Russia deep in debt after losing the Crimean War. Critics mocked "Seward's Folly," named after the Secretary of State who negotiated the deal, but just 15 years after the purchase, huge deposits of gold were unearthed in the Panhandle's Gastineau Channel. Prospectors quickly struck gold in rivers such as the Yukon, Charley, Fortymile, and Klondike.

The Trans-Alaska Pipeline, running 800mi. through the heart of the Alaskan wilderness, has had a revolutionary effect on the state's political, social, and economic landscape since its construction in 1977. In August of 1998, the federal government gave the go-ahead for drilling in about one-fifth of the National Petroleum Reserve's 23 million acres. Environmentalists argue that drilling will disrupt the pristine wilderness, while oil companies want the entire area to be opened.

For more comprehensive coverage of Alaska and its arctic allures, see *Let's Go: Alaska & the Pacific Northwest, Including Western Canada 2000.*

## HIGHLIGHTS OF ALASKA

■ **Natural Wonders.** Denali National Park (p. 928) is the state's crown jewel. Wrangell-St. Elias National Park (p. 927) houses massive glaciers, while Glacier Bay National Park (p. 935) basks in a symphony of sea and ice.
■ **Wildlife.** Cruises out of Seward into Kenai Fjords National Park (p. 926) are stuffed with opportunities to view sea critters.
■ **Recreation.** Southeast Alaska's grandest features include kayaking in Misty Fiords National Monument (p. 933), climbing Deer Mountain in Ketchikan (p. 931), and hiking the West Glacier Trail in Juneau (p. 934).

## ⊠ PRACTICAL INFORMATION

**Capital:** Juneau.

**Visitor Info: Alaska Division of Tourism,** P.O. Box 110801, Juneau 99811-0801 (907-465-2010; www.dced.state.ak.us/tourism). **Alaska Department of Fish & Game, Division of Wildlife Conservation,** P.O. Box 25526 Juneau, AK 99802-5526 (907-465-4190; www.state.ak.us/local/akpages/FISH.GAME/wildlife/wildmain.htm).

**Postal Abbreviation:** AK. **Sales Tax:** 0%.

## CLIMATE

Weather varies from the coast inland. Anchorage temperatures range from 8°F in winter to 65°F in summer. In Alaska's interior, the temperature ranges from around 70°F in summer to -30°F and lower in winter. Progressing farther north, summer days and winter nights become longer. North of the Arctic Circle, the sun does not set at all on the nights around the summer solstice in late June, nor does it rise on the days around the winter solstice in December.

## ⊡ GETTING AROUND

The **Alaska Railroad Corporation (ARRC)** (800-544-0552), covers 470mi. from Seward to Fairbanks, with stops in Anchorage and Whittier. The **Alaska Marine Hwy.,** P.O. Box 25535, Juneau 99802-5535 (800-642-0066), remains the most practical and enjoyable way to explore much of the Panhandle, Prince William Sound, and the

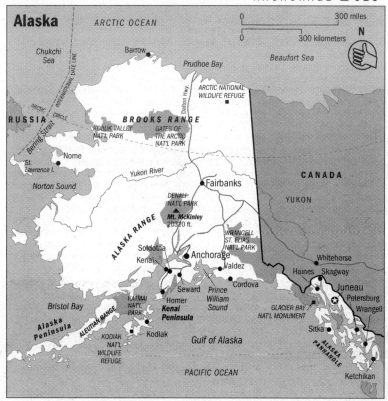

Kenai Peninsula. The **AlaskaPass,** P.O. Box 351, Vashon, WA 98070-0351 (800-248-7598 or 206-463-6550), offers unlimited access to Alaska's railroad, ferry, and bus systems (15 days $699; 30 days $949; 21 non-consecutive days over a 45-day period $999). Most of the state's major **highways** are known by their name as often as their number (George Parks Hwy.=Rt. 3=The Parks). Driving to and through Alaska is not for the faint of car; highways reward drivers with stunning views and access to true wilderness, but they barely scratch the surface of the massive state. See p. 908 for the two major highway approaches into the state from points south. For Alaska's most remote destinations, **air travel** is an expensive necessity. Intrastate airlines and charter services, many of them based at the busy Anchorage airport, transport passengers and cargo to virtually every village in Alaska. Many are listed in the relevant **Practical Information** sections.

# ANCHORAGE

Alaska's only metropolis, Anchorage is home to 254,000 people—two-fifths of the state's population. As far north as Helsinki and almost as far west as Honolulu, the city achieved its large size (2000 sq. mi.) by hosting three major economic projects: the Alaska Railroad, WWII military developments, and the Trans-Alaska Pipeline. Anchorage serves as a good place to get oriented and stock up on supplies before journeying to the breathtaking wilderness just outside.

## 🛈 PRACTICAL INFORMATION

Downtown Anchorage is laid out in a grid: Numbered **avenues** run east-west, with addresses designated east or west from **C St.** North-south **streets** are lettered alphabetically to the west and named alphabetically to the east of **A St.** The rest of Anchorage spreads out along major highways.

Most Alaskan airstrips can be reached from **Anchorage International Airport** (266-2437) either directly or through a connection in Fairbanks; the *Daily News* lists second-hand tickets. **Yellow Cab** (272-2422) charges about $15 from the airport to the downtown hostel (24hr.). **Alaska Railroad,** 411 W. 1st Ave. (265-2494, outside AK 800-544-0552), runs to Denali (8hr., $102); Fairbanks (12hr., $154); and Seward (4hr., in summer only, $50). Flagstops anywhere along route; wave the bus down with a white cloth. (Ticket window open M-F 5:30am-5pm, Sa-Su 5:30am-1pm.) **Grayline Alaska** (800-544-2206) sends buses daily to Seward (4hr., $40); Valdez (10hr., $66); and Portage (2hr., $40); and 3 times per week to Haines ($189) and Skagway ($209), both overnight. **Parks Hwy. Express** (479-3065, in AK 888-600-6001) runs buses daily to Denali ($30) and Fairbanks ($49). **Alaska Marine Hwy.,** 605 W. 4th Ave. (800-642-0066), sells ferry tickets (open in winter M-F 9am-5:30pm). **People Mover Bus** (343-6543), in the Transit Center on 6th Ave. between G and H St., sends local buses all over the Anchorage area. (Runs M-F 6am-10pm; restricted schedule Sa-Su; $1, ages 5-18 50¢, over 65 25¢; tokens 90¢; day passes $2.50. Office open M-F 8am-5pm.) **Airport Car Rental,** 502 W. Northern Lights Blvd. (277-7662) charges $45 per day, with unlimited mi. (Must be 21+; under 25 surcharge $5 per day; cash or credit card deposit required. Open M-F 8am-8pm, Sa-Su 9am-6pm.)

The **Log Cabin Visitor Information Center** (274-3531, events 276-3200), on W. 4th Ave. at F St., sells a 50¢ bike guide (open daily June-Aug. 7:30am-7pm; May and Sept. 8am-6pm; Oct.-Apr. 9am-4pm). The **Alaska Public Lands Information Center,** Old Federal Building, 605 W. 4th Ave. (271-2737 or 271-2738), between F and G St., combines the Park, Forest, State Parks, and Fish and Wildlife Services under one roof (open daily 9am-5:30pm). **Challenge Alaska** (344-7399) refers services for the disabled. **Internet access: Surf City Cafe,** 415 L. St. (12¢ per min.). **Post Office:** W. 4th Ave. and C St., on the lower level in the yellow mall (open M-F 10am-5:30pm). **ZIP code:** 99510. **Area code:** 907.

# ACCOMMODATIONS AND FOOD

**Alaska Private Lodgings** (258-1717; call M-Sa 8am-7pm) or the **Anchorage reservation service** (272-5909) arrange out-of-town B&Bs (from $65). Two of the best campgrounds in **Chugach State Park** (354-5014) are **Eagle River** ($15; 12½mi. from town) and **Eklutna** ($10; 36½mi. northeast of town) along Glenn Hwy. Both fill up early, especially on weekends.

◙ **Spenard Hostel,** 2845 W. 42nd Pl., is comfortable, clean, and welcoming. Take bus #36 or #7 from downtown, or #6 from the airport down Spenard to Turnagain Blvd.; 42nd Pl. is the first left from Turnagain. (248-5036. 3 kitchens, free local calls, bike rental $5, laundry, lockers, Denali Shuttle drop-off/pick-up. Beds or tent sites $15. No curfew or lockout. Chore requested. Check-in 9am-1pm and 7-11pm. 6-night max. stay.) **Qupqugiaq Inn,** 640 W. 36th Ave., between Arctic Blvd. and C St, has well-lit rooms with locks. Take bus #9. (563-5633. Common lounge and kitchen, shared bath, cable TV. No smoking or alcohol. Singles from $39; doubles $49. Check-in noon-7pm and 10pm-2am.) **Anchorage International Youth Hostel (HI-AYH),** 700 H St. at 7th St., 1 block south of the city bus station on the edge of downtown—you can't beat the location, but facilities are only adequate. (276-3635. Kitchens, TV, balconies, lockers, and laundry. $15, nonmembers $18. Lockout noon-5pm. Curfew 1am; reception until 2am. Chore requested. 5-night max. stay in summer. Pay by 11am or lose your spot. Book in advance.)

◙ **Moose's Tooth,** 3300 Old Seward (bus #2 or 36), serves pizza (small spinach $9) and brews as hearty as the climbers who tackle the nearby peak. (258-2537. Local bands Th; open mic M 9-11pm. Open M-Th 11am-midnight, F-Sa noon-1am, Su noon-midnight.) **Twin Dragon,** 612 E. 15th Ave. near Gambel (bus #11), offers an all-you-can-eat buffet of marinated meats and vegetables, hot off the giant grill. (Lunch $7; BBQ and Chinese food buffet $1.; 276-7535. Open M-Sa 11am-midnight, Su 1pm-midnight.) **Side Street Espresso,** 412 G St., is a gathering hole for the hip and

## DOES THE WORD "MUSH" MEAN ANYTHING TO YOU?

Charlie Darwin would have liked these odds: snow, wind, and frigid cold, separating the women from the girls. The celebrated Iditarod dog sled race begins in Anchorage on the first weekend in March. Dogs and their drivers ("mushers") traverse a 1150mi. trail over two mountain ranges, along the mighty Yukon River, and over the frozen Norton Sound to Nome. The Iditarod Trail began as a dog sled supply route from Seward on the southern coast to interior mining towns. The race commemorates the 1925 rescue of Nome, when drivers ferried 300,000 units of life-saving diptheria serum from Nenana, near Fairbanks, to Nome. Today, up to 70 contestants speed each year from Anchorage to Nome, competing for a $450,000 purse but surprisingly willing to help fellow mushers in distress. The fastest time up to now was recorded by Doug Swingley—9 days, 2hr. You can visit the **Iditarod Headquarters** at Mi. 2.2 Knik Rd. in Wasilla.

the yup, with political salons, frequent acoustic music, a decent book exchange, and bound copies of local writers' efforts. (Cappuccino $2.25; Thai iced tea $1.50. 258-9055. Open M-Sa 7am-5pm, Su 8am-5pm.)

## SIGHTS, OUTDOORS, AND NIGHTLIFE

Near town off Northern Lights Blvd., **Earthquake Park** recalls the 1964 Good Friday quake, the strongest ever recorded in North America, registering 9.2 on the Richter scale. At the **Anchorage Museum of History and Art,** 121 W. 7th Ave., at A St., permanent Native Alaskan artifacts and art mingle with national and international works. (343-6061. Open daily Su-F 9am-9pm, Sa 9am-6pm; Sept.-May Tu-Sa 10am-6pm, Su 1pm-5pm. Tours daily at 10, 11am, 1, and 2pm. $5, seniors $4.50, under 18 free.) At the **Alaska Zoo,** Mi. 2 on O'Malley Rd., Binky the polar bear mauled an Australian tourist in 1994 and became a local hero. *Let's Go does not recommend attempting to endear yourself to locals by maiming tourists.* (346-3242. Open daily 9am-6pm. $7, seniors $6, ages 12-18 $4, 3-11 $3. Bus #2 there, #91 back.)

The 11mi. **Tony Knowles Coastal Trail** is arguably one of the best urban bike paths in the country; in the winter, it's groomed for **cross-country skiing.** The serene **Chugach State Park,** cornering the city to the north, east, and south, has **public use cabins** (800-280-2267; $25 per night; $8.25 reservation fee) and 25 established **day hiking** trails. A 15min. drive from the city center, **Flattop Mountain** (4500 ft.) is the most frequently climbed mountain in Alaska, providing an excellent view of the inlet, the Aleutian Chain, and on the rare clear day, Denali. Parking at the trailhead costs $5, or take bus #92 to Hillside Rd. and Upper Huffman Rd. From there, the trailhead is a ¾mi. walk along Upper Huffman Rd., then right on Toilsome Hill Dr. for 2mi.; it's a 2mi. hike to the summit. Less frequented hikes branch from the **Powerline Trail,** which begins at the same parking lot as the Flattop Trail. The **Middle Fork Loop,** ¾mi. off of Powerline, leads a gentle 12mi. through spruce woods and open tundra. The **Eklutna Lakeside Biking Trail** extends 13mi. one-way from the Eklutna Campground, off Mi. 26 of the Glenn Hwy. (Rt. 1). A relatively flat dirt road, the trail follows the blue-green Eklutna Lake for 7mi. before entering a steep river canyon, ending at the base of the Eklutna River. **Nancy Lake State Recreation Area,** just west of the Parks Hwy. (Rt. 3) at Mi. 67.3, and just south of **Willow,** contains the **Lynx Lake Canoe Loop,** which takes 2 days and weaves through 8mi. of lakes and portages, with designated campsites along the way. The loop begins at Mi. 4.5 of the Nancy Lake Parkway, at the Tanaina Lake Canoe Trailhead. For **canoe rental** or **shuttle service** in the Nancy Lake Area, call **Tippecanoe** (495-6688; canoes $25 1st day, $70 per week; shuttle free for backpackers).

The brew pub revolution has hit Anchorage, and microbrews gush from taps like oil through the pipeline. At **Bernie's Bungalow Lounge,** 626 D St., relax in one of many wingback chairs or couches as you sip your lemon drop martini ($5), puff on a

ALASKA

cigar, and play a round of croquet in a hotspot frequented by the young and retro (276-8808; open M-Th 2pm-2:30am, F-Sa 2pm-3am, Su noon-2:30am). **Chilkoot Charlie's,** 2435 Spenard Rd., at Fireweek, bus #7 has cavernous dance floors and top 40/ rock music. "Koots" is the place to dance into the night. Dollar drink specials until 10pm. Escalating cover from 8pm ($2-5; open Su-Th 10:30am-2:30am, F-Sa 11am-3am). The cry for good live music is answered daily at 9:30pm at **Blues Central,** 825 Northern Lights Blvd., at the corner of Artic St.; take bus #9. (Microbrews $4.50, gutter cocktails $3. 272-1341. Open M-F 11am-2am, Sa-Su 5pm-2am. Cover Tu-Th $2, F-Sa $3, Su free.)

# SEWARD AND KENAI FJORDS

Seward is yet another of Alaska's super-scenic coastal towns, drawing hikers, kayakers, sailors, anglers, and cruise lines. Giving visitors a glimpse at Alaska's coastal and underwater goings-on, is the **Alaska SeaLife Center,** at the end of downtown between 3rd and 4th Ave. (224-3080 or 800-224-2525. Open May-Sept. daily 8am-8pm; in winter W-Su 10am-5pm. $12.50, seniors $11.25, ages 7-12 $10.) Next door, the **Chugach Heritage Center,** 501 Railway Ave., houses a theater and a gallery of Native Alaskan art. Half-hour performances every hour serve to educate the public and to preserve native culture. (224-5065. Open Tu-Su 10am-8pm. $8, ages 4-16 $6.50.)

Seward serves as gateway to the waterways and yawning ice fields of **Kenai Fjords National Park. Exit Glacier,** the only road-accessible glacier in the park, lies 9mi. west on a spur from Mi. 3.7 of the Seward Hwy. (Rt. 9). A **shuttle** (224-8747) runs here 4 times daily from downtown Seward (round-trip $10); parking for the day is $5. Beyond this glacier, boat cruises are the easiest and most popular way to see the park. **Kenai Fjords Tours** are informative and amusing. (224-8068 or 800-478-8068; 6-9½hr.; $100-139, children $50-60). **Major Marine Tours** brings along a ranger to explain wildlife and glacier facts, and serves a salmon, halibut, and shellfish dinner for $10 extra (224-8030 or 800-764-7300; 8hr.; $99). **Wildlife Quest** is the only outfit with speedy catamarans (5½hr.; $99, children $49; includes free pass to SeaLife Center). **Sunny Cove Sea Kayaking** (345-5339) offers a joint trip with Kenai Fjords Tours, including the wildlife cruise, a salmon bake, kayaking instruction, and a 2½hr. wilderness paddle ($139).

🖾 **Kate's Roadhouse,** 5½mi. outside town on the Seward Hwy., has huge continental breakfasts with home-baking and a quietly sleeping pig in the sitting room. (224-5888. Free shuttle service, laundry, bedding, and towels. Shared baths. Clean dorms $17, private rooms $59, 4 private cabins with electricity, cable TV, and heat $29-49.) **Ballaine House Lodging,** 437 3rd Ave. at Madison St., 2 blocks from downtown, is bright, clean, and well-furnished, with pleasant rooms and a scrumptious breakfast. (224-2362. Singles $60; doubles $84; lower rates without breakfast. Free laundry with notice. Pick-up and drop-off.) You can camp at the **Munical Waterfront Campground,** along Ballaine Rd. between Railway Ave. and D St. (Sites $6; RV sites $10, hookups $15. 2-week max stay. Check-out 4pm. Open May 15-Sept. 30.) **Miller's Daughter,** 1215 4th Ave., has organic, fat-free, and herbivore-friendly food (tuna salad sandwich $4.50; 224-6091; open daily 7am-7pm).

Seward is 127mi. south of Anchorage on the scenic **Seward Hwy. (Rt. 9).** Most services and outdoor outfits cluster in the small boat harbor on **Resurrection Bay.** Across from the visitor center at the **Alaska Railroad** depot, trains leave for Anchorage at 6:45am in summer (800-544-0552; 4½hr.; $50, ages 2-11 $25). **Seward Bus Lines,** 1914 Seward Hwy. (224-3608), runs to Anchorage (1 per day at 9am, $30; airport service $5). The **Alaska Marine Hwy.** (224-5485, reservations 800-642-0066) docks at 4th Ave. and Railway St., running three per month in summer to Valdez (11hr., $58) and Homer (25hr., $96). The **Seward Chamber of Commerce** (224-8051) is at Mi. 2 on the Seward Hwy. (open M-F 8am-5pm, Sa-Su 9am-4pm). **Kenai Fjords National Park Visitor Center** (224-3175, info 224-2134) is at the small-boat harbor (open daily 8am-7pm; in winter M-F 9am-5pm). **Post Office:** (224-3001), at 5th Ave. and Madison St. (open M-F 9:30am-4:30pm, Sa 10am-2pm). **ZIP code:** 99664. **Area code:** 907.

# WRANGELL-ST. ELIAS

**Wrangell-St. Elias National Park** is the largest national park in the U.S. (13.2 million acres). Beyond towering peaks and extensive glaciers, Wrangell teems with wildlife. With only two rough roads that penetrate its interior, and almost no established trails, the park's inaccessibility keeps many tourists away. **Ranger stations** lurk exclusively outside the park boundaries in **Copper Center** (822-7261), south of Glennallen (open 8am-6pm); **Yakutat** (784-3295; open 8am-5pm), in the east; **Chitina** (823-2205; open daily 10am-6pm) in the west; and **Slana** (822-5238; open 8am-5pm), on the park's northern boundary. They have the lowdown on all the must-knows and go-sees of the park, and sell invaluable topographical maps (entire park $9; quadrants $4). **Backcountry Connection** (822-5292 or 800-478-5292) runs **buses** daily from Glennallen (4hr.; 7am; $65, round-trip $105) and Chitina (3hr.; 8:30am; $50, round-trip $90) to McCarthy. **Charter flights** from McCarthy or Nabesna start at around $60 per person (one-way).

One of the park's access routes is the scenic **Nabesna Rd.**, extending a grueling 46mi. (1½hr.) from the Richardson Hwy. (Rt. 4) into the park's northern portion. The turn-off for the road is at **Slana** (rhymes with "bandana"), 65mi. southwest of Tok on the Tok Cutoff. **Nabesna**, at the end of the 42mi. road, is little more than a mining ghost town, where the **End-of-the-Road Bed and Breakfast** (822-5312, last-ditch messages 822-3426) has bunks ($20), singles ($55), and doubles ($65).

The more harrowing **McCarthy Rd.** plunges 60mi. (3hr.) into the park from Chitina (CHIT-nuh) to the western edge of the Kennicott River, where travelers must cross a footbridge and walk ½mi. into the town of **McCarthy.** Free parking is available another ½mi. back before the river. Deep in the heart of the park, McCarthy and its sister town **Kennicott** are quiet today, but abandoned log-hewn buildings and forgotten roads bear witness to a boom town past. **Wrangell Mountain Air** (554-4411 or 800-478-1160) flies to McCarthy daily from Chitina at 9:05am and 2:45pm (round-trip $130). Regular **shuttle buses** run the 5mi. from McCarthy to Kennicott; the river's tram station carries schedules, with copies posted throughout both towns (10am-8:30pm; round-trip $10). The newly opened **Kennicott River Lodge and Hostel**, P.O. Box 83225, Fairbanks 99708 (554-4441, in winter 479-6822), right before the footbridge at Mi. 58.7 (look for sign), offers several pine-fresh cabins ($25; no linens) with comfortable beds and a striking view of Kennicott River and Glacier. The only indoor alternative across the bridge is the **McCarthy Lodge** (554-4402; singles $95; doubles $110). Non-guests can shower ($5) at the lodge, or breakfast (7am-10am; $4-9) and sup ($15-23, served at 7pm; reservations required) in a rustic dining room with antique-covered walls (open daily 7am-10pm; bar opens at 5pm). **Camping** is free at the lot ½mi. back along the road toward Chitina (pit toilets, no water). Scrumptious, cheap feasts are served at **Roadside Potato Head**, in a colorfully decorated van by the tram station (554-1234; burritos $6; open daily 11am-9pm).

This is the place for flightseeing in Alaska. Even a short flight to 16,390 ft. Mt. Blackburn and the surrounding glaciers offers soul-stunning views. **Wrangell Mountain Air** (554-4411, reservations 800-478-1160) makes a 35min. tour of the amazing icefalls of the **Kennicott** and **Root Glaciers** ($50). The best bargain, a 70min. trip,

---

# OLD PILOTS AND BOLD PILOTS, BUT NO OLD BOLD PILOTS

Alaska has the highest per capita ownership of small planes, the greatest number of pilots, the greatest number of float planes, and in Anchorage, one of the nation's busiest airports. Throughout much of the interior, small planes aren't simply the best way to get there—they're the only way. Some of the state's most colorful lore is steeped in aviation—like the story of Alaska's 3rd governor, who broke both ankles crash-landing his small plane to avoid endangering the children playing on the airstrip. Tales of unusual landings are as common as tales of unusual cargo: Bush pilots have been known to transport canoes, beer, furniture, and even moose to the farthest reaches of the state.

ALASKA

goes up the narrow **Chitistone Canyon** to view the thundering **Chitistone Falls,** over 15 glaciers, and five mountain peaks ($95). There is a 2-person minimum on all flights. **Copper Oar** (800-523-4453), at the end of the McCarthy Rd., runs a 2hr. **white-water rafting** trip down the Class III Kennicott River ($45). **St. Elias Alpine Guides** (in McCarthy 554-4445; in Anchorage 888-933-5427) lead a variety of guided hikes and explorations. The park maintains **no trails** around McCarthy; consult with a ranger station before setting out. Ranger stations need a **written itinerary** for independent overnight trips. **Area code:** 907.

# DENALI NATIONAL PARK AND PRESERVE

9000 sq. mi. of snow-capped peaks, braided streams, and glacier-carved valleys, interrupted only by a lone gravel road, **Denali National Park and Preserve** is not a place made for humans; nevertheless, more than a million visitors invite themselves here year after year. And why not? Such untamed, beautiful wilderness is hard to find. Visitors to the park are guests of grizzly bears, moose, caribou, wolves, Dall sheep, raptors, and wildflowers. Denali's 20,320 ft. centerpiece, called Mt. McKinley by the U.S. Geological Survey, but known to locals as Denali or "the Mountain" is the world's tallest mountain from base to peak. Mid to late Aug. is the best time to visit—fall colors peak, berries ripen, mosquito season is virtually over, and Sept. snows have not yet arrived.

**⚐ PRACTICAL INFORMATION.** The **George Parks Hwy.** (Rt. 3) makes for smooth and easy traveling to the park entrance north from Anchorage (240mi., 4hr.) or south from Fairbanks (120mi., 3hr.). Leading east away from the park, the gravel **Denali Hwy.** (Rt. 8) starts 27mi. south of the park entrance at Cantwell, and proceeds 136mi. to Paxson (closed in winter). The **Alaska Railroad** (683-2233 or 800-544-0552) makes regular stops at Denali Station (open daily 10am-5pm), 1½mi. from the park entrance, and runs out to Fairbanks (1 per day; 4½hr.; $54; bikes $10) and Anchorage (1 per day; 8hr.; $102, bikes $20); reserve ahead. **Parks Hwy. Express** (479-3065) runs to the park from Anchorage (4hr., $30) and from Fairbanks (3hr., $20). The **Alaska Backpacker Shuttle** (344-8775) runs between Anchorage and Denali ($40, bikes $5).

Only the first 14mi. of the park road are accessible by private vehicle; the remaining 75mi. of dirt road can be reached only by shuttle bus, camper bus, or bicycle. **Shuttle buses** leave from the visitor center (daily 5am-6pm), pause at the well-nigh inevitable sighting of any major mammal ("MOOOOOSE!"), and turn back at various points along the park road, such as **Toklat,** Mi. 53 ($12.50); **Eielson,** Mi. 66 ($21); **Wonder Lake,** Mi. 85 ($27); and **Kantishna,** Mi. 89 ($31). (Ages 13-16 ½-price; under 13 free. Most buses are wheelchair accessible.) **Camper buses** ($15.50) transport only those visitors with **campground permits** and **backcountry permits,** and move faster than the shuttle buses (depart daily at 6:40, 8:40, 10:40am, 2:40, 4:40pm). Buses stop to pick up along the way. Unlike private vehicles, bikes *are* permitted on all 89mi. of park roads.

All travelers must stop at the **Denali Visitors Center** (683-2294), ½mi. from the Parks Hwy. (Rt. 3), for orientation. Park rangers collect the **entrance fee** ($5 per person, families $10; good for 1 week). Most park privileges are first come, first served; conduct all business at the visitor center as early in the day as possible. (Open daily mid-Apr. to Sept. 7am-8pm. Lockers 50¢.) **Denali Outdoor Center** (683-1925), at Mi. 238.9, just north of the park entrance, rents bikes (½-day $25; full-day $40; 5 or more days $35 per day). **Healy Clinic** (683-2211) is 13mi. north of the park entrance (open May-Sept. M-F 9am-5pm; nurse on call 24hr.). **Post Office:** (683-2291), next to Denali Hotel, 1mi. from the visitors center (open May-Sept. M-F 8:30am-5pm, Sa 10am-1pm; Oct.-Apr. M-Sa 10am-1pm). **ZIP code:** 99755. **Area code:** 907.

**▛▟ ACCOMMODATIONS AND FOOD.** To reach the **Denali Hostel,** go 9.6mi. north of the park entrance, turn left onto Otto Lake Rd., and continue straight 1.3mi. past the golf course (don't veer left). It's the 2nd house on the right, with a beautiful setting (oh, the sunsets!), international clientele, helpful owners, clean rooms, full kitchen, TV room, showers, and coin-operated laundry. (683-1295. Shuttle to the park and Alaska Railroad. Beds $23. Linen $3. Check-in 5:30-10pm. No curfew. No credit cards. Reservations recommended. Open May-Sept.)

Campers must obtain a permit from the visitor center, and may stay for up to 14 nights in the park's 7 campgrounds, which line the park road ($6-12). Call 800-622-7275 for advance reservations (272-7275 from Anchorage); first come, first served sites are distributed rapidly at the visitor center. **Riley Creek** is the only campground open year-round, and has the only dump station. All campgrounds within the park are wheelchair accessible, except for **Igloo Creek** and **Sanctuary River.**

Once you board that park bus, there is no food available anywhere. At **Black Bear Coffee House,** 1mi. north of the park entrance, the coffee is hot and strong, the muffins are fresh, and the staff is all smiles. (Veggie sandwich with hot cup of soup $7. 683-1656. Open May-Sept. daily approx. 7am-10pm.) **Denali Smoke Shack,** north of park entrance at Mi. 238.5, serves real Alaskan barbecue and a large vegetarian menu. (683-7665. Cajun chicken sandwich $8. Open daily 5:30am-10:30am and noon-midnight. Bar open noon-2am.) **Lynx Creek Pizza,** 1mi. north of the park entrance has cheese-heavy pizza with a great crust (14in. pie from $16.75) and a salad bar (683-2547; open daily 11am-11pm).

**◪ THE OUTDOORS.** The best way to experience Denali is to get off the bus and explore the land. Beyond Mi. 14, the point which only shuttle and camper buses can cross, there are **no trails.** You can begin day hiking from anywhere along the park road by riding the shuttle bus to a suitable starting point and asking the driver to let you off. It's rare to wait more than 30min. to flag a ride back. **Primrose Ridge,** beginning at Mi. 16 on the right side of the road, is bespangled with wildflowers and has spectacular views of the Alaska Range and the carpeted emerald valley below. A walk north from Mi. 14 along the **Savage River** provides a colorful, scenic stroll through this valley. The **Rock Creek Trail** runs 2½mi. from the hotel toward Park Headquarters (where the dog-sled demonstrations are held) but suffers from road noise. The more challenging **Mt. Healy Overlook Trail** starts from the hotel parking lot and climbs to an impressive view at 3400 ft. (5mi. round-trip; 1700 ft. elevation gain; 3-4hr.) **Discovery hikes** are guided 3-5hr. hikes, departing on special buses from the visitor center. Topics vary; a ranger might lead you on a cross-country scramble or a moose trail excursion. The hikes are free but require reservations and a bus ticket. More sedate 45min. **tundra walks** leave from Eielson Visitor Center daily at 1:30pm. More guided talks and walks are posted at the visitor center.

There are no trails in the backcountry. While day hiking is unlimited and requires no permit, only 2-12 backpackers can camp at one time in each of the park's 43 units. Overnight stays in the backcountry require a **free permit,** available no earlier or later than 1 day in advance at the **backcountry desk** in the visitor center. The **quota board** there reports which units are still available. Type-A hikers line up outside as early as 6:30am to grab permits for popular units. Talk to rangers and research your choices with the handy *Backcountry Description Guides* and *The Backcountry Companion,* available at the visitor center bookstore. The visitor center sells essential topographic maps ($4). All but 2 zones require that food be carried in **bear resistant food containers (BRFC),** available for free at the backcountry desk. These are bulky things; be sure to leave space in your backpack (LSIYB). With the park's cool, often drizzly weather and its many rivers, streams, and pools, your feet will get wet. **Hypothermia** can set in quickly and quietly; talk with rangers about prevention and warning signs.

# FAIRBANKS

Fairbanks stands unchallenged as North American civilization's northernmost hub—witness such landmarks as the "World's Northernmost Woolworth's," "World's Northernmost Denny's," and "World's Northernmost Southern Barbecue." From here, adventuresome travelers can drive, fly, or float to the Arctic Circle and into the tundra. Most do not make the long and arduous trip to Fairbanks merely to stay put; any road leads out of town into utter wilderness in minutes.

**ALASKA**

**⚡ PRACTICAL INFORMATION.** Most tourist destinations lie within the square formed by **Airport Way, College Rd., Cushman Blvd.,** and **University Way.** The city center lies north of the intersection of Cushman and Airport Way. Fairbanks is a **bicycle-friendly** city, with wide shoulders, multi-use paths, and sidewalks. The **airport** is 5mi. from downtown on Airport Way. **Alaska Railroad,** 280 N. Cushman St. (456-4155), runs trains down south. (Mid-May to mid-Sept., 1 per day to Anchorage ($154) via Denali ($54). Mid-Sept. to mid-Oct. and Feb. to mid-May, 1 per week to Anchorage ($120). Ages 2-11 ½-price. Depot open M-F 7am-3pm, Sa-Su 7am-11am.) **Parks Hwy. Express** (479-3065 or 888-600-6001) runs daily to Denali ($20, round-trip $35) and Anchorage (about 9hr.; $55, round-trip $100) and 3 per week to Glenallen ($45, round-trip $85) and Valdez ($60, round-trip $110). **Municipal Commuter Area Service (MACS)** (459-1011), at 5th and Cushman St., runs 2 routes (red and blue) through downtown and its surroundings. (Fare $1.50; students, seniors, and disabled 75¢; under 5 free. Day pass $3.) **Fairbanks Taxi:** (452-3535). **U-Save Auto Rental,** 3245 College Rd. (479-7060), charges $30 per day, and 26¢ per mi. after 100mi. (must be 21+ with credit card; under 25 extra $3 per day plus $500 deposit).

**Visitor Information:** 550 1st Ave. (456-5774 or 800-327-5774), at Cushman (open daily 8am-8pm; Labor Day-Memorial Day M-F 8am-5pm). **Alaska Public Lands Information Center (APLIC):** 250 Cushman St. #1A, 99707 (456-0527), at 3rd. St. in the basement of the Federal building (open daily 9am-6pm; in winter Tu-Sa 10am-6pm). **Internet access: Gulliver's New and Used Books,** in the Campus Corner Mall (474-9574; open M-Sa 9am-10pm, Su 9am-6pm; free). **Post Office:** 315 Barnette St. (452-3203; open M-F 9am-6pm, Sa 10am-2pm). **ZIP code:** 99707. **Area code:** 907.

**⚑⚏ ACCOMMODATIONS AND FOOD. Grandma Shirley's Hostel,** 510 Dunbar St., is the Fairbanks Überhostel. From the Steese Expwy., turn right onto the Trainor Gate Rd., then left at E. St., and right on Dunbar St. (451-9816. $16.25. Spectacular kitchen, showers, TV room, big backyard, and free bike use. Two co-ed rooms, 10 and 4 beds.) **Billie's Backpackers Hostel,** 2895 Mack Blvd., is a somewhat cluttered but welcoming place to meet many international travelers. Take Westwood Way 1 block off College to Mack Rd. (479-2034. Shower and kitchen in each room. Beds $18. Breakfast $7; all-you-can-eat dinner $10. Tent sites $10 per person.) **Chena River State Campground,** off Airport Way on University Ave., is landscaped, clean, and on a quiet stretch of the Chena River. (56 sites. $10. In summer, 5-night max. stay per vehicle. Dump station $5.)

An artery-blocking good time fills Airport Way and College Rd. **Sam's Club,** 48 College Rd., is good for stocking up on groceries (451-4800; open M-Sa 9am-8pm, Su 10am-7pm). **Lemon Grass,** 388 Old Chena Pump Rd., in the mall behind the Red Fox pumps Thai pop and hip-hop and serves good food (456-2200; Tom kha $3.50; open Tu-Su 11am-4pm and 5-9pm). **Wolf Run Dessert & Coffee House,** 3360 Wolf Run, just off University Way near Geist, offers scrumptious desserts, plush chairs, and a stone hearth fireplace with rocking chair (458-0636; espresso $1, peanut butter pie $4.25; open Tu-Th 11am-10pm, F-Sa 11am-midnight, Su noon-8pm).

**⚏⚑ SIGHTS, OUTDOORS, AND NIGHTLIFE.** The **University of Alaska Museum,** a 10min. walk up Yukon Dr. from the Wood Center, features a thorough look at the Aleut/Japanese evacuation during WWII, indigenous crafts, and Blue Babe, a 36,000 year-old steppe bison recovered from the permafrost. (474-7505. Open June-Aug. daily 9am-7pm; May and Sept. daily 9am-5pm; Oct.-Apr. M-F 9am-5pm, Sa-Su noon-5pm. $5, seniors $4.50, ages 13-18 $3.) **Georgeson Botanical Gardens,** on Tanana Dr. west of the museum, grows tulips (late June through July) overlooking Fairbanks and the Alaska Range (474-1944). Stand upwind of the Large Animal Research Station, which offers a rare chance to see baby musk oxen and other arctic animals up close; take Farmer's Loop to Ballaine Rd. and turn left on Van Kovich; the farm is 1mi. up on the right. (474-7207. Tours June-Aug. Tu, Sa 11am and 1:30pm, Th 1:30pm; Sept. Sa 1:30pm. $5, students $2, seniors $4.)

**Moose Mountain,** 20min. northeast of town, has over 20 downhill skiing trails. (479-4732. Lift tickets $25; college students, seniors, military, and ages 13-17 $20; ages 7-12 $15; over 70 or under 6 free. $5 off after 1pm or if the temperature is below 0°F.) Maps for **multi-use trails** are available at the Wood Center, in the UAF Activities Office. **Cross-country skiing trails** cross the UAF campus. The **Chena River State Recreation Area** has a variety of multi-use trails. Maps are available at the Public Lands Information Center (see **Practical Information,** above).

**Howling Dog Saloon,** 11½mi. north on the Steese Hwy. (Rt. 6) toward Fox, at the intersection of the Old and New Steese Hwys., is, as the manager says "rough, tough, and good-lookin.'" Volleyball, pool, and horseshoe games go on until 4am or so (457-8780; live music W-Sa; open May-Oct. Su-Th 4pm-around 2am, F-Sa 4pm-around 4am). In mid-July, Fairbanks citizens don old-time duds and whoop it up for **Golden Days,** a celebration of Felix Pedro's 1902 discovery that sparked the Fairbanks gold rush. Although its relation to the actual gold rush days is questionable, the **rubber duckie race** is one of the biggest events (452-1105).

# SOUTHEAST ALASKA

Southeast Alaska sometimes goes by "the Panhandle" or "the southeast." It spans 500mi. from the basins of Misty Fiords National Monument to Skagway at the foot of the Chilkoot Trail. The waterways weaving through the Panhandle, collectively known as the Inside Passage, make up an enormous saltwater soup spiced with islands, inlets, fjords, and the ferries that flit among them. The absence of roads in the steep coastal mountains has helped Panhandle towns maintain their small size and hospitable personalities. The **Alaska Marine Hwy.** system (see p. 922) provides the cheapest, most exciting way to explore the Inside Passage.

# KETCHIKAN

Ketchikan is the first stop in Alaska for cruise ships and would-be cannery workers. An average of nearly 12½ ft. of rainfall a year can not deter visitor's delight in the fabulous proximity to Tongass National Forest (one third of which lies in the Ketchikan area) and the stunning Misty Fiords National Monument. Ketchikan also offers numerous native and historical attractions and a revamped historical district. Unfortunately, much of Ketchikan's native population remains economically and psychologically depressed—salmon fishing and timber industries and their workers have fallen on increasingly hard times.

## ⓘ PRACTICAL INFORMATION

Ketchikan rests on **Revillagigedo Island** (ruh-VIL-ya-GIG-a-doe). Upon reaching Ketchikan from Canada, **roll back your watch** by an hour to get in step with Alaska Time. The town caters to the elite and its attractions are extremely spread out, making bike rental a wise option. A small **ferry** runs from the airport, across from Ketchikan on Gravina Island, to just north of the state ferry dock (every 15min., in winter every 30min.; $2.50). **Alaska Airlines** (225-2141 or 800-426-0333; open M-F 9:30am-5pm) makes daily flights to Juneau ($95-140). **Alaska Marine Hwy.** (225-6181) sends wheelchair-accessible boats from the far end of town on N. Tongass Hwy. to Wrangell ($24), Juneau ($74), and Skagway ($98). The main bus route runs a loop between the airport parking lot near the ferry terminal at one end, and Dock and Main St. downtown at the other. ($1, students, seniors, and children 75¢. Runs every 30min. M-F 5:15am-9:45pm; 1 per hr. Sa 6:45am-8:45pm, Su 8:45am-3:45pm.) **Taxi: Sourdough Cab** (225-5544; 24hr.).

**Ketchikan Visitors Bureau:** 131 Front St. (225-6166 or 800-770-3300), at the cruise ship docks downtown (open daily 8am-5pm). **Southeast Alaska Visitors Center (SEAVC)** (228-6220) 50 Main St., provides trip-planning service, plus info on public lands around Ketchikan, including Tongass and Misty Fiords. The beautiful new ecology and native history exhibit is worth the $4. (Free in off season. Open Apr.-Sept. daily 8am-5pm; Oct.-Mar. Tu-Sa 8:30am-4:30pm.) **Post Office:** (225-9601), by the ferry terminal (open M-F 8:30am-5pm). **ZIP code:** 99901. **Area code:** 907.

## ACCOMMODATIONS AND FOOD

The **Ketchikan Reservation Service** (800-987-5337; fax 247-5337) provides info on B&Bs (singles from $60). Because of boardwalk stairs, these accommodations aren't wheelchair accessible. The **Ketchikan Youth Hostel (HI-AYH)**, is at Main and Grant St. in the First Methodist Church. The social scene is skimpy since the doors close at 11pm sharp. Bring a sleeping bag for the foam mats. (225-3319. Common area, showers, kitchen, and free tea, coffee, and cookies every night. $8, nonmembers $11. 4-night max. stay when full. Lockout 9am-6pm. Lights out 11pm-7am. Call ahead if arriving on a late ferry. Make reservations. Open June-Aug.) **Eagle View Bed & Breakfast and Backpacker Bunks,** 2303 5th Ave., is reached via Jefferson Ave. uphill from Tongass, turn right on 5th Ave.; it's a big brown house at the end of the street. Not as cheap as the hostel, but the B&B has free use of a kitchen, TV, sauna, BBQ, and hammocks. (225-5461. 1mi. uphill from the ferry docks. Laundry $2.50 per load. Doubles $25; 2 tent sites $15 per person. )

Campgrounds usually have stay limits of a week or two, and are really out of the way. There is no public transportation from the town to the campgrounds, so plan on hiking, biking, or paying an exorbitant cab fare. **Signal Creek** and **3 C's Campgrounds** sit across the street from each other on Ward Lake Rd. Drive north on Tongass Ave. and turn right at the sign for Ward Lake, approximately 5mi. from the ferry terminal ($8; 28 spaces, water, and pit toilets; 7-night max. stay; open May-Sept.). Anyone can camp for up to 30 days in **Tongass National Forest,** but may not return for 6 months after that time. Any clearing is free.

The freshest seafood swims in **Ketchikan Creek;** in summer, anglers frequently hook king salmon from the docks by Stedman St. **The Pizza Mill,** 808 Water St., through the tunnel, is 2 blocks north of downtown. (225-6646. Personal pizzas with 2 toppings $5.50. 12 in. pizza $12. Open Su-W 11am-11pm, Th-Sa 11am-3am.) **Burger Queen,** 518 Water St., is 1 block past the tunnel. The regal veggie burgers, chicken troika sandwiches, and guacamole cheddar burgers ($2-8) please the pickiest. (225-6060. Open in summer M-Sa 11am-8pm; in winter until 4pm.)

## ◉ SIGHTS AND THE OUTDOORS

Ketchikan's primary cultural attraction is the **Saxman Totem Park,** the largest totem park in Alaska, 2½mi. southwest of town on Tongass Hwy. *($8 by cab, or a short ride on the Hwy. bike path. Open M-F 9am-5pm, Sa-Su when a cruise ship is in.)* The **Totem Heritage Center,** on the hill above downtown, houses 33 well-preserved totem poles from Tlingit, Haida, and Tsimshian villages. It is the largest collection of authentic, pre-commercial totem poles in the U.S., but only a few are on display. *(601 Deermount St. 225-5900. Open daily May-Sept. 8am-5pm. $4, under 13 free.)* A $7 combination ticket also provides admission to the **Deer Mountain Fish Hatchery and Raptor Center,** across the creek. *(225-9533. Open daily May-Sept. 8am-4:30pm.)*

From Ketchikan, a trail up 3001 ft. **Deer Mountain** makes a good dayhike. Walk up the hill past the city park on Fair St.; the marked trailhead branches off to the left just behind the dump. The ascent is steep but manageable, and on a rare clear day the walk yields sparkling views of the sea and surrounding islands. While most hikers stop at the 2½mi. point, the trail continues above the treeline to the summit along an 8mi. route that passes Blue Lake and leads over John Mountain to Little Silvis Lake and the Beaver Falls Fish Hatchery. This portion of the trail is poorly marked, and snow and ice are common on the peaks even in the summer; only experienced and well-prepared hikers should attempt it. An A-frame cabin between Deer Mountain and John Mountain can be reserved through the Forest Service desk at SEAVC (see p. 931). The trail emerges 13mi. from Ketchikan at the Beaver Falls power station parking lot.

A less strenuous, more family-oriented hike is the **Perseverance Lake Trail.** The trail begins approximately 100 ft. before the entrance to the Three C's Campground, and makes a leisurely 2¼mi. climb to Perserverance Lake. The trail passes through muskeg, old-growth sitka spruce, hemlock, and cedar, and the lake is great for trout fishing. For cold swimming, a sandy beach, and picnic tables, head to **Ward Lake** at the Signal Creek Campground. A 1¼mi. trail circles the grassy pond. Bikers can explore surrounding logging roads.

Defy the laws of rainy weather and gravity at **Kave Sport's indoor climbing gym.** Over 2300 sq. ft. of climbing walls challenge beginners and expert climbers alike. *(615 Stedman Ave. 225-5283. Open M-F 6am-10pm, Sa 8am-8pm, Su noon-6pm. $8 per day. Equipment rental up to $9.)*

## NEAR KETCHIKAN: MISTY FIORDS

The jagged peaks, plunging valleys, and dripping vegetation of **Misty Fiords National Monument,** 20mi. east of Ketchikan, make biologists dream and outdoors enthusiasts drool. Only accessible by kayak, boat, or float plane, the 2.3-million-acre park offers superlative camping, kayaking, hiking, and wildlife-viewing. **Camping** is permitted throughout the park, and the Forest Service maintains four first come, first served shelters (free) and 14 cabins ($25). Contact the **Misty Fiords Ranger Station** (225-2148), 3031 Tongass Ave., Ketchikan, and ask ahead at the SEAVC (see p. 931). Kayaking neophytes might contact **Alaska Cruises,** 220 Front St., Box 7814 (225-6044); they'll drop off both kayaker and kayak at the head of Rudyard Bay during one of four weekly sightseeing tours ($175 per person). **Area code:** 907

# JUNEAU

Alaska's state capital has an air of modernity and progressiveness usually not found in the rural fishing villages of Southeast Alaska. Accessible only by water and air, Juneau is the second-busiest cruise ship port in the U.S., after Miami. Hordes of travelers come to Juneau for the Mendenhall Glacier, numerous hiking trails, and close access to Glacier Bay. Be prepared to share the beauty.

## 🛈 PRACTICAL INFORMATION

**Franklin St.** is the main drag downtown. **Glacier Hwy.** connects downtown, the airport, the residential area of the Mendenhall Valley, and the ferry terminal. The ferry and airport are both annoyingly far from the glacier and downtown. **Juneau International Airport,** 9mi. north of Juneau on Glacier Hwy., is served by **Alaska Airlines** (789-0600 or 800-426-0333), on S. Franklin St. at 2nd St. in the Baranov Hotel, which flies to Anchorage ($114-236); Sitka ($98); Ketchikan ($140); and Gustavus ($42). **Capital Transit** (789-6901) runs buses from downtown to the airport and Mendenhall Glacier, with hourly express service downtown (M-F 8:10am-5:10pm). The closest stop to the ferry is at Auke Bay, 2mi. from the terminal (runs M-Sa 7am-10:30pm, Su 9am-5:30pm; fare $1.25; exact change required). **MGT Ferry Express** (789-5460) meets all ferries and runs to downtown hotels or to the airport ($5; call 6-8pm 1 day prior). **Alaska Marine Hwy.,** 1591 Glacier Ave. (465-3941 or 800-642-0066), docks at the Auke Bay terminal, 14mi. from the city on the Glacier Hwy., and runs to Ketchikan ($74); Sitka ($26); and Bellingham, WA ($226). **Taku Cab** (586-2121) runs from downtown to Mendenhall Glacier ($15), the ferry ($20), and the airport ($15).

**Davis Log Cabin Visitor Center,** 134 3rd St., (888-581-2201 or 586-2201), at Seward St., is a great source of pamphlets and maps (open M-F 8:30am-5pm, Sa-Su 9am-5pm; Oct.-May M-F 8:30am-5pm). **National Forest and Park Services,** 101 Egan Dr. (586-8751), at Willoughby in Centennial Hall, provide info on hiking and fishing in the area, and reservations for Forest Service cabins in Tongass National Forest (open M-F 8am-5pm). Find **Internet access** at the **library,** at Admiral Way and S. Franklin St. **Post Office:** 709 W. 9th St. (586-7987; open M-F 9am-5pm, Sa 9am-1pm for parcel pick-up only). **ZIP code:** 99801. **Area code:** 907.

## ACCOMMODATIONS AND FOOD

The **Alaska B&B Association** (586-2959), can help find a room downtown (from $65). On a steep hill, lovely **Juneau International Hostel (HI-AYH)**, 614 Harris St., at 6th St., enforces strict rules in a prime location. (586-9559. 48 beds. $7, nonmembers $10. Kitchen. Wash $1.25, dry 75¢. Lockout 9am-5pm and 11pm curfew. 3-night max. stay if they're full. $10 deposit mailed in advance serves as a reservation. No phone reservations.) **Alaskan Hotel**, 167 Franklin St., right downtown, has been meticulously restored to original 1913 decor. (586-1000, in the lower 48 800-327-9347. Kitchenettes and TVs. Hot tub with radio $13-26.25 per hr. Rooms $67-84; rates lower in winter. Free luggage storage for guests. Wash or dry $1.) **Mendenhall Lake Campground** is about 6mi. from the ferry terminal on Montana Creek Rd.; take Glacier Hwy. north 9mi. to Mendenhall Loop Rd., continue 3½mi., and take the right fork. Bus drivers will stop within 2mi. of camp (7am-10:30pm). The 60 sites have stunning views of the glacier and convenient trails to go even closer. (Fireplaces, water, flush toilets, showers, picnic tables, free firewood. Sites $8, seniors $4. 14-night max. stay. No reservations. Open May 15-Sept. 30.)

**Armadillo Tex-Mex Cafe**, 431 S. Franklin St., shelters locals in the heart of the cruise ship district with fast, saucy service and hot, spicy food. (586-1880. 2 enchiladas $6. Free chips and salsa. Open M-Sa 11am-10pm, Su 4-10pm.) **Myriad Cafe**, 230 Seward St., is an all-organic, vegetarian- and vegan-friendly fare: the fish is macrobiotic, the meat hormone- and antibiotic-free, and the breakfast menu even comes with tofu options. (586-3433. Salads and pasta from $6. Brown rice sushi $1.35, with seafood $1.75. Internet access $8 per hr. Open daily 9am-9pm, breakfast served Sa-Su until 5pm.)

## 🎇 SIGHTS AND OUTDOORS

The excellent **Alaska State Museum** leads through the history and culture of Alaska's four major native groups: Tlingit, Athabascan, Aleut, and Inuit. *(395 Whittier St. 465-2901. $4, seniors and children free. Open May 18-Sept. 17 M-F 9am-6pm, Sa-Su 10am-6pm; Sept. 18-May 17 Tu-Sa 10am-4pm.)* The hexagonal and onion-domed 1894 **St. Nicholas Russian Orthodox Church,** on 5th St. between N. Franklin and Gold St., holds rows of icons and a glorious altar. Services, held Saturday at 6pm and Sunday at 10am, are conducted in English, Old Slavonic, and Tlingit. *($1 donation requested. Open daily in summer 9am-5pm.)*

The **West Glacier Trail** begins off Montana Creek Rd., by the Mendenhall Lake Campground. The 5-6hr. walk yields stunning views of **Mendenhall Glacier** from the first step to the final outlook. The 3½mi., one-way trail parallels the glacier through western hemlock forest and up a rocky cairn-marked scramble to the summit of 4226 ft. **Mt. McGinnis**. At the end of Basin Rd., the easy **Perseverance Trail** leads to the ruins of the Silverbowl Basin Mine and booming waterfalls. The **Granite Creek Trail** branches off the Perseverance Trail and follows its namesake to a beautiful basin, 3¾mi. from the trailhead. The summit of Mt. Juneau lies 3mi. farther along the ridge and, again, offers terrific views. The shorter, steeper **Mt. Juneau Trail,** which departs from Perseverance Trail about 1mi. from the trailhead, opens up similar vistas. Many trails are well-maintained and excellent for **mountain biking.** Check with **Mountain Gears** for their difficulty rankings and suggestions. Biking off-road is sometimes prohibited.

**Tracy Arm**, a mini-fjord near Juneau, is known as "the poor man's Glacier Bay," offering much of the same spectacular beauty and wildlife as the national park at well under half the cost. **Auk Nu Tours** is the biggest tour company. *(76 Egan Dr. 800-820-2628. Lunch included. $100).* **Wilderness Swift Charters** might be worth the extra $25: their small boats take only 6 passengers, offer a smoked salmon lunch, and the chance to stop and listen to whales sing on an underwater microphone. *(463-4942.)* **Kayak Express,** 4107 Blackberry St. (780-4591), and **Alaska Discovery,** 5449 Shuane Dr. (780-6226 or 800-586-1911), provide rental kayaks, pickups and drop-off in Glacier Bay and elsewhere, and **guided kayak tours** in about the same price range as the tour boats. In winter, the **Eaglecrest Ski Area,** on Douglas Island, offers decent alpine skiing. *(155 S. Seward St. 586-5284 or 586-5330. $24 per day, ages 12-17 $17, under 12 $12; ski rental $20, children $14.)* The Eaglecrest **ski bus** departs from the Baranov Hotel at 8:30am and returns from the slopes at 5pm on winter weekends and holidays. *(Round-trip $6.)*

## GLACIER BAY NATIONAL PARK

Glacier Bay was once referred to by explorer Jean François de Galaup de la Perouse as "perhaps the most extraordinary place in the world." Crystal monoliths, broken off from glaciers, float peacefully in fjords, while humpback whales maneuver the maze of the icy blue depths. Glacier Bay National Park encloses nine tidewater glaciers, as well as the **Fairweather Mountains,** the highest coastal range in the world. (Eat your heart out, Norway.) Charter flights, tours, and cruise ships all probe Glacier Bay, providing close encounters with glaciers, rookeries, whales, and seals. The bay itself is divided into two inlets: the westward **Tarr Inlet** advances as far as the **Grand Pacific** and **Margerie Glaciers,** while the eastward **Muir Inlet** ends at the **Muir** and **Riggs Glaciers.**

Glacier Bay provides a rare opportunity to see geological and ecological processes radically compressed. A mere two centuries ago, the **Grand Pacific Glacier** covered the entire region under a sheet of ancient ice. Severe earthquakes separated the glacier from its terminal moraine (the silt and debris that insulates advancing ice from the relatively warm surrounding seawater), and the glacier retreated 45mi. in 150 years—light speed in glacial time. As a result, the uncovered ground is virgin territory, colonized by pioneering vegetation.

Getting to **Bartlett Cove,** the principal access point to the bay, is relatively easy: a plane or ferry takes visitors to **Gustavus,** and from there a taxi or shuttle (about $12) goes to **Glacier Bay Lodge** (697-2230 or 800-451-5952; open M-F 11:30am-2pm and 4-9pm) and the **Visitor Information Center,** both steps from the cove. The few ways to see the glaciers are expensive. Sightseers take one of a range of packages on a sightseeing cruise boat; backcountry travelers are dropped off by the same ship for their trips. Visitors should contact **Glacier Bay National Park** P.O. Box 140, Gustavus 99826 (697-2230) for assistance in planning a backcountry trip. Glacier Bay is becoming *the* destination for extended kayak trips in the region. The only **food** available at Bartlett Cove is at the dining room in the lodge, which is rather expensive, so trippers bring provisions with them. (Open daily 6-9am, 11:30-2:30pm, and 4:30-10pm.)

**Wilderness camping** and **hiking** are permitted throughout the park, though there are no trails except the two near the lodge, and hiking is very difficult in most of the park because of thick alder brush. Backcountry hiking and kayaking is possible in the **Dry Bay** area (the northwest corner of the park), as is **rafting** down the **Alsek River.** For info on these activities contact the Yakutat District Office of the National Park Service, P.O. Box 137, Yakutat, AK 99689 (784-3295).

ALASKA

DISTANCE CHART

# DISTANCES (MI.) AND TRAVEL TIMES (BY BUS)

| | Atlanta | Boston | Chic. | Dallas | D.C. | Denver | L.A. | Miami | N. Orl. | NYC | Phila. | Phnx. | St. Lou. | Sa. Fran. | Seattle | Trnto. | Vanc. | Mont. |
|---|---|---|---|---|---|---|---|---|---|---|---|---|---|---|---|---|---|---|
| Atlanta | | 1108 | 717 | 783 | 632 | 1406 | 2366 | 653 | 474 | 886 | 778 | 1863 | 560 | 2492 | 2699 | 959 | 2825 | 1240 |
| Boston | 22hr. | | 996 | 1794 | 442 | 1990 | 3017 | 1533 | 1542 | 194 | 333 | 2697 | 1190 | 3111 | 3105 | 555 | 3242 | 326 |
| Chicago | 14hr. | 20hr. | | 937 | 715 | 1023 | 2047 | 1237 | 928 | 807 | 767 | 1791 | 302 | 2145 | 2108 | 537 | 2245 | 537 |
| Dallas | 15hr. | 35hr. | 18hr. | | 1326 | 794 | 1450 | 1322 | 507 | 1576 | 1459 | 906 | 629 | 1740 | 2112 | 1457 | 2255 | 1763 |
| D.C. | 12hr. | 8hr. | 14hr. | 24hr. | | 1700 | 2689 | 1043 | 1085 | 225 | 139 | 2350 | 845 | 2840 | 2788 | 526 | 3292 | 665 |
| Denver | 27hr. | 38hr. | 20hr. | 15hr. | 29hr. | | 1026 | 2046 | 1341 | 1785 | 1759 | 790 | 860 | 1267 | 1313 | 1508 | 1458 | 1864 |
| L.A. | 45hr. | 57hr. | 39hr. | 28hr. | 55hr. | 20hr. | | 2780 | 2005 | 2787 | 2723 | 371 | 1837 | 384 | 1141 | 2404 | 1285 | 2888 |
| Miami | 13hr. | 30hr. | 24hr. | 26hr. | 20hr. | 39hr. | 53hr. | | 856 | 1346 | 1214 | 2368 | 1197 | 3086 | 3368 | 1564 | 3505 | 1676 |
| New O. | 9hr. | 31hr. | 18hr. | 10hr. | 21hr. | 26hr. | 38hr. | 17hr. | | 1332 | 1247 | 1535 | 677 | 2331 | 2639 | 1320 | 2561 | 1654 |
| NYC | 18hr. | 4hr. | 16hr. | 31hr. | 5hr. | 35hr. | 53hr. | 26hr. | 27hr. | | 104 | 2592 | 999 | 2923 | 2912 | 496 | 3085 | 386 |
| Phila. | 18hr. | 6hr. | 16hr. | 19hr. | 3hr. | 33hr. | 50hr. | 23hr. | 23hr. | 2hr. | | 2511 | 904 | 2883 | 2872 | 503 | 3009 | 465 |
| Phoenix | 40hr. | 49hr. | 39hr. | 19hr. | 43hr. | 17hr. | 8hr. | 47hr. | 30hr. | 45hr. | 44hr. | | 1503 | 753 | 1510 | 2069 | 1654 | 2638 |
| St. Louis | 11hr. | 23hr. | 6hr. | 13hr. | 15hr. | 17hr. | 35hr. | 23hr. | 13hr. | 19hr. | 16hr. | 32hr. | | 2113 | 2139 | 810 | 2276 | 1128 |
| San Fran. | 47hr. | 60hr. | 41hr. | 47hr. | 60hr. | 33hr. | 7hr. | 59hr. | 43hr. | 56hr. | 54hr. | 15hr. | 45hr. | | 807 | 2630 | 951 | 2985 |
| Seattle | 52hr. | 59hr. | 40hr. | 40hr. | 54hr. | 25hr. | 22hr. | 65hr. | 50hr. | 55hr. | 54hr. | 28hr. | 36hr. | 16hr. | | 2623 | 146 | 2964 |
| Toronto | 21hr. | 11hr. | 10hr. | 26hr. | 11hr. | 26hr. | 48hr. | 29hr. | 13hr. | 11hr. | 13hr. | 48hr. | 14hr. | 49hr. | 48hr. | | 4563 | 655 |
| Vancv. | 54hr. | 61hr. | 42hr. | 43hr. | 60hr. | 27hr. | 24hr. | 67hr. | 54hr. | 57hr. | 56hr. | 30hr. | 38hr. | 18hr. | 2hr. | 53hr. | | 4861 |
| Montreal | 23hr. | 6hr. | 17hr. | 28hr. | 12hr. | 39hr. | 53hr. | 32hr. | 31hr. | 7hr. | 9hr. | 53hr. | 23hr. | 56hr. | 55hr. | 7hr. | 55hr. | |

# INDEX

## A

Uinta National Forest, UT
695
Underground Railroad 9
United Indians of All Tribes
Foundation, WA 861
United States Air Force
Academy, CO 673
United States Olympic Team,
CO 671
Universal Studios, CA 771
Universal Studios, FL 433
Universities
Amherst 142
Arizona 734
Brown 144
College of William & Mary
309
Columbia 208
Cornell 244
Duke 353
Florida 456
Harvard 126
Haskell Indian Nations, KS
560
Indiana 491
Iowa 549
Kansas 559
Mary Washington, VA 306
Massachusetts Institute of
Technology 126
Massachusetts-Amherst
142
McGill, PQ 171
Michigan 476
Middlebury 108
New York 218
North Carolina at Chapel
Hill 350
Ohio State 464
Oregon (U of O) 891
Pennsylvania 266
Stanford, CA 826
Texas at Austin 590
Toronto 187
Tuskegee 387
UCLA 767
University of Texas at El
Paso 608
Vermont 106
Virginia 314
Washington 860
Williams 141
Wisconsin 513
Yale 149
Upper Peninsula, MI 484–
487
**Utah** 690–709
Arches 700
Bryce Canyon 704
Canyonlands 702
Capitol Reef 703

Cedar City 707
Dinosaur and Vernal 696
Hovenweep 708
Moab 698
Natural Bridges 708
Park City 695
Salt Lake City 690–695
Timpanogos Cave 695
Zion 706

**V**

Vail, CO 666
Valley Forge, PA 267
Valley of Fire State Park 688
Valley of the Gods, UT 709
Vancouver Island, BC 904–
906
Vancouver, BC 897–903
Vanderbilt, George 10
Vashon Island, WA 864
vegetarians 86
Venice, CA 768
Ventura 797
**Vermont** 103–112
Brattleboro 111
Burlington 104–107
Champlain Valley 107
Stowe 108–110
White River Junction 110
Vernal, UT 696
Vespucci, Amerigo 7
Veterans Day 31
Vicksburg, MS 394
Victoria Day 31
Victoria, BC 904
views, nice
Ketchikan, AK 932
**Virginia** 300–318
Charlottesville 312–315
Fredericksburg 304–307
Historic Triangle 307–310
Jamestown 309
Richmond 301–304
Shenandoah National Park
315–317
Virginia Beach 310–312
Williamsburg 307–310
Yorktown 309
Virginia Beach, VA 310–312
Visa 43
Voodoo Museum, LA 404
Voyageurs National Park, MN
529

**W**

Wadsworth-Longfellow,
Henry 91
Waffle House, GA 375

Walden Pond, MA 129
Walker, MN 527
Wall Drug, SD 538
Wall Street, NY 216
Wall, SD 538
Wallowa Mountains, OR 895
Walnut Canyon National
Monument, AZ 718
Warren, Chief Justice Earl 8
**Washington** 852–879
Bellingham 866
Cascade Range 873–878
Marblemount 877
Mt. Rainier National Park
874
Mt. St. Helens 873
Olympia 865
Olympic National Park 870
Olympic Peninsula 869–
872
Orcas Island 868
Port Townsend 869
Ross Lake 877
San Juan Islands 867–
869
Seattle 853–864
Sedro Woolley 877
Spokane 878
Twisp 878
Vashon Island 864
Winthrop 877
Washington, Booker T. 387
**Washington, D.C**
Arlington National
Cemetery, VA 300
**Washington, D.C.** 286–300
FBI 296
Holocaust Museum 295
Iwo Jima Memorial 300
Korean War Memorial 295
Library of Congress 293
Lincoln Memorial 294
National Archives 296
National Postal Museum
293
Smithsonian 293
Supreme Court 293
The Mall 293
The Mint 295
U.S. Capitol 292
Vietnam Memorial 294
Washington Monument
294
Washington, George 8, 300
Watergate, D.C. 296
Waterton Lakes National
Park, AB 631
Waterton-Glacier Peace Park,
MT and AB 627–632
Wayne, John 549
Webster, Noah 148

# X

X

Not many words begin with "x"

# Y

# Z

Z

Your life has a limit but knowledge has none. If you use what is limited to pursue what has no limit, you will be in danger. If you understand this and still strive for knowledge, you will be in danger for certain! -Chuang Tzu

# ABOUT LET'S GO

## FORTY YEARS OF WISDOM

As a new millennium arrives, *Let's Go: Europe*, now in its 40th edition and translated into seven languages, reigns as the world's bestselling international travel guide. For four decades, travelers criss-crossing the Continent have relied on *Let's Go* for inside information on the hippest backstreet cafes, the most pristine secluded beaches, and the best routes from border to border. In the last 20 years, our rugged researchers have stretched the frontiers of backpacking and expanded our coverage into Asia, Africa, Australia, and the Americas. We're celebrating our 40th birthday with the release of *Let's Go: China*, blazing the traveler's trail from the Forbidden City to the Tibetan frontier; *Let's Go: Perú & Ecuador*, spanning the lands of the ancient Inca Empire; *Let's Go: Middle East*, with coverage from Istanbul to the Persian Gulf; and the maiden edition of *Let's Go: Israel*.

It all started in 1960 when a handful of well-traveled students at Harvard University handed out a 20-page mimeographed pamphlet offering a collection of their tips on budget travel to passengers on student charter flights to Europe. The following year, in response to the instant popularity of the first volume, students traveling to Europe researched the first full-fledged edition of *Let's Go: Europe*, a pocket-sized book featuring honest, practical advice, witty writing, and a decidedly youthful slant on the world. Throughout the 60s and 70s, our guides reflected the times. In 1969 we taught travelers how to get from Paris to Prague on "no dollars a day" by singing in the street. In the 80s and 90s, we looked beyond Europe and North America and set off to all corners of the earth. Meanwhile, we focused in on the world's most exciting urban areas to produce in-depth, fold-out map guides. Our new guides bring the total number of titles to 48, each infused with the spirit of adventure and voice of opinion that travelers around the world have come to count on. But some things never change: our guides are still researched, written, and produced entirely by students who know first-hand how to see the world on the cheap.

## HOW WE DO IT

Each guide is completely revised and thoroughly updated every year by a well-traveled set of over 250 students. Every spring, we recruit over 180 researchers and 70 editors to overhaul every book. After several months of training, researcher-writers hit the road for seven weeks of exploration, from Anchorage to Adelaide, Estonia to El Salvador, Iceland to Indonesia. Hired for their rare combination of budget travel sense, writing ability, stamina, and courage, these adventurous travelers know that train strikes, stolen luggage, food poisoning, and marriage proposals are all part of a day's work. Back at our offices, editors work from spring to fall, massaging copy written on Himalayan bus rides into witty, informative prose. A student staff of typesetters, cartographers, publicists, and managers keeps our lively team together. In September, the collected efforts of the summer are delivered to our printer, which turns them into books in record time, so that you have the most up-to-date information available for your vacation. Even as you read this, work on next year's editions is well underway.

## WHY WE DO IT

We don't think of budget travel as the last recourse of the destitute; we believe that it's the only way to travel. Living cheaply and simply brings you closer to the people and places you've been saving up to visit. Our books will ease your anxieties and answer your questions about the basics—so you can get off the beaten track and explore. Once you learn the ropes, we encourage you to put *Let's Go* down now and then to strike out on your own. You know as well as we that the best discoveries are often those you make yourself. When you find something worth sharing, please drop us a line. We're Let's Go Publications, 67 Mount Auburn St., Cambridge, MA 02138, USA (email: feedback@letsgo.com). For more info, visit our website, http://www.letsgo.com.

**Next time, make your *own* hotel arrangements.**

Yahoo! Travel

# READER QUESTIONNAIRE

Name: _____

Address: _____

City: _____ State: _____ Country: _____

ZIP/Postal Code: _____ E-mail: _____ How old are you? ____

And you're...?   in high school   in college   in graduate school
               employed   retired   between jobs

**Which book(s) have you used?** _____

**Where have you gone with Let's Go?** _____

**Have you traveled extensively before?**  yes  no

**Had you used Let's Go before?**  yes  no    **Would you use it again?**  yes  no

**How did you hear about Let's Go?** friend   store clerk   television
                           review   bookstore display
                           ad/promotion   internet   other: _____

**Why did you choose Let's Go?** reputation   budget focus   annual updating
                         wit & incision   price   other: _____

**Which guides have you used?** Fodor's   Footprint Handbooks   Frommer's $-a-day
                      Lonely Planet   Moon Guides   Cognoscenti Maps
                      Rough Guides   UpClose   other: _____

**Which guide do you prefer? Why?** _____

**Please rank the following in your Let's Go guide:** (1=needs improvement, 5=perfect)

| | | | | | | |
|---|---|---|---|---|---|---|
| packaging/cover | 1 2 3 4 5 | food | 1 2 3 4 5 | maps | 1 2 3 4 5 |
| cultural introduction | 1 2 3 4 5 | sights | 1 2 3 4 5 | directions | 1 2 3 4 5 |
| "Essentials" | 1 2 3 4 5 | entertainment | 1 2 3 4 5 | writing style | 1 2 3 4 5 |
| practical info | 1 2 3 4 5 | gay/lesbian info | 1 2 3 4 5 | budget resources | 1 2 3 4 5 |
| accommodations | 1 2 3 4 5 | up-to-date info | 1 2 3 4 5 | other: _____ | 1 2 3 4 5 |

**How long was your trip?**  one week  two wks.  three wks.  a month  2+ months

**Why did you go?** sightseeing  adventure travel  study abroad  other: _____

**What was your average daily budget, not including flights?** _____

**Do you buy a separate map when you visit a foreign city?**  yes  no

**Have you used a Let's Go Map Guide?**  yes  no  **If you have, which one?** _____

**Would you recommend them to others?**  yes  no

**Have you visited Let's Go's website?**  yes  no

**What would you like to see included on Let's Go's website?** _____

**What percentage of your trip planning did you do on the web?** _____

**What kind of Let's Go guide would you like to see?** recreation (e.g., skiing)  phrasebook
                 spring break  adventure/trekking  first-time travel info  Europe altas

**Which of the following destinations would you like to see Let's Go cover?**
       Argentina  Brazil  Canada  Caribbean  Chile  Costa Rica  Cuba
       Morocco  Nepal  Russia  Scandinavia  Southwest USA  other: _____

**Where did you buy your guidebook?**  independent bookstore  college bookstore
       travel store  Internet  chain bookstore  gift    other: _____

Please fill this out and return it to **Let's Go, St. Martin's Press,** 175 Fifth Ave., New York, NY 10010-7848. All respondents will receive a free subscription to **The Yellowjacket**, the Let's Go Newsletter. You can find a more extensive version of this survey on the web at http://www.letsgo.com.

Los Angeles

# L.A. Westside

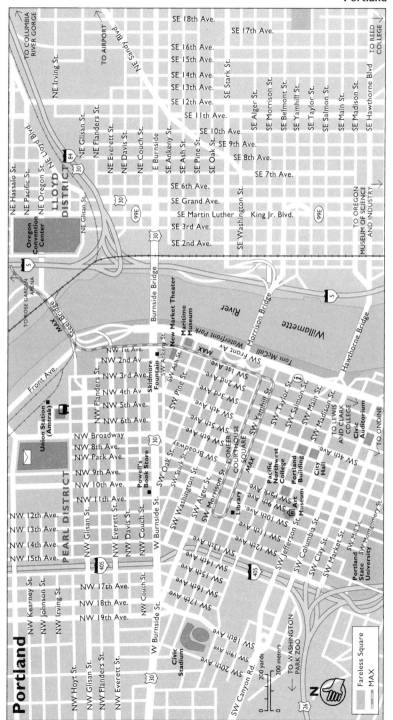

# Portland

# Seattle

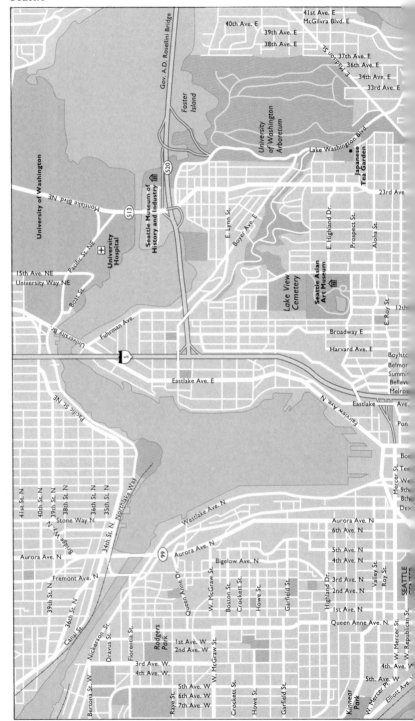

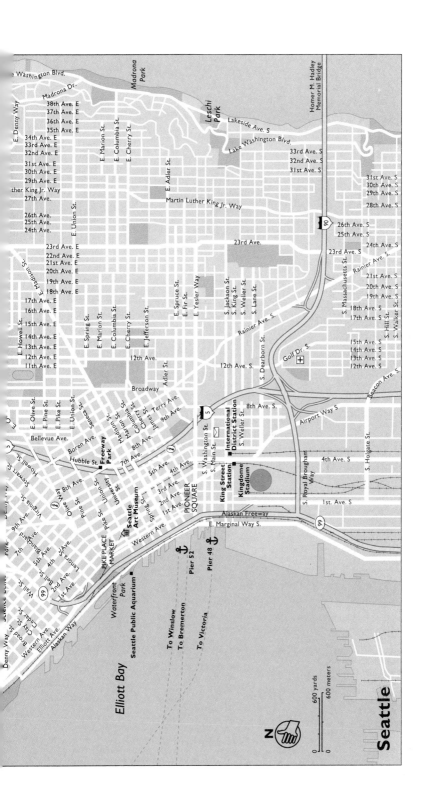

Vancouver

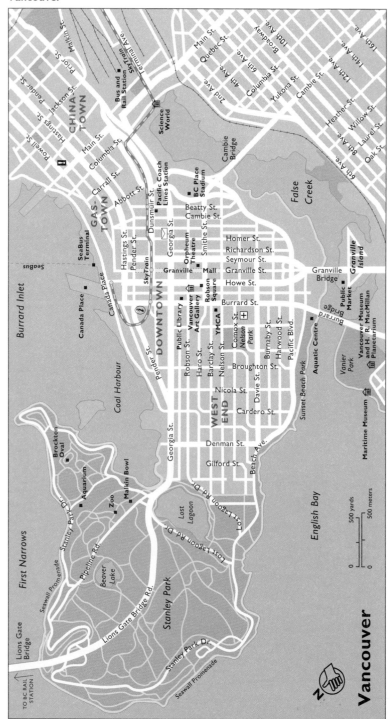

Downtown Washington, D.C.

# Central Washington, D.C.

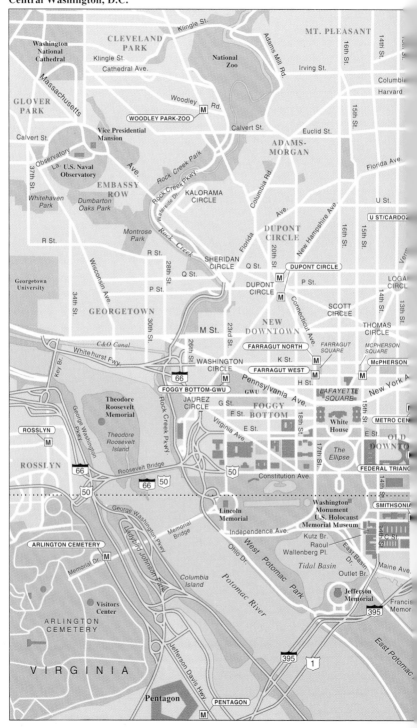

# Central Washington, D.C.

# The Mall Area, Washington, D.C.

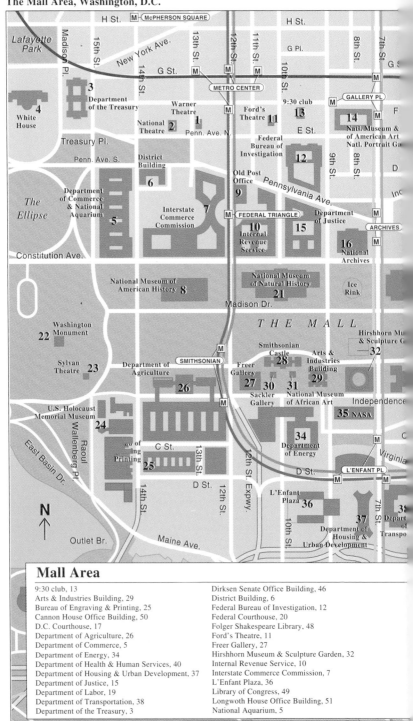

## Mall Area

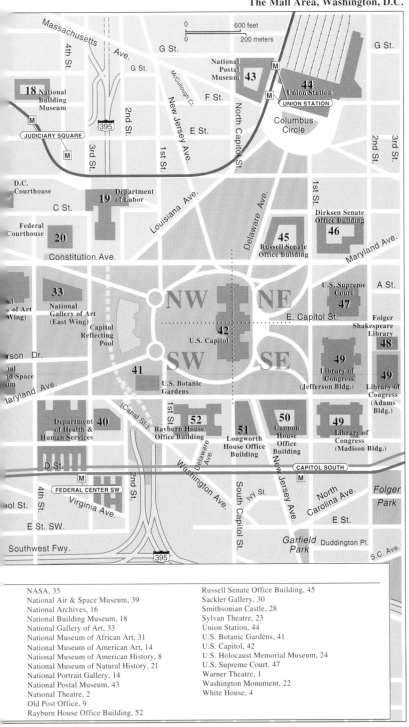

# The Mall Area, Washington, D.C.

# White House Area, Foggy Bottom, and Nearby Arlington

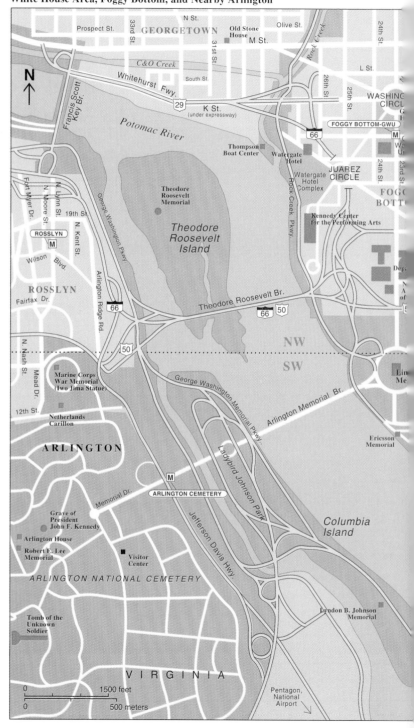

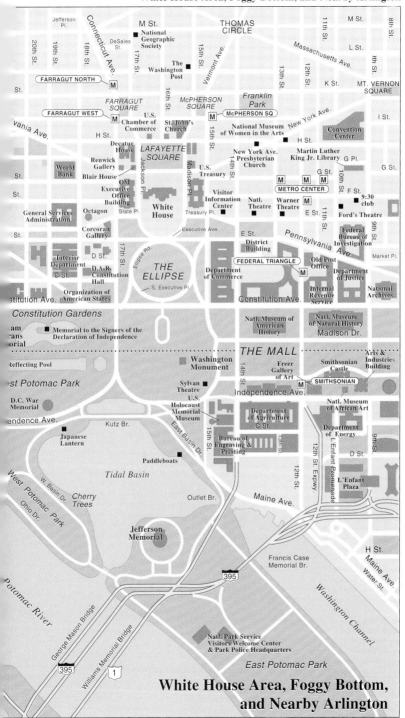

# White House Area, Foggy Bottom, and Nearby Arlington

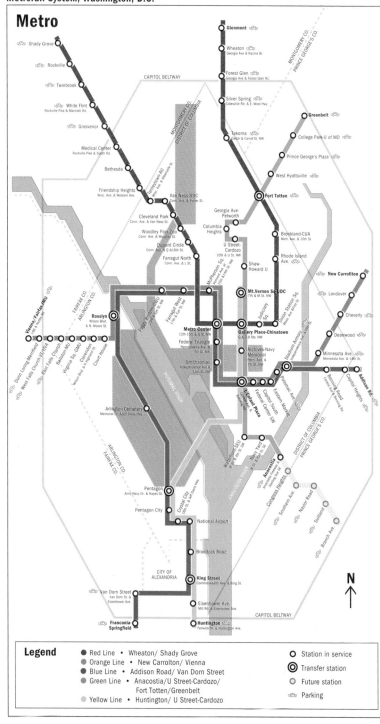

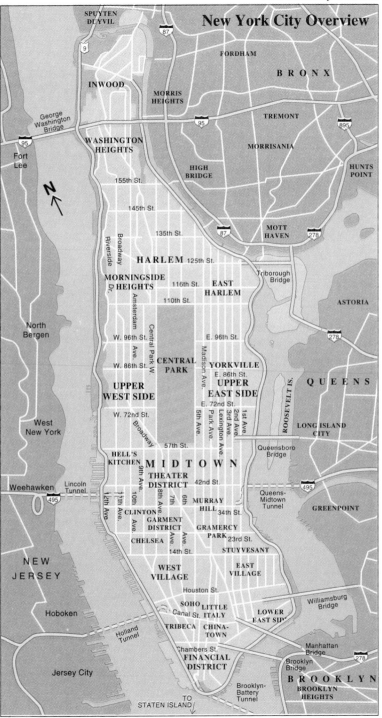

New York City Subways

Subways

Stops are not served by all trains at all times.
Refer to Transit Authority map for descriptions
of express, local, and limited service.

LEGEND

K,B   Line
168 St   Terminal

# Downtown Manhattan

# Downtown Manhattan

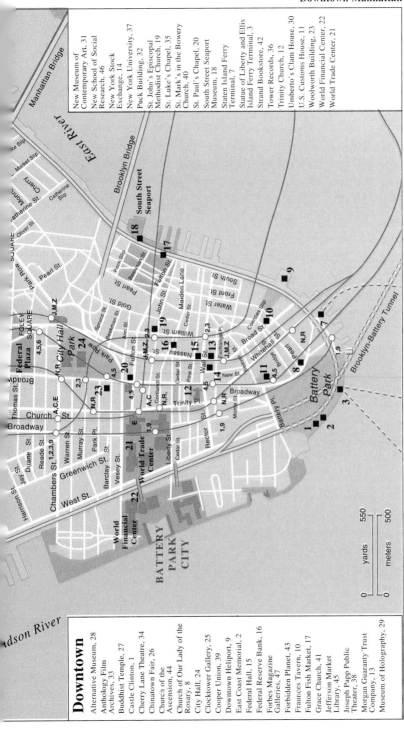

New Museum of Contemporary Art, 31
New School of Social Research, 46
New York Stock Exchange, 14
New York University, 37
Puck Building, 32
St. John's Episcopal Methodist Church, 19
St. Luke's Chapel, 35
St. Mark's in the Bowery Church, 40
St. Paul's Chapel, 20
South Street Seaport Museum, 18
Staten Island Ferry Terminal, 7
Statue of Liberty and Ellis Island Ferry Terminal, 3
Strand Bookstore, 42
Tower Records, 36
Trinity Church, 12
Umberto's Clam House, 30
U.S. Customs House, 11
Woolworth Building, 23
World Financial Center, 22
World Trade Center, 21

## Downtown

Alternative Museum, 28
Anthology Film Archives, 33
Buddhist Temple, 27
Castle Clinton, 1
Cherry Lane Theatre, 34
Chinatown Fair, 26
Church of the Ascension, 44
Church of Our Lady of the Rosary, 8
City Hall, 24
Clocktower Gallery, 25
Cooper Union, 39
Downtown Heliport, 9
East Coast Memorial, 2
Federal Hall, 15
Federal Reserve Bank, 16
Forbes Magazine Galleries, 47
Forbidden Planet, 43
Fraunces Tavern, 10
Fulton Fish Market, 17
Grace Church, 41
Jefferson Market Library, 45
Joseph Papp Public Theater, 38
Morgan Guaranty Trust Company, 13
Museum of Holography, 29

# Midtown Manhattan

East River

Queens-Midtown Tunnel

FDR Dr.

Queensboro Bridge

TURTLE BAY

United Nations

First Ave.

Second Ave.

Third Ave.

Second Ave.

Third Ave.

Citicorp Center

Lexington Ave.

Park Ave.

Park Ave.

Madison Ave.

Grand Central Terminal

MURRAY HILL

Museum of Modern Art

Fifth Ave.

Rockefeller Center

New York Public Library

Empire State Building

Grand Army Plaza

Park South

Central

Carnegie Hall

Bryant Park

Broadway

Seventh Ave.

GARMENT DISTRICT

HERALD SQUARE

TIMES SQUARE

Eighth Ave.

Eighth Ave.

COLUMBUS CIRCLE

New York Convention & Visitors Bureau

Port Authority Bus Terminal

General Post Office

Ninth Ave.

Ninth Ave.

Dyer Ave.

Tenth Ave.

Tenth Ave.

HELL'S KITCHEN

Lincoln Tunnel

Eleventh Ave.

Twelfth Ave.

W. 60th St. W. 59th St. W. 58th St. W. 57th St. W. 56th St. W. 55th St. W. 54th St. W. 53rd St. W. 52nd St. W. 51st St. W. 50th St. W. 49th St. W. 48th St. W. 47th St. W. 46th St. W. 45th St. W. 44th St. W. 43rd St. W. 42nd St. W. 41st St. W. 40th St. W. 39th St. W. 38th St. W. 37th St. W. 36th St. W. 35th St. W. 34th St.

E. 56th St. E. 55th St. E. 54th St. E. 53rd St. E. 52nd St. E. 51st St. E. 50th St. E. 49th St. E. 48th St. E. 47th St. E. 46th St. E. 45th St. E. 44th St. E. 43rd St. E. 42nd St. E. 41st St. E. 40th St.

E. 60th St. E. 59th St. E. 58th St. E. 57th St.

E. 39th St. E. 38th St. E. 37th St. E. 36th St. E. 35th St. E. 34th St. E. 33rd St.

A,B,C,D 1,2,3,9
N,R
B,Q
N,R
4,5,6
N,R
B,Q
C,E
A,C,E
1,2,3,9
N,R
B,D,E
B,D,F,Q
1,2,3, N,R,9
1,2,3, N,R,9 7
4,5, 6,S 7
E,F
6
7
B,D,F, Q,7
N,R
N,R,Q
6

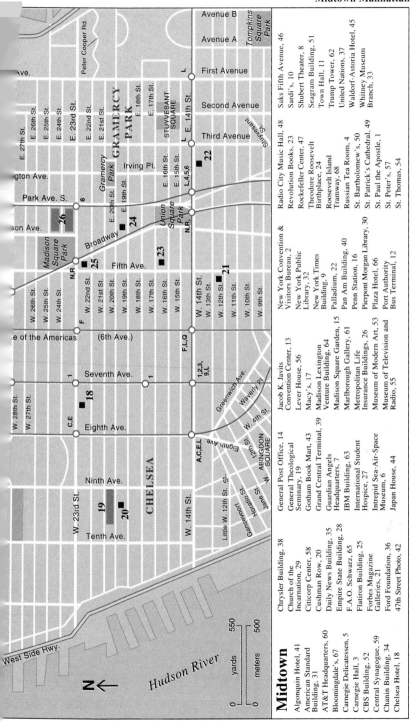

# Uptown

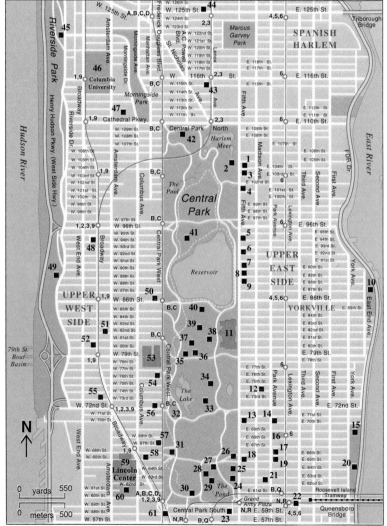